McGraw Hill Education

DISCOVER MCGRAW-HILL NETWORKS™

AN AWARD-WINNING SOCIAL STUDIES PROGRAM DESIGNED TO FULLY SUPPORT YOUR SUCCESS.

- » Aligned to the National Council for the Social Studies Standards
- » Engages students with interactive resources and compelling stories
- » Provides rigorous, differentiated instruction for every learning style
- » Facilitates targeted learning to drive toward assessment success

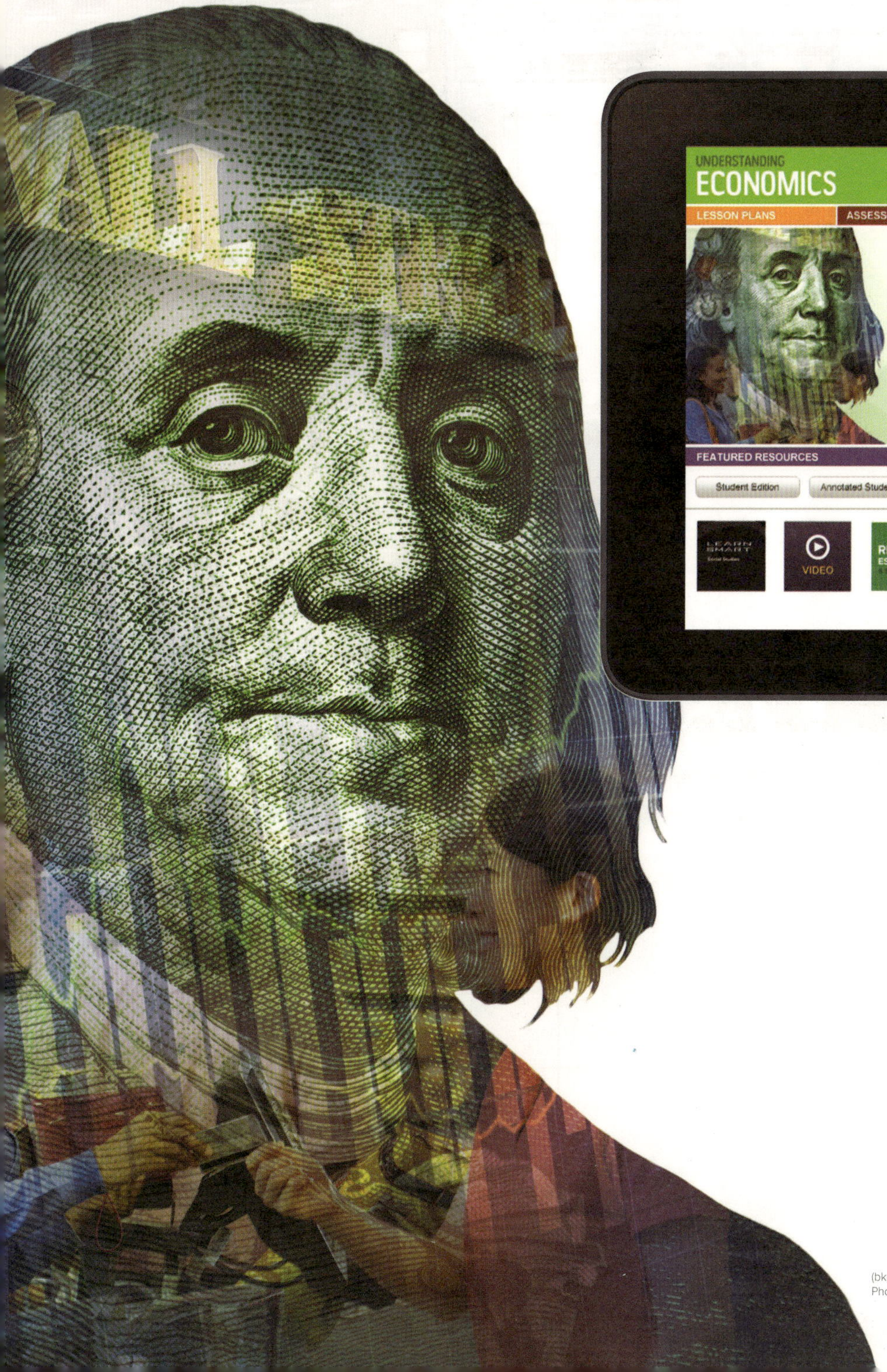

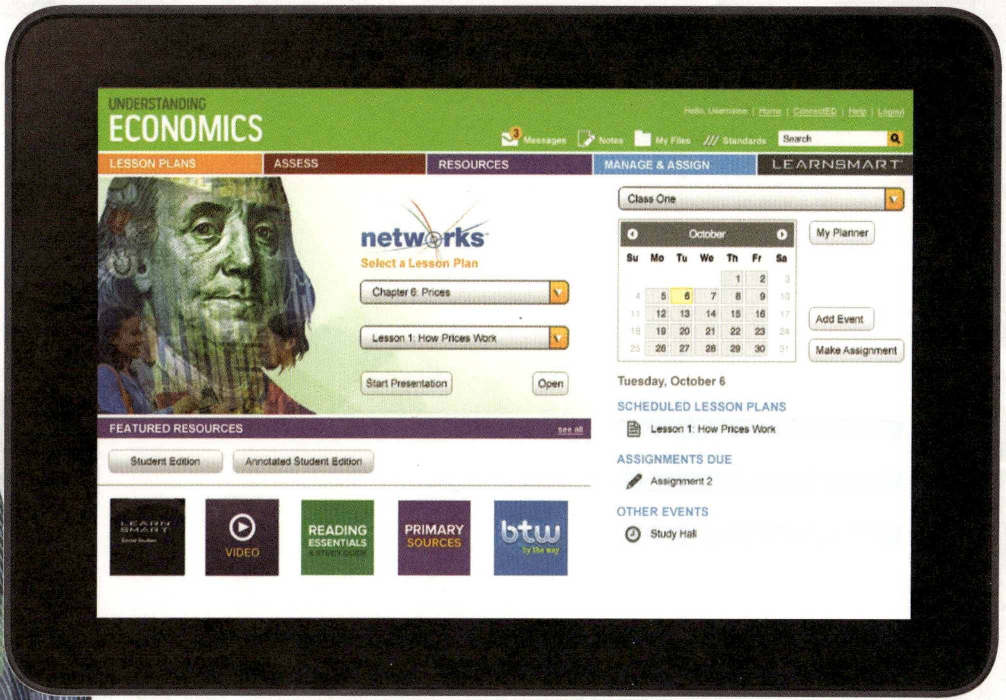

networks™

(bkgd)Panama/Alamy; (t to b, l to r)George Hammerstein/Corbis/Glow Images;©TongRo Image Stock/Alamy; (2)Aaron Roeth Photography; (3)instamatics/E+/Getty Images; (4)Blend Images - Ariel Skelley/Brand X Pictures/Getty Images

UNDERSTANDING IS THE FOUNDATION OF ACHIEVEMENT

McGraw-Hill Networks Social Studies programs provide thorough support for developing reading and writing comprehension for all students.

BUILD UNDERSTANDING WITH:

- » Essential and Guiding Questions to focus on key ideas
- » Reading strategies, vocabulary support, and Foldables® to increase comprehension
- » Abundant primary sources and document-based questions to deepen critical thinking skills

SUPPORT ENGLISH LANGUAGE LEARNERS THROUGH:

- » Student Edition online
- » English-Spanish glossary in every program
- » Additional Spanish resources and instructional support available

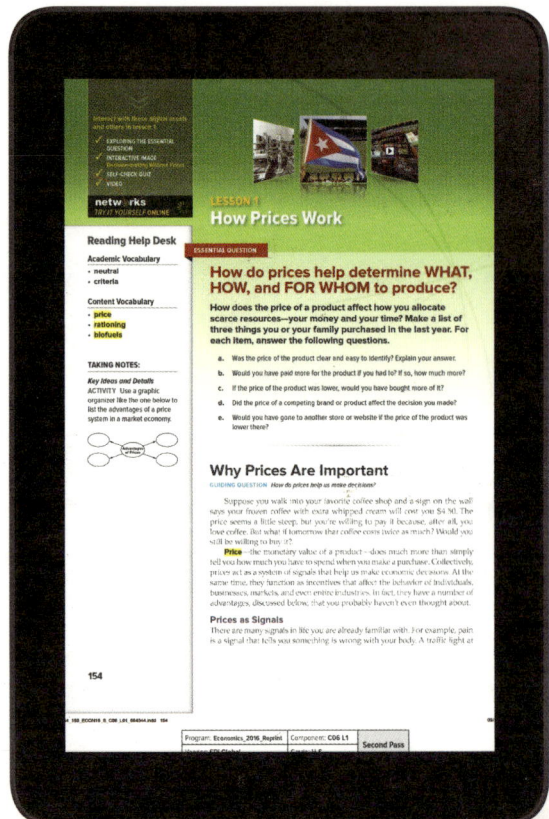

networks

FOCUS TIME AND EFFORT ON DESIRED OUTCOMES

LEARNSMART®

LearnSmart® with SmartBook™ will take your assessment prep to the next level. A proven adaptive learning program, LearnSmart® offers an interactive environment that helps students learn faster, study more efficiently, and retain more knowledge.

» Pinpoint where students are excelling or where more support is needed
» Differentiate instruction for students and report on year-long progression
» Compare student-to-student, class-to-class, and teacher-to-teacher results
» Provide detailed reports on essential data at the class, school, or district level

SPEND YOUR TIME TEACHING YOUR WAY.

EVERYTHING YOU NEED IN ONE EASY-TO-USE TEACHER LESSON CENTER.

- **MANAGE** your classes
- **ORGANIZE** your resources
- **CUSTOMIZE** to fit all students' needs
- **DIFFERENTIATE** so all students succeed
- **ASSESS** with confidence

DISCOVER IT ALL ONLINE!

1. Go to connected.mcgraw-hill.com
2. Enter your username and password
3. Click on your book
4. Select your chapter and lesson, or explore the Resource Library

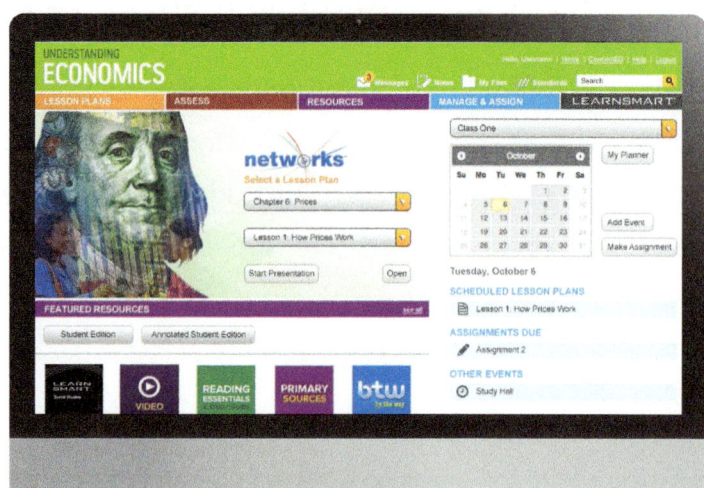

GO ONLINE AND START EXPLORING!

MHEDUCATION.COM/PREK-12

TEACHER EDITION

UNDERSTANDING ECONOMICS

Curriculum Knowledge Center
CEHHS
University of Michigan-Dearborn

Gary E. Clayton, Ph.D.

Cover photo credits: (bkgd) Panama/Alamy; (t to b, l to r) George Hammerstein/Corbis/Glow Images; ©TongRo Image Stock/Alamy; (2)Aaron Roeth Photography; (3)instamatics/E+/Getty Images; (4)Blend Images - Ariel Skelley/Brand X Pictures/Getty Images

McGraw-Hill networks™ meets you anywhere—takes you everywhere. Go online.
1. Go to connected.mcgraw-hill.com.
2. Enter your User Name and Password from your teacher.
3. Click on your book.
4. Select your chapter and lesson, or explore the Resource Library.

About the Cover: Benjamin Franklin, whose engraved image appears on the $100 bill, is well known as one of America's Founders. Franklin helped write the Declaration of Independence and U.S. Constitution, and he was a famous diplomat, author, inventor, and printer. He might also be considered one of the first U.S. monetarists—in 1729 he promoted increasing the money supply as a way to stimulate the economy. Franklin's image on the cover is superimposed with other images symbolizing economic activity: Wall Street's importance in stock markets, voluntary exchange of goods and services for payment, and coins that make up part of M1 (a measure of our money supply).

Used with permission. *Voluntary National Content Standards in Economics*, 2ⁿᵈ Edition. Copyright © 2010 Council for Economic Education, New York, NY. All rights reserved. For more information visit www.councilforeconed.org or call 1-212-730-7007.

mheducation.com/prek-12

Copyright © 2018 McGraw-Hill Education

All rights reserved. No part of this publication may be reproduced or distributed in any form or by any means, or stored in a database or retrieval system, without the prior written consent of McGraw-Hill Education, including, but not limited to, network storage or transmission, or broadcast for distance learning.

Send all inquiries to:
McGraw-Hill Education
8787 Orion Place
Columbus, OH 43240

ISBN: 978-0-07-668136-5
MHID: 0-07-668136-X

Printed in the United States of America

3 4 5 6 7 8 QVS 22 21 20 19 18

AUTHOR/CONSULTANTS AND REVIEWERS

AUTHOR

Gary E. Clayton, Ph.D., is Professor and Chair of the Economics and Finance Department at Northern Kentucky University. He received his Ph.D. in economics from the University of Utah and an honorary doctorate from the People's Friendship University of Russia in Moscow. Dr. Clayton has authored several textbooks and a number of articles, has appeared on numerous radio and television programs, and was a guest commentator for economic statistics on NPR's Marketplace. Dr. Clayton won the Freedoms Foundation Leavey Award for Excellence in Private Enterprise Education in 2000. Other awards include a national teaching award from the National Council on Economic Education (NCEE), NKU's 2005 Frank Sinton Milburn Outstanding Professor award, and the Excellence in Financial Literacy Education award from the national Institute for Financial Literacy® in 2009. Dr. Clayton has taught international business and economics to students in England, Austria, and Australia. In 2006 he helped organize a micro loan development project in Uganda.

CONTRIBUTING AUTHOR

Jay McTighe has published articles in a number of leading educational journals and has coauthored ten books, including the best-selling *Understanding by Design* series with Grant Wiggins. Mr. McTighe also has an extensive background in professional development and is a featured speaker at national, state, and district conferences and workshops. He received his undergraduate degree from the College of William and Mary, earned a Masters degree from the University of Maryland, and completed postgraduate studies at Johns Hopkins University.

ACADEMIC CONSULTANTS

Julie Heath, Ph.D.
Chair, Department of Economics
University of Memphis
Memphis, Tennessee

Jane S. Lopus, Ph.D.
Director, Center for Economic Education
California State University, East Bay
Hayward, California

Mark J. Perry, Ph.D.
Professor of Finance and Economics
University of Michigan—Flint
Flint, Michigan

TEACHER REVIEWERS

Lorraine Dumerer
R.L. Turner High School
Carrollton-Farmers Branch
 Independent School District
Carrollton, Texas

Lisa Ellison
Kokomo High School
Kokomo School Corporation
Kokomo, Indiana

Matt Pedlow
Jackson Public School District
Jackson High School
Jackson, Michigan

Alice Temnick
United Nations International School
New York, NY

Mike Wallace
Gateway School District
Gateway High School
Monroeville, Pennsylvania

Tom Woodruff
Rogers Public School District
Rogers High School
Rogers, Arkansas

CONTENTS

How to Use the Teacher Edition..xxvi
How to Use the Online Student Edition..................................xxxiv
How to Use the Online Teacher Edition..................................xl
Correlation to the Council for Economic Education's Voluntary National Content Standards
   in Economics..xlviii
Voluntary National Content Standards in Economics......................liv
Understanding by Design®...lviii
Reading Strategies...lxii
Primary Sources Strategies...lxiv
Meeting the Diverse Needs of Our Students..............................lxvi
Performance Assessment Strategies: Project-Based Learning..............lxx
Test-Taking Strategies...lxxii
Academic Vocabulary..lxxiv
Why Teach with Technology?...lxxvi
College and Career Readiness...lxxviii
Scavenger Hunt...lxxx

UNIT ONE Thinking Like an Economist.................................1

What is Economics?...3

ESSENTIAL QUESTION
In what ways do people cope with the problem of scarcity?

Economic Perspectives – Budgeting Lifestyles – 5
   Basic Elements of Budgets...4

LESSON 1 Scarcity and the Science of Economics......................6

Biography Adam Smith (1723–1790)....................................9
Case Study Drought and Scarcity in the
   United States: 2012...13

LESSON 2 Our Economic Choices......................................14

Exploring the Essential Question......................................19

LESSON 3 Using Economic Models.....................................21

Exploring the Essential Question......................................25

Careers Retail Business Manager....................................27
Global Economy & You The Shift to a Service
   Economy..28
Debates Should fracking be allowed to continue even
   though it uses our water resources?................................30

iv

Economic Systems and Decision Making 35

ESSENTIAL QUESTION

How does an economic system help a society deal with the fundamental problem of scarcity?

Economic Perspectives – Economic Systems Around the World 36

LESSON 1 Economic Systems 38

Careers Physician's Assistant 41

Exploring the Essential Question 46

Case Study What Does Your Day Look Like? The 9 to 5 in Traditional, Command, and Market Economies .. 47

LESSON 2 Mixed Economies 48

Biography Karl Marx (1818–1883) 50

Debates Should government provide health care? 54

LESSON 3 The Global Transition to Capitalism 56

Global Economy & You Confronting Pollution 60

The American Free Enterprise System 69

ESSENTIAL QUESTIONS

• *What are the benefits of a free enterprise economy?*

• *What are the major economic and social goals of the American free enterprise system?*

Economic Perspectives – Starting Your Own Business 70

LESSON 1 American Free Enterprise Capitalism 72

Exploring the Essential Question 77

Careers Franchise Operator 78

Case Study Public versus Private Ownership 81

LESSON 2 Roles and Responsibilities in a Free Enterprise Economy 82

Exploring the Essential Question 85

LESSON 3 Evaluating Economic Performance 87

Global Economy & You The Richest Countries in the World 88

Biography Brian Linton (1986–) 90

Exploring the Essential Question 90

Debates Should students be financially rewarded for good grades? 92

CONTENTS

UNIT TWO Understanding Markets 97

Demand 99

ESSENTIAL QUESTIONS
- How does demand help societies determine WHAT, HOW, and FOR WHOM to produce?
- What are the causes of a change in demand?

Economic Perspectives – Law of Demand 100

LESSON 1 What is Demand? 102

Biography Carl Menger (1840–1921) 105

Case Study Holiday Demand 107

LESSON 2 Factors Affecting Demand .. 108

Exploring the Essential Question 110

Global Economy & You Demand for Goods 111

Careers Retail Buyer 112

LESSON 3 Elasticity of Demand 114

Exploring the Essential Question 119

Debates Should it be legal to raise prices on basic terms needed for survival during natural disasters or other emergencies? 120

Supply 125

ESSENTIAL QUESTIONS
- What are the basic differences between supply and demand?
- Why is the production function useful for making business decisions?
- How do companies determine the most profitable way to operate?

Economic Perspectives – Law of Supply 126

LESSON 1 What is Supply? 128

Global Economy & You The Global Economy and Your Cup of Coffee 131

Exploring the Essential Question 133

LESSON 2 The Theory of Production ... 136

Biography Daniel Akerson (1948–) 138

Exploring the Essential Question 139

Debates Do multinational corporations have a duty to keep their base of operations in their home countries? 140

LESSON 3 Cost, Revenue, and Profit Maximization 142

Exploring the Essential Question 144

Careers Painting Contractor 145

Case Study The Nearly Instant Snowboard 147

There's More Online! Videos • Animations • Games • Interactive Maps, Images, Graphs, Charts...and more

Prices 151

ESSENTIAL QUESTIONS
- How do prices help determine WHAT, HOW, and FOR WHOM to produce?
- What factors affect prices?

Economic Perspectives – Supply Affects Prices.. 152

LESSON 1 How Prices Work 154

Exploring the Essential Question 156

Exploring the Essential Question 159

LESSON 2 The Effects of Prices 160

Global Economy & You Price Differences Around the World... 163

Exploring the Essential Question 164

Case Study Supply, Demand, and the Cost of Super Bowl Advertising 167

LESSON 3 Social Goals, Prices, and Market Efficiency 168

Biography Milton Friedman (1912–2006) 170

Careers Cost Estimator 172

Debates Is it a good idea to raise the minimum wage? 174

Market Structures 179

ESSENTIAL QUESTIONS
- How do varying market structures impact prices in a market economy?
- Why do markets fail?
- How does the government attempt to correct market failures?

Economic Perspectives – Monopolies & Oligopolies 180

LESSON 1 Competition and Market Structures 182

Global Economy & You From Monopoly to Oligopoly 187

Exploring the Essential Question 189

Debates Do current copyright laws do more harm than good? 190

LESSON 2 Market Failures 192

Biography Joseph Stiglitz (1943–) 193

Exploring the Essential Question 194

Case Study Coming to America 197

LESSON 3 The Role of Government 198

Exploring the Essential Question 200

Careers Consumer Advocate Lawyer 202

vii

CONTENTS

UNIT THREE Business and Labor 207

Business Organization 209

ESSENTIAL QUESTIONS
- How are businesses formed and how do they grow?
- How does a market economy support nonprofit organizations?

Economic Perspectives – Bankrolling Start-Ups 210

LESSON 1 Forms of Business Organizations 212

Careers Corporate Auditor 216
Exploring the Essential Question 219
Case Study Powder Pollution 222

LESSON 2 Business Growth and Expansion 223

Biography Friedrich August von Hayek (1899–1992) 225
Exploring the Essential Question 225
Debates Is it ethical for businesses to outsource jobs to foreign countries when there is high unemployment in the United States? 230

LESSON 3 Nonprofit Organizations 232
Exploring the Essential Question 234
Global Economy & You Economic Analysis on a Global Scale 235

Labor and Wages 241

ESSENTIAL QUESTIONS
- What features of the modern day labor industry are the result of union action?
- What factors lead to higher wages for a worker?

Economic Perspectives – Are You Union? 242

LESSON 1 The Labor Movement 244
Biography Cèsar Chávez (1927–1993) 246
Exploring the Essential Question 249

LESSON 2 Wages and Labor Disputes 252
Careers National Labor Relations Board Administrative Law Judge 255
Exploring the Essential Question 256
Case Study Homestead Strike 258

LESSON 3 Employment Trends and Issues 259
Global Economy & You Worker Productivity 264
Debates In most cases, are senior business executives worth what they are paid? 266

There's More Online! Videos • Animations • Games • Interactive Maps, Images, Graphs, Charts...and more

UNIT FOUR Money, Banking, and Finance 271

Money and Banking 273

ESSENTIAL QUESTIONS
- What features of the modern day labor industry are the result of union action?
- What factors lead to higher wages for a worker?

Economic Perspectives – Polymer Banknotes: Currency of the Future 274

LESSON 1 The Evolution, Functions, and Characteristics of Money 276

Global Economy & You The Dollar in Decline 279

Biography Thomas J. Curry (1957–) 280

Exploring the Essential Question 280

LESSON 2 The Development of Modern Banking 282

Exploring the Essential Question 287

Case Study Currency Design 289

LESSON 3 Banking Today 290

Careers Financial Clerks 293

Exploring the Essential Question 294

Debates Should the gold standard have been abandoned and should it be brought back? 296

Financial Markets 301

ESSENTIAL QUESTIONS
- What is the role of savings in the financial system?
- What options are available for investing your money?

Economic Perspectives – Stocks and Bonds 302

LESSON 1 Savings and the Financial System 304

Exploring the Essential Question 307

LESSON 2 Financial Assets and Their Markets 310

Global Economy & You Trading Around the World 311

Biography Suze Orman (1951–) 313

Exploring the Essential Question 316

Case Study The New York and the National Stock Exchanges 317

LESSON 3 Investing in Equities and Options 318

Careers Stockbroker and Investment Banker 319

Exploring the Essential Question 322

Debates Is the illegal practice of insider trading punished too severely in the United States? 326

ix

CONTENTS

UNIT FIVE Economic Performance 331

Evaluating the Economy 333

ESSENTIAL QUESTION
How do we determine the economic and social well-being of the United States?

Economic Perspectives — Examining the U.S. Census 334

LESSON 1 Measuring the Nation's Output and Income 336

Global Economy & You Population and World Trade 338

Exploring the Essential Question 341

Debates Can the U.S. economy succeed without a big manufacturing base? 344

LESSON 2 Population Growth and Trends 346

Careers Social Worker 350

Exploring the Essential Question 351

Case Study Our Need for Forests 352

LESSON 3 Poverty and the Distribution of Income 353

Biography John Kenneth Galbraith (1908-2006) 357

Exploring the Essential Question 358

Economic Instability 363

ESSENTIAL QUESTION
What are the causes and consequences of instability in the economy?

Economic Perspectives — What is an Economic Bubble? 364

LESSON 1 Business Cycles and Economic Instability 366

Exploring the Essential Question 368

Biography Irene Rosenfeld (1953-) 371

Case Study A Greek Tragedy 374

LESSON 2 Inflation 375

Global Economy & You The Worldwide Domino Effect of U.S. Inflation 377

Exploring the Essential Question 378

LESSON 3 Unemployment 382

Careers Human Resources Specialist 385

Exploring the Essential Question 387

Debates Is economic stability the key to world peace? 390

There's More Online! Videos • Animations • Games • Interactive Maps, Images, Graphs, Charts...and more

UNIT SIX Government and the Economy 395

CHAPTER 14 Taxes and Government Spending 397

ESSENTIAL QUESTION
How does the government collect revenue, and on what is that revenue spent?

Economic Perspectives – Money In, Money Out: Federal Revenue and Expenditures 398

LESSON 1 Taxes 400

Exploring the Essential Question 408

Careers Tax Attorney 409

Case Study From the President's Point of View .. 411

LESSON 2 Federal Government Finances 412

Biography Daniel Werfel (1971-) 415

Exploring the Essential Question 417

LESSON 3 State and Local Government Finances 423

Global Economy & You High Taxes—Are You Sure? 425

Exploring the Essential Question 429

Debates Should the rich pay higher taxes? 430

CHAPTER 15 Fiscal Policy 435

ESSENTIAL QUESTIONS
• *How does the government promote the economic goals of price stability, full employment, and economic growth?*
• *How do we know if macroeconomic equilibrium has been achieved?*

Economic Perspectives – The Limitations of Supply & Demand Side Economics 436

LESSON 1 Demand-Side Policies 438

Biography John Maynard Keynes (1883-1946) .. 440

Careers Credit Counselor 442

Exploring the Essential Question 443

Case Study Then and Now—the New Deal's Tennessee Valley Authority (TWA) 444

LESSON 2 Supply-Side Policies 445

Exploring the Essential Question 447

LESSON 3 Macroeconomic Equilibrium .. 450

Global Economy & You The National Debt 454

Debates Should the government make major changes in federal spending and taxation to deal with the growing national debt? 456

xi

CONTENTS

CHAPTER 16 Monetary Policy 461

ESSENTIAL QUESTION
How does the government promote the economic goals of price stability, full employment, and economic growth?

Economic Perspectives – The Lesser Known Parts of the Federal Reserve 462

LESSON 1 Structure and Responsibilities of the Fed 464

Exploring the Essential Question 468

Case Study Changes in the U.S. Economy: Growth in Government Spending 469

LESSON 2 Monetary Policy 470

Biography Janet L. Yellen (1946–) 475

Exploring the Essential Question 476

LESSON 3 Economics and Politics 478

Global Economy & You The Global Effects of the Fed's Actions 479

Careers Chief Plant Engineer, U.S. Mint 480

Exploring the Essential Question 481

Debates Should the Federal Reserve Bank be abolished? 484

UNIT SEVEN The Global Economy 489

CHAPTER 17 Resources for Global Trade 491

ESSENTIAL QUESTION
How does trade benefit all participating parties?

Economic Perspectives – What is the World Trade Organization? 492

LESSON 1 Absolute and Comparative Advantage 494

Biography Paul Krugman (1953-) 498

Exploring the Essential Question 498

Case Study Three Ways 9/11 Affected the Economy 500

LESSON 2 Barriers to International Trade 501

Careers Foreign Service Agricultural Attaché ... 502

Exploring the Essential Question 505

LESSON 3 Foreign Exchange and Trade Deficits 508

Global Economy & You The Big Mac Index 510

Exploring the Essential Question 512

Debates Should the euro be abolished? 514

xii

Global Economic Development 519

ESSENTIAL QUESTIONS
- Why is the economic health of all nations important in a global economy?
- What are the challenges associated with globalization?

Economic Perspectives – Micro-Lending: Building Economies One Small Loan at a Time 520

LESSON 1 Economic Development 522

Exploring the Essential Question 529

Case Study A Solar-Powered Nepal 530

LESSON 2 Globalization: Characteristics and Trends 531

Global Economy & You How Much Did Your T-Shirt Cost to Make? 532

Exploring the Essential Question 533

Careers World Bank Staff 538

LESSON 3 Global Problems and Economic Incentives 540

Biography Thomas Robert Malthus (1766-1834) . . 546

Exploring the Essential Question 548

Debates Are the world's wealthiest nations obligated to aid in the economic development of poor nations? 550

Personal Financial Literacy 555

ESSENTIAL QUESTIONS
- How can financial institutions help you increase and better manage your money?
- What are the different types of business organizations?
- How can you take control of your own money?

Economic Perspectives – FAFSA: Free Application for Federal Student Aid 556

LESSON 1 Financial Institutions and Your Money 558

LESSON 2 Business Organizations and Your Money 568

LESSON 3 Personal Money Decisions . . 574

Databank 587
Reference Atlas 603
Glossary/Glosario 617
Index 663

FEATURES

Economic Perspectives

Budgeting Lifestyles	4
Economic Systems around the World	36
Starting Your Own Business	70
Law of Demand	100
Law of Supply	126
Supply Affects Prices	152
Monopolies & Oligopolies	180
Bankrolling Start-Ups	210
Are You Union?	242
Polymer Banknotes: Currency of the Future	274
Stocks and Bonds	302
Examining the U.S. Census	334
What is an Economic Bubble?	364
Money In, Money Out: Federal Revenue and Expenditures	398
The Limitations of Supply & Demand Side Economics	436
The Lesser Known Parts of the Federal Reserve	462
What is the World Trade Organization?	492
Micro-Lending: Building Economies One Small Loan at a Time	520
FAFSA: Free Application for Federal Student Aid	556

Debates

Should fracking be allowed to continue even though it uses our water resources?	30
Should government provide health care?	54
Should students be financially rewarded for good grades?	92
Should it be legal to raise prices on basic terms needed for survival during natural disasters or other emergencies?	120
Do multinational corporations have a duty to keep their base of operations in their home countries?	140
Is it a good idea to raise the minimum wage?	174
Do current copyright laws do more harm than good?	190
Is it ethical for businesses to outsource jobs to foreign countries when there is high unemployment in the United States?	230
In most cases, are senior business executives worth what they are paid?	266
Should the gold standard have been abandoned and should it be brought back?	296
Is the illegal practice of insider trading punished too severely in the United States?	326
Can the U.S. economy succeed without a big manufacturing base?	344
Is economic stability the key to world peace?	390
Should the rich pay higher taxes?	430
Should the government make major changes in federal spending and taxation to deal with the growing national debt?	456
Should the Federal Reserve Bank be abolished?	484
Should the euro be abolished?	514
Are the world's wealthiest nations obligated to aid in the economic development of poor nations?	550

Case Study

Drought and Scarcity in the United States: 2012	13
What Does Your Day Look Like? The 9 to 5 in Traditional, Command, and Market Economies	47
Public versus Private Ownership	81
Holiday Demand	107
The Nearly Instant Snowboard	147
Supply, Demand, and the Cost of Super Bowl Advertising	167
Coming to America	197
Powder Pollution	222
Homestead Strike	258
Currency Design	289
The New York and the National Stock Exchanges	317
Our Need for Forests	352
A Greek Tragedy	374
From the President's Point of View	411
Then and Now—the New Deal's Tennessee Valley Authority (TVA)	444
Changes in the U.S. Economy: Growth in Government Spending	469
Three Ways 9/11 Affected the Economy	500
A Solar-Powered Nepal	530

FEATURES

THE GLOBAL ECONOMY & YOU

The Shift to a Service Economy	**28**
Confronting Pollution	**60**
Purchasing Power Around the World	**88**
Demand for Goods	**111**
The Global Economy and Your Cup of Coffee	**131**
Price Differences Around the World	**163**
From Monopoly to Oligopoly	**187**
Economic Analysis on a Global Scale	**235**
Worker Productivity	**264**
The Dollar in Decline	**279**
Trading Around the World	**311**
Population and World Trade	**338**
The Worldwide Domino Effect of U.S. Inflation	**377**
High Taxes—Are You Sure?	**425**
The National Debt	**454**
The Global Effects of the Fed's Actions	**479**
The Big Mac Index	**510**
How Much Did Your T-Shirt Cost to Make?	**532**

BIOGRAPHY

Adam Smith (1723–1790)	**9**
Karl Marx (1818–1883)	**50**
Brian Linton (1986–)	**90**
Carl Menger (1840–1921)	**105**
Daniel Akerson (1948–)	**138**
Milton Friedman (1912–2006)	**170**
Joseph Stiglitz (1943–)	**193**
Friedrich August von Hayek (1899–1992)	**225**
Cèsar Chávez (1927–1993)	**246**
Thomas J. Curry (1957–)	**280**
Suze Orman (1951–)	**313**
John Kenneth Galbraith (1908–2006)	**357**
Irene Rosenfeld (1953–)	**371**
Daniel Werfel (1971–)	**415**
John Maynard Keynes (1883–1946)	**440**
Janet L. Yellen (1946–)	**475**
Paul Krugman (1953–)	**498**
Thomas Robert Malthus (1766–1834)	**546**

CAREERS

Retail Business Manager	**27**
Physician's Assistant	**41**
Franchise Business Owner	**78**
Retail Buyer	**112**
Painting Contractor	**145**
Cost Estimator	**172**
Consumer Advocate Lawyer	**202**
Corporate Auditor	**216**
National Labor Relations Board Administrative Law Judge	**255**
Financial Clerks	**293**
Stockbroker and Investment Banker	**319**
Social Worker	**350**
Human Resources Specialist	**385**
Tax Attorney	**409**
Credit Counselor	**442**
Chief Plant Engineer, U.S. Mint	**480**
Foreign Service Agricultural Attachè	**502**
World Bank Staff	**538**

Political Cartoons

There's No Such Thing as a Free Lunch	**12**
Command Economy	**52**
Economic and Social Goals	**89**
Expectations and Demand	**113**
Negative Marginal Returns	**139**
When Markets Talk	**173**
Product Differentiation	**185**
Credit Unions and Banks	**233**
Labor Unions	**248**
Federal Reserve Note	**284**
Bull Markets and Bear Markets	**324**
GDP and National Economic Health	**339**
The Wage-Price Spiral	**379**
Taxes	**401**
The Federal Reserve	**477**
International Trade	**504**
Sources of Energy	**547**

MAPS, CHARTS, AND GRAPHS

CHAPTER 1
Figure 1.1 Scarcity **7**
Figure 1.2 The Factors of Production **15**
Figure 1.3 Production Possibilities Curve **16**
Figure 1.4 Opportunity Cost **17**
Figure 1.5 Decision Making Grid **18**
Figure 1.6 Which are the responsibilities of the consumer? **20**
Figure 1.7 Economic Growth **22**
Figure 1.8 Education Pays **23**
Figure 1.9 The Circular Flow of Economic Activity ... **25**

CHAPTER 2
Disadvantages of Command Economy **42**
Figure 2.1 Comparing Economic Systems **44**
Figure 2.2 Characteristics of Mixed Economies **49**
Figure 2.3 Economic Systems and Per Capita GDP .. **62**

CHAPTER 3
American Small Businesses **74**
Figure 3.1 Characteristics of Free Enterprise Capitalism **75**

CHAPTER 4
Figure 4.1 The Price of Burritos **103**
Figure 4.2 Individual and Market Demand Curves .. **104**
Figure 4.3 A Change in the Quantity Demanded ... **109**
Figure 4.4 A Change in Demand **110**
Figure 4.5 Demand Elasticity and the Total Expenditures Test **116**
Figure 4.6 Determinants of Demand Elasticity **118**

CHAPTER 5
Figure 5.1 Supply of Burritos **129**
Figure 5.2 Individual and Market Supply Curves ... **130**
Colombian Coffee Production and U.S. Coffee Prices, 1990–2012 .... **131**
Figure 5.3 A Change in Supply **132**
Figure 5.4 Elasticity of Supply **134**
Figure 5.5 Short-Run Production **137**
Figure 5.6 Production, Costs, Revenues, and Profits .. **143**

CHAPTER 6
Figure 6.1 Market Equilibrium **161**
Figure 6.2 Surplus and Shortage **162**
iPhone Prices Across the Globe **163**
Figure 6.3 Changes in Price **165**
Figure 6.4 Price Ceilings & Price Floors **169**
Figure 6.5 Price Ceiling: Rent Control **171**

CHAPTER 7
Figure 7.1 Pure Competition and Profit Maximization **183**
Figure 7.2 Characteristics of Market Structures ... **186**
Figure 7.3 Using Cost-Benefit Analysis **195**
Figure 7.4 Federal Regulatory Agencies **201**

CHAPTER 8
Figure 8.1 Business Organizations **213**
Figure 8.2 Stock Ownership **217**
Figure 8.3 Corporate Structure **218**
Ponca City, OK Pollution **222**
Figure 8.4 Growth Through Reinvestment **224**
Figure 8.5 Types of Mergers **225**
Figure 8.6 Conglomerate Structure **227**

CHAPTER 9
Figure 9.1 Trade (Craft) and Industrial Unions **245**
Figure 9.2 Right-to-Work, State by State **249**
Figure 9.3 Union Membership and Representation by Industry **250**
Figure 9.4 Market Theory of Wage Determination .. **253**
Figure 9.5 Median Weekly Earnings by Occupation and Union Affiliation **254**
Figure 9.6 Union Membership as a Percentage of Employed Workers **260**
Figure 9.7 Median Female Income as a Percentage of Male Income **261**
Figure 9.8 Gender and Income Distribution of Men and Women by Occupation **262**
Labor Productivity in U.S. Dollars, 2011 .... **264**
Figure 9.9 The Minimum Wage **265**

CHAPTER 10
Trade-Weighted Value of the Dollar **279**
Figure 10.1 State and National Banks **288**
Figure 10.2 Fractional Reserves and the Money Supply **291**
Figure 10.3 Typical Consumer Fees Charged by Banks **292**

CHAPTER 11
Figure 11.1 Overview of the Financial System **305**
Figure 11.2 The Power of Compound Interest **308**
Figure 11.3 Risk and Return **309**
Trading Across the World **311**

There's More Online! Videos • Animations • Games • Interactive Maps, Images, Graphs, Charts...and more

Figure 11.4 Bond Ratings ... 312
Figure 11.5 Financial Assets and their Markets ... 315
Figure 11.6 How to Interpret How Stocks are Performing ... 320
Figure 11.7 How Much Money Will You Have at Retirement? ... 323

CHAPTER 12
Figure 12.1 Estimating Total Annual Output ... 337
Figure 12.2 Circular Flow of Economic Activity ... 342
Figure 12.3 Center of Population ... 348
Figure 12.4 Projected Distribution of the Population by Age and Gender ... 349
Figure 12.5 Poverty Guidelines ... 354
Figure 12.6 Poverty in the United States: Total Number and Rate ... 354
Figure 12.7 The Distribution of Income ... 355

CHAPTER 13
Figure 13.1 Business Cycles ... 367
Figure 13.2 The Index of Leading Economic Indicators ... 372
Figure 13.3 Constructing the Consumer Price Index ... 376
Figure 13.4 Inflation Erodes the Value of the Dollar ... 380
Figure 13.5 The Unemployment Rate ... 384
Figure 13.6 Measuring Consumer Discomfort ... 388

CHAPTER 14
Figure 14.1 Shifting the Incidence of a Tax ... 402
Figure 14.2 Three Types of Taxes ... 405
Figure 14.3 The Value-Added Tax ... 407
Figure 14.4 Income Tax Table for Single Individuals ... 408
Real GDP Growth, 2007–2012 ... 411
State and Local Government Revenues and Expenditures ... 411
Figure 14.5 Federal Budget for Fiscal Year 2016 ... 414
Figure 14.6 The Federal Deficit and the National Debt ... 418
Figure 14.7 Two Views of the National Debt ... 419
Figure 14.8 State Government Revenues and Expenditures ... 424
Taxes as a Share of Gross Domestic Product, 2011 ... 425
Figure 14.9 Local Government Revenues and Expenditures ... 427

CHAPTER 15
Aggregate Output-Expenditure Model ... 439
Figure 15.1 Personal Income Tax Rates and Receipts ... 446
Figure 15.2 Comparing Supply-Side and Demand-Side Policies ... 448
Figure 15.3 The Aggregate Supply Curve ... 451
Figure 15.4 Aggregate Demand Curve ... 451
Figure 15.5 The Economy in Equilibrium ... 452
Figure 15.6 Fiscal Policy and Aggregate Demand ... 453
Figure 15.7 Supply Side Policies and Aggregate Supply ... 455

CHAPTER 16
Figure 16.1 Structure of the Federal Reserve System ... 465
Increase in Government Spending ... 469
Figure 16.2 Fractional Reserves and the Monetary Supply ... 471
Figure 16.3 Short-Run Impact of Monetary Policy ... 472
Figure 16.4 The Reserve Requirement as a Tool of Monetary Policy ... 474
Figure 16.5 Monetary Policy Tools ... 476
The Global Effects of the Fed's Action ... 479

CHAPTER 17
Figure 17.1 American Dependence on Trade ... 495
Figure 17.2 U.S. Merchandise Trade by Area ... 496
Figure 17.3 The Gains from Trade ... 497
Figure 17.4 Foreign Exchange Rates ... 509
The Big Mac Index ... 510
Figure 17.5 Flexible Exchange Rates ... 511
Figure 17.6 International Value of the Dollar ... 512

CHAPTER 18
Figure 18.1 The Corruption Perception Index ... 526
Figure 18.2 Map of European Union ... 534
Figure 18.3 ASEAN ... 535
Figure 18.4 COMESA ... 536
Figure 18.5 OPEC ... 537
Figure 18.6 World Population Growth Rates ... 541
Figure 18.7 World Population Growth Rates by Country ... 542
Figure 18.8 Energy Flows in the United States ... 545

CHAPTER 19
Figure 19.1 Building Your Budget ... 559
Figure 19.2 Simple vs. Compound Interest ... 561
Figure 19.3 How to Write a Check ... 563
Figure 19.4 Capacity to Repay Debt ... 564
Figure 19.5 Credit Basics ... 565
Figure 19.6 How Do You Score? ... 566
Figure 19.7 Common Investments ... 571
Figure 19.8 Reading Stock Market Reports ... 572
Figure 19.9 Unemployment and Earnings ... 575

PRIMARY SOURCES

CHAPTER 1

"Why the Grass Should Not Always Be Greener," by Rusty Todd, *Wall Street Journal*, June 2013 ..... **30**

"Hydraulic Fracturing and Water Resources: Separating the Frack from the Fiction," by Heather Cooley and Kristina Donnelly, Pacific Institute **31**

William Pentland, "The Coming Food Crisis: Blame Ethanol," *Forbes*, July 28, 2012 ..... **34**

CHAPTER 2

Art Kellermann, Associate Dean for Health Policy, Emory University **54**

From Clare Boothe Luce Policy Institute's Policy Express Paper, "Who Should Pay for Health Care?" by Sally Pipes **55**

Karl Marx, *Wage-Labor and Capital* **68**

CHAPTER 3

State Senator Fletcher Hartsell (R-Cabarrus, NC). WRAL News **92**

Bob Brooks and Sam Goldstein, psychologists **93**

Mike Debonis, *Washington Post*, July 10, 2013 ..... **96**

CHAPTER 4

Mark Perry, Professor of Economics, University of Michigan **120**

Chris Christie, New Jersey Governor in the aftermath of Hurricane Sandy **121**

Carl Menger, *Principles of Economics* **124**

CHAPTER 5

Andy Grove, former Chief Executive Officer of Intel **140**

Jagdish Bhagwati, Professor of Economics and Law, Columbia University **141**

Elizabeth Weise, "Ethanol pumping up food prices," *USA Today*, February 14, 2011 ..... **150**

CHAPTER 6

President Barack Obama, State of the Union Address, February 12, 2013 ..... **174**

Ellen Sauerbrey, "SAUERBREY: Raising minimum wage hurts those it claims to help," *The Washington Times*, March 18, 2013 ..... **175**

M.L. Johnson, "Cranberry farmers struggle as surplus drops prices," *Businessweek*, May 6, 2013 ..... **178**

CHAPTER 7

Sandra Aistars, executive director of The Copyright Alliance, "On Empowering Artists," *The Huffington Post*, The Blog, February 28, 2013 ..... **190**

Kyle Wiens, co-founder and CEO, iFixit, "Forget the Cellphone Fight—We Should Be Allowed to Unlock Everything We Own," *Wired*, March 18, 2013 ..... **191**

Statement of Thomas M. Hoenig, Director of the FDIC, June 26, 2013 ..... **206**

CHAPTER 8

Daniel Griswold, director of the Center for Trade Policy Studies at the Cato Institute **230**

Lou Dobbs, anchor and managing editor of *Lou Dobbs Tonight*, CNN **231**

Joanne Ostrow, *The Denver Post*, Jan. 15, 2013 ..... **240**

CHAPTER 9

Donald Delves, founder and president of the Delves Group **266**

Nell Minow, editor and co-founder of *The Corporate Library* **267**

Todd Stottlemyer, National Federation of Independent Business **270**

CHAPTER 10

The Library of Economics and Liberty **296**

Barry Eichengreen, "A Critique of Pure Gold" **297**

Allie Bidwell, "Congress Approves Student Loan Deal," *U.S. News and World Report*, August 1, 2013 ..... **300**

CHAPTER 11

Robert W. McGee, Florida International University **326**

Arthur Levitt, chairman of the Securities and Exchange Commission, February 27, 1998 ..... **327**

Mark Mobius, *Bonds: An Introduction to the Core Concepts* **330**

CHAPTER 12

Office of United States Trade Representative, Executive Office of the President **344**

Council on Competitiveness **345**

Joseph E. Stiglitz, "Of the 1%, by the 1%, for the 1%," *Vanity Fair*, May 2011 ..... **362**

There's More Online! Videos • Animations • Games • Interactive Maps, Images, Graphs, Charts...and more

CHAPTER 13

Dr. Jean Ping, chairperson of the African Union Commission, at the Third Africa-Europe Summit in Tripoli **390**

President Barack Obama, "Nobel Lecture: A Just and Lasting Peace," December 2009 .... **391**

Federal Reserve Governor Sarah Bloom Raskin, April 18, 2013 .... **394**

CHAPTER 14

President Barack Obama, 2011 .... **430**

Robert Murphy, the Mises Institute. From "Soak-the-Rich Taxes: Fail!" by Robert P. Murphy. Mises Daily: Thursday, November 4, 2010.................... **431**

Lawrence Haas, "Sorry, the Federal Deficit Isn't a Spending Problem,"*The Fiscal Times*, February 3, 2011............................... **434**

CHAPTER 15

Alan Greenspan, former Federal Reserve Board Chairman **456**

President Franklin D. Roosevelt. Franklin D. Roosevelt: "Address Before the American Retail Federation, Washington, D.C.," May 22, 1939. Online by Gerhard Peters and John T. Woolley, The American Presidency Project.................... **457**

Douglas Elmendorf, "Economic Stimulus: What characteristics make fiscal stimulus most effective?" Tax Policy Center, February 7, 2008. From *The Tax Policy Briefing Book: A Citizen's Guide for the 2012 Election and Beyond*, by the Staff and Affiliates of the Tax Policy Center **460**

CHAPTER 16

Congressman Ron Paul. Interview with Jennifer Schonberger, "Should We Abolish the Federal Reserve," *The Motley Fool*, September 25, 2009 .. **484**

Deputy Secretary Neil Wolin, Remarks to the American Bar Association's Banking Law Committee, November 13, 2009 .... **485**

Ben S. Bernanke, former Federal Reserve Board Chairman, in a speech at a conference sponsored by the National Bureau of Economic Research, Cambridge, Massachusetts, July 10, 2013 .... **488**

CHAPTER 17

George Soros, Chairman of Soros Fund Management................................... **514**

Guy Verhofstadt, former prime minister of Belgium, "The euro and Europe," *The Economist*, July 26, 2011 .... **515**

Alan J. Auerbach and Maurice Obstfeld, "Too much focus on the yuan?" *Vox*, October 23, 2010 .... **518**

CHAPTER 18

President Barack Obama, speech before the United Nations General Assembly, September 23, 2010 .. **550**

Nancy Birdsall, Dani Rodrik, and Arvind Subramanian, "How to Help Poor Countries," *Foreign Affairs*, July/August 2005............................... **551**

"The Gated Globe," *The Economist*, October 12, 2013.............................. **554**

networks ONLINE RESOURCES

Interactive Maps, Charts, and Graphs

Chapter 1
Lesson 1 Figure 1.1 Scarcity
Lesson 2 Figure 1.2 The Factors of Production
Lesson 2 Figure 1.3 Production Possibilities Curve
Lesson 2 Figure 1.4 Opportunity Cost
Lesson 2 Figure 1.5 Decision Making Grid
Lesson 2 Figure 1.6 Which are the responsibilities of the consumer?
Lesson 3 Figure 1.7 Economic Growth
Lesson 3 Figure 1.8 Education Pays
Lesson 3 Figure 1.9 The Circular Flow of Economic Activity

Chapter 2
Lesson 1 Figure 2.1 Comparing Economic Systems
Lesson 2 Figure 2.2 Characteristics of Mixed Economies
Lesson 2 The Spectrum of Mixed Economies
Lesson 3 Asian Economies in Transition

Chapter 3
Lesson 1 Figure 3.1 Characteristics of Free Enterprise Capitalism

Chapter 4
Lesson 1 Figure 4.1 The Price of Burritos
Lesson 1 Figure 4.2 Individual and Market Demand Curves
Lesson 2 Figure 4.3 A Change in the Quantity Demanded
Lesson 2 Figure 4.4 A Change in Demand
Lesson 3 Figure 4.5 Demand Elasticity and the Total Expenditures Test
Lesson 3 Figure 4.6 Determinants of Demand Elasticity

Chapter 5
Lesson 1 Figure 5.1 Supply of Burritos
Lesson 1 Figure 5.2 Individual and Market Supply Curves
Global Economy & You Colombian Coffee Production and U.S. Coffee Prices, 1990–2012
Lesson 1 Figure 5.3 A Change in Supply
Lesson 1 Figure 5.4 Elasticity of Supply
Lesson 2 Figure 5.5 Short-Run Production
Lesson 3 Figure 5.6 Production, Costs, Revenues, and Profits

Chapter 6
Lesson 2 Figure 6.1 Market Equilibrium
Lesson 2 Figure 6.2 Surplus and Shortage
Global Economy & You Map iPhone Prices Across the Globe
Lesson 2 Figure 6.3 Changes in Price
Lesson 3 Figure 6.4 Price Ceilings & Price Floors
Lesson 3 Figure 6.5 Price Ceiling: Rent Control
Lesson 3 Figure 6.6 Price Floor: Minimum Wage

Chapter 7
Lesson 1 Figure 7.1 Pure Competition and Profit Maximization
Lesson 1 Figure 7.2 Characteristics of Market Structures
Lesson 2 Figure 7.3 Using Cost-Benefit Analysis
Lesson 3 Figure 7.4 Federal Regulatory Agencies

Chapter 8
Lesson 1 Figure 8.1 Business Organizations
Lesson 1 Figure 8.2 Stock Ownership
Lesson 1 Figure 8.3 Corporate Structure
Lesson 2 Figure 8.4 Growth Through Reinvestment
Lesson 2 Figure 8.5 Types of Mergers
Lesson 2 Figure 8.6 Conglomerate Structure

Chapter 9
Lesson 1 Figure 9.1 Trade (Craft) and Industrial Unions
Lesson 1 Figure 9.2 Right-to-Work, State by State
Lesson 1 Figure 9.3 Union Membership and Representation by Industry
Lesson 2 Figure 9.4 Market Theory of Wage Determination
Lesson 2 Figure 9.5 Median Weekly Earnings by Occupation and Union Affiliation
Lesson 3 Figure 9.6 Union Membership as a Percentage of Employed Workers
Lesson 3 Figure 9.7 Median Female Income as a Percentage of Male Income
Lesson 3 Figure 9.8 Gender and Income Distribution of Men and Women by Occupation
Global Economy & You Labor Productivity in U.S. Dollars, 2011
Lesson 3 Figure 9.9 The Minimum Wage

Chapter 10
Global Economy & You The Dollar in Decline
Lesson 1 Three Functions of Money
Lesson 2 Figure 10.1 State and National Banks
Lesson 3 Figure 10.2 Fractional Reserves and the Money Supply
Lesson 3 Figure 10.3 Typical Consumer Fees Charged by Banks

Chapter 11
Lesson 1 Figure 11.1 Overview of the Financial System
Lesson 1 Figure 11.2 The Power of Compound Interest
Lesson 1 Figure 11.3 Risk and Return
Global Economy & You Trading Across the World
Lesson 2 Figure 11.4 Bond Ratings
Lesson 2 Figure 11.5 Financial Assets and their Markets
Lesson 3 Figure 11.6 How to Interpret How Stocks are Performing
Lesson 3 Figure 11.7 How Much Money Will You Have at Retirement?

Chapter 12
Lesson 1 Figure 12.1 Estimating Total Annual Output
Lesson 1 Figure 12.2 Circular Flow of Economic Activity
Lesson 2 Figure 12.3 Center of Population
Lesson 2 Population Growth and Challenges
Lesson 2 Figure 12.4 Projected Distribution of the Population by Age and Gender
Lesson 3 Figure 12.5 Poverty Guidelines
Lesson 3 Figure 12.6 Poverty in the United States: Total Number and Rate
Lesson 3 Figure 12.7 The Distribution of Income

Chapter 13
Lesson 1 Figure 13.1 Business Cycles
Lesson 1 Figure 13.2 The Index of Leading Economic Indicators

Explore these assets as well as all assets from the Student Edition online!

Lesson 2 Figure 13.3 Constructing the Consumer Price Index
Lesson 2 Figure 13.4 Inflation Erodes the Value of the Dollar
Lesson 3 Figure 13.5 The Unemployment Rate
Lesson 3 Figure 13.6 Measuring Consumer Discomfort

Chapter 14
Lesson 1 Figure 14.1 Shifting the Incidence of a Tax
Lesson 1 Figure 14.2 Three Types of Taxes
Lesson 1 Figure 14.3 The Value-Added Tax
Lesson 1 Figure 14.4 Income Tax Table for Single Individuals
Lesson 2 Figure 14.5 Federal Budget for Fiscal Year 2016
Lesson 2 Figure 14.6 The Federal Deficit and the National Debt
Lesson 2 Impacts of the National Debt
Lesson 2 Figure 14.7 Two Views of the National Debt
Lesson 3 Figure 14.8 State Government Revenues and Expenditures
Global Economy & You Taxes as a Share of Gross Domestic Product, 2011
Lesson 2 Figure 14.9 Local Government Revenues and Expenditures

Chapter 15
Lesson 1 Figure 15.1 Personal Income Tax Rates and Receipts
Lesson 2 Figure 15.2 Comparing Supply-Side and Demand-Side Policies
Lesson 3 Figure 15.3 The Aggregate Supply Curve
Lesson 3 Figure 15.4 Aggregate Demand Curve
Lesson 3 Figure 15.5 The Economy in Equilibrium
Lesson 3 Figure 15.6 Fiscal Policy and Aggregate Demand
Lesson 3 Figure 15.7 Supply Side Policies and Aggregate Supply

Chapter 16
Lesson 1 Figure 16.1 Structure of the Federal Reserve System
Lesson 1 Responsibilities of the Federal Reserve
Lesson 2 Figure 16.2 Fractional Reserves and the Monetary Supply
Lesson 2 Figure 16.3 Short-Run Impact of Monetary Policy
Lesson 2 Figure 16.4 The Reserve Requirement as a Tool of Monetary Policy
Lesson 3 Figure 16.5 Monetary Policy Tools

Chapter 17
Lesson 1 Figure 17.1 American Dependence on Trade
Lesson 1 Figure 17.2 U.S. Merchandise Trade by Area
Lesson 1 Figure 17.3 U.S. The Gains from Trade
Lesson 1 Increased Political Stability
Lesson 3 Figure 17.4 Foreign Exchange Rates
Lesson 3 The Big Mac Index
Lesson 3 Figure 17.5 Flexible Exchange Rates
Lesson 3 Figure 17.6 International Value of the Dollar

Chapter 18
Lesson 1 Figure 18.1 The Corruption Perception Index
Lesson 2 Figure 18.2 Map of European Union
Lesson 2 Figure 18.3 ASEAN
Lesson 2 Figure 18.4 COMESA
Lesson 2 Figure 18.5 OPEC
Lesson 3 Figure 18.6 World Population Growth Rates
Lesson 3 Figure 18.7 World Population Growth Rates by Country
Lesson 3 Figure 18.8 Energy Flows in the United States

Chapter 19
Lesson 1 Figure 19.1 Building Your Budget
Lesson 1 Figure 19.2 Simple vs. Compound Interest
Lesson 1 Figure 19.4 Capacity to Repay Debt
Lesson 1 Figure 19.6 How Do You Score?
Lesson 2 Figure 19.7 Common Investments
Lesson 2 Figure 19.8 Reading Stock Market Reports
Lesson 2 Figure 19.9 Unemployment and Earnings

Interactive Debates

Chapter 1: Should fracking be allowed to continue even though it uses our water resources?
Chapter 2: Should government provide health care?
Chapter 3: Should students be financially rewarded for good grades?
Chapter 4: Should it be legal to raise prices on basic terms needed for survival during natural disasters or other emergencies?
Chapter 5: Do multinational corporations have a duty to keep their base of operations in their home countries?
Chapter 6: Is it a good idea to raise the minimum wage?
Chapter 7: Do current copyright laws do more harm than good?
Chapter 8: Is it ethical for businesses to outsource jobs to foreign countries when there is high unemployment in the United States?
Chapter 9: In most cases, are senior business executives worth what they are paid?
Chapter 10: Should the gold standard have been abandoned and should it be brought back?
Chapter 11: Is the illegal practice of insider trading punished too severely in the United States?
Chapter 12: Can the U.S. economy succeed without a big manufacturing base?
Chapter 13: Is economic stability the key to world peace?
Chapter 14: Should the rich pay higher taxes?
Chapter 15: Should the government make major changes in federal spending and taxation to deal with the growing national debt?
Chapter 16: Should the Federal Reserve Bank be abolished?
Chapter 17: Should the euro be abolished?
Chapter 18: Are the world's wealthiest nations obligated to aid in the economic development of poor nations?

Interactive Case Study

Chapter 1: Drought and Scarcity in the United States: 2012
Chapter 2: What Does Your Day Look Like? The 9 to 5 in Traditional, Command, and Market Economies
Chapter 3: Public versus Private Ownership
Chapter 4: Holiday Demand
Chapter 5: The Nearly Instant Snowboard
Chapter 6: Supply, Demand, and the Cost of Super Bowl Advertising
Chapter 7: Coming to America

networks ONLINE RESOURCES

Chapter 8: Powder Pollution
Chapter 9: Homestead Strike
Chapter 10: Currency Design
Chapter 11: The New York and the National Stock Exchanges
Chapter 12: Our Need for Forests
Chapter 13: A Greek Tragedy
Chapter 14: From the President's Point of View
Chapter 15: Then and Now—the New Deal's Tennessee Valley Authority (TVA)
Chapter 16: Changes in the U.S. Economy: Growth in Government Spending
Chapter 17: Three Ways 9/11 Affected the Economy
Chapter 18: A Solar-Powered Nepal

Interactive Images

Chapter 1
Lesson 1 Figure 1.1 Scarcity
Lesson 1 WHAT to Produce
Lesson 2 Figure 1.3 Production Possibilities Curve
Lesson 2 Figure 1.4 Opportunity Cost
Lesson 2 Figure 1.5 Decision Making Grid
Lesson 3 Figure 1.8 Education Pays
Lesson 3 Figure 1.9 The Circular Flow of Economic Activity
Lesson 3 Free Enterprise at Work

Chapter 2
Lesson 1 Traditional Economy
Lesson 1 Command Economy
Lesson 1 Disadvantages of Command Economy
Lesson 1 Effects of the Global Economy
Lesson 1 Figure 2.1 Comparing Economic Systems
Lesson 2 Figure 2.2 Characteristics of Mixed Economies
Lesson 3 Adjusting to Economic Change
Lesson 3 The European Union

Chapter 3
Lesson 1 Profit Motive
Lesson 1 Figure 3.1 Characteristics of Free Enterprise Capitalism
Lesson 1 A Variety of Goods
Lesson 1 Disadvantages of Free Enterprise
Lesson 2 Role of the Consumer

Chapter 4
Lesson 1 Figure 4.1 The Demand for Burritos
Lesson 1 Figure 4.1 Individual and Market Demand Curves
Lesson 1 Individual and Market Demand Curves
Lesson 2 Figure 4.4 A Change in Demand
Lesson 3 Figure 4.5 Demand Elasticity and the Total Expenditures Test
Lesson 3 Figure 4.6 Determinants of Demand Elasticity

Chapter 5
Lesson 1 Figure 5.1 Supply of Burritos
Lesson 1 Figure 5.2 Individual and Market Supply Curves
Lesson 1 Figure 5.3 A Change in Supply
Lesson 1 Figure 5.4 Elasticity of Supply
Lesson 1 Supply and Prices: Blizzard Kills and Buries Cows

Lesson 2 Automation: Unemployment vs. Profitability
Lesson 3 Figure 5.6 Production, Costs, Revenues, and Profits
Lesson 3 e-Commerce

Chapter 6
Lesson 1 Decision-making Without Prices
Lesson 1 What happens when there is...rationing in the United States
Lesson 2 Figure 6.1 Market Equilibrium
Lesson 2 Estimating Prices
Lesson 2 Figure 6.2 Surplus & Shortage
Lesson 2 Figure 6.3 Changes in Price
Lesson 3 Figure 6.4 Price Ceilings and Price Floors
Lesson 3 Figure 6.5 Price Ceiling
Lesson 3 Figure 6.6 Price Floor—Minimum Wage

Chapter 7
Lesson 1 Figure 7.1 Pure Competition and Profit Maximization
Lesson 1 Figure 7.2 Characteristics of Market Structures
Lesson 2 Figure 7.3 Using Cost-Benefit Analysis
Lesson 3 Federal Regulatory Agencies

Chapter 8
Lesson 1 Figure 8.1 Business Organizations
Lesson 1 Figure 8.2 Stock Ownership
Lesson 1 Figure 8.3 Corporate Structure
Lesson 2 Figure 8.4 Growth Through Reinvestment
Lesson 2 Figure 8.5 Types of Mergers
Lesson 3 Figure 8.6 Conglomerate Structure

Chapter 9
Lesson 1 Figure 9.1 Trade (Craft) and Industrial Unions
Lesson 1 Figure 9.2 Right-to-Work State by State
Lesson 1 Figure 9.3 Union Membership and Representation by Industry
Lesson 2 Figure 9.4 Market Theory of Wage Determination
Lesson 3 Figure 9.5 Median Weekly Earnings by Occupation and Union Affiliation
Lesson 3 Figure 9.6 Union Membership as a Percentage of Employed Workers
Lesson 3 Figure 9.7 Median Female Income as a Percentage of Male Income
Lesson 3 Figure 9.8 Gender and Income Distribution of Men and Women by Occupation
Lesson 3 Figure 9.9 The Minimum Wage

Chapter 10
Lesson 1 The History of Money
Lesson 1 Three Functions of Money
Lesson 2 Figure 10.1 State and National Banks
Lesson 2 Run on the Bank
Lesson 3 Figure 10.2 Fractional Reserve and the Money Supply
Lesson 3 Wall Street Mayhem
Lesson 3 Figure 10.3 Typical Consumer Fees Charged by Banks

Chapter 11
Lesson 1 Figure 11.1 Overview of the Financial System
Lesson 1 Comparing Financial Institutions
Lesson 1 Figure 11.2 The Power of Compound Interest

Lesson 1 Figure 11.3 Risk and Return
Lesson 2 Figure 11.4 Bond Ratings
Lesson 2 Figure 11.5 Financial Assets and Their Markets
Lesson 3 Figure 11.6 How to Interpret How Stocks are Performing
Lesson 3 Figure 11.7 How Much Money Will You Have at Retirement?

Chapter 12
Lesson 1 Figure 12.1 Estimating Total Annual Output
Lesson 1 Figure 12.2 Circular Flow of Economic Activity
Lesson 1 The Output Expenditure Model
Lesson 2 Figure 12.3 Center of Population, 1790–2000
Lesson 2 Population Growth and Challenges
Lesson 2 Figure 12.4 Projected Distribution of the Population by Age and Gender, 2015
Lesson 3 Figure 12.5 Poverty Guidelines
Lesson 3 Figure 12.6 Poverty in the United States: Total Number and Rate
Lesson 3 Figure 12.7 The Distribution of Income
Lesson 3 How an Enterprise Zone Attempts to Revitalize an Area

Chapter 13
Lesson 1 Figure 13.1 Business Cycles
Lesson 1 Great Depression
Lesson 1 Figure 13.2 The Index of Leading Economic Indicators
Lesson 2 Figure 13.3 Constructing the Consumer Price Index
Lesson 2 Hyperinflation
Lesson 2 Figure 13.4 Inflation Erodes the Value of the Dollar
Lesson 3 Figure 13.5 The Unemployment Rate
Lesson 3 Figure 13.6 Measuring Consumer Discomfort

Chapter 14
Lesson 1 Figure 14.1 Shifting the Incidence of a Tax
Lesson 1 Figure 14.2 Three Types of Taxes
Lesson 1 Figure 14.3 The Value-Added Tax
Lesson 1 History of Tax Reform
Lesson 1 Figure 14.4 Income Tax Table for Single Individuals
Lesson 2 Figure 14.5 Federal Budget for Fiscal Year 2016
Lesson 2 Figure 14.6 The Federal Deficit and the National Debt
Lesson 2 Impacts of the National Debt
Lesson 2 Figure 14.7 Two Views of the National Debt
Lesson 3 Figure 14.8 State Government Revenues and Expenditures
Lesson 3 Figure 14.9 Local Government Revenues and Expenditures

Chapter 15
Lesson 1 Aggregate Output-Expenditure Model
Lesson 1 Figure 15.1 Personal Income Tax Rates and Receipts
Lesson 2 Reagan Deregulation
Lesson 2 Figure 15.2 Comparing Supply-Side and Demand-Side Policies
Lesson 3 Figure 15.3 The Aggregate Supply Curve
Lesson 3 Figure 15.4 Aggregate Demand Curve
Lesson 3 Figure 15.5 The Economy in Equilibrium
Lesson 3 Great Recession of 2008–2009
Lesson 3 Figure 15.6 Fiscal Policy and Aggregate Demand
Lesson 3 Figure 15.7 Supply Side Policies and Aggregate Supply

Chapter 16
Lesson 1 Figure 16.1 Structure of the Federal Reserve System
Lesson 1 Consumer Protections from the Federal Reserve System
Lesson 2 Figure 16.2 Fractional Reserves and the Monetary Supply
Lesson 2 Figure 16.3 Short-Run Impact of Monetary Policy
Lesson 2 Figure 16.4 The Reserve Requirement as a Tool of Monetary Policy

Chapter 17
Lesson 1 Figure 17.1 American Dependence on Trade
Lesson 1 Figure 17.2 U.S. Merchandise Trade by Area
Lesson 1 Figure 17.3 The Gains from Trade
Lesson 1 Increased Political Stability
Lesson 2 The WTO
Lesson 3 Figure 17.4 Foreign Exchange Rates
Lesson 3 Figure 17.5 Flexible Exchanges Rates
Lesson 3 Figure 17.6 International Value of the Dollar

Chapter 18
Lesson 1 Figure 18.1 The Corruption Perception Index
Lesson 2 Figure 18.2 The European Union
Lesson 2 Figure 18.3 ASEAN
Lesson 2 Figure 18.4 COMESA
Lesson 2 Figure 18.5 OPEC
Lesson 3 Figure 18.6 World Population Growth Rates: 1950–2050
Lesson 3 Figure 18.7 World Population Growth Rates by Country: 1970 and 2013
Lesson 3 Renewable Resources: Alternative to Fossil Fuels
Lesson 3 Figure 18.8 Energy Flows in the United States

Chapter 19
Lesson 1 Figure 19.1 Building your Budget
Lesson 1 Figure 19.2 Simple vs. Compound Interest
Lesson 1 Figure 19.3 How to Write a Check
Lesson 1 Figure 19.5 Credit Basics
Lesson 2 Figure 19.8 Reading Stock Market Reports
Lesson 3 Figure 19.9 Unemployment and Earnings

Interactive Self-Check Quizzes

Chapter 1   Three Quizzes, One Per Lesson
Chapter 2   Three Quizzes, One Per Lesson
Chapter 3   Three Quizzes, One Per Lesson
Chapter 4   Three Quizzes, One Per Lesson
Chapter 5   Three Quizzes, One Per Lesson
Chapter 6   Three Quizzes, One Per Lesson
Chapter 7   Three Quizzes, One Per Lesson
Chapter 8   Three Quizzes, One Per Lesson
Chapter 9   Three Quizzes, One Per Lesson
Chapter 10 Three Quizzes, One Per Lesson
Chapter 11 Three Quizzes, One Per Lesson
Chapter 12 Three Quizzes, One Per Lesson
Chapter 13 Three Quizzes, One Per Lesson
Chapter 14 Three Quizzes, One Per Lesson
Chapter 15 Three Quizzes, One Per Lesson
Chapter 16 Three Quizzes, One Per Lesson
Chapter 17 Three Quizzes, One Per Lesson
Chapter 18 Three Quizzes, One Per Lesson

networks ONLINE RESOURCES

Lesson Presentations

Access pre-built lesson presentations or create customized presentations using resources you upload to fit your classroom.

Research and Writing Skills

How to Find Main Ideas and Details
How to Find Resources on the Internet
How to Make an Outline
How to Manage Your Time
How to Paraphrase
How to Sequence Events
How to Summarize Information
Prewriting, Drafting, and Revising Skills
How to Use What You Find on the Internet
How to Write a Letter
Creating a Bibliography: CMS Style
Creating a Bibliography: MLA Style

Critical Thinking Skills

How to Analyze the News
How to Analyze Documents and Photos
How to Analyze Visuals
How to Compare and Contrast
How to Distinguish Fact from Opinion
How to Identify Cause and Effect
How to Make Inferences and Draw Conclusions
How to Predict

McGraw-Hill Assessment

Access pre-built lesson quizzes (1 per lesson) and chapter tests (2 per chapter) or create customized assessments for use in print or online and track results with robust reporting tools. Pre-built quizzes and tests are also available in the Chapter Tests and Lesson Quizzes blackline master.

21st Century Skills

Buying a Car
Saving and Investing: Make your money grow
Insurance: Protect yourself
Paying Taxes: Simplify the annual event
Renting an Apartment: Know what to look for
Using a Checking Account
Getting a Job
How to Analyze the News
How to Recognize Historical Perspective
How to Plan a Service Project
Your Education: Jump-Start Your Future!

Digital Worksheets

Simulations
- **Chapter 1** What Is Economics? Teaching Strategies—Disaster Aid
- **Chapter 2** Economic Systems and Decision Making Teaching Strategies
- **Chapter 3** American Free Enterprise Teaching Strategies—What solution to this problem will satisfy entrepreneurs, consumers, and government officials?
- **Chapter 4** Demand Teaching Strategies—New Markets
- **Chapter 5** Supply Teaching Strategies—Starting a Business
- **Chapter 6** Prices Teaching Strategies—Will Work for Pay?
- **Chapter 7** Market Structures Teaching Strategies—Competition, Collusion, and Price Fixing
- **Chapter 8** Business Organizations Teaching Strategies—Crowdfunding
- **Chapter 9** Employment, Labor, and Wages Teaching Strategies—How are Labor and Wage Conflicts Resolved?
- **Chapter 10** Money and Banking Teaching Strategies—Too Big to Fail Simulation
- **Chapter 11** Financial Markets Teaching Strategies
- **Chapter 12** Evaluating the Economy Teaching Strategies—Who Are We?
- **Chapter 13** Economic Instability Teaching Strategies—The Auto Industry and Unemployment
- **Chapter 14** Taxes and Government Spending Teaching Strategies—Influences on Tax Law
- **Chapter 15** Fiscal Policy Teaching Strategies—Advertising Supply-Side and Demand-side Economics
- **Chapter 16** Monetary Policy Teaching Strategies—Keeping on an Even Keel
- **Chapter 17** Resources for Global Trade Teaching Strategies—Buy American?
- **Chapter 18** Global Economic Development Teaching Strategies—Micro-Entrepreneurs

Math Practice for Economics
- **Chapter 1** Graphing
- **Chapter 2** Computing Per Capita Gross Domestic Product (GDP)
- **Chapter 3** Economic Freedom and Competition
- **Chapter 4** Recognizing Factors That Affect Demand
- **Chapter 5** Production, Costs, Revenues, and Profits
- **Chapter 6** Analyzing Price
- **Chapter 7** Comparing Prices Among Competitors

networks — Explore these assets as well as all assets from the Student Edition online!

Chapter 8   Calculating the Monetary Effects of Mergers
Chapter 9   Minimum Wage vs. Standard of Living
Chapter 10 Handling a Checking Account
Chapter 11 Analyzing an NYSE Euronext Listing
Chapter 12 Examining U.S. Poverty Thresholds
Chapter 13 Investing Your Money
Chapter 14 Progressive and Regressive Taxes
Chapter 15 Comparing the Effects of Changing Tax Policy
Chapter 16 Calculating Reserves and Money Supply
Chapter 17 The Cost of a Pair of Shoes
Chapter 18 Population Growth

Personal Finance Activities
Chapter 1   What to Spend Money On
Chapter 2   Who Needs Insurance?
Chapter 3   Comparing Credit Card Offers
Chapter 4   Tracking Spending
Chapter 5   Assessing the Competition
Chapter 6   The Cost of Minimum Payments
Chapter 7   Calculating Gas Mileage
Chapter 8   Evaluating Stocks
Chapter 9   Saving up for Purchases
Chapter 10 Cash, Debit, or Credit?
Chapter 11 Risk and Return
Chapter 12 A Living Wage
Chapter 13 Changing Jobs
Chapter 14 Pay Day
Chapter 15 Tracking your Spending
Chapter 16 Help from the Fed
Chapter 17 Calculating Exchange Rates
Chapter 18 Global Economic Development—Get a Job

Enrichment Activities
Chapter 1   What Is Economics?—Big Box Stores: Good or Bad for Local Economies?
Chapter 2   Economic Systems and Decision Making—A New Economic Model?
Chapter 3   The American Free Enterprise System—The Disadvantages of Free Enterprise
Chapter 4   Demand—Analyzing Dairy Prices
Chapter 5   Supply—The Ultimate in Cost Savings—and Profits?
Chapter 6   Prices—Rationing During Scarcity
Chapter 7   Market Structures—Energy Markets and Climate Change
Chapter 8   Business Organizations—Stockholders Flex Their Muscles
Chapter 9   U.S. Labor Movements and Song
Chapter 10 Money and Banking—The Financial Crisis and the FDIC
Chapter 11 Financial Markets—A History of Treasury Securities
Chapter 12 Evaluating the Economy—Income and Wealth Inequality in America
Chapter 13 Business Cycles and Economic Instability—Calculating the Consumer Price Index

Chapter 14 Taxes and Government Spending—Lobbying, Taxes, and the American Electoral System
Chapter 15 Fiscal Policy—Examining John Maynard Keynes and Demand-Side Economics
Chapter 16 Assessing the Fed's Action
Chapter 17 NAFTA Twenty Years Later
Chapter 18 Global Economic Development

Reteaching Activities
Chapter 1   What is Economics?
Chapter 2   Economic Systems and Decision Making
Chapter 3   Role of the Government
Chapter 4   Demand
Chapter 5   Supply
Chapter 6   Prices
Chapter 7   Market Structures
Chapter 8   Business Organizations
Chapter 9   Employment, Labor, and Wages
Chapter 10 Money and Banking
Chapter 11 Financial Markets
Chapter 12 Evaluating the Economy
Chapter 13 Economic Instability—The Unemployment Rate
Chapter 14 Taxes and Government Spending
Chapter 15 Economic Models and Political Parties
Chapter 16 Monetary Policy
Chapter 17 The United States Trade Deficit
Chapter 18 Global Economic Development

Reading Support
These activities are available for each chapter:
Assessing Background Knowledge
Vocabulary Activity

This activity is available for each lesson:
Guided Reading Activity

Differentiation, Intervention, and Remediation
These activities are available for each chapter:
Hands-On Chapter Projects with Technology-Based Online Extensions
Reinforcing Economic Skills
Chapter Summaries

HOW TO USE THE TEACHER EDITION

TO THE TEACHER Welcome to the McGraw-Hill **networks** Teacher Edition—a new approach to the Teacher Edition based on the principles of *Understanding By Design*®.

Planning the Unit and the Chapter

Understanding By Design®
All Networks programs have been created using the approach developed by Jay McTighe, coauthor of *Understanding By Design*®.
- The main goal is to focus on the desired results before planning each chapter's instruction.
- The Unit and Chapter Planners list the Enduring Understandings and the Essential Questions that students will learn and use as they study the chapters.
- Identifying the Predictable Misunderstandings will help you anticipate misconceptions students might have as they read the chapters.
- Every chapter provides assessment options to help you measure student understanding.
- Information in the Unit Planner is expanded upon in the Chapter Planners.

Standards
Each Chapter Planner identifies the Council of Economic Educators standards that are covered in the chapter.

Pacing Guide
Time management suggestions for teaching the chapter are provided.

Skill-Based Activities
Each lesson includes a variety of print-based and digital activities designed to teach a range of skills, including:

- **C** Critical Thinking Skills
- **V** Visual Skills
- **R** Reading Skills
- **T** Technology Skills
- **W** Writing Skills

Differentiated Instruction
Activities are designed to meet the needs of:
- **BL** Beyond Level
- **AL** Approaching Level
- **ELL** English Language Learners

In addition, activities are designed to address a range of *learning styles*.

xxvi How to Use the Teacher Edition

Planning the Unit and the Chapter (continued)

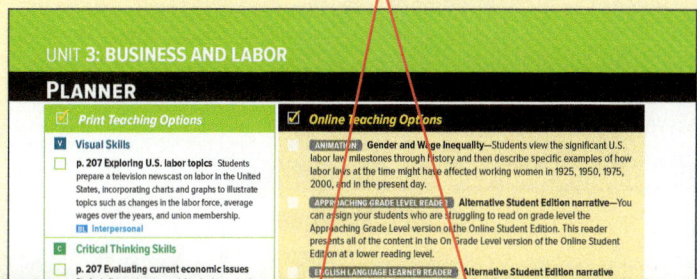

Don't forget! You can customize all your Lesson Plans online.

Student Objectives
Using *Understanding By Design®* as the framework, the planners outline the content and skills that students will be expected to know.

Planners
The Unit and Chapter Openers and Lesson Planners provide a snapshot of the resources available to enhance and extend learning. The activities are organized by skill type, level, and learning style.

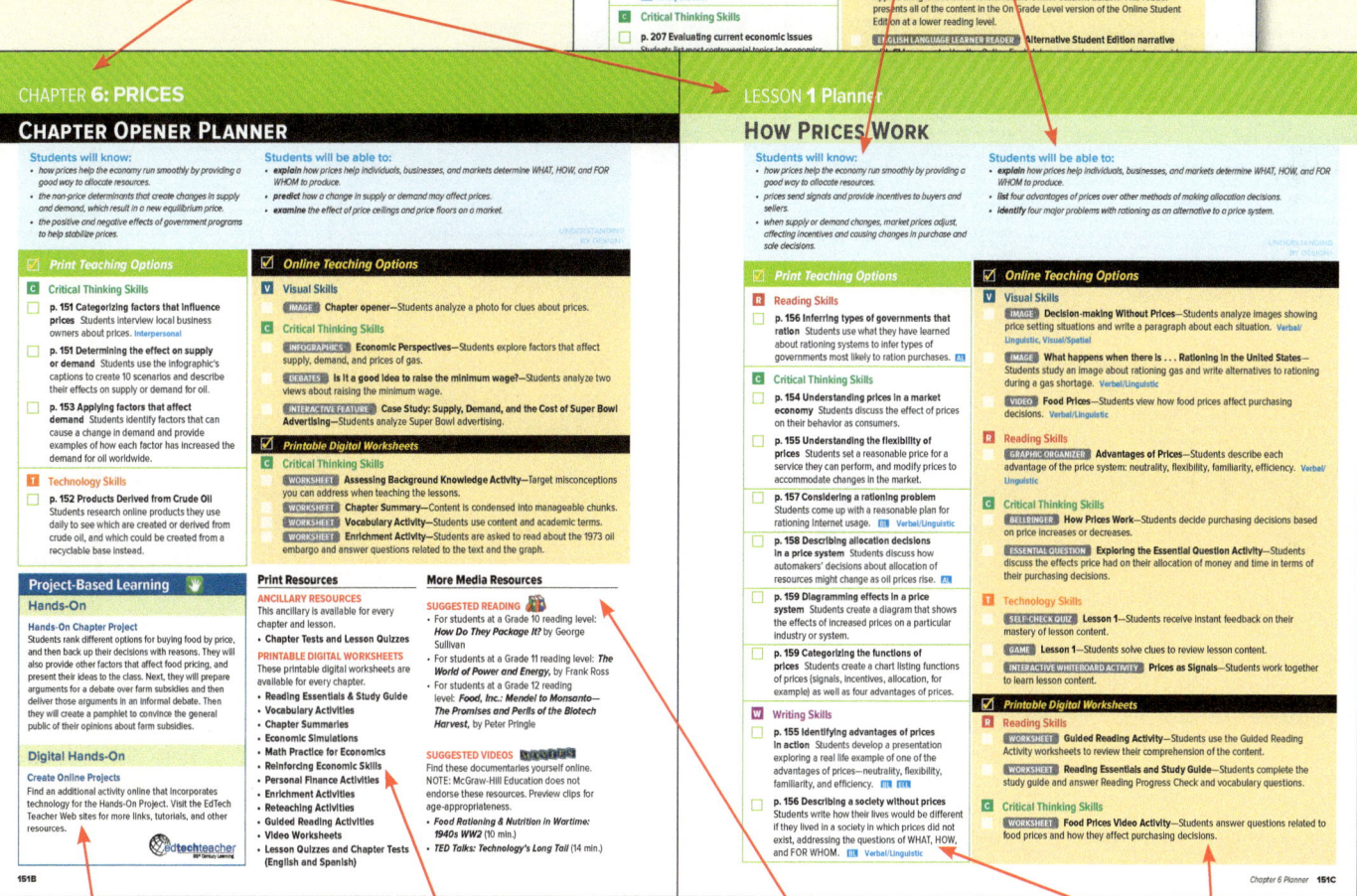

Project-Based Learning
Cumulative projects bring the subject to life for the student and help you assess your students' level of understanding. The program includes Hands-On Projects with technology-based extensions.

Print Resources
Every chapter includes printable worksheets and materials to build vocabulary and improve reading comprehension.

Make It Relevant
Enrich and extend the content with videos and books.

Print and Digital Options
Each planner has two columns listing print-based activities and online digital assets.

Digital assets include:
- interactive maps
- photos
- games
- slide shows
- whiteboard activities
- lesson videos
- worksheets

How to Use the Teacher Edition **xxvii**

HOW TO USE THE TEACHER EDITION

Using the Wraparound Resources and Activities

STUDENT EDITION PAGES AND WRAPAROUND ACTIVITIES
The entire Student Edition appears in the Teacher Edition. Activities and recommended resources appear in the side and bottom margins of the Teacher Edition, at point of use.

Introduce the Content
Each unit and chapter begins with activities to engage students' interest in the chapter's content.

Intervention and Remediation
Each Chapter Planner concludes with intervention and remediation strategies for every lesson, as well as Online Resources that can be used to help students understand the content.

Author Letter
Each chapter begins with the author's perspective about key concepts found in the chapter.

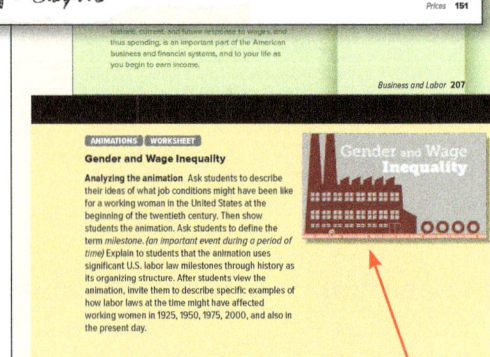

Unit Videos
Each unit features a short video animation that introduces students to an important concept found within one of the chapters.

Using the Wraparound Resources and Activities (continued)

Don't forget! You can customize all your Lesson Plans online.

Economic Perspectives

These two pages of the Chapter Opener are designed to help students learn more about an important economic concept through a real-world example. Students get the opportunity to apply their growing economic knowledge to their daily life.

The Teacher Edition contains activities and discussion questions for these features.

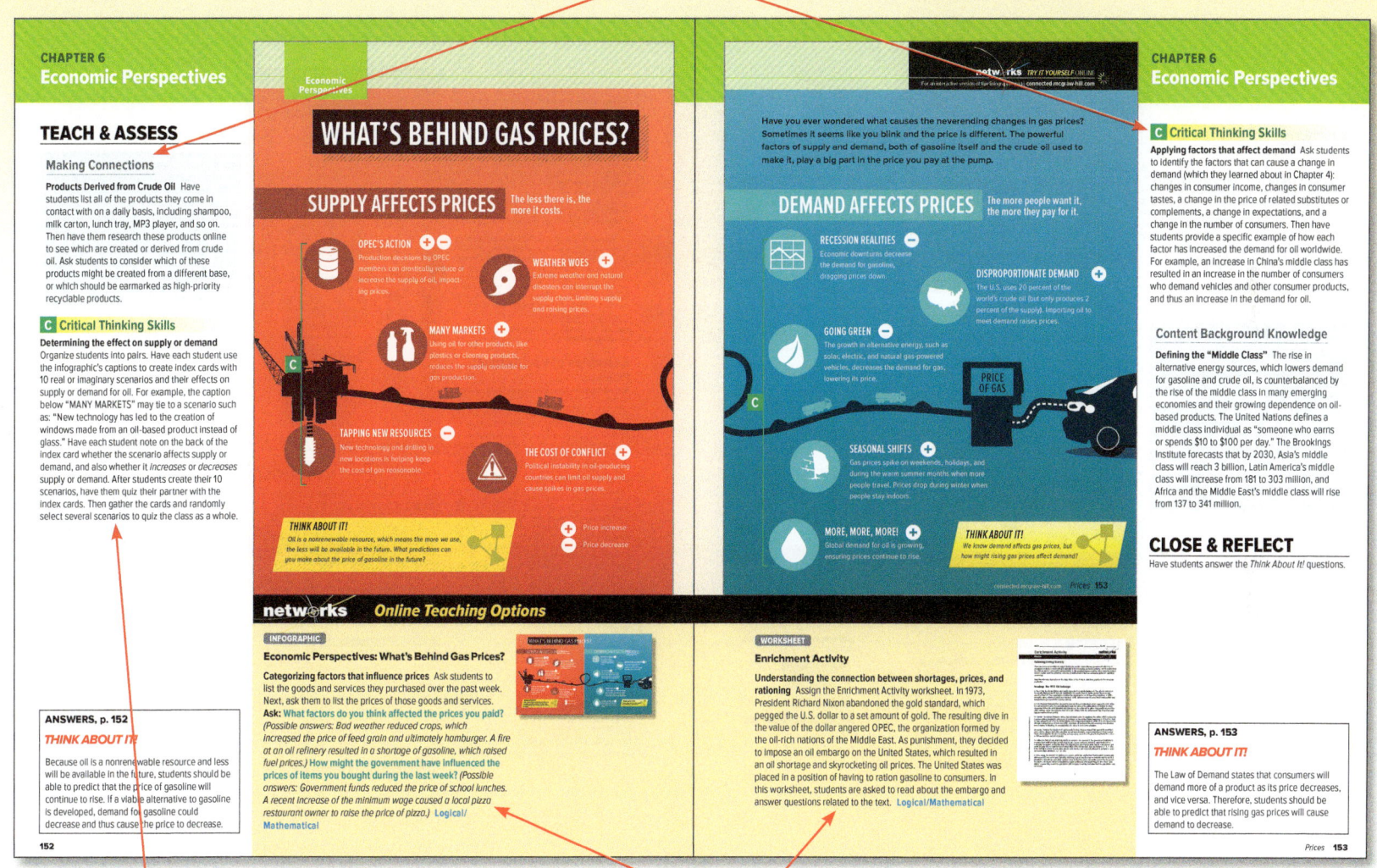

Print-Based Activities

Activities in the margins correspond to the text in the Student Edition. These activities are coded to indicate their level and the learning style they support.

Online Digital Activities

Online digital activities for the lesson appear at the bottom of each page. The gray icon indicates the type of activity available in the online Teacher Center. Activities include interactive whiteboard activities, videos, interactive maps, images, and worksheets. Activities can be projected or used on your classroom whiteboard. Worksheets can be edited and printed, or assigned online, depending on student access to technology.

How to Use the Teacher Edition   xxix

HOW TO USE THE TEACHER EDITION

Using the Wraparound Resources and Activities (continued)

ENGAGE
Every lesson begins with an Engage activity designed to motivate students and focus their attention on the lesson topic.

Guiding Questions
Guiding Questions in the Student Edition point out key knowledge that students need to acquire to be able to answer the chapter's Essential Question.

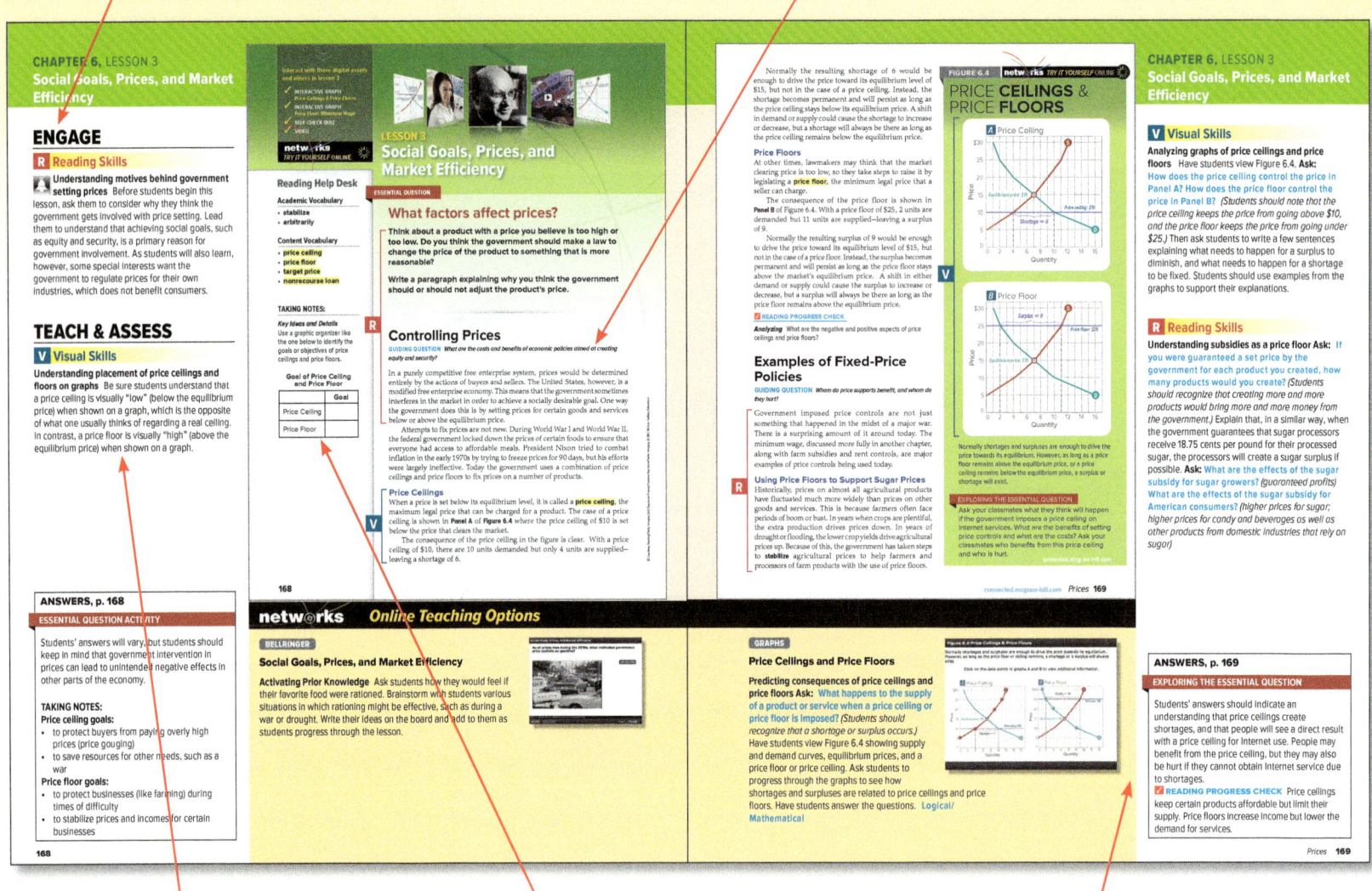

TEACH & ASSESS
Teach & Assess is the core of the lesson. It contains activities, lecture notes, background information, and discussion questions to teach the lesson.

Reading Help Desk
- Content Vocabulary
- Academic Vocabulary
- Note-Taking Activity and Graphic Organizer

Answers
Answers to questions and activities in the Student Edition appear in the bottom corner of the Teacher Edition pages.

xxx   How to Use the Teacher Edition

Using the Wraparound Resources and Activities (continued)

Don't forget! You can customize all your Lesson Plans online.

Brackets
Brackets on the Student Edition page correspond to teaching strategies and activities in the Teacher Edition. As you teach the lesson, the brackets show you where to use these activities and strategies.

Reading Progress Check
A Reading Progress Check appears at the end of each topic in the Student Edition to help gauge student reading comprehension.

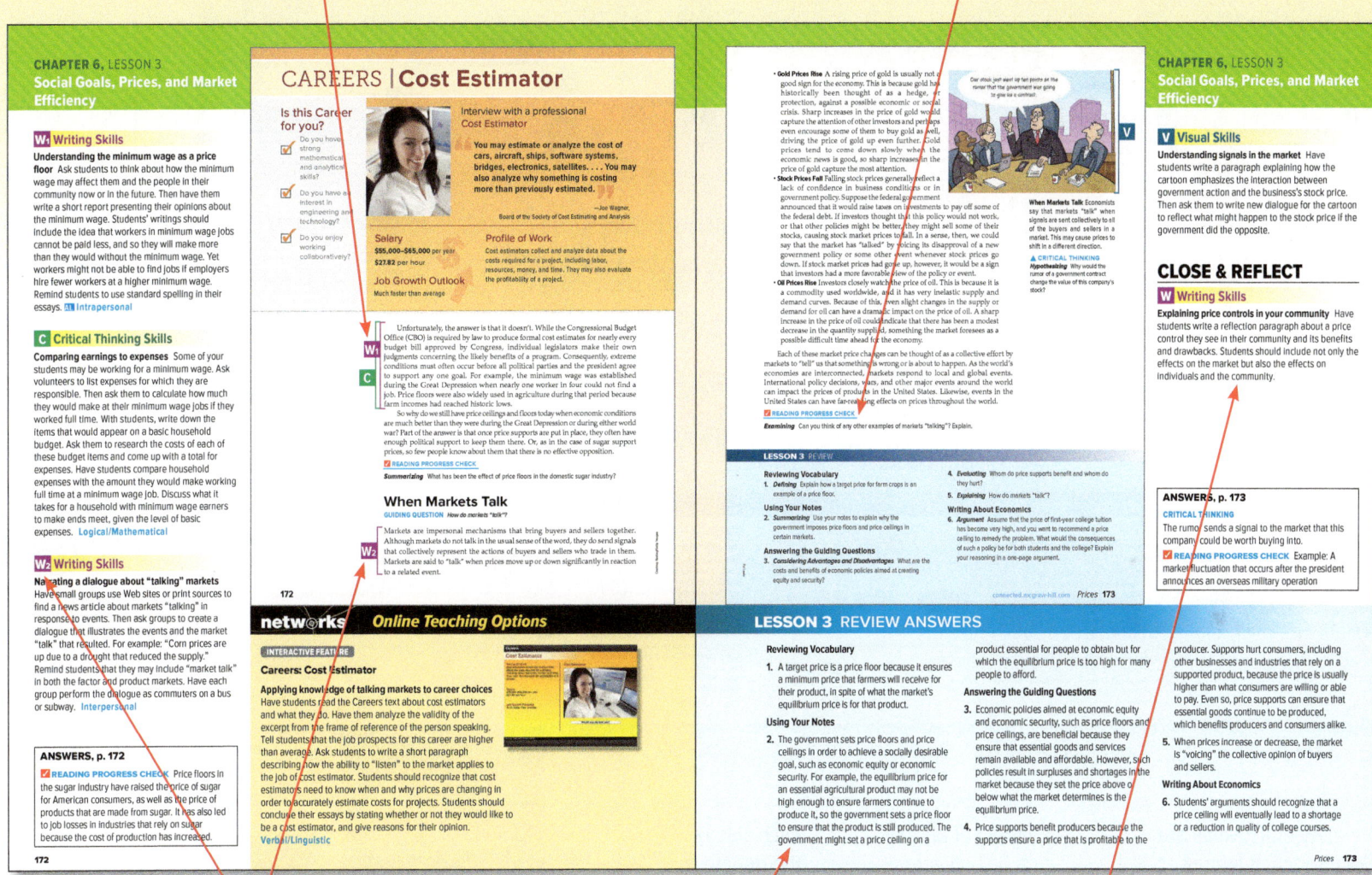

Letters
The letters on the reduced Student Edition page identify the type of activity. See the key on the first planning page of each chapter to learn about the different types of activities.

Lesson Review Answers
Answers to the lesson Review appear at the bottom of the last page of each lesson.

CLOSE & REFLECT
Each lesson ends with activities designed to help students link the content to the lesson's Guiding Questions and the chapter's Essential Questions.

How to Use the Teacher Edition **xxxi**

HOW TO USE THE TEACHER EDITION

Special Features

Debates
This program includes Debates features which present two sides of an important economic issue. Each Debate features a summary of the controversy, primary source excerpts outlining both sides of the argument and other supporting materials.

Case Study
This program also includes a Case Study feature focusing on a real-world economic story. The Case Study presents a story summary as well as a variety of illustrations and data.

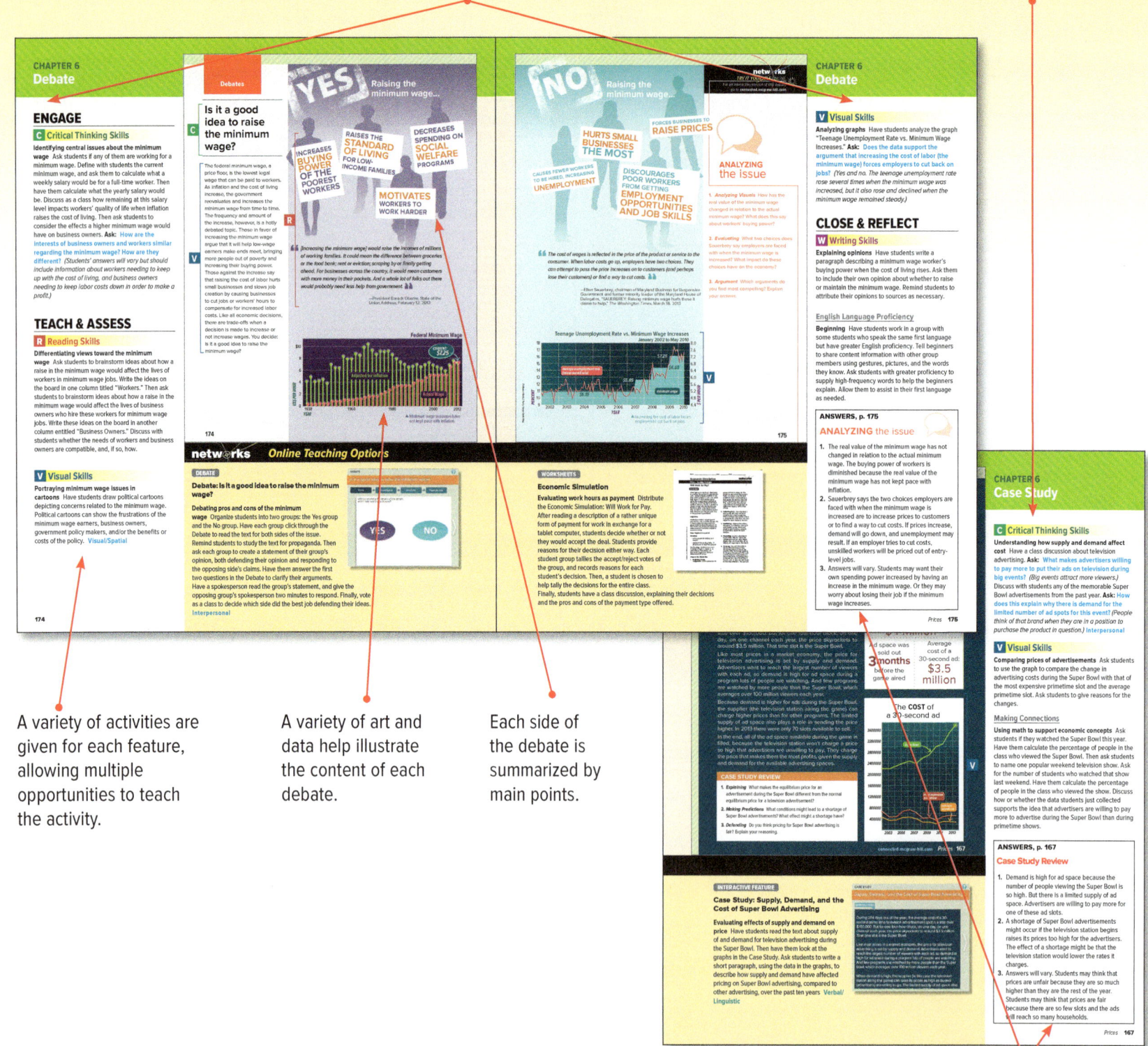

A variety of activities are given for each feature, allowing multiple opportunities to teach the activity.

A variety of art and data help illustrate the content of each debate.

Each side of the debate is summarized by main points.

Questions assess students' understanding of the information in the feature.

Using the Wraparound Resources and Activities (continued)

Don't forget! You can customize all your Lesson Plans online.

Brackets
Brackets on the Student Edition page correspond to teaching strategies and activities in the Teacher Edition. As you teach the lesson, the brackets show you where to use these activities and strategies.

Reading Progress Check
A Reading Progress Check appears at the end of each topic in the Student Edition to help gauge student reading comprehension.

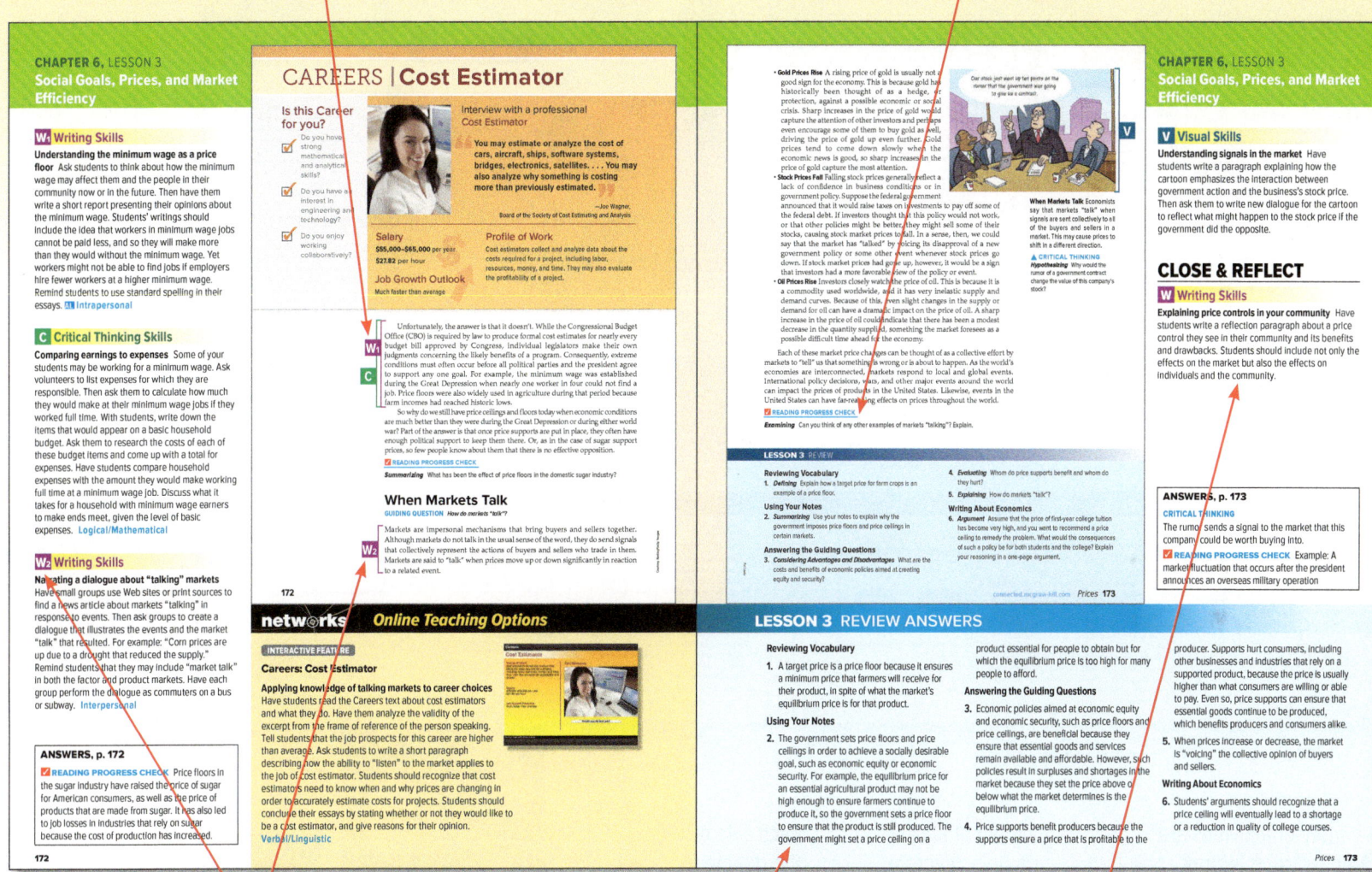

Letters
The letters on the reduced Student Edition page identify the type of activity. See the key on the first planning page of each chapter to learn about the different types of activities.

Lesson Review Answers
Answers to the lesson Review appear at the bottom of the last page of each lesson.

CLOSE & REFLECT
Each lesson ends with activities designed to help students link the content to the lesson's Guiding Questions and the chapter's Essential Questions.

How to Use the Teacher Edition **xxxi**

HOW TO USE THE TEACHER EDITION

Special Features

Debates
This program includes Debates features which present two sides of an important economic issue. Each Debate features a summary of the controversy, primary source excerpts outlining both sides of the argument and other supporting materials.

Case Study
This program also includes a Case Study feature focusing on a real-world economic story. The Case Study presents a story summary as well as a variety of illustrations and data.

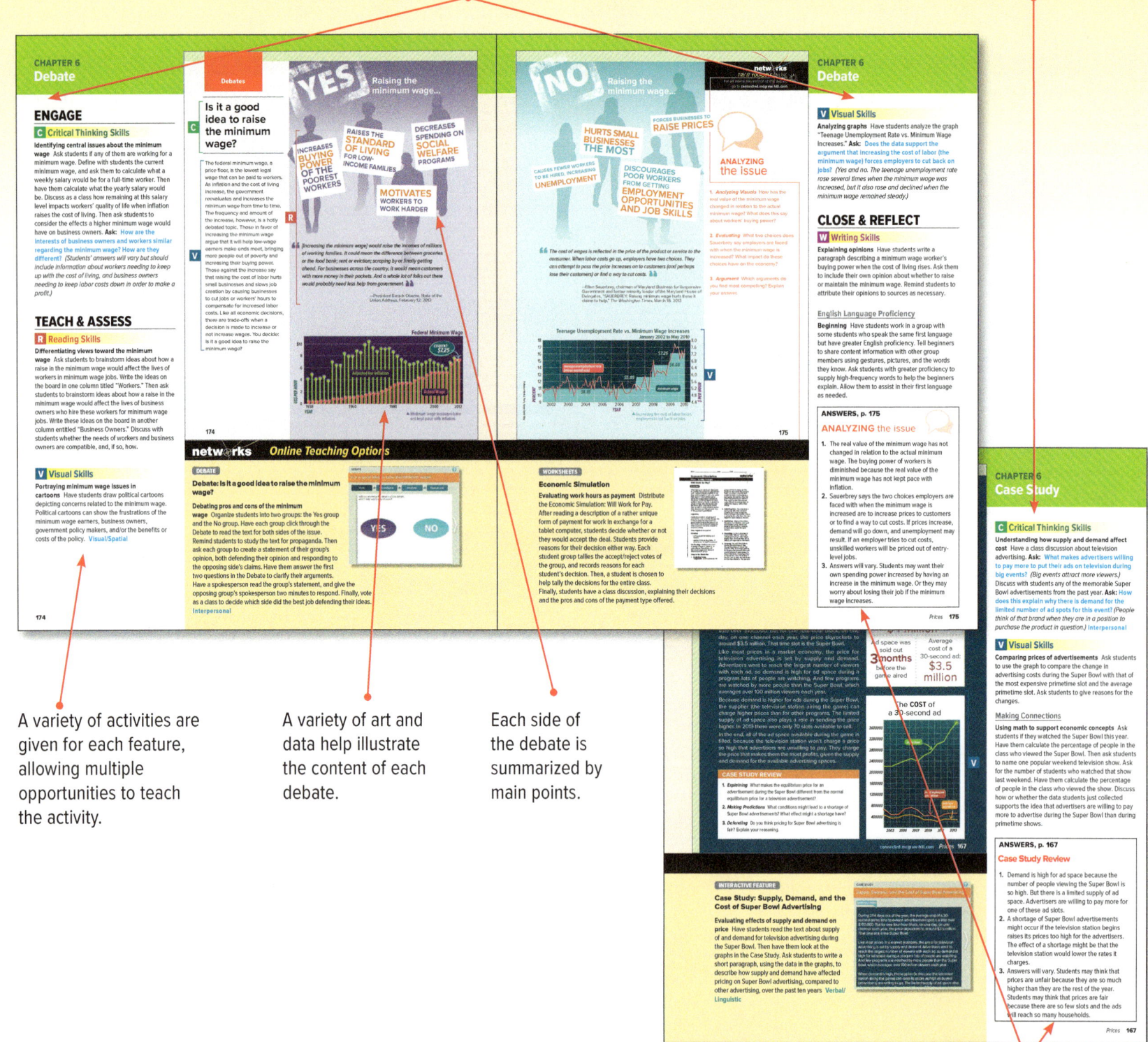

A variety of activities are given for each feature, allowing multiple opportunities to teach the activity.

A variety of art and data help illustrate the content of each debate.

Each side of the debate is summarized by main points.

Questions assess students' understanding of the information in the feature.

Activities and Assessment

Study Guide
Each chapter ends with a highly visual Study Guide that helps summarize the key concepts taught within each chapter.

Chapter Activities
Each chapter ends with the following:
- Critical Thinking Questions
- 21st Century Skills Activity
- Building Financial Literacy Activities
- Analyzing Visuals Questions

Chapter Assessment
Each chapter ends with the following:
- Answering the Essential Question Activities
- Analyzing Primary Sources Questions and Activities

Online Assessment Options
Digital assessment opportunities are available for every chapter.

Assessment Answers
Answers to the chapter assessment questions

Don't forget! You can customize all your Lesson Plans online.

How to Use the Teacher Edition xxxiii

HOW TO USE THE ONLINE STUDENT EDITION

TO THE STUDENT
Welcome to McGraw-Hill Education's **Networks** online student learning center. Here you will access your online student edition as well as many other learning resources.

1) LOGGING ON TO THE STUDENT LEARNING CENTER

Using your internet browser, go to connected.mcgraw-hill.com

Enter your username and password or

Create a New Account using the redemption code your teacher gave you.

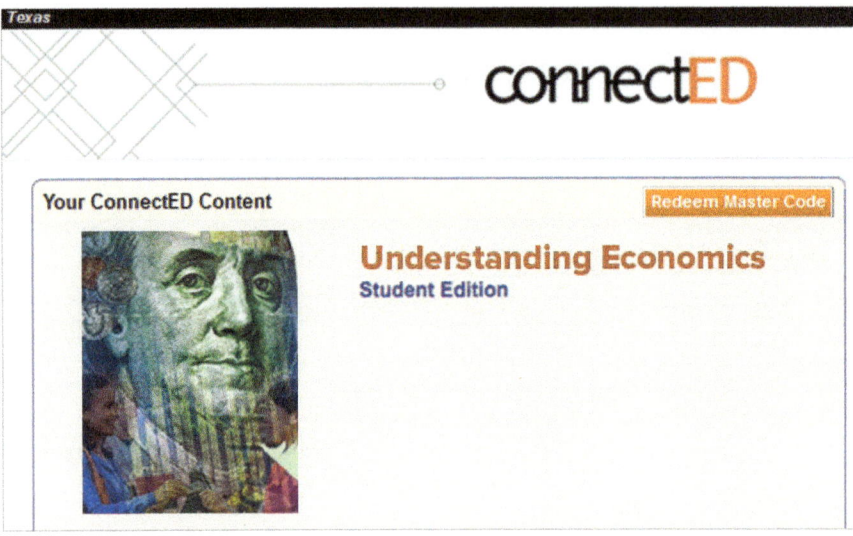

2) SELECT YOUR PROGRAM

Click your program to launch the home page of your online student learning center.

xxxiv

HOW TO USE THE ONLINE STUDENT EDITION

Using Your Home Page

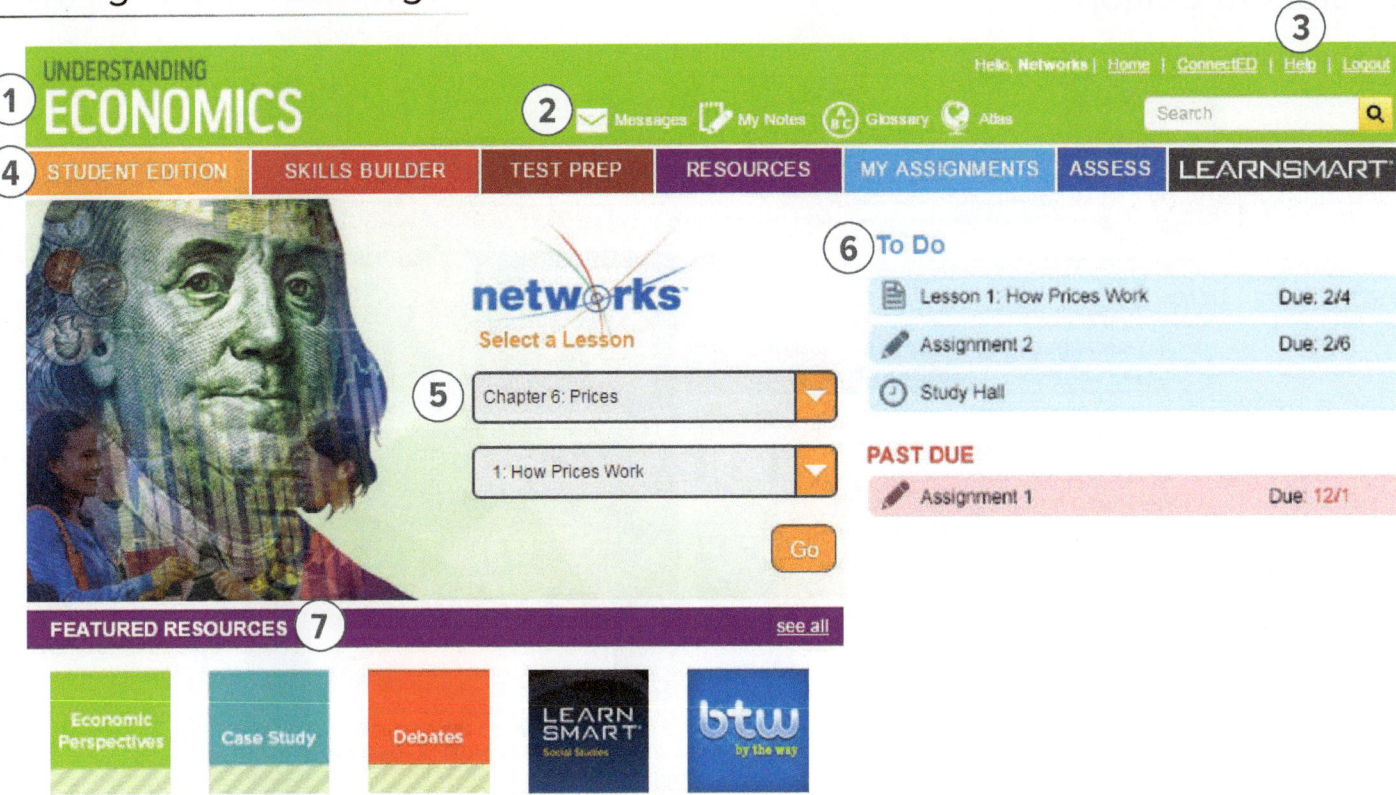

① **HOME PAGE**

To return to your Home Page at any time, click the networks logo in the top left corner of the page.

② **QUICK LINKS MENU**

Use this menu to access:
- Messages
- My Notes (your personal notepad)
- Glossary
- Atlas
- Correlations

③ **HELP**

For videos and assistance with the various features of the networks system, click help.

④ **MAIN MENU**

Use the menu bar to access:
- The Online Student Edition
- Skills Builder (for activities to improve your skills)
- Test Prep
- Resource Library
- Assignments
- Assessments
- LearnSmart

⑤ **ONLINE STUDENT EDITION**

Go to your online student edition by selecting the chapter and lesson and then click Go.

⑥ **ASSIGNMENTS**

Recent assignments from your teacher will appear here. Click the assignment to see the details.

⑦ **RESOURCE LIBRARY**

Click on the featured resources or click *see all* to browse the Resource Library.

HOW TO USE THE ONLINE STUDENT EDITION

Using Your Online Student Edition

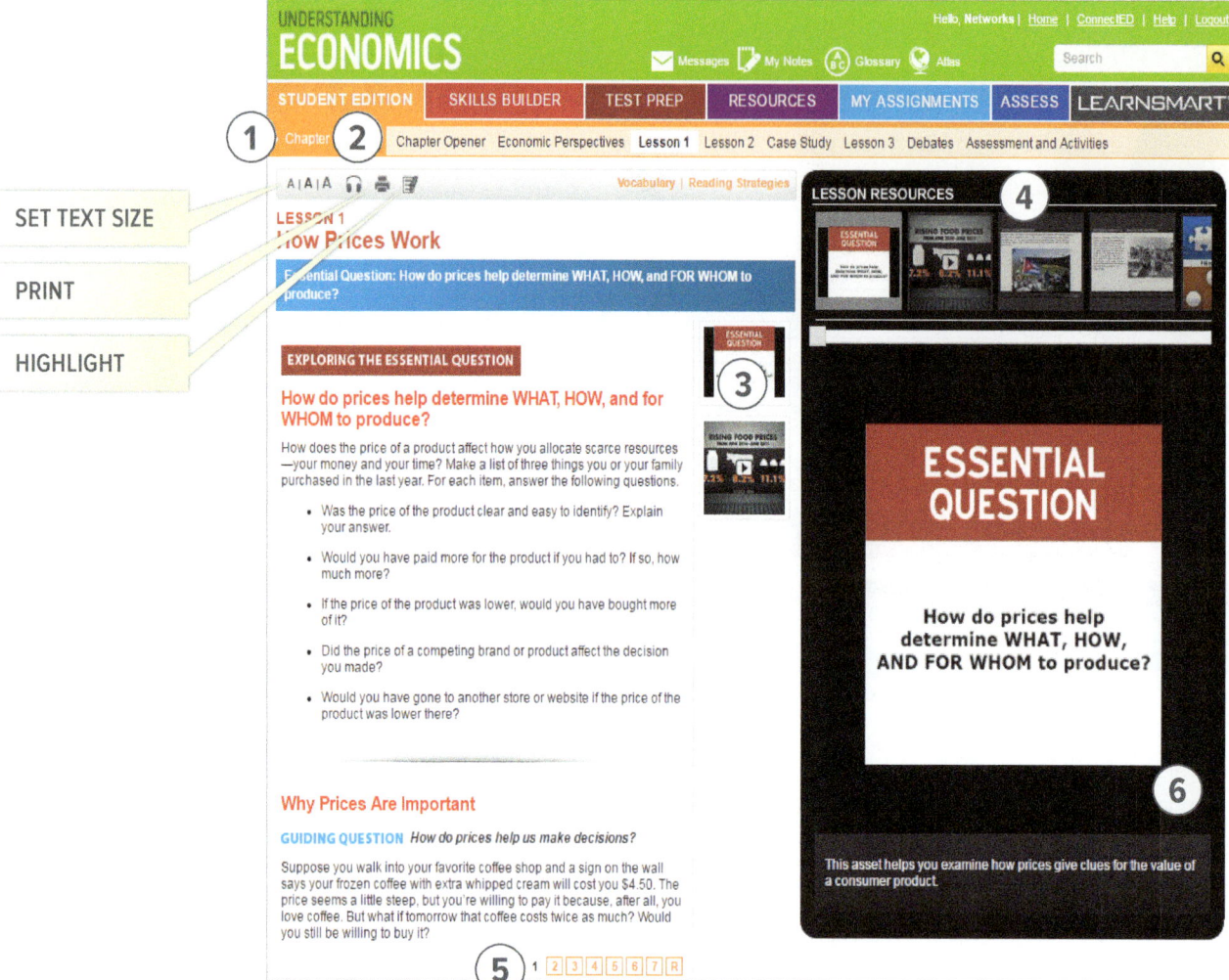

1 LESSON MENU

• Use the tabs to open the different lessons and special features in a chapter or unit.

• Clicking on the unit or chapter title will open the table of contents.

2 AUDIO EDITION

Click on the headphones symbol to have the page read to you. MP3 files for downloading each lesson are available in the Resource Library.

3 RESOURCES FOR THIS PAGE

Resources appear in the middle column to show that they go with the text on this page. Click the images to open them in the Viewer.

4 LESSON RESOURCES

Use the carousel to browse the interactive resources available in this lesson. Click on a resource to open it in the viewer below.

5 CHANGE PAGES

Click here to move to the next page in the lesson.

6 RESOURCE VIEWER

Click on the image that appears in the viewer to launch an interactive resource, including:

• Lesson Videos
• Interactive Photos and Slideshows
• Interactive Maps
• Interactive charts and graphs
• Games
• Self-Check Quizzes for each lesson

HOW TO USE THE ONLINE STUDENT EDITION

Reading Support in the Online Student Edition

Your Online Student Edition contains several features to help improve your reading skills and understanding of the content.

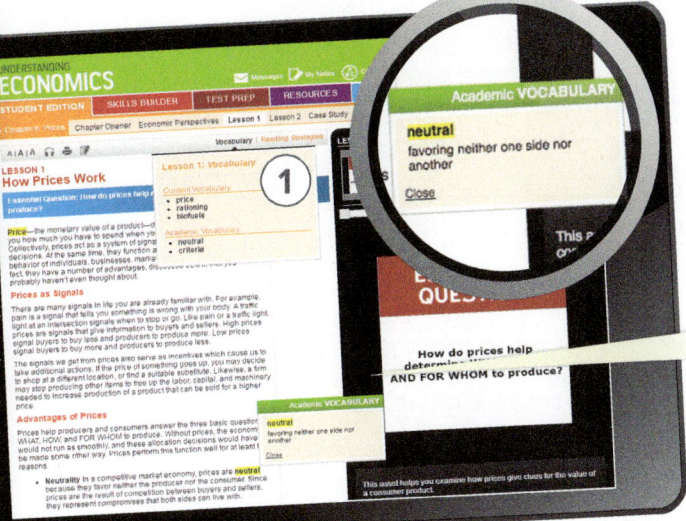

1 LESSON VOCABULARY

Click Vocabulary to bring up a list of terms introduced in this lesson.

VOCABULARY POP-UP

Click on any term highlighted in yellow to open a window with the term's definition.

2 NOTES

Click My Notes to open the note-taking tool. You can write and save any notes you want in the Lesson Notes tab.

Click on the Guided Notes tab for Guided Reading Questions. Answering these questions will help you build a set of notes about the lesson.

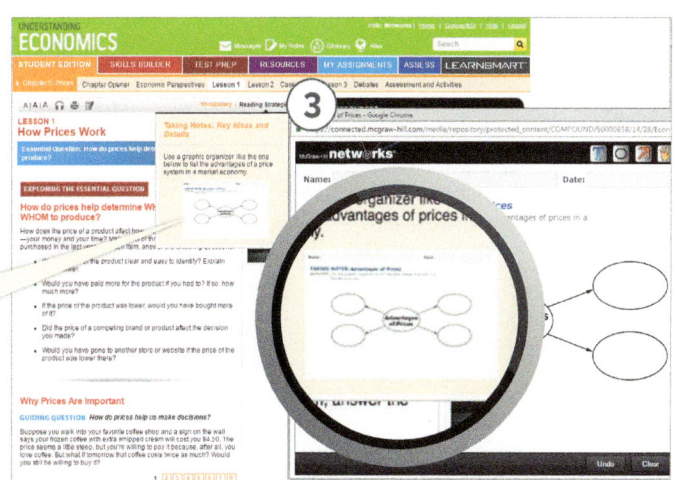

3 GRAPHIC ORGANIZER

Click Reading Strategies to open a note-taking activity using a graphic organizer.

Click the image of the graphic organizer to make it interactive. You can type directly into the graphic organizer and save or print your notes.

xxxvii

HOW TO USE THE ONLINE STUDENT EDITION

Using Interactive Resources in the Online Student Edition

Each lesson of your online student edition contains many resources to help you learn the content and skills you need to know for this subject.

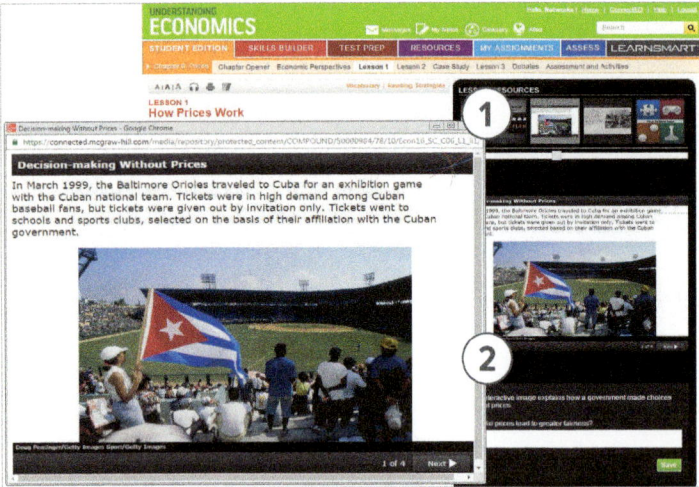

1 LAUNCHING RESOURCES

Clicking a resource in the viewer launches an interactive resource.

2 QUESTIONS AND ACTIVITIES

When a resource appears in the viewer, there are usually 1 or 2 questions or activities beneath it. You can type and save your answers in the answer boxes and submit them to your teacher.

3 INTERACTIVE MAPS

When you encounter a digital map asset, click on the image in the viewer to launch the asset. Most of the maps in this program have different layers of information displayed. Click through the asset to find all of the data.

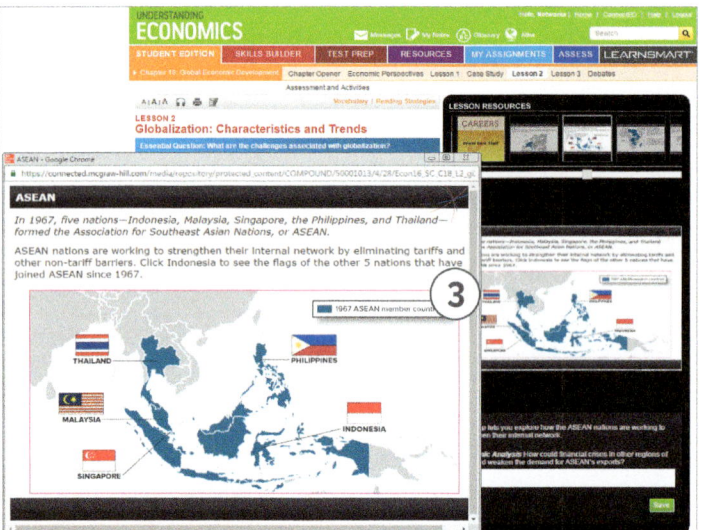

4 CHAPTER FEATURE

Each chapter begins with a feature called *Economic Perspectives*. They include interactive data and visuals to help you understand a main topic of the chapter's content.

Click within each digital infographic to discover all of the information. Each feature is unique and designed to present its own set of data in an exciting and visual experience.

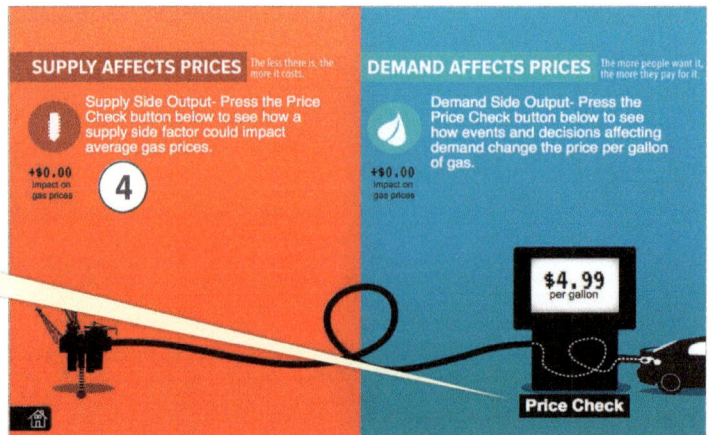

HOW TO USE THE ONLINE STUDENT EDITION

Activities and Assessment

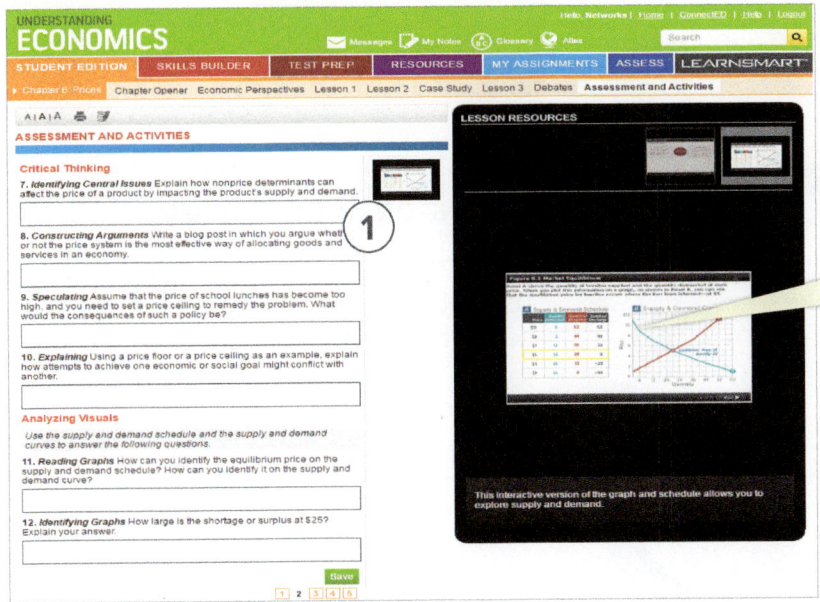

1 CHAPTER ASSESSMENT AND ACTIVITIES

At the end of each chapter is the Assessment and Activities tab. Here you can test your understanding of what you have learned. You can type and save answers in the answer boxes and submit them to your teacher.

When a question or activity uses an image or graph or map, it will appear in the viewer.

Finding Other Resources

There are hundreds of additional resources available in the Resource Library. Click the tab Resources to enter the library.

2 RESOURCE LIBRARY

Click the Resources tab to find videos, games, biographies, careers, the Reading Essentials and Study Guides, and many other interactive resources and worksheets.

You can search the Resource Library by Lesson or Keyword.

Click the star to mark a resource as a favorite.

xxxix

HOW TO USE THE ONLINE TEACHER EDITION

TO THE TEACHER
Welcome to McGraw-Hill Education's **networks**™ online teacher lesson center. Here you will access your online lesson plans, worksheets, tests and quizzes, and many other teaching resources.

① LOGGING ON TO THE TEACHER LESSON CENTER

Using your Internet browser, go to connected.mcgraw-hill.com.

Enter your username and Password or

Create a New Account using the redemption code.

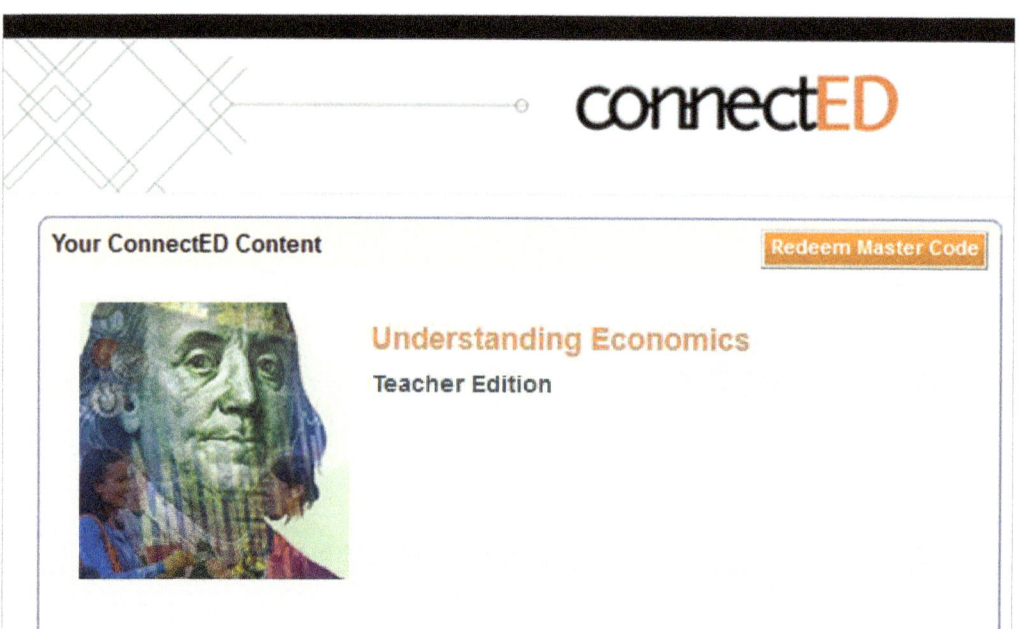

② SELECT YOUR PROGRAM

Click your program to launch the home page of your online teacher lesson center.

xl *Go Online!* connected.mcgraw-hill.com

HOW TO USE THE ONLINE TEACHER EDITION

Using Your Home Page

Your home page provides quick access to all of your teaching resources.

1 MAIN MENU

Use the menu bar to:
- Access Lesson Plans
- Link to the McGraw-Hill Assessment to edit and create your own tests and quizzes
- Manage your classroom and send assignments to students
- Access LearnSmart

2 HOME PAGE

To return to your home page at any time, click the title in the top left corner of the page.

3 QUICK LINKS MENU

Use this menu to access:
- Messages from your students
- Notes (your personal notepad)
- My Files (you can upload your own files to use with the lesson plans)
- Correlations

4 HELP

For videos, professional development, and assistance with the features of networks™, click Help.

5 RESOURCE LIBRARY

Click on the featured resources or click *see all* to browse the Resource Library.

6 STUDENT EDITION

Click to open the online student edition.

7 ANNOTATED STUDENT EDITION

Click to open the student edition showing sample answers to questions and activities.

8 SEARCH

Search Networks by entering Keywords into the Search box.

9 CALENDAR

Create classes and then use the planner to track lesson plans, events, and assignments.

10 LESSON SELECTOR

To open a lesson plan, select the chapter, then choose the chapter materials you need:
- Lesson Plans (lecture notes, activities, and resources for each lesson)
- Activities to help introduce and wrap-up the chapter
- Activities and resources to help with Intervention and Remediation
- Activities to support Gifted and Talented students

Go Online! connected.mcgraw-hill.com

HOW TO USE THE ONLINE TEACHER EDITION

Using Your Online Lesson Plans

Each lesson plan is divided into sections that follow the teaching cycle: Engage, Teach and Assess, Close and Reflect. Each section includes lecture notes, activities, questions, prompts, and links to lesson resources. Click the arrow beside each section to open it.

1) ACTIVITIES AND WORKSHEETS

Within each section of the lesson is a list of interactive activities, printable worksheets, and other resources. Click each activity to launch it.

2) LECTURE NOTES

If you click Customize, you can edit, revise, and rearrange these notes to suit your needs and save them as a custom lesson plan. You can also print copies of the lecture notes.

3) LEVELED AND DIFFERENTIATED ACTIVITIES

Activities within each lesson are identified if they are appropriate for Approaching Level (AL) or Beyond Level (BL) students, and whether they are appropriate for English Language Learners (ELL).

Go Online! connected.mcgraw-hill.com

HOW TO USE THE ONLINE TEACHER EDITION

(4) TEACHING WITH THE STUDENT EDITION

Lesson plans also contain activities and questions for using the student edition content within the lesson. The activities are coded by the type of skills they help to develop.

(5) LESSON PRESENTATIONS

Click the Start button next to LESSON PRESENTATION, and then select Launch Presentation to launch a pre-built presentation. Each presentation is made up of a series of slides showing resources, interactive activities, and worksheets suitable for whole-class instruction. Select Launch Editor to create or edit a customized version of your lesson presentation.

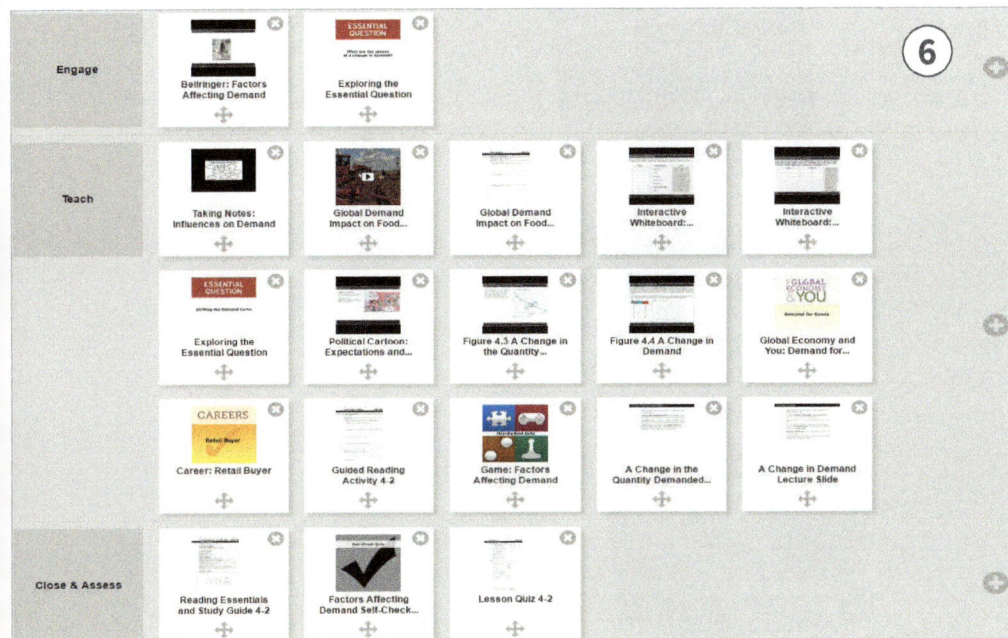

(6) CUSTOMIZING YOUR PRESENTATIONS

To customize your presentations, grab the arrow at the bottom of a tile to move the tile to a different location. Click the x in the top right corner to remove an item. Click the + at far right to add new items. If you want to return to the original lesson presentation, select "Reset Presentation."

Go Online! connected.mcgraw-hill.com **xliii**

HOW TO USE THE ONLINE TEACHER EDITION

Finding Resources

1) USING CHAPTER RESOURCES AT A GLANCE

At the top of the lesson, select the chapter you want to search, and then select Chapter Resources at a Glance. Open the sections below to locate resources for the whole chapter or for specific lessons. Answer keys are also available for chapter and lesson activities.

2) TYPES OF RESOURCES

All of the resources for a particular chapter or lesson are listed. You can quickly identify available worksheets, activities, projects, and options to review, assess, remediate, and differentiate.

3) LAUNCH RESOURCES

Click on the image of each resource to launch it and view its content.

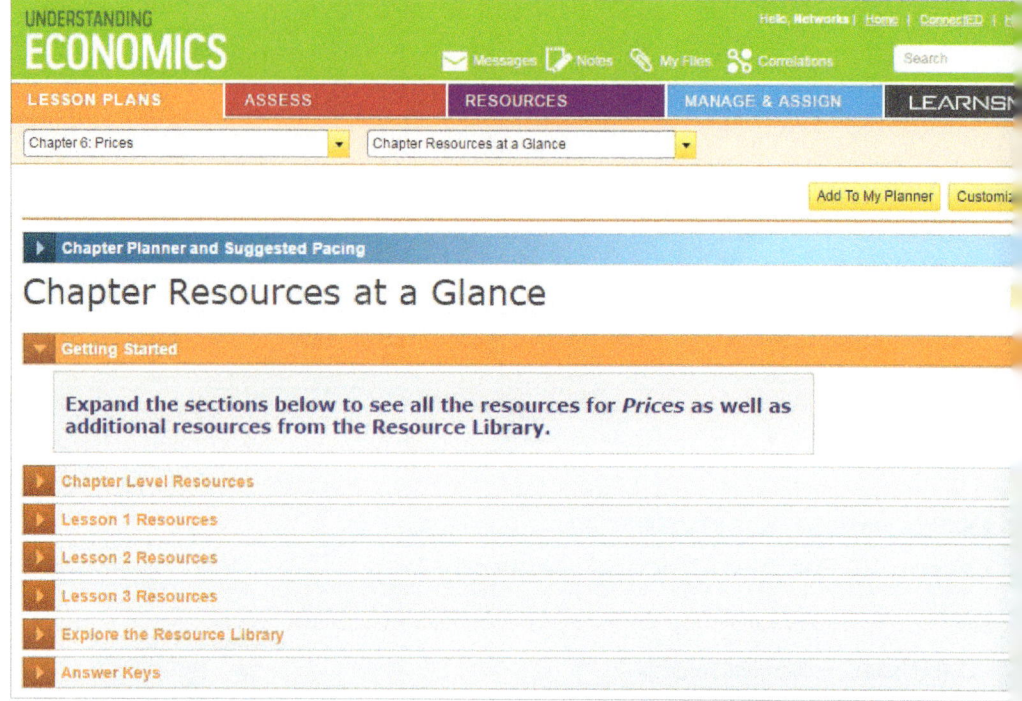

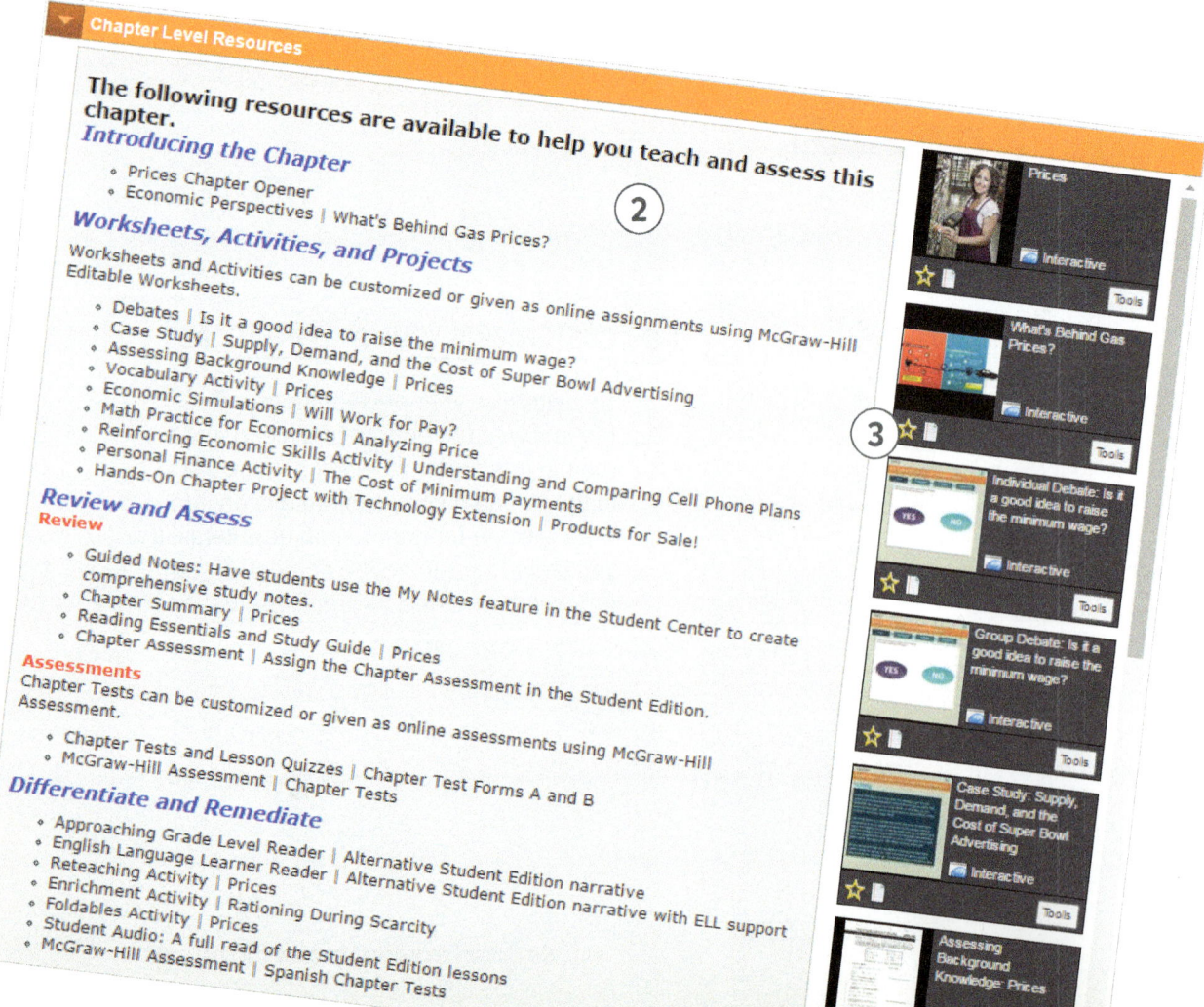

HOW TO USE THE ONLINE TEACHER EDITION

4 RESOURCE LIBRARY

Hundreds of additional resources are available in the Resource Library. Click the Resources tab to enter the library.

5 RESOURCE MENU

Click the tabs in the Resource menu to find hundreds of assets, including Economic Perspectives, Case Studies, Debates, Biographies, Charts and Graphs, Professional Development materials, and printable files of the Reading Essentials and Study Guide workbook.

6 SEARCH

You can search the Resource Library by lesson or keyword.

7 UPLOAD YOUR OWN RESOURCES

Click My Files in the Resource Menu. Then click Upload New Files. Locate files on your computer and upload them into My Files for use in your own custom lesson plans and presentations.

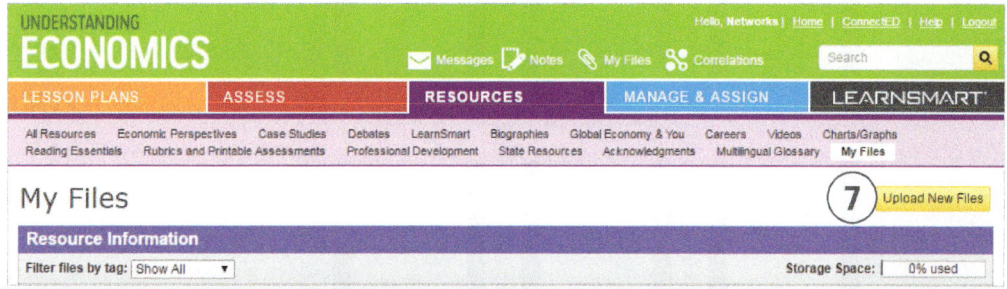

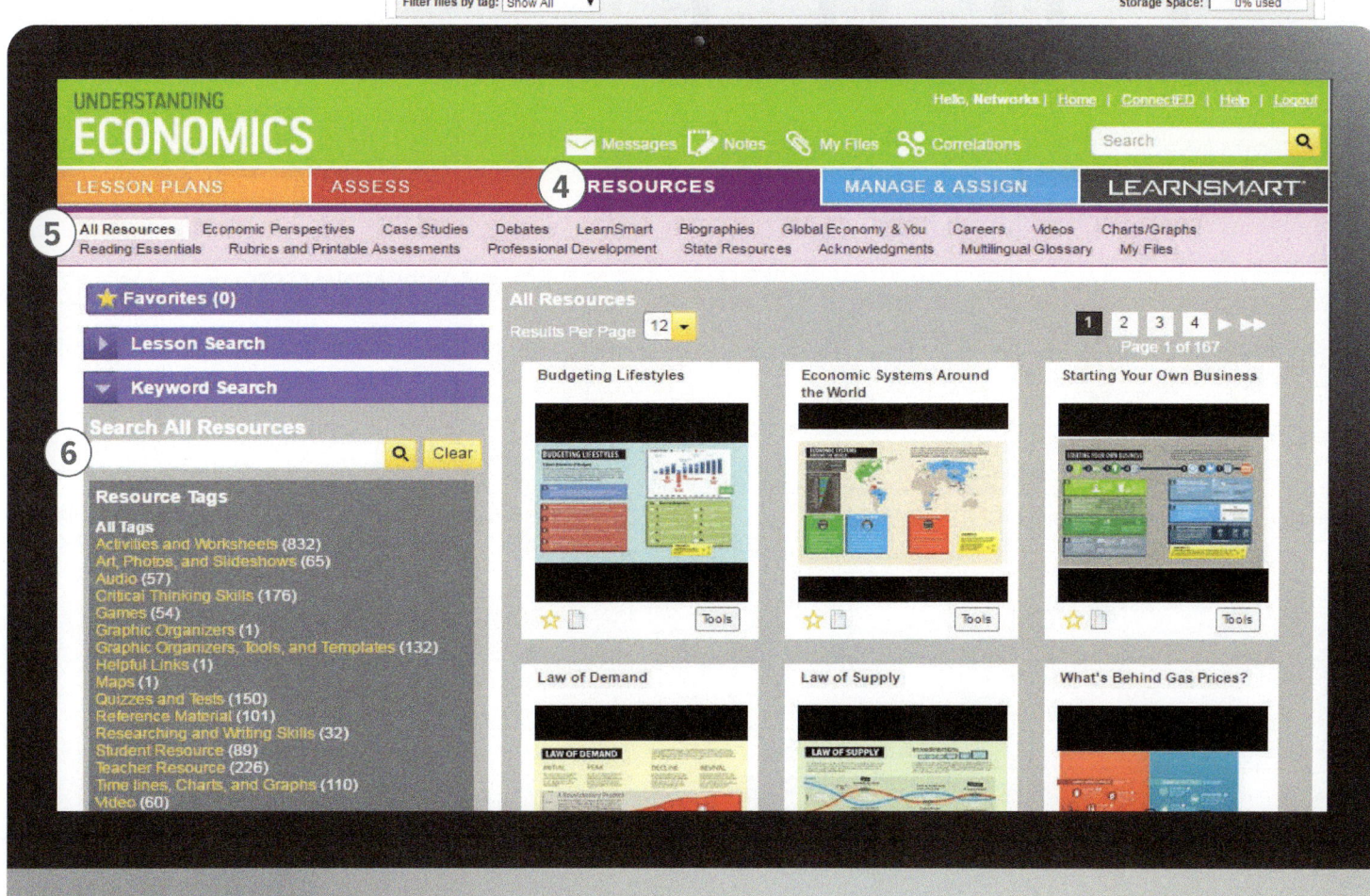

Go Online! connected.mcgraw-hill.com

HOW TO USE THE ONLINE TEACHER EDITION

Using the McGraw-Hill Online Assessment Center

All of your chapter tests and lesson quizzes are available in the McGraw-Hill Online Assessment Center. There are hundreds of tech-enhanced questions and hundreds more traditional questions. You can use the existing test questions, edit them to meet classroom needs, or create your own questions and tests from scratch.

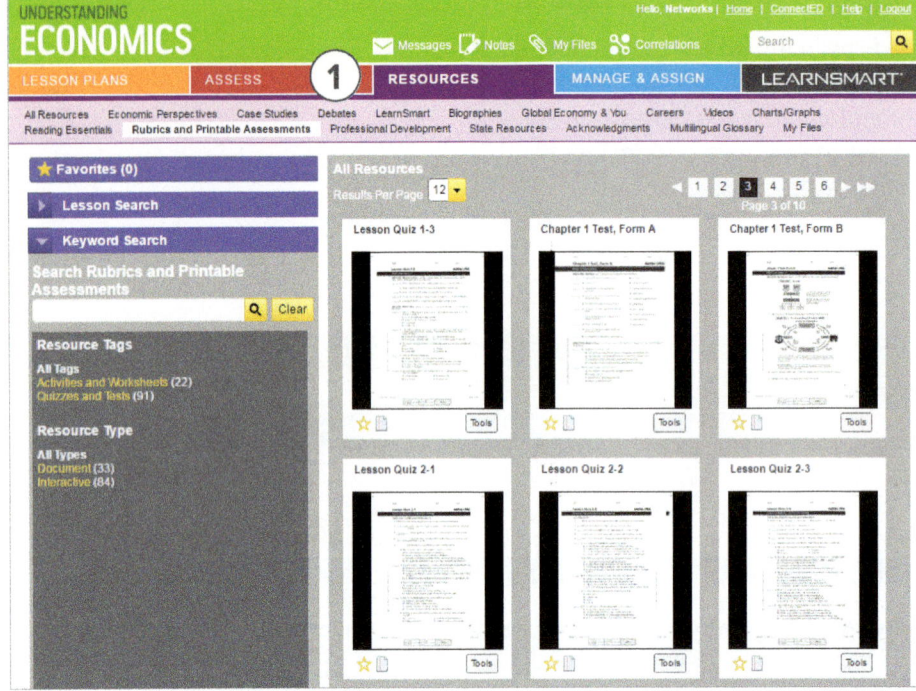

1) ASSESS

In the RESOURCES tab, click on the Rubrics and Printable Assessments subtab for test preparation activities and rubrics, and to access printed tests and quizzes.

2) LAUNCH McGraw-Hill Assessment

Click on the ASSESS tab to access the McGraw-Hill Online Assessment Center. Then click My Test Library and My Tests to open the *Understanding Economics* test and quiz banks.

3) SELECTING BANKS

Clicking on any bank will open it and give you the option to Preview, Assign to Class, Print, and other choices.

4) CREATING TESTS

Click New Test and select your test settings. Then add questions from the Question Banks or write new questions. Question types include Multiple Choice, Multi-Select, Select Text, Matching, Bucketing, Ordering, and Image Labels in addition to more traditional question types.

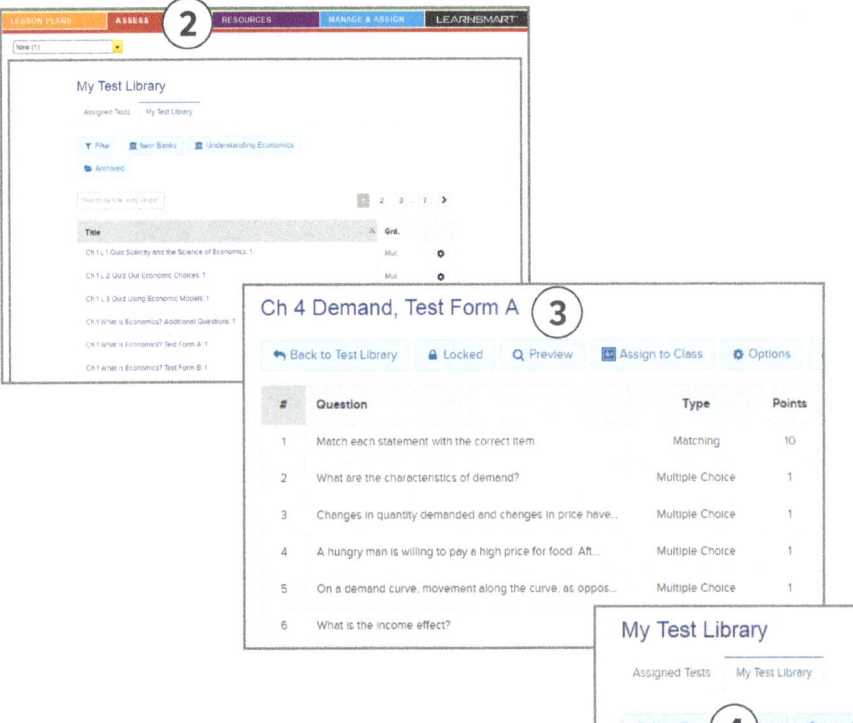

HOW TO USE THE ONLINE TEACHER EDITION

① MANAGE YOUR CLASS

Click Manage and Assign to set up your classes, send assignments to students, and check student messages.

② ASSIGNING DIFFERENT READING LEVELS FOR THE ONLINE STUDENT EDITION

After classes are set up in your Manage and Assign center, you can assign an Approaching Level edition of the text narrative to individual students. The Approaching Level text is written two levels below the regular student edition text.

An English Language Learner edition of the text is also provided. The ELL edition uses the Approaching Level text but includes additional activities and support to help English language learners.

Adaptive Learning

LEARNSMART®
Using revolutionary adaptive technology, LearnSmart® builds a learning experience unique to each student's individual needs.

③ ADAPTIVE LEARNING AND ASSESSMENT

LearnSmart® provides additional adaptive practice for students with varying needs.

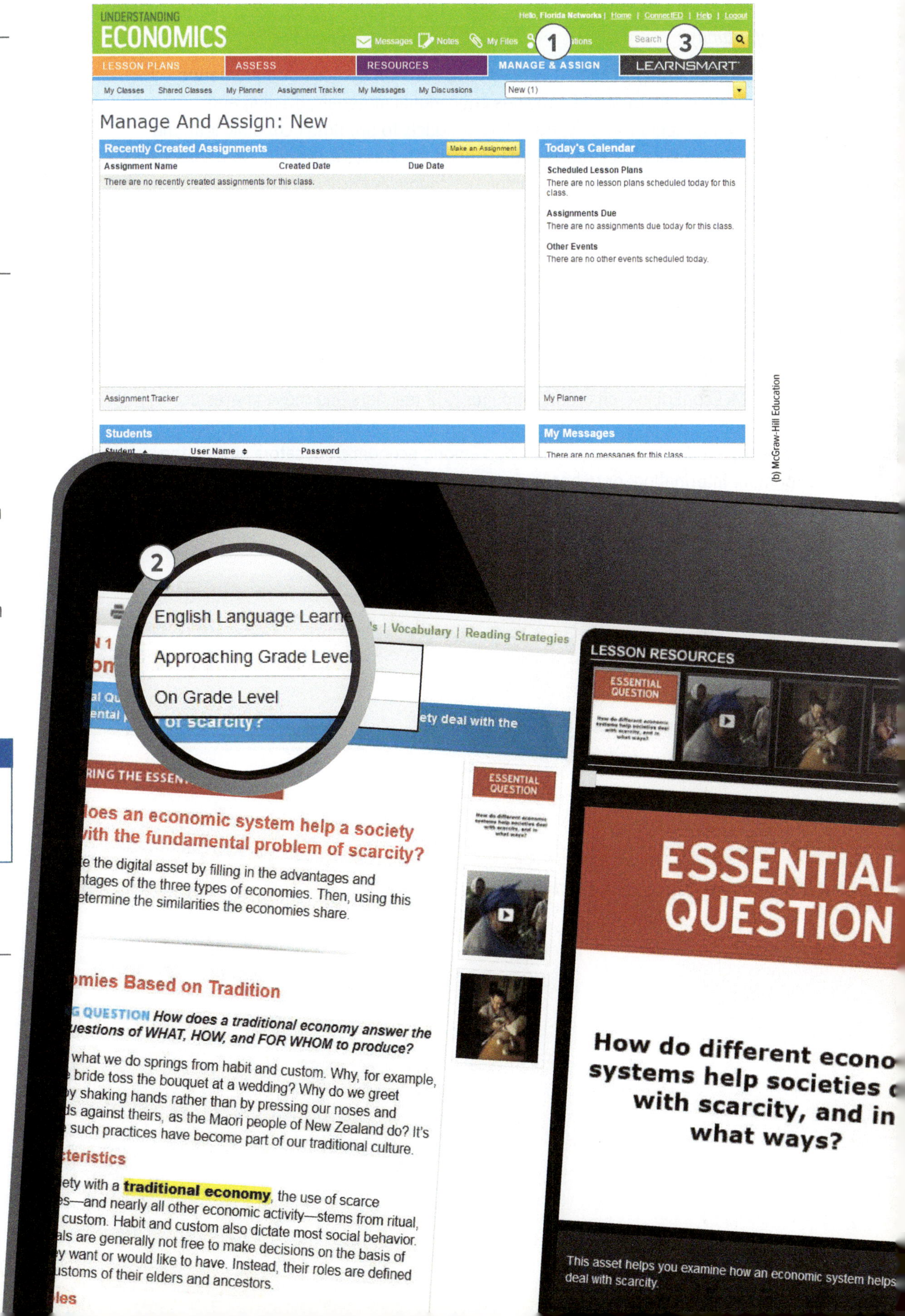

Council for Economic Education

Teaching Opportunity®

The Council for Economic Education (CEE) is an organization dedicated to promoting financial and economic literacy. CEE provides educational materials, training and professional development programs, and other products to promote economic learning and sound decision making. CEE has also developed *Voluntary National Content Standards in Economics* to be used in designing a complete economics curriculum.

The Council for Economic Education was founded in 1949 on the idea that "there is no aspect of education more important than that which makes all our citizens intelligent and truly informed about the economic system in which they live and work." Today, CEE advocates economic and personal finance education in the United States at the local, state, national, and international levels. In the United States, CEE reaches 150,000 teachers each year. Internationally, CEE delivers programs in more than 30 countries.

CEE sponsors MyEconEdLink, an organization for K-12 teachers and those interested in economics education. MyEconEdLink provides educational materials, conferences and workshops, and facilitates communication among economic educators around the world. For more information, or to become a member of MyEconEdLink, visit http://www.councilforeconed.org/resources/community/.

Text Correlation to the Voluntary National Content Standards in Economics

In 1994 the United States Congress designated economics as one of the nine core subjects to be taught in America's schools. As a result, the Council for Economic Education developed the *Voluntary National Content Standards in Economics* for use in economics curricula.

Understanding Economics provides extensive coverage for the 20 voluntary content standards. For a complete discussion of the standards, you can reach the Council for Economic Education online at www.councilforeconed.org, or at 1-800-338-1192.

For each standard, the student will understand:	*Understanding Economics* Chapter and Lesson Coverage
[1] Scarcity	
Productive resources are limited. Therefore, people cannot have all the goods and services they want; as a result, they must choose some things and give up others.	**Chapter 1** Lesson 1 Scarcity and the Science of Economics Lesson 2 Our Economic Choices Lesson 3 Using Economic Models **Chapter 2** Lesson 1 Economic Systems Lesson 2 Mixed Economies Lesson 3 The Global Transition to Capitalism **Chapter 18** Lesson 3 Global Problems and Economic Incentives
[2] Decision Making	
Effective decision making requires comparing the additional costs of alternatives with the additional benefits. Many choices involve doing a little more or a little less of something: few choices are "all or nothing" decisions.	**Chapter 1** Lesson 1 Scarcity and the Science of Economics Lesson 2 Our Economic Choices Lesson 3 Using Economic Models **Chapter 2** Lesson 1 Economic Systems Lesson 2 Mixed Economies **Chapter 3** Lesson 3 Evaluating Economic Performance **Chapter 4** Lesson 1 What Is Demand? Lesson 2 Factors Affecting Demand? **Chapter 5** Lesson 3 Cost, Revenue, and Profit Maximization **Chapter 6** Lesson 1 How Prices Work **Chapter 15** Lesson 3 Macroeconomic Equilibrium **Chapter 19** Lesson 1 Financial Institutions and Your Money Lesson 2 Business Organizations and Your Money

Text Correlation to the Voluntary National Content Standards in Economics

For each standard, the student will understand:	*Understanding Economics* Chapter and Lesson Coverage
[3] Allocation	
Different methods can be used to allocate goods and services. People acting individually or collectively must choose which methods to use to allocate different kinds of goods and services.	**Chapter 2** 　　Lesson 2　Mixed Economies **Chapter 6** 　　Lesson 1　How Prices Work 　　Lesson 3　Social Goals, Prices, and Market Efficiency **Chapter 14** 　　Lesson 1　Taxes
[4] Incentives	
People usually respond predictably to positive and negative incentives.	**Chapter 6** 　　Lesson 1　How Prices Work **Chapter 14** 　　Lesson 1　Taxes **Chapter 18** 　　Lesson 3　Global Problems and Economic Incentives
[5] Trade	
Voluntary exchange occurs only when all participating parties expect to gain. This is true for trade among individuals or organizations within a nation, and among individuals or organizations in different nations.	**Chapter 17** 　　Lesson 1　Absolute and Comparative Advantages 　　Lesson 2　Barriers to International Trade 　　Lesson 3　Foreign Exchange and Trade Deficits **Chapter 18** 　　Lesson 2　Globalization: Characteristics and Trends
[6] Specialization	
When individuals, regions, and nations specialize in what they can produce at the lowest cost and then trade with others, both production and consumption increase.	**Chapter 17** 　　Lesson 1　Absolute and Comparative Advantages
[7] Markets and Prices	
A market exists when buyers and sellers interact. This interaction determines market prices and thereby allocates scarce goods and services.	**Chapter 6** 　　Lesson 1　How Prices Work 　　Lesson 2　The Effects of Prices **Chapter 7** 　　Lesson 1　Competition and Market Structures 　　Lesson 2　Market Failures
[8] Role of Prices	
Prices send signals and provide incentives to buyers and sellers. When supply or demand changes, market prices adjust, affecting incentives.	**Chapter 4** 　　Lesson 1　What is Demand? 　　Lesson 2　Factors Affecting Demand 　　Lesson 3　Elasticity of Demand **Chapter 5** 　　Lesson 1　What is Supply? 　　Lesson 2　The Theory of Production 　　Lesson 3　Cost, Revenue, and Profit Maximization **Chapter 6** 　　Lesson 1　How Prices Work 　　Lesson 2　The Effects of Prices 　　Lesson 3　Social Goals, Prices, and Market Efficiency **Chapter 18** 　　Lesson 3　Global Problems and Economic Incentives

For each standard, the student will understand:	*Understanding Economics* Chapter and Lesson Coverage
[9] Competition and Market Structure	
Competition among sellers usually lowers costs and prices, and encourages producers to produce what consumers are willing and able to buy. Competition among buyers increases prices and allocates goods and services to those people who are willing and able to pay the most for them.	**Chapter 3** Lesson 1 American Free Enterprise Capitalism **Chapter 7** Lesson 1 Competition and Market Structure Lesson 2 Market Failures
[10] Institutions	
Institutions evolve and are created to help individuals and groups accomplish their goals. Banks, labor unions, markets, corporations, legal systems, and not-for-profit organizations are examples of important institutions. A different kind of institution, clearly defined and enforced property rights, is essential to a market economy.	**Chapter 8** Lesson 1 Forms of Business Organizations Lesson 3 Nonprofit Organizations **Chapter 9** Lesson 1 The Labor Movement **Chapter 16** Lesson 1 Structures and Responsibilities of the Fed Lesson 2 Monetary Policy **Chapter 19** Lesson 1 Financial Institutions and Your Money
[11] Money and Inflation	
Money makes it easier to trade, borrow, save, invest, and compare the value of goods and services. The amount of money in the economy affects the overall price level. Inflation is an increase in the overall price level that reduces the value of money.	**Chapter 3** Lesson 3 Evaluating Economic Performance **Chapter 10** Lesson 1 The Evolution, Functions, and Characteristics of Money Lesson 2 The Development of Modern Banking **Chapter 13** Lesson 2 Inflation
[12] Interest Rates	
Interest rates, adjusted for inflation, rise and fall to balance the amount saved with the amount borrowed, which affects the allocation of scarce resources between present and future uses.	**Chapter 10** Lesson 1 The Evolution, Functions, and Characteristics of Money **Chapter 16** Lesson 2 Monetary Policy **Chapter 19** Lesson 1 Financial Institutions and Your Money
[13] Income	
Income for most people is determined by the market value of the productive resources they sell. What workers earn primarily depends on the market value of what they produce.	**Chapter 9** Lesson 2 Wages and Labor Disputes Lesson 3 Economic Trends and Issues **Chapter 12** Lesson 3 Poverty and the Distribution of Income
[14] Entrepreneurship	
Entrepreneurs take on the calculated risk of starting new businesses, either by embarking on new ventures similar to existing ones or by introducing new innovations. Entrepreneurial innovation is an important source of economic growth.	**Chapter 1** Lesson 2 Our Economic Choices **Chapter 3** Lesson 2 Roles and Responsibilities in a Free Enterprise Economy **Chapter 7** Lesson 2 Market Failures **Chapter 8** Lesson 2 Business Growth and Expansion

Text Correlation to the Voluntary National Content Standards in Economics

For each standard, the student will understand:	*Understanding Economics* Chapter and Lesson Coverage
[15] Economic Growth	

Investment in factories, machinery, new technology, and in the health, education, and training of people stimulates economic growth and can raise future standards of living.	**Chapter 1**
	    Lesson 3 Using Economic Models
	Chapter 16
	    Lesson 1 Demand-Side Policies
	    Lesson 2 Supply-Side Policies
	    Lesson 3 Economics and Politics
	Chapter 17
	    Lesson 1 Absolute and Comparative Advantage
	Chapter 18
	    Lesson 1 Economic Development

[16] Role of Government and Market Failure	

There is an economic role for government in a market economy whenever the benefits of a government policy outweigh its costs. Governments often provide for national defense, address environmental concerns, define and protect property rights, and attempt to make markets more competitive. Most government policies also have direct or indirect effects on people's incomes.	**Chapter 2**
	    Lesson 1 Economic Systems
	    Lesson 2 Mixed Economies
	    Lesson 3 The Global Transition to Capitalism
	Chapter 3
	    Lesson 2 Roles and Responsibilities in a Free Enterprise Economy
	    Lesson 3 Evaluating Economic Performance
	Chapter 6
	    Lesson 3 Social Goals, Prices, and Market Efficiency
	Chapter 7
	    Lesson 2 Market Failures
	    Lesson 3 The Role of Government
	Chapter 15
	    Lesson 1 Taxes
	    Lesson 2 Federal Government Finances
	    Lesson 3 State and Local Government Finances
	Chapter 16
	    Lesson 1 Structure and Responsibilities of the Fed
	    Lesson 2 Monetary Policy
	    Lesson 3 Economics and Politics
	Chapter 18
	    Lesson 3 Global Problems and Economic Incentives

[17] Government Failure	

Costs of government policies sometimes exceed benefits. This may occur because of incentives facing voters, government officials, and government employees, because of actions by special interest groups that can impose costs on the general public, or because social goals other than economic efficiency are being pursued.	**Chapter 7**
	    Lesson 2 Market Failures
	Chapter 16
	    Lesson 2 Monetary Policy
	    Lesson 3 Economics and Politics
	Chapter 17
	    Lesson 2 Barriers to International Trade

For each standard, the student will understand:	*Understanding Economics* Chapter and Lesson Coverage
[18] Economic Fluctuations	

Fluctuations in a nation's overall levels of income, employment, and prices are determined by the interaction of spending and production decisions made by all households, firms, government agencies, and others in the economy. Recessions occur when overall levels of income and employment decline.	**Chapter 12**
	    Lesson 1 Measuring the Nation's Output and Income
	    Lesson 2 Population Growth and Trends
	Chapter 13
	    Lesson 1 Business Cycles and Economic Instability
	    Lesson 2 Inflation
	    Lesson 3 Unemployment
	Chapter 15
	    Lesson 3 Macroeconomic Equilibrium
	Chapter 16
	    Lesson 3 Economics and Politics
	Chapter 18
	    Lesson 1 Economic Development

[19] Unemployment and Inflation	

Unemployment imposes costs on individuals and the overall economy. Inflation, both expected and unexpected, also imposes costs on individuals and the overall economy. Unemployment increases during recessions and decreases during recoveries.	**Chapter 12**
	    Lesson 3 Poverty and the Distribution of Income
	Chapter 13
	    Lesson 1 Business Cycles and Economic Instability
	    Lesson 2 Inflation
	    Lesson 3 Unemployment

[20] Fiscal and Monetary Policy	

Federal government budgetary policy and the Federal Reserve System's monetary policy influence the overall levels of employment, output, and prices.	**Chapter 15**
	    Lesson 1 Demand-Side Policies
	    Lesson 2 Supply-Side Policies
	    Lesson 3 Macroeconomic Equilibrium
	Chapter 16
	    Lesson 1 Structure and Responsibilities of the Fed
	    Lesson 2 Monetary Policy
	    Lesson 3 Economics and Politics

Used with permission. *Voluntary National Content Standards in Economics*, 2nd Edition. Copyright © 2010 Council for Economic Education, New York, NY. All rights reserved. For more information visit www.councilforeconed.org or call 1-212-730-7007.

Voluntary National Content Standards in Economics

Understanding Economics incorporates the 20 **Voluntary National Content Standards** developed and revised by the **Council for Economic Education**.

Standard 1 Scarcity	
Productive resources are limited. Therefore, people cannot have all the goods and services they want; as a result, they must choose some things and give up others.	**Related concepts:** Capital Resources, Capital Goods, Choice, Consumer Economics, Consumers, Goods, Human Resources, Natural Resources, Limited Resources, Opportunity Cost, Producers, Production, Productive Resources, Scarcity, Service, Wants, Entrepreneurship, Inventors, Entrepreneur, Factors of Production
Standard 2 Decision Making	
Effective decision making requires comparing the additional costs of alternatives with the additional benefits. Many choices involve doing a little more or a little less of something: few choices are "all or nothing" decisions.	**Related concepts:** Decision Making, Profit Motive, Benefit, Costs, Marginal Analysis, Marginal Benefits, Marginal Cost, Profit, Profit Maximization, Cost/Benefit Analysis
Standard 3 Allocation	
Different methods can be used to allocate goods and services. People acting individually or collectively must choose which methods to use to allocate different kinds of goods and services.	**Related concepts:** Economic Systems, Market Structure, Supply, Command Economy, Market Economy, Traditional Economy, Command Economy
Standard 4 Incentives	
People usually respond predictably to positive and negative incentives.	**Related concepts:** Choice, Incentive, Scarce Resources
Standard 5 Trade	
Voluntary exchange occurs only when all participating parties expect to gain. This is true for trade among individuals or organizations within a nation, and among individuals or organizations in different nations.	**Related concepts:** Barriers to Trade, Barter, Exports, Imports, Voluntary Exchange, Exchange, Exchange Rate, Free Trade
Standard 6 Specialization	
When individuals, regions, and nations specialize in what they can produce at the lowest cost and then trade with others, both production and consumption increase.	**Related concepts:** Economic Specialization, Division of Labor, Production, Productive Resources, Specialization, Factor Endowments, Gains from Trade, Relative Price, Transaction Cost, Factors of Production, Full Employment, Comparative Advantage, Absolute Advantage

Standard 7 Markets and Prices

A market exists when buyers and sellers interact. This interaction determines market prices and thereby allocates scarce goods and services.

Related concepts: Price, Market Price, Market Structure, Markets, Price Floors, Price Stability, Equilibrium Price, Quantity Demanded, Quantity Supplied, Relative Price, Exchange Rate, Shortage, Surplus

Standard 8 Role of Prices

Prices send signals and provide incentives to buyers and sellers. When supply or demand changes, market prices adjust, affecting incentives.

Related concepts: Non-price Determinants, Price Floor, Price Stability, Supply, Demand, Determinants of Demand, Determinants of Supply, Law of Demand, Law of Supply, Price Ceiling, Substitute Good, Price, Incentive, Market-clearing Price

Standard 9 Competition and Market Structure

Competition among sellers usually lowers costs and prices, and encourages producers to produce what consumers are willing and able to buy. Competition among buyers increases prices and allocates goods and services to those people who are willing and able to pay the most for them.

Related concepts: Market Structure, Non-price Competition, Levels of Competition. Collusion

Standard 10 Institutions

Institutions evolve and are created to help individuals and groups accomplish their goals. Banks, labor unions, markets, corporations, legal systems, and not-for-profit organizations are examples of important institutions. A different kind of institution, clearly defined and enforced property rights, is essential to a market economy.

Related concepts: Legal and Social Framework, Mortgage, Borrower, Interest, Labor Union, Legal Forms of Business, Legal Foundations of a Market Economy, Nonprofit Organization, Property Rights, Banking, Financial Institutions

Standard 11 Money and Inflation

Money makes it easier to trade, borrow, save, invest, and compare the value of goods and services. The amount of money in the economy affects the overall price level. Inflation is an increase in the overall price level that reduces the value of money.

Related concepts: Exchange, Money Management, Money Supply, Currency, Definition of Money, Money, Characteristics of Money, Functions of Money, Goods and Services, Inflation, Deflation, Consumer Price Index (CPI)

Standard 12 Interest Rates

Interest rates, adjusted for inflation, rise and fall to balance the amount saved with the amount borrowed, which affects the allocation of scarce resources between present and future uses.

Related concepts: Interest Rate, Monetary Policy, Real vs. Nominal Risk, Risk, Investing, Savers, Savings

Voluntary National Content Standards in Economics

Standard 13 Income	
Income for most people is determined by the market value of the productive resources they sell. What workers earn primarily depends on the market value of what they produce.	**Related concepts:** Human Resources, Derived Demand, Functional Distribution of Income, Labor, Labor Market, Marginal Resource Product, Personal Distribution of Income, Wage, Aggregate Demand (AD), Aggregate Supply (AS), Demand, Price of Inputs, Functional Distribution
Standard 14 Entrepreneurship	
Entrepreneurs take on the calculated risk of starting new businesses, either by embarking on new ventures similar to existing ones or by introducing new innovations. Entrepreneurial innovation is an important source of economic growth.	**Related concepts:** Taxation, Costs, Costs of Production, Entrepreneur, Risk, Taxes, Cost/Benefit Analysis, Innovation, Entrepreneurship, Inventors, Incentives
Standard 15 Economic Growth	
Investment in factories, machinery, new technology, and in the health, education, and training of people stimulates economic growth and can raise future standards of living.	**Related concepts:** Incentive, Interest Rate, Opportunity cost, Production, Technological Changes, Trade-off, Trade-offs Among Goals, Human Capital, Intensive Growth, Investment, Physical Capital, Productivity, Risk, Standard of Living, Economic Efficiency, Economic Equity, Economic Freedom, Economic Growth, Economic Security, Poverty, Investing, Business, Businesses and Households, Factors of Production, Health and Nutrition, Savers, Savings, Stock Market
Standard 16 Role of Government and Market Failure	
There is an economic role for government in a market economy whenever the benefits of a government policy outweigh its costs. Governments often provide for national defense, address environmental concerns, define and protect property rights, and attempt to make markets more competitive. Most government policies also have direct or indirect effects on people's incomes.	**Related concepts:** Externalities, Income, Natural Monopoly, Redistribution of Income, Role of Government, Taxation, Transfer Payments, Bonds, Distribution of Income, Income Tax, Maintaining Competition, Monopolies, Negative Externality, Non-clearing Markets, Positive Externality, Negative Externality, Property Rights, Public Good, Maintaining Regulation, Taxes, Regulation, Government Expenditures, Government Revenues
Standard 17 Government Failure	
Costs of government policies sometimes exceed benefits. This may occur because of incentives facing voters, government officials, and government employees, because of actions by special interest groups that can impose costs on the general public, or because social goals other than economic efficiency are being pursued.	**Relative concepts:** Cost/Benefit Analysis, Benefit, Costs, Special Interest Group, Barriers to Trade, Role of Government

Standard 18 Economic Fluctuations

Fluctuations in a nation's overall levels of income, employment, and prices are determined by the interaction of spending and production decisions made by all households, firms, government agencies, and others in the economy. Recessions occur when overall levels of income and employment decline.

Related concepts: Gross Domestic Product (GDP), Macroeconomic Indicators, Nominal Gross Domestic Product (GDP), Per Capital Gross Domestic Product (GDP), Potential Gross Domestic (GDP), Real Gross Domestic Product (GDP), Deflation, Labor Force, Unemployment, Unemployment Rate, Inflation, Imports, Exports, Net Exports, Recession, Depression, Consumer Price Index (CPI)

Standard 19 Unemployment and Inflation

Unemployment imposes costs on individuals and the overall economy. Inflation, both expected and unexpected, also imposes costs on individuals and the overall economy. Unemployment increases during recessions and decreases during recoveries.

Related concepts: Types of Unemployment, Causes of Inflation, Consumer Price Index (CPI), Deflation, Labor force, Unemployment, Unemployment Rate, Inflation

Standard 20 Fiscal and Monetary Policy

Federal government budgetary policy and the Federal Reserve System's monetary policy influence the overall levels of employment, output, and prices.

Related concepts: Inflation, National Debt, Tools of the Federal Reserve, Discount Rate, Federal Budget, Fiscal Policy, Monetary Policy, Open Market Operations, Reserve Requirements, Budget, Budget Deficit, Central Banking System, Budget Surplus, Causes of Inflation, Taxes, Role of Government, Revenues, Expenditures, Federal Reserve System

professional development

UNDERSTANDING BY DESIGN®
by Jay McTighe

Understanding by Design® (UbD®) offers a planning framework to guide curriculum, assessment, and instruction. Its two key ideas are contained in the title: 1) focus on teaching and assessing for understanding and transfer, and 2) design curriculum "backward" from those ends. UbD is based on seven key tenets:

1. UbD is a way of thinking purposefully about curricular planning, not a rigid program or prescriptive recipe.

2. A primary goal of UbD is developing and deepening student understanding: the ability to make meaning of learning via "big ideas" and transfer learning.

3. Understanding is revealed when students autonomously make sense of and transfer their learning through authentic performance. Six facets of understanding—the capacity to explain, interpret, apply, shift perspective, empathize, and self assess—serve as indicators of understanding.

4. Effective curriculum is planned "backward" from long-term desired results though a three-stage design process (Desired Results, Evidence, Learning Plan). This process helps to avoid the twin problems of "textbook coverage" and "activity-oriented" teaching in which no clear priorities and purposes are apparent.

5. Teachers are coaches of understanding, not mere purveyors of content or activity. They focus on ensuring learning, not just teaching (and assuming that what was taught was learned); they always aim and check for successful meaning making and transfer by the learner.

6. Regular reviews of units and curriculum against design standards enhance curricular quality and effectiveness.

7. UbD reflects a continuous improvement approach to achievement. The results wof our designs—student performance—inform needed adjustments in curriculum as well as instruction.

Three Stages of Backward Design

In UbD, we propose a 3-stage "backward design" process for curriculum planning. The concept of planning "backward" from desired results is not new. In 1949 Ralph Tyler described this approach as an effective process for focusing instruction. More recently, Stephen Covey, in the best selling book, *Seven Habits of Highly Effective People*, reports that effective people in various fields are goal-oriented and plan with the end in mind. Although not a new idea, we have found that the deliberate use of backward design for planning curriculum units and courses results in more clearly defined goals, more appropriate assessments, more tightly aligned lessons, and more purposeful teaching.

Backward planning asks educators to consider the following three stages:

Stage 1 – Identify Desired Results

What should students know, understand, and be able to do? What content is worthy of understanding? What "enduring" understandings are desired? What essential questions will be explored?

In the first stage of backward design we consider our goals, examine established Content Standards (national, state, province, district), and review curriculum expectations. Since there is typically more "content" than can reasonably be addressed within the available time, teachers must make choices. This first stage in the design process calls for setting priorities.

More specifically, Stage 1 of UbD asks teachers to identify the "big ideas" that we want students to come to understand, and then to identify or craft companion essential questions. Big ideas reflect transferable concepts, principles and processes that are key to understanding the topic or subject. Essential questions present open-ended, thought-provoking inquiries that are explored over time.

More specific knowledge and skill objectives, linked to the targeted Content Standards and Understandings, are also identified in Stage 1. An important point in UbD is to recognize that factual knowledge and skills are not taught for their own sake, but as a means to larger ends. Ultimately, teaching should equip learners to be able to use or transfer their learning; i.e., meaningful performance with content. This is the "end" we always want to keep in mind.

Stage 2 – Determine Acceptable Evidence

How will we know if students have achieved the desired results? What will we accept as evidence of student understanding and proficiency? How will we evaluate student performance?

Backward design encourages teachers and curriculum planners to first "think like an assessor" before designing specific units and lessons. The assessment evidence we need reflects the desired results identified in Stage 1. Thus, we consider in advance the assessment evidence needed to document and validate that the targeted learning has been achieved. Doing so invariably sharpens and focuses teaching.

In Stage 2, we distinguish between two broad types of assessment—Performance Tasks and Other Evidence. The performance tasks ask students to apply their learning to a new and authentic situation as means of assessing their understanding. In UbD, we have identified six facets of understanding for assessment purposes[1]. When someone truly understands, they:

- Can **explain** concepts, principles and processes; i.e., put it in their own words, teach it to others, justify their answers, show their reasoning.
- Can **interpret**; i.e., make sense of data, text, and experience through images, analogies, stories, and models.
- Can apply; i.e., effectively use and adapt what they know in new and complex contexts.
- Demonstrate **perspective**; i.e., can see the big picture and recognize different points of view.
- Display **empathy**; i.e., perceive sensitively and "walk in someone else's shoes."
- Have **self-knowledge**; i.e., show metacognition, use productive habits of mind, and reflect on the meaning of their learning and experience.

These six facets do not present a theory of how people come to understand something. Instead, the facets are intended to serve as indicators of how understanding is revealed, and thus provide guidance as to the kinds of assessments we need to determine the extent of student understanding. Here are two notes regarding assessing understanding through the facets:

1) All six facets of understanding need not be used all of the time in assessment. In social studies, Empathy and Perspective may be added when appropriate.

2) Performance Tasks based on one or more facets are not intended for use in daily lessons. Rather, these tasks should be seen as culminating performances for a unit of study.

In addition to Performance Tasks, Stage 2 includes Other Evidence, such as traditional quizzes, tests, observations, and work samples to round out the assessment picture to

Examples of Essential Questions in Social Studies	
Understandings or Big Ideas	**Essential Questions**
History involves interpretation, and different people may interpret the same events differently.	Whose "story" is this? How do we know what <u>really</u> happened in the past?
The geography, climate, and natural resources of a region influence the culture, economy, and lifestyle of its inhabitants.	How does <u>where</u> we live influence <u>how</u> we live?
History often repeats itself. Recognizing the patterns of the past can help us better understand the present and prepare for the future.	Why study the past? What does the past have to do with today?
Governments can change based on the changing needs of their people, the society, and the world.	What makes an effective government? Why do/should governments change?

[1] Wiggins, G. and McTighe, J. and (1998, 2005). *Understanding By Design.* Alexandria, VA: The Association for Supervision and Curriculum Development.

professional development

UNDERSTANDING BY DESIGN®
(continued)

determine what students know and can do. A key idea in backward design has to do with alignment. In other words, are we assessing everything that we are trying to achieve (in Stage 1) or only those things that are easiest to test and grade? Is anything important slipping through the cracks because it is not being assessed? Checking the alignment between Stages 1 and 2 helps insure that *all* important goals are appropriately assessed.

Stage 3 – Plan Learning Experiences and Instruction

How will we support learners in coming to an understanding of important ideas and processes? How will we prepare them to autonomously transfer their learning? What enabling knowledge and skills will students need in order to perform effectively and achieve desired results? What activities, sequence, and resources are best suited to accomplish our goals?

In Stage 3 of backward design, teachers now plan the most appropriate learning activities to help students acquire important knowledge and skills, come to understand important ideas and processes, and transfer their learning in meaningful ways. When developing a plan for learning, we propose that teachers consider a set of instructional principles, embedded in the acronym W.H.E.R.E.T.O. These design elements provide the armature or blueprint for instructional planning in Stage 3 in support of our goals of understanding and transfer.

Each of the W.H.E.R.E.T.O. elements is presented in the form of questions to consider.

W = *How will I help learners know – What they will be learning? Why this is worth learning? What evidence will show their learning? How will their performance be evaluated?*

Learners of all ages are more likely to put forth effort and meet with success when they understand the learning goals and see them as meaningful and personally relevant. The "W" in W.H.E.R.E.T.O. reminds teachers to clearly communicate the goals and help students see their relevance. In addition, learners need to know the concomitant performance expectations and assessments through which they will demonstrate their learning so that they have clear learning targets and the basis for monitoring their progress toward them.

H = *How will I hook and engage the learners?*

There is wisdom in the old adage: "Before you try to teach them, you've got to get their attention." The best teachers have always recognized the value of "hooking" learners through introductory activities that "itch" the mind and engage the heart in the learning process, and we encourage teachers to deliberately plan ways of hooking their learners to the topics they teach. Examples of effective hooks include provocative essential questions, counter-intuitive phenomena, controversial issues, authentic problems and challenges, emotional encounters, and humor. One must be mindful, of course, of not just coming up with interesting introductory activities that have no carry-over

value. The intent is to match the hook with the content and the experiences of the learners—by design—as a means of drawing them into a productive learning experience.

> **E** = *How will I equip students to master identified standards and succeed with the transfer performances? What learning experiences will help develop and deepen understanding of important ideas?*

Understanding cannot be simply transferred like a load of freight from one mind to another. Coming to understand requires active intellectual engagement on the part of the learner. Therefore, instead of merely covering the content, effective educators "uncover" the most enduring ideas and processes in ways that engage students in constructing meaning for themselves. To this end, teachers select an appropriate balance of constructivist learning experiences, structured activities, and direct instruction for helping students acquire the desired knowledge, skill, and understanding. While there is certainly a place for direct instruction and modeling, teaching for understanding asks teachers to engage learners in making meaning through active inquiry.

> **R** = *How will I encourage the learners to rethink previous learning? How will I encourage on-going revision and refinement?*

Few learners develop a complete understanding of abstract ideas on the first encounter. Indeed, the phrase "coming to understand" is suggestive of a process. Over time, learners develop and deepen their understanding by thinking and re-thinking, by examining ideas from a different point of view, from examining underlying assumptions, by receiving feedback and revising. Just as the quality of writing benefits from the iterative process of drafting and revising, so too do understandings become more mature. The "R" in W.H.E.R.E.T.O. encourages teachers to explicitly include such opportunities.

> **E** = *How will I promote students' self-evaluation and reflection?*

Capable and independent learners are distinguished by their capacity to set goals, self-assess their progress, and adjust as needed. Yet, one of the most frequently overlooked aspects of the instructional process involves helping students to develop the metacognitive skills of self-evaluation, self-regulation, and reflection. The second "E" of WHERETO reminds teachers to build in time and expectations for students to regularly self-assess, reflect on the meaning of their learning, and set goals for future performance.

> **T** = *How will I tailor the learning experiences to the nature of the learners I serve? How might I differentiate instruction to respond to the varied needs of students?*

"One size fits all teaching" is rarely optimal. Learners differ significantly in terms of their prior knowledge and skill levels, their interests, talents, and preferred ways of learning. Accordingly, the most effective teachers get to know their students and tailor their teaching and learning experiences to connect to them. A variety of strategies may be employed to differentiate *content* (e.g., how subject matter is presented), *process* (e.g., how students work), and *product* (e.g., how learners demonstrate their learning). The logic of backward design offers a cautionary note here: the Content Standards and Understandings should *not* be differentiated (except for students with Individualized Education Plans—I.E.P.s). In other words, differentiate means keeping the end in mind for all.

> **O** = *How will I organize the learning experiences for maximum engagement and effectiveness? What sequence will be optimal given the understanding and transfer goals?*

When the primary educational goals involve helping students acquire basic knowledge and skills, teachers may be comfortable "covering" the content by telling and modeling.

However, when we include understanding and transfer as desired results, educators are encouraged to give careful attention to how the content is organized and sequenced. Just as effective story tellers and filmmakers often don't begin in the "beginning," teachers can consider alternatives to sequential content coverage. For example, methods such as the Case Method, Problem or Project-Based Learning, and Socratic Seminars immerse students in challenging situations, even before they may have acquired all of the "basics." They actively engage students in trying to make meaning and apply their learning in demanding circumstances without single "correct" answers.

Conclusion

Many teachers who are introduced to the backward design process have observed that while the process makes sense in theory, it often feels awkward in use. This is to be expected since the principles and practices of UbD often challenge conventional planning and teaching habits. However, with some practice, educators find that backward design becomes not only more comfortable, but a way of thinking. The resources found in this program support teaching and assessing for understanding and transfer.

professional development

READING STRATEGIES: HOW CAN I HELP MY STUDENTS READ AND UNDERSTAND THE TEXT?

Social studies teachers do not have to be reading teachers to help students read and understand their texts. Often poor readers lack interest in the topic, have trouble concentrating, cannot understand a word or sentence, or are confused as to how the information fits together. These problems can frustrate the student and the teacher, but there are strategies that can be used to improve comprehension and retention of information. Using these reading strategies not only helps poor readers, but also strengthens the reading skills of strong readers.

Activate Prior Knowledge

Activating prior knowledge provides opportunities for students to discover and articulate what they already know about key concepts and ideas. It stimulates student interest and prepares students to incorporate new information into a larger picture. In addition, it helps the teacher to determine a starting place for instruction.

✓ Write the topic on the board and have students brainstorm what they know about it. Record their responses on the board.

✓ Ask general or specific questions about the topic and see how students respond to them.

✓ Present an anticipation guide. An anticipation guide provides a series of statements about an idea or topic. Students read each statement and tell whether they agree or disagree, based on their prior understandings and experiences.

✓ Use a K-W-L-H or K-W-L chart to activate prior knowledge and set reading purposes. Students identify what they already know (or think they **know**) and what they **want** to find out about the topic. After reading, students complete the chart.

K	W	L	H
What I **Know**	What I **Want** to Find Out	What I **Learned**	**How** I Can Learn More

Set Reading Purposes

Reading is a purposeful activity. We read to find answers to specific questions, to satisfy curiosity, and to be entertained.

✓ Have students preview the reading selection. Tell students to read the title, headings, and subheadings. Draw students' attention to diagrams, tables, and other visuals and their captions. Discuss how these will help comprehension.

✓ Prompt students to predict what they might learn in the selection, based on their preview. Invite them to list additional questions they hope to answer through the reading. Have them identify possible problems, such as unfamiliar words or ideas, to watch for as they read.

✓ Discuss the need to "shift gears" in reading speed and attention when reading. Support students as they plan how best to read a selection—slowly to watch for new vocabulary and ideas or quickly to review previously learned ideas. They can also discuss new information with a buddy as they read.

Vocabulary Development

Vocabulary knowledge and reading comprehension are closely related.

✓ Before students read, preteach vocabulary that is crucial for understanding key topics and concepts.

✓ Relate new vocabulary to known words and ideas. After introducing a word and its definition, have students name synonyms or related words they know.

✓ If a student encounters an unfamiliar word while reading, have him or her try to pronounce it aloud. Sometimes saying the word will trigger one's memory of its meaning.

✓ As students read, help them use prefixes (word parts added to the beginning of base words), suffixes (word parts added to the end of base words), and roots (word elements from which other words are formed) as clues to decipher the meaning of words.

- Encourage students to use the context of surrounding words and sentences to determine a word's meaning.
- If context clues and structural analysis fail to help a student understand an important word as they read, have students find the definition in a glossary or dictionary. If the word is not critical for understanding, have students note the word and read on. Later, have students reread the word in context. If the meaning is still unclear, have students consult the dictionary.

Common Prefixes	Meanings	Examples
un–, dis–, non–, im–, and il–	"not" or "the opposite of"	unwrapped, dishonest, nonprofit, immortal, illogical
re–	"again" or "back"	reheat
post–	"after"	postwar
uni–	"one"	unicycle

Common Suffixes	Meanings	Examples
–ship, –hood	"state of" or "condition of"	friendship, neighborhood
–ment	"act of" or "state of"	management
–ish	"like"	childish
–ous	"full of" or "like"	joyous

Taking Notes

Taking notes challenges readers to determine what is most important and to organize information in a way that makes sense. Note taking can also help students stay focused as they read. Reviewing notes can build students' retention of important information.

- Have students take notes after they have read long paragraphs in the section rather than the entire chapter. This helps them focus on important ideas and details and prevents them from losing track of the flow of information.
- Remind students that as they take notes on the section, they should not take a long time to do it. Students should read, think, write, and move on.
- Have students take notes using note cards. Notes should be recorded in the students' own words and labeled with the page number where the entire text appears.
- To use notes to review a passage, have students read through the notes, highlighting the most important information. As they review, encourage students to annotate their notes, making connections between related ideas, and clarifying difficult concepts.

Summarizing

Summarizing demands that students identify the most important ideas and details to create a streamlined version of the text.

- After reading the section, have students recall as much of the information as possible. If the main idea and its supporting details are presented in a certain order, make sure students can recall that organization.
- As they summarize, students should try to answer as many of the following questions as possible: *who, what, where, when, why,* and *how.*
- If the section does not have a main idea that is clearly stated, have students create one that is concise but comprehensive. Have students state the main idea in a topic sentence at the beginning of their summaries.
- Sometimes summaries seem disconnected when details are left out. Students should use connector words such as "and" or "because," along with introductory or closing statements, to make ideas more connected.

Dr. Elizabeth Pryor offers some advice below, gleaned from her years of teaching experience.

Classroom Advice

Reading Comprehension: Be Aware, Reread, and Connect

Many students think silent reading means just looking at words and saying them in their heads. They do not make the connection that reading is supposed to make sense! Have you ever read a paragraph or a page and then said to yourself, "What was that?" As a good reader, you were aware of your lack of understanding. Poor readers, on the other hand, just keep on reading the words, unaware that they do not understand them.

What strategies do good readers use when this happens? Most reread the text they did not understand. Before rereading I study key words I might have missed. When I reread, sometimes I "whisper read" so I can hear the text as well as read it. As I reread, I try to connect what I am reading with something I already know. If I reread and still don't understand, I read it a third (or fourth) time. Each rereading increases comprehension.

In summary, **Be aware** of understanding as you read, **reread**, and **connect** the reading to what you already know. **BARC!**

professional development

PRIMARY SOURCE STRATEGIES

A primary source is direct evidence of an event, idea, period, or development. It is an oral or written account obtained from actual participants in an event. Examples of primary sources include the following:

- ✓ official documents (records, statistics)
- ✓ political declarations, laws, and rules for governance
- ✓ speeches and interviews
- ✓ diaries, memoirs, and oral histories
- ✓ autobiographies
- ✓ recipes and cookbooks
- ✓ advertisements and posters
- ✓ letters

Physical objects, such as tools and dishes, can be primary sources; so can visual evidence in the form of fine art, photographs, maps, films, and videos. Primary sources can also include songs and audio recordings.

Why Use Primary Sources in Your Classroom?

Using primary sources to teach transforms the study of social studies from a passive process to an active one. Students become investigators—finding clues, formulating hypotheses and drawing inferences, making judgments, and reaching conclusions. Bringing primary sources into the classroom stimulates students to think critically about events, issues, and concepts rather than just memorizing dates, names, and generalizations reached by others. Thinking critically then becomes a habit that can work towards making students good citizens.

Choosing Primary Sources

- ✓ Provide exposure to a variety of source types, including historic photographs, folk or popular music, financial records, or household

accounts, as well as letters, journals, and historic documents.

- ✓ When choosing print sources, consider the interests and reading levels of your students. Many texts contain challenging vocabulary and unfamiliar sentence structure. You can create a reader's guide that defines key vocabulary and paraphrases the main points of the reading.
- ✓ Some documents may be too long. Decide whether using an excerpt will provide enough information for students to draw conclusions.
- ✓ Depending upon the topic and your instructional objectives, you may need to provide several different primary sources to expose students to a variety of perspectives.
- ✓ Decide how students will access the primary sources: through the Internet, the library, a museum, or other print resources. Consider the possibility of an Internet virtual field trip for students. Moving from link to link, students can visit museum sites and other Web pages to view artifacts; interpret economic or census data; and read journals, letters, and official documents.

How Do I Introduce Students to Primary Sources?

Carefully explain the nature of primary sources when you introduce them to students. Although primary sources contain valuable clues, be sure to alert students that primary sources contain biases and prejudices and must be approached with caution. Every primary source reflects the creator's point of view to some degree. Students must consider the authorship and why the primary source was written.

Using Primary Sources in the Classroom

Primary sources provide a rich source of inspiration for a variety of instructional strategies. They can be used to spark interest in a new topic, foster deeper exploration into a region, a historical era, or assess students' understanding of social studies concepts and facts.

- ✓ **Prereading Activities** Present a primary source for students to study at the beginning of a new chapter or topic. Have students analyze the source, using the questions and guidelines presented. Then have students make predictions about what they might learn in the upcoming lessons. A primary source that presents a point of view or information that conflicts with students' prior knowledge can be a powerful motivator to learn new material.

- ✓ **Exploring Information** Provide a variety of print and digital primary sources related to a topic or time period. Have students contrast the items, analyzing the information, making inferences, and drawing conclusions about the period.

Interpreting a Primary Source

Before students interpret a primary source, they need to know the context into which the source fits. Then they can use questions, and guidelines, such as those below, to help them analyze and interpret the primary source.

Print Sources
- Who created the source, and what was the purpose for doing so?
- Did the writer personally experience or witness the event(s)?
- At what point did the writer record the information—as it happened or afterward? How long after?
- Who was the intended audience?
- Was the writer trying to record facts, express an opinion, or persuade others to take action?
- What is the author's main message?
- What values does the document convey?
- What bias does it reflect?
- What information about the topic can you gather from this document?
- Compare this document with what you know about the topic. Does it confirm those ideas or introduce a new perspective?
- How might other accounts about this topic support or modify the message this source delivers?

Visual Sources
- Who created the source, and what was the purpose for doing so?
- What does the image show?
- What mood does the image convey?
- Who or what dominates the image or catches your eye?
- How does the view impact the message?
- What details can you learn from the image?
- What is excluded from view?
- What bias does the visual reflect?
- What information about the topic can you gather from this visual?
- How might other visuals about this topic support or modify the message this one delivers?

Audio Sources
- Who created the source? What was the purpose for creating this source?
- What is the main idea of the audio?
- What mood does the recorder's voice convey?
- What bias does the audio text reflect?
- What information about the topic can you gather from this audio source?
- Compare the information in this source with what you already know about the topic. Does it confirm those ideas or introduce a new perspective?
- How might other sources about this topic support or modify the message that this one delivers?

✓ **Evaluation Activities** Have students evaluate a primary source and tell how it supports or refutes what they learned in the text, or have students read a primary source document that provides one perspective on a topic and have students write their own account, presenting another perspective or opinion.

Following is a step-by-step activity suggested by educator Leslie Espinosa. This activity is especially beneficial when a less-proficient reader is paired with a more-proficient reader.

Classroom Activity

Reading and Understanding Primary Sources

1. Before class make a list of student reading partners. Make sure one of the two is a good reader.
2. Have students read a primary source document (or part of a primary source document), taking turns as they go. They should "mark" any words that they do not understand.
3. After each paragraph, the student pair should stop and paraphrase what it says in their own words.
4. Students should look up unfamiliar words they've marked and create an illustrated dictionary entry for each term (over the course of the year or semester).
5. Ask student pairs to present their paraphrased primary source to the rest of the class.

Professional Development lxv

professional development

MEETING THE DIVERSE NEEDS OF OUR STUDENTS
by Douglas Fisher, Ph.D.

Today's classroom contains students from a variety of backgrounds with a variety of learning styles, strengths, and challenges. As teachers we are facing the challenge of helping students reach their educational potential. With careful planning, you can address the needs of all students in the social studies classroom. The basis for this planning is universal access. When classrooms are planned with universal access in mind, fewer students require specific accommodations.

What Is a Universal Access Design for Learning?

Universal design was first conceived in architectural studies when business people, engineers, and architects began making considerations for physical access to buildings. The idea was to plan the environment in advance to ensure that everyone had access.

As a result, the environment would not have to be changed later for people with physical disabilities, people pushing strollers, workers who had injuries, or others for whom the environment would be difficult to negotiate. The Center for Universal Design at www.design.ncsu.edu/cud defines Universal Design as:
The design of products and environments to be usable by all people, to the greatest extent possible, without the need for adaptation or specialized design.

Universal Design and Access in Education

Researchers, teachers, and parents in education have expanded the development of built-in adaptations and inclusive accommodations from architectural space to the educational experience, especially in the area of curriculum.

In 1998, the National Center to Improve the Tools of Educators (NCITE), with the partnership of the Center for Applied Special Technology (CAST), proposed an expanded definition of universal design focused on education:
In terms of learning, universal design means the design of instructional materials and activities that allows the learning goals to be achievable by individuals with wide differences in their abilities to see, hear, speak, move, read, write, understand English, attend, organize, engage, and remember.

How Does Universal Design Work in Education?

Universal design and access, as they apply to education and schooling, suggest the following:

✓ **Inclusive Classroom Participation**
Curriculum should be designed with all students and their needs in mind. The McGraw-Hill social studies print and online texts and materials were designed with a wide range of students in mind. For example, understanding that English learners and students who struggle with reading would be using this text, vocabulary is specifically taught and reinforced. Similarly, the teacher-support materials provide multiple instructional points to be used depending on the needs of the students in the class. Further, the text is written such that essential questions and guiding questions are identified for all learners.

✓ **Maximum Text Readability**
In universally designed classrooms that provide access for all students, texts use direct language, clear noun-verb agreements, and clear construct-based wording. In addition to these factors, the McGraw-Hill social studies texts use embedded definitions

for difficult terms, provide for specific instruction in reading skills, use a number of visual representations, and include note-taking guides.

✓ **Adaptable and Accommodating**
The content in this textbook can be easily translated, read aloud, or otherwise changed to meet the needs of students in the classroom. The lesson and end-of-chapter activities and assessments provide students with multiple ways of demonstrating their content knowledge while also ensuring that they have practice with thinking in terms of multiple-choice questions. Critical thinking and analysis skills are also practiced.

How Is Differentiated Instruction the Key to Universal Access?

To differentiate instruction, teachers must acknowledge student differences in background knowledge and current reading, writing, and English language skills. They must also consider student learning styles and preferences, interests, and needs, and react accordingly. There are a number of general guidelines for differentiating instruction in the classroom to reach all students, including:

✓ **Link Assessment With Instruction**
Assessments should occur before, during, and after instruction to ensure that the curriculum is aligned with what students do and do not know. Using assessments in this way allows you to plan instruction for whole groups, small groups, and individual students. Backward planning, where you establish the assessment before you begin instruction, is also important.

✓ **Clarify Key Concepts and Generalizations**
Students need to know what is essential and how this information can be used in their future learning. In addition, students need to develop a sense of the big ideas—ideas that transcend time and place.

✓ **Emphasize Critical and Creative Thinking**
The content, process, and products used or assigned in the classroom should require that students think about what they are learning. While some students may require support, additional motivation, varied tasks, materials, or equipment, the overall focus on critical and creative thinking allows for all students to participate in the lesson.

✓ **Include Teacher- and Student-Selected Tasks**
A differentiated classroom includes both teacher- and student-selected activities and tasks. At some points in the lesson or day, the teacher must provide instruction and assign learning activities. In other parts of the lesson, students should be provided choices in how they engage with the content. This balance increases motivation, engagement, and learning.

How Do I Support Individual Students?

The vast majority of students will thrive in a classroom based on universal access and differentiated instruction. However, wise teachers recognize that no single option will work for all students and that there may be students who require unique systems of support to be successful.

Classroom Activity

Display a map of imperialism in Africa around 1914. Discuss with students the map's general information and have them list each country under the European power that controlled it.

To differentiate this activity:

- Have students imagine they are living in the early 1900s. Have them write a letter to a British newspaper about colonial rule in Africa.
- Have students record the number of African countries under European rule. Have them take the data and create a bar graph that shows which European powers were the most active colonizers at the time.
- Have students compose a song or poem about European rule in Africa, from an African's point of view.
- Have students choose a country of modern Africa to research. Have them write a three-page paper discussing how that country was affected by colonialism and how it has changed since the days of European rule.

professional development

MEETING THE DIVERSE NEEDS OF OUR STUDENTS
(continued)

Tips For Instruction

The following tips for instruction can support your efforts to help all students reach their maximum potential.

- ✓ Survey students to discover their individual differences. Use interest inventories of their unique talents so you can encourage contributions in the classroom.
- ✓ Be a model for respecting others. Adolescents crave social acceptance. The student with learning differences is especially sensitive to correction and criticism, particularly when it comes from a teacher. Your behavior will set the tone for how students treat one another.
- ✓ Expand opportunities for success. Provide a variety of instructional activities that reinforce skills and concepts.
- ✓ Establish measurable objectives and decide how you can best help students who meet them.
- ✓ Celebrate successes and make note of and praise "work in progress."
- ✓ Keep it simple. Point out problem areas if doing so can help a student effect change. Avoid overwhelming students with too many goals at one time.
- ✓ Assign cooperative group projects that challenge all students to contribute to solving a problem or creating a product.

How Do I Reach Students With Learning Disabilities?

- ✓ Provide support and structure. Clearly specify rules, assignments, and responsibilities.
- ✓ Practice skills frequently. Use games and drills to help maintain student interest.
- ✓ Incorporate many modalities into the learning process. Provide opportunities to say, hear, write, read, and act out important concepts and information.
- ✓ Link new skills and concepts to those already mastered.
- ✓ If possible, allow students to record answers on audio.
- ✓ Allow extra time to complete assessments and assignments.
- ✓ Let students demonstrate proficiency with alternative presentations, including oral reports, role plays, art projects, and musical presentations.
- ✓ Provide outlines, notes, or recordings of lecture material.
- ✓ Pair students with peer helpers, and provide class time for pair interaction.

How Do I Reach Students With Behavioral Challenges?

- ✓ Provide a structured environment with clear-cut schedules, rules, seat assignments, and safety procedures.
- ✓ Reinforce appropriate behavior and model it for students.
- ✓ Cue distracted students back to the task through verbal signals and teacher proximity.
- ✓ Set goals that can be achieved in the short term. Work for long-term improvement in the big areas.

How Do I Reach Students With Physical Challenges?

- ✓ Openly discuss with the student any uncertainties you have about when to offer aid.
- ✓ Ask parents or therapists and students what special devices or procedures are needed and whether any special safety precautions need to be taken.
- ✓ Welcome students with physical challenges into all activities, including field trips, special events, and projects.
- ✓ Provide information to assist class members and adults in their understanding of support needed.

How Do I Reach Students with Visual Impairments?

- ✓ Facilitate independence. Modify assignments as needed.
- ✓ Teach classmates how and when to serve as visual guides.
- ✓ Limit unnecessary noise in the classroom if it distracts the student with visual impairments.
- ✓ Provide tactile models whenever possible.

- ✓ Foster a spirit of inclusion. Describe people and events as they occur in the classroom. Remind classmates that the student with visual impairments cannot interpret gestures and other forms of nonverbal communication.
- ✓ Provide recorded lectures and reading assignments for use outside the classroom.
- ✓ Team the student with a sighted peer for written work.

How Do I Reach Students With Hearing Impairments?

- ✓ Seat students where they can see your lip movements easily and where they can avoid any visual distractions.
- ✓ Avoid standing with your back to the window or light source.
- ✓ Use an overhead projector so you can maintain eye contact while writing information for students.
- ✓ Seat students where they can see speakers.
- ✓ Write all assignments on the board, or hand out written instructions.
- ✓ If the student has a manual interpreter, allow both student and interpreter to select the most favorable seating arrangements.
- ✓ Teach students to look directly at each other when they speak.

How Do I Reach English Learners?

- ✓ Remember, students' ability to speak English does not reflect their academic abilities.
- ✓ Try to incorporate the students' cultural experience into your instruction. The help of a bilingual aide may be effective.
- ✓ Avoid any references in your instruction that could be construed as cultural stereotypes.
- ✓ Preteach important vocabulary and concepts.
- ✓ Encourage students to preview text before they begin reading, noting headings.
- ✓ Remind students not to ignore graphic organizers, photographs, and maps since there is much information in these visuals.
- ✓ Use memorabilia and photographs whenever possible to build background knowledge and understanding. An example of this would be coins in a foreign currency or a raw cotton ball to reinforce its importance in history.

How Do I Reach Gifted Students?

- ✓ Make arrangements for students to take selected subjects early and to work on independent projects.
- ✓ Ask "what if" questions to develop high-level thinking skills. Establish an environment safe for risk taking in your classroom.
- ✓ Emphasize concepts, theories, ideas, relationships, and generalizations about the content.
- ✓ Promote interest in the past by inviting students to make connections to the present.
- ✓ Let students express themselves in alternate ways such as creative writing, acting, debates, simulations, drawing, or music.
- ✓ Provide students with a catalog of helpful resources, listing such things as agencies that provide free and inexpensive materials, appropriate community services and programs, and community experts who might be called upon to speak to your students.
- ✓ Assign extension projects that allow students to solve real-life problems related to their communities.

Classroom Activity

Students respond eagerly to a subject when they can relate it to their own experiences. With the growing number of students who come from other world regions, explaining geography through a global theme (such as volcanoes) can give them a worldwide as well as a regional perspective. To develop this awareness, display a large world map. Have students use the library or the Internet to research the latitude and longitude of 15 major volcanoes around the world. Ask them to mark these locations on the map and answer the following questions:

- What patterns do you see in volcanic activity?
- What causes volcanic activity?
- Where in the world are volcanoes most active?

As a follow-up, suggest students use the Internet to find legends about the origins of some of the world's volcanoes. Encourage students to share what they find with the class.

professional development

PERFORMANCE ASSESSMENT STRATEGIES: PROJECT-BASED LEARNING

In response to the growing demand for accountability in the classroom, educators must use multiple assessment measures to accurately gauge student performance. In addition to quizzes, tests, essay exams, and standardized tests, assessment today incorporates a variety of performance-based measures, such as project-based learning.

Project-based learning is a way of teaching and learning in which students apply and acquire knowledge, and develop skills by investigating complex questions or challenges over an extended period of time. Students use their creativity and collaboration skills to communicate their ideas. These activities also help students become aware of diverse audiences for their work. Project-based learning can include an individual product, a group product, or a combination of both.

Teachers may allow students to choose the type of project to complete so that the project is more meaningful to them. McGraw-Hill offers a Hands-On Chapter Project for every chapter. A few examples of these activities include creating a graphic novel, writing a magazine cover story, and writing and illustrating or finding images for a travel journal. In addition to these more traditional activities, McGraw-Hill also provides a Digital Hands-On Project for every chapter. These fun and challenging projects include creating online maps,

podcasts, and virtual speaking avatars. Links, tutorials, and guides, other resources for each project are included.

What Are Some Typical Performance-Based Assessments?

There are many kinds of performance-based assessments. They all share one common characteristic—they challenge students to create products that demonstrate what they know and their ability to apply it.

Writing

Performance-based writing assessments challenge students to apply their knowledge of social studies in a variety of contexts. Writing activities are most often completed by an individual rather than by a group.

- ✓ **Journals** Students write from the perspective of a historical character or a citizen of a particular historical era.
- ✓ **Letters** Students write a letter from one historical figure to another or from a historical figure to a family member or another audience.
- ✓ **Position Papers or Editorials** Students explain a controversial issue and present their own opinion and recommendations, supported with strong evidence and convincing reasons.
- ✓ **News articles** Students write a variety of stories from the perspective of a reporter living in a particular historical time period. This could also involve writing letters to the editor.
- ✓ **Biographies and Autobiographies** Students write about historical figures either from the third person point of view (biography) or from the first person (autobiography).
- ✓ **Creative Stories** Students integrate historical events into a piece of fiction, incorporating the customs, language, and geography of the period.
- ✓ **Poems and Songs** Students follow the conventions of a particular type of song or poem as they tell about a historical event or person.
- ✓ **Research Reports** Students synthesize information from a variety of sources into a well-developed research report.

Oral Presentations

Oral presentations allow students to demonstrate their social studies literacy before an audience. Oral presentations are often group efforts, although this need not be the case.

- ✓ **Simulations** Students hold simulations, or reenactments, of actual events, such as trials, acts of civil disobedience, battles, speeches, and so forth.
- ✓ **Debates** Students debate opposing viewpoints of a historical policy or issue. Students can debate from a contemporary perspective or in a role in which they assume a viewpoint held by a historical character.
- ✓ **Interviews** Students conduct a mock interview of a historical character or bystander.
- ✓ **Oral Reports** Students present the results of research efforts in a lively oral report. This report may be accompanied by visuals.
- ✓ **Skits and Plays** Students use historical events as the basis for a play or skit. Details should accurately reflect customs and the setting of the period.

Visual Presentations

Visual presentations allow students to demonstrate their social studies understandings in a variety of visual formats. Visual presentations can be either group or individual projects.

- ✓ **Models** Students make models to demonstrate or represent a process, place, event, battle, artifact, or custom.
- ✓ **Museum Exhibit** Students create a rich display of material around a topic. Typical displays might include models, illustrations, photographs, videos, writings, and audiotaped explanations.
- ✓ **Graphs or Charts** Students analyze and represent historical data in a line graph, bar graph, table, or other chart format.
- ✓ **Drawings** Students represent or interpret a historical event or period through illustration, including political cartoons.
- ✓ **Posters and Murals** Posters and murals may include maps, time lines, diagrams, illustrations, photographs, collages, and written explanations that reflect students' understandings of historical information.
- ✓ **Quilts** Students sew or draw a design for a patchwork quilt that shows a variety of perspectives, events, or issues related to a key topic.
- ✓ **Videos** Students film a video to show historical fiction or to preserve a simulation of a historical event.
- ✓ **Multimedia Presentations or Slide Shows** Students create a computer-generated multimedia presentation containing historical information and analysis.

How Are Performance Assessments Scored?

There are a variety of ways used to evaluate performance tasks. Some or all of the following methods may be used.

- ✓ **Scoring Rubrics** A scoring rubric is a set of guidelines for assessing the quality of a process and/or product. It establishes criteria used to distinguish acceptable responses from unacceptable ones, generally along a scale from excellent to poor. Rubrics clearly outline expectations for behaviors and outcomes. Rubrics may be used as guidelines as the students prepare their products. They are also commonly used for self-assessment.
- ✓ **Models of Excellent Work** Teacher-selected models of excellent work concretely illustrate expectations and help students set goals for their own projects.
- ✓ **Student Self-Assessment** Students can assess themselves using a variety of methods. Students can rank their work in relation to the model, use a scoring rubric, and write their own goals. Students can then evaluate how well they have met the goals they set for themselves. Regardless of which method or methods students use, they should be encouraged to evaluate their behaviors and processes, as well as the finished product.
- ✓ **Peer or Audience Assessment** Many of the performance tasks target an audience other than the classroom teacher. If possible, an audience of peers should give feedback to the student or group. Have the class create rubrics for specific projects together.
- ✓ **Observation** As students carry out their performance tasks, you may want to formally observe students at work. Start by developing a checklist, identifying all the specific behaviors and understandings you expect students to demonstrate. Then observe students as they carry out performance tasks, and check off the behaviors as you observe them.
- ✓ **Interviews** As a form of ongoing assessment, you may want to conduct interviews with students, asking them to analyze, explain, and assess their participation in performance tasks.

professional development

TEST-TAKING STRATEGIES

It's not enough for students to learn social studies facts and concepts—they must be able to show what they know in a variety of test-taking situations.

How Can I Help My Students Do Well on Objective Tests?

Objective tests may include multiple choice, true/false, and matching questions. Applying the following strategies can help students do their best on objective tests.

Multiple-Choice Questions

✓ Students should read the directions carefully to learn what answer the test requires—the best answer or the right answer. This is especially important when answer choices include "all of the above" or "none of the above."

✓ Advise students to watch for negative words in the questions, such as *not, except, unless, never,* and so forth. If the question contains a negative, the correct answer choice is the one that does not fit.

✓ Students should try to mentally answer the question before reading the answer choices.

✓ Students should read all the answer choices and cross out those that are obviously wrong. Then they should choose an answer from those that remain.

True/False Questions

✓ It is important that students read the entire question before answering. For an answer to be true, the entire statement must be true. If one part of a statement is false, the answer should be marked *False*.

✓ Remind students to watch for words like *all, never, every,* and *always*.

Analyze:	To **analyze** means to systematically and critically examine all parts of an issue or event.
Classify or Categorize:	To **classify** or **categorize** means to put people, things, or ideas into groups, based on a common set of characteristics.
Compare and Contrast:	To **compare** is to show how things are similar, or alike. To contrast is to show how things are different.
Describe:	To **describe** means to present a sketch or impression. Rich details, especially details that appeal to the senses, flesh out a description.
Discuss:	To **discuss** means to systematically write about all sides of an issue or event.
Evaluate:	To **evaluate** means to make a judgment and support it with evidence.
Explain:	To **explain** means to clarify or make plain.
Illustrate:	To **illustrate** means to provide examples or to show with a picture or other graphic.
Infer:	To **infer** means to read between the lines or to use knowledge and experience to draw conclusions, make a generalization, or form a prediction.
Justify:	To **justify** means to prove or to support a positions with specific facts and reasons.
Predict:	To **predict** means to tell what will happen in the future, based on an understanding of prior events and behaviors.
State:	To **state** means to briefly and concisely present information.
Summarize:	To **summarize** means to give a brief overview of the main points of an issue or event.
Trace:	To **trace** means to present the steps or stages in a process or event in sequential or chronological order.

Statements containing these words are often false.

Matching Questions

✓ Students should read through both lists before they mark any answers.

✓ Unless an answer can be used more than once, students should cross out each choice as they use it.

✓ Using what they know about grammar can help students find the right answer. For instance, when matching a word with its definition, the definition is often the same part of speech (noun, verb, adjective, and so forth) as the word.

How Can I Help My Students Do Well on Essay Tests?

Essay tests require students to provide thorough and well-organized written responses, in addition to showing what they know. Help students use the following strategies on essay tests.

Read the Question

The key to writing successful essay responses lies in reading and interpreting questions correctly. Teach students to identify and underline key words in the questions, and to use these words to guide them in understanding what the question asks. Help students understand the meaning of some of the most common key words, listed in the chart.

Plan and Write the Essay

After students understand the question, they should follow the writing process to develop their answer. Encourage students to follow the steps below to plan and write their essays.

1. Map out an answer. Make lists, webs, or an outline to plan the response.

2. Decide on an order in which to present the main points.

3. Write an opening statement that directly responds to the essay question.

4. Write the essay. Expand on the opening statement. Support key points with specific facts, details, and reasons.

5. Write a closing statement that brings the main points together.

6. Proofread to check for spelling, grammar, and punctuation.

How Can I Help My Students Prepare for Standardized Tests?

Students can follow the steps below to prepare for standardized assessments they are required to take.

 Read About the Test Students can familiarize themselves with the format of the test, the types of questions that will be asked, and the amount of time they will have to complete the test. Emphasize that it is very important for students to budget their time during test-taking.

 Review the Content Consistent study throughout the school year will help students build social studies knowledge and understanding. If there are specific objectives or standards that are tested on the exam, help students review these facts or skills to be sure they are proficient.

 Practice Provide practice, ideally with actual released tests, to build students' familiarity with the content, format, and timing of the real exam. Students should practice all the types of questions they will encounter on the test—multiple choice, short answer, true or false, and extended response.

 Pace Students will need to pace themselves differently depending on how the test is administered. If the test is time, students should not allow themselves to become stuck on any one question. As students practice, they should try to increase the number of questions they can answer correctly. If the test is untimed, students should work slowly and carefully. If students have trouble with an item, they should mark it and come back to it later.

 Analyze Practice Results Help students improve test-taking performance by analyzing their test-taking strengths and weaknesses. Spend time discussing students' completed practice tests, explaining why particular answers are right or wrong. Help students identify what kinds of questions they had the most difficulty with. Look for patterns in errors and then tailor instruction to review the appropriate test-taking skills or social studies content.

Below is an example of an activity from experienced instructor Tara Musselwhite to incorporate assessment review in the classroom.

Classroom Advice

Frequently reviewing graded tests is a great way for students to assess their test-taking skills. It also gives teachers the opportunity to teach test-taking strategies and review content. As the class rereads each test question, guide students to think logically about their answer choices. Show students how to:

1. Read each question carefully to determine its meaning.
2. Look for key words in the question to support their answers.
3. Recognize synonyms in the answer choices that may match phrases in the question.
4. Narrow down answer choices by eliminating ones that don't make sense.
5. Anticipate the answer before looking at the answer choices.
6. Circle questions of which they are unsure and go back to them later. Sometimes a clue will be found in another question on the test.

professional development

ACADEMIC VOCABULARY
How Can I Help My Students Learn Academic Vocabulary?

What Is Academic English?

Academic English is the language used in academics, business, and courts of law. It is the type of English used in texts, and contains linguistic features associated with academic disciplines like social studies. Proficiency in reading and using academic English is especially related to long-term success in all parts of life.

By reinforcing academic English, teachers can help learners to access authentic, academic texts—not simplified texts that dummy down the content. In this way, they can provide information that will help build their students' background knowledge rapidly.

What Is Academic Vocabulary?

Academic vocabulary is based on academic English. By the time children have completed elementary school, they must have acquired the knowledge needed to understand academic vocabulary. How many words should they acquire to be able to access their texts? A basic 2,000-word vocabulary of high-frequency words makes up 87% of the vocabulary of academic texts. Eight hundred other academic words comprise an additional 8% of the words. Three percent of the remaining words are technical words. The remaining 2% are low-frequency words. There may be as many as 123,000 low-frequency words in academic texts.

Why Should Students Learn Academic Vocabulary?

English learners who have a basic 2,000-word vocabulary are ready to acquire most general words found in their texts.

Knowledge of academic words and general words can significantly boost a student's comprehension level of academic texts. Students who learn and practice these words before they graduate from high school are more likely to master academic material with increased confidence and speed.

They waste less time and effort in guessing words or consulting dictionaries than those who only know the basic 2,000 words that characterize general conversation.

How Do I Include Academic Vocabulary and Academic English in My Teaching?

Teachers can provide students with academic vocabulary and help students understand the academic English of their text.

To develop academic English, learners must have already acquired basic proficiency in everyday English.

Academic English should be taught within contexts that make sense. In terms of instruction, teaching academic English includes providing students with access to core curriculum—in this case social studies.

Academic English arises in part from social practices in which academic English is used. The acquisition of academic vocabulary and grammar is necessary to advance the development of academic English.

Tips for Teaching Academic Vocabulary

✓ **Expose Students to Academic Vocabulary** You do not need to call attention to words students are learning because they will acquire them subconsciously.

✓ **Do Not Correct Students' Mistakes When Using the Vocabulary Words** All vocabulary understanding and spelling errors will disappear once the student reads more.

✓ **Help Students Decode the Words Themselves** Once they learn the alphabet, they should be able to decode words. Decoding each word they don't recognize will help them more than trying to focus on sentence structure. Once they can recognize the words, they can read "authentic" texts.

✓ **Do Not Ignore the English Learner in This Process** They can learn academic vocabulary before they are completely fluent in oral English.

Guidelines for Teaching Academic Vocabulary

1. Direct and planned instruction
2. Models—that have increasingly difficult language
3. Attention to form—pointing out linguistic features of words

✓ **Helping Students Build Academic Vocabulary Leads to Broader Learning** Students who have mastered the basic academic vocabulary are ready to acquire words from the rest of the groups. To help determine which words are in the 2,000-word basic group, refer to *West's General Service List of English Words, 1953*. The list is designed to serve as a guide for teachers and as a checklist and goal list for students.

Classroom Activity

Writing About Modern America

Give students a brief writing assignment. Ask them to write a short essay about one of the topics listed below in the left column. Have students use as many of the academic vocabulary words in the right column as they can in their essay. When completed, ask student volunteers to share their writing. Note what academic vocabulary words they use.

Topic	Academic Vocabulary
The challenges of reducing poverty in America	sufficient minimum medical income
Recent technological advances	innovate technology media potential data transmit

professional development

WHY TEACH WITH TECHNOLOGY?
by Tom Daccord and Justin Reich, EdTechTeacher

✓ **Technology is transforming the practice of historians and should transform history classrooms as well.** While printed documents, books, maps, and artwork constitute the bulk of the historical record before 1900, the history of the last century is also captured in sound and video recording and in Web sites and other Internet resources. Today's students need to learn how to analyze and build arguments using these multimedia records as well as traditional primary sources.

✓ **So many of the sources that helped historians and history teachers fall in love with the discipline are now available online.** In recent decades, universities, libraries, archives, and other institutions have scanned and uploaded many vast treasure troves of historical sources. The Internet-connected classroom increasingly has access to the world's historical record, giving students a chance to develop critical thinking skills as well as learning historical narratives.

✓ **Whoever is doing most of the talking or most of the typing is doing most of the learning, and the more people listening the better.** Technology allows us to transfer the responsibility for learning from teachers to students, and to put students in the driver's seat of their own learning. Students who are actively engaged in creating and presenting their understandings of history are learning more than students passively listening. Technology also allows students to publish their work to broader audiences of peers, parents, and even the entire Internet-connected world. Students find the opportunities challenging, exciting, and engaging.

✓ **The more ways students have to engage with content, the more likely they are to remember and understand that content.** The Internet can provide students and teachers with access to text documents, images, sounds and songs, video, simulations, and games. The more different ways students engage with historical content, the more likely they are to make meaning of that material.

✓ **Students live in a technology-rich world, and classrooms should prepare students for that world.** When students spend most of their waking hours connected to a worldwide, online network of people, resources, and opportunities, they experience dissonance and disappointment in entering a "powered-down" school. Many students will leave school to go on to workplaces completely transformed by technology, and teachers have a responsibility to prepare students for these environments.

Integrating Technology Effectively

Ben Shneiderman, in his book *Leonardo's Laptop,* lays out a four-part framework for teaching with technology: Collect-Relate-Create-Donate. This framework is a helpful blueprint for designing projects and learning experiences with technology.

Collect Students should begin a project by collecting the resources necessary to produce a meaningful presentation of their understanding. In some cases, students might collect these resources through textbook reading and teacher lecture, but students should also collect resources from online collections, school

For More Information
Visit the EdTechTeacher Web sites for more links, tutorials, and other resources.

Teaching With Technology

In addition to the many other online resources in this program, EdTech Teacher has created digital project-based learning activities for every chapter. These can be used independently or with the print chapter-based hands-on activities. These cumulative projects bring geography to life and reveal student understanding through performance assessment. The digital hands-on projects integrate technology with instruction. Students use software and the Internet to create projects that are fun and challenging.

library Web sites, and online searches.

Relate Technology greatly facilitates the process of students working together socially. The ability to collaborate is essential to the workplace and civic sphere of the future. In creating technology projects, students should have the chance to work together, or at least to comment on each other's work, using blogs, wikis, podcasts, and other collaborative publishing tools.

Create Using multimedia publishing tools, students should have the opportunity to design presentations and performances of their historical understanding. They should make historical arguments in linear text, as well as through images, audio and video recordings, and multimedia presentations.

Donate Finally, students should create work not just for their teachers, but for broader audiences. Students who have a chance to share their work with their peers, their families, their community, and the Internet-connected world find that opportunity rewarding. Today's students experience very few barriers to expression in their networked lives, and they crave these opportunities in schools.

Learn More about Teaching with Technology

EdTechTeacher has several Web sites designed to help social studies and geography teachers learn more about teaching with technology. The Best of History Web Sites (www.besthistorysites.net) is the Internet's authoritative directory of social studies-related resources, Web sites, games, simulations, lesson plans, and activities. Teaching History with Technology (www.thwt.org) has a series of white papers, tutorials, and guides for enriching teaching strategies (lecturing, discussion, presentations, assessments, and so forth) with educational technology. EdTechTeacher (www.edtechteacher.org) has additional teaching resources and information about learning opportunities such as free webinars and other professional development workshops.

Tom Daccord and Justin Reich are co-Directors of EdTechTeacher. Together they authored Best Ideas for Teaching With Technology: A Practical Guide for Teachers by Teachers.

Guidelines for Successful Technology Projects

1) **Plan for problems.** Things can go wrong when working with technology, and learning how to deal with these challenges is essential for students, and for their teachers. As you start using technology in the classroom, try to have an extra teacher, aide, student-teacher, or IT staff member in the room with you to help troubleshoot problems. When things do go wrong, stay calm, and ask your students to help you resolve challenges and make the most of class time. Always have a back up, "pencil and paper" activity prepared in case there are problems with computers or networks. Over time, teachers who practice teaching with technology experience fewer and fewer of these problems, but they can be very challenging the first time you experience them!

2) **Practice from multiple perspectives.** Whenever you develop a technology project, try to do everything that students will do from a student's perspective. If you create a blog or wiki with a teacher account, create a student account to test the technology.

3) **Adapt to your local technology resources, but don't let those resources keep you from using technology.** Some schools have excellent and ample technology resources—labs, laptop carts, and ipads—that make completing technology projects straightforward. Other schools have fewer resources, but virtually every student can get access to a networked computer in school, at the library or at home, especially if you give them a few nights to do so. Many technology activities are described as if you could complete them in a few class periods, but if resources are limited, you might consider spreading the activity out over a few days or weeks to give students the chance to get online.

4) **Plan with a partner.** Going it alone can be scary. If possible, have another teacher in your department or on your team, design and pilot technology projects with you to help solve the challenges that crop up whenever trying out new pedagogies.

5) **It's harder, then it gets easier.** Learning new teaching strategies is always hard. With technology, however, once you get past the initial learning curve there are all sorts of ways technology can make teaching more efficient and simultaneously make learning more meaningful for students.

professional development

COLLEGE AND CAREER READINESS

Why Is College & Career Readiness Crucial?

- Only 70% of American students receive a high school diploma.
- Of that 70% of high school graduates, one-third of those who make it to college require remedial help.
- Over 90% of new jobs that will be available to students in the 21st century will require some postsecondary education.
- Most employers today cannot compete successfully without a workforce that has solid academic skills.
- The average difference in salary between someone with a high school degree and someone with postsecondary credentials can be $1 million over their lifetimes.

What Is College & Career Readiness?

Students are college and career ready when they have the level of preparation needed to academically, socially, and cognitively complete a postsecondary course of study without remediation. Students are prepared when they can enter the workforce at a level at which they are in line for promotion and career enhancement.

The ultimate goal of the college and career readiness initiative is to maintain America's competitive edge in the global economy of today. The workforce of the 21st century is an increasingly global, knowledge-based economy that demands the ability to:

- Think critically
- Solve problems
- Create and innovate
- Communicate
- Collaborate
- Learn new skills
- Use ICT (information and communications technology)

Explain College & Career Readiness to Students

One of the first steps you should take is to provide students with a framework that will help them see the relevancy of what they do in school. The three principal elements of College and Career Readiness (CCR) are:

- an understanding of core academic skills and the ability to apply them in educational and employment settings
- familiarity with skills valued by a broad range of employers such as communication, critical thinking, and responsibility
- mastery of the technologies and skill sets associated with a career pathway

Once students have been exposed to these elements, it is critical for them to see how they relate to their own plans for continuing education and career choice. Mention that CCR is more than just a personal issue, and it affects the country and our quality of life.

Most students—as well as many adults—consider work to be an obligation that they must perform in order to have money. Earning a salary is, of course, a central benefit of working, but so is the sense of satisfaction that comes from doing a job well. Moreover, every job contributes to the quality of life in our communities and our nation. Being prepared to pursue an education or get a job after high school is the hallmark of a good citizen.

Recognize That All Careers Are Important

Without question, the greatest challenge faced by educators, parents, and the public is recognizing that all jobs are important. When you discuss careers, be generous with your reflections and encourage your students to do the same. Be sure to mention the enormous variety of opportunities available to them in diverse fields. The more that students can recognize the

rich possibilities of whatever career they pursue, the more likely they will be to enjoy success and personal satisfaction.

Students typically have a relatively narrow perspective on the careers and jobs available to them. As part of the discussion of careers, broaden this perspective by reviewing some opportunities that your students might not be aware of. An interesting place to start is in the high profile industries of sports and entertainment.

Many students dream of being celebrities and have no idea about how unlikely this is. What they don't realize is that for every professional athlete, singer, or movie star, there are a hundred or more fascinating careers including sports trainers, writers, administrative assistants, drivers, and a seemingly endless list of other jobs. Not surprisingly, students usually respond positively when they learn that just in case they are not the next superstar in sports or entertainment, there are other opportunities that will allow them to achieve their dream in a slightly different way.

Students can explore careers in many ways; one way is by reviewing the 16 career clusters. Career clusters are groups of similar occupations and industries. They were developed by the U.S. Department of Education as a way to organize career planning. Students can visit the Career Center at http://ccr.mcgraw-hill.com/ to begin their explorations.

Make It Clear That There Are Various Paths To Success

A surprisingly small percentage of adults reach their careers through a direct and well-planned strategy. Familiarizing students with the various paths to success provides them with a realistic view of what life is like after high school and college. It may also give them an anchor in their own lives in the future when they find that they are wandering, which most of them will inevitably do.

Divergence from a direct path to a career is almost inevitable, and in many cases, is a desirable and enriching experience. Helping students to recognize this will make their future challenges seem less intimidating.

Have students investigate and discuss the career paths of people they know personally and by reputation, including celebrities. This discussion will promote engagement while showing the twists and turns that usually lead to success. Be sure to include some common but less-known paths, like the college benefits associated with military service or the arrangements nurses might make with a hospital to exchange tuition payments for a commitment of several years.

Make college and career readiness a regular part of interactive classroom discussions.

Unlike many other school subjects, a critical aspect of college and career readiness is its focus is on the future of each student, not the content of a course. Perhaps the best way to have students recognize this is to be sure that the time you spend discussing students' future pathways is truly interactive, with at least as much commentary from students as there is from you or other adult participants.

Because students are more willing to participate in discussions that have personal meaning to them, consider using these questions as starting points. These are "self-mentoring" questions that will help students clarify their thinking.

- What is something you really want to do in the next 10 years?
- How do you plan to get there?
- What is your back-up plan?
- What is something that you have done that made you proud?
- In which postsecondary courses do you think you would do best? Why do you think this?
- Imagine that you are going into the military. This choice involves activities that are hard physically and mentally. How would you handle these challenges?
- When you can't make up your mind about something important, what do you do?

HAVE STUDENTS EXPLORE COLLEGE AND CAREER READINESS ON THEIR OWN AT http://ccr.mcgraw-hill.com.

SCAVENGER HUNT

Understanding Economics contains a wealth of information. The trick is to know where to find it. If you go through this scavenger hunt, either alone, with a fellow student, or with your teachers or parents, you will quickly learn how the textbook is organized and how to get the most out of your reading and study time. Let's get started!

1. How many units and chapters are in the book? **7 units and 19 chapters**

2. What is the difference between the glossary and the index? **glossary defines vocabulary, in both English and Spanish; index provides page references**

3. Each chapter features primary sources—articles and quotes related to the content of the section. Where can you find primary sources used within this textbook? **Debates features and Analyzing Primary Sources questions in the Chapter Assessment**

4. How can you explore how the ideas discussed in this textbook relate to you? **Exploring the Essential Question activities and Global Economy & You**

5. If you want to quickly find all the charts, graphs, and tables that relate to supply or demand, where in the front of the book do you look? **Table of Contents**

6. What is the quickest way to find information on detailed, specific topics such as gross domestic product and the national debt? **look in the index**

7. Where can you find the main points for the topic Market Structure summed up visually? **the Study Guide for Chapter 7**

8. Where can you find a list of the Content Vocabulary words for Chapter 12, Lesson 2, and how are they indicated in the text? **listed in the Reading Help Desk, and boldfaced and highlighted in yellow in the text**

9. There is more material to help you learn online. Where in this textbook can you find some of the extra digital assets available for each lesson listed? **The "Try It Yourself Online" box at the top of every lesson.**

10. Which of the book's special features provides information about how the global economy affects you and your community? **The Global Economy & You**

UNIT 1
THINKING LIKE AN ECONOMIST Planner

UNDERSTANDING BY DESIGN®

Enduring Understandings
- Resources are limited, so people must make choices.
- Economic systems shape the way individuals, businesses, and government interact.
- Entrepreneurs, consumers, and the government play an important role in the American free enterprise system.

Essential Questions
- In what ways do people cope with the problem of scarcity?
- How does an economic system help a society deal with the fundamental problem of scarcity?
- What are the benefits of a free enterprise economy?

Students will Know:
- societies must make choices about what, how, and for whom to produce.
- land, labor, capital, and entrepreneurs are the four factors of production.
- the value of a good or service depends on its scarcity and utility.
- the different economic systems used to allocate scarce goods and resources.
- most countries have mixed economies.
- *the terms* free enterprise, free market, *and* capitalism *are synonymous terms to describe the U.S. economic system.*
- *the basic characteristics of the U.S. free enterprise system, including private property, incentives, economic freedom, competition, and the limited role of government.*

Students will be able to:
- **explain** why all societies face the problem of scarcity.
- **identify** three basic choices that are faced by all societies.
- **compare and contrast** the characteristics of traditional, command, and market economies.
- **explain** why mixed economies exist.
- **explain** how the American economy incorporates the five main characteristics of a free enterprise economy.
- **describe** the disadvantages of a free enterprise economy.
- **analyze** the role of entrepreneurs in a free enterprise economy.
- **express** the role of the consumer in a free enterprise economy.
- **explain** who determines the role of government in the American free enterprise system.

Predictable Misunderstandings
Students may think:
- *Scarcity can be corrected simply by producing more of the scarce products.*
- *Value is determined by an item's usefulness.*
- *All capitalistic countries have the same type of economy.*
- *Individuals have little control over the types and quality of goods and services produced.*
- *America has a pure free enterprise economy.*

Assessment Evidence
Performance Tasks:
- *Hands-On Chapter Projects with Technology Extensions*
- *Economic Simulations*
- *Math Practice for Economics*
- *Personal Finance Activities*
- *Reinforcing Economic Skills Activities*

Other Evidence:
- *Guided Reading Activities*
- *Vocabulary Activities*
- *Lesson Quizzes*
- *Chapter Tests, Forms A and B*

SUGGESTED PACING GUIDE—Semester
Introducing the Unit . . . . ½ Day
Chapter 1: What Is Economics? . . . . 5 Days
Chapter 2: Economic Systems and Decision Making . . . . 5 Days
Chapter 3: The American Free Enterprise System . . . . 5 Days

---

Key for Using the Teacher Edition

SKILL-BASED ACTIVITIES

Types of skill activities found in the Teacher Edition.
- **V** **Visual Skills** require students to analyze maps, graphs, charts, and photos.
- **R** **Reading Skills** help students practice reading skills and master vocabulary.
- **C** **Critical Thinking Skills** help students apply and extend what they have learned.
- **W** **Writing Skills** provide writing opportunities to help students comprehend the text.
- **T** **Technology Skills** require students to use digital tools effectively.

*Letters are followed by a number when there is more than one of the same type of skill on the page.

DIFFERENTIATED INSTRUCTION

All activities are written for the on-level student unless otherwise marked with the leveled labels below.
- **BL** Beyond Level
- **AL** Approaching Level
- **ELL** English Language Learners

All students benefit from activities that utilize different learning styles. Many activities are marked as below when a particular learning style is highlighted.

Intrapersonal
Logical/Mathematical
Visual/Spatial
Verbal/Linguistic
Naturalist
Kinesthetic
Auditory/Musical
Interpersonal

UNIT 1: THINKING LIKE AN ECONOMIST

PLANNER

☑ Print Teaching Options

V Visual Skills

☐ **p. 1 Gathering information** Students create a television-viewing log chronicling the number and types of economics-related items presented on the nightly news. **Visual/Spatial**

C Critical Thinking Skills

☐ **p. 1 Examining opinions on employment roles** Students give their opinions about whether they would rather be a manager of a large company or the owner of a small company, and why. **Interpersonal**

☐ **p. 1 Identifying wants** Students interview partners and point out that wants are purchased in the marketplace and cost money that most people must earn by selling their labor, or working. Students learn that we trade our productive efforts to satisfy our wants. **Verbal/Linguistic**

☐ **p. 2 Analyzing primary and secondary sources** Students learn to identify primary and secondary sources. Then they practice analyzing the credibility of primary and secondary sources by researching a primary and a secondary source for one of the opinions in a Debate feature. Students present their findings to the class and members agree or disagree that the sources found are credible. **Logical/Mathematical Verbal/Linguistic**

☑ Online Teaching Options

☐ **ANIMATION** **The Free Enterprise System**—Students will identify the three elements of the free enterprise system.

☐ **APPROACHING GRADE LEVEL READER** **Alternative Student Edition narrative**—You can assign your students who are struggling to read on grade level the Approaching Grade Level version of the Online Student Edition. This reader presents all of the content in the On Grade Level version of the Online Student Edition at a lower reading level.

☐ **ENGLISH LANGUAGE LEARNER READER** **Alternative Student Edition narrative with ELL support**—Use the Online English Language Learner reader to provide additional reading support for ELL students. You can find this tool in the Online Student Edition.

☑ Printable Digital Worksheets

R Reading Skills

☐ **WORKSHEET** **Guided Reading Activity**—Students use the Guided Reading Activities worksheets to review their comprehension of the content.

☐ **WORKSHEET** **Reading Essentials and Study Guide**—Students complete the study guide and answer Reading Progress Check and vocabulary questions.

C Critical Thinking Skills

☐ **WORKSHEET** **The Free Enterprise System Animation Activity**—Students answer questions about the three elements of the free enterprise system. **Verbal/Linguistic**

☐ **WORKSHEET** **Assessing Background Knowledge Activity**—Students should complete the Assessing Background Knowledge Activity before they study each chapter. Students' responses will give you a good idea of the kinds of misconceptions you can address when teaching the lessons.

☐ **WORKSHEET** **Chapter Summary**—Summaries are provided for each chapter and thoroughly condense core content into manageable chunks.

☐ **WORKSHEET** **Vocabulary Activity**—Students apply their knowledge of content and academic vocabulary words.

UNIT 1
Thinking Like an Economist

CHAPTER 1
What is Economics?

ESSENTIAL QUESTION
In what ways do people cope with the problem of scarcity?

CHAPTER 2
Economic Systems and Decision Making

ESSENTIAL QUESTION
How does an economic system help a society deal with the fundamental problem of scarcity?

CHAPTER 3
The American Free Enterprise System

ESSENTIAL QUESTIONS
What are the benefits of a free enterprise economy?

What are the major economic and social goals of the American free enterprise system?

IT MATTERS BECAUSE ...

Economics influences the lives of everyone on Earth. Economics affects your life when you earn money and then decide to spend your money to buy something you need or want. You might buy clothes, food, electronics, sports equipment, or any of the other hundreds of items available to buy. You probably didn't realize it, but the process of deciding what to buy and how much to pay for it applies some of the basic elements of thinking like an economist. Understanding the fundamentals of how economists think will help you make better choices in your own economic decisions.

UNIT 1
Thinking Like an Economist

ENGAGE

🔔 **Examining opinions on employment roles** Ask: *How would you feel about owning your own company? Explain.* (Answers will vary.) Tell students that in a phone survey, the Gallup organization questioned a random sample of approximately 1,000 teenagers across the country on their thoughts about entrepreneurship. The sample ranged in age from 14 to 19 years and was evenly divided between males and females. Almost 7 out of every 10 respondents said that they wanted to be entrepreneurs. Asked if they would rather be a manager of a large company or the owner of a small company, most chose the latter. Discuss students' opinions on the subject. **AL** *Verbal/Linguistic, Interpersonal*

Identifying wants Have pairs of students interview their partners to obtain the following information: (1) Give an example of a want. (2) What inputs are necessary to produce the want? *(factors of production—land, labor, capital, and entrepreneurship)* (3) Do you have any part in the process necessary to get your want? (Does the student work?) (4) What can you do to get your want? After the interviews, ask the class what is necessary to obtain their wants. Point out that wants are purchased in the marketplace and cost money that most people must earn by selling their labor, or working. In other words, we trade our productive efforts to satisfy our wants.
BL *Verbal/Linguistic*

Gathering information Have students create a television-viewing log chronicling the number and types of economics-related items presented on the nightly news. Suggest that some students watch national newscasts on the networks, that others watch national newscasts on cable (such as CNN or MSNBC), and that still others watch local newscasts. Students should record the date, the subject of the item, and the length of time devoted to the item. When study of the unit is completed, have students compare and discuss their logs, noting how much news related to economics was presented. *Logical/Mathematical*

ANIMATIONS **WORKSHEET**

The Free Enterprise System

Analyzing the animation Have a student read the title of the animation. Tell students there are three important related elements in a free enterprise system. After viewing the animation, have class members identify the three elements. *(entrepreneurs, consumers, government)* Divide the class into small groups and have each group create a skit that includes the three elements.
BL *Kinesthetic, Logical/Mathematical*

UNIT 1
Thinking Like an Economist

DEVELOP YOUR SKILLS ONLINE

Analyzing Primary and Secondary Sources

Tell students that historians and economists use primary and secondary sources to understand previous events. Explain to students that *primary sources* are artifacts or eyewitness accounts, such as photographs, letters, journals, autobiographies, legal documents, drawings, and other objects. *Secondary sources* are interpretations of an event produced well after the event took place. Tell students that textbooks, for example, are secondary sources.

Ask: What might be a drawback of primary sources? *(Primary sources provide valuable information but may not give a complete account of an event. A letter from an immigrant might describe a difficult journey, for example, but it may not tell you how many people immigrated.)* Remind students that sometimes the author or creator of a primary source often has a specific point of view that might affect their material. **Ask: Why should a researcher always question the intentions of the author?** *(The author or creator's viewpoint might not have been objective, or balanced.)* **Why do you think a historian might wish to research several first-person accounts of a past event?** *(A historian needs to research several accounts of the same event to determine whether the source has unfairly flattered or criticized an event or person.)* **Is a biography a primary or secondary source?** *(A biography is a secondary source because the author is writing about someone else.)*

To practice analyzing the credibility of primary and secondary sources, have small groups research a primary and a secondary source for one of the opinions in a Debate feature. Have each group present to the class their findings and whether group members agree or disagree that the sources found are credible. **AL** Logical/Mathematical Verbal/Linguistic

---

Develop your Skills Online

Analyzing Primary and Secondary Sources

Primary and secondary sources are important sources of information about economic conditions both past and present. But it's important to be able to analyze and evaluate the validity of economic information in both types of sources. Use these tips to analyze primary and secondary sources for bias, propaganda, point of view, and frame of reference.

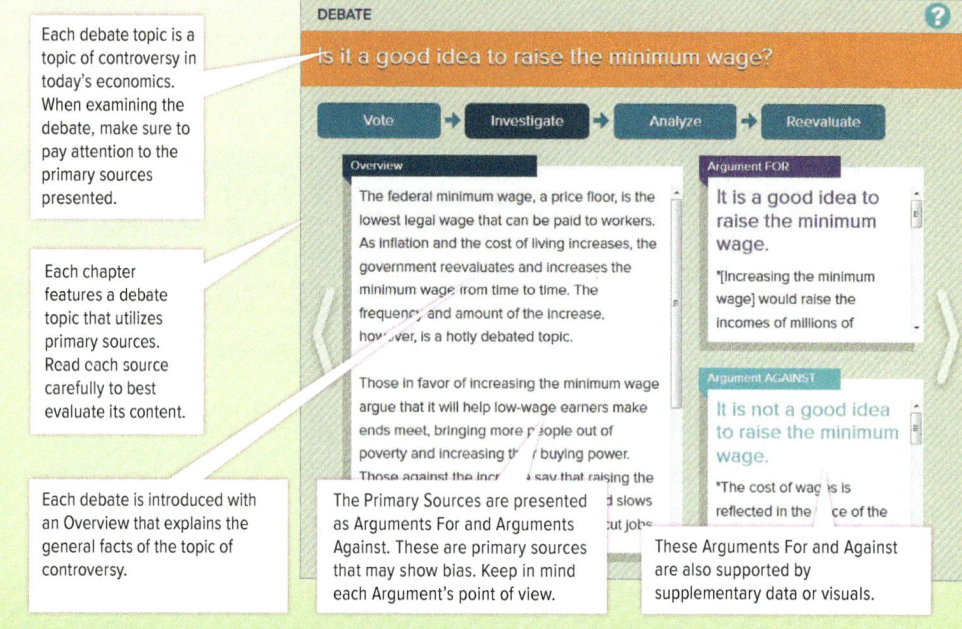

networks Online Teaching Options

DEBATES

SAMPLE Debate: Should students be financially rewarded for good grades?

Evaluating information for validity Have students view the Debate and call on a student to summarize the main arguments in favor of rewarding students for good grades. Invite the class to add more reasons. Then ask another student to summarize the reasons opposing student rewards. Ask the class to provide additional reasons to support this view. Then point out the sources of the two excerpts. Have students consider the point of view from the state senator and psychologists, and ask whether these occupations add validity to their arguments. Why or why not? **Interpersonal**

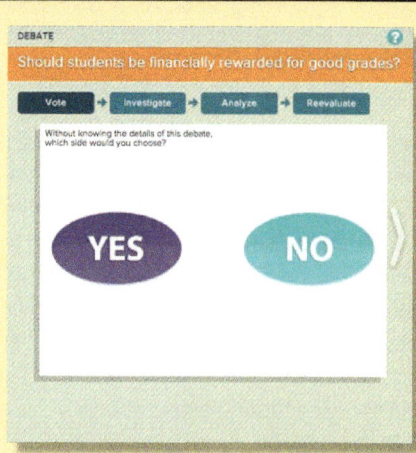

CHAPTER 1
What Is Economics? Planner

UNDERSTANDING BY DESIGN®

Enduring Understanding
- *Resources are limited, so people must make choices.*

Essential Questions
- *In what ways do people cope with the problem of scarcity?*

Predictable Misunderstandings
Students may think:
- *Scarcity can be corrected simply by producing more of the scarce products.* Explain that scarcity results from almost unlimited needs and wants.
- *Value is determined by an item's usefulness.* Explain that although utility, or satisfaction, is one of the necessary elements, value also depends on the item's scarcity, or availability.
- *The cost of making one choice instead of another (opportunity cost) applies only to businesses such as manufacturers.* Explain that opportunity costs apply to everyone and should be investigated before any major decision is made.

Assessment Evidence
Performance Tasks:
- *Hands-On Chapter Project with Technology Extension*

Other Evidence:
- *Guided Reading Activities*
- *Vocabulary Activity*
- *Lesson Quizzes*
- *Self-Check Quizzes*
- *Chapter Assessment*
- *Chapter Tests, Forms A and B*

SUGGESTED PACING

Introducing the Chapter....... ½ Day	Debate .... ½ Day
Lesson 1: Scarcity and the Science of Economics................. 1 Day	Lesson 3: Using Economic Models .... 1 Day
Case Study .... ½ Day	Study Guide, Chapter Assessment, and Wrap-Up .... ½ Day
Lesson 2: Our Economic Choices .... 1 Day	

TOTAL 5 Days

Key for Using the Teacher Edition

SKILL-BASED ACTIVITIES

Types of skill activites found in the Teacher Edition.

- **V** **Visual Skills** require students to analyze maps, graphs, charts, and photos.
- **R** **Reading Skills** help students practice reading skills and master vocabulary.
- **C** **Critical Thinking Skills** help students apply and extend what they have learned.
- **W** **Writing Skills** provide writing opportunities to help students comprehend the text.
- **T** **Technology Skills** require students to use digital tools effectively.

*Letters are followed by a number when there is more than one of the same type of skill on the page.

DIFFERENTIATED INSTRUCTION

All activities are written for the on-level student unless otherwise marked with the leveled labels below.

- **BL** Beyond Level
- **AL** Approaching Level
- **ELL** English Language Learners

All students benefit from activities that utilize different learning styles. Many activities are marked as below when a particular learning style is highlighted.

- Intrapersonal
- Logical/Mathematical
- Visual/Spatial
- Verbal/Linguistic
- Naturalist
- Kinesthetic
- Auditory/Musical
- Interpersonal

Council for Economic Education

Below are the Council for Economic Education Voluntary National Content Standards in Economics covered in the *What Is Economics?* chapter.

Content Standard 1: Productive resources are limited. Therefore, people cannot have all the goods and services they want; as a result, they must choose some things and give up others.

Content Standard 2: Effective decision making requires comparing the additional costs of alternatives with the additional benefits. Many choices involve doing a little more or a little less of something: few choices are "all or nothing" decisions.

Content Standard 3: Different methods can be used to allocate goods and services. People acting individually or collectively must choose which methods to use to allocate different kinds of goods and services.

CHAPTER 1: WHAT IS ECONOMICS?

CHAPTER OPENER PLANNER

Students will know:
- societies do not have enough productive resources to satisfy everyone's wants and needs, so they must make choices about what, how, and for whom to produce.
- land, labor, capital, and entrepreneurs are the four factors necessary to produce goods and services.
- productivity is most important for economic growth.

Students will be able to:
- *explain* why all societies face the problem of scarcity.
- *identify* three basic choices that are faced by all societies.
- *describe* the four basic factors of production.
- *evaluate* trade-offs and opportunity costs to choose wisely or make the best decision.
- *compare* the factor and labor markets and their roles in the circular flow of economic activity.

UNDERSTANDING BY DESIGN

☑ Print Teaching Options

V Visual Skills

☐ **p. 3 Scarcity and Time** Students keep a log of how their hours are spent and create a graph.

☐ **p. 5 Finding the Best Price** Students price items by store and brand to find the "best buy."

C Critical Thinking Skills

☐ **p. 3 Understanding the importance of choice** Students imagine they have $100 to spend.

☐ **p. 4 Analyzing the process behind making choices** Students choose how their needs and wants will be met on a monthly income of $350.

☐ **p. 5 Applying opportunity cost** Students identify opportunity **cost for purchases.**

☑ Online Teaching Options

V Visual Skills

☐ **IMAGE** Chapter Opener—Students view a buyer in an economic transaction.

C Critical Thinking Skills

☐ **INFOGRAPHICS** Economic Perspectives—Students identify items as a fixed expense, planned expense, variable expense, and/or financed payment.

☐ **DEBATES** Should fracking be allowed to continue even though it uses our water resources?—Students analyze two views and supporting evidence about fracking.

☐ **INTERACTIVE FEATURE** Case Study: Drought and Scarcity in the United States: 2012—Students analyze how drought affected the United States in 2012.

☑ Printable Digital Worksheets

C Critical Thinking Skills

☐ **WORKSHEET** Personal Finance Activity—Students decide what their needs and wants are, and how to allocate their money accordingly.

☐ **WORKSHEET** Enrichment Activity—Students read about "big box" stores' effect on the independent retail sector.

Project-Based Learning

Hands-On

WORKSHEET Hands-On Chapter Project

Students plan how to start a business by deciding the type of business to open, researching the demographics of a location, creating a business plan, and discussing options for raising the capital necessary to open the business.

Digital Hands-On

Create Online Projects

Find an additional activity online that incorporates technology for the Hands-On Project. Visit the EdTech Teacher Web sites for more links, tutorials, and other resources.

Print Resources

ANCILLARY RESOURCE

This ancillary is available for every chapter and lesson.

- Chapter Tests and Lesson Quizzes

PRINTABLE DIGITAL WORKSHEETS

These printable digital worksheets are available for every chapter.

- Reading Essentials & Study Guide
- Vocabulary Activities
- Chapter Summaries
- Economic Simulations
- Math Practice for Economics
- Reinforcing Economic Skills
- Personal Finance Activities
- Hands-On Chapter Projects
- Enrichment Activities
- Reteaching Activities
- Guided Reading Activities
- Video Worksheets
- Lesson Quizzes and Chapter Tests (English and Spanish)

More Media Resources

SUGGESTED READING

- For students at a Grade 10 reading level: *Oprah Winfrey: Rising Above, Reading Out,* by Henry Billings and Melissa Billings
- For students at a Grade 11 reading level: *Influential Economists,* by Marie Bussing-Bunks
- For students at a Grade 12 reading level: *How Cool Is Comics Lit,* by Charles McGrath

SUGGESTED VIDEOS

Find these documentaries yourself online. NOTE: McGraw-Hill Education does not endorse these resources. Preview clips for age-appropriateness.

- *The Ka-Ching Dynasty* (26 min.)
- *TED Talks: The 6 Killer Apps of Prosperity* (20 min.)

LESSON 1 Planner

SCARCITY AND THE SCIENCE OF ECONOMICS

Students will know:
- societies do not have enough productive resources to satisfy everyone's wants and needs, so they must make choices about what, how, and for whom to produce.
- the value of a good or service depends on its scarcity and utility.

Students will be able to:
- *explain* why all societies face the problem of scarcity.
- *categorize* the various types of goods and services.
- *identify* three basic choices that are faced by all societies.
- *summarize* the four reasons people study economics.

UNDERSTANDING BY DESIGN®

✓ Print Teaching Options

R Reading Skills

- ☐ **p. 7 Understanding the source of scarcity** Students consider how limited resources and unlimited wants create scarcity.
- ☐ **p. 9 Identifying Adam Smith's point of view** Students identify Adam Smith's view of wealth, material possessions, and people.
- ☐ **p. 10 Determining cause and effect of making choices** Students answer questions about limited resources and unlimited wants.
- ☐ **p. 11 Describing how societies answer the basic economic questions** Students pose WHAT, HOW, and FOR WHOM to produce.

C Critical Thinking Skills

- ☐ **p. 6 Recognizing the prevalence of economics** Students note how economics affects their lives.
- ☐ **p. 7 Responding to scarcity** Students name a scarce resource and how it has affected them.
- ☐ **p. 8 Categorizing Needs and Wants** Students categorize wants and needs as a durable, nondurable, consumer, or capital good. **BL**
- ☐ **p. 8 Identifying types of goods** Students identify what to ask before making purchases.
- ☐ **p. 9 Applying TINSTAAFL** Students examine ads that support TINSTAAFL. **BL** Visual/Spatial
- ☐ **p. 10 Considering HOW to produce** Groups produce a playground with varying labor.
- ☐ **p. 12 Analyzing the behavioral aspect of economics** Students analyze an economics article for bias or normative statements. **BL**

W Writing Skills

- ☐ **p. 8 Making inferences about value** Students consider why some goods are more valuable.
- ☐ **p. 11 Explaining key elements of economics** Students explain how the four key elements of economics are interrelated.
- ☐ **p. 12 Identifying the central concept of scarcity** Students write a paragraph that explains the fundamental economic problem.

✓ Online Teaching Options

V Visual Skills

- ☐ **BELLRINGER Identifying a Limited Resource**—Students view photographs and decide which photograh shows a limited resource. Visual/Spatial
- ☐ **SLIDE SHOWS Scarcity**—Students view scarce resources and write a paragraph identifying the choices we have to make due to scarcity. Visual/Spatial
- ☐ **VIDEO Republic of Happiness**—Students view a video about Bhutan's Gross National Happiness principle. Verbal/Linguistic

R Reading Skills

- ☐ **GRAPHIC ORGANIZER Scarcity**—Students describe items they think should be produced to address actual or potential scarcity in each goods category: Nondurable, Durable, Capital and Consumer. Logical/Mathematical
- ☐ **LECTURE SLIDES WORKSHEET The Scope of Economics**—After viewing the Lecture Slides and main ideas of the lesson, students complete the Guided Reading Activity. Logical/Mathematical

C Critical Thinking Skills

- ☐ **ESSENTIAL QUESTION Exploring the Essential Question Activity**—Students consider how they would handle the problem of need versus scarcity.
- ☐ **BIOGRAPHY Biography of Adam Smith**—Students discuss Adam Smith's ideas.
- ☐ **IMAGE WHAT to Produce**—Students relate how a focus group helps companies decide WHAT to produce and take part in a classroom focus group.

T Technology Skills

- ☐ **SELF-CHECK QUIZ Lesson 1**—Students receive instant feedback on their mastery of lesson content.
- ☐ **GAME Lesson 1**—Students solve clues to review lesson content.
- ☐ **INTERACTIVE WHITEBOARD ACTIVITY Needs vs. Wants**—Students work together to learn lesson content.

✓ Printable Digital Worksheets

R Reading Skills

- ☐ **WORKSHEET Guided Reading Activity**—Students use the Guided Reading Activity worksheets to review their comprehension of the content.
- ☐ **WORKSHEET Reading Essentials and Study Guide**—Students complete the study guide and answer Reading Progress Check and vocabulary questions.

C Critical Thinking Skills

- ☐ **WORKSHEET Republic of Happiness Video Activity**—Students answer questions about the Bhutanese economy, what elements it has adopted from the West, and its relationship to nature.

LESSON 2 Planner

OUR ECONOMIC CHOICES

Students will know:
- land, labor, capital, and entrepreneurs are the four factors necessary to produce goods and services.
- entrepreneurs take the risk to combine productive resources to produce goods and services.
- how a production possibilities curve can be used to determine the most efficient allocation of resources.

Students will be able to:
- **describe** the four basic factors of production.
- **identify** production alternatives using a production possibilities curve.
- **explain** the concept of opportunity cost, including the opportunity cost of idle resources.
- **evaluate** trade-offs and opportunity costs to choose wisely or make the best decision.
- **list** the rights and responsibilities of consumers.

UNDERSTANDING BY DESIGN®

☑ Print Teaching Options

V Visual Skills
- ☐ **p. 15 Building vocabulary** Students define and illustrate the four factors of production.

R Reading Skills
- ☐ **p. 19 Muckrakers** Students consider how muckrakers heralded consumerism by reading *The Jungle* or *Unsafe at Any Speed*.

C Critical Thinking Skills
- ☐ **p. 14 Examining their personal economic decisions** Students consider whether they are compulsive or careful in how they spend money.
- ☐ **p. 15 Determining factors of production** Students brainstorm the factors of production in a T-shirt business. **BL** Logical/Mathematical
- ☐ **p. 16 Synthesizing wants and the factor of labor** Students interview partners about wants and production inputs. **AL** Logical/Mathematical
- ☐ **p. 16 Understanding production possibilities** Students select a product and create a production possibilities curve for it.
- ☐ **p. 17 Applying opportunity cost** Students figure the opportunity cost of accepting a summer manufacturing or landscaping job.
- ☐ **p. 20 Evaluating alternatives** Students explain trade-offs after winning $100. **AL** Intrapersonal

W Writing Skills
- ☐ **p. 16 Identifying factors of production** Students create quiz cards about the 4 factors.
- ☐ **p. 18 Understanding opportunity costs and trade-offs** Students write a short essay about the costs and benefits of using a product.

T Technology Skills
- ☐ **p. 18 College Tuition Trade-Offs** Students consider the costs and benefits of attending college or immediately entering the workforce.
- ☐ **p. 19 Learning about the consumer right of safety** Students research consumer Web sites.

☑ Online Teaching Options

V Visual Skills
- ☐ **VIDEO** Risky Business—Students view a video about the challenges producers face. Logical/Mathematical
- ☐ **CHART** Factors of Production—Students identify a community or state producer and consider its access to all four factors of production. Verbal/Linguistic
- ☐ **GRAPHS** Production Possibilities Curve—Students discuss how a business uses a production possibilities curve. Logical/Mathematical
- ☐ **GRAPH** Opportunity Cost—Students see how the production of one good affects the production of a different good. Visual/Spatial
- ☐ **CHARTS** Decision-Making Grid—Students consider buying expensive shoes.

R Reading Skills
- ☐ **GRAPHIC ORGANIZER** Our Economic Choices—Students fill in the columns: Choices Producers Make, Production Possibilities, Choices Consumers Make.
- ☐ **INTERACTIVE WHITEBOARD ACTIVITY** Consumer Responsibilities—Students identify statements that show consumer responsibilities. Logical/Mathematical

C Critical Thinking Skills
- ☐ **ESSENTIAL QUESTION** Exploring the Essential Question—Students decide what option is a good economic choice for dealing with scarcity. Logical/Mathematical
- ☐ **INTERACTIVE WHITEBOARD ACTIVITY** Consumer Responsibilities—Students identify statements that are consumer responsibilities. Logical/Mathematical

W Writing Skills
- ☐ **BELLRINGER** Making Good Economic Choices—Students describe an incident in which they were affected by scarcity of an item. Verbal/Linguistic

T Technology Skills
- ☐ **SELF-CHECK QUIZ** Lesson 2—Students receive instant feedback on their quiz.
- ☐ **GAME** Lesson 2—Students solve clues to review lesson content.
- ☐ **INTERACTIVE WHITEBOARD ACTIVITY** How to Deal with Scarcity—Students work together to learn lesson content.

☑ Printable Digital Worksheets

R Reading Skills
- ☐ **WORKSHEET** Guided Reading Activity—Students review lesson content.

C Critical Thinking Skills
- ☐ **WORKSHEET** Risky Business—Students answer questions about the challenges producers face.

LESSON 3 Planner

USING ECONOMIC MODELS

Students will know:
- productivity is the most important factor to economic growth.
- the economic activity in markets connects individuals and businesses.
- effective decision making requires comparing the additional costs of alternatives with the additional benefits.
- simple economic models can be used to understand complex economic systems.

Students will be able to:
- **describe** the importance of economic growth and the factors that make economic growth possible.
- **compare** the factor market and the labor market and their roles in the circular flow of economic activity.
- **discuss** the use of economic models to explain economic activity.
- **analyze** the benefits of an action or plan using a cost-benefit analysis.
- **explain** how the study of economics can help people make better economic choices.

UNDERSTANDING BY DESIGN®

☑ Print Teaching Options

V Visual Skills

- ☐ **p. 22** Students create a production possibilities curve.
- ☐ **p. 25** Interpreting the roles of resource owners in the circular flow
- ☐ **p. 25** Interpreting the roles of firms in the circular flow *Visual/Spatial*
- ☐ **p. 25** Students review how the rest of the world interacts in the circular flow.

R Reading Skills

- ☐ **p. 26** Students consider how economists might gather data to make an economic model.

C Critical Thinking Skills

- ☐ **p. 21** Students consider how economics helps them plan their future.
- ☐ **p. 22** Students discuss how economic growth would be affected if productivity declined.
- ☐ **p. 23** Students tie education and technology to economic growth. **AL**
- ☐ **p. 23** Demonstrating division of labor and specialization Groups create booklets.
- ☐ **p. 24** Contrasting factor and product markets
- ☐ **p. 25** Providing real-world examples Students create real-world circular-flow models.
- ☐ **p. 26** Creating a circular-flow model Students put themselves in a circular flow diagram.
- ☐ **p. 27** Students describe a subjective and an objective decision they made recently.
- ☐ **p. 27** Contrasting costs and benefits of economic decisions

W Writing Skills

- ☐ **p. 23** Students write their spending and/or saving choices if their money doubled.
- ☐ **p. 28** Students compare a country's poverty rate and personal income to the U.S.

☑ Online Teaching Options

V Visual Skills

- ☐ **GRAPHS** **Education Pays**—Students consider the relationship between increased level of education and increased salary. *Visual/Spatial*
- ☐ **SLIDE SHOWS** **Circular Flow of Economic Activity**—Students consider how they have participated in the circular flow of economic activity. *Logical/Mathematical*
- ☐ **VIDEO** **Decision Making**—Students watch a video about economic decisions.
- ☐ **INTERACTIVE FEATURE** **Careers: Retail Business Manager**
- ☐ **IMAGES** **Free Enterprise at Work**—Students discuss characteristics found in a free enterprise economy. *Visual/Spatial*

R Reading Skills

- ☐ **GRAPHIC ORGANIZER** **Characteristics that Affect Economic Growth**—Students identify characteristics, such as population, that affect economic growth.

C Critical Thinking Skills

- ☐ **BELLRINGER** **Supply & Demand Model for Movie DVDs**—Students identify alternatives if the price of DVDs suddenly increased. *Logical/Mathematical*
- ☐ **ESSENTIAL QUESTION** **Exploring the Essential Question**—Students consider ways consumers and productions can obtain their wants and needs.
- ☐ **INTERACTIVE FEATURE** **Global Economy & You: Shifting from Manufacturing to Service**—Students review primary, secondary, and tertiary economic activity.

T Technology Skills

- ☐ **SELF-CHECK QUIZ** **Lesson 3**—Students receive instant feedback on quizzes.
- ☐ **GAME** **Lesson 3**—Students solve clues to review lesson content.
- ☐ **INTERACTIVE WHITEBOARD ACTIVITY** **Factor and Product Markets**—Students work together to learn lesson content.

☑ Printable Digital Worksheets

R Reading Skills

- ☐ **WORKSHEET** **Vocabulary Activity**—Students use content and academic terms.
- ☐ **WORKSHEET** **Reteaching Activity**—Students use this activity worksheet to review and reteach chapter content.

C Critical Thinking Skills

- ☐ **WORKSHEET** **Decision Making Video Activity**—Students make a conclusion and an inference about economic decisions. *Intrapersonal*

CHAPTER 1 What Is Economics?

INTERVENTION AND REMEDIATION STRATEGIES

LESSON 1 Scarcity and the Science of Economics

Reading and Comprehension

Have students determine the meaning of a word in context. After reading the section of text under the heading "Why We Have Scarcity," have students write a definition of the word *economics*. After you have reviewed their definitions, ask them to write a short paragraph using the word *economics*.

Text Evidence

Have students read the section of text under the heading "Our Needs and Wants." To have students determine the central ideas of the text, write the following questions on the board for them to write and answer in their notebooks. **Ask: What are some needs that all people share?** *(food, clothing, shelter)* **What are some wants that you have?** *(Answers will vary, but could include a new cell phone, a notebook computer, or a video game).* Discuss answers with students.

LESSON 2 Our Economic Choices

Reading and Comprehension

To have students determine the meaning of a word in context, have them write the word *land* in their notebooks. Tell students that in relation to economics, this word has a specific meaning. Write on the board aspects of *land* in relation to economics: deserts, fertile fields, forests, sunshine, and climate. Tell students that *land* means natural resources. Have students write a sentence using the word *land* as it is used in economics.

Text Evidence

Have students read the section under "Consumer Responsibilities." To determine the central idea of the text, ask students to write a list of two things that a responsible consumer should do when purchasing an item. *(Answers may include: Do research and find the best deal before buying a product; deal ethically with the store after you buy an item.)*

LESSON 3 Using Economic Models

Reading and Comprehension

To have students determine the meaning of a phrase as used in the text, have them consider the term *economic interdependence*. Tell students that we rely on others and others rely on us to provide most of the goods and services we use. Have students think of one item that they use and write a short paragraph explaining how they rely on others for that item.

Text Evidence

Have students read the text in the first paragraph under the heading "Circular Flow of Economic Activity." Ask them to then examine the figure showing circular flow. Tell students to determine the central ideas of the text in relation to what *markets* are in economics. **Ask: What is the role markets play in the circular flow?** *(Students should realize that markets are a location of exchange, and that markets allow buyers and sellers to exchange a specific product or factor of production.)* Have them write a short paragraph explaining the importance of markets in economics.

Online Resources

Assessing Background Knowledge Use this worksheet to pre-assess students' background knowledge before they start the chapter.

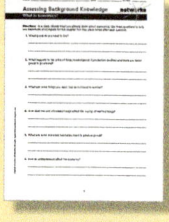

Chapter Summaries Have students use the summary as a pre-reading activity or as a post-reading review to check the main ideas covered in each lesson.

Guided Reading Activities Have students complete these activities as they read each lesson. They provide reading notes the student can use for review and to prepare for assessments.

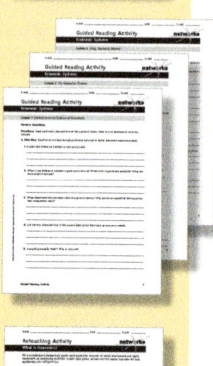

Reteaching Activities Have students complete the Reteaching Activity for remedial practice and review of vital content.

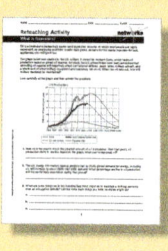

Self-Check Quizzes These quizzes provide instant feedback on areas the students may need to re-read to understand a main idea.

Reading Essentials and Study Guide This resource offers writing and reading activities for the approaching-level student.

Approaching Grade Level Reader This reader presents all of the content of the Online Student Edition but at a lower reading level.

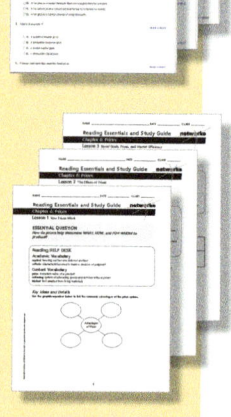

English Language Learner Reader Provide additional reading support for ELL students. Find this tool online.

What is Economics?

ESSENTIAL QUESTION
- In what ways do people cope with the problem of scarcity?

networks
www.connected.mcgraw-hill.com
There's More Online about economics.

CHAPTER 1

Economic Perspectives
Budgeting Lifestyles

Lesson 1
Scarcity and the Science of Economics

Lesson 2
Our Economic Choices

Lesson 3
Using Economic Models

CHAPTER 1
What Is Economics?

ENGAGE

Call students' attention to the photo and ask them to describe what it shows. Guide them to recognize that a shopper is exchanging money for a product or a *good*. **Ask: How does this image symbolize the chapter titled *What Is Economics?*** *(The activity shown in the photo—the exchange of money for a good—shows a buyer in a basic economic transaction. The shopper represents a consumer.)* In a discussion, lead students to think about the fact that there are different kinds of goods—durable, nondurable, and consumer—and to recognize the difference between goods and services.

Understanding the importance of choice Ask students to imagine that they have $100 to spend. Have them make a list of the items they would like to buy and the approximate price of each. Have them add up the prices and, if the total exceeds $100, remove items so they do not exceed their budget. Lead students in a discussion of their choices and the thought process that led them to those choices. Conclude by pointing out that *choice* is a key concept in economics. **Intrapersonal**

Making Connections

Scarcity and Time Time is a precious resource. To help students grasp the concept of time as a scarce resource, have them keep a one-week log of how all their hours (168) are spent. Ask students to divide these hours into categories such as sleep, school, studying, eating, entertainment, travel, preparation, shopping, and so on. Then have students enter the information in a database and convert it into a circle graph. Students should compare their graphs.

Letter from the Author
Dear Economics Teacher,

Economics is one of those topics that seems to intimidate everyone. That's a shame because the topics at the core of the science—scarcity, supply and demand, employment or unemployment, international trade—are things that affect every one of us, even the author of this text! The good news, however, is that economics isn't really all that difficult. That's probably because we spend most of our time studying how we affect the world and how it affects us. Scarcity is the first issue we study, followed by strategies and behaviors to combat it. What could be more interesting, or more important, than this?

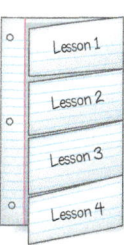

Go to the Foldables® library for a cumulative chapter-based Foldable® activity that your students can use to help take notes and prepare for assessment.

CHAPTER 1
Economic Perspectives

TEACH & ASSESS

C Critical Thinking Skills

Analyzing the process behind making choices Tell students to suppose they are freshmen at college and have a part-time job that earns $350 a month. They live in a dorm and have a paid meal plan at the college cafeteria. Have students identify three needs they will have. Then have them identify three wants they might have as college freshmen. Finally, have students work out how those needs (not already paid for) and wants could be managed on $350 a month. **AL**

Content Background Knowledge

Disposable vs. Discretionary Income Income can be both disposable and discretionary. *Disposable* income is the money a person has left after all taxes have been paid. People spend their disposable income on many kinds of goods and services. First, they buy the necessities: food, clothing, and housing. Any leftover income, which can be saved or spent on extras such as luxury items or entertainment, is called *discretionary* income.

Economic Perspectives

BUDGETING LIFESTYLES

5 Basic Elements of Budgets

Budgets help people keep track of the money they have coming in and how they spend that money over time. Budgets can be done with pencil and paper or by using specialized software. Whichever format you choose, using a budget to manage your money helps prevent debt and unpaid bills from piling up. Examining your finances regularly helps you achieve your life goals, because your financial choices are planned with those goals in mind.

1 Income
This is the source of all household spending. Make sure you work with the net income (income AFTER taxes are removed) for accurate calculations of what you can actually afford. Gross income is the money earned BEFORE all taxes and deductions are removed.

2 Fixed Expenses *Examples: rent, utilities, insurance, tuition, car payment*
These are necessary costs that usually occur monthly or annually. Failure to pay these can result in eviction from your home, loss of services, or repossession.

3 Planned Expenses *Examples: vacation, major purchase such as a car, a house, more education*
These are purchases or investments that you're planning for over a long period of time.

4 Variable Expenses *Examples: groceries, clothing, fuel, vehicle expenses, pet-related expenses*
These necessities must be paid for regularly, but in more unpredictable amounts.

5 Financed Payments *Examples: payments for credit cards, loans, or lines of credit*
Make these payments in full each month to avoid paying more due to high interest rates or late payment fees.

---

networks Online Teaching Options

INFOGRAPHIC

Economic Perspectives: Budgeting Lifestyles

Identifying needs and wants Display the Economic Perspectives feature and start a discussion about needs and wants. Ask students to think about the things they will *need* and the things they will *want* if they are going away to college after high school. Have student pairs list these needs and wants in a two-column chart. Then have them label each item as a fixed expense, planned expense, variable expense, and/or financed payment.
Visual/Spatial, Interpersonal

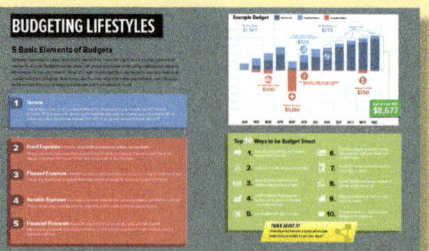

CHAPTER 1
Economic Perspectives

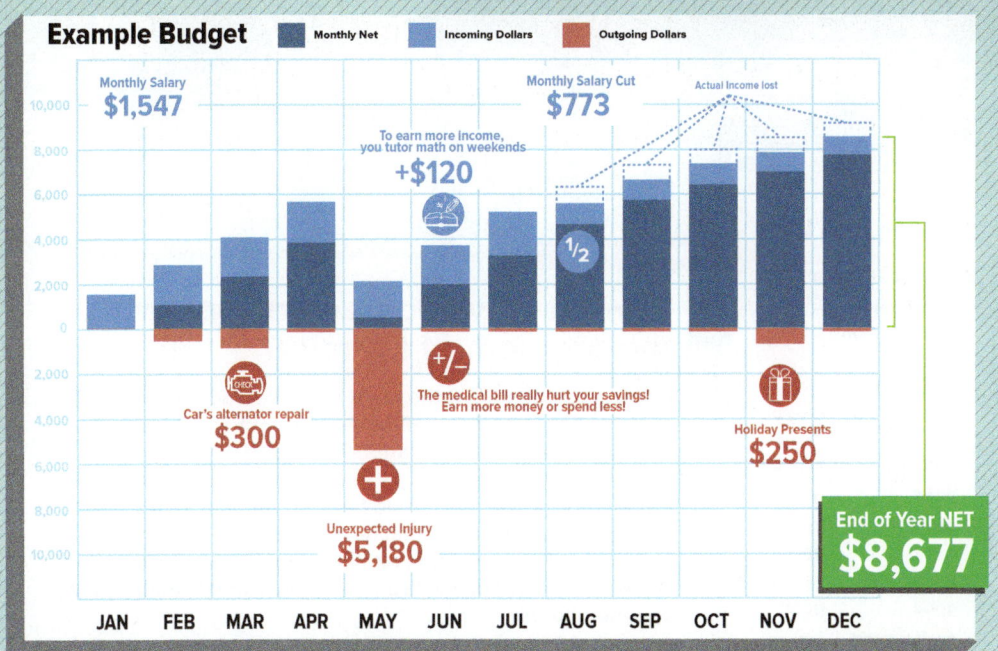

C Critical Thinking Skills

Applying opportunity cost to budgets Ask students to list purchasing choices they have made recently. Then ask them to explain the concept of opportunity costs and identify the opportunity cost for each of their purchases. Encourage students to share and compare their lists.

Making Connections

Finding the Best Price Organize students into groups, and have groups develop lists of 10 common household items. Then have the groups visit at least three stores where these items are available, and price the items by store and brand. Have groups include store brand and generic product prices where applicable. Ask the groups to organize their data into tables, and then have them compare their tables to see which is the "best buy" for each item.

CLOSE & REFLECT

Have students answer the *Think About It!* questions.

WORKSHEET

Personal Finance Activity: What to Spend Money On

Considering spending habits Have students complete the Personal Finance Activity, which will give them a chance to decide what their needs and wants are, and to allocate their money accordingly. At the end of this activity, they will be able to look at their own spending habits more objectively. **Logical/Mathematical, Interpersonal**

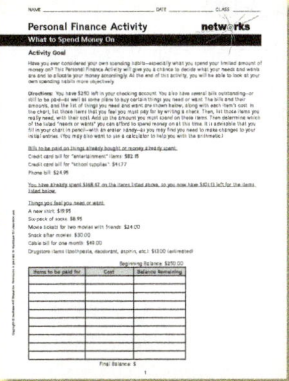

ANSWERS, p. 5

THINK ABOUT IT!

Students should realize that by listing all of their income and expenses in an accurate list, the mystery of where their money is going is gone. By then halting any spending for frivolous or spontaneous wants, funds will be available for necessary basic needs.

CHAPTER 1, LESSON 1
Scarcity and the Science of Economics

ENGAGE

C Critical Thinking Skills

Recognizing the prevalence of economics Before students begin the lesson, write the following sentence on the board: *Economics affects our lives every day.* Have a student read the sentence aloud. In a class discussion, ask students whether they think the sentence is true or false. Have students give reasons for their opinions. Lead students to identify the ways economics affects their lives every day. List their answers on the board.

Interact with these digital assets and others in lesson 1
- ✓ INTERACTIVE IMAGE — WHAT to Produce
- ✓ SLIDESHOW — Scarcity
- ✓ SELF-CHECK QUIZ
- ✓ VIDEO

networks — TRY IT YOURSELF ONLINE

LESSON 1
Scarcity and the Science of Economics

ESSENTIAL QUESTION

C In what ways do people cope with the problem of scarcity?

A storm has damaged the main highway leading to your town, so there have been no deliveries of essential, or even nonessential, items to neighborhood stores. Some people are running out of certain things they need or want. Others have lost electric power, and some have no running water. Below is a list of things you have that some of your neighbors are looking for. For each item, explain at least one way you think is best (and perhaps fairest) to distribute these items among your neighbors.

a. One loaf of bread
b. One bicycle
c. An assortment of handyman tools in one toolbox
d. One bottle of aspirin
e. One half-full bottle of antiseptic and 10 cotton balls
f. Two one-gallon jugs of bottled water
g. One cellular smart phone
h. Three blankets
i. Ten towels
j. One MP3 player

Reading Help Desk

Academic Vocabulary
- transferable
- accumulation
- intangible
- comprehensive

Content Vocabulary
- scarcity
- economics
- need
- want
- good
- durable good
- nondurable good
- consumer good
- capital good
- service
- value
- paradox of value
- utility
- wealth
- gross domestic product

TAKING NOTES:

Key Ideas and Details
ACTIVITY Use a graphic organizer like this one to list goods needed to address actual or potential scarcity in each category.

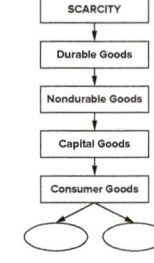

Scarcity—The Basic Economic Problem

GUIDING QUESTION Why do all societies face the problem of scarcity?

You may wonder if the study of economics is worth your time and effort, but it helps us in many ways—especially in our roles as individuals, as members

---

ANSWERS, p. 6

ESSENTIAL QUESTION ACTIVITY

Students' answers will vary. After reviewing the problem presented in the Essential Question activity, have students make a T-chart. On one side, have students list each of the items, and on the other side a possible person to receive that item. For example, would a neighbor with three children merit the loaf of bread? Would an elderly woman receive one of the blankets? Have students present their charts in a class discussion.

TAKING NOTES: Answers in the graphic organizer will vary. Have students define the types of goods before providing two examples of scarcity for each. Sample answers for first oval might be: Washing machine, burritos, lathe, shoes. Sample answers for second oval might be: Vehicle, writing paper, robot welder, and shirt.

---

networks — Online Teaching Options

BELLRINGER

Scarcity and the Science of Economics

Identifying a limited resource Show the Bellringer photographs as students enter the classroom. Tell students that today they are going to consider limited resources in their lives. Explain that we all have limited resources, and the nation has limited resources as well. Have students look at the photos and decide which one shows a limited resource. *(The forest symbolizes limited resources, whereas the housing development symbolizes unlimited wants.)* In a discussion, point out that *all* resources and products face scarcity. Because people have unlimited wants, no amount of a resource or product could ever fulfill all of those wants. **Visual/Spatial**

of our communities, and as global citizens. The good news is that economics is not just useful; it can be interesting as well. Don't be surprised to find that the time you spend on this topic will be well spent.

Why We Have Scarcity

Have you ever noticed that very few people are satisfied with the things they have? For example, someone without a home may want a small one; someone else with a small home may want a larger one; someone with a large home may want a mansion. Whether they are rich or poor, most people seem to want *more* than they already have. In fact, if each of us were to make a list of all the things we want, it would most likely include more things than our country could ever hope to produce.

This is why we have scarcity, and this is why scarcity is the fundamental economic problem facing all societies. **Scarcity** is the condition that results from society not having enough resources to produce all the things people would like to have. As **Figure 1.1** shows, scarcity affects almost every decision we make. This is where economics comes in. **Economics** is the study of how people try to satisfy seemingly unlimited and competing needs and wants through the careful use of relatively scarce resources.

scarcity fundamental economic problem facing all societies resulting from a combination of scarce resources and people's virtually unlimited needs and wants

economics social science dealing with how people satisfy seemingly unlimited and competing needs and wants with the careful use of scarce resources

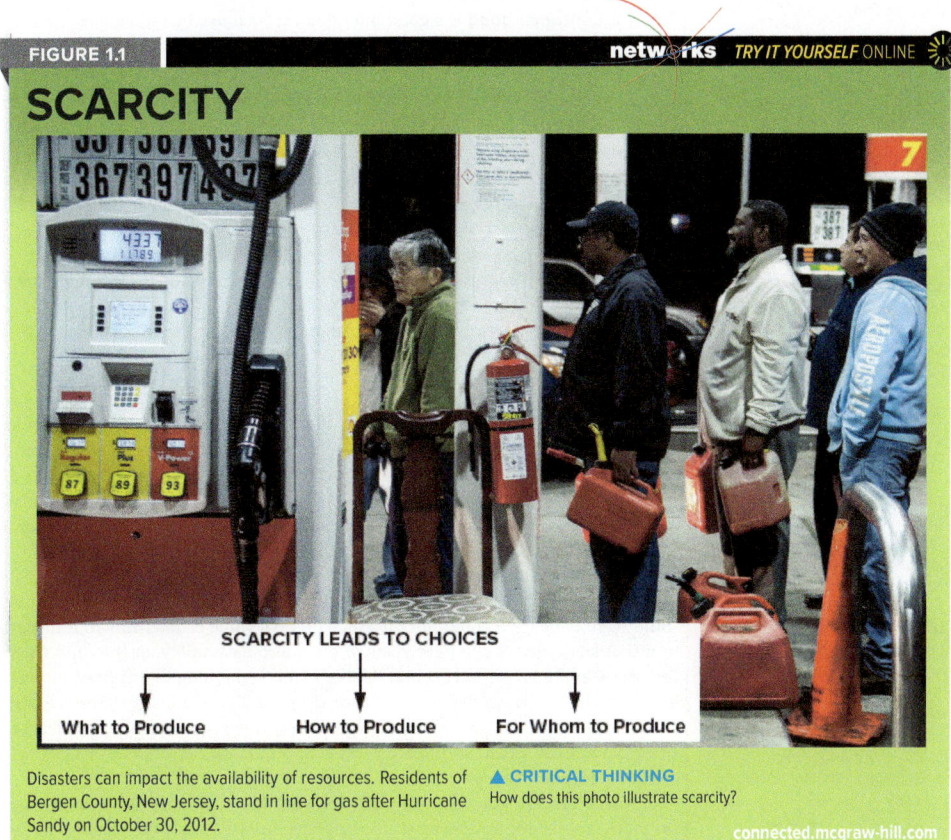

FIGURE 1.1

SCARCITY

SCARCITY LEADS TO CHOICES
- What to Produce
- How to Produce
- For Whom to Produce

Disasters can impact the availability of resources. Residents of Bergen County, New Jersey, stand in line for gas after Hurricane Sandy on October 30, 2012.

▲ **CRITICAL THINKING**
How does this photo illustrate scarcity?

CHAPTER 1, LESSON 1
Scarcity and the Science of Economics

TEACH & ASSESS

R Reading Skills

Understanding the source of scarcity Ask: **What effect do limited resources and unlimited wants have on the economy?** *(They create scarcity.)* AL

C Critical Thinking Skills

Responding to scarcity Have students explain why scarcity is a basic economic problem faced by every society. To reinforce this point, ask: **Name a resource that you have noticed is less abundant than in previous years. How has this change affected your family's use of the resource?** *(Answers will vary but may include water, electricity, or gasoline. Students' families may use these resources carefully, such as by carpooling or conserving water.)* AL **Verbal/Linguistic**

SLIDE SHOW

Scarcity

Understanding scarcity in daily life Have students view Figure 1.1. Ask students to identify the scarce resources shown in it. Have students select one of the scarce resources and write a paragraph identifying the choices we have to make because that resource is scarce. Have students share their paragraphs in class.
Visual/Spatial

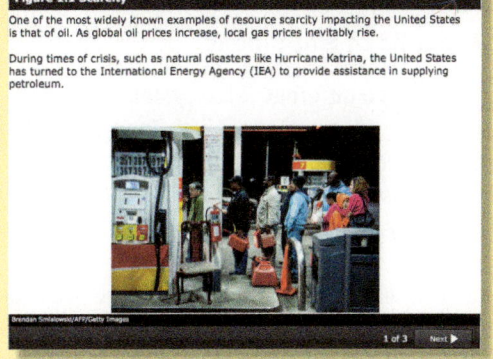

ANSWERS, p. 7

CRITICAL THINKING
Sample answer: A line of people waiting to fill multiple gas cans instead of filling vehicles reveals that the gasoline is limited. Body posture and several anxious expressions reveal concern over whether the consumers' needs will be met with the limited amount of gas.

CHAPTER 1, LESSON 1
Scarcity and the Science of Economics

Making Connections

Categorizing Needs and Wants Have students list all of the products they come in contact with on a daily basis, including shampoo, shoes, backpack, desk, MP3 player, and so on. Ask students to identify which of these products are needs and which are wants. Then have them label each product as a durable, nondurable, consumer, or capital good. Ask students to defend their categorizations. **BL**

C Critical Thinking Skills

Identifying types of goods Have students list two additional examples for each type of good: durable, nondurable, consumer, and capital. **Ask: When purchasing a particular good, what questions could you ask yourself to help identify the best product?** *(Possible answers: How much will I use a particular product? How long do I want a particular product to last?)* **Interpersonal**

W Writing Skills

Making inferences about value **Ask: Why do you think some goods are more valuable than others?** *(To have monetary value, a good must be scarce and have utility for the person purchasing it. Some goods that have utility are more scarce than others, which makes them more valuable.)* Have students write a brief essay describing an item they personally consider valuable and explaining why it falls under the concept of scarcity. *(It was made with limited resources and has utility for the purchaser.)* **AL Verbal/Linguistic**

---

need basic requirement for survival, including food, clothing, and shelter

want something we would like to have but is not necessary for survival

transferable capable of being passed from one person to another

good tangible economic product that is useful, transferable to others, and used to satisfy wants and needs

durable good good that lasts for at least three years when used regularly

nondurable good item that wears out, is used up, or lasts for fewer than three years when used regularly

consumer good good intended for final use by consumers other than businesses

capital good tool, equipment, or other manufactured good used to produce other goods and services; a factor of production

service work or labor performed for someone; economic product that includes haircuts, home repairs, and forms of entertainment

value monetary worth of a good or service as determined by the market

paradox of value apparent contradiction between the high value of a nonessential item and the low value of an essential item

utility ability or capacity of a good or service to be useful and give satisfaction to someone

wealth sum of tangible economic goods that are scarce, useful, and transferable from one person to another; excludes services

Our Needs and Wants

Economists often talk about people's needs and wants. A **need** is a basic requirement for survival, such as food, clothing, and shelter. A **want** is simply something we would like to have but is not necessary for survival. Food, for example, is needed for survival. But because many foods will satisfy the need for nourishment, the range of things represented by the term *want* is much broader than that represented by the term *need*.

Our needs and wants are usually expressed in terms of economic products—goods and services that are useful, relatively scarce, and **transferable** to others. These products generally fall into two groups. The first one is a **good**—a useful, tangible item, such as a book, car, or MP3 player, that can be used to satisfy a need or want. Goods are then divided into categories, depending on their use—and some goods, such as an automobile, can belong to two groups at the same time:

- A **durable good** is one that lasts three years or more when used on a regular basis. Durable goods include tools such as robot welders and tractors, and consumer goods such as automobiles.
- A **nondurable good** is an item that lasts for fewer than three years when used on a regular basis. Food, writing paper, and most clothing items are examples of nondurable goods.
- A **consumer good** is a good intended for final use by individuals, such as shoes, a shirt, or an automobile.
- A **capital good** is a tool or good such as machinery or equipment that is used by businesses to produce other products.

The other type of economic product is a **service**, or work that is performed for someone. Services include haircuts, home repairs, and forms of entertainment such as concerts. They also include the work that doctors, lawyers, and teachers perform. The difference between a good and a service is that a good is tangible, or something that can be touched, while a service is not.

Most goods and services have something called **value**, a term that refers to a worth that can be expressed in dollars and cents. But why does something have value, and why are some things more valuable than others? To answer these questions, it helps to review a problem Adam Smith, a Scottish social philosopher, faced back in 1776.

The Paradox of Value

Philosophers talked about value for hundreds of years, but they were unable to explain the concept satisfactorily. They were puzzled by the fact that some necessities, such as water, had a very low monetary value. On the other hand, some nonnecessities, such as diamonds, had a very high value. This contradiction was called the **paradox of value**. Adam Smith, our earliest economist, was one of the first to explain the essence of value in his famous book *The Wealth of Nations*, which was published in 1776.

Economists knew that scarcity was necessary for something to have value. Still, scarcity by itself could not fully explain how value is determined. It turned out that for something to have value, it must also have **utility**, or the capacity to be useful and provide satisfaction. Utility is not something that is fixed or even measurable, like weight or height. Instead, the utility of a good or service may vary from one person to the next. One person may get a great deal of satisfaction from a home computer; another may get very little. One person may enjoy a rock concert; another may not.

Adam Smith argued that for something to have value that can be expressed in monetary terms, it must be scarce *and* have utility. This is the solution to the

8

---

networks Online Teaching Options

VIDEO **WORKSHEET**

Republic of Happiness

Evaluating a different value system in Bhutan Have students review the video worksheet first. Then, after viewing the video, lead students to identify the Gross National Happiness principle in Bhutan. Have students complete the worksheet. Use their answers as a springboard for a discussion of Bhutan's values, which are a blend of economic development, spiritual values, and cultural values. Help students to analyze and explain how the Bhutanese regard nature and well-being as more important than consumerism and profits. Ask students to predict whether Bhutan's values might be affected by globalization. Then point out to students how they have used description, analysis, explanation, and prediction—the scope of economics as discussed later on pages 11–12—in their discussion. **Verbal/Linguistic**

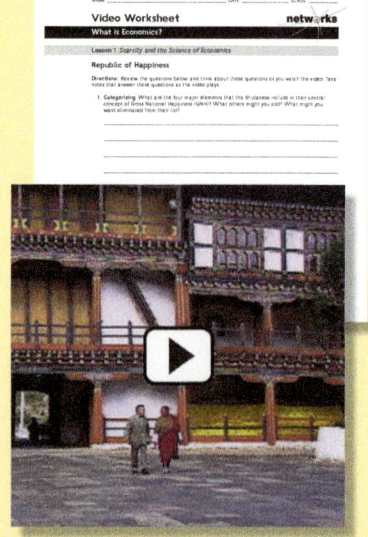

Video Supplied by BBC Worldwide Learning

paradox of value. Diamonds are scarce and have utility; thus they possess a value that can be stated in monetary terms. Water has utility but is not scarce enough in most places to give it much value. Therefore, water is less expensive, or has less monetary value, than diamonds. The emphasis on monetary value is important to economists. Unlike moral or social value, which is the topic of other social sciences, the value of something in terms of dollars and cents is a concept that everyone can easily understand.

Wealth

Wealth is another important concept. In an economic sense, **wealth** is the **accumulation** of products that are tangible, are scarce, have utility, and are transferable from one person to another. A nation's wealth comprises all tangible items—including natural resources, factories, stores, houses, motels, theaters, furniture, clothing, books, highways, video games, and even basketballs—that can be exchanged.

While goods are counted as wealth, services are not, because they are **intangible**. However, this does not mean that services are not useful or valuable. Indeed, when Adam Smith published his famous book *The Wealth of Nations* in 1776, he was referring specifically to the abilities and skills of a nation's people as the source of its wealth. For Smith, if a country's material possessions were taken away, its people, through their efforts and skills, could restore these possessions. On the other hand, if a country's people were taken away, its wealth would deteriorate.

TINSTAAFL

The problem of scarcity has another important consequence. Because resources are limited, everything we do has a cost—even when it seems as if we are getting something "for free." For example, do you really get a free meal when you use a "buy one, get one free" coupon? The business that gives it away still has to pay for the resources that went into the meal, so it usually tries to recover these costs by charging more for its other products. In the end, you may actually be the one who pays for the "free" lunch! Realistically, most things in life are not free, because someone has to pay for producing them in the first place. Economists use the term *TINSTAAFL* to describe this concept. TINSTAAFL means "There Is No Such Thing As A Free Lunch."

✓ **READING PROGRESS CHECK**

Contrasting What is the difference between a need and a want?

Questions All Societies Face

GUIDING QUESTION What basic choices are faced by all societies?

Because we live in a world of relatively scarce resources, we have to make careful choices about the way we use these resources. In addition to the origin of scarcity shown in Figure 1.1, the figure also presents three basic questions we need to answer as we make these choices.

WHAT to Produce

The first question is WHAT to produce. For example, should a society direct most of its resources to the production of military equipment or to other items such as food, clothing, or housing? Suppose the decision is to produce housing. Should the limited resources be used to build low-income, middle-income, or upper-income housing? A society cannot produce everything its people want, so it must decide WHAT to produce.

BIOGRAPHY

Adam Smith
ECONOMIST 1723–1790

Adam Smith, the father of economics, was educated at Oxford University and taught at Glasgow University. Smith wrote his most influential book, *The Wealth of Nations* (1776), in his native Scotland. Smith used historical and illustrative examples to critique economic theory. His insightful analyses elevated economics to the status of science. Smith's ideas rested on free market principles. He believed in the "invisible hand" of the market: The ideal economic system is shaped by the interaction of economic actors and should not be under government control. Everyone acting in his or her own "rational self-interest" improves the economy and general welfare. Smith believed that markets function best within social systems that rein in market-distorting forces, such as monopolies. He therefore criticized cutthroat, "dog-eat-dog" capitalism.

▲ **CRITICAL THINKING**
1. *Finding the Main Idea* On the basis of his writings in *The Wealth of Nations*, what do you think is Smith's central idea about what makes an economy function optimally?
2. *Evaluating* Why do you think Smith had a negative view of monopolies as undermining the free market? How do you think Smith might view today's multinational corporations? Explain your answer.

connected.mcgraw-hill.com   *What is Economics?* **9**

CHAPTER 1, LESSON 1
Scarcity and the Science of Economics

R Reading Skills

Identifying Adam Smith's point of view Ask: **What was Adam Smith's view of the relationship between a country's wealth, its material possessions, and its people?** *(Adam Smith believed that a nation's wealth consisted of material possessions and its people. If material possessions were taken away, the people could restore the possessions. If a country's people were taken away, the nation's wealth would deteriorate.)* **AL** **Verbal/Linguistic**

C Critical Thinking Skills

Applying TINSTAAFL Ask students to bring in examples of advertisements or flyers that promote *free* goods or services. Then have them analyze the fine print that negates the reality of "free" and supports the concept of TINSTAAFL. Ask students to identify ways the businesses in the advertisements recover their costs. **BL** **Visual/Spatial**

BIOGRAPHY

Adam Smith

Becoming familiar with Adam Smith's theories Display the digital biography feature of Adam Smith. Lead students in a discussion about Adam Smith and the "invisible hand" of the market. Ask: **What is the "invisible hand"?** *(Lead students to conclude that competition and self-interest—among both producers and consumers—is the invisible hand.)* For students who may not infer this answer, point out Smith's aversion to monopolies, which is the opposite of competition. Then have students answer the questions. **Visual/Spatial**

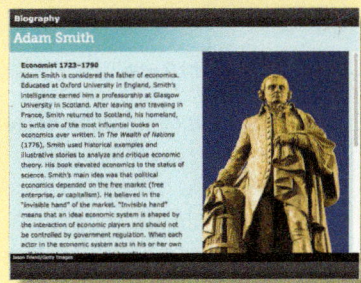

ANSWERS, p. 9

✓ **READING PROGRESS CHECK** A need is a basic requirement for survival. A want is something we would like to have, but it is not necessary for survival.

CRITICAL THINKING
1. Smith's central idea about what makes an economy function optimally is the lack of government control over the economy—that everyone acting in his or her own "rational self-interest" instead provides an "invisible hand" in shaping the market.
2. Smith's negative view of monopolies stemmed from their control over a market and restricting choice for consumers. Smith's view of today's multinational corporations might be mixed: he would appreciate the trade among nations, but he might be critical of the monopolization of an industry in a particular country.

What Is Economics? **9**

CHAPTER 1, LESSON 1
Scarcity and the Science of Economics

R Reading Skills

Determining cause and effect of making choices Ask: **What effect do limited resources and unlimited wants have on the economy?** *(They create scarcity and cause societies to have to make choices.)* Ask: **What problems do you think societies might face in choosing WHAT, HOW, and FOR WHOM to produce?** *(Answers may include the problem of meeting many needs with limited resources.)* **AL** Verbal/Linguistic

C Critical Thinking Skills

Considering HOW to produce Organize students into groups of 2, 3, 4, 5, 6, and 7 (adjust as necessary, with one group having only two people, and each successive group adding another person). Ask each group to devise and write down/illustrate a process for constructing a playground castle, using only the number of people in the group. Each group has an unlimited budget for capital goods. Each person in the group must have a task in the process. Upon completion, have groups compare HOW they plan to produce with varying numbers of people. Point out the similarity to Japan's and Mexico's situation discussed in the text. **BL**
Kinesthetic, Logical/Mathematical

ANSWERS, p. 10

CRITICAL THINKING

Focus groups allow entrepreneurs to determine what consumers want, and it is the desires of consumers that drive WHAT is produced.

R In some countries, the decision of WHAT to produce is made by the government. For example, in North Korea, the government has almost complete control over this decision. As a result, large quantities of military goods are produced rather than consumer goods for the people. In the United States, however, spending decisions made by consumers largely determine the answer to the WHAT to produce question.

HOW to Produce
A second question is HOW to produce. Should factory owners use automated production methods that require more machines and fewer workers, or should they use fewer machines and more workers? If a community has many unemployed people, using more workers might be better. On the other hand, in countries where machinery is widely available, automation can often lower production costs. Lower costs make manufactured items less expensive and, therefore, available to more people.

C Japan and Mexico provide a good example of this. In Japan, more than half the population is older than 45 years of age. With relatively fewer young people working, they have highly automated factories that require fewer workers. In Mexico, however, the population is much younger, so production techniques rely less on automation with robots and use people instead.

FOR WHOM to Produce
The third question is FOR WHOM to produce. After a society decides WHAT and HOW to produce, it must decide who will receive the things produced. If a society decides to produce housing, for example, should it be the kind of housing that is wanted by low-income workers, middle-income professional people, or

For WHOM to Produce
Entrepreneurs who are considering creating a new product may have focus groups for their target audience to get an overall understanding of their needs and wants.

▼ **CRITICAL THINKING**
Economic Analysis How do focus groups answer the question of WHAT to produce?

10

---

networks Online Teaching Options

IMAGES

WHAT to Produce

Examining how companies determine what to produce Have students view the photograph. Tell students that companies often use focus groups to help them decide which products to manufacture and to limit market risks. Leaders of a focus group ask a group of consumers what they like or do not like about a potential product. Simulate a focus group in the class. Show students a product such as a pair of running shoes or a computer notebook. Ask students what they like or dislike about that product and then take a poll on whether a company should risk manufacturing it. **Interpersonal**

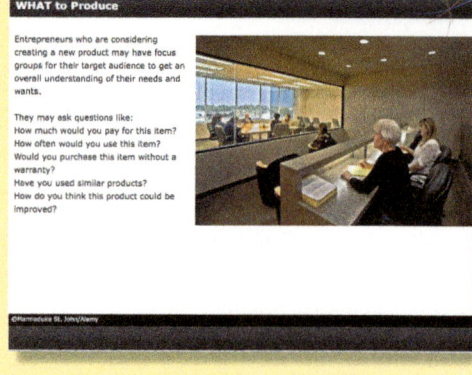

the very rich? If there are not enough houses for everyone, a society has to make a choice about who will receive the existing supply. These questions concerning WHAT, HOW, and FOR WHOM to produce are never easy for any society to answer. Nevertheless, they must be answered as long as there are not enough resources to satisfy people's seemingly unlimited wants and needs.

R

☑ **READING PROGRESS CHECK**

Analyzing Why are societies faced with the three basic questions of WHAT, HOW, and FOR WHOM?

The Scope of Economics

GUIDING QUESTION *Why do we study economics?*

Economics is the study of human efforts to satisfy seemingly unlimited and competing wants through the careful use of relatively scarce resources. Economics is also a *social science* because it deals with the behavior of people as they deal with this basic issue. The four key elements of this study are description, analysis, explanation, and prediction.

Description
One part of economics describes economic activity. For example, we often hear about **gross domestic product** (GDP)—the monetary value of all final goods, services, and structures produced within a country's borders in a 12-month period. GDP is the most **comprehensive** measure of a country's total output and a key measure of a nation's economic health. Economics also describes jobs, prices, trade, taxes, and government spending. Description allows us to know what the world looks like. However, description is only part of the picture, because it leaves many important "why" and "how" questions unanswered.

Analysis
Economics analyzes the economic activity that it describes. Why, for example, are the prices of some items higher than others? Why do some people earn higher incomes than others? How do taxes affect people's desire to work and save? When analyzing primary sources or secondary sources, take into account the bias of the author. After accounting for that source author's individual point of view, you are more likely to provide an accurate analysis of the evidence.

Explanation
Economics also involves explanation. After economists analyze a problem and understand why and how things work, they need to communicate this knowledge to others. Like all scientists, this explanation should be based in careful research that properly attributes ideas to source material so that other economists can evaluate and duplicate the work for accuracy. If we all have a common understanding of the way our economy works, some economic problems will be easier to address or fix in the future. When it comes to GDP, you will soon discover that economists spend much of their time explaining why the measure is, or is not, performing in the manner that is expected.

Prediction
Finally, economics is concerned with prediction. For example, we may want to know whether our incomes will rise or fall in the near future. Because economics is the study of both what is happening and what tends to happen, it can help predict what may happen in the future, including the most likely effects of different actions. The study of economics helps us become more informed citizens and

W

SKILLS PRACTICE
As you move through this course, keep a list of the academic and economic words you come across. Before you share information with classmates, choose some of these words to use.

accumulation gradual collection of goods

intangible not physical; something that cannot be touched

gross domestic product monetary value of all final goods, services, and structures produced within a country's national borders during a one-year period

comprehensive covering many or all areas

CHAPTER 1, LESSON 1
Scarcity and the Science of Economics

R Reading Skills

Describing how societies answer the basic economic questions Have students use the examples in the text to describe how various countries answer the WHAT, HOW, and FOR WHOM basic economic questions. **AL** Verbal/Linguistic

English Language Proficiency

Advanced As you introduce a new vocabulary word, activate students' prior knowledge. Ask them if and where they have seen or read the word before. Tell them to write the word in the center circle of a concept web and write word associations in surrounding circles. Then define or have a student define the word. Tell students to add to their concept webs with the definition in mind.

W Writing Skills

Explaining key elements of economics Have students write an essay naming the four key elements of economics and explaining how they are interrelated. In a class discussion, have students share their essays. **AL** Verbal/Linguistic

---

POLITICAL CARTOON

TINSTAAFL

Determining the cost of a free lunch Have students write a paragraph calculating the "real" cost of the "free sandwich" and explaining how the cartoon emphasizes the economic reality of TINSTAAFL.

ANSWERS, p. 11

☑ **READING PROGRESS CHECK** We live in a world of relatively scarce resources and we have to make choices regarding how to use those resources.

CHAPTER 1, LESSON 1
Scarcity and the Science of Economics

C Critical Thinking Skills

Analyzing the behavioral aspect of economics
Remind the class that economics is a behavioral science. Have students consider how economists might account for human factors—such as emotions, trends, biases, and personal convictions—when studying economics. **Ask: Do these factors always affect people in the same way? How do these factors make the study of economics more difficult?** *(Answers should demonstrate an understanding of the many variable human factors involved when studying economic issues and problems.)* Then ask students to find an economics article online and analyze its validity for bias or normative statements: those that typically involve value judgments, are not supported by economic models, use words such as *should,* and make a recommendation that may have unpredictable consequences or cannot be tested for accuracy. **BL**

CLOSE & REFLECT

W Writing Skills

Identifying the central concept of scarcity Have students write a paragraph that identifies and explains the fundamental economic problem that all societies face. Students should share their paragraphs in a class discussion.

ANSWERS, p. 12

CRITICAL THINKING
The man spent money in gas as well as time spent driving out of his way for months.

✓ **READING PROGRESS CHECK** Economics deals with the behavior of people as they deal with the basic issue of scarcity.

This cartoon shows someone who does not clearly understand the principle of "There's No Such Thing As A Free Lunch."

▶ **CRITICAL THINKING**
Distinguishing Fact from Opinion Explain how this man's lunch may not have been truly "free," even if he didn't have to hand over any money today.

better decision makers. Because of this, it is important to realize that good economic choices are the responsibility of all citizens in a free and democratic society.

By way of summary, economics deals with all these questions, and sometimes even more. It is also a dynamic science in that the subjects it studies—individuals such as ourselves and the economy as a whole—are always changing. Fortunately, the methods and the tools—the graphs and models of the economy—are well-suited to the task. This is something that gives the economist a certain amount of confidence when explaining or describing events, and we hope it gives you confidence as well.

✓ **READING PROGRESS CHECK**

Explaining Why is economics considered to be a social science?

LESSON 1 REVIEW

Reviewing Vocabulary
1. *Describing* What is the difference between a good that is a need and a good that is a want? Provide one example of each.

Using Your Notes
Refer to the graphic organizer at the beginning of this lesson to answer this question.
2. *Explaining* Which categories of goods used by ordinary people are most affected by scarcity? Use examples from two of these categories and explain how the scarcity of these goods might arise and how this scarcity would affect most people.

Answering the Guiding Questions
3. *Analysis/Synthesis/Evaluation* Why do all societies face the problem of scarcity?

4. *Knowledge/Comprehension/Application* What basic choices are faced by all societies?
5. *Analysis/Synthesis/Evaluation* Why do we study economics?

Writing About Economics
6. *Argument* Do you think there are any policies or steps that a society can take to avoid scarcity, at least in terms of supplying all the needs of its population? Write an argument for or against the concept that scarcity can be prevented by a society. If you argue that this is possible, describe the steps that can be taken to achieve this. If you argue that this is not possible, explain what makes it impossible.

LESSON 1 REVIEW ANSWERS

Reviewing Vocabulary
1. A good that is a need is necessary for survival, such as food, water, shelter, clothing, medical care, and so on. A want is not essential to life but makes life easier or more interesting, such as a radio or TV.

Using Your Notes
2. Consumer goods are affected the most by scarcity. Answers will vary but may mention that natural disasters may cause shortages of food (consumer good) or limit access to or transportation of building materials for homes (durable goods).

Answering the Guiding Questions
3. All societies face scarcity because all have unlimited wants and needs with limited resources.
4. Each society must decide WHAT to produce, HOW to produce it, and FOR WHOM to produce it.
5. People study economics to become more informed citizens and better decision makers.

Writing About Economics
6. Arguments will vary. Students who argue that it is possible to reduce scarcity may suggest keeping stores of goods in reserve to be used when a disaster occurs. Students who argue that it is impossible to reduce scarcity may point to the uncertainty of events that lead to shortages. Point out that scarcity is a human condition—unlimited wants—restricted by limited resources.

Case Study

DROUGHT & SCARCITY in the UNITED STATES: 2012

For an interactive version of this case study go to connected.mcgraw-hill.com

The worst drought in half a century struck the United States in 2012. The Midwest was hit especially hard, and large amounts of vital crops were lost. Corn yields were the lowest they had been since 1995, because more than half the corn crop died due to lack of rain. Production of soybeans, wheat, and other agricultural commodities suffered, too, but to a lesser extent.

The lack of rain persisted throughout the growing season. In mid-June, about 16 percent of farms and 20 percent of croplands were badly affected by the drought. By mid-August, these numbers had increased to 43 percent of farms and 57 percent of farmland affected.

Drastic reductions in the supply of agricultural commodities had the expected effect on prices. Corn prices rose by approximately $1.00 extra per bushel. Because corn is also used in many other products, this resulted in higher prices for other consumer goods.

Ethanol, a form of alcohol made from corn, is added to gasoline to reduce polluting auto emissions. As the drought of 2012 intensified, people began to question the wisdom of using a vital food commodity as fuel. Much of the corn the U.S. produces is used as feed for animals that humans consume. During a drought, diverting corn away from food for use as fuel causes food prices to increase even more.

Drought often brings scorching temperatures. August 2012 was the hottest month on record (at that time) in the United States. The heat that accompanied the drought was so intense it seriously damaged infrastructure in some affected areas: railroad tracks warped and buckled from the heat and highway asphalt melted and became impassable. Damage to infrastructure reduces the nation's economic output by limiting the production and transport of goods.

It was in 2013 that many drought-related food prices increased. Consumers saw price increases of about 5 percent for beef, 4.5 percent for dairy, and 6.9 percent for eggs.

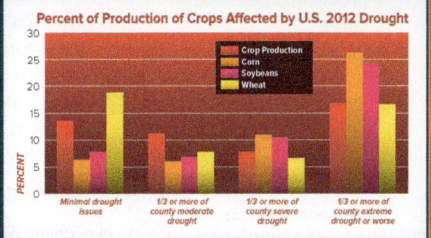

Percent of Production of Crops Affected by U.S. 2012 Drought

CASE STUDY REVIEW

1. **Explaining** Why does a natural disaster (drought, flood) in an agricultural region almost always result in higher prices for commodities and consumer goods?
2. **Making Connections** What other areas of a country's infrastructure might be vulnerable to extreme weather, such as drought or floods? How does infrastructure damage affect the overall economy?
3. **Analyzing** How did ethanol use affect the shortage of corn available to consumers during and after the drought of 2012? Do you think that commodities in one sector should be used in another economic sector? How might the concept of needs and wants affect your analysis of this issue?

CHAPTER 1
Case Study

V Visual Skills

Sequencing information Ask students to read the Case Study and then create a one-page time line of the drought events. Be sure students include the rise in consumer prices in 2013 on the time line.
Visual/Spatial

C Critical Thinking Skills

Understanding cause and effect Have students design a cause-and-effect chart showing how a natural disaster can affect consumer prices. Remind students to include not only the effect on agricultural products, but also on the higher transportation costs if the disaster interrupts waterways or infrastructure.
BL Logical/Mathematical, Visual/Spatial

T Technology Skills

Researching other natural disasters' effects on prices Have students research another natural disaster that recently affected agricultural areas in the world, and subsequently prices for agricultural products. Ask students to use graphs and charts to present their research to the class. Remind students to be sure to attribute their information to source materials. **BL Kinesthetic**

ANSWERS, p. 13

Case Study Review

1. Natural disasters kill a portion of the crops, so there is less supply to meet demand. Prices go up when demand exceeds supply.
2. Infrastructure is damaged when an earthquake destroys buildings and bridges, or when a drought disrupts ferry or water transport services. When infrastructure is damaged, producers cannot get their goods to markets. This reduces economic activity.
3. Using corn to produce ethanol made the food shortage worse because there was less corn to begin with, and a significant percentage of it was diverted from food use to fuel use. Students may argue that commodities in one sector should not be used in another, citing the ethanol example and unknown consequences in other sectors. Other students may argue that if commodities are not essential for living, then it is acceptable for them to be used in other sectors.

---

networks Online Teaching Options

INTERACTIVE FEATURE

Case Study: Drought and Scarcity in the United States: 2012

Assessing a drought's impact on the economy Have students view the Case Study showing how crops were affected by the drought in 2012. Discuss the graph with the class, noting that different degrees of drought have a range of effects on crop production. Have students write a paragraph comparing and contrasting the effects of an area with minimal drought issues with the effects an extreme drought has on an area. Discuss the paragraphs in class. **Visual/Spatial**

CHAPTER 1, LESSON 2
Our Economic Choices

ENGAGE

C Critical Thinking Skills

🔔 **Examining personal economic decisions**
Before students begin the lesson, ask them to think about how they make economic decisions. Are they compulsive in the way they spend their money? Or are they careful in how they spend their money? Have they ever made a budget only to fail to follow that budget? Have students rate themselves regarding the way they spend their money.

Interact with these digital assets and others in lesson 2
- ✓ INTERACTIVE CHART Decision-Making Grid
- ✓ INTERACTIVE WHITEBOARD ACTIVITY Consumer Responsibilities
- ✓ SELF-CHECK QUIZ
- ✓ VIDEO

netw❂rks TRY IT YOURSELF ONLINE

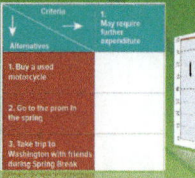

LESSON 2
Our Economic Choices

Reading Help Desk

Academic Vocabulary
- transformed

Content Vocabulary
- factors of production
- land
- capital
- labor
- entrepreneurs
- production possibilities curve
- opportunity cost
- trade-offs
- consumerism

TAKING NOTES:
Key Ideas and Details
Use a graphic organizer like the one below to identify ways that choices can be made to cope with the problem of scarcity.

Our Economic Choices		
Choices Producers Make	Production Possibilities	Choices Consumers Make

ESSENTIAL QUESTION

In what ways do people cope with the problem of scarcity?

You and your brother need new laptops for school, which starts next week. You both researched the models of new laptops and both decide to buy the same model. You go to an electronics warehouse store to buy the laptops. The store advertised a closeout sale on the brand and model of the laptops you and your brother want to buy. When you get to the store, the clerk tells you the specific model of laptop that was on sale has sold out. He shows you and your brother a new model that has more features than the model you wanted, and it is $75 more in price. What options do you and your brother have? Decide what you would do in these circumstances and explain your choice.

a. Buy the new model at $75 more in price
b. Ask to see another model of laptop that is nearer in price to the model that was on sale
c. Decide not to buy a laptop at a store and check into buying a laptop online
d. Decide to go to another electronics store
e. Ask to see the most inexpensive laptop the store sells

The Choices Producers Make

GUIDING QUESTION *Why must producers make production choices?*

It helps to think of our economy as being made up of two broad groups—producers and consumers. Of course we also have government, but more on that later; let's turn our attention to producers first.

Producers include all kinds of businesses, from individual artists who sell their creations at art shows to giant corporations whose annual revenue is in the billions of dollars. All of these producers have one thing in common: they all use what economists call "factors of production." The **factors of production**,

14

---

netw❂rks *Online Teaching Options*

BELLRINGER

Making Good Economic Choices

Considering choices Display the Bellringer. Tell students that they will consider how scarcity affects the value of an item, and what economic choices they make when an item they want is not available. Have students write a paragraph describing an incident in which they were affected by scarcity of an item and what choices they made. **Verbal/Linguistic**

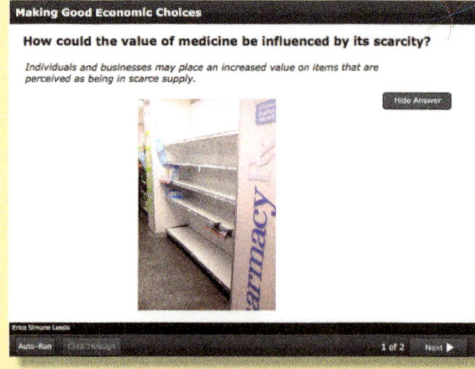

ANSWERS, p. 14

ESSENTIAL QUESTION ACTIVITY

Answers will vary depending on what students will do in the circumstances. Students should explain their choices.
TAKING NOTES: Sample answers: **Choices Producers Make:** what factors of production to use or not use **Production Possibilities:** how to combine factors of production to get the maximum output; what the opportunity costs are **Choices Consumers Make:** what trade-offs to make; what the opportunity costs are

or resources required to produce the things we would like to have, are land, capital, labor, and entrepreneurs. As shown in **Figure 1.2**, all four are required to produce goods and services.

Land

In economics, **land** refers to the "gifts of nature," or natural resources not created by people. *Land* includes deserts, fertile fields, forests, mineral deposits, livestock, sunshine, and the climate necessary to grow crops. Because a finite amount of natural resources are available at any given time, economists tend to think of land as being fixed, or in limited supply. Changing world events and market speculation can easily affect the prices of limited natural resources such as oil and metals.

Sometimes newer methods of production can be used to extract more resources out of the ground. For example, relatively new "fracking" techniques are used to recover natural gas locked in underground shale deposits, but the natural gas was already there before the new mining methods were developed.

Capital

A second factor of production is **capital**, sometimes called *capital goods*—the tools, equipment, machinery, and factories used in the production of goods and services. Capital is unique because it is the result of production. A bulldozer, for example, is a capital good used in construction. When it was built in a factory, it was the result of production involving other capital goods. The computers in your school that are used to produce the service of education also are capital goods.

factors of production productive resources needed to produce goods; the four factors are land, capital, labor, and entrepreneurship

land natural resources or "gifts of nature" not created by human effort; one of the four factors of production

capital tools, equipment, and factories used in the production of goods and services; one of the four factors of production

FIGURE 1.2

FACTORS OF PRODUCTION

Land
Labor
Capital
Entrepreneur

In order to create a product, four factors of production are needed.

◀ **CRITICAL THINKING**
Economic Analysis What four factors of production are necessary to bring clothing to consumers?

connected.mcgraw-hill.com

What is Economics? **15**

CHAPTER 1, LESSON 2
Our Economic Choices

TEACH & ASSESS

V Visual Skills

Building vocabulary Explain that in the context of economics, words such as *capital* and *labor* have meanings different from those with which students may be most familiar. Ask students to write the four factors of production in their personal economics glossary and draw several illustrations that demonstrate the economic meaning of each term as defined in the text. **ELL** Visual/Spatial

C Critical Thinking Skills

Determining factors of production Have students brainstorm the factors of production that would be required to establish a business that designs and sells T-shirts. Encourage students to be as thorough as possible when brainstorming their lists.
BL Logical/Mathematical

IMAGES

Factors of Production

Identifying the key factors of production
Discuss with the class the crucial importance of producers in any economy. Tell students that all producers use the four factors of production. After the class has viewed the images, have students identify a producer in their community or in their state and discuss whether they think that producer has ample access to all four factors of production. Finally, have students research contributions of entrepreneurs, inventors, and other key individuals from various gender, social, and ethnic backgrounds in the development of the United States. Verbal/Linguistic

ANSWERS, p. 15

CRITICAL THINKING
Land, capital, labor, and entrepreneurs

CHAPTER 1, LESSON 2
Our Economic Choices

C1 Critical Thinking Skills

Synthesizing wants and the factor of labor Have pairs of students interview their partners to obtain the following information: (1) Give an example of a want. (2) What inputs are necessary to produce the want? *(factors of production—land, labor, capital, and entrepreneurship)* (3) Do you have any part in the process necessary to get your want? *(Does the student work?)* (4) What can you do to get your want? After the interviews, ask the class what is necessary to obtain their wants. Point out that wants are purchased in the marketplace and cost money that most people must earn by selling their labor, or working. In other words, we trade our productive efforts to satisfy our wants. **AL Logical/Mathematical**

W Writing Skills

Identifying factors of production On index cards, have students list an item on the front and identify which factor of production it is on the back—"corn" and "land," for example. Assign students to create five examples for each factor, for a total of 20 index cards. Encourage students to quiz each other with their index cards. **AL Verbal/Linguistic**

C2 Critical Thinking Skills

Understanding production possibilities Ask students to select a product that they like or use. Have students imagine a scenario in which it would be beneficial for a company making that product to construct a production possibilities curve. *(Sample: A company is producing CD players and MP3 players. It is thinking of eliminating CD players, but it wants to see all the production possibilities before making its decision.)* Then have students create a sample production possibilities curve for the company. **BL Logical/Mathematical**

ANSWERS, p. 16

✓ **READING PROGRESS CHECK** There would be a scarcity of items.

CRITICAL THINKING
Producing any combination of goods and services outside the frontier requires more resources than the society currently has. It may help to think of the frontier as a barrier beyond which current production cannot take place because of limited resources.

Labor

A third factor of production is **labor**—people with all their efforts, abilities, and skills. This category includes all people except a unique group of individuals called entrepreneurs, whom we single out because of their special role in the economy. Historically, factors such as birthrates, immigration, famine, war, and disease have had a dramatic impact on the quantity and quality of labor.

Entrepreneurs

A fourth factor of production is the people responsible for much of the change and progress in our economy. These individuals are **entrepreneurs**, risk-takers in search of profits who do something new with existing resources. Entrepreneurs are often thought of as being the driving force in an economy because they are the people who start new businesses or bring new products to market.

Henry Ford is one example of an entrepreneur. His introduction of the moving assembly line in 1913 revolutionized the way cars were produced. Steve Jobs was another entrepreneur who **transformed**, or dramatically changed the nature of, the personal computer, cell phone, and music distribution industries.

labor people with all their abilities and efforts; one of the four factors of production; does not include the entrepreneur

entrepreneurs risk-taking individuals who introduce new products or services in search of profits; one of the four factors of production

transformed to change the nature of something

production possibilities curve diagram representing all possible combinations of goods and/or services an economy can produce when all productive resources are fully employed

✓ **READING PROGRESS CHECK**

Interpreting What would happen if one of the factors of production were missing?

Production Possibilities

GUIDING QUESTION *How does a production possibilities curve illustrate the decisions made in an economy?*

Everything we make requires the four factors of production. The individual artist requires materials that come from nature, such as pigments in paints (land); uses paintbrushes and easels (capital); spends many hours creating the art (labor); and makes the effort to promote the finished products (entrepreneurship). Giant corporations do the same, only on a much larger scale.

Even the service called *education* uses all four factors of production. The desks and lab equipment used in schools are capital goods. Teachers and other employees provide the labor. Land includes the property where the school is located as well as the iron ore and timber used to make the building. Finally, educational publishers are entrepreneurs. They create the materials that help teachers present the subject matter.

Identifying Possible Alternatives

Economists use the **production possibilities curve**, sometimes also called the frontier, to illustrate all possible combinations of output. A production possibilities curve is a diagram that represents various combinations of goods and services an economy can produce when all its resources are efficiently used. In the example in **Figure 1.3**, a mythical country called Alpha produces two goods—cars and clothing.

FIGURE 1.3 networks *TRY IT YOURSELF* ONLINE

PRODUCTION POSSIBILITIES CURVE

The Production Possibilities Curve

[Graph with Cars on y-axis (0–80) and Clothing on x-axis (0–500), showing points a, d, e, b, c on a curve]

The production possibilities curve, or frontier, shows the different combinations of two products that can be produced if all resources are fully employed.

▲ **CRITICAL THINKING**
Why can production only take place on or inside the frontier?

connected.mcgraw-hill.com

16

---

networks Online Teaching Options

GRAPHS

Production Possibilities Curve

Understanding a production possibilities curve Tell students that the production possibilities curve is called the *frontier*. Have students view Figure 1.3 Production Possibilities Curve. **Ask: Why can production take place on or inside the frontier?** *(Student answers should demonstrate an understanding that a frontier indicates the maximum combination of goods and services that can be produced.)* **Why will a firm have to eventually choose a combination of two points?** *(Student answers should demonstrate an understanding that a firm has to choose only two points on or inside the frontier because every firm's resources are limited.)* **Logical/Mathematical**

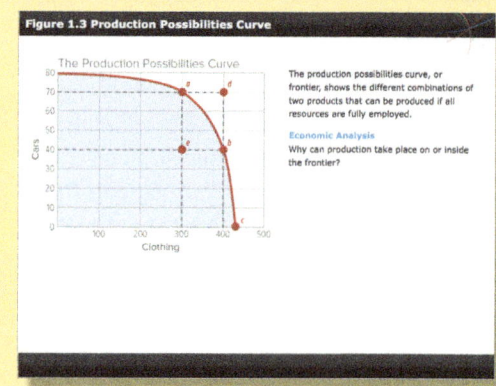

Figure 1.3 Production Possibilities Curve

The production possibilities curve, or frontier, shows the different combinations of two products that can be produced if all resources are fully employed.

Economic Analysis
Why can production take place on or inside the frontier?

Even though Alpha produces only two goods, the country has a number of alternatives available to it, which is why the figure is called a production *possibilities* frontier. For example, it could choose to use all of its resources to produce 70 units of cars and 300 units of clothing, which is shown as point **a** in Figure 1.3. Or it could shift some of its resources out of car production and into clothing, thereby moving output to point **b**. Alpha could even choose to produce at point **c**, which represents all clothing and no cars, or at point **e**, which is inside the frontier. Choosing an option inside the frontier results in less than maximum production and doesn't fully use resources. Although Alpha has many alternatives, eventually it will have to settle on a single combination such as point **a**, point **b**, or any other point on or inside the curve, because its resources are limited.

Fully Employed Resources
All points that lie on the curve, such as **a**, **b**, and **c**, represent maximum combinations of output that are possible if all resources are fully employed. To illustrate, suppose that Alpha is producing at point **a**, and the people would like to move to point **d**, which represents the same amount of cars, but more clothing. As long as all resources are fully employed at point **a**, there are no extra resources available to produce the extra clothing. Therefore, point **d** cannot be reached, nor can any other point outside the curve. This is why the figure is called a production possibilities frontier—to indicate the maximum combinations of goods and services that can be produced.

Opportunity Cost
People often think of cost in terms of dollars and cents. To an economist, however, cost means more than the price tag on a good or service. Instead, economists think broadly in terms of **opportunity cost**, the value of the next best alternative given up. For example, suppose that Alpha was producing at point **a** and that it wanted to move to point **b**. This is clearly possible as long as point **b** is not outside the production possibilities frontier. However, Alpha will have to give something up in return. As shown in **Figure 1.4**, the opportunity cost of producing the 100 additional units of clothing is the 30 units of cars given up.

As you can see, opportunity cost applies to almost all activities, and it is not always measured in terms of dollars and cents. For example, you need to balance the time you spend doing homework and the time you spend with your friends. If you decide to spend extra hours on your homework, the opportunity cost of this action is the time that you cannot spend with your friends. You normally have a number of trade-offs available whenever you make a decision, and the opportunity cost of the choice you make is the value of the next best alternative that you give up.

The Opportunity Cost of Idle Resources
If some resources were not fully employed, then it would be impossible for Alpha to reach its maximum potential production. Suppose that Alpha was producing at point **b** when workers in the clothing industry went on strike. Clothing production would

opportunity cost cost of the next best alternative use of money, time, or resources, when one choice is made rather than another

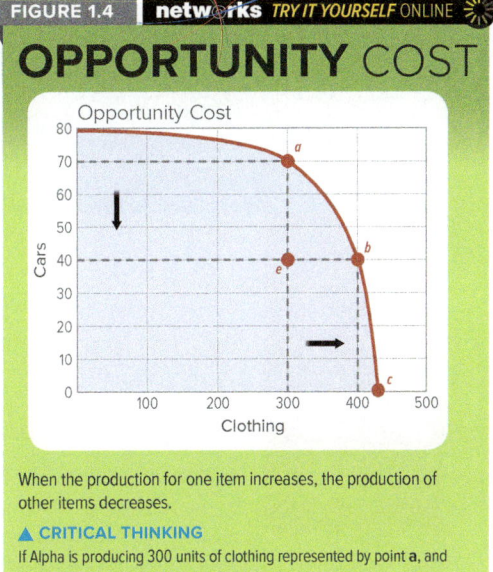

FIGURE 1.4

OPPORTUNITY COST

When the production for one item increases, the production of other items decreases.

▲ CRITICAL THINKING
If Alpha is producing 300 units of clothing represented by point **a**, and if it then decides to produce the amount of clothing at point **c**, what would be the opportunity cost in cars?

CHAPTER 1, LESSON 2
Our Economic Choices

Making Connections

Governments, Choice, and Opportunity Cost
Explain to students that governments, like individuals and businesses, must also make choices about which programs to support with their limited funding. If resources are devoted to increasing the size of the police force, for example, those same resources cannot also be used to improve education or build dams. Point out that governments cannot simply raise taxes to pay for everything they want to provide, because a dollar spent in taxes is a dollar the household cannot use to spend for food or clothing or gasoline—another opportunity cost. Have students explain why choice is a basic economic problem faced by every society.

C Critical Thinking Skills

Applying opportunity cost Tell students that Gerard has two choices for a summer job—a manufacturing job that pays $10.25 per hour, or a landscaping job that pays $8.65 per hour. At the landscaping company, he could work and have lunch with three of his closest friends. **Ask: For one 40-hour workweek, what would be the opportunity cost, in dollars, of accepting the landscaping job?** *($64.00)* **What would be the opportunity cost of accepting the manufacturing job?** *(not working or eating lunch with his friends every day)* **Logical/Mathematical**

English Language Proficiency

Advanced After you introduce content vocabulary, ask students about their prior experiences to deepen their understanding of meanings in English. For example, if the word is *opportunity*, ask them what types of opportunities they have experienced. Then pair them to discuss times they have witnessed or read about opportunities.

GRAPHS

Opportunity Cost

Understanding opportunity cost Tell students there are opportunity costs in all economic choices. In Figure 1.4, students will see how the production of one good affects the production of a different good. Have students click on the Opportunity Cost graph. **Ask: What happens when the production of one item increases?** *(The production of the other item decreases.)* **Visual/Spatial**

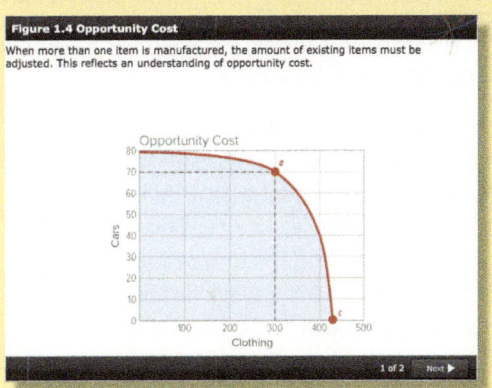

ANSWERS, p. 17

CRITICAL THINKING
When the production of one item increases, the production of another decreases. If Alpha starts at point **a**, which represents 70 cars and 300 units of clothing, and moves to point **c**, then the opportunity cost of the additional units of clothing will be the 70 cars given up. If it instead starts at point **b** and shifts its production to point **a**, the opportunity cost of getting 30 additional cars would be 100 units of clothing given up.

CHAPTER 1, LESSON 2
Our Economic Choices

W Writing Skills

Understanding opportunity costs and trade-offs Instruct students to think of a recent economic choice they made and the trade-offs involved in that choice. Then direct them to write a short persuasive essay in which they explain their choice and the costs and benefits of using the product. **AL**
Verbal/Linguistic

Making Connections

College Tuition Trade-Offs As many high school students approach graduation, they must weigh the trade-offs of attending college or immediately entering the workforce. In making the choice, high school graduates must weigh both the cost of attending college as well as the potential earning power they will gain by acquiring a college education. According to the National Center for Education Statistics, one year of tuition, room, and board for an undergraduate at a 4-year institution averaged $22,092 in 2011. However, the earning power of workers with a college degree is double (or higher) than that of workers with a high school diploma or GED. Have students visit the National Center for Education Statistics Web site and evaluate the validity of its economic information for bias.

ANSWERS, p. 18

✓ READING PROGRESS CHECK It represents various combinations of goods and services an economy can produce when all its resources are in use.

CRITICAL THINKING
Consumers can select and customize their own criteria and compare a number of different alternatives to make the choice best for them.

---

fall, causing total output to change to point **e**. The opportunity cost of the unemployed resources would be the 100 units of lost clothing production.

Production at point **e** could also be the result of other idle resources, such as factories or land that are available but not being used. As long as some resources are idle, the country cannot produce on its frontier—which is another way of saying that it cannot reach its full production potential.

✓ READING PROGRESS CHECK

Synthesizing How can the production possibilities frontier be used to illustrate economic growth?

The Choices Consumers Make

GUIDING QUESTION Why is it important to evaluate trade-offs and opportunity costs when making choices?

In a world where "there is no such thing as a free lunch," there are alternatives and costs to everything we do. Choices can be made by society as a whole, or by individuals in the society. Either way, the alternatives and their opportunity costs are important, so it pays to examine these concepts closely.

Trade-Offs

Making the right decision, or at least the best decision from a limited group of alternatives, is not always easy. This is because every decision we make has its **trade-offs**, or alternative choices that are given up in favor of the choice we select. Because of this, it helps to have a consistent strategy, or a plan to make the best decision. For example, suppose that you have decided to spend some of the money you earned last summer, but you have not decided how to spend it.

trade-offs alternative that must be given up when one choice is made rather than another

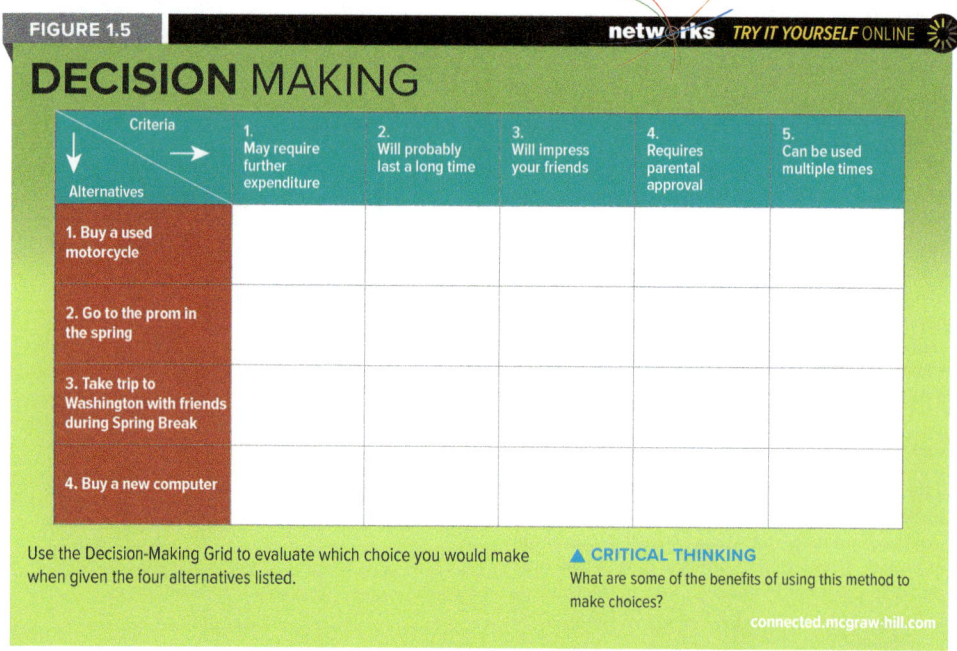

FIGURE 1.5 **DECISION MAKING**

Use the Decision-Making Grid to evaluate which choice you would make when given the four alternatives listed.

▲ **CRITICAL THINKING**
What are some of the benefits of using this method to make choices?

18

---

networks Online Teaching Options

CHARTS

Decision-Making Grid

Learning to make wise purchases Have students view Figure 1.5 Decision-Making Grid. Ask them to think about a large purchase they may have made recently. How did they decide to make that purchase? Did they research their options? Filling in the projected chart throughout the discussion, lead students to think about the positive and negative aspects of buying a pair of expensive running shoes. **Visual/Spatial**

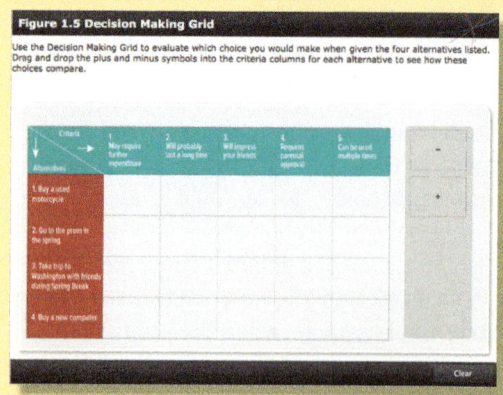

One way to help make a decision is to construct a model such as the grid in **Figure 1.5**, with the alternatives listed in the first column and the criteria in the first row.

If all of the alternatives have the same dollar cost, then all that remains to be done is to evaluate each one with a "+" if it satisfies the criterion, or with a "–" if it does not. These evaluations may differ from one person to the next, but in the case of Figure 1.5, the best alternative is to buy a new computer because it satisfies more criteria than any other alternative.

The decision-making grid is a good way to analyze an economic problem because it forces you to consider a number of alternatives and the criteria you will use to evaluate the alternatives. Finally, it makes you evaluate each alternative on the basis of the criteria you selected.

Opportunity Cost for Consumers

Producers are not the only ones that face opportunity costs; these costs apply to consumers as well. The decision-making grid also shows the opportunity cost of making a decision like buying a computer. This is because the next best alternative use of time or money would be to buy a used motorcycle. So again, the opportunity cost of doing something is not measured in terms of dollars and cents. Instead, economists think of the next best alternative given up—which would be the purchase of a motorcycle, because it is the second best choice in terms of meeting all of the criteria. In contrast to the opportunity cost, which is the next best choice, the trade-offs are all of the other alternatives that could have been chosen.

Even time has an opportunity cost, and you cannot necessarily put a monetary value on it. The opportunity cost of reading this economics book, for example, is the history paper or math homework that you could not do at the same time.

EXPLORING THE ESSENTIAL QUESTION

Consumers deal with the scarcity of items frequently, especially when a new electronics gadget first comes on the market. Long lines at electronic stores occur and people even camp out overnight in front of the stores to make sure that when the stores open with the new gadget for sale, they will get one of those gadgets. Do you agree that this is a good way to deal with the scarcity of an electronics item? Describe whether you agree or not and give your reasons.

Consumer Rights

In a world of giant corporations, it may seem as if the individual consumer is the "little guy" who often gets overlooked. Collectively, of course, consumers as a group help decide WHAT producers should make, and therefore where a country will be on its production possibilities frontier. For example, if consumers decide that they want more clothing and fewer cars, they will help move the economy from point **a** on the production possibilities curve in Figure 1.3 to point **b**.

Consumers were given some protection in 1962 when President John F. Kennedy sent a message to Congress outlining the first four consumer rights listed below. President Richard Nixon later added the fifth consumer right:

- **The right to safety**—protection against goods that are dangerous to life and health
- **The right to be informed**—to receive information that can be used for reasoned choices and protection against fraud
- **The right to choose**—the right to be protected in markets where competition may not always exist

EXPLORING THE ESSENTIAL QUESTION

Imagine you are an entrepreneur who has made a huge profit selling Product A. However, even though Product A is still selling well, you have an idea to produce another product, Product B. Product A is selling 300 units and requires very little in the way of resources and is garnering a nice profit. Product B seems like it would do well, but your market research shows you probably would only be able to sell 100 units. To help you decide if it's worth putting your resources toward Product B, create a hypothetical production possibilities curve and write a one-page essay explaining why or why not it would be a good decision to only produce Product A or produce both. Compare your essay and graph with a classmate's to analyze how they have created their production possibilities curve.

CHAPTER 1, LESSON 2
Our Economic Choices

Content Background Knowledge

Muckrakers It can be said that muckrakers in the late 1800s and early 1900s heralded consumerism. Upton Sinclair's *The Jungle*, written in 1906, exposed the unsanitary conditions in the meat-packing industry, and led to the establishment of government inspection agencies. Ralph Nader's book *Unsafe at Any Speed: The Designed-In Dangers of the American Automobile*, published in 1965, also influenced consumer safety—this time regarding the auto industry. Have students read one or both of these books and evaluate the validity of their economic information for propaganda.

T Technology Skills

Learning about the consumer right of safety
Assign student groups a product safety topic (auto safety, car seat safety, playground equipment safety, and so on). Have each group research their topic on the Internet from various consumer safety organizations. Have student groups prepare and present a PowerPoint® presentation with the information they find. **BL** Verbal/Linguistic

INTERACTIVE WHITEBOARD ACTIVITIES

Consumer Responsibilities

Examining your responsibilities as a consumer Display Figure 1.6—Responsibilities of the Consumer. Tell students to read through the statements and identify those that are consumer responsibilities. Have students debate any statements in disagreement. **Logical/Mathematical**

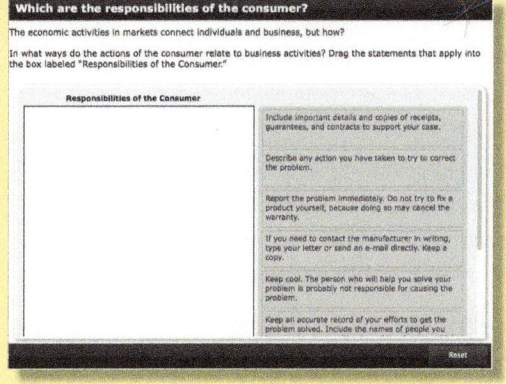

ANSWERS, p. 19

EXPLORING THE ESSENTIAL QUESTION

Students' essays and production possibilities curves will vary, depending on the amount of profit students surmise Product B will garner. Ask students to replace Product A and B with real products to help in understanding. For example, Product A could be an existing cell phone that is popular and profitable but becoming outmoded, whereas Product B is a newer version that does not have consumer loyalty yet.

EXPLORING THE ESSENTIAL QUESTION

Answers will vary. Sample answer: *Yes*, this is a good way to deal with scarcity of a new electronics gadget. Consumers with the willingness, money, and time to wait in long lines should obtain the product.

CHAPTER 1, LESSON 2
Our Economic Choices

CLOSE & REFLECT

C Critical Thinking Skills

Evaluating alternatives Have students imagine that they have won $100 in a raffle. Ask them how the knowledge of trade-offs and opportunity cost can help them decide what to do with the money.

AL Intrapersonal

ANSWERS, p. 20

CRITICAL THINKING
Sample answer: All of the consumer actions listed relate back to the business. In addition, the consumer actions help future consumers.

✓ **READING PROGRESS CHECK** Consumers would probably make many bad economic choices.

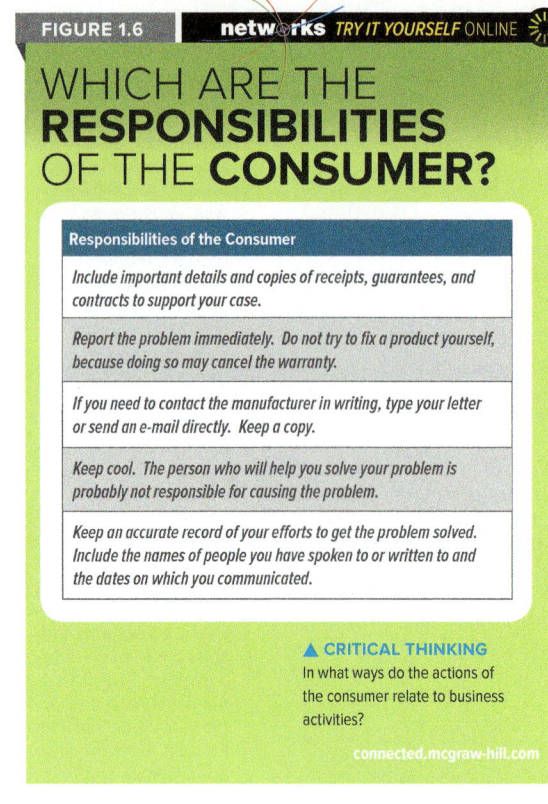

FIGURE 1.6 networks TRY IT YOURSELF ONLINE

WHICH ARE THE RESPONSIBILITIES OF THE CONSUMER?

Responsibilities of the Consumer

Include important details and copies of receipts, guarantees, and contracts to support your case.

Report the problem immediately. Do not try to fix a product yourself, because doing so may cancel the warranty.

If you need to contact the manufacturer in writing, type your letter or send an e-mail directly. Keep a copy.

Keep cool. The person who will help you solve your problem is probably not responsible for causing the problem.

Keep an accurate record of your efforts to get the problem solved. Include the names of people you have spoken to or written to and the dates on which you communicated.

▲ **CRITICAL THINKING**
In what ways do the actions of the consumer relate to business activities?

connected.mcgraw-hill.com

- **The right to be heard**—the guarantee that consumer interests will be considered when laws are being written
- **The right to redress**—the ability of consumers to receive adequate payment from producers if they are harmed by their products

These consumer rights were part of a movement called **consumerism** that began in the 1960s. The movement was an attempt to educate buyers about purchases they make and to demand better and safer products from producers.

Consumer Responsibilities

The consumer rights listed above were responsible for a number of laws that worked to protect consumers. At the same time, it was recognized that consumers have responsibilities as well as rights.

These responsibilities are listed in **Figure 1.6** and basically require consumers to behave ethically when dealing with producers and other merchants. For example, an ethical consumer is expected to do his or her homework when searching for a product. This includes searching for the store with the lowest price and reading the full information about the product, including the operating instructions and other disclosure requirements, before making a purchase.

The availability of online shopping makes many of these steps easier. For example, it is possible to search for the seller with the lowest price, and many sites even list comments by consumers who have already purchased the product. In addition, there are a number of sites that do comparison tests, and some even recommend preferred sellers to make purchasing something easier.

consumerism a social movement that was aimed at promoting the interests of consumers

✓ **READING PROGRESS CHECK**

Determining Cause and Effect How do you think our society would be different if citizens did not study economics?

LESSON 2 REVIEW

Reviewing Vocabulary
1. *Explaining* Explain what the term *labor* means.

Using Your Notes
2. *Describing* Use your notes in the graphic organizer to describe how the four factors of production interrelate.

Answering the Guiding Questions
3. *Examining* Why must producers make production choices?
4. *Describing* How does a production possibilities curve illustrate a society's potential output choices in an economy?

5. *Considering Advantages and Disadvantages* Why is it important to evaluate trade-offs and opportunity costs when making choices?

Writing About Economics
6. *Informative/Explanatory* Think about how scarcity affects your school community. Write an essay in which you formulate some ideas about how the school administration could deal with that scarcity.

20

LESSON 2 REVIEW ANSWERS

Reviewing Vocabulary

1. The term *labor* means all the abilities and skills of people in a society.

Using Your Notes

2. Answers will vary but should identify the four factors of production: land, which is a natural resource; capital, the tools and machinery and equipment used in producing goods; labor, people with their efforts and skills; and entrepreneurs, who are risk-taking people in search of profits.

Answering the Guiding Questions

3. Producers must make production choices because of scarcity, or limited factors of production.

4. The production possibilities curve shows the maximum combinations of goods and services an economy can produce when all its productive resources are fully employed.

5. Evaluating trade-offs—or alternative choices—and opportunity costs—or the next best alternative use of money, time, or resources—helps one make a good decision.

Writing About Economics

6. Answers will vary but should include one or two specific scarcity issues—such as limited classroom space or computers available, limited time spent on athletic fields or weight room, ratio of teachers to students—as well as one or two ideas of how to deal with that scarcity.

Interact with these digital assets and others in lesson 3

- INTERACTIVE CHART Prices
- INTERACTIVE IMAGE Effects of Hurricane Sandy
- SELF-CHECK QUIZ
- VIDEO

networks TRY IT YOURSELF ONLINE

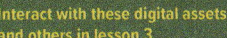

LESSON 3
Using Economic Models

Reading Help Desk

Academic Vocabulary
- mechanism
- assumptions

Content Vocabulary
- economic growth
- productivity
- human capital
- division of labor
- specialization
- economic interdependence
- market
- factor markets
- product markets
- economic model
- cost-benefit analysis
- free enterprise economy
- standard of living

TAKING NOTES:

Key Ideas and Details
ACTIVITY Use a graphic organizer like the one below to identify six characteristics that affect economic growth.

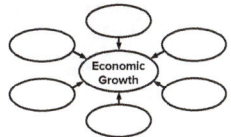

ESSENTIAL QUESTION

In what ways do people cope with the problem of scarcity?

Think about one thing you want or need but can't have because it is too expensive. Then write two paragraphs explaining your answers to these two questions:

- What steps could businesses take to make this item less costly to produce and therefore more affordable for customers?
- What could you do as a consumer to better afford it?

Economic Growth

GUIDING QUESTION *Why is economic growth important?*

Economic growth occurs when a nation's total output of goods and services increases over time. Economic growth is important for two reasons. First, because of scarcity, everybody currently wants more goods and services than they have now. Second, if the population is growing, there will be even more people wanting goods and services to satisfy their wants and needs in the future.

Economic Growth Requires Risks and Sacrifices

Investing in new physical capital or human resources can increase future productivity and capital, but investments like these may also require us to limit our current consumption. This is the dilemma of opportunity costs that everyone faces. Not consuming today in order to have the ability to consume tomorrow is not without risk. For example, are businesses making the right investment decisions today to meet consumer demands in the future? Have you picked the right major in college, or will the field you are studying no longer be as necessary by the time you graduate?

No one knows the exact answers to these questions, which is why there is an element of risk. However, we do know what will happen if nothing is done today—and that is very little growth or progress. You probably already know someone who has wasted a few years by living for today without investing for tomorrow. Chances are also good that you don't want to end up living like them.

connected.mcgraw-hill.com **What Is Economics?** 21

CHAPTER 1, LESSON 3
Using Economic Models

ENGAGE

C Critical Thinking Skills

Demonstrating an understanding of the scope of economics Before students begin the lesson, tell them they have seen how economics plays a role in our everyday lives. Now ask students to think about how understanding economics can play a role in planning their future. Point out that job markets change over time. **Ask: Have you thought about the type of work you will do after you have finished high school and college? What job markets have grown in the last year?** *(Answers should show that students are aware of changing job markets.)* **What influence does economic growth have on the changing job markets?** *(Answers should include that economic growth in various industries greatly influences the job market.)*

ANSWERS, p. 21

ESSENTIAL QUESTION ACTIVITY

Students' answers will vary. Tell students to think about one expensive item they want or perhaps even need. For example, they might need a car to get to their part-time job, but a car is expensive. Lead a discussion in which the class completes the answers in the activity. Students should understand that businesses could take steps to lower production costs of a car. Students also should understand that, as consumers, they can take steps such as saving their money to afford a car.

TAKING NOTES:
Risk and Sacrifice
Productivity
Human Capital
Division of Labor
Specialization
Economic Interdependence

---

networks Online Teaching Options

BELLRINGER

Supply & Demand Model for Movie DVDs

Understanding an economic model of price affecting demand Display the Bellringer: Supply & Demand Model for Movie DVDs. Tell students that, as consumers, how they react to the price of items affects the supply of those items. For example, if they often buy movie DVDs, but the price of movie DVDs goes up, their and other consumers' reactions to that event affects the supply of movie DVDs. Have students list three things they would do if they usually buy movie DVDs but the price of them suddenly increased. **Logical/Mathematical**

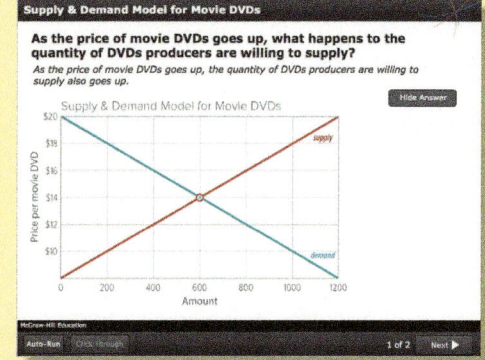

What Is Economics? **21**

CHAPTER 1, LESSON 3
Using Economic Models

TEACH & ASSESS

C Critical Thinking Skills

Drawing conclusions about productivity Ask: **How would economic growth be affected if productivity declined?** *(Productivity affects output, and output affects growth, so economic growth would slow as the output of goods declines.)* **AL** **Verbal/Linguistic**

V Visual Skills

Illustrating human capital Write "human capital" on the board, and have students provide examples of the concept. Encourage them to think of their personal skills and abilities, their health, how they learn, and what motivates them. Then have students create a personal production possibilities curve that shows an expansion in their production frontier with more education. **AL** **Kinesthetic**

ANSWERS, p. 22

CRITICAL THINKING

Having more productive resources or increased productivity make it possible for the economy to grow.

Describing Economic Growth

Economists have a number of ways to show economic growth, but the easiest way is to use the production possibilities curve (frontier). The production possibilities curve displays various combinations of goods and services that can be produced when all factors of production are fully employed. Over time, however, changes may cause the production possibilities frontier to expand. The population may grow, the stock of capital may expand, technology may improve, or productivity may increase. If any of these changes occur, then our mythical country called Alpha will be able to produce a little more of everything in the future.

The effect of economic growth is shown in **Figure 1.7**. Economic growth, made possible by having more resources or increased productivity, causes the production possibilities frontier to expand outward. Economic growth will eventually allow Alpha to produce at point **d**, which it could not do earlier.

C Increases in Productivity

Everyone in a society benefits when scarce resources are used efficiently. This is described by the term **productivity**, a measure of the amount of goods and services produced with a given amount of resources in a specific period of time.

Productivity goes up whenever more can be produced with the same amount of resources. For example, if a company produced 5,000 pencils in an hour, and then it produced 5,100 in the next hour with the same amount of land, labor, and capital, then productivity went up in the second hour. Productivity is often discussed in terms of labor, but it applies to all factors of production.

V The Importance of Human Capital

A major contribution to productivity comes from investments in **human capital**, the sum of people's skills, abilities, health, knowledge, and motivation. Individuals can invest in their own education by completing high school, going to technical school, or attending college. Businesses can invest in

economic growth increase in a nation's total output of goods and services over time

productivity measure of the amount of output produced in a specific time period with a given amount of resources; normally refers to labor, but can apply to all factors of production

human capital sum of people's skills, abilities, health, and motivation

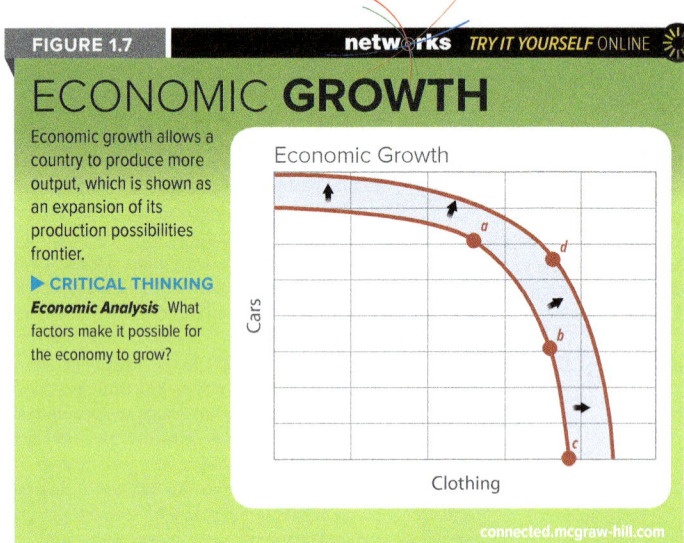

FIGURE 1.7

ECONOMIC GROWTH

Economic growth allows a country to produce more output, which is shown as an expansion of its production possibilities frontier.

▶ **CRITICAL THINKING**
Economic Analysis What factors make it possible for the economy to grow?

---

networks Online Teaching Options

GRAPHS

Economic Growth

Analyzing economic growth on a graph As students view Figure 1.7, point out that opportunity cost still plays a role in economic growth. Producers must make a choice about how to use their limited resources. The major difference is that the economy produces more with more resources, *or* it produces more with the same amount of resources but with more efficient productivity caused by better human capital and technology. **Visual/Spatial**

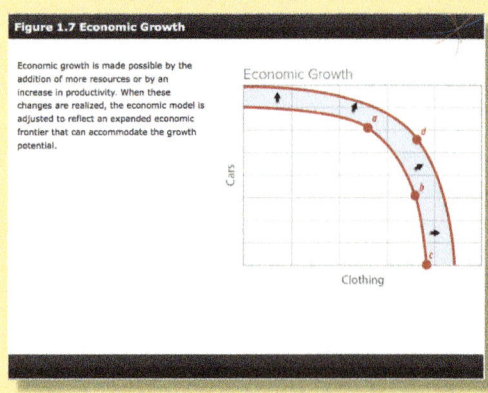

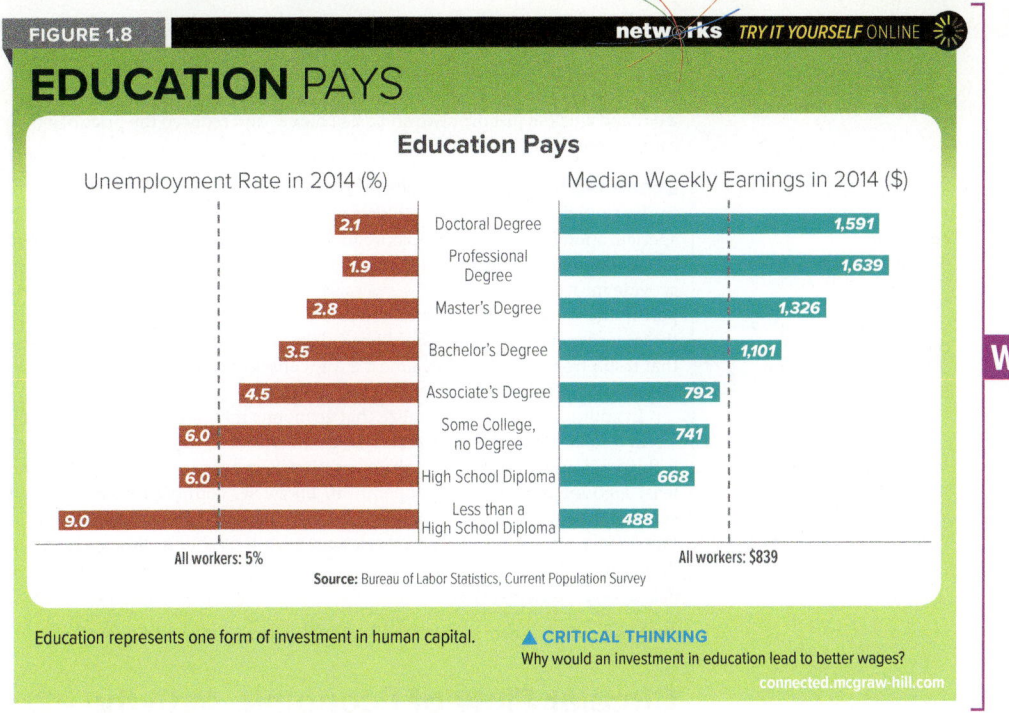

FIGURE 1.8

EDUCATION PAYS

Education represents one form of investment in human capital.

▲ CRITICAL THINKING
Why would an investment in education lead to better wages?

training and other programs that improve the skills of their workers. Government can invest in human capital by providing financial aid for education and health care.

Figure 1.8 shows that investments in education can have substantial payoffs. According to the table, high school graduates earn substantially more than nongraduates, and college graduates make even more than high school graduates. In addition, higher levels of education generally lead to lower levels of joblessness. Educational investments require that we make a sacrifice today so we can have a better life in the future, and few investments generate higher returns.

Division of Labor and Specialization

The division of labor and specialization can also improve productivity. **Division of labor** is a way of organizing work so that each worker or work group completes a separate part of the overall task. A worker who performs a few tasks many times a day is likely to be more proficient than a worker who performs several different tasks in the same period.

The division of labor has another advantage: it makes specialization possible. **Specialization** takes place when factors of production perform only tasks they can do better or more efficiently than others. For example, the assembly of a product may be broken down into a number of separate tasks to be performed by different workers (division of labor). When each worker is assigned to perform the specific task he or she does best, the result is specialization.

division of labor division of work into a number of separate tasks to be performed by different workers

specialization assignment of tasks to the workers, factories, regions, or nations that can perform them most efficiently

What is Economics? 23

CHAPTER 1, LESSON 3
Using Economic Models

W Writing Skills

Changing economic choices Direct students to write an essay in which they explain how their economic choices might change if they found themselves with twice the amount of financial resources they currently have. Ask them to consider whether they would allocate more money to spending and/or saving and encourage them to explain the reasoning behind their decisions.
Intrapersonal

C1 Critical Thinking Skills

Predicting consequences of increased education
Ask: What might happen if individuals do not invest in their own education? *(Possible answer: They will have trouble getting a job and earning a living.)* How do educated workers, combined with new technology, increase economic growth? *(Human capital combined with new technology increases productivity without increasing resources, so the economy grows.)* **AL**

C2 Critical Thinking Skills

Demonstrating division of labor and specialization
Organize students into groups of 2, 3, and 4. Provide the group of 2 with notebook paper, 1 ruler, 1 pencil, 1 scissors, and 1 stapler. Provide the group of 3 with notebook paper, 1 ruler, 2 pencils, 2 scissors, and 1 stapler. Provide the group of 4 with notebook paper, 2 rulers, 2 pencils, 2 scissors, and 2 staplers. Ask each group to construct small booklets (3 inches x 3 inches) with 12 pages each and 5 staples on the side. Each group should construct as many booklets as they can in five minutes. After the time is up, compare the productivity of the groups. Discuss how division of labor and specialization increased the productivity (and economic growth) of the groups with more people and more capital resources.
Kinesthetic

GRAPHS

Education Pays

Examining the relationship between education and salary Have students view Figure 1.8 Education Pays. Ask them to consider the relationship between increased level of education and increased salary. **Ask: What happens to income as education level rises?** *(income increases)* **How is continuing to stay in school related to planning for the future?** *(Answers should demonstrate that attaining a higher degree increases lifelong earning potential.)* **Visual/Spatial**

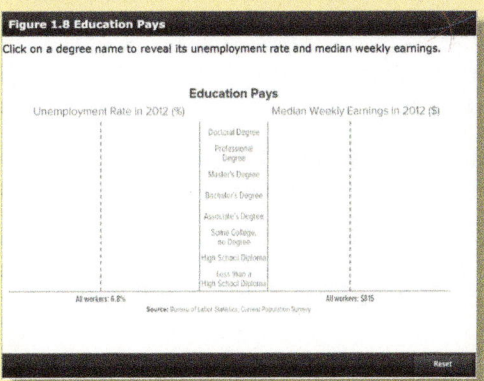

ANSWERS, p. 23

CRITICAL THINKING
Education provides knowledge and skills that employers value, and they will pay higher wages for those skills.

What Is Economics? 23

CHAPTER 1, LESSON 3
Using Economic Models

W Writing Skills

Applying the concept of interdependence Have students list examples of ways they are dependent on others or how others are dependent on them. Then have students circle which of their examples show economic interdependence and explain why.
ELL Intrapersonal

C Critical Thinking Skills

Contrasting factor and product markets Ask: **What are the major differences between factor markets and product markets?** *(In factor markets, factors of production are bought and sold, and individuals earn wages and salaries in exchange for their labor. In product markets, producers sell goods and services to individuals who purchase items using the income they earned in the factor markets.)* Have students write a paragraph giving examples of a factor market and a product market. **AL** Verbal/Linguistic

---

One example of the advantages offered by the division of labor and specialization is Henry Ford's use of the moving assembly line in automobile manufacturing in 1913. Having each worker add one part to the car, rather than a few workers assembling the entire vehicle, cut the assembly time of a car from a day and a half to just over two and a half hours—and reduced the price of a new car by more than 50 percent.

Economic Interdependence

In the United States, increases in productivity due to the division of labor and specialization have yet another consequence: a remarkable degree of **economic interdependence**. This means that we rely on others, and others rely on us, to provide most of the goods and services we consume. As a result, events in one part of the world often have a dramatic impact elsewhere. This does not mean that interdependence is necessarily bad. The gains in productivity and income that result from specialization almost always offset the costs associated with the loss of self-sufficiency.

In addition, economists realize that economic interdependence makes the world a safer place. For example, most of the places in the world where there is the possibility of war or other hostile action exist between countries with the least amount of economic cooperation. Likewise, countries with the most economic cooperation and interdependence, such as the United States and Japan, have the strongest political relations even though the cultures are quite different.

economic interdependence mutual dependence of the economic activities of one person, company, region, or nation on those of another person, company, region, or nation

✓ **READING PROGRESS CHECK**

Analyzing What role does specialization play in the productivity of an economy?

Circular Flow of Economic Activity

GUIDING QUESTION *How do businesses and individuals participate in both the product market and the factor market in an economy?*

Another popular model is the circular flow diagram, an illustration used to show how markets connect people and businesses in the economy. The key feature of this circular flow is the **market**, a location or other **mechanism** that allows buyers and sellers to exchange a specific product. Markets may be local, national, or global—and they can even exist in cyberspace.

There are many markets in an economy as large as ours, and certainly among the most important are the markets that make up our financial system. Because they are so important, and because they are discussed in a separate chapter, they are not illustrated in the simple circular flow diagram in **Figure 1.9**. Instead, it helps to think of financial markets as providing the "lubrication" in the economic engine of capitalism, much the same way an automotive engine provides the oil that lubricates its individual parts so that they work smoothly together.

market meeting place or mechanism through which buyers and sellers of an economic product come together; may be local, regional, national, or global

mechanism process or means by which something can be accomplished

Factor Markets

As shown in Figure 1.9, individuals earn their incomes in **factor markets**, where all of the factors of production are bought and sold. This is where entrepreneurs hire labor for wages and salaries, acquire land in return for rent, and borrow money to operate their businesses. The concept of a factor market is a simplified but realistic version of the real world. For example, you participate in the factor market when you sell your labor to an employer in exchange for the wages the employer pays you.

factor markets markets in which productive resources are bought and sold

---

networks Online Teaching Options

WORKSHEET

What Is Economics? Vocabulary Activity

Building vocabulary Present the Vocabulary worksheet. After students answer the questions, have them put each term in a logical placement on a circular flow of economic activity.

ANSWERS, p. 24

✓ **READING PROGRESS CHECK** Specialization can improve productivity.

FIGURE 1.9

CIRCULAR FLOW OF ECONOMIC ACTIVITY

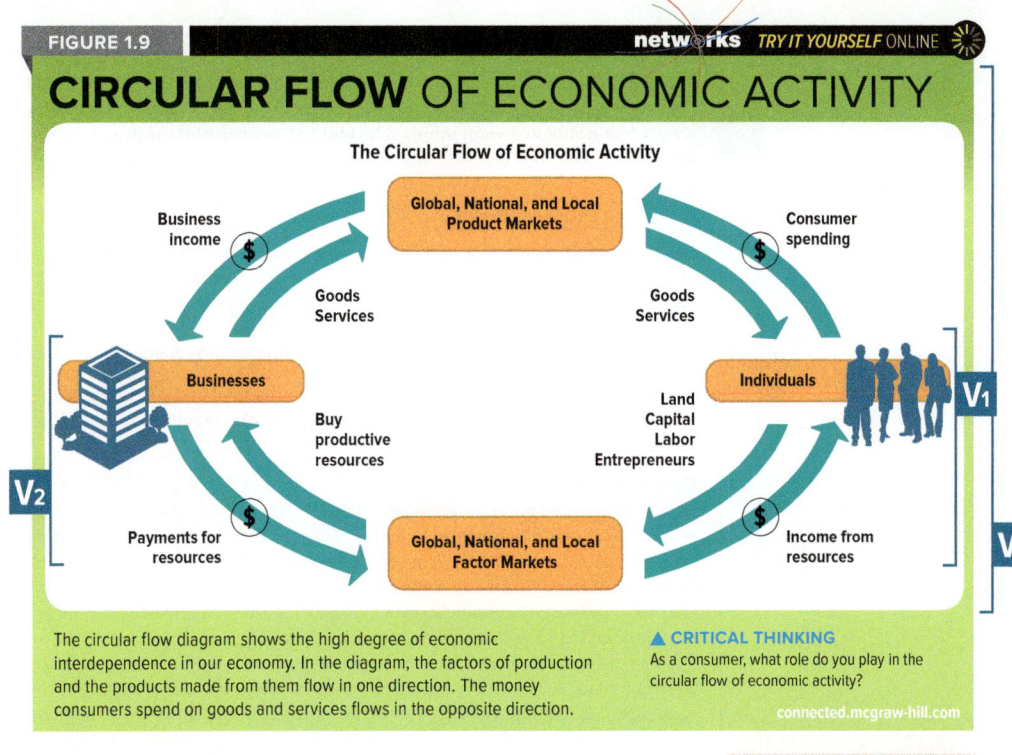

The circular flow diagram shows the high degree of economic interdependence in our economy. In the diagram, the factors of production and the products made from them flow in one direction. The money consumers spend on goods and services flows in the opposite direction.

▲ **CRITICAL THINKING**
As a consumer, what role do you play in the circular flow of economic activity?

Product Markets

After individuals receive income from the resources they sell in a factor market, they spend it in **product markets**. These are markets where producers sell their goods and services. Thus, the wages, salaries, and other income that individuals receive in the factor markets return to businesses in the product markets. Businesses then use this money to produce more goods and services, and the cycle of economic activity repeats itself.

Products are sold almost everywhere you look. For example, you are participating in the product market whenever you put money into a soft drink machine: the money goes in, and the soda comes out. The money doesn't go back to the producer immediately, of course, because it probably won't be picked up until the machine is serviced and refilled by the distributor. When your currency does get back to the producer, it will be used to purchase more factors of production to make drinks for the soda machine again.

Many markets are becoming more electronic. Some cities have parking meters—not to mention gas stations and soda machines—that accept credit cards. The electronic transfer of funds is quicker and more efficient for the seller, who gets the money immediately and without theft or other losses. Other parking meter systems have "pay-by-cell" technologies that allow you to find an unused parking meter, or even add money from a distance.

The Role of Markets

The circular flow diagram is unique in that it has no starting or ending point. You can start with the individuals going to work, or you can start with businesses

EXPLORING THE ESSENTIAL QUESTION

You have been asked to talk to a class about the way a local firm relates to the circular flow diagram. Prepare a one-paragraph outline for each of the following points:

- What does the firm sell in the product market? What will the firm do with the revenue it gets from these sales?

- What does the firm buy in the factor market? Where does the firm get the money to make the purchases in the factor market?

C

product markets market in which goods and services are bought and sold

What is Economics? 25

CHAPTER 1, LESSON 3
Using Economic Models

V1 Visual Skills

Interpreting the roles of resource owners in the circular flow Have students review Figure 1.9 The Circular Flow of Economic Activity. **Ask: Who owns the productive resources in the diagram, and what roles do they play in the circular flow?** *(Individuals; They provide labor, land, capital, and ideas to businesses in the factor markets. They purchase goods and services from businesses in the product markets.)* **Visual/Spatial**

V2 Visual Skills

Interpreting the roles of firms in the circular flow Ask: What roles do firms play in the circular flow of economic activity? *(They pay for the resources and labor of individuals in the factor markets. They create goods and services for sale in the product markets.)* **Visual/Spatial**

V3 Visual Skills

Explaining a global aspect of the circular flow Have students review the Circular Flow diagram. **Ask: How does the rest of the world interact in the circular flow of economic activity for the United States?** *(Students may note that migrant workers take part in the factor markets, or that multinational corporations create goods and services for sale in the global product markets.)* **Visual/Spatial**

C Critical Thinking Skills

Providing real-world examples Ask students to create a circular-flow model with real-world examples of businesses, factor markets, individuals, and product markets. **Visual/Spatial**

SLIDE SHOWS

Circular Flow of Economic Activity

Understanding the circular flow of economic activity Have students view Figure 1.9 The Circular Flow of Economic Activity. Tell them that this is a model that shows how people and businesses are connected in the global, national, and local economy. **Ask: Where do you fit into this model?** *(consumer spending and possibly labor)* **How do you think you have participated in the circular flow of economic activity in the past month?** *(Answers should demonstrate that every time students purchase an item, they are participating in the circular flow of economic activity.)* **Logical/Mathematical**

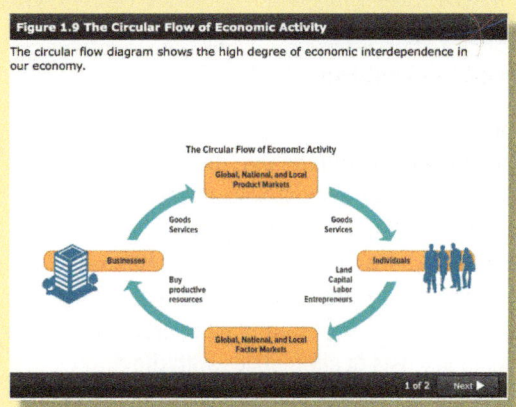

ANSWERS, p. 25

CRITICAL THINKING

As an individual spending on goods and services in product markets.

EXPLORING THE ESSENTIAL QUESTION

Answers will vary. Students should include the resources the firms would need from the factor markets, as well as the products the firms will try to sell in the product markets.

What Is Economics? 25

CHAPTER 1, LESSON 3
Using Economic Models

C Critical Thinking Skills

Creating a circular-flow model Have students think about their own economic activities. Tell students to construct a circular flow diagram that represents their own placement. Compare diagrams for students with and without jobs. **Visual/Spatial**

R Reading Skills

Understanding the basis of economic models
Explain that economic models attempt to explain and predict phenomena based on information that has been gathered over time. A good model incorporates all of the known information, and it can be used to predict future outcomes. Models can be tested for their usefulness, and discarded if they do not work. Ask students to think about the ways in which economists might gather the data they use to study specific parts of the economy. Then direct students to make a list of these methods. Students may suggest methods such as statistical analysis, polling and interviews, and surveys or questionnaires. Ask students if they think using "common sense" is a valid method for gathering data for an economic model. **Logical/Mathematical**

Making Connections

Models Models are used in many disciplines. Biologists use models to show what protein synthesis and DNA looks like. Psychologists use models to explain the functioning of the human brain and animal responses. Military analysts also use computer models to predict the outcomes of various strategies in a war. Even fashion models are, in fact, models. With the introduction of mass production of clothing, producers needed to develop standardized sizes, so they used "models" to represent different proportions. Ask students if they can think of other disciplines that utilize models.

ANSWERS, p. 26

✓ **READING PROGRESS CHECK** The wages and salaries that people receive from businesses in the factor markets return to businesses in the product markets.

---

taking their final products to the product markets to sell. In fact, you can start anywhere you want because, like a circle, it has no beginning and no ending.

C The important thing to realize is that individuals and businesses are *connected* by markets. For example, you probably have never visited the factory that made your athletic shoes or your automobile, and the makers of those two products have never met you. Even so, you and the producers are connected through markets.

✓ **READING PROGRESS CHECK**

Explaining What roles do factor markets and product markets play in the economy?

Thinking Like an Economist

GUIDING QUESTION How can simple models help us understand a complex economy?

Economists study how people satisfy seemingly unlimited and competing wants through the careful use of scarce resources. Economists therefore are concerned with strategies that will help people make good choices.

economic model simplified version of a complex concept or behavior expressed in the form of a graph, figure, equation, or diagram

Economic Models

One strategy is to build an **economic model**, a simplified equation, graph, or figure that shows how something works. This can mean transferring statistical information to a written or visual form for clarity thereby reducing complex situations to their most basic elements. The production possibility curve in this chapter and the circular flow diagram in Figure 1.9 are examples of how complex economic activity can be explained by a simple model.

R In reality, of course, any economy represented by a simple production possibility curve is able to produce more than two goods or services, but the concepts of trade-offs and opportunity costs are easier to illustrate if only two products are examined. As a result, simple models such as these are sometimes all economists need to analyze or describe an actual situation.

Keep in mind that models can always be revised to make them better. If an economic model helps us to make a prediction that turns out to be right, the model can be used again. If the prediction is wrong, the model might be changed to make a better prediction the next time.

assumptions something taken for granted; something we think is true

It is also important to realize that models are based on **assumptions**, or things we think are true. In general, the quality of a model is no better than the assumptions on which it is based, but a model with a few reasonable assumptions is usually easier to understand. In the case of the production possibilities curve, we assumed that only two goods could be produced. This made the model easier to illustrate and still allowed us to discuss the concepts of trade-offs and opportunity costs.

cost-benefit analysis comparison of the cost of an action to its benefits

Cost-Benefit Analysis

The second strategy is to use **cost-benefit analysis**, a way of comparing the benefits of an action to the expected costs. Cost-benefit analysis can be used to evaluate a single course of action or to make a choice between two alternatives.

For example, if you are trying to analyze a single course of action such as whether or not to go to a basketball game, you would simply compare all of the expected benefits to the anticipated cost. The benefits could include enjoyment, time with friends, and cheering on your favorite team. The cost could include time away from studying, the price of admission and parking, and loss of sleep. If the benefits exceeded the costs, you would go to the game. If it did not, you would choose to do something else.

26

---

networks Online Teaching Options

VIDEO **WORKSHEET**

Decision Making

Understanding economic decision making
Have students watch the Decision Making video and complete the accompanying worksheet. Ask them to identify one decision they made recently—such as what education to pursue after high school or whether to buy a particular brand of running shoes—and enumerate the additional costs of alternatives with the additional benefits of that decision.
Intrapersonal

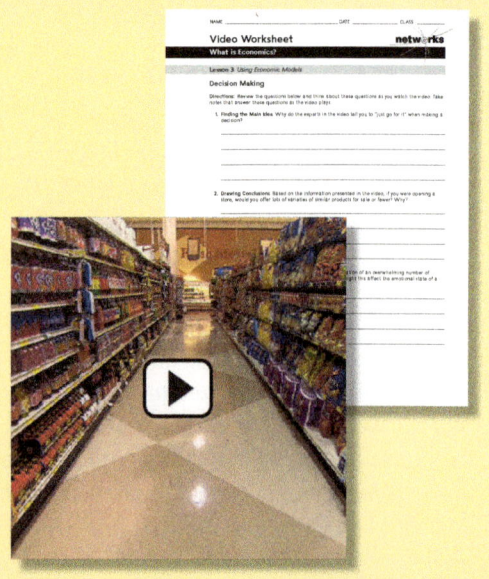

CAREERS | Retail Business Manager

Is this Career for you?

 Do you have strong mathematical and analytical skills?

 Do you have an interest in hiring, training, and managing staff?

 Do you have an interest in working with customers and coworkers to sell things in a product market?

Interview with a Retail Business Manager

"I do the ordering, the markdowns, etc. And I'm constantly writing employee reviews and meeting with the people I supervise, making sure they are progressing the way we need them to progress."

—Rob Corbett
Manager, Scheels All Sports

Salary
$105,260 per year
$50.60 per hour

Job Growth Outlook
Average

Profile of Work
Retail business managers have a broad responsibility for all aspects of a business's financial and operational success. They must be able to evaluate products and personnel effectively in order to make sound, market-based decisions that will affect the direction the business takes and the success it achieves in the product market.

Or suppose that you have to choose between two video games, A and B, which you like equally. If B costs less, it would be the better choice because you would get more satisfaction per dollar spent. However, if the benefits of A and B were different, you could still divide the benefits by the costs and then choose the one with the highest ratio.

Take Small Steps

Finally, incrementalism is the third and final strategy that can help you make good choices. Incrementation simply means to take small, but careful steps toward the final goal. This is especially useful if you are unsure of the exact amount of an activity you want to experience.

You probably do this already without even knowing it. If presented with a hot beverage, you start with a small sip to make sure that it's not too hot. If you are presented with a new food, a small bite is the best way to see if you want another. If any of these small steps are successful, then you can do it again. Eventually the cost of another step will be greater than the benefit, so you stop drinking the beverage or eating the food.

 READING PROGRESS CHECK

Explaining How does cost-benefit analysis help make economic decisions?

The Road Ahead

GUIDING QUESTION How does the study of economics help you make better choices?

The study of economics does more than explain how people deal with scarcity. Economics also includes the study of how things are made, bought, sold, and

connected.mcgraw-hill.com   *What is Economics?* **27**

CHAPTER 1, LESSON 3
Using Economic Models

C1 Critical Thinking Skills

Categorizing types of decisions Ask: **What is the difference between a subjective decision and an objective decision?** *(Subjective decisions can be affected by emotions, bias, personal convictions, and so on. Objective decisions are not influenced by outside factors.)* Have students write a paragraph describing a subjective decision they made recently, and a paragraph describing an objective decision they made. **Intrapersonal**

C2 Critical Thinking Skills

Contrasting costs and benefits of economic decisions Ask students to think about a recent economic decision they made. In a paragraph, have them contrast the benefits they received for taking that action with the costs of that action. Have them consider whether the benefits are immediate benefits or long-range, lasting benefits. Encourage volunteers to share their paragraphs in class.
Intrapersonal

INTERACTIVE FEATURE

Careers—Retail Business Manager

Examining a career in retail managerial work Have students view the Careers feature and discuss the quote from the retail business manager. Tell them that retail business managers decide what a store carries and puts on sale, and they have responsibility for all aspects of a retail store's financial and operational success. Lead a discussion about the character traits a retail manager should exhibit. Ask students to identify successful retail businesses in their community or state. Have students share any experiences they have had working for those businesses, such as a part-time job. **Verbal/Linguistic**

ANSWERS, p. 27

 READING PROGRESS CHECK It is a way of comparing the benefits of an action to the expected costs.

CHAPTER 1, LESSON 3
Using Economic Models

W1 Writing Skills

Analyzing standard of living Have students research to find out what elements are used to measure a country's standard of living (for example, poverty rate and personal income). Have students use their findings to comment on the standard of living in the United States. **BL** Verbal/Linguistic

W2 Writing Skills

Evaluating economic decisions Ask students to consider several of their past economic decisions, such as buying a gift or finding a job, and write a journal entry entitled: *How can studying economics help me make better decisions?* Verbal/Linguistic

Content Background Knowledge

A New Economic Situation Economic models do not always accurately predict economic behavior. For example, economists in the 1970s were surprised when the traditional methods of fighting inflation—reducing the money supply and raising taxes—failed to bring prices under control. Even more surprising, the high inflation was accompanied by an economic slowdown. This situation was so unusual that economists had to create a new term—stagflation—to describe it.

ANSWERS, p. 28

CRITICAL THINKING

Most students will answer *Yes*. People's need for goods is limited, but people will continue to want and need more services. They may want a new cell phone every year, a new car every few years, but the demand for Internet service, health care, information, and entertainment is virtually unlimited.

---

free enterprise economy market economy in which privately owned businesses have the freedom to operate for a profit with limited government intervention

used. It provides insight as to how incomes are earned and spent, how jobs are created, and how the economy works on a daily basis. The study of economics also gives us a better understanding of the workings of a **free enterprise economy**—one in which consumers and privately owned businesses, rather than the government, make the majority of the WHAT, HOW, and FOR WHOM decisions.

Topics and Issues

The study of economics will provide you with a working knowledge of the economic incentives, laws of supply and demand, price systems, economic institutions, and property rights that make the U.S. economy function. Along the way, you will learn about topics such as unemployment, the business cycle, inflation, and economic growth. You will also examine the role of business, labor, and government in the U.S. economy, as well as the relationship between the U.S. economy and the international community.

standard of living quality of life based on ownership of necessities and luxuries that make life easier

All of these topics have a bearing on our **standard of living**—our quality of life based on the ownership of the necessities and luxuries that make life easier. As you study economics, you will learn how to measure the value of our production and how productivity helps determine our standard of living. You also will find that the way the American people make economic decisions is not the only way to make these decisions. Economists have identified three basic kinds of economic systems, that we will analyze.

THE GLOBAL ECONOMY & YOU

The Shift to a Service Economy

Most of the world's developed countries are undergoing an important shift from an economy based on the production of goods to one primarily built on services. In less-developed economies, most employment takes place in manufacturing, construction, agriculture, and mining. As these economies grow and people's incomes increase, basic needs are satisfied and people demand more services such as health care, education, entertainment, and banking. In developing economies such as those of China, Brazil, Mexico, and India, rapid growth means incomes are rising, and a strong service industry is developing. In advanced economies, such as those of the United States, Japan, and Western Europe, service industries have become even more dominant. In the United States, the service sector is expected to create more than 90 percent of all new jobs between 2012 and 2022. As more economies grow, this global shift to service economies will continue to accelerate.

EMPLOYMENT BY SECTOR
service · industry · agriculture

Source: The World Bank 2007 World Development Indicators, Employment by Economic Activity; http://data.worldbank.org/sites/default/files/wdi07fulltext.pdf

▲ **CRITICAL THINKING**
Making Predictions Would you expect this trend toward a service-based economy to continue? Why?

28

---

networks Online Teaching Options

INTERACTIVE FEATURE

Global Economy & You: Shifting from Manufacturing to Service

Assessing the global shift from market to service economies Have students view the Global Economy & You feature. Explain that economists often divide economic activities into three categories. Primary activities are those jobs that directly access raw materials. Farming, fishing, and mining are examples of primary activities. Secondary activities are jobs that involve changing raw materials into finished products through some form of manufacturing. Tertiary activities are the service-sector jobs. People in these occupations do not create a finished good but instead perform a service, such as waiting tables. Explain that the service sector includes everything from garbage collecting to running a corporation.

Economics for Citizenship

The study of economics helps us become better decision makers—in our personal lives as well as in the voting booth. Economic issues are often debated during political campaigns, so we need to understand the issues before deciding which candidate to support.

Most of today's political issues have important economic consequences. For example, is it important to balance the federal budget? How can we best keep inflation in check? What methods can we use to strengthen our economy? The study of economics will not provide you with clear-cut answers to these questions, but it will give you a better understanding of the issues involved.

Understanding the World Around Us

The study of economics helps us understand the complex world around us. This is particularly useful because the world is not as orderly as your economics textbook, for example. Your book is neatly divided into sections for study, and the information in those sections remains relatively constant. In contrast, society is dynamic, and technology and other innovations always lead to changes.

Economics provides a framework for analysis—a structure that helps explain how things are organized. Because this framework describes the incentives that influence behavior, it helps us understand why and how the world changes.

In practice, the world of economics is complex and the road ahead is bumpy. As we study economics, however, we will gain a much better appreciation of how we affect the world and how it affects us.

✓ READING PROGRESS CHECK

Determining Cause and Effect How do you think the study of economics will make your life better?

In a free-enterprise economy, consumers and privately-owned businesses, rather than the government, make most of the decisions about what goods and services are produced, and at what prices. Even though businesses operate next door to each other, they are independent. The economic decisions of a music store owner have little impact on the business of his neighborhood pizzeria.

▲ CRITICAL THINKING

Identifying You want to open a small store near your home. What does the city government do to help business owners, and what does it do to hinder them?

LESSON 3 REVIEW

Reviewing Vocabulary

1. *Defining* Explain how productivity relates to market growth.

Using Your Notes

2. *Summarizing* Use your notes to identify key components of economic growth and to explain how they function in an economy.

Answering the Guiding Questions

3. *Explaining* Why is economic growth important?

4. *Examining* How do businesses and individuals participate in both the product market and the factor market in an economy?

5. *Analyzing* How can simple models help us understand a complex economy?

6. *Explaining* How does the study of economics help you make better choices?

Writing About Economics

7. *Informative/Explanatory* As a member of a school service organization, you have heard several proposals on how to best support a community food bank. All of the proposals are worthwhile, but your organization has limited dollars and volunteer hours available for the project. How would you suggest your organization should proceed in order to make the best decision? Write one or two paragraphs explaining your approach and how it would help in the decision-making process.

CHAPTER 1
Debate

ENGAGE

C1 Critical Thinking Skills

Examining the issue Show students photos or Web sites of a fracking site, including the equipment and the process—such as the pump and the pool of run-off water. Then show them photos of a natural gas site that uses the standard drilling method of extracting natural gas. Lead students in a discussion of the difference between the process of fracking (extracting natural gas from underground shale) and the standard drilling process of finding underground wells of natural gas. Have students vote whether they are for fracking or against fracking. Record students' votes for comparison later.

TEACH & ASSESS

C2 Critical Thinking Skills

Analyzing political action Have students use the library or Internet to research any fracking-related actions the federal government has taken in the past year. In an essay, have them analyze whether they think the action, or no action, is a good or bad energy policy for the nation.

R Reading Skills

Debating the issue Divide the class into groups and assign half of the groups to support fracking, and the other half to oppose fracking. As students read the text for their own side of the debate, ask them to write three reasons the text gives to support their point of view. Have them look at the other side's argument as well, and write three reasons that support the other side's point of view. Have students analyze the validity of the information from the primary sources for point of view, and then ask students to write a rebuttal sentence for each of the opposing side's reasons. Appoint a moderator to run the debate. Groups should take turns presenting the Yes and No arguments related to fracking. **BL**
Verbal/Linguistic

Content Background Knowledge

Hydraulic Fracturing Modern-day fracking can be traced back to 1947 when it was first used in Kansas. The process is called hydraulic fracturing. Groups in favor of the process claim that natural gas production has increased more than 90 percent because of fracking. Fracking methods and materials vary, but it is estimated that most sites are fractured from 8 to 40 times before they become inactive.

Debates

C1 Should fracking be allowed to continue even though it uses our water resources?

R

Fracking is a process of removing natural gas from underground shale. Under high pressure, water, chemicals, and sand are pumped deep underground. The pressure causes the shale to crack and release the natural gas inside.

The current fracking process has been in use since 1999 and has had good results. In 2011, the United States supplied 95 percent of its natural gas needs using the fracking method.

Economically, extracting natural gas from domestic sources diminishes U.S. reliance on foreign governments. It also lowers energy costs and adds thousands of jobs in the United States in the energy industries.

Many people think fracking is a creative solution to the problem the United States has faced—the scarcity of domestic natural gas and oil to generate the energy to meet its growing needs, mainly for electricity. Others point out that fracking uses large amounts of water resources—water resources needed by farmers for irrigation to grow food and water used to generate energy through a system of dams.

YES Use our water resources for fracking.

PRODUCTION OF ENERGY IS USUALLY A WATER-INTENSIVE PROCESS.

WATER DEMANDS FOR FRACKING ARE LESS THAN THOSE FOR OTHER MEANS OF ENERGY PRODUCTION.

MOST FRACKING USES BRACKISH WATER, SO IT DOES NOT AFFECT THE POTABLE WATER SUPPLY.

C2 FRACKING IS A SOLUTION TO ENERGY NEEDS. ACCORDING TO THE U.S. DEPARTMENT OF ENERGY, MORE NATURAL GAS WILL BE EXTRACTED BY FRACKING IN THE FUTURE.

> "Objections to the amount of water used in fracking verge on trivial given that electricity generation and irrigation account for more than 70% of water used nationwide. By the time the mighty Colorado River reaches Mexico, for example, it is reduced to nearly a trickle by all the dams and irrigation outlets upstream."
>
> —"Why the Grass Should Not Always Be Greener," by Rusty Todd, *Wall Street Journal*, June 2013

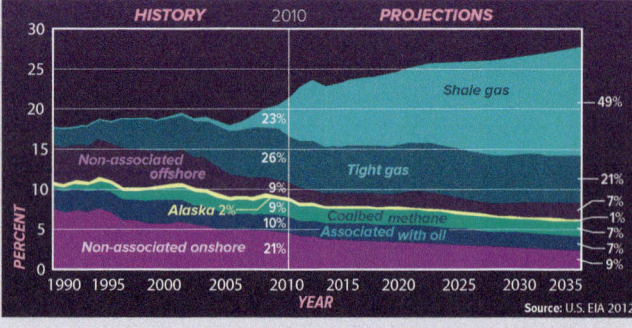

Sources of Natural Gas

---

networks Online Teaching Options

DEBATE

Debate: Should fracking be allowed to continue even though it uses our water resources?

Comparing alternatives Tell students that part of the debate on fracking is the basic question of how we will use natural resources to get the fuel our society needs to generate energy. **Ask: What source does the government think will be tapped in the future for natural gas?** *(extracting natural gas from shale)* **Does this mean there will be more fracking or less fracking in the future?** *(more fracking)* Have students discuss whether using large amounts of natural gas obtained from fracking as an energy source is good national energy policy. Then have students view the graph showing people's concerns about fracking. Have students list two negatives and two positives of the process of fracking. Discuss the lists in class. **Verbal/Linguistic**

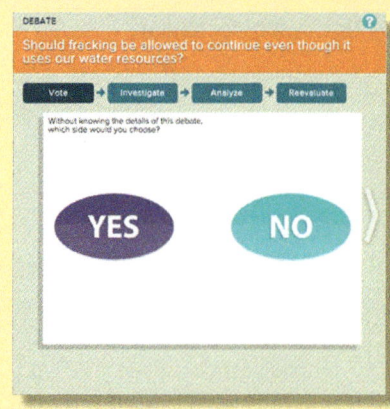

NO Do not use our water resources for fracking.

networks TRY IT YOURSELF ONLINE
For an interactive version of this debate go to **connected.mcgraw-hill.com**

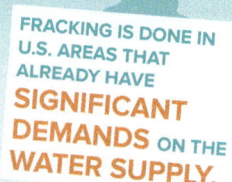

FRACKING IS DONE IN U.S. AREAS THAT ALREADY HAVE **SIGNIFICANT DEMANDS** ON THE **WATER SUPPLY**.

FRACKING **POLLUTES** THE WATER IT USES, AND MUCH OF IT **CANNOT BE RETURNED** TO ITS SOURCE.

FRACKING IS A **MAJOR USE** OF WATER RESOURCES.

INCREASING RELIANCE ON FRACKING FOR ENERGY OVERALL MEANS **MORE DEMANDS ON** THE U.S. WATER **SUPPLY**.

ANALYZING the issue

1. Explaining How are the issues of fracking and water resources connected?

2. Identifying Perspectives How is the perspective of Mr. Todd different from the perspective of the report from the Pacific Institute?

3. Drawing Conclusions With which side of the debate about fracking and the water resources it uses do you agree? Give reasons for your opinion.

"More and better data are needed on the volume of water required for hydraulic fracturing and the major factors that determine the volume, such as well depth and the nature of the geological formation. Additional analysis is needed on the cumulative impacts of water withdrawals on local water availability, especially given that water for hydraulic fracturing can be a consumptive use of water. Finally, more research is needed to identify and address the impacts of these large water withdrawals on local water quality."

—Pacific Institute, www.pacinst.org, "Hydraulic Fracturing and Water Resources: Separating the Frack from the Fiction" by Heather Cooley and Kristina Donnelly

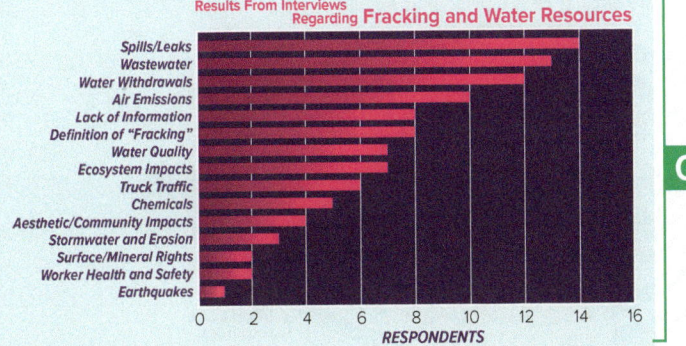

Results From Interviews Regarding Fracking and Water Resources

31

CHAPTER 1
Debate

C Critical Thinking Skills

Researching local energy sources Have small student groups use reliable online sources to learn how energy is generated in their state or region. Is it coal-based, oil-based, natural-gas based, or a combination? Have students make a chart showing the fuels used in their state or region in the last five years to generate energy. When groups present their charts, lead a class discussion about whether the ongoing use of that energy source is good or bad energy policy. **BL Logical/Mathematical**

English Language Proficiency

Advanced High Encourage students to monitor their oral language production and employ self-corrective techniques. Tell them that as they are speaking, they should be aware of whether or not they are phrasing ideas correctly and in the best possible way. Model self-corrective techniques they can use when they realize they should or could have stated something better.

CLOSE & REFLECT

W Writing Skills

Summarizing Have students vote again on whether they are for fracking or against fracking. Compare these votes to their earlier votes. Then have students summarize the fracking controversy in a paragraph, and discuss which aspects of the debate they think are valid and which are not.

GRAPHIC ORGANIZERS

Table

Preparing and defending arguments Divide the class into groups for and against the issue, and distribute the graphic organizer. Ask students to follow these steps: 1. Write *Arguments* as the header for the first column. Have students list four reasons that support their position. 2. Write *Counterarguments* as the second column header. Have students come up with points their opponents could use to minimize their arguments. 3. Write *Refutations* as the final column header. Have students write down ways that they can refute, or prove the opponents' counter-arguments are wrong, in a fair and logical manner. 4. Have students rank arguments from strongest to weakest, based on how easy they are to defend against counterarguments. 5. Students should agree on the top three arguments and use them in their debate presentation. **Interpersonal, Visual/Spatial**

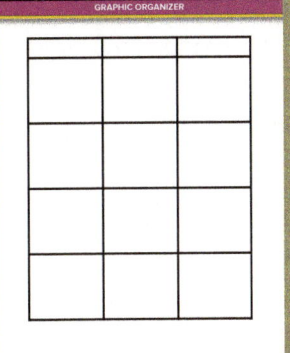

ANSWERS, p. 31

ANALYZING the issue

1. Fracking uses large amounts of water in the process of breaking open underground shale.
2. Mr. Todd thinks the issue of the water resources used in fracking is trivial and not important. The Pacific Institute report states that more study of the issue is needed—therefore it is not trivial.
3. Students should state their opinions about the issue and specific reasons for those opinions.

What Is Economics? **31**

Chapter 1
Study Guide

C Critical Thinking Skills

Assessing Ask students to think about needs that all people have, and then consider people's most common wants. Have a volunteer record students' responses on the board. Then lead a class discussion about the most significant wants that people seek to acquire. **Ask: How do you think people determine what their most important wants will be?** *(Answers will vary, but students may suggest that people determine what these wants will be based on factors such as the items' practicality, affordability, status, value, utility, and so on.)*

W Writing Skills

Developing a portfolio Have students start an Economics Portfolio in which they store their writing activities for this and subsequent chapters. Ask students to also create and continue developing a Personal Economics Glossary in which they list, define, exemplify, and possibly illustrate the economics terms they encounter in this textbook and in daily newscasts.

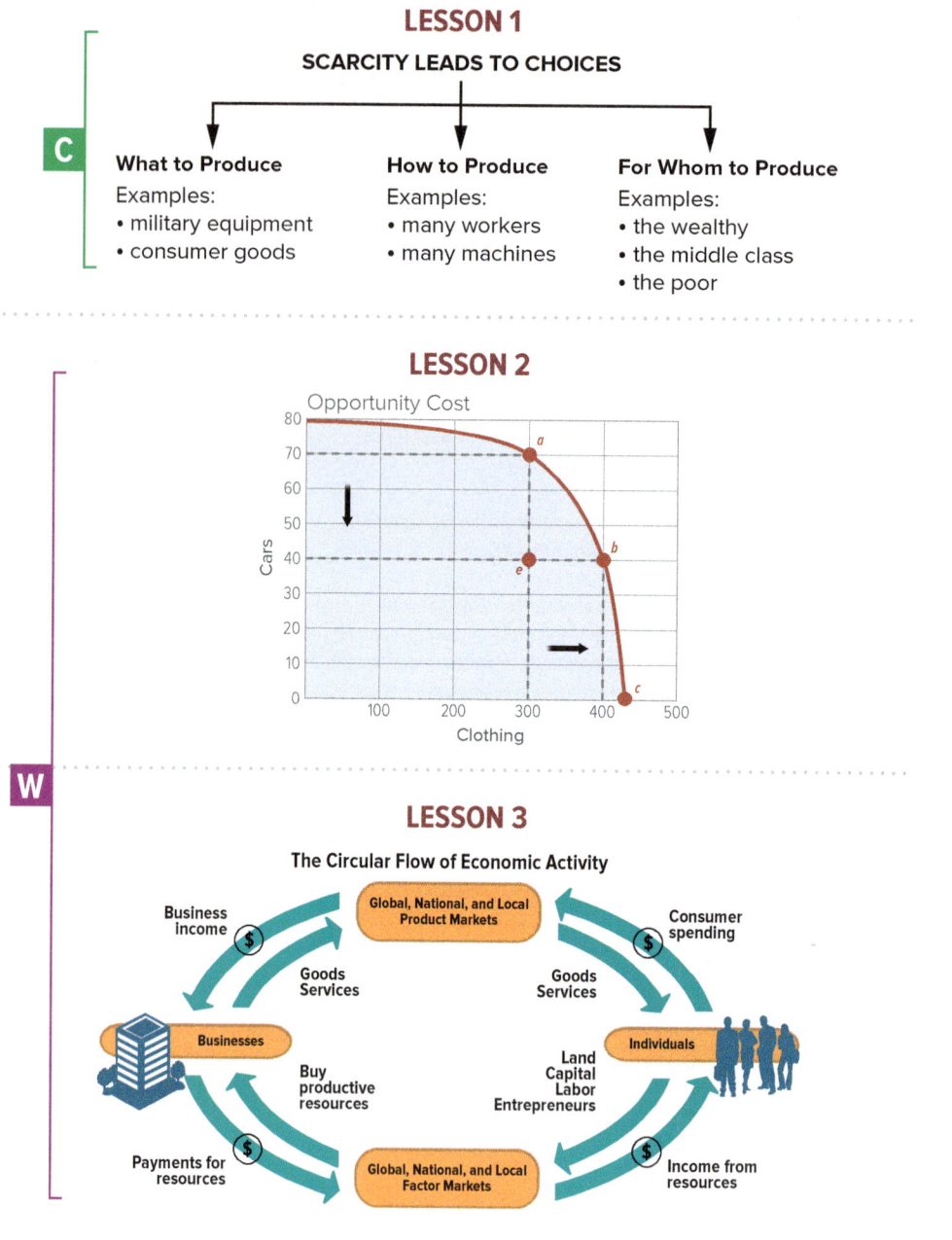

WORKSHEET

Hands-On Chapter Project with Technology Extension

Students will plan how to start a business. They will begin by deciding the type of business to open in a vacant storefront on a popular shopping street. They will also research the demographics of the population in the area and the types of stores already located in the vicinity. Students will create a business plan that includes the estimated cost of opening the business: rent and utilities for the store; cost of producing or acquiring goods; any costs for employees; advertising costs, etc. Finally, students will discuss options for raising the capital necessary to open the business.

Find an additional activity online that incorporates technology for this project. Visit the EdTech Teacher Web sites for more links, tutorials, and other resources.

CHAPTER 1 Assessment

Directions: On a separate sheet of paper, answer the questions below. Make sure you read carefully and answer all parts of the questions.

Lesson Review

Lesson 1

1. **Differentiating** Why would expanding the nation's communications network be considered an increase in wealth, while improving the education of its people would not be considered an increase in wealth?

2. **Explaining** One of the basic economic questions is for whom products are produced. In our society, how would that question be answered for a common consumer product such as a cell phone? Explain.

Lesson 2

3. **Recalling** How did Adam Smith describe workers as a part of the free enterprise system?

4. **Identifying** Identify an example of each of the four factors of production that are required to produce a pencil.

5. **Making Connections** After paying tuition and rent, a college student has $100 left over. The student is sick and could get medical attention. The cost of the office visit is $40, plus he will have to spend $60 on medicine. Alternatively, the student could spend the money on food and hope he will get over what is making him sick. What should the student choose? Explain the opportunity costs of the decision.

Lesson 3

6. **Analyzing** Why does planning for economic growth, stability, full employment, and efficiency involve both risks and sacrifices?

7. **Explaining** How does productivity relate to economic growth?

8. **Analyzing** How are the roles of resource owners and firms explained by the circular flow diagram of economic activity?

Critical Thinking

9. **Analyzing** Analyze and explain the paradox of value as it relates to two products: bread, which has low monetary value, and a ticket to a concert by a popular band, which has a high monetary value.

10. **Constructing Arguments** Is it possible in the real world for an entrepreneur to operate a business in which all of the factors of production are always fully employed? Why or why not?

11. **Making Connections** Evaluate government rules as stated in the lists of consumer rights and consumer responsibilities. In one or two paragraphs, explain how these guidelines benefit businesses as well as consumers.

12. **Explaining** Explain why no economic model to analyze economic concepts or issues will ever be entirely reliable.

Analyzing Visuals

Use the production possibilities curve to answer the following questions.

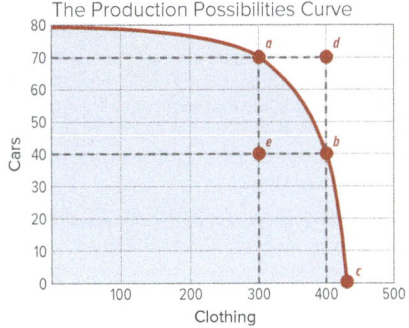

The Production Possibilities Curve

13. **Interpreting** Interpret this production possibilities curve by describing what is occurring at point e.

14. **Applying** Assume that there is a natural disaster that destroys many homes. People have lost many of their possessions, including clothing. Suddenly a need has arisen for 500 units of clothing. Alpha is willing to give up cars for more clothing. Is this extra production of clothing possible? Explain your answer based on this production possibilities curve.

15. **Reading Graphs** If the country of Alpha produces the maximum number of cars—about 80—how many units of clothing could it produce? Explain your answer.

If You've Missed Question	1	2	3	4	5	6	7	8	9	10	11	12	13	14	15
Go to page	9	10	9	15	17	21	22	24	8	16	19	26	16	16	16

Chapter 1 Assessment Answers

Lesson Review

Lesson 1

1. Wealth is defined as tangible goods; a communications network is an example of a tangible good. An education is not tangible, so it is not considered part of a nation's wealth.

2. A cell phone is produced for whomever can afford to buy it. Our government does not dictate who can buy a phone or control the price to make it available to certain classes. However, demand from people with varying levels of income may influence the manufacturer's decision to target the product at a high-end or low-end market.

Lesson 2

3. Smith claimed people can be an economical asset in a free enterprise system.

4. Sample answer: Land: the tree; Capital: a saw; Labor: the person who used the saw; Entrepreneur: the business person who formed the pencil company.

5. Students may choose either option. The opportunity cost of choosing medical care is the loss of food and the resultant hunger that choice would cause; the opportunity cost of choosing food would be feeling sicker longer and perhaps not being able to function well in school.

Lesson 3

6. Investing in the physical or human capital needed for economic growth requires sacrificing some current consumption opportunities today. The risk is that the sacrifices of today may not have the anticipated results in the future.

7. Productivity can promote growth by enabling more goods to be produced by the same amount of productive factors.

8. The circular flow diagram demonstrates how resource owners, such as individuals, sell their labor for wages. Resource owners then spend the wages to purchase goods and services produced by the businesses.

Critical Thinking

9. The paradox is that bread is a food, which is essential for life, yet it is relatively inexpensive, while a concert ticket can be expensive. Bread has high utility but is not scarce enough to have great monetary value. The concert ticket is scarce and has high utility for some people, so its monetary value is high.

10. Under normal circumstances, yes, an entrepreneur could employ all of the factors of production. But workers sometimes get sick, power outages or machine breakdowns occur, and other events may interfere with attempts to fully employ resources.

11. Rights and responsibilities help ensure fairness. Businesses have incentives to deliver quality goods and services. Satisfied customers are more likely to return and make further purchases.

12. Every model is based on assumptions, which may or may not be true. In addition, assumptions that are true today may not be true tomorrow due to changes in the variables on which the assumptions are based.

Analyzing Visuals

13. Production is at less than full capacity. Fewer cars and less clothing are produced than could be produced if all resources were being fully used.

14. Alpha cannot produce 500 units of clothing because that point lies outside the production possibilities curve, meaning that the resources are not available to produce those extra units of clothing.

15. Alpha could not produce any clothing because all of its available resources would be utilized to produce the cars.

Chapter 1 Assessment Answers

Answering the Essential Question

16 Students should recognize that scarcity is a basic economic problem faced by every society and that societies, as well as individuals, make economic decisions based on it. Production is limited by the scarcity of the factors of production. Individuals are limited by income in what they can purchase. Both individuals and businesses make decisions to purchase and produce goods based on the benefits, risks, and trade-offs involved in their decisions.

21st Century Skills

17 Answers will vary, but the student should create a functional chart to evaluate the benefits and trade-offs in making the choice between the alternatives. Criteria used for the chart will vary. The student should provide a reasonable explanation for his or her final choice.

18 Student reports will vary, but students should accurately describe how technology was used to create a more efficient workplace and how that efficiency made the company more competitive or profitable.

19 Students should do research to collect and evaluate data showing how small businesses have affected the economy. Their results should demonstrate that small businesses have created a large percentage of the new jobs in the U.S. and have contributed substantially to the growth of GDP.

Building Financial Literacy

20 a., b. Answers will vary somewhat, but students should demonstrate an understanding of the four factors of production and how scarcity affects both the production and consumption of goods and services.

Analyzing Primary Sources

21 The drought reduces the amount of corn that can be raised for food in the United States, leaving less to export. As a result, food shortages are occurring in countries that normally import corn from the United States.

22 By requiring corn to be used for ethanol, the government may be creating a food shortage that may lead to malnutrition among the poor of the world.

CHAPTER 1 Assessment

Directions: On a separate sheet of paper, answer the questions below. Make sure you read carefully and answer all parts of the questions.

ANSWERING THE ESSENTIAL QUESTION

Review your answers to the introductory questions at the beginning of each lesson. Then answer the Essential Question on the basis of what you learned in the chapter. Have your answers changed?

16 *Summarizing* In what ways do people cope with the problem of scarcity?

21st Century Skills

17 *Problem Solving* Assume you have $50 to spend and are considering spending it on one of the following items:
- dinner with a friend—$50
- concert ticket—$30
- new shirt—$50

Create an economic model to evaluate the trade-offs among the different choices. Draw a decision-making grid and list the alternatives in the first column and the criteria you will use to compare the choices along the first row. Complete the chart and make a choice, explaining why you decided on that alternative.

18 *Identifying Cause and Effect* Do research to identify one company that has used technology to increase its productivity. Write a few paragraphs in which you analyze how increased productivity relates to the growth of the company. Be sure to cite your sources.

19 *Creating and Using Graphs* The role of entrepreneurs in our economy can be effectively measured by how small businesses contribute to our economy. Do Internet research to learn how small businesses have affected our employment and GDP or the financial markets (the DOW Industrial Averages or Standard and Poor's) over the past several decades. Record your findings in a chart or graph and summarize your results in a brief paragraph.

Building Financial Literacy

20 *Explaining* You have been offered a large sum of money in order to start a new business in your community.

  a. How will the four factors of production affect your decision of what kind of business to begin and where you will locate it?

  b. How will your new business affect your community and the choices they have?

Analyzing Primary Sources

Read the excerpt and answer the questions that follow.

PRIMARY SOURCE

" A series of spikes in global food prices resulted in riots in 2008 and contributed to violent uprisings in North Africa and the Middle East in 2011. The culprit is a matter of considerable and frequently heated debate, but the most commonly cited candidates include market speculators, global warming and aggressive government renewable fuel mandates. "

—William Pentland, "The Coming Food Crisis: Blame Ethanol," *Forbes,* July 28, 2012

Pentland's article goes on to describe how analysts at the New England Complex Systems Institute theorize that food shortages due to drought in the U.S. Midwest could result in a worldwide crisis far worse than anything seen yet. The analysts concluded that the drought could increase the effect of market speculation and policies surrounding corn-to-ethanol conversion, with a devastating effect on the global food crisis. The increase in food prices may mean that many people worldwide will suffer malnutrition and death.

21 *Identifying Cause and Effect* Analyze the impact of the drought in the United States on its trading partners.

22 *Considering Advantages and Disadvantages* Explain the opportunity costs of the "aggressive government renewable fuel mandates."

If You've Missed Question	16	17	18	19	20	21	22
Go to page	7	18	22	16	14	24	17

34

---

networks Online Assessment Options

WORKSHEET

Chapter Tests and Lesson Quizzes

Chapter 1 Tests Forms A and B Have students complete the Chapter Tests and Lesson Quizzes to assess student understanding throughout the chapter. Print and online assessment tools offer chapter and lesson evaluation through a variety of question formats, including document-based questions.

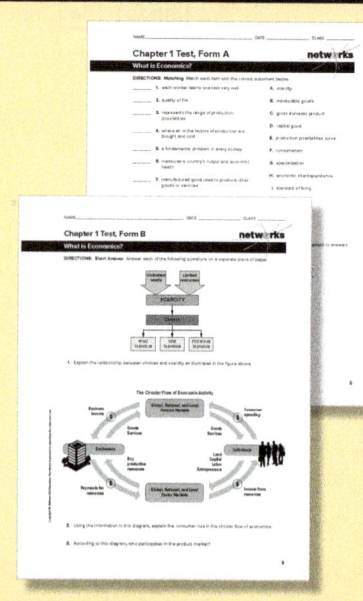

CHAPTER 2
Economic Systems and Decision Making Planner

UNDERSTANDING BY DESIGN®

Enduring Understanding
- *Economic systems shape the way individuals, businesses, and government interact.*

Essential Questions
- *How does an economic system help a society deal with the fundamental problem of scarcity?*

Predictable Misunderstandings
Students may think:
- *Many of the command economies of the past were communist economies.* Explain that there has never been a true communist economy.
- *All capitalistic countries have the same type of economy.* Countries that endorse private enterprise are capitalistic to some extent, but most economies are "mixed economies."

Assessment Evidence
Performance Task
- *Hands-On Chapter Project with Technology Extension*

Other Evidence
- *Guided Reading Activities*
- *Vocabulary Activity*
- *Lesson Quizzes*
- *Self-Check Quizzes*
- *Chapter Assessment*
- *Chapter Tests, Forms A and B*

SUGGESTED PACING

Introducing the Chapter . . . . ½ Day	Lesson 3: The Global Transition to Capitalism . . . . 1 Day
Lesson 1: Economic Systems . . . . 1 Day	
Case Study . . . . ½ Day	Study Guide, Chapter Assessment and Wrap-Up . . . . ½ Day
Lesson 2: Mixed Economies . . . . 1 Day	
Debate . . . . ½ Day	

TOTAL 5 Days

Key for Using the Teacher Edition

SKILL-BASED ACTIVITIES

Types of skill activites found in the Teacher Edition.

- **V** Visual Skills require students to analyze maps, graphs, charts, and photos.
- **R** Reading Skills help students practice reading skills and master vocabulary.
- **C** Critical Thinking Skills help students apply and extend what they have learned.
- **W** Writing Skills provide writing opportunities to help students comprehend the text.
- **T** Technology Skills require students to use digital tools effectively.

*Letters are followed by a number when there is more than one of the same type of skill on the page.

DIFFERENTIATED INSTRUCTION

All activities are written for the on-level student unless otherwise marked with the leveled labels below.

- **BL** Beyond Level
- **AL** Approaching Level
- **ELL** English Language Learners

All students benefit from activities that utilize different learning styles. Many activities are marked as below when a particular learning style is highlighted.

Intrapersonal **Naturalist**
Logical/Mathematical **Kinesthetic**
Visual/Spatial **Auditory/Musical**
Verbal/Linguistic **Interpersonal**

Council for Economic Education

Below are the Council for Economic Education Voluntary National Content Standards in Economics covered in the *Economic Systems and Decision Making* chapter.

Content Standard 2: Effective decision making requires comparing the additional costs of alternatives with the additional benefits. Many choices involve doing a little more or a little less of something: few choices are "all or nothing" decisions.

Content Standard 3: Different methods can be used to allocate goods and services. People acting individually or collectively must choose which methods to use to allocate different kinds of goods and services.

CHAPTER 2: ECONOMIC SYSTEMS AND DECISION MAKING

CHAPTER OPENER PLANNER

Students will know:
- the different economic systems used to allocate scarce goods and resources.
- most countries have mixed economies.
- the characteristics of socialism and communism.
- the transition from one economic system to another involves struggle.
- capitalism takes on different forms in different countries.

Students will be able to:
- **compare and contrast** the characteristics of traditional, command, and market economies.
- **discuss** the advantages and disadvantages of mixed economies.
- **analyze** the problems faced by economies during their transition to a capitalist economy.
- **explain** why capitalism is different in different countries.

UNDERSTANDING BY DESIGN®

☑ Print Teaching Options

V Visual Skills
- ☐ **p. 36 Summarizing a map** Students identify free enterprise, mixed, and command systems.
- ☐ **p. 36 Analyzing a map** Students identify particular regions and their economies.

C Critical Thinking Skills
- ☐ **p. 35 Comparing economic systems**
- ☐ **p. 35 Predicting Career Changes** Students consider jobs in a command economy.
- ☐ **p. 37 Brainstorming characteristics of economic systems**

W Writing Skills
- ☐ **p. 37 Creating an illustrated time line** Students consider nationalizing resources.

☑ Online Teaching Options

V Visual Skills
- ☐ **IMAGE** Chapter opener—Students look for clues about economic systems.

C Critical Thinking Skills
- ☐ **INFOGRAPHICS** Economic Perspectives—Students identify and compare countries that have a mixed economy, a command economy, and a free-enterprise economy.
- ☐ **DEBATES** Should government provide healthcare?—Students analyze two views about government providing healthcare.
- ☐ **INTERACTIVE FEATURE** Case Study: What Does Your Day Look Like? The 9 to 5 in Traditional, Command, and Market Economies

☑ Printable Digital Worksheets

C Critical Thinking Skills
- ☐ **WORKSHEET** Assessing Background Knowledge Activity—Target misconceptions you can address when teaching the lesson.
- ☐ **WORKSHEET** Enrichment Activity—Students read about a new economic model for business.

Project-Based Learning

Hands-On

WORKSHEET Hands-On Chapter Project
Student groups act as consultants to an American business that is seeking to expand both its production facilities and its product sales to a place that has a different economic system.

WORKSHEET Economic Simulation
Students determine the value of different items and discuss how their value might change when viewed by people in different economic systems.

Digital Hands-On

Create Online Projects

Find an additional activity online that incorporates technology for the Hands-On Project. Visit the EdTech Teacher Web sites for more links, tutorials, and other resources.

Print Resources

ANCILLARY RESOURCE
This ancillary is available for every chapter and lesson.
- Chapter Tests and Lesson Quizzes

PRINTABLE DIGITAL WORKSHEETS
These printable digital worksheets are available for every chapter and lesson.
- Reading Essentials & Study Guide
- Vocabulary Activities
- Chapter Summaries
- Economic Simulations
- Math Practice for Economics
- Reinforcing Economic Skills
- Personal Finance Activities
- Hands-On Chapter Projects
- Enrichment Activities
- Reteaching Activities
- Guided Reading Activities
- Video Worksheets
- Lesson Quizzes and Chapter Tests (English and Spanish)

More Media Resources

SUGGESTED READING
- For students at a Grade 10 reading level: *China: A Study of an Economically Developing Country,* by Julia Waterlow
- For students at a Grade 11 reading level: *The Haunted Land: Facing Europe's Ghosts After Communism,* by Tina Rosenberg
- For students at a Grade 12 reading level: *Small Is Beautiful: Economics as if People Mattered,* by E. F. Schumacher

Review suggested books before assigning them.

SUGGESTED VIDEOS MOVIES
Find these documentaries yourself online. NOTE: McGraw-Hill Education does not endorse these resources. Preview clips for age-appropriateness.
- *China: The Orient Excess* (25 min.)
- *The World's Richest City* (25 min.)

LESSON 1 Planner

ECONOMIC SYSTEMS

Students will know:
- how scarcity of economic resources requires each form of government to make decisions about how goods and services are to be produced and distributed.
- the different economic systems used to allocate scarce goods and resources.
- people acting individually or collectively must choose which methods to use to allocate different kinds of goods and services.
- how the various economic systems answer the following questions: What to produce? How to produce it? For whom to produce it?

Students will be able to:
- **compare and contrast** the characteristics of traditional, command, and market economies.
- **list** the advantages and disadvantages of traditional, command, and market economies.

UNDERSTANDING BY DESIGN®

☑ Print Teaching Options

R Reading Skills

- ☐ **p. 38 Using context clues** Students explain the meaning of *custom*. **AL Verbal/Linguistic**
- ☐ **p. 43 Analyzing a command economy**
- ☐ **p. 46 Finding solutions to disadvantages** Students brainstorm how government might remedy disadvantages of a market economy.
- ☐ **p. 46 Summarizing the lesson**

C Critical Thinking Skills

- ☐ **p. 38 Identifying traditions in society and in the economy** Students identify traditional economic actions in the U.S. **AL**
- ☐ **p. 39 Drawing conclusions about change in a traditional economy** **AL Logical/Mathematical**
- ☐ **p. 40 Drawing inferences about economic choices** Students count how many economic decisions went into putting a meal on the table.
- ☐ **p. 42 Demonstrating limitations of choice** Students act as a planning committee in a command economy.
- ☐ **p. 42 Synthesizing data** Students compare graphs about North and South Korea.

W Writing Skills

- ☐ **p. 39 Writing a narrative about living in a traditional economy**
- ☐ **p. 39 Summarizing a traditional economic system**
- ☐ **p. 44 Summarizing a command economic system**
- ☐ **p. 45 Writing about the benefits of a market economy** Students write an essay explaining the benefits of a market economy.
- ☐ **p. 45 Comparing incentives** Students summarize role incentives play in a market economy versus a traditional and command system.

☑ Online Teaching Options

V Visual Skills

- ☐ **IMAGE The Traditional Economy of the Inuit**—Students compare and contrast Inuit economic activity with the U.S. economy. **Interpersonal**
- ☐ **VIDEO Cabbage Bartering in Russia**—Students consider the barter process.
- ☐ **IMAGES Command Economy**—Students examine who allocates and receives resources in a command economy. **Visual/Spatial**
- ☐ **IMAGES Disadvantages of a Command Economy**—Students analyze differences between North and South Korea. **Logical/Mathematical**

R Reading Skills

- ☐ **INTERACTIVE FEATURE Careers**—Students investigate health care services.
- ☐ **GRAPHIC ORGANIZER Market vs. Command Economy**—Students compare and contrast the market economy with the command economy. **Logical/Mathematical**

C Critical Thinking Skills

- ☐ **BELLRINGER Economic Systems**—Students draw conclusions about Cuba.
- ☐ **ESSENTIAL QUESTION Exploring the Essential Question**—Students complete a chart listing advantages and disadvantages of each economic system.
- ☐ **IMAGES Effects of the Global Economy**—Students discuss how the tsunami and nuclear disaster affected tourism in Japan. **Verbal/Linguistic**

T Technology Skills

- ☐ **SELF-CHECK QUIZ Lesson 1**—Students receive instant feedback on answers.
- ☐ **GAME Lesson 1**—Students solve clues to review lesson content.
- ☐ **INTERACTIVE WHITEBOARD ACTIVITY Economic Systems**—Students work together to learn lesson content.

☑ Printable Digital Worksheets

R Reading Skills

- ☐ **WORKSHEET Guided Reading Activity**—Students review lesson content.
- ☐ **WORKSHEET Reading Essentials and Study Guide**—Students complete the study guide and answer Reading Progress Check and vocabulary questions.

C Critical Thinking Skills

- ☐ **WORKSHEET Cabbage Bartering in Russia Video Activity**—Students answer questions about bartering in Russia when the Soviets governed.

LESSON 2 Planner

MIXED ECONOMIES

Students will know:
- a country's standard of living depends upon its ability to produce goods and services.
- most countries have mixed economies.
- countries modify their economic systems in order to meet the needs of the people or accomplish economic or political goals.

Students will be able to:
- **explain** why mixed economies exist.
- **name** examples of mixed economies in the world today.
- **discuss** the advantages and disadvantages of mixed economies.

UNDERSTANDING BY DESIGN®

✓ Print Teaching Options

R Reading Skills

☐ **p. 51 Making connections between economies** Students summarize the goals and stages of communism.

☐ **p. 52 Comparing mixed market economies** Students discuss similarities and differences among the free enterprise system, socialism, and communism. **Interpersonal**

☐ **p. 53 Assessing socialism** Students discuss why socialism might be less efficient than capitalism. **Logical/Mathematical**

☐ **p. 53 Summarizing the lesson** Students create an outline of the lesson.

C Critical Thinking Skills

☐ **p. 48 Predicting advantages and disadvantages** Students define *mixed economy* and predict what they will learn in the lesson. **Verbal/Linguistic**

☐ **p. 49 Identifying traditional, command, and market features in the U.S. economic system** Students discuss the United States as a mixed economy. **Logical/Mathematical**

☐ **p. 50 Identifying socialist countries and services** Students research two socialist countries. **Verbal/Linguistic**

☐ **p. 51 Drawing inferences about economies** Students identify characteristics of mixed socialist states and why Western countries oppose them. **BL Logical/Mathematical**

☐ **p. 52 Hypothesizing about economies and political systems** Students consider why mixed economies thrive more often in democracies.

W Writing Skills

☐ **p. 50 Writing a persuasive essay about economic systems** Students argue which type of economy is superior.

☐ **p. 53 Presenting a panel discussion about China** Students present a panel discussion on economic changes in China.

✓ Online Teaching Options

V Visual Skills

☐ **CHARTS Characteristics of Mixed Economies**—Students drag countries onto a Venn diagram. **Visual/Spatial**

☐ **VIDEO Communist Russia, A Great Economic Experiment**—Students view a video and summarize phases and challenges of the Russian economy.

R Reading Skills

☐ **BIOGRAPHY Karl Marx**—Students read and discuss why Marx became an influential figure. **Interpersonal, Verbal/Linguistic**

☐ **GRAPHIC ORGANIZER Advantages and Disadvantages of a Mixed Economy**—Students complete a table with information about mixed economies. **Visual/Spatial**

C Critical Thinking Skills

☐ **BELLRINGER Mixed Economies**—Students discuss what they know about socialism and a mixed economy. **Verbal/Linguistic**

☐ **ESSENTIAL QUESTION Exploring the Essential Question**—Students identify actions that can minimize effects of scarcity.

☐ **INTERACTIVE WHITEBOARD The Spectrum of Mixed Economies**—Students drag countries onto a continuum between communism and capitalism. **Kinesthetic**

T Technology Skills

☐ **SELF-CHECK QUIZ Lesson 2**—Students receive instant feedback on answers.

☐ **GAME Lesson 2**—Students solve clues to review lesson content.

☐ **INTERACTIVE WHITEBOARD ACTIVITY Identifying Mixed Economies**—Students work together to learn lesson content.

✓ Printable Digital Worksheets

R Reading Skills

☐ **WORKSHEET Guided Reading Activity**—Students review their comprehension.

☐ **WORKSHEET Reading Essentials and Study Guide**—Students complete the study guide and answer Reading Progress Check and vocabulary questions.

C Critical Thinking Skills

☐ **WORKSHEET Communist Russia: A Great Economic Experiment Video Activity**—Students investigate the changing economy of Russia.

☐ **WORKSHEET Reteaching Activity**—Students analyze similarities and differences among economic systems. **Visual/Spatial, Intrapersonal**

☐ **WORKSHEET Enrichment Activity**—Students discuss a workers' plight and eventual ownership of a new company. **Intrapersonal**

LESSON 3 Planner

THE GLOBAL TRANSITION TO CAPITALISM

Students will know:
- the characteristics of socialism and communism.
- the transition from one economic system to another involves struggle.
- capitalism takes on different forms in different countries.

Students will be able to:
- **analyze** the problems faced by economies during their transition to a capitalist economy.
- **evaluate** the success of various countries and regions that are currently making the transition to capitalism.
- **explain** why capitalism is different in different countries.

UNDERSTANDING BY DESIGN®

✓ Print Teaching Options

V Visual Skills
- ☐ p. 62 Predicting the future of North Korea
- ☐ p. 64 Creating a poster Students advertise Singapore as favorable for businesses.

R Reading Skills
- ☐ p. 57 Demonstrating understanding of vouchers
- ☐ p. 58 Determining desirable qualities for transitioning
- ☐ p. 58 Defining *glasnost* Students explain how *glasnost* influenced economic changes.
- ☐ p. 60 Using academic vocabulary Students tie isolationism to economic development.
- ☐ p. 61 Sequencing events Students sequence Eastern Europe's economic history since 1980.
- ☐ p. 64 Understanding geopolitics Students discuss why Taiwan has a separate government.

C Critical Thinking Skills
- ☐ p. 56 Inferring outcomes of transitioning economies
- ☐ p. 57 Making inferences about transitioning to capitalism
- ☐ p. 59 Comparing economic plans Students compare Stalin's and Mao's economic plans.
- ☐ p. 63 Hypothesizing about possible outcomes Students consider a different Korean economy.
- ☐ p. 65 Contrasting economic history of nations

W Writing Skills
- ☐ p. 57 Writing a narrative Students write a story about the fall of communism.
- ☐ p. 58 Writing about the Five-Year Plan
- ☐ p. 63 Writing a report Students describe a Japanese company.

T Technology Skills
- ☐ p. 62 Creating line graphs Students research Japan's annual GDP figurets since 1950.

✓ Online Teaching Options

V Visual Skills
- ☐ **VIDEO** The Silk Road—Students watch a video of China transitioning to a capitalist economy. *Visual/Spatial*
- ☐ **INTERACTIVE FEATURE** Global Economy & You—Students analyze China's transition to capitalism and pollution. *Visual/Spatial, Naturalist*
- ☐ **IMAGE** Adjusting to Economic Change—Students compare shopping in China to U.S. shoppers. *Visual/Spatial*
- ☐ **IMAGE** The European Union—Students view an EU map and study the EU's recent challenges. *Visual/Spatial, Logical/Mathematical*
- ☐ **IMAGE** South Korean Manufacturing, Asian Economies in Transition—Students analyze South Korea's economy and a Japanese keiretsu. *Visual/Spatial*
- ☐ **INFOGRAPHIC** Economic Perspectives—Students contrast per capita incomes by type of economy. *Visual/Spatial, Logical/Mathematical*

R Reading Skills
- ☐ **GRAPHIC ORGANIZER** How Governments Promote Growth—Students list how governments promote economic growth in capitalist and transitioning countries.

C Critical Thinking Skills
- ☐ **BELLRINGER** Global Transition to Capitalism—Students identify specific countries moving to capitalism. *Visual/Spatial*
- ☐ **ESSENTIAL QUESTION** Exploring the Essential Question—Students identify ramifications of expanding production or increasing the price of smart phones.

T Technology Skills
- ☐ **SELF-CHECK QUIZ** Lesson 3—Students receive instant feedback on answers.
- ☐ **GAME** Lesson 3—Students solve clues to review lesson content.
- ☐ **INTERACTIVE WHITEBOARD ACTIVITY** Transition to Capitalism—Students work together to learn lesson content.

✓ Printable Digital Worksheets

R Reading Skills
- ☐ **WORKSHEET** Reteaching Activity—Students review and reteach content and vocabulary. This worksheet can be used with struggling students.
- ☐ **WORKSHEET** Chapter Summary—Student groups "teach" the class.

C Critical Thinking Skills
- ☐ **WORKSHEET** The Silk Road Video Activity—Students make inferences about economic decisions.
- ☐ **WORKSHEET** Math Practice for Economics—Students compute per capita GDP for various countries.

CHAPTER 2 Economic Systems and Decision Making

INTERVENTION AND REMEDIATION STRATEGIES

LESSON 1 Economic Systems

Reading and Comprehension

Divide the different types of economic systems among students. Ask each student to review his or her system and to write a paragraph explaining what makes that system successful (or not) in the modern world. Tell them to use facts and reasons from the text to support their ideas. After completing their paragraphs, ask the students that wrote about each system to share their ideas in a class discussion.

Text Evidence

Review how to use text evidence to support ideas and statements. Then pose these directives:

- Find evidence in the text to support this statement: An advantage of the traditional economy is that people generally know for whom they are producing goods. *(When an Inuit hunter is successful, the hunter shares the meat with the entire village.)*
- Find evidence in the text to support this statement: An advantage of the command economy is that the central government can set a new economic direction and bring about rapid change. *(The Soviet Union changed from an agricultural society to an industrial society in just a few decades.)*
- Find evidence in the text to support this statement: An advantage of the market economy is that it can adjust gradually to change. *(In 2005, gasoline prices were low, so people bought gas-guzzling SUVs. When gas prices rose sharply, SUV sales dropped and people bought fuel-efficient small cars.)*

LESSON 2 Mixed Economies

Reading and Comprehension

Divide students into three groups and assign one of the questions below to each group. Have groups answer the questions and find details to support their responses. Then ask students to share their answers and reasons with the class.

- Can a mixed economy operate without private ownership of productive resources? Why or why not?
- How are mixed socialism and communism alike and different?
- Why are most of the world's economies transitioning to mixed economies?

Text Evidence

Ask students to write one or two paragraphs that answer this question: **How does a mixed economy respond to the problem of scarcity? Give details from the text to support your answer.** Have students compare their responses in small group discussions.

LESSON 3 The Global Transition to Capitalism

Reading and Comprehension

Tell students to imagine that they have a friend living in a communist country. Recently, that country's central government has come under pressure from its citizens to adopt a capitalism system. The government appears ready to take that step. Have students write a letter to their friend telling him or her what to expect as this transition takes place.

Text Evidence

Have students work in pairs and find the answer to this question: **What are the three most important reasons that countries are transitioning to capitalism? Explain your answers, citing details from the text.** Have each pair of students present their answer and reasons in a group discussion.

Online Resources

Assessing Background Knowledge Use this worksheet to pre-assess students' knowledge before they start the chapter.

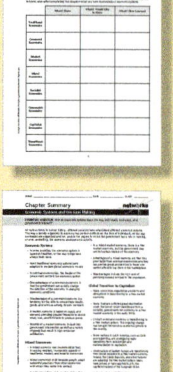

Chapter Summaries Have students use the summary as a pre-reading activity or as a post-reading review to check the main ideas covered in each lesson.

Guided Reading Activities Have students complete these activities as they read each lesson. They provide reading notes the student can use for review and to prepare for assessments.

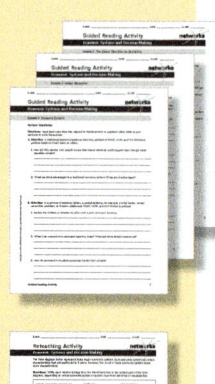

Reteaching Activities Have students complete the Reteaching Activity for remedial practice and review of vital content.

Self-Check Quizzes These quizzes provide instant feedback on areas the students may need to re-read to understand a main idea.

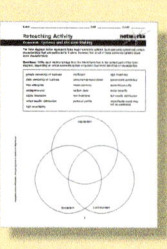

Reading Essentials and Study Guide This resource offers writing and reading activities for the approaching-level student.

Approaching Grade Level Reader This reader presents all of the content of the Online Student Edition but at a lower reading level.

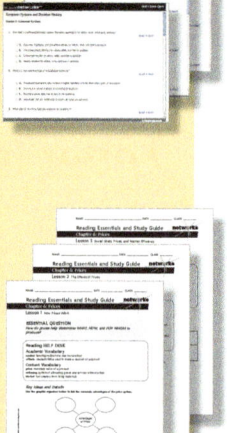

English Language Learner Reader Provide additional reading support for ELL students. Find this tool in the Online Student Edition.

Economic Systems and Decision Making

ESSENTIAL QUESTION
- How does an economic system help a society deal with the fundamental problem of scarcity?

networks
www.connected.mcgraw-hill.com
There's More Online about economic systems and decision making.

CHAPTER 2

Economic Perspectives
Economic Systems Around the World

Lesson 1
Economic Systems

Lesson 2
Mixed Economies

Lesson 3
The Global Transition to Capitalism

Letter from the Author

Dear Economics Teacher,

The core issue of scarcity is still with us in this chapter, but now our attention turns to the way in which countries have molded themselves to deal with the problem. For example, most western economies like the one in the United States have market-based systems that include some government involvement, whereas other countries have command or socialist-type economies. The world is changing, however, and many economies are in transition because they seek something that we already have—efficient markets that make effective use of relatively scarce resources.

Gary E. Clayton

CHAPTER 2
Economic Systems and Decision Making

ENGAGE

🔔 Call students' attention to the photo and ask them to describe what it shows. Guide them to recognize that an engineer (or other worker) is adjusting valves in an industrial complex or refinery.
Ask: Why is this image a good one to symbolize the chapter titled *Economic Systems and Decision Making*? *(Economic systems answer the WHAT, HOW, and FOR WHOM decisions of a society. Depending on what type of system a country has, energy and other resources are distributed according to who owns or obtains the resources and who has the money to pay for them.)* In a discussion, lead students to understand that in a market or capitalist economic system, private companies or individuals, not the state, have property rights and own these resources. **Visual/Spatial**

Comparing economic systems Organize students into groups and ask them to identify and briefly describe some economies that are very different from our U.S. economy. Examples might be those in China, Cuba, or Venezuela. Guide a discussion of main differences in how these economies operate and their effects on consumers compared to how our economy functions. List these points on the board. Tell students that economists have divided all economies into three major categories that students will learn about in this lesson. Challenge students to decide which category the economies they have just discussed will fit into as they read the lesson. **Interpersonal**

Making Connections

Predicting Career Changes Have students make a list of choices they have regarding their future career (where to work, what to do, whether to attend higher education, and so on). Then have students consider what could change in those choices if they moved to a country with a command economy. **Interpersonal**

FOLDABLES Study Organizer

Go to the Foldables® library for a cumulative chapter-based Foldable® activity that your students can use to help take notes and prepare for assessment.

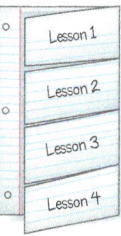

CHAPTER 2
Economic Perspectives

TEACH & ASSESS

V1 Visual Skills

Summarizing a map **Ask: What does the map show?** *(Countries of the world that use one of the three primary economic systems: free enterprise, mixed, and command.)* Ask students to identify countries that use each of these systems.
AL Visual/Spatial

V2 Visual Skills

Analyzing a map **Ask: Are most command economies and/or mixed economies concentrated in a particular region or continent?** *(No, they are dispersed, except for North American countries, which are free enterprise.)* Point out that although the map indicates several countries that operate under these three different economic systems, in reality most of them are gradually introducing changes by allowing market-driven practices. Have students select a country not highlighted on the map and research its economic system. **AL** Visual/Spatial

Economic Perspectives

ECONOMIC SYSTEMS AROUND THE WORLD

The economic systems of most countries typically reflect one of three predominant economic structures:
- 🟩 FREE ENTERPRISE
- 🟦 MIXED SYSTEM
- 🟥 COMMAND/SOCIALISTIC

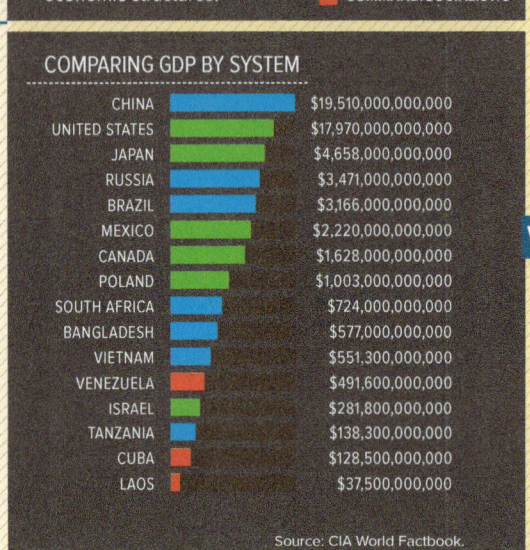

COMPARING GDP BY SYSTEM

CHINA	$19,510,000,000,000
UNITED STATES	$17,970,000,000,000
JAPAN	$4,658,000,000,000
RUSSIA	$3,471,000,000,000
BRAZIL	$3,166,000,000,000
MEXICO	$2,220,000,000,000
CANADA	$1,628,000,000,000
POLAND	$1,003,000,000,000
SOUTH AFRICA	$724,000,000,000
BANGLADESH	$577,000,000,000
VIETNAM	$551,300,000,000
VENEZUELA	$491,600,000,000
ISRAEL	$281,800,000,000
TANZANIA	$138,300,000,000
CUBA	$128,500,000,000
LAOS	$37,500,000,000

Source: CIA World Factbook.

FREE ENTERPRISE

Private citizens own and use the factors of production to generate profits. But even these countries do not have a purely free-enterprise system as the government also plays some role in regulating production and profits.

MIXED ECONOMY

Mixed economies have characteristics of the other two systems. South Africa has a stock exchange and a strong private sector, both typical of free enterprise economies. But, the national electric service is government controlled, typical of command economies.

networks Online Teaching Options

INFOGRAPHIC

Economic Perspectives: Economic Systems Around the World

Gaining a spatial perspective of economic systems Display the map. **Ask: What countries have a mixed economy (considered socialist)?** *(Brazil, Russia, China, South Africa, Tanzania, Vietnam, or Bangladesh.)* **What command economy is geographically closest to the U.S.?** *(Cuba)* **Where are three other command economies?** *(Venezuela, Laos, North Korea.)* **Where are free-enterprise economies?** *(Students may suggest the United States, Canada, Mexico, Poland, or Israel.)* Have students physically point out the countries they name on the map. Call students' attention to the inset box and compare GDP by country and economic system. Have student volunteers read aloud the descriptions of the three systems. **Visual/Spatial**

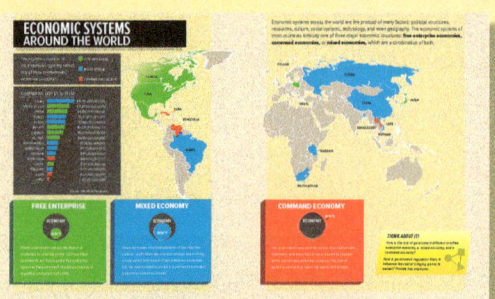

CHAPTER 2
Economic Perspectives

Economic systems across the world are the product of many factors: political structures, resources, culture, social systems, technology, and even geography. The economic systems of most countries embody one of three major economic structures: **free enterprise economies, command economies,** or **mixed economies,** which are a combination of both.

COMMAND ECONOMY

The government owns all of the factors of production and determines how these factors are combined to produce goods and services within the economy. This type of system is increasingly rare in the twenty-first century.

THINK ABOUT IT!

How is the role of government different in a free enterprise economy, a mixed economy, and a command economy?

How is government regulation likely to influence the cost of bringing goods to market? Provide two examples.

Economic Systems and Decision Making 37

WORKSHEET

Economic Simulation

Gaining a perspective of values in differing economic systems Distribute the Economic Simulation to groups. Students will determine the value of different items and discuss how those items' value might change when viewed/used by people living in societies with different economic systems. Students assign value to each item as representatives of a capitalist society, a socialist society, and a command-economy society. **Visual/Spatial**

W Writing Skills

Creating an illustrated time line Have students select either Venezuela or the Republic of South Africa to research regarding their state ownership of oil and the national electric service, respectively. Ask them to create an illustrated time line highlighting the major events that led to the state-ownership of these resources. **BL Visual/Spatial**

C Critical Thinking Skills

Brainstorming characteristics of economic systems Challenge students to brainstorm the characteristics of a free enterprise economic system. List their ideas on the board. Then ask them to describe a mixed or socialist economic system and list those ideas on the board. Finally, have students describe the characteristics of a command economic system and add those ideas on the board. Tell students to consult the list as they learn more about these systems.

CLOSE & REFLECT

Have students answer the *Think About It!* questions.

ANSWERS, p. 37

THINK ABOUT IT!

1. The role of government in a command economy is all-encompassing and controlling. In a free-enterprise system, government's role is mostly to regulate for fairness. In mixed economies, government's role is more involved than in free-enterprise systems but less involved than in command systems; government may control some public services but allow the private sector to function without too much oversight.

2. Government regulation adds to the cost of production. Examples may include the auto industry's requirements to test and retest functionality and safety features of vehicles. Dairy or egg farmers must follow strict health and environmental regulations regarding sterilization and agricultural run-off.

Economic Systems and Decision Making **37**

CHAPTER 2, LESSON 1
Economic Systems

ENGAGE

C Critical Thinking Skills

Identifying traditions in society and in the economy Before students begin the lesson, ask them to identify and briefly describe some traditions that Americans follow in society. The textbook identifies the bridal tradition of tossing the bouquet and the social tradition of shaking hands. Students may offer holiday traditions and customs, or even the custom of driving on the right side of the road. List students' suggestions on the board. Then have students consider traditional *economic* actions in the United States or in their families. **Ask: What is the traditional tipping percentage? How many students will carry on a family members' occupation? Does one family member by habit or tradition take out the trash or wash dishes or babysit?** Point out that although the United States as a whole does not have a traditional economy, economic traditions and customs are still evident. **AL**

TEACH & ASSESS

R Reading Skills

Using context clues Ask: What does the term *custom* mean as it is used in the text? *(an action that has been done by others in the past)* **What words and phrases provide clues to this meaning?** *(Possible answers: "habit," "the bride tosses the bouquet at a wedding," "traditional culture")* **AL**
Verbal/Linguistic

ANSWERS, p. 38

ESSENTIAL QUESTION ACTIVITY

Traditional economies produce and distribute according to custom. Command economies produce and distribute by decree according to a central governing authority. In market economies, production is based on what consumers want, and those who have demand (can pay) receive the distributed goods and services.

TAKING NOTES

Market Economy: Citizens make most decisions; expanded private property rights; limited government interference. Both: Can make changes quickly; may not provide enough basic goods or services. Command Economy: central authority makes most decisions; limited private property rights; affordable basic goods and services.

Interact with these digital assets and others in lesson 1
- ✓ INTERACTIVE CHART Comparing Economic Systems
- ✓ INTERACTIVE IMAGE Traditional Economy of the Inuit
- ✓ SELF-CHECK QUIZ
- ✓ VIDEO

networks
TRY IT YOURSELF ONLINE

LESSON 1
Economic Systems

Reading Help Desk

Academic Vocabulary
- stagnation
- emphasizing

Content Vocabulary
- traditional economy
- economic systems
- command economy
- socialism
- market
- market economy
- capitalism

TAKING NOTES:

Key Ideas and Details
ACTIVITY As you read the lesson, complete a graphic organizer like the one below to identify ways in which a market economy differs from, and is similar to, a command economy.

Market Economy
Similarities
Command Economy

ESSENTIAL QUESTION

How does an economic system help a society deal with the fundamental problem of scarcity?

Compare and contrast the three main types of economic systems, focusing on the basic elements of production and distribution of goods and services.

Economies Based on Tradition

GUIDING QUESTION *How does a traditional economy answer the basic questions of WHAT, HOW, and FOR WHOM to produce?*

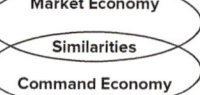

Much of what we do springs from habit and custom. Why, for example, does the bride toss the bouquet at a wedding? Why do we greet people by shaking hands rather than by pressing our noses and foreheads against theirs, as the Maori people of New Zealand do? It's because such practices have become part of our traditional culture.

Characteristics

In a society with a **traditional economy**, the use of scarce resources—and nearly all other economic activity—stems from ritual, habit, or custom. Habit and custom also dictate most social behavior. Individuals are generally not free to make decisions on the basis of what they want or would like to have. Instead, their roles are defined by the customs of their elders and ancestors.

Examples

Many societies—such as the central African Mbuti, the Australian Aborigines, and other indigenous peoples around the world—have traditional economies. The Inuit of Northern Canada in the nineteenth century provide an especially interesting case of a traditional economy.

For generations, Inuit parents taught their children how to survive in a harsh climate by making tools, fishing, and hunting. Their children, in turn, taught these skills to the next generation. When the Inuit hunted, it was traditional to share the spoils of the hunt with other families. If a walrus or bear was taken, hunters divided the kill evenly into as many portions as there were

---

networks **Online Teaching Options**

BELLRINGER

Economic Systems

Analyzing a command system Use the Bellringer photograph to initiate a class discussion about how different societies answer the basic economic questions in different ways. Then have students examine the photograph and note the quantity of items shown. Guide students to understand that Cuba operates under a different kind of economic system in which the central government makes most of the economic decisions. The majority of Cubans either go without certain goods and services or learn to devise alternative solutions to their needs. **Visual/Spatial, Verbal/Linguistic**

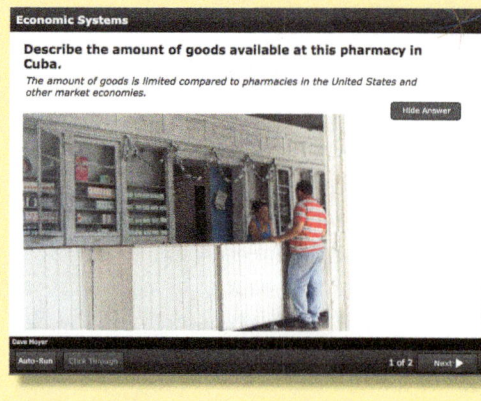

heads of families in the hunting party. The hunter most responsible for the kill had first choice, the second hunter to help with the kill chose next, and so on. Because the Inuit shared freely and generously with one another, members of the hunting party later shared their portions with other families who had not participated.

As a result, the hunter had the honor of the kill and the respect of the village, rather than a physical claim to the entire animal. Because of this tradition of sharing, and as long as skilled hunters lived in the community, a village could survive the long, harsh winters. This custom was partially responsible for the Inuit's survival for thousands of years.

Advantages

The main advantage of a traditional economy is that everyone knows which role to play. Little uncertainty exists over WHAT to produce. If you are born into a family of hunters, you hunt. If you are born into a family of farmers, you farm. Likewise, little uncertainty exists over HOW to produce, because you do things much the same way your parents did. Finally, the answer to the FOR WHOM question is determined by the customs and traditions of the society. In some societies, you alone might be responsible for providing for your immediate family. In others, such as the Inuit, you would share the spoils of your hunt with all the families of the village. In other words, tradition dictates how people live their lives.

Disadvantages

The main drawback of a traditional economy is that it tends to discourage new ideas and new ways of doing things. The strict roles in a traditional society have the effect of punishing people who act differently or break the rules. The lack of progress due to the lack of new ideas and new ways of doing things leads to economic **stagnation** and a lower standard of living than in other **economic systems**.

✓ READING PROGRESS CHECK

Describing What are the advantages and disadvantages of a traditional economy?

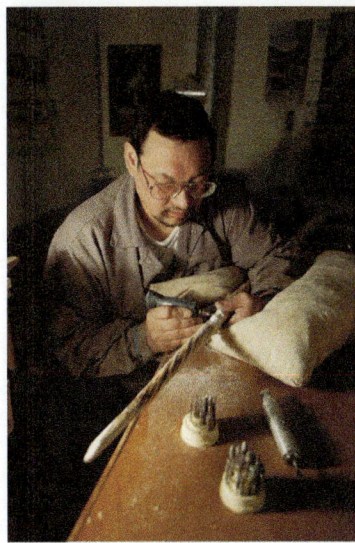

An Inuit hunter gets the choice of first cuts from a successful hunt and then the others in the community get to share in the kill as well. This rewards the skill of the hunter and also ensures that everyone in the traditional economy benefits.

▲ CRITICAL THINKING
Identifying There are advantages and disadvantages to an Inuit traditional economy. Name one advantage and one disadvantage of an Inuit traditional economy and provide an example of each.

Economies Based on Command

GUIDING QUESTION *How does a command economy answer the basic questions of WHAT, HOW, and FOR WHOM to produce?*

In a **command economy**, a central authority makes the major decisions about WHAT, HOW, and FOR WHOM to produce. A command economy can be headed by a king, a dictator, a president, a tribal leader, or anyone else who makes the major economic decisions.

A modern, and somewhat more liberal, version of the command economy is socialism. **Socialism** is an economic and political system in which the government owns some, but not all, of the factors of production. As such, the government plays a major role in answering most of the major WHAT, HOW, and FOR WHOM questions.

Characteristics

In a pure command economy, the central governing authority makes all of the major economic decisions. This means that the government decides if houses or apartments will be built. It also decides on the best way to build them and on who will receive them.

traditional economy economic system in which the allocation of scarce resources, and other economic activity, is the result of ritual, habit, or custom

stagnation lack of movement

economic systems organized way a society provides for the wants and needs of its people

command economy economic system characterized by a central authority that makes most of the major economic decisions

socialism economic system in which government owns some factors of production and has a role in determining what and how goods are produced

connected.mcgraw-hill.com   Economic Systems and Decision Making   **39**

VIDEO   WORKSHEET

Cabbage Bartering in Russia

Understanding bartering Show the video Cabbage Bartering in Russia and discuss the process of bartering. Explain that bartering was more common in traditional economies than in advanced mixed economies like that of the United States, but emphasize that bartering is still used. Ask students to describe instances of bartering they know about. Ask students to discuss the disadvantages of bartering in a complex modern economy.   **Visual/Spatial, Logical/Mathematical**

CHAPTER 2, LESSON 1
Economic Systems

W1 Writing Skills

Writing a narrative about living in a traditional economy Have students write a short story about a young person who lives in a traditional economy. Stories should include a description of the trade that the person learns from his or her parents. Invite students to illustrate their stories with drawings or magazine images.   **Intrapersonal**

C Critical Thinking Skills

Drawing conclusions about change in a traditional economy Ask: **Why do you think leaders in traditional economies discourage or even punish change?** *(Possible answer: Leaders might fear that an outside influence will hurt the community's culture.)*   **AL Logical/Mathematical**

W2 Writing Skills

Summarizing a traditional economic system Have students summarize in a chart the basic characteristics of a traditional economic system in regard to property rights, incentives, economic freedom, competition, and the role of government.   **Logical/Mathematical**

ANSWERS, p. 39

CRITICAL THINKING
A main advantage of a traditional Inuit economy is that everyone knows their roles, like the hunters who know which choice they will get after a successful hunt. A disadvantage is that new ways of doing things are discouraged. Thus, if others in the community wanted the first cuts, that would not be possible without breaking the rules and possibly punishment.

✓ **READING PROGRESS CHECK** Advantages: little uncertainty, everyone knows what to do; Disadvantages: new ideas and new ways of doing things are discouraged, lack of progress leads to economic stagnation and lower standard of living

Economic Systems and Decision Making   **39**

CHAPTER 2, LESSON 1
Economic Systems

C Critical Thinking Skills

Drawing inferences about economic choices Have students write what their families ate or used for breakfast or dinner, including products, brands, containers, and utensils. Have students count how many economic decisions/choices went into putting the meal on the table. Discuss what it would be like to be responsible for making sure that each family member had what he or she wanted to eat every day. **AL Intrapersonal**

Sometimes the central authority is generous with the country's wealth and spreads it around for the benefit of all. In other cases, much of the country's wealth is plundered and kept for the exclusive benefit of its leader. Such countries often have a culture in which citizens must use bribery to obtain the smallest portions of everyday commodities.

Most command economies severely limit private property rights. That means that people are not allowed to own their homes, businesses, and other productive resources, although they may have some personal items like clothing and tools. Because of this, the government owns most of the resources in the economy.

Socialist economies share many of the same characteristics of pure command economies; only fewer resources are owned or controlled by the central authority. Under socialism, the stated objective of the government is to serve the needs of its people, not just enhance the welfare of its leaders. Most socialist economies tend to be larger than economies directed by pure tradition, which makes it harder for the government to own and direct everything.

C Regardless of how the wealth is produced and shared, both pure command as well as socialist economies share a common trait—the major economic decisions are made by the government and not necessarily *for* the people.

Examples

Modern examples of pure command economies are limited to a handful of dictatorships and small tribal economies around the world. North Korea is perhaps the world's last leading example of a command economy where everything—even the media and tourism—is either owned or controlled by the government.

What Happens in a . . .

Command Economic System

This Cuban marketplace represents all of the common characteristics of a command economy. The government has the most influence in determining WHAT types of products are sold, the method for HOW those products are sold, and FOR WHOM those products are sold. The preferences of the consumer do not carry as much impact as is true in the United States' market economy.

▲ **CRITICAL THINKING**
Identifying The number of command economies is limited for a number of reasons. What is one major disadvantage of the Cuban command economy?

---

networks Online Teaching Options

IMAGES

Command Economy

Examining a command economy Have students view the Cuban marketplace and read the captions. **Ask: Who allocates resources in a command economy?** *(the government)* **How do people in command economies often get items that the government has not sanctioned, or for which it has not allocated resources?** *(through the black market)* **Visual/Spatial**

ANSWERS, p. 40

CRITICAL THINKING

Students should respond with at least one disadvantage from the following: that the government can choose to produce products that the general population does not necessarily want or need; that choices are limited in the marketplace and that the quality of the products are not that good; that a large decision-making bureaucracy hinders efficient production; that individual incentives to work are limited because everybody's wages are about the same; or that businesses do not have the freedom to pursue the profit motive.

CAREERS | Physician's Assistant

Is this career for you?

 Do you have an interest in health care?

 Do you enjoy helping people?

 Are you detail oriented?

Interview with a Physician's Assistant

"But the real knowledge, the most valuable thing we can take from this place, is our human experience.... It comes from the mistakes we made and from the little victories that lifted us back up. It comes from the relationships and the bonds that we formed. It comes from the patients we helped and it comes from the ones we couldn't."

—Harrison Reed, PA

Salary
Median salary: $90,930 per year
$43.72 per hour

Job Growth Outlook
The growth potential is much higher than average.

Profile of Work
Physician assistants, also known as PAs, practice medicine under the direction of physicians and surgeons. They are formally trained to examine patients, diagnose injuries and illnesses, and provide treatment. Physician's assistants help offer superior services in a decentralized health care system.

More important are the small and shrinking number of countries based on socialism, a group that includes Cuba and Vietnam, as well as Venezuela under former president Hugo Chavez. The former socialist country of the Soviet Union, or USSR, is another example, but it collapsed in 1991. Countries such as Denmark, Sweden, and Norway are no longer described as socialist because they have completed a transition to capitalism, even though they still have a few socialist features like free universal education and health services.

Advantages

A major strength of a command system is that it can change direction drastically. The former Soviet Union went from a rural agricultural society in 1910 to an industrial nation in a few decades by **emphasizing** the growth of heavy industry. During this period, the central planners shifted resources on a massive scale from farming and consumer goods to industrial production.

emphasizing stressing

Another major advantage of a socialist command economy is that it allows most citizens to receive some goods and services that they would otherwise not be able to afford. Cubans, for example, have access to universal health care. Likewise, President Chavez tried to provide basic food, commodities, and electricity at below-market rates to Venezuelan citizens during his time in office.

The same is true of North Korea and the former Soviet Union, where many public services—including health, education, and transportation—were available to everyone at little or no cost. Because there were many low-income citizens in these countries, these services would not have been affordable otherwise.

CHAPTER 2, LESSON 1
Economic Systems

Making Connections

Drawing Conclusions about North Korea's Economy Have students identify characteristics of life in North Korea. **Ask: How are these a result of a command economy? Explain.** *(The government dictates where human and other resources are directed. The government wants only certain people to live in the city, possibly to keep more people working in agriculture in rural areas. North Korean industry produces only enough cars for military and government personnel, but not enough for consumers. These decisions are made by the government rather than the economy. Economic freedom is virtually nonexistent.)* **Logical/Mathematical**

English Language Proficiency

Advanced High Have students use a four square graphic to deepen understanding of basic and grade-level vocabulary. Tell them to write a target word in a circle in the center of the square and the definition in the upper left corner of the square. In the upper right corner, have them write some characteristics of the item named or described by the word. Tell them to compare and contrast by listing examples of the concept in the lower left corner and nonexamples in the lower right corner. Then have them review the information with a partner.

INTERACTIVE FEATURE

Careers: Physician's Assistant

Examining the career of a physician's assistant Have students read the Physician's Assistant feature. Then guide a discussion on this career by asking: **Why does a physician's assistant need to be detail oriented? What are the advantages of this career? What are the disadvantages?** Encourage students to discuss whether they think this career is right for them. Explain that the need for medical personnel is expanding rapidly as the American population ages and the Affordable Care Act extends health insurance to more people. Ask students to investigate the growing need for health care services and then to discuss how these changes will affect the demand for physician's assistants. Ask them to consider how these changes will affect how health care is delivered and the changing roles of health care professionals. **Verbal/Linguistic**

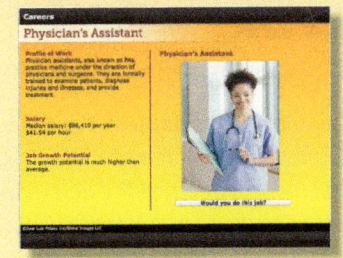

CHAPTER 2, LESSON 1
Economic Systems

C1 Critical Thinking Skills

Demonstrating limitations of choice Have students suppose that they are the planning committee of a command economy. Tell them that only enough fertilizer and pesticides exist to plant five crops this year. Students must list the five crops that will receive the resources. Have students compare their lists and discuss the limitations for consumers caused by a command economy. **AL** Verbal/Linguistic

C2 Critical Thinking Skills

Synthesizing data Ask students to study the data shown in the North Korea and South Korea circle graphs, and then compare the data to the per capita GDP of the two countries. Invite students to find out what percentages of the U.S. economy are based on agriculture, services, and industry. Then ask students why an economy based on services and industry rather than agriculture leads to a higher GDP per capita. Logical/Mathematical

Disadvantages

Command economies have several major disadvantages. The first is that leaders of command economies usually provide for themselves at the expense of the general population. The result is that high government officials have nice cars, houses, and plenty of food while the average citizen may be forced to go without.

In the socialist former Soviet Union, for example, generations of people were forced to go without basic consumer goods and adequate housing. Similarly, the current North Korean government puts a strong emphasis on defense spending while their people have suffered years of hunger. At times, the government even had to accept food aid from international sources because of disastrous agricultural policies.

A second disadvantage of command or socialist economies is the loss of the individual freedom to choose. For example, someone who does not want the services of national health ends up paying for it anyway because it has been made available to others. Even the choices of where and how to live can be affected. In Cuba, doctors are required to live in the same buildings where they provide their services, a practice unheard of in the United States.

Free state-controlled media such as radio and TV are another common feature of most socialist countries, but the programming is usually limited to the propaganda content that the government wants its people to see, not what the people would choose to see. In North Korea, living conditions in other parts of the world are not shown, because the government wants its people to think that they live in a modern, advanced society.

A third disadvantage is the production of low-quality goods. Workers who are unhappy with where and how they are supposed to work are often given quotas to fill as a way to stimulate production. This sometimes causes the workers to focus on filling their quotas rather than on producing quality goods.

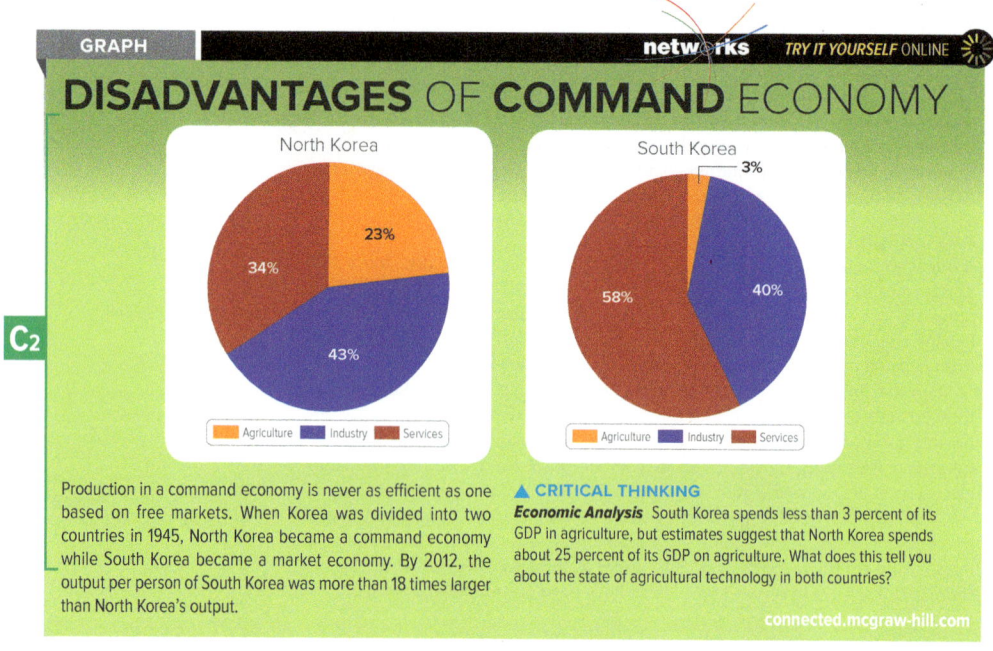

Production in a command economy is never as efficient as one based on free markets. When Korea was divided into two countries in 1945, North Korea became a command economy while South Korea became a market economy. By 2012, the output per person of South Korea was more than 18 times larger than North Korea's output.

▲ **CRITICAL THINKING**
Economic Analysis South Korea spends less than 3 percent of its GDP in agriculture, but estimates suggest that North Korea spends about 25 percent of its GDP on agriculture. What does this tell you about the state of agricultural technology in both countries?

networks Online Teaching Options

GRAPHS

Disadvantages of a Command Economy

Comparing economies Have students click through the feature until they view the graphs. Then ask them to describe the differences they see between the two countries shown. Ask them to explain what this reveals about the economic development of these two countries as well as the impact on consumers. Emphasize that North Korea has a command economy, whereas South Korea has a market economy. Discuss what the graphs show about the basis of the economic development of the two countries. Logical/Mathematical

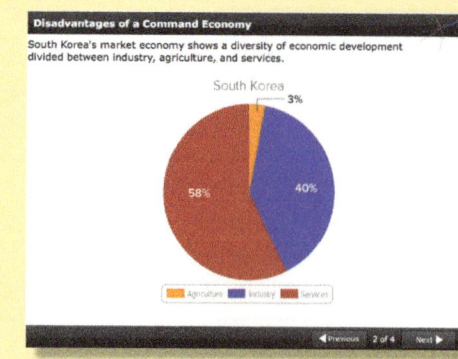

ANSWERS, p. 42

CRITICAL THINKING

Agricultural technology is much less efficient in North Korea, or much more efficient in South Korea.

In March of 2011, Japan was struck by a tsunami which disabled a nuclear reactor and released radioactivity into the environment. Nearby cities were contaminated and became unlivable. Because of the economic interdependence of nations, there were global economic consequences. Some automobile parts made in Japan were not available for assembly in the United States. Many seafood exports came to a halt. Tourists decided to visit Thailand and neighboring countries rather than Japan.

◀ CRITICAL THINKING
Analyzing Cause and Effect
How do you think the production of Korean automobiles or electronic goods like video games, music devices, and televisions could have been affected by the Japanese tsunami?

At one time in the former Soviet Union, quotas for electrical motors were measured in tons of output. Soviet workers then filled their quotas by producing the world's heaviest electrical motors. The Soviets also made some of the most beautiful chandeliers in the world. However, the quotas for those were also measured in terms of weight, so the chandeliers were also some of the heaviest in the world. Many were so heavy that they could not be safely secured to the ceiling—and some would occasionally fall to the floor.

A fourth disadvantage is that an economy with major elements of command requires a large decision-making bureaucracy. In the former Soviet Union, an army of clerks, planners, and other administrators was needed to make the production and distribution plans for even the most basic products. This structure slowed decision making and raised the cost of production.

In Venezuela—a modern economy tending toward socialism under Chavez—entire industries in the agricultural, financial, oil, and steel sectors were taken over by the government to pay for "low-cost" food and electricity provided to everyone. These industries also required supervision by planners, and many of the planners were politicians who were making decisions to satisfy political goals, regardless of the economic impact of their decisions.

A fifth disadvantage is that rewards for individual initiatives are rare in both command and socialist economies. In the early years of the Soviet Union, all workers were paid about the same, regardless of their occupation or how hard they worked in each profession. Doctors were paid about the same as factory workers, and most factory workers were paid about the same regardless of how much each worker produced. As a result of this heritage, wages today are still relatively uniform in many other modern socialist countries.

The result—and a very important one—is that economies with relatively uniform wages for different occupations and effort do not provide much incentive for people to learn or work. Why, for example, would you bother to go to college or take the time to learn a difficult skill if you could not be rewarded for it?

Yet a sixth disadvantage is that a planning bureaucracy often lacks the flexibility to promptly deal with major problems, or even minor day-to-day ones. As a result, command economies tend to lurch from one crisis to the next—or collapse completely, as did the former Soviet Union.

CHAPTER 2, LESSON 1
Economic Systems

R Reading Skills

Analyzing a command economy Ask: **Why is it difficult in a command economy for the people to change how the central governing authority manages the economy?** *(Possible answer: The governing authority has all or most of the power, whereas the people have very little power.)* **Logical/Mathematical**

IMAGES

Effects of the Global Economy

Identifying causes and effects of economic events Display the image and read (or have students read) the onscreen text. Ask students how the tsunami and nuclear disaster affected tourism in Japan. Invite them to speculate about how these events may have affected tourism in other Asian nations. Ask students to draw conclusions about how a major disaster can affect the immediate economy of the region or nation where it occurs, as well as how it might affect other nations. Ask them to consider whether scientific, technological, or other positive developments might have similar but opposite repercussions. **Verbal/Linguistic**

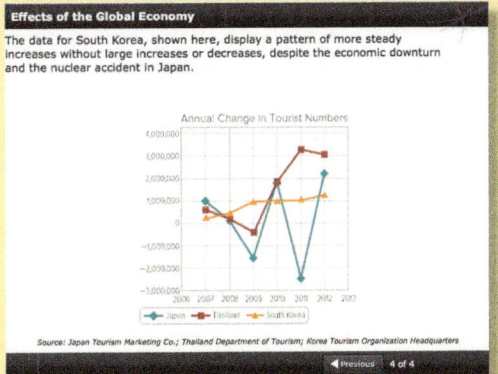

ANSWERS, p. 43

CRITICAL THINKING
Korean electronic goods—such as televisions, music devices, and video games—as well as automobiles are major exports and major competitors with Japanese products. It would be reasonable to expect a surge in production of all these Korean products.

CHAPTER 2, LESSON 1
Economic Systems

W Writing Skills

Summarizing a command economic system Have students summarize in a chart the basic characteristics of a command economic system in regard to property rights, incentives, economic freedom, competition, and the role of government. **Logical/Mathematical**

C Critical Thinking Skills

Researching global connections Challenge students to research how major economic developments in one country affected other countries. Students might, for example, investigate how the development of personal computers, cell phones, solar energy technology, or hybrid automotive technology affected local and global economies. **BL Verbal/Linguistic**

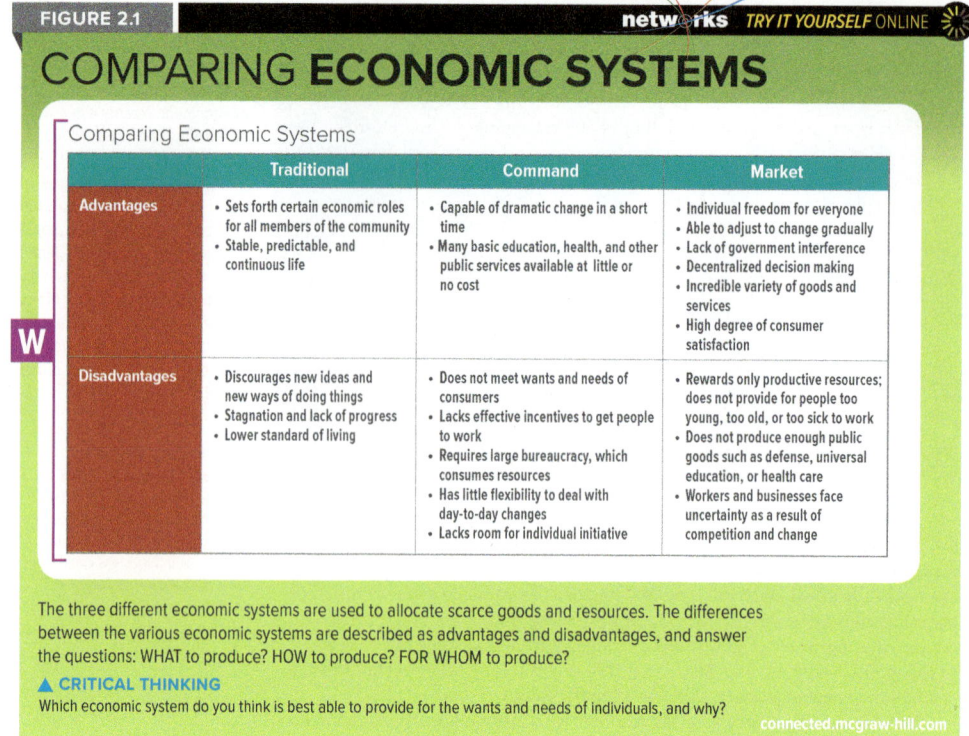

FIGURE 2.1 COMPARING ECONOMIC SYSTEMS

	Traditional	Command	Market
Advantages	• Sets forth certain economic roles for all members of the community • Stable, predictable, and continuous life	• Capable of dramatic change in a short time • Many basic education, health, and other public services available at little or no cost	• Individual freedom for everyone • Able to adjust to change gradually • Lack of government interference • Decentralized decision making • Incredible variety of goods and services • High degree of consumer satisfaction
Disadvantages	• Discourages new ideas and new ways of doing things • Stagnation and lack of progress • Lower standard of living	• Does not meet wants and needs of consumers • Lacks effective incentives to get people to work • Requires large bureaucracy, which consumes resources • Has little flexibility to deal with day-to-day changes • Lacks room for individual initiative	• Rewards only productive resources; does not provide for people too young, too old, or too sick to work • Does not produce enough public goods such as defense, universal education, or health care • Workers and businesses face uncertainty as a result of competition and change

The three different economic systems are used to allocate scarce goods and resources. The differences between the various economic systems are described as advantages and disadvantages, and answer the questions: WHAT to produce? HOW to produce? FOR WHOM to produce?

▲ **CRITICAL THINKING**
Which economic system do you think is best able to provide for the wants and needs of individuals, and why?

Almost all countries are connected by foreign trade, so it is possible for a problem in one part of the world to be quickly transmitted to another. Something like rapidly rising oil prices because of a hurricane in the Gulf of Mexico is bound to have a worldwide impact on countries as far away as Finland or Mongolia. A small economy directed by a central planning authority would not be able to react quickly to events like these.

Finally, pure command economies tend to stay relatively small because they have such a hard time making all of the decisions necessary for growth and change to take place. It is easy for a ruler to make all of the major decisions in a small tribal economy, but when the economy reaches the size of a small country, too many decisions are needed to make it grow satisfactorily. When the economy gets to the size of the former Soviet Union, it is so hard to coordinate the decisions that the country collapses without any outside pressure.

Goods and services are never free, even if the country has an economy directed by socialism. This is because the universal problem of *TINSTAAFL*, or There Is No Such Thing As A Free Lunch, still applies to socialist economies. In more developed European countries such as Denmark, Sweden, and Norway, programs like free education and national health care are funded with high domestic tax rates. As a result, the tax rates in these countries are higher than those in the United States.

☑ **READING PROGRESS CHECK**

Analyzing What are the major problems with a command economy?

---

networks Online Teaching Options

CHARTS

Comparing Economic Systems

Comparing economic systems Have students read and click through Figure 2.1 Comparing Economic Systems. When students finish reading the advantages and disadvantages of each type of system, they will drag the labels to the correct columns. **Verbal/Linguistic**

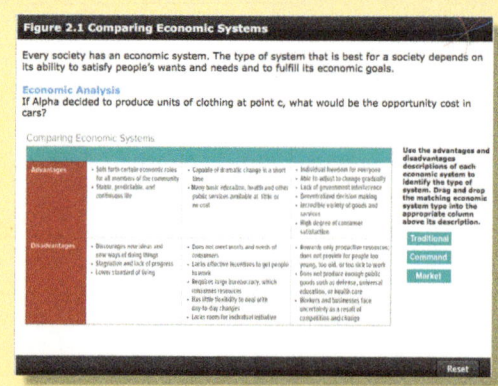

ANSWERS, p. 44

CRITICAL THINKING
Answers will vary. Students should be able to defend their answers.

☑ **READING PROGRESS CHECK** A command economy ignores consumer wants and needs; gives incentive to fill quotas instead of making good products; needs a large bureaucracy; cannot handle minor problems; rarely rewards individual initiative.

CHAPTER 2, LESSON 1
Economic Systems

Economies Based on Markets

GUIDING QUESTION *How does a market economy answer the basic questions of WHAT, HOW, and FOR WHOM to produce?*

A **market** is an arrangement where buyers and sellers interact to determine the prices and quantities of goods and services. A market might be in a physical location, such as a farmer's market, or on a Web site, such as eBay. Regardless of its form, a market can exist as long as a mechanism is in place for buyers and sellers to interact. A **market economy** is one where the WHAT, HOW, and FOR WHOM questions are primarily answered by people who make supply and demand decisions in their own best interests.

Characteristics

A market economy is characterized by a great deal of freedom. People can spend their money on the products they want most, which is like casting dollar "votes" for those products. This tells producers which products people want most, thus helping answer the question of WHAT to produce. Businesses are free to find the best production methods when deciding HOW to produce. Finally, the income that consumers earn and spend in the market determines FOR WHOM to produce.

Market economies also feature the private ownership of resources. A market economy is often described as being based on **capitalism**—an economic system where private citizens own and use the factors of production for their own profit or gain. The term *capitalism* draws attention to the private ownership of resources, while the term *market economy* focuses on where the goods and services are exchanged. As a result, the two terms focus on different features of the same economic system.

Examples

Many of the most prosperous economies in the world, such as Australia, Canada, Great Britain, Japan, Singapore, South Korea, parts of Western Europe, and the United States, are based on markets and capitalism. While there are significant differences among them, these economies share the common elements of markets and the private ownership of productive resources to seek profits.

Advantages

The first advantage of a market economy is its high degree of individual freedom. People are free to spend their money on almost any good or service they choose. People also are free to decide where and when they want to work, or if they want to invest further in their own education and training. At the same time, producers are free to decide what they want to produce, whom they want to hire, which inputs they want to use, and the way they want to produce.

The second advantage of a market economy is that it adjusts gradually to change over time. Before 2005, for example, gasoline prices were low, so people tended to buy large gas-guzzling SUVs. When the price of gas rose sharply in that year, SUV sales fell, and smaller, more fuel-efficient vehicles became popular. The decision that individuals made themselves—not decisions made by government planners—helped the economy adjust to change.

A third advantage is the relatively small degree of government interference. Except for certain concerns such as justice and national defense, the government normally tries to stay out of the way of buyers and sellers.

A fourth advantage is that decision making is decentralized. Billions, if not trillions, of individual economic decisions are made daily. Collectively, consumers make the decisions that direct scarce resources into the uses they favor most, so everyone has a voice in the way the economy runs.

market meeting place or arrangement through which buyers and sellers interact to determine price and quantity of an economic product; may be local, regional, national, or global

market economy economic system in which supply, demand, and the price system help people allocate resources and make the WHAT, HOW, and FOR WHOM to produce decisions; same as free enterprise economy

capitalism economic system in which private citizens own and use the factors of production in order to generate profits

---

Making Connections

Market Advantages Help students to make connections to the advantages of the market economy. **Ask: How many brands of breakfast cereals are there in your supermarket?** *(By one count, there may be at least 150 different brands.)* Invite a student to research what is found on the shelves of grocery stores in Cuba or another command economy. **What products have you seen that were very popular and then faded away over time?** *(Sample answer: Blackberry cell phones faded away because they did not adapt to competition and market changes. CDs are fading away because of newer technology, such as MP3s.)* **What economic decisions have you made this past week?** *(Sample answers: what to buy for lunch, which clothing item to buy, whether to buy a music single by one artist rather than another)*

W1 Writing Skills

Comparing incentives Have students summarize in a paragraph the role that incentives play in a market economy, and how this role differs from its role in a traditional system and a command economic system. **Logical/Mathematical**

W2 Writing Skills

Writing about the benefits of a market economy Have students write an essay explaining why each of the following examples are considered benefits of a market economy:

- freedom of consumers and producers, a variety of goods
- responsive prices
- investment opportunities. **BL** **Verbal/Linguistic**

WORKSHEET

Guided Reading Activity

Summarizing economic systems Ask students to complete the Guided Reading Activity worksheet for Lesson 1. When students finish, read the questions and ask volunteers to read their responses. Encourage discussion among students who have different responses.
Verbal/Linguistic

CHAPTER 2, LESSON 1
Economic Systems

R Reading Skills

Finding solutions to disadvantages Organize students into small groups, and have them brainstorm answers to the following question: **How might the government help remedy some of the disadvantages of a market economy?** *(Possible answers: provide universal health care; help the sick and the elderly through programs such as Medicare and Social Security; offer unemployment insurance to reduce insecurity)*

CLOSE & REFLECT

R Reading Skills

Summarizing the lesson Have students review what they have learned about the traditional, command (socialism and communism), and market (free enterprise) economic systems. Ask students to describe the chief characteristics of each system, the advantages of each system, and the disadvantages of each system. Then have students identify countries with a free enterprise system and give three economic facts about it.

ANSWERS, p. 46

 READING PROGRESS CHECK The main benefits of a market economy are freedom, consumers tell businesses what to produce through spending, and private ownership of resources.

A fifth advantage of the market economy is the variety of goods and services that are produced. You can find ultrasound devices to keep the neighbor's dog out of your yard, or download video and street maps to your cell phone, or even use your cell phone as a flashlight. In short, if a product can be imagined, it is likely to be produced in hopes that people will buy it.

A sixth advantage is the high degree of consumer satisfaction. In a market economy, the choice one group makes does not affect the choices of other groups. If 51 percent of the people want to buy classical music, and 49 percent want to buy rap music, people in both groups can still get what they want.

Yet another advantage of a market economy is that goods are usually privately owned, and privately owned goods last longer than goods owned by others. For example, who would take better care of a new car or truck—the person who owns it, or the person who drives one owned by his or her boss? The answer almost always is that the owner is the one who takes better care of his or her property. In a world of relatively scarce resources, it makes sense to have an economic system that has this feature.

EXPLORING THE ESSENTIAL QUESTION
Compare and contrast the three main types of economic systems, focusing on the basic elements of production and distribution of goods and services.

Disadvantages

The market economy does not provide for everyone. Some people may be too young, too old, or too sick to earn a living or to care for themselves. These people would have difficulty surviving in a pure market economy without assistance from family, government, or charitable groups.

A market economy also may not provide enough of some basic goods and services. For example, private markets do not adequately supply all of the roads, libraries, universal education, or comprehensive health care people would like to have. This is because private producers concentrate on providing products they can sell for a profit.

Finally, a market economy has a high degree of uncertainty. Workers might worry that their company will move to another country in search of lower labor costs. Employers may worry that someone else will produce better or less expensive products, thereby taking their customers.

✓ **READING PROGRESS CHECK**

Identifying What are the main benefits of a market economy?

LESSON 1 REVIEW

Reviewing Vocabulary
1. *Defining* Define capitalism.
2. *Summarizing* What are the functions of an economic system?

Using Your Notes
Refer to the graphic organizer at the beginning of this lesson to answer this question.

3. *Comparing* Use your notes to describe the differences between a market economy and a command economy.

Answering the Guiding Questions

4. *Explaining* How does a traditional economy answer the questions of WHAT, HOW, and FOR WHOM to produce?

5. *Explaining* How does a command economy answer the questions of WHAT, HOW, and FOR WHOM to produce?

6. *Explaining* How does the economic freedom that defines a market economy help answer the questions of WHAT, HOW, and FOR WHOM to produce?

Writing About Economics

7. *Informative/Explanatory* Choose elements from at least two of the main economic systems and explain why these elements combined would contribute to a mixed system that could be more effective than one that was a pure traditional, command, or market system.

LESSON 1 REVIEW ANSWERS

Reviewing Vocabulary

1. Capitalism is an economic system in which private citizens own and use the factors of production for their own profit or gain.

2. Economic systems are organized ways a society provides for the wants and needs of its people by answering the questions of WHAT, HOW, and FOR WHOM to produce.

Using Your Notes

3. In a market economy, people are free to make their own decisions; in a command economy, a central authority makes decisions. A market economy has a high degree of freedom; a command economy has a low degree of freedom. A market economy allows for individual ownership of resources; in a command economy, a central authority owns the resources.

Answering the Guiding Questions

4. In a society with a traditional economy, the use of scarce resources—and nearly all other economic activity—stems from ritual, habit, or custom.

5. In a pure command economy, a central authority makes the major decisions about WHAT, HOW, and FOR WHOM to produce.

6. Because consumers and business operators have more freedom to make choices about what goods and services to produce and purchase, their motivations help signal to the market what the economy should provide.

Writing About Economics

7. Students should highlight characteristics and advantages of at least two of the main economic systems working together to be more effective as a mixed system.

Case Study

What Does YOUR DAY LOOK LIKE? THE 9 TO 5 IN Traditional, Command, & Market Economies

Maori, like this fisherman, still practice some traditional economic methods.

The Maori, the indigenous people of New Zealand, had a traditional economy that depended on fishing, gathering, and subsistence farming. Fishing was done with lines and nets, and birds and small animals were trapped. Getting food was difficult and time consuming.

Goods and services were exchanged through gift giving, and generosity was highly valued. Men and women divided labor: Men farmed, hunted, and fished for the family's food supply. Women weeded, cooked, and wove clothing. Skilled craftspeople became known as carvers or builders.

North Korea is a command economy. In Pyongyang, the capital, life is relatively easy in comparison with the poverty found throughout the rural areas of the country. North Korean citizens cannot enter or leave the capital without a permit and must be a member of an approved resident family or have performed some exceptional service for the Communist Party to maintain a residence in Pyongyang.

Power outages are frequent, and food shortages, although less frequent than outside the city, do occur. Almost all cars belong to the government or military. Martial music and propaganda are continuously broadcast over loudspeakers.

The people of the United Kingdom live in a market economy. Life there provides many options not available in traditional or command economies. Large department stores offer a great variety of goods and services. Housing options range from small apartments to large mansions. Four out of five households have cars. Over 65 percent of British citizens own their own homes, and the price of a home averages £165,000 (or about $262,000).

The average annual individual income in the United Kingdom is £30,000 (approximately $47,000). About 75 percent of British jobs are in service industries—hotels, restaurants, travel, shopping, computers, and finances. British workers do not have to work more than 48 hours a week if they choose not to, but about 22 percent of them do work longer. Workers in the United Kingdom get at least 24 paid holidays a year.

The United Kingdom uses a modern, mixed economy.

CASE STUDY REVIEW

1. **Drawing Conclusions** Why do work roles in a traditional economy tend to be limited?
2. **Summarizing** Why do market economies, like that of the United Kingdom, provide more consumer products than other types of economies?

CHAPTER 2 Case Study

C1 Critical Thinking Skills

Assessing life in the United States Ask students to consider what it's like to live an ordinary life in the United States. Draw a two-column chart on the board and write the questions that follow in the first column. Ask each question and guide students to arrive at a rating between 1 and 10 for each question, with 1 = poor and 10 = excellent. Record responses in the second column titled "Assessing Life in the U.S."

- How would you rate the availability of goods in the United States?
- How would you rate the likelihood, for the average American, of earning a living in the United States?
- How would you rate the quality of infrastructure (electricity, gas, clean drinking water, roadways)?
- How would you rate the average quality of housing in the United States?

Save student ratings. **Interpersonal**

C2 Critical Thinking Skills

Drawing conclusions about bartering Remind students that there is no common system of valuing goods in a barter system, so buyers and sellers must continually work out price negotiations. To give students an appreciation of the logistical difficulties of barter, list five daily items on the board—such as one gallon of milk, one gallon of gasoline, one loaf of bread, one downloadable song, and one book. Then have students negotiate the price of each item. For example, how many downloadable songs equal one gallon of milk? **Logical/Mathematical, Interpersonal**

C3 Critical Thinking Skills

Comparing nations Ask students to look again at the "Assessing Life in the U.S." chart they completed earlier. Add three more columns to the chart and have students answer the same four questions (with the same 1–10 ratings) about the Maori, North Korea, and the United Kingdom. Ask students to defend their ratings.

ANSWERS, p. 47

Case Study Review

1. Economies that focus on subsistence and are based on habit, rituals, and roles tend to provide limited and proscribed options for work.
2. In a market economy, if a product can be imagined, it is likely to be produced in hopes that people will buy it. Also, in a market economy, the choice one group makes does not affect the choices of other groups.

---

networks Online Teaching Options

INTERACTIVE FEATURE

Case Study: What Does Your Day Look Like?

Comparing and evaluating economic systems Display the Case Study and pause on the photograph of the Maori fisher. Ask students to read the text describing the Maori way of life and tell how it reflects a traditional economy. Continue in the same way for the North Korean command economy and the United Kingdom market economy.

Ask: Which country would you prefer to live in? Why? *(Most students will choose the United Kingdom because more goods would be available, and citizens would not have to work as hard merely to survive.)* **Visual/Spatial**

CHAPTER 2, LESSON 2
Mixed Economies

ENGAGE

C Critical Thinking Skills

Predicting advantages and disadvantages
Before students begin to study the lesson, ask them to work in pairs and write a definition for *mixed economy*. Then have students predict what they will learn in the text about the advantages and disadvantages of a mixed economy. Ask pairs to add their predictions under their definition. Remind students to check their predictions as they read the text. **Verbal/Linguistic**

Interact with these digital assets and others in lesson 2
- ✓ INTERACTIVE CHART — Characteristics of Mixed Economies
- ✓ INTERACTIVE WHITEBOARD — Spectrum of Mixed Economies
- ✓ SELF-CHECK QUIZ
- ✓ VIDEO

networks TRY IT YOURSELF ONLINE

Reading Help Desk

Academic Vocabulary
- allocation

Content Vocabulary
- mixed economies
- Great Depression
- communism

TAKING NOTES:

Key Ideas and Details
ACTIVITY Use a graphic organizer like the one below to identify the advantages and disadvantages of a mixed economy. Add lines and boxes as needed under each category.

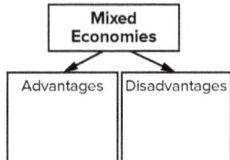

LESSON 2
Mixed Economies

ESSENTIAL QUESTION

How does an economic system help a society deal with the fundamental problem of scarcity?

Suppose your region experiences a scarcity of timber for building. In a mixed economy, what would you most likely see happen?

a. People would rely on the government to provide more timber.
b. Entrepreneurs would offer timber at high prices.
c. The government would redistribute timber from those who have a lot to those who don't have any.

C Even though there are several different kinds of economies, there are more **mixed economies**—economic systems where tradition, government, and markets each answer some of the WHAT, HOW, and FOR WHOM questions—than any other kind. Sometimes there is so much overlapping that it's hard to know exactly what kind of economy it is.

Characteristics of a Mixed Economy

GUIDING QUESTION *What makes an economy mixed?*

Textbooks like to use neat categories like traditional, market, and command or socialist economies; but the real world is not so orderly.

Why Mixed Economies Exist

Mixed economies exist for several reasons. One is that the three major types of economic systems identified by economists—traditional, command, and market—are extreme cases that are useful for classification and descriptive purposes, whereas there is much more diversity in the real world. A second reason for diversity is that a seismic domestic event like a revolution or a period of severe economic decline may invite change. A third reason is that nations tend to evolve over time, shedding some policies that do not work and adding new ones that do.

---

networks Online Teaching Options

BELLRINGER

Mixed Economies

Activating prior knowledge Use this activity to reveal students' prior knowledge of socialism and a mixed economy. Write these questions on the board and encourage a class discussion:

- What is the primary characteristic of socialism?
- Would you expect socialist countries to have high taxes or low taxes? Explain.
- What are some socialist countries?
- What, do you think, is a mixed economy?
- Is a mixed economy related to socialism? Explain.

Verbal/Linguistic

ANSWERS, p. 48

ESSENTIAL QUESTION ACTIVITY

Answer b is correct.
TAKING NOTES: Advantages: Can give flexibility in economic choices; can provide help for needy citizens; can let voters make decisions.
Disadvantages: Can cause higher taxes for social programs; can limit social services; can lower quality of services; can make government less efficient

Perhaps the most famous example of a revolution affecting economic change took place after Joseph Stalin's rise to power in Russia in 1929. Stalin's iron control of the political apparatus transformed a largely peasant and emerging industrial society into a massive command economy. By the 1950s, the Soviet Union was a major industrial and military superpower. Until its collapse in 1991, the economic success of the Soviet Union's socialist economy was something that many emerging countries copied, even though they may have started with significant components of traditional or market economy structures.

Meanwhile, well before the **Great Depression**—the worst period of economic decline in U.S. history that lasted from approximately 1929 to 1939—the United States had become a powerful industrial economy based on free market principles. Conditions were so harsh in the 1930s that a number of non-free market programs were created, including unemployment insurance, the minimum wage, Social Security, price supports in agriculture, and even bank deposit insurance. This was an example of a predominantly capitalistic market economy evolving into a mixed market economy, an evolution that took place because a democratic political system allowed people to demand changes to the way workers and consumers were treated.

The WHAT, HOW, and FOR WHOM Decisions

When we consider political parties and economic systems at the same time, the picture often becomes muddied. For example, the conventional name of North Korea is the Democratic People's Republic of Korea—despite the fact that there is no democracy there at all. The same is true for Laos, or the Lao People's Democratic Republic, which is also not a democracy because it is ruled by the communist Pathet Lao party.

mixed economies economic system that has some combination of traditional, command, and market economies; also see modified free enterprise economy

Great Depression worst period of economic decline in U.S. history, lasting from approximately 1929 to 1939

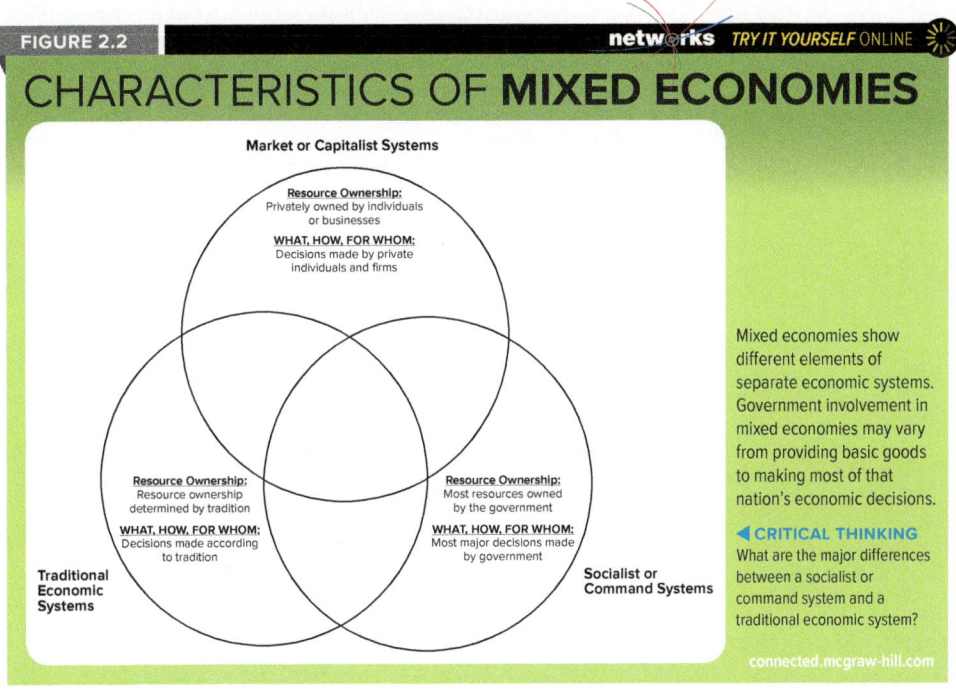

FIGURE 2.2
CHARACTERISTICS OF MIXED ECONOMIES

Mixed economies show different elements of separate economic systems. Government involvement in mixed economies may vary from providing basic goods to making most of that nation's economic decisions.

◀ **CRITICAL THINKING**
What are the major differences between a socialist or command system and a traditional economic system?

CHARTS

Characteristics of Mixed Economies

Identifying characteristics of mixed economies Have students view Figure 2.2 Characteristics of Mixed Economies. After reading the information about resource ownership and who makes the WHAT, HOW, and FOR WHOM decisions, students should drag each listed country into its correct placement on the diagram. Provide additional countries for students to categorize. **Visual/Spatial**

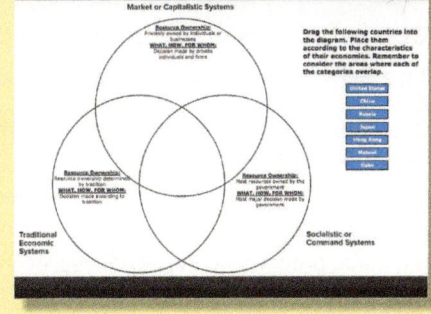

CHAPTER 2, LESSON 2
Mixed Economies

TEACH & ASSESS

C Critical Thinking Skills

Identifying traditional, command, and market features in the U.S. economic system Discuss the United States as a mixed economy. Point out that it combines elements of a traditional economy, command economy, and market economy. **Ask: What are some features of the traditional, command, and market economies in the United States?** *(Sample answers: traditional economy: some children follow parents' occupation; command economy: U.S. Postal Service, Social Security, Affordable Care Act; market economy: businesses that operate with minimal government interference)* **Logical/ Mathematical**

Content Background Knowledge

Social Security Act The Great Depression was a wake-up call for economists and government leaders who had taken a laissez-faire approach toward the economy. The old, the sick, and the poor were the hardest hit when the economy crashed. To help create a buffer for the elderly segment of the population, in 1935 the government passed the Social Security Act, which provided minimal levels of support for older Americans. Contributions were first collected in 1937, and benefits were first paid out in 1940. Today, Social Security is one of the most popular federal social programs, one that continues to provide security for older Americans and that is particularly important in times of economic downturns. In the 2007–2008 financial crisis, for example, many people lost their jobs and large portions of their retirement investments. Retired persons and those approaching retirement were particularly hard-hit by this development because they had little time to recoup those earnings. Social Security provided an important buffer that kept many from falling into poverty. Its creation was one of many steps the United States has taken towards becoming a mixed economy.

ANSWERS, p. 49

CRITICAL THINKING
In a socialist or command system, resources are owned by the government, and the government makes major economic decisions. In a traditional economic system, resource ownership and economic decisions are determined by the culture's traditions or customs.

CHAPTER 2, LESSON 2
Mixed Economies

W Writing Skills

Writing a persuasive essay about economic systems Have students write several paragraphs arguing why they believe that a market economy, command economy, or mixed economy is superior. Require students to use standard punctuation in their paragraphs. **BL Intrapersonal, Verbal/Linguistic**

C Critical Thinking Skills

Identifying socialist countries and services Have students conduct research to identify two countries that operate under socialism today and make a list of the basic services their governments provide. **Verbal/Linguistic**

ANSWERS, p. 50

☑ **READING PROGRESS CHECK** The main characteristics of a mixed economy include private individuals owning only some of the productive resources, while the government owns and uses the rest. In addition, government is involved in the economy in a regulatory capacity and in providing some safety net features for vulnerable citizens.

A nation's involvement in the three major economic decisions can vary considerably. Some countries have governments that intervene only in certain key industries and leave the rest to markets. Other countries have governments that intervene much more. In the case of socialism, the more socialist a country claims to be, the more likely the possibility that its government makes all of the three major economic decisions, often with the claim that they are made for the benefit of its people. When this happens, a mixed socialist economy can turn into a socialist command economy.

Often the distinguishing characteristics of a socialist economy is that it has one-party rule. The party that rules claims to make its decisions on behalf of all citizens, but it often makes decisions on behalf of the ruling party, which is why many socialist economies are also described as command economies.

Shared Characteristics of Mixed Economies

Because there are so many characteristics that a mixed economy can have, it is difficult to describe them all. However, some of the possible combinations are shown in **Figure 2.2**.

Perhaps the most distinguishing feature of a market or capitalist economy is the private ownership of productive resources and the freedom to use them as the owner sees fit. In this system, the **allocation** of these resources happens entirely in a free market comprised of self-directed individuals.

allocation distribution

Under socialism, private individuals own some of the productive resources, while the government owns and uses the rest. The extent of government-owned resources varies from one socialist country to the next, with most socialist countries being the ones with the most government ownership of resources. For example, in the former Soviet Union, none of the resources were privately owned because the government owned them all.

Yet another shared characteristic under socialism is that the more socialistic the country, the more likely the political system is to be communist. For example, four of the most socialistic countries today are Cuba, China, Laos, and Vietnam–all of which are communist and have no democracy.

In a traditional economy, almost all of the major decisions are made according to tradition, making progress and change very difficult. However, when people from a traditional economy come into contact with other cultures, they often adopt technologies and ways of doing things that can benefit them. When the Inuit of Northern Canada saw that rifles were more effective hunting tools than spears, rifles were readily accepted. Likewise, acceptance of markets and limited resource ownership may have been accepted in the same way.

The mixed economies would be represented by the overlapping segments in the center of the diagram in Figure 2.2. Those economies with the most significant components of markets and capitalism are likely to be the most economically developed of the group.

☑ **READING PROGRESS CHECK**

Explaining What are the main characteristics of a mixed economy?

Examples of Mixed Economies

GUIDING QUESTION *Why are most economies in the world today considered mixed economies?*

Mixed economies share characteristics with all three economic systems—market, socialist, and traditional. Even so, it is sometimes difficult to describe them as uniquely belonging to one type of economic system or another.

50

---

networks Online Teaching Options

INTERACTIVE WHITEBOARD ACTIVITIES

Characteristics of Socialism and Communism
The Spectrum of Mixed Economies

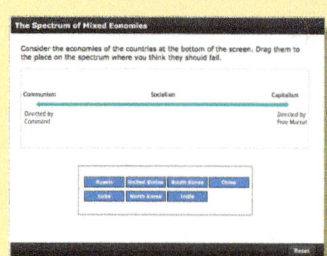

Categorizing mixed economies Display the interactive whiteboard activity, Characteristics of Socialism and Communism. Ask students to place the descriptions into the proper categories. Invite students to add more descriptors regarding property rights, incentives, economic freedom, competition, and the role of government. Then have students analyze and complete the Spectrum of Mixed Economies activity. **Interpersonal, Kinesthetic**

Communist Economies

The communist philosophy was first laid out by the economic historian and social scientist Karl Marx and his colleague Friedrich Engels in the 1800s. Marx viewed all of history as a class struggle between workers and property owners—a struggle that would lead to alternating periods of depression, such as the one the United States had in the 1930s, and periods of prosperity. Marx thought that the working class would eventually rise up and overthrow the property owners. Society would then eventually reach a theoretical ideal called **communism**, a state of economic and political affairs where everyone would contribute according to his or her abilities and consume according to his or her needs.

In this ideal community, no government would be needed and could therefore be eliminated. In order to get there, however, Marx thought that a society would pass through a period of socialism that would require a strong government that served the needs of the people. This is why so many of the so-called communist governments in China, the former Soviet Union, Cuba, and other places around the world frequently described themselves as being socialist, as if they were stepping-stones needed to reach the eventual ideal of communism.

In a communist system, labor is organized for the common advantage of the community, and everyone consumes according to his or her needs. In practice, however, communist governments have become so involved in dictating the everyday economic decisions of WHAT, HOW, and FOR WHOM that they are frequently called command economies.

As for a true communist economy, there are none in the world today, and there have never been any in the past. Communism still remains a theoretical ideal in the minds of many revolutionaries, even though in practice it has never been reached.

Mixed Socialism

According to Karl Marx, socialism is the stage of economic and political system necessary for a country to reach the ideal of communism. Under socialism, the government owns and controls some, but not all, of the basic productive resources. In most socialist economies, the government provides some of the basic needs of its people, such as education, jobs, transportation, and health care.

There are a number of mixed socialist economies today. China has a mixture of traditional, command, and market economies. While tradition has a strong influence in rural areas, the government makes many of the major economic decisions and owns the major factors of production.

Cuba and North Korea are similar to the former Soviet Union, where a socialist government once controlled almost all resources. The Soviet Union's ownership and control of resources were so extensive that some economists thought of the country as much of a command economy as it was a socialistic one.

Venezuela made a dramatic turn toward socialism when Hugo Chavez became president in 1999. He embarked on a policy of land and wealth redistribution, along with nationalization of domestic and even multinational corporations. Firms that were nationalized included telephone, electric utilities, leading steel companies, food processing plants, and even banks. Most of the nationalization was done by either confiscating or purchasing firms from their former owners. President Chavez died in 2013 before his nationalization was complete, leaving an economy that had a mix of socialism, capitalism, and tradition.

Mixed Market Economies

There are many examples of mixed market economies, especially in democratic countries, where people have the ability to influence the makeup of the economy. In Norway, the government owns the basic petroleum industry. It then uses the revenue from selling oil to other nations to keep its domestic gas prices low,

---

BIOGRAPHY

Karl Marx
ECONOMIC PHILOSOPHER
(1818–1883)

The German philosopher Karl Marx was the author of a pamphlet called *The Communist Manifesto*. In it he laid out ideas that would become known as Marxism. Later he wrote *Das Kapital*, in which he explained the theory of capitalism. Marx studied many philosophers and was drawn to some of the most radical groups. He later moved to Paris and spent time among the working classes. And although he thought they were "utterly crude and unintelligent," he liked how they worked together. In his manuscript from this time, he wrote, "The brotherhood of man is no mere phrase with them, but a fact of life, and the nobility of man shines upon us from their work-hardened bodies." This experience helped shape his ideas about how the working class would rise up and take control through revolution.

▲ **CRITICAL THINKING**
Making Inferences What did Marx see in the working class that made him think it had the power to rise up in revolution?

communism economic and political system in which factors of production are collectively owned and directed by the state; a theoretically classless society in which everyone works for the common good

---

CHAPTER 2, LESSON 2
Mixed Economies

R Reading Skills

Making connections between economies Have students summarize the goals and stages of communism. **Ask: How is the traditional economy of the nineteenth-century Inuit similar to the theoretical goals of communism?** *(The Inuit system provided for a sharing of food so that no one in the group would go hungry. Theoretically, communism operates the same way, allowing everyone to consume according to his or her needs.)*
AL Interpersonal, Logical/Mathematical

C Critical Thinking Skills

Drawing inferences about economies Ask students to identify the characteristics of the mixed socialist states of China, Cuba, North Korea, and the former Soviet Union. List student responses on the board. **Ask: If these countries provide important services and seek the good of the people, why do many people, especially those in Western countries, strongly oppose them?** *(Students may point to the limitations on economic and personal freedom. Mention also that the goods and services provided are usually substandard or limited by shortages for all citizens except those in the highest level of the ruling party.)* **BL** Logical/Mathematical

---

BIOGRAPHY

Karl Marx

Analyzing the philosophy of Karl Marx Have students read the biography of Karl Marx. Then divide students into groups to discuss these questions:

- Why do you think Marx became such an influential figure?
- Why were his ideas about the working class popular?
- Do you think these ideas still arouse interest among certain classes or groups of people?

After students discuss their answers to these questions, assemble the class and have groups share their ideas and conclusions. **Interpersonal, Verbal/Linguistic**

ANSWERS, p. 51

CRITICAL THINKING
Marx saw a brotherhood among the working class. Their loyalty to one another inspired him to believe they had great power.

CHAPTER 2, LESSON 2
Mixed Economies

R Reading Skills

Comparing mixed market economies Guide a discussion of the similarities and differences among the free enterprise system, socialism, and communism based on these basic characteristics of economic systems: property rights, incentives, economic freedom, competition, and the role of government. Then have students focus on the countries with mixed market economies. **Ask: What are one or two characteristics that countries with mixed market economies share?** *(social welfare programs, limited government involvement in industry, many free-market elements)* **Intrapersonal**

C Critical Thinking Skills

Hypothesizing about economies and political systems **Ask: Why do mixed economies seem to thrive more often in democracies than in less open societies?** *(People in democracies have a greater say in who controls resources and how much the government acts to support social programs.)* **What kinds of reasons might Chinese authorities and rulers of other command economies have for allowing increased private ownership of resources?** *(Possible answers: Private ownership of resources leads to the incentive to produce more, resulting in a larger tax base to support the state and state officials. Authorities may also want to avoid civil unrest.)*

This cartoon shows one of the disadvantages to a command economy.

▶ **CRITICAL THINKING**
Identifying Central Issues Which of the disadvantages of a command economy is shown here? Explain your answer.

finance education, maintain roads, and provide social welfare for its citizens. Because the government controls one major industry, it is a mixed economy based on capitalism and markets with some elements of socialism.

Sweden was once known as the "socialist state that works" because of its combination of a strong private economy and the broadest range of social programs in the free world. However, the population objected to the high taxes needed to support its social programs, so the country cut back on these expenditures in the 1980s. It is now a mixed market economy because it has not given up all of its socialist programs.

Because of generous welfare benefits in Denmark, Germany, and France, these countries also qualify as having mixed market economies. In fact, any country that provides significant welfare benefits would qualify, especially if the benefits received by citizens were paid for with taxpayer's money. South Korea, India, and Thailand also have mixed economies that combine traditional economies with elements of command and market economies.

Finally, the United States also falls into the category of being a mixed market economy. This is because many of our free market features are combined with traditional and socialist elements. As for tradition, many children follow their parents into their parents' occupations. As for elements of socialism, the United States has federal programs that make disability payments to people injured on the job or programs that provide nationwide health and retirement payments to millions of people. Programs like these apply to large groups and are paid for with taxpayer dollars but the programs by themselves do not make the United States a socialist economy.

☑ **READING PROGRESS CHECK**

Explaining How can you explain the range of mixed economies in the world?

Evaluating Mixed Economies

GUIDING QUESTION *Which members of society benefit from a mixed economy?*

Mixed economies are a fact of life and can be found all over the globe, and they offer advantages and disadvantages to those who live in them.

52

networks Online Teaching Options

VIDEO WORKSHEET

Communist Russia, A Great Economic Experiment

Analyzing a video about Communist Russia
As students view the video *Communist Russia, A Great Economic Experiment*, ask them to study the phases Russia underwent when the economy was taken over by Communists, and then again when the Soviet Union collapsed. When they finish watching the video, ask them to summarize the phases and their changes. Ask them whether they think the last part of the title, "A Great Economic Experiment," is an accurate description of what Russia underwent. **Verbal/Linguistic**

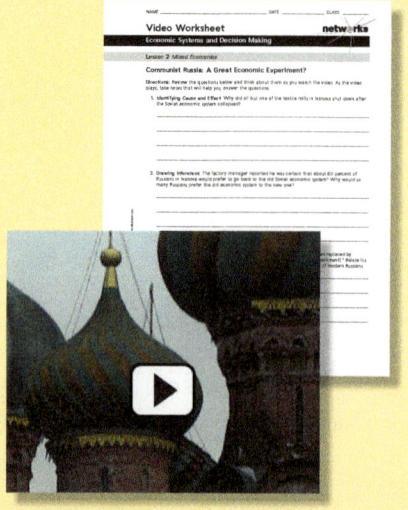

ANSWERS, p. 52

CRITICAL THINKING
The disadvantage shown is that of lack of choice. Because the consumer's desires are not impacting production decisions, consumers do not have as many choices as in a mixed economy.

☑ **READING PROGRESS CHECK** The range of mixed economies in the world is due to the extent to which each of the economies has characteristics of market, socialist, and traditional systems.

Advantages of Mixed Economies

Countries that have mixed economies seem to have them because of the benefits the mixed components offer. For example, during the 1970s China's economic growth was poor in comparison with its neighboring countries Japan, South Korea, and Hong Kong. Shortly after Chairman Mao Zedong's death in 1976, China's leaders undertook a modernization of China's economy that involved a heavy dose of capitalism, or "capitalism with Chinese characteristics" as it was often described.

China became one of the fastest growing economies in the world and, according to the U.S. Central Intelligence Agency, the world's largest economy. To maintain its growth, China has endorsed various capitalist measures such as markets, competition, profit, and international trade. Still, China is controlled by its communist party, and the government owns all factors of production.

These changes would not have happened if they did not benefit Chinese authorities, so the fact that they are happening is evidence that they are beneficial to its leadership. Similar changes are also happening all over the world, including the countries of North Korea, Cuba, and even in the former Soviet Union.

The advantages of mixed economies are not restricted to communist-controlled command economies. In the democratic countries of northern Europe, countries like Sweden, Denmark, Germany, and Norway have maintained extensive socialistic programs that offer generous education, employment, and health benefits even though their economies are based on capitalism and free markets. In the United States, socialist-sounding programs like widespread health insurance exist side-by-side with competitive markets and the ownership of private property.

Disadvantages of Mixed Economies

Mixed economies with a strong component of socialism tend to provide more services to consumers than do traditional command economies. For example, Germany and the Scandinavian countries offer a wide range of social benefits that includes medical coverage, free education, and even generous vacation time. The problem is that these programs are not free, so the countries must find a way to pay for them.

One way to cover the costs of these programs is through taxation. As a result, personal income taxes are higher in almost all major European countries than they are in the United States. The other way to cover these costs is to produce less of something else. So, the cost of generous welfare programs can be absorbed by shifting resources away from other projects.

✓ **READING PROGRESS CHECK**

Identifying Who are the people that benefit from the structure of a mixed economy?

LESSON 2 REVIEW

Reviewing Vocabulary
1. *Defining* Explain in your own words the allocation of goods under the ideal of communism. Name some countries that display elements of communism in their economies.

Using Your Notes
2. *Explaining* Use your notes to cite details that support the idea that mixed economies have both advantages and disadvantages.

Answering the Guiding Questions
3. *Explaining* What makes an economy mixed?
4. *Evaluating* Why are most economies in the world today considered mixed economies?
5. *Describing* Which members of society benefit from a mixed economy?

Writing About Economics
6. *Persuasive/Explanatory* Research the term *scarcity*. In a five-paragraph essay, define scarcity and explain why scarcity can be considered a fundamental problem in an economy. Next write a persuasive essay taking a position on the following statement: *Scarcity is the primary driving force behind a movement away from socialist and command economies and toward a mixed economy.* Give examples from the lesson to explain your answer.

CHAPTER 2, LESSON 2
Mixed Economies

W Writing Skills

Presenting a panel discussion about China Ask students to work in groups to research the economic changes that have taken place in China during the past twenty years. Have them plan and present a panel discussion on their findings. Remind students to evaluate the validity of economic information from secondary sources for propaganda. Encourage students to include graphs and other visuals in their panel discussions. **BL** Interpersonal, Kinesthetic

R Reading Skills

Assessing socialism Ask: **Why might socialism be less efficient than capitalism?** *(Possible answers: People are not rewarded for hard work. Central planners cannot efficiently make the number of economic decisions needed to serve current population levels.)* Logical/Mathematical

CLOSE & REFLECT

R Reading Skills

Summarizing the lesson Have students analyze the economic information of this lesson by creating a summary outline, using the main heads to organize their details.

ANSWERS, p. 53

✓ **READING PROGRESS CHECK** A mixed economy can benefit both the government and people who are in need of assistance, such as the elderly and the sick.

LESSON 2 REVIEW ANSWERS

Reviewing Vocabulary
1. Students should note that under communism, goods are distributed to all people, and everyone consumes according to their needs. Cuba, Laos, North Korea, and Vietnam are some of the countries students can mention while answering this question.

Using Your Notes
2. Advantages of a mixed economy: grows faster and protects the most vulnerable citizens; Disadvantages of mixed economy: cost of services leads to high taxes

Answering the Guiding Questions
3. When one type of economy comes in contact with another type of economy, a government adjusts to economic demands from the market and from citizens.
4. Most economies are considered mixed because most have some portion of the means of production under government control. Most economic systems also have some element of the market or capitalism.
5. The most vulnerable members of society benefit from a mixed economy because they are offered some social safety net.

Writing About Economics
6. Students should write that scarcity is a situation that arises because people have unlimited wants but limited resources. Their persuasive essay should take a clear side on the issue of the role scarcity plays in a move away from socialism and toward market economic systems.

CHAPTER 2
Debate

ENGAGE

C1 Critical Thinking Skills

Evaluating the costs of health care Initiate a discussion of the cost of health care, helping students to recognize that the cost is high and can affect people in many different ways. Begin the discussion by asking questions such as:

- What happens when someone is seriously sick or injured?
- Who pays for this medical care?
- What happens if someone cannot afford the treatment and does not have insurance?

Ask students to consider reasons for saving part of their paycheck each payday. Then have them prioritize those reasons or these uses of savings: to purchase a house, to pay for college, to buy a car, to cover unexpected medical costs. (Most students will not be saving for medical issues.) **Ask: Why do most young people not save for health care?** *(Most young people view health insurance as an expensive luxury they can do without.)* **Interpersonal**

TEACH & ASSESS

C2 Critical Thinking Skills

Evaluating the government's role in health care Divide the class into two teams and assign each team the Yes or the No side of the issue debated in the feature. Allow the teams to meet and discuss their arguments. Urge them to list facts, evidence, reasons, and other arguments that support their position. Encourage them to consider counterarguments as well. Then ask teams to debate the topic in class. Limit the time each team has to present their supporting arguments and in rebuttal. Have the class vote on the winner of the debate.

C3 Critical Thinking Skills

Identifying perspectives Have students interview a family member, their doctor, a businessperson, or a political leader about the role the government should play in health care. Explain that their purpose is to gather information that reflects another point of view. Tell students to prepare ahead of time by writing a list of questions. Have students write a summary of their interview and then share their results in class discussion.

Debates

C1 Should government provide health care?

Some 47 million Americans currently live without insurance to cover their health care costs. About 80 percent of them come from poor working families. Just 2 percent of the uninsured, mostly young adults, have no health insurance. The prevailing view among this age group is that health insurance is a luxury they can do without.

C3
Most Americans agree that everyone should have access to affordable health coverage. They disagree on how to make that happen. Some reformers call for government-paid health care funded by taxes. Others believe that free market compeition driven by consumer choice can deliver health care at the lowest possible cost. The role government should play in providing health coverage for all Americans remains a controversial issue, despite the fact that every other industrialized nation has some form of universal insurance. While examining each position on whether the government should provide health care, analyze and evaluate the validity of the statements for propaganda. Be sure to also consider the debaters' frame of reference when evaluating their arguments.

C2
YES The government should provide health care.

- MORE PEOPLE WOULD HAVE ACCESS TO AFFORDABLE HEALTH CARE.
- MORE PEOPLE WOULD RECEIVE CARE BEFORE SERIOUS PROBLEMS DEVELOP THAT ARE EXPENSIVE TO TREAT.
- HEALTH CARE WILL BECOME MORE EFFICIENT.
- HEALTH CARE WILL BE LESS EXPENSIVE.

> Medicare could pay 30 percent less to doctors and hospitals and everybody would get better. But it won't happen on its own because one person's waste is another person's revenue stream. That's why we need a cop on the beat, and the only cop with the clout to get the healthcare industry to play by the rules is the federal government.
>
> —Art Kellermann, Associate Dean for Health Policy, Emory University

Where Americans Get Their Health Insurance
- UNINSURED 16%
- OTHER PUBLIC PLANS 1%
- MEDICARE 13%
- MEDICAID 16%
- INDIVIDUAL POLICY 5%
- EMPLOYER'S INSURANCE PLAN 49%

Source: The Kaiser Family Foundation

54

---

networks Online Teaching Options

DEBATE

Debate: Should government provide health care?

Analyzing health care Display the Debate activity and invite students to speculate how people who fall into the uninsured category pay their health care costs. **Ask: What happens if people cannot afford to pay their health care bills?** *(Answers will vary, but students may mention bankruptcy or heavy borrowing, and should recognize that these actions can have serious effects on the individual and his or her family. In addition, many people who previously could not afford health insurance used emergency room facilities, the costs of which were covered by taxpayer dollars.)* Then lead the class in examining the line graph. Encourage a discussion of the trends, their causes, and whether or not they represent a positive or a negative development. Have students give reasons for their opinions. **Visual/Spatial**

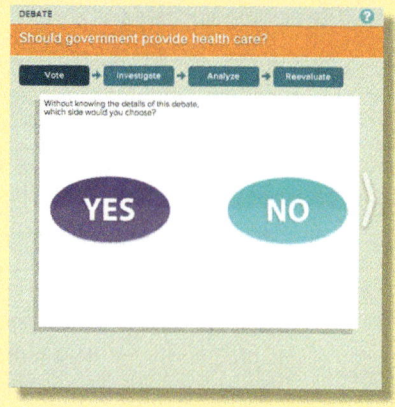

> *Imagine that you paid a set annual fee to get all your meat and fish at one market, and there was no limit on what you could take for your use. The easiest way for the grocer to keep costs in line with annual fees and discourage waste, abuse, or overuse would be to ration availability.... This same form of rationing is often used in government single-payer health care systems by limiting the number of costly medical procedures available and forcing patients to get on a waiting list for them.*

—From Clare Boothe Luce Policy Institute's Policy Express Paper, "Who Should Pay for Health Care?" by Sally Pipes

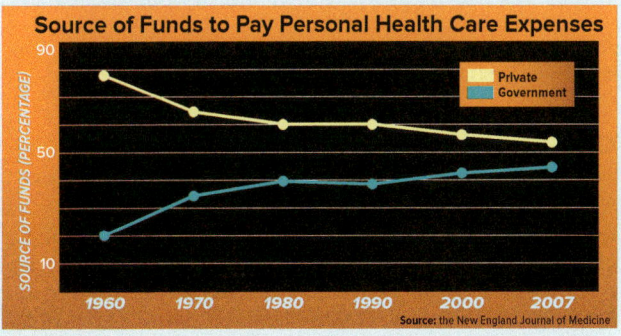

ANALYZING the issue

1. **Analyzing Visuals** How has the source of funds used to pay for Americans' health care changed in the last 50 years? Does this trend argue for or against government-paid health care?

2. **Exploring Issues** How do you think government-paid health care would affect the cost of health care and access to it? Explain why.

3. **Evaluating** In each argument, do you feel there is use of propaganda to compel people to one position or the other?

CHAPTER 2
Debate

English Language Proficiency

Intermediate List new expressions such as common idioms that are used during classroom instruction and interactions. In addition, write these phrases from the Debate's primary sources on the board: "cop on the beat," "play by the rules," "get on a waiting list." Have students illustrate each idiom using the literal meaning of its words and its actual common meaning.

CLOSE & REFLECT

C Critical Thinking Skills

Exploring issues Remind students that the government's role in health care has had a long history and includes legislation such as Medicare and Medicaid. Despite these developments, the debate continues. Guide students in discussing why this issue is so difficult to resolve. List their ideas on the board.

ANSWERS, p. 55

ANALYZING the issue

1. Although private funds remain the main source of payment, it is declining as a percentage, and government payment is increasing. Some may argue that this trend supports a move to a government-paid system, while others may argue that it is no reason to completely abandon private payment. Either argument should demonstrate reasoned judgment.

2. Some may contend that government-provided health care would be cheaper because private insurance companies would not be involved. Others might argue that government inefficiencies might raise the costs of care. Some may claim that if everyone had government-provided insurance, access to care would increase because people could afford to get treatment. Others may contend that such improved access would lead to rationing.

3. Some may favor government-paid insurance, while others may oppose it. In either case, arguments should draw on the points raised in the debate and show reasoned judgment in evaluating them, as well as how the use of propaganda may influence a person's opinion one way or another.

GRAPHIC ORGANIZER

Problem-Solution

Discussing solutions to problems in health care Organize students into groups of three or four and give each group the graphic organizer. Ask them to follow these steps in completing the activity:

1. Brainstorm a list of problems associated with the health care industry.
2. Choose the three biggest problems and enter them on the problem-solution chart.
3. Discuss the solution to each problem. Some problems may have more than one solution.
4. Enter the solutions the group suggests for each problem on the chart.

Have groups share their ideas with the class. **Interpersonal, Visual/Spatial**

Economic Systems and Decision Making **55**

CHAPTER 2, LESSON 3
The Global Transition to Capitalism

ENGAGE

C Critical Thinking Skills

🔔 **Inferring outcomes of transitioning economies** Before students begin the lesson, ask them to list some reasons that countries with command and socialist economies are shifting to capitalist economies. **Ask:** *Do you think this transition will be easy or quick? Why or why not?* (Answers will vary, but students may mention the difficulties of shifting to capitalist economies that allow more personal freedom but fewer services provided by government.)

ANSWERS, p. 56

ESSENTIAL QUESTION ACTIVITY

Help students understand the two main choices inherent in the questions. Expanding production of smart phones may require a large, time-consuming adjustment to the factory, whereas increasing the price of the smart phones is a quick decision that could reduce the shortage in the short run. Guide students to understand than an increased price, however, will also cause some customers to purchase smart phones elsewhere. These same customers may not return to buy students' smart phones after their factory expansion is completed. Point out that these are the types of decisions and choices new capitalist countries face.

TAKING NOTES: Russia: restructured the economy, gave more independence to businesses, and encouraged small businesses; privatized through vouchers; created a stock market. **China:** privatized some industries, introduced market reforms, gave more independence to state-owned companies. **Chile:** privatized airlines and utilities; used pension funds to give capital to new businesses; increased foreign trade. **Japan:** developed a loyal, dedicated workforce; developed new technologies, improved productivity through capital-intensive methods; subsidizes certain industries to help make them competitive. **South Korea:** opened its markets to world trade; focused on gaining experience in a few industries at a time, slowly expanding from toys to textiles to heavy industry and automobiles.

Interact with these digital assets and others in lesson 3
- ✓ INTERACTIVE IMAGE — Manufacturing in South Korea
- ✓ SLIDESHOW — The European Union
- ✓ SELF-CHECK QUIZ
- ✓ VIDEO

networks TRY IT YOURSELF ONLINE

LESSON 3
The Global Transition to Capitalism

Reading Help Desk

Academic Vocabulary
- undertaking
- isolationism

Content Vocabulary
- GDP per capita
- privatization
- vouchers
- Five-Year Plan
- Gosplan
- collectivization
- perestroika
- Great Leap Forward
- nationalization
- Solidarity
- European Union (EU)
- black market
- capital-intensive
- *keiretsu*
- population density

TAKING NOTES:

Key Ideas and Details
ACTIVITY Use a graphic organizer like this one to list how governments promote economic growth in capitalist and transitional countries.

How Governments Promote Growth

Country	
Russia	
China	
Chile	
Japan	
South Korea	

ESSENTIAL QUESTION

How does an economic system help a society deal with the fundamental problem of scarcity?

Suppose you run a company that makes and sells smart phones. If the stores in which your phones are sold cannot stock enough phones to meet customer demand, what would you do? Would you produce more phones or fewer phones? Would you change the price of your phones? Explain your decisions.

The dominant economic trend of our lifetime has been the transition of communist and socialist economic systems to capitalism. It has been a transition of epic proportions, and it shows few signs of slowing down. As countries make the transition, the final form of capitalism they adopt will reflect many of their own cultural and social values. That is one reason why so many different faces of capitalism exist in the world today.

Some of the former transitioning countries, such as Chile, Russia, and the former Soviet bloc countries of Eastern Europe, have almost completed their transition to capitalism. Because of their previous history as command or socialist countries, however, the **GDP per capita**, or GDP per person, in those countries is still lower than those in other capitalist countries.

Problems of Transition

GUIDING QUESTION *In what ways does the mind-set of a country's citizens have to change in order to transition to capitalism?*

 When an economy becomes large and complex, a capitalist market-based system is the most efficient way to organize production and provide the necessary economic incentives. Even so, economies that are not capitalist often find that the transition to capitalism is difficult.

56

---

networks *Online Teaching Options*

BELLRINGER

Global Transition to Capitalism

Activating prior knowledge about capitalist countries Discuss the questions on the Bellringer. Ask students to identify the specific countries moving to capitalism as shown on the map. Then ask students to select several countries shown as NOT moving to capitalism on the Bellringer, particularly countries in the regions of South Asia, Southeast Asia, Southwest Asia, and Africa. Have students research to learn what types of economies some of these countries have. **Visual/Spatial**

Why Capitalism?

Simply put, capitalism is the most powerful engine for generating wealth the world has ever seen. Because of capitalism, countries or regions as culturally diverse as Germany, Japan, Singapore, South Korea, Sweden, the United States, and the special administrative region of Hong Kong have greatly increased their productivity and have experienced exceptional economic growth.

This growth has improved nearly everyone's standard of living, the quality of life based on the ownership of necessities and luxuries that make life easier. In a world that is becoming increasingly connected by the media, people everywhere are aware of—and even begin to want—some of the wealth that capitalism in other countries can generate.

In contrast, the collapse of the Soviet Union indicates that communism as an economic system has reached an evolutionary dead end. Pure capitalism can be harsh and may not be attractive to everyone, but in democratic nations, people can modify capitalism to meet more of their economic and social goals. However, there is no guarantee that countries attempting a transition to capitalism will be able to do it smoothly, or that they can do it at all. This is because there are so many hurdles to negotiate.

Privatization of State-Owned Property

A key feature of capitalism is the ownership of private property. In order for the transition to capitalism to take place, **privatization**, or the conversion of state-owned factories and other property to private ownership, must be accomplished. Privatization is important because entrepreneurs want to be rewarded for **undertaking** business ventures involving risk. Private property is also important because people take better care of property they actually own.

In Poland, Hungary, and the Czech Republic, this transition was accomplished by using vouchers. **Vouchers** were certificates that could be used to purchase government-owned property. In practice, vouchers were either given to the citizens of a country or sold at very low prices. State-owned companies could then be converted to corporations, and the corporate stock could be auctioned for vouchers. As vouchers were exchanged for certificates of ownership, the ownership of state-owned enterprises was transferred to private hands.

Loss of Political Power

Under communism, the Communist Party was the ruling class. When countries transitioned to capitalism, the party feared that it would lose much of its political power as a new class of entrepreneurs and capitalists took over.

In countries such as Czechoslovakia, Hungary, and Poland, the Communist Party leaders who were ousted from office lost their power before their country's industry was privatized. In these countries, the voucher system worked reasonably well to redistribute wealth to new leaders.

In other countries, Communist leaders grabbed a large share of vouchers and thus a large portion of ownership in many privatized companies. In the most blatant cases, some of which occurred in Russia after the collapse of the Soviet Union, the ownership of companies was directly transferred to politicians who were influential during the transition period.

As a result, former political leaders traded their political power for economic power in the form of resource ownership, and so the old ruling group simply became the new ruling group. In the case of Russia, the members of the old ruling party had a difficult time actually giving up their power.

GDP per capita gross domestic product on a per person basis; can be expressed in current or constant dollars

privatization conversion of state-owned factories and other property to private ownership

undertaking entering into an activity

vouchers certificates that could be used to purchase government-owned property during privatization

Economic Systems and Decision Making 57

CHAPTER 2, LESSON 3
The Global Transition to Capitalism

TEACH & ASSESS

R Reading Skills

Demonstrating understanding of vouchers Ask: **What are two goods or services that vouchers are used for in the United States?** *(Possible answers: food [food stamps], schools, and housing in some areas; gift cards are a form of voucher)* **BL**
Verbal/Linguistic

C Critical Thinking Skills

Making inferences about transitioning to capitalism Ask: **Why might nations resist making the transition to capitalism?** *(Possible answers: government leaders fear a loss of political power and control over the population; fear of economic chaos during the transition; difficulty of losing the mindset of devotion to anti-capitalist ideology)*
Verbal/Linguistic

W Writing Skills

Writing a narrative Have students use reliable print or online sources to research the story of an individual who lived in an Eastern European nation during the fall of communism. Ask students to write a narrative story based on that individual and how he or she adjusted during the transition to a new economic system. Remind students to base their fictional story on facts about the time period. Require students to use standard grammar in their narratives. **Verbal/Linguistic**

VIDEO **WORKSHEET**

The Silk Road

Understanding China's transition to a new economy Have students view the video. Guide students in discussing the challenges and incentives experienced by the Chinese people while transitioning from a command to a capitalist economy. Have students do additional research to learn about the historic Silk Road. Ask them to report on how it affected both China and other parts of Asia and Europe. Have them compare and contrast what is happening in China today with the impact of the Silk Road many centuries ago. **Visual/Spatial**

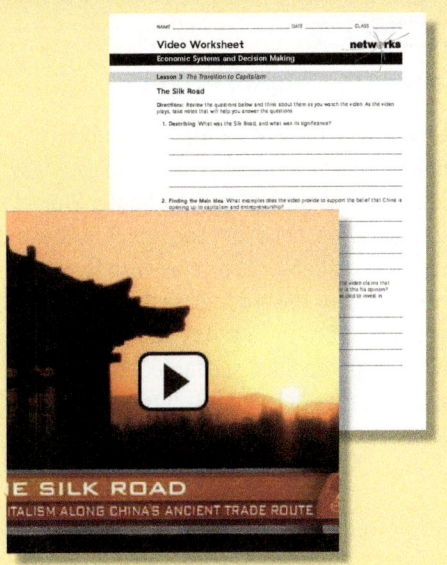

CHAPTER 2, LESSON 3
The Global Transition to Capitalism

R1 Reading Skills

Determining desirable qualities for transitioning
Ask: *According to the text, what qualities should people in nations making the transition to capitalism develop? (Answers may include patience, perseverance, and self-reliance.)*
BL Logical/Mathematical

W Writing Skills

Writing about the Five-Year Plan Instruct students to consult reliable print or online sources to research Joseph Stalin's first Five-Year Plan in the Soviet Union. Ask students to write a report explaining the historical context, goals, and results of the plan.
BL Verbal/Linguistic

R2 Reading Skills

Defining *glasnost* Inform students that in addition to *perestroika*, Gorbachev also introduced *glasnost* policy in the Soviet Union. Have students research the meaning of that word and write a paragraph explaining how glasnost influenced the economic changes that occurred during the final years of the Soviet Union. **BL** Verbal/Linguistic

---

ANSWERS, p. 58

✓ **READING PROGRESS CHECK** State-owned properties must be privatized. People must adjust to a different set of incentives.

58

Responding to New Incentives

People in countries that transition to capitalism have to adjust to a whole new set of incentives. They have to learn how to make decisions on their own, take initiative, interpret prices, and fend for themselves in free markets. Many of these adjustments are enormous, often even prohibitive.

For example, workers used to getting the same salary regardless of how hard or how often they come to work have to learn that they will get fired if they do a poor job. Factory managers have to learn to pay back loans they took out from banks, and they have to learn to pay their bills on time.

Underestimating the Costs

Too many countries that want the advantages of capitalism focus on its benefits, but they don't fully consider its costs. Yet the costs can hinder or even prevent a country's successful transition.

The costs of capitalism during the Great Depression, for example, included instability, unemployment, and social unrest. At that time, the United States did not have the economic policies and social welfare programs needed to lessen the devastation. Now that such assistance exists in the United States, most economists agree that another Great Depression will not occur here.

The same cannot be said for the countries in transition. They have not yet developed the automatic stabilizers and the social welfare nets that cushion the instabilities of capitalism. During transition, nations will experience the instabilities of early capitalism long before they experience the benefits.

✓ **READING PROGRESS CHECK**

Summarizing What are the main problems for a nation transitioning to capitalism?

Countries and Regions in Transition

GUIDING QUESTION *What are the common features of the transition to capitalism?*

Despite the transitional problems, most nations and regions all over the globe are moving toward capitalism. Some have a little further to go than others, but may eventually get there; others appear to have gone about as far as they ever will go.

Russia

To see why the transition to capitalism has been so difficult for Russia, it helps to understand how the economy was managed during the Soviet era. During that period, the government controlled economic activity with Five-Year Plans. The first **Five-Year Plan**—a comprehensive, centralized economic plan designed to achieve rapid industrialization—was introduced by Joseph Stalin in 1927.

The **Gosplan** was the central authority that devised the plans and directed overall economic activity. It tried to manage the economy by assigning production quotas to all Soviet industries. Central planning also extended to agriculture with the introduction of **collectivization**—the forced common ownership of all agricultural and industrial enterprises. Planners then sought to ensure the growth of the economy simply by increasing the quotas given to the farms and factories.

Despite its efforts, central planning eventually failed. The Soviet economy had become too complex and large to be managed by a single planning bureaucracy. Shortages appeared everywhere, workers were often unpaid, and many people lacked the incentives to work.

After Mikhail Gorbachev assumed power in 1985, he introduced **perestroika**, the restructuring of the Soviet economy. Under the restructuring, plant managers had more freedom to pursue profits, and small business was encouraged.

Five-Year Plan comprehensive, centralized economic plan used by the Soviet Union and China to coordinate development of agriculture and industry

Gosplan central planning authority in the former Soviet Union that devised and directed Five-Year Plans

collectivization forced common ownership of factors of production; used in the former Soviet Union in agriculture and manufacturing

perestroika fundamental restructuring of the Soviet economy; policy introduced by Gorbachev

58

---

networks Online Teaching Options

WORKSHEETS

Hands-On Chapter Project

Researching and reporting on economic systems Divide students into groups and have them complete the Hands-On Chapter Project titled "Location, Location, Location." Follow the discussion guidelines. You may wish to direct more questions toward their research into transitioning economies. Ask students if they have considered the disadvantages as well as the advantages of locating a business in these economies. **Interpersonal**

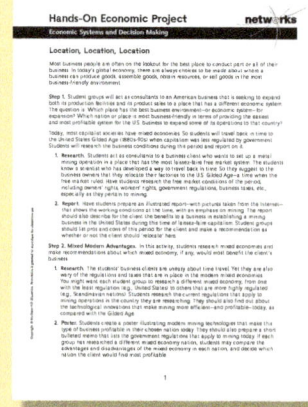

Gorbachev's successor, Russian president Boris Yeltsin, accelerated privatization after the fall of the Soviet Union. The government distributed vouchers to citizens so that they could purchase ownership shares in companies being privatized. Eventually Russia opened a stock market, which made the ownership of capital by private individuals a reality in a country that once preached the evils of private property.

Under the first regime of President Vladimir Putin, privatization began to slow. Under the guise of fighting corruption, Putin used his power to regain centralized control of key energy and mineral industries. The period of transition to capitalism is now over for Russia. Under the second presidency of Putin, the country can be described as having a market-based economy with the exception of energy, natural resource, and defense-related industries, which the government controls.

China

The People's Republic of China became a communist economy in 1949. That year the Chinese Communist Party, under the leadership of Mao Zedong, gained control of the country. Over the next few decades, China modeled itself after the Soviet Union, adopting a series of Five-Year Plans to manage its growth.

In 1958 Chinese leaders instituted the **Great Leap Forward**, an attempt to revolutionize industrial and agricultural production almost overnight. This ambitious and radical Five-Year Plan forced farmers off their land to live and work on large, state-owned communal farms.

The Great Leap Forward was a disaster. The agricultural experiment failed, and the economy never came close to achieving the planned degree of industrialization. Other plans followed, but by the late 1970s China finally decided to abandon the Soviet model.

By the early 1980s, the influence of other successful market economies in Asia—especially in Hong Kong—was too much for China to ignore. Guangdong Province, one of China's provinces just north of Hong Kong, copied many of the free market practices of the region and was even allowed to officially experiment with capitalism.

Today China is privatizing some industries, introducing market reforms, and otherwise acting in a capitalistic manner. The progress made so far is remarkable as it now is the world's largest economy. China's transition was made possible because of its willingness to replace communist ideology and control with capitalistic practices.

China's transition to capitalism is not yet complete; it has implemented the reforms on a gradual basis and still has a long way to go. Many prices are still regulated and many industries are state owned, although many state-owned firms have been given more autonomy.

Great Leap Forward
China's second Five-Year Plan, begun in 1958, which forced collectivization of agriculture and rapid industrialization

In this photo, Chinese shoppers look for good bargains at a store. The shift toward a market-based system has given shoppers like these more choices and more ways to spend their earnings.

▼ **CRITICAL THINKING**
What are some of the benefits and challenges that people in China face now that their economy is becoming more market-based?

CHAPTER 2, LESSON 3
The Global Transition to Capitalism

C Critical Thinking Skills

Comparing economic plans Ask: **How were Joseph Stalin's economic plans and Mao Zedong's economic plans similar?** *(Both included five-year plans, both wanted to rapidly industrialize, both featured planning and common ownership, and both eventually failed.)* **Logical/Mathematical**

English Language Proficiency

Intermediate Encourage students to communicate by defining or describing when exact English words are not known. Model examples such as, "If I did not know the word for *privatization*, I might call it 'taking factories owned by government and giving them to private citizens.'" When students use such circumlocutions, provide the missing word and encourage them to practice it.

IMAGES

Adjusting to Economic Change

Visualizing China's transition to a new economy Have students view the image. Guide students in comparing and contrasting the situation shown with the same type of event in the United States. *(The situation shown—the group of shoppers in a department store—is no different than a department store in the United States, except that prices are in yuan instead of dollars.)* **Visual/Spatial**

ANSWERS, p. 59

CRITICAL THINKING
Benefits include the incentive to gain profits and improve standard of living, a greater variety of products available, and more economic freedom. Challenges include some remaining price regulations, continued state-owned firms, pollution and other environmental problems, and the challenges inherent in having to learn to think and act independently regarding purchasing and other economic decisions.

CHAPTER 2, LESSON 3
The Global Transition to Capitalism

R Reading Skills

Using academic vocabulary Ask: How might a policy of isolationism affect a nation's economic development? *(Answers may include limited foreign investment, fewer grants from other nations, and less trade with other nations.)* **BL Verbal/Linguistic**

EXPLORING THE ESSENTIAL QUESTION

Imagine that you are an industrial worker in a city in China. What would you put in an e-mail to a relative in the United States explaining how China's transition to capitalism is affecting your work and your daily life?

isolationism national policy of avoiding international alliances and economic interactions

At the same time, China is faced with some problems that may slow its growth. The population is aging, which will eventually leave the country with a shortage of younger workers. Pollution of the air and water is another major problem, and was so severe that China had to take drastic steps to reduce air pollution during the Beijing Olympic Games in 2008. To reduce air pollution, approximately 300,000 heavy trucks were banned during the Olympics, while half of the city's 3.5 million vehicles were only allowed to drive every other day. Plus, in 2013, over 13,000 dead and decaying pigs were discovered floating down a major river that flowed into Shanghai. Even though the river supplies the city with about one-fifth of its water supply, government officials described the water quality as being "normal."

Latin America

In the past, many Latin American countries followed a path of economic development that combined socialism and **isolationism**. Chile, however, took major steps to foster the growth of capitalism when it privatized airlines, telephone services, and utilities. The country even used the billions deposited in its pension funds to supply capital to new entrepreneurs. As a result, many industries prospered, and Chile now exports copper, paper and pulp, fruit, and chemicals.

Today Chile has one of the strongest market-oriented economies in the region. It is extensively engaged in foreign trade and has some of the strongest financial institutions in the region. The conversion to a free market economy is now complete and has been a resounding success.

THE GLOBAL ECONOMY & YOU

Confronting Pollution

The rapid industrial growth that has accompanied China's transition to capitalism is the reason that China has overtaken the United States as the world's largest economy. However, this growth has caused China many of the problems the United States faced when it industrialized more than a century ago. Among the most troubling is pollution.

Some 70 percent of the energy that powers China's industries comes from burning coal. The resulting air pollution kills almost 500,000 people annually. Sixteen of the world's 20 most polluted cities are in China. In addition, the water in nearly two-thirds of China's cities is severely polluted by toxic chemicals and other contaminants. Although China has recently strengthened its environmental-protection laws, the nation's local governments often ignore them for fear that complying will stifle economic growth.

Coal also fueled U.S. industrialization in the late 1800s. The resulting smoke darkened the skies of the nation's major cities. In the United States, the first air pollution laws appeared on the local level. Pittsburgh passed a smoke-reduction law in 1869 and Cincinnati did so in 1881. But as in China, they were not enforced. Not until 1955, after 20 people died and nearly 7,000 became seriously ill in an incident in Pennsylvania, did Congress pass the first federal law to control air pollution.

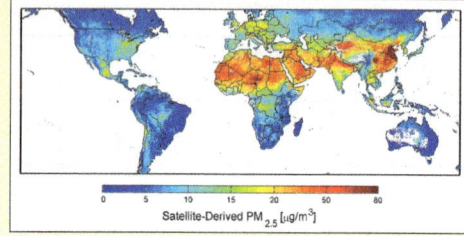

Satellite-Derived PM$_{2.5}$ [μg/m³]

The United States once faced a water pollution problem not unlike the one in China today. In the late 1800s, U.S. factories began dumping chemicals and other industrial wastes into the nation's waterways. But here, too, the federal government was slow to act. Not until a highly polluted river in Cleveland actually caught fire in 1969 was Congress motivated to respond with the nation's first water-pollution control law in 1972.

▲ **CRITICAL THINKING**
Hypothesizing Why might environmental issues be more likely to plague industrializing countries that are transitioning to capitalism?

---

networks Online Teaching Options

INTERACTIVE FEATURE

Global Economy & You: Confronting Pollution

Evaluating consequences of industrialization
Display the Global Economy & You feature. Have students read the text and then discuss China's process of transitioning from communism to capitalism. Click on the map to reveal the wind currents that are carrying China's air pollution to all parts of the globe. Then discuss the questions. Point out that the effects of economic as well as environmental events in one country are rarely limited to the country itself.
Ask: What other areas of the world have very high levels of pollution? *(much of South Asia and North Africa)* Explain that some of these areas are not highly industrialized. **Ask: Why do these areas have so much pollution?** *(Winds carry China's pollution to some areas. Dense populations with few environmental regulations cause high levels of pollution in other areas.)* **Visual/Spatial, Naturalist**

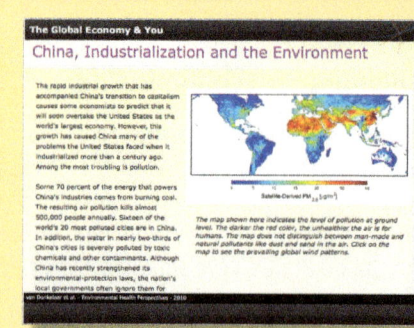

ANSWERS, p. 60

CRITICAL THINKING
As government-owned industries are privatized, government loses direct control over their operations. If their new private owners place competition for profit over protecting the environment, government might be reluctant to intervene for fear of violating property rights and stifling economic growth.

Argentina has similarly embarked on a program to remove government from the everyday business of running the economy. The country is rich in natural resources, and it has a highly literate population and a diversified industrial base. At first the government sold state-owned oil fields, petrochemical plants, and a number of other businesses to private companies. Since 2000 it experienced both high rates of growth and a major crisis in its banking sector. Instability in the political sector, however, along with **nationalization**, the conversion of private property to government ownership, of several major energy companies has halted the full transition to capitalism.

Finally, one country clearly resisting the transition to capitalism is Venezuela. Under President Hugo Chavez, who ruled as president until his death in March 2013, the economy was being transformed into a socialist state. However, the transition to socialism was not smooth, because of a housing crisis, rapidly rising prices, and electricity and food shortages. President Chavez's successor promised to continue the socialist policies, but the private sector is in turmoil and it remains to be seen if the trend toward socialist policies will continue.

Eastern Europe

The nations of Eastern Europe, especially those that were unwilling members of the former Soviet bloc, were eager to shed communism and embrace capitalism.

The struggle for freedom began in Poland with **Solidarity**, the independent and sometimes illegal labor union established in 1980. Solidarity was influential in securing a number of political freedoms in Poland. Eventually, the Communist Party lost power, and interest in capitalism grew. In 2004 Poland joined the **European Union (EU)**, the association of European nations created in 1993 to develop a single market with full economic and political cooperation.

Hungary also made a successful transition to a market economy. It was considered the most "Western" Communist bloc country with a thriving **black market**—a market in which entrepreneurs and merchants sell goods illegally. Hungary's experience with these markets helped ease the transition to capitalism. It too became a full member of the European Union in 2004.

Finally, the Czech and Slovak Republics, along with Estonia, Latvia, Lithuania, and Slovenia, were all granted admission to the EU in 2004. These countries, along with Bulgaria and Romania, which joined in 2007, made great strides toward capitalism after the collapse of the Soviet Union. All of these

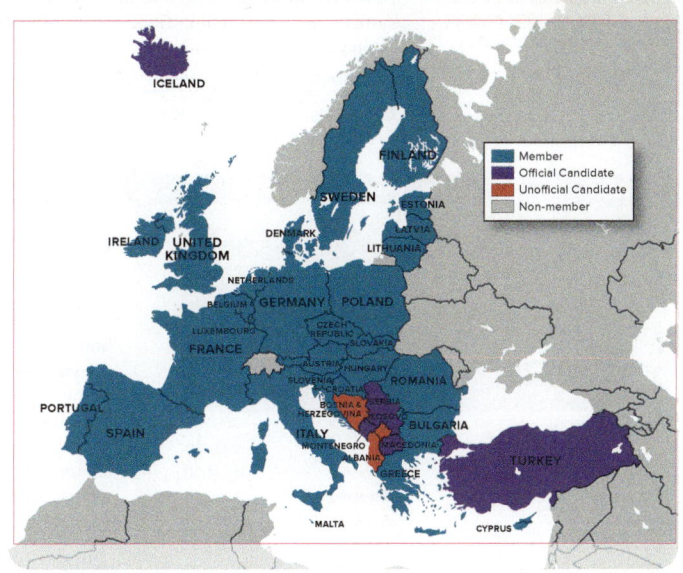

Since 1993, the European Union has expanded its membership to include several Eastern European nations that transitioned from communism to capitalism.

▲ **CRITICAL THINKING**
Evaluating What is remarkable about the growth of the European Union as a free trade area in the last decade of the twentieth century?

nationalization shift of an economy, or part of an economy, from private ownership to government ownership

Solidarity independent Polish labor union founded in 1980 by Lech Walesa

European Union (EU) successor of the European Coal and Steel Community established in 1993 by the Maastricht Treaty

black market market in which goods and services are sold illegally

INTERACTIVE FEATURE

The European Union

Understanding Eastern Europe's transition to a new economy Ask students what they know about the European Union. Have students view the images and ask them where the member countries are located. Point out that some of these countries are in Eastern Europe. Remind students that these countries were part of the former Soviet Union and as such had command economies. Invite students to discuss how the transition to capitalism would have subjected these countries to many challenges. Explain that many of these transitional struggles continue. Guide a discussion of how the transition affects both the countries themselves and also the Western European members who have long had capitalist economies. **Visual/Spatial, Logical/Mathematical**

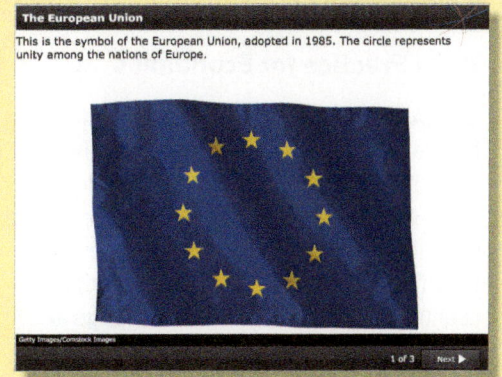

The European Union
This is the symbol of the European Union, adopted in 1985. The circle represents unity among the nations of Europe.

CHAPTER 2, LESSON 3
The Global Transition to Capitalism

R Reading Skills

Sequencing events in a time line Have students select a nation of Eastern Europe that was formerly part of the Soviet bloc. Ask students to create a time line that includes the major events in that nation's economic history since 1980. **Logical/Mathematical**

ANSWERS, p. 61

CRITICAL THINKING
Many of the countries in the European Union transitioned from communism to capitalism in a relatively short period of time. Point out to students that this map shows countries that made up the free-trade area called the European Coal and Steel Community (ECSC). The ECSC consisted of Belgium, France, Germany, Italy, Luxembourg, and the Netherlands. It coordinated iron and steel production, and the ECSC's cooperation evolved into the EU. The countries that signed the Maastricht Treaty establishing the European Union in 1993 included: Belgium, Denmark, France, Germany, Greece, Ireland, Italy, Luxembourg, Netherlands, Portugal, Spain, and United Kingdom.

CHAPTER 2, LESSON 3
The Global Transition to Capitalism

V Visual Skills

Predicting the future of North Korea Ask: **What does this table suggest about the economic future of North Korea?** *(Possible answer: The nation will soon begin making the transition to capitalism.)* **Logical/Mathematical**

T Technology Skills

Creating line graphs Instruct students to use reliable sources to find Japan's annual GDP figures since 1950. Ask students to create a line graph based on their findings. **BL Logical/Mathematical**

---

capital-intensive production process requiring large amounts of capital in relation to labor.

countries thus completed one of the more remarkable transitions of economic systems in history—going from communism to capitalism in a relatively short period of time.

✓ **READING PROGRESS CHECK**

Comparing How were the transitions similar and different between Russia and the Eastern European countries?

FIGURE 2.3 — ECONOMIC SYSTEMS AND PER CAPITA GDP

Economic Systems and Per Capita GDP

Country	Economic System	Per Capita GDP
Singapore	Capitalist	$85,700
Norway	Capitalist	$68,400
Hong Kong	Capitalist	$57,000
United States	Capitalist	$56,300
Sweden	Capitalist	$48,000
Taiwan	Capitalist	$47,500
Germany	Capitalist	$47,400
Denmark	Capitalist	$45,800
France	Capitalist	$41,000
Japan	Capitalist	$38,200
Korea, South	Capitalist	$36,700
Czech Republic	Capitalist	$31,500
Slovenia	Former Transition	$30,900
Estonia	Capitalist	$28,700
Lithuania	Capitalist	$28,000
Poland	Capitalist	$26,400
Hungary	Former Transition	$26,000
Latvia	Capitalist	$24,500
Chile	Capitalist	$23,800
Russia	Capitalist	$23,700
Argentina	Capitalist	$22,400
Venezuela	Socialist	$16,000
Thailand	Capitalist	$16,100
China	Transition	$14,300
Cuba	Socialist	$10,200
India	Transition	$6,300
Vietnam	Socialist	$6,100
Laos	Socialist	$5,400
Korea, North	Command	$1,800

Source: CIA World Factbook, 2016

Countries that have had longer experience with capitalism also have higher per capita GDPs.

▲ **CRITICAL THINKING**
Economic Analysis Why is Russia's per capita GDP lower than that of Hungary or Poland?

Other Faces of Capitalism

GUIDING QUESTION Why is capitalism different in different countries?

Some former socialist or communist countries are still making the transition to capitalism. Many other countries have had successful capitalist economic societies for some time. This is one reason that so many other countries are trying to make the transition. As **Figure 2.3** shows, capitalist countries have much higher per capita incomes than other countries.

Japan

Japan, like the United States, has a capitalist economy based on markets, prices, and the private ownership of capital. There are several reasons for Japan's success. One is that Japan has a loyal and dedicated workforce. At many companies, employees even arrive early for work to take part in group calisthenics and meditation with the intent on making their day more productive.

Another reason is the ability and willingness of the Japanese to develop new technologies. Because of its small and aging population, Japan has worked to boost productivity by developing techniques that are **capital-intensive**—methods of production that use large amounts of capital for every person employed—rather than labor-intensive. As a result, Japan is recognized as the world leader in the area of industrial robots.

The feature that really sets Japan apart from the United States is the degree to which Japan's government is involved in the day-to-day activities of the private sector. The country's Ministry of International Trade and Industry (MITI), for example, is a government body that identifies promising export markets for Japanese firms. The ministry then provides subsidies to industries to make them competitive in those areas.

---

networks — Online Teaching Options

WORKSHEET

Math Practice for Economics

Computing GDP per capita Have students use the Math Practice for Economics worksheet to compute per capita GDP for the countries shown in the worksheet table. Review how to read the table if necessary. Ask: **What does *per capita* mean?** *(per person)* Have students compare countries and per capita incomes. **Logical/Mathematical**

ANSWERS, p. 62

✓ **READING PROGRESS CHECK** Similar: all privatized their state-owned industries; Different: transition in Eastern Europe was faster and more complete

CRITICAL THINKING
Russia has a much larger population than Hungary or Poland.

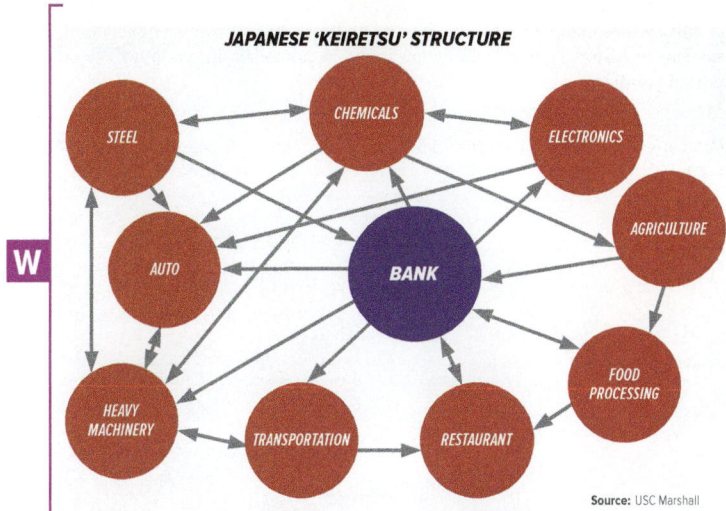

JAPANESE 'KEIRETSU' STRUCTURE

Source: USC Marshall

A *keiretsu* is a form of business organization that is unique to Japan. A keiretsu is a complex web of diverse companies that share investment sources and leadership groups. The various companies hold shared portions of stock ownership in each other, centered on a core bank. The structure helps the connected companies weaken the impact of stock market declines and helps prevent hostile takeover efforts. This system provides stability and unity that helps a keiretsu's companies work together for long-term economic growth.

◀ **CRITICAL THINKING**
Comparing How is the keiretsu similar to a U.S. company's board of directors? How is it different?

keiretsu independently owned group of Japanese firms joined and governed by an external board of directors in order to regulate competition

Despite Japan's successes, it experienced economic stagnation that began in the 1990s. Part of the reason is that most large Japanese firms belong to a **keiretsu** (kay • reht • soo), a tightly knit group of firms governed by an external board of directors. The role of the keiretsu is to ensure that competition does not threaten individual firms. A similar agreement in the United States among competing firms would be illegal under our antitrust laws.

Modest economic growth returned in 2003 and continued until 2008, when Japan entered the global economic slump of 2008–2009. Before it could fully recover, in 2011 a massive tsunami hit Japan and destroyed a major nuclear reactor and caused the loss of nearly 20,000 lives. Since then, public opinion turned against nuclear power and almost all of its 50 nuclear reactors were shut down two years later.

All of this, with the possible exception of the 2011 tsunami, is an ironic turn of events because the world looked to Japan as the very model of growth in the 1980s.

South Korea

One of the most successful nations in Asia is South Korea. In the mid-1950s, after it became divided from North Korea, South Korea was one of the poorest countries in Asia. It needed to rebuild an economy torn up by war. The country also had the highest **population density**—number of people per square mile of land area—in the world.

The South Korean government began by opening its markets to world trade. At first, the government focused on only a few industries. This allowed its people to gain experience producing and exporting for world markets. Businesses in the South Korean economy began to produce inexpensive toys and consumer goods. As they became skilled in production and exports, businesses next moved into textiles such as shirts, dresses, and sweaters. They then invested in heavy industry, such as shipbuilding and steel manufacturing.

Today, South Korea is a major producer of consumer and electronic goods such as home appliances and televisions. The country also has become a leading producer of automobiles. The South Korean experience shows that capitalism can change a badly war-damaged economy into a well-developed, highly industrial one in just a few generations.

population density number of people per square mile of land area

connected.mcgraw-hill.com   *Economic Systems and Decision Making*   **63**

CHAPTER 2, LESSON 3
The Global Transition to Capitalism

W Writing Skills

Writing a report Have students select a Japanese company that interests them. Ask students to write a report describing the company's plants, work force, products, and customer base. **Verbal/Linguistic**

C Critical Thinking Skills

Hypothesizing about possible outcomes Ask: **How do you think Korea's economy would be different today if North Korea had won the Korean War?** *(Possible answer: The entire peninsula would be struggling economically. The economic boom that took place in South Korea would not have occurred.)*
How do you think Korea's economy would be different today if South Korea had won the Korean War? *(Possible answer: The entire peninsula would be thriving economically. The economic boom would have surpassed that which actually occurred in South Korea.)* **Logical/Mathematical**

IMAGES

Asian Economies in Transition

Analyzing Asian economies Have students analyze the diagram of the Japanese keiretsu. Ask: **What is advantageous about the keiretsu form of business organization?** *(The structure helps weaken the impact of stock market declines and helps prevent hostile takeover efforts.)* Check students' prior knowledge about mergers. Ask: **What type of merger is similar to a keiretsu?** *(vertical merger, or conglomerate)* **Visual/Spatial**

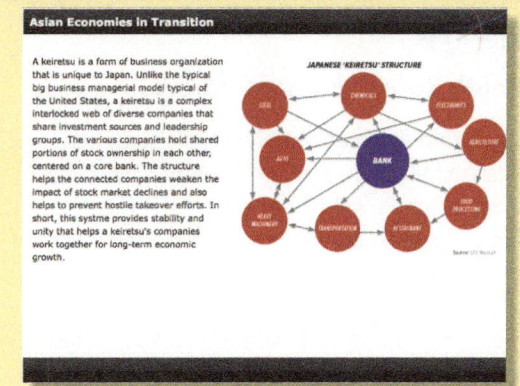

ANSWERS, p. 63

CRITICAL THINKING

The keiretsu is similar to a company's board of directors in that it consists of a group of individuals who make decisions regarding the company's future. It is different because the various companies hold joint shares of stock in each other all centered on a core bank. This type of interlocking ownership is prohibited in the United States because it reduces competition.

Economic Systems and Decision Making   **63**

CHAPTER 2, LESSON 3
The Global Transition to Capitalism

V Visual Skills

Creating a poster Have students review the text about Singapore. Ask students to draw a poster that advertises the country as a favorable location for multinational businesses. Before they start this project, encourage students to consult outside sources to learn more about the incentives Singapore offers to prospective companies.
AL Visual/Spatial

R Reading Skills

Understanding geopolitics Ask: Why does Taiwan have a separate government from the People's Republic of China? *(During the Chinese Civil War, the defeated Nationalist regime fled to Taiwan and set up a separate government.)*

South Korea's biggest export commodities are semiconductors, wireless telecommunications equipment, and other digital products. This has helped South Korea's economy grow to the point where it is now the 12th largest economy in the world.

▲ **CRITICAL THINKING**
Drawing Conclusions How has South Korea become economically successful?

South Korea, like other nations of the capitalist world, recovered slowly from the worldwide slump in 2008–2009, but it shows no signs of retreating from its commitment to capitalism. Its major industries are in the export sector, and so its recovery and future economic growth are closely tied to the continued recovery of other capitalist systems in the world.

Singapore

Singapore is a small island nation about 3.5 times larger than Washington, D.C. Despite its small size, its GDP ranks about 40th in the world, and it has a per capita income almost 20 percent higher than that of the United States. The lure of generous tax breaks, government subsidies, and government-sponsored training of employees has attracted thousands of multinational firms to Singapore. Efforts to develop its own technologies through spending on research and development accounted for a significant part of its strong economic growth.

The government of Singapore has focused on a few select industries, including telecommunications services, software, and biotechnology. The government has spent millions on laboratories, attracting top scientists from all over the world. Pharmaceuticals and medical technology are now leading industries, and Singapore is Southeast Asia's leading financial and high-tech hub.

The high rates of recent economic growth, its corruption-free environment, and its sound capitalist structure are all reasons for Singapore's remarkable performance.

Taiwan

Taiwan, formerly known as Formosa, is located off the coast of the much larger People's Republic of China. The population of Taiwan is about 23 million, and the per capita income is almost 80 percent of that of the United States.

64

net**w**orks   *Online Teaching Options*

IMAGES

South Korean Manufacturing

Analyzing Asian economies Have students analyze the image of South Korean manufacturing. **Ask: What are South Korea's biggest export commodities?** *(semiconductors and wireless telecommunications equipment)* **What ranking is South Korea's economy?** *(South Korea is the 12th largest economy in the world.)* Visual/Spatial

ANSWERS, p. 64

CRITICAL THINKING
South Korea has become economically successful by producing digital products.

Planning has always been a feature of the Taiwanese economy, with the government trying to identify those industries most likely to grow in the future. Most of these plans target high-tech industries such as telecommunications, consumer electronics, semiconductors, precision machinery, aerospace, and pharmaceuticals. Government guidance of investment and foreign trade is decreasing, and the country has signed a number of international trade agreements with capitalist nations, which should help boost growth.

Taiwan was one of the early economic powers in Asia, but some experts have warned that the centralized planning process will hamper future economic growth. Another concern is the looming presence of the People's Republic of China, which regards Taiwan as a "renegade province" and vows eventual unification. Despite its early start, the per capita GDP in Taiwan has fallen behind those of Hong Kong and Singapore.

Sweden

Sweden is now a mature industrial nation even though it was once known for its broad range of social welfare programs. The Swedish economy—with its generous maternity, education, disability, and old-age benefits—was thought to be the model of European socialism.

Social benefits were expensive, however, and to pay for them, the highest tax brackets reached 80 percent. This meant that a person who earned an additional $100 would keep only $20. Many athletes and celebrities even left the country to avoid high taxes.

Eventually the heavy tax burden, the high costs of the welfare state, and massive government deficits cut into Sweden's economic growth and led to the defeat of the Socialist Party. After a new government committed to a free market economy, it reduced the role of the public sector, lowered taxes, and privatized many government-owned businesses.

Today Sweden features a mix of high-tech capitalism and liberal welfare benefits. The welfare system attracts other residents of the EU because of the liberal benefits they can collect, something that contributes to a relatively high unemployment rate. Despite the taxes required to support the welfare system, Sweden generates a GDP per capita about three-quarters the size of that in the United States.

✓ **READING PROGRESS CHECK**

Explaining How did Japan, Singapore, and South Korea manage to become some of the more successful economies of the late twentieth century?

LESSON 3 REVIEW

Reviewing Vocabulary
1. *Explaining* How are vouchers used in the privatization process?

Using Your Notes
2. *Summarizing* Use your notes to summarize how government promotes economic growth in capitalist countries and in those transitioning to capitalism.

Answering the Guiding Questions
3. *Describing* How must a country's citizens' understanding of economic incentives change in order to transition to capitalism?

4. *Summarizing* What are the common features of the transition to capitalism?

5. *Differentiating* Why is capitalism different among countries?

Writing About Economics
6. *Informative/Explanatory* How have Russia and China dealt with the problem of scarcity in the past? How effective have they been? Why would transitioning to capitalism help them to solve this problem?

CHAPTER 2, LESSON 3
The Global Transition to Capitalism

C Critical Thinking Skills

Contrasting economic history of nations Ask: **How does Sweden's recent economic history differ from that of the nations of Eastern Europe?** *(Possible answer: In Sweden, citizens voted the socialists out of power; in Eastern Europe, people overthrew the communist governments.)*
AL Logical/Mathematical

CLOSE & REFLECT

R Reading Skills

Drawing conclusions from the lesson Ask students to review each subsection of the lesson and to write one or two important conclusions that can be drawn from it. Ask students to share their conclusions in class discussion.

ANSWERS, p. 65

✓ **READING PROGRESS CHECK** In all three, the government opened the economy to international trade, often by identifying promising industries and then subsidizing their development.

LESSON 3 REVIEW ANSWERS

Reviewing Vocabulary
1. The government distributes these vouchers to citizens so that they can gain a share of ownership of businesses that were once state-owned.

Using Your Notes
2. Governments in capitalist countries identify desirable markets and industries and then use subsidies and other means to help related businesses compete in them. Governments in transitioning countries promote the privatization of state-owned businesses and give more operational autonomy to those that remain state-owned.

Answering the Guiding Questions
3. They have to adjust to a new set of incentives. They must learn how to make decisions on their own, to work hard and do a good job, to take initiative, to interpret prices, and to generally fend for themselves in free markets.

4. State-owned property is privatized. Government gives up a measure of power and control on one hand and provides aid to certain industries on the other.

5. Each of these countries has a unique history and culture that has affected its development. Government policies, including involvement in the economy and its relationship with certain industries, have also been different from country to country.

Writing About Economics
6. Both countries once tried to boost production through central planning. Government tried to control economic activity by formulating a series of Five-Year Plans to guide their management of the economy. But managing a large, complex economy proved difficult, and when the plans failed to meet preset quotas, shortages resulted. Transitioning to capitalism lets free market forces set supply. When a shortage develops, privately owned producers are free to adjust to the unmet demand by producing more.

Chapter 2
Study Guide

C Critical Thinking Skills

Visualizing a market economy List the advantages and disadvantages of the market economic system on a sheet of paper. Organize students into several groups, and give each group a copy of the list. Ask groups to search newspapers and magazines and to watch television news programs to locate examples of each of the listed advantages and disadvantages. Suggest that groups present their findings in a pictorial essay titled "Market Economies: Advantages and Disadvantages." Call on group representatives to share their essays with the class. **Visual/Spatial, Kinesthetic**

W Writing Skills

Evaluating traditional elements of a market economy In American retail stores, consumers may either accept the posted price or decide to shop for a better price elsewhere. However, in certain markets—used cars for example—buyer and seller may bargain or haggle to agree on the price. Have students keep journal entries of the various advertised prices of a few selected makes and model years of used cars over a period of two weeks. Ask students to write a few lines in answer to the following: What risks do buyer and seller each assume when the buyer must "make an offer"?

STUDY GUIDE

ECONOMIC SYSTEMS
LESSON 1

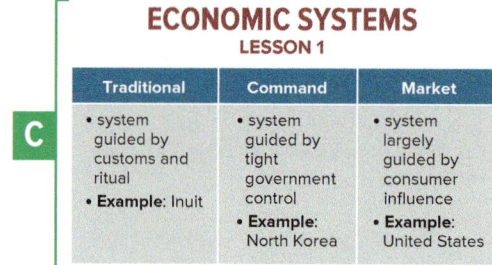

MIXED ECONOMIES
LESSON 2

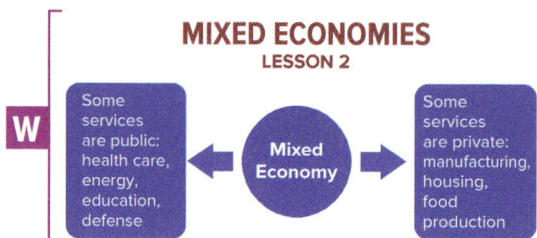

THE GLOBAL TRANSITION TO CAPITALISM
LESSON 3

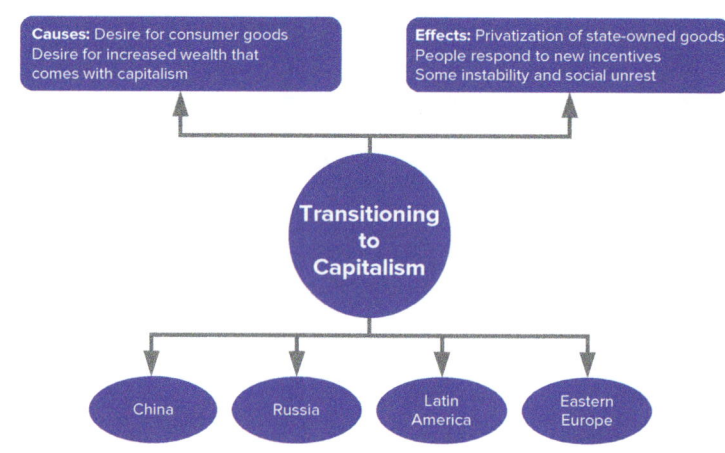

networks Online Assessment Options

WORKSHEET

Reinforcing Economic Skills Activity

Analyzing a business in crisis Assign the Reinforcing Economic Skills Activity worksheet. Students will use the skill of making comparisons to compare five factors of economic systems as they apply to the United States and the former Soviet Union.

# CHAPTER 2 Assessment

Directions: On a separate sheet of paper, answer the questions below. Make sure you read carefully and answer all parts of the questions.

Lesson Review

Lesson 1

1. **Draw Conclusions** What are some of the ways that people benefit from an economy that moves away from a command economy and more toward a socialist or market economy?

2. **Cause and Effect** What are some of the reasons that a traditional economy can lead to economic stagnation?

Lesson 2

3. **Compare and Contrast** How is a mixed economy different from a capitalist economy?

4. **Analyze** According to Karl Marx, what is the ultimate goal of a communist system?

Lesson 3

5. **Describe** What were some of the ways that the voucher system of privatization of public property was abused in the change from communism to capitalist societies?

6. **Compare and Contrast** What were the advantages of the Five-Year Plans of China and Russia? What were the disadvantages?

Critical Thinking

7. **Cause and Effect** How does the price of gas change behavior in a market economy? How is behavior changed in a command economy based on output measurements?

8. **Speculating** The strength of the economy of Singapore is based largely on its lack of corruption and generous government support for new businesses. How do you suppose its neighbors view the small island nation?

9. **Explaining** Describe the economy of Norway. What elements of its economy are based on socialism?

Analyzing Visuals

Use the visual below to answer the following questions.

10. **Identifying** Who are the people that do not benefit from a market economy? What needs go unmet?

11. **Predicting** Based on the advantages and disadvantages list, which type of economic system will likely grow fastest?

12. **Identifying** Which type of economic system would be able to most quickly address a natural disaster or other major social problem?

Comparing Economic Systems

	Traditional	Command	Market
Advantages	• Sets forth certain economic roles for all members of the community • Stable, predictable, and continuous life	• Capable of dramatic change in a short time • Many basic education, health, and other public services available at little or no cost	• Individual freedom for everyone • Able to adjust to change gradually • Lack of government interference • Decentralized decision making • Incredible variety of goods and services • High degree of consumer satisfaction
Disadvantages	• Discourages new ideas and new ways of doing things • Stagnation and lack of progress • Lower standard of living	• Does not meet wants and needs of consumers • Lacks effective incentives to get people to work • Requires large bureaucracy, which consumes resources • Has little flexibility to deal with day-to-day changes • Lacks room for individual initiative	• Rewards only productive resources; does not provide for people too young, too old, or too sick to work • Does not produce enough public goods such as defense, universal education, or health care • Workers and businesses face uncertainty as a result of competition and change

Need Extra Help?

If You've Missed Question	1	2	3	4	5	6	7	8	9	10	11	12
Go to page	44	39	49	50	57	59	51	64	44	46	39	39

TAKE THIS TEST ONLINE AT connected.mcgraw-hill.com

Critical Thinking Questions

7. Answers may vary. In a market economy, when gas prices are low, people buy larger cars that use more gas. When gas prices increase, drivers purchase smaller vehicles that get more miles to the gallon. In a command economy, workers produce not according to the best product, but according to output measurements. So if a factory is measured by tons of product, workers will produce heavy products.

8. Singapore's neighbors likely envy its success. Many neighboring countries have larger populations and a higher percentage of people involved in agriculture, even subsistence agriculture, so those countries face problems not encountered by citizens of Singapore.

9. Norway's government owns the petroleum industry. Industry profits are used to benefit all Norwegians by providing low gas prices, good roads, low-cost education, and social welfare. This economy is considered "mixed" because the government owns part of the means of production in the society.

Analyzing Visuals

10. The poor, sick, old, or very young do not benefit from a market economy. Their needs for health care, education, or welfare often go unmet if government services do not supply a safety net.

Chapter 2 Assessment Answers

Lesson Review

Lesson 1

1. People benefit from greater personal choices, more availability to own property, and a chance to earn greater money based on hard work.

2. Traditional economies are rooted in consistency. They are unlikely to try new things or to take advantage of capitalist opportunities. This leads to missed opportunities to grow an economy and eventually results in stagnation.

Lesson 2

3. In a mixed economy the government controls some systems in the economy, whereas in a capitalist economy the government plays a very small role.

4. The ultimate goal of a communist system is to organize for the common advantage of the community, with everyone consuming according to their needs.

Lesson 3

5. In some countries, property was privatized by distributing vouchers as political favors.

6. Both countries saw the advantage of the plans to quickly industrialize their economic systems and to move beyond an agrarian society. The disadvantage is that both countries reaped disastrous results.

11. The market system will likely grow fastest because entrepreneurs and businesses take advantage of market incentives.

12. The command economy would be able to most quickly address a natural disaster or other major social problem, because all decisions are made by a central authority and dramatic change is possible in a short time.

Chapter 2
Assessment Answers

Answering the Essential Question

13 An economic system deals with the problem of scarcity by addressing the questions of WHAT, HOW, and FOR WHOM to produce.

21st Century Skills

14 Students' presentations should identify the advantages of the free-enterprise system to South Korea. They should use persuasive language to convince their audience. The call to action should show understanding of the benefit of increased sales to South Korea.

15 Editorials should show understanding that capitalist systems allow a greater disparity between rich and poor. They should recognize that freedom allows opportunity for individuals to gain an economic advantage over others.

16 Students should show an understanding that taxes are used to pay for government services. They should recognize the benefit of those services and then make a judgment about their value to a society.

Building Financial Literacy

17 Students in a public school would likely treat their books and materials with less respect than they would treat their own purchased materials.

18 This difference in respect indicates that humans are motivated by ownership and achieving financial and material success.

Analyzing Primary Sources

19 The following quote is evidence of the emotional impact that the palace will have on the community: ". . . the occupant of the relatively little house will always find himself more uncomfortable, more dissatisfied. . . ."

20 Karl Marx argued that the masses would rise up to take power from the rich. An economic system based on the communist ideal—which Marx outlines in the *Communist Manifesto* and *Das Kapital*—would more effectively address the tension between the owners of the small houses and the owners of the large houses.

21 Traditional: community members would share the palace equally. Command: the palace would be built only when all people were given a palace in which to live. Market: members have the ability to work hard to earn the money to build their own palaces.

68

CHAPTER 2 Assessment

Directions: On a separate sheet of paper, answer the questions below. Make sure you read carefully and answer all parts of the questions.

ANSWERING THE ESSENTIAL QUESTION

Review your answers to the introductory question at the beginning of each lesson. Then answer the Essential Question on the basis of what you learned in the chapter. Have your answers changed?

13 **Understanding Relationships** How does an economic system help a society deal with the fundamental problem of scarcity?

21st Century Skills

14 **Presentation Skills** The economy of South Korea is closely tied to the growth and strength of other capitalist countries of the world. Research the exports of South Korea. Then make a multimedia presentation designed to promote those products to the recovering nations that might be or become customers for South Korea's exports.

15 **Create and Analyze Arguments and Draw Conclusions** Write an editorial for or against the following statement: People should give up the freedom to make choices in exchange for free, guaranteed, and universally available services, such as housing, education, employment, and health care.

16 **Decision Making** Write a blog post in which you evaluate whether you would like to pay higher taxes and get more government services or the reverse: pay lower taxes and get fewer government services. Explain your reasons.

Building Financial Literacy

Understanding how individuals react to the ownership of goods helps us understand the role of goods in a society.

17 **Comparing and Contrasting** How would you expect students at a public school to treat their books and other school property? How would that differ at a school in which students purchase their own books and materials for school?

18 **Analyzing** How can you explain this difference and what does it say about the human relationship to money?

Analyzing Primary Sources

Read the excerpt and answer the questions that follow.

PRIMARY SOURCE

" A house may be large or small; as long as the neighboring houses are likewise small, it satisfies all social requirement for a residence. But let there arise next to the little house a palace, and the little house shrinks into a hut. The little house now makes it clear that its inmate has no social position at all to maintain, or but a very insignificant one; and however high it may shoot up in the course of civilization, if the neighboring palace rises in equal or even in greater measure, the occupant of the relatively little house will always find himself more uncomfortable, more dissatisfied, more cramped within his four walls. "

—Karl Marx, *Wage-Labor and Capital*

19 **Examining Primary Sources** Carefully review the language used by Marx in this primary source. What evidence of propaganda or bias can you find in his descriptive choices that increased the emotional impact of this statement? Does Marx's use of these words affect the validity of his economic argument? Quote at least two sentences from the passage when constructing your answer.

20 **Explaining** Use what you know about Karl Marx to explain how he would resolve the tension between the small and large houses mentioned in the excerpt.

21 **Categorizing** Consider what you know about different market systems to analyze how the situation described in the excerpt would be resolved in command, traditional, and market economic systems. In what way would each economic system resolve the matter differently? Explain why.

Need Extra Help?

If You've Missed Question	13	14	15	16	17	18	19	20	21
Go to page	38	63	56	53	46	46	50	50	38

68

---

networks Online Assessment Options

WORKSHEET

Chapter Tests and Lesson Quizzes

Chapter 2 Tests Forms A and B Have students complete the Chapter Tests and Lesson Quizzes to assess student understanding throughout the chapter. Print and online assessment tools offer chapter and lesson evaluation through a variety of question formats, including document-based questions.

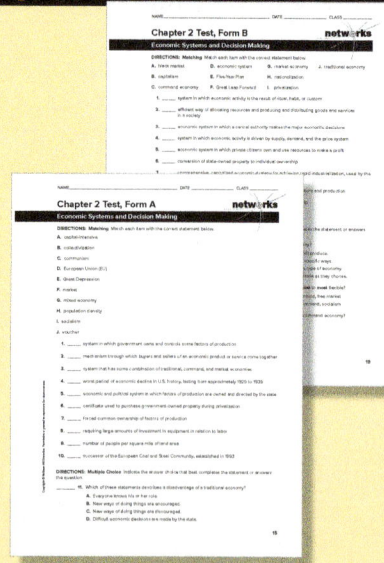

CHAPTER 3
The American Free Enterprise System Planner

Council for Economic Education

Below are the Council for Economic Education Voluntary National Content Standards in Economics covered in *The American Free Enterprise System* chapter.

Content Standard 2: Effective decision-making requires comparing the additional costs of alternatives with the additional benefits. Many choices involve doing a little more or a little less of something; few choices are "all or nothing" decisions.

Content Standard 8: Prices send signals and provide incentives to buyers and sellers. When supply or demand changes, market prices adjust, affecting incentives.

Content Standard 14: Entrepreneurs take on the calculated risk of starting new businesses, either by embarking on new ventures similar to existing ones or by introducing new innovations. Entrepreneurial innovation is an important source of economic growth.

Content Standard 16: There is an economic role for government in a market economy whenever the benefits of a government policy outweigh its costs. Governments often provide for national defense, address environmental concerns, define and protect property rights, and attempt to make markets more competitive. Most government policies also have direct or indirect effects on peoples' incomes.

UNDERSTANDING BY DESIGN®

Enduring Understanding
- Entrepreneurs, consumers, and the government play an important role in the American free enterprise system.

Essential Questions
- What are the benefits of a free enterprise economy?
- What are the major economic and social goals of the American free enterprise system?

Predictable Misunderstandings
Students may think:
- *Individuals have little control over the types and quality of goods and services produced.* Explain that consumers "vote" by spending their money.
- *America has a pure free enterprise economy.* Explain that Americans have allowed some government intervention to provide economic growth, among other goals. This results in a mixed or modified free enterprise economy.

Assessment Evidence
Performance Task
- Hands-On Chapter Project with Technology Extension

Other Evidence
- Guided Reading Activities
- Vocabulary Activity
- Lesson Quizzes
- Self-Check Quizzes
- Chapter Assessment
- Chapter Tests, Forms A and B

SUGGESTED PACING

Introducing the Chapter:	½ Day
Lesson 1: American Free Enterprise Capitalism	1 Day
Case Study	½ Day
Lesson 2: Roles and Responsibilities in a Free Enterprise Economy	1 Day
Lesson 3: Evaluating Economic Performance	1 Day
Debate	½ Day
Study Guide, Chapter Assessment and Wrap-Up	½ Day
TOTAL	**5 Days**

Key for Using the Teacher Edition

SKILL-BASED ACTIVITIES
Types of skill activites found in the Teacher Edition.

V **Visual Skills** require students to analyze maps, graphs, charts, and photos.

R **Reading Skills** help students practice reading skills and master vocabulary.

C **Critical Thinking Skills** help students apply and extend what they have learned.

W **Writing Skills** provide writing opportunities to help students comprehend the text.

T **Technology Skills** require students to use digital tools effectively.

*Letters are followed by a number when there is more than one of the same type of skill on the page.

DIFFERENTIATED INSTRUCTION
All activities are written for the on-level student unless otherwise marked with the leveled labels below.

BL Beyond Level
AL Approaching Level
ELL English Language Learners

All students benefit from activities that utilize different learning styles. Many activities are marked as below when a particular learning style is highlighted.

Intrapersonal
Logical/Mathematical
Visual/Spatial
Verbal/Linguistic
Naturalist
Kinesthetic
Auditory/Musical
Interpersonal

CHAPTER 3: THE AMERICAN FREE ENTERPRISE SYSTEM

Chapter Opener Planner

Students will know:
- the terms *free enterprise, free market,* and *capitalism* are synonymous terms to describe the U.S. economic system.
- the basic characteristics of the U.S. free enterprise system.
- entrepreneurs, consumers, and the government play important roles in a free enterprise economy.

Students will be able to:
- **summarize** the opportunities and benefits for individuals in the American free enterprise economy.
- **analyze** the role of entrepreneurs in a free enterprise economy.
- **express** the role of the consumer in a free enterprise economy.
- **consider the advantages and disadvantages** of government intervention in the American free enterprise system.
- **list** economic and social goals of the American free enterprise system.

UNDERSTANDING BY DESIGN®

☑ Print Teaching Options

C Critical Thinking Skills

- ☐ **p. 69 Analyzing starting a business** Students explore challenges that entrepreneurs face.
- ☐ **p. 69 Proof in the Numbers** Students explore the creation of wealth for U.S. franchise owners.
- ☐ **p. 70 Considering business rights and protections** Students discuss business rights that encourage entrepreneurs.
- ☐ **p. 70 Applying business steps** Students apply business steps to small businesses.
- ☐ **p. 71 Analyzing business responsibilities and duties** Students identify legal restrictions and responsibilities of businesses.
- ☐ **p. 71 Evaluating effects of regulations** Students consider eliminating government regulations.

☑ Online Teaching Options

V Visual Skills

- ☐ **IMAGES** Chapter opener—Students analyze a photo for free enterprise clues.

C Critical Thinking Skills

- ☐ **INFOGRAPHICS** Economic Perspectives—Students explore steps detailing facts about opening a successful business.
- ☐ **DEBATES** Should students be financially rewarded for good grades?—Students summarize arguments for and against rewarding students for good grades.
- ☐ **INTERACTIVE FEATURE** Case Study: Public Versus Private Ownership—Students give reasons the government should or should not have built the TVA.

☑ Printable Digital Worksheets

C Critical Thinking Skills

- ☐ **WORKSHEET** Math Practice for Economics—Students graph economic freedom and competition.
- ☐ **WORKSHEET** Enrichment Activity—Students analyze the growing income gap.

Project-Based Learning

Hands-On

Hands-On Chapter Project
In this project, students will explore the interconnectedness of the five elements of the free enterprise system. They will look at how consumers, entrepreneurs, and the government factor into this system, and then create a model or poster showing how the parts of the free enterprise system relate to one another.

Digital Hands-On

Create Online Projects

edtechteacher
21st Century Learning

Find an additional activity online that incorporates technology for the Hands-On Project. Visit the EdTech Teacher Web sites for more links, tutorials, and other resources.

Print Resources

ANCILLARY RESOURCE
This ancillary is available for every chapter and lesson.
- Chapter Tests and Lesson Quizzes

PRINTABLE DIGITAL WORKSHEETS
These printable digital worksheets are available for every chapter and lesson.
- Reading Essentials & Study Guide
- Vocabulary Activities
- Chapter Summaries
- Economic Simulations
- Math Practice for Economics
- Reinforcing Economic Skills
- Personal Finance Activities
- Enrichment Activities
- Reteaching Activities
- Guided Reading Activities
- Video Worksheets
- Lesson Quizzes and Chapter Tests (English and Spanish)

More Media Resources

SUGGESTED READING
- For students at a Grade 10 reading level: *That One Man's Profit Is Another's Loss,* by Michel de Montaigne
- For students at a Grade 11 reading level: *The Haunted Land: Facing Europe's Ghosts After Communism,* by Tina Rosenberg
- For students at a Grade 12 reading level: *Small is Beautiful: Economics as if People Mattered,* by E. F. Schumacher

SUGGESTED VIDEOS
Find these documentaries yourself online. NOTE: McGraw-Hill Education does not endorse these resources. Preview clips for age-appropriateness.
- *The dot.com Bubble* (27 min.)
- *Money as Debt* (47 min.)
- *TED Talks: The Post-Crisis Consumer* (16 min.)

LESSON 1 Planner

AMERICAN FREE ENTERPRISE CAPITALISM

Students will know:
- the terms free enterprise, free market, and capitalism are synonymous terms to describe the U.S. economic system.
- the basic characteristics of the U.S. free enterprise system, including private property, incentives, economic freedom, competition, and the limited role of government.
- how clearly defined and enforced property rights are essential to a market economy.

Students will be able to:
- **explain** how the American economy incorporates the five main characteristics of a free enterprise economy.
- **summarize** the opportunities and benefits for individuals in the American free enterprise economy.
- **describe** the disadvantages of a free enterprise economy.

UNDERSTANDING BY DESIGN®

✓ Print Teaching Options

V Visual Skills
- ☐ **p. 75 Analyzing free enterprise capitalism** Students use Adam Smith's concept of competition as the invisible hand.

R Reading Skills
- ☐ **p. 72 Identifying terms for the U.S. economy**
- ☐ **p. 73 Understanding essential concepts of free enterprise** Students list characteristics of a free enterprise capitalist economy.
- ☐ **p. 74 Inferring causes of economic activity** Students discuss why it is necessary for people to keep the rewards they earn.
- ☐ **p. 79 Explaining why firms combine** Students discuss why suppliers tend to combine.

C Critical Thinking Skills
- ☐ **p. 72 Personalizing free enterprise capitalism** Students discuss how small businesses illustrate free enterprise capitalism.
- ☐ **p. 73 Appreciating private property rights** Students rate the five characteristics of free enterprise capitalism in order of importance.
- ☐ **p. 75 Comparing and contrasting industries** Students explain why the government allows different levels of competition. **Verbal/Linguistic**
- ☐ **p. 76 Relating free enterprise to democracy** Students discuss why capitalism works best in a democracy. **Logical/Mathematical**
- ☐ **p. 76 Drawing conclusions about economic changes** Students identify how free enterprise capitalism adjusts to change. **Verbal/Linguistic**
- ☐ **p. 77 Debating the profit motive** Students discuss whether the motivation to create wealth always leads to positive results.
- ☐ **p. 79 Identifying causes of uneven economic growth** Students discuss why economic growth in free enterprise capitalism is often uneven.
- ☐ **p. 80 Business Regulations** Students explain government regulations small businesses face.

✓ Online Teaching Options

V Visual Skills
- ☐ **IMAGES** **Profit Motive**—Students view graphs of small business statistics.
- ☐ **TIME LINE** **A Variety of Goods**—Students discuss advantages and disadvantages of having many choices, and the effect of competition on choices.
- ☐ **VIDEO** **Ford Struggles to Stay Profitable**—Students view characteristics and benefits of free enterprise capitalism displayed by Ford and its customers.
- ☐ **IMAGES** **Disadvantages of Free Enterprise**—Students discuss whether capitalism contributes to the gap between the rich and the poor.

R Reading Skills
- ☐ **GRAPHIC ORGANIZERS** **Benefits and Disadvantages of Free Enterprise**— Students compare the benefits and disadvantages of free enterprise.

C Critical Thinking Skills
- ☐ **BELLRINGER** **American Free Enterprise Capitalism**—Students discuss incentives to start a business. **Visual/Spatial**
- ☐ **ESSENTIAL QUESTION** **Exploring the Essential Question**—Students discuss how new products emerge in a free enterprise system. **Verbal/Linguistic**
- ☐ **INTERACTIVE FEATURE** **Characteristics of Free Enterprise Capitalism**—Students discuss characteristics of free enterprise and give real-world examples.
- ☐ **INTERACTIVE FEATURE** **Careers: Franchise Operator**—Students discuss character traits that a franchise owner must exhibit. **Interpersonal**

T Technology Skills
- ☐ **SELF-CHECK QUIZ** **Lesson 1**—Students receive instant feedback on answers.
- ☐ **GAME** **Lesson 1**—Students solve clues to review lesson content.
- ☐ **INTERACTIVE WHITEBOARD ACTIVITY** **Private Enterprise: Skateboard Shop**— Students work together to learn lesson content.

✓ Printable Digital Worksheets

R Reading Skills
- ☐ **WORKSHEET** **Guided Reading Activity**—Students use the Guided Reading Activity worksheets to review their comprehension of the content.
- ☐ **WORKSHEET** **Reading Essentials and Study Guide**—Students complete the study guide and answer Reading Progress Check and vocabulary questions.

C Critical Thinking Skills
- ☐ **WORKSHEET** **Ford Struggles to Stay Profitable Video Activity**—Students answer questions related to characteristics and benefits of free enterprise capitalism displayed by Ford and its customers.

LESSON 2 Planner

ROLES AND RESPONSIBILITIES IN A FREE ENTERPRISE ECONOMY

Students will know:
- the function of profit in a market economy as an incentive for entrepreneurs to accept the risks of business failure.
- entrepreneurs, consumers, and the government play important roles in a free enterprise economy.
- that government laws establish the rules and institutions in which markets operate.

Students will be able to:
- **analyze** the role of entrepreneurs in a free enterprise economy.
- **express** the role of the consumer in a free enterprise economy.
- **explain** who determines the role of government in the American free enterprise system.
- **consider** the advantages and disadvantages of government intervention in the American free enterprise system.

UNDERSTANDING BY DESIGN®

☑ Print Teaching Options

V Visual Skills

☐ **p. 83 Diagramming the effects of entrepreneurs** Students create a visual summary of entrepreneurs as catalysts.

☐ **p. 85 Analyzing misleading advertising** Students identify the government agency set up to protect consumers from misleading claims.

R Reading Skills

☐ **p. 83 Understanding the importance of entrepreneurs** Students discuss why economic freedom is vital to a free-market economy.

☐ **p. 83 Understanding consumer sovereignty** Students discuss why consumers ultimately control what is produced. *Logical/Mathematical*

☐ **p. 86 Defining a mixed economy**

C Critical Thinking Skills

☐ **p. 82 Analyzing the role of the entrepreneur** Students explain what an entrepreneur is.

☐ **p. 82 Hypothesizing about a start-up business** Students describe start-up costs and benefits as business owners. *Interpersonal*

☐ **p. 84 Applying consumer sovereignty to real numbers** Students vote on which products they would buy, and discuss consumer influences.

☐ **p. 84 Identifying consumer rights and responsibilities**

☐ **p. 85 Evaluating the cost of government actions** Students discuss situations when costs of government actions outweigh the benefits.

☐ **p. 85 Identifying government restrictions** Students evaluate restrictions government places on the use of individual property.

W Writing Skills

☐ **p. 85 Writing about government's changing role**

☐ **p. 86 Evaluating government regulations** Students write arguments for and against government's role as regulator.

☑ Online Teaching Options

V Visual Skills

☐ **VIDEO Creativity Helping Workers**—Students view innovations in entrepreneurship. *Interpersonal*

☐ **IMAGES Role of the Consumer**—Students discuss similarities between the consumer and the entrepreneur. *Logical/Mathematical*

☐ **CHARTS Government Regulatory Agencies**—Students match the description with the correct agency, explaining how regulations affect consumers. *Logical/Mathematical*

R Reading Skills

☐ **GRAPHIC ORGANIZERS Roles and Responsibilities**—Students identify the roles of the entrepreneur, consumer, and government in the economy. *Verbal/Linguistic*

C Critical Thinking Skills

☐ **BELLRINGER Roles and Responsibilities in a Free Enterprise Economy**—Students cite examples of a business that moved into their area and increased competition, and discuss the effects. *Logical/Mathematical*

☐ **ESSENTIAL QUESTION Exploring the Essential Question**—Students match entrepreneurs, consumers, and the government with their roles in the economy. *Logical/Mathematical*

T Technology Skills

☐ **SELF-CHECK QUIZ Lesson 2**—Students receive instant feedback on their mastery of lesson content.

☐ **GAME Lesson 2**—Students solve clues to review lesson content.

☐ **INTERACTIVE WHITEBOARD ACTIVITY Free Enterprise Economy**—Students work together to learn lesson content.

☑ Printable Digital Worksheets

R Reading Skills

☐ **WORKSHEET Reteaching Activity**—Students review the lesson, explaining their answers and discussing any misunderstandings.

☐ **WORKSHEET Guided Reading Activity**—Students use the Guided Reading Activity worksheets to review their comprehension of the content.

☐ **WORKSHEET Reading Essentials and Study Guide**—Students complete the study guide and answer Reading Progress Check and vocabulary questions.

C Critical Thinking Skills

☐ **WORKSHEET Creativity Helping Workers Video Activity**—Students answer questions about entrepreneurship.

☐ **WORKSHEET Economic Simulation**—Students work in groups to take the roles of entrepreneurs, consumers, and government officials resolving dilemmas.

LESSON 3 Planner

EVALUATING ECONOMIC PERFORMANCE

Students will know:
- the U.S. economic and social goals may change over time.
- the costs and benefits of policies related to the economic goals.

Students will be able to:
- **list** economic and social goals of the American free enterprise system.
- **explain** why economic and social goals may change over time.
- **explain** how conflict among economic goals is resolved in the American free enterprise system.

UNDERSTANDING BY DESIGN®

✓ Print Teaching Options

V Visual Skills

☐ **p. 88 Creating a poster about economic security** Students create a poster to illustrate the costs and benefits of providing economic security. *Visual/Spatial*

R Reading Skills

☐ **p. 88 Defining and applying *equity*** Students write a paragraph about the difference between equity and equality, and the costs and benefits of U.S. economic policies related to equity.

C Critical Thinking Skills

☐ **p. 87 Discussing clashing goals** Students describe situations where economic goals clash with social goals, and debate priorities in these cases.

☐ **p. 87 Determining costs and benefits of economic freedom** Students list opposing aspects of American economic freedom.

☐ **p. 87 Determining cause and effect** Students discuss the effect efficiency has on the number of goods available. *Logical/Mathematical*

☐ **p. 89 Exploring conflicting goals** Students explore how the goal of protecting the environment might conflict with the goals of efficiency or full employment. *Naturalist*

☐ **p. 90 Understanding trade-offs** Students explore the issue of trade-offs, opportunity costs, and political solutions.

☐ **p. 90 Constitutional Economic Rights** Students scan the U.S. Constitution to find and discuss economic concepts regarding property rights and taxation, as well as limits on individuals and on the government.

☐ **p. 91 Analyzing changes in the U.S. economy** Students discuss ways that Americans have modified the free enterprise economy.

W Writing Skills

☐ **p. 91 Finding the main ideas** Students write a summary of the lesson and exchange summaries with a partner to compare the main ideas.

✓ Online Teaching Options

V Visual Skills

☐ **INTERACTIVE FEATURE Global Economy & You**—Students explore graphs showing per capita income and discuss the discrepancy between the richest and the poorest countries. *Visual/Spatial*

☐ **POLITICAL CARTOON Political Cartoon**—Students discuss the economic goals that clash in the cartoon. *Visual/Spatial*

☐ **VIDEO American Entrepreneurs in China**—Students watch a video and discuss American entrepreneurs in China.

R Reading Skills

☐ **GRAPHIC ORGANIZER U.S. Economic Goals**—Students brainstorm a list of economic goals they think most Americans share. *Interpersonal*

☐ **BIOGRAPHY Brian Linton**—Students discuss the value of Brian Linton's business model. *Interpersonal*

C Critical Thinking Skills

☐ **BELLRINGER Evaluating Economic Performance**—Students review the characteristics of the three types of economic systems. *Interpersonal*

☐ **ESSENTIAL QUESTION Exploring the Essential Question**—Students discuss the chart comparing economies.

T Technology Skills

☐ **SELF-CHECK QUIZ Lesson 3**—Students receive instant feedback on their mastery of lesson content.

☐ **GAME Lesson 3**—Students solve clues to review lesson content.

☐ **INTERACTIVE WHITEBOARD ACTIVITY Economic and Social Goals**—Students work together to learn lesson content.

✓ Printable Digital Worksheets

R Reading Skills

☐ **WORKSHEET Guided Reading Activity**—Students use the Guided Reading Activity worksheets to review their comprehension of the content.

☐ **WORKSHEET Reading Essentials and Study Guide**—Students complete the study guide and answer Reading Progress Check and vocabulary questions.

☐ **WORKSHEET Reteaching Activity**—Students use this activity worksheet to review and reteach chapter content and vocabulary. This worksheet can be used with struggling students who need additional help with difficult content concepts.

C Critical Thinking Skills

☐ **WORKSHEET American Entrepreneurs in China Video Activity**—Students answer questions about American entrepreneurs in China.

Chapter 3 Planner **69E**

CHAPTER 3 The American Free Enterprise System

INTERVENTION AND REMEDIATION STRATEGIES

LESSON 1 American Free Enterprise Capitalism

Reading and Comprehension

Divide students into groups of three and assign each of the students in the groups one section of the lesson. Ask students to carefully study their section of text and to take notes on the main ideas and most important details. Then have students meet in their groups and present a verbal outline of their section to their partners.

Text Evidence

Present this scenario to students: A friend has been reading about command economies and has become persuaded that this economic system offers the best hope for economic and social equality. As evidence of her argument, she points to the growing gap between rich and poor in capitalist countries and the disastrous effects of the Great Recession. These issues, she argues, can be managed far better in a command economy. Ask students to write a rebuttal to this argument. Tell them to back up their arguments by citing specific details from the text.

LESSON 2 Roles and Responsibilities in a Free Enterprise Economy

Reading and Comprehension

Ask students to write answers to these three questions:

Why are entrepreneurs important to the free enterprise economy?

How are the dollars that consumers spend in the marketplace like votes that decide what is and what is not produced?

What is one example of how the government acts as a protector, as a provider, and as a regulator?

Ask students to share their answers in a class discussion.

Text Evidence

Remind students that the free enterprise economy is comprised of three elements: the entrepreneur, the consumer, and the government. Ask students to write an essay in which they rank these three elements by their importance, or the power they bring to bear on the economy. In their essays, students should support their ranking by citing specific evidence from the text.

LESSON 3 Evaluating Economic Performance

Reading and Comprehension

Ask students to choose any two of the economic goals and write a paragraph explaining how they can come into conflict and the opportunity costs they involve. Have them share their ideas in class.

Text Evidence

Ask students to choose four of the economic and social goals discussed in the text and explain in a brief essay what that goal is and why it is important to Americans. Remind them to cite textual evidence to support their answers.

Online Resources

Assessing Background Knowledge Use this worksheet to pre-assess students' knowledge before they start the chapter.

Chapter Summaries Have students use the summary as a pre-reading activity or as a post-reading review to check the main ideas covered in each lesson.

Guided Reading Activities Have students complete these activities as they read each lesson. They provide reading notes the student can use for review and to prepare for assessments.

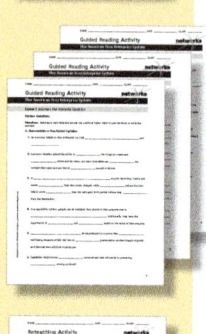

Reteaching Activities Have students complete the Reteaching Activity for remedial practice and review of vital content.

Self-Check Quizzes These quizzes provide instant feedback on areas the students may need to re-read to understand a main idea.

Reading Essentials and Study Guide This resource offers writing and reading activities for the approaching-level student.

Approaching Grade Level Reader This reader presents all of the content of the Online Student Edition but at a lower reading level.

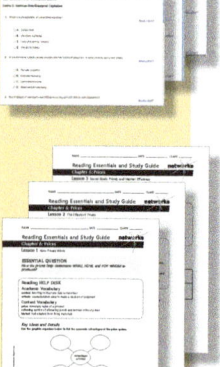

English Language Learner Reader Provide additional reading support for ELL students. Find this tool in the Online Student Edition.

The American Free Enterprise System

ESSENTIAL QUESTIONS
- What are the benefits of a free enterprise economy?
- What are the major economic and social goals of the American free enterprise system?

networks
www.connected.mcgraw-hill.com
There's More Online about the American free enterprise system.

CHAPTER 3

Economic Perspectives
Starting Your Own Business

Lesson 1
American Free Enterprise Capitalism

Lesson 2
Roles and Responsibilities in a Free Enterprise Economy

Lesson 3
Evaluating Economic Performance

Letter from the Author

Dear Economics Teacher,

Nothing in this textbook is more important than the American free enterprise system, yet it is sometimes difficult for students to appreciate how special it really is! The problem is that students are already familiar with core features like prices, competitive markets, supply and demand, private property, freedom of choice, and the profit motive. I've always found that the best ways to get the benefits of the free enterprise system across to students is to draw their attention to a comparison of our own economy to some of the other economic systems that were discussed in Chapter 2. Hopefully this tip will work as well for you as it did for me.

Gary E. Clayton

CHAPTER 3
The American Free Enterprise System

ENGAGE

Call students' attention to the photo and ask them to describe what it shows. Guide them to recognize that these two entrepreneurs are cutting the ribbon to mark the opening of their new business. **Ask: Why is this image a good one to symbolize the chapter titled *The American Free Enterprise System*?** *(These two women are celebrating the opening of their new business, which marks the achievement of an important goal in their lives. Entrepreneurs represent the foundation of the American free enterprise system because they lead the way in building our economy.)*

Analyzing starting a business Invite students to explain whether they would like to own their own business. Encourage them to tell what kind of business they would like to own and why. **Ask: Why do people want to own a business?** *(Sample answer: to work for themselves, to become wealthy)* **What risks do they take?** *(Sample answer: failure of the business, loss of investment)* Encourage students to talk about the challenges and incentives that face every entrepreneur.

Making Connections

Proof in the Numbers To help students appreciate the impact of the free enterprise system on the creation of wealth, **ask:**

- How many fast-food restaurant chains can you name?
- How often do you eat at McDonald's?
- How many people are employed at these companies?

Tell students that most of these companies started as a single store and then grew. By 2012, McDonald's alone had more than 14,000 stores in the United States and about 33,000 stores worldwide. Ask students to speculate on the impact these stores have on the creation of wealth for U.S. franchise owners. Emphasize that this is all possible because of the free enterprise system.

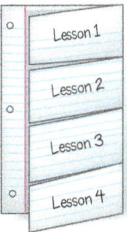

Go to the Foldables® library for a cumulative chapter-based Foldable® activity that your students can use to help take notes and prepare for assessment.

CHAPTER 3
Economic Perspectives

TEACH & ASSESS

C1 Critical Thinking Skills

Considering business rights and protections Discuss the steps with students. Point out that in some other economic systems, people do not have these choices. **Ask: What business rights encourage entrepreneurs to start and own businesses in the United States?** *(Sample answers: Property rights such as real estate ownership, copyright laws, and patents assure an owner that a successful business location, idea, or invention cannot be taken away. The right to hire employees ensures an owner that he or she can compete with other businesses to hire the best employees. The right to dissolve a business reassures a business owner that he or she can get out of a business if it is not profitable.)* **Logical/Mathematical**

C2 Critical Thinking Skills

Applying business steps Divide students into groups of three or four and ask them to discuss how each of these steps would apply to a certain kind of small business, such as a restaurant, clothing store, or construction company. **Ask: What additional responsibilities would these particular businesses need to face?** Call on groups to share their ideas. **Interpersonal**

Economic Perspectives
STARTING YOUR OWN BUSINESS

1. **2. inc** **3.** **4.**

1. Create a business plan
Decide what good or service to provide.

Of the 5.8 million employer firms in the U.S., 89.7% had fewer than 20 workers

276,788 — In 2012, 276,788 patents were granted in the U.S.
2,992 — 2,992 patents were granted in the UK.

2. Decide on a business structure
This legal structure will determine your business' tax status.

☑ C-corporation   ☐ S-corporation
☐ Partnership   ☐ Trust   ☐ Nonprofit
☐ Sole proprietorship

3. Determine a location
This could be almost anywhere: your home, a garage, a separate building… or the back of a truck.

Over half of all U.S. businesses are based in an owner's home.

.com — More entrepreneurs are creating online businesses, which have much lower overhead costs.

4. Come up with a finance plan
So many options: personal savings, loans from loved ones, bank loans, grants, or even credit cards!

Every year, about **600,000** businesses start up in the U.S.

Venture capitalists only fund about 300 new businesses every year.

Over 80% of new businesses in the U.S. are funded by personal savings or with the help of family and friends.

---

networks — Online Teaching Options

INFOGRAPHIC

Economic Perspectives: Starting Your Own Business

Analyzing how to start a business Guide students in discussing each of the steps shown on the infographic. For each step, **ask: Why is this step essential in order for business owners to succeed?** Have students read through the infographic, noting whether any of the facts surprise them. Discuss why or why not.
Logical/Mathematical

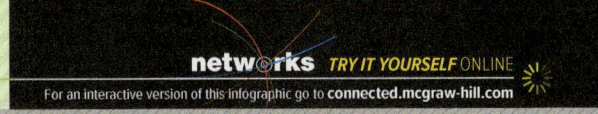

For an interactive version of this infographic go to connected.mcgraw-hill.com

For many people, starting their own business is the ultimate achievement of the American dream. Before establishing a new business, however, there are a few steps that must be taken. Building a business involves decision making, planning, structuring, and laying the legal groundwork before the first product is sold.

CHAPTER 3
Economic Perspectives

C1 Critical Thinking Skills

Analyzing business responsibilities and duties
Point out that many of the legal licenses and permits identified in number 6 are needed to protect society as well as the economy. For example, environmental laws are in place to protect society from pollution, and health regulations protect restaurant and food store patrons. Ask students to identify some examples of the legal restrictions and responsibilities of businesses. **Logical/Mathematical**

5. Register your business name and build a Web site
Build an identity: reserve a domain name/URL, build a Web site, and create a logo.

ONLY 25% HAVE A WEBSITE
In 2012, 75% of American businesses (and 58% of small businesses) did not have a web site.

#1 - iPad 3
#2 - Samsung Galaxy S3
#3 - iPad Mini

In 2012, 97% of Americans searched for products and services online

6. Obtain a business license, permits & an employer ID number (EIN)
The permits you'll need are determined by the type of business you start. Also, make sure you register for federal, state, and local taxes!

12-3456789

C2 Critical Thinking Skills

Evaluating the effects of regulations Have students discuss their responses to the Think About It! question. Then ask them to consider whether their responses mean the regulation should be eliminated. **Ask: What would be the consequence for the economy or society if that regulation were abolished?** *(Students may say that, although the regulation might, in some circumstances, cause a business to fail, its overall benefits outweigh the damage done to any single business.)* **Logical/Mathematical**

7. Set up an accounting system
Open a separate bank account just for your business. Use it to track business expenses and revenues. Careful, clear financial records are important to business success.

49% 5 Years or less
34% 10 Years or less
26% 15 Years or less

Business survival rates

THINK ABOUT IT!
Follow the steps provided to begin creating your own small business. Then write a short essay that evaluates which of these regulations are the easiest to accomplish and which are the most challenging. Identify which step you think is most critical to your business' early success.

CLOSE & REFLECT
Have students answer the *Think About It!* questions.

connected.mcgraw-hill.com   The American Free Enterprise System 71

WORKSHEET

Hands-On Chapter Project

Setting up a mock business If you have not already assigned the Chapter 1 Hands-On Project, do so now. Students will plan how to start a business. They will begin by deciding the type of business to open in a vacant storefront on a popular shopping street. They will also research the demographics of the population in the area and the types of stores already located in the vicinity. Students will create a business plan that includes the estimated cost of opening the business: rent and utilities for the store; cost of producing or acquiring goods; any costs for employees; advertising costs, etc. Finally, students will discuss options for raising the capital necessary to open the business.

ANSWERS, p. 71

THINK ABOUT IT!

In their essays, students should evaluate which step is the easiest to accomplish and which is the most challenging. Discuss as a class which step they think is most critical to their businesses' early success.

CHAPTER 3, LESSON 1
American Free Enterprise Capitalism

ENGAGE

C Critical Thinking Skills

Personalizing free enterprise capitalism Ask students to think about family members, neighbors, or other people they know who own a small business. **Ask: Why can Americans start businesses? What kind of businesses do they own? Who are their competitors? What role does the government play in how they run their businesses or in the products they sell?** Guide a discussion of how these small businesses illustrate free enterprise capitalism.

TEACH & ASSESS

R Reading Skills

Identifying terms for the U.S. economy Ask: What three terms are synonymous terms that describe the U.S. economic system? *(free enterprise, free market, and capitalism)* **ELL** Verbal/Linguistic

---

ANSWERS, p. 72

ESSENTIAL QUESTION ACTIVITY

Students' answers will vary. Review the characteristics of a command economy. Discuss whether a manufacturer in a command economy would have any incentive to invest large amounts of money in developing innovative products. Why or why not? *(Possible answer: No, because command economies allow little or no competition, so manufacturers are not compelled to make newer or better products to survive.)*
TAKING NOTES: Benefits of Free Enterprise: Individual freedom, a variety of goods, adapts to change, promotes progress, creates wealth.
Disadvantages of Free Enterprise: Uneven growth, growing gap between rich and poor, suppliers tend to combine to avoid competition, large supply-side tendencies, rights and responsibilities required of businesses.

72

Interact with these digital assets and others in lesson 1
✓ INTERACTIVE CHART
  Free Enterprise Capitalism
✓ INTERACTIVE IMAGE
  Disadvantages of Free Enterprise Capitalism
✓ SELF-CHECK QUIZ
✓ VIDEO

networks
TRY IT YOURSELF ONLINE

LESSON 1
American Free Enterprise Capitalism

Reading Help Desk

Academic Vocabulary
- incentive

Content Vocabulary
- free enterprise
- voluntary exchange
- private property rights
- profit
- profit motive
- competition
- biofuels
- Great Recession

TAKING NOTES:

Key Ideas and Details
ACTIVITY Use a graphic organizer like the one below to compare the benefits and disadvantages of a free enterprise economic system.

Benefits of Free Enterprise	Disadvantages of Free Enterprise

ESSENTIAL QUESTION

What are the benefits of a free enterprise economy?

Think of a product that you use that was developed or modified as a result of some change in the marketplace.

1. Would this product have been developed in a command economy? Why or why not?

2. How does this product demonstrate a strength of the free enterprise system?

Characteristics of Free Enterprise Capitalism

GUIDING QUESTION *How does the American economy incorporate the main characteristics of a free enterprise economy?*

Capitalism is an economic system in which private citizens, like yourself or perhaps other members of your family, own and use the factors of production to make products and generate profits. If the products can be bought and sold in markets without government regulation or interference, we have a condition called *free markets*.

If an economy has both capitalism and free markets, we say that the economy is based on free enterprise. Under **free enterprise**, resources are privately owned, and competition is allowed to flourish with a minimum of government interference. Because the terms are so similar, people often use the terms *free enterprise, free market,* and *capitalism* interchangeably to describe the economic system of the United States. A capitalistic free enterprise economy has five important characteristics: economic freedom, voluntary exchange, private property rights, the profit motive, and competition. Many of these features may already be familiar to you, but they are so important to the success of our economy and the way we live that it's important to review them.

Economic Freedom
Economic freedom means more than being able to buy the things you want. It means that you have the freedom to choose your occupation, your employer,

72

---

networks Online Teaching Options

BELLRINGER

American Free Enterprise Capitalism

Analyzing business ownership and competition Have students view the Bellringer image and read the two questions aloud. Discuss student answers. Ask students which of these two responses would most strongly influence their decision to start a business. **Ask: What other incentives might someone have to become an entrepreneur?** *(Possible response: the desire to own a business and be one's own boss)* Encourage students to rank these incentives from least to most important.
Visual/Spatial

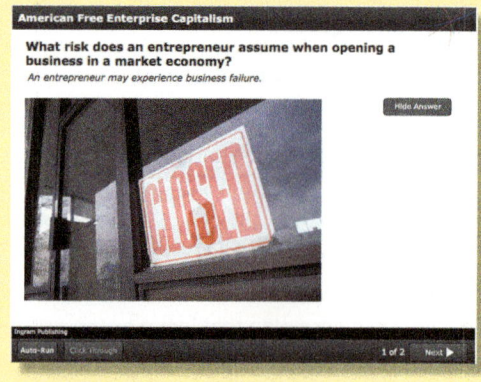

and your job location. You can even leave your current job and move on to another job that offers greater opportunity.

Businesses also enjoy considerable economic freedom. They are free to hire the workers of their choice, and they are free to produce the products they think will be the most profitable. Businesses can make as many items as they want, sell them wherever they please, and normally charge whatever price they choose. In short, they are generally free to risk success or failure.

Think how much different life would be under a different economic system. There are few choices under a traditional economic system because you would be doing the same things, in the same way as your elders did. Under a command economy, you would be doing what the leaders want, not what you want. Under a system guided by socialism, you would be working for the benefit of the state and you would be guided by the directions given to you by the state. Only a free market capitalist system would give you the type of freedom you enjoy today.

Voluntary Exchange

A second characteristic of capitalism is **voluntary exchange**—voluntary act of buyers and sellers freely and willingly engaging in market transactions. A voluntary transaction benefits both the buyer and the seller, or the exchange would never occur.

For example, when buyers spend their money on a product, they act on a belief that the item they purchase is of greater value than the money they give up—or they would not make the purchase. When sellers exchange their products for cash, they believe that the money they receive is more valuable than the product they sell—otherwise they would not make the sale.

In a command or mixed socialist economy, the state would have a bigger role in deciding WHAT and FOR WHOM to produce, thus bypassing the decisions that could have been made in markets. This would result in fewer markets and fewer buyers and sellers that would benefit from voluntary exchange.

Private Property

Another major feature of capitalism is **private property rights**, which allow people to own and control their possessions as they wish. People have the right to use or even abuse their property as long as they do not interfere with the rights of others.

Private property gives people the **incentive** to work, save, and invest. When people are free to do as they wish with their property, they are not afraid to accumulate, improve, use, or lend it. They also know they can keep any rewards they might earn. The Due Process clause of the Fourteenth Amendment to the U.S. Constitution protects private property rights of the American people. That clause states that the State cannot " deprive any person of life, liberty, or property, without due process of law."

Private property makes borrowing possible and investing attractive. If you own property, you can use the property as collateral, or security, if you need to take out a loan. Or if you want to invest in a business or in another private enterprise, there will be a record of your transaction, which will prove that you are an owner. Both of these features—borrowing and investing—are much more difficult in a command or a socialist economy, if they happen at all.

Profit Motive

Under free enterprise capitalism, people are free to risk any part of their wealth in a business venture. If it goes well, they will earn rewards for their efforts. If it goes poorly, they could lose their investment. **Profit** is the extent to which the

free enterprise an economic system in which privately owned businesses have the freedom to operate for a profit with limited government intervention

voluntary exchange act of buyers and sellers freely and willingly engaging in market transactions; a characteristic of capitalism and free enterprise

private property rights fundamental feature of capitalism, which allows individuals to own and control their possessions as they wish; includes both tangible and intangible property

incentive something that motivates

profit difference between the revenue from sales and the full opportunity cost of resources involved in producing the sales

---

CHAPTER 3, LESSON 1
American Free Enterprise Capitalism

R Reading Skills

Understanding essential concepts of free enterprise Read aloud the five characteristics of a free enterprise capitalist economy. Then have students explain in their own words what they think each of the characteristics means. Have students give examples of economic freedom. **ELL** Verbal/Linguistic

C Critical Thinking Skills

Appreciating private property rights Ask students to rate the five characteristics of free enterprise capitalism in order of importance. Lead them to understand that without private property rights, the other characteristics are meaningless. **ELL** Verbal/Linguistic

---

ESSENTIAL QUESTION

Exploring the Essential Question

Analyzing change in free enterprise economies Ask students to name some products that have been developed or modified because of changes in the marketplace. To stimulate discussion, mention computers and cell phones. Discuss how a variety of new products emerges quickly in a free enterprise system with each new change in technology or consumer interest. Then follow up by asking the questions on the screen. **Verbal/Linguistic**

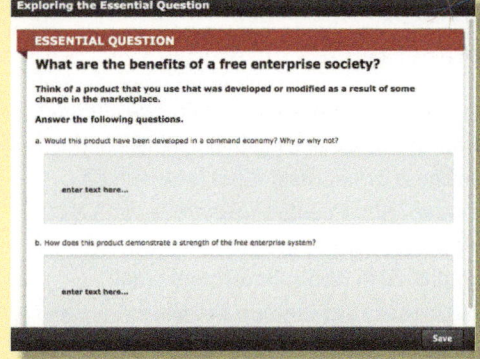

CHAPTER 3, LESSON 1
American Free Enterprise Capitalism

R Reading Skills

Inferring causes of economic activity **Ask: Why is it economically efficient and necessary for people to keep the rewards they earn?** *(Possible answer: If they can keep their rewards, they will work harder and be willing to take risks.)* **Logical/Mathematical**

Content Background Knowledge

Limited Private Property Rights Explain to students that although private property rights are essential to free enterprise capitalism, our society has decided that the right must be limited. Laws and regulations have been created to override property rights in certain situations. The Fifth Amendment defines eminent domain, or the power of government to take private property for public use, stating "nor shall private property be taken for public use without just compensation." Rent control, zoning laws, workers' compensation laws, and minimum wage laws are all examples of the government limiting private property rights. For example, the owner of a house designed by Frank Lloyd Wright in Phoenix wanted to demolish the house and build two new houses on the property. The city balked at losing the famous house and declared it a historic building, meaning it could not be torn down. Invite students to debate the issue of private property rights versus the limited role of government in protecting the interests of society.

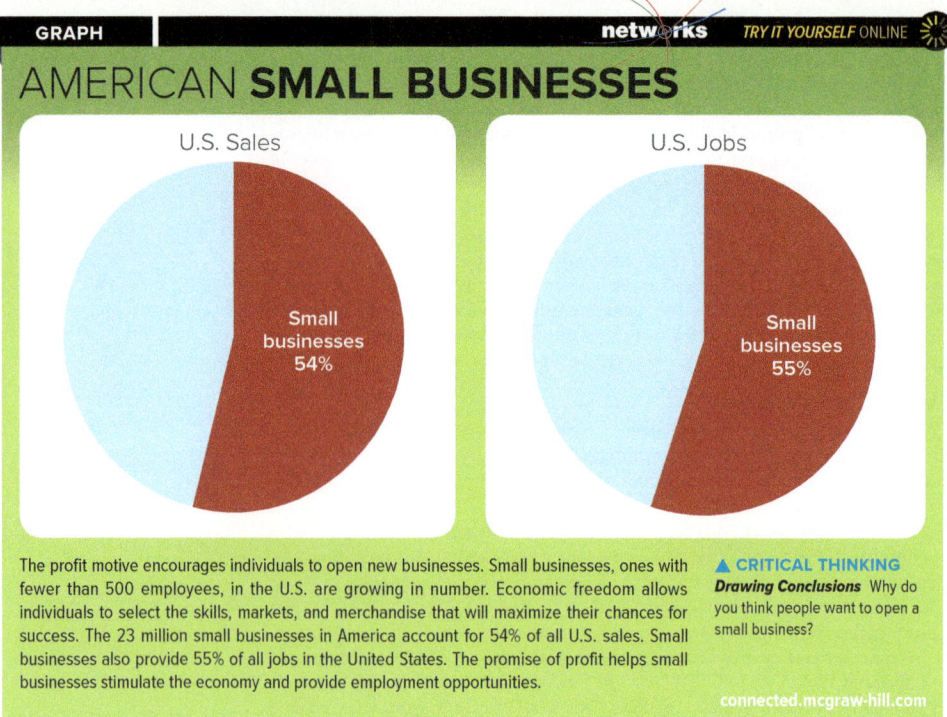

GRAPH

AMERICAN SMALL BUSINESSES

U.S. Sales — Small businesses 54%
U.S. Jobs — Small businesses 55%

The profit motive encourages individuals to open new businesses. Small businesses, ones with fewer than 500 employees, in the U.S. are growing in number. Economic freedom allows individuals to select the skills, markets, and merchandise that will maximize their chances for success. The 23 million small businesses in America account for 54% of all U.S. sales. Small businesses also provide 55% of all jobs in the United States. The promise of profit helps small businesses stimulate the economy and provide employment opportunities.

▲ **CRITICAL THINKING**
Drawing Conclusions Why do you think people want to open a small business?

profit motive driving force that encourages people and organizations to improve their material well-being; characteristic of capitalism and free enterprise

revenue from sales exceeds the full opportunity cost of the resources involved in producing the products sold. The **profit motive**—the incentive to improve one's material well-being—is largely responsible for the growth of a free enterprise system.

The freedom to seek profits helps to guarantee that there is a never-ending stream of products, new and old, being offered in markets to attract consumers' dollars. Some products are offered by firms entering industries for the first time; other firms may be leaving one industry and entering another. Not all succeed, but the lure of profits is the single most important thing that assures us of a never-ending supply of goods and services.

In a command economy, there would be no profit motive to encourage businesses to produce, because the WHAT to produce question would be guided by the central planning authorities. These central authorities would be much more likely to keep underperforming ventures operating for political reasons rather than letting them fail so that resources could move to other activities where they could be better used.

competition the struggle among sellers to attract consumers

Competition

Capitalism thrives on **competition**—the struggle among sellers to attract consumers with the best products at the lowest prices. Competition is possible because individual businesses and entrepreneurs have the freedom to produce the products they think will be the most profitable. Free enterprise capitalism allows competition to flourish, benefiting both producers and consumers alike.

networks Online Teaching Options

IMAGES

Profit Motive

Examining the profit motive Have students view the image and captions of the small business owner. **Ask: What is the profit motive?** *(the incentive to improve one's material well-being)* Then have students click to the circle graphs. **Ask: About how many small businesses are there in the United States?** *(23 million)* **About what percentage of jobs in the United States are related to small businesses?** *(55 percent)* **Visual/Spatial**

Open for Business
The profit motive encourages individuals to open new businesses. Small businesses in the U.S. are growing in number.

ANSWERS, p. 74

CRITICAL THINKING
Because they think that the rewards of profit and personal freedom will outweigh the risks of business.

Competition benefits consumers by assuring them that unpopular products will cease to be produced if consumers do not buy them. Competition also benefits consumers by assuring them that producers are always working to bring newer, better, and less expensive products to market.

Competition benefits the economy by ensuring that the most efficient producers of a product will survive, while the least efficient producers will be forced to shut down, or try to produce different products. In a world of scarce resources, competition helps to assure that these resources are used as efficiently as possible.

☑ **READING PROGRESS CHECK**

Explaining How do private property rights serve as an incentive in a free enterprise economy?

Benefits of Free Enterprise Capitalism

GUIDING QUESTION *How does a free enterprise economy provide opportunities for individuals?*

Individual Freedom

Individual freedom is almost the same as the "economic freedom" described earlier, so in some ways the two overlap—with economic freedom being both a characteristic and a benefit of capitalism. This is true of capitalism in the United States, but it is also true of other parts of the world like Singapore and northern Europe where capitalism and democracy are the strongest.

Our individual freedom is evident in many different ways, from choices we make in the market to choices we make in the voting booth. Strong and stable democratic traditions are also present in countries with free enterprise capitalism, both of which help reinforce the other.

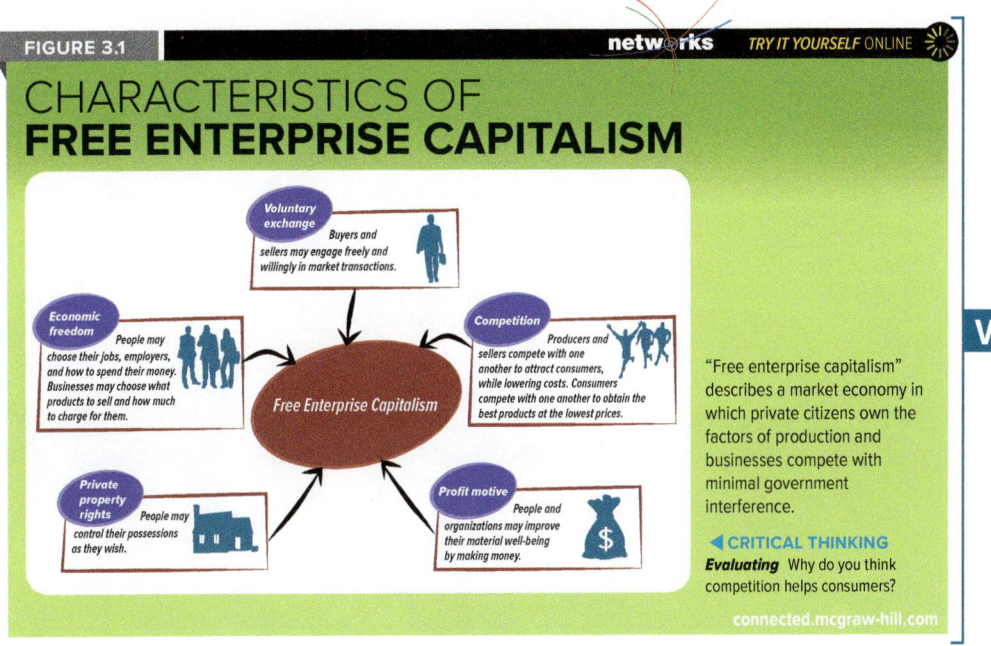

FIGURE 3.1

CHARACTERISTICS OF FREE ENTERPRISE CAPITALISM

- **Voluntary exchange** — Buyers and sellers may engage freely and willingly in market transactions.
- **Economic freedom** — People may choose their jobs, employers, and how to spend their money. Businesses may choose what products to sell and how much to charge for them.
- **Competition** — Producers and sellers compete with one another to attract consumers, while lowering costs. Consumers compete with one another to obtain the best products at the lowest prices.
- **Private property rights** — People may control their possessions as they wish.
- **Profit motive** — People and organizations may improve their material well-being by making money.

"Free enterprise capitalism" describes a market economy in which private citizens own the factors of production and businesses compete with minimal government interference.

◄ **CRITICAL THINKING**
Evaluating Why do you think competition helps consumers?

The American Free Enterprise System 75

CHAPTER 3, LESSON 1
American Free Enterprise Capitalism

C Critical Thinking Skills

Comparing and contrasting industries Tell students that some industries, such as fast-food restaurants, are highly competitive, whereas others have little competition (for example, some cities have a single cable TV provider). Have students identify one example of a competitive industry and one example of an industry with little competition. Ask them to explain why the government allows two industries to have different levels of competition. **Verbal/Linguistic**

V Visual Skills

Analyzing free enterprise capitalism Ask: **Which characteristic of free enterprise in the illustration holds the other characteristics together?** *(competition)* Have students explain why, using Adam Smith's concept of competition as the invisible hand that guides the market. **AL Visual/Spatial**

INTERACTIVE FEATURE

Characteristics of Free Enterprise Capitalism

Describing the characteristics of free enterprise capitalism Have students view Figure 3.1 and read each of the characteristics in turn. Discuss the characteristics and ask students to give real-world examples of each. Challenge students to discuss these questions: **How has Adam Smith's philosophy impacted the U.S free enterprise system? Why is voluntary exchange vital to strong free enterprise capitalism? Why does the federal government sometimes intervene in our economy to promote or protect competition? What effect does the ability to choose jobs and employers have on the success of the free enterprise system? How would a lack of private property rights affect economic conditions in a command economy? Verbal/Linguistic**

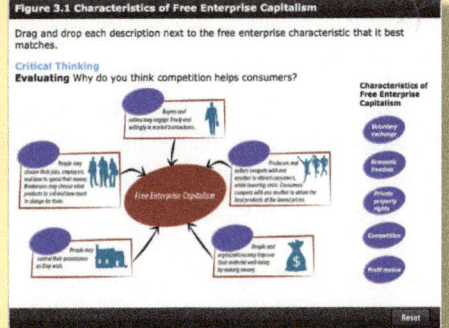

ANSWERS, p. 75

☑ **READING PROGRESS CHECK** When people are free to do as they wish with their property, they are not afraid to accumulate, improve, use, or lend it. They also know they can keep any reward they might earn.

CRITICAL THINKING
Competition helps to ensure that producers are always working to bring newer, better, and less expensive products to market.

The American Free Enterprise System 75

CHAPTER 3, LESSON 1
American Free Enterprise Capitalism

C1 Critical Thinking Skills

Relating free enterprise to democracy **Ask: Why would it be impossible to have free enterprise capitalism without a strong democratic tradition?** *(Possible answer: Free enterprise capitalism depends upon the rights that democracy guarantees to people, such as economic freedom for both consumers and producers, the voluntary exchange of goods and services, private property rights, and the ability to pursue profits.)* **Logical/Mathematical**

C2 Critical Thinking Skills

Drawing conclusions about economic changes
Ask students to identify changes they are witnessing in the economy, such as lower prices for electronic goods or increased prices for concert tickets. Ask them to discuss the causes of these changes and to explain how they demonstrate the ability of free enterprise capitalism to adjust to change. **Verbal/Linguistic**

ANSWERS, p. 76
CRITICAL THINKING
Students may infer that toothpaste companies have either merged or become oligopolies that prevent barriers to entry.

C1 Freedom is something we should value every day, from the time we get up until the time we go to bed. Many of the choices we make—from the type of food we buy to the choices we make about our occupation, our employer, and our job location—would not be possible without an economy based on free enterprise capitalism.

A Variety of Goods
Market economies everywhere are renowned for producing a huge variety of goods of almost all shapes, colors, and sizes, depending on the type of product.

Take shoes for example. Whenever you go into a store, there is an incredible variety of colors, styles, shapes, and sizes. If the store is big enough, there may be aisles and aisles of shoes—and the variety of shoes in those aisles changes from one season to the next. Go to a different store, and you can find the same thing, only this time the brands, colors, styles, and shapes may all be different. All of this comes about because of competition, but think how different things would be in a different type of economy.

Under a command economy as in the former Soviet Union, the central planners would solve the problem of shoe production this way: First they would get an estimate of the number of men, women, and children in the economy. Then they would decide how many pairs of shoes each would get in a year's time. When it came to deciding how many styles and colors they would produce, the easiest thing to do would be to make a small number of styles with a limited number of colors. The result, as far as the consumer was concerned, was a handful of styles that were produced mostly in one color—black.

Since the 1950s, hundreds of toothpaste brands have appeared on the market. In the U.S., 412 kinds of toothpaste were available in 2003, but by 2011 that had fallen to 352 kinds of toothpaste.

▼ **CRITICAL THINKING**
Suggest a possible reason why the number of brands of toothpaste has declined in recent years.

C2 Adapting to Change
Market economies adjust daily to the forces of change. The adjustment takes place mainly through the price system, and a change in the price of one product can affect changes in other industries. Consider the way the rising cost of oil on

76

---

networks Online Teaching Options

TIME LINE

A Variety of Goods

Examining the impact of competition on product availability Display the image showing the large variety of toothpastes available. Ask students to describe the differences among brands that they have used. Then tell them that the number of toothpaste brands have grown radically over time. Have them examine the time line and discuss the developments. **Ask: What effect do you think these developments had on the proliferation of toothpaste varieties?** *(The developments enabled manufacturers to differentiate their products so they could offer more varieties and compete more successfully.)* **What are the benefits of having a variety of goods available? What might be some disadvantages of having so many choices? Would such a variety of goods be available if there were little or no competition?** **Verbal/Linguistic**

international markets has affected our economy. One of the most visible changes has been increased gas mileage for new car models. Because there has been growing emphasis on fuel efficiency, the automakers have thought of ways to achieve this criterion. More efficient gasoline engines and lighter-weight materials for car bodies have been developed to improve efficiency. Some of the improvement is also due to extensive wind tunnel testing to reduce wind drag.

Other changes have also taken place because of the rising price of oil. Wind farms have popped up all over the country to turn wind into electricity. Solar energy is also being harnessed, along with **biofuels**, fuels whose energy is derived from renewable plant and animal materials, vegetable oils, and municipal and industrial wastes. Buildings are now becoming much more energy efficient, costing less to heat and cool. All of these developments have been driven by the higher price of oil.

These adjustments are often difficult to observe day by day, but when observed year by year or even decade by decade, the changes are significant. In the end, it is the market economy, with its emphasis on ever-changing prices, that helps us adjust to change.

Think about how different things would be if we had a command economy in a time of rising oil prices. In a command economy, central planners might try to keep everyone happy by giving them the same amount of oil that they had been using. That might seem to work at first, but soon the government would be producing or buying oil on international markets at one price, and then distributing it to consumers at a much lower price. Government budgets would make up the difference, but none of the energy-efficient changes would take place because the quantity of oil consumed would remain relatively constant. If oil quantities did suddenly change, the central planners might dictate solutions like not driving on weekends or other short-term fixes, rather than encouraging the innovation necessary to create fuel-efficient cars.

Promoting Progress

In a free market capitalist economy, if business and entrepreneurs are allowed to freely enter markets and compete for the dollars that consumers are willing to spend, the result will be economic progress in the form of a continuing supply of newer and better products. For proof of this progress, consider the recent development in the markets that affect you the most.

For example, consider the cell phone industry, which seems to have newer and better products almost monthly. Cell phones are now available from a number of different companies in a variety of sizes and shapes. The phones also have a number of different features that change almost daily—including apps that allow your phone to be used as a street map with GPS connections, an MP3 player, a game player, and a flashlight; the list goes on and on. Computer tablets have also evolved rapidly, as have many other consumer products.

All this progress is possible because of the intense competition among firms to get the business of consumers. The competition takes the form of better products and, usually, lower prices—both of which promote progress.

Creation of Wealth

Economists think of wealth as the accumulation of products that are tangible, are scarce, have utility, and are transferable from one person to another. The creation of wealth is exactly what happens when more and better products are produced in a free market capitalist system.

The Gross Domestic Product—the dollar value of all final goods, services, and structures produced within a country's borders in a 12-month period—of the U.S. economy is the second-largest in the world, having recently been surpassed

EXPLORING THE ESSENTIAL QUESTION

In a free enterprise economy, businesses may be subject to government regulation, but they are not controlled by the government. Consider this situation: A business called Beta becomes very successful. It moves into a larger space. Then it opens more and more stores around the city, and offers lower prices than its competitors. Many of the competing firms begin to go out of business, and eventually, Beta is the only store where people can shop. Should the government prevent Beta's domination of the market so that there are other places where people can buy the things they want?

Write a paragraph explaining your answer.

biofuels fuel made from wood, peat, municipal solid waste, straw, corn, tires, landfill gases, fish oils, and other waste

connected.mcgraw-hill.com   *The American Free Enterprise System* **77**

CHAPTER 3, LESSON 1
American Free Enterprise Capitalism

C Critical Thinking Skills

Debating the profit motive Point out to students that the desire to create wealth drives the free enterprise system. Ask students whether this motivation always leads to positive results for the economy or society. **BL** Verbal/Linguistic

VIDEO / WORKSHEET
Ford Struggles to Stay Profitable

Analyzing free enterprise at Ford Have students watch the video and identify characteristics and benefits of free enterprise capitalism displayed by Ford and its customers. *(competition, profit motive, voluntary exchange, variety of goods, economic freedom, ease and efficiency of adapting to change)* **Ask: What part of the Ford organization is not characterized strictly by market forces?** *(union members' salaries)* **Visual/Spatial**

Video Supplied by BBC Worldwide Learning

ANSWERS, p. 77

EXPLORING THE ESSENTIAL QUESTION

Students' opinions will vary. Require students to offer explanations that support their opinions.

The American Free Enterprise System **77**

CHAPTER 3, LESSON 1
American Free Enterprise Capitalism

English Language Proficiency

Advanced High As students gain proficiency in English, make a point of using new language structures in your oral instruction. After such language structures have been used, ask questions to check for understanding. Repeat information using the new language structures and ask students to paraphrase. Then have them use the new language structure to tell you something from their own knowledge.

C Critical Thinking Skills

Comparing franchises and independent businesses Ensure that students understand the similarities and differences between owning a franchise and owning an independent business by asking them to name a locally-owned, independent business and a well-known franchise. Then draw a comparison-contrast chart on the board and have students write details in the chart to compare these businesses. **AL Logical/Mathematical**

ANSWERS, p. 78

 READING PROGRESS CHECK The free enterprise system can adjust to changing economic conditions through the price system. The ability of market economies to change prices allows for adjustments that keep free enterprise running smoothly in the face of short- and long-term fluctuations.

---

by China, which has a population more than four times larger than the population of the United States.

There is no question that an economic system based on free market capitalism is the most efficient wealth-generating system the world has ever seen. The success of the United States has not been lost on other nations. It is one of the main reasons that so many other nations have a free market capitalist system—or are transitioning to one.

 READING PROGRESS CHECK

Explaining How does the free enterprise system allow for the ability to more easily adapt to changing economic conditions?

Disadvantages of Free Enterprise Capitalism

GUIDING QUESTION *What are the weak points of the free enterprise economy?*

Free enterprise capitalism is not without some drawbacks. Of course they may seem relatively minor when compared to problems with other types of economies, but still, they exist.

CAREERS | Franchise Business Owner

Is this Career for you?

 Can you adapt easily to the changes inherent in the free enterprise system?

C Does the thought of being an entrepreneur appeal to you?

 Do you have a knack for providing excellent service?

 Would you enjoy the freedom of running your own business?

Interview with a Franchise Business Owner

"In this highly competitive world, there is always fear in the beginning about making your business succeed and be profitable. I learned early on that you have to make yourself strong, so that fear doesn't become an obstacle in achieving your goals. Also, finding the right team of people to serve our customers is always a key focus."

—Anita Shah, franchise owner, Dunkin' Donuts and Baskin-Robbins

Salary
$55,000-$75,000 per year

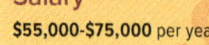

Job Growth Potential
Modest

Profile of Work

Franchise business owners are entrepreneurs who purchase the right to sell a well-known product. In exchange, they receive support and guidance from the brand owner and the benefit of selling a product consumers already know. While success is not guaranteed, the success rate of a franchise is higher than that of an independent start-up business.

78

---

networks Online Teaching Options

INTERACTIVE FEATURE

Career: Franchise Operator

Evaluating a career as a franchise owner Have students view the Careers feature, and ask a student to read the quoted text and the Profile of Work aloud. **Ask: What are some character traits that a franchise owner must exhibit?** *(Sample answer: risk-taker, patience, effective judge of potential employees)* **What are some franchises that operate nearby?** *(Sample answers: McDonalds, Ace Hardware, Dunkin' Donuts, Baskin Robbins)* Encourage students to discuss what they know about these businesses and to list some of the advantages and disadvantages (costs and benefits) they see in owning such a business. Then read and discuss the rest of the feature. **Interpersonal**

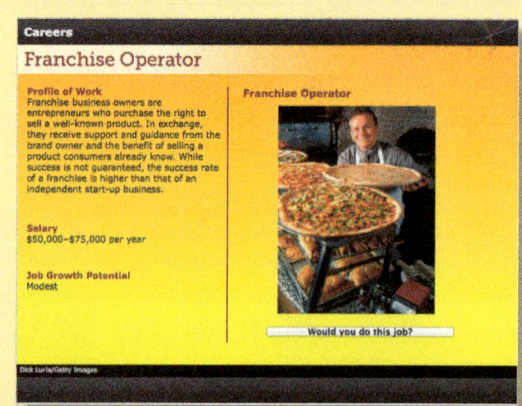

Uneven Economic Growth

The growth of free enterprise capitalism is not always smooth and uninterrupted. Sometimes the growth is relatively fast, and at other times it takes a step back. Most recently, the U.S. economy went through what is now called the **Great Recession**, which started in December of 2007 and lasted until mid-2009. During this 18-month period, the nation's Gross Domestic Product actually shrank about 4.5 to 5 percent!

Periods of uneven economic growth are not pleasant, but they do remove some of the "fat" or unneeded activities in businesses and public services. Even with these painful periods, free market capitalist systems still outperform other economic systems like traditional, command, or socialist economies by a wide margin.

Growing Gaps Between Rich and Poor

Another disadvantage of free enterprise capitalism is that the rich seem to get richer while the poor seem to stay poor. While this will be discussed in greater detail in a later chapter, federal statistics on income support this observation.

Some of this is due to the fact that some people—if they are able to devise a product that meets the consumer's economic need—can grow very rich in a very short period of time. There may not be many solutions to this issue. Tax policies and social welfare programs that divert income from the wealthy to the poor are opposed by many Americans who believe them to be socialist in nature. Still, if the gap gets too wide, voters may demand that government do something about it.

Large "Supply-Side" Tendencies

Economists know that free enterprise economies work best when there are a large number of players—buyers and sellers—on both sides of the market.

This is not a problem on the buyers side of the market where the number of participants seems to grow as more and more people start to search for and buy products along with millions of others. Your parents may have done most of their shopping for clothing, books, medicine, and other products in a small local market with a few thousand other buyers. You, however, may well join millions of other buyers on the Internet in purchasing the same products nationally.

The supply side of the market is completely different because suppliers tend to combine with other suppliers in order to avoid competition—or to "become more efficient" by eliminating some overlapping operations. For example, the Carnival Corporation is a company that owns Carnival Cruise Lines, Holland America, Princess Cruises, Seabourn in North America, and also Costa Cruises

Minimum wage workers protested for higher wages in 2013. The widening gap between rich and poor is a disadvantage of free enterprise capitalism.

▲ **THINK ABOUT IT**
In general, free enterprise capitalism rewards those individuals who have invested in their education with higher paying jobs. Minimum wage jobs do not require an extensive or expensive education, so the people who rely upon minimum wages for a living are at an economic disadvantage. Who are these disadvantaged minimum wage workers?

Great Recession severe economic downturn that lasted from late 2007 through mid-2009

CHAPTER 3, LESSON 1
American Free Enterprise Capitalism

C Critical Thinking Skills

Identifying causes of uneven economic growth
Ask: Why is economic growth in free enterprise capitalism often uneven? *(Possible answer: Unlike command or even socialist economies in which production and the cost of goods are largely controlled by the government, free enterprise capitalism is controlled by the market, so many variables—such as consumer confidence and changes in the cost or availability of resources—can affect economic growth.)* **Logical/Mathematical**

R Reading Skills

Explaining why firms combine Ask: Why do suppliers tend to combine in a capitalist economy? *(Suppliers who combine operations face less competition and can make higher profits.)* Ask students to explain why the government does not do more to discourage or prevent firms from combining. **AL Verbal/Linguistic**

IMAGES

Disadvantages of Free Enterprise

Analyzing the minimum wage Display the image and read the text with students. Ask students if they think that free enterprise capitalism contributes to this gap between the rich and the poor. Urge students to give reasons for their responses. Then encourage them to offer solutions. Point out that some cities and states have raised the minimum wage in their jurisdictions higher than the federal minimum. **Ask: What is the minimum wage where you live?** *(If students do not know, or if your city or state has a higher minimum wage than the federal minimum, ask a student to do research to learn about the wage and to report back to class.)* **Logical/Mathematical**

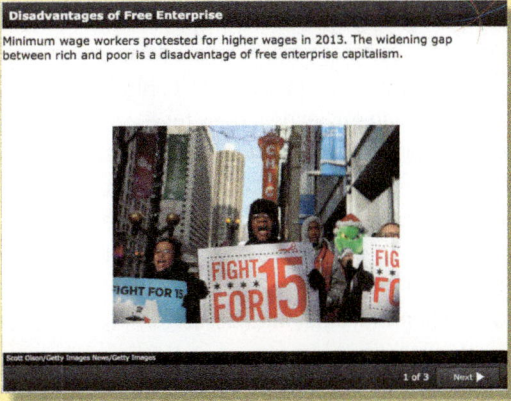

ANSWERS, p. 79

CRITICAL THINKING
Answers will vary, but many minimum wage earners work in fast food restaurants and child care facilities.

CHAPTER 3, LESSON 1
American Free Enterprise Capitalism

Making Connections

Business Regulations Ask students to name some examples of local businesses that they visit. Discuss the range of government regulations that such businesses are subject to. **Ask: Apart from regulations discussed in the text, what are some other government regulations that apply to businesses?** *(Sample answer: Businesses must get licenses to operate, restaurants are subject to food handling regulations, all businesses must adhere to certain safety regulations for employees.)* **ELL** **Verbal/Linguistic**

CLOSE & REFLECT

R Reading Skills

Summarizing the lesson Have students work in pairs and review the lesson by writing two main ideas for each subsection. Then guide a class discussion. Ask students to share their main ideas and explain why they think those ideas are important to understanding the lesson.

ANSWERS, p. 80

✓ **READING PROGRESS CHECK** Supply-side tendencies can result in the suppliers combining efforts to avoid competition. This can result in the consumer having fewer purchasing and cost options.

---

in Southern Europe. You have to wonder how intense the competition between these companies really is if they are all part of the same company.

When similar firms combine, the result is fewer participants on the supply side of the market. Meanwhile, the participants on the demand side of the market are now focused on a diminished number of suppliers. This is one of the results of capitalism, and it is one that makes competitive markets less efficient. It is one of the reasons that the government may step in if there appear to be too few firms in an industry—but the government does not often prevent the general tendency of firms to combine and reduce competition.

Rights and Responsibilities of Business

You may not realize it, but corporations have most of the same rights as individuals. They can sue and be sued, they can enter into contracts, and they can own property, just like you can. About the only thing that corporations can't do that you can do is vote.

In addition to these rights, businesses also have many responsibilities, most of which are due to government regulations that limit the scope of their activities. For example, the federal Immigration and Nationality Act (INA) requires that all employees be treated equally. This makes it illegal for businesses to have a "U.S. citizens only" hiring policy, unless citizenship is required by a federal, state, or local law, or by government contract.

Other government regulations protect consumers against harm from products on the market, ranging from baby seats and cribs to ignition switches on automobiles. These broad-ranging regulations are required by the Consumer Product Safety Commission, which was established in 1972. Requirements like these are unique to free enterprise capitalism because they are not found in other types of economic systems like traditional, command, or socialist economies. Instead, these policies exist because consumers have the power at the ballot box to force their representatives to enact some regulations on businesses. The result is that "free enterprise" is slightly less free than the term suggests.

✓ **READING PROGRESS CHECK**

Explaining How do the "supply-side tendencies" in a free enterprise economy tend to work to the disadvantage of the consumer?

LESSON 1 REVIEW

Reviewing Vocabulary
1. ***Defining*** Explain how the Great Recession illustrated one of the weaknesses of a free enterprise economy.

Using Your Notes
2. ***Summarizing*** Use your notes to compare the benefits and disadvantages of a free enterprise economic system.

Answering the Guiding Questions
3. ***Explaining*** How does the American economy incorporate the main characteristics of a free enterprise economy?
4. ***Summarizing*** How does a free enterprise economy's freedom of producers provide benefits for individual consumers?
5. ***Analyzing*** What are the weak points, or economic costs, that are part of a free enterprise economy?

6. ***Identifying*** What regulation was established in 1972 to ensure that businesses take responsibility for the products they produce?

Writing About Economics
7. ***Argument*** During the Great Recession, many people lost a great deal of their personal wealth. Some firms went out of business. Unemployment rose quickly. The United States' free enterprise system has periodically experienced poor economic times. Why then, don't Americans embrace more government control of the economy? Write a one-page argument stating and defending your point of view, making sure to consider the costs and the benefits of the disposal of business property within the free enterprise system.

LESSON 1 REVIEW ANSWERS

Reviewing Vocabulary
1. The Great Recession demonstrated the large swings in growth and contraction that characterize a free market economy.

Using Your Notes
2. Benefits: individual freedom; variety of goods and services; an economy adaptive to change, promotes progress, and creates wealth. Disadvantages: a gap between the rich and poor, and a tendency for suppliers to combine, thereby reducing competition.

Answering the Guiding Questions
3. The American economy allows individuals to purchase what they want, work where they want, and change jobs when they want. Businesses can make whatever products they wish and sell them at any price. Buyers and sellers can exchange money for products, but no one is forced to buy or sell. People and corporations own property and can do buy it, sell it, use it to borrow money, or to make a profit. People have the right to make a profit. Most businesses operate in competition with other businesses.

4. Individuals can own property and use the property as they wish to make a profit and build wealth. They can buy and sell any products they wish. If they discover a new product or a better way to make a product, they can begin selling the product to gain an edge in the marketplace.

5. The individual economic freedom in free enterprise can also mean widespread income gaps as not everyone is guaranteed economic success.

6. The Consumer Product Safety Commission was established to protect consumers from poor manufacturing and to make sure that products met quality and safety standards.

Writing About Economics
7. Students should demonstrate an understanding of both the benefits and the weaknesses of the free enterprise economy.

Case Study

For an interactive version of this case study go to connected.mcgraw-hill.com

PUBLIC VERSUS PRIVATE OWNERSHIP

There has long been debate over the merits of public versus private enterprise ownership. Often, the argument is made that public ownership is essential when the benefits of development are vital to the public interest but too risky or expensive for private ventures. This fairly describes many of the publicly owned businesses in the United States, such as the National Aeronautics and Space Administration (NASA), Ginnie Mae (which ensures that capital is available for home mortgages), and many municipal sanitation and water departments. Another example is the Tennessee Valley Authority (TVA).

In 1933, the federal government created the TVA to build hydroelectric dams on the Tennessee River and its tributaries, primarily to control flooding and generate electric power. At that time, people in most urban areas enjoyed the benefits of electric power. But it was rare in rural areas, especially in poorer regions such as the Tennessee Valley. Power companies were slow to bring electricity to these areas because it was expensive to string wire to all these remote sites, and the citizens were too poor to pay for it. The TVA, underwritten by the federal government, was considered the solution.

The project was controversial from the beginning. Many people were suspicious of government involvement in private enterprise. Power companies believed the government should stay out of private enterprise. Others believed it was the government's duty to ensure the availability of affordable power and to provide a means for poor people of the region to improve their standard of living. Court battles took place, finally reaching the Supreme Court. The Court ruled that the government had the legal authority to build the dams and sell and distribute electricity.

Today, the TVA operates 29 hydroelectric dams—as well as nuclear and conventional power-generating facilities in the valley—and is America's largest public power provider.

The map above shows the extent of the hydroelectric dams built in the Tennessee River valley. The Big Ridge Lake recreational area is one example of a community benefit to the Tennesse Valley Authority project that was not related to electrification services.

CASE STUDY REVIEW

1. **Analyzing** Why would privately owned power companies oppose the government's plan to build the TVA's hydroelectric dams?
2. **Defending** Do you think that the government has a legitimate role in providing goods and services to consumers? Under what circumstances?

connected.mcgraw-hill.com   The American Free Enterprise System

CHAPTER 3, LESSON 2
Roles and Responsibilities in a Free Enterprise System

ENGAGE

C1 Critical Thinking Skills

Analyzing the role of the entrepreneur Before students begin the lesson, ask them to explain what an entrepreneur is. **Ask:**

- What does an entrepreneur do?
- What makes the role of entrepreneur challenging?
- What makes the role of entrepreneur rewarding?
- How does an entrepreneur relate to consumers and to the government?

Encourage students to take notes about the responses to these questions and to refer back to them as they read more about the roles of entrepreneurs, consumers, and government in the U.S. economy. **Logical/Mathematical**

TEACH & ASSESS

C2 Critical Thinking Skills

Hypothesizing about a start-up business Have students work in pairs to describe a business that a teenager could open. Then tell pairs to answer these questions about their business: **What are the start-up costs? How much time would you need to devote to the business? Who are your target customers? What benefits will you gain as the business owner?** Have partners present their information to the class. **Interpersonal**

ANSWERS, p. 82
ESSENTIAL QUESTION ACTIVITY

Answers will vary.
TAKING NOTES Role: Entrepreneur; **Responsibilities:** Organize and manage resources such as land, capital, and labor to seek a profit. **Role:** Consumer; **Responsibilities:** Use purchasing decisions to determine the types of goods and services that will be offered in the market. **Role:** Government; **Responsibilities:** Protect private property rights and consumers, Provide services, Regulate marketplace, Act as a consumer of goods and services

---

Interact with these digital assets and others in lesson 2
- ✓ WHITEBOARD ACTIVITY Government Regulatory Agencies
- INTERACTIVE IMAGE Role of the Consumer
- ✓ SELF-CHECK QUIZ
- ✓ VIDEO

networks TRY IT YOURSELF ONLINE

LESSON 2
Roles and Responsibilities in a Free Enterprise Economy

Reading Help Desk

Academic Vocabulary
- catalyst
- regulator

Content Vocabulary
- entrepreneur
- consumer sovereignty
- mixed economy
- modified free enterprise economy

TAKING NOTES:

Key Ideas and Details
ACTIVITY As you read the lesson, complete a graphic organizer like the one below to identify the roles and responsibilities in a free enterprise system.

Roles	Responsibilities

ESSENTIAL QUESTION

What are the benefits of a free enterprise economy?

We often think of the American free enterprise economy as having several distinct "players" that ensure its success. These players include entrepreneurs, consumers, and the government. How do you fit in? How does the system benefit you? As a student, you may find that you need extra spending money to cover your school and your living expenses. You may begin thinking about becoming an entrepreneur by creating a small business that will earn you money. You may also decide to look into getting a job. Or you may visit your school's financial aid office to see if there is some form of government student aid, such as a loan, grant, or work-study program.

Answer the following questions:

1. What might I do as an entrepreneur? What type of business or service might I be able to offer for a fee?
2. What type of part-time job might I like that is available near my school?
3. What type of financial aid might be available to me through my school?

The Role of the Entrepreneur

GUIDING QUESTION *Why are entrepreneurs essential to the success of a free enterprise economy?*

The **entrepreneur** is the person who organizes and manages the land, capital, and labor in order to seek the reward called profit. Entrepreneurs are important because they are the ones who start new businesses such as restaurants, automobile repair shops, and Internet cafes, among other types of businesses. Entrepreneurs are usually people who want to "be their own boss" and are willing to take risks to make their dreams come true.

Most entrepreneurs fail, but others survive and manage to stay in business with varying degrees of success. A few, and only a very few, manage to become

---

networks *Online Teaching Options*

BELLRINGER

Roles and Responsibilities in a Free Enterprise Economy

Analyzing business ownership and competition Have students view the Bellringer image and read the questions aloud. Discuss student responses. Encourage students to cite examples from their own community in which a business moved into an area and increased competition. **Ask: What have you observed when a firm has gone out of business? How does it affect competition, prices, and the variety of choices available to consumers?** *(Answers will vary, but students should recognize that with less competition, they may have noticed higher prices, and they probably had fewer choices.)* **Logical/Mathematical**

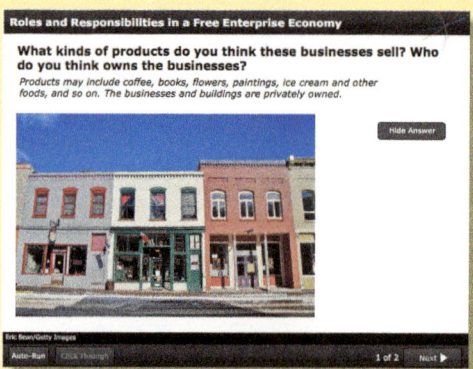

fantastically wealthy. Well-known entrepreneurs like Mark Zuckerberg, Jeff Bezos, and Steve Jobs changed the way we communicate, shop, and work.

Despite the high rate of failure among entrepreneurs, the dream of success is often too great to resist. The entrepreneur is both the spark plug and the **catalyst** of the free enterprise economy. When entrepreneurs are successful, everybody benefits. Entrepreneurs are rewarded with profits, a growing business, and the satisfaction of a job well done. Workers across the country are rewarded with more and better-paying jobs. Consumers are rewarded with new and better products. The government is rewarded with a higher level of economic activity and larger tax receipts that can be used to build roads, schools, and libraries and to provide other services for people not even connected to the original entrepreneur.

It does not stop there. Successful entrepreneurs attract other firms to the industry who rush in to "grab a share" of the profits. To remain competitive and stay in business, the original entrepreneur may have to improve the quality of the product or cut prices, which means that customers can buy more for less. In the end, the entrepreneur's search for profits can lead to a chain of events that brings new products, greater competition, more production, higher quality, and lower prices for consumers.

Because of the entrepreneur, businesses in our economy have become enormously successful. Today, our Gross Domestic Product is the largest in the world and our economy is largely responsible for generating more wealth than any other nation on earth. None of this would have been possible without the entrepreneur.

entrepreneur risk-taking individual in search of profits; one of four factors of production

catalyst something that stimulates activity among people or forces

✓ **READING PROGRESS CHECK**

Analyzing Why are entrepreneurs considered both spark plugs and catalysts of the free enterprise economy?

The Role of the Consumer

GUIDING QUESTION *What role do consumers play in a free enterprise system?*

Consumers have power in the economy because they ultimately determine WHAT to produce. If consumers like a new product, the producer will be rewarded with profits. If consumers do not buy the new product, the firm may lose money or even go out of business. The term **consumer sovereignty** recognizes the role of the consumer as sovereign, or ruler, of the market. The phrase "the customer is always right" reflects this power.

In recent years, producers have had outstanding successes with products ranging from fast foods to social media platforms. Other products, for example, including Harley Davidson perfume, flower-flavored PEZ, and Dr. Care's aerosol toothpaste (which kids discovered they could spray around the bathroom), were rejected by consumers and are no longer produced.

In addition, as people are exposed to new ideas and products, consumers want the benefits. For example, when desktop computers were introduced, it wasn't long before American consumers were purchasing more desktop computers than televisions, even though computers were barely known just 35 years ago.

Then, computer laptops became more popular than desktop computers. Finally, computer tablets became more popular than laptops. Today, consumers buy products made all over the world and frequently use the Internet to research products and make purchases.

consumer sovereignty role of consumer as ruler of the market in determining the types of goods and services produced

CHAPTER 3, LESSON 2
Roles and Responsibilities in a Free Enterprise System

V Visual Skills

Diagramming the effects of entrepreneurs Have students create a visual summary of all the effects of entrepreneurs as catalysts in the economy. Students might create a tree or interlocking concept web or illustrate a graphic novel. **BL** Kinesthetic, Visual/Spatial

R1 Reading Skills

Understanding the importance of entrepreneurs
Ask: Why is the entrepreneur and his or her economic freedom so important to the health of the free-market economy? *(Entrepreneurs create jobs, contribute to growing the economy, pay taxes, and provide consumers with more and better products. They attract additional firms into their industry, which creates competition and thereby reduces prices and improves the quality and variety of products.)* **AL** Logical/Mathematical

R2 Reading Skills

Understanding consumer sovereignty
Ask: Why do consumers ultimately control what is produced? *(Consumers buy the products; if they like a product, they purchase more of it and reward the firm with profit so more products are made. If they do not like the product, the firm will not make a profit and so will stop producing the item.)* **AL** Logical/Mathematical

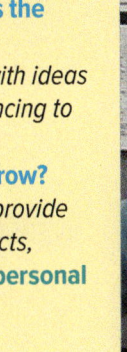

VIDEO **WORKSHEET**

Creativity Helping Workers

Analyzing entrepreneurial opportunities Have students view the video. **Ask:** How does the ability to "rent" equipment promote entrepreneurship? *(It enables people with ideas to start a business even if they lack financing to purchase equipment.)* How does entrepreneurship help the economy grow? *(Whenever small businesses start, they provide jobs and new, perhaps innovative products, which will stimulate competition.)* **Interpersonal**

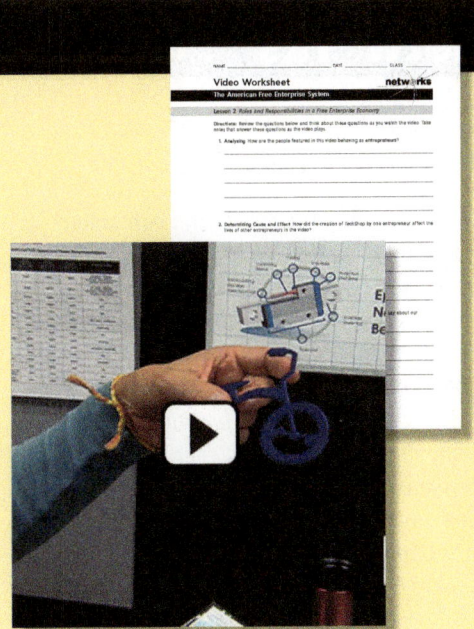

ANSWERS, p. 83

✓ **READING PROGRESS CHECK** Entrepreneurs are spark plugs because they start businesses. They are catalysts because their businesses can stimulate other activity among people and other businesses.

CHAPTER 3, LESSON 2
Roles and Responsibilities in a Free Enterprise System

C1 Critical Thinking Skills

Applying consumer sovereignty to real numbers
Have students bring to class advertisements of technology, entertainment, and clothing products; or have students create illustrations of products they think would be popular. Hold up each image, and by a show of hands have students vote whether they would purchase the item if they had the money to do so. Keep track of the votes as a percentage for and against each item. Apply that percentage to the total U.S. population of around 330 million, or to a specific age category of the U.S. population (for example, 21.2 million 15-to-19 year olds). Help students understand that a consumer "vote" for a product can lead to huge wealth for producers.
Interpersonal

C2 Critical Thinking Skills

Identifying consumer rights and responsibilities
Have students develop a list of consumer rights and responsibilities as they apply to the purchase, use, and disposal of personal property. **Logical/Mathematical**

What is the role of . . .

AS APPLE INTRODUCES NEW DEVICES, LOYAL CONSUMERS **VOICE THEIR APPROVAL** BY WAITING ANXIOUSLY FOR THE NEWEST PRODUCT TO BE RELEASED.

The Consumer in the United States

Making Their Voice Heard

Consumers have influence and power in a free enterprise economic system. Because they have to choose between a wide variety of products, the economic choices they make give all consumers a collective voice in what should be produced and sold. A crowd of people waiting for the release of a brand new product is a powerful demonstration of this influence in action. Just as people "vote" with their dollars for products and services they want, they also do so by investing time and effort in obtaining them.

▲ **CRITICAL THINKING**
Explain how the concept of consumer sovereignty can impact the types of products available, using the example of a computer game.

C2 Think of the dollars that consumers spend in the marketplace as "votes" that give them a say in what is, and what is not, produced. Because of this, consumers play an important role in the American free enterprise economy.

 READING PROGRESS CHECK

Recalling What is the role of the consumer in the free market economy?

84

---

networks Online Teaching Options

IMAGES

Role of the Consumer

Understanding the role of the consumer
Have students view the Role of the Consumer image and read the question. Discuss their answers. **Ask: How is a consumer like an entrepreneur?** *(Both the consumer and the entrepreneur enable the economy to grow: the entrepreneur by creating products and competition, and the consumer by expressing demand and stimulating business development. Both put money into the market, which creates jobs and promotes economic growth with its related benefits.)* **Logical/Mathematical**

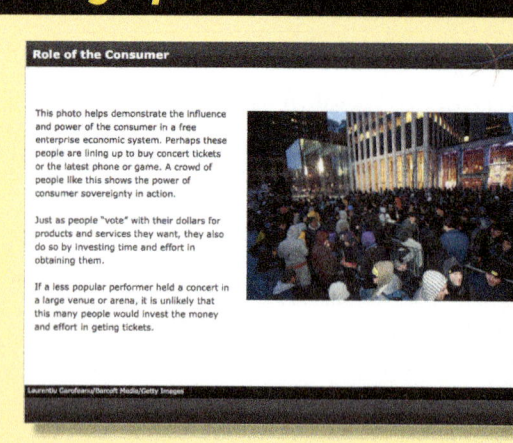

ANSWERS, p. 84

CRITICAL THINKING
A computer game that many people want becomes a bestseller, with many consumers willing to pay for it. One that is less popular may not be profitable enough for its maker to continue offering it.

✓ **READING PROGRESS CHECK** The consumer plays the role of "judge" in a free enterprise system by determining which products and services succeed by purchasing the products and services that best meet their needs.

The Role of Government

GUIDING QUESTION *How is the role of government determined in the American free enterprise system?*

The role of government—whether national, state, or local—stems from the desires, goals, and aspirations of its citizens. Government has become involved in the economy because its citizens want it that way. Consequently, government has become a protector, provider, **regulator**, and consumer. In general, the role of government in the economy is justified whenever its benefits outweigh its costs.

regulator someone or something that controls activities

Protector
As protector, the U.S. government makes laws such as those against false and misleading advertising, unsafe food and drugs, environmental hazards, and unsafe automobiles. It also enforces laws against abuses of individual freedoms. The U.S. Constitution even gives the government the right to protect the private property rights of American citizens.

Provider
All levels of government provide goods and services for its citizens. The national government supplies a system of justice and national defense. It provides subsidies to parts of the economy, such as agriculture. In addition, it gives funding to state and local governments for programs such as road construction. State governments provide education, highways, and public welfare. Local governments provide parks, libraries, sanitation, and transportation services.

Regulator
In its role as a regulator, the national government is charged with preserving competition in the marketplace. It also oversees communications, interstate commerce, and even entire industries such as banking and nuclear power. State governments oversee insurance rates and automobile registrations, while local governments regulate economic activity with building and zoning permits.

The regulatory role of government is often controversial. Most businesses do not like to be told how to run their affairs. Consumers, however, do not always know when they are at risk from hazards, such as potential poisoning from unsafe food preparation or false and misleading advertising from some companies. As a result, they want the government to monitor and regulate such activities.

> **EXPLORING THE ESSENTIAL QUESTION**
>
> If you wanted to start your own small business, how might the federal, state, or local government help you in your endeavor? List a few government programs or services that might be helpful to an entrepreneur trying to start his or her own business for the first time.

Consumer
The tasks of protecting, providing, and regulating are expensive. This means all levels of government, like any business, consume scarce resources to fulfill their role. Government has grown so much in recent years that it spends more than all private businesses combined.

✓ **READING PROGRESS CHECK**

Summarizing What role does the government play in a free enterprise system?

CHAPTER 3, LESSON 2
Roles and Responsibilities in a Free Enterprise System

C1 Critical Thinking Skills

Evaluating the cost of government actions
Ask: *In what situations do you think the cost of government actions outweigh the benefits? (Some might think certain actions, like enforcing a national minimum wage, will cost jobs and raise the prices of goods or services.)* **Verbal/Linguistic**

V Visual Skills

Analyzing misleading advertising Have students search for examples of advertising that could be misleading. Ask them to create a poster showing the examples they find and to add captions that explain why each ad might be misleading. Finally, have them add the government agency that is set up to protect consumers from misleading claims. **AL Visual/Spatial**

C2 Critical Thinking Skills

Identifying and evaluating government restrictions Have students identify examples of restrictions that the government places on the use of individual property. List these examples on the board. Then have students, by a show of hands, evaluate whether each restriction is valid or invalid. Encourage students to explain their reasoning. **Verbal/Linguistic**

W Writing Skills

Writing about government's changing role Have students select one of the economic roles of the government and research whether the role has changed over time. Students should write a report about their findings. Encourage them to use visuals such as charts and graphs. **Verbal/Linguistic**

CHARTS
Government Regulatory Agencies

Identifying government agencies Have students view the Government Regulatory Agencies chart and read the text. Call on volunteers to match the description with the correct agency. As they do, ask students to expand on the description by explaining how these regulations directly affect consumers. For example, the FDA oversees all medicines to ensure they are effective in doing what they are supposed to do, are not dangerous, and are produced in a responsible manner. **Logical/Mathematical**

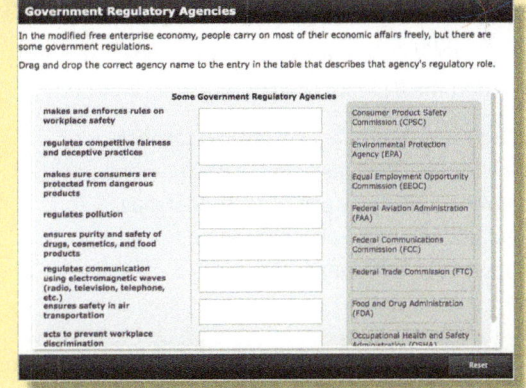

ANSWERS, p. 85

EXPLORING THE ESSENTIAL QUESTION

Sample Answer: The Small Business Administration provides guidance as well as loans to help entrepreneurs get started.

✓ **READING PROGRESS CHECK** The government acts as a protector, a provider, regulator, and consumer in a free enterprise economy.

CHAPTER 3, LESSON 2
Roles and Responsibilities in a Free Enterprise System

R Reading Skills

Defining a mixed economy   Ask: What makes the U.S. economy a mixed, or modified free enterprise economy? *(People and businesses can carry on economic affairs freely but are subject to some government regulation and intervention.)*
AL Verbal/Linguistic

W Writing Skills

Evaluating government regulations Ask students to work individually or in pairs to summarize government's role as regulator in our modified free enterprise economy. Have them write four arguments in support of government regulations on the use of individual and business property, and four arguments opposing government regulations. In class discussion, have students share their ideas. Verbal/Linguistic

CLOSE & REFLECT

R Reading Skills

Reviewing the lesson Ask students to write one question about each subsection. Collect the questions and have students answer them in a class review.

ANSWERS, p. 86

✓ **READING PROGRESS CHECK** Americans want government to play a role in the economy because the private sector cannot provide services like national defense or a system of laws.

An attraction of a free enterprise economic system is that it empowers the individual. A small business owner has more freedom to make economic decisions and profit from success. Consumers have a wider variety of products and services to purchase.

Mixed or Modified Free Enterprise

GUIDING QUESTION *Why has the free enterprise system been modified to include some government intervention?*

mixed economy economic system that has some combination of traditional, command, and market economies; also see modified free enterprise economy

modified free enterprise economy free enterprise market economy where people carry on their economic affairs freely, but are subject to some government intervention and regulation; also see mixed economy

Perhaps an unintended consequence of government's role as protector, provider, regulator, and consumer is the emergence of the **mixed economy,** or **modified free enterprise economy.** In this economy, people and businesses carry on their economic affairs freely, but they are subject to some government intervention and regulation.

Some people prefer to have no government involvement in the economy, but this is not possible. After all, some services, such as national defense and a system of laws and justice, cannot be supplied by the private sector alone.

Unfortunately, there is no clear answer to the question of how much government involvement is necessary, and so it has become one of the great unsolved questions of our time. The issue is in the news almost daily, and it has become a rallying cry for both individual politicians and political parties. If this issue is ever resolved, it will be done by the voting public. Until then, just remember that we have a mixed or modified free enterprise economy because the majority of people want it that way.

✓ **READING PROGRESS CHECK**

Explaining Why do Americans want government to play a role in the economy?

LESSON 2 REVIEW

Reviewing Vocabulary
1. *Defining* Explain how consumer sovereignty operates in the marketplace to determine the success or failure of an entrepreneur.

Using Your Notes
2. *Summarizing* Use the information you jotted down in the graphic organizer to describe how government helps business provide the goods and services that people need and want.

Answering Guiding Questions
3. *Analyzing* Why are entrepreneurs essential to the success of a free enterprise economy?
4. *Making Connections* What role do consumers play in a free enterprise system?

5. *Applying* How is the role of government determined in the American free enterprise system?
6. *Explaining* Why has the free enterprise system been modified to include some government intervention?

Writing About Economics
7. *Identifying Perspective* What perspective is presented in this lesson about government's role in the free enterprise system? Do you agree or disagree that there are some areas of the free market in which government has a legitimate role to play to rein in business excesses and to ensure consumer safety? Describe your perspective on this issue and compare and contrast it with the perspective presented in this lesson. Use examples to support your argument.

LESSON 2 REVIEW ANSWERS

Reviewing Vocabulary
1. An entrepreneur will be successful in his or her new business if the business provides a good or service that is new and wanted by consumers or if the good or service is of better quality at a better price than that of competitors.

Using Your Notes
2. The government maintains the infrastructure that businesses need to create and transport goods; it defends the nation, and thus businesses, against foreign aggression; it subsidizes vital goods, such as agricultural products; it writes and enforces some regulations on businesses to protect consumers against unfair practices or unsafe products.

Answering the Guiding Questions
3. Entrepreneurs create new businesses that provide new jobs; they often develop innovative products and services that may spread through the economy and open up opportunities for even more new businesses.
4. Consumers play the crucial role of "judge" by purchasing the products and services that best meet their needs. In this way, consumers determine which products are sold and which businesses succeed.

5. The public and legislators decide if government is needed to subsidize vital products, to ensure the safety of products or fairness in business practices (regulation), and to provide the infrastructure in which businesses can operate.
6. Government intervention is needed to ensure fair competition and to protect the public safety; for example, in pharmaceutical and vehicle safety.

Writing About Economics
7. Students may argue for or against varying degrees of government involvement. Students should provide a cogent, logical argument supported by real examples.

Interact with these digital assets and others in lesson 3

✓ BIOGRAPHY
  Brian Linton
✓ POLITICAL CARTOON
  Economic and Social Goals
✓ SELF-CHECK QUIZ
✓ VIDEO

networks
TRY IT YOURSELF ONLINE

LESSON 3
Evaluating Economic Performance

Reading Help Desk

Academic Vocabulary
- adverse
- accommodate

Content Vocabulary
- minimum wage
- Social Security
- Medicare
- inflation
- fixed income

TAKING NOTES:

Key Ideas and Details
ACTIVITY Use a graphic organizer like the one below to summarize the goals of the U.S. economy.

ESSENTIAL QUESTION

What are the major economic and social goals of the American free enterprise system?

C1 We all have personal goals; even businesses and governments have goals. Living in the United States, we have goals for our free enterprise economic system. What do you think are some of the major economic and social goals most people in the United States share? Identify one of these goals and write a paragraph discussing whether you agree or disagree with that goal.

Economic and Social Goals

GUIDING QUESTION *Why might our economic goals change over time?*

In the United States, people share many broad economic and social goals. While it might be difficult to find all of our goals listed in any one place, they are repeated many times in statements made by friends, relatives, community leaders, and elected officials. We can categorize those statements into seven major economic and social goals.

Economic Freedom

C2 Americans traditionally place a high value on the freedom to make their own economic decisions. They like to choose their own occupations, employers, and uses for their money. Business owners like the freedom to choose when, where, and what they produce. This belief in economic freedom, like the belief in political freedom, is one of the cornerstones of American society.

Economic Efficiency

C3 Most people recognize that resources are scarce and that factors of production must be used wisely. If resources are wasted, fewer goods and services can be produced, fewer wants and needs can be satisfied, and fewer resources can be left for future generations. Because economic decision making needs to be efficient, economic efficiency is also one of our major goals.

connected.mcgraw-hill.com   *The American Free Enterprise System* **87**

CHAPTER 3, LESSON 3
Evaluating Economic Performance

ENGAGE

C1 Critical Thinking Skills

Discussing clashing goals Before students begin the lesson, invite students to describe situations where economic goals clash with social goals. For example, it might be in our economic interest to allow a firm to build a factory in a community because it will provide jobs. At the same time, building the factory might create noise pollution or traffic jams that would diminish the quality of the neighborhood. Encourage a debate about priorities in these cases.

TEACH & ASSESS

C2 Critical Thinking Skills

Determining costs and benefits of economic freedom Ask students to list opposing aspects of American economic freedom, such as freedom to develop a business versus the freedom to live in a business-free zone. **AL**

C3 Critical Thinking Skills

Determining cause and effect Ask: *What effect does efficiency have on the number of goods available? (Higher efficiency produces a greater number of goods with the original amount of resources.)* **Logical/Mathematical.**

BELLRINGER

Evaluating Economic Performance

Identifying market characteristics in the U.S. economy
Display the Bellringer chart and review the characteristics of the three types of economic systems. After students respond to the first question, **ask: How do you know?** *(Sample answer: Individuals make most economic decisions; they own the factors of production; they have a high degree of individual freedom; they have access to a large variety of goods and services; people have little incentive to engage in unprofitable ventures; and people experience a high degree of economic uncertainty.)* **What are some examples of traditional and command economies?** *(Sample answers: traditional: Inuit; command: Cuba)* Read and discuss the other questions. **Interpersonal**

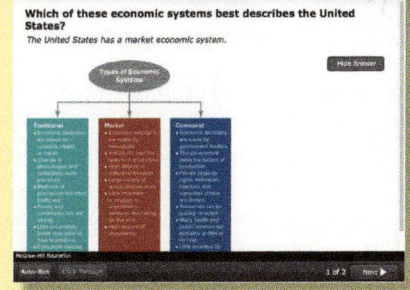

ANSWERS, p. 87

ESSENTIAL QUESTION ACTIVITY

Answers will vary. Ask a student to give an example and encourage other students to agree or disagree and explain why.

TAKING NOTES: Economic freedom, economic efficiency, economic equity, economic security, full employment, price stability, economic growth

The American Free Enterprise System **87**

CHAPTER 3, LESSON 3
Evaluating Economic Performance

R Reading Skills

Defining and applying *equity* **Ask: What is the difference between** *equity* **and** *equality*? (*Equity* means "*fairness*"; *equality* means "*the same*.") Have students write a paragraph using each word and describing the costs and benefits of U.S. economic policies related to the economic goal of equity. **Verbal/Linguistic**

V Visual Skills

Creating a poster about economic security
Ask students to create a poster about the economic goal of security. Students can use magazine and newspaper photos to illustrate the costs and benefits of providing economic security. Have students write a short caption explaining how each photo represents the goal. **AL Visual/Spatial**

Economic Equity

Americans have a strong tradition of justice, impartiality, and fairness. Many people, for example, believe in equal pay for equal work. As a result, it is illegal to discriminate on the basis of age, sex, race, religion, or disability in employment. At the national and state levels, we have established the **minimum wage**—the lowest legal wage that can be paid to most workers. While not everyone supports it, the minimum wage does put a floor on the amount of income that some workers earn.

In the interest of fairness, most people believe that advertisers should not be allowed to make false claims about their products. Many states even have "lemon laws," which allow new car buyers to get their money back for a car with too many defects.

minimum wage lowest legal wage that can be paid to most workers

adverse unfavorable or harmful

Social Security federal program of disability and retirement benefits that covers most working people

Medicare federal health insurance program for senior citizens, regardless of income

Economic Security

Americans desire protection from such **adverse** economic events as layoffs and illnesses, injuries, or disabilities that prevent them from being able to work. As a result, many states have set up unemployment compensation programs to help workers who lose their jobs through no fault of their own.

At the national level, Congress has set up **Social Security**—a federal program of disability and retirement benefits that covers most working people. Today, more than 90 percent of all American workers participate in the Social Security system. Most retirees and some widows, people with disabilities, and others are also eligible for benefits. **Medicare**, a federal health insurance program for senior

THE GLOBAL ECONOMY & YOU

Purchasing Power Around the World

The map shown here indicates one measure of wealth—the average per capita income. But it does not take into account the disparity between the wealthy and the poor within a country, or how these compare from one country to another. A different way to look at wealth and poverty is to examine the percentage of income or consumption that the wealthy or the poor control.

In most of these cases, the wealthy control a great deal of the country's income or consumption, whereas the poor control only a small amount. This is something to keep in mind when looking at the measures of economic security—how much of a nation's population controls the majority of its wealth? How might income and consumption be spread out among all sectors of society? Keep in mind that using PPP (purchasing power parity) helps economists to compare GDP (gross domestic product) per capita in different countries by its purchasing power.

Answering these questions can help nations establish and reach their economic and social goals.

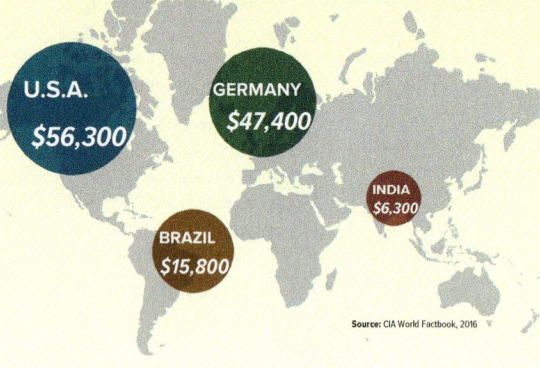

AVERAGE PER CAPITA INCOME
- U.S.A. $56,300
- GERMANY $47,400
- BRAZIL $15,800
- INDIA $6,300

Source: CIA World Factbook, 2016

▲ **CRITICAL THINKING**
Analyzing What goals might one of these countries add to their economic and social plans based on the data you see here?

networks Online Teaching Options

INTERACTIVE FEATURE

Global Economy & You

Reading maps and graphs Have students view the Global Economy & You feature. **Ask: What does the map show?** *(how the per capita GDP of countries compare)* Have students identify those that have the highest per capita GDP. Then read the text aloud and discuss the question. Move to the graph. **Ask: About how much is the average per capita income of the richest 10 percent of Americans?** *($150,000)* **What is the average per capita income of the poorest 10 percent of Americans?** *($10,000)* Have students reveal the graphs for Brazil, Germany, and India, and discuss the discrepancy between the richest and the poorest. **Visual/Spatial**

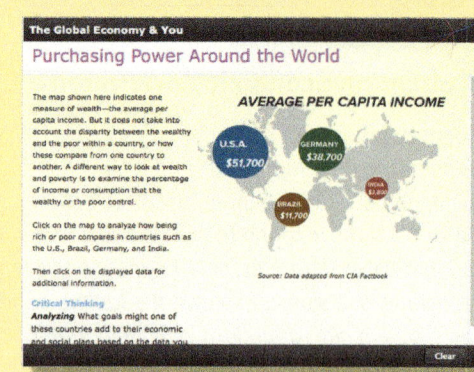

ANSWERS, p. 88

CRITICAL THINKING

Answers will vary. Students may conclude that for Brazil and India, goals may need to address economic security, full employment, and economic growth. For the United States and Germany, with their high average per-capita incomes, the goal may address economic equity.

This cartoon indicates that not all social and economic goals can be achieved at the same time.

▲ CRITICAL THINKING
Evaluating Explain why the protestors may not understand economics.

citizens, regardless of income, is another program that provides economic security to elderly Americans.

Full Employment
When people work, they earn income by producing goods and services for others. Without jobs, people cannot support themselves or their families, nor can they produce output for others. As a result, most people want their economic system to provide as many jobs as possible. The goal of full employment even became law when Congress passed the Employment Act of 1946 in an effort to avoid the widespread joblessness that the country faced in the Great Depression.

Price Stability
Another goal is to have stable prices. If **inflation**—a rise in the general level of prices—occurs, workers need more money to pay for food, clothing, and shelter. People who live on a **fixed income**—an income that does not increase over time, even though prices do—find that bills are harder to pay and planning for the future is more difficult.

High rates of inflation can even discourage business activity. During times of high inflation, interest rates on loans tend to increase along with the price of goods and services. If interest rates get too high, they can discourage both borrowing and spending by businesses. Price stability adds a degree of certainty to the future for businesses and consumers alike.

inflation rise in the general level of prices

fixed income income that does not increase over time

connected.mcgraw-hill.com   The American Free Enterprise System **89**

CHAPTER 3, LESSON 3
Evaluating Economic Performance

C Critical Thinking Skills

Exploring conflicting goals Ask: **How might the goal of protecting the environment conflict with the goals of efficiency or full employment?** *(Possible answer: Protecting the environment might mean limiting the use of resources such as timber, which would cost jobs, or regulating the amount of pollution that firms could produce, which might drive some firms out of business.)* **Naturalist**

English Language Proficiency

Beginning Identify cognates among basic vocabulary words heard during classroom instruction and interactions, such as *describe* and *describir*, or research and *investigar*. Write pairs of cognates under the same image showing the action or object. Have students repeat each cognate. Have beginning English speakers work in mixed groups with students who speak their first language but are more proficient in English. Groups should make cards, each with a cognate in their first language on one side and the English counterpart on the other side. Then they should use the cards to practice the pronunciation and meaning of the English words.

POLITICAL CARTOON

Political Cartoon

Evaluating conflicting economic goals Have students study the political cartoon and interpret its meaning. Discuss the economic goals that clash in the cartoon, and why. Encourage students to work in pairs to create different messages on the demonstrators' signs in the cartoon. The messages should represent economic goals that clash. **Visual/Spatial**

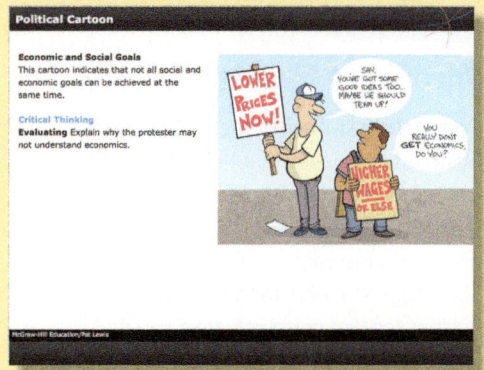

ANSWERS, p. 89

CRITICAL THINKING

Guide students to understand that providing higher wages often results in businesses raising the prices of their products in order to continue making a profit. In addition, lower prices on goods may result in some businesses reducing their labor force, which means *no* wages instead of higher wages.

CHAPTER 3, LESSON 3
Evaluating Economic Performance

C Critical Thinking Skills

Understanding trade-offs Further explore the issue of trade-offs, opportunity costs, and political solutions with students. For example, guide students in exploring the trade-offs and opportunity costs surrounding the issue of tariffs versus economic freedom. You might have them create a chart showing the costs and benefits of implementing a particular stand on the issue. **ELL** Logical/Mathematical

Making Connections

Constitutional Economic Rights Have students scan the U.S. Constitution to find economic concepts regarding property rights and taxation, as well as limits on individuals and the government. Discuss the Framers' original intent and how the role of government in the American economic system has changed over time. Verbal/Linguistic

---

ANSWERS, p. 90

EXPLORING THE ESSENTIAL QUESTION

Students should suggest that a high unemployment rate leads to less consumer spending and stagnant economic growth. A low unemployment rate indicates more production, more consumer spending, and perhaps inflation.

✓ READING PROGRESS CHECK
Students' answers should include such themes as economic security and certainty and economic freedom.

CRITICAL THINKING
Answers will vary. Many students will agree that UBB will sell more items because of its conservation connection. Many consumers want to support the economic goal of economic equity by becoming more pro-environment, and UBB's message lets customers "help." Ask students to provide reasons for their responses.

BIOGRAPHY

Brian Linton
ENTREPRENEUR (1986–)

Brian Linton turned his love of the ocean into a thriving company. While a college student, he spent summers driving from Florida to Maine selling jewelry imported from Thailand. He would donate some of his profits to groups working on cleaning up oceans. But for Linton, the disconnect between the sale of items and the actual conservation work was too great.

After some thought about how to adjust his business model, Linton started a company called United By Blue. As described on the company's website, "For every product sold, UBB removes one pound of trash from oceans and waterways through company organized and hosted cleanups." On the website is a Trash Ticker that records the number of pounds of trash the company has cleaned up. The company organizes community cleanups throughout the United States.

▶ **CRITICAL THINKING**
Drawing Conclusions Do you think United By Blue will sell more items because of its conservation connection? Give reasons for your answer.

Economic Growth

A major goal of most Americans is economic growth. Most people hope to have a better job, a newer car, their own home, and a number of other things in the future. Overall growth enables more people to have more goods and services. Because the nation's population is likely to increase, economic growth is necessary to meet everyone's needs.

EXPLORING THE ESSENTIAL QUESTION

Read over the seven economic and social goals. One of the major goals is full employment. Look up the U.S. unemployment rate in the 21st century. How are the unemployment rate and economy related? Describe in a paragraph how you think the unemployment rate and economy interact.

Future Goals

The seven goals discussed so far are the ones on which most people seem to agree. As our society evolves, however, it is possible that new goals will develop. Do people feel that a cleaner environment is important enough to be added to the list of goals? Should we add the preservation of endangered species such as the California Channel Islands fox? In the end, we are the ones who decide on the goals that are most important to us, and it is entirely possible that our goals will change in the future.

✓ **READING PROGRESS CHECK**

Interpreting What major themes can you identify in the list of seven economic goals?

Resolving Trade-Offs Among Goals

GUIDING QUESTION *How are conflicts among economic goals resolved?*

There are two significant issues with goals. One is that they sometimes are in conflict; the other is that there are opportunity costs associated with achieving them. Fortunately, our democratic system can help us deal with both problems.

For example, a policy that keeps foreign-made shoes out of the country could help achieve the goal of full employment in the domestic shoe industry, but it could work against individual freedom by restricting international trade and giving people fewer options for shoe buying. Or, as another example, supporters of an increase in the minimum wage argue that it is the equitable, or "right," thing to do. Opponents argue that an increase in the minimum wage could cause fewer workers to be hired. They argue that the minimum wage restricts the freedom of employers to determine what wages they think are fair for their workers.

Both of these issues also involve opportunity costs. The opportunity cost of keeping foreign-made shoes out of the country may be fewer choices and higher prices in local stores. The opportunity cost of an increase in the minimum wage may be higher unemployment and higher prices in the stores that pay workers minimum wage.

How are the trade-offs among goals resolved? If it is a political issue, and most are, then voters can compare the opportunity costs to the benefits, and then vote for political candidates who support their position. If the majority of voters feel that foreign-made shoes provide lower prices and more selection, they would probably support policies that permit them to be imported. If the

---

networks Online Teaching Options

BIOGRAPHY

Brian Linton Biography

Connecting to environmentally-focused businesses Have students view the Brian Linton biography feature and ask a volunteer to read the text aloud. Guide students in discussing the value of this business model. Encourage students to think of other kinds of businesses that could effectively use environmental objectives to grow a business while benefiting both the business and the environment. Interpersonal

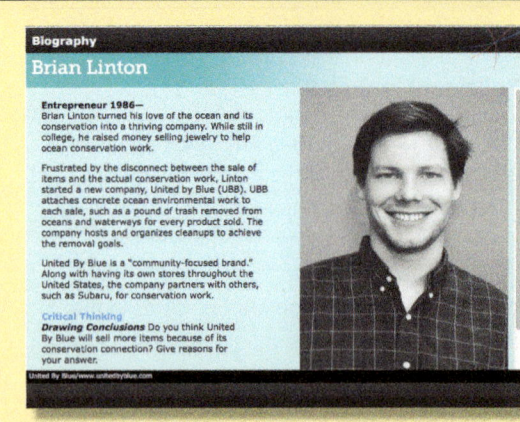

The space shuttle *Discovery* represents an economic decision. Constructing and operating the shuttle comes from public funds. Are the jobs created by the existence of the shuttle and the discoveries made through its operation worth the expense? These are the types of economic choices that are evaluated.

majority of voters feel that the minimum wage is too low, then they can vote for the candidates who support raising it.

Fortunately, the economic system of the United States is flexible enough to allow choices, **accommodate** compromises, and still satisfy the majority of Americans. This is because a democratic government reflects the will of a majority of its people. As a result, many government functions reflect people's desire to modify the economic system to achieve their economic goals. A program such as Social Security, as well as laws dealing with child labor and the minimum wage, reveal how Americans have modified their free enterprise economy. Attempts to achieve or modify these goals are yet another reason we have a mixed or modified free enterprise economy.

accommodate to allow for

☑ **READING PROGRESS CHECK**

Explaining Why do trade-offs among goals exist?

LESSON 3 REVIEW

Reviewing Vocabulary
1. *Defining* Explain what inflation is.

Using Your Notes
2. *Summarizing* Use your notes to explain the seven economic and social goals most Americans share.

Answering the Guiding Questions
3. *Hypothesizing* Why might our economic goals change over time?
4. *Evaluating* How are conflicts among economic goals resolved?

Writing About Economics
5. *Informative/Explanatory* What are some new economic and social goals that you think Americans will share as the 21st century develops? Identify a new goal and explain how it will affect American economics.

CHAPTER 3, LESSON 3
Evaluating Economic Performance

C Critical Thinking Skills

Analyzing changes in the U.S. economy
Ask: What are some ways that Americans have modified the free enterprise economy? *(Possible answers: Government provides social goods; products such as cigarettes and alcohol have age restrictions; only drugs approved by the FDA can legally be sold.)* **Verbal/Linguistic**

CLOSE & REFLECT

W Writing Skills

Finding the main ideas Ask students to write a two- or three-paragraph summary of the lesson. When they finish, have them exchange summaries with a partner and compare the main ideas each chose to include.

LESSON 3 REVIEW ANSWERS

Reviewing Vocabulary
1. Inflation is a rise in prices and particularly affects those on a fixed income.

Using Your Notes
2. Students should list and explain these goals: 1. Economic Freedom; 2. Economic Efficiency; 3. Economic Equity; 4. Economic Security; 5. Full Employment; 6. Price Stability; 7. Economic Growth.

Answering the Guiding Questions
3. Students should include in their answers that economic goals evolve over time as new issues and concerns arise (for example, climate change). Resolving these issues could mean changing or adjusting our economic goals.
4. Conflicts over economic issues are often resolved by voters voting for the candidate who shares their views. Also, the U.S. economic system is flexible, and it accommodates compromises that satisfy the majority of Americans.

Writing About Economics
5. Student answers will vary but should include one of the issues facing the United States today, such as climate change, terrorism, or high unemployment among young people. Answers should explain how resolving any of those issues might affect the U.S. economy.

ANSWERS, p. 91

☑ **READING PROGRESS CHECK** Sometimes goals are in conflict, and there are opportunity costs associated with achieving goals

CHAPTER 3
Debate

ENGAGE

C1 Critical Thinking Skills

Expressing opinions on financial rewards for students Introduce the Debate feature by telling students that some educators and community leaders have suggested the possibility of paying students who earn good grades in class, on tests, and for reading books. Invite students to offer their opinions on the subject. Then conduct a survey by asking students to vote yes or no on the proposal: "Should students be financially rewarded for good grades?" Record the results of the survey on the board. **Interpersonal**

TEACH & ASSESS

C2 Critical Thinking Skills

Evaluating the arguments Ask students to analyze the arguments presented in the feature. Have them consider these questions:

- Which arguments are most compelling?
- Which quotations make the strongest arguments? Why?
- What is the point of view of each argument? Does the point of view make the argument more or less valid?

In a class discussion, have volunteers share their ideas. Then poll the class by asking which argument is strongest. **Logical/Mathematical**

Making Connections

Personal Rewards Ask students if they have ever been rewarded for winning a tournament, completing some challenging task, or accomplishing some goal. Invite them to share their experiences. **Ask: Is being paid for good performance in school the same or different? Why or why not?** **Logical/Mathematical**

English Language Proficiency

Beginning On cards, write words from the Debate feature ranging from the familiar to the unfamiliar, such as "tenet," "proposed," "cash," "controversial," "intrinsic," and "arbitrary." State a sentence that uses accessible language but leave out one of the words. Have students repeat the sentence after you and fill in the blank by saying the missing word. As needed, prompt by holding up the card.

Debates

C1 Should students be financially rewarded for good grades?

C2 Students who do not do well in school are less likely to succeed as adults who can contribute to and benefit within the United States' capitalist economic system. This system is based largely on the tenet of financial reward for effort and achievement. Students who fail in school are less able to compete for jobs and participate in a meaningful economic way.

Some educators have proposed—and some have even experimentally instituted—programs in which students are paid cash money if they get good grades, do well on tests, or read more books. However, this approach is highly controversial.

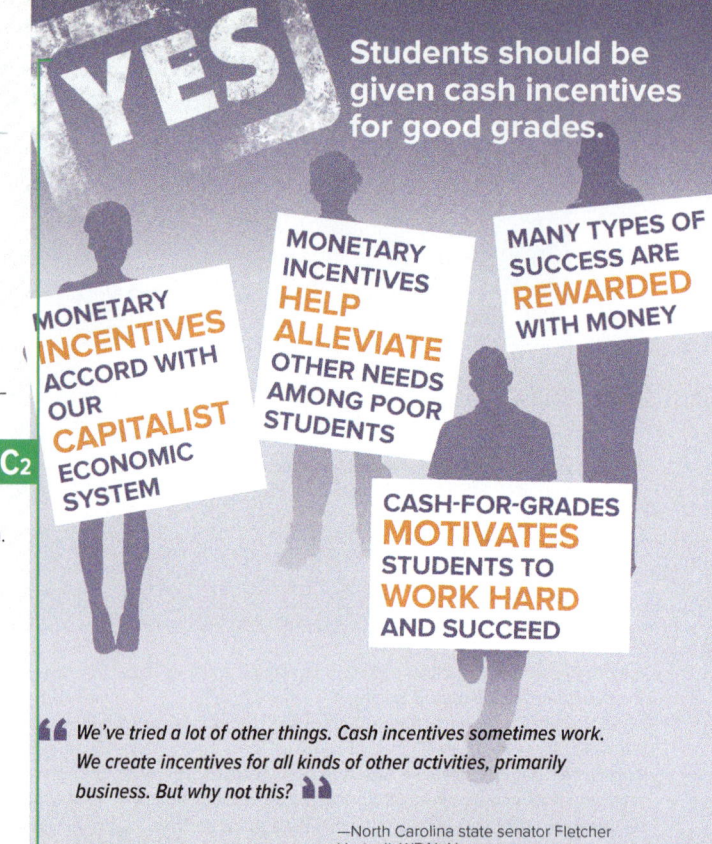

YES Students should be given cash incentives for good grades.

- MONETARY INCENTIVES ACCORD WITH OUR CAPITALIST ECONOMIC SYSTEM
- MONETARY INCENTIVES HELP ALLEVIATE OTHER NEEDS AMONG POOR STUDENTS
- MANY TYPES OF SUCCESS ARE REWARDED WITH MONEY
- CASH-FOR-GRADES MOTIVATES STUDENTS TO WORK HARD AND SUCCEED

"We've tried a lot of other things. Cash incentives sometimes work. We create incentives for all kinds of other activities, primarily business. But why not this?"
—North Carolina state senator Fletcher Hartsell; WRAL News

▲ Providing cash as a motivator for good school grades is a controversial method for improving educational performance.

networks Online Teaching Options

DEBATE

Debate: Should students be financially rewarded for good grades?

Evaluating information for validity Have students view the Debate and call on a student to summarize the main arguments in favor of rewarding students for good grades. Invite the class to add more reasons. Then ask another student to summarize the reasons opposing student rewards. Ask the class to provide additional reasons to support this view. Then point out the sources of the two excerpts. Have students consider the point of view from the state senator and psychologists, and ask whether these occupations add validity to their arguments. Why or why not? **Interpersonal**

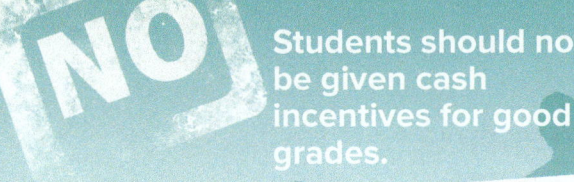

NO Students should not be given cash incentives for good grades.

TAXPAYERS SHOULDN'T PAY FOR STUDENT FINANCIAL INCENTIVES

HOW MUCH EACH GRADE OR BOOK READ IS WORTH WOULD BE AN ARBITRARY DESIGNATION

LEARNING HAS INTRINSIC, NOT MONETARY, WORTH

FINANCIAL REWARD TEACHES STUDENTS THAT THINGS THAT DON'T PAY CASH ARE NOT WORTH DOING

networks
TRY IT YOURSELF ONLINE
For an interactive version of this debate go to connected.mcgraw-hill.com

" Intrinsic motivation—participating at school for the sheer pleasure of learning—is soon eclipsed by the promise of external rewards, and a child's natural enthusiasm for learning may be dampened. It doesn't really teach kids the reward of learning for learning's sake. "

—Bob Brooks and Sam Goldstein, psychologists

▲ Critics of the method of paying for good grades believe that it sends the wrong message to students preparing for the adult world.

ANALYZING the issue

1. **Identifying Perspectives** How do the two quotes differ in their arguments for and against paying students cash for reading or getting better grades and test scores? Use examples from the quotes in your answer.

2. **Applying** What aspects of the American capitalist system might have given rise to the idea that students should be financially compensated for working hard at school? Do you think this is a legitimate application of the free enterprise, capitalist system? Why or why not?

3. **Defending** Which of these arguments do you support? Analyze the validity of the economic information presented in these sources for point of view and compare with your own point of view. Use information from the quotes and your personal experience to support your argument.

93

CHAPTER 3
Debate

C Critical Thinking Skills

Researching arguments Point out that the arguments presented in this feature are not the only ones that could be made to support or oppose the proposition. Challenge students to choose a position on the issue and to do research to find more arguments. Tell them to find facts, quotations, and other details to support their arguments. Have students share their new arguments with the class, attributing the new information as appropriate to authors. **BL** Logical/Mathematical

CLOSE & REFLECT

Re-evaluating opinions Refer back to the results of the survey you conducted while introducing the feature. Ask students if they have changed their minds after studying the arguments. Encourage them to explain why they did or did not alter their opinions.

ANSWERS, p. 93

ANALYZING the issue

1. The quotes in favor of cash incentives focus on a system that is well organized and on the educational gains such a program has achieved where it has been implemented. The quotes against these incentives stress that learning should occur and be valued for its own sake, that learning may stop once cash payments stop, and that the money could be better used to improve school buildings and reduce class sizes.

2. The capitalist concept that entrepreneurs and businesses are motivated by profit lends itself to the notion that students will respond to cash incentives to learn. Students may think that this is a legitimate and effective application of the capitalist system. Other students may disagree and argue that learning is not a "good" or "service" but a preparation for life—economic and noneconomic—and should not be monetized.

3. Some students may argue from experience that their lack of money makes it more difficult to set aside time for school work and that therefore cash compensation would help them do better in school. They may contend that learning has a cash value, just like most everything else. Other students may think that learning cannot be valued monetarily, or that the money used for cash incentives could, in fact, be better used to reduce class size and renovate old schools.

GRAPHIC ORGANIZERS

Table

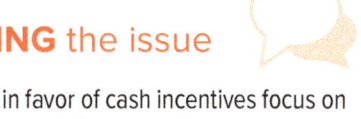

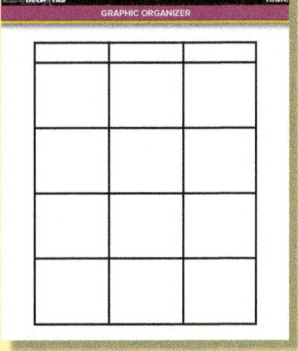

Preparing and defending arguments Divide the class into groups for and against the issue, and distribute the graphic organizer. Ask students to follow these steps:

1. Write *Arguments* for the first column. Have students list four reasons that support their position.
2. Write *Counterarguments* as the second column header. Have students come up with points their opponents could use to minimize their arguments.
3. Write *Refutations* as the final column header. Have students write ways they can refute, or prove the opponents' counterarguments are wrong.
4. Have students rank arguments from strongest to weakest, based on how easy they are to defend against counterarguments. **Visual/Spatial**

The American Free Enterprise System 93

Chapter 3
Study Guide

C1 Critical Thinking Skills

Determining importance Ask: **Which event in American history was most significant in developing and enhancing the U.S. economic system? Why?** *(Possible answer: the writing of the U.S. Constitution; it established the rights and protections that enable the U.S. economic system to function)*

C2 Critical Thinking Skills

Evaluating Have students list what they think are the top five problems that exist in the U.S. economy today. Have a volunteer write the suggested problems on the board. Have other volunteers identify what role the government would play if it took on the problem. Conduct a poll to find which problems students think are the most important.
Verbal/Linguistic, Interpersonal

W Writing Skills

Personal Writing Direct students to choose one of the economic and social goals and write about a personal experience involving the goal.
Intrapersonal

STUDY GUIDE

LESSON 1

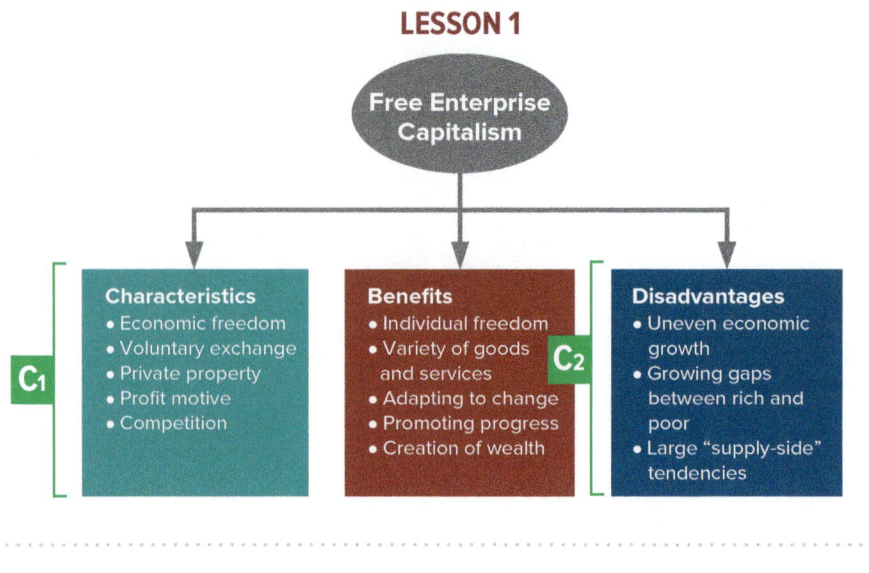

LESSON 2

LESSON 3

American Economic and Social Goals
1. Economic Freedom
2. Economic Efficiency
3. Economic Equity
4. Economic Security
5. Full Employment
6. Price Stability
7. Economic Growth

networks Online Assessment Options

WORKSHEET

Hands-On Chapter Project with Technology Extension In this project, students will explore the interconnectedness of the five elements of the free enterprise system. They will look at how consumers, entrepreneurs, and the government factor into this system, and then create a model or poster showing how the parts of the free enterprise system relate to one another.

  Find an additional activity online that incorporates technology for this project. Visit the EdTech Teacher Web sites for more links, tutorials, and other resources.

CHAPTER 3 Assessment

Directions: On a separate sheet of paper, answer the questions below. Make sure you read carefully and answer all parts of the questions.

Lesson Review

Lesson 1
1. **Comparing** Name some alternatives to a free enterprise system and describe their limitations.
2. **Assessing** Explain how our free enterprise system encourages competition.

Lesson 2
3. **Analyzing** What role does the consumer play in the free enterprise system?
4. **Identifying** What does a catalyst do in a free enterprise system?

Lesson 3
5. **Explaining** What does the minimum wage do?
6. **Drawing Conclusions** How might government programs increase people's economic security?

Analyzing Visuals
Use the illustration to answer the following questions.

7. **Interpreting** Of all the characteristics of free enterprise capitalism shown in the illustration, which one do you think is the most important to the success of the economic system? Why?

8. **Predicting** Based on the illustration of the cornerstones of free enterprise capitalism, what effect do you think a drop in housing prices would have on the overall economy?

Critical Thinking

9. **Identifying Central Issues** Explain how incentives and the limited role of government function in a free enterprise system.
10. **Constructing Arguments** Write a blog post in which you argue that a mixed free enterprise economy either limits or encourages economic growth.
11. **Explaining** Cite an example that illustrates the "supply-side" tendencies of the free enterprise system.

21st Century Skills

12. **Identifying Cause and Effect** Write an essay identifying the costs and benefits of government policies related to our American economic goals.
13. **Research Skills** Using the Internet or resources in the library, identify a nation that is moving from a restricted economy to a free enterprise economy. In a multimedia presentation, report on the current economic status of that nation and the problems related to its transition.

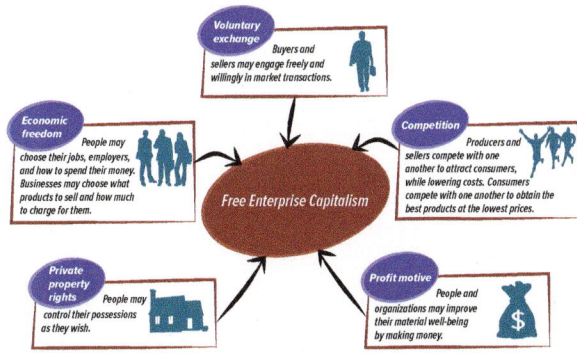

Need Extra Help?

If You've Missed Question	1	2	3	4	5	6	7	8	9	10	11	12	13
Go to page	73	74	83	83	88	88	72	72	73	86	79	85	72

Chapter 3 Assessment Answers

Lesson Review

Lesson 1

1. Two alternatives to a free enterprise system are a command economy and socialism. In a command economy, people can do only what the leaders decide. In socialism, the government owns most of the means of production and distribution.

2. Competition thrives because businesses and entrepreneurs have the freedom to produce the products they think will be the most profitable. Having a variety of goods allows consumers to enjoy economic freedom

Lesson 2

3. The consumer determines what gets produced by purchasing products and rewarding the businesses that make them. The success of a business is dependent on the customers/consumers.

4. A catalyst stimulates activity among people or forces. Successful entrepreneurs are catalysts in a free enterprise system.

Lesson 3

5. The minimum wage puts a floor on the amount of income that some workers earn.

6. Government programs can provide a safety net to keep people from becoming destitute. The U.S. government established Social Security, which is a program of disability and retirement benefits. The U.S. government also established Medicare, a health insurance program for senior citizens.

Analyzing Visuals

7. Competition is the most important to the success of the economic system. Competition benefits the economy because it ensures that the most efficient producers of a product will survive and the least efficient producers will either cease producing or produce different products.

8. Students should indicate that a drop in housing prices would have a big impact on the economy as property rights and ownership are one of the cornerstones of free enterprise capitalism.

Critical Thinking

9. Incentives such as private property rights encourage people to work, save, and invest in buying property such as a home. The U.S. Constitution protects private property rights and prevents government from interfering in the people's private property rights.

10. The argument that a mixed free enterprise economy limits economic growth should include the idea that when people and businesses are subject to government intervention and regulation, it can inhibit market growth. The argument that it does not limit economic growth should point to the success of the U.S. economy, which now is a mixed free enterprise economy.

11. There is a tendency for suppliers to combine in order to avoid competition. That means there is less competition and fewer choices for consumers. An example is the Carnival Corporation, which owns most of the cruise ships serving the U.S. people.

21st Century Skills

12. Students should indicate that the American goal of economic equity brought about the establishment of the minimum wage. Many argue that the minimum wage hinders business growth by determining wages to be paid to workers.

13. Students may include nations such as India, Malaysia, and China as examples.

Chapter 3
Assessment Answers

14. Answers will vary, but could include government regulations on automobile mileage for cars sold in the state or nationally, or smoking regulations.

15. The U.S. Constitution protects the private property rights of the American people in the Due Process clause of the Fourteenth Amendment.

Answering the Essential Questions

16. Students should include specific benefits and specific choices that they have because of the free enterprise economy.

17. Students should indicate that the desire for economic security brought about the government establishing Social Security and Medicare. In addition, the goal of full employment has brought about the government to pass legislation to avoid widespread unemployment.

Building Financial Literacy

18. Students should include specific answers that explain the degree in which economic security and equity are part of their financial goals. Students should also include a plan showing how they intend to reach their financial goals.

Analyzing Primary Sources

19. Students should include the idea that the requirement would compel Wal-Mart to increase the wages they pay their workers, causing them to make less profits. This fact may have made the company decide that the costs of new stores (opportunity cost) were not worth the profit they expected (benefit).

20. The goal was to secure more wages for workers. Students should include the reasons they think the impact was positive or negative. Negative impact: Washington, D.C., lost the chance to have a Wal-Mart in its district that would provide consumers with good buying choices. Positive impact: Washington, D.C., is better off without a Wal-Mart, as it drives out small business owners who cannot compete with Wal-Mart's prices.

21. Students should indicate that large retailers would probably not build stores in those locations. The large retailers have many choices where to build stores.

CHAPTER 3 Assessment

Directions: On a separate sheet of paper, answer the questions below. Make sure you read carefully and answer all parts of the questions.

14. Understanding Relationships Among Events Use the Internet or a newspaper to find an example of a recently established federal or state government regulation. In an essay, explain how that regulation will affect businesses in your state.

15. Identifying Where does the U.S. Constitution provide the basis for our understanding of the protection of private property rights?

ANSWERING THE ESSENTIAL QUESTIONS

Review your answers to the introductory questions at the beginning of each lesson. Then answer the Essential Questions on the basis of what you learned in the chapter. Have your answers changed?

16. Summarizing Write an essay summarizing the benefits of our free enterprise economy and the impact they have on your economic choices.

17. Understanding Relationships How have changes in American economic and social goals modified our free enterprise economy?

Building Financial Literacy

18. Decision Making Setting personal financial goals helps in making good economic decisions. Describe your short-term and longer-term financial goals and explain how they address economic security.

Analyzing Primary Sources

Read the excerpts and answer the questions that follow.

In July of 2013, the giant retailer Wal-Mart planned to build three stores in Washington, D.C. The D.C. Council, however, imposed requirements that large retailers must pay their employees 50 percent more than minimum wage. The Council passed the wage-hike bill despite Wal-Mart's prior warning that the requirement could cause the store to forego its plans.

PRIMARY SOURCE

" 'Nothing has changed from our perspective,' Wal-Mart spokesman Steven Restivo said in a statement after the vote, reiterating that the company will abandon plans for three unbuilt stores and 'review the financial and legal implications' of not opening three others under construction."

—Mike Debonis, *Washington Post*, July 10, 2013

19. Hypothesizing Why do you think the new wage requirements caused Wal-Mart to change its plans?

20. Considering Advantages and Disadvantages What was the goal of the D.C. Council in imposing wage requirements on large retailers? Do you think the impact will be positive or negative?

21. Making Predictions If local governments are successful in imposing wage requirements on large retailers, what do you think the large retailers will do?

Need Extra Help?

If You've Missed Question	14	15	16	17	18	19	20	21
Go to page	85	73	75	90	88	90	90	90

---

networks Online Assessment Options

WORKSHEET

Chapter Tests and Lesson Quizzes

Chapter 3 Tests Forms A and B Have students complete the Chapter Tests and Lesson Quizzes to assess student understanding throughout the chapter. Print and online assessment tools offer chapter and lesson evaluation through a variety of question formats, including document-based questions.

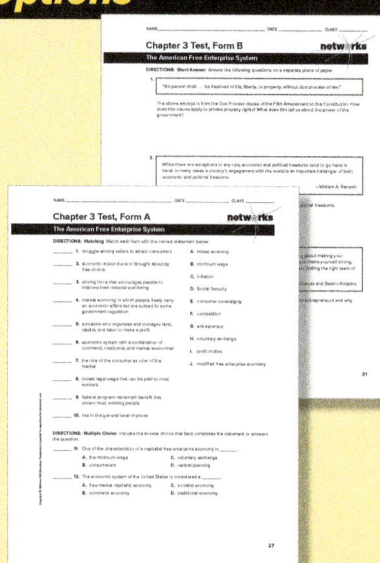

UNIT 2
UNDERSTANDING MARKETS Planner

UNDERSTANDING BY DESIGN®

Enduring Understanding
- Demand influences WHAT, HOW, and FOR WHOM goods are produced.
- Supply in a market economy is determined by what produces the greatest amount of profit.
- The interaction of buyers and sellers in a market economy determines market prices and thereby allocates scarce goods and services.
- Profit inspires people to take risks with their resources.

Essential Questions
- How does demand help societies determine WHAT, HOW, and FOR WHOM to produce?
- What are the causes of a change in demand?
- What are the basic differences between supply and demand?
- Why is the production function useful for making business decisions?
- How do prices help determine WHAT, HOW, and FOR WHOM to produce?
- How do varying market structures impact prices in a market economy?
- How does the government attempt to correct market failures?

Students will know:
- the Law of Demand: quantity demanded of a product varies inversely with its price.
- the factors that cause a change in demand.
- the difference between elastic demand and inelastic demand for a product.
- supply is the amount of a product offered for sale at all possible prices that could prevail in the market, and several factors cause a change in supply.
- the three stages of production, and how to set price and output.
- the basic characteristics of monopoly, oligopoly, monopolistic competition, and pure competition.

Students will be able to:
- **explain** how demand helps societies determine WHAT, HOW, and FOR WHOM to produce, as well as the price level.
- **explain** how income and substitutes affect quantity demanded as well as the elasticity of demand for a product.
- **describe** the basic differences between supply and demand using supply and demand curves.
- **discuss** how the signals sent by prices help people make economic decisions.
- **describe** factors that affect competition and success or failure in a market.
- **make** connections between past government laws and today's modified free enterprise economic system.

Predictable Misunderstandings
Students may think:
- Demand is an individual's desire to own a product.
- Productivity goes up when more workers are added.
- All monopolies are harmful to an economic system.
- Lack of competition helps a company succeed and prevents market failure.

Assessment Evidence
Performance Task:
- Hands-On Chapter Projects with Technology Extensions
- Economic Simulations
- Math Practice for Economics
- Personal Finance Activities
- Reinforcing Economic Skills Activities

Other Evidence:
- Guided Reading Activities
- Vocabulary Activities
- Lesson Quizzes
- Chapter Tests, Forms A and B

SUGGESTED PACING GUIDE—Semester
Introducing the Unit	½ Day
Chapter 4: Demand	5 Days
Chapter 5: Supply	3½ Days
Chapter 6: Prices	5 Days
Chapter 7: Market Structures	5 Days

Key for Using the Teacher Edition

SKILL-BASED ACTIVITIES

Types of skill activities found in the Teacher Edition.

- **V** **Visual Skills** require students to analyze maps, graphs, charts, and photos.
- **R** **Reading Skills** help students practice reading skills and master vocabulary.
- **C** **Critical Thinking Skills** help students apply and extend what they have learned.
- **W** **Writing Skills** provide writing opportunities to help students comprehend the text.
- **T** **Technology Skills** require students to use digital tools effectively.

*Letters are followed by a number when there is more than one of the same type of skill on the page.

DIFFERENTIATED INSTRUCTION

All activities are written for the on-level student unless otherwise marked with the leveled labels below.

- **BL** Beyond Level
- **AL** Approaching Level
- **ELL** English Language Learners

All students benefit from activities that utilize different learning styles. Many activities are marked as below when a particular learning style is highlighted.

- Intrapersonal
- Logical/Mathematical
- Visual/Spatial
- Verbal/Linguistic
- Naturalist
- Kinesthetic
- Auditory/Musical
- Interpersonal

UNIT 2: UNDERSTANDING MARKETS

Planner

☑ Print Teaching Options

Critical Thinking Skills

☐ **p. 97 Discussing factors that influence prices** Students discuss factors that influence demand, such as advertising for a particular brand name, thus affecting the price.

Writing Skills

☐ **p. 97 Analyzing local competition** Students select a business that they patronize in their community and write a short analysis of the business by responding to several questions. **Intrapersonal, Logical/Mathematical, Interpersonal**

☐ **p. 97 Explaining reasons for high demand** Students research and write about a product or service for which they believe there will be a high demand in the twenty-first century. **Verbal/Linguistic, Visual/Spatial**

☐ **p. 98 Practicing analyzing economic information** Students learn the steps to analyze information and then practice analysis of economic information on the digital and interactive features and graphics in the online Student Edition. **Logical/Mathematical, Verbal/Linguistic**

☑ Online Teaching Options

☐ **ANIMATION Types of Markets**—Students view the animation about different types of markets and then create a poster showing the markets they participate in as employees and as consumers spending their pay. **Verbal/Linguistic, Visual/Spatial**

☐ **APPROACHING GRADE LEVEL READER Alternative Student Edition narrative**—You can assign your students who are struggling to read on grade level the Approaching Grade Level version of the Online Student Edition. This reader presents all of the content in the On Grade Level version of the Online Student Edition at a lower reading level.

☐ **ENGLISH LANGUAGE LEARNER READER Alternative Student Edition narrative with ELL support**—Use the Online English Language Learner reader to provide additional reading support for ELL students. You can find this tool in the Online Student Edition.

☑ Printable Digital Worksheets

Reading Skills

☐ **WORKSHEET Guided Reading Activity**—Students use the Guided Reading Activities worksheets to review their comprehension of the content.

☐ **WORKSHEET Reading Essentials and Study Guide**—Students complete the study guide and answer Reading Progress Check and vocabulary questions.

Critical Thinking Skills

☐ **WORKSHEET Types of Markets Animation Activity**—Students answer questions about the types of markets they participate in. **Verbal/Linguistic**

☐ **WORKSHEET Assessing Background Knowledge Activity**—Students should complete the Assessing Background Knowledge Activity before they study each chapter. Students' responses will give you a good idea of the kinds of misconceptions you can address when teaching the lessons.

☐ **WORKSHEET Chapter Summary**—Summaries are provided for each chapter and thoroughly condense core content into manageable chunks.

☐ **WORKSHEET Vocabulary Activity**—Students apply their knowledge of content and academic vocabulary words.

UNIT 2
Understanding Markets

IT MATTERS BECAUSE...
Did you know that every time you spend money on something, you're casting a vote? These "dollar votes" help decide what products you see on the shelves at the store and even how much those products cost. Whenever you buy or sell something, whether it's a pineapple or a plane ticket, you are participating in a market. All transactions between buyers and sellers take place in markets and, even though they come in many different shapes and sizes, all markets have similar characteristics. Understanding how markets are structured, how they operate, and the factors that influence the choices buyers and sellers make will help you help you make better decisions with your "dollar votes."

CHAPTER 4
Demand

ESSENTIAL QUESTIONS

How does demand help societies determine WHAT, HOW, and FOR WHOM to produce?

What are the causes of a change in demand?

CHAPTER 5
Supply

ESSENTIAL QUESTION

How do companies determine the most profitable way to operate?

CHAPTER 6
Prices

ESSENTIAL QUESTIONS

How do prices help determine WHAT, HOW, and FOR WHOM to produce?

What factors affect prices?

CHAPTER 7
Market Structures

ESSENTIAL QUESTIONS

How do varying market structures impact prices in a market economy?

Why do markets fail?

How does the government attempt to correct market failures?

UNIT 2
Understanding Markets

ENGAGE

Discussing factors that influence prices
Ask: *How much does a baseball glove cost? (Answers should vary, suggesting that prices for baseball gloves differ widely.) Why might prices differ? (Possible answers: brand name, type of glove, type of store, quality of leather)* Suggest to students that the price of a baseball glove depends on demand for that glove relative to supply. In turn, other factors influence demand, such as advertising for a particular brand name, thus affecting the price.

Analyzing local competition Ask students to select a business that they patronize in their community. Have them write a short analysis of the business by responding to the following questions: (1) What is the name and location of the business? (2) Why do you purchase from this business? *(for example: convenience, price, service, quality of product)* (3) What is the competition for the business? *(for example: nearby stores, malls, catalog orders, online stores)* (4) How does the business compete? *(for example: price competition, sales, advertising, special services)* Have students share their analyses with the class. **Intrapersonal, Logical/Mathematical, Interpersonal**

Explaining reasons for high demand
Have students research and write about a product or service for which they believe there will be a high demand in the twenty-first century. Students should explain why they think such a high demand will exist, and then use the Internet and financial magazines to make predictions about the product's or service's potential growth. Have students create charts and graphs to support their positions. **Verbal/Linguistic, Visual/Spatial**

ANIMATIONS | WORKSHEET

Types of Markets

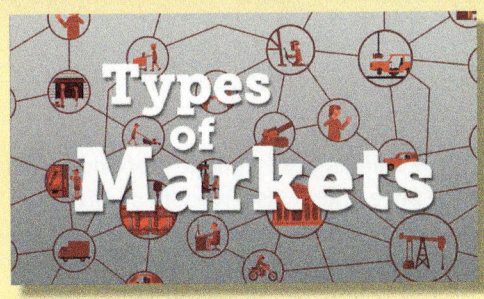

Analyzing the animation Have students view the animation about different types of markets. Then have them choose a job that they either currently do or want to do. Have them create a poster showing the markets they participate in as employees and as consumers spending their pay. The poster should also show the markets in which employers participate. The markets should be connected in a web diagram with arrows that show the connections between markets, and each market should be labeled. Students should illustrate each market with images that represent the activities found in them. **Verbal/Linguistic, Visual/Spatial**

UNIT 2
Understanding Markets

DEVELOP YOUR SKILLS ONLINE

Practicing Analyzing Economic Information
Have students practice analysis of economic information on the digital and interactive features and graphics in the Online Student Edition. Students should explore digital activities that involve the manipulation of data on graphs to show how a change in one set of data affects another set of data. Remind students to use the following steps to analyze information:

- Identify the topic that is being discussed.
- Examine how the information is organized. What are the main points?
- Summarize the information in your own words, and then make a statement of your own based on your understanding of the topic and on what you already know.

To help students practice analyzing economic information, have them choose an interactive graph to explore, and then write an evaluation paragraph about what happens to the data when they manipulate the graph. Students should identify the data on the graph at the start of the activity, and then explain what happens when they change the data using the interactivity feature on the graph.

Develop your Skills Online

Analyzing Economic Information
Using Interactive Graphs

Economists often use models of economic data and economic theory to better understand the complexities of an economic system. Common models used by economists are graphs that highlight how different types of data affect individuals and/or various segments of the economy. This economics program provides interactive graphs that allow you to examine how manipulating the data changes the results of the overall model.

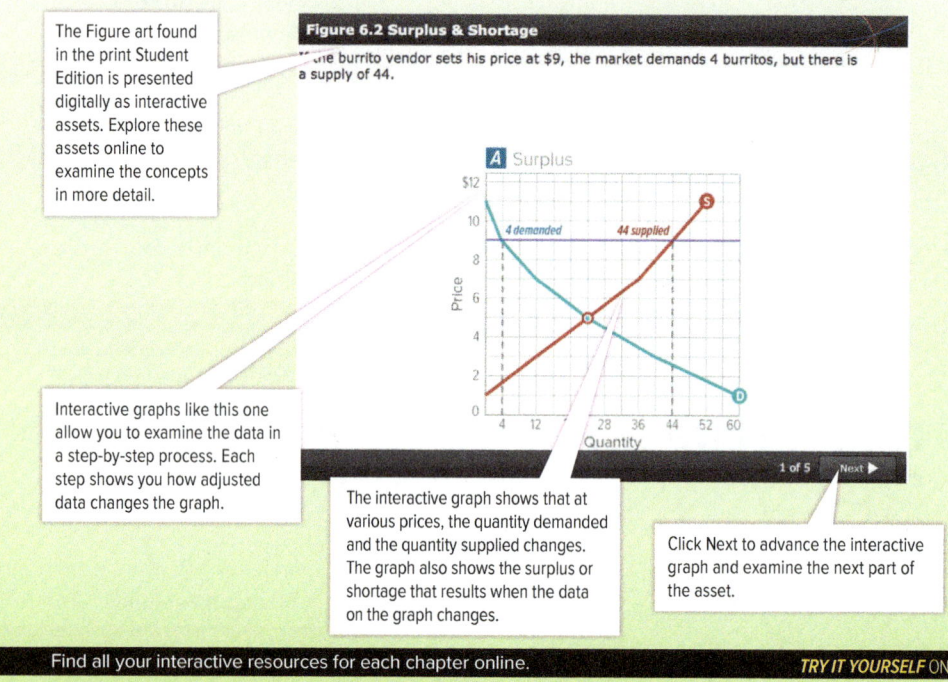

Find all your interactive resources for each chapter online.

networks **Online Teaching Options**

GRAPHS

SAMPLE: Price Ceilings and Price Floors

Predicting consequences of price ceilings and price floors Ask: **What happens to the supply of a product or service when a price ceiling or price floor is imposed?** *(Students should recognize that a shortage or surplus occurs.)* Have students view Figure 6.4 showing supply and demand curves, equilibrium prices, and a price floor or price ceiling. Ask students to progress through the graphs to see how shortages and surpluses are related to price ceilings and price floors. Have students answer the questions. **Logical/Mathematical**

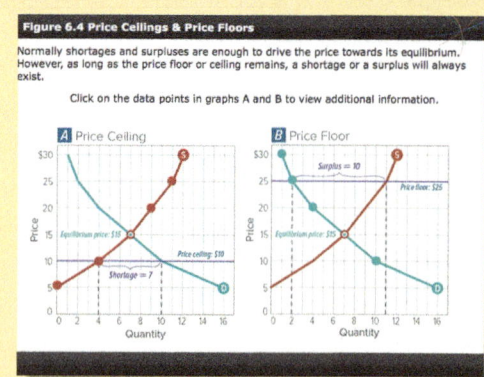

CHAPTER 4
Demand Planner

UNDERSTANDING BY DESIGN®

Enduring Understanding
- *Demand influences WHAT, HOW, and FOR WHOM goods are produced.*

Essential Questions
- *How does demand help societies determine WHAT, HOW, and FOR WHOM to produce?*
- *What are the causes of a change in demand?*

Predictable Misunderstandings
Students may think:
- *Demand is an individual's desire to own a product.* Explain that demand includes desire to own a product, but also includes the consumer's willingness to buy the product and the ability to pay for it.
- *Changes in the quantity of a product demanded by consumers depends on many different variables.* Explain that only a change in price can change the quantity demanded, but other factors determine the elasticity of demand for the product.

Assessment Evidence
Performance Task
- *Hands-On Chapter Project with Technology Extension*

Other Evidence
- *Guided Reading Activities*
- *Vocabulary Activity*
- *Lesson Quizzes*
- *Self-Check Quizzes*
- *Chapter Assessment*
- *Chapter Tests, Forms A and B*

SUGGESTED PACING

Introducing the Chapter: ½ Day	Lesson 3: Elasticity of Demand . . 1 Day
Lesson 1: An Introduction to Demand . . . 1 Day	Debate . . . ½ Day
Case Study . . . ½ Day	Study Guide, Chapter Assessment and Wrap-Up . . . ½ Day
Lesson 2: Factors Affecting Demand . . . 1 Day	

TOTAL 5 Days

Key for Using the Teacher Edition

SKILL-BASED ACTIVITIES
Types of skill activites found in the Teacher Edition.

V **Visual Skills** require students to analyze maps, graphs, charts, and photos.

R **Reading Skills** help students practice reading skills and master vocabulary.

C **Critical Thinking Skills** help students apply and extend what they have learned.

W **Writing Skills** provide writing opportunities to help students comprehend the text.

T **Technology Skills** require students to use digital tools effectively.

*Letters are followed by a number when there is more than one of the same type of skill on the page.

DIFFERENTIATED INSTRUCTION
All activities are written for the on-level student unless otherwise marked with the leveled labels below.

BL Beyond Level
AL Approaching Level
ELL English Language Learners

All students benefit from activities that utilize different learning styles. Many activities are marked as below when a particular learning style is highlighted.

Intrapersonal
Logical/Mathematical
Visual/Spatial
Verbal/Linguistic
Naturalist
Kinesthetic
Auditory/Musical
Interpersonal

Council for Economic Education

Below are the Council for Economic Education Voluntary National Content Standards in Economics covered in the *Demand* chapter.

Content Standard 8: Prices send signals and provide incentives to buyers and sellers. When supply or demand changes, market prices adjust, affecting incentives.

CHAPTER 4: DEMAND

CHAPTER OPENER PLANNER

Students will know:
- demand is the desire, ability, and willingness to buy a product or service.
- the Law of Demand, which states that the quantity demanded of a product varies inversely with its price.
- the difference between elastic demand and inelastic demand for a product.

Students will be able to:
- **explain** how demand helps societies determine WHAT, HOW, and FOR WHOM to produce.
- **paraphrase** the Law of Demand.
- **apply** the total expenditures test to determine the elasticity of a product.

UNDERSTANDING BY DESIGN®

☑ Print Teaching Options

R Reading Skills
- ☐ p. 100 Predicting changes in demand

C Critical Thinking Skills
- ☐ p. 99 Identifying factors that affect demand
- ☐ p. 99 Demand Decisions Students describe an "overpurchase" because of a low price.
- ☐ p. 100 Understanding relationships between price and quantity demanded

W Writing Skills
- ☐ p. 101 Explaining purchasing decisions

☑ Online Teaching Options

V Visual Skills
- ☐ **IMAGE** Chapter opener—Students analyze a photo for factors affecting demand.

C Critical Thinking Skills
- ☐ **INFOGRAPHICS** Economic Perspectives—Students discuss the Law of Demand and the importance of substitutions. *Verbal/Linguistic*
- ☐ **DEBATES** Should it be legal to raise prices on basic items needed for survival during natural disasters or other emergencies?
- ☐ **INTERACTIVE FEATURE** Case Study: Holiday Demand—Students analyze how prices change based on fads and expectations.

☑ Printable Digital Worksheets
- ☐ **WORKSHEET** Math Practice for Economics—Students read about the Law of Diminishing Marginal Utility.

Project-Based Learning

Hands-On

WORKSHEET Hands-On Chapter Project
Students examine the work at a warehouse for a chain of superstores in the center of the United States. They form groups that serve as suppliers for departments in the store, and ensure that the supply in the stores meets the changing demands of the customers. Students explore different scenarios that will require them to make decisions as a group about supplying products for their department, and create presentations about their decisions. Finally, they create a job description for the manager of a superstore warehouse, using what they have learned about responding to customer demand.

Digital Hands-On

Create Online Projects

Find an additional activity online that incorporates technology for the Hands-On Project. Visit the EdTech Teacher Web sites for more links, tutorials, and other resources.

Print Resources

ANCILLARY RESOURCE
This ancillary is available for every chapter and lesson.
- Chapter Tests and Lesson Quizzes

PRINTABLE DIGITAL WORKSHEETS
These printable digital worksheets are available for every chapter and lesson.
- Reading Essentials & Study Guide
- Vocabulary Activities
- Chapter Summaries
- Economic Simulations
- Math Practice for Economics
- Reinforcing Economic Skills Activities
- Personal Finance Activities
- Enrichment Activities
- Reteaching Activities
- Guided Reading Activities
- Video Worksheets
- Lesson Quizzes and Chapter Tests (English and Spanish)

More Media Resources

SUGGESTED READING
- For students at a Grade 10 reading level: *Exploring Careers,* by U.S. Department of Labor
- For students at a Grade 11 reading level: *The Success of the Navajo Arts and Crafts Enterprise,* by Lenora Begay Trahant
- For students at a Grade 12 reading level: *Business Builders in Fast Food,* by Nathan Aaseng

SUGGESTED VIDEOS
Find these documentaries yourself online. NOTE: McGraw-Hill Education does not endorse these resources. Preview clips for age-appropriateness.
- *Merchants of Cool* (53 min.)
- *Secret History of the Credit Card* (60 min.)

LESSON 1 Planner

WHAT IS DEMAND?

Students will know:
- demand is the desire, ability, and willingness to buy a product or service.
- the Law of Demand, which states that the quantity demanded of a product varies inversely with its price.

Students will be able to:
- **name** the variables that determine demand for a product.
- **explain** how demand helps societies determine WHAT, HOW, and FOR WHOM to produce.
- **paraphrase** the Law of Demand.
- **interpret the significance** of diminishing marginal utility on the price consumers are willing to pay for additional units of a product.

UNDERSTANDING BY DESIGN®

☑ Print Teaching Options

V Visual Skills

- ☐ **p. 103 Creating demand schedules and graphs** Students list prices for a product, constructing a demand schedule and graphing data. **Logical/Mathematical**

- ☐ **p. 105 Creating a cartoon about marginal utility** Students create cartoons that show diminishing marginal utility. **AL ELL Visual/Spatial**

R Reading Skills

- ☐ **p. 102 Activating prior knowledge about demand** Students discuss how answering WHAT, HOW, and FOR WHOM can establish demand.

- ☐ **p. 102 Understanding math terms** Students discuss the word *variable*.

C Critical Thinking Skills

- ☐ **p. 104 Reinforcing demand's downward slope** Students discuss the demand curve's downward slope. **AL ELL Logical/Mathematical**

- ☐ **p. 105 Creating a market demand curve** Students acquire price data to create a market demand curve for a product. **BL Logical/Mathematical**

- ☐ **p. 106 Theorizing about marginal utility** Students discuss the problems of measuring marginal utility.

W Writing Skills

- ☐ **p. 104 Observing the Law of Demand** Students write about a time when they observed the Law of Demand in action. **Verbal/Linguistic**

- ☐ **p. 105 Testing the Law of Demand** Students decide how many soft drinks they would buy at several different prices, and write a generalization about the Law of Demand. **Verbal/Linguistic**

- ☐ **p. 106 Explaining buying decisions** Students write a reflection paragraph describing two different decisions they made regarding purchases.

☑ Online Teaching Options

V Visual Skills

- ☐ **GRAPHS Demand for Burritos**—Students explore a graph and explain how demand is illustrated. **Visual/Spatial**

- ☐ **VIDEO Fear of Buying**—Students watch a video about consumer fears during a recession.

R Reading Skills

- ☐ **GRAPHIC ORGANIZERS Relationship between Price and Demand**—Students describe the relationship between price and demand, and give specific examples. **Logical/Mathematical**

- ☐ **BIOGRAPHY Carl Menger**—Students read and discuss what made Carl Menger's theory of demand different.

C Critical Thinking Skills

- ☐ **BELLRINGER Introduction to Demand**—Students explore the Market Demand Curve for Movie DVDs. **Visual/Spatial**

- ☐ **ESSENTIAL QUESTION Exploring the Essential Question Activity**—Students write about the ways in which an advertisement makes people want to buy a product.

- ☐ **GRAPHS Individual and Market Demand Curves**—Students predict what a market demand curve will look like and explore individual demand curves.

T Technology Skills

- ☐ **SELF-CHECK QUIZ Lesson 1**—Students receive instant feedback on their mastery of lesson content.

- ☐ **GAME Lesson 1**—Students solve clues to review lesson content.

- ☐ **INTERACTIVE WHITEBOARD ACTIVITY Diminishing Marginal Returns**—Students work together to learn lesson content.

☑ Printable Digital Worksheets

R Reading Skills

- ☐ **WORKSHEET Guided Reading Activity**—Students use the Guided Reading Activity worksheets to review their comprehension of the content.

- ☐ **WORKSHEET Reading Essentials and Study Guide**—Students complete the study guide and answer Reading Progress Check and vocabulary questions.

C Critical Thinking Skills

- ☐ **WORKSHEET Economic Simulation**—Students do market research to decide what types of clothing to sell in another country.

- ☐ **WORKSHEET Fear of Buying Video Activity**—Students answer questions related to consumer behavior during a recession, creating a summary of the video.

LESSON 2 Planner

FACTORS AFFECTING DEMAND

Students will know:
- only a change in price can cause a change in quantity demanded.
- the factors that cause a shift in demand include consumer tastes, substitutes, complements, expectations, and the number of consumers.

Students will be able to:
- **specify** the factor that causes a change in the quantity demanded.
- **explain** how the income and substitution effects change quantity demanded.
- **list** non-price factors that affect demand.

UNDERSTANDING BY DESIGN®

☑ Print Teaching Options

C Critical Thinking Skills

- ☐ **p. 108 Reinforcing the effect of price on quantity demanded** Students compare a seesaw to the relationship between price and quantity demanded. *Logical/Mathematical*

- ☐ **p. 108 Analyzing the relationship of price and quantity demanded** Student plot quantity demanded at a current income and after purchasing power increases. *Visual/Spatial*

- ☐ **p. 109 Understanding the income and substitution effects** Students determine whether quantity demanded goes up or down based on various scenarios.

- ☐ **p. 109 Income Effect** Students apply the income effect to their purchasing decisions.

- ☐ **p. 110 Change in Demand** Students explore a crop destruction's effects on price, substitutes, and complementary products.

- ☐ **p. 111 Explaining shifts in demand** Students explain what would happen to demand in various situations.

- ☐ **p. 112 Understanding changes in number of consumers** Students predict demand curve movement for toys if the birthrate declined.

W Writing Skills

- ☐ **p. 109 Applying the substitution effect** Students list substitutes they would buy if prices of original goods rose. *Intrapersonal*

- ☐ **p. 112 Understanding changes in expectations** Students explain how a rumor or unfavorable report affects demand.

- ☐ **p. 113 Applying changes in quantity demanded and demand** Students write how price, real income, or the substitution effect determined their quantity demanded; and how tastes or expectations affected demand.

T Technology Skills

- ☐ **p. 111 Graphing changes in consumer tastes** Students illustrate changes in demand on schedules and graphs. **BL** *Kinesthetic*

☑ Online Teaching Options

V Visual Skills

- ☐ **GRAPHS Change in the Quantity Demanded**—Students analyze a graph about change in quantity demanded. *Visual/Spatial*

- ☐ **VIDEO Global Demand Impact on Food Prices**—Students view a video on global demand and its impact on food prices.

- ☐ **GRAPHS Change in Demand**—Students analyze how a change in consumer tastes shift the demand curve for a product. *Visual/Spatial*

- ☐ **POLITICAL CARTOON "Expectations"**—Students analyze a political cartoon about demand and consumer expectations.

R Reading Skills

- ☐ **INTERACTIVE FEATURE Global Economy & You**—Students read about a store that did not take into account consumer tastes. *Intrapersonal*

C Critical Thinking Skills

- ☐ **BELLRINGER Factors Affecting Demand**—Students discuss factors affecting demand. *Logical/Mathematical*

- ☐ **ESSENTIAL QUESTION Exploring the Essential Question**—Students brainstorm ideas about what makes a business decide to produce a particular product. *Logical/Mathematical*

- ☐ **ESSENTIAL QUESTION Exploring the Essential Question**—Students nonprice factors that affect demand. *Logical/Mathematical*

T Technology Skills

- ☐ **SELF-CHECK QUIZ Lesson 2**—Students receive instant feedback on their mastery of lesson content.

- ☐ **GAME Lesson 2**—Students solve clues to review lesson content.

- ☐ **INTERACTIVE WHITEBOARD ACTIVITY Recognizing Substitutes and Complements**—Students work together to learn lesson content.

☑ Printable Digital Worksheets

R Reading Skills

- ☐ **WORKSHEET Guided Reading Activity**—Students use the Guided Reading Activity worksheets to review their comprehension of the content.

- ☐ **WORKSHEET Reading Essentials and Study Guide**—Students complete the study guide and answer Reading Progress Check and vocabulary questions.

C Critical Thinking Skills

- ☐ **WORKSHEET Global Demand Impact on Food Prices**—Students answer questions about global demand and its impact on food prices.

LESSON 3 Planner

ELASTICITY OF DEMAND

Students will know:
- the difference between elastic demand and inelastic demand for a product.
- the determinants of demand elasticity.

Students will be able to:
- **summarize** the three cases of demand elasticity.
- **apply** the total expenditures test to determine the elasticity of a product.
- **identify** determinants of demand elasticity.

UNDERSTANDING BY DESIGN®

☑ Print Teaching Options

V Visual Skills

☐ **p. 116 Modeling elasticity** Students explore elasticity on four graphs, performing total expenditures tests. **BL** Visual/Spatial

R Reading Skills

☐ **p. 114 Introducing elasticity** Students associate meaning of *elastic* and *inelastic* by exploring how a rubber band stretches.
AL ELL Verbal/Linguistic

☐ **p. 118 Identifying products' elasticity** Students identify which type of demand elasticity soft drinks, salt, steak, electric power have, and why. Logical/Mathematical

C Critical Thinking Skills

☐ **p. 114 Identifying elasticity** Students list 10 household goods and services that have elastic and inelastic demand. **AL**

☐ **p. 117 Identifying components of elasticity** Students note whether quantity demanded responds to price changes, amount of income used, "delayable," or available substitutes. **BL** Logical/Mathematical

☐ **p. 119 Applying knowledge of elasticity to personal purchases** Students write about spending changes given what they know about prices, demand, and elasticity.

W Writing Skills

☐ **p. 115 Creating dialogue about elasticity of food purchases** Students write a conversation or lyrics about rising food prices, substitutions, and demand elasticity. Auditory/Musical

☐ **p. 118 Writing about elasticity** Students write about someone who has inelastic demand for a product but is faced with a significant price change. **BL** Verbal/Linguistic

☑ Online Teaching Options

V Visual Skills

☐ **GRAPHS Demand Elasticity and the Total Expenditures Test**—Students explore the effects of elasticity on total expenditures. Visual/Spatial

☐ **VIDEO Energy Prices Lead to Biofuel Use**—Students watch a video about changes in energy prices leading to biofuel use.

R Reading Skills

☐ **GRAPHIC ORGANIZER Types of Elasticity**—Students describe and compare types of elasticity. Verbal/Linguistic

C Critical Thinking Skills

☐ **BELLRINGER Elasticity of Demand**—Students answer which of the three types of elasticity equals 1.

☐ **ESSENTIAL QUESTION Exploring the Essential Question**—Students discuss what factors could influence the decision to buy or not buy a product.

☐ **CHARTS Determinants of Demand Elasticity**—Students explore decisions that determine whether a product is elastic. Logical/Mathematical

T Technology Skills

☐ **SELF-CHECK QUIZ Lesson 3**—Students receive instant feedback on their mastery of lesson content.

☐ **GAME Lesson 3**—Students solve clues to review lesson content.

☐ **INTERACTIVE WHITEBOARD ACTIVITY Demand Elasticity**—Students work together to learn lesson content.

☑ Printable Digital Worksheets

R Reading Skills

☐ **WORKSHEET Guided Reading Activity**—Students use the Guided Reading Activity worksheets to review their comprehension of the content.

☐ **WORKSHEET Reading Essentials and Study Guide**—Students complete the study guide and answer Reading Progress Check and vocabulary questions.

☐ **WORKSHEET Reteaching Activity**—Students use this activity worksheet to review and reteach chapter content and vocabulary. This worksheet can be used with struggling students who need additional help with difficult content concepts.

C Critical Thinking Skills

☐ **WORKSHEET Personal Finance**—Students track expenses and assess each item they have purchased for demand elasticity.

☐ **WORKSHEET Energy Prices Lead to Biofuel Use Video Activity**—Students answer questions about changes in energy prices leading to biofuel use.

CHAPTER 4 Demand

INTERVENTION AND REMEDIATION STRATEGIES

LESSON 1 An Introduction to Demand

Reading and Comprehension

Have students write a paragraph describing what demand is, and have them provide two examples to support their definition. Then have students select the topic sentence from five paragraphs in this lesson and rewrite them in their own words.

Text Evidence

Have students explore the individual demand curves and the market demand curve in the text. Then have them write a short report explaining how the market curve is created, and why it looks the way that it does. Have them explain in their report what factors might make the market curve change, citing evidence from the text.

LESSON 2 Factors Affecting Demand

Reading and Comprehension

Have students write a summary paragraph stating the key factor—price—that affects quantity demanded. Then ask them to write one sentence describing an example of their own quantity demanded for a product changing because of price. Finally, ask each student to choose a good they would buy more of if the price of school lunches, for example, were cut in half and they had more income to spend on other goods. Have students plot their quantity demanded at their current income and after their purchasing power increased.

Text Evidence

Have students write a sentence stating what factors affect demand. *(changes in consumer income and consumer tastes, the changes in prices of related goods such as substitutes and complements, changes in expectations, and changes in the total number of consumers)* Then have them provide one example of each effect from the text to support their statement.

LESSON 3 Elasticity of Demand

Reading and Comprehension

Have students write in their own words the questions that must be asked to determine elasticity of a product. Then have them use those questions to evaluate a product they buy.

Text Evidence

Have students find examples of products in the text that are elastic. Then have them find examples of products that are inelastic. Have them write one sentence for each product that explains why it is elastic or inelastic, using evidence from the text to support their statements.

Online Resources

Assessing Background Knowledge Use this worksheet to pre-assess students' knowledge before they start the chapter.

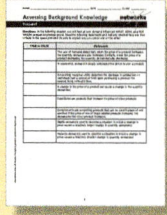

Chapter Summaries Have students use the summary as a pre-reading activity or as a post-reading review to check the main ideas covered in each lesson.

Guided Reading Activities Have students complete these activities as they read each lesson. They provide reading notes the student can use for review and to prepare for assessments.

Reteaching Activities Have students complete the Reteaching Activity for remedial practice and review of vital content.

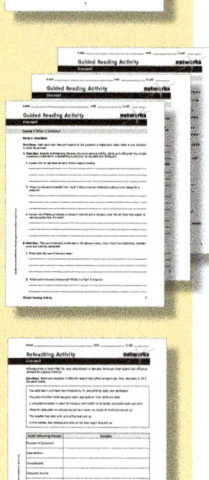

Self-Check Quizzes These quizzes provide instant feedback on areas the students may need to re-read to understand a main idea.

Reading Essentials and Study Guide This resource offers writing and reading activities for the approaching-level student.

Approaching Grade Level Reader This reader presents all of the content of the Online Student Edition but at a lower reading level.

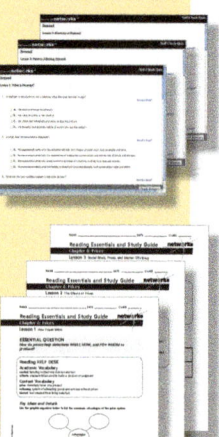

English Language Learner Reader Provide additional reading support for ELL students. Find this tool in the Online Student Edition.

Demand

ESSENTIAL QUESTIONS
- How does demand help societies determine WHAT, HOW, and FOR WHOM to produce?
- What are the causes of a change in demand?

networks
www.connected.mcgraw-hill.com
There's More Online about demand.

CHAPTER 4

Economic Perspectives
Law of Demand

Lesson 1
What is Demand?

Lesson 2
Factors Affecting Demand

Lesson 3
Elasticity of Demand

CHAPTER 4
Demand

ENGAGE

 Call students' attention to the photo and ask them to describe what it shows. Guide them to recognize that people are waiting in line to buy popular items at a store. **Ask: Why is this image a good one to symbolize the chapter titled Demand?** *(Demand is the desire, ability, and willingness to buy a product, and the people in the photo are an example of what consumers will do to get a popular product.)* In a discussion, lead students to understand that several factors, including price and consumer taste, affect demand for a product. **Visual/Spatial**

Identifying factors that affect demand Discuss the factors that affect consumer purchases of a product. Point out that there are several factors. **Ask: What makes you want to buy a product?** *(Sample answers: popularity of the product, consumer tastes, trends, price of the product)* **What encourages consumers to buy more of a product?** *(Lower prices encourage more buying.)* **Verbal/Linguistic**

Making Connections

Demand Decisions Have students describe to the class a time when they decided to buy more of a product than they needed right away because of a low price. **Ask: Did the low price of a product make you buy more than you needed? Was it a good purchasing decision?** *(Sample answer: I bought more paper for the printer than I needed; it was a good decision because I use the paper and paid less for it than I would have if I had waited to buy later.)*

Letter from the Author

Dear Economics Teacher,

Here's a chapter that students should have no trouble relating to—the topic of demand. It's also a great chapter to use when explaining how to read graphs, which will be especially helpful to the visual learner. One of the strengths of economics is that simple concepts can be presented in so many different ways: in written text, visually with charts and graphs, or even mathematically in the form of equations. And with all of the variables that economists have to consider, the relationship between the variables of price and quantity are sound and unchallenged—and a great way to introduce students to one of the few unequivocal economic concepts.

Go to the Foldables® library for a cumulative chapter-based Foldable® activity that your students can use to help take notes and prepare for assessment.

Gary E. Clayton

CHAPTER 4
Economic Perspectives

TEACH & ASSESS

R Reading Skills

Predicting changes in demand Have students read through the infographic. Then ask them to predict how demand might change for the products described in the infographic, and what factors might cause this change in demand. Have them write a short paragraph describing their predictions.
Verbal/Linguistic

W Writing Skills

Describing purchasing decisions and demand Have students write a journal entry describing a product they want to buy but cannot afford. Have them describe in their journal entry a strategy for eventually purchasing the product, either by saving money or by waiting for the product's price to go down. **Verbal/Linguistic**

C Critical Thinking Skills

Understanding relationships between price and quantity demanded Have students draw a demand curve for each product in the infographic. Students can make up the actual data (how many smart phones are purchased between them and their friends, and the prices of the phones, for example). **Logical/Mathematical, Visual/Spatial**

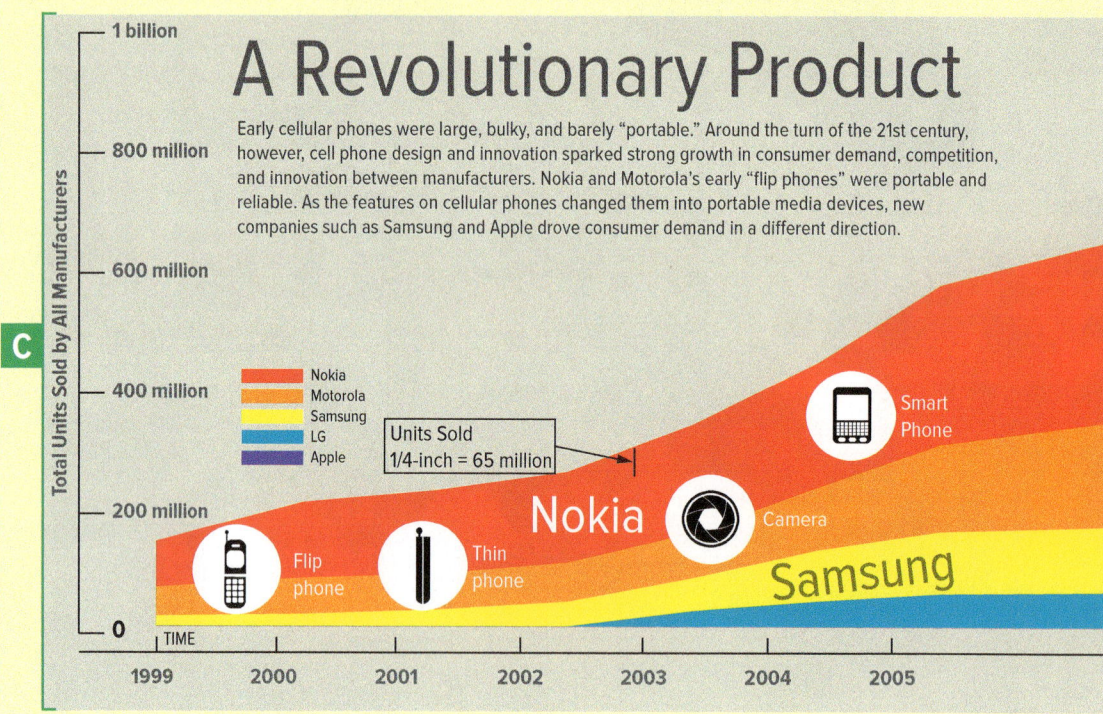

Economic Perspectives

LAW OF DEMAND

INITIAL
R When a new product is introduced, the number of buyers may be small. The number of buyers and the demand may increase as positive opinions collect. Setting an affordable price can also attract new buyers.

PEAK
W If a product gets into the market ahead of other products and captures consumer loyalty, it can lead to significant sales and profit gains. Especially when demand is growing and competition is minimal, a product may experience its highest levels of demand.

A Revolutionary Product
Early cellular phones were large, bulky, and barely "portable." Around the turn of the 21st century, however, cell phone design and innovation sparked strong growth in consumer demand, competition, and innovation between manufacturers. Nokia and Motorola's early "flip phones" were portable and reliable. As the features on cellular phones changed them into portable media devices, new companies such as Samsung and Apple drove consumer demand in a different direction.

networks Online Teaching Options

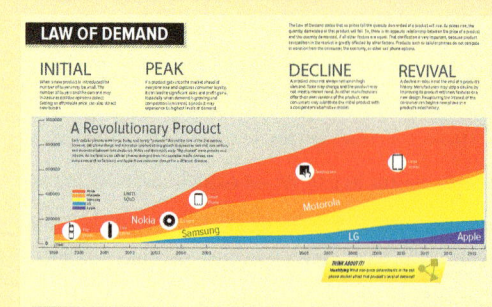

INFOGRAPHIC

Economic Perspectives: Law of Demand

Understanding the Law of Demand Have students state the Law of Demand. Then have them study the feature and discuss the importance of substitutions. Ask them to give an example describing how the Law of Demand changed their purchasing decisions as the price of a new product decreased after other firms entered the market and provided choices.
Verbal/Linguistic

100

CHAPTER 4
Economic Perspectives

The Law of Demand states that as prices fall, the quantity demanded of a product will rise. As prices rise, the quantity demanded of that product will fall. So, there is an opposite relationship between the price of a product and the quantity demanded, if all other factors are equal. That clarification is very important, because product competition in the market is greatly affected by other factors. Products such as cellular phones do not compete in isolation from the consumer, the economy, or other cell phone options.

DECLINE
A product does not always remain in high demand. Tastes may change and the product may not meet a market need. As other manufacturers offer their own versions of the product, new consumers may substitute the initial product with a competitor's alternative model.

REVIVAL
A decline in sales is not the end of a product's history. Manufacturers may stop a decline by improving their products with new features or a new design. Recapturing the interest of the consumer can begin a new phase in a product's sales history.

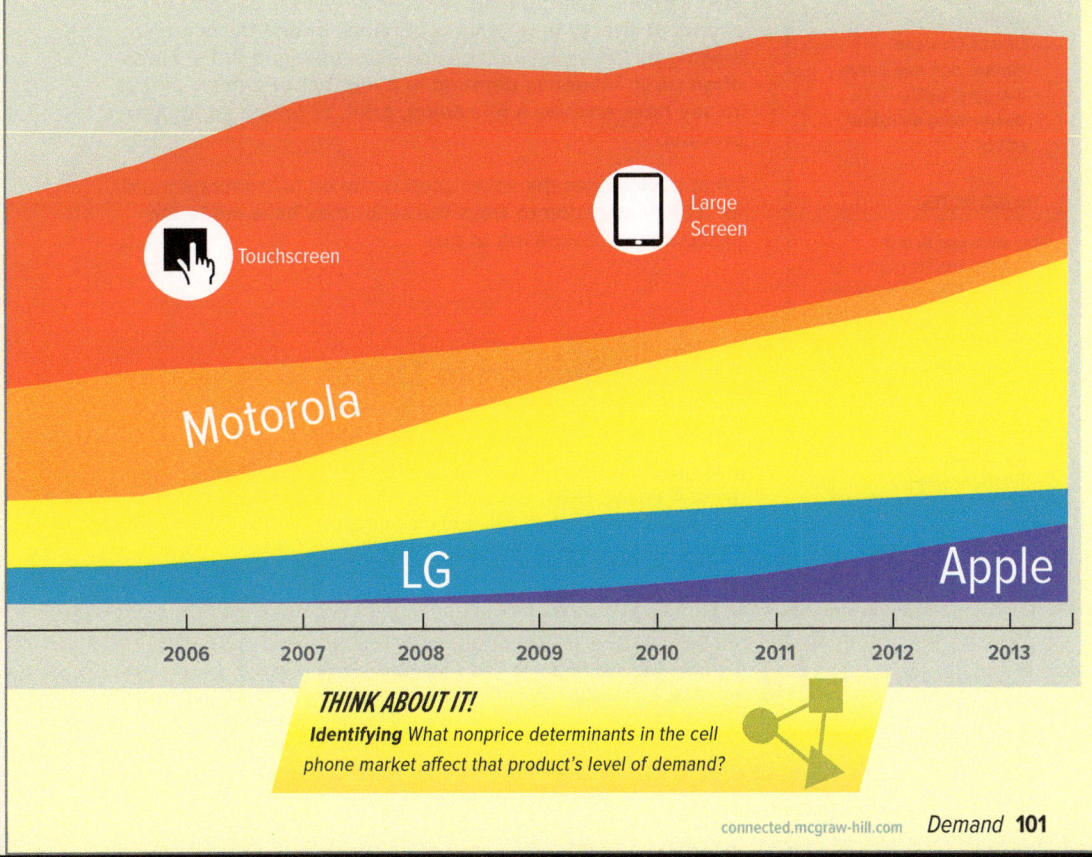

THINK ABOUT IT!
Identifying What nonprice determinants in the cell phone market affect that product's level of demand?

Content Background Knowledge

The S Curve Explain that the infographic shows a typical S curve, which researchers use to show the growth of a particular phenomenon over units of time. The growth of the phenomenon is measured on the Y- or vertical axis, and units of time are expressed on the X- or horizontal axis. The S curve shows the starting point of the phenomenon, its rapid growth as it takes off and becomes more popular, and the period when it levels off as fewer new people begin to purchase it.

W Writing Skills

Explaining purchasing decisions Have students create a table tracking the price of an item they waited to buy because of price. Have them write a short paragraph explaining when they decided to finally purchase the item, and what factors guided their decision. Remind students to use economic-related terminology correctly. **Logical/Mathematical**

CLOSE & REFLECT

Have students answer the *Think About It!* questions.

WORKSHEET

Math Practice for Economics

Applying factors affecting quantity demanded to real-life situations Read through the worksheet with students and answer any questions they may have about the Law of Diminishing Marginal Utility, the Real Income Effect, and the Substitution Effect. Then have students answer the questions on the worksheet. Finally, have students create one additional problem for the Law of Diminishing Marginal Utility, using an example from real life, and calculate answers for the problem they create.
Logical/Mathematical

ANSWERS, p. 101

THINK ABOUT IT!

Non-price determinants included consumers tastes or fads, expectations, the availability of substitutes, the amount of income required to purchase a cell phone, and how many consumers overall demanded cell phones.

CHAPTER 4, LESSON 1
What Is Demand?

ENGAGE

R1 Reading Skills

Activating prior knowledge about demand
Before students begin the lesson, ask them to recall the three questions societies ask in order to make production decisions: WHAT, HOW, and FOR WHOM. **Ask:** How can these questions be adjusted to establish demand for a product? *(Sample answer: Companies need to know what people need or want to buy, how much consumers would pay for the product, and for whom the advertising should be targeted—who the customers are.)*

TEACH & ASSESS

R2 Reading Skills

Understanding math terms Explain that the word *variable* is a math term referring to quantities that may change. In a relationship between variables, one is often unknown and changes as the other variable changes. These variables could be time and money, age and height, hours studying and grades earned, and so on. In economics, the variables are often price and quantity. However, economists also study seemingly unrelated factors—like unemployment levels and birthrates—to try to identify relationships. Explain that in a causal relationship, the variable that is the *causative* factor is called the *independent variable*. The responding variable is called the *dependent variable*.

ANSWERS, p. 102

ESSENTIAL QUESTION ACTIVITY

Answers will vary. Have students write a short paragraph about the ways in which the advertisement makes people want to buy the product. Or have students suggest three ways in which they would change the advertisement to make it more compelling to encourage consumers to buy the product.

TAKING NOTES
Price Increases → Demand <u>decreases</u>
Price Decreases → Demand <u>increases</u>

Interact with these digital assets and others in lesson 1

✓ INTERACTIVE GRAPH
   Price of Burritos
✓ INTERACTIVE GRAPH
   Individual and Market
   Demand Curves
✓ SELF-CHECK QUIZ
✓ VIDEO

networks
TRY IT YOURSELF ONLINE

LESSON 1
What Is Demand?

Reading Help Desk

Academic Vocabulary
- prevail
- inversely

Content Vocabulary
- demand
- microeconomics
- demand schedule
- incentive
- demand curve
- Law of Demand
- market demand curve
- marginal utility
- diminishing marginal utility

TAKING NOTES:

Key Ideas and Details
ACTIVITY Use the graphic organizer below to identify the relationship between price and demand

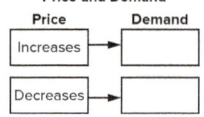

Relationship between Price and Demand

Price	Demand
Increases	
Decreases	

ESSENTIAL QUESTION

How does demand help societies determine WHAT, HOW, and FOR WHOM to produce?

R1 **Demand** describes the various amounts of a product that someone is willing and able to buy over a range of possible prices at one point in time. **Microeconomics** is the part of economic theory that deals with behavior and decision making by individual units, such as people and firms. Firms often try to influence demand in a number of different ways. To see how, analyze a television, print, or online ad for a product.

What devices has the seller used in the ad to create demand for it? Pay attention to ways the seller may have made the product more appealing to buy.

An Introduction to Demand

GUIDING QUESTION *What is the relationship between the price of an item and the quantity demanded?*

In a market economy, people and firms act in their own best interest to answer the basic WHAT, HOW, and FOR WHOM questions. Demand is central to this process, so an understanding of the concept of demand is essential if we are to understand how the economy works.

Demand Illustrated

R2 Fortunately, the calculation of demand comes down to only two variables—the price of a product and the quantity available at a given point in time. For example, we might want to know how many people would choose to see a movie on a given afternoon if the ticket price were $5. Or we might want to know how many would choose to view it if the price were $10. To keep things simple, economists employ a simple assumption called *ceteris paribus*, or other things held constant. So if the price changes from $5 to $10, or to any

102

---

networks *Online Teaching Options*

BELLRINGER

Introduction to Demand

Understanding the effect of price on demand Have students explore the Market Demand Curve for Movie DVDs in the Bellringer. Have students answer the questions. Then have a class discussion about how price affects demand for a product. **Ask:** How does price affect the number of DVDs people are willing to buy? *(Sample answer: The higher the price, the fewer DVDs people are willing to buy.)*
Visual/Spatial

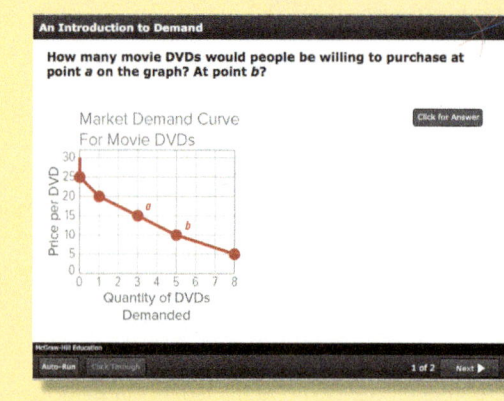

other price, we assume that nothing else changes. By assuming *ceteris paribus*, we rule out any changes in other factors such as the number of other movies playing, how easy it is to purchase tickets, and whether it's a holiday weekend.

An Individual's Demand Schedule

To see how an economist would analyze individual demand, look at **Panel A** in **Figure 4.1**. It shows the amount of burritos that a consumer, whom we'll call Mike, would be willing and able to purchase over a range of possible prices that go from $1 to $10. The information in Panel A is known as a **demand schedule**.

The demand schedule shows the various quantities demanded of a particular product at all prices that might **prevail** in the market at a given time.

As you can see, Mike would not buy any burritos at a price of $9 or $10, but he would buy one if the price fell to $6, and he would buy two if the price were $4, and so on. Just like the rest of us, he is generally willing to buy more units of a product at lower prices. Of course, these numbers may not be entirely realistic but are intended to keep the example simple. For Mike, prices are an **incentive**, a motivating influence that causes him to act. When the price goes up, he will buy less, and when the price goes down, he will buy more. His income, hunger, and many other factors will feed into his desire, willingness, and ability to buy. But if all of those are held constant, then a change in price will be the single incentive that affects the quantity he will buy.

The Individual's Demand Curve

The demand schedule in Panel A of Figure 4.1 can also be shown graphically as the downward-sloping line in **Panel B**. If we transfer each of the price-quantity

demand combination of quantities that someone would be willing and able to buy over a range of possible prices at a given moment

microeconomics branch of economic theory that deals with behavior and decision making by small units such as individuals and firms

demand schedule listing showing the quantity demanded at all possible prices that might prevail in the market at a given time

prevail to predominate

incentive something that motivates

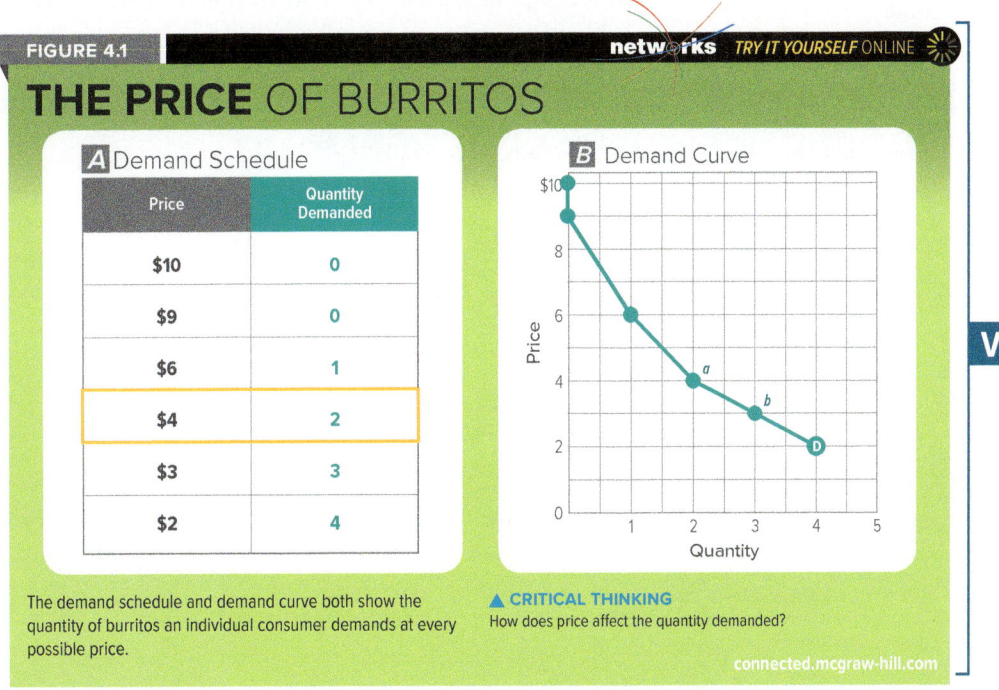

FIGURE 4.1

THE PRICE OF BURRITOS

A Demand Schedule

Price	Quantity Demanded
$10	0
$9	0
$6	1
$4	2
$3	3
$2	4

B Demand Curve

The demand schedule and demand curve both show the quantity of burritos an individual consumer demands at every possible price.

▲ **CRITICAL THINKING**
How does price affect the quantity demanded?

Demand 103

CHAPTER 4, LESSON 1
What Is Demand?

C Critical Thinking Skills

Reinforcing demand's downward slope Have a class discussion reinforcing the demand curve's downward slope. Many students misread the *X*-axis as price instead of quantity, and so misunderstand that quantity demanded is at its highest when the curve extends far and low to the right. **AL** **ELL** Logical/Mathematical

W Writing Skills

Observing the Law of Demand Have students write about a time when they observed the Law of Demand in action. Students can write about purchases they have made or purchases they have observed others making. Remind students to use standard sentence structure when writing. Verbal/Linguistic

---

demand curve graph showing the quantity demanded at each and every possible price that might prevail in the market at a given time

Law of Demand rule stating that more will be demanded at lower prices and less at higher prices; an inverse relationship between price and quantity demanded

inversely in the opposite way

market demand curve demand curve that shows the quantities demanded by everyone who is willing and able to purchase a product at all possible prices at one moment in time

marginal utility additional satisfaction or usefulness obtained from acquiring or consuming one more unit of a product

diminishing marginal utility decrease in additional satisfaction or usefulness as additional units of a product are acquired

observations in the demand schedule to the graph, we can then connect the points to form the curve. Economists call this a **demand curve**, which shows the quantity demanded at each price that might prevail in the market.

For example, point **a** in Panel B shows that Mike would purchase two burritos at a price of $4 each, while point **b** shows that he will buy three at a price of $3. The demand schedule and the demand curve show the same information—one in a table and the other as a graph.

✓ **READING PROGRESS CHECK**

Interpreting How do people react to a change in the price of an item? How does this illustrate the concept of demand?

The Law of Demand

GUIDING QUESTION *Why do economists think of demand as a "law"?*

The prices and quantities in Figure 4.1 point out an important feature of demand: for practically every good or service that we might buy, higher prices are associated with smaller amounts demanded. Conversely, lower prices are associated with larger amounts demanded. This is known as the **Law of Demand**, which states that the quantity demanded varies **inversely** with its price. When the price of something increases, the quantity demanded decreases. Likewise, when the price goes down, buyers have an incentive to purchase more, and so the quantity demanded goes up.

Why We Call It a "Law"

Economics is a social science—a study of the way we behave when things around us change. In all of the sciences, we speak of "laws" when a theory

FIGURE 4.2 INDIVIDUAL AND MARKET DEMAND CURVES

The market demand curve shows the quantities demanded by everyone in the market who is interested in purchasing a product, such as burritos, at a given point in time.

▲ **CRITICAL THINKING**
How does the market demand curve differ from an individual's demand curve?

---

networks Online Teaching Options

GRAPHS

Individual and Market Demand

Reading graphs that show individual and market demand Have students explore the individual demand curves in the activity, but before they look at the market demand curve, ask them to predict what it will look like. **Ask:** *If both of the individual curves slope down, what should the market curve do? Why?* (Sample answer: The market curve will also slope down, because it is an average of the data used to create the two individual curves.)

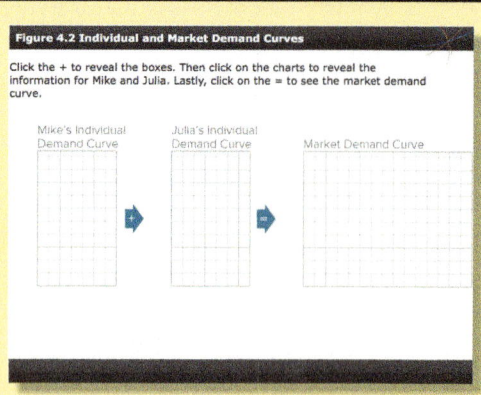

ANSWERS, p. 104

✓ **READING PROGRESS CHECK** People usually buy more if the price decreases or buy less if it increases. Demand is the desire, ability, and willingness to buy a product; all of these tend to increase as the price decreases. With few exceptions, desire and ability or willingness to buy a product decrease if the price increases.

CRITICAL THINKING
It shows the quantity demanded by everyone—in this case, Mike and Julia—for all prices that might prevail in a market at a specific time. Mike's and Julia's quantities demanded were added together for each price point.

proves true after repeated tests and it fits within our larger understanding of the field. The inverse relationship between price and quantity demanded appears in study after study, with people almost always stating that they would buy more of an item if its price went down, and less if the price went up.

Second, common sense and simple observation are consistent with the Law of Demand. This is how people behave in everyday life—people buy more ice cream at lower prices than they do at higher prices; it's the main reason that grocery stores put products on sale.

The Market Demand Curve

The market demand curve shows the quantities demanded by everyone who is interested in purchasing the product, as in the example with the movie tickets. **Figure 4.2** shows the market demand curve for Mike and his friend Julia, the only two people in the market whom (for simplicity) we assume to be willing and able to purchase burritos.

To get the market demand curve, all we do is add together the number of burritos that Mike and Julia would purchase at every possible price. Then, we simply plot the prices and quantities on a separate graph. To illustrate, point **a** in Figure 4.2 represents the two burritos that Mike would purchase at $4, plus the one that Julia would buy at the same price. Likewise, point **b** represents the quantity of burritos that both would purchase at $3.

Of course, an actual market demand curve would represent thousands, if not millions, of people, and the range of prices would have to be high enough to include everyone. Other than that, there are no meaningful differences between individual and market demand curves. Both are downward sloping, and both represent the number of items that would be purchased at a given time and place with all other things being unchanged.

✓ **READING PROGRESS CHECK**

Explaining How does the market demand curve reflect the Law of Demand?

Demand and Marginal Utility

GUIDING QUESTION *How does the principle of diminishing marginal utility explain the price we would be willing to pay for another unit of a good or service?*

As you learned earlier, economists use the term *utility* to describe the amount of usefulness or satisfaction that someone gets from the use of a product. **Marginal utility**—the *extra* usefulness or *additional* satisfaction a person gets from acquiring or using one more unit of a product—is an important extension of this concept because it explains so much about demand.

The reason we buy something in the first place is because we feel that the product is useful and will give us utility, or satisfaction. However, as we use more and more of a product, we usually encounter **diminishing marginal utility**. That means that the extra satisfaction we get from using additional quantities of the product begins to decline.

Because of our diminishing satisfaction—our diminishing marginal utility—as we consume every additional unit, we usually are not willing to pay as much for the second, third, and fourth unit, and so on, as we did for the first. This is why our demand curve is downward-sloping, and this is why Mike and Julia won't pay as much for the second burrito as they did for the first.

Diminishing satisfaction happens to all of us. For example, if you are very thirsty, you might be willing to pay a high price for a bottle of water. Once you

BIOGRAPHY

Carl Menger
ECONOMIST
(1840–1921)

Carl Menger was born into a wealthy family in what is now Poland. Soon after earning a PhD from the Jagiellonian University of Kraków in 1867, he took a position as a professor of economic theory at the University of Vienna in Austria, where he taught until 1903.

Menger pioneered the idea of marginal utility in economic thought, arguing that a good's value—and thus its price—is determined by how well it satisfies a consumer's wants. His thinking challenged traditional views that value derives from the cost of the labor needed to produce the good. Critics derided Menger and his students, calling them the "Austrian School," to emphasize their departure from the mainstream. Today, the Austrian School is a widely-accepted body of economic theory and Menger is highly regarded as its founder.

▶ **CRITICAL THINKING**
Identifying What new insights did Menger contribute to economic theory?

connected.mcgraw-hill.com   *Demand* **105**

CHAPTER 4, LESSON 1
What Is Demand?

W Writing Skills

Testing the Law of Demand Ask students how many soft drinks they would buy at 25 cents a can, at 50 cents, at $1, at $1.50, and so on. Note the prices and quantities on the board. Then ask students to write a generalization about the Law of Demand based on these figures. **Verbal/Linguistic**

C Critical Thinking Skills

Creating a market demand curve In a general class discussion, brainstorm a list of products that class members buy. Organize the class into small groups, and tell each group to imagine that they are forming a business. Students should then choose from the list a product that they would like to sell, and set a range of three to five possible prices they might charge for it. Group members should then survey ten classmates to see what quantities they would buy at each of the prices. Have each group compile the data into a demand schedule. Then direct the groups to use their demand schedules to graph a market demand curve for their product. **BL Logical/Mathematical**

V Visual Skills

Creating a cartoon about marginal utility Have students create cartoons that show diminishing marginal utility. For example, several storyboards could show a spectator at a ball game, purchasing three hotdogs for $3.25 each. The spectator has enough after buying three hotdogs, and thus the value placed on additional satisfaction from a fourth hot dog would be less than $3.25. According to what will give the spectator the most satisfaction, he or she will save or spend the $3.25 on something else. Eventually, the spectator receives no additional satisfaction, even if the vendor offered the product at zero price. **AL ELL Visual/Spatial**

ANSWERS, p. 105

✓ **READING PROGRESS CHECK** The market demand curve shows the quantities demanded by everyone who might want to purchase a product. It shows how the Law of Demand works in relation to prices and quantity purchased.

CRITICAL THINKING
He pioneered the theory of marginal utility—that a good's value and price are determined by how well it satisfies a consumer's wants.

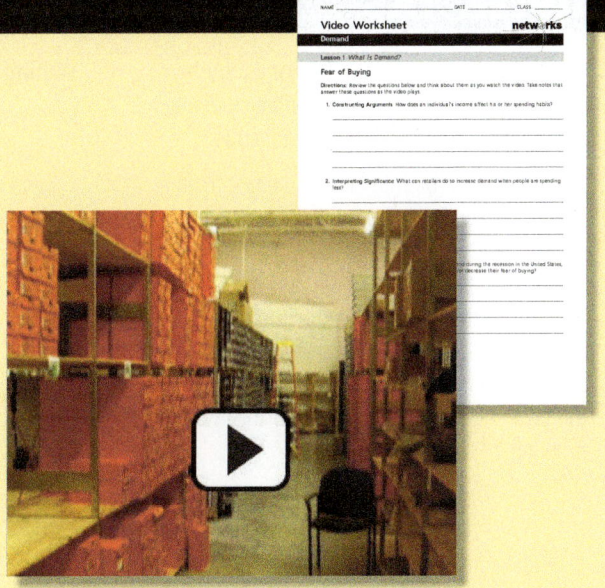

VIDEO   **WORKSHEETS**

Fear of Buying

Describing the effects of a recession on demand Have students watch the video about consumer fears during a recession. Then have students write a summary of the video, describing how consumers' fears affect their buying behavior, and the chain reaction involved along the supplier chain.

CHAPTER 4, LESSON 1
What Is Demand?

C Critical Thinking Skills

Theorizing about marginal utility Have a class discussion about marginal utility. **Ask:** *What problems might economists have in trying to measure marginal utility?* (Sample answer: Marginal utility is difficult to measure because it is subjective. If 20 people were asked how much satisfaction they received from a second soft drink, for example, each one might give a different answer.)

CLOSE & REFLECT

W Writing Skills

Explaining buying decisions Have students write a reflection paragraph describing two different decisions they made regarding purchases: one decision to buy a product, and one decision not to buy a product. Have them explain what affected their decisions: price, need, utility, or other factors.

ANSWERS, p. 106

✓ **READING PROGRESS CHECK** As we consume more and more of something, we get less additional satisfaction out of each additional amount we consume. Getting less satisfaction decreases our willingness to pay as much for another unit.

Consumer demand is influenced by less measurable factors, such as advertising.

consume it and are less thirsty, the second bottle will give you less satisfaction and so you might not be willing to pay the same price as you did for the first.

C ✓ READING PROGRESS CHECK

Describing How does the principle of diminishing marginal utility explain the way we feel about paying the same price for another unit of a good or service?

LESSON 1 REVIEW

Reviewing Vocabulary
1. How does marginal utility affect demand?

Using Your Notes
2. Use your notes to explain how prices affect demand.

Answering the Guiding Questions
3. *Identifying* What is the relationship between the price of an item and the quantity demanded?
4. *Explaining* Why do economists use the term *law* when they describe demand?
5. *Making Connections* How does the principle of marginal utility explain the price we would be willing to pay for another unit of a good or service?

Writing About Economics
6. *Informative/Explanatory* Research an example of how decreased market demand for a product has affected its price. Why did demand decrease? Did the product become unnecessary or obsolete? Did the producer or its competitors offer a newer or better version? How did sellers try to increase demand for the product?

106

LESSON 1 REVIEW ANSWERS

Reviewing Vocabulary
1. A product's marginal utility motivates a consumer to demand more of the product.

Using Your Notes
2. As price increases, demand decreases. As price decreases, demand increases.

Answering the Guiding Questions
3. The quantity demanded varies inversely with its price. As the price of the item goes up, demand for it goes down. When the price goes down, buyers have an incentive to purchase more of the item.
4. It states an unchanging behavior. Everyday observation, as well as study after study, confirms the relationship it establishes.
5. The usefulness or satisfaction we get from a product gives us an incentive to acquire more of it. But as we acquire more and more units, the extra satisfaction we get from using them begins to decline. As a result, our demand for the product declines, and we are not willing to pay as much for the additional units as we did for the first unit.

Writing About Economics
6. Students' responses should address all elements of the question, should include and apply the concepts of incentive, price, and demand, and should demonstrate an accurate understanding of these concepts and their relationships.

Case Study

For an interactive version of this case study go to connected.mcgraw-hill.com

HOLIDAY DEMAND

Every year, it's much the same. The holiday season's "hot" toy, the one that kids just have to have, flies off shelves in stores across the nation. Consumers run from store to store and feverishly search the Internet, only to face the same devastating news: "The item you want is out of stock."

What causes this "demand madness" that strikes around the holidays? Some people blame Shirley Temple. In 1934, when the child actress was just 6 years old, the Ideal Toy Company captured her likeness and distinctive curly locks on the world's first celebrity doll. Demand for the doll skyrocketed when her breakout film *Bright Eyes* was released just before Christmas. Sales eventually hit $45 million.

Another possible culprit is the family-run toy company that began selling small plastic features to stick on potatoes in 1952. Mr. Potato Head was the first toy advertised on television, prompting a chorus of "Can I have that?" and "I want that!" from America's children.

One entrepreneur's idea of selling rocks as "pets" became the hot holiday toy of 1975. He sent a press release to every major media outlet. By the time the holiday came, consumers were buying more than 100,000 Pet Rocks a day. The fad ended after just six months, but more than 5 million were sold.

After the first *Star Wars* movie appeared in 1977, one toymaker couldn't produce enough Star Wars action figures to meet the demand. In a stroke of marketing genius, panicked parents were offered an Early Bird Certificate instead. On the holiday, children opened a package that contained no toy, but instead had information about the figure they would receive in a few weeks.

Will you be caught up in the frenzy this year? Parents can find it hard to resist when their child insists that this season's new toy is the only toy she or he wants.

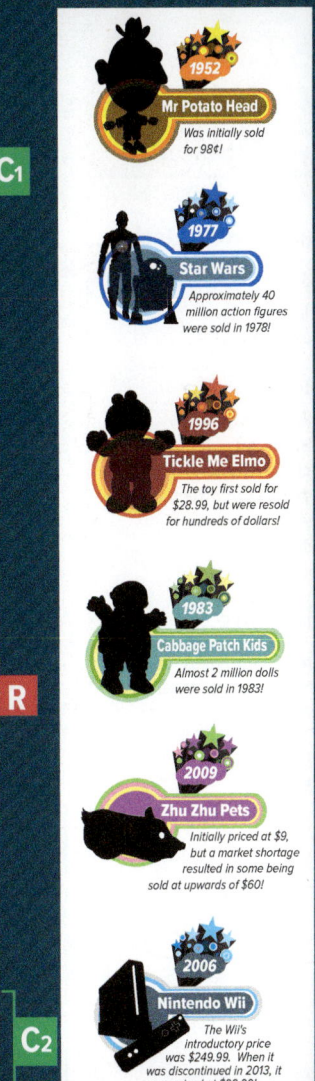

1952 Mr Potato Head Was initially sold for 98¢!

1977 Star Wars Approximately 40 million action figures were sold in 1978!

1996 Tickle Me Elmo The toy first sold for $28.99, but were resold for hundreds of dollars!

1983 Cabbage Patch Kids Almost 2 million dolls were sold in 1983!

2009 Zhu Zhu Pets Initially priced at $9, but a market shortage resulted in some being sold at upwards of $60!

2006 Nintendo Wii The Wii's introductory price was $249.99. When it was discontinued in 2013, it was priced at $99.99!

CASE STUDY REVIEW

1. **Making Generalizations** What common factor turned all four products into "hot" toys? Explain.
2. **Making Predictions** What effect do you think seasonal demand might have on the price of goods? Explain why.

CHAPTER 4
Case Study

C1 Critical Thinking Skills

Assessing demand for toys Have students brainstorm a list of toys that were popular when they were younger. Ask students to count, by a show of hands, who had each of five popular toys on the list. Then have a class discussion relating the difficulty their parents may have had in acquiring each toy.
Interpersonal

R Reading Skills

Identifying reasons for high demand Have students read the Case Study. Then have them write a paragraph describing why there was such a high demand for the toys mentioned, and what factors might lower the demand. Ask them to include in their paragraphs information about the toy's demand elasticity *at the time* and the determinants of the elasticity. **Verbal/Linguistic**

C2 Critical Thinking Skills

Comparing demand for toys Have students brainstorm a list of items that were popular during the last holiday season. Have each student choose one item to research online, and compare the demand for that item during the holiday season with the demand for one toy mentioned in the Case Study. Ask students to write possible reasons for any differences in the demand for the two items.
BL Logical/Mathematical

Content Background Knowledge

Toys: Big Business About $21.5 billion is spent annually on toys in the United States—about $280 per child. Mattel and Hasbro hold more than 40 percent of the toy market.

---

networks Online Teaching Options

INTERACTIVE FEATURE

Case Study: Holiday Demand

Analyze the effect of novelty and advertising on demand Have students read the Case Study. **Ask: What did all of the toys have in common at the time they were popular?** *(Sample answers: They were all new; they were all either associated with a movie or widely advertised.)* Then have students create a graph showing the trend in demand for popular toys over the past several decades. Ask students to write a paragraph stating their theory about how and why the demand has changed. **Visual/Spatial**

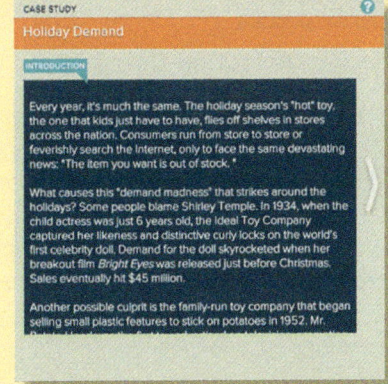

ANSWERS, p. 107

CASE STUDY REVIEW

1. The demand for each toy increased not only because of the holiday season, but also because the toy was promoted by a popular movie or an advertising campaign.
2. The price might go up while demand for the product is higher, and it might go down again once the season is over and demand falls.

CHAPTER 4, LESSON 2
Factors Affecting Demand

ENGAGE

C1 Critical Thinking Skills

🔔 **Reinforcing the effect of price on quantity demanded** Before students begin the lesson, draw a seesaw on the board. **Ask: How does a seesaw illustrate the relationship between price and quantity demanded?** *(As price goes up, quantity demanded goes down. As price goes down, quantity demanded goes up.)* **Logical/Mathematical**

TEACH & ASSESS

C2 Critical Thinking Skills

Analyzing the relationship of price and quantity demanded Have students work together in pairs. Ask each pair to choose a good they would buy more of if the price of school lunches, for example, were cut in half and they had more income to spend on other goods. Have students plot their quantity demanded at their current income and after their purchasing power increased. **Visual/Spatial**

ANSWERS, p. 108

ESSENTIAL QUESTION ACTIVITY

Answers will vary. Businesses find out what consumers need/want by doing market research and finding out what is popular/what consumers use. Have students explain how they would, as new entrepreneurs, decide what product to sell and how to advertise that product.

TAKING NOTES
Changes in quantity demanded: Income effect, Substitution effect
Changes in demand: Consumer tastes, Number of consumers, Substitutes, Complements

---

Interact with these digital assets and others in lesson 2
- ✓ INTERACTIVE GRAPH Change in Quantity Demanded
- ✓ INTERACTIVE GRAPH A Change in Demand
- ✓ SELF-CHECK QUIZ
- ✓ VIDEO

networks TRY IT YOURSELF ONLINE

Reading Help Desk

Academic Vocabulary
- principle
- illustrated

Content Vocabulary
- change in quantity demanded
- income effect
- substitution effect
- change in demand
- substitutes
- complements

TAKING NOTES:
Key Ideas and Details
ACTIVITY Many factors affect demand. Using a mind map with "demand" at the center, illustrate the various influences on demand.

LESSON 2
Factors Affecting Demand

ESSENTIAL QUESTION

What are the causes of a change in demand?

Demand for many products and services changes constantly. It's up to businesses to determine what consumers will want and when in order to meet market demand.

What factors in your own life have an effect on your interest in acquiring a particular product? Make a list and compare it with a friend's list. How do your factors differ? If you were a business looking at these factors, how might you adjust production?

A Change in the Quantity Demanded

GUIDING QUESTION *What is the effect of a change in price on quantity demanded?*

C1 Let's say the price of a product changes and all other factors remain the same. In that case, the demand curve doesn't move, but the quantity demanded changes. But sometimes the entire demand curve shifts due to a factor other than price, such as an advertising campaign or a change in consumer income. Look at **Figure 4.3** to see what happens when only the price changes and everything else remains constant. Point **a** on the demand curve shows that at $5, 24 burritos are sold. When the price falls to $3, the number of burritos purchased goes up to 40. On the other hand, when the price goes up, fewer burritos are demanded. This movement from point **a** to point **b** or from **b** to **a** is a **change in quantity demanded**—a change that is graphically represented as a movement *along* the demand curve. This result is a well-established **principle** in economics.

Only Price Changes the Quantity Demanded

C2 A change in quantity demanded can be caused by only one event—a change in price. Lots of other things can affect the demand curve, but price is the only factor that can cause a movement along the demand curve, as we see in Figure 4.3.

---

networks **Online Teaching Options**

BELLRINGER

Factors Affecting Demand

Identifying the factors that affect demand
Introduce the factors that affect demand by asking students to brainstorm ideas about what makes them decide whether to buy a product.
Ask: What stops you from buying a product? What makes you want to buy a product?
(Sample answers: The product is too expensive, out of fashion, or of poor quality. The product is affordable, popular, or necessary for survival.) Then have students view the Bellringer and answer the questions. **Logical/Mathematical**

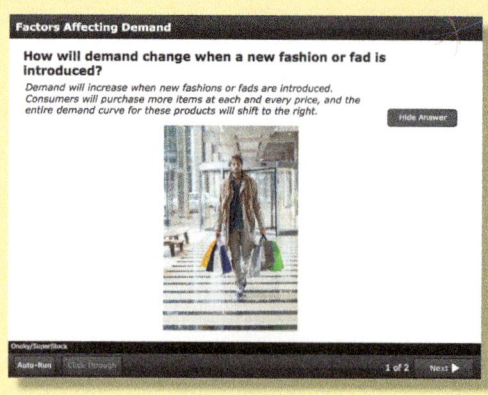

FIGURE 4.3

CHANGE IN THE QUANTITY DEMANDED

Only a change in price can cause a change in quantity demanded. When the price goes down, the quantity demanded increases. When the price goes up, the quantity demanded decreases. Both changes appear as a movement along the demand curve.

▶ **CRITICAL THINKING**
Why do price and quantity demanded move in opposite directions?

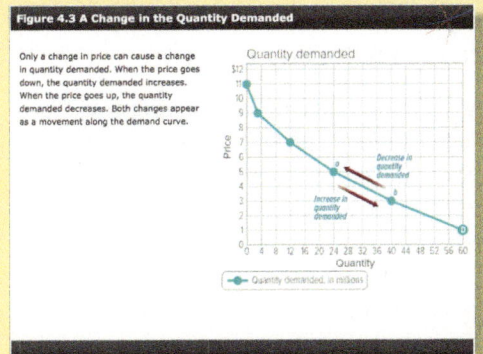

CHAPTER 4, LESSON 2
Factors Affecting Demand

Making Connections

Income Effect Ask students to consider how their purchasing decisions might be affected if they require two fill-ups per month for their vehicle, and the price of gasoline rises. Explain that if the price of gasoline rises, but students' income does not, they obviously cannot continue buying the same amount of gas AND everything else they normally purchase. The real income effect can work in the opposite direction, too. If they are already buying two fill-ups a month and the price of gasoline drops in half, their real income then increases. They will have more purchasing power and will probably increase their spending on other goods.

C Critical Thinking Skills

Understanding the income and substitution effects Organize students in teams of three to play the "Up or Down?" game. Select two teams and give each team a flash card on which a large arrow is drawn. Present scenarios—for example, the price of DVDs goes up, but income remains the same—then ask: "Will quantity demanded for DVDs go up or go down?" Team members should display their flash cards with the arrow pointing in the correct direction. If any team member displays the flash card incorrectly, that team is disqualified, and a new team joins the game. Continue until all teams have competed.

W Writing Skills

Applying the substitution effect Ask students to list five goods they use. Then have them list other goods they would buy more of if the prices of the original goods rose and the substitution effect took hold. **Intrapersonal**

The Income Effect

When the price of a product drops, consumers pay less and, as a result, have some extra income to spend. For example, we can see from Figure 4.3 that consumers spent $120 to buy 24 burritos when the price was $5 per burrito. If the price drops to $3, they would spend only $72, or $3 times 24, on the same quantity, leaving them $48 "richer" because of the lower price. They may even spend some of this extra income on more burritos. As a result, part of the increase from 24 to 40 units purchased, shown as the movement from point **a** to point **b** on the demand curve, comes about because consumers feel richer.

If the price had gone up, consumers would have felt a bit poorer and would have bought fewer burritos. This illustrates the **income effect**: the change in quantity demanded because of a change in price that alters consumers' income.

The Substitution Effect

When the price of a burrito drops from $5 to $3, burritos become less expensive than before, in comparison with other goods and services. As a result, consumers tend to replace a more costly item—say, pizza—with a less costly one—more burritos. The **substitution effect** is the change in quantity demanded because of a shift in relative prices. Together, the income and substitution effects explain why consumers increase their consumption of burritos from 24 to 40 when the price drops from $5 to $3.

Whenever a price change causes a change in quantity demanded, we see a movement *along* the demand curve, as **illustrated** in Figure 4.3. Regardless of whether the quantity demanded increases or decreases, the demand curve itself does not shift.

✓ **READING PROGRESS CHECK**

Describing How is a change in the quantity demanded illustrated on the demand curve?

---

change in quantity demanded movement along the demand curve showing that a different quantity is purchased in response to a change in price

principle a fundamental law or idea

income effect that portion of a change in quantity demanded caused by a change in a consumer's income when the price of a product changes

substitution effect the portion of a change in quantity demanded that is due to a change in the relative price of the good

illustrated shown with an image or example

GRAPHS

Change in the Quantity Demanded

Understanding changes along a demand curve Have students view the graph and answer the question. Then have them write a paragraph using the concept illustrated by the graph to describe a specific example of an item's change in price increasing or decreasing the quantity demanded. **Visual/Spatial**

ANSWERS, p. 109

CRITICAL THINKING

If people buy something at a lower price, they have more money to buy a larger quantity. The quantity demanded increases when the price decreases because people have enough money to buy more.

✓ **READING PROGRESS CHECK** A change in quantity demanded causes movement along the demand curve. Quantity demanded increases when the price decreases.

CHAPTER 4, LESSON 2
Factors Affecting Demand

Making Connections

Change in Demand To increase students' understanding of the effects of a change in demand, use the following scenario: A disease destroys much of the coffee crop in South America. **Ask:** How might this affect the price of coffee? *(The price increases.)* How might this affect the demand for substitute products? *(Demand for substitute drinks, such as tea or soft drinks, should increase.)* How might this affect the demand for complementary products? *(Demand for complementary products, such as sugar or coffee creamer, should decrease.)* Have students illustrate these changes using a demand schedule or graph. **Logical/Mathematical, Kinesthetic**

ANSWERS, p. 110

CRITICAL THINKING
It certainly is possible for several things to be happening at the same time. For example, tomorrow our demand for a product might be affected by both an increase in our income and a decrease in our preference for the product. These two changes might operate in a way to cancel each other out, but anything is possible.

A Change in Demand

GUIDING QUESTION *What factors, excluding price, affect demand?*

Sometimes other factors change while the price remains the same. When this happens, people may decide to buy *different* amounts of a product at the *same* price. This is known as a **change in demand**. As a result, the entire demand curve shifts to the right to show an increase in demand, or to the left to show a decrease in demand. This is different than a *change in quantity demanded*, which is a movement along the demand curve caused by a change in price.

Demand can change because of changes in various factors, including consumer income, consumer tastes, future expectations, the number of consumers, and the price of related goods such as substitutes or complements.

Consumer Income

Consider the way in which an increase in the minimum wage might affect the market demand schedule and curve in **Figure 4.4**. When people earn more, they are usually willing to buy different amounts at all possible prices. We can now add a third column to **Panel A** to show these increases. At a price of $9, for example, consumers are now willing to buy 16 burritos instead of 3. At a price of $7, consumers are now willing to buy 28 burritos instead of 12, a change shown by movement from point **a** to point **a´**. When the rest of the information in the schedule is transferred to the graph in **Panel B**, the demand curve will have increased, or shifted to the right.

change in demand different amounts of a product are demanded at every price, causing the demand curve to shift to the left or to the right

EXPLORING THE ESSENTIAL QUESTION
What change in each factor that influences demand would cause the demand curve to shift to the left or right?

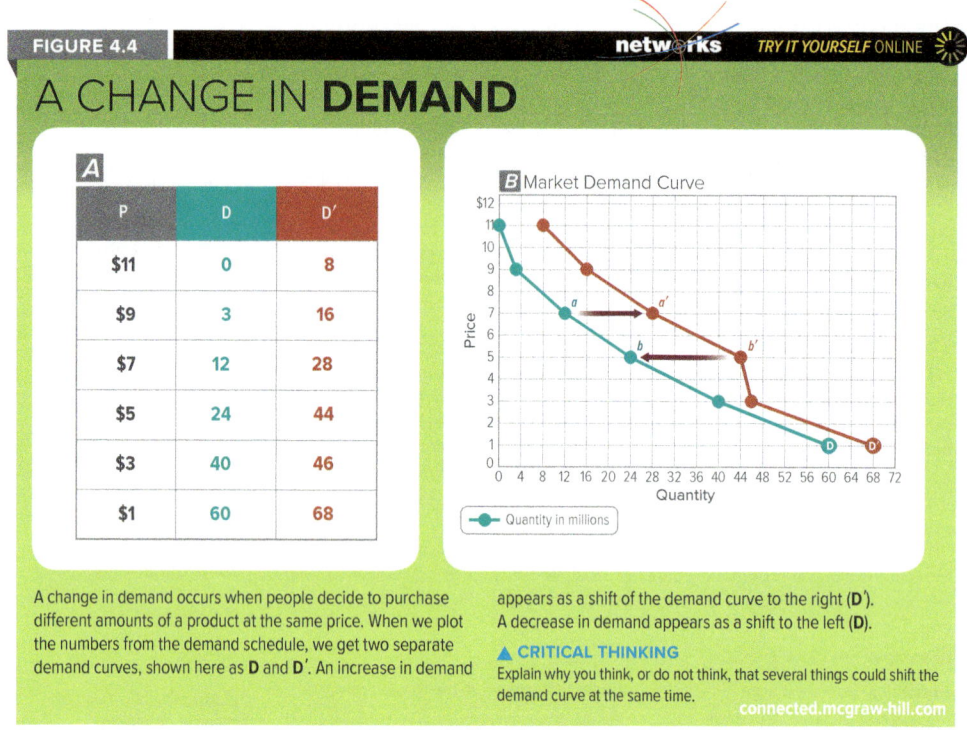

FIGURE 4.4 A CHANGE IN DEMAND

A change in demand occurs when people decide to purchase different amounts of a product at the same price. When we plot the numbers from the demand schedule, we get two separate demand curves, shown here as D and D´. An increase in demand appears as a shift of the demand curve to the right (D´). A decrease in demand appears as a shift to the left (D).

▲ **CRITICAL THINKING**
Explain why you think, or do not think, that several things could shift the demand curve at the same time.

connected.mcgraw-hill.com

110

networks Online Teaching Options

GRAPHS

Change in Demand

Interpreting shifts in the demand curve Have students explore the interactive graph and answer the question. Then discuss how a change in consumer tastes might shift the demand curve for this product, and compare that change to the change in quantity demanded created by the income effect. **Visual/Spatial**

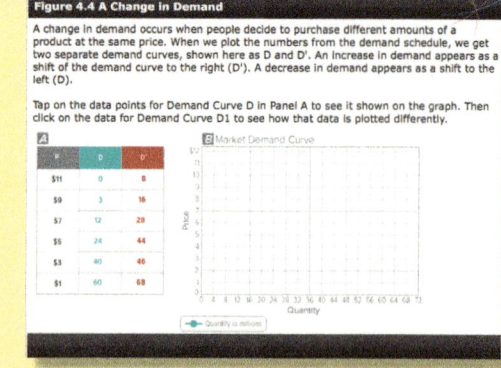

A decrease in consumer income would have the opposite effect. Instead of buying 3 burritos at $9, they might buy 2. Similarly, instead of buying 12 burritos at $7, they might buy 9, and so on down the column. Once these new quantities are plotted, the demand curve will have shifted to the left, showing a decrease in demand.

Consumer Tastes

Consumers often change their minds about which products to buy. Advertising, fashion trends, peer group pressure, and even changes in the season can affect consumer choices. For example, when a product is successfully advertised, its popularity increases and people tend to buy more of it at all possible prices. As a result, the demand curve shifts to the right.

On the other hand, people will buy less of a product if they get tired of it, or if they have a reason to worry about whether it's a good choice. This is exactly what happens when a rumor or unfavorable report about a product appears. When fewer people want the product at all possible prices, the demand curve shifts to the left, showing a decrease in demand.

substitutes competing products that can be used in place of one another; products related in such a way that an increase in the price of one increases the demand for the other

Substitutes

A change in the price of related products can cause a change in demand. Some products are known as **substitutes** because they can be used in place of other products. For example, if people treat butter and margarine as substitutes, an

THE GLOBAL ECONOMY & YOU

Demand for Goods

If a multinational business does not understand and adjust to cultural variations from one place to another, demand for its goods could drop. When Wal-Mart opened its first store in Argentina, it made no changes in its usual strategy. The new store offered cuts of meat, cosmetics, and clothes for the American market. Even the design of the store was based on American buying habits, with long and narrow aisles. Argentinean consumers, however, liked different cuts of meat, cosmetics more suited to European tastes, and smaller, tighter clothes. They shopped daily, which made the narrow aisles more crowded than in the United States, where consumers tend to shop weekly. Sales were a disaster. Wal-Mart changed its strategy before opening its next store, and demand improved significantly.

▶ **CRITICAL THINKING**
Making Predictions If you were in charge of opening a new store in a different country, what factors would you consider before you opened for business?

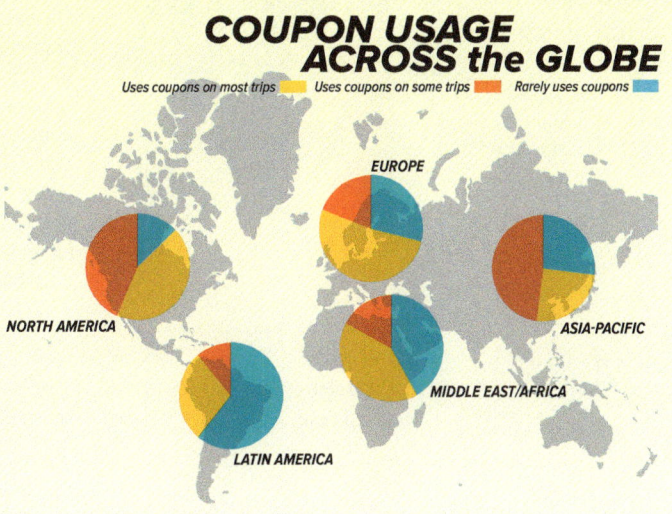

COUPON USAGE ACROSS the GLOBE
Uses coupons on most trips · Uses coupons on some trips · Rarely uses coupons

NORTH AMERICA · EUROPE · ASIA-PACIFIC · MIDDLE EAST/AFRICA · LATIN AMERICA

CHAPTER 4, LESSON 2
Factors Affecting Demand

C Critical Thinking Skills

Explaining shifts in demand Ask students to explain what would happen to the demand for DVDs in the following situations: (1) There is an overall increase in wages. (2) A chain of appliance stores puts all DVD players on sale. (3) The price of movie tickets increases dramatically. *(Demand for DVDs would increase in all situations. Wage increases give consumers more income to buy more DVDs. Demand for DVD players and DVDs would increase, as they are complementary goods. Demands for DVDs would increase because DVDs and movie tickets are substitute goods.)* Conclude by asking students to present other situations that might lead to an increase in demand for DVDs. **Logical/Mathematical**

T Technology Skills

Graphing changes in consumer tastes Ask student pairs to think of three situations in which consumer tastes for a product changed. Have pairs work together to illustrate the changes in demand on schedules and graphs. **BL Kinesthetic**

INTERACTIVE FEATURE

Global Economy & You

Understanding the effect of consumer tastes on demand Have students read the description of how Wal-Mart did not take into account consumer tastes when it opened a store in Argentina. Then have them write a journal entry from the perspective of a person from Argentina who walks into a store and sees the products Wal-Mart is trying to sell. **Intrapersonal**

ANSWERS, p. 111

CRITICAL THINKING
Student answers will vary but should indicate that they would do research to find out what customers in different countries like and are used to for a shopping experience. They would then adjust their store layouts and products accordingly.

CHAPTER 4, LESSON 2
Factors Affecting Demand

W Writing Skills

Understanding changes in expectations Have students write a short story about how a rumor or an unfavorable report affects the demand of a product or service. For example, students might imagine how a report of an imminent hurricane would affect the sale of bottled water at each and every price. **Verbal/Linguistic**

C Critical Thinking Skills

Graphing changes in expectations Have students think of a product they delayed purchasing because of the expectation that a new version of the product would soon be available. Ask students to graph the change in the direction of the demand curve for the product.

---

increase in the price of butter will cause an increase in the demand for margarine. Likewise, an increase in the price of margarine would cause the demand for butter to increase, shifting the demand curve for butter to the right.

In general, the demand for a product tends to increase if the price of its substitute goes up. The demand for a product tends to decrease if the price of its substitute goes down.

Complements

complements products that increase the use of other products; products related in such a way that an increase in the price of one reduces the demand for both

Other related goods are known as **complements**, because the use of one increases the use of the other. Personal computers and software are two complementary goods. When the price of computers decreases, consumers buy more computers *and* more software. If the price of computers spirals upward, consumers would buy fewer computers and less software.

In general, an increase in the price of a good usually leads to a decrease in the demand for its complement. A decrease in the price of a good tends to increase the demand for its complement.

W C Expectations

The way people think about the future can also affect demand. For example, suppose that a company announces a technological breakthrough in the cost and quality of televisions. Even if these new products might not be available for a year, some consumers might hold off buying a TV today because of their

CAREERS | Retail Buyer

Is this Career for you?

 Do you have strong decision-making skills?

 Are you a good negotiator?

 Do you have good instincts about buying trends in a particular specialty?

 Do you understand what factors affect demand in various markets?

Salary
$58,360 per year
$28.06 per hour

Job Growth Outlook
Slower than average

Interview with a Retail Buyer

"The selection of styles is done in conformance with planned assortment requirements, unit and size breakdown requirements, quality and finish. Fashion buyers must understand the market and contribute to the overall buying strategy in financial, styling and distribution terms. Fashion buyers must be imaginative, creative, perceptive and objective kind of people."

—Jill Heller, Boutique Retailer

Profile of Work

Wholesale and retail buyers purchase goods for resale to consumers. Buyers who work for large organizations usually specialize in one or two lines of merchandise. Buyers who purchase items that will be sold to customers largely decide which products their organization will offer. They must predict which products will appeal most to their customers. If they are wrong, their company's profits and reputation could suffer.

112

networks Online Teaching Options

VIDEO **WORKSHEETS**

Global Demand Impact on Food Prices

Understanding the impact of demand on food prices Have students watch the video. **Ask:** *What is the effect of higher demand on food prices?* (Food prices go up.) Then have students answer the questions on the worksheet. For the last question, have students write a paragraph predicting what will happen to demand as food prices continue to rise.

expectations. The new expectations would cause fewer TVs to be purchased at every price, and the demand curve would shift to the left.

Of course, expectations can also have the opposite effect. Imagine if the weather service forecasts a bad year for crops. People might stock up on some foods today, before these items actually became scarce. The willingness to buy more today because of expected shortages later on would cause an increase in current demand, shown by a shift of the demand curve to the right.

Although we can predict the change in demand caused by a change in the price of a good's substitute or complement, we can't predict the effect of a change in expectations without additional details.

Number of Consumers

A change in income, tastes, expectations, and prices of related products affects *individual* demand schedules and curves—and hence the *market* demand curve. The market demand curve can also change if there is a change in the number of consumers.

Generally, when more consumers enter the market, market demand increases, and the curve shifts to the right. Suppose that a building near a store that sells burritos needs repairs. A large group of workers comes to the neighborhood. Many of them buy burritos for lunch. We would add the number of burritos that they buy at all possible prices to those the store used to sell. When the work is finished and the construction workers leave, market demand might decrease, with the market demand curve shifting to the left.

☑ **READING PROGRESS CHECK**

Explaining How do changes in consumer income and tastes affect movements of the demand curve?

This cartoon shows how expectations about the future may affect consumer demand.

▲ **CRITICAL THINKING**
Contrasting Explain which consumer is allowing their expectations about the future to affect demand and how.

LESSON 2 REVIEW

Reviewing Vocabulary
1. Explain the income effect.
2. How do complements affect demand?

Using Your Notes
3. Are there more factors that have an impact on change in demand or on change in quantity demanded?

Answering the Guiding Questions
4. What is the effect of a change in price on quantity demanded?

5. What factors, excluding price, affect demand?

Writing About Economics
6. Identify which of the following factors creates a movement of the entire demand curve and which creates movement along the demand curve:
   a. Consumer income
   b. Price
   c. Consumer taste
   d. Number of consumers

CHAPTER 4, LESSON 2
Factors Affecting Demand

C Critical Thinking Skills

Understanding changes in number of consumers
Ask: What eventually would happen to the demand curve for toys if the birthrate declined? Why? *(The demand curve would shift to the left, because there would be a decline in demand for toys at each and every price.)* **Logical/Mathematical**

CLOSE & REFLECT

W Writing Skills

Applying changes in quantity demanded and demand Have students write an example from personal experience of how price, their real income, or the substitution effect determined their ability to buy a good or service. Then have them provide an example of how their consumer tastes or an expectation affected their demand for a product. **Intrapersonal**

ANSWERS, p. 113

CRITICAL THINKING
The hesitant shopper is expecting the arrival of the newer phone, so she is not buying a phone now, decreasing the demand.

☑ **READING PROGRESS CHECK** Changes in consumer income and tastes can cause the demand curve to shift right or left depending on the change. With more income, demand can increase. With less income, demand decreases. A change in taste can cause demand to increase or decrease.

LESSON 2 REVIEW ANSWERS

Reviewing Vocabulary
1. When price changes affect consumers' spending power and, as a result, consumers demand more or less of a good or service, we call this the income effect.
2. If two products are complements, an increase in the price of one of the two reduces the demand for both products.

Using Your Notes
3. Many factors contribute to changes in demand. Price is the main factor that determines the quantity demanded.

Answering the Guiding Questions
4. A change in price results in a change in quantity demanded. When prices go up, quantity demanded goes down, and vice versa.
5. Factors affecting demand include consumer income, expectations, tastes, substitutes, complements, and the number of consumers.

Writing About Economics
6. Consumer income: An increase in consumer income can shift the demand curve to the right. Price: Price is plotted along the demand curve. It does not shift the curve itself. Consumer tastes: As consumer tastes make a product more appealing, the demand curve shifts to the right. Number of consumers: When more consumers enter a market, the curve shifts to the right.

CHAPTER 4, LESSON 3
Elasticity of Demand

ENGAGE

R Reading Skills

🔔 **Introducing elasticity** Before students begin the lesson, help them understand the meaning of *elastic* and *inelastic* by showing them a rubber band and how it stretches. Extend their understanding by pointing out that the prefix *in-* means "without." **Ask:** Which stretches or changes more—something that is elastic or inelastic? *(something that is elastic)* **ELL AL** Verbal/Linguistic

TEACH & ASSESS

C Critical Thinking Skills

Identifying elasticity Have students list 10 goods and services in their households that have elastic and inelastic demand. Have them put these items in a chart. Ask them to save the chart for a later activity. **AL** Logical/Mathematical.

ANSWERS, p. 114

ESSENTIAL QUESTION ACTIVITY

Direct students to understand that pricing decisions are based on the elasticity of demand for a product.

TAKING NOTES
Elastic Demand: Price change causes a relatively larger change in demand
Inelastic Demand: Price change causes a relatively smaller change in demand
Unit Elastic Demand: Price change causes a proportional change in demand

114

Interact with these digital assets and others in lesson 3
✓ INTERACTIVE GRAPHS
  Demand Elasticity and the Total Expenditures Test
✓ INTERACTIVE GRAPH
  Determinants of Demand Elasticity
✓ SELF-CHECK QUIZ
✓ VIDEO

networks TRY IT YOURSELF ONLINE

LESSON 3
Elasticity of Demand

Reading Help Desk

Academic Vocabulary
- technical
- adequate

Content Vocabulary
- elasticity
- demand elasticity
- elastic
- inelastic
- unit elastic

TAKING NOTES:

Key Ideas and Details
ACTIVITY Use the graphic organizer below to describe the characteristics of elastic, inelastic, and unit elastic demand.

Types of Elasticity	
Demand Type	Description
Elastic Demand	
Inelastic Demand	
Unit Elastic Demand	

ESSENTIAL QUESTION

What are the causes of a change in demand?

Prices change all the time, but sometimes the consequences can be surprising. For example, if you had a store and wanted to increase your revenue, would you want to increase or decrease the price of your goods? Believe it or not, your total revenue could decrease in either or both cases! Let's examine the relationship between prices and changes in quantity demanded to see why.

R Because quantity demanded depends on its price, economists use a concept called elasticity. **Elasticity** is a measure of responsiveness that describes the way a dependent variable changes in response to a change in an independent variable. In economics, price is almost always the independent variable, or the variable that causes the quantity demanded to change.

Pick a product that five of your friends use. Select three prices for the product with one being reasonable, and two others being one-third higher and one-third lower. Now, ask your friends how much they would spend on the product at each price. If you sold the product, which price would you use and why?

Three Cases of Demand Elasticity

GUIDING QUESTION *How do we measure the three cases of demand elasticity?*

C We already know that consumers react to a change in price by changing quantity demanded. For example, in Figure 4.3, consumers increased quantity demanded from 24 to 40 when we lowered the price of burritos from $5 to $3. This response is known as **demand elasticity**, the extent to which a change in price causes a change in quantity demanded. Demand elasticity has three outcomes:

- **Elastic Demand** Demand is **elastic** when a change in price causes a *relatively larger* change in quantity demanded. This is shown in **Panel A** of **Figure 4.5**. As we move from point **a** to point **b**, we see that price

114

---

networks *Online Teaching Options*

BELLRINGER

Elasticity of Demand

Understanding differences in elasticity of demand Point out that an elastic band stretches or changes when you pull on it. Have students view the Bellringer activity and answer the question about which of the three elasticities equals 1. Then, after students answer the question about products that are elastic and products that are inelastic, ask them to state where on the continuum they would place each product.

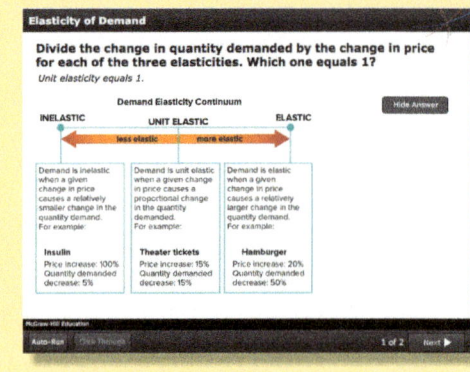

declines by one-third, or from $3 to $2. At the same time, the quantity demanded doubles from two to four units. Demand between $3 and $2 is elastic, because the percentage change in quantity demanded is relatively larger than the percentage change in price. The demand for products like green beans, corn, or other garden vegetables tends to be elastic, because consumers have options and do not need any one vegetable urgently. If the price goes up, consumers can buy other vegetables. But if it goes down, they may switch from other vegetables.

- **Inelastic Demand** Demand is **inelastic** when a given change in price causes a *relatively smaller change* in quantity demanded. This is shown in **Panel B** of Figure 4.5, where a one-third drop in price from point **a´** to **b´** causes quantity demanded to increase by 25 percent, or from two to two and one-half units. For example, an increase in the price of a cancer drug may not bring about much change in the quantity demanded if patients don't have other options. Even if the price were cut in half, the quantity demanded might not increase if patients didn't need a higher dosage.
- **Unit Elastic Demand** Demand is **unit elastic** when a given change in price causes a *proportional change* in quantity demanded. For example, **Panel C** of Figure 4.5 shows that a drop in price from **a″** to **b″** causes an equal percentage increase in quantity demanded. Examples of unit elasticity are difficult to find because the demand for most products is either elastic or inelastic. Unit elasticity is more like a middle ground that separates the other two categories of price elasticity of demand: elastic and inelastic.

To summarize, to measure the elasticity of demand, compare the percentage change in the dependent variable—quantity demanded—to the percentage change in the independent variable—price. Relatively smaller changes in quantity demanded indicate inelastic demand. Relatively larger changes in quantity demanded indicate elastic demand. Changes that are proportional to the change in price are unit elastic.

✓ **READING PROGRESS CHECK**

Comparing What is the difference between elastic and inelastic demand?

The Total Expenditures Test

GUIDING QUESTION *How does the total expenditures test help determine demand elasticity?*

To estimate elasticity, compare the *direction* of a price change to the *direction* of the change in total revenue, or total expenditures. This is sometimes called the total revenue or total expenditures test. A few examples will make this clear.

Determining Total Expenditures

We find total expenditures (or total revenue) by multiplying the price of a product by the quantity demanded for any point along the demand curve. What consumers consider spending is revenue to the seller, so the two terms mean essentially the same thing. To illustrate, the total expenditure under point **a** in Panel A of Figure 4.5 is $6 to either the buyer or the seller. Likewise, the total expenditure under point **b** in Panel A is $8, or four units at $2 each.

Estimating Elasticity

The relationship between a change in price and the change in total expenditures is shown in the last panel of Figure 4.5.

For example, in Panel A of Figure 4.5, the price decrease changes quantities enough to increase total expenditures from $6 to $8, an example of elastic demand because price and revenue changes move in opposite directions.

elasticity a measure of responsiveness that tells us how a dependent variable, such as quantity demanded or quantity supplied, responds to a change in an independent variable such as price

demand elasticity the extent to which a change in price causes a change in the quantity demanded; demand elasticity has three cases: elastic, inelastic, or unit elastic

elastic type of elasticity in which a change in the independent variable (usually price) results in a larger change in the dependent variable (usually quantity demanded or supplied)

inelastic case of demand elasticity where the percentage change in the independent variable (usually price) causes a less than proportionate change in the dependent variable (usually quantity demanded or supplied)

unit elastic elasticity where a change in the independent variable (usually price) generates a proportional change of the dependent variable (quantity demanded or supplied)

CHAPTER 4, LESSON 3
Elasticity of Demand

V Visual Skills

Modeling elasticity On the board, draw four graphs like the ones shown below. Add prices and quantities to the first two graphs and have students perform a total expenditures test for them. Point out the change in quantity demanded for each change in price. Reinforce that the more vertical the demand curve, the more inelastic the demand. Ask students to provide examples of products that fit each situation shown on the graphs. **BL** Visual/Spatial

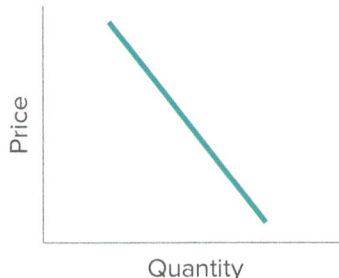

Inelastic demand

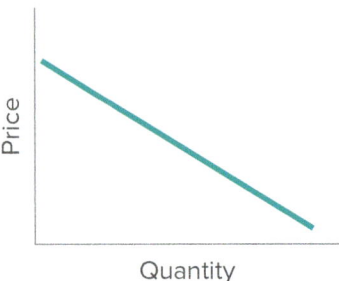

Elastic demand

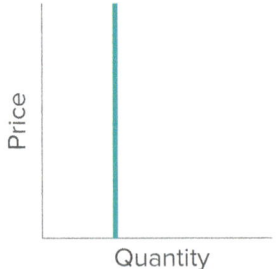

Perfectly Inelastic Demand

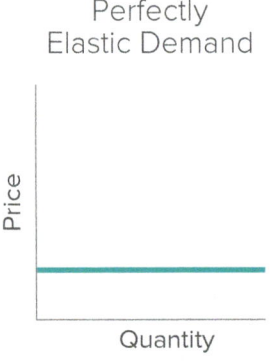

Perfectly Elastic Demand

In Panel B of Figure 4.5, the same decrease in price causes a decrease in revenue—an example of inelastic demand.

In Panel C of Figure 4.5, the decrease in price neither increases nor decreases total receipts. This is because at point **a″**, two units are demanded at a price of $3 for total receipts of $6, while at **b″**, three units are demanded at a price of $2 for total receipts of $6. When total receipts do not change even though there is a change in price, we have a case of unit elasticity.

Note that the same relationships between a change in price and a change in total receipts hold if the price moves in the other direction. If price goes up from $2 to $3 in Panel A of Figure 4.5, then total revenue goes down—so the change in price and the change in revenue move in opposite directions. Or if the price goes up in Panel B, revenue also moves up.

We could summarize the changes among these relationships in the following way:

- **Elastic demand**—a change in price and a change in revenue move in <u>opposite</u> directions
- **Unit elastic demand**—there is <u>no change in revenue</u> regardless of the change in price
- **Inelastic demand**—a change in price and a change in revenue move in the <u>same</u> direction

Business Sales

technical related to a particular subject such as art, science, or trade

While this discussion about elasticity may seem **technical**, knowledge of demand elasticity is extremely important to most businesses. Suppose, for example, that you run your own business and want to do something that will raise your revenues. You could try to stay open longer, or you could try to advertise in order

FIGURE 4.5

DEMAND ELASTICITY AND THE TOTAL EXPENDITURES TEST

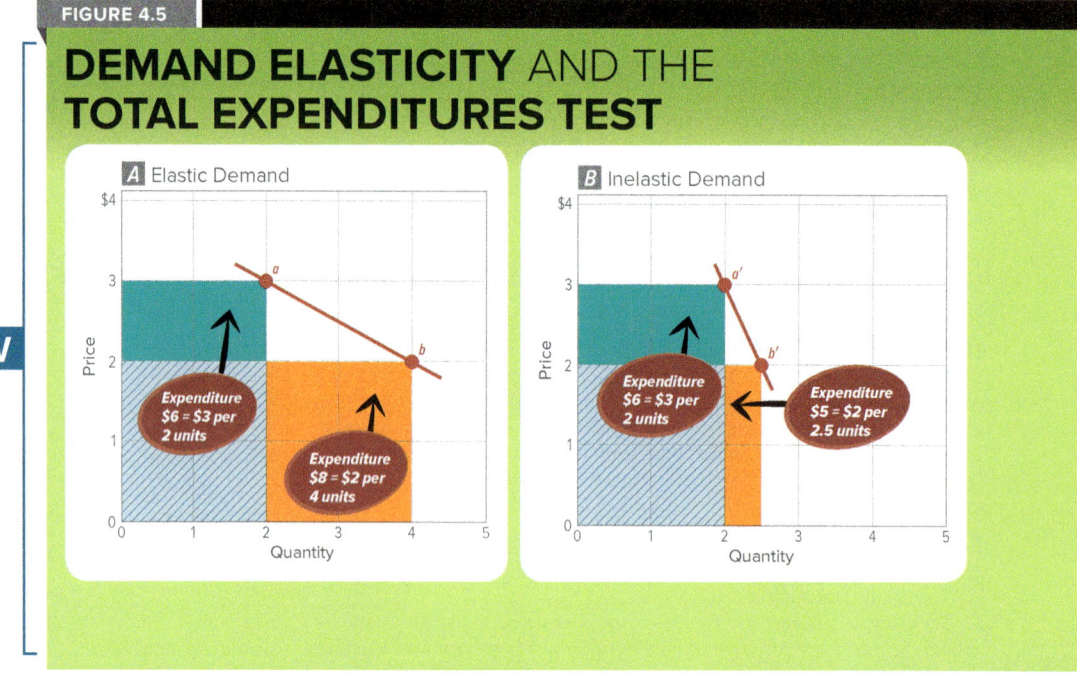

GRAPHS

Demand Elasticity and the Total Expenditures Test

Describing the effects of elasticity on expenditures Have students use Figure 4.5 to explore the effects of elasticity on total expenditures when the price changes for a product. Then ask them to think of a product that fits the scenario illustrated in each graph, and write a few sentences about each product to describe its elasticity. Visual/Spatial

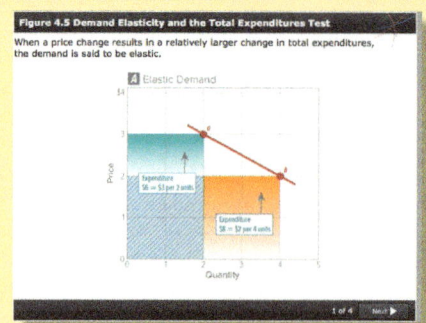

to increase sales. You might, however, also be tempted to raise the price of your product in order to increase total revenue from sales.

This might actually work in the case of medical services, because the demand for this product is generally inelastic (and an increase in price is associated with an increase in revenue). However, what would happen if you sold a product with elastic demand, such as burgers? If you raised the price, your total revenue—which is the same as expenditures by the consumer—would go down instead of up. That's exactly what you didn't want!

Many businesses experiment with different prices when they introduce a new product to the market. Knowing the demand elasticity for a new product will allow a business to set (or change) the price to maximize total revenues.

✓ READING PROGRESS CHECK

Explaining What happens to the total expenditures for a product with elastic demand when its price goes up?

Determinants of Demand Elasticity

GUIDING QUESTION *What factors determine a product's demand elasticity?*

What makes the elasticity for a specific good? To find out, ask the following three questions. The answers will give you a reasonably good, if not exact, idea.

Can the Purchase Be Delayed?

Sometimes consumers cannot postpone the purchase of a product. This tends to make demand inelastic, meaning that the quantity of the product demanded is not especially sensitive to changes in price.

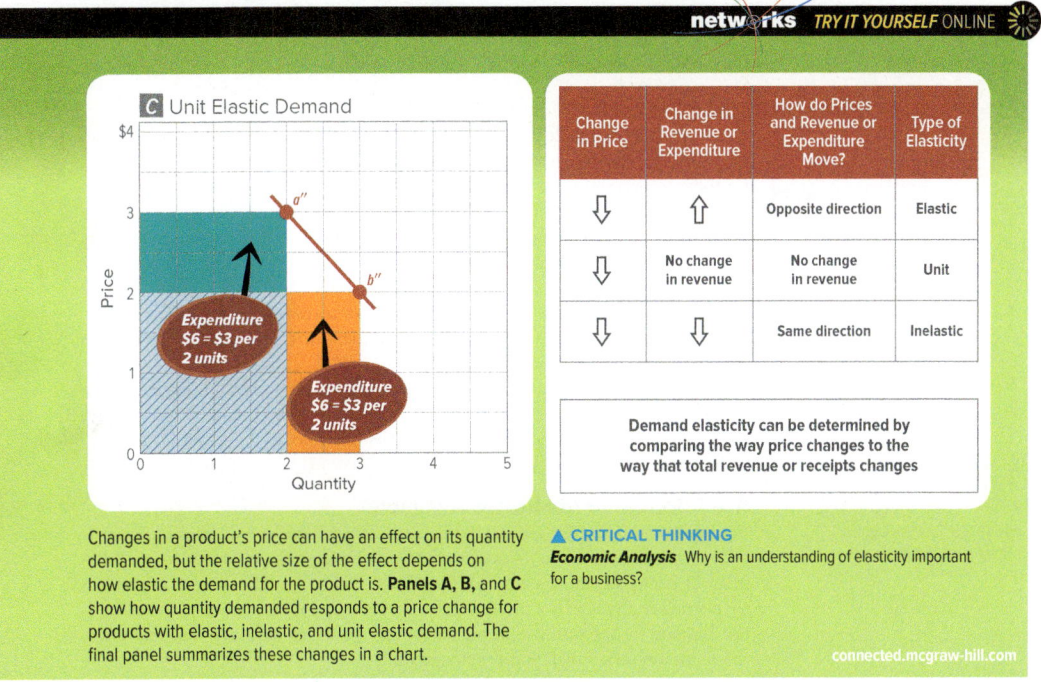

Changes in a product's price can have an effect on its quantity demanded, but the relative size of the effect depends on how elastic the demand for the product is. **Panels A, B,** and **C** show how quantity demanded responds to a price change for products with elastic, inelastic, and unit elastic demand. The final panel summarizes these changes in a chart.

▲ CRITICAL THINKING
Economic Analysis Why is an understanding of elasticity important for a business?

Energy Prices Lead to Biofuel Use

Studying the effects of price increases on consumer behavior
Have students watch the video on biofuel use, a substitution response to high energy prices. Then have students write a paragraph describing how lower prices for these new sources of energy and the consumer response will affect the revenue of standard or traditional energy providers. **Verbal/Linguistic**

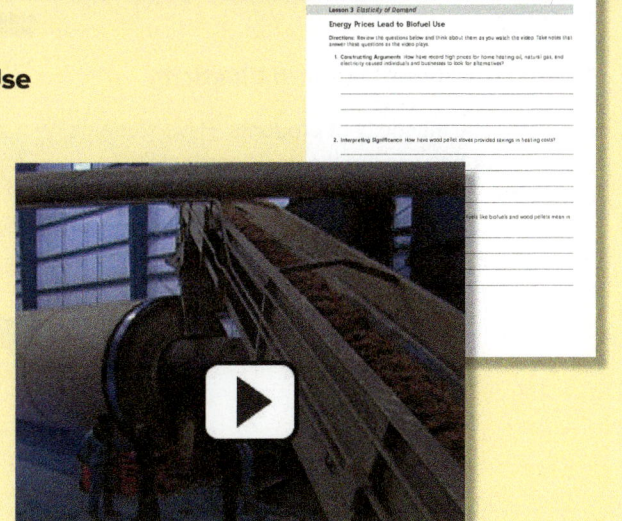

CHAPTER 4, LESSON 3
Elasticity of Demand

C Critical Thinking Skills

Identifying components of elasticity Have students procure the chart they created earlier, with the 10 goods and services in their households that have elastic and inelastic demand. Now have them note whether the quantity demanded for each item responds to changes in price, amount of income used to purchase the item, whether the item's purchase can be delayed (necessity), or available substitutes. Explain that those items that do respond with a change in quantity demanded have elastic demand. **BL Logical/Mathematical**

Content Background Knowledge

Demand Elasticity in the Teenager Market
The government uses elasticity to decide whether a tax on an undesirable product will affect the demand for that product. However, not all products have the same elasticity for all markets. For example, in one study the demand for tobacco products was shown to be inelastic. Users would purchase the same amount of these products, regardless of the price. But this study did not take into account differences between age groups. A tax on tobacco products has been found to have an impact on teenage tobacco use. Teenagers change their purchasing behavior when the price of tobacco goes up, so the demand for tobacco in this market is elastic.

ANSWERS, p. 117

✓ **READING PROGRESS CHECK** Total expenditures decrease because people buy less of the product when the price increases.

CRITICAL THINKING
A business will often try to increase its total revenue from sales by increasing the prices of its products. However, this only works if the demand for its products is inelastic. If demand is elastic, higher prices will reduce total revenues. If demand is unit elastic, the change in price will not affect total revenues.

CHAPTER 4, LESSON 3
Elasticity of Demand

R Reading Skills

Identifying products' elasticity Ask: **What type of demand elasticity do each of these products have—and why: Soft drinks?** *(elastic; because substitutes exist)* **Salt?** *(inelastic; because the percentage of a person's total budget devoted to the purchase of salt is relatively small)* **Steak?** *(elastic; because substitutes exist)* **Electric power?** *(inelastic; the purchase cannot be delayed in the short term)* **Logical/Mathematical**

W Writing Skills

Writing about elasticity Have students write a short story about someone who has inelastic demand for a product but is faced with a significant price change. Students can write about a product such as medicine but could also invent examples of their own, such as the gas needed to get to a job interview on time or a specific gift for an important person. **BL Verbal/Linguistic**

ANSWERS, p. 118

CRITICAL THINKING

The purchase usually can be delayed, there are usually adequate substitutes, and the purchase is likely to take up a large portion of the budget. For all these reasons, demand for a luxury good would tend to be elastic.

FIGURE 4.6
DETERMINANTS OF DEMAND ELASTICITY

Products and Their Elasticity

Determinants of elasticity If yes: elastic If no: inelastic	Fresh tomatoes, corn, or green beans	Gasoline from a particular station	Gasoline in general	Services of medical doctors	Insulin	Butter
Can purchase be delayed?	Yes	Yes	No	No	No	Yes
Are adequate substitutes available?	Yes	Yes	No	No	No	Yes
Does purchase use a large portion of income?	No	Yes	Yes	Yes	No	No
Types of elasticity	Elastic	Elastic	Inelastic	Inelastic	Inelastic	Elastic

The elasticity of demand can usually be estimated by examining the answers to three key questions. All three do not have to be the same in order to determine elasticity, and in some cases the answer to a single question is so important that it alone might override the answers to the other two.

▲ **CRITICAL THINKING**
Economic Analysis If you applied the three questions to a luxury product, what would be the elasticity of demand for that product?

For example, people who need to take medication on a regular schedule will pay higher prices rather than delay buying and using the product. The demand for tobacco products also tends to be inelastic because the product is addictive. As a result, a sharp increase in price will lower the quantity purchased by consumers, but not by very much. The change in quantity demanded is also likely to be relatively small for these products when their prices go down instead of up.

But if the price of coffee, chips, or gasoline from a particular station increased, consumers could delay buying any of these items without suffering any great inconvenience.

Figure 4.6 summarizes some of these observations. If the answer to the question "Can the purchase be delayed?" is yes, then the demand for the product is likely to be elastic. If the answer to the question is no, then demand is likely to be inelastic.

Are Adequate Substitutes Available?

adequate just enough to satisfy a requirement

If **adequate** substitutes are available, consumers can switch back and forth between the product and its substitute to take advantage of the best price. If the price of beef goes up, buyers can switch to chicken. With enough substitutes, even small changes in the price of a product will cause people to switch, making the demand for the product elastic. However, the fewer the available substitutes, the more inelastic the demand tends to be.

118

---

networks Online Teaching Options

CHART

Determinants of Demand Elasticity

Analyzing the elasticity of products Have students use Figure 4.6 to explore the decisions that determine whether a product is elastic. Then have them write a paragraph describing what determines whether a product is elastic or inelastic, using the information from the chart to support their statements. **Logical/Mathematical**

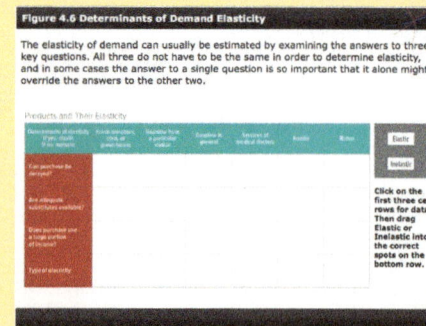

Sometimes only a single adequate substitute is needed to make demand elastic. For example, in the past there were few substitutes for sending a letter through the post office. Today, most people use e-mail or send instant messages on their cell phones. Because of all these alternatives, it is more difficult for the U.S. Postal Service to increase its total revenues by raising the price of a first-class stamp.

Note that the size of the market is also important. For example, the demand for gasoline or tobacco products at a particular station tends to be elastic because consumers can buy gas or tobacco at another location. If we ask about the demand for gasoline or tobacco in general, however, demand is much more inelastic because there are few adequate substitutes for either.

Does the Purchase Use a Large Portion of Income?

The third factor is the amount of income required to make the purchase. If the amount is large, then demand tends to be elastic. If the amount of income is small, demand tends to be inelastic.

Finally, you may have noticed that the answers to our three questions are not always "yes" or "no" for each of the products shown in Figure 4.6. Some products are easy to classify, since each of the answers is "yes" or "no." However, we have to use our judgment on others. For example, the demand for the services of medical doctors and products tends to be inelastic, even though they tend to require a large portion of people's income. This is because most people prefer to receive medical care right away or from a particular provider rather than taking the time to look for adequate substitutes.

EXPLORING THE ESSENTIAL QUESTION

Remember the survey you invented at the beginning of the lesson? Take a look at your survey results and answer the following questions:

How would the results be different if the product you were selling were tomatoes or another type of food? How would the results be different if your product were a car or something very expensive to maintain? If you wanted to increase your revenue from sales, would you increase your price or lower it?

✓ **READING PROGRESS CHECK**

Identifying Can you think of other goods with inelastic demand? Why is the demand for those goods inelastic?

LESSON 3 REVIEW

Reviewing Vocabulary
1. *Defining* Give examples of goods that you consider to be elastic and inelastic.

Using Your Notes
2. *Compare and Contrast* Use your notes to explain why some goods have elastic demand and some goods have inelastic demand.

Answering the Guiding Questions
3. *Explaining* How do we measure the three cases of demand elasticity?
4. *Evaluating* How does the total expenditures test help determine demand elasticity?
5. *Describing* What factors determine a product's demand elasticity?

Writing About Economics
6. *Persuasive/Explanatory* Make a list of three items you or members of your family have purchased in the past week. Using what you know about demand elasticity, write a paragraph about each item to explain whether your demand for the item you purchased is elastic or inelastic. Explain whether or not there are adequate substitutes, whether the purchase might have been delayed, or whether the purchase uses a large portion of your income.

CHAPTER 4, LESSON 3
Elasticity of Demand

CLOSE & REFLECT

C Critical Thinking Skills

Applying knowledge of elasticity to personal purchases Have students write a reflection paragraph stating what questions they should ask themselves as they make purchases, and what factors influence their purchases. Have them explain any changes they might make to their spending habits, given what they know about prices, demand, and elasticity.

ANSWERS, p. 119

EXPLORING THE ESSENTIAL QUESTION

Tomatoes have elastic demand, so as a tomato seller you cannot raise prices. An increase in the price of tomatoes would result in decreased demand because there are substitutes for tomatoes and the purchase can be delayed. A vehicle or other expensive item also has elastic demand. An increase in the price of a vehicle would result in decreased demand because there are substitutes, the purchase can be delayed, and the purchase requires a large portion of income.

✓ **READING PROGRESS CHECK** Answers will vary but should include goods like milk, eggs, and bread. Consumers have some choices in those goods, but if all the types of milk, eggs, and bread get more expensive, consumers will pay more for them because they are basic staples.

LESSON 3 REVIEW ANSWERS

Reviewing Vocabulary

1. Many food goods have elasticity since substitutes are easily found. Medicine and cigarettes are inelastic since they are necessary (to some people) and have few substitutes.

Using Your Notes

2. Some goods have demand elasticity because there are adequate substitutes and because their purchase can be delayed. Other goods do not have elasticity because they are a requirement for living and have no good substitutes.

Answering the Guiding Questions

3. We measure the three cases of demand elasticity by looking at the relative change in demand as it responds to a change in price.

4. By finding out what the total expenditures are for a product, a business is able to determine the demand elasticity. This is important in fixing an appropriate price for an item.

5. Factors include whether the purchase can be delayed, whether there are adequate substitutes, and the amount of income required to make the purchase.

Writing About Economics

6. Students should identify three consumer products and should clearly explain the elasticity of each one.

CHAPTER 4
Debate

ENGAGE

C1 Critical Thinking Skills

Hypothesizing about prices in a crisis Have students think of a recent natural disaster. **Ask: If you were one of the victims of this disaster, what would you do if the price for survival items such as food and water rose to a level you could not afford? Would you think this was fair?** *(Sample answers: I would have to rely on relatives or friends for food and water; I would be upset; it is not fair to take advantage of people who are suffering.)* **Verbal/Linguistic**

TEACH & ASSESS

C2 Critical Thinking Skills

Discussing the ethics of price gouging Have a class discussion about raising prices in different circumstances. **Ask: What is the difference between raising prices when demand goes up under normal circumstances and raising prices during a natural disaster or crisis?** *(Sample answer: Raising prices when demand goes up is a normal business practice, but raising prices to take advantage of people in trouble is unethical.)* **Verbal/Linguistic**

Making Connections

Personal Perspective Have students write a first-person journal entry in the voice of a victim of a flood who needs to purchase items for survival. If students use information from the Debate feature, remind them to attribute their ideas to the authors.

Debates

C1 Should it be legal to raise prices on basic items needed for survival during natural disasters or other emergencies?

C2 Imagine that the news is warning of a natural disaster such as a hurricane or a blizzard. You need food or water, gasoline for a generator, or diapers for a baby. You hike to the nearest store only to find that prices have doubled. The store owners are *price gouging*. Many states prohibit raising prices—under extraordinary circumstances—on essential goods such as food, water, gas, batteries, generators, and flashlights. The laws set strict restrictions and harsh penalties for any business that raises prices more than 10 percent to 25 percent above normal prices.

If you found high prices just before or after a major event, would you be angry at the owner for trying to make an extra buck? When evaluating these debates, be careful to keep in mind any potential bias from the person or organization represented in the primary source. Do they have other motives that affect their point of view that alters the validity of their information?

YES

PEOPLE WHO CAN **CUT BACK** WILL USE LESS AND LEAVE **MORE PRODUCTS** FOR THOSE WHO CANNOT ADJUST THEIR **CONSUMPTION**

HIGHER PRICES **ENCOURAGE** PEOPLE TO **PREPARE** FOR THE NEXT DISASTER

HIGHER PRICES KEEP PEOPLE FROM **BUYING MORE THAN THEY NEED**

SELLERS ARE **ATTRACTED** BY HIGH PRICES AND **BRING MORE GOODS** INTO THE AREA

❝ Anti-price gouging laws are really guaranteed shortage laws. ❞
—Mark Perry, Professor of Economics, University of Michigan

▲ Business owners are also affected by the high demand during emergencies. They need to maintain a profit to stay in business if deliveries are cut off.

120

---

networks Online Teaching Options

DEBATE

Debate: Should it be legal to raise prices on basic items needed for survival during natural disasters or other emergencies?

Analyzing the ethics of price gouging Organize students into two groups: the Yes group and the No group. Have each group click through the Debate to read the text for both sides of the issue. Ask each group to create a statement of their group's opinion, both defending their opinion and responding to the opposing side's claims. Have them answer the first two questions in the Debate activity to clarify their arguments. Have a spokesperson for each group read the group's statement, and give the opposing group's spokesperson two minutes to respond. Finally, vote as a class to decide which side did the best job defending their ideas. **Verbal/Linguistic**

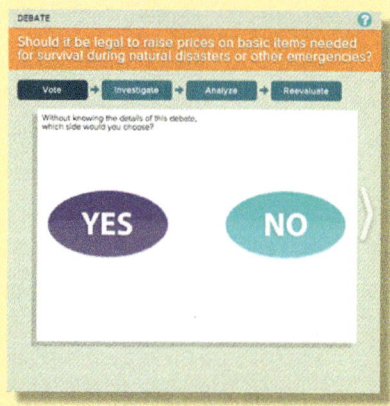

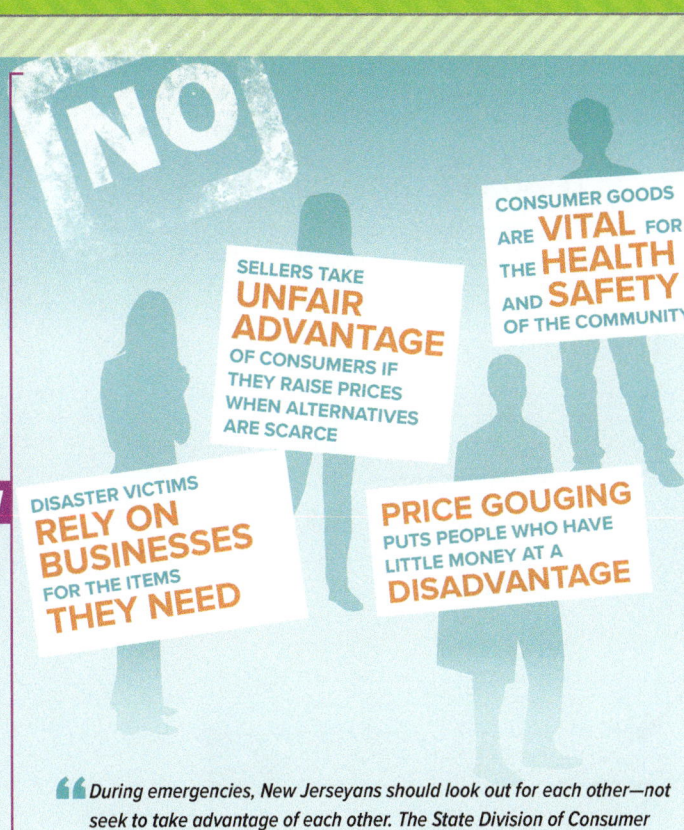

> *During emergencies, New Jerseyans should look out for each other—not seek to take advantage of each other. The State Division of Consumer Affairs will look closely at any and all complaints about alleged price gouging. Anyone found to have violated the law will face significant penalties.*
>
> —New Jersey governor Chris Christie, in the aftermath of Hurricane Sandy

▲ During emergencies, critical supplies can be low. Consumers should not need to struggle with price gouging.

ANALYZING the issue

1. **Analyze** How does demand for goods change after a natural disaster?

2. **Evaluating** What impact does an anti-price gouging law have on an economic system?

3. **Argument** Which argument do you find most compelling? Explain your answer.

121

CHAPTER 4
Debate

W Writing Skills

Arguing the ethics of price gouging Have students read the Debate feature and evaluate the validity of the sources for point of view. Then have students form pairs and write a dialogue between a person who supports the Yes side and a person who supports the No side of the Debate. Ask students to present their dialogues to the class. **Verbal/Linguistic**

CLOSE & REFLECT

W Writing Skills

Describing opinions about price-gouging Have students write a reflection paragraph explaining how their opinion about price-gouging has either changed or become stronger after analyzing this Debate.

English Language Proficiency

Intermediate During class debates, provide opportunities for students to seek clarification of spoken language. When a student has spoken, ask, "Does anyone have any questions about what (student name) just said?" When you are giving directions or providing instruction, stop frequently and ask, "Any questions?"

GRAPHIC ORGANIZERS

K-W-L-H Chart

Using charts to organize learning Distribute the K-W-L-H graphic organizer to student groups of three or four. Tell students that they will use the K-W-L-H organizer to organize their learning as they review the Debate. Ask them to follow these steps to complete the activity:

1. Read the first paragraph of the Debate.
2. Fill out the "What I Know" and "What I Want to Know" sections of the organizer.
3. Read the remaining primary sources and paragraphs of the Debate.
4. Fill out the "What I Learned" and "How I Can Learn More" sections of the organizer.

Ask student groups to share their ideas with the class. **Verbal/Linguistic**

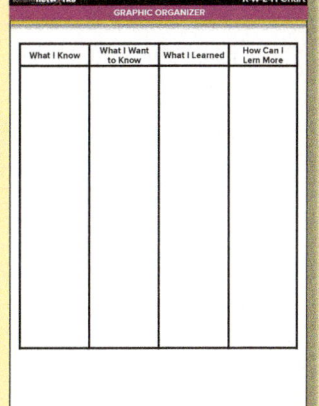

ANSWERS, p. 121

ANALYZING the issue

1. Demand for essential goods increases dramatically after a disaster, but supply is often diminished.
2. Anti-price-gouging laws prevent the economic system from working normally. This decreases supply, and shortages result.
3. Students should show understanding of the human cost of price gouging as well as the economic system that makes price gouging reasonable.

Demand **121**

Chapter 4
Study Guide

W Writing Skills

Personal Writing Tell students to write a report in which they choose three products that they currently purchase and describe how a change in each determinant of demand would affect the amount of the good that they purchase. **Verbal/Linguistic**

C Critical Thinking Skills

Assessing Ask students to think about the goods that they purchase. Using information from the text, have them make a judgment as to which good has the most elastic demand and the most inelastic demand. Have students write a paragraph about each good, explaining why the good has certain demand characteristics.

STUDY GUIDE

LESSON 1

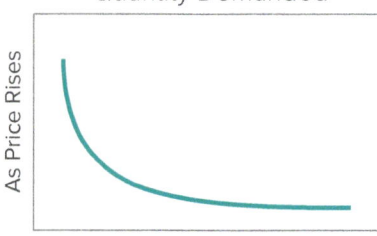

Raising the Price Reduces Quantity Demanded

LESSON 2

LESSON 3

networks Online Assessment Options

WORKSHEET

Economic Simulation

Students will do market research to decide what types of clothing to sell in a clothing store in one of several countries. They will use factors that are involved in making clothing purchasing decisions in these specific countries to do their research. Finally, they will share their findings with classmates and, in groups, develop two or three products that they will propose to the company to sell in their clothing store.

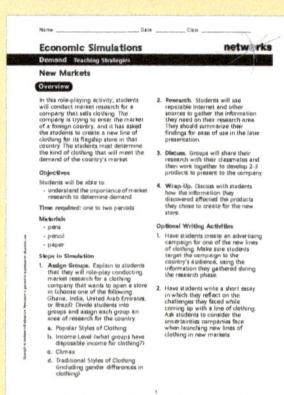

122

CHAPTER 4 Assessment

Directions: On a separate sheet of paper, answer the questions below. Make sure you read carefully and answer all parts of the questions.

Lesson Review

Lesson 1

1. **Cause and Effect** Identify the Law of Demand and give an example of the law in action.

2. **Draw Conclusions** Explain the rule of marginal utility and how it works in real life.

Lesson 2

3. **Evaluate** How can a change in income shift a demand for goods?

4. **Cause and Effect** What is likely to happen when consumers hear reports that make them worry about a product's safety? Explain the possible effect on demand and price.

Lesson 3

5. **Describe** If demand for a product is inelastic, what would you predict will happen to demand when its price rises?

6. **Making Connections** Explain why the demand for a brand new digital device might be elastic or inelastic. How might that elasticity change over time once the device is no longer brand new?

Analyzing Visuals

Use the visual below to answer the following questions.

7. **Analyzing** When consumers have more money to spend, how does the demand for burritos change? Draw a chart like the one below. Compare your chart with a classmate's and analyze the differences in two supply-and-demand graphs. How does your classmate's chart compare with your supply-and-demand model?

8. **Reading Graphs** If you are selling burritos at $7 each, how much more money would you make if your customers had higher incomes?

9. **Applying** With high-income burrito buyers, at what price would you make the most money?

Critical Thinking

10. **Identifying Central Issues** Demand includes the desire, ability, and willingness to buy a product. Explain in a paragraph why each one of these factors must be present to create demand.

11. **Speculating** How do the number of consumers in a marketplace affect demand? How do the number of consumers affect prices?

12. **Interpreting** Explain why it is reasonable to say that "total revenue" is the same as "total expenditures."

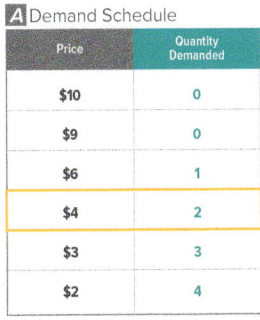

A Demand Schedule

Price	Quantity Demanded
$10	0
$9	0
$6	1
$4	2
$3	3
$2	4

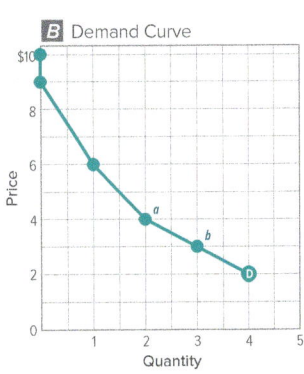

B Demand Curve

Need Extra Help?

If You've Missed Question	1	2	3	4	5	6	7	8	9	10	11	12
Go to page	104	105	110	111	115	117	110	110	110	103	113	115

Chapter 4 Assessment Answers

Lesson Review

Lesson 1

1. The Law of Demand states that more will be demanded at lower prices and less at higher prices. For example, fewer cars are demanded when the price of cars goes up.

2. Marginal utility is the extra usefulness a person gets from acquiring another unit of a product. For example, a person is likely to enjoy the second and third beverage less than the first, a case of diminishing marginal utility.

Lesson 2

3. A shift in income is a non-price factor that can change the demand for goods. When people have more money, they may be able to afford to buy more.

4. Negative reports about a product's safety will decrease demand, and less of the product will be purchased regardless of price.

Lesson 3

5. Demand will stay the same.

6. The demand would probably be inelastic when the device is first introduced if there are no substitutes for it. As time passes, the demand elasticity would increase if substitutes become available.

Analyzing Visuals

7. With more income, a consumer demands a greater quantity. When all consumers have more income, the demand curve shifts to the right.

8. According to the graph, no complete burritos are purchased at $7 each. With higher incomes, consumers will purchase more, according to the income effect.

9. Students should note that the seller will make the most money by charging $3 per burrito. As the graph shows, at point b the seller makes $9. Any other combination results in less money earned.

Critical Thinking

10. Sample answer: To create demand, consumers must wish for a product. Second, they must have the ability to buy it, meaning they have access to sellers and enough money for the purchase. Third, they must be willing to spend their money this way.

11. When the number of consumers increases, demand also increases, which is likely to lead to higher prices.

12. While a consumer spends money, that money becomes revenue for a seller. Therefore, expenditures and revenues are equal.

Chapter 4
Assessment Answers

Answering the Essential Questions

13 Students should show understanding of how price determines demand for a product. They should demonstrate understanding of the non-price influences on demand.

21st Century Skills

14 Students should show understanding that some goods are necessary for living and will be purchased in the same amount regardless of price, while other goods have greater demand elasticity and will be in lesser demand as the price increases.

15 Students should show understanding that sellers may be influenced to sell higher priced goods out of a sense of corporate citizenship. That seller would need to convince his buyers that the social benefit is worth the extra costs.

16 Students should conduct research and record their results. They should write a paragraph to summarize their inferences about the demand for goods in areas with differing income levels.

Building Financial Literacy

17 a. Products that might see seasonal changes in demand include clothing, such as coats, clothing, and swimwear; household goods such as air conditioners or heaters; and tools such as hedge trimmers or snow shovels.

b. Negative advertisements about a competitor's product could decrease demand for it. Positive ads for your product could increase demand.

Analyzing Primary Sources

18 Menger writes, "In considering the goods he will acquire in trade, each man takes account only of their use value to himself." This indicates his understanding that each individual values goods differently from other individuals.

19 As the exchanges become more complex, individuals will need to find a means of exchange that does not involve direct barter.

CHAPTER 4 Assessment

Directions: On a separate sheet of paper, answer the questions below. Make sure you read carefully and answer all parts of the questions.

ANSWERING THE ESSENTIAL QUESTIONS

Review your answers to the introductory questions at the beginning of each lesson. Then answer the Essential Questions on the basis of what you learned in the chapter. Have your answers changed?

13 **Understanding Relationships** How does demand help societies determine WHAT, HOW, and FOR WHOM to produce? What are the causes of a change in demand?

21st Century Skills

14 **Create and Analyze Arguments and Draw Conclusions** Think about the goods you and your family buy every week. Select 10 items and analyze whether market demand for each is likely to be elastic or inelastic. Rank the items in order from most elastic to least. Then write a paragraph explaining your analysis.

15 **Citizenship** Some businesses think about good citizenship when they decide what to sell. For example, a business might sell organic food or recycled carpeting, even though those products might be more expensive than goods that are more damaging to the environment. Use the Law of Demand to explain why these sellers might be successful.

16 **Research Skills** You learned that sellers can charge higher prices in areas where consumers have greater income. Visit or call stores in affluent areas and others in less-affluent areas to compare the prices of goods that you might buy yourself. What do the differences tell you about demand?

Building Financial Literacy

17 **Recognizing Behavior** For a business owner, understanding how the demand for goods changes with consumer tastes is critical to success. Answer the following questions from the seller's perspective.

a. What products are likely to sell more or less depending on the season?

b. What kind of advertising could change the demand for the goods you sell or goods sold by your competitors?

Analyzing Primary Sources

Read the excerpt and answer the questions that follow.

PRIMARY SOURCE

" *In the early stages of trade, when economizing individuals are only slowly awakening to knowledge of the economic gains that can be derived from exploitation of existing exchange opportunities, their attention is, in keeping with the simplicity of all cultural beginnings, directed only to the most obvious of these opportunities. In considering the goods he will acquire in trade, each man takes account only of their use value to himself. Hence the exchange transactions that are actually performed are restricted naturally to situations in which economizing individuals have goods in their possession that have a smaller use value to them than goods in the possession of other economizing individuals who value the same goods in reverse fashion. A has a sword that has a smaller use value to him than B's plough, while to B the same plough has a smaller use value than A's sword—at the beginning of human trade, all exchange transactions actually performed are restricted to cases of this sort.* "

—Carl Menger, *Principles of Economics*

18 **Citing Source** Where in this passage does Menger begin to explain his ideas about marginal utility? Quote at least one sentence.

19 **Finding Resolution** Menger describes early trading situations. What might happen as trade becomes more complex?

Need Extra Help?

If You've Missed Question	13	14	15	16	17	18	19
Go to page	102	115	118	109	110	105	105

124

---

networks Online Assessment Options

WORKSHEET

Chapter Tests and Lesson Quizzes

Chapter 4 Tests Forms A and B Have students complete the Chapter Tests and Lesson Quizzes to assess student understanding throughout the chapter. Print and online assessment tools offer chapter and lesson evaluation through a variety of question formats, including document-based questions.

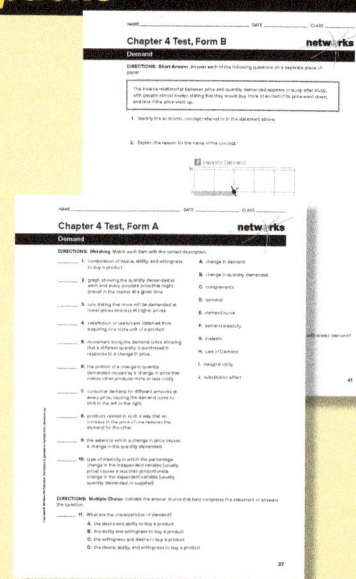

CHAPTER 5
Supply Planner

UNDERSTANDING BY DESIGN®

Enduring Understanding
- Supply in a market economy is determined by what produces the greatest amount of profit.

Essential Questions
- What are the basic differences between supply and demand?
- Why is the production function useful for making business decisions?
- How do companies determine the most profitable way to operate?

Predictable Misunderstandings
Students may think:
- *A change in supply is the same as a change in quantity supplied.* Explain that a change in quantity supplied occurs only when price changes.
- *Productivity goes up when more workers are added.* Explain that while this is true to a certain extent, lack of motivation or training can result in lower productivity. In addition, after a certain number of employees are hired, adding more employees results in negative marginal returns.

Assessment Evidence
Performance Tasks:
- Hands-On Chapter Project with Technology Extension

Other Evidence:
- Guided Reading Activities
- Vocabulary Activity
- Lesson Quizzes
- Self-Check Quizzes
- Chapter Assessment
- Chapter Tests, Forms A and B

SUGGESTED PACING GUIDE

Introducing the Chapter. . . . . ½ Day	Lesson 3: Cost, Revenue, and Profit Maximization. . . . . ½ Day
Lesson 1: What Is Supply? . . . . . ½ Day	Case Study . . . . ½ Day
Lesson 2: The Theory of Production . . . . ½ Day	Study Guide, Chapter Assessment and Wrap-Up . . . . . ½ Day
Debate . . . . ½ Day	

TOTAL TIME 3½ Days

Key for Using the Teacher Edition

SKILL-BASED ACTIVITIES

Types of skill activites found in the Teacher Edition.

V **Visual Skills** require students to analyze maps, graphs, charts, and photos.

R **Reading Skills** help students practice reading skills and master vocabulary.

C **Critical Thinking Skills** help students apply and extend what they have learned.

W **Writing Skills** provide writing opportunities to help students comprehend the text.

T **Technology Skills** require students to use digital tools effectively.

*Letters are followed by a number when there is more than one of the same type of skill on the page.

DIFFERENTIATED INSTRUCTION

All activities are written for the on-level student unless otherwise marked with the leveled labels below.

BL Beyond Level
AL Approaching Level
ELL English Language Learners

All students benefit from activities that utilize different learning styles. Many activities are marked as below when a particular learning style is highlighted.

Intrapersonal
Logical/Mathematical
Visual/Spatial
Verbal/Linguistic
Naturalist
Kinesthetic
Auditory/Musical
Interpersonal

Council for Economic Education

Below are the Council for Economic Education Voluntary National Content Standards in Economics covered in the *Supply* chapter.

Content Standard 2: Effective decision making requires comparing the additional costs of alternatives with the additional benefits. Many choices involve doing a little more or a little less of something: few choices are "all or nothing" decisions.

Content Standard 8: Prices send signals and provide incentives to buyers and sellers. When supply or demand changes, market prices adjust, affecting incentives.

CHAPTER 5: SUPPLY

CHAPTER OPENER PLANNER

Students will know:
- supply is the amount of a product offered for sale at all possible prices that could prevail in the market.
- the factors that cause a change in supply.
- the three stages of production and their characteristics.
- how firms determine price and output through marginal analysis.

Students will be able to:
- **describe** the basic differences between supply and demand.
- **list** factors that can cause a change in supply.
- **summarize** the three cases of supply elasticity.
- **summarize** the three stages of production.
- **differentiate** among fixed, variable, total, and marginal costs.

UNDERSTANDING BY DESIGN®

☑ Print Teaching Options

R Reading Skills

☐ **p. 126 Identifying surpluses and shortages** Students identify an overstock and shortage.

C Critical Thinking Skills

☐ **p. 125 Identifying examples of supply** Students define *supply* and discuss examples.

☐ **p. 125 The Right Price** Students explore how firms make supply and price decisions.

☐ **p. 126 Analyzing a supply curve about labor and wages** Students create a supply schedule of labor they would supply at various wages.

T Technology Skills

☐ **p. 127 Summarizing the Law of Supply** Students create multimedia about how the Law of Supply affects business decisions. **BL**

☑ Online Teaching Options

V Visual Skills

☐ **IMAGES** Chapter opener—Students relate a warehouse worker to supply.

C Critical Thinking Skills

☐ **INFOGRAPHICS** Economic Perspectives—Students discuss the Law of Supply.

☐ **DEBATES** Do multinational corporations have a duty to keep their base of operations in their home countries?

☐ **INTERACTIVE FEATURE** Case Study: The Nearly Instant Snowboard—Students analyze how 3-D printing affects suppliers' costs and inventories.

☑ Printable Digital Worksheets

C Critical Thinking Skills

☐ **WORKSHEET** Chapter Summary—Content is condensed into manageable chunks.

☐ **WORKSHEET** Vocabulary Activity—Students use content and academic terms.

☐ **WORKSHEET** Enrichment Activity—Students create a multimedia presentation about their own hypothetical business.

Project-Based Learning

Hands-On

WORKSHEET Hands-On Chapter Project
Paper Airplane Production Students will imagine that they are working in a paper airplane factory with limited space. In groups, they will explore the stages of production as more and more workers produce paper airplanes in a limited space. Students will then use the data they collected to plot their company's production function and calculate the effects on revenue.

Digital Hands-On

Create Online Projects

Find an additional activity online that incorporates technology for the Hands-On Project. Visit the EdTech Teacher Web sites for more links, tutorials, and other resources.

Print Resources

ANCILLARY RESOURCES
This ancillary is available for every chapter and lesson.
- Chapter Tests and Lesson Quizzes

PRINTABLE DIGITAL WORKSHEETS
These printable digital worksheets are available for every chapter and lesson.
- Reading Essentials & Study Guide
- Vocabulary Activities
- Chapter Summaries
- Economic Simulations
- Math Practice for Economics
- Reinforcing Economic Skills
- Personal Finance Activities
- Enrichment Activities
- Reteaching Activities
- Guided Reading Activities
- Video Worksheets
- Lesson Quizzes and Chapter Tests (English and Spanish)

More Media Resources

SUGGESTED READING
- For students at a Grade 10 reading level: ***Networking to Find a Job,*** by Stuart Schwartz & Craig Conley
- For students at a Grade 11 reading level: ***Futurelife: The Biotechnology Revolution,*** by Alvin Silverstein & Virginia Silverstein
- For students at a Grade 12 reading level: ***Our Own Devices: The Past and Future of Body Technology,*** by Edward Tenner

SUGGESTED VIDEOS
Find these documentaries yourself online. NOTE: McGraw-Hill Education does not endorse these resources. Preview clips for age-appropriateness.
- ***The Diamond Empire*** (90 min.)
- ***Britain's Bad Housing*** (45 min.)
- ***TED Talks: The Era of Open Innovation*** (19 min.)

LESSON 1 Planner

WHAT IS SUPPLY?

Students will know:
- supply is the amount of a product offered for sale at all possible prices that could prevail in the market.
- the factors that cause a change in supply.
- the three types of supply elasticity.

Students will be able to:
- *describe* the basic differences between supply and demand.
- *explain* why supply and demand curves slope in opposite directions.
- *compare* a change in quantity supplied to a change in supply.
- *list* factors that can cause a change in supply.
- *summarize* the three cases of supply elasticity.

UNDERSTANDING BY DESIGN

✓ Print Teaching Options

V Visual Skills
- ☐ **p. 129 Comparing supply and demand curves** Students discuss how the supply curve compares to the demand curve.

R Reading Skills
- ☐ **p. 132 Examining cost of resources** Students reflect how the cost of resources affects supply.

C Critical Thinking Skills
- ☐ **p. 128 Relating the profit incentive to supply** Students discuss firms' incentive for profits.
- ☐ **p. 130 Illustrating the Law of Supply** Students create a schedule and graph from classroom data.
- ☐ **p. 131 Emphasizing quantity supplied** Students discuss what causes a change in quantity supplied versus a change in supply.
- ☐ **p. 131 Analyzing changes in supply** Students find a news story about nonprice change in supply.
- ☐ **p. 132 Predicting movement of supply curves** Students determine which direction the supply curve will move for different scenarios.
- ☐ **p. 133 Examining number of sellers** Students represent suppliers in the music industry by humming.
- ☐ **p. 133 Explaining changes in supply** Students explain what would happen to the supply of tires.
- ☐ **p. 134 Demonstrating elasticity** Students view a demonstration of elasticity.
- ☐ **p. 134 Inelastic Holiday Supply** Students think of products with inelastic holiday supply.
- ☐ **p. 135 Identifying examples of firms with various supply elasticity**

W Writing Skills
- ☐ **p. 129 Explaining supply** Students explain why supply involves a direct (rather than inverse) relationship between prices and quantity.
- ☐ **p. 134 Defining supply elasticity** Students define *supply elasticity*.

✓ Online Teaching Options

V Visual Skills
- ☐ **GRAPHS** **Supply of Burritos**—Students explore a graph showing Law of Supply.
- ☐ **GRAPHS** **Individual and Market Supply Curves**—Students discuss the differences and similarities between individual and market supply curves.
- ☐ **GRAPHS** **A Change in Supply**—Students discuss what happens to the supply curve with a change in supply, listing possible causes. **Verbal/Linguistic**
- ☐ **VIDEO** **Bad Weather**—Students watch how the world cotton supply decreased.
- ☐ **GRAPH** **Elasticity of Supply**—Students create a hypothetical product that illustrates one type of supply elasticity. **BL** **Logical/Mathematical**

R Reading Skills
- ☐ **GRAPHIC ORGANIZERS** **Supply, Price, and Demand**—Students explain how supply and price react to changes in demand. **Logical/Mathematical**

C Critical Thinking Skills
- ☐ **BELLRINGER** **What Is Supply?**—Students discuss what happens to the quantity supplied of running shoes if the price increases. **Verbal/Linguistic**
- ☐ **ESSENTIAL QUESTION** **Exploring the Essential Question Activity**—Students explore factors affecting the supply of T-shirts offered for sale.
- ☐ **INTERACTIVE FEATURE** **Global Economy & You**—Students analyze what affects the supply and price of coffee beans. **BL** **Visual/Spatial, Logical/Mathematical**

T Technology Skills
- ☐ **SELF-CHECK QUIZ** **Lesson 1**—Students receive instant feedback on answers.
- ☐ **GAME** **Lesson 1**—Students solve clues to review lesson content.
- ☐ **INTERACTIVE WHITEBOARD ACTIVITY** **Increasing Supply**—Students work together to learn lesson content.

✓ Printable Digital Worksheets

R Reading Skills
- ☐ **WORKSHEET** **Guided Reading Activity**—Students review their comprehension.
- ☐ **WORKSHEET** **Reading Essentials and Study Guide**—Students complete the study guide and answer Reading Progress Check and vocabulary questions.

C Critical Thinking Skills
- ☐ **WORKSHEET** **Bad Weather Video Activity**—Students answer questions related to how the world cotton supply decreased.
- ☐ **WORKSHEET** **Personal Finance**—Students identify part-time businesses they would like to start, labeling which have elastic or inelastic supply.

LESSON 2 Planner

THE THEORY OF PRODUCTION

Students will know:
- technological change and investments in capital goods and human capital may increase labor productivity but have significant opportunity costs and economic risks.
- the three stages of production and their characteristics.
- the stages of production determine the most profitable number of workers a firm can hire.

Students will be able to:
- **explain** how production affects supply elasticity.
- **explain** how the production function is used to make business decisions.
- **discuss** total and marginal product at different production periods.
- **summarize** the three stages of production.

UNDERSTANDING BY DESIGN®

✓ Print Teaching Options

V Visual Skills

☐ **p. 137 Creating a production function** Students create a production function schedule for a hypothetical business.
BL Logical/Mathematical

☐ **p. 138 Illustrating stages of production** Students depict how marginal product changes in the three stages of production for a product.
AL Visual/Spatial

C Critical Thinking Skills

☐ **p. 136 Predicting how to measure the production function of a business** Students identify elements used for measuring the production function of a business. Verbal/Linguistic

☐ **p. 137 Relating labor to the short run** Students discuss why a short-run production function is useful for measuring effects of changes in labor. **AL** Logical/Mathematical, Verbal/Linguistic

☐ **p. 137 Determining the effect of changing one variable** Students discuss the interconnectedness of variables in a business.
BL Verbal/Linguistic

☐ **p. 138 Determining cause and effect** Students create a graph to answer: How does a change in inputs affect production? **BL** Visual/Spatial

☐ **p. 139 Productivity of labor** Students analyze a business's costs and benefits in providing incentives to increase labor productivity.

W Writing Skills

☐ **p. 138 Describing stages of production** Students describe how the three stages of production are different. **AL** Verbal/Linguistic, Interpersonal

☐ **p. 139 Summarizing concepts** Students write a summary of the production function, including the concept of marginal production.

✓ Online Teaching Options

V Visual Skills

☐ **VIDEO Oil Companies**—Students view the video and express their opinions about the way oil companies handle supply. Interpersonal

☐ **GRAPHS Short-Run Production**—Students discuss how companies hire workers based on marginal product rather than total product. **BL** Verbal/Linguistic

R Reading Skills

☐ **GRAPHIC ORGANIZERS Production Function**—Students take notes about production. **AL** Verbal/Linguistic

☐ **BIOGRAPHY Daniel Akerson**—Students read and provide an opinions on Akerson's quote about leadership. **AL** Verbal/Linguistic, Interpersonal

C Critical Thinking Skills

☐ **BELLRINGER Theory of Production**—Students discuss factors that affect changes in short-run and long-run production periods. **AL** Verbal/Linguistic

☐ **ESSENTIAL QUESTION Exploring the Essential Question**—Students discuss actions companies take when sales increase or decrease. **AL** Verbal/Linguistic

T Technology Skills

☐ **SELF-CHECK QUIZ Lesson 2**—Students receive instant feedback on their mastery of lesson content.

☐ **GAME Lesson 2**—Students solve clues to review lesson content.

☐ **INTERACTIVE WHITEBOARD ACTIVITY Production Periods**—Students work together to learn lesson content.

✓ Printable Digital Worksheets

R Reading Skills

☐ **WORKSHEET Guided Reading Activity**—Students use the Guided Reading Activity worksheets to review their comprehension of the content.

☐ **WORKSHEET Reading Essentials and Study Guide**—Students complete the study guide and answer Reading Progress Check and vocabulary questions.

C Critical Thinking Skills

☐ **WORKSHEET Oil Companies Video Activity**—Students answer questions about the way oil companies handle supply. Interpersonal

LESSON 3 Planner

COST, REVENUE, AND PROFIT MAXIMIZATION

Students will know:
- *marginal product* is the extra output or change in total product caused by adding one more unit of variable input.
- the difference between a fixed cost and a variable cost and the effect these costs have on how a business operates.
- how firms determine price and output through marginal analysis.

Students will be able to:
- **differentiate** among fixed, variable, total, and marginal costs.
- **explain** the differences in average, total, and marginal revenue.
- **describe** the cost advantages of e-commerce.
- **identify** the relationship between profit maximization and break-even analysis.

UNDERSTANDING BY DESIGN®

☑ Print Teaching Options

V Visual Skills
- ☐ **p. 145 Analyzing a table** Students analyze a table for negative returns, greatest total profit, and total fixed costs. **Logical/Mathematical**

R Reading Skills
- ☐ **p. 143 Defining business costs** Students define *fixed, variable, total,* and *marginal costs*.
- ☐ **p. 146 Summarizing business costs and revenues** Students answer: How could this chapter help a person starting a business?

C Critical Thinking Skills
- ☐ **p. 142 Identifying measures of cost** Students list the costs a hypothetical business has.
- ☐ **p. 143 Categorizing costs** Students put costs of running the school in the proper categories of fixed and variable costs. **AL Interpersonal**
- ☐ **p. 143 Prioritizing marginal cost** Students explain whether they agree with: *The most useful measure of cost is marginal cost.*
- ☐ **p. 143 Analyzing costs** Students list costs involved in operating a contracting business.
- ☐ **p. 144 Analyzing costs and revenue** Students decide if a business should hire a new worker.
- ☐ **p. 145 Balancing marginal cost and marginal revenue** Students decide steps to take if marginal cost is less than marginal revenue.
- ☐ **p. 146 Understanding the break-even point** Students research a company that has failed and discuss the reasons. **BL**

W Writing Skills
- ☐ **p. 144 Explaining measures of revenue** Students write about which measure of revenue is most important for business success.

T Technology Skills
- ☐ **p. 145 Showing constitutional support** Students research laws that affect businesses' drive to maximize profits.

☑ Online Teaching Options

V Visual Skills
- ☐ **GRAPHS Production, Costs, Revenue, and Profits**—Students study how revenues and profits are affected by costs.
- ☐ **VIDEO Rising Price of Gasoline**—Students watch a video and discuss why a moving company would be hard hit by an increase in gasoline prices.
- ☐ **IMAGE e-commerce**—Students compare costs of maintaining an online store versus a brick and mortar store. **Logical/Mathematical**

R Reading Skills
- ☐ **INTERACTIVE FEATURE Painting Contractor Career**—Students read and discuss the advantages and disadvantages of having a contracting business.
- ☐ **GRAPHIC ORGANIZERS Cost, Revenue, and Profit Maximization**—Students find the information businesspeople must gather to balance costs and revenue.

C Critical Thinking Skills
- ☐ **BELLRINGER Cost, Revenue, and Profit Maximization**—Students discuss whether the assembly line photo shows a maximized labor force. **AL**
- ☐ **ESSENTIAL QUESTION Exploring the Essential Question**—Students brainstorm ways a business determines the most profitable way to operate. **AL**
- ☐ **GRAPHS Production, Costs, Revenues, and Profits**—Students compute marginal revenue. **BL Logical/Mathematical**

T Technology Skills
- ☐ **SELF-CHECK QUIZ Lesson 3**—Students receive instant feedback on answers.
- ☐ **GAME Lesson 3**—Students solve clues to review lesson content.
- ☐ **INTERACTIVE WHITEBOARD ACTIVITY Production, Costs, Revenues, and Profits**—Students work together to learn lesson content.

☑ Printable Digital Worksheets

R Reading Skills
- ☐ **WORKSHEET Guided Reading Activity**—Students review their comprehension.
- ☐ **WORKSHEET Reading Essentials and Study Guide**—Students complete the study guide and answer Reading Progress Check and vocabulary questions.
- ☐ **WORKSHEET Reteaching Activity**—Students review difficult content concepts.

C Critical Thinking Skills
- ☐ **WORKSHEET Rising Price of Gasoline Video Activity**—Students answer questions about a moving company hard hit by an increase in gasoline prices.

CHAPTER 5 Supply
INTERVENTION AND REMEDIATION STRATEGIES

LESSON 1 What Is Supply?

Reading and Comprehension

Have students write a summary of the essential points discussed in the lesson. Summaries should include that all businesses, or producers, have to decide how much product to supply and at what price; various factors can cause a change in supply; and if there is a change in price, there will be a change in quantity supplied.

Text Evidence

Review how to use text evidence to support ideas and statements. Then pose these directives: Businesses can show on a graph various quantities supplied at every possible price. Find evidence in the text to support this statement. *(A supply curve is a graph that shows the quantities supplied at each and every possible price in the market.)* Technology can change the productivity and price of a product. Find evidence in the text to support this statement. *(The introduction of a new machine or industrial process can lower the cost of production, which increases productivity.)*

LESSON 2 The Theory of Production

Reading and Comprehension

Have students answer the two questions below and find details to support their responses. Then ask students to share their answers and reasons with the class. In analyzing production, what time period is usually focused on? *(When economists analyze production, they focus on the short run, a production period so brief that only the amount of the variable input—usually labor—can be changed.)* What question does every business face in the short run? *(In the short run, every firm faces the question of how many workers to hire.)*

Text Evidence

Have students answer the following question in a paragraph: *Of the three stages of production, what stage do most firms usually operate in? Explain why.* Have students compare their answers in small group discussions.

LESSON 3 Cost, Revenue, and Profit Maximization

Reading and Comprehension

You are thinking of starting a business in selling used books. Write a brief essay outlining what research you will do before deciding whether to launch the business.

Text Evidence

Direct student pairs to write an essay discussing three reasons most businesses are selling their products through e-commerce. Have pairs share their essays in class discussion.

Online Resources

Assessing Background Knowledge Use this worksheet to pre-assess students' knowledge before they start the chapter.

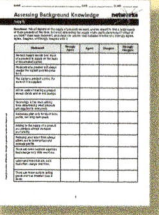

Chapter Summaries Have students use the summary as a pre-reading activity or as a post-reading review to check the main ideas covered in each lesson.

Guided Reading Activities Have students complete these activities as they read each lesson. They provide reading notes the student can use for review and to prepare for assessments.

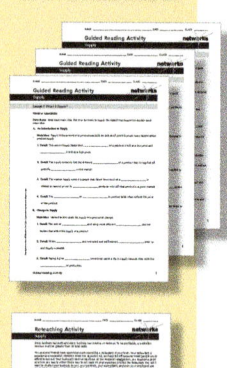

Reteaching Activities Have students complete the Reteaching Activity for remedial practice and review of vital content.

Self-Check Quizzes These quizzes provide instant feedback on areas the students may need to re-read to understand a main idea.

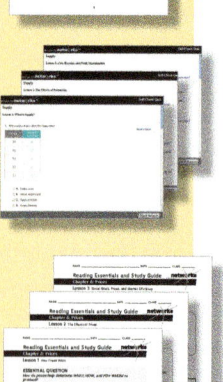

Reading Essentials and Study Guide This resource offers writing and reading activities for the approaching-level student.

Approaching Grade Level Reader This reader presents all of the content of the Online Student Edition but at a lower reading level.

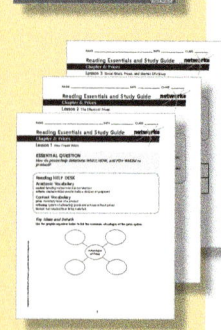

English Language Learner Reader Provide additional reading support for ELL students. Find this tool in the Online Student Edition.

Supply

ESSENTIAL QUESTIONS
- What are the basic differences between supply and demand?
- Why is the production function useful for making business decisions?
- How do companies determine the most profitable way to operate?

networks
www.connected.mcgraw-hill.com
There's More Online about supply.

CHAPTER 5

Economic Perspectives
Law of Supply

Lesson 1
What is Supply?

Lesson 2
The Theory of Production

Lesson 3
Cost, Revenue, and Profit Maximization

Letter from the Author

Dear Economics Teacher,

This chapter on supply, like the one on demand, is the second chapter to use many graphs. This occurs because supply is the other half of a market, which we'll examine in the next chapter. The graphs are simple, but we can't expect to understand how markets work without understanding the fundamental building blocks of a market—supply and demand. This chapter also demonstrates the systematic way of thinking that economists use when they try to explain how the economy works. Because of this, it might be a good time to remind students that economics is, after all, a social *science*.

Gary E. Clayton

CHAPTER 5
Supply

ENGAGE

Call students' attention to the photo and ask them to describe what it shows. Guide them to recognize that a warehouse worker is seen among stacks of products. **Ask: Why is this image a good one to symbolize the chapter *Supply*?** *(The quantity of a product to supply or to offer for sale is something all businesses must decide. It is the basic element of business in a market economy.)* In a class discussion, lead students to understand that in a market or capitalist economic system, private companies, not the state, decide all supply issues.

Identifying examples of supply Discuss what supply is with the class. Tell students that supply is the amount of product offered for sale at all possible prices in a market. **Ask: What are some examples of products offered for sale at all possible prices?** *(Sample answers: produce in supermarkets; electronics such as cell phones and computer notebooks; cars; clothing)* **AL** Verbal/Linguistic

Making Connections

The Right Price Tell students that because products are supplied for sale at all possible prices, sometimes buying an item can be a complex process. This is especially true when purchasing an expensive item like electronics, kitchen appliances, or a car. **Ask: How do firms make decisions about their supply of products and the prices they charge for them?** *(Students may suggest that a firm's production of goods and the price for those goods are determined by demand.)* Have students write a description of how they or their family or friend went about purchasing an expensive item. Descriptions should include whether students bought the item online or in a physical store as well as any differences they found in the price of the good. **Verbal/Linguistic**

FOLDABLES
Study Organizer

Go to the Foldables® library for a cumulative chapter-based Foldable® activity that your students can use to help take notes and prepare for assessment.

Supply **125**

CHAPTER 5
Economic Perspectives

TEACH & ASSESS

R Reading Skills

Identifying surpluses and shortages Have students identify where a surplus (overstock) and product shortage occur in the feature. **Ask: Why did a surplus occur?** *(because more producers entered the market, and the quantity supplied exceeded quantity demanded; producers may have set the price too high)* **Why did a shortage occur?** *(because quantity demanded exceeded quantity supplied, which may have occurred after a product upgrade or when producers set the price too low)* **Visual/Spatial**

C Critical Thinking Skills

Analyzing a supply curve about labor and wages Have students read the information about wages and hours, and study the backward-bending supply curve. Ask students whether they agree or disagree with the premise. Have students create a supply schedule showing the quantity of labor hours they would be willing to supply at various wages.
AL Verbal/Linguistic

Economic Perspectives

LAW OF SUPPLY

The Law of Supply states that producers will offer an increased supply of an item as its price rises. This law demonstrates how change in price affects the behavior of producers in the market. Supply can also be impacted by competition. New product models can result in changes to price, supply, and product demand.

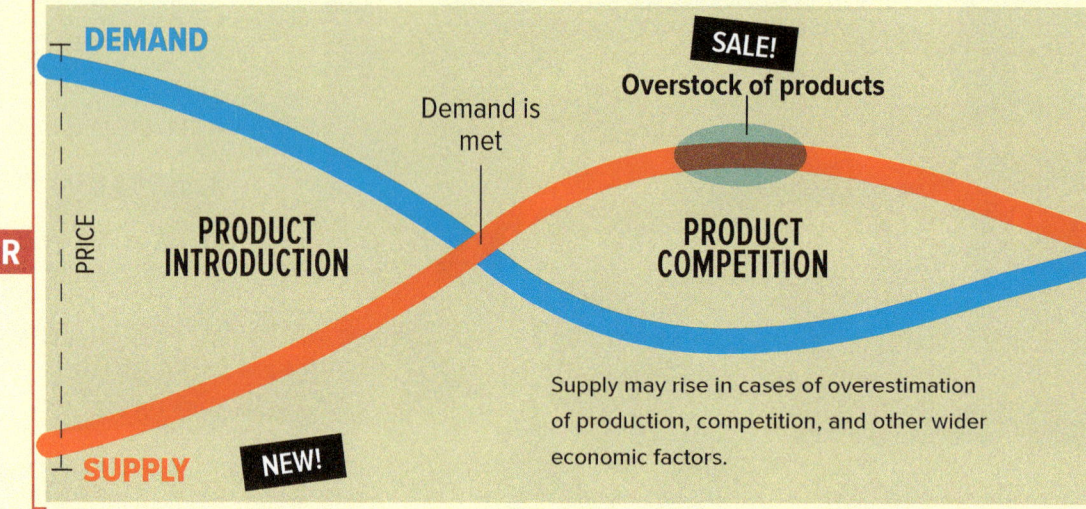

Supply may rise in cases of overestimation of production, competition, and other wider economic factors.

Wages and Hours: The highest earners work fewer hours?

There is an exception to the Law of Supply. Economists consider the backward-bending supply curve of labor (wage rates on the Y-axis and the supply of labor on the X-axis) to have a different dynamic than the one predicted by the Law of Supply. When wages are rising, more people are willing to work more hours. They will reach an equilibrium point where earnings are so high that they feel they can afford to work less. Work hours decrease.

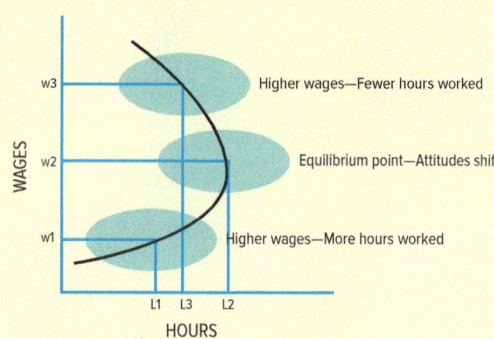

---

networks Online Teaching Options

INFOGRAPHIC

Economic Perspectives: Law of Supply

Analyzing how costs affect supply Have students view the Economic Perspectives feature while discussing the Law of Supply in a market economy. Review that the Law of Supply states that the quantity supplied of a product increases as potential earnings increase.
Ask: What, besides the profit motive, affects supply? *(costs)* **What is the difference between variable costs and fixed costs?** *(Variable costs change as production changes. Variable costs include the cost of resource inputs and overtime wages, for example. Fixed costs are unchanging costs, or those that businesses pay even if they do not produce a single item, such as rent or insurance.)*

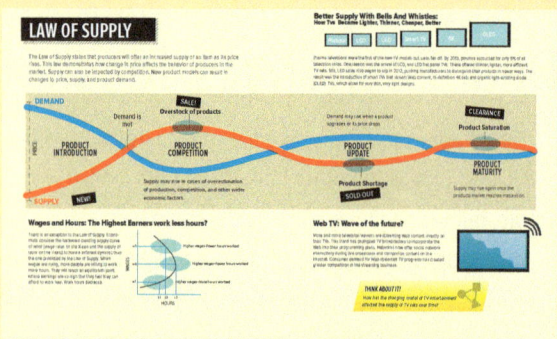

126

CHAPTER 5
Economic Perspectives

Better Supply With Bells And Whistles:
How Tvs Became Lighter, Thinner, Cheaper, Better

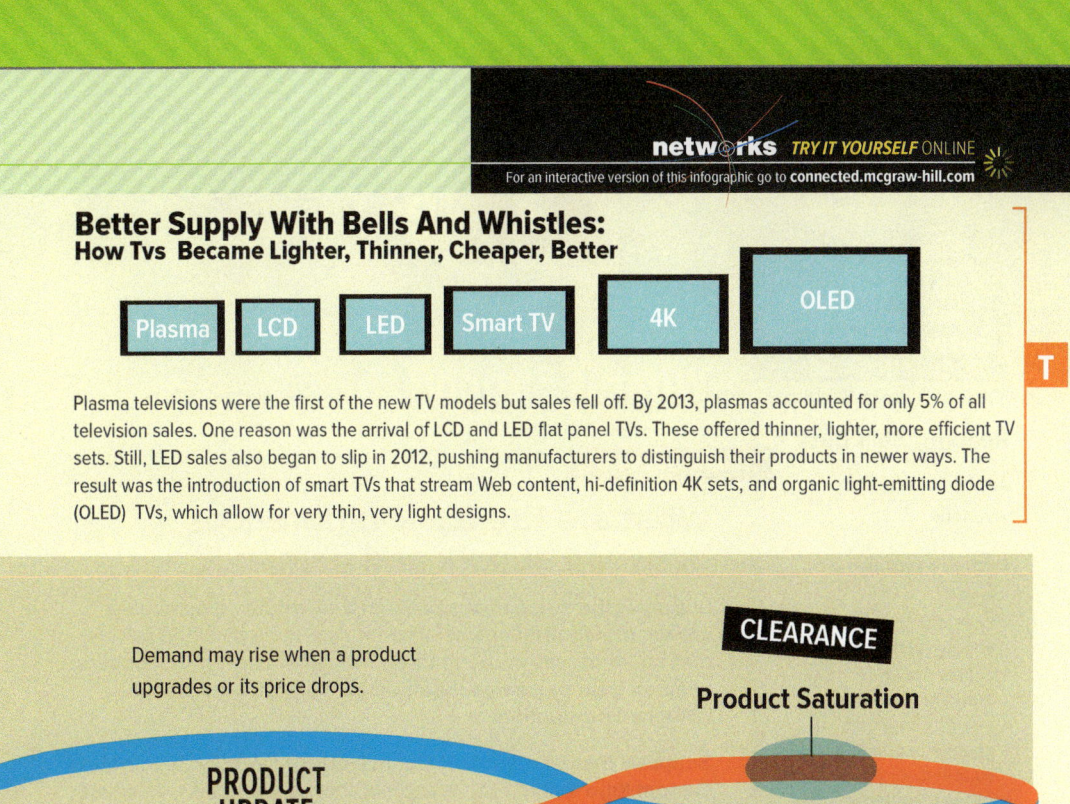

Plasma televisions were the first of the new TV models but sales fell off. By 2013, plasmas accounted for only 5% of all television sales. One reason was the arrival of LCD and LED flat panel TVs. These offered thinner, lighter, more efficient TV sets. Still, LED sales also began to slip in 2012, pushing manufacturers to distinguish their products in newer ways. The result was the introduction of smart TVs that stream Web content, hi-definition 4K sets, and organic light-emitting diode (OLED) TVs, which allow for very thin, very light designs.

Demand may rise when a product upgrades or its price drops.

PRODUCT UPDATE — Product Shortage — SOLD OUT

CLEARANCE — Product Saturation

PRODUCT MATURITY

Supply may rise again once the product market reaches maturation.

Web TV: Wave of the future?

More and more television viewers are streaming Web content directly on their TVs. This trend has prompted TV broadcasters to incorporate the Web into their programming plans. Networks now offer social network interactivity during live broadcasts and companion content on the Internet. Consumer demand for Web-streamed TV programs has created greater competition in the streaming business.

THINK ABOUT IT!
How has the changing model of TV entertainment affected the supply of TV sets over time?

T Technology Skills

Summarizing the Law of Supply Have students create a multimedia program that summarizes the Law of Supply. For their summary, tell students to research online and take notes, focusing on one business and showing how the Law of Supply influences the decisions, costs, and other issues that are part of that business. Have students transfer their notes into a media presentation. **BL Visual/Spatial**

CLOSE & REFLECT

Have students answer the *Think About It!* questions.

WORKSHEET

Economic Simulation

Determining how much to supply and at what price
Provide students with the Economic Simulation: Starting a Business. Students will work in groups, with each group forming a business to sell one type of merchandise to the public. Students must plan where they will get necessary resources and how much they cost. They must determine costs, including costs of labor and marketing, and how much they must sell (and at what price) to break even or make a profit.

ANSWERS, p. 127

THINK ABOUT IT!

As new models are introduced, competitors change their production to match the new technology and the overall supply increases, causing surpluses (overstock). As yet another model or product update occurs, supply does not keep up with demand, and shortages occur until competitors again change production. The cycle continues with each new model.

CHAPTER 5, LESSON 1
What Is Supply?

ENGAGE

C Critical Thinking Skills

 Relating the profit incentive to supply Before students begin the lesson, ask them why firms in a free enterprise economy sell products. *(to earn profits)* **Ask:** *How might the firms' incentive for greater profits affect and be affected by a growing community?* *(New stores and restaurants—suppliers—may move into the area. The new businesses have based their decision on the increased demand of the growing community.)* **AL Verbal/Linguistic**

Content Background Knowledge

Supply in a Command Economy Tell students that in a capitalist economy, business owners decide on the quantity of products to manufacture and supply. Factored into their decisions are the availability of materials to make the product, manufacturing costs, the selling price, and consumer demand. In a command economy, the state decides what is manufactured, how much is manufactured, and the selling price of a product. Consumer demand has little effect on supply.

ANSWERS, p. 128

ESSENTIAL QUESTION ACTIVITY

Essays should include information about the Law of Supply—that producers will supply more at high prices than at low prices.

TAKING NOTES:
Demand increases: Supply and price increase
Demand decreases: Supply and price decrease

128

Interact with these digital assets and others in lesson 1
✓ INTERACTIVE GRAPH Individual and Market Supply Curves
✓ INTERACTIVE GRAPH Elasticity of Supply
✓ SELF-CHECK QUIZ
✓ VIDEO

networks TRY IT YOURSELF ONLINE

Reading Help Desk

Academic Vocabulary
- various

Content Vocabulary
- supply
- Law of Supply
- supply schedule
- supply curve
- market supply curve
- quantity supplied
- change in quantity supplied
- change in supply
- subsidy
- supply elasticity

TAKING NOTES:

Key Ideas and Details
ACTIVITY Use the graphic organizer below. In the Effect column, explain how supply and price react to demand.

Supply, Price, and Demand	
Cause	Effect
Demand increases	
Demand decreases	

LESSON 1
What Is Supply?

ESSENTIAL QUESTION

What are the basic differences between supply and demand?

Supply is the amount of a product that would be produced, grown, or acquired and offered for sale at all possible prices that could prevail in the market. Demand is how much buyers want an item or service. Sometimes, though, other factors influence production.

Suppose that as a Student Council officer, your job is to obtain custom logo T-shirts for every member of your class. Because you want to get the best possible price, you plan to make inquiries, meet with suppliers, and finally ask for bids. You are also going to ask for quotes at three different price levels, but you want the same quality shirt to be supplied at each price. You haven't done the work yet, and you only have a $1,000 budget, but the more you think about it, the more you think that you can predict the outcome.

On the basis of what you know about the **Law of Supply**, write a brief essay explaining the economic principles occurring here.

An Introduction to Supply

GUIDING QUESTION *Why do supply and demand curves slope in opposite directions?*

All producers must decide how much of a product to offer for sale at **various** prices—a decision made according to what is best for the individual seller. What is best depends upon the cost of producing the goods or services. These results can be illustrated in the form of a table or a graph.

The Supply Schedule

The **supply schedule** is a listing of the various quantities of a particular product that a producer would supply at all possible prices in the market. **Panel A** of **Figure 5.1** presents a hypothetical supply schedule for burritos at

128

---

networks Online Teaching Options

BELLRINGER

The Law of Supply

Exploring the supply of goods and services in the economy Have students view the Bellringer. Tell students to think about the relationship between the prices of goods and the supply of those goods. Ask students to imagine that they make running shoes, and the price for those shoes increases. What would happen to the quantity supplied of the running shoes? Have them write a short paragraph explaining their answers. **Verbal/Linguistic**

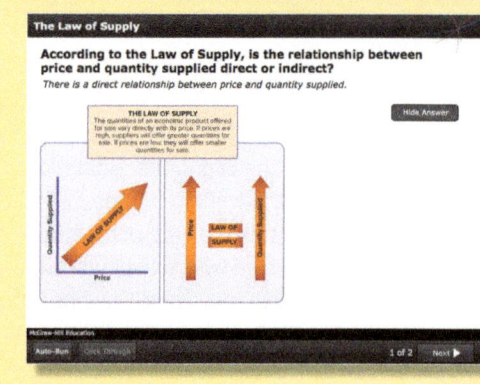

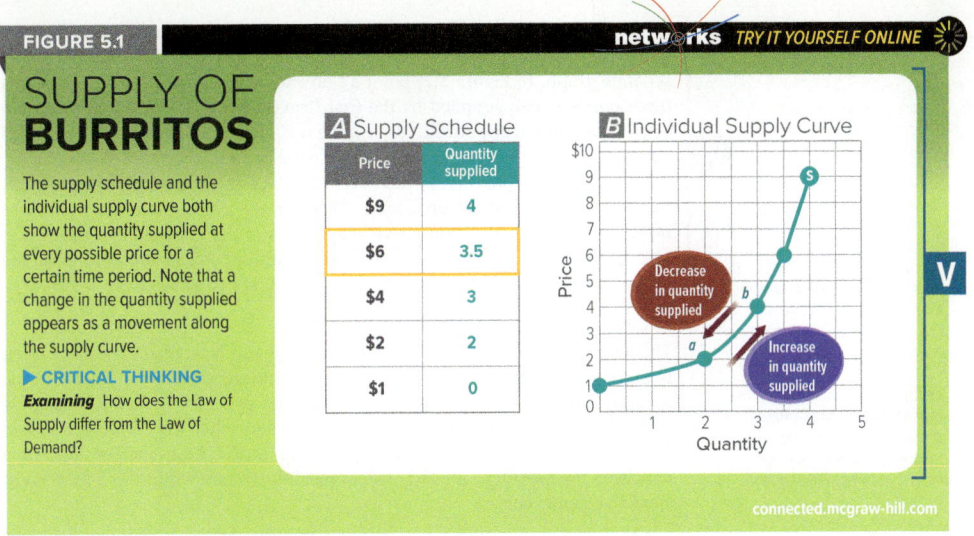

FIGURE 5.1

SUPPLY OF BURRITOS

The supply schedule and the individual supply curve both show the quantity supplied at every possible price for a certain time period. Note that a change in the quantity supplied appears as a movement along the supply curve.

▶ **CRITICAL THINKING**
Examining How does the Law of Supply differ from the Law of Demand?

a certain price. It shows the quantities of burritos that will be supplied at various prices, all other things being equal. If you compare it to the demand schedule in Panel A of Figure 4.1, you will see that the two are remarkably similar.

The main difference between Figure 5.1 and Figure 4.1 is that for supply, the quantity goes up when the price increases, rather than down as in the case of demand. This is because a high price is an incentive for a producer to offer more, whereas a low price is an incentive to produce less.

The Individual Supply Curve

The data presented in the supply schedule can also be illustrated graphically as the upward-sloping line in **Panel B** of Figure 5.1. To draw it, all we do is transfer each of the price-quantity observations in the schedule over to the graph, and then connect the points to form the curve. The result is a **supply curve**, a graph showing the various quantities supplied at all possible prices that might prevail in the market at any given time. Of course the prices and quantities in Figure 5.1 are a bit unrealistic, but the numbers are used to keep the graph simple.

The main thing to remember is that all normal supply curves have a positive slope that goes up when you read the diagram from left to right. This shows that if the price goes up, the quantity supplied will go up too.

While the supply schedule and curve in Figure 5.1 represent the voluntary decisions of a single, hypothetical producer of burritos, remember that supply is a very general concept. In fact, you are a supplier whenever you look for a job and offer your services for sale. Your economic product is your labor, and you would probably be willing to supply more labor for a higher wage than you would for a lower one.

The Market Supply Curve

The supply schedule and curve in Figure 5.1 show the information for a single producer. Frequently, however, we are more interested in the **market supply curve**, the supply curve that shows the quantities offered at various prices by all producers that offer the product for sale in a given market.

supply amount of a product a producer or seller would be willing to offer for sale at all possible prices in a market at a given point in time

Law of Supply principle that more will be offered for sale at higher prices than at lower prices

various different

supply schedule a table showing the quantities that would be produced or offered for sale at each and every possible price in the market at a given point in time

supply curve a graph that shows the quantities supplied at each and every possible price in the market

market supply curve supply curve that shows the quantities offered at various prices by all firms that sell the same product in a given market

---

CHAPTER 5, LESSON 1
What Is Supply?

TEACH & ASSESS

V Visual Skills

Comparing supply and demand curves Ask: **How does the supply curve compare to the demand curve you read about in the previous chapter?** *(The supply curve slopes in the opposite direction.)* **AL** **ELL** Visual/Spatial

W Writing Skills

Explaining supply Have students write a paragraph explaining why the concept of supply involves a direct relationship rather than an inverse relationship between prices and quantity.

GRAPHS

Supply of Burritos

Reading an individual supply curve Have students view Figure 5.1 Supply of Burritos. Tell students that the graph shows an example of the Law of Supply. It shows the quantity of burritos supplied at every possible price. Direct students to the Supply Schedule. Ask: **What happens to the quantity supplied of burritos if the price increases?** *(The quantity supplied increases.)* Direct students to the Individual Supply Curve. Ask: **How is an increase in quantity supplied reflected in the supply curve?** *(An increase in quantity supplied is shown as a movement upward.)* Have students continue through the graphic to see how factors can change the shape of a supply curve. **Visual/Spatial**

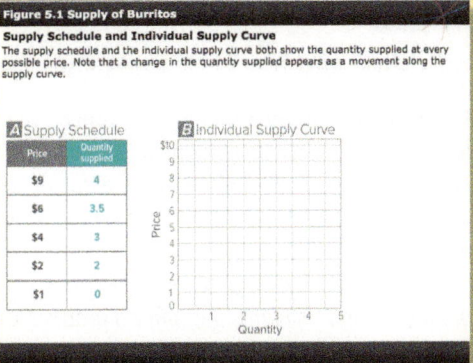

ANSWERS, p. 129

CRITICAL THINKING

For the Law of Supply, quantity varies directly with the price, rather than inversely as with the law of demand.

CHAPTER 5, LESSON 1
What Is Supply?

W Writing Skills

Understanding supply's relationship to price Have students imagine that they manufacture sneakers. At some point in the manufacturing process, assume the price of a pair of sneakers increases to $400. Have each student write a paragraph explaining why he or she is choosing to supply more sneakers. **AL** Verbal/Linguistic

C Critical Thinking Skills

Illustrating the Law of Supply Draw a two-column table on the board with "Pay Per Hour" and "Students Willing to Work" as column headings. In the "Pay" column, list the figures $1 through $10. State that you need help to clean the classroom. Ask who would be interested in the job at a wage of $1 an hour. Record the number in the "Students Willing to Work" column, and then repeat the process for all other hourly rates. Tells students that they have created a supply schedule and provided an example of the Law of Supply. Have students use the data in the supply schedule to construct a supply graph. **ELL** Visual/Spatial

---

ANSWERS, p. 130

CRITICAL THINKING

It would shift to the right because another firm would be adding additional units of output, in this case burritos, to the ones already being offered by the first two suppliers.

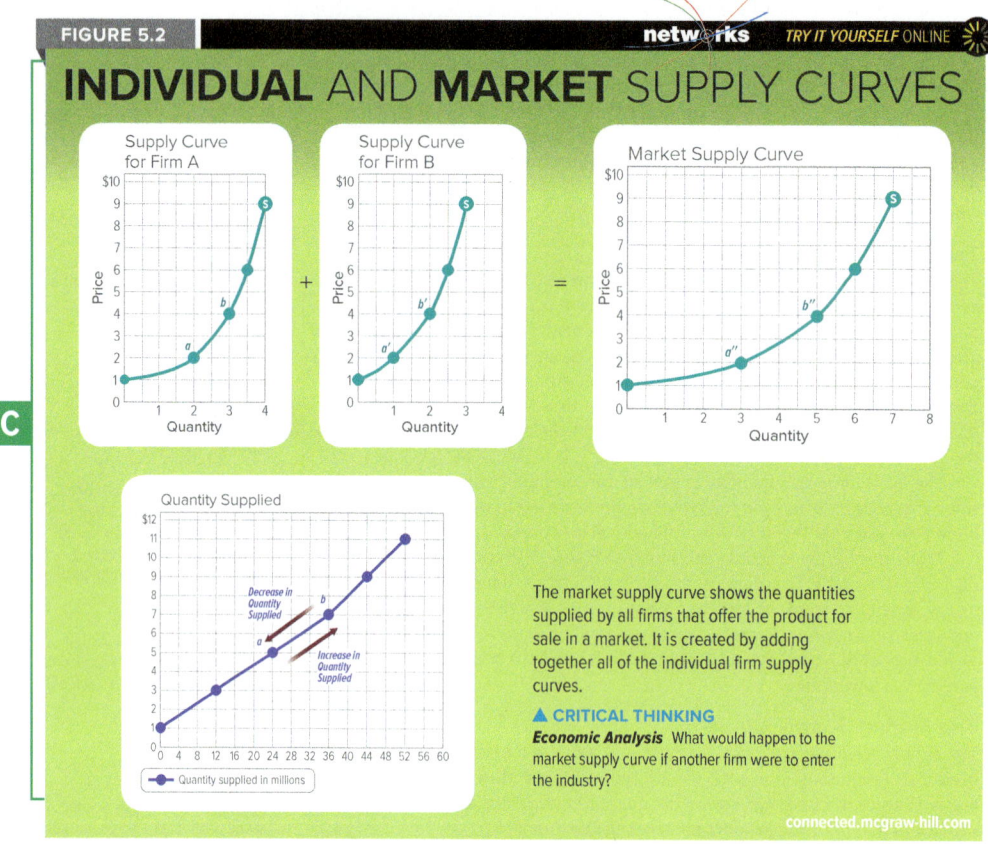

To obtain the data for the market supply curve, add the number of burritos that all individual businesses would produce, and then plot those numbers on a separate graph. In **Figure 5.2**, point **a"** on the market supply curve represents three burritos—two supplied by the first firm and one by the second—that are offered for sale at a price of $2. In the same way, point **b"** on the curve represents a total of five burritos offered for sale at a price of $4.

Of course two producers seldom represent all of the producers in a market, but if we could add all producers together we might have a much more representative market supply curve like the one in the final panel of Figure 5.2. This figure has a wide range of prices and quantities because it represents all the producers in the market, not just two as in the first two panels.

quantity supplied specific amount offered for sale at a given price; point on the supply curve

change in quantity supplied change in the amount offered for sale in response to a price change; movement along the supply curve

A Change in Quantity Supplied

The **quantity supplied** is the amount that a single producer or all producers bring to market at any given price. A **change in quantity supplied** is the change in the amount offered for sale in response to a change in price. In Figure 5.2, the supply curve **S** shows 24 million burritos are supplied when the price is $5, and 36 million are supplied when the price goes up to $7. These changes illustrate a change in the quantity supplied, which—just like demand—shows as a movement *along* the supply curve.

FIGURE 5.2
INDIVIDUAL AND MARKET SUPPLY CURVES

The market supply curve shows the quantities supplied by all firms that offer the product for sale in a market. It is created by adding together all of the individual firm supply curves.

▲ **CRITICAL THINKING**
Economic Analysis What would happen to the market supply curve if another firm were to enter the industry?

---

networks Online Teaching Options

GRAPHS

Individual and Market Supply Curves

Analyzing individual and market supply curves Direct students to Figure 5.2 Individual and Market Supply Curves. **Ask: How are individual supply curves and market supply curves different?** *(Individual supply curves illustrate information from a single firm. Market supply curves illustrate information from all firms that offer a product for sale.)* **How are individual supply curves and market supply curves the same?** *(In both, a change in quantity supplied only takes place if there is a change in price. In both, a change in quantity supplied is shown as movement along the curve—not a shift of the curve.)*

Note that the change in quantity supplied can be an *increase* or a *decrease*, depending on whether more or less of a product is offered. For example, the movement from **a** to **b** in Figure 5.3 shows an increase because the number of products offered for sale goes from 24 million to 36 million when the price goes up. If the movement along the supply curve had been from point **b** to point **a**, there would have been a decrease in quantity supplied because the number of products offered for sale went down.

In a market economy, producers react to changing prices in just this way. Take oil as an example. If the price of oil falls, the producer may offer less for sale or even leave the market altogether if the price falls too low. If the price rises, the producer may offer more oil for sale to take advantage of the better prices.

It makes no difference whether we are talking about an individual supply curve or a market supply curve. In either case, a change in quantity supplied *only* takes place if there is a change in price. Also, a change in quantity supplied will not shift the supply curve to the left or the right—only the amount of output offered for sale along an original supply curve is affected by the change in price.

✓ **READING PROGRESS CHECK**

Synthesizing How might a producer of bicycles adjust quantity supplied when prices decrease?

Change in Supply

GUIDING QUESTION What might happen to make a producer decrease the supply of a product?

Sometimes something happens to cause a **change in supply**, a situation where suppliers offer different amounts of a product for sale at all possible prices in the market.

change in supply different amounts offered for sale at each and every possible price in the market; shift of the supply curve

THE GLOBAL ECONOMY & YOU

The Global Economy and Your Cup of Coffee

Have you ever noticed that the price of a cup of coffee at your favorite coffee shop changes? Coffee beans are a major product in the global marketplace. In the world market, the value of coffee beans is second to the value of oil. Colombia is the second largest country producing coffee beans (after Brazil), and the United States is a major importer of Colombian coffee beans.

The price change in your local coffee shop is based on the supply of coffee beans, which in turn influences world coffee bean prices. Because coffee beans are an agricultural product, there are many variables in the coffee bean market. Agricultural products are susceptible to many problems outside of the farmer's control. In the last few years, for example, Colombia's coffee bean growers have experienced many setbacks. Weather-related problems, such as heavy rains, have affected crops. Growers cannot control the weather. Another problem is that disease attacked the coffee bean crops. Both of these problems led to a decrease in the supply of Colombian coffee beans. A decrease in supply in an agricultural product usually means an increase in price. Since the United States is a large importer of Colombian coffee beans, consumers at U.S. coffee shops have felt the effects of these agricultural setbacks.

▲ **CRITICAL THINKING**
Hypothesizing Weather affects coffee bean crops; farmers cannot control the weather. What effect do you think climate change could have on coffee output?

connected.mcgraw-hill.com **Supply** 131

CHAPTER 5, LESSON 1
What Is Supply?

C1 Critical Thinking Skills

Emphasizing quantity supplied **Ask:** *What causes a change in quantity supplied?* (a change in the price of the product) *What do you think will cause a change in supply?* (something other than price)

C2 Critical Thinking Skills

Analyzing changes in supply Ask students to find a news story about a nonprice change in supply—an increase or a decrease—of a basic resource, such as oil or wheat. Have them explain the cause(s) for the change and analyze how the change will affect price. Then ask students to identify businesses whose costs may be affected by the change.
BL Verbal/Linguistic

INTERACTIVE FEATURE

The Global Economy & You

Evaluating the global economy and coffee Have students view the Global Economy & You feature. **Ask:** *In your experience, how has the price of a cup of coffee changed in the past year or so?* (Responses should include when and where students have purchased coffee as well as changes in prices. Students who are not coffee drinkers may instead mention the experiences of friends or family members.) *How do you think the price of the cup of coffee you buy at the local coffee shop is affected by the global market for coffee?* (It is directly tied to the supply and price of coffee beans on the global market.) *What affects the supply of coffee beans?* (many variables, including weather and disease of the plants) Have students research online the price of coffee in the United States in the past year and create a graph showing their findings. **BL** Visual/Spatial, Logical/Mathematical

---

ANSWERS, p. 131

✓ **READING PROGRESS CHECK** A producer of bicycles might make a change in quantity supplied and offer fewer bicycles for sale.

CRITICAL THINKING
Weather-related problems could reduce coffee output, which would affect coffee prices.

Supply **131**

CHAPTER 5, LESSON 1
What Is Supply?

C Critical Thinking Skills

Predicting movement of supply curves Organize students into teams of three to play the Supply Curve Game. Choose two teams and give each team two flashcards—one saying LEFT and the other saying RIGHT. Present scenarios such as the following: If a new tax is placed on DVDs, will the supply curve for DVDs shift left or right? *(left)* If new technology leads to an easier way to manufacture DVDs, will the supply curve for DVDs shift left or right? *(right)* Team members should display their flashcards with the correct answer. If any team member displays the flashcard incorrectly, that team is disqualified and a new team joins the game. Continue the game until all teams have competed. **Interpersonal**

R Reading Skills

Examining cost of resources Ask: **How does the cost of resources affect supply?** *(When the cost of resources decreases, supply increases. When the cost of resources increases, supply decreases.)* Have students create an illustration that reflects how the cost of resources affects supply. **AL** **Visual/Spatial**

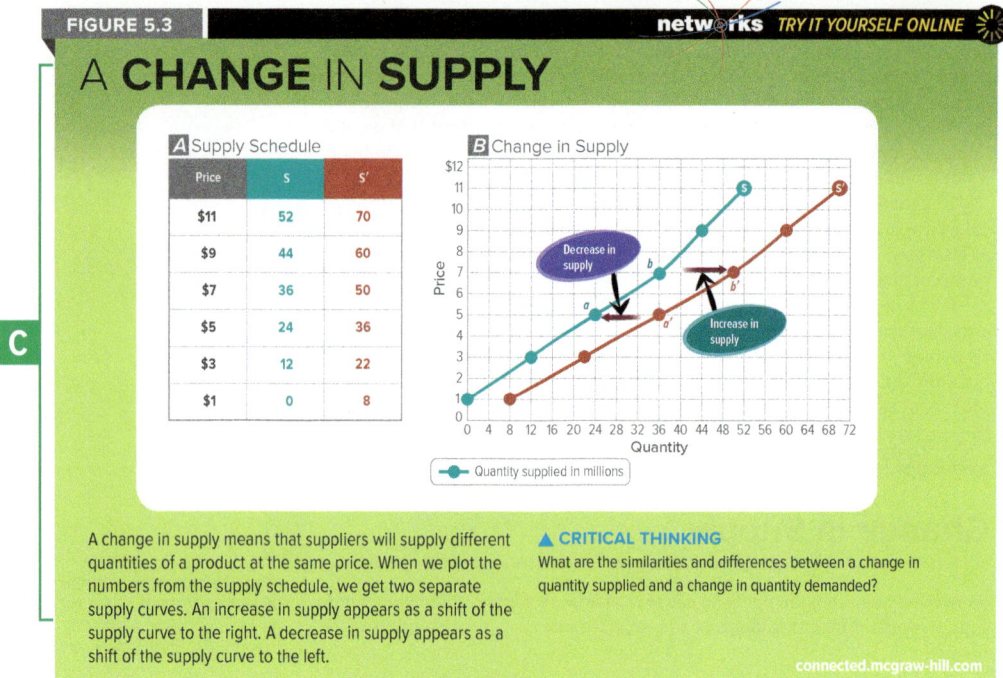

FIGURE 5.3
A CHANGE IN SUPPLY

A change in supply means that suppliers will supply different quantities of a product at the same price. When we plot the numbers from the supply schedule, we get two separate supply curves. An increase in supply appears as a shift of the supply curve to the right. A decrease in supply appears as a shift of the supply curve to the left.

▲ **CRITICAL THINKING**
What are the similarities and differences between a change in quantity supplied and a change in quantity demanded?

Comparing a Change in Quantity Supplied to a Change in Supply

The change in quantity supplied in Figure 5.3 is not the same as the change in supply. This is because the change in quantity supplied occurs only when there is a change in price. When we have a change in supply, we are looking at situations where all quantities change even though the price remains the same.

For example, the supply schedule in the figure shows that producers are now willing to offer more burritos for sale at every price. Where 24 million burritos were offered at a price of $5, now there are 36 million offered. Where 36 million were offered at a price of $7 before, 50 million are now offered, and so on for every price that could prevail in the market.

When both old and new quantities supplied are plotted in the form of a graph, it appears as if the supply curve has shifted to the right, showing an *increase in supply*. For a *decrease in supply* to occur, fewer products would be offered for sale at all possible prices, and so the supply curve would shift to the left.

Factors that Can Cause a Change in Supply

Changes in supply, whether they are increases or decreases, can occur for the reasons discussed below.

- **Cost of Resources** A change in the cost of productive inputs such as land, labor, and capital can cause a change in supply. Supply might increase because of a lower cost of inputs such as labor or packaging, enabling suppliers to produce more at every price—thereby shifting the supply curve to the right.
  An increase in the cost of inputs has the opposite effect. A higher cost of inputs would force producers to offer fewer products for sale at every price—shifting the supply curve to the left.

---

networks *Online Teaching Options*

GRAPHS

Change in Supply

Understanding a shift of the supply curve Have students view Figure 5.3 A Change in Supply. Tell students that a change in supply means that different amounts of a product are offered for each and every possible price in the market.
Ask: **Looking at the graph, what happens to the supply curve if there is a change in supply?** *(The entire supply curve shifts.)* Lead students to consider what they think causes a change in supply. Have students make a list of those causes, and come back to the list during class discussion. **Verbal Linguistic**

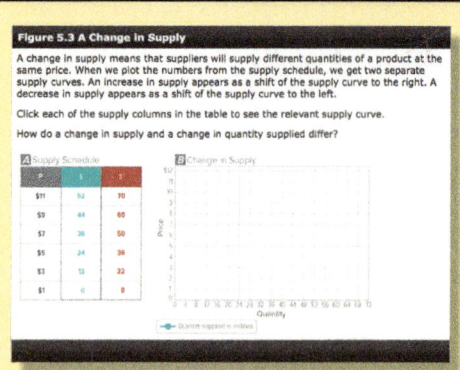

ANSWERS, p. 132

CRITICAL THINKING
Similarities: Both are caused by a change in price.
Differences: a change in quantity <u>supplied</u> is a movement along (up or down) a stationary supply curve; it is not a movement of the supply curve. A change in quantity <u>demanded</u> is a movement along (up or down) a stationary demand curve; it is not a movement of the demand curve.

- **Productivity** Productivity increases whenever more output is produced with the same amount of inputs. When management trains or motivates its workers, productivity usually goes up because more is produced with the same amount of inputs—resulting in a supply curve that shifts to the right.

  But if workers fall behind on training, become unmotivated, or are unhappy, then productivity could decrease. Fewer goods would be produced at every possible price—shifting the supply curve to the left.

- **Technology** The introduction of a new machine or industrial process can lower the cost of production, which increases productivity. For example, improvements in jet aircraft fuel efficiencies have lowered the fuel cost of air passenger service. When production costs go down, a firm can produce more at every possible price—thereby shifting its supply curve to the right.

  New technologies do not always work at first, of course, and so at first the supply curve may briefly shift to the left. However, firms expect new technologies to be beneficial, or they would not have adopted them in the first place.

- **Taxes** Firms view taxes as a cost of production, just like raw materials and labor. This is one reason why businesses almost always lobby for lower taxes. If a company pays fewer taxes, it can produce more at each possible price—shifting its supply curve to the right.

  However, if taxes go up, its production costs go up and it will produce less at each and every price—thereby shifting its supply curve to the left.

- **Subsidies** A **subsidy** is a payment to an individual, business, or other group to encourage or protect a certain type of economic activity. Today, many farmers in the milk, cotton, corn, wheat, sugar, and soybean industries receive subsidies to support their incomes—which shifts the supply curves of their products to the right.

  When subsidies are repealed, production costs go up, and firms will either leave the market entirely or produce less at each possible price—something that shifts their supply curves to the left.

- **Government Regulations** If government decides to reduce its regulations on business, production costs go down and firms are able to produce more output at all possible prices—thereby shifting individual supply curves to the right.

  More often, however, government increases its regulations, which raise a typical business's cost of production. For example, when the government requires new auto safety features such as air bags, emission controls, or higher collision safety standards, cars cost more to produce. Manufacturers then adjust to the higher production costs by producing fewer cars at every possible price—shifting the market supply curve to the left.

- **Number of Sellers** Most markets are fairly active, with firms entering and leaving all the time. You often see this where you live, especially when one store closes and another opens in its place. Whenever an industry grows because more firms are coming in, the market supply curve shifts to the right. Or if the industry is shrinking because firms are leaving, fewer products are offered for sale at the same prices as before, which shifts the market supply curve to the left. A change in the number of sellers is different from the other factors listed above, because this is the only factor that can affect the market supply curve without affecting the supply curve of any individual firm.

- **Expectations** Expectations can affect the decisions a firm makes. These expectations may affect anything from the cost of inputs to the demand for the firm's products. Unless we know more about these expectations, however, it is not possible to make any generalizations about the way in which they affect a firm's supply curve.

subsidy government payment to encourage or protect a certain economic activity

EXPLORING THE ESSENTIAL QUESTION

How do government regulations affect supply and demand? In a paragraph, explain how a government regulation to increase bicycle safety might affect supply and demand. The new government regulation requires bicycle manufacturers to put a chain guard on bicycles they make. Would that affect the supply of bicycles? Give reasons for your answer.

Supply 133

VIDEO WORKSHEET

Bad Weather

Evaluating how weather can affect resources and supply
Have the class view the video. **Ask: What caused the decrease in the world cotton supply?** *(rain and flooding)* Discuss the causal chain resulting from bad weather: a decrease in cotton as a resource, which causes a shortage and an increase in its price; an increase in the cost of producing cotton cloth (and other goods dependent on cotton), which forces producers to offer fewer products for sale at every price; which moves the supply curve to the left.
Logical/Mathematical

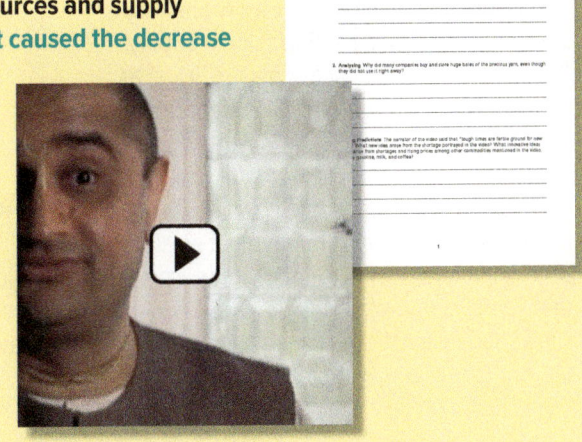

CHAPTER 5, LESSON 1
What Is Supply?

R Reading Skills

Examining productivity Ask: How can management increase productivity? *(by training and motivating workers)* **AL**

C1 Critical Thinking Skills

Explaining changes in supply Ask students to explain what would happen to the supply of high-performance tires in the following situations: (1) The cost of rubber—an important raw material used in the making of tires—increases. *(Supply decreases because the cost of inputs has increased.)* (2) Several new businesses enter the high-performance tire market. *(Supply increases because as more and more firms enter an industry, greater quantities of the product are supplied at each and every price.)* (3) Government imposes a tax on automobile parts—including tires. *(Supply decreases because taxes cause the cost of production to rise.)* (4) New technology increases efficiency in the tire-making process. *(Supply increases because increased efficiency means lower production costs.)*
BL Logical/Mathematical

C2 Critical Thinking Skills

Examining number of sellers Choose five students to represent suppliers in the music industry, and have them hum. Then add two more students to the group and ask what change occurred. *(Suppliers were added, and the humming became greater.)* Create a graph on the board and have a volunteer chart the change, noting that the market supply curve shifted right. Then have some students leave the group of suppliers. Ask the class how the change affected the supply of hums offered for sale. *(It decreased.)* Have a volunteer chart the change, noting that the market supply curve shifted left.
ELL Auditory/Musical

ANSWERS, p. 133

EXPLORING THE ESSENTIAL QUESTION

It probably would affect the supply of bicycles because production costs would increase. The manufacturer has to re-tool the bicycle-making process to add the chain guard. That takes time, so the supply of bicycles would be affected. This plus the cost of the chain guard itself would increase production costs. The manufacturer would pass this cost on to the consumer and undoubtedly, anticipating a decrease in demand due to price increase, reduce the overall production of bicycles.

Supply 133

CHAPTER 5, LESSON 1
What Is Supply?

W Writing Skills

Defining supply elasticity Have students define *supply elasticity* in their own words. *(Possible answer: Elastic supply means a change in price leads to a larger change in output. Unit elastic means any change in price causes a proportional change in quantity supplied. Inelastic means a change in price causes a smaller change in quantity supplied.)* Have students present their definitions in a class discussion. **AL Verbal/Linguistic**

C Critical Thinking Skills

Demonstrating elasticity Bring three different strengths of rubber bands to class. Demonstrate elastic supply with the more relaxed band, adding that there is a larger increase in output. Demonstrate inelastic supply with the tightest band, adding that there is a smaller increase in output. Demonstrate unit elastic with the medium-strength band, adding that the change in output is similar in proportion to price increase. Have students make a drawing of the three different strengths of rubber bands and label them. **ELL Visual/Spatial**

Making Connections

Inelastic Holiday Supply Toy manufacturers may face a temporary inelasticity of supply if a toy turns out to be more popular than expected during the holiday buying season and it cannot be manufactured quickly enough to satisfy the seasonal demand. That was the situation in December 1996, when the Tickle Me Elmo doll turned out to be the hottest toy of the season. The toy, regularly priced at $23.99, was advertised in newspapers for as much as $500. Some customers said they would pay *any* price to buy the toy in time for Christmas. Ask students to think of other toys or products whose supply was inelastic during a holiday season.

ANSWERS, p. 134

✓ **READING PROGRESS CHECK** because many individual suppliers make up the market supply

CRITICAL THINKING the nature of production and the speed at which the producer can react to price changes

---

As you can see, there are many factors that can cause a change in supply and consequently cause the market supply curve to shift to the left or to the right. However, *only a change in price*—which was discussed in the previous section—can cause a change in quantity supplied, which is a movement along a stationary supply curve.

✓ **READING PROGRESS CHECK**

Explaining Why do factors that cause a change in individual supply also affect the market supply curve?

Elasticity of Supply

GUIDING QUESTION *How does the production of a product affect the elasticity of supply?*

supply elasticity responsiveness of quantity supplied to a change in price

Just as demand has elasticity, so does supply. **Supply elasticity** is a measure of the degree to which the quantity supplied responds to a change in price.

As you might imagine, there is very little difference between supply and demand elasticities. If quantities of a product are being purchased, the concept is demand elasticity. If quantities of a product are being produced and offered for sale, the concept is supply elasticity.

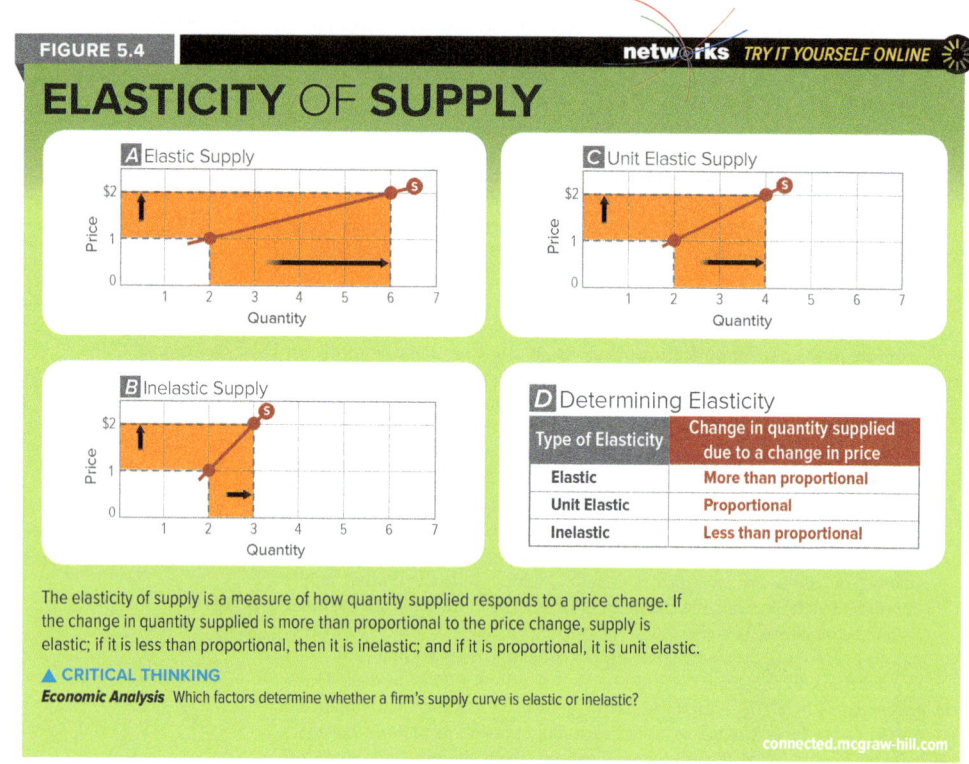

FIGURE 5.4 ELASTICITY OF SUPPLY

The elasticity of supply is a measure of how quantity supplied responds to a price change. If the change in quantity supplied is more than proportional to the price change, supply is elastic; if it is less than proportional, then it is inelastic; and if it is proportional, it is unit elastic.

▲ **CRITICAL THINKING**
Economic Analysis Which factors determine whether a firm's supply curve is elastic or inelastic?

---

networks Online Teaching Options

GRAPHS

Elasticity of Supply

Analyzing supply elasticity on graphs Have students view Figure 5.4 Elasticity of Supply. Tell students that supply has elasticity just as demand has elasticity. Have a student read the definition of supply elasticity in the text *(a measure of the degree to which the quantity supplied responds to a change in price)*. Divide the class into three groups and assign one type of elasticity to each group. Ask each group to create a presentation using a hypothetical product that illustrates the type of supply elasticity they were assigned. Require each group to include a graph that shows supply elasticity, unit elasticity, or inelasticity. Have groups share their presentations. **BL Logical/Mathematical**

Three Cases of Supply Elasticity

Supply and demand each have three cases of elasticity. The three examples of supply elasticity are illustrated in **Figure 5.4**. In each case, we look to see how the quantity supplied, the dependent variable, responds to a change in price, which is the independent variable.

- **Elastic Supply** The supply curve in **Panel A** is elastic because the change in price causes a proportionally larger change in quantity supplied. Doubling the price from $1 to $2 causes the quantity supplied to triple from two to six units. Again, the prices and numbers are unrealistically simple, but that is to make the diagrams easier to understand.
- **Inelastic Supply Panel B** shows an inelastic supply curve. In this case, a change in price causes a proportionally smaller change in quantity supplied. When the price doubles from $1 to $2, a 100 percent increase, the quantity supplied goes up only 50 percent, or from two units to three units.
- **Unit Elastic Supply Panel C** shows a unit elastic supply curve. Here, a doubling, or a 100 percent change, in price causes a proportional change in the quantity supplied. As the price goes from $1 to $2, the quantity supplied also doubles.

What Determines Supply Elasticity?

The elasticity of a producer's supply curve depends on the nature of its production. If a firm can adjust to new prices quickly, then supply is likely to be elastic. If the nature of production is such that adjustments take much longer, then supply is more likely to be inelastic.

The supply curve for nuclear power, for example, is inelastic in the short run. No matter what price is being offered, electric utilities will find it difficult to increase nuclear power output because of the huge amount of engineering, capital, and technology needed—not to mention the issue of extensive government regulation—before nuclear production can be increased.

However, the supply curve is likely to be elastic for many toys, candy, and other products that can be made quickly without large amounts of capital and skilled labor. If consumers are willing to pay more for any of these products, most producers will be able to gear up quickly to significantly increase production.

Unlike demand elasticity, only production considerations determine supply elasticity. If a firm can react quickly to a changing price, then supply is likely to be elastic. If the firm takes longer to react to a change in price, then supply is likely to be inelastic.

✓ **READING PROGRESS CHECK**

Comparing How are the elasticities of supply and demand similar? How do they differ?

LESSON 1 REVIEW

Reviewing Vocabulary
1. *Defining* Explain in your own words the term *Law of Supply*.

Using Your Notes
2. *Summarizing* Use your notes to identify the costs of producing a product.

Answering the Guiding Questions
3. *Explaining* Why do supply and demand curves slope in opposite directions?
4. *Evaluating* What might happen to make a producer decrease his or her supply of a product?
5. *Describing* How is the elasticity of supply affected by the way a product is produced?

Writing About Economics
6. *Informative/Explanatory* Research an example of an item with decreasing supply and increasing demand that occurred in the United States within the last five years. What caused the supply of the item to decrease? When demand increased, what happened to the price of the item? What is the current status of the supply and demand of the item? Write a two-page essay about your findings.

connected.mcgraw-hill.com *Supply* 135

CHAPTER 5, LESSON 1
What Is Supply?

C Critical Thinking Skills

Identifying examples of firms with various supply elasticity Ask students to think of types of businesses that experience elastic supply *(coffee shops, copy centers, restaurants)* and inelastic supply *(nuclear power plants, auto manufacturers)*. Then have them explain why a coffee shop, for example, can adjust supply more quickly than a large manufacturer. *(Every day, as more and more customers arrive, the owner can buy more beans, filters, water, and cups to meet consumer demand. She can even hire more workers quickly and increase quantity supplied. It takes much longer for a large manufacturer to adjust production amounts.)* **Verbal/Linguistic**

CLOSE & REFLECT

W Writing Skills

Summarizing the Law of Supply Have students select a business and write an essay describing a hypothetical example of how that business can be affected by the Law of Supply. Remind students to use standard spelling in their essays.

ANSWERS, p. 135

✓ **READING PROGRESS CHECK** The elasticities of supply and demand are similar in that both are a change in quantity demanded or supplied proportional (or not) to price. Unlike demand elasticity, however, supply elasticity is determined only by production issues. Demand elasticity is determined by how much income is used, whether there are substitutes available, and whether the purchase can be delayed.

LESSON 1 REVIEW ANSWERS

Reviewing Vocabulary
1. Student answers should include that the Law of Supply means suppliers will normally offer more for sale at high prices and less at lower prices.

Using Your Notes
2. Production costs include the costs of land, labor, capital, technology, taxes, and government regulations.

Answering the Guiding Questions
3. They slope in opposite directions because high prices cause the supply to go up. But high prices cause the demand to go down.
4. A decrease in supply may be caused by an increased cost in resources; low worker productivity; adjustments to new technology; high taxes; few or no subsidies; increased government regulations; a reduction in the number of sellers; and fearful expectations.
5. It depends on the type of product. If a company can adjust production to new prices quickly, then there is elasticity of supply. If the company cannot make production adjustments quickly, then the supply is likely to be inelastic.

Writing About Economics
6. Students should identify an item and provide credible sources for the information they include in their essay. Encourage students to include a graph or table in their essay. Student essays should answer each of the questions listed.

Supply 135

CHAPTER 5, LESSON 2
The Theory of Production

ENGAGE

C Critical Thinking Skills

🔔 **Predicting how to measure the production function of a business** Before students begin the lesson, ask them to write a list of business elements that might be part of measuring the production function of a business. **Ask: Why do you think labor and the technology used in production are important in measuring the production function?** *(They are resource inputs that affect quantity supplied.)* Then have students predict what they will learn in the text about measuring the production function. Ask students to share their lists. Remind students to check their predictions as they read the text. **Verbal/Linguistic**

English Language Proficiency

Advanced High Before students read the production function text with challenging language, explain how asking and answering questions can help enhance and confirm understanding of text. Have them preview the title, headings, visuals, and vocabulary of the lesson. Model generating questions before reading. Use a think-aloud to model how to pause during reading, pose a question, and continue reading to find the answer. Provide a graphic such as a QAR chart to use before and during reading. Have students discuss answers to their questions with a peer.

ANSWERS, p. 136

ESSENTIAL QUESTION ACTIVITY

Students may understand that labor is usually the easiest factor of production to change—to increase or decrease. Have students consider the difficulty of changing the factor of land (resources) in a bread factory, or changing the factor of capital in a steel mill.

TAKING NOTES
Production time: short term, long term
Measurements: marginal product, total product

Interact with these digital assets and others in lesson 2
✓ INTERACTIVE IMAGE
  Automation: Unemployment vs. Profitability
✓ BIOGRAPHY
  Daniel Akerson
✓ SELF-CHECK QUIZ
✓ VIDEO

networks
TRY IT YOURSELF ONLINE

LESSON 2
The Theory of Production

Reading Help Desk

Academic Vocabulary
- hypothetical
- contributes

Content Vocabulary
- production function
- short run
- long run
- total product
- marginal product
- stages of production
- diminishing returns

TAKING NOTES:

Key Ideas and Details
ACTIVITY Use the graphic organizer below to describe the production function.

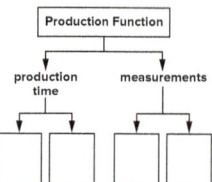

ESSENTIAL QUESTION

Why is the production function useful for making business decisions?

Companies change the mix of their productive inputs all the time—and you may have been part of this without even knowing it! For example, have you or one of your friends ever worked in the fast food industry? How many times have you or your friend been called in to work when the business got busy, or been sent home when sales slowed?

In a paragraph or two, explain why labor is often considered a variable factor of production. Are any other factors of production as easy to change? Why or why not?

The Production Function

GUIDING QUESTION *Why is marginal product an important concept for business owners to understand?*

C | Production is usually illustrated with a **production function**—a figure that shows how total output changes when the amount of a single variable input (usually labor) changes while all other inputs are held constant. The production function can be illustrated with a schedule, such as the one in columns one and two of **Panel A** of **Figure 5.5**, or with a graph like the one in **Panel B**.

Both panels list **hypothetical** output as the number of workers changes from zero to 12. According to the numbers in Panel A, if no workers are used, there is no output. If the number of workers goes up by one, output rises to seven. Add another worker, and total output rises to 20. Use three workers, and total output rises to 38, and so on. Next, we use this information to construct the production function that appears as the graph in Panel B, where the number of variable inputs is shown on the horizontal axis, and total production is shown on the vertical axis.

The Production Period

When economists analyze production, they focus on the **short run**, a production period so brief that only the amount of the variable input can be

---

networks **Online Teaching Options**

BELLRINGER

Theory of Production

Analyzing the theory of production Use this activity to reveal students' prior knowledge of the theory of production. Have students view the Bellringer and answer these questions: **What are some inputs that change the production of an item?** *(the cost of resources such as the cost of land, labor and capital; new technology; and taxes and government regulations.)* **In analyzing production, does the change in the total number of workers (labor) affect a short-run production period or a long-run production period?** *(short-run production period)* **What are some elements that might be changed in a long-run production period?** *(Long-run changes are factors such as changes in the technology used in production or the acquisition or sale of land used for production.)* Have students discuss their answers. **AL Verbal/Linguistic**

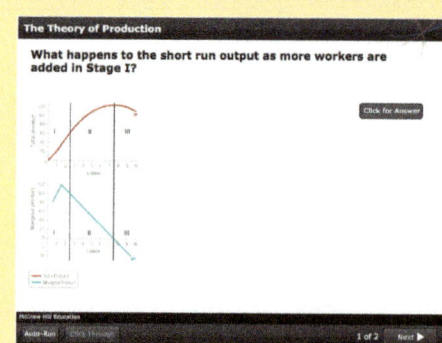

changed. The production function in Figure 5.5 reflects the short run because only the total number of workers changes. No changes occur in the amount of machinery, technology, or land used. Thus, any change in output must be caused by a change in the number of workers.

Other changes take place in the **long run**, a production period long enough for the firm to adjust the quantities of *all* its productive resources, including capital.

For example, a firm that reduces its labor force today may also have to close down some factories later on. These factory closings are long-run changes because the amount of capital used for production changes slowly.

Total Product
The second column in Panel A of Figure 5.5 shows **total product**, or the total output produced by the firm. As you read down the column, you will see that zero units of total output are produced with zero workers, seven are produced with one worker, and so on.

Again, this is a short-run relationship, because the figure assumes that only the amount of labor varies while the amount of other resources used remains unchanged. Now that we have total product, we can easily see how we get our next measure.

Marginal Product
The measure of output shown in the third column of Panel A in Figure 5.5 is an important concept in economics. The measure is **marginal product**, the *extra* output or change in total product caused by adding one more unit of variable input.

production function graphic portrayal showing how a change in the amount of a single variable input affects total output

hypothetical assumed but not proven

short run production period so short that only variable inputs (usually labor) can be changed

long run production period long enough to change amount of variable and fixed inputs used in production

total product total output or production by a firm

marginal product extra output due to the addition of one more unit of input

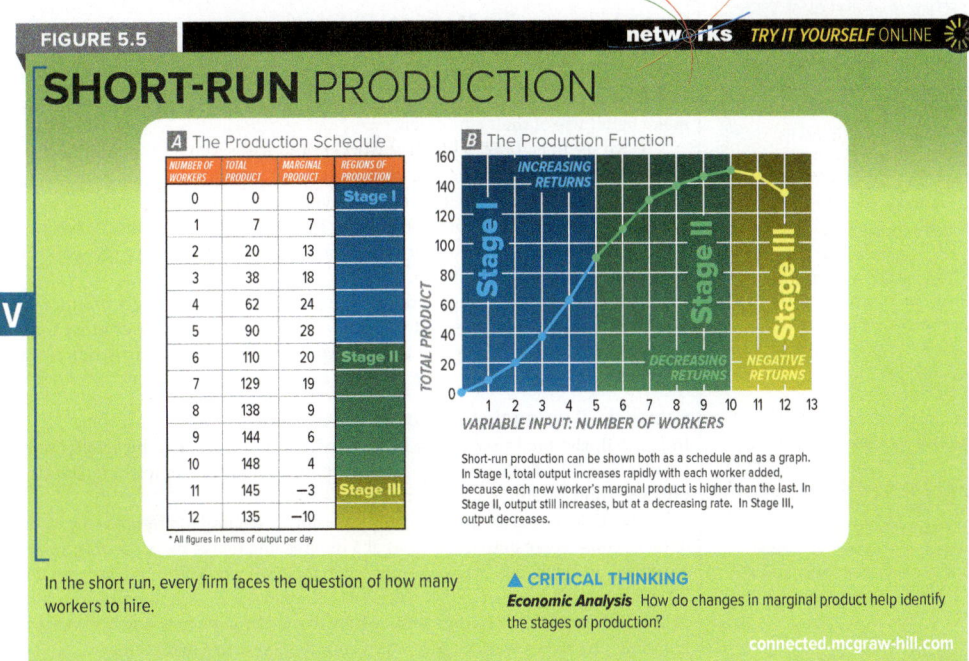

FIGURE 5.5 SHORT-RUN PRODUCTION

In the short run, every firm faces the question of how many workers to hire.

▲ **CRITICAL THINKING**
Economic Analysis How do changes in marginal product help identify the stages of production?

CHAPTER 5, LESSON 2
The Theory of Production

C1 Critical Thinking Skills

Relating labor to the short run Ask: **Why is a short-run production function useful for measuring effects of changes in labor?** *(Output resulting from changes in labor can be evaluated using shorter periods, such as on a daily basis. Output resulting from changes in other variables, such as land or capital, requires longer periods of evaluation.)* **AL** Logical/Mathematical, Verbal/Linguistic

C2 Critical Thinking Skills

Determining the effect of changing one variable Tell students it is important to understand the interconnectedness of variables in a business. Write this question on the board: *How does changing one variable affect the other variable inputs of a company?* To reinforce the concept of changing just one variable, have students draw a before-and-after diagram. The "before" diagram should show 3 units of labor, 5 units of land, and 6 units of capital. The "after" diagram should have a change in the number of units of just one of the categories—land, labor, or capital. Students should realize that changing one variable will eventually cause the other variables to change because output has changed. **BL** Verbal/Linguistic

V Visual Skills

Creating a production function Ask: **Why is the use of the production function important in business?** *(It allows businesses to gauge whether additional input will result in extra output.)* Have students make up a hypothetical business and create a production function schedule for that business. **BL** Logical/Mathematical

---

GRAPHS

Short-Run Production

Understanding returns in the production function Display Figure 5.5. Explain that few decisions in life are "all or nothing" decisions. For example, students do not ask themselves how many movies they want to see in their lifetime. They decide whether they want to see *one* movie *tonight*. Point out that, in a similar way, most economic decisions are about whether we should have "one more" of something. Marginal analysis describes how people make decisions based on "one more" unit. Explain that in economics, *marginal* means "one more," or "extra," or "additional." Point out the Marginal Product column in the production schedule, and explain that firms look at this column, not Total Product, to decide how many workers to hire in order to maximize profits. Walk students through the stages on both the schedule and graph. **BL** Verbal/Linguistic

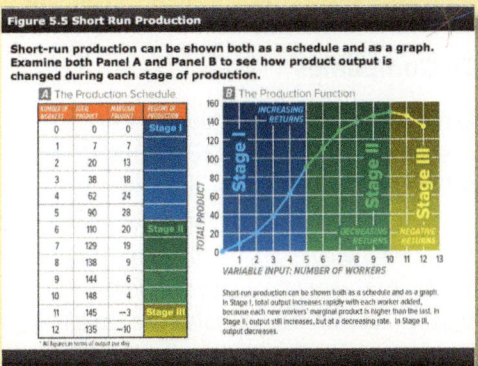

ANSWERS, p. 137

CRITICAL THINKING When each worker's marginal product is increasing, the company is in Stage I. When it is increasing, but at a decreasing rate, the company is in Stage II. When there are negative returns in marginal product, the company is in Stage III.

CHAPTER 5, LESSON 2
The Theory of Production

C Critical Thinking Skills

Determining cause and effect Have students work in small groups to formulate an answer to the following question: How does a change in inputs affect production? Encourage students to create schedules or graphs to illustrate their answer. Have each small group present their answer to the class.
BL Visual/Spatial

W Writing Skills

Describing stages of production Have students write several paragraphs describing how the three stages of production are different. Remind students to use economics-related terminology correctly. After students have written their paragraphs, put three columns on the board identified as Stage 1, Stage 2, and Stage 3. Fill in the columns with suggestions from students in a class discussion.
AL Verbal/Linguistic, Interpersonal

V Visual Skills

Illustrating stages of production Have students choose a specific product and create a visual presentation depicting how the marginal product changes in the three stages of production. Ask students to explain their visuals to the class.
AL Visual/Spatial

BIOGRAPHY

Daniel Akerson
GENERAL MOTORS CEO (1948–)

Daniel Akerson led one of the greatest turnarounds in American business history. After decades as the world's leading car manufacturer, General Motors had grown oversized and inefficient. When it fell into bankruptcy in 2009, the U.S. government lent the carmaker $49.5 billion to keep it afloat. In 2010, Akerson was named GM's CEO and given the task of turning the carmaker around.

Before this, Akerson had worked in telecommunications and private equity, but never in the automotive industry. Akerson explained, "It's all about leadership. I don't think you have to be a subject-matter expert."

Tough decisions were made, including the decision to fire 47,000 people who could no longer be used productively. Akerson fought to change GM's culture and increase efficiencies. By 2012, GM had profits of $4.9 billion.

▲ **CRITICAL THINKING**
Making Decisions In order to survive, GM closed 14 plants and fired 47,000 workers. As it returned to profitability and sales increased, workers had to be hired back. At what point would Akerson decide that no more workers could be added to the workforce at a particular plant?

As we see in the figure, the marginal product, or extra output, of adding the first worker is seven. Likewise, the marginal product of adding the second worker is 13. This is because seven units of output are produced with the first worker, and 20 units are produced by adding the second worker. So, the extra or *marginal* output of adding the second worker is 13. If you look down the column, you will see that the marginal product for every worker is different, with some even being negative.

Finally, note that the sum of the marginal products is equal to the total product. For example, the marginal product of the first and second workers is 7 plus 13, or 20—the same as the total product for two workers. Likewise, the sum of the marginal products of the first three workers is 7 plus 13 plus 18, or 38—the total output for three workers.

☑ **READING PROGRESS CHECK**

Analyzing Why does the production function represent short-run production?

Stages of Production

GUIDING QUESTION How do companies use the stages of production to determine the most profitable number of workers to hire?

In the short run, every firm faces the question of how many workers to hire. To answer this question, let us take another look at Figure 5.5, which shows three distinct **stages of production**: Stage I, which is called increasing returns; Stage II, which is called diminishing returns; and Stage III, which is called negative returns.

Each of these stages gets its name from the way marginal product changes as more workers are added.

Stage I—Increasing Marginal Returns

Stage I of the production function is the phase in which the marginal product of each additional worker increases. This happens because as more workers are added, they can cooperate with each other or specialize in certain operations to make better use of their equipment.

As we see in Figure 5.5, the first worker produces seven units of output. The second is even more productive, with a marginal product of 13 units, bringing total production to 20. As long as each new worker **contributes** more to total output than the worker before, total output rises at an increasing rate. According to the figure, the first five workers are in Stage I, because these are the workers with increasing marginal returns.

When it comes to hiring workers, companies do not knowingly produce in Stage I. When a firm learns that each new worker increases output more than the last, it is motivated to hire yet another worker. As a result, the firm soon finds itself producing in the next stage, Stage II, of production.

Stage II—Decreasing Marginal Returns

In Stage II, the total production keeps growing, but it does so by smaller and smaller amounts. Each additional worker, then, is making a diminishing, but still positive, contribution to total output.

Stage II illustrates the principle of decreasing or **diminishing returns**—the stage of production where output increases at a diminishing rate as more variable inputs are added. In Figure 5.5, Stage II begins when the sixth worker is hired, because the 20-unit marginal product of that worker is less than the 28-unit marginal product of the fifth worker. The stage ends when the tenth worker is added, because marginal products are no longer positive for workers after that point.

138

---

networks — Online Teaching Options

VIDEO | **WORKSHEETS**

Oil Companies

Assessing issues Have students view the video. **Ask: Why were oil companies not drilling in the existing leases, and therefore limiting supply, as noted in the video?** *(At the time, big oil companies stated that oil reserves were not available in the existing lease areas. Officials believed oil companies were limiting the supply to create shortages and therefore keep prices high.)* Have students discuss how oil companies handle supply. **Ask: Do the companies' actions aid or hinder the U.S. consumer of oil?** **BL** Verbal/Linguistic

ANSWERS, p. 138

☑ **READING PROGRESS CHECK** The production function illustrates the changes of one variable in a brief period, or in the short run.

CRITICAL THINKING
Akerson would make that decision when the marginal product began to slow or decrease.

"I DON'T UNDERSTAND IT... TWO WORKERS CAN MAKE TWICE AS MUCH PRODUCT AS ONE WORKER, BUT TWO THOUSAND WORKERS AREN'T MAKING ANYTHING!"

This cartoon shows an exaggerated example of negative marginal returns.

◀ **CRITICAL THINKING**
Making Connections Which stage of production was the factory owner experiencing when he went from one worker to two workers? How can you tell?

Stage III—Negative Marginal Returns

If the firm hires too many workers, they will get in each other's way or otherwise interfere with production, causing total output to fall. Stage III, then, is where the marginal product of each additional worker is negative. For example, the 11th worker has a marginal product of *minus* three, and the 12th's is *minus* 10, causing output to fall.

EXPLORING THE ESSENTIAL QUESTION
Most firms operate within Stage II, but is this always the best choice? How would the diminishing returns of adding each extra employee affect what the business must charge for each item or service?

Because most companies would not hire workers if their negative marginal return combined to negatively affect the company's total production, the number of workers a firm hires will only be found in Stage II. As we will see in the next section, the exact number of workers to be hired also depends on the revenue from the sale of the output. For now, however, we can say that the firm with the production function shown in Figure 5.5 will hire from 6 to 10 workers.

✓ **READING PROGRESS CHECK**

Analyzing Why would a firm be motivated to hire more workers than are found in Stage I of the production function?

stages of production phases of production that consist of increasing, decreasing, and negative returns

contributes gives time, money, or effort

diminishing returns stage of production where output increases at a decreasing rate as more units of variable input are added

---

LESSON 2 REVIEW

Reviewing Vocabulary
1. *Explaining* Why don't economists consider the effects of changes to technology when focusing on the short run?
2. *Calculating* When does marginal product equal total product?

Using Your Notes
3. *Summarizing* Using your notes, explain why a manager needs to know both total product and marginal product when making business decisions.

Answering the Guiding Questions
4. *Explaining* Why is marginal product an important concept for business owners to understand?

5. *Analyzing* How can the stages of production be used to determine the most profitable number of workers to hire?

Writing About Economics
6. *Informative/Explanatory* Company XYZ has developed a new product that is selling briskly. The company has added several workers, and the chief operating officer has asked you whether even more workers should be hired. Create a hypothetical production function schedule or graph for this company and write a one-page essay explaining how this schedule demonstrates the value of knowing each worker's marginal product.

CHAPTER 5, LESSON 2
The Theory of Production

Making Connections

Productivity of Labor Productivity is measured in different ways. The productivity of labor is gauged by output per hour worked. Because a higher rate of output per hour worked will lead to increased profits, businesses are constantly seeking ways to boost labor productivity. The methods businesses use to achieve this goal include providing attractive working environments, offering pay incentives and bonuses, subsidizing further education so that workers gain new skills, investing in modern capital equipment, and building or purchasing larger, more efficient plants. Have students research and analyze a local business's costs and benefits in providing these incentives to increase labor productivity. Have students present the consequences of the business's economic decisions in a brief oral report.

CLOSE & REFLECT

W Writing Skills

Summarizing concepts Have students use their own words to write a summary of the production function including the concept of marginal production. Encourage students to share their summaries. Remind students that the most important economic concept for business managers to understand is that of marginal product.

ANSWERS, p. 139

CRITICAL THINKING
He was experiencing Stage I of production—increasing marginal returns—because the increased number of workers was causing a large increase in output.

EXPLORING THE ESSENTIAL QUESTION
Students should recognize that the principle of diminishing returns suggests that in Stage II, the cost of producing each item would be greater for each additional input and therefore the price charged would have to be increased. Some students may argue that the overall cost of other production factors, such as the fixed costs of a lease, supply and distribution chain, and utilities might alter this conclusion and make it more cost effective to add the extra employees despite the diminishing returns.

✓ **READING PROGRESS CHECK** A firm could still make more profit overall by hiring workers in Stage II of the production function. It is in Stage III that it becomes harmful to hire more workers because the marginal product becomes negative.

LESSON 2 REVIEW ANSWERS

Reviewing Vocabulary
1. Changes in technology cannot be made quickly, so they do not affect production in the short run.
2. Marginal product equals total product with the first worker.

Using Your Notes
3. Students should understand that a business manager wants to maximize total product. To do that efficiently, he or she must know how adding each extra unit of input affects marginal product and thereby how it contributes to total product.

Answering the Guiding Questions
4. As long as marginal product continues to rise, the business is operating profitably.
5. In Stages I and II, each additional worker hired continues to add to production, although returns are diminishing in Stage II. At Stage III, adding employees causes negative marginal returns.

Writing About Economics
6. Students should include a production function and how it demonstrates the relationship between hiring extra employees and marginal and total product.

CHAPTER 5
Debate

ENGAGE

C1 Critical Thinking Skills

Expressing opinions on multinational corporations Start a discussion about multinational corporations and ask students if they think these companies have a duty to keep their headquarters and base of operations in their home countries. Have students give reasons for their responses. Log the responses to note whether any students change their opinions after they read the feature. **Verbal/Linguistic**

TEACH & ASSESS

R Reading Skills

Researching government involvement Direct small groups to research actions taken by the executive or legislative branch of the federal government in the last three years to encourage multinational corporations to keep their manufacturing facilities in the United States. Have groups create a multimedia presentation focusing on one action and present it to the class. **BL Verbal/Linguistic**

C2 Critical Thinking Skills

Proposing solutions Have students view the graph "Where the Jobs Are." Ask: **Does the graph support the argument made by Professor Bhagwati?** *(No, it supports the argument made by Grove.)* Have students brainstorm solutions to the problem of multinational corporations moving jobs to other countries. Remind students that problem solving includes these steps: identify the problem, gather information, list and consider options, consider advantages and disadvantages, choose and implement a solution, and evaluate the effectiveness of the solution. **Logical/Mathematical**

English Language Proficiency

Intermediate As spoken language becomes increasingly complex and elaborated, provide linguistic support for students during class debates. Provide sentence frames that allow students with intermediate proficiency to answer questions about lesson content and contribute to the discussions.

Debates

C1 Do multinational corporations have a duty to keep their base of operations in their home countries?

A multinational corporation is a corporation that does business in more than one country. It sells products or services internationally, and often has offices or factories in different countries, choosing them on the basis of labor costs, tax advantages, and other criteria.

Multinational corporations have existed from the beginning of international trade and today number more than 40,000. Many have larger incomes than those of some of the host countries in which they do business. Although a well-established component of the global economy, multinationals are sometimes at the center of controversy because of their willingness to locate their bases of operation outside of their home countries, taking with them some of the taxes, jobs, and influence that they have at home and shifting them to another country.

YES Multinational companies that stay in their home country accomplish the following:

- CREATE MORE GOOD JOBS FOR FELLOW CITIZENS
- KEEP INVESTMENT DOLLARS AT HOME
- INCREASE COMPETITION WITHIN THE COUNTRY
- PAY MORE TAXES IN THE COUNTRY IN WHICH THEY BEGAN

"You could say, as many do, that shipping jobs overseas is no big deal because the high-value work—and much of the profits—remain in the U.S. That may well be so. But what kind of a society are we going to have if it consists of highly paid people doing high-value-added work—and masses of unemployed?"

—Andy Grove, former Chief Executive Officer of Intel

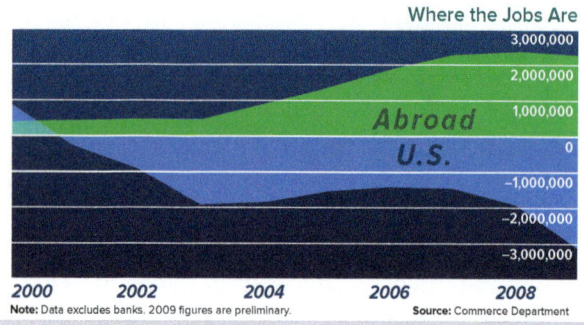

Where the Jobs Are
Note: Data excludes banks. 2009 figures are preliminary. Source: Commerce Department

140

---

networks Online Teaching Options

DEBATE

Debate: Do multinational corporations have a duty to keep their base of operations in their home countries?

Examining issues Have students view the Debate feature and read the text describing multinational corporations. Ask: **What is the controversy surrounding multinational corporations?** *(Answers should include that many U.S. multinationals are locating their base of operations outside of the United States, where taxes and wages are lower.)* **What does the graph show about jobs in the U.S.?** *(It shows that multinational corporations are moving jobs out of the United States.)* Have students select either the pro or con side of the debate and write a speech advocating their side. **Verbal/Linguistic Logical/Mathematical**

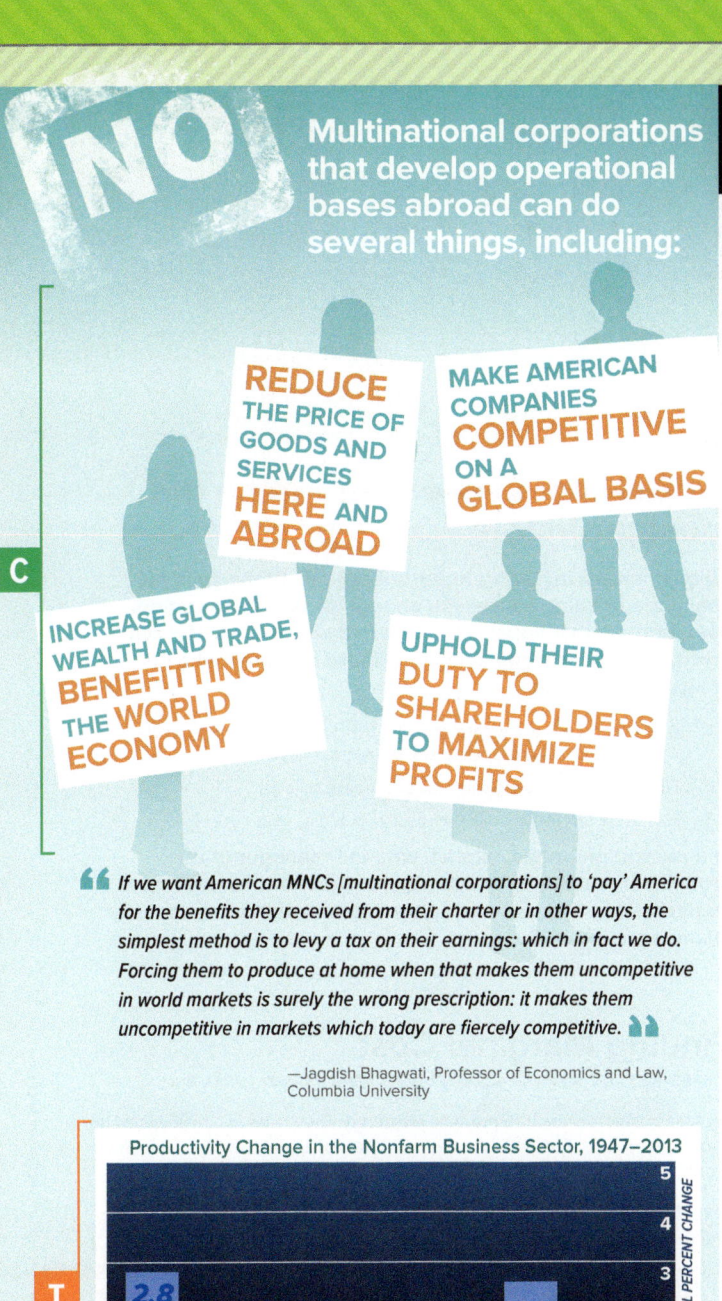

NO Multinational corporations that develop operational bases abroad can do several things, including:

- REDUCE THE PRICE OF GOODS AND SERVICES HERE AND ABROAD
- MAKE AMERICAN COMPANIES COMPETITIVE ON A GLOBAL BASIS
- INCREASE GLOBAL WEALTH AND TRADE, BENEFITTING THE WORLD ECONOMY
- UPHOLD THEIR DUTY TO SHAREHOLDERS TO MAXIMIZE PROFITS

" If we want American MNCs [multinational corporations] to 'pay' America for the benefits they received from their charter or in other ways, the simplest method is to levy a tax on their earnings: which in fact we do. Forcing them to produce at home when that makes them uncompetitive in world markets is surely the wrong prescription: it makes them uncompetitive in markets which today are fiercely competitive. "

—Jagdish Bhagwati, Professor of Economics and Law, Columbia University

Productivity Change in the Nonfarm Business Sector, 1947–2013

Period	Average Annual Percent Change
1947–73	2.8
1973–79	1.2
1979–90	1.5
1990–2000	2.2
2000–07	2.6
2007–13	1.6

Source: U.S. Bureau of Labor Statistics

networks TRY IT YOURSELF ONLINE
For an interactive version of this debate go to connected.mcgraw-hill.com

ANALYZING the issue

1. **Analyzing Visuals** How does the graph reinforce the argument made by Grove?

2. **Evaluating** Explain Bhagwati's argument that requiring multinationals to maintain a strong base of operations in the United States makes them less competitive in the world market. How would this affect American consumers in the long run?

3. **Defending** Which arguments do you find most compelling? Explain your answer.

CHAPTER 5
Debate

C Critical Thinking Skills

Summarizing points of view Ask students to write two paragraphs explaining and summarizing the Yes and No points of view on multinational corporations. **Verbal/Linguistic**

T Technology Skills

Researching the issue Have students research a multinational corporation in your state or region that moved its manufacturing to another country. If there are no relevant corporations in your state or region, students can broaden the scope geographically. Groups should gather information about what the corporation does or manufactures, and the reasons the corporation moved its facilities. Remind students to analyze the validity of the publicly stated reasons in regard to propaganda and/or point of view. Direct students to create a multimedia presentation conveying what their research shows. **BL Logical/Mathematical**

CLOSE & REFLECT

W Writing Skills

Examining benefits in host countries After discussing the effects of multinational corporations on U.S. jobs and workers, ask students to consider the political and social benefits of having U.S. multinational corporations in other countries. **ELL**

GRAPHIC ORGANIZERS

Table

Preparing and defending arguments Divide the class into groups for and against the issue, and distribute the graphic organizer. Ask students to follow these steps in preparing their arguments:

1. Write *Arguments* as the header for the first column. Have students list four reasons that support their position in this column.
2. Write *Counterarguments* as the second column header. Have students come up with points their opponents could use to minimize their arguments and write them in this column.
3. Write *Refutations* as the final column header. Have students write down ways they can refute, or prove the opponents' counterarguments are wrong.
4. Have students review the graphic organizer and rank arguments from strongest to weakest, based on how easy they are to defend against counterarguments.

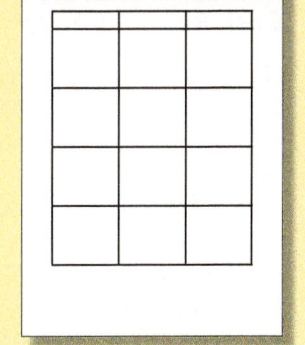

ANSWERS, p. 141

ANALYZING the issue

1. The graph shows that as more jobs have shifted to other countries, there have been fewer jobs in the United States.
2. If corporations have to pay people in the United States more, and if they are forced to remain in the United States even if they could operate more cheaply elsewhere, it will cost them more to keep their business going. Higher costs mean less competitiveness in the world market. To counter that, the corporations would likely close (reducing options for consumers) or pass the higher costs on to consumers.
3. Answers will vary but should demonstrate understanding of both sides of the debate.

Supply 141

CHAPTER 5, LESSON 3
Cost, Revenue, and Profit Maximization

ENGAGE

C Critical Thinking Skills

Identifying measures of cost Before students begin the lesson, tell them that every business has costs. Present a hypothetical business (a cupcake factory, for example) and ask students to brainstorm and list the types of costs the business would have. Many students will list the costs of various raw materials (cupcake ingredients and packaging, for example). Lead students to also consider the fixed costs the business faces. Point out that businesses have two categories of costs—fixed costs and variable costs. **AL Logical/Mathematical**

Making Connections

Cost vs. Price In everyday usage, the words *cost* and *price* are often used interchangeably. For example, when someone says, "The cost of living is going up," he or she is comparing the prices of goods and services today with prices during an earlier time. For economists, however, the terms *price* and *cost* are distinct. Economists define *price* as the amount consumers are willing and able to pay for goods and services. *Cost* is expressed in terms of opportunity cost, or that which is given up to do something else. To accountants, cost entails all the expenses directly related to doing business, whereas business managers define it as anything that reduces profits. Have students write a brief paragraph on how they and their peers use the two terms as consumers.

English Language Proficiency

Intermediate Model asking questions using Who, What, Where, When, How, and Why. Provide, or have students make, words cards with high-frequency, high-need concrete vocabulary. Provide, or have them make, another set of cards with the question starter words. Group students and have them take turns drawing a question word and a high-frequency word and using both words in a question.

ANSWERS, p. 142

ESSENTIAL QUESTION ACTIVITY

Students should conclude that companies need to look at all costs to determine the most profitable way to operate.

TAKING NOTES
Costs: fixed, variable, total, marginal
Revenue: average, total, marginal

Interact with these digital assets and others in lesson 3
- ✓ INTERACTIVE GRAPH Production, Costs, Revenues, and Profits
- ✓ INTERACTIVE IMAGE e-Commerce
- ✓ SELF-CHECK QUIZ
- ✓ VIDEO

networks TRY IT YOURSELF ONLINE

LESSON 3
Cost, Revenue, and Profit Maximization

Reading Help Desk

Academic Vocabulary
- generates
- conducted

Content Vocabulary
- fixed costs
- overhead
- variable cost
- total cost
- marginal cost
- average revenue
- total revenue
- marginal revenue
- profit-maximizing quantity of output
- break-even point
- e-commerce

TAKING NOTES:

Key Ideas and Details
ACTIVITY Use the graphic organizer below to describe information business people must gather in order to balance costs and revenue.

Costs	Revenue
___	___
___	___
___	___

ESSENTIAL QUESTION

How do companies determine the most profitable way to operate?

All businesses, including nonprofit organizations, face the challenge of being successful enough to stay in operation. Even better, most hope to operate in a way that maximizes profits. What decisions does a business need to make to achieve these goals?

C
1. What are the costs of the lease, the utility bills, the purchase and repair of equipment, and other daily expenses for doing business?
2. What is the cost of paying employee salaries and benefits?
3. What is the cost of producing each good or providing each service?

In a paragraph or two, explain why the manager of this organization needs to answer these questions to develop a business plan that will enable the organization to continue in business.

Finding Marginal Cost

GUIDING QUESTION *What is the difference between a fixed cost and a variable cost?*

Because businesses want to produce efficiently, they need to consider several measures of cost. But which is the most useful if they want to maximize profits? To find out, we will examine them one by one.

Fixed Costs

The first measure is **fixed costs**—the costs that an organization incurs even if there is little or no activity. When it comes to this measure of costs, it makes no difference whether the business produces nothing, very little, or a large amount. Total fixed costs, sometimes called **overhead**, remain the same.

Fixed costs include salaries paid to executives, interest charges on bonds, rent payments on leased properties, and state and local property taxes. Fixed costs also include depreciation—the charge for the gradual wear and tear on capital goods because of their use over time. A machine, for example, will not last forever, because its parts will wear out slowly and eventually break.

---

networks *Online Teaching Options*

BELLRINGER

Cost, Revenue, and Profit Maximization

Identifying ways to maximize business profits
Click on the Bellringer and project the image of workers on an assembly line. Discuss with students what the image shows about the production of this factory. **Ask: How can a business maximize profits through its labor force?** *(A firm must hire the appropriate number of workers in order to sustain productivity and maximize profits.)*
Why is maximizing the labor force important?
(The amount of wages and the number of workers on the payroll affects profits, so if a business lowers wages or cuts the number of workers, it can maximize profits assuming it maintains productivity.) Have students write a paragraph discussing whether they think this photo shows a maximized labor force. **AL Verbal/Linguistic**

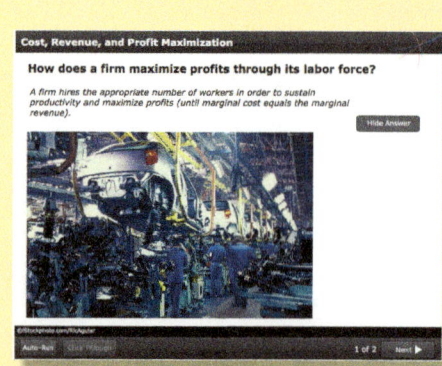

FIGURE 5.6
PRODUCTION, COSTS, REVENUES, AND PROFITS

When we add the costs and revenues to the production schedule, we can find the firm's profits. Note that fixed costs don't change. Of all measures, marginal costs and marginal revenue are the most important because they are used to determine the level of production that generates the maximum level of profits.

▶ **CRITICAL THINKING**
Economic Analysis How important do you think fixed costs are to the business owner?

Regions of production	Production Schedule			Costs					Revenues		Profit
	Number of workers	Total product	Marginal product	Total fixed cost	Total variable cost	Total cost	Marginal cost		Total revenue	Marginal revenue	Total profit
	0	0	0	$50	$0	$50	—		$0	—	–$50
Stage I	1	7	7	50	90	140	$12.86		105	$15	–35
	2	20	13	50	180	230	6.92		300	15	70
	3	38	18	50	270	320	5.00		570	15	250
	4	62	24	50	360	410	3.75		930	15	520
	5	90	28	50	450	500	3.21		1,350	15	850
	6	110	20	50	540	590	4.50		1,650	15	1,060
	7	129	19	50	630	680	4.74		1,935	15	1,210
Stage II	8	138	9	50	720	770	10.00		2,070	15	1,300
	9	144	6	50	810	860	15.00		2,160	15	1,300
	10	148	4	50	900	950	22.50		2,220	15	1,270
Stage III	11	145	–3	50	990	1,040	—		2,175	15	1,135
	12	135	–10	50	1,080	1,130	—		2,025	15	895

connected.mcgraw-hill.com

Suppose fixed costs are $50 for the firm with the hypothetical production function shown in Figure 5.5 in the previous lesson. To keep all of our numbers together, **Figure 5.6** shows the same production function in the first three columns, along with total fixed costs in column four. As you can see, the total fixed cost is $50 for every level of output, even if nothing is produced.

Variable Costs
The second measure is **variable cost**, the cost that changes when the business's rate of operation or output changes. While fixed costs are generally associated with machines and other capital goods, variable costs are usually associated with labor and raw materials. For example, wage-earning workers may be laid off or asked to work overtime as output changes. Other examples of variable costs include electric power to run machines and freight charges to deliver the final product.

For most businesses, the largest variable cost is labor. If a business wants to hire one worker to produce seven units of output per day, and if the worker costs $90 per day, the total variable cost is $90. If the business wants to hire a second worker to produce additional units of output, then its total variable cost is $180, and so on. These are the numbers shown in column five of the figure.

Total Cost
Figure 5.6 shows the total cost of production, which is the sum of the fixed and variable costs. Total cost takes into account all the costs a business faces in the course of its operations. If the business decides to use six workers costing $90 each to produce 110 units of total output, then its **total cost** will be $590—the sum of $50 in fixed costs plus $540 (or $90 times six) of variable costs.

Marginal Cost
Variable, fixed, and total costs are necessary to compute the most useful measure of cost, **marginal cost**—the *extra* cost incurred when producing one more unit of output.

To find marginal cost, we have to divide the additional cost of adding each worker by the additional output the worker generates. To find the marginal cost of the first worker, we divide the additional cost of $90 by the additional output of 7 to get $12.86. To find the marginal cost of the second worker, we divide the additional

fixed costs costs of production that do not change when output changes

overhead broad category of fixed costs that includes interest, rent, taxes, and executive salaries

variable cost production cost that varies as output changes; labor, energy, raw materials

total cost sum of variable cost plus fixed cost; all costs associated with production

marginal cost extra cost of producing one additional unit of production

Supply **143**

CHART
Production, Costs, Revenue, and Profits

Computing marginal costs Tell students to study Figure 5.6 and the text to get an idea of how revenues and profits are affected by costs. **Ask:** What is the most useful measure of cost? *(marginal cost)* What types of costs must businesses compute to find marginal cost? *(fixed costs, variable costs, and total costs)* What does marginal cost represent? *(the extra cost incurred when producing one more unit of output)*

CHAPTER 5, LESSON 3
Cost, Revenue, and Profit Maximization

TEACH & ASSESS

R Reading Skills

Defining business costs **Ask:** What are four types of costs that affect a business's decisions about production? *(fixed, variable, total, marginal)* Have students define each cost and use the terms in a sentence. **AL** Verbal/Linguistic

C1 Critical Thinking Skills

Categorizing costs Review with students the difference between fixed costs and variable costs. Then invite the school principal to the class to discuss the cost of running the school. After the principal's talk, ask students to make charts using Fixed Costs and Variable Costs as headings. Have students place in the proper category the various costs noted by the principal. **AL** Interpersonal

C2 Critical Thinking Skills

Analyzing costs Ask students to list some of the costs that might be involved in operating a contracting business. *(Possible answers: office space, employees, tools, electricity, Internet access, etc.)* **Ask:** Which of these can be reduced or eliminated in order to cut costs? *(Students should think critically about what is essential to running a contracting business.)* **BL** Logical/Mathematical

C3 Critical Thinking Skills

Prioritizing marginal cost Write on the board the following statement: *The most useful measure of cost is marginal cost.* Ask students to consider whether they agree or disagree with this statement, and why. Have students write a brief essay explaining their position and their reasons for it. In a class discussion, have students share their views. Verbal/Linguistic

---

ANSWERS, p. 143

CRITICAL THINKING

The business owner certainly has to earn enough revenue to pay the fixed costs; after that, however, the measure of fixed costs has limited value because fixed costs remain regardless of the level of output.

Supply **143**

CHAPTER 5, LESSON 3
Cost, Revenue, and Profit Maximization

W Writing Skills

Explaining measures of revenue Explain that businesses have three types of measures to determine their revenues. List the three types of revenue measures on the board: average revenue, total revenue, and marginal revenue. Emphasize that one of these measures is the most important one for determining the success of a business. Have students identify that measure and write a paragraph naming it, describing it, and explaining it. **Verbal/Linguistic**

C Critical Thinking Skills

Analyzing costs and revenue Explain that a leaf-raking business is considering hiring a new worker. The only cost to the business would be the worker's wage, which is $90 per day. The worker can rake four yards per day, and customers are charged a price of $20 per yard. **Ask: Should the business hire the worker?** *(No. The marginal cost to hire the worker—$90 in wages—would be higher than the marginal revenue the firm would earn—4 yards X $20 = $80.)* **Verbal/Linguistic**

ANSWERS, p. 144

☑ **READING PROGRESS CHECK** No, because fixed costs remain the same regardless of whether the firm produces nothing, very little, or a large amount.

EXPLORING THE ESSENTIAL QUESTION

Nothing would happen to your fixed costs, because fixed costs remain the same regardless of the level of output.

☑ **READING PROGRESS CHECK** The word *marginal* stands for the extra revenue from the sale of every additional unit of output.

144

---

cost of $90 by the additional output of 13 to get $6.92, and so on. All of these values are shown in column seven of Figure 5.6. As we will see next, marginal revenue is the most useful measure of revenue because it helps us with profit maximization.

☑ **READING PROGRESS CHECK**

Analyzing If a firm's total output increases, will the fixed costs increase? Explain.

Finding Marginal Revenue

GUIDING QUESTION *Why is marginal revenue more important than the average revenue?*

The second important measure a business needs to find is its marginal revenue. Before we get to it, however, we deal with two other measures of revenue.

Average Revenue

average revenue average price that every unit of output sells for

The **average revenue** is simply the average price that every unit of output sells for. For example, if the company whose costs and revenues represented by the table in Figure 5.6 sells every unit of output for $15, its average revenue is $15. This would remain unchanged at $15 if it sold 10, 100, or 1,000 units. Of all the revenue measures, average revenue is the least useful, even though it is perhaps the easiest to understand. For this reason, the table in Figure 5.6 does not have a column for average revenue.

Total Revenue

total revenue total amount earned by a firm from the sale of its products; average price of a good sold times the quantity sold

The **total revenue** is all the revenue that a business receives. In the case of the firm shown in Figure 5.6, total revenue, shown in column eight, is equal to the number of units sold multiplied by the average price of $15 per unit. So, if one worker is hired and seven units are produced and sold at $15 each, the total revenue is $105. If 10 workers are hired and their 148 units of total output sell for $15 each, then total revenue is $2,220. The calculation is the same for any level of output in the table. Total revenue is shown in column eight of Figure 5.6.

EXPLORING THE ESSENTIAL QUESTION

Imagine you run a company that manufactures widgets. Last week, you had $1,000 in total costs and revenue of $1,000. If you want to hire 10 more workers at $110 a day, what would happen to your total fixed cost?

Marginal Revenue

marginal revenue extra revenue from the sale of one additional unit of output

The most important measure of revenue is **marginal revenue**, the extra revenue a business receives from the production and sale of one additional unit of output. You can find the marginal revenue in Figure 5.6 by dividing the change in total revenue by the change in total output, or by the marginal product.

For example, when the business employs five workers, it produces 90 units of output and **generates** $1,350 of total revenue. If a sixth worker is added, output increases by 20 units and total revenues increase to $1,650. If we divide the change in total revenue ($300) by the marginal product (20), we have marginal revenue of $15.

generates produces or brings into being

As long as every unit of output sells for $15, the marginal revenue earned by the sale of one more unit will always be $15. For this reason, the marginal revenue appears to be constant at $15 for every level of output in Figure 5.6. In reality, this is not always the case, as businesses often find that marginal revenue varies, especially if they sell some of their output at different prices.

☑ **READING PROGRESS CHECK**

Explaining What does the word "marginal" in the term "marginal revenue" stand for?

Profit Maximization and Break-Even

GUIDING QUESTION *What cost advantage does e-commerce offer businesses?*

The fixed costs of building a store are usually much lower, so marginal costs will also be much lower and profits higher.

144

---

networks Online Teaching Options

VIDEO **WORKSHEETS**

Rising Price of Gasoline

Examining the rising price of gasoline
Have students view the video. Lead a class discussion about why a moving company would be hard hit by an increase in gasoline prices. Include in the discussion the various fixed costs (wages, utilities, and truck payments, for example) and variable costs (prices of gasoline and paper) faced by the moving company. **Logical/Mathematical**

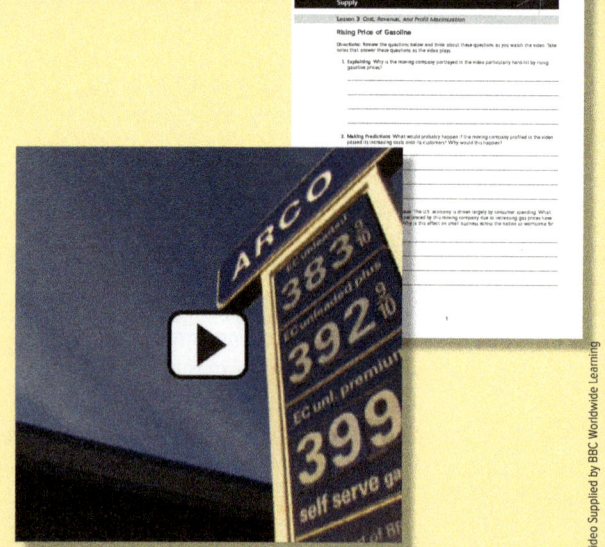

CAREERS | Painting Contractor

Is this Career for you?

 Do you have the mathematical skills to complete a marginal analysis?

 Do you have strong leadership abilities?

 Are you a good decision-maker?

 Are you interested in materials, methods, and tools?

Interview with a professional painting contractor

"If you don't understand your numbers—gross profit, labor percent, overhead costs, etc.—then the likelihood of having a successful business is close to zero. It may sound cliché, but cash is king, debt is the executioner and 'numbers' are the axe."

—Joe Brindle, President, Custom Coatings Incorporated, Hickory, NC

Salary
Median pay: $83,860
$40.32 per hour

Job Growth Outlook
Average

Profile of Work
Most painting contractors own their own businesses, so they have to be on top of the "numbers." They need to be proficient at completing a regular marginal analysis so they know whether their revenue covers the costs of doing business, while leaving them with a profit. If not, contractors need to adjust the prices they quote when bidding on jobs or find a way to reduce their costs while maintaining quality of service.

Profit Maximization

Suppose the firm in Figure 5.6 wanted to experiment to find the level of output which maximized profits. The business would hire the sixth worker, for example, because the extra output would cost only $4.50 to produce while generating $15 in new revenues. This means that each of the 20 additional units produced would generate $10.50 of profit, increasing total profits from $850 to $1,060.

Having made a profit with the sixth worker, the business would hire the seventh and eighth workers for the same reason. While the addition of the ninth worker neither adds to nor takes away from total profits, the firm would have no incentive to hire the tenth worker. If it did, it would find that profits would go down, and it would go back to using nine workers.

Eventually, the **profit-maximizing quantity of output**—the volume of production where marginal cost and marginal revenue are equal—is reached, as shown in the last column in Figure 5.6. Other levels of output may generate equal profits, but none will be more profitable.

The firm in Figure 5.6 found this level of output by using trial and error, but it could have saved some time by looking for the level of output, 144 units using nine workers, where marginal cost in column seven is exactly equal to marginal revenue in column nine. This is why we computed the marginal cost and revenue measures in the first place.

profit-maximizing quantity of output level of production where marginal cost is equal to marginal revenue

Break-Even Analysis

Sometimes a firm may not be able to sell enough to maximize its profits right away, so it may want to know how much it must sell just to cover its costs. This

connected.mcgraw-hill.com   Supply **145**

CHAPTER 5, LESSON 3
Cost, Revenue, and Profit Maximization

T Technology Skills

Showing constitutional support Tell students that the U.S. Constitution established a climate for profit maximizing by supporting property rights, enforcing contracts, giving the federal government control over monetary matters, and not creating trade barriers among states. Have students research the Constitution and laws that affect businesses' drive to maximize profits, and then create a multimedia report to present to the class. Remind students to use standard punctuation when writing. **BL Visual/Spatial, Auditory/Musical**

V Visual Skills

Analyzing a table Direct students' attention back to Figure 5.6 Production, Costs, and Revenues.
Ask: What is the most number of workers that can be hired before negative returns cause output to fall? *(10)* How many new workers will give the greatest total profit? *(8)* Why do the numbers in the total fixed cost column stay the same? *(Fixed costs remain the same regardless of the level of production or services offered.)* **Logical/Mathematical**

C Critical Thinking Skills

Balancing marginal cost and marginal revenue Remind students that when the marginal cost is equal to the marginal revenue, profit-maximizing quantity of output is reached. **Ask:** What steps can a company take if marginal cost is less than marginal revenue? *(Possible answers: expand output by hiring workers, increasing production)* How would these steps help equalize marginal cost and marginal revenue? *(Expanding output would increase marginal cost, eventually increasing it enough to become equal to marginal revenue.)* **BL Logical/Mathematical**

INTERACTIVE FEATURE

Painting Contractor Career

Examining careers Have students view the Career and read the primary source. **Ask:** What does Joe Brindle think is the most important aspect of a business that an owner has to understand? *(the numbers: gross profit, overhead costs, labor percentage)* What numbers does he fail to mention? *(He fails to mention many other costs and revenues, but lead students to answer 'marginal revenues.')* Have students discuss the advantages and disadvantages of having a contracting business. **Verbal/Linguistic**

Supply **145**

CHAPTER 5, LESSON 3
Cost, Revenue, and Profit Maximization

C Critical Thinking Skills

Understanding the break-even point Ask: **What might happen if a business does not know its break-even point?** *(If a business does not understand how much revenue it must generate to cover its total operating costs, it may lose money and fail.)* Ask students to research a company that has failed in the last two years, and in a brief essay discuss the reasons for the failure. **BL** **Verbal/Linguistic**

Making Connections

e-commerce E-commerce is convenient, provides access to many products, and allows customers to compare features and prices of a product. Some people dislike e-commerce because it does not provide personal customer service. Also, customers cannot physically examine the product until it is delivered to their home. Have students discuss their shopping preference—e-commerce or stores—and explain the pros and cons of each.

CLOSE & REFLECT

Summarizing business costs and revenues Have students answer the question: How could this chapter help a person who is starting a business?

ANSWERS, p. 146

✓ **READING PROGRESS CHECK**
An e-commerce store conducts business over the Internet and has much less overhead than a traditional business that has higher fixed costs.

---

break-even point production level where total cost equals total revenue; production needed if the firm is to recover its costs

is when the firm needs to find its **break-even point**, the level of production that generates just enough revenue to cover its total operating costs.

For example, the firm in Figure 5.6 could not cover all its costs if it employed one worker and produced seven units. This is because total costs were $140, while total revenue only amounted to $105. However, if it employed two workers and could sell 20 units, the company would cover all of its costs. The result is that two workers would have to be hired to break even. Or if the number of workers in the first column were in thousands, the break-even point would be more than one but less than two.

However, the break-even point only tells the firm how much it has to produce to cover its costs. Most businesses want to do more—they want to maximize the amount of profits they can make, not just cover their costs. To do this, they would have to compute their marginal costs and marginal revenues to find the level of output where they were equal.

Costs and Business Operation

For reasons largely related to costs, stores are increasingly selling online, making it one of the fastest-growing areas of business today. Stores do this because the overhead, or the fixed costs of operation, on the Internet is so low. Another reason is that a firm does not need as much inventory. And if a business can lower its fixed or variable costs, it also helps its break-even point by lowering the amount of sales it needs to cover its total costs.

e-commerce electronic business or exchange conducted over the Internet

conducted handled by way of

People engaged in **e-commerce**—an electronic business **conducted** over the Internet—do not need to spend a large sum of money to rent a building and stock it with inventory. Instead, for just a fraction of the cost of a typical store, the e-commerce business owner can purchase Web access along with an e-commerce software package that provides everything from Web catalog pages to ordering, billing, and accounting software. Then, the owner of the e-commerce business store inserts pictures and descriptions of the products for sale into the software and loads the program.

When customers visit the "store" on the Web, they see a range of goods for sale. In some cases, the owner has the merchandise in stock; in other cases, the merchant simply forwards the orders to a distribution center that handles the shipping. Either way, the fixed costs of operation are significantly lower than they would be in a typical retail store—and the break-even point of sales is much lower.

✓ **READING PROGRESS CHECK**

Contrasting What are the differences between an e-commerce store and a traditional business?

LESSON 3 REVIEW

Reviewing Vocabulary
1. *Explaining* What is the difference between marginal revenue and total revenue?

Using Your Notes
2. *Summarizing* Using your notes, explain the relationship between costs and revenue.

Answering the Guiding Questions
3. *Contrasting* What is the difference between a fixed cost and a variable cost?
4. *Contrasting* What is the difference between average revenue and marginal revenue?

5. *Contrasting* What cost advantage does e-commerce offer businesses?

Writing About Economics
6. *Informative/Explanatory* ABC Company has been breaking even all year. The board of directors has hired a new manager and charged her with the responsibility of maximizing profits. How does the manager determine what steps to take to make the firm profitable?

LESSON 3 REVIEW ANSWERS

Reviewing Vocabulary
1. Total revenue is all the revenue a company receives. Marginal revenue is the extra revenue received from selling one more unit.

Using Your Notes
2. If costs exceed revenue, the company loses money. If costs and revenue are equal, the company breaks even, but does not earn a profit. It's necessary to find a balance in which revenue exceeds costs to achieve a profit.

Answering the Guiding Questions
3. A fixed cost does not change regardless of how much a business produces. A variable cost changes as the business produces more, hires more workers, or cuts back on production.

4. Average revenue is the average price of each unit of output. Marginal revenue is the extra revenue received from the production and sale of one additional unit of output.

5. An e-commerce business does not require a physical store or many of the other fixed costs of a traditional store, so its fixed costs and break-even point are lower.

Writing About Economics
6. Students should understand that the manager cannot simply try to maximize revenue, but rather must balance it against the cost of producing a product. She will begin by determining marginal costs and marginal revenues and finding the point where these two values are equal. Consider the concepts of marginal revenue, total revenue, and fixed and variable costs.

Case Study

The NEARLY INSTANT SNOWBOARD

Three-dimensional printing has been around since the 1980s. The price and quality finally became practical for small-business and personal use. These printers work much like a desktop printer, only instead of ink, they eject plastic, wax, paper, titanium, gold, or one of a large number of other materials in very fine layers that build up to form a three-dimensional object. More and more businesses are using 3-D printing for design and manufacture.

Burton Snowboards in Burlington, VT, uses 3-D printing to design new snowboards. This change has dramatically cut the time needed for developing a new board from two years to one year. Moreover, the technology prints out a prototype of the new board that can be held and examined from every perspective. It can even be ridden down a snow slope and checked out for performance characteristics. When the snowboard doesn't quite come out as hoped, the designers can go back to their computers, tweak the design, and print out a revised version. In the past, the company designed the board first, then devoted time and resources to tooling up a production line to produce a working prototype, and only then could they actually test the board.

A few years ago, a rider had an idea for adding a "wing" to a snowboard. Burton created a design for the idea, printed out a prototype, and handed it over to the rider for a test ride the next day.

This design and development technology produces cost savings in other ways, too. For example, instead of waiting until production can manufacture a finished board for use in marketing and advertising materials, the photographers may now work with the 3-D prototype. The catalog and other promotional materials are ready to go even before the production line starts rolling out the new snowboards, producing faster sales and earlier delivery dates.

This collection of red plastic parts shows the intricacy of the parts created by a 3-D printer. Using these printing machines can help companies create items faster.

CASE STUDY REVIEW

1. **Analyzing** How can 3-D printing enable Burton to develop better boards than more traditional methods?
2. **Speculating** Think about the implications of 3-D printing. How might this technology affect the broader U.S. economy as it becomes more widely used?

CHAPTER 5
Case Study

C1 Critical Thinking Skills

Predicting outcomes of 3-D printing Ask students to predict how the development of three-dimensional printing could change the way businesses develop a new product. Discuss whether students think this change would be positive or negative. Have them give reasons for their answers. **Verbal/Linguistic**

W Writing Skills

Researching current 3-D printing Have students research different ways 3-D printing is being used in businesses in the United States today. Included in the research should be information about how 3-D printers impact suppliers' inventories and other variable costs. Students should display their findings in a class presentation. **Visual/Spatial**

C2 Critical Thinking Skills

Assessing 3-D printing Discuss with students how 3-D printing would be useful for some industries but not for others. Have them write a paragraph assessing the ways it could be used and the positive and negative aspects of using it. **AL Verbal/Linguistic**

Making Connections

Printing Chocolate In 2014, Hershey's announced that it would enter the 3-D printing world by supplying the company 3D Systems with chocolate for the printer. Ask students what products they would be interested in creating from a 3-D printer if they owned one. The starting price for consumer 3-D printers is about $1,000.

C3 Critical Thinking Skills

Summarizing Have students write a news report about 3-D printing that will appear in e-news on the Internet. Direct students to explain the invention and its current uses, and predict its future uses.

ANSWERS, p. 147

Case Study Review

1. The designs can be tested and modified much faster and more efficiently than in the past, so a higher level of fine-tuning of the board can be achieved.
2. Answers will vary, but students may say it will allow manufacturers and designers to become more innovative and reduce the costs of production while producing higher-quality products. They may also recognize that it may displace some workers by making design and production operations more efficient, requiring fewer workers.

---

networks Online Teaching Options

INTERACTIVE FEATURE

Case Study: The Nearly Instant Snowboard

Explaining the benefits of 3-D printing Have students view the Nearly Instant Snowboard feature. Discuss some of the benefits of this new process. Ask: **What are some cost-saving aspects of this invention?** *(The invention saves time and costs incurred in producing an experimental model.)* Have students write a paragraph explaining how the snowboarding industry can benefit from using 3-D printing. **Logical/Mathematical**

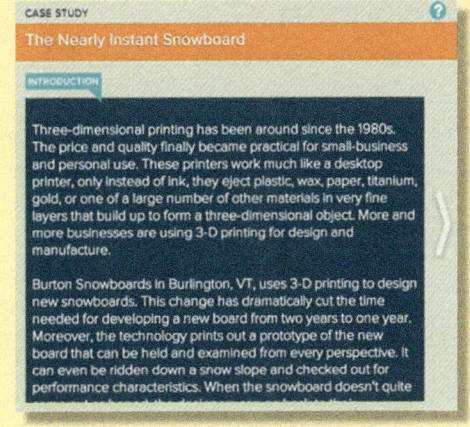

Chapter 5
Study Guide

V | Visual Skills

Contrasting Have students look at the production function and describe the shape of the curve as it goes from one stage to the next. Then have them explain the reason that the curve changes in this way. *(Students should be able to verbalize that the curve rises sharply during Stage I, rises more gently in Stage II, and slopes downward in Stage III. The sharp rise in Stage I indicates increases at a consistently higher rate. Stage II indicates slower increases at a higher rate. Stage III indicates decreases.)* **AL**

C | Critical Thinking Skills

Problem Solving Remind students that when the marginal cost is equal to the marginal revenue, profit-maximizing quantity of output is reached.
Ask: What steps can a company take if marginal cost is less than marginal revenue? *(Expand output by hiring workers, increasing production, and so on.)* **How would that help equalize marginal cost and marginal revenue?** *(Expanding output would increase marginal cost, eventually increasing it to become equal with marginal revenue.)*

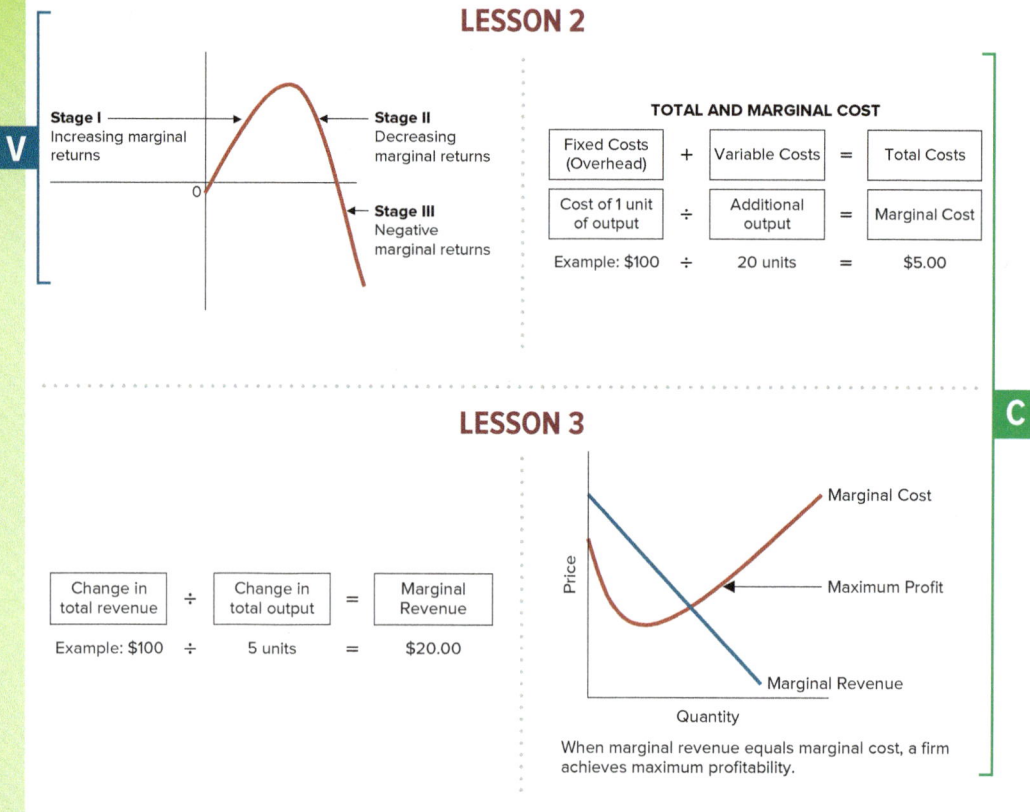

networks Online Teaching Options

WORKSHEET

Economic Simulation

The Economic Simulation worksheet asks students to work in groups, with each group forming a business to sell one type of merchandise to the public. Groups must plan where they will get necessary resources and how much they cost. They must research the competition. They also will determine costs of the business, including cost of labor and marketing, and how much they must sell (and at what price) to break even or to make a profit. Students will gain an understanding of how costs and prices, as well as competition, affect running a business.

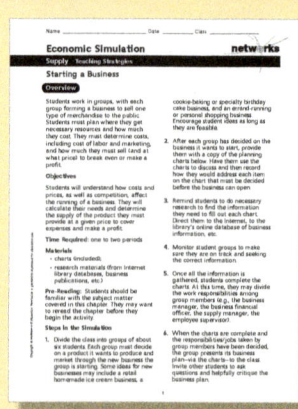

CHAPTER 5 Assessment

Directions: On a separate sheet of paper, answer the questions below. Make sure you read carefully and answer all parts of the questions.

Lesson Review

Lesson 1

1. **Explaining** Why does a normal supply curve always increase, from left to right, on a supply graph?

2. **Describing** Imagine that several large new electric power supplies have been developed in your region, putting a greatly increased quantity of electricity on the market. Describe what happens to a supply curve for electricity.

Lesson 2

3. **Explaining** How can a manager use the production function to decide whether to add an input to increase production?

4. **Analyzing** Why do most firms operate in Stage II of the three stages of production?

Lesson 3

5. **Analyzing** Why is it necessary to know fixed, variable, and total costs to determine marginal cost?

6. **Contrasting** Why is it more important for a manager to know marginal revenue than average revenue?

7. **Explaining** A business manufacturer has continued producing bicycles until the marginal cost reached $200, at which marginal revenue also reached $200. What would be the effect of producing an additional bicycle? Explain.

Critical Thinking

8. **Analyzing** Imagine that a friend operates her own business performing live music at weddings. If the price she can charge for her performances increases, will she do more performances or fewer? Why?

9. **Making Decisions** Assume that you own a food truck specializing in hamburgers and hot dogs. The opportunity has arisen to operate at the local minor league ballpark this summer. All vendors at the park charge twice as much as you do now. How will supply elasticity affect the price you'll charge and the quantity of burgers and hot dogs you can serve? How many people will you hire to help you? Explain the basis for your decisions.

10. **Analyzing** An entrepreneur has purchased rights to produce and sell an innovative new product. She has limited start-up funds for the business. Should she open an e-business or a traditional store? Explain your answer.

Analyzing Visuals

Use the supply schedule and individual supply curve to answer the following questions.

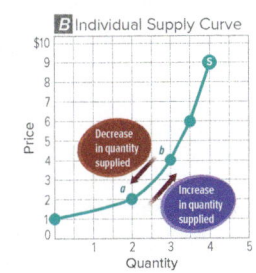

11. **Analysis** How many burritos will the producer supply at the price of $1? In your opinion, what is the reason for that quantity?

12. **Applying** Producers want to get the best price for their product. What stops them from charging the highest price possible?

ANSWERING THE ESSENTIAL QUESTIONS

Review your answers to the introductory questions at the beginning of each lesson. Then answer the Essential Questions on the basis of what you learned in the chapter. Have your answers changed?

13. **Contrasting** What are the basic differences between supply and demand?

Need Extra Help?

If You've Missed Question	1	2	3	4	5	6	7	8	9	10	11	12	13
Go to page	129	129	136	138	142	144	145	131	136	146	129	129	128

Chapter 5 Assessment Answers

Lesson Review

Lesson 1

1. In almost every situation, a supplier will produce more goods as the price for goods increases.

2. As the quantity of a product increases, the supply curve shifts to the right.

Lesson 2

3. A manager can use the production function to see the effect of adding or subtracting one variable input on the total output. As a result, the manager can determine if that will increase or decrease profitability, or keep it the same.

4. Students should recognize that although adding each input produces less output than the previous input, a state of diminishing returns, the firm continues to produce more total output.

Lesson 3

5. Total costs can only be determined by adding up the variable and fixed costs. Marginal cost is the change in total cost brought about by adding one unit of input.

6. Average revenue is the average price that every unit of output sells for. Marginal revenue is the extra revenue gained by producing one additional unit of output, which tells the manager whether to increase or reduce production or to maintain current production levels.

7. The manufacturer would either make the same or less profit because the point where marginal cost equals marginal revenue represents the point of maximum profit.

Critical Thinking Questions

8. Students should recognize that as prices increase, so does supply. Therefore, the performer will probably play at more weddings.

9. Students should demonstrate an understanding of how supply elasticity affects how much food they can prepare and at what price, as well as how the limits of work space and appliances for food preparation in a food truck will limit the number of employees that can be hired.

10. Students should demonstrate understanding that the cost of setting up an e-business is much lower than operating a traditional store. As a result, the break-even point will be reached sooner, allowing the entrepreneur to conserve her start-up funds.

Analyzing Visuals

11. The producer would supply no burritos at $1. Students should note that either the producer would not make enough profit at that price, or sell at a loss.

12. As shown in the previous chapter, consumer demand tapers off at higher prices for most products.

Answering the Essential Questions

13. Students should understand that as demand increases, the supply will increase and as demand decreases, supply will decrease. They should also note that for supply, as quantity goes up when the price goes up, demand for a product goes down as price goes up.

Chapter 5
Assessment Answers

14 Production function helps managers decide how much to increase the input of factors of production to maximize productivity and profit.

15 They compute their marginal costs to their marginal revenue and find the level of output where they are equal.

21st Century Skills

16 Sample answers: The cost of resources could go up for unforeseen reasons, such as higher transportation costs or a war that causes scarcity of materials needed in the components. A government might impose new taxes on the components. A technology breakthrough in manufacturing of the components could give his competitors the advantage.

17 The firm can hire 15 workers before marginal product becomes negative. The optimal number to employ is 14.

18 Students should recognize that the owner would want to know how much each new employee would contribute to total production and whether adding the employee would increase, maintain, or reduce productivity and to what extent. The owner might get this information by determining the productivity of the current staff and then estimating how much each additional employee would contribute.

Building Financial Literacy

19 a. Variable items: any lemons ordered in addition to those on hand. Fixed costs: space rental fee, the original lemon order, paper cups, miscellaneous items.

b. Your break-even point will be $550.

c. Your point of profit maximization will be 1,000 cups of lemonade sold for $1,000.

d. The fundraiser does not have labor costs. Students may also note that it does not have other fixed costs, such as taxes, utilities, and other overhead costs.

Analyzing Primary Sources

20 The cost of resources due to drought, floods, and a mandate to use corn for ethanol. The factors will cause the supply curve to shift to the left.

21 The supply is inelastic. Despite prices that almost doubled, the supply did not increase, or increased only modestly.

22 Students should support their opinions with valid arguments.

150

CHAPTER 5 Assessment

Directions: On a separate sheet of paper, answer the questions below. Make sure you read carefully and answer all parts of the questions.

14 *Explaining* Why is the production function useful for making business decisions?

15 *Describing* How do companies determine the most profitable way to operate?

21st Century Skills

16 *Identifying Cause and Effect* A young entrepreneur is planning to manufacture electronic consumer products. He has identified sources for electronic components at very competitive prices. What factors might cause a change in the supply of these components that could endanger the profitability of the firm?

17 *Economics* A manufacturer has ten employees who produce 100 units of a product. Management hires one more employee who adds eight units to the total. Hiring another worker adds six units to the total. Hiring one more worker adds four units to the total. If the trend continues, how many total employees can the firm add before marginal product is negative? What is the optimal number of workers the company should employ?

18 *Problem Solving* A small business owner must decide whether or not to hire additional employees. Assuming that the owner can sell all the products produced at the current price and that wages for new workers would be the same as for current workers, what information would the business owner want to have to make this hiring decision? How could the owner get the information needed?

Building Financial Literacy

19 *Analyzing* You are organizing a lemonade stand for a club's fund-raising event. You have recruited volunteers to work in the booth. The club will provide: tables, tablecloths, and two large signs. You have paid $150 to rent the space for your booth. You have ordered 1,000 lemons for $200—enough for 1,000 cups of lemonade, which you will sell for $1.00 per cup. The vendor can deliver more as you need them, but you can't return those you've already accepted. You have purchased 2,000 paper cups for $100. Miscellaneous items cost an additional $100.

a. What are the variable costs in this enterprise? The fixed costs?

b. What will be your break-even point if you do not order additional lemons?

c. At what point will you maximize profits?

d. How does this fund-raising event differ from a for-profit business?

Analyzing Primary Sources

Read the excerpt and answer the questions that follow.

The cost of food was rising in early 2011, which concerned the governments of some developing nations. American prices remained stable, but that was headed for change:

PRIMARY SOURCE

"*The immediate causes of the rise are clear: bad harvests due to drought in Russia, China, and Argentina and floods in Australia, among other things. But a longer-term cause may come as a surprise: 24% of the U.S. corn crop is now mandated to go to ethanol, taking slack out of the world food market and making price shocks more likely, agricultural economists say.*"

—Elizabeth Weise, "Ethanol pumping up food prices," *USA Today*, February 14, 2011

Corn yields in 2010 were lower than expected and U.S. corn reserves were the lowest in a decade. Corn prices were more than $6.00 a bushel. About 5 billion bushels of corn was demanded each year for ethanol production.

20 *Identifying Cause and Effect* What factors are causing a change in the supply of corn that can be used for food? Would these factors cause the supply curve to shift to the right or to the left?

21 *Analyzing* Based on the information, do you think the supply of corn is elastic, inelastic, or unit elastic?

22 *Analyzing* Do you think this primary source's information is propaganda? Explain your answer.

Need Extra Help?

If You've Missed Question	14	15	16	17	18	19	20	21	22
Go to page	136	142	131	138	142	142	132	134	132

150

---

networks *Online Assessment Options*

WORKSHEET

Chapter Tests and Lesson Quizzes

Chapter 5 Tests Forms A and B Have students complete the Chapter Tests and Lesson Quizzes to assess student understanding throughout the chapter. Print and online assessment tools offer chapter and lesson evaluation through a variety of question formats, including document-based questions.

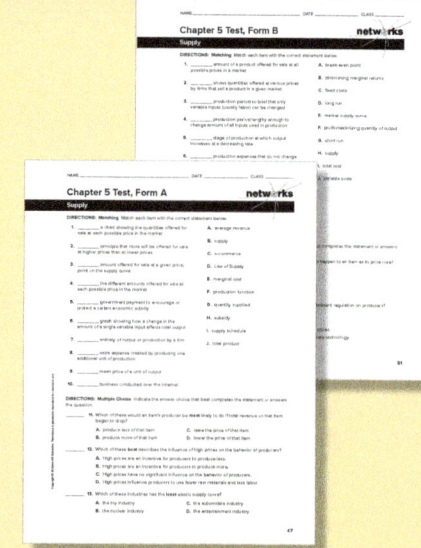

CHAPTER 6
Prices Planner

UNDERSTANDING BY DESIGN®

Enduring Understanding
- The interaction of buyers and sellers in a market economy determines market prices and thereby allocates scarce goods and services.

Essential Questions
- How do prices help determine WHAT, HOW, and FOR WHOM to produce?
- What factors affect prices?

Predictable Misunderstandings
Students may think:
- *Using a price ceiling to make a product affordable is good for both the economy and society in general.* Explain that price ceilings may have unexpected outcomes. Point out the example in the chapter of controlling rents using price ceilings. In the end, fixing prices interferes with a market's natural ability to adjust to changing supply and demand.
- *Rising gold prices are a sign of a good economy.* Explain that rising gold prices are not a good sign because gold is seen as protection against economic crisis. A sharp increase in the price of gold would get attention, possibly causing more people to buy gold, which would drive the price up even further. In a good economy, the price of gold tends to decrease slowly.

Assessment Evidence
Performance Task
- Hands-On Chapter Project with Technology Extension

Other Evidence
- Guided Reading Activities
- Vocabulary Activity
- Lesson Quizzes
- Self-Check Quizzes
- Chapter Assessment
- Chapter Tests, Forms A and B

SUGGESTED PACING GUIDE
Introducing the Chapter: . . . . . . ½ Day	Lesson 3: Social Goals, Prices, and Market Efficiency . . . 1 Day
Lesson 1: How Prices Work . . . . . 1 Day	Debate . . . . ½ Day
Lesson 2: The Effects of Prices . . 1 Day	Study Guide, Chapter Assessment and Wrap-Up . . . . ½ Day
Case Study . . . . ½ Day	

TOTAL 5 Days

Key for Using the Teacher Edition

SKILL-BASED ACTIVITIES

Types of skill activites found in the Teacher Edition.

- **V** Visual Skills require students to analyze maps, graphs, charts, and photos.
- **R** Reading Skills help students practice reading skills and master vocabulary.
- **C** Critical Thinking Skills help students apply and extend what they have learned.
- **W** Writing Skills provide writing opportunities to help students comprehend the text.
- **T** Technology Skills require students to use digital tools effectively.

*Letters are followed by a number when there is more than one of the same type of skill on the page.

DIFFERENTIATED INSTRUCTION

All activities are written for the on-level student unless otherwise marked with the leveled labels below.

- **BL** Beyond Level
- **AL** Approaching Level
- **ELL** English Language Learners

All students benefit from activities that utilize different learning styles. Many activities are marked as below when a particular learning style is highlighted.

Intrapersonal	Naturalist
Logical/Mathematical	Kinesthetic
Visual/Spatial	Auditory/Musical
Verbal/Linguistic	Interpersonal

Council for Economic Education

Below are the Council for Economic Education Voluntary National Content Standards in Economics covered in the *Prices* chapter.

Content Standard 7: A market exists when buyers and sellers interact. This interaction determines market prices and thereby allocates scarce goods and services.

Content Standard 8: Prices send signals and provide incentives to buyers and sellers. When supply or demand changes, market prices adjust, affecting incentives.

CHAPTER 6: PRICES

CHAPTER OPENER PLANNER

Students will know:
- how prices help the economy run smoothly by providing a good way to allocate resources.
- the non-price determinants that create changes in supply and demand, which result in a new equilibrium price.
- the positive and negative effects of government programs to help stabilize prices.

Students will be able to:
- *explain* how prices help individuals, businesses, and markets determine WHAT, HOW, and FOR WHOM to produce.
- *predict* how a change in supply or demand may affect prices.
- *examine* the effect of price ceilings and price floors on a market.

UNDERSTANDING BY DESIGN

☑ Print Teaching Options

C Critical Thinking Skills

☐ **p. 151 Categorizing factors that influence prices** Students interview local business owners about prices. *Interpersonal*

☐ **p. 151 Determining the effect on supply or demand** Students use the infographic's captions to create 10 scenarios and describe their effects on supply or demand for oil.

☐ **p. 153 Applying factors that affect demand** Students identify factors that can cause a change in demand and provide examples of how each factor has increased the demand for oil worldwide.

T Technology Skills

☐ **p. 152 Products Derived from Crude Oil** Students research online products they use daily to see which are created or derived from crude oil, and which could be created from a recyclable base instead.

☑ Online Teaching Options

V Visual Skills

☐ **IMAGE** Chapter opener—Students analyze a photo for clues about prices.

C Critical Thinking Skills

☐ **INFOGRAPHICS** Economic Perspectives—Students explore factors that affect supply, demand, and prices of gas.

☐ **DEBATES** Is it a good idea to raise the minimum wage?—Students analyze two views about raising the minimum wage.

☐ **INTERACTIVE FEATURE** Case Study: Supply, Demand, and the Cost of Super Bowl Advertising—Students analyze Super Bowl advertising.

☑ Printable Digital Worksheets

C Critical Thinking Skills

☐ **WORKSHEET** Assessing Background Knowledge Activity—Target misconceptions you can address when teaching the lessons.
☐ **WORKSHEET** Chapter Summary—Content is condensed into manageable chunks.
☐ **WORKSHEET** Vocabulary Activity—Students use content and academic terms.
☐ **WORKSHEET** Enrichment Activity—Students are asked to read about the 1973 oil embargo and answer questions related to the text and the graph.

Project-Based Learning

Hands-On

Hands-On Chapter Project
Students rank different options for buying food by price, and then back up their decisions with reasons. They will also provide other factors that affect food pricing, and present their ideas to the class. Next, they will prepare arguments for a debate over farm subsidies and then deliver those arguments in an informal debate. Then they will create a pamphlet to convince the general public of their opinions about farm subsidies.

Digital Hands-On

Create Online Projects
Find an additional activity online that incorporates technology for the Hands-On Project. Visit the EdTech Teacher Web sites for more links, tutorials, and other resources.

Print Resources

ANCILLARY RESOURCES
This ancillary is available for every chapter and lesson.
- Chapter Tests and Lesson Quizzes

PRINTABLE DIGITAL WORKSHEETS
These printable digital worksheets are available for every chapter.
- Reading Essentials & Study Guide
- Vocabulary Activities
- Chapter Summaries
- Economic Simulations
- Math Practice for Economics
- Reinforcing Economic Skills
- Personal Finance Activities
- Enrichment Activities
- Reteaching Activities
- Guided Reading Activities
- Video Worksheets
- Lesson Quizzes and Chapter Tests (English and Spanish)

More Media Resources

SUGGESTED READING
- For students at a Grade 10 reading level: *How Do They Package It?* by George Sullivan
- For students at a Grade 11 reading level: *The World of Power and Energy,* by Frank Ross
- For students at a Grade 12 reading level: *Food, Inc.: Mendel to Monsanto—The Promises and Perils of the Biotech Harvest,* by Peter Pringle

SUGGESTED VIDEOS
Find these documentaries yourself online. NOTE: McGraw-Hill Education does not endorse these resources. Preview clips for age-appropriateness.
- *Food Rationing & Nutrition in Wartime: 1940s WW2* (10 min.)
- *TED Talks: Technology's Long Tail* (14 min.)

LESSON 1 Planner

HOW PRICES WORK

Students will know:
- how prices help the economy run smoothly by providing a good way to allocate resources.
- prices send signals and provide incentives to buyers and sellers.
- when supply or demand changes, market prices adjust, affecting incentives and causing changes in purchase and sale decisions.

Students will be able to:
- **explain** how prices help individuals, businesses, and markets determine WHAT, HOW, and FOR WHOM to produce.
- **list** four advantages of prices over other methods of making allocation decisions.
- **identify** four major problems with rationing as an alternative to a price system.

UNDERSTANDING BY DESIGN®

☑ Print Teaching Options

R Reading Skills

☐ **p. 156 Inferring types of governments that ration** Students use what they have learned about rationing systems to infer types of governments most likely to ration purchases. **AL**

C Critical Thinking Skills

☐ **p. 154 Understanding prices in a market economy** Students discuss the effect of prices on their behavior as consumers.

☐ **p. 155 Understanding the flexibility of prices** Students set a reasonable price for a service they can perform, and modify prices to accommodate changes in the market.

☐ **p. 157 Considering a rationing problem** Students come up with a reasonable plan for rationing Internet usage. **BL** Verbal/Linguistic

☐ **p. 158 Describing allocation decisions in a price system** Students discuss how automakers' decisions about allocation of resources might change as oil prices rise. **AL**

☐ **p. 159 Diagramming effects in a price system** Students create a diagram that shows the effects of increased prices on a particular industry or system.

☐ **p. 159 Categorizing the functions of prices** Students create a chart listing functions of prices (signals, incentives, allocation, for example) as well as four advantages of prices.

W Writing Skills

☐ **p. 155 Identifying advantages of prices in action** Students develop a presentation exploring a real life example of one of the advantages of prices—neutrality, flexibility, familiarity, and efficiency. **BL ELL**

☐ **p. 156 Describing a society without prices** Students write how their lives would be different if they lived in a society in which prices did not exist, addressing the questions of WHAT, HOW, and FOR WHOM. **BL** Verbal/Linguistic

☑ Online Teaching Options

V Visual Skills

☐ **IMAGE Decision-making Without Prices**—Students analyze images showing price setting situations and write a paragraph about each situation. Verbal/Linguistic, Visual/Spatial

☐ **IMAGE What happens when there is . . . Rationing in the United States**—Students study an image about rationing gas and write alternatives to rationing during a gas shortage. Verbal/Linguistic

☐ **VIDEO Food Prices**—Students view how food prices affect purchasing decisions. Verbal/Linguistic

R Reading Skills

☐ **GRAPHIC ORGANIZER Advantages of Prices**—Students describe each advantage of the price system: neutrality, flexibility, familiarity, efficiency. Verbal/Linguistic

C Critical Thinking Skills

☐ **BELLRINGER How Prices Work**—Students decide purchasing decisions based on price increases or decreases.

☐ **ESSENTIAL QUESTION Exploring the Essential Question Activity**—Students discuss the effects price had on their allocation of money and time in terms of their purchasing decisions.

T Technology Skills

☐ **SELF-CHECK QUIZ Lesson 1**—Students receive instant feedback on their mastery of lesson content.

☐ **GAME Lesson 1**—Students solve clues to review lesson content.

☐ **INTERACTIVE WHITEBOARD ACTIVITY Prices as Signals**—Students work together to learn lesson content.

☑ Printable Digital Worksheets

R Reading Skills

☐ **WORKSHEET Guided Reading Activity**—Students use the Guided Reading Activity worksheets to review their comprehension of the content.

☐ **WORKSHEET Reading Essentials and Study Guide**—Students complete the study guide and answer Reading Progress Check and vocabulary questions.

C Critical Thinking Skills

☐ **WORKSHEET Food Prices Video Activity**—Students answer questions related to food prices and how they affect purchasing decisions.

LESSON 2 Planner

THE EFFECTS OF PRICES

Students will know:
- the non-price determinants that create changes in supply and demand, which result in a new equilibrium price.
- shortages of a product usually result in price increases in a market economy; surpluses usually result in price decreases.

Students will be able to:
- **discuss** how price can affect a seller's decision to produce a product.
- **predict** how a change in supply or demand may affect prices.
- **describe** the relationship between prices and competitive markets.

UNDERSTANDING BY DESIGN®

☑ Print Teaching Options

V Visual Skills

☐ **p. 161 Evaluating the validity of a graph** Students compare data in a graph with their knowledge of current burrito prices. **AL**

R Reading Skills

☐ **p. 161 Understanding the importance of "voluntary"** Students write a short paragraph explaining why the actions of buyers and sellers in a market can be considered voluntary.

C Critical Thinking Skills

☐ **p. 160 Understanding prices** Students brainstorm a list of products and estimate a reasonable price for each product.

☐ **p. 162 Identifying suppliers' motivation** Students will discuss the fact that there are marketing firms hired specifically by companies to poll consumers about the price they would pay for the company's product. **AL**

☐ **p. 163 Price Adjustments** Students deliver a short oral report describing the market forces that caused a product they have purchased to drop in price.

☐ **p. 163 Identifying surpluses and shortages** Students examine situations surrounding the surplus or shortage of three products they choose, and how sellers could avoid the surplus or shortage. **AL**

☐ **p. 164 Explaining factors that affect equilibrium prices** Students explain how nonprice determinants of supply and demand could affect the equilibrium price of a product.

☐ **p. 166 Summarizing causes and effects of shortages** Students write a paragraph stating what would happen if there were a shortage in a product they use.

W Writing Skills

☐ **p. 165 Writing a narrative about effects on prices** Students write a short story about an entrepreneur who must deal with supply fluctuations and their effect on prices. **BL**

☑ Online Teaching Options

V Visual Skills

☐ **VIDEO How to Negotiate Prices for Everything**—Students view a video on how to negotiate prices using supply and demand.

☐ **GRAPHS Market Equilibrium**—Students use an interactive graph to explore supply, demand, and equilibrium prices.

☐ **GRAPHS Surplus and Shortage**—Students explore an interactive graph to see how prices create shortages and surpluses and write a paragraph about their results.

R Reading Skills

☐ **GRAPHIC ORGANIZERS Cause and Effect of Surplus and Shortage**—Students use the graphic organizer to identify the causes and effects of surpluses and shortages. *Verbal/Linguistic*

C Critical Thinking Skills

☐ **BELLRINGER How Prices Work**—Students conclude that prices rise for shortage items with a large quantity demanded.

☐ **ESSENTIAL QUESTION Exploring the Essential Question**—Students use prior knowledge of prices, supply, and demand to decide whether a price is too high, too low, or just right.

☐ **INTERACTIVE FEATURE Global Economy & You**—Students read a text and click to see differences in iPhone® prices across the globe, predicting how Internet purchasing will affect prices in the future. *Visual/Spatial*

☐ **GRAPH Changes in Prices**—Students explore supply and demand curves to predict changes in the equilibrium price. *Visual/Spatial, Logical/Mathematical*

T Technology Skills

☐ **SELF-CHECK QUIZ Lesson 2**—Students receive instant feedback on their mastery of lesson content.

☐ **GAME Lesson 2**—Students solve clues to review lesson content.

☐ **INTERACTIVE WHITEBOARD ACTIVITY Supply and Demand: Burritos**—Students work together to learn lesson content.

☑ Printable Digital Worksheets

R Reading Skills

☐ **WORKSHEET Guided Reading Activity**—Students use the Guided Reading Activity worksheets to review their comprehension of the content.

☐ **WORKSHEET Reading Essentials and Study Guide**—Students complete the study guide and answer Reading Progress Check and vocabulary questions.

C Critical Thinking Skills

☐ **WORKSHEET How to Negotiate Prices for Everything Video Activity**—Students use the worksheet to answer questions about a video on negotiating prices.

LESSON 3 Planner

SOCIAL GOALS, PRICES, AND MARKET EFFICIENCY

Students will know:
- how government wage and price controls create shortages and surpluses and prevent prices from allocating goods and services.
- the positive and negative effects of government programs to help stabilize prices.

Students will be able to:
- **examine** the effect of price ceilings and price floors on a market.
- **evaluate** government efforts to achieve social goals by interfering with the natural flow of supply and demand in a free enterprise system.
- **identify** events that may cause markets to "talk."

UNDERSTANDING BY DESIGN®

☑ Print Teaching Options

V Visual Skills

☐ **p. 168 Understanding placement of price ceilings and floors on graphs** Students understand that a price ceiling is visually "low" while a price floor is visually "high" on graphs.

☐ **p. 169 Analyzing graphs of price ceilings and price floors** Students explore graphs to show how price ceilings and floors control prices.

R Reading Skills

☐ **p. 168 Understanding motives behind government setting prices** Students consider why government is involved with price setting.

☐ **p. 169 Understanding subsidies as a price floor** Students explore subsidies to understand them as price floors.

☐ **p. 170 Analyzing Milton Friedman's impact** Students analyze who most benefited from Friedman's ideas. **Interpersonal**

C Critical Thinking Skills

☐ **p. 171 Understanding rent control as a price ceiling** Students prepare a short dialogue simulating a landlord and a tenant in front of a rent control board. **Verbal/Linguistic**

☐ **p. 172 Comparing earnings to expenses** Students compare household expenses with the amount they would make working full time at a minimum wage job. **Logical/Mathematical**

☐ **p. 170 Debating a Friedman philosophy** Students discuss a quote by Milton Friedman.

W Writing Skills

☐ **p. 172 Understanding the minimum wage as a price floor** Students present their opinions about the minimum wage. **Intrapersonal**

☐ **p. 172 Narrating a dialogue about "talking" markets** Students find a news article about markets "talking" in response to events.

☐ **p. 173 Explaining price controls in your community** Students write about the benefits and drawbacks of a price control in their community.

☑ Online Teaching Options

V Visual Skills

☐ **GRAPHS** **Price Ceilings and Price Floors**—Students explore the graphs to see how shortages and surpluses are related to price ceilings and price floors.

☐ **GRAPHS** **Price Ceiling**—Students explore a graph to show how the quantity of apartments demanded is affected by where the price ceiling is set.

☐ **GRAPHS, MAP** **Price Floor**—Students explore a graph and a map showing how the price floor affects minimum wage across the United States.

☐ **VIDEO** **Raising Minimum Wage**—Students watch a video about the pros and cons of raising the minimum wage.

R Reading Skills

☐ **GRAPHIC ORGANIZERS** **Goal of Price Ceiling and Price Floor**—Students brainstorm ideas about why price ceilings and floors are set. **Verbal/Linguistic**

☐ **BIOGRAPHIES** **Milton Friedman**—Students infer what Friedman would say about rent control.

C Critical Thinking Skills

☐ **BELLRINGER** **Social Goals, Prices, and Market Efficiency**—Students brainstorm situations in which rationing might be effective, such as during a war or drought.

☐ **ESSENTIAL QUESTION** **Exploring the Essential Question**—Students discuss the effects government setting prices.

W Writing Skills

☐ **INTERACTIVE FEATURE** **Careers**—Students analyze the job of cost estimator.

T Technology Skills

☐ **SELF-CHECK QUIZ** **Lesson 3**—Students assess mastery of lesson content.

☐ **GAME** **Lesson 3**—Students solve clues to review lesson content.

☐ **INTERACTIVE WHITEBOARD ACTIVITY** **Prices Review**—Students work together to learn lesson content.

☑ Printable Digital Worksheets

R Reading Skills

☐ **WORKSHEET** **Guided Reading Activity**—Students review their comprehension of the content.

☐ **WORKSHEET** **Reading Essentials and Study Guide**—Students complete the study guide and answer Reading Progress Check questions.

☐ **WORKSHEET** **Reteaching Activity**—This can be used with struggling students who need additional help with difficult content concepts.

C Critical Thinking Skills

☐ **WORKSHEET** **Raising Minimum Wage Video Activity**—Students answer questions about the pros and cons of raising the minimum wage.

CHAPTER 6 Prices

INTERVENTION AND REMEDIATION STRATEGIES

LESSON 1 How Prices Work

Reading and Comprehension

Before students read the text, have them scan through the lesson and write down the Reading Progress Check questions about how prices work. Tell students to leave space underneath each question to write notes. Ask them to take notes related to each subsection under its corresponding question. When they get to the end of each subsection, ask them to answer the corresponding Reading Progress Check question using their notes.

Text Evidence

Ask students to write down each Guiding Question and underline key words or a phrase in each question. Have students scan the text for these key words and phrases. Ask them to write one sentence from the text that includes these key words and phrases and helps to answer each Guiding Question.

LESSON 2 The Effects of Prices

Reading and Comprehension

Have students read the text of the lesson. As they read, ask them to pause after each subsection and write one question about the effects of prices. Then have them switch questions with a partner and answer their partner's questions. Finally, have each student check their partner's answers.

Text Evidence

Have students work with a partner. Ask each student to find an example in the text of how prices affect the behavior of consumers, and rewrite that example in their own words. Then have students switch examples and ask them to find the original example in the text that goes with the rewritten example.

LESSON 3 Social Goals, Prices, and Market Efficiency

Reading and Comprehension

Have students read through the text of the lesson. Then ask them to use each content vocabulary word in a sentence that expresses an idea stated in the lesson. The sentences should be mostly in the students' words, rather than sentences taken verbatim from the text.

Text Evidence

Have students write down an example from the text of a product that has a price floor. Then have them write down an example from the text of a product that has a price ceiling. Finally, have them write down the three markets in the text that "talk," and give evidence from the text that explains what the markets "say."

Online Resources

Assessing Background Knowledge Use this worksheet to pre-assess students' knowledge before they start the chapter.

Chapter Summaries Have students use the summary as a pre-reading activity or as a post-reading review to check main ideas covered in each lesson.

Guided Reading Activities Have students complete these activities as they read each lesson. They provide reading notes the student can use for review and to prepare for assessments.

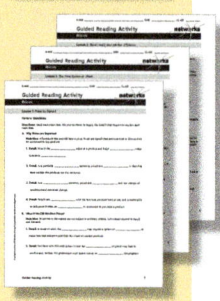

Reteaching Activities Have students complete the Reteaching Activity for remedial practice and review of vital content.

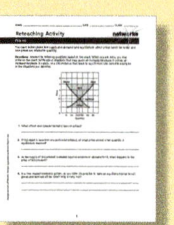

Self-Check Quizzes These quizzes provide instant feedback on areas the students may need to re-read to understand a main idea.

Reading Essentials and Study Guide This resource offers writing and reading activities for the approaching-level student.

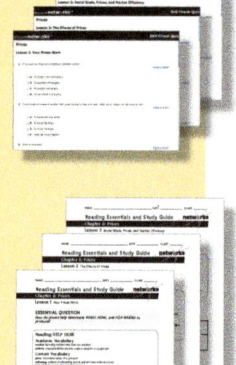

Approaching Grade Level Reader This reader presents all of the content of the Online Student Edition but at a lower reading level.

English Language Learner Reader Provide additional reading support for ELL students. Find this tool in the Online Student Edition.

Prices

ESSENTIAL QUESTIONS
- How do prices help us make decisions?
- What factors affect prices?

networks
www.connected.mcgraw-hill.com
There's More Online about prices.

CHAPTER 6

Economic Perspectives
What's behind gas prices?

Lesson 1
How Prices Work

Lesson 2
The Effects of Prices

Lesson 3
Social Goals, Prices, and Market Efficiency

CHAPTER 6
Prices

ENGAGE

Call students' attention to the photo and ask them to describe what it shows. Guide them to recognize that a store clerk is electronically scanning the price of a product. **Ask: How does this image symbolize the chapter titled *Prices*?** *(Answers may vary, but students should recognize that almost everything consumers purchase in the United States has a price that has been determined through market forces.)* In a discussion, lead students to understand that prices are the result of the interaction of supply and demand.

Categorizing factors that influence prices
Organize the class into pairs. Have each pair interview a local business owner about the factors that influence the prices of certain items he or she sells. Ask students to present the results of their interviews to the class. **Interpersonal**

Making Connections

Ceteris Paribus Remind students that *ceteris paribus* is a Latin term meaning "all other things held equal." When economists look at the causes and effects of economic activity, they make the assumption that nothing is changing except for the variable they are studying. For example, the *ceteris paribus* assumption states that when the price of apples increases, people will buy fewer apples. This implies that the prices of pineapples, oranges, bananas, and other fruits remained the same, or "held equal." In real life, however, perhaps the prices of other fruits rose even *higher* than the price of apples did. In this situation, consumers might purchase even MORE apples.

FOLDABLES
Study Organizer

Go to the Foldables® library for a cumulative chapter-based Foldable® activity that your students can use to help take notes and prepare for assessment.

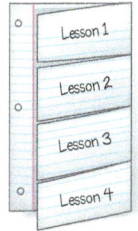

Letter from the Author
Dear Economics Teacher,

Finally, we are able to put supply and demand together to make a market! It's our third chapter that relies heavily on graphs, but by now students should be comfortable with them. The reason we need so many graphs, of course, is to show how prices are determined as well as what happens to prices when there is a change in either supply or demand. Sometimes the forces are strong, and at other times they are weaker—but either way these forces are the key to how a market system is able to determine prices without involving government. It's too bad everything isn't so simple.

Gary E. Clayton

CHAPTER 6
Economic Perspectives

TEACH & ASSESS

Making Connections

Products Derived from Crude Oil Have students list all of the products they come in contact with on a daily basis, including shampoo, milk carton, lunch tray, MP3 player, and so on. Then have them research these products online to see which are created or derived from crude oil. Ask students to consider which of these products might be created from a different base, or which should be earmarked as high-priority recyclable products.

C Critical Thinking Skills

Determining the effect on supply or demand
Organize students into pairs. Have each student use the infographic's captions to create index cards with 10 real or imaginary scenarios and their effects on supply or demand for oil. For example, the caption below "MANY MARKETS" may tie to a scenario such as: "New technology has led to the creation of windows made from an oil-based product instead of glass." Have each student note on the back of the index card whether the scenario affects supply or demand, and also whether it *increases* or *decreases* supply or demand. After students create their 10 scenarios, have them quiz their partner with the index cards. Then gather the cards and randomly select several scenarios to quiz the class as a whole.

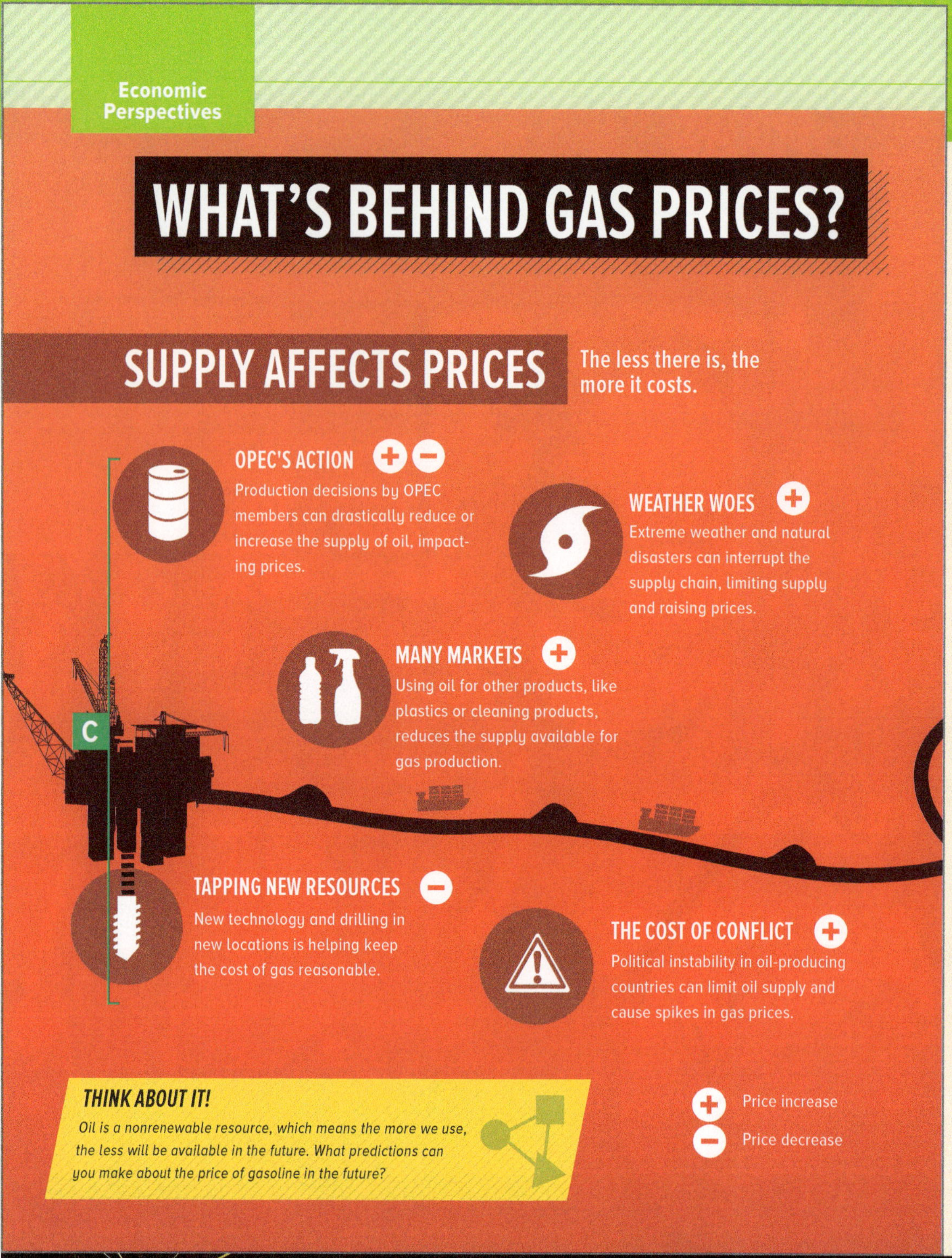

Economic Perspectives

WHAT'S BEHIND GAS PRICES?

SUPPLY AFFECTS PRICES
The less there is, the more it costs.

OPEC'S ACTION (+)(−)
Production decisions by OPEC members can drastically reduce or increase the supply of oil, impacting prices.

WEATHER WOES (+)
Extreme weather and natural disasters can interrupt the supply chain, limiting supply and raising prices.

MANY MARKETS (+)
Using oil for other products, like plastics or cleaning products, reduces the supply available for gas production.

TAPPING NEW RESOURCES (−)
New technology and drilling in new locations is helping keep the cost of gas reasonable.

THE COST OF CONFLICT (+)
Political instability in oil-producing countries can limit oil supply and cause spikes in gas prices.

THINK ABOUT IT!
Oil is a nonrenewable resource, which means the more we use, the less will be available in the future. What predictions can you make about the price of gasoline in the future?

(+) Price increase
(−) Price decrease

---

networks Online Teaching Options

INFOGRAPHIC

Economic Perspectives: What's Behind Gas Prices?

Categorizing factors that influence prices Ask students to list the goods and services they purchased over the past week. Next, ask them to list the prices of those goods and services. **Ask: What factors do you think affected the prices you paid?** *(Possible answers: Bad weather reduced crops, which increased the price of feed grain and ultimately hamburger. A fire at an oil refinery resulted in a shortage of gasoline, which raised fuel prices.)* **How might the government have influenced the prices of items you bought during the last week?** *(Possible answers: Government funds reduced the price of school lunches. A recent increase of the minimum wage caused a local pizza restaurant owner to raise the price of pizza.)* **Logical/Mathematical**

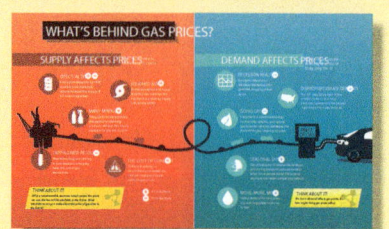

ANSWERS, p. 152

THINK ABOUT IT!

Because oil is a nonrenewable resource and less will be available in the future, students should be able to predict that the price of gasoline will continue to rise. If a viable alternative to gasoline is developed, demand for gasoline could decrease and thus cause the price to decrease.

For an interactive version of this infographic go to **connected.mcgraw-hill.com**

CHAPTER 6
Economic Perspectives

Have you ever wondered what causes the neverending changes in gas prices? Sometimes it seems like you blink and the price is different. The powerful factors of supply and demand, both of gasoline itself and the crude oil used to make it, play a big part in the price you pay at the pump.

DEMAND AFFECTS PRICES
The more people want it, the more they pay for it.

RECESSION REALITIES ⊖
Economic downturns decrease the demand for gasoline, dragging prices down.

DISPROPORTIONATE DEMAND ⊕
The U.S. uses 20 percent of the world's crude oil (but only produces 2 percent of the supply). Importing oil to meet demand raises prices.

GOING GREEN ⊖
The growth in alternative energy, such as solar, electric, and natural gas-powered vehicles, decreases the demand for gas, lowering its price.

SEASONAL SHIFTS ⊕
Gas prices spike on weekends, holidays, and during the warm summer months when more people travel. Prices drop during winter when people stay indoors.

MORE, MORE, MORE! ⊕
Global demand for oil is growing, ensuring prices continue to rise.

THINK ABOUT IT!
We know demand affects gas prices, but how might rising gas prices affect demand?

connected.mcgraw-hill.com   Prices **153**

C Critical Thinking Skills

Applying factors that affect demand Ask students to identify the factors that can cause a change in demand (which they learned about in Chapter 4): changes in consumer income, changes in consumer tastes, a change in the price of related substitutes or complements, a change in expectations, and a change in the number of consumers. Then have students provide a specific example of how each factor has increased the demand for oil worldwide. For example, an increase in China's middle class has resulted in an increase in the number of consumers who demand vehicles and other consumer products, and thus an increase in the demand for oil.

Content Background Knowledge

Defining the "Middle Class" The rise in alternative energy sources, which lowers demand for gasoline and crude oil, is counterbalanced by the rise of the middle class in many emerging economies and their growing dependence on oil-based products. The United Nations defines a middle class individual as "someone who earns or spends $10 to $100 per day." The Brookings Institute forecasts that by 2030, Asia's middle class will reach 3 billion, Latin America's middle class will increase from 181 to 303 million, and Africa and the Middle East's middle class will rise from 137 to 341 million.

CLOSE & REFLECT

Have students answer the *Think About It!* questions.

WORKSHEET

Enrichment Activity

Understanding the connection between shortages, prices, and rationing Assign the Enrichment Activity worksheet. In 1973, President Richard Nixon abandoned the gold standard, which pegged the U.S. dollar to a set amount of gold. The resulting dive in the value of the dollar angered OPEC, the organization formed by the oil-rich nations of the Middle East. As punishment, they decided to impose an oil embargo on the United States, which resulted in an oil shortage and skyrocketing oil prices. The United States was placed in a position of having to ration gasoline to consumers. In this worksheet, students are asked to read about the embargo and answer questions related to the text. **Logical/Mathematical**

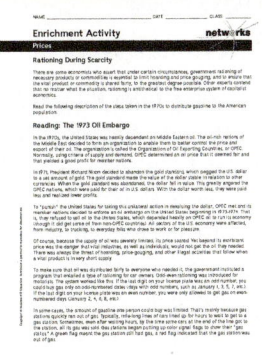

ANSWERS, p. 153

THINK ABOUT IT!

The Law of Demand states that consumers will demand more of a product as its price decreases, and vice versa. Therefore, students should be able to predict that rising gas prices will cause demand to decrease.

Prices **153**

CHAPTER 6, LESSON 1
How Prices Work

ENGAGE

C Critical Thinking Skills

🔔 **Understanding prices in a market economy** Before students begin the lesson, ask them to discuss the effect of prices on their behavior as consumers. Have volunteers come up with two examples from their own purchasing behavior: one example of purchasing an item based on the price, and one example of deciding not to purchase an item based on the price. Then explain that changing prices and the resulting change in behavior of consumers and producers balances a market economy.

Interact with these digital assets and others in lesson 1.

- ✓ EXPLORING THE ESSENTIAL QUESTION
- ✓ INTERACTIVE IMAGE Decision-making Without Prices
- ✓ SELF-CHECK QUIZ
- ✓ VIDEO

networks TRY IT YOURSELF ONLINE

LESSON 1
How Prices Work

ESSENTIAL QUESTION

Reading Help Desk

Academic Vocabulary
- neutral
- criteria

Content Vocabulary
- price
- rationing
- biofuels

TAKING NOTES:

Key Ideas and Details
ACTIVITY Use a graphic organizer like the one below to list the advantages of a price system in a market economy.

How do prices help determine WHAT, HOW, and FOR WHOM to produce?

How does the price of a product affect how you allocate scarce resources—your money and your time? Make a list of three things you or your family purchased in the last year. For each item, answer the following questions.

a. Was the price of the product clear and easy to identify? Explain your answer.
b. Would you have paid more for the product if you had to? If so, how much more?
c. If the price of the product was lower, would you have bought more of it?
d. Did the price of a competing brand or product affect the decision you made?
e. Would you have gone to another store or website if the price of the product was lower there?

Why Prices Are Important

GUIDING QUESTION *How do prices help us make decisions?*

Suppose you walk into your favorite coffee shop and a sign on the wall says your frozen coffee with extra whipped cream will cost you $4.50. The price seems a little steep, but you're willing to pay it because, after all, you love coffee. But what if tomorrow that coffee costs twice as much? Would you still be willing to buy it?

Price—the monetary value of a product—does much more than simply tell you how much you have to spend when you make a purchase. Collectively, prices act as a system of signals that help us make economic decisions. At the same time, they function as incentives that affect the behavior of individuals, businesses, markets, and even entire industries. In fact, they have a number of advantages, discussed below, that you probably haven't even thought about.

Prices as Signals

There are many signals in life you are already familiar with. For example, pain is a signal that tells you something is wrong with your body. A traffic light at

---

networks   *Online Teaching Options*

BELLRINGER

How Prices Work

Activating Prior Knowledge Have students work in groups to complete the Bellringer activity. Then provide a print or online catalog to students. Have them work in pairs to choose two items they would like to purchase—one inexpensive and one expensive. Ask how they would decide whether or not to buy each item, and how that decision would change if the price increased or decreased.

ANSWERS, p. 154

ESSENTIAL QUESTION ACTIVITY

Students' answers will vary depending on the product selected and the students' own experiences, but students should recognize that prices influence their decisions about what and how much to buy.

TAKING NOTES: Answers in the graphic organizer should include: Neutrality, Flexibility, Familiarity, and Efficiency.

an intersection signals when to stop or go. Like pain or a traffic light, prices are signals that give information to buyers and sellers. High prices signal buyers to buy less and producers to produce more. Low prices signal buyers to buy more and producers to produce less.

The signals we get from prices also serve as incentives which cause us to take additional actions. If the price of something goes up, you may decide to shop at a different location, or find a comparable substitute. Likewise, a firm may stop producing other items to free up the labor, capital, and machinery needed to increase production of a product that can be sold for a higher price.

Advantages of Prices

Prices help producers and consumers answer the three basic questions of WHAT, HOW, and FOR WHOM to produce. Without prices, the economy would not run as smoothly, and these allocation decisions would have to be made some other way. Prices perform this function well for at least four reasons.

- **Neutrality** In a competitive market economy, prices are **neutral** because they favor neither the producer nor the consumer. Since prices are the result of competition between buyers and sellers, they represent compromises that both sides can live with.
- **Flexibility** Prices in a market economy help provide flexibility. Unforeseen events such as natural disasters and war affect the prices of many items. For example, when Hurricane Sandy destroyed much of the northeast United States in October 2012, oyster harvesters in the Chesapeake Bay were unable to work for several days. This caused the price of oysters to temporarily spike in places as far away as Georgia. Buyers and sellers then reacted to the new level of prices and adjusted their consumption and production accordingly, helping the system function smoothly again. The

price the monetary value of a product

neutral favoring neither one side nor another

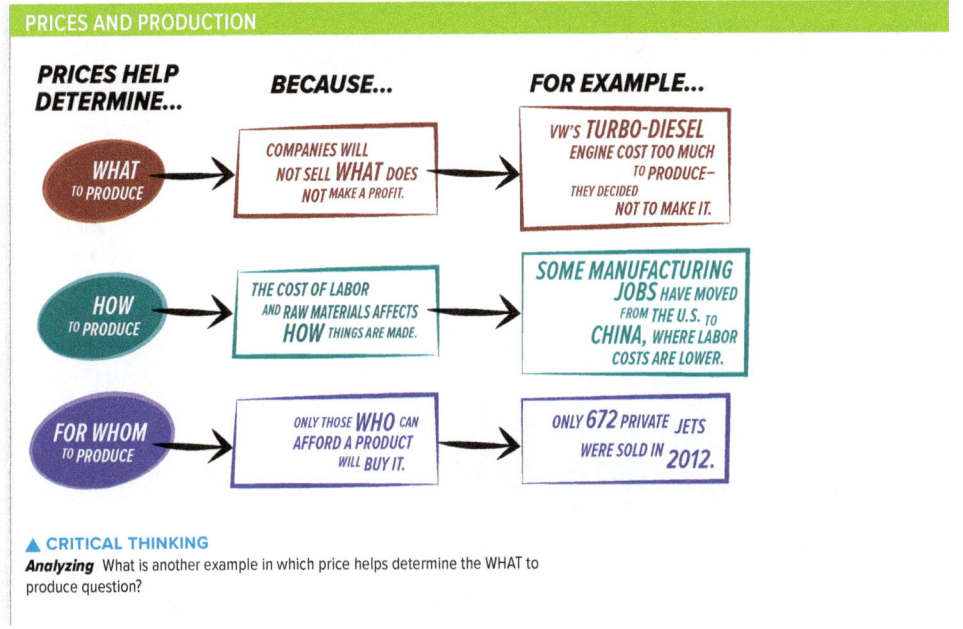

PRICES AND PRODUCTION

▲ CRITICAL THINKING
Analyzing What is another example in which price helps determine the WHAT to produce question?

Prices **155**

CHAPTER 6, LESSON 1
How Prices Work

TEACH & ASSESS

W Writing Skills

Identifying advantages of prices in action
Organize students into groups and assign each group one of the advantages of prices—neutrality, flexibility, familiarity, and efficiency. Direct groups to identify a real-life example of their assigned advantage in operation. Have groups develop a brief presentation showcasing their example. Presentations could take the form of an illustrated lecture, a television or radio news story, or a small exhibit. **BL** **ELL** **Kinesthetic**

C Critical Thinking Skills

Understanding the flexibility of prices Discuss as a class the advantages that using prices offers to both buyers and sellers. Then ask each student to choose a simple service he or she could perform after school to earn income; for example, babysitting, pet care, lawn moving, or computer repair. **Ask:** How would you go about setting an hourly price for your service in order to be competitive? Have students set a reasonable price. Then, to simulate the flexibility of prices, ask students to think of changing conditions that might affect that price; for example, the addition of another child to babysit, or a reduction in the amount of lawn to mow. Have students set what they consider reasonable prices to accommodate these changes. **Logical/Mathematical**

ESSENTIAL QUESTION

Exploring the Essential Question

Understanding prices and allocation of resources Ask students to think of a product they or their families purchased in the last year. Ask students to write down the approximate price of the item, as well as their reasons for deciding on that purchase. Explain to students that pricing affects not only their purchasing decisions but also the allocation of production resources by companies. Then have students work in groups to discuss and answer the questions in the activity. Finally, have each group present to the class the effects price had on their allocation of money and time in terms of their purchasing decisions.

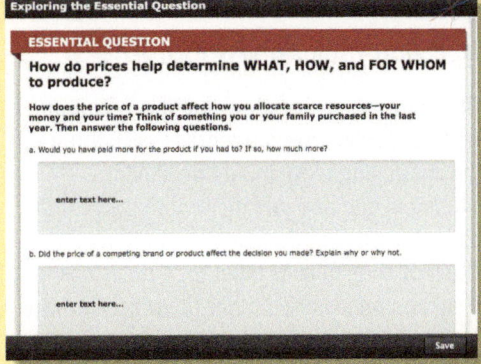

ANSWERS, p. 155

CRITICAL THINKING
Answers will vary. Producers of a popular product or fad, such as a particular athletic shoe, will profit as long as the cost to produce the item remains lower than the price to consumers.

Prices **155**

CHAPTER 6, LESSON 1
How Prices Work

W Writing Skills

Describing a society without prices Have students consider how their lives would be different if they lived in a society in which prices did not exist. Ask them to write a short story using standard sentence structure describing this fictional society. Tell students that they should include in their stories how the society addresses the questions of WHAT, HOW, and FOR WHOM. **BL** Verbal/Linguistic

R Reading Skills

Inferring types of governments that ration Have students use what they have learned from the text about rationing systems to infer what types of governments are most likely to ration purchases. **Ask: What types of governments do you think are most likely to make allocations based on rationing? Why?** (Totalitarian; those types of governments generally control purchasing decisions) **AL**

ANSWERS, p. 156

☑ **READING PROGRESS CHECK** People make purchasing decisions based on prices; this results in the allocation of goods and services.

EXPLORING THE ESSENTIAL QUESTION

Students' answers will vary, but they will most likely say that if the price increased, they would produce more in order to make more money from a popular product.

156

---

ability of the price system to absorb unexpected "shocks" is one of the strengths of prices in a market economy.

- **Familiarity** Most people have known about prices all their lives. As a result, prices are familiar and easy to understand. There is no ambiguity over a price—if something costs $1.99, then we know exactly what we have to pay to get it. This allows people to make decisions quickly and efficiently, with a minimum of time and effort.
- **Efficiency** Finally, prices have no cost of administration. Competitive markets tend to help products find their own prices without outside help or interference. No bureaucrats need to be hired, no committees formed, no laws passed, or other decisions made. Even when prices adjust from one level to another, the changes are usually so gradual that people hardly notice.

☑ **READING PROGRESS CHECK**

Summarizing What decisions do prices help consumers and producers make?

What If We Did Not Have Prices?

GUIDING QUESTION *Are prices the best way to allocate resources?*

Have you ever thought about how our economy would function without prices? Without knowing the prices of goods or services, how would we decide WHAT to produce? Without knowing the cost of productive inputs, how would we answer the HOW to produce question? Finally, how would we decide FOR WHOM to produce? Would intelligence, good looks, or even political connections determine the allocation?

criteria characteristics used to make a decision or judgment

rationing system of allocating goods and services without prices

EXPLORING THE ESSENTIAL QUESTION

Imagine you run a company that makes and sells skateboards. If the price of skateboards started to increase, would you choose to make more skateboards or fewer skateboards? Explain your decision.

These questions may seem far-fetched, but even command economies need **criteria** to answer these questions. For example, when the Baltimore Orioles played an exhibition baseball game in Cuba in 1999, there were not enough stadium seats for all the local baseball fans who wanted to attend. Cuba's Prime Minister at the time, Fidel Castro, then solved the FOR WHOM question by giving the seats to Communist Party members—whether they were baseball fans or not.

Rationing

Without prices, another system must be used to decide who gets what. One method is rationing—a system under which government decides everyone's "fair" share. Under such a system, people receive a ration coupon, a ticket or a receipt that entitles the holder to obtain a certain amount of a product. The coupon can be given to people outright, or the government can charge a modest fee. **Rationing** was used widely during World War II, but has not had widespread use since then. This is because the problems with rationing are more extensive than most people realize.

In 1999 the Baltimore Orioles visited Cuba to play against the Cuban national team. The Cuban government rationed the number of tickets made available to the people of Cuba.

156

---

networks *Online Teaching Options*

IMAGES

Decision-making Without Prices

Understanding decision-making with and without prices Ask students to click through the image and read about two similar situations that had one major difference: the setting of prices. Discuss with students which situation they think is most fair—decisions based on prices or on other factors—and why. Ask students to write a short paragraph explaining their opinion, using details from the image's captions to support their ideas. **Verbal/Linguistic, Visual/Spatial**

Problems with Rationing

In the mid-1970s, the country faced an energy crisis that quadrupled the price of oil. State governments implemented a simple form of rationing to deal with gasoline shortages in 1973. Drivers whose license plates ended in an odd number could buy gas on odd days, while drivers with even-number plates could buy gas on even numbered days. In 1974 the national government started to make plans for further gasoline rationing involving coupons, but the plans were never implemented, largely because of the following problems:

- **Perceived Fairness** The debate over fairness began immediately. People in small towns thought they should have more coupons than people in big cities, because big cities had better mass transit systems.

What happens when there is . . .

RESIDENTS OF **NEW YORK CITY** LINED UP FOR THEIR **RATIONED SHARE OF GASOLINE** AFTER HURRICANE SANDY PRODUCED **SHORTAGES IN 2012**

Rationing in the United States

Wartime Rationing 1942–1945

During World War II, the federal government rationed food, gasoline, and even clothing. This was done to ensure that the raw materials or the finished products for these items were guaranteed for military use.

The vast majority of Americans supported U.S. involvement in World War II after Japan attacked Pearl Harbor in December 1941. As a result, most Americans readily complied with the rationing and restrictions the government put in place, even though it eliminated the market-driven forces of supply and demand.

Rationing Today

Modern-day rationing in the United States is uncommon and is usually a temporary response to an unexpected crisis or shortage.

In late 2012 New England states implemented temporary gas rationing after Hurricane Sandy made it difficult to deliver enough gasoline to the area residents. In 2013 a nationwide helium shortage meant the gas was conserved for use in essential medical and manufacturing industries. As a result, party supply stores received only a small ration of helium for use in balloons.

▲ **CRITICAL THINKING**

Making Predictions Do you think it is a good idea for the government to implement rationing during a crisis or shortage? What might be the result if the economy relied on the price system instead of rationing?

CHAPTER 6, LESSON 1
How Prices Work

C Critical Thinking Skills

Describing allocation decisions in a price system
Ask students to discuss how automakers' decisions about allocation of resources might change as oil prices rise. Students should consider the types of vehicles automakers produce and their relative consumption of fuel, as well as consumers' willingness to purchase these vehicles. AL

English Language Proficiency

Advanced Pair students and have partner 1 retell the lesson in his or her own words while partner 2 takes notes. Next, have partners write a summary based on the notes. Then have the pair turn to another pair. Partner 2 will retell the summary while the other pair checks the summary to see if anything important was left out.

ANSWERS, p. 158

☑ **READING PROGRESS CHECK** Price system: people make their own purchasing decisions based on the prices of goods and services. Rationing system: government agency decides what and how many goods and services people will receive.

People with older cars thought they should have more coupons, because their cars were less fuel-efficient than newer ones. However, people with newer cars thought that this would penalize them for having bought more expensive, fuel-efficient ones. Couples with several cars thought they should have more coupons because they had more cars, but couples with one car thought that would not be fair to them. Consequently, making a distribution system that everyone thought would be fair seemed almost hopeless.

- **Administrative Expense** The administrative cost of rationing is another major issue. Someone has to pay for the printing and distribution costs of the coupons, and that includes the salaries of workers. Every community would also need "review boards" so that someone could listen to those who thought they should have more coupons. In 1974, nearly 5 billion gasoline ration coupons were printed just in case the government decided to go ahead with a rationing program. The tentative plans, never carried out, were to ship the coupons to every post office in every city or town in the country so that everyone would have access to them after the "fairness" problem was resolved.
- **Distorted Incentives** Rationing programs are specifically designed to take the place of supply and demand. The one in 1974 that was designed to keep the cost of gasoline low for consumers would have distorted market incentives in three different ways: Energy companies would have been discouraged from producing more gasoline. Automobile companies would have had less incentive to produce more fuel-efficient vehicles. And, consumers would have had less incentive to reduce unnecessary driving to save gasoline. None of these incentives solved the basic problem of too little supply and too much demand.
- **Abuse and Misuse** Finally, no matter how much care was taken, some coupons would have been stolen, sold, or counterfeited. The 1974 gasoline coupons had another unique problem. To make them difficult to counterfeit, each carried a high-quality portrait of President Washington like the one on a dollar bill. Unfortunately the likeness was so good that a ration coupon could also be used in a dollar-changing machine. This gave anyone with a coupon the option to use it for a gallon of gas that cost about sixty cents, or to use it in a coin changer to get four quarters.

As you can imagine, the problems with rationing are extremely difficult to solve. The many problems surrounding the 1974 gasoline rationing coupons were the reason that they were never issued and later destroyed.

☑ **READING PROGRESS CHECK**

Contrasting What are the differences between the price system and rationing?

Prices as a System

GUIDING QUESTION *How do prices connect markets in an economy?*

Although the price system is not perfect, most economists believe it is the most efficient way to allocate resources. This is because prices do more than help individuals make decisions; they also help allocate resources both within and between markets.

Consider the way in which higher prices rippled through markets today, causing changes both large and small. Because the demand for gas is basically inelastic, high gas prices mean that people have to spend a greater part of their income on gas, leaving them with less money to spend elsewhere. If enough

---

networks — Online Teaching Options

VIDEO WORKSHEET

Food Prices

Understanding how food prices affect purchasing decisions
Ask students to read the video worksheet to preview the questions before viewing the video. Then have students watch the video and answer the questions. As a class, discuss the answers. Ask volunteers to relate personal or family experiences with rising food prices and purchasing decisions. **Verbal/Linguistic**

drivers believe that higher gas prices are likely to be permanent, they may buy more fuel-efficient cars, including hybrids that run on both electricity and gasoline. Many others may instead decide to rely more on their city mass-transit systems, or do without automobiles altogether.

Over time, the impact of higher gas prices will spill over to the farm and consumer food sectors. Farmers will benefit if they sell more of their grain to companies that make gasahol, a blend of 90 percent unleaded gasoline and 10 percent grain alcohol. But, whenever more grain is used in fuels, less is available to make flour—which raises the price of bread. Other companies may make major investments in **biofuels**—fuels whose energy is derived from renewable plant and animal materials, vegetable oils, and municipal and industrial wastes—in hopes of developing adequate substitutes for gasoline.

The ultimate impact of higher gas prices is to cause productive resources, like raw materials and workers, to shift out of some industries and into others: out of wheat production for flour and bread and into wheat production for gasahol; out of gas-guzzling automobiles and into fuel-efficient hybrids; out of other industries and into renewable fuels. Although the adjustment process is painful for many individuals and companies, it is a natural and necessary shift of resources for a market economy.

biofuels a fuel created from living materials

EXPLORING THE ESSENTIAL QUESTION

Think of an example of a product or technology that no longer exists or that is not as common as it once was. Then answer the following questions.

a. Why do you think this product or technology is no longer produced?

b. For what other product or industry might the resources that formerly produced this product now be used?

c. What do you think happened to the price of this product before producers stopped making it?

In the end, prices do more than convey information to buyers and sellers in a market: they also help allocate resources between markets. This is why economists think of prices as a "system"—part of an informational network—that links all markets in the economy.

✓ **READING PROGRESS CHECK**

Identifying How do prices help allocate resources between markets?

LESSON 1 REVIEW

Reviewing Vocabulary

1. *Defining* Explain in your own words how the terms *rationing* and *price* are related.

Using Your Notes

2. *Summarizing* Use your notes to explain why the price system is an efficient allocator of economic resources.

Answering the Guiding Questions

3. *Explaining* How do prices help us make decisions?
4. *Evaluating* Are prices the best way to allocate resources?
5. *Describing* How do prices connect markets in an economy?

Writing About Economics

6. *Informative/Explanatory* Research an example of rationing that took place in either the United States or another country. Under what circumstances was rationing implemented? How was it implemented? What effect did rationing have on the economy? Was rationing an effective way to allocate goods and services in this particular situation? Write a two-page essay to explain your findings.

CHAPTER 6, LESSON 1
How Prices Work

C Critical Thinking Skills

Diagramming effects in a price system Have students create a diagram that shows the effects of increased prices on a particular industry or system. For example, a drought may reduce grain feed, which increases its overall price, which increases the price of beef and milk, which increases the price of other products dependent on beef and milk. In contrast, products not affected by grain prices (substitutes) hold prices steady and become more attractive to consumers. As more consumers purchase those products, other suppliers enter the market and draw even more consumers away from beef and milk products, eventually lowering demand. Challenge students to create at least ten system "links" in the diagram.

CLOSE & REFLECT

C Critical Thinking Skills

Categorizing the functions of prices Have students create a chart listing the various functions of prices (signals, incentives, and allocation, for example) as well as the four advantages of prices. On the chart, have them give examples of each function and advantage, either from the text or from their personal experiences.

ANSWERS, p. 159

EXPLORING THE ESSENTIAL QUESTION

Answers will vary, but students should recognize that the price of the product most likely dropped before the product ceased to be produced.

✓ **READING PROGRESS CHECK** Price increases lower demand, which causes manufacturers to shift resources to more profitable markets.

LESSON 1 REVIEW ANSWERS

Reviewing Vocabulary

1. *Rationing* is a system to allocate goods and services without the use of *prices*.

Using Your Notes

2. Prices are neutral, which means they are equally fair to both consumers and producers; flexible, which means they can adapt to changing economic conditions; familiar, which means everyone understands how they work; and efficient, because the market determines prices largely on its own and without administration.

Answering the Guiding Questions

3. Prices help producers determine what and how much to produce. Prices help consumers determine what and how much to buy. When prices are high for a product, producers will produce more of that product, but consumers will buy less of it. When prices are low for a product, producers will produce less of that product, but consumers will buy more.

4. Students' answers will vary, but they may say that yes, prices are the fairest way to allocate resources because they naturally adjust to the supply and demand for a product in the market, are efficient and inexpensive to use, and are neutral for buyers and sellers.

5. Prices connect markets because changes in one market create a ripple effect that is felt through prices in another market. For example, if there is a shortage of a raw material, it not only would raise the price of the raw material, it would raise the price of the products made from that material.

Writing About Economics

6. Answers will vary, but students should evaluate the situation objectively with the costs and benefits of both prices and rationing in mind.

CHAPTER 6, LESSON 2
The Effects of Prices

ENGAGE

C Critical Thinking Skills

Understanding prices Ask students to read the list of products and prices under the Exploring the Essential Question head. Discuss the prices as a class, product by product, and ask students to brainstorm reasons why each price is too high, too low, or just right. Then ask them to brainstorm a list of other products and estimate a reasonable price for each product. **Ask: How do you know the price for each product is reasonable?** *(Students' answers will vary, but should include details about seeing prices posted in advertisements or seeing products available in a variety of places at similar prices.)*

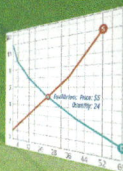

Interact with these digital assets and others in lesson 2
- INTERACTIVE GRAPH Market Equilibrium
- INTERACTIVE GRAPH Surplus & Shortage
- INTERACTIVE IMAGE Evaluating Prices
- SELF-CHECK QUIZ
- VIDEO

networks TRY IT YOURSELF ONLINE

Reading Help Desk

Academic Vocabulary
- voluntary
- fluctuate

Content Vocabulary
- economic model
- equilibrium price
- equilibrium quantity
- surplus
- shortage

TAKING NOTES:

Key Ideas and Details
ACTIVITY Use a graphic organizer like the one below to identify the causes and effects of surpluses and shortages.

Cause and Effect of Surplus and Shortage
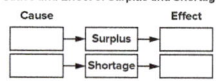

LESSON 2
The Effects of Prices

ESSENTIAL QUESTION

What factors affect prices?

You are the owner of a general store that sells a wide variety of products. A new employee has just finished putting price tags on several of the products and you are checking his work. For each of the following products, decide whether you think the price is too high, too low, or just right. Explain your decision for each.

C
- a. $7.99 for a new bicycle
- b. $1.00 for a can of corn
- c. $44 for a Frisbee
- d. $99 for a burrito
- e. $35 for a wristwatch
- f. $2 for a pair of socks

How Prices Adjust

GUIDING QUESTION *How does price affect a seller's decision to produce a product?*

Have you ever tried to buy something and had to haggle over the price? The transaction probably went something like this: the seller started by quoting a price that seemed unrealistically high. You countered with an offer that the seller thought was too low. Then you bargained until you settled on a price that was agreeable to both of you.

Of course you don't have to argue with sellers over the price of every product you buy. However, prices for almost all goods and services in a market economy represent compromises between buyers and sellers to reach a final price.

Markets and Prices

In a market economy, buyers and sellers have exactly the opposite goals: buyers want to find good deals at low prices, and sellers hope for high prices and large profits. Neither can get exactly what they want, so some adjustment is necessary to reach a compromise. In this way, everyone who participates has a hand in determining prices.

---

networks Online Teaching Options

BELLRINGER

What Factors Affect Prices

Activating Prior Knowledge Ask students to think of a time when they wanted something that was not immediately available, but later was found elsewhere. **Ask: Had the price of the item increased, decreased, or remained the same when you found it later?** Make a list of reasons why, based on student suggestions.

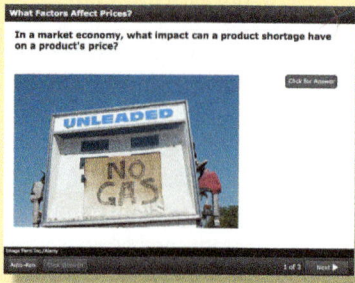

ANSWERS, p. 160

ESSENTIAL QUESTION ACTIVITY

Answers will vary, but students are likely to say that a is too low, c and d are too high, and b, e, and f are about right. They may say that they came to these conclusions based on their familiarity with the prices for these products in their own lives.

TAKING NOTES: Cause 1: Quantity higher than demand at a given price, Effect 1: Lower price; Cause 2: Quantity lower than demand at a given price, Effect 2: Higher price

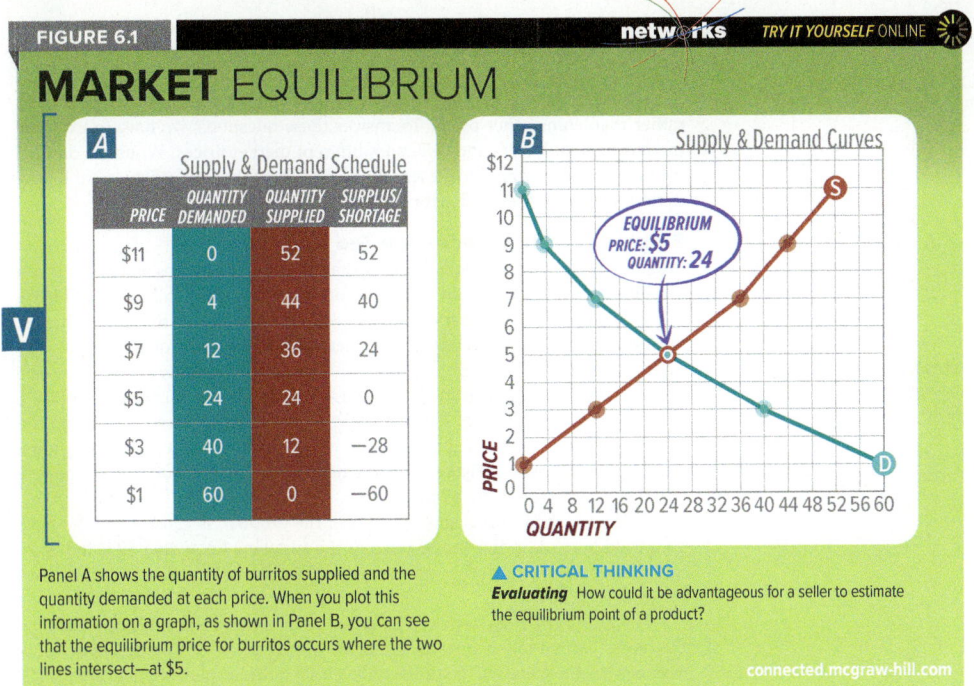

FIGURE 6.1

MARKET EQUILIBRIUM

A Supply & Demand Schedule

PRICE	QUANTITY DEMANDED	QUANTITY SUPPLIED	SURPLUS/ SHORTAGE
$11	0	52	52
$9	4	44	40
$7	12	36	24
$5	24	24	0
$3	40	12	−28
$1	60	0	−60

B Supply & Demand Curves

EQUILIBRIUM PRICE: $5 QUANTITY: 24

Panel A shows the quantity of burritos supplied and the quantity demanded at each price. When you plot this information on a graph, as shown in Panel B, you can see that the equilibrium price for burritos occurs where the two lines intersect—at $5.

▲ CRITICAL THINKING
Evaluating How could it be advantageous for a seller to estimate the equilibrium point of a product?

For example, how do we know that the price of a cell phone is fair to both the producer and the consumer? Most economists would argue that as long as the process is competitive and the transaction is voluntary, then the price will be just about right or the sale would not take place. Because transactions in a market economy are **voluntary**, the compromise that settles the differences between buyers and sellers must be to the benefit of both, or the phone would not be sold.

Supply and Demand

So, how does a market arrive at a compromise price that is "just about right"? To see how this process works, we'll put the burrito demand curve from Figure 4.3 and the burrito supply curve from Figure 5.3 together in **Figure 6.1**. This figure is the most popular "tool" used by economists and represents what most people simply call "supply and demand." The figure is also an **economic model** that can be used to analyze behavior and predict outcomes.

As we know from previous chapters, the data in Figure 6.1 show the market demand for and supply of burritos at various prices. **Panel A** shows this information in the form of a schedule, while **Panel B** shows both the market demand curve and the supply curve that are in the schedule. However, both curves can be combined into one diagram because the vertical and horizontal axes are identical in Figure 4.3 and Figure 5.3.

Note that the supply and demand curves intersect at a specific point. The price associated with this point is called the **equilibrium price**, the price at which the number supplied equals the number demanded. The equilibrium price is also called the *market clearing price* because it is the price at which there is neither a surplus nor a shortage. The **equilibrium quantity** is also associated with this price because the quantity supplied is equal to the quantity purchased.

voluntary done or brought about by free choice

economic model a simplified version of a complex behavior expressed in the form of an equation, graph, or illustration

equilibrium price price where quantity supplied equals quantity demanded

equilibrium quantity quantity of output supplied that is equal to the quantity demanded at the equilibrium price

CHAPTER 6, LESSON 2
The Effects of Prices

C Critical Thinking Skills

Identifying suppliers' motivation Ask: Do you think it is common for sellers to offer a new product at a price well above what turns out to be the equilibrium price? Why or why not? *(Answers will vary. Students responding "yes" may reason that sellers, wanting to maximize profits, will sell a product at as high a price as buyers are willing to pay. If the initial price turns out to be too high, sellers can later lower the price.)* Explain that there are marketing firms hired specifically by companies to poll consumers about the price they would pay for the company's product. **AL**

English Language Proficiency

Advanced Have students use a graphic novel treatment to retell the surplus and shortage information in the lesson. First, have them write one main idea in each frame of the strip. Then have them draw pictures to support the idea. Group students and have them use their graphic treatments to retell the information to one another.

This price, $5 in both Panels A and B of Figure 6.1, helps sellers decide how many productive and financial resources must be allocated to the production of that product.

But how does the market reach this equilibrium, and why does it settle at $5 rather than some other price? To answer these questions, we have to examine the reactions of buyers and sellers to different market prices. When we do this, we assume that neither buyers nor the sellers know the final price, so we'll have to find it by using trial and error.

Surpluses—When Prices Are Too High

We start on Day 1 with sellers thinking that the price of burritos will be $9. If you examine the supply schedule in Panel A or the supply curve in Panel B of Figure 6.1, you can see that suppliers will offer 44 burritos for sale at that price. Buyers, however, only want 4 burritos at that price, leaving a surplus of 40 burritos.

surplus situation where quantity supplied is greater than quantity demanded at a given price.

A **surplus** is a situation in which the quantity supplied is greater than the quantity demanded at a given price. The 40-burrito surplus at the end of Day 1 is shown in column four of Panel A in Figure 6.1 as the difference between the quantity supplied and the quantity demanded at the $9 price. It is also shown graphically in **Panel A** of **Figure 6.2** as the horizontal distance between the supply and demand curves at the $9 price.

A surplus shows up as unsold units of the product. Because suppliers have 40 unsold burritos at the end of the day, the suppliers know that $9 is too high. Suppliers also know that they have to lower the price if they want to attract more buyers.

Therefore, the price tends to go down as a result of the surplus. Of course the model cannot tell us how far the price will go down, but we can reasonably assume that the price will go down only a little if the surplus is small, and much more if the surplus is larger.

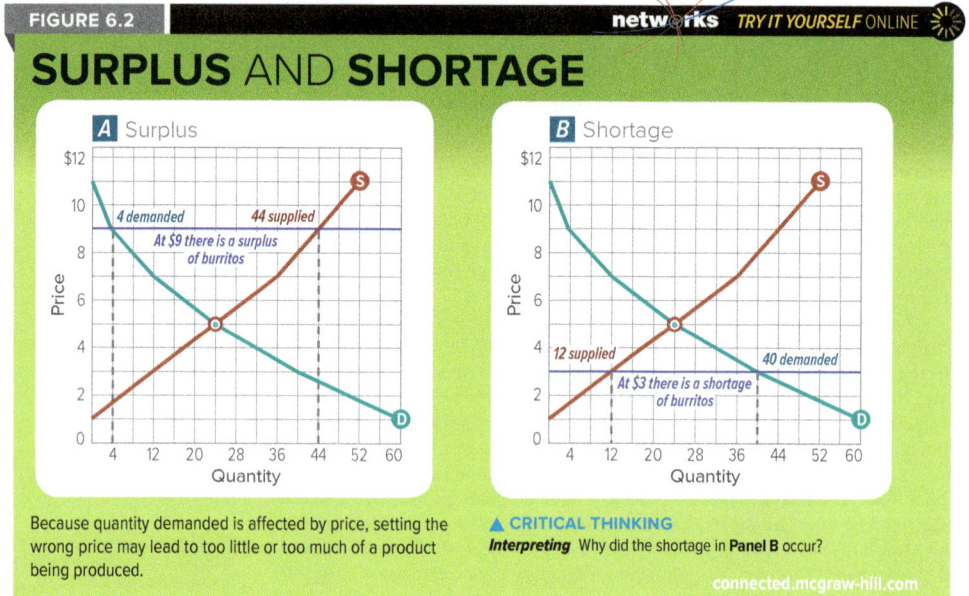

FIGURE 6.2

SURPLUS AND SHORTAGE

A Surplus

B Shortage

Because quantity demanded is affected by price, setting the wrong price may lead to too little or too much of a product being produced.

▲ **CRITICAL THINKING**
Interpreting Why did the shortage in **Panel B** occur?

162

---

networks Online Teaching Options

GRAPHS

Surplus and Shortage

Understanding shortages and surpluses on a graph Have students view Figure 6.2 showing supply and demand graphs—one with a price that creates a shortage, and the other with a price that creates a surplus. Ask students to select any price on the graphs, note the quantity supplied and the quantity demanded at that price, and calculate the resulting shortage or surplus. Then have them write a paragraph using standard grammar describing the reasons for their results. **Verbal/Linguistic**

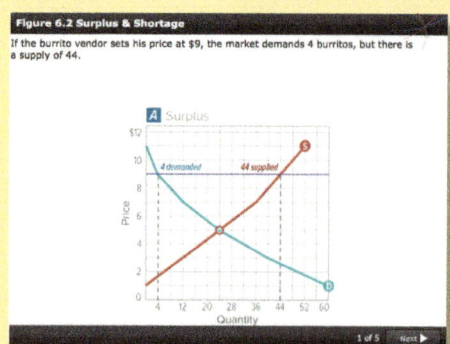

ANSWERS, p. 162

CRITICAL THINKING The shortage in Panel B occurred because the price was too low. Quantity demanded was greater than quantity supplied.

Surpluses can occur in all types of markets. For example, the clearance section at a department store is full of surplus products. Another example of a surplus happens when the government tries to help farmers by setting a price for a farm product that is higher than the market-clearing equilibrium price. Naturally, farmers respond by producing more than consumers want to buy at that price, and then the government has to decide how to deal with the surplus.

Shortages—When Prices are Too Low
Burrito sellers are more cautious on Day 2, so they anticipate a much lower price of $3. At that price, the quantity they are willing to supply changes to 12 burritos. However, as Panel B in Figure 6.2 shows, this price turns out to be too low. At a market price of $3, only 12 burritos are supplied and 40 are demanded—leaving a shortage of 28 burritos.

A **shortage** is a situation in which the quantity demanded is greater than the quantity supplied at a given price. When a shortage happens, sellers have no more burritos to sell, and they end the day wishing they had charged a higher price.

As a result of the shortage, the price will go up. While our model does not show exactly how much the price will go up, we can assume that the next price will be less than $9, which we already know is too high.

Shortages could happen in any market. Suppose, for example, that hospital administrators decide to decrease the salaries of nurses. At lower salaries, fewer nurses would enter or remain in the profession and the quantity supplied could easily be less than the quantity demanded—leading to a shortage of nurses.

shortage situation where quantity supplied is less than quantity demanded at a given price

THE GLOBAL ECONOMY & YOU

Price Differences Around the World
Have you ever shopped for a product online and noticed the price is different from country to country? In addition to taxes, subsidies, import fees, and the cost of doing business, in many cases prices are set on the basis of the amount consumers are willing to pay. In other words, where consumers are willing to pay more, the price will be higher. This *perceived value* can contribute to drastic price differences from one country to the next. One example is Apple's iPhone. In Japan, the price is more than double what American consumers pay for the same product.

▶ **CRITICAL THINKING**
Hypothesizing In recent years it has become easier to purchase products from other countries through the Internet. How might this affect price differences among countries in the long run?

iPHONE PRICES ACROSS the GLOBE

- $649 USA
- $989 Brazil
- $783 UK
- $751 Ireland
- $904 Russia
- $722 South Africa
- $656 Hong Kong
- $1601 Japan
- $835 Australia
- $849 New Zealand

connected.mcgraw-hill.com   Prices 163

CHAPTER 6, LESSON 2
The Effects of Prices

C Critical Thinking Skills

Identifying surpluses and shortages Have students think of three products that exemplify a surplus or shortage. Explain that almost any sale or clearance item can be an example of a surplus, whereas rain checks or sold-out items signal a shortage. Using the specific products students identify, lead a discussion in which students examine the situation surrounding the surplus or shortage, and what the sellers could have done differently to avoid the surplus or shortage. AL

Making Connections

Price Adjustments Have students reflect upon the items they have purchased in their lifetimes. Ask them to identify a product that, although too expensive when it first came out, became affordable after the price eventually dropped. Have students deliver a short oral report describing the market forces that caused this situation. Tell them to create and include in their presentation a supply-and-demand graph showing how their quantity demanded changed in response to price and the quantity supplied.

INTERACTIVE FEATURE

The Global Economy & You: Price Differences Around the World

Hypothesizing about price differences around the world Have students read the text and click to see the differences in iPhone® prices across the globe. Then ask students how they think the ability to purchase items all over the world using the Internet has affected prices currently and in the future. Have students support their ideas with details about the effects of supply and demand on prices. **Visual/Spatial**

ANSWERS, p. 163

CRITICAL THINKING
The transparency that the Internet brings to consumers will help to equalize prices among countries. The more information that consumers have, the more competitive the prices among suppliers.

Prices   163

CHAPTER 6, LESSON 2
The Effects of Prices

C Critical Thinking Skills

Explaining factors that affect equilibrium prices
Have each student choose a nonprice determinant of supply (cost of resources, productivity, technology, taxes and subsidies, expectations, government regulations, and number of sellers) and a nonprice determinant of demand (changes in income, tastes, prices of related products, expectations, the number of consumers) and explain how a combination of these factors could affect the equilibrium price of a product.

EXPLORING THE ESSENTIAL QUESTION

Imagine that you are the owner and operator of a burrito food truck. What tools and strategies would you use to correctly forecast the price of burritos to avoid surpluses or shortages?

fluctuate to rise and fall uncertainly

C

Equilibrium—When the Price Is Just Right

If the new price is $7 on Day 3, the result will be a surplus of 24 burritos. This surplus will cause the price to drop again, but probably not below $3, which already proved to be too low. However, if the price drops to $5, the market will have found its equilibrium price. As we saw earlier, the equilibrium price is the price that "clears the market" by leaving neither a surplus nor a shortage. Also note that Panel B in both Figures 6.1 and 6.2 shows 24 as the equilibrium quantity of output at the equilibrium price of $5.

Although our economic model of the market cannot show exactly how long it will take to reach equilibrium, or if the exact equilibrium price will ever be reached, the **fluctuations** of prices due to surpluses and shortages will always be pushing the price in that direction. Whenever the price is too high, the surplus will tend to force the price down. Whenever the price is too low, the shortage will tend to force the price up. As a result, the market tends toward its own equilibrium.

The supply and demand for burritos affects the price you pay for them, but keep in mind that many different markets are connected in an economy. As a result, price adjustments that take place in other markets play a role in the price you pay for the products you buy. For example, a change in the price of black beans affects not only the income of black bean farmers and distributors, but also the income of the burrito vendor who uses black beans in his product. If the price of black beans is too high, the burrito vendor might raise his prices in order to stay profitable, or he might choose to use a different kind of bean in his product, which would in turn affect the income of his suppliers.

Think of how much more difficult it would be to reach an equilibrium price and quantity of output if we did not have markets to help us. Competitive markets have the advantage of giving us prices that are neutral, flexible, understood by everybody, and free of administrative costs. It would be difficult to find another system that works equally well at reaching the equilibrium price of $5 and the equilibrium quantity of 24 units. When competitive markets reach equilibrium and if nothing else changes, prices and quantities will be stable because there are no surpluses or shortages.

✓ **READING PROGRESS CHECK**

Summarizing How do surpluses and shortages help establish the equilibrium price and quantity of output?

Why Prices Change

GUIDING QUESTION How do changes in supply and demand affect prices?

Once a market has found its equilibrium price and quantity, things could still change. This is because the market supply curve and the market demand curve are influenced by a variety of factors, any of which could change at any time.

Economists use their market models of supply and demand to explain how prices are determined and why prices change. A change in price can be caused by changes in supply, changes in demand, or changes in both. Elasticity is also important when predicting how prices are likely to change.

Changes in Supply

An excellent example of how supply changes affect price can be seen in agriculture, which often experiences wide swings in prices from one year to the next. A farmer may keep up with all the latest developments and have the best advice experts can offer, but the farmer can never be sure what price to expect for the crop. For example, a corn farmer may plant 500 acres of corn, hoping for

164

---

networks — Online Teaching Options

VIDEO **WORKSHEET**

How to Negotiate Prices for Everything

Applying supply and demand to price negotiations Have students view the video. **Ask: What is the most important thing you need to do before approaching a credit card, cable, or phone company to lower your interest rate or monthly bill?** *(research competitors' prices)* Ask students to go to some of the Internet sites given in the video to do research on prices for three items: a hospital procedure, a hotel reservation, and a cell phone plan.

ANSWERS, p. 164

EXPLORING THE ESSENTIAL QUESTION

Students' answers will vary. Forecasting tools and strategies may include tabulating the number of customers each day, their food preferences, and which items they purchase before and after pay day (usually mid-month and end-of-month).

✓ **READING PROGRESS CHECK** Surpluses cause sellers to lower prices while shortages cause sellers to raise prices. This process continues until there are no surpluses or shortages and an equilibrium price is reached.

a price of $5 a bushel. However, the farmer also knows that the actual price may end up being anywhere from $2 to $10.

Weather is one of the main reasons for variations in agricultural prices. If it rains too much after planting, the seeds may rot or be washed away and the farmer must replant. If it rains too little, the seeds may not sprout. Even if the weather is perfect during the growing season, rain can still interfere with the harvest. The weather, then, often causes a change in supply.

The result, shown in **Panel A** of **Figure 6.3**, is that the supply curve for agricultural products can shift, causing the price to increase or decrease. For example, at the beginning of the season, the farmer may expect supply to look like curve **S**. If a bumper, or record, crop is harvested, however, supply may look like S^1, giving the farmer a much lower price for his product. If severe weather strikes, supply may look like S^2, giving the farmer a much higher price for his crop. In either case the price of corn is likely to change dramatically.

Changes in Demand

A change in demand, like a change in supply, can affect the price of a good or service. All of the factors that affect individual demand—changes in income, tastes, prices of related products, expectations, and the number of consumers—also affect the market demand for goods and services. One example is the demand for gold.

In **Panel B** of Figure 6.3, a small increase in demand, illustrated by a shift from **D** to D^1, causes a large increase in the price. This is exactly what happened in late 2012 when uncertainty over economic growth and unstable political situations around the world encouraged people to buy gold. The rapid increase in demand

FIGURE 6.3 CHANGES IN PRICES

A Change in Supply: Corn Prices

B Change in Demand: Gold Prices

A shift in supply or demand can cause a change in price for a product. Panel A illustrates how a change in supply due to weather can cause a large change in food prices. Panel B shows that a large price change will also take place if there is a change in demand.

▲ **CRITICAL THINKING**
Identifying What would happen to the equilibrium price of concert tickets for a band if the band became wildly popular? Explain your answer.

connected.mcgraw-hill.com

Prices **165**

CHAPTER 6, LESSON 2
The Effects of Prices

W Writing Skills

Writing a narrative about effects on prices Have students identify a business, other than farming, that sometimes experiences fluctuations in supply (for example, gas stations and grocery stores). Ask students to write a short story using standard grammar about an entrepreneur in that business who must deal with supply fluctuations. In their stories, tell students to explain the nonprice factors that caused the fluctuations and how they affected supply and prices. **BL Verbal/Linguistic**

Content Background Knowledge

Graphing Conventions Remind students that on economic graphs, price is always on the Y-axis, and quantity is always on the X-axis. Graphs such as the ones shown in Figure 6.3 are models, and therefore do not have specific quantities on the X-axis. Reinforce that quantity increases from left to right.

GRAPHS

Changes in Prices

Identifying effects on prices Have students work in pairs, with both partners identifying the equilibrium price of D and S on graph A. *($5)* Then have Student 2 look away from the graph, and have Student 1 state whether the supply curve moves right or left. Have Student 2 predict what happens to the equilibrium price, whether it increases or decreases, and then view the graph to confirm the prediction. Have partners do the same with graph B, identifying the initial equilibrium price at D and S *($1,000)*, and then Student 2 noting whether the demand curve moves right or left. Student 1 predicts what happens to the equilibrium price.

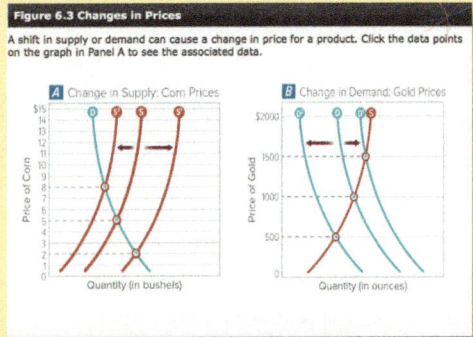

ANSWERS, p. 165

CRITICAL THINKING The equilibrium price would increase. Demand would increase, driving prices up.

Prices **165**

CHAPTER 6, LESSON 2
The Effects of Prices

CLOSE & REFLECT

C Critical Thinking Skills

Summarizing causes and effects of shortages
Have students write a paragraph stating what would happen if there were a shortage in a product they use. Students should what factors could cause the shortage. Then they should explain how the shortage would affect the price of the product. Finally, they should give solutions to deal with the shortage, and ways to get the price of the item back to its equilibrium level.

ANSWERS, p. 166

✓ **READING PROGRESS CHECK** Elasticity limits the changes in prices that occur for a good when its supply or demand fluctuates.

---

drove the price of gold to over $1,800 an ounce, when 10 years earlier it was about $300 an ounce.

Changes in Supply *and* Demand

In most cases, price is affected by both supply and demand changing at the same time. For example, Hurricanes Katrina and Rita tore through the Gulf of Mexico in 2005, destroying or disabling hundreds of oil-drilling platforms, refineries, and storage facilities. This caused the supply of oil to decrease (or shift to the left), driving the price of gasoline higher.

To make matters worse with respect to gasoline prices, 2006 and 2007 were years of relatively strong economic growth, so the demand for oil and gasoline shifted to the right just after the supply of oil had shifted to the left. The result was a near doubling of oil prices and a sharp increase in gas prices that peaked in 2008.

Prices and Competitive Markets

Economists like to see competitive markets because the price system is more efficient when markets are competitive. A purely competitive market requires a set of ideal conditions and outcomes that are seldom found, but fortunately markets don't have to be perfect to be useful. As long as prices are allowed to adjust to new levels in response to the pressures exerted by surpluses and shortages, prices will perform their role as signals to both consumers and producers.

Trying to achieve the ideal model of a competitive market is the basis for considerable government policy. For example, to increase the number of competitors in a market, laws have been passed to prevent companies from becoming too large. Other laws were passed that require firms to disclose information to help consumers decide if they want to buy something. Further laws have been passed to prevent firms from taking unfair advantage of consumers. All of this is done in order to make markets more competitive.

The great advantage of competitive markets is that they allocate resources efficiently. As sellers compete to meet consumer demands, they are forced to lower the prices of their goods. This encourages them to keep their costs down. At the same time, competition among buyers helps prevent prices from falling too far. This means that both consumers and producers have a role in determining the market's equilibrium price.

✓ **READING PROGRESS CHECK**

Explaining How does the elasticity of a product affect changes in its price?

LESSON 2 REVIEW

Reviewing Vocabulary
1. ***Explaining*** How is the equilibrium price of a product related to the equilibrium quantity, and how can these values be determined?

Using Your Notes
2. ***Determining Cause and Effect*** Use your notes to describe an example of a surplus and an example of a shortage, including what may have caused them.

Answering the Guiding Questions
3. ***Describing*** How does price affect a seller's decision to produce a product?

4. ***Summarizing*** How do changes in supply and demand affect prices?

Writing About Economics
5. ***Informative/Explanatory*** Select a product that appears in a newspaper or online ad of several different stores. Note the various prices and indicate whether any of these prices are sale prices. What does the information tell you about the equilibrium price of the product you selected? Write a paragraph explaining your answer.

166

LESSON 2 REVIEW ANSWERS

Reviewing Vocabulary

1. When the quantity supplied for a product is equal to the quantity demanded for the product, that quantity is the equilibrium quantity. The price of the product at the equilibrium quantity is the equilibrium price. At the equilibrium price and quantity, there is neither a surplus nor a shortage of the product.

Using Your Notes

2. Answers will vary, but students may mention items they have seen in the clearance section at a store as an example of a surplus. As an example of a shortage, they may mention a time they wanted to buy something and it was sold out. Students might mention a lack of demand or too much demand as the cause of the surplus or shortage, or they might mention ineffective pricing.

Answering the Guiding Questions

3. If the price consumers are willing to pay for a product is high, producers will produce more of it. If the price consumers are willing to pay is low, producers will produce less or even none of it.

4. When demand for a product increases, the price increases. When demand for a product decreases, the price decreases. When supply of a product increases, the price decreases. When supply of a product decreases, the price increases.

Writing About Economics

5. Answers will vary. Students should note whether the prices are sale prices, and if so, deduce that the store is experiencing a surplus.

Case Study

SUPPLY, DEMAND, and the COST of SUPER BOWL ADVERTISING

During 364 days out of the year, the average cost of a 30-second prime time television advertisement spot is a little over $100,000. But for one four-hour block, on one day, on one channel each year, the price skyrockets to around $3.5 million. That time slot is the Super Bowl.

Like most prices in a market economy, the price for television advertising is set by supply and demand. Advertisers want to reach the largest number of viewers with each ad, so demand is high for ad space during a program lots of people are watching. And few programs are watched by more people than the Super Bowl, which averages over 100 million viewers each year.

Because demand is higher for ads during the Super Bowl, the supplier (the television station airing the game) can charge higher prices than for other programs. The limited supply of ad space also plays a role in sending the price higher. In 2013 there were only 70 slots available to sell.

In the end, all of the ad space available during the game is filled, because the television station won't charge a price so high that advertisers are unwilling to pay. They charge the price that makes them the most profits, given the supply and demand for the available advertising spaces.

ONE YEAR in Super Bowl Ads (2013)

Number of viewers: **108.4 million**

Percent of U.S. households tuned in: **46.3%**

Number of 30-second advertising spots sold: **70**

Top price paid for one 30-second ad: **$4 million**

Ad space was sold out **3 months** before the game aired

Average cost of a 30-second ad: **$3.5 million**

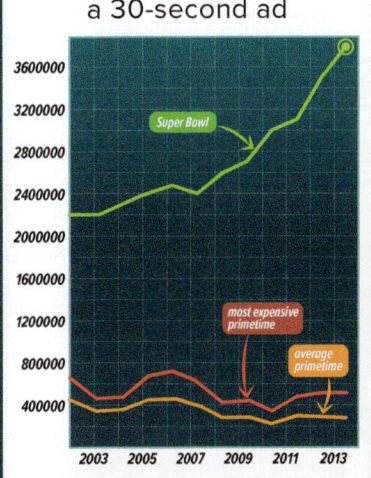

The COST of a 30-second ad

CASE STUDY REVIEW

1. **Explaining** What makes the equilibrium price for an advertisement during the Super Bowl different from the normal equilibrium price for a television advertisement?
2. **Making Predictions** What conditions might lead to a shortage of Super Bowl advertisements? What effect might a shortage have?
3. **Defending** Do you think pricing for Super Bowl advertising is fair? Explain your reasoning.

CHAPTER 6
Case Study

C Critical Thinking Skills

Understanding how supply and demand affect cost Have a class discussion about television advertising. **Ask: What makes advertisers willing to pay more to put their ads on television during big events?** *(Big events attract more viewers.)* Discuss with students any of the memorable Super Bowl advertisements from the past year. **Ask: How does this explain why there is demand for the limited number of ad spots for this event?** *(People think of that brand when they are in a position to purchase the product in question.)* **Interpersonal**

V Visual Skills

Comparing prices of advertisements Ask students to use the graph to compare the change in advertising costs during the Super Bowl with that of the most expensive primetime slot and the average primetime slot. Ask students to give reasons for the changes.

Making Connections

Using math to support economic concepts Ask students if they watched the Super Bowl this year. Have them calculate the percentage of people in the class who viewed the Super Bowl. Then ask students to name one popular weekend television show. Ask for the number of students who watched that show last weekend. Have them calculate the percentage of people in the class who viewed the show. Discuss how or whether the data students just collected supports the idea that advertisers are willing to pay more to advertise during the Super Bowl than during primetime shows.

ANSWERS, p. 167

Case Study Review

1. Demand is high for ad space because the number of people viewing the Super Bowl is so high. But there is a limited supply of ad space. Advertisers are willing to pay more for one of these ad slots.
2. A shortage of Super Bowl advertisements might occur if the television station begins raises its prices too high for the advertisers. The effect of a shortage might be that the television station would lower the rates it charges.
3. Answers will vary. Students may think that prices are unfair because they are so much higher than they are the rest of the year. Students may think that prices are fair because there are so few slots and the ads will reach so many households.

INTERACTIVE FEATURE

Case Study: Supply, Demand, and the Cost of Super Bowl Advertising

Evaluating effects of supply and demand on price Have students read the text about supply of and demand for television advertising during the Super Bowl. Then have them look at the graphs in the Case Study. Ask students to write a short paragraph, using the data in the graphs, to describe how supply and demand have affected pricing on Super Bowl advertising, compared to other advertising, over the past ten years **Verbal/Linguistic**

CHAPTER 6, LESSON 3
Social Goals, Prices, and Market Efficiency

ENGAGE

R Reading Skills

Understanding motives behind government setting prices Before students begin this lesson, ask them to consider why they think the government gets involved with price setting. Lead them to understand that achieving social goals, such as equity and security, is a primary reason for government involvement. As students will also learn, however, some special interests want the government to regulate prices for their own industries, which does not benefit consumers.

TEACH & ASSESS

V Visual Skills

Understanding placement of price ceilings and floors on graphs Be sure students understand that a price ceiling is visually "low" (below the equilibrium price) when shown on a graph, which is the opposite of what one usually thinks of regarding a real ceiling. In contrast, a price floor is visually "high" (above the equilibrium price) when shown on a graph.

ANSWERS, p. 168

ESSENTIAL QUESTION ACTIVITY

Students' answers will vary, but students should keep in mind that government intervention in prices can lead to unintended negative effects in other parts of the economy.

TAKING NOTES:
Price ceiling goals:
- to protect buyers from paying overly high prices (price gouging)
- to save resources for other needs, such as a war

Price floor goals:
- to protect businesses (like farming) during times of difficulty
- to stabilize prices and incomes for certain businesses

Interact with these digital assets and others in lesson 3

- INTERACTIVE GRAPH Price Ceilings & Price Floors
- INTERACTIVE GRAPH Price Floor: Minimum Wage
- SELF-CHECK QUIZ
- VIDEO

networks TRY IT YOURSELF ONLINE

LESSON 3
Social Goals, Prices, and Market Efficiency

Reading Help Desk

Academic Vocabulary
- stabilize
- arbitrarily

Content Vocabulary
- price ceiling
- price floor
- target price
- nonrecourse loan

TAKING NOTES:

Key Ideas and Details
Use a graphic organizer like the one below to identify the goals or objectives of price ceilings and price floors.

Goal of Price Ceiling and Price Floor	
	Goal
Price Ceiling	
Price Floor	

price ceiling the highest legal price that can be charged for a product

price floor the lowest legal price that can be paid for a product

stabilize to make steady or unchanging

ESSENTIAL QUESTION

What factors affect prices?

Think about a product with a price you believe is too high or too low. Do you think the government should make a law to change the price of the product to something that is more reasonable?

Write a paragraph explaining why you think the government should or should not adjust the product's price.

R Controlling Prices

GUIDING QUESTION *What are the costs and benefits of economic policies aimed at creating equity and security?*

In a purely competitive free enterprise system, prices would be determined entirely by the actions of buyers and sellers. The United States, however, is a modified free enterprise economy. This means that the government sometimes interferes in the market in order to achieve a socially desirable goal. One way the government does this is by setting prices for certain goods and services below or above the equilibrium price.

Attempts to fix prices are not new. During World War I and World War II, the federal government locked down the prices of certain foods to ensure that everyone had access to affordable meals. President Nixon tried to combat inflation in the early 1970s by trying to freeze prices for 90 days, but his efforts were largely ineffective. Today the government uses a combination of price ceilings and price floors to fix prices on a number of products.

Price Ceilings

When a price is set below its equilibrium level, it is called a **price ceiling**, the maximum legal price that can be charged for a product. The case of a price ceiling is shown in **Panel A** of **Figure 6.4** where the price ceiling of $10 is set below the price that clears the market.

V The consequence of the price ceiling in the figure is clear. With a price ceiling of $10, there are 10 units demanded but only 4 units are supplied—leaving a shortage of 6.

---

networks Online Teaching Options

BELLRINGER

Social Goals, Prices, and Market Efficiency

Activating Prior Knowledge Ask students how they would feel if their favorite food were rationed. Brainstorm with students various situations in which rationing might be effective, such as during a war or drought. Write their ideas on the board and add to them as students progress through the lesson.

Normally the resulting shortage of 6 would be enough to drive the price toward its equilibrium level of $15, but not in the case of a price ceiling. Instead, the shortage becomes permanent and will persist as long as the price ceiling stays below its equilibrium price. A shift in demand or supply could cause the shortage to increase or decrease, but a shortage will always be there as long as the price ceiling remains below the equilibrium price.

Price Floors

At other times, lawmakers may think that the market clearing price is too low, so they take steps to raise it by legislating a **price floor**, the minimum legal price that a seller can charge.

The consequence of the price floor is shown in **Panel B** of Figure 6.4. With a price floor of $25, 2 units are demanded but 11 units are supplied—leaving a surplus of 9.

Normally the resulting surplus of 9 would be enough to drive the price toward its equilibrium level of $15, but not in the case of a price floor. Instead, the surplus becomes permanent and will persist as long as the price floor stays above the market's equilibrium price. A shift in either demand or supply could cause the surplus to increase or decrease, but a surplus will always be there as long as the price floor remains above the equilibrium price.

✓ **READING PROGRESS CHECK**

Analyzing What are the negative and positive aspects of price ceilings and price floors?

Examples of Fixed-Price Policies

GUIDING QUESTION *Whom do price supports benefit, and whom do they hurt?*

Government imposed price controls are not just something that happened in the midst of a major war. There is a surprising amount of it around today. The minimum wage, discussed more fully in another chapter, along with farm subsidies and rent controls, are major examples of price controls being used today.

Using Price Floors to Support Sugar Prices

Historically, prices on almost all agricultural products have fluctuated much more widely than prices on other goods and services. This is because farmers often face periods of boom or bust. In years when crops are plentiful, the extra production drives prices down. In years of drought or flooding, the lower crop yields drive agricultural prices up. Because of this, the government has taken steps to **stabilize** agricultural prices to help farmers and processors of farm products with the use of price floors.

FIGURE 6.4

PRICE CEILINGS & PRICE FLOORS

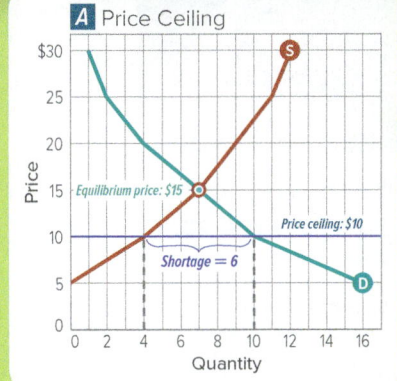

Normally shortages and surpluses are enough to drive the price towards its equilibrium. However, as long as a price floor remains above the equilibrium price, or a price ceiling remains below the equilibrium price, a surplus or shortage will exist.

EXPLORING THE ESSENTIAL QUESTION

Ask your classmates what they think will happen if the government imposes a price ceiling on Internet services. What are the benefits of setting price controls and what are the costs? Ask your classmates who benefits from this price ceiling and who is hurt.

connected.mcgraw-hill.com

CHAPTER 6, LESSON 3
Social Goals, Prices, and Market Efficiency

V Visual Skills

Analyzing graphs of price ceilings and price floors Have students view Figure 6.4. **Ask: How does the price ceiling control the price in Panel A? How does the price floor control the price in Panel B?** *(Students should note that the price ceiling keeps the price from going above $10, and the price floor keeps the price from going under $25.)* Then ask students to write a few sentences explaining what needs to happen for a surplus to diminish, and what needs to happen for a shortage to be fixed. Students should use examples from the graphs to support their explanations.

R Reading Skills

Understanding subsidies as a price floor Ask: If you were guaranteed a set price by the government for each product you created, how many products would you create? *(Students should recognize that creating more and more products would bring more and more money from the government.)* Explain that, in a similar way, when the government guarantees that sugar processors receive 18.75 cents per pound for their processed sugar, the processors will create a sugar surplus if possible. **Ask: What are the effects of the sugar subsidy for sugar growers?** *(guaranteed profits)* **What are the effects of the sugar subsidy for American consumers?** *(higher prices for sugar; higher prices for candy and beverages as well as other products from domestic industries that rely on sugar)*

GRAPHS

Price Ceilings and Price Floors

Predicting consequences of price ceilings and price floors Ask: What happens to the supply of a product or service when a price ceiling or price floor is imposed? *(Students should recognize that a shortage or surplus occurs.)* Have students view Figure 6.4 showing supply and demand curves, equilibrium prices, and a price floor or price ceiling. Ask students to progress through the graphs to see how shortages and surpluses are related to price ceilings and price floors. Have students answer the questions. **Logical/Mathematical**

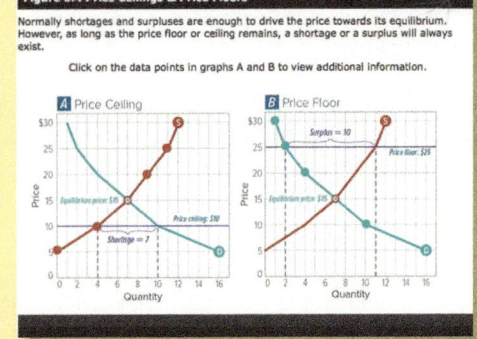

ANSWERS, p. 169

EXPLORING THE ESSENTIAL QUESTION

Students' answers should indicate an understanding that price ceilings create shortages, and that people will see a direct result with a price ceiling for Internet use. People may benefit from the price ceiling, but they may also be hurt if they cannot obtain Internet service due to shortages.

✓ **READING PROGRESS CHECK** Price ceilings keep certain products affordable but limit their supply. Price floors increase income but lower the demand for services.

CHAPTER 6, LESSON 3
Social Goals, Prices, and Market Efficiency

Content Background Knowledge

Commodity Credit Corporation (CCC)
The control on sugar prices is not the first time the federal government has used a target price as a price floor to assist growers. During the Great Depression, the federal government established the Commodity Credit Corporation (CCC), an agency in the Department of Agriculture, to help farmers. The agency set a price floor, and paid farmers the difference between that price and the market price of their products to keep prices stable.

R Reading Skills

Analyzing Milton Friedman's impact Have students read the biography feature and discuss the importance of economist Milton Friedman. Explain that Friedman, a fervent believer in individual freedom, advocated free markets with minimal government involvement. In his book *Capitalism and Freedom*, he argued for a flat tax rate and the elimination of deductions, such as those for mortgage interest. As mentioned in the biography, he also opposed agricultural subsidies, price controls, and the minimum wage. Ask students to analyze who most benefitted from Friedman's ideas. **Interpersonal**

C Critical Thinking Skills

Debating a Friedman philosophy Provide students with this quote by Milton Friedman: "I am in favor of cutting taxes under any circumstances and for any excuse, for any reason, whenever it's possible."
Ask: What do you think Friedman meant by "whenever it's possible"? How "possible" would it be now? Point out that Friedman was not in favor of fiscal irresponsibility; he wanted reductions in spending to accompany tax cuts. **Interpersonal**

ANSWERS, p. 170

CRITICAL THINKING
Friedman opposed price controls because they caused producers to stop or slow production.

BIOGRAPHY

Milton Friedman
ECONOMIST 1912–2006
American economist and educator Milton Friedman made enormous contributions to our understanding of income, unemployment, the role of money, free markets, and many other areas of economics. Friedman voiced his opposition to government control of prices, including agricultural subsidies and the minimum wage. He famously said, "We economists don't know much, but we do know how to create a shortage. If you want to create a shortage of tomatoes . . . just pass a law that retailers can't sell tomatoes for more than two cents per pound. Instantly you'll have a tomato shortage." In addition to an influential teaching career, Friedman wrote several prominent books and advised both Presidents Nixon and Reagan on economic policy. Friedman received the Nobel Prize for Economics in 1976.

▲ **CRITICAL THINKING**
Drawing Conclusions Based on Friedman's quote about tomatoes, why do you think he opposed price controls?

The sugar industry provides just one example of how the government can stabilize farm prices with the use of price floors. Beginning in 1981, and reauthorized by the 2008 Farm Act, the government set target prices on sugar derived from sugar cane. A **target price** is a price floor the government thinks is fair for a particular product. To ensure that farmers receive the target price for their products, the government sets up a loan system.

For example, in 2013 the government set a loan rate of 18.75 cents per pound on cane sugar. A processor of sugar cane could take out a loan from the United States Department of Agriculture (USDA) at this rate as long as it pledged its sugar as collateral, or security, for the loan. After the sugar was processed, the processor had two options:

1. The sugar could be sold on the open market at a higher price than the target price, and then the proceeds of the sale could be used to repay the USDA loan.
2. Or, if the market price of sugar fell below the target price, the processor could keep the proceeds of the loan and let the USDA take possession of the sugar.

Because the loan does not have to be repaid, it is called a **nonrecourse loan**—a loan that carries neither a penalty nor further obligation to repay. Either way, the processor is guaranteed to get at least 18.75 cents per pound for the processed sugar, which is why it is a price floor that helps to stabilize farm income.

In addition to stabilizing agricultural incomes, the price supports in sugar have helped domestic sugar producers compete with foreign sugar producers. The price supports have also saved a number of jobs in the sugar production industry.

Unfortunately, the sugar support policies have also raised the price of sugar for the American consumer. Since the first Farm Act that introduced this type of policy in 1981, U.S. sugar prices have been about twice as high as world sugar prices, something that has cost American consumers billions of dollars. The higher cost of domestic sugar has also been a problem for domestic industries that use sugar, like makers of candy, sweets, and beverages. These domestic industries have lost jobs as a result of higher sugar prices.

Agricultural price supports are just one example of a nation trying to achieve one economic goal—economic security—at the expense of another—full employment. As you can see, setting a legal price too high to achieve a socially desirable goal has its consequences.

Using Price Ceilings to Control Rents

Rent control is an example of a price ceiling because it sets a maximum price that can be charged for certain types of housing. During World War II the country used rent controls to keep housing prices from rising uncontrollably. Today rent controls are used in New York City to make housing more affordable for many middle- and low-income consumers. **Figure 6.5** shows how rent control works.

Let us assume that without rent controls, the free market would establish rents at $1,500 a month, with an equilibrium quantity of two million apartments at that rate. If the government wants to promote the social goals of equity and security for people who cannot afford these rents, it can **arbitrarily** establish a price ceiling at $1,000 a month.

No doubt potential renters would like the $1,000 price and would demand 2.4 million apartments. Landlords, on the other hand, only want to supply 1.6 million units at that price—leaving a shortage of 0.8 million, or 800,000 apartments. This shortage would persist as long as the price ceiling remains below the equilibrium price.

170

---

networks *Online Teaching Options*

GRAPHS

Price Ceiling

Reading graphs to understand price ceilings Have students view Figure 6.5 showing a price ceiling of $1,000 for rent control. Have students write a short explanation of what happens when the price is set to equilibrium and when it is lowered below equilibrium. *(Students should note that quantity supplied and quantity demanded are the same at equilibrium, and quantity supplied is less than quantity demanded if the price is set lower than equilibrium, creating a shortage of apartments. Students should also mention that more people will demand apartments at lower-than-equilibrium prices, because the price is so low.)* **Verbal/Linguistic**

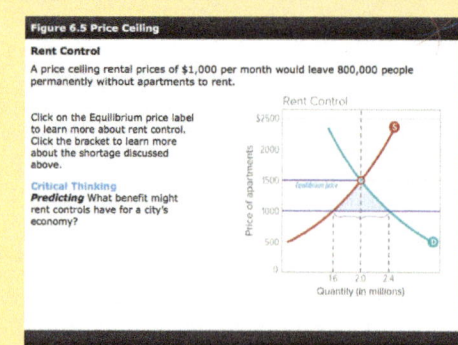

Are people better off? Perhaps not. Clearly the 800,000 potential renters who could not get apartments are unhappy. Also, landlords are unhappy because they are being forced to accept a lower price for their rental units. Because of this, the landlords want to rent fewer units than they would under free market conditions. More than likely, they would convert some of the nicer apartments to high-priced condos or offices—leaving the less desirable ones to be rented. They would also cut back on basic repairs and upkeep on the units they rent, which allows the buildings to deteriorate.

The only people who are better off are the 1.6 million renters who were able to get the apartments for $1,000 a month. But even they may eventually become unhappy when they discovered that their landlords were neglecting upkeep on their buildings. Meanwhile, there are long lines of people waiting to get the low-cost rental units. All of this results in a situation where prices no longer allocate apartments. Instead, landlords deal with the shortage by using long waiting lists or by resorting to nonprice criteria, such as excluding renters with children and pets.

Is the landlord's behavior unreasonable? After all, what would you do if you owned rental units in a city with rent controls? If you could not increase rents to keep up with repairs and city building taxes, you might do what other landlords do, and that is lower your costs by providing the absolute minimum upkeep. You may even tear some buildings down to make way for more profitable shopping centers, factories, parking garages, or high-rise office buildings. All of this contributes to the gradual movement of productive resources out of the rental market and into other activities. This is just one example of how rent controls distort the economy's allocation of productive assets.

In the end, government attempts to achieve two of our seven economic goals—economic equity and economic security—will be in conflict with another goal—economic efficiency. Whether or not the tradeoff is worth it depends on the way voters evaluate the costs and benefits of the action, and then express their satisfaction or frustration in the voting booth.

Government and Social Goals

The American free enterprise system has seven broad economic and social goals that most people seem to share: economic freedom, economic efficiency, economic equity, economic security, full employment, price stability, and economic growth. However, we also know that these goals are often in conflict with one another. As a result, legislation to achieve any one goal almost always conflicts with other economic goals—which makes effective government policy-making difficult.

So, how does government decide which of the seven economic goals to promote? And, how does government evaluate the costs and benefits of a specific policy to see if it should be supported rather than another?

FIGURE 6.5

PRICE CEILING: RENT CONTROL

Rent Control graph showing Equilibrium price at $1,500 and Rent control as a price ceiling at $1,000. At a price ceiling $1,000 there is a shortage of 800,000 apartments.

A price ceiling rental price of $1,000 per month would leave 800,000 people permanently without apartments to rent.

▲ **CRITICAL THINKING**
Predicting Which consumers might benefit if a city introduces rent controls?

target price price floor for agricultural products set by the government to stabilize farm prices

nonrecourse loan loan that carries neither penalty nor further obligation to repay

arbitrarily randomly or by chance

CHAPTER 6, LESSON 3
Social Goals, Prices, and Market Efficiency

C Critical Thinking Skills

Understanding rent control as a price ceiling
Have students prepare a short dialogue simulating a landlord and a tenant in front of a rent control board. Students should include the economic reasoning behind each person's justification for or against rent control. **Verbal/Linguistic**

GRAPHS

Price Floor

Reading graphs and maps to understand price floors Ask students to study Figure 6.6 showing the price floor of $7.25 for the federal minimum wage. Be sure students understand that supply on this graph refers to workers willing to supply their labor. Tell students they can click on the map to see state minimum wages as well. Ask students to choose three states' minimum wages and apply them to the graph's price and quantity. Then have them write a few sentences explaining what happens to supply and demand for jobs at a particular state's wage. Students should explain whether there is a surplus or shortage of jobs at that rate, and how that affects the labor market. **Logical/Mathematical**

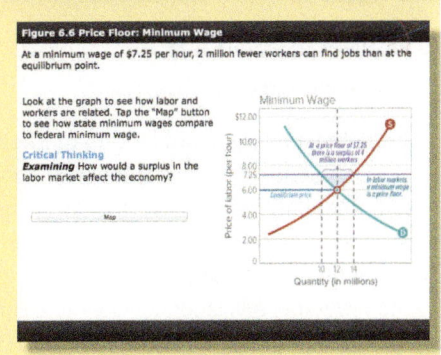

ANSWERS, p. 171

CRITICAL THINKING
People with lower incomes would benefit from rent-control policies.

CHAPTER 6, LESSON 3
Social Goals, Prices, and Market Efficiency

W1 Writing Skills

Understanding the minimum wage as a price floor Ask students to think about how the minimum wage may affect them and the people in their community now or in the future. Then have them write a short report presenting their opinions about the minimum wage. Students' writings should include the idea that workers in minimum wage jobs cannot be paid less, and so they will make more than they would without the minimum wage. Yet workers might not be able to find jobs if employers hire fewer workers at a higher minimum wage. Remind students to use standard spelling in their essays. **AL** Intrapersonal

C Critical Thinking Skills

Comparing earnings to expenses Some of your students may be working for a minimum wage. Ask volunteers to list expenses for which they are responsible. Then ask them to calculate how much they would make at their minimum wage jobs if they worked full time. With students, write down the items that would appear on a basic household budget. Ask them to research the costs of each of these budget items and come up with a total for expenses. Have students compare household expenses with the amount they would make working full time at a minimum wage job. Discuss what it takes for a household with minimum wage earners to make ends meet, given the level of basic expenses. Logical/Mathematical

W2 Writing Skills

Narrating a dialogue about "talking" markets Have small groups use Web sites or print sources to find a news article about markets "talking" in response to events. Then ask groups to create a dialogue that illustrates the events and the market "talk" that resulted. For example: "Corn prices are up due to a drought that reduced the supply." Remind students that they may include "market talk" in both the factor and product markets. Have each group perform the dialogue as commuters on a bus or subway. Interpersonal

---

ANSWERS, p. 172

✓ **READING PROGRESS CHECK** Price floors in the sugar industry have raised the price of sugar for American consumers, as well as the price of products that are made from sugar. It has also led to job losses in industries that rely on sugar because the cost of production has increased.

172

CAREERS | Cost Estimator

Is this Career for you?
- ✓ Do you have strong mathematical and analytical skills?
- ✓ Do you have an interest in engineering and technology?
- ✓ Do you enjoy working collaboratively?

Interview with a professional Cost Estimator

"You may estimate or analyze the cost of cars, aircraft, ships, software systems, bridges, electronics, satellites.... You may also analyze why something is costing more than previously estimated."

—Joe Wagner,
Board of the Society of Cost Estimating and Analysis

Salary
$55,000–$65,000 per year
$27.82 per hour

Job Growth Outlook
Much faster than average

Profile of Work
Cost estimators collect and analyze data about the costs required for a project, including labor, resources, money, and time. They may also evaluate the profitability of a project.

W1 / C

Unfortunately, the answer is that it doesn't. While the Congressional Budget Office (CBO) is required by law to produce formal cost estimates for nearly every budget bill approved by Congress, individual legislators make their own judgments concerning the likely benefits of a program. Consequently, extreme conditions must often occur before all political parties and the president agree to support any one goal. For example, the minimum wage was established during the Great Depression when nearly one worker in four could not find a job. Price floors were also widely used in agriculture during that period because farm incomes had reached historic lows.

So why do we still have price ceilings and floors today when economic conditions are much better than they were during the Great Depression or during either world war? Part of the answer is that once price supports are put in place, they often have enough political support to keep them there. Or, as in the case of sugar support prices, so few people know about them that there is no effective opposition.

✓ **READING PROGRESS CHECK**

Summarizing What has been the effect of price floors in the domestic sugar industry?

When Markets Talk

GUIDING QUESTION *How do markets "talk"?*

W2

Markets are impersonal mechanisms that bring buyers and sellers together. Although markets do not talk in the usual sense of the word, they do send signals that collectively represent the actions of buyers and sellers who trade in them. Markets are said to "talk" when prices move up or down significantly in reaction to a related event.

---

networks Online Teaching Options

INTERACTIVE FEATURE

Careers: Cost Estimator

Applying knowledge of talking markets to career choices
Have students read the Careers text about cost estimators and what they do. Have them analyze the validity of the excerpt from the frame of reference of the person speaking. Tell students that the job prospects for this career are higher than average. Ask students to write a short paragraph describing how the ability to "listen" to the market applies to the job of cost estimator. Students should recognize that cost estimators need to know when and why prices are changing in order to accurately estimate costs for projects. Students should conclude their essays by stating whether or not they would like to be a cost estimator, and give reasons for their opinion. Verbal/Linguistic

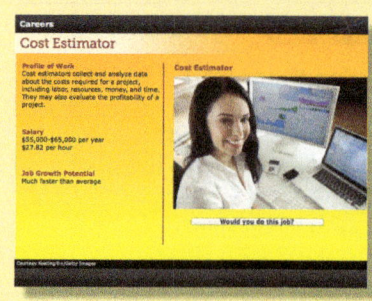

- **Gold Prices Rise** A rising price of gold is usually not a good sign for the economy. This is because gold has historically been thought of as a hedge, or protection, against a possible economic or social crisis. Sharp increases in the price of gold would capture the attention of other investors and perhaps even encourage some of them to buy gold as well, driving the price of gold up even further. Gold prices tend to come down slowly when the economic news is good, so sharp increases in the price of gold capture the most attention.
- **Stock Prices Fall** Falling stock prices generally reflect a lack of confidence in business conditions or in government policy. Suppose the federal government announced that it would raise taxes on investments to pay off some of the federal debt. If investors thought that this policy would not work, or that other policies might be better, they might sell some of their stocks, causing stock market prices to fall. In a sense, then, we could say that the market has "talked" by voicing its disapproval of a new government policy or some other event whenever stock prices go down. If stock market prices had gone up, however, it would be a sign that investors had a more favorable view of the policy or event.
- **Oil Prices Rise** Investors closely watch the price of oil. This is because it is a commodity used worldwide, and it has very inelastic supply and demand curves. Because of this, even slight changes in the supply or demand for oil can have a dramatic impact on the price of oil. A sharp increase in the price of oil could indicate that there has been a modest decrease in the quantity supplied, something the market foresees as a possible difficult time ahead for the economy.

Each of these market price changes can be thought of as a collective effort by markets to "tell" us that something is wrong or is about to happen. As the world's economies are interconnected, markets respond to local and global events. International policy decisions, wars, and other major events around the world can impact the prices of products in the United States. Likewise, events in the United States can have far-reaching effects on prices throughout the world.

☑ **READING PROGRESS CHECK**

Examining Can you think of any other examples of markets "talking"? Explain.

When Markets Talk Economists say that markets "talk" when signals are sent collectively to all of the buyers and sellers in a market. This may cause prices to shift in a different direction.

▲ **CRITICAL THINKING**
Hypothesizing Why would the rumor of a government contract change the value of this company's stock?

CHAPTER 6, LESSON 3
Social Goals, Prices, and Market Efficiency

V Visual Skills

Understanding signals in the market Have students write a paragraph explaining how the cartoon emphasizes the interaction between government action and the business's stock price. Then ask them to write new dialogue for the cartoon to reflect what might happen to the stock price if the government did the opposite.

CLOSE & REFLECT

W Writing Skills

Explaining price controls in your community Have students write a reflection paragraph about a price control they see in their community and its benefits and drawbacks. Students should include not only the effects on the market but also the effects on individuals and the community.

LESSON 3 REVIEW

Reviewing Vocabulary
1. *Defining* Explain how a target price for farm crops is an example of a price floor.

Using Your Notes
2. *Summarizing* Use your notes to explain why the government imposes price floors and price ceilings in certain markets.

Answering the Guiding Questions
3. *Considering Advantages and Disadvantages* What are the costs and benefits of economic policies aimed at creating equity and security?

4. *Evaluating* Whom do price supports benefit and whom do they hurt?

5. *Explaining* How do markets "talk"?

Writing About Economics
6. *Argument* Assume that the price of first-year college tuition has become very high, and you want to recommend a price ceiling to remedy the problem. What would the consequences of such a policy be for both students and the college? Explain your reasoning in a one-page argument.

ANSWERS, p. 173

CRITICAL THINKING
The rumor sends a signal to the market that this company could be worth buying into.

☑ **READING PROGRESS CHECK** Example: A market fluctuation that occurs after the president announces an overseas military operation

---

LESSON 3 REVIEW ANSWERS

Reviewing Vocabulary
1. A target price is a price floor because it ensures a minimum price that farmers will receive for their product, in spite of what the market's equilibrium price is for that product.

Using Your Notes
2. The government sets price floors and price ceilings in order to achieve a socially desirable goal, such as economic equity or economic security. For example, the equilibrium price for an essential agricultural product may not be high enough to ensure farmers continue to produce it, so the government sets a price floor to ensure that the product is still produced. The government might set a price ceiling on a product essential for people to obtain but for which the equilibrium price is too high for many people to afford.

Answering the Guiding Questions
3. Economic policies aimed at economic equity and economic security, such as price floors and price ceilings, are beneficial because they ensure that essential goods and services remain available and affordable. However, such policies result in surpluses and shortages in the market because they set the price above or below what the market determines is the equilibrium price.

4. Price supports benefit producers because the supports ensure a price that is profitable to the producer. Supports hurt consumers, including other businesses and industries that rely on a supported product, because the price is usually higher than what consumers are willing or able to pay. Even so, price supports can ensure that essential goods continue to be produced, which benefits producers and consumers alike.

5. When prices increase or decrease, the market is "voicing" the collective opinion of buyers and sellers.

Writing About Economics
6. Students' arguments should recognize that a price ceiling will eventually lead to a shortage or a reduction in quality of college courses.

CHAPTER 6
Debate

ENGAGE

C Critical Thinking Skills

Identifying central issues about the minimum wage Ask students if any of them are working for a minimum wage. Define with students the current minimum wage, and ask them to calculate what a weekly salary would be for a full-time worker. Then have them calculate what the yearly salary would be. Discuss as a class how remaining at this salary level impacts workers' quality of life when inflation raises the cost of living. Then ask students to consider the effects a higher minimum wage would have on business owners. **Ask: How are the interests of business owners and workers similar regarding the minimum wage? How are they different?** (Students' answers will vary but should include information about workers needing to keep up with the cost of living, and business owners needing to keep labor costs down in order to make a profit.)

TEACH & ASSESS

R Reading Skills

Differentiating views toward the minimum wage Ask students to brainstorm ideas about how a raise in the minimum wage would affect the lives of workers in minimum wage jobs. Write the ideas on the board in one column titled "Workers." Then ask students to brainstorm ideas about how a raise in the minimum wage would affect the lives of business owners who hire these workers for minimum wage jobs. Write these ideas on the board in another column entitled "Business Owners." Discuss with students whether the needs of workers and business owners are compatible, and, if so, how.

V Visual Skills

Portraying minimum wage issues in cartoons Have students draw political cartoons depicting concerns related to the minimum wage. Political cartoons can show the frustrations of the minimum wage earners, business owners, government policy makers, and/or the benefits or costs of the policy. **Visual/Spatial**

Debates

C Is it a good idea to raise the minimum wage?

V The federal minimum wage, a price floor, is the lowest legal wage that can be paid to workers. As inflation and the cost of living increase, the government reevaluates and increases the minimum wage from time to time. The frequency and amount of the increase, however, is a hotly debated topic. Those in favor of increasing the minimum wage argue that it will help low-wage earners make ends meet, bringing more people out of poverty and increasing their buying power. Those against the increase say that raising the cost of labor hurts small businesses and slows job creation by causing businesses to cut jobs or workers' hours to compensate for increased labor costs. Like all economic decisions, there are trade-offs when a decision is made to increase or not increase wages. You decide: is it a good idea to raise the minimum wage?

R **YES** Raising the minimum wage...
- INCREASES BUYING POWER OF THE POOREST WORKERS
- RAISES THE STANDARD OF LIVING FOR LOW-INCOME FAMILIES
- DECREASES SPENDING ON SOCIAL WELFARE PROGRAMS
- MOTIVATES WORKERS TO WORK HARDER

"[Increasing the minimum wage] would raise the incomes of millions of working families. It could mean the difference between groceries or the food bank; rent or eviction; scraping by or finally getting ahead. For businesses across the country, it would mean customers with more money in their pockets. And a whole lot of folks out there would probably need less help from government."

—President Barack Obama, State of the Union Address, February 12, 2013

Federal Minimum Wage — CURRENT: $7.25 — Minimum wage increases have not kept pace with inflation.

networks Online Teaching Options

DEBATE

Debate: Is it a good idea to raise the minimum wage?

Debating pros and cons of the minimum wage Organize students into two groups: the Yes group and the No group. Have each group click through the Debate to read the text for both sides of the issue. Remind students to study the text for propaganda. Then ask each group to create a statement of their group's opinion, both defending their opinion and responding to the opposing side's claims. Have them answer the first two questions in the Debate to clarify their arguments. Have a spokesperson read the group's statement, and give the opposing group's spokesperson two minutes to respond. Finally, vote as a class to decide which side did the best job defending their ideas. **Interpersonal**

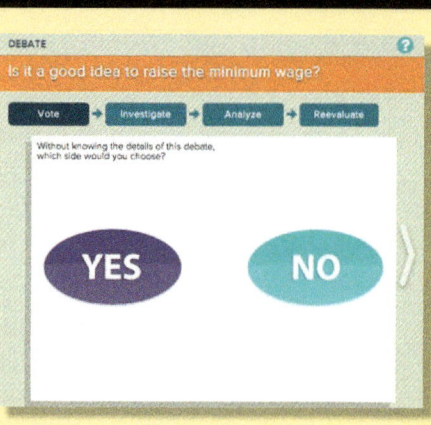

NO Raising the minimum wage...
- HURTS SMALL BUSINESSES THE MOST
- FORCES BUSINESSES TO RAISE PRICES
- CAUSES FEWER WORKERS TO BE HIRED, INCREASING UNEMPLOYMENT
- DISCOURAGES POOR WORKERS FROM GETTING EMPLOYMENT OPPORTUNITIES AND JOB SKILLS

> The cost of wages is reflected in the price of the product or service to the consumer. When labor costs go up, employers have two choices. They can attempt to pass the price increases on to customers (and perhaps lose their customers) or find a way to cut costs.

—Ellen Sauerbrey, chairman of Maryland Business for Responsive Government and former minority leader of the Maryland House of Delegates, "SAUERBREY: Raising minimum wage hurts those it claims to help," *The Washington Times*, March 18, 2013

ANALYZING the issue

1. *Analyzing Visuals* How has the real value of the minimum wage changed in relation to the actual minimum wage? What does this say about workers' buying power?

2. *Evaluating* What two choices does Sauerbrey say employers are faced with when the minimum wage is increased? What impact do these choices have on the economy?

3. *Argument* Which arguments do you find most compelling? Explain your answer.

Teenage Unemployment Rate vs. Minimum Wage Increases
January 2002 to May 2010

▲ Increasing the cost of labor forces employers to cut back on jobs.

CHAPTER 6
Debate

Visual Skills

Analyzing graphs Have students analyze the graph "Teenage Unemployment Rate vs. Minimum Wage Increases." **Ask: Does the data support the argument that increasing the cost of labor (the minimum wage) forces employers to cut back on jobs?** *(Yes and no. The teenage unemployment rate rose several times when the minimum wage was increased, but it also rose and declined when the minimum wage remained steady.)*

CLOSE & REFLECT

Writing Skills

Explaining opinions Have students write a paragraph describing a minimum wage worker's buying power when the cost of living rises. Ask them to include their own opinion about whether to raise or maintain the minimum wage. Remind students to attribute their opinions to sources as necessary.

English Language Proficiency

Beginning Have students work in a group with some students who speak the same first language but have greater English proficiency. Tell beginners to share content information with other group members using gestures, pictures, and the words they know. Ask students with greater proficiency to supply high-frequency words to help the beginners explain. Allow them to assist in their first language as needed.

ANSWERS, p. 175

ANALYZING the issue

1. The real value of the minimum wage has not changed in relation to the actual minimum wage. The buying power of workers is diminished because the real value of the minimum wage has not kept pace with inflation.

2. Sauerbrey says the two choices employers are faced with when the minimum wage is increased are to increase prices to customers or to find a way to cut costs. If prices increase, demand will go down, and unemployment may result. If an employer tries to cut costs, unskilled workers will be priced out of entry-level jobs.

3. Answers will vary. Students may want their own spending power increased by having an increase in the minimum wage. Or they may worry about losing their job if the minimum wage increases.

WORKSHEETS

Economic Simulation

Evaluating work hours as payment Distribute the Economic Simulation: Will Work for Pay. After reading a description of a rather unique form of payment for work in exchange for a tablet computer, students decide whether or not they would accept the deal. Students provide reasons for their decision either way. Each student group tallies the accept/reject votes of the group, and records reasons for each student's decision. Then, a student is chosen to help tally the decisions for the entire class. Finally, students have a class discussion, explaining their decisions and the pros and cons of the payment type offered.

Chapter 6
Study Guide

T Technology Skills

Developing a graph Ask students to create a graph showing market demand and supply curves based on the following figures:

Price	Demand	Supply
$22	60,000	20,000
$24	50,000	28,000
$26	44,000	32,000
$28	36,000	36,000
$30	30,000	40,000
$32	24,000	46,000

Ask: Which prices will result in surpluses? *($30 and $32)* **Which prices will result in shortages?** *($22, $24, and $26)*

W Writing Skills

Defending Have students take on the roles of Congress members participating in a floor debate about a bill that would raise the minimum wage by $1.00 per hour. Direct students to write a speech expressing their views on the bill. Students may wish to suggest a modification to the bill rather than accepting or rejecting it outright. Remind students that the speech is intended to win the support of other members. *Verbal/Linguistic*

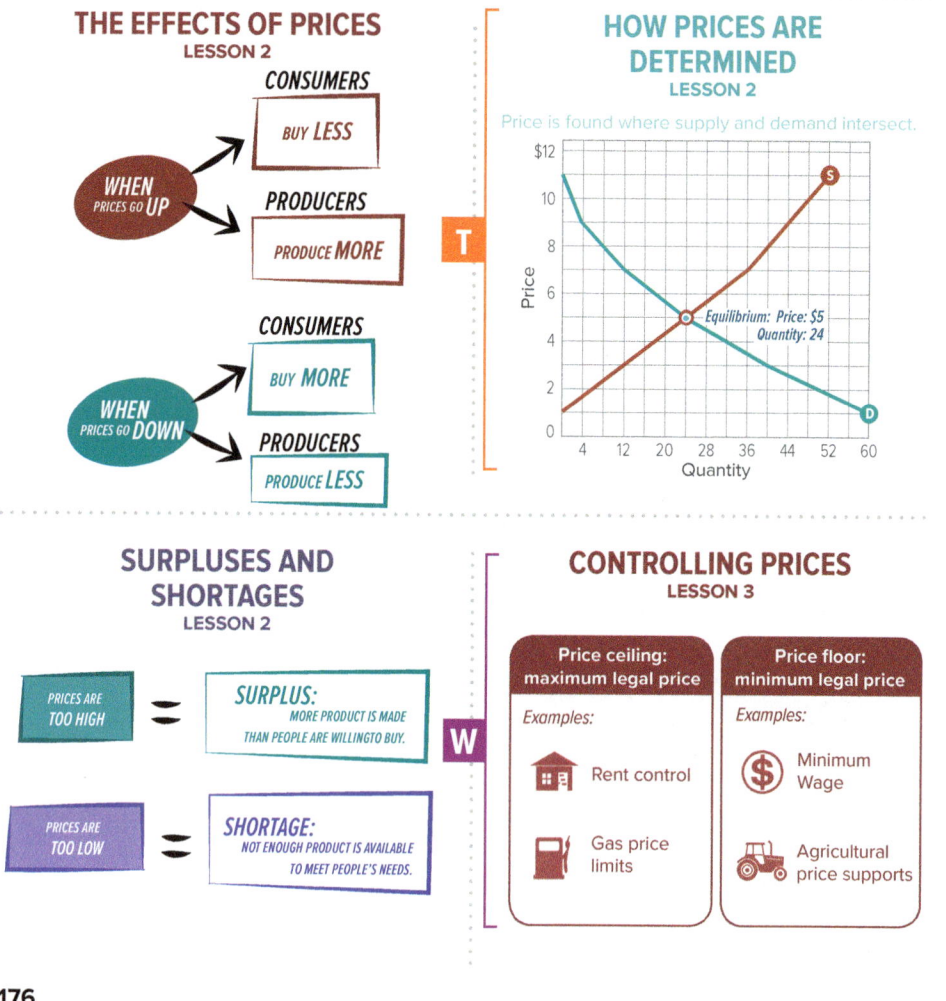

Hands-On Chapter Project with Technology Extension

Students will work in groups to rank different options for buying food by price, and then support their decisions with reasons. They will also provide other factors that affect food pricing, and present their ideas to the class. Next, they will prepare arguments for a debate over farm subsidies and then deliver those arguments in an informal debate. They will also decide which arguments are most compelling. Finally, they will work in groups to first discuss perspectives of various groups on farm subsidies, and then create a pamphlet to convince the general public of their opinions about farm subsidies.

 Find an additional activity online that incorporates technology for this project. Visit the EdTech Teacher Web sites for more links, tutorials, and other resources.

CHAPTER 6 Assessment

Directions: On a separate sheet of paper, answer the questions below. Make sure you read carefully and answer all parts of the questions.

Lesson Review

Lesson 1
1. **Describing** In what ways do prices help us allocate goods and services?
2. **Specifying** What alternative exists to the price system? What challenges does this alternative present?

Lesson 2
3. **Inferring** What is the result of a price that is set above the equilibrium price? Below the equilibrium price?
4. **Identifying** How are quantity supplied and quantity demanded affected by changes in prices? Give an example of how these quantities might change if the price decreases.

Lesson 3
5. **Explaining** Why does a price ceiling set below the equilibrium price result in a shortage?
6. **Drawing Conclusions** What is a goal of the federal minimum wage? Who benefits from it?

Critical Thinking
7. **Identifying Central Issues** Explain how non-price determinants can affect the price of a product by impacting the product's supply and demand.
8. **Constructing Arguments** Write a blog post in which you argue whether or not the price system is the most effective way of allocating goods and services in an economy.
9. **Speculating** Assume that the price of school lunches has become too high, and you need to set a price ceiling to remedy the problem. What would the consequences of such a policy be?
10. **Explaining** Using a price floor or a price ceiling as an example, explain how attempts to achieve one economic or social goal might conflict with another.

Need Extra Help?

If You've Missed Question	1	2	3	4	5	6	7	8	9	10	11	12	13
Go to page	155	156	162	162	168	172	158	156	170	171	161	161	161

Analyzing Visuals

Use the supply and demand schedule and the supply and demand curves to answer the following questions.

A Supply & Demand Schedule

PRICE	QUANTITY DEMANDED	QUANTITY SUPPLIED	SURPLUS/SHORTAGE
$11	0	52	52
$9	4	44	40
$7	12	36	24
$5	24	24	0
$3	40	12	−28
$1	60	0	−60

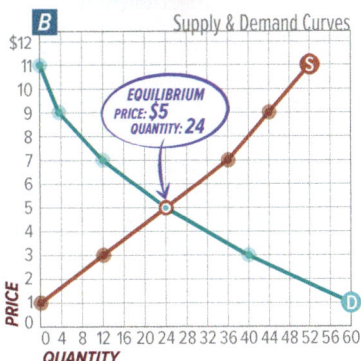

11. **Reading Graphs** How can you identify the equilibrium price on the supply and demand schedule? How can you identify it on the supply and demand curve?
12. **Identifying Graphs** How large is the shortage or surplus at $25? Explain your answer.
13. **Predicting** If the price started at $5 today, what would happen to the price tomorrow? Why?

CHAPTER 6 Assessment Answers

Lesson Review

Lesson 1
1. Prices determine who in the market receives a good or service based on who can afford or is willing to pay a particular price for the good or service.
2. Rationing is an alternative to the price system, but it presents challenges such as perceived fairness, high cost of administration, potential for abuse, and a distortion of incentives to produce.

Lesson 2
3. A price set above the equilibrium price results in a surplus because people buy less of a product than is produced. A price set below the equilibrium price results in a shortage because people want to buy more of a product than is available.
4. Changes in prices affect how much people are willing to buy and how much producers are willing to produce. A high price causes consumers to buy less but producers to produce more. A low price causes consumers to buy more but producers to produce less. Examples will vary.

Lesson 3
5. A price ceiling results in a shortage because more people are willing to buy a product at the lower price, but producers are not willing to produce as much of the product. As a result, there is not enough of the product available to meet the demand, and the product runs out before everyone who wants to buy it is able to.
6. The goal of the federal minimum wage is to ensure that workers are not underpaid. Workers in low-paying jobs benefit most from the minimum wage.

Critical Thinking
7. Nonprice determinants give consumers and producers additional reasons to produce or consume more or less. For example, if a product becomes popular because of a celebrity endorsement, the supply and the demand might increase. Bad weather might decrease the supply of a farm product. A bad product review might decrease the demand for a product.
8. Students' answers will vary but they should demonstrate an understanding of the benefits and consequences of both the price system and rationing.
9. Students' answers will vary. Students should consider the fact that a price ceiling has benefits for the consumer but may have detrimental effects for the businesses providing the goods, can result in a shortage, and may eventually result in lower quality for the consumer.
10. Students' answers will vary depending on the example chosen, but they should demonstrate an understanding of how attempts to achieve one goal can result in a negative impact on other people or industries.

Analyzing Visuals
11. On the supply and demand schedule, the equilibrium price is found where the quantity demanded and the quantity supplied are equal. On the supply and demand curve, it is found where the supply and demand lines intersect.
12. There is a surplus of 32, which results from a quantity supplied of 40, minus a quantity demanded of 8.
13. The price would not change, because $5 is the equilibrium price that both suppliers (producers) and demanders (consumers) agree upon. Hitting the equilibrium price on the first day is rare; normally producers will adjust prices slightly in response to consumer demand.

Chapter 6
Assessment Answers

Answering the Essential Questions

14 Prices help producers determine what and how much to produce. Prices help consumers determine what and how much to buy. When prices are high for a product, producers will produce more of that product, but consumers will buy less of it. When prices are low for a product, producers will produce less of that product, but consumers will buy more.

15 The demand and supply of a product are the primary determinants of prices; however, other factors can affect prices, including the popularity of a product, the weather, or prices of related products.

21st Century Skills

16 Students should recognize benefits and costs of government intervention in the price system.

17 Presentations should show how consumers respond to price increases and note differences in consumer responses between products with inelastic and elastic demand.

18 Students' graphs should include prices that are lower and higher than the equilibrium price, and should show that lower prices create a shortage, while higher prices create a surplus.

Building Financial Literacy

19a Students might suggest: comparing the price of the car at several dealers, finding the value of the car online, and talking to dealers to see how much they are willing to come down on price.

19b Students should recognize the relationship between the price and their budget constraints.

Analyzing Primary Sources

20 Canadian cranberries increased the supply of cranberries available to Americans, which drove the price down and meant U.S. cranberry farmers received less for their product.

21 The goal was to ensure economic security for American cranberry farmers that year. Students may list a variety of impacts, including hurting Canadian cranberry growers, a reduction of competition, keeping American growers in business, or an unintended reliance of American cranberry growers on government assistance.

22 The price of cranberries may increase because as more cranberries are sent to international markets, the domestic supply will decrease.

CHAPTER 6 Assessment

Directions: On a separate sheet of paper, answer the questions below. Make sure you read carefully and answer all parts of the questions.

ANSWERING THE ESSENTIAL QUESTIONS

Review your answers to the introductory questions at the beginning of each lesson. Then answer the Essential Questions on the basis of what you learned in the chapter. Have your answers changed?

14 **Summarizing** How do prices help us make decisions?

15 **Understanding Relationships** What factors affect prices?

21st Century Skills

16 **Defending** Under what circumstances, if any, do you think it is appropriate for the government to interfere in the market by manipulating prices? Write a one-page position statement, supporting your opinion with examples.

17 **Presentation Skills** Make a list of three products with elastic demand and three products with inelastic demand. Conduct a survey in which you ask 20 people how they would respond to an increase in prices for each of the products. Create a multimedia presentation to explain how consumers respond to price changes based on your findings.

18 **Creating and Using Graphs** Research the price of a product. Using the price you found as the equilibrium price, create an imaginary supply and demand schedule showing how the quantity supplied and the quantity demanded for the product changes at various prices. Then, graph your results.

Building Financial Literacy

19 **Decision Making** Knowing how to evaluate prices will help you make better decisions when choosing how to allocate your scarce resources—your time and money.

  a. What strategies might you use to ensure you are getting the best price for a product? Make a list of ways to "shop around" for the best price on a car.

  b. Identify a product you hope to purchase sometime in the next year. Describe how you would compare the price of the product against your budget to make a purchasing decision.

Need Extra Help?

If You've Missed Question	14	15	16	17	18	19	20	21	22
Go to page	162	164	168	164	161	164	164	171	165

178

Analyzing Primary Sources

Read the excerpt and answer the questions that follow.

PRIMARY SOURCE

"*Farmers in Wisconsin, the leading cranberry producer, have been working for years to expand their acreage at the request of Ocean Spray and other processors who expected to see strong growth in overseas sales of juice and sweetened, dried cranberries. Growth has been slower than expected, however, as nations continue to struggle with the Great Recession and its aftermath, said Tom Lochner, executive director of the Wisconsin State Cranberry Growers Association. Growth of 2 percent to 3 percent overseas, coupled with flat demand in the U.S., left farmers with a huge excess of cranberries this fall after an unexpected jump in production in Canada, he said.*"

—M.L. Johnson, "Cranberry farmers struggle as surplus drops prices," *Businessweek*, May 6, 2013

The U.S. Department of Agriculture had predicted that the crop would be worth about $48 per 100 pounds, but it announced it would buy $5 million worth of cranberry products to use in food assistance programs. Cranberry farmers knew that they had to boost sales in addition to getting help from the government. The industry's marketing group introduced cranberries in Europe with good success. Next, the group plans to focus on introducing cranberries in Asia.

20 **Identifying Cause and Effect** Why did an increase in Canadian cranberries negatively impact cranberry farmers in the United States?

21 **Considering Advantages and Disadvantages** What was the goal of the U.S. Department of Agriculture's decision to buy $5 million worth of cranberries? What impacts, positive and negative, might the decision have on producers and consumers?

22 **Making Predictions** If the cranberry industry is successful in making its fruit popular in new markets, what will happen to the price of cranberries? Explain your answer.

---

networks Online Assessment Options

WORKSHEET

Chapter Tests and Lesson Quizzes

Chapter 6 Tests Forms A and B Have students complete the Chapter Tests and Lesson Quizzes to assess student understanding throughout the chapter. Print and online assessment tools offer chapter and lesson evaluation through a variety of question formats, including document-based questions.

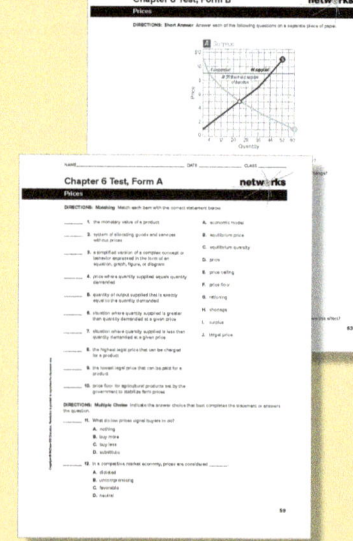

CHAPTER 7
Market Structures Planner

UNDERSTANDING BY DESIGN®

Enduring Understanding
- Profit inspires people to take risks with their resources.

Essential Questions
- How do varying market structures impact prices in a market economy?
- Why do markets fail?
- How does the government attempt to correct market failures?

Predictable Misunderstandings
Students may think:
- *All monopolies are harmful to an economic system.* Explain that some monopolies can be beneficial, especially if a company can offer its products at a lower cost because it produces them in such large volume or provides them to so many people (economy of scale).
- *Lack of competition helps a company succeed and prevents market failure.* Explain that lack of competition tends to cause a company to reduce its efforts to use resources carefully, which leads to wastefulness and other issues. Lack of competition is one of the five major reasons for market failure.

Assessment Evidence
Performance Task
- Hands-On Chapter Project with Technology Extension

Other Evidence
- Guided Reading Activities
- Vocabulary Activity
- Lesson Quizzes
- Self-Check Quizzes
- Chapter Assessment
- Chapter Tests, Forms A and B

SUGGESTED PACING

Introducing the Chapter: ½ Day	Case Study ½ Day
Lesson 1: Competition and Market Structures 1 Day	Lesson 3: The Role of Government 1 Day
Debate ½ Day	Study Guide, Chapter Assessment and Wrap-Up ½ Day
Lesson 2: Market Failures 1 Day	

TOTAL 5 Days

Key for Using the Teacher Edition

SKILL-BASED ACTIVITIES
Types of skill activites found in the Teacher Edition.

V Visual Skills require students to analyze maps, graphs, charts, and photos.

R Reading Skills help students practice reading skills and master vocabulary.

C Critical Thinking Skills help students apply and extend what they have learned.

W Writing Skills provide writing opportunities to help students comprehend the text.

T Technology Skills require students to use digital tools effectively.

*Letters are followed by a number when there is more than one of the same type of skill on the page.

DIFFERENTIATED INSTRUCTION
All activities are written for the on-level student unless otherwise marked with the leveled labels below.

BL Beyond Level
AL Approaching Level
ELL English Language Learners

All students benefit from activities that utilize different learning styles. Many activities are marked as below when a particular learning style is highlighted.

Intrapersonal
Logical/Mathematical
Visual/Spatial
Verbal/Linguistic
Naturalist
Kinesthetic
Auditory/Musical
Interpersonal

Council for Economic Education

Below are the Council for Economic Education Voluntary National Content Standards in Economics covered in the *Market Structures* chapter.

Content Standard 9: Competition among sellers usually lowers costs and prices, and encourages producers to produce what consumers are willing and able to buy. Competition among buyers increases prices and allocates goods and services to those people who are willing and able to pay the most for them.

Content Standard 16: There is an economic role for government in a market economy whenever the benefits of a government policy outweigh its costs. Governments often provide for national defense, address environmental concerns, define and protect property rights, and attempt to make markets more competitive. Most government policies also have direct or indirect effects on people's incomes.

CHAPTER 7: MARKET STRUCTURES

CHAPTER OPENER PLANNER

Students will know:
- the basic characteristics of the four market structures: monopoly, oligopoly, monopolistic competition and pure competition.
- ways that firms engage in price and non-price competition

Students will be able to:
- **discuss** the usefulness of studying pure competition even though there are no purely competitive markets.
- **name** the conditions for pure competition and perfect competition.

UNDERSTANDING BY DESIGN

☑ Print Teaching Options

V Visual Skills
- ☐ **p. 180 Summarizing the infographic** Students summarize characteristics, examples, and behaviors of monopolies and oligopolies.
- ☐ **p. 181 Analyzing the infographic** Students analyze different types of market structures.

C Critical Thinking Skills
- ☐ **p. 179 Comparing market structures** Student decide on one item to sell in a class store and discuss how competition influences the market.
- ☐ **p. 179 NIMBY** Students discuss the concept of "Not In My Back Yard" (NIMBY).
- ☐ **p. 181 Researching local market structures** Students note how competition and market structure affected local business decisions.

W Writing Skills
- ☐ **p. 180 Examining monopolies** Students note characteristics and examples of the four types of monopolies.

Project-Based Learning

Hands-On

WORKSHEET Hands-On Chapter Project
Groups will research antitrust cases, examining the arguments on both sides of the case and what led to the case. Students will present their findings to the class, considering which type of market structure was evident in their case. Then students will discuss the similarities between the cases groups presented, and why the government felt the need to intervene in these situations.

Digital Hands-On

Create Online Projects

Find an additional activity online that incorporates technology for the Hands-On Project. Visit the EdTech Teacher Web sites for more links, tutorials, and other resources.

☑ Online Teaching Options

V Visual Skills
- ☐ **IMAGE Chapter opener**—Students analyze a photo for clues about government regulations and market structures.

C Critical Thinking Skills
- ☐ **INFOGRAPHICS Economic Perspectives**—Students find examples of monopolies and oligopolies.
- ☐ **DEBATES Do current copyright laws do more harm than good?**—Students analyze the effects of piracy and discuss their views on music copyright.
- ☐ **INTERACTIVE FEATURE Case Study: Coming to America**—Students discuss government incentives for establishing businesses in the U.S.

☑ Printable Digital Worksheets

C Critical Thinking Skills
- ☐ **WORKSHEET Enrichment Activity**—Students read about energy markets and their effect on climate change.
- ☐ **WORKSHEET Chapter Summary**—Content is condensed into manageable chunks.
- ☐ **WORKSHEET Vocabulary Activity**—Students use content and academic terms.

Print Resources

ANCILLARY RESOURCE
This ancillary is available for every chapter and lesson.
- Chapter Tests and Lesson Quizzes

PRINTABLE DIGITAL WORKSHEETS
These printable digital worksheets are available for every chapter and lesson.
- Reading Essentials & Study Guide
- Vocabulary Activities
- Chapter Summaries
- Economic Simulations
- Math Practice for Economics
- Reinforcing Economic Skills
- Personal Finance Activities
- Enrichment Activities
- Reteaching Activities
- Guided Reading Activities
- Video Worksheets
- Lesson Quizzes and Chapter Tests (English and Spanish)

More Media Resources

SUGGESTED READING
- For students at a Grade 10 reading level:
  Hearing the Pitch: Evaluating All Kinds of Advertising, by Carlienne Frisch
- For students at a Grade 11 reading level:
  Government and the Environment: Tracking the Record, by Thomas G. Aylesworth
- For students at a Grade 12 reading level:
  Foreign Oil Dependence, by James Haley

SUGGESTED VIDEOS MOVIES
Find these documentaries yourself online. NOTE: McGraw-Hill Education does not endorse these resources. Preview clips for age-appropriateness.
- *The Supermarket That's Eating Britain* (30 min.)
- *Wal-Mart: The High Cost of Low Price* (1 hour 38 min.)

LESSON 1 Planner

COMPETITION AND MARKET STRUCTURES

Students will know:
- the basic characteristics of the four market structures: monopoly, oligopoly, monopolistic competition and pure competition.
- ways that firms engage in price and non-price competition
- how changes in the level of competition in different markets can affect price and output levels.
- the pursuit of self-interest in competitive markets usually leads to choices and behavior that also promote the national level of well-being.

Students will be able to:
- *discuss* the usefulness of studying pure competition even though there are no purely competitive markets.
- *name* the conditions for pure competition and perfect competition.
- *explain* the role of advertising in a monopolistic competition.
- *summarize* ways in which monopolistic competitors compete for customers.
- *explain* why markets dominated by oligopolies result in high prices for consumers.
- *describe* the interdependent behavior of oligopolists.
- *summarize* the characteristics of the four major types of monopolies.

UNDERSTANDING BY DESIGN®

☑ Print Teaching Options

V Visual Skills
- ☐ p. 183 **Analyzing graphs** Students discuss differences between marginal cost & revenue.

R Reading Skills
- ☐ p. 183 **Summarizing characteristics of pure competition**
- ☐ p. 185 **Identifying monopolistic competition characteristics** AL Verbal/Linguistic
- ☐ p. 186 **Understanding the literal meaning of** *oligopoly* Students research word origins.
- ☐ p. 188 **Comparing monopolies and oligopolies**

C Critical Thinking Skills
- ☐ p. 182 **Analyzing economic freedom** Students tie laissez-faire to the American Revolution.
- ☐ p. 183 **Speculating about pure competition conditions** AL
- ☐ p. 185 **Identifying examples of monopolistic competition** Students explain the effectiveness of advertisements.
- ☐ p. 186 **Determining cause and effect** Students determine what happens when an oligopolistic firm makes a product change. AL
- ☐ p. 187 **Writing about oligopolies** Students argue for their preferred brand.
- ☐ p. 188 **Identifying natural monopolies**
- ☐ p. 189 **Speculating about patents**
- ☐ p. 189 **Relating technology and monopoly**

W Writing Skills
- ☐ p. 183 **Comparing competition to democracy**
- ☐ p. 184 **Writing about pure competition**
- ☐ p. 184 **Creating an ad about pure competition**

☑ Online Teaching Options

V Visual Skills
- ☐ GRAPHS **Pure Competition and Profit Maximization**—Students explore supply, demand, marginal cost, and marginal revenue under pure competition.
- ☐ INTERACTIVE FEATURES **Global Economy & You**—Students discuss the breakup of AT&T's monopoly. Visual/Spatial
- ☐ VIDEO **Google Wants to Stop Microsoft Merging**—Students watch the video about Google's desire to stop Microsoft from buying Yahoo. Visual/Spatial

R Reading Skills
- ☐ GRAPHIC ORGANIZERS **Characteristics of Different Market Structures**—Students describe market structures. Verbal/Linguistic
- ☐ GRAPHIC ORGANIZERS **Venn Diagram**—Students compare pure and monopolistic competition.

C Critical Thinking Skills
- ☐ BELLRINGER **Competition and Market Structure**—Students examine a post office and a steel mill regarding market structures. Verbal/Linguistic
- ☐ ESSENTIAL QUESTION **Exploring the Essential Question Activity**—Students discuss a gas station monopoly. Logical/Mathematical

T Technology Skills
- ☐ SELF-CHECK QUIZ **Lesson 1**—Students receive instant feedback on answers.
- ☐ GAME **Lesson 1**—Students solve clues to review lesson content.
- ☐ INTERACTIVE WHITEBOARD ACTIVITY **Monopolistic Competition vs. Oligopoly**—Students work together to learn lesson content.

☑ Printable Digital Worksheets

R Reading Skills
- ☐ WORKSHEET **Guided Reading Activity**—Students review their comprehension.
- ☐ WORKSHEET **Reading Essentials and Study Guide**—Students complete the study guide and answer Reading Progress Check and vocabulary questions.

C Critical Thinking Skills
- ☐ WORKSHEET **Google Wants to Stop Microsoft Merging Video Activity**—Students answer questions about merger prevention.
- ☐ WORKSHEET **Personal Finance Activity**—Students calculate gas mileage.
- ☐ WORKSHEET **Math Practice for Economics**—Students compare competitors in the candy industry.

LESSON 2 Planner

MARKET FAILURES

Students will know:
- markets can sometimes fail because of inadequate competition, inadequate information, resource immobility, public goods, and externalities.
- externalities exist when some of the costs or benefits associated with production and consumption fall on someone other than the producers or consumers of the product.
- externalities indicate a market failure and can be corrected with government action.

Students will be able to:
- **state** the factors that reduce competition in a market.
- **discuss** the five main causes of market failures.
- **evaluate** methods to reduce harmful spillovers and to encourage helpful spillovers.

UNDERSTANDING BY DESIGN

☑ Print Teaching Options

R Reading Skills

☐ **p. 192 Activating prior knowledge about perfect competition** Students discuss the conditions necessary for perfect competition.

☐ **p. 193 Defining and categorizing public goods** Students discuss a public good, and define non-rival consumption and non-exclusive ownership. **ELL AL**

☐ **p. 196 Identifying government involvement in externalities** Students discuss ways the government handles externalities or spillovers.

☐ **p. 196 Drawing conclusions from the lesson** Students review the lesson and write conclusions.

C Critical Thinking Skills

☐ **p. 192 Drawing conclusions about failed businesses** Students list failed businesses or products and explain why they failed. **AL** Interpersonal

☐ **p. 193 Demonstrating the importance of adequate information** Students find and compare interest rates on credit cards. **BL** Logical/Mathematical

☐ **p. 193 Providing examples of externalities** Students identify negative and positive externalities.

☐ **p. 194 Understanding frame of reference for market failure** Students evaluate the validity of economic information.

☐ **p. 194 Pollution Solution** Students find examples of pollution and report on proposed solutions.

☐ **p. 195 Devising a plan** Students identify an externality and devise a plan for benefiting from it or correcting it.

☑ Online Teaching Options

V Visual Skills

☐ **CHARTS Cost-Benefit Analysis**—Students click on different project headings to see cost-benefit ratios. Logical/Mathematical

☐ **VIDEO Blu-ray vs. HD DVDs**—Students view a video about the failure of the HD DVD format. Verbal/Linguistic

R Reading Skills

☐ **GRAPHIC ORGANIZERS Causes of Market Failure**—Students identify the causes of market failures. Logical/Mathematical

☐ **BIOGRAPHY Joseph Stiglitz**—Students read about Joseph Stiglitz's economic ideas. Interpersonal, Verbal/Linguistic

C Critical Thinking Skills

☐ **BELLRINGER Market Failures**—Students discuss what they know about market failures. Visual/Spatial, Verbal/Linguistic

☐ **ESSENTIAL QUESTION Exploring the Essential Question**—Students discuss how the 2007 housing market failure affected the economy.

T Technology Skills

☐ **SELF-CHECK QUIZ Lesson 2**—Students receive instant feedback on their mastery of lesson content.

☐ **GAME Lesson 2**—Students solve clues to review lesson content.

☐ **INTERACTIVE WHITEBOARD ACTIVITY Natural and Geographic Monopolies**—Students work together to learn lesson content.

☑ Printable Digital Worksheets

R Reading Skills

☐ **WORKSHEET Guided Reading Activity**—Students use the Guided Reading Activity worksheets to review their comprehension of the content.

☐ **WORKSHEET Reading Essentials and Study Guide**—Students complete the study guide and answer Reading Progress Check and vocabulary questions.

☐ **WORKSHEET Blu-ray vs. HD DVDs Video Activity**—Students answer questions about the failure of the HD DVD format. Verbal/Linguistic

☐ **WORKSHEET Enrichment Activity**—Students examine externalities associated with energy production. Visual/Spatial

LESSON 3 Planner

THE ROLE OF GOVERNMENT

Students will know:
- laws and regulations adopted in the United States to promote competition among firms.
- in the United States, the federal government enforces antitrust laws and regulations to try to maintain effective levels of competition; however, laws and regulations can also have unintended effects of reducing competition.
- providing public goods and promoting transparency can improve economic efficiency.
- because the government is involved in certain aspects of our economy, it is a modified version of free enterprise.

Students will be able to:
- **analyze** government regulations that attempt to ensure competition.
- **explain** how transparency and public disclosure affect consumer decisions.
- **make connections** between past government laws and regulations and today's modified free enterprise economic system in the United States.

UNDERSTANDING BY DESIGN®

✓ Print Teaching Options

R Reading Skills

- ☐ **p. 200 Identifying regulations** Students discuss why companies are required to explain methods for computing interest.
- ☐ **p. 201 Taking notes about federal regulatory agencies** Students quiz each other about federal agencies and their functions. **AL**
- ☐ **p. 203 Recalling terms that describe the U.S. economic system** Students identify synonyms for the U.S. economic system. **AL**

C Critical Thinking Skills

- ☐ **p. 198 Discussing U.S. market structures**
- ☐ **p. 199 Defining and evaluating cease and desist orders** Students discuss whether issuing these orders are a justifiable government role.
- ☐ **p. 200 Researching through the SEC** Students research a company in the EDGAR database.
- ☐ **p. 201 Researching local zoning laws** Students create a map showing zones and effects on starting a neighborhood business. **BL**
- ☐ **p. 202 Predicting the future role of government**
- ☐ **p. 202 Constructing arguments about government regulation** Students debate the following: *The government is too involved in regulating our economy.* **Verbal/Linguistic**
- ☐ **p. 203 Analyzing frame of reference** Students analyze the validity of a statement by the author.

W Writing Skills

- ☐ **p. 202 Evaluating start-up regulations** Students search online for ordinances and rate them as beneficial or intrusive. **Verbal/Linguistic**

✓ Online Teaching Options

V Visual Skills

- ☐ **INTERACTIVE FEATURES** Careers—Students explore the career of consumer advocate lawyer. **Logical/Mathematical**
- ☐ **CHARTS** Federal Regulatory Agencies—Students discuss the roles of the various federal regulatory agencies. **Visual/Spatial, Logical/Mathematical**
- ☐ **VIDEO** Role of Government—Students watch a video about competition in the credit card market. **Visual/Spatial**

R Reading Skills

- ☐ **GRAPHIC ORGANIZER** Government Regulations and Competition Monitoring—Students identify how government ensures competition and prevents business failure. **Verbal/Linguistic**
- ☐ **GRAPHIC ORGANIZER** Concept Web—Students express information about anti-monopoly legislation. **Verbal/Linguistic**

C Critical Thinking Skills

- ☐ **BELLRINGER** Role of Government—Students discuss monopolies and the government role in regulating or breaking them up. **Verbal/Linguistic**
- ☐ **ESSENTIAL QUESTION** Exploring the Essential Question—Students discuss the main causes of market failure. **Verbal/Linguistic**

T Technology Skills

- ☐ **SELF-CHECK QUIZ** Lesson 3—Students receive instant feedback on answer.
- ☐ **GAME** Lesson 3—Students solve clues to review lesson content.
- ☐ **INTERACTIVE WHITEBOARD ACTIVITY** The Role of Government—Students work together to learn lesson content.

✓ Printable Digital Worksheets

R Reading Skills

- ☐ **WORKSHEET** Guided Reading Activity—Students review their comprehension.
- ☐ **WORKSHEET** Reading Essentials and Study Guide—Students complete the study guide and answer Reading Progress Check and vocabulary questions.
- ☐ **WORKSHEET** Reteaching Activity—Reteach chapter content and vocabulary.

C Critical Thinking Skills

- ☐ **WORKSHEET** Role of Government Video Activity—Students answer questions about competition in the credit card market. **Visual/Spatial**

CHAPTER 7 Market Structures

INTERVENTION AND REMEDIATION STRATEGIES

LESSON 1 Competition and Market Structures

Reading and Comprehension

Divide the different types of market structures among students. Ask each student to review his or her structure and to write a paragraph explaining what makes that system successful (or not) in the real world. Tell them to use facts and reasons from the text to support their ideas. After completing their paragraphs, ask the students to share their ideas in a class discussion.

Text Evidence

Have students work in pairs and find the answer to this question: **What are the two most important reasons the United States today has few monopolies? Explain your answers, citing details from the text.** Have each pair of students present their answer and reasons in a group discussion.

LESSON 2 Market Failures

Reading and Comprehension

Ask students to imagine that a tornado (or other locally possible natural disaster) has caused major damage to several local businesses. Local government officials are considering offering no-interest loans and tax incentives to the companies to rebuild. Have students write a blog entry detailing their opinion of whether or not the businesses should be helped to survive or allowed to fail. Post all blog entries to a class Web site, and ask students to post responses to at least three of their classmates' blogs.

Text Evidence

Review how to use text evidence to support ideas and statements. Then pose these directives:

- Public utilities are regulated to prevent waste and abuse of resources. Find evidence in the text to support this statement. *(This is one of the reasons that public utilities such as electricity are regulated by the government—to make sure that the firms do not use their monopoly status to waste or abuse resources.)*

- Private markets are inefficient at supplying public goods. Find evidence in the text to support this statement. *(When left to itself, the market either does not supply these items at all, or it supplies them inadequately.)*

- Market prices do not reflect the cost of negative externalities, like air pollution. *(Externalities are market failures because their costs and benefits are not reflected in the market prices that buyers and sellers pay.)*

LESSON 3 The Role of Government

Reading and Comprehension

Divide students into three groups and assign one of the questions below to each group.

Have groups answer the questions and find details to support their responses. Then ask students to share their answers and reasons with the class.

- Why did the U.S. pass the Federal Trade Commission Act?
- Should all monopolies be broken up? Why or why not?
- How does the government help keep natural gas prices low? Why does it do this?

Text Evidence

Ask students to write one or two paragraphs responding to this question: **How does the government react to fix market failure? Give details from the text to support your answer.** Have students compare their responses in small group discussions.

Online Resources

Assessing Background Knowledge Use this worksheet to pre-assess students' background knowledge before they start the chapter.

Chapter Summaries Have students use the summary as a pre-reading activity or as a post-reading review to check main ideas covered in each lesson.

Guided Reading Activities Have students complete these activities as they read each lesson. They provide reading notes the student can use for review and to prepare for assessments.

Reteaching Activities Have students complete the Reteaching Activity for remedial practice and review of vital content.

Self-Check Quizzes These quizzes provide instant feedback on areas the students may need to re-read to understand a main idea.

Reading Essentials and Study Guide This resource offers writing and reading activities for the approaching-level student.

Approaching Grade Level Reader This reader presents all of the content of the Online Student Edition but at a lower reading level.

English Language Learner Reader Provide additional reading support for ELL students. Find this tool in the Online Student Edition.

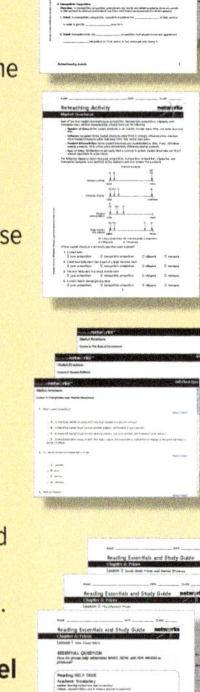

179F

Market Structures

ESSENTIAL QUESTIONS
- How do varying market structures impact prices in a market economy?
- Why do markets fail?
- How does the government attempt to correct market failures?

networks
www.connected.mcgraw-hill.com
There's More Online about market structures.

CHAPTER 7

Economic Perspectives
Monopolies & Oligopolies

Lesson 1
Competition and Market Structures

Lesson 2
Market Failures

Lesson 3
The Role of Government

Letter from the Author

Dear Economics Teacher,

By now we've established the value of markets—the fact that they are neutral, efficient, and about the only way to allocate goods and services in an advanced economy like ours. A market is efficient not just because it is a market, however. It often takes another party like the courts or the government to make sure the markets stay competitive. Unfortunately, many businesses expend a considerable amount of time, money, and energy to establish a non-competitive edge. Challenge your students to be on the lookout for such activities, and post them in a conspicuous place. The results will surprise you!

CHAPTER 7
Market Structures

ENGAGE

Have students examine the photo and ask them to describe what it shows. Guide them to recognize that two workers are working in a manufacturing facility. **Ask: How might this image represent what you will learn in a chapter titled Market Structures?** *(Market structures influence economic behaviors and outcomes. In the past, self-interest in competitive markets led to unsafe factory workplaces. Today, government regulations ensure that these workers have a safe workplace environment.)* In a discussion, lead students to understand that even in free market economic systems, government regulations promote economic competition and efficiency while also protecting workers and consumers. **Visual/Spatial**

Comparing market structures Organize the class into six different groups. Tell students to imagine that they are opening a class store. Have each group decide on one item their group will sell. Examples might include computers, athletic shoes, cars, or pizzas. Write each item on the board. If no two items are similar, **ask: How does having no competition influence the market for these items?** *(If demand is high, sellers can set the prices as high as they wish. With no competition, standards for quality may not have to be as high. Sellers may not need to advertise.)* If two or more items are similar, **ask: How does competition influence the market for these items?** *(Buyers can chose which item they wish to buy based on price or differences between the products. Sellers may need to advertise to attract buyers.)* This chapter will discuss the four different market structures that reflect unique competitive conditions. **Interpersonal**

Making Connections

NIMBY Discuss this scenario that personalizes "Not In My Back Yard" (NIMBY): A developer has acquired the vacant land across the street from your house and plans to build a shopping mall on the property. How might you benefit from the mall? How might it negatively impact your life? List benefits and downsides on the board and discuss as a class. **Intrapersonal**

FOLDABLES
Study Organizer

Go to the Foldables® library for a cumulative chapter-based Foldable® activity that your students can use to help take notes and prepare for assessment.

CHAPTER 7
Economic Perspectives

TEACH & ASSESS

V Visual Skills

Summarizing the infographic Ask: **What does the infographic show?** *(characteristics, examples, and behaviors of monopolies and oligopolies)* **Visual/Spatial**

W Writing Skills

Examining monopolies Have students examine the characteristics of the four types of monopolies. Ask them to create a graphic organizer with the four types, a description of the characteristics of each type, and an example of each type. **Visual/Spatial**

Economic Perspectives

MONOPOLIES & OLIGOPOLIES

The Sherman Act (1890) was passed by Congress to prevent anticompetitive behavior in the marketplace. Based on Congress' ability to regulate interstate commerce, the law prohibits the formation of trusts, which consolidate stockholder shares from different companies into one corporate entity.

NATURAL MONOPOLY
occurs when the nature of an industry does not allow for multiple companies to do business. (Example: sewage industry – competition not practical because homes/homeowners cannot accommodate multiple sewage lines)

GEOGRAPHIC MONOPOLY
occurs when a single company in a particular area offers a certain good or service. (Example: a general store in a small town is the only place citizens can buy eggs and milk in that area)

TECHNOLOGICAL MONOPOLY
occurs when one company holds the sole patent on a particular technology. (Example: a pharmaceutical company owns the patent for the cure to a specific disease)

GOVERNMENT MONOPOLY
occurs when a government has by law reserved a specific business for one of its own agencies. (Example: distribution of running water is run by city government)

Examples:

Railroads

By the late 1800s, a few railroad companies dominated transportation across the United States. Railroad companies joined to totally control prices and competition, leaving the country vulnerable to their exorbitant prices (since everyone relied on the railroads to either transport or receive goods). In 1887, the federal government created the Interstate Commerce Commission to regulate American commerce.

Cable TV

Cable television is a natural monopoly because the cost of entering the market (i.e., installing new cable lines) prevents effective competitors from entering the market. Most communities are serviced by one cable company. Telecomm firms AT&T and Verizon also provide cable television service. Satellite television is another alternative. Despite potentially changing the game, telecomm and satellite television haven't decreased costs for consumers.

Telephone

Until 1984, AT&T was the single provider of U.S. telephone service (and most equipment) under what was known as the Bell System. In 1974, the Department of Justice filed an antitrust lawsuit against AT&T under the Sherman Antitrust Act. In 1984, the final settlement broke up the Bell System into seven independent Regional Bell Operating Companies ("Baby Bells"), which enabled competition and innovation in telecommunications.

---

networks **Online Teaching Options**

INFOGRAPHIC

Economic Perspectives: Monopolies & Oligopolies

Gaining a perspective of market structures Before students view the infographic, check their prior knowledge of market structures. **Ask:**

- **What market structure is theoretical?** *(pure competition)*
- **What market structures are found in the real world?** *(oligopoly, monopoly, monopolistic competition)*
- **What is an example of a monopolistically competitive product?** *(Sample answers: toothpaste, soda, shampoo)*

Have students use the infographic to find their own examples of monopolies and oligopolies. **Visual/Spatial**

CHAPTER 7
Economic Perspectives

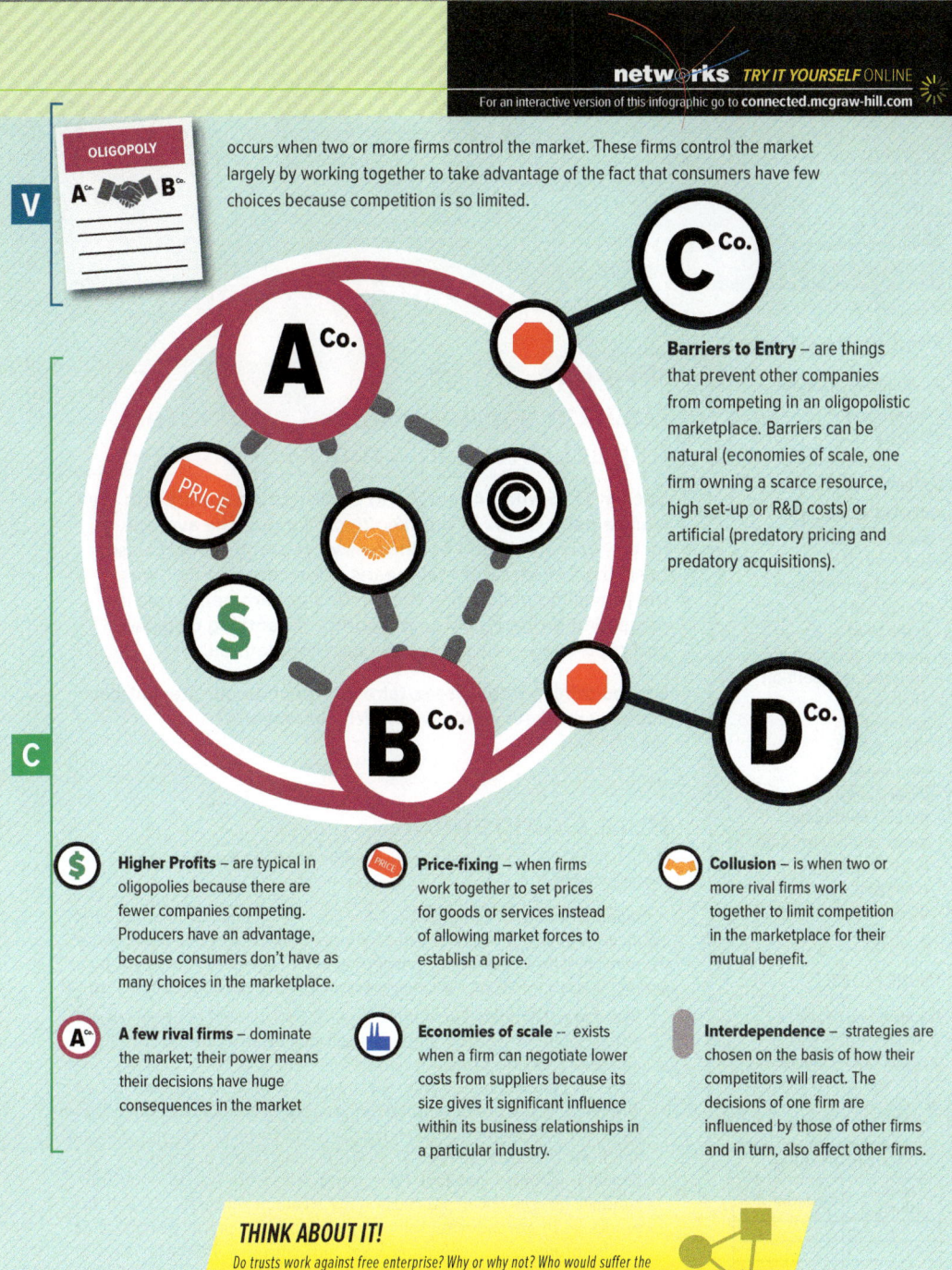

occurs when two or more firms control the market. These firms control the market largely by working together to take advantage of the fact that consumers have few choices because competition is so limited.

Barriers to Entry – are things that prevent other companies from competing in an oligopolistic marketplace. Barriers can be natural (economies of scale, one firm owning a scarce resource, high set-up or R&D costs) or artificial (predatory pricing and predatory acquisitions).

Higher Profits – are typical in oligopolies because there are fewer companies competing. Producers have an advantage, because consumers don't have as many choices in the marketplace.

A few rival firms – dominate the market; their power means their decisions have huge consequences in the market

Price-fixing – when firms work together to set prices for goods or services instead of allowing market forces to establish a price.

Economies of scale – exists when a firm can negotiate lower costs from suppliers because its size gives it significant influence within its business relationships in a particular industry.

Collusion – is when two or more rival firms work together to limit competition in the marketplace for their mutual benefit.

Interdependence – strategies are chosen on the basis of how their competitors will react. The decisions of one firm are influenced by those of other firms and in turn, also affect other firms.

THINK ABOUT IT!
Do trusts work against free enterprise? Why or why not? Who would suffer the most if monopolies and oligopolies were unregulated? Why?

V Visual Skills

Analyzing the infographic Ask: In which market structure does the seller control the market price and supply quantity? *(monopoly)* Which market structure has two or more sellers? *(oligopoly)* **Visual/Spatial**

C Critical Thinking Skills

Researching local market structures Have students select a company that recently opened for business in their area. Ask students to write a brief report on the goods or services that company provides, and note which other businesses provide the same goods and services in the area. Have students apply information from the infographic to determine which market structure the business follows. Instruct students to conclude their reports by explaining why they think the owners of the business decided to open in that particular location and how the market structure may have influenced the decision. **Ask:** How are competition and the profit motive related? *(People open businesses to earn profits. Competition forces entrepreneurs to keep prices low enough to attract customers. However, prices must remain high enough to ensure profits.)* Ask for volunteers to share the names of the companies they selected. Discuss as a class how each new business could affect the market for the goods and services that it sells. **Visual/Spatial, Interpersonal**

CLOSE & REFLECT

Have students answer the *Think About It!* questions.

WORKSHEET

Economic Simulation

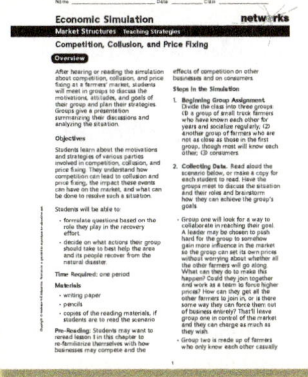

Analyzing collusion and price fixing Have students use the Economic Simulation "Competition, Collusion, and Price Fixing" to learn about the motivations and strategies involved in competition, collusion, and price fixing at a farmers' market. Students will understand how competition can lead to collusion and price fixing, the impact these events can have on the market, and what can be done to resolve such a situation. **Intrapersonal, Interpersonal**

ANSWERS, p. 181

THINK ABOUT IT!

Trusts do work against free enterprise. Consumers suffer the most if monopolies and oligopolies are unregulated. If unregulated, monopolies and oligopolies can control the prices that consumers pay, as well as control the prices of their suppliers.

CHAPTER 7, LESSON 1
Competition and Market Structures

ENGAGE

C Critical Thinking Skills

 Analyzing economic freedom Before students read the information about Adam Smith in the introductory information, ask them to consider the date of publication of his *Wealth of Nations* (1776). **Ask: What else was occurring at that time?** *(American Revolution)* Point out that Smith was Scottish, not American. Lead students to understand that revolutionary ideas were not confined geographically, nor were they limited to purely political spheres. The text describes *laissez-faire* as the prevailing philosophy of the time. **Ask: Why would people in 1776 be interested in limiting the government's role in the economy? Are laissez-faire attitudes still prevalent in the U.S. economy? When do people welcome government interference, and when do they resist it?** Lead students to understand that as economies became more complex, government influence became more acceptable to maintain fair markets and to protect both businesses and individuals. Then have students brainstorm and analyze recent changes in the basic characteristics of the U.S. economy. **BL**

Making Connections

A Perfectly Competitive Market The grain market for number two yellow corn is close to perfectly competitive. Many farmers grow this corn, and there are many buyers. The farmers do not advertise or band together to control price. There is open communication about the market price. But entry into the market is limited because it takes a sizeable investment to grow grain.

ANSWERS, p. 182

ESSENTIAL QUESTION ACTIVITY

Answers will vary. Many will say that a total laissez-faire approach would not work because government is still necessary for protecting property rights, enforcing contracts, settling disputes, and protecting consumers from unscrupulous business practices.

TAKING NOTES

Pure or perfect competition: Large number of buyers and sellers; identical markets; no market barriers. **Monopolistic competition:** Like pure competition, but products are similar instead of identical. **Oligopoly:** Large sellers dominate and have the ability to affect prices. **Monopoly:** Single producer; no competition; nearly impossible to enter market.

182

Interact with these digital assets and others in lesson 1
- ✓ INTERACTIVE GRAPH Pure Competition and Profit Maximization
- ✓ INTERACTIVE GRAPH Characteristics of Market Structures
- ✓ SELF-CHECK QUIZ
- ✓ VIDEO

networks TRY IT YOURSELF ONLINE

Reading Help Desk

Academic Vocabulary
- theoretical
- equate

Content Vocabulary
- market structure
- pure competition
- industry
- perfect competition
- monopolistic competition
- product differentiation
- nonprice competition
- oligopoly
- collusion
- price-fixing
- monopoly
- laissez-faire
- natural monopoly
- geographic monopoly
- technological monopoly
- government monopoly

TAKING NOTES:

Key Ideas and Details
ACTIVITY Use the graphic organizer below to compare the characteristics of different market structures.

Characteristics of Different Market Structures

Market Structure	Characteristics

182

LESSON 1
Competition and Market Structures

ESSENTIAL QUESTION

How do varying market structures impact prices in a market economy?

Back in 1776 when Adam Smith published *An Inquiry into the Nature and Causes of the Wealth of Nations*, the average factory was small, and businesses were competitive. Laissez-faire, the French term that means "allow them to do," was the prevailing philosophy that limited government's role in protecting property, enforcing contracts, settling disputes, and protecting firms against foreign competition.

C Do you think a total laissez-faire approach to our present-day complex markets would work? Why or why not?

Pure Competition

GUIDING QUESTION *Why do we study pure competition even though there are no purely competitive markets?*

A **market structure** is a classification that describes the nature and degree of competition among firms in the same industry. Markets are often described by the number of firms and the amount of competition in them. For example, **pure competition** is a *theoretical* market structure with three necessary conditions:

- **Very Large Numbers** There must be a very large number of buyers and sellers, none of which is large enough or powerful enough to single-handedly affect the price.
- **Identical Products** Buyers and sellers deal in identical products. With no difference in the products, there is no need for brand names. With no differences between products, one seller's merchandise is just as good as another's, so there is no need to advertise, which keeps prices low.
- **Freedom of Entry and Exit** Buyers and sellers are free to enter into, conduct, or get out of business. This freedom makes it difficult for producers in any **industry**, the group of firms that produce identical or similar products, to keep the market to themselves. Producers have to keep prices competitive, or new firms could take away some of their business.

---

networks Online Teaching Options

BELLRINGER

Competition and Market Structure

Activating prior knowledge Have students first examine the image of the post office. **Ask: What services does the U.S. Postal Service provide? What private companies compete with the post office? What unique services does the post office provide that the competitors do not?** Explain to students that the USPS has a government-regulated monopoly on first class mail. It is illegal for private companies such as UPS or FedEx to deliver first class mail. Government restrictions are designed to make the postal service more efficient. Next, have students examine the image of the steel mill. **Ask: What barriers would exist for a startup business to enter this market?** Guide students to understand that entering this market would require a large investment to buy land, buildings, equipment, and raw materials. **Visual/Spatial**

When a fourth and fifth condition—perfect knowledge by all buyers and all sellers of all conditions in the market, along with perfect mobility of resources—are added to the first three, we have **perfect competition**. Perfect competition is, as the term implies, "perfect" in every respect with no complications. However, it is also a theoretical condition because there are no markets in the world today with all five necessary conditions.

Because no markets exhibit all of these conditions, both terms—*pure* and *perfect*—are often used interchangeably. After all, competition in either purely competitive or perfectly competitive markets would be enough to ensure that prices would be kept close to cost and quality uniform.

Profit Maximization

Under pure competition, market supply and demand set the equilibrium price for the product. Because the price is determined in the market, and because each firm by itself is too small to influence the market price, the pure competitor is often called a "price taker." The firm then must find the level of output it can produce that will maximize its profits.

To understand how this is done, it helps to examine **Figure 7.1**. In fact, the firm in Figure 7.1 is the same one that appeared earlier in Figure 5.6. While the number of workers is not shown in Figure 7.1, its total production, marginal cost, and marginal revenue are the same in both figures. The only difference is that Figure 5.6 shows the data in the form of a table, while Figure 7.1 shows the same numbers in the form of a graph.

The graph in **Panel A** shows that supply and demand set the equilibrium market price at $15 per unit of output. Because the firm in **Panel B** receives $15 for the first and every additional unit it sells, the market price is the same as the firm's marginal revenue (MR).

market structure market classification according to number and size of firms, type of product, and type of competition; nature and degree of competition among firms in the same industry

pure competition a theoretical market structure that requires three major conditions: very large numbers of buyers and sellers, identical products, and freedom of entry and exit

theoretical existing only in theory; not practical

industry group of firms producing similar or identical products

perfect competition theoretical market structure characterized by a large number of well-informed independent buyers and sellers who exchange identical products and have freedom of entry and exit

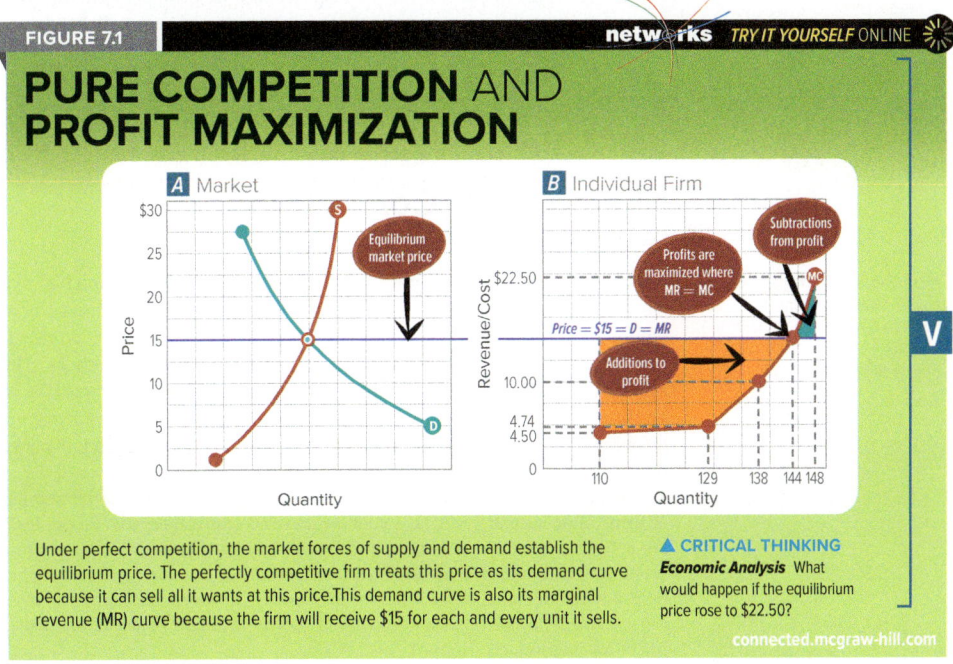

FIGURE 7.1 PURE COMPETITION AND PROFIT MAXIMIZATION

Under perfect competition, the market forces of supply and demand establish the equilibrium price. The perfectly competitive firm treats this price as its demand curve because it can sell all it wants at this price. This demand curve is also its marginal revenue (MR) curve because the firm will receive $15 for each and every unit it sells.

▲ **CRITICAL THINKING**
Economic Analysis What would happen if the equilibrium price rose to $22.50?

GRAPHS

Pure Competition and Profit Maximization

Analyzing graphs of profit maximization Display Figure 7.1. Direct students to Panel A. **Ask:** *Where do the supply and demand curves intersect?* ($15) Explain that the purely competitive firm treats this price as its demand curve and its marginal revenue (MR) because the firm will receive $15 for each and every unit it sells. Direct students to panel B. Point to the larger shaded area to the left. **Ask:** *What does this area show?* (additions to profit) Next, point to the smaller shaded area to the right. **Ask:** *What does this area show?* (subtractions from profit) *Where are profits maximized?* (at the intersection of marginal cost [MC] and marginal revenue [MR]) **Visual/Spatial, Logical/Mathematical**

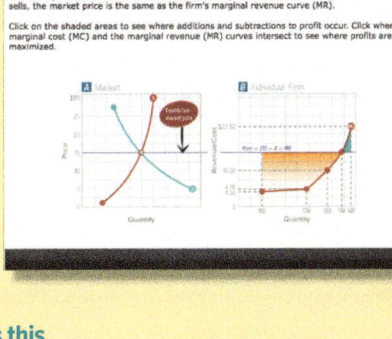

CHAPTER 7, LESSON 1
Competition and Market Structures

TEACH & ASSESS

C Critical Thinking Skills

Speculating about pure competition conditions
Ask: *What would happen if consumers did not have easy access to information about products and services?* (Possible answer: Sellers could raise prices, exploiting consumers' lack of knowledge.) **AL**

W Writing Skills

Comparing competition to democracy Have students write a one-page essay about the role of economic competition in a political democracy. Students might attempt to link the freedom of interaction that occurs under perfect competition with the political freedoms granted in a democracy, or they might note that economic competition implies equality of opportunity. Remind students to use standard grammar. **BL** Verbal/Linguistic

R Reading Skills

Summarizing characteristics of pure competition Have students write in their own words the reasons why perfect competition keeps prices low. (Summaries should include the following: no need for advertising, no reason for one seller to charge a higher price, buyers will always purchase from the seller with the lowest price, and new sellers can enter the market easily.)

V Visual Skills

Analyzing graphs **Ask:** *In Figure 7.1, what is the difference between marginal cost and marginal revenue at the quantity of 129?* ($10.26) *What would happen if the firm in the graph tried to charge a price greater than $15?* (Consumers would buy from other firms, and sales for the firm in the graph would drop.) Visual/Spatial

---

ANSWERS, p. 183

CRITICAL THINKING The new price of $22.50 would be the new MR, and since profit is maximized at the quantity of output where MR = MC, output increases to 148 to maximize profits.

CHAPTER 7, LESSON 1
Competition and Market Structures

W1 Writing Skills

Writing about pure competition Have students write a paragraph using the following as a topic sentence: It is practically impossible to meet all the conditions for perfect competition. **AL**

W2 Writing Skills

Creating an ad about pure competition Organize students into groups. Tell groups that their task is to write a 45-second to 1-minute radio advertisement that explains the benefits and provides examples of perfect competition. Suggest that groups listen to examples of radio ads before undertaking the task. Call on groups to "broadcast" their advertisements to the class. **BL** Auditory/Musical

---

Marginal Analysis Again

When it comes to determining the profit-maximizing quantity of output in Figure 7.1, the logic of marginal analysis is the same as before. For example, Panel B in the figure tells us that the firm would make a profit on the 110th unit of output because it would cost only $4.50 to produce and could be sold for $15.

As long as the marginal cost of producing one more unit of output is less than the marginal revenue from the sale of that output, the firm would continue to expand its output.

W1 Given its marginal cost and marginal revenue conditions, the firm shown in Figure 7.1 would find it profitable to hire enough workers to expand production until 144 units of output are produced. Of course, total output would continue to go up if the firm expanded production beyond 144 units. However, total profits would start to go down because the marginal cost of production would then become increasingly larger than the $15 marginal revenue from sales.

In the end, the profit-maximizing quantity of output is found where the marginal cost of production is equal to the marginal revenue from sales, or where MC = MR. This occurs at 144 units of output. Other levels of output may generate equal profits, but none will generate more. This is exactly the same result we reached when we examined Figure 5.6 earlier, only this time we come to the same conclusion by examining a graph rather than looking at a table.

Less Than Pure Competition

Understanding pure competition is important because economists use it to evaluate other, less competitive, market structures that lack one or more of the conditions required for pure competition. Specifically, these structures are monopolistic competition, oligopoly, and monopoly.

W2 Most firms and industries in the United States today fall into one of these categories. Firms in each of these categories face less competition, and as a result, firms supply lower quantities of their products and charge higher prices. This is why purely competitive markets are theoretically ideal situations that can be used to evaluate other market structures.

✓ **READING PROGRESS CHECK**

Describing What are the conditions required for perfect competition?

Monopolistic Competition

GUIDING QUESTION *What role does advertising play in monopolistic competition?*

monopolistic competition
market structure having all conditions of pure competition except for identical products; a form of imperfect competition

Sometimes a market features **monopolistic competition**, a market structure that has all of the conditions of pure competition except for identical products. Under monopolistic competition, products are generally similar and include things such as designer clothing, cosmetics, gourmet food, and even shoes. The *monopolistic* aspect describes the seller's efforts to convince consumers that its product is unique enough to be worthy of a higher price. The *competition* aspect is a reminder that if sellers raise the price too much, customers will ignore minor differences and change brands.

Because a monopolistic competitor faces competition from a large number of firms in its industry, it must somehow convince consumers that its products are better than the products produced by other firms. The use of a brand name is one way to do this. If a monopolistic competitor can convince consumers that its products are safer, more reliable, trustworthy, or even more popular than those made by other firms, the consumer may be willing to pay slightly higher prices for its products.

184

---

networks Online Teaching Options

GRAPHIC ORGANIZER

Venn Diagram

Comparing and contrasting two market structures Give each student a copy of the graphic organizer. Have them label the left circle "Pure Competition" (PC) and the right circle "Monopolistic Competition" (MC). Characteristics they should consider as similar or different include:
- Number of firms in the industry *(similar—PC: Many; MC: Many)*
- Influence over price *(different—PC: None; MC: Limited)*
- Product differentiation *(different—PC: None; MC: Fair amount)*
- Advertising *(different—PC: None; MC: Fair amount)*
- Ease of entry into market *(similar—PC: Easy; MC: Easy)*

Lead a class discussion of their findings, considering why pure competition and monopolistic competition can share two important characteristics while being different in the other three.

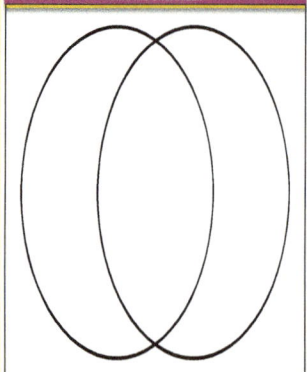

ANSWERS, p. 184

✓ **READING PROGRESS CHECK** Large number of buyers and sellers; identical markets; no market barriers

POLITICAL CARTOON: PRODUCT DIFFERENTIATION

> FOLKS, SURE THIS POCKETKNIFE IS A BETTER DEAL THAN ANY OTHER BECAUSE IT HAS A SCREWDRIVER, A LEATHER PUNCH, AND A PAIR OF SCISSORS...
>
> ...BUT THAT'S NOT ALL! IT ALSO CONTAINS A FLASHLIGHT, A MAGNETIC COMPASS, A CLOCK, A THERMOMETER AND AN ATTENTION-GETTING EMERGENCY WHISTLE!
>
> 80 - CALL NOW! 1-800-55

This cartoon describes an example of an advertisement that attempts to influence consumers by differentiating this pocketknife from the others in the marketplace.

◀ **CRITICAL THINKING**
Evaluating Which market structure is involved here? How can you tell?

How Monopolistic Competitors Compete

Monopolistic competition is characterized by **product differentiation**—real or perceived differences between competing products in the same industry. Almost all of the items produced today are differentiated in one way or another.

To make their products stand out, monopolistic competitors try to make consumers aware of product differences. They usually do this with **nonprice competition**—the use of advertising, giveaways, or other promotions designed to convince buyers that the product is somehow unique or fundamentally better than its competitors'.

In a monopolistically competitive industry, advertising is important. This explains why producers of designer clothes spend so much on advertising and promotion. If a seller can differentiate a product in the mind of the buyer, the firm may be able to raise the price above its competitors' prices. But because advertising is expensive, it raises the cost of doing business for the monopolistic competitor, and hence the price the consumer pays.

product differentiation
real or imagined differences between competing products in the same industry

nonprice competition
competition based on a product's appearance, quality, or design, rather than its price

Profit Maximization

The profit-maximizing behavior of the monopolistic competitor is the same as that of the perfect competitor, when producing where MC = MR. The marginal revenue curve will be a bit different for the monopolistic competitor, but that's all. As a result, the monopolistic competitor will adjust its production until its marginal cost is equal to its marginal revenue. If the firm can convince consumers that its product is better, then it can charge a higher price. If not, the firm will charge less. However, MC = MR still determines the profit maximizing quantity of output.

Finally, it is easy for firms to enter the monopolistically competitive industry. Because each new firm makes a product only a little different from others in the

---

CHAPTER 7, LESSON 1
Competition and Market Structures

R Reading Skills

Identifying monopolistic competition characteristics Ask: *In which market structures is product differentiation important?* (monopolistic competition and oligopoly) *In which market structure do firms have limited influence over price?* (monopolistic competition) **AL** Verbal/Linguistic

C1 Critical Thinking Skills

Providing examples of monopolistic competition List the following products on the board: soda, bottled water, perfume, aspirin. Ask students to name their favorite brands of these items and explain their choices. Point out that this is an illustration of product differentiation, because student preferences were based on slight differences among brands, swayed most likely by advertising. In addition, point out that monopolistic competitors also use advertising to influence consumers' *perceptions* of price. For example, the price of a good may be expressed as $9.99 instead of $10.00. Verbal/Linguistic

C2 Critical Thinking Skills

Identifying examples of monopolistic competition Ask students to think of advertising jingles that have influenced them to buy a product. Have each student sing, hum, or identify one such song and explain its effectiveness. **AL** Auditory/Musical

---

POLITICAL CARTOON

Product Differentiation

Analyzing the cartoon Have students study the political cartoon and interpret its meaning. Discuss the ways the salesperson has differentiated his product. Discuss how this cartoon exemplifies monopolistic competition. Ask students to create their own political cartoons with a similar theme: advertising a product with many more uses than its original one.

ANSWERS, p. 185

CRITICAL THINKING This is an example of monopolistic competition. Although other similar products are available, the seller of the pocketknife is trying to convince consumers that his product is unique.

CHAPTER 7, LESSON 1
Competition and Market Structures

R Reading Skills

Understanding the literal meaning of *oligopoly*
Have students research the origins and meaning of the two parts of the word *oligopoly* and then explain its meaning. *(It is a Greek word. From* oligoi, *meaning "few, small, little" and* polein, *meaning "to sell." Hence, oligopoly means "few sellers.")*

C Critical Thinking Skills

Determining cause and effect Ask: **What is the effect of a company in an oligopoly making a product change?** *(The other companies in the oligopoly will make the same change.)* **AL**

English Language Proficiency

Intermediate Provide or have students make cards containing vocabulary words used routinely in classroom communication. Write cloze sentences on the board. As you write each sentence, have students hold up the card with the word that completes the sentence.

ANSWERS, p. 186

CRITICAL THINKING monopolistic competition and oligopoly

✓ **READING PROGRESS CHECK** They are the same; the firm still maximizes profits at the output at which marginal cost equals marginal revenue.

186

FIGURE 7.2
CHARACTERISTICS OF MARKET STRUCTURES

	Number of firms in industry	Influence over price	Product differentiation	Advertising	Entry into market	Examples
Pure competition	Many	None	None	None	Easy	Perfect: None Near: Truck farming
Monopolistic competition	Many	Limited	Fair amount	Fair amount	Easy	Gas stations Women's clothing
Oligopoly	Few	Some	Fair amount	Some	Difficult	Automobiles Aluminum
Pure monopoly	One	Extensive	None	None	Almost impossible	Perfect: None Near: Water

The term *market structure* refers to the nature and degree of competition among firms operating in the same industry. Individual market structures, listed on the left, are determined by the five characteristics listed in the columns above.

▲ **CRITICAL THINKING**
Economic Analysis In what market structures does nonprice competition play a role?

connected.mcgraw-hill.com

industry, the result is a large number of firms producing a variety of similar products. **Figure 7.2** summarizes all of these characteristics.

✓ **READING PROGRESS CHECK**

Comparing How is profit maximization in a monopolistic firm different from that of a pure competitor?

Oligopoly

GUIDING QUESTION *Why do markets dominated by oligopolies result in higher prices for the consumer than would exist in perfect competition?*

oligopoly market structure in which a few large sellers dominate the market and have the ability to affect prices in the industry; form of imperfect competition

R **Oligopoly** is a market structure in which a few very large sellers dominate the industry. The product of an oligopolist may have distinct features, as do the many makes and models of cars in the auto industry; or it may be standardized, as in the steel industry. As a result, oligopoly, also summarized in Figure 7.2, is less competitive than is monopolistic competition.

In the United States, many markets are already oligopolistic, and many more are becoming so. For example, three companies dominate the fast-food industry and five companies dominate the cellular telephone service industry. A few large corporations control other industries, such as the domestic airline and automobile industries.

Interdependent Behavior

C Because oligopolists are generally large and because they usually produce similar products, whenever one firm acts, the other firms in the industry may follow—or they run the risk of losing customers. The ability to act together is partly due to the fact that there are so few firms in the industry.

186

---

networks Online Teaching Options

CHARTS

Characteristics of Market Structures

Using tables and charts Direct students' attention to Figure 7.2 and have them compare and contrast the characteristics of different market structures. Click on the different market structures to see their characteristics. Ask: **Which two market structures have the least product differentiation?** *(pure competition, pure monopoly)* **Why do pure competition and pure monopoly have no perfect examples?** *(These markets are only theoretical. Market conditions and government regulation prevent real world examples.)* **Visual/Spatial**

The tendency of oligopolists to act together often shows up in their pricing behavior, such as copying a competitor's price reduction in order to attract new customers or not lose existing customers. For example, if Ford or General Motors announces zero-interest financing or thousands of dollars back on each new car purchased, its competitors may match the promotion almost immediately.

How Oligopolies Compete

Oligopolists also compete using nonprice competition, for example, by enhancing their products with new or different features. Automobile companies do this every year when they introduce new models. If an oligopolist finds a way to enhance a product, its competitors are at a slight disadvantage for a period of time. After all, it takes longer to match a new physical attribute for a product than it does to match a price cut.

It is possible that the interdependent behavior takes the form of collusion instead of competition. **Collusion** is a formal agreement to set specific prices or to otherwise behave in a cooperative manner. One form of collusion is **price-fixing**, or agreeing to charge the same or similar prices for a product that are higher than those determined under competition. The firms also might agree to divide the market so that each is guaranteed to sell a certain amount. Because collusion usually restrains trade, it is against the law in the United States.

collusion illegal agreement among producers to fix prices, limit output, divide markets, or otherwise agree to reduce competition

price-fixing illegal agreement by firms to charge a uniform price for a product

THE GLOBAL ECONOMY & YOU

From Monopoly to Oligopoly

Multinational corporations are often huge companies that employ thousands of workers and make billions of dollars a year. Large and powerful as they are, however, these companies are almost always oligopolies that operate in competition with similar firms. A few of these firms once operated as monopolies without competition, but for various reasons have lost this market dominance.

One of the best-known monopolies was AT&T. It was considered a natural monopoly under the Graham-Willis Act of 1921, which permitted the company to be the sole provider of all long-distance telephone service. AT&T also operated local phone service in many places and manufactured almost all U.S. phone equipment. For a century, its dominance of the telephone market was almost complete. Its monopoly ended in 1984, however, after a protracted legal battle with the government. AT&T was broken into seven companies that operated as oligopolies providing regional service, while AT&T retained its long-distance service.

Another firm that had monopoly power is Microsoft, which produces the software for the operating system used in most PCs. When the government looked into Microsoft's monopolistic hold on the industry in the late 1990s, federal judge Thomas Penfield Jackson declared that "Microsoft enjoys so much power in the market . . . that if it wished to exercise this power . . . it could charge a price for Windows substantially above that which could be charged in a competitive market." While the government closely monitored Microsoft's business practices, it never went so far as to break up the company. Instead, the market has been restoring competition. Microsoft continues its hold on the PC market, but mobile devices are taking over a fast-growing segment of the data communications business, and Apple owns a large piece of this business.

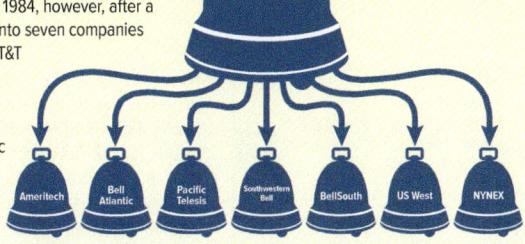

▲ **CRITICAL THINKING**
Drawing Inferences Why is it sometimes difficult for monopolies to hold onto their dominance of a market?

connected.mcgraw-hill.com   Market Structures **187**

INTERACTIVE FEATURE

The Global Economy & You

Exploring how monopolies became oligopolies Display the Global Economy & You feature "From Monopoly to Oligopoly." Have students read the text and then discuss the breakup of AT&T's monopoly. **Ask: Why do you think the government ended the AT&T monopoly?** *(Possible answers: other companies wanted into the market, the government wanted to encourage competition and innovation)* **Do you think breaking up the AT&T monopoly was effective?** *(Possible answers: Yes, there are many competitors in the phone market, and phone products and services are always evolving. No, AT&T is still a large, powerful company that has great influence on the national market.)* **Visual/Spatial**

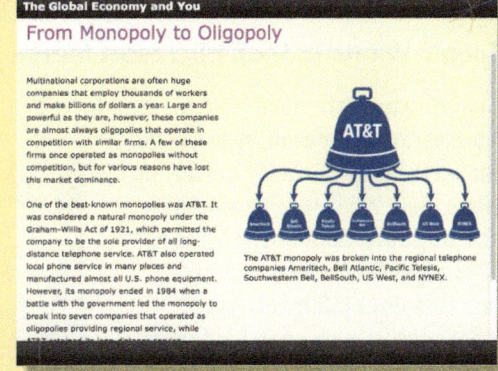

CHAPTER 7, LESSON 1
Competition and Market Structures

C Critical Thinking Skills

Writing about oligopolies Have students choose a product made by an oligopoly and write a brief essay in which they argue for the superiority of their preferred brand. For example, students may argue that McDonald's has the best cheeseburgers, based on taste, price, and convenience. **AL Verbal/Linguistic**

Making Connections

A Local Oligopoly Have students work in groups and identify a business in the community that is part of an oligopoly. Have students observe the business and research it. Then have groups present an oral report describing the competitive strategies employed by the business. Students might evaluate advertisements for effectiveness and purpose. They also might evaluate product quality of their producer versus that of other producers or observe strategies such as location and price. Students should evaluate the business's place in the oligopoly. For example, does it distribute a good made under oligopoly conditions? (car dealership, gas station) Or does it actually produce a good or service under oligopoly conditions? (one of two or three doctors in town; one of two or three Italian restaurants in town) **BL Logical/Mathematical**

ANSWERS, p. 187

CRITICAL THINKING The government often steps in to reduce the power of monopolies. Changes in the market and in technology may also provide new competition over time.

Market Structures **187**

CHAPTER 7, LESSON 1
Competition and Market Structures

R Reading Skills

Comparing monopolies and oligopolies Ask: **How is a monopoly different from an oligopoly?** *(An oligopoly exists when only a few producers compete in a market. A monopoly exists when only one producer of a product or service exists.)* **AL**

C Critical Thinking Skills

Identifying natural monopolies Have students list some natural monopolies on the board. Then have students choose one of the monopolies and draw a picture or make a collage that illustrates what the community would look like if the product or service was supplied by competitors instead of a regulated monopoly. **ELL** *Visual/Spatial*

ANSWERS, p. 188

✓ **READING PROGRESS CHECK** Because they produce similar products and each firm has the ability to influence price, oligopolists tend to follow each other's lead in prices to avoid losing customers over price.

EXPLORING THE ESSENTIAL QUESTION, p. 189

Discuss the question on page 189. Most students will say that they would expect to pay more than normal for the gas. Some may say the price is not reasonable because it costs the station owner the same or only somewhat more than what owners are paying in more competitive areas. Most students will say there are no practical solutions since the customer traffic in the remote place is not sufficient to attract competition and it would not be appropriate for the government to step in and regulate the prices.

Profit Maximization

The oligopolist, like all other firms, maximizes its profits when it finds the quantity of output at which its marginal cost is equal to its marginal revenue, or where MC = MR. The oligopolist will then charge the price consistent with this level of sales.

Because nonprice competition is expensive, and because the oligopolist has so few competitors, the product's final price is likely to be higher than it would be under monopolistic competition, and much higher than it would be under pure competition. Expenses associated with nonprice competition are passed on to the consumer.

✓ **READING PROGRESS CHECK**

Explaining Why do oligopolists frequently appear to act together?

Monopoly

GUIDING QUESTION *Why are some types of monopolies considered acceptable while others are not?*

monopoly market structure characterized by a single producer; form of imperfect competition

The opposite of pure competition is monopoly. A **monopoly** is a market structure with only one seller of a particular product. This situation—like that of pure competition—is an extreme case. In fact, the American economy has few, if any, cases of pure monopoly—although the local cable TV operator or telephone company that your parents grew up with have been monopolies in the past. When people talk about monopolies today, they usually mean near-monopolies, because there usually seems to be some competition.

laissez-faire philosophy that government should not interfere with business activity

In a **laissez-faire** economy, monopolies might be more common because government would play little role in controlling their development. However, we have few monopolies today because Americans traditionally have disliked them and have tried to outlaw them. Another reason is that new technologies often introduce products that compete with existing monopolies. The development of the fax machine allowed businesses to send electronic letters that competed with the U.S. Postal Service. Later, e-mail and texting displaced the fax.

Types of Monopolies

Sometimes the nature of a good or service dictates that society would be served best by a monopoly. At other times, the market may only be big enough to support a single firm. Consequently, we can recognize several types of monopolies.

natural monopoly market structure in which average costs of production are lowest when all output is produced by a single firm

- **Natural monopoly** A **natural monopoly** is one in which a single firm can produce the product more cheaply than any number of competing firms could. This includes public utility companies, because it would be wasteful to duplicate the networks of pipes and wires that distribute water, natural gas, and electricity throughout a city. The government often gives a public utility the exclusive right to do business in a certain area without competition. In return, the companies accept a certain amount of government regulation.

geographic monopoly market structure in which a firm has a monopoly because of its location or the small size of the market

- **Geographic Monopoly** A **geographic monopoly** is a monopoly based on the absence of other sellers in a certain geographic area. A drugstore operating in a town too small to support two or more such businesses would be a geographic monopoly if it offered services that could not be provided by other businesses. Similarly, the owner of the only gas station on a lonely interstate highway exit ramp also has a type of geographic monopoly.

networks Online Teaching Options

VIDEO | **WORKSHEETS**

Google Wants to Stop Microsoft Merging

Analyzing a video Have students view the video. Guide students in discussing the reasons why Google wanted to stop Microsoft from buying Yahoo. Ask: **What type of market structures are Google and Yahoo?** *(oligopoly)* **What type of market structure does Microsoft have?** *(monopoly)* **How do search engines make money?** *(through advertising)* **How much money is at stake in the online search engine advertising market?** *($30–$40 billion, which is expected to double)* *Visual/Spatial*

- **Technological Monopoly** A **technological monopoly** is one based on ownership or control of a manufacturing method, process, or other scientific method. The government may grant a *patent*—an exclusive right to manufacture, use, or sell any new and useful invention for a specific period—to the inventor. Inventions are covered for 20 years; after that, they become public property available for the benefit of all. Art and literary works are protected through a *copyright*—the exclusive right of authors or artists to publish, sell, or reproduce their work for their lifetime plus 70 years.
- **Government Monopoly** A **government monopoly** is a monopoly owned and operated by the government. Government monopolies are often found at all levels of government. In most cases, they involve products or services that private industry cannot adequately supply. Many towns and cities have monopolies that oversee water use. Some states control alcoholic beverages by requiring that they be sold only through state stores. The federal government controls the processing of weapons-grade uranium for military and national security purposes.

Profit Maximization

Monopolies maximize profits the same way other firms do: they **equate** marginal cost (MC) with marginal revenue (MR) to find the profit-maximizing quantity of output. Even so, there are reasons why the monopolist is likely to charge a higher price, and produce a smaller quantity of output, than will the oligopolist, monopolistic competitor, or perfect competitor.

First, the monopolist is usually much larger than the other types of firms. This is because only one firm—the monopolist—supplies the product. Second, because of the lack of competition, the monopolist is less likely to keep its own costs under control, which means that it may be more likely to charge a higher price. If the monopolist is successful in charging a higher price, less will be produced and supplied to the market. The combination of a higher price and smaller amount of output is one measure of the inefficiency of a monopoly.

✓ **READING PROGRESS CHECK**

Analyzing Why might it be a good idea to support a natural monopoly?

EXPLORING THE ESSENTIAL QUESTION

Imagine that you are traveling and run low on gas in an out-of-the-way location, and there is only one gas station for the next 30 miles. How much would you expect to pay for the gas? Do you think this price is reasonable? Are there any practical solutions to this geographic monopoly?

technological monopoly market structure in which a firm has a monopoly because it owns or controls a manufacturing method, process, or other scientific advantage

government monopoly monopoly created and/or owned by the government

equate to represent as equal or equivalent

LESSON 1 REVIEW

Reviewing Vocabulary
1. *Explaining* Why might oligopolies sometimes be tempted to act in collusion?

Using Your Notes
2. *Contrasting* What are two major differences between pure competition and each of the following: monopolistic competition, an oligopoly, a monopoly?

Answering the Guiding Questions
3. *Explaining* How can you describe examples of pure competition? Why do we study pure competition even though there are no purely competitive markets?
4. *Describing* What role does advertising play in monopolistic competition?
5. *Explaining* Why do markets dominated by oligopolies result in high prices for the consumer?
6. *Explaining* Why are some types of monopolies considered acceptable while others are not?

Writing About Economics
7. *Argument* XYZ Corporation operated in oligopolistic competition with only two competitors. For different reasons, the two competitors left the industry, leaving XYZ in a monopolistic situation. XYZ immediately doubled its prices for a nearly essential consumer product. Should the government intervene to regulate prices? Why or why not?

connected.mcgraw-hill.com   Market Structures **189**

CHAPTER 7, LESSON 1
Competition and Market Structures

C1 Critical Thinking Skills

Speculating about patents Ask students to describe the effect they think the patent system of the United States has had on the number of inventions produced by American inventors. Why? Students may point out the importance of the incentive to earn profits and create wealth from the sale of one's own inventions; this incentive, which came about because of the patent system, likely increased the number of inventions. **BL Interpersonal**

C2 Critical Thinking Skills

Relating technology and monopoly Ask students to list ways they use current technology. Then have them write a short report explaining how the use of a particular technology relates to the concept of monopoly. Examples include: placing an order with Amazon.com weakens a geographic monopoly of a local bookstore; using a computer with Windows strengthens the Microsoft monopoly; paying for and downloading a song onto an MP3 player abides by the song's copyright protection. **BL Verbal/Linguistic**

CLOSE & REFLECT

Summarizing Have students create a visual presentation of the four market structures: their characteristics, how they differ from one another, and an example of each type.

ANSWERS, p. 189

✓ **READING PROGRESS CHECK** Natural monopolies exist because one firm can produce the service or product at lower cost than more than one firm. Encouraging competition would result in higher prices.

LESSON 1 REVIEW ANSWERS

Reviewing Vocabulary
1. Oligopolies produce generally similar products and often compete on a nonprice basis, leading them to act interdependently. This interdependence entices them to act together to set prices or cooperate closely for the benefit of all of the firms.

Using Your Notes
2. Sample answer: Unlike a pure competition, monopolistic competition has similar but identical products and higher prices; an oligopoly is dominated by large sellers who operate interdependently, and it is difficult to enter the market; a monopoly is comprised of one seller who has no competition.

Answer the Guiding Questions
3. Purely competitive markets are theoretically ideal situations to use in evaluating other market structures; real world examples do not exist. Existing firms face less competition, ask higher prices, and offer fewer products than would be the case in purely competitive markets.
4. Advertising is used to differentiate one product from all others to attract consumers and sell at higher prices.
5. Oligopolies often compete on a nonprice basis, which is expensive. The costs are passed on to consumers.
6. The nature of circumstances dictates that society is best served by a monopoly, such as natural, geographic, technological, and government monopolies.

Writing About Economics
7. Students should recognize that a monopoly operates in a situation where it is very difficult for competitors to enter the market, so it is unlikely that competition will ever force the company to reduce prices. Since it produces a near-essential product, students may argue that the only choice is to have the government regulate the industry.

CHAPTER 7
Debate

ENGAGE

C1 Critical Thinking Skills

Understanding copyright laws Start a discussion of copyright laws, helping students understand that copyright laws are designed to protect intellectual property. To begin the discussion, **ask:**

- What is copyright law?
- What are some examples of intellectual property?
- How do people commonly infringe on copyright law?
- How can creators keep people from pirating their work?

Ask students to brainstorm reasons people pirate copyrighted materials. Write answers on the board, then have students vote on the top three reasons. **Ask: Why do many people pirate movies, music, and videogames when they know it is illegal?** *(Most people assume that they will not get caught or prosecuted.)* **Interpersonal**

TEACH & ASSESS

R Reading Skills

Identifying the basis of intellectual property protection Ask: Where in the U.S. Constitution does American copyright law originate? *(Article I, Section 8)* Point out to students that Article I, Section 8 lists the powers granted to Congress. Clause 8 reads: "To promote the Progress of Science and useful Arts, by securing for limited Times to Authors and Inventors the exclusive Right to their respective Writings and Discoveries." **Verbal/Linguistic**

C2 Critical Thinking Skills

Analyzing emerging technology Ask students to research how online music streaming services have impacted the music industry. You may wish to have student pairs research different aspects of the topic, such as how the services deal with copyright law, how streaming has affected sales, and how the music industry has responded to these services. Have students write a summary of their research and then share their findings in a class discussion. **Verbal/Linguistic, Interpersonal**

Debates

C1 Do current copyright laws do more harm than good?

You've heard about copyright law, but what is it, and is it important? Today's copyright laws are based on the Copyright Act of 1976, although copyright law goes back much further and is based on Article 1, Section 8, of the U.S. Constitution. It is designed to protect intellectual property. To be protected, a work must be original and in a fixed or tangible form. Copyright protection provides the creator of the work with exclusive protection for the author's lifetime plus 70 years.

In the digital age, it is easy to share works. Suppose you purchase a hit single and make a copy to share with a friend. Under current copyright law, that is piracy. Copying a movie from a DVD or copying an article from an Internet site and including it in a blog are also examples of piracy. There is no question that people "steal" or pirate copyrighted material all the time. The exact extent of the problem is unknown, but it is widely believed to be extensive. The question is: would it be better just to eliminate copyright altogether, or does copyright still provide important legal protection?

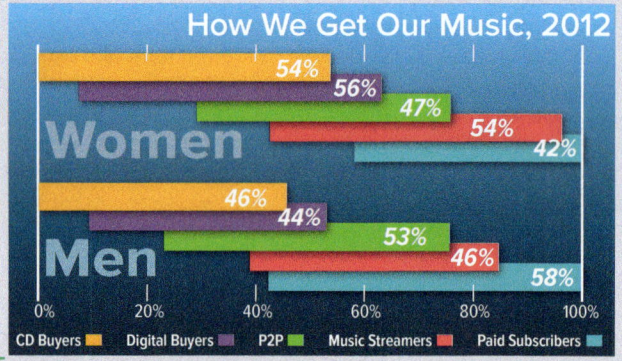

190

---

networks Online Teaching Options

DEBATE

Do current copyright laws do more harm than good?

Analyzing copyright law Display the Debate feature and direct students to analyze the first graph. **Ask: What may happen to artists if 65% of their music is acquired illegally?** *(Answers will vary, but students may say that artists may suffer financially. They may need to find other revenue sources, such as increased touring, to make up for the loss of sales. They may leave the music business entirely.)* Now lead the class in examining the second graph. Ask students to describe what the graph shows. Encourage a discussion of the increases in overall sales, despite the decrease in physical CD sales and the prevalence of piracy. Have students share their thoughts on the Debate issue. **Visual/Spatial**

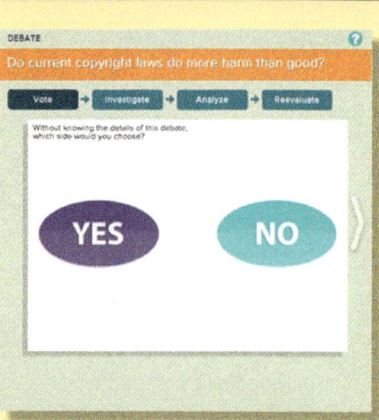

NO Government copyright laws have no place in the U.S. free enterprise system and should be abolished.

SHARING A MUSIC FILE OR DIGITAL BOOK IS THE SAME AS LOANING A CD OR BOOK TO A FRIEND

PIRACY HASN'T STALLED CREATIVITY; MOVIES STILL GET MADE AND SOFTWARE DEVELOPED

FILE SHARING GIVES EVERYONE ACCESS TO INFORMATION, STIMULATING **CREATIVITY**

THE ECONOMY DOESN'T SUFFER; MONEY SAVED ON MUSIC GETS **SPENT** ELSEWHERE

networks TRY IT YOURSELF ONLINE
For an interactive version of this debate go to connected.mcgraw-hill.com

ANALYZING the issue

> This is a property rights issue, and current copyright law gets it backwards, turning regular people—like students, researchers, and small business owners—into criminals. Fortune 500 telecom manufacturer Avaya, for example, is known for suing service companies, accusing them of violating copyright for simply using a password to log in to their phone systems. That's right: typing in a password is considered 'reproducing copyrighted material.'

—Kyle Wiens, co-founder and CEO, iFixit, "Forget the Cellphone Fight—We Should Be Allowed to Unlock *Everything* We Own," *Wired*, March 18, 2013

1. **Evaluating** In the first quotation, Aistars takes the position that the creators of a work have the most at stake in this controversy. Wiens takes the opposite position, that consumers have the most at stake. Who makes the stronger case? Why do you think so?

2. **Analyzing** One of the con arguments states that the economy won't suffer if copyright law is eliminated. The argument is that when someone is given a shared file rather than spending money to buy it, the money isn't lost to the economy; it's simply redirected to buy something else, such as a pizza. Is this a fair argument? Why or why not?

3. **Defending** Which arguments do you find most compelling? Explain your answer.

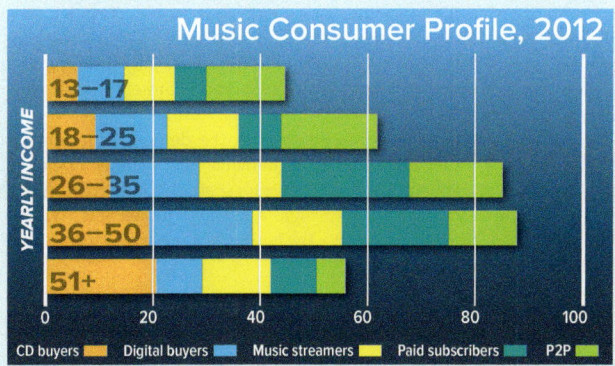

Music Consumer Profile, 2012
YEARLY INCOME: 13–17, 18–25, 26–35, 36–50, 51+
CD buyers, Digital buyers, Music streamers, Paid subscribers, P2P

CHAPTER 7
Debate

C Critical Thinking Skills

Evaluating government's role in intellectual property protection Divide the class into two teams and assign each team the Yes or the No side of the issue. Allow teams to prepare their arguments. Remind students that, for every fact or excerpt they quote, they need to attribute the information to their source. Encourage them to consider counterarguments as well. Then ask teams to debate the topic. Limit the time each team has to present their supporting arguments and in rebuttal. Have the class vote on the winner of the debate. **Verbal/Linguistic**

Making Connections

Pay or Piracy? Ask students to analyze the validity of each primary source in the Debate from its frame of reference. **Ask: What organization does each speaker represent?** *(The Copyright Alliance;* Wired*)* Have students determine their own frame of reference, reflecting on how they personally acquire music. Ask whether anyone is interested in becoming an actor or musical artist, and whether a lack of potential royalties (due to pirated movies and music) would deter them from following that career path. **Intrapersonal, Auditory/Musical**

CLOSE & REFLECT

Exploring issues Remind students that the debate over intellectual property rights will continue as technology constantly evolves. Meanwhile, the government will continue trying to keep up with rapid changes to the market, attempting to maintain a fair balance in protecting both creators and consumers. Lead students in a discussion of why this problem will never have an easy solution. **Verbal/Linguistic, Interpersonal**

GRAPHIC ORGANIZERS

Table

Preparing and defending arguments Divide the class into groups for and against the issue, and distribute the graphic organizer. Ask students to follow these steps in preparing their arguments:

1. Write Arguments as the header for the first column. Have students list four reasons that support their position.
2. Write Counterarguments as the second column header. Have students come up with points their opponents could use to minimize their arguments and write them in this column.
3. Write Refutations as the final column header. Have students write down ways that they can refute, or prove the opponents' counterarguments are wrong.
4. Have students review the graphic organizer and rank arguments from strongest to weakest, based on how easy they are to defend against counterarguments.

ANSWERS, p. 191

ANALYZING the issue

1. Students should recognize that this issue affects both creators and consumers and that however the copyright issue is finally resolved, one group will benefit while the other will be harmed. Students should give arguments to support their position.
2. Students should recognize that the money will stay in the economy, but spending the money on a creative work may not have the same effect as if it were spent on something else.
3. Students should give facts and reasons based on the debate to support their response.

CHAPTER 7, LESSON 2
Market Failures

ENGAGE

C Critical Thinking Skills

Drawing conclusions about failed businesses Before students begin the lesson, ask them to list some familiar businesses or products that no longer exist. Examples might include Blockbuster Video or VHS tapes. **Ask: Why do you think these businesses and products failed?** *(Answers will vary, but students should indicate that these businesses were weak or did not keep up with evolving changes/technology, and thus were bypassed. Products may have failed because they were replaced by newer technology, or consumer tastes may have changed, resulting in reduced demand.)* **AL** **Interpersonal**

TEACH & ASSESS

R Reading Skills

Activating prior knowledge about perfect competition **Ask: What are the conditions necessary for perfect competition?** *(many buyers and sellers acting independently, identical products, good information, freedom of entry into industry)*

ANSWERS, p. 192

ESSENTIAL QUESTION ACTIVITY

Answers will vary. Students may cite imprudent mortgage lending practices, lack of accountability in mortgage finance, deregulation that led to risky financial activities, fragmented government regulation, credit rating agencies that gave AAA status to subprime securities, and so on.
TAKING NOTES: inadequate competition, not enough information, resources can't or won't move, too few public goods, externalities or spillover effects

192

Interact with these digital assets and others in lesson 2
✓ BIOGRAPHY Joseph Stiglitz
✓ INTERACTIVE TABLE Using Cost-Benefit Analysis
✓ SELF-CHECK QUIZ
✓ VIDEO

networks
TRY IT YOURSELF ONLINE

LESSON 2
Market Failures

Reading Help Desk

Academic Vocabulary
- sustain

Content Vocabulary
- market failure
- public good
- spillover effects
- externalities
- cost-benefit analysis

TAKING NOTES:

Key Ideas and Details
ACTIVITY Use the graphic organizer below to identify the main causes of market failures.

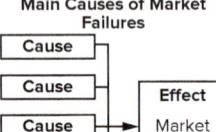

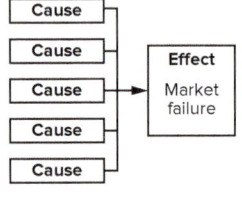

market failure condition where any of the requirements for a competitive market—usually adequate competition, knowledge of prices and opportunities, mobility of resources, and competitive profits—leads to an inefficient allocation of resources characterized by too much or too little being produced

192

ESSENTIAL QUESTION

Why do markets fail?

When a company fails, we see a market at work—weeding out weak firms and rewarding the strong ones. Sometimes, however, a whole market or industry fails and healthy companies go down with it. In 2007, the nation's housing market failed, causing countless homeowners, builders, realtors, and mortgage lenders financial hardship or ruin.

Investigate the failure of this market and write a report applying what you learn in this lesson to explain it.

Causes of Market Failures

GUIDING QUESTION *What factors reduce competition in a market?*

A **market failure** occurs whenever a flaw in the market system prevents an efficient allocation of resources. As you will learn, five main causes of market failures—situations causing too much or too little production—exist.

Not Enough Competition

Over time, mergers and combinations of companies result in larger and fewer firms dominating an industry. The decrease in competition tends to reduce the efficient use of scarce resources. For example, why would a firm with few or no competitors have the incentive to use its resources carefully? Inadequate competition, the first of five causes of market failures, may also enable a business to influence politicians in order to get special treatment that enriches its managers and owners.

Inadequate competition can occur on both the demand side and the supply side of the market. If we look at the demand side, there is little or no competition if the government is the only buyer for space shuttles, hydroelectric dams, super computers, M1 tanks, or high-technology fighter jets. When a market has only one or just a few buyers, the buyer has more power to influence the market price.

Not Enough Information

Not having enough information is the second of five main causes of market failures. This means that everyone—consumers, businesspeople, and

---

networks Online Teaching Options

BELLRINGER

Market Failures

Activating prior knowledge Use the Bellringer to reveal students' prior knowledge of market failures. Write these questions on the board and encourage a class discussion:

- What is a market failure?
- What market failure does this photograph represent?
- What is an economic bubble? A housing bubble?

Divide students into small groups and ask them to discuss the photo and accompanying questions. After a few minutes, ask groups to share their responses. Guide a class discussion. **Visual/Spatial, Verbal/Linguistic**

government officials—must have adequate information about market conditions if resources are to be allocated efficiently. However, if the information is available to only one side of the market, then the market will not be efficient.

For example, how efficient would the market for health insurance be if insurance companies had access to a person's health history before that person bought a policy? Because insurance companies prefer to sell policies to healthy people, people with above-average health problems would have a much more difficult time getting health insurance. The result would be profitable insurance companies and a population with significant, and uninsured, health issues.

Resources That Can't, or Won't, Move

A third cause of market failures, and a difficult problem for any economy, is called "resource immobility." This means that land, capital, labor, and entrepreneurs cannot, or will not, move to markets where they can earn higher returns. Instead, they tend to stay put and sometimes remain unemployed for long periods of time.

This often happens when a large auto assembly plant, steel mill, or mine closes, leaving thousands of workers without jobs. Some workers could find jobs in other cities if they were willing to move, but not all of them can. Some of the newly unemployed may not be able to sell their homes. Others may not want to move away from friends and relatives. As a result, the number of people without jobs goes up and tax collections from workers go down. This was the unfortunate situation for thousands of auto workers in Detroit and nearby manufacturing states because of the 2008–2009 economic decline when the U.S. auto industry nearly collapsed.

Too Few Public Goods

The fourth market failure occurs when markets do not produce the right amount of public goods. A **public good** is a product that is collectively consumed by everyone, and whose use by one individual does not diminish the satisfaction or value available to others. Examples are highways, parks, flood control measures, national defense, and police and fire protection.

Private markets do not supply public goods efficiently because there is not enough profit to be made by producing them. This leaves government to produce them, but government does not usually spend enough money on them even though everyone seems to agree that production, repair, and/or expansion are needed. For example, how many highways and bridges in your community are in need of expansion or repair?

Consider the failure to reinforce the floodwalls in New Orleans prior to Hurricane Katrina. Everyone knew that the floodwalls could not **sustain** a direct hit from a hurricane, but they were not strengthened even though they are public goods funded by government expenditures. When the floodwalls were breached by Katrina, New Orleans sustained massive damages. According to the National Weather Service, Katrina was "the costliest U.S. hurricane on record."

Externalities or Spillover Effects

The fifth reason that markets fail is the failure to compensate for **spillover effects**, or uncompensated side effects that either benefit or harm a third party not involved in the activity that caused it. Spillover effects are also called **externalities** and mean the same thing.

Spillover effects cause market failures when the costs and benefits of a new activity are not reflected in the market prices that users pay. For example, think of what happens when an airport expands its flights on a certain route from two days a week to five without changing the price of the flights:

BIOGRAPHY

Joseph Stiglitz
ECONOMIST (1943–)

Joseph Stiglitz taught economics before becoming head of President Bill Clinton's Council of Economic Advisers and chief economist at the World Bank. He returned to teaching in 2001 as professor of economics at Columbia University.

Stiglitz's research focuses on how unequal information affects markets. He found that information—and the lack of it—helps to determine supply, demand, and price. For example, a loan applicant knows more about his company's project than the lender he approaches to finance it. How risky is the project? If the financial institution finds information that makes the project appear to have a high risk level, it might charge a higher rate or even refuse to make the loan.

In 2001, Stiglitz shared the Nobel Prize in Economics with two other economists who did similar research.

▲ **CRITICAL THINKING**
Applying What do Stiglitz's findings suggest about how information inequalities might affect a market for used cars?

Market Structures

CHAPTER 7, LESSON 2
Market Failures

C1 Critical Thinking Skills

Demonstrating the importance of adequate information Have students use the Internet to find the interest rates being offered on five different credit cards. Have students imagine they have made a credit purchase of $1,000, and then identify the rate that is best for the borrower and the rate that is most profitable for the lender. Ask students why the "fine print" is important and how difficult it was to find. **BL** Logical/Mathematical

R Reading Skills

Defining and categorizing public goods Ask: **What is a public good?** (products that are paid for and consumed collectively such as highways, national defense, police and fire protection) **Why does the market NOT supply public goods?** (There is no profit to be made by producing them.) Explain to students that public goods have two unique characteristics: non-rival consumption and non-exclusive ownership. **Non-rival consumption** means that one person's use of the good does not prevent another person from using the same good. If you are watching a fireworks show with your friend, for example, your viewing does not prevent your friend from also seeing the fireworks. **Non-exclusive ownership** means that after a good is provided, it is difficult or impossible to keep those who have not paid from receiving the product. If your town charges admission to the park for a fireworks show, for example, it cannot prevent people outside the park from looking into the sky to see the show. List items on the board (e.g., national defense, theater, lighthouse, baseball game, sidewalks) and have students categorize them as private or public goods. **ELL** **AL**

C2 Critical Thinking Skills

Providing examples of externalities Ask: **What is an example of a negative externality that you have encountered?** (Possible answer: being awakened early by construction noise from a neighbor's yard) **What is an example of a positive externality?** (Possible answer: enjoyment of the neighbor's improved landscaping)

ANSWERS, p. 193

CRITICAL THINKING The seller knows more about the car than the buyer does. Buyers might not be willing to buy or pay high prices for used cars they know little about. Sellers may have to lower the price or even provide buyers with a guarantee if they do not provide information about the car's history.

BIOGRAPHY

Joseph Stiglitz Biography

Analyzing the impact of Joseph Stiglitz Have students read the biography of Joseph Stiglitz. Then organize students into groups to discuss these questions: **What economic theory earned Stiglitz a Nobel Prize in Economics? How do Stiglitz's ideas reflect what you have learned about market structures? How can information inequalities affect individual businesses? How do they affect the greater market? How can consumers, business people, and government officials correct information inequalities to prevent market failures?** After students discuss their answers to these questions, assemble the class and have groups share their ideas and conclusions. **Interpersonal, Verbal/Linguistic**

CHAPTER 7, LESSON 2
Market Failures

C Critical Thinking Skills

Understanding frame of reference for market failure When students have finished reading the subsection "Causes of Market Failures," have them evaluate the validity of economic information in the text for frame of reference. Explain that many market failures are not viewed as such until long after the effects become evident. Have students brainstorm historical examples of market failure due to inadequate competition, inadequate information, resource immobility, too few public goods, and externalities or spillover effects.

Making Connections

Pollution Solution Have students use print or online resources to find five specific examples of historical or current pollution (for example, the smog in Los Angeles, the Cuyahoga River in Cleveland, and so on) and research solutions to the pollution. Students should report on solutions the government and private citizens have proposed or have begun working on to remedy the problems.

---

public good economic products that are consumed collectively, such as highways, national defense, police and fire protection

sustain to support or hold up

spillover effects uncompensated side effects that either benefit or harm a third party not involved in the activity that caused it

externalities uncompensated side effects that affect an uninvolved third party

---

- The added noise would generate additional and uncompensated discomfort and annoyance to the airport's neighbors. This is an example of a **negative spillover**, or **negative externality**—the uncompensated harm, cost, or inconvenience suffered by a third party because of other's actions.
- This might also generate benefits or advantages to the families of travelers if the travelers were able to spend more time at home or on other activities. This is an example of a **positive spillover**, or **positive externality**, an unreimbursed benefit received by someone who was not involved in the activity that generated the benefit.

The issue of compensation is important to both spillovers. Clearly the airport does not compensate the neighbors who are inconvenienced by the noise. Likewise, families benefiting from more time spent with their travelers do not compensate the airport for the new flights.

As long as the prices that travelers pay for air travel do not reflect the negative or positive spillovers that airport flight route changes generate, we will have a market failure. The question becomes: How should we deal with spillovers?

☑ **READING PROGRESS CHECK**

Analyzing What type of market flaw do you think is most likely to cause a market failure?

Dealing with Spillovers

GUIDING QUESTION How can externalities or spillovers be both good and bad?

The problem with spillovers is that they distort market outcomes—equilibrium prices and quantities—that then affect other decisions made by consumers and producers. While the spillover effects might be small, they may still affect the decisions made in the market. Overall, this makes the economy less efficient.

Taxing Harmful Spillovers

Pollution is a negative spillover, and it is difficult to correct because unregulated firms often have an incentive to pollute. Take the historical example of firms that were located near rivers because of convenient transportation. The firms also used the rivers as a giant waste disposal system, which helped keep their production costs lower than if they had to pay for the waste disposal. This led to lower market prices for the final product, more purchases, and then even more pollution. Who was affected by the negative spillovers from the pollution? It was the people who lived downstream from the polluting firms who "paid" for the pollution in the form of lower water quality—even if they did not buy or ever use the products.

How could we deal with this type of pollution? This is where the government may need to step in. Of course, the government could simply make pollution illegal, and it often does. The government could also set pollution standards, as it does for automobile emissions. Another answer might be to tax firms for the pollution they discharge into the air or water. The tax then becomes a cost of production, which ends up raising the price of the product for the consumers who buy it. Higher prices would put the cost of pollution on the users of the product, rather than uninvolved third parties. The tax would also cause less to be purchased, which in turn would cause less pollution.

Each of these solutions requires some degree of government involvement, and sometimes government is reluctant to act. Nevertheless, we need to realize that negative spillovers are already hurting people, and that correcting the spillovers may lead to a more efficient allocation of resources and less pollution.

EXPLORING THE ESSENTIAL QUESTION

Identify a public good that you think is needed in your community. Then write a tweet for your Twitter followers about why local taxpayers should support it.

ANSWERS, p. 194

☑ **READING PROGRESS CHECK** Answers will vary. Students may refer to not enough competition, not enough information, resources that can't or won't move, too few public goods, and externalities.

EXPLORING THE ESSENTIAL QUESTION

Student tweets should accurately identify a needed public good, and should demonstrate an understanding of market failure in taking a position on tax increases.

---

networks Online Teaching Options

VIDEO | **WORKSHEETS**

Blu-ray vs. HD DVDs

Analyzing a video As students view the video, ask them to identify some factors that ultimately would lead to the failure of the HD DVD format. Have interested students research Blu-ray sales since the demise of HD DVD. **Verbal/Linguistic**

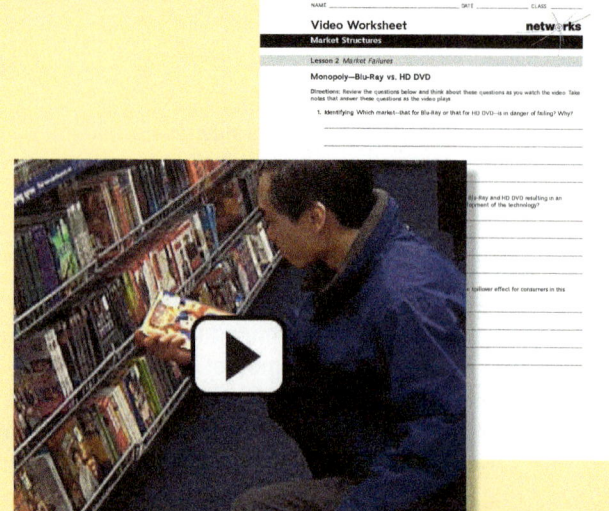

Subsidizing Helpful Spillovers

Spillovers can also be positive. A classic example is health and public education. A community with a healthy and well-educated workforce will attract more industry and more economic development. This will generate higher tax receipts, and help many enjoy a higher standard of living. For these and other reasons, it often makes sense for government to subsidize the cost of public or private education.

The benefits of positive spillovers are why state and local governments pay for the cost of primary and secondary public education. When it comes to higher education, however, state governments only pay for part of the cost, leaving the rest to be paid by students in the form of tuition. Given education's value to the community, many economists feel that government subsidies to higher education should be larger. This is expensive, however, so government tends to underfund higher education even though higher subsidies may make sense.

As for public health, consider the role of government when it started requiring smallpox immunization shots to young children in the 1950s. The cost of the shots was relatively minimal, while the elimination of smallpox has been a benefit to millions of people. This resulted in a much healthier population that could work, produce, and pay taxes on their incomes many years later.

Using Cost-Benefit Analysis

A reasonable way for government to evaluate competing projects that have positive spillovers would be to use **cost-benefit analysis**. Cost-benefit analysis is a strategy that evaluates the costs and benefits of various projects to find the one that has the highest ratio of benefits to costs. This is widely used in business to evaluate competing projects and is also a strategy used by government.

For example, the costs and benefits of three competing public goods projects are shown in **Figure 7.3**. Project A promises the most benefits but is also the

cost-benefit analysis calculation that compares the cost of an action to its benefits

---

FIGURE 7.3

USING COST-BENEFIT ANALYSIS

Costs and Benefits of Competing Public Goods Projects

	Project A	Project B	Project C
Benefits:	$150	$140	$78
Costs:	$100	$70	$60
Benefits/Costs:	$1.5	$2.0	$1.3

Cost-benefit analysis is a strategy that evaluates the costs and benefits of various projects to find the one that has the highest ratio of benefits to costs. This is widely used in businesses to evaluate competing projects.

▲ **CRITICAL THINKING**
Making Decisions Based on the cost-benefit analysis, assuming the city can only fund one project, which project should the city government fund?

CHAPTER 7, LESSON 2
Market Failures

C Critical Thinking Skills

Devising a plan Have students work in groups to identify a positive or negative externality and devise a plan for benefiting from it or correcting it.

English Language Proficiency

Intermediate Ask students to explain or retell the information about dealing with spillovers. As needed, ask questions prompting students to be more specific or give more detail. As more English is acquired, ask for more detail and specificity.

CHARTS

Cost-Benefit Analysis

Using tables and charts Have students preview Figure 7.3. Click on the different project headings to see their cost-benefit ratios. **Ask:**

- Which project has the highest benefits? *(Project A)* The lowest? *(Project C)*
- Which project has the highest cost? *(Project A)* The lowest? *(Project C)*
- What is the cost-benefit ratio for each project? *(Project A: 1.5, Project B: 2.0, Project C: 1.3)*

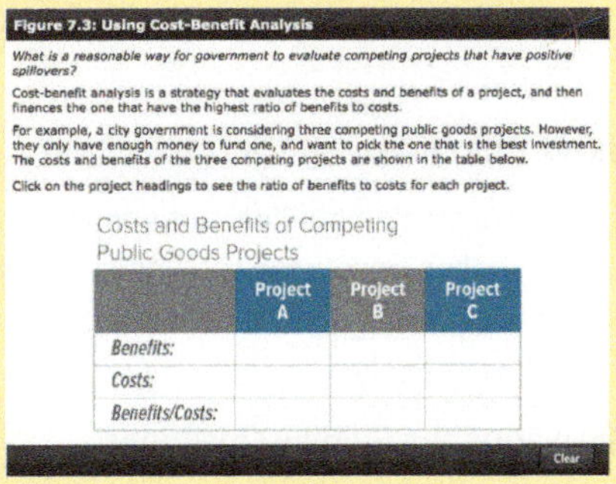

ANSWERS, p. 195

CRITICAL THINKING The city government should fund Project B. Although it is not the cheapest project, nor does it offer the highest benefit value, it has the best cost-benefit ratio (2.0), meaning that it will generate $2 for every $1 invested.

CHAPTER 7, LESSON 2
Market Failures

R Reading Skills

Identifying government involvement in externalities Ask: **What are two ways the government handles externalities or spillovers?** *(The government taxes negative externalities and subsidizes positive externalities.)* **What regulations has government enacted against industrial pollution and automobile emissions?** *(Answers may include setting pollution standards through legislation; issuing regulations that require firms to dispose of pollution in a particular way; imposing fines on firms that do not comply; imposing taxes on polluting firms, the cost of which is ultimately passed on to users of the firm's products.)*

CLOSE & REFLECT

R Reading Skills

Drawing conclusions from the lesson Have students review each subsection of the lesson and write one or two important conclusions that can be drawn from it. Ask students to share their conclusions in class discussion.

---

most expensive. Project C is the least expensive and promises the fewest benefits. So, which project should be financed?

If we were to assume that the city could fund any one of these projects and wanted to use cost-benefit analysis to make the selection, we would set up a ratio of benefits to costs for each project as is done in the bottom row of the figure. Then, we would look for the project that has the highest ratio of benefits to costs. This ratio is the highest for Project B, even though B is neither the cheapest project to pursue nor the one with the most benefits. However, the ratio of 2.0 tells us that the project would generate $2 of benefits for every dollar spent, whereas Project A generates $1.50 and Project C generates $1.30 for the same dollar spent.

While this is a reasonable strategy, there may well be other factors that also influence the government's decision. In the case of New Orleans' floodwalls, it was all too easy to postpone the necessary expenditures because they would have resulted in either higher taxes or in not providing other public goods. This is the situation today with the many overdue repairs that are needed on our nation's highways and bridges.

A Role for Government

Whenever we want to deal with positive or negative spillovers, the case for government action is greatly increased. Ideally, we would like to charge individual firms that pollute, or subsidize specific activities such as education and immunization against disease. Realistically, the costs of something like pollution or the benefits of something like higher education or immunization shots are so thinly spread across the population that we could never assign exact costs or benefits to specific firms or individuals. As a result, government has to deal with these issues as well as it can with general laws, taxes, and subsidies.

Of course, it is unrealistic to think that we will ever be able to effectively deal with all of the spillovers caused by something like an airport expansion. It is not unrealistic, however, to think that we can deal with many of the major ones like pollution, transportation, health, and education. We need to recognize that some degree of government involvement will be required, which is one of the reasons that we have a modified free enterprise economy today.

✓ **READING PROGRESS CHECK**

Explaining If externalities are negative, is there a potential role for government intervention?

LESSON 2 REVIEW

Reviewing Vocabulary
1. *Defining* Explain why externalities can cause market failures.

Using Your Notes
2. *Summarizing* Use your notes to identify the main causes of market failures.

Answering the Guiding Questions
3. *Analyzing Cause and Effect* What factors reduce competition in a market?
4. *Explaining* How can externalities or spillovers be both good and bad?

Writing About Economics
5. *Informative/Explanatory* Identify an action or situation in your community that resulted in an externality. Describe the externality and explain why it was positive or negative.

196

LESSON 2 REVIEW ANSWERS

Reviewing Vocabulary
1. Their costs and benefits are not reflected in the market prices that buyers pay.

Using Your Notes
2. Inadequate competition; not enough information; resources can't or won't move; too few public goods; externalities or spillover effects

Answering the Guiding Questions
3. On the supply side, mergers and combinations of companies result in fewer firms competing in a market. Fewer buyers reduce competition on the demand side of the market.

4. Economic activities can benefit some third parties who were not involved in them and at the same time harm other third parties.

Writing About Economics
5. The situations, actions, and externalities that students describe may vary, but their descriptions, classifications, and explanations should demonstrate an understanding of externalities and how they can be both positive and negative.

ANSWERS, p. 196

✓ **READING PROGRESS CHECK** Yes, negative externalities often result in government intervention. Factories that caused pollution, for example, did not willingly institute clean measures until Congress legislated them.

Case Study

COMING to AMERICA

South Korean automaker Kia was the world's seventh-largest car company in 2003. It wanted to do better. So Kia decided to make cars in the United States, where it had already sold a million vehicles in just nine years since entering the U.S. market.

Mississippi wanted Kia. So did Georgia, whose governor went to South Korea in 2003 to sell the state. Among Georgia's attractions were its excellent rail and highway network, its thriving seaports at Brunswick and Savannah, and its location within a two-hour flight or a two-day truck haul of 80 percent of the U.S. market.

In 2006, Kia officials decided on the town of West Point, once one of Georgia's top textile centers. But with the mills long closed, it now had one of the highest unemployment rates in the state. Kia saw in these jobless Georgians the nucleus of a highly motivated workforce.

To seal the deal, Georgia officials agreed to build a state job center dedicated to training Kia's workers. The state also paid for a railroad spur to connect the factory with a nearby railroad line, since 80 percent of the cars it produced would ship by rail. These incentives came on top of nearly $400 million in state and local tax breaks over a 20-year period. At the last minute, Mississippi more than doubled Georgia's offer. But Kia remained committed to West Point.

Construction of Kia's first American plant began in 2008, and in just over a year, cars began rolling off the assembly line. By 2012, some 3,000 workers were producing more than 360,000 vehicles a year—in comparison with 240,000 at the average U.S. auto plant. Kia celebrated record sales and 18 straight years of increases in U.S. market share.

CASE STUDY REVIEW

1. **Identifying** What factors caused Kia to choose Georgia for its first American plant?
2. **Speculating** Why might Kia have believed that manufacturing cars in the United States would boost its sales?
3. **Evaluating** Was locating a manufacturing facility in the United States a good business move for Kia? Explain why or why not.

The new Kia Motors plant in West Point, Georgia, was beneficial to the Georgia economy and also helped Kia manufacture its cars more efficiently.

CHAPTER 7 Case Study

R1 Reading Skills
Activating prior knowledge about the auto industry
Ask: What market structure is the U.S. auto industry? *(oligopoly)*

C1 Critical Thinking Skills
Problem solving in corporate decision-making
Have students identify one positive externality and one negative externality in the Kia plant Case Study. In a short oral or written report, students should create a governmental response plan to correct for both externalities.

R2 Reading Skills
Drawing conclusions about government incentives Ask: Why would officials extend tax breaks over 20 years? *(Possible answers: to encourage Kia to maintain the plant over the long term; to spread the $400 million out over time to avoid drastically affecting tax revenues)*

C2 Critical Thinking Skills
Evaluating alternative outcomes Provide students with a U.S. map. Have them locate key points of interest in this Case Study: West Point, Brunswick, and Savannah. Ask students to estimate a two-day truck haul from West Point; then, using a compass, create a rough map of where 80 percent of the U.S. auto market would be. Discuss with students whether it would be cost efficient for Kia to also reach the other 20 percent of the market. **Logical/Mathematical**

ANSWERS, p. 197

Case Study Review
1. Georgia's excellent highway and rail network, its seaports, its proximity to 80 percent of the U.S. market, nearly $400 million in tax-break incentives, a railroad spur, and a state job center to train its workers.
2. Students' speculations may include that closer proximity to consumers would have reduced Kia's cost of shipping cars to market, a savings that could be passed on in more attractive pricing to potential buyers. Students may also speculate that American-made Kias might be more attractive to American consumers opposed to buying a "foreign" car.
3. Most students will likely judge it a good move, as evidenced by the factory's highly productive workforce and the company's increasing market share and record U.S. sales.

INTERACTIVE FEATURE

Case Study: Coming to America

Identifying government enticements to business
Encourage classroom discussion by asking the following questions:

- Why did Kia want to open a plant in the United States? *(They wanted to sell more cars in the U.S.)*
- What did the governor of Georgia expect to gain for his state? *(jobs, economic growth)*
- What negative and positive externalities might the new plant have created? *(negative: pollution, traffic congestion; positive: stimulation of local businesses, a better-educated workforce)*
- What incentives did Georgia offer to entice Kia to build there? *(workforce training, railroad spur, tax incentives)* **Verbal/Linguistic**

CHAPTER 7, LESSON 3
The Role of Government

ENGAGE

C Critical Thinking Skills

🔔 **Discussing U.S. market structures** Before students begin the lesson, discuss the United States as a mix of market structures: pure competition, monopolistic competition, oligopoly, and monopoly. **Ask: Why is the U.S. economic structure not pure competition?** *(Sample answers: Pure competition is rare, the U.S. market has very diverse products, buyers are not always well-informed, high financial barriers exist to entering certain businesses, the government regulates the economy to prevent market failures.)* Stress that this lesson will discuss the role of government in steering the economy to be more competitive.
Logical/Mathematical

English Language Proficiency

Beginning Display and discuss images of common environmental print, such as logos of common businesses, labels on food products, restroom signs, traffic signs, and directional signs in parking lots. Discuss the meanings of known words in this context. Discuss exceptions such as different ways of indicating gender on restroom doors. Have students give examples of environmental print they have seen around school or the community. Provide periodicals with advertising in the classroom and encourage students to circle words they know in familiar ads. Provide newspapers and encourage students to circle words they know in headlines and advertisements.

ANSWERS, p. 198

ESSENTIAL QUESTION ACTIVITY

Answers will vary. Be sure students understand the causes of market failure *(inadequate competition; not enough information; resources cannot or will not move; too few public goods; externalities or spillover effects)* and the history of the TARP program before answering the questions.

TAKING NOTES
Monopolies: Break up monopolies and restore competition, Prevent formation, Regulate existing monopolies
Consumers: Corporate transparency, Consumer agencies
Regulations: Zoning, Agency oversight

Interact with these digital assets and others in lesson 3
✓ TABLE Federal Regulatory Agencies
✓ CAREERS Consumer Advocate Lawyer
✓ SELF-CHECK QUIZ
✓ VIDEO

netw⚡rks
TRY IT YOURSELF ONLINE

Reading Help Desk

Academic Vocabulary
- restrained
- intervention

Content Vocabulary
- trusts
- price discrimination
- cease and desist order
- economies of scale
- public disclosure
- mortgage
- foreclosure

TAKING NOTES:

Key Ideas and Details
ACTIVITY As you read this lesson, fill out the graphic organizer below to help you understand government's role in helping to ensure competition and prevent business failure in the economy.

LESSON 3
The Role of Government

ESSENTIAL QUESTION

C How does the government attempt to correct market failures?

In September 2008, the United States experienced the gravest financial crisis since the Great Depression of the 1930s. The nation's biggest banks had incurred so much debt that they were in danger of failing.

To prevent the failure of the financial market, the federal government crafted the Toxic Asset Relief Program (TARP), an emergency bailout for the banks. TARP provided billions of dollars in loans to financial institutions facing bankruptcy. Even so, banks severely cut back on lending, which affected, for one, the automobile industry. The U.S. government then set up loan programs to keep the auto industry from failing.

By 2013, most of the bailout money was repaid and both the financial and automobile markets were improved. Even so, some economists argued that failing industries should be allowed to fail because that is the way independent free markets work. Other economists contended that although government noninterference in the market is preferred, in extreme cases, the government should act as the "rescuer of last resort" to prevent economic catastrophe.

Do you think the government was justified in stepping in to help solve the financial crisis? With which economists do you agree, and why? Write a short essay explaining the extent of the role you believe government should have played in the financial crisis of 2008.

198

---

netw⚡rks   Online Teaching Options

BELLRINGER

Role of Government

Activating prior knowledge Use the Bellringer to stimulate students' prior knowledge of monopolies and the government role in regulating them or breaking them up. Remind students of the Global Economy & You feature in Lesson 1: From Monopoly to Oligopoly, which discussed the breakup of the AT&T monopoly. Lead a class discussion of the graphic and accompanying questions.

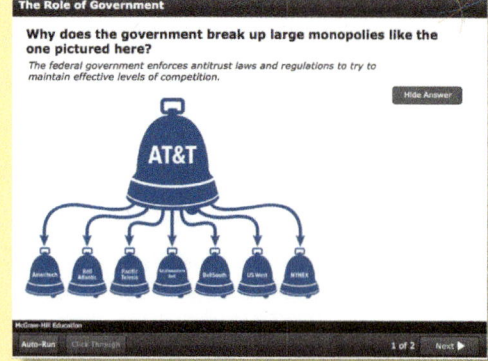

Ensuring Competition

GUIDING QUESTION *Why are some government regulations beneficial for consumers?*

There are several ways in which government can help maintain competitive markets. One is by attacking monopolies, in an attempt to break them up into smaller firms that can compete against each other. A second is to expand laws against monopolies and other actions in restraint of trade to prevent monopolies from forming. A third is to leave the monopolies in place, but to regulate their activities rather than prohibit them.

Breaking Up Monopolies

In the late 1800s, competition was threatened by the growing use of monopolies and **trusts**—combinations of firms designed to restrict competition or control prices in a particular industry. The most important monopoly at the time was Standard Oil Company, which was owned by John D. Rockefeller and controlled 90 percent of the domestic oil industry. Because it was so big and powerful, it could set almost any price it wanted for its products.

The government tried to restore competition in 1890 by passing the Sherman Antitrust Act "to protect trade and commerce against unlawful restraint and monopoly." The Sherman Act was the nation's first significant law against monopolies and other restraints that suppressed competition. Standard Oil was sued under the Sherman Act, and when the case reached the Supreme Court in 1911, it was forced to break up into 34 separate companies.

trusts illegal combinations of corporations or companies organized to suppress competition

Preventing Monopolies from Forming

The Sherman Act laid down broad foundations for maintaining competition. However, the act was not specific enough to stop many other practices that **restrained** competition. As a result, Congress passed the Clayton Antitrust Act in 1914 to give the government more power over monopolies. This act outlawed **price discrimination**—the practice of selling the same product to different consumers at different prices—if it substantially lessens competition.

The Federal Trade Commission Act was passed in the same year to enforce the Clayton Antitrust Act. The act set up the Federal Trade Commission (FTC) and gave it the authority to issue cease and desist orders. A **cease and desist order** is an FTC ruling requiring a company to stop an unfair business practice, such as price fixing, which reduces or limits competition among firms.

In 1936, Congress passed the Robinson-Patman Act in an effort to strengthen the Clayton Act, particularly the provisions that dealt with price discrimination. Under this act, companies could no longer offer special discounts to some customers while denying them to others.

restrained limited the activity or growth of

price discrimination practice of charging different customers different prices for the same product

cease and desist order ruling requiring a company to stop an unfair business practice that reduces or limits competition

Regulating Existing Monopolies

Not all monopolies are bad, and for that reason, not all should be broken up. Sometimes a firm can benefit from **economies of scale**, a situation in which the average cost of production falls as the firm gets larger. If a natural monopoly can benefit from these economies, it makes sense for the government to let the firm expand, and then regulate its activities so that it cannot take unfair advantage of consumers.

Local and state governments regulate many monopolies, such as cable television companies, water, and electric utilities. If a public utility wants to raise rates, it must argue its case before a public utility commission or other government agency.

economies of scale increasingly efficient use of personnel, plant, and equipment that lowers the average cost of production as a firm becomes larger

✓ **READING PROGRESS CHECK**

Describing Why are some government regulations beneficial for consumers?

CHAPTER 7, LESSON 3
The Role of Government

TEACH & ASSESS

R Reading Skills

Activating prior knowledge Tell students that the late nineteenth century was a time when giant corporations dominated much of the American economy. **Ask:** *Aside from Standard Oil, what were two other industrial giants in the late 1800s?* (Possible answers: Carnegie Steel; American Tobacco Company; Union Pacific)

Content Background Knowledge

Sherman Antitrust Act The first law to fight monopolies, the Sherman Antitrust Act, was enacted in 1890 as a response to growing concern over the power of trusts. Enforcement was left to the courts, and judges considered the language of the act too vague to make big companies change the way they did business. As a result, the number of trusts increased following passage of the act. It took another 14 years before the first major lawsuit, *Northern Securities v. United States,* was filed. Laws have become stronger since then, but price collusion still is a problem. In May 2006, three computer memory chip manufacturers were accused of fixing prices over a three-year period. This increased the price of chips for computer manufacturers, and thus the price of computers for consumers. The chipmakers agreed to pay $160 million to settle the case.

C Critical Thinking Skills

Defining and evaluating cease and desist orders Inform students that a cease and desist order has two parts. First, business must *cease*, or stop, the unfair practice. Secondly, they must *desist*, or not take up that practice again. In the example of price fixing, sellers must stop the immediate actions in which they are conspiring to set prices. Any further price fixing is punishable by law. Have students discuss whether they think issuing cease and desist orders are a justifiable role of government. **Verbal/Linguistic**

ANSWERS, p. 199

✓ **READING PROGRESS CHECK** Some government regulations benefit consumers by ensuring that, for example, food is safe to eat, and that appliances, cars, and other goods work properly and are not dangerous for consumers to use.

GRAPHIC ORGANIZER

Concept Web

Recognizing government roles in regulating competition Have students create a concept web to express the information about anti-monopoly legislation. The inner circle should read "Anti-Monopoly Legislation." Bubbles tied to the inner circle should list the four acts (Sherman Antitrust Act, Clayton Antitrust Act, Federal Trade Commission Act, Robinson-Patman Act), and then each of those bubbles should have a connecting bubble explaining the act.

CHAPTER 7, LESSON 3
The Role of Government

C Critical Thinking Skills

Researching through the SEC Have students visit www.sec.gov and read the section that introduces the SEC. Then have them choose a company, find it in the EDGAR database, and record five pieces of information that they learn there. **BL**

R Reading Skills

Identifying regulations Have students identify ordinances and regulations required for establishing various types of businesses. For example, ask students to consider what ordinances and regulations a veterinary clinic/animal boarding center must meet upon establishment (noise ordinance; regulations regarding animal wastes, medications, and the number of animals per cage; and so on). Ask students to identify what ordinances or regulations exist to establish a daycare center, a skating rink, a restaurant, or any other business students may be interested in establishing. Then have students consider the regulations that apply to the establishment of financial institutions. **Ask: Why do credit card companies and banks explain in great detail the method for computing monthly interest, the length of the loan, the size of the payments, and other lending terms?** *(They are required to do so by the Consumer Financial Protection Bureau and other federal agencies.)* **Why must pharmaceutical companies list side effects as well as benefits of a particular drug?** *(They are required to do so by law.)*

Making Connections

Identity Theft A more recent consumer protection provided by government is helping people recover from identity theft. Have students go to IdentityTheft.gov to learn ways to protect their identity, and how to report identity theft.

ANSWERS, p. 200
EXPLORING THE ESSENTIAL QUESTION

Students may state that some transparency is warranted, especially when it comes to consumer product safety (e.g., food, appliances, cars). Students may recognize that proprietary information should remain exempt from transparency rules to maintain a company's or entrepreneur's competitive advantage. Students may argue that experience shows that limited transparency does not result in market failure.

Competition, Consumer Protection, and Regulation

GUIDING QUESTION *How does the government promote economic efficiency?*

The government also has other, perhaps more indirect, ways to deal with practices that are in restraint of trade. It can promote public disclosure by companies to consumer groups. It can introduce brand-new agencies or bureaus to protect existing consumer activities.

Promoting Transparency

Efficient and competitive markets need adequate information. *Transparency* is a term used to indicate that information and actions are not hidden and instead are easily available for review.

public disclosure requirement forcing a business to reveal information about its products or its operations to the public

Public disclosure, the requirement that businesses reveal certain information to the public, is an important way to do this. For example, every time you buy a can of food at the grocery store you can see a list of contents on the back. Or if you want information on a company, you can check with the Securities and Exchange Commission (SEC). In general, the SEC requires corporations that sell stock to the public to disclose financial and operating information on a regular basis to both their shareholders and the SEC. The data are stored in a free database that can be accessed by anyone on the Internet.

Disclosure requirements also exist for consumer lending. If you obtain a credit card or borrow money to buy a car, the lender will explain in writing the method for computing the monthly interest, the length of the loan, the size of the payments, and other lending terms. This is not an act of kindness on the lender's part. Federal law requires these disclosures. Finally, "truth-in-advertising" laws are enforced by the Federal Trade Commission (FTC) to prevent sellers from making false claims about their products.

Consumer Financial Protection Bureau

One of the major causes of the Great Recession of 2008-2009 was the millions of low-quality home mortgages that could not be repaid. A **mortgage** is a legal document that pledges ownership of a home to a lender as security for repayment of borrowed money. When consumers stopped making their monthly mortgage payments, they lost their homes to foreclosure. **Foreclosure** is the situation in which a lender reclaims a home because the borrower has defaulted on the previously agreed-upon payments. This caused millions of people to lose their homes and forced lenders to lose billions of dollars, which helped pull the economy down.

In the spirit of disclosure and in hopes of preventing another situation like this, Congress established the Consumer Financial Protection Bureau (CFPB) in 2011 to provide oversight and guidance in the financial lending industry. For example, one early action was the development of an "Ability-to-Repay" rule, which was designed to assure both borrowers and lenders of reliable mortgage repayment conditions whenever a loan was made. Other actions included prescribing rules for debt-collection policies and issuing guidance to debt collectors for following existing debt-collection laws.

Finally, almost all government documents, studies, and reports of a financial, economic, or commercial nature are available on the Internet. This adds a considerable amount of transparency, if someone wants to take the time to look it up.

Federal Regulatory Agencies in Our Lives

There are literally hundreds of federal agencies that affect almost everything we do. The short list in **Figure 7.4** touches on some of the major ones, but certainly not all.

EXPLORING THE ESSENTIAL QUESTION

Limits to Transparency?
Since regulatory agencies were first formed, businesses have argued against what they considered "excessive" transparency. Should restaurant menus include information about their food's fat content and calories? Should food packagers disclose exactly how "natural" the "natural flavorings" are in their products? Should foods whose genetic properties have been altered by scientists be labeled as "genetically modified" food?

What do you think? Should the requirements for transparency be limited? If so, in what cases? Do you think greater transparency is linked to market failure? What types of transparency do you want or not want? Write a short essay explaining your point of view.

200

---

networks Online Teaching Options

VIDEO **WORKSHEET**

The Role of Government

Analyzing and evaluating a video Show The Role of Government video and guide students in discussing competition in the credit card market.
Ask: What is the issue? *(antitrust lawsuit against Visa and Mastercard, who are accused of preventing banks from offering American Express cards to consumers)* **What evidence did the Visa spokesperson give that supports the idea that competition is still viable for any credit card company?** *(He stated that credit card companies send out 4 billion solicitations each year and have access to consumers without going through banks.)* **Visual/Spatial**

Most of us are aware of things such as reports from the National Weather Service and automobile recalls issued by the National Highway Traffic Safety Administration (NHTSA). Likewise, you have probably heard about high-profile product recalls of baby cribs or car seats that can fail to protect young children. You also may have heard about various food products that have been recalled by the Food and Drug Administration (FDA) because they are suspected of carrying *E. coli* bacteria.

However, many other activities by federal agencies are probably not known to the average consumer. For example, how many people know if their bank is audited by the FDIC in an effort to make it safer? Likewise, most people are probably unaware of the airport inspections and pilot training programs that the Federal Aviation Administration oversees. Finally, how many people know about the proposed merger by Microsoft and Yahoo! that was prevented by the Federal Trade Commission because the FTC thought that a combination of the two companies would give them an unfair advantage in the market?

Zoning and Other Local Ordinances

Not all of the regulations in our lives are at the federal level. Many regulations at the local level also affect us.

Zoning, for example, is a way of controlling land use and is in effect almost everywhere. In 1926, the U.S. Supreme Court legitimized zoning as a way to promote and protect the health, safety, and welfare of the people in a community. Zoning divides a municipality into small parcels in which the location, construction, and intensity of residential, commercial, and industrial activities are regulated.

For example, residential zoning laws are usually designed to stabilize and maintain the characteristics of neighborhoods. This is done by specifying things

mortgage legal document that pledges ownership of a home to a lender as security for repayment of borrowed money

foreclosure process in which a lender reclaims the property due to a lack of payment by the borrower

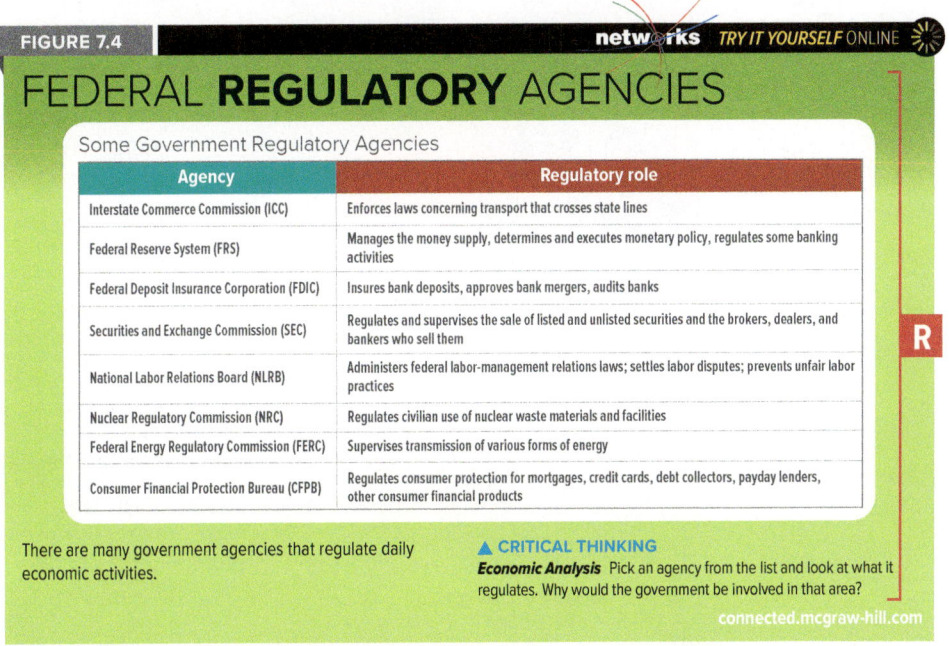

FIGURE 7.4

FEDERAL REGULATORY AGENCIES

Some Government Regulatory Agencies

Agency	Regulatory role
Interstate Commerce Commission (ICC)	Enforces laws concerning transport that crosses state lines
Federal Reserve System (FRS)	Manages the money supply, determines and executes monetary policy, regulates some banking activities
Federal Deposit Insurance Corporation (FDIC)	Insures bank deposits, approves bank mergers, audits banks
Securities and Exchange Commission (SEC)	Regulates and supervises the sale of listed and unlisted securities and the brokers, dealers, and bankers who sell them
National Labor Relations Board (NLRB)	Administers federal labor-management relations laws; settles labor disputes; prevents unfair labor practices
Nuclear Regulatory Commission (NRC)	Regulates civilian use of nuclear waste materials and facilities
Federal Energy Regulatory Commission (FERC)	Supervises transmission of various forms of energy
Consumer Financial Protection Bureau (CFPB)	Regulates consumer protection for mortgages, credit cards, debt collectors, payday lenders, other consumer financial products

There are many government agencies that regulate daily economic activities.

▲ **CRITICAL THINKING**
Economic Analysis Pick an agency from the list and look at what it regulates. Why would the government be involved in that area?

CHAPTER 7, LESSON 3
The Role of Government

W Writing Skills

Evaluating start-up regulations Tell students to suppose that they are setting up a business of their choice. Have them search online for ordinances and regulations that apply to the establishment of their type of business. (Steer students toward small businesses and the Small Business Administration Web site.) Ask students to summarize the ordinances and regulations applicable to their start-up, rating them as beneficial or intrusive. **Verbal/Linguistic**

C1 Critical Thinking Skills

Constructing arguments about government regulation Select teams to debate the following proposition: *The government is too involved in regulating our economy.* Have teams develop their arguments, rebuttals, and counterarguments using information found in Lesson 3 and additional library or Internet research. **Verbal/Linguistic**

C2 Critical Thinking Skills

Predicting the future role of government
Ask: **Do you think the role of government in the U.S. economy will change over time? If so, do you think the government will have a larger or smaller role?** *(Require students to provide supporting evidence for their opinions.)* **Logical/Mathematical**

---

such as the minimum size of lots that can be used for homes, as well as the maximum height and size of structures on these lots. An area designated for commercial use might specify things such as the type and sizes of retail establishments and the parking requirements for each. An area zoned for industrial use might allow for medium to heavy manufacturing facilities, along with rail access.

W Despite their good intentions, cities and communities evolve over time, and zoning laws may or may not keep up with the changes. A city that had a vibrant residential downtown or neighborhoods 50 years ago may have suffered from a population flight to the suburbs, leaving empty homes, storefronts, and hotels. Now, the zoning changes needed to help these areas regain their former status may not be in place, or may not be possible, because some people in those areas are afraid of even more change. Other people argue that zoning laws infringe on their freedom to make choices and oppose all zoning laws for that reason.

C2 C1 Most of these topics are too broad to examine in detail here. However, it should be clear that local government regulations, as well as federal ones, can have a major impact on our lives.

✓ **READING PROGRESS CHECK**

Describing How does increasing transparency help the U.S. economy?

CAREERS | Consumer Advocate Lawyer

Is this Career for you?

 Are you strongly motivated to dedicate yourself and your career to public service?

 Do you have an interest in consumer protection laws and policies?

 Are you willing to relocate to Washington, D.C.?

Interview with a Consumer Advocate Lawyer

"Our job is to go after unfair and deceptive practices that affect commerce and ... consumers."

— Delores Gardner Thompson, George Washington University Law School, Class of 1997

Salary
As of 2012, the median salary for a lawyer in the United States was $113,530 per year.

Job Growth Potential
In general, the job outlook for lawyers between 2010 and 2020 is good. The number of job openings for lawyers is expected to grow by about 10 percent during this decade.

Profile of Work
Depending on the consumer advocate lawyer's area of expertise, she might spend her working day processing consumer complaints about business practices or investigating misleading advertising or marketing practices. A business continuity planning lawyer might work with a team to make policy recommendations to protect consumers from fraud or prepare legal cases against businesses that violate consumer protection regulations.

202

---

networks | Online Teaching Options

INTERACTIVE FEATURE

Career: Consumer Advocate Lawyer

Researching a career as consumer advocate lawyer Have students analyze the Career feature to learn about a career as a consumer advocate lawyer with the Bureau of Consumer Protection. Instruct students to research three other careers within the Federal Trade Commission. Have them summarize the work profiles, and then create a graph summarizing the salaries and job growth potential of the careers. Encourage students to share their findings with the class. **Logical/Mathematical**

ANSWERS, p. 202

✓ **READING PROGRESS CHECK** Transparency makes it more difficult for companies to engage in fraud, such as price fixing or overcharging customers for goods or services.

Modified Free Enterprise

GUIDING QUESTION *Why is the U.S. economy considered a modified free enterprise economy?*

The U.S. economy has changed slowly but steadily over the years. One of the outcomes of this evolution is the rise of the modified free enterprise economy. In short, many of the things we do and many of the things we buy are in some way indirectly affected by many of these federal agencies discussed above. This even includes law such as zoning ordinances that affect people's property rights and their ability to exercise their personal economic freedom.

In the late 1800s, the freedom to pursue self-interests allowed some people to seek economic gain at the expense of others. Under the label of competition, a few larger firms used their power to take advantage of smaller ones. In some industries, less competitive market structures, such as monopolies, eroded competition, and the economy became less efficient.

Because of these developments, Congress passed laws to prevent "evil monopolies" and to protect the rights of workers. It also passed food and drug laws to protect people from false advertising claims and harmful products. Even public utilities faced significant government regulation to prevent the price-gouging of consumers. Collectively, these actions have resulted in a modification of free enterprise.

Some economists believe that concern is shifting to increased economic efficiency and the role of the government in promoting it. Markets are important, but we recognize that markets can fail in several different ways. When this happens, the government has been given the power and can take steps to remedy the situation.

In addition to occasional interventions to keep markets reasonably competitive, the government can make the economy more efficient by supplying public goods and promoting transparency. People will continue to debate the proper role of government, but it turns out that markets alone cannot provide all of our wants and needs.

Over the years, government's role in the economy has received increasing scrutiny as concern over consumer protection has expanded to include the promotion of economic competition and efficiency. As a result of this government **intervention**, we now have a modified free enterprise economy, or an economy based on markets with varying degrees of government regulation. The arrival of a modified free enterprise economy didn't just happen, it happened because people wanted it that way.

intervention involvement in a situation to alter the outcome

✓ **READING PROGRESS CHECK**

Summarizing Why do we use the term *modified* to describe the American free enterprise economy?

LESSON 3 REVIEW

Reviewing Vocabulary
1. *Explaining* Why would the Federal Trade Commission issue a cease and desist order to a company that was found to be engaged in price discrimination?

Using Your Notes
Use the information you jotted down in the graphic organizer to answer this question.
2. *Summarizing* How does the regulation of monopolies and agency oversight of business practices help protect consumers?

Answering the Guiding Questions
3. *Evaluating* Why are some government regulations beneficial for consumers?

4. *Application* How does the government promote economic efficiency?
5. *Synthesis* Why is the U.S. economy considered a free enterprise economy?

Writing About Economics
6. *Argument* To what extent should the government intervene to ensure economic efficiency? Do you agree with some economists that the government should not be allowed to regulate free enterprise for the good of the consumer? If not, in what circumstances should the government get involved?

CHAPTER 7, LESSON 3
The Role of Government

R Reading Skills

Recalling terms that describe the U.S. economic system Ask students to recall the three terms that are synonymous in describing the U.S. economic system. *(free enterprise, free market, capitalism)* **Ask: What is another term that can now be applied to the U.S. economic system?** *(modified free enterprise)* **AL**

C Critical Thinking Skills

Analyzing frame of reference Have students analyze the validity of this statement by the author: "In addition to occasional interventions to keep markets reasonably competitive, the government can make the economy more efficient by supplying public goods and promoting transparency." **Ask: What is the author's frame of reference for making this statement?** *(The author previously cited instances of monopolistic industries during times when public goods were not available and transparency was missing.)*

CLOSE & REFLECT

Summarizing Have students summarizr the U.S. government's policies, both historical and current, toward economic competition.

ANSWERS, p. 203

✓ **READING PROGRESS CHECK** We use the term modified to indicate that we recognize that ours is not a pure free enterprise system, because the government does have a limited role to play in the economy.

LESSON 3 REVIEW ANSWERS

Reviewing Vocabulary
1. The FTC would issue the order for the company to stop this practice of charging different customers different prices because that is an unfair business practice and distorts the functioning of the free market.

Using Your Notes
2. Monopolies tend to control prices because they have little or no competition. This unfairly raises prices for consumers who have nowhere else to go to buy a monopolistic product. Agency oversight ensures that businesses engage in fair competition and that their products are safe to use.

Answering the Guiding Questions
3. Some government regulations benefit consumers by ensuring that, for example, food is safe to eat and that appliances, cars, and other goods work properly and are not dangerous for consumers to use.

4. Government mandates public disclosure, or transparency, on the part of businesses who sell to consumers. This regulation lets the government, other businesses, and other companies see if there is fraud or other noncompetitive practices.

5. It is a free enterprise economy because, despite limited government involvement, individuals and businesses are free to compete in an open and fair marketplace.

Writing About Economics
6. Students may argue that in extreme circumstances, some limited government intervention is needed. Other students may argue that government interference prevents the market from correcting itself, which in the long run may be self-defeating.

Chapter 7
Study Guide

C1 Critical Thinking Skills

Categorizing Organize students into groups of three—with one group member representing monopolies; another, oligopolies; and the third, monopolistic competition. Each member of each group should clip business advertisements and articles that characterize his or her market structure. As a group, have students compare the ads (and businesses) that each person collected. Have students defend their reasoning behind placing a particular company in its particular grouping.

C2 Critical Thinking Skills

Surveying Have students conduct an informal survey of family members, friends, students, and teachers on government's role in the economy. Suggest that they ask such questions as the following: Is there too much or not enough government regulation? Which regulatory agencies, if any, should be curtailed, expanded, or abolished? Have students share their survey results with the class.

STUDY GUIDE

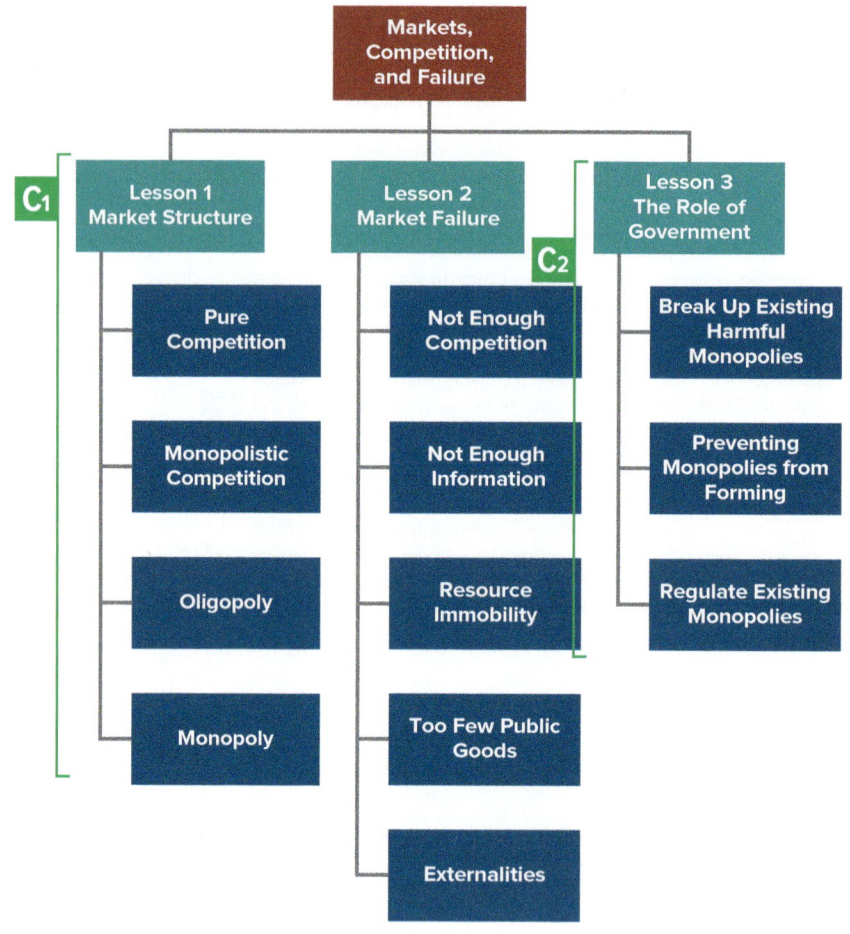

networks Online Assessment Options

WORKSHEET

Hands-On Chapter Project with Technology Extension

Groups will research antitrust cases, examining the arguments on both sides of the case and what led to the case. Students will present their findings to the class, considering which type of market structure was evident in their case. Then students will discuss the similarities between the cases groups presented, and why the government felt the need to intervene in those situations.
Interpersonal

Find an additional activity online that incorporates technology for this project. Visit the EdTech Teacher Web sites for more links, tutorials, and other resources.

CHAPTER 7 Assessment

Directions: On a separate sheet of paper, answer the questions below. Make sure you read carefully and answer all parts of the questions.

Lesson Review

Lesson 1

1. **Explaining** Why do natural and geographical monopolies arise, and why are they often good for the economy and for consumers?

2. **Identifying** What is collusion among oligopolies, and how does it tend to reduce competition and harm consumers by imposing higher prices?

Lesson 2

3. **Drawing Conclusions** Why might the lack of competition resulting from business mergers tend to lead to market failures?

4. **Describing** Why is government intervention often crucial when dealing with both positive and negative externalities?

Lesson 3

5. **Discussing** How does transparency improve competition and benefit consumers?

6. **Interpreting** How can a modified free enterprise system change over time in terms of the degree to which it is considered "modified"?

Critical Thinking

7. **Evaluating** Which of the four market structures encourages the greatest competition and benefits for other businesses and consumers? Explain your answer in terms of price competition and the effect of that business type on the overall economy.

8. **Analyzing** How may negative externalities lead to market failures? Should government correct the failures caused by externalities? Describe an example of negative externality and defend your position about the government's role in correcting the situation.

9. **Assessing** Is it possible that absolute transparency among businesses might make monopolistic businesses more acceptable? Or do monopolies almost always have a negative effect on the economy because of reduced competition?

Building Financial Literacy

10. **Planning** You and a friend have developed a new smartphone app. Will you market it to the public? Will you sell your idea to existing app companies? What are the pros and cons with each method? Which path gives your product the best chance to compete with other apps? Explain which path you would choose.

11. **Contrasting** In what way does renting a home or apartment prove to be more beneficial than owning a home in an area affected by a negative externality, such as increased pollution? What negative effects might a renter have to deal with? How might a renter prepare in advance for the possibility of a negative event?

ANSWERING THE ESSENTIAL QUESTIONS

Review your answers to the introductory questions at the beginning of each lesson. Then answer the Essential Questions on the basis of what you learned in the chapter. Have your answers changed?

12. **Displaying** One concept in this chapter is that businesses take risks and that companies are more generously rewarded for taking risks that turn out positively, but they may fail if the risks they take have negative results. Choose one type of market structure in this chapter (monopolistic competition, oligopoly, or monopoly). Create a flow chart that shows the relationship of risk-taking for this type of market structure and the consequences of failure if the risk proves to be too great. Include government interventions that might correct the market failure and help keep businesses afloat.

13. **Identifying Cause and Effect** How do the following circumstances sometimes lead to market failure? Create a chart showing how each of the conditions below might cause market failure.

    a. Inadequate competition
    b. Negative externalities
    c. Resource immobility

Need Extra Help?

If You've Missed Question	1	2	3	4	5	6	7	8	9	10	11	12	13
Go to page	188	187	192	196	200	203	182	193	199	182	194	182	192

Chapter 7 Assessment Answers

Lesson Review

Lesson 1

1. Natural and geographical monopolies arise from the circumstances in which a market exists. Natural monopolies may be beneficial because they have a lower cost of production, which is concentrated and more efficient. Geographical monopolies may be beneficial because the company's location may make its goods production more efficient and less costly.

2. When companies collude, they secretly agree to set prices that are beneficial to them and their profits. They cooperate instead of competing. Price-fixing sets prices higher than they would be in a truly competitive environment, and this hurts consumers, who have to pay more.

Lesson 2

3. Mergers lead to the creation of larger companies that may dominate the market. This domination reduces competition and may also lead to inefficient use of resources.

4. Difficulty in applying a cost-benefit analysis to these events makes government intervention vital. Negative externalities, such as pollution, are often diffuse and are thus better handled by the government. Similarly, education is a diffuse or widespread endeavor best handled by the government.

Lesson 3

5. Transparency reduces the likelihood of fraud that might give a company an unfair advantage. Consumers benefit because they know that the company is producing quality goods at a reasonable price.

6. The economic system can change over time as the degree of government intervention, regulation, and oversight of companies, sectors, or the economy as a whole changes.

Critical Thinking

7. Pure and monopolistic competition are most beneficial for consumers. Monopolies and oligopolies provide benefits for firms.

8. Students should choose one actual negative externality and describe the roles of the private sector or business and that of government in ameliorating the problem. They should then defend a position about the degree of government intervention in the event.

9. Students should exhibit understanding of a monopoly and transparency.

Building Financial Literacy

10. Students should present a decision and give reasons—in terms of cost, profit, feasibility, marketing, etc.—for their choice.

11. Students should present the pros and cons of renting in light of a negative externality.

Answering the Essential Questions

12. Students should create a flow chart for a monopolistic competition, oligopoly, or monopoly. The chart should show two strands: risk-taking that leads to reward, and risk-taking that leads to failure. On the negative side, the chart should include a separate strand showing the various ways government might intervene to prevent or correct a market failure and keep the business or sector afloat.

13. Students should briefly discuss how each circumstance might cause market failure. They may mention that inadequate competition may lead to overpricing and shoddy production, that negative externalities might overwhelm a market's ability to continue to operate profitably, and that resource immobility may deprive the market of materials needed to continue production and stay in business.

Chapter 7
Assessment Answers

14 Student essays should explain or compare the structures of monopolies and oligopolies. They should mention the absolute hold a monopoly has on the price of its good(s), that oligopolies may compete in terms of price but that price-fixing is often a problem.

21st Century Skills

15 Students should identify the innovation and superior quality of products produced by oligopolistic companies as their main source of competition.

16 Students' essays should cite reliable studies and articles, and present brief synopses of the main points. Interpreting opinion and recognizing and synthesizing facts should be evident regardless of the point of view students embrace.

17 Answers will vary, but should relate what they find to concepts of market failure, competition, spillover effects, and cost benefit analysis.

Analyzing Primary Sources

18 Students should understand that Mr. Hoenig wants to keep commercial banks from speculating with depositors' money. Banks that do this should lose their FDIC safety net. This would prevent another bailout because the FDIC, which is partly funded by the government, is depositors' insurance and would not have to pay back non-insured money that is at risk or is lost by the bank.

19 Mr. Hoenig perceives that FDIC insurance would be tapped to bail out banks that use insured deposits to make risky investments. If those investments fail, the FDIC would have to replace depositors' lost money. The FDIC might run out of money if the amount of insured money used to gamble on risky investments was too high.

20 Students should recognize this as a fact. Mr. Hoenig is not stating what he thinks should or might be, or stating his personal feelings about it, but is explaining what actually happened that caused the financial crisis he is testifying about.

Analyzing Visuals

21 They would supply fewer units at the new equilibrium price.

22 Each firm would take up a larger portion of the market, and could act more as a "price maker" than a "price taker."

CHAPTER 7 Assessment

Directions: On a separate sheet of paper, answer the questions below. Make sure you read carefully and answer all parts of the questions.

14 *Identifying Central Issues* How does market structure affect competition and prices? Write a short essay in which you compare monopolies and oligopolies in terms of their structure. Explain how these structures affect competition in the marketplace and price setting. Include examples of the types of competition market-dominating businesses can and do engage in to attract consumers.

21st Century Skills

15 *Identifying Cause and Effect* Why do monopolies and oligopolies often engage in nonprice competition? What are the primary types of competition these market structures engage in?

16 *Identifying Perspectives and Differing Interpretations* Some markets struggle to provide public goods because the profit margin is very low. Providing adequate housing for the nonworking poor is one such problem. Some experts say that government subsidies can help builders and/or landlords make a modest profit on low-income housing. Other experts insist that in a free enterprise economy, all sectors must be subject to market forces, competition, and unsubsidized profit. Write a short essay where you explain your point of view against the evidence you research for each side.

17 *Understanding Relationships Among Events* Research different reactions to the bank bailout after the financial crisis of 2008. Pick one of the viewpoints you find and write a short paragraph describing the argument. How does it fit in with what you have learned? Do you agree with the author? Be sure to cite your source.

Analyzing Primary Sources

PRIMARY SOURCE

"*Keeping [broker-dealer activities] inside the safety net exposes the FDIC Deposit Insurance Fund and the taxpayer to loss. Therefore, activities that should be placed outside the safety net and thus subject to market forces are: most derivative activities; proprietary trading; and trading for customer accounts, or market making. Allowing customer trading makes it easy to game the system by 'concealing' proprietary trading as part of it. Also, prime brokerage services require the ability to trade, and essentially allow companies to finance their activities with highly unstable, uninsured, wholesale 'deposits' that come with implied protection. This combination of factors, as we have recently witnessed, leads to unstable markets and government bailouts.*"

—Thomas M. Hoenig, Director of the FDIC, June 26, 2013

18 *Identifying* What limitations does Mr. Hoenig suggest be put on commercial banks that would help prevent another financial crisis and possible bank bailout?

19 *Analyzing Primary Sources* What risk does Mr. Hoenig perceive to the FDIC if the safety net is extended to banks that invest in high-risk securities?

20 *Distinguishing Fact from Opinion* Mr. Hoenig states that "Allowing customer trading makes it easy to game the system. . . . " Is Mr. Hoenig stating a fact or opinion?

Analyzing Visuals

Use the graphs below to answer the following questions.

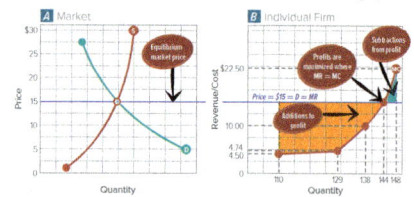

21 *Interpreting* What would be the effect on the quantity supplied by the individual firm in Panel B if the equilibrium market prices fell to $10 per unit of output?

22 *Analyzing* The figure above is based on pure competition. How would the market dynamic change if there are fewer firms in the market?

Need Extra Help?

If You've Missed Question	14	15	16	17	18	19	20	21	22
Go to page	186	186	195	196	196	196	196	183	183

networks Online Assessment Options

WORKSHEET

Chapter Tests and Lesson Quizzes

Chapter 7 Tests Forms A and B Have students complete the Chapter Tests and Lesson Quizzes to assess student understanding throughout the chapter. Print and online assessment tools offer chapter and lesson evaluation through a variety of question formats, including document-based questions.

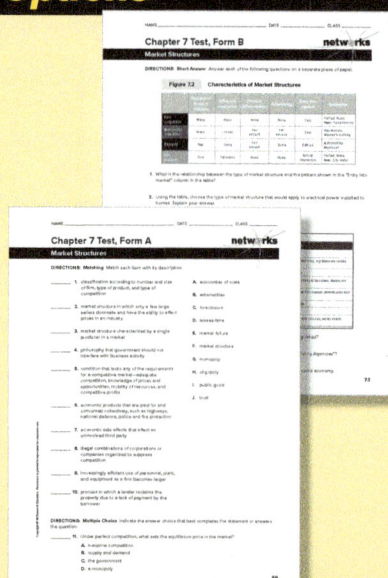

UNIT 3
BUSINESS AND LABOR Planner

UNDERSTANDING BY DESIGN®

Enduring Understandings
- Individuals and groups work independently and cooperatively to achieve goals.
- Disputes over ideas, resources, values, and politics can lead to change.

Essential Questions
- How are businesses formed and how do they grow?
- How does a market economy support nonprofit organizations?
- What features of the modern day labor industry are the result of union action?
- What factors lead to higher wages for a worker?

Students will know:
- the characteristics, advantages, and disadvantages of sole proprietorships, partnerships, and corporations in the United States economy.
- economic institutions such as labor unions, nonprofit organizations, and cooperatives evolve in market economies to help members and clients accomplish their goals.
- the major events in the rise and subsequent development of the labor movement, including the national labor unions.
- how supply of and demand for labor affect wages.
- how the earnings of workers are determined by the market value of the product produced and workers' productivity.
- the reasons for the decline in labor union influence in the United States.

Students will be able to:
- **describe** how various types of businesses are formed and how they grow.
- **discuss** the purpose of labor unions.
- **analyze** the effect of union action on the modern labor industry.
- **identify** the different types of union arrangements that exist today and state reasons for the decline of union influence.
- **list** three major causes for pay discrimination in the labor market.

Predictable Misunderstandings
Students may think:
- Sole proprietors are not responsible for financial risk if the business fails.
- Stockholders in a corporation do not have to pay individual income tax on their profits.
- Union methods are limited to calling strikes, pickets, or boycotts.

Assessment Evidence
Performance Task
- Hands-On Chapter Projects with Technology Extensions
- Economic Simulations
- Math Practice for Economics
- Personal Finance Activities
- Reinforcing Economic Skills Activities

Other Evidence:
- Guided Reading Activities
- Vocabulary Activities
- Lesson Quizzes
- Chapter Tests, Forms A and B

Key for Using the Teacher Edition

SKILL-BASED ACTIVITIES
Types of skill activities found in the Teacher Edition.
- **V Visual Skills** require students to analyze maps, graphs, charts, and photos.
- **R Reading Skills** help students practice reading skills and master vocabulary.
- **C Critical Thinking Skills** help students apply and extend what they have learned.
- **W Writing Skills** provide writing opportunities to help students comprehend the text.
- **T Technology Skills** require students to use digital tools effectively.

*Letters are followed by a number when there is more than one of the same type of skill on the page.

DIFFERENTIATED INSTRUCTION
All activities are written for the on-level student unless otherwise marked with the leveled labels below.
- **BL** Beyond Level
- **AL** Approaching Level
- **ELL** English Language Learners

All students benefit from activities that utilize different learning styles. Many activities are marked as below when a particular learning style is highlighted.

Intrapersonal
Logical/Mathematical
Visual/Spatial
Verbal/Linguistic
Naturalist
Kinesthetic
Auditory/Musical
Interpersonal

SUGGESTED PACING GUIDE—Semester
Introducing the Unit . . . . ½ Day
Chapter 8: Business Organization . . . . . . 5 Days
Chapter 9: Labor and Wages . . . . 5 Days

UNIT 3: BUSINESS AND LABOR

Planner

☑ Print Teaching Options

■ Visual Skills

☐ **p. 207 Exploring U.S. labor topics** Students prepare a television newscast on labor in the United States, incorporating charts and graphs to illustrate topics such as changes in the labor force, average wages over the years, and union membership.
BL Interpersonal

■ Critical Thinking Skills

☐ **p. 207 Evaluating current economic issues** Students list most controversial topics in economics today, and explain their point of view on topics such as employment, labor unions, the minimum wage, pay equity, business growth, and determining fair wages.
Interpersonal

☐ **p. 209 Evaluating information and making inferences** Students develop and practice the skills of evaluating information and making inferences while reading point-of-view text such as the Case Study features.

■ Writing Skills

☐ **p. 207 Researching state and national occupation and wage data** Students visit the Bureau of Labor Statistics Web site and click on a selected career. Then students write the number of national and state workers in the occupation and the mean annual wage for the occupation at both levels.
Logical/Mathematical

☑ Online Teaching Options

☐ **ANIMATION Gender and Wage Inequality**—Students view the significant U.S. labor law milestones through history and then describe specific examples of how labor laws at the time might have affected working women in 1925, 1950, 1975, 2000, and in the present day.

☐ **APPROACHING GRADE LEVEL READER Alternative Student Edition narrative**—You can assign your students who are struggling to read on grade level the Approaching Grade Level version of the Online Student Edition. This reader presents all of the content in the On Grade Level version of the Online Student Edition at a lower reading level.

☐ **ENGLISH LANGUAGE LEARNER READER Alternative Student Edition narrative with ELL support**—Use the Online English Language Learner reader to provide additional reading support for ELL students. You can find this tool in the Online Student Edition.

☑ Printable Digital Worksheets

■ Reading Skills

☐ **WORKSHEET Guided Reading Activity**—Students use the Guided Reading Activities worksheets to review their comprehension of the content.

☐ **WORKSHEET Reading Essentials and Study Guide**—Students complete the study guide and answer Reading Progress Check and vocabulary questions.

■ Critical Thinking Skills

☐ **WORKSHEET Gender and Wage Inequality Animation Activity**—Students answer questions about labor milestones (1912: Massachusetts minimum wage laws; 1923: Supreme Court ruling in Adkins v. Children's Hospital; 1938: the Fair Labor Standards Act; 1963: The Equal Pay Act; 1978: amendment to the Civil Rights Act protects women from job loss due to pregnancy; 2009: the Lily Ledbetter Fair Pay Restoration Act) for women. **Verbal/Linguistic**

☐ **WORKSHEET Assessing Background Knowledge Activity**—Students should complete the Assessing Background Knowledge Activity before they study each chapter. Students' responses will give you a good idea of the kinds of misconceptions you can address when teaching the lessons.

☐ **WORKSHEET Chapter Summary**—Summaries are provided for each chapter and thoroughly condense core content into manageable chunks.

☐ **WORKSHEET Vocabulary Activity**—Students apply their knowledge of content and academic vocabulary words.

UNIT 3
Business and Labor

CHAPTER 8
Business Organizations

ESSENTIAL QUESTIONS
How are businesses formed and how do they grow?

How does a market economy support nonprofit organizations?

CHAPTER 9
Labor and Wages

ESSENTIAL QUESTIONS
What features of the modern labor industry are the result of labor action?

What factors lead to higher wages for a worker?

WHY IT MATTERS BECAUSE ...

You may have seen the topics of labor markets, jobs reports, and employment data reported in the news. The state of the U.S. labor force is intricately related to our economy. In fact, job creators, business owners, and economists all use reports about these topics to assess the state of our economy. Understanding our labor force's historic, current, and future response to wages, and thus spending, is an important part of the American business and financial systems, and to your life as you begin to earn income.

ANIMATIONS | **WORKSHEET**

Gender and Wage Inequality

Analyzing the animation Ask students to describe their ideas of what job conditions might have been like for a working woman in the United States at the beginning of the twentieth century. Then show students the animation. Ask students to define the term *milestone*. *(an important event during a period of time)* Explain to students that the animation uses significant U.S. labor law milestones through history as its organizing structure. After students view the animation, invite them to describe specific examples of how labor laws at the time might have affected working women in 1925, 1950, 1975, 2000, and also in the present day.

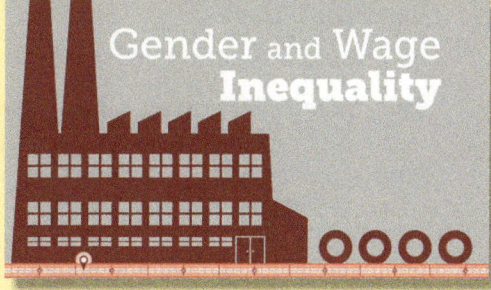

UNIT 3
Business and Labor

ENGAGE

 Researching state and national occupation and wage data Tell students that in Unit 3, they will learn about different types of businesses, jobs, and wages. Give each student an index card. On the top line, have students write a career title they are considering. Below the title, draw a vertical line down the center of the card. Have students visit the Bureau of Labor Statistics (http://stats.bls.gov/oes/current/oes_nat.htm) and click on the selected career. Have students label the left side of the card "National" and write the number of American workers in the occupation and the mean annual wage for the occupation.

Students can also find *state* information at the Bureau of Labor Statistics (http://stats.bls.gov/oes/current/oessrcst.htm). Students may select their state and the occupation. Have students label the right column of their card as "State" and write the number of state workers in the occupation and the mean annual wage. Have students compare the national and state average wages for the career. **Logical/Mathematical**

Evaluating current economic issues Have each student list what he or she thinks are the three most controversial topics in economics today. Call on volunteers to share their lists with the class, noting new issues on the board as they are offered. Invite each student to explain their point of view as they read each topic on their lists. Circle topics such as employment, labor unions, the minimum wage, pay equity, business growth, determining fair wages, and so on. Then point out that the circled issues will be discussed at some length in Unit 3. **Interpersonal**

Exploring U.S. labor topics Have students work in groups of five to prepare a two-minute newscast on labor in the United States. Some students might act as reporters, others might play experts or "people on the street," and still others might take the role of news anchors. Suggest that students incorporate charts to illustrate topics such as changes in the labor force, average wages over the years, union membership, and so on. Then allow time in class for groups to "broadcast" their news programs. **BL**

UNIT 3
Business and Labor

DEVELOP YOUR SKILLS ONLINE

Evaluating Information and Making Inferences

Remind students that when they are reading point-of-view text such as the Case Study features, they will need to evaluate what they are reading and then "read between the lines," or use clues to figure out something that is not stated directly in the text. Help students develop and practice the skills of evaluating information and making inferences.

When evaluating information to determine its reliability, tell students to ask themselves the following questions as they read:

- Is there bias? In other words, does the source unfairly present just one point of view, ignoring any arguments against it?
- Is the information published in a credible, reliable publication?
- Is the author or speaker identified? Is he or she an authority on the subject?
- Is the information up-to-date?
- Is the information backed by facts and other sources? Does it seem to be accurate?
- Is it well-written and well-edited? Writing that has errors in spelling, grammar, and punctuation is likely to be careless in other ways as well.

After students have finished reading text from a lesson or feature, have them follow these steps to make inferences:

- Read carefully for stated facts and ideas.
- Summarize the information and list important facts.
- Consider information that might be missing, and ask why.
- Apply related information that they may already know.
- Use their knowledge and insight to develop some logical conclusions.

Develop your Skills Online

Attribute Ideas and Information to Source Materials and Authors

The subject of economics is full of data, much of it numerical and statistical. But the interpretation of that data is what keeps the subject fresh and new for students and for each real-world circumstance. A good student understands the necessity of carefully studying the work of other researchers. And students must learn how to give credit to authors as part of the research process. In this way, other students can evaluate the research conducted and verify it. Attributing information to your sources also maintains honesty in the scientific process.

Each chapter has a Case Study asset with information on a chapter-specific topic. The content of this asset is chosen from select sources and authors.

Click through the Case Study asset to examine the Introduction and the source materials chosen for each topic.

Case Study assets provide information in text or visual form. Examine each source carefully so that you understand the ideas presented within.

Use the note-taking pane to help you attribute the ideas and information presented in the asset. You may cut and paste from the sources or type your own notes.

Each Case Study asset also gives you assessment questions to evaluate for each content topic.

Find all your interactive resources for each chapter online.

Chapter 8 Business Organizations

Chapter 9 Labor and Wages

Online Teaching Options

INTERACTIVE FEATURE

SAMPLE Case Study: Homestead Strike

Sequencing events in the Homestead Strike Have students read about the Homestead Strike. Draw a time line on the board and, as students call out events of the strike, place them in order on the time line. Then view and discuss the feature as a class, inviting students to describe what they see in the images and relate them to the sequence of events. Draw a three-column chart on the board with the headings "Management," "Strikers," and "Government." Create two rows: "Right" and "Wrong." Have students decide which actions on the part of each of the three participants involved were right and which were wrong. In cases of disagreement, have students support their viewpoints. Finally, have students determine, if possible, whether the outcome was a positive or a negative one and why. **Verbal/Linguistic**

CHAPTER 8
Business Organization Planner

UNDERSTANDING BY DESIGN®

Enduring Understanding
- Individuals and groups work independently and cooperatively to achieve goals.

Essential Questions
- How are businesses formed and how do they grow?

Predictable Misunderstandings
Students may think:
- *Sole proprietors are not responsible for financial risk if the business fails.* Explain that sole proprietors are personally responsible for their business debts. If the business fails and leaves behind large debts, the sole proprietor's personal possessions can be liquidated to pay the debts.
- *Stockholders in a corporation do not have to pay individual income tax on their profits.* Explain that corporate profits are actually taxed twice. The corporation itself pays tax on the profits. Then the stockholders pay tax on their dividends, which counts as personal income.

Assessment Evidence
Performance Task
- Hands-On Chapter Project with Technology Extension

Other Evidence
- Guided Reading Activities
- Vocabulary Activity
- Lesson Quizzes
- Self-Check Quizzes
- Chapter Assessment
- Chapter Tests, Forms A and B

SUGGESTED PACING

Introducing the Chapter . . . . . . ½ Day	Debate . . . . ½ Day
Lesson 1: Forms of Business Organization . . . . 1 Day	Lesson 3: Nonprofit Organizations . . . . 1 Day
Case Study . . . . ½ Day	Study Guide, Chapter Assessment, and Wrap-Up. . . . . . ½ Day
Lesson 2: Business Growth and Expansion . . . . 1 Day	

TOTAL 5 Days

Key for Using the Teacher Edition

SKILL-BASED ACTIVITIES
Types of skill activites found in the Teacher Edition.

V Visual Skills require students to analyze maps, graphs, charts, and photos.

R Reading Skills help students practice reading skills and master vocabulary.

C Critical Thinking Skills help students apply and extend what they have learned.

W Writing Skills provide writing opportunities to help students comprehend the text.

T Technology Skills require students to use digital tools effectively.

*Letters are followed by a number when there is more than one of the same type of skill on the page.

DIFFERENTIATED INSTRUCTION
All activities are written for the on-level student unless otherwise marked with the leveled labels below.

BL Beyond Level
AL Approaching Level
ELL English Language Learners

All students benefit from activities that utilize different learning styles. Many activities are marked as below when a particular learning style is highlighted.

Intrapersonal
Logical/Mathematical
Visual/Spatial
Verbal/Linguistic
Naturalist
Kinesthetic
Auditory/Musical
Interpersonal

Council for Economic Education

Below are the Council for Economic Education Voluntary National Content Standards in Economics covered in the *Business Organization* chapter.

Content Standard 10: Institutions evolve and are created to help individuals and groups accomplish their goals. Banks, labor unions, markets, corporations, legal systems, and not-for-profit organizations are examples of important institutions. A different kind of institution, clearly defined and enforced property rights, is essential to a market economy.

CHAPTER 8: BUSINESS ORGANIZATION

CHAPTER OPENER PLANNER

Students will know:
- the characteristics, advantages, and disadvantages of sole proprietorships, partnerships, and corporations in the United States economy.
- investing in new physical or human capital can increase future productivity and consumption.
- economic institutions, such as labor unions, nonprofit organizations and cooperatives, evolve in market economies to help members and clients accomplish their goals.

Students will be able to:
- **describe** how various types of businesses are formed and how they grow.
- **discuss** the advantages and disadvantages of sole proprietorships, partnerships, corporations, and franchises.
- **summarize** the advantages companies gain by merging with other companies.
- **explain** why the values of nonprofit organizations and cooperatives are difficult to analyze.

UNDERSTANDING BY DESIGN®

☑ Print Teaching Options

V Visual Skills
- ☐ **p. 210 Analyzing crowdfunding Web sites** Students assess crowdfunding presentations.

R Reading Skills
- ☐ **p. 210 Understanding business incubators** Students discuss what incubators provide.
- ☐ **p. 211 Analyzing venture capitalists and angel investors** Students describe their differences.

C Critical Thinking Skills
- ☐ **p. 209 Mom & Pop vs. Big Box** Students compare small businesses to superstores.
- ☐ **p. 211 Assessing motivations of entrepreneurs and investors** Students analyze factors that motivate people to start or invest in a businesses.

☑ Online Teaching Options

V Visual Skills
- ☐ IMAGES **Chapter opener**—Students look for clues about business organization.

C Critical Thinking Skills
- ☐ INFOGRAPHICS **Economic Perspectives**—Students discuss the four methods of raising capital for new businesses.
- ☐ DEBATES Is it ethical for businesses to outsource jobs to foreign countries when there is high unemployment in the United States?
- ☐ INTERACTIVE FEATURE **Case Study: Powder Pollution**—Students analyze how a factory was stopped from polluting.

☑ Printable Digital Worksheets

C Critical Thinking Skills
- ☐ WORKSHEET **Economic Simulation**—Students calculate a hypothetical start-up.
- ☐ WORKSHEET **Personal Finance Activity**—Students interpret a graph about stocks.
- ☐ WORKSHEET **Enrichment Activity**—Students read about stockholders.

Project-Based Learning

Hands-On

Hands-On Chapter Project
In this activity, students work in groups, each of which is starting a business with a different structure (sole proprietorship, partnership, corporation). Students outline the organizational structure of their business and thus create a kind of informal business plan. Each organizational structure and business plan should follow the structure of that group's particular business type.

Digital Hands-On

Create Online Projects

Find an additional activity online that incorporates technology for the Hands-On Project. Visit the EdTech Teacher Web sites for more links, tutorials, and other resources.

Print Resources

ANCILLARY RESOURCE
This ancillary is available for every chapter and lesson.
- Chapter Tests and Lesson Quizzes

PRINTABLE DIGITAL WORKSHEETS
These printable digital worksheets are available for every chapter and lesson.
- Reading Essentials & Study Guide
- Vocabulary Activities
- Chapter Summaries
- Economic Simulations
- Math Practice for Economics
- Reinforcing Economic Skills
- Personal Finance Activities
- Enrichment Activities
- Reteaching Activities
- Guided Reading Activities
- Video Worksheets
- Lesson Quizzes and Chapter Tests (English and Spanish)

More Media Resources

SUGGESTED READING
- For students at a Grade 10 reading level: *Top Entrepreneurs and Their Businesses*, by Robert B. Pile
- For students at a Grade 11 reading level: *Be Your Own Boss: Small Businesses*, by Ernestine Glesecke
- For students at a Grade 12 reading level: *Business Builders in Cosmetics*, by Jacqueline C. Kent

SUGGESTED VIDEOS MOVIES
Find these documentaries yourself online. NOTE: McGraw-Hill Education does not endorse these resources. Preview clips for age-appropriateness.
- *Design the New Business* (40 min.)
- *China or Bust* (50 min.)

LESSON 1 Planner

FORMS OF BUSINESS ORGANIZATION

Students will know:
- the characteristics, advantages, and disadvantages of sole proprietorships, partnerships, and corporations in the United States economy.
- incorporation allows firms to accumulate sufficient financial capital to make large-scale investments and achieve economies of scale. Incorporation also reduces the risk to investors by limiting stockholders' liability to their share of ownership of the corporation.

Students will be able to:
- **describe** how various types of businesses are formed and how they grow.
- **discuss** the advantages and disadvantages of sole proprietorships, partnerships, corporations, and franchises.

UNDERSTANDING BY DESIGN®

☑ Print Teaching Options

R Reading Skills

- ☐ **p. 212 Using context clues** Students define *sole proprietorship.*
- ☐ **p. 217 Defining corporate terms** Students explain a dividend and a stockholder.
- ☐ **p. 218 Corporate Regulation** Students research muckraking journalists' exposés.
- ☐ **p. 219 Analyzing disadvantages of corporations**
- ☐ **p. 220 Discovering the many types of franchises**

C Critical Thinking Skills

- ☐ **p. 212 Comparing proprietorships and partnerships**
- ☐ **p. 213 Recognizing qualities of sole proprietorships**
- ☐ **p. 214 Balancing costs and revenue through inventory** Students discuss how sole proprietors make a profit. *Logical/Mathematical*
- ☐ **p. 215 Identifying valuable partnership qualities**
- ☐ **p. 216 Forming a faux partnership** Students draw up an agreement for a partnership.
- ☐ **p. 217 Sequencing steps to incorporation**
- ☐ **p. 220 Documenting and debating franchises' effects on small businesses** Students note the effects franchises have on "mom & pop" stores.
- ☐ **p. 220 Franchises in the United States** Students discuss the growth of franchising.

W Writing Skills

- ☐ **p. 213 Writing a business narrative** Students write about starting a business. *Verbal/Linguistic*
- ☐ **p. 215 Understanding partnership disadvantages**
- ☐ **p. 219 Researching and writing about types of corporations**

☑ Online Teaching Options

V Visual Skills

- ☐ **GRAPH Analyzing Pie Charts**—Students identify the number, sales, and net income for each business type. *Logical/Mathematical*
- ☐ **GRAPH The Corporate Structure**—Students discuss corporate hierarchy.
- ☐ **GRAPH Stock Ownership**—Students identify characteristics of corporations.
- ☐ **VIDEO Branding Ford**—Students draw conclusions about the effects of using recognizable brand names. *Logical, Linguistic*

R Reading Skills

- ☐ **GRAPHIC ORGANIZER Forms of Business Organizations**—Students describe characteristics, advantages, and disadvantages of business organizations.
- ☐ **GRAPHIC ORGANIZER Concept Web**—Students list details about a partnership.

C Critical Thinking Skills

- ☐ **BELLRINGER Forms of Business Organization**—Students discuss the costs, risks, and benefits of running a franchise.
- ☐ **ESSENTIAL QUESTION Exploring the Essential Question**—Students compare the benefits and disadvantages of a sole proprietorship with those of a partnership.
- ☐ **INTERACTIVE FEATURE Careers: Corporate Auditor**—Students discuss whether they are interested in this career.

T Technology Skills

- ☐ **SELF-CHECK QUIZ Lesson 1**—Students receive instant feedback on their mastery of lesson content.
- ☐ **GAME Lesson 1**—Students solve clues to review lesson content.
- ☐ **INTERACTIVE WHITEBOARD ACTIVITY Business Types: Advantages and Disadvantages**—Students work together to learn lesson content.

☑ Printable Digital Worksheets

R Reading Skills

- ☐ **WORKSHEET Guided Reading Activity**—Students use the Guided Reading Activity worksheets to review their comprehension of the content.
- ☐ **WORKSHEET Reading Essentials and Study Guide**—Students complete the study guide and answer Reading Progress Check and vocabulary questions.

C Critical Thinking Skills

- ☐ **WORKSHEET Branding Ford Video Activity**—Students answer questions about Ford's branding of its cars.

LESSON 2 Planner

BUSINESS GROWTH AND EXPANSION

Students will know:
- business owners can use their profits to update and expand their firms.
- mergers allow firms to quickly grow in size.
- investing in new physical or human capital can increase future productivity and consumption, but such investments require the sacrifice of current consumption and entail economic risks.

Students will be able to:
- *explain* why many business owners choose to reinvest their profits.
- *summarize* the advantages companies gain by merging with other companies.
- *identify* ways new businesses can find start-up funds.

UNDERSTANDING BY DESIGN®

☑ Print Teaching Options

V Visual Skills
- ☐ p. 229 **Launching a start-up** Students create a poster about a start-up and its funding.

R Reading Skills
- ☐ p. 224 **Understanding business choices** Students discuss a business's cash flow.
- ☐ p. 224 **Researching a reinvesting business**
- ☐ p. 225 **Considering Hayek's views** Students review Friedrich Hayek's principles.
- ☐ p. 226 **Understanding conglomerate motives**
- ☐ p. 226 **Contrasting conglomerates and multinationals**

C Critical Thinking Skills
- ☐ p. 223 **Making decisions about how to grow your business**
- ☐ p. 223 **Applying depreciation**
- ☐ p. 224 **Writing about wise reinvestment** Students write guidelines for reinvesting profits.
- ☐ p. 225 **Evaluating types of mergers** Students find a vertical and horizontal merger.
- ☐ p. 226 **Justifying a merger** Students discuss whether two stores should merge.
- ☐ p. 226 **Appreciating merger issues**

W Writing Skills
- ☐ p. 225 **Writing about a proposed merger**
- ☐ p. 227 **Identifying advantages and disadvantages of multinationals**
- ☐ p. 228 **Making your case for funding**
- ☐ p. 228 **Researching incubators, venture capitalists, and angel investors**

T Technology Skills
- ☐ p. 228 **Researching government involvement in start-up funding**

☑ Online Teaching Options

V Visual Skills
- ☐ **GRAPH** **Growth Through Reinvestment**—Students consider the process of growth through reinvestment.
- ☐ **CHART** **Types of Mergers**—Students explain the difference between two types of mergers. **Verbal/Linguistic**
- ☐ **VIDEO** **Cadbury**—Students view a video about Cadbury's merger with Kraft.

R Reading Skills
- ☐ **GRAPHIC ORGANIZER** **Models for Business Growth**—Students complete information about mergers and reinvestment.
- ☐ **INTERACTIVE WHITEBOARD ACTIVITY** **Investment Options**—Students analyze investment options.
- ☐ **BIOGRAPHY** **Friedrich August von Hayek**—Students summarize Friedrich August von Hayek's economic ideas.

C Critical Thinking Skills
- ☐ **BELLRINGER** **Business Growth and Expansion**—Students discuss why two companies might decide to merge.
- ☐ **ESSENTIAL QUESTION** **Exploring the Essential Question**—Students show the advantages and disadvantages of merging or expanding.

T Technology Skills
- ☐ **SELF-CHECK QUIZ** **Lesson 2**—Students receive instant feedback on their mastery of lesson content.
- ☐ **GAME** **Lesson 2**—Students solve clues to review lesson content.
- ☐ **INTERACTIVE WHITEBOARD ACTIVITY** **Investment Options**—Students work together to learn lesson content.

☑ Printable Digital Worksheets

R Reading Thinking SKILLS
- ☐ **WORKSHEET** **Guided Reading Activity**—Students use the Guided Reading Activity worksheets to review their comprehension of the content.
- ☐ **WORKSHEET** **Reading Essentials and Study Guide**—Students complete the study guide and answer Reading Progress Check and vocabulary questions.

C Creative Thinking SKILLS
- ☐ **WORKSHEET** **Cadbury Video Activity**—Students answer questions about Cadbury's takeover by Kraft.

LESSON 3 Planner

NONPROFIT ORGANIZATIONS

Students will know:
- labor unions, nonprofit organizations and cooperatives evolve to help members and clients accomplish their goals.
- decision-making in small and large firms, labor unions, educational institutions, and not-for-profit organizations has different goals and faces different rules and constraints.
- the government provides some goods and services while helping to make sure the economy runs smoothly.

Students will be able to:
- *explain* why the values of nonprofit organizations and cooperatives are difficult to analyze.
- *categorize* cooperatives according to their purpose.
- *discuss* the purpose of labor unions.
- *describe* the activities of professional associations and business associations.

UNDERSTANDING BY DESIGN®

☑ Print Teaching Options

R Reading Skills

☐ **p. 233 Identifying types of cooperatives** Students discuss how and why cooperatives help members.

☐ **p. 237 Summarizing the lesson** Students summarize the roles of nonprofits.

C Critical Thinking Skills

☐ **p. 232 Identifying nonprofit organizations** Students describe why service organizations are important and funded.

☐ **p. 233 Evaluating cooperatives' usefulness** Students identifying needs and interests served by a new cooperative.

☐ **p. 235 Analyzing the Better Business Bureau** Students identifies information that a local BBB provides to help them make good consumer decisions.

☐ **p. 236 Categorizing roles of government** Students identify the direct and indirect roles of government.

☐ **p. 236 Explaining and defending a point of view** Students debate the effect on those who receive government payments.

W Writing Skills

☐ **p. 234 Learning about professional associations** Students write a brochure about a professional or business association.
Interpersonal

T Technology Skills

☐ **p. 233 Comparing credit unions and commercial banks** Students research a local or state credit union and a national commercial bank.

☑ Online Teaching Options

V Visual Skills

☐ **POLITICAL CARTOON** **Credit Unions and Banks**—Students discuss advantages and disadvantages for the owners and customers of credit unions and banks.

☐ **VIDEO** **Ithaca Promotes Currency**—Students view how using a local currency helped local businesses.

R Reading Skills

☐ **GRAPHIC ORGANIZER** **Types of Nonprofit Organizations**—Students summarize the benefits of various nonprofit organizations.

C Critical Thinking Skills

☐ **BELLRINGER** **Nonprofit Organizations**—Students discuss working conditions before nonprofit labor unions formed.

☐ **ESSENTIAL QUESTION** **Exploring the Essential Question**—Student discuss nonprofit issues.

T Technology Skills

☐ **SELF-CHECK QUIZ** **Lesson 3**—Students receive instant feedback on their mastery of lesson content.

☐ **GAME** **Lesson 3**—Students solve clues to review lesson content.

☐ **INTERACTIVE WHITEBOARD ACTIVITY** **Government as a Nonprofit Organization**—Students work together to learn lesson content.

☑ Printable Digital Worksheets

R Reading Skills

☐ **WORKSHEET** **Guided Reading Activity**—Students use the Guided Reading Activity worksheets to review their comprehension of the content.

☐ **WORKSHEET** **Reading Essentials and Study Guide**—Students complete the study guide and answer Reading Progress Check and vocabulary questions.

☐ **WORKSHEET** **Reteaching Activity**—Students use this activity worksheet to review and reteach chapter content and vocabulary. This worksheet can be used with struggling students who need additional help with difficult content concepts.

C Critical Thinking Skills

☐ **WORKSHEET** **Ithaca Promotes Currency Video Activity**—Students draw conclusions about the shop-local program in Ithaca.

CHAPTER 8 Business Organization
INTERVENTION AND REMEDIATION STRATEGIES

LESSON 1 Forms of Business Organization

Reading and Comprehension

Have students reread lesson 1 and create an outline of the information they read in this lesson. Ensure that students use correct outline form and that they have understood what they read by including the main points in their outlines. Students may share their outlines with each other.

Text Evidence

Review with students the concept of liability—or the risk the business owner assumes for the debts and damages that may occur because of the business. Have students find evidence in the text that describes the degree of liability for each type of business structure described. Once they have found the textual evidence, have them make a list in which they organize each business type from greatest personal liability for the owner (at the top) to least liability (at the bottom).

LESSON 2 Business Growth and Expansion

Reading and Comprehension

Have students reread the lesson section about mergers. Then have them create a chart, with a business they would like to own in the center circle. Have them draw lines from this center circle to other boxes or circles in which they describe other businesses that their business might merge with in order to grow and expand. Students should explain why and how the newly acquired business would improve the original business's profits and competitiveness.

Text Evidence

Review with students the concept of cash flow and its relation to profits. Have students find the part of the text that explain how cash flow can be used for reinvestment. Encourage students to explain how they would reinvest cash flow to expand a business they would like to own some day.

LESSON 3 Nonprofit Organizations

Reading and Comprehension

Review the concept of nonprofit organizations with students, and have them read the introductory paragraphs that explain them. Encourage students to describe some nonprofit organizations they know about that exist in their city or town. These may be business or professional organizations, as well as charitable organizations. Encourage students to think of a social need in their community and have them describe the type of nonprofit organization they might start to help address this need. Students may consult the text to familiarize themselves with types of nonprofits so they can decide which type would work best.

Text Evidence

Ask: Why would workers take money from their paycheck to pay dues to a labor union? *(Sample answer: Because labor unions represent worker interests with management.)* Have students find the section of the text that describes the functions of labor unions. Have students write a short paragraph or make a list of the benefits workers derive from being members of a labor union.

Online Resources

Assessing Background Knowledge Use this worksheet to pre-assess students' background knowledge before they start the chapter.

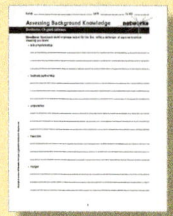

Chapter Summaries Have students use the summary as a pre-reading activity or as a post-reading review to check the main ideas covered in each lesson.

Guided Reading Activities Have students complete these activities as they read each lesson. They provide reading notes the student can use for review and to prepare for assessments.

Reteaching Activities Have students complete the Reteaching Activity for remedial practice and review of vital content.

Self-Check Quizzes These quizzes provide instant feedback on areas the students may need to re-read to understand a main idea.

Reading Essentials and Study Guide This resource offers writing and reading activities for the approaching-level student.

Approaching Grade Level Reader This reader presents all of the content of the Online Student Edition but at a lower reading level.

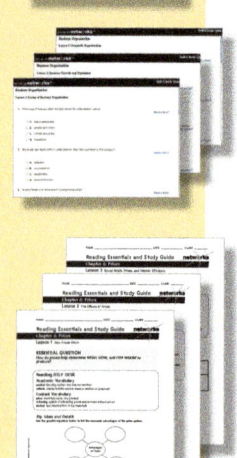

English Language Learner Reader Provide additional reading support for ELL students. Find this tool online.

Business Organization

ESSENTIAL QUESTIONS
- How are businesses formed and how do they grow?
- How does a market economy support nonprofit organizations?

networks
www.connected.mcgraw-hill.com
There's More Online about business organization.

CHAPTER 8

Economic Perspectives
Bankrolling Start-Ups

Lesson 1
Forms of Business Organization

Lesson 2
Business Growth and Expansion

Lesson 3
Nonprofit Organizations

Letter from the Author
Dear Economics Teacher,

We've talked a lot about producers, but the discussion has usually been in the abstract. This now changes as we examine how firms are structured and how they operate. This topic of business organizations will be important for students, because at some time in their future they will likely be working for one. The topic will also be important when students become investors, because they will want to know as much as they can about the companies that are using their investment dollars. Knowing in advance how a business operates and what it thinks is important will help students make better sense of the many business decisions they will encounter.

CHAPTER 8
Business Organization

ENGAGE

Call students' attention to the photo and ask them to describe what it shows. Guide them to recognize that it shows a man and possibly his son in a small grocery store. **Ask: What relationship do you think these two people have to this store?** *(Sample answer: They probably own this store, as the store appears to be a small, family-owned one and not a mega-store.)* **What type of business structure—a sole proprietorship or a corporation—do you think this business has? Why?** *(Sample answer: It is probably a sole proprietorship owned by the man in the apron. Sole proprietorships are the most common form of business structure for family)*

Distinguishing small and large businesses Have students use Internet or other sources to find photos of large, corporate supermarkets, especially interior views that can be compared to the chapter opening photograph. Encourage students to describe the look of the supermarket and to distinguish its features from those shown in the photo of the family-owned grocery. Have students discuss the benefits to consumers and communities of each type of business structure. **Visual/Spatial**

Making Connections

Mom & Pop vs. Big Box Encourage students to express their point of view regarding the advantages and disadvantages of small, local, family-owned businesses, such as groceries, pharmacies, and other specialty shops. Bring up personal service, personalized (even homemade) goods, and keeping money earned by the community *in* the community. Explain that superstores are most often headquartered outside the community, so nearly all the money spent in the store leaves the community.

Go to the Foldables® library for a cumulative chapter-based Foldable® activity that your students can use to help take notes and prepare for assessment.

CHAPTER 8
Economic Perspectives

TEACH & ASSESS

R Reading Skills

Understanding business incubators Ask: **Who establishes business incubators?** *(local governments, universities)* **What do incubators provide to entrepreneurs?** *(training, advocacy, support, resources, capital and/or connections to capital)* **Verbal/Linguistic**

V Visual Skills

Analyzing crowdfunding Web sites Have students find and evaluate crowdfunding presentations on one or more Web sites. Have them assess those sites they think are most effective in terms of the way they are worded, the way the text is presented, the way visuals are used, and so on. Have them discuss or list the common characteristics of effective advertising and effective crowdfunding presentations. **Verbal/Linguistic**

Economic Perspectives

BANKROLLING START-UPS

R

Incubators
Business incubators are organizations established by local governments or universities. Incubators give entrepreneurs training, advocacy, and support and resources to help launch businesses. Incubators may also have capital to invest or can provide connections to potential funding sources. Some incubators are called accelerators, which focus on speeding the growth of developed businesses.

According to one source—
Over **182** "accelerators" around the world have nurtured more than **3,000** start-up companies.

V

Crowdfunding
This new funding method gets small contributions from a large "crowd" of individuals. Crowdfunding is typically done on the Web, where investors can give to an online Web site. Crowdfunding lends itself well to short-term, project-oriented campaigns.

By 2013, crowdfunding campaigns around the world were expected to raise a total of **$5.1 billion**.

STARTUP, INC.

---

networks Online Teaching Options

INFOGRAPHIC

Economic Perspectives: Bankrolling Start-Ups

Understanding various methods of bankrolling start-ups Have students view the infographic and help them identify the four methods of raising capital for new businesses. Invite volunteers to read the explanation of each: incubators, crowdfunding, venture capitalists, and angel investors. Discuss the factoids that accompany each description, and invite students to differentiate among the methods of bankrolling. **Visual/Spatial, Verbal/Linguistic**

CHAPTER 8
Economic Perspectives

networks TRY IT YOURSELF ONLINE
For an interactive version of this infographic go to connected.mcgraw-hill.com

Small businesses are the heart and soul of the American economy. In 2013, the U.S. featured almost 28 million small businesses (those employing less than 500 people). This accounted for over half of all workers. Starting a business takes money and depending on the business' needs, entrepreneurs use different methods to raise the funds to get their business running.

Venture Capitalists
These financiers use managed pools of funds to aid new business ventures that seem profitable. Venture capitalists typically require entrepreneurs to present a proposal for funding. In return for their investment, venture capitalists get a portion of the business revenues. These investors also have a hand in company decisions. Venture capitalists may also assist in the company's initial public offering (IPO) to gather public sale of stock.

In 2010, **11%** of private sector jobs in the U.S. were at venture-backed companies. Venture capital-backed firms generated revenue that was equivalent to **21%** of U.S. GDP.

Angel Investors
These are wealthy individuals who fund start-up companies. Angel investors differ from venture capitalists because they invest their own money and are driven by motives beyond financial returns. Angel investors often help develop the new business and stay connected to them. A group of angel investors pooling their resources are called angel networks or angel groups.

In 2011, **12.2%** of angels were women but by 2012, that number was nearly double at **21%**.

THINK ABOUT IT!
If you were starting a new business, which method would you use to raise capital to fund your venture? Why?

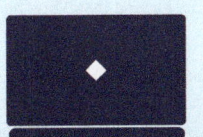

Business Organization **211**

C Critical Thinking Skills

Assessing motivations of entrepreneurs and investors Encourage students to think about and discuss the notion that only money motivates a person to start a business or invest in a business. Ask students to suggest other motivations for starting and investing in business. Students may describe other factors—such as personal satisfaction, being one's own boss, expressing one's creativity, being part of a new wave of innovation—as being the major motivator. **AL** Intrapersonal

R Reading Skills

Analyzing venture capitalists and angel investors
Ask: **What are venture capitalists?** *(financiers who use managed pools of funds to aid new potentially profitable business ventures)* **What do venture capitalists receive in exchange for their investment?** *(a portion of the business's revenues and involvement in company decisions)* **How do angel investors differ from venture capitalists?** *(Angel investors are wealthy individuals who fund start-up companies with their own money, not by pooling funds with others. They are motivated beyond financial returns.)* Verbal/Linguistic

T Technology Skills

Researching angel investors Have students key "angel investor" into a search engine. Ask students to select a Web site and write a summary of information found on it. Verbal/Linguistic

CLOSE & REFLECT

Have students answer the *Think About It!* questions.

WORKSHEET

Economic Simulation

Understanding crowdfunding Have students define the concept of crowdfunding (*a means of using the Internet to raise funds to start or expand a small business*) and how it can be used by individuals and small groups to raise money for a start-up company. Assign the simulation and monitor groups as they calculate how much money they need to raise, making sure they include all possible expenses in their business plan. They should also deduct from the investment amount any funds they or their friends or relatives will contribute to the start-up. After groups have created the online presentation of text and visuals for their hypothetical start-up, have them share it with the class. Ask for suggestions that might make each presentation more appealing to the investing public. Visual/Spatial, Verbal/Linguistic

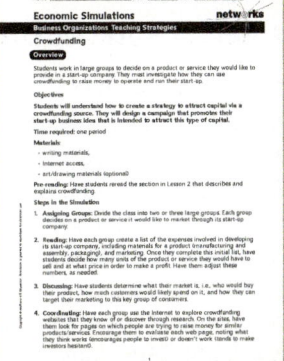

ANSWERS, p. 211

THINK ABOUT IT!

Answers will vary. Require students to include reasons and evidence for their decisions.

Business Organization **211**

CHAPTER 8, LESSON 1
Forms of Business Organization

ENGAGE

C Critical Thinking Skills

Comparing proprietorships and partnerships Before students begin the lesson, ask if any have ever operated a sole proprietorship or partnership. Prompt them with examples: lemonade stand, lawn-mowing business, babysitting service. Have students explain why the sole proprietorship type of business organization is best for an informal business. Using the lemonade stand as an example, have students discuss the advantages and disadvantages of running a business on your own (sole proprietorship) or with a friend as a business partner (partnership). **AL Verbal/Linguistic**

TEACH & ASSESS

R Reading Skills

Using context clues Tell students that the word *sole* in the term *sole proprietorship* is an adjective than means "one and only" or "single." **Ask: What are other terms that use sole as an adjective?** *(Possible answers: sole ownership, sole survivor, sole heir)*

ANSWERS, p. 212

ESSENTIAL QUESTION ACTIVITY

Sole Benefits: ease of startup, owner keeps all profits. Drawbacks: unlimited liability, difficulty of raising capital. Partnership: ease of startup and attracting capital. Cons include potential conflicts among partners and limited life.
TAKING NOTES: **Sole proprietorship** Formed: single individual. Grows: adding a small number of employees. Adv: easy to set up; management is simple; owner keeps all profits. Disadv: unlimited liability; hard to raise capital; difficult to carry enough inventory. **Partnership** Formed: legal agreement between partners. Grows: adding partners. Adv: ease of startup, easier to attract capital. Disadv: responsible for other partners' actions; potential conflicts among partners; limited life. **Corporation** Formed: charter. Grows: sale of stock or issue of bonds. Adv: easier to raise capital; limited liability; unlimited life. Disadv: double taxation; charters expensive; owners have little voice. **Franchise** Formed: franchisee leases from a franchisor. Grows: add new customers. Adv: known product line; national advertising; professional advice. Disadv: initial high cost; must be renewed; no ownership at end of franchise agreement

---

Interact with these digital assets and others in lesson 1
- ✓ INTERACTIVE GRAPH Stock Ownership
- ✓ INTERACTIVE GRAPH Corporate Structure
- ✓ SELF-CHECK QUIZ
- ✓ VIDEO

networks TRY IT YOURSELF ONLINE

LESSON 1
Forms of Business Organization

ESSENTIAL QUESTION

How are businesses formed and how do they grow?

There are three main forms of business organization in the economy today—the sole proprietorship, the partnership, and the corporation. A hybrid form of business called the franchise is also popular and combines investment opportunities with ownership. Each offers its owners significant advantages and disadvantages.

C Samantha sells homemade cupcakes on the sidewalk in front of her house as a sole proprietor. She does all the work, makes all the sales, and keeps all the profits. If she instead makes and sells cupcakes with her best friend and if they share the profits from the cupcakes business, they would be operating as a partnership.

Write a paragraph outlining the benefits and drawbacks Samantha faces as a sole proprietor and the pros and cons she'd encounter if she ran her cupcake business with her best friend, as a partnership.

Reading Help Desk

Academic Vocabulary
- comprise
- entity

Content Vocabulary
- sole proprietorship
- unlimited liability
- inventory
- limited life
- partnership
- general partnership
- limited partnership
- corporation
- charter
- stock
- stockholders
- dividend
- common stock
- preferred stock
- bond
- principal
- interest
- double taxation
- franchise
- franchisor
- franchisee

TAKING NOTES:

Key Ideas and Details
ACTIVITY Use the graphic organizer to show the different characteristics of the four types of business organizations.

Forms of Business Organizations

Business type	How It's formed	How It grows	Advantages	Disadvantages
Sole proprietorship				
Partnership				
Corporation				
Franchise				

Sole Proprietorships

GUIDING QUESTION What makes a sole proprietorship the easiest form of business to start?

R The most common form of business organization in the United States is the **sole proprietorship** or **proprietorship**—a business owned and run by a single individual. Because proprietorships are basically one-person operations, they **comprise** the smallest form of business. As **Figure 8.1** shows, they are also relatively profitable. While they only account for about 4 percent of total sales, they bring in about 16 percent of the total profits earned by all businesses.

Forming a Proprietorship

The sole proprietorship is the easiest form of business to start because it involves almost no requirements except for occasional business licenses and

212

---

networks Online Teaching Options

BELLRINGER

Forms of Business Organization

Evaluating franchises Write the following on the board and have students discuss the costs, risks, and benefits of running a franchise.
Start-Up Costs and Ongoing Fees: Total investment: $101,575–$338,075; Franchise fee: $35,000–$128,000; Ongoing royalty fee: $1.5K–12.5K/mo.; Term of franchise agreement: 10 years, renewable. **Financial Requirements:** Net worth: $500,000; Liquid cash available: $350,000. **Support:** Training: Available at headquarters: 3–5 days, At franchisee's location: 2 days. Ongoing support: Newsletter, meetings, Toll-free phone line, Grand opening, Internet, Field operations/evaluations, Purchasing cooperatives. Marketing support: Co-op advertising, Ad slicks, National media.

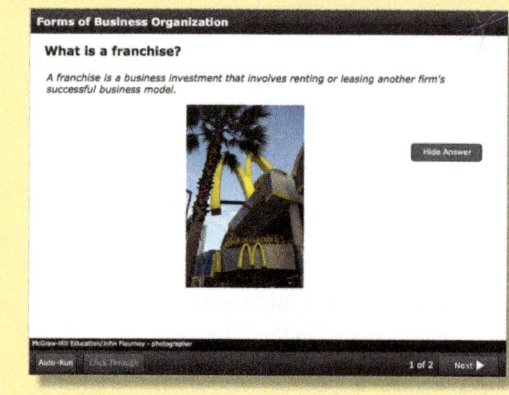

fees. Most proprietorships are ready for business as soon as they set up operations. You could start a proprietorship simply by putting up a lemonade stand in your front yard. Someone else could decide to mow lawns or open a restaurant. A proprietorship can be run on the Internet, out of a garage, or from an office in a professional building.

Advantages

As you have just learned, a sole proprietorship is easy to start up. If someone has an idea or an opportunity to make a profit, he or she only has to decide to go into business and then do it.

Ease of management, the second advantage, also is relatively simple. Decisions do not require the approval of a co-owner, boss, or other "higher-up." This flexibility means that the proprietor can make an immediate decision if a problem or opportunity comes up.

A third advantage is that the owner can keep the profits of successful management without having to share them with other owners. The owner also has to accept the possibility of a loss, but the lure of profits makes people willing to take risks.

Fourth, the proprietorship does not have to pay separate business income taxes because the business is not recognized as a separate legal **entity**. The owner still must pay individual income taxes on profits earned by the sole proprietorship, but the business itself is not taxed separately.

Suppose, for example, Mr. Winters owns and operates a small hardware store in a local shopping center and a small auto repair business in his garage next to his home. Because neither business depends on the other, and because the only thing they have in common is Mr. Winters's ownership, the two businesses are separate and distinct economic activities. For tax purposes, however, everything is lumped together at the end of the year. When Mr. Winters files his personal income taxes, the profits from both businesses are combined with any wages and salaries from other sources. He does not pay taxes on either of the businesses separately.

A fifth advantage of the proprietorship is the psychological satisfaction many people get from being their own bosses. These people often have a strong desire to see their name in print, have dreams of great wealth or community status, or simply want to make their mark in history.

A sixth advantage is that it is easy to get out of business. All the proprietor has to do is pay any outstanding bills and then stop offering goods or services for sale.

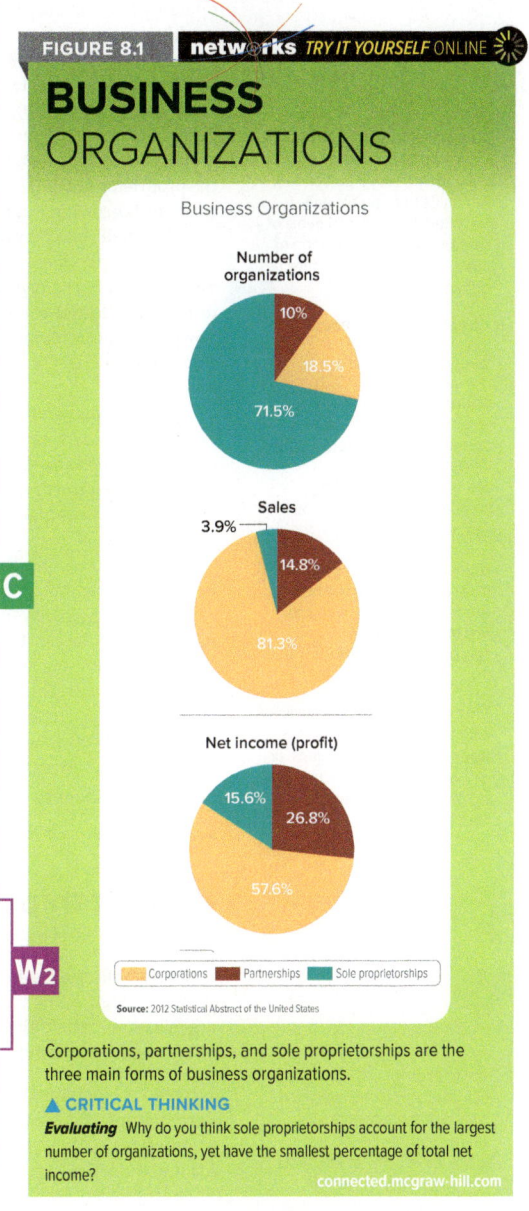

FIGURE 8.1

BUSINESS ORGANIZATIONS

Business Organizations

Number of organizations
- 10% Corporations
- 18.5% Partnerships
- 71.5% Sole proprietorships

Sales
- 3.9%
- 14.8%
- 81.3%

Net income (profit)
- 15.6%
- 26.8%
- 57.6%

Source: 2012 Statistical Abstract of the United States

Corporations, partnerships, and sole proprietorships are the three main forms of business organizations.

▲ **CRITICAL THINKING**
Evaluating Why do you think sole proprietorships account for the largest number of organizations, yet have the smallest percentage of total net income?

CHAPTER 8, LESSON 1
Forms of Business Organization

C Critical Thinking Skills

Balancing costs and revenue through inventory
Discuss the need for a sole proprietor, like any other business, to make a profit by balancing how much is spent on inventory, or products bought to sell to customers, and income, or how much money is made on these sales. Because of high personal risk, a sole proprietor must carefully calibrate how much money he or she spends on goods to have on hand to sell to customers. **Ask: Why might a sole proprietor not want to maintain a large inventory of parts, supplies, or products?** *(Students should recognize that the risk is too great that some of these products or supplies might not be sold, and then the sole proprietor would not have enough cash to pay the business's bills.)* **What are some other disadvantages of sole proprietorships?** *(owner has unlimited liability, hard to raise capital, and difficult to hire enough people)* **BL** Logical/Mathematical

English Language Proficiency

Beginning Pair students to study vocabulary used routinely in written materials about types of business organizations. Guide pairs as they make two sets of cards with vocabulary words you assign. One set will show the written words. The other set will have a picture or definition for each word. One partner is to hold up a word card and read the word aloud. The other partner will find the corresponding picture or definition card. When all cards have been matched, partners switch roles.

ANSWERS, p. 214

✓ **READING PROGRESS CHECK** A sole proprietor has total liability, or risk, for things that go wrong in the business, as well as having all the responsibilities and doing all the work without any help.

214

---

sole proprietorship unincorporated business owned and run by a single person who has rights to all profits and unlimited liability for all debts of the firm; most common form of business organization in the United States

comprise to be composed of

entity unit or being

unlimited liability requirement that an owner is personally and fully responsible for all losses and debts of a business; applies to proprietorships, and general partnerships

inventory stock of goods held in reserve; includes finished goods waiting to be sold and raw materials to be used in production

limited life situation in which a firm legally ceases to exist when an owner dies or quits, or a new owner is added; applies to sole proprietorships and partnerships

partnership unincorporated business owned and operated by two or more people who share the profits and have unlimited liability for the debts and obligations of the firm

Disadvantages

The main disadvantage of a proprietorship is that the owner of the business has **unlimited liability**. This means that the owner is personally and fully responsible for all losses and debts of the business. If the business fails, the owner's personal possessions may be taken away to satisfy business debts.

As an example, let us revisit the earlier case of Mr. Winters, who owns and operates two businesses. If the hardware business should fail, his personal wealth, which includes the automobile repair shop, may be legally taken away to pay off debts arising from the hardware store.

A second disadvantage of a proprietorship is the difficulty of raising financial capital. Generally, a large amount of money is needed to set up a business, and even more may be required for its expansion. However, banks and other lenders are often reluctant to lend money to new or very small businesses. As a result, the proprietor often has to raise financial capital by tapping savings, using credit cards, or borrowing from friends and family.

The small size of a proprietorship can also be a disadvantage. A retail store, for example, may need to hire several employees just to stay open during normal business hours. It may also have to carry a minimum **inventory**—a stock of finished goods and parts in reserve—to satisfy customers or to keep production flowing smoothly. Because of limited financial capital, the proprietor may not be able to hire enough personnel or stock enough inventory to operate the business efficiently.

A fourth disadvantage is that the proprietor often has limited managerial experience. The owner-manager of a small company may be an inventor who is highly qualified as an engineer but lacks the "business sense" or the time needed to oversee the growth of the company. This owner may have to hire others to do the types of work—manufacturing, sales, and accounting—at which he or she is not an expert.

A fifth disadvantage is the difficulty of attracting qualified employees. Because proprietorships tend to be small, employees often have to be skilled in several areas. In addition, many top graduates are more likely to be attracted to positions with larger, better-established firms than smaller, less-known ones. This is especially true when larger firms offer fringe benefits—employee benefits such as paid vacations, sick leave, retirement, and health or medical insurance—in addition to wages and salaries.

A sixth disadvantage of the sole proprietorship is **limited life**. This means that the firm legally ceases to exist when the owner dies, quits, or sells the business.

✓ **READING PROGRESS CHECK**

Describing What are the major disadvantages of a sole proprietorship?

Partnerships

GUIDING QUESTION *How is responsibility shared in a partnership?*

A **partnership** is a business that is jointly owned by two or more persons. As shown in Figure 8.1, partnerships are the least numerous form of business organization in the United States, accounting for the second smallest proportion of sales and net income.

Types of Partnerships

Partnerships share many of the same strengths and weaknesses of a sole proprietorship. While there are several types of partnerships, the most important fall into the following categories:

214

---

networks Online Teaching Options

GRAPHIC ORGANIZER

Forms of Business Organizations

Analyzing characteristics, advantages, and disadvantages of sole proprietorships Have students view the graphic organizer. Ask them to define *Sole proprietorship* and describe its key characteristics, advantages, and disadvantages. Fill in the appropriate boxes as students provide suggestions. *(How it's formed: a single individual; How it grows: slowly adding a small number of employees; Advantages: easy to set up, management is simple, and owner keeps all profits; Disadvantages: owner has unlimited liability, hard to raise capital, and difficult to hire enough people and carry enough inventory)* Verbal/Linguistic

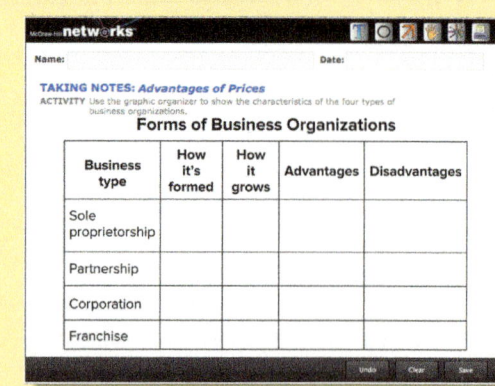

- The **general partnership** is the most common form of partnership. In it, all partners are responsible for the management and financial obligations of the business.
- In the **limited partnership**, at least one partner is not active in the daily running of the business and has limited responsibility for the debts and obligations of the business.

Forming a Partnership
Like a proprietorship, a partnership is relatively easy to start. While a partnership can be started with just a handshake, formal legal papers are usually drawn up to specify arrangements between partners. Although not always required, these papers state ahead of time how the expected profits (or possible losses) will be divided.

The partnership papers may also state the way future partners can be added to the business, and the way the property of the business will be distributed if the partnership ends.

Advantages
Like the sole proprietorship, one advantage of the partnership is its ease of start-up. Even the start-up costs of the partnership, which normally involve attorney fees and a filing fee, are minimal if they are spread over several partners.

Ease of management is another advantage. Each partner usually brings a different area of expertise to the business; one might have a talent for marketing, another for production, another for bookkeeping and finance, and so on. While partners normally agree ahead of time to consult with each other before making major decisions, partners generally have a great deal of freedom to make minor ones.

A third advantage is the lack of separate taxes on a partnership's income. As in the case of a proprietorship, the partners earn profits from the firm and then pay individual income taxes on them quarterly, or at the end of the year. Partners have to submit separate schedules to the Internal Revenue Service detailing their profits from the partnership, but this is for informational purposes only and does not give a partnership any separate legal status.

Fourth, partnerships can usually attract financial capital more easily than proprietorships. This is because they are generally larger and have a better chance of getting a bank loan. The existing partners could also take in new partners who bring financial capital with them as part of their price for joining.

A fifth advantage of partnerships is the more efficient operations that come with their slightly larger size. In some areas, such as medicine and law, a relatively small firm with three or four partners might be just the right size for the market. Other partnerships, such as accounting or investment firms, may have hundreds of partners offering services throughout the United States.

Disadvantages
This is where the two types of partnerships differ. The *general partnership* has the disadvantage that each partner is fully responsible for the acts of all other partners. If one partner causes the firm to suffer a huge loss, each partner is fully and personally responsible for the loss. This is similar to the unlimited liability feature of a proprietorship, but it is more complicated because more owners are involved. As a result, most people in business are extremely careful when they choose a business partner.

In the case of the *limited partnership*, a limited partner's responsibility for the debts of the business is limited by the size of his or her investment in the firm. If the business fails and debts remain, the limited partner loses only the original investment, leaving the general partners to make up the rest. So, if a limited

general partnership form of partnership where all partners are jointly responsible for management and debts

limited partnership form of partnership where one or more partners are not active in the daily running of the business, and whose liability for the partnership's debt is restricted to the amount invested in the business

---

CHAPTER 8, LESSON 1
Forms of Business Organization

C Critical Thinking Skills
Identifying valuable partnership qualities Have students work in pairs, with each pair first listing the advantages of partnerships. *(ease of startup, ease of management, and easier to attract capital)* Then ask each pair to create a list of qualities they think are most important in forming a successful business partnership. Have students share their lists and why they think the characteristics they chose are important. **Ask: What characteristics did most or all of you list as being important in a business partner? Why did you value this quality so highly in terms of its relationship to running a business? What role do your own abilities play in your choice of a partner's qualities?** **AL** Interpersonal

W Writing Skills
Understanding partnership disadvantages Ask students to discuss the disadvantages of forming partnerships. *(partners may be responsible for the acts of other partners, potential conflicts among partners, and limited life of partnership)* To help illustrate the difficulties of partnerships, ask students to answer the following questions in a brief essay: What problems might occur if you were assigned to do a graded team project with one other student? Would there be more or fewer problems if more students were assigned to each team? Explain. **AL** Verbal/Linguistic

---

GRAPHIC ORGANIZER
Concept Web
Using diagrams to distinguish local partnerships Have students select a partnership that recently opened for business in their area and write this company's name in the center oval of the diagram. Ask students to research or visit the partnership and list details about that partnership in the surrounding circles of the diagram. For example, note whether it is a general or limited partnership, the number of partners, each partner's area of expertise, and so on.

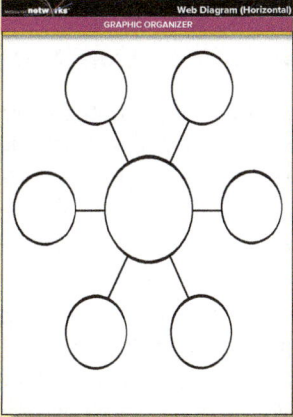

Curriculum Knowledge Center
CEHHS
University of Michigan-Dearborn

CHAPTER 8, LESSON 1
Forms of Business Organization

C Critical Thinking Skills

Forming a faux partnership Organize students into groups of three or four. Inform groups that they have decided to set up a painting and decorating company as a partnership. Have each group draw up an agreement among the partners. Point out that the agreement should address such issues as the role each partner plays in providing capital and running the company, how each partner will share in the profits and losses of the company, and what will happen to the partnership and its assets or debts if one or more partners dies or decides to leave. Call on group representatives to share their agreements with the class. **Verbal/Linguistic**

---

partner contributed $50,000 to a partnership, and if the partnership was sued and subsequently owed tens of millions, the most the limited partner could lose would be $50,000.

A second disadvantage is that the partnership, like the proprietorship, has limited life. When a partner dies or leaves, the partnership must be dissolved and reorganized as a new partnership if the remaining partners want to stay in business. However, the new partnership may reach an agreement with the older partnership and keep its old name, trademark, and other features of the business.

C A third disadvantage is the potential for conflict between partners. Sometimes partners discover that they do not get along, so they have to either learn to work together or leave the business. If the partnership is large, these types of problems can easily develop, even though initially everyone thought they would get along.

☑ **READING PROGRESS CHECK**

Contrasting What is the main difference between a general partnership and a limited partnership?

corporation form of business organization recognized by law as a separate legal entity with all the rights and responsibilities of an individual, including the right to buy and sell property, enter into legal contracts, and to sue and be sued

Corporations

GUIDING QUESTION *Why do corporations collectively earn more profits than proprietorships or partnerships?*

Corporations account for about one-fifth of the businesses in the United States, as shown in Figure 8.1, although they are responsible for a majority of all sales. A **corporation** is a form of business organization recognized by law as a separate legal entity with all the rights of an individual. This status gives the corporation

---

CAREERS | Corporate Auditor

Is this Career for you?

 Do you enjoy working with numbers, and do you have strong analytical skills?

 Do you pay close attention to detail, and are you organized?

 Are you interested in technology and complex mathematical computer programs?

Interview with a Corporate Auditor

"The profession of internal auditing will continue to grow as long as there's imagination in the minds of internal auditors. We have so many possibilities."

—Paul Sobel, Chairman of the Board, Institute of Internal Auditors

Salary
$62,000–$65,000 per year

Job Growth Potential
About average, with a projected growth rate of 13 percent between 2012 and 2022

Profile of Work
Auditors examine the financial statements of corporations to make sure that they are accurate and comply with relevant laws and regulations. After carefully studying the corporation's accounts, an auditor will make recommendations about how to reduce costs, enhance revenues, increase profits, or further comply with business regulations.

216

---

networks | Online Teaching Options

INTERACTIVE FEATURE

Careers: Corporate Auditor

Evaluating a corporate career Have students view the Corporate Auditor Career feature. Have volunteers read aloud one section of the feature. Then ask for a show of hands in answer to each of the three questions under "Is this career for you?" Invite students to explain why they would or would not want to pursue this career. Encourage students to discuss what might make this type of job attractive to them. **Ask: What qualities do you have that you might develop to make you a good corporate auditor?** *(develop stronger number and computer skills, become more organized, etc.)*

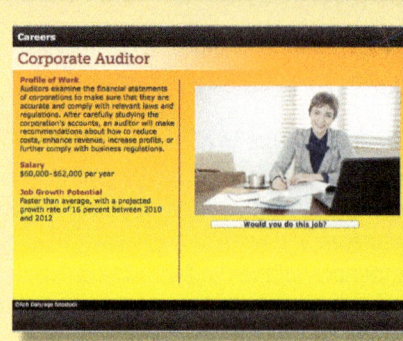

ANSWERS, p. 216

☑ **READING PROGRESS CHECK** In a general partnership, each partner is equally responsible for the business's debts. In a limited partnership, a partner's responsibility is limited to the size of his or her investment in the business.

the right to buy and sell property, to enter into legal contracts, and to sue and be sued. In fact, the corporation can do almost anything you can do except vote.

Forming a Corporation

Unlike a sole proprietorship or partnership, a corporation is a very formal and legal arrangement. People who want to *incorporate*, or form a corporation, must file for permission from the national government or the state where the business will have its headquarters. If approved, a **charter**—a government document that gives permission to create a corporation—is granted. The charter states the company's name, address, purpose, and other features of the business.

The charter also specifies the number of shares of **stock**, or ownership certificates, in the firm. These shares are sold to investors, called stockholders or shareholders. As shown in **Figure 8.2**, **stockholders** then own a part of the corporation. The money gained from the sale of stock is used to set up the corporation. If the corporation is profitable, it may eventually issue a **dividend**—a check that transfers a portion of the corporate earnings—to each stockholder.

Corporate Structure

When investors purchase stock, they become owners with certain ownership rights. The extent of these rights depends on the type of stock purchased: common or preferred.

- **Common stock** represents basic ownership of a corporation. Each share of common stock usually has one vote to elect a board of directors. The directors, in turn, set broad policies and goals for the corporation, and also hire a professional management team to run the business.
- **Preferred stock** represents *nonvoting* ownership shares of the corporation. Preferred stockholders cannot vote for the directors, but they receive their dividends before common stockholders receive theirs. If a corporation goes out of business, preferred stockholders get their investment back before common stockholders do.

In theory, a stockholder who owns a majority of a corporation's common stock can elect enough board members to control the company. In some cases, the common stockholder might elect himself or herself, or even other family members, to the board of directors.

In practice, however, this is not done very often because most corporations are so large and the number of shares held by the typical stockholder is so small. Most small stockholders either do not vote, or they turn their votes over to someone else. This is done with the use of a proxy, a ballot that gives a stockholder's representative the right to vote on corporate matters.

Although corporations differ in size, they generally organize in similar ways. As **Figure 8.3** shows, the day-to-day operations of a corporation are divided into different departments headed by vice presidents, who in turn report to the president of the company. Neither the president nor the other employees of the corporation have direct contact with the owners, or shareholders, of the company.

FIGURE 8.2

STOCK OWNERSHIP

If a corporation has 200 shares of stock, and you could divide the firm into 200 equal parts, the owner of a single share of stock would own 1/200th of the corporation.

▲ **CRITICAL THINKING**
Evaluating In what ways is the ownership and management of a corporation different from that of a sole proprietorship or a partnership?

connected.mcgraw-hill.com

charter written government approval to establish a corporation; includes company name, address, purpose of business, number of shares of stock, and other features of the business

stock certificate of ownership in a corporation; can be either common or preferred stock

stockholders people who own a share or shares of stock in a corporation; same as shareholders

dividend check paid to stockholders, usually quarterly, representing a portion of corporate profits

common stock most basic form of corporate ownership, generally with one vote per share for stockholders

preferred stock form of stock with no voting privileges; has a higher claim on corporate income and assets than does common stock

Business Organization **217**

CHAPTER 8, LESSON 1
Forms of Business Organization

C Critical Thinking Skills

Sequencing steps to incorporation Have students create a sequencing chart in which they show the steps involved in forming a corporation. *(General steps: Filing for permission from the federal or state government. Selling stock to investors, according to the charter. Establishing the company with the money gained from stock sales.)* Then have students explain how corporations raise money through the sale of stocks. **AL Logical/Mathematical**

R Reading Skills

Defining corporate terms Ask: **What is the relationship between a dividend and a stockholder?** *(A dividend is a check that stockholders receive as a portion of the corporate earnings.)*

DIAGRAM

Stock Ownership

Understanding stockholding Have students view Figure 8.2 Stock Ownership. Have volunteers provide characteristics of corporations. *(Possible answers: Corporations are owned by their stockholders, also called shareholders. Corporations are required to hold annual stockholder meetings at which stockholders can ask questions or make comments directly to the board, the president or director, and other high-level executives about the running of the corporation. Stockholders also get to vote on various proposals made at the meeting that affect the running and profitability of the corporation.)* **Visual/Spatial**

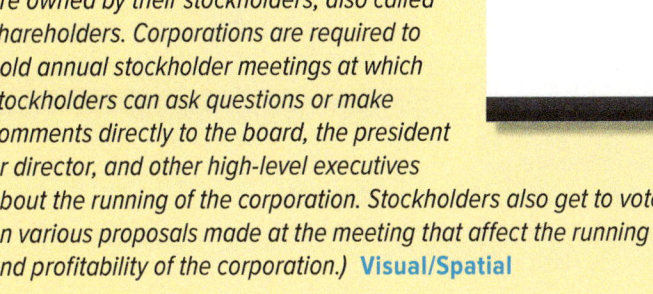

ANSWERS, p. 217

CRITICAL THINKING

In a sole proprietorship, the owner makes all decisions. In a partnership, two or more partners must come to agreement when making business decisions. In a corporation, stockholders may have a voice in how the corporation is operated.

Business Organization **217**

CHAPTER 8, LESSON 1
Forms of Business Organization

C Critical Thinking Skills

Charting the corporate ladder Have students create a step-chart in which they work their way up the corporate ladder. At each step, beginning as a lower-level employee, students should note what job they might be interested in. For example, they may start as a sales employee in Domestic sales, then move up to Manager of Domestic Sales, then to Vice President of Sales, etc. Encourage students to discuss or note how their jobs and responsibilities change at each level **Logical, Intrapersonal.**

Content Background Knowledge

Corporate Regulation State charters issued during the 1800s for the most part greatly restricted the powers of corporations. By the end of the century, however, courts and legislatures, yielding to pressure from business interests, began to ease controls on corporate activities. Exposés of business corruption by muckraking journalists at the turn of the century stirred demands for renewed restrictions. As a result, federal and state governments passed laws and ordinances regulating practically every aspect of corporate operations. Invite students to research and report on one of the muckraking events, such as Upton Sinclair and America's meat-packing industry, or Ida Tarbell and Standard Oil. Have students present their findings in oral presentations.

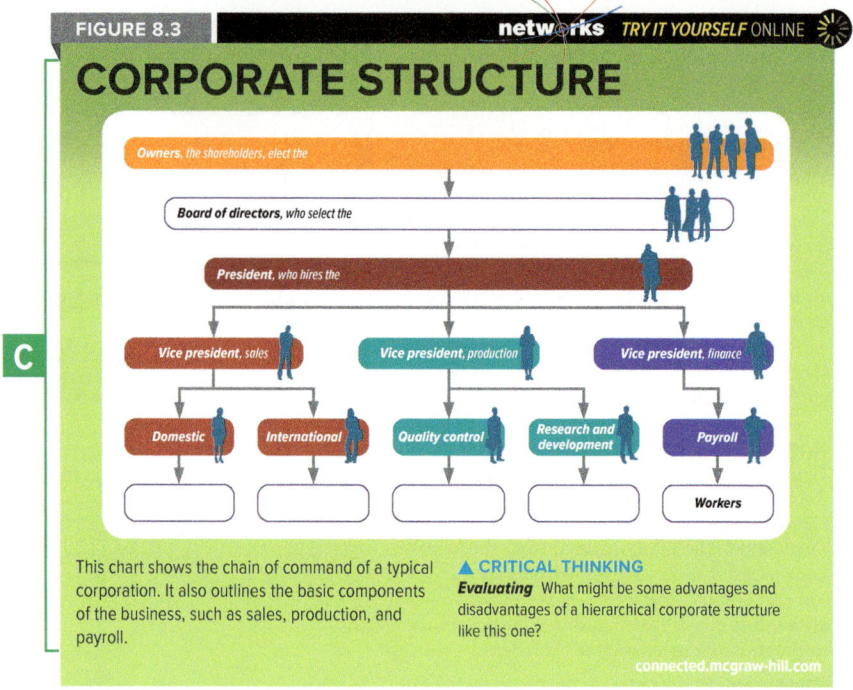

FIGURE 8.3

CORPORATE STRUCTURE

This chart shows the chain of command of a typical corporation. It also outlines the basic components of the business, such as sales, production, and payroll.

▲ CRITICAL THINKING
Evaluating What might be some advantages and disadvantages of a hierarchical corporate structure like this one?

connected.mcgraw-hill.com

bond formal contract to repay borrowed money and interest on the borrowed money at regular future intervals

principal amount borrowed when getting a loan or issuing a bond

interest payment made for the use of borrowed money; usually paid at periodic intervals for long-term bonds or loans

limited liability requirement in which a corporation, but not its owners, is responsible for all losses and debts of the business

Advantages

The typical corporation has two important advantages over the proprietorship or partnership. The first is the ease of raising financial capital; it can usually sell additional stock to investors. The revenue from the sale of stock can then be used to finance or expand operations. A corporation may also borrow money from investors by issuing bonds. A **bond** is a written promise to repay the amount borrowed at a later date. The amount borrowed is known as the **principal**. The corporation also pays **interest**, the price paid for the use of the lender's money.

The second important advantage is that the corporation provides **limited liability** for its owners. This means that the corporation itself, not its owners, is fully responsible for its debts and other obligations. To illustrate, suppose a corporation cannot pay its debts and goes out of business. Because of limited liability, stockholder losses are limited to the money they invested in the corporation's stock. Even if other debts remain, stockholders are not responsible for them.

Many firms incorporate just to take advantage of the limited liability. For example, suppose Mr. Winters, who owns the hardware store and the auto repair business, now decides to set up each business as a separate corporation. If the hardware business should fail, his personal wealth, which includes stock in the automobile repair business, is safe. Mr. Winters may lose all the money invested in the hardware business, but that would be the extent of his loss.

From a broader economic perspective, limited liability enables firms to undertake potentially profitable ventures that are inherently risky. This is why a business will use the corporate form of organization if it wants to introduce potentially risky products like medicines or a nuclear power plant.

218

networks Online Teaching Options

CHARTS

Corporate Structure

Analyzing corporate structure Have students view Figure 8.3 Corporate Structure. Point out that a corporation has a hierarchical structure, with the greatest power and responsibility found at the top of the corporate "pyramid" and with decreasing power and responsibility the lower down on the pyramid you go. **Ask: What skill(s) is most important for the top tier of corporate officers to have?** *(Sample answers: managerial, delegative, etc.)* **How might the performance and efficiency of lower-level employees affect the entire corporate structure?** *(Sample answer: If employees do not work well, the entire structure is compromised.)* **Verbal/Linguistic, Visual/Spatial**

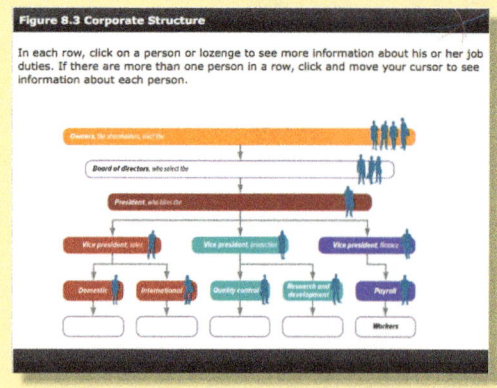

ANSWERS, p. 218

CRITICAL THINKING

Advantages: This structure makes it easy to see to whom each employee reports and whom each employee supervises. Employees have defined roles, and the responsibilities of each can be easily seen. Disadvantages: Decision-making can be slowed if too many decisions require the approval of a handful of managers at the top. Also, the corporate structure may stifle innovation if employees are not allowed to collaborate with others outside of their areas.

218

A third advantage of a corporation is that the corporation's board of directors can hire professional managers to run the firm. This means that the corporation's owners, its stockholders, can own a portion of the corporation without having to know much about the business itself.

Another advantage is unlimited life, meaning that the corporation continues to exist even when shareholders sell their ownership shares of stock to someone else. Because the corporation is recognized as a separate legal entity, the name of the company stays the same, and the corporation continues to do business.

This leads to a fifth advantage, the ease of transferring ownership of the corporation. If a shareholder no longer wants to be an owner, he or she simply sells the stock to someone else who then becomes the new owner. As a result, it is easier for the owner of a corporation to find a new buyer than it is for the owner of a sole proprietorship or a partnership.

Disadvantages

Because the law recognizes the corporation as a separate legal entity, it must keep detailed sales and expense records so that it can pay taxes on its profits. This leads to the first disadvantage, the **double taxation** of corporate profits. Profits are taxed the first time when the corporation pays income taxes. The profits are taxed a second time when shareholders pay taxes on their dividends.

For example, suppose a corporation pays a 25 percent income tax on profits of $100, or taxes of $25, and sends the rest of its profits to shareholders as dividends. The shareholders must pay a 20 percent tax on $75 of dividends or $15. In the end, the $100 profit that the corporation earned was actually taxed twice—first at 25 percent and then at 20 percent. Actual tax laws are much more complicated than this, but the double taxation of corporate profits is a fact of life for shareholders.

Another disadvantage of the corporate structure is the difficulty and expense of getting a charter. Depending on the state, attorney's fees and filing expenses can cost several thousand dollars. This may be a minor expense for a large corporation, but it is more of a burden for smaller ones.

A third disadvantage of the corporation is that its owners, the shareholders, have little voice in how the business is run. Shareholders vote for the board of directors, and the directors turn day-to-day operations over to a professional management team. The result is a separation of ownership and management.

Finally, the fourth disadvantage is that corporations are subject to more government regulations than other forms of business. Corporations must register with the state in which they are chartered. If a corporation wants to sell its stock to the public, it must register with the federal Securities and Exchange Commission (SEC). Corporations also have to provide financial reports on sales and profits to the general public on a regular basis. Even an attempt to buy or combine with another business may require federal government approval.

double taxation feature of taxation that allows stockholders' dividends to be taxed both as corporate profit and as personal income

EXPLORING THE ESSENTIAL QUESTION

A few years ago, as a hobby, you began to repair your friends' bicycles. Word spread, and your friends' friends began paying you to help them repair their bikes. Now you are repairing bikes, and designing and building new bikes as well. Consider the following:

- If you decided to form a partnership, which form of partnership would you choose?
- In which circumstances might you choose to incorporate instead of partnering?
- If you eventually grew your business into a corporation, what do you think would attract a stockholder to invest?

CHAPTER 8, LESSON 1
Forms of Business Organization

W Writing Skills

Researching and writing about types of corporations Have students find and read articles (online or in newspapers or magazines) about public and privately held corporations. Have students write two short paragraphs in which they explain what each is, and then identify and describe one of each type of corporation. Some students may also want to research and write about a company that transitions from a private company to a corporation via an Initial Public Offering (IPO) of stock (as Facebook did).
BL Verbal/Linguistic

R Reading Skills

Analyzing disadvantages of corporations Discuss with students the disadvantages of corporations. *(double taxation, difficulty and expense of getting a charter, and owners have little say in how the corporation is run)* Be sure students understand the difference between common and preferred stockholders.

GRAPHIC ORGANIZER

Forms of Business Organizations

Analyzing characteristics, advantages, and disadvantages of corporations Have students complete the third category of the interactive graphic organizer by defining *Corporation* and identifying the key characteristics, advantages, and disadvantages of corporations. Fill in the appropriate boxes as students provide suggestions. *(How it's formed: a government document called a charter; How it grows: sale of stock or issue of bonds; Advantages: easier to raise capital, limited liability, and unlimited life; Disadvantages: double taxation, difficulty and expense of getting a charter, and owners have little say in how corporation is run)* **Verbal/Linguistic**

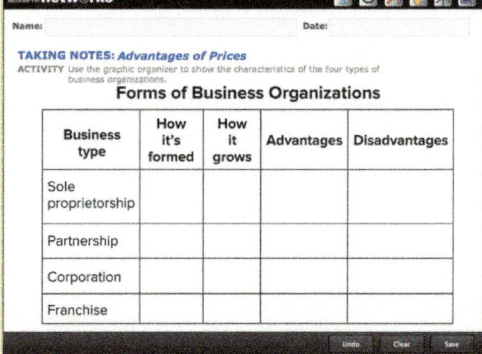

ANSWERS, p. 219

EXPLORING THE ESSENTIAL QUESTION

Answers will vary.

✓ **READING PROGRESS CHECK** Why do many business owners prefer corporations over other forms of business organization? *(In a corporation, the individual has little or no liability or risk if the business has debts or fails.)*

CHAPTER 8, LESSON 1
Forms of Business Organization

C Critical Thinking Skills

Documenting and debating franchises' effects on small businesses Have students research the effects that the proliferation and popularity of franchises have had on "mom and pop" stores. Encourage students to take notes during their research. Then have the class debate the pros and cons of franchises in terms of (1) their potential for allowing individuals to buy into already successful businesses, and (2) their impact on the creation and success of other types of individually owned small businesses. **Verbal/Linguistic, Logical/Mathematical**

R Reading Skills

Discovering the many types of franchises Have students use online or print sources to find out as much as possible about the immense variety of franchises that people can invest in and run as a business. Students should make a list of at least a dozen categories of franchises. Have them also list the brand names/business names of one or more franchises under each category.

Making Connections

Franchises in the United States The inventor and entrepreneur Isaac Singer began the practice of franchising in the United States. In the mid-1800s, Singer signed agreements with several merchants that allowed them to market his sewing machines. The interstate highway system caused the practice of franchising to explode in the 1950s. Increasing automobile ownership took more Americans on the road, where they looked for familiar motels, restaurants, and gas stations they knew and trusted. Time students to see how fast they can name 30 franchises familiar in the United States today.

Franchises

GUIDING QUESTION *What are the advantages and disadvantages of investing in a franchise for both the franchisee and franchisor?*

C You are probably more familiar with the franchise than any other form of business. For example, if you have ever been in Subway, Jiffy Lube, 7-Eleven, Supercuts, McDonald's, Pizza Hut, Hardee's, or Dunkin' Donuts, you have been in a franchise. Franchises account for about 4 percent of all businesses, but they are heavily concentrated in retail commercial areas where they are highly visible.

franchise business investment that involves renting or leasing another successful business model

franchisor creator and owner of the business model that is rented or leased by investors

franchisee person that invests in the business model of the franchisor with his or her own money and start-up costs

The Franchise
Technically, a **franchise** is a temporary business investment that involves renting or leasing another firm's successful business model. Before we see how this works, we need to identify both participants in a franchise:

- The **franchisor** is the actual owner of the business that lets other investors rent or lease its name, business profile, and way of doing business.
- The **franchisee** is the investor who rents or leases the business model from the franchisor and then hopes to recoup his or her investment by selling the franchisor's goods or services.

Becoming an "Owner"
People who buy a franchise are usually investors who always wanted to go into business but never did. Or they may already own a business but are looking to earn more income. For example, take Mr. Winters, our sole proprietor who has a small hardware store in a local shopping center. Business had been slow at the store, and so he was thinking of buying a franchise.

R After some research, he found more than a thousand franchisors that offered everything from day-care centers to hotels to restaurants. The one that caught his attention, though, was a franchise opportunity from Clamp-On Tools, a respected brand name in the tool and hardware industry. The franchise required an initial investment of $300,000, most of which used to remodel his store and bring it up to Clamp-On standards. He would then have to pay an initial franchise fee of $15,000, along with a monthly royalty fee of $110 for the 10-year term of the franchise. In return, Mr. Winters would be selling name-brand items, have access to a full range of hardware-store supplies, and benefit from company support that included advertising, training meetings, toll-free support lines, and field operations and evaluations.

While these terms sounded steep, Clamp-On had more than 3,000 stores in the United States and another 1,200 in Canada and the rest of the world, so Mr. Winters thought that the franchise agreement would be profitable. Still, he wasn't too happy about Clamp-On's requirements that he have a positive net worth of $40,000 and another $80,000 of liquid cash (basically, cash, bank accounts, and savings accounts) on hand, because he knew that Clamp-On expected him to be able to survive in months when sales were slow. Still, it sounded attractive.

Advantages of a Franchise
Mr. Winters knew what the advantages were for him; he would be catapulted into a nationwide network that had a respected product, a deep product line, excellent quality standards, nationwide advertising, and professional advice whenever he needed it. With a bit of luck, he hoped to see some annual profits after the start-up costs were recouped. However, there were advantages to the franchisor as well.

networks Online Teaching Options

VIDEO WORKSHEET

Branding Ford

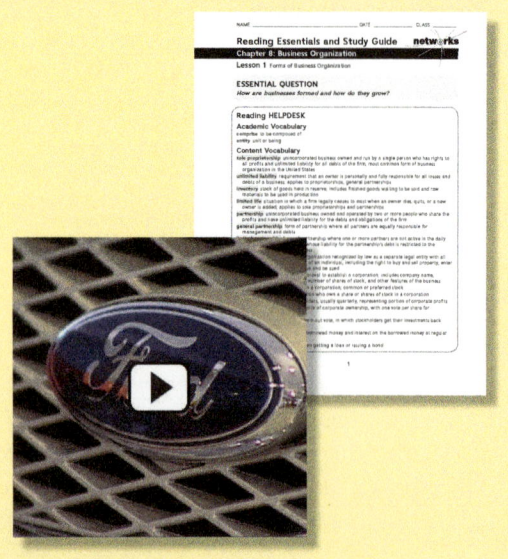

Drawing conclusions Have students watch the video. Discuss the consumers' reactions to products with older, more recognizable names. **Ask: How does a "tried and true" name for a product that has a reputation for reliability affect consumer attitudes and company sales?** Encourage students to draw conclusions about the effects of using recognizable brand names on the development and marketing of new, innovative products. How might a company use its brand to help it market new products?
Logical, Linguistic

For example, Clamp-On would be able to add one more location to its nationwide network without having to build a single new brick-and-mortar building. This is because Mr. Winters was providing one for them—something that greatly reduced the financial risk of Clamp-On's expansion. There were other potential risk reductions as well because liabilities for employee or employer misconduct (sexual harassment, safety code violations, etc.) would be the sole responsibility of Mr. Winters, not Clamp-On. The up-front franchise payment would help Clamp-On's profitability, as would the monthly royalty fee. Finally, by requiring Mr. Winters to make a substantial investment at the beginning, Clamp-On felt that he would be highly motivated to make the franchise work.

Disadvantages of a Franchise

Mr. Winters was clearly aware of the investment he would have to make for a Clamp-On tool and hardware store. Still, other franchises were a lot more expensive, and they seemed to work. For example, the start-up costs alone for a McDonald's could be as high as $2 million or even $15 million for a Hampton Inn & Suites. He also knew that there would be a substantial cost if he wanted to terminate the franchise before the 10 years were up. The main thing that bothered him, however, was knowing that owning a franchise is not the same as purchasing a business for the purpose of ownership. He knew that if he went with Clamp-On, he was likely to have 10 years of profits—but then nothing in year 10 except for the right to renew the franchise.

✓ **READING PROGRESS CHECK**

Evaluating Why do many business owners prefer corporations over other forms of business organization?

LESSON 1 REVIEW

Reviewing Vocabulary

1. *Explaining* What are shareholders, and what is the difference between the preferred and common stock they buy? What type of business entity issues these types of stocks?

2. *Explaining* How does the owner's liability to losses differ in a general partnership and a limited partnership?

Using Your Notes

Use the information you jotted down in the graphic organizer to answer this question.

3. *Contrasting* Which of the three types of business do you think has the greatest advantages and fewest disadvantages in comparison with the others? Explain your answer.

Answering the Guiding Questions

4. *Evaluating* What makes a sole proprietorship the easiest form of business to start?

5. *Explaining* How is responsibility shared in a partnership?

6. *Summarizing* Why do corporations generally have the largest profits of any form of business?

7. *Applying* Imagine you're considering becoming a franchisee, but you haven't yet decided if it's the right kind of business for you. On the basis of what you've read about franchises, which factors would you consider in order to reach a decision?

Writing About Economics

8. *Explanatory* Which of the business types discussed in this chapter would grow the most over time (about a decade or so)? What accounts for the different rates of growth—of both profits and expansion—for each business type? Why would some businesses be more aggressive in pursuing rapid growth than others? Explain your answers.

CHAPTER 8, LESSON 1
Forms of Business Organization

CLOSE & REFLECT

C Critical Thinking Skills

Summarizing the lesson Ask students to suggest a type of business they would like to run, what organization they would like it to have, and why this structure would best ensure the business's success.

ANSWERS, p. 221

✓ **READING PROGRESS CHECK** They prefer corporations because in this organization the individuals involved have no liability if the business loses money or fails.

LESSON 1 REVIEW ANSWERS

Reviewing Vocabulary

1. Shareholders buy stock in a corporation. Those who hold common stock can vote for the corporate board. Those who hold preferred stock have no vote. Corporations issue and sell stock.

2. In a general partnership, liability is shared equally. In a limited partnership, some partners may have liability equal to their share of the business.

Using Your Notes

3. Students should support their answers with details of advantages over other types of business.

Answering the Guiding Questions

4. It has few requirements other than paying fees and obtaining licenses, if necessary.

5. In a general partnership, all partners share responsibility equally. In a limited partnership, one or more partners will share less of the responsibility.

6. They can often benefit from economies of scale to gain market share.

7. Advantages to consider: profiting from a brand with an established identity; training and advertising in place. Disadvantages: expensive to start and maintain franchise fees; must follow the franchise's rules.

Writing About Economics

8. If the business is successful, students may determine that a corporation may grow most over time because of its ability to raise capital via issuing stock. The capital could be used to expand the business. However, some students may decide that a franchise that is very successful might grow more than some corporations, as more and more franchises are opened and do well. Students should support their choice with details from the chapter.

CHAPTER 8
Case Study

C Critical Thinking Skills

Making decisions about industry and pollution
Guide students to a discussion of factory location, including the issue of workers at the factory living within a reasonable commuting distance from it. Encourage students to talk about how to balance, or reconcile, the need for convenience in terms of getting to work with the possible harm factory pollution might do.

V Visual Skills

Investigating spatial location Have students look at the map and compare it to a more detailed map. **Ask: Is Ponca City near a large urban area, such as Tulsa?** *(No, it appears to be in a rural area.)* **Why would the jobs at the plant be so important to residents of Ponca City?** *(There are often few jobs available in rural areas.)* Discuss with students why, in a rural area, one might have to live near one's place of work. Using this logic, have students evaluate the validity of information in the feature for point of view.

Content Background Information

Clean Air Act In 1970, the United States Congress passed, and President Nixon signed, the Clean Air Act, which set "acceptable" standards for pollutants in the air. The Clean Air Act can require polluters to remove toxic materials from their emissions or reduce or eliminate polluting emissions. It is because of this act that the citizens of Ponca City received a settlement from the polluting factory in their city.

ANSWERS, p. 222

Case Study Review

1. Students should mention that the company released carbon black into the air at night or on weekends when ODEQ agents were not working and could not check on the emissions. Also, both the company and the ODEQ used the chemical reaction of carbon black with atmospheric chemicals to deny that carbon black itself (in its pure form) was a problem coming from the factory.
2. Students should use details from the narrative to show how the corporation avoided responsibility and transparency. Students should connect regulation in the public interest with a company's efforts to find loopholes.

Case Study

For an interactive version of this case study go to **connected.mcgraw-hill.com**

POWDER POLLUTION

V

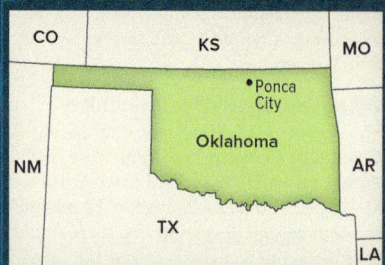

C The residents of Ponca City often found their cars, streets, trees, and lawns coated with a thin film of fine black powder.

Three miles from the town's center, a chain-link fence was all that separated the residents from the source of the powder—the Continental Carbon factory, which produced "carbon black," a substance used to strengthen tires and other rubber products.

Many of Ponca City's children developed asthma, and the black dust in the air made their asthma worse. Farmers who grew crops anywhere near that chain-link fence saw some of their crops die. Even worse, carbon black can cause cancer and diseases of the heart and lungs, according to the U.S. Centers for Disease Control.

The Environmental Protection Agency (EPA) felt that the company was in violation of Clean Air Act regulations, and ordered the Oklahoma Department of Environmental Quality (ODEQ) to review resident complaints. The ODEQ discovered that Continental Carbon released carbon black late at night or on weekends, when the ODEQ agents were off duty. But once carbon black enters the air, it combines chemically with other atmospheric chemicals. This changes it from pure carbon black—which can be traced to the factory—into a new and different compound. These chemical reactions allowed Continental Carbon and the ODEQ to claim that, technically, there was no carbon black pollution from the factory.

Residents disagreed, and in 2002, plant workers, residents, and farmers began working together to stop the pollution. Public pressure built against the company, and in 2005, the residents filed a lawsuit against Continental Carbon.

In 2009, Continental Carbon agreed to pay the residents in and around Ponca City close to $20 million in damages. The company paid to relocate those living nearest the fence. The outcome pleased many residents, but some residents were not satisfied—although the company paid millions in damages, it never admitted that it was responsible for any type of pollution.

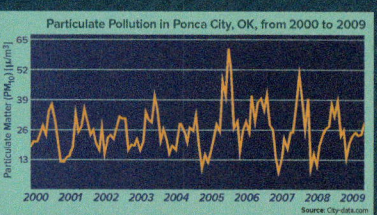

Ponca City became a center of discussion on government regulation of industry when particulate pollution in the city became an obvious problem.

CASE STUDY REVIEW

1. *Identifying Cause and Effect* How did the timing of Continental Carbon's release of carbon black, as well as this substance's natural interaction with chemicals in the air, allow the company to continue to violate the Clean Air Act for years after complaints were filed by citizens?
2. *Evaluating Central Issues* How do the events in the Ponca City story relate to the issue of a business's economic responsibilities? And how do government regulations enacted in the public interest restrict corporate use of its property?

222

---

networks Online Teaching Options

INTERACTIVE FEATURE

Case Study: Powder Pollution

Analyzing pollution data Have students click on the map and then examine the graph, which shows the level of black carbon particulates in the air in Ponca City, OK, from 2000–2009. **Ask: How much does the level of particulates vary?** *(from less than 13 to 65 microns per square meter)* Explain that these are the years Continental Carbon paid residents for damages. **Ask: What was the highest level of particulates recorded during this period? What was the minimum number of particulates in the air during all these years?** *(Highest level: about 62; level never dipped below about 8)* **How did particulate levels in Ponca City compare with national levels during this period?** *(Ponca City had consistently higher levels of particulates during this period.)*

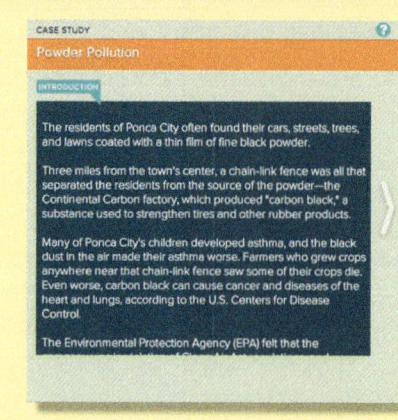

CHAPTER 8, LESSON 2
Business Growth and Expansion

LESSON 2
Business Growth and Expansion

Interact with these digital assets and others in lesson 2
- ✓ INTERACTIVE CHART Growth Through Reinvestment
- ✓ INTERACTIVE GRAPH Conglomerate Structure
- ✓ SELF-CHECK QUIZ
- ✓ VIDEO

networks TRY IT YOURSELF ONLINE

Reading Help Desk

Academic Vocabulary
- merger
- internally

Content Vocabulary
- income statement
- net income
- depreciation
- cash flow
- horizontal merger
- vertical merger
- conglomerate
- multinational
- incubators
- venture capitalist
- angel investors
- crowdfunding

TAKING NOTES:

Key Ideas and Details
ACTIVITY Use a graphic organizer like the one below to describe the characteristics of two business growth models.

Models for Business Growth

Growth Model	Description
Reinvestment and Internal Growth	
Mergers and Acquisitions	

income statement report showing a business's sales, expenses, and profits for a certain period, usually three months or a year

ESSENTIAL QUESTION
How are businesses formed and how do they grow?

With two friends you started a business—Healthy Foods—selling four types of healthy sandwiches to fellow students out of the back of your van. You each contributed $50 to start the business. After three months, Healthy Foods has made $900. You and your friends must decide what to do with that extra money. If you invest the profits back into the business and add more types of sandwiches, or buy several more coolers to store beverages, or advertise, Healthy Foods is likely to grow. But Beta Burger, your new competition, has talked about joining forces by merging the businesses.

How would you prefer to grow your business: by reinvesting the profits you and your friends made, or by merging with Beta Burger? Explain.

Growth Through Reinvestment

GUIDING QUESTION *Why would business owners choose to reinvest profits?*

Most businesses use financial statements to keep track of their business operations. One of the most important of those is the **income statement**—a report showing a business's sales, expenses, net income, and cash flows for a period of time, such as three months or a year. We can use the income statement to show how a business can use some of the revenue it receives from sales to grow through reinvestment.

Estimating Cash Flows

An income statement such as the one in **Figure 8.4** shows a firm's **net income**—the funds left over after all of the firm's expenses, including taxes, are subtracted from its sales. These expenses include the cost of inventory, wages and salaries, interest payments, and all other payments the firm must make as part of its normal business operations. One of the most important of these payments is **depreciation**—a noncash charge the firm takes for the general wear and tear on its capital goods.

connected.mcgraw-hill.com **Business Organization 223**

ENGAGE

C1 Critical Thinking Skills

Making decisions about how to grow your business Have students read the text describing a new and successful business. The business is so successful that the owners have made more profit than they had expected. But there is a catch: their business faces competition from another business. Have students work in small groups to decide how they think this business should grow. Have them work together to list reasons they should merge with the competing business. Then have them list reasons that they should expand by investing their profits within the business (i.e., not merge). When groups are done, have them compare the reasons they put in each list. **Ask: What is your (each group's) final decision: to merge or not to merge?** *(Sample answer: We decided not to merge because we want to be different from Beta Burger.)* Discuss which path to growth was most popular among students.

TEACH & ASSESS

C2 Critical Thinking Skills

Applying depreciation To help students understand the concept of depreciation, have them name capital goods needed in a clothing manufacturing business. (Possible answers: machines that make patterns, cut the material, and sew the garments) Explain that the machines gradually deteriorate, or depreciate, with use. **ELL**

---

networks Online Teaching Options

BELLRINGER
Business Growth and Expansion

Introducing mergers Use the Bellringer to encourage students to discuss and explain why two companies might decide it is in the self-interest of both to merge. **Ask: Based on the photograph, which two companies merged to form a single company?** *(Kinko's and Federal Express)* **How might the services provided by each company be complemented or enhanced by this merger? How does a merger of this type allow the reach of each company to expand?** Invite students to work in small groups to create a list of services that are improved by the melding of the shipping company and the copy company. Encourage them also to note any negative impacts, if any, on services provided due to this merger. **Verbal/Linguistic**

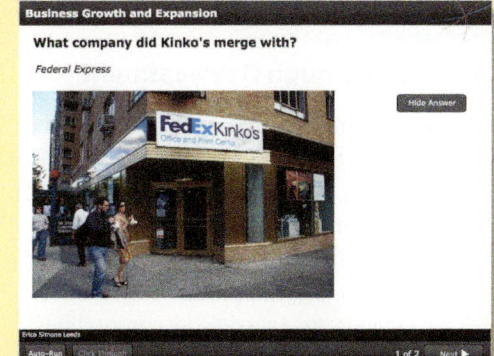

ANSWERS, p. 223

ESSENTIAL QUESTION ACTIVITY

Answers will vary.

TAKING NOTES
Reinvestment and Internal Growth: The company grows internally through the reinvestment of net profits to improve and expand operations.
Mergers and Acquisitions: The company grows by joining together with another organization and taking advantage of pooled resources to grow.

Business Organization **223**

CHAPTER 8, LESSON 2
Business Growth and Expansion

R1 Reading Skills

Understanding business choices Ask: **What are two things a business can do with its cash flow?** (pay shareholder dividends [corporations only] or invest in a new plant, equipment, or technologies)

R2 Reading Skills

Researching a reinvesting business Have students research one specific business that has successfully reinvested its cash flow. Students should read about the type of reinvestments made and the results. Then encourage a class discussion on the different ways a company can reinvest its profits to successfully expand its business. **BL**

C Critical Thinking Skills

Writing about wise reinvestment Have students think about the different ways a company can reinvest its profits: for example, for advertising, for promotions, for opening many new stores, or for building a new factory, and so on. Have students write "A Guide to Reinvestment" in which they propose guidelines for businesses about smart ways to reinvest cash flow. For example, a very small business should not reinvest all its profits in promotions or advertising, but perhaps should reinvest in broadening its product line. Students should take time to think about a business of their choosing and the wisest ways this business should reinvest its cash flow. Student guidelines should explain why some reinvestments are foolish for this business and why other reinvestments are wise for this business. Have students share their guidelines with the class to generate discussion. **Verbal/Linguistic**

ANSWERS, p. 224

✓ READING PROGRESS CHECK Reinvesting cash flow allows the business owner to allocate resources to those parts of the business that would do best in helping the business expand.

CRITICAL THINKING
Increasing dividends will reduce the amount of cash available for reinvestment, which will make it difficult for the business to buy new equipment and technologies. Over time, this could reduce the ability of the business to stay up to date and to remain competitive with other businesses.

224

---

net income measure of business profits determined by subtracting all expenses, including taxes, from revenues

depreciation gradual wear on capital goods

cash flow total amount of new funds the business generates from operations; broadest measure of profits for a firm because it includes both net income and noncash charges

merger combination of two or more business enterprises to form a single firm

horizontal merger combination of firms producing the same kind of product

vertical merger combination of firms involved in different steps of manufacturing, marketing, or sales

Depreciation is called a *noncash* charge because the money stays in the firm rather than being paid to someone else. For example, interest may be paid to a bank, wages may be paid to employees, or payments may be made to suppliers to provide some of the inputs used in production. Current tax laws allow the firm to treat depreciation two different ways. First, it is treated as an expense, which lowers the amount of income subject to taxes. Although it is treated as an expense because the capital goods used in production have lost value, it does not reduce the cash on hand. Because of this, firms usually prefer to take as much depreciation as possible to reduce the taxes they pay. As you can see in the figure, an increase in depreciation would lower the earnings before tax and the taxes owed.

The **cash flow**—the sum of net income and noncash charges such as depreciation—is the *bottom line*, a more comprehensive measure of a firm's profits. This is because the cash flow represents the total amount of after-tax income generated from operations.

Reinvesting Cash Flows

If a business has a positive cash flow, the firm can then decide how to allocate it. If the business is a corporation, the board of directors may declare a dividend to be paid directly to shareholders as a reward for their investments. The remainder of the funds could then be reinvested in a new plant, equipment, or technologies. If the business is a proprietorship or partnership, the owners could keep some of the cash flow as a reward for risk-taking and then reinvest the rest.

When cash flows are reinvested in a business, the firm can produce new or additional products. This generates additional sales and an even larger cash flow during the next sales period. As long as the firm has positive cash flows, and as long as the reinvested funds are larger than the wear and tear on equipment, the firm will grow.

Finally, the concept of cash flow is also important to investors. In fact, if investors want to know about the financial health of a firm, a positive cash flow is one of the first things they look for.

✓ READING PROGRESS CHECK

Summarizing What is the benefit of reinvesting cash flow in a business?

Growth Through Mergers

GUIDING QUESTION *What advantages are gained through business mergers?*

Another way a business can expand is by engaging in a **merger**—a combination of two or more businesses to form a single firm. When two companies merge, one gives up its separate legal identity. For public-recognition purposes, however, the name of the new company may reflect the identities of both. When Chase National Bank and Bank of Manhattan merged, the new company was called the Chase Manhattan Bank of New York.

FIGURE 8.4 networks TRY IT YOURSELF ONLINE

GROWTH THROUGH REINVESTMENT

Growth Through Reinvestment

First quarter income statement

Sales of goods and services	$1,000
Less: Cost of goods sold	400
Wages and salaries	250
Interest payments	50
Depreciation	100
Earnings before tax	**$200**
Less: Taxes at (40%)	80
Net income	**$120**
Plus: Depreciation	100
Cash flow	**$220**

Reinvestment is needed to keep a company up-to-date and to ensure continuing profitability.

▲ **CRITICAL THINKING**
Evaluating What might be the long-term effects if a business chooses to increase dividends?

connected.mcgraw-hill.com

---

networks Online Teaching Options

DIAGRAM

Growth Through Reinvestment

Understanding the sequence and results of reinvestment Display the Growth Through Reinvestment interactive graphic. Explain that the process of growth through reinvestment applies to all businesses, including partnerships and sole proprietorships. Point out, however, that dividends are paid only by corporations.
Ask: **What must happen in a business for cash flow to increase?** (Sample answer: Sales/profits must rise.)

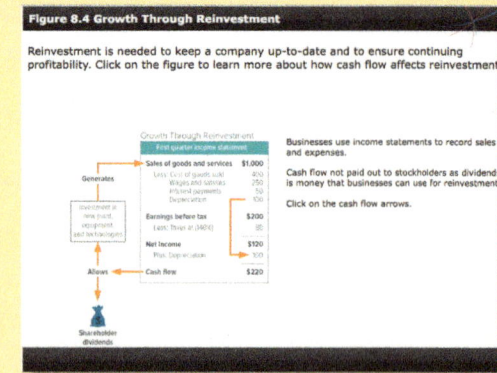

FIGURE 8.5
TYPES OF MERGERS

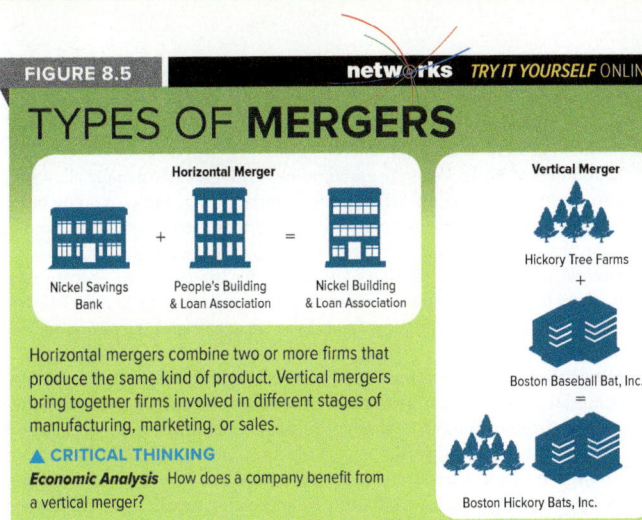

Horizontal mergers combine two or more firms that produce the same kind of product. Vertical mergers bring together firms involved in different stages of manufacturing, marketing, or sales.

▲ **CRITICAL THINKING**
Economic Analysis How does a company benefit from a vertical merger?

BIOGRAPHY

Friedrich August von Hayek
ECONOMIST (1899–1992)

Winner of the 1974 Nobel Prize in Economics, Austrian Friedrich Hayek attended the University of Vienna. He promoted laissez-faire, which put him in opposition to economist John Maynard Keynes. Hayek is well known for explaining the business cycle, and his work continues to be influential. He saw the price system as a network that controlled the economy. If a central bank tampered with it—by keeping interest rates low, for example—the economy would experience unsustainable growth, according to Hayek. He argued that central planning couldn't effectively control the "economic calculation," or the price system that happens naturally in the free market. Hayek taught at the University of Chicago, and his views influenced British Prime Minister Margaret Thatcher and U.S. president Ronald Reagan.

▶ **CRITICAL THINKING**
Hypothesizing Write a paragraph discussing whether you think Hayek would approve of a government sponsored economic stimulus. Give reasons for your view.
Analyzing Write a short essay explaining how Hayek's view of the importance of a free price system fits in with his laissez-faire philosophy.

Later it changed its name to the Chase Manhattan Corporation to reflect its geographically expanding business. Finally, after merging with JP Morgan, it settled on JPMorgan Chase. Likewise, Procter & Gamble kept the brand name "Gillette" after it bought the company.

Types of Mergers
There are two types of mergers, both of which are illustrated in **Figure 8.5**. The first is a **horizontal merger**, which takes place when firms that produce the same kind of product join forces. One such example is the bank merger of JP Morgan and Chase Manhattan to form JPMorgan Chase.

When companies involved in different stages of manufacturing, marketing, or sales join together, it results in a **vertical merger**. One example of a vertical merger is the formation of the U.S. Steel Corporation. At one time it mined its own ore, shipped it across the Great Lakes, smelted it, and made steel into many different products. Vertical mergers take place when companies seek to protect against the potential loss of suppliers.

EXPLORING THE ESSENTIAL QUESTION
Research a horizontal merger that occurred in the last three years in the United States. Using reliable sources for facts, write two paragraphs describing the merger and the reasons for the horizontal structure. What benefits are expected from the merger?

Reasons for Merging
Mergers take place for many reasons, but most of them are to improve the company's performance in the eyes of the shareholder.

- **Faster Growth** Some companies find that they cannot grow as fast as they would like by only using **internally** generated funds. But by merging with another firm, the company's size and sales appear to grow faster.

CHAPTER 8, LESSON 2
Business Growth and Expansion

W Writing Skills

Writing about a proposed merger Ask students to consider two companies that could improve if they merged. Have students write a paragraph describing the type of merger it should be, and how the merger would benefit consumers in terms of the quality and range of products offered.

R Reading Skills

Considering Hayek's views Have students offer their opinion on Friedrich Hayek's economic principles and how, if implemented, they would affect the lives of today's U.S. citizens.

C1 Critical Thinking Skills

Evaluating types of mergers Have students research examples of vertical and horizontal mergers. Encourage them to find one example of each in which the merger worked out well and in which it did not work out well. Have students discuss if the benefits or problems were related to the type of merger or to a mistaken idea about how the merger would improve business.

Making Connections

Hayek Friedrich von Hayek, who lived through World War II, was deeply influenced by Hitler's dictatorship. Have students relate those events to von Hayek's idea that government intervention in the economy leads to tyranny, but markets unhindered by government *prevent* tyranny.

C2 Critical Thinking Skills

Analyzing Hayek's impact Have students analyze Friedrich Hayek's impact on the U.S. free enterprise system.

CHARTS

Types of Mergers

Distinguishing types of mergers Display Figure 8.5, which shows the different types of mergers: vertical and horizontal. Have volunteers read each set of captions and then use them to explain the difference between the two types of mergers. **Ask: What do you think are the benefits of each type of merger?** (Sample answer: For horizontal mergers, the business may take over competitors. For vertical mergers, the business may take over companies that they formerly had to pay for needed services but now they get these services for less money because they own the companies that provide them.) **Verbal/Linguistic**

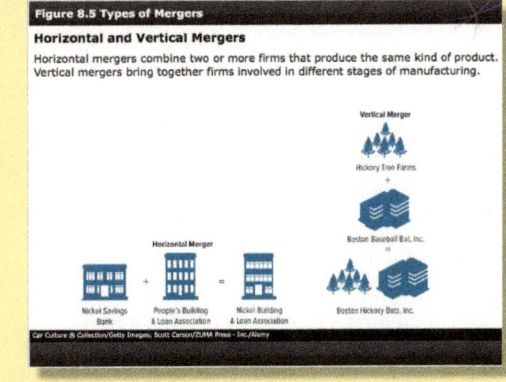

ANSWERS, p. 225

CRITICAL THINKING
Vertical mergers take place when companies seek to protect against the loss of suppliers.

EXPLORING THE ESSENTIAL QUESTION
Answers should include some of the six reasons for mergers.

CRITICAL THINKING
Answers should center on Hayek's disapproval of government's intervention into market affairs.

CHAPTER 8, LESSON 2
Business Growth and Expansion

C1 Critical Thinking Skills

Justifying a merger **Ask:** Would a store that sells snowboards merge with a store that sells surfboards? Would this be a responsible use of both businesses? Explain. *(Possible response: A store in a cold climate would sell many snowboards but few surfboards. A store on the coast would sell many surfboards but few snowboards. Merging would likely not be responsible, as most places warm enough for surfing do not get cold enough for snow, and vice versa.)*

C2 Critical Thinking Skills

Appreciating merger issues Discuss with students the likelihood that sensitive negotiations are required before a merger can take place because both parties must reach an agreement about the terms of the merger. **Ask:** What types of issues do you think must be decided before two separate companies decide to merge into one company? *(Sample answer: Allocation of responsibilities, division of profits, shared [or not] decision making, etc.)*

R1 Reading Skills

Understanding conglomerate motives
Ask: What is the main reason for conglomerate mergers? *(diversification for safety; to avoid "putting all eggs into one basket")*

R2 Reading Skills

Contrasting conglomerates and multinationals
Ask: How can a multinational corporation also be a conglomerate? *(If a multinational makes unrelated products, it is a conglomerate.)* Ask students to list the differences of conglomerates and multinationals. *(Possible answer: Differences include that they have a different scope, with multinationals operating in different countries, paying taxes in the countries where it has operations, and being a citizen of several countries at the same time.)*
Verbal/Linguistic

- **Synergy** This is the idea that when firms combine, they will take the best characteristics of each to become a better and stronger company. This is like the argument that one and one makes three, which is always tempting for management and shareholders.
- **Economies of Scale** When firms combine, the larger size usually allows for lower cost of production, whether in manufacturing, sales, or some other aspect of business. For example, two banks that merge can close some of their branch locations if they formerly competed against each other.
- **Diversification** Some mergers are driven by the desire to acquire new product lines. When a telecommunications company such as AT&T buys a cable TV company, it can offer faster Internet access and telephone service in a single package.
- **Elimination of Rivals** Sometimes firms merge to catch up with, or even eliminate, rivals. Royal Caribbean Cruises acquired Celebrity Cruise Lines in a horizontal merger to double in size to become the second-largest cruise line behind Carnival.
- **Change or Lose Corporate Identity** A merger may help a company change or lose a corporate identity. When ValuJet merged with AirWays to form AirTran Holdings Corporation, AirTran hoped the name change would help the public forget ValuJet's tragic Everglades crash in 1996 that claimed 110 lives even though the new company flew the same planes and routes as the original one. Sometimes one company will purchase or acquire another for the same reasons that firms merge. The difference between an acquisition and a merger, however, is that a merger usually involves an exchange of stock or a consolidation as a new company. In the case of an acquisition or a buyout, however, the firm that makes the purchase uses its own cash or stock—and the company being bought loses its own identity.

Conglomerates

A corporation may become so large through mergers and acquisitions that it turns into a conglomerate. A **conglomerate** is a firm that typically has at least four businesses, each making unrelated products, none of which are responsible for a majority of its sales. For example, the largest of 3M Company's six business segments illustrated in **Figure 8.6** accounts for about one-third of its sales.

Diversification is one of the main reasons for conglomerate mergers. Some firms hope to protect their overall sales and profits by not "putting all their eggs in one basket." Isolated economic events, such as bad weather or a sudden change of consumer tastes, may affect some product lines but not all of them at the same time.

In recent years, the number of conglomerates in the United States has declined. In Asia, however, conglomerates remain strong. Samsung, LG, and Hyundai-Kia are still dominant in South Korea, as are Mitsubishi, Panasonic, and Sony in Japan.

Multinationals

Other large corporations have become international in scope. A **multinational** is a corporation that has manufacturing or service operations in a number of different countries. In effect, it is a citizen of several countries at one time. A multinational is likely to pay taxes in each country where it has operations and is subject to the laws of each. General Motors, Nabisco, British Petroleum, Royal Dutch Shell, Mitsubishi, and Sony are examples of multinational corporations that have attained worldwide economic importance.

internally existing or occurring from within

conglomerate firm with four or more businesses making unrelated products, with no single business responsible for a majority of its sales

multinational corporation producing and selling without regard to national boundaries and whose business activities are located in several different countries

---

networks Online Teaching Options

GRAPHIC ORGANIZER

Models for Business Growth

Taking notes to model business growth
Use the graphic organizer to help students understand how mergers compare to reinvestment as a means of business expansion. Have students discuss what mergers are and how they differ from reinvestment as a means of business expansion. Then have students complete the graphic organizer, describing both forms of business expansion. **Ask:** Which form of business expansion would likely produce the most immediate and dramatic effect on the original business? *(Sample answer: A merger, because as soon as it is finalized it adds another company to the first company.)*

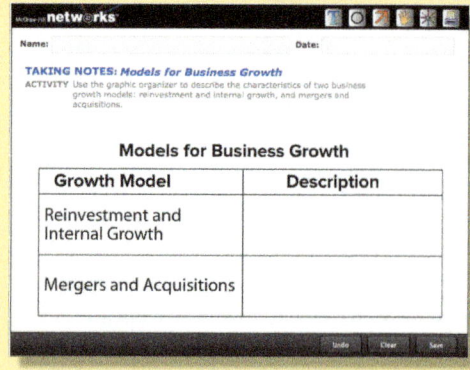

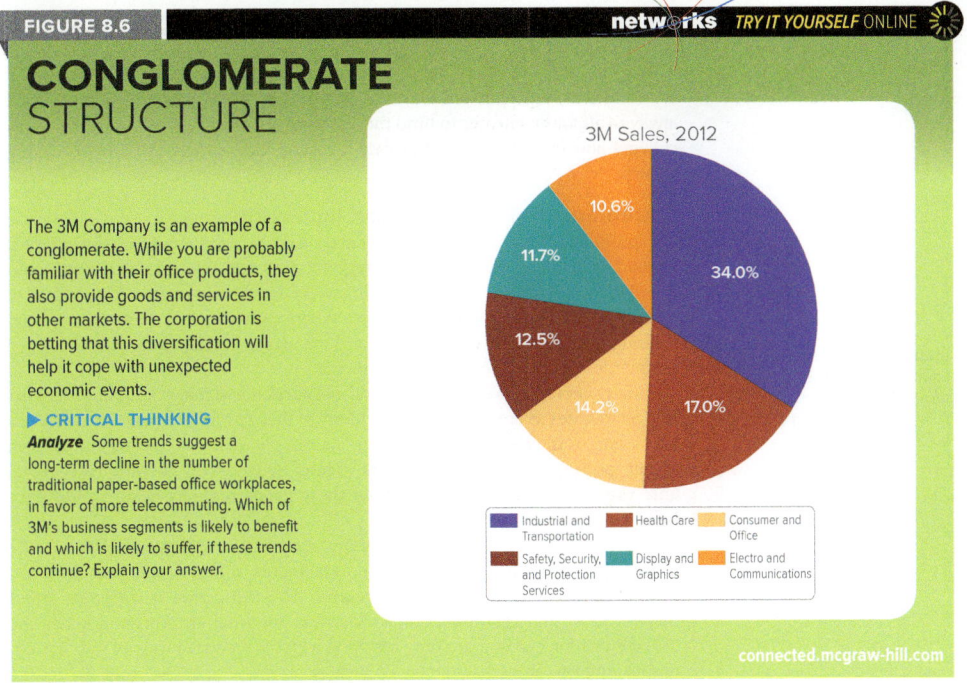

FIGURE 8.6

CONGLOMERATE STRUCTURE

The 3M Company is an example of a conglomerate. While you are probably familiar with their office products, they also provide goods and services in other markets. The corporation is betting that this diversification will help it cope with unexpected economic events.

▶ **CRITICAL THINKING**
Analyze Some trends suggest a long-term decline in the number of traditional paper-based office workplaces, in favor of more telecommuting. Which of 3M's business segments is likely to benefit and which is likely to suffer, if these trends continue? Explain your answer.

Multinational corporations are important because they have the ability to move resources, goods, services, and financial capital across national borders. For example, a multinational with its headquarters in Canada could sell bonds in France. The proceeds could then be used to expand a plant in Mexico that makes products for sale in the United States. A multinational may also be a conglomerate if it makes unrelated products, but it is more likely to be called a multinational if it conducts operations in several different countries.

Multinationals are usually welcome in a nation because they transfer new technologies and generate new jobs in areas where jobs are needed. Multinationals also produce tax revenues for the host country, which helps that nation's economy.

At times, multinationals have been known to abuse their power by paying low wages to workers, exporting scarce natural resources, or interfering with the development of local businesses. Some critics point out that multinational corporations are able to demand tax, regulatory, and wage concessions by threatening to move their operations to another country. Other critics are concerned that multinationals may alter traditional ways of life and business customs in the host country.

Most economists, however, welcome the lower-cost production and higher-quality output that global competition brings. They also believe that the transfer of technology that eventually takes place will raise the standard of living for everyone. On balance, the advantages of multinationals far outweigh the disadvantages.

✓ **READING PROGRESS CHECK**
Explaining What are the different types of mergers that happen within businesses?

CHAPTER 8, LESSON 2
Business Growth and Expansion

W Writing Skills

Identifying advantages and disadvantages of multinationals Have students create a chart identifying the advantages and disadvantages of multinationals. *(Advantages: resources, goods, services, and financial capital are moved across national borders; new technologies and new jobs are transferred where needed; tax revenues produced for host country; lower-cost production and higher-quality output; raises standard of living for many in host country. Disadvantages: pay low wages to workers; export scarce natural resources from host country; interfere with local businesses; may demand concessions; may alter traditional ways of life in host country; working conditions may be unhealthy and dangerous; may utilize child labor; may harm environment with lax pollution laws.)*

English Language Proficiency

Advanced Model using a graphic organizer to take notes on spoken information. For example, teach students to use a two-column Table Notes organizer with questions such as Who, What, Where, When, Why, and How about start-up incubators, venture capitalists, angel investors, and crowdfunding. Put these questions in the left column. Model taking notes in the right column by answering the question in the left column.

INTERACTIVE FEATURE

Conglomerate Structure

Analyzing a conglomerate After students click through Figure 8.6, have them research another conglomerate, such as General Electric. Encourage students to find out how GE grew its business through mergers with smaller companies. Students may want to make a list or a poster that shows the many and varied types of businesses GE is involved in—many of which involved mergers with companies already in that type of business. **Verbal/Linguistic, Visual/Spatial**

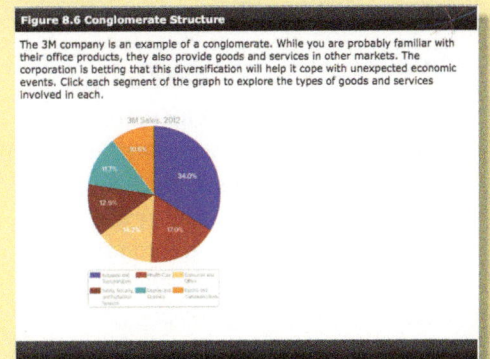

ANSWERS, p. 227

CRITICAL THINKING
Student answers may vary. One possibility is that the Electro and Communications segment might benefit and the Consumer and Office segment might suffer.

✓ **READING PROGRESS CHECK** The two main types of mergers are horizontal mergers and vertical mergers.

CHAPTER 8, LESSON 2
Business Growth and Expansion

T Technology Skills

Researching government involvement in start-up funding Have students use the Internet to find out the degree to which the government (federal and state) subsidizes new and innovative ideas that lead to start-up companies by financing research and development at public universities and other publicly funded "incubators." Students may want to research public funding in your state or public funding of a particular industry. They may even want to learn about public funding, even indirect funding, that led to the formation of a small start-up company that eventually grew into a massively profitable corporation. Encourage students to share their findings with the class. **Logical/Mathematical**

W₁ Writing Skills

Researching incubators, venture capitalists, and angel investors Have students key "financial incubator," "venture capitalist," and/or "angel investor" into a search engine. Ask students to select a Web site and write a summary of information found on it. Students should share their findings with the class.

W₂ Writing Skills

Making your case for funding Have students think of a small business they would like to start. Then encourage them to list reasons why other students, acting as venture capitalists, should invest in their start-up business. Students may list points highlighting how innovative and ultimately profitable their new business will be. Then give student volunteers five minutes each to pitch their business idea to the "venture capitalists" in the class. At the end, all students may offer constructive critiques of each pitch and explain why they were or were not persuaded to invest in each business presented. **Auditory/Musical, Verbal/Linguistic**

228

Entrepreneurial Funding for Start-Ups

GUIDING QUESTION *What are the different ways businesses can find start-up funds?*

Businesses are so important to the health of regions and countries that we don't always wait for businesses to fund their own growth and expansion. Many states, colleges and universities, and private investors have stepped in and are trying to help.

Entrepreneurial Education and Incubators

The problem with starting a new business isn't just about having a good idea. Instead, it is often about having enough funding and managerial ability to put the idea into action. To fill this gap, many states and universities have begun to promote start-up **incubators**, or places where potential entrepreneurs can get training in accounting, engineering, and managerial skills, along with potential financing, to give life to a business concept.

Many universities even have specialized curricula so that graduating students can get degrees in entrepreneurship. Many of these programs have competitions at the end of their studies where students can compete for start-up funds from either public or private investors. Many will never become successful entrepreneurs, of course, but without these programs they never would have had a chance to try.

Historically, there have been many cooperative ventures between elite universities and top companies, with agreements and products that enriched both parties if the ideas were successful. The thing that is different about incubators is that the education needed for potential entrepreneurs and the possibilities for funding are now reaching a much broader range of individuals, not just top researchers who may do little or no teaching in exchange for getting research grants.

incubators places where entrepreneurs can receive the training and other assistance to build a successful start-up business

Venture Capitalists

A **venture capitalist** is a provider of investment funds to a new or unproven business in exchange for an equity (ownership) share. Venture capitalists are usually well known in the start-up community, and a rigorous presentation is usually required to secure funding. In return, the venture capitalist may expect as much as a 25 percent annual return on his or her investment, and require ownership of at least half the company. These terms may seem rigorous, but they are often necessary to offset expected losses on other start-ups that the venture capitalist supports.

The venture capitalist will also offer helpful expertise and can introduce the entrepreneur to other industry firms to help solve problems. The venture capitalist will help the entrepreneur with an initial public offering (IPO) of corporate stock in hopes of getting the company off the ground. If the IPO is successful, the venture capitalist might sell his or her shares and then go look for another start-up to fund.

venture capitalist provider of investment funds to a start-up business in exchange for partial ownership of the business

Angel Investors

Angel investors like to fund the start-ups of family, friends, or others whose business ideas have potential, but could not otherwise obtain enough seed money. The term "angel" is due to the fact that they are usually more interested in helping the individual survive than getting a substantial return on their investment. Because of this, the financing terms are much more generous and forgiving than would be the terms of any other type of funding.

angel investors informal and usually affluent investors who provide funds to less-promising start-ups

228

networks Online Teaching Options

VIDEO **WORKSHEET**

Cadbury

Making inferences about mergers Have students watch the video. Discuss the reason this merger occurred. **Ask:** **What did Kraft not understand about Cadbury and its customers when it pushed through the merger?** *(It did not understand the nostalgia and resistance to change among Cadbury's loyal customers.)* **What can you infer about the different motivations of stockholders and the customers regarding this merger?** *(Stockholders anticipated more dividends; customers were opposed because they feared a decline in product quality.)*

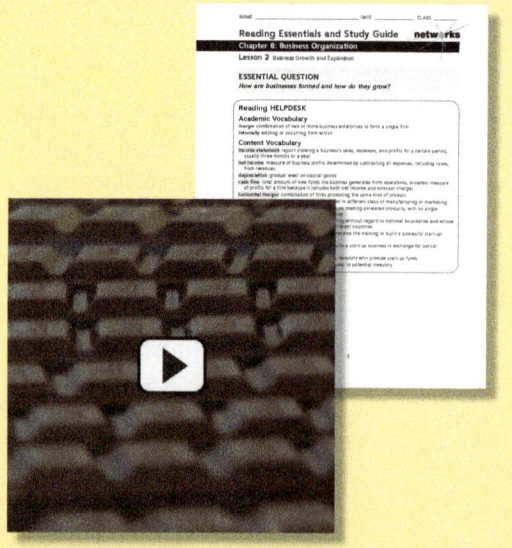

While there is no set pattern or model for angel lending, support is usually in the form of a one-time injection of funds, although even that might change over time. Some angel investors are organized as "clubs" and pool their funds; others are organized more formally and require a "piece of the business" if it becomes successful. Wealthy investors often mentor the companies they help fund. They hope that the success of the companies will improve life for the whole community.

Crowdfunding

One of the newest ways for an entrepreneur to secure financing is through **crowdfunding**, also known as crowdsourcing, the making of a direct funding appeal to a "crowd" of possibly interested investors on a social networking platform. For example, if a potential entrepreneur has an idea that he or she wants to promote to an interest group, the promotion can be made for very little cost. All that is required is a good idea, a successful crowdfunding strategy, a suitable media platform, and a crowd willing to listen and, of course, contribute.

Crowdfunding had its roots in Facebook and LinkedIn, when people would solicit advice on things like how to become a more effective speaker. More recently, crowdfunding is being used to solicit funds for start-up investment projects. A number of the earliest crowdfunding sites, such as Kickstarter, Fundable, and Crowdfunder, have had varying degrees of success, but are still evolving as the technology and methods are likely to undergo considerable evolution.

Until then, the $5.7 million raised by Kickstarter in a little more than 10 hours from over 90,000 backers to bring the cult favorite Veronica Mars back to life on the big screen will be one of the success stories that every crowdfunding entrepreneur would love to match.

crowdfunding using social networking to appeal to potential investors

✓ **READING PROGRESS CHECK**

Explaining What are the advantages and disadvantages of seeking financial start-up from a venture capitalist?

CHAPTER 8, LESSON 2
Business Growth and Expansion

CLOSE & REFLECT

V Visual Skills

Launching a start-up business Have students decide on a start-up business they would like to get off the ground. Have them create a poster or other visual aid that shows what product or service the business will provide, how they will get funding to get the business up and running, and what type of merger, if any, they might consider later when their business is a success.

ANSWERS, p. 229

✓ **READING PROGRESS CHECK** The advantages are that the venture capitalists will offer business expertise to the start-up, introduce the entrepreneur to other industry companies to help solve problems, and help the entrepreneur with an initial public offering (IPO). The disadvantages are that the venture capitalists often require a significant ownership share of the business and expect significant returns on the investment.

LESSON 2 REVIEW

Reviewing Vocabulary
1. **Explaining** Why is cash flow a more comprehensive measure of a company's profits than net income?

Using Your Notes
Refer to the graphic organizer for this question.
2. **Explaining** Your business partner has decided he wants to merge your business—Healthy Foods—with former competitor Beta Burger. He's told you about the advantages, but you've got your doubts. What possible disadvantages about the merger would you explain to your partner before you both make your decision?

Answering the Guiding Questions
3. **Describing** Why would business owners choose to reinvest profits?

4. **Summarizing** What advantages are gained through business mergers?

5. **Explaining** What are the different ways businesses can find start-up funds?

Writing About Economics
6. **Argument** Assume you and a friend have an outstanding business idea for a social media product and want to find some start-up funds to start a business. You and your friend disagree on which way to find start-up funds. Choose one of the funding sources discussed in the lesson, and in a one-page essay present your argument for your choice. Be sure to give reasons for your choice and what you predict the outcome will be.

LESSON 2 REVIEW ANSWERS

Reviewing Vocabulary
1. Cash flow includes noncash charges, such as depreciation. increase cash flows. Also, investors look at cash flow before investing, and a solid cash flow attracts more investors.

Using Your Notes
2. Answers should center on (1) arguments over what the business will be called from then on, (2) the risk of combining different, possibly clashing, company cultures, and (3) the lack of any guarantee that the customers will like the new, merged business.

Answering the Guiding Questions
3. Profits help fuel innovation, such as new product development, which can further

4. Some advantages include faster growth, lower production costs, the acquisition of new product lines, the elimination of rivals, and the reinvention of a corporate identity.

5. Businesses can find start-up funds by getting involved with an incubator, by finding venture capitalists and angel investors, and by using social media to crowdfund.

Writing About Economics
6. Answers should include one of the ways to find start-up funds discussed in the lesson: incubators, venture capitalists, angel investors, or crowdfunding. Students should give reasons for their choice and include what they predict the outcome of their choice will be.

CHAPTER 8
Debate

ENGAGE

C1 Critical Thinking Skills

Understanding unemployment in a recession Explain to students that beginning in the fall of 2008, the United States entered a Great Recession after financial institutions teetered on the brink of collapse due to excessively risky investments. At one point in the months following the onset of the Great Recession, unemployment topped 10 percent. Many people became jobless when the companies they worked for went out of business. (The banking crisis dried up credit needed by many businesses.) Then invite students to discuss the impact of outsourcing on the slow rate of job growth in the United States.
Ask: What could have been done to spur businesses to create more jobs for the unemployed during this crisis? Discuss whether the government should have done something to entice these corporations to bring jobs back to the United States. **Logical/Mathematical, Verbal/Linguistic**

TEACH & ASSESS

V Visual Skills

Researching working conditions in developing nations Have students find images of working conditions in developing nations where many MNCs have outsourced jobs. Students should look for images that show different types of jobs in different industries. Discuss the socioeconomic benefits of outsourcing to these countries. **AL ELL Visual/Spatial**

C2 Critical Thinking Skills

Assessing consumers' responsibility for sustaining outsourcing Have students discuss the following conundrum: Americans earn less as jobs are outsourced overseas to low-wage countries. Because they have less money, Americans tend to buy cheaper goods, which are made overseas by low-wage workers. This perpetuates the cycle of outsourcing American jobs, lowering U.S. workers' wages, and slowing the creation of domestic jobs.
Ask: Do you think American consumers who buy imports are responsible for their own predicament? What might American consumers do to reverse or slow down this trend? *(Sample answer: consumer cooperatives may sell only U.S.-made goods at lower prices)* Encourage students to be innovative in their ideas for solving this problem. **Logical/Mathematical**

Debates

C1 Is it ethical for businesses to outsource jobs to foreign countries when there is high unemployment in the United States?

Among today's businesses, it is not uncommon for companies to outsource certain business functions. They may do so to save money on internal staffing. They may also wish to take advantage of third-party suppliers that have expertise in certain functions.

One aspect of outsourcing that has attracted much attention in recent years is the outsourcing of certain jobs to overseas companies. While the practice of foreign outsourcing can provide much-needed cost savings, many Americans are concerned that U.S. jobs are being lost to overseas workers. These concerns are especially pressing during periods of high unemployment, when jobs are scarce and laid-off workers are desperately searching for new positions.

In this type of economic climate, is it ethical for businesses to continue to outsource jobs to countries outside of the United States?

YES Outsourcing jobs and investing in foreign countries...

- **IMPROVES THE OVERALL ECONOMY BY CREATING PROFITABLE BUSINESSES**
- **CAUSES SOME BUSINESSES TO OUTSOURCE CERTAIN JOBS IN ORDER TO COMPETE**
- **MAKES COMPANIES MORE PROFITABLE BY REDUCING LABOR COSTS**

V MANY OUTSOURCED JOBS ARE LOWER-PAYING POSITIONS THAT AMERICANS DON'T WANT

> *The phenomenon of foreign outsourcing creates tangible benefits for the U.S. economy and American workers. Whatever negative impact it has had on specific firms and workers has been limited and is far outweighed by the benefits.*
>
> —Daniel Griswold, director of the Center for Trade Policy Studies at the Cato Institute

C2 Outsourcing Benefits
- Focus on core business
- Cost savings
- Increased efficiency
- Staffing flexibility
- Specialized expertise

---

networks Online Teaching Options

DEBATE

Debate: Is it ethical for businesses to outsource jobs to foreign countries when there is high unemployment in the United States?

Debating an ethical issue Have a volunteer read aloud the question to be debated. Have two other students read the suggested arguments in favor of (*pro*) and against (*con*) the debate question. Organize students into two groups, each to debate one side of the issue. Give students 10–15 minutes to prepare their arguments. Then allow 15–20 minutes for debate. Each side gets three minutes to present an argument; the other side gets two minutes to rebut it. Sides take turns presenting arguments and rebuttals. Have students discuss which side was most persuasive on the issue.

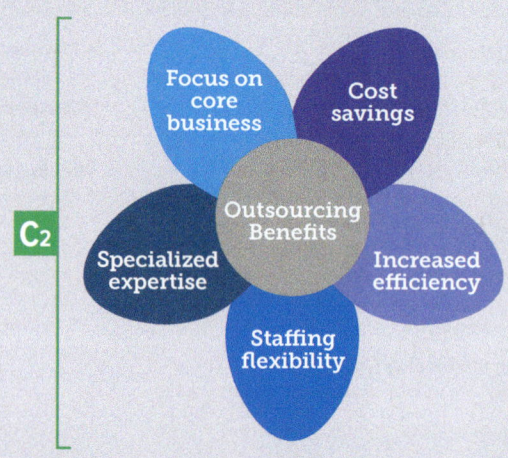

NO Outsourcing jobs and investing in foreign countries...

- CAUSES U.S. EMPLOYEES IN SOME SECTORS TO HAVE FEWER JOB PROSPECTS
- MAY BE OFFSET BY AN INCREASE IN MANAGEMENT AND OVERSIGHT COSTS
- MAY CAUSE PRODUCT QUALITY TO SUFFER DUE TO LANGUAGE AND CULTURAL BARRIERS
- MAY CAUSE COMPANIES TO LOSE CONTROL OVER PROPRIETARY INFORMATION

networks
TRY IT YOURSELF ONLINE
For an interactive version of this debate go to connected.mcgraw-hill.com

> "One: How many more jobs must we lose before they become concerned about our middle class and our strength as a consumer market? Two: When will the U.S. have to quit borrowing foreign capital to buy foreign goods that support European and Asian economies while driving us deeper into debt? Three: What jobs will our currently 15 million unemployed workers fill, where and when?"
>
> —Lou Dobbs, anchor and managing editor of *Lou Dobbs Tonight*, CNN

FROM 1999 TO 2010, AMERICAN COMPANIES ADDED 3X AS MANY NEW OVERSEAS JOBS AS NEW U.S. JOBS

ANALYZING the issue

1. **Analyzing Visuals** How has the number of jobs in America and the number of jobs outsourced changed? What does this mean to the American worker?

2. **Identifying** What are some of the tangible benefits of outsourcing that Griswold refers to, and what are some of the negative impacts Dobbs refers to?

3. **Argument** Which argument do you find most compelling: jobs at home or outsourcing jobs abroad? Explain your answer.

DEBATE

Analyzing outsourcing Focus on the graphic above about outsourcing. **Ask: How many more jobs are U.S. multinational corporations (MNCs) creating overseas than they are creating in the United States?** *(three times as many)* Have students discuss the types of jobs most likely to be outsourced, and then have students talk about the relationship between global computer use and the outsourcing of high-skilled jobs. Tell students that even physicians' jobs are being outsourced, as lower-paid doctors who can do the same work via computer from low-wage countries overseas take the jobs of American radiologists and other specialists. Have students brainstorm a list of jobs that cannot be outsourced. Encourage them to talk about what characteristics, if any, these jobs share. **Logical/Mathematical, Verbal/Linguistic**

CHAPTER 8
Debate

R Reading Skills

Learning about the changing middle class Have students find sources (online or in newspapers or magazines) that describe how the Great Recession and long-term unemployment affected the middle class in the United States. Have students write a report about what has happened to the middle class and its likely effects on the U.S. economy, particularly in terms of demand for goods and services. **BL Verbal/Linguistic**

CLOSE & REFLECT

Summarizing the issues Have students write a summary outlining the issues debated here. The summary should be unbiased. The students may then write one or two paragraphs that set out their opinion on the issue of outsourcing jobs at a time of high unemployment. Students should use examples and evidence in making a cogent, logical, and well-expressed argument for their viewpoint.

English Language Proficiency

Intermediate Ask students yes and no questions about the debate topic, such as "Do you believe that....?" After they answer, offer a sentence starter such as "I think that," and encourage students to express an opinion or idea in a sentence. Then encourage students to elaborate with more detail about their opinions.

ANSWERS, p. 231

ANALYZING the issue

1. The number of jobs in America has decreased and the number of jobs outsourced has increased.
2. Tangible benefits include cost savings to consumers; and businesses' increased efficiency, staffing flexibility, specialized expertise, and the ability to focus on core business. Negative impacts include a weakening of the middle class, going deeper into debt as a country, and 15 million unemployed workers.
3. Students should clearly state which side of the argument they're leaning toward and should justify their positions. Arguments for jobs at home may include emotional appeals about family members affected by outsourcing, or general appeals to economic equity (fairness) or economic security, two of the U.S. economy's seven overarching socioeconomic goals. Arguments for outsourcing or offshoring may include appeals to economic freedom and economic efficiency, also two goals.

CHAPTER 8, LESSON 3
Nonprofit Organizations

ENGAGE

C Critical Thinking Skills

Identifying nonprofit organizations Before students begin the lesson, have them name several national nonprofit service organizations. Then ask them if they are aware of any nonprofits that operate only in their state, city, or locality. Encourage students to think of and name or describe local or state nonprofit groups. Prompt them to think about groups devoted to improving education, the environment, housing, food, helping the poor, the ill, or the disabled, and so on. Encourage students who are familiar with one of these organizations to describe why their work is important and, if possible, to explain how they are funded. Encourage interested students to contact a local nonprofit to find out what it does and how it is supported.

ANSWERS, p. 232

ESSENTIAL QUESTION ACTIVITY

Students' answers should include that nonprofit organizations, as the name suggests, do not profit from their work. Yet they must somehow find the money they need to function and provide services like for-profit businesses.

TAKING NOTES
Community Organization: incorporated to take advantage of unlimited life and limited liability; use revenues to benefit the community
Cooperative: voluntary association that performs an economic activity to benefit its members
Labor Union: organization of workers that represent their interest in employment matters and bargain with management
Professional Organization: members of a profession working together to improve conditions, skill levels, and perceptions of profession
Business Associations: group of businesses that promote shared interests, either in a specific community or specific kind of business
Government: directly provides some goods and services; ensures fairness and efficiency in the market

---

Interact with these digital assets and others in lesson 3
✓ POLITICAL CARTOON Credit Unions and Banks
✓ GLOBAL ECONOMY AND YOU Economic Analysis on a Global Scale
✓ SELF-CHECK QUIZ
✓ VIDEO

networks TRY IT YOURSELF ONLINE

LESSON 3
Nonprofit Organizations

ESSENTIAL QUESTION

How does a market economy support nonprofit organizations?

Reading Help Desk

Academic Vocabulary
- analyze
- devote

Content Vocabulary
- nonprofit organization
- cooperative, or co-op
- credit union
- labor union
- collective bargaining
- chamber of commerce
- Better Business Bureau

TAKING NOTES:

Key Ideas and Details
ACTIVITY Use the graphic organizer below to identify types of nonprofit organizations and the benefits they offer.

Types of Nonprofit Organizations

Organization	Benefit

Most businesses use scarce resources to produce goods and services in hopes of earning a profit for their owners. Other organizations operate on a "not-for-profit" basis. A **nonprofit organization** works in a businesslike way to promote the collective interests of its members rather than to seek financial gain for its owners.

There are hundreds of thousands of nonprofit organizations in the United States today. The American Red Cross, the United Way, the Smithsonian Institution, the Girl Scouts, and even the U.S. Olympic Committee are just a few of the better-known national nonprofits, but there are many more in almost every community in the country.

Pick a nonprofit organization that you know of and answer the following questions about it:

a. What is the purpose of this organization?
b. How does it make money to fund its purpose?
c. How is this nonprofit organization different from for-profit businesses? How is it the same?
d. Why do you think the government doesn't require this organization to pay taxes?

Community Organizations and Cooperatives

GUIDING QUESTION *Why is the value of community organizations and cooperatives difficult to measure?*

Community Organizations
Community organizations include schools, churches, hospitals, welfare groups, and adoption agencies. Many of these organizations are legally

---

networks *Online Teaching Options*

BELLRINGER

Nonprofit Organizations

Describing industrial working conditions prior to unionization Use the Bellringer to initiate a discussion about how unions, as nonprofit organizations, formed in response to the terrible conditions in which men, women, and even young children worked in in the United States, and elsewhere. Have students look closely at the photograph and note details that reveal these working conditions.

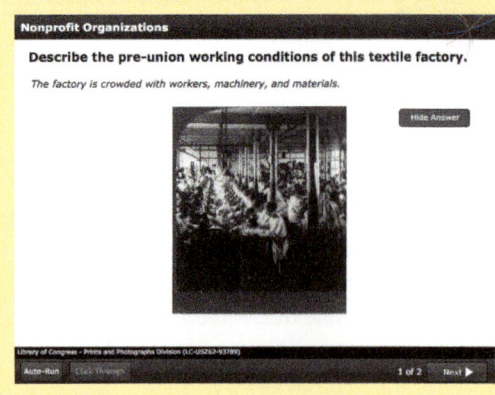

incorporated to take advantage of unlimited life and limited liability. They are similar to profit-seeking businesses but do not issue stock, pay dividends, or pay income taxes. If their activities produce revenues in excess of expenses, they use the surplus to further their work.

Like profit-seeking businesses, nonprofit organizations use scarce factors of production. The results of their efforts are difficult to **analyze**, however, because the value of their contributions is difficult to measure. Even so, the large number of nonprofits shows that they are an important part of our economic system.

Cooperatives

A common type of nonprofit organization is the **cooperative, or co-op**. A cooperative is a voluntary association formed to carry on some kind of economic activity that will benefit its members. Cooperatives fall into three major categories: consumer, service, and producer.

- **Consumer cooperative** A consumer co-op is a voluntary association that buys bulk amounts of goods such as food or clothing that can be sold to members at prices lower than those charged by regular businesses. Members usually **devote** several hours a week or month to the operation to help keep costs down.
- **Service cooperative** A service co-op provides services such as insurance, credit, or child care to its members, rather than goods. A **credit union**, a financial organization that accepts deposits from, and makes loans to, employees of a particular company or government agency, is a service co-op.
- **Producer cooperative** A producer co-op is mostly made up of producers like farmers and helps members promote or sell their products directly to markets, consumers, or companies that use the members' products. Some co-ops, such as the Ocean Spray cranberry co-op, market their products directly to consumers.

✓ **READING PROGRESS CHECK**

Explaining How does a cooperative work?

nonprofit organization economic institution that operates like a business but does not seek financial gain; schools, churches, and community-service organizations are examples

analyze to break down into parts to study how each part relates to another

cooperative, or co-op nonprofit association performing some kind of economic activity for the benefit of its members

devote give time or attention

credit union nonprofit service cooperative that accepts deposits, makes loans, and provides other financial services

POLITICAL CARTOON: CREDIT UNIONS AND BANKS

Credit unions and banks are both corporations that help consumers handle financial issues.

◀ **CRITICAL THINKING**
Evaluate Give at least one advantage of a bank and one advantage of a credit union.

CHAPTER 8, LESSON 3
Nonprofit Organizations

R Reading Skills

Identifying types of cooperatives Have students create a three-column chart defining the three types of cooperatives and providing several examples of each. Then have students describe how and why cooperatives help the people who belong to them. Explain that a person must often pay a small membership fee to join a cooperative. Tell students to include reasons people are willing to pay that fee (such as lower prices members pay at a cooperative store, or the benefits members get from joining a service or producer cooperative).

C Critical Thinking Skills

Evaluating cooperatives' usefulness Encourage students to discuss how each type of cooperative helps its members. **Ask: Why are cooperatives, such as health food cooperatives or credit unions, beneficial to people who live near them and are members?** *(Sample answer: They are beneficial because they understand local needs and problems, are more responsive to the issues facing local residents, and look out for members' interests.)* Invite students to describe cooperatives that may exist in your area. If few or none exist, encourage them to suggest what local needs and interests might be served if a particular type of cooperative was started. **Verbal, Logical/Mathematical**

T Technology Skills

Comparing credit unions and commercial banks Have students find the Web site of a credit union in your locality or state. Tell students to take notes about information on the site, such as interest rates paid for savings, interest rates charged for loans and mortgages, special programs designed for local use, etc. Then have students find similar information for a national commercial bank. Have students compare the information and create a two-column chart in which they contrast information for the two types of banks.

ANSWERS, p. 233

✓ **READING PROGRESS CHECK** Cooperatives are voluntary organizations that allow members to collaborate to provide services or to buy or sell products that would be more expensive or less successful if members had to do it as individuals.

CRITICAL THINKING
Answers may vary. Banks are large institutions that can absorb risk better than credit unions. Credit unions are smaller but are intended primarily to serve members' needs without trying to reward shareholders. Thus, interest rates are often lower for credit union members.

POLITICAL CARTOON

Credit Unions and Banks

Comparing and contrasting banks and credit unions Have students view the political cartoon, and ask volunteers to explain the differences between credit unions and banks. Then organize students into small groups and have each group complete a Venn diagram comparing the two. Then have students discuss the advantages and disadvantages of each type of bank: for those who own the financial institution as well as for the public users of each type. Remind students that banks are larger and may be able to offer more services, but they are operated to earn profits for shareholders. Credit unions are intended for the benefit of their members, not shareholders, but are often smaller and offer a more limited range of services. **Logical/Mathematical, Visual/Spatial**

CHAPTER 8, LESSON 3
Nonprofit Organizations

W Writing Skills

Learning about professional associations Have students set up an appointment to interview (in person, by phone, or by e-mail) a professional (doctor, lawyer, teacher, police officer, etc.) in their local community. Students should prepare questions to ask about a professional or business association to which the interviewee belongs. Have them ask what the association provides or does, including disseminating information about licensing, training, standards, and promoting members' financial interests and services. Students should summarize the information in a brochure. **Interpersonal**

Content Background Knowledge

First Successful U.S. Cooperative The first successful cooperative in the United States—the Philadelphia Contributionship for the Insurance of Houses from Loss of Fire—was organized by Benjamin Franklin in 1751. It is still operating today, making it the oldest continuously operative cooperative in the country.

Labor, Professional, and Business Organizations

GUIDING QUESTION *How do some nonprofit organizations promote the interests of workers and consumers?*

Nonprofit organizations are not just limited to co-ops and civic groups. Many other groups also organize this way to promote the interests of their members.

Labor Unions

One important group is the **labor union**, an organization of workers formed to represent its members' interests in various employment matters. The union participates in **collective bargaining** when it negotiates with management over issues such as pay, working hours, health-care coverage, vacations, and other job-related matters. Unions also lobby for laws that will benefit or protect their workers.

The largest labor union in the United States is the National Education Association (NEA), which represents public school teachers, administrators, and substitute educators. While the NEA is an independent union, approximately 57 other unions representing approximately 12 million workers have joined the American Federation of Labor–Congress of Industrial Organizations (AFL-CIO). The AFL-CIO is an association of unions that includes workers in a variety of different jobs.

labor union organization that works for its members' interests concerning pay, working hours, health coverage, fringe benefits, and other job-related matters

collective bargaining process of negotiation between union and management representatives over pay, benefits, and job-related matters

EXPLORING THE ESSENTIAL QUESTION

A union of public-transportation employees goes on strike for higher wages. People who depend upon buses and trains must find alternative ways of getting around. The employees don't go back to work until they have gotten a large raise. How do the actions of the union affect the economy?

W Professional Associations

Some workers belong to professional societies, trade associations, or academies. Such professional associations consist of people in a specialized occupation interested in improving the working conditions, skill levels, and public perceptions of the profession.

The American Medical Association (AMA) and the American Bar Association (ABA) are examples of organizations that include members of specific professions. These groups influence the licensing and training of their members, set standards for conduct, and are actively involved in political issues that affect them. Other professional associations represent bankers, teachers, college professors, police officers, and hundreds of other professions.

Business Associations

Businesses also organize to promote their collective interests. Most communities have a local **chamber of commerce**, an organization that promotes the welfare of its member businesses. The typical chamber sponsors activities ranging from educational programs to lobbying for favorable business legislation.

chamber of commerce nonprofit organization of local businesses whose purpose is to promote their interests

Industry or trade associations represent specific kinds of businesses. Trade associations are interested in shaping the government's policy on such economic issues as free enterprise, imports and tariffs, the minimum wage, and new construction.

234

---

networks Online Teaching Options

GRAPHIC ORGANIZER

Types of Nonprofit Organizations

Summarizing the benefits of different nonprofit organizations Have students fill out the graphic organizer for the following nonprofit organization types: government, community organizations, cooperatives, labor unions, professional organizations, and business organizations. All students in the class may participate in suggesting what should be listed in the table.

Ask: Why is the government considered a nonprofit organization? *(Sample answer: Because the government provides funding and services but does not make a profit from them.)* Encourage students to list the different ways the government, as a nonprofit entity, helps businesses and individuals. Urge students to recognize the government's role in education, research and development, distribution of needed goods and services, and so on.

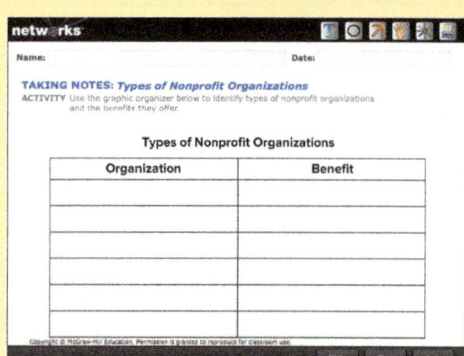

ANSWERS, p. 234

EXPLORING THE ESSENTIAL QUESTION

Answers should note the negative effects (prohibiting people who use public transportation from getting to work) and/or the positive effects (increasing workers' wages and thereby putting more money into the economy).

234

Some business associations help protect the consumer. The **Better Business Bureau** is a nonprofit organization sponsored by local businesses. It provides general information on companies and maintains records of consumer inquiries and complaints.

Better Business Bureau business-sponsored nonprofit organization providing information on local companies to consumers

✓ **READING PROGRESS CHECK**

Summarizing How do professional associations help their members?

THE GLOBAL ECONOMY & YOU

Economic Analysis on a Global Scale

The International Monetary Fund (IMF) is a global organization with 188 participating countries as members. Its goal is to help member nations manage the opportunities and challenges that come from the globalization of the world's economy.

As with national or local nonprofit organizations in the United States, the IMF works to support the capabilities of its members. The IMF may provide financial analysis of economic trends to help countries forecast potential opportunities to pursue or crises to address. The IMF offers research on global and regional economic development and provides technical assistance to countries trying to manage their economies. The IMF may also provide loans to help countries survive financial missteps. It sometimes makes loans to help countries fight poverty.

▲ **CRITICAL THINKING**
Drawing Inferences The map shows the entire European Union, of which 19 countries are part of the eurozone. Why is the work of the IMF important to U.S. citizens?

This support helps stabilize and strengthen a world where economies are growing more intertwined every year. Today, if one nation or region faces an economic crisis, the consequences can usually be felt in all parts of the world. In 2011, for example, Cyprus—an island nation in the Mediterranean Sea—found itself with a massive national debt that threatened the survival of the eurozone, of which it is a part. The eurozone is an economic group of member nations that have adopted the euro as their currency. The IMF, along with other lenders, provided Cyprus with a $13.4 billion loan, but there were strings attached. Cyprus had to make significant reforms to change how its banking system worked and to implement measures to control its debt. The IMF and others helped Cyprus design a plan to meet those goals.

The IMF is an example of a global organization that provides its members access to resources that member states may lack. Other large international organizations include the International Committee of the Red Cross, the World Trade Organization, the United Nations Children's Fund, and the World Health Organization.

connected.mcgraw-hill.com   Business Organization **235**

CHAPTER 8, LESSON 3
Nonprofit Organizations

C Critical Thinking Skills

Analyzing the Better Business Bureau Have students use online or other sources to find out what their local or state Better Business Bureau does, particularly in terms of helping consumers and the public. Encourage students to use the information provided to choose the best automobile repair shop in their area. Have them explain the types of information that the BBB might be able to provide that would help them make this and similar types of consumer decisions.

ANSWERS, p. 235

✓ **READING PROGRESS CHECK** They promote the welfare of members by, for example, representing them in collective bargaining, providing training in skills, and lobbying for favorable laws.

CRITICAL THINKING
Students should recognize that the United States is engaged in a global economic community and that the welfare of other nations directly affects the welfare of the United States. If the economy of one nation fails, international trade and the stability of banking systems can be disrupted, causing a downturn in the American market. That, in turn, can affect jobs and the financial well-being of individual citizens. Global economies today are increasingly interconnected, so a financial crisis in one country can quickly affect the financial health of other nations. For this reason, the ability of the IMF to provide Cyprus with financing and policy advice in response to the crisis benefited the citizens of the United States and other countries, too.

INTERACTIVE FEATURE

Economic Analysis on a Global Scale

Researching Cyprus and the IMF Have students type "Cyprus + economic crisis" into a search engine and select one of the links that appears. Ask students to create a time line of ten events that led to the crisis in Cyprus. Then have students do a search for "International Monetary Fund" and summarize one IMF intervention in recent years.

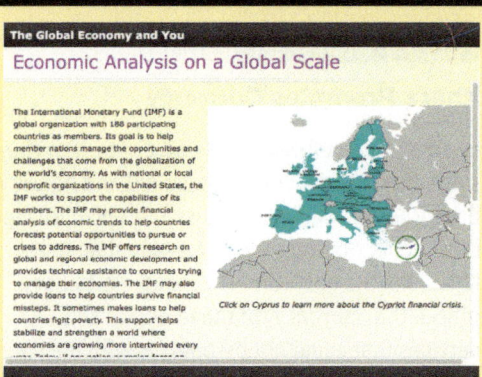

Business Organization **235**

CHAPTER 8, LESSON 3
Nonprofit Organizations

C1 Critical Thinking Skills

Categorizing the economic roles of government Have students create a two-column chart titled "The Role of Government in a Market Economy," with one column headed "Direct Role" and the other column headed "Indirect Role." Tell students to fill in each column with examples. *(Sample direct roles: Tennessee Valley Authority, U.S. Postal Service; Sample indirect roles: college scholarships, Social Security payments)* **Verbal/Linguistic, Logical/Mathematical**

C2 Critical Thinking Skills

Explaining and defending a point of view Have students discuss and debate the question: What effect do you think receiving payments from the government has on those who receive these payments? Include among the recipients corporations that get subsidies for producing goods, agricultural businesses that get subsidies for growing certain crops, the elderly who receive Social Security benefits, the disabled who get disability benefits, the unemployed who get unemployment insurance benefits, and so on. Encourage students to use logical arguments and evidence to support their point of view. Further, have students explain why they may have one point of view for one type of government payment and another when the payment goes to a different party. **Verbal/Linguistic**

Government

GUIDING QUESTION *How does the government operate as a nonprofit organization?*

Although you may not realize it, your local, state, or national government functions as a nonprofit economic organization. Sometimes government plays a direct role in the economy, while at other times the role is indirect.

Direct Role of Government

Many government agencies produce and distribute goods and services to consumers, giving government a direct role in the economy. The role is "direct" because the government supplies a good or service that competes with those provided by private businesses. Here are three examples of government's direct role in the economy:

- **Tennessee Valley Authority (TVA)** The TVA supplies electric power to most of Tennessee and parts of Alabama, Georgia, Kentucky, North Carolina, Virginia, and Mississippi. This supplier competes directly with privately-owned power companies.
- **Federal Deposit Insurance Corporation (FDIC)** The FDIC insures deposits in our nation's banks. Because the insurance the FDIC supplies could be provided by privately-owned insurance companies, the FDIC is an example of the direct role of government.
- **U.S. Postal Service (USPS)** The USPS originally was called the Post Office Department, but the USPS became a government corporation in 1970. The USPS competes directly with private firms like Federal Express (FedEx) and the United Parcel Service (UPS).

Many federal agencies are organized as government-owned corporations. These corporations charge for their products and the revenue goes back into the "business." Unlike private corporations, however, Congress covers any losses the public corporation may incur.

Bank transactions are backed by the FDIC, which ensures that consumers' money is safe in banks in the United States.

networks Online Teaching Options

VIDEO **WORKSHEET**

Ithaca Promotes Currency

Evaluating a solution Have students view the video. Discuss with students what the city of Ithaca did and how it went about doing it. Encourage students to discuss their point of view about a locality creating its own currency. Stress that although Ithaca had its own currency, people also used official U.S. currency for those goods and services that could not be paid for with the local dollars. Encourage students to discuss how using a local currency helped local businesses. *(It kept currency and economic activity within the community and supported local shops and entrepreneurs.)*

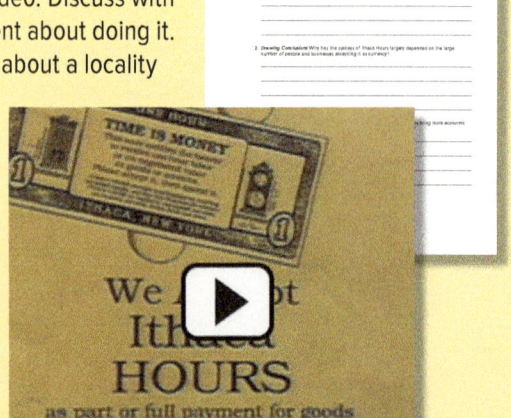

State and local governments also play a direct role in the economy. State governments provide colleges and universities, retirement plans, and statewide police protection. Local governments provide police and fire protection, rescue services, and schools. At the same time, all levels of government help develop and maintain roads and parks.

Indirect Role of Government

The government plays an indirect role when it acts as an umpire to help the market economy operate smoothly and efficiently, or when it gives a group of consumers a boost in purchasing power that they might not otherwise have. This role is "indirect" because a government action does not encourage direct competition with private sector producers, but still has an impact on the economy. Some examples of government's indirect role are listed below:

- **Antitrust laws** Laws like the Sherman Antitrust Act of 1890 were passed to make monopolies and combinations in restraint of trade illegal. The impact is indirect because it prevents firms from doing some things, like combining to make a monopoly, without directly competing with them.
- **College scholarships** Government grants or scholarships to students may encourage more students to go to college. These funds will have the long-run impact of creating a workforce that will be more productive, earn more income, and pay more taxes than a less-educated one.
- **Social Security payments** People who receive Social Security checks get purchasing power that helps keep them out of poverty. The government's role is indirect because it boosts purchasing power of recipients without competing directly with other sectors of the economy.

Payments and funds generated from indirect government actions often give recipients a purchasing power they otherwise might not have had as well as the power to "vote" by making their demands known in the market. This power influences the production of goods and services, which in turn affects the allocation of scarce resources.

✓ **READING PROGRESS CHECK**

Evaluating Do you think one government role is more important than another? Why?

CHAPTER 8, LESSON 3
Nonprofit Organizations

CLOSE & REFLECT

R Reading Skills

Summarizing the lesson Have students summarize the many different but important roles nonprofit organizations of all types play in our economy and in our lives. Invite students to discuss how their life might be different if nonprofit organizations (including the government and its programs) did not exist.

ANSWERS, p. 237

✓ **READING PROGRESS CHECK** Student answers will vary. Sample answer: I think the provision of a social safety net, such as Social Security, Medicare, and unemployment insurance, is the most important government role. Students should recognize that the government influences the economy directly by setting up nonprofit businesses that compete with private businesses and indirectly to influence the marketplace.

LESSON 3 REVIEW

Reviewing Vocabulary
1. *Explaining* How does the Better Business Bureau (BBB) benefit consumers? How might complaints filed with the BBB affect a company's relationship with its customers or potential customers?

Using Your Notes
Refer to the graphic organizer to answer this question.

2. *Examining* Use your notes to explain how nonprofit organizations are an important part of the economy.

Answering the Guiding Questions
3. *Explaining* Why is the value of community organizations and cooperatives difficult to measure?

4. *Describing* How do some nonprofit organizations promote the interests of workers and consumers?

5. *Describing* How does the government operate as a nonprofit organization?

Writing About Economics
6. *Informative/Explanatory* Select a specific nonprofit organization, either one mentioned in the text or another that you know about. In a paragraph, describe the organization. Who are the members? Who benefits from it and how? How does the local or national economy support this organization?

connected.mcgraw-hill.com Business Organization **237**

LESSON 3 REVIEW ANSWERS

Reviewing Vocabulary
1. The Better Business Bureau provides information on local companies to consumers so they know where to find goods and services and where they can make inquiries and make complaints. If a company's BBB profile includes substantial complaints, current and potential customers may go elsewhere. However, negative complaints with the BBB may encourage a business to better serve its customers.

Using Your Notes
2. Students should recognize that nonprofits influence the economy in numerous ways, including improving the skills and bargaining power of workers and businesspeople and addressing social ills, like poverty.

Answering the Guiding Questions
3. Many of the services they provide do not have a clear monetary value, and any revenue they make in excess of costs are put back into the organization.

4. They provide a variety of services. For example, labor unions represent members in collective bargaining; professional associations improve skill levels and public perceptions of the profession; business associations sponsor educational programs and lobby for favorable business legislation.

5. The government operates as a nonprofit by setting up agencies or businesses that provide services or products to the public. If a business brings in more money than it spends, the revenue goes back into the business.

Writing About Economics
6. Students should identify one nonprofit organization and identify its members and who benefits from it. Students should explain one or more ways in which our economy benefits from the nonprofit.

Chapter 8
Study Guide

C1 Critical Thinking Skills

Problem-Solving Remind students that sole proprietorships and partnerships are the two main types of unincorporated businesses in the United States. **Ask: What conditions might lead a sole proprietor to change the business to a partnership?** *(Possible answers include needing more business capital, wanting more help in running the business, or wanting to spend less time on the business.)* **What conditions might lead to a partnership to change the business to a sole proprietorship?** *(Possible answers include needing to earn more money by not sharing profits with a partner, not getting along with a partner, or wanting to shrink the business.)*

C2 Critical Thinking Skills

Drawing Conclusions Have students consider reinvestment. **Ask: How can reinvesting in new technology increase a business's profits?** *(Possible answer: New technology can lead to more efficient processes that increase production. Increased production results in higher profits.)*

STUDY GUIDE

C1

	Advantages	Disadvantages
Sole Proprietorship	• Ease of startup/shut down • Simple management • Owner keeps profit • No separate business tax • Personal satisfaction	• Unlimited liability • Inefficient • Hard to find employees • Limited life
Partnership	• Ease of start up • Ease of management • No separate business tax • Efficient operations • Ease of financing	• High liability • Limited life • Conflict between partners
Corporation	• Easy to raise capital • Limited liability • Professional managers • Unlimited life • Easy to transfer ownership	• Double taxation • Difficult to set up • Owners don't run firm • Government regulations

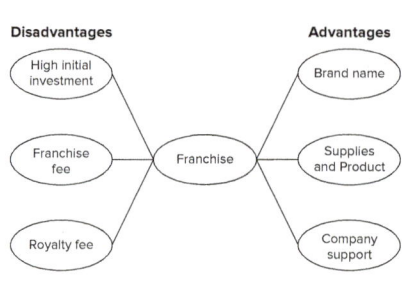

C2

 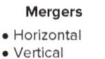

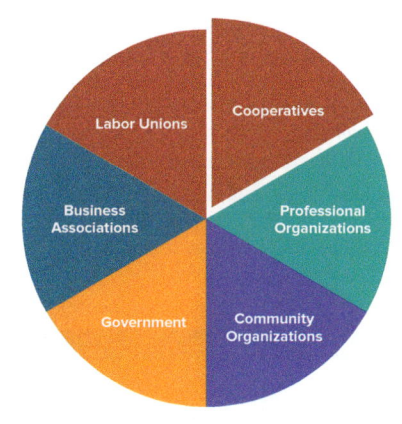

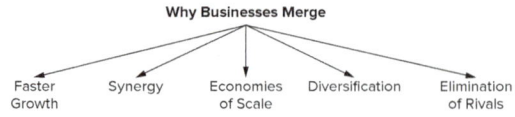

238

---

networks Online Assessment Options

WORKSHEET

Hands-On Chapter Project with Technology Extension

In this activity, students work in groups, each of which is starting a business with a different structure (sole proprietorship, partnership, and corporation). Students outline the organizational structure of their business and thus create a kind of informal business plan. Each organizational structure and business plan should follow the structure of that group's particular business type.

Find an additional activity online that incorporates technology for this project. Visit the EdTech Teacher Web sites for more links, tutorials, and other resources.

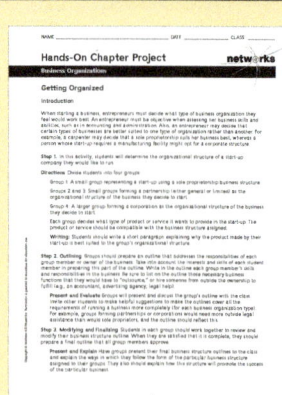

CHAPTER 8 Assessment

Directions: On a separate sheet of paper, answer the questions below. Make sure you read carefully and answer all parts of the questions.

Lesson Review

Lesson 1

1. **Explaining** Imagine that you want to start a landscaping business. Why might you choose to enter the business in partnership rather than as a sole proprietor?

2. **Describing** During the early 2000s, energy giant Enron was shaken by financial mismanagement and scandal. It filed for bankruptcy and, after losing virtually all of its customers, went out of business. What would have been the extent of stockholders' liabilities? Explain.

Lesson 2

3. **Analyzing** Your landscaping business is flourishing, but you realize that it's mainly a nine-month business; it dies out during the winter. A friend has a business clearing snow from parking lots and driveways, a great wintertime business. You and your friend decide to merge your businesses. What kind of merger is it, vertical or horizontal? Explain.

4. **Analyzing** A young entrepreneur has a great idea for a start-up and has secured funding from a venture capitalist. The venture capitalist wants 15 percent of the company and expects a 20 percent return on his investment. Is this a good deal for the entrepreneur? Why or why not?

Lesson 3

5. **Describing** What are some economic benefits to a city of having active professional associations?

6. **Evaluating** Should the government take a direct role in the economy? Explain your answer and give one or more examples.

7. **Explaining** How might your family benefit from joining a cooperative?

Critical Thinking

8. **Synthesizing** Two years ago, an entrepreneur began a start-up. Since then it has been very successful, but the entrepreneur doesn't think it is growing quickly enough. In one or more paragraphs, identify and explain some strategies she might consider to build it faster.

Need Extra Help?

If You've Missed Question	1	2	3	4	5	6	7	8	9	10	11	12
Go to page	212	218	225	228	234	236	233	224	212	236	224	224

9. **Considering Advantages and Disadvantages** A recent graduate of a business school has decided to start a luxury chauffeur service in his town. He has the financial support of friends and family to get the enterprise going. He wonders what type of business organization to form. What advice would you give him? Explain your answer.

10. **Evaluating** The federal government created the Tennessee Valley Authority at a time when many people living in rural areas did not have electricity because private companies could not make a profit by stringing lines to serve so few people. Times have changed; now private companies can profit from serving rural customers. Should the government get out of the business of competing with private power companies? Explain your answer.

Analyzing Visuals

Use the income statement to answer the following questions about cash flow.

11. **Explaining** Why is depreciation added to net income to arrive at cash flow?

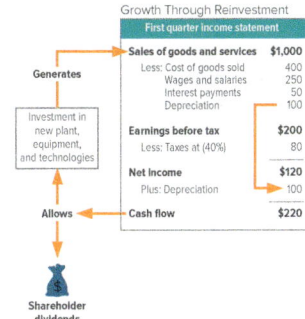

12. **Applying** How much can the firm reinvest into the business? Why would the owner want to reinvest the money?

Chapter 8 Assessment Answers

Lesson Review

Lesson 1

1. A partnership has greater financial resources, and responsibility for running the business can be shared.

2. Stockholders would have lost all value of the shares of stock they held in Enron. That would have been the extent of their losses because in a corporation, individual stockholders' liability is limited to the loss of their investment.

Lesson 2

3. It is a horizontal merger. Both firms are in a similar business.

4. This is probably a reasonable deal for the entrepreneur. The venture capitalist is risking a lot of money by investing in an unproven startup. Some venture capitalists ask for as much as half of a business and expect a higher rate of return.

Lesson 3

5. Students should address some of the reasons outlined in the lesson: (1) professional associations improve the knowledge and skill levels of the professionals working in the city, (2) they organize to promote better working conditions and to enhance public perception of the profession, (3) they provide licensing and certification to individuals in the profession, and (4) they often influence legislation that affects them.

6. Students may say the government should act directly in cases in which a service or product is needed that businesses cannot or do not provide because it is unprofitable to do so. Examples might include the TVA and postal service.

7. Students might suggest they might join a food cooperative so they could purchase food at lower prices, a service cooperative in order to get a car loan at a lower interest rate, or a producer co-op to get better prices when they sell their family's produce.

Critical Thinking Questions

8. Students should identify a variety of strategies based on the content of the chapter that may help the entrepreneur build her business more quickly. Possible solutions might include mergers, selling stock or bonds to raise capital, or reinvesting earnings.

9. Students should demonstrate an understanding of the advantages and disadvantages of the different business organizations. They may recommend a corporation because of the limited liability of owners, or they may recommend that since the graduate has support from friends and family (angel investors), he may have a greater chance with venture capitalists as well.

10. Students should demonstrate an understanding of why and how the government sometimes takes a direct role in the economy. Students take either position on whether the government should get out of the business but should give reasons for their response.

Analyzing Visuals

11. Depreciation is a noncash charge. It is deducted from the firm's revenue as an expense, but it is not paid out—that is, its value has not immediately been "spent" or lost. The deduction is therefore added back in to show the cash flow.

12. The firm can reinvest the total amount of the cash flow, $220. The owner might choose to reinvest the money in order to help the company grow.

Chapter 8
Assessment Answers

Answering the Essential Questions

13 Students should demonstrate knowledge of business organizations and also business structures and how entrepreneurs use them to establish and grow businesses.

14 Students should demonstrate an understanding of the primary contributions of nonprofits, which should include references to the types of nonprofits described in the text: community organizations, cooperatives, labor unions, professional associations, etc.

21st Century Skills

15 Students may say the partners should incorporate. It will reduce their liability and allow them to more easily raise funds to finance the expansion.

16 Students should present the argument that investments require sacrifice of current consumption, but investing in new physical and human capital can increase future productivity and consumption.

17 The co-op is a nonprofit comprised of farmers who have joined together to market and promote their produce. The commercial grain elevator is privately owned, buys from farmers, and sells the grain for a profit on the open market. The co-op does not make a profit or pay taxes, so the farmer may earn more by selling his grain through the co-op.

Building Financial Literacy

18 a. Students should demonstrate an understanding of the advantages and disadvantages of partnerships and sole proprietorships. b. Students should consider incorporating as one option. They may also say the owner could retain the proprietorship and hire a manager. Students should analyze the advantages of the different options, make a recommendation, and explain their reasons.

Analyzing Primary Sources

19 The merger gives RMPBS access to the Latino audience and a stronger newsroom and has increased its audience to 70,000. The merger will enable expansion through the growing Latino audience and by enhancing its skills.

20 The enterprises made a horizontal merger. All are in broadcasting and serve similar audiences.

240

CHAPTER 8 Assessment

Directions: On a separate sheet of paper, answer the questions below. Make sure you read carefully and answer all parts of the questions.

ANSWERING THE ESSENTIAL QUESTIONS

Review your answers to the introductory questions at the beginning of each lesson. Then answer the Essential Questions on the basis of what you learned in the chapter. Have your answers changed?

13 *Explaining* How are businesses formed and how do they grow?

14 *Explaining* How does a market economy support nonprofit organizations?

21st Century Skills

15 *Decision Making* Twenty years ago, two entrepreneurs formed a partnership and opened a shop selling frozen yogurt. The business now has two stores in different parts of the city. The partners want to open stores in three other cities. Should they continue their partnership or incorporate?

16 *Create and Analyze Arguments and Draw Conclusions* A consultant has advised a manufacturer to increase his investment in robots and other technology because it will increase productivity. The owner worries about the cost of upgrading and knows that his employees don't have the skills to operate the new technology. If you were the consultant, what arguments would you present to support your recommendations?

17 *Compare and Contrast* A soybean farmer in Illinois has the opportunity to sell his beans through a farmers' co-op or he can sell them directly to a large commercial grain elevator. How are these two operations alike and different? Where is the farmer most likely to earn the bigger profit? Why?

Building Financial Literacy

18 *Analyzing* A young entrepreneur began providing customers with one-on-one, in-home computer reapair. He has hired several employees, but he still can't keep up with demand. Management isn't his strongest skill. A friend has proposed joining the business as a manager.

   a. Considering only business reasons, should the owner take on his friend as a partner?

   b. What other options does he have for growing the business? Which should he choose? Why?

Analyzing Primary Sources

When organizations join forces and partner or merge, they often have access to resources they previously didn't, along with other benefits. Read the excerpt and answer the questions that follow.

Public media in Colorado are hoping to find strength in numbers. Rocky Mountain PBS on Tuesday signed a merger agreement with the investigative reporting service I-News and with public radio station KUVO (89.3 FM), designed to "redefine public media" in Colorado, RMPBS president and CEO Doug Price said. . . .

PRIMARY SOURCE

"For the I-News Network, the merger means a ready infrastructure at RMPBS so the reporting team can focus on journalism, rather than the business model, said I-News executive director Laura Frank.

For jazz, blues, news station KUVO, the merger means access to the business acumen of RMPBS, already evident in clearing hurdles to technical improvements for the station, and stability in an uncertain era. . . .

For RMPBS, the deal provides access via KUVO to the growing Latino audience, and a weightier newsroom with the five I-News staffers.

The deal makes RMPBS 'the fastest growing public media operation in the country,' Price said. The membership of RMPBS has grown from 47,000 in 2010 to 63,000 now and, counting KUVO's numbers, will reach 70,000 post-merger. . . ."

—By Joanne Ostrow, *The Denver Post*, Jan. 15, 2013

19 *Analyzing Primary Sources* How has Rocky Mountain PBS benefited from the merger? How will these benefits enable RMPBS to grow?

20 *Classifying* What kind of merger has taken place among these three enterprises? Explain.

Need Extra Help?

If You've Missed Question	13	14	15	16	17	18	19	20
Go to page	212	232	212	224	233	212	216	225

240

---

networks *Online Assessment Options*

WORKSHEET

Chapter Tests and Lesson Quizzes

Chapter 8 Tests Forms A and B Have students complete the Chapter Tests and Lesson Quizzes to assess student understanding throughout the chapter. Print and online assessment tools offer chapter and lesson evaluation through a variety of question formats, including document-based questions.

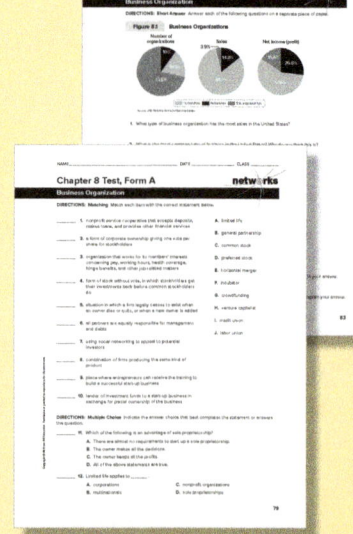

CHAPTER 9
Labor and Wages Planner

UNDERSTANDING BY DESIGN®

Enduring Understanding
- *Disputes over ideas, resources, values, and politics can lead to change.*

Essential Question
- *What features of the modern labor industry are the result of union action?*

Predictable Misunderstandings
Students may think:
- *Union methods are limited to calling strikes, pickets, or boycotts.* Explain that the first method used by modern unions is negotiation with company management. If negotiations fail, strikes, pickets, or boycotts may be employed to place pressure on employers.
- *People who go to work for a company that has unionized must join the union in order to work for the company.* Explain that there are several types of union agreements. A closed shop, in which employees must belong to the union to be hired, is usually illegal. Other types of agreements allow employees to join the union after they are hired or even allow workers to be hired without joining the union at all.

Assessment Evidence
Performance Task
- *Hands-On Chapter Project with Technology Extension*

Other Evidence
- *Guided Reading Activities*
- *Vocabulary Activity*
- *Self-Check Quizzes*
- *Lesson Quizzes*
- *Chapter Assessment*
- *Chapter Tests, Forms A and B*

SUGGESTED PACING

Introducing the Chapter:	½ Day
Lesson 1: The Labor Movement	1 Day
Lesson 2: Wages and Labor Disputes	1 Day
Case Study	½ Day
Lesson 3: Employment Trends and Issues	1 Day
Debate	½ Day
Study Guide, Chapter Assessment, and Wrap-Up	½ Day

TOTAL TIME   5 Days

Key for Using the Teacher Edition

SKILL-BASED ACTIVITIES

Types of skill activites found in the Teacher Edition.

V **Visual Skills** require students to analyze maps, graphs, charts, and photos.

R **Reading Skills** help students practice reading skills and master vocabulary.

C **Critical Thinking Skills** help students apply and extend what they have learned.

W **Writing Skills** provide writing opportunities to help students comprehend the text.

T **Technology Skills** require students to use digital tools effectively.

*Letters are followed by a number when there is more than one of the same type of skill on the page.

DIFFERENTIATED INSTRUCTION

All activities are written for the on-level student unless otherwise marked with the leveled labels below.

BL Beyond Level
AL Approaching Level
ELL English Language Learners

All students benefit from activities that utilize different learning styles. Many activities are marked as below when a particular learning style is highlighted.

Intrapersonal
Logical/Mathematical
Visual/Spatial
Verbal/Linguistic
Naturalist
Kinesthetic
Auditory/Musical
Interpersonal

Council for Economic Education

Below are the Council for Economic Education Voluntary National Content Standards in Economics covered in the *Labor* and *Wages* chapter.

Content Standard 10: Institutions evolve and are created to help individuals and groups accomplish their goals. Banks, labor unions, markets, corporations, legal systems, and not-for-profit organizations are examples of important institutions. A different kind of institution, clearly defined and enforced property rights, is essential to a market economy.

Content Standard 13: Income for most people is determined by the market value of the productive resources they sell. What workers earn depends, primarily, on the market value of what they produce and how productive they are.

CHAPTER 9: LABOR AND WAGES

CHAPTER OPENER PLANNER

Students will know:
- the major events in the rise of the labor movement, including the national labor unions.
- the union arrangements in which unionized workers can participate today.
- how supply of and demand for labor affect wages.
- the methods used by labor unions and management to resolve labor disputes.

Students will be able to:
- **analyze** the effect of union action on the modern labor industry.
- **discuss** the options available for solving labor disputes.
- **state** reasons for the decline of union influence.
- **list** three major causes for pay discrimination in the labor market.
- **consider the advantages and disadvantages** of having a federal minimum wage.

UNDERSTANDING BY DESIGN

☑ Print Teaching Options

R Reading Skills

☐ **p. 242 Evaluating right to work opinions** Students consider views on labor.

C Critical Thinking Skills

☐ **p. 241 Planning labor costs for a new business** Students make decisions to set up a new business.

☐ **p. 242 Characterizing the local area** Students consider which local businesses are unionized or would benefit by having a union negotiate for workers. *Logical/Mathematical*

☐ **p. 243 Discussing unionization of college athletics** Students research and report on the Northwestern University football players' attempt to unionize in 2014 and opponents' views.

☑ Online Teaching Options

V Visual Skills

☐ **IMAGES Chapter opener**—Students analyze a photo for clues about labor laws.

C Critical Thinking Skills

☐ **INFOGRAPHICS Economic Perspectives**—Students discuss how right-to-work laws support the American free enterprise system.

☐ **DEBATES Are senior business executives worth what they are paid?**—Students study discuss the incomes of senior business executives.

☐ **INTERACTIVE FEATURE Case Study: Homestead Strike**—Students learn about the fight among union workers, employers, and the government.

☑ Printable Digital Worksheets

C Critical Thinking Skills

☐ **WORKSHEET Economic Simulation**—Students take part in a simulated mediation.

☐ **WORKSHEET Assessing Background Knowledge Activity**—Target misconceptions you can address when teaching the lessons.

Project-Based Learning

Hands-On

WORKSHEET Hands-On Chapter Project
Students act as consultants for a union with declining membership. It is their job to research aspects of the decline and make recommendations for reversing that trend. Each group will focus on a different factor: government actions, changes in workforce demographics, union membership across industries and change over time, or the effect of free trade on unions. Group members will summarize their findings and present their recommendation report to the class, who will act as union members.

Digital Hands-On

Create Online Projects

Find an additional activity online that incorporates technology for the Hands-On Project. Visit the EdTech Teacher Web sites for more links, tutorials, and other resources.

Print Resources

ANCILLARY RESOURCE
This ancillary is available for every chapter and lesson.
- Chapter Tests and Lesson Quizzes

PRINTABLE DIGITAL WORKSHEETS
These printable digital worksheets are available for every chapter and lesson.
- Reading Essentials & Study Guide
- Vocabulary Activities
- Chapter Summaries
- Economic Simulations
- Math Practice for Economics
- Reinforcing Economic Skills
- Personal Finance Activities
- Enrichment Activities
- Reteaching Activities
- Guided Reading Activities
- Video Worksheets
- Lesson Quizzes and Chapter Tests (English and Spanish)

More Media Resources

SUGGESTED READING
- For students at a Grade 10 reading level: ***The Rise of Industry: 1860–1900,*** by Christopher Collier & James Lincoln Collier
- For students at a Grade 11 reading level: ***The Great Depression,*** by Jacqueline Farrell
- For students at a Grade 12 reading level: ***The Great Depression and the New Deal: America's Economic Collapse and Recovery,*** by Anne E. Schraff

SUGGESTED VIDEOS
Find these documentaries yourself online. NOTE: McGraw-Hill Education does not endorse these resources. Preview clips for age-appropriateness.
- *Wage Crisis* (26 min.)
- *Richie Rich Gets Richer* (28 min.)
- *TED Talks: What Will Future Jobs Look Like?* (14 min.)

LESSON 1 Planner

THE LABOR MOVEMENT

Students will know:
- the major events in the rise of the labor movement, including the national labor unions.
- the major events in the conflicts between labor and management since the Civil War, including tactics employed by both sides such as strikes, injunctions, black list, and boycotts.
- the union arrangements in which unionized workers can participate today.

Students will be able to:
- **analyze** the effect of union action on the modern labor industry.
- **summarize** union activity from Colonial times to the 1930s.
- **evaluate** the strength of the labor movement since the 1930s.
- **identify** the different types of union arrangements that exist today.

UNDERSTANDING BY DESIGN

✓ Print Teaching Options

V Visual Skills

- **p. 248 Sequencing information about the AFL-CIO** Students make a time line of key events in the relationship of the AFL and CIO.
- **p. 249 Illustrating American labor** Students create a collage illustrating the U.S. labor force.

R Reading Skills

- **p. 247 Inferring the effects of the labor movement** Students infer why the Great Depression changed attitudes toward unions.
- **p. 250 Summarizing the reading** Students summarize the characteristics of closed, union, modified union, and agency shops. **AL**
- **p. 251 Researching the contributions of women and minorities** Students study women and minority groups in the labor movement.
- **p. 251 Understanding the main idea** Students state the changes that labor unions made for American workers today.

C Critical Thinking Skills

- **p. 244 Comparing working conditions** Students list characteristics of a particular job and describe its working conditions. **BL ELL**
- **p. 245 Determining cause and effect** Students discuss why unions have strong bargaining power. **Logical/Mathematical**
- **p. 246 Defending a position** Students decide what caused better working conditions and wages for American workers. **BL**
- **p. 248 Researching the labor movement culture** Students research the role of songs in the struggles to unionize workers.

W Writing Skills

- **p. 245 Researching the U.S. job market** Students write about changes in the U.S. job market and predict how the market will change by 2050. **Verbal/Linguistic**

✓ Online Teaching Options

V Visual Skills

- **INTERACTIVE FEATURE** Trade and Industrial Unions—Students summarize the difference between trade or craft unions and industrial unions. **Verbal/Linguistic**
- **MAPS** The Right-to-Work, State-by-State in the United States—Students create a pros and cons chart about right-to-work laws. **Logical/Mathematical**
- **BIOGRAPHY** César Chávez—Students learn about César Chávez, who founded the United Farm Workers union. **Verbal/Linguistic**
- **POLITICAL CARTOON** Two Views of Trade Unions—Students discuss the benefits and drawbacks of organized labor in the U.S. **Verbal/Linguistic**

R Reading Skills

- **GRAPHIC ORGANIZER** Time Line—Students summarize the history of the labor unions in the United States. **Verbal/Linguistic**

C Critical Thinking Skills

- **BELLRINGER** The Labor Movement—Students discuss the Pullman strike of 1894.
- **ESSENTIAL QUESTION** Exploring the Essential Question—Students describe their workplace experiences.
- **ESSENTIAL QUESTION** Exploring the Essential Question—Students discuss what a workday would be like without unions.
- **CHARTS** Union Membership and Representation by Industry—Students read about union membership and representation.

T Technology Skills

- **SELF-CHECK QUIZ** Lesson 1—Students receive instant feedback on their mastery of lesson content.
- **GAME** Lesson 1—Students solve clues to review lesson content.
- **INTERACTIVE WHITEBOARD ACTIVITY** Budgeting and Prices—Students work together to learn lesson content.

✓ Printable Digital Worksheets

R Reading Skills

- **WORKSHEET** Guided Reading Activity—Students use the Guided Reading Activity worksheets to review their comprehension of the content.
- **WORKSHEET** Reading Essentials and Study Guide—Students complete the study guide and answer Reading Progress Check and vocabulary questions.

LESSON 2 Planner

WAGES AND LABOR DISPUTES

Students will know:
- how supply of and demand for labor affect wages.
- the characteristics that are most likely to increase wages and nonwage benefits, including skill, productivity, education, occupation, and mobility.
- how the earnings of workers are determined by the market value of the product produced and workers' productivity.
- the methods used by labor unions and management to resolve labor disputes.

Students will be able to:
- **explain** why different people earn different wages.
- **discuss** the options available for solving labor disputes.
- **consider** the advantages and disadvantages of having a federal minimum wage.

UNDERSTANDING BY DESIGN

✓ Print Teaching Options

V Visual Skills

- **p. 253 Using line graphs** Students show how labor supply and demand would change under two scenarios. **BL** Logical/Mathematical

- **p. 256 Charting the collective bargaining process** Students create a flowchart to show the collective bargaining process. **AL** Visual/Spatial

C Critical Thinking Skills

- **p. 254 Classifying different types of jobs** Students list ten jobs, their labor categories (skilled, unskilled, semiskilled, professional), and factors affecting supply and demand.

- **p. 255 Evaluating wage practices** Students discuss whether they believe job seniority should warrant higher wages.

- **p. 256 Supporting an argument** Students write about a fictional strike from the union's and management's perspectives. **BL** Verbal/Linguistic

W Writing Skills

- **p. 252 Preparing to read** Students review content vocabulary.

- **p. 253 Creating job advertisements** Students write ads for jobs in the four categories of labor. **ELL** Verbal/Linguistic

- **p. 257 Assessing criteria for settling a dispute** Students decide when a U.S. president should get involved in a labor-management dispute.

- **p. 257 Explaining how wages are determined and how labor disputes are resolved** Students choose one of these topics to write about.

T Technology Skills

- **p. 256 Conducting online research about strikes** Students report on a recent strike, the steps taken to end the disagreement, and the resolution. Auditory/Musical

✓ Online Teaching Options

V Visual Skills

- **VIDEO** **Discrimination Lawsuit**—Students view a video of female employees who bring a class action suit against Walmart.

R Reading Skills

- **GRAPHIC ORGANIZERS** **Resolving Labor Disputes**—Students explain the ways labor disputes are resolved. Verbal/Linguistic

C Critical Thinking Skills

- **BELLRINGER** **Wages and Labor Disputes**—Students consider why unions and management would rather negotiate a settlement than have a strike.

- **ESSENTIAL QUESTION** **Exploring the Essential Question**—Students discuss questions about solving labor disputes.

- **GRAPHS** **Market Theory of Wage Determination**—Students discuss how supply and demand affect wages for roofers and professional athletes.

T Technology Skills

- **SELF-CHECK QUIZ** **Lesson 2**—Students receive instant feedback on their mastery of lesson content.

- **GAME** **Lesson 2**—Students solve clues to review lesson content.

- **INTERACTIVE WHITEBOARD ACTIVITY** **Supply and Demand: Burritos**—Students work together to learn lesson content.

✓ Printable Digital Worksheets

R Reading Skills

- **WORKSHEET** **Guided Reading Activity**—Students use the Guided Reading Activity worksheets to review their comprehension of the content.

- **WORKSHEET** **Reading Essentials and Study Guide**—Students complete the study guide and answer Reading Progress Check and vocabulary questions.

C Critical Thinking Skills

- **WORKSHEET** **Discrimination Lawsuit Video Activity**—Students gather information about a class action suit.

LESSON 3 Planner

EMPLOYMENT TRENDS AND ISSUES

Students will know:
- the reasons for the decline in labor union influence in the United States.
- men are generally paid more than women because of difference in skills, the types of jobs they choose, and discrimination.
- unless adjusted, the minimum wage will lose purchasing power any time there is inflation.

Students will be able to:
- **state** reasons for the decline of union influence.
- **list** three major causes for pay discrimination in the labor market.
- **consider the advantages and disadvantages** of having a federal minimum wage.

UNDERSTANDING BY DESIGN®

☑ Print Teaching Options

R Reading Skills
- ☐ **p. 261 Applying observation to make predictions** Students consider why women receive lower pay than men.
- ☐ **p. 265 Predicting future trends** Students predict employment trends of the next 25 years.

C Critical Thinking Skills
- ☐ **p. 259 Characterizing the local job market** Students categorize available local jobs and write a summary about the local job market.
- ☐ **p. 262 Helping women to join the workforce** Students consider what companies can do to employ women in higher-paying occupations.
- ☐ **p. 262 Understanding figurative terms** Students define *glass ceiling*. **ELL**
- ☐ **p. 263 Evaluating government practices** Students discuss the fairness of a minority-owned business getting work before others.
- ☐ **p. 264 Researching workers' benefits** Students write to a human resources department to learn about fringe benefits.

W Writing Skills
- ☐ **p. 260 Analyzing the reasons for declining union membership** Students explain the decline in union membership. **ELL** **Visual/Spatial**
- ☐ **p. 260 Exploring employment issues** Students research a topic relevant to union workers and write a dialogue. **BL**
- ☐ **p. 263 Assessing social progress** Students respond to a quote by Shirley Chisholm regarding discrimination. **BL**
- ☐ **p. 264 Taking a stand on a living wage** Students support their position on whether a "living wage" standard should be adopted.

T Technology Skills
- ☐ **p. 262 Looking for jobs for women** Students research advancement prospects for women.

☑ Online Teaching Options

V Visual Skills
- ☐ **BELLRINGER** **Employment Trends and Issues**—Students explain how gender relates to wage inequality. **Visual/Spatial**
- ☐ **CHARTS** **Median Weekly Earnings by Occupation and Union Affiliation**—Students discuss how being part of union could affect income.
- ☐ **GRAPHS** **Union Membership as a Percentage of Employed Workers**—Students learn about events that have affected union membership.
- ☐ **GRAPHS** **Gender and Income Distribution of Men and Women by Occupation**—Students analyze the gender wage disparity by occupation. **Visual/Spatial**
- ☐ **GRAPHS** **Median Female Income as a Percentage of Male Income**—Students study discrepancy in earnings between men and women. **Visual/Spatial**
- ☐ **VIDEO** **Masculinity**—Students watch a video about how society views men in terms of roles and responsibilities.
- ☐ **GRAPHS** **Minimum Wage**—Students see how inflation affects minimum wage.

C Critical Thinking Skills
- ☐ **ESSENTIAL QUESTION** **Exploring the Essential Question**—Students discuss two different wage policies

T Technology Skills
- ☐ **SELF-CHECK QUIZ** **Lesson 3**—Students receive instant feedback on their mastery of lesson content.
- ☐ **GAME** **Lesson 3**—Students solve clues to review lesson content.
- ☐ **INTERACTIVE WHITEBOARD ACTIVITY** **Social Goals**—Students work together to learn lesson content.

☑ Printable Digital Worksheets

R Reading Skills
- ☐ **WORKSHEET** **Guided Reading Activity**—Students use the Guided Reading Activity worksheets to review their comprehension of the content.
- ☐ **WORKSHEET** **Reading Essentials and Study Guide**—Students complete the study guide and answer Reading Progress Check and vocabulary questions.

C Critical Thinking Skills
- ☐ **WORKSHEET** **Masculinity Video Activity**—Students write a summary of the video they viewed on masculinity.
- ☐ **WORKSHEET** **Personal Finance Activity**—Students examine the connection between the minimum wage and the standard of living. **Logical/Mathematical**

Chapter 9 Planner **241E**

CHAPTER 9 Labor and Wages
INTERVENTION AND REMEDIATION STRATEGIES

LESSON 1 The Labor Movement

Reading and Comprehension

After students have read the lesson, have them work in pairs to complete a time line of events described in The Labor Movement. Then have pairs compare their time line with that of another pair. Tell them to settle any differences by referring to the lesson.

Text Evidence

Have students reread the sections on Union Activities and Employer Resistance. Tell them to make a two-column chart and label the columns "Union Actions" and "Employer Actions." Tell them to list the actions each side uses to try to win a dispute. Then have them use their notes to write a summary of the information in the two sections, including definitions of the different types of tactics unions and employers use.

LESSON 2 Wages and Labor Disputes

Reading and Comprehension

After students have read the lesson, ask them to look again at the section on Wage Determination. Remind them that there are four explanations for why people are paid different wages. Have students work in pairs to write one sentence summarizing each explanation.

Text Evidence

Have students reread the section on Resolving Labor Disputes. Tell them to decide which options are preferred and which should be avoided. *(Students should determine that collective bargaining, mediation, and arbitration are preferred, whereas injunction, seizure, and presidential intervention are undesirable. Fact-finding occurs when feelings are already antagonistic, and it is not binding; students may place it in either category.)* Have students explain their classification based on evidence from the text.

LESSON 3 Employment Trends and Issues

Reading and Comprehension

Have students identify the three reasons why women are paid less than men. Ask them to explain how they found the reasons in the text. *(Students should identify (1) differences in skills and experience, (2) uneven gender distribution among occupations, and (3) gender discrimination. The subheadings of the first three sections under the heading "Lower Pay for Women" should have helped them locate the information.)*

Text Evidence

Point out that laws have been passed that were meant to remedy wage and salary discrimination against women and minorities. Have students find the names and dates of those laws. *(Equal Pay Act of 1963; Civil Rights Act of 1964)* **Ask: Were these laws successful?** Tell students to support their answers with evidence from the text. *(Students should note that these acts were passed over 50 years ago, but that, according to the graphs shown and to the text itself, women are still being paid less today.)*

Online Resources

Assessing Background Knowledge Use this worksheet to pre-assess students' background knowledge before they start the chapter.

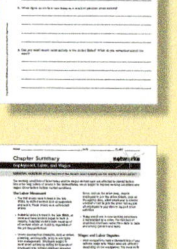

Chapter Summaries Have students use the summary as a pre-reading activity or as a post-reading review to check the main ideas covered in each lesson.

Guided Reading Activities Have students complete these activities as they read each lesson. They provide reading notes the student can use for review and to prepare for assessments.

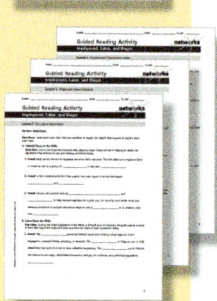

Reteaching Activities Have students complete the Reteaching Activity for remedial practice and review of vital content.

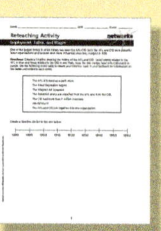

Self-Check Quizzes These quizzes provide instant feedback on areas the students may need to re-read to understand a main idea.

Reading Essentials and Study Guide This resource offers writing and reading activities for the approaching-level student.

Approaching Grade Level Reader This reader presents all of the content of the Online Student Edition but at a lower reading level.

English Language Learner Reader Provide additional reading support for ELL students. Find this tool online.

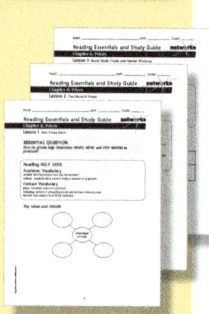

Labor and Wages

ESSENTIAL QUESTIONS
- What features of the modern labor industry are the result of union action?
- What factors lead to higher wages for a worker?

networks
www.connected.mcgraw-hill.com
There's More Online about labor and wages.

CHAPTER 9

Economic Perspectives
Are You Union?

Lesson 1
The Labor Movement

Lesson 2
Wages and Labor Disputes

Lesson 3
Employment Trends and Issues

Letter from the Author

Dear Economics Teacher,

Some people might wonder why the topic of "labor" and the discussion of organized labor's history is so important. The short answer is that labor includes the work we do, and the compensation of labor is the income we receive. As for the tumultuous history of organized labor, the alternating periods of turmoil and calm are primarily responsible for many of our most important labor laws. The struggle between labor and management continues today, and we can make better sense of it if we know a little bit about its history. It's also one of the most interesting chapters of American economic development.

CHAPTER 9
Labor and Wages

ENGAGE

Call students' attention to the photo and ask them to describe the woman, what kind of equipment she is wearing, and what she is doing. **Ask: Why is this image a good one to symbolize the chapter titled *Employment, Labor, and Wages?*** *(In the U.S. today, the workforce is protected by labor laws and by agreements between companies and labor unions. These protections apply to hours and wages, but also to gender and racial equality as well as workplace safety. The woman's protective goggles are an example of the latter.)* Invite students to share what they already know about labor laws and union activities.

Planning labor costs for a new business Form students into groups of five or six. Have each group imagine that they are setting up a new business. Tell them to decide (1) what sort of business they will develop, (2) what job each of them will have in the business, and (3) what each of them will be paid per year. Tell them that they can spend no more than $200,000 on salaries for the first year. When they are finished, have each group share their decisions. Use their work as a basis for discussing what sorts of choices they made about jobs and salaries and the factors that influenced their decisions. Tell them that in this chapter they will learn more about the job market, pay, and working conditions, as well as how pay and conditions are negotiated.

Making Connections

Scholarship Supply and Demand   Ask: Would you rather win an academic scholarship or a sports scholarship to college? Why? Guide students to realize that sports scholarships frequently pay all a student's expenses. Explain that scholarships, like wages and salaries, are dependent on a variety of factors, including the law of supply and demand.

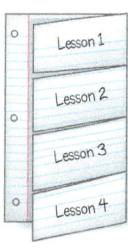

Go to the Foldables® library for a cumulative chapter-based Foldable® activity that your students can use to help take notes and prepare for assessment.

CHAPTER 9
Economic Perspectives

TEACH & ASSESS

R Reading Skills

Understanding words in context Point out to students that the word *labor* can mean "work"—both the noun and the verb. However, it can also mean "workers" or "employees," and it can refer to all the workers or employees in a company or even in an entire country. **Ask: How is the word *labor* used in the first paragraph?** *(Students should recognize that the word is used in the latter meaning.)* **ELL** Verbal/Linguistic

C Critical Thinking Skills

Characterizing the local area Have students consider which businesses in their local area are unionized or would benefit by having a union negotiate for workers. Discuss whether students have ever seen a strike or picket, or knows someone who has experienced either of these two union activities. Ask students whether they have ever utilized a boycott to protest against a company's policies. Logical/Mathematical

---

Economic Perspectives

ARE YOU UNION?

R The earliest unions in the United States were actually guilds of workers specializing in certain skills, like carpentry, shoemaking and cabinetry. The first organized labor group was the Federal Society of Journeymen Cordwainers (shoemakers), which formed in Philadelphia in 1794. Craft unions set standard wages for their services and protected themselves from workplace exploitation in an organized fashion. Over the next several decades American trade unions faced twists and turns as they maneuvered the world of politics while trying to stay true to their mission.

The Birth of the Union

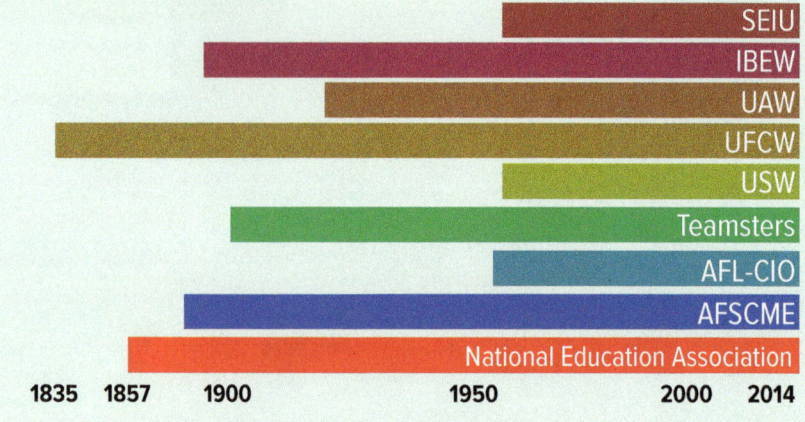

SEIU
IBEW
UAW
UFCW
USW
Teamsters
AFL-CIO
AFSCME
National Education Association

1835   1857   1900   1950   2000   2014

Union Tools

C

Strike: Union-organized work stoppage designed to gain concessions from an employer

Picket: Demonstration or march outside a place of business to protest a company's actions or policies

Boycott: Protest in the form of refusal to buy, including attempts to convince others to take their business elsewhere

Lockout: Refusal to let employees work until they agree to management demands

---

networks Online Teaching Options

INFOGRAPHIC

Economic Perspectives: Are You Union?

Identifying characteristics of unions Provide students with the full names of the unions: American Federation of State, County, and Municipal Employees (AFSCME); American Federation of Labor and the Committee of Industrial Organizations (AFL-CIO); International Brotherhood of Teamsters (Teamsters); United Auto Workers or "International Union, United Automobile, Aerospace and Agricultural Implement Workers of America" (UAW); International Brotherhood of Electrical Workers (IBEW); United Steel Workers or "United Steel, Paper and Forestry, Rubber, Manufacturing, Energy, Allied Industrial and Service Workers International Union" (USW); United Food and Commercial Workers International Union (UFCW); Service Employees International Union (SEIU). Point out that the National Education Association, founded in 1857, is the largest public-sector union in the U.S. Verbal/Linguistic

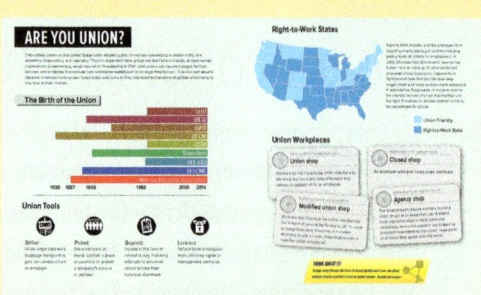

CHAPTER 9
Economic Perspectives

Right-to-Work States

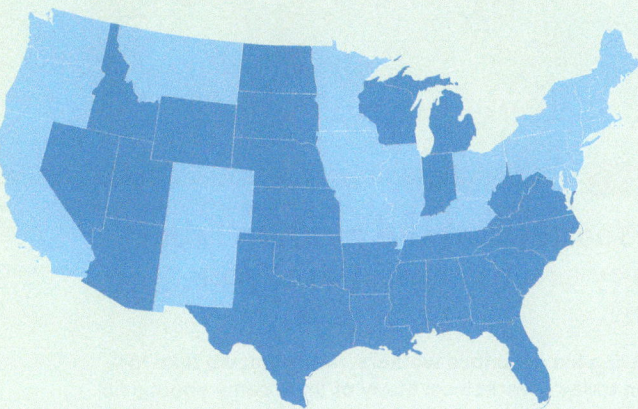

Right-to-Work statutes prohibit employers from requiring employees to join unions (including paying dues) as criteria for employment. In 2016, 26 states had right-to-work laws on the books—and as many as 19 other states had proposed similar legislation. Opponents of right-to-work laws feel that the laws keep wages lower and make workers more vulnerable to exploitation. Proponents of the laws point to the financial burden of union membership and the right of workers to choose whether or not to be represented by unions.

R

☐ Union Friendly
■ Right-to-Work State

Union Workplaces

 Authorization for representation
Union shop
Workers do not have to be union members to be hired, but must join soon afterward and remain unionized while an employee

C

 Authorization for representation
Modified union shop
Workers don't have to be union members to be hired and cannot be forced to join in order to keep their jobs. However, if a worker chooses to join a union, they must remain a member while employed.

 Authorization for representation
Closed shop
An employer who only hires union members

 Authorization for representation
Agency shop
The shop doesn't require workers to join a union to get or to keep their job. Workers must pay union dues to fund collective bargaining. Nonunion workers are subject to contracts negotiated by the union, regardless of whether they agree with the terms.

THINK ABOUT IT!
Categorizing Examine the Union Tools and identify which ones are direct methods of action and which ones are indirect actions. Explain your answer.

connected.mcgraw-hill.com   Labor and Wages **243**

R Reading Skills

Evaluating right-to-work opinions Have students read the paragraph about Right-to-Work States. Ask: **What do right-to-work statutes prohibit?** *(They prohibit employers from requiring employees to join unions and pay dues as a criteria for employment.)* **Why do opponents of right-to-work laws oppose them?** *(Opponents feel that the laws keep wages lower and make workers more vulnerable to exploitation.)* **Why do proponents like right-to-work laws?** *(Proponents believe union membership is a financial burden to workers, and they believe workers should be able to choose whether or not to be represented by unions.)* Tell students that some states appeal the constitutionality of court decisions regarding right-to-work statutes, so the right-to-work states shown on the map may change over time.

C Critical Thinking Skills

Discussing unionization of college athletics Have students research Northwestern University football players' attempt to unionize in 2014. Ask students to report what the players wanted and why; how being granted employee status opened the possibility of unionizing; and opponents' views. Discuss the issue in class, comparing college athletes and professional athletes, and then have students consider alternative solutions to the college athletes' concerns. **BL**

CLOSE & REFLECT

Have students answer the *Think About It!* questions.

WORKSHEET
Economic Simulation

Resolving a labor dispute Assign the Economic Simulation worksheet: How Are Labor and Wage Conflicts Resolved? This role play will require students to read and assimilate the background information and to review Lessons 1 and 2 in this chapter. Allow time during class for the three groups to research and plan their strategies. Encourage students to keep notes on their negotiation points to refer to during the simulated mediation. **Interpersonal, Kinesthetic, Verbal/Linguistic**

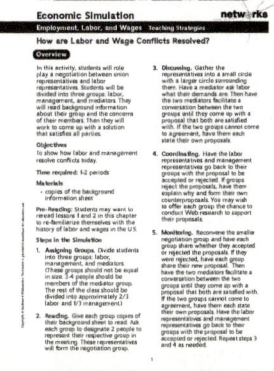

ANSWERS, p. 243

THINK ABOUT IT!

Strikes and pickets are direct methods of action. Boycotts and lockouts are indirect methods of action.

Labor and Wages **243**

CHAPTER 9, LESSON 1
The Labor Movement

ENGAGE

C Critical Thinking Skills

Comparing working conditions Point out that different types of jobs have different working conditions and that different countries have different laws regarding working conditions. With students' help, write on the board a number of different types of jobs (for example, factory work, retail sales, office work, restaurant work, mining, computer programming, medical work). Ask students to form small groups. Each group should pick one of the types of work and create a list of characteristics of a job in that area, including working hours, workplace hazards, and type of pay. Ask the groups to share their descriptions with the class and discuss similarities and differences. If any students are familiar with workers' situations in other countries, invite them to contribute to the discussion. If relevant, ask the following question. **Ask: How are working conditions in other countries like or unlike those in the U.S.?** *(Students may note that conditions in some other countries are like conditions in the U.S. before modern labor laws were passed; they may also note that workers in some countries have more generous vacations, sick leave, and maternity leave than workers in the U.S.)*
BL ELL Interpersonal

ANSWERS, p. 244

ESSENTIAL QUESTION ACTIVITY

Answers will vary. All of these workers' rights technically apply to today's typical workforce. Students may note, however, that freelance or part-time workers do not have weekends off or work an eight-hour day or have paid vacation or sick days. Immigrant labor may not receive minimum wages or overtime pay.

TAKING NOTES

Student time lines should also include the 1877 railroad strike; the 1886 Haymarket riot; the 1914 Clayton Antitrust Act; the 1935 Wagner Act; the 1947 Taft-Hartley Act; and the formation in 1955 of the AFL-CIO.

LESSON 1
The Labor Movement

Reading Help Desk

Academic Vocabulary
- legislation
- prohibited

Content Vocabulary
- craft union
- industrial union
- strike
- picket
- boycott
- lockout
- company unions
- Great Depression
- right-to-work law
- independent unions
- closed shop
- union shop
- modified union shop
- agency shop
- civilian labor force

TAKING NOTES:

Key Ideas and Details
ACTIVITY Use the graphic organizer below to track the developments and changes in the U.S. labor movement.

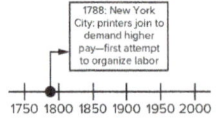

ESSENTIAL QUESTION

What features of the modern labor industry are the result of union action?

The following list describes workers' rights that we take for granted in today's workplace. Many of them came about as a result of the historical and ongoing struggle between workers and employers. Write a paragraph explaining why you think these features apply or do not apply to today's workforce.

- Weekends off from work
- The eight-hour work day
- Basic, enforced safety measures at the workplace
- Paid vacation (or sick days)
- Days off for national holidays
- Extra pay for working overtime
- Minimum wage guarantee

Colonial Times to the 1930s

GUIDING QUESTION For what purposes did early unions form?

Today, only one out of every nine working Americans is a member of a labor union. Even so, unions are important because they played a major historical role in helping to create the **legislation** that affects our pay and working conditions today. As you read about the history of the labor movement, think about the sequence of events that have given workers the benefits they enjoy in today's labor market.

Early Union Development

In 1778 printers in New York City joined together to demand higher pay. This was the first attempt to organize labor in America. Before long, unions of shoemakers, carpenters, and tailors developed, each hoping to negotiate

244

---

networks Online Teaching Options

BELLRINGER

The Labor Movement

Exploring major events in the rise of the labor movement Show students the image of the federal troops during the Pullman strike of 1894. Explain that, in order to convince the railroad companies to meet their demands, strikers prevented trains from traveling to their destinations. One of the effects of this was that letters and other mail could not be distributed. Since the postal service was a part of the U.S. government, federal troops were sent in to ensure mail would be delivered. Invite students to share their ideas about which side was right—those who were fighting for better pay, shorter hours, and safer working conditions or those who wanted to ensure that travelers, goods, and mail reached their destinations safely.

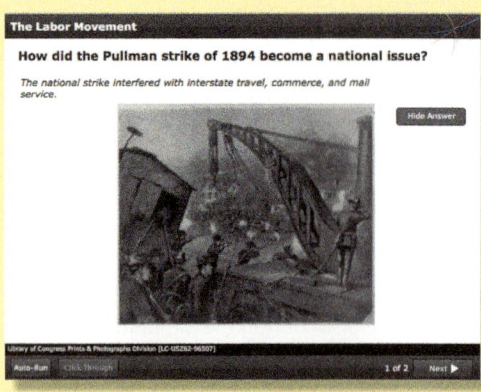

agreements that covered hours, pay, and working conditions. While only a small fraction of all workers belonged to unions, most unions were made up of skilled workers and possessed strong bargaining power.

Until about 1820, most of America's workforce was made up of farmers, small business owners, and the self-employed. Soon immigrants began to arrive in great numbers. Because they provided a supply of cheap, unskilled labor, they posed a threat to the unions that were working to preserve existing wage and labor standards.

In addition, public opinion was largely against union activity, and some parts of the country even banned labor unions. Labor organizers often were viewed as troublemakers, and many workers believed they could better negotiate with their employers on a one-to-one basis.

Civil War to the 1930s

The Civil War led to higher prices and a greater demand for goods and services. Manufacturing expanded, and the farm population declined. Hourly workers in industrial jobs made up about one-fourth of the country's working population.

Working conditions in some industries were difficult, and hostile attitudes toward unions slowly began to soften. Many of the cultural and linguistic differences between immigrants and American-born workers began to fade, and the labor force became more unified.

Types of Unions

In the industrial post–Civil War period, the two main types of labor unions shown in **Figure 9.1** dominated. The first was the **craft union** or trade union, an association of skilled workers who perform the same kind of work. The Cigar

legislation laws enacted by the government

craft union labor union whose members perform the same kind of work; same as trade union

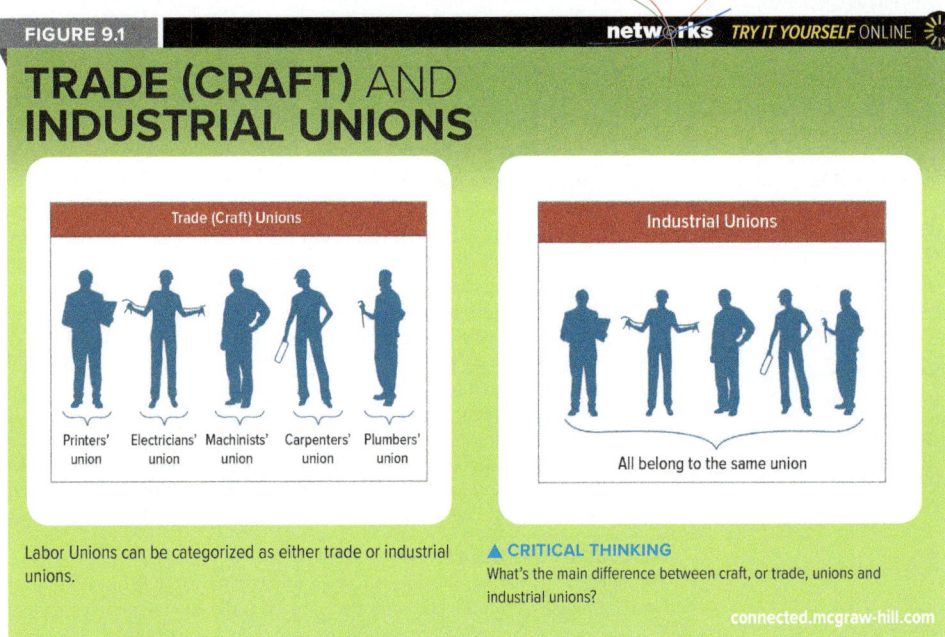

FIGURE 9.1

TRADE (CRAFT) AND INDUSTRIAL UNIONS

Labor Unions can be categorized as either trade or industrial unions.

▲ CRITICAL THINKING
What's the main difference between craft, or trade, unions and industrial unions?

CHAPTER 9, LESSON 1
The Labor Movement

C Critical Thinking Skills

Defending a position Write the following question on the board: **Were better working conditions and wages for American workers the result of labor union activity or the increased demand for skilled labor?** Call on volunteers to offer evidence supporting either side of the question. BL

English Language Proficiency

Advanced High Teach students to identify basic text structures used in their reading materials. Point out that the text structure is determined by the purpose of the chapter, section, or paragraph. Explain that students can use text structure as a clue to the author's purpose. Give examples of language specific to each structure, such as signal words. Then have students practice identifying text structures as sequence, main idea/detail, cause/effect, comparison/contrast, or problem/solution.

BIOGRAPHY

César Chávez
UNION ORGANIZER (1927–1993)

César Chávez grew up in a family in which everyone who was able had to labor in the farm fields. A witness to the injustices of workers with no recourse, Chávez became a labor activist and union organizer.

Chávez believed in the power of organizing. The union he started merged with other unions to form the United Farm Workers union (UFW) in 1966, which eventually gave migrant farm workers the power to negotiate better wages and working conditions. By 1970, the UFW negotiated a union contract for grape pickers. Chávez organized boycotts and peaceful protests. He fasted for weeks to pressure growers to negotiate with the UFW to help farm workers.

César Chávez died in 1993 while defending the UFW against a lawsuit brought by lettuce growers.

▶ **CRITICAL THINKING**
Identifying Cause and Effect
How do you think César Chávez's early life influenced his commitment to unionizing migrant farm workers in California?
Drawing Inferences What problems do you think Chávez had to face and overcome in trying to organize migrant workers?

Makers' Union, begun by union leader Samuel Gompers, is an example of this type of union.

The second type of union was the **industrial union**—an association of workers in the same industry, regardless of the job each individual worker performs. The development of basic mass-production industries such as steel and textiles provided the opportunity to organize this kind of union. Because many of the workers in these industries were unskilled and could not join trade unions, they organized as industrial unions instead.

Union Activities
Unions tried to help workers by negotiating for higher pay, job security, and better hours and working conditions. If an agreement could not be reached, workers would **strike**, or refuse to work until certain demands were met. Unions also pressured employers by having the striking workers **picket**, or parade in front of the employer's business carrying signs about the dispute. The signs might ask other workers not to seek jobs with the company, or they might ask customers and suppliers to show union support by taking their business elsewhere.

If striking and picketing did not force a settlement of the dispute, a union could organize a **boycott**—a mass refusal to buy products from targeted employers or companies. When a boycott was effective, it hurt the company's business.

Employer Resistance
Employers resented the strikes, pickets, and boycotts, so they fought unions in a number of ways. Sometimes the owners called for a **lockout**, a refusal to let employees work until they agreed to management demands.

Lockouts, once relatively rare, have been increasingly used by management. In 2011, the National Football League locked its players out for 130 days. In the same year, the National Basketball Association locked its players out for 161 days. The New York City Opera even locked out its singers and orchestra briefly in 2012.

At other times, management has responded to a strike, or the threat of a strike, by hiring all new workers to replace those on strike. Some owners even set up **company unions**—unions organized, supported, or run by employers—to head off efforts by others to organize their workers.

The Ludlow Massacre
Perhaps nothing typified such struggles more than a strike in Colorado. The United Mine Workers of America had organized a strike against a coal mining company owned by John D. Rockefeller to demand better pay and working conditions. When the company forced workers out of company-owned homes, the miners and their families moved into tents set up by the union.

The strike, expected to end after a few days, instead lasted 14 months. At times, fights broke out between striking miners and company guards. The mining company also hired a private detective agency and received assistance from the Colorado National Guard.

One fight in spring 1914 turned into an all-day battle and a devastating fire. In the end, dozens of people were killed, including 2 women and 11 children. The violence, quickly called the Ludlow massacre, sparked rioting in other coal-mining communities. The resulting conflict eventually claimed nearly 200 lives.

Attitude of the Courts
Throughout this period, the courts had an unfavorable attitude toward unions. Under English common law, unions were considered conspiracies against

---

ANSWERS, p. 246

CRITICAL THINKING

1. Students should recognize that Chavez's experience as a child, in a poor family of migrant farm workers, who worked at the whim of the landowners, gave him first-hand experience of the suffering and the needs of these workers.

2. Students might infer that migrant farm workers would be hard to organize because they frequently move from place to place and work for different farm owners in different places. Because the workers were poor and dependent on the farm owners, they probably didn't feel that they had a choice. Chávez used protests, boycotts, and personal fasting to show the workers his commitment to organizing them to gain their rights.

---

networks Online Teaching Options

BIOGRAPHY
César Chávez

Examining a 20th century labor movement Show students the image of César Chávez. Ask whether any of them have heard of Chávez and to explain what they know. Make sure that they are aware that Chávez was a migrant farm worker who founded a union and organized nonviolent protests. Then have them click on the image to read more about Chávez and how he founded the United Farm Workers union. Point out that many people in the mid-20th century supported his union by boycotting farm products.

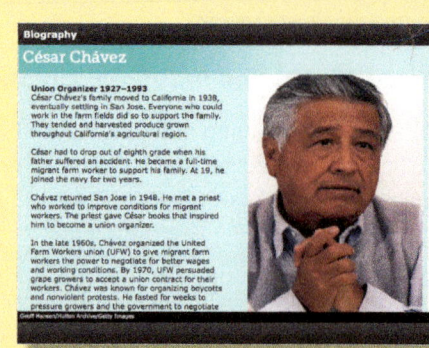

business and were prosecuted in the United States. Even the Sherman Antitrust Act of 1890, aimed mainly at curbing monopolies, was used to keep labor in line.

For example, in 1902 the United Hatters Union called a strike against a Danbury, Connecticut, hat manufacturer that had rejected a union demand. The union decided to apply pressure on stores to not stock hats made by the Danbury firm. The hat manufacturer, charging a conspiracy in restraint of trade under the Sherman Act, filed a damage suit that went all the way to the Supreme Court. The Supreme Court ruled that the union had organized an illegal boycott in restraint of trade, thereby dealing a severe blow to organized labor.

The Danbury Hatters case and several subsequent antiunion decisions pushed organized labor to call for relief. The passage of the Clayton Antitrust Act of 1914 helped to remedy the threat to unions by expressly exempting labor unions from prosecution under the Sherman Act.

✓ READING PROGRESS CHECK

Recalling How did unions change from their beginning in the eighteenth century through the early part of the twentieth century?

Labor Since the 1930s

GUIDING QUESTION *Have labor laws since the 1930s strengthened or weakened the union movement, and why?*

During the 1930s, times were especially hard for working people. Jobs were scarce, and people lacked unemployment insurance. In response, Congress passed a series of laws that supported organized labor. Although a backlash against labor followed, these laws provided the most important labor protections that are still in effect today.

Labor in the Great Depression

The **Great Depression**—the worst period of economic decline and stagnation in the history of the United States—began with the collapse of the stock market in October 1929. Economic output reached bottom in 1933 and did not recover to its 1929 level until 1939. At times, as many as one in four workers was without a job. Others kept their jobs but saw pay cuts. In 1929, the average hourly manufacturing wage was 55 cents. By 1933, it plummeted to 5 cents in some areas.

The Great Depression brought misery to millions, but it also changed attitudes toward the labor movement. Common problems united factory workers, and union promoters renewed their efforts to organize workers.

Pro-Union Legislation

New legislation soon aided labor. The Norris-LaGuardia Act of 1932 prevented federal courts from issuing rulings against unions engaged in peaceful strikes, picketing, or boycotts. This forced companies to negotiate directly with their unions during labor disputes.

The National Labor Relations Act, or Wagner Act, of 1935 established the right of unions to have collective bargaining. The act also created the National Labor Relations Board (NLRB), giving it the power to police unfair labor practices. The NLRB also could oversee and certify union election results. If a fair election resulted in a union as the employees' bargaining agent, employers had to recognize and negotiate with it.

The Fair Labor Standards Act of 1938 applied to businesses that engage in interstate commerce. The law set the first minimum wage and established time-and-a-half pay for overtime, which—by 1940—was defined as more than 40 hours per week. The act also **prohibited** oppressive child labor, defined as any

industrial union labor union whose members perform different kinds of work in the same industry

strike union-organized work stoppage designed to gain concessions from an employer

picket demonstrate or march before a place of business to protest a company's actions or policies

boycott protest in the form of refusal to buy, including attempts to convince others to take their business elsewhere

lockout management refusal to let employees work until company demands are met

company unions unions organized, supported, or run by an employer

Great Depression worst period of economic decline in U.S. history, lasting from approximately 1929 to 1939

prohibited prevented or forbade

CHAPTER 9, LESSON 1
The Labor Movement

R Reading Skills

Inferring the effects of the labor movement
Ask: *In what way did the Great Depression change attitudes toward union activities? Why do you think this change occurred?* (Possible answer: Common problems united factory workers, and many people may have sympathized with out-of-work laborers. Economic hardships were widespread and shared.) **Verbal/Linguistic**

ESSENTIAL QUESTION

Exploring the Essential Question

Understanding the need for labor laws Display the words, "If you don't come in Sunday, don't come in Monday." Ask students to explain what these words imply. *(People worked seven days a week.)* Point out that people also worked more than eight hours each day. Tell students to imagine that, instead of coming to school each day, they had to go to work and that their boss had these words on the gate to the factory. Invite them to discuss how they might feel and what they might do. To spur the discussion, ask questions like these: **What do you think would happen if you got sick? When would you spend time with your family? How do you think you would feel after work? If someone came to you and invited you to join a group fighting for shorter working hours and one day off each week, what would you do?**

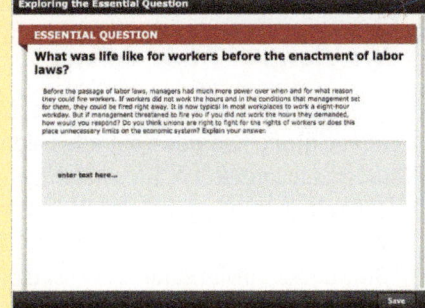

ANSWERS, p. 247

✓ **READING PROGRESS CHECK** Students' answers should recognize that the first union in 1778 was small and local, and but workers' response to poor working conditions and pay spurred widespread demand. The difficult working conditions during the Civil War were followed by the rise of the craft and trade unions, with early industrial unions organizing strikes and picket lines. Students should also mention the roles of early legislation, the courts, and employer resistance in shaping union development.

CHAPTER 9, LESSON 1
The Labor Movement

C Critical Thinking Skills

Researching the labor movement culture Tell students that labor and union songs make up a significant part of American folk music. Have volunteers prepare a presentation about the role of music in the struggles to unionize workers over the last 100 years or so. Encourage musically talented students to perform selections from the labor songbook. **Auditory/Musical**

V Visual Skills

Sequencing information about the AFL-CIO Have students make a time line of key events in the relationship of the AFL and the CIO. Events should include the formation of the groups, their merger, and their split. **Verbal/Linguistic**

ANSWERS, p. 248

CRITICAL THINKING

Students could mention any number of workers' benefits—eight-hour workday, safe working environment, and so on—that resulted from labor unions' collective bargaining and other efforts. A drawback could state that higher wages for American unionized laborers result in higher prices for products.

TWO VIEWS OF TRADE UNIONS

This cartoon portrays two exaggerated views of labor unions.

▶ **CRITICAL THINKING**
Analyze Identify and explain at least one benefit and one drawback to labor unions.

labor for a child under 16 and work that is hazardous to the health of a child under 18.

Antiunion Backlash

The union movement had grown strong by the end of World War II, but then public opinion shifted again. Some people feared that communists had secretly entered the unions. Others were concerned over production losses due to the increased number of strikes. People began to think that management, not labor, was the victim.

Growing antiunion feelings led to the Labor-Management Relations Act, or Taft-Hartley Act, of 1947. The act had a tough antiunion provision known as Section 14(b) that allows individual states to pass **right-to-work laws**. A right-to-work law is a state law making it illegal to force workers to join a union as a condition of employment.

right-to-work law state law making it illegal to require a worker to join a union

If a state does not have a right-to-work law, new workers may be required to join an existing union as a condition of employment. If a state has a right-to-work law, then new hires can decide for themselves whether or not they want to join the union. Today, the states shown in **Figure 9.2** have taken advantage of Section 14(b) to pass right-to-work laws.

Other legislation was aimed at stopping criminal influences that had begun to emerge in the labor movement. The most important law was the Labor-Management Reporting and Disclosure Act, or Landrum-Griffin Act, of 1959.

This act required unions to file regular financial reports with the government. It also limited the amount of money union officials could borrow from the union.

The AFL-CIO

The American Federation of Labor (AFL) began in 1886 as an organization of craft or trade unions. It later added several industrial unions. The craft and industrial unions, however, did not always agree, and so eight of the industrial unions formed a separate group headed by John L. Lewis, the president of the United Mine Workers of America.

The AFL and Lewis did not get along, so Lewis and his industrial unions were expelled in 1935 and formed the Congress of Industrial Organizations

248

---

netw⊙rks *Online Teaching Options*

POLITICAL CARTOON

Two Views of Trade Unions

Assessing the value of labor unions Display the political cartoon giving two views of trade unions and ask several students to interpret it. Then have students complete the activity individually. Create a two-column chart on the board, labeling one column "Benefits" and the other "Drawbacks." Invite students to list their answers in the chart. Use their answers as a basis for a class discussion on the role of organized labor in the United States today. **Verbal/Linguistic**

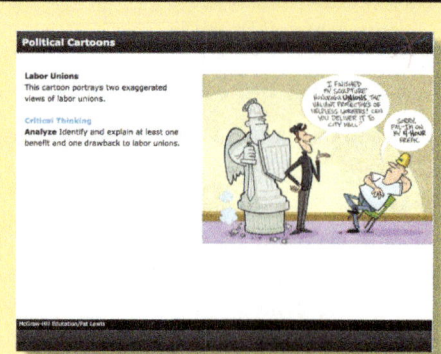

FIGURE 9.2

RIGHT-TO-WORK, STATE BY STATE

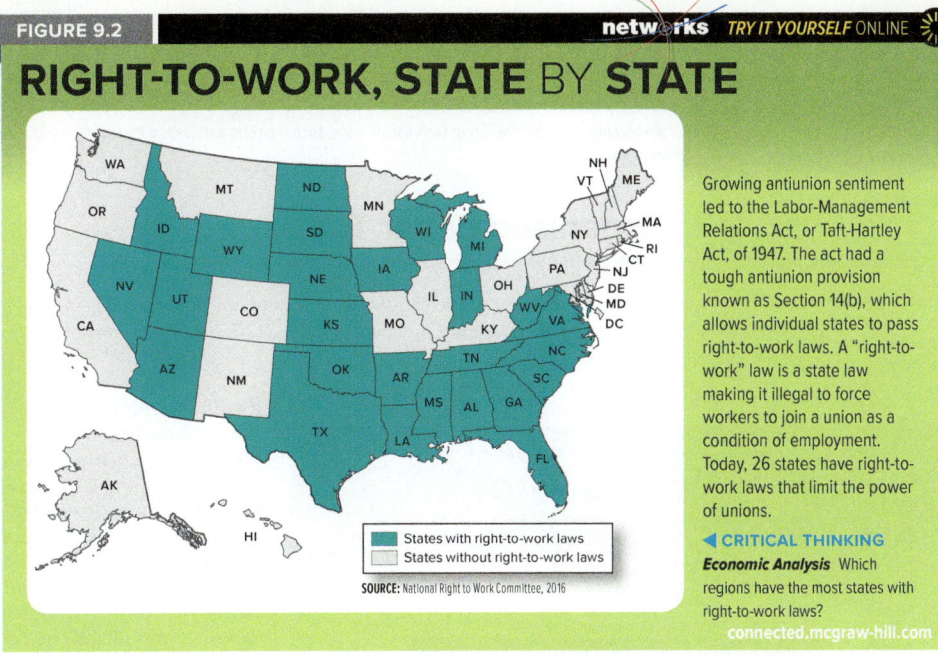

Growing antiunion sentiment led to the Labor-Management Relations Act, or Taft-Hartley Act, of 1947. The act had a tough antiunion provision known as Section 14(b), which allows individual states to pass right-to-work laws. A "right-to-work" law is a state law making it illegal to force workers to join a union as a condition of employment. Today, 26 states have right-to-work laws that limit the power of unions.

◀ **CRITICAL THINKING**
Economic Analysis Which regions have the most states with right-to-work laws?

connected.mcgraw-hill.com

(CIO). The CIO quickly organized unions in industries that had not been unionized before, such as the steel and automobile industries. By the 1940s, the CIO had nearly 7 million members.

As the CIO grew stronger, it began to challenge the dominance of the AFL. In 1955, the AFL and the CIO joined to form the American Federation of Labor and Congress of Industrial Organizations (AFL-CIO). By 2005, however, disagreement over the best way to spend union funds resulted in a breakup of the AFL-CIO. The breakaway unions formed the rival Change to Win Coalition.

This split did not seem to weaken the political influence of organized labor. The remaining AFL-CIO unions focused their efforts on lobbying politicians. The Change to Win Coalition focused its efforts on recruiting new union members.

EXPLORING THE ESSENTIAL QUESTION

Before the passage of labor laws, managers had much more power over when and for what reason they could fire workers. If workers did not work the hours and in the conditions that management set for them, they could be fired right away. It is now typical in most workplaces to work a five-day workweek. But if management threatened to fire you if you did not work the hours they demanded, how would you respond? Do you think unions are right to fight for the rights of workers or does this place unnecessary limits on the economic system? Explain your answer.

Independent Unions

Although the AFL-CIO and the Change to Win Coalition are still major forces, other unions are also important in the labor movement. Many of these are —unions that do not belong to either the AFL-CIO or to

independent unions labor union not affiliated with the AFL-CIO or the Change to Win Coalition

---

CHAPTER 9, LESSON 1
The Labor Movement

V Visual Skills

Illustrating American labor Organize students into several groups, and have each group create a collage illustrating the U.S. labor force. Have group members collect pictures of people at work from magazines, newspapers, and other media. Inform groups that jobs should range from blue-collar to white-collar and should include service workers. Have groups use these images to create their collages. Point out that collages should show diversity in terms of occupations, types of employees, and types of locations. Have groups display their finished collages around the classroom. Then use the collages to help students learn the content. You might ask students to categorize the types of work shown in the collages or speculate on the likelihood of jobs shown being outsourced or offshored. **AL Kinesthetic, Visual/Spatial**

MAPS

Right-to-Work, State by State

Exploring how laws can limit union power Display the interactive map and have students determine whether their state has right-to-work laws. Lead a discussion about the benefits and drawbacks of such laws. Then, create a two-column chart on the board and have students fill it in with the pros and cons of right-to-work laws. **Logical/Mathematical**

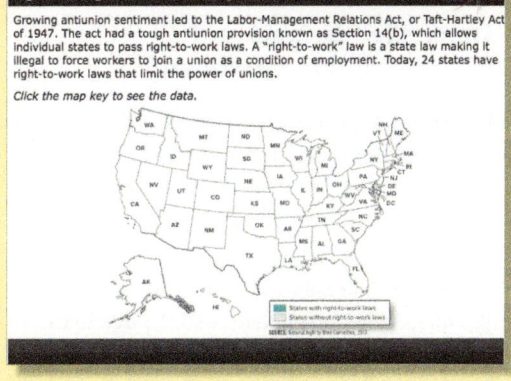

ANSWERS, p. 249

CRITICAL THINKING

Students should recognize that the Midwest and the South have the most states with right-to-work laws.

EXPLORING THE ESSENTIAL QUESTION

Answers will vary but students should show that they understand the continued conflict between labor and management. If jobs are difficult to get, a worker might have to abide by management's rules so as not to lose the job, and a union might be perceived as a way to counterbalance the power of management. However, if students have a negative view of unions, they might talk about trying to negotiate with management individually.

CHAPTER 9, LESSON 1
The Labor Movement

C Critical Thinking Skills

Formulating questions Have students write five questions based on the information in the table Union Membership and Representation by Industry. Then have them exchange work with a partner and answer each other's questions.

R Reading Skills

Summarizing the reading Have students review the information about closed shops, union shops, modified union shops, and agency shops. Then have them make a T-chart listing characteristics of each arrangement. **AL**

---

closed shop arrangement under which workers must join a union before they are hired; usually illegal

union shop arrangement under which workers must join a union after being hired

modified union shop arrangement under which workers have the option to join a union after being hired

agency shop arrangement under which nonunion members must pay union dues

the Change to Win Coalition—such as the Major League Baseball Players Association. Other examples of independent unions are the Fraternal Order of Police and the U.S. Airline Pilots Association.

✓ **READING PROGRESS CHECK**

Analyzing Why did the Great Depression have such a strong and lasting impact on the labor movement?

Organized Labor Today

GUIDING QUESTION How do the types of union arrangements differ?

Unionized workers participate in several kinds of union arrangements. In addition, union participation in the labor force varies widely from one industry to another.

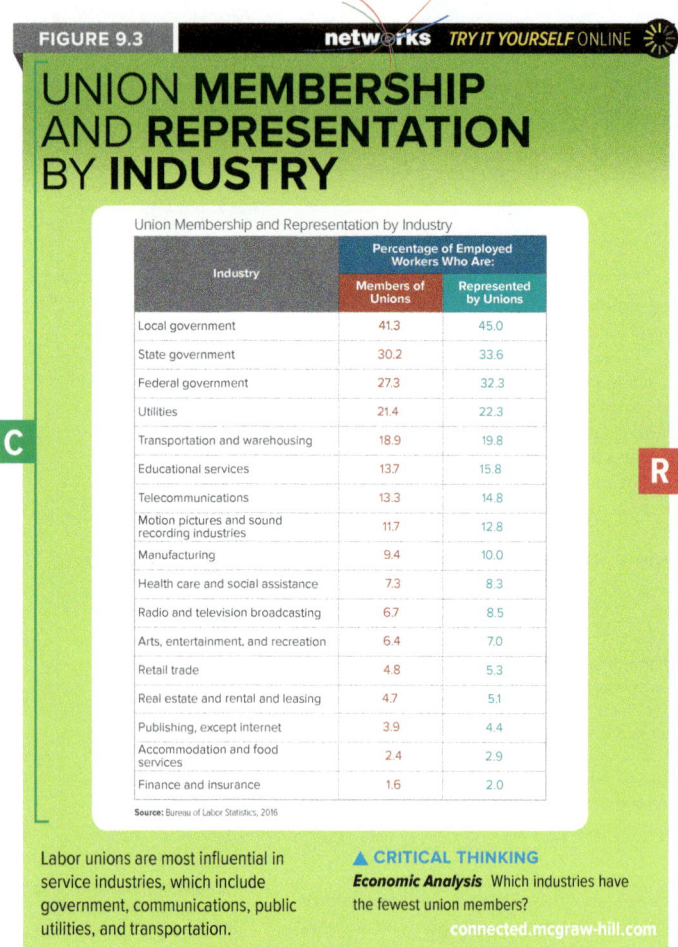

FIGURE 9.3

UNION MEMBERSHIP AND REPRESENTATION BY INDUSTRY

Union Membership and Representation by Industry

Industry	Percentage of Employed Workers Who Are:	
	Members of Unions	Represented by Unions
Local government	41.3	45.0
State government	30.2	33.6
Federal government	27.3	32.3
Utilities	21.4	22.3
Transportation and warehousing	18.9	19.8
Educational services	13.7	15.8
Telecommunications	13.3	14.8
Motion pictures and sound recording industries	11.7	12.8
Manufacturing	9.4	10.0
Health care and social assistance	7.3	8.3
Radio and television broadcasting	6.7	8.5
Arts, entertainment, and recreation	6.4	7.0
Retail trade	4.8	5.3
Real estate and rental and leasing	4.7	5.1
Publishing, except internet	3.9	4.4
Accommodation and food services	2.4	2.9
Finance and insurance	1.6	2.0

Source: Bureau of Labor Statistics, 2016

Labor unions are most influential in service industries, which include government, communications, public utilities, and transportation.

▲ **CRITICAL THINKING**
Economic Analysis Which industries have the fewest union members?

connected.mcgraw-hill.com

Kinds of Union Arrangements

The most restrictive kind of union arrangement is the **closed shop**, in which an employer agrees to hire only union members. This arrangement was common until the Taft-Hartley Act of 1947 made the closed shop illegal for all companies involved in interstate commerce. Because most firms in the United States today are directly or indirectly engaged in interstate commerce, few, if any, closed shops exist today.

Another union arrangement is the **union shop**, where workers do not have to belong to the union to be hired, but must join soon afterward and remain a member for as long as they keep their jobs.

Another union arrangement is the **modified union shop**. Under this arrangement, workers do not have to belong to a union to be hired and cannot be made to join one to keep their jobs. If workers voluntarily join the union, however, they must remain members for as long as they hold their jobs.

An **agency shop** is a union arrangement governed by a security agreement that does *not* require a worker to join a union as a condition to get or

---

networks Online Teaching Options

CHARTS

Union Membership and Representation by Industry

Exploring organized labor today Have students view Figure 9.3 and point out that unions represent more people than just their members. Ask them to think about this fact as they read the information in the activity. Then, have them click through to read the details it provides. When they have read it, have them work in pairs to create summaries of what they learned. Invite pairs to share their summaries with the class.

ANSWERS, p. 250

✓ **READING PROGRESS CHECK** Because so many people were out of work and in desperate need, the attitude toward labor changed during the Great Depression. Common problems united workers, especially those in factories, to organize and form unions. Legislation that provided for worker protections was enacted during the Depression, such as the Fair Labor Standards Act, which is still in effect.

CRITICAL THINKING
Retail, real estate, publishing, food services, and finance

keep a job. It *does* require the worker to pay union dues to help pay for collective bargaining costs. Nonunion workers also are subject to the contract terms negotiated by the union, whether or not they agree with the terms.

An agency shop is also known as "fair share." Unions like to use this term to remind everyone that the dues the nonmembers pay to the union are used on behalf of all the workers, whether they are union members or not.

Unionized Workers in the Labor Force

Today, the United States has a population of about 320 million people. Approximately half of the people belong to the **civilian labor force**—men and women 16 years old and over who are either working or actively looking for a job. The civilian classification excludes the prison population, other institutionalized persons, and members of the armed forces.

civilian labor force noninstitutionalized part of the population, aged 16 and over, either working or looking for a job

Noteworthy features of unionized working people in the labor force:

- One out of every nine working Americans is either unionized or represented by a union.
- More men than women are union members, regardless of age.
- More workers over the age of 45 are unionized than younger workers.
- African Americans are more likely than other workers to belong to unions, while Asian Americans are the least likely to be union members.
- Union membership among full-time workers is more than twice as high as membership among part-time workers.
- Industries with the *highest* rates of unionization are *local governments, state governments*, and the *federal government*, as shown in **Figure 9.3**.

Finally, union membership rates also differ considerably by state. In the three *most* unionized states—Alaska, Hawaii, and New York—at least one in five workers is unionized. In the three states that are the *least* unionized—Arkansas, North Carolina, and South Carolina—approximately 1 worker out of 30 is unionized.

✓ **READING PROGRESS CHECK**

Contrasting How do the types of union arrangements differ?

LESSON 1 REVIEW

Reviewing Vocabulary

1. **Explaining** How do a strike and a boycott differ?
2. **Explaining** In what way might a modified union shop weaken the bargaining power that workers have in a union shop?

Using Your Notes

As you read the lesson, use the time line to help you understand developments and changes in the U.S. labor movement.

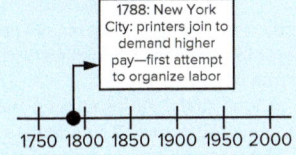

U.S. Labor Movement

1788: New York City: printers join to demand higher pay—first attempt to organize labor

3. **Evaluating** Which time period in U.S. history since 1750 has seen the greatest advancement in organized labor? Explain.

Answering the Guiding Questions

4. **Identifying Central Issues** For what purposes did early unions form?
5. **Evaluating** Have labor laws since the 1930s strengthened or weakened the union movement, and why?
6. **Contrasting** How do the types of union arrangements differ?

Writing About Economics

7. **Argument** In your opinion, do unions have a useful, even necessary, role to play in the modern American economy? How do you think unions affect the current economy? In what ways might the economy be improved if unions were stronger, or how might the economy be weakened by more unionization? Defend your point of view with facts and evidence in a one-page paper.
8. **Expository** In a short answer essay, identify what regulation was passed in 1890 and how it applied to the establishment of businesses?

CHAPTER 9, LESSON 1
The Labor Movement

R Reading Skills

Researching the contributions of women and minorities Organize students into several groups. Have groups investigate the roles that women and minority groups played in the development of the American labor movement. Then have them use their findings to create a brochure or poster that might accompany a museum exhibit on minorities and organized labor in the United States. Suggest that brochures or posters include an overview of the exhibit and several exhibit items (for example, paintings, photographs, charts, or graphs) accompanied by explanatory captions. Have groups present their brochures or posters to the class.
Interpersonal

CLOSE & REFLECT

R Reading Skills

Understanding the main idea Have students review the lesson and create a main-idea statement about the changes that labor unions made for American workers today.

ANSWERS, p. 251

✓ **READING PROGRESS CHECK** Students should highlight the differences between the closed shop (workers must join a union), a union shop (workers must join a union after they are hired), a modified union shop (workers are free to join a union if they choose), and an agency shop (nonunion members must pay union dues).

LESSON 1 REVIEW ANSWERS

Reviewing Vocabulary

1. Strikes are walkouts by employees. A boycott involves the public refusing to buy a product made by the firm to force the company to negotiate with workers.
2. If too few workers join the union, the modified union shop has less clout in its negotiations. In a union shop, all workers join the union and so have more power in negotiating with the employer.

Using Your Notes

3. Students may suggest that the post-Depression era saw the greatest advancement for organized labor. Some of the most powerful and enduring industrial unions were formed at this time, as well as the strongest labor laws.

Answering the Guiding Questions

4. Most early unions formed to press for better pay and safer working conditions.
5. Students may recognize that from the 1930s through the World War II, the strength of unions grew, but after that there was a backlash, particularly the right-to-work laws enacted in many states.
6. Students should describe the differences among the various union shops: closed, agency, union, and modified union.

Writing About Economics

7. Students should use facts or evidence to support their viewpoint. Students may argue that unions help the economy by putting more money in workers' pockets, thus increasing demand for more goods. Or they may argue that union demands for higher wages cause employers to reduce worker hours or fire workers they feel they cannot afford to pay at the higher wage level.
8. The Sherman Antitrust Act of 1890 was a regulation that kept the establishment of businesses from creating a monopoly in the market.

CHAPTER 9, LESSON 2
Wages and Labor Disputes

ENGAGE

W Writing Skills

Preparing to read Before students begin the lesson, ask them to review the content vocabulary on the first page of the lesson. If they are unsure of the meaning of any of the words, have them look them up in the glossary or a dictionary. Then have them write three sentences using at least two words from the list in each sentence. Invite students to share their sentences with the class.

ANSWERS, p. 252

ESSENTIAL QUESTION ACTIVITY

Some ways that labor-management disputes may be resolved before resulting in work stoppage or a deadlock include collective bargaining, mediation, arbitration, fact-finding, and presidential intervention. Students' opinions on whether the government or other third party should become involved will vary. Ask students to provide reasons for their opinions.

TAKING NOTES
Collective bargaining
Mediation
Arbitration
Fact finding
Injunction and seizure
Presidential intervention

Interact with these digital assets and others in lesson 2
- ✓ INTERACTIVE GRAPH
  Wage Theory of Price Determination
- ✓ INTERACTIVE CHART
  Median Weekly Earnings
- ✓ SELF-CHECK QUIZ
- ✓ VIDEO

networks TRY IT YOURSELF ONLINE

LESSON 2
Wages and Labor Disputes

ESSENTIAL QUESTION

What factors lead to higher wages for a worker?

Labor disputes are not uncommon, and most occur over pay and working conditions. If a dispute results in an actual work stoppage, both sides stand to lose enormous sums of money.

As a result, and regardless of the reason for the dispute, the deliberations to end it are usually intense. Fortunately, there are several ways to resolve a dispute before it turns into a deadlock.

Think about some ways such disputes might be resolved. Should the government, or some other third party, intervene? How?

Reading Help Desk

Academic Vocabulary
- anticipate
- distorted

Content Vocabulary
- wage rate
- market theory of wage determination
- equilibrium wage rate
- theory of negotiated wages
- seniority
- signaling theory
- collective bargaining
- grievance procedure
- mediation
- arbitration
- fact-finding
- injunction
- seizure

TAKING NOTES:

Key Ideas and Details
ACTIVITY Use the graphic organizer below to identify the different ways that labor disputes are resolved.

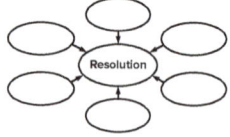

Wage Determination

GUIDING QUESTION *Why do different people earn different wages?*

Most occupations have a **wage rate**, a standard amount of pay given for work performed. Wage rates usually differ from one occupation to the next, and sometimes even within the same occupation. There are four explanations as to why this happens.

Noncompeting Categories of Labor

One explanation recognizes four broad categories of labor that have different levels of knowledge and skills. The highest pay goes to people in jobs that require the most skills and training; the lowest pay goes to jobs with the least skills and training. Because workers in one category do not compete directly with those in other categories, wages differ in each of the following noncompeting grades:

- **Unskilled labor**—consists of workers in jobs that do not require people with special training and skills. People in these jobs work primarily with their hands at tasks such as picking fruit or mopping floors.
- **Semiskilled labor**—workers in jobs that require enough mechanical skills to operate machines for which they need a minimum amount of training. These workers may operate basic equipment such as cleaning equipment, lawnmowers, and other machines that call for a modest amount of training.

---

networks Online Teaching Options

BELLRINGER

Wages and Labor Disputes

Exploring union participation today Point out that unions not only represent the interests of groups of workers, but also those of individual workers. Use the Bellringer to introduce the important concepts of *mediation*, *collective bargaining*, and *arbitration*. **Ask: Why do you think both unions and management prefer to negotiate rather than strike?** (Students should recognize that striking means people are out of work, and unions must help support them. At the same time, the company is not producing or performing at peak, so it is losing income. Moreover, since others—including the public—may rely on the company for goods and/or services, a strike hurts everyone and affects public perception of both the company and the union.)

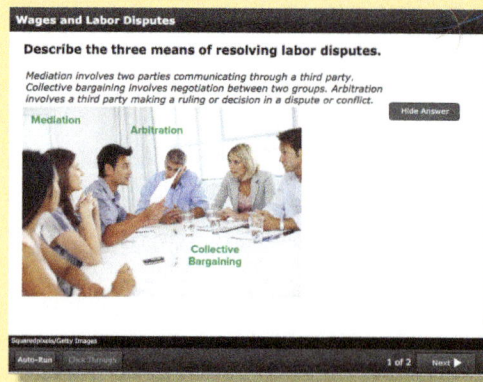

- **Skilled labor**—consists of workers with higher investments in education and training who operate complex equipment and perform most of their tasks with little supervision. Examples include carpenters, electricians, tool and die makers, computer technicians, and computer programmers.
- **Professional labor**—consists of individuals who have the highest level of knowledge-based education and managerial skills. Examples include teachers, doctors, scientists, lawyers, and top managers such as corporate executives.

Of course, there are no distinct boundaries between these categories of labor, but in general, average wages are different for each.

Market Theory of Wage Determination

Another explanation for the differences in pay many people receive is based on the **market theory of wage determination**. This theory states that the supply and demand for a worker's skills and services determine the wage or salary.

For example, if there is a low demand for roofers but a relatively large supply, the result would be relatively low wages for roofers. If conditions are reversed, so that the demand is high and supply is low, then wages would be much higher. This describes the market for the services of professional athletes. In this market, a small supply of talent combined with relatively high demand results in higher wages.

You can see this interaction of supply and demand in **Figure 9.4**. In each market, the intersection of supply and demand determines the **equilibrium wage rate**—the wage rate that leaves neither a surplus nor a shortage in the labor market.

wage rate prevailing pay scale for work performed in an occupation in a given area or region

market theory of wage determination explanation stating that the supply and demand for a worker's skills and services determine the wage or salary

equilibrium wage rate wage rate leaving neither a surplus nor a shortage of workers in the market

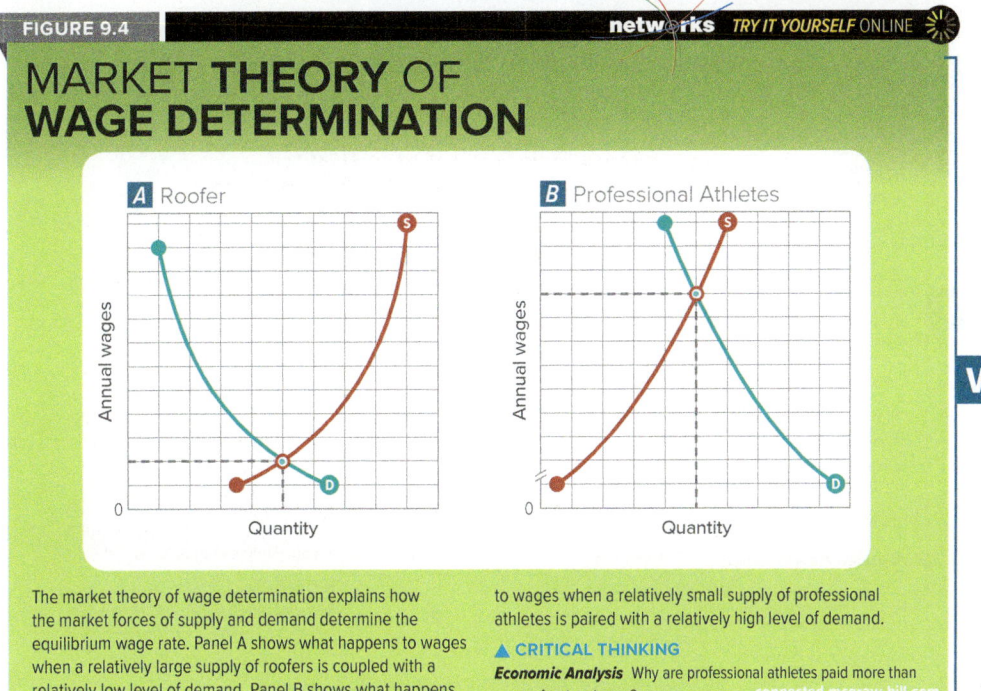

FIGURE 9.4 — MARKET THEORY OF WAGE DETERMINATION

The market theory of wage determination explains how the market forces of supply and demand determine the equilibrium wage rate. Panel A shows what happens to wages when a relatively large supply of roofers is coupled with a relatively low level of demand. Panel B shows what happens to wages when a relatively small supply of professional athletes is paired with a relatively high level of demand.

▲ **CRITICAL THINKING**
Economic Analysis Why are professional athletes paid more than nonprofessional ones?

CHAPTER 9, LESSON 2
Wages and Labor Disputes

TEACH & ASSESS

W Writing Skills

Creating job advertisements List the four categories of labor on the board. Have students write a brief newspaper advertisement for a job in each category. If necessary, brainstorm several types of jobs in each skill category. Then have students read and compare their advertisements.
ELL Verbal/Linguistic

V Visual Skills

Using line graphs Have students draw two line graphs showing (1) how the labor supply would change in a highly remote location if very high wages were offered to prospective employees, and (2) how the demand for labor would change in an industrial firm that just invested in robotics. **BL**
Logical/Mathematical

GRAPHS

Market Theory of Wage Determination

Understanding wage determination Display and discuss the graphs for roofers and professional athletes. Form students into groups to discuss and agree on an answer to the Economic Analysis question. Use the groups' answers as the basis for a class discussion. Then have the groups complete the activity.

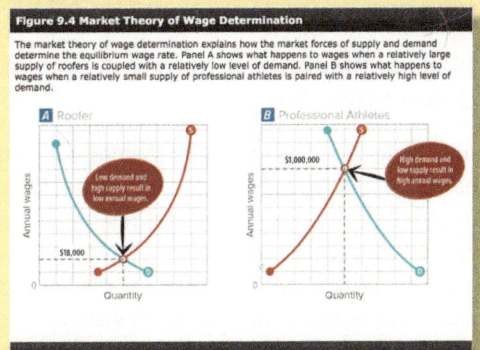

ANSWERS, p. 253

CRITICAL THINKING

There is high demand and low supply for professional athletes, so their pay (where S and D intersect) is high.

CHAPTER 9, LESSON 2
Wages and Labor Disputes

C Critical Thinking Skills

Classifying different types of jobs Call on students to identify different types of jobs, and list their responses on the board. Then ask students to make a three-column chart in their notebooks, using "Jobs," "Labor Category," and "Factors Affecting Supply and Demand" as column headings. Direct students to select 10 jobs from the list and enter them in the first column. In the second column, have them note whether the jobs are unskilled, semiskilled, skilled, or professional. In the third column, have them note what factors might affect how supply and demand determine wages.

V Visual Skills

Researching occupational groupings Work with students to help them understand the differences among the occupational groupings in Figure 9.5, especially among similar-sounding ones, such as "Healthcare practitioner and technical occupations" and "Healthcare support occupations" or "Protective service occupations" and "Personal care and service occupations." Have students go to the Bureau of Labor Statistics Web site to research the groupings further. **Verbal/Linguistic**

ANSWERS, p. 254

CRITICAL THINKING
They accrue more for lower paid occupations.

Exceptions to the market theory may appear to exist at certain times. Some unproductive workers may receive high wages because of family ties or political influence. Or some highly skilled workers may receive low wages because of discrimination based on their race or gender. An exception does not negate the validity of supply and demand; however, it is just that—an exception.

Theory of Negotiated Wages

C The third approach to wage rate determination recognizes the power of unions. The **theory of negotiated wages** states that the bargaining strength of organized labor is a factor that helps to determine wages. A strong union, for example, may have the power to force higher wages on some firms because the firms would not be able to afford work interruptions in case of a threatened strike.

Figure 9.5 helps validate the theory of negotiated wages. While only 12 major occupational groups are shown, the figure is typical in that almost all workers represented by unions receive median weekly salaries that are higher than those of nonunion workers.

theory of negotiated wages explanation of wage rates based on the bargaining strength of organized labor

FIGURE 9.5

MEDIAN WEEKLY EARNINGS BY OCCUPATION AND UNION AFFILIATION

Occupations	Median Weekly Earnings of Workers Who Are:	
	Represented by Unions	Non-Union
Architecture and engineering occupations	1,399	1,427
Computer and mathematical occupations	1,327	1,434
Healthcare practitioner and technical occupations	1,194	1,014
Education, training, and library occupations	1,074	860
Construction and extraction occupations	1,064	695
Installation, maintenance, and repair occupations	1,051	799
Protective service occupations	1,029	687
Office and administrative support occupations	821	639
Building & grounds cleaning and maintenance	628	469
Healthcare support occupations	546	495
Personal care and service occupations	521	496
Food preparation and serving-related occupations	512	436

Source: Bureau of Labor Statistics, 2016

The graph shows that weekly earnings are slightly higher for the majority of workers who are represented by unions.

◀ **CRITICAL THINKING**
Economic Analysis Do the earnings benefits of unionization accrue more to higher paid occupations or lower paid occupations?

254

---

networks Online Teaching Options

CHARTS

Median Weekly Earnings by Occupation and Union Affiliation

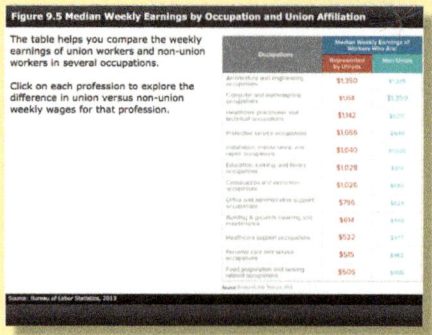

Analyzing the effect of union membership on earnings Display Figure 9.5, and allow students time to get an overview of its contents. Then review the chart's contents line by line as a group, clicking on the occupations to show whether union or non-union workers' earnings are higher. As you review each line, ask students to characterize the job categories and give examples of jobs in each. For example, the category "Architecture and engineering occupations" includes people who design buildings and bridges, whereas the category "Construction and extraction occupations" includes people who construct buildings and bridges. Invite students to speculate on why the wage levels are what they are for each group.

Most union workers also benefit from **seniority**—the length of time a person has been on the job. Because of their seniority, some workers receive higher wages than others who perform similar tasks, even if they do not have better skills.

seniority length of time a person has been on a job

Signaling Theory

The fourth explanation for differences in wage rates is based on **signaling theory**. This theory states that employers are willing to pay more to people with certificates, degrees, and other indicators that "signal" superior knowledge or ability. For example, a sales firm might prefer to hire a college graduate with a major in history than a high school graduate who excelled in business courses. While this may seem odd, some firms view the college degree as a signal that the individual possesses the intelligence, perseverance, and maturity to succeed.

You might hear from friends that they did not need their college degree to do the job they currently have—as if their education was not important. But this view overlooks signaling theory, which helps explain why they got the job in the first place.

signaling theory theory that employers are willing to pay more for people with certificates, diplomas, degrees, and other indicators of superior ability

✓ **READING PROGRESS CHECK**

Explaining What is the difference between the market theory of wage determination and the theory of negotiated wages?

CAREERS | National Labor Relations Board Administrative Law Judge

Is this Career for you?

 Are you interested in developing a thorough knowledge of the law?

 Are you a good listener?

 Are you a logical, decisive, and impartial thinker?

 Can you speak and write clearly and precisely?

Salary
Median pay: $91,880
$44.17 per hour

Job Growth Potential
Faster than average

Interview with an Administrative Law Judge

"I enjoy being able to make an impact on a very limited, yet purposeful area of law—an area that can affect so many different people (employees and employers alike). The record I create and ultimately my decisions, if appealed to a higher court, can create and set the precedent for all employers, employees, and legal professionals to follow."

—Judge Noell F. Allen, Administrative Law Judge

Profile of Work

An administrative law judge is not a member of the judicial branch, but holds an administrative position and makes decisions and recommendations in cases involving government programs or related matters. A National Labor Relations Board administrative judge hears cases involving labor law and issues written decisions. A decision can be appealed to the directors of the NLRB in Washington, DC. If the board upholds the ruling, it can set legal precedent for similar rulings in the future.

CHAPTER 9, LESSON 2
Wages and Labor Disputes

C Critical Thinking Skills

Evaluating wage practices **Ask:** Do you think job seniority should be rewarded with higher wages? Explain. *(Students answering "yes" may cite the greater experience of workers with seniority, whereas those saying "no" may say that seniority alone does not indicate better job performance.)*

English Language Proficiency

Advanced High Have students listen to recordings of content information delivered in complex English, such as the Discrimination Lawsuit video presented on page 256. Ask questions to be sure students comprehend. If students fail to demonstrate understanding, repeat the information using the same complex English, and invite volunteers to paraphrase it in simpler language.

INTERACTIVE FEATURE

Careers: National Labor Relations Board Administrative Law Judge

Experiencing labor conflict Have students read the Careers feature. Explain that even the most detailed and comprehensive work agreement cannot spell out all the specific issues and problems that might occur after it has been signed by all parties. Give students a chance to act as labor relations judges by providing them with this scenario: A particular worker has been reassigned to a less pleasant job within a company. Was this reassignment for legitimate business reasons? Or, as the worker suspects, was he or she assigned because of a personality conflict with a particular manager? Have students present the grievance before a "judge," who must rule on the grievance.

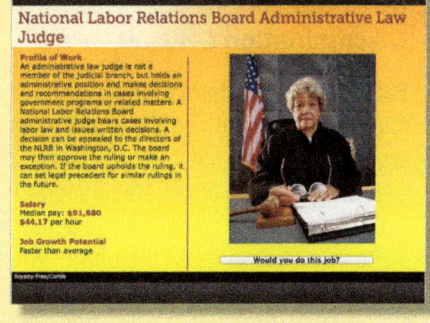

ANSWERS, p. 255

✓ **READING PROGRESS CHECK** The market theory of wage determination posits that wages are determined by supply and demand for workers' services. The theory of negotiated wages posits that wages are determined by negotiation between a labor union and management.

CHAPTER 9, LESSON 2
Wages and Labor Disputes

V Visual Skills

Charting the collective bargaining process Review the text on collective bargaining with students. Ensure that students understand that when conflicts arise between labor and management, mediation and arbitration may be used to find compromises. Then ask students to create a flowchart showing the collective bargaining process. Call on volunteers to display and explain their flowcharts. **AL Visual/Spatial**

C Critical Thinking Skills

Supporting an argument Have students write two statements to be submitted to the arbitrator about a fictional local strike that is about to be settled by binding arbitration. One statement should be from the perspective of the union. The other entry should be written from the point of view of management. **BL Verbal/Linguistic**

T Technology Skills

Conducting online research about strikes Have students use online resources to research a recent strike in your state. Have them note the reasons for the work stoppage, the procedures used to end the dispute, and the resolution. Have students present their findings in the form of a radio news report that lasts two to three minutes. Invite volunteers to "broadcast" their reports to the class. **Auditory/Musical**

ANSWERS, p. 256

EXPLORING THE ESSENTIAL QUESTION

Students will most likely use experience and customer satisfaction as their main arguments to get a raise. If the neighbor can't or won't pay more, students might consider trying to get a job, whether mowing lawns or doing other work, that pays more, or they might decide that they should take the job anyway because they need the money, and the neighbor is likely to hire someone else to do it.

---

collective bargaining process of negotiating between union and management representatives over pay, benefits, and job-related matters

anticipate to expect or be sure of in advance

grievance procedure provision in a contract outlining the way future disputes and grievance issues will be resolved

mediation process of resolving a dispute by bringing in a neutral third party to help both sides reach a compromise

arbitration agreement by two parties to place a dispute before a third party for a binding settlement; also called binding arbitration

EXPLORING THE ESSENTIAL QUESTION

Imagine that you agree to mow your neighbor's lawn for a set price. You agree to the price and do the work once a week all summer. The next summer, you think you should get paid more for the job, and you want to ask for more money. What arguments would you make that would be most likely to get you more money? What will you do if your neighbor refuses to pay more? Explain your answer.

fact-finding agreement between union and management to have a neutral third party collect facts about a dispute and present nonbinding recommendations

distorted not truthfully represented

Resolving Labor Disputes

GUIDING QUESTION *What options are available for solving labor disputes?*

When organized labor negotiates with management, disputes are bound to happen. Both sides can use collective bargaining to minimize such disputes. If this fails, they can turn to mediation, arbitration, fact-finding, injunction and seizure, or in extreme cases, presidential intervention.

Collective Bargaining

Labor-management relations usually require **collective bargaining**—negotiations that take place between labor and management over issues such as pay, working hours, health care coverage, and other job-related matters. During collective bargaining, elected union officials represent workers, and company officials in charge of labor relations represent management. Collective bargaining requires compromise from both parties, and the discussions over issues may go on for months.

If the negotiations are successful, both parties agree on basic issues such as pay, working conditions, and benefits. Because it is difficult to **anticipate** future problems, a **grievance procedure**—a provision for resolving issues that may come up later—may also be included in the final contract.

Normally, the union and management are able to reach an agreement because the costs of failure are so high. Workers, for example, still have to make regular payments on car loans and mortgages, and companies don't want to lose customers to other businesses. In short, everyone has a big stake in resolving labor issues.

Mediation

One way to resolve differences is through **mediation**, the process of bringing in a neutral third person or persons to help settle a dispute. The mediator's primary goal is to find a solution that both parties will accept. A mediator must be unbiased so that neither party benefits at the expense of the other. If the mediator has the confidence and trust of both parties, he or she will be able to learn what concessions each side is willing to make.

In the end, the mediator recommends a compromise to both sides. Neither side has to accept a mediator's decision, although it often helps break the deadlock.

Arbitration

Another popular way to resolve differences is through **arbitration**, a process in which both sides agree to place their differences before a third party whose decision will be accepted as final. Because both sides must agree to any final decision the arbitrator makes, this type of negotiation is also called binding arbitration.

Arbitration is finding its way into areas beyond labor-management relations. Today, for example, most credit card companies require disputes with cardholders to be resolved by an arbitrator rather than in the courts. This means that a credit card holder can no longer sue the credit card company in the event of a dispute because the matter goes to arbitration instead.

Fact-Finding

A third way to resolve a dispute is through **fact-finding**, an agreement between union and management to have a neutral third party collect facts about a dispute and present nonbinding recommendations. This process can be especially useful in situations where each side has deliberately **distorted** the issues to win public

256

---

networks Online Teaching Options

VIDEO **WORKSHEET**

Discrimination Lawsuit

Examining a discrimination lawsuit Explain to students that when negotiation fails, one option workers have is to sue their employer. Tell them that when a group of people join together to bring a suit, this is called a class action suit. Write these headings on the board: Why the Women Sued, Arguments on Both Sides, Supreme Court's Decision and Why. Then have students view the video and fill in the information. *(The U.S. Supreme Court ruled that women suing Walmart were too diverse to file a class action lawsuit. They must each file suit independently.)*

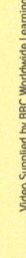

support, or when one side simply does not believe the claims made by the other side. Neither labor nor management has to accept the recommendations of the fact-finding committee.

Injunction

A fourth way to settle labor-management disputes is through injunction or seizure. During a dispute, one of the parties may request an **injunction**—a court order instructing one side to act, or not act. If issued against a union, the injunction may direct the union not to strike. If issued against a company, it may direct the company not to lock out its workers.

injunction court order issued to prevent a company or union from taking or not taking action during a labor dispute

Many labor disputes involve an injunction. For example, after professional baseball players ended their strike and went back to work in 1995, the owners promptly called a lockout. The players then got an injunction against the owners, and the 1995 baseball season began—but without a labor agreement.

Seizure

Under extreme circumstances, the government may resort to **seizure**—a temporary takeover of operations—while the government negotiates with the union. This occurred in 1946 when the government seized the bituminous (high-quality black) coal industry. While operating the mines, government officials worked out a settlement with the miners' union.

seizure temporary government takeover of a company to keep it running during a labor-management dispute

Presidential Intervention

The president of the United States may enter a labor-management dispute by publicly appealing to both parties to resolve their differences. While rarely used, this can be effective if the appeal has broad public support. The president also can fire federal workers. In 1981, President Ronald Reagan fired striking air traffic controllers because they were federal employees who had gone on strike despite having taken an oath not to do so.

The president also has emergency powers that can be used to end some strikes. When pilots from American Airlines went on strike in 1997 during a peak travel weekend, President Bill Clinton used a 1926 federal law, the Railway Labor Relations Act, to order an end to the strike less than 30 minutes after it began.

☑ **READING PROGRESS CHECK**

Summarizing In what ways can labor and management resolve disputes?

LESSON 2 REVIEW

Reviewing Vocabulary

1. *Defining* How does the market theory of wage determination explain the difference in pay rates?

2. *Explaining* Under what circumstances might management and labor turn to arbitration to settle a dispute?

Using Your Notes

3. *Evaluating* What would be the most preferable way for both labor and management to resolve a labor dispute? What would be the last resort for solving a dispute? Explain your answer.

Answering the Guiding Questions

4. *Explaining* Why do different people earn different wages?

5. *Describing* What options are available for solving labor disputes?

Writing About Economics

6. *Informative/Explanatory* What plan can you make for yourself that will help you earn the highest wages during your working life? Explain your response.

connected.mcgraw-hill.com Labor and Wages **257**

CHAPTER 9, LESSON 2
Wages and Labor Disputes

W Writing Skills

Assessing criteria for settling a dispute Have students work in pairs to write a list of criteria that a U.S. president should follow in deciding whether to intervene in a labor-management dispute.

CLOSE & REFLECT

W Writing Skills

Explaining how wages are determined and how labor disputes are resolved Divide students into two groups. Have each student in the first group create a one-minute lesson explaining how wages are determined, and each student in the second group create a one-minute lesson explaining how labor disputes are resolved. Tell them to make sure their speeches explain these processes: they should not simply list terms. Then pair a student from one group with a student from the other, and have them deliver their lessons to each other. In each pair, the "student" should take notes and ask at least one question of the "teacher" based on the one-minute lesson.

ANSWERS, p. 257

☑ **READING PROGRESS CHECK** Labor and management disputes are resolved through collective bargaining, mediation, arbitration, fact finding, injunctions, seizure, and presidential intervention.

LESSON 2 REVIEW ANSWERS

Reviewing Vocabulary

1. Wages are determined by the supply and demand for workers in particular jobs.

2. Management and labor might use arbitration when they are unable to reach a compromise by themselves and are willing to let an outside arbitrator make the decision.

Using Your Notes

3. Collective bargaining would be the preferred method of resolving a dispute, because the two parties would negotiate and reach a compromise they are both willing to accept. Presidential intervention would be the least preferred method, because both parties would lose control of the situation and would be coerced into accepting the president's decision.

Answering the Guiding Questions

4. Four theories explain why people earn different wages: the theory of noncompeting categories of labor, market theory of wage determination, theory of negotiated wages, and signaling theory.

5. Labor disputes can be settled by collective bargaining, mediation, arbitration, fact-finding, injunction, seizure, and presidential intervention.

Writing About Economics

6. Students will probably identify getting a good education or training in a career that is in high demand as the most effective way to get a high-paying job. They should cite the signaling theory and the market theory of wage determination to support their responses.

Labor and Wages **257**

CHAPTER 9
Case Study

R Reading Skills

Locating specific information in the text Ask: **What decision did the steel plant managers make that sparked the strike?** *(They cut wages.)* **Why did they make this decision?** *(The price of steel dropped steeply, reducing their income.)* Use students' answers to explore management's motivations.

C1 Critical Thinking Skills

Speculating on results Ask: **What would happen to a family if the wage-earners' pay were cut?** Use students' answers to explore strikers' motivations.

C2 Critical Thinking Skills

Discussing causes and effects of the Homestead Strike Ask students to brainstorm a list of causes associated with the Homestead Strike. Choose up to four primary causes and write them on the board. Then discuss the effects of the Homestead Strike and add them to the board. Ask students to consider ways the strike could have been avoided.
Interpersonal, Visual/Spatial

ANSWERS, p. 258

Case Study Review

1. Management was exerting its right to decide how they will run their business by deciding how much to pay workers and whether they would operate their plant. Workers were exerting their rights by deciding what salary they were willing to work for, by choosing to join a union, and by going on strike as a way to extract their demands.
2. Students should recognize that the bases of today's disputes are similar to those in Homestead: wages and the right to organize. Today's disputes are generally peaceful and are settled through negotiations rather than violence. Students should recognize that unlike the situation at Homestead, the government now takes a more balanced view to protecting the rights of both workers and management.
3. Some students will say the government had the responsibility to stop the violence and to protect the rights of business owners. Other students will say the government ignored workers' rights and should have allowed the two sides to settle their dispute on their own. In either case, students should give reasons for their views.

Case Study

THE HOMESTEAD STRIKE

In the mid- and late 1800s, a time when unions were first organizing, clashes between labor and management were not uncommon, and sometimes, they got entirely out of hand. One such instance occurred at Andrew Carnegie's steel plant in Homestead, Pennsylvania, in 1892.

R The event was triggered by a general downturn in the economy that led to a steep drop in steel prices. At Andrew Carnegie's steel plant in Homestead, Pennsylvania, the decision was made to cut wages. The workers protested, of course. Many were members of the Amalgamated Association of Iron and Steel Workers, one of the strongest unions of this time, but the contract expired that June. Plant manager Henry C. Frick, with Carnegie's blessing, was determined to enforce the wage cut and break the union **C1** while he was at it. He refused to negotiate with the union, offering to negotiate only with individual workers. When the union refused, Frick closed the plant down. The workers went on strike.

C2 Frick then hired 300 Pinkerton agents (private security guards) to guard the plant. As they approached Homestead by river barge, word swept through town. Workers and sympathizers gathered on the banks of the river and a deadly gun battle broke out. The fight ended with three Pinkerton agents and seven workers dead and the surrender of the Pinkerton agents. This initial victory by the workers quickly turned sour for them when the Pennsylvania governor called in 8,500 National Guard soldiers to put an end to the violence.

With peace restored, Frick called in strikebreakers—workers willing to cross the strikers' picket lines and work in the plant. Four months later, their resources exhausted, the workers gave in and returned to their jobs. The union was broken. It was 26 years before unions regained any power in the steel industry.

During the Homestead Riot, strikers fought against private detectives.

The Pennsylvania state militia marches into the area to restore order.

CASE STUDY REVIEW

1. *Identifying* What rights was management exerting at Carnegie's steel plant? What rights were the strikers exerting?
2. *Comparing and Contrasting* In what ways are today's labor-management disputes similar to and different from the dispute at Homestead? Explain your answer.
3. *Evaluating* Should the government have gotten involved in this strike? Explain.

---

networks Online Teaching Options

INTERACTIVE FEATURE

Case Study: Homestead Strike

Sequencing events in the Homestead Strike
Have students read about the Homestead Strike. Draw a time line on the board and, as students call out events of the strike, place them in order on the time line. Then view and discuss the feature as a class, inviting students to describe what they see in the images and relate them to the sequence of events. Organize students into three groups. Assign each group a role: workers, management, and government. Have each group research the Homestead Strike and prepare a case in support of their demands and interests. Then have them role-play a negotiation between the groups. You may choose to have the government representatives serve as mediators. **Verbal/Linguistic**

Interact with these digital assets and others in lesson 3

- ✓ INTERACTIVE CHART Union Membership as a Percentage of Employed Workers
- ✓ INTERACTIVE GRAPH The Minimum Wage
- ✓ SELF-CHECK QUIZ
- ✓ VIDEO

netw rks
TRY IT YOURSELF ONLINE

Reading Help Desk

Academic Vocabulary
- trend
- equivalent

Content Vocabulary
- giveback
- two-tier wage system
- glass ceiling
- set-aside contract
- minimum wage
- current dollars
- real or constant dollars
- base year

TAKING NOTES:

Key Ideas and Details
ACTIVITY Complete the graphic organizer below to explain why women face an income gap, relative to men.

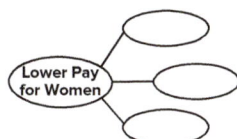

LESSON 3
Employment Trends and Issues

ESSENTIAL QUESTION

What factors lead to higher wages for a worker?

Important issues abound in today's labor market. While some workers are faced with layoffs when factories close, other industries have problems filling all their available jobs. This is especially true for those positions that pay only federal or state minimum wages, such as some resort jobs and jobs in the fast food industry.

Difficulty in filling enough minimum wage jobs is just one issue facing the national economy. Workers have seen a decline of unions, which limits their ability to influence wages, while women have to deal with differences in pay in the labor market.

Survey a fast food restaurant or other low-wage employer in your community to find out how many jobs are unfilled in that outlet and what pay is being offered for any open positions. Ask about employee turnover. What factors are at work in that employer's labor situation?

Decline of Union Influence

GUIDING QUESTION *Do you think union influence will continue to decline?*

A significant **trend** in today's economy is the decline in union membership and influence. As **Figure 9.6** shows, 35.5 percent of nonfarm workers—or about one of every three workers—were union members in 1945. This number has dropped since then to about 11.3 percent—or less than one in every nine workers—in 2013.

connected.mcgraw-hill.com **Labor and Wages 259**

CHAPTER 9, LESSON 3
Employment Trends and Issues

ENGAGE

C Critical Thinking Skills

🔔 **Characterizing the local job market** Before students begin the lesson, ask students to list jobs available locally online or in a local newspaper. Have them categorize these jobs in a chart and write three sentences summarizing their conclusions about the local job market based on their categorizations. Have them share their charts and summaries with the class. **Verbal/Linguistic, Visual/Spatial**

BELLRINGER

Employment Trends and Issues

Exploring wage inequality in the United States Display the image of the two banks. Explain that they convey information about wage inequality in the United States. **Ask: What does each bank represent?** *(Students should realize that the pink bank represents women and the blue bank represents men.)* Have students explain what the difference in bank size suggests about wage inequality. Explain that in this lesson they will learn more about gender issues and other labor-related matters. **Visual/Spatial**

ANSWERS, p. 259

ESSENTIAL QUESTION ACTIVITY

Surveys and survey results will vary. Tell students that some companies have wage policies that reward workers for experience, further education, and loyalty by increasing their pay, whereas other companies have wage policies that accentuate keeping labor costs low. Have students work through the activity and discuss their answers as a class.

TAKING NOTES
Human Capital Differences: differences in experience and education
Gender and Occupation: uneven distribution of women and men among occupations
Discrimination: difficulty in getting raises and promotions because of the glass ceiling

Labor and Wages **259**

CHAPTER 9, LESSON 3
Employment Trends and Issues

TEACH & ASSESS

W1 Writing Skills

Analyzing the reasons for declining union membership Have students create a cause-and-effect graphic organizer that explains the reasons for the decline in union membership. *(Causes that explain the falling union influence should include antiunion activities by management, more women and teenagers in the labor force, and rising prices of union-made goods.)* **ELL** Visual/Spatial

W2 Writing Skills

Exploring employment issues Instruct students to write and then perform for the class a dialogue between two unionized workers. The workers might be discussing a proposed giveback, a company bankruptcy, or a two-tier wage system. Have students research their topic, consider how two workers might feel about it, and then write and perform their dialogues. **BL** Verbal/Linguistic

---

ANSWERS, p. 260

CRITICAL THINKING

Union membership during the last decade has declined slightly.

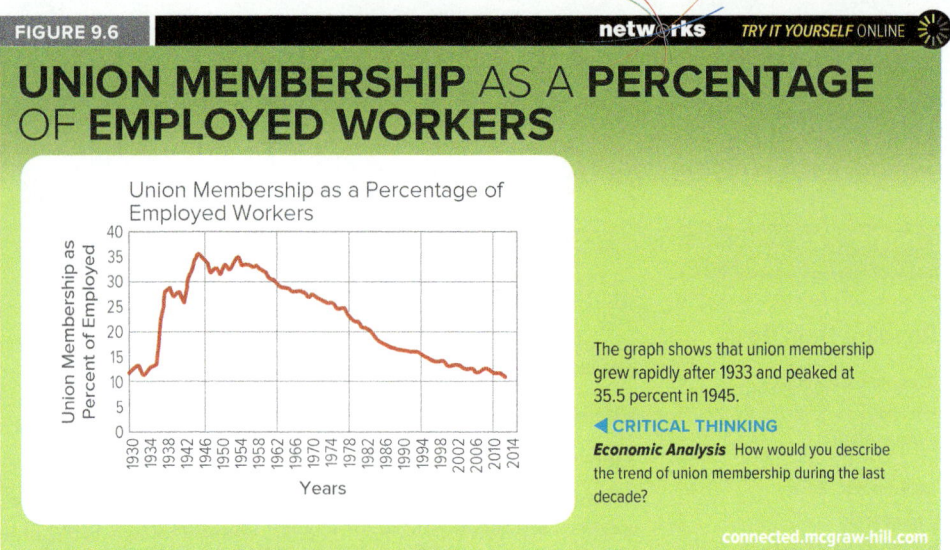

FIGURE 9.6

UNION MEMBERSHIP AS A PERCENTAGE OF EMPLOYED WORKERS

The graph shows that union membership grew rapidly after 1933 and peaked at 35.5 percent in 1945.

◀ **CRITICAL THINKING**
Economic Analysis How would you describe the trend of union membership during the last decade?

Reasons for Union Decline

Several reasons account for this decline. The first is that many employers have made a determined effort to keep unions out of their businesses. Some companies hire consultants to map out legal strategies to fight unions. Others try to head off the formation of a union by making workers part of the management team, adding employees to the board of directors, or setting up profit-sharing plans to reward employees.

W1 A second reason for union decline is that new additions to the labor force—especially women and teenagers—traditionally have had little loyalty to organized labor. In addition, more Americans are working in part-time jobs to help make ends meet. People who work a second job have less time to join or even support a union.

Yet another reason is that unions have had to deal with the consequences of their success. When union wages are higher than those of nonunion workers, as you saw in Figure 9.5, union-produced goods become more expensive than those produced by nonunion or foreign workers. Consumers then buy the less expensive products and some unionized plants are forced to close.

Renegotiating Union Wages

Because unions have generally kept their wages above those of comparable nonunion workers, union wages have been under pressure to come down. In fact, in recent years, there have been almost as many news reports of unions fighting to maintain wage levels as there were reports of union wages rising. One way employers have been able to reduce union wages is by asking for givebacks **W2** from union workers. A **giveback** is a wage, fringe benefit, or work rule given up when a labor contract is renegotiated.

Some companies were able to get rid of labor contracts by claiming bankruptcy. If a company can show that wages and fringe benefits contributed significantly to its fiscal problems, federal bankruptcy courts usually allow management to terminate union contracts and renegotiate lower wage scales.

trend a pattern or general tendency

giveback wage, fringe benefit, or work rule given up when renegotiating a contract

260

---

networks Online Teaching Options

GRAPHS

Union Membership as a Percentage of Employed Workers

Exploring changes in union membership
Display Figure 9.6 and make sure students understand what it shows by examining the labels on the axes, the title, and the introductory caption. Then have students click through the decades to learn more about events that have affected union membership. **Ask: Why do you think union membership continues to decline? Explain.** Have each student write a newspaper editorial taking a stand on whether workers should join unions. Tell them to support their arguments with data from this graph and the Median Weekly Earnings by Occupation and Union Affiliation chart. **Verbal/Linguistic**

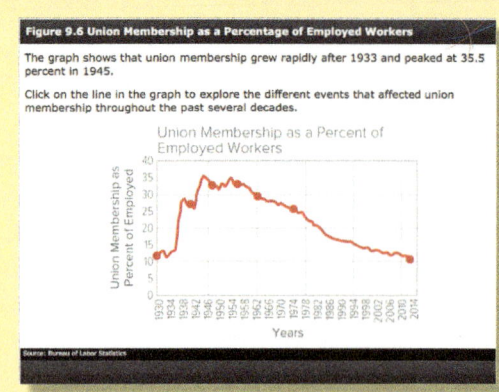

Another way to reduce union salary scales is with a **two-tier wage system**—a system that keeps high wages for current workers, but has a lower wage for newly hired workers. This practice has become widespread and often has union approval.

✓ **READING PROGRESS CHECK**

Identifying Why do successful unions create problems for themselves?

Lower Pay for Women

GUIDING QUESTION *What are the causes of pay discrimination in the labor market?*

two-tier wage system wage scale paying newer workers a lower wage than others already on the job

Overall, women face a substantial gap between their income and the income received by men. As **Figure 9.7** shows, women's income has been only a fraction of men's income over a 50-year period. Because of this glaring difference, people often ask, "Why is this, and what can or should be done about it?"

Human Capital Differences

It turns out that about one-third of the male-female income gap is due to differences in the skills and experience that women bring to the labor market. For example, women tend to drop out of the labor force to raise families more often than men. Working women also tend to have lower levels of education than their male counterparts. If these two factors—experience and education—were the same for men and women, about one third of the wage gap would disappear.

Gender and Occupation

Approximately another one-third of the wage gap is due to the uneven distribution of men and women among various occupations. For example, more

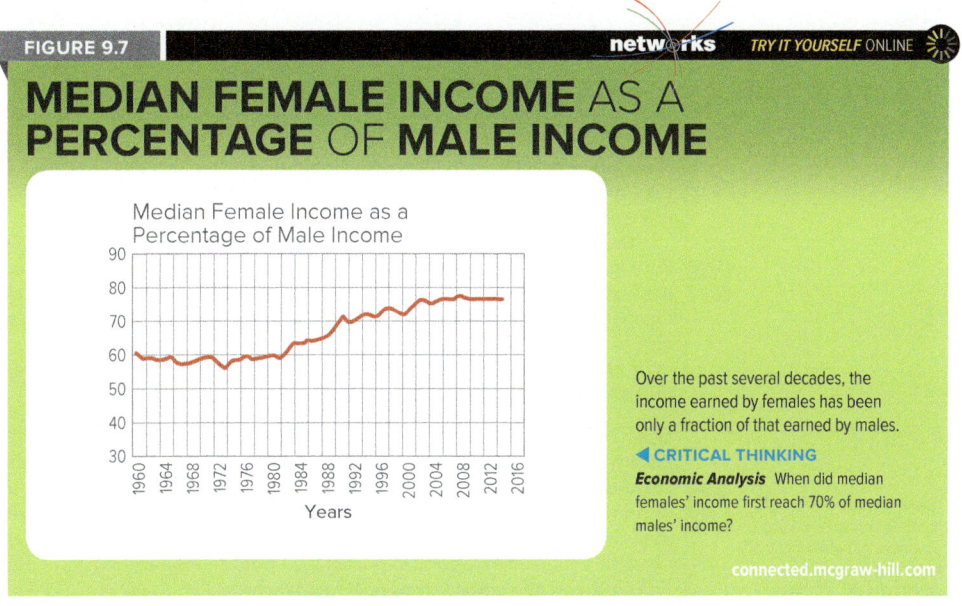

FIGURE 9.7

MEDIAN FEMALE INCOME AS A PERCENTAGE OF MALE INCOME

Over the past several decades, the income earned by females has been only a fraction of that earned by males.

◀ **CRITICAL THINKING**
Economic Analysis When did median females' income first reach 70% of median males' income?

Labor and Wages **261**

CHAPTER 9, LESSON 3
Employment Trends and Issues

T Technology Skills

Looking for jobs for women Have students use an Internet search engine to find a report on jobs that experts feel will offer good advancement prospects for women in the years ahead. Point out that reliable sites will include those sponsored by government agencies, colleges and universities, foundations, and professional and educational organizations. Have students share their reports and discuss issues that arise. Conclude by asking students why these particular jobs are considered promising for women and whether they agree with the experts on their choices.

C1 Critical Thinking Skills

Helping women to join the workforce Ask: **How could companies increase the number of women in higher-paying occupations such as construction and engineering?** *(Possible answer: provide day care and family leave opportunities)*

C2 Critical Thinking Skills

Understanding figurative terms Have students think about the term *glass ceiling*. Ask: **If a ceiling were made of glass, what would happen?** *(Possible answers: You could see through it. It would be hard to break it. It would hurt to break it.)* Have students look at the definition of the term *glass ceiling* in the text. Ask whether they can think of anyone who has tried to break through the glass ceiling and invite them to identify that person and explain whether or not she was successful and why.
ELL

ANSWERS, p. 262

CRITICAL THINKING

The jobs that men occupy more than women tend to have the highest pay rates.

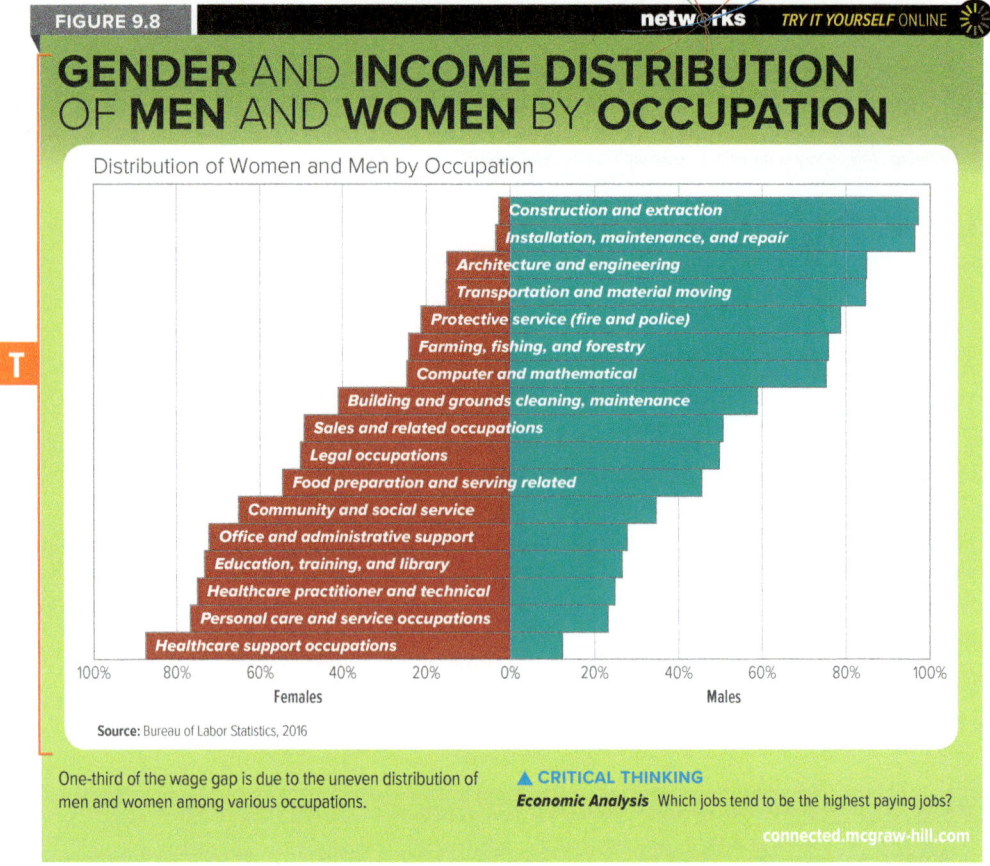

FIGURE 9.8
GENDER AND INCOME DISTRIBUTION OF MEN AND WOMEN BY OCCUPATION

One-third of the wage gap is due to the uneven distribution of men and women among various occupations.

▲ **CRITICAL THINKING**
Economic Analysis Which jobs tend to be the highest paying jobs?

men than women work in higher-paying construction and engineering trades. Likewise, more women than men work in lower-paying household service and office occupations.

The distribution of men and women in various occupations as reported by the Bureau of Labor Statistics is shown in **Figure 9.8**. As long as wages for occupations in construction, installation, maintenance, and repair are higher than wages for personal care and healthcare support occupations, on average, men will earn more than women.

In which occupational area is employment most evenly distributed between men and women?

Discrimination

Finally, the remaining one-third of the gap cannot be explained by specific reasons. Economists attribute this portion of differences in income to discrimination that women face in the labor market. In fact, women and minorities often encounter difficulties in getting raises and promotions, an experience sometimes referred to as reaching a **glass ceiling**—an invisible barrier that obstructs their advancement up the corporate ladder.

glass ceiling seemingly invisible barrier hindering advancement of women and minorities in a white male-dominated organization

262

---

networks Online Teaching Options

GRAPHS

Gender and Income Distribution of Men and Women by Occupation

Analyzing the relationship between gender and occupation Display Figure 9.8 showing the percentage of men and women in various occupations. Make sure students understand the structure of the chart: women's share of each occupation is on the left, and men's share is on the right. Point out that the chart shows almost no women work in construction and extraction trades, and that few men work in health care support occupations. Ask students to recall which occupations are paid highest. Encourage them to refer to the Median Weekly Earnings by Occupation and Union Affiliation chart to refresh their memories. Ask: **How does this distribution affect women's wages?** *(Students should understand that the occupations in which workers tend to be male are also the occupations that tend to have higher wages.)* **Visual/Spatial**

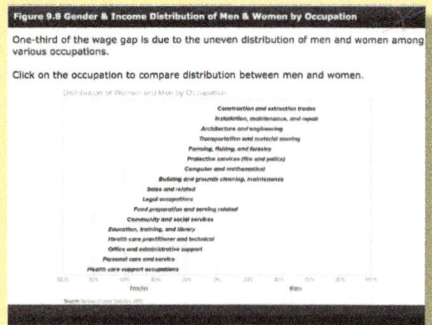

Legal Remedies

Two federal laws are designed to fight wage and salary discrimination. The first is the Equal Pay Act of 1963, which prohibits wage and salary discrimination for jobs that require **equivalent** skills and responsibilities. This act applies only to men and women who work at the same job in the same business establishment. This means, for example, that men and women with equal educations who teach the same accounting classes in the same college or university should have approximately the same salaries.

The second law is the Civil Rights Act of 1964. Title VII of this act prohibits discrimination in all areas of employment on the basis of gender, race, color, religion, and national origin. The law applies to employers with 15 or more workers.

The Civil Rights Act also set up the Equal Employment Opportunity Commission (EEOC). The EEOC investigates charges of discrimination, issues guidelines and regulations, conducts hearings, and collects statistics. The government can sue companies that show patterns of discrimination.

equivalent equal in value

Market Remedies

Another way to overcome unfair hiring practices is by reserving some market activity for minority groups. One example is the government **set-aside contract**, a guaranteed contract reserved for a targeted group. The federal government, for example, requires that a certain percentage of defense contracts be reserved exclusively for minority-owned businesses. Some state governments do the same for state contracts.

Many set-aside programs include a "graduation" clause that "promotes" minority-owned businesses out of the program once they reach a certain size or have received set-aside contracts for a certain number of years. Such limits are set because the program is intended to give these firms an initial boost, not a permanent subsidy.

set-aside contract guaranteed contract or portion of a contract reserved for a targeted group, usually a minority

✓ **READING PROGRESS CHECK**

Synthesizing What are similarities between the Equal Pay Act and set-aside contracts?

The Federal Minimum Wage

GUIDING QUESTION *What would happen if there were no minimum wage?*

The **minimum wage**—the lowest wage that can be paid by law to most workers—was intended to prevent the exploitation of workers and to provide some degree of equity and security to those who lacked the skills needed to earn a decent income. First set at $.25 per hour in 1939, the federal minimum wage had increased to $7.25 by 2009.

minimum wage lowest legal wage that can be paid to most workers

Debate Over the Minimum Wage

The minimum wage has always been controversial. Supporters of the minimum wage argue that the objectives of equity and security are consistent with U.S. economic goals. Besides, they say, the wage is not very high in the first place. Opponents object to the minimum wage on the grounds of economic freedom, another economic goal. This group also believes that it discriminates against young people and is one of the reasons that many teenagers cannot find jobs.

Some parts of the country have instituted their own minimum wages. For example, 19 states have minimum wage laws that require a higher hourly rate than the federal minimum wage. In addition, some cities like Los Angeles have a "living wage" that is also higher than the federal minimum wage. Any company doing business with the city is required to pay its workers at least that amount.

connected.mcgraw-hill.com **Labor and Wages 263**

CHAPTER 9, LESSON 3
Employment Trends and Issues

W Writing Skills

Assessing social progress Share with students this quotation from member of Congress Shirley Chisholm, the first African American woman in Congress and the first woman to run for president: "I've always met more discrimination being a woman than being black." Have students write a paragraph responding to this quotation. Then have them write which form of discrimination they feel is closer to being eliminated from our society and why. **BL**

C Critical Thinking Skills

Evaluating government practices Have students write a response to this question: **Do you think it is right for a minority-owned business to receive a contract to do business, even if a non-minority-owned company could do the same work for less money?** Have students justify their answers. *(Answers will vary but should be well supported.)*

VIDEO **WORKSHEET**

Masculinity

Exploring the definition of masculinity
Remind students that men tend to be paid more than women and to work in higher paid occupations—despite the fact that women tend to be better educated than men. Fewer males are applying to or graduating from college, due in part to a change in what is viewed as masculine behavior. This is also creating a shift in how men are viewed in society and their roles and responsibilities. Ask students to write a summary of the video after viewing it.

Video Supplied by BBC Worldwide Learning

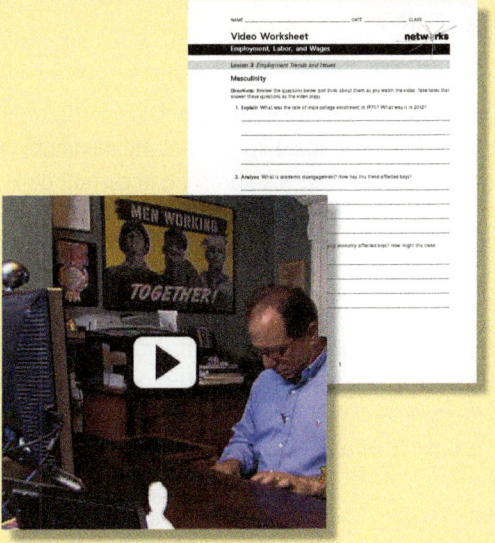

ANSWERS, p. 263

✓ **READING PROGRESS CHECK** Both are designed to favor underrepresented groups in the economy, and both are enforced by government.

Labor and Wages 263

CHAPTER 9, LESSON 3
Employment Trends and Issues

W Writing Skills

Taking a stand on a living wage Have students write a letter to a city official on the subject of a "living wage." Have them take and support a position on whether or not your community should adopt a "living wage" standard. Have volunteers read their letters to the class.

C Critical Thinking Skills

Researching workers' benefits Point out that wages often include fringe benefits, such as paid vacation time. Organize students into groups, and have each group write to the human resources department of a local company to discover what fringe benefits it offers. As a class, compare students' findings.

THE GLOBAL ECONOMY & YOU

Worker Productivity

American workers produce more value for their employers each year than workers in any other developed nation. And only Norwegians produce more per hour on the job.

Worker productivity can be calculated in two ways. One way measures the average value of goods and services produced by each worker in an economy during one calendar year. In other words, how much of a nation's total Gross Domestic Product (GDP) the average worker produces. The other way of measuring productivity calculates output per hour. This statistic accounts for differences in hours of labor. For example, the average U.S. worker works about 1,800 hours each year, while the average Norwegian works only about 1,400 hours. In China, South Korea, and several other Asian countries, the average exceeds 2,200 hours per year.

Here's how American workers compared to their counterparts in some other industrialized or industrializing countries in the most recent year for which data is available.

Labor Productivity in U.S. Dollars, 2011

Country	Productivity per person employed	Productivity per hour worked
Norway	$ 103,678	$ 72.87
United States	$ 105,969	$ 62.14
Japan	$ 73,515	$ 42.48
South Korea	$ 63,978	$ 29.03
Mexico	$ 35,579	$ 17.13
Brazil	$ 19,764	$ 10.54
China	$ 16,778	Not available
India	$ 9,691	Not available

Source: *Knoema.com*

▲ **CRITICAL THINKING**
Constructing Arguments Do you think that the United States should be placed ahead of Norway on this labor productivity chart? Explain why or why not.

---

current dollars dollar amounts or prices that are not adjusted for inflation

real or constant dollars dollar amounts or prices that have been adjusted for inflation

base year year serving as a point of comparison for other years in a price index or other statistical measure

Current Dollars

Figure 9.9 illustrates the minimum wage in **current dollars**, or dollars not adjusted for inflation, from 1939 to 2013. In this view the minimum wage appears to have increased dramatically over time. However, the figure does not account for inflation, which erodes the purchasing power of the minimum wage.

Inflation

To compensate for inflation, economists like to use **real or constant dollars**—dollars that are adjusted in a way that removes the distortion of inflation. This involves the use of a **base year**—a year that serves as a comparison for all other years.

Although the computations may seem complex, the results are not. Using constant base-year prices, Figure 9.9 also shows that the minimum wage had relatively more purchasing power in 1968 than in any other year. As long as the base year serves as a common denominator for comparison purposes, the results would be the same regardless of the base year used.

The figure also shows that the purchasing power of the minimum wage goes up whenever the wage increases faster than inflation, or down whenever inflation increases faster than the minimum wage. This was the case after 2009 when the minimum wage remained fixed at $7.25 per hour while prices continued to go up. If you look at the last four years in the constant-year line, you can see that the wage actually purchased a little less each year because of inflation. As long as the minimum wage remains unchanged at $7.25 and inflation continues, the purchasing power of the wage will continue to decline.

264

---

networks Online Teaching Options

GRAPHS

Minimum Wage

Understanding the minimum Display Figure 9.9 analyzing the minimum wage. Explain that the minimum wage is shown in three ways: expressed in current dollars, adjusted for inflation, and as a percentage of the average wage for workers in manufacturing. **Ask: Why did the minimum wage adjusted for inflation drop between 1997 and 2006, even though the minimum wage remained at $5.15 an hour?** *(Because prices rose over this time period, the purchasing power of the minimum wage declined.)* **In what year would you have wanted to be earning the minimum wage? Why?** *(Most students will choose 1968 because the minimum wage adjusted for inflation was at its highest level.)* Have students answer the Economic Analysis question and share their answers. **Logical/Mathematical**

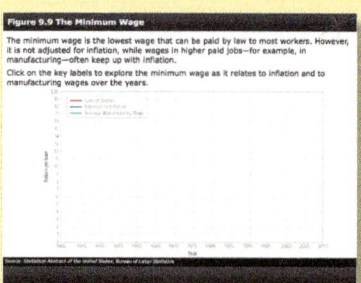

ANSWERS, p. 264

CRITICAL THINKING

Some students may argue that U.S. workers should be placed above Norwegian workers because U.S. workers produce more value over the course of a year. Other students may argue that Norwegian workers are more productive because they work fewer hours but produce almost as much annually as do U.S. workers, giving them, on average, higher hourly productivity.

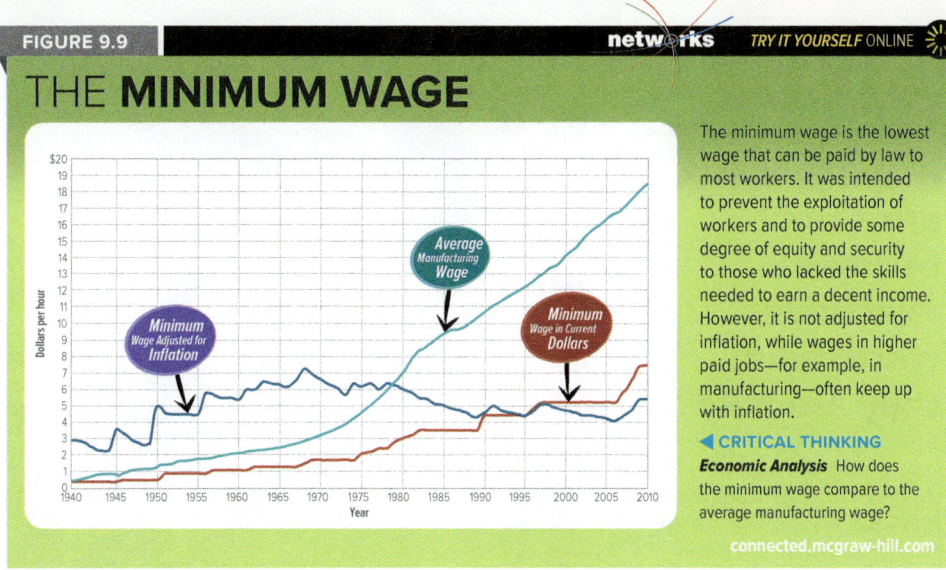

FIGURE 9.9

THE MINIMUM WAGE

The minimum wage is the lowest wage that can be paid by law to most workers. It was intended to prevent the exploitation of workers and to provide some degree of equity and security to those who lacked the skills needed to earn a decent income. However, it is not adjusted for inflation, while wages in higher paid jobs—for example, in manufacturing—often keep up with inflation.

◀ **CRITICAL THINKING**
Economic Analysis How does the minimum wage compare to the average manufacturing wage?

connected.mcgraw-hill.com

Manufacturing Wages

The third data line in Figure 9.9 shows the minimum wage as a percentage of the average manufacturing wage. In 1968, the minimum wage was $1.60 and the average manufacturing wage $3.01, or 53.2 percent of the manufacturing wage. The ratio peaked in 1968 and then slowly declined. As long as the minimum wage stays fixed and manufacturing wages go up, this ratio will continue to decline.

The minimum wage will certainly be raised again. What is not certain is when this will happen. When the minimum wage becomes unacceptably low to voters and their elected officials, Congress will increase it. Some people even want to link the minimum wage to inflation, so that the wage will automatically rise when prices rise.

✓ **READING PROGRESS CHECK**

Summarizing What is the difference between measures of the minimum wage in current dollars and real or constant dollars?

LESSON 3 REVIEW

Reviewing Vocabulary
1. **Explaining** How and why would set-aside contracts affect the glass ceiling?

Using Your Notes
2. **Evaluating** Use your notes to explain why women face an income gap when compared to men.

Answering the Guiding Questions
3. **Making Predictions** Do you think union influence will continue to decline? Why or why not?
4. **Identifying** What are the causes of pay discrimination in the labor market?
5. **Speculating** What would happen if there were no minimum wage?

Writing About Economics
6. **Argument** Imagine that you are a union member employed by a company that wants to adopt a two-tier wage system. Prepare some remarks for your next union meeting to convince your fellow union members to support or oppose making this change in your union's contract with your employer.

CHAPTER 9, LESSON 3
Employment Trends and Issues

CLOSE & REFLECT

R Reading Skills

Predicting future trends Ask students to predict the major employment trends of the next 25 years and their effects, using facts and concepts from the lesson to support their predictions.

ANSWERS, p. 265

CRITICAL THINKING
The minimum wage ranges from a third to a half of the manufacturing wage.

✓ **READING PROGRESS CHECK** Current dollars are not adjusted for inflation; real dollars are adjusted in a way that removes the distortion of inflation.

LESSON 3 REVIEW ANSWERS

Reviewing Vocabulary
1. They would remove the glass ceiling because they would provide women opportunities for economic growth.

Using Your Notes
2. Differences in skills and experiences; fewer women in higher-paying jobs and more in low-paying jobs; discrimination and the glass ceiling are all reasons why the income gap exists.

Answering the Guiding Questions
3. Most students will likely predict that unions will continue to decline, citing the continuing trend; new additions to the labor force, for example, more women and teenagers, who traditionally have little loyalty to organized labor; and current pressures on unions for givebacks and to keep wages down.
4. Causes may include race- and gender-related occupational, educational, and skill variables.
5. Students might consider the potential impact on wage and employment levels, poverty rates, and other socioeconomic factors, and should recognize that free-market forces would set wages.

Writing About Economics
6. Students should show reasoned judgment and demonstrate understanding of the two-tier system, unions and their relationship with employers, and the current state of the organized labor movement.

CHAPTER 9
Debate

ENGAGE

C1 Critical Thinking Skills

Evaluating pay scales Create a sample pay scale on the board for a fictional corporation as follows: worker—$25,000/year, supervisor—$35,000/year, manager—$55,000/year, director—$80,000/year, vice-president—$250,000/year, president—$900,000/year, CEO—$9,000,000/year. Point out that there might be a number of companies in the corporation, each with its own president. Ask students whether they find this a fair pay scale and to explain their answers. Explain that CEOs and similar top-level managers frequently make extremely high salaries. **Logical/Mathematical**

TEACH & ASSESS

C2 Critical Thinking Skills

Supporting generalizations with details Have students read the lists of points under the headings "Yes" and "No." Then have students form pairs. Assign each pair one of the arguments under one of the headings; for example, "Senior executives... have skills that other employees lack." Students should think of at least three details that support their assigned generalization. Have students share their details with the class. **Verbal/Linguistic**

Content Background Knowledge

Golden Parachutes In addition to their high salaries and high annual bonuses, top executives also receive high severance packages when they leave their jobs. These pay packages are known as *golden parachutes* and include things like retirement income, company stock, and cash severance pay. They are typically set in the contract that is signed when the executive enters the position. For example, when James J. Mulva left his job in 2012 after a decade as CEO of ConocoPhillips, his "parachute" amounted to roughly $156 million.

Debates

C1 In most cases, are senior business executives worth what they are paid?

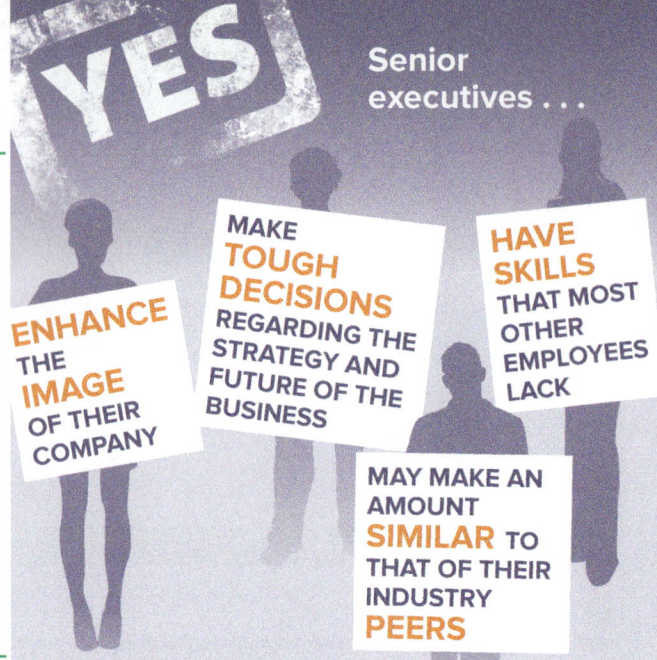

In many companies, senior business executives make more than 300 times the amount of the average employee. Often, their compensation adds up to millions of dollars per year between salary, stock options, bonuses, and incentives. Even directors of charities often make more than $100,000 per year.

These executives come under scrutiny when they continue to accept high compensation while their companies experience financial difficulties. For example, during the economic downturn that began in 2007, leaders of some Standard & Poor's 500 companies came under fire as they walked away from floundering companies—or stayed with them—with millions in their pockets. So are these executives productive enough to merit their compensation?

Leaders of huge corporations face difficult decisions regarding business strategies and operations. Even leaders of small companies often work long hours to strategize and maintain their company's image in the business world.

So you decide: Are senior business executives worth what they are paid?

> *We don't spend enough time talking about how we're going to structure pay to improve the productivity of the rest of the employees. I'm not saying we need to pay less attention to executive pay, but we need to pay a lot more attention to worker pay, and that's where boards of directors can focus more of their attention.*
> —Donald Delves, founder and president of the Delves Group

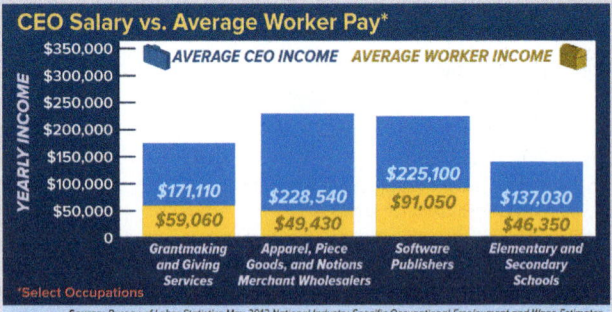

networks Online Teaching Options

DEBATE

Debate: In most cases, are senior business executives worth what they are paid?

Analyzing numerical data Display the graph showing CEO compensation vs. that of average workers. Have students study the graph and ask questions about it. Go through the same process with the graph showing the ratio of the highest paid to median workers in one industry. Then have students write two sentences about each graph; each sentence should focus on a trend or specific comparison. Invite students to share their sentences as a basis for class discussion. Then have them read the information in the activity about executive pay.
Logical/Mathematical

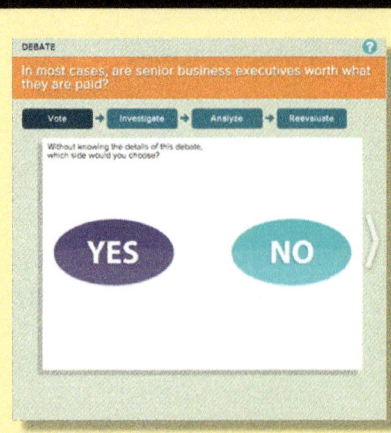

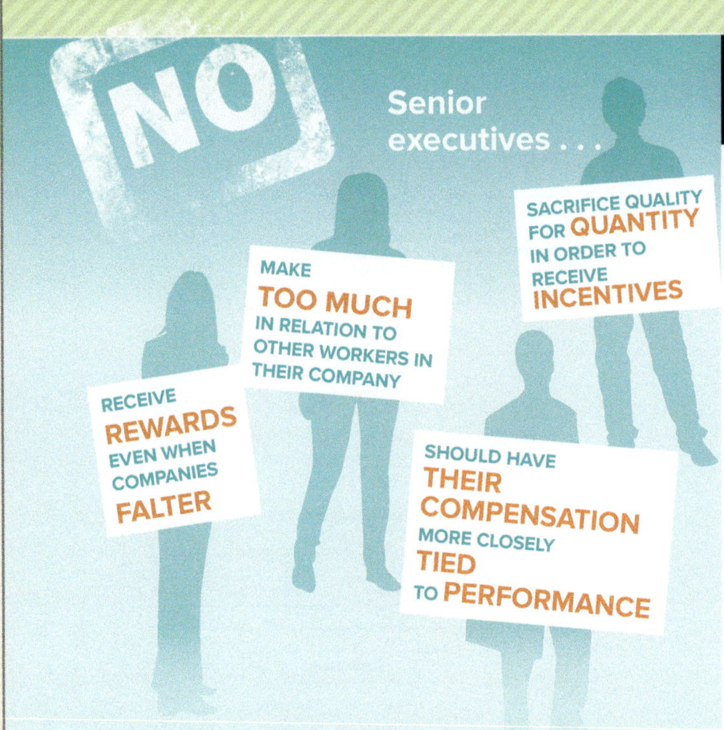

NO

Senior executives...

- MAKE **TOO MUCH** IN RELATION TO OTHER WORKERS IN THEIR COMPANY
- SACRIFICE QUALITY FOR **QUANTITY** IN ORDER TO RECEIVE **INCENTIVES**
- RECEIVE **REWARDS** EVEN WHEN COMPANIES **FALTER**
- SHOULD HAVE THEIR **COMPENSATION** MORE CLOSELY **TIED** TO **PERFORMANCE**

> "Excessive executive compensation of the past decade is both a symptom and a cause of the current economic mess. And the post-meltdown awards are all but guaranteed to continue to create perverse incentives that will reward management and further damage the interests of shareholders and every other participant in the economy."
>
> —Nell Minow, editor and co-founder of *The Corporate Library*

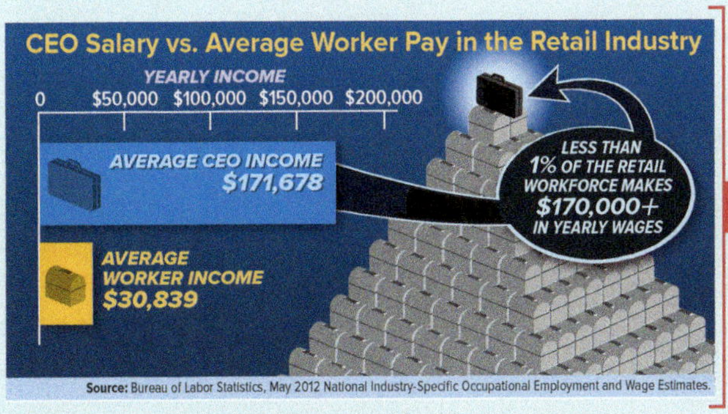

CEO Salary vs. Average Worker Pay in the Retail Industry

YEARLY INCOME

- AVERAGE CEO INCOME: $171,678
- AVERAGE WORKER INCOME: $30,839
- LESS THAN 1% OF THE RETAIL WORKFORCE MAKES $170,000+ IN YEARLY WAGES

Source: Bureau of Labor Statistics, May 2012 National Industry-Specific Occupational Employment and Wage Estimates.

ANALYZING the issue

1. **Analyzing Visuals** How has executive compensation changed in relation to average worker compensation?

2. **Exploring Issues** Why might some people think that CEOs should be compensated more than they currently are? How might an economist argue against this position?

3. **Evaluating** Which arguments do you find most compelling? Explain your answer.

CHAPTER 9
Debate

R Reading Skills

Researching case studies Have interested students research the pay of individual CEOs. Have others find the annual income of other well-known people, such as the U.S. president, a big-city mayor, a well-known athlete, a famous movie star, and the UN secretary-general. Then have them create a bar graph comparing their findings. **Logical/Mathematical**

CLOSE & REFLECT

W Writing Skills

Supporting an argument Have students write a one- to two-page essay arguing for their own position on the issue of executive pay. Remind them to state their position clearly and to support it logically, using specific details. Suggest that they remember to also acknowledge an opposing argument in their essay and explain why it is flawed. Tell them to cite any sources they use and include a reference list.

DEBATE

Debate

Debating the pay of senior business managers After students have worked through the activity, create two debate teams. One team should argue that senior business executives are worth what they are paid, and the other should argue that they are not. Explain the structure of the debate. Then allow teams time to decide on a strategy, assign debate roles, and perform research to find further support for their positions. Remind students to attribute source information to authors. Tell them to plan their statements carefully. Poll the audience before the debate and again afterwards to determine which team has been more persuasive. **Verbal/Linguistic**

ANSWERS, p. 267

ANALYZING the issue

1. It has increased to the point that a senior business executive makes 300 times the amount of the average employee.
2. Senior business executives often work long hours and face stressful, difficult decisions in exchange for their high salaries. Economists might argue that executive salaries are commensurate with the supply of and demand for people in those positions.
3. Answer will vary. In either case, arguments should draw on the points raised in the debate and show reasoned judgment in evaluating them.

Chapter 9
Study Guide

C1 Critical Thinking Skills

Debating Organize students into two groups to debate the following: Should professional athletes, rock singers, and movie stars command high salaries for their labor? Suggest that students analyze societal values in the debate. **Interpersonal**

C2 Critical Thinking Skills

Evaluating Ask: Why do you think women typically make less money for doing the same work as men? Have students conduct research to find out in which lines of work men's and women's wages are most equal, and in which lines of work they are most unequal. Guide students in a discussion of the possible reasons and what can be done to ensure that people are paid equally for equal work, regardless of gender. **Verbal/Linguistic**

STUDY GUIDE

LESSON 1

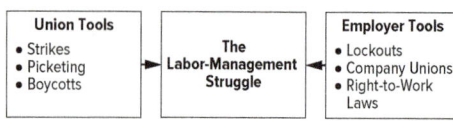

LESSON 1

Least Restrictive → Agency Shop → Modified Union Shop → Union Shop → Closed Shop ← Most Restrictive

LESSON 2

Collective Bargaining Fails → Mediation, Arbitration, Injunction, Seizure → Conflict ends

LESSON 2

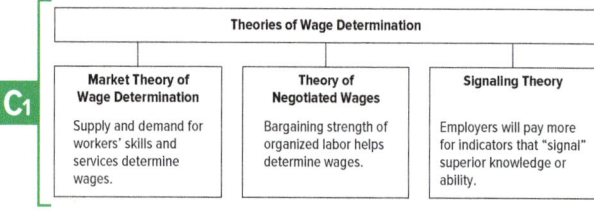

LESSON 3

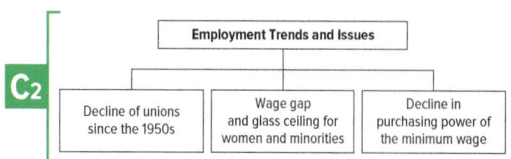

---

networks Online Assessment Options

WORKSHEET

Hands-On Chapter Project with Technology Extension

In this activity, students will work in groups to act as consultants for a union with declining membership. It is their job to research aspects of the decline in membership and make recommendations for reversing that trend. Each group will focus on a different factor: government actions, changes in workforce demographics, union membership across industries and change over time, or the effect of free trade on unions. Group members will summarize their individual findings, and the group will present their recommendation report to the class, who will act as union members.

edtechteacher 21st Century Learning — Find an additional activity online that incorporates technology for this project. Visit the EdTech Teacher Web sites for more links, tutorials, and other resources.

CHAPTER 9 Assessment

Directions: On a separate sheet of paper, answer the questions below. Make sure you read carefully and answer all parts of the questions.

Lesson Review

Lesson 1

1 **Differentiating** How do trade unions and industrial unions differ?

2 **Identifying** What methods have unions historically used to obtain their goals?

Lesson 2

3 **Analyzing** Why do skilled and professional workers generally receive higher wages than unskilled and semiskilled workers?

4 **Specifying** What role does fact-finding play in the arbitration and mediation process between labor and management?

Lesson 3

5 **Naming** Identify three methods employers have used to reduce their labor costs when dealing with unions.

6 **Explaining** Why is it necessary to consider inflation when evaluating the adequacy of the current minimum wage?

Critical Thinking

7 **Making Connections** Why has the union movement in the United States gone through cycles of weak influence and strong support? Write a short essay that uses events and examples to explain these trends.

8 **Identifying Central Issues** Why would collective bargaining, mediation, and arbitration be better than strikes, lockouts, and injunctions as ways of settling wage disputes?

9 **Analyzing** Some people believe that market forces are a better mechanism for wage determination than are negotiated wages. Do you agree or disagree? Explain why.

10 **Constructing Arguments** Write an op-ed article explaining why the government should or should not attempt to intervene when some workers in a company receive lower pay than others in the same job.

Analyzing Visuals

Use the map to answer the following questions.

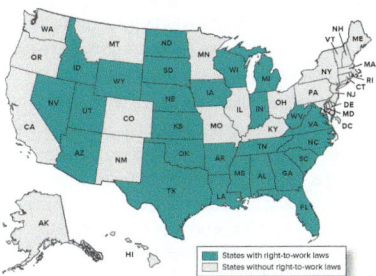

States with right-to-work laws
States without right-to-work laws

SOURCE: National Right to Work Committee, 2016.

11 **Synthesizing** Given that West Virginia and Wisconsin recently addressed right-to-work laws, do you think the map will change more in the future?

12 **Identifying** What are some of the factors that lead to the passage of right-to-work laws?

ANSWERING THE ESSENTIAL QUESTIONS

Review your answers to the introductory questions at the beginning of each lesson. On the basis of what you have learned in the chapter, write a short essay that explains how unions have affected our overall economy. Use the chapter's Essential Questions as springboards to frame your ideas.

13 **Assessing** What features of the modern labor industry are results of union action? Discuss with a classmate which of these features they believe are no longer necessary in today's workforce or should no longer be enforced. Remember to evaluate your classmate's frame of reference as well as their specific answer.

14 **Synthesizing** What factors lead to higher wages for a worker?

21st Century Skills

15 **Create and Analyze Arguments and Draw Conclusions** Earlier in our nation's history, many workers were paid for each good they produced rather than by the number of hours they worked. This pay structure, called "piecework," is still

Need Extra Help?

If You've Missed Question	1	2	3	4	5	6	7	8	9	10	11	12	13	14	15
Go to page	245	246	252	256	260	263	246	256	254	257	248	248	244	252	264

Chapter 9 Assessment Answers

Lesson Review

Lesson 1

1 The members of a trade union all have the same skill or craft. Members of an industrial union all work in the same industry regardless of their skill or the job they do.

2 strikes, picketing, and boycotts

Lesson 2

3 Skilled and professional workers generally have knowledge that is in higher demand or shorter supply than that possessed by unskilled and semiskilled workers.

4 It provides the arbitrator or mediator with an undistorted view of information and issues in a dispute between an employer and a union.

Lesson 3

5 givebacks, two-tiered wage systems, bankruptcy

6 Inflation can reduce the buying power of the minimum wage, which might make an increase in the minimum wage necessary.

Critical Thinking

7 Responses should connect the influence of low wages and poor working conditions, strikes and other labor tools, and the pro-union laws of the 1930s, such as the Norris-LaGuardia Act and the Wagner Act (NLRA), to explain cycles of strong support. They should cite factors such as company unions, labor violence and public backlash, early court attitudes toward unions, anti-labor legislation such as Taft-Hartley and right-to-work laws, and recent declines in union membership to explain cycles of weak union influence.

8 Collective bargaining, mediation, and arbitration all bring some form of negotiated or compromise settlement between workers and employers. Strikes, lockouts, and injunctions all produce clear victors and unhappy losers.

9 Students' views will vary but should demonstrate understanding of the impact of negotiation and market theories on wage determination.

10 Students' answers should cite personal characteristics such as skill or education level, race, and gender as wage determinates. Worker actions to improve law wages should center on improving their education or skill set, which government actions include minimum wage laws, set-asides, and laws barring wage discrimination.

Analyzing Visuals

11 Students' answers will vary, but should note that union membership has steadily fallen since the 1940s.

12 Public opinion turned against unions because of concerns about production losses due to increased strikes and fears of communists infiltrating union membership.

Answering the Essential Questions

13 Student responses should focus on higher wages and better working conditions.

14 Student responses should consider skill levels and labor supply (market theory of wage determination), seniority and union factors (theory of negotiated wages), and signaling theory.

21st Century Skills

15 Some students may argue that workers should be paid only for what they produce and note that this system rewards hard work and also benefits employers. Some may see the system as exploitative of workers, while others may view hourly wages as a disincentive to productivity.

Chapter 9
Assessment Answers

16. Some students may support the principle of a minimum wage, while others may find government actions to prevent wage discrimination based on race or gender to be acceptable. Still others may argue against government intervention and for allowing free markets to set wages.

17. Charts should show strikes, boycotts, picketing, injunctions and lockouts as adversarial and categorize collective bargaining and mediation as collaborative. Some students may classify arbitration as collaborative and others as adversarial.

Building Financial Literacy

18. Students' answers will vary, but should include the average entry-level pay for each occupation they have chosen. Students' charts should also include the minimum education or training required by the occupation as well as the outlook for the job market in each occupation selected. Students' answers should compare the pay for two occupations that require some post-high school education with two different occupations that require only a high school education or less. In their charts, students should calculate the total differences in earnings over a 40-year career.

19. Students' responses should fulfill all requirements of the activity and demonstrate reasoned judgment in the conclusions they draw regarding their needs and wants.

Analyzing Primary Sources

20. He says that it will cause employers to cut hours and number of employees and result in fewer job opportunities for workers.

21. They can either absorb the higher costs or keep them the same by cutting hours and the number of employees. In either case he suggests that these choices will have a harmful effect on the economy.

CHAPTER 9 Assessment

Directions: On a separate sheet of paper, answer the questions below. Make sure you read carefully and answer all parts of the questions.

sometimes practiced today. Given that American workers are among the most productive in the world, do you think such a system would result in higher pay for workers and higher productivity for companies? Explain and support your views in a one-page paper.

16. *Identifying Perspectives and Differing Interpretations* Under what circumstances, if any, do you think it is appropriate for the government to intervene in the labor market by setting wages? Consider the rationale for government intervention and historically, how such intervention has affected the economy. Then write a position paper supporting your argument with examples from the chapter.

17. *Creating and Using Charts* Create a chart of the methods by which labor unions and management resolve labor disputes. Organize your chart in a way that lets you categorize each method as collaborative or adversarial. Then on a separate sheet of paper explain why you categorized each method as you did.

Building Financial Literacy

18. *Planning* Knowing what an occupation pays, the education or training it requires, and the demand for that type of work can help you to make better career decisions for your future. The Bureau of Labor Statistics (BLS) in the U.S. Department of Labor has a website where you can find much of this information.

   a. Identify some professional or skilled occupations that interest you. Research them on the BLS website. What is the average entry-level pay for each? What is the minimum education or training each requires? What is the outlook for the job market in each occupation? Make a chart and record this information.

   b. It is said that people with education or training beyond high school will earn much more money in their lifetime than people without them. Use the BLS website to test this assumption by comparing the pay for two occupations that require some post-high school education with two occupations that require only a high school education or less. Calculate the total differences in earnings over a 40-year career and record your findings in a chart.

19. *Calculating* Knowing what your wants and needs cost and calculating how much income is required to meet them can help you to achieve financial stability.

   a. Make a list of your current financial obligations. Add to it your costs of everyday living, such as money you need for recreation, transportation, food, and so on. Project these expenses on a monthly basis.

   b. Now add to your expense list wants you hope to fulfill in the near future—perhaps a new video game or television, or a car. If any of these purchases would be paid for over time, add their projected monthly payments to your list.

   c. Total the monthly cost of your wants and needs. Then calculate how many hours you would have to work every month at a job that pays minimum wage. Does the number exceed the time you have available? Now recalculate your time and income requirements based on only the list you made in part a. Does the difference in outcomes provide an incentive to rethink your part b wants list? Explain why or why not.

Analyzing Primary Sources

Read the excerpt to answer the questions that follow.

PRIMARY SOURCE

"Every increase in the minimum wage raises the overall costs of small-business owners, and they must react to stay in business. If faced with a minimum-wage hike, most independent business owners say they would respond by cutting workers' hours, reducing the number of employees, and leaving jobs vacant. This is because it's not always possible for small businesses to pass on increased costs to their customers by raising prices."

—Todd Stottlemyer, National Federation of Independent Business

20. *Expressing* Why does Stottlemyer believe that raising the minimum wage is not good for workers?

21. *Exploring Issues* What choices does Stottlemyer say employers are faced with when the minimum wage is increased? What impact could these choices have on the economy?

Need Extra Help?

If You've Missed Question	16	17	18	19	20	21
Go to page	247	256	252	263	264	264

---

networks Online Assessment Options

WORKSHEET

Chapter Tests and Lesson Quizzes

Chapter 9 Tests Forms A and B Have students complete the Chapter Tests and Lesson Quizzes to assess student understanding throughout the chapter. Print and online assessment tools offer chapter and lesson evaluation through a variety of question formats, including document-based questions.

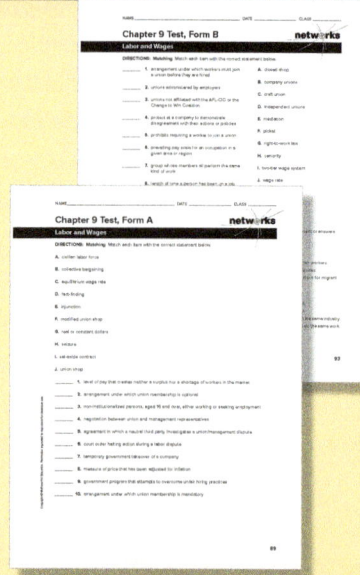

UNIT 4
MONEY, BANKING, AND FINANCE Planner

UNDERSTANDING BY DESIGN®

Enduring Understandings
- Money makes it easier to trade, borrow, save, invest, and compare the value of goods and services.
- Resources are limited, so people must make choices.

Essential Questions
- How has money evolved to meet the needs of people everywhere?
- How did the creation of the Fed improve our banking system?
- How has technology affected the way we use money today?
- What is the role of savings in the financial system?
- What options are available for investing your money?

Students will know:
- the basic functions and characteristics of money.
- the role of the Federal Reserve, banks, and other financial institutions in the economy of the United States.
- the major methods of accessing funds in checking, savings, and credit accounts.
- the role of financial institutions in saving, borrowing, and capital formation.
- the characteristics, advantages, and risks of various investment options.
- financial assets can be bought and sold through stockbrokers, mutual funds, 401(k) plans and in the future as well as in the present.

Students will be able to:
- **summarize** the development of money in the United States.
- **explain** why the National Banking System was created.
- **compare** the available types of financial assets.
- **explain** how investors make money using futures contracts.

Predictable Misunderstandings
Students may think:
- Money in the United States has always been backed by the federal government.
- When money is deposited in a bank, the bank keeps the money or deposits it at the Fed.
- Students' personal savings have no effect on the overall financial system.
- Investing requires thousands of dollars.

Assessment Evidence
Performance Task
- Hands-On Chapter Projects with Technology Extensions
- Economic Simulations
- Math Practice for Economics
- Personal Finance Activities
- Reinforcing Economic Skills Activities

Other Evidence:
- Guided Reading Activities
- Vocabulary Activities
- Lesson Quizzes
- Chapter Tests, Forms A and B

Key for Using the Teacher Edition
SKILL-BASED ACTIVITIES
Types of skill activities found in the Teacher Edition.
- **V** **Visual Skills** require students to analyze maps, graphs, charts, and photos.
- **R** **Reading Skills** help students practice reading skills and master vocabulary.
- **C** **Critical Thinking Skills** help students apply and extend what they have learned.
- **W** **Writing Skills** provide writing opportunities to help students comprehend the text.
- **T** **Technology Skills** require students to use digital tools effectively.

*Letters are followed by a number when there is more than one of the same type of skill on the page.

DIFFERENTIATED INSTRUCTION
All activities are written for the on-level student unless otherwise marked with the leveled labels below.
- **BL** Beyond Level
- **AL** Approaching Level
- **ELL** English Language Learners

All students benefit from activities that utilize different learning styles. Many activities are marked as below when a particular learning style is highlighted.

Intrapersonal
Logical/Mathematical
Visual/Spatial
Verbal/Linguistic
Naturalist
Kinesthetic
Auditory/Musical
Interpersonal

SUGGESTED PACING GUIDE—Semester
Introducing the Unit . . . . ½ Day
Chapter 10: Money and Banking . . . . 5 Days
Chapter 11: Financial Markets . . . . 5 Days

UNIT 4: MONEY, BANKING, AND FINANCE

Planner

☑ Print Teaching Options

C Critical Thinking Skills

☐ **p. 271 Evaluating barter and money** Students discuss what it would be like if trading were the only way to get what one wanted. Then students explore how difficulties with currency are resolved with modern payment methods. **Verbal/Linguistic**

☐ **p. 271 Discussing the role of banking and financial institutions** Students discuss some ways in which banking and the financial markets enable the economy to grow. **Interpersonal**

☐ **p. 272 Using a problem-solving approach** Students practice using a problem-solving approach to solve a problem regarding money and/or banking by implementing and evaluating a solution. **Verbal/Linguistic, Visual/Spatial**

W Writing Skills

☐ **p. 271 Analyzing the Fed's performance** Students research to learn about the beginning of the Federal Reserve in 1913, and to identify specific problems the Fed was created to solve, and to determine what solutions resulted. **Interpersonal**

☑ Online Teaching Options

☐ **ANIMATION** **The American Banking System**—Students share experiences in opening a checking account, making deposits, taking out a loan, or using an ATM. They explain how making a deposit produces economic growth by putting money into the economy.

☐ **APPROACHING GRADE LEVEL READER** **Alternative Student Edition narrative**— You can assign your students who are struggling to read on grade level the Approaching Grade Level version of the Online Student Edition. This reader presents all of the content in the On Grade Level version of the Online Student Edition at a lower reading level.

☐ **ENGLISH LANGUAGE LEARNER READER** **Alternative Student Edition narrative with ELL support**—Use the Online English Language Learner reader to provide additional reading support for ELL students. You can find this tool in the Online Student Edition.

☑ Printable Digital Worksheets

R Reading Skills

☐ **WORKSHEET** **Guided Reading Activity**—Students use the Guided Reading Activities worksheets to review their comprehension of the content.

☐ **WORKSHEET** **Reading Essentials and Study Guide**—Students complete the study guide and answer Reading Progress Check and vocabulary questions.

C Critical Thinking Skills

☐ **WORKSHEET** **The American Banking System Animation Activity**—Students understand how a portion of the deposit is lent by a bank to other customers who spend it puts in motion a cycle of buying and selling of goods and services, which in turn creates jobs, pays wages, and further stimulates the economy.

☐ **WORKSHEET** **Assessing Background Knowledge Activity**—Students should complete the Assessing Background Knowledge Activity before they study each chapter. Students' responses will give you a good idea of the kinds of misconceptions you can address when teaching the lessons.

☐ **WORKSHEET** **Chapter Summary**—Summaries are provided for each chapter and thoroughly condense core content into manageable chunks.

☐ **WORKSHEET** **Vocabulary Activity**—Students apply their knowledge of content and academic vocabulary words.

UNIT 4
Money, Banking, and Finance

CHAPTER 10
Money and Banking

ESSENTIAL QUESTIONS

How has money evolved to meet the needs of people everywhere?

How did the creation of the Fed improve our banking system?

How has technology affected the way we use money today?

CHAPTER 11
Financial Markets

ESSENTIAL QUESTIONS

What is the role of savings in the financial system?

What options are available for investing your money?

IT MATTERS BECAUSE...

Money may be the driving force behind our market economy, but have you ever wondered how it has led us to this point? Better yet, how has our economic past evolved to meet your present and future monetary needs? This unit is designed to describe the functions of money in our economy, help you examine what roles you play in our market and financial systems, and ultimately further your understanding of how money contributes to economic growth.

ANIMATIONS | **WORKSHEET**

The American Banking System

Analyzing the animation Prior to showing students the animation, ask if any of them have used a bank. Encourage students to share experiences in opening a checking account, making deposits, taking out a loan, or using an ATM. Point out that all of these activities help promote economic development. Have students view the animation. Ask them to explain how making a deposit produces economic growth by putting money into the economy. Ensure students understand how a portion of the deposit is lent by the bank to other customers who spend it, thereby putting in motion a cycle of buying and selling of goods and services, which in turn creates jobs, pays wages, and further stimulates the economy.

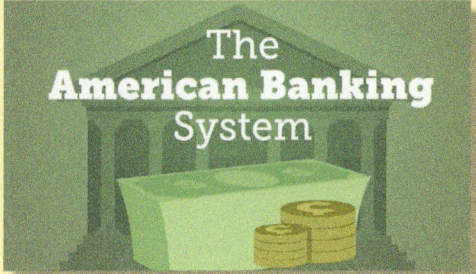

UNIT 4
Money, Banking, and Finance

ENGAGE

Evaluating barter and money Ask students if they ever trade things, such as helping someone with homework in exchange for a movie ticket or a share of a pizza. Encourage discussion. **Ask:**

- What would it be like if trading were the only way you could get what you want?
- What is inconvenient about trading one item or service for another?
- How does money solve this problem?
- What is inconvenient about money? How is that problem being solved?

Then guide a discussion about how money can sometimes be inconvenient. For example, we have to go to a bank to get it. It can be lost or stolen. It is difficult to use to purchase goods from a merchant who is not local. **Ask: How are these difficulties solved?** *(Sample answers: credit cards, checks, wire transfers, electronic payments)* Point out that in this unit, students will read more about money and the role it plays in our economy.
Verbal/Linguistic

Discussing the role of banking and financial institutions **Ask: What are some ways in which banking and the financial markets enable the economy to grow?** *(Possible answers: They provide savings, investment, and borrowing resources for consumers as well as financing for new businesses and for the expansion of existing businesses. They circulate and expand the money supply, enable the exchange of goods and services, and provide a uniform currency.)* As students read this unit, encourage them to look for more details about how the banking and financial markets function and promote economic growth in the United States.
Interpersonal

Analyzing the Fed's performance Have students research to learn about the beginning of the Federal Reserve in 1913. Ask them to identify specific problems the Fed was created to solve, and to determine what solutions resulted. Have them decide if the Fed continues to fulfill its mission today. Finally, have them write an essay evaluating the Fed's performance over time. **Interpersonal**

UNIT 4
Money, Banking, and Finance

DEVELOP YOUR SKILLS ONLINE

Using a Problem-Solving Approach

Help students practice using a problem-solving approach to solve a problem regarding money and/or banking by implementing and evaluating a solution. Remind them to:

(1) identify a problem,

(2) gather information,

(3) list and consider options,

(4) consider advantages and disadvantages,

(5) choose and implement a solution, and

(6) evaluate the effectiveness of the solution.

Have students work individually to complete the activity. Then ask students to work in small groups of three or four and compare their work.

Verbal/Linguistic, Visual/Spatial

Develop your Skills Online

networks TRY IT YOURSELF ONLINE
Try using interactive graphs online at connected.mcgraw-hill.com

Use a Problem-Solving Process
with Infographics

Economists use data to build their economic models. But data is not only numbers and statistical charts. Some data can be found in highly visual pieces known as infographics. This economics program uses interactive infographics to help you learn more about data in the real world. You can find these Economic Perspective infographics at the start of each chapter of this program.

Each chapter in this program is introduced by an Economic Perspectives infographic. These vibrant assets enliven your study of that chapter's content.

Each Economic Perspective is structured in a unique fashion to best highlight the data of that chapter's topic.

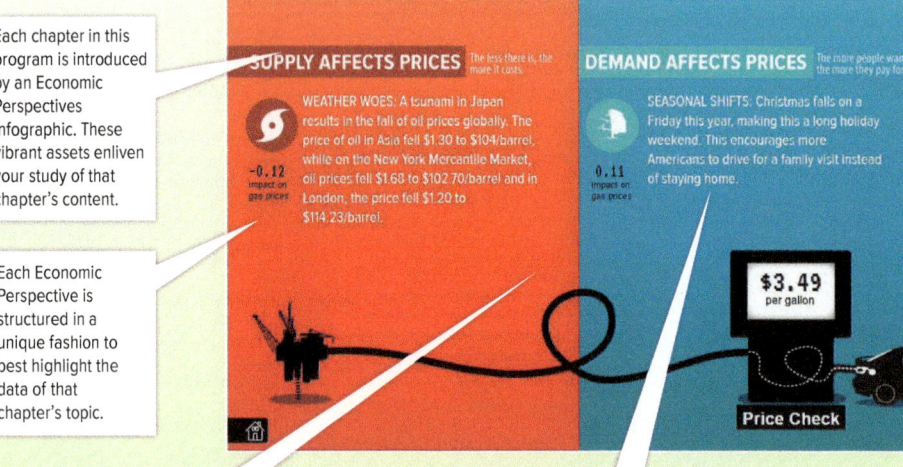

By clicking through the online screens of these digital infographics, you are shown many different kinds of data in a variety of ways.

Interpreting the different types of data often requires that you conduct a problem-solving process to break down the data and examine it step-by-step.

Find all your interactive resources for each chapter online.   **TRY IT YOURSELF ONLINE**

Chapter 10 Money and Banking
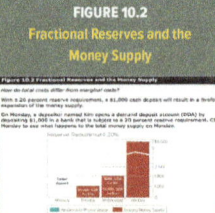
FIGURE 10.2 Fractional Reserves and the Money Supply

Chapter 11 Financial Markets and Investing
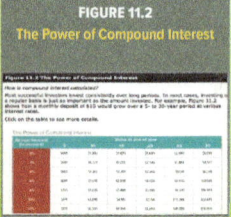
FIGURE 11.2 The Power of Compound Interest

Chapter 11 Financial Markets and Investing

CAREERS Stockbroker and Investment Banker

272

---

networks Online Teaching Options

WORKSHEET

SAMPLE: Economic Simulation

Solving financial problems In this Economic Simulation, students represent the major players of the 2008 financial crisis. Government leaders, the largest banks, and the opposing party will engage in a dialogue about how to stave off an even greater financial disaster. They will be studying and enacting the events of October 2008. Finally, students will decide whether they agree with the decisions actually made.

CHAPTER 10
Money and Banking Planner

UNDERSTANDING BY DESIGN®

Enduring Understanding
- Money makes it easier to trade, borrow, save, invest, and compare the value of goods and services.

Essential Questions
- How has money evolved to meet the needs of people everywhere?
- How did the creation of the Fed improve our banking system?
- How has technology affected the way we use money today?

Predictable Misunderstandings
Students may think:
- *Money in the United States has always been backed by the federal government.* Explain that before the Civil War, the federal government left banking up to individual states.
- *When money is deposited in a bank, the bank keeps the money or deposits it at the Fed.* Explain that the bank is required to keep only 20 percent of the money deposited. The bank is free to lend the remaining 80 percent and charge interest on it.

Assessment Evidence
Performance Task
- Hands-On Chapter Project with Technology Extension

Other Evidence
- Guided Reading Activities
- Vocabulary Activity
- Lesson Quizzes
- Self-Check Quizzes
- Chapter Assessment
- Chapter Tests, Forms A and B

SUGGESTED PACING

Introducing the Chapter: ½ Day	Case Study ½ Day
Lesson 1: The Evolution, Functions, and Characteristics of Money 1 Day	Lesson 3: Banking Today 1 Day
	Debate ½ Day
Lesson 2: The Development of Modern Banking 1 Day	Study Guide, Chapter Assessment and Wrap-Up ½ Day

TOTAL 5 Days

Council for Economic Education

Below are the Council for Economic Education Voluntary National Content Standards in Economics covered in the *Money and Banking* chapter.

Content Standard 11: Money makes it easier to trade, borrow, save, invest, and compare the value of goods and services. The amount of money in the economy affects the overall price level. Inflation is an increase in the overall price level that reduces the value of money.

Key for Using the Teacher Edition

SKILL-BASED ACTIVITIES

Types of skill activites found in the Teacher Edition.

V **Visual Skills** require students to analyze maps, graphs, charts, and photos.

R **Reading Skills** help students practice reading skills and master vocabulary.

C **Critical Thinking Skills** help students apply and extend what they have learned.

W **Writing Skills** provide writing opportunities to help students comprehend the text.

T **Technology Skills** require students to use digital tools effectively.

*Letters are followed by a number when there is more than one of the same type of skill on the page.

DIFFERENTIATED INSTRUCTION

All activities are written for the on-level student unless otherwise marked with the leveled labels below.

BL Beyond Level
AL Approaching Level
ELL English Language Learners

All students benefit from activities that utilize different learning styles. Many activities are marked as below when a particular learning style is highlighted.

Intrapersonal
Logical/Mathematical
Visual/Spatial
Verbal/Linguistic
Naturalist
Kinesthetic
Auditory/Musical
Interpersonal

CHAPTER 10: MONEY AND BANKING

CHAPTER OPENER PLANNER

Students will know:
- the basic functions and characteristics of money.
- the role of banks and other financial institutions in the economy of the United States (wording based on Indiana standard)

Students will be able to:
- **compare** the characteristics of modern money with the basic characteristics of all money.
- **evaluate** bank services to determine which bank would work best for them individually.

UNDERSTANDING BY DESIGN®

☑ Print Teaching Options

R Reading Skills

☐ **p. 274 Examining polymer currency** Students discuss benefits of higher-cost polymer bills and research people shown on the currencies in the infographic.

C Critical Thinking Skills

☐ **p. 273 Analyzing our need for banks** Students discuss how banks function.

☐ **p. 275 Assessing security in technology** Students discuss hacking, identity theft, and how to minimize security risks associated with the use of banking technology. **BL**

T Technology Skills

☐ **p. 274 Examining the technology in currency** Students identify other currency technologies in currency and discuss how these technologies limit counterfeiting.

☑ Online Teaching Options

V Visual Skills

☐ **IMAGE Chapter opener**—Students analyze a photo for clues about banking.

C Critical Thinking Skills

☐ **INFOGRAPHICS Economic Perspectives**—Students explore polymer currency.

☐ **DEBATES Should the gold standard have been abandoned and should it be brought back?**

☐ **INTERACTIVE FEATURE Case Study: Currency Design**—Students discuss how counterfeiting affects the economy.

☑ Printable Digital Worksheets

C Critical Thinking Skills

☐ **WORKSHEET Math Practice for Economics**—Students read about handling a checking account.

☐ **WORKSHEET Enrichment Activity**—Students answer questions about the crisis of 2008, TARP, and the FDIC.

☐ **WORKSHEET Assessing Background Knowledge**—Target misconceptions early.

☐ **WORKSHEET Chapter Summary**—Content is condensed into manageable chunks.

☐ **WORKSHEET Vocabulary Activity**—Students use content and academic terms.

Project-Based Learning

Hands-On

WORKSHEET Hands-On Chapter Project
Student groups create and pitch to the government, their client, a proposal for an advertising campaign to convince the public to accept the discontinuance of Federal Reserve notes and substitute an all-digital monetary system based on the use of credit and debit cards, EFTs, and online banking.

Digital Hands-On

Create Online Projects

Find an additional activity online that incorporates technology for the Hands-On Project. Visit the EdTech Teacher Web sites for more links, tutorials, and other resources.

Print Resources

ANCILLARY RESOURCE
This ancillary is available for every chapter and lesson.
- Chapter Tests and Lesson Quizzes

PRINTABLE DIGITAL WORKSHEETS
These printable digital worksheets are available for every chapter and lesson.
- Reading Essentials & Study Guide
- Vocabulary Activities
- Chapter Summaries
- Economic Simulations
- Math Practice for Economics
- Reinforcing Economic Skills
- Personal Finance Activities
- Enrichment Activities
- Reteaching Activities
- Guided Reading Activities
- Video Worksheets
- Lesson Quizzes and Chapter Tests (English and Spanish)

More Media Resources

SUGGESTED READING
- For students at a Grade 10 reading level: *From Seashells to Smart Cards: Money and Currency*, by Ernestine Giesecke
- For students at a Grade 11 reading level: *Money Business: Banks and Banking,* by Ernestine Giesecke
- For students at a Grade 12 reading level: *The House of Morgan: An American Banking Dynasty and the Rise of Finance*, by Ron Chernow

SUGGESTED VIDEOS
Find these documentaries yourself online. NOTE: McGraw-Hill Education does not endorse these resources. Preview clips for age-appropriateness.
- *I Want the Earth (plus 5%)* (45 min.)
- *The Money Fix* (1 hr. 19 min.)

LESSON 1 Planner

THE EVOLUTION, FUNCTIONS, AND CHARACTERISTICS OF MONEY

Students will know:
- money was invented to facilitate the exchange of goods and services.
- the role of money and financial institutions in a market economy.
- the basic functions and characteristics of money.

Students will be able to:
- **summarize** the development of money in the United States.
- **list** four characteristics of money.
- **describe** the three functions of money.
- **compare** the characteristics of modern money with the basic characteristics of all money.
- **name** the components of money in the United States today.

UNDERSTANDING BY DESIGN®

☑ Print Teaching Options

V Visual Skills

☐ **p. 280 Creating graphs** Students illustrate: "Currency, like almost everything else, loses its value whenever there is too much of it."

R Reading Skills

☐ **p. 276 Defining and demonstrating barter** Students define "mutual coincidence of wants," and mock barter.

☐ **p. 278 Determining cause and effect** Students discuss why Continental dollars became worthless.

☐ **p. 280 Describing the functions and characteristics of fiat money** Students answer: How and why does the dollar bill qualify as money? **BL** Verbal/Linguistic

☐ **p. 280 Appreciating the positive aspects of currency** Students discuss how paper currency is better than coins and how debit cards are better than paper currency. Verbal/Linguistic

C Critical Thinking Skills

☐ **p. 276 Discussing currency** Students consider how government, schools, or other services could function without money. Verbal/Linguistic

☐ **p. 277 Evaluating barter** Students discuss how effective a bartering system would be today.

☐ **p. 277 Comparing commodity, fiat, and representative money** Students describe characteristics of commodity, fiat, and representative money.

☐ **p. 279 Evaluating the usefulness of money** Students evaluate functions and characteristics of commodity and representative money.

W Writing Skills

☐ **p. 278 Creating a chart about early money** Students identify coins that colonists used.

☐ **p. 281 Writing about money** Students explain the different types of money and the definitions the federal government uses for the money supply. Verbal/Linguistic

☑ Online Teaching Options

V Visual Skills

☐ **SLIDE SHOW** **The History of Money**—Students view images of early money. Verbal/Linguistic

☐ **INTERACTIVE FEATURE** **Global Economy & You**—Students discuss the declining value of the dollar. Logical/Mathematical

☐ **VIDEO** **The Cost of Making a Penny**—Students watch the video and discuss whether the penny should be eliminated.

R Reading Skills

☐ **BIOGRAPHY** **Thomas J. Curry**—Students read about Thomas J. Curry and discuss the OCC and the National Banking system. Interpersonal

C Critical Thinking Skills

☐ **BELLRINGER** **Evolution, Functions, and Characteristics of Money**—Students discuss how the low value of money results in inflation. Interpersonal

☐ **ESSENTIAL QUESTION** **Exploring the Essential Question**—Students match payment methods.

T Technology Skills

☐ **SELF-CHECK QUIZ** **Lesson 1**—Students receive instant feedback on their mastery of lesson content.

☐ **GAME** **Lesson 1**—Students solve clues to review lesson content.

☐ **INTERACTIVE WHITEBOARD ACTIVITY** **Types of Money**—Students work together to learn lesson content.

☑ Printable Digital Worksheets

R Reading Skills

☐ **WORKSHEET** **Guided Reading Activity**—Students use the Guided Reading Activity worksheets to review their comprehension of the content.

☐ **WORKSHEET** **Reading Essentials and Study Guide**—Students complete the study guide and answer Reading Progress Check and vocabulary questions.

C Critical Thinking Skills

☐ **WORKSHEET** **The Cost of Making a Penny Video Activity**—Students answer questions about whether the penny should be eliminated. Logical/Mathematical

LESSON 2 Planner

THE DEVELOPMENT OF MODERN BANKING

Students will know:
- the role of banks and other financial institutions in the economy of the United States.
- the Federal Reserve is the nation's central bank.
- the national banking system was created to standardize currency and banking practices in the United States.

Students will be able to:
- *explain* why the National Banking System was created.
- *consider* the advantages and disadvantages of being on a gold standard.
- *explain* how the Federal Reserve System strengthened the National Banking System.
- *describe* the process of establishing a new bank.

UNDERSTANDING BY DESIGN®

✓ Print Teaching Options

V Visual Skills

- ☐ **p. 283 Designing currency** Students redesign forms of U.S. currency.
- ☐ **p. 285 Comparing and contrasting gold and silver certificates** Students list differences between gold and silver certificates.
- ☐ **p. 288 Finding the main idea** Students explore the growth of state and national banks in U.S. history. **Verbal/Linguistic**

R Reading Skills

- ☐ **p. 282 Skimming for information** Students find out what happened to currency by the end of the Revolutionary War. **Verbal/Linguistic**
- ☐ **p. 283 Identifying causes of banking changes** Students identify the major event in U.S. history that changed commercial banking.
- ☐ **p. 284 Defining *legal tender*** Students use the term *legal tender*. **ELL Verbal/Linguistic**
- ☐ **p. 284 Identifying events in the banking system** Students identify steps the National Bank took to create a new banking system and establish its currency. **Verbal/Linguistic**
- ☐ **p. 287 Analyzing banking problems and Fed solutions** Students identify problems with the nation's banking system and the Fed's solutions.

C Critical Thinking Skills

- ☐ **p. 282 Discussing bank regulation** Students speculate on how unregulated banking can cause turmoil. **Verbal/Linguistic**
- ☐ **p. 285 Understanding the gold standard** Students discuss preferences for paper currency or gold. **Logical/Mathematical**
- ☐ **p. 286 Evaluating advantages and disadvantages of the gold standard** Students explain the gold standard.
- ☐ **p. 287 Making predictions** Students predict how the Great Depression impacted banking.
- ☐ **p. 287 Analyzing Depression-era songs for propaganda** Students evaluate economic information in Depression-era songs.

✓ Online Teaching Options

V Visual Skills

- ☐ **VIDEO Small Business Frustrated by Banks**—Students view a video about frustrations of small businesses who operate using credit. **Visual/Spatial**
- ☐ **IMAGES Run on the Bank!**—Students discuss why and how a run on the bank could occur. **Visual/Spatial**
- ☐ **GRAPHS State and National Banks**—Students discuss data about the growth of banks.

R Reading Skills

- ☐ **GRAPHIC ORGANIZER Development of the National Banking System**—Students take notes about changes in the national banking system. **Visual/Spatial**
- ☐ **GRAPHIC ORGANIZER Vertical Main Idea**—Students show main ideas and supporting details for "The Gold Standard." **Visual/Spatial**
- ☐ **GRAPHIC ORGANIZER Cause-and-Effect**—Students identify what led the United States to abandon the gold standard. **Visual/Spatial**

C Critical Thinking Skills

- ☐ **BELLRINGER The Development of Modern Banking**—Students discuss how abandoning the gold standard would stimulate economic growth. **Verbal/Linguistic**
- ☐ **ESSENTIAL QUESTION Exploring the Essential Question**—Students read statements about banking. **Verbal/Linguistic**

T Technology Skills

- ☐ **SELF-CHECK QUIZ Lesson 2**—Students receive instant feedback on their mastery of lesson content.
- ☐ **GAME Lesson 2**—Students solve clues to review lesson content.
- ☐ **INTERACTIVE WHITEBOARD ACTIVITY Federal Reserve Districts**—Students work together to learn lesson content.

✓ Printable Digital Worksheets

R Reading Skills

- ☐ **WORKSHEET Guided Reading Activity**—Students use the Guided Reading Activity worksheets to review their comprehension of the content.
- ☐ **WORKSHEET Reading Essentials and Study Guide**—Students complete the study guide and answer Reading Progress Check and vocabulary questions.
- ☐ **WORKSHEET Reteaching**—Students complete the worksheet as they review the section, explaining their answers and discussing any misunderstandings. **Logical/Mathematical**

C Critical Thinking Skills

- ☐ **WORKSHEET Small Business Frustrated by Banks**—Students answer questions about the frustrations of small businesses who operate using credit. **Visual/Spatial**

LESSON 3 Planner

BANKING TODAY

Students will know:
- the major methods of accessing funds in checking, savings, and credit accounts.
- the advantages and disadvantages of using credit cards.
- the technological developments in banking that have made it easier to access money and track spending.
- major changes in financial services industry regulation that have resulted from changes in technology.

Students will be able to:
- **evaluate** bank services to determine which bank would work best for them individually.
- **explain** why saving and becoming creditworthy are good ideas for everyone.

UNDERSTANDING BY DESIGN®

✓ Print Teaching Options

R Reading Skills

- **p. 291 Analyzing the role of interest in allocating savings** Students discuss the difference between a savings deposit and a CD.
- **p. 292 Discussing bank functions** Students weigh advantages of paying by electronic or paper check rather than cash.
- **p. 292 Understanding banking fees** Students explain fees typically charged by banks.
- **p. 293 Examining risks, costs, and benefits of accounts** Students show each type of account and its risks, costs, and benefits. **ELL**

C Critical Thinking Skills

- **p. 290 Hypothesizing on sources of bank profits** Students write ways they think a bank makes money. **Logical/Mathematical**
- **p. 290 Understanding bank profits** Students determine how shareholders in a bank earn profits. **AL**
- **p. 291 Identifying effects of fractional reserve requirements** Students identify how the Fed uses fractional reserve requirements.
- **p. 291 Understanding bank risks** Students consider risks banks take when allocating savings to its most productive use.
- **p. 293 Categorizing pros and cons of debit and credit** Students provide pros and cons of using debit and credit cards.
- **p. 294 Understanding credit card company profits** Students discuss how credit card companies earn profits.
- **p. 294 Brainstorming ways to save** Students identify methods to develop the habit of saving.
- **p. 295 Recognizing consequences of creditworthiness** Students share ways to improve a personal credit score.
- **p. 295 Summarizing the lesson** Students write main ideas and supporting details.

✓ Online Teaching Options

V Visual Skills

- **IMAGES** **Wall Street Mayhem**—Students read about banking practices that led to the Great Depression.
- **CHART** **Fractional Reserve and the Money Supply**—Students discuss how the fractional reserve process affects the economy. **Logical/Mathematical**
- **VIDEO** **Credit Cards**—Students watch a video about the advantages and disadvantages of using credit. **Verbal/Linguistic**
- **CHART** **Typical Consumer Fees Charged by Banks**—Students estimate the average monthly cost of having a checking or savings account. **Interpersonal**

R Reading Skills

- **INTERACTIVE FEATURE** **Careers: Financial Clerk**—Students read about the job of financial clerk. **Verbal/Linguistic**

C Critical Thinking Skills

- **BELLRINGER** **Banking Today**—Students learn about the 2009 banking crisis.
- **ESSENTIAL QUESTION** **Exploring the Essential Question**—Students discuss pros and cons of getting a credit card. **Verbal/Linguistic**

T Technology Skills

- **SELF-CHECK QUIZ** **Lesson 3**—Students receive instant feedback on answers.
- **GAME** **Lesson 3**—Students solve clues to review lesson content.
- **INTERACTIVE WHITEBOARD ACTIVITY** **Advantages and Disadvantages of Banking Products**—Students work together to learn lesson content.

✓ Printable Digital Worksheets

R Reading Skills

- **WORKSHEET** **Guided Reading Activity**—Students review their comprehension.
- **WORKSHEET** **Reading Essentials and Study Guide**—Students complete the study guide and answer Reading Progress Check and vocabulary questions.
- **WORKSHEET** **Reteaching Activity**—Students review content and vocabulary.

C Critical Thinking Skills

- **WORKSHEET** **Math Practice for Economics**—Students view a checking account.
- **WORKSHEET** **Reinforcing Economic Skills**—Students explore bank services.
- **WORKSHEET** **Personal Finance Activity**—Students analyze the pros and cons of using cash, debit cards, and credit cards.

CHAPTER 10 Money and Banking

INTERVENTION AND REMEDIATION STRATEGIES

LESSON 1 The Evolution, Functions, and Characteristics of Money

Reading and Comprehension

Write these questions on the board:
- What advantages does the use of money have over the barter system?
- How does fiat money differ from commodity money?
- What are the four main characteristics of money?
- How does the U.S. dollar perform the three essential functions of money?

Allow students a few minutes to find the answers to the questions. Then explore the answers in class discussion.

Text Evidence

Read the following scenario aloud to students:

An alien spaceship lands on Earth. The aliens have been observing Earth for centuries and have finally decided it would be safe to land and share knowledge about our two civilizations. One of the travelers visits your school. In telling about the alien economy, the visitor holds up a large piece of iron ore and explains that this is the money they use. He asks what we use, and someone holds up a paper dollar. In surprise, the alien asks how this can possibly be used as a medium of exchange.

Tell students to write a dialogue with the alien in which they explain how our money works and describe why iron would never work as money on our planet. In your dialogue, cite details from the text to support your ideas.

LESSON 2 The Development of Modern Banking

Reading and Comprehension

Organize students into groups of three and ask students in each group to divide up the sections of the lesson. Tell students to read and take notes on the main ideas and important details in their assigned sections. Then have each student "teach" his or her section to the other members of the group.

Text Evidence

Tell students that members of Congress have occasionally introduced legislative bills that would eliminate the Federal Reserve. Ask students to investigate a member of Congress who has done this and to write a letter to that individual arguing why they think the Fed is a vital component of our financial system. Tell them to cite facts and examples from the text to support their argument.

LESSON 3 Banking Today

Reading and Comprehension

Have students review the lesson and write two questions about important ideas in each section. Then ask students to work in small groups and to ask their questions and discuss the answers. Assemble the class and encourage students to ask any questions that groups were unable to answer.

Text Evidence

Tell students that a friend has inherited several thousand dollars. Her broker advised her to invest it in a particular bank corporation, telling her that it was both a safe investment and one that could yield good profits in the years to come. Your friend is skeptical. She thinks of banks as useful service companies and wonders if they have the potential to earn much. Ask students to write an essay explaining how banks earn money and why they can be very profitable. Have students cite details from the text to support their ideas.

Online Resources

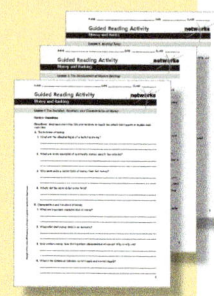

Assessing Background Knowledge Use this worksheet to pre-assess students' background knowledge before they start the chapter.

Chapter Summaries Have students use the summary as a pre-reading activity or as a post-reading review to check the main ideas covered in each lesson.

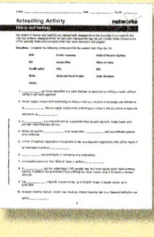

Guided Reading Activities Have students complete these activities as they read each lesson. They provide reading notes the student can use for review and to prepare for assessments.

Reteaching Activities Have students complete the Reteaching Activity for remedial practice and review of vital content.

Self-Check Quizzes These quizzes provide instant feedback on areas the students may need to re-read to understand a main idea.

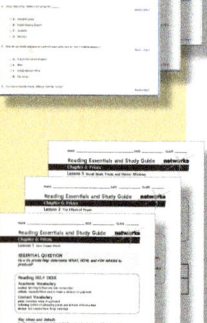

Reading Essentials and Study Guide This resource offers writing and reading activities for the approaching-level student.

Approaching Grade Level Reader This reader presents all of the content of the Online Student Edition but at a lower reading level.

English Language Learner Reader Provide additional reading support for ELL students. Find this tool online.

Money and Banking

ESSENTIAL QUESTIONS
- How has money evolved to meet the needs of people everywhere?
- How did the creation of the Fed improve our banking system?
- How has technology affected the way we use money today?

networks
www.connected.mcgraw-hill.com
There's More Online about money and banking.

CHAPTER 10

Economic Perspectives
Polymer Banknotes: Currency of the Future

Lesson 1
The Evolution, Functions, and Characteristics of Money

Lesson 2
The Development of Modern Banking

Lesson 3
Banking Today

Letter from the Author

Dear Economics Teacher,

Students find money and banking fascinating when they understand these topics. Most people think about money but don't give much thought to the way it evolved, or to the characteristics it possesses. Most of our money today is in the form of computerized bookkeeping entries. Who could have considered that so many different societies would have devised so many different, but extremely useful, forms of money—sea shells, Native American wampum, tobacco, or gold coins? It almost seems as if money was something that begged to be invented. Well, invented it was, and now we have to understand it and learn to manage it.

CHAPTER 10
Money and Banking

ENGAGE

Call students' attention to the photo and ask them to describe what it shows. Guide them to recognize that this bank customer is withdrawing cash from an automated teller machine (ATM). **Ask: Why is this image a good one to symbolize the chapter titled *Money and Banking*?** *(Banks help us manage our money. The ATM is giving the customer access to her money when she needs it.)* In a discussion, lead students to understand that banks are central to our free enterprise economic system. They serve businesses and individuals, helping the circular flow of money and offering other financial assets.

Analyzing our need for banks Guide a discussion of how banks function in our economy. **Ask:**

- **How do banks help us use the money we earn?** *(Banks allow us to save money and to earn interest on the savings, help us invest our money, and give us access to money when we need it.)*
- **How do banks help companies do business?** *(Sample answers: Banks protect the money businesses earn; they loan money to companies for expansion; they distribute payroll to employees.)*

Making Connections

Banks Help students appreciate the everyday importance of banking. **Ask: What banks can you name?** *(Sample answers: Bank of America, Wells Fargo)* Guide students to the conclusion that there are many banks in every community. Most of the ones we think of first are "brick and mortar" banks—the ones we see on many corners—but there are many that operate online. Ask students to name some of these banks. *(Ally Bank and Charles Schwab Bank are examples of Internet banks. Students may also correctly name some of the same banks they identified as brick-and-mortar banks.)*

FOLDABLES Study Organizer

Go to the Foldables® library for a chapter-based Foldable® activity that your students can use to help take notes and prepare for assessment.

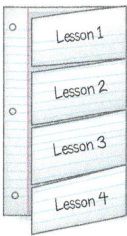

CHAPTER 10
Economic Perspectives

TEACH & ASSESS

R Reading Skills

Examining polymer currency Ask: **What is another name for polymer?** *(plastic)* Discuss with students why proponents support the printing of the higher-cost polymer bills. Ask: **How many countries were using polymer banknotes by 2014?** *(nearly 60 countries)* Have students research the people shown on the currencies in the infographic. **Visual/Spatial**

T Technology Skills

Examining the technology in currency Challenge students to identify other technologies in currency they know of or have read about. Ask them to discuss how these technologies are limiting counterfeiting. **Interpersonal**

Content Background Knowledge

Photocopying Dilemma Advanced color photocopying technology in the 1990s created a dilemma for the U.S. Bureau of Engraving and Printing, the department that prints currency and tries to stay ahead of counterfeiters. The 1996 Series Notes had watermarks and color-shifting ink that would not be reproduced by photocopy machines. The redesigned $100 bill introduced in 2013 has additional security features, including a special placement of text that forms a "constellation" code, which the government and large photocopier companies agreed upon. This code alerts photocopy machines to add black stripes to the image, thus preventing the currency from being copied cleanly.

Economic Perspectives

POLYMER BANKNOTES: CURRENCY OF THE FUTURE

R Polymer banknotes are made from thin, flexible polypropylene film. They last longer than their paper counterparts and can even survive the washing machine. (They do, however, melt under extreme heat.) Proponents say that the higher cost of producing polymer bills is offset by the fact that they last 2-3 times longer than paper bills, producing them requires less energy and they can be recycled. More important, polymer bills are harder to counterfeit.

Why Polymer Is Better:

Safer
The new features are very hard to copy

Resistant
Plastic won't absorb like paper will

Longer-lasting
Polymer notes last 2-3x as long as paper

Cleaner
The note's surface will resist germs

Greener
Can easily be recycled for reuse

Polymer catches on

T Polymer banknotes are becoming the currency format of choice for more and more countries around the world. As of 2014, nearly 60 countries used polymer or polymer-paper bank notes. China began issuing polymer bills in 2000. In 2002, Mexico became the first North American country to adopt polymer banknotes, followed by Canada in 2011.

China    **Mexico**    **Canada**

---

networks Online Teaching Options

INFOGRAPHIC

Polymer Banknotes: Currency of the Future

Analyzing polymer currency Have students view the infographic. Ask if any of them have seen polymer banknotes. Ask: **What are the advantages of using polymer?** *(safer, resistant, longer-lasting, cleaner, greener)* **What printing methods and other devices has Australia used on its currency to make counterfeiting more difficult?** *(microprinting, registration device, raised ink, offset print, fluorescent ink, shadow image, transparent window)* **Visual/Spatial**

CHAPTER 10
Economic Perspectives

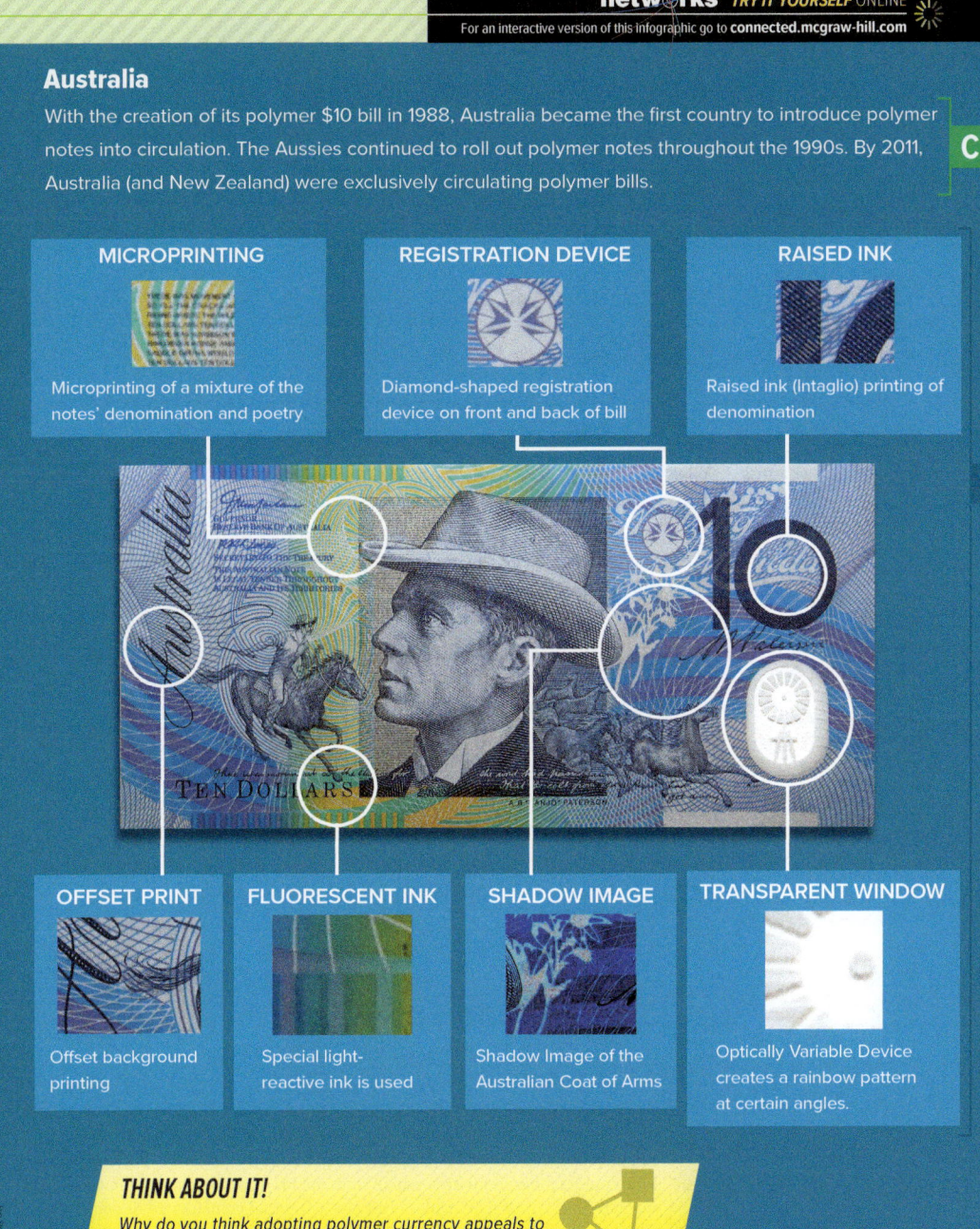

Australia
With the creation of its polymer $10 bill in 1988, Australia became the first country to introduce polymer notes into circulation. The Aussies continued to roll out polymer notes throughout the 1990s. By 2011, Australia (and New Zealand) were exclusively circulating polymer bills.

MICROPRINTING — Microprinting of a mixture of the notes' denomination and poetry

REGISTRATION DEVICE — Diamond-shaped registration device on front and back of bill

RAISED INK — Raised ink (Intaglio) printing of denomination

OFFSET PRINT — Offset background printing

FLUORESCENT INK — Special light-reactive ink is used

SHADOW IMAGE — Shadow Image of the Australian Coat of Arms

TRANSPARENT WINDOW — Optically Variable Device creates a rainbow pattern at certain angles.

THINK ABOUT IT!
Why do you think adopting polymer currency appeals to the governments of developing countries?

C Critical Thinking Skills

Assessing security in technology Ask students what they know about the security risks associated with the use of technology for money and banking transactions. Remind students that news stories periodically tell of hackers who have accessed customer passwords and personal data, putting their identities and financial data at risk. Invite students to discuss how and why this happens and what can be done to limit hacking. **Interpersonal**

V Visual Skills

Designing a new currency Ask students to design their own currency, including at least three of the seven features shown on the Australia banknote. **Kinesthetic**

CLOSE & REFLECT
Have students answer the *Think About It!* questions.

WORKSHEET
Hands-On Chapter Project

Evaluating the need for paper currency In this activity, student groups will act as members of advertising agencies who are competing for a government advertising contract. The groups will create a proposal for an advertising campaign to convince the public to accept the discontinuance of Federal Reserve notes. In its place, the government wants to substitute an all-digital monetary system based on the use of credit and debit cards, EFTs, and online banking. Students will pitch their proposals to the client. Introduce the chapter project by **asking, Do we need currency?** Encourage a brief discussion to review what students have learned about currency in our society and about the availability of electronic options. Then explain the project and assign students to groups to complete the activity. **Interpersonal**

ANSWERS, p. 275

THINK ABOUT IT!

Answers will vary, but students should mention that although polymer currency is more expensive to produce, it lasts 2-3 times longer than paper bills, producing them requires less energy, they can be recycled, and—more important—they are harder to counterfeit.

CHAPTER 10, LESSON 1
The Evolution, Functions, and Characteristics of Money

ENGAGE

C Critical Thinking Skills

🔔 **Discussing currency** Ask: **What kinds of money do you know about?** *(dollars, bitcoin, Canadian dollars, euros, and so on)* Point out that although most purchases are completed using alternative methods of payment, such as credit cards and electronic transfers, the measure of value is still in familiar dollars or similar currency. Guide students to discuss how currency fuels the economic system. Encourage them to consider how government, schools, or other services could function without money. **Verbal/Linguistic**

TEACH & ASSESS

R Reading Skills

Defining and demonstrating barter Have students define the phrase "mutual coincidence of wants." *(a situation where two people want exactly what the other has and are willing to trade what they have for it)* Then distribute index cards with various products written on them. For example, one students receives 10 cards, each with "1 egg" written on it. Another student receives one card identified as "1 pair of boots." A third student's 5 cards each state "1 hour of electricity." After students receive their cards, have them barter for several rounds to obtain what they want. Find out how many students actually achieved their bartering goal. **Interpersonal, Verbal/Linguistic**

ANSWERS, p. 276

ESSENTIAL QUESTION ACTIVITY

Different payment methods may include debit cards, checks, traveler's checks, credit cards, gift cards, smart cards, and so on. These are forms of money because they serve as a medium of exchange, a measure of value, and a store of value. Alternative payment methods can be exchanged for currency, or Federal Reserve notes, if necessary.
TAKING NOTES: Portability, Durability, Divisibility, Scarcity

---

Interact with these digital assets and others in lesson 1
✓ SLIDESHOW The History of Money
✓ INTERACTIVE GRAPH Three Functions of Money
✓ SELF-CHECK QUIZ
✓ VIDEO

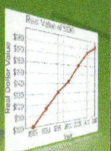

netw rks
TRY IT YOURSELF ONLINE

Reading Help Desk

Academic Vocabulary
- revolution

Content Vocabulary
- Federal Reserve System (Fed)
- Federal Reserve notes
- barter economy
- commodity money
- fiat money
- specie
- monetary unit
- medium of exchange
- measure of value
- store of value
- demand deposit accounts (DDAs)
- M1
- M2

TAKING NOTES:

Key Ideas and Details
ACTIVITY Use the graphic organizer below to identify the characteristics of money.

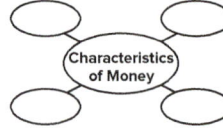

276

LESSON 1
The Evolution, Functions, and Characteristics of Money

ESSENTIAL QUESTION

How has money evolved to meet the needs of people everywhere?

Money is not just something you spend. It's like a tool or a device that serves everyone's best interest. Money has been developed by different societies at different times all over the world. The need for money has become as accepted as the need for laws and government.

Today, our money is managed by the **Federal Reserve System (Fed)**, the privately owned, publicly controlled, central bank of the United States. The Fed issues paper currency known as **Federal Reserve notes**, the most visible part of our money supply.

Think about how people pay for their purchases.

- What are some different payment methods?
- Are these also forms of money? Explain.
- What is the connection between Federal Reserve notes and other payment methods?

The Evolution of Money

GUIDING QUESTION *Why did money replace the barter system?*

Take a moment to think what life would be like in a **barter economy**, a moneyless economy that relies on trade. The exchange of goods and services would be more difficult because the products some people have to offer are not always acceptable to others, or easy to divide for payment. For example, how could a milkman with a pail of milk obtain a pair of shoes if the cobbler wanted a basket of fish? Unless there is a "mutual coincidence of wants"—a situation in which two people want exactly what the other has and are willing to trade what they have for it—it is difficult for trade to take place.

---

netw rks *Online Teaching Options*

BELLRINGER

Evolution, Functions, and Characteristics of Money

Examining options for currency Display the Bellringer photo and discuss question 2 about the low value of money. Explain that this results in a decline of purchasing power, or inflation. Tell students that in some countries, this decline in purchasing power has led to hyperinflation, in which currency essentially becomes meaningless. **Ask: What might happen in a society in which the currency has little value?** *(Possible answer: People might turn to bartering or use another country's currency. Social unrest may escalate.)* **Interpersonal**

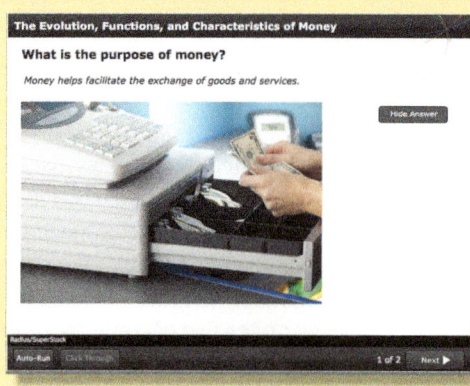

Life is simpler in an economy with money. The milkman sells the milk for cash and then exchanges that cash for a pair of shoes. The cobbler takes the cash and looks for someone selling fish. Money, as it turns out, makes life easier for everybody in ways we may have never considered.

Money in Colonial America

The money used by early settlers in the American colonies was similar to that found in early societies. Some of it consisted of **commodity money**—money that has an alternative use as an economic good, or commodity. Many products—including corn, hemp, gunpowder, and musket balls—served as commodity money. They could be used to settle debts and make purchases. At the same time, colonists could consume these products, if necessary.

Commonly accepted commodity money was tobacco, for which the Governor of Colonial Virginia set a value of three English shillings per pound in 1618. Two years later, the colonists used some of this commodity money to bring wives to the colonies.

Other colonies established **fiat money**—money by government decree. For example, in 1637, Massachusetts established a monetary value for wampum—a form of currency the Wampanoag Native Americans made out of white and purple mussel shells. The Wampanoag and the settlers used these shells in trade. White shells were more plentiful than purple ones, so one English penny was made equal to six white or three purple shells. The colonial settlers could even pay their taxes with wampum.

Early Paper Currency

Paper currency was another popular form of fiat money in the colonies. Some state laws allowed individuals to print their own paper currency if they promised to redeem the currency for gold or silver. Some states even printed money in the form of tax anticipation notes and used them to pay salaries, buy supplies, and meet other government expenditures until they received taxes and could redeem the notes.

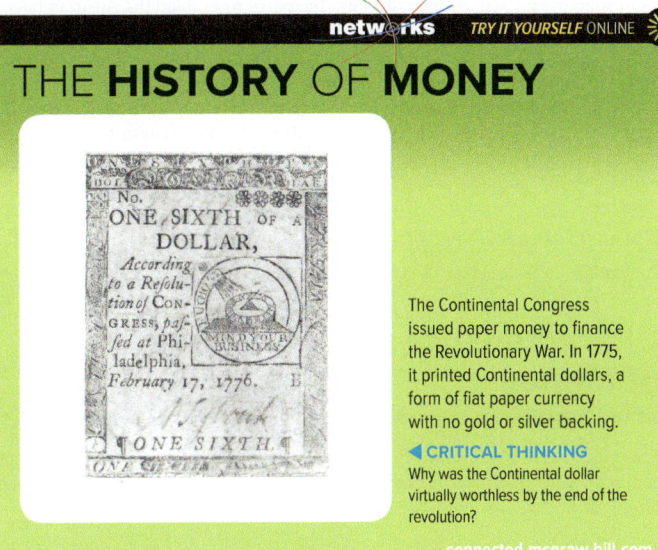

THE HISTORY OF MONEY

The Continental Congress issued paper money to finance the Revolutionary War. In 1775, it printed Continental dollars, a form of fiat paper currency with no gold or silver backing.

◀ CRITICAL THINKING
Why was the Continental dollar virtually worthless by the end of the revolution?

Federal Reserve System (Fed) privately owned, publicly controlled, central bank of the United States

Federal Reserve notes paper currency issued by the Fed that eventually replaced all other types of federal currency

barter economy moneyless economy that relies on trade or barter

commodity money money that has an alternative use as an economic good; gunpowder, flour, corn, etc.

fiat money money by government decree; has no alternative value or use as a commodity

---

CHAPTER 10, LESSON 1
The Evolution, Functions, and Characteristics of Money

C1 Critical Thinking Skills

Evaluating barter   Ask: How effective would a bartering system be in today's economy? Explain. *(Students should point out that it would be inefficient and, on a national scale, ineffective. Bartering typically works only in small societies with fairly simple economic systems.)*

C2 Critical Thinking Skills

Comparing commodity, fiat, and representative money   Ask: How does money become valuable? To answer this question, have students describe the characteristics of commodity, fiat, and representative money. Then ask them to give examples of each. Commodity money has inherent value, which means it would have value even it were not used as money. People valued commodities such as salt, cacao beans, fur, and gold before they used these items as money. Representative money, such as government notes, had value because it represented silver or gold that the nation's central bank held in vaults. The bearer of the note could trade it for actual silver or gold. Debit cards or gift cards are current examples of representative money. The modern U.S. dollar has fiat value. This means it has value because the government says it has value, and requires that it be accepted to pay all debts.

SLIDE SHOW

The History of Money

Asking and answering questions about money Have students view the slide show, pausing long enough on each slide to write a question or a comment based on the text. After completing the slide show, collect the questions and replay the slide show. Discuss the questions and comments as a class. You may wish to have students do research to find the answers to questions that go beyond the content of the show. **Verbal/Linguistic**

ANSWERS, p. 277

CRITICAL THINKING

By the end of the war, nearly one-quarter *billion* Continental dollars had been printed. Money, like almost everything else, loses its value whenever there is too much of it, so a volume that large would cause the Continental dollar to lose value.

CHAPTER 10, LESSON 1
The Evolution, Functions, and Characteristics of Money

R Reading Skills

Determining cause and effect **Ask: Why were the Continental dollars virtually worthless at the end of the Revolutionary War?** *(They were not backed by gold or silver, and there were too many in circulation.)*

W Writing Skills

Creating a chart about early money Have students create a two-column chart with the headings "Name of Coin" and "Country of Origin." Students should complete their charts by identifying coins that the colonists used and the countries those coins represented. *(shillings from England, talers from Australia, pesos from Spain)* **Ask: Why were so many foreign coins in circulation in the colonies?** *(Answers should include the concept that the colonies were populated with people from various countries.)* **Visual/Spatial**

ANSWERS, p. 278

☑ **READING PROGRESS CHECK** Commodity money could be exchanged for goods and services just like fiat money. Unlike fiat money, it could also be used by the owner. Fiat money was more easily transportable than commodity money, but unlike commodity money, it had no intrinsic value.

---

revolution an overthrow of government

specie money in the form of gold or silver coins

R The Continental Congress issued paper money to finance the Revolutionary War. In 1775, it printed Continental dollars, a form of fiat paper currency with no gold or silver backing. By the end of the war, nearly one-quarter billion Continental dollars had been printed—a volume so large that it was virtually worthless by the end of the **revolution**.

Specie in the Colonies

Colonists also used modest amounts of **specie**—or money in the form of silver or gold coins. These included English shillings, Austrian talers, and various European coins that immigrants brought to the colonies. Coins were the most desirable form of money, not only because of their mineral content, but because they were in limited supply. By 1776, only $12 million in specie circulated in the colonies, compared to nearly $500 million in paper currency.

The most popular coin in the colonies was the Spanish peso, which came to America through trade and piracy. Long before the American Revolution had begun, the Spanish were mining silver in Mexico. They melted silver into bullion—ingots or bars of precious metals—or minted it into coins for shipment to Spain. When the Spanish treasure ships left the West Indies (Cuba and the present-day Caribbean Islands) on their way to Spain, they often became victims of Caribbean pirates who spent their stolen treasure in America's southern ports.

W The "triangular trade" among the colonies, Africa, and the Caribbean brought more pesos to America. Traders took molasses and pesos from the Caribbean to the colonies. There they sold the molasses to be made into rum and spent their pesos on other goods. The rum was shipped to Africa, where it was traded for enslaved Africans. The enslaved Africans were taken to the Caribbean to be sold for pesos and more molasses or to be shipped to the colonies. The trade cycle started anew when molasses and pesos were taken to the colonies.

From "Talers" to "Dollars"

monetary unit standard unit of currency in a country's money supply; American dollar, British pound, etc.

Spanish pesos were known as "pieces of eight," because they were divided into eight subparts known as "bits." Because the pesos resembled the Austrian talers, they were nicknamed "talers," which in German sounded exactly like the word *dollars*. This term became so popular that the dollar became the basic **monetary unit**, or standard unit of currency, in the U.S. money system.

Rather than dividing the dollar into eighths as the Spanish had done with the peso, it was decided to divide it into tenths, which was easier to understand. Still, some of the terminology associated with the Spanish peso remains, as when people sometimes call a 25-cent coin—one quarter of a dollar—"two bits."

☑ **READING PROGRESS CHECK**

Comparing Compare the costs and benefits of commodity money and fiat money.

Characteristics and Functions of Money

GUIDING QUESTION *What are the requirements needed for something to be used as money?*

The study of early money is useful because it helps us understand the characteristics that give money its value. In fact, any substance can serve as money if it possesses four main characteristics.

278

---

networks Online Teaching Options

VIDEO   WORKSHEET

The Cost of Making a Penny

Evaluating the functions of a penny Before showing the video, **ask: Do you think the penny fulfills the functions of money: a useful medium of exchange, measure of value, and store of value? Why or why not?** *(Many students will say it is not needed, that a penny does not buy anything.)* Invite discussion, and then show the video. When students have viewed the video, ask them if the penny should be eliminated. Then ask them which facts or ideas had the greatest influence on their opinion of what to do with the penny. **Logical/Mathematical**

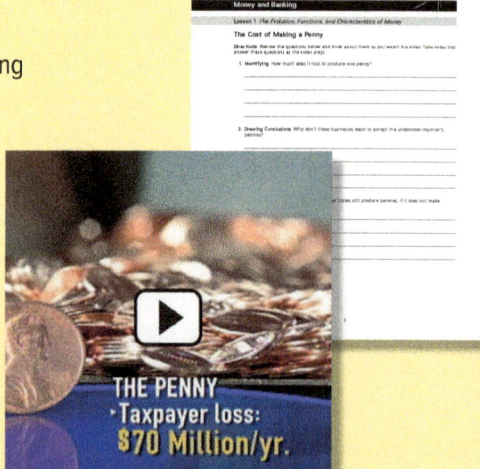

Characteristics of Money

First, money must be *portable*, or easily transferred from one person to another, to make the exchange of money for products easier. Most money in early societies was very portable—including shells, wampum, tobacco, and compressed blocks of tea.

Second, money must also be reasonably *durable* so it does not deteriorate when it is handled. Most colonial money was quite durable, especially monies like musket balls and wampum. Even the fiat paper money of the colonial period was durable in the sense that it could be easily replaced by new bills when old ones became worn.

Third, money should be easily *divisible* into smaller units so that people can use only as much as they need for a transaction. Most early money was highly divisible. Blocks of tea or cheese were cut with a knife. Bundles of tobacco leaves could easily be broken apart. Even Spanish pesos were cut with a knife into eighths to make "bits" for payment.

Finally, money must be available, but only in *limited supply*. Stones used as money on the Yap Islands, for example, were carried in open canoes from other islands 400 miles away. Because navigation was uncertain and the weather was unpredictable, only one canoe in 20 completed the round trip, so there was only a limited supply of stones.

THE GLOBAL ECONOMY & YOU

The Dollar in Decline

It seems as if the decline in the American dollar has been going on for decades. There are many causes for this recent decline. One is the U.S. budget deficit, which has grown due to government borrowing in order to operate all its programs. The second is the Fed's increase in our domestic money supply.

Here's how it happened: The government spends more than it takes in each year. To cover the deficit, it sells government bonds. Because the deficit is so large, and because it has been going on so long, the U.S. now has trillions of dollars in outstanding bonds. To help the government finance its deficit, and to help stimulate economic growth during and after the Great Recession, the Federal Reserve has been buying up bonds with its currency. Where does the currency come from? The Fed prints it. Remember, the dollar is fiat currency—and to have value it has to be scarce. But by printing more and more money, the Fed has caused the dollar to become less scarce, and its value relative to other currencies has declined.

Because the dollar is now worth less than, say, the euro, American goods are more competitively priced for sale in Europe than they have been in the past—which will help boost our exports. Conversely, goods priced in euros cost us more than they did a few years ago—which should help reduce imports into the United States. Together, these two forces will help the U.S. balance of payments, and hopefully affect the international value of the dollar.

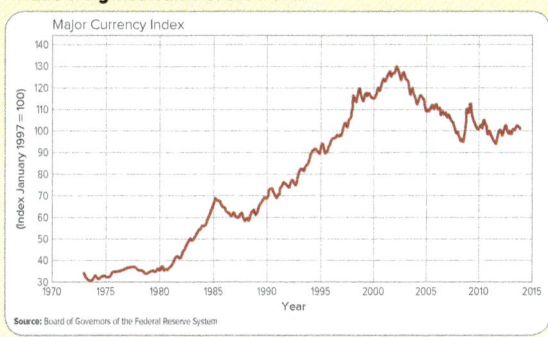

Trade-Weighted Value of the Dollar

Source: Board of Governors of the Federal Reserve System

▲ **CRITICAL THINKING**

Analyzing The forces of supply and demand help set the international value of the dollar. If you want to take a trip to Europe, should you take more or fewer dollars than you might have taken ten years ago?

connected.mcgraw-hill.com Money and Banking **279**

WORKSHEET

Assessing Background Knowledge

Charting knowledge about money Ask students to write answers in the "What I Know" and "What I Would Like to Know" columns in the chart. Then guide a discussion of their answers by encouraging volunteers to tell how they answered each question. Have students complete the third column of the chart ("What I Have Learned") after finishing Lesson 3. **Verbal/Linguistic**

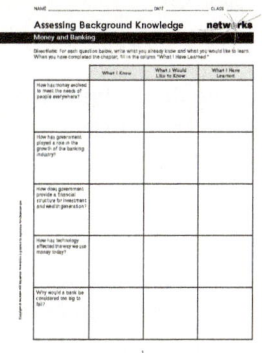

CHAPTER 10, LESSON 1
The Evolution, Functions, and Characteristics of Money

C Critical Thinking Skills

Evaluating the usefulness of money Have students select one form of commodity money (cowrie shells, for example) and one form of representative money (gold certificates, for example) and describe how the two items do or do not fulfill the three functions and four characteristics of money. **BL**

English Language Proficiency

Intermediate When you ask a question, have students rearrange the words in the question to answer in a complete statement. For example, to the question, "What is commodity money, and what types of products served as commodity money?" students answer, "Commodity money is money that has another use as a good or product, and the types of products that served as commodity money included corn, hemp, gunpowder, and tobacco." As students increase in accuracy and ease, invite them to rearrange or add words to create a variety of sentence types with the same meaning but different word order. For example, student can move a phrase and answer, "Commodity money, such as corn, hemp, gunpowder, and tobacco, had use as money and as a product."

ANSWERS, p. 279

CRITICAL THINKING

Someone visiting Europe would want to take more dollars because goods and services will be more expensive there due to the decline in the value of the dollar. A European visiting America would find the United States less expensive because the decline in the value of the dollar in relation to the euro would make things less expensive here.

CHAPTER 10, LESSON 1
The Evolution, Functions, and Characteristics of Money

V Visual Skills

Creating graphs Have students create a graph to illustrate the following sentence: "Currency, like almost everything else, loses its value whenever there is too much of it." *(Students should demonstrate understanding of supply and demand graphs.)* **Visual/Spatial**

R1 Reading Skills

Describing the functions and characteristics of fiat money On the board, draw a two-column chart with "Functions and Characteristics" and "The Dollar" as column headings. In the first column, list the three functions and four characteristics of money. Then have students view a dollar bill. Ask them to identify how the dollar fulfills each function and demonstrates each characteristic. Note their responses in the appropriate row in the chart. Have students use the information in the chart to write a paragraph answering the following question: How and why does the dollar bill qualify as money? **BL Verbal/Linguistic**

R2 Reading Skills

Appreciating the positive aspects of currency
Ask: How is paper currency an improvement over coins? *(Paper currency is produced in higher denominations and is much more portable.)* How are debit cards an improvement over paper currency? *(Answers may include that they are safer than having large amounts of currency in a wallet or purse; they are convenient; they are accepted for the exact amount of the purchase.)* **Verbal/Linguistic**

BIOGRAPHY

Thomas J. Curry
COMPTROLLER OF THE CURRENCY (1957–)

As Comptroller of the Office of the Currency (OCC) since 2012, Thomas J. Curry heads one of the most powerful offices overseeing the U.S. economy. The OCC was formed in 1863 with the mission of regulating the National Banking System. Today the OCC supervises about two-thirds of all commercial banking assets, including more than 2,000 national banks and saving associations, 50 federal branches, and the agencies of foreign banks operating in the U.S. In his appointed position as Head of the OCC, Curry helps maintain the viability of these banks and ensures the nation has sufficient currency liquidity to lend, trade, and conduct the business of the U.S. economy.

Curry received a law degree from the New England School of Law in 1981. In 1982, he served in the Massachusetts Secretary of State's office as an attorney. From 1990 to 1991 and from 1995 to 2003, he was the Commissioner of Banks for Massachusetts. He also serves as the Director of the Federal Deposit Insurance Corporation (FDIC), beginning in 2004.

▲ **CRITICAL THINKING**
Drawing Conclusions Why does the federal government need a bureau to oversee banking operations?

Money, like almost everything else, loses its value whenever there is too much of it. This was a major problem for most types of commodity money. In Virginia, the price of tobacco went from 36 pennies a pound to 1 penny a pound after everyone started growing their own tobacco. Wampum even lost its value when settlers used industrial dyes to turn white shells into purple—thereby doubling their value. Most paper currency in the colonial period also lost its value when too much was printed.

Three Functions of Money

Any substance that is portable, durable, divisible, and limited in supply can serve as money. If it does, it will serve three roles in the economy.

- **Medium of exchange**—A medium of exchange is something accepted by all parties as payment for goods and services. Throughout history, people have used various materials as a medium of exchange, including colored shells, tobacco, gold, silver, and even salt.
- **Measure of value**—Money serves as a measuring stick used to express the worth of something in terms that most people understand. In the United States, this worth is expressed in dollars and cents.
- **Store of value**—The feature of money that allows purchasing power to be saved until needed. For example, you can spend your money on something now, or wait and spend your money later.

The modern money we use today serves all of these functions.

Characteristics of Modern Money

While our modern money may seem to be quite different from earlier forms of money, it shares the same fundamental characteristics and functions of money. For example,

- **Portability**—Modern money is *portable*. Our currency is lightweight, is convenient, and can be easily transferred from one person to another. The same applies to the use of checks or electronic deposits in a bank.
- **Durability**—Modern money is reasonably durable. Metallic coins last about 20 years under normal use. Paper currency is also reasonably *durable*, with a $1 bill lasting about 18 months in circulation. The introduction of the Sacagawea dollar coin was an attempt to make the money supply even more durable by replacing the $1 bill with longer-lasting coins.
- **Divisibility**—Modern money is *divisible*. The penny, the smallest denomination of coin, is small enough for almost any purchase. In addition, people can write checks for the exact amount of a purchase.
- **Scarcity**—Modern money is in *limited supply*. This is because the Fed monitors the size of the money supply and takes steps to keep it from growing too fast.

EXPLORING THE ESSENTIAL QUESTION

In what way is our modern money an improvement over money used during the Colonial period? Is there any way in which Colonial money was superior to our money today?

ANSWERS, p. 280

CRITICAL THINKING
Students should recognize that without oversight, the banking industry would be affected by the same dangers of unregulated business that can affect other industries, including unfair competition, monopolies, and so forth.

EXPLORING THE ESSENTIAL QUESTION
Students should note that Colonial money took many forms, from talers to pesos to commodity money, which would have made trade more complex. Modern money, on the other hand, takes one form, so trade is simple. The advantage of Colonial money is that commodity dollars had intrinsic value. If nothing else, it could be eaten or otherwise used.

---

networks Online Teaching Options

BIOGRAPHY

Thomas J. Curry

Discussing the Comptroller of the Office of the Currency Ask a student to read the biography of Thomas J. Curry aloud. **Ask:**

- **What does the OCC do?** *(The Office of the Currency, or OCC, regulates the National Banking System, ensures the viability of the banks in the OCC, and makes certain there is enough currency so the economy can function smoothly.)*
- **What is the National Banking System?** *(A federal agency that oversees about two-thirds of all commercial banks and savings associations in the United States, as well as foreign banks operating in this country.)*
- **What is Thomas Curry's background and experience?** *(He has a degree in law, served as Commissioner of Banks for Massachusetts, and as Director of the FDIC.)* **Verbal/Linguistic**

The fact that our money supply works so well contributes to the success of the American economy. Our money supply continues to evolve under the supervision of the Fed.

Components of Modern Money

Today, the money supply has several different components. Some are in the form of Federal Reserve notes, and some in the form of metallic coins issued by the United States Mint. Other components include **demand deposit accounts (DDAs)**, or funds deposited in a bank that can be accessed by writing a check or using a debit card.

The Fed has two measures of our money supply. **M1** is the narrow definition that includes coins and currency, traveler's checks, DDAs, and checking accounts held at depository institutions. These forms of money all function as a medium of exchange. **M2** is a broader measure that includes M1 along with forms of money that serve as a store of value, components including savings deposits, time deposits, and money market funds.

Think of how these different components made our money supply more useful to us! For example, coins have always been useful, but paper currency was an improvement over coins, because paper currency could be produced in higher denominations and was much more portable. Checking accounts were an improvement over coins and paper currency because checks can be written in any amount and can be easily mailed, making it easier to transfer money. In addition, a cancelled check serves as a receipt for the transaction. Also, a lost check can be cancelled by a bank, unlike missing coins or bills that might never be seen again.

Funds transferred electronically—for example, when a company pays its employees by transferring funds directly into their bank accounts—are faster, simpler, less expensive, and usually more convenient than checks. These changes are likely to continue in unpredictable ways, making money safer and more useful.

✓ **READING PROGRESS CHECK**

Explaining How does modern money reflect the functions and characteristics of money?

medium of exchange money or other substance generally accepted as payment for goods and services; one of the three functions of money

measure of value one of the three functions of money that allows it to serve as a common denominator to measure value

store of value one of the three functions of money allowing people to preserve value for future use

demand deposit accounts (DDAs) account whose funds can be removed from a bank or other financial institution by writing a check or using a debit card

M1 narrow definition of money supply conforming to money's role as medium of exchange; components include coins, currency, checks, other demand deposits, traveler's checks

M2 broad definition of money supply conforming to money's role as a medium exchange and a store of value; components include M1 plus savings deposits, time deposits, and money market funds

CHAPTER 10, LESSON 1
The Evolution, Functions, and Characteristics of Money

W Writing Skills

Writing about money Have each student write a paragraph explaining the different types of money, such as traveler's checks, DDAs, checks, and currency, and the definitions the federal government uses for the money supply. **Verbal/Linguistic**

CLOSE & REFLECT

W Writing Skills

Summarizing the lesson Ask students to review the chapter and to write an outline of its content. They can use the headings to organize their outlines and add important details under each.

LESSON 1 REVIEW

Reviewing Vocabulary

1. *Explaining* How can commodity money provide a measure of value?

Using Your Notes
Use the graphic organizer for this question.

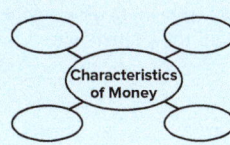

2. *Examining* Why is it important for money to be divisible?

Answering the Guiding Questions

3. *Explaining* Why did money replace the barter system?

4. *Describing* What are the qualifications for something to be used as money?

Writing About Economics

5. *Informative/Explanatory* Often, the U.S. Treasury evaluates the usefulness of the penny and considers whether to discontinue it. On the basis of your understanding of the function of money, why do you think it was created in the first place? Does it still have a purpose in the modern economy? Explain your answers.

connected.mcgraw-hill.com   Money and Banking   **281**

LESSON 1 REVIEW ANSWERS

Reviewing Vocabulary

1. Commodity money provides a measure to value other goods or services. One service might be worth one pound of tobacco, while another service might be worth more or less.

Using Your Notes

2. It's necessary to be able to divide money so that it can be used to purchase items of lesser value as well as those of greater value.

Answering the Guiding Questions

3. Life is simpler with money because it is easier to buy and sell, so you can get what you need and sell your own goods and services.

4. To serve as money, it must be easily portable, durable, divisible, and in limited supply.

Writing About Economics

5. Students should recognize that the penny was first created in order to satisfy the need of people to divide money in order to purchase items of lesser value. Students my disagree about its current purpose because very little can now be purchased with a penny.

ANSWERS, p. 281

✓ **READING PROGRESS CHECK** It is portable, durable, divisible, and in limited supply. It functions as a medium of exchange, a measure of value, and a way to store value.

CHAPTER 10, LESSON 2
The Development of Modern Banking

ENGAGE

C Critical Thinking Skills

Discussing bank regulation Before students begin the lesson, ask them to recall what they know about the financial crisis during the Great Recession of 2008–2009. Explain that the economic problems of this period were in part due to lack of necessary regulations of the banking industry. Point out that earlier in our history, banks were almost completely unregulated. Ask students to speculate on how unregulated banking can cause turmoil in the economy. **Verbal/Linguistic**

TEACH & ASSESS

R Reading Skills

Skimming for information Ask: What happened to Continental dollars by the end of the Revolutionary War? *(They had become worthless.)* **Verbal/Linguistic**

ANSWERS, p. 282

ESSENTIAL QUESTION ACTIVITY

Statement b is true about our banking system.

TAKING NOTES: Sample answers: Event 1—Continental currency worthless; Event 2—State currencies not uniform, overprinted, counterfeited; Event 3—Greenbacks printed

---

Interact with these digital assets and others in lesson 2

✓ INTERACTIVE GRAPH
  State and National Banks
✓ INTERACTIVE IMAGE
  Run on the Bank
✓ SELF-CHECK QUIZ
✓ VIDEO

networks
TRY IT YOURSELF ONLINE

Reading Help Desk

Academic Vocabulary
- clauses
- initially

Content Vocabulary
- state bank
- legal tender
- national bank
- national currency
- Gold Certificates
- Silver Certificates
- gold standard
- central bank
- bank run
- bank holiday
- Federal Deposit Insurance Corporation (FDIC)

TAKING NOTES:

Key Ideas and Details
ACTIVITY Use the graphic organizer below to identify the key developments that led to the modern banking system. Add and fill in boxes as needed.

Development of the National Banking System

LESSON 2
The Development of Modern Banking

ESSENTIAL QUESTION

How did the creation of the Fed improve our banking system?

Understanding the evolution of our banking system is important because it helps us understand the features of modern banking. Today we have a managed money supply that is accepted by everyone simply because people have faith in it. Which of the following is true about our banking system today?

a. Most of our money circulates as coins and paper currency.
b. Today's money is not backed by gold or silver.
c. Our banking system is shifting away from electronic bookkeeping.

Early Banking in America

GUIDING QUESTION Why was the national banking system developed?

Banking practices in the United States have seen many changes. At one time, banking was virtually unregulated. This led to abuses, and even affected the type of money we use.

Privately Issued Bank Notes

During the Revolutionary War, nearly 250 million Continental dollars were printed. But by the end of the Revolution, Continental currency had become worthless, and people did not trust the government to issue anything except coins. Accordingly, Article 1, Section 8, of the United States Constitution states:

PRIMARY SOURCE

The Congress shall have power . . .

To coin money, regulate the value thereof, and of foreign coin, and fix the standard of weights and measures;

---

networks Online Teaching Options

BELLRINGER

The Development of Modern Banking

Discussing the gold standard Display the Bellringer and read the questions aloud to students. Discuss students' responses. Guide a discussion of how abandoning the gold standard would stimulate economic growth. Encourage all answers, and urge students to keep these ideas in mind as they read the lesson. **Verbal/Linguistic**

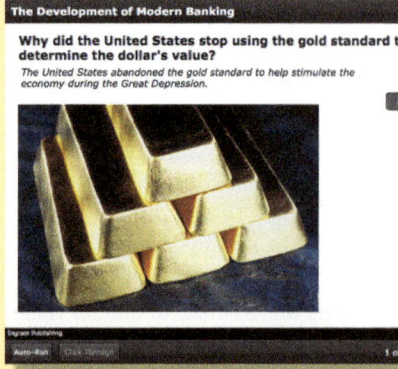

To provide for the punishment of counterfeiting the securities and current coin of the United States; . . .

To make all laws which shall be necessary and proper for carrying into execution the foregoing powers, and all other powers vested by this Constitution in the government of the United States, or in any department or officer thereof.

Article 1, Section 10, further states:

No State shall . . . coin money; emit bills of credit; make any thing but gold and silver coin a tender in payment of debts. . . .

Because of these **clauses**, the federal government did not print paper currency until the Civil War. Instead, the printing, distribution, and regulation of the paper money supply were left to the discretion of privately owned banks and other companies that wanted to build canals, railroads, and other ventures.

Growth of State Banks

The new Constitution left the printing of paper currency to individual states. By 1811 the country had about 100 state banks. A **state bank** receives its operating charter from a state government.

Banks issued their own currency by printing their notes at local printing shops. The banks then put these notes in circulation with the assurance that people could exchange them for gold or silver if they ever lost faith in the bank or its currency.

At first, most banks printed only the amount of currency they could reasonably back with their gold and silver reserves. Others, however, were not as honest and printed large amounts of paper currency in remote areas to make it difficult for people to redeem their currency.

clauses a stipulation, usually in a legal document

state bank a bank that receives its charter from the state in which it operates

Problems with Currency

Even when banks were honest, problems with their currency arose. First, each bank issued its own currency in different sizes, colors, and denominations. As a result, hundreds of different kinds of notes could be in circulation in any given city.

Second, banks were tempted to issue too many notes because they could print more money whenever they wanted. Third, counterfeiting became a major problem. With so many different types of notes in circulation, some counterfeiters did not even bother to copy notes issued by existing banks. Instead, they just made up fictitious ones.

By the beginning of the Civil War, more than 1,600 banks were issuing more than 10,000 different kinds of paper currency. Each bank was supposed to have backing for its notes in the form of gold or silver, but this was seldom the case. As a result, when people tried to use their notes, merchants would often check the latest listing of good and bad currencies before deciding whether to accept them.

Politically powerful local bankers resisted any calls for a better system until an event that would forever change commercial banking in the United States—the Civil War.

Greenbacks

To fight the Civil War, both the Union and the Confederacy needed to raise enormous sums. Congress tried to borrow money by selling bonds, but failed to raise as much money as the Union war effort required. So Congress decided to print paper currency for the first time.

CHAPTER 10, LESSON 2
The Development of Modern Banking

V Visual Skills

Designing currency Have students redesign forms of U.S. currency. Ask students to brainstorm a list of national leaders, prestigious citizens, or well-known places that they think should be honored on currency. You might suggest that they research foreign currencies for design ideas. Post students' designs in the classroom. **AL** Visual/Spatial, Kinesthetic

R Reading Skills

Identifying causes of banking changes Ask: What major event in U.S. history changed commercial banking forever? *(the Civil War)* Verbal/Linguistic

Content Background Knowledge

National Banks Explain to students that national banks are private banks that are members of the Federal Reserve System. As such, they participate in the auctioning of U.S. Treasury bonds and in transactions with the Fed. They must also be members of the Federal Deposit Insurance Corporation (FDIC). Emphasize that although a national bank is similar to the central banks that operate in some countries, a U.S. national bank is not owned by the government. It operates as an independent business within the bounds of federal regulations.

ESSENTIAL QUESTION

Exploring the Essential Question

Activating prior knowledge Read each of the statements and call on a student to provide the "yes" or "no" answer. Ask the class if they agree. Encourage students to explain their answers. Record the total number of "yes" and "no" answers on the board for each statement and save the responses to review later in the lesson. Verbal/Linguistic

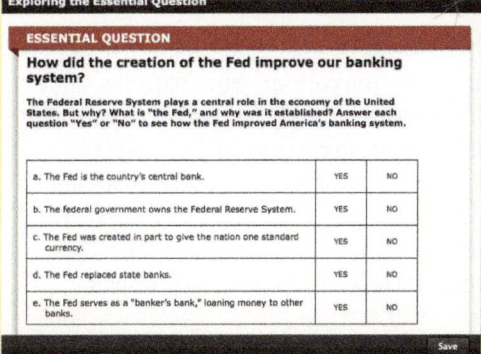

CHAPTER 10, LESSON 2
The Development of Modern Banking

R1 Reading Skills

Defining *legal tender* To help students understand the term *legal tender*, tell them that there are several different meanings for the word *tender*. In the case of money, it means "the thing offered." Money is the thing offered in payment of a debt, and because it is "legal" it must be accepted as payment. Ask students to write a sentence using the term *legal tender*. Then have student pairs check the accuracy of each other's sentences. **ELL** Verbal/Linguistic

R2 Reading Skills

Identifying events in the banking system Ask: **What steps did the National Bank take to create a new banking system and establish its currency?** *(issued its own notes called national currency; implemented bank inspections; set high standards for the industry; placed a 10 percent tax on privately owned bank notes)* Verbal/Linguistic

---

ANSWERS, p. 284

CRITICAL THINKING The gold standard limited the amount of currency in circulation to a specific amount of gold. Because the paper currency was relatively scarce, it kept its value.

---

legal tender currency that must be accepted for payment by decree of government

national bank a commercial bank chartered by the National Banking System

national currency currency backed by government bonds and issued by commercial banks in the National Banking System

initially originally; at the beginning

In 1861 it authorized the printing of $60 million in new currency that had no gold or silver backing. Congress simply declared that the notes were **legal tender**—and must be accepted as payment. These new notes were soon dubbed "greenbacks" because of the green ink on the reverse side, which made them easy to distinguish from state notes, which were usually blank on the back.

The National Banking System

As the war dragged on, people feared that the greenbacks—like the Continental dollars used almost a century earlier to finance the Revolutionary War—might become worthless. When the greenbacks did lose some of their value, people avoided using them, forcing Congress to find another way to pay for the war.

In 1863, Congress enacted the National Currency Act, which created a National Banking System (NBS) made up of national banks. A **national bank** is a privately owned bank that receives its operating charter from the federal government. These banks issued their own notes, called **national currency**, or national bank notes, backed with bonds that the banks bought from the federal government. The government hoped that rigorous bank inspections and other high standards would give people confidence in the new banking system and its currency. The new system also would help the Union cause because banks that joined the NBS had to buy Union bonds.

Initially, only a few state-chartered banks joined the system, because it was easier for them to print their money at local printers. Finally, in 1865, the federal government forced state banks to become part of the National Banking System by placing a 10 percent tax on all privately issued bank notes. Because state-chartered banks could not afford the tax, they withdrew their notes, leaving only the greenbacks and currency issued by the NBS in circulation.

Thus, the need to finance the Civil War changed paper money from issues by state banks to issues backed by the federal government.

Other Federal Currencies

The 10 percent tax greatly simplified the money supply as state banks withdrew more than 10,000 different sizes and denominations. Before long, though, new types of federal currency appeared.

The shift from valuing currency based on a gold standard allowed federal currency to adjust to the needs of the economy more quickly.

▶ **CRITICAL THINKING**
How did the use of a gold standard keep the money supply tight?

---

networks Online Teaching Options

POLITICAL CARTOON

Federal Reserve Note

Analyzing the cartoon Have students study the political cartoon and interpret its meaning. Ask students to compare and contrast the characteristics of Federal Reserve Notes (fiat money) with gold certificates (representative money). Students should include the mention of fractional reserves in their comparisons.

In the same year, the NBS was created, the government issued **Gold Certificates**—paper currency backed by gold placed on deposit with the United States Treasury. At first, these certificates were printed in large denominations for use exclusively by banks, but by 1882, they were also available in smaller denominations to the general public.

In 1878, the government introduced **Silver Certificates**—paper currency backed by silver placed on reserve with the Treasury. This increased demand for silver, pleasing silver miners. The government was already circulating silver dollar coins, but they were too big to be convenient and the public was happy to have an alternative.

Gold Certificates paper currency backed by gold; issued in 1863 and popular until recalled in 1934

Silver Certificates paper currency backed by, and redeemable for, silver from 1878 to 1968

✓ **READING PROGRESS CHECK**

Explaining Why did the government issue greenbacks in the year 1861?

The Gold Standard

GUIDING QUESTION *What does it take for a country to be on a gold standard?*

Gold coins had been a small part of the country's money supply ever since the colonial period. The California gold rush in the late 1840s greatly increased the amount of gold coins in circulation, and by the end of the Civil War, gold coins seemed to be everywhere.

However, the country did not go on a **gold standard**—when the basic unit of currency is equivalent to, and can be exchanged for, a specific amount of gold—until Congress passed the Gold Standard Act in 1900.

gold standard a system in which the basic unit of currency is equivalent to, and can be exchanged for, a specific amount of gold

Going on the Gold Standard

The Gold Standard Act of 1900 defined a dollar as equivalent to 1/20.67 of an ounce of gold. People continued to use greenbacks, Gold Certificates, Silver Certificates, National Bank Notes, and other federal currencies that specified the number of dollars they represented. But now they could exchange these notes for gold at the Treasury whenever they wanted.

Because people liked the convenience of paper currency and usually did not demand gold, the government could hold much less gold than the currency represented. This is generally true when countries go on a gold standard.

Advantages of a Gold Standard

A gold standard has two major advantages. First, people may feel more secure about their currency. Second, the standard is supposed to prevent the government from creating too much money, because gold is a limited resource. And if paper currency is relatively scarce, it should keep its value.

Since it is rare that all of a country's paper notes would be redeemed at the same time, the United States never held a gold reserve equal to the value of its notes.

The bank runs of the Great Depression were both the *result* of panic—depositors fearing they would lose their savings—and a *cause* of panic. Runs led to failures, reinforcing fears. Government officials knew they had to do something. Account holders, worried that their bank might fail, rushed to withdraw money. Ironically, it was the runs themselves that caused many banks to fail. The first bank runs of the Great Depression occurred in 1930.

▲ **CRITICAL THINKING**
How did the government respond to bank runs during the Great Depression?

CHAPTER 10, LESSON 2
The Development of Modern Banking

V Visual Skills

Comparing and contrasting gold and silver certificates Have students use a graphic organizer to list the differences between gold certificates and silver certificates. *(Gold certificates were issued in 1863, backed by gold, placed on deposit with the U.S. Treasury, and printed in large denominations used by banks and small denominations used by the general public. Silver certificates were issued in 1878, backed by silver, placed on reserve with the Treasury, and used by the public.)* **ELL** Visual/Spatial

C Critical Thinking Skills

Understanding the gold standard Point out that as a result of the Gold Standard Act of 1900, people could exchange their greenbacks and other paper currency for gold if they chose. **Ask: Why didn't people prefer gold?** *(Sample answer: Gold is heavy and more difficult to carry around than paper money.)* **Why was it important to people that they had the right to exchange their paper currency for gold?** *(Gold had a fixed value, whereas paper money was only valuable because it was backed by gold, or by the decree of the government.)* Logical/Mathematical

---

IMAGES

Run on the Bank!

Understanding a bank panic Ask students to view the photograph and read the captions. **Ask: Why were people in such a panic to withdraw their money?** *(They were afraid the banks would close and they would lose all their savings.)* **Would such a bank run occur today? Why or why not?** *(Most students would say such a run would be unlikely today because funds deposited with banks are insured by the federal government.)* Visual/Spatial

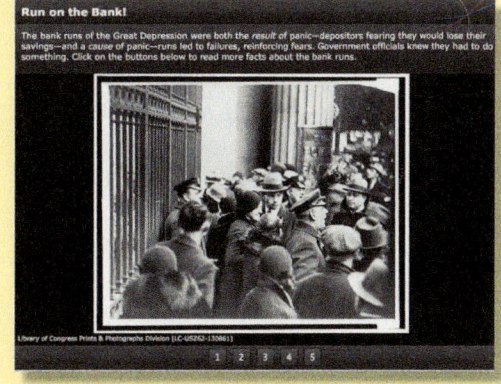

ANSWERS, p. 285

✓ **READING PROGRESS CHECK** To raise money for the Civil War

CRITICAL THINKING President Roosevelt declared a bank holiday in 1933, and Congress passed legislation to strengthen the banking industry. The Banking Act of 1933 created the Federal Deposit Insurance Corporation (FDIC) to insure depositors' savings.

CHAPTER 10, LESSON 2
The Development of Modern Banking

C Critical Thinking Skills

Evaluating advantages and disadvantages of the gold standard Ask: Do you think the advantages or the disadvantages of the gold standard are more important? Explain. *(Some students may say the advantages are more important because having paper currency backed by gold would give people more confidence in their financial system, plus people may prefer to know that the government cannot just print money when it wants. Others may say the disadvantages are more important because a limited supply of money could be disastrous for a growth economy.)*

Making Connections

Current Advocates of the Gold Standard Tell students that even today, there are many people who advocate a gold standard. Guide students in speculating on reasons that people might have for preferring a gold standard today given our current economic circumstances. Discuss and evaluate these ideas as a class. You might encourage interested students to do research and identify additional reasons cited by present-day advocates. Have them share their findings with the class.
Logical/Mathematical

English Language Proficiency

Advanced High Pair students and have pairs listen to the video Small Business Frustrated by Banks. Tell students to pause the recording after particularly complex language, and discuss the point that was just made. Students should verify that they both understand the information before moving forward in the recording.

ANSWERS, p. 286

☑ **READING PROGRESS CHECK** Advantages: People feel more secure, and the government is prevented from creating too much money. Disadvantages: Because money must be backed by gold, a limited supply of gold can slow the growth of the economy. Also, if many people decide to convert currency to gold at the same time, the government can be drained of gold reserves.

286

Disadvantages of a Gold Standard
A growing economy needs its money supply to grow as well, and so, under a gold standard, increasing its stocks of gold. If gold is scarce, the growth of the money supply may slow, and perhaps stop, limiting economic growth. That is one major disadvantage of the gold standard.

Another risk is that a large number of people may decide to convert their currency at the same time, and drain the gold reserves.

Abandoning the Gold Standard
During the Depression years, many banks failed, and almost one person in four did not have a job. In such uncertain times, people began redeeming their paper currency for gold. Foreign governments with large dollar holdings did the same, and the gold stock held by the U.S. government rapidly shrank.

In 1933, President Roosevelt issued a series of orders that effectively denied the gold standard to the American people. Executive orders required all citizens to surrender their gold coins to the Federal Reserve System at the rate of one ounce of gold for $20.67 of Federal Reserve Notes. The next step was to raise the price of gold from $20.67 to $35 an ounce. By 1935, U.S. citizens could no longer redeem dollars for gold, but foreign governments were allowed to do so at the higher $35/oz. price.

After World War II, some European countries wanted to build their gold stocks, so they started to redeem their dollar holdings for gold, again severely draining U.S. reserves. The official price of $35/oz. lasted until August 15, 1971, when President Nixon took the final step and declared that the United States would no longer redeem any dollars for gold. Ever since, the price of gold has fluctuated with changes in supply and demand.

☑ **READING PROGRESS CHECK**

Describing What are the advantages and disadvantages of the gold standard?

Creation of the Fed

GUIDING QUESTION *How did the Fed strengthen the National Banking System?*

The national banking system also needed to evolve during the gold-standard years. Despite a huge number of banks, the system was having difficulty circulating enough currency for the growing nation. Checking accounts were becoming popular, but many banks had trouble adapting to the challenge. And even minor recessions were causing them major problems.

The Federal Reserve System
Reform came in 1913 when Congress created the Federal Reserve System, now often called the "Fed," as the nation's central bank. A **central bank** is a banker's bank, which can lend to other banks in times of need.

The Fed was set up in some ways like a corporation. Any bank that joined had to purchase shares of stock in the system. All national banks were required to do so, and state-chartered banks were eligible to buy shares as well. As shareholders—or part-owners—banks own the Federal Reserve System, not the federal government.

The Fed's own currency, called Federal Reserve Notes, eventually replaced all other types of federal currency. Because the Fed had the resources to lend to other banks during periods of difficulty, it became the nation's first true central bank.

central bank a bank that can lend to other banks in times of need, or a "bankers' bank"

---

networks Online Teaching Options

VIDEO | WORKSHEET

Small Business Frustrated by Banks

Understanding one role of banks Have students view the video to learn about the role of banks and other financial institutions in the economy of the United States. In particular, students will learn about the frustrations of small businesses who operate using credit. Discuss the point of view of the entrepreneur and the bank's representative. Then have students complete the worksheet.
Visual/Spatial

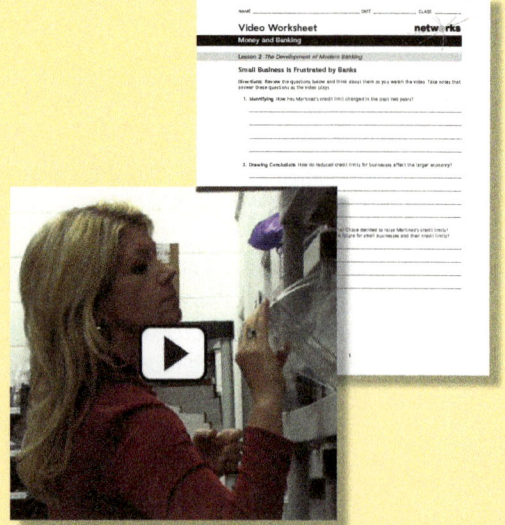

EXPLORING THE ESSENTIAL QUESTION

The establishment of the Fed aimed to solve several problems in the nation's banking system. Match the problems listed on the top with the solutions offered by the Fed listed on the bottom.

Problems:
a. There were many national banks and no centralized system for keeping them strong.
b. Banks were vulnerable to failure because of lack of reserves.
c. The nation was operating with several different forms of national currency.

Solutions:
a. The Fed had the ability to loan money to banks that were in trouble.
b. Federal Reserve notes replaced all other types of federal currency.
c. The Fed served as a central bank, which strengthened the nation's banking system.

Banking in the Great Depression

Despite the creation of the Fed, many banks were only marginally sound during the 1920s. One reason was that the number of banks had soared between the Civil War and 1921, when the total exceeded 31,000. Although some consolidation occurred over the next decade, there were still too many small struggling banks at the start of the Great Depression in 1929.

As **Figure 10.1** shows, a staggering number of bank failures occurred. By 1934 more than 10,000 banks had closed or merged with stronger banks. If account holders became worried about their bank, they would rush to withdraw money before it failed—creating a **bank run**. These runs caused many banks to fail.

On March 5, 1933, President Roosevelt announced a **bank holiday**—a brief period during which every bank in the country was required to close. Several days later, after Congress passed legislation to strengthen the banking industry, most banks were allowed to reopen.

Federal Deposit Insurance

When banks failed during the Great Depression, depositors lost most or even all their savings because deposits were not insured. The Banking Act of 1933 corrected this by creating the **Federal Deposit Insurance Corporation (FDIC)** to insure customer deposits in case of a bank failure. At first, the FDIC insured customer deposits to a maximum of $2,500 but today the limit is $250,000 per customer per bank. If an account holds more than this amount, the depositor may go to court and sue the bank owners to recover the rest.

After the FDIC was created, people worried less about the safety of their deposits, which reduced the number of bank runs. If a bank was in danger of collapse, the FDIC could do one of the following:

1. Seize the bank,
2. Sell it to a stronger one, or
3. Liquidate it and pay off the depositors.

If the bank was sold, the sale was done in secrecy to prevent panic and to keep shareholders from selling worthless stock to unsuspecting investors.

bank run sudden rush by depositors to withdraw all deposited funds, generally in anticipation of bank failure or closure

bank holiday brief period during which all banks or depository institutions are closed to prevent bank runs

Federal Deposit Insurance Corporation (FDIC) The United States government institution that provides deposit insurance on the depositor's account

---

CHAPTER 10, LESSON 2
The Development of Modern Banking

R Reading Skills

Analyzing banking problems and Fed solutions
Have students create a problems-solutions diagram in their notes. Ask them to identify at least three problems with the nation's banking system that were addressed by the creation of the Fed, and what the Fed's solutions were.

C1 Critical Thinking Skills

Making predictions Before students read this section, **Ask:** How do you think the Great Depression impacted banking? *(Students will likely predict that the Depression devastated the banking industry.)* Have students continue reading to check the accuracy of their predictions. **Logical/Mathematical**

C2 Critical Thinking Skills

Analyzing Depression-era songs for propaganda
Have students listen to songs from the Great Depression that touch upon the poverty and misery of the era. Examples include "Brother, Can You Spare a Dime?" (performed by Bing Crosby), "I Ain't Got No Home" (by Woody Guthrie), and "Eleven Cent Cotton, Forty Cent Meat" (by Bob Miller). Discuss the subject matter in the songs, especially whom the singers seem to blame for their poor conditions. Have each student write a paragraph analyzing and evaluating the validity of economic information in the songs for propaganda. **Auditory/Musical**

GRAPHS

State and National Banks

Reading a graph Have students view the State and National Banks graph and ask a student to read the text. **Ask:**

- **When did the number of banks begin to grow most rapidly?** *(about 1880)*
- **When did the greatest number of banks exist?** *(about 1920)*
- **How many banks were there in 1920 altogether?** *(about 31,000)*
- **What kinds of banks have always been most common?** *(state charter banks)*
- **What has been the trend in the number of banks in recent decades?** *(downward)*
- **When was the last time the U.S. had so few banks?** *(about the 1880s)* **Visual/Spatial**

Figure 10.1 State and National Banks
The number of banks in the United States grew rapidly after 1880 and peaked in 1921. A period of mergers and consolidations took place from 1921 to 1929, after which the Great Depression took its toll. The number of banks remained relatively constant from 1933 to 1985, when another wave of mergers took place.

ANSWERS, p. 287

EXPLORING THE ESSENTIAL QUESTION

Problem a: solution c; Problem b: solution a; Problem c: solution b.

CHAPTER 10, LESSON 2
The Development of Modern Banking

V Visual Skills

Finding the main idea Review with students the line graph that shows the growth of state and national banks in U.S. history. **Ask: What statement relates the main idea of the graph?** *(Possible answer: The number of state and national banks has decreased since 1921.)* Verbal/Linguistic

CLOSE & REFLECT

R Reading Skills

Summarizing the lesson Ask students to review the lesson and write questions based on the text. In class discussion, call on students to ask their questions. Call on other students to give the answers and to locate details from the lesson.

ANSWERS, p. 288

CRITICAL THINKING Answers will vary, but students should understand that dramatic advancements in computer hardware and software capabilities have transformed banking—an information- and number-intensive industry. Enhanced information processing has made individual units (branches and companies) able to handle more of the overall demand, thus enabling fewer companies to handle that demand, thus enabling merged companies to operate effectively.

✓ **READING PROGRESS CHECK** To insure customer deposits in case of bank failure

---

FIGURE 10.1
STATE AND NATIONAL BANKS

The number of banks in the United States grew rapidly after 1880 and peaked in 1921. A period of mergers and consolidations took place from 1921 to 1929, after which the Great Depression took its toll. The number of banks remained relatively constant from 1933 to 1985, when another wave of mergers took place.

▶ **CRITICAL THINKING**
Economic Analysis How do you think technology played a role in bank mergers after 1985?

State and National Banks
- State Charter
- National Charter
- All Banks

1921: MORE THAN 31,000 STATE AND FEDERALLY CHARTERED BANKS EXIST IN THE COUNTRY.

1934: FIVE YEARS AFTER THE DEPRESSION BEGINS, APPROXIMATELY 14,100 BANKS REMAIN.

2014: FEWER THAN 6,000 BANKS ARE LEFT AFTER MERGERS THAT BEGAN IN 1985.

Source: FDIC

Federal Reserve Notes
The Federal Reserve Notes that were first introduced in 1914 have become the most visible component of our money supply. All of the other federal currencies—National Bank Notes, Silver Certificates, Gold Certificates, and even the U.S. Notes, or "greenbacks"—have slowly retired and were replaced by Federal Reserve Notes.

During the early gold standard years, every dollar of Federal Reserve Notes was backed by $0.25 gold reserves. As the note issue grew, and as the government was having difficulty in keeping enough gold to back the notes, the 25 percent reserve was reduced and eventually removed.

A Better Monetary System
Today, in part thanks to the Fed, we have a uniform currency and a more efficient payment system, as well as a sound central bank.

One concern is the fact that some banks have become so large that they cannot be allowed to fail, a problem the Fed was not designed to manage.

✓ **READING PROGRESS CHECK**
Describing What is the purpose of the FDIC?

LESSON 2 REVIEW

Reviewing Vocabulary
1. ***Defining*** Explain in your own words the difference between a national bank and a central bank.

Using Your Notes
2. ***Explaining*** Use your notes to explain the chain of events that led to the creation of the Federal Reserve System.

Answering the Guiding Questions
3. ***Explaining*** Why was the National Banking System developed?

4. ***Evaluating*** What must a country do to establish a gold standard?

5. ***Drawing Conclusions*** How did the Fed strengthen the National Banking System?

Writing About Economics
6. ***Informative/Explanatory*** The FDIC was created in large part to restore public confidence in the nation's banking system. Write a paragraph explaining what can happen when the public loses that confidence. Cite examples from the text to support your points.

LESSON 2 REVIEW ANSWERS

Reviewing Vocabulary
1. A national bank is a commercial bank that receives its charter from the federal government. A central bank is a federally backed "banker's bank" that can loan money to banks in need.

Using Your Notes
2. Answers should include the lack of standard currency through the 1800s, the problems with the gold standard, the changing payment methods, and the instability of banks that led to the creation of the Federal Reserve System.

Answering the Guiding Questions
3. The National Banking System was developed to restore the public's confidence in the nation's banking system and to sell bonds to help fund the war.

4. A country needs to have the appearance that currency can be redeemed for gold.

5. The Fed helped restore confidence in the banking system, because it could provide loans to help banks that were in trouble.

Writing About Economics
6. Students should show understanding that the nation's banking system depends on the participation of the public. If people don't feel confident that the national currency will hold its worth, they will avoid using it and the system will break down.

Case Study

MODERN CURRENCY DESIGN

The Federal Reserve Board is responsible for designing the U.S. paper currency. The currency must be easily identifiable and difficult to counterfeit, with security features that are hard to reproduce.

The Fed released the first standardized design in 1929. In 1990, it introduced a special "thread" as well as "microprinting," tiny print hidden in certain areas of the note. Both made it difficult to produce convincing counterfeit currency even with advanced copy machines.

In 1996, all currency notes went through a major redesign for the first time since 1929. Since then, the Fed has released new currency designs on different notes every few years. Each redesign includes new security features aimed at staying ahead of counterfeiters. The latest redesign, issued in October 2013, is a $100 bill. You can view the new currency and its features here: http://www.newmoney.gov

The new $100 includes many older security features such as watermarking, microprinting, and a security thread, but it also introduces some new ones. For example, a new blue vertical ribbon includes 3D images of a bell inside an inkwell. The bell inside the inkwell changes colors from copper to green as the note is tilted.

Counterfeiting is not just an American problem, however. The infographic at the start of this chapter shows how other countries have taken on the challenge of currency security.

CASE STUDY REVIEW

1. **Analyzing Visuals** Using the government Web site URL compare the front of the new $100 bill with the first one issued by the Fed in 1914. Identify the security features that have been added since 1914.
2. **Exploring Issues** Why is it important for the government to prevent counterfeiting? What could happen if a significant amount of counterfeit money got into circulation?

For an interactive version of this case study go to connected.mcgraw-hill.com

---

CHAPTER 10 Case Study

Critical Thinking Skills

Considering the risks of counterfeiting Tell students that counterfeiting can be a serious problem for an economy. Remind them of the problems discussed in the text that occurred during pre-Civil War days. Explain that modern technology plus law enforcement efforts to foil counterfeiting have greatly reduced the problem, but ongoing efforts are needed to keep up with counterfeiters. Point out that counterfeiting is a serious federal criminal offense punishable by a stiff fine and up to 15 years in prison. Ask students why people try to counterfeit currency, even knowing the penalties are high if they get caught. **Interpersonal**

Reading Skills

Answering questions Tell students that for many decades, there were many different sources of legal bills in the U.S., and they all looked different. When the Fed was created, it began to standardize currency, but for many years each branch of the Fed still printed its own bills. **Ask: When did the Fed finally establish one design for all bills?** *(1929)* **Verbal/Linguistic**

Critical Thinking Skills

Defining terms Write these words on the board: thread, microprinting, counterfeiter, watermark, 3D image, inkwell. Guide a discussion of the meaning of each word and ask students to share sentences using the word. **ELL Verbal/Linguistic**

Content Background Knowledge

Counterfeit Coins The Euro zone has a particular problem with counterfeiting, including one that is not rampant in the U.S.: the counterfeiting of coins. Partly this issue arises because euro coins are minted in denominations as high as 2 euros, making it worth the trouble to counterfeit them.

ANSWERS, p. 289

Case Study Review

1. Students should note security features such as watermarks, microprinting, 3D ribbon, and the bell in the inkwell.
2. Students should note that if counterfeit money is in circulation, the value of real currency may decrease. Also, payees might stop accepting currency if they have no way of telling whether it is valid or counterfeit.

---

networks Online Teaching Options

INTERACTIVE FEATURE
Case Study: Modern Currency Design

Analyzing how counterfeiting affects the value of money Display the Case Study and ask a student to read the text. **Ask: How does the presence of counterfeit money affect the economy?** *(Possible answers: It increases the money supply, thereby reducing the value of money. It creates distrust in financial exchanges, so economic activity slows. It makes people question the value of the currency.)* Have students display the security features of the new $100 bill. Discuss how each of these features helps make the bill more difficult to copy. **Ask: Will these security features prevent U.S. currency from being counterfeited? Why?** *(Students may suggest that it will make it much more difficult to produce convincing counterfeit bills. They may suggest, however, that new technologies may help counterfeiters catch up with ways to overcome the newer security measures.)* **Logical/Mathematical**

CHAPTER 10, LESSON 3
Banking Today

ENGAGE

C1 Critical Thinking Skills

 Hypothesizing on sources of bank profits Before students begin the lesson, **ask:** How does a bank get its money? Have students write three or four ways in which they think a bank makes money. Discuss their answers, and then tell them to look for more answers to this question as they read the lesson. **Logical/Mathematical**

TEACH & ASSESS

C2 Critical Thinking Skills

Understanding bank profits Emphasize to students that a bank is, in many ways, just another business. It is financed by stockholders and generally organized like other companies. **Ask: How do shareholders in a bank earn profits?** *(They may receive dividends from the corporation, and the value of their stocks may increase if the bank is successful.)* **AL**

ANSWERS, p. 290

ESSENTIAL QUESTION ACTIVITY

Sample answers: Positive aspects of electronic payments include convenience and efficiency. Negative aspects include the necessity of reviewing your payments online to reconcile your bank account statement.
TAKING NOTES: Checking Accounts/DDAs, Saving Accounts and Time deposits, Debit cards, Electronic Funds Transfer, Credit cards, Smart cards

---

Interact with these digital assets and others in lesson 3
✓ INTERACTIVE IMAGE
  Wall Street Mayhem
✓ INTERACTIVE CHART
  Typical Consumer Fees
  Charged by Banks
✓ SELF-CHECK QUIZ
✓ VIDEO

networks
TRY IT YOURSELF ONLINE

Reading Help Desk

Academic Vocabulary
- products

Content Vocabulary
- credit union
- corporation
- stock
- shareholder
- state-chartered bank
- certificates of deposit/CDs
- reserve requirement

TAKING NOTES:

Key Ideas and Details
ACTIVITY Use the graphic organizer below to identify the customer services most banks offer.

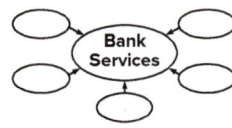

credit union nonprofit service cooperative that accepts deposits, makes loans, and provides other financial services

products things that are sold

corporation form of business organization recognized by law as a separate legal entity with all the rights and responsibilities of an individual, including the right to buy and sell property, enter into legal contracts, sue and be sued

290

LESSON 3
Banking Today

ESSENTIAL QUESTION

How has technology affected the way we use money today?

Your parents pay the household bills electronically. Your grandmother, however, pays her household bills by putting paper checks into the mail. Each method has its positive and negative sides. Make a T-chart with the top of one column entitled "Electronic payments" and the other "Paper checks." List the positive and negative aspects for each type of payment.

C1 A commercial bank is like any other business in that it is in business to make a profit. A bank or depository institution like a **credit union** is similar to many other businesses in that its "**products**," or the things it sells, are all services. A bank is also a bit different in that most of the money it loans has been borrowed from others.

How a Bank Gets Its Money

GUIDING QUESTION *How does a bank become established?*

Although banks are engaged in a number of different activities, the primary one is lending money, which they mainly get as deposits from individual consumers and businesses. To legally accept those deposits, a bank must be established properly.

Issuing Stock

Most banks are established as a **corporation**, for two reasons. First, a corporation can raise funds by selling **stock** to anyone who wants to be a part owner, or **shareholder**, in the bank. Second, a corporation is responsible for **C2** its debt, but none of its shareholders are. This is called "limited liability." If the corporation gets in trouble, its shareholders are protected.

When people decide to start a bank, they hire attorneys to complete and file the legal papers to establish a corporation. Usually the founders reserve some of the initial shares of stock for themselves and sell the remaining shares to others. To set up a **state-chartered bank**, they must follow state laws specifying the minimum amount of financial capital that a founder must contribute.

---

networks *Online Teaching Options*

BELLRINGER

Banking Today

Identifying causes and effects Remind students that the United States experienced a disastrous banking crisis in 2009. Discuss the situation and its ramifications. Help students create a cluster diagram on the board showing how it impacted all parts of the economy. Display the Bellringer and discuss the question. **Verbal/Linguistic**

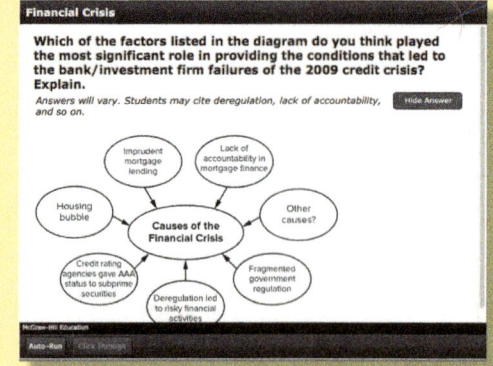

Consumer and Business Deposits

Once a bank is ready to begin operations, it accepts deposits and will pay interest on them. The rate of interest must be very close to rates paid by competing financial institutions, which might be savings and loans, credit unions, or other banks.

Most of its competitors will pay very little, if any, interest on checking deposits, and slightly more on longer-term savings deposits. The new bank might also be offering **certificates of deposit, or CDs**, which despite the name, actually are not deposits. Instead, they are considered loans from a consumer to the bank.

Fractional Reserves Expand Bank Deposits

When a bank receives a new deposit or CD, it must keep some of it as part of the bank's reserves. **Figure 10.2** shows how this process works for a $1,000 deposit, from a new customer called Kim, which is subject to a 20 percent reserve requirement established by the Fed.

As long as the bank keeps 20 percent of the deposit, it is free to lend the remaining $800. Let's say it lends the money to Bill, and Bill puts that money into a checking account for convenience. Bill could use an account at another bank or the lending bank. Either way, the $800 becomes a new deposit subject to a 20 percent **reserve requirement**—leaving $640 that can be loaned to a new customer.

This process of depositing, lending, and then depositing again can continue until the total amount of new loans reaches $5,000. Because the bank charges interest every time it makes a new loan, but must also keep reserves, it can charge interest on $4,000 of loans for every $1,000 deposited. The reserves could be kept in the bank, or at the Fed.

The bank may continue attracting deposits and making loans until it is "loaned out," or unable to make any more loans. If the Fed lowers the reserve requirement to 10 percent, every new loan can be as much as 90 percent of each deposit. On the other hand, if the Fed raises the requirement to 25 percent, the bank will need to find more reserves to back the existing loans.

Finally, the bank will have to report its reserves and its demand deposits to the Fed on a regular basis. Banks are heavily regulated by the Fed, the Comptroller of the Currency, the FDIC, and possibly even some state banking officials. Bankers are not very happy about this, but the regulation has prevented massive failures like those we saw during the Great Depression.

Loans, Investments, and Fees

Loans to consumers and businesses are an important part of a bank's profits. For example, a bank might pay 2 percent on deposits, and lend the balance after reserves at 6 percent for home repairs or mortgages. The difference between these two rates—2 percent and 6 percent—is the "spread," 4 percent. The spread creates profits that the bank may use to pay its employees and other bills.

A bank will also earn money on its investments, which could cover a wide range of activities. If a bank has extra funds that are not loaned out, it could buy U.S bonds, for example.

stock certificate of ownership in a corporation; common or preferred stock

shareholder person who owns a share or shares of stock in a corporation; same as stockholders

state-chartered bank bank that receives its charter from the state in which it operates

certificates of deposit/CDs receipt showing that an investor has made an interest-bearing loan to a financial institution

reserve requirement formula used to compute the amount of a depository institution's required reserves

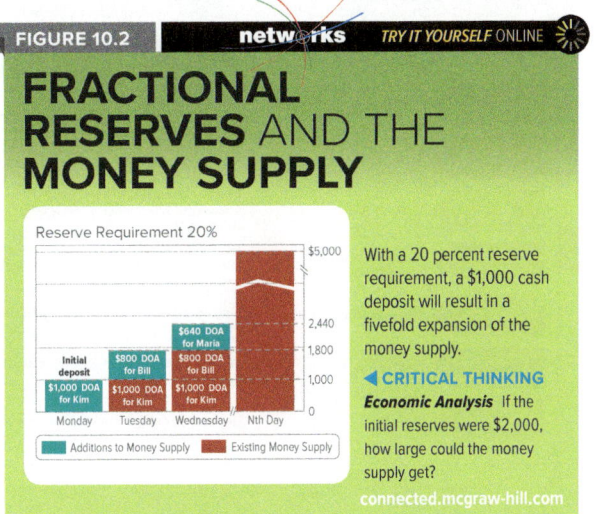

FIGURE 10.2

FRACTIONAL RESERVES AND THE MONEY SUPPLY

With a 20 percent reserve requirement, a $1,000 cash deposit will result in a fivefold expansion of the money supply.

◀ **CRITICAL THINKING**
Economic Analysis If the initial reserves were $2,000, how large could the money supply get?

CHAPTER 10, LESSON 3
Banking Today

R Reading Skills

Analyzing the role of interest in allocating savings
Ask: *What is the difference between a deposit into a savings account and a certificate of deposit?* (A savings deposit is an amount of money a consumer places into a bank savings account in exchange for interest on the amount. The savings can be withdrawn at any time. A CD is a loan made by the consumer to the bank. It cannot be withdrawn for a specific amount of time.) *Why would consumers relinquish their savings to the bank for long periods of time?* (CDs earn higher rates of interest.) **ELL** Verbal/Linguistic

C1 Critical Thinking Skills

Identifying effects of fractional reserve requirements **Ask:** *How can the Federal Reserve use fractional reserve requirements to manage the economy?* (By increasing the reserve, the Fed can reduce the amount of money flowing into the economy, thereby slowing economic growth. By reducing the reserve, the Fed can increase the amount of money flowing into the economy, thereby stimulating economic growth.) Tell students that this is not an ideal tool for managing the economy because of its other effects. For example, changing the reserve requirements impacts the stability of the bank and can directly impact bank profits.
BL Verbal/Linguistic

C2 Critical Thinking Skills

Understanding bank risks Have students consider the risks banks take when allocating savings to its most productive use. **Ask:** *What are some of these risks?* (investing bank profits in subprime financial assets; loaning more than the fractional reserve requirement allows; providing loans that are later defaulted)

GRAPHS

Fractional Reserves and the Money Supply

Analyzing the fractional reserve Display Figure 10.2 and have a student read the text aloud. Walk through the additions to the money supply and discuss the Economic Analysis question. **Ask:** *How does the fractional reserve practice help the economy?* (Students should understand that by putting more money into the market, it provides more resources for consumers and businesses to make purchases and expand business operations, which create economic growth.) Guide a discussion of how increasing the fractional reserve would slow the economy. **Logical/Mathematical**

ANSWERS, p. 291

CRITICAL THINKING
$10,000

CHAPTER 10, LESSON 3
Banking Today

R1 Reading Skills

Discussing bank functions Guide a discussion of students' banking needs. **Ask: What functions of banks do you currently utilize? Does it matter if your bank is near to you? Why?** *(Most students will say it doesn't matter because most banking needs can be met electronically.)* **What are the advantages of paying by electronic or paper check rather than cash?** *(Checks provide evidence that payment has been made and accepted.)* **Verbal/Linguistic**

R2 Reading Skills

Understanding banking fees Call on different students to explain each of the fees typically charged by banks. As a class, discuss whether the fee can be avoided and how. **Verbal/Linguistic**

Finally, the category of fees is also a significant source of bank funds. For example, there may be fees for maintaining an account, application fees when applying for a loan, withdrawal fees for using an automated teller machine (ATM) from another bank, fees for overdrawing your checking account, and fees for bouncing checks. A modest list of typical fees appears in **Figure 10.3**. Fees can be especially difficult for customers who keep minimal balances in their accounts or are late paying bills.

✓ **READING PROGRESS CHECK**

Explaining What are the different ways banks can make money?

Selecting a Bank

GUIDING QUESTION *Why have so many different methods evolved for accessing money?*

Almost everyone will need the services of a bank sometime, so it is never too early to shop around.

Evaluating Your Needs

You begin by thinking about which banking services you need. For example, does your employer pay only by check, or also pay workers electronically, depositing funds directly in a bank? You might consider the second option, especially if a bank you like offers lower fees to customers who receive direct deposit paychecks.

Next, consider the bills you normally pay. Do you actually go to various locations to pay monthly charges for car loans, food, rent, gas, and electric bills—or can these bills be paid by mail or even electronically?

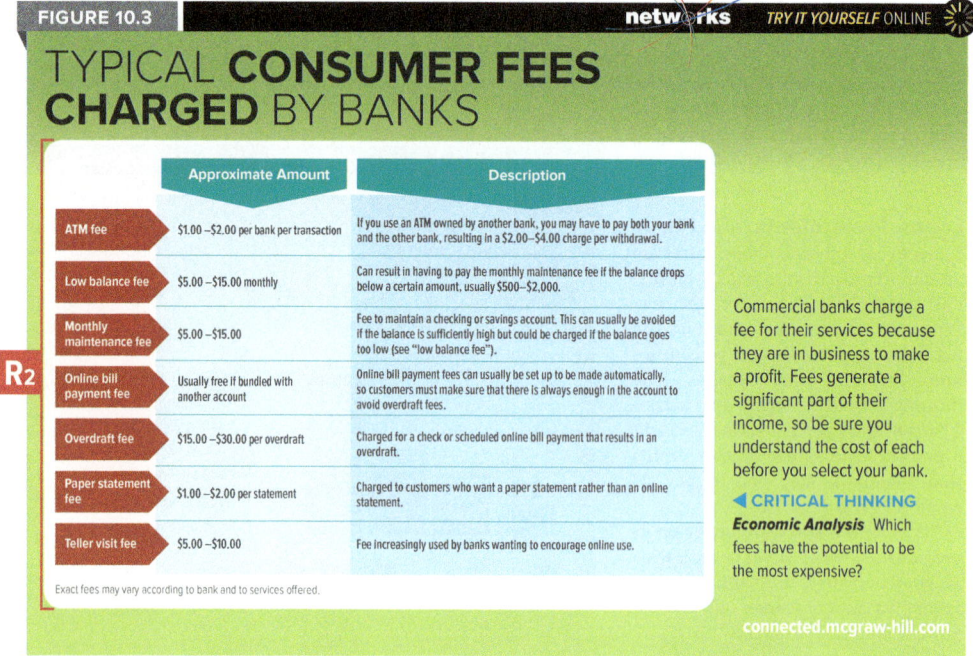

FIGURE 10.3

TYPICAL CONSUMER FEES CHARGED BY BANKS

Commercial banks charge a fee for their services because they are in business to make a profit. Fees generate a significant part of their income, so be sure you understand the cost of each before you select your bank.

◀ **CRITICAL THINKING**
Economic Analysis Which fees have the potential to be the most expensive?

292

---

networks Online Teaching Options

CHARTS

Typical Consumer Fees Charged by Banks

Evaluating the costs of banking Display Figure 10.3 and highlight and discuss each type of fee with students. Then ask students to work individually to estimate the average monthly cost of having a checking or savings account based on their likely needs. Guide students in discussing what they learn about the costs of banking and then about the benefits versus the costs of banking. **Interpersonal**

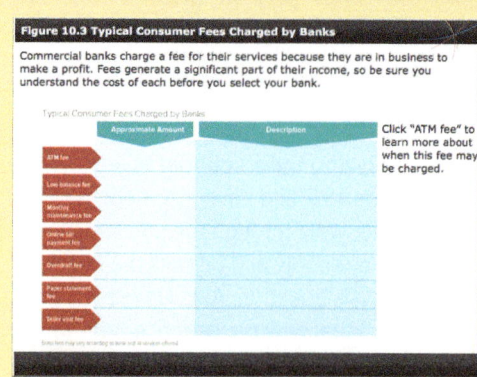

ANSWERS, p. 292

✓ **READING PROGRESS CHECK** Banks can charge fees for checking accounts, for ATM withdrawals, and for bounced checks. They can also make money by charging fees for applying for a loan, by charging withdrawal fees, and for maintaining an account.

CRITICAL THINKING

Student answers will vary depending on the frequency with which they use particular services. The overdraft fee has the potential to be the most expensive because it is assessed per overdraft, while other fees, such as the low balance fee, are assessed on a monthly basis.

If your bills can be paid by mail, then having a regular checking account makes sense. If they can be paid electronically, you might want a bank that will make it easy for you to do so. Cash might work better for you if you pay your bills in person, but remember that cancelled checks and electronic records are excellent evidence that a payment has been made and accepted.

Banking Services

Banks offer a variety of services. You may not need to use all of them immediately, but it's good to know about what you might do later on.

- **Checking accounts or DDAs**—This is one of the most useful services. Checking accounts let you make purchases in any amount up to the limit of your deposit, and let you make a payment by mail. The bank has to honor the withdrawal on demand, or when presented with a check, so they are also known as DDAs for "Demand Deposit Accounts." Because they generate a lot of paper, the banking industry is steadily moving toward electronic banking. Right now, for example, your check may be processed by a cashier and handed right back to you—with the rest of the "paperwork" done electronically. Many banks also prefer to present your monthly summary electronically, rather than put a paper copy in the mail.

- **Savings accounts and Time deposits**—Savings accounts and time or "term" deposits restrict withdrawals. You may be able to make a certain number of withdrawals from a savings account, and fewer on time deposits. In return, a bank will usually pay slightly higher interest rates on money that you can't withdraw at will. If you close your account, you can have your money back, but you will forfeit most of the interest you expected to earn. Opening a savings account will help you get into the habit of saving, and build a credit rating if you want to apply for a credit card. Your best strategy might be to open a savings account and add to it with regular deposits—even if your deposits are small. You may be surprised how small amounts can build up over time and serve you in emergencies.

- **Debit cards**—A debit card looks just like a credit card, but it is electronically tied to your checking account. To make a purchase, you simply swipe the card, which is faster than writing a check. Because the money is transferred immediately from your account to the merchant's account, there is a lot less

CHAPTER 10, LESSON 3
Banking Today

R Reading Skills

Examining risks, costs, and benefits of accounts
Organize students into small groups and assign each group one of the banking services and types of accounts described in the text. Have pairs develop a graphic organizer to visually display the type of account and the risks, monetary costs, and benefits of maintaining the account. Have students share their organizers with the class. **ELL** Visual/Spatial

C Critical Thinking Skills

Categorizing pros and cons of debit and credit
Ask students to explain what they believe are the obligations of borrowing money. Write their responses on the board. Tell students to create a chart with three column headings: Type of Card, Positives, Negatives. In column one, students should list credit cards and debit cards. Then have them provide detailed pros and cons of using each. Finally, ask students to use their charts in a class discussion on ways to avoid credit card debt and ways to eliminate credit card debt.

CAREERS | Financial Clerks

Is this Career for you?

 Do you have strong customer service skills?

 Do you have basic math skills?

 Are you detail oriented?

Profile of Work
Tellers work in bank branches. Approximately 27 percent of tellers work a part-time schedule. They process bank transactions for customers such as cashing checks, collecting loan payments and depositing money.

Salary
$24,100 per year
$11.59 per hour

Job Growth Outlook
No change is expected in job growth, which is at 1 percent. However, job prospects are deemed excellent as many workers leave these jobs.

connected.mcgraw-hill.com   Money and Banking   293

INTERACTIVE FEATURE

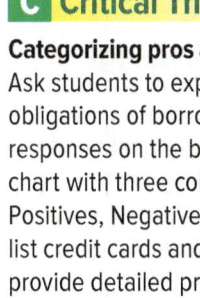

Career: Financial Clerks

Examining a career as a financial clerk Have students read the Financial Clerk feature. **Ask:**

- **What are customer service skills?** *(skills needed to work with the bank's customers to answer questions, solve problems, and provide general support)*

- **Why does a financial clerk need to have good customer service skills?** *(Financial clerks work mostly with the bank's customers; to satisfy the customers, good customer service skills are needed.)*

- **What are the advantages of this career?** *(Possible answers: It allows you to work part-time; job prospects are excellent.)*

- **What are the disadvantages?** *(Possible answers: No change is expected in job growth; typical pay rate is low.)*

Encourage students to discuss whether they think this career is right for them.
Verbal/Linguistic

CHAPTER 10, LESSON 3
Banking Today

C1 Critical Thinking Skills

Understanding credit card company profits Ask: **How do credit card companies earn profits from credit cards?** *(They charge interest on the unpaid balance.)* **What might cause credit card companies to go out of business?** *(if all of their card holders paid their entire balances on time)* **Do you think credit card companies are worried about that occurring? Why or why not?** *(No; American consumers have a long tradition of spending more than they can pay for.)*

Content Background Knowledge

The First Credit Cards The concept of making purchases on credit dates back to ancient times. The credit card, however, is a more recent phenomenon. Diners Club issued the first "plastic money" in 1950. Holders of the Diners Club card could use it to charge meals at 27 restaurants in New York City. In 1958, Bank of America issued the first bank credit card: the BankAmericard (now Visa). The concept gradually gained popularity. By 1965 there were five million credit cards in use. Three decades later, Americans owned nearly 1.4 billion credit cards.

C2 Critical Thinking Skills

Brainstorming ways to save After discussing why it is a good idea to save, divide students into small groups and challenge them to identify some methods they can use to develop the habit of saving. For example, they might prioritize savings by taking a percentage out of every paycheck before accounting for any other expenses. Have groups share their ideas in class. Ask a student to make a master list of the ideas and distribute it to the class.
Interpersonal

ANSWERS, p. 294

EXPLORING THE ESSENTIAL QUESTION

Student answers should include that a high school student could abuse the privilege of having a credit card or debit card and how they can accrue high credit card debt if they choose that option. Students should give reasons why they agree with the older brother or why they do not agree with him.

✓ **READING PROGRESS CHECK** Having a checking account lets you make purchases in any amount up to the limit of your deposit and enables you to make payments through the mail or electronically.

EXPLORING THE ESSENTIAL QUESTION

It is your birthday, and your uncle has given you a new, crisp one-hundred-dollar bill. You decide to open a checking account with the money. You go to the bank with your older brother, a recent college graduate who just started working as a reporter. At the bank, you are given a debit card and the option of a credit card. Your older brother says he thinks you'd be better off without a credit card. In a few paragraphs, explain your older brother's caution by comparing and contrasting the positive and negative aspects of debit cards. Be sure to include in your answer whether you agree or disagree with your brother's advice.

---

paperwork for you, the bank, and the merchant. Merchants like debit cards because the purchase will not go through if there is not enough money in your DDA, and they don't have to deal with bounced checks. However, your risk of losses on a lost or stolen debit card is not limited, as they are with a credit card. A stranger could have access to all of your money! The risk and the cost of fraud lie directly on consumers.

- **Credit cards**—A credit card allows you to borrow money directly from a bank up to a previously determined limit. You are usually allowed to pay the loan back in a 20- to 30-day grace period without having to pay any interest. If you fail to pay the loan off on time, interest can be charged on the borrowed funds at rates often approximating 20–25 percent. Credit cards are one of a bank's most profitable services. Most credit card holders fail to pay the account in full before the end of the grace period. Because the monthly interest rate is so high, a careless consumer can easily end up with the equivalent of a perpetual, or never-ending, loan from the bank on a relatively small balance.

- **Smart card**—A smart card is similar to a credit card in size and appearance, but has a built-in microprocessor instead of a magnetic security strip. The microprocessor has many more safety features and is therefore safer than a credit card. The information on the card includes much more data about you and can be used as an identification card as well as for electronic purchases from a merchant. Smart cards are widely used in Europe and are just beginning to gain acceptance in the United States. Because they require an entirely different type of card reader, the changeover from the magnetic strip technology to embedded microchips will be slower than many people would like.

- **Electronic Funds Transfer (EFT)**—This term generally describes any system that uses computer and electronic technology in place of checks and other paper transactions. Some EFT services include those provided by ATMs that let you bank any time, direct deposits of payrolls by companies, pay-by-phone systems, debit card purchases, electronic check conversions that convert a paper check into an electronic payment at a store, or virtually any other transaction that involves the electronic movement of funds. The term applies to so many different situations that it no longer describes a unique activity.

Banks also offer a number of other services, from providing safety-deposit boxes for storing valuables to helping new corporations issue stock to investors. Whether or not you are a regular consumer, if you are an emerging entrepreneur of a full-fledged business, any one of your local bankers would be more than happy to visit you and help assess your needs. Remember that competition in banking is like competition anywhere else—talk to more than one banker to get the best services at the best price.

✓ **READING PROGRESS CHECK**

Explaining What are some of the benefits of having a checking account?

Rounding Out Your Financial Literacy

GUIDING QUESTION *How do smart banking practices contribute to your own financial literacy?*

There are many components to financial literacy, and a sound knowledge of banking fundamentals is one of them. Developing your own creditworthiness is another important component, as the relationship you have with your commercial bank or other financial institution will be key.

Why You Should Save

Get into the habit of saving, and do it as if your savings will be your only source of retirement income. If you have a Demand Deposit Account (DDA) with a bank, it

294

---

networks Online Teaching Options

VIDEO | WORKSHEET

Credit Cards

Comprehending credit Have students view the video and take notes on the advantages and disadvantages of using credit. Then ask students to complete the accompanying worksheet. **Verbal/Linguistic**

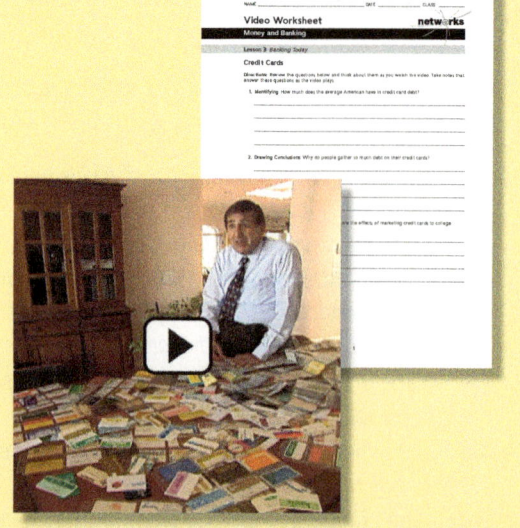

will gladly make arrangements to have a small amount automatically deducted from your checking account and placed in savings where your money will earn a little more interest—and will be a little less convenient to access. Or if your employer can make automatic deposits in a credit union, consider that option as well.

Saving on a regular basis will do more than provide a modest pool of funds for future use. It will also demonstrate that you have the discipline and patience to embark on a career-long path to financial success. No one will expect a young person such as you to have a lot of savings, but a demonstrated track record of discipline and success will open up many other opportunities in life.

Pay Attention to the Details

You already know that banks offer a wide range of "products" or services to their customers. You also know that banks and depository institutions charge fees for almost all of them, which is understandable because banks are in business to make a profit. What you should do, however, is carefully consider which services you need, and which fees you really need to pay.

Banks in the same community often charge different rates for their services, so you should try to learn all you can about these alternatives. Then, decide which are most important to you. Finally, shop around for the best prices.

Only a few of the fees listed in Figure 10.3 are likely to apply to you right now, but over time many of them will. Also, some of them are assessed monthly, but others such as overdraft charges can occur several times a month. Some services, such as on-line bill payments, are often offered at no cost to attract new customers. The bottom line: avoid unnecessary fees.

Making Yourself Creditworthy

Your "creditworthiness" is your financial standing today based on the credit history you created. While you may not have a credit history now, you can begin to build one at a store by purchasing an item on lay-away and keeping up with the payments. Or better yet, you can build a good financial relationship with a bank.

Eventually, your creditworthiness may allow you to have bigger and more expensive things, such as a car, a home, or a comfortable retirement. In the meantime, keeping yourself out of debt will have its own rewards. When people find themselves in trouble with their credit card debt, they run into a constant need to earn enough income to pay for past expenditures.

It is hard to put a price on peace of mind, but nothing in life is free. If you want creditworthiness, do not expect to get it without discipline on your side. But you should feel that the investment has been well worthwhile!

✓ **READING PROGRESS CHECK**

Explaining Why should you make creditworthiness a goal for your future?

LESSON 3 REVIEW

Reviewing Vocabulary

1. *Defining* Explain what a state-chartered bank is.

Using Your Notes

2. *Summarizing* Use your notes to explain the services banks provide.

Answering the Guiding Questions

3. *Explaining* How does a bank become established?

4. *Evaluating* Why have so many different methods evolved for accessing money?

5. *Explaining* How do smart banking practices contribute to your own financial literacy?

Writing About Economics

6. *Informative/Explanatory* Write a short paragraph explaining how you handle money for purchases. Include whether you have a bank account, the type of account, and what technology you use. If you do not have a bank account, explain what you do instead.

CHAPTER 10, LESSON 3
Banking Today

C Critical Thinking Skills

Recognizing consequences of creditworthiness Tell students that good or bad credit has many consequences beyond getting or not getting a credit card. Point out that if they have a poor credit rating, they will pay higher interest rates on loans or may be denied a loan. They also might have difficulty renting an apartment and will pay more for car insurance than someone with a better credit rating. Ask students to research ways to improve one's personal credit score and, as a result, become a low-risk borrower. Have students share their lists in class. **BL** Verbal/Linguistic

CLOSE & REFLECT

W Writing Skills

Summarizing the lesson Have each student write one main idea for each section of the lesson and three or more details that support it.

ANSWERS, p. 295

✓ **READING PROGRESS CHECK** Being creditworthy enables you to eventually buy large items such as a car or a home or to finance a college education.

LESSON 3 REVIEW ANSWERS

Reviewing Vocabulary

1. A state-chartered bank is a bank that, upon forming, receives its charter from the state in which it operates. The laws of the state would be followed in forming the bank.

Using Your Notes

2. Banks provide checking accounts, savings accounts and time deposits, debit cards, credit cards, smart cards, and electronic funds transfers.

Answering the Guiding Questions

3. A bank is usually organized as a corporation. The corporation raises funds by selling stock.

4. Customers need a variety of methods to access money in the electronic age. Many employers, for example, pay workers by electronically depositing their paychecks into workers' checking accounts. Overall, the banking industry is moving toward using less paper, such as paper checks, and doing all customer banking electronically.

5. Smart banking practices help you develop your own creditworthiness. Considering carefully what services you need from banks and which banking fees you really need to pay helps you save.

Writing About Economics

6. Students should describe what type of banking accounts they have and what electronic transactions they perform. If students do not have a bank account, they should describe how they handle their money transactions, such as being paid from their part-time job in cash and paying for everything with cash.

CHAPTER 10
Debate

ENGAGE

C1 Critical Thinking Skills

Expressing initial opinions of the gold standard
Introduce the Debate feature by pointing out that one of the most long-standing debates in economics is over the gold standard. Ask students to share what they already know about the gold standard and what it means for the economy. **Ask: Should the United States go back on the gold standard?** Encourage students to declare their opinions and to offer reasons. Then direct them to study the arguments presented in the Debate.

TEACH & ASSESS

R Reading Skills

Recognizing causes and effects Read the quotation from the "Yes" argument to students. **Ask: What is fiat money?** *(Money that has value only because the government says it does.)* Guide a discussion of how this value can fluctuate depending upon the government and the country.
AL ELL Verbal/Linguistic

C2 Critical Thinking Skills

Evaluating opinions on gold Read the two quotations aloud, and ask students to explain the contradictory views they present. Ask students to weigh the other information they have studied in this Debate and then explain which point of view they think is more accurate and to explain why.
Logical/Mathematical

Debates

C1 Should the gold standard have been abandoned and should it be brought back?

R Though the United States abandoned the last remnant of the gold standard system in 1971, some people argue that we should restore it. Why? The gold standard limits the power of government to print money and cause inflation. It also establishes fixed exchange rates in international trade.

A few nations now control the global gold supply, and a gold standard would give them power to affect economies throughout the world. Also, gold is not endlessly available, and linking the money supply to gold limits how much economies can grow.

The United States flourished under an international gold standard with a fixed-exchange system from the 1940s into the 1960s. By the end of the 1970s, however, the dollar had grown weaker. Other countries had built strong economies, and inflation had made the dollar less popular. When the United States stopped exchanging dollars for gold, the fixed exchange rate system ended.

YES We should return to the gold standard

- A GOLD STANDARD WOULD LOWER INFLATION RATES AND SLOW THE RISE IN CONSUMER PRICES
- A GOLD STANDARD LIMITS THE GOVERNMENT FROM PRINTING FIAT MONEY
- A GOLD STANDARD WOULD RESTRICT THE GOVERNMENT FROM INCREASING THE NATIONAL DEBT
- A GOLD STANDARD WOULD REDUCE THE U.S. TRADE DEFICIT

C2 " *Although the last vestiges of the gold standard disappeared in 1971, its appeal is still strong. Those who oppose giving discretionary powers to the central bank are attracted by the simplicity of its basic rule. Others view it as an effective anchor for the world price level.* "
—The Library of Economics and Liberty

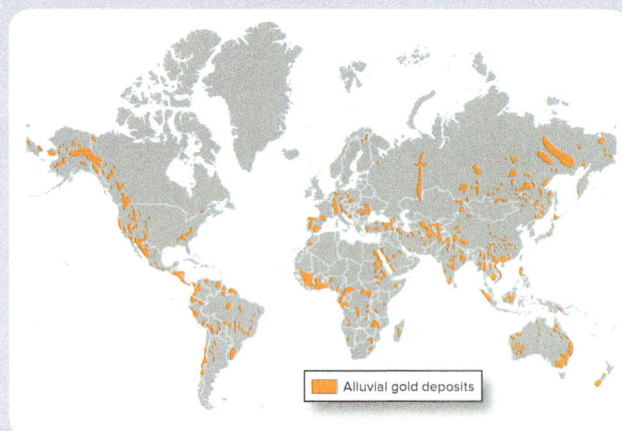
Alluvial gold deposits

---

networks Online Teaching Options

DEBATE

Debate: Should the gold standard have been abandoned and should it be brought back?

Identifying the advantages and disadvantages of gold
Have students read the text. **Ask: What are the advantages of the gold standard?** *(It limits the power of a government to print money, thereby controlling inflation. It creates a fixed exchange rate for international trade.)* **What are the disadvantages of the gold standard?** *(A few countries can control the supply, giving them economic power over other nations. Gold is a limited resource, so tying money to it limits economic growth.)*
AL Logical/Mathematical

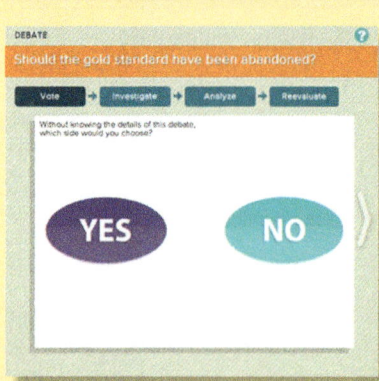

NO
We should not return to the gold standard

networks
TRY IT YOURSELF ONLINE
For an interactive version of this debate go to **connected.mcgraw-hill.com**

- GOLD STANDARDS CAN CAUSE DEFLATION, WHICH DESTABILIZES THE ECONOMY
- A GOLD STANDARD WOULD PREVENT THE FEDERAL RESERVE FROM AIDING THE ECONOMY DURING RECESSIONS
- THE VALUE OF GOLD FLUCTUATES AND THIS WOULD NOT PROVIDE ECONOMIC STABILITY
- THE VALUE OF MONEY IN A GLOBAL WORLD COULD BE CONTROLLED ONLY BY GOLD-PRODUCING COUNTRIES

> As the economy grows, the price level will have to fall. The same amount of gold-backed currency has to support a growing volume of transactions, something it can do only if the prices are lower, unless the supply of new gold by the mining industry magically rises at the same rate as the output of other goods and services. If not, prices go down, and real interest rates become higher.

—Barry Eichengreen, "A Critique of Pure Gold"

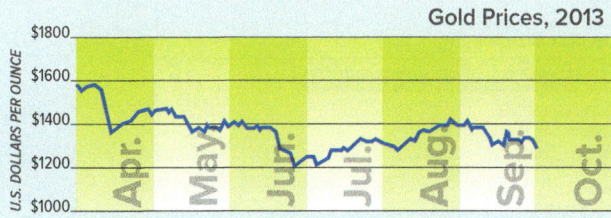
Gold Prices, 2013

ANALYZING the issue

1. **Analyzing Visuals** Look carefully at the world map showing the location of current gold mines in the world. If the world returned to an international gold standard, would the United States be the major source of gold? If not, what areas of the world would be the sources of gold?

2. **Exploring Issues** How do you think the return to the gold standard would affect the countries that have large, active gold mines?

3. **Evaluating** Which arguments do you find most compelling? Explain your answer.

297

CHAPTER 10
Debate

V Visual Skills

Comparing and contrasting arguments on the gold standard Help students see the differing arguments more clearly by drawing a T-chart on the board. At the head of one column, write "Yes," and at the top of the other write "No." Have students identify arguments from the text that are for and against the gold standard. **AL** Visual/Spatial

CLOSE & REFLECT

C Critical Thinking Skills

Re-examining first opinions of the gold standard Ask students to recall their position on the gold standard prior to studying the arguments presented in this feature. Have them write one or two paragraphs telling whether their opinion changed and giving their reasons.

DEBATE

Debate

Using a graph to answer questions Direct students' attention to the graph showing gold prices over time. **Ask: How would the fluctuating price of gold affect the value of the dollar if the U.S. were on the gold standard?** *(The value of the dollar would move when the value of gold increased or decreased.)* **How do changes in the price of gold influence the dollar, since the U.S. does not follow the gold standard?** *(Gold will fluctuate independently of the dollar, just like any other good.)* Invite students to debate how this is good or bad for the economy.
Interpersonal

ANSWERS, p. 297

ANALYZING the issue

1. The United States would not be a major source of gold. Areas of the world that would be sources of gold include Russia, East Asia, and Africa.
2. It would mean that these countries would be the dominant economies in the global economy.
3. Students should state which arguments they agree with and their reasons.

Money and Banking **297**

Chapter 10
Study Guide

W Writing Skills

Identifying characteristics Call students' attention to the portion of the Study Guide listing characteristics of money. Discuss with students the meaning of each characteristic. Then ask students to write a paragraph in which they explain how the money used in the United States meets each of these characteristics.

C Critical Thinking Skills

Analyzing "new" money Call on students to name objects that might be used as money today if there were no dollar bills or coins. List at least 10 responses on the board. Then organize students into small groups and direct each group to apply the characteristics and functions of money to the listed objects. Have groups select the object that would best serve as money based on their analyses.
Verbal/Linguistic

R Reading Skills

Researching U.S. money Assign each student or group a particular time period in U.S. history. Instruct each group to use online resources to research the various types of currency found in the United States during their assigned period. Encourage students to use simple outlines or graphic organizers to record their findings. Direct them to include a fun fact to help them provide context for their time period. For example, in the frontier areas during the colonial period, hunters often left their deerskins at trading posts until they could pick them up at a later date. As proof of ownership, the hunters would obtain a receipt, which they could exchange among themselves or use at the trading post for supplies. The receipts, worth about a dollar because of the value of the hides, were called "bucks"—hence, the common name for the dollar.

298

STUDY GUIDE

LESSON 1

History of Money in American Colonies
- Commodity money—money that has an alternative use as an economic good
- Fiat money—currency made usable by government decree that has no value or use other than as money
- Specie—money in the form of silver or gold coins

Characteristics and Functions of Money
- Characteristics
  - Portable
  - Durable
  - Divisible
  - Limited Supply
- Functions
  - Medium of Exchange
  - Measure of Value
  - Store of Value

Federal Reserve Definitions of Money Supply
- M1—Coins, Currency, Traveler's Checks, DDAs, and Checking Accounts
- M2—All of M1 plus Savings Deposits and Time Deposits

LESSON 2

Types of Money in Colonial America
- Continental dollars—issued by the Continental Congress
- State bank—issued money—in circulation before the Civil War
- Greenbacks—authorized by Congress to pay for Civil War
- Gold Certificates—issued by National banking system, 1863
- Silver Certificates—issued by National banking system, 1878
- Federal Reserve notes—issued by the Federal Reserve, 1913

The Gold Standard
- Established in 1900 with Gold Standard Act
- Abandoned in 1933 for Federal Reserve notes
- Gold standard for Federal Reserve notes phased out in 1970s

LESSON 3

How a Bank Earns Money
- Issuing stock
- Consumer and Business deposits
- Loans, investments, and fees

Bank Services
- Checking accounts or DDAs
- Savings accounts and Time Deposits
- Debit cards
- Credit cards
- Smart cards
- Electronic fund transfers

Financial Literacy
- Save regularly
- Pay attention to financial details
- Establish your credit worthiness

298

---

networks Online Assessment Options

WORKSHEET

Reinforcing Economic Skills: Choosing a Bank

Evaluating a bank Guide a discussion of each of the questions on the worksheet with students. Ensure that they understand the purpose and benefits of each of the services discussed and how they affect households. Tell students to consider their personal banking needs as they weigh their responses to the questions. After students complete their research, have them meet in small groups to compare their results.
Verbal/Linguistic

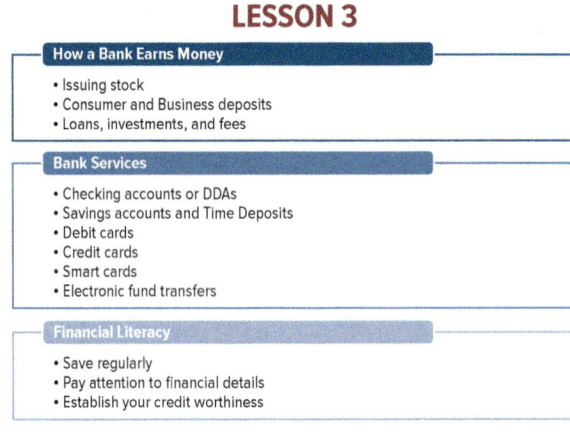

CHAPTER 10 Assessment

Directions: On a separate sheet of paper, answer the questions below. Make sure you read carefully and answer all parts of the questions.

Lesson Review

Lesson 1

1 **Identifying** Explain what specie was used in the North American colonies.

2 **Specifying** Name three ways the money in the United States today meets people's needs.

Lesson 2

3 **Inferring** Why was the issuing of Silver Certificates in 1878 a positive step in establishing a national currency?

4 **Identifying** Beginning in 1933, what happened to the Gold Standard?

5 **Comparing** Considering the evolution of currency in our country, what were some of the negative aspects of previously used currency? What are the positive aspects of the currency we use today?

Lesson 3

6 **Explaining** How does a bank earn money?

7 **Drawing Conclusions** How does the system of reserve requirements expand bank deposits?

Critical Thinking

8 **Identifying Central Issues** Identify how the U.S. government established a system in 1933 to protect a customer's bank deposits.

9 **Constructing Arguments** Write a blog post in which you state whether the Fed is the most effective way of maintaining monetary stability.

10 **Speculating** Assume that you inherited $5,000. Would you spend it or deposit it in a savings or checking account? Would you buy a CD or investigate other investment possibilities?

11 **Explaining** Defining the terms commodity money and fiat money, explain how both were used in colonial America and why the limitations of commodity money led to the development of fiat money.

Analyzing Visuals

Use the graph below to answer the following questions.

12 **Reading Graphs** What banking activities occurred in the years just prior to the Great Depression?

13 **Identifying Graphs** Compare and contrast the number of state-chartered banks in 2010 with the totals in 1879 and 1890.

14 **Predicting** What has happened to the number of banks since 1985? Do you think this trend will continue?

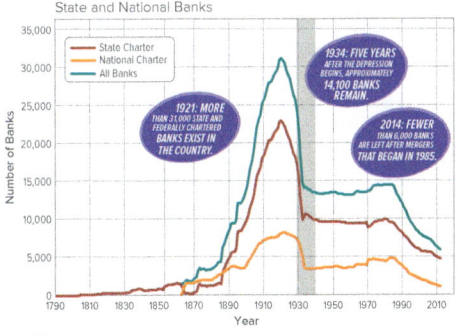

Need Extra Help?

If You've Missed Question	1	2	3	4	5	6	7	8	9	10	11	12	13	14
Go to page	278	280	285	286	283	291	291	286	286	293	277	288	288	288

---

7 When a bank receives a new deposit, it must, by law, keep some of it as a reserve. The reserve requirement is now 20 percent. But it can lend out the remainder and earn profits that allow the bank to expand.

Critical Thinking

8 The U.S. government established Federal Deposit Insurance to make sure that customers do not lose all of their deposits when a bank fails.

9 If making the *pro*-Federal Reserve case, students should cite the advantages of uniform currency, a more efficient payment system, and a sound central bank. Students making the *con*-Federal Reserve case should mention that some people think the Fed wields too much power and manipulates the economy in dangerous ways.

10 Students should give reasons for why they decide to invest, spend, or save the money they inherited, demonstrating the pros and cons of various choices.

11 Commodity money is money that has an alternative use as an economic good, such as flour or corn. Fiat money is money created by a government by decree. Since commodity money did not meet the needs of the colonists, some colonies established fiat money. In Massachusetts the colony established Wampanoag—white and purple mussel shells to use in trade.

Chapter 10 Assessment Answers

Lesson Review

Lesson 1

1 Silver and gold coins used in the colonies included English shillings; Austrian talers; and various European coins, including the popular Spanish peso.

2 Money today is portable, durable, divisible, and scarce.

Lesson 2

3 Paper currency backed by silver dollars became popular because the public wanted an alternative to the bulky silver dollars.

4 In 1933, President Roosevelt took steps to remove the U.S. economy from the gold standard but made an exception for dollars held by foreign governments. In 1971, President Nixon took the final step and stated that the U.S. would not redeem dollars for gold.

5 Prior to the creation of the Fed, banks issued their own currency, resulting in hundreds of different kinds of notes that could be in circulation in any given city. Sometimes this currency could be fraudulent and worthless. We now have uniform currency that is backed by the Fed.

Lesson 3

6 Banks earn money by selling shares in the bank, through consumer and business deposits, by using the fractional reserves system to make loans, through investments, and by charging fees.

Analyzing Visuals

12 Many banks were formed in the 1920s before the Great Depression.

13 The number of state-chartered banks in 2010 is the same as in 1890; for 1879, there are fewer state-chartered banks than in 2010.

14 Student answers should state that the number of banks since 1985 has declined. If they think that trend will continue, they must give reasons, such as the fact that banks are merging more since 1985. If they think the trend will stop or reverse, they must explain why.

Chapter 10
Assessment Answers

Answering the Essential Questions

15 Student answers should include two of the following: it established a central bank, provided enough currency for a growing United States, enabled customers to use a checking system, and unified currency when the Federal Reserve issued notes.

16 Students answers should include that technology has affected the use of money globally by enabling funds to be transferred electronically.

21st Century Skills

17 Student answers should include reasons for their opinions, such as the possibility that mergers create huge banks that, if they fail, could bring down the economy.

18 Presentations will vary but students should outline the services and fees offered by a local bank and by an online bank.

19 Students should use a credible source such as statistics from the state government and remember to also cite the resource.

Building Financial Literacy

20 a. Students' lists should include using the Internet to find information about banking services and fees. Visiting a local bank and talking with a representative should also be included. b. Student answers should include some type of financial plan with goals, although they each might have different financial goals.

Analyzing Primary Sources

21 Answers should include that college and graduate students vote; nearly all U.S. voters think students need support to pay for higher education; and many voters cited government help to big banks as a reason to help students.

22 Answers should include that it would relieve students of massive debt when they graduate. Negative responses might state that students will make poor decisions and accumulate more debt in the student loan program.

23 Students should give reasons for their opinion: Congress will always act to limit interest rates on student loans because students vote and everyone supports the idea of young people getting a higher education.

CHAPTER 10 Assessment

Directions: On a separate sheet of paper, answer the questions below. Make sure you read carefully and answer all parts of the questions.

ANSWERING THE ESSENTIAL QUESTIONS

Review your answers to the introductory questions at the beginning of each lesson. Then answer the Essential Questions on the basis of what you learned in the chapter. Have your answers changed?

15 *Summarizing* In a one-page essay, explain two ways the establishment of the Federal Reserve System changed the monetary system in the United States.

16 *Understanding Relationships* Write a short essay discussing one way in which technology has affected the use of money in the global world today.

21st Century Skills

17 *Defending* Are bank mergers good or bad for the U.S. economy? Write a one-page position statement, supporting your opinion with your reasoning.

18 *Presentation Skills* Investigate the services and fees of two banks. Bank 1 has a branch in your neighborhood or town, and Bank 2 is an online bank. Make a multimedia presentation outlining their services and fees and present it to the class.

19 *Creating and Using Graphs* Use the Internet or a newspaper to find the number of state-chartered banks in your state for each year of the last 10 years. Use the data you collect to create a graph showing whether the number of state-chartered banks in your state increased or decreased in the last 10 years.

Building Financial Literacy

20 *Decision Making* Adopting a financial plan that involves banking services is an important part of your financial literacy. You also need to understand fees for banking services and know how to find the highest interest rates for your accounts.

a. What strategies might you use to ensure you get the most services at low fees? Make a list of ways to "shop around" for the best bank for your needs. Include online banks.

b. Describe your financial plan to meet your five-year financial goals—such as paying for college, buying a car or a house or condo, or taking a trip. What action will you take each year to reach those goals?

Analyzing Primary Sources

Read the excerpt and answer the questions that follow.

In 2013, Congress passed legislation to lower interest rates on student loans. Before the bill passed, interest rates on student loans ran as high as nearly 8 percent.

PRIMARY SOURCE

"*The bill passed by Congress would lower interest rates for all types of student loans, at least for the near future. Undergraduate loans issued for the coming school year would carry a rate of 3.86 percent, while graduate and PLUS loans would be offered at 5.4 percent and 6.4 percent, respectively.*"

—Allie Bidwell, "Congress Approves Student Loan Deal," *U.S. News and World Report*, August 1, 2013

21 *Explaining* Why do you think Congress wanted to limit interest rates on student loans?

22 *Considering Advantages and Disadvantages* What impact, positive and negative, might the decision have on college and graduate students?

23 *Making Predictions* Do you think that in the future Congress will always act to limit interest rates on student loans?

Need Extra Help?

If You've Missed Question	15	16	17	18	19	20	21	22	23
Go to page	286	293	287	292	290	292	291	291	291

---

networks Online Assessment Options

WORKSHEET

Chapter Tests and Lesson Quizzes

Chapter 10 Tests Forms A and B Have students complete the Chapter Tests and Lesson Quizzes to assess student understanding throughout the chapter. Print and online assessment tools offer chapter and lesson evaluation through a variety of question formats, including document-based questions.

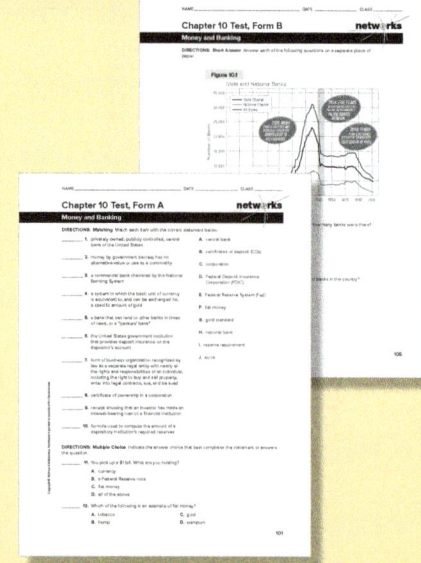

CHAPTER 11
Financial Markets Planner

UNDERSTANDING BY DESIGN®

Enduring Understanding
- *Resources are limited, so people must make choices.*

Essential Questions
- *What is the role of savings in the financial system?*
- *What options are available for investing your money?*

Predictable Misunderstandings
Students may think:
- *Their personal savings has no effect on the overall financial system.* Explain that by saving, each individual makes funds available for other people to use, which is an important part of the financial system and economic growth.
- *Investing requires thousands of dollars.* Explain that some forms of investment, such as CDs and government savings bonds, require relatively small initial investments. Government savings bonds are available for as little as $25.

Assessment Evidence
Performance Task
- *Hands-On Chapter Project with Technology Extension*

Other Evidence
- *Guided Reading Activities*
- *Vocabulary Activity*
- *Self-Check Quizzes*
- *Lesson Quizzes*
- *Chapter Assessment*
- *Chapter Tests, Forms A and B*

SUGGESTED PACING

Introducing the Chapter. . . . . . . ½ Day	Case Study . . . . ½ Day
Lesson 1: Savings and the Financial System . . . . 1 Day	Lesson 3: Investing in Equities and Options . . . . 1 Day
Lesson 2: Financial Assets and Their Markets. 1 Day	Debate . . . . ½ Day
	Study Guide, Chapter Assessment, and Wrap-Up . . . . ½ Day

Total 5 Days

Key for Using the Teacher Edition

SKILL-BASED ACTIVITIES
Types of skill activites found in the Teacher Edition.

V Visual Skills require students to analyze maps, graphs, charts, and photos.
R Reading Skills help students practice reading skills and master vocabulary.
C Critical Thinking Skills help students apply and extend what they have learned.
W Writing Skills provide writing opportunities to help students comprehend the text.
T Technology Skills require students to use digital tools effectively.

*Letters are followed by a number when there is more than one of the same type of skill on the page.

DIFFERENTIATED INSTRUCTION
All activities are written for the on-level student unless otherwise marked with the leveled labels below.

BL Beyond Level
AL Approaching Level
ELL English Language Learners

All students benefit from activities that utilize different learning styles. Many activities are marked as below when a particular learning style is highlighted.

Intrapersonal
Logical/Mathematical
Visual/Spatial
Verbal/Linguistic

Naturalist
Kinesthetic
Auditory/Musical
Interpersonal

Council for Economic Education

Below are the Council for Economic Education Voluntary National Content Standards in Economics covered in the *Financial Markets* chapter.

Content Standard 10: Institutions evolve and are created to help individuals and groups accomplish their goals. Banks, labor unions, markets, corporations, legal systems, and not-for-profit organizations are examples of important institutions. A different kind of institution, clearly defined and enforced property rights, is essential to a market economy.

Content Standard 15: Investment in factories, machinery, new technology, and in the health, education, and training of people can raise future standards of living.

CHAPTER 11: FINANCIAL MARKETS

CHAPTER OPENER PLANNER

Students will know:
- the role of financial institutions in saving, borrowing, and capital formation.
- how the amount of savings in an economy is the basis of capital formation.
- the basic considerations when investing money, including the risk-return relationship.
- investment risk can be reduced through diversification.

Students will be able to:
- *explain* the role of savings in the financial system.
- *identify* the four parts of the financial system.
- *consider the advantages and disadvantages* of a risky investment.
- *name* four basic investment considerations.
- *discuss* the importance of portfolio diversification.
- *evaluate* stock performance using standard measures of performance.

UNDERSTANDING BY DESIGN

☑ Print Teaching Options

R Reading Skills
- ☐ p. 302 **Defining basic investment terms** Students define *savings*, *risk*, and *return*.

C Critical Thinking Skills
- ☐ p. 301 **Identifying financial markets** Students discuss various stock exchanges.
- ☐ p. 302 **Analyzing investing** Students select an investment and defend it.

W Writing Skills
- ☐ p. 303 **Illustrating bond transaction roles** Students show the role of investor, broker, firm.

T Technology Skills
- ☐ p. 301 **Stock Values** Students list how stocks affect lives.

☑ Online Teaching Options

V Visual Skills
- ☐ **IMAGES** Chapter opener—Students analyze a photo about financial markets.

C Critical Thinking Skills
- ☐ **INFOGRAPHICS** Economic Perspectives—Students identify ways that bonds differ from stocks. Visual/Spatial
- ☐ **DEBATES** Is the illegal practice of insider trading punished too severely in the United States? Students analyze two views about insider trading.
- ☐ **INTERACTIVE FEATURE** Case Study: The New York and the National Stock Exchanges—Students describe differences in trading in stock exchanges.

☑ Printable Digital Worksheets

C Critical Thinking Skills
- ☐ **WORKSHEET** Enrichment Activity—Students compare and contrast types of investments.

Project-Based Learning

Hands-On

Hands-On Chapter Project
Student groups will work together to determine the best way to invest $10,000 they have won in a competition. They will first research ways of investing the money and analyze the risk-return relationship for the investment(s) or asset(s) they select. Together, group members will decide on the best investments. Each group will design a pamphlet or poster explaining their investment choices and present it to the class.

Digital Hands-On

Create Online Projects

Find an additional activity online that incorporates technology for the Hands-On Project. Visit the EdTech Teacher Web sites for more links, tutorials, and other resources.

Print Resources

ANCILLARY RESOURCES
This ancillary is available for every chapter and lesson.
- Chapter Tests and Lesson Quizzes

PRINTABLE DIGITAL WORKSHEETS
These printable digital worksheets are available for every chapter and lesson.
- Reading Essentials & Study Guide
- Vocabulary Activities
- Chapter Summaries
- Economic Simulations
- Math Practice for Economics
- Reinforcing Economic Skills
- Personal Finance Activities
- Enrichment Activities
- Reteaching Activities
- Guided Reading Activities
- Video Worksheets
- Lesson Quizzes and Chapter Tests (English and Spanish)

More Media Resources

SUGGESTED READING
- For students at a Grade 10 reading level: *Everyday Banking: Consumer Banking*, by Ernestine Giesecke
- For students at a Grade 11 reading level: *Taxpayers Will Get a Return on Investment*, by John Harrington
- For students at a Grade 12 reading level: *Business Builders in Real Estate*, by Nathan Aaseng

SUGGESTED VIDEOS MOVIES
Find these documentaries yourself online. NOTE: McGraw-Hill Education does not endorse these resources. Preview clips for age-appropriateness.
- *The Wall Street Code* (60 min.)
- *Money and Speed: Inside the Black Box* (48 min.)

LESSON 1 Planner

SAVINGS AND THE FINANCIAL SYSTEM

Students will know:
- the role of financial institutions in saving, borrowing, and capital formation.
- how the amount of savings in an economy is the basis of capital formation.
- the types of accounts available to consumers from financial institutions and the risks, monetary costs, and benefits of maintaining these accounts.

Students will be able to:
- **explain** the role of savings in the financial system.
- **identify** the four parts of the financial system.
- **consider the advantages and disadvantages** of a risky investment.
- **name** four basic investment considerations.

UNDERSTANDING BY DESIGN®

☑ Print Teaching Options

V Visual Skills

☐ **p. 305 Identifying methods of saving** Students list and describe methods of saving.

☐ **p. 307 Comparing and contrasting financial intermediaries** Students compare finance companies, life insurance companies, and pension funds. **Visual/Spatial**

R Reading Skills

☐ **p. 305 Recognizing and defining academic language** Students use *intermediary* in relation to the financial system. **ELL**

C Critical Thinking Skills

☐ **p. 304 Identifying personal roles in the financial system** Students identify as consumers who save or borrow. **Interpersonal**

☐ **p. 305 Understanding economic growth** Students relate savings, borrowing, and growth.

☐ **p. 306 Assessing information** Students poll people about their savings and produce a graph.

☐ **p. 308 Understanding compound interest** Students discuss the steps of compounding.

W Writing Skills

☐ **p. 306 Explaining the financial system** Students summarize the parts of the financial system. **BL Verbal/Linguistic**

☐ **p. 307 Analyzing financial motivations** Students analyze advertisements for financial companies. **BL Visual/Spatial, Interpersonal**

☐ **p. 308 Advertising sensible investment practices** Students develop a public-service campaign that encourages sensible investing.

☐ **p. 309 Explaining the financial system and the economy** Students explain the choices for investing savings. **BL Verbal/Linguistic**

☐ **p. 309 Summarizing** Students write an explanation of why savings must occur to grow the economy.

☑ Online Teaching Options

V Visual Skills

☐ **VIDEO College Debt**—Students watch a video about college debt.

R Reading Skills

☐ **GRAPHIC ORGANIZER Financial Intermediaries**—Students identify common financial intermediaries: bank, credit union, finance company, life insurance company, pension fund. **Logical/Mathematical**

C Critical Thinking Skills

☐ **BELLRINGER Savings and the Financial System**—Students identify trends in the prime rate.

☐ **ESSENTIAL QUESTION Exploring the Essential Question**—Students discuss the part they play in the financial system.

T Technology Skills

☐ **SELF-CHECK QUIZ Lesson 1**—Students receive instant feedback on their mastery of lesson content.

☐ **GAME Lesson 1**—Students solve clues to review lesson content.

☐ **INTERACTIVE WHITEBOARD ACTIVITY The Financial System**—Students work together to learn lesson content.

☑ Printable Digital Worksheets

R Reading Skills

☐ **WORKSHEET Guided Reading Activity**—Students review their comprehension of the content.

C Critical Thinking Skills

☐ **WORKSHEET Reading Essentials and Study Guide**—Students complete the study guide and answer Reading Progress Check and vocabulary questions.

☐ **WORKSHEET College Debt Video Activity**—Students answer questions related to college debt and how it affects savings and financial systems.

LESSON 2 Planner

FINANCIAL ASSETS AND THEIR MARKETS

Students will know:
- a bond is a long-term investment, with the price determined by supply, demand, and the buyer's assessment of repayment risk.
- the characteristics, advantages, and risks of various investment options.
- financial assets are grouped into different markets depending on their maturity and liquidity.

Students will be able to:
- **discuss** the factors that determine the value of a bond.
- **compare** the available types of financial assets.
- **explain** the difference between a capital market and a money market.
- **categorize** financial assets into the primary or secondary market.

UNDERSTANDING BY DESIGN®

☑ Print Teaching Options

V Visual Skills
- ☐ **p. 315 Evaluating capital and money markets** Students compare certificate of deposits and corporate bonds. **AL**

R Reading Skills
- ☐ **p. 311 Understanding bonds** Students explain the process of making money from a bond purchase.
- ☐ **p. 312 Understanding bond ratings** Students explain how bond ratings.
- ☐ **p. 315 Identifying money market mutual funds** Students explain how money market mutual funds are created.

C Critical Thinking Skills
- ☐ **p. 310 Identifying investment options** Students create an outline of investment terms.
- ☐ **p. 311 Identifying bond categories** Students create flash cards about bond components, prices, yields, or ratings. **BL Visual/Spatial**
- ☐ **p. 313 Researching types of bonds** Students conduct interviews about various bonds.
- ☐ **p. 314 Comparing financial assets** Students compare the advantages and disadvantages of different bonds.
- ☐ **p. 316 Summarizing financial assets and their markets** Students list characteristics of financial assets and their markets.

W Writing Skills
- ☐ **p. 312 Explaining a bond's ratings** Students research the rating of a bond they might buy.
- ☐ **p. 314 Contrasting Treasury notes and Treasury bills** Students contrast returns. **AL**
- ☐ **p. 314 Comparing investment options** Students compare safety vs. risks and returns.

T Technology Skills
- ☐ **p. 312 Following bond interest rates** Students follow interest rates on bonds for a week.

☑ Online Teaching Options

V Visual Skills
- ☐ **VIDEO Price of Oil**—Students view a video on the price of oil.
- ☐ **GRAPHS Bond Ratings**—Students use an interactive graph to explore bond ratings.
- ☐ **GRAPHS Financial Assets and Their Markets**—Students explore financial assets and their markets.

R Reading Skills
- ☐ **GRAPHIC ORGANIZERS Financial Assets**—Students describe financial assets. **Verbal/Linguistic**

C Critical Thinking Skills
- ☐ **BELLRINGER Financial Assets and Their Markets**—Students conclude that finance companies are just one type of financial intermediary that connects savers to borrowers.
- ☐ **ESSENTIAL QUESTION Exploring the Essential Question**—Students decide how to invest an inheritance.

T Technology Skills
- ☐ **SELF-CHECK QUIZ Lesson 2**—Students receive instant feedback on their mastery of lesson content.
- ☐ **GAME Lesson 2**—Students solve clues to review lesson content.
- ☐ **INTERACTIVE WHITEBOARD ACTIVITY Investments and Risk**—Students work together to learn lesson content.

☑ Printable Digital Worksheets

R Reading Skills
- ☐ **WORKSHEET Guided Reading Activity**—Students review their comprehension of the content.
- ☐ **WORKSHEET Reading Essentials and Study Guide**—Students complete the study guide and answer Reading Progress Check and vocabulary questions.

C Critical Thinking Skills
- ☐ **WORKSHEET Price of Oil Video Activity**—Students answer questions about on oil prices. **Visual/Spatial**

LESSON 3 Planner

INVESTING IN EQUITIES AND OPTIONS

Students will know:
- investment risk can be reduced through diversification.
- financial assets can be bought and sold in the future as well as in the present.
- investors can purchase stock through stockbrokers on exchanges, through mutual funds, or through 401(k) plans.

Students will be able to:
- **discuss** the importance of portfolio diversification.
- **evaluate** stock performance using standard measures of performance.
- **explain** how investors make money using futures contracts.

UNDERSTANDING BY DESIGN®

☑ Print Teaching Options

R Reading Skills

- ☐ **p. 321 Defining and assessing mutual funds** Students explain how a mutual fund benefits investors.
- ☐ **p. 322 Sequencing information about 401(k)s** Students show the steps of investing in a 401(k) plan.
- ☐ **p. 324 Defining market terminology** Students describe kinds of markets. **Verbal/Linguistic**
- ☐ **p. 325 Defining a futures contract** Students define and explain futures contracts.

C Critical Thinking Skills

- ☐ **p. 318 Analyzing investment options** Students list investment options with which they are familiar.
- ☐ **p. 319 Examining factors that affect equities** Students consider how trading shares affects their price. **Logical/Mathematical**
- ☐ **p. 320 Researching stocks** Students find current stock prices and dividends during the past year. **Visual/Spatial**
- ☐ **p. 322 Identifying characteristics of financial assets** Students play the game "Investment—What Am I?"
- ☐ **p. 325 Examining a call option** Students consider call options and their risks.
- ☐ **p. 325 Defending or refuting a statement** Students defend or refute: The best indicator of how the economy is performing is the stock market.

W Writing Skills

- ☐ **p. 321 Investing wisely in the stock market** Students convince investors to practice portfolio diversification. **BL Visual/Spatial**
- ☐ **p. 323 Choosing an information source** Students review information about measures of stock performance. **AL Verbal/Linguistic**
- ☐ **p. 324 Researching and describing corporate value** Students study and follow a stock.
- ☐ **p. 325 Assessing a futures contract** Students analyze investing in futures.

☑ Online Teaching Options

V Visual Skills

- ☐ **GRAPHS How to Interpret How Stocks Are Performing**—Students interpret stock performance. **Logical/Mathematical**
- ☐ **GRAPHS How Much Money Will You Have at Retirement?**—Students explore a graph to show how much money an individual will have at retirement.
- ☐ **VIDEO Recession**—Students watch a video about recessions.

R Reading Skills

- ☐ **GRAPHIC ORGANIZERS Characteristics of Stock Markets**—Students brainstorm characteristics of stock markets. **Verbal/Linguistic**

C Critical Thinking Skills

- ☐ **BELLRINGER Investing in Equities and Options**—Students explain whether relying on a 401(k) is the best option for retirement.
- ☐ **ESSENTIAL QUESTION Exploring the Essential Question**—Students discuss investment options available to individuals.

W Writing Skills

- ☐ **INTERACTIVE FEATURE Careers**—Students discuss the traits and interests of a stockbroker or investment banker. **Verbal/Linguistic**

T Technology Skills

- ☐ **SELF-CHECK QUIZ Lesson 3**—Students receive instant feedback on their mastery of lesson content.
- ☐ **GAME Lesson 3**—Students solve clues to review lesson content.
- ☐ **INTERACTIVE WHITEBOARD ACTIVITY News and Investments**—Students work together to learn lesson content.

☑ Printable Digital Worksheets

R Reading Skills

- ☐ **WORKSHEET Guided Reading Activity**—Students use the Guided Reading Activity worksheets to review their comprehension of the content.
- ☐ **WORKSHEET Reading Essentials and Study Guide**—Students complete the study guide and answer Reading Progress Check and vocabulary questions.
- ☐ **WORKSHEET Reteaching Activity**—Students use this activity worksheet to review and reteach chapter content and vocabulary. This worksheet can be used with struggling students who need additional help with difficult content concepts.

C Critical Thinking Skills

- ☐ **WORKSHEET Recession Video Activity**—Students answer questions about effects of the recession.

CHAPTER 11 Financial Markets

INTERVENTION AND REMEDIATION STRATEGIES

LESSON 1 Savings and the Financial System

Reading and Comprehension

Tell students to write a paragraph explaining the importance of savings to the financial system. Tell them to use facts and reasons from the text to support their ideas. After completing their paragraphs, ask students to share their ideas in a class discussion.

Text Evidence

Review how to use text evidence to support ideas and statements. Then ask students to find evidence in the text to support the following statements:

- People can save money in many different ways. (People can save in a number of ways. They can open a savings account, buy a bond, or purchase a certificate of deposit.)
- A financial system is a connection of savers, investors and financial institutions. (A financial system is a network of savers, investors, and financial institutions that work together to transfer savings to investment uses.)
- Credit unions are formed for the benefit of its members. (Credit unions are owned by and operated for the benefit of its members.)

LESSON 2 Financial Assets and their Markets

Reading and Comprehension

Organize the class into three groups and assign one of the questions below to each group. Have groups answer the questions and use details to support their responses. Then ask students to share their answers and reasons with the class.

- What are bonds and who issues them?
- What are two kinds of financial assets that people can invest in?
- For how long is money loaned in a money market?

Text Evidence

Have students write one or two paragraphs in answering this question: What are two sources for checking the quality of bonds? Give details from the text to support your answer. Have students share their answers in class discussion.

LESSON 3 Investing in Equities and Options

Reading and Comprehension

Have students write an essay summarizing the way a person can buy shares of stock (also called equities) in the today's digital age. Students should share their summaries in small group discussion.

Text Evidence

Have students answer the question: What stock indicators do many investors consult to check the overall performance of stocks? Students should cite details from the text in their answer.

Online Resources

Assessing Background Knowledge Use this worksheet to pre-assess students' background knowledge before they start the chapter.

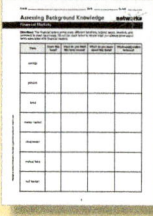

Chapter Summaries Have students use the summary as a pre-reading activity or as a post-reading review to check the main ideas covered in each lesson.

Guided Reading Activities Have students complete these activities as they read each lesson. They provide reading notes the student can use for review and to prepare for assessments.

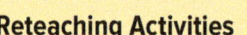

Reteaching Activities Have students complete the Reteaching Activity for remedial practice and review of vital content.

Self-Check Quizzes These quizzes provide instant feedback on areas the students may need to re-read to understand a main idea.

Reading Essentials and Study Guide This resource offers writing and reading activities for the approaching-level student.

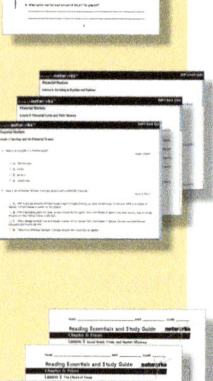

Approaching Grade Level Reader This reader presents all of the content of the Online Student Edition but at a lower reading level.

English Language Learner Reader Provide additional reading support for ELL students. Find this tool online.

Financial Markets

ESSENTIAL QUESTIONS
- What is the role of savings in the financial system?
- What options are available for investing your money?

networks
www.connected.mcgraw-hill.com
There's More Online about financial markets.

CHAPTER 11

Economic Perspectives
Stocks and Bonds

Lesson 1
Savings and the Financial System

Lesson 2
Financial Assets and Their Markets

Lesson 3
Investing in Equities and Options

CHAPTER 11
Financial Markets

ENGAGE

Ask students to describe what the photograph shows. Guide them to recognize that a stockbroker is on the phone and behind him are computer line graphs showing stock market activity.
Ask: Why is this image a good one to symbolize the chapter titled *Financial Markets*? *(Financial markets operate around the world in a fast-paced environment; many agreements and orders to buy or sell shares are conveyed over the telephone. Computer graphs are an intricate part of measuring activity in financial markets.)* In a discussion, lead students to understand that in a market or capitalist economic system, the federal government may regulate financial markets but does not control them.

Identifying financial markets Discuss with the class the various stock exchanges they have heard about. They might mention the stock exchanges in New York and some may be familiar with the stock exchange in Hong Kong. Tell students that many countries have stock exchanges in their capital cities. Point out that all global exchanges function in a similar manner to conduct the business of buying and selling stocks and bonds. Challenge students to consider how financial markets affect businesses in their community. **BL Logical/Mathematical**

Making Connections

Effects of Stock Values Have students make a list of the ways in which the rise and fall of stock values affect their lives, even though they probably do not trade stocks. *(affects prices in stores, affects overall strength or weakness of the economy, affects the job market)* Point out to students that it is important to understand financial markets, because they have such far-reaching effects.

Letter from the Author

Dear Economics Teacher,

If money is like the oil that keeps an engine running smoothly, financial markets are the parts of the engine that move to oil to the places where it is needed most. Financial markets are places you can save your money, or borrow if you need it—and who doesn't when it's time to buy a car or a house? An economy is stronger when it has a variety of markets that move money to places where it is needed most. That's the beauty of a market economy: because of markets, the economy tends to "run itself" far better than if the major economic decisions were to be made by government planners.

Gary E. Clayton

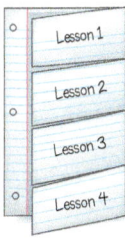

Go to the Foldables® library for a cumulative chapter-based Foldable® activity that your students can use to help take notes and prepare for assessment.

Financial Markets **301**

CHAPTER 11
Economic Perspectives

TEACH & ASSESS

R Reading Skills

Defining basic investment terms Write the words *savings, risk,* and *return* on the board. Tell students these are key words to understanding financial markets. Have the class discuss and define the words, and write the class definitions on the board. Have students write sentences using each word.
ELL Verbal/Linguistic

C Critical Thinking Skills

Analyzing investing Tell students that investing is a key element of the financial system in the United States. Explain that every investment has some degree of risk, but that there are levels of investing. One can invest conservatively, moderately, or in a risky manner. Have students select a level of investment they might use as a guide to investing their savings and write a one-page essay defending it.
AL Verbal/Linguistic Logical/Mathematical

W Writing Skills

Creating an investing narrative Tell students that all stock transactions start with one thing: money. People invest in order to gain a financial return on that money. Have student pairs write a narrative describing a hypothetical incident that illustrates the maxim, "people invest to make money on their money." Have students read their narrative to the class. **BL** Verbal/Linguistic

---

Economic Perspectives

STOCKS AND BONDS

R Bonds are securities that represent the small piece of debt incurred when a company "borrows" money from an individual. Companies issue bonds (i.e., sell debt) to raise capital for expansion, improvements or any other costs that the business may be facing. Each bond is like an IOU, representing a small debt.

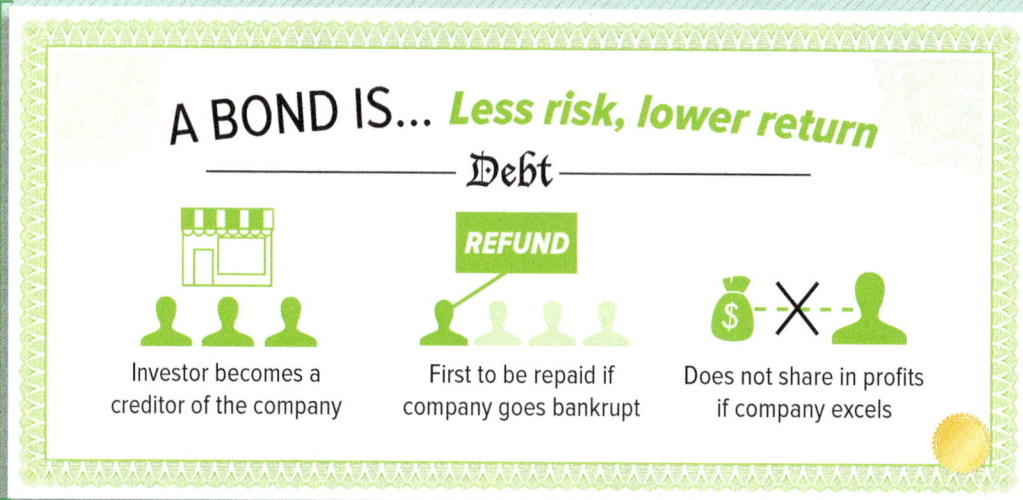

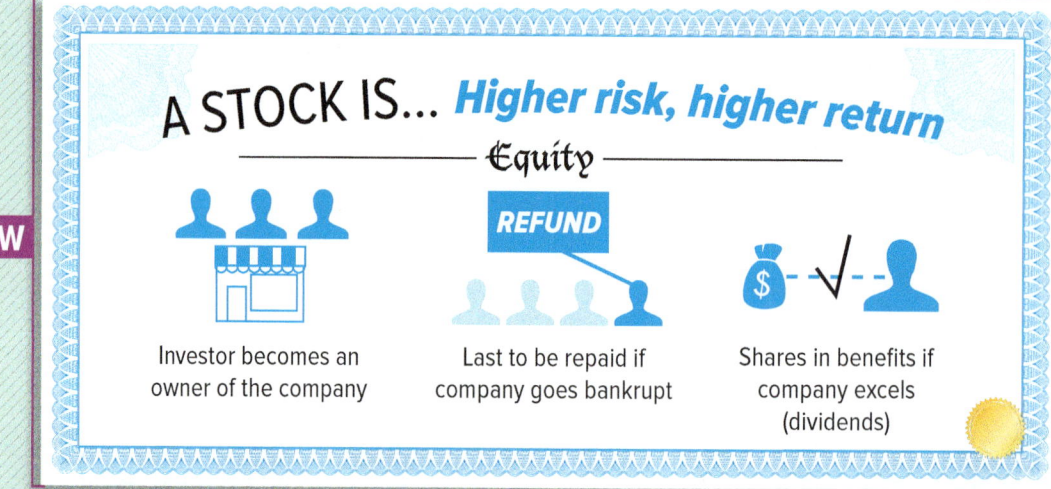

networks Online Teaching Options

INFOGRAPHIC

Economic Perspectives: Stocks and Bonds

Examining the stock market Tell students that because financial markets have a great impact on our lives, it is wise to understand them. Most students will have heard of stock markets, major financial markets in which individuals and companies buy and sell equities. Have a volunteer read the opening paragraph about bonds.
Ask: What are three ways that bonds differ from stocks? *(Bonds are loans from investors to companies or government. Bonds have less risk and lower returns than stocks. A bondholder is first to be repaid if the company goes bankrupt. Bondholders do not share in the company's profits. Depending on the type of bond purchased, the investor may receive intermittent interest payments.)* Review the kinds of bonds. **Visual/Spatial**

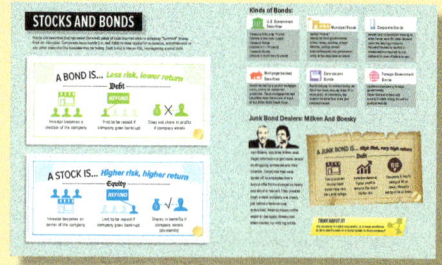

networks TRY IT YOURSELF ONLINE
For an interactive version of this infographic go to connected.mcgraw-hill.com

Kinds of Bonds:

 U.S. Government Securities
Treasury Bills, aka "T-bills" (mature in less than 1 year)
Treasury Notes (mature in 1 – 10 years)
Treasury Bonds (mature in more than 10 years)

 **Municipal Bonds**
Called "munis"
Issued by local governments (cities, states, counties, school districts, publicly owned airports/seaports, any government entity at the state level or below)

 Corporate Bonds
Issued by a corporation looking to raise funds; specific risks depend upon the issuing company
Secured (backed by assets) or unsecured (not secured by any collateral in case of failure to pay)

 **Mortgage-backed Securities**
Bonds backed by a pool of mortgage loans, usually on residential properties. These mortgage-backed securities were the source of much of the 2008-2009 Credit Crisis.

 Zero-coupon Bonds
Bonds that pay no interest during the life of the bond; maturity takes 10 or more years. At maturity, the investor receives face value plus credited interest.

 Foreign Government Bonds
Issued and backed by foreign governments
Have risks associated with country's credit rating, as well as political stability

Junk Bond Dealers: Milken and Boesky

Ivan Boesky and Mike Milken used illegal information to get inside details on struggling companies and their finances. Sometimes they were tipped off by employees that a buyout offer from a stronger company was about to happen. They invested when a weak company was cheap, just before a takeover was announced. When company profits began to rise again, Boesky and Milken cashed out with big profits.

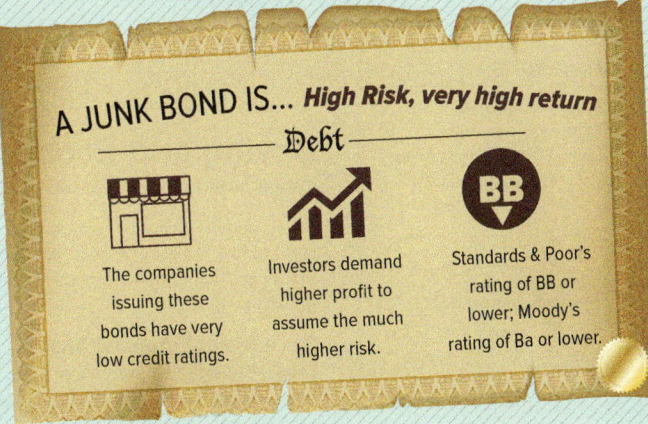

A JUNK BOND IS... High Risk, very high return — Debt

- The companies issuing these bonds have very low credit ratings.
- Investors demand higher profit to assume the much higher risk.
- Standards & Poor's rating of BB or lower; Moody's rating of Ba or lower.

 THINK ABOUT IT!
If a company is highly successful, is it more profitable to be a stock owner or a bond holder in that company?

Financial Markets **303**

CHAPTER 11
Economic Perspectives

W Writing Skills

Illustrating bond transaction roles Have students create illustrations showing the role of the investor, broker, and firm or government in a bond purchase. Require students to write extensive captions on their illustrations. **Visual/Spatial**

CLOSE & REFLECT

Have students answer the *Think About It!* questions.

WORKSHEET

Personal Finance Activity: Risk and Return

Comparing and contrasting investments Tell students that this worksheet will help them compare and contrast the many types of investments, ranging from savings accounts to stocks. Have student pairs complete a paper copy of the worksheet. Then have pairs share their answers with the class.

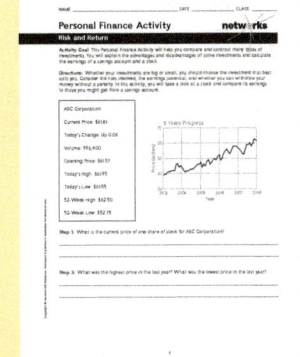

ANSWERS, p. 303

THINK ABOUT IT!

If a company is highly successful, it is more profitable to be a stock owner. A stock provides higher returns than bonds—when a company is successful.

CHAPTER 11, LESSON 1
Savings and the Financial System

ENGAGE

C Critical Thinking Skills

Identifying personal roles in the financial system Before students begin the lesson, ask them to brainstorm about ways they are part of the financial system—as a consumer who either saves or borrows. Take a poll to see whether there are more students who save or more students who borrow. Point out that using credit cards is a method of borrowing money. Then have students create a flow chart that shows how a student's college fund savings account in a local bank might help build a new school in the community. **AL** Interpersonal

Making Connections

Savings or Lottery? Ask: **What's the surest method of accumulating $1 million—saving or gambling?** Many Americans think that their best chance of amassing even half that sum is winning the lottery. Actually, the chances of winning a big lottery jackpot are somewhere between 10 million and 20 million to one. However, an investment of $50 a week—the amount that many Americans spend on the lottery—at 9 percent interest over 40 years would grow to just a little under $1,022,000.

ANSWERS, p. 304

ESSENTIAL QUESTION ACTIVITY

Students should recognize that they are a part of the system whenever they save money or borrow money to make a purchase. They may have or use a credit card, and they may have a savings account and/or a college fund. They should recognize that their role will expand as they finish school and begin working.

TAKING NOTES

Banks and credit unions: accept deposits and lend money; **Finance companies:** make loans to consumers and buy installment contracts from merchants who sell goods on credit; **Life insurance companies:** collect cash through insurance premiums and loan surplus funds to others; **Pension funds:** collect contributions from employees, pay out benefits, and invest holdings in stocks and bonds

304

Interact with these digital assets and others in lesson 1
- ✓ INTERACTIVE IMAGE Comparing Financial Institutions
- ✓ INTERACTIVE GRAPH The Risk-Return Relationship
- ✓ SELF-CHECK QUIZ
- ✓ VIDEO

networks TRY IT YOURSELF ONLINE

LESSON 1
Savings and the Financial System

Reading Help Desk

Academic Vocabulary
- compensation

Content Vocabulary
- savings
- certificate of deposit (CD)
- financial assets
- financial intermediaries
- financial system
- credit union
- finance company
- premium
- pension
- pension fund
- diversification
- risk

TAKING NOTES:

Key Ideas and Details
ACTIVITY Use a graphic organizer like the one below to identify and describe at least four financial intermediaries.

ESSENTIAL QUESTION

What is the role of savings in the financial system?

For an economy to grow it must produce the factor of production called capital—the equipment, tools, and machinery used in production. This happens when **savings**—the dollars that become available when people abstain from consumption—are made available to borrowers.

It turns out that consumers like you are a big part of this process.

- What part do you play in this process?
- When are you a borrower?
- When are you a saver?
- How will your role change as you grow older and finish your education?

Saving and Economic Growth

GUIDING QUESTION *What is your role in the circular flow of finance?*

When people save, they make funds available for others to use. Businesses can borrow these savings to produce new goods and services, build new plants and equipment, and create more jobs. Saving thus makes economic growth possible.

Savers and Financial Assets

People can save in a number of ways. They can open a savings account, buy a bond, or purchase a **certificate of deposit (CD)**—a document showing that an interest-bearing loan has been made to a bank or other financial institution. In each case, savers obtain a receipt or record of the funds they place with others.

Economists call these documents **financial assets**—claims on the property and the income of the borrower. The documents are assets because they are

304

---

networks *Online Teaching Options*

BELLRINGER

Savings and the Financial System

Analyzing the prime rate trend Have students view the Bellringer. Remind students that the prime rate is directly related to the discount rate that the Federal Reserve charges on loans to financial institutions. Also point out that interest rates *earned* on deposits will be lower than the prime rate charged to borrowers. Ask: **What does the graph show?** *(The graph shows the prime interest rates back to 1956.)* **What trend is indicated on the graph for interest rates?** *(Interest rates are dropping.)* **AL** Visual/Spatial Logical/Mathematical

FIGURE 11.1

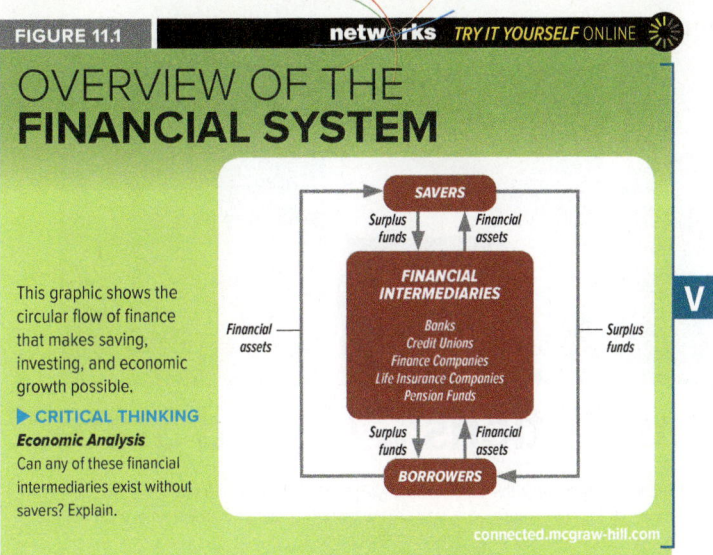

OVERVIEW OF THE FINANCIAL SYSTEM

This graphic shows the circular flow of finance that makes saving, investing, and economic growth possible.

▶ **CRITICAL THINKING**
Economic Analysis
Can any of these financial intermediaries exist without savers? Explain.

---

property that has value. They represent claims on the borrower because they specify the amount loaned and the terms at which the loan was made.

For example, you have an extra $500 from a summer job and you want to put it in a bank for safekeeping. If you put the money in a savings account, you will get a receipt for your deposit. Or if you put it in a CD—which is technically treated as a loan to the bank—you will get a different receipt. Either way, both receipts signify that you have put $500 in the bank, and you have a claim on the property and the income of that institution for $500.

The Circular Flow of Finance

Figure 11.1 shows the circular flow of finance that makes saving, investing, and economic growth possible. This illustration of the financial system has four parts:

- **Savings** The first part consists of savers who provide the savings that borrowers will use. A saver might be someone like you who wants to put a weekly paycheck in a bank or credit union; it might be a city government that is making contributions into an employee retirement fund; or it could be a corporation that is investing surplus cash until it is needed to meet a payroll.
- **Financial intermediaries** The second part consists of **financial intermediaries**—institutions such as banks, credit unions, life insurance companies, pension funds, and finance companies that collect the funds that savers provide so that they can be loaned to borrowers.
- **Borrowers** The third part consists of borrowers who use those funds for various purposes. A business might borrow so that it can produce capital equipment needed for economic growth, or it might want to produce goods and services to sell to consumers. A university might borrow so that it can build student housing. An individual might borrow so that he can buy a car or a house.
- **Financial assets** The fourth part consists of the financial assets—bonds, certificates of deposits, and other documents that show that borrowing has taken place and that there is a claim on the income and assets of the borrower.

savings the dollars that become available for investors to use when others save

certificate of deposit (CD) receipt showing that an investor has made an interest-bearing loan to the financial institution

financial assets stocks or documents that represent a claim on the income and property of the borrower; CDs, bonds, Treasury bills, mortgages

financial intermediaries institutions that channel savings to investors; banks, insurance companies, savings and loan associations, credit unions

---

CHAPTER 11, LESSON 1
Savings and the Financial System

TEACH & ASSESS

V Visual Skills

Identifying methods of saving Have students examine the overview of the financial system. Then ask students to identify and describe methods of saving with which they are familiar. Have students work in pairs or small groups to create tables listing these methods and briefly describing how they work. **Ask: Why do you think governments and institutions want people to save money?** *(Savings in an economy are the basis of capital formation.)*
BL Logical/Mathematical

C Critical Thinking Skills

Understanding economic growth Write the following terms on the board: *savings, borrowing, growth*. Ask students to imagine that they have borrowed money to build a new home. Have students name others who would benefit from building the house. *(building contractors, suppliers, architects, and so on)* Mention that the money students borrowed benefited the economy as a whole, because it generated economic activity. Then point out that all this was made possible by others' savings. Conclude by asking students to write a generalization about the relationship between the three terms on the board.
AL Logical/Mathematical

R Reading Skills

Recognizing and defining academic language Help students interpret the meaning of the word *intermediaries*. Explain that the prefix *inter-* means "between or among" and the word *mediate* means "to work between two parties." Have students write a short paragraph using the word in relation to the financial system. Encourage students to share their paragraphs. **ELL** Verbal/Linguistic

---

INTERACTIVE FEATURE

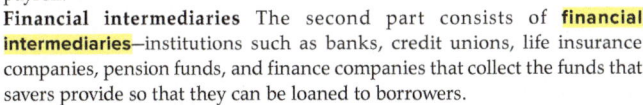

Overview of the Financial System

Analyzing the circular flow of finance
Have students view Figure 11.1 to examine and discuss the basics of saving and investing money. Have students identify the four parts of the financial system and trace and explain the role of savers, borrowers, financial intermediaries, and financial assets in the circular flow of money in the financial system. **Ask: Can any financial intermediaries exist without savers? Explain.** *(Answers should include that financial intermediaries depend upon savers to operate, because they cannot loan money if they do not have deposits or investors.)* Ask students to create another circular-flow model of finance with real-world examples.
AL Visual/Spatial

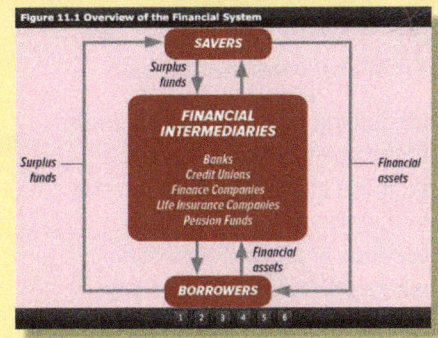

ANSWERS, p. 305

CRITICAL THINKING

Students should recognize that financial intermediaries depend upon savers to operate, since they cannot loan cash if they do not have deposits, investors, or save it themselves.

CHAPTER 11, LESSON 1
Savings and the Financial System

W Writing Skills

Explaining the financial system Have students write a one-page essay paragraph summarizing the parts of the financial system. Tell students to write for readers who are unfamiliar with the financial system and to answer the question: *How does the financial system benefit both borrowers and savers?* (Students should conclude that the financial system ensures that savers will have outlets in which to invest their savings. It also provides a source of financial capital that businesses and other borrowers can draw from to fuel future economic growth.) Remind students to use economic-related terminology correctly and to use standard grammar, spelling, sentence structure, and punctuation. **BL** Verbal/Linguistic

C Critical Thinking Skills

Assessing information Organize students into small groups. Direct each group member to conduct an informal poll among family members, neighbors, and friends to discover how many people save and for what reasons. Encourage students to survey people of both genders who represent a range of ages, ethnic groups, and income levels. Then instruct students to combine their results with those of other group members and work together to produce a wall chart or graph that displays their findings. Invite each group to present their finished visuals to the class and discuss the results of their research. **AL** Logical/Mathematical, Visual/Spatial

---

What are the different types of...

Financial Institutions in the United States?

Banks are the most familiar type of financial institutions in the United States, and they are most likely where you have placed your money. Banks offer a variety of investment options that will help you grow your money.

Credit unions function similarly to banks but are nonprofit organizations that operate for the benefit of its members. They are usually connected to a single employer and work to aid that employer's staff.

Finance companies make loans directly to consumers. They may charge more than banks or credit unions, but they offer better credit terms.

▲ **CRITICAL THINKING**
Interpreting What are the main differences between banks, credit unions, and finance companies in how they serve the financial system?

financial system network of savers, investors, and financial institutions that work together to transfer savings to investment uses

Collectively, these four parts make up the **financial system**—a network of savers, investors, financial institutions, and financial assets that work together to transfer savings from savers to investors.

Financing Capital Formation

Capital formation depends on saving and borrowing. When households borrow, they invest some of the funds in homes. When businesses borrow, they invest some of the funds in tools, equipment, and machinery. When governments borrow, they invest some of the funds in highways, hospitals, universities, and other public goods.

In the end, everyone benefits from an efficient financial system. The smooth flow of funds through the system helps ensure that savers have an outlet for their savings. Borrowers, in turn, will have a source of financial capital that can be invested in capital goods needed for future economic growth.

Financial Intermediaries

The main financial institutions in our economic system are listed in Figure 11.1. A brief description of each shows how they work to bring savers and borrowers together.

- **Banks** There are fewer than 6,000 banks in the country, but many of them have branch locations in shopping malls and grocery stores. Banks are the most visible of all financial intermediaries. Banks offer checking accounts, saving accounts, and CDs as a way of attracting deposits from consumers, but their most profitable customers are usually commercial businesses. Most banks offer other consumer products such as credit cards, but fees for overdrafts and late credit card payments are major profit items.

---

networks Online Teaching Options

GRAPHIC ORGANIZER | IMAGES

Financial Intermediaries

Identifying financial intermediaries Project the interactive graphic organizer and Comparing Financial Institutions. **Ask:** *What is one common financial intermediary, where people save and borrow money, that can be found in almost every community?* (bank) Have a student write in *bank* in the diagram. Continue filling in the rest of the diagram with identifiers and characteristics as students click through the images during class discussion. (credit union, finance company, life insurance company, pension fund) **AL** Logical/Mathematical

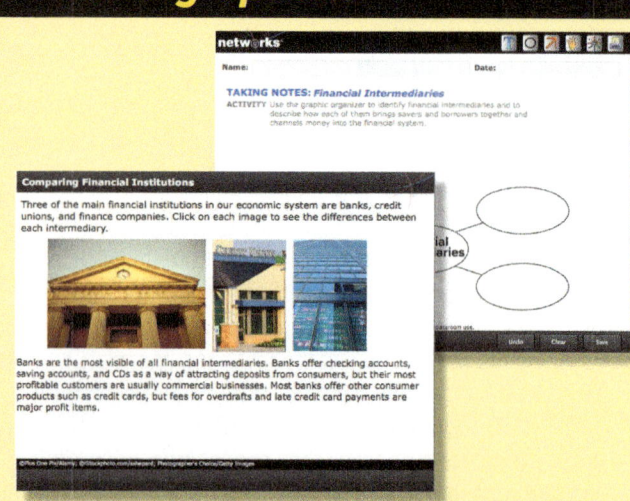

ANSWERS, p. 306

CRITICAL THINKING

A bank accepts deposits and makes loans to all consumers. A credit union accepts deposits and makes loans only to members. A finance company specializes in making loans directly to consumers. Because finance companies make some risky loans, they charge more than banks or credit unions.

- **Credit Unions** A **credit union** is a nonprofit service cooperative that accepts deposits, makes loans, issues CDs, and offers checking accounts. Credit unions are owned by, and operated for, the benefit of its members. Most of the country's approximately 7,200 credit unions are small, and most are organized around a single employer (municipal workers, teachers, or employees at a large company), so periodic contributions can be deducted from a worker's paycheck. If you are a member of a credit union, it may seem just like a bank, but if you are not a member, you won't be able to use any of its services.
- **Finance Companies** A **finance company** is a firm that specializes in making loans directly to consumers. It also buys installment contracts from merchants who sell goods on credit. Many merchants, for example, cannot afford to wait years for a customer to pay off high-cost items purchased on an installment plan, so the merchant will sell a customer's installment contract to a finance company for a lump sum. This allows the merchant to advertise easy credit terms without actually accepting the full risks of the loan. The finance company then carries the loan full term, or takes customers to court if they do not pay. Because finance companies make some risky loans, they charge more than commercial banks or credit unions.
- **Life Insurance Companies** A life insurance company provides financial protection for a spouse, children, or other dependents in the event of a person's death. The **premium** is the periodic fee that the insured pays for this policy. Because insurance companies collect premiums on a regular basis, they often have surplus cash to lend. Large businesses can often go directly to a life insurance company to get a loan. An individual consumer can sometimes borrow against an insurance policy that he or she holds with a company.
- **Pension Funds** A **pension fund** is a fund that collects periodic contributions from a firm's employees. The fund then makes regular payments called a **pension** to workers who become eligible for retirement or disability benefits. During the 30- to 40-year lag between the time the savings are deposited and the time a worker needs to use them, the money is usually invested in high-quality corporate stocks and bonds.

All financial intermediaries accept deposits or contributions from individuals, businesses, and/or governments, and in each case, the accumulated funds are loaned out to other borrowers. This is how savings in a strong financial system can be made available for use by others in the economy.

✓ **READING PROGRESS CHECK**

Comparing and Contrasting How do finance companies, life insurance companies, and pension funds channel savings to borrowers?

Basic Investment Considerations

GUIDING QUESTION What are the advantages and disadvantages of a risky investment?

You may want to participate in the financial system by saving, or by investing in CDs, bonds, and other financial assets. Before you do so, however, you should be aware of some basic investment considerations.

Consistency

Most successful investors invest consistently over long periods. In most cases, investing on a regular basis is just as important as the amount invested. For example, **Figure 11.2** shows how a monthly deposit of $10 would grow over a 5- to 30-year period at various interest rates. Even at modest rates, the balance in the account accumulates quickly. Because $10 is a small amount, imagine

EXPLORING THE ESSENTIAL QUESTION

Banks, credit unions, and finance companies need savers to survive. Life insurance companies rely on people buying life insurance, and pension funds need people to contribute to pensions. Explain what would happen if people stopped using these financial intermediaries.

credit union nonprofit service cooperative that accepts deposits, makes loans, and provides other financial services

finance company firm that makes loans directly to consumers and specializes in buying installment contracts from merchants who sell on credit

premium monthly, quarterly, semiannual, or annual price paid for an insurance policy

pension fund fund that collects and invests income until payments are made to eligible recipients

pension regular allowance for someone who has worked a certain number of years, reached a certain age, or who has suffered from an injury

CHAPTER 11, LESSON 1
Savings and the Financial System

R Reading Skills

Comparing and contrasting Lead students in a brief discussion of the similarities and differences between *consistency* and *simplicity*. Guide students to understand that both concepts are basic considerations that can help protect investors. Have students create Venn diagrams summarizing how these ideas are alike and different.
ELL Visual/Spatial, Verbal/Linguistic

W Writing Skills

Advertising sensible investment practices
Call on volunteers to identify and explain the factors that people should consider when investing. Note their responses on the board. Then organize students into small groups and ask them to develop a public-service advertising campaign that encourages sensible investment practices. Groups might create a print advertisement, a tape of a radio commercial, or storyboards for a television campaign. Have groups present their campaign ideas to the class. Visual/Spatial, Verbal/Linguistic

C Critical Thinking Skills

Understanding compound interest Walk through the steps of compounding interest with students. Explain that compound interest is different than simple interest. For example, if you deposited $10,000 and earned simple interest of 5%, you would earn $500 a year for a total of $1,500 interest in 3 years. In contrast, if you deposited $10,000 and earned compound interest of 5% annually, you would earn $500 the first year. But in the second year, you would earn interest not on $10,000 but on $10,500—your original deposit plus the first year's interest—which would total $525. In the third year, you would earn interest on $11,025, which is $551.25. With compound interest, then, your initial $10,000 would grow to $11,576.26 in three years, instead of $11,500 with simple interest. Explain that this amount may seem like a minor difference, but it can become a major difference as the balance grows over the years. **AL** Logical/Mathematical

---

ANSWERS, p. 308

CRITICAL THINKING
$439

---

how much larger the account would grow with larger deposits! That is why many investment advisers tell people to save something every month.

Simplicity

Most analysts advise people to stay with what they understand. Thousands of investments are available, and many are quite complicated. Knowing a few fundamental principles can help you make good choices among these options. Successful investors suggest that you should:

- Ignore any investment that seems too complicated, or one that you don't understand.
- Ignore any investment that seems too good to be true, because it probably is.

A few investors do get lucky, but most build wealth because they invest regularly, and they avoid the investments that seem too far out of the ordinary.

Importance of Diversification

While you should do everything you can to understand the characteristics, strengths, and weaknesses of financial assets, it is also important to diversify your investments. **Diversification** means spreading your funds over a wide variety of investments so that losses on a particular one have a limited impact on the entire portfolio. This means that buying 100 shares of 10 different stocks is better than buying 1,000 shares of one stock *even* if the cost is the same.

Better yet, you might spread your risk by buying fewer stocks in all, and using some of the remaining funds on CDs or government bonds. That way, a downturn in all stock prices would not affect the value of the CDs and bonds in your portfolio. So the more you have to invest, the more you should diversify.

diversification the technique of spreading funds over a large number of investments to reduce the portfolio's overall risk

---

FIGURE 11.2

THE POWER OF COMPOUND INTEREST

The Power of Compound Interest

Annual Interest (in percent)	Value at end of year						
	5	10	15	20	25	30
0%	$600	$1,200	$1,800	$2,000	$2,500	$3,600
2%	$630	$1,327	$2,097	$2,948	$3,888	$4,927
4%	$663	$1,472	$2,461	$3,668	$5,141	$6,940
6%	$698	$1,639	$2,908	$4,620	$6,930	$10,045
8%	$735	$1,829	$3,460	$5,890	$9,510	$14,904
10%	$774	$2,048	$4,145	$7,594	$13,268	$22,605
12%	$817	$2,300	$4,996	$9,893	$18,788	$34,950

Most successful investors invest consistently over long periods. In most cases, investing on a regular basis is just as important as the amount invested. For example, Figure 11.2 shows how a monthly deposit of $10 would grow over a 5- to 30-year period at various interest rates.

▲ **CRITICAL THINKING**
Economic Analysis How much interest is earned after the first 10 years at 6 percent?

---

networks   Online Teaching Options

CHARTS

The Power of Compound Interest

Understanding compound interest Project Figure 11.2. Tell students that the chart shows the results of compound interest. Click through the activity, having a volunteer read the text. Tell students that in an account earning compound interest, the sooner savers invest their money, the more money the investment makes. Also, investing on a regular basis increases the money made on an initial investment. Have students answer the questions in the activity. **Ask:** What is the value of the account after 10 years at 6 percent interest? *($1,639)* What is the value of the account at 10 percent interest after 20 years? *($7,594)*
Logical/Mathematical

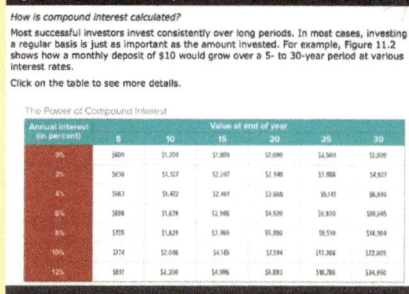

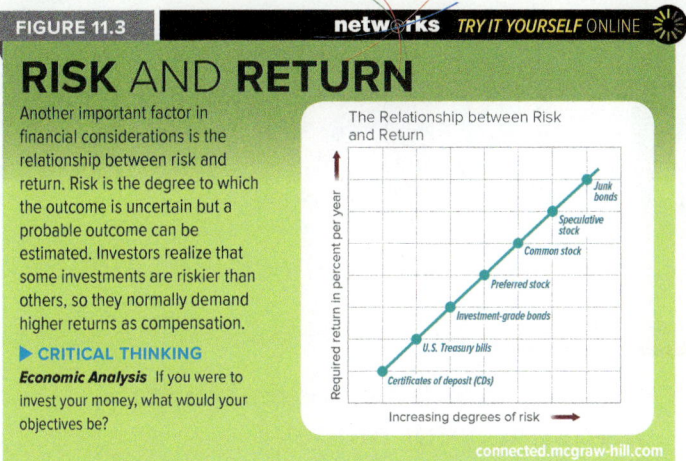

FIGURE 11.3

RISK AND RETURN

Another important factor in financial considerations is the relationship between risk and return. Risk is the degree to which the outcome is uncertain but a probable outcome can be estimated. Investors realize that some investments are riskier than others, so they normally demand higher returns as compensation.

▶ **CRITICAL THINKING**
Economic Analysis If you were to invest your money, what would your objectives be?

The Risk-Return Relationship

Another important factor is the relationship between risk and return. **Risk** is the degree to which the outcome is uncertain but a probable outcome can be estimated. Investors realize that some investments are riskier than others, so they normally demand higher returns as **compensation**. This relationship between increasing risks and returns is illustrated in **Figure 11.3**.

As an investor, you must consider the level of risk that you can tolerate. If you are comfortable with high levels of risk, then you may want to purchase risky investments that promise high returns. Otherwise, consider lower-risk investments instead.

Investment Objectives

Finally, you need to consider your reason for investing. For example, if you want to cover living expenses during random periods of unemployment, you might want to buy financial assets that can easily be converted into cash. If you want to save for retirement, another type of financial asset might work better.

Investors have a large number of stocks, financial assets, and other investments from which to choose. The investor's knowledge of the risk and return characteristics of each, along with his or her own needs, is important when making these decisions.

✓ **READING PROGRESS CHECK**

Identifying If you were to invest your money, what would your objectives be?

risk a situation in which the outcome is not certain, but the probabilities can be estimated

compensation something, such as money, given or received as an equivalent for goods or services, injury, debt, or high risk

---

LESSON 1 REVIEW

Reviewing Vocabulary
1. *Contrasting* What is the difference between a savings account and a certificate of deposit?
2. *Defining* Explain the relationship between risk and return.

Using Your Notes
3. *Contrasting* What are the main differences between credit unions, banks, and life insurance companies in how they serve the financial system?

Answering the Guiding Questions
4. *Describing* What is your role in the circular flow of finance?

5. *Identifying* What are the advantages and disadvantages of a risky investment?

Writing About Economics
6. *Informative/Explanatory* Assume that America has been going through a long period of financial prosperity. People are confident in their jobs, and saving has become a low priority for many people and for businesses. What would be the long-term consequences of this action for individuals and businesses? Explain how this situation would affect economic growth.

CHAPTER 11, LESSON 1
Savings and the Financial System

W Writing Skills

Explaining the financial system and the economy Point out to students that many factors should be considered before investing savings. **Ask: What is the basic source component of the financial system?** *(savings)* Have students write a one-page essay explaining the financial system with its many choices for investing savings. Students should assume readers of their essays know little about choices for investing savings. Ask students to share their essays in class discussion.
BL Verbal/Linguistic

CLOSE & REFLECT

W Writing Skills

Summarizing To make sure students understand the importance of savings to the financial system and the economy, have them write an explanation of why savings must occur to grow the economy. Discuss their explanations in class.

ANSWERS, p. 309

CRITICAL THINKING
Answers will vary. Ask volunteers to discuss their financial objectives.

✓ **READING PROGRESS CHECK** Students will have different goals but should understand how the risk and return relationship will affect those goals.

LESSON 1 REVIEW ANSWERS

Reviewing Vocabulary

1. With a savings account, the bank issues a receipt for the deposit. With a certificate of deposit, the bank issues a type of receipt showing you have loaned money to the bank.

2. Risk is the degree to which the outcome of an investment is underlaid. Typically, higher returns can be expected from a high-risk investment, whereas safer investments pay lower returns.

Using Your Notes

3. A bank accepts deposits and makes loans to all consumers. A credit union accepts deposits and makes loans only to members. A life insurance company insures people's lives and accepts premiums in payment for this service. Surplus from the premiums is loaned directly to businesses.

Answering the Guiding Questions

4. Students should recognize that they are savers whenever they put money into a checking or savings account and borrowers whenever they use a credit card.

5. Risky investments usually offer greater opportunities for high returns but they may also lose some or all of their value.

Writing About Economics

6. Students should recognize that if people and businesses stopped saving, it would disrupt the circular flow of finance by reducing the availability of cash that could be loaned to businesses and individuals. This might slow economic growth and deprive individuals of the means for financing new homes, cars, and so on. Students might recognize that a lack of cash for loans would drive interest rates for available loans higher.

CHAPTER 11, LESSON 2
Financial Assets and Their Markets

ENGAGE

C Critical Thinking Skills

🔔 **Identifying investment options** Tell students that in this lesson they will learn about bonds and certificates of deposit—their risks, yields, ratings, and markets in which they are sold. Have students browse through the lesson and create an outline of major and minor headings, leaving space to add details under the minor headings. Ask students to also list vocabulary terms off to the side of their outline, similar to a Cornell note-taking style. As students encounter a vocabulary term, remind them to add the definition to their notes.

AL Logical/Mathematical

English Language Proficiency

Intermediate To help students speak using grade-level content area vocabulary in context, list these vocabulary words on the board: *bond, par value, maturity, coupon rate, current yield, junk bonds, municipal bonds, tax-exempt, savings bonds, EE savings bonds, beneficiary, Treasury notes, Treasury bonds, Treasury bills, IRAs, capital market, money market, primary market, secondary market.* Ask students questions about the content of Lesson 2. Tell them to use at least one of the words from the board in each answer.

ANSWERS, p. 310

ESSENTIAL QUESTION ACTIVITY

Safe investments include municipal bonds, savings bonds, EE savings bonds, Treasury notes, Treasury bonds, Treasury bills, and long-term mutual funds. Riskier assets include corporate bonds and stocks.

TAKING NOTES
Sample answers: Bonds (municipal, savings, corporate); Treasuries (Treasury notes, Treasury bonds, Treasury bills); Stocks; Certificates of deposit (CDs)

Interact with these digital assets and others in lesson 2
✓ INTERACTIVE CHART Bond Ratings
✓ INTERACTIVE CHART Financial Assets and Their Markets
✓ SELF-CHECK QUIZ
✓ VIDEO

networks TRY IT YOURSELF ONLINE

LESSON 2
Financial Assets and Their Markets

Reading Help Desk

Academic Vocabulary
- offset

Content Vocabulary
- bond
- par value
- maturity
- coupon rate
- current yield
- junk bonds
- municipal bonds
- tax-exempt
- savings bonds
- EE savings bonds
- beneficiary
- Treasury notes
- Treasury bonds
- Treasury bills
- Individual Retirement Accounts (IRAs)
- capital market
- money market
- primary market
- secondary market

TAKING NOTES:

Key Ideas and Details
ACTIVITY Use a graphic organizer like the one below to identify and describe at least four financial assets.

ESSENTIAL QUESTION

What options are available for investing your money?

You have inherited a few thousand dollars from a relative. What do you do with this money? You don't want to put it under your mattress for safekeeping. You want it to work for you; that is, you want to increase the amount of money you have. To do that, you must put the money in something that pays interest. You know that some investments are safe, because there is little or no chance that you will lose your original investment. Others are risky, because you may lose your original sum. The point to remember is that the safer the investment, the lower the return, or the less your money earns. Name at least one safe and one risky investment option you can use to help your money grow.

Bonds as Financial Assets

GUIDING QUESTION *What factors determine a bond's value?*

Bonds are popular financial assets, and we hear about them all the time. Governments and businesses issue bonds when they need to borrow funds for long periods. A **bond** is a formal long-term contract that requires repayment of borrowed money and interest on the borrowed funds at regular intervals over time.

Increasingly, bonds are taking on an international flavor with companies in one country issuing bonds in another. Although this may seem complex, the main components of a bond are relatively simple.

Bond Components
A bond has three main components:
- **Par value** Par value is the amount borrowed and consequently the amount that must be paid back to the lender by the time the bond reaches its maturity.

310

---

networks **Online Teaching Options**

BELLRINGER

Financial Assets and Their Markets

Identifying financial institutions in the financial system Have students view the Bellringer.
Ask: **What does the word *bailout* refer to in the headline?** *(The Obama administration did not let the largest finance companies fail during the recession.)* **Why do you suppose the issue of saving finance companies is related to the lesson on financial assets?** Explain that finance companies are just one type of financial intermediary that connects savers to borrowers. In this lesson, students are going to examine the options available for investing their money.
AL Logical/Mathematical

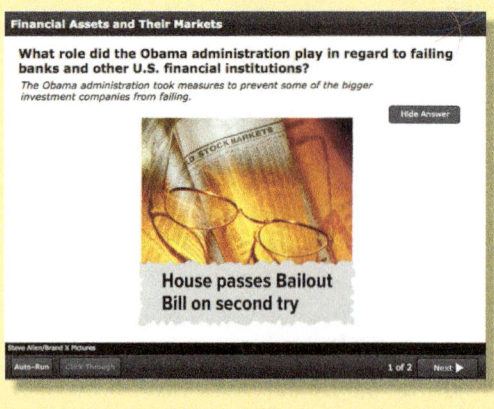

- **Maturity** Maturity refers to the life of a bond. If the bond has a 30-year maturity, then the issuer of the bond has 30 years to repay the lender.
- **Coupon rate** Coupon rate is the rate of interest that is paid on the par value. A bond with a 5 percent coupon rate will pay 5 percent of the par value annually, usually in two semiannual payments.

Suppose a corporation sells a 6 percent, 20-year, $1,000 par value bond that pays interest semiannually. The coupon payment to the bond holder is $30 semiannually (.06 times $1000, divided by 2). When the bond reaches maturity after 20 years, the company retires the debt by paying the holder the par value of $1,000.

Bond Prices

An investor views the bond as a financial asset that will pay $30 twice a year for 20 years, plus a final par value payment of $1,000. Investors can offer $950, $1,000, $1,100, or any other amount for this future payment stream. An investor may consider changes in future interest rates, the risk that the company will default, and other factors before deciding what to offer. Supply and demand among buyers and sellers will then establish the final price of the bond.

bond formal contract to repay borrowed money and interest on the borrowed money at regular future intervals

par value principal of a bond or total amount borrowed

maturity life of a bond or length of time funds are borrowed

coupon rate stated interest on a corporate, municipal or government bond

THE GLOBAL ECONOMY & YOU

Trading Around the World

Computer trading of stocks and bonds makes it possible for individual traders to trade on exchanges all around the world. So, if traders cannot find attractive investments in U.S. markets, they can always look for buying or selling opportunities in other countries—or even on other continents.

Most professional traders that deal with international markets work for an investment bank or brokerage firm. These firms manage their clients' money by buying and selling securities in hopes of securing a profit. This requires traders to closely monitor stock and bond prices around the world.

Other traders may be self-employed and operate a small business out of their home. Most use sophisticated computer software to analyze a vast array of data about global stocks and bonds. These professionals have programmed their computer models to look for certain indicators that will tell them what to buy or sell, and when to do it.

Online brokerage firms provide some computer-based analytical tools, but they may not provide individual traders with access to stocks on every international market. Instead, most offer access to several of the largest and most popular global stock indices like the DJIA (US), FTSE (UK), DAX (Germany), CAC (France), Nikkei (Japan), and the Hang Seng (Hong Kong).

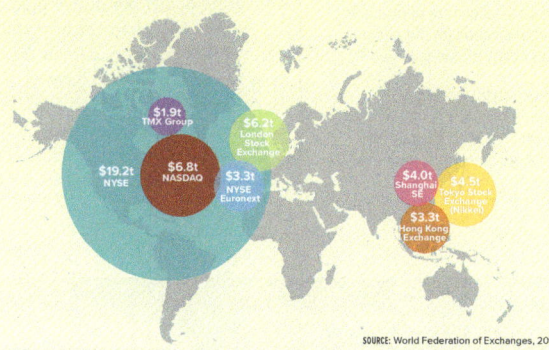

SOURCE: World Federation of Exchanges, 2015

▲ **CRITICAL THINKING**
Drawing Inferences What can you infer about the effects that globally traded stocks and bonds might have on an economy in trouble, or one that is experiencing a temporary downturn? What, if anything, might be done about these effects?

Online stock trading of international stocks has not yet gone 24/7, but investors can still trade "after hours" by posting "buy" or "sell" orders to be executed when markets open, or when stocks or bonds hit a certain price. For traders who want 24/7 action, major currencies like the U.S. dollar, the euro, the Japanese yen, or the Australian dollar are sold around the clock, 168 hours a week.

connected.mcgraw-hill.com   Financial Markets **311**

CHAPTER 11, LESSON 2
Financial Assets and Their Markets

TEACH & ASSESS

C Critical Thinking Skills

Identifying bond categories Organize students into groups of four. Assign each group member one of the following categories: bond components, bond prices, bond yields, or bond ratings. Have members create flash cards with questions about their assigned category. Then have group members quiz one another using the flash cards.
BL Visual/Spatial

R Reading Skills

Understanding bonds Ask: What are you doing when you purchase a bond? *(You are lending money to the borrower. The borrower may be a corporation or a government—federal, state, or local—that issues the bonds.)* **Generally, how does one make money from purchasing a bond?** *(The bond issuer pays periodic interest payments—often semiannually—to the bondholder. After a set period of time—the maturity—the bond itself, or par value, is repaid.)*

INTERACTIVE FEATURE

Global Economy & You

Examining world stock markets Have students view the Global Economy & You feature. **Ask: What does computer trading of stocks and bonds enable an investor to do if the U.S. market is on the downswing?** *(U.S. traders can look for buying opportunities around the world.)* Have students discuss how the circular-flow financial model they discussed in Lesson 1 is affected by the rest of the world. Then have students explain whether they think global trading has more advantages or more disadvantages. Ask for reasons supporting their point of view. **AL** Logical/Mathematical

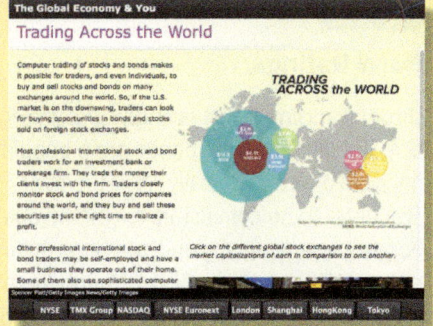

ANSWERS, p. 311

CRITICAL THINKING

Students should explain that as investments follow trends (e.g., an upswing in a chart), investors pile into that trend. Students may infer that this electronic movement of assets into or out of an economy in a temporary downturn or other condition may exacerbate that condition and make it harder for the economy to recover.

CHAPTER 11, LESSON 2
Financial Assets and Their Markets

W Writing Skills

Explaining a bond's ratings Direct students to research the rating of a bond they might consider purchasing. **Ask: Why would you want to find a bond's ratings?** *(to make sure that the issuing agency has a good credit rating)* Have them find the Standard & Poor's and Moody's ratings for the bond and research how these corporations evaluated the bond. **BL** Verbal/Linguistic

T Technology Skills

Following bond interest rates Explain that many newspapers and Web sites post interest rates for both corporate and government bonds. Televised financial shows also offer the interest rates daily. Ask students to select three bonds or types of bonds and follow their interest rates for a week. Students may make spreadsheets or graphs to present their findings. Logical/Mathematical

R Reading Skills

Understanding bond ratings Direct students' attention to the bond ratings table. Discuss words in the table such as *speculative* and *default*. Explain to students that these terms have other meanings, but here they are being used to describe bonds. Working in pairs, have students look up the meanings of the words in relation to bonds. Pairs should write a sentence using each word. **ELL** Verbal/Linguistic

---

ANSWERS, p. 312

CRITICAL THINKING

Students should explain that lower rated bonds pay more because they're riskier.

Bond Yields

In order to compare bonds, investors usually compute the bond's **current yield**, the annual interest divided by the purchase price. If an investor paid $950 for the bond described above, the current yield would be $60 divided by $950, or 6.32 percent. If the investor paid $1,100 for the bond, the current yield would be $60 divided by $1,100, or 5.46 percent.

It may appear as if the issuer fixes the return on a bond when the bond is first issued. However, the interest received, and the price paid, determine the actual current yield of each bond. The result is that the bond yield, like the bond price, is determined by supply and demand.

Bond Ratings

Because the creditworthiness, or financial health, of corporations and governments differ, all 6 percent, 20-year, $1,000 bonds will not cost the same.

There are no guarantees that the issuer will be around in 20 years to redeem the bond. Therefore, investors will pay more for bonds with an impeccable credit rating. However, investors will pay less for a similar bond if it is issued by a corporation with a low credit rating.

Fortunately, investors have a way to check the quality of bonds. Two major corporations, Standard & Poor's and Moody's, publish bond ratings. They rate bonds on a number of factors, including the basic financial health of the issuer, the expected ability of the issuer to make the future coupon and principal payments, and the issuer's past credit history.

Bond ratings, shown in **Figure 11.4**, use letters scaled from AAA, which represents the highest investment grade, to D, which generally stands for default. If a bond is in default, the issuer has not kept up with the interest or other required payments. These ratings are widely publicized, and investors can find the rating of any bond they plan to purchase.

Bonds with high ratings sell at higher prices than the bonds with lower ratings. A 6 percent, 20-year, $1,000 par value bond with an AAA-grade rating may sell for $1,100 and have a current yield of 5.45 percent ($60/$1,100 = 0.0545 or 5.45 percent). Another 6 percent, 20-year, $1,000 par value bond issued by a different company may have a BBB-grade rating, and may therefore sell for only $950 because of a higher risk. The second bond, however, has a higher current yield of 6.32 percent ($60/$950 = 0.0632 or 6.32 percent). This is consistent with

current yield bond's annual coupon interest divided by purchase price; measure of a bond's return

offset to balance higher levels of risk with a larger payoff

junk bonds exceptionally risky bond with a Standard & Poor's rating of BB or lower that carries a high rate of return as compensation for the higher possibility of non-payment

municipal bonds a type of investment, often tax exempt, issued by state and local governments; known as munis

FIGURE 11.4
BOND RATINGS

Investors have a way to check the quality of bonds. Two major corporations, Standard & Poor's and Moody's, publish bond ratings. They rate bonds on a number of factors, including the basic financial health of the issuer, the expected ability of the issuer to make the future coupon and principal payments, and the issuer's past credit history.

▶ **CRITICAL THINKING**
Economic Analysis How do bond ratings affect the price of bonds?

	Standard & Poor's	Moody's	
High investment grade	AAA	Aaa	Best quality
High grade	AA	Aa	High quality
Upper medium grade	A	a	Upper medium grade
Medium grade	BBB	Baa	Medium grade
Lower medium grade	BB	Ba	Possesses speculative elements
Speculative	B	B	Generally not desirable
Vulnerable to default	CCC	Caa	Poor, possibly in default
Subordinated to other debt rated CCC	CC	Ca	Highly speculative, often in default
Subordinated to CC debt	C	C	Income bonds not paying income
Bond in default	D	D	Interest and principal payments in default

Source: Standard & Poor's; Moody's

312

---

networks Online Teaching Options

CHARTS

Bond Ratings

Understanding bond ratings Display Figure 11.4. Tell students that bonds are a popular financial asset, especially for retirement accounts. To help investors check the quality of bonds, two major corporations publish bond ratings. Have students click through the activity.
Ask: What are some factors considered in the bond ratings? *(Answers should include some of the following: the basic financial health of the issuer, the expected ability of the issuer to make the future coupon and principal payments, and the issuer's past credit history.)* **What is the range of the ratings?** *(The ratings range from best quality to a company having bonds in default.)* **AL** Logical/Mathematical

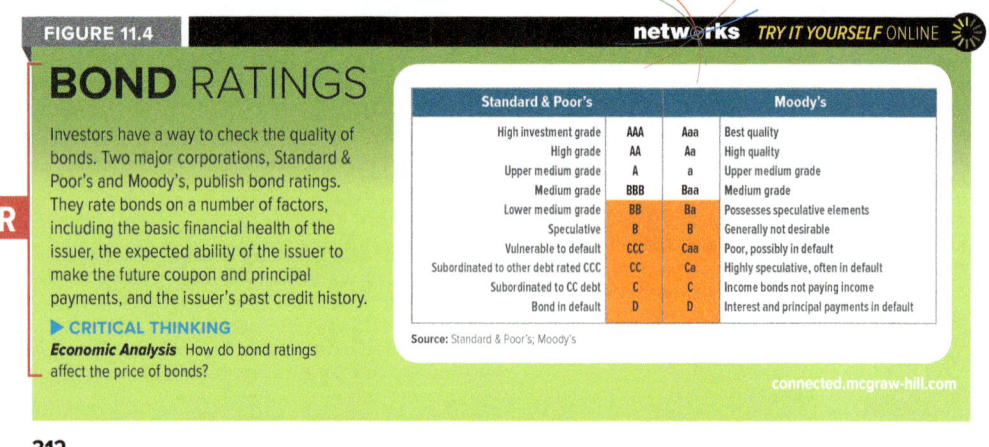

Figure 11.4 Bond Ratings
Investors have a way to check the quality of bonds. Two major corporations, Standard & Poor's and Moody's, publish bond ratings. They rate bonds on a number of factors, including the basic financial health of the issuer, the expected ability of the issuer to make the future coupon and principal payments, and the issuer's past credit history.

Click on the name of each corporation to get a brief background of the company.

the basic risk-return relationship, which states that investors require higher returns to **offset** increased levels of risk.

Bonds issued by the U.S. government are considered to be the safest of all financial assets because they have almost no risk of ever being in default. Because of this, these bonds also have the lowest yields.

✓ READING PROGRESS CHECK

Describing What factors determine a bond's value?

Financial Assets and Their Characteristics

GUIDING QUESTION *Which financial assets are the safest?*

The modern investor has a wide range of financial assets from which to choose. These include certificates of deposit, bonds, and Treasury notes and bills. They vary in cost, maturity, and risk.

Certificates of Deposit

Certificates of deposit (CDs) are a common investment. Many people think of them as just another type of account with a bank, but they are loans that investors make to financial institutions. Because banks and other borrowers count on the use of these funds for a certain time period, they usually impose a penalty if people try to cash in their CDs early.

CDs are attractive to small investors because they can cost as little as $500 or $1,000. Investors can also select the length of maturity, giving them an opportunity to tailor the expiration date to future expenditures such as college tuition, a vacation, or some other expense. Some banks issue CDs in almost any denomination and for various lengths of time.

Finally, the CDs issued by commercial banks, savings banks, and savings associations are included in the $250,000 FDIC insurance limit. The National Credit Union Association insures most CDs issued by credit unions.

Corporate Bonds

Corporate bonds are an important source of corporate funds. Some individual corporate bonds have par value as low as $1,000, but par value of $10,000 are more common. When investors buy a bond, they first determine the level of risk they can afford, and then they narrow their search to bonds with the same risk ratings.

Bond ratings are shown in Figure 11.4. The highest investment grade bonds carry ranking of triple or double A, while **junk bonds**—exceptionally risky bonds with a Standard & Poor's rating of BB or lower, or a Moody's rating of Ba or lower—carry the highest rates of return to compensate for the highest possibility of default.

Investors may purchase corporate bonds as long-term investments, but these and most other bonds can be quickly sold if investors need cash for other purposes. The Internal Revenue Service considers the interest, or coupon, payments on corporate bonds as taxable income, a fact investors must consider when they invest in bonds.

Municipal Bonds

Municipal bonds, or "munis," are bonds issued by state and local governments. States issue bonds to finance highways, state buildings, and some public works. Cities issue bonds to pay for baseball parks and football stadiums, or to fund

BIOGRAPHY

Suze Orman
FINANCIAL ADVISOR (1951–)

Suze Orman's family was not rich. After leaving college, Orman waitressed for $400 a week. Dreaming of opening a restaurant, she invested her money with a stockbroker who put it into risky investments. Orman lost everything. Orman became determined to learn about investing. She got a trainee job with a brokerage and did so well that in the year 1987 she started her own brokerage firm.

Orman's media career began on a local radio show. Listeners really liked her. Many wrote asking for investment advice. In the 1990s, Orman responded by writing a series of investment books; some became best sellers.

The weekly Suze Orman Show started on TV in 2003 and became an instant hit. Orman has appeared on other TV shows and writes an investment column for a magazine.

▲ **CRITICAL THINKING**
Identifying Cause and Effect What experience compelled Suze Orman to learn about finance and become a broker?
Hypothesizing Why do you think the broker Orman hired put all her money into risky investments? What do you think his intentions were?

CHAPTER 11, LESSON 2
Financial Assets and Their Markets

C Critical Thinking Skills

Comparing financial assets Divide the class into groups of four students each. Assign each group a financial asset such as municipal bonds, Treasury bills, certificates of deposits, or corporate bonds. Have two members of each group prepare a list of advantages of investing in their assigned asset, and the other two members write a list of disadvantages of investing in their assigned asset. Have students come together with each group explaining its assets advantages and disadvantages to the rest of the class. **BL** Interpersonal, Verbal/Linguistic

Content Background Knowledge

Savings Bonds After the attack on Pearl Harbor in 1941, the government implemented savings bonds called *war bonds* to increase public funding for the war effort. These bonds were issued in denominations of $10, $25, $50, $75, $100, $200, $500, $1,000, $10,000, and $100,000, and could be purchased at 75 percent of the face amount. Public figures urged citizens to buy war bonds, and department stores encouraged customers to accept war stamps in place of change. Even movie stars urged the public to buy more bonds.

W1 Writing Skills

Contrasting Treasury notes and Treasury bills Have students write a compare-and-contrast paragraph about how investors receive returns on their investments in Treasury notes and Treasury bills. Students' paragraphs should explain that periodic interest is added directly to Treasury note accounts, whereas Treasury bills are sold on a discount basis. **AL** Logical/Mathematical, Verbal/Linguistic

W2 Writing Skills

Comparing investment options Have students work in groups of three or four to select three investment options and compare their levels of safety vs. risks, and their potential returns. Have students develop their own rating systems to evaluate these investment options. They may wish to include corresponding visual symbols with their ratings. Have students consider any of the following: government or corporate bonds, equities, certificates of deposit, and Treasury bills. Discuss group findings in class. **BL** Logical/Mathematical

---

libraries, parks, and other civic improvements. Because governments have the power to tax, and will be able to pay interest and principal for any bonds they issue, municipal bonds are generally regarded as safe investments.

Most municipal bonds are **tax-exempt**, meaning that the federal government does not tax the interest paid to investors. In some cases, the states issuing the bonds also exempt the interest payments from state taxes. The tax-exempt feature also allows the government agencies to pay a lower rate of interest, thereby lowering the government's cost of borrowing.

Government Savings Bonds

C **Savings bonds**, or **EE savings bonds**, are low-denomination, non-transferable bonds issued by the U.S. government. Investors can buy them directly from the U.S. Treasury over the Internet. All an investor has to do is open an account, and the bonds will be issued electronically to the investor's account. The electronic bonds sell at face value, so you pay $50 for a $50 bond, or $10,000 for a $10,000 bond, and interest is added later.

Investors often buy bonds for their heirs by designating a **beneficiary**, or someone who inherits the ownership of the financial asset if the purchaser dies. A grandmother, for example, may buy EE saving bonds in her name and designate a grandchild as the beneficiary. When she dies, the beneficiary automatically takes ownership of the savings bond without having to pay any inheritance taxes.

Treasury Notes and Bonds

When the federal government borrows funds for periods lasting longer than one year, it issues Treasury notes and bonds. **Treasury notes** are United States government obligations with maturities of 2 to 10 years, while **Treasury bonds** have maturity dates of 20–30 years. Both pay interest every 6 months until they mature. The only collateral that secures both is the faith and credit of the U.S. government.

Treasury notes and bonds come in denominations of $100, which means that small investors can afford to buy them. The notes and bonds are issued electronically, and investors purchase them directly from the U.S. Treasury. Since the investors' accounts are computerized, the Treasury adds the periodic interest payments directly to these accounts rather than mailing checks to the investors.

Treasury Bills

Federal government borrowing generates other financial assets known as **Treasury bills**. A Treasury bill, also called a T-bill, is a short-term obligation with a maturity of 4, 13, 26, or 52 weeks and a minimum denomination of $100.

T-bills do not pay interest directly; instead, they are sold on a discount basis. For example, an investor may pay an auction price of $970 for a 26-week bill that matures at $1,000. The $30 difference between the amount paid and the amount received is the interest, or the investor's return. Because the investor receives $30 profit on a $970 investment, the semiannual return of $30 divided by $970 is 3.1 percent.

Individual Retirement Accounts

W2 Many employees invest money in **Individual Retirement Accounts (IRAs)**, long-term, tax-sheltered time deposits that can be set up as part of an individual retirement plan. For example, an unmarried worker may decide to deposit $4,000 annually in such an account.

The worker then deducts these deposits from his or her taxable income, thereby sheltering $4,000 from the individual income tax. Taxes on the interest

---

tax-exempt not subject to tax by federal or state governments

savings bonds low-denomination, non-transferable bond issued by the federal government, usually through payroll savings plans

EE savings bonds low-denomination, non-transferable bond issued by the federal government, usually through payroll savings plans

beneficiary person designated to take ownership of an asset if the owner of the asset dies

Treasury notes United States government obligation with a maturity of 2 to 10 years

Treasury bonds United States government bond with maturity of 30 years

Treasury bills short-term United States government obligation with a maturity of 4, 13, 26, or 52 weeks and a minimum denomination of $100

Individual Retirement Accounts (IRAs) retirement account in the form of a long-term time deposit, with annual contributions not taxed until withdrawn during retirement

---

networks Online Teaching Options

WORKSHEET

Financial Markets Reteaching Activity

Summarizing financial markets Project the worksheet and tell students that it summarizes information about financial markets. Lead the class in discussion to fill out the columns. After the columns are filled in, have student pairs write answers to the questions on the worksheet. Reassemble the class and discuss the answers. **AL** Verbal/Linguistic

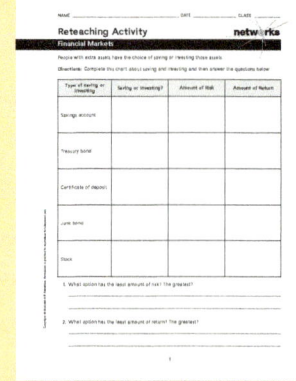

and the principal will eventually have to be paid when the worker reaches retirement. However, the tax-deferment feature gives the worker an incentive to save today, postponing the taxes until the worker is retired and probably in a lower tax bracket.

☑ READING PROGRESS CHECK

Analyzing What features of a government bond appeal most to you?

Markets for Financial Assets

GUIDING QUESTION *Why is there overlap among markets for financial assets?*

Investors often refer to markets according to the characteristics of the financial assets traded in them. These markets overlap to a considerable degree.

Capital Markets

Investors speak of the **capital market** when they mean a market in which money is loaned for more than one year. Long-term CDs and corporate and government bonds that take more than a year to mature belong in this category. Capital market assets are shown in the right-hand column of **Figure 11.5**.

capital market market in which financial capital is loaned and/or borrowed for more than one year

Money Markets

Investors refer to the **money market** when they mean a market in which money is loaned for period of less than one year. The financial assets that belong to the money market are shown in the left-hand column of Figure 11.5.

Note that a person who owns a CD with a maturity of one year or less is involved in the money market. If the CD has a maturity of more than one year, the person is involved in the capital market as a supplier of funds.

Many investors purchase money market mutual funds, which are funds created when investor deposits are pooled so that stocks or bonds can be purchased. Money market mutual funds usually pay slightly higher interest rates than banks.

money market a market in which financial capital is loaned and/or borrowed for one year or less

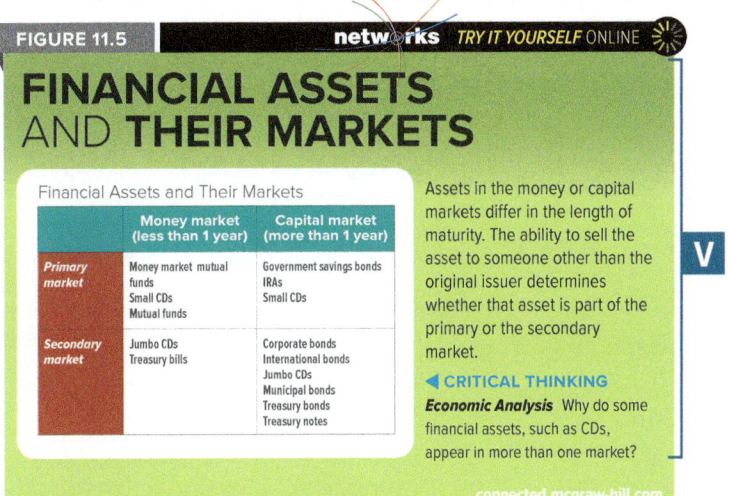

FIGURE 11.5

FINANCIAL ASSETS AND THEIR MARKETS

Financial Assets and Their Markets

	Money market (less than 1 year)	Capital market (more than 1 year)
Primary market	Money market mutual funds Small CDs Mutual funds	Government savings bonds IRAs Small CDs
Secondary market	Jumbo CDs Treasury bills	Corporate bonds International bonds Jumbo CDs Municipal bonds Treasury bonds Treasury notes

Assets in the money or capital markets differ in the length of maturity. The ability to sell the asset to someone other than the original issuer determines whether that asset is part of the primary or the secondary market.

◀ CRITICAL THINKING
Economic Analysis Why do some financial assets, such as CDs, appear in more than one market?

connected.mcgraw-hill.com

CHAPTER 11, LESSON 2
Financial Assets and Their Markets

R Reading Skills

Identifying money market mutual funds
Ask: **How are money market mutual funds created?** *(when financial managers pool the deposits of their customers to purchase stocks or bonds)*

Content Background Knowledge

Money Market Mutual Funds Money market mutual funds are popular investment tools. They can be either a capital market investment (matures in more than one year) or a money market investment (matures in less than one year). The purpose of a money market mutual fund is to give investors a safe place to easily invest cash assets. Although they usually have low returns, they carry low risk. Money market fund shares are always worth at least one dollar. The rate of interest that the shares can earn changes.

V Visual Skills

Evaluating capital and money markets Direct students' attention to the Financial Assets and Their Markets chart. Ask: **Why might an investor choose a certificate of deposit (CD) over a corporate bond?** *(CDs often have a shorter maturity, are less risky, and may require less investment money.)* **What financial asset appears in more than one market?** *(CDs)* **What is the difference between a government savings bond and a Treasury bond?** *(The government savings bond is in the primary market and cannot be transferred, and the Treasury bond is in the secondary market and can be transferred.)* **What information about IRAs does the chart provide?** *(The chart shows that IRAs take more than one year to mature and can be sold or repurchased only the original issuer.)*
Visual/Spatial

CHARTS

Financial Assets and Their Markets

Comparing and contrasting money and capital markets Display Figure 11.5. Tell students that assets in the money and capital markets differ in the length of maturity. Ask: **What are some assets that mature in less than a year?** *(money market mutual funds, Treasury bills)* **What are some assets that mature after more than a year?** *(government savings bonds and municipal bonds)* The primary market of an asset means that the asset cannot be transferred. Only the original issuer, such as the government when issuing government savings bonds, can sell or repurchase an asset. Ask: **What determines whether an asset is in the secondary market?** *(An asset can be sold to someone other than the original issuer.)* **What are some assets that mature in less than a year and are in the secondary market?** *(Treasury bills, Jumbo CDs)* AL Logical/Mathematical, Verbal/Linguistic

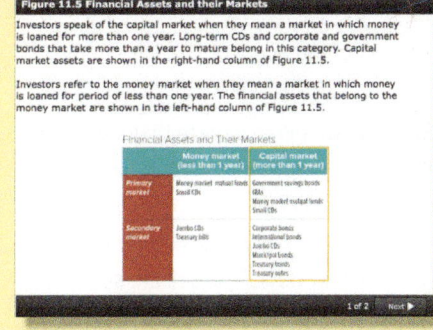

ANSWERS, p. 315

☑ **READING PROGRESS CHECK** Students may explain that the safety or lack of risk in a government bond appeals to them most.

CRITICAL THINKING
Some financial assets, such as CDs, appear in more than one market because some can and some cannot be sold to someone else.

CHAPTER 11, LESSON 2
Financial Assets and Their Markets

CLOSE & REFLECT

C Critical Thinking Skills

Summarizing financial assets and their markets
Have student pairs review the lesson and list the characteristics of the different financial assets discussed and their markets. Pairs should use their lists in a class discussion that summarizes the key points of the lesson.

ANSWERS, p. 316

EXPLORING THE ESSENTIAL QUESTION

Student pie charts will vary by proportion or percentage of pie given to each type of financial instrument, but student charts should show that (1) Conservative Strategy charts have more safe investments (bonds, treasuries) and fewer stocks; (2) Moderate Strategy charts may have equal bonds and stocks; and (3) Aggressive Strategy charts have more stocks, junk bonds, etc., than safe treasuries or similar bonds.

✓ **READING PROGRESS CHECK** In a primary market, only the initial issuer can sell the asset; in a secondary market, all assets can be sold. In a capital market, money is lent for more than one year; in a money market, money is lent for less than one year.

EXPLORING THE ESSENTIAL QUESTION

As you begin your working life, you will want to save and invest some of your earnings to have money for retirement, to accumulate a down payment for a house, or other important purchase. What strategy do you think you'll be comfortable with in distributing your money among different types of investment? There are basically three investment strategies based on an investor's risk tolerance. A conservative allocation is low risk. A moderate allocation has medium risk. An aggressive allocation has greater risk. The different strategies allocate different proportions of your money to different types of investment, depending on your strategy.

Research the three investment strategies, or risk tolerances. Create a pie chart for each investment strategy. Show an approximate allocation (in bonds, stocks, treasuries, junk bonds, etc.) for each investment strategy.

Primary Markets

Another way to view financial markets is to focus on the liquidity of a newly created financial asset. One market for financial assets is the **primary market**, a market where only the original issuer can sell or repurchase a financial asset. Government savings bonds and IRAs are in this market because neither of them can be transferred. Small CDs are also in the primary market because investors tend to cash them early if they need money, rather than trying to sell them to someone else.

primary market market in which only the original issuer can sell or repurchase a financial asset; government savings bonds, IRAs, small CDs

Secondary Markets

If a financial asset can be sold to someone other than the original issuer, it then becomes part of the **secondary market**, where existing financial assets can be resold to new owners.

The major difference between the primary and secondary market is the liquidity that the secondary market provides to its investors. If a strong secondary market exists for a financial asset, investors know that the asset can be liquidated quickly and without penalty, other than the fee for handling the transaction.

secondary market market in which all financial assets can be sold to someone other than the original issuer; corporate bonds, government bonds

✓ **READING PROGRESS CHECK**

Contrasting How are capital and money markets different? How do primary and secondary markets differ?

LESSON 2 REVIEW

Reviewing Vocabulary

1. *Describing* In general, which bond would pay a higher interest rate on your investment: a Treasury bond or a junk bond? Why?

2. *Explaining* What benefit to investors does investing in the secondary market have over investing in a primary market?

Reviewing Your Notes

Use the information you jotted down in the graphic organizer to answer this question.

3. *Describing* Describe two different types of financial assets and explain how they differ from each other.

Answering the Guiding Questions

4. *Describing* What factors determine a bond's value?

5. *Assessing* Which financial assets are the safest?

6. *Explaining* Why is there overlap among markets for financial assets?

Writing About Economics

7. *Narrative* Write a two-paragraph narrative. In paragraph one, describe a person who is wise to invest money conservatively, or in low-risk investments. What types of investments would they be? Describe this person's circumstances and investment goals. In the second paragraph, describe a person who would be wise to invest money in an aggressive, high-risk portfolio. What types of investments would this person buy? What might this person's circumstances and investment goals be? Explain why each is wise in making very different types of investments, on the basis of each one's situation and goals.

LESSON 2 REVIEW ANSWERS

Reviewing Vocabulary

1. Students explain that the junk bond would pay more because it's riskier.

2. Students should state that the secondary market allows anyone who holds an asset to sell it to someone else.

Using Your Notes

3. Students may describe any two of the following: bonds, stocks, CDs, treasuries, etc., and provide at least one difference between the two chosen.

Answering the Guiding Questions

4. The risk of the bond, or financial stability of the issuer, is the main determinant of value.

5. Students should recognize that those insured by or backed by the U.S. government are safest.

6. Students should mention that different markets may be able to sell the same or similar assets.

Writing About Economics

7. Student narratives should describe someone, such as a retiree, who needs to have a safe source of income or savings; so conservative investments are wise in this situation. Someone looking to grow his or her money quickly would be wise to put some of it into more risky investments that pay more.

CHAPTER 11
Case Study

Case Study

THE NEW YORK and the NATIONAL STOCK EXCHANGES

The New York Stock Exchange (NYSE) is one of the largest and the most influential stock exchanges in the world. It began in 1792 when 24 stockbrokers met under a buttonwood tree to establish a set of rules for buying and selling the bonds and shares of company stock. The Buttonwood Agreement was signed by all present, who then regularly met under the Wall Street tree. In 1817, the Buttonwood Agreement was updated to establish the New York Stock & Exchange Board—shortened to the New York Stock Exchange in 1863.

In 2006 the NYSE merged with a publicly traded electronic exchange, to become the NYSE Group, Inc. In 2008, NYSE merged with a European exchange to become NYSE Euronext. It also incorporated the American Stock Exchange (AMEX) to become the world's largest exchange group.

Now a new electronic age of computer-based trading has taken over. Brokers still trade on the floor, but the old days of shouting stockbrokers and using hand gestures to buy or sell stocks or bonds have diminished. Anyone with a computer and Internet access—from high-powered financial institutions to ordinary individuals with online brokerage accounts—can trade electronically at the NYSE.

The National Stock Exchange operates purely in digital trades.

The National Stock Exchange (NSE) is less well known than the NYSE. The NSE was established in Cincinnati in 1865 and was long known as the Cincinnati Stock Exchange (CSE). As the exchange grew and traded more widely, it opened a second office in Chicago, and a new name had to be found to announce its more widespread influence. In 2003, the CSE was rechristened the National Stock Exchange.

The NSE is unique in that all trades are conducted electronically. The NSE went totally electronic in 1980; by 1986, it had completely automated all transactions. Using its own very advanced trading software has made physical trading by brokers unnecessary and has helped keep down the cost of trading. In 2006, the NSE introduced BLADE, a state-of-the-art electronic trading technology. BLADE can complete trades in microseconds and is highly cost effective.

The NYSE Euronext is located in New York City.

The NSE currently maintains its primary headquarters in New Jersey. Of course, because of its innovative trading technology, the new NSE has no trading floor. Though many equities and bonds can be traded on the NSE, it is best known for its trading in exchange-traded funds, or ETFs.

CASE STUDY REVIEW

1. **Comparing and Contrasting** How are the NYSE and the NSE similar in how they trade? In what ways are they different?

2. **Drawing Inferences** What actions taken by the NYSE led to its becoming the world's largest exchange? What can you infer from this about the nature of financial activity in the world today?

C1 Critical Thinking Skills

Examining stock markets Have students state terms that relate to the New York and National stock exchanges. Make a master list on the board from the discussion. Have volunteers select an item from the list and expand on it. Ask other students to give their impressions of the terms and where they received those impressions. *(movies, documentaries, parents, and so on)* **AL** Verbal/Linguistic

R Reading Skills

Explaining NYSE history Have students read the Case Study and find the information about the Buttonwood Agreement of 1792. Have them re-read that information. Tell students to write a short essay describing the Buttonwood Agreement and its importance. Encourage students to include an illustration with their essays and to share their essays and illustrations. **ELL** Verbal/Linguistic

C2 Critical Thinking Skills

Identifying new exchange memberships Tell students that membership in the NYSE Euronext exchange has been limited to 1,366 seats since 1953. Today, if a company wants to join the exchange, it must purchase a membership from a current exchange member. Have student groups research how much the membership seats have sold for in the last five years and the companies that bought those membership seats. Have students make a chart summarizing the information.

T Technology Skills

Examining stock market glitches To examine the pitfalls of a computerized exchange, have students research computer glitches the New York and National stock exchanges have experienced in the last ten years and create a report. Tell them to describe the safeguards that have been installed to prevent such glitches from recurring. **BL**

ANSWERS, p. 317

Case Study Review

1. Students should explain that both use a lot of electronic, computer-based trading, but that the NSE uses this exclusively.
2. Students should state that the NYSE has engaged in more mergers with other stock exchanges, and this has allowed them to expand and become powerful. Students should infer that it is the global nature of markets and asset trading that has allowed the NYSE to expand so much.

INTERACTIVE FEATURE

Case Study: The New York and the National Stock Exchanges

Identifying characteristics of the New York Stock Exchange Have students view the Case Study. Have a volunteer read the text.
Ask: What is the major difference in trading in the stock exchanges today from trading in the mid-twentieth century? *(Computers are used extensively to initiate trading and to monitor trading.)* **Ask:** How is the National Stock Exchange different from NYSE Euronext? *(All trades are conducted electronically.)* **AL** Visual/Spatial

CHAPTER 11, LESSON 3
Investing in Equities and Options

ENGAGE

C Critical Thinking Skills

Analyzing investment options Before students begin the lesson, tell them that every investment has some degree of risk. Ask students to list the various investment options with which they are familiar. Lead them to identify three options: savings accounts, government bonds, and corporate stocks. **Ask: Do you think these options carry high risk or low risk?** *(Student answers should include that savings accounts carry low risk; buying government bonds carries a low risk; and buying corporate stocks often is a higher risk.)*

ANSWERS, p. 318

ESSENTIAL QUESTION ACTIVITY

Equities and futures may earn potentially higher returns than government bonds. People may purchase bonds because they feel somewhat secure about their investments without becoming experts in the stock market.

TAKING NOTES

NYSE Euronext: Originally known as New York Stock Exchange (NYSE) until it merged with Euronext (a major European equities and securities market) in 2007; Until recently, the oldest, largest, and most prestigious of the organized stock exchanges in the United States

AMEX-NASDAQ: Originally known as American Stock Exchange (AMEX) until it merged with a major over-the-counter market in 2008; Attracted many smaller and lesser-known firms; sells other financial assets such as options and futures

---

Interact with these digital assets and others in lesson 3

✓ INTERACTIVE TABLE
How to Interpret How Stocks Are Performing
✓ INTERACTIVE GRAPH
How Much Money Will You Have at Retirement?
✓ VIDEO

networks
TRY IT YOURSELF ONLINE

Reading Help Desk

Academic Vocabulary
- implication

Content Vocabulary
- equities
- stockbroker
- Efficient Market Hypothesis (EMH)
- portfolio diversification
- mutual fund
- net asset value (NAV)
- 401(k) plan
- vesting
- stock or securities exchange
- Dow Jones Industrial Average (DJIA)
- Standard & Poor's 500 (S&P 500)
- bull market
- bear market
- spot market
- futures contract
- option
- call option
- put option

TAKING NOTES:

Key Ideas and Details
ACTIVITY Use the graphic organizer below to identify and describe the different stock markets.

Stock Market	Characteristics

LESSON 3
Investing in Equities and Options

ESSENTIAL QUESTION

What options are available for investing your money?

Government bonds rank among the safest financial assets, though returns may be modest. **Equities** and futures are at the opposite end of the risk spectrum. They often offer the lure of strong returns—along with the risk of a complete loss.

C Purchasing stock used to be complicated and required professional help. With computers and the Internet, today anyone can easily invest in stocks, mutual funds, or even options.

Apart from an individual's personal tolerance for risk, a person may have many reasons for choosing either bonds or equities.

- What specific reasons might someone have for choosing to invest in equities or futures rather than government bonds?
- Under what circumstances might a person prefer bonds?

Stock Prices and Efficient Markets

GUIDING QUESTION *Why is portfolio diversification important?*

Equities, or shares of common stocks that represent ownership of corporations, form another type of financial asset available to investors.

Buying or Selling Equities

There are different ways to buy shares of stock, more commonly referred to as equities. An investor may want to use a **stockbroker**—a person who buys or sells equities for his or her clients. Stockbrokers offer recommendations and advice as part of the service they perform. In return, they earn a fee based on the size of the investor's transaction, whether it is a purchase or a sale.

The investor can also open an Internet account with a discount brokerage firm and bypass the services of a stockbroker. This method allows the investor to buy, sell, and monitor his or her stock portfolio from a personal computer or even a cell phone. The discount brokerages charge much less for every transaction and they may even offer overviews and summaries of developments in key industries that appear to have more promise than others.

---

networks *Online Teaching Options*

BELLRINGER

Investing in Equities and Options

Examining investing in equities Project the Bellringer activity. Tell students that this lesson focuses on buying stocks, or *equities*. Point out that many Americans invest in stocks in 401(k) pension plans through their place of employment. **Ask: Is relying on a 401(k) the best option for individual retirement funding?** *(Students should realize there is a risk even in 401(k) retirement plans.)* Encourage students to express their own ideas of what is a good option for building an individual retirement fund.

AL Logical/Mathematical

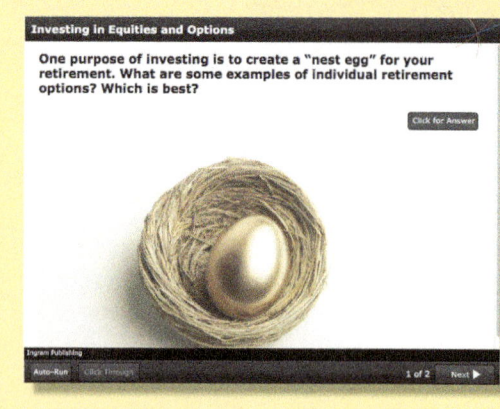

Even more important is the range of tools that the online discount brokers offer. Do you want companies that offer only high-paying dividends? No problem—just sort the 10,000-plus stocks in the market to find the ones that offer the highest-paying dividends! Alternatively, maybe you prefer companies that carry very little or no debt. Run another sort and you can find a list of those also. You can also combine the sorts to find the companies that pay the highest dividends *and* have the least amount of debt. Then, generate a series of charts showing 1-, 3-, or 10-year stock price histories to help you narrow your choice.

Diagnostic tools like this, plus the low fees that discount brokers charge, are just some of the reasons why Internet brokerage firms have become so popular.

equities stocks that represent ownership shares in corporations

stockbroker person who buys or sells securities for investors

Supply, Demand, and Share Values
The value of almost all stocks goes up and down daily, sometimes gaining or losing a few cents a share and at other times gaining or losing much more. This is due to a change in the supply of or the demand for the shares of stock.

CAREERS | Stockbroker and Investment Banker

Is this Career for you?
☑ Are you interested in learning about investments and financial tools?

☑ Can you communicate ideas and information clearly so others will understand?

☑ Are you willing to devote long hours to analyzing companies and their business practices?

Interview with a Stockbroker
" If you want to own something that you think you want to own for the next five to 10 years, don't get caught in the trap of instantaneous success and affirmation of the success of your investments. When you buy a stock, if it goes up the next day, it doesn't mean you're right. If it falls it doesn't mean you're wrong either. "

—David Rolfe, Chief Investor Officer at Wedgewood Partners

Salary
Median pay: **$70,190**
$33.75 per hour

Job Growth Potential
About as Fast as Average

Profile of Work
An investment banker is someone who helps companies raise funds by issuing securities, such as stocks and bonds, and selling them. Investment bankers also advise companies on mergers, acquisitions, and other transactions and prepare the necessary documents. A stockbroker operates as a kind of go-between for buyers and sellers of securities. The sellers might be investment bankers or corporations. The buyers might be individuals, investment companies, mutual funds, and pension funds, among many others. Both bankers and stockbrokers must thoroughly analyze the financial strengths and weaknesses of the companies they are representing. Sometimes, this can be exhausting work that involves long hours, but highly successful brokers and bankers can earn very good incomes.

CHAPTER 11, LESSON 3
Investing in Equities and Options

C Critical Thinking Skills

Researching stocks Organize students into small groups. Have groups conduct research to find three companies that produce products or services that students use, such as computers, cell phones, and backpacks. Groups should then continue researching to find the current stock price of these companies, as well as the dividend during the past year. Have each group present its three companies to the class in a visual. Ask the class to identify the two companies that would have been the best investments for the year. **AL** *Visual/Spatial*

T Technology Skills

Graphing stocks Have student pairs look at the past five days' NYSE Euronext listings for the four stocks in the table displayed in Figure 11.6. Then have students create a graph showing the number of shares traded (in 100s) and the closing prices for the last five days for each of the four stocks. **BL** *Logical/Mathematical, Visual/Spatial*

ANSWERS, p. 320

CRITICAL THINKING

Fedex Corp.

Investor expectations are influential because they affect both the supply of and demand for stocks. If investors think that the price of a share of stock will go up, they will try to buy shares before others do. However, if everyone tries to buy shares at the same time, share prices will go up because of the overall increase in demand.

The same thing happens in reverse if investors think that the share prices are likely to go down. If enough investors decide to sell, then the collective action of everyone selling at the same time will increase the supply of shares, and stock prices will fall.

Many investors follow their companies closely, hoping to be the first to detect a likely change in the demand for the company's stock. For example, if a company announces an expensive product recall or a potentially damaging lawsuit, the investor may try to sell his or her shares before others sell theirs—and collectively change the price of the company's shares.

How Is Your Stock Performing?

If you are interested in how an individual stock is doing, a listing like the one in **Figure 11.6** can be found in most daily papers. Stock summaries on the Internet vary widely in format and detail, but the following summary of the most basic symbols applies to Internet listings as well:

- **52 Weeks**—The high and low prices for the past 12 months. During that period, a single share of Estée Lauder sold for as much as $42.01 and for as little as $29.98. We are not told when the high and low prices occurred, only that they did.
- **Stock (SYM)**—A unique and easily remembered character string usually selected by the corporation.
- **DIV**—The company's annual dividend that is paid in four equal installments. The FDX annual dividend is $0.32, so each quarterly check is $0.08 per share.

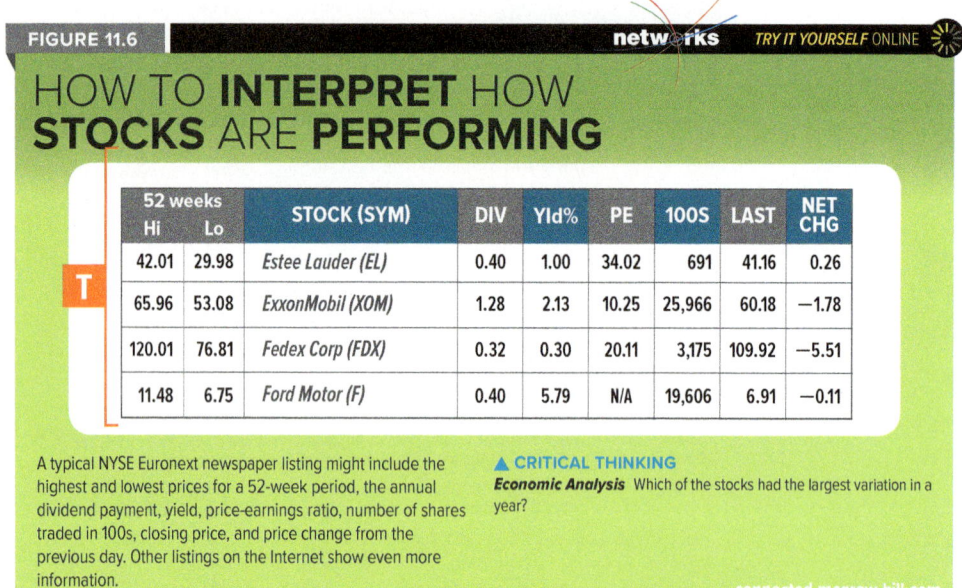

FIGURE 11.6

HOW TO INTERPRET HOW STOCKS ARE PERFORMING

52 weeks Hi	52 weeks Lo	STOCK (SYM)	DIV	Yld%	PE	100S	LAST	NET CHG
42.01	29.98	Estee Lauder (EL)	0.40	1.00	34.02	691	41.16	0.26
65.96	53.08	ExxonMobil (XOM)	1.28	2.13	10.25	25,966	60.18	—1.78
120.01	76.81	Fedex Corp (FDX)	0.32	0.30	20.11	3,175	109.92	—5.51
11.48	6.75	Ford Motor (F)	0.40	5.79	N/A	19,606	6.91	—0.11

A typical NYSE Euronext newspaper listing might include the highest and lowest prices for a 52-week period, the annual dividend payment, yield, price-earnings ratio, number of shares traded in 100s, closing price, and price change from the previous day. Other listings on the Internet show even more information.

▲ **CRITICAL THINKING**
Economic Analysis Which of the stocks had the largest variation in a year?

---

networks Online Teaching Options

CHARTS

How to Interpret How Stocks Are Performing

Examining how stocks perform Have students view Figure 11.6. Click on each column heading and have a volunteer read the explanation.
Ask: Which stock had the largest range of high/low prices for the past 12 months? *(Fedex Corp)* Which stock paid the highest annual dividend? *(ExxonMobil)* Discuss with the class which stock they think would be a good investment. **AL** *Logical/Mathematical*

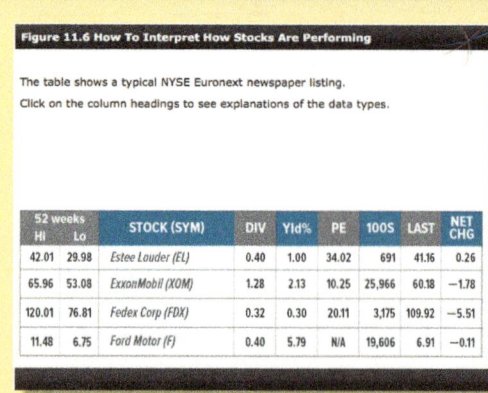

- **Yld%**—Think of this as being roughly similar to the interest return on a bank deposit. Therefore, if you bought one company's share at the closing price of $6.91, you would receive a $0.40 annual dividend. The dividend yield is DIV/LAST, or $0.40/$6.91 = 0.0579, or 5.79 percent.
- **PE**—This symbol stands for the ratio of last share price to annual earnings per share. It is used as a measure of valuation and tells us how much an investor is willing to pay to get $1 of current earnings. The PE is also referred to as a "multiple," because it tells us how much an investor is willing to pay for a dollar of earnings. PEs can also change if the value in either the numerator or the denominator changes. Two years after Ford returned to profitability, for example, its stock price rose to $17.41, and its earnings per share rose to $1.51, giving it a PE ratio of 11.52. (Values not shown in Figure 11.6)
- **100s**—Volume of shares traded that day in hundreds.
- **LAST**—Tells us the final, or closing, price for a share of stock that day.
- **NET CHG**—Tells us how the most recent closing price compared to the previous closing price. FedEx closed at $109.92, which was $5.51 lower than the previous day's closing price.

Finally, some stock listings may have more columns of information than you see in Figure 11.6, and others may have fewer. The number of columns that you see in a newspaper depends on the amount of space available, and the amount of data (or number of columns) that the newspaper has purchased.

Stock Market Efficiency

Most large equity markets with a large number of buyers and sellers are reasonably competitive. However, there is no sure way to invest in stocks and always make a profit. Stock prices can vary considerably from one company to the next, and the price of any stock can change dramatically from one day to the next. Because of this, investors are always looking to find the best ones to buy or sell, as well as those to avoid. All of this attention makes the market more competitive.

Many stock market experts support the **Efficient Market Hypothesis (EMH)**—the argument that stocks are usually priced correctly and that bargains are hard to find because stocks are followed closely by so many investors. The theory states that each stock is constantly analyzed by many different professional analysts in a large number of stock investment companies. If the analysts observe anything that might affect the fortunes of the companies they watch, they buy or sell the stocks immediately. This in turn causes stock prices to adjust almost immediately to new market information.

The main **implication** for the investor is that if all stocks are priced correctly because of all the attention they get from thousands of stock analysts, it does not matter which ones you purchase. Of course, you might get lucky and pick a stock about to go up, or you might get unlucky and pick a stock about to go down, but over time, these gains and losses will even out. Because of this, **portfolio diversification**—the practice of holding a large number of different stocks so that increases in some stocks can offset declines in others—is a popular strategy.

You can diversify your own stock portfolio if you hold stocks issued by as few as 10 unrelated companies. However, a better way to protect the value of your stock portfolio is to invest in a mutual fund, which holds stock issued by hundreds or even thousands of companies.

Mutual Funds

A **mutual fund** is a company that sells shares of securities to individual investors. It invests the money it receives in a diversified portfolio of stocks and bonds issued by hundreds or even thousands of different companies. With such a large portfolio, the mutual fund reaps the maximum gains of diversification.

Efficient Market Hypothesis (EMH) argument that stocks are always priced about right, and that bargains are hard to find because they are closely watched by so many investors

implication something suggested to be naturally understood

portfolio diversification strategy of holding different investments to minimize risk

mutual fund company that sells shares of a portfolio of securities, e.g., stocks and bonds issued by other companies

---

CHAPTER 11, LESSON 3
Investing in Equities and Options

W Writing Skills

Investing wisely in the stock market Ask students to write a brochure in which they attempt to convince potential investors in the stock market to practice portfolio diversification. Encourage students to highlight the benefits of diversification, outline risks to avoid, and propose a general strategy through which an investor might wisely assemble a diverse stock portfolio.
BL Logical/Mathematical

R Reading Skills

Defining and assessing mutual funds Discuss with students that a mutual fund is a company that invests in a large portfolio of stocks and sometimes bonds. **Ask: How does the large size of a typical mutual fund benefit potential investors?** *(The large size provides diversification, allowing investors to avoid risking the investment of all their funds in one or a few companies. Mutual funds hire a staff of experts to monitor market conditions and analyze many stocks and bonds before deciding which ones to buy or sell. This offers investors the benefit of contributing funds to a number of carefully chosen investments.)* Have students write a sentence using the term *mutual fund*. **AL** Verbal/Linguistic

---

WORKSHEET

Math Practice for Economics

Analyzing an NYSE Euronext Listing Distribute copies of the Math Practice for Economics worksheet, and have students study the NYSE Euronext listing and answer the questions.

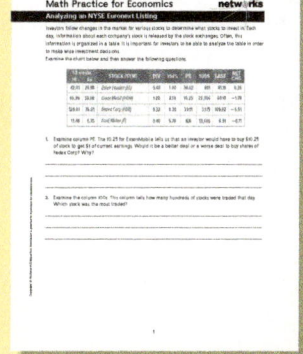

CHAPTER 11, LESSON 3
Investing in Equities and Options

C Critical Thinking Skills

Identifying characteristics of financial assets
Have students play the game "Investment—What Am I?" Have students use index cards to write three clues to the identity of each financial asset—one asset per index card. Organize students into teams. Have a quiz leader read clues from an asset card to a specified team. If the team correctly identifies the asset after the first clue, it receives three points. If it identifies the asset after two clues, it receives two points, and one point if the identification is made after three clues. If the team fails to identify the asset after three clues, then another team may attempt to. **BL**

R Reading Skills

Sequencing information about 401(k)s Ask students to show the steps of investing in a 401(k) plan. Tell students to construct a sequence graphic organizer under the assumption that the company will match employees' contributions to the plan. Have students distribute imaginary retirement funds among three different financial assets and explain why they chose those assets and those percentages of funds. **Visual/Spatial**

Content Background Knowledge

401(k) Plans The U.S. government created 401(k) plans in 1978. The plan gets its name from the section of the Internal Revenue Code that created it. One advantage of the plan is that it is portable—employees can change jobs and keep their 401(k) plans. Another advantage is that employees can decide how to invest the money in the plan. Before 401(k) plans became available, many employees had either pension plans or profit-sharing plans invested by their employers. In an employee left the job or was fired, rights to pensions or profit-sharing sometimes ceased.

ANSWERS, p. 322

EXPLORING THE ESSENTIAL QUESTION

Possible answer: Some investors may have personal knowledge of certain companies and feel confident in their growth over time. Other investors may prefer having more control over what investments they have.

---

net asset value (NAV) the market value of a mutual fund share determined by dividing the value of the fund by the number of shares issued

Mutual funds also receive dividends from many of the companies in their portfolio, which they can pass on to the mutual fund's shareholders.

About the only thing a mutual fund cannot do is protect its investors against swings in the stock market as a whole. So, if the market tends to rise or fall for several days in a row, almost all of the stock in the mutual fund's portfolio will rise or fall as well.

Stockholders can also sell their mutual fund shares for a profit, just like other stocks. The market value of a mutual fund share is called the **net asset value (NAV)**—the net value of the mutual fund divided by the number of shares issued by the mutual fund.

Mutual funds allow people to invest in the market without risking all they have in one or a few companies. The large size of the typical mutual fund makes it possible for the fund to hire a staff of experts to monitor market conditions and analyze many different stocks and bonds before deciding which ones to buy or sell. Mutual funds are also very liquid and this makes it easy for investors to add to or withdraw funds from their mutual fund accounts.

EXPLORING THE ESSENTIAL QUESTION

Many people prefer buying shares in mutual funds to taking on the responsibility of choosing and investing in individual stocks. This makes them feel secure about their investments without becoming experts in the stock market or spending time learning about the companies they will invest in. Nonetheless, many other people choose to do it on their own, perhaps working with a stockbroker, to identify and purchase individual stocks.

Why might some people prefer to invest in particular stocks on their own rather than relying on a mutual fund?

401(k) Plans

401(k) plan a tax-deferred investment and savings plan that acts as a personal pension fund for employees

The need for retirement planning has increased the popularity of the **401(k) plan**—a tax-deferred investment and savings plan that acts as a personal pension fund for employees. To contribute to the plan, a company's employees authorize regular payroll deductions. The deductions are then pooled and invested in mutual funds or other investments approved of by the company.

Contributing to a plan lowers today's taxable income because you don't have to pay income taxes on the contributions until you withdraw them. An added benefit of a 401(k) plan is that most employers typically match a portion of an employee's contributions.

For example, if your employer matches your contribution at the rate of 50 cents on the dollar, you have an immediate 50 percent return on the investment. To see how, suppose you deposit $100 in a 401(k), and your employer matches it with a $50 contribution. This will leave you with $150 in the fund, for an immediate gain of $50 on your initial investment.

Because the 401(k) was designed to provide retirement income to savers, there is a penalty if you take your money out before age 59½. Currently, the penalty is 10 percent of the funds you withdraw, and that is in addition to the ordinary income taxes that you will have to pay on the withdrawn funds.

vesting the length of time you need to work at the company before you can take the employer's matching contribution with you

Finally, pay attention to the plan's **vesting**—the length of time you need to work at the company before you can take the employer's matching contribution with you. For example, suppose your company matches at a rate of 50 cents on the dollar, and that the plan won't be vested until you work for three years. If you contribute $1,000 annually for each of three years, the company will have matched your $3,000 contribution with another $1,500. Because the plan is now vested, you can take $4,500 with you if you decide to leave.

322

---

networks Online Teaching Options

WORKSHEETS

Hands-on Chapter Project

Analyzing investment choices In this activity, student groups will work together to determine the best way to invest $10,000 that they have won in a competition. They will first research ways of investing the money and analyze the risk-return relationship for the investment(s) or asset(s) they select. Together, group members will decide on the best investments. Each group will design a pamphlet or poster explaining their investment choices and present it to the class.

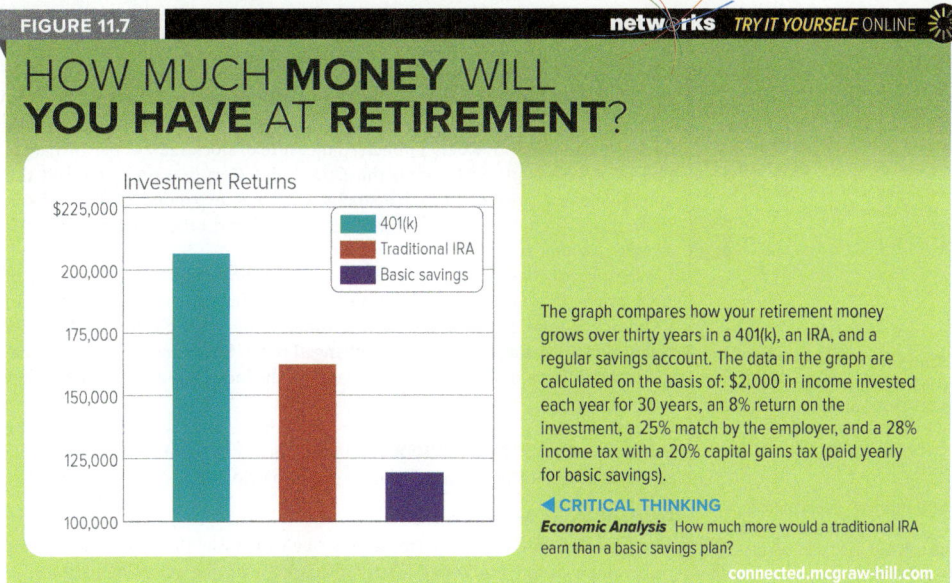

FIGURE 11.7

HOW MUCH MONEY WILL YOU HAVE AT RETIREMENT?

The graph compares how your retirement money grows over thirty years in a 401(k), an IRA, and a regular savings account. The data in the graph are calculated on the basis of: $2,000 in income invested each year for 30 years, an 8% return on the investment, a 25% match by the employer, and a 28% income tax with a 20% capital gains tax (paid yearly for basic savings).

◀ CRITICAL THINKING
Economic Analysis How much more would a traditional IRA earn than a basic savings plan?

However, if you work a day less than three years before you go to a different job, the employer's matching contribution stays with the employer and you lose $1,500. The money you contributed is still yours, but now you have to start over again with a new employer contribution.

✓ READING PROGRESS CHECK

Explaining What determines the value of a stock?

Stock Markets and Their Performance

GUIDING QUESTION How is stock market performance evaluated?

Stocks, like almost everything else, are traded in markets. Investors follow these markets daily because the performance of the market is likely to affect their stocks.

Stock Exchanges

Historically, investors would gather at an organized **stock or securities exchange**, a place where buyers and sellers meet to trade stocks. An organized exchange gets its name from the way it conducts business. Members pay a fee to join, and trades can only take place on the floor of the exchange.

Until recently, the oldest, largest, and most prestigious of the organized stock exchanges in the United States was the New York Stock Exchange (NYSE). Over the years, the Exchange grew to be the most prestigious stock exchange in the United States.

Another national stock exchange was the American Stock Exchange (AMEX). In an attempt to broaden its appeal to investors, the AMEX attracted many smaller and lesser-known firms. It also started selling other financial assets such as options and futures to broaden its product line.

In 2008, the NYSE merged with Euronext, a major European equities and securities market, and is now known as NYSE Euronext. The AMEX was acquired by NYSE Euronext and has since lost its identity as a separate exchange.

stock or securities exchange physical place where buyers and sellers meet to exchange securities

---

CHAPTER 11, LESSON 3
Investing in Equities and Options

W Writing Skills

Choosing an information source Have students review the information in the text about measures of stock performance. Then have them choose one of the measures and write a paragraph detailing why they think their chosen measure would be the most reliable. Remind students to support their responses with facts from the text. **AL** Verbal/Linguistic

Content Background Knowledge

NYSE Before 1792, no organized market for trading securities existed. In May of that year, individuals who wanted to trade in securities met in New York City, only a short walk from the present site of the NYSE. At first, only U.S. bonds and a few stocks were traded on the NYSE, but trading activity increased as the 1800s progressed, reflecting economic growth and expansion. In 1867, the NYSE introduced the stock ticker, a machine that records purchases and sales of stock. This innovation helped accommodate the growth brought about by the Industrial Revolution. Nearly 100 years later, electronic data processing automated a large part of the transfer of trading information.

VIDEO | WORKSHEET

Recession

Examining the recession Tell students this video shows what happened to 401(k) plans during the recession. Lead a class discussion after viewing the video. **Ask:** What did 401(k) plans replace for employees? *(The 401(k) plans replaced pension plans that were previously offered by companies.)* Why did companies stop offering pension plans? *(Many companies found that offering 401(k) plans to their employees was cheaper than offering pension plans.)* After viewing the video do you think having a 401(k) is a good idea for a retirement plan? *(Possible answers include yes, no, and it is a good idea to have a mix of various types of investments for a retirement plan.)*

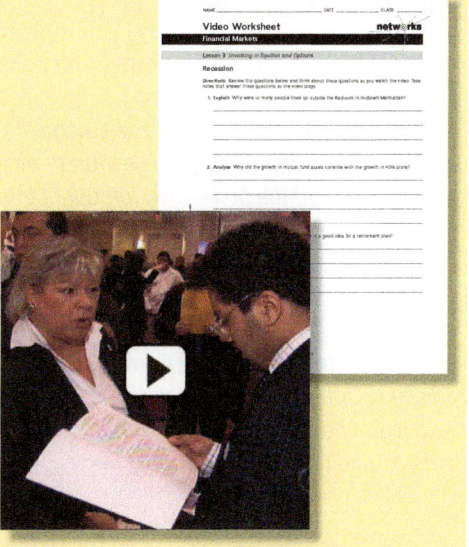

ANSWERS, p. 323

CRITICAL THINKING
About $40,000 more

✓ **READING PROGRESS CHECK** The number of outstanding shares to be traded, a company's profitability, and expectations for the company's growth

CHAPTER 11, LESSON 3
Investing in Equities and Options

W Writing Skills

Researching and describing corporate value
Have students select a major corporation and investigate the goods or services it produces, how many employees it has, where it is located, and what its prospects are for future growth. Instruct students to consult Standard and Poor's, Moody's, or Value Line for information. After students have studied the corporation and followed the stock, have them write a letter to a friend describing the stock from the viewpoint of a prospective investor interested in buying shares of the corporation. Call on students to read their letters to the class. **BL**

R Reading Skills

Defining market terminology Tell students that two terms used to describe which way the market is moving are *bull market* and *bear market*. Have a volunteer read the two paragraphs describing each kind of market. Discuss with students ways they can remember the definitions of these terms, such as a bull's horns tossing something *up* into the air, and a *bull market* is a strong market with the prices moving *up*. A bear can grab and wrestle another animal *down* to the ground, and a bear *market* is one in which the prices of stocks are falling *down*. Have students write a paragraph describing a *bull market* and a *bear market* in their own words.
ELL Verbal/Linguistic

Content Background Knowledge

Closure of Stock Exchanges Stock exchanges rarely close for emergencies. In the twenty-first century, the New York Stock Exchange has closed just twice. The exchange was closed for four days after the 9/11 terrorist attack on the World Trade Center in 2001. It was closed again on October 29, 2012 for Hurricane Sandy, which hit New York City and the New Jersey shore and left thousands of people homeless and millions of people without power.

ANSWERS, p. 324

CRITICAL THINKING
Student answers may vary. One possible answer is that during a bear market, the demand for stocks is lower. Many stocks will lose value to the point where some are significantly undervalued. As investors realize there are potential bargains, the demand for the stocks, and thus their prices, will rise.

324

Dow Jones Industrial Average (DJIA) an index of 30 representative stocks used to monitor price changes in the overall stock market

Standard & Poor's 500 (S&P 500) an index of 500 stocks used to monitor prices on the NYSE, American Stock Exchange, and the OTC market

bull market period during which stock market prices move up for several months or years in a row

Measures of Performance
Because they are concerned about the performance of their stocks, most investors consult one of two popular indicators. When these indicators go up, stocks in general also go up. When they go down, stocks in general go down.

The first of these indicators is the **Dow Jones Industrial Average (DJIA)**, the most popular and widely publicized measure of stock market performance. The DJIA began in 1884, when the Dow Jones Corporation published the average closing price of 11 active stocks. Coverage expanded to 30 stocks in 1928. Since then, some stocks have been added and others deleted, but the sample remains at 30. **W**

Because of these changes, the DJIA is no longer a mathematical average of stock prices. In addition, the evolution of the DJIA has obscured the meaning of a "point" change in the index. At one time, a one-point change in the DJIA meant that an average share of stock changed by $1. Since this is no longer true, it is better to focus on the percentage change of the index rather than the number of points.

Investors also use another popular benchmark of stock performance, the **Standard & Poor's 500 (S&P 500)**. It uses the price changes of 500 representative stocks as an indicator of overall market performance.

Bull vs. Bear Markets
Investors often use colorful terms to describe which way the market is moving. **R** For example, a **bull market** is a "strong" market with the prices moving up for

This cartoon describes the tendency for market fluctuations to be cyclical in nature.

▲ **CRITICAL THINKING**
Making Connections Explain one reason why a prolonged bear market is often followed by a bull market.

324

---

networks Online Teaching Options

POLITICAL CARTOON

Associating stock market terms Have students study the political cartoon and interpret its meaning.
Ask: What is happening in the cartoon? *(The bear has obviously been "riding" the market-bicycle for a long time, and the bull is now impatient to have his turn. Similarly, the U.S. economy went through an extended period of contraction during the Great Recession, and the stock market remained shaky for a long time.)* What do you think happens after there is a prolonged bull market? *(Answers may include that in a bull market, the price of stocks might go so high above market value that the demand for stocks drops and a bear market could begin.)* **AL** Visual/Spatial

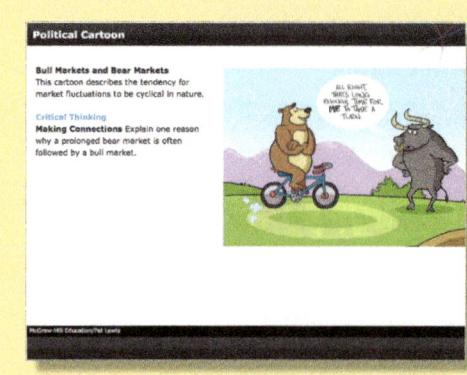

several months or years in a row. One of the strongest bull markets in history began in 1988 when stock prices rose more than 500 percent by 2000.

A **bear market** is a "mean" or "nasty" market, with the prices of equities falling sharply for several months or years in a row. The most spectacular bear market since the 1930s was during the Great Recession of 2008–2009, when the DJIA lost more than one-half its value.

bear market period during which stock market prices move down for several months or years in a row

✓ **READING PROGRESS CHECK**

Contrasting What is the difference between the Dow Jones Industrial Average and Standard & Poor's 500?

Trading in the Future

GUIDING QUESTION *Why do we have futures contracts?*

Most buying and selling takes place in the present, or in a **spot market**. In this market, a transaction is made immediately at the prevailing price.

The spot price of gold in London, for example, is the price as it exists in that city at that moment. Sometimes the exchange takes place later, rather than right away. This occurs with a **futures contract**—an agreement to buy or sell at a specific future date at a predetermined price. For example, you may agree to buy gold at $1,258 an ounce in six months, hoping that the actual price will be higher when the date arrives.

A futures contract can be written on almost anything, including the size of the S&P 500 or the level of future interest rates. In most cases, the profit or loss on the contract is settled with a cash payment rather than the buyer taking delivery.

An **option** is a special type of futures contract that gives the buyer the right to cancel the contract. For example, you may pay $5 today for a **call option**—the right to *buy* something at a specific future price. If the call option gives you the right to purchase 100 shares of stock at $70 a share, and if the price drops to $30, you tear up the option and buy the stock elsewhere for $30. If the price rises to $100, you execute the option, buy the stock for $70, and resell it for $100—or take a cash settlement.

You could also buy a **put option**—the right to sell something at a specific future price. The put option, like the call option, gives the buyer the right to tear up the contract if the actual future price is not advantageous to the buyer.

spot market market in which a transaction is made immediately at the prevailing price

futures contract an agreement to buy or sell at a specific date in the future at a predetermined price

option contract giving investors an option to buy or sell commodities, equities, or financial assets at a specific future date using a price agreed upon today

call option futures contract giving investors the option to cancel a contract to buy commodities, equities, or financial assets

put option futures contract giving investors the option to cancel a contract to sell commodities, equities, or financial assets

✓ **READING PROGRESS CHECK**

Explaining Why might a contract that takes place in the future be an advantage to the buyer or seller?

LESSON 3 REVIEW

Reviewing Vocabulary
1. *Defining* What is a futures contract?

Using Your Notes
2. *Contrasting* What is the main difference between the NYSE Euronext and the AMEX-NASDAQ?

Answering the Guiding Questions
3. *Explaining* Why is portfolio diversification important?
4. *Describing* How do we track stock market performance?
5. *Explaining* Why do we have futures contracts?

Writing About Economics
6. *Argument* A friend has just come into a large sum of money and is planning to invest all of it in one or two stocks that she is confident will quickly increase in value. Present an argument in favor of diversifying her investment in a range of stocks rather than just one or two.

connected.mcgraw-hill.com   Financial Markets 325

LESSON 3 REVIEW ANSWERS

Reviewing Vocabulary
1. An agreement to buy or sell at a specific future date at a predetermined price

Using Your Notes
2. NYSE Euronext conducts stock exchanges only on the floor of the exchange. AMEX-Nasdaq conducts exchanges in an over-the-counter market.

Answering the Guiding Questions
3. Diversification helps reduce the likelihood of significant drops in the investors' investments.
4. Stock market performance is tracked by referring to two indicators: the Dow Jones Industrial Average or the Standard & Poor's 500.
5. A futures contract allows investors to lock in a price to buy or sell a stock to make investing more predictable and reduce the risk of serious loss.

Writing About Economics
6. Students should demonstrate an understanding of the Efficient Market Hypothesis in arguing for diversification, pointing out that stocks are generally priced close to their value, so finding a stock with an unrecognized value is rare. Portfolio diversification, on the other hand, will provide some protection against extreme loss in value.

CHAPTER 11, LESSON 3
Investing in Equities and Options

R Reading Skills

Defining a futures contract Tell students that most buying and selling of stocks takes place in the present. It is possible, however, to agree to buy a stock at a later date. This agreement is called a *futures contract*. Have student pairs read the definition of a *futures contract* in the text. Discuss the meaning with the class. Have students write the term and the sentence in their personal economic glossaries. **ELL** Verbal/Linguistic

W Writing Skills

Assessing a futures contract Ask students to write a brief essay discussing whether they would invest in a futures contract with their savings. Tell them to explain why they would or would not make such an investment. Remind students to consider the risk-reward relationship. Discuss student essays in class. **AL** Logical/Mathematical

C Critical Thinking Skills

Examining a call option Review with students that there is a special type of futures contract that gives the buyer the right to cancel the contract. It is called a *call option*. Have a student read aloud the text about call options. **Ask: How does a call option protect a buyer? Explain.** *(It protects a buyer from having to pay too high a price for a futures contract. It does this by allowing the buyer to cancel the contract if the price drops below the contract price.)* In discussion, encourage students to share their opinions regarding whether they would engage in call options or consider the risk too high. **BL** Logical/Mathematical

CLOSE & REFLECT

Defending or refuting a statement Ask students to defend or refute the following statement: The best indicator of how the economy is performing is the stock market.

ANSWERS, p. 325

✓ **READING PROGRESS CHECK** The Dow Jones Industrial Average is a measure of the stock performance of a sample of 30 companies. Standard & Poor's 500 monitors the price of 500 stocks.

✓ **READING PROGRESS CHECK** The buyer may want to lock in a good price today in case it goes up in the future; the seller may want to lock in a price today in case it goes down in the future.

Financial Markets **325**

CHAPTER 11
Debate

ENGAGE

C1 Critical Thinking Skills

Examining insider trading Ask students if they have seen TV news stories about insider trading. Have students brainstorm and list what they know about insider trading and the punishment for it. In class discussion, have students share their lists. Explain that there is a debate over whether the punishments for insider training are too severe. Ask students to consider what they think about the issue.
AL Verbal/Linguistic

TEACH & ASSESS

C2 Critical Thinking Skills

Debating Organize a debate by dividing the class in half. Have one half formulate an argument for the Yes side, and the other half formulate an argument for the No side. Have the groups each select a student to be the debater. Have the selected students debate their views before the class.
Verbal/Linguistic

R Reading Skills

Defining terms Write the terms *pending acquisition* and *publically announced* on the board. Discuss with students what these terms mean. Have students write short paragraphs explaining in their own words what the terms mean. ELL Verbal/Linguistic

---

Debates

C1 Is the illegal practice of insider trading punished too severely in the United States?

Insider trading is the practice of trading stocks, bonds, or other securities on the basis of knowledge of the corporation from inside, non-public sources in violation of a person's obligations to the company or stockholders. Examples may include buying or selling stocks on the basis of information about changes to management that have not been publically announced or a pending acquisition that may change the prospects of the company for good or for bad. This kind of information can easily affect the value of the securities. Someone who has this knowledge before it goes public has an advantage not enjoyed by most other investors.

The federal government has made this form of insider trading illegal. Penalties vary and include a fine, imprisonment, an injunction against continuing the practice, or reimbursement for the profits gained from the transaction.

Laws that punish insider trading are controversial. Some believe insider trading should be dealt with harshly; others ask, "What's the big deal?" Decide for yourself.

YES Insider trading is punished too severely in the United States

- INSIDER TRADING WILL NOT CHANGE THE DOW OR S&P 500 RESULTS
- UNCOVERING INSIDER TRADING IS EXPENSIVE; THERE ARE MORE IMPORTANT ISSUES
- SOME INVESTORS WILL ALWAYS HAVE BETTER INFORMATION THAN OTHERS.
- INSIDERS SPREAD INFORMATION, MAKING THE MARKET MORE EFFICIENT

> "If the sellers are hurt by having an inside trader in the market, it is difficult to measure the damage, and it appears that there is no damage. In fact, the academic literature recognizes that insider trading does not result in any harm to any identifiable group (Manne, 1985) and those who sell to inside traders may actually be helped rather than harmed because they received a better price."
>
> —Robert W. McGee, Florida International University

326

---

networks Online Teaching Options

DEBATE

Debate: Is the illegal practice of insider trading punished too severely in the United States?

Expressing views on insider trading Have students view the Debate feature. As you click through the feature, have volunteers read the text. Explain that some people think those guilty of insider trading should be dealt with harshly, but others think it is "no big deal" and believe the punishment is too severe. Have students express their initial views on this issue. AL Verbal/Linguistic

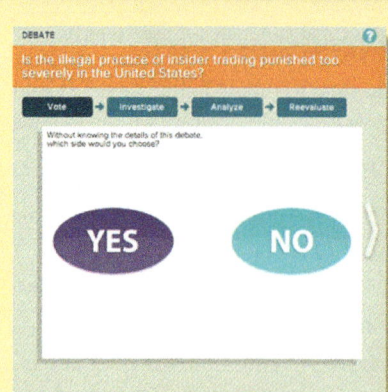

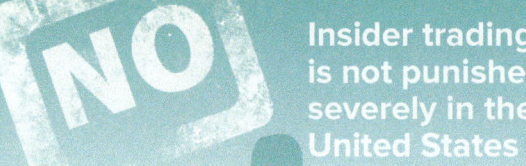

CHAPTER 11
Debate

C Critical Thinking Skills

Identifying perspectives Have students interview a variety of people about their views of insider trading. Students could interview a banker, a stockbroker, a computer analyst, a retired police officer—anyone who might have investments in the stock market. Students should prepare a list of questions before the interview. Have students explain to these people that they are gathering information about different points of view on the issue. After the interviews, have students write a summary of the interviews and share them with the class. **BL** Interpersonal, Verbal/Linguistic

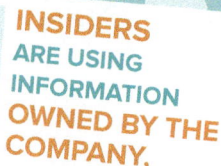

ANALYZING the issue

1. **Evaluating** In the first quotation, McGee makes the case that insider trading doesn't do any harm to other investors. In the second quotation, Arthur Levitt says it does do harm by damaging the trust people have in the market. Who makes the strongest case? Why do you think so?

2. **Analyzing** One of the pro arguments states that insider trading will not affect the market value of a firm as it is measured by the DJIA or S&P 500. Does this claim seem valid to you? Why or why not?

3. **Defending** Which arguments do you find most compelling? Explain your answer.

CLOSE & REFLECT

C Critical Thinking Skills

Summarizing the insider trading debate Have students make a T-chart with one column labeled *Yes* and the other column labeled *No*. Have them list the appropriate views in each column.

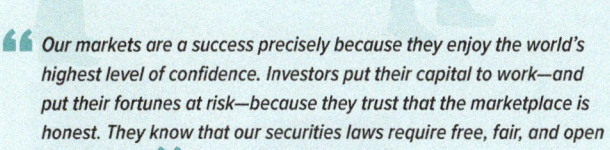

"Our markets are a success precisely because they enjoy the world's highest level of confidence. Investors put their capital to work—and put their fortunes at risk—because they trust that the marketplace is honest. They know that our securities laws require free, fair, and open transactions."

—Arthur Levitt, chairman of the Securities and Exchange Commission, February 27, 1998

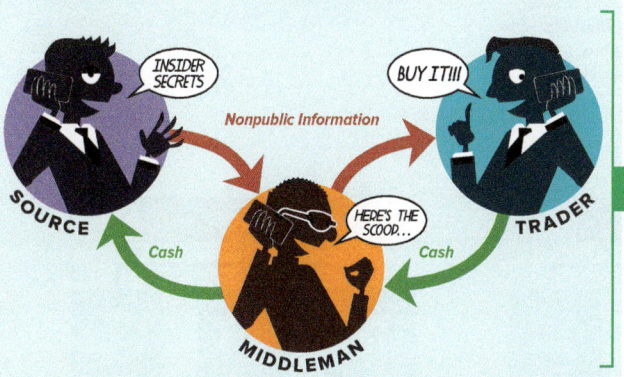

DEBATE

Debate

Assessing opinions about insider trading Point out the Yes and No excerpts in the Debate feature. Have a volunteer read the Yes quote. **Ask: What is the main point of Robert McGee's view?** *(He states that it appears sellers or buyers are not damaged by insider trading.)* Have a volunteer read the No quote. **Ask: What is the main point of Arthur Levitt's quote?** *(The markets are successful because investors can trust that the marketplace is honest.)* Tell students to write a brief essay describing the position with which they agree. Have students share their essays in class discussion. **AL** Verbal/Linguistic Logical/Mathematical

ANSWERS, p. 327

ANALYZING the issue

1. Students may be more persuaded by one argument than the other but should give specific reasons for their response.
2. Student answers will depend upon their interpretation of arguments on the effects of insider trading. They should give reasons for their responses.
3. Students may choose any of the arguments but should explain why they feel the argument is most compelling and demonstrate a clear understanding of insider trading.

Chapter 11
Study Guide

C1 Critical Thinking Skills

Applying the financial system Ask students to review the graphic showing the financial system and the flow of funds throughout this system. Instruct them to consider how this system works to meet the needs of both borrowers and lenders. **Ask: How might a transaction involving a life insurance company progress throughout the financial system?** *(Possible answer: The people in a household would pay a life insurance company cash premiums for the protection the company offers. The life insurance company could then take these surplus funds and lend them to a business that needed funding for growth.)* **Logical/Mathematical**

C2 Critical Thinking Skills

Evaluating risks Have students write a personal essay in which they reflect on the potential risks involved in each type of equity and future shown in the graphic organizer at the bottom of the page. Students should identify which types of investments would be most appealing to them and discuss the reduction in risk offered by investments such as mutual funds and call options. **Verbal/Linguistic**

STUDY GUIDE

LESSON 1
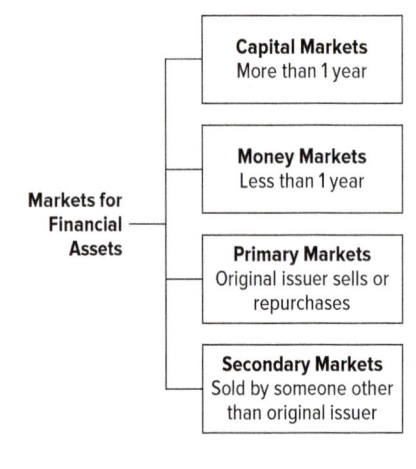

LESSON 2
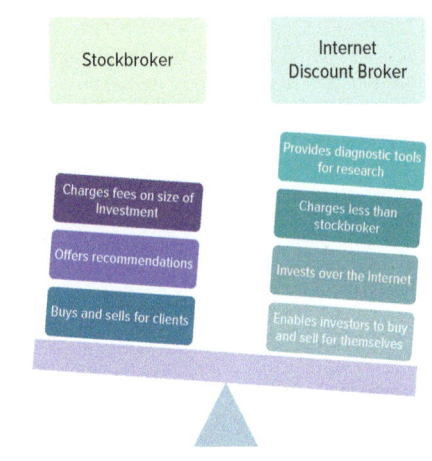

LESSON 3
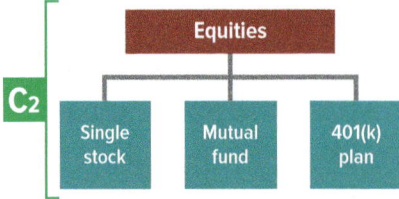
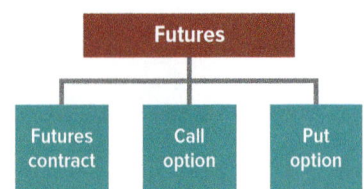

328

networks Online Assessment Options

WORKSHEET

Financial Markets Reteaching Activity

Summarizing financial markets Project the worksheet and tell students that it summarizes information about financial markets. Lead the class in discussion to fill out the columns. After the columns are filled in, have student pairs write answers to the questions on the worksheet. Reassemble the class and discuss the answers. **Verbal/Linguistic**

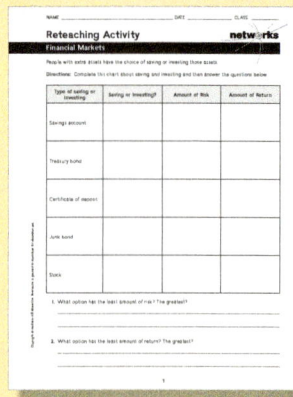

CHAPTER 11 Assessment

Directions: On a separate sheet of paper, answer the questions below. Make sure you read carefully and answer all parts of the questions.

Lesson Review

Lesson 1

1. **Describing** How are financial assets created in a free enterprise system?
2. **Explaining** What is the role of the major nondepository financial institutions in the financial system?

Lesson 2

3. **Calculating** You purchase a 4 percent, 10-year, $1,000 par value corporate bond. Interest is paid semi-annually. How much interest are you paid after six months? What will be the par value of the bond after 10 years?
4. **Explaining** How do CDs appear in multiple markets?

Lesson 3

5. **Contrasting** What are some major advantages of using an online brokerage rather than a stockbroker?
6. **Explaining** Why is portfolio diversification an important investment strategy?
7. **Analyzing** Under what circumstances will an investor make money after signing a futures contract?

Critical Thinking

8. **Synthesizing** As a financial planner, you have been approached by a new client for investment advice. The client, Ms. Abrams, wants to buy her first house. She knows it will take a few years of saving and investing and wants to get started. She is also concerned about her future and wants to begin investing some money for retirement. Devise a general investment plan for Ms. Abrams. Keep in mind her mid-term goal of buying a house and her long-term goal of preparing for retirement.

9. **Considering Advantages and Disadvantages** You have set a goal of saving $4,000 every year, beginning the year you finish school and start working and lasting until you retire. You are considering these three investment instruments: an IRA, stocks, and certificates of deposit. Which will likely produce the best long-term returns? Explain your answer.

10. **Supporting Perspectives** Why might someone want to buy stock during a bear market?

Analyzing Visuals

Use the graph to answer the following questions about risk and return.

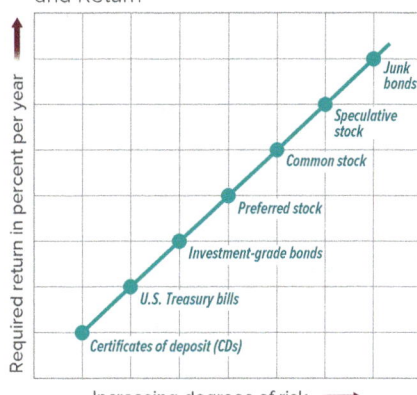

The Relationship between Risk and Return

11. **Explaining** What is the risk and return relationship between certificates of deposit and U.S. Treasury bills? Why is this the case?
12. **Analyzing** If municipal bonds were added to this graph, where would they be placed? Explain.

Need Extra Help?

If You've Missed Question	1	2	3	4	5	6	7	8	9	10	11	12
Go to page	304	306	311	313	318	321	325	322	322	325	313	313

Chapter 11 Assessment Answers

Lesson Review

Lesson 1

1. Financial assets are created when a lender/investor receives a receipt like a CD showing he has a claim on the borrower for an amount lent under specific terms.

2. Finance companies lend directly to consumers and buy up installment contracts. Life insurance companies lend surplus funds. Pension funds invest money until payments are made to eligible recipients.

Lesson 2

3. You will be paid $20 interest every six months. After ten years, the par value of the bond will be $1,000.

4. Small CDs are in the primary market because investors tend to cash them in early. Long-term CDs belong in the capital market. A CD with maturity of less than one year belongs in the money market. If the CD can be sold to someone else, it would be found in the secondary market.

Lesson 3

5. An online brokerage costs less, allows easy access from a personal computer or mobile device, provides overviews and summaries of developments, and offers tools that allow the investor to identify stocks that meet the investor's criteria.

6. Diversification helps protect a portfolio from wild swings in market value by evening out gains and losses among stocks.

7. The investor will only make money if the price of the stock exceeds the target price stated on the contract.

Critical Thinking Questions

8. Students may recommend various investment instruments but their plan should be consistent with the mid-term and long-term goals of the client.

9. Students should choose the IRA because taxes will be deferred on funds invested in an IRA whereas taxes are not deferred on the earnings of stocks or CDs.

10. During a bear market, stocks have fallen so buying stocks at that time creates the opportunity that profit can be made when a bull market returns and prices go up.

Analyzing Visuals

11. Both are safe investments, but CDs are considered safer because they are issued by banks and insured by the FDIC. Treasury bonds may have higher yields and are also quite safe since they are secured by the federal government.

12. Municipal bonds are guaranteed by states or cities so they would be placed between U.S. Treasury bills and Investment grade bonds. They are not quite as secure as U.S. Treasury bills, which are guaranteed by the U.S. government, but are more secure than investment grade bonds that are guaranteed by corporations.

Chapter 11 Assessment Answers

Answering the Essential Questions

13 Students should demonstrate understanding of how savings fuels the financial system by supplying financial institutions with funds that are then loaned to individuals and businesses to finance purchases.

14 Students should demonstrate understanding of the wide range of investment possibilities including government and corporate bonds, CDs, IRAs, money markets, stocks, futures, and options.

21st Century Skills

15 Students may suggest any of a number of investments including a bank savings account, bonds, or mutual funds. They should demonstrate an understanding of the short-term duration of the investment and the risk-return relationship.

16 Students should demonstrate an awareness in the difference in risk between the two bonds, the potential returns, and their willingness to accept risk.

17 Some students may recommend selling the fund and putting the money in a CD or money market fund until the market stabilizes. Other students may have different recommendations. Students should demonstrate understanding of the investment options, market performance, and long-term goals.

Building Financial Literacy

18 Students should choose three stocks and analyze their performance. They should provide valid reasons for purchasing the stock on a short- or long-term basis.

Analyzing Primary Sources

19 Bonds provide a new methods to raise funds without raising taxes, which is usually an unpopular decision.

20 Corporations can issue bonds to raise capital for further investment without multiplying the number of owners and points of view—as stocks do. Governments appreciate the way that bonds help raise needed revenue without raising taxes. For these reasons, a financial advisor may encourage the use of bonds because they provide an influx of money without other consequences that may be viewed as negative by the bond issuer.

330

CHAPTER 11 Assessment

Directions: On a separate sheet of paper, answer the questions below. Make sure you read carefully and answer all parts of the questions.

ANSWERING THE ESSENTIAL QUESTIONS

Review your answers to the introductory questions at the beginning of each lesson. Then answer the Essential Questions on the basis of what you learned in the chapter. Have your answers changed?

13 **Explaining** What is the role of savings in the financial system?

14 **Explaining** What options are available for investing your money?

21st Century Skills

15 **Decision Making** Your aunt has given you $10,000 for your college education. You don't need it right now, but you don't want to just let it sit in your checking account where it doesn't earn any interest. Given that you won't need the money until you enter college, what should you do with it? Explain your answer.

16 **Compare and Contrast** You are considering investing in bonds. You have located two corporate bonds. One is AAA-rated, has a par value of $1,000, and has a coupon rate of 5 percent. The other is a CCC bond with a par value of $900 and a coupon rate of 8 percent. Considering your risk tolerance, which is the better value? Why?

17 **Compare and Contrast** Tom has been working for several years and recently invested some of his savings in a stock mutual fund. This will be part of his retirement savings, which he will not need for at least 30 years. Last week, however, it has become apparent that Congress cannot agree on a budget and large portions of the government may have to be shut down until the issue is resolved. Financial experts fear the Dow may drop and the economy may even fall into a recession. What should Tom do about his investment? Explain your answer.

Building Financial Literacy

18 **Planning** You have been working and saving for the past two years and have accumulated $10,000. You want to invest it in stocks. Research the performance of three stocks listed on the NYSE or NASDAQ. Then create a short presentation describing the best investment choice. Imagine that you are going to pitch this stock to others, to convince them to invest with you. In order to make the most effective presentation, include persuasive information on these points:

- Reasons you chose the stock
- Stock performance
- Factors influencing the gain/loss in value
- Analysis of why you would hold your stock for either the short term or the long term

Analyzing Primary Sources

Read the excerpt and answer the questions that follow.

PRIMARY SOURCE

"Bonds do not dilute ownership percentages as new stock would. The interest that corporations pay on bonds can also be less costly than dividends. In the case of governments, which cannot issue equity, bonds offer an alternative to raising taxes or fees."

—Mark Mobius, *Bonds: An Introduction to the Core Concepts*

19 **Analyzing Primary Sources** What makes bonds an attractive option for government?

20 **Analyzing** Under what conditions might a financial adviser advise investing in bonds even in the situation described in the article? What would be the reasons for the advice?

Need Extra Help?

If You've Missed Question	13	14	15	16	17	18	19	20
Go to page	304	310	313	312	321	318	313	313

330

---

networks Online Assessment Options

WORKSHEET

Chapter Tests and Lesson Quizzes

Chapter 11 Tests Forms A and B Have students complete the Chapter Tests and Lesson Quizzes to assess student understanding throughout the chapter. Print and online assessment tools offer chapter and lesson evaluation through a variety of question formats, including document-based questions.

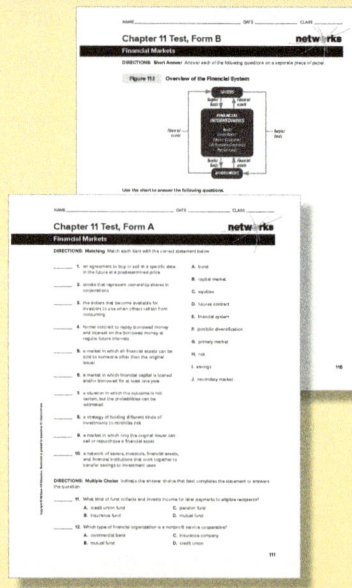

UNIT 5
ECONOMIC PERFORMANCE Planner

UNDERSTANDING BY DESIGN®

Enduring Understandings
- Economics provides strategies, theories, and analytical tools to deal with everyday problems.
- Learning about the past helps us understand the present and make decisions about the future.

Essential Questions
- How do we determine the economic and social well-being of the United States?
- How do population trends impact the economy?
- What are the causes and consequences of instability in the economy?

Students will know:
- fluctuations in a nation's overall levels of income, employment, and prices are determined by the interaction of spending and production decisions made by all households, firms, government agencies, and others in the economy.
- methods used to measure overall economic activity, including the Gross Domestic Product (GDP) and the Consumer Price Index (CPI).
- the reasons for income inequality and how the government has attempted to alleviate it.
- the stages of the business cycle and the characteristics of each.
- the methods used by economists to forecast business cycles, including leading economic indicators and econometric models.
- in the long-run, inflation results from increases in a nation's money supply that exceed increases in its output of goods and services.
- the consequences of unemployment, such as uncertainty, political instability, and social problems.

Students will be able to:
- **discuss** what the GDP and other economic indicators tell us about the economy.
- **discuss** the distribution of income in the United States.
- **explain** why ups and downs in the business cycle are considered normal.
- **discuss** inflation and the unemployment rate and understand information they provide.

Predictable Misunderstandings
Students may think:
- The gross domestic product (GDP) is based on current prices.
- Economic instability affects only the workforce and unemployment rates.
- The unemployment rate exaggerates the problem of unemployment.

Assessment Evidence
Performance Task
- Hands-On Chapter Projects with Technology Extensions
- Economic Simulations
- Math Practice for Economics
- Personal Finance Activities
- Reinforcing Economic Skills Activities

Other Evidence:
- Guided Reading Activities
- Vocabulary Activities
- Lesson Quizzes
- Chapter Tests, Forms A and B

Key for Using the Teacher Edition
SKILL-BASED ACTIVITIES

Types of skill activities found in the Teacher Edition.
- **V** **Visual Skills** require students to analyze maps, graphs, charts, and photos.
- **R** **Reading Skills** help students practice reading skills and master vocabulary.
- **C** **Critical Thinking Skills** help students apply and extend what they have learned.
- **W** **Writing Skills** provide writing opportunities to help students comprehend the text.
- **T** **Technology Skills** require students to use digital tools effectively.

*Letters are followed by a number when there is more than one of the same type of skill on the page.

DIFFERENTIATED INSTRUCTION
All activities are written for the on-level student unless otherwise marked with the leveled labels below.
- **BL** Beyond Level
- **AL** Approaching Level
- **ELL** English Language Learners

All students benefit from activities that utilize different learning styles. Many activities are marked as below when a particular learning style is highlighted.

Intrapersonal
Logical/Mathematical
Visual/Spatial
Verbal/Linguistic
Naturalist
Kinesthetic
Auditory/Musical
Interpersonal

SUGGESTED PACING GUIDE—Semester
Introducing the Unit . . . . ½ Day
Chapter 12: Evaluating the Economy . . . . 5 Days
Chapter 13: Economic Instability . . . . 5 Days

UNIT 5: ECONOMIC PERFORMANCE

PLANNER

☑ Print Teaching Options

Critical Thinking Skills

☐ **p. 331 Analyzing measures of economic performance** Students identify and explain what issues (unemployment rate, inflation, poverty, etc.) indicate about the performance of the American economy. **Verbal/Linguistic**

☐ **p. 331 Comparing macroeconomic statistics** Students select a country and look up macroeconomic statistics about it: real GDP, the size of the population, the unemployment rate, and the inflation rate. Students then discuss the differences among countries' statistics. **Interpersonal, Visual/Spatial**

☐ **p. 332 Recognizing bias** Students follow steps to learn how to recognize bias. Then they have the opportunity to develop the skill of recognizing bias and explaining a point of view on an economic issue after reading a biography feature in the text. **Interpersonal**

☑ Online Teaching Options

☐ **ANIMATION** **Inflation and the Economy**—Students do research to find historic data on inflation and the consumer price index.

☐ **APPROACHING GRADE LEVEL READER** **Alternative Student Edition narrative**—You can assign your students who are struggling to read on grade level the Approaching Grade Level version of the Online Student Edition. This reader presents all of the content in the On Grade Level version of the Online Student Edition at a lower reading level.

☐ **ENGLISH LANGUAGE LEARNER READER** **Alternative Student Edition narrative with ELL support**—Use the Online English Language Learner reader to provide additional reading support for ELL students. You can find this tool in the Online Student Edition.

☑ Printable Digital Worksheets

Reading Skills

☐ **WORKSHEET** **Guided Reading Activity**—Students use the Guided Reading Activities worksheets to review their comprehension of the content.

☐ **WORKSHEET** **Reading Essentials and Study Guide**—Students complete the study guide and answer Reading Progress Check and vocabulary questions.

Critical Thinking Skills

☐ **WORKSHEET** **Inflation and the Economy Animation Activity**—Students answer questions about periods of high inflation, relatively low inflation, and the consumer price index.

☐ **WORKSHEET** **Assessing Background Knowledge Activity**—Students should complete the Assessing Background Knowledge Activity before they study each chapter. Students' responses will give you a good idea of the kinds of misconceptions you can address when teaching the lessons.

☐ **WORKSHEET** **Chapter Summary**—Summaries are provided for each chapter and thoroughly condense core content into manageable chunks.

☐ **WORKSHEET** **Vocabulary Activity**—Students apply their knowledge of content and academic vocabulary words.

UNIT 5
Economic Performance

IT MATTERS BECAUSE …

In our market economy, economic growth significantly affects our daily lives. Jobs, monetary policies, production and trade, the prices of goods and spending levels . . . all these things and more can add up and make or break an individual's potential to achieve the "American Dream." Understanding how economic mechanisms work to measure our collective economic and social well-being will help you make better economic decisions now and in the future.

CHAPTER 12
Evaluating the Economy

ESSENTIAL QUESTIONS

How do we determine the economic and social well-being of the United States?

How do population trends impact the economy?

What steps can we take to deal with poverty?

CHAPTER 13
Economic Instability

ESSENTIAL QUESTION

What are the causes and consequences of instability in the economy?

Economic Performance 331

UNIT 5
Economic Performance

ENGAGE

 Analyzing measures of economic performance Ask: **What issues measure the performance of the national economy?** *(Possible answers: number of unemployed, inflation, number of people living in poverty, health of the housing market)* Call on volunteers to share their ideas with the rest of the class. On the board, list the items that students mentioned. Ask students to explain what they think these issues indicate about the performance of the American economy. Conclude by mentioning that many of these issues will be discussed in this unit.
Verbal/Linguistic

Comparing macroeconomic statistics
Ask each student to select a country and look up macroeconomic statistics about it. Have them find real GDP, the size of the population, the unemployment rate, and the inflation rate. On a long sheet of paper, draw a scale of per capita real GDP. Have students mark on the scale where their countries are situated. On another large sheet of paper, draw a scaled graph with the inflation rate on the vertical axis and the unemployment rate on the horizontal axis. Have students mark the positions of their countries on that graph. Discuss the differences among the countries' statistics.
Interpersonal, Visual/Spatial

ANIMATIONS **WORKSHEET**

Inflation and the Economy

Analyzing the animation Have students do research to find historic data on inflation and the consumer price index. Data are available for every year since 1913. **Ask:**

- During what periods was inflation high?
- During what periods was inflation relatively low?
- By how much has the consumer price index risen since 2000? Since 1950? Since 1913?

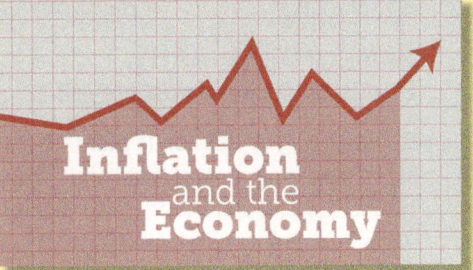

Unit 5 **331**

UNIT 5
Economic Performance

DEVELOP YOUR SKILLS ONLINE

Recognizing Point of View

Help students learn to recognize that a person's point of view, or bias, influences the way he or she interprets and writes about events. Tell students that recognizing bias helps them judge the accuracy of what they hear or read. Teach students to follow these steps to learn how to recognize bias:

- Examine the author's identity, especially his or her views and particular interests.
- Identify statements of fact.
- Identify any expressions of opinion or emotion. Look for words that have positive or negative overtones for clues about the author's feelings on a topic.
- Determine the author's point of view.
- Determine how the author's point of view is reflected in the work.

Provide students with the opportunity to develop the skill of recognizing bias and explaining a point of view on an economic issue. After reading a Biography feature in the text, have students write brief responses to these questions:

- **What is the economist's point of view?**
- **What facts and other details are given to explain or otherwise support that view?**
- **What experiences has the economist had that may have contributed to the point of view?**

In class, discuss these questions. Encourage students to share their ideas and reasons.
Interpersonal

Develop your Skills Online

Explain a Point of View
on an Economic Issue

Economists are people too and those people bring their own individual experiences, beliefs, and points of view to their study of economics and to their interpretation of economic data. This economics program provides biographic information on famous economic theorists, pioneers in the subject, and current key individuals in today's economic system. By reading these biographies and considering the points of view of these individuals, you can make better judgments on the accuracy of their economic actions.

Each chapter features a Biography asset on a noteworthy economist, an entrepreneur, or some other important contributor to the study of economics.

Each Biography asset examines some key moments and economic contributions provided by these individuals.

These Biography assets give you the opportunity to consider the unique points of view that economists bring to topics and controversies.

The Biography feature in the printed Student Edition is also provided as a digital asset in the Online Student Center. You may also answer the Critical Thinking questions online.

Find all your interactive resources for each chapter online.

Chapter 12 Evaluating the Economy

Chapter 13 Economic Instability

---

networks Online Teaching Options

BIOGRAPHY

SAMPLE BIOGRAPHY:
Friedrich August von Hayek

Summarizing an economic point of view
Display the biography of Friedrich August von Hayek. Have students read it and then invite volunteers to summarize his economic ideas.
Ask: How would von Hayek view social programs such as Social Security and Medicare? *(Sample answer: He would oppose them because they imply government intervention in the economy.)* **Ask: What do you think von Hayek's opinion would be of Adam Smith's idea of the invisible hand always at work guiding and correcting markets?** *(Sample answer: He would agree because he believed in absolute free market capitalism.)*

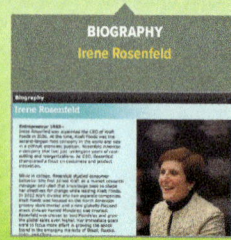

CHAPTER 12
Evaluating the Economy Planner

UNDERSTANDING BY DESIGN®

Enduring Understanding
- *Economics provides strategies, theories, and analytical tools to deal with everyday problems.*

Essential Questions
- *How do we determine the economic and social well-being of the United States?*
- *How do population trends impact the economy?*

Predictable Misunderstandings
Students may think:
- *The gross domestic product (GDP) is based on current prices.* Explain that although this is true for current GDP, economists generally use real GDP instead because it accounts for inflation. Real GDP *per capita* provides an even more accurate portrait.

- *Income is the same as wealth.* Income is a "flow variable" that measures a value over a period of time. Wealth is a "stock variable" that measures a value at one point in time.

Assessment Evidence
Performance Task
- *Hands-On Chapter Project with Technology Extension*

Other Evidence
- *Guided Reading Activities*
- *Vocabulary Activity*
- *Lesson Quizzes*
- *Self-Check Quizzes*
- *Chapter Assessment*
- *Chapter Tests, Forms A and B*

SUGGESTED PACING

Introducing the Chapter: ½ Day	Case Study ½ Day
Lesson 1: Measuring the Nation's Output and Income 1 Day	Lesson 3: Poverty and the Distribution of Income 1 Day
Debate ½ Day	Study Guide, Chapter Assessment and Wrap-Up ½ Day
Lesson 2: Population Growth and Trends 1 Day	

TOTAL 5 Days

Key for Using the Teacher Edition

SKILL-BASED ACTIVITIES

Types of skill activites found in the Teacher Edition.

V Visual Skills require students to analyze maps, graphs, charts, and photos.

R Reading Skills help students practice reading skills and master vocabulary.

C Critical Thinking Skills help students apply and extend what they have learned.

W Writing Skills provide writing opportunities to help students comprehend the text.

T Technology Skills require students to use digital tools effectively.

*Letters are followed by a number when there is more than one of the same type of skill on the page.

DIFFERENTIATED INSTRUCTION

All activities are written for the on-level student unless otherwise marked with the leveled labels below.

BL Beyond Level
AL Approaching Level
ELL English Language Learners

All students benefit from activities that utilize different learning styles. Many activities are marked as below when a particular learning style is highlighted.

Intrapersonal
Logical/Mathematical
Visual/Spatial
Verbal/Linguistic
Naturalist
Kinesthetic
Auditory/Musical
Interpersonal

Council for Economic Education

Below are the Council for Economic Education Voluntary National Content Standards in Economics covered in the *Evaluating the Economy* chapter.

Content Standard 3: Allocation Different methods can be used to allocate goods and services. People acting individually or collectively must choose which methods to use to allocate different kinds of goods and services.

Content Standard 18: Economic Fluctuations Fluctuations in a nation's overall levels of income, employment, and prices are determined by the interaction of spending and production decisions made by all households, firms, government agencies, and others in the economy. Recessions occur when overall levels of income and employment decline.

CHAPTER 12: EVALUATING THE ECONOMY

CHAPTER OPENER PLANNER

Students will know:
- methods used to measure overall economic activity, including Gross Domestic Product (GDP) and the Consumer Price Index (CPI).
- how fertility, life expectancy, and net migration influence population trends.
- the reasons for income inequality.

Students will be able to:
- **discuss** what GDP tells us about the economy.
- **explain** why so many different methods are needed to measure national income.
- **describe** how the population of the United States is counted.
- **analyze** the effect of an aging population on the U.S. economy.
- **discuss** the distribution of income in the United States.
- **list** reasons for income inequality.

UNDERSTANDING BY DESIGN®

☑ Print Teaching Options

V Visual Skills
- ☐ p. 334 Making inferences about the map
  Students discuss the census regions.

R Reading Skills
- ☐ p. 334 Researching local demographics
  Students use the U.S. Census Web site to examine demographic features.

C Critical Thinking Skills
- ☐ p. 333 Evaluating our economic well-being
  Students consider how they feel about our economic situation.
- ☐ p. 333 The Local Economy's Well-Being
  Students draw conclusions about the national economy.
- ☐ p. 334 Locating a business Students determine where they should open a business.

☑ Online Teaching Options

V Visual Skills
- ☐ IMAGE Chapter opener—Students analyze a photo for clues about the economy.

C Critical Thinking Skills
- ☐ INFOGRAPHICS Economic Perspectives—Students evaluate population groups and demographic information about the U.S. Census.
- ☐ DEBATES Can the U.S. economy succeed without a big manufacturing base?—Students analyze two views about the need for a big manufacturing base.
- ☐ INTERACTIVE FEATURE Case Study: Our Need for Forests—Students analyze the issue of deforestation.

☑ Printable Digital Worksheets

C Critical Thinking Skills
- ☐ WORKSHEET Economic Simulation—Students create their own census questions.
- ☐ WORKSHEET Personal Finance Activity—Students budget with poverty-level figures.
- ☐ WORKSHEET Math Practice for Economics—Students answer questions about the Census Bureau's measure of poverty.
- ☐ WORKSHEET Enrichment Activity—Students read about income and wealth inequality.

Project-Based Learning

Hands-On

Hands-On Chapter Project
In this activity, students work in groups. They are employed by a local business and their boss is concerned about poverty in the area. She has suggested that the company do several service days during the year. The boss has asked each team to develop a proposal describing where the employees should spend those service days. Teams will present their proposal to all of the company employees (the class), who will select the proposal to carry out.

Find an additional activity online that incorporates technology for the Hands-On Project. Visit the EdTech Teacher Web sites for more links, tutorials, and other resources.

Print Resources

ANCILLARY RESOURCE
This ancillary is available for every chapter and lesson.
- Chapter Tests and Lesson Quizzes

PRINTABLE DIGITAL WORKSHEETS
These printable digital worksheets are available for every chapter and lesson.
- Reading Essentials & Study Guide
- Vocabulary Activities
- Chapter Summaries
- Economic Simulations
- Math Practice for Economics
- Reinforcing Economic Skills
- Personal Finance Activities
- Enrichment Activities
- Reteaching Activities
- Guided Reading Activities
- Video Worksheets
- Lesson Quizzes and Chapter Tests (English and Spanish)

More Media Resources

SUGGESTED READING
- For students at a Grade 10 reading level:
  Poverty in America, by Milton Meltzer
- For students at a Grade 11 reading level:
  Population: Opposing Viewpoints, by Charles F. Hohm & Lori Justine Jones
- For students at a Grade 12 reading level:
  Poverty: Opposing Viewpoints, by Karen Balkin

SUGGESTED VIDEOS
Find these documentaries yourself online. NOTE: McGraw-Hill Education does not endorse these resources. Preview clips for age-appropriateness.
- *Money and Life* (86 min.)
- *Aftermath of a Crisis* (48 min.)
- *TED Talks: The Death of Innovation, The End of Growth* (12 min.)

LESSON 1 Planner

MEASURING THE NATION'S OUTPUT AND INCOME

Students will know:
- fluctuations in a nation's overall levels of income, employment, and prices are determined by the interaction of spending and production decisions made by all households, firms, government agencies, and others in the economy.
- methods used to measure overall economic activity, including Gross Domestic Product (GDP) and the Consumer Price Index (CPI).

Students will be able to:
- **discuss** what GDP tells us about the economy.
- **list** variations of GDP to account for inflation and population changes.
- **explain** what GDP does not tell us about the economy.
- **name** five different measures that are used to measure national income.
- **explain** why so many different methods are needed to measure national income.

UNDERSTANDING BY DESIGN®

☑ Print Teaching Options

V Visual Skills
- ☐ p. 342 Understanding the circular flow of economic activity

R Reading Skills
- ☐ p. 337 Defining terms Students define *gross*, *domestic*, and *comprehensive*.
- ☐ p. 338 Examining the underground economy
- ☐ p. 340 Comparing GDP and GNP
- ☐ p. 342 Identifying economic effects of consumers on the circular flow chart
- ☐ p. 343 Explaining the foreign sector

C Critical Thinking Skills
- ☐ p. 337 Understanding sampling techniques
- ☐ p. 338 Understanding exclusions from GDP
- ☐ p. 338 Predicting outcomes Students consider why used items are not counted in GDP.
- ☐ p. 339 Synthesizing information about per capita GDP
- ☐ p. 341 Analyzing DPI Students compute their disposable personal income (DPI).
- ☐ p. 341 Defining measures of income
- ☐ p. 342 Classifying household consumption

W Writing Skills
- ☐ p. 340 Interpreting the strengths and weaknesses of GDP
- ☐ p. 342 Writing about depreciation
- ☐ p. 343 Noting the importance of imports and exports

T Technology Skills
- ☐ p. 339 Creating a per capita GDP graph
- ☐ p. 341 Researching and graphing PI

☑ Online Teaching Options

V Visual Skills
- ☐ **POLITICAL CARTOON** GDP and National Economic Health—Students explain the analogy between Uncle Sam and a medical patient.
- ☐ **CHART** Estimating Gross Domestic Product—Students discuss the *expenditure* and *income* approach.
- ☐ **VIDEO** Engineers Outsourcing—Students watch a video about how outsourcing jobs affects the U.S. GDP.
- ☐ **CHART** Circular Flow of Economic Activity—Students discuss government actions that affect the circular flow.
- ☐ **CHART** Output Expenditure Model—Students examine the equation for calculating GDP.

R Reading Skills
- ☐ **GRAPHIC ORGANIZER** Types of GDP—Students identify the three types of GPD.
- ☐ **GRAPHIC ORGANIZER** Main Idea Chart—Students organize the measures of national income.

C Critical Thinking Skills
- ☐ **BELLRINGER** Measuring the Nation's Output and Income—Students identify items not included in GDP.
- ☐ **ESSENTIAL QUESTION** Exploring the Essential Question—Students categorize goods and services as part of GDP.
- ☐ **INTERACTIVE FEATURE** Global Economy & You—Students decide whether NAFTA is good for the U.S. economy.
- ☐ **ESSENTIAL QUESTION** Exploring the Essential Question—Students calculate PI and DPI.

T Technology Skills
- ☐ **SELF-CHECK QUIZ** Lesson 1—Students receive instant feedback on their answers.
- ☐ **GAME** Lesson 1—Students solve clues to review lesson content.

☑ Printable Digital Worksheets

R Reading Skills
- ☐ **WORKSHEET** Guided Reading Activity—Students review their comprehension.
- ☐ **WORKSHEET** Reading Essentials and Study Guide—Students complete the study guide and answer Reading Progress Check and vocabulary questions.

C Critical Thinking Skills
- ☐ **WORKSHEET** Engineers Outsourcing Video Activity—Students answer questions about outsourcing engineers.

LESSON 2 Planner

POPULATION GROWTH AND TRENDS

Students will know:
- the country's population has shifted from a fast-growing, mostly rural population to a slower-growing, mostly urban one.
- how fertility, life expectancy, and net migration influence population trends.

Students will be able to:
- *identify* the sources of income for each sector of the economy.
- *describe* how the population of the United States is counted.
- *interpret the significance* of regional population change in the economy.
- *analyze* the effect of an aging population on the U.S. economy.

UNDERSTANDING BY DESIGN®

✓ Print Teaching Options

V Visual Skills
- ☐ **p. 349 Using population pyramids** Students examine a population pyramid and predict what it will look like in 2030. *Logical/Mathematical*

R Reading Skills
- ☐ **p. 350 Creating word webs** Students create word webs for *fertility, life expectancy,* and *net immigration levels.* *Verbal/Linguistic*

C Critical Thinking Skills
- ☐ **p. 346 Hypothesizing about the census** Students discuss the importance of the census.
- ☐ **p. 347 Hypothesizing a method** Students speculate on how the center of population is found. *Logical/Mathematical*
- ☐ **p. 348 Synthesizing information** Students discuss reasons Americans are moving to the Sun Belt. *Verbal/Linguistic*
- ☐ **p. 349 Identifying examples of population trends** Students list ways population trends are used. *Verbal/Linguistic*
- ☐ **p. 350 Total Fertility Rate** Students discuss the TFR as a way to make regional comparisons and predictions.
- ☐ **p. 351 Making predictions about population growth** Students predict factors that might change the expected low population growth of the U.S. *Verbal/Linguistic*

W Writing Skills
- ☐ **p. 347 Writing a letter** Students e-mail the U.S. Census Bureau for steps on how census information is analyzed.
- ☐ **p. 349 Predicting the effects of population changes** Students review how aging population will personally affect them. *Intrapersonal*
- ☐ **p. 351 Evaluating the lesson** Students identify the population trend they feel will have the greatest effect on the nation and on their community over the next 25 years.

✓ Online Teaching Options

V Visual Skills
- ☐ **MAP** **Center of Population map**—Students discuss the population shift and how the population center will move in coming decades. *Visual/Spatial*
- ☐ **GRAPH** **Projected Distribution of the Population by Age and Gender, 2015**—Students speculate about the dependency ratio based on the data for their age group. *Logical/Mathematical*
- ☐ **INFOGRAPHIC** **Population Growth and Challenges**—Students consider how changes may affect them. *Logical/Mathematical*
- ☐ **VIDEO** **Happiness Income**—Students examine a study about helping others.

C Critical Thinking Skills
- ☐ **BELLRINGER** **Population Growth and Trends**—Students explore how longer life expectancy might affect them. *Interpersonal*
- ☐ **ESSENTIAL QUESTION** **Exploring the Essential Question**—Students consider U.S. population changes.
- ☐ **INTERACTIVE FEATURE** **Careers**—Students consider a career in social work. *Verbal/Linguistic*

T Technology Skills
- ☐ **SELF-CHECK QUIZ** **Lesson 2**—Students receive instant feedback on their answers.
- ☐ **GAME** **Lesson 2**—Students solve clues to review lesson content.
- ☐ **INTERACTIVE WHITEBOARD ACTIVITY** **Social Security**—Students work together to learn lesson content.

✓ Printable Digital Worksheets

R Reading Skills
- ☐ **WORKSHEET** **Guided Reading Activity**—Students review their comprehension of the content.
- ☐ **WORKSHEET** **Reading Essentials and Study Guide**—Students complete the study guide and answer Reading Progress Check and vocabulary questions.

C Critical Thinking Skills
- ☐ **WORKSHEET** **Economic Simulation**—Students create their own census form to gather information about the U.S. population and to uncover new demographic data that reflects changes in our society and technology.
- ☐ **WORKSHEET** **Happiness Income Video Activity**—Students answer questions about spending money on oneself versus spending on others to gain happiness.

LESSON 3 Planner

POVERTY AND THE DISTRIBUTION OF INCOME

Students will know:
- the gap in the distribution of income is widening every year.
- the reasons for income inequality.
- how the government has attempted to alleviate poverty through anti-poverty programs.

Students will be able to:
- **define** poverty.
- **discuss** the distribution of income in the United States.
- **list** reasons for income inequality.
- **evaluate** current and proposed antipoverty programs.

UNDERSTANDING BY DESIGN®

☑ Print Teaching Options

V Visual Skills
- ☐ **p. 355 Analyzing graphs and making predictions** Students predict how the income gap will impact U.S. society and the economy.

R Reading Skills
- ☐ **p. 353 Using context clues to learn word meaning** Students discuss *relative poverty*.
- ☐ **p. 355 Summarizing information in a table** Students summarize the Distribution of Income.

C Critical Thinking Skills
- ☐ **p. 353 Expressing opinions about poverty** Students discuss whether poverty can be viewed solely as an economic issue.
- ☐ **p. 354 Making a budget on the poverty threshold**
- ☐ **p. 356 Explaining the effect of rising health care costs**
- ☐ **p. 357 Evaluating efforts to eliminate poverty**
- ☐ **p. 358 Evaluating the administration of welfare programs** Students debate whether private companies should administer Medicaid.
- ☐ **p. 359 Considering problems and solutions of the negative income tax**
- ☐ **p. 359 Predicting the end of poverty** Students decide if income inequality will be fixed.

W Writing Skills
- ☐ **p. 355 Writing about education and poverty** Students propose a solution for the problem.
- ☐ **p. 356 Writing a short story** Students write about the effect of one of the nine factors affecting income inequality. **Verbal/Linguistic**
- ☐ **p. 357 Writing a persuasive essay** Students react to this statement: The government has a responsibility to help through income and general assistance.
- ☐ **p. 358 Writing a report on a social service program** Students research social services.

☑ Online Teaching Options

V Visual Skills
- ☐ **CHART** **Poverty Guidelines**—Students speculate on the poverty line.
- ☐ **GRAPH** **Poverty in the United States**—Students give reasons why the poverty rate has scarcely changed in 40 years.
- ☐ **GRAPH** **Distribution of Income**—Students describe the Lorenz Curve.
- ☐ **IMAGE** **Enterprise Zone Attempts to Revitalize an Area**—Students discuss what combinations make the community viable. **Verbal/Linguistic**
- ☐ **VIDEO** **Hard Time Generation**—Students discuss ways government has attempted to alleviate poverty. **Visual/Spatial**

R Reading Skills
- ☐ **GRAPHIC ORGANIZER** **Factors that Contribute to Poverty**—Students detail key factors that contribute to poverty. **Visual/Spatial**
- ☐ **BIOGRAPHY** **John Kenneth Galbraith**—Students read about Galbraith's philosophy.

C Critical Thinking Skills
- ☐ **BELLRINGER** **Enterprise Zones**—Students identify the benefits of enterprise zones.
- ☐ **ESSENTIAL QUESTION** **Exploring the Essential Question**—Students identify government antipoverty programs.

T Technology Skills
- ☐ **SELF-CHECK QUIZ** **Lesson 3**—Students receive instant feedback on their answers.
- ☐ **GAME** **Lesson 3**—Students solve clues to review lesson content.
- ☐ **INTERACTIVE WHITEBOARD ACTIVITY** **Reasons for Inequality**—Students work together to learn lesson content.

☑ Printable Digital Worksheets

R Reading Skills
- ☐ **WORKSHEET** **Guided Reading Activity**—Students review their comprehension.
- ☐ **WORKSHEET** **Reading Essentials and Study Guide**—Students complete the study guide and answer Reading Progress Check and vocabulary questions.
- ☐ **WORKSHEET** **Reteaching Activity**—Students use this activity worksheet to review and reteach chapter content and vocabulary.

C Critical Thinking Skills
- ☐ **WORKSHEET** **Hard Time Generation**—Students answer questions about living in poverty.
- ☐ **WORKSHEET** **Use the Enrichment Activity**—Students consider income and wealth inequality.

CHAPTER 12 Evaluating the Economy

INTERVENTION AND REMEDIATION STRATEGIES

LESSON 1 Measuring the Nation's Output and Income

Reading and Comprehension

Have students refer to the text and answer these questions:

- What does GDP measure?
- How do economists use GDP to assess how the economy is doing?
- What is the difference between real and current GDP?
- What is the difference between GDP and GNP?
- What are two other measures of income and what do they measure?
- What are the four sectors of the economy?
- How do economists use the output-expenditure model?

Text Evidence

Ask students to write an essay explaining how economists measure the economic and social well-being of Americans. Have them tell which is the best economic measure of well-being and ask them to explain why. Remind students to cite details from the text to support their ideas.

LESSON 2 Population and Growth Trends

Reading and Comprehension

Have students work in pairs and write three questions about each of the main sections of the lesson. Then have pairs exchange questions and find the answers. When students have completed the task, call on pairs to share some of their questions. Guide a class discussion of the answers.

Text Evidence

Tell students that the 2010 Census cost approximately $13 billion dollars, or about $97 per household. Then ask them to imagine that an editorial in their local newspaper complained that this is too much to spend and that most of the information gathered has no meaningful use. The writer wants the government to do a simple counting of the population, which will cost much less, rather than gathering all the details about how much education people have, how big their household is, and so on. "We just need to know how many of us there are," the writer says. Ask students to write their own letter-to-the-editor explaining why the census is necessary and why all the information is valuable. Have students cite facts and other details to support their claims.

LESSON 3 Poverty and the Distribution of Income

Reading and Comprehension

Divide students into groups of three and assign each of the students in the groups one of the sections of the lesson. Ask students to prepare an outline of their section of text. The outline should include the main ideas and the most important details. Then have students meet in their groups and use their outlines to present an oral review of their section.

Text Evidence

Ask students: **Should current antipoverty programs be expanded, trimmed down, or changed in some way?** Have students write an essay giving their response. Tell them to explain their reasoning, citing details from the text to support their ideas. Tell them to assume that current trends that have led to growing income inequality will continue for the foreseeable future.

Online Resources

Assessing Background Knowledge Use this worksheet to pre-assess students' background knowledge before they start the chapter.

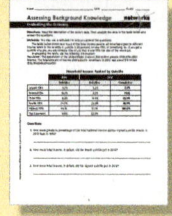

Chapter Summaries Have students use the summary as a pre-reading activity or as a post-reading review to check the main ideas covered in each lesson.

Guided Reading Activities Have students complete these activities as they read each lesson. They provide reading notes the student can use for review and to prepare for assessments.

Reteaching Activities Have students complete the Reteaching Activity for remedial practice and review of vital content.

Self-Check Quizzes These quizzes provide instant feedback on areas the students may need to re-read to understand a main idea.

Reading Essentials and Study Guide This resource offers writing and reading activities for the approaching-level student.

Approaching Grade Level Reader This reader presents all of the content of the Online Student Edition but at a lower reading level.

English Language Learner Reader Provide additional reading support for ELL students. Find this tool online.

Evaluating the Economy

ESSENTIAL QUESTION
How do we determine the economic and social well-being of the United States?

networks
www.connected.mcgraw-hill.com
There's More Online about evaluating the economy.

CHAPTER 12

Economic Perspectives
Examining the U.S. Census

Lesson 1
Measuring the Nation's Output and Income

Lesson 2
Population Growth and Trends

Lesson 3
Poverty and the Distribution of Income

Letter from the Author

Dear Economics Teacher,

Most developed nations, and that includes our own, have a bias for growth. Of course, we know that resources are limited and that they must be used carefully, but we also know that scarcity is something that affects everyone. Economists like to think of the economy as analogous to a giant pie that can be divided into slices for everyone. If you are like most people, you probably want a bigger slice in the future. This requires economic growth, because without it there's no way for everyone to get a larger slice. This makes the goal of economic growth a lot more reasonable.

Gary E. Clayton

CHAPTER 12
Evaluating the Economy

ENGAGE

Call students' attention to the photograph. **Ask: What is happening?** *(A home lender is placing a foreclosure sign on a home that has been foreclosed.)* **Under what circumstances does a lender foreclose on a home?** *(A home is foreclosed when the owners fail to make their mortgage payments, and the lender takes the home back to recoup its investment.)* Point out that foreclosures occurred frequently throughout the country during and in the aftermath of the economic crisis of 2008–2009. **Ask: What does this tell you about the economic and social well-being of people at this time?** *(Students should infer that many people were probably out of work, their personal financial situations were desperate, and they could not make mortgage payments.)* **Visual/Spatial**

Evaluating our economic well-being Point out that we have mainly focused on objective, measurable aspects of the economy so far. Tell students that *subjective* issues relate to how we *feel* about our economic situation. Ask these questions:

- **How do you feel about the economic well-being of our country? Why?**
- **Is there a widening income gap between the rich, poor, and middle class? Is this a problem?**
- **Is our country headed in the right direction in economic terms?** **Interpersonal**

Making Connections

The Local Economy's Well-Being Ask students what economic activities or conditions in their community tell them about the economy. Stimulate discussion by asking questions such as:

- **Are stores and other businesses putting "help-wanted" signs in their windows?**
- **Are there lines at the unemployment office?**
- **Do you know people who have been laid off?**
- **Have you noticed more people out shopping in stores and malls?**

Guide students in drawing conclusions from these personal observations about the state of the local and national economy.

Study Organizer

Go to the Foldables® library for a cumulative chapter-based Foldable® activity that your students can use to help take notes and prepare for assessment.

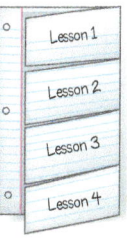

CHAPTER 12
Economic Perspectives

TEACH & ASSESS

R Reading Skills

Researching local demographics Have students use the U.S. Census Web site to learn more about the area they live in. Have them report to the class about the average age, the ethnic mix, employment statistics, and other demographic features. Invite them to use charts and graphs to support their report. **BL** Logical/Mathematical

V Visual Skills

Making inferences about the map Discuss the census regions shown on the map. **Ask: Why are some regions so much larger than others?** *(The large geographic regions are sparsely populated relative to the smaller regions. High population density areas are the smaller regions.)* **In which census region do you live? What is the central city of your region?**

C Critical Thinking Skills

Locating a business Have students form small groups. Tell each group to decide on a type of business they would like to develop, and to determine where in the country they should open their first factory, office, or store. Have them share their ideas with the class, explaining the demographic reasons they chose that type of business (what age market they are targeting) and the factors that led them to decide where to open it first (densely populated or sparsely populated). **BL** Interpersonal, Logical/Mathematical

---

Economic Perspectives

EXAMINING THE U.S. CENSUS

The first U.S. census took place in 1790 during George Washington's administration, under the direction of Secretary of State Thomas Jefferson. It gathered information on the original 13 states, plus the districts of Kentucky, Maine, Vermont, and Tennessee. According to the U.S. Constitution, it was a nationwide survey to be held every ten years. The law required that every household be surveyed; both free persons and enslaved persons were recorded. There have been 23 censuses to date, most recently in 2010. Between censuses the U.S. Census Bureau calculates estimates based on most recent data.

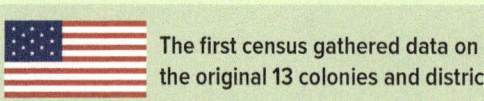

The first census gathered data on the original 13 colonies and districts.

Since **1790**

Every **10** Years

Census Regions Today

For Census purposes, the nations is divided into the geographic areas shown below. Each region has a central city, indicated by the star on the map.

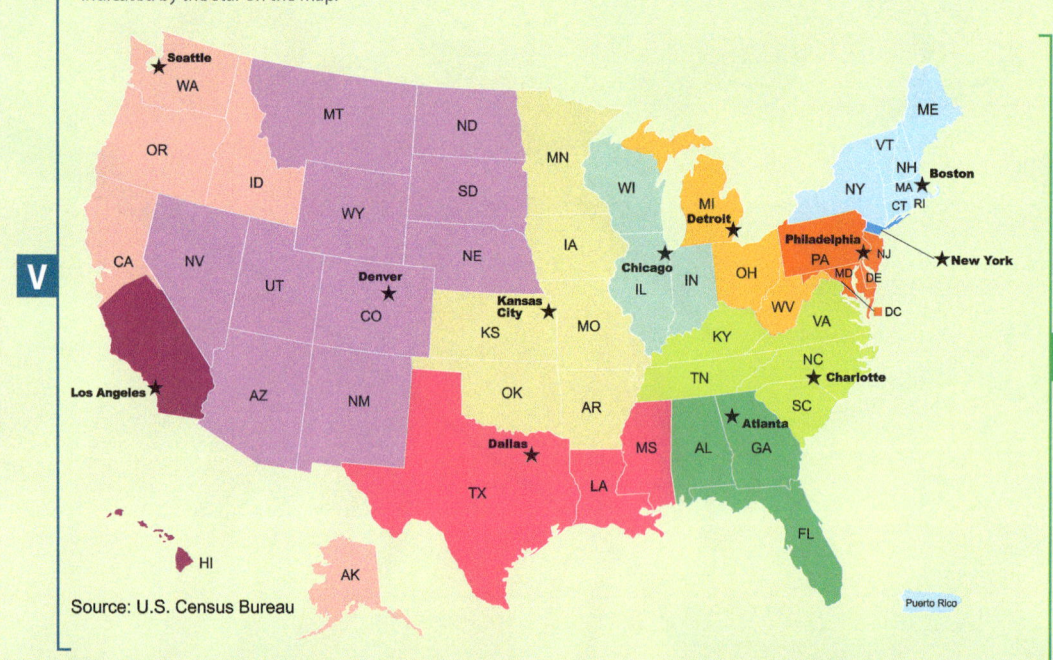

Source: U.S. Census Bureau

---

networks Online Teaching Options

INFOGRAPHIC

Economic Perspectives: Examining the U.S. Census

Evaluating perspectives Tell students that the 2010 Census revealed the U.S. population to be nearly 309 million. (For comparison, the *world's* total population reached seven billion in the fall of 2011.) Have students read and evaluate the descriptions of the "generations" in the graphic. Discuss whether students think the descriptions are fair or biased, and why. Ask students to create a visual time line of events that highlight and/or symbolize each generation mentioned in the graphic. **Visual/Spatial**

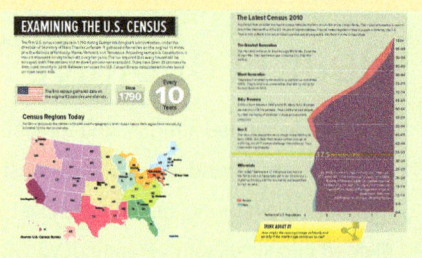

334

The Latest Census 2010

Population data provides the most accurate measure of where people live in the United States. This critical information is used to determine membership in the U.S. House of Representatives. Beyond measuring the number of people in America, the U.S. Census also collects information about businesses and geographic distribution in the United States.

The Greatest Generation
The men and women who lived through World War II and the Korean War. Their worldview was influenced by Cold War politics.

Silent Generation
They were frustrated by the social and political turmoil of the 1960s. They turned in a conservative direction by voting for Richard Nixon in 1968.

Baby Boomers
Children born between 1945 and 1961. Many Baby Boomers were active in 1960s protests. Their childhood was shaped by mass marketing of American culture and economic prosperity.

Gen X
This part of the population came of age in the 1980s and early 1990s. Gen Xers often have a cynical distrust of authority, but don't always challenge that authority. They often celebrate diversity.

Millennials
Also called "Generation Y," this group was born in the 1980s and reached adulthood in the 21st century. Digital technology and the Internet have shaped their formative years.

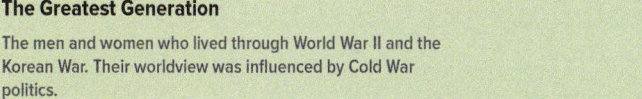

37.5 Median Age in 2010

By 2010, the median age in the United States was 37.5 years old. It had increased 1.9 years since 2000. Between 1990 and 2000, the median age had increased by 2.4 years. This aging trend was the result of the aging of the large Baby Boomer generation, birth rate stabilization, and longer life expectancy.

■ Female
■ Male

Percent of U.S. Population 4 3 2 1 0

THINK ABOUT IT!
How might the country change politically and socially if the median age continues to rise?

WORKSHEET

Math Practice for Economics

Analyzing census information regarding poverty Distribute copies of the worksheet. Explain that the U.S. Census began measuring the number of Americans living in poverty in 1959. Since 1980, the Census has measured the number of people living in poverty every year. Students will study a chart and answer questions about whether the U.S. Census Bureau's measure of Americans living in poverty truly reflects the number of Americans who are impoverished. **Logical/ Mathematical**

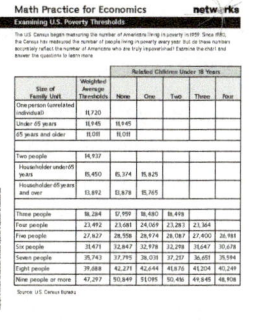

CHAPTER 12
Economic Perspectives

Content Background Knowledge

Reapportionment and Redistricting Remind students that the number of U.S. Representatives a state has is based on population data gathered every 10 years through the U.S. Census. If a state gains or loses population, its representatives may have to be reapportioned according to the new population figures. Reapportionment often requires that a state go through a process called redistricting. State legislatures are responsible for redistricting when a state experiences changes in population. The main requirement in redistricting is that each district be roughly equal in population. But the redistricting process sometimes becomes a highly charged political issue. Draw the four diagrams below on the board, and tell students to notice that in each, the Xs and the Os never move. Imagine that the Xs are Republican voters and the Os are Democratic voters. If Republicans control the state legislature, they might draw district lines as shown in figure (b). This would group Republican supporters, and result in controlling more districts.

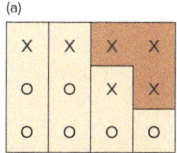
(a)

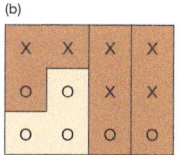
(b)

X controls one district.   X controls three districts.

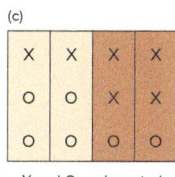
(c)

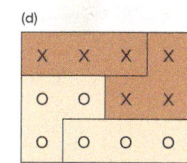
(d)

X and O each control two districts.   X and O each control two districts.

CLOSE & REFLECT
Have students answer the *Think About It!* questions.

ANSWERS, p. 335

THINK ABOUT IT!

Answers will vary, but students should understand that a higher median age means that fewer working age people are paying into the Social Security system, whereas more people are approaching the age where they can start applying for their contributions. Fewer resources for younger people, such as elementary schools, may need to be constructed and utilized, whereas more senior centers and perhaps nursing homes will need to be created.

CHAPTER 12, LESSON 1
Measuring the Nation's Output and Income

ENGAGE

R Reading Skills

Comparing and contrasting economic terms Before students begin the lesson, ask them to compare the terms *macroeconomics* and *microeconomics*. Point out that *macro-* means "very large" and *micro-* means "extremely small." **Ask:**

- **What does microeconomics deal with?** *(The specific financial concerns of a business, organization, or individual, and the economic relationships among them. The price of a company's products or of particular commodities in the market are topics within microeconomics.)*
- **What is the subject of macroeconomics?** *(The overall economy of a state, country, or the world and the events that drive that economy on a large scale. The study of a nation's income, output, and consumption are topics within macroeconomics.)* **Verbal/Linguistic**

ANSWERS, p. 336

ESSENTIAL QUESTION ACTIVITY

1. No
2. Yes
3. No
4. Yes
5. Yes

TAKING NOTES:
Current GDP
Real GDP
GDP per capita

Interact with these digital assets and others in lesson 1

✓ INTERACTIVE GRAPH
  Circular Flow of Economic Activity
✓ INTERACTIVE IMAGE
  The Output Expenditure Model
✓ SELF-CHECK QUIZ
✓ VIDEO

networks
TRY IT YOURSELF ONLINE

Reading Help Desk

Academic Vocabulary
- excluded

Content Vocabulary
- gross domestic product (GDP)
- intermediate products
- Secondhand sales
- Nonmarket transactions
- underground economy
- base year
- real GDP
- current GDP
- real GDP per capita
- gross national product (GNP)
- net national product (NNP)
- national income (NI)
- personal income (PI)
- disposable personal income (DPI)
- household
- unrelated individual
- family
- net exports of goods and services
- output-expenditure model

TAKING NOTES:

Key Ideas and Details
ACTIVITY Use the graphic organizer below to identify the three types of GDP.

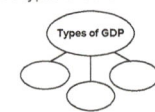

LESSON 1
Measuring the Nation's Output and Income

ESSENTIAL QUESTION

How do we determine the economic and social well-being of the United States?

You have probably heard of the U.S. GDP. It defines the total market value of all final goods and services produced in the United States during a one-year period. But it doesn't measure all goods and services. It doesn't measure the goods or services used to make other products already counted in the GDP. It also doesn't measure nonmarket transactions—activities that you do around the house that are not involved in a market, such as washing the car. Read the questions below and answer with a yes or no to indicate whether you think the good or service is counted in the GDP.

1. You clean out the basement of your house.
2. Your mother buys flour and sugar to make bread.
3. The bakery in town buys flour and sugar to make bread.
4. The bakery sells loaves of bread.
5. You buy new tires for your bicycle.

GDP—The Measure of National Output

GUIDING QUESTION *What does GDP tell us about the economy?*

Macroeconomics is the branch of economics that deals with the economy as a whole. Macro, as it is often called, makes use of a comprehensive set of measures in the National Income and Product Accounts (NIPA) to keep track of the nation's production, consumption, saving, investment, and income.

---

networks Online Teaching Options

BELLRINGER

Measuring the Nation's Output and Income

Discussing exclusions from GDP Have students view the Bellringer and discuss the questions. Then encourage students to discuss other intermediate products not included in GDP. Have students differentiate among secondhand sales, nonmarket transactions, and transactions in the underground economy, and discuss why these items are not included in GDP. **Interpersonal**

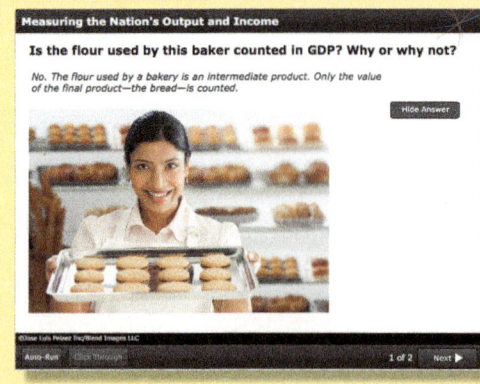

Gross domestic product (GDP) is one of these comprehensive measures of national output. It is defined as the total market value of all final goods and services produced within a country's borders during a 12-month period.

Measuring Current GDP

The measurement of GDP is fairly easy to understand. All we have to do is multiply all of the final goods and services produced in a 12-month period by their prices, and then add them up to get the total dollar value of production.

Figure 12.1 provides a conceptual example. The first column contains three product categories—goods, services, and structures—used in the NIPA. The third category, structures, includes residential housing, apartments, and buildings for commercial purposes. The total number of final goods, services, and structures produced in the year is listed in the quantity column, and the price column shows the average of each product. To get GDP, we simply multiply the quantity of each good by its price and then add the results, as is done in the last column of the table.

Of course, it is not possible to record every single good, service, and structure produced during the year, so government statisticians instead use scientific sampling techniques to estimate the quantities and prices of the individual products. To keep the report as current as possible, they estimate GDP quarterly, or every three months, and then revise the numbers for months after that. As a result, it takes several months to discover how the economy actually performed.

gross domestic product (GDP) dollar value of all final goods, services, and structures produced within a country's national borders during a one-year period

intermediate products products that are components of other final products already included in the GDP; for example, new tires and radios for use on new cars

Some Things Are Excluded

Because GDP is a measure of final output, **intermediate products**—goods used to make other products that are already counted in GDP—are **excluded**. If you

FIGURE 12.1

ESTIMATING TOTAL ANNUAL OUTPUT

Estimating Gross Domestic Product

	Product	Quantity (millions)	Price (per 1 unit)	Dollar value (millions)
Goods	Automobiles	6	$25,000	$150,000
	Replacement tires	10	$60	$600
	Shoes	55	$50	$2,700
	...*	...*	...*	...*
Services	Haircuts	150	$8	$1,200
	Income tax filings	30	$150	$4,500
	Legal advice	45	$200	$9,000
	...*	...*	...*	...*
Structures	Single family	3	$175,600	$525,000
	Multifamily	5	$300,000	$1,500,000
	Commercial	1	$1,000,000	$1,000,000
	...*	...*	...*	...*

Note: *...other goods, services, and structures.

Total GDP = $18 trillion

Gross domestic product is the total dollar value of production within a country's borders in a 12-month period. It can be found by multiplying all of the goods and services produced by their prices, and then adding them up.

▲ **CRITICAL THINKING**
Economic Analysis How is the dollar value for each of the products on the table calculated?

connected.mcgraw-hill.com

connected.mcgraw-hill.com   *Evaluating the Economy*   **337**

CHAPTER 12, LESSON 1
Measuring the Nation's Output and Income

TEACH & ASSESS

R Reading Skills

Defining terms Have each student, without using the textbook or a dictionary, write economic definitions of *gross*, *domestic*, and *comprehensive*. Then have students explain the meanings to partners. Finally, have pairs check their definitions in a dictionary. **ELL** Verbal/Linguistic

W Writing Skills

Writing quiz questions about GDP Have students create a five-question quiz about gross domestic product based on the information in this lesson. Questions should cover the main points about GDP. Have students exchange quizzes with a partner. **AL** Verbal/Linguistic

C Critical Thinking Skills

Understanding sampling techniques Ask: **Why do scientific sampling techniques give an accurate picture of the economy, even though economists do not record every single good and service produced?** *(Sampling techniques are created to draw out an exact representative picture of the nation's economic activity, which includes some estimation.)* Logical/Mathematical

---

CHARTS

Estimating Gross Domestic Product

Estimating GDP Display Figure 12.1. Point out that economists calculate GDP in one of two ways. First, there is the *expenditure* approach. Economists add up all of the money *spent* by consumers, businesses, the government, and the foreign sector on new goods and services produced within the United States. There is also the *income* approach to calculating GDP, which will be discussed in the next subsection. In this approach, economists add up all of the money that people *earned* in the country. Both approaches result in nearly the same total amount.

ANSWERS, p. 337

CRITICAL THINKING
The dollar value is calculated by multiplying the number of units by the price per unit.

Evaluating the Economy   **337**

CHAPTER 12, LESSON 1
Measuring the Nation's Output and Income

C1 Critical Thinking Skills

Understanding exclusions from GDP Ask students which of the following items would be counted in the U.S. GDP for 2015: (a) A house built in 1998 and sold to new owners in 2015; (b) A Toyota vehicle produced in Japan and sold to an American family; (c) An illegal purchase of pirated copies of movies; (d) A Ford vehicle produced in Michigan and sold to a family in Canada; (e) A historical home purchased by the local library. *(Answer d is correct. A car produced in the United States is part of the U.S. GDP, regardless of who purchased it. Answers a and e are incorrect because the houses are not new goods in 2015. Answer b is incorrect because a car imported from Japan is not counted toward the U.S. GDP. Answer c is incorrect because illegal goods are not counted in GDP.)* **Verbal/Linguistic**

C2 Critical Thinking Skills

Predicting outcomes Ask: **What would happen if a nation counted the sales of used items in its GDP? Of nonmarket transactions?** *(GDP totals would be artificially inflated; the inaccurate information would prevent the nation from effectively measuring its economic growth.)* **Logical/Mathematical**

R Reading Skills

Examining the underground economy
Ask students to analyze ways to decrease the amount of activity in the underground economy. Note suggestions on the board. *(Suggestions may include lower taxes, increased policing of underground economic activities, or harsher penalties for those taking part in underground economic activities.)*

ANSWERS, p. 338

CRITICAL THINKING

The influx of cheaper international produce will drive down the price of the local produce, because although consumers may be willing to pay more for local produce, *how much* depends on the comparison with the international price. If the difference is too high, all but the most devoted localvores will purchase the international produce.

---

buy new replacement tires for your automobile, for example, the tires are counted in GDP because they were intended for final use by the customer and not combined with other parts to make a different product. However, tires on a new car are not counted separately because their value is already built into the price of the vehicle. Other goods, such as flour and sugar, are part of GDP if they are bought for final use by the consumer. However, if a baker buys them to make bread for sale, only the value of the bread is counted.

Secondhand sales—the sales of used goods—are also excluded from GDP because no new production is involved when products already in existence are transferred from one owner to another. Although the sale of a used car, a house, or an MP3 player may give others cash that they can use on new purchases, only the original sale is included in GDP.

Nonmarket transactions—economic activities that do not generate expenditures in the market—are also excluded. For example, GDP does not take into account the value of your services when you mow your own lawn or do your own home repairs. However, these activities would be counted if they were done for pay by someone outside the home. For this reason, services that homemakers provide are excluded from GDP even though they would amount to billions of dollars annually if actually purchased in the market.

Finally, transactions that occur in the **underground economy**—economic activities that are not reported for legal or tax collection purposes—are not counted in GDP. Some of these activities are illegal, such as gambling, smuggling,

excluded not counted or included

Secondhand sales sales of used goods; category of activity not included in GDP computation

Nonmarket transactions economic activity not taking place in the market, and therefore, not included in GDP; examples include services of homemakers and work done around the home

---

THE GLOBAL ECONOMY & YOU

Population and World Trade

In the twenty-first century, growth is the fundamental characteristic of the relationship between population and world trade. The United Nations projects that by 2025, 8.1 billion people will live on the planet. More people on the planet mean more markets, and more markets mean more trading in goods and services.

Some people claim that this overall growth in world trade helps people in all countries because trade activity creates jobs and means more money is available for a nation to spend on health care and education. The United States government promotes world trade and joins with other nations in international trade agreements, such as NAFTA, the North American Free Trade Agreement, which has created the world's largest free trade area. Many of the goods and services you buy, including food products such as vegetables, are available in the U.S. because of NAFTA.

Those against such international trade agreements claim the agreements do not increase the GDP per capita in developing nations, but rather benefit a small percentage of the population. But if the trend continues, as the population increases, world trade will increase, and there will be fewer locally produced goods and services for you to buy in the U.S.

▲ CRITICAL THINKING
Hypothesizing How do you think the influx of food products such as vegetables from other countries will affect local produce farms? What do you think it will do to the price of the locally produced vegetables?

338

---

networks Online Teaching Options

INTERACTIVE FEATURE

Global Economy & You

Evaluating world trade Have students read the Global Economy & You feature. Ask them if they think NAFTA and similar agreements that encourage trade are good or bad for the U.S. economy. Encourage debate and ask students to give reasons and facts to support their opinions. Ask students to do research to locate trade statistics showing the impact of NAFTA on employment and economic growth. Have students share their findings with the class.
Interpersonal

GDP AND NATIONAL ECONOMIC HEALTH

This cartoon describes the reliance on statistics such as GDP as ways to measure economic health of nations.

◀ **CRITICAL THINKING**
Identifying Perspectives Name at least one assumption that is made when considering GDP as a measure of national economic health.

prostitution, and the drug trade. Other activities are legal, such as those in farmers' markets or bake sales, but the cash payments are not always reported.

Current GDP vs. Real GDP

Because of the way it is computed, GDP can appear to increase whenever prices go up. For example, if the number of automobiles, replacement tires, and other products in Figure 12.1 stays the same from one year to the next while prices go up, GDP will go up. Therefore, in order to make accurate comparisons over time, GDP must be adjusted for inflation.

To do so, economists use a set of constant prices in a **base year**—a year that serves as the basis of comparison for all other years. For example, if we compute GDP for several years in a row using only prices that existed in 2009, then any increases in GDP must be due to changes in the quantity column and cannot be caused by changes in the price column.

This measure is called **real GDP**, or GDP measured with a set of constant base year prices. In contrast, the terms GDP, nominal GDP, and **current GDP** all mean that the output in any given year was measured using the actual prices that existed in that year. Because these prices change from one year to the next, GDP would appear to grow faster if the values were not adjusted for inflation.

GDP per Capita

There may be times when we want to adjust GDP for population. For example, we may want to see how the economy of a country is growing over time, or how the total annual output of one country compares to that of another. If so, we use **real GDP per capita**, or real GDP divided by the population, to get the amount of output on a per-person basis. Per capita GDP can be computed on a current or constant basis.

underground economy unreported legal and illegal activities that do not show up in GDP statistics

base year year serving as point of comparison for other years in a price index or other statistical measure

real GDP gross domestic product after adjustments for inflation; same as GDP in constant dollars

current GDP gross domestic product measured in current prices, unadjusted for inflation

real GDP per capita gross domestic product on a per person basis

connected.mcgraw-hill.com *Evaluating the Economy* 339

CHAPTER 12, LESSON 1
Measuring the Nation's Output and Income

C Critical Thinking Skills

Synthesizing information about per capita GDP
Ask: Why is per capita GDP a better measure of a country's prosperity than total GDP? *(Per capita GDP describes the average prosperity of each person, while total GDP says nothing about the share of the prosperity of an individual person. Larger countries may have higher total GDPs, but if the individual's per capita GDP is lower than that of an individual in a smaller country, the first individual has a lower standard of living.)* **Logical/Mathematical**

T Technology Skills

Creating a per capita GDP graph Have students use graphing tools to create a bar graph of the 30 countries with the highest GDP per capita. Ask interested students to further research a world cartogram showing GDP per capita and to reconstruct it for the classroom wall. Remind students to attribute their cartogram information to source materials. **Logical/Mathematical**

POLITICAL CARTOON

GDP and National Economic Health

Interpreting a political cartoon Show students the cartoon and ask a student to read it aloud. Point out that the cartoon is making an analogy by comparing one thing to another.
Ask: What is the cartoon comparing? *(The health of the economy with the health of a person.)* **How would you explain the analogy?** *(A doctor checks a person's health by measuring his or her temperature. An economist measures an economy's health by measuring its GDP.)* **Visual/Spatial**

ANSWERS, p. 339

CRITICAL THINKING

For GDP to be considered as an accurate indicator of national economic health, several assumptions need to be made. Students should reply with at least one of the following assumptions: that second-hand sales, non-market sales, and other transactions in the underground economy do not contribute much to the economy; that GDP is being referenced against a base year to eliminate any misleading effects of inflation; and that the types of products and changes in their quality are not of interest.

CHAPTER 12, LESSON 1
Measuring the Nation's Output and Income

W Writing Skills

Interpreting the strengths and weaknesses of GDP
Have students write a short essay, intended for younger students, that explains the strengths and weaknesses of GDP as a measure of the nation's economic health. Remind them to provide a general background of the subject and use language and examples that younger people would readily understand. Have volunteers read their explanations to the class. **Verbal/Linguistic**

R Reading Skills

Comparing GDP and GNP Ask: **What is the difference between GDP and GNP?** *(GDP measures the total value of all final goods and services produced within a country. GNP is the measure of the total value of the goods and services produced by a nation's citizens, no matter whether the goods and services are produced in the home country or in other countries.)* **Verbal/Linguistic**

Making Connections

Students' Contributions to NI Ask: **How do you and your family affect the measurements that economists use to evaluate the U.S. economy?** *(Wages that students, siblings, parents, and other family members earn are counted as personal income. This total is then added to the national income for the United States.)* **Verbal/Linguistic**

ANSWERS, p. 340

✓ **READING PROGRESS CHECK** The GDP measures the dollar value of all final goods, services, and structures produced within a country's national borders during a one-year period. It is important because it gives us a good idea of how our economy is performing.

What GDP Does Not Tell Us

GDP is one of the most useful statistics we have because it tells us how well our economy is performing. However, there are several things that GDP does not tell us. For example:

- **Composition of output**—GDP tells us nothing about the types of products being produced. If GDP increases by $10 billion, for example, we know that production is growing and that income is being generated, so we are likely to view the growth as a good thing. However, we might feel differently if we discovered that the extra output consisted entirely of military nerve gas stockpiles rather than new highways, libraries, and parks.
- **Quality of life impacts**—The impact of production may have a negative impact on the quality of life. The construction of 10,000 new homes may at first appear to be good for the economy. However, if the new homes harmed a wildlife refuge, or had other negative impacts on the environment, the value of the homes might be viewed differently.
- **Nonmarket activities**—Because GDP does not count work around the home that a spouse or homemaker may provide, GDP understates the total amount of productive activity in the economy.
- **Improved product quality**—GDP is not designed to keep track of changes in product quality. For example, a $1,000 computer today may be far better than a $1,000 computer five years ago—but both would contribute the same amount of value to GDP.

GDP is, by definition, the total market value of all final goods and services produced within a country's borders during a 12-month period. It is nothing more, and it is nothing less. We have to look at other measures to see how the production of new goods and services impacts the above issues; GDP is not designed to tell us anything about them.

A Measure of Economic Performance and Well-Being

Even though GDP was never intended to be a measure of welfare, there is reason to believe that GDP does contribute to our overall well-being. For example, we know that voluntary transactions in a market occur only when both parties to the transaction think they are better off after they have made the transaction. This means that every time a new product is produced and sold, there are at least two parties that feel they are better off—the buyer and the seller.

When we extend this to the trillions of new products produced and sold in a given year, it is easy to see why changes in GDP can be considered an indicator of changes in our country's overall economic well-being, as well as our economic health. If more things are produced and sold, there are more individuals who feel better off.

✓ **READING PROGRESS CHECK**

Explaining What does GDP measure, and why is it important?

Measures of National Income

GUIDING QUESTION *Why is national income measured in several different ways?*

Whenever business activity creates output, it generates jobs and income for someone. GDP, then, is like a two-sided coin, where one side represents output and the other side an equal amount of income. If we want to see how much output is produced, we look at one side of the coin. If we want to see how much income is generated, we look at the other side of the coin.

340

---

networks Online Teaching Options

VIDEO WORKSHEETS

Engineers Outsourcing

Analyzing how outsourcing affects GDP Display the video and have students complete the accompanying worksheet. Ask: **How does outsourcing jobs affect U.S. GDP?** *(The income earned from the outsourced jobs is not counted in U.S. GDP. As a result, the economic growth for this particular engineering sector occurs in India, not the United States.)*

While GDP is the largest and most important measure in the NIPA, we can also use the NIPA to generate the five measures of income described below.

Gross National Product
Our first measure of the country's total income is called **gross national product (GNP)**—the market value of goods and services produced by labor and property supplied by U.S. residents, regardless of where they are located. This is very similar to GDP, but there are significant differences between GDP and GNP. The best and easiest thing to remember is that GDP is a measure of total national *output*, while GNP is a measure of total national *income*.

Net National Product
The second measure of national income is **net national product (NNP)**, or GNP less depreciation. Depreciation is also called *capital consumption allowances*. It represents the capital equipment that wore out or became obsolete during the year.

National Income
The third measure in the NIPA is **national income (NI)**. National income is the income that is left after all taxes except the corporate profits tax are subtracted from NNP. Examples of these taxes, also known as *indirect business taxes*, are excise taxes, property taxes, licensing fees, customs duties, and general sales taxes.

Personal Income
The fourth measure of the nation's total income is **personal income (PI)**—the total amount of income going to consumers before individual income taxes are subtracted. To go from national to personal income, several adjustments must be made. For example, personal income does not include payments into the Social Security fund by working people. It would, however, include the Social Security checks that retired individuals receive.

Disposable Personal Income
The fifth measure of income in the NIPA is **disposable personal income (DPI)**—the total income the consumer sector has at its disposal after personal income taxes. Although it is the smallest measure of income, it is important because it reflects the actual amount of money consumers are able to spend.

At the individual level, your disposable income is equal to the amount of money received from your employer after taxes and Social Security have been taken out. When you look at the paystub you receive every week or so from your employer, you are looking at your share of the nation's DPI.

✓ **READING PROGRESS CHECK**

Summarizing What are the different measures of national income?

Economic Sectors and Circular Flows
GUIDING QUESTION *What are the four components of GDP?*

It helps to think of the macroeconomy as consisting of several different parts, or sectors. These sectors receive various components of the national income, which they then use to purchase the total output. These sectors are part of the circular flow of economic activity illustrated in **Figure 12.2**.

Income generated by production flows to the consumer (C), investment (I), government (G), and net foreign (X − M) sectors, where X stands for exports and M for imports. These sectors then use the income to purchase the nation's output.

---

gross national product (GNP) the market value of goods and services produced by labor and property supplied by U.S. residents

net national product (NNP) gross national product minus depreciation charges for wear and tear on capital equipment; measure of net annual production generated with labor and property supplied by a country's citizens

national income (NI) net national product less indirect business taxes; measure of a nation's income

personal income (PI) total amount of income going to the consumer sector before individual income taxes are paid

disposable personal income (DPI) personal income less individual income taxes; total income available to the consumer sector after income taxes

---

EXPLORING THE ESSENTIAL QUESTION

You are applying for a part-time job at a local coffee shop. You plan to work 15 hours a week. You will be paid every two weeks with all taxes taken out of your check. The pay per hour is the minimum wage in your state, which is $8 an hour. You will pay 10 percent of each paycheck in taxes and Social Security. Do the math and figure what your personal income (PI) will be and what your disposable personal income (DPI) will be every two weeks.

a. PI: $240; DPI: $236

b. PI: $260; DPI $256

c. PI $240; DPI $216

d. PI $320; DPI $300

CHAPTER 12, LESSON 1
Measuring the Nation's Output and Income

C1 Critical Thinking Skills

Defining measures of income Randomly assign one of the five income measures to students until all students have an assignment. Have them write a description of their assigned measure that answers the following questions: What does the measure show? What is added or subtracted to find the measure? To whom would this measure be most valuable? Why?

T Technology Skills

Researching and graphing PI Tell students that the Census Bureau collects information on personal income (PI) for large metropolitan areas. Then ask groups to use the most recent *Statistical Abstract of the United States* to find the top 10 metropolitan areas in terms of PI. Have them note how PI has changed for these metropolitan areas over time. Then have groups present their findings in annotated graph form. **Logical/Mathematical**

C2 Critical Thinking Skills

Analyzing DPI Review with students how to find disposable personal income (DPI). Then ask them to compute their weekly or monthly DPI, and have them estimate how they "dispose" of this amount. Relate the ability to do so to the characteristics of the U.S. free enterprise system and the value it places on private property. **Logical/Mathematical**

Content Background Knowledge

Three Kinds of Consumption National income accounting records three classifications of consumption in the consumer sector. Durable goods have an average life of more than three years—automobiles, furniture, appliances, etc. Nondurable goods have an average life of less than three years—shampoo, food, gas, clothing, etc. Services, such as financial or legal advice, health care, and haircuts, make up the final classification of consumption. Some classifications seem arbitrary. A well-made coat, for example, may last 10 years, but as an item of clothing it would be regarded as a nondurable good.

ANSWERS, p. 341

EXPLORING THE ESSENTIAL QUESTION

c. PI: $240; DPI: $216

✓ **READING PROGRESS CHECK** The different measures of national income are Gross National Product (GNP), Net National Product (NNP), National Income (NI), Personal Income (PI), and Disposable Personal Income (DPI).

ESSENTIAL QUESTION

Exploring the Essential Question

Determining PI and DPI Show students the Exploring the Essential Question slide and have a student read the first scenario. Ask students to work individually to find the answer. Discuss the answer as a class and clarify any misunderstandings. Have students work through the remaining scenarios in the same fashion. **Logical/Mathematical**

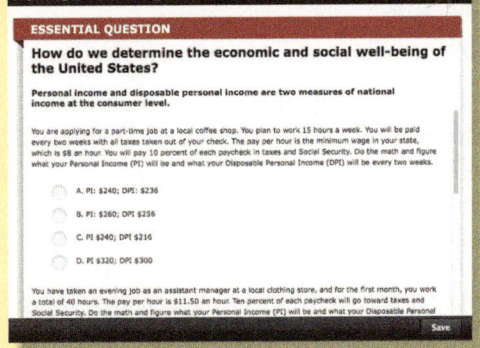

CHAPTER 12, LESSON 1
Measuring the Nation's Output and Income

V Visual Skills

Understanding the circular flow of economic activity Ask: **What expenditures make up gross domestic product?** *(personal consumption expenditures, government purchases of goods and services, and investment expenditures)*
Verbal/Linguistic

R Reading Skills

Identifying economic effects of consumers Ask students to suggest ways that consumers as a whole can affect the nation's economy. *(buying decisions, savings patterns, living arrangements, and so on)* Also ask them to identify the section of the circular flow chart where these activities are located. *(the bottom of the chart)*
Logical/Mathematical

C Critical Thinking Skills

Classifying household consumption Ask students which of the following would NOT be counted as consumption: (a) Children buy popcorn at the zoo. (b) Two students buy movie tickets. (c) General Motors buys new robots for its assembly line. (d) A dog owner pays for a kennel stay. (e) A new college graduate buys his first car. *(Answer c would NOT be counted as consumption. Robots used in an assembly line are considered capital. When General Motors buys new robots, the purchase is counted as business investment—not household consumption.)*

W Writing Skills

Writing about depreciation Have students write a narrative describing an item they or their family owned that experienced depreciation. Narratives should first analyze the benefits of the use of the personal property, and then explain the rate of the depreciation and approximate estimates of the value of the item before, during, and after depreciation. **Verbal/Linguistic**

ANSWERS, p. 342

CRITICAL THINKING
Personal income is on an individual level and does not include payments into the Social Security fund. It equals the amount of income people receive after all taxes and Social Security are withheld.

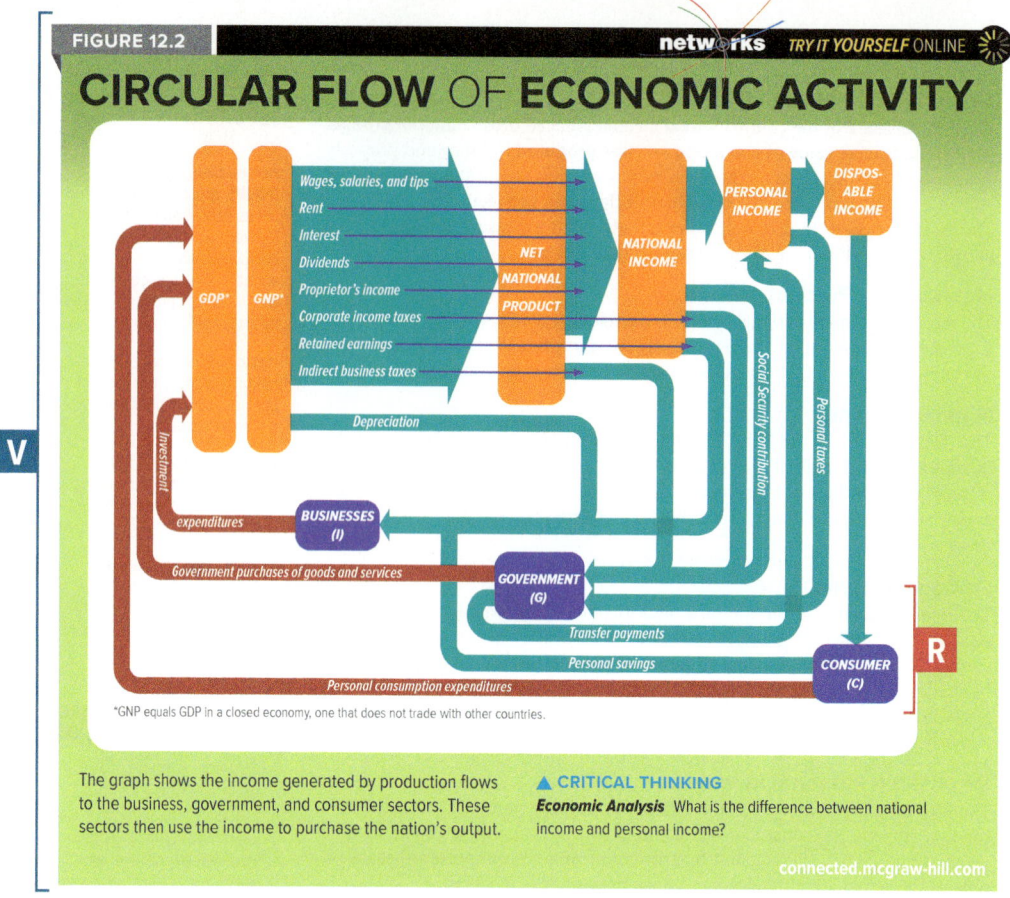

FIGURE 12.2
CIRCULAR FLOW OF ECONOMIC ACTIVITY

*GNP equals GDP in a closed economy, one that does not trade with other countries.

The graph shows the income generated by production flows to the business, government, and consumer sectors. These sectors then use the income to purchase the nation's output.

▲ **CRITICAL THINKING**
Economic Analysis What is the difference between national income and personal income?

---

household basic unit of consumer sector consisting of all of the people who occupy a house, apartment, or separate living quarters

unrelated individual person living alone or with nonrelatives even though that person may have relatives living elsewhere

family two or more people living together that are related by blood, marriage, or adoption

Consumer Sector

The largest sector in the economy is the consumer, or **household**, sector. Its basic unit, the household, consists of all of the people who occupy a house, apartment, or room that constitutes separate living quarters. Households include related family members and all others—such as lodgers, foster children, and employees—who share the living quarters.

A household also can consist of an **unrelated individual**—a person who lives alone even though he or she may have family living elsewhere. Finally, a household can be a **family**—a group of two or more people related by blood, marriage, or adoption who are living together in a household.

The consumer sector, shown as **C** in Figure 12.2, receives its income in the form of disposable personal income. This is the income that is left over after all of the depreciation, business and income taxes, and FICA payments are taken out, and after any income received in transfer payments is added back in.

Investment Sector

The next sector of the macroeconomy is the business, or investment, sector, which is labeled **I** in Figure 12.2. This sector is made up of proprietorships,

342

---

networks Online Teaching Options

CHARTS

Circular Flow of Economic Activity

Understanding the circular flow of economic activity Have students view Figure 12.2 and read the text aloud. Click on GNP to call out the production flows to business, government, and consumer sectors. Ask: **What government actions affect the circular flow?** *(Social Security contributions are calculated there, and business taxes and personal taxes flow there.)* **How is disposable personal income used?** *(personal savings and personal consumption)* **Where do personal consumption expenditures go?** *(They become part of GDP and GNP and then flow back into the economy in the form of wages, rent, interest, and so on.)*
Visual/Spatial

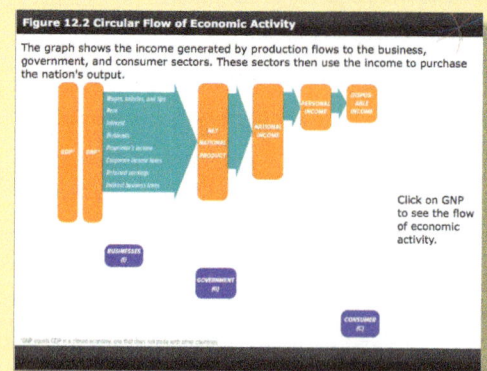

partnerships, and corporations that are responsible for producing the nation's output. The income of this sector comes from the retained earnings—the profits not paid out to owners—that are subtracted from NI and the depreciation or capital consumption allowances that are subtracted from GNP.

Government Sector
The third sector is the public, or government, sector, which includes all local, state, and federal levels of government. Shown as **G** in Figure 12.2, this sector receives its income from indirect business taxes, corporate income taxes, Social Security contributions, and individual income taxes.

Net Foreign Sector
The fourth sector of the macroeconomy is the net foreign sector, which includes all consumers and producers outside the United States. The foreign sector buys many U.S. goods—such as tractors, airplanes, and agricultural products—and services—such as insurance—that make up our GDP. In return, the foreign sector supplies other products—such as Japanese cars, South Korean steel, and Brazilian shoes—to U.S. consumers. For this reason, the foreign sector's purchases are called **net exports of goods and services** and are abbreviated as (X − M) to reflect the difference between exports and imports.

This sector does not have a specific source of income. Instead, it represents the difference between the dollar value of goods sent abroad and that of goods purchased from abroad. If the two are reasonably close, the foreign sector appears to be small, even when large numbers of goods and services are traded.

The Output-Expenditure Model
The consumption part of the circular flow can also be represented algebraically as the **output-expenditure model**. When written as

$$GDP = C + I + G + (X - M)$$

the expression says that GDP is equal to the sum of aggregate demand for output by the consumer, investment, government, and net foreign sectors.

Economists use the output-expenditure model to represent the macroeconomic version of total spending by all sectors of the economy.

net exports of goods and services net expenditures by the output-expenditure model's foreign sector; equal to total exports less total imports

output-expenditure model macroeconomic model describing aggregate demand by the consumer, investment, government, and foreign sectors; GDP = C + I + G + F

✓ **READING PROGRESS CHECK**
Describing How does the foreign sector fit into the output-expenditure model?

LESSON 1 REVIEW

Reviewing Vocabulary
1. *Defining* Explain the differences between PI and DPI.

Using Your Notes
2. *Summarizing* Use your notes to explain the three types of GDP.

Answering the Guiding Questions
3. *Explaining* What does GDP tell us about the economy?
4. *Discussing* Why is national income measured in several different ways?
5. *Describing* What are the four components of GDP?

Writing About Economics
6. *Informative/Explanatory* Write a two-page essay comparing the current GDP and the real GDP. What role does government play in measuring the real GDP? Use text from the lesson and research in the library or on the Internet for more information about the government role in measuring the real GDP.

connected.mcgraw-hill.com   Evaluating the Economy **343**

CHAPTER 12, LESSON 1
Measuring the Nation's Output and Income

R Reading Skills

Explaining the foreign sector *Ask:* **Why might the foreign sector appear to be insignificant when, in fact, large numbers of goods and services may be traded?** *(If imports and exports are about equal, the foreign sector of the economy will appear small.)* **Logical/Mathematical**

W Writing Skills

Noting the importance of imports and exports Direct students to locate an article on foreign trade from a current online source. Ask students to summarize the article in one or two paragraphs and then write a conclusion that analyzes the impact of U.S. imports and exports on the United States and the foreign country. Have students evaluate the validity of the online source for bias before presenting their summaries to the class.

CLOSE & REFLECT

Outlining the lesson Ask students to create an outline of the lesson, using the headings to help organize their work. Tell them to include all important details in their outlines.

ANSWERS, p. 343

 READING PROGRESS CHECK The foreign sector represents a country's total exports minus total imports and is one of the four factors that when added together equal a country's GDP, according to the output-expenditure model.

LESSON 1 REVIEW ANSWERS

Reviewing Vocabulary
1. The PI (personal income) is the total amount of income going to consumers before individual income taxes are subtracted. The DPI (disposable personal income) is the total income the consumer sector has at its disposal after personal income taxes.

Using Your Notes
2. The three types of GDP are the real GDP, the current GDP, and the real GDP per capita.

Answering the Guiding Questions
3. The GDP tells us the dollar value of all final goods, services, and structures produced within a country's national boarders during a one-year period. In addition, it is an indicator of changes in the country's overall economic well-being and economic health.
4. Looking at national income from several different perspectives helps us see how the income associated with the output produced is generated.
5. The four components of GDP are the consumer sector, investment sector, government sector, and net foreign sector.

Writing About Economics
6. Student answers should include that government economists adjust the current GDP for inflation. The economists use a set of constant prices in a base year, or a year that serves as a comparison.

Evaluating the Economy **343**

CHAPTER 12
Debate

ENGAGE

C1 Critical Thinking Skills

Weighing the importance of manufacturing Tell students that for many years the U.S. economy has been shifting more and more from a base in manufacturing to one in service industries. **Ask: Why is this shift important?** *(Answers will vary, but students may say that manufacturing jobs typically pay more than many service industry jobs.)* Tell students that many economists, business leaders, and government officials argue that the U.S. economy cannot succeed long-term with a service-based economy. Ask them to study this debate and decide for themselves. **Logical/Mathematical**

TEACH & ASSESS

C2 Critical Thinking Skills

Evaluating pay in manufacturing and services Emphasize to students that there are a wide range of service and manufacturing jobs. Some jobs in both categories pay well, but others do not. Ask students to give examples in both categories of jobs that pay well and jobs that do not pay so well. Encourage students to research to learn more about wages and salaries in manufacturing and services. **Verbal/Linguistic**

Content Background Knowledge

Manufacturing Misconception Point out that there is a common misperception about the decline in manufacturing in the United States. Although jobs in manufacturing have dropped precipitously since 1970, manufacturing output has actually increased just as dramatically due to vastly improved workplace efficiency largely accomplished through advances in technology. Between 1970 and 2010, the value of U.S. manufacturing increased steadily from about $1,300 billion to about $2,800 billion per year in 2000 dollars. Meanwhile, manufacturing employment dropped, almost as steadily, from about 17.5 million jobs in 1970 to about 11.5 million jobs in 2010. Discuss with students whether this actually represents a decline in manufacturing or an increase in efficiency that masks an increase in manufacturing.

Debates

C1 Can the U.S. economy succeed without a big manufacturing base?

The question of whether a big manufacturing base is needed to have a growing economy rather than a services-based economy has been around for decades. Since the financial crises in the first decade of the twenty-first century, the question is revived.

The U.S. and Great Britain's services-based economies in this century have struggled, while the economies of countries with a manufacturing-based economy, such as Germany and China, have grown. Those who say a big manufacturing base is necessary point to how manufacturing has a multiplying effect on the economy. Those who argue a manufacturing base is unnecessary in the twenty-first century point to the growth of the U.S. services sector and the increase in jobs in that sector.

YES U.S. service-based economy is sufficient because...

- U.S. SERVICES ACCOUNT FOR A MAJORITY OF U.S. GDP
- JOBS IN U.S. SERVICES SECTOR INCREASE
- U.S. SERVICES SECTOR GENERATES THE WORLD'S LARGEST SERVICES TRADE
- COUNTRIES LIKE INDIA HAVE A GROWING ECONOMY BASED ON THE SERVICES SECTOR

> Service industries account for 68 percent of U.S. GDP and four out of five U.S. jobs. This dynamic services economy generates the largest services trade in the world.... Whether it is telecommunications, financial services, computer services, retail distribution, environmental services, audiovisual services, express delivery, or any other services sector, services trade is interconnecting our world, lowering costs for consumers and businesses, enhancing competition and innovation, improving choice and quality, attracting investment, diffusing knowledge and technology, and allowing for the efficient allocation of resources.

—Office of United States Trade Representative, Executive Office of the President

C2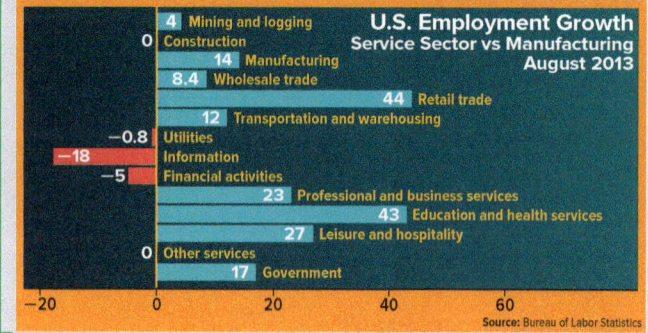

U.S. Employment Growth Service Sector vs Manufacturing August 2013
- Mining and logging: 4
- Construction: 0
- Manufacturing: 14
- Wholesale trade: 8.4
- Retail trade: 44
- Transportation and warehousing: 12
- Utilities: −0.8
- Information: −18
- Financial activities: −5
- Professional and business services: 23
- Education and health services: 43
- Leisure and hospitality: 27
- Other services: 0
- Government: 17

Source: Bureau of Labor Statistics

344

---

net**w**orks *Online Teaching Options*

DEBATE

Debate: Can the U.S. economy succeed without a big manufacturing base?

Evaluating arguments Ask students to read and study the Debate feature. Then call on a student to read the Yes quotation aloud. **Ask: What are the main points of the Yes argument?** *(American service industries account for 68 percent of GDP, and four out of five jobs. They generate the largest services trade in the world. Service industries connect the world, lower consumer and business costs, increase competition and innovation, improve choice and quality, attract investment, spread knowledge and technology, and use resources efficiently.)* Then review the bulleted list of arguments. Next, have a student read the No argument aloud and **ask: What are the main points of the No argument?** *(Manufacturing drives innovation and job creation; automation and technology make manufacturing more efficient.)* Review the arguments for a stronger manufacturing base. Then ask students which arguments are stronger. **Interpersonal**

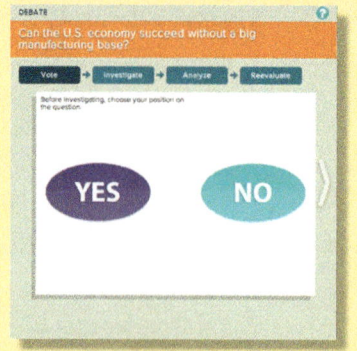

NO A manufacturing base is needed for economic growth because...

- MANUFACTURING HAS THE **LARGEST MULTIPLIER EFFECT** ON THE ECONOMY
- SLOW MANUFACTURING GROWTH **HURTS** A COUNTRY'S ABILITY TO EXPORT
- EVEN SERVICE-BASED ECONOMIES HAVE **STRONG MANUFACTURING FOUNDATIONS**
- **INABILITY** TO **EXPORT** GOODS LEADS TO BALANCE-OF-PAYMENT **DIFFICULTIES**

networks
TRY IT YOURSELF ONLINE
For an interactive version of this debate go to connected.mcgraw-hill.com

> "Our call for a robust manufacturing sector stems not from a nostalgic yearning for the past, but a clear-eyed determination to forge a dynamic future for Americans through a new era of production excellence. Manufacturing remains a driver of innovation and job creation, even as automation and technology make manufacturing more efficient. The United States must implement sound policies to [grow] the manufacturing sector."
> —Council on Competitiveness

ANALYZING the issue

1. **Analyzing Visuals** How has growth of the services sector affected employment in the United States?

2. **Evaluating** According to the U.S. Manufacturing Competitiveness Initiative (USMCI), what effect does a strong manufacturing base have on the overall economy?

3. **Argument** Which arguments do you find most compelling? Explain your answer.

▲ The manufacturing industry has a multiplier effect on the whole economy.

CHAPTER 12
Debate

R Reading Skills

Defining terms **Ask:** What is the multiplier effect? *(the result of investing in an activity that creates more value than the original resource or amount invested)* What are some examples of the multiplier effect? *(Possible example: Investing in an auto plant creates jobs paying a certain amount at the plant but also creates paying jobs in auto parts suppliers, tire manufacturers, and so on.)* **Verbal/Linguistic**

CLOSE & REFLECT

W Writing Skills

Writing an essay Ask students to write a brief essay stating their opinion on the Debate issue: Can the U.S. economy succeed without a big manufacturing base? Tell them to cite details from what they learned during the study of this feature.

DEBATE

Debate

Using graphs Direct students' attention to the graph. Ask students to list the categories and their accompanying data. **Ask:** How many jobs were created in manufacturing? How many jobs were created in financial activities? Which categories experienced the highest growth in employment? **Visual/Spatial**

ANSWERS, p. 345

ANALYZING the issue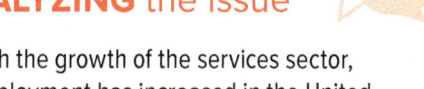

1. With the growth of the services sector, employment has increased in the United States.
2. According to the USMCI, manufacturing drives innovation and job creation.
3. Student answers should give specific reasons for their opinion, such as: a strong manufacturing base provides exports and helps reduce the trade deficit; or a strong service sector means more jobs for Americans.

CHAPTER 12, LESSON 2
Population Growth and Trends

ENGAGE

C Critical Thinking Skills

🔔 **Hypothesizing about the census** Ask students why the Framers of the Constitution may have considered a census so vital to the United States that it needed to be included in the Constitution.
Ask: *Given its importance, what kinds of information do you think should be collected in the census? (Students may suggest information on age, sex, national origin, education level, size of family, and so on.)* Ask students to explain why this information might be useful. **Verbal/Linguistic**

Interact with these digital assets and others in lesson 2
✓ INTERACTIVE MAP Center of Population, 1790–2000
✓ INFOGRAPHIC Future Population Growth
✓ SELF-CHECK QUIZ
✓ VIDEO

networks
TRY IT YOURSELF ONLINE

LESSON 2
Population Growth and Trends

Reading Help Desk

Academic Vocabulary
- residence

Content Vocabulary
- census
- urban population
- rural population
- center of population
- infrastructure
- baby boom
- population pyramid
- dependency ratio
- demographers
- fertility rate
- life expectancy
- net immigration

TAKING NOTES:

Key Ideas and Details
ACTIVITY Use the graphic organizer below to identify the listed changes in the United States.

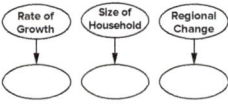

ESSENTIAL QUESTION

How do we determine the economic and social well-being of the United States?

The population of the United States has been in a state of continual change throughout our history. Consider these changes that have occurred in recent decades:

- The average age of the population has gotten older.
- The population is shifting from the northeastern United States toward the southwestern United States.
- Productivity has increased in large part because of technology.

How will these changes affect the economy of the United States in the years to come?

a. The burden on working people to support retired workers will decrease.
b. Demand for resources will change with population changes.
c. Technological growth will decline.
d. None of these things will impact the overall economy.

Population in the United States

GUIDING QUESTION *What changes has the U.S. population experienced since 1790?*

C Population is important for a number of reasons. First, a country's population is the source of its labor, one of the four factors of production. Second, the population is the primary consumer of the nation's output and has a direct effect on how much is produced. Because of this, the size, composition, and rate of growth of a country's population have an impact on macroeconomic performance.

346

---

networks **Online Teaching Options**

BELLRINGER

Population Growth and Trends

Discussing the effects of population trends
Show students the Bellringer and discuss the two questions. Guide students in exploring other economic effects of this information. Elicit responses by asking the following questions. **Ask:** *How might longer life expectancy affect GDP? How will it affect the cost of health care? In what other ways might it affect you?* **Interpersonal**

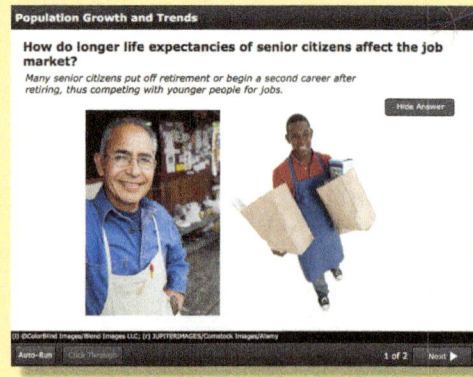

ANSWERS, p. 346

ESSENTIAL QUESTION ACTIVITY

Answer b is correct.
TAKING NOTES:
Rate of Growth: Declining; growth is now less than 1.0% annually
Size of Household: Declining; about 2.6 people per household
Regional Change: Population shifting to the western and southern parts of the country

The Constitution of the United States requires the government to periodically take a **census**, an official count of all people living in the United States, including their place of **residence**. Because the official census occurs every 10 years, it is called the *decennial census.*

The original use of the census was to apportion the number of representatives that each state elects to Congress. Today, the census gives us a wealth of data about our nation, and we even use it to make projections into the future.

Counting the Population

The federal government conducted the first census in 1790. Throughout the 1800s, the government created temporary agencies each decade to do the counting. In 1902, Congress permanently established the U.S. Census Bureau. Today, the Bureau works year round, conducting monthly surveys relating to the size and other characteristics of the population.

When the Census Bureau conducted the last decennial census, it used the household as its primary survey unit. In this census, about five in every six households received a "short form," which took just a few minutes to fill out. The remaining households received a "long form," which included more questions and served to generate a more detailed profile of the population. Bureau employees also used different methods to count special groups, such as homeless persons, who do not normally conform to the household survey unit.

The Census Bureau tabulates and presents its data in a number of ways. One such classification considers the size of the **urban population**—people living in incorporated cities, villages, or towns with 2,500 or more inhabitants. The **rural population** makes up the remainder of the total, including those people who live in sparsely populated areas along the fringes of cities.

Growth and Regional Change

The population of the United States has grown considerably since colonial times. The rate of growth, however, has slowly declined. Between 1790 and 1860, the population grew at a compounded rate of about 3.0 percent a year. From the beginning of the Civil War until 1900, the average fell to 2.2 percent. From 1900 to the beginning of World War II, the rate dropped to 1.4 percent. After a brief rise at the end of World War II, the rate of increase continued to decline slowly but steadily, and today the rate of population growth is less than 1.0 percent annually.

The census also shows a steady trend toward smaller households. During colonial times, household size averaged about 5.8 people. By 1960, the average had fallen to 3.3, and today it is about 2.6 people. The figures reflect a worldwide trend toward smaller families in industrialized countries. The figures also show that more individuals are living alone today than ever before.

An important population shift began in the 1970s with a migration to the western and southern parts of the United States. These regions have grown quite rapidly, while most of the older industrial areas in the north and east have grown more slowly or even lost population. As people have left the crowded, industrial Northeast for warmer, more spacious parts of the country, the population in southern and western states has been increasing steadily.

Another indicator of population shift is the **center of population**—the point where the country would balance if it could be laid flat and everyone weighed the same. In 1790, the center was 23 miles east of Baltimore, Maryland. Since then, as you can see in **Figure 12.3**, it has moved farther west. By the 2010 decennial census, the center of population had reached a point about 2.7 miles northeast of Plato, Missouri.

census complete count of population, including place of residence

residence the place where a person lives

urban population those people living in incorporated cities, towns, and villages with 2,500 or more inhabitants

rural population those people not living in urban areas, including sparsely populated areas along the fringes of cities

center of population point where the country would balance if it were flat and everyone weighed the same

---

CHAPTER 12, LESSON 2
Population Growth and Trends

TEACH & ASSESS

W Writing Skills

Writing a letter Have students write a business letter or e-mail to the U.S. Census Bureau requesting information on how census information is gathered and analyzed. Have volunteers share their letters.
ELL Verbal/Linguistic

R Reading Skills

Skimming for information Students who have trouble reading a passage may benefit from skimming it before reading to develop a timeframe for the events or ideas that are presented. Have students skim the subsection "Growth and Regional Change" for time markers, such as "Between 1790 and 1860" and "From the beginning of the Civil War until 1900." Ask students to point out other similar markers in other subsections. **AL** Verbal/Linguistic

C Critical Thinking Skills

Hypothesizing a method Ask students to speculate on how the center of population is found. *(Many students will recognize that the area of the country is compared mathematically with the population and the population's location to find the theoretical center.)* Logical/Mathematical

---

WORKSHEETS

Economic Simulation

Conducting a census Tell students that they will be creating their own census form to gather relevant information about the U.S. population and to uncover new demographic data that reflects changes in our society and technology. As preparation for the task, ask students to review the section of text that explains the census. Then organize students into groups and instruct them in the steps of the simulation. Verbal/Linguistic

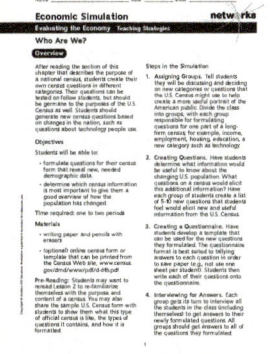

CHAPTER 12, LESSON 2
Population Growth and Trends

C Critical Thinking Skills

Synthesizing information   Ask: What are some reasons Americans are moving to the Sun Belt, the name for the western and southern parts of the United States? Have students discuss suggested reasons. Then ask them to rank the reasons in importance for (1) most people, and (2) themselves. *(Possible reasons may include climate, job opportunities, or desire to be near relatives. Students' rankings will vary.)* **Verbal/Linguistic**

English Language Proficiency

Advanced Before students read Lesson 2, provide them with a graphic organizer such as one with questions in the left column and spaces to write notes in the right. Tell them to prepare to summarize by identifying key information that could be included in a summary. Then have students retell content in a round-table discussion. Each student takes a turn retelling a sentence until the group has completed a full retelling of the text.

FIGURE 12.3

CENTER OF POPULATION, 1790–2010

The center of the population is the point where the country would balance if the map were flat and every person weighed the same.

▲ **CRITICAL THINKING**
Economic Analysis Why has the center moved since the first census was conducted in 1790?

Consequences of Growth

Changes in population can distort some macroeconomic measures, such as GDP and GNP. As a result, both measures are often expressed on a per capita, or per person, basis. One result is GDP per capita, which is determined by dividing GDP by the population. GDP per capita is especially useful when making comparisons over time or comparisons between countries.

Population growth can have several consequences. If a nation's population grows faster than its output, the country could end up with more mouths than it can feed. On the other hand, if a nation's population grows too slowly, there may not be enough workers to sustain economic growth. In addition, a growing population puts more demand on resources.

When a growing population shifts toward certain areas, such as cities or suburbs, it puts different pressures on existing resources. In Atlanta, Georgia, for example, urban sprawl and traffic congestion have become major problems. In heavily populated areas of Arizona, Nevada, and southern California, adequate supplies of fresh water have become major concerns.

Because it takes a long time to plan and construct a country's **infrastructure**—the highways, levees, mass transit, communications systems, electricity, water, sewer, and other public goods needed to support a population—we need to pay attention to future population trends. If we neglect them, even modest shifts in the population can cause enormous problems in the future.

infrastructure the highways, levees, mass transit, communications, power, water, sewerage, and other public goods needed to support a population

☑ **READING PROGRESS CHECK**

Explaining What have been the major population changes since the first census in 1790?

348

---

networks Online Teaching Options

MAPS

Center of Population

Examining the historic shift in population
Display Figure 12.3 and read and discuss the opening text. **Ask: Why do you think the population center shifted west from 1790 to 1850?** *(The U.S. expanded its borders. As the population grew along the eastern seaboard, people moved west into the lightly populated lands.)* **Where do you think the population center will shift to after 1850? Why?** Click on 1850 and then 1910 to show the advance of the population center. Read and discuss the text. Invite students to speculate on how they think the population center will move in the coming decades. **Visual/Spatial**

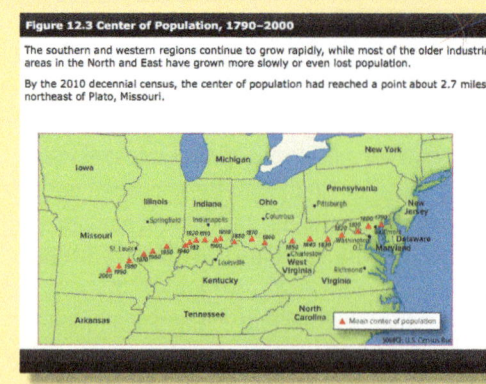

Figure 12.3 Center of Population, 1790–2000
The southern and western regions continue to grow rapidly, while most of the older industrial areas in the North and East have grown more slowly or even lost population.

By the 2010 decennial census, the center of population had reached a point about 2.7 miles northeast of Plato, Missouri.

ANSWERS, p. 348

CRITICAL THINKING
The center of population has moved to the west because, over time, more and more people are moving from the northeast to the southwestern United States.

☑ **READING PROGRESS CHECK** The population has grown enormously, households have become smaller, and the center of population has shifted toward the West and South.

Projected Population Trends

GUIDING QUESTION What effect will the aging population have on the economy?

Population trends are important to many groups. Political leaders watch population shifts to see how voting patterns may change. Community leaders are interested because changes in local population affect services such as sanitation, education, and fire protection. Businesses use census data to help determine markets for products and sales territories.

Age and Gender

When making its projections, the Census Bureau assumes that the aging generation of baby boomers will drive many characteristics of the population. People born during the **baby boom**, the high birthrate years from 1946 to 1964, make up a sizable portion of the current population. As shown in **Figure 12.4**, people born during this time span created a significant bulge in the **population pyramid**, a type of bar graph that shows the breakdown of population by age and gender.

The bulge in the middle of the pyramid for ages 55 to 74 represents the baby boomers in the year 2020. A second, minor bulge represents the children born to the baby boom generation. As years pass, more births add to the bottom of the pyramid and push earlier groups upward into higher age brackets.

Soon, more and more baby boomers will reach their retirement years and want to collect pensions, Social Security, and Medicare benefits. Because most of these payments are transfer payments, they will place a heavy burden on the younger and relatively smaller working population. The burden becomes evident with changes in the **dependency ratio**—the ratio of the population under 15 and over 65 to the population aged 15 to 65. The dependency ratio was 49.4 in 2010, but according to Census Bureau projections, it will rise to 65.9 by 2030, and to 70.9 by 2090.

Finally, if you compare the left side of the population pyramid with the right, you will see that women tend to outlive men. Separate population pyramids can also be created for any racial or ethnic group.

baby boom historically high birthrate years in the United States from 1946 to 1964

population pyramid diagram showing the breakdown of population by age and gender

dependency ratio ratio of the population aged under 15 or 65 and over to the population aged 15 to 65

Race and Ethnicity

The Census Bureau also makes projections for racial and ethnic groups. In 2000, whites were the largest component of the total population. The numbers of African Americans, Hispanic Americans, Asian Americans, and Native Americans followed in that order.

FIGURE 12.4

PROJECTED DISTRIBUTION OF THE POPULATION BY AGE AND GENDER, 2015

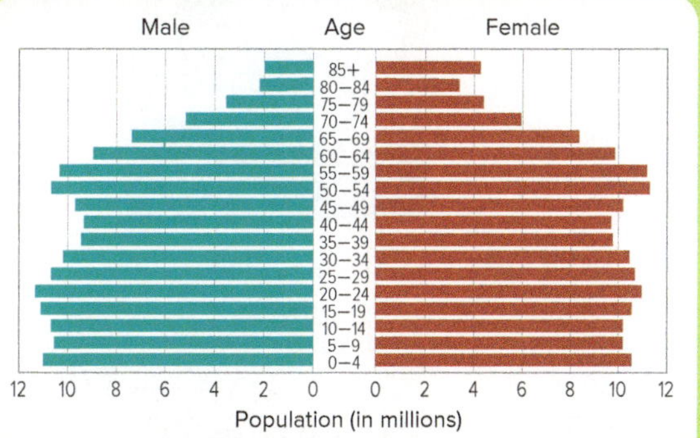

Source: U.S. Census Bureau, Population Division.

Population pyramids are one way to show the distribution of population. In this pyramid, the population is divided by age and gender. In 2020, baby boomers will be represented by the age brackets 55 through 74.

▲ **CRITICAL THINKING**
Economic Analysis To which age bracket do the greatest number of males belong? To which age bracket do the greatest number of females belong?

GRAPHS

Projected Distribution of the Population by Age and Gender, 2015

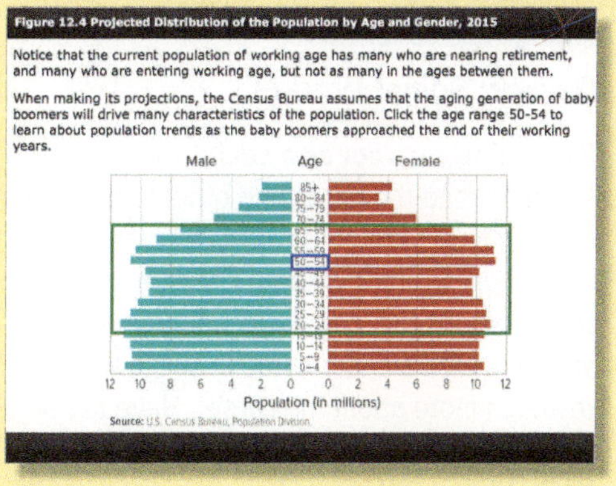

Identifying effects of population change
Have students view Figure 12.4—the population pyramid—and guide a discussion of what it reveals about our population. Tell students that the Baby Boom generation is made up of those persons born between 1946 and 1964. **Ask:** How old will the oldest Baby Boomers be in 2015? *(69)* How old are the youngest of the Baby Boomers in 2015? *(51)* What effect will this generation have on later generations as they retire? *(Possible answer: Later generations will have to pay taxes and work in careers that will care for these older adults.)* Have students find their age group on the graph. Ask students to speculate about the dependency ratio based on the data. **Logical/Mathematical**

CHAPTER 12, LESSON 2
Population Growth and Trends

C Critical Thinking Skills

Identifying examples of population trends Have students list three ways in which population trends are used. Then have them give examples of each trend from history or current events, either locally or nationally. **Verbal/Linguistic**

W Writing Skills

Predicting the effects of population changes Have students review the information on the effects of age on the population. Then have them write a few paragraphs on how these population changes will affect them personally. Have students share their ideas with the class. **Intrapersonal**

V Visual Skills

Using population pyramids Provide students with these vocabulary terms related to population pyramids: *Cohort:* An age cohort is a group of people in a 5-year age bracket, such as 50–54. Each bar on this population pyramid shows a cohort. *Elderly dependent population:* People aged 65 and over who are dependent on those in their working years of 15–64. *Youth dependent population:* People aged 15 and younger who are dependent on those in their working years of 15–64. *Sex ratio:* The sex ratio is the ratio of males to females. For example, there are more females than males in the 80–84 age cohort largely because women live longer than men. *Growth rate:* The shape of the pyramid shows the population's growth rate. For example, a pyramid looking like this one—more like a column than a pyramid—is a slow growing population. In contrast, a population pyramid with a wide base shows a rapid growth rate. A third type, with a narrow base, shows a declining population growth rate. **Ask:** How do you think this population pyramid will look in the year 2030? Give reasons to support your predictions. *(Likely changes include the baby boom "bulge" moving higher on the pyramid, another minor bulge to represent the children of the large baby boomer cadre, and more people living longer due to advances in health care.)* **Logical/Mathematical**

ANSWERS, p. 349

CRITICAL THINKING

The greatest number of males belong to the 20–24 age bracket. The greatest number of females belong to the 50–54 age bracket.

CHAPTER 12, LESSON 2
Population Growth and Trends

Making Connections

Total Fertility Rate The base of a population pyramid reveals fertility. The total fertility rate (TFR) is the average number of children born to a woman throughout her childbearing years. "Replacement fertility" is the level of fertility at which each successive generation of women produces enough children to ensure that the same number of females survives to have offspring themselves. TFR is a better way to make regional comparisons and predictions for the future. TFRs are high in rapid-growth countries like Chad. They are lower in the United States, which has slower or stable growth. TFRs are lowest in countries such as Italy, which has declining growth. Ask students how many siblings they have. Do students think the number of children in their family is average for a family in your area? Does the number of children in their family vary from previous generations?

R Reading Skills

Creating word webs To help students understand the material in the subsection on population growth, have them create word webs for each of the three factors that affect population growth: *fertility, life expectancy,* and *net immigration levels*. Have students contribute their ideas to webs on the board. AL **Verbal/Linguistic**

Differences in fertility rates, life expectancies, and immigration rates will change the racial statistics dramatically in the future. By 2050, the Asian and Hispanic portions of the population are expected to nearly double. The number of African Americans will also increase. The white non-Hispanic population is expected to remain a majority of the total population at just under 50 percent.

Future Population Growth

According to **demographers**—people who study the growth, density, and other characteristics of population—three major factors affect population growth. These factors are fertility, life expectancy, and net immigration levels.

demographers people who study growth, density, and other characteristics of the population

fertility rate number of births that 1,000 women are expected to undergo in their lifetime

life expectancy average remaining life span in years of a person who has reached a specified age

- **Fertility**—The **fertility rate** is the number of births that 1,000 women are expected to undergo in their lifetime. A fertility rate of 2,119, for example, translates to 2.119 births per woman. According to the Census Bureau, this rate is projected as the most likely fertility rate for the United States. That rate is barely above the replacement population rate—the rate at which the number of births in a population offsets the number of deaths so that the size of the population neither increases nor decreases.
- **Life expectancy**—The second factor, **life expectancy**, is the average remaining life span of a person who has reached a given age. The Census Bureau predicts that life expectancy at birth will go from about 77.7 years today to 83.9 years by 2050.

CAREERS | Social Worker

Is this Career for you?

 Do you have a passion for helping people improve their lives?

 Are you a problem-solver?

 Are you an empathetic listener who understands how people can become overwhelmed by everyday issues?

 Are you an emotionally balanced person who can deal with frustration and stress?

Salary
Median pay: **$44,200**
$21.25 per hour

Job Growth Potential
Faster than Average

Interview with a Social Worker

"You need an understanding that people go through their own experiences and have their own perspective.... Sometimes on the surface, it could seem that the main problem is not having a job or not being able to pay their bills, but when you explore the problem with the client, you might find that there are layers of self-doubt or low self-esteem or depression or anxiety that are barriers for their development. You have to look at what's underneath the surface and help the clients understand how to do the same thing."

—Susan Engel, Social Worker

Profile of Work
Social workers counsel individuals and help them find ways to solve the challenges of everyday life. Clients may be children, the elderly, the homeless, the sick, or anyone who needs guidance and assistance. The social worker may simply listen and advise, but frequently takes a more active role in finding government resources, treatment, educational opportunities, or therapy to help the person resume a healthy and vibrant life. Social workers may work for state agencies, for private social service agencies, for rehabilitation centers, or in clinical environments.

350

---

networks Online Teaching Options

INTERACTIVE FEATURE

Career: Social Worker

Examining a career as a social worker Have students read the quote and other text on the Careers feature. **Ask: What appeals to you about this career? Why? What does not appeal to you about this career? Why?** Encourage students who are interested in social work to research more about the career. Have them share what they learn with the class.
Verbal/Linguistic

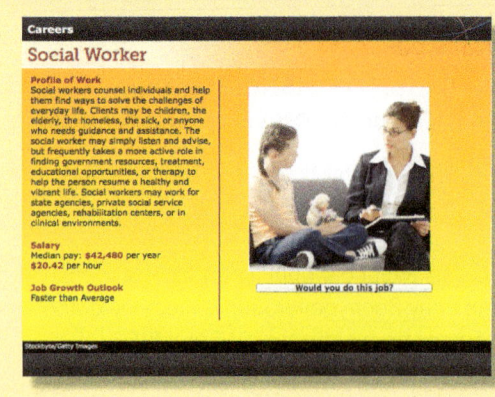

- **Net immigration**—The third factor is **net immigration**—the overall change in population caused by people moving into and out of the country. The Census Bureau recently estimated a net immigration rate of about 1.4 million per year or higher. This figure is based on 1,040,000 immigrants—those entering the country—and 160,000 emigrants—those leaving the country—in the future.

Taking into account these three factors, analysts expect the rate of population growth in the United States to continue to decline. The growth rate, at about 0.75 percent today, is likely to decrease further until the year 2050. At that time, the resident United States population is expected to be about 440 million people.

Most of the demographic factors examined in this section point to a population that is likely to grow more slowly in the future. While this may seem like a matter for concern, it is important to note that increases in productivity can easily offset the negative effects of declining population growth. If slightly fewer people produce significantly more on average, then total output will continue to grow.

Future Population Challenges

The larger concern is the age composition of the future population. As the population matures, a greater percentage of people reach retirement age. This will cause an increase in the demand for medicines, medical facilities, retirement homes, and other products that are needed for the retired and the elderly. At the same time, there may be a declining need for schools, playgrounds, and other facilities as the young become a smaller percentage of the population.

These changes tend to be gradual, and their impact on the economy can be anticipated with some degree of certainty. One of the major advantages of a market economy is that it accommodates change with the least amount of disruption of daily life.

✓ **READING PROGRESS CHECK**

Summarizing Why is the rate of population growth declining?

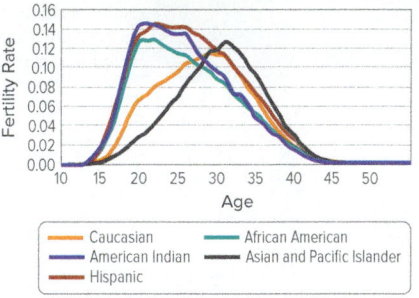

POPULATION INFOGRAPHIC

Source: U.S. Census Bureau, Population Division.

The U.S. Census Bureau periodically produces projections of the United States resident population. These projections are produced using assumptions about demographic components of change (future births, deaths, and net immigration). Changing population demographics puts pressure on existing resources.

▲ **CRITICAL THINKING**
Hypothesizing What role does a population's fertility rate play in its larger economic picture?

net immigration net population change after accounting for those who leave as well as enter a country

EXPLORING THE ESSENTIAL QUESTION

Which will have a greater impact on the economy: a slowing fertility rate or an increasing life expectancy? Why do you think so?

LESSON 2 REVIEW

Reviewing Vocabulary
1. *Explaining* Why do economists pay a great deal of attention to the baby boom generation?
2. *Defining* What is the dependency ratio?

Using Your Notes
3. *Contrasting* What effect will the slowing rate of population growth in the United States have on the economy?

Answering the Guiding Questions
4. *Describing* What changes has the U.S. population experienced since 1790?

5. *Explaining* What effects will the aging population have on the economy?

Writing About Economics
6. *Argument* A friend is concerned that the declining birth rate will be a disaster for your generation and those that follow because so much of the country's economic prosperity will rest on the shoulders of a smaller and smaller proportion of working adults. You disagree that it will be a disaster. Explain your reasons.

connected.mcgraw-hill.com   Evaluating the Economy 351

CHAPTER 12, LESSON 2
Population Growth and Trends

C Critical Thinking Skills

Making predictions about population growth Have students predict factors that might alter the expected low population growth of the U.S. over the next 50 years. *(Possible answer: a higher immigration rate due to ecological, economic, or social chaos in other countries)*

CLOSE & REFLECT

Evaluating Have students identify the population trend they feel will have the greatest effect on the nation in the next 25 years.

ANSWERS, p. 351

CRITICAL THINKING
Fertility rates can help economists predict what the work force will look like in the future. They also help indicate where resources need to go—whether to childcare programs or nursing homes.

EXPLORING THE ESSENTIAL QUESTION
Some students may argue that the increasing life expectancy will have a greater impact because there will be more elderly people who will contribute little to the economy but require more social services. Others may argue that the declining fertility rate will have a greater impact because there will be fewer people to work and produce foods and services and to fuel the economy through saving, investing, and spending on consumer goods.

✓ **READING PROGRESS CHECK** The fertility rate is declining, people are having fewer children, and net immigration is not as high as in the past.

LESSON 2 REVIEW ANSWERS

Reviewing Vocabulary
1. This generation represents a large portion of the current population. As they age, they will cause changes to the economy.
2. The ratio of the population aged under 15 and over 65 to the population aged 15 to 65.

Using Your Notes
3. Fewer people will be in the working-age class, with the result that there will be fewer people working to support more children and elderly.

Answering the Guiding Questions
4. The population has grown considerably, but the rate has slowly declined. Households have gotten smaller from an average of 5.8 people per household to 2.6 people. The population has migrated toward the southwest.
5. As baby boomers retire, they will require payment of pensions, Social Security, and Medicare benefits, which will place a heavy burden on the younger and smaller working population.

Writing About Economics
6. Students may suggest that the market economy will gradually adjust to the changes in the make-up of the population. They may also cite the development of new technologies that will keep productivity increasing to compensate for relatively fewer workers.

CHAPTER 12
Case Study

W1 Writing Skills

Writing an editorial about deforestation Ask students to take a position on deforestation and to write an editorial stating their opinion on the issue and asking the audience to take some action. Have students share their editorials in class or post them on the class or school Web site.

V Visual Skills

Using a map Call students' attention to the map. **Ask:** What areas of the world are at greatest risk for deforestation? *(South America, central and west Africa, Indonesia and Papua New Guinea, Cambodia, North Korea)* Point out that many of these regions include some of the world's poorest countries. **Ask:** How might a country's economic situation influence deforestation and the nation's ability to manage it? *(Poor nations and poor people are focused more on getting enough to eat and improving lives in the short term. Saving the environment or other long-term goals are secondary priorities.)* **Visual/Spatial**

W2 Writing Skills

Finding a solution to deforestation Have students read the final paragraph aloud and discuss what the scientists say about overcrowding and the need that drives people to carve small farms out of forests. Tell students to consider the validity of their point of view: that small farmers are trying to find a way to survive. Ask students to consider what can or should be done to solve the problem of deforestation in light of the needs of these people. Ask students to write an essay stating their opinion on this issue and suggesting one or more solutions.
Verbal/Linguistic

ANSWERS, p. 352

Case Study Review

1. Students should recognize that this alternative also has economic and social costs. The people would have to turn to other means of earning a living, which could impact their personal lives as well as the economies of the countries where they live.
2. Sample answer: Increases in carbon dioxide will increase global warming, which will increase economic costs of storm damage, flooding of coastal regions, and so on. As forests are destroyed, the costs of lumber and other forest products will increase.

352

Case Study

For an interactive version of this case study go to connected.mcgraw-hill.com

OUR NEED for FORESTS

Population growth provides many economic benefits. Without population growth, our workforce may not be able to produce the goods and services we want or to pay enough taxes to care for an aging population. But population growth also creates challenges. One of the most significant ongoing problems in many parts of the world is deforestation. According to the World Wildlife Fund, between 46 and 58 million square miles of forest are destroyed every year. Much of that loss is tied directly or indirectly to the demands of an increasing population.

Forests are vital for many reasons. For example, they are crucial to maintaining biological diversity. They absorb carbon dioxide, which keeps it out of the atmosphere where it would contribute to global warming. Forests provide timber, medicines, and other resources through sustainable forest practices, while also creating jobs. So when vast forest acreages are lost, everyone suffers.

There are many causes for deforestation. What often gets the most blame is the clearing of land to make way for cattle ranches and for the non-sustainable harvesting of forest products. Because of the demands of growing populations in distant parts of the world, this forest-clearing occurs on an industrial scale in places such as the Amazon rain forest of South America and in West Africa. The world's population demands more lumber and more beef, and these "unused" rain forests are prime targets for businesses seeking to fill these demands.

But in places like Guatemala and Ecuador, seemingly more innocent practices resulting from population growth are having what many scientists view as an even greater impact on forests. As population pressures overcrowd existing farmlands, people turn to the forests where they clear-cut and burn lands to establish small farms. The next generation of farmers does the same. Over time, vast swaths of forest are eliminated.

Logging in Malaysia has decimated the forests in that country, just as it has in South and Central America.

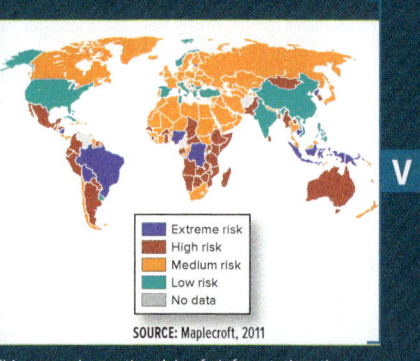
Extreme risk / High risk / Medium risk / Low risk / No data
SOURCE: Maplecroft, 2011
This map shows the risk of deforestation that countries face today.

CASE STUDY REVIEW

1. **Speculating** What if people were prohibited from clearing land in the Central American forests for farm use? How would they earn a living? How would this affect their lives and the economy of these countries?
2. **Analyzing** How does the loss of forests in South America affect the economy of the United States?

352

---

networks — Online Teaching Options

INTERACTIVE FEATURE

Case Study: Our Need for Forests

Debating the value of a forest Display the photograph of the stark landscape of a leveled forest, and ask students what may have happened. Elicit that it was deliberately cleared so the land could be used for development. Then have students read the text. Ask students to list the benefits of a forest. Then have them list the reasons people clear the land. Encourage a new discussion of the benefits of a sustainable forest versus the needs of developers. **Ask:** Is a landscape such as this worth more covered with a living, sustainable forest or for use as grazing land or farms? *(Encourage students to debate any differences of opinion.)* **Naturalist**

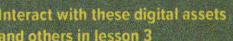

Interact with these digital assets and others in lesson 3

✓ INTERACTIVE GRAPH
  The Distribution of Income
✓ INTERACTIVE IMAGE
  How a Free Enterprise Zone Works
✓ SELF-CHECK QUIZ
✓ VIDEO

networks
TRY IT YOURSELF ONLINE

LESSON 3
Poverty and the Distribution of Income

Reading Help Desk

Academic Vocabulary
- impact • stagnant
- uniform

Content Vocabulary
- poverty threshold
- poverty guidelines
- Lorenz curve • welfare
- food stamps • Medicaid
- Earned Income Tax Credit (EITC)
- enterprise zones
- workfare
- negative income tax

TAKING NOTES:

Key Ideas and Details
ACTIVITY As you read, complete the graphic organizer below to keep track of the factors contributing to poverty in the United States.

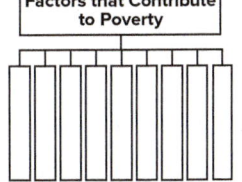

Factors that Contribute to Poverty

poverty threshold
annual dollar income used to determine poverty

ESSENTIAL QUESTION

How do we determine the economic and social well-being of the United States?

Which of the following are factors in the poverty level in the U.S.?

- Educational opportunities
- Availability of skilled employment
- Income distribution
- Discrimination

Poverty

GUIDING QUESTION *How is poverty defined?*

Poverty is one of the most difficult problems we have in our economy. We can define it, and we can explain some of the major reasons for it. Doing something about it, however, has challenged us ever since the mid-1900s. Poverty is a relative measure that depends on prices, the standard of living, and the incomes that others earn. What may seem like poverty to one person may seem like riches to another, so we first need to understand how poverty is defined.

Defining Poverty

People are classified as living in poverty if their incomes fall below a predetermined level, or threshold. The **poverty threshold** is the benchmark used to evaluate the income that people receive. If they have incomes below the threshold, they are considered to be in poverty even if they have supplements such as food stamps, subsidized housing, and Medicaid.

The Social Security Administration developed the thresholds in 1964 using two studies done by the U.S. Department of Agriculture in the 1950s. The first study developed four nutritionally adequate food plans for individuals and families of different sizes. The least expensive food plan was then selected as the food budget that would keep people out of poverty.

connected.mcgraw-hill.com **Evaluating the Economy** 353

CHAPTER 12, LESSON 3
Poverty and the Distribution of Income

ENGAGE

C Critical Thinking Skills

Expressing opinions about poverty
Tell students that poverty and income inequality are the focus of this lesson. **Ask:** From an economic point of view, how big a problem is poverty? Why? After students discuss this question, **ask:** Can poverty be viewed solely as an economic issue? Why or why not? **Verbal/Linguistic**

R Reading Skills

Using context clues to learn word meaning
Refer students to the first paragraph in their text after the subhead *Poverty*. Point out the word *relative* in the fourth sentence. Then "think out loud" in this way to demonstrate how the text first uses a term and then explains its meaning: "The text says poverty is a relative measure. I'm not sure what that means, but as I continue reading, I find out. *Relative* means something like 'different things to different people.' The text is saying that a certain amount of money could make someone well off in one country, but leave him or her poor in another." Have students look for more examples of this text structure as they read this subsection. **AL** **Verbal/Linguistic**

BELLRINGER

Enterprise Zones

Identifying one antipoverty measure
Tell students that poverty remains one of our nation's most critical and intractable problems. Have students discuss some of the antipoverty programs funded by the U.S. government. Then have students view the Bellringer activity and answer the questions. **Interpersonal**

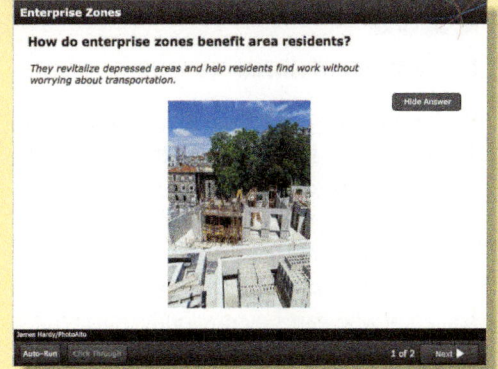

ANSWERS, p. 353

ESSENTIAL QUESTION ACTIVITY

Students should understand that all of the elements listed are factors in the poverty level in the United States.

TAKING NOTES
Education
Wealth
Tax law changes
Decline of unions
More service jobs
Advances in technology
Monopoly power
Discrimination
Changing family structure

Evaluating the Economy **353**

CHAPTER 12, LESSON 3
Poverty and the Distribution of Income

TEACH & ASSESS

C Critical Thinking Skills

Making a budget on the poverty threshold
Organize students into groups of four. Explain that each group represents a family of four (2 adults and 2 children under age 18) living on the 2013 poverty threshold—an annual income of $23,624, or about $454 per week. Have each group develop a detailed family budget, making certain that their budget is balanced. After several groups have shared their budgets, have students discuss what they felt were difficult choices, how much discretionary income they had left, and other issues related to the difficulty of living at the poverty threshold.

V Visual Skills

Analyzing poverty data Have students read the caption for Figure 12.6 and analyze the "Number in poverty" line. **Ask: About how many people lived in poverty in 1960?** *(about 40 million people)* **In 1970?** *(about 24 million people)* **In 2008?** *(about 40 million people)* Now have students analyze the "Poverty rate" line. **Ask: What was the approximate poverty rate in 1960?** *(about 22 percent)* **In 1970?** *(about 12 percent)* **In 2008?** *(about 13 percent)* Finally, ask students to discuss this question: **Why do you think that the poverty rate has scarcely changed in over 40 years?** *(Encourage students to offer ideas and give their reasons.)*
Logical/Mathematical

English Language Proficiency

Advanced High Have students work in groups to brainstorm a list of social and grade-appropriate poverty topics about which most students have strong ideas or opinions. Have a recorder list the topics. Assign each student to choose a topic and deliver a persuasive speech to the class, supporting the opinions, ideas, and feelings with reasons, facts, and examples.

ANSWERS, p. 354

CRITICAL THINKING
Poverty guidelines are used to determine eligibility for government programs.

CRITICAL THINKING
The poverty rate was lowest around 1974; highest, around 2008.

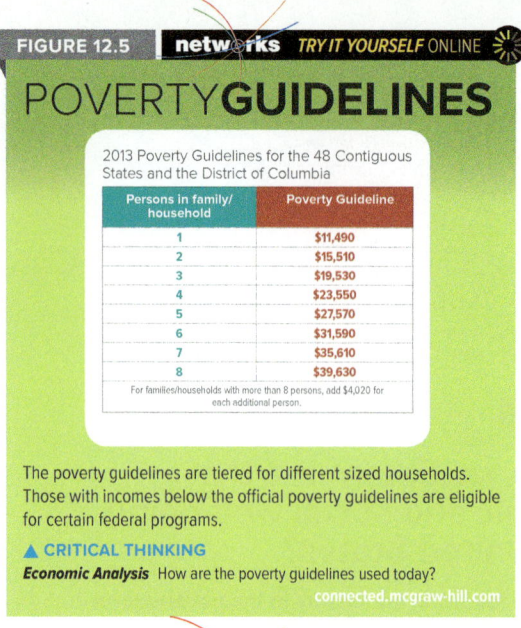

FIGURE 12.5

POVERTY GUIDELINES

2013 Poverty Guidelines for the 48 Contiguous States and the District of Columbia

Persons in family/household	Poverty Guideline
1	$11,490
2	$15,510
3	$19,530
4	$23,550
5	$27,570
6	$31,590
7	$35,610
8	$39,630

For families/households with more than 8 persons, add $4,020 for each additional person.

The poverty guidelines are tiered for different sized households. Those with incomes below the official poverty guidelines are eligible for certain federal programs.

▲ **CRITICAL THINKING**
Economic Analysis How are the poverty guidelines used today?

connected.mcgraw-hill.com

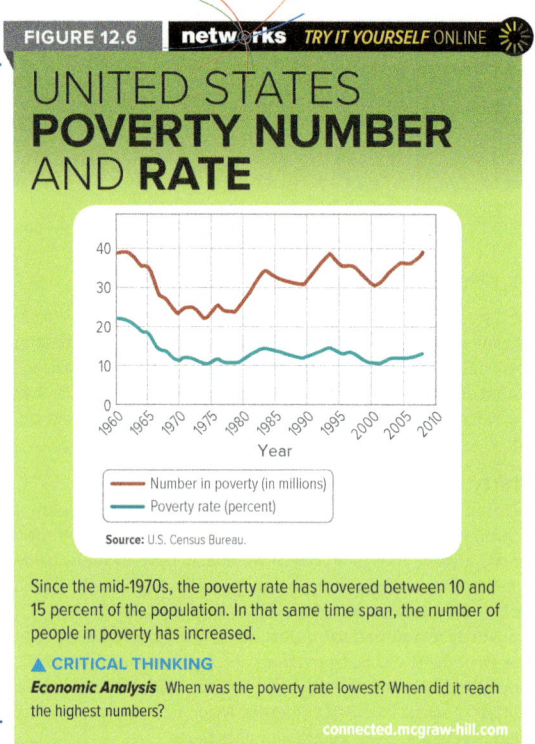

FIGURE 12.6

UNITED STATES POVERTY NUMBER AND RATE

Source: U.S. Census Bureau.

Since the mid-1970s, the poverty rate has hovered between 10 and 15 percent of the population. In that same time span, the number of people in poverty has increased.

▲ **CRITICAL THINKING**
Economic Analysis When was the poverty rate lowest? When did it reach the highest numbers?

connected.mcgraw-hill.com

The second study found that families typically spend one-third of their total income on food. To obtain the threshold, the Social Security Administration simply took the least expensive food budget of the four food plans and multiplied it by three. Today the thresholds are adjusted upward every year by an amount just enough to offset increases in inflation.

For administrative purposes, the poverty thresholds are then simplified to appear as **poverty guidelines**, or administrative guides used to determine eligibility for certain federal programs such as the Food Stamps Program and Head Start. **Figure 12.5** shows the guidelines that were established for 2013.

Historical Poverty Trends

The most recent official poverty rate for the country, shown in **Figure 12.6**, was 15.0 percent, representing about 46,496,000 people. While the poverty rate was essentially unchanged for several years in a row prior to that, the four years of modest economic growth since the Great Recession have barely dented the poverty rate.

While not shown in the figure, the poverty rate for children under the age of 18 was closer to 22 percent for the most recent year. Also, the poverty rate for people age 65 and older was closer to 9 percent. Children, then, are the most vulnerable of all groups in poverty.

Distribution of Income

In addition to determining the actual number of people in poverty, economists are interested in finding out how income is distributed among households. To do so, the incomes of all households are ranked from highest to lowest, and the ranking is divided into quintiles, or fifths. Then the total amount of the nation's income earned by each quintile is calculated.

The table in **Panel A** of **Figure 12.7** shows household income quintiles for three different years. As before, only money income is counted, while other aid such as Medicaid or food stamps is excluded. Using the most recent year in the figure as our example, the percentage of income earned by each quintile is added to the other quintiles. These incomes are plotted as a Lorenz curve. The **Lorenz curve**, which shows how the actual distribution of income varies from an equal distribution, appears in **Panel B**.

To illustrate, in 2012 the 3.2 percent of total income received by the lowest quintile is plotted in Panel B. This amount is added to the 8.3

---

networks Online Teaching Options

CHARTS

Poverty Guidelines

Understanding poverty levels Display Figure 12.5 and ask a student to read the text aloud. Invite students to speculate on what the government considers the poverty line for a single person. Then click on 1 person. Compare that amount to student estimates. Point out that someone who earns even slightly above this amount is not considered living in poverty, according to federal guidelines. Hypothesize that a single person earns $11,500 per year. **Ask: What must be purchased with this income?** *(Sample answer: food, housing, medicine, transportation to work)* Discuss the challenges the individual faces in meeting basic needs. Continue on to households of other sizes. **Logical/Mathematical**

percent the next quintile earns. This process continues until the cumulative amounts of all quintiles are plotted.

If all households received exactly the same income—so that 40 percent of the households earn 40 percent of the total income, and so on—the Lorenz curve would appear as a diagonal line running from one corner of the graph to the other. Because all households do not receive the same income, however, the Lorenz curve is not a diagonal. As you can see in the figure, the distribution of income recently has become more unequal than it was in 1990.

A Lorenz curve can also be shown for groups other than households. These include Lorenz curves for individuals, families, or even occupations.

✓ **READING PROGRESS CHECK**

Describing How were poverty thresholds developed?

Reasons for Income Inequality

GUIDING QUESTION *Which factors are most important in unequal income distribution and why?*

There are at least nine, if not more, reasons why incomes vary. Education and wealth are among the most important of these reasons.

Education

One of the most important reasons for income inequality is the difference in individuals' educational levels. People's income normally goes up as they get more education. However, in the last 30 years, the gap between well-educated and poorly educated workers has widened. This has caused wages for highly skilled workers to soar, while wages for the less skilled have remained about the same.

You saw proof of the importance of education in Figure 1.8. This figure shows that, on average, someone who has earned a college degree makes more than twice as much as someone without a high school diploma. In addition, a person without a high school diploma will be without a job nearly three times more often than someone with a college degree. The conclusion is that education pays, and it is one of the best ways to avoid poverty.

Wealth

Income also varies because some people hold more wealth than others, and the distribution of wealth is even more unequal than the distribution of income. When wealth holders are ranked from highest to lowest in 2007, the year before the Great Recession, the top 1 percent held 34.6 percent of all the wealth in the country. The bottom 80 percent of people in the country had about 15 percent of the total wealth. After the recession, the percentage share held by the top 1 percent increased to 37.1 percent, while the share held by the bottom 80 percent of the population fell to 12.3 percent.

poverty guidelines administrative guidelines used to determine eligibility for certain federal programs

Lorenz curve graph showing how much the actual distribution of income differs from an equal distribution among the five quintiles

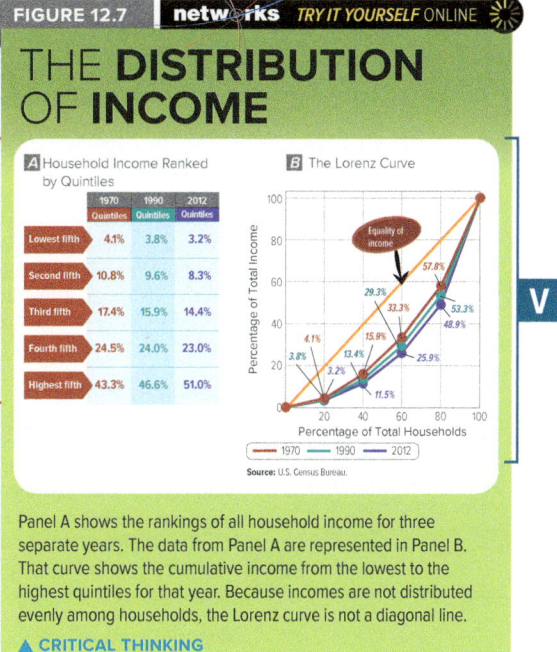

FIGURE 12.7

THE DISTRIBUTION OF INCOME

Panel A shows the rankings of all household income for three separate years. The data from Panel A are represented in Panel B. That curve shows the cumulative income from the lowest to the highest quintiles for that year. Because incomes are not distributed evenly among households, the Lorenz curve is not a diagonal line.

▲ **CRITICAL THINKING**
Economic Analysis What trend can you identify in these data?

CHAPTER 12, LESSON 3
Poverty and the Distribution of Income

W Writing Skills

Writing an essay about education and poverty Have students write an essay addressing the problem of a lack of education among many poor people and proposing a solution the government could take to address the problem. Have volunteers share their solutions. **Verbal/Linguistic**

R Reading Skills

Summarizing information in a table Have students write a paragraph summarizing the information in the Distribution of Income, Panel A. Then ask them why the information was presented in a table, rather than as text. *(A graphic presentation saves space and is easier to read.)* **AL Visual/Spatial**

V Visual Skills

Analyzing graphs and making predictions Have students analyze the Distribution of Income figure and use the data to formulate statements. *(Possible statement: The income gap between the richest and poorest citizens of the United States is widening.)* Have students contribute to a class list of predictions about (1) whether the income gap will continue to grow, stay the same, or lessen; and (2) how a continuing or growing gap between rich and poor will affect U.S. society and the economy. **Logical/Mathematical**

GRAPHS

Distribution of Income

Interpreting data about income inequality Ask students to study Figure 12.7 showing household income by quintiles. **Ask: How much of the nation's total household income was received by the poorest quintile in 2012?** *(3.2 percent)* **How has this percentage changed since 1970?** *(It dropped from 4.1 percent.)* **How has the percentage of total household income received by the richest quintile changed since 1970?** *(It has increased from 43.3 percent to 51 percent.)* Now discuss the Lorenz Curve. **Ask: What does the grid on the graph indicate?** *(the percentage of the nation's total income earned by each percentage of total households)* 80 percent of households earned only 48.9 percent of all income in 2012.

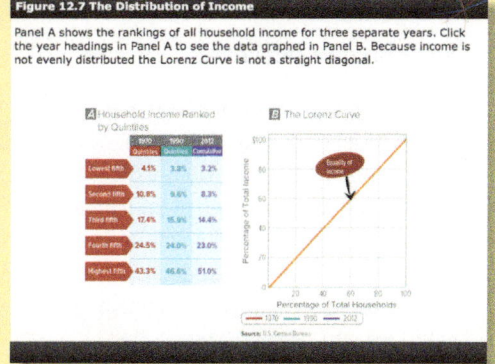

ANSWERS, p. 355

✓ **READING PROGRESS CHECK** The Social Security Administration developed the poverty thresholds by developing alternative food plans, then selecting the least expensive one as the food budget that would keep people out of poverty. The cost of the food for this budget was then multiplied by 3 to establish the threshold.

CRITICAL THINKING

Income inequality increased during the period depicted.

CHAPTER 12, LESSON 3
Poverty and the Distribution of Income

V Visual Skills

Creating a cause-and-effect chart Have students create a cause-and-effect chart about the influence of wealth on life choices. Ask volunteers to re-create their charts on the board. *(Charts should illustrate that wealth, as distinct from income, allows people to send children to expensive schools, start businesses for children, choose not to work, and live off investments.)* **Visual/Spatial**

W Writing Skills

Writing a short story Have students write a short story about the effect of one of the nine factors affecting income inequality (education, wealth, tax law changes, decline of unions, more service jobs, advances in technology, monopoly power, discrimination, and changing family structure) on a family living in poverty. **Verbal/Linguistic**

C Critical Thinking Skills

Explaining the effect of rising health care costs
Ask: Do you think having more doctors might slow the rise in health care costs? Why or why not? *(Answers will vary. Students saying "yes" may cite the law of supply and demand, arguing that raising the supply of doctors would lower their cost; students saying "no" might claim that most of the expense in health care is not due to a lack of doctors but to expensive drugs, equipment, and other factors.)* **ELL Logical/Mathematical**

---

impact effect

This inequality has a dramatic **impact** on people's ability to earn income. Wealthy families can send their children to expensive colleges and universities. The wealthy also can afford to set their children up in businesses where they can earn a better income. Even if the very wealthy choose not to work, they can make investments that will earn additional income.

Tax Law Changes
In recent years, Congress has changed many tax laws, reducing taxes for almost all Americans. Marginal tax rates on high incomes, however, have been reduced more than rates on lower incomes, adding to the growing inequality of income.

The 15 percent tax rate that applies to most dividend payments, for example, is the same as the second-lowest rates the poorest Americans pay. To illustrate, an individual with $8,000,000 of stock that pays a 5 percent dividend would pay only a 15 percent tax rate on those dividends. The rate jumps to 20 percent after that, but someone with $8,000,000 of dividend-paying stock still pays the same percentage rate on those dividends as someone who earns only $20,000 a year.

Decline of Unions
As heavy manufacturing declined in the United States, union membership fell, especially among less-skilled workers, adding to the growing income gap. High school graduates who once followed their parents into high-paying factory jobs can no longer do so. This leaves them to find other work, often for much less pay.

The people who would have followed their parents into high-paying factory jobs are also the ones less likely to increase their education beyond high school. Their failure to secure more education to offset the loss of high-paying factory jobs is an additional factor that has caused the distribution of income to widen.

More Service Jobs
A structural change in the U.S. economy saw industry convert from goods production to service production. This event widened the income differential. Because wages are typically lower in service industries, such as restaurants, movie theaters, and clothing stores, annual incomes also tend to be lower.

Advances in Technology
Advances in technology mean that many service jobs require fewer skills than before. A cashier at a fast-food restaurant, for example, no longer needs to know how to accurately add several separate purchases to reach a total, or make change for a $10 bill when somebody places an order. Instead, the register computes the total and tells the cashier how much change to give the customer.

When fewer skills are required to do a job, it stands to reason that the wages paid for the job will be low, and even **stagnant** over time.

stagnant not changing

Monopoly Power
Another factor is the degree of monopoly power that some groups have. As you may recall, unions have been able to obtain higher wages for their members in the past. Some white-collar workers—clerical, business, or professional workers who generally are salaried—also have a degree of monopoly power if they can affect the number of workers in their industry.

welfare government or private agency programs that provide general economic and social assistance to needy individuals

The American Medical Association, for example, has successfully limited the number of people entering the profession by restricting medical school certifications. This has been a major factor in driving up the incomes of doctors.

uniform even or consistent

Discrimination
Discrimination also affects the distribution of income. Women might not be promoted to higher-paid executive positions because male executives simply

---

networks Online Teaching Options

WORKSHEETS

Enrichment Activity

Examining causes for income inequality To help students better understand the factors that have led to increased income inequality in the United States, assign the Income and Wealth Inequality in America Enrichment worksheet. Read the introduction with students, and then ask students to work individually to study the reading and the graph and to answer the questions. When students finish, guide a class discussion of the activity. **Verbal/Linguistic**

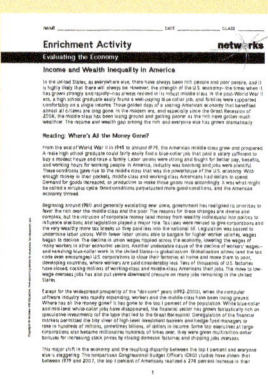

are not accustomed to women in roles of power. Some unions might deny membership to immigrants or ethnic minorities.

Although workplace discrimination is illegal, it still occurs. When it does, it causes women and minority groups to be crowded into other labor markets where oversupply drives wages down.

Changing Family Structure

A final reason for the growing income gap concerns the changing structure of the American family. The shift from two-parent families to single-parent families and other household living arrangements tends to decrease the average family income. This and the other factors mentioned above contribute to the trend of the rich getting richer and the poor getting poorer.

Mobility Between Quintiles

As difficult as the above issues appear to be at any given time, we must not lose sight of the fact that there is significant movement between quintiles during the course of one's lifetime. Someone just starting out in life may find him or herself in the lowest quintile, but as time goes on, he or she rises into the second, third, fourth, or maybe even the fifth quintile—only to fall again during retirement years. This moderates the issue of poverty, but does not excuse it.

✓ READING PROGRESS CHECK

Synthesizing Which factors are most important in unequal income distribution? Why?

Antipoverty Programs

GUIDING QUESTION *To what extent should the government financially support those in poverty?*

Over the years, the federal government has tried a number of programs to help the needy. Most come under the general heading of **welfare**—economic and social assistance from the government or private agencies because of need.

Reducing poverty has been difficult. As Figure 12.6 shows, even the record economic expansions of the 1980s and 1990s failed to make a significant dent in the percentage of Americans living in poverty. Some of the following programs clearly helped reduce the percentage living in poverty from the record-high levels in the early 1960s, but progress after that has been extremely difficult.

Income Assistance

Programs that provide direct cash assistance to those in need fall into the category of income assistance. One such program is the Temporary Assistance for Needy Families (TANF), which began in 1997. Although provisions and benefits vary from state to state, many families qualify for modest cash payments because of the death, continuous absence, or permanent disability of a parent. More recently, Congress voted to tighten provisions of the law and toughen work standards for two-parent households.

Another income assistance program is the Supplemental Security Income (SSI), which makes cash payments to blind or disabled people or to people age 65 and older. Originally, the states administered the program, but because benefits varied so much from state to state, the federal government took it over to ensure more **uniform** coverage.

General Assistance

Programs that assist poor people but do not provide direct cash assistance fall into the category of general assistance.

BIOGRAPHY

John Kenneth Galbraith

ECONOMIST
(1908–2006)

Shaped by his experiences during the Great Depression, liberal economist John Kenneth Galbraith believed in the government's ability to solve problems. Galbraith was seen by other economists as an iconoclast—a person willing to challenge accepted belief. In his classic *The Affluent Society*, Galbraith argued that the U.S. economy had resulted in individual wealth, while public projects such as education and highways were underfunded. He argued that government regulation of prices would steer Americans away from spending money on things they didn't need and help them refocus on attaining an education or appreciating culture.

Galbraith was a major force in directing the Democratic Party's economic platform. Under President Roosevelt, he administered wage and price controls in the Office of Price Administration. President Johnson's "war on poverty" incorporated many of Galbraith's ideas.

▲ CRITICAL THINKING
Making Inferences Which viewpoint made Galbraith an iconoclast to other economists?

connected.mcgraw-hill.com   *Evaluating the Economy* 357

CHAPTER 12, LESSON 3
Poverty and the Distribution of Income

C Critical Thinking Skills

Evaluating the administration of welfare programs
Have students discuss this statement: Welfare programs such as Medicaid and food stamps would be administered more effectively and cheaply by private companies. Have students offer support for their responses. **Verbal/Linguistic**

W Writing Skills

Writing a report on a social service program Have students identify one social service program available in your state. Then have them research it using your state's official Web site and write a short report on the program. Have them explain the goal of the program, its cost and history, and some of its activities. Have students share their reports with the class. Conclude with a discussion of other programs students think the state should offer to alleviate poverty and provide security. **Verbal/Linguistic**

---

food stamps government-issued coupons that can be exchanged for food

Medicaid joint federal-state medical insurance for low-income people

EXPLORING THE ESSENTIAL QUESTION

Which statement best describes the goals of many antipoverty programs?

1. To prevent the needy from having to work at low-paying jobs.
2. To provide financial assistance and help people find jobs to support themselves.
3. To encourage poor students to stay in school.

Earned Income Tax Credit (EITC) federal tax credits and cash payments for low-income workers

enterprise zones areas free of local, state, and federal tax laws as well as other operating restrictions

workfare program requiring welfare recipients to work in exchange for benefits

---

- **Supplemental Nutrition Assistance Program (SNAP)**—More commonly known as "food stamps," SNAP is a program that serves millions of Americans. The **food stamps** themselves are government-issued coupons that can be redeemed for food and may be given or sold to eligible low-income people. For example, if a person pays 40 cents for a $1 food stamp, that person can get a dollar's worth of food for a fraction of its cost. The program, which became law in 1964, is different from other programs because eligibility is based solely on income.

- **Medicaid**—Another general assistance program is **Medicaid**, a joint federal-state medical insurance program for low-income people. Under the program, the federal government pays a majority of health-care costs, and state governments cover the rest. Medicaid serves millions of Americans, including children, the visually impaired, and the disabled.

Social Service Programs

Over the years, individual states have developed a variety of social service programs to help the needy. These include areas such as child abuse prevention, foster care, family planning, job training, child welfare, and day care. Although states control the kinds of services the programs provide, the federal government may match part of the cost. To be eligible for matching funds, a state must file an annual service plan with the federal government. If the plan is approved, the state is free to select issues it wishes to address, set the eligibility requirements and decide how the programs are to be carried out. As a result, the range of services and the level of support may vary from state to state.

Tax Credits

Many working Americans qualify for special tax credits. The most popular is the **Earned Income Tax Credit (EITC)**, which provides federal tax credits and even cash to low-income workers. The credit is applied first to federal income taxes. Low-income workers can take the remainder of the credit in cash if the credit is larger than the taxes owed.

While the EITC was designed as a tax credit, it was also designed to encourage people to get a job and go to work. After all, you can't even file for the EITC unless you are working. The credit has proven to be popular, with millions of working families receiving benefits annually.

Enterprise Zones

Special **enterprise zones** are areas where companies can locate free of some local, state, and federal tax laws and other operating restrictions. Many enterprise zones are established in run-down or depressed areas. This benefits area residents because they can find work without worrying about transportation.

Nearly everyone agrees that a growing economy helps alleviate poverty. The enterprise zone concept is an attempt to focus some of that growth directly in the areas that need it most by making more employment opportunities available.

Workfare Programs

Because of rising welfare costs, many state and local governments require individuals who receive welfare to provide labor in exchange for benefits. **Workfare** is a program in which welfare recipients work for their benefits. People on workfare often assist law enforcement officials or sanitation and highway crews, work in schools or hospitals, or perform other types of community service work.

In some cases, companies can even earn federal tax credits when they hire workers directly from the welfare rolls. Under these circumstances, the employment is a win-win situation for employer and employee.

---

networks — Online Teaching Options

VIDEO WORKSHEET

Hard Time Generation

Analyzing a video Have students view the video. Guide students in discussing the ways government has attempted to alleviate poverty. Have students view the video a second time. Afterwards, have them work in pairs and write down additional questions about the video. Guide a class discussion of these questions.
AL Interpersonal, Visual/Spatial

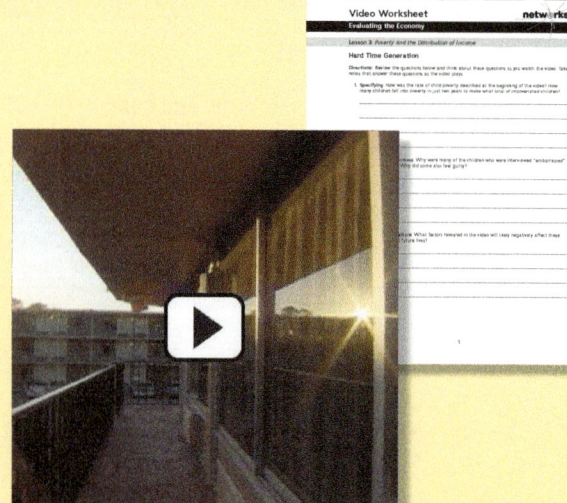

ANSWERS, p. 358

EXPLORING THE ESSENTIAL QUESTION

Students should select statement 2.

Negative Income Tax

The **negative income tax** is a proposed type of tax that would make cash payments to certain groups below the poverty line. While the program is not in use today, the proposal is attractive because cash payments would take the place of existing welfare programs rather than supplementing them. Also, everyone would qualify for the program, not just working people, as with the EITC.

Under the negative income tax, the federal government sets an income level below which people would not have to pay taxes. Then the government would pay a certain amount of money to anyone who earned less than that amount. For example, suppose that an individual's tax liability was computed using the following formula:

$$\text{taxes} = (25\% \text{ of income}) - \$8{,}000$$

Under this formula, a person with no income would have a tax of minus $8,000—which is another way of saying that the person will receive $8,000 from the government. If the person earned exactly $12,000, then the taxes would be $3,000 minus $8,000, so they would receive $5,000 for a total of $17,000 ($5,000 from the tax formula plus the $12,000 in earned income). Under this formula, a person would have to make $32,000 before he or she actually paid any taxes.

The negative income tax differs from other antipoverty programs in two respects. First, it is a market-based program designed to encourage people to work. The objective is to make the minimum payment large enough to be of some assistance, yet small enough so that people are better off working. Then, when people do go to work, the taxes they pay need to be low enough to not discourage them from working. Second, the negative income tax would be cost-effective because it would take the place of other, more costly, welfare programs. In addition, government would save on administrative costs.

negative income tax tax system that would make cash payments in the form of tax refunds to individuals when their income falls below certain levels

An Extremely Difficult Problem

We might ask how the U.S. economy has done as a result of all these programs since the mid-1970s. The answer, unfortunately, is that poverty has been a remarkably difficult problem to solve even during periods of strong economic growth. Because economic growth by itself is not enough, there are sound reasons to try to reduce the problem of poverty. Not only would millions of Americans be better off, but everyone else in the economy would be better off as well. After all, if too many people find themselves without the capacity to earn and spend, there will be fewer people to purchase the products that our economy produces.

☑ **READING PROGRESS CHECK**

Summarizing What are the benefits of the EITC to a working person?

LESSON 3 REVIEW

Reviewing Vocabulary

1. *Explaining* Explain in your own words how enterprise zones are intended to help the poverty problem.
2. *Explaining* Explain how poverty guidelines are used.

Using Your Notes

3. *Summarizing* Use your notes to summarize the factors that contribute to poverty in the United States.

Answering the Guiding Questions

4. *Explaining* How is poverty defined?

5. *Evaluating* Which factors are most important in unequal income distribution and why?
6. *Describing* To what extent should the government financially support those in poverty?

Writing About Economics

7. *Persuasive/Explanatory* Write a five-paragraph essay that explores the following question: Do you think a workfare program is the best way to address income inequalities within our economy? Why or why not?

connected.mcgraw-hill.com   *Evaluating the Economy* 359

Chapter 12
Study Guide

W Writing Skills

Designing a business Refer students to the diagram in the center of this page. Review the three factors that influence population growth. Then have students write a paragraph describing a business they could start, based on one of the factors as it affects today's society and the future. Have volunteers share their business descriptions and explain why they made their particular choice. You may also want to have students discuss businesses they expect would not be successful, based on current trends in fertility, life expectancy, and immigration. **Interpersonal**

C Critical Thinking Skills

Categorizing Refer students to the diagram at the bottom of this page and review each cause, if necessary. **Ask: Which of the causes of income inequality do you feel could best be solved by government? By the private sector? By a government-private sector combination? Explain your answers.** (Answers will vary but should be logical and well supported.) **Verbal/Linguistic**

STUDY GUIDE

LESSON 1

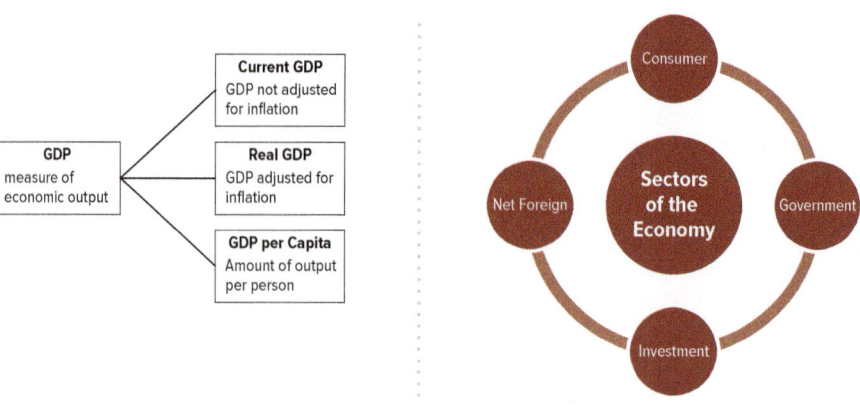

LESSON 2

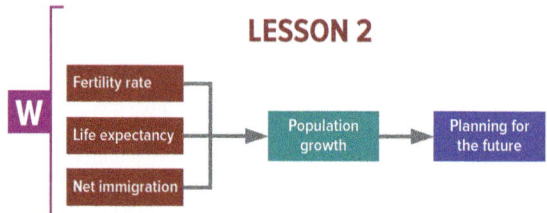

LESSON 3

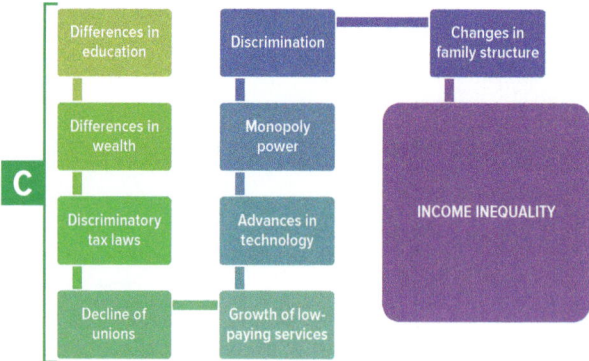

networks Online Assessment Options

WORKSHEET

Personal Finance Activity

Students will fill in a monthly budget chart based on their own anticipated income after finishing school, and then based on a person living at the poverty level in order to understand the challenges an impoverished person faces in trying to survive.

CHAPTER 12 Assessment

Directions: On a separate sheet of paper, answer the questions below. Make sure you read carefully and answer all parts of the questions.

Lesson Review

Lesson 1

1 **Explaining** What is the source of income for the four sectors of the economy?

2 **Identifying** How might government actions affect the circular flow of economic activity?

Lesson 2

3 **Interpreting** In what way is the census an important tool for economists?

4 **Explaining** How might the age composition of the future population impact our economy?

5 **Explaining** What effect will changes in productivity have on the economy in the future?

Lesson 3

6 **Identifying** What are the main causes of inequality in the distribution of income?

7 **Explaining** How do enterprise zones benefit residents of run-down or depressed areas?

Critical Thinking

8 **Evaluating** Research the GDP per capita for several countries. What can you learn about the country's wealth from those figures?

9 **Analyzing** How do the different measures of output and income allow us to assess the economy of a nation?

10 **Evaluating** During a major downturn in the economy, your local community is considering implementing a workfare program. Do you think this program will be more or less effective than a basic welfare program? Explain your answer.

11 **Assessing** Suppose you were told that you would earn $95,000 per year by the time you were 30. Explain why this information would say little about the standard of living you might enjoy. What other information would you need before you could evaluate how well you could live when you are 30?

Use the graph below to answer the following questions about income inequality.

Analyzing Visuals

12 **Analyzing Visuals** In 1990, 60 percent of households fell what percentage below the equality of income level? How much below equality of income was this group in 2012?

13 **Summarizing** According to this graph, summarize the changes in income inequality between 1990 and 2012.

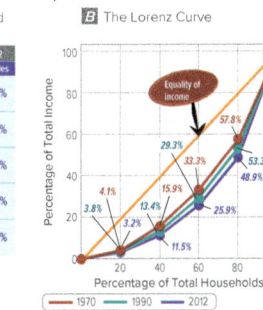

A Household Income Ranked by Quintiles

Quintiles	1970 Quintiles	1990 Quintiles	2012 Quintiles
Lowest fifth	4.1%	3.8%	3.2%
Second fifth	10.8%	9.6%	8.3%
Third fifth	17.4%	15.9%	14.4%
Fourth fifth	24.5%	24.0%	23.0%
Highest fifth	43.3%	46.6%	51.0%

B The Lorenz Curve

Source: U.S. Census Bureau.

Need Extra Help?

If You've Missed Question	1	2	3	4	5	6	7	8	9	10	11	12	13
Go to page	341	343	348	349	351	355	358	339	336	358	355	355	355

TAKE THIS TEST ONLINE AT connected.mcgraw-hill.com   **Evaluating the Economy** 361

Chapter 12 Assessment Answers

Lesson Review

Lesson 1

1 Consumer sector: disposable personal income; investment sector: retained earnings; government sector: indirect business taxes, corporate income taxes, Social Security contributions, and personal taxes from the consumer sector; foreign sector: does not have a specific source of income

2 Answers might include that government purchases and provides goods and services, regulates economic activity, and collects taxes.

Lesson 2

3 The census enables economists to identify population trends that can be used to predict changes in economy that may cause problems if not addressed.

4 Younger workers will carry a heavy burden as the economy must support a larger proportion of older, retired workers through pensions, Social Security, and Medicare benefits.

5 Students may say that increased productivity through technology can easily offset the changes caused by an aging population.

Lesson 3

6 Education, wealth, monopoly power, decline of unions, increase in service jobs, discrimination, changes in tax laws, and changing family structures can all contribute to inequality in the distribution of income.

7 Enterprise zones provide local employment opportunities where employees don't have to worry about transportation. The zones pump dollars into the local economy.

Analyzing Visuals

12 In 1990 the bottom three quintiles (60% of households) held 29.3% of income, so they were 30.7% below the income equality level. In 2012, these same quintiles fell 34.1% below the income equality level.

13 Income inequality has increased for all households between 1990 and 2012.

Critical Thinking

8 GDP per capita gives one a better idea of the standard of living in a country.

9 Possible answer: Economists use a variety of factors because no single measurement captures the entire picture of the growth and performance of a nation's economy.

10 Students should understand that both workfare and welfare are programs to aid those living in poverty. Workfare requires welfare recipients to exchange some of their labor for benefits. Students' assessments of effectiveness will vary, but they should give reasons and details to support their positions.

11 Students should take into account inflation, cost of living, income distribution, tax burden, and other factors that influence standard of living.

Chapter 12
Assessment Answers

Answering the Essential Questions

14 Students should demonstrate an understanding of various measurements used in determining economic and social well-being, including GDP, GNP, DPI, NI, and so on.

15 Students should demonstrate an understanding of how shifts in population, changes in the makeup of the population, and other population trends affect GDP, infrastructure, the dependency ratio, and other economic factors.

16 Students may suggest ways of improving income assistance, Medicare, social services, the EITC, enterprise zones, workfare, use of the negative income tax, or other alternatives.

21st Century Skills

17 Students should respond that GDP is a measure of economic growth; workers and consumers benefit when the economy grows. Moreover, when a product is purchased, two parties, the buyer and the seller, feel they are better off. As a result, an improved GDP does indirectly measure improved well-being for individuals.

18 Students should recognize that longer life expectancies means more older people relying on Medicare and Social Security; declining birthrates means fewer people in the workforce to produce taxes to pay for these programs.

19 Students may suggest addressing any of the factors that influence income inequality. They should give reasons for their choice.

20 Circular flow diagrams will vary. Students should carefully track the different entry and exit points of income and expense.

Building Financial Literacy

21 Students should recognize that income inequality affects their lives, including what college they can attend and how they will pay for it, the type of housing they can afford, and maintaining a comfortable standard of living.

Analyzing Primary Sources

22 If people had more opportunities, they would earn more and income inequality would diminish.

23 Research and education would create opportunities that would provide more high-quality jobs for workers who are now suffering from lack of opportunity and low wages.

362

CHAPTER 12 Assessment

Directions: On a separate sheet of paper, answer the questions below. Make sure you read carefully and answer all parts of the questions.

ANSWERING THE ESSENTIAL QUESTIONS

Review your answers to the introductory questions at the beginning of each lesson. Then answer the Essential Question on the basis of what you learned in the chapter. Have your answers changed?

14 **Explaining** How do we determine the economic and social well-being of the United States?

15 **Explaining** How do population trends impact the economy?

16 **Analyzing** What steps can we take to deal with poverty?

21st Century skills

17 **Create and Analyze Arguments and Draw Conclusions** After listening to a newscast reporting higher than expected GDP for the past year, a friend has commented that it doesn't matter. GDP, she says, only shows that business is doing well. It doesn't really tell anything about how well ordinary people are doing or whether their well-being has improved. How would you respond?

18 **Understanding Relationships Among Events** How will longer life expectancies and declining birthrates make some programs, such as Social Security and Medicare, more difficult to fund?

19 **Problem Solving** What is the most important step that can be taken to reduce income inequality? Explain your answer.

20 **Building Economic Models** Review the example of the circular flow of economic activity shown in Figure 12.2. Then create your own economic model showing the circular flow of a simpler economy, such as your parents' income. How does their income come in and how is it divided and delivered to other segments of the economy around you?

Building Financial Literacy

21 **Analyzing** Imagine that you must teach a younger class about income inequality and its consequences. Prepare teaching notes. In your notes, cover the effects of income inequality on the following matters:
- Attending college
- Renting or purchasing a home
- Maintaining a desirable standard of living

Analyzing Primary Sources

Read the excerpt and answer the questions that follow.

PRIMARY SOURCE

"Some people look at income inequality and shrug their shoulders. So what if this person gains and that person loses? What matters, they argue, is not how the pie is divided but the size of the pie."

—Joseph E. Stiglitz, "Of the 1%, by the 1%, for the 1%," *Vanity Fair*, May 2011

But Stiglitz goes on to explain why this way of looking at the matter is wrong. First, income inequality means less opportunity for this country's most valuable resource—its people. Lack of income can hamper a person's ability to take advantage of opportunities that may present themselves. Second, those things that lead to inequality often lead to more inequality. For example, the power of monopolies may tempt our young people to pursue careers in finance instead of other areas that could help stimulate the economy. Finally, Stiglitz notes that our modern economy would benefit most from the types of investments that would help not only advance us as a nation but also provide more opportunity for more people: research, education, infrastructure.

22 **Analyzing Primary Sources** How is income inequality related to limited opportunities?

23 **Drawing Conclusions** How would expanded investment in research and education help reduce income inequality?

Need Extra Help?

If You've Missed Question	14	15	16	17	18	19	20	21	22	23
Go to page	336	348	357	336	349	357	342	355	355	355

362

---

networks Online Assessment Options

WORKSHEET

Chapter Tests and Lesson Quizzes

Chapter 12 Tests Forms A and B Have students complete the Chapter Tests and Lesson Quizzes to assess student understanding throughout the chapter. Print and online assessment tools offer chapter and lesson evaluation through a variety of question formats, including document-based questions.

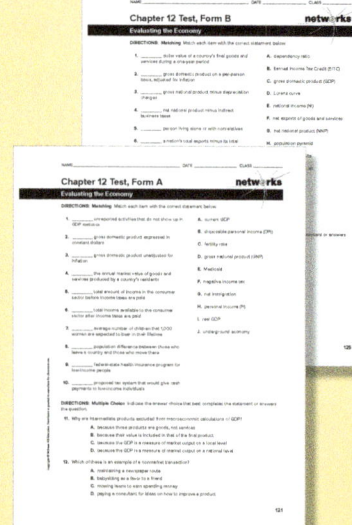

CHAPTER 13
Economic Instability Planner

UNDERSTANDING BY DESIGN®

Enduring Understanding
- Learning about the past helps us understand the present and make decisions about the future.

Essential Questions
- What are the causes and consequences of instability in the economy?

Predictable Misunderstandings
Students may think:
- *Economic instability affects only the workforce and unemployment rates.* Explain that economic instability touches every area of our lives. It can lead to a higher crime rate and cause marital disputes. It can also affect political decisions.
- *The unemployment rate exaggerates the problem of unemployment.* Explain that, if anything, the unemployment rate underestimates the problem, because it only counts people who are actively looking for work. It does not include people who have tried and failed to find work and have therefore become discouraged or given up.

Assessment Evidence
Performance Task
- *Hands-On Chapter Project with Technology Extension*

Other Evidence
- *Guided Reading Activities*
- *Vocabulary Activity*
- *Lesson Quizzes*
- *Self-Check Quizzes*
- *Chapter Assessment*
- *Chapter Tests, Forms A and B*

SUGGESTED PACING

Introducing the Chapter: ...... ½ Day	Lesson 3: Unemployment ...... 1 Day
Lesson 1: Business Cycles and Economic Instability .... 1 Day	Debate .... ½ Day
Case Study .... ½ Day	Study Guide, Chapter Assessment and Wrap-Up .... ½ Day
Lesson 2: Inflation .... 1 Day	
	TOTAL 5 Days

Council for Economic Education

Below are the Council for Economic Education Voluntary National Content Standards in Economics covered in the *Economic Instability* chapter.

Content Standard 11: Money makes it easier to trade, borrow, save, invest, and compare the value of goods and services. The amount of money in the economy affects the overall price level. Inflation is an increase in the overall price level that reduces the value of money.

Content Standard 18: Fluctuations in a nation's overall levels of income, employment, and prices are determined by the interaction of spending and production decisions made by all households, firms, government agencies, and others in the economy. Recessions occur when overall levels of income and employment decline.

Content Standard 19: Unemployment imposes costs on individuals and the overall economy. Inflation, both expected and unexpected, also imposes costs on individuals and the overall economy. Unemployment increases during recessions and decreases during recoveries.

Content Standard 20: Federal government budgetary policy and the Federal Reserve System's monetary policy influence the overall levels of employment, output, and prices.

Key for Using the Teacher Edition

SKILL-BASED ACTIVITIES
Types of skill activites found in the Teacher Edition.

V Visual Skills require students to analyze maps, graphs, charts, and photos.

R Reading Skills help students practice reading skills and master vocabulary.

C Critical Thinking Skills help students apply and extend what they have learned.

W Writing Skills provide writing opportunities to help students comprehend the text.

T Technology Skills require students to use digital tools effectively.

*Letters are followed by a number when there is more than one of the same type of skill on the page.

DIFFERENTIATED INSTRUCTION
All activities are written for the on-level student unless otherwise marked with the leveled labels below.

BL Beyond Level
AL Approaching Level
ELL English Language Learners

All students benefit from activities that utilize different learning styles. Many activities are marked as below when a particular learning style is highlighted.

Intrapersonal
Logical/Mathematical
Visual/Spatial
Verbal/Linguistic
Naturalist
Kinesthetic
Auditory/Musical
Interpersonal

CHAPTER 13: ECONOMIC INSTABILITY

CHAPTER OPENER PLANNER

Students will know:
- the stages of the business cycle and the characteristics of each.
- the different causes of inflation and who gains and losses because of inflation.
- the consequences of unemployment, such as uncertainty, political instability, and social problems.

Students will be able to:
- **list** five potential causes of the business cycle.
- **identify** the causes of the Great Depression.
- **name** two methods used to predict business cycles.
- **explain** how the consumer price index is used to calculate inflation.
- **discuss** the unemployment rate and the information it provides.
- **list** types of unemployment.
- **discuss** the effects of economic instability on consumers.

UNDERSTANDING BY DESIGN®

☑ Print Teaching Options

V Visual Skills
- ☐ **p. 364 Diagramming consequences of instability** Students show the downward spiral caused by the dot.com and housing bubbles.

R Reading Skills
- ☐ **p. 364 Identifying economic terms** Students learn about IPOs.

C Critical Thinking Skills
- ☐ **p. 363 Understanding the effects of instability** Students illustrate the general effects of economic instability.
- ☐ **p. 365 Sequencing the dot.com and housing bubbles** Students put events on a time line.
- ☐ **p. 365 Proposing solutions for the future** Students brainstorm solutions to economic instability.

☑ Online Teaching Options

V Visual Skills
- ☐ **IMAGE Chapter opener**—Students discuss causes and consequences of economic instability.

C Critical Thinking Skills
- ☐ **INFOGRAPHICS Economic Perspectives**—Students learn about the dot.com and housing bubbles.
- ☐ **DEBATES Is economic stability the key to world peace?**
- ☐ **INTERACTIVE FEATURE Case Study: A Greek Tragedy**—Students analyze the recession in Greece.

☑ Printable Digital Worksheets

C Critical Thinking Skills
- ☐ **WORKSHEET Chapter Summary**—Content is condensed into manageable chunks.
- ☐ **WORKSHEET Vocabulary Activity**—Students use content and academic terms.
- ☐ **WORKSHEET Assessing Background Knowledge Activity**—Target misconceptions you can address when teaching the lessons.
- ☐ **WORKSHEET Enrichment Activity**—Students use knowledge of the Consumer Price Index.

Project-Based Learning

Hands-On

WORKSHEET Hands-On Chapter Project
In this activity, student groups create graphs that show leading economic indicators over the past ten years, and create a talk show that makes predictions about the future of the business cycle.

Digital Hands-On

Create Online Projects

Find an additional activity online that incorporates technology for the Hands-On Project. Visit the EdTech Teacher Web sites for more links, tutorials, and other resources.

Print Resources

ANCILLARY RESOURCE
This ancillary is available for every chapter and lesson.
- Chapter Tests and Lesson Quizzes

PRINTABLE DIGITAL WORKSHEETS
These printable digital worksheets are available for every chapter and lesson.
- Reading Essentials & Study Guide
- Vocabulary Activities
- Chapter Summaries
- Economic Simulations
- Math Practice for Economics
- Reinforcing Economic Skills
- Personal Finance Activities
- Enrichment Activities
- Reteaching Activities
- Guided Reading Activities
- Video Worksheets
- Lesson Quizzes and Chapter Tests (English and Spanish)

More Media Resources

SUGGESTED READING
- For students at a Grade 10 reading level: *The New Deal and the Great Depression in American History,* by Lisa A. Wroble
- For students at a Grade 11 reading level: *Free to Choose: A Personal Statement,* by Milton Friedman & Rose Friedman
- For students at a Grade 12 reading level: *Voices of Protest: Huey Long, Father Coughlin and the Great Depression,* by Alan Brinkley

SUGGESTED VIDEOS MOVIES
Find these documentaries yourself online. NOTE: McGraw-Hill Education does not endorse these resources. Preview clips for age-appropriateness.
- *The Plague of the Black Debt* (48 min.)
- *Europe on the Brink* (23 min.)
- *TED Talks: How We Can Predict the Next Financial Crisis* (17 min.)

LESSON 1 Planner

BUSINESS CYCLES AND ECONOMIC INSTABILITY

Students will know:
- the stages of the business cycle and the characteristics of each
- recessions occur when overall levels of income and employment decline.
- the methods used by economists to forecast business cycles, including leading economic indicators and econometric models.

Students will be able to:
- **explain** why ups and downs in the business cycle are considered normal.
- **list** five potential causes of the business cycle.
- **identify** the causes of the Great Depression.
- **describe** the reforms that were made as a result of the Great Depression.
- **discuss** the impacts of the Great Recession of 2008–09 on the economy.
- **name** two methods used to predict business cycles.

UNDERSTANDING BY DESIGN®

☑ Print Teaching Options

V Visual Skills

☐ **p. 366 Visualizing the business cycle** Students diagram the business cycle.

☐ **p. 368 Illustrating business cycle causes** Students create a collage. **ELL Visual/Spatial**

R Reading Skills

☐ **p. 367 Understanding business cycle terms** Students analyze a business cycle diagram.

☐ **p. 373 Activating prior knowledge in econometric model** Students review terms.

C Critical Thinking Skills

☐ **p. 368 Recognizing causes of business cycles** Students list causes of business cycles and examples. **Visual/Linguistic**

☐ **p. 369 Applying the effects of the Great Depression** Students calculate the effect of the Great Depression on their current income.

☐ **p. 371 Understanding the FDIC** Students consider FDIC benefits in the 1930s and today.

☐ **p. 373 Drawing conclusions from economic data** Students predict the effect of a recession on their personal lives.

☐ **p. 373 Organizing economic data** Students chart concepts of recession and expansion.

W Writing Skills

☐ **p. 367 Describing the effects of a downturn** Students describe the chain reaction of economic instability. **Verbal/Linguistic**

☐ **p. 369 Summarizing the stock market crash and its effects**

☐ **p. 372 Writing letters to the editor** Students describe how instability has affected them.

☐ **p. 372 Applying knowledge of economic predictions** Students explain the statistics that predict changes in GDP.

☑ Online Teaching Options

V Visual Skills

☐ **BELLRINGER Economic Instability**—Students identify an example of an economic bubble and discuss how it happened.

☐ **GRAPH Business Cycles**—Students define terms that describe the rise and fall of the business cycle.

☐ **VIDEO Stock Market Crash**—Students discuss and compare the stock market crash of 1929 with current economic situations.

☐ **SLIDE SHOW Great Depression**—Students view images of the Great Depression.

☐ **GRAPH Index of Leading Economic Indicators**—Students explore economic indicators.

R Reading Skills

☐ **BIOGRAPHIES Irene Rosenfeld**—Students consider the relevance of Irene Rosenfeld's ideas during times of economic instability.

C Critical Thinking Skills

☐ **GRAPHIC ORGANIZER Government Steps to Manage the Economy**—Students complete the graphic organizer, research a specific step, and write a short report.

T Technology Skills

☐ **SELF-CHECK QUIZ Lesson 1**—Students receive instant feedback on their mastery of lesson content.

☐ **GAME Lesson 1**—Students solve clues to review lesson content.

☐ **INTERACTIVE WHITEBOARD ACTIVITY Causes of the Business Cycle**—Students work together to learn lesson content.

☑ Printable Digital Worksheets

R Reading Skills

☐ **WORKSHEET Guided Reading Activity**—Students use the Guided Reading Activity worksheets to review their comprehension of the content.

☐ **WORKSHEET Reading Essentials and Study Guide**—Students complete the study guide and answer Reading Progress Check and vocabulary questions.

C Critical Thinking Skills

☐ **WORKSHEET Stock Market Crash Video Activity**—Students answer questions related to the causes and effects of the 1929 stock market crash.

LESSON 2 Planner

INFLATION

Students will know:
- inflation is an increase in the overall price level that reduces the value of money.
- inflation, both expected and unexpected, imposes costs on individual and the overall economy.
- the different causes of inflation and who gains and loses because of inflation.

Students will be able to:
- **explain** how the consumer price index is used to calculate inflation.
- **list** the causes of inflation.
- **state** the consequences of inflation.
- **explain** why creditors are hurt more than debtors by inflation.

UNDERSTANDING BY DESIGN®

☑ Print Teaching Options

V Visual Skills
- ☐ **p. 379 Illustrating cost-push inflation** Students sequence phrases to illustrate cost-push theory.

R Reading Skills
- ☐ **p. 375 Using word parts to define *inflation*** Students write definitions of *inflation*.

C Critical Thinking Skills
- ☐ **p. 376 Calculating a fictional CPI** Students calculate the cost of a market basket. Logical/Mathematical
- ☐ **p. 377 Calculating the CPI and rate of inflation** Students use consumer price index formulas.
- ☐ **p. 378 Researching hyperinflation** Students explain hyperinflations effect on consumers.
- ☐ **p. 378 Understanding demand-pull inflation** Students consider a demand-pull scenario and discuss the implications.
- ☐ **p. 379 Making inferences about inflation** Students explain the relationship between inflation and unemployment.
- ☐ **p. 380 Analyzing effects of inflation** Students evaluate inflation on people within a community.
- ☐ **p. 380 Using graphs to explore the effects of inflation** Students review the purchasing power of a dollar.
- ☐ **p. 381 Analyzing purchasing power** Students calculate purchasing power over time.

W Writing Skills
- ☐ **p. 380 Persuasive writing about the effects of inflation** Students request a raise based on inflation.
- ☐ **p. 381 Predicting effects of inflation on purchasing power**

T Technology Skills
- ☐ **p. 376 Market Basket Categories** Students categorize goods and services in market basket categories.

☑ Online Teaching Options

V Visual Skills
- ☐ **BELLRINGER** **Stagflation**—Students describe the characteristics of stagflation.
- ☐ **VIDEO** **Inflation Jumped**—Students view the effects of consumer activity on inflation. AL
- ☐ **POLITICAL CARTOON** **Wage-Price Spiral**—Students describe a cause and an effect of economic instability.
- ☐ **SLIDE SHOW** **Hyperinflation**—Students learn about historical and recent hyperinflation.

R Reading Skills
- ☐ **INTERACTIVE FEATURE** **Global Economy & You**—Students explore the effect of inflation on the value of the U.S. dollar.

C Critical Thinking Skills
- ☐ **ESSENTIAL QUESTION** **Exploring the Essential Question**—Students consider the effect of inflation on saving money.
- ☐ **GRAPH** **Inflation Erodes the Value of the Dollar**—Students consider data about the effects of inflation.

W Writing Skills
- ☐ **GRAPHIC ORGANIZER** **Causes and Effects of Inflation**—Students chart causes of inflation.

T Technology Skills
- ☐ **SELF-CHECK QUIZ** **Lesson 2**—Students receive instant feedback on their mastery of lesson content.
- ☐ **GAME** **Lesson 2**—Students solve clues to review lesson content.
- ☐ **INTERACTIVE WHITEBOARD ACTIVITY** **Causes and Effects of Inflation**—Students work together to learn lesson content.

☑ Printable Digital Worksheets

R Reading Skills
- ☐ **WORKSHEET** **Guided Reading Activity**—Students review their comprehension of the content.
- ☐ **WORKSHEET** **Reading Essentials and Study Guide**—Students complete the study guide and answer Reading Progress Check and vocabulary questions.

C Critical Thinking Skills
- ☐ **WORKSHEET** **Inflation Jumped Video Activity**—Students answer questions about inflation.

LESSON 3 Planner

UNEMPLOYMENT

Students will know:
- the unemployment rate is an imperfect measure of unemployment.
- unemployment can be caused by people changing jobs, by seasonal fluctuations in demand, by changes in the skills needed by employers, or by cyclical fluctuations in the level of national spending.

Students will be able to:
- **discuss** the unemployment rate and the information it provides.
- **identify** a method to defend against unemployment.
- **list** types of unemployment.
- **discuss** the effects of economic instability on consumers.

UNDERSTANDING BY DESIGN®

✓ Print Teaching Options

R Reading Skills

- **p. 383 Defining the civilian labor force** Students consider the people included and not included in the labor force.
- **p. 383 Figuring the unemployment rate** Students research the current unemployment rate.
- **p. 383 Identifying weaknesses of the unemployment rate**
- **p. 386 Connecting outsourcing to unemployment**
- **p. 389 Tying unemployment to social problems**

C Critical Thinking Skills

- **p. 384 Extrapolating from the unemployment rate** Students consider the interdependence of various elements of the economy.
- **p. 385 Researching job opportunities and benefits** Students research steps they could take if they became unemployed.
- **p. 386 Analyzing local unemployment** Students determine the most common type of unemployment in their community.
- **p. 387 Analyzing types of unemployment** Students classify unemployment for various situations.
- **p. 387 Identifying types of unemployment** Students illustrate the types of unemployment.
- **p. 388 Drawing conclusions about the GDP gap** Students research a Web site and interpret the data. *Logical/Mathematical*
- **p. 389 Theorizing about war and unemployment** Students tie war to unemployment.

W Writing Skills

- **p. 384 Describing the move from underemployment to full employment** Students interview an underemployed person.
- **p. 389 Reflecting on prospects for employment** Students write a plan of action for gaining employment after graduation.

✓ Online Teaching Options

V Visual Skills

- **VIDEO Foodstamps**—Students view the video to learn about the government foodstamps program.

C Critical Thinking Skills

- **BELLRINGER Unemployment**—Students brainstorm the impact if unemployment did not exist.
- **ESSENTIAL QUESTION Exploring the Essential Question**—Students present various community approaches to economic instability.

W Writing Skills

- **INTERACTIVE FEATURE Unemployment Rate**—Students explain how the unemployment rate is tied to recession.
- **INTERACTIVE FEATURE Careers: Human Resource Specialist**—Students write a mock interview between an employer and a prospective employee.
- **GRAPHIC ORGANIZER Sources of Unemployment**—Students compare two sources of unemployment.
- **GRAPH Measuring Consumer Discomfort**—Students describe financial discomfort for a person.

T Technology Skills

- **SELF-CHECK QUIZ Lesson 3**—Students receive instant feedback on their mastery of lesson content.
- **GAME Lesson 3**—Students solve clues to review lesson content.
- **INTERACTIVE WHITEBOARD ACTIVITY Sources of Unemployment**—Students work together to learn lesson content.

✓ Printable Digital Worksheets

R Reading Skills

- **WORKSHEET Guided Reading Activity**—Students review their comprehension of the content.
- **WORKSHEET Reading Essentials and Study Guide**—Students complete the study guide and answer Reading Progress Check and vocabulary questions.
- **WORKSHEET Reteaching Activity**—Students use this activity worksheet to review and reteach chapter content and vocabulary.

C Critical Thinking Skills

- **WORKSHEET Economic Simulation**—Students try to save the auto industry.
- **WORKSHEET Personal Finance**—Students create a plan to change jobs.
- **WORKSHEET Foodstamps Video Activity**—Students take notes about the effects of poverty on a family.

Chapter 13 Planner **363E**

CHAPTER 13 Economic Instability

INTERVENTION AND REMEDIATION STRATEGIES

LESSON 1 Business Cycles and Economic Instability

Reading and Comprehension

Have students read the first lesson and identify the vocabulary words in the lesson. Then have them use the vocabulary words in a summary of the lesson's content. Finally, have students create a chart with the columns "Recession" and "Expansion," and list lesson terms and concepts in each column. Some terms will be used in both columns.

Text Evidence

Have students scan the lesson to find evidence in the text that shows the reasons why the Great Depression occurred. Sample evidence: An enormous gap in the distribution of income was one important cause. Poverty prevented workers from stimulating the economy by spending. The rich had the income but often used it for such nonproductive activities as stock market speculation. Easy credit also played a role. Many people borrowed heavily in the late 1920s to buy stocks. Then, as interest rates rose, it was difficult for them to repay their loans. . . .

LESSON 2 Inflation

Reading and Comprehension

Have students write a sentence that defines each of the following words: *inflation, stagflation,* and *hyperinflation.* Then have them write a paragraph that compares and contrasts the three terms. Finally, have students predict the effects of inflation on their own purchasing power by writing a report about how they will change their spending habits if inflation continues to rise.

Text Evidence

Have students find evidence in the text that shows the steps for calculating the Consumer Price Index. Sample evidence: The first step we have to take is to select a market basket. . . . The next step is to find the average price of each item in the market basket. To do so, every month, employees of the U.S. Census Bureau sample prices on nearly 80,000 items in stores across the country. They then add up the prices to find the total cost of the market basket. . . . The last step in the process is to make the numbers in the table easier to interpret by converting the dollar cost of a market basket to an index value. This is done by dividing the cost of every market basket by the base-year market basket cost.

LESSON 3 Unemployment

Reading and Comprehension

Have students explain the difference between underemployment and unemployment. Have students think of mnemonic devices to help them remember the various kinds of unemployment.

Text Evidence

Have students find evidence in the text that shows who is included in unemployment records. Sample evidence: In the middle of any given month, about 1,500 specialists from the Bureau of the Census begin their monthly survey of about 60,000 households in nearly 2,000 counties, covering all 50 states. Census workers are looking for the unemployed—people available for work who made a specific effort to find a job during the past month and who, during the most recent survey week, worked less than one hour for pay or profit. People are also classified as unemployed if they worked in a family business without pay for less than fifteen hours a week.

Online Resources

Assessing Background Knowledge Use this worksheet to pre-assess students' background knowledge before they start the chapter.

Chapter Summaries Have students use the summary as a pre-reading activity or as a post-reading review to check the main ideas covered in each lesson.

Guided Reading Activities Have students complete these activities as they read each lesson. They provide reading notes the student can use for review and to prepare for assessments.

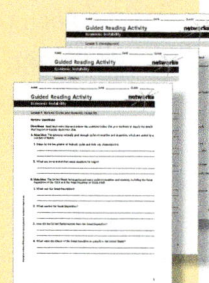

Reteaching Activities Have students complete the Reteaching Activity for remedial practice and review of vital content.

Self-Check Quizzes These quizzes provide instant feedback on areas the students may need to re-read to understand a main idea.

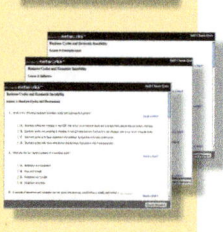

Reading Essentials and Study Guide This resource offers writing and reading activities for the approaching-level student.

Approaching Grade Level Reader This reader presents all of the content of the Online Student Edition but at a lower reading level.

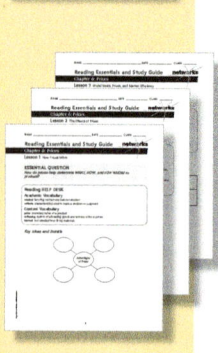

English Language Learner Reader Provide additional reading support for ELL students. Find this tool online.

Economic Instability

ESSENTIAL QUESTION
What are the causes and consequences of instability in the economy?

networks
www.connected.mcgraw-hill.com
There's More Online about economic instability.

CHAPTER 13

Economic Perspectives
What Is an Economic Bubble?

Lesson 1
Business Cycles and Economic Instability

Lesson 2
Inflation

Lesson 3
Unemployment

CHAPTER 13
Economic Instability

ENGAGE

Call students' attention to the photo and ask them to describe what it shows. Guide them to recognize that a previously unemployed person has obtained a new position. **Ask: Why might this image be used on the chapter titled *Economic Instability*?** *(Economic instability is caused by changes in spending, innovations, external shocks, and changes in government policy. In this instance, a person who was laid off during a time of economic instability has obtained a new job.)* Have students create a one-page dialogue between the two people in the photo that uses the theme of causes and consequences of economic instability.

Understanding the effects of instability

Have students create a chart with three headings: Government, Community, and Family. Then have them brainstorm a list of the general effects of economic on each of these three categories. In a discussion, lead students to understand that a number of factors contribute to economic instability, at the government level as well as at the consumer level.

Making Connections

Local Instability Have students write a paragraph describing how economic instability has affected a person or business in their community. Then ask them to identify what they think caused the instability.

Go to the Foldables® library for a cumulative chapter-based Foldable® activity that your students can use to help take notes and prepare for assessment.

Letter from the Author

Dear Economics Teacher,

The consequences of economic instability are among the most painful we experience. The problems usually start small, with prices rising faster than incomes, or businesses that cut back on the number of hours employees work. Little problems can then turn into bigger ones, like periods of high inflation, or weeks and months of unemployment. This hits us right in the pocketbook and eventually causes problems for everyone in the family. Economists don't know how to prevent all of these problems, but it helps to know how small problems start, and it helps to know what we can do about them.

Gary E. Clayton

CHAPTER 13
Economic Perspectives

TEACH & ASSESS

R Reading Skills

Identifying economic terms Ask: **What is an IPO?** *(Initial Public Offering, or the first sales of stock in a company)* **Why did investors rush to fund start-up technology companies, even those without realistic potential for profits?** *(Investors saw the Internet as a golden opportunity to reach consumers through networks; they did not consider how the networks would generate cash flow.)*
Verbal/Linguistic

V Visual Skills

Diagramming consequences of instability Have students create a cause-and-effect diagram showing the downward economic spiral caused by the dot.com and housing bubbles. Have students begin with "economic uncertainty," followed by actions and non-actions that resulted from that. *(Sample responses: decline in consumer purchases, reduced production, lost jobs, higher unemployment, decrease in tax revenues, government spends less on schools and roads, and so on)*
ELL Verbal/Linguistic

Economic Perspectives

WHAT IS AN ECONOMIC BUBBLE?

The Online Gold Rush: The Dot-Com Bubble of 2000

WHO?
Investors wanted to get in on the ground floor of a new market: the Internet. They bought stock in unproven companies --- often for inflated prices they only considered because they hoped for higher returns on their investments.

WHAT?

$5 Trillion

R Tech and Internet start-up companies multiplied as the Internet's scope expanded. Start-ups sold stock to the public (at inflated share prices) through initial public offerings (IPOs) to capitalize on investor demand and maximize profit.

WHEN?
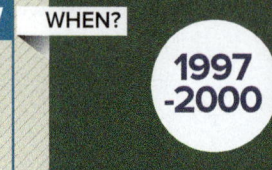
1997-2000

The Dot-Com Bubble expanded in the late 1990s and burst in early 2000 when the value of Internet stocks plunged. This was a catalyst for the 2000 stock market crash that ultimately cost investors nearly $5 trillion and precipitated the 2001 recession.

WHY?
Despite the fact that many start-ups didn't have business plans, earnings, or even realistic potential for profit, investors rushed to fund them because they saw the Internet as a golden opportunity.

HOW?

Analysts focused on the reach Internet companies had through their online networks, instead of scrutinizing how those networks would generate cash flow. Many greatly over-valued the stock of Internet start-ups when they calculated earnings models.

---

networks *Online Teaching Options*

INFOGRAPHIC

Economic Perspectives: What Is an Economic Bubble?

Tracing economic instability through bubbles
Have students explore the infographic. Then have them discuss the question, "What do you think was the single largest cause of the housing bubble?" using words from the infographic to describe their opinion.
Verbal/Linguistic

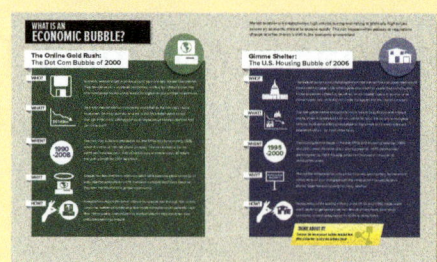

364

CHAPTER 13
Economic Perspectives

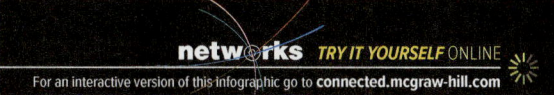

Market bubbles are created when high-volume buying and selling at artificially high prices causes an economic market to expand rapidly. This can happen when policies or regulations change or when there's a shift in the economic environment.

Gimme Shelter:
The U.S. Housing Bubble of 2006

WHO?  The federal government passed legislation that relaxed financial sector restrictions. Banks and mortgage underwriters gave easy credit to unqualified home buyers. Home appraisers inflated home values, which caused buyers to borrow more. Home buyers took on introductory-rate mortgages that they could not repay.

WHAT?  The real estate market ballooned as more people bought homes at inflated prices. When foreclosures hit an unsustainable level, the subprime mortgage industry (institutions offering mortgages to higher-risk borrowers) collapsed catastrophically --- i.e., the bubble burst.

WHEN?  **1995-2008** The housing bubble began in the late 1990s and expanded between 2000 and 2005, when the demand for housing grew. By 2007, demand was declining and by 2008, housing prices had dropped in 24 out of 25 metropolitan areas.

WHY? 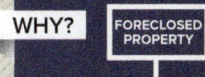 The market stalled and housing prices dropped, leaving many homeowners owing more on their mortgage than the value of their house (negative equity). Sales fell and housing inventory piled up.

HOW?  Deregulation of the lending industry in the 1980s and 1990s made credit much easier to get (sometimes with little down payment), even when borrowers couldn't demonstrate an ability to repay loans.

THINK ABOUT IT!
Compare the two economic bubbles detailed here. What similarities can you find between them?

Economic Instability

C1 Critical Thinking Skills

Sequencing the dot.com and housing bubbles Have students read and discuss the text on the Economic Perspectives feature. Then ask them to sequence the events on a time line. Have them place the economic events above the time line. Underneath the time line, ask students to add *political* and *social* events that help put the economic events in context. **BL** Verbal/Linguistic

C2 Critical Thinking Skills

Proposing solutions for the future Ask students to write letters to their representatives in Congress describing possible solutions to prevent another Great Recession. Have volunteers read their letters aloud. Discuss the various solutions the students identified. **BL** Verbal/Linguistic

CLOSE & REFLECT

Have students answer the *Think About It!* questions.

WORKSHEET

Reinforcing Economic Skills

Identifying cause and effect Have students read and discuss the text on the Reinforcing Economic Skills worksheet, which analyzes five causes and effects of the Great Recession of 2008. Students will look for logical relationships between events, and then complete a table by listing five effects mentioned in the excerpt, and identifying the cause of each. Verbal/Linguistic

ANSWERS, p. 365

THINK ABOUT IT!

Both had a high volume of buying and selling at artificially high prices.

CHAPTER 13, LESSON 1
Business Cycles and Economic Instability

ENGAGE

Visual Skills

 Visualizing the business cycle Before students begin the lesson, draw a wavy line (to represent the business cycle) on the board. Ask volunteers to come to the board and write these terms in the appropriates places on the line: peak/boom, trough, expansion/recovery, contraction/recession. Correct any errors, and ask students to draw the labeled diagram in their notes.

English Language Proficiency

Advanced As students read Lesson 1, with its increasingly complex English, teach students to use a Cornell Notes graphic organizer. Tell them to follow these procedures: (1) As they read, write key terms and main ideas in a right-hand column headed *Notes*. (2) After they read, write questions about the notes in a left-hand column headed *Questions*. (3) Cover the notes and quiz a partner about the questions. (4) Use the notes to write a summary in a bottom-channel column headed *Summary*.

ANSWERS, p. 366

ESSENTIAL QUESTION ACTIVITY

Students may write that a parent might fear losing a job; that, during a downturn, groceries might be more expensive and that the family might have to start buying cheaper or generic-brand items; that allowances might be cut; or that family vacations might be scaled back. If the student lives in a family that owns a business, he or she might indicate that his or her parents might feel compelled to institute layoffs or hiring freezes during downturns. The student may also indicate that unpredictability, in general, may compel a family to preemptively save for the lean times.

TAKING NOTES
Social Security
Minimum wage
Unemployment programs
Securities and exchange commission
Federal deposit insurance corporation

366

Interact with these digital assets and others in lesson 1
✓ INTERACTIVE GRAPH Business Cycles
✓ SLIDESHOW The Great Depression
✓ SELF-CHECK QUIZ
✓ VIDEO

netw⊙rks
TRY IT YOURSELF ONLINE

LESSON 1
Business Cycles and Economic Instability

Reading Help Desk

Academic Vocabulary
- series

Content Vocabulary
- business cycles
- business fluctuations
- recession
- peak
- trough
- expansion
- trend line
- depression
- depression scrip
- leading economic indicator
- Dow-Jones Industrial Average (DJIA)
- leading economic index (LEI)
- econometric model

TAKING NOTES:

Key Ideas and Details
ACTIVITY Use a graphic organizer like the one below to identify steps the government took after the Great Depression to help avoid another severe downturn.

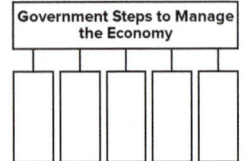
Government Steps to Manage the Economy

ESSENTIAL QUESTION

What are the causes and consequences of instability in the economy?

Our economy is in a constant state of flux. Stock prices go up and down. Unemployment rises and falls. Even worse, sometimes these events take steep dives or go into prolonged downturns that go on for months or longer, and no one seems to know how much longer these events will continue. The economy appears unpredictable and characterized by instability.

Think about the causes and consequences of unpredictability in the economy. What are three ways that this unpredictability affects you and your family personally, on a day-to-day basis?

Business Cycles: Characteristics and Causes

GUIDING QUESTION *Why are ups and downs in the business cycle normal?*

Economic growth is something that is beneficial to almost everyone, but we cannot take it for granted. Sometimes **business cycles**—regular ups and downs of real GDP—interrupt economic growth. **Business fluctuations**—the rise and fall of real GDP over time in an irregular manner—interrupt growth at other times. We can describe the basic features of an expansion or a recession, or the "phases of the business cycle," as they are sometimes called. When it comes to identifying the actual causes, though, no one theory seems to explain all past events or predict future ones, because each seems to be a little different from the last.

366

---

netw⊙rks Online Teaching Options

BELLRINGER

Economic Instability

Describing economic bubbles Have students view the Bellringer and read the questions. **Ask: What do you think causes a bubble in an industry?** *(Sample answer: artificially inflated prices that suddenly become lower)* Have students name an example of an industry that has experienced a bubble in recent years and discuss how it happened.

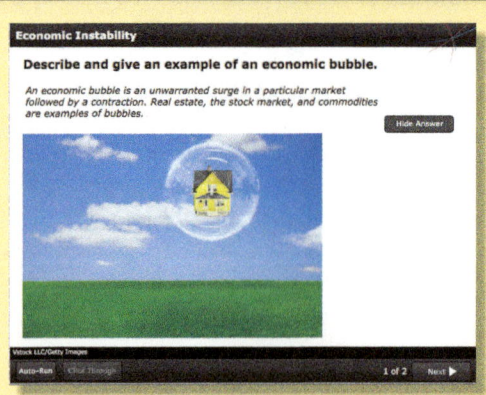

Phases of the Business Cycle

A business cycle has two distinct phases, both of which are discussed below and illustrated in **Figure 13.1**.

- **Recession**—The first phase is **recession**, a period during which real GDP—GDP measured in constant prices—declines for at least two quarters in a row, or six consecutive months. The recession begins when the economy reaches a **peak**—the point where real GDP stops going up. It ends when the economy reaches a **trough**—the turnaround point where real GDP stops going down.
- **Expansion**—When the declining real GDP bottoms out, the economy moves into the second phase, called **expansion**—a period of recovery from a recession that involves increased real GDP, industrial production, real income, and employment lasting several years or more. Expansion continues until the economy reaches a new peak. When it does, the current business cycle ends and a new one begins.

If periods of recession and expansion did not occur, the economy would follow a steady growth path called a **trend line**. As Figure 13.1 shows, the economy departs from, and then returns to, its trend line as it passes through phases of recession and expansion. To make it easier to read, recessions in figures such as this are usually shaded to separate them from periods of expansion.

If a recession becomes very severe, it may turn into a **depression**—a state of the economy with large numbers of people out of work, acute shortages, and excess capacity in manufacturing plants. Most experts agree that the Great Depression of the 1930s was the only depression the United States experienced during the twentieth century.

Causes of the Business Cycle

A business cycle begins when the economy reaches a peak and begins to slide into a recession. The question, then, is what stops the economy from growing and turns an expansion into a contraction? Economists have offered several possible causes.

business cycles systematic changes in real GDP marked by alternating periods of expansion and contraction

business fluctuations changes in real GDP marked by alternating periods of expansion and contraction that occur on an irregular basis

recession decline in real GDP lasting at least two quarters or more

peak point in time when real GDP stops expanding and begins to decline

trough point in time when real GDP stops declining and begins to expand

expansion period of uninterrupted growth of real GDP, industrial production, real income, and employment lasting for several years or more; recovery from recession

trend line growth path the economy would follow if it were not interrupted by alternating periods of recession and recovery

depression state of the economy with large numbers of unemployed, declining real incomes, overcapacity in manufacturing plants, and general economic hardship

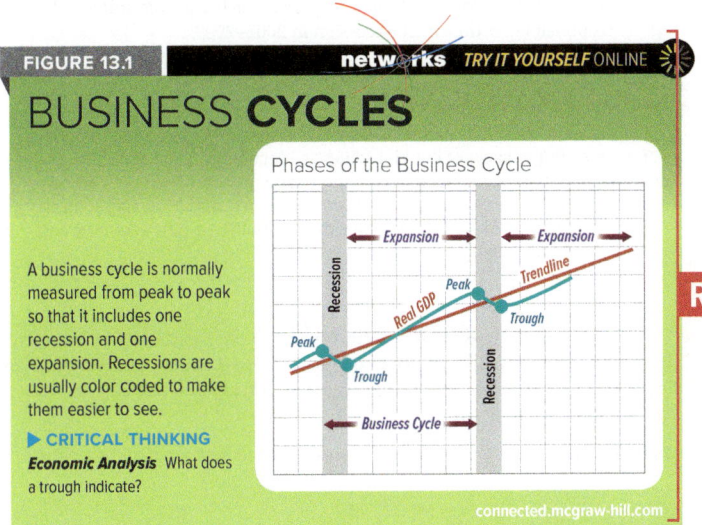

FIGURE 13.1 BUSINESS CYCLES

A business cycle is normally measured from peak to peak so that it includes one recession and one expansion. Recessions are usually color coded to make them easier to see.

▶ **CRITICAL THINKING**
Economic Analysis What does a trough indicate?

Economic Instability 367

CHAPTER 13, LESSON 1
Business Cycles and Economic Instability

TEACH & ASSESS

W Writing Skills

Describing the effects of a downturn Remind students that during a recession, people may lose their jobs. Newly unemployed people must conserve their resources—this means that they spend much less than when they were employed. When spending does not take a place, a chain reaction is set off that affects the whole economy. Ask students to write a short paragraph describing the chain reaction that is set off when a large factory is closed in a small town, throwing hundreds of people out of work. **Verbal/Linguistic**

R Reading Skills

Understanding business cycle terms Have students look at the Business Cycle graph.
Ask: Where is real GDP in relation to the trend line after a recession? *(below the trend line)* What is the name of the phase when GDP is rising? *(expansion)* What are the positives and negatives for people when the economy hits a trough? *(Negatives: the economy has reached a low point, people experience hard times; Positives: GDP has stopped falling, recovery will soon follow)*
Verbal/Linguistic

GRAPHS

Business Cycles

Analyzing business cycles Have students look at Figure 13.1 showing the rise and fall of the business cycle. Point out the words that describe the parts of the cycle. Have students write the words down and define them.
Ask: As you look at the graph, how would you describe a trough? *(Sample answer: A trough occurs when the GDP stops declining and starts to increase again.)* Have students answer the question on the activity. Then have them write a paragraph describing the entire business cycle, using the words that they defined at the beginning of the activity.

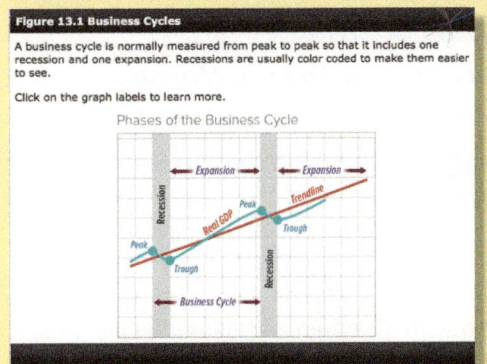

ANSWERS, p. 367

CRITICAL THINKING
A trough indicates that real GDP has stopped declining and has begun to increase.

CHAPTER 13, LESSON 1
Business Cycles and Economic Instability

C Critical Thinking Skills

Recognizing causes of business cycles Have students create a two-column chart, and ask them to list the causes of business cycles in the left column. Then have them do research online to find examples of stories in the news that exemplify each cause. Students should place the news headlines in the right side of the chart next to the appropriate cause. Examples of economics headlines may include: "Unemployment is up," "Consumer confidence is down," "President proposes jobs package," "Congress seeks tax cut," "New housing starts are down," "The Fed raises key interest rates," "U.S. stocks drop after Fed action," and so on. **Visual/Spatial**

V Visual Skills

Illustrating business cycle causes Have students create a collage about one or more of the causes of the business cycle. Collage items might include photos of a factory or government shutdown that affects workers, images of foreclosure signs on homes, a map of a war in the Middle East, and so on. **ELL Visual/Spatial**

- **External shocks**—One potential cause of business cycles is external shocks, such as an increase in oil prices, wars, or international conflicts. Some shocks drive the economy up, as when Great Britain discovered North Sea oil in the 1970s. Other shocks can be negative, as when high oil prices hit the United States in mid-2005. Either way, the shocks may temporarily knock the economy off its long-term growth trend.
- **Changes in investment spending**—Changes in capital expenditures are also important. When the economy is expanding, businesses expect future sales to be high, so companies may build new plants or buy new equipment to replace older equipment. At first, this generates jobs and income, but after a while, businesses may decide they have expanded enough. If they then cut back on their capital investments, layoffs and eventually recession may result.
- **Changes in monetary policy**—Some economists point to the Federal Reserve System's policies on interest rates. For example, loans are easy to get when "easy money" policies—Fed policies that promote low interest rates—are in effect. Easy money encourages the private sector to borrow and invest, which stimulates the economy for a short time. When the stimulus stops, however, the economy stops growing and recession sets in.
- **Fiscal-policy shocks**—Fiscal policy, the use of federal government spending and revenue-collection measures, have also been blamed. If a change in either spending or taxation suddenly occurs, it may affect decisions somewhere else in the economy. For example, threats by elected officials to shut down government because of policies they disagree with may cause uncertainty and worry in other parts of the economy.
- **Speculation and "bubbles"**—Expectations about the future have always been important. Speculation over the expected profitability of Internet stocks in 2000 became known as the "dot-com bubble." When the bubble burst, the stock market crashed and the economy went into a mild recession in 2001. The bursting of the subsequent housing bubble in 2006–2007 negatively affected consumer buying power and was largely responsible for the Great Recession in 2008–2009.

> **EXPLORING THE ESSENTIAL QUESTION**
>
> Many events, such as speculation on the value of stocks or even the bursting of the housing or Internet bubbles, directly affect only a limited number of people, but indirectly affect others in the economy, sort of like how dropping a rock into a pond sends ripples far beyond the drop point. How might these isolated economic events send ripples throughout the entire economy and bring about recessions?

Finally, in many cases, several factors seem to work together to create a cycle. In these situations, a disturbance in one part of the economy seems to have an impact somewhere else, causing an expansion to begin or a recession to end.

☑ **READING PROGRESS CHECK**

Summarizing What are thought to be the causes of business cycles?

368

---

networks Online Teaching Options

GRAPHIC ORGANIZER

Government Steps to Manage the Economy

Analyzing steps taken after the Great Depression Have students read about the stock market crash and the steps the government took to ensure that it would not happen again. Then have them fill in the graphic organizer with the five steps the government took after the Great Depression. *(Social Security, minimum wage, unemployment programs, Securities and Exchange Commission, Federal Deposit Insurance Corporation)* Finally, have them choose one of the steps to research, writing a short report about the step's history, how it helped economic stability, its costs, and how it is used now. **Verbal/Linguistic**

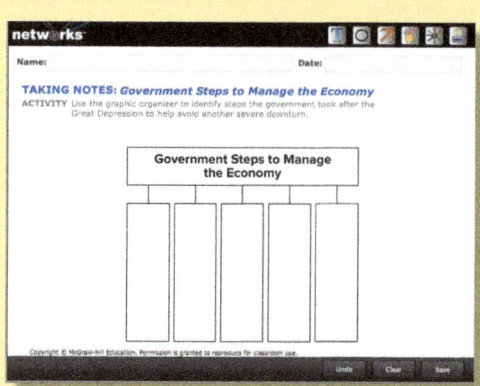

ANSWERS, p. 368

EXPLORING THE ESSENTIAL QUESTION

Students should recognize that all parts of the economy are linked and that changes to one sector will affect other sectors. They should provide concrete examples, such as how lower stock prices may influence a corporation's nationwide hiring and firing policies and thus how unemployment could influence a family's day-to-day activities. Students may also recognize how these events influence consumer confidence and how that affects the economy.

☑ **READING PROGRESS CHECK** External shocks, changes in investment spending, changes in monetary policy, fiscal policy shocks, and speculation bubbles

This front page shows some of the reaction to the stock market crash, known as "Black Tuesday," that marked the beginning of the Great Depression, the worst economic downturn in American history.

◀ CRITICAL THINKING
Summarizing What impact did the Great Depression have on the United States?

Business Cycles in the United States

GUIDING QUESTION *How did the Great Depression change the role of government in the economy?*

Economic activity in the United States followed an irregular course throughout the twentieth century. The worst downturn was the Great Depression of the 1930s. Business cycles have been milder since then, but they are still important.

The Great Depression

The stock market crash on October 29, 1929, known as "Black Tuesday," marked the beginning of the Great Depression, one of the darkest periods in American history. Between 1929 and 1933, real GDP declined nearly 50 percent, from approximately $103 billion to $55 billion. At the same time, the number of people out of work rose nearly 800 percent—from 1.6 million to 12.8 million. During the Depression's worst years, one out of every four workers was unemployed. Even workers with jobs suffered. The average manufacturing wage, which was 55 cents an hour in 1929, plunged to 5 cents an hour by 1933.

Many banks across the country failed. Federal bank-deposit insurance did not exist at the time, so depositors were not protected. To slow panic withdrawals, the federal government declared a "bank holiday" in March 1933 and closed every bank in the country. The closure lasted for only a few days, but about one-quarter of the banks never reopened.

The Federal Reserve System allowed the size of the money supply to fall by about one-third. Official paper currency was in such short supply that people began using **depression scrip**—unofficial currency that towns, counties, chambers of commerce, and other civic bodies issued. Billions of dollars of this scrip were used to pay salaries for teachers, firefighters, police officers, and other municipal employees.

depression scrip currency issued by towns, chambers of commerce, and other civic bodies during the Great Depression of the 1930s

Causes of the Great Depression

An enormous gap in the distribution of income was one important cause. Poverty prevented workers from stimulating the economy by spending. The rich had the income but often used it for such nonproductive activities as stock market speculation.

CHAPTER 13, LESSON 1
Business Cycles and Economic Instability

W Writing Skills

Summarizing the stock market crash and its effects
Have students write a summary of what happened the day the stock market crashed in 1929 and how the relationship between the American public and the government changed after the crash. Or have students consult historical sources to research how the stock market crash affected individuals on "Black Tuesday." Students may research a broker, a stockholder, the manager of a publicly held firm, or a vendor on Wall Street. **Verbal/Linguistic**

C Critical Thinking Skills

Applying the effects of the Great Depression
Have students calculate how their weekly income (from allowance or work) would change if it fell by the same rate that manufacturing wages dropped between 1929 and 1933. **Ask: How would you economize if this happened to you?** *(Possible answers: cut back on entertainment expenses; ride a bicycle instead of drive)* **Logical/Mathematical**

SLIDE SHOW

Great Depression

Writing a narrative about the Great Depression
Have students view the Great Depression slide show. As they view the slides, ask a volunteer to read aloud the captions for each slide. Have students take notes on the slides. Then have students write a journal entry describing the day that one of the people in front of the bank could not get his or her life savings out of the bank. Have students describe that person's feelings and the economic impact on that person's life.

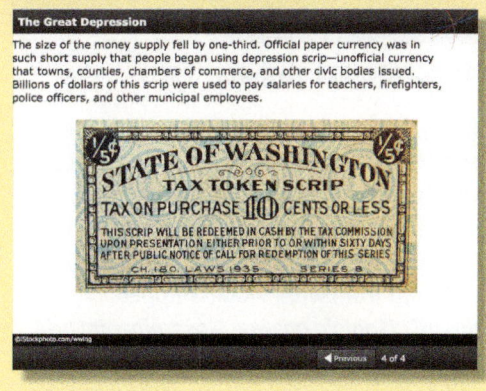

ANSWERS, p. 369

CRITICAL THINKING
Answers include massive unemployment, a 50 percent drop in GDP, and substantial, long-lasting government programs to ease suffering and bring greater stability to the economy.

CHAPTER 13, LESSON 1
Business Cycles and Economic Instability

R Reading Skills

Researching Social Security Have students go online to research how the Social Security program works, who it benefits, and challenges it faces. Explain that some government officials have proposed privatizing and/or dismantling Social Security. Have students research reasons for these proposals, and then moderate a class debate on whether Social Security has outlived its purpose.

Content Background Knowledge

Monetary Policy and the Great Depression

Monetarists view the Great Depression differently from Keynesian economists. Monetarists do not deny that a lack of business investment in the early 1930s reduced aggregate demand. However, they feel that the fall in aggregate demand resulted from the reduced amount of money in circulation. According to monetarists, the Fed should have greatly increased the amount of money in the economy. Instead, the steps taken by the Fed cut the money supply by one-third between 1929 and 1933. By its actions, the monetarists claim, the Fed turned what would have been just another recession into an economic disaster.

Because of the Great Depression, millions of American workers were unemployed. The federal government stepped in to provide work programs and financial support to both employ labor and to provide money to stimulate the economy.

▶ **CRITICAL THINKING**
Was it the influence of the federal government's stimulus efforts that helped to end the Great Depression?

Easy credit also played a role. Many people borrowed heavily in the late 1920s to buy stocks. Then, as interest rates rose, it was difficult for them to repay their loans. When the crunch came, heavily indebted people had nothing to fall back on.

Global economic conditions also played a part. During the 1920s, the United States made many loans to foreign countries to help support international trade. When these loans suddenly were harder to get, foreign buyers purchased fewer American goods, and U.S. exports fell sharply.

International trade wars intensified the deteriorating situation. The U.S. put high tariffs, or fees, on foreign goods coming into the U.S. to protect domestic jobs. Foreign countries then retaliated by putting high tariffs on the goods we sold to them, which hurt manufacturing jobs in our industries.

Recovery and Legislative Reform

The Great Depression finally ended ten years after it started, when real GDP returned to its 1929 high. The economy recovered partly because of increased government spending and partly on its own. The massive spending during World War II added another huge stimulant that further propelled the economy after 1940.

The country was so shaken by the Great Depression that a number of reforms were established from 1933 to 1940 both to protect people and to prevent another such disaster. While all of the changes are too numerous to mention, here are some of the more important ones:

- **Social Security**—The Social Security Act was passed in 1935 as a way to help people provide for their own retirement.
- **Minimum wage**—The minimum wage, originally set at 25 cents an hour in 1938, was designed to guarantee most workers a minimum hourly wage.
- **Unemployment programs**—Several new unemployment programs gave relief to people who were temporarily out of work.
- **Securities and Exchange Commission (SEC)**—In 1934, the SEC was created to require companies that offered securities for sale to fully disclose the truth about their business, the securities they were selling,

370

networks *Online Teaching Options*

VIDEO   WORKSHEETS

Stock Market Crash

Analyzing the Stock Market Have students watch the Stock Market Crash video. Discuss whether they think the same thing could happen again today. **Ask: What makes the results of the stock market crash of 1929 different from what would happen today?** *(Sample answer: Governmental programs are in place to protect bank deposits, provide for retirement, and provide some funding for the unemployed.)* Then have students answer the questions on the worksheet.

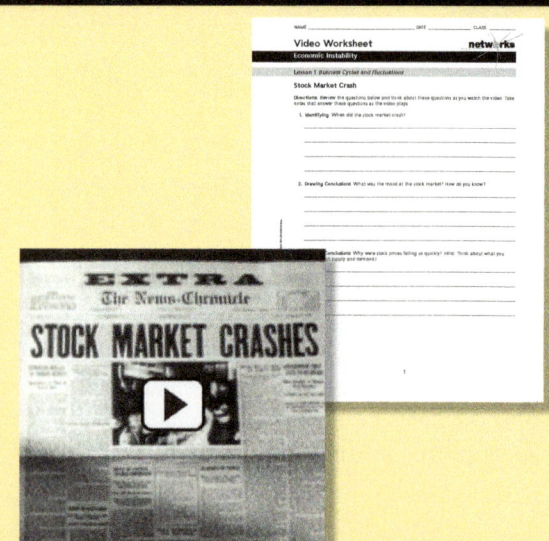

ANSWERS, p. 370

CRITICAL THINKING
The economy recovered partly because of government stimulus efforts, but mostly it recovered because of the massive spending during World War II.

and the risks involved in investing. The SEC regulated securities markets and made stock ownership by the public much safer.
- **Federal Deposit Insurance Corporation (FDIC)**—The FDIC was created to provide modest bank insurance for depositors in 1933. Such safeguards were not available during the Great Depression, when many banks failed and depositors lost their life savings.

In all, the period from 1933 to 1940 saw the establishment of many federal regulations and institutions to make working, banking, investing, and retirement safer. The reforms of the 1930s seemed to help, and most economists today think that they provide enough stimulus and protection to make another Great Depression unlikely.

Business Cycles after World War II
Business cycles became much more moderate after World War II, with shorter recessions and longer periods of expansion. During this time, the average length of recessions was about ten months, while expansions averaged about fifty-four months.

After the early 1980s, recessions occurred less frequently. A record-setting peacetime expansion during the Reagan administration began in November 1982 and lasted for almost eight years. That was followed by a longer, and even more prosperous, expansion during the Clinton years from 1991 to 2001. In fact, this period of uninterrupted economic growth is the longest peacetime expansion in U.S. history.

Aside from a very brief and mild recession in 2001, our most recent recession began with the housing market collapse that began in 2007.

The Great Recession of 2008–2009
The Great Recession of 2008–2009 started in December of 2007 and lasted until June of 2009. With a duration of 18 months, it was the longest and deepest recession in the United States since the Great Depression of the 1930s. Real GDP dropped about 4.5 percent during this period and did not recover its 2007 high until mid-2011, nearly four years later.

The impact on workers was perhaps the most devastating of all, with the percentage of working people who were unemployed more than doubling between October 2007 and October 2009. By a different measure, more than 8,159,000 people lost their jobs over the same two-year period. Finally, while the economy added a few thousand jobs every month after the recovery began, it took almost six and a half years before the total number of people employed in December 2007 was reached.

During the Great Depression, as the economy failed many banks across the country also failed. Crowds gathered outside of banks to get their deposits before it all disappeared. Since then the Federal Deposit Insurance Corporation was created to safeguard more of people's money.

BIOGRAPHY

Irene Rosenfeld
ENTREPRENEUR (1953–)

Irene Rosenfeld was appointed the CEO of Kraft Foods in 2006. At the time, Kraft Foods was the second-largest food company in the world and was in a difficult economic position. Rosenfeld inherited a company that had just undergone years of cost-cutting and reorganizations. As CEO, Rosenfeld championed a focus on customers and product innovation.

While in college, Rosenfeld studied consumer behavior. She first joined Kraft as a market research manager and used that knowledge base to shape her directives for change while leading Kraft Foods. In 2012 Kraft divided into two separate companies. Kraft Foods was focused on the North American grocery store market and a new globally-focused snack division named Mondelez was created. Rosenfeld was chosen to lead Mondelez and grow the global sales even higher. Her immediate goals were to focus more effort in growing the snack brand in the emerging markets of Brazil, Russia, India, and China.

Rosenfeld earned her doctorate, her Master of Science, and her bachelor's degree from Cornell University in New York.

▲ **CRITICAL THINKING**
Drawing Conclusions Why do you think it was helpful for Rosenfeld to apply her studies in consumer behavior to a company such as Kraft Foods?

CHAPTER 13, LESSON 1
Business Cycles and Economic Instability

C Critical Thinking Skills

Understanding the FDIC Have students visit www.fdic.gov to find out the basic insurance coverage provided by the FDIC on deposits. Ask students to speculate on whether the amount of insurance is enough for today and whether it would have made a difference in the 1930s. **Ask: How does the FDIC reduce the possibility of runs on banks?** *(People know that even if their bank fails, the government will give them a certain amount of their money back.)*

Making Connections

Easy Credit and the Great Recession Easy credit played a role in causing both the Great Depression and the Great Recession. For example, in 2007 the mortgage securities market fell into crisis. The housing market slumped. Combined with loan delinquencies from borrowers with poor credit ratings, this slump caused more than two dozen mortgage lenders to go bankrupt. These bankruptcies in turn dragged the housing market down further and helped cause the 2008–2009 recession. Have students calculate monthly mortgage payments on a $100,000 30-year loan at 6.125 percent interest. *($607.61)* Next have students calculate monthly mortgage payments on a $100,000 15-year loan at 5.5 percent interest. *($817.08)*
Ask: What are the advantages and disadvantages of each type of loan? *(The monthly payments on the 30-year loan are lower, but the total financing costs will be greater over the duration of the loan. The monthly payments on the 15-year loan are higher, but the total financing charge will be lower because the loan will be paid off much faster.)*

BIOGRAPHY
Biography: Irene Rosenfeld

Analyzing business policies Have students read the biography of Irene Rosenfeld, and discuss her focus on customers. Have them consider how her ideas are especially relevant during times of economic instability. *(Students should note that during recessions, consumers reduce purchases. The competition for limited consumer dollars is fierce.)* Then ask students to describe how Kraft snack foods (the Mondelez brand) may need to be adjusted for markets in Brazil, Russia, India, and China.

ANSWERS, p. 371

CRITICAL THINKING
Because of the nature of Kraft's consumer-targeted food products, having a sense of the consumer should be valuable in determining what types of products to produce.

CHAPTER 13, LESSON 1
Business Cycles and Economic Instability

W1 Writing Skills

Writing letters to the editor Have students write a letter to the editor of a newspaper, describing how economic instability has affected their community, and making a suggestion for how to improve the local economy for people who are suffering the most.

Content Background Knowledge

Major Economic Indicators Discuss with students the 10 individual leading indicators that make up the LEI. These include:

1. Average weekly hours for production workers in manufacturing
2. Weekly initial claims for unemployment insurance
3. New orders for consumer goods
4. Speed with which companies make deliveries (the busier a company, the longer it will take to fill orders)
5. Number of contracts and orders for plants and equipment
6. Number of building permits issued for private housing units
7. Stock prices as measured by the S&P Index
8. Changes in money supply in circulation
9. Changes in interest rates
10. Changes in consumer expectations

W2 Writing Skills

Applying knowledge of economic predictions Have students research other statistics that predict changes in GDP. Then have them write a one-page essay explaining why economists consider those statistics to be important factors in determining the future state of the economy.

ANSWERS, p. 372

✓ READING PROGRESS CHECK Answers include massive unemployment, a 50 percent drop in GDP, and substantial, long-lasting government programs to ease suffering and bring greater stability to the economy.

CRITICAL THINKING
If the LEI peaks, or begins to turn down while the economy is still growing, economists think that a recession may begin sometime in the next three to fifteen months.

W1 The devastation of the recession extends well beyond the percentage of people unemployed or the number of people working. Many people who lost their jobs after October 2007 also lost their houses and their cars when they couldn't make their monthly payments. Others were forced to use their retirement savings or went even further into debt just to cover everyday living expenses.

The economic havoc wrought by the Great Recession of 2008–2009 served as a harsh reminder of how seemingly small changes in the economy can have a painful, widespread impact.

✓ READING PROGRESS CHECK

Inferring What impact did the Great Depression have on the United States?

Predicting the Next Business Cycle

GUIDING QUESTION *How do leading economic indicators help us predict downturns and upturns in the economy?*

series group of related things or events

Economists use several methods to predict business cycles. Some use the statistical **series** known as the leading economic index. Others make use of a tool called econometric modeling.

leading economic indicator statistical series that normally turns down before the economy turns down or turns up before the economy turns up

W2 **Using Leading Economic Indicators**

A change in a single statistic often indicates a change in future GDP. For example, the length of the average workweek may change just before a recession begins if people work fewer hours. This makes the measure a **leading economic indicator**—a statistical series that normally changes direction before the economy changes its direction.

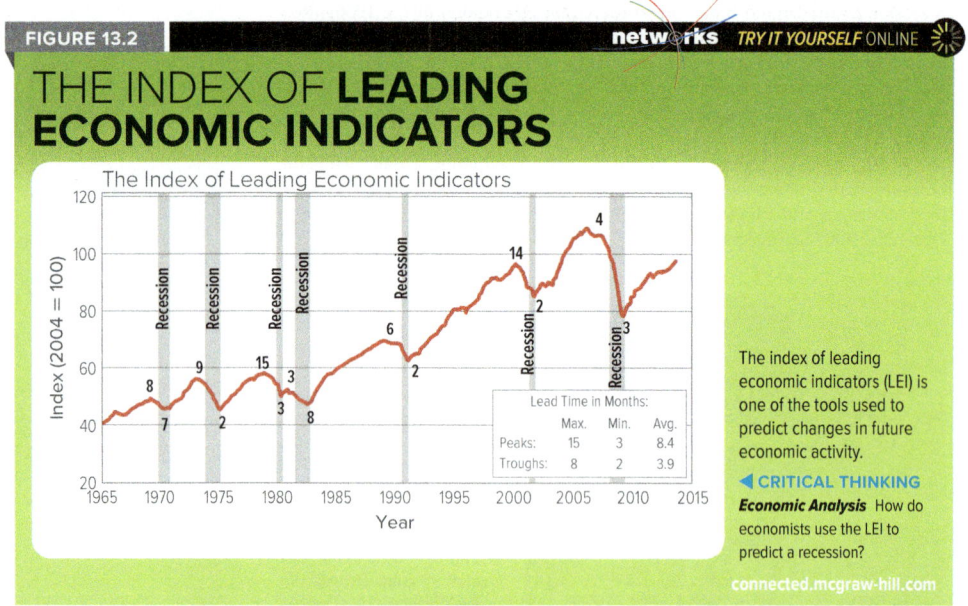

FIGURE 13.2 THE INDEX OF LEADING ECONOMIC INDICATORS

The index of leading economic indicators (LEI) is one of the tools used to predict changes in future economic activity.

◀ **CRITICAL THINKING**
Economic Analysis How do economists use the LEI to predict a recession?

---

networks Online Teaching Options

GRAPHS

Index of Leading Economic Indicators

Analyzing the index of leading economic indicators Have students explore Figure 13.2, clicking to reveal the peaks and troughs for each time period. Then have them write a definition for the terms *leading economic indicator* and *leading economic index (LEI)*. **Ask:** How do economists use the LEI to predict a recession? *(Sample answer: If the LEI peaks, or begins to turn down while the economy is still growing, economists think that a recession may begin sometime in the next three to fifteen months.)*

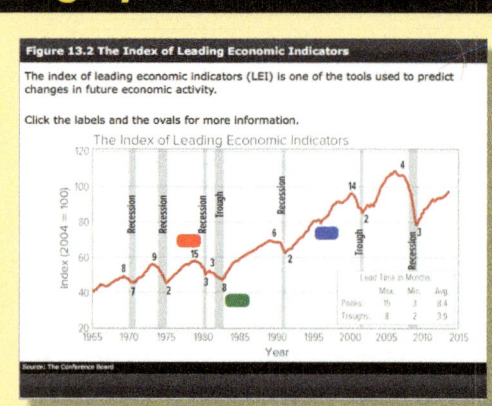

One such leading indicator is the **Dow Jones Industrial Average (DJIA)**, a statistical series of 30 stock prices that represents daily changes of all stocks in major markets. The DJIA did a fairly good job predicting the last two recessions, but did not do quite as well before that. Because no single series has proven completely reliable, economists like to combine several individual series into an overall index. This is the approach used by the **leading economic index (LEI)**, a monthly statistical series that uses a combination of 10 individual indicators to forecast changes in real GDP and the general direction of the U.S. economy.

The LEI is shown in **Figure 13.2**. As you can see, the LEI turned down before each of the seven recessions shown in the figure. The average time between a dip in the index and the onset of a recession is about eight or nine months. However, the warning time for the Great Recession, perhaps because of its severity, was closer to 20 months.

Using Econometric Models

An **econometric model** is a mathematical model that uses algebraic equations to describe how the economy behaves. Most models start with an "output-expenditure" model:

$$GDP = C + I + G + (X - M)$$

To see how we use it, suppose that a survey of consumers (the C in the equation) revealed that households annually spend a fixed amount of money called **a**, along with 95 percent of their disposable personal income, or DPI. We could express this as $C = a + .95(DPI)$ and then substitute this equation into the output-expenditure model to get:

$$GDP = a + .95(DPI) + I + G + (X - M)$$

This process is repeated until each of the terms in the model is expanded and the equation is broken down into smaller and smaller components. To find GDP, forecasters put in the latest values for the variables on the right side of the equation and then solve for GDP.

Over time, actual changes in the economy are compared to the model's predictions. The model is then updated by changing some of the equations. In the end, some models give reasonably good forecasts for up to nine months into the future.

Dow Jones Industrial Average (DJIA) an index of 30 representative stocks used to monitor price changes in the overall stock market

leading economic index (LEI) monthly statistical series that uses a combination of ten individual indicators to forecast changes in real GDP

econometric model macroeconomic expression used to describe how the economy is expected to perform in the future

✓ **READING PROGRESS CHECK**
Analyzing Why are short-term econometric models more accurate than long-term models?

LESSON 1 REVIEW

Reviewing Vocabulary
1. *Identifying* What is the period between the peak and the trough of a business cycle called?

Using Your Notes
Refer to the graphic organizer at the beginning of the lesson to answer this question.
2. *Explaining* How does the Securities and Exchange Commission work to prevent a repeat of the Great Depression?

Answering the Guiding Questions
3. *Explaining* Why are ups and downs in the business cycle normal?

4. *Describing* How did the Great Depression change the role of government in the economy?
5. *Describing* How do leading economic indicators help us predict downturns and upturns in the economy?

Writing About Economics
6. *Argument* The Great Depression led to many reforms to our economic system, leading many economists to say that a repeat of that disastrous event is extremely unlikely. Do you agree or disagree? Give details to explain your answer.

connected.mcgraw-hill.com   Economic Instability 373

CHAPTER 13, LESSON 1
Business Cycles and Economic Instability

C Critical Thinking Skills

Drawing conclusions from economic data Have students write a paragraph describing how they might change their post-graduation plans if economists predicted a recession soon after they graduate.

R Reading Skills

Activating prior knowledge in econometric models Have students review the terms they already know in the econometric model called the output-expenditure model. **Ask: What are the components of the output-expenditure model?** (GDP = gross domestic product; C = consumption expenditures; I = investment spending; G = government expenditures; X = exports; M = imports; X – M = net exports) Have students write these terms down as a reference.

CLOSE & REFLECT

C Critical Thinking Skills

Organizing economic data Have students create a chart with the columns "Recession" and "Expansion," and list lesson terms and concepts in each column. Some terms will be used in both columns.

ANSWERS, p. 373

✓ **READING PROGRESS CHECK** Data used for longer-term models become increasingly speculative. Despite trying, no one can perfectly predict the future, especially the further out into it we imagine.

LESSON 1 REVIEW ANSWERS

Reviewing Vocabulary
1. recession

Using Your Notes
2. The SEC regulates companies soliciting funds from investors so that investors can have greater faith in their investments.

Answering the Guiding Questions
3. Many events that affect the business cycle are unexpected and naturally occurring, such as shortages or surpluses, changes in investment spending, and speculation.

4. Because the Great Depression was so severe and affected so many people, the government stepped in to relieve suffering and to provide more economic stability to prevent recurrences. These remedies include Social Security, the Securities and Exchange Commission, and the Federal Deposit Insurance Corporation (FDIC).

5. Leading economic indicators provide warning signs that usually precede a downturn or upturn in the economy.

Writing About Economics
6. Most students will say a repeat of the Great Depression is unlikely because of establishment of the SEC, FDIC, unemployment programs, and other changes to our economic system.

Economic Instability 373

CHAPTER 13
Case Study

W Writing Skills

Writing a dialogue about the effects of economic crises Have students use the Case Study text and research on the Great Recession of 2008 to write a dialogue between a young Greek person and a young American person who have gone through this economic crisis. Have the dialogue focus on what life is like now in their respective countries, comparing and contrasting their country's recovery or lack of recovery, as related to their everyday lives. **Verbal/Linguistic**

R Reading Skills

Identifying economic problems Have students read the Case Study and make a list of words and phrases that describe difficulties in Greece's economy. Ask them to define these words and phrases, and then use them in their answers to the questions on the activity. **ELL Verbal/Linguistic**

Making Connections

Other Economic Crises? Have students research the economic situations in one of the other countries mentioned in the activity: Spain, Portugal, or Ireland. Then have them write a paragraph stating how these countries risk having a crisis similar to that of Greece occur. **Verbal/Linguistic**

C Critical Thinking Skills

Considering solutions Have students write a paragraph stating what they think Greece's government could do to have a positive effect on the country's economy.

ANSWERS, p. 374
Case Study Review

1. Years of rampant government spending and high budget deficits left Greece unable to pay its bills when a severe world recession hit.
2. rising prices, high unemployment, falling wages, falling consumer spending, a shrinking economy, and the inability to pay its public debt
3. Responses should indicate that the quality of life has been adversely affected, noting the high unemployment, high prices, frequent strikes, and other crisis-related unrest.

374

Case Study

A GREEK TRAGEDY

For an interactive version of this case study go to **connected.mcgraw-hill.com**

W High prices are just one of the economic problems that have devastated Greece in recent years—for some segments of the workforce, unemployment rates have skyrocketed. (Nearly 60 percent of Greece's youth population is unemployed.) As a result, the economic crisis has created a **R** series of cause-and-effect relationships that include a reduction in consumer spending by an annual rate of nearly 9 percent, as well as causing the country's gross domestic product (GDP) to shrink by more than 20 percent since the crisis began in 2007. The overall effect of the economic decline has an effect on many countries in the European Union as well. **C**

Greece's prolonged crisis is largely the consequence of years of unrestrained government spending and spiraling budget deficits. For example, public sector wages rose 50 percent between 1999 and 2007. The government also ran up huge debts paying for the 2004 Athens Olympics. When the global Great Recession hit in 2007, the country's debt levels were already so high that it could no longer pay its bills.

An even greater economic crisis would have resulted if Greece didn't pay its debts, so the European Union loaned Greece billions of dollars to help the country pay its creditors. However, the loans came on the condition that Greece drastically cut spending and reduce its deficit. This requirement fell hardest on the Greek people because the government could not afford aid programs for those who lost their jobs or had their wages drastically cut.

Frequent strikes, bombings, and other disruptions in response to the cuts have added to Greece's problems. Greece's future remains a matter of concern, and many fear that other countries such as Spain, Ireland, and Portugal—each of which has similar economic challenges—could follow Greece into economic chaos.

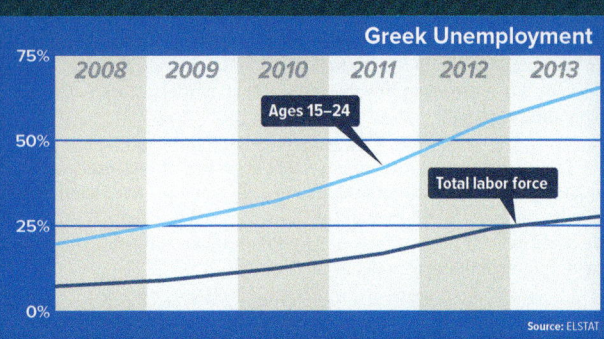
During the global recession, Greece's unemployment rose rapidly.

CASE STUDY REVIEW

1. **Specifying** What behavior by Greece's government brought on that nation's economic crisis?
2. **Identifying** What economic issues and problems does Greece face?
3. **Making Connections** How do you think Greece's economic problems have affected the quality of life for Greeks?

374

---

networks Online Teaching Options

INTERACTIVE FEATURE

Case Study: A Greek Tragedy

Comparing and contrasting causes and effects of economic crises Have students read about the economic crisis in Greece in the Case Study. Then have them read the text on the Reinforcing Economic Skills worksheet, and fill in the cause-and-effect table for both the United States and Greece. Finally, have students write a compare-and-contrast paragraph about the two countries and their plights during the Great Recession.

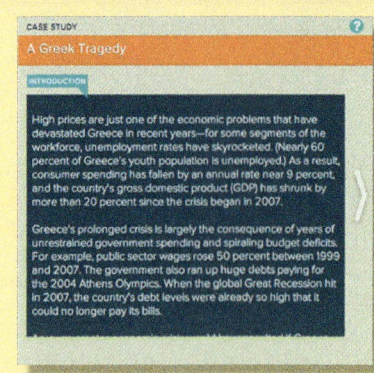

LESSON 2
Inflation

ESSENTIAL QUESTION

What are the causes and consequences of instability in the economy?

Pretend that a month ago you created a list of five goods and services that high school students commonly consume. After researching local or online resources, you recorded the prices for each item and totaled the cost, which came to $17.50. Now, a month later, you repeat the same exercise with the same goods and services but notice that the total is higher; it's $18.11.

a. Which is this change an example of: inflation or deflation?

b. What is the monthly inflation or deflation rate for this group of items (known as a "market basket")? That is, what monthly percentage change was there?

Measuring Prices and Inflation

GUIDING QUESTION How is the consumer price index used to calculate inflation?

Macroeconomic instability is not limited to fluctuations in the level of national output (GDP) or national income (GNP). Changes in prices can be equally disruptive to the economy. When the general level of prices rises, the economy is experiencing **inflation**. A decline in the general level of prices is called **deflation**. Both situations are harmful to the economy and should be avoided whenever possible.

To understand inflation, we must first examine how it is measured. This involves the **construction** of a **price index**—a statistical series used to measure changes in the level of prices over time. We will focus on the popular **consumer price index (CPI)**, a comprehensive statistical series that tracks monthly changes in the prices paid by consumers for a representative "basket" of goods and services.

The Market Basket

The first step we have to take is to select a **market basket**—a representative selection of commonly purchased goods and services. The CPI uses the prices

Reading Help Desk

Academic Vocabulary
- construction
- recover

Content Vocabulary
- inflation
- deflation
- price index
- consumer price index (CPI)
- market basket
- base year
- creeping inflation
- hyperinflation
- stagflation
- producer price index (PPI)
- implicit GDP price deflator
- demand-pull inflation
- cost-push inflation
- creditors
- debtors

TAKING NOTES:
Key Ideas and Details
ACTIVITY Use a graphic organizer like the one below to differentiate these two main explanations for inflation.

	Causes	Effects
Demand-Pull Inflation		
Cost-Push Inflation		

Economic Instability 375

CHAPTER 13, LESSON 2
Inflation

ENGAGE

R Reading Skills

🔔 **Using word parts to define inflation** Before students begin the lesson, have them examine the word *inflation*. **Ask: What word do you recognize as the root of the word *inflation*? What does this root word mean?** *(Sample answer: inflate; to expand or increase in size)* Have students use the meaning of the root word to help them write a definition for inflation. Then have them compare that definition to the one in the text. Finally, explain the difference between inflation and inflation rates. Inflation means that "prices are increasing." Inflation *rates* tell you "by how much."

BELLRINGER

Stagflation

Understanding stagflation Have students look at the Bellringer activity. **Ask: What do you think "stagflation" means?** *(Sample answer: inflation plus stagnant economy)* Then have students describe in complete sentences the characteristics of an economy experiencing stagflation.

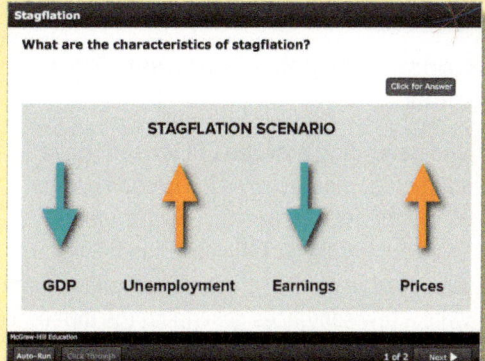

ANSWERS, p. 375

ESSENTIAL QUESTION ACTIVITY
1. inflation
2. 3.48%

TAKING NOTES
Demand-pull
Cause: All sectors of the economy try to buy more goods and services than the economy can produce
Effect: Creates shortages, "pulling" prices up
Cost-push
Cause: Rising input costs, especially energy and organized labor, drive up the cost of products for manufacturers
Effect: The rising costs of production "pushes" prices up

Economic Instability 375

CHAPTER 13, LESSON 2
Inflation

TEACH & ASSESS

C Critical Thinking Skills

Calculating a fictional CPI Have students work together in groups of five or six. Ask students to create a market basket for their group. Each basket should include 20 items that students typically buy. Totaling the prices of the items, students should figure the current cost of their group's market basket. Ask students to then calculate the total cost of the basket for the next three years if prices rise by 4 percent each year. Have students determine the CPI for the third year using the current market basket cost as the base year. Make copies of each group's basket list and distribute them to the other groups. Have students compare baskets and, as a class, create a composite market basket. **Logical/Mathematical**

Making Connections

Market Basket Categories Tell students that a market basket includes the average prices of about 300 goods and services from these categories:

- Food And Beverages
- Housing
- Apparel
- Transportation
- Medical Care
- Recreation
- Education and Communication
- Other goods and services

After writing these categories on the board, have students visit the Bureau of Labor Statistics Web site to see what types of items—such as car insurance, pet products, and funeral expenses—are included in each category. Ask students to consider several goods and services that had to be added to the market basket in the past several decades *(various technology products, for example)*. **Ask: Which of the following is NOT used to calculate the CPI? (a) price of a dozen eggs; (b) cost of a movie theater ticket; (c) hours worked per week; (d) base year; (e) money spent on college tuition.** *(Answer c is correct, meaning that hours worked per week are NOT included in the CPI or used to calculate it.)*

ANSWERS, p. 376

CRITICAL THINKING
A CPI of 167.1 means that consumer prices in August 1999 were 167.1 percent higher, or 1.671 times higher, than they were in the 1982–84 base period.

---

inflation sustained rise in the general level of prices of goods and services

deflation sustained decrease in the general level of the prices of goods and services

construction creation by assembling individual parts

price index statistical series used to measure changes in the price level over time

consumer price index (CPI) index used to measure price changes for a market basket of frequently used consumer items

market basket representative collection of goods and services used to compile a price index

base year year serving as point of comparison for other years in a price index or other statistical measure

---

of approximately 300 goods and services, such as those shown in **Figure 13.3**. While this may seem like a small number, these items are scientifically selected to represent the types of purchases that most consumers make.

The next step is to find the average price of each item in the market basket. To do so, every month, employees of the U.S. Census Bureau sample prices on nearly 80,000 items in stores across the country. They then add up the prices to find the total cost of the market basket. The hypothetical results of such a monthly activity are shown in Figure 13.3 for three separate periods.

A **base year**—a year that serves as the basis of comparison for all other years—is then selected. While almost any year will do, the Bureau of Labor Statistics (BLS) in the U.S. Department of Commerce currently uses average prices as they existed from 1982 to 1984. While this is likely to be updated in the future, it is still the most popular base year used for prices today.

The Consumer Price Index

The last step in the process is to make the numbers in the table easier to interpret by converting the dollar cost of a market basket to an index value. This is done by dividing the cost of every market basket by the base-year market basket cost. For example, the $4,190 cost for August 2013 is divided by the $1,792 base-period cost to get 2.338, or 233.8 percent. The index number for August—233.8—represents the level of prices in comparison to the base-period prices.

In practice, all of the conversions are understood to be a percentage of the base-period cost even though the % sign or the word percent is not used. For example, prices in August 2013 are 233.8 percent of those in the base period, which is another way of saying that prices have more than doubled. A different base year would give a different index number. However, to avoid confusion, the base year is changed only infrequently.

FIGURE 13.3

CONSTRUCTING THE CONSUMER PRICE INDEX

Item	Price Base Period 1982–84	Price 1998	Price 2009
Toothpaste	1.40	1.49	3.80
Milk (1 gal.)	1.29	1.29	3.20
Peanut butter (2-lb. jar)	2.50	2.65	4.70
Lightbulb (60 watt)	0.45	0.48	0.65
---	---	---	---
Automobile tune up	40.00	42.00	84.75
Total market basket price	$1,792	$2,925	$3,868
Current market basket cost / Base market basket cost	$1,792 / $1,792 = 1.000	$2,925 / $1,792 = 1.632	$3,868 / $1,792 = 2.158
Index number (%)	100.0(%)	163.2 (%)	215.8 (%)
Average salary			

Every month the Bureau of Labor Statistics (BLS) checks price changes of commonly used consumer items in some 300 general categories—called the market basket.

▲ **CRITICAL THINKING**
Economic Analysis How do we interpret a CPI of 167.1?

376

---

networks Online Teaching Options

CHARTS

Constructing the Consumer Price Index

Understanding how the CPI is used Have students explore Figure 13.3 to see how the consumer price index works with a market basket of products. Then have them answer the question on the activity. Finally, have them write a few sentences describing the difference between the CPI for August 2012 and August 2013. **Logical/Mathematical**

Because so many prices are sampled all over the country, the BLS publishes specific consumer price indexes for selected cities and large urban areas, as well as one for the economy as a whole.

Measuring Inflation

Now that we have the price index, we can find the annual percentage change in the price level, which is how inflation is measured. To use some data that is more current, the CPI in August of 2012 is 230.4 and exactly 233.8 one year later. To find the annual *percentage change*, we would divide the change in the CPI by the beginning value of the CPI in the following manner:

$$\frac{233.8 - 230.4}{230.4} = \frac{3.4}{230.4} = 0.0148 = 1.48\%$$

In other words, the rate of inflation was 1.48 percent for the 12-month period.

The rate of inflation tends to change over long periods of time. In the last 20 years, the United States could be described as having **creeping inflation**—inflation in the range of 1 to 3 percent per year. When inflation is this low, it is generally not seen as much of a problem. However, inflation can rise to the point where it gets out of control. **Hyperinflation**—inflation in the range of 500 percent a year and above—does not happen very often. When it does, it is generally the last stage before a total monetary collapse.

creeping inflation relatively low rate of inflation, usually 1 to 3 percent annually

hyperinflation abnormal inflation in excess of 500 percent per year; last stage of monetary collapse

THE GLOBAL ECONOMY & YOU

The Worldwide Domino Effect of U.S. Inflation

U.S. inflation is not just a problem in the United States. The effects of U.S. inflation rates are felt around the world. Those world effects, in turn, affect consumers in the United States.

When inflation causes prices to rise in the United States, the number of goods and services that each dollar will buy decreases. When this occurs, the dollar's exchange rate—its value compared to the currencies of other countries—also falls. This change is important because the exchange rate determines how much goods made in the United States will sell for in other countries. It also determines how much Americans will pay for goods made in those countries.

Suppose you want to buy a car imported from Germany. If inflation lowers the dollar's exchange rate against the German euro, it will take more dollars to match the selling price of the car. For you, this means you will have to pay more for the car. It might also mean that you pay more interest if you get a loan to purchase that car, because creditors sometimes raise interest rates to recover costs lost from the decreasing value of the money they lend to debtors.

At the same time, U.S. inflation makes U.S. exports less expensive overseas. That's because the dollar's decreased value and the lower exchange rate mean that fewer euros, for example, will be needed to equal the item's selling price. This may be good for the foreign buyers of U.S. products. But it hurts the makers of similar products in those countries, possibly leading to job loss and a lower GDP.

▲ **CRITICAL THINKING**
Identifying Cause and Effect In what specific ways might inflation in the United States affect how the German carmaker does business?

CHAPTER 13, LESSON 2
Inflation

C1 Critical Thinking Skills

Researching hyperinflation Have students research a country that has experienced hyperinflation and write several paragraphs explaining the upheaval citizens experience. For example, Zimbabwe at one time had hyperinflation in which a roll of toilet paper cost $145,750 (69 cents in U.S. dollars).

R Reading Skills

Determining the importance of the CPI Have students visit the Bureau of Labor Statistics Web site (www.bls.gov) and locate the Frequently Asked Questions for the CPI. Ask students to select a question and then write a paragraph explaining why it is important for economists and/or consumers to know the answer.

C2 Critical Thinking Skills

Understanding demand-pull inflation Provide the following scenario to students: When corn was demanded for ethanol fuel, there was a shortage of corn for animal feed. The shortage resulted in higher prices for corn, which resulted in higher prices for animal feed, which resulted in higher prices for steak. **Ask: Which type of inflation does this situation exemplify? Explain.** *(Demand-pull inflation; It results when all sectors in the economy try to buy more goods than the economy can produce. Prices are "pulled up" by excessive demand.)*

ANSWERS, p. 378

EXPLORING THE ESSENTIAL QUESTION

(C) $447.
(Year 1: $5,000 × .029 = 145
Year 2: $5,145 × .029 = 149.20
Year 3: $5,294.20 × .029 = 153.53
Additional amount to save = $447.73)

☑ **READING PROGRESS CHECK** A market basket is a selection of commonly used consumer goods and services and their current prices. The consumer price index (CPI) uses a market basket of 300 goods and services to measure price-level fluctuations from year to year.

C1: The record for hyperinflation was set in Hungary during World War II. At that time, huge amounts of currency were printed to pay the government's bills. By the end of the war, it was claimed that 828 *octillion* (828,000,000,000,000,000,000,000,000,000) pengös equaled 1 prewar pengö.

An economy also may experience **stagflation**, a period of stagnant economic growth coupled with inflation. Stagflation was a concern in the 1970s, a time of rising prices coupled with high unemployment. Even today, some people worry that the high price of oil could cause prices to go up and economic growth to slow down.

Other Price Indexes

A price index can be constructed for any segment of the economy in exactly the same way. The agricultural sector, for example, constructs a separate price index for the products it buys (diesel fuel, fertilizer, and herbicides) and then compares it to the prices it gets for its products.

The **producer price index (PPI)** is a monthly series that reports prices received by domestic producers. Prices in this series are recorded when a producer sells its output to the very first buyer. This sample consists of about 100,000 commodities, using 1982 as the base year. Although it is compiled for all commodities, it is broken down into various subcategories, including farm products, fuels, chemicals, rubber, pulp and paper, and processed foods.

The **implicit GDP price deflator**, used to measure changes in GDP, is another series. This series is used less frequently because the figures for real GDP, or GDP already adjusted for price increases, are provided when GDP is announced.

Finally, these are just a few of the many price indexes that the government maintains. Even so, the CPI is by far the most popular and the one we watch most often.

☑ **READING PROGRESS CHECK**

Analyzing How is a market basket used to measure the price level?

EXPLORING THE ESSENTIAL QUESTION

R: You've decided to save $5,000 over three years in order to buy a car. But you heard that the annual inflation rate was 2.9 percent. So you know that the car you like today that costs $5,000 will actually cost more in three years. About how much extra money, beyond the $5,000, should you also save in order to afford the car you want?

a. $279
b. $323
c. $447

stagflation combination of stagnant economic growth and inflation

producer price index (PPI) index used to measure prices received by domestic producers; formerly called the wholesale price index

implicit GDP price deflator index used to measure price changes in gross domestic product.

demand-pull inflation explanation that prices rise because all sectors of the economy try to buy more goods and services than the economy can produce

Causes of Inflation

GUIDING QUESTION *Why is there no single cause of inflation?*

Economists have offered several explanations for the causes of inflation. Nearly every period of inflation is due to one or more of the following causes: demand-pull, cost-push, wage-price spiral, or excessive monetary growth.

Demand-Pull

C2: According to the explanation called **demand-pull inflation**, all sectors in the economy try to buy more goods and services than the economy can produce. As consumers, businesses, and governments converge on stores, they cause shortages, which drive up prices. Thus prices are "pulled" up by excessive demand. This could happen, for example, if consumers decided to use their credit cards and go into debt to buy things they otherwise could not afford.

A similar explanation blames inflation on excessive spending by the federal government. After all, the government also borrows and then spends billions of dollars, thus putting upward pressure on prices. Unlike the demand-pull explanation, which cites the excess demand on all sectors of the economy, this explanation holds only the federal government's deficit spending responsible for inflation.

---

networks *Online Teaching Options*

VIDEO **WORKSHEETS**

Inflation Jumped

Summarizing effects of consumer activity on inflation Have students brainstorm ways in which consumer activity affects inflation. Then have them watch the video. Finally, have them offer their ideas in a class discussion summarizing the effects of consumer activity on inflation mentioned in the video.

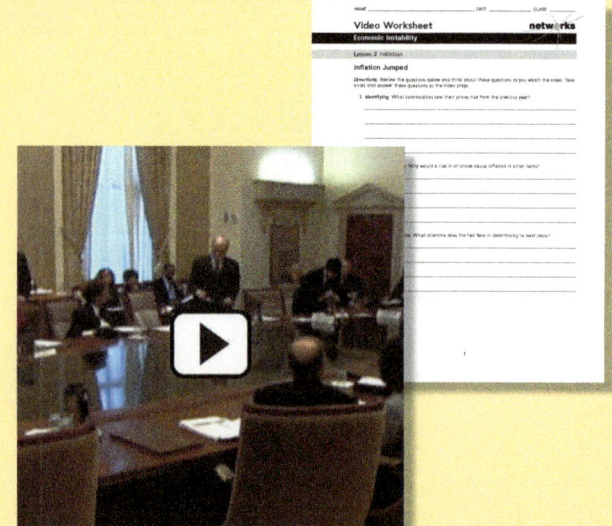

Cost-Push

The **cost-push inflation** explanation claims that rising input costs, especially energy and organized labor, drive up the cost of products for manufacturers and thus cause inflation. This situation might occur, for example, when a strong national union wins a large wage contract, forcing manufacturers to raise prices to **recover** the increase in labor costs.

Another cause of cost-push inflation could be a sudden rise in the international price of oil, which can raise the price of everything from plastics and gasoline to shipping costs and airline fares. Such an increase in prices occurred during the 1970s, when prices for crude oil went from $5 to $35 a barrel. It happened again in 2008, when the price of oil surged to over $140 a barrel.

cost-push inflation explanation that rising input costs, especially energy and organized labor, drive up the cost of products for manufacturers and thus cause inflation

recover to get back

Wage-Price Spiral

A more neutral explanation does not blame any particular group or event for rising prices. According to this view, a self-perpetuating spiral of wages and prices becomes difficult to stop.

The spiral might begin when higher prices force workers to ask for higher wages. If they get the higher wages, producers try to recover that cost with higher prices. As each side tries to improve its relative position with a larger increase than before, the rate of inflation keeps rising.

Excessive Monetary Growth

The most popular explanation for inflation is excessive monetary growth. This occurs when the money supply grows faster than real GDP. According to this view, any extra money or additional credit created by the Federal Reserve System will increase someone's purchasing power. When people spend this additional money, they cause a demand-pull effect that drives up prices.

THE WAGE-PRICE SPIRAL

This cartoon describes one mechanism that can lead to inflation, a wage-price spiral.

◀ **CRITICAL THINKING**
Making Predictions How might a wage-price spiral come to an end and stop triggering inflation?

connected.mcgraw-hill.com   Economic Instability **379**

POLITICAL CARTOON

The Wage-Price Spiral

Analyzing a political cartoon Have students write a paragraph explaining how the cartoon emphasizes the wage-price spiral cause of inflation. Then ask them to draw their own cartoon emphasizing one of the other causes of inflation. **Verbal/Linguistic**

CHAPTER 13, LESSON 2
Inflation

V Visual Skills

Illustrating cost-push inflation Point out that some economists illustrate the cost-push theory of inflation with a circle of arrows. Draw a circle, and provide students with the following phrases out of order. Have students use arrows and the phrases to illustrate the process of cost-push inflation around the circle. 1. Workers demand higher wages to balance the decline in their purchasing power. 2. Large unions receive wage increases. 3. Businesses pay higher wages, causing their costs to increase. 4. Businesses raise prices to maintain profits. 5. Consumers pay higher prices for goods. (which points back to number 1) **Visual/Spatial**

C Critical Thinking Skills

Making inferences about inflation Ask: **Which type of inflation might be accompanied by unemployment? Explain.** *(Sample answer: Cost-push inflation. With demand-pull inflation, there is a higher level of spending and therefore no reason to lay people off. With cost-push inflation, a rise in prices can reduce the amount being bought, which would cause production and employment to be cut back.)*

Content Background Knowledge

The Gold Standard Remind students that when the money supply was linked to the gold supply, price levels usually did not vary. Inflation was not a persistent economic problem during the nation's gold standard years. Major gold discoveries, however, could abruptly increase the money supply and price levels. When gold was discovered in California in the mid-1800s, a monetary shock jolted the U.S. economy. Because the gold standard left economies vulnerable to such instability and was costly to maintain, most nations abandoned it in the twentieth century. Today governments use monetary policies to regulate the money supply.

ANSWERS, p. 379

CRITICAL THINKING

Student answers will vary. One possible way that the spiral could end is that a business may find that it has increased prices so much that there is no longer demand for the product. In this case, the business may fail, or may need to cut costs somehow to be able to offer the products at a lower cost. Unfortunately, a common way to cut costs in such situations is to lay off workers.

Economic Instability **379**

CHAPTER 13, LESSON 2
Inflation

C1 Critical Thinking Skills

Analyzing effects of inflation Have students evaluate how a sharp increase in inflation might affect the following people: 1. A person who has just withdrawn a considerable amount from a savings account. *(Money will have less value, or buying power, than when it was initially saved.)* 2. A doctor on staff at a large hospital. *(Work will be largely unaffected, because demand for medical services is relatively inelastic.)* 3. A retired autoworker on a fixed pension. *(Fixed incomes are susceptible to a loss of purchasing power.)* 4. A borrower about to repay a loan. *(The money paid back will have less value than that borrowed.)*

W Writing Skills

Persuasive writing about the effects of inflation Have students imagine that they have worked at the same part-time job for the past three years. During that time, their wages have remained the same. Have students write a letter to their boss asking for a raise. Students should use information about inflation to justify their request. Remind students to use standard grammar, spelling, sentence structure, and punctuation.

C2 Critical Thinking Skills

Using graphs to explore the effects of inflation Have students review the Inflation Erodes the Value of the Dollar graph. **Ask: In what year was the purchasing power of the dollar equal to 10 percent of its value in 1947?** *(2007)* **In which decade did the purchasing power of the dollar decline by the greatest amount?** *(1970s)* **Visual/Spatial**

ANSWERS, p. 380

✓ **READING PROGRESS CHECK** Students may choose demand-pull inflation, cost-push inflation, wage-price spiral, or excessive monetary growth. In any case, students should cite information in the text to support their answers, and should draw connections among the different explanations.

CRITICAL THINKING
When the purchasing power of the dollar rose, the price level declined.

Advocates of this explanation point out that inflation cannot be maintained without a growing money supply. For example, if the price of gas goes up sharply, but the amount of money people have remains the same, then consumers will simply have to buy less of something else. While the price of gas may rise, the prices of other things will fall—because producers usually decrease their prices when demand decreases—leaving the overall price level unchanged.

✓ **READING PROGRESS CHECK**

Explaining Which explanation do you think gives the most reasonable cause of inflation? Why?

Consequences of Inflation

GUIDING QUESTION *Whom does inflation hurt the most?*

While low levels of inflation may not be a problem, inflation can have a disruptive effect on an economy if it gets too high, variable, or uncertain.

Reduced Purchasing Power

As you can see from **Figure 13.4**, purchasing power of the dollar has fluctuated considerably in the hundred years since 1913. Most of the fluctuations took place between 1913 and 1933, when the country was on the gold standard. After 1933, the declining purchasing power of the dollar was entirely due to inflation.

This happens because the dollar buys less whenever prices rise, and thus it loses value over time. This may not be a problem for everyone, but decreasing purchasing power can be especially hard on retired people or those with fixed incomes because their money buys a little less each month. Those not on fixed incomes are better able to cope. They can increase their fees or wages to better keep up with inflation.

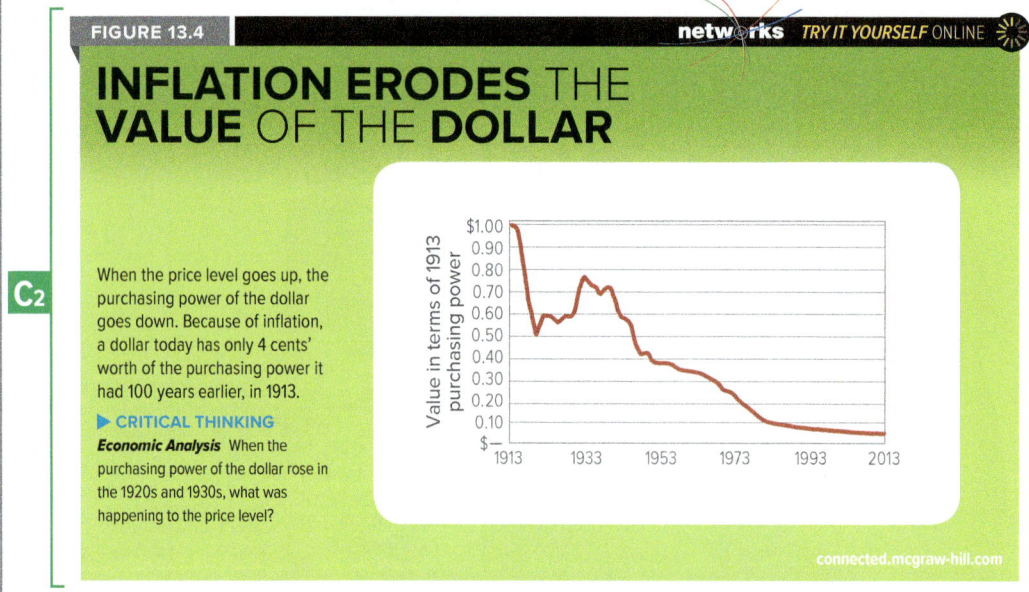

FIGURE 13.4

INFLATION ERODES THE VALUE OF THE DOLLAR

When the price level goes up, the purchasing power of the dollar goes down. Because of inflation, a dollar today has only 4 cents' worth of the purchasing power it had 100 years earlier, in 1913.

▶ **CRITICAL THINKING**
Economic Analysis When the purchasing power of the dollar rose in the 1920s and 1930s, what was happening to the price level?

380

---

networks *Online Teaching Options*

GRAPH

Inflation Erodes the Value of the Dollar

Using a graph to understand the effects of inflation on the dollar Have students view Figure 13.4 and build a graph with data about the dollar's purchasing power. Then have them write a short story interpreting the effects of this erosion of purchasing power on three generations of a family over the period shown on the graph. **Verbal/Linguistic**

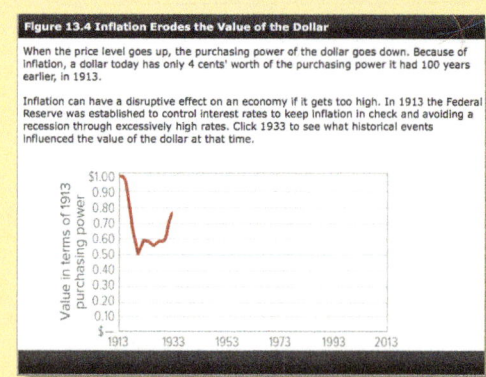

Distorted Spending Patterns

Inflation has a tendency to make people change their spending habits. For example, when prices went up in the early 1980s, interest rates—the cost of borrowed money—also went up. This caused spending on durable goods, especially housing and automobiles, to fall dramatically.

To illustrate, suppose that a couple wanted to borrow $100,000 over 20 years to buy a house. At a 7 percent interest rate, their monthly mortgage payments would be $660.12. At 14 percent, their payments would be $1,197.41. In 1981 some mortgage rates reached 18 percent, which meant a monthly payment of $1,517.32 for the same size loan! As a result of the high interest rates in that period, the homebuilding industry almost collapsed.

Encouraged Speculation

Inflation tempts some people to speculate in an attempt to take advantage of rising prices. For example, when interest rates were low from 2001 to 2005, many unqualified buyers were able to purchase high-priced homes. Interest rates did go up in 2006 and 2007, but they never went as high as they did in the early 1980s. Even so, many of the unqualified buyers defaulted on, or didn't pay, their mortgage payments, which helped drive the economy into recession.

Some people actually make money on speculative ventures like this, but even speculators lose money on deals from time to time. For the average consumer, a large loss could have devastating consequences.

Distorted Distribution of Income

During long inflationary periods, **creditors**, or people who lend money, are generally hurt more than **debtors**, or borrowers, because earlier loans are repaid later with dollars that buy less.

Suppose that you borrow $100 to buy bread that costs $1 a loaf. This means that you could buy 100 loaves of bread today with that loan money. If inflation set in, and if the price of bread doubled by the time you paid back the loan, the lender could buy only 50 loaves of bread with the money you repaid, because each loaf now would cost $2. This is why the creditor is hurt more than the borrower when inflation takes place.

creditors persons or institutions to whom money is owed

debtors persons or institutions that owe money

✓ **READING PROGRESS CHECK**

Identifying Why is inflation especially hard on people with fixed incomes?

LESSON 2 REVIEW

Reviewing Vocabulary

1. Write a sentence that illustrates the relationship between the terms *inflation* and *debtors*.
2. Explain why creditors prefer creeping inflation over hyperinflation.

Using Your Notes

3. Use your notes from the graphic organizer you created at the beginning of this lesson to explain two main explanations for inflation and how they contribute to the wage-price spiral.

Answering the Guiding Questions

4. *Examining* How is the consumer price index used to calculate inflation?

5. *Analyzing* Why is monetary expansion considered to be the primary cause of inflation?

6. *Exploring Issues* Whom does inflation hurt the most? Explain why.

Writing About Economics

7. *Argument* Government spending has long been a major political issue. High spending by government contributes to economic growth, but it also contributes to inflation. Proposals to cut government spending that have come before Congress in recent years have been hotly debated. Write a letter to your member of Congress that makes an economic argument for or against cuts in government spending, and use some of the content vocabulary from this lesson in your argument.

connected.mcgraw-hill.com   Economic Instability 381

CHAPTER 13, LESSON 2
Inflation

C Critical Thinking Skills

Analyzing purchasing power Have students use the Internet to find out the current maximum monthly Social Security payment. Then have students calculate how much purchasing power (in dollars) the payment would lose in one year if the inflation rate is 3 percent, 4 percent, and 6 percent. **Logical/Mathematical**

CLOSE & REFLECT

W Writing Skills

Predicting effects of inflation on purchasing power Have students predict the effects of inflation on their own purchasing power by writing a report about how they will change their spending habits if inflation continues to rise.

ANSWERS, p. 381

✓ **READING PROGRESS CHECK** It reduces the purchasing power of their income. In other words, a dollar becomes less valuable and therefore buys less.

LESSON 2 REVIEW ANSWERS

Reviewing Vocabulary

1. Sample sentence: When inflation rates are high, debtors repay loans with money that is worth less than when they borrowed it.
2. The money they loan will not decline in value as much by the time the loan is repaid.

Using Your Notes

3. In demand-pull inflation, shortages that result from excessive demand pull prices up. In cost-push inflation, increased production costs push prices up. So when prices of goods and services go up, workers seek wage increases in order to pay for items, and this causes more cost-push inflation because manufacturers increase the prices of their products to recover the costs of higher wages. This results in prices spiraling further upward.

Answering the Guiding Questions

4. The current prices of a "market basket" of representative goods and services are compared to the prices of those goods and services in a "base year." The difference between the total current prices and the base-year prices is divided by the total base-year prices to produce a percentage price increase, which is expressed as the consumer price index.
5. Excessive monetary growth increases people's purchasing power, and when people spend this additional money they cause a demand-pull effect that drives up prices.
6. Inflation hurts those living on low or fixed incomes the most because, as prices rise, the value of their savings or income decreases.

Writing About Economics

7. Students' letters should take a clear position for or against limits on government spending; should demonstrate understanding of the relationship between government spending, inflation, and economic growth; and should recognize the effects of both on society.

CHAPTER 13, LESSON 3
Unemployment

ENGAGE

V Visual Skills

 Demonstrating instability Before students begin the lesson, place a set of scales in front of the class. Inform students that the scales represent the economy. Move the scales by adding weights to either side. At the same time, mention that a condition called inflation can upset the economic stability. Balance the scales, then set them in motion again, pointing out that unemployment too can cause the economy to become unstable. Tell students that in this lesson they will learn about different approaches to tackle unemployment.

TEACH & ASSESS

C Critical Thinking Skills

Considering unemployment Ask: **Why do you suppose unemployment is considered a barometer of the economy?** *(because unemployment tends to rise during recessions and drop during periods of expansion)* Be sure students understand how to correctly interpret an unemployment graph. A downward trend line on an unemployment graph is positive.

ANSWERS, p. 382
ESSENTIAL QUESTION ACTIVITY

Students should provide reasons why their choice is the best one.
TAKING NOTES
Frictional Unemployment
Structural Unemployment
Technological Unemployment
Cyclical Unemployment
Seasonal Unemployment

382

Interact with these digital assets and others in lesson 3
- ✓ INTERACTIVE GRAPH The Unemployment Rate
- ✓ INTERACTIVE GRAPH Measuring Consumer Discomfort
- ✓ SELF-CHECK QUIZ
- ✓ VIDEO

networks TRY IT YOURSELF ONLINE

LESSON 3
Unemployment

Reading Help Desk

Academic Vocabulary
- confined
- fundamental
- unfounded

Content Vocabulary
- civilian labor force
- unemployed
- unemployment rate
- long-term unemployed
- frictional unemployment
- structural unemployment
- outsourcing
- technological unemployment
- cyclical unemployment
- seasonal unemployment
- GDP gap
- misery index

TAKING NOTES:

Key Ideas and Details
ACTIVITY Use a graphic organizer like the one below to identify the sources of unemployment.

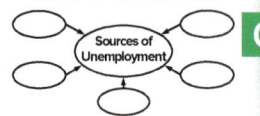
Sources of Unemployment

ESSENTIAL QUESTION

What are the causes and consequences of instability in the economy?

V In periods of economic instability, just about every community in the nation feels the consequences and has to adapt. Which of the following do you think is the best approach for a community to address economic instability that's hurting the local economy? In a paragraph, explain why you think your choice is the best one.

1. A committee could be organized of local businesspeople, and a petition asking for federal government aid could be sent to the congressional representative of the community's district.
2. Businesses experiencing difficulty could apply to banks for loans and raise the prices of their products to pay off the loans.
3. Community leaders and local government officials could brainstorm ways to attract consumers to buy at local businesses.
4. Representatives from businesses, banks, and the local government could meet regularly to monitor economic developments in the community and work together to find ways to help those businesses having difficult times.

Measuring Unemployment

GUIDING QUESTION *Who is not included in the labor force?*

C Most Americans identify strongly with their work. If you were to ask someone to describe themselves, most likely they would tell you their occupation, such as a cook, a teacher, or a sales associate. These individuals, along with approximately half of the people in the United States, belong to the labor force, and at any given time, millions are without jobs. Sometimes this is because they choose not to work, as when they have quit one job to look for another. In most cases, however, people are out of work for reasons largely out of their control.

382

---

networks   Online Teaching Options

BELLRINGER

Unemployment

Activating prior knowledge about unemployment Have students brainstorm ideas about what would happen if unemployment benefits did not exist.
Ask: **What does history reveal about the effects on a country's economy without unemployment benefits?** *(Sample answer: The Great Depression showed that the cost of high unemployment without benefits was harmful to the economy. It was in the government's best interest to create an unemployment benefits program.)* Then have students read through the Bellringer activity and answer the questions.

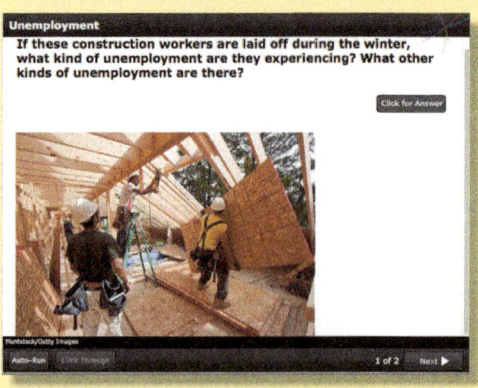

To understand the severity of joblessness, we need to know how it is measured and what is overlooked. The measure of joblessness is the unemployment rate, one of the most closely watched and politically charged statistics in the economy.

Civilian Labor Force

The Bureau of Labor Statistics defines the **civilian labor force**, more commonly called the labor force, as the sum of all persons age sixteen and above who are either employed or actively seeking employment. This measure excludes members of the military. Since only people able to work are included in the labor force, those persons who are **confined** to jail or reside in mental health facilities are also excluded.

Unemployed Persons

The process of deciding whether someone is able to work, willing to work, or even at work is more complicated than most people realize. In the middle of any given month, about 1,500 specialists from the Census Bureau begin their monthly survey of about 60,000 households in nearly 2,000 counties, covering all 50 states. Census workers are looking for the **unemployed**—people available for work who made a specific effort to find a job during the past month and who, during the most recent survey week, worked less than one hour for pay or profit. People are also classified as unemployed if they worked in a family business without pay for less than fifteen hours a week.

After the census workers collect their data, they turn it over to the Bureau of Labor Statistics for analysis and publication. These data, which include the unemployment rate, are then released to the American public on the first Friday of every month.

Unemployment Rate

Unemployment is normally expressed in terms of the **unemployment rate**, or the number of unemployed individuals divided by the total number of persons in the civilian labor force. The monthly unemployment rate is expressed as a percentage of the entire labor force. For example, in September 2009 the unemployment rate was calculated as follows:

$$\frac{\text{Number of unemployed persons}}{\text{Civilian labor force}} = \frac{9{,}474{,}000}{155{,}694{,}000} = 0.061 = 6.1\%$$

Monthly changes in the unemployment rate, often as small as one-tenth of 1 percent, may seem minor even though they have a huge impact on the economy. With a civilian labor force of approximately 155.6 million people, a one-tenth of 1 percent rise in unemployment would mean that nearly 154,800 people had lost their jobs. This number is more than the current population of major American cities such as Kansas City, Kansas; Syracuse, New York; Springfield, Massachusetts; Sunnyvale, California; Padadena, Texas; or Savannah, Georgia.

Variations in the unemployment rate can be seen in **Figure 13.5**. In general, it tends to rise just before a recession begins and then continues to rise sharply during the recession. If the recession is severe enough, as it was during the Great Recession of 2008–2009, it can double. Finally, when the rate finally starts to go back down, it may take five or more years for it to reach its previous low.

Uneven Burden of Unemployment

The burden of the unemployment rate does not fall evenly on everyone. Instead, the unemployment rate differs for people of different ages, races, and sexes. In addition, differences in work experience, education, training, and skills play a role, as does discrimination.

civilian labor force noninstitutionalized part of the population, aged sixteen and over, either working or looking for a job

confined kept within

unemployed state of working for less than one hour per week for pay or profit in a non-family-owned business, while being available and having made an effort to find a job during the past month

unemployment rate ratio of unemployed individuals divided by total number of persons in the civilian labor force, expressed as a percentage

CHAPTER 13, LESSON 3
Unemployment

R1 Reading Skills

Defining the civilian labor force Ask: Who is included in the civilian labor force? *(people age 16 and above who are employed or are actively seeking employment)* Who is not included in the civilian labor force? *(members of the military, people confined to jail or in mental health facilities)*

R2 Reading Skills

Figuring the unemployment rate Ask: How is the unemployment rate figured? *(It is the number of unemployed individuals divided by the total number of persons in the civilian labor force.)* Have students research the current unemployment rate.

R3 Reading Skills

Identifying weaknesses of the unemployment rate Have students identify some of the weaknesses of the unemployment rate, or how it understates employment conditions. Lead students to understand that it does not count those who have given up looking for work, nor does it count part-time or underemployed workers.

WORKSHEETS

Economic Simulation

Simulating an unemployment problem in the auto industry
In the simulation, students will try to tackle the unemployment problem and save the auto industry. Each group will use their own perspective to approach the crisis facing the auto industry, combat unemployment, hasten job creation, and maintain economic stability in an efficient and cost-effective way. **Interpersonal**

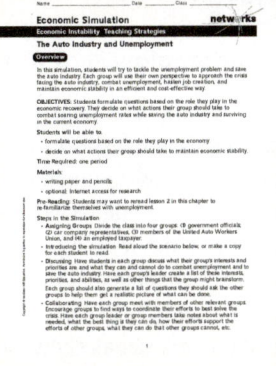

CHAPTER 13, LESSON 3
Unemployment

C Critical Thinking Skills

Extrapolating from the unemployment rate Tell students that economists look at a variety of events in order to assess the state of the economy and to predict what will be happening in the months ahead. Several key measurements are especially important in helping them understand the economy. Have students consider the indicator "employment."
Ask: What does a high unemployment rate say about how the economy is doing? *(Students should recognize that high unemployment means businesses are not doing well enough to hire workers. Students may also recognize that when fewer people are working, there will be fewer consumers buying goods and services, further slowing the economy.)* Follow-up with similar considerations about production and GDP. Then draw the circular flow diagram on the board and discuss how this model shows the interdependence of all the elements in the economy. Explain that when one part of the economy falters, it affects all of the other parts. **Visual/Spatial**

W Writing Skills

Describing the move from underemployment to full employment Have students identify an individual with a part-time job who wants to gain full-time work. Ask students to describe this person's story through a personal interview. Ask students to write a paper narrating the person's work experience, goals, and struggles to remove him or herself from the category of "underemployed."

ANSWERS, p. 384

CRITICAL THINKING

The number of unemployed declined significantly between 1993 and 2001. Keep in mind that on this graph, an upward movement is negative for the economy, meaning more unemployed workers. A downward movement is positive, meaning fewer unemployed workers.

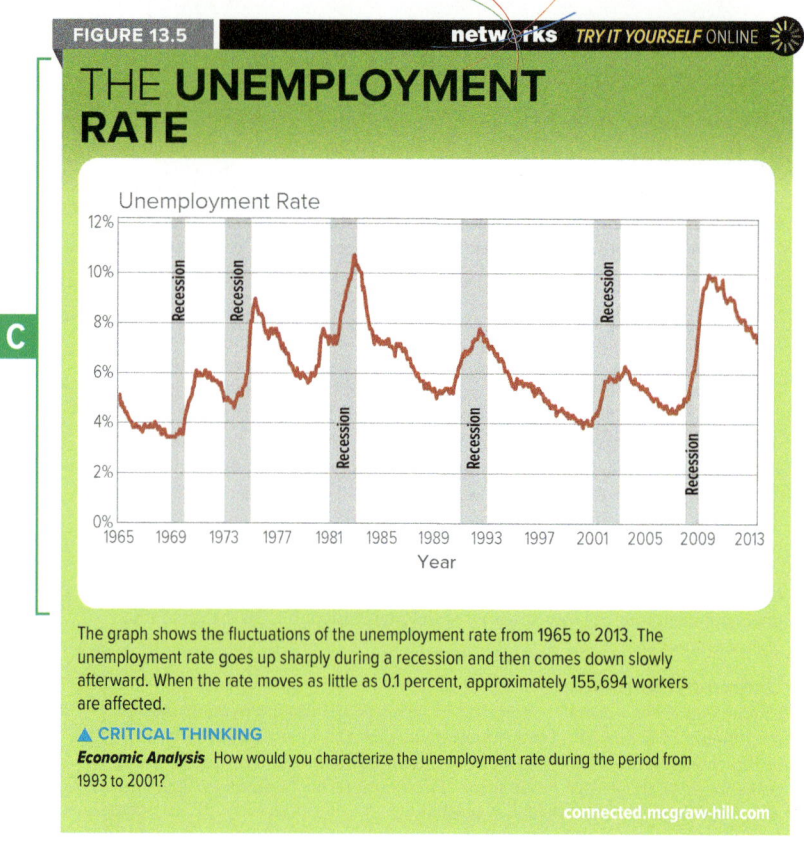

FIGURE 13.5

THE UNEMPLOYMENT RATE

The graph shows the fluctuations of the unemployment rate from 1965 to 2013. The unemployment rate goes up sharply during a recession and then comes down slowly afterward. When the rate moves as little as 0.1 percent, approximately 155,694 workers are affected.

▲ **CRITICAL THINKING**
Economic Analysis How would you characterize the unemployment rate during the period from 1993 to 2001?

For example, the unemployment rate for adult women is just slightly lower than the rate for adult men, but the rate for teenagers is normally about three to four times higher than the rate for either adult men or adult women. Likewise, the unemployment rate for African Americans, regardless of gender, is about twice as high as the rate for Caucasians, and Asians have the lowest rate of all.

Finally, about one-third of all unemployed persons—regardless of sex, age, or race—are the **long-term unemployed**, or workers who have been without a job for twenty-seven weeks or more. These are the workers most likely to give up looking for a job and eventually end up leaving the labor force altogether.

long-term unemployed workers who have been unemployed for twenty-seven weeks or more

Underemployment

It might seem that a measure as comprehensive as the unemployment rate would include all of the people who are without a job. If anything, however, the unemployment rate understates employment conditions for two reasons.

First, the unemployment rate does not count those too frustrated or discouraged to look for work. During recessionary periods, these labor force "dropouts" may include nearly a million people. Although they are not working and probably would like to find work, these people are not classified as

---

networks *Online Teaching Options*

GRAPH

The Unemployment Rate

Using a graph to show how unemployment is tied to recessions Have students explore Figure 13.5 showing unemployment rates across a period of time that includes several recessions. Then have them write a paragraph explaining how the unemployment rate is tied to recessions. If time permits, have students do research on one of the recessions shown in the graph. Have them write a one-page paper describing what happened to spark the recession, and how the unemployment rate was affected during the recession. **Logical/Mathematical**

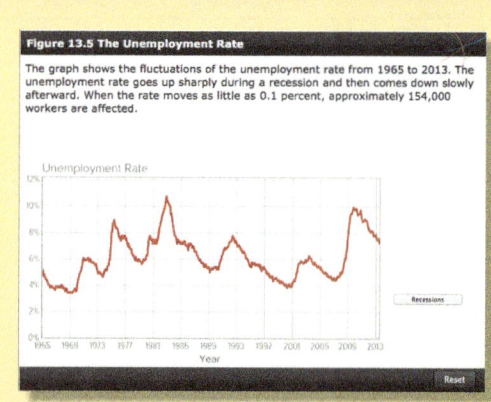

unemployed because they did not actively seek a job within the previous survey period.

Second, people are considered employed even when they only hold part-time jobs. For example, suppose a worker lost a high-paying job requiring forty hours a week and replaced it with a minimum-wage job requiring one hour a week. Although that worker would work and earn less, he or she would still be considered employed. In other words, being employed means working some, not just working full time.

Defending Against Unemployment

People often ask what they can do to protect themselves against unemployment, but the solutions are not always easy. For example, you cannot do much about your race or gender, but you can do something about your education. After all, the unemployment rate for everyone goes down as the level of education goes up!

This is important because it is easier for a person to get more education or skills while they are young than to do so when they are older. All a young person has to do is to stay in school longer to earn a diploma, or go to a community or technical college to earn a two-year degree. If circumstances permit, a four-year college degree gives even more protection against unemployment. Pursuing a diploma or an advanced degree is more challenging as you get older, so it is a good idea to get your education while you are young.

✓ **READING PROGRESS CHECK**

Summarizing How do we calculate the monthly unemployment rate?

CHAPTER 13, LESSON 3
Unemployment

C Critical Thinking Skills

Researching job opportunities and benefits Ask students to suppose that they were hired for a job and were pleased with the position. Explain that after five years, however, the company had to lay them off. Ask students to research steps they could take to find another similar position and/or receive unemployment benefits while they looked for another position.

Content Background Knowledge

Growing Occupations According to the Bureau of Labor Statistics, the fastest growing occupations between 2012 and 2022 are: industrial organizational psychologists, personal care aides, insulation workers, interpreters and translators, diagnostic medical sonographers, helpers (brickmasons, blockmasons, stonemasons, and tile and marble setters), occupational therapy assistants, genetic counselors, physical therapist assistants, physical therapist aides, skincare specialists, physician assistants, segmental pavers, electricians, information security analysts, occupational therapy aides, health specialties teachers, medical secretaries, and physical therapists.

CAREERS | Human Resources Specialist

Is this career for you?

 Do you have strong decision-making skills?

 Do you have good listening skills?

 Do you enjoy meeting and talking with new people from different backgrounds?

Interview with a professional
Human Resources Specialist

"Challenging work supported by great coworkers. Great work-life flexibility."

—Cisco Systems human resources manager

Salary
$55,640 per year
$26.75 per hour

Job Growth Outlook
Slower than average

Profile of Work
Human resources specialists recruit, interview, and place workers. They match employers with job applicants who have the skills and qualifications to meet the employers' needs. They work in nearly every industry—many are employed by individual companies, and others work for staffing and human resources firms. Many attend job fairs to meet and interview job applicants.

connected.mcgraw-hill.com   *Economic Instability* **385**

INTERACTIVE FEATURE

Career: Human Resource Specialist

Understanding relationships between human resource specialists and prospective employees
Have students read the Profile of Work and other text about the job responsibilities of a human resources specialist. Then have them write a mock interview dialogue between a human resources specialist for a company in their town and a prospective employee who has been out of work for two years. **Verbal/Linguistic**

ANSWERS, p. 385

✓ **READING PROGRESS CHECK** The unemployment rate is calculated by dividing the total number of persons in the civilian labor force by the ratio of unemployed individuals.

CHAPTER 13, LESSON 3
Unemployment

C Critical Thinking Skills

Analyzing local unemployment **Ask:** Which type of unemployment do you think is most common in your community? Explain. *(Answers will vary.)* Have students conduct research to find out which type of unemployment is actually most common in their community. Discuss their findings as a class.

R Reading Skills

Connecting outsourcing to unemployment
Ask: What type of unemployment is caused by outsourcing? *(structural unemployment)*

English Language Proficiency

Advanced High Provide a list of abstract and content-based vocabulary. Assign each student to prepare and deliver a news report about a topic related to unemployment. Tell students to use the words in the oral report.

Sources of Unemployment

GUIDING QUESTION *Why are some types of unemployment unavoidable?*

Economists have identified several kinds of unemployment. The nature and cause of each kind affects how much the unemployment rate can be reduced.

Frictional Unemployment

frictional unemployment unemployment caused by workers changing jobs or waiting to go to new ones

A common type of unemployment is **frictional unemployment**, the situation where workers are between jobs for one reason or another. This is usually a short-term condition, and workers suffer little economic hardship. This type of unemployment is natural and results from the constant changes in the economy that prevent qualified workers from immediately finding job openings.

As long as workers have the freedom to choose or change occupations, some people will always be leaving their old jobs to look for better ones. Because there are always some workers doing this, the economy will always have some frictional unemployment.

Structural Unemployment

structural unemployment unemployment caused by a fundamental change in the economy that reduces the demand for some workers

fundamental basic; an essential part

outsourcing hiring outside firms to perform non-core operations to lower operating costs

A more serious type of unemployment is **structural unemployment**, when economic progress, a change in consumer tastes and preferences, or a **fundamental** change in the operations of the economy reduces the demand for workers and their skills. In the early 1900s, for example, technological and economic progress resulted in the development of the automobile, which soon replaced horses and buggies and left highly skilled buggy-whip makers out of work. Later, when automobile drivers decided that they could lower the price of a fill-up by pumping the gas themselves, there was a sharp drop in the demand for gas station attendants.

Another development, **outsourcing**—the hiring of outside firms to perform non-core operations to lower operating costs—has become popular. Outsourcing was first used when firms found that they could have other companies perform some routine internal operations, such as the preparation of weekly paychecks. Later, improvements in technology made it possible for companies to move some of their customer service operations abroad where wages are much lower. For example, if you call your cell phone or cable company, or a computer software maker for customer assistance, your call is likely to be routed to an English-speaking worker in the Philippines or India rather than a U.S. office.

Sometimes the government contributes to structural unemployment. Congress's decision to close military bases in the 1990s is a prime example. Military bases are much larger than most private companies, and the impact of the base closings was concentrated in selected regions and communities. A few areas were able to attract new industry that hired some of the unemployed workers, but most workers either developed new skills or moved to other locations to find jobs.

Technological Unemployment

technological unemployment unemployment caused by technological developments or automation that make some workers' skills obsolete

A third kind of unemployment is **technological unemployment**, unemployment that occurs when workers are replaced by machines or automated systems that make their skills obsolete. Technological unemployment is closely related to structural unemployment, although the technological changes are not always as broad in scale or as influential on society as cars replacing buggies.

One example is the reduced need for bank tellers by commercial banks because of the increased use of automated teller machines (ATMs). Another example would be the introduction of word-processing programs whose spell-checking, formatting, and text-manipulation functions have greatly reduced the

---

networks — Online Teaching Options

WORKSHEET

Personal Finance Activity

Planning for a job change Have students read the introduction to the activity on the worksheet. Then have a class discussion about what it takes to move on from a job that you do not like. **Ask:** What can you do to be proactive about finding a new job? *(Sample answer: I can look for a new job without leaving my old job; I can ask for new responsibilities at my old job that might prepare me for my new career; I can do research about jobs that interest me and try to gain qualifications that will allow me to move in that direction).* Then have students prepare a timeline for the actions they will take to move from their old job to a new job. **Interpersonal**

CHAPTER 13, LESSON 3
Unemployment

demand for typists. Finally, many workers have been replaced by computerized programs on the Internet that take orders, process payments, and arrange for shipping directly to the consumer.

EXPLORING THE ESSENTIAL QUESTION

Your older sister was laid off from her job as a bank teller a month ago. The bank where she worked laid off many bank tellers because of automation. She's thinking about looking for the same teller jobs at other banks, but you don't think that's a good idea. What kind of advice would you give your sister? Describe your advice and your reasoning for it in one or two paragraphs.

Cyclical Unemployment

A fourth kind of unemployment is **cyclical unemployment**, unemployment directly related to swings in the business cycle. During a recession, for example, many people put off buying durable goods such as automobiles and refrigerators. As a result, some industries must lay off workers until the economy recovers.

If we look at Figure 13.5, we can see that the unemployment rate rose dramatically whenever the economy was in recession. For example, during the Great Recession, more than 8 million jobs were lost. Laid-off workers may eventually get their jobs back when the economy improves, but it usually takes five or more years of economic growth before the unemployment rate returns to where it was before the recession. In the meantime, the pain of unemployment is a fact of life for those who are out of work.

cyclical unemployment unemployment directly related to swings in the business cycle

Seasonal Unemployment

Finally, a fifth kind of unemployment is **seasonal unemployment**, unemployment resulting from seasonal changes in the weather or in the demand for certain products or jobs. Many carpenters and builders, for example, have less work in the winter because some tasks, such as replacing a roof or digging a foundation, are harder to do in cold weather. Department store sales clerks often lose their jobs after the December holiday season is over.

The difference between seasonal and cyclical unemployment relates to the period of measurement. Cyclical unemployment takes place over the course of the business cycle, which may last three to five years. Seasonal unemployment takes place every year, regardless of the general health of the economy.

seasonal unemployment unemployment caused by annual changes in the weather or other conditions that prevail at certain times of the year

✓ **READING PROGRESS CHECK**

Interpreting Which categories of unemployment do you think are the most troublesome for the U.S. economy? Why?

Costs of Instability

GUIDING QUESTION *How can economic instability affect you?*

Recession, inflation, and unemployment are all forms of instability that hinder economic growth. These problems can occur separately or at the same time. Fears about these conditions are not **unfounded**, because economic instability carries enormous costs that can be measured in economic as well as human terms.

unfounded not based on fact

GDP Gap

One measure of the economic cost of unemployment is the **GDP gap**—the difference between the actual GDP and the potential GDP that could be

GDP gap difference between what the economy can and does produce; annual opportunity cost of unemployed resources

connected.mcgraw-hill.com   Economic Instability   **387**

C1 Critical Thinking Skills

Analyzing types of unemployment Have students identify the type of unemployment for the following situations: An autoworker is laid off during a recession. *(cyclical unemployment)* A college graduate is looking for her first job. *(Looking for a first job is frictional unemployment.)* A steelworker loses her job when her company moves to Mexico. *(Lack of demand for a particular skill is an example of structural unemployment.)* A snowplow operator is laid off after winter. *(seasonal unemployment)* A new father quits his job to become a stay-at-home dad. *(People who choose not to work are not unemployed.)* An accountant quits her job to look for a better one. *(Voluntarily quitting one's job is frictional unemployment.)* A photographer loses his job because his skill as a slide developer becomes obsolete. *(technological unemployment)*

C2 Critical Thinking Skills

Identifying types of unemployment Have students design a poster showing the types of unemployment. Have them include a specific example of each type. Then have them present their poster to the class.

ANSWERS, p. 387

EXPLORING THE ESSENTIAL QUESTION

Student answers should touch on why going for the same type of job at the same type of place is probably not the best idea; if automation has made many of the sister's job functions obsolete, then it would stand to reason that other banks are laying off as well, or will be in the near future. On the positive side, the student should briefly describe a more promising alternative. For example, the student could advise the sister to take classes at a local college or community center, and emphasize the importance of career education and training early in life. In any case, students should provide reasons for their suggestions that incorporate what they've learned in the lesson.

✓ **READING PROGRESS CHECK** Student answers should indicate that they understand that some unemployment causes are difficult to fix, such as structural unemployment, technological unemployment, cyclical unemployment, and seasonal unemployment.

VIDEO **WORKSHEET**

Food Stamps

Understanding the costs of instability Have students brainstorm government programs available for people who are unemployed or underemployed. Then have them watch the video about families who need to use food stamps to buy groceries. **Verbal/Linguistic**

Video Supplied by BBC Worldwide Learning

Economic Instability **387**

CHAPTER 13, LESSON 3
Unemployment

C1 Critical Thinking Skills

Drawing conclusions about the GDP gap Have students visit the U.S. Bureau of Economic Analysis Web site (www.bea.gov). Ask them to select one or more tables that include information about the GDP gap. Instruct students to write a paragraph that describes what the data reveal about the GDP gap. Students should also explain why economists would be interested in that information. **Logical/Mathematical**

C2 Critical Thinking Skills

Making inferences A workforce is said to be at full employment when the unemployment rate is around 4 or 5 percent. **Ask: Why will the unemployment rate never be 0?** *(Some people will always be looking for new or different work.)*

---

produced if all resources were fully employed. In other words, the gap is a type of opportunity cost—a measure of output not produced because of unemployed resources.

If we were to illustrate the gap with a production-possibilities curve, the amount that could be produced would be at a point on the frontier. The amount actually produced would be represented by a point inside the frontier. The distance between the two would be the GDP gap.

In a more dynamic sense, the business cycle may cause the size of this gap to vary over time. The scale of GDP is such that if GDP declines even a fraction of a percentage point, the amount of lost production and income could be enormous. For example, suppose that an economy with a $13.5-trillion-dollar GDP declines by just one-tenth of one percent. This translates into $13.5 billion in lost output!

misery index unofficial statistic that is the sum of monthly inflation and the unemployment rate

Misery Index

Figure 13.6 shows the **misery index**, sometimes called the discomfort index—the sum of the monthly inflation and unemployment rates. As the figure shows, the index usually reaches a peak either during or immediately following a recession.

FIGURE 13.6 MEASURING CONSUMER DISCOMFORT

The graph shows the fluctuations of an unofficial measure of consumer discomfort called the misery index. The misery index is compiled by adding the monthly inflation and unemployment rates.

▲ **CRITICAL THINKING**
Economic Analysis When did the misery index reach its highest point?

---

networks Online Teaching Options

GRAPH

Measuring Consumer Discomfort

Understanding causes of financial discomfort
Have students use Figure 13.6 to explore fluctuations in consumer discomfort. Then have students pick an era when the discomfort was high, and write a journal entry in the voice of a person from that time, describing events that caused financial discomfort to that person.
Verbal/Linguistic

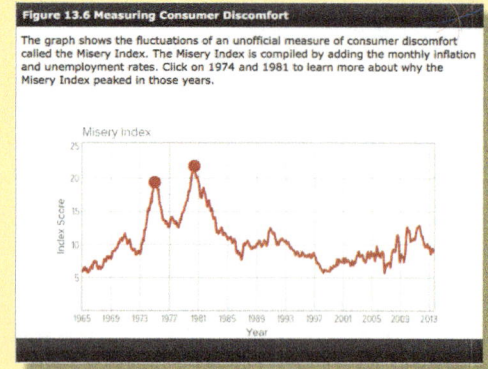

ANSWERS, p. 388
CRITICAL THINKING
1981

Although it is not an official government statistic, the misery index provides a reasonable indicator of consumer suffering during periods of high inflation and high unemployment.

Uncertainty

When the economy is unstable, a great deal of uncertainty exists. Workers may not buy something because of concern over their jobs. This uncertainty translates into many consumer purchases that are not made, causing unemployment to rise as jobs are lost.

Workers are not the only ones affected by uncertainty. The owner of a business that is producing at capacity may decide against an expansion even though new orders are arriving daily. Instead, the producer may try to raise prices, which increases inflation. Even government may decide to spend less on schools and roads if it is not sure of its revenues.

Political Instability

Politicians also suffer the consequences of economic instability. When times are difficult, voters are dissatisfied, and incumbents are often voted out of office. For example, many experts believe that Barack Obama's victory over his Republican opponent in November 2008 was due in part to the pain inflicted by the Great Recession.

Events like the government shutdown of 2013 are a significant cause of economic instability. If too much economic instability exists, as during the Great Depression of the 1930s, some voters are willing to vote for radical change. As a result, economic instability adds to the political instability of our nation.

Community and Domestic Matters

Recession, inflation, and unemployment can also lead to higher rates of crime and poverty. They also contribute to domestic problems such as marital instability and divorce, especially when individuals or families face uncertainty because lost jobs and income make it difficult to pay the bills. Thus all of us have a stake in reducing economic instability.

✓ **READING PROGRESS CHECK**

Identifying What makes the GDP gap a type of opportunity cost?

LESSON 3 REVIEW

Reviewing Vocabulary
1. *Defining* Explain what the misery index is, whether it is official or not, and when it usually reaches a peak.

Using Your Notes
2. *Interpreting* Use your notes to identify what types of unemployment would affect part-time sales clerks.

Answering the Guiding Questions
3. *Examining* Who is not included in the labor force?
4. *Explaining* Why are some types of unemployment unavoidable?
5. *Assessing* How can economic instability affect you?

Writing About Economics
6. *Informative/Explanatory* Write an essay explaining how, as a member of the workforce, you cope with economic instability. What specific steps can you now take and plan to take in the future that would help protect your job and your income?

CHAPTER 13, LESSON 3
Unemployment

C Critical Thinking Skills

Theorizing about war and unemployment Have a class discussion about war and unemployment. **Ask: How might a war contribute to both inflation and unemployment?** *(Government wartime spending increases could contribute to inflation; the rising costs of the war could cause a rise in uncertainty, which would reduce consumer spending and increase unemployment.)*

R Reading Skills

Tying unemployment to social problems
Ask: What social problems are associated with unemployment? *(Answers will vary, but students may mention a disruption of families, reduce a person's self-respect, and a rise in crime.)*

CLOSE & REFLECT

W Writing Skills

Reflecting on prospects for employment Have students research the employment prospects for recent college graduates. Have them use their research to develop a plan of action for gaining employment after graduation.

ANSWERS, p. 389

✓ **READING PROGRESS CHECK** It is an opportunity cost because it measures output not produced.

LESSON 3 REVIEW ANSWERS

Reviewing Vocabulary
1. The misery index is an unofficial index which is the sum of the monthly inflation and unemployment rates.

Using Your Notes
2. Student answers should show that they understand the different types of unemployment sources. Their answers should include structural unemployment, technological unemployment, cyclical unemployment, and seasonal unemployment.

Answering the Guiding Questions
3. People in the military and those confined to jail or mental health facilities are not included in the labor force.
4. Some types of unemployment that are unavoidable are seasonal unemployment, cyclical unemployment, structural unemployment, and technological unemployment.
5. Student answers should show an awareness that economic instability is a reality in the twenty-first century. Their answers could include that their plans for after high school are affected by economic insecurity and that the work skills they will focus on are affected by economic insecurity.

Writing About Economics
6. Student essays should demonstrate an awareness that there are ways to cope with economic insecurity. They can be careful in the work skills they choose to acquire, the industry they intend to work in, and how they handle their income.

CHAPTER 13
Debate

ENGAGE

C Critical Thinking Skills

Gathering information about reasons for wars Have students identify recent wars. **Ask: Where and when have wars occurred over the past fifty years?** *(Sample answers: Vietnam in the 1960s through 1975, Bosnia in the early 1990s, the Persian Gulf in the early 1990s, Afghanistan beginning in 2001)* Have students suggest causes of war in general, and list these causes on the board. Then ask students to analyze the list and evaluate what the main causes appear to be for the wars they identified. **Verbal/Linguistic**

TEACH & ASSESS

R Reading Skills

Identifying the causes and effects of war Ask students to choose one phrase from each side of the argument that states the main cause of war. Have students note each side's frame of reference. Then ask students to explain in their own words what effect that cause has on the daily lives of people whose countries are at war.

W Writing Skills

Arguing sides of the debate on reasons for war Have students rewrite one of the sides of the argument in their own words, using examples from daily life that support what they think is important for maintaining world peace.

Debates

C Is economic stability the key to world peace?

Almost 400 conflicts and wars took place around the globe during 2012. What was at the root of these conflicts? How can we reduce the threat of future wars? There are many answers to these questions.

R

Most experts agree that each conflict is different and is governed by multiple causes and circumstances. But if the world community got together, combined resources, and sought to put an end to regional and international conflicts, what would it target?

W

Some experts say economic instability and related issues are the source of most wars. Others disagree, arguing that other challenges, such as ethnic or religious rivalries, injustice, terrorism, and nationalism are the basis of the majority of wars. Review the arguments and come to your own conclusions.

YES Economic development is key to world peace because...

- POVERTY AND LACK OF ECONOMIC OPPORTUNITY CAUSE VIOLENCE
- UNEMPLOYMENT AND IDLENESS BREED DISCONTENT
- TRADE LESSENS THE THREAT OF WAR
- INEQUALITY CAUSES DISAGREEMENTS WHICH CAN LEAD TO WARFARE

> Everyone is however aware that there can be no peace without development, as insecurity and violence feed on poverty, injustice, and inequalities.
>
> —Dr. Jean Ping, chairperson of the African Union Commission, at the Third Africa-Europe Summit in Tripoli

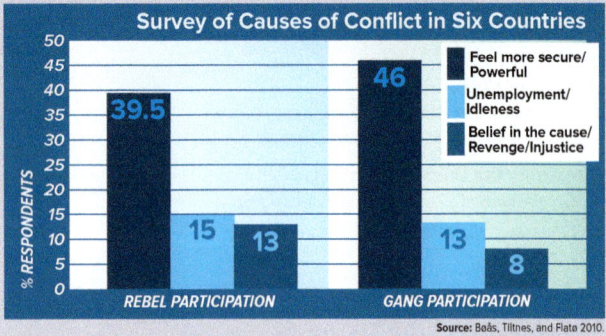

Survey of Causes of Conflict in Six Countries

Rebel Participation: 39.5 (Feel more secure/Powerful), 15 (Unemployment/Idleness), 13 (Belief in the cause/Revenge/Injustice)
Gang Participation: 46, 13, 8

Source: Baås, Tiltnes, and Flatø 2010.

390

---

networks Online Teaching Options

DEBATE

Debate: Is economic stability the key to world peace?

Exploring issues related to wars Have students choose a war to research; in particular, researching causes of the war. Then have them read the Debate feature. Finally, have them write a journal entry in the voice of a person who has gone through the war they researched, explaining reasons for the war, and supporting one side of the Debate about economic reasons for war. **Verbal/Linguistic**

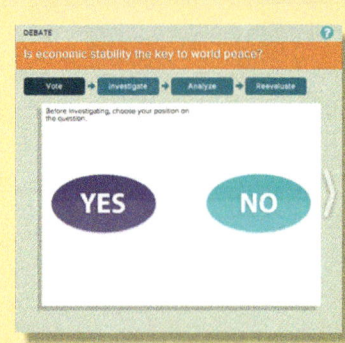

NO Economic stability is not the key to world peace because...

- ECONOMIC DEVELOPMENT CAN ONLY OCCUR AFTER PEACE IS ESTABLISHED
- PEOPLE WANT DEMOCRACY; ECONOMICS WILL COME LATER
- REDUCING ETHNIC RIVALRIES AND EXTREMISM MUST COME FIRST
- INJUSTICE IS A ROADBLOCK TO ANY ECONOMIC IMPROVEMENTS

"I believe that peace is unstable where citizens are denied the right to speak freely or worship as they please; choose their own leaders or assemble without fear. Pent-up grievances fester, and the suppression of tribal and religious identity can lead to violence."

—President Barack Obama, "Nobel Lecture: A Just and Lasting Peace," December 2009

networks
TRY IT YOURSELF ONLINE
For an interactive version of this debate go to connected.mcgraw-hill.com

ANALYZING the issue

1. **Analyzing** According to his Nobel Prize speech, what does President Barack Obama believe are the primary causes of war? Do you agree or disagree? Why?

2. **Making Generalizations** Review the second graph, "Causes of Conflict 2012." What generalization can you make from these data about why conflicts break out? In other words, what do many of these reasons have in common?

3. **Defending** Which side of the argument do you find most compelling? Explain your answer.

Causes of Conflict 2012
Source: Conflict Barometer 2012, Heidelberg Institute for International Conflict Research

391

CHAPTER 13
Debate

C Critical Thinking Skills

Debating the causes and effects of war Have students form two debate teams. Assign one team the Yes argument in the debate, and the other the No argument. Have each team read the feature and research real-life examples that support its argument. Then have a representative from each team present arguments to the class. Each team should also allow two minutes of questions by the other team. Finally, students should vote to decide which team supported its argument the best. **Verbal/Linguistic**

W Writing Skills

Narrating the causes and effects of war Have students write a dialogue between two people who have opposing views in this Debate. The dialogue should address the issues that each side believes are the main causes of war, and give examples of the effects of those causes.

Making Connections

Quotes about War Ask students to enter "causes of war quotes" into a search engine, and then click on one of the sites that result from their search. Have students select a quote they find interesting or that summarizes their opinions. Ask them to create a poster or mobile with the quotations and source material. **Ask:** Do any of the quotations tie war to economics? Explain. **AL Kinesthetic**

CLOSE & REFLECT

C Critical Thinking Skills

Drawing conclusions about the causes of war Have students take the side they defended in the Debate, or the war that they described, and write a paragraph about what can maintain peace.

> **ANSWERS, p. 391**
>
> **ANALYZING the issue**
>
> 1. President Obama believes that violence and war occur when societies don't have freedom of speech, religious freedom, democracy, or freedom of assembly. Students may agree or disagree but should give reasons for their views.
> 2. Students might suggest that most wars result from a desire for power or control, including control of political authority, borders, resources, and people.
> 3. Students should give facts and reasons based on the debate to support their response.

GRAPHIC ORGANIZER

Cause-and-Effect Chart

Recognizing economic causes and effects of wars Organize students into small groups of three or four and give each group the graphic organizer. Ask them to follow these steps to complete the activity:

1. Brainstorm a list of causes associated with the outbreak of wars.
2. Choose up to four primary causes and enter them on the cause-and-effect diagram.
3. Discuss the effects of wars and add them to the diagram. Have groups share their ideas with the class. **Interpersonal, Visual/Spatial**

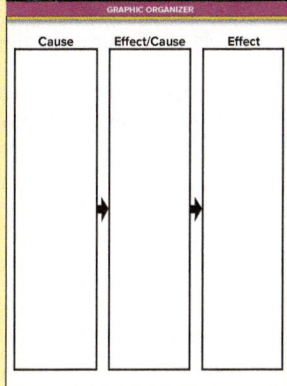

Economic Instability 391

Chapter 13
Study Guide

W Writing Skills

Illustrating inflation Have students create a poster representing the different types of inflation. An example of an item for the poster could be a photo of customers in a store frantically trying to buy a popular toy before its price increases. Ask students to include captions identifying each type of inflation.
Interpersonal

C Critical Thinking Skills

Creating a commercial to ease underemployment Point out to students that unemployment benefits do not cover the underemployed, or those people who are working in jobs that do not utilize their training. Ask students to do research on Web sites that help unemployed and underemployed find jobs or improve their skills in fields that are experiencing a labor shortage. Have students create a commercial presenting the options available to someone who is unemployed, or someone who cannot readily find employment in their chosen field. Students might post their commercials on the class or school Web site or share their information in a class presentation.

STUDY GUIDE

LESSON 1

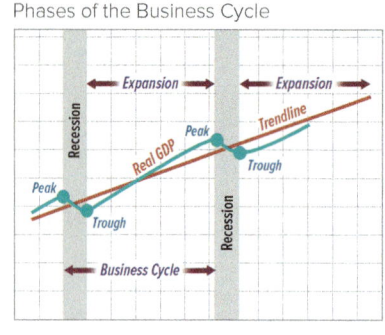
Phases of the Business Cycle

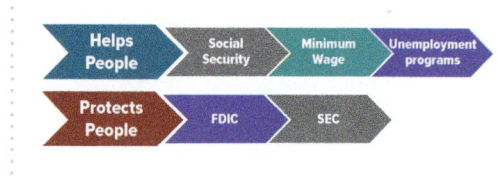

LESSON 2

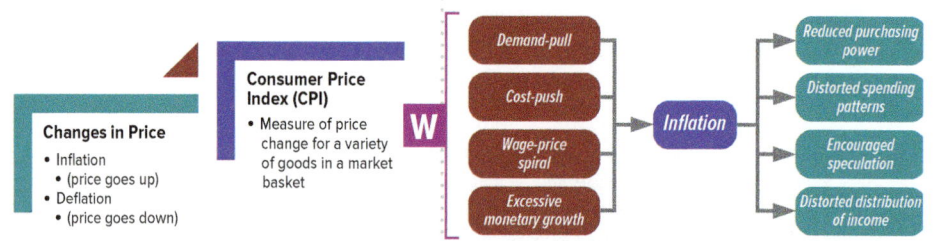

LESSON 3

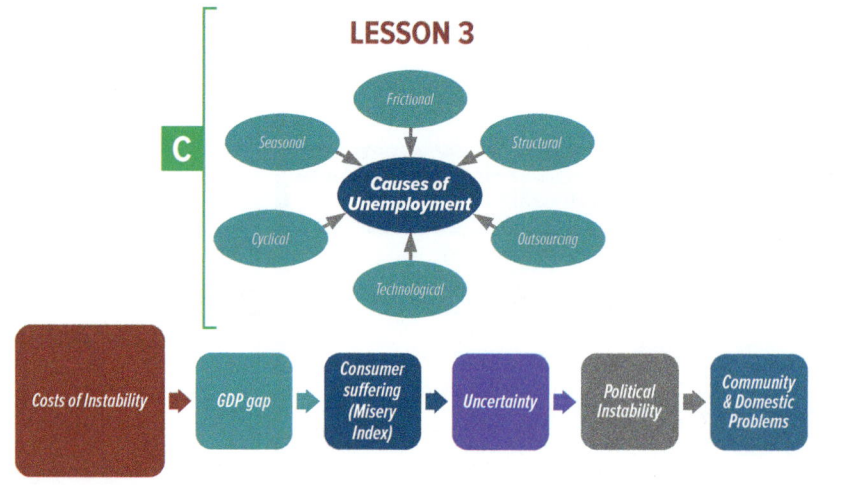

392

networks Online Teaching Options

WORKSHEET

Hands-on Chapter Project with Technology Extension

In this activity, student groups will create graphs that show leading economic indicators over the past ten years, and create a talk show that makes predictions about the future of the business cycle.

Find an additional activity online that incorporates technology for this project. Visit the EdTech Teacher Web sites for more links, tutorials, and other resources.

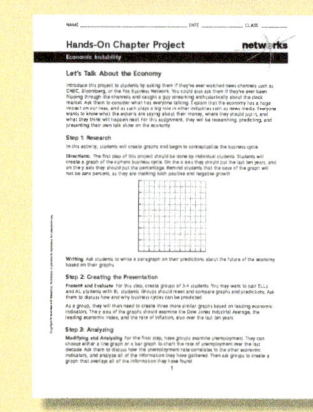

392

CHAPTER 13 Assessment

Directions: On a separate sheet of paper, answer the questions below. Make sure you read carefully and answer all the parts of the questions.

Lesson Review

Lesson 1

1. **Explaining** Describe the business cycle and explain what causes changes in it.

2. **Identifying Cause and Effect** What post-Depression reforms kept the economy from reaching Depression-level lows during the Great Recession of 2008–2009? Give two examples.

Lesson 2

3. **Comparing and Contrasting** What are the differences among creeping inflation, hyperinflation, and stagflation?

4. **Analyzing** How does inflation affect consumers?

Lesson 3

5. **Interpreting** How does education affect employment?

6. **Comparing and Contrasting** What makes structural and technological unemployment more serious than frictional unemployment?

Critical Thinking

7. **Speculating** How could an economy avoid severe economic downturns (recessions or depressions) over long periods of time?

8. **Drawing Conclusions** How could creditors avoid being hurt more than borrowers during periods of high inflation?

9. **Explaining** Describe some effects of economic instability. Which are human and which are economic effects, and why?

Analyzing Visuals

Use the visual below to answer the following questions.

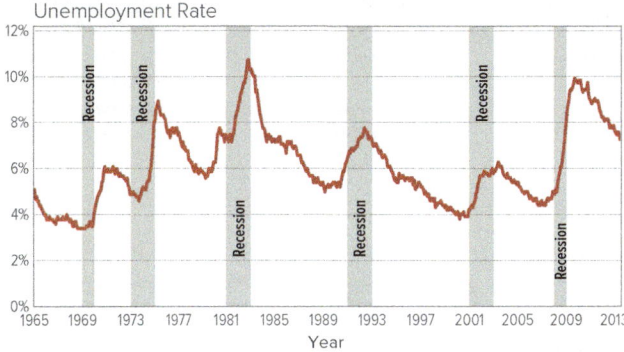

Unemployment Rate

10. **Identifying** During what periods did the United States have recessions? How do you know?

11. **Predicting** Based on the pattern shown in the graph, what will the unemployment rate do after 2013?

12. **Identifying** What does the graph show about the U.S. economy overall?

ANSWERING THE ESSENTIAL QUESTION

Review your answers to the introductory questions at the beginning of each lesson. Then answer the Essential Question on the basis of what you learned in the chapter. Have your answers changed?

13. **Identifying Cause and Effect** What are the causes and consequences of instability in the economy?

Need Extra Help?

If You've Missed Question	1	2	3	4	5	6	7	8	9	10	11	12	13
Go to page	367	370	377	380	383	386	368	381	387	367	367	367	387

Chapter 13 Assessment Answers

Lesson Review

Lesson 1

1. Students should include details about the business cycle, including how it indicates recession and expansion of the economy. There are many causes of changes, including external shocks, changes in investment spending, changes in monetary policy, fiscal policy shocks, and speculation bubbles. Students should list at least two of these.

2. Students should mention two of the reforms listed and how they helped. Social Security kept retirees from being destitute. Minimum wage laws prevented businesses from dropping their wages too low. Unemployment programs helped those who were out of work. The FDIC helped banks stay in business and protected the money of many citizens.

Lesson 2

3. Creeping inflation is slow inflation over time, such as U.S. economic growth of 1 to 3 percent per year. Hyperinflation is inflation of more than 500 percent in a year—it signals monetary collapse of an economy because it is out of control. Stagflation is part inflation and part stagnation—the economy inflates, but growth does not keep pace with inflation.

4. Inflation gives consumers less purchasing power (if their income does not keep pace with inflation) and causes consumers to change their spending habits, spending less when prices rise and more when they fall. It also encourages some consumers to speculate.

Lesson 3

5. People who have more education tend to be employed. The higher the education level, the less likely a person is to be unemployed.

6. Structural unemployment is the result of a significant change in the economy, like a shift away from horses to cars. Technological unemployment is similar and comes from a shift in technology that makes some workers unnecessary. The unemployment that results is harder to overcome than frictional unemployment (which is usually temporary) because the unemployed have to develop new skills and look for different types of jobs.

Critical Thinking

7. Students should indicate an understanding that such avoidance might require more government intervention in an economy. People would most likely have to give up some of their freedom of choice in order to have a more stable economy.

8. Creditors could lend to fewer people, start with high interest rates, or raise their interest rates to keep pace with inflation.

9. Effects of economic instability include GDP gap (not using all of production possibilities), increase in the misery index, uncertainty, political instability, more crime and poverty. The misery index, uncertainty, political instability, and crime are human effects that can lead to further economic effects like poverty and a greater GDP gap.

Analyzing Visuals

10. The United States had recessions during the peaks shown on the graph. When there is a recession, unemployment increases, hence the peaks.

11. Students should indicate an understanding of the graph pattern of peaks and troughs. Since 2013 is at least part of a trough, students should write that unemployment will continue to decrease and then increase again, or just that it will increase.

12. The graph shows that the economy goes in cycles of peaks and troughs.

Answering the Essential Question

13. Causes include overall changes in the economy—what is produced, how quickly it grows, how much people choose to invest and where, and so on. Consequences include unemployment, inflation, and so on.

Chapter 13
Assessment Answers

21st Century Skills

14. Students should use proper economic terminology and compare data effectively. The causes of inflation are described in Lesson 2.

15. Students should indicate that more government intervention into the market would likely be necessary to smooth out the cycle. Solutions proposed may include greater regulation of financial markets, fiscal policy in an attempt to stimulate growth, or monetary policy in order to control inflation or manage the money supply. In any case, the student should also include the potential disadvantages of such top-down intervention, which may include the greater intrusion of the government into individual purchasing decisions.

16. Students should include all of the types of unemployment and should speak from personal experience as much as possible. Possible effects include short- or long-term unemployment, retraining, further education, and so on.

Building Financial Literacy

17. Students may suggest building up their education and skill base, choosing fairly safe investments, following a budget, choosing a career in a field that's growing, finding low interest rates for any necessary loans, and so on. A personal savings plan may demonstrate an understanding of putting a certain amount away (10 percent, 20 percent, etc.) for larger future expenses, closer budgeting of day-to-day expenses, and a prioritization of which purchases are more important, immediate, or necessary than others.

Analyzing Primary Sources

18. Students should point to Raskin's arguments regarding the difficulties of maintaining employment, lack of job and income growth, rise in inequality, and lack of wealth beyond a mortgage.

19. Students should use proper economic terminology with regard to business cycles. They should point to the economic recession and the cyclical nature of business to explain that the economy will recover over time, but inequality will persist because of the factors Raskin mentions.

20. People have responded to the recession by curtailing their spending and focusing on reducing debt. Students may predict that that response will elongate the recession because a lack of spending slows economic growth.

394

CHAPTER 13 Assessment

Directions: On a separate sheet of paper, answer the questions below. Make sure you read carefully and answer all parts of the questions.

21st Century Skills

14. Presentation Skills Choose a cause of inflation. Create a graph or chart showing data related to that cause of inflation and present your graphic to the class. Be sure to explain how the parts of the graph or chart are related and why you think this cause of inflation is significant.

15. Create and Analyze Arguments and Draw Conclusions Write a blog post arguing that ups and downs in the business cycle are not necessary. Include in your argument a solution to those ups and downs. How would you change the economy to smooth out the cycle? What are the possible disadvantages of your approach?

16. Compare and Contrast Create a chart that compares the different types of unemployment (frictional, structural, technological, cyclical, seasonal). Identify any types that have affected people you know, and write a paragraph explaining the consequences of those types of unemployment. If you don't know anyone who has experienced unemployment, write a paragraph about the effects of the different types of unemployment.

Building Financial Literacy

17. Planning You should plan ahead for the inevitable ups and downs that the economy faces. What steps can you take to ensure that you are not overly affected by the downturns of the business cycle? If you were to design a personal savings program that allowed you to both buy some of the things you want now and save for the future, what would that program look like?

Analyzing Primary Sources

Read the excerpt and answer the questions that follow.

PRIMARY SOURCE

"Compounding the effect of falling house prices on household wealth and credit was the fact that these low- to middle-income households are also composed of some of the groups that have historically borne the brunt of downturns in the labor market. During recessions, the young, the less educated, and minorities are more likely to experience flat or declining wages, reduced hours, and unemployment. While this disparity is not a new phenomenon, dealing with a loss in labor income during the most recent recession was a heightened challenge to households that had mortgage obligations and no other forms of wealth to cushion the blow. . . .

[Households] have come to realize that house prices will not rise indefinitely and that their labor income prospects are less rosy than they had believed. As a result, they are curtailing their spending in an effort to rebuild their nest eggs and may also be trimming their budgets in order to bring their debt levels into alignment with their new economic realities. . . .

[T]here is also some evidence to suggest that the factors that contributed to the rise in inequality and the stagnation of wages in the bottom half of the income distribution, such as technological change that favors those with a college education and globalization, are still at play in the recovery—and perhaps may have accelerated. About two-thirds of all job losses in the recession were in middle-wage occupations—such as manufacturing, skilled construction, and office administration jobs—but these occupations have accounted for less than one-fourth of subsequent job growth."

—Federal Reserve Governor Sarah Bloom Raskin, April 18, 2013

18. Examining Primary Sources What evidence in the passage supports the idea that people with middle or low incomes suffered more than the wealthy during the Great Recession? Quote at least one sentence from the passage.

19. Explaining Use what you know about economic cycles to explain the results of the Great Recession that Raskin describes.

20. Predicting According to Raskin, how have people responded to the recession? What effects do you think that response will have?

Need Extra Help?

If You've Missed Question	14	15	16	17	18	19	20
Go to page	378	367	386	372	371	371	372

394

---

networks Online Assessment Options

WORKSHEET

Chapter Tests and Lesson Quizzes

Chapter 13 Tests Forms A and B Have students complete the Chapter Tests and Lesson Quizzes to assess student understanding throughout the chapter. Print and online assessment tools offer chapter and lesson evaluation through a variety of question formats, including document-based questions.

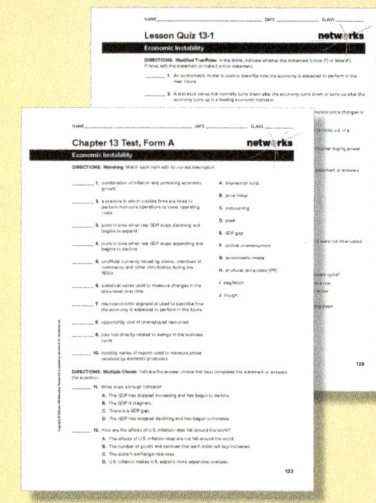

UNIT 6
GOVERNMENT AND THE ECONOMY Planner

UNDERSTANDING BY DESIGN®

Enduring Understanding
- Governments are formed to maintain order and regulate activities in a geographic area.

Essential Questions
- How does the government collect revenue, and on what is that revenue spent?
- How does the government promote the economic goals of price stability, full employment, and economic growth?
- How do we know if macroeconomic equilibrium has been achieved?

Students will know:
- the types of taxes at the local, state, and national levels; the economic importance of each type of taxes; the basis on which they are levied; and the categories to which each type belongs—proportional, progressive, and regressive.
- the factors involved in making city, state, and national budgets, and the ways that tax revenue is used in the community.
- how the government uses fiscal policy to promote the economic goals of price stability, full employment, and economic growth.
- the government runs a budget deficit when its expenditures exceed its revenues.
- the structure and functions of the Federal Reserve System.

Students will be able to:
- **discuss** the three general criteria for effective taxes; the two principles of taxation in use in the United States; the three types of taxes; and the effects of taxes on resources, behavior, productivity, and growth in a society.
- **summarize and explain** tax reform attempts since 1981, the process of determining an annual federal budget, sources of revenue, categories of government expenditures, and the difficulties of reducing the national debt.
- **evaluate and describe** the goals, methods, and limitations of demand-side policies as well as supply-side policies.
- **explain** how monetary policy works, the tools the Fed uses to expand and contract the money supply, and the principle of monetary expansion under a fractional reserve system.
- **discuss** the importance of timing in the use of monetary policy.

Predictable Misunderstandings
Students may think:
- The country may go bankrupt if the national debt becomes too high.
- Property tax applies only to homeowners.
- The federal government can solve most economic problems by adjusting the level of government-sector spending.
- Government interventions can be temporary measures that are repealed as soon as the economy stabilizes.
- The Federal Reserve System is an agency of the federal government.

Assessment Evidence
Performance Task
- Hands-On Chapter Projects with Technology Extensions
- Economic Simulations
- Math Practice for Economics
- Personal Finance Activities
- Reinforcing Economic Skills Activities

Other Evidence:
- Guided Reading Activities
- Vocabulary Activities
- Lesson Quizzes
- Chapter Tests, Forms A and B

Key for Using the Teacher Edition

SKILL-BASED ACTIVITIES

Types of skill activites found in the Teacher Edition.
- **V** **Visual Skills** require students to analyze maps, graphs, charts, and photos.
- **R** **Reading Skills** help students practice reading skills and master vocabulary.
- **C** **Critical Thinking Skills** help students apply and extend what they have learned.
- **W** **Writing Skills** provide writing opportunities to help students comprehend the text.
- **T** **Technology Skills** require students to use digital tools effectively.

*Letters are followed by a number when there is more than one of the same type of skill on the page.

DIFFERENTIATED INSTRUCTION

All activities are written for the on-level student unless otherwise marked with the leveled labels below.
- **BL** Beyond Level
- **AL** Approaching Level
- **ELL** English Language Learners

All students benefit from activities that utilize different learning styles. Many activities are marked as below when a particular learning style is highlighted.

Intrapersonal
Logical/Mathematical
Visual/Spatial
Verbal/Linguistic
Naturalist
Kinesthetic
Auditory/Musical
Interpersonal

SUGGESTED PACING GUIDE—Semester

Introducing the Unit . . . . ½ Day
Chapter 14: Taxes and Government Spending . . . . 5 Days
Chapter 15: Fiscal Policy . . . . 5 Days
Chapter 16: Monetary Policy . . . . 5 Days

UNIT 6: GOVERNMENT AND THE ECONOMY PLANNER

PLANNER

✓ Print Teaching Options

C Critical Thinking Skills

☐ **p. 395 Connecting the cost of public goods and services with taxes** Students list public goods and services that they use, such as road maintenance and police protection, that are funded by government. Then they look at deductions from their paychecks to see how much money is deducted by each level of government.

☐ **p. 395 Understanding fractional reserves** Students start with 10 pennies and walk through the actions that banks take in loaning out fractional reserves. Students see how the deposits increase the amount of money in circulation.

☐ **p. 396 Evaluating economic data using graphs, charts, and tables** Students recognize the differences among line graphs, bar graphs, and circle graphs. Students practice using graphs, charts, and tables by doing research on their city or town's revenue and expenditures, and then creating bar graphs or circle graphs that show where the revenue comes from and on what the money is spent.

W Writing Skills

☐ **p. 395 Proposing methods to stimulate the economy** Students act as economic advisers reporting to the president. They investigate different methods that might be used to stimulate the economy. **Verbal/Linguistic**

✓ Online Teaching Options

☐ **ANIMATION Taxes and You**—Students research the types of taxes that people in their community typically must pay.

☐ **APPROACHING GRADE LEVEL READER Alternative Student Edition narrative**—You can assign your students who are struggling to read on grade level the Approaching Grade Level version of the Online Student Edition. This reader presents all of the content in the On Grade Level version of the Online Student Edition at a lower reading level.

☐ **ENGLISH LANGUAGE LEARNER READER Alternative Student Edition narrative with ELL support**—Use the Online English Language Learner reader to provide additional reading support for ELL students. You can find this tool in the Online Student Edition.

✓ Printable Digital Worksheets

R Reading Skills

☐ **WORKSHEET Guided Reading Activity**—Students use the Guided Reading Activities worksheets to review their comprehension of the content.

☐ **WORKSHEET Reading Essentials and Study Guide**—Students complete the study guide and answer Reading Progress Check and vocabulary questions.

C Critical Thinking Skills

☐ **WORKSHEET Taxes and You Animation Activity**—Students answer questions about the types of taxes that people in their community typically must pay.

☐ **WORKSHEET Assessing Background Knowledge Activity**—Students should complete the Assessing Background Knowledge Activity before they study each chapter. Students' responses will give you a good idea of the kinds of misconceptions you can address when teaching the lessons.

☐ **WORKSHEET Chapter Summary**—Summaries are provided for each chapter and thoroughly condense core content into manageable chunks.

☐ **WORKSHEET Vocabulary Activity**—Students apply their knowledge of content and academic vocabulary words.

UNIT 6

Government and the Economy

CHAPTER 14
Taxes and Government Spending

ESSENTIAL QUESTIONS

How does the government collect revenue, and on what is that revenue spent?

How do we know if macroeconomic equilibrium has been achieved?

CHAPTER 15
Fiscal Policy

ESSENTIAL QUESTION

How does the government promote the economic goals of price stability, full employment, and economic growth?

CHAPTER 16
Monetary Policy

ESSENTIAL QUESTION

How does the government promote the economic goals of price stability, full employment, and economic growth?

IT MATTERS BECAUSE...

The monetary policy of the United States has an impact on the lives of everyone in the U.S. as well as others around the globe. The Federal Reserve System is responsible for establishing this policy, which affects our money and the lending practices of banks. Understanding how the actions of the Federal Reserve System and our government influence the nation's money supply can help you understand the role of money in your life and in our global economy.

UNIT 6
Government and the Economy

ENGAGE

Connecting the cost of public goods and services with taxes Ask: **What are some positive uses of tax money?** *(Students might mention education and public safety improvements.)* Tell students that local, state, and federal taxes pay for items that are public goods and services. Ask students to list public goods and services that they use, such as road maintenance and police protection. Ask students to look at deductions from their paychecks or a generic paycheck to see how much money is deducted by each level of government. Tell students that in this unit they will learn more about the ways that the government makes and spends money.

Proposing methods to stimulate the economy Organize students into several groups, and ask them to imagine they are panels of economic advisers reporting to the president. Then provide the following hypothetical situation: Recently, the national economy has been in a recession, with unemployment at 7 percent and rising, inflation at 4 percent, investment at low levels, and economic growth close to 1.5 percent. The president has asked for recommendations on how to stimulate the economy. Have groups investigate the different methods that might be used, starting with the information in this unit. Ask groups to prepare a written report listing their recommendations.

Understanding fractional reserves Begin this activity by giving a student 10 pennies. This Student One deposits the pennies in Bank A. (The "bank" is another student.) Set the reserve requirement at "1 penny" of each new deposit. Ask: **How many pennies can be loaned out?** *(9 pennies)* Then have Bank A loan the pennies to Student Two. Ask: **How many pennies are in the money supply now?** *(19: 10 deposited in Bank A and 9 on loan to Student Two)* Have Student Two "make a purchase at the cost of 9 pennies" from a third student, who then deposits the money in Bank B. Ask: **How many pennies are in the money supply now?** *(28 pennies)* Then have Bank B loan out 8 pennies. Again take a count of the money supply. *(36 pennies are in the money supply: 10 in Bank A, 9 loaned out from Bank A, 9 deposited in Bank B, and 8 loaned out)* Continue until students grasp the concept.

ANIMATIONS **WORKSHEET**

Taxes and You

Analyzing the animation Have students view the animation on how taxation affects them directly. Then ask them to research the types of taxes that people in their community typically must pay. Have them create a fictional character who owns a house and has a job in their community. Have them make up a value for the house and property using average property values in their community, and a yearly income for the job using the average salary for people in their community. Then direct them to create a table showing what their fictional character pays in taxes for each type of tax. For sales taxes, have students estimate an average amount spent per year on items that would be subject to the sales tax.

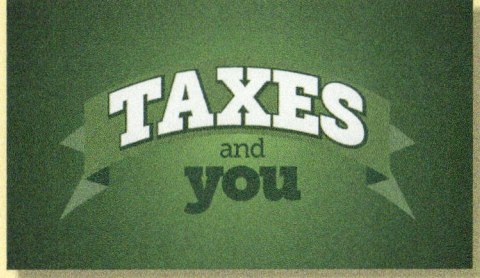

UNIT 6
Government and the Economy

DEVELOP YOUR SKILLS ONLINE

Evaluating Economic Data Using Graphs, Charts, and Tables

Have students practice evaluating economic data using the interactive graphs, charts, and tables. Begin by helping students recognize the differences among line graphs, bar graphs, and circle graphs:

- Line graphs are drawings that compare numerical values. They often are used to compare changes over time or differences between places, groups of items, or other related events.
- Bar graphs are often used to show changes over time or to compare quantities between similar categories of information.
- Circle graphs usually show the relationship of parts to a whole.

Remind students that they may wish to use a table or a chart to organize and display information. Tables and charts are often used to show comparisons between similar categories of information. Tables usually compare statistical or numerical data. Tabular data is presented in columns and rows. Charts often show a wider variety of information than tables.

To practice using graphs, charts, and tables, have students do research on their city or town's revenue and expenditures. Have them create bar graphs or circle graphs that show where the revenue comes from, and on what the money is spent. Have students write a summary of what the graphs show, evaluating their town's financial situation and making suggestions for possible changes or improvements.

Develop your Skills Online

networks TRY IT YOURSELF ONLINE
Try using interactive graphs online at connected.mcgraw-hill.com

Evaluate Economic Data
Using Charts, Tables, Graphs, and Maps.

Economists need to be comfortable viewing and interpreting data in a variety of visual formats. The data could be displayed in a simple table of numbers, or presented as a type of graph, or even placed alongside a map to make a comparison to geographic data. This economics program provides many opportunities to interpret and evaluate data using all of these types of visual presentations.

Each Chapter Assessment features a series of Analyzing Visuals questions that are based on a visual presentation of economic data.

Each visual to be evaluated will feature questions that test your ability to examine the economic data.

Sometimes the Analyzing Visual will be a table of data that needs to be evaluated.

Other chapter assessments may present a visual infographic or a line graph. Answering these questions will improve your ability to examine and interpret data.

Analyzing Visuals
Use the supply and demand schedule and the supply and demand curve to answer the following questions.

A Supply & Demand Schedule

Price	Quantity Demanded	Quantity Supplied	Surplus/ Shortage
$11	0	52	52
$9	4	44	40
$7	12	36	24
$5	24	24	0
$3	40	12	−28
$1	60	0	−60

Find all your interactive resources for each chapter online.   **TRY IT YOURSELF** ONLINE

Chapter 14 Taxes and Government Spending
ANALYZING VISUALS
Assessment, question 11

11 *Analyzing* The two graphs show what happens when the government places a $1.00 tax on a product. Which panel shows an incidence of tax in which the consumer pays more of the tax than the producer?

Chapter 15 Fiscal Policy
ANALYZING VISUALS
Assessment, questions 11 and 12

11 *Analyzing Visuals* What change in fiscal policy could explain the change in aggregate demand from AD¹ to AD²? Explain your answer.

12 *Analyzing Visuals* Which aggregate demand curve represents the higher-performing economy? How can you tell?

Chapter 16 Monetary Policy
ANALYZING VISUALS
Assessment, questions 11 and 12

11 *Identifying Graphs* In Graph A, Monetary Expansion, by the Fed's keeping interest rates low, what is the total addition to the money supply?

12 *Reading Graphs* In Graph B, Monetary Contraction, what happened on Tuesday to the amount of money added to the money supply? Why is that less than in Graph A?

396

---

networks **Online Teaching Options**

CHARTS

SAMPLE: Circular Flow of Economic Activity

Understanding the circular flow of economic activity Have students view Figure 12.2 and read the text aloud. Click on GNP to call out the production flows to business, government, and consumer sectors.
Ask: What government actions affect the circular flow? *(Social Security contributions are directed there, and business taxes and personal taxes flow there.)* **How is disposable personal income used?** *(personal savings and personal consumption)* **Where do personal consumption expenditures go?** *(They become part of GDP and GNP and then flow back into the economy in the form of wages, rent, interest, and so on.)* **Visual/Spatial**

Figure 12.2 Circular Flow of Economic Activity
The graph shows the income generated by production flows to the business, government, and consumer sectors. These sectors then use the income to purchase the nation's output.

Click on GNP to see the flow of economic activity.

CHAPTER 14
Taxes and Government Spending

UNDERSTANDING BY DESIGN®

Enduring Understanding
- Governments are formed to maintain order and regulate activities in a geographic area.

Essential Questions
- How does the government collect revenue, and on what is that revenue spent?

Predictable Misunderstandings
Students may think:
- *The country may go bankrupt if the national debt becomes too high.* Explain that most of the national debt is debt we owe to ourselves, and that the government does not necessarily have to pay off its debts within any given time frame. It often just issues new bonds to pay off the old ones.
- *Property tax applies only to homeowners.* Explain that the items included in the tax may vary from place to place, but property tax usually includes both tangible and intangible items. Furniture, stocks, bonds, and bank accounts are also property and are taxed in most locations.

Assessment Evidence
Performance Task
- Hands-On Chapter Project with Technology Extension

Other Evidence
- Guided Reading Activities
- Vocabulary Activity
- Lesson Quizzes
- Self-Check Quizzes
- Chapter Assessment
- Chapter Tests, Forms A and B

Council for Economic Education

Below are the Council for Economic Education Voluntary National Content Standards in Economics covered in the *Taxes and Government Spending* chapter.

Content Standard 16: There is an economic role for government in a market economy whenever the benefits of a government policy outweigh its costs. Governments often provide for national defense, address environmental concerns, define and protect property rights, and attempt to make markets more competitive. Most government policies also have direct or indirect effects on people's incomes.

SUGGESTED PACING

Introducing the Chapter: ½ Day	Lesson 3: State and Local Government Finances . . . . 1 Day
Lesson 1: Taxes . . . . 1 Day	Debate . . . . ½ Day
Case Study . . . . ½ Day	Study Guide, Chapter Assessment and Wrap-Up . . . . ½ Day
Lesson 2: Federal Government Finances . . . . 1 Day	

TOTAL 5 Days

Key for Using the Teacher Edition

SKILL-BASED ACTIVITIES

Types of skill activites found in the Teacher Edition.

V Visual Skills require students to analyze maps, graphs, charts, and photos.

R Reading Skills help students practice reading skills and master vocabulary.

C Critical Thinking Skills help students apply and extend what they have learned.

W Writing Skills provide writing opportunities to help students comprehend the text.

T Technology Skills require students to use digital tools effectively.

*Letters are followed by a number when there is more than one of the same type of skill on the page.

DIFFERENTIATED INSTRUCTION

All activities are written for the on-level student unless otherwise marked with the leveled labels below.

BL Beyond Level
AL Approaching Level
ELL English Language Learners

All students benefit from activities that utilize different learning styles. Many activities are marked as below when a particular learning style is highlighted.

Intrapersonal
Logical/Mathematical
Visual/Spatial
Verbal/Linguistic

Naturalist
Kinesthetic
Auditory/Musical
Interpersonal

CHAPTER 14: TAXES AND GOVERNMENT SPENDING

CHAPTER OPENER PLANNER

Students will know:
- to be effective, taxes must be equitable, easy to understand, and efficient.
- taxes can be levied on the basis of benefits received or the ability to pay.
- all taxes can be broken down into proportional, progressive, and regressive.
- the major revenue categories.

Students will be able to:
- **summarize** tax reform attempts since 1981.
- **explain** the process of determining an annual federal budget.
- **list** major federal expenditures.
- **discuss** the effect of a federal deficit on the national debt.
- **list** sources of revenue and largest expenditure categories at the state government level.
- **list** sources of revenue and largest expenditure categories at the local government level.

UNDERSTANDING BY DESIGN®

☑ Print Teaching Options

C Critical Thinking Skills

☐ **p. 397 Categorizing government spending**
Students brainstorm categories of government spending.

☐ **p. 399 Describing the results of budget cuts**
Students debate which programs should receive priority in the event of budget cuts.

☐ **p. 398 Summarizing taxes** Students create a T-chart to summarize the benefits and drawbacks of paying taxes.

W Writing Skills

☐ **p. 398 Explaining the need for revenue**
Students create a dialogue about the need for a revenue source.

☑ Online Teaching Options

V Visual Skills

☐ **IMAGE** **Chapter opener**—Students analyze a photo for clues about government expenditures.

C Critical Thinking Skills

☐ **INFOGRAPHICS** **Economic Perspectives**—Students compare and contrast federal revenues and expenditures.

☐ **DEBATES** **Should the rich pay higher taxes?**—Students analyze opposing opinions about taxing the rich.

☐ **INTERACTIVE FEATURE** **Case Study: From the President's Point of View**—Students discuss governmental financial planning and budgeting.

☑ Printable Digital Worksheets

C Critical Thinking Skills

☐ **WORKSHEET** **Assessing Background Knowledge Activity**—Target misconceptions to address when teaching the lessons.

☐ **WORKSHEET** **Chapter Summary**—Content is condensed into manageable chunks

☐ **WORKSHEET** **Vocabulary Activity**—Students use content and academic terms.

☐ **WORKSHEET** **Enrichment Activity**—Students review the effect of lobbying on taxes.

Project-Based Learning

Hands-On

Hands-On Chapter Project
Students work in groups, acting as reporters for a national online newspaper covering government policy. They will research information about taxation and spending in the past fiscal year, analyze this information, and create an infographic to easily convey the information to readers. Students will present their infographics in a poster gallery to be reviewed by their peers.

Digital Hands-On

Create Online Projects

Find an additional activity online that incorporates technology for the Hands-On Project. Visit the EdTech Teacher Web sites for more links, tutorials, and other resources.

Print Resources

ANCILLARY RESOURCE
This ancillary is available for every chapter and lesson.
- Chapter Tests and Lesson Quizzes

PRINTABLE DIGITAL WORKSHEETS
These printable digital worksheets are available for every chapter and lesson.
- Reading Essentials & Study Guide
- Vocabulary Activities
- Chapter Summaries
- Economic Simulations
- Math Practice for Economics
- Reinforcing Economic Skills
- Personal Finance Activities
- Enrichment Activities
- Reteaching Activities
- Guided Reading Activities
- Video Worksheets
- Lesson Quizzes and Chapter Tests (English and Spanish)

More Media Resources

SUGGESTED READING
- For students at a Grade 10 reading level:
Your Money at Work: Taxes, by Ernestine Giesecke
- For students at a Grade 11 reading level:
Other Revenue Sources Should Be Pursued, by William Straus
- For students at a Grade 12 reading level:
Careers Inside the World of the Government, by Sue Hurwitz

SUGGESTED VIDEOS MOVIES
Find these documentaries yourself online. NOTE: McGraw-Hill Education does not endorse these resources. Preview clips for age-appropriateness.
- *The Tax Free Tour* (53 min.)
- *TED Talks: Government—Investor, Risk-Taker, Innovator* (14 min.)

LESSON 1 Planner

TAXES

Students will know:
- to be effective, taxes must be equitable, easy to understand, and efficient.
- taxes can be levied on the basis of benefits received or the ability to pay.
- all taxes can be broken down into three categories—proportional, progressive, and regressive.

Students will be able to:
- **discuss** the effects of taxes on resources, behavior, productivity, and growth in a society.
- **describe** the three general criteria for effective taxes.
- **summarize** the two principles of taxation that are currently in use in the United States.
- **name** the three types of taxes that exist in the United States today.
- **analyze** the potential effects of alternative tax approaches.
- **summarize** tax reform attempts since 1981.

UNDERSTANDING BY DESIGN®

☑ *Print Teaching Options*

V Visual Skills
- ☐ p. 402 Visualizing the incidence of a tax
- ☐ p. 402 Graphing the incidence of a local tax

R Reading Skills
- ☐ p. 401 Connecting tax deductions and sin taxes to consumer behavior
- ☐ p. 401 Understanding the effects of taxes on productivity and growth
- ☐ p. 404 Determining ability-to-pay
- ☐ p. 405 Calculating the Medicare tax
- ☐ p. 408 Understanding the alternative minimum tax
- ☐ p. 410 Understanding the un-permanent tax cuts of 2011

C Critical Thinking Skills
- ☐ p. 400 Identifying perspectives about taxes
- ☐ p. 404 Applying the benefit principle of taxation
- ☐ p. 405 Hypothesizing a progressive sales tax
- ☐ p. 407 Predicting the consequences of a VAT
- ☐ p. 407 Evaluating tax goals and side effect
- ☐ p. 409 Comparing and contrasting tax reforms
- ☐ p. 410 Evaluating the fairness of the income tax system

W Writing Skills
- ☐ p. 400 Explaining the effects of taxes on resource allocation
- ☐ p. 403 Describing the three criteria of effective taxes
- ☐ p. 404 Comparing and contrasting the two principles of taxation
- ☐ p. 408 Explaining how to calculate individual income tax

☑ *Online Teaching Options*

V Visual Skills
- ☐ **GRAPHS** Shifting the Incidence of a Tax—Students explore the effects of demand on the incidence of a tax.
- ☐ **POLITICAL CARTOON** Taxes—Students view a cartoon about taxes.
- ☐ **VIDEO** Taxing Times—Students watch a video about the amount of taxes paid by different segments.
- ☐ **SLIDE SHOW** History of Tax Reform—Students write a summary of a tax reform.
- ☐ **INTERACTIVE FEATURE** Careers: Tax Attorney—Students research a job description.

C Critical Thinking Skills
- ☐ **BELLRINGER** Taxes—Students apply criteria for effective taxation.
- ☐ **ESSENTIAL QUESTION** Exploring the Essential Question—Students discuss services which may or may not be paid for by taxes.
- ☐ **CHARTS** Three Types of Taxes—Students contrast tax types on various groups.
- ☐ **CHARTS** Value-Added Tax—Students compare the effects of types of taxes.
- ☐ **CHARTS** Income Tax Table for Single Individuals—Students calculate the difference between two types of taxes.

W Writing Skills
- ☐ **GRAPHIC ORGANIZER** Economic Impact of Taxes—Students write about the effect of taxes on spending and saving behaviors.

T Technology Skills
- ☐ **SELF-CHECK QUIZ** Lesson 1—Students receive instant feedback on answers.
- ☐ **GAME** Lesson 1—Students solve clues to review lesson content.
- ☐ **INTERACTIVE WHITEBOARD ACTIVITY** What Would a Flat Tax Look Like?

☑ *Printable Digital Worksheets*

C Critical Thinking Skills
- ☐ **WORKSHEET** Math Practice—Students learn about progressive and regressive taxes.
- ☐ **WORKSHEET** Reinforcing Economic Skills—Students classify proposed taxes as progressive, proportional, and regressive.
- ☐ **WORKSHEET** Taxing Times Video Activity—Students answer questions about ability to pay.
- ☐ **WORKSHEET** Personal Finance Activity—Students explore paycheck deductions.

LESSON 2 Planner

FEDERAL GOVERNMENT FINANCES

Students will know:
- the major revenue categories and their respective proportions of local, state and federal budgets.
- when the government runs a budget deficit, it must borrow to finance that deficit.

Students will be able to:
- **explain** the process of determining an annual federal budget.
- **list** major federal expenditures.
- **discuss** the effect of a federal deficit on the national debt.
- **explain** how the transfer of purchasing power between generations affects future generations.
- **describe** the difficulties involved with reducing the national debt.

UNDERSTANDING BY DESIGN

✓ Print Teaching Options

V Visual Skills
- ☐ p. 418 Comparing the deficit and the debt
- ☐ p. 419 Examining the growth of the national debt

R Reading Skills
- ☐ p. 412 Defining fiscal and calendar years
- ☐ p. 413 Summarizing the federal budget process
- ☐ p. 414 Identifying the purpose of indexing
- ☐ p. 415 Understanding the necessity of government borrowing
- ☐ p. 415 Identifying excise taxes as regressive
- ☐ p. 416 Defining earmarks
- ☐ p. 417 Predicting the future of Medicare and Medicaid costs
- ☐ p. 418 Understanding the difference between the deficit and the debt
- ☐ p. 421 Understanding the line-item veto

C Critical Thinking Skills
- ☐ p. 414 Identifying reasons for borrowing
- ☐ p. 415 Calculating Social Security Taxes
- ☐ p. 415 Expressing opinions on corporate income taxes
- ☐ p. 416 Differentiating between mandatory and discretionary spending
- ☐ p. 420 Analyzing the national debt owed to foreigners
- ☐ p. 422 Hypothesizing about the difficulties of debt reduction

W Writing Skills
- ☐ p. 416 Offering opinions about user fees
- ☐ p. 420 Writing about the impact of the national debt

✓ Online Teaching Options

V Visual Skills
- ☐ **GRAPHS** Federal Budget for Fiscal Year 2014—Students use figures on the graph to write an equation for the federal deficit.
- ☐ **GRAPHS** Federal Budget for Fiscal Year 2014—Students use figures from the graph to create a poster.
- ☐ **GRAPHS** Two Views of the National Debt—Students discuss the concept of public debt.
- ☐ **CHARTS** Impact of the National Debt—Students sequence events.
- ☐ **VIDEO** Balancing Government Budgets—Students watch a video about local government budgets.

R Reading Skills
- ☐ **BIOGRAPHY** Daniel Werfel—Students read about Werfel's efforts to reduce the deficit.

C Critical Thinking Skills
- ☐ **BELLRINGER** Federal Government Finances—Students discuss federal spending and the federal deficit.
- ☐ **ESSENTIAL QUESTION** Exploring the Essential Question—Students analyze categories of federal spending.
- ☐ **GRAPHS** The Federal Deficit and The National Debt—Students explain the results of the decision not to use surplus to pay off national debt.

T Technology Skills
- ☐ **SELF-CHECK QUIZ** Lesson 2—Students receive instant feedback on their mastery of lesson content.
- ☐ **GAME** Lesson 2—Students solve clues to review lesson content.
- ☐ **INTERACTIVE WHITEBOARD ACTIVITY** Government Spending—Students examine expenditures and calculate their percentage of the budget.

✓ Printable Digital Worksheets

R Reading Skills
- ☐ **WORKSHEET** Guided Reading Activity—Students review their comprehension of the content.
- ☐ **WORKSHEET** Reading Essentials and Study Guide—Students complete the study guide and answer Reading Progress Check and vocabulary questions.

C Critical Thinking Skills
- ☐ **WORKSHEET** Balancing Government Budgets Video Activity—Students analyze efforts to balance local government budgets.
- ☐ **WORKSHEET** Influences on Tax Law Economic Simulation Activity—Students defend a tax law.

LESSON 3 Planner

STATE AND LOCAL GOVERNMENT FINANCES

Students will know:
- the ways that tax revenue is used in the community.
- the factors involved in making city, state, and national budgets.

Students will be able to:
- **list** sources of revenue at the state government level.
- **name** the largest state government expenditure categories.
- **list** sources of revenue at the local government level.
- **discuss** local variations in spending.

UNDERSTANDING BY DESIGN®

✓ Print Teaching Options

V Visual Skills

☐ **p. 426 Creating a poster about state government spending** Students illustrate various categories of state government spending. *Visual/Spatial*

R Reading Skills

☐ **p. 427 Reading graphs to understand local government expenditures** Students analyze the amount of spending for specified categories.

C Critical Thinking Skills

☐ **p. 423 Contrasting expenses covered by federal and local government** Students create a chart about federal and local services.

☐ **p. 424 Drawing conclusions from sales tax records** Students record sales tax paid on purchases.

☐ **p. 424 Comparing and contrasting state taxes** Students compare state tax rates of two states. *Logical/Mathematical*

☐ **p. 425 Researching behavior of taxpayers** Students interview various taxpayers.

☐ **p. 426 Making generalizations about higher education** Students tie state government with benefits of supporting education.

☐ **p. 427 Exploring property taxes** Students research property tax assessment in their community. *Logical/Mathematical*

☐ **p. 428 Comparing local utility revenues** Students identify utility rates for various communities.

W Writing Skills

☐ **p. 426 Writing persuasively about a balanced budget amendment** Students write a speech for or against a balanced budget amendment.

☐ **p. 427 Creating a speech about budgetary issues** Students propose a shift in spending within a local budget. *Verbal/Linguistic*

☐ **p. 429 Explaining the need for more expenditures** Students write a proposal for funding.

✓ Online Teaching Options

V Visual Skills

☐ **GRAPHS** **State Government Revenues and Expenditures**—Students view federal government allocated at the state level.

☐ **VIDEO** **Congress and Education Spending**—Students watch a video about earmarks.

☐ **GRAPHS** **Local Government Revenues and Expenditures**—Students discuss how funding from the state government allocated at the local level.

C Critical Thinking Skills

☐ **BELLRINGER** **State and Local Government Finances**—Students list pros and cons of privatizing parking.

☐ **ESSENTIAL QUESTION** **Exploring the Essential Question**—Students research services local government provides.

☐ **INTERACTIVE FEATURE** **Global Economy & You feature**—Students explore the need for higher taxes to provide needed services.

☐ **GRAPHIC ORGANIZERS** **Sources of State and Local Revenue**—Students write a paragraph comparing and contrasting two sources of state government revenue.

☐ **GRAPHS** **Local Government Revenues and Expenditures**—Students categorize spending.

T Technology Skills

☐ **SELF-CHECK QUIZ** **Lesson 3**—Students receive instant feedback on their answers.

☐ **GAME** **Lesson 3**—Students solve clues to review lesson content.

☐ **INTERACTIVE WHITEBOARD ACTIVITY** **Why Balance the Budget?**—Students work together to learn lesson content.

✓ Printable Digital Worksheets

R Reading Skills

☐ **WORKSHEET** **Guided Reading Activity**—Students review their comprehension of the content.

☐ **WORKSHEET** **Reading Essentials and Study Guide**—Students complete the study guide and answer Reading Progress Check and vocabulary questions.

☐ **WORKSHEET** **Reteaching Activity**—Students review and reteach chapter content.

C Critical Thinking Skills

☐ **WORKSHEET** **Congress and Education Spending Video Activity**—Students answer questions about earmarks.

CHAPTER 14 Taxes and Government Spending

INTERVENTION AND REMEDIATION STRATEGIES

LESSON 1 Taxes

Reading and Comprehension

Have students read the first lesson and identify the vocabulary words in the lesson. Have them define the vocabulary words and note the context in which they appear. Then have them summarize the lesson, using the vocabulary words.

Text Evidence

Have students look for two types of alternative taxes. Then have them define each type. Finally, have them look for evidence in the text that shows an example of each type of tax, and write the example next to their definition.

LESSON 2 Federal Government Finances

Reading and Comprehension

Have students write a definition for the word *budget*. Then have them read the section on how the federal budget is developed. Finally, have them compare the use of the word *budget* in the text with the way they use it in their everyday life.

Text Evidence

Have students find evidence in the text that the largest category of federal spending has changed from national defense to Social Security.

LESSON 3 State and Local Government Finances

Reading and Comprehension

Have students read the sections on state and local expenditures. Then have them explain what the word *expenditures* means. Finally, have them make a list of state expenditures, and a list of local ones.

Text Evidence

Have students read the sections on state and local revenues. Have them look for the word *intergovernmental*. Ask them to define the word. Then have them find evidence in the text that both state and local governments receive intergovernmental funds.

Online Resources

Assessing Background Knowledge Use this worksheet to pre-assess students' background knowledge before they start the chapter.

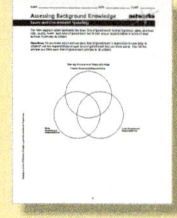

Chapter Summaries Have students use the summary as a pre-reading activity or as a post-reading review to check the main ideas covered in each lesson.

Guided Reading Activities Have students complete these activities as they read each lesson. They provide reading notes the student can use for review and to prepare for assessments.

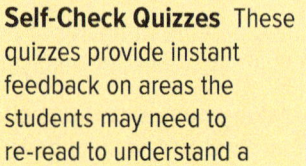

Reteaching Activities Have students complete the Reteaching Activity for remedial practice and review of vital content.

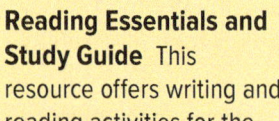

Self-Check Quizzes These quizzes provide instant feedback on areas the students may need to re-read to understand a main idea.

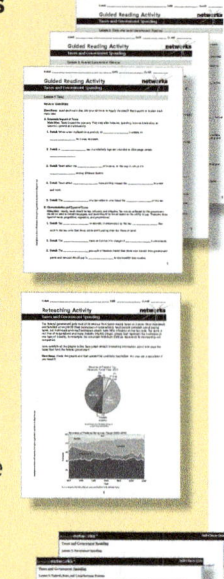

Reading Essentials and Study Guide This resource offers writing and reading activities for the approaching-level student.

Approaching Grade Level Reader This reader presents all of the content of the Online Student Edition but at a lower reading level.

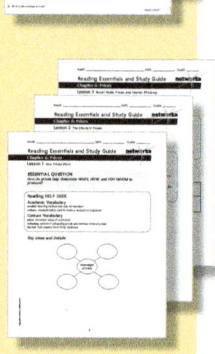

English Language Learner Reader Provide additional reading support for ELL students. Find this tool online.

Taxes and Government Spending

ESSENTIAL QUESTION
How does the government collect revenue, and on what is that revenue spent?

networks
www.connected.mcgraw-hill.com
There's More Online about taxes and government spending.

CHAPTER 14

Economic Perspectives
Money In, Money Out: Federal Revenue and Expenditures

Lesson 1
Taxes

Lesson 2
Federal Government Finances

Lesson 3
State and Local Government Finances

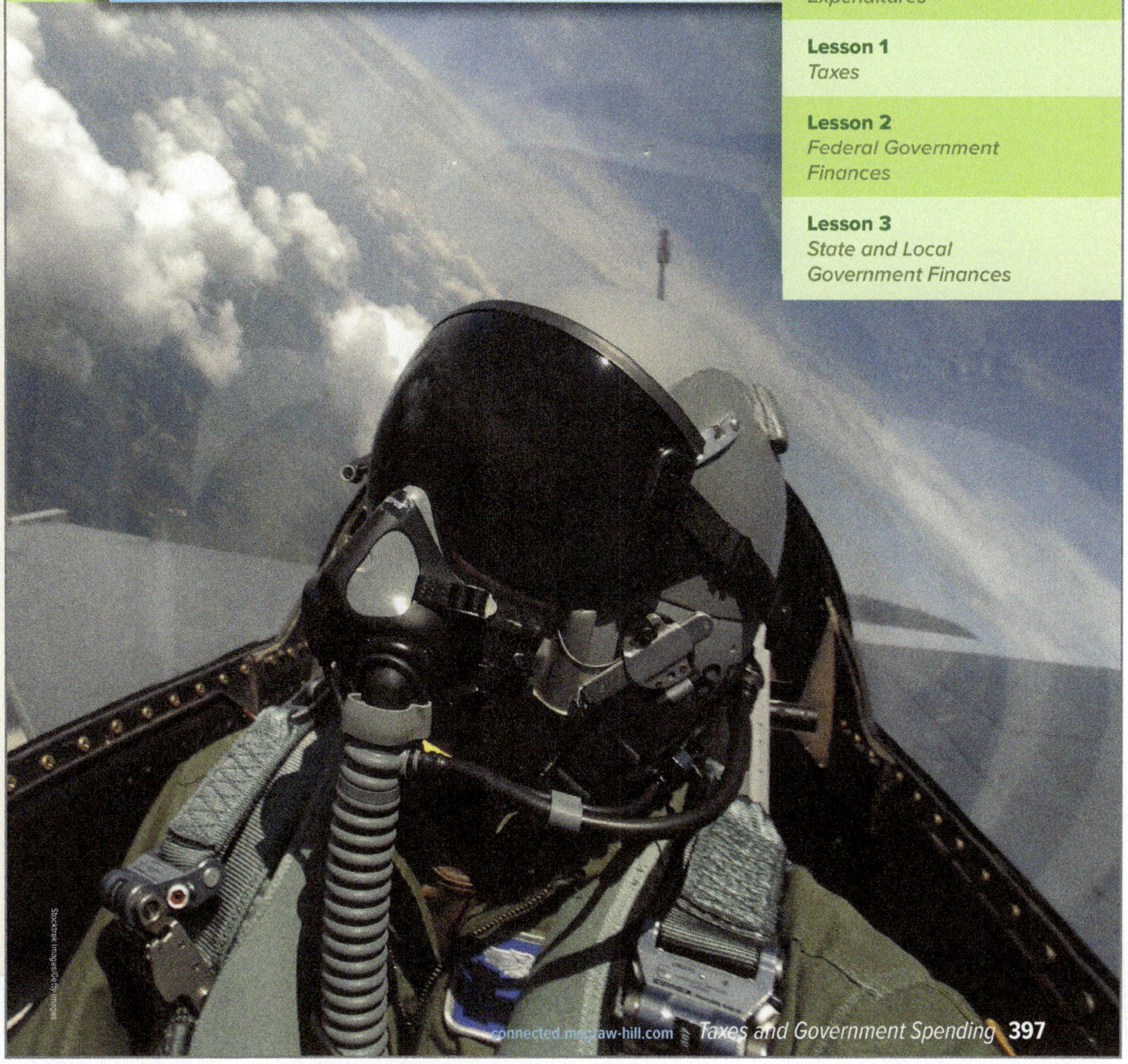

CHAPTER 14
Taxes and Government Spending

ENGAGE

Call students' attention to the photo and ask them to describe what it shows. Guide them to recognize that the pilot is flying a U.S. military airplane. **Ask: Why is this image a good one to symbolize the chapter titled *Taxes and Government Spending*?** *(The government spends a great deal of its revenue on the military.)* In a discussion, lead students to understand that taxes and government spending fluctuate from year to year, and are modified according to the country's needs as well as the state of the economy. **Visual/Spatial**

Categorizing government spending Ask: Where do taxpayer dollars go? *(Sample answer: the military, roads, social programs, government salaries)* Have students brainstorm other categories of government spending and list the categories on the board. Ask students to guess what percentage of the budget funds each category, and write the percentages on the board. Update the categories and percentages as you work through the chapter.

Making Connections

Government Support Have students consider the goods and services in their lives that are supported by federal, state, and local revenues. **Ask: Why does government pay for these services? What would you do if the services disappeared or were not government funded?**

Letter from the Author

Dear Economics Teacher,

When I teach government and taxes, I try to remind people that everyone is entitled to their own opinion, but *not* to their own set of facts. So the first order of business is to master some of the basic facts regarding taxes, and then evaluate whether the spending is consistent with the actions we want our government to take. After all, government can do some things better than we can do by ourselves. So be sure to let your students discuss government finances, but first tied to the facts, and then listen to the opinions.

Gary E. Clayton

FOLDABLES
Study Organizer

Go to the Foldables® library for a cumulative chapter-based Foldable® activity that your students can use to help take notes and prepare for assessment.

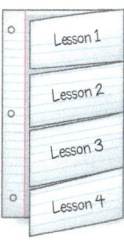

CHAPTER 14
Economic Perspectives

TEACH & ASSESS

Content Background Information

Budget Categories Many of the federal revenue and expenditure labels in the infographic fall under more general category titles in the official budget. For example, the "insurance" taxes shown (Old Age and Survivors, Disability, Hospital, and Unemployment Insurance Taxes) often fall under the general category of "Social Insurance and Retirement Receipts."

W Writing Skills

Explaining the need for revenue Have students choose one of the revenue sources in the infographic and create a dialogue between two people about the revenue source. Dialogues should discuss the need for the revenue source and whether it should be increased or reduced.
Verbal/Linguistic

C Critical Thinking Skills

Summarizing taxes Have students summarize in a T-chart the benefits and drawbacks of paying taxes.
BL *Verbal/Linguistic*

Economic Perspectives

MONEY IN, MONEY OUT: FEDERAL REVENUE AND EXPENDITURES*

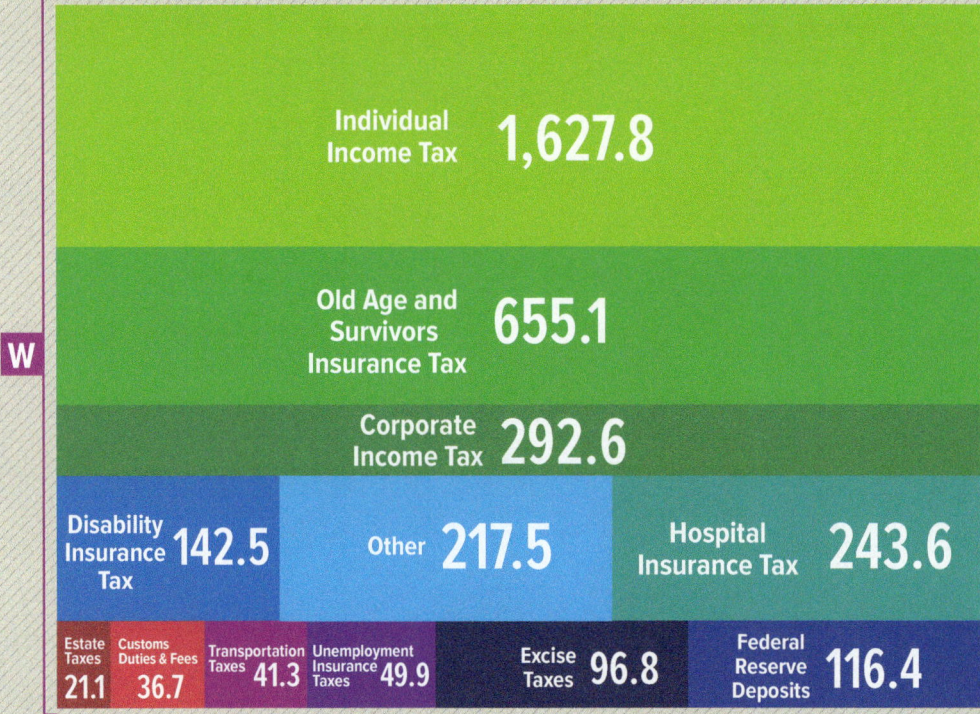

Revenue (in billions of dollars)

- Individual Income Tax: 1,627.8
- Old Age and Survivors Insurance Tax: 655.1
- Corporate Income Tax: 292.6
- Disability Insurance Tax: 142.5
- Other: 217.5
- Hospital Insurance Tax: 243.6
- Estate Taxes: 21.1
- Customs Duties & Fees: 36.7
- Transportation Taxes: 41.3
- Unemployment Insurance Taxes: 49.9
- Excise Taxes: 96.8
- Federal Reserve Deposits: 116.4

*Fiscal Year 2016 **Source:** Office of Management and Budget

Taxes support the costs of operating the government. Therefore taxes are the primary source of revenue for the federal government. The individual income tax on salary, which is the largest part of revenue, was created by the 16th Amendment in 1913. However, the roots of the individual income tax go back to Congress's passage of the Revenue Act of 1861.

---

networks Online Teaching Options

INFOGRAPHIC

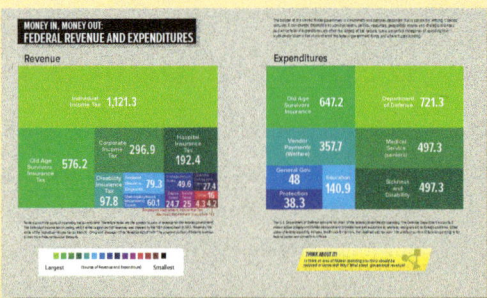

Economic Perspectives: Money In, Money Out: Federal Revenue and Expenditures

Identifying federal revenues and expenditures
Have students explore the infographic about federal revenues and expenditures for Fiscal Year 2016. Discuss with students the priorities evident from the largest-to-smallest federal expenditures. Have students voice their opinions about whether these priorities should change, and why or why not. Then have students compare the largest-to-smallest revenues and expenditures in the infographic to the bar graphs in Figure 14.5, which show revenues and expenditures in percentage form for Fiscal Year 2016 (estimated). Prompt students to notice that interest payments are not included as expenditures in the infographic. *Logical/Mathematical*

CHAPTER 14
Economic Perspectives

networks TRY IT YOURSELF ONLINE
For an interactive version of this infographic go to connected.mcgraw-hill.com

The budget of the United States government is a mammoth and complex document that is constantly shifting. Created annually, it can change depending on administrations, politics, resources, geopolitical events, and strategic alliances. And while federal expenditures are often the subject of hot debate, there are certain categories of spending that traditionally claim a lion's share of what the federal government funds and where it gets funding.

Expenditures (in billions of dollars)

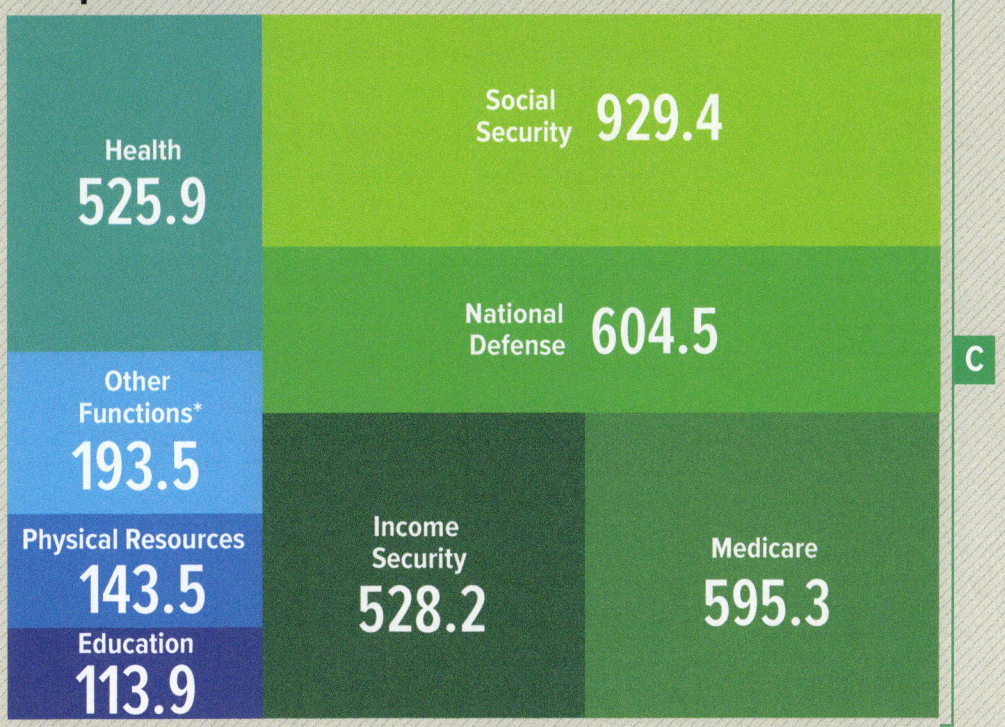

- Health: 525.9
- Social Security: 929.4
- National Defense: 604.5
- Other Functions*: 193.5
- Physical Resources: 143.5
- Income Security: 528.2
- Medicare: 595.3
- Education: 113.9

*Includes International Affairs; General Science, Space, and Technology; Agriculture; Administration of Justice; General Government; and Allowances.

Social Security and the U.S. Department of Defense accounts for much of the federal government's spending. Other significant areas of federal spending include income security; health care for seniors, the disabled, and the poor; and education.

THINK ABOUT IT!
Is there an area of federal spending you think should be reduced or increased? Why? What about government revenue?

Taxes and Government Spending **399**

C Critical Thinking Skills

Describing the results of budget cuts Point out to students that when revenues decrease, cuts are made in the federal budget. Have students think of a program that might be subject to budget cuts. Then have them debate whether that program or other programs should have priority. **Verbal/Linguistic**

Content Background Knowledge

Protective Services Point out to students the overlapping nature of some items and categories in the federal budget. For example, the category of protective services includes the U.S. Forest Service Law Enforcement and Investigations (Dept. of Agriculture), National Oceanic and Atmospheric Administration Fisheries Office for Law Enforcement (Dept. of Commerce), National Security Agency Police (NSA), the Department of Army Police, Office of Criminal Investigations Police (Dept. of Health and Human Services), the Federal Protective Service (Dept. of Homeland Security), Office of Border Patrol (Dept. of Homeland Security), U.S. Marshals Service (Dept. of Justice), Federal Aviation Administration (Dept. of Transportation), Bureau of Engraving and Printing Police (Dept. of Treasury), U.S. Supreme Court Police (Judicial Branch), NASA Security Services, U.S. Postal Police, Amtrak Police, Federal Reserve Police, the National Zoological Park Police, and the Federal Bureau of Prisons, which employs more than 38,000 workers who oversee the operation of federal prisons.

CLOSE & REFLECT

Have students answer the *Think About It!* questions.

WORKSHEET

Hands-on Chapter Project

Understanding taxation and spending Distribute the Hands-on Chapter Project worksheet. Students work in groups, acting as reporters for a national online newspaper covering government policy. They will research information about taxation and spending in the past fiscal year, analyze this information, and create an infographic to easily convey the information to readers. Students will present their infographics in a poster gallery to be reviewed by their peers. **Visual/Spatial, Logical/Mathematical**

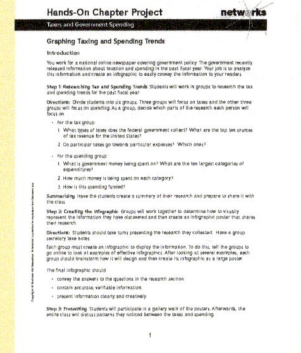

ANSWERS, p. 399

THINK ABOUT IT!

Answers will vary. Have students provide reasons for their opinions.

Taxes and Government Spending **399**

CHAPTER 14, LESSON 1
Taxes

ENGAGE

C Critical Thinking Skills

Identifying perspectives about taxes Direct students to think about varying perspectives of taxes by asking the following questions. **Ask: Should tax dollars support public schools? If so, why should people who do not have children in public schools have taxes deducted from their paychecks to pay for schools? How are national parks and museums supported? Why should people who do not use the parks and museums have taxes deducted from their paychecks to support them?**

TEACH & ASSESS

W Writing Skills

Explaining the effects of taxes on resource allocation **Ask: How do taxes impact resource allocation?** *(by raising the prices on goods and services, which makes people buy less, causing some industries to reduce production, causing labor and other resources to move to other industries)* Have students diagram a chain of events in which an item is taxed, showing the specific effects of consumers buying fewer numbers of the item, and including examples of the movement of resources. **Verbal/Linguistic**

English Language Proficiency

Advanced As English used in text and classroom instruction become increasingly complex, provide frequent opportunities for students to demonstrate comprehension. Ask questions during class instruction, and provide them for written text. Emphasize questions that consult high-order understanding.

ANSWERS, p. 400

ESSENTIAL QUESTION ACTIVITY

Students' paragraphs will vary but should include different ways the government collects taxes (corporate and individual income, sales, customs duties, and so on) and which tax methods are fairest to everyone.

TAKING NOTES:
Behavior adjustment
Income redistribution
Productivity
Resource Allocation

Interact with these digital assets and others in lesson 1
✓ INTERACTIVE CHART
  The Value-Added Tax
  SLIDESHOW
  History of Tax Reform
✓ SELF-CHECK QUIZ
  VIDEO

TRY IT YOURSELF ONLINE

LESSON 1
Taxes

Reading Help Desk

Academic Vocabulary
- validity
- evolved
- concept
- controversial

Content Vocabulary
- sin tax
- distribution of income
- incidence of a tax
- tax loopholes
- individual income tax
- Internal Revenue Service (IRS)
- sales tax
- tax return
- ability-to-pay
- proportional tax
- average tax rate
- Medicare
- progressive tax
- marginal tax rate
- regressive tax
- flat tax
- value-added tax (VAT)
- alternative minimum tax
- capital gains

TAKING NOTES:

Key Ideas and Details
ACTIVITY As you read the section, complete the graphic organizer below by listing the economic impact of taxes.

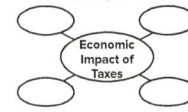

Economic Impact of Taxes

ESSENTIAL QUESTION

How does the government collect revenue, and on what is that revenue spent?

How many different ways does the government collect revenue from taxpayers, and which of those methods do you feel are the fairest to everyone?

Prepare a two paragraph summary with the different ways government collects taxes in the first paragraph. In the second paragraph devote the text to the ways that you think are the most efficient or the fairest to everyone.

An enormous amount of money is required to run all levels of government—and the need seems to be growing every year. Taxes are the primary way to do this, and taxes affect the things we do in more ways than you think.

Economic Impact of Taxes

GUIDING QUESTION *How do taxes affect the decisions you make?*

Taxes and other governmental revenues influence the economy by affecting everything from resource allocation to the nation's productivity and growth. In addition, the burden of a tax does not always fall on the party being taxed.

Resource Allocation

Whenever a tax is placed on a good or service, it raises the product's price to the consumer. It should come as no surprise, then, that people react to the higher price in a predictable manner—they buy less. When sales fall, some firms cut back on production, which means that some resources—land, capital, and labor—will have to go to other industries to be employed. So something as simple as a tax can easily affect the allocation of resources in the economy.

---

netw⚡rks *Online Teaching Options*

BELLRINGER

Taxes

Understanding effective taxes Bring in copies of federal income tax forms for students to view, and have students apply the three criteria of effectives taxes to the forms. Then have them look at the Bellringer activity. Discuss ways to make the federal income tax more efficient and simple. **Verbal/Linguistic**

Behavior Adjustment

Taxes are sometimes used to encourage or discourage certain types of activities. For example, homeowners can use interest payments on mortgages as tax deductions—a practice that encourages home ownership. Interest payments on other consumer debt, such as credit cards, are not deductible—a practice that makes credit card use less attractive.

A so-called **sin tax**—a relatively high tax designed to raise revenue while reducing consumption of a socially undesirable product such as liquor or tobacco—is another example of how a tax can change behavior. For the tax to be effective, however, it has to be reasonably uniform from one city or state to the next so that consumers do not have alternative sales outlets that allow them to avoid the tax.

Income Redistribution

Taxes are collected because the government needs to pay for its spending. The **distribution of income**—the way in which income is allocated among families, individuals, or other groups—is always affected by taxes. You probably think that your income goes down if you pay a lot of taxes, but it may go up if you receive a lot of transfer payments.

In an ideal world, the money that government spends would only cover public goods like highways, schools, national defense, and even a system of laws and courts that would be impractical for individuals to purchase by themselves. Unfortunately, the world is not perfect and so taxes do affect the incomes that people have. This is one reason why we should attempt to understand the nature of taxes and the impacts they have on our society.

Productivity and Growth

Taxes can affect productivity and economic growth by changing the incentives to save, invest, and work. For example, some people think that taxes are already too high. Why, they argue, should they work to earn additional income if they have to pay out some of it in taxes?

While these arguments have **validity**, it is difficult to tell if we have reached the point where taxes are too high. While we do not have exact answers to these questions, we do know that there must be some level of taxes at which productivity and growth would suffer.

sin tax a relatively high tax designed to raise revenue while reducing consumption of a socially undesirable product

distribution of income the way in which income is allocated among families, individuals, or other groups

validity justification

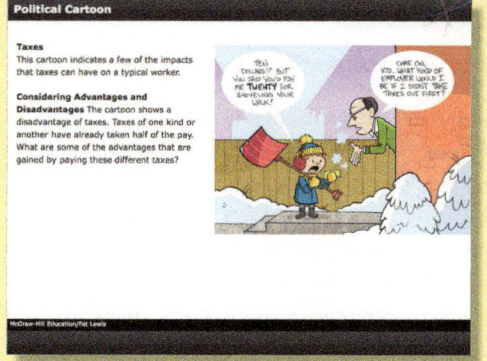

This cartoon indicates a few of the impacts that taxes can have on a typical worker.

◀ **CRITICAL THINKING**
Considering Advantages and Disadvantages The cartoon shows a disadvantage of taxes. Taxes of one kind or another have already taken half of the pay. What are some of the advantages that are gained by paying these different taxes?

CHAPTER 14, LESSON 1
Taxes

V1 Visual Skills

Graphing the incidence of a local tax Tell students that they are going to determine the economic importance of a tax in their community. Have students choose a product and determine its demand elasticity. Next, have them draw, on a single graph, hypothetical supply and demand curves for their chosen product. Tell students to assume a 10 percent tax has been placed on their product. Have students use their supply and demand curves to determine where the incidence of tax will fall. *(If demand is inelastic, the burden of tax will fall on consumers; if demand is elastic, the burden will be shared by producers and consumers.)* Point out that when a community decides to place a tax on a product, it must consider the elasticity of the product and who will ultimately pay the tax.
Visual/Spatial, Logical/Mathematical

V2 Visual Skills

Visualizing the incidence of a tax Have students look at the graphs showing the effects of elastic and inelastic demand on the incidence of taxes.
Ask: What is the difference in curve D from Panel A to Panel B? *(Curve D in Panel B is at a sharper vertical angle than curve D in Panel A.)* **How do the shapes of the curves illustrate the concepts of elastic and inelastic demand?** *(In Panel A, the curve is more relaxed or flexible and is described as elastic. In Panel B, the curve is at a sharper angle and is more rigid; it is described as inelastic.)*
Visual/Spatial

ANSWERS, p. 402

✓ **READING PROGRESS CHECK** Taxes may encourage or discourage certain behaviors among businesses and consumers. Firms may choose certain business practices to reduce their tax burden. Higher prices for products may discourage consumers from purchasing some products, resulting in lost sales to businesses.

CRITICAL THINKING
The consumer

Incidence of a Tax

Finally, there is the matter of who actually pays the tax. This is known as the **incidence of a tax**—or the final burden of the tax. This can happen if we have an *indirect tax*—a tax that can be shifted to others. Examples would be a business property tax or a sales tax. For example, suppose that a city wants to tax a local electric utility to raise revenue. If the utility is able to raise its rates, consumers will likely bear some of the burden of the tax in the form of higher utility bills. This is not the case for a *direct tax*, or one that cannot be shifted to others. An example of a direct tax is the personal income tax or a driver's license fee.

Supply and demand analysis can help us analyze the incidence of a tax. To illustrate, **Figure 14.1** shows an *elastic* demand curve in **Panel A** and an *inelastic* demand curve in **Panel B**. Both panels have identical supply curves labeled **S**. Now, suppose that the government levies a $1 tax on the producer, thereby shifting the supply curve up by the amount of the tax.

In Panel A, the product's market price increases by 60 cents, which means that the producer must have absorbed the other 40 cents of the tax. In Panel B, however, the same tax on the producer results in a 90-cent increase in price, which means that the producer absorbed only 10 cents of the tax. The figure clearly shows that it is much easier for a producer to shift the incidence of a tax to the consumer if the consumer's demand curve is relatively inelastic.

incidence of a tax the final burden of the tax

✓ **READING PROGRESS CHECK**

Summarizing How do taxes affect businesses and consumers?

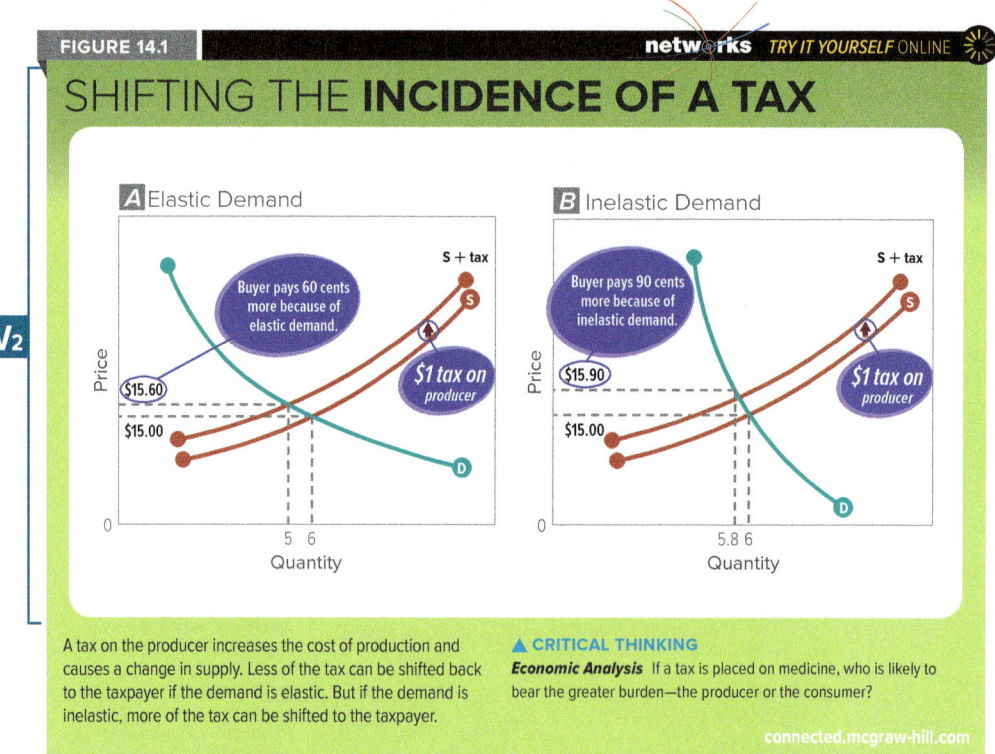

FIGURE 14.1 SHIFTING THE INCIDENCE OF A TAX

A tax on the producer increases the cost of production and causes a change in supply. Less of the tax can be shifted back to the taxpayer if the demand is elastic. But if the demand is inelastic, more of the tax can be shifted to the taxpayer.

▲ **CRITICAL THINKING**
Economic Analysis If a tax is placed on medicine, who is likely to bear the greater burden—the producer or the consumer?

Online Teaching Options

GRAPHS

Shifting the Incidence of a Tax

Analyzing the incidence of a tax Have students click on Figure 14.1 to explore the effects of demand on the incidence of a tax. Then ask them who bears the greater burden of a tax on medicine: the producer or the consumer. *(consumer)* Ask them to support their reasoning using the information about elastic demand versus inelastic demand. **Verbal/Linguistic**

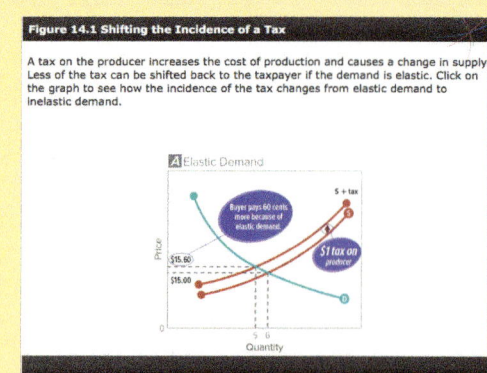

Characteristics and Types of Taxes

GUIDING QUESTION *What makes a tax effective?*

The U.S. Constitution states that "The Congress shall have the Power to lay and collect Taxes, Duties, Imposts, and Excises, to pay the Debts and provide for the common Defence and general Welfare of the United States . . ." in Article I, Section 8. Like it or not, some amount of taxation is needed to pay the nation's bills, so we want to make them as fair and as effective as possible. To do so, taxes must meet three criteria: equity, simplicity, and efficiency.

Criteria for Effective Taxes

People generally recognize three criteria for effective taxes—equity, simplicity, and efficiency. No single tax has all three characteristics, as the following examples will show.

- **Equity** or fairness—the first criterion—means that taxes should be impartial and just. Problems, however, arise when we ask *what is fair?* For example, you might believe that everyone should pay the same amount, but someone else may think that wealthier people should pay more than those earning less.

  Unfortunately, there is no overriding guide to make taxes completely equitable. However, it does make sense to avoid **tax loopholes**—exceptions or oversights in the tax law that allow some people or businesses to avoid paying taxes. Loopholes are fairness issues, and most people oppose them on the basis of equity.

- **Simplicity** means that tax laws should be written so that both taxpayers and tax collectors can understand them. This is because people seem more willing to tolerate taxes when they understand them.

  A **sales tax**—a general tax levied on most consumer purchases—is much simpler. The sales tax is paid at the time of purchase, and the amount of the tax is computed and collected by the merchant. Some goods such as food and medicine may be exempt, but if a product is taxed, then everyone who buys the product pays the tax. In contrast, the **individual income tax**—the federal tax on people's earnings—is a prime example of a complex tax. The entire federal code is thousands of pages long and even the simplified instructions from the **Internal Revenue Service (IRS)**, the branch of the U.S. Treasury Department in charge of collecting taxes, are lengthy and difficult to understand. In contrast, the first income tax forms in 1913 were only 4 pages long, including all forms and instructions.

- **Efficiency** means that a tax should be relatively easy to administer and reasonably successful at generating revenue. The individual income tax is fairly efficient when income taxes are collected. Because most payrolls are computerized, an employer can easily withhold a portion of an employee's pay and send it to the IRS. At the end of the year, the employer notifies each employee of the amount of tax withheld so that the employee can settle any under- or overpayment with the IRS.

- The taxpayer does this by filing a **tax return**—an annual report to the IRS summarizing total income, deductions, and taxes withheld—on or before April 15. Any difference between the amount already paid and the amount actually owed is settled at that time, a process that usually requires an enormous amount of a worker's time and effort.

tax loopholes exceptions or oversights in the tax law allowing taxpayer to avoid taxes

sales tax general state or city tax levied on a product at the time of sale

individual income tax tax levied on the wages, salaries, and other income of individuals

Internal Revenue Service (IRS) branch of the U.S. Treasury Department that collects taxes

tax return annual report filed with local, state, or federal government detailing income earned and taxes owed

---

CHAPTER 14, LESSON 1
Taxes

Content Background Knowledge

Taxing Income In the United States, the idea of taxing income goes back to the 1740s when the colony of Massachusetts Bay taxed the "faculties" (earning power) of individuals and the "returns and gains" of tradespeople and craftspeople.

W Writing Skills

Describing the three criteria of effective taxes
Tell students to create a chart with three columns. Have them use as a heading for each column one of the three criteria of effective taxes: equity, simplicity, and efficiency. Then have students write a description of each criterion under its heading. Finally, have students write one successful example of each criterion working, and one example of the criterion not working. **Verbal/Linguistic**

Making Connections

Paying Taxes Ask students to raise their hands if they pay taxes. Ask a student whose hand was not raised if he or she buys clothing, gasoline, food, or magazines, and point out that in almost all states such articles are taxed when they are purchased. Ask another student whose hand was not raised if he or she attends music concerts or sporting events, and point out that the cost of the ticket probably includes a special entertainment tax. Then have students make a list of goods or services they may have purchased in the last week on which they paid a tax. Have students compare and discuss their lists. **AL ELL Intrapersonal**

WORKSHEETS

Reinforcing Economic Skills

Classifying taxes Distribute the worksheet to students. Explain that, as citizens who will be paying taxes, it is important that students know the differences among types of taxes and the impact taxes have on both individuals and businesses. Students will classify proposed taxes into three categories: progressive, proportional, and regressive.
Logical/Mathematical

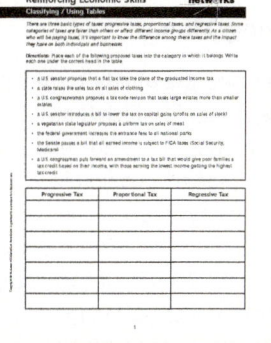

CHAPTER 14, LESSON 1
Taxes

C Critical Thinking Skills

Applying the benefit principle of taxation To curtail pollution, governments are levying more taxes based on the benefit principle. France was the first nation to levy a direct pollution tax, which requires manufacturers to pay tax on every unit of pollution they discharge. Tell students to imagine that they are environmental consultants whom world leaders ask for tax suggestions. **Ask: Whom would you recommend the leaders of Mexico City tax to raise money for cleaning up air pollution from vehicles?** *(tax car dealers who sell cars without antipollution devices)* **Whom would you recommend Canadian leaders tax to combat the acid rain caused by U.S. factories?** *(a tax on goods coming into Canada from the United States, the factors that caused acid rain)* **Naturalist**

W Writing Skills

Comparing and contrasting the two principles of taxation Have students compare and contrast the benefit principle with the ability-to-pay principle, giving examples of each principle in action to support their ideas. **Verbal/Linguistic**

R Reading Skills

Determining ability-to-pay Ask: How is the amount each person has to pay determined under the ability-to-pay principle? *(The amount each person pays depends on how much income each earns.)*

Other taxes, like those collected in toll booths on state highways, are much less efficient. The state has to invest millions of dollars in heavily reinforced booths that span the highway just to collect a dollar or two from every passing vehicle. The cost to commuters, besides the toll, is the lost time and the wear and tear on their automobiles as they brake for toll booths along the road.

evolved developed gradually

Two Principles of Taxation

Taxes in the United States are based on two principles that have **evolved** over the years. These principles are the benefit principle and the ability-to-pay principle.

- **Benefit principle** This principle of taxation states that those who benefit from government goods and services should pay in proportion to the amount of benefits they receive.

  Gasoline taxes are a good example of this principle. Because the gas tax is built into the price of gasoline, people who drive more than others pay more gas taxes—and therefore pay for more of the construction and upkeep of our nation's highways. Taxes on truck tires operate on the same principle. Since heavy vehicles like trucks are likely to put the most wear and tear on roads, a tire tax links the cost of highway upkeep to the user.

  Despite its attractive features, the benefit principle has two limitations. The first is that those who receive government benefits like subsidized housing may also be the ones who can least afford to pay for them. Even though they are often required to pay a certain amount based on their income, they cannot pay in proportion to the benefits they receive.

  The second limitation is that benefits are often hard to measure. After all, the people who buy the gas are not the only ones who benefit from the roads built with gas taxes. Owners of property, like hotels and restaurants along the way, are also likely to benefit from the roads that the gas tax helps provide.

ability-to-pay principle of taxation based on belief that taxes should be paid according to level of income regardless of benefits received

- **Ability-to-pay** This principle is based on the belief that people should be taxed according to their ability to pay, regardless of the benefits they receive. An example is the individual income tax, which requires people with higher incomes to pay more than those who earn less.

  This principle assumes that people with higher incomes suffer less discomfort paying taxes than people with lower incomes. For example, a family of four with an annual taxable income of $20,000 needs every cent to pay for necessities. At an average tax rate of about 13 percent, this family pays $2,599–a huge amount for them. A family of four with taxable income of $100,000 can afford to pay a higher average tax rate with much less discomfort.

Three Types of Taxes

Three general types of taxes exist in the United States today—proportional, progressive, and regressive. As **Figure 14.2** shows, each type of tax is classified according to the way in which the tax burden changes as income changes. To calculate the tax burden, we divide the amount that someone pays in taxes by their taxable income.

proportional tax (or flat) tax in which percentage of income paid in tax is the same regardless of the level of income

- A **proportional tax** imposes the same percentage rate of taxation on everyone, regardless of income. If the income tax rate is 20 percent, an individual with $10,000 in taxable income pays $2,000 in taxes. A person with $100,000 in taxable income pays $20,000.

average tax rate total taxes paid divided by the total taxable income

If the percentage tax rate is constant for all levels of taxable income, the **average tax rate**—total tax paid divided by the total taxable income—also is constant, regardless of income.

---

networks Online Teaching Options

VIDEO **WORKSHEET**

Taxing Times

Analyzing the ability-to-pay principle Have students watch the video. Then have a class discussion about the percentage that companies and the wealthy pay in taxes, compared to that of low- and middle-income individuals. **Ask: How does the ability-to-pay principle of taxation apply to what you saw in the video?** *(Wealthy individuals and corporations do not pay what they are able, whereas lower income individuals pay more than they are able.)* **Interpersonal Logical/Mathematical**

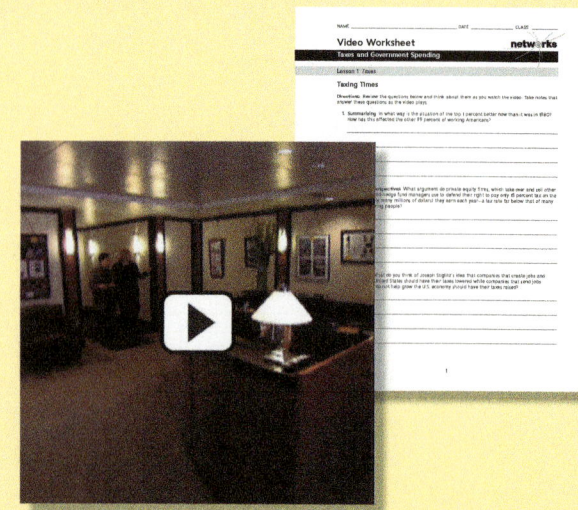

CHAPTER 14, LESSON 1
Taxes

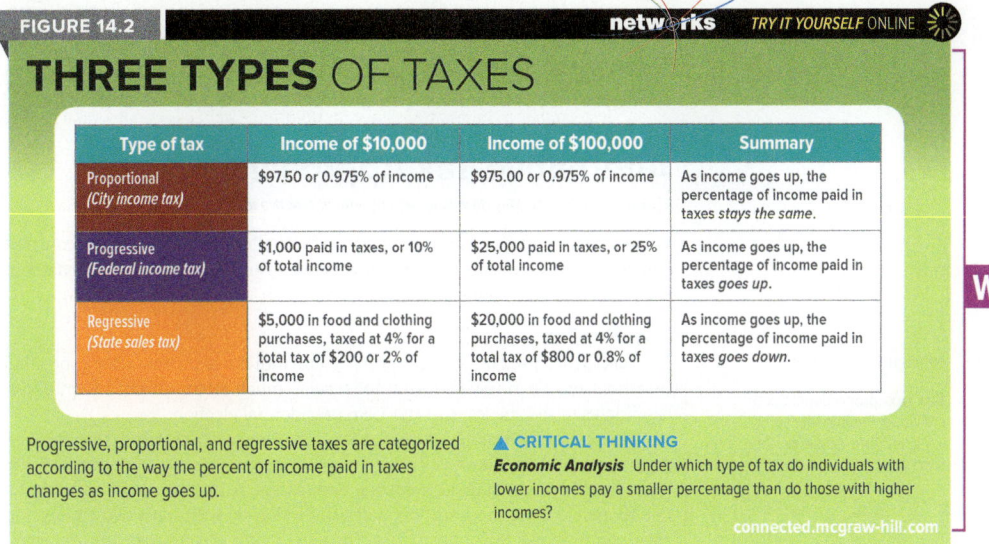

FIGURE 14.2

THREE TYPES OF TAXES

Type of tax	Income of $10,000	Income of $100,000	Summary
Proportional (City income tax)	$97.50 or 0.975% of income	$975.00 or 0.975% of income	As income goes up, the percentage of income paid in taxes *stays the same*.
Progressive (Federal income tax)	$1,000 paid in taxes, or 10% of total income	$25,000 paid in taxes, or 25% of total income	As income goes up, the percentage of income paid in taxes *goes up*.
Regressive (State sales tax)	$5,000 in food and clothing purchases, taxed at 4% for a total tax of $200 or 2% of income	$20,000 in food and clothing purchases, taxed at 4% for a total tax of $800 or 0.8% of income	As income goes up, the percentage of income paid in taxes *goes down*.

Progressive, proportional, and regressive taxes are categorized according to the way the percent of income paid in taxes changes as income goes up.

▲ **CRITICAL THINKING**
Economic Analysis Under which type of tax do individuals with lower incomes pay a smaller percentage than do those with higher incomes?

The tax that funds **Medicare**—a federal health-care program available to all senior citizens, regardless of income—is a proportional tax at 1.45 percent of income, with no limit on the amount of income taxed. Other than this, few proportional taxes are used in the United States.

- A **progressive tax** is a tax that imposes a higher percentage rate of taxation on higher incomes than on lower ones. This tax uses a progressively higher **marginal tax rate**, the tax rate that applies to the next dollar of taxable income.

For example, suppose the law required everyone to pay a rate of 10 percent on all taxable income up to $8,900, and then a rate of 15 percent on all income after that. If someone had taxable income of $7,000, or even $7,499, this person would continue to pay 10 percent on the very next dollar earned. However, if the same person had taxable income of $8,901, the marginal tax rate would be 15 percent on the next, or $8,901st dollar earned. In either case, the marginal tax is always the tax that is paid on the very next dollar of taxable income.

- A **regressive tax** is a tax that imposes a *higher* percentage rate of taxation on low incomes than on high incomes. For example, a person in a state with a 4 percent sales tax and an annual income of $10,000 may spend $5,000 on food and clothing and pay sales taxes of $200 (or .04 times $5,000). A person with an annual income of $100,000 may spend $20,000 on food and clothing and pay state sales taxes of $800 (or .04 times $20,000).

On a percentage basis, the person with the lower income pays 2 percent (or $200 divided by $10,000) of income in sales taxes, while the person with the higher income pays 0.8 percent (or $800 divided by $100,000). As a result, the 4 percent sales tax is regressive because the individual with the higher income pays a smaller percentage of income in sales taxes than does the individual with the lower income. Most states use

Medicare a federal health-care program for senior citizens, regardless of income

progressive tax tax where percentage of income paid in tax rises as level of income rises

marginal tax rate tax rate that applies to the next dollar of taxable income

regressive tax tax where percentage of income paid in tax goes down as income rises

---

W Writing Skills

Explaining principles of taxation and tax types
Have students work in groups to create pamphlets that explain the two principles of taxation and the three tax types to consumers. Have them use illustrations to clarify the concepts for consumers, and make the information user-friendly by using standard grammar and sentence structure.
Verbal/Linguistic, Visual/Spatial

R Reading Skills

Calculating the Medicare tax Ask: **What type of tax is the tax that funds Medicare?** *(proportional)* **How is the Medicare tax calculated?** *(The tax is 1.45 percent of income, no matter how high the income.)* Have students create a graph showing the Medicare tax paid for five different levels of income.
Logical/Mathematical

C Critical Thinking Skills

Hypothesizing a progressive sales tax Ask: **What would happen if a state sales tax became progressive?** *(Sample answer: People who made more money would have to pay higher sales taxes than people who made less money.)* **Is it possible to administer a sales tax as a progressive tax? What problems might arise?** *(Sample answer: It would be next to impossible, because people would have to carry some kind of identification that shows how much income they make; people would have to give too much personal information at the point of purchase; it would unfairly mark people who made less money and might cause discrimination.)*

CHART

Three Types of Taxes

Understanding types of taxes Have students explore Figure 14.2. Ask: **Which type of tax most heavily impacts people with higher incomes?** *(progressive tax)* As a class, answer the question in the activity, and then compare and contrast the impact of each type of tax on people with the lowest incomes versus those with the highest incomes. **Logical/Mathematical**

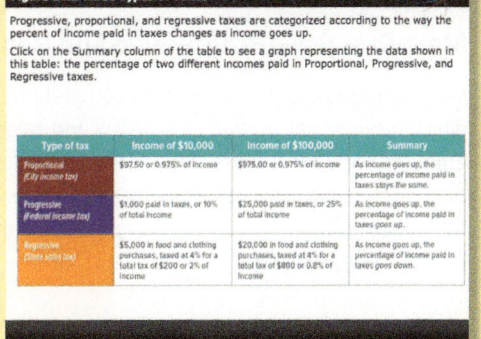

ANSWERS, p. 405

CRITICAL THINKING
Progressive tax

CHAPTER 14, LESSON 1
Taxes

W Writing Skills

Arguing for or against a flat tax Have students write a persuasive essay arguing either for or against a flat income tax. If they are arguing for a flat tax, they must provide reasons why this type of tax would be beneficial, but they must also state what the drawbacks would be, and why the benefits outweigh the drawbacks. If they are arguing against the flat tax, they must provide reasons why the drawbacks would outweigh the benefits.

T Technology Skills

Polling for tax opinions Have students poll 10 adults for their opinion about whether the United States should convert to a flat tax policy. Ask students to combine their findings into a spreadsheet, and from that create a bar graph. Students may create bar graphs for age spreads and by gender. Share the results with the class.

Making Connections

Historical View of Income Taxes Show students that the fairness of income taxes has been debated for thousands of years by reading the following quote from Plato (circa 428–348 B.C.): "When there is an income tax, the just man will pay more and the unjust less on the same amount of income." **Ask: Based on this quote, do you think Plato would prefer a flat tax on income or the current progressive income tax system?** *(Students should mention that, under the present system, taxpayers can use loopholes to pay less than others with the same income. As a result, Plato would probably prefer the flat tax.)*

ANSWERS, p. 406

☑ **READING PROGRESS CHECK** The income tax is progressive because it is based on income—the higher one's income, the greater the percent of income is taxed.

---

sales taxes as a way to generate significant state income. In every case, however, the sales tax is the most regressive tax used in the country today.

☑ **READING PROGRESS CHECK**

Synthesizing Is the income tax progressive, proportional, or regressive? Explain.

Alternative Tax Approaches

GUIDING QUESTION Why do lawmakers consider alternative taxes?

The need for new tax revenues and the desire to alter the tax burden is a constant source of new proposals. Because of this, we hear a lot about two alternatives: the flat tax and the value-added tax.

The Flat Tax

concept general idea

flat tax proportional tax on individual income after a specified threshold has been reached

The **concept** of a **flat tax**—a proportional tax on individual income after a specified threshold has been reached—did not receive much attention until Republican candidates raised the issue in the 1996 presidential election.

The primary advantage of the flat tax is the simplicity it offers to the taxpayer. A person would still have to fill out an income tax return every year but could skip many current steps, such as itemizing deductions. A second advantage is that a flat tax would close most tax loopholes if it did away with most deductions and exemptions. Finally, a flat tax reduces the need for tax accountants, tax preparers, and even a large portion of the IRS. As a result, Americans would no longer have to spend an estimated 7 billion hours every year preparing tax returns.

W
T

However, a flat tax has several disadvantages. First, it would remove many of the incentives built into the current tax code, especially those that encourage home ownership and charitable contributions. For example, the tax code now allows homeowners to deduct interest payments on home mortgages, something that lowers the cost of financing a home. The tax code also allows charitable deductions which benefit many churches, museums, and welfare agencies. Other incentives that might be lost include deductions for education, training, and child care.

Another problem is that no one knows exactly what rate is needed to replace the revenue collected under the current tax system. In 1996, supporters of the flat tax argued that a 15 percent rate would work. Other estimates by the U.S. Treasury put the tax closer to 23 percent—which represents more of a burden on low-income earners because their taxes would increase in comparison with current rates.

Finally, there is no clear answer as to whether a flat tax would further stimulate economic growth. After all, the extraordinary growth of the American economy in the 1990s, the longest period of peacetime prosperity in our history, took place when progressive tax brackets were higher than they were any time since 1987.

The Value-Added Tax

controversial disputed

value-added tax (VAT) tax on the value added at every stage of the production process

Another **controversial** proposal is to adopt the equivalent of a national sales tax by taxing consumption rather than income. This could be done with a **value-added tax (VAT)**—a tax placed on the value that manufacturers add at each stage of production. The United States currently does not have a VAT, although it is widely used in Europe.

To see how the VAT works, consider how the tax impacts the manufacturing and sale of wooden baseball bats in **Figure 14.3**. First, loggers cut the trees and sell the timber to lumber mills. The mills process the logs for sale to bat manufacturers. The manufacturers then shape the wood into baseball bats. After the bats are painted or varnished, they are sold to a wholesaler. The wholesaler sells them to retailers, who sell them to consumers. As the figure shows, a VAT tax is levied at each stage of production.

---

net works Online Teaching Options

WORKSHEET

Math Practice—Progressive and Regressive Taxes

Calculating taxes Have students complete the worksheet, which requires calculating income tax and sales tax, in both real amounts and percentages. Students will understand the difference between progressive and regressive taxes, and know that federal income tax is an example of a progressive tax.

Logical/Mathematical

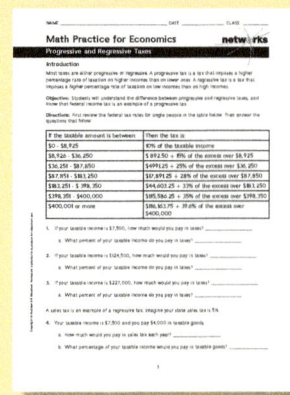

FIGURE 14.3

THE VALUE-ADDED TAX

		No taxes		With a 10% value-added tax	
		Value added	Cumulative value	Value added with a 10% VAT	Cumulative with VAT
Step 1	Loggers fell trees and sell the timber to the mills for processing.	$1	$1	$1 + $.10 = $1.10	$1.10
Step 2	Mills cut the timber into blanks that will be used to make bats.	$1	$2	$1 + $.10 = $1.10	$2.20
Step 3	Bat manufacturers shape and paint or varnish the bats and sell them to wholesalers.	$5	$7	$5 + $.50 = $5.50	$7.70
Step 4	Wholesalers sell the bats to retail outlets where consumers can buy them.	$1	$8	$1 + $.10 = $1.10	$8.80
Step 5	Retailers put the bats on the shelves and wait for consumers.	$2	$10	$2 + $.20 = $2.20	$11.00
Step 6	Consumers buy the bats for:		$10		$11.00

The VAT is like a national sales tax added to each stage of production. As a result, it is built into the final price of a product and is less visible to consumers. The third and fifth columns show the value added at each stage, and the fourth and sixth columns show the cumulative values.

▲ **CRITICAL THINKING**
Economic Analysis Is a VAT regressive, proportional, or progressive? Why?

The VAT has several advantages. First, it is hard to avoid because it is built into the price of the product being taxed. Second, the tax incidence is widely spread, which makes it harder for a single firm to shift the burden of the tax to another group. Third, the VAT is easy to collect, because firms make their VAT payments directly to the government. Consequently, even a relatively small VAT can raise a tremendous amount of revenue, especially when it is applied to a broad range of goods and services. Finally, some supporters claim that the VAT would encourage people to save more than they do now. After all, if none of your money is taxed until it is spent, you might think more carefully about purchases, and possibly decide to spend less—and save more.

The main disadvantage of the VAT is that it tends to be virtually invisible. In the baseball bat example, consumers may be aware that bat prices went from $10 to $11, but they might attribute this to a shortage of good wood, higher wages, or some other factor. In other words, it is difficult for taxpayers to be vigilant about higher taxes if they cannot see them.

 READING PROGRESS CHECK

Describing Explain how a value-added tax works.

Tax Reform Highlights

GUIDING QUESTION *Why is the tax code continually revised?*

Tax reform has received considerable attention recently. Since 1981, there have been more changes in the tax code than at any other time in our nation's history.

Tax Reform in 1981

When Ronald Reagan was elected president in 1980, he believed that high taxes were the main stumbling block to economic growth. In 1981, he signed the

---

CHAPTER 14, LESSON 1
Taxes

C1 Critical Thinking Skills

Predicting the consequences of a value-added tax Have a class discussion about the consequences of a federal value-added tax. Ask students if they have ever shopped at a factory outlet mall. Discuss the concept of outlet malls—manufacturers selling directly to the public through their own store.
Ask: How do you think a federal value-added tax would affect the trend of factory outlet malls? Would the number of malls increase, decrease, or remain the same? On what do you base your prediction? *(Students may note that a value-added tax could increase the number of factory outlet malls. Outlet malls could sell products more cheaply because they could circumvent the retailers' tax that increases prices.)*

C2 Critical Thinking Skills

Evaluating tax goals and side effects Explain that, theoretically, any tax action or tax reform is undertaken to advance an accepted social goal; for example, to promote freedom through a strong military, or to decrease unemployment through public projects. Whether these social goals have actually been advanced is often a source of debate. Even the most effective use of taxation sometimes produces totally unforeseen side effects. Write the following list on the board. For each tax action, ask students to tell (a) what they think the goal is, and (b) what, if any, unexpected side effects (positive or negative) might result. 1. Property taxes are used to fund public education. 2. Business taxes are decreased. 3. High taxes are levied on cigarettes and alcohol. 4. Sales tax is no longer allowed as a deduction on federal income tax returns. 5. Income tax rates are lowered for most people. 6. High import taxes are imposed on foreign-made cars. 7. Corporate tax rates are lowered.

CHART

The Value-Added Tax

Comparing a sales tax with a value-added tax
Have students explore Figure 14.3 to see how the tax is applied for each step in the production process of a baseball bat. Then have them apply your state sales tax on the final product (cumulative value) and compare the price with a cumulative value-added tax.
Logical/Mathematical

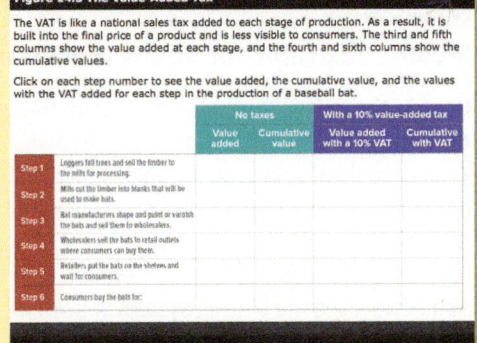

ANSWERS, p. 407

CRITICAL THINKING
Regressive, because the percentage of a consumer's income paid goes down as their income goes up.

 READING PROGRESS CHECK A VAT taxes a product at each stage of its production. The tax is thereby built into the purchase price for the end-user. Because it is collected from the producer at each stage of production, it is invisible to the consumer.

CHAPTER 14, LESSON 1
Taxes

R1 Reading Skills

Understanding the alternative minimum tax
Ask: What is the alternative minimum tax? *(It is a personal income tax rate that applies to cases in which taxes paid by the very rich would otherwise fall below a certain level because of tax loopholes or other circumstances.)* Have students explain what makes the alternative minimum tax differ from the personal income tax.

R2 Reading Skills

Explaining the tax reform of 1997 **Ask: What were the two forces that created the tax reform in 1997? Explain.** *(One force was economic; the government had unexpectedly high tax revenues in 1997. The other force was political; the Republicans had gained a majority in Congress. They reduced the tax on capital gains and lowered inheritance taxes.)*

W1 Writing Skills

Understanding the reaction to capital gains tax changes **Ask: How was the capital gains tax changed in 1997?** *(It was reduced from 28 to 20 percent.)* Who benefited most from this change? *(the top 20 percent of earners)* Have students write a letter to the editor of a newspaper in the voice of a person who is one of the bottom 20 percent of earners, explaining how this tax change affects all earners. **Interpersonal**

W2 Writing Skills

Explaining how to calculate individual income tax
Have students write a simple guide to calculating income tax for an individual, using the Income Tax Table for Single Individuals. First, students should explain what income taxes are used for. Then students should invent an adjusted income (after deductions) to use as an example, and write steps for calculating the tax on that income. Students should use the Tax Table to illustrate their guide. **Visual/Spatial, Logical/Mathematical**

ANSWERS, p. 408

EXPLORING THE ESSENTIAL QUESTION

Any of the goals are acceptable. Have students provide supporting details for the topic they select.

CRITICAL THINKING

Because the marginal tax rates (10%, 15%, 25%, 28%, 33%, 35%, and 39.6%) increase as income increases.

EXPLORING THE ESSENTIAL QUESTION

How does the government collect revenue, and on what is that revenue spent?

Tax laws have been reformed many times and for a variety of reasons. Which of the following are possible goals of tax reform? Explain your answers.

- To address inequities in the tax code
- To reduce surplus revenue
- To boost economic growth

alternative minimum tax personal income tax rate that applies to cases where taxes would otherwise fall below a certain level

Economic Recovery Tax Act, which included large tax reductions for individuals and businesses.

Before the Recovery Act, the individual tax code had 16 marginal tax brackets ranging from 14 to 70 percent. The act lowered the marginal rates in all brackets, capping the highest marginal tax at 50 percent. In comparison, today's tax code, shown in **Figure 14.4**, has seven marginal brackets ranging from 10 to 39.6 percent.

Tax Reform: 1986, 1993

By the mid-1980s, the idea that the tax code favored the rich and powerful was gaining momentum. In 1983, there were numerous calls for tax reform when people discovered that more than 3,000 millionaires paid no income taxes.

In 1986, Congress passed sweeping tax reform that made it difficult for the very rich to avoid taxes altogether. The **alternative minimum tax**—the personal income tax rate that applies whenever the amount of taxes paid falls below a designated level—was strengthened. Under this provision, people had to pay a minimum tax of 20 percent, regardless of other circumstances or loopholes in the tax code.

As the United States entered the 1990s, the impact of 10 years of tax cuts was beginning to show. Government spending was growing faster than revenue, and the government had to borrow more. The resulting tax reform of 1993 was driven more by the need for the government to drive down the deficit than to overhaul the tax brackets. As a result, two top marginal tax brackets of 35 and 39.6 percent were added.

Tax Reform in 1997

The forces that created tax reform were both economic and political. On the economic side, the government found itself with unexpectedly high tax revenues in 1997. The two new marginal tax brackets of 35 and 39.6 percent that had been added in 1993, along with the closure of some tax loopholes, meant that most people paid more taxes than before.

On the political side, the Republicans had gained a firm majority in Congress and now saw a need to fulfill a commitment to their supporters. They reduced the tax on **capital gains**—profits from the sale of an asset held for 12 months or longer—from 28 to 20 percent. The new law also lowered inheritance taxes.

Some people thought that these tax cuts favored the wealthy, and even the government agreed. An analysis by the U.S. Treasury Department determined that nearly half of the benefits went to the top 20 percent of wage and income earners. The lowest 20 percent received less than 1 percent of the tax reductions. With all its changes, the 1997 federal tax law became the most complicated ever.

FIGURE 14.4

INCOME TAX TABLE FOR SINGLE INDIVIDUALS, 2016

If taxable income is over...	But not over...	The tax is:
$0	$9,275	10% of the taxable income
$9,275	$37,650	$927.50 plus 15% of the amount over $9,275
$37,650	$91,150	$5,183.75 plus 25% of the amount over $37,650
$91,150	$190,150	$18,558.75 plus 28% of the amount over $91,150
$190,150	$413,350	$46,278.75 plus 33% of the amount over $190,150
$413,350	$415,050	$119,934.75 plus 35% of the amount over $413,350
$415,050	No limit	$120,529.75 plus 39.6% of the amount over $415,050

According to the individual tax table, a single individual with $10,000 of taxable income would pay .10($9,275) + .15 ($725) = $927.50 + $108.75 = $1,036.25 in taxes.

▲ **CRITICAL THINKING**
Economic Analysis Why is the individual income tax a progressive tax?

connected.mcgraw-hill.com

408

---

networks Online Teaching Options

CHARTS

Income Tax Table for Single Individuals

Contrasting marginal tax brackets with flat tax brackets Have students explore Figure 14.4. Then have them write a paragraph explaining the difference between this system of taxation and a flat tax system. Have students calculate the difference between the tax for an income of $200,000 using the bracket system of taxation ($49,529.25) and a flat tax percentage of 15% ($30,000). **Ask: Who benefits more from the bracket system, the person with the lower income or the person with the higher income?** **Logical/Mathematical**

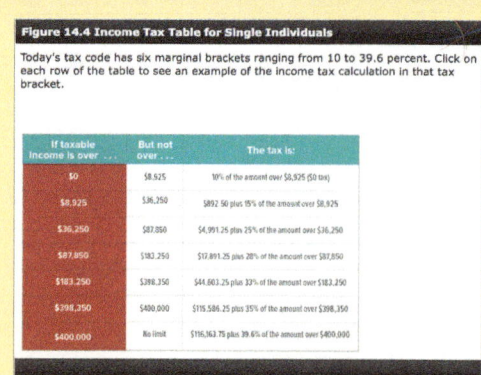

Tax Reform in 2001

By 2001, politicians faced a new issue: the federal government was actually collecting more taxes than it was spending. These surpluses were projected to continue to the year 2010.

Surpluses could have been used to repay some of the money the government borrowed in the 1980s or to fund new federal spending. With broad Republican support, President Bush backed a massive $1.35 billion tax cut to "give the money back to the people." The "temporary" 10-year tax cut was due to expire in 2011. The main feature of the 2001 tax reform was to reduce the top four marginal tax brackets of 27, 30, 35, and 39.6 percent to 25, 28, 33, and 35 percent by 2006. The law also introduced a 10 percent tax bracket and eliminated the estate tax on the wealthiest 2 percent of taxpayers by 2010.

Tax Reform in 2003

Slow economic growth in 2002 convinced the Bush administration and Congress to accelerate many of the 2001 tax reforms. Specifically, the top four marginal tax brackets were reduced immediately rather than in 2006.

For lower income taxpayers, the top end of the 10 percent bracket was increased modestly. The child tax credit was also expanded from $600 to $1,000.

capital gains profits from the sale of an asset held for 12 months or longer

CHAPTER 14, LESSON 1
Taxes

W Writing Skills

Explaining the tax reform of 2001 Ask students to choose one way in which tax reforms in 2001 changed the tax structure, and have them write an explanation of what reformers expected the change to accomplish.

C Critical Thinking Skills

Comparing and contrasting tax reforms Have students choose two tax reforms from their text to research. Direct them to write a one-page essay comparing and contrasting the changes brought about by each reform and the effects that each reform had on the economy.

Content Background Knowledge

The Sixteenth Amendment and Tax Deadline Explain to students that tax brackets are not the only aspect of the taxation system that has been reformed more than once. On February 3, 1913, Congress adopted the 16th Amendment and instituted the income tax. It originally set March 1 as the deadline for filing taxes. Five years later, with the Revenue Act of 1918, Congress moved the date to March 15. That date was the deadline for the next 37 years. In 1955 the deadline was changed to April 15, which is the present due date—for most years, that is. By law, filing and payment deadlines that fall on Saturday, Sunday, or legal holidays are set for the next business day. Therefore, in certain years, the deadline date might be April 17 or April 18. In those years, taxpayers have an extra day or two to file their returns.

CAREERS | Tax Attorney

Is this Career for you?

- Do you enjoy doing research?
- Are you a problem solver?
- Are you interested in finance and tax law?
- Are you willing to work long hours to help people navigate complex legal issues?

Interview with a Tax Lawyer

> I usually work on 6–10 matters per day, so there are lots of diverse issues. It could be anything from disputes to planning estates, to any assortment of business questions. I represent a lot of smaller businesses and privately held businesses and consult on various issues like transferring the business, selling businesses, getting money to start a new business, and employment or contract issues.

—Craig S. Lair, Tax Attorney

Salary
Median pay: **$112,760** per year
$54.21 per hour

Job Growth Potential
About the same as average

Profile of Work
Tax lawyers are experts in tax laws and regulations. They use their knowledge to help individuals, small businesses, and large corporations comply with the Internal Revenue Service's (IRS) regulations. Tax lawyers help their clients navigate the complex world of tax-related issues and advise them on how much tax they need to pay on income and profits. Like all lawyers, tax lawyers tend to work long hours. Much of their work time is spent doing research and preparing documents.

connected.mcgraw-hill.com **Taxes and Government Spending 409**

SLIDE SHOW

History of Tax Reform

Exploring the history of U.S. tax reforms
Have students explore the slide show about the history of tax reform in the United States. Then have them choose one of the events and do further research on it. Have them write a summary about the event, describing what led to it, how it unfolded, and what effects it has had on the tax system in the United States.

Verbal/Linguistic

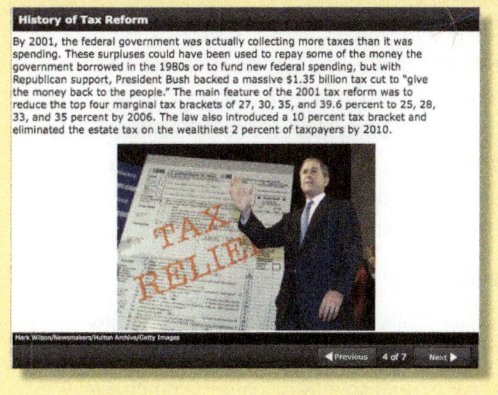

CHAPTER 14, LESSON 1
Taxes

R Reading Skills

Understanding the un-permanent tax cuts of 2011
Ask: What factors prevented the tax cuts of the Bush administration from becoming permanent? *(The 2008 election of Democrat Barack Obama and Democratic control of the Senate and House of Representatives helped bring an end to the tax cuts. In addition, the severe recession of 2008–2009 reduced tax revenues and increased government expenditures, making keeping the tax cuts impossible.)*

CLOSE & REFLECT

Evaluating the fairness of the income tax system
Have students create a poster that represents their opinion of the fairness of the U.S. income tax system. The poster should include images with captions that describe aspects of the system they find fair or unfair. Students do not have to have one opinion about all aspects of the system. For example, they may find certain aspects to be fair and others to be unfair, and may write about and illustrate both opinions on their posters. Finally, have students display their posters in a gallery. **Visual/Spatial, Verbal/Linguistic**

ANSWERS, p. 410

✓ READING PROGRESS CHECK
Tax reform is a political as well as an economic issue. Taxes need to keep up with revenue in order not to increase the debt, but politicians have different ideas about how taxes affect the overall economy. This creates changes in tax code based on who has political power.

Finally, the 20 percent capital gains tax bracket was reduced from 20 to 15 percent.

The 2003 tax cuts put the federal government back in the same deficit spending situation as in 1993. A series of tax cuts reduced taxes in upper income brackets, and government was spending more than it collected in taxes.

The "Permanent" Tax Cuts of 2011

In 2002 and 2003, many congressional Republicans were hoping to preserve the tax cuts that had been made during the Bush administration. As a result, there was considerable talk about making them "permanent," even though the government was running record budget deficits.

R When Barack Obama was elected president in 2008, the Democrats also gained control of the Senate and the House of Representatives. This left the future of the Bush tax cuts in the hands of the newly-elected Democrats.

Then, the Great Recession of 2008–2009 reduced federal government tax revenues. As the government increased its spending with the Obama administration stimulus efforts, the federal deficit grew rapidly. The resulting record federal deficit for 2009 ended the hope of those wanting to make the Bush tax cuts permanent.

Tax Reform in 2013

Over the next few years, the economy grew slowly in the wake of the Great Recession, with weak tax collections from individuals and businesses, and slow growth of real GDP. Politicians argued over making the Bush tax cuts permanent, but the Democrats held the White House and the Senate, so the two top tax brackets, shown in Figure 14.4, were added.

Tax reform is never done, of course, and so the progressive income tax brackets in Figure 14.4 were again targeted by conservatives who believed that higher rates of economic growth cannot be achieved without lower tax rates. No one knows for sure, of course, but higher economic growth of real GDP is something that all politicians support, so additional changes to the personal income tax code are bound to happen.

✓ READING PROGRESS CHECK

Inferring Why have tax reforms occurred so frequently in recent years?

LESSON 1 REVIEW

Reviewing Vocabulary
1. *Defining* Explain the purpose of a sin tax and its function as governmental restriction on the use of individual property.
2. *Defining* Explain the difference among a proportional tax, a progressive tax, and a regressive tax.

Using Your Notes
3. *Explaining* Use your notes to explain the economic impact of taxes as described in this lesson.

Answering the Guiding Questions
4. *Exploring Issues* How do taxes affect the decisions you make? In your answer provide examples of how this type of financial restriction of your earned property impacts your economic choices. Evaluate the benefits and drawbacks of this type of restriction.

5. *Synthesizing* What makes a tax effective?
6. *Evaluating* Why do lawmakers consider alternative taxes?
7. *Drawing Conclusions* Why is the tax code continually revised?

Writing About Economics
8. *Argument* Write a five-paragraph essay explaining which of the two principles of taxation—the benefit principle or the ability-to-pay principle—you think is more equitable. Be sure to include in your answer how the two principles differ from one another.

LESSON 1 REVIEW ANSWERS

Reviewing Vocabulary
1. The purpose is to discourage harmful behaviors. The restriction makes the personal behavior more expensive.
2. Proportional: same percentage regardless of income; progressive: rate of taxation increases as income rises; regressive: rate of taxation decreases as income rises

Using Your Notes
3. Taxes on goods and services generally are passed to the consumer, which increases the cost and may discourage consumers from buying more. A decline in economic activity can affect production, which may lead to fewer employment opportunities.

Answering the Guiding Questions
4. Answer will vary, but students should note that taxes increase the cost of goods or services, and so may discourage purchases or require substitutes.
5. Equity, simplicity, and efficiency
6. As the country grows, there is a need for more government services. These services are financed by tax revenue. To find ways to increase revenue, alternative methods of taxation are often proposed and considered.
7. Tax reform is a political as well as an economic issue. Politicians have different ideas about how taxes affect the overall economy.

Writing About Economics
8. Students should support their arguments with logical reasoning and facts from the chapter.

Case Study

From the PRESIDENT'S POINT OF VIEW

For an interactive version of this case study go to connected.mcgraw-hill.com

One of the more important publications documenting the state of our economic system is published each year under the title *Economic Report of the President*. The 2013 report runs for 456 pages and interprets and analyzes virtually every aspect of America's economic activity at both the federal and state levels.

This important document originated in 1946 on the heels of World War II. Congress, fearful the country might fall back into the financial disaster of the Great Depression, wanted to learn what was happening with the economy. It established the President's Council of Economic Advisors and directed it to undertake a detailed analysis of the economy. The *Report* is issued annually.

The *Report* presents an enormous quantity of information in text, tables, and graphs detailing what is driving or putting a drag on the economy as well as projecting trends going forward. In 2013, it included information on the following:

- Trends in personal income, employment, jobs, and worker skills
- International trade and American competitiveness
- Costs and quality of health care
- Annual economic goals for the country
- A plan for following through on the economic goals

Many graphs and tables add detailed, visual information about the economy. Study the graph "Real GDP, 2007–2012." It shows quarterly changes in GDP. Notice the dip in the graph, which indicates the Great Recession of 2008–2009.

Now consider the table "State and Local Government Revenues and Expenditures." All categories of revenue and expenditures increased, but notice how it reflects changes in priorities as well. For example, in 1950, more was spent on highways than on public welfare. In 2010, much more was spent on welfare than on highways. You can see how this kind of information helps the president and Congress keep tabs on the economy and make changes to help promote growth.

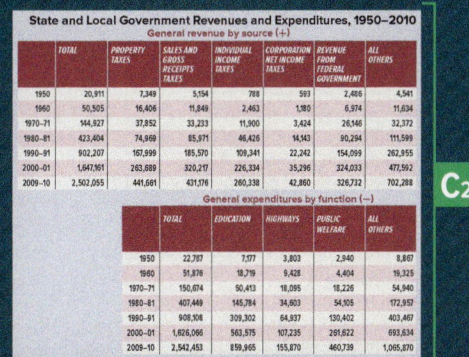

CASE STUDY REVIEW

1. **Analyzing** Look at the table "State and Local Government Revenues and Expenditures," and notice the general revenue columns for individual income taxes and corporation net income taxes. Between 1950 and 2010, which source of revenue shows the greatest increase?

2. **Drawing Conclusions** Why is it important to have such a detailed report on the economy? How does it help the president and Congress make decisions about taxes and expenditures?

CHAPTER 14, LESSON 2
Federal Government Finances

ENGAGE

C Critical Thinking Skills

Making predictions about federal spending categories Have students read the list showing four possible combinations of federal spending that make up the largest part of the government's budget. **Ask: What do you already know about federal spending categories?** *(Sample answer: The federal government pays for the military, for Medicare, for social programs, and for educational loans.)* Have students select one of the answers and write it down. By a show of hands, have students vote on the prioritization of items in the list. **Verbal/Linguistic**

TEACH & ASSESS

R Reading Skills

Defining fiscal and calendar years Ask: What is the difference between a fiscal year and a calendar year? *(The calendar year begins on January 1 and ends on December 31, whereas a fiscal year can begin anywhere in the year and extend one full year.)* **What are the beginning and end dates of the government's fiscal year?** *(The government's fiscal year begins on October 1 and ends on September 30.)* Point out to students that a fiscal year is a financial planning period that lasts for a full year, but may or may not coincide with the calendar year.

ANSWERS, p. 412
ESSENTIAL QUESTION ACTIVITY

Answer c is correct.
TAKING NOTES:
Individual Income Taxes
Borrowing
Payroll Taxes
Corporate Income Taxes
Excise Taxes, Estate, and Gift Taxes
Customs duties and miscellaneous fees

Interact with these digital assets and others in lesson 2

✓ **INTERACTIVE GRAPH** The Federal Deficit and the National Debt
✓ **INTERACTIVE TABLE** Impact of the National Debt
✓ **SELF-CHECK QUIZ**
✓ **VIDEO**

networks
TRY IT YOURSELF ONLINE

Reading Help Desk

Academic Vocabulary
- coincide
- instituted

Content Vocabulary
- fiscal year • indexing
- appropriations bill
- continuing budget resolution • Medicaid
- budget deficit
- budget surplus
- customs duty
- payroll tax • FICA
- corporate income tax
- excise tax • estate tax
- gift tax • public sector
- user fee • national debt
- earmarks, or pork
- transfer payments
- private sector
- crowding-out effect
- sequester
- line-item veto
- spending caps
- entitlements
- debt ceiling

TAKING NOTES:

Key Ideas and Details
ACTIVITY Use the graphic organizer below to identify ways the federal government raises revenues.

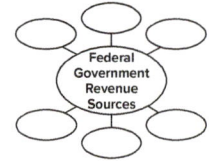

LESSON 2
Federal Government Finances

ESSENTIAL QUESTION

How does the government collect revenue, and on what is that revenue spent?

The federal government collects huge revenues and spends that money for the welfare of the people and the nation. You have probably seen discussions and debates about how the government spends its money. Before reading the lesson, think about what you know about how the government spends its revenue. From the list below, select the answer that you think best describes the largest expenditures of the federal government.

a. The government spends the largest portion of its revenue on Social Security, national defense, education, and student loans.

b. The government spends the largest portion of its revenue on scientific research at universities, national defense, and Medicare and Medicaid.

c. The government spends the largest portion of its revenue on national defense, Social Security, Medicare and Medicaid, and programs to support those unable to support themselves.

d. The government spends the largest portion of its revenue on Medicare, Medicaid, Social Security, and unemployment benefits.

Federal government finances are complex. Finances start with the preparation of a budget, and include both revenue sources and approval of expenditures. This is an annual process, and it is always difficult to accomplish everything in such a short period of time.

Establishing the Federal Budget

GUIDING QUESTION *How does the federal government determine an annual budget?*

The federal budget spans a **fiscal year**—a 12-month financial planning period that may or may not **coincide** with the calendar year. The government's fiscal year starts on October 1 and expires on September 30 of the following calendar year.

---

networks Online Teaching Options

BELLRINGER

Federal Government Finances

Analyzing changes in federal spending and the federal deficit Have students brainstorm world events that may have impacted federal spending over the past two decades. **Ask: What types of interactions with other countries might cause the federal government to reevaluate how it spends revenues?** *(Sample answer: Wars and responses to terrorism result in an increase in military spending and either a decrease in spending in other areas or an increase in the federal deficit.)* Then have students look at the Bellringer activity and answer the questions about federal spending and the federal deficit in relation to the events of September 11, 2001. Finally, have a class discussion on whether the spending and deficit responses were reasonable at the time, and whether they continue to be reasonable. **Verbal/Linguistic**

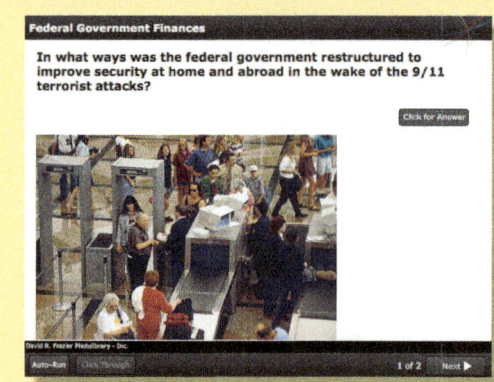

Executive Formulation

The president's Office of Management and Budget (OMB), part of the executive branch, is responsible for preparing the federal budget. However, the president's budget is only a request, and Congress can approve, modify, or disapprove it. By law, the budget must be sent to both houses of Congress by the first Monday in February. After that, the process slows considerably.

Congressional Action

Once the House of Representatives receives the president's budget request, it breaks down the budget into 12 major expenditure categories and assigns each to a separate House subcommittee. Each of the subcommittees then prepares an **appropriations bill**, an act of Congress that allows federal agencies to spend money for a specific purpose. Subcommittees hold hearings, debate, and vote on each bill. An approved bill is sent to the full House Appropriations Committee. If it passes there, the bill is sent to the entire House for a vote.

The Senate acts on the budget after the House has approved it. The Senate may approve the bill as sent by the House, or it may draft its own version. If differences exist between the House and the Senate versions, a joint House–Senate conference committee tries to work out a compromise bill. During this process, the House and the Senate often seek advice from the Congressional Budget Office (CBO). The CBO is a nonpartisan congressional agency that evaluates the impact of legislation and projects future revenues and expenditures that will result from the legislation.

Final Approval

If the House and Senate both approve the compromise bill, they send it to the president for signature. Because Congress literally took apart, rewrote, and put back together the president's budget, the final version may not resemble the original proposal. In many cases, a bill may have changed considerably, with items added to the president's original budget.

If the budget was altered too much, the president can veto the bill and force Congress to come up with a budget closer to the original version. However, once signed by the president, the budget becomes the official document for the next fiscal year that starts on October 1. Or if there is no agreement on funding, Congress can pass a **continuing budget resolution**, which is an agreement to fund a government agency at existing, reduced, or even expanded levels. Because of spending disagreements in Congress, continuing resolutions have been used frequently since 2001.

The 2016 Fiscal Year Budget

The federal budget shown in **Figure 14.5** is called the fiscal year (FY) 2016 budget because 9 of the 12 calendar months fall within the year 2016. The figure shows $3,336 billion (or $3.3 trillion) of revenue and $3,952 billion (or $3.9 trillion) of spending, leaving a **budget deficit**—a negative balance that results when expenditures exceed revenues—of about $616 billion. If expenditures were less than revenues, the result would be a **budget surplus**.

As the year goes on, the size of the deficit or surplus is likely to change significantly. This is because unforeseen events like changes in business conditions that affect tax collections, or changes in the political will to conduct spending, are likely to occur.

✓ **READING PROGRESS CHECK**

Describing Why does it take so long for the federal budget to be approved?

---

fiscal year 12-month financial planning period that may coincide with the calendar year; October 1 to September 30 for the federal government

coincide to happen or exist at the same time or in the same position

appropriations bill legislation authorizing spending for certain purposes

continuing budget resolution an agreement to fund a government agency at certain levels

budget deficit a negative balance after expenditures are subtracted from revenues

budget surplus a positive balance after expenditures are subtracted from revenues

---

CHAPTER 14, LESSON 2
Federal Government Finances

TEACH & ASSESS

C Critical Thinking Skills

Comparing family budgets to the federal budget Have students make a list of how their family's purchasing decisions are similar to and different from the government's budget-making process. (Possible similarities: Both spend money on a variety of different items; both try to base spending decisions on projected income. Possible differences: The federal government receives income from a variety of different sources as opposed to one or two incomes; many people are involved in the federal budget-making process, whereas one or two people usually make a family's budget decisions.) **Logical/Mathematical**

R Reading Skills

Summarizing the federal budget process Have students create a tree diagram summarizing the possible steps that the budget can go through before it can become the official document for the fiscal year. **Visual/Spatial**

WORKSHEETS

Assessing Background Knowledge

Assessing expenditures for levels of government
Have students think about the items they have already listed as federal government expenditures and put them in one of the circles on the Venn diagram. Have them label the circle "Federal Government Responsibilities." Have students label the other two circles "State Government Responsibilities" and "Local Government Responsibilities." Then have students fill in those circles with categories of expenditures they think belong to state and local governments, as opposed to the federal government. Finally, have them list responsibilities they think the three levels of government share. Tell students to keep the worksheet handy for later use. **Visual/Spatial**

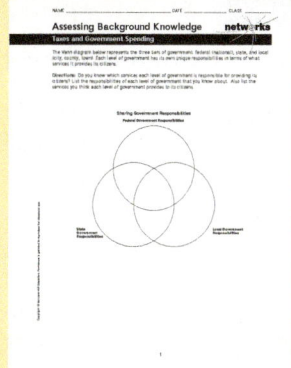

ANSWERS, p. 413

✓ **READING PROGRESS CHECK**

The president draws up the budget, and sends it to Congress for approval. First the House and then the Senate have to agree on it. During this process, members debate and make changes. Both the House and the Senate have to approve the bill, and then it goes to the president. If the budget is too altered, the president might veto it and force the Senate and House to come up with a budget closer to the original budget.

CHAPTER 14, LESSON 2
Federal Government Finances

R Reading Skills

Identifying the purpose of indexing Ask: **How does the government account for inflation in calculating tax brackets?** *(The government indexes the tax brackets, raising them each year to account for inflation.)* Point out to students that if a pay raise accounts for inflation only, a worker's purchasing power does not improve, and it is therefore not fair for that worker to be bumped up into a higher tax bracket because of that pay raise.

C Critical Thinking Skills

Identifying reasons for borrowing Have a class discussion about borrowing as a source of federal revenue. Ask: **Why has the federal government become more reliant on borrowing as a source of revenue?** *(increased spending on Social Security and Medicare on the aging population; increased spending on national defense after 2/11/2001; lower tax rates since the 1980s; lower tax collections during and after the Great Recession)* Have students suggest ways that the balance of revenue resources could change in the future.

V Visual Skills

Creating circle graphs from bar graphs
Have students use the information in the Federal Budget for Fiscal Year 2016 graph to create two circle graphs. Ask students to compare the original figure against the graphs they created and then write a paragraph explaining which format they believe presents the data most effectively, and why. **Visual/Spatial**

ANSWERS, p. 414

CRITICAL THINKING
Mandatory: Social Security; Discretionary: national defense

---

payroll withholding system method of automatically removing deductions from a paycheck

indexing adjustment of tax brackets to offset the effects of inflation

payroll tax tax on wages and salaries to finance Social Security and Medicare costs

FICA Federal Insurance Contribution Act; tax levied on employers and employees to support Social Security and Medicare

corporate income tax tax on corporate profits

excise tax general revenue tax levied on the manufacture or sale of selected items

estate tax tax on the transfer of property when a person dies

gift tax tax on donations of money or wealth that is paid by the donor

Federal Government Revenue Sources

GUIDING QUESTION *What are the main sources of government revenue?*

The federal government gets its revenue from a number of sources. Taxes are the primary source of revenue, but borrowing also plays a big part. As shown in Figure 14.5, the four largest sources of government revenue are individual income taxes, borrowing (the deficit), Social Security taxes, and corporate income taxes.

Individual Income Taxes

Today, the individual income tax accounts for about one-third of all federal government revenue. In most cases, the tax is collected through a **payroll withholding system**, a system that requires an employer to automatically deduct income taxes from a worker's paycheck and send them directly to the IRS.

The tax code is also indexed because inflation can push a worker into a higher tax bracket. **Indexing** is an upward revision of the tax brackets to keep workers from paying more in taxes just because of inflation. Workers might otherwise move into a higher tax bracket when they receive a pay raise that only makes up for inflation.

Borrowing

Borrowing by the federal government is a large source of federal revenue. Borrowing has always been an important source of revenue, but four things have dramatically increased reliance on it. The first was increased government spending on Social Security and Medicare as our population aged. The second was the sharply increased spending on national defense after the

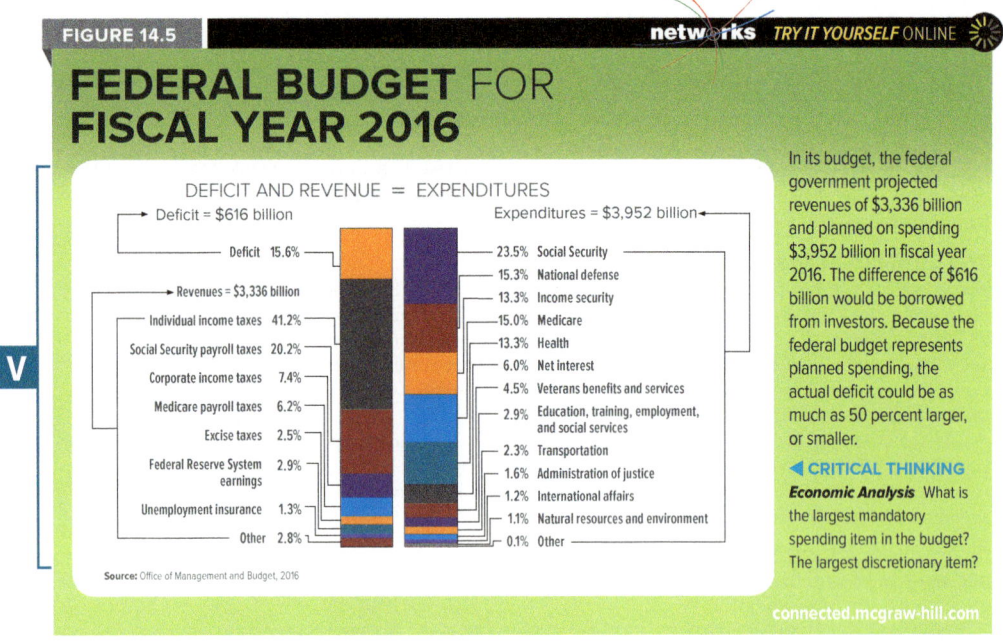

FIGURE 14.5

FEDERAL BUDGET FOR FISCAL YEAR 2016

In its budget, the federal government projected revenues of $3,336 billion and planned on spending $3,952 billion in fiscal year 2016. The difference of $616 billion would be borrowed from investors. Because the federal budget represents planned spending, the actual deficit could be as much as 50 percent larger, or smaller.

◄ **CRITICAL THINKING**
Economic Analysis What is the largest mandatory spending item in the budget? The largest discretionary item?

414

---

networks Online Teaching Options

GRAPHS

Federal Budget for Fiscal Year 2016

Analyzing the components of a budget
Have students look at Figure 14.5 showing the categories in the federal budget for FY2016. Point out that a budget includes not only expenditures (money going out) and revenues (money coming in), but also the difference between the two, which is either a deficit or a surplus. Have students write an equation that shows how the amount of the deficit is calculated, using the figures on the graph. **Logical/Mathematical**

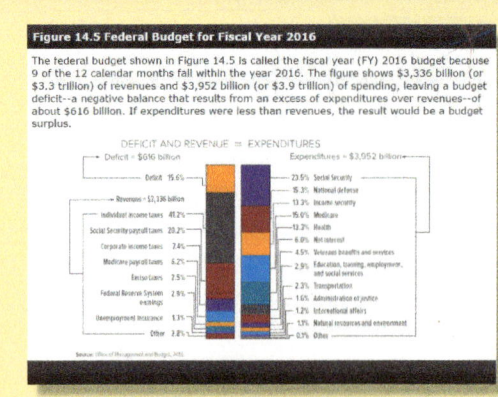

9/11/2001 terrorist attack. The third was the steady passage of lower tax rates since the 1980s, and the fourth was the lower tax collections during and after the Great Recession.

Even without these major events, the government would still need to borrow. This is because tax revenues fluctuate, and so the government never knows exactly how much it will have, or how much it will need to spend in any given year. Therefore, if the government does not collect enough money in taxes and user fees, or if it has more expenses than it can fund, it simply borrows the rest by selling bonds to investors.

Figure 14.5 shows that the federal government has become dependent on this source of funds, with the amount of money borrowed almost double the amount of taxes collected from private corporations.

Payroll Taxes

Another important federal revenue source is the Social Security Payroll Tax, also called the **payroll tax.** It is deducted directly from paychecks. The official name is **FICA,** the Federal Insurance Contributions Act tax, which is levied on employers and employees equally to pay for Social Security and Medicare.

In 2014, the Social Security component of FICA was 6.2 percent of wages and salaries up to $117,000. Above that amount, Social Security taxes are not collected, regardless of income. This means that a person with taxable income of $117,000 pays the same Social Security tax—$7,254—as does someone who earns $1,000,000,000.

In 1965, Congress added Medicare to the Social Security program. The Medicare component of FICA is taxed at a flat rate of 1.45 percent. Unlike Social Security, there is no cap on the amount of income taxed, which makes it a proportional tax.

Corporate Income Taxes

The fourth-largest source of federal revenue is the **corporate income tax**—the tax a corporation pays on its profits. The corporation is taxed separately from individuals because the corporation is recognized as a separate legal entity.

Corporations pay a slightly progressive tax, but the actual tax rate that corporations pay is much lower because of numerous tax breaks given to business. To cite just one example, in 2013 a U.S. Senate subcommittee found that Apple Computer, one of the world's most profitable corporations, used a complex network of international corporations to avoid paying any taxes to the American government—or to any other national governments for that matter—on $30 billion of profits. On top of that, the subcommittee concluded that Apple did not violate the U.S. tax code and therefore acted lawfully.

Excise, Estate, and Gift Taxes

The **excise tax**—a tax on the manufacture or sale of items such as gasoline and liquor—is the fifth-largest source of federal government revenue. Federal excise taxes are levied on telephone services, tires, gasoline, legal betting, and coal. Because low-income families spend larger portions of their incomes on some of these goods than do high-income families, excise taxes tend to be regressive.

An **estate tax** is the tax on the transfer of property when a person dies. The estate includes everything a person owned. Estate taxes can range from 18 to 50 percent of the value of the estate, although estates worth less than $3,500,000 are exempt. Because the exemption is so high, fewer than 2 percent of all estates pay any tax at all.

A **gift tax** is a tax on the transfer of money or wealth and is paid by the person who makes the gift. The gift tax is used to make sure that wealthy people

BIOGRAPHY

Daniel Werfel
GOVERNMENT (1971–)

Daniel Werfel (he goes by the name of Danny) was appointed commissioner of the Internal Revenue Service (IRS) in May 2013, a time when the agency was facing investigations by Congress and continuing federal budgetary problems. President Obama said of his appointment, "Throughout his career working in both Democratic and Republican administrations, Danny has proven an effective leader who serves with professionalism, integrity, and skill."

Werfel rose through the ranks as a civil servant, worked in the Justice Department as an attorney, and more recently, worked in the White House Office of Management and Budget for both President Obama and President George W. Bush. Werfel is a government leader who has experience directing government's large efforts, including the Obama administration's implementation of the federal budget cuts known as sequestration. He holds a law degree from the University of North Carolina at Chapel Hill and a master's degree in public policy from Duke University.

▲ **CRITICAL THINKING**
Drawing Conclusions On the basis of Werfel's experience, do you think he was a good appointment to lead the IRS? Give your reasons.

CHAPTER 14, LESSON 2
Federal Government Finances

R1 Reading Skills

Understanding the necessity of government borrowing Ask: **Could the government stop borrowing money altogether? Why or why not?** (No; because tax revenues fluctuate and circumstances may require more funding in a given year) **How does the federal government borrow?** (It sells bonds.)

C1 Critical Thinking Skills

Calculating Social Security taxes Ask: **Which tax pays for Social Security and Medicare?** (FICA, also known as the payroll tax) **Who pays this tax?** (employers and employees) Have students calculate the amount a person with a salary of $100,000 would pay in 2014 for the Social Security component of this tax. (6.2% of $100,000, or $6,200) **Logical/Mathematical**

C2 Critical Thinking Skills

Expressing opinions on corporate income taxes Ask: **Why can some corporations get away with paying little or no taxes to the government?** (A series of tax breaks for businesses can be used to lower a corporation's tax payments, sometimes to the point of not even having to pay taxes.) Have students write an opinion essay stating whether or not they agree with the idea that corporations pay lower taxes than individuals do, and providing reasons and examples to support their opinion. **Verbal/Linguistic**

R2 Reading Skills

Identifying excise taxes as regressive Ask: **Why do excise taxes tend to be regressive?** (Many of the goods that have a federal excise tax are items that low-income families spend large portions of their incomes on.)

BIOGRAPHY

Biography: Daniel Werfel

Evaluating the role of the IRS Commissioner
Have students read the biography of Daniel Werfel. Then have them do more research on him and his life. Ask students to write a biographical essay about Mr. Werfel, including a description of his role in the IRS and his efforts to reduce the deficit.
Verbal/Linguistic

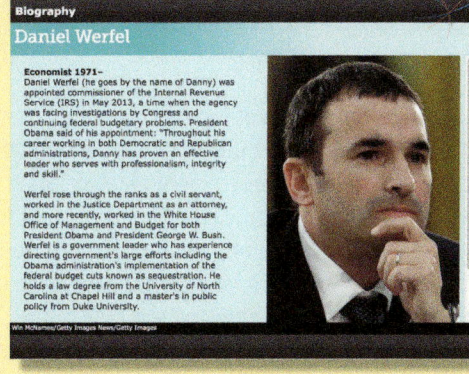

ANSWERS, p. 415

CRITICAL THINKING
Student answers should show an understanding that Werfel's government experience should be helpful in his running the IRS, even when it is being investigated by Congress.

CHAPTER 14, LESSON 2
Federal Government Finances

W1 Writing Skills

Defining types of taxation Have students write, in their own words, a definition of and an example for each type of tax at the federal level.
Verbal/Linguistic

W2 Writing Skills

Offering opinions about user fees Have students write a journal entry giving their opinion of user fees charged for things such as entry into national parks. Tell them to include whether they think the fees are equitable and why some people may be more comfortable with the fees because they are not called "taxes." **Verbal/Linguistic**

R Reading Skills

Defining earmarks Ask: **What is another word for "earmarks"?** *(pork)* Have students write two sentences, one defining the word "earmarks" and the other giving a possible example of this type of spending. **Logical/Mathematical**

C Critical Thinking Skills

Differentiating between mandatory and discretionary spending Direct students to create a T-chart labeled "Mandatory spending" and "Discretionary spending." Have them list the definition of each term in the appropriate column on the chart, as well as examples of each type of spending. **Logical/Mathematical**

ANSWERS, p. 416

✓ **READING PROGRESS CHECK** Corporations are taxed separately from individuals because a corporation is recognized as a separate legal entity.

---

customs duty tax on imported products

user fee fee paid for the use of a good or service; form of a benefit tax

do not try to avoid taxes by giving away their estates before they die. Figure 14.5 shows that estate and gift taxes account for only a small fraction of total federal government revenue.

Other Revenue Sources

A **customs duty** is a charge levied on goods brought into the United States from other countries. Many types of goods are covered, ranging from automobiles to silver ore. The duties are relatively low and produce little federal revenue today.

Before the enactment of the income tax amendment, however, they were the largest income source for the federal government.

Finally, a fraction of federal revenue is collected through various miscellaneous fees. One example of a miscellaneous fee is a **user fee**—a charge levied for the use of a good or service. User fees were widely promoted by President Ronald Reagan, who wanted to find revenue sources that did not involve taxes.

User fees include entrance charges at national parks, as well as the fees ranchers pay when their animals graze on federal land. These fees are essentially taxes based on the benefit principle, because only the individuals who use the services pay them. People also seem more comfortable with them since they are not called "taxes."

✓ **READING PROGRESS CHECK**

Explaining Why are corporations taxed separately from individuals?

Federal Government Expenditures

GUIDING QUESTION *How does the federal government determine an annual budget?*

public sector that part of the economy made up of the local, state, and federal governments

earmarks, or pork a line item budget expenditure that circumvents normal budget building processes and procedures and benefits a small number of people or businesses

Spending by the **public sector**—the part of the economy consisting of federal, state, and local governments—was relatively low prior to the Great Depression. Since then, attitudes have shifted and spending has increased sharply. Some of the spending was in the form of **earmarks, or pork**, a term used to describe a line-item budget expenditure that circumvents normal budget-building procedures. More recently, most spending has been for things like national defense, highways, parks, and a number of other categories.

Social Security

The largest category of expenditures in the federal budget is for payments to aged and disabled Americans through the Social Security program. Retired persons receive benefits from the Old-Age and Survivors Insurance (OASI) program. Those unable to work receive payments from disability insurance (DI) programs.

mandatory spending federal spending authorized by law that continues without the need for annual approvals of Congress

Spending for Social Security is sometimes called **mandatory spending**, or spending authorized by law that continues without the need for annual approvals by Congress. This is because the total Social Security payments in any given year are dependent on the number of people eligible for Social Security and the level of benefits already approved by Congress. Unless changes to the program are made, Social Security will continue to be the largest category of federal expenditure as our population continues to get older and more people reach retirement.

National Defense

For much of the late 1900s, national defense comprised the largest category of spending, although it is now exceeded by Social Security. National defense includes military spending by the Department of Defense and defense-related atomic energy activities, such as the development of nuclear weapons and the disposal of nuclear wastes.

416

---

networks *Online Teaching Options*

WORKSHEETS

Reteaching Activity

Analyzing two views of federal revenues Have students study the two graphs showing the different categories of revenue the federal government receives. Ask: **Which one shows change over time?** *(the line graph)* **Which revenue sources have diminished since 1950?** *(excise taxes and corporate taxes)* **Which large revenue source is missing from the graphs?** *(borrowing)* **Visual/Spatial**

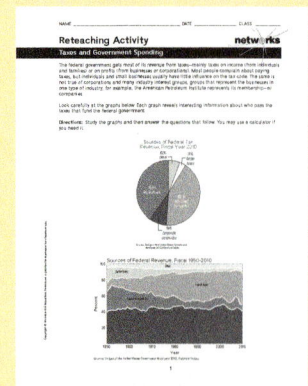

CHAPTER 14, LESSON 2
Federal Government Finances

Defense expenditures are called **discretionary spending**—spending that must be approved by Congress in the annual budgetary process. Unlike Social Security payments, which normally go up as the population gets older, annual defense expenditures can go up, down, or remain the same, depending on the will of the president and Congress.

Income Security

Income security consists of a wide range of programs that includes unemployment assistance, food and nutrition assistance, and retirement benefits for both federal civilian employees and retired military. Other programs are designed to support people unable to fully care for themselves. The vast majority of these expenditures are **transfer payments**—payments for which the government receives neither goods nor services in return.

Other transfer payments include Social Security, unemployment compensation, welfare, aid for people with disabilities, child care, foster care, and adoption assistance. Those unable to support themselves receive Supplemental Security Income (SSI), subsidized housing, federal child support, Temporary Assistance for Needy Families (TANF), and food stamps. Most income security expenditures are mandatory and therefore do not need congressional authorization every year.

Medicare and Medicaid

Medicare began in 1966 and is another mandatory program for senior citizens, regardless of income. It provides an insurance plan that covers major hospital costs. Medicare also offers optional insurance that provides additional coverage for doctor and laboratory fees, outpatient services, and some medical equipment costs.

In recent years, Medicare expenditures have risen dramatically as the population has aged and the cost of caring for the elderly has gone up. Given the increasing cost of medicine and current population trends, increases in this category of expenditure are expected to continue.

Health-care services for low-income people, disease prevention, and consumer safety account for a significant part of the federal budget. **Medicaid**, for example, is a joint federal-state medical insurance program for low-income persons. Because the payments have already been determined by Congress, this is one of the mandatory expenditure programs. Other mandatory programs include health-care services for working and retired federal employees.

Some programs in this category are discretionary. The Occupational Safety and Health Administration (OSHA), which monitors occupational safety and health in the workplace, is one such program. Other discretionary programs include AIDS and breast cancer research, substance abuse treatment, and mental health services.

Other broad categories of the federal budget include education, training, employment, and social services; veterans' benefits; transportation; administration of justice; and natural resources and the environment. They include both mandatory and discretionary spending.

✓ **READING PROGRESS CHECK**

Summarizing What steps are involved in establishing the federal budget?

From Deficits to Debt

GUIDING QUESTION *How do annual budget deficits add up to the national debt?*

Historically, a remarkable amount of **deficit spending**—or spending in excess of revenues collected—has characterized the federal budget. Sometimes the

---

discretionary spending spending for federal programs that must receive annual authorization

transfer payments payments for which the government receives neither goods nor services in return

EXPLORING THE ESSENTIAL QUESTION

Let us suppose that you have started a part-time job at the local coffee shop. You are working 15 hours a week and get paid the minimum wage in your state. You get paid every two weeks. Write a paragraph describing the taxes you will pay to the federal government every two weeks. Describe any issues you have with paying these taxes and why.

Medicaid joint federal-state medical insurance program for low-income people

deficit spending annual government spending in excess of taxes and other revenues

---

Making Connections

Domestic Policies Supported by Taxes Explain that domestic policies (in contrast to foreign policies) are those that occur at home and affect the American people as a whole. The Preamble to the U.S. Constitution includes the following domestic goals of government: "to insure domestic Tranquility," "to promote the general Welfare," and "to secure the Blessings of Liberty." Accordingly, federal taxes support public programs providing for citizens' income security, health care, environmental protection, energy policy, Homeland security policy, and immigration policy. Ask students to identify other important uses of national taxes.

C Critical Thinking Skills

Speculating about spending Have a discussion about goods and services the government provides. **Ask: Why do you think some people object to the government providing certain goods and services?** *(Answers may include a concern about higher taxes and a belief that the private sector can provide goods more efficiently.)* Ask students to name goods and services they think government should provide more or less of, and have them give reasons for their selections. **Verbal/Linguistic**

R Reading Skills

Predicting the future of Medicare and Medicaid costs Ask: Why are Medicare and Medicaid costs rising so dramatically? *(The population is aging and the cost of medical care is rising.)* Have students predict what costs will do in the future, given what they have read about medical care and the population.

ANSWERS, p. 417

EXPLORING THE ESSENTIAL QUESTION

Student answers should show that they understand they will pay FICA taxes. In discussing any issues they have with paying FICA, they should show recognition of the employer contribution to both Social Security and Medicare and the benefits their families may be receiving, and the benefits they expect to receive later in their lives.

✓ **READING PROGRESS CHECK** The president draws up a budget, sends the budget to the House, which then may alter it. The House sends it to the Senate. If the Senate alters the budget, it is then reconciled with the House budget. When the House and Senate agree, the budget goes to the president, who either signs or vetoes it.

WORKSHEETS

Influences on Tax Law Simulation

Demonstrating influences on tax policy Students will role play various groups that influence federal tax policy. Divide the class into three groups. Group One students are members of an industry lobbying group that represents defense contractors and seeks tax breaks for them. Group Two students enact the role of members of Congress. Group Three students represent ordinary citizens who have come to Congress to convince lawmakers to make the tax code more progressive in the interest of middle-class citizens and to limit or eliminate unfair tax breaks for corporations. **Verbal/Linguistic**

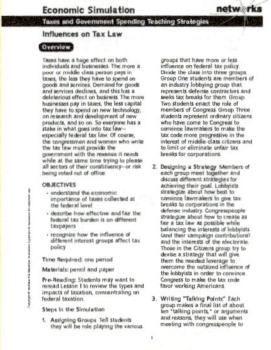

CHAPTER 14, LESSON 2
Federal Government Finances

R1 Reading Skills
Understanding the difference between the deficit and the debt Ask: **How does a deficit happen?** *(The government spends more than it collects in revenues for a year, and so it must borrow to make up the difference.)* **How is the national debt calculated?** *(by adding up all outstanding federal notes, bonds, and other debt obligations for that year, and then adding that figure to the existing debt)* Logical/Mathematical

R2 Reading Skills
Understanding the budget and national debt Ask: **What would happen to the national debt if the government achieves a balanced budget for the year?** *(The amount of the national debt will not change.)*

V Visual Skills
Comparing the deficit and the debt Ask: **How is the information in the two graphs in Figure 14.6 related?** *(The amount in Panel A is the federal deficit for each year, and adds to or subtracts from the amounts—the total national debt—in Panel B.)* Logical/Mathematical

ANSWERS, p. 418
CRITICAL THINKING
Because the national debt is the sum of all deficits. If another deficit is added, regardless of how small, national debt grows larger.

---

government plans deficit spending. At other times, revenues drop and expenditures rise at the same time, as they did during and after the Great Recession, causing a single annual deficit to reach the trillions.

Deficits Add to the Debt
Panel A of **Figure 14.6** shows the history of the federal budget deficit since 1965. During that period, the federal budget showed a surplus only five times. The first was in 1969, and the last four occurred in the years 1998 to 2001. When the federal government runs a deficit, it must finance the revenue shortage by borrowing. It does this by selling U.S. Treasury notes and other securities to the public. If we add up all outstanding federal notes, bonds, and other debt obligations, we have a measure of the **national debt**—the total amount borrowed from investors to finance the government's deficit spending.

As **Panel B** in Figure 14.6 shows, the national debt grows whenever the government runs a deficit. If the federal budget runs a surplus, then some of the borrowed money is repaid and the amount of total debt goes down, as it did from 1998 to 2001. If the federal government achieves a **balanced budget**—an annual budget in which expenditures equal revenues—the national debt will not change.

A Growing Public Debt
The national debt has grown almost continuously since 1900 when the debt was $1.3 billion. By 1929 it had reached $16.9 billion, and by 1940 it was $50.7 billion. By 2014 the total national debt had reached almost $18 trillion.

Some of this debt is money that the government owes itself. For example, approximately $5 trillion of this debt is in government **trust funds**—special accounts used to fund specific types of expenditures such as Social Security and Medicare. When the government collects the FICA or payroll taxes, it puts the revenues in these trust accounts. The money is then invested in government securities until it is paid out.

national debt the total amount borrowed from investors to finance the government's deficit spending

balanced budget annual budget in which expenditures equal revenues

trust funds special account used to hold revenues designated for a specific expenditure such as Social Security, Medicare, or highways

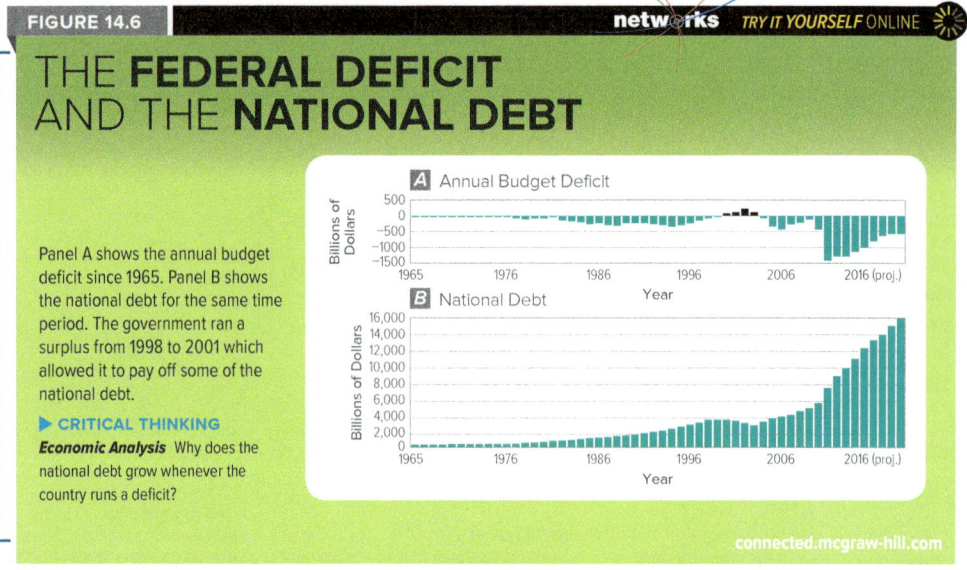

FIGURE 14.6
THE FEDERAL DEFICIT AND THE NATIONAL DEBT

Panel A shows the annual budget deficit since 1965. Panel B shows the national debt for the same time period. The government ran a surplus from 1998 to 2001 which allowed it to pay off some of the national debt.

▶ **CRITICAL THINKING**
Economic Analysis Why does the national debt grow whenever the country runs a deficit?

---

networks Online Teaching Options

GRAPHS
The Federal Deficit and the National Debt

Explaining choices in spending Have students explore Figure 14.6 showing the national debt and the federal deficit. Ask: **Why is part of the federal deficit graph in black?** *(During those years, there was a surplus.)* Have students write an explanatory paper about the decision not to use the surplus to pay off the national debt, and the results of that decision. Logical/Mathematical

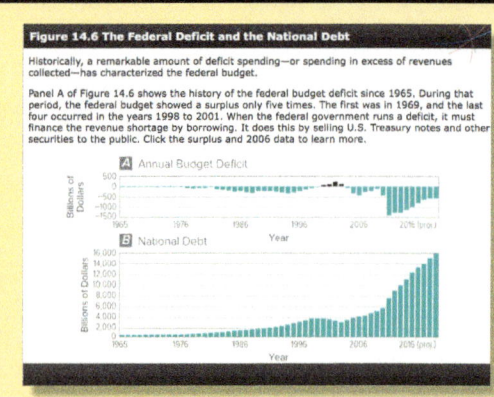

Because trust fund balances represent money the government owes to itself, most economists tend to disregard this portion of the debt. Instead, they view the public portion of the debt—which amounted to about $13 trillion in 2014—as the economically relevant part of the debt.

Figure 14.7 presents two alternative views of the total national debt held by the public. **Panel A** shows the debt as a percentage of GDP. In **Panel B**, the national debt is computed on a **per capita**, or per person, basis. Both measures are relatively large by historical standards.

per capita per person basis; total divided by population

Public vs. Private Debt

Despite the size of the public debt, several important differences between public and private debt mean that the country can never go bankrupt. One is that we owe most of the national debt to ourselves—whereas private debt is owed to others.

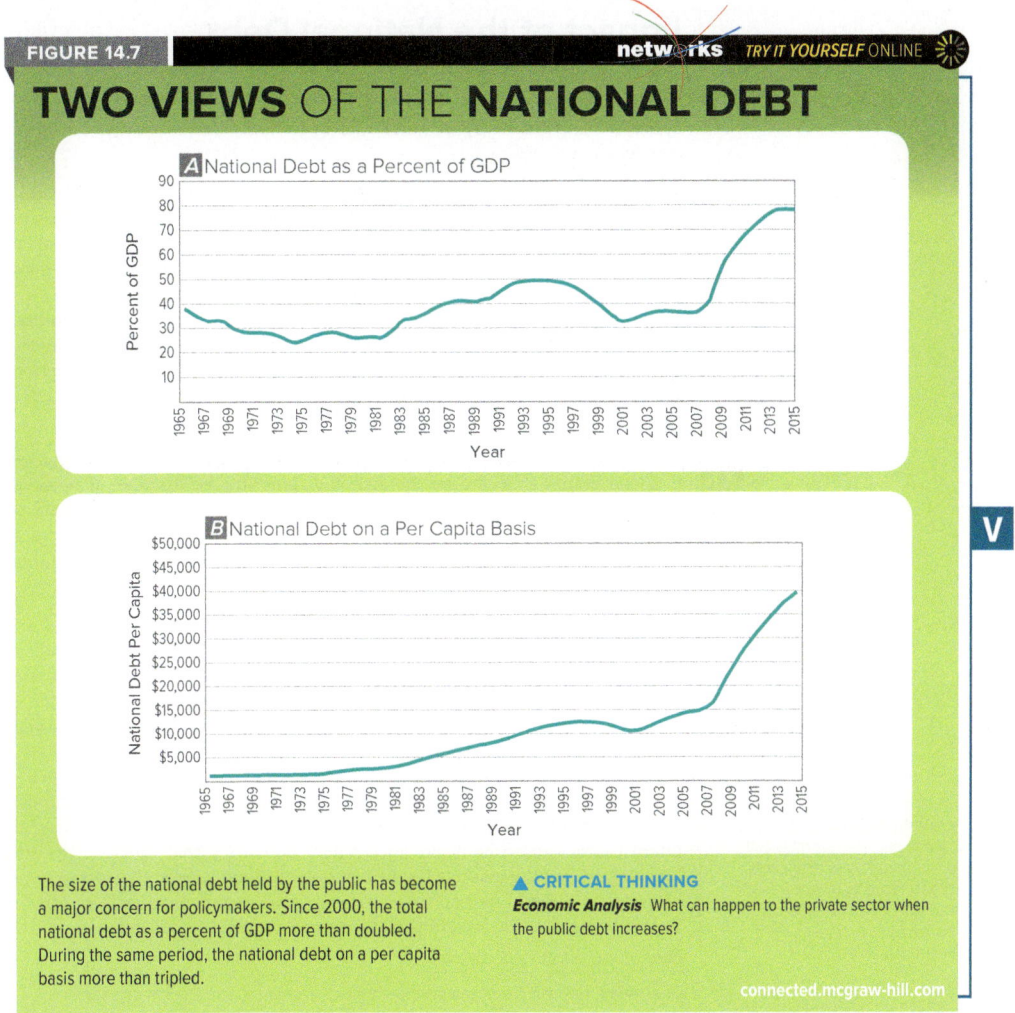

FIGURE 14.7

TWO VIEWS OF THE NATIONAL DEBT

A. National Debt as a Percent of GDP

B. National Debt on a Per Capita Basis

The size of the national debt held by the public has become a major concern for policymakers. Since 2000, the total national debt as a percent of GDP more than doubled. During the same period, the national debt on a per capita basis more than tripled.

▲ **CRITICAL THINKING**
Economic Analysis What can happen to the private sector when the public debt increases?

CHAPTER 14, LESSON 2
Federal Government Finances

V Visual Skills

Examining the growth of the national debt
Have students look at the two graphs in Figure 14.7. **Ask: Is the debt better or worse today than it was in 2000?** *(Worse; the debt today is a higher percentage of GDP, and the per capita debt is higher.)* Have students list reasons why they think the debt grew since 2001. *(Students should mention the high deficits incurred because of the tax rate decreases; the numerous wars fought since 2001; the Great Recession, which increased unemployment benefits while reducing tax collections; costly natural disasters; and so on. The increased deficits all added to the national debt.)*

English Language Proficiency

Intermediate To enhance and confirm understanding, have students take a close look at visual support before they read the text. Tell them to work in pairs, using graphs, illustrations, and other visuals to form questions about the selection and predict answers. After reading, have partners compare their original predictions with the answers they found, and discuss how their ideas changed or stayed the same.

GRAPHS

Two Views of the National Debt

Explaining the impact of debt on individuals
Have students look at the two representations of the national debt in Figure 14.7, expressed as a percentage of the GDP and the debt per capita. Then have them discuss how public debt is different from private debt, and explain why the country can never go bankrupt.
Verbal/Linguistic

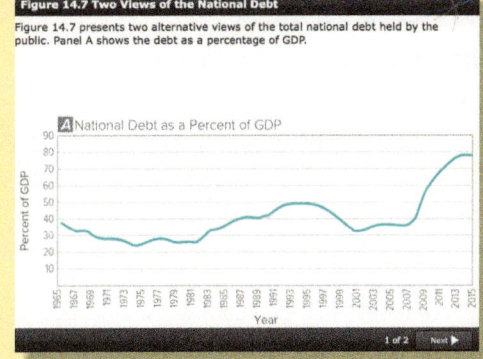

ANSWERS, p. 419

CRITICAL THINKING
Students should recognize that generally, when the public debt increases, taxes increase and people have less money for themselves.

CHAPTER 14, LESSON 2
Federal Government Finances

C Critical Thinking Skills

Analyzing the national debt owed to foreigners Instruct students to use reliable print or online resources to analyze the public debt owed to foreigners. Ask students to prepare a statistical summary of this portion of the debt. Students should include the different companies and nations to which the government owes money, along with the corresponding amounts. **Logical/Mathematical**

W Writing Skills

Writing about the impact of the national debt Have students summarize the three effects of the national debt given in the text *(transferring purchasing power, reducing economic incentives, and causing a crowding-out effect)*. Ask students to draw visual aids (diagrams or cartoons) to help them remember the causes and effects of the national debt in these three situations. **Verbal/Linguistic, Kinesthetic**

Making Connections

Interest Payments on the National Debt 1800–1900 Point out to students that the federal government has been paying off a debt since 1789. Most years, just the interest on the debt has been in the millions. Give students these figures listing how much the federal government paid in interest on the debt for every tenth year between 1800 and 1900: 1800: $3 million; 1810: $3 million; 1820: $5 million; 1830: $2 million; 1840: (information unavailable); 1850: $4 million; 1860: $3 million; 1870: $129 million; 1880: $96 million; 1890: $36 million; 1900: $40 million. Ask students to put this information on a time line and hypothesize why the interest on the debt increased by 4300 percent between 1860 and 1870. *(Students will likely answer that the debt increased by that amount because of the costs of the Civil War and Reconstruction.)* **Logical/Mathematical**

ANSWERS, p. 420

✓ **READING PROGRESS CHECK** Public debt is money that the government owes mostly to us, the people; private debt is money that private citizens owe to others.

✓ **READING PROGRESS CHECK** Government borrowing increases the national debt, which increases taxes. Also, if the government appears to spend money in a careless manner, government borrowing can reduce private economic incentives.

Another difference is repayment. When private citizens borrow, they usually plan to repay the debt by a specific date. When the government borrows, it gives little thought to repayment and issues new bonds to pay off the old bonds.

A third difference has to do with purchasing power. When private individuals repay debts, they give up purchasing power because they have less money to buy goods and services. However, the federal government does not always give up purchasing power, because the taxes collected from some groups are simply transferred to others. The exception is the 34 percent of the public debt owned by foreigners. When payments are made to investors outside the United States, some purchasing power is temporarily diverted from the U.S. economy.

✓ READING PROGRESS CHECK

Contrasting What is the main difference between public and private debt?

Impact of the National Debt

GUIDING QUESTION *How does the transfer of purchasing power between generations affect you?*

Even though we owe most of the national debt to ourselves, it affects the economy by transferring purchasing power, reducing economic incentives, and causing a crowding-out effect.

Transferring Purchasing Power

private sector *that part of the economy made up of private individuals and businesses*

The national debt can cause a transfer of purchasing power from the **private sector**—the part of the economy made up of private individuals and privately owned businesses—to the public sector. In general, when the public debt increases, taxes increase and people have less money for themselves.

Purchasing power can also be transferred from one generation to another. If the government borrows today and leaves the repayment to future taxpayers, then today's adults will consume more and their children less. The accumulation of debt by one generation can thus reduce the economic well-being of the next.

Reducing Economic Incentives

Government borrowing can reduce private economic incentives if it appears to spend money in a careless manner. A community, for example, may use a federal grant to purchase expensive equipment that its citizens would not want to pay for themselves. If the taxpayers that benefit from a project would not want to fund it themselves, it is unlikely that other taxpayers would want their taxes to go to such projects.

Crowding Out

When the federal government uses deficit spending, it must borrow money in financial markets. This is a supply-and-demand situation in the markets where money can be borrowed. If the demand for funds increases without a corresponding increase in the supply of funds available for borrowing, the price of borrowed money—the interest rate—will go up, forcing borrowers to pay more.

crowding-out effect *higher than normal interest rates and diminished access to financial capital faced by private investors when government increases its borrowing in financial markets*

Because the government borrows so much, it can compete with businesses and individuals such as potential home buyers for the supply of available funds. This competition can cause a **crowding-out effect**—the higher-than-normal interest rates caused by heavy government borrowing that squeezes private borrowers out of the market. The firm or potential homeowner that would have been able to borrow funds at 5 percent for an investment or home may no longer be able to afford those investments if interest rates rise to 7 percent.

✓ READING PROGRESS CHECK

Describing How can the government's role as a borrower impact economic incentives?

420

---

networks *Online Teaching Options*

INTERACTIVE FEATURE

Impact of the National Debt

Making connections to the impact of the national debt The chart explores the impact of the national debt on economic incentives and taxes. Have students drag and drop the events into the appropriate columns of the activity. Then ask them to answer the question: How can the government's role as a borrower impact economic incentives? **Logical/Mathematical**

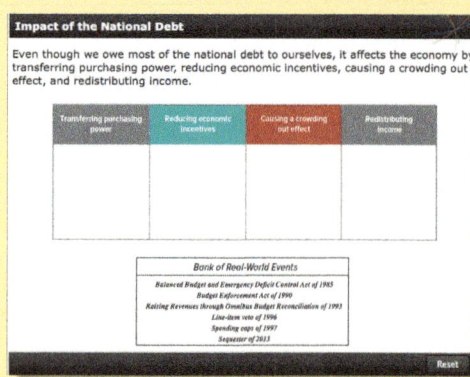

Reducing Deficits and the Debt

GUIDING QUESTION Why is it difficult to reduce the national debt?

Because federal budget deficits add to the debt, we have to first address the federal budget deficit. Concern over deficit spending since the 1980s has led to a number of attempts to control it.

Early Legislative Failures

One of the first significant attempts to control the federal deficit took place when Congress tried to mandate a balanced budget. The legislation was formally called the Balanced Budget and Emergency Deficit Control Act of 1985, or Gramm-Rudman-Hollings (GRH) after its sponsors.

Despite high hopes, GRH failed for two reasons. First, Congress discovered that it could get around the law by passing spending bills that took effect two or three years later. Second, the economy started to decline in 1990, triggering a suspension of budget cuts when the economy was weak.

In 1990, Congress passed the Budget Enforcement Act (BEA). The BEA's main feature was a **"pay-as-you-go" provision**—a requirement that new spending proposals must be offset by reductions elsewhere in the budget. If no agreement on the reductions could be reached, then automatic, across-the-board spending cuts would be **instituted**.

Congress soon discovered that cutting spending was more difficult than it had thought, so it suspended the provision in order to increase spending.

In 1996, Congress gave the president a **line-item veto**—the power to cancel specific budget items without rejecting the entire budget—but the Supreme Court declared it unconstitutional. This was followed by the Balanced Budget Agreement of 1997, which featured rigid **spending caps**—legal limits on annual discretionary spending—to assure that Congress balanced the budget by 2002. However, the caps required politically unpopular cuts in many programs such as health, science, and education, so the caps were also abandoned.

Raising Revenues

Raising revenues is another way to reduce deficits. President Clinton's Omnibus Budget Reconciliation Act of 1993 was an attempt to trim $500 billion from the deficit over a five-year period. The act featured a combination of spending reductions and tax increases that made the individual income tax more progressive—especially for the wealthiest 1.2 percent of taxpayers.

Higher tax rates, along with strong economic growth, combined to produce four consecutive years of federal budget surpluses from 1998 through 2001. But in 2001, Congress expected annual surpluses to last for another 10 years. Rather than pay down the debt, Congress cut tax rates while also increasing spending, which made the situation worse.

Unexpected Spending

In 2001, terrorist attacks during the Bush administration led to unplanned government spending on homeland security and wars in Iraq and Afghanistan. Because this was also the first year of President Bush's tax cuts, and because economic activity was low, the federal government had fewer tax revenues to spend. As a result, record federal budget deficits returned in 2002.

In addition, spending was difficult to reduce because the federal budget had so many **entitlements**—broad social programs with established eligibility requirements to provide health, nutritional, or income supplements to individuals. People are entitled to draw benefits if they meet the eligibility requirements. Although most entitlements are classified as mandatory spending,

"pay-as-you-go" provision requirement that new spending proposals or tax cuts must be offset by reductions elsewhere

instituted put into action

line-item veto power to cancel specific budget items without rejecting the entire budget

spending caps limits on annual discretionary spending

entitlements program or benefit using established eligibility requirements to provide health, nutritional, or income supplements to individuals

---

CHAPTER 14, LESSON 2
Federal Government Finances

C Critical Thinking Skills

Researching legislative efforts Have students use print or online resources to find out more information about one of the legislative efforts to reduce the deficit and the debt. Ask students to use their findings to write a report expanding upon the text's description of their selected topic.

Making Connections

The Federal Budget Ask students to find a recent newspaper article about the federal budget. Summarize the article and write a caption explaining how the article relates to this lesson.
Verbal/Linguistic

R1 Reading Skills

Understanding the line-item veto Ask: **How would the line-item veto have helped the president balance the budget?** *(It would have given the president the power to cancel specific budget items—earmarks, or pork—without rejecting the entire budget.)*

R2 Reading Skills

Identifying spending issues of 2001 Have students discuss the circumstances that overturned the budget surpluses of 1998–2001. Be sure students understand the increase in government spending due to the terrorist attacks of 2001 and the existence of so many entitlements, combined with cuts in tax rates, led to record federal budget deficits. Ask: **Do you think a pay-as-you-go provision or debt ceiling can reduce the national debt?** *(Students should provide support for their opinions.)*

VIDEO **WORKSHEET**

Balancing Local Government Budgets

Evaluating efforts to balance local government budgets Have students watch the video about a variety of efforts to balance local government budgets. Then have students pick one effort from the video to critique. Have them write a description of the problem, the effort to fix the problem, and a suggestion for a different or better way to reduce the expense or raise revenue. **Verbal/Linguistic**

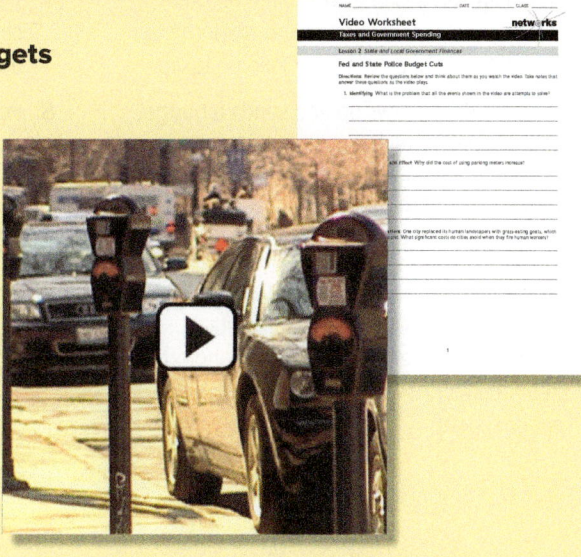

CHAPTER 14, LESSON 2
Federal Government Finances

C1 Critical Thinking Skills

Hypothesizing about the difficulties of debt reduction Ask: **Why is it so difficult to reduce the national debt?** Have students write a one-page explanation to answer the question, and have them provide examples to explain their answers.

C2 Critical Thinking Skills

Constructing arguments about debt Have students write a short dialogue between two people who have opposing views about the reduction of government programs to reduce expenditures and lower debt. **Verbal/Linguistic**

CLOSE & REFLECT

Considering taxation and debt Have students discuss whether they believe they will see the eradication of national debt within their lifetime. Ask: **Is such a goal even desirable?** Verbal/Linguistic

---

ANSWERS, p. 422

✓ **READING PROGRESS CHECK**
The attempt by some House Representatives to repeal the Affordable Care Act, which they do not like, and their willingness to shut down the government and nearly force the government to default on its commitments to repay its debts, shows the deep divide in Washington on how to allocate federal spending.

---

sequester a law that required automatic budget cuts

Congress can revise them. Still, this is difficult to do for members of Congress because the programs are so popular.

Sequester
In 2011, President Obama and Congress agreed to a deficit reduction measure that would start in 2013. It featured a **sequester**, which required automatic and arbitrary budget cuts that would begin in 2013 if Congress could not agree on significant deficit reductions before then. The cuts affected all discretionary programs such as education, energy, medical research, and even national defense.

The sequester was specifically designed to be so unattractive that Democrats and Republicans would prefer to get together and agree on a better way to reduce the deficit. When 2013 arrived, however, Congress was unable to agree on a deficit reduction program, and so the automatic sequester cuts took place. The result was that some spending reductions occurred, but almost everyone was unhappy with them. Congress was also unable to agree on measures to reduce the deficit and so the federal debt continued to rise, although at a slower rate. Finally, by late 2013 the federal debt reached the legal limit established earlier by Congress.

debt ceiling total amount of money the federal government is allowed to borrow

Enforcing the Debt Ceiling
The **debt ceiling** is the total amount of money that the U.S. government is authorized to borrow to meet existing commitments like Social Security, Medicare, interest on the national debt, military salaries, and payment of tax refunds. The ceiling, also called the debt limit, does not authorize spending on new programs. Instead, it only permits borrowing for expenditures that have already been authorized by Congress and the president.

As you saw in Figure 14.5, interest payments on the federal debt are the sixth largest expenditure item in the federal budget. If interest rates go up, this expenditure will get larger and the government will either have to run a bigger deficit or cut additional spending elsewhere.

✓ **READING PROGRESS CHECK**

Describing How have the budget and spending crises of the Obama administration illustrated the partisan disagreements of how to allocate federal spending?

LESSON 2 REVIEW

Reviewing Vocabulary
1. *Explaining* What is a transfer payment made by the government?

Using Your Notes
2. *Identifying* Use your notes to describe an example of a government revenue source that is not a tax.

Answering the Guiding Questions
3. *Explaining* How does the collection of taxes allow our government to help its citizens and keep them safe?
4. *Describing* What are the main sources of government revenue?
5. *Summarizing* How does the federal government determine an annual budget?
6. *Assessing* How do annual budget deficits add up to the national debt?
7. *Hypothesize* How does the transfer of purchasing power between generations affect you?
8. *Draw Conclusions* Why is it difficult to reduce the national debt?

Writing About Economics
9. *Informative/Explanatory* Using research sources, write an essay describing one federal budget debate that occurred in the last three years and that affected the whole country. Use credible sources to explain the two sides of the debate and how it was resolved.

LESSON 2 REVIEW ANSWERS

Reviewing Vocabulary
1. A transfer payment is a payment to a party in which the government receives neither goods nor services, such as Social Security payments.

Using Your Notes
2. Students should identify borrowing, customs duties, and user fees.

Answering the Guiding Questions
3. The U.S. Constitution allows Congress to lay and collect taxes for providing national and for the general welfare of its citizens.
4. The main sources of government revenue are individual income taxes, borrowing, payroll taxes, and corporate income taxes.
5. The president draws up and sends a budget to the House, which may alter it. The House sends it to the Senate. Its version, reconciled with the House budget, goes to the president, who signs or vetoes it.
6. The deficit is the amount spent above the annual budget. Adding up all deficits—outstanding federal notes, bonds, and other debt obligations— results in the national debt.
7. The accumulation of debt by one generation can reduce the economic well-being of the next.
8. People do not want programs they like to be cut, there are legislative failures to agree on spending cuts, and unexpected spending, such as that incurred after the 2001 terrorist attacks, is sometimes necessary.

Writing About Economics
9. Student answers should show an understanding of the highly charged politics of both sides of the controversy surrounding the issue of federal spending and federal debt.

CHAPTER 14, LESSON 3

State and Local Government Finances

Interact with these digital assets and others in lesson 3
- ✓ INTERACTIVE GRAPH
  State Government Revenues and Expenditures
- ✓ INTERACTIVE GRAPH
  Local Government Revenues and Expenditures
- ✓ SELF-CHECK QUIZ
- ✓ VIDEO

networks TRY IT YOURSELF ONLINE

LESSON 3
State and Local Government Finances

Reading Help Desk

Academic Vocabulary
- constituents
- implemented
- considerably

Content Vocabulary
- intergovernmental revenue
- balanced budget amendment
- intergovernmental expenditures
- property tax
- tax assessor
- natural monopolies

TAKING NOTES:

Key Ideas and Details
ACTIVITY Use the graphic organizer below to identify the sources of state and local revenue.

Revenue Sources
- State
- Local

ESSENTIAL QUESTION

How does the government collect revenue, and on what is that revenue spent?

It's impossible to ignore the role that government plays in our everyday lives. Public lands, public utilities, law enforcement, and firefighters are all evidence of our interaction with government. Take a few minutes to consider just how interwoven government at the local and state levels is with our daily lives.

What are some of the services that your local and state governments provide? List as many as you can think of.

Now think about the cost of paying all the salaries, providing maintenance on state and local property, and of providing all the other services you have identified.

How does the government get the revenue to pay for all of these services?

The amount of net spending by state and local governments amounts to an ever-increasing portion of our GDP, the dollar measure of all final goods and services produced in a country in a year. In fact, state and local government expenditures together are larger than all federal government spending.

It wasn't always this way, but sometimes politicians have a hard time saying "no" when it comes to taking care of their **constituents** and the interests of their home districts.

ENGAGE

C Critical Thinking Skills

Contrasting expenses covered by federal and local government Have students review services that are covered by federal dollars by writing a list of these services on one side of a T-chart. Then have them read the opening pages of the lesson and write a list of services covered by local government dollars on the other side of the T-chart. Finally, have them write a short paragraph describing how the group of local expenses as a whole differs from the expenses covered by federal dollars. **Verbal/Linguistic**

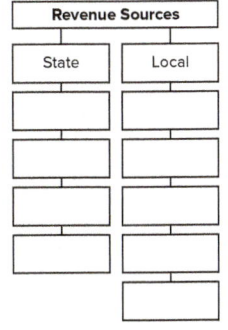

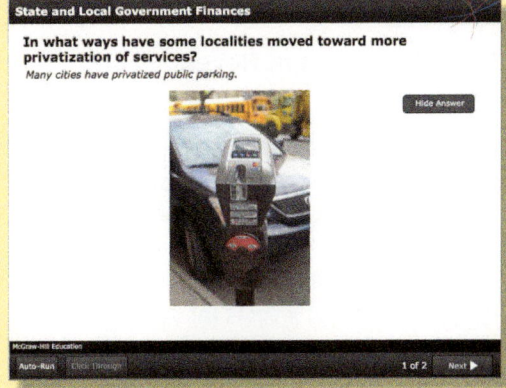

BELLRINGER

State and Local Government Finances

Comparing benefits of private and public services Have students view the Bellringer activity. Then ask them to create a T-chart with the benefits of privatizing parking on one side, and the drawbacks on the other.
Logical/Mathematical

ANSWERS, p. 423

ESSENTIAL QUESTION ACTIVITY

Students should recognize the large range of services state and local governments provide, including items such as maintenance of streets, parks, and public spaces; running schools and libraries; ensuring public safety and public health; trash collection; water systems; and others. Students may be aware of many revenue sources, including sales and income taxes as well fees from items such as drivers' licenses.

TAKING NOTES
State:
Intergovernmental Revenues
Sales Taxes
Individual Income Taxes
Other Revenues
Local:
Intergovernmental Revenues
Sales Taxes
Other Revenues
Property Taxes
Utility Revenues

CHAPTER 14, LESSON 3
State and Local Government Finances

TEACH & ASSESS

C1 Critical Thinking Skills

Drawing conclusions from sales taxes records Have students keep a record of the total amount of sales taxes they pay on purchases during a week. **Ask: Did sales taxes play a role in your purchasing decisions? How would your spending behavior have differed if there were no sales tax?** *(Answers will vary but should reflect the personal impact of sales taxes.)* **Logical/Mathematical**

C2 Critical Thinking Skills

Comparing and contrasting state taxes Have students identify their state's tax rates and research the rates of taxes in neighboring states. Then have them create a chart to compare and contrast their tax level with that of neighboring states. **Logical/Mathematical**

ANSWERS, p. 424

CRITICAL THINKING In addition to intergovernmental revenue, employee retirement, and sales taxes states have access to many other sources of revenue. These sources include tuition and fees collected from state-owned colleges, universities, and technical schools; corporate income taxes; and hospital fees.

State Government Revenue Sources

GUIDING QUESTION *Where do states get most of their revenue?*

State governments collect their revenues from several sources. **Figure 14.8** shows the relative proportions of these sources, the largest of which are examined below.

Intergovernmental Revenues

The largest source of state revenue consists of **intergovernmental revenue**—funds collected by one level of government that are distributed to another level of government for expenditures. States receive the majority of these funds from the federal government to help fund the state's expenditures for welfare, education, highways, health, and hospitals.

Employee Retirement

State employees contribute to their own retirement funds. In recent years, they have been asked to contribute an even larger share of their income to these retirement funds, which accounts for the relative size of this category. State workers would include some faculty and staff at smaller colleges, some workers at public schools, and most highway and public safety officials.

Sales Taxes

Most states also have **implemented** sales taxes to add to their revenue. A sales tax is a general tax levied on consumer purchases of nearly all products. The tax is a percentage of the purchase price, which is added to the final price the consumer pays. Merchants collect the tax at the time of sale. The taxes are then turned over to the proper state government agency on a monthly or other periodic basis.

constituents persons who are represented by an elected official

intergovernmental revenue funds that one level of government receives from another level of government

implemented put into effect

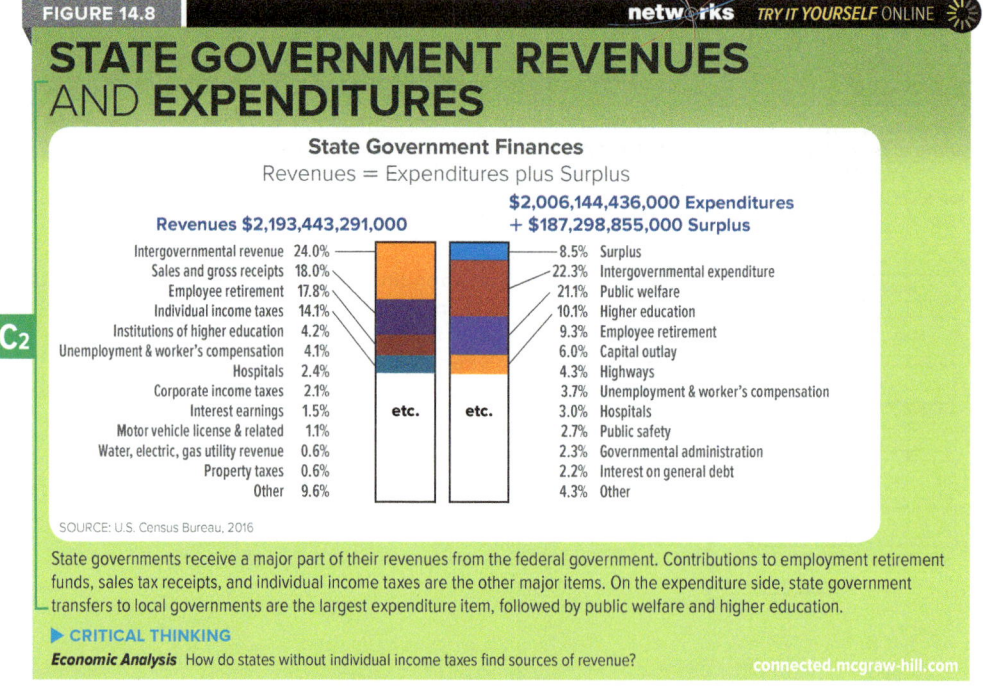

FIGURE 14.8

STATE GOVERNMENT REVENUES AND EXPENDITURES

State Government Finances
Revenues = Expenditures plus Surplus

Revenues $2,193,443,291,000

$2,006,144,436,000 Expenditures + $187,298,855,000 Surplus

Revenues		Expenditures	
Intergovernmental revenue	24.0%	Surplus	8.5%
Sales and gross receipts	18.0%	Intergovernmental expenditure	22.3%
Employee retirement	17.8%	Public welfare	21.1%
Individual income taxes	14.1%	Higher education	10.1%
Institutions of higher education	4.2%	Employee retirement	9.3%
Unemployment & worker's compensation	4.1%	Capital outlay	6.0%
Hospitals	2.4%	Highways	4.3%
Corporate income taxes	2.1%	Unemployment & worker's compensation	3.7%
Interest earnings	1.5%	Hospitals	3.0%
Motor vehicle license & related	1.1%	Public safety	2.7%
Water, electric, gas utility revenue	0.6%	Governmental administration	2.3%
Property taxes	0.6%	Interest on general debt	2.2%
Other	9.6%	Other	4.3%

SOURCE: U.S. Census Bureau, 2016

State governments receive a major part of their revenues from the federal government. Contributions to employment retirement funds, sales tax receipts, and individual income taxes are the other major items. On the expenditure side, state government transfers to local governments are the largest expenditure item, followed by public welfare and higher education.

▶ **CRITICAL THINKING**
Economic Analysis How do states without individual income taxes find sources of revenue?

networks Online Teaching Options

GRAPHS

State Government Revenues and Expenditures

Categorizing state government expenditures Have students explore the higher education category of expenditures on Figure 14.8. **Ask: How much does it cost for you to go to a state college or university, compared to what it costs for someone from out of state?** *(Answers will vary according to location.)* If students do not know the difference in rates, have them do research to find out. Have students write a short report on the difference in rates, and explain that some of the expenses for students are subsidized by state funding. **Verbal/Linguistic**

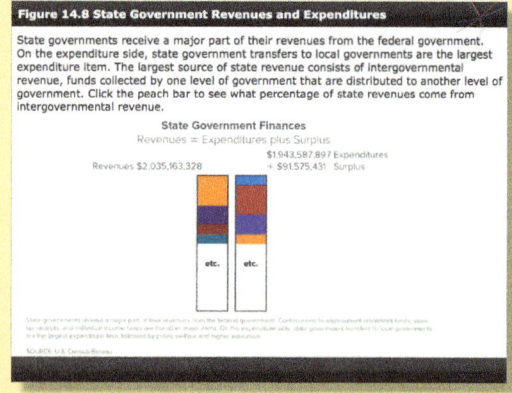

Most states allow merchants to keep a small portion of what they collect to compensate for their time and bookkeeping costs. The sales tax is one of the largest sources of revenue for states, although five states—Alaska, Delaware, Montana, New Hampshire, and Oregon—do not have a general sales tax.

Individual Income Taxes

All but seven states—Alaska, Florida, Nevada, South Dakota, Texas, Washington, and Wyoming—rely on the individual income tax for revenue. The tax brackets in each state vary **considerably**, and taxes can be progressive in some states and proportional in others.

considerably to a noticeable or significant extent

Other Revenues

States rely on a variety of other revenue sources, including interest earnings on surplus funds; tuition and fees collected from state-owned colleges, universities, and technical schools; corporate income taxes; and hospital fees. While the percentages for revenue sources in Figure 14.8 are representative of most states, wide variations among states exist. For example, Alaska is the only state without either a general sales tax or an income tax, so it has to rely on other taxes and fees for its operating revenue.

✓ **READING PROGRESS CHECK**

Contrasting How do states without individual income taxes find sources of revenue?

THE GLOBAL ECONOMY & YOU

High Taxes—Are You Sure?

If you've drawn a paycheck, you've probably been amazed, and discouraged, to see how much was withheld in taxes before you received it. Plus, you have to pay sales tax on many of the things you buy. If you own a car, in some states you might also have to pay personal property taxes on it. Later, if you buy a home, you'll pay property taxes on it. It all adds up to an enormous piece of your income going straight to your local, state, or federal government.

Before you get too upset, consider all the things you get in return, such as police and fire protection, streets and highways, schools, parks, health care, and much more. And if that doesn't make you feel better, imagine how you'd feel if you lived in one of the other industrialized nations of the world. Comparatively, our taxes are very low.

One measure of a country's tax burden is the ratio of its tax revenues to gross domestic product (GDP). Despite the criticism over high taxes in the United States, our federal government's revenue as a percentage of GDP is much lower than people realize. Denmark is often ranked first as the country with the world's highest taxes. In comparison with other countries in the industrialized world, the United States falls well toward the bottom of the list in the lowest tax-revenue-to-GDP ratios.

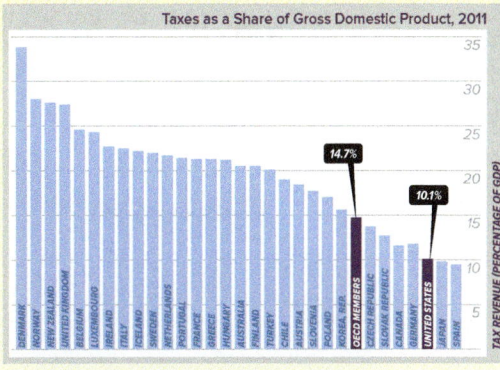

▲ CRITICAL THINKING

Drawing Inferences Why do you think the United States ranks so low in its tax rate in comparison with other industrialized nations?

CHAPTER 14, LESSON 3
State and Local Government Finances

C Critical Thinking Skills

Researching behavior of taxpayers To learn more about how taxes affect the behavior of taxpayers, divide the class into groups of three students to interview a variety of taxpayers in your community, including small-business owners, high school students with part-time jobs, large-business managers, and retired people. Instruct students to ask their subjects to name federal, state, and local taxes that they pay. Students should then ask their subjects to describe how paying taxes affects their economic behavior—hiring new workers, expanding a business, buying products, saving, and so on. Have each group of students compile and summarize their findings, making special note of any differences among the four groups of taxpayers interviewed. Invite a volunteer from each group to share their findings with the class. **Verbal/Linguistic, Interpersonal**

INTERACTIVE FEATURE

Global Economy & You

Making connections with government spending Display the Global Economy & You feature. Have students read the feature and look at the graph. Ask: **Why do many other countries have higher taxes?** *(They provide more services than our government provides for its citizens.)* Then have them write an opinion paper stating whether or not they would be willing to pay higher taxes if they could be sure that the government would use the money to provide needed services. **Verbal/Linguistic**

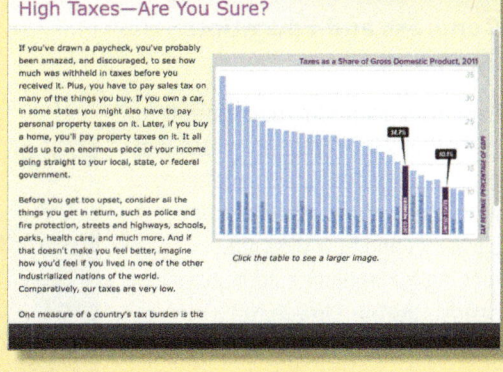

ANSWERS, p. 425

✓ **READING PROGRESS CHECK** States use a variety of revenue sources, including sales taxes, intergovernmental revenue, interest earnings, corporate income taxes, and property taxes.

CRITICAL THINKING Students may suggest that other countries provide more government and social services.

CHAPTER 14, LESSON 3
State and Local Government Finances

V Visual Skills

Creating a poster about state government spending Have students create a poster illustrating the different categories of spending by their state government. Tell students that they may use images clipped from magazines, their own drawings, or a combination of both. **Visual/Spatial**

W Writing Skills

Writing persuasively about a balanced budget amendment Ask students to research the arguments for and against a balanced budget amendment in their state. Instruct them to write a speech arguing why their state should or should not adopt such an amendment. If their state already has a balanced budget amendment, direct students to write a speech about why their state should keep or repeal the amendment. Have students deliver their speeches to the class. **Verbal/Linguistic**

C Critical Thinking Skills

Making generalizations about higher education Ask: How do you think state governments benefit from supporting higher education? *(Possible answer: A well-educated population is better able to support itself and create businesses, which helps the economy to grow.)*

ANSWERS, p. 426

CRITICAL THINKING Answers will vary. Students may suggest that local and state revenues would not cover the cost of larger projects, or that other expenditures such as schools and hospitals have first priority over city and state funds.

426

State Government Expenditures

V GUIDING QUESTION *What are the largest state government expenditure categories?*

Individual states, like the federal government, also have expenditures. Like the federal government, states must approve spending before distributing funds.

The Budget Process

At the state level, the process of creating a budget and getting approval for spending can take many forms. For example, some states such as Kentucky have biannual budgets, or budgets that cover two years at a time. In most states, the process is loosely modeled after that of the federal government. Unlike the federal government, however, some states have a **balanced budget amendment**—a constitutional provision requiring that annual spending not exceed revenues.

Under this provision, states often must cut spending when revenue drops. A reduction in revenue may occur if sales taxes or state income taxes fall because of a decline in the general level of economic activity.

balanced budget amendment constitutional amendment requiring government to spend no more than it collects in taxes and other revenues, excluding borrowing

intergovernmental expenditures funds that one level of government transfers to another level for spending

Intergovernmental Expenditures

As Figure 14.8 shows, the largest category of state spending is **intergovernmental expenditures**—funds that one level of government transfers to another level for spending. These funds come from state revenue sources such as sales taxes, and they are distributed to counties, cities, and other local communities to cover a variety of educational and other municipal expenditures.

Public Welfare

The second-largest category of state expenditures is public welfare. These payments take the form of cash assistance, payments for medical care, spending to maintain welfare institutions, and other welfare expenditures.

Higher Education

State governments have traditionally taken responsibility for the large task of funding state colleges and universities. In most states, the tuition that students pay covers only a portion of higher education expenses. States usually budget funds to pay the remainder of the cost. Today, the cost of higher education is the third-largest category of expenditure.

Cities and states receive funds from the federal government—otherwise known as intergovernmental revenue—to help pay for larger projects like road construction.

▼ **CRITICAL THINKING**
Analysis Why would city and state governments rely on federal funds for such projects?

Employee Retirement

Many states have their own insurance and retirement funds for state employees. The money in these funds is is invested until employees retire, become unemployed, or are injured on the job. Contributions to these funds make this category a significant expenditure. Their main beneficiaries are teachers, legislators, highway workers, police, and other state employees.

Other Expenditures

The expenditures in the remaining state budget categories are relatively small. As Figure 14.8 shows, states spend money on a wide range of

426

---

networks *Online Teaching Options*

VIDEO **WORKSHEETS**

Congress and Education Spending

Exploring issues in educational spending Have students watch and discuss the video. Then have them write a letter to the editor about earmarks and how they affect funding for legitimate educational needs. **Verbal/Linguistic**

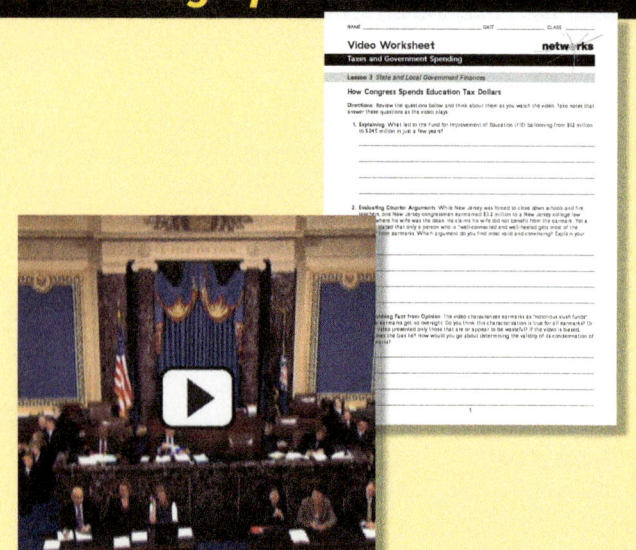

activities including corrections; utilities such as electricity, gas, and water; hospitals; and parks and recreation. Highways and road improvements are possible exceptions because they may require larger amounts of state money.

✓ READING PROGRESS CHECK

Explaining How does a balanced budget amendment work?

Local Government Revenue Sources

GUIDING QUESTION *How are local government revenue sources different from those of federal and state governments?*

Like state governments, local governments have a variety of revenue sources, as shown in **Figure 14.9**. These sources include taxes and funds from state and federal governments. The main categories are discussed below.

Intergovernmental Revenues

Local governments receive the largest part of their revenues—slightly more than one-third—in the form of intergovernmental transfers from state governments. These funds are generally intended for education and public welfare. A much smaller amount comes directly from the federal government, mostly for urban renewal.

Property Taxes

The second-largest source of revenue for local governments is the **property tax**—a tax on tangible and intangible possessions. Such possessions usually include real estate, buildings, furniture, farm animals, stocks, bonds, and bank accounts. Most states also assess a property tax on automobiles.

The property tax that raises the most revenue is the tax on real estate. Taxes on other personal property, with the exception of automobiles, are seldom

property tax tax on tangible and intangible possessions such as real estate, buildings, furniture, stocks, bonds, and bank accounts

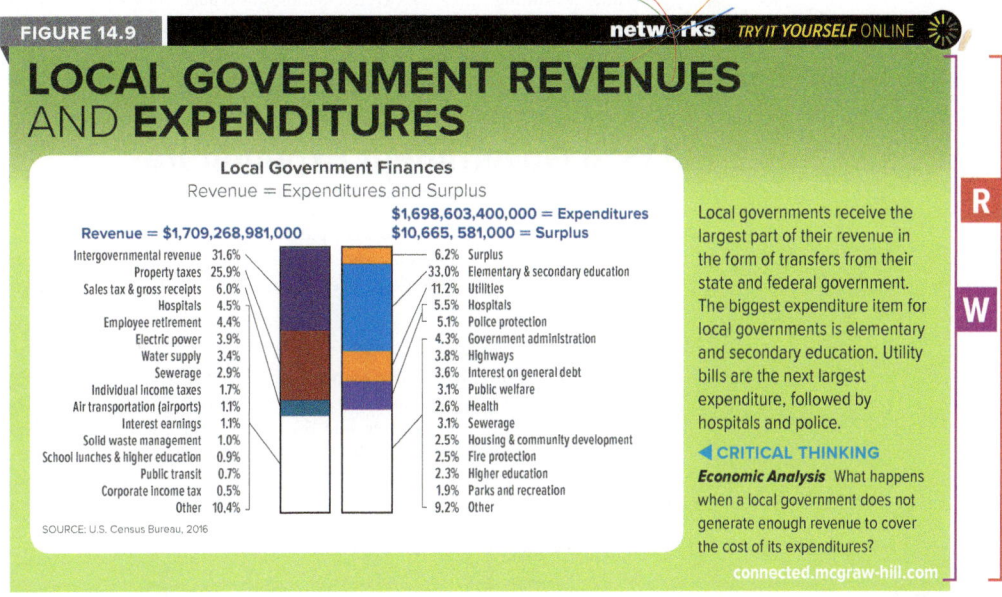

FIGURE 14.9

LOCAL GOVERNMENT REVENUES AND EXPENDITURES

Local Government Finances
Revenue = Expenditures and Surplus

Revenue = $1,709,268,981,000
$1,698,603,400,000 = Expenditures
$10,665,581,000 = Surplus

Revenue		Expenditures	
Intergovernmental revenue	31.6%	Surplus	6.2%
Property taxes	25.9%	Elementary & secondary education	33.0%
Sales tax & gross receipts	6.0%	Utilities	11.2%
Hospitals	4.5%	Hospitals	5.5%
Employee retirement	4.4%	Police protection	5.1%
Electric power	3.9%	Government administration	4.3%
Water supply	3.4%	Highways	3.8%
Sewerage	2.9%	Interest on general debt	3.6%
Individual income taxes	1.7%	Public welfare	3.1%
Air transportation (airports)	1.1%	Health	2.6%
Interest earnings	1.1%	Sewerage	3.1%
Solid waste management	1.0%	Housing & community development	2.5%
School lunches & higher education	0.9%	Fire protection	2.5%
Public transit	0.7%	Higher education	2.3%
Corporate income tax	0.5%	Parks and recreation	1.9%
Other	10.4%	Other	9.2%

SOURCE: U.S. Census Bureau, 2016

Local governments receive the largest part of their revenue in the form of transfers from their state and federal government. The biggest expenditure item for local governments is elementary and secondary education. Utility bills are the next largest expenditure, followed by hospitals and police.

◀ **CRITICAL THINKING**
Economic Analysis What happens when a local government does not generate enough revenue to cover the cost of its expenditures?

connected.mcgraw-hill.com

Taxes and Government Spending **427**

GRAPHS

Local Government Revenues and Expenditures

Making connections between state and local government revenues Have students explore Figure 14.9. **Ask: What do you think "intergovernmental revenue" means in this graph, compared to the state graph?** *(It is revenue given from the state to local governments.)* Have students create a pie chart showing how much of local government's funding comes from the state government. Then have them write a caption for their pie graph, describing what the state funds are used for in the local community. **Visual/Spatial**

CHAPTER 14, LESSON 3
State and Local Government Finances

C Critical Thinking Skills

Exploring property taxes Have students explore problems with property taxes. **Ask: What is the main disadvantage of property taxes?** *(It is difficult to assign value to personal property.)* Then have students research how property taxes are assessed in their community and write a paragraph explaining how their community handles the assessments and collections. **Logical/Mathematical**

R Reading Skills

Reading graphs to understand local government expenditures Have students analyze the Local Government Revenues and Expenditures graph to calculate the dollar amounts that local governments spend on education (all levels) and police protection. *(Elementary and secondary education plus higher education: $599.6 billion; Police protection: $86.6 billion)* **Logical/Mathematical**

W Writing Skills

Creating a speech about budgetary issues Have students analyze the spending allocations in the Health bar of the Local Government Revenues and Expenditures graph. Ask students to prepare a persuasive speech advocating a different allocation of funds that would provide more funding for fire protection. Students should explain how the other percentages would be adjusted to make this possible. Have students theorize about possible effects of cutting these expenditures. Ask students to give their speeches to the class. **Verbal/Linguistic**

ANSWERS, p. 427

✓ **READING PROGRESS CHECK** When revenue drops below spending levels, spending must, according to state law, be curtailed.

CRITICAL THINKING When a local government is unable to generate enough revenue to meet spending needs, a deficit is created.

CHAPTER 14, LESSON 3
State and Local Government Finances

C Critical Thinking Skills

Comparing local utility revenues Have students identify the local usage rates for a utility such as electric power or water. Then have them research the rates for other cities or counties in their state, including areas with high populations and those with low populations. Ask students to write a report proposing reasons for any differences they find. *(Answers will vary according to students' location, but potential reasons for differences include the source of power generation—coal, oil, alternative—and the distance of the community from the source.)* **Logical/Mathematical**

ANSWERS, p. 428

✓ **READING PROGRESS CHECK** the tax on real estate

---

tax assessor person who examines and values property for tax purposes

natural monopolies market structure in which average costs of production are lowest when all output is produced by a single firm

---

collected because of the problem of valuation. For example, how would the **tax assessor**—the person who assigns value to property for tax purposes—know the reasonable value of everyone's wedding silver, furniture, clothing, or other tangible property? Instead, most communities find it more efficient to hire one or more individuals to assess the value of a few big-ticket items such as buildings and motor vehicles.

Sales Taxes
Many cities have their own sales taxes. Merchants collect these taxes along with the state sales taxes at the point of sale. While these taxes typically are much lower than state sales taxes, they are the third most important source of local government revenue.

Utility Revenues
The fourth-largest source of local revenue is the income from public utilities that supply water, electricity, sewerage, and even telecommunications. Because of economies of scale, many of these companies are **natural monopolies**.

A community needs only one set of electrical power lines or underground water pipes, for example, so one company usually supplies all of the services. When people pay their utility bills, the payments are counted as a source of revenue for local governments if the utility was government owned.

Other Revenues
Figure 14.9 shows a variety of ways in which local governments collect their remaining revenue. Some local governments receive a portion of their funds from hospital fees. Others may collect income taxes from individuals and profits taxes from corporations. Still another revenue source for local governments is the interest on invested funds.

If local governments spend more than they collect in revenues, they can borrow from investors. While borrowed funds are usually small in comparison with those of the federal government, they can form an important source of local government funding. Still, the revenue sources available in general are much more limited than those available to the state and federal levels of government.

✓ **READING PROGRESS CHECK**

Recalling Which property tax earns the most revenue for local governments?

Local Government Expenditures

GUIDING QUESTION *On what do local governments spend money?*

Local governments include counties, parishes, townships, municipalities, tribal councils, school districts, and other special districts. The different categories of expenditures made by these local governments are illustrated in Figure 14.9.

The Budget Process
At the local level, power to approve spending often rests with the mayor, the city council, the county judge, or some other elected representative or body. The methods used to approve spending and the dates of the fiscal year itself are likely to vary considerably from one local government to the next.

Generally, the amount of revenue collected from property taxes, city income taxes, and other local sources is relatively small and limits the spending of local agencies. Some local governments are even bound by state requirements to avoid deficit spending.

---

networks — Online Teaching Options

GRAPHS

Local Government Revenues and Expenditures

Reading graphs to analyze local government spending Have students explore the "spending" portion of Figure 14.9. Then have them form small "town meeting" groups to discuss the spending categories. Have the groups decide if the division of spending makes sense, and have them create an oral presentation to be delivered by the leader of each group. The presentation should state the group's decision and back it up with details about spending categories, as well as local community needs. **Logical/Mathematical**

Figure 14.9 Local Government Revenues and Expenditures

Local governments receive the largest part of their revenue in the form of transfers from their state and federal government. The biggest expenditure item for local governments is elementary and secondary education. Utility bills are the next largest expenditure, followed by hospitals and police.

Like state governments, local governments have a variety of revenue. These sources include taxes and funds from state and federal governments.

Local governments receive the largest part of their revenues in the form of intergovernmental transfers from state governments. Click the Purple bar to see the percentage of local revenue that comes from intergovernmental transfers.

CHAPTER 14, LESSON 3
State and Local Government Finances

Elementary and Secondary Education
Local governments have primary responsibility for elementary and secondary education. Expenditures budgeted in this category include administrators' and teachers' salaries, wages for maintenance and cafeteria workers, textbooks, and other supplies. School districts also pay for the construction and upkeep of all school buildings. Schools account for more than one-third of all local government spending, making it the largest item in most local budgets.

Utilities
Public utilities that are owned by the government serve communities by providing services such as sewerage, electricity, natural gas, and water. For most local governments, spending on these utilities amounts to the second-largest expenditure and consumes about 11 percent of local spending.

In the typical community, the majority of expenditures on utilities are for schools, libraries, civic centers, and administrative buildings. Street lighting and traffic lights account for other utility expenditures.

Hospitals
Many local communities have their own hospital. The increasing cost of health care is one of the reasons that hospitals rank so high on the list of local government expenditures. However, state governments also contribute to the construction and maintenance of local hospitals, which helps keep the cost down.

Police and Fire Protection
Most communities maintain a full-time, paid police force. Many have fire departments with paid, full-time firefighters as well. However, some communities, especially those with smaller populations and limited budgets, maintain volunteer fire departments to keep the cost down.

Other Expenditures
Government administration, highway and street repair expenditures, interest on borrowed money, and public welfare absorb most of the remaining spending. Other categories include housing, health, higher education, parks, and corrections.

✓ **READING PROGRESS CHECK**

Synthesizing Which local expenditures would you categorize as mandatory spending, and why?

EXPLORING THE ESSENTIAL QUESTION
State and local governments generally take responsibility for different categories of services. For example, state government usually funds universities while local government usually supports elementary and secondary education. Why do you think state and local governments have assumed these specific responsibilities?

CLOSE & REFLECT

W Writing Skills

Explaining the need for more expenditures Have students create a program for which they need government funding, and write a proposal to convince government leaders that the program is necessary for their community. **Verbal/Linguistic**

LESSON 3 REVIEW

Reviewing Vocabulary
1. *Describing* What role does a tax assessor play in determining property taxes?

Using Your Notes
2. *Drawing Inferences* How can state governments use revenue to influence local expenditures? Does the federal government have this same influence at the state level? Explain.

Answering the Guiding Questions
3. *Explaining* Where do states get most of their revenue?
4. *Identifying* What are the largest state government expenditure categories?
5. *Explaining* How are local government revenue sources different from those of federal and state governments?

Writing About Economics
6. *Argument* Some states have balanced budget amendments. What effect will this have on the services they provide? Do you agree or disagree that a balanced budget amendment is appropriate at the state level? Explain your reasoning.
7. *Explaining* What does the U.S. Constitution say about taxation and for what purpose are the taxes collected? Why is this important to the economic well-being of our nation?

ANSWERS, p. 429

EXPLORING THE ESSENTIAL QUESTION

Students should recognize that many of the services funded at the state level are those that extend across multiple county and local jurisdictions. For example, universities serve students from across the state, whereas elementary and secondary schools serve residents of a local area.

✓ **READING PROGRESS CHECK** Students may say that education, utilities, and public safety and health are the most important.

LESSON 3 REVIEW ANSWERS

Reviewing Vocabulary
1. The tax assessor determines the value of property that will be taxed.

Using Your Notes
2. Students should understand that because local governments get a large share of their revenue from their state government, the state can influence how they spend it. Likewise, the federal government can influence state spending through its intergovernmental expenditures to the states.

Answering the Guiding Questions
3. States get most of their money from intergovernmental sources.
4. The largest expenditure categories include intergovernmental expenditures, public welfare, insurance and retirement benefits for state employees, and higher education.
5. Local governments get a much larger portion of their revenue from intergovernmental sources, property taxes, and utility revenues.

Writing About Economics
6. Students may favor or disapprove of balanced budget amendments, but they should demonstrate understanding of how they work and their impact on a state's responsibility to provide services.
7. The U.S. Constitution states that Congress has the power to lay and collect taxes for the purpose of paying the nation's debts, as well as providing a fund for defense and the general welfare of its citizens.

CHAPTER 14
Debate

ENGAGE

C1 Critical Thinking Skills

Introducing taxation principles Ask: **Should the rich pay higher taxes?** Have students discuss the issue, pointing out that the higher rate under discussion applies to income earned from investments, not salaries. Explain that wealthy people are taxed at a lower rate on their investments than they are on their income. Have a class discussion about the taxation principle of ability-to-pay as it relates to taxing the rich.
Interpersonal

TEACH & ASSESS

C2 Critical Thinking Skills

Debating the issue Organize a classroom debate. Divide the class into two groups and assign one group to support the issue and the other group to oppose it. As students read the text for their own side of the debate, ask them to write three reasons the text gives to support their opinion. Have them look at the other side's argument as well, and write three reasons that support the other side's argument. Ask students to write a rebuttal sentence for each of the opposing side's reasons, arguing against those reasons. Appoint a moderator to run the debate. Groups should take turns presenting to the class the Yes and No arguments related to higher taxes for the rich. **BL Verbal/Linguistic**

W Writing Skills

Constructing arguments about taxing the rich Have students read the feature and take a side on the Debate issue. Have them write a persuasive paragraph stating their opinion about taxing the rich at a higher level. Encourage them to provide details from the feature and their own research to support their opinion. Remind students to analyze the validity of authors' sources for bias, and to cite their sources. **Verbal/Linguistic**

Debates

Should the rich pay higher taxes?

C1 The question of whether the wealthiest Americans should pay more taxes has been debated for years. Federal tax laws offer many tax breaks for people who earn most of their money through investments, resulting in a lowered tax rate. The people who qualify for this tax break are generally very wealthy. Yet, their income is taxed at a lower rate than salaried income, which often falls into a higher tax bracket.

C2 Some politicians, including President Obama, have proposed changing the tax code so that the wealthy pay a more equitable share of taxes. Supporters of this idea argue that the wealthy should do their part to support the nation, while opponents say that the rich have a right to keep what they earn.

Even some of the wealthiest Americans, such as Warren Buffet and Bill Gates, have spoken in support of raising taxes on the wealthy. But those who oppose this action believe that it is unfair to those who have worked hard to earn their success.

W While reading the evidence, analyze the validity of the economic information from these primary sources and the data presented. Pay attention to the frame of reference of both points of view when considering which side is more persuasive.

YES The rich should pay higher taxes.

THE VERY RICH **CAN AFFORD TO PAY** HIGHER TAXES WITHOUT SACRIFICING THEIR LIFESTYLES

IT IS POSSIBLE TO BE VERY RICH IN THE UNITED STATES DUE TO THE EDUCATIONAL AND OTHER OPPORTUNITIES PROVIDED BY THE GOVERNMENT; THEREFORE WEALTHY PEOPLE **SHOULD DO THEIR PART** TO HELP SUPPORT THE COUNTRY

IT IS **MORALLY WRONG** THAT WEALTHY PEOPLE PAY A SMALLER PORTION OF THEIR INCOME IN TAXES THAN MIDDLE- AND LOWER-INCOME PEOPLE

HISTORICALLY, PAYING HIGHER TAXES **HAS NOT PREVENTED** THE WEALTHY FROM CONTINUING TO INVEST AND CREATE JOBS

" Warren Buffett's secretary shouldn't pay a higher tax rate than Warren Buffett. There is no justification for it. It is wrong that in the United States of America, a teacher or a nurse or a construction worker who earns $50,000 should pay higher tax rates than somebody pulling in $50 million. "
—President Barack Obama, 2011

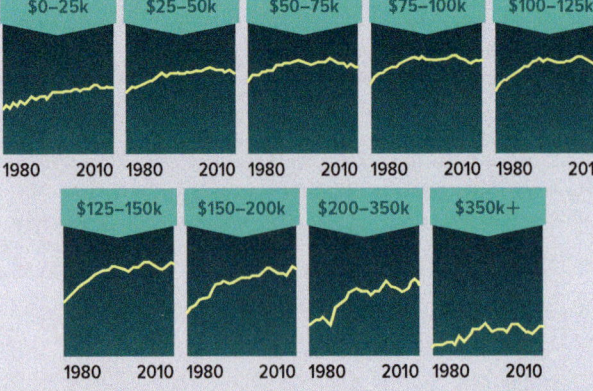

Share of Income Claimed by Taxes, per Tax Bracket

$0–25k | $25–50k | $50–75k | $75–100k | $100–125k
$125–150k | $150–200k | $200–350k | $350k+

networks Online Teaching Options

DEBATE

Debate: Should the rich pay higher taxes?

Defending opinions about taxing the rich Have students conduct a town meeting about taxing the rich. Have a volunteer play Warren Buffett, who has expressed the need for rich people to pay more because they *can* pay more. Assign one-half of the class to defend the opinion that rich people should keep their money because the free-enterprise system allows for the incentive to create wealth, and the other half of the class defend the opinion that rich people should pay more. Students should use the Debate feature to prepare their opinions about taxing the rich. **Interpersonal, Verbal/Linguistic**

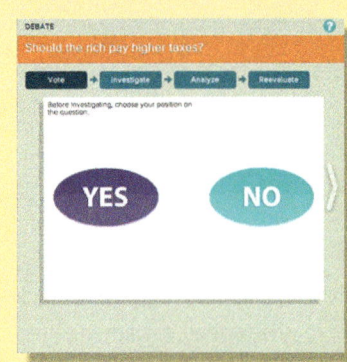

NO The rich should not pay higher taxes.

networks TRY IT YOURSELF ONLINE
For an interactive version of this debate go to **connected.mcgraw-hill.com**

- WEALTHY PEOPLE WILL BE **LESS LIKELY** TO **INVEST** IN NEW ENTERPRISES THAT COULD CREATE JOBS
- INCREASING THE TAX BURDEN ON THE WEALTHY **VIOLATES PRIVATE PROPERTY RIGHTS**
- PLACING A HIGHER TAX BURDEN ON THE WEALTHY WILL **TAKE THEIR MONEY** OUT OF THE PRIVATE SECTOR, WHERE IT WOULD GO FURTHER TO BOOST THE ECONOMY AND CREATE JOBS
- THE GOVERNMENT **SHOULD FOCUS** ON **REDUCING** WASTEFUL **SPENDING** RATHER THAN INCREASING TAXES ON ANYONE

> For those who believe in private-property rights, soaking the rich is an immoral policy. But it is also economically counterproductive. The federal and state governments won't solve their fiscal problems until they cut spending. At best, confiscating more from the wealthy will simply postpone the day of reckoning.

—"Soak-the-Rich Taxes Fail!" by Robert P. Murphy. Mises Daily: Thursday, November 4, 2010. http://mises.org/daily/author/380/Robert-P-Murphy

ANALYZING the issue

1. **Analyzing** In which income bracket do people pay the highest share of their income in taxes?

2. **Drawing Conclusions** Why would the very wealthy pay a lower proportion of their income in payroll taxes?

3. **Argument** Which arguments do you find most compelling? Explain your answer.

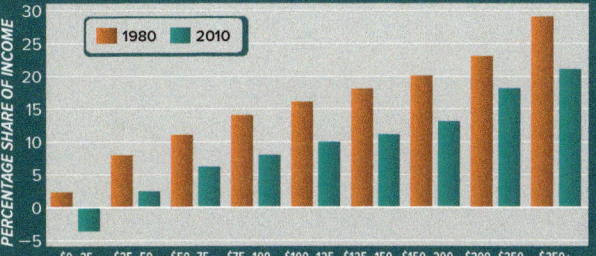

Share of Income Paid in Federal Income Taxes (1980, 2010) by amount per tax bracket (in thousands of dollars): $0–25, $25–50, $50–75, $75–100, $100–125, $125–150, $150–200, $200–350, $350+

CHAPTER 14
Debate

V Visual Skills

Creating political cartoons Have students create political cartoons about the rich paying taxes. Students should use details from the feature as well as their own observations to support their ideas. **Visual/Spatial**

Content Background Knowledge

Bill Gates Bill Gates, the founder of Microsoft, is one of the richest people in the world, and he is also one of the most generous. He has stated publicly that poverty can be ended in this century. He and his wife, Melinda, run a charitable foundation that has given more than $28 billion in aid.

CLOSE & REFLECT

W Writing Skills

Summarizing the issue Have students summarize the controversy in a paragraph, and discuss which aspects of the Debate they think are valid and which are not. **Verbal/Linguistic**

431

GRAPHIC ORGANIZER
Table

Posing questions about taxing the rich Distribute the graphic organizer. Have students use it to write four questions about taxing the rich in column 1. Then have each student interview at least two people, asking the four questions about the rich's ability and willingness to pay more taxes. Have them use information in the Debate feature to prepare their questions, and tell them to write their respondents' answers in columns 2 and 3 of the graphic organizer. Have students share their responses.
Interpersonal, Verbal/Linguistic

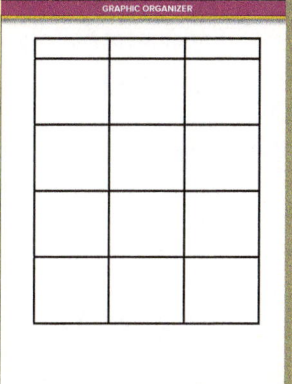

ANSWERS, p. 431

ANALYZING the issue

1. According to the second chart, those who make over $350,000 per year pay the highest proportion of their income in taxes.
2. Because they earn more of their income from investments than from wages, and investments are taxed at a lower rate.
3. Students should choose one side of the argument and defend their position logically with data based on the text.

Taxes and Government Spending **431**

Chapter 14
Study Guide

W1 Writing Skills

Developing a political cartoon about taxes Have students create their own political cartoon about taxes—including an allusion to one of the three criteria for effective taxes, one of the two principles of taxation, and/or one of the three types of taxes.
Visual/Spatial

W2 Writing Skills

Writing about the national debt Have students explore the impact of the national debt on economic incentives and taxes. Then have them write a song or poem about the effect the national debt is having on the prosperity of the country, using their answer to the question to inspire their lyrics. Have students perform their poem or song for the class.

V Visual Skills

Identifying expenditures Direct students to travel around their area and identify examples of federal, state, and local spending (at least five examples for each). Possible ideas include an interstate highway, a state park, and an elementary school. Instruct students to create a collage illustrating their finds. Students may use photographs they have taken or their own drawings. *Visual/Spatial*

STUDY GUIDE

LESSON 1

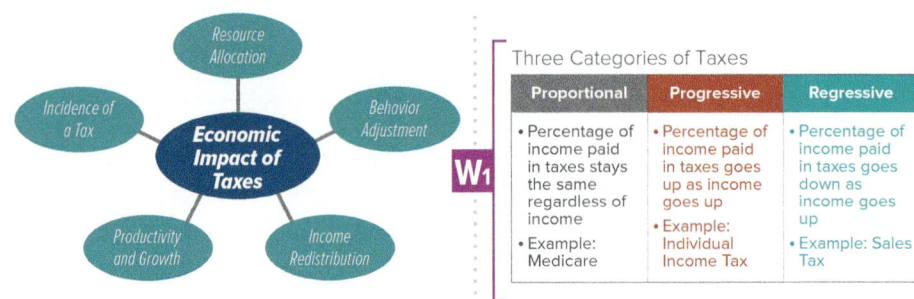

LESSON 2

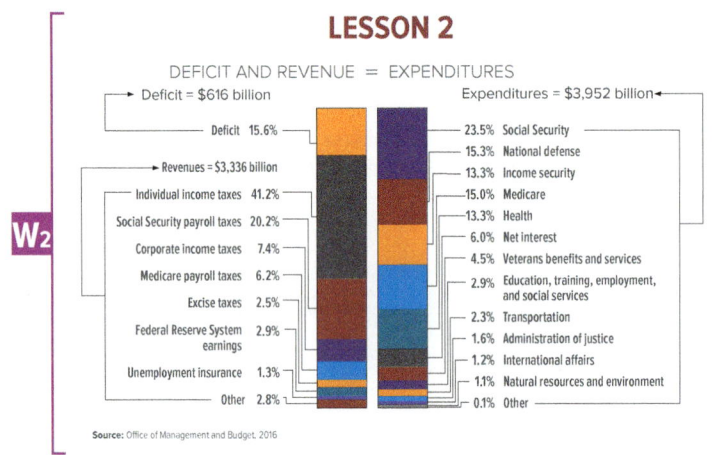

LESSON 3

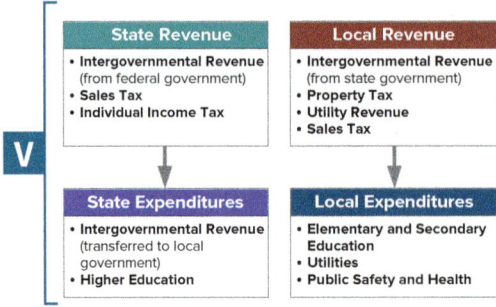

networks *Online Teaching Options*

WORKSHEET

Enrichment Activity

Evaluating lobbying, taxes, and the American electoral system
Assign the Enrichment Activity worksheet. Have students use the last research question to write a paper about what they think is the best solution to the problem of manipulation and corruption of the tax system by corporate lobbyists. Have them use the text in the worksheet as a starting point for research into activities of lobbyists for specific companies, as well as solutions that people have proposed to combat the problem of corruption.

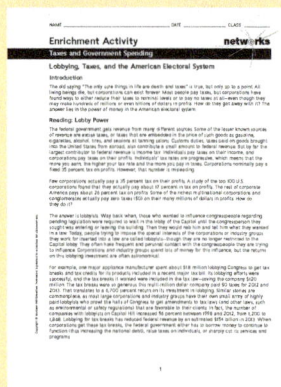

CHAPTER 14 Assessment

Directions: On a separate sheet of paper, answer the questions below. Make sure you read carefully and answer all parts of the questions.

Lesson Review

Lesson 1

1. **Explaining** How can government use taxes to reallocate the use of resources in the economy?
2. **Explaining** Why is a sales tax considered a regressive tax?
3. **Evaluating** A city is considering placing a 3 percent tax on food purchased at grocery stores. Using the three criteria for effective taxes, evaluate this proposal, and explain your reasoning.

Lesson 2

4. **Explaining** What taxes make up FICA? Which is a proportional tax? Explain.
5. **Summarizing** What did certain members of Congress do in 2013 to try to prevent implementation of the Affordable Care Act? What was the ultimate effect for the economy?

Lesson 3

6. **Identifying** What are the two largest sources of revenue for both state and local governments?
7. **Explaining** How might balanced budget laws affect local governments?

Critical Thinking

8. **Comparing and Contrasting** If you were an elected official and recognized the need to increase revenue to support additional services, which of the following taxes would you prefer to use: individual income, sales, VAT, or flat taxes? Explain.
9. **Problem Solving** Few members of Congress would deny that America's massive debt and continued deficit spending are enormous problems. So far, their efforts to fix the problem haven't succeeded. Considering all you know about taxes, expenditures, and the history of efforts to control the budget, what solution would you offer? Write a proposal that you might submit to your congressional representative.

10. **Evaluating** Both state and local governments get a large portion of their revenues from intergovernmental revenues. Is this an effective means for getting revenue for essential government programs, or is there a better way? Explain your answer.

Analyzing Visuals

Use the visual below to answer the following questions about shifting the incidence of a tax.

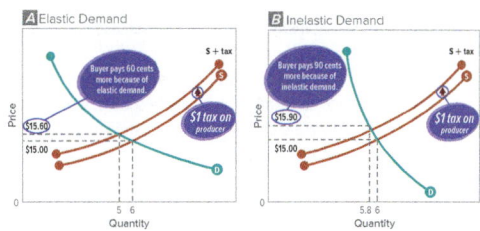

11. **Analyzing** The two graphs show what happens when the government places a $1.00 tax on a product. Which panel shows an incidence of tax in which the consumer pays more of the tax than the producer?
12. **Drawing Conclusions** Is Panel A more likely to describe the tax on a medicine or on snack food? Explain your answer.

ANSWERING THE ESSENTIAL QUESTION

Review your answers to the introductory questions at the beginning of each lesson. Then answer the Essential Question on the basis of what you learned in the chapter. Have your answers changed?

13. **Explaining** How does the government collect revenue, and on what is that revenue spent?

Need Extra Help?

If You've Missed Question	1	2	3	4	5	6	7	8	9	10	11	12	13
Go to page	400	405	403	415	422	424	427	406	418	424	402	402	414

Chapter 14 Assessment Answers

Lesson Review

Lesson 1

1. Increasing taxes on certain goods causes the price to go up and consumers may buy fewer of those goods. Suppliers will then allocate fewer resources to those goods; the resource will then shift to other businesses.
2. People with higher incomes pay a smaller percentage of their income in sales taxes than do those with lower incomes.
3. Students should demonstrate understanding of the three criteria of effective taxes: equity, simplicity, efficiency. They may decide that the tax is not equitable but would be simple and efficient.

Lesson 2

4. Social Security and Medicare make up FICA. Medicare is a proportional tax, because the same percentage of income is taxed regardless of how much or little is earned.
5. Conservative members of Congress attempted to prevent raising the debt ceiling, thereby shutting down the government and risking nonpayment of federal debt in hopes the president would allow repeal of the ACA. The ploy didn't work, but it resulted in the government paying higher interest rates on borrowed money.

Lesson 3

6. intergovernmental revenues
7. Students should recognize that balanced budget laws require governments to spend no more than they receive in revenue. It can mean that in times of declining revenue, local government will have to reduce services.

Critical Thinking

8. Students should demonstrate an understanding of the different kinds of taxes and their advantages and disadvantages.
9. Students should demonstrate an understanding of the complexity of the federal debt and deficit and the competing and contradictory interests of members of Congress and of the public with regard to taxes and government programs.
10. Students may agree or disagree but should demonstrate an understanding of intergovernmental revenues, how they influence spending, and alternative ways of raising revenues.

Analyzing Visuals

11. Panel B
12. It describes a snack food because an increase in the tax will reduce some demand for the product. Medicines are more essential and people will be more likely to buy them even if the price increases.

Answering the Essential Question

13. Students should demonstrate understanding of the different kinds of revenues collected by federal, state, and local governments and of the types of programs the revenue is spent on.

Chapter 14
Assessment Answers

21st Century Skills

14 Answers will vary. Encourage students to be aware of frame of reference and use of propaganda

15 Students should understand that a large enough increase in taxes would reduce the sales of these products. They may or may not agree with this approach to reducing obesity.

16 Students should demonstrate an understanding of the causes and effects of our current deficit spending and also of the effects of a balanced budget amendment on the economy and government services and programs.

17 Students should demonstrate an understanding of sales and property taxes, the criteria for effective taxes, and the principles of taxation.

Building Financial Literacy

18 Students should demonstrate an understanding of the advantages and disadvantages of the flat tax and how it will affect deductions and the incomes of people in different income categories.

Analyzing Primary Sources

19 Haas is not making the point that the deficit is not a problem, but rather that it is a solvable problem; we just have to decide if we want to solve it by decreasing expenditures, increasing revenues, or a combination of both. Students may agree or disagree but should give reasons for their opinions.

20 The current large deficit was created by two political decisions during the Bush administration to cut taxes, rather than by unregulated expenditures or other events that affected the economy.

CHAPTER 14 Assessment

Directions: On a separate sheet of paper, answer the questions below. Make sure you read carefully and answer all parts of the questions.

21st Century Skills

14 **Evaluating** Working with a classmate, examine each other's answers to the Exploring the Essential Question activity in Lesson 2. How does your classmate answer the question about paying taxes out of your part-time wages? Keep in mind that this classmate's paragraph represents a secondary source. When evaluating your classmate's answer, be aware of the frame of reference or any use of propaganda they used when answering the question.

15 **Problem Solving** Because of the increase in obesity rates in your city, the city council is proposing a significant increase in the sales tax on sugared soft drinks and some other high-calorie snacks. Would such a tax reduce the consumption of these foods? Would you support such a tax? Explain.

16 **Identifying Cause and Effect** Congress has been squabbling about deficit spending for decades. Recently, a block of representatives banded together and introduced an amendment to the U.S. Constitution that would require the federal government to adhere to a balanced budget. Your representative is a member of that block of legislators. What would you tell your representative about what this amendment would mean for the country?

17 **Create and Analyze Arguments and Draw Conclusions** A friend who is very interested in politics and economics has said that sales and property taxes are neither a fair nor an efficient means of raising revenues. He believes that state and local governments should eliminate these two forms of taxation. What is your response?

Building Financial Literacy

18 **Analyzing** A family friend is running for the House of Representatives on a tax-reform platform. She believes implementing a flat tax may be the best way to straighten out the tax system, but she is not sure how people will react to her proposal or whether they will understand it. She has asked you to describe your response to her idea. Write a few paragraphs. Do you approve of a flat tax? What will be the benefits? The disadvantages? In your response, consider these issues:

- its effect on interest payments on home mortgages and home ownership
- its effect on low-income and high-income taxpayers
- deductions for education, training, and childcare

Analyzing Primary Sources

Read the excerpt and answer the questions that follow.

PRIMARY SOURCE

"Frankly, if you want to blame our looming deficits on policy changes, you would look not to spending but, rather, taxes—specifically, to President Bush's huge tax cuts of 2001 and 2003 that Congress recently extended until 2012 and will likely extend either wholly or in large measure again after that.

Simply letting the Bush tax cuts expire would reduce annual deficits to about 3 percent of GDP (which is considered economically sustainable) over the next decade, though they would start rising again later on due to soaring health care costs.

Does that mean "the deficit problem is a revenue problem?" No, it means the deficit is what it always is—a mismatch between revenues and spending. Policymakers can address it by cutting spending, raising revenues, or some combination of the two. What they choose to do is a political matter, nothing more and nothing less."

—Lawrence Haas, "Sorry, the Federal Deficit Isn't a Spending Problem" (All rights reserved. This column first appeared on February 3, 2011, in *The Fiscal Times,* which also owns the copyright.)

19 **Analyzing Primary Sources** Lawrence Haas makes our deficit spending sound like there's no problem at all. Is this the case, or does he mean something else? Do you agree? Explain.

20 **Exploring Issues** Why is the deficit a political matter?

Need Extra Help?

If You've Missed Question	14	15	16	17	18	19	20
Go to page	417	406	421	424	406	417	418

---

networks Online Assessment Options

WORKSHEET

Chapter Tests and Lesson Quizzes

Chapter 14 Tests Forms A and B Have students complete the Chapter Tests and Lesson Quizzes to assess student understanding throughout the chapter. Print and online assessment tools offer chapter and lesson evaluation through a variety of question formats, including document-based questions.

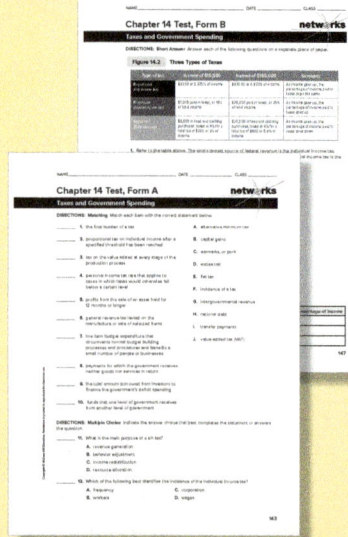

CHAPTER 15
Fiscal Policy Planner

UNDERSTANDING BY DESIGN®

Enduring Understanding
- *Governments are formed to maintain order and regulate activities in a geographic area.*

Essential Questions
- How does the government promote the economic goals of price stability, full employment, and economic growth?
- How do we know if macroeconomic equilibrium has been achieved?

Predictable Misunderstandings
Students may think:
- *Government interventions can be temporary measures that are repealed as soon as the economy stabilizes.* Explain that programs such as entitlements and unemployment benefits are difficult to remove because people are reluctant to give them up.
- *The federal government can solve most economic problems by adjusting the level of government-sector spending.* Explain that lags between the time a problem occurs and the time the government responds partly nullify the effects. Also, demand-side (Keynesian) policies are ineffective against inflation and unemployment.

Assessment Evidence
Performance Task
- *Hands-On Chapter Project with Technology Extension*

Other Evidence
- *Guided Reading Activities*
- *Vocabulary Activity*
- *Lesson Quizzes*
- *Self-Check Quizzes*
- *Chapter Assessment*
- *Chapter Tests, Forms A and B*

SUGGESTED PACING

Introducing the Chapter: ½ Day	Lesson 3: Macroeconomic Equilibrium .... 1 Day
Lesson 1: Demand-Side Policies .... ½ Day	Debate .... ½ Day
Case Study .... ½ Day	Study Guide, Chapter Assessment and Wrap-Up ..... ½ Day
Lesson 2: Supply-Side Policies .... 1 Day	

TOTAL 5 Days

Key for Using the Teacher Edition

SKILL-BASED ACTIVITIES

Types of skill activites found in the Teacher Edition.

- **V** Visual Skills require students to analyze maps, graphs, charts, and photos.
- **R** Reading Skills help students practice reading skills and master vocabulary.
- **C** Critical Thinking Skills help students apply and extend what they have learned.
- **W** Writing Skills provide writing opportunities to help students comprehend the text.
- **T** Technology Skills require students to use digital tools effectively.

*Letters are followed by a number when there is more than one of the same type of skill on the page.

DIFFERENTIATED INSTRUCTION

All activities are written for the on-level student unless otherwise marked with the leveled labels below.

- **BL** Beyond Level
- **AL** Approaching Level
- **ELL** English Language Learners

All students benefit from activities that utilize different learning styles. Many activities are marked as below when a particular learning style is highlighted.

Intrapersonal	Naturalist
Logical/Mathematical	Kinesthetic
Visual/Spatial	Auditory/Musical
Verbal/Linguistic	Interpersonal

Council for Economic Education

Below are the Council for Economic Education Voluntary National Content Standards in Economics covered in the *Fiscal Policy* chapter.

Content Standard 17: Costs of government policies sometimes exceed benefits. This may occur because of incentives facing voters, government officials, and government employees, because of actions by special interest groups that can impose costs on the general public, or because social goals other than economic efficiency are being pursued.

Content Standard 18: Fluctuations in a nation's overall levels of income, employment, and prices are determined by the interaction of spending and production decisions made by all households, firms, government agencies, and others in the economy. Recessions occur when overall levels of income and employment decline.

Content Standard 19: Unemployment imposes costs on individuals and the overall economy. Inflation, both expected and unexpected, also imposes costs on individuals and the overall economy. Unemployment increases during recessions and decreases during recoveries.

Content Standard 20: Federal government budgetary policy and the Federal Reserve System's monetary policy influence the overall levels of employment, output, and prices.

Chapter 15 Planner **435A**

CHAPTER 15: FISCAL POLICY

CHAPTER OPENER PLANNER

Students will know:
- fiscal policies are decisions to change spending and taxation levels by the federal government.
- how the government uses fiscal policy to promote the economic goals of price stability, full employment, and economic growth.

Students will be able to:
- evaluate the effects of Keynesian economics.
- describe the combined effect of the Keynesian multiplier and accelerator on the GDP.
- explain the goals and methods of demand-side policies.
- discuss the limitations of demand-side policies.

UNDERSTANDING BY DESIGN

✓ Print Teaching Options

R Reading Skills

☐ **p. 436 Understanding terminology** Students define flat income tax and payroll tax.

☐ **p. 436 Categorizing pros and cons** Students pros/cons of supply-side and demand-side policies.

C Critical Thinking Skills

☐ **p. 435 Assessing fiscal policies** Students explain a fiscal policy the government has enacted recently.

☐ **p. 437 Analyzing policy** Students explain the main idea of each policy.

W Writing Skills

☐ **p. 436 Comparing and contrasting policies** Students contrats Russia's supply-side policies with China's demand-side policies.

✓ Online Teaching Options

V Visual Skills

☐ **IMAGE Chapter opener**—Students analyze a photo about fiscal policy symbols.

C Critical Thinking Skills

☐ **INFOGRAPHICS Economic Perspectives**—Students summarize fiscal policies that shaped Russia and China.

☐ **DEBATES Should the government make major changes in federal spending and taxation to deal with the growing national debt?**—Students analyze two positions on government debt.

☐ **INTERACTIVE FEATURE Case Study: Then and Now—the New Deal's Tennessee Valley Authority (TVA)**—Students analyze government involvement in economic development.

✓ Printable Digital Worksheets

C Critical Thinking Skills

☐ **WORKSHEET Reinforcing Economic Skills**—Students compare demand-side and supply-side economics.

☐ **WORKSHEET Economic Simulation**—Students create a commercial for a supply-side or demand-side policy.

☐ **WORKSHEET Assessing Background Knowledge Activity**—Target misconceptions you can address when teaching the lessons.

Project-Based Learning

Hands-On

WORKSHEET Hands-On Chapter Project
In this activity, students will work in groups as committees on fiscal policy that work for the U.S. president. Students will research past fiscal policies and determine whether they were effective. They will then present this information to the president, who wants to start a new program to fulfill the economic goals of the United States. Student groups will devise their own method of presentation for this information.

Digital Hands-On

Create Online Projects

Find an additional activity online that incorporates technology for the Hands-On Project. Visit the EdTech Teacher Web sites for more links, tutorials, and other resources.

Print Resources

ANCILLARY RESOURCE
This ancillary is available for every chapter and lesson.
- Chapter Tests and Lesson Quizzes

PRINTABLE DIGITAL WORKSHEETS
These printable digital worksheets are available for every chapter and lesson.
- Reading Essentials & Study Guide
- Vocabulary Activities
- Chapter Summaries
- Economic Simulations
- Math Practice for Economics
- Reinforcing Economic Skills
- Personal Finance Activities
- Enrichment Activities
- Reteaching Activities
- Guided Reading Activities
- Video Worksheets
- Lesson Quizzes and Chapter Tests (English and Spanish)

More Media Resources

SUGGESTED READING
- For students at a Grade 10 reading level: *Considering a Job Offer*, by Stuart Schwartz & Craig Conley
- For students at a Grade 11 reading level: *In Search of Excellence: Lessons From America's Best-Run Companies*, by Thomas J. Peters & Robert H. Waterman
- For students at a Grade 12 reading level: *Presidential Leadership: Rating the Best and Worst in the White House*, by James Taranto

SUGGESTED VIDEOS
Find these documentaries yourself online. NOTE: McGraw-Hill Education does not endorse these resources. Preview clips for age-appropriateness.
- *For Sale: The American Dream* (25 min.)
- *The Ascent of Money Episode 4: Risky Business* (50 min.)

LESSON 1 Planner

DEMAND-SIDE POLICIES

Students will know:
- demand-side policies are designed to affect total demand through taxing, government spending, and automatic stabilizers.

Students will be able to:
- **evaluate** the effects of Keynesian economics.
- **describe** the combined effect of the Keynesian multiplier and accelerator on the GDP.
- **explain** the goals and methods of demand-side policies.
- **discuss** the limitations of demand-side policies.

UNDERSTANDING BY DESIGN

☑ Print Teaching Options

V Visual Skills

- **p. 439 Understanding the combined effect of the multiplier and accelerator** Students diagram the downward spiral of GDP.
- **p. 442 Identifying lags and their effects** Students sequence lags in a business cycle.

R Reading Skills

- **p. 438 Understanding fiscal policy basics** Students identify government actions to influence or stabilize the economy.
- **p. 438 Understanding the purpose of Keynesian theory**
- **p. 439 Connecting the aggregate output-expenditure model to Keynesian economics**
- **p. 440 Understanding two approaches to demand-side policies** Students explain direct and indirect approaches of government involvement.
- **p. 440 Justifying the short-term budget deficit** Students explain how Keynes justified a temporary but necessary government deficit.

C Critical Thinking Skills

- **p. 438 Personalizing fiscal policy** Students explain how they are affected by fiscal policy.
- **p. 440 Defining "demand-side"** Students explain the purpose of demand-side policy.
- **p. 441 Identifying automatic stabilizers**
- **p. 441 Identifying points of view on entitlement programs**
- **p. 443 Applying Keynes's theory** Students describe recent deficit spending.
- **p. 443 Analyzing government spending categories** Students cut government spending.

W Writing Skills

- **p. 441 Arguing for or against Keynesian policies** Students write about Keynesian policies in the economy. Verbal/Linguistic
- **p. 442 Elaborating on limitations of demand-side policies**

☑ Online Teaching Options

V Visual Skills

- **CHARTS Aggregate Output-Expenditure**—Students explore the model. Visual/Spatial
- **VIDEO California Raises Taxes Due to Deficit**—Students discuss government spending, taxes, and budget deficits. Verbal/Linguistic

R Reading Skills

- **GRAPHIC ORGANIZER Limitations of Demand-Side Policies**—Students take notes on the limitations of demand-side policies. Verbal/Linguistic

C Critical Thinking Skills

- **BELLRINGER Demand-Side Policies**—Students discuss the historical trend of government spending since 1930.
- **ESSENTIAL QUESTION Exploring the Essential Question**—Students explain whether the federal student loan program is an example of Keynesian economics.

T Technology Skills

- **SELF-CHECK QUIZ Lesson 1**—Students receive instant feedback on their answers.
- **GAME Lesson 1**—Students solve clues to review lesson content.
- **INTERACTIVE WHITEBOARD ACTIVITY The Trend Toward Increased Government Spending**—Students work together to learn lesson content.

☑ Printable Digital Worksheets

R Reading Skills

- **WORKSHEET Guided Reading Activity**—Students use the Guided Reading Activity worksheets to review their comprehension of the content.
- **WORKSHEET Reading Essentials and Study Guide**—Students complete the study guide and answer Reading Progress Check and vocabulary questions.

C Critical Thinking Skills

- **WORKSHEET California Raises Taxes Due to Deficit Video Activity**—Students answer questions about California tax increases and budget deficits.

LESSON 2 Planner

SUPPLY-SIDE POLICIES

Students will know:
- supply-side economics focuses on policies that increase production through less government and lower taxes.
- supply-side policies focus on economic growth rather than stability.

Students will be able to:
- **compare and contrast** supply-side and demand-side policies.
- **discuss** the limitations of supply-side policies.
- **compare** the aggregate supply curve for the economy to the supply curves of individual producers.

UNDERSTANDING BY DESIGN®

☑ Print Teaching Options

V Visual Skills

☐ **p. 449 Creating a political cartoon about deregulation** Students illustrate a concept related to supply-side economics. Visual/Spatial

R Reading Skills

☐ **p. 445 Understanding supply-siders' key goal** Students describe a key goal for supply-siders and how they hope to achieve it.

☐ **p. 446 Tracing the lower-tax argument** Students explain the argument used by supply-siders when promoting lower tax rates.

☐ **p. 447 Understanding the Laffer curve** Students compare the Laffer curve against income tax receipt history.

C Critical Thinking Skills

☐ **p. 445 Analyzing the government's economic goal strategies** Students give the current government a passing or failing grade in each goal.

☐ **p. 446 Understanding terminology for supply-side policies** Students explain why supply-side policies were called "trickle-down economics". Verbal/Linguistic

☐ **p. 448 Analyzing opinions about tax cuts** Students interview people about income taxes. Interpersonal

☐ **p. 449 Comparing demand-side and supply-side policies** Students explain the similarities between the two policies.

☐ **p. 449 Expressing opinions on supply-side economics** Students state whether they support the idea of using supply-side economics. Verbal/Linguistic

W Writing Skills

☐ **p. 447 Evaluating the impacts of deregulation** Students research the deregulation of an industry. Verbal/Linguistic

☐ **p. 448 Creating a dialogue about supply-side policy effects** Students address a drawback of supply-side economics in their community. Interpersonal

☑ Online Teaching Options

V Visual Skills

☐ **VIDEO Bush and Obama Tax Cuts**—Students view a video on tax policies made by Presidents Bush and Obama.

☐ **GRAPH Personal Income Tax Rates and Receipts**—Students explore personal income tax rates and receipts.

☐ **GRAPHS Comparing Supply-Side and Demand-Side Policies**—Students explore an interactive graph that compares the two policies.

R Reading Skills

☐ **GRAPHIC ORGANIZERS Supply-Side Economics**—Students identify the characteristics of supply-side economics. Verbal/Linguistic

C Critical Thinking Skills

☐ **BELLRINGER Supply-Side Policies**—Students examine three economic goals of the federal government.

☐ **ESSENTIAL QUESTION Exploring the Essential Question**—Students discuss the government's success with attaining economic goals.

T Technology Skills

☐ **SELF-CHECK QUIZ Lesson 2**—Students receive instant feedback on their mastery of lesson content.

☐ **GAME Lesson 2**—Students solve clues to review lesson content.

☐ **INTERACTIVE WHITEBOARD ACTIVITY Supply-Side vs. Demand-Side Economics**—Students work together to learn lesson content.

☑ Printable Digital Worksheets

R Reading Skills

☐ **WORKSHEET Guided Reading Activity**—Students use the Guided Reading Activity worksheets to review their comprehension of the content.

☐ **WORKSHEET Reading Essentials and Study Guide**—Students complete the study guide and answer Reading Progress Check and vocabulary questions.

C Critical Thinking Skills

☐ **WORKSHEET Bush and Obama Tax Cuts Video Activity**—Students answer questions about a video on Bush and Obama tax cuts. Verbal/Linguistic, Visual/Spatial

LESSON 3 Planner

MACROECONOMIC EQUILIBRIUM

Students will know:
- the government runs a budget deficit when its expenditures exceed its revenues.
- the national debt is the accumulated sum of all of the government's past annual deficits and surpluses.
- the measures taken by Congress to reduce deficits and the national debt.

Students will be able to:
- **compare** the aggregate supply curve for the economy to the supply curves of individual producers.
- **explain** how aggregate demand is related to individual demand.
- **explain** how aggregate demand and aggregate supply can be used together to achieve or manipulate macroeconomic equilibrium.

UNDERSTANDING BY DESIGN®

☑ Print Teaching Options

R Reading Skills

- ☐ **p. 451 Understanding price level and aggregate supply** Students explain why the term *price level* is used instead of *price*.
- ☐ **p. 453 Comparing aggregate demand and the market demand curve** Students identify causes of a decrease in aggregate demand.
- ☐ **p. 453 Relating inflation and recessions to macro equilibrium**
- ☐ **p. 453 Understanding how demand-side policies affect AD**
- ☐ **p. 454 Understanding how supply-side policies affect AS**
- ☐ **p. 455 Finding real examples of AS and AD** Students scan for stories that might cause a change in aggregate supply or demand.

C Critical Thinking Skills

- ☐ **p. 450 Evaluating equilibrium** Students discuss the state of equilibrium. *Interpersonal*
- ☐ **p. 451 Assessing the aggregate demand curve** Students explain why the aggregate demand curve a hypothetical curve.
- ☐ **p. 452 Analyzing causes of increases in aggregate supply** Students identify factors that increase aggregate supply.
- ☐ **p. 452 Relating underemployment to aggregate supply** Students explain the impact underemployment has on aggregate supply.
- ☐ **p. 453 Predicting changes in aggregate demand** Students explain how increased competition would affect aggregate demand.
- ☐ **p. 455 Creating policy changes** Students design a policy change and create a brochure.

W Writing Skills

- ☐ **p. 451 Defining *aggregate*** Students use the word *aggregate*. **ELL** *Verbal/Linguistic*
- ☐ **p. 452 Creating questions about aggregate demand** Students write a five-question quiz.

☑ Online Teaching Options

V Visual Skills

- ☐ **GRAPHS** **The Aggregate Supply Curve**—Students explore a graph of the aggregate supply curve. *Logical/Mathematical*
- ☐ **GRAPHS** **Aggregate Demand Curve**—Students explore a graph of the aggregate demand curve. *Logical/Mathematical*
- ☐ **GRAPHS** **The Economy in Equilibrium**—Students write a summary of how the graph shows changes in the economy. *Logical/Mathematical, Verbal/Linguistic*
- ☐ **GRAPHS** **Fiscal Policy and Aggregate Demand**—Students write a paragraph describing a benefit and drawback of demand-side fiscal policy.
- ☐ **GRAPHS** **Supply Side Policies and Aggregate Supply**—Students use graph to explain what could prevent the equilibrium point from being lower.
- ☐ **VIDEO** **America's Debt**—Students watch a video about America's debt crisis.

R Reading Skills

- ☐ **GRAPHIC ORGANIZER** **Increase in Aggregate Supply**—Students take notes on factors that could lead to an increase in aggregate supply. *Verbal/Linguistic*

C Critical Thinking Skills

- ☐ **BELLRINGER** **Macroeconomic Equilibrium**—Students look at the supply and demand curves and locate the equilibrium price. *Verbal/Linguistic*
- ☐ **ESSENTIAL QUESTION** **Exploring the Essential Question**—Students brainstorm events that could lead to an economic downturn. *Verbal/Linguistic*

T Technology Skills

- ☐ **SELF-CHECK QUIZ** **Lesson 3**—Students receive instant feedback on answers.
- ☐ **GAME** **Lesson 3**—Students solve clues to review lesson content.
- ☐ **INTERACTIVE WHITEBOARD ACTIVITY** **Shifts in the Aggregate Supply Curve**—Students work together to learn lesson content.

☑ Printable Digital Worksheets

R Reading Skills

- ☐ **WORKSHEET** **Guided Reading Activity**—Students review their comprehension.
- ☐ **WORKSHEET** **Reading Essentials and Study Guide**—Students complete the study guide and answer Reading Progress Check and vocabulary questions.

C Critical Thinking Skills

- ☐ **WORKSHEET** **America's Debt Video Activity**—Students use the worksheet to answer questions America's debt crisis.

CHAPTER 15 Fiscal Policy

INTERVENTION AND REMEDIATION STRATEGIES

LESSON 1 Demand-Side Policies

Reading and Comprehension

Have students write definitions for the words multiplier and accelerator as they relate to the lesson topic. Then have them think of other ways the words could be used in other contexts. Finally, have them use each word in a sentence to explain Keynes's economic theory.

Text Evidence

Tell students to write a definition for the word limitation. Have students create a concept web in which the middle oval states "Limitations of Demand-Side Economics." Next, have them scan the lesson for examples of limitations of demand-side economics. Finally, have them put the examples they found in the text into ovals that branch out from the center oval.

LESSON 2 Supply-Side Policies

Reading and Comprehension

Ask students to review the definition of the word supply. Then ask them to predict what group supply-side policies target. Finally, have them write a definition, in their own words, for supply-side policies.

Text Evidence

Have students read through the lesson once. Then point out that supply-side economics proposes two methods to stimulate the economy. Challenge students to name these two methods: decreasing the role of government and lowering federal taxes. Finally, have students find evidence in the text that describes a benefit and a drawback of each of these two methods.

LESSON 3 Macroeconomic Equilibrium

Reading and Comprehension

Have students look up the word aggregate in a dictionary and then infer what the definitions of aggregate supply and aggregate demand might be. Review with students the definition of equilibrium as it relates to supply and demand. Have them write, in their own words, a definition of the term macroeconomic equilibrium. Ask students to compare their definitions with the one in the textbook, and correct any errors.

Text Evidence

Have students write the terms aggregate supply curve and aggregate demand curve. Then have them scan the text to find evidence that shows which problems in our economy these two curves can help explain: inflation and recessions.

Online Resources

Assessing Background Knowledge Use this worksheet to pre-assess students' background knowledge before they start the chapter.

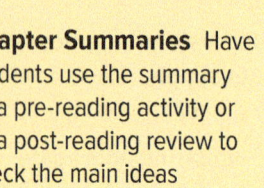

Chapter Summaries Have students use the summary as a pre-reading activity or as a post-reading review to check the main ideas covered in each lesson.

Guided Reading Activities Have students complete these activities as they read each lesson. They provide reading notes the student can use for review and to prepare for assessments.

Reteaching Activities Have students complete the Reteaching Activity for remedial practice and review of vital content.

Self-Check Quizzes These quizzes provide instant feedback on areas the students may need to re-read to understand a main idea.

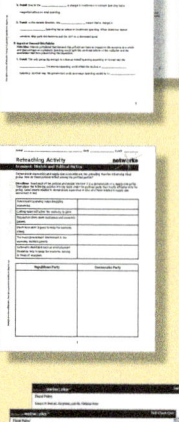

Reading Essentials and Study Guide This resource offers writing and reading activities for the approaching-level student.

Approaching Grade Level Reader This reader presents all of the content of the Online Student Edition but at a lower reading level.

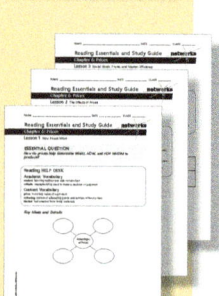

English Language Learner Reader Provide additional reading support for ELL students. Find this tool online.

Fiscal Policy

ESSENTIAL QUESTIONS
- How does the government promote the economic goals of price stability, full employment, and economic growth?
- How do we know if macroeconomic equilibrium has been achieved?

networks
www.connected.mcgraw-hill.com
There's More Online about fiscal policy.

CHAPTER 15

Economic Perspectives
The Limitations of Supply & Demand Side Economics

Lesson 1
Demand-Side Policies

Lesson 2
Supply-Side Policies

Lesson 3
Macroeconomic Equilibrium

CHAPTER 15
Fiscal Policy

ENGAGE

Call students' attention to the photo and ask them to describe what it shows. Guide them to recognize that the man in the photo is standing in front of the Capitol in Washington, D.C., dressed very casually with a dollar bill taped over this mouth. **Ask: Why is this image a good one to symbolize the chapter titled *Fiscal Policy*?** *(Fiscal policy is the use of taxes and government spending to keep the country producing output at full capacity. The dollar taped over the man's mouth symbolizes "money talks" in Congress, referring to the protester's belief that special interests have derailed government's fiscal priorities away from the middle class.)* In a discussion, lead students to understand that fiscal policy is designed to promote the economic goals of price stability, full employment, and economic growth, but it does not always accomplish those goals.

Assessing fiscal policies Have students think of one fiscal policy the government has enacted recently. **Ask: What were the benefits and drawbacks of this policy?** *(Students may answer that the policy benefited one group of people financially, but did not benefit another group.)*
Verbal/Linguistic, Interpersonal

Making Connections

Gathering public opinion about fiscal policy
Have students choose a family member or member of the community to interview. Have them ask the interviewee how recent changes in taxation or government spending have affected their employment, their spending, and their overall sense of financial stability. Have students present their interview questions and answers to the class.
Verbal/Linguistic, Interpersonal

Go to the Foldables® library for a cumulative chapter-based Foldable® activity that your students can use to help take notes and prepare for assessment.

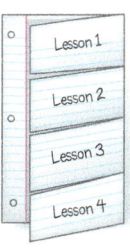

Letter from the Author

Dear Economics Teacher,

This chapter is about the spending and taxing decisions that government can do to stimulate the economy—or slow it down if it grows too fast. Business cycles are a fact of life, and when a downturn hits us, we need to do everything we can to keep it from getting worse. Fortunately, the government can moderate the situation by using demand-side or supply-side policies. Using the right policies, however, requires that government policymakers have a correct understanding of the situation. If they don't, the wrong policies can make the situation worse.

Gary E. Clayton

CHAPTER 15
Economic Perspectives

TEACH & ASSESS

R1 Reading Skills

Categorizing pros and cons Have students create a T-chart, with one side containing pros of supply-side policies, and the other side containing pros of demand-side policies. Then have them create a second T-chart identifying cons of each policy.
Verbal/Linguistic

W Writing Skills

Comparing and contrasting policies Have students write a one-page report comparing and contrasting the effects of supply-side policies and demand-side policies on the economies of Russia and China. After students view the infographic, have them do online research to find tax revenues and debt as a percentage of GDP for Russia, China, and the United States from 2000 to the present. Have students present this information in graphic form. Discuss whether supply-side or demand-side policies seem to be creating more economic growth.
Verbal/Linguistic, Logical/Mathematical

R2 Reading Skills

Understanding terminology Ask students to find the terms *flat income tax* and *payroll tax* in the infographic. Have them review Chapter 14 and write a few sentences defining the terms.
Verbal/Linguistic

Economic Perspectives

THE LIMITATIONS OF SUPPLY & DEMAND SIDE ECONOMICS

What is Supply-Side Economics?

R1 Supply-side economics sees production (which supplies goods and services) as the most important driver of economic growth. Supply-side economics was developed by former *Wall Street Journal* writer Jude Wanniski, who encouraged Ronald Reagan to adopt supply-side ('trickle-down') economics in his 1980s presidential campaigns.

Supply-side says...

W

Keep government out of the economy!

Lower taxes for the wealthy will trigger investment & saving

Limit monetary policy – keep the Fed in check!

Prosperity for the wealthy will 'trickle down' to everyone!

Russia: Taxation the Supply-side Way

R2 As Russia moved away from Communism, it embraced supply-side oriented tax policies. In 2000, those with the highest incomes paid an income tax rate of 30% --- plus the 40.5% payroll tax levied on all income levels by the Russian government. In 2001, new president Vladimir Putin adopted a 13% flat income tax and reduced the payroll tax. In the first year after the change, government revenue from income taxes increased 26% because more people paid their taxes. In the two years after Putin's new tax policies, growth of the Russian economy more than tripled.

---

networks *Online Teaching Options*

INFOGRAPHIC

Economic Perspectives: The Limitations of Supply & Demand-Side Economics

Analyzing the fiscal policies of Russia and China
Before students view the infographic, have them brainstorm definitions of *supply-side* and *demand-side*. Then have students view the infographic and summarize the fiscal policies that shaped Russia and China in the early 2000s. Poll students about their opinions on U.S. tax policies and debt. Ask how many believe the United States should follow the Russian path or Chinese path. Keep the poll and discuss again after students read the chapter. **Verbal/Linguistic**

CHAPTER 15
Economic Perspectives

What is Demand-Side Economics? (Keynesian Economics)

British economist John Maynard Keynes introduced this economic philosophy in 1936. Demand-side economics (also called Keynesian economics) states that the total demand of households, businesses, and government are the most important driver of the economy.

Demand-side says...

Government stimulus encourages investment

Lower taxes for middle & lower classes will trigger spending

Use policy to promote employment and price stability

Middle class spending spreads money throughout the economy!

China: Demand-side Ups And Downs

In the 21st century, China's mammoth economy has welcomed market competition as its goods-hungry middle class swells into the hundreds of millions. Still, Chinese officials are concerned about the country's rising debt --- and slow economic growth. In the early 2000s, China's debt remained at around 130% of its GDP; after the 2008 financial crisis, China's debt skyrocketed to over 200% of GDP. Historically, such rapidly growing debt has been an omen of economic crisis, and complicating matters is China's massive but little-regulated 'shadow banking' system, which operates outside of formal banking.

THINK ABOUT IT!
Which economic philosophy has been most influential in the past ten years?

C Critical Thinking Skills

Analyzing policy Have students read through the infographic and study the icons and their captions. Then have students explain the main idea of each policy in a separate sentence: The _____ policy benefits the _____ because it limits/triggers/encourages _____. **Verbal/Linguistic, Logical/Mathematical**

CLOSE & REFLECT

Have students answer the *Think About It!* questions.

WORKSHEET

Reinforcing Economic Skills

Summarizing demand-side and supply-side policies Distribute copies of the worksheet. Students will read a passage about demand-side and supply-side economics, and then compare the two theories by determining whether certain attributes apply to each theory.

ANSWERS, p. 437

THINK ABOUT IT!

Answers will vary. Government stimulus money kept the banking and auto industries alive after the Great Recession, so some students will cite demand-side policies as more influential. But Russia's economy more than tripled under Putin's new supply-side tax policies, so some students will cite supply-side policies as more influential.

CHAPTER 15, LESSON 1
Demand-Side Policies

ENGAGE

C Critical Thinking Skills

Personalizing fiscal policy Before students begin the lesson, ask them to define the word *fiscal* (relating to government taxes and spending) **Ask: How are you personally affected by fiscal policy?** (If students receive a paycheck, taxes have been deducted. The government decides tax rates, which affects how much money people have available to spend, which affects the economy.) **Verbal/Linguistic**

TEACH & ASSESS

R1 Reading Skills

Understanding fiscal policy basics Ask: What two actions does the government take to influence or stabilize the economy—otherwise known as fiscal policy? (The government either adjusts taxes or government spending—or both.)

R2 Reading Skills

Understanding the purpose of Keynesian theory Ask: What was Keynesian economics designed specifically to do? (lower unemployment and raise output by stimulating aggregate demand) Point out that aggregate demand (and aggregate supply) is a conceptual measure because it is impossible to calculate a true measure.

English Language Proficiency

Intermediate Before students read the challenging language in this lesson, write several topic-related sentences on sentence strips. Use a different structure for each sentence. Cut the sentence strips so that a single word or phrase appears on its own piece of paper. Give groups a set of sentence parts to arrange in a sentence. Then have each group member read the sentence aloud.

ANSWERS, p. 438

ESSENTIAL QUESTION ACTIVITY

Students may cite the drawback of adding to the federal deficit by government funding unemployment payments and job-training services.

TAKING NOTES:
Problem of lead and lag times
Increased dependency on government
Burden of taxes outweighs benefits
Deficit spending adds to national debt

438

Interact with these digital assets and others in lesson 1
- POLITICAL CARTOON Keynesian Policies
- INTERACTIVE GRAPH Tax Rates and Receipts
- SELF-CHECK QUIZ
- VIDEO

networks TRY IT YOURSELF ONLINE

LESSON 1
Demand-Side Policies

Reading Help Desk

Academic Vocabulary
- unstable

Content Vocabulary
- fiscal policy
- Keynesian economics
- multiplier
- accelerator
- automatic stabilizers
- unemployment insurance
- entitlements

TAKING NOTES:

Key Ideas and Details
ACTIVITY Use the graphic organizer below to identify the limitations of Demand-Side Policies.

438

ESSENTIAL QUESTION

C How does the government promote the economic goals of price stability, full employment, and economic growth?

High unemployment has a major impact on the U.S. economy. Since the Great Depression, state and federal governments have provided assistance to those who lose their jobs while they look for new work. These programs have benefits and drawbacks. In three paragraphs, identify and explain one drawback related to government unemployment payments and job-training and job-hunting services.

Keynesian Economics

GUIDING QUESTION *How were Keynes's ideas different from what is in practice today?*

R1 Whenever the economy is performing poorly, people tend to look for solutions from their elected representatives in Washington. They may look for changes in **fiscal policy**—the federal government's attempt to influence or stabilize the economy through taxing and government spending.

R2 Activist fiscal policies are derived from **Keynesian economics**, an approach designed to lower unemployment and raise output by stimulating aggregate demand. John Maynard Keynes, a British economist and the most important economic philosopher since Adam Smith, put forth these theories in 1936 and dominated the thinking of economists until the 1970s.

In the 1930s, Keynes offered his basic macroeconomic framework, which has come to be known as the aggregate output-expenditure model, or GDP = C + I + G + (X − M). In this model, "C" stands for household or consumer spending, "I" for the investment or business sector, and "G" for the government. In the last group, the net foreign sector, "M" stands for imports and "X" for exports. GDP stands for gross domestic product, the total output of the economy.

---

networks Online Teaching Options

BELLRINGER

Demand-Side Policies

Connecting government spending to the deficit Have students study the graph in the Bellringer. Have a class discussion about the historical trend of government spending since 1930. **Ask: How does an increase in government spending affect the deficit?** (It raises it.) **What is a positive effect of government spending?** (Lead students to understand that during economic downturns, government spending offsets the lack of spending—or demand—in other sectors of the economy.)

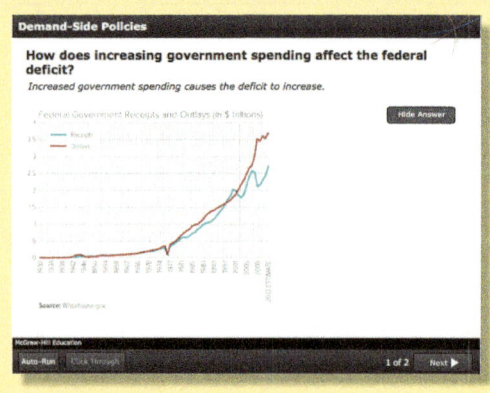

Depression-Era Economics

Keynes was writing in Great Britain during the worldwide depression in the 1930s that included the Great Depression in the United States.

When Keynes created his equation, he reasoned that any change in GDP on the left side could be traced to changes on the right side. The question was, which of the four components was causing the instability, and by how much?

According to Keynes, the impact of the net foreign sector (X – M) was so small that it could be ignored. The government sector (G) was not the problem either, because its expenditures were normally stable over time. Spending by the consumer sector (C), was the most stable of all. So that led Keynes to argue that **unstable** spending by the business, or investment, sector (I) was to blame for the decline of GDP during those years.

The Multiplier

Keynes correctly deduced that spending by the investment sector was not only unstable but had a magnified effect on GDP, rippling through the economy and becoming stronger as it went along. If investment spending declined by $50 billion, for example, many workers would lose their jobs. These workers in turn would spend less and pay fewer taxes. Soon, the amount of spending by all sectors in the economy would be down by more than the initial decline in investment.

This effect is called the **multiplier**: a change in investment spending will have a magnified effect on total spending. In fact, studies say that in today's economy, the multiplier is about 2. So if investment spending goes down by $50 billion, the decline in overall spending could reach $100 billion. The multiplier also works in the other direction. An increase in spending by $50 billion would increase overall spending by twice that amount.

fiscal policy use of government spending and revenue collection measures to influence the economy

Keynesian economics government spending and taxation policies suggested by John Maynard Keynes to stimulate the economy; synonymous with fiscal policies or demand-side economics

unstable unsteady

multiplier change in overall spending caused by a change in investment spending

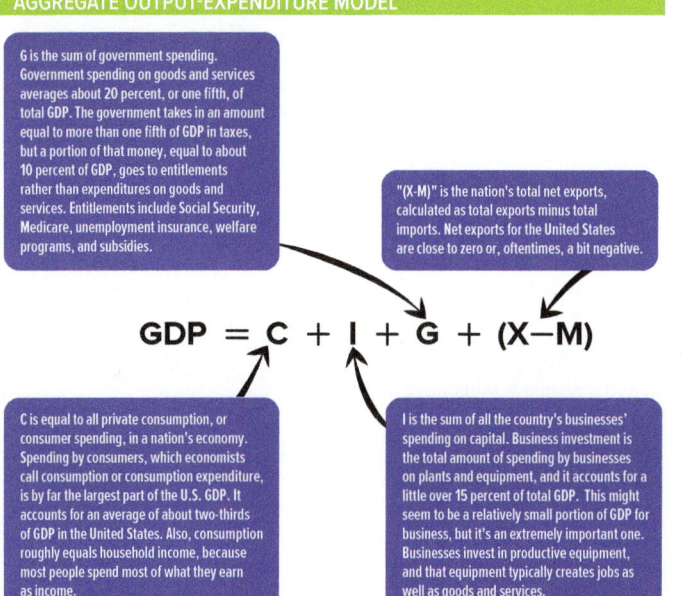

AGGREGATE OUTPUT-EXPENDITURE MODEL

G is the sum of government spending. Government spending on goods and services averages about 20 percent, or one fifth, of total GDP. The government takes in an amount equal to more than one fifth of GDP in taxes, but a portion of that money, equal to about 10 percent of GDP, goes to entitlements rather than expenditures on goods and services. Entitlements include Social Security, Medicare, unemployment insurance, welfare programs, and subsidies.

"(X–M)" is the nation's total net exports, calculated as total exports minus total imports. Net exports for the United States are close to zero or, oftentimes, a bit negative.

C is equal to all private consumption, or consumer spending, in a nation's economy. Spending by consumers, which economists call consumption or consumption expenditure, is by far the largest part of the U.S. GDP. It accounts for an average of about two-thirds of GDP in the United States. Also, consumption roughly equals household income, because most people spend most of what they earn as income.

I is the sum of all the country's businesses' spending on capital. Business investment is the total amount of spending by businesses on plants and equipment, and it accounts for a little over 15 percent of total GDP. This might seem to be a relatively small portion of GDP for business, but it's an extremely important one. Businesses invest in productive equipment, and that equipment typically creates jobs as well as goods and services.

$$GDP = C + I + G + (X-M)$$

The size of a nation's economy is the total value of the spending on goods and services in the nation in a year. According to this model, GDP, the total output of the economy, is consumed by four sectors: C being the household or consumer sector; I being the investment or business sector; G being the government sector; and the net foreign sector where M stands for imports and X for exports.

◀ **CRITICAL THINKING**
Making Predictions Based on the model, if a nation's imports increase while all other variables stay the same, what will the impact be on GDP? Explain why using the equation for the model.

CHAPTER 15, LESSON 1
Demand-Side Policies

C Critical Thinking Skills

Defining "demand-side" Ask: **Why is demand-side policy referred to as "demand-side"?** *(The purpose is to increase demand—or spending—for goods and services, which in turn will increase production, reduce unemployment, increase tax receipts, and so on.)* **Logical/Mathematical**

R1 Reading Skills

Understanding two approaches to demand-side policies Ask: **What are the direct and indirect approaches of government involvement in demand-side policies?** *(The direct approach is to put money directly into the economy through spending. The indirect approach is to lower taxes in order to encourage businesses and consumers to spend more.)*

W Writing Skills

Writing a story about John Maynard Keynes today Direct students to review the main economic ideas of John Maynard Keynes. Ask students to write a story in which Keynes uses a time machine to travel to the United States today. Instruct students to include in their stories Keynes's likely reactions to, and opinions about, the current economic situation in this country. **Verbal/Linguistic, Intrapersonal**

R2 Reading Skills

Justifying the short-term budget deficit Ask: **How did Keynes justify a temporary but necessary government deficit in fiscal policy?** *(He assumed that when the economy recovered, tax collections would rise and the debt could be paid back.)*

ANSWERS, p. 440

✓ READING PROGRESS CHECK Keynesian economics says that the government should play a large role in stimulating the economy.

CRITICAL THINKING
Students answers should show an awareness that generally Keynesian theory has been followed by U.S. economic policy with significant departures since the 1970s and that a debate continues today.

440

BIOGRAPHY

John Maynard Keynes
ECONOMIST (1883–1946)

The English economist John Maynard Keynes inspired a school of economic thought that government spending to achieve full employment helps end a recession or depression.

He was educated at the University of Cambridge. Until the Great Depression of the 1930s, Keynes was considered a conventional economist. In 1936 he wrote *The General Theory of Employment, Interest and Money*, in which he stressed that consumers did not cause shifts in the business cycle. Instead, governments, businesses, and investors did. During World War II, the United State and most of Europe used his economic theories.

After the war he was a representative at the Bretton Woods Conference (1944), where the World Bank and International Monetary Fund were established. His final work was in 1945, when he negotiated a loan from the United States to Britain for rebuilding that war-torn nation.

▲ **CRITICAL THINKING**
Drawing Conclusions Do you think the current economic policy of the United States generally follows theories Keynes advocated, or are people starting to question Keynesian theories? Give reasons for your thinking.

The Accelerator

Keynes also identified an **accelerator**: the change in investment spending caused by a change in total spending. As overall spending drops, investors become more cautious and invest less, and overall spending goes down even more.

When the multiplier and the accelerator combine, they push GDP down deeper and faster in a downward spiral, as people saw clearly during the worldwide depression. On top of that, when consumers also became more cautious and tried to save, they pushed GDP down as well or kept it low.

✓ READING PROGRESS CHECK

Analyzing What does Keynesian economics say is the economic role of the government?

Impact of Demand-Side Policies

GUIDING QUESTION *What are the goals of demand-side policies?*

So Keynes concluded that the problem during the Great Depression was a *lack* of spending. Perhaps an increase in spending would drive GDP back up, fighting the combined effects of the multiplier and accelerator.

Role of Government

His solution was relatively simple. Only the government was big enough to step in and offset changes in investment-sector spending. After all, spending by the consumer sector, C, was relatively stable. And spending by the net foreign sector, (X – M), was too small to make much of a difference. This left only the government sector, G, to offset the decline in the business sector, or I, spending.

The G sector could spend to offset the decline in spending by businesses. In a more indirect approach, the government could encourage businesses and consumers to spend by lowering taxes and other measures.

How Deficit Spending Works

Suppose there was a $50 billion decline in business spending. According to Keynesian doctrine, the government could spend $10 billion to build a dam, give $20 billion in grants to cities to fix up poor neighborhoods, and spend another $20 billion in other ways. As G increased to offset the decrease in I, the overall sum of C + I + G + (X – M) would remain unchanged.

Or if, instead of spending the $50 billion, the government reduced tax rates, and consumers and businesses spent the $50 billion not collected in taxes they could offset the initial decline in investment spending, and the sum of C + I + G + (X – M) would again not change.

Either way, the government would run the risk of a short-term budget deficit, and need to borrow to make up the difference. In Keynes's view, that deficit was unfortunate but necessary to stop further declines in economic activity. However, when the economy recovered, tax collections would rise, and the debt could be paid back. This justification for *temporary* federal deficits was one of the lasting contributions of Keynesian economics and a major departure from the economic thinking of the time.

"Priming the Pump"

By the 1960s, economists talked confidently about "priming the pump," a term used to suggest that only a relatively small amount of government spending was needed to initiate a bigger round of overall spending in the economy.

The economy had come through the Great Depression of the 1930s, and the massive government spending during World War II had driven the U.S. economy to new heights. Econometric models involving multiplier-accelerator interactions were popular. But the limitations of demand-side economics were not yet fully understood.

440

---

networks Online Teaching Options

BIOGRAPHY

Biography: John Maynard Keynes

Expressing opinions on Keynes's ideas Have students read the biography of John Maynard Keynes. Ask: **Do you think the current economic policy of the United States generally follows theories Keynes advocated, or are people starting to question Keynesian theories? Explain.** *(Student answers should show an awareness that Keynesian theory has generally been followed by U.S. economic policy, but with significant departures since the 1970s, and that a debate continues today.)* Then have students write a one-page opinion essay on whether they think the United States should return to some of Keynes's ideas that have been abandoned since the 1970s. **Verbal/Linguistic**

Automatic Stabilizers

Another key component of demand-side policies is the role of **automatic stabilizers**, which are programs that automatically trigger government spending on certain benefits when economic growth slows down. The benefits are approved by Congress before problems arise. They keep purchasing power for the recipients from falling below a floor, helping the economy by keeping up demand while providing a safety net for individuals.

One important automatic stabilizer is the progressive income tax. For example, if your father loses his job or works fewer hours because of cutbacks and earns less, he may end up in a lower tax bracket, paying fewer taxes. That leaves him with more money to spend than he would have otherwise had.

He may also receive **unemployment insurance**—insurance that workers who lose their jobs through no fault of their own can collect from individual states for a limited amount of time. This insurance cannot be collected by people who are fired because of misconduct or simply quit without good reasons.

Most **entitlements**—broad social programs that use established eligibility requirements to provide income supplements—function as automatic stabilizers. For example, people who can't work because of significant disabilities or retire by a certain age established in the law are entitled to checks from Social Security.

Automatic stabilizers, along with today's entitlement programs, are Keynesian in the sense that they are intended to put a floor on consumer purchasing power when economic times are difficult. They are also intended to react quickly to difficult economic situations because the relief does not have to wait for Congress to act in response to a crisis. For example, people who become unemployed can receive help in a matter of weeks.

✓ **READING PROGRESS CHECK**

Summarizing How did the Great Depression experience affect economists' views?

Limitations of Demand-Side Policies

GUIDING QUESTION *Why has the government typically been unable to reduce spending after business spending has recovered?*

Keynes envisioned the role of government spending as a counterbalance to changes in investment spending. In his theoretical framework, the government could increase its spending to offset declines in investment spending and decrease its spending whenever the business sector recovered. In practice, however, things are not so simple. The government has not been able to respond as quickly and flexibly as it would ideally.

The Problem of Leads and Lags

Spending is delayed for three reasons.

- The *recognition* lag—it takes time to understand how the economy is changing. Because it takes many months to collect reliable data, six months or more might pass before everyone recognizes that GDP has stopped growing.
- The *legislative* lag—it also takes time to agree on the solution to an economic downturn. It often takes a year or more to pass relatively simple laws that require modest expenditures. Members of Congress are likely to fight over, and consequently delay, spending programs big enough to offset a significant decline in business spending—especially when they insist that some of that spending be in their own states and districts.

accelerator change in investment spending caused by a change in overall spending

automatic stabilizers programs that automatically provide government benefits during an economic downturn; unemployment, insurance, and entitlement programs

unemployment insurance government program providing payments to the unemployed; an automatic stabilizer

entitlements program or benefit using established eligibility requirements to provide health care, food, or income supplements to individuals

---

VIDEO / WORKSHEET

California Raises Taxes Due to Deficit

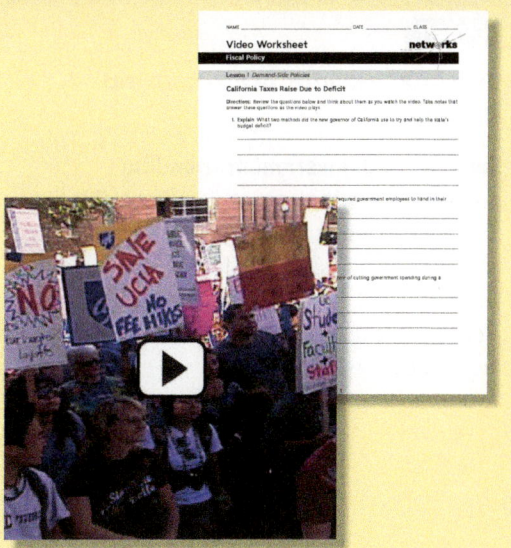

CHAPTER 15, LESSON 1
Demand-Side Policies

V Visual Skills

Identifying lags and their effects Direct students to draw a timeline of 48 months (4 years). Have them suppose that a peak in the business cycle just occurred, and now a contraction will set in. Have students chart the possible recognition, legislative, and implementation lags on the timeline. **Kinesthetic**

W1 Writing Skills

Elaborating on limitations of demand-side policies Have students choose one of the limitations of demand-side policies *(leads and lags, increased dependency on government, reaching a tipping point of the burden of taxes)*, and write an e-mail to the writer of an economics blog about the effects of that limitation. **Verbal/Linguistic**

W2 Writing Skills

Arguing for or against Keynesian policies Direct students to write and then perform a speech arguing for or against a greater application of Keynesian policies in the U.S. economy. Instruct students to use the information in the text as well as reliable Internet or library resources that provide factual material to strengthen their arguments. If students argue for Keynesian policies, make sure they address the limitations of these policies and provide solutions to counteract those limitations. **Verbal/Linguistic**

- The *implementation* lag—this is the amount of time it takes for an approved spending project or tax cut to actually pump money into the economy and create jobs. For example, a law authorizing a new highway or bridge might lead to years of planning, surveying, buying properties in the way, construction, and paving, with money trickling out along the way.

With all of these lags, how then is it possible to implement government spending with enough *lead* time to offset the likely problems of an impending recession? Most recessions are over well before the legislative lag is overcome. All the lags together might add up to 4–5 years—when even the Great Recession of 2008–2009 lasted only 18 months.

Increased Dependency on Government
An equally significant problem is the possibility, and some say probability, that people will become increasingly dependent on the federal government, rather than on their own skills and initiative. For example, if people count on unemployment checks, they may be less likely to search for a new job or start a business.

Even if the government can increase federal spending effectively to counter a weak economy, cutting back later is much more difficult.

CAREERS | Credit Counselor

Is this Career for you?
Do you have an interest in helping people work through financial crises?

 Are you a problem-solver?

 Can you speak directly and honestly with clients, even about bad news?

 Are you good at math and finance or willing to learn?

Salary
Median pay: $43,670
$21.00 per hour

Job Growth Potential
About average

Interview with a Credit Counselor

"Basically what we do is we're not trying to get the creditors' money back. That's not our purpose. Our purpose is to help you by giving you the tools that you need in order to gain control so that you can sleep at night, so that eventually you could start saving money, so that you can get out of debt, so that you can have an emergency fund, so that you don't have to constantly be worrying about this same problem over and over again."

—Tina Powis-Dow, Director of Education and Marketing, Consumer Credit Counseling Service

Profile of Work
A credit counselor helps people who have fallen into debt. A counselor analyzes a client's income, spending habits, job situation, and sources of debt, and helps the client arrive at a reasonable plan for getting back on sound financial footing. In extreme cases, this might involve recommending that the client file for bankruptcy. On other occasions, the credit counselor might negotiate with creditors on behalf of the debtor to develop a workable repayment arrangement. Some credit counselors will continue to work with clients to help them learn money-management skills.

442

---

networks | Online Teaching Options

GRAPH

Personal Income Tax Rates and Receipts

Summarizing government spending patterns Have students explore Panel B in Figure 15.1 on page 446, showing government receipts from 2000 to 2005. Have them write a sentence summarizing the pattern shown in the chart. *(Tax receipts decreased as personal income increased.)* **Visual/Spatial**

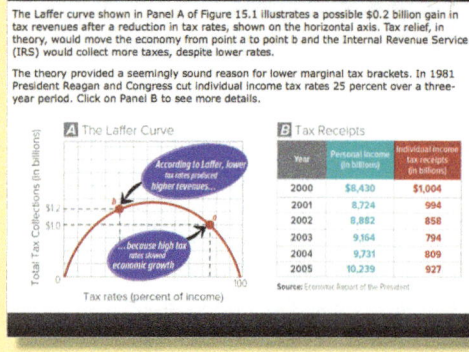

Reaching a "Tipping Point"

Eventually, it's likely that a tipping point will arrive when people decide that the burden of taxes needed to finance government expenditures will outweigh the benefits. No one knows exactly when this will happen because massive shifts in public opinion take place slowly and are hard to measure.

Most observers feel that the point was approaching with the arrival of supply-side economics when Ronald Reagan was elected president in 1981. Others think that the tipping point might have occurred when conservative politicians like Steve Forbes campaigned on a 17% flat-tax platform that promised lowered government spending in 1996.

Even others point to the rise of the conservative Tea Party movement whose strong opposition to government spending on the Affordable Care Act (ACA) in 2013 helped shut down the government and brought the country to the edge of default.

EXPLORING THE ESSENTIAL QUESTION

After you graduate from high school you plan on getting more education—either training in technology or attending college. Both types of post–high school education are expensive, and you need a loan. You explore the student loan program run by the government. Write a paragraph explaining whether or not you think the government student loan program is an example of Keynesian economics. Give your reason.

The Keynesian Legacy

Keynes died in 1946 just after the world emerged from the depths of the Great Depression and the aftermath of World War II. The economic stimulus provided by wartime spending was driving the U.S. economy to new heights, but Keynes never had time to think about the consequences of too much stimulation.

Even after the economy recovers, politicians have never been able to fully cut back on government spending instituted during a decline in business investment. People who personally benefit like the stimulus provided by other taxpayers, and they usually want more of it rather than less. To be popular with their constituents, politicians tend to vote for more and more government spending.

✓ **READING PROGRESS CHECK**

Analyzing Why are Keynes's ideas important in the study of economics?

LESSON 1 REVIEW

Reviewing Vocabulary

1. *Defining* Explain what the main idea of Keynesian economics says about the cause of economic cycles.

2. *Summarizing* Use your notes to summarize how dependency on government is a limitation of economic demand-side policies.

Answering the Guiding Questions

3. *Analyzing* How were Keynes's ideas different from what is in practice today?

4. *Assessing* What are the goals of demand-side policies?

5. *Explaining* Why has the government typically been unable to reduce spending after business spending recovered?

Writing About Economics

6. *Informative/Explanatory* Research a specific government program in effect in the 21st century that reflects Keynesian economics. Under what circumstances was the program initiated? How has it been implemented? What effect does the program have on the economy? Do you think the program is effective? Write a two-page essay to explain your findings.

Fiscal Policy **443**

CHAPTER 15, LESSON 1
Demand-Side Policies

C **Critical Thinking Skills**

Applying Keynes's theory Ask: **Does the federal government's recent pattern of deficit spending match Keynes's ideas? Why or why not?** *(No; Keynes advocated temporary federal deficits, whereas the federal government's current deficits are ongoing.)* **Verbal/Linguistic**

CLOSE & REFLECT

Analyzing government spending categories Have students list which categories of government spending they think could be cut, and which categories they think should continue to exist in order to stimulate the economy. **Verbal/Linguistic**

LESSON 1 REVIEW ANSWERS

Reviewing Vocabulary

1. The main idea of Keynesian economics is that government, business, and investments all contribute to unstable economic cycles.

Using Your Notes

2. If people become economically dependent on government, they may become less entrepreneurial and bring fewer of the advantages of new businesses.

Answering the Guiding Questions

3. Keynes's ideas are still practiced in some U.S. government fiscal policies. Keynes's ideas were dominant until the 1970s.

4. To reverse or slow a downturn in the economy and promote growth

5. Many people benefit from the government stimulus programs and are reluctant to give them up.

Writing About Economics

6. Students should demonstrate an awareness of current government programs such as the stimulus program initiated to resolve the Great Recession and Social Security and Medicare. They should select one program and explain its origin, main features, and effects, and whether it is effective and why.

ANSWERS, p. 443

EXPLORING THE ESSENTIAL QUESTION

Students should show that they understand that a program such as the student loan program is an example of Keynesian economics. It is an example of the government stimulating the economy by making post–high school education more accessible to people who otherwise could not afford it.

✓ **READING PROGRESS CHECK** Keynesian economic ideas have greatly influenced the economy in the twentieth and twenty-first centuries.

Fiscal Policy **443**

CHAPTER 15
Case Study

R Reading Skills

Listing the benefits provided by the TVA Have students write a list of the benefits provided by the TVA to the public. Next to each benefit, have students write whether the benefit continues to be provided by the TVA today. They may research the TVA online to confirm the benefits it now provides. **Verbal/Linguistic**

C Critical Thinking Skills

Differentiating public versus private funding
Ask: What is the difference between public funding and private funding? *(Public funding comes from the government, whereas private funding comes from individuals and companies.)* Then have students discuss how the TVA was funded when it began, and how it is funded now. **Verbal/Linguistic**

Making Connections

Local Utilities Have students list utilities in their local community that provide benefits similar to those that the TVA provides, or other public businesses such as bus service. Then have them choose one of these businesses to research, and have them write a one-page description of the benefits this organization provides. Students should include any government funding this organization receives, or special government oversight or regulations. **Verbal/Linguistic**

ANSWERS, p. 444

Case Study Review

1. The TVA was first funded by the federal government. In the twenty-first century it is completely self-financed.
2. Students should show knowledge that Keynesian economists would have been in favor of the TVA in 1933. Students should explain that strict Keynesians—those who strongly believe in a strong economic role for government—would probably not be in favor of how the TVA has evolved into a self-financing corporation.

Case Study

THEN & NOW—
THE NEW DEAL'S
TENNESSEE VALLEY AUTHORITY (TVA)

During the depths of the Great Depression in 1933, the U.S. Congress established and funded the Tennessee Valley Authority in order to serve a poverty-stricken area of approximately 80,000 square miles, including most of Tennessee and parts of Alabama, Georgia, Kentucky, Mississippi, North Carolina, and Virginia.

The area needed electrical power and much more. Besides supplying power, the TVA helped control floods and erosion; it even provided inoculations for the population against smallpox and typhoid. While power companies criticized the new Authority as unconstitutional, most hailed the New Deal program as an innovative way to solve big problems.

By 1959, the power program was self-financing, and today it is the nation's largest public power provider. Continuing its legacy of innovation, the TVA is now committed to providing cleaner and lower-cost energy. It has developed a new strategy to reduce pollutants, and has reduced sulfur dioxide emissions by 90 percent.

Federal funding for its environmental and economic development programs ended in 1999, but those programs also continue, and in the first decade of the 21st century the TVA ranked among the nation's top 10 utilities for promoting economic development.

CASE STUDY REVIEW

1. **Explaining** How was the TVA first funded, and how is it funded now?
2. **Analyzing** Do you think strict Keynesian economists would have been in favor of the TVA in 1933 and how it has evolved? Explain your answer.

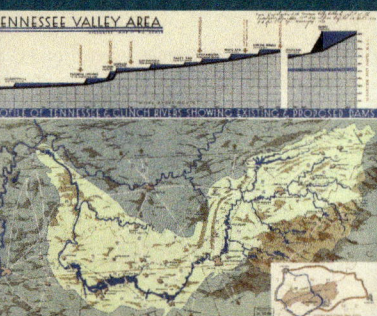
The TVA improved a wide region of the southeastern United States.

Pre-TVA, the South did not have much electricity outside of cities.

The massive federal program generated lots of jobs and lots of economic benefits.

---

networks Online Teaching Options

INTERACTIVE FEATURE

Case Study: Then & Now—The New Deal's Tennessee Valley Authority (TVA)

Making connections between the TVA and Keynesian economics Have students read the Case Study about the TVA. **Ask:** What do Keynesian economists believe government should do regarding economic development? *(Government should fund economic development in order to stimulate the economy.)* Then have students write a statement in the voice of a Keynesian economist describing what he or she thinks about the creation of the TVA. **Verbal/Linguistic**

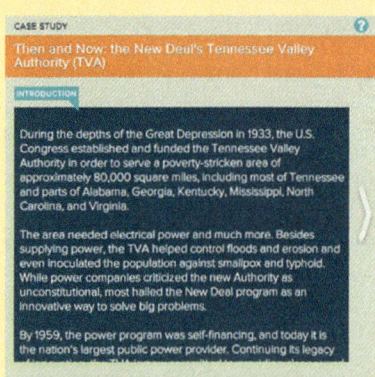

CHAPTER 15, LESSON 2
Supply-Side Policies

Interact with these digital assets and others in lesson 2
- ✓ SLIDESHOW Reagan Deregulation
- ✓ INTERACTIVE GRAPH Comparing Supply-Side and Demand-Side Policies
- ✓ SELF-CHECK QUIZ
- ✓ VIDEO

networks TRY IT YOURSELF ONLINE

LESSON 2
Supply-Side Policies

Reading Help Desk

Academic Vocabulary
- promote

Content Vocabulary
- supply-side policies
- Laffer curve
- deregulation

TAKING NOTES:

Key Ideas and Details
ACTIVITY Use the graphic organizer below to identify strategies or methods supply-siders used and the purpose that led to these actions.

Supply-Side Economics
Strategy	Purpose

ESSENTIAL QUESTION

How does the government promote the economic goals of price stability, full employment, and economic growth?

Three ongoing goals of the federal government are to promote economic growth, employment, and price stability. Over many decades, our strategies to achieve these goals have evolved as new economic theories emerged and conditions changed. Considering current economic conditions, answer these questions:

- How well are we now achieving the goals of price stability, employment, and economic growth?
- What steps is the government taking to advance these goals?
- What more could, or should, the government do?

Goals of Supply-Side Policies

GUIDING QUESTION *In what ways are supply-side and demand-side policies different?*

It is easy to see the development of supply-side economics as an alternative to demand-side economics.

Supply-side policies target producers, who are also suppliers, to stimulate their output, and therefore provide jobs. Supply-side theory became a political force after conventional demand-side economics seemed to falter in the 1970s, although many of the individual policies advocated by supply-siders were already popular.

Origins of Supply-Side Economics

In the 1970s demand-side policies did not seem to be controlling two of the nation's biggest economic problems—growing unemployment and inflation. Many Americans, including politicians, were ready to try something else.

ENGAGE

C Critical Thinking Skills

Analyzing the government's economic goal strategies Write on the board the three ongoing goals of the government: economic growth, employment, price stability. Have students discuss whether the current government gets a passing or failing grade in each goal. **Ask:** What goal of demand-side policy is missing from this list? *(a safety net)* **Verbal/Linguistic**

TEACH & ASSESS

R Reading Skills

Understanding supply-siders' key goal Ask: What is a key goal for supply-siders? *(to reduce the economic role of the federal government)* How do supply-siders hope to reduce the government's involvement? *(by cutting the number of agencies and by cutting federal spending)*

BELLRINGER

Supply-Side Policies

Activating prior knowledge about economic growth Have students view the Bellringer. Then have a class discussion about possible ways to stimulate economic growth. **Ask:** How could tax cuts stimulate economic growth? *(People would spend more of their money because they would get to keep more of it instead of paying it out in taxes.)* How could tax cuts hurt the economy? *(There would be less revenue to pay for programs that benefit people.)*

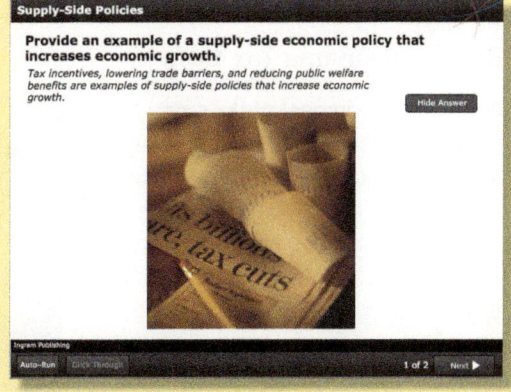

ANSWERS, p. 445

ESSENTIAL QUESTION ACTIVITY

Answers will vary.

TAKING NOTES:
Strategies:
Reduce size of government
Reduce taxes
Deregulate industry
Purposes:
Stimulate economic growth
Reduce unemployment
Control inflation
Increase government revenue

CHAPTER 15, LESSON 2
Supply-Side Policies

R Reading Skills

Tracing the lower-tax argument Ask: **What argument do supply-siders use when promoting lower tax rates?** *(They believe that lower tax rates allow individuals to keep more of the money they earn, which encourages them to work harder, providing more money to spend, leading to businesses producing more to meet greater demand.)*

C Critical Thinking Skills

Understanding terminology for supply-side policies Ask: **Why do you think supply-side policies were called "trickle-down economics"?** *(The tax cuts and relaxed regulations were designed to increase the productivity of manufacturers and the wealthy, who in turn would create more jobs for the middle and lower classes. The benefits of supply-side policies were thus intended to "trickle down" to all elements of society.)* **Verbal/Linguistic**

Content Background Knowledge

President Reagan's Impact The impact of President Reagan's economic policies remains the subject of intense debate, just as it was in the 1980s. Supporters point out that Reagan's tax cuts and deregulation efforts sparked a full recovery for the U.S. economy, which was mired in a severe downturn when he took office in 1981. Inflation, interest rates, and unemployment fell during the Reagan years, and the economy entered the longest period of continual expansion in American history. Reagan's supply-side policies also created record budget deficits and a staggering national debt, however. Critics also maintain that real wages declined during the Reagan years and that the growth of other leading world economies outpaced that of the United States in the 1980s.

ANSWERS, p. 446

CRITICAL THINKING Over that period, personal income increased, but individual income tax receipts decreased.

---

supply-side policies economic policies designed to stimulate the economy by removing government regulations and lowering marginal tax rates to increase production

The change came in 1981 when Ronald Reagan was elected president. Supply-side policies, which suited his conservative politics, soon became the hallmark of his administration.

A Smaller Role for Government

A key goal for supply-siders is to reduce the economic role of the federal government, which they argue dampens production and slows growth. One strategy is to cut the number of agencies. Another is to cut federal spending.

President Reagan tried to shrink the federal government, but his efforts were largely unsuccessful. Instead, he worked to lower tax rates in hopes that a growing federal deficit would force Congress to accept less spending.

Lower Federal Taxes

Supply-siders also target the federal tax burden on individuals and businesses. Lower tax rates, they argue, allow individuals to keep more of the money they earn, which encourages them to work harder. In the long run, they will have more money to spend, and businesses will produce more to meet greater demand.

Government revenues, they argue, also increase, because the additional business activity will be taxed.

During the 1980s, optimistic supply-siders even argued that lower individual income tax rates would stimulate the economy so much that the government could collect even more taxes than before.

This idea is expressed mathematically in the **Laffer curve**—a possible relationship between federal income tax rates and tax revenues.

Laffer curve a hypothetical, or possible, relationship between federal income tax rates and tax revenues

FIGURE 15.1

PERSONAL INCOME TAX RATES AND RECEIPTS

A The Laffer Curve

According to Laffer, lower tax rates produced higher revenues...

...because high tax rates slowed economic growth

B Tax Receipts

Year	Personal income (in billions)	Individual income tax receipts (in billions)
2000	$8,430	$1,004
2001	8,724	994
2002	8,882	858
2003	9,164	794
2004	9,731	809
2005	10,239	927

Source: Economic Report of the President

The Laffer curve is a hypothetical relationship between federal income tax rates and tax revenues. Panel A illustrates a possible $0.2 billion gain in tax revenues after a reduction in tax rates, shown on the horizontal axis. Tax relief, in theory, would move the economy from point **a** to point **b** and the Internal Revenue Service (IRS) would collect more taxes, despite lower rates.

▲ **CRITICAL THINKING**
Economic Analysis How does personal income in 2000 and 2005 compare to individual income tax receipts during the same years?

connected.mcgraw-hill.com

446

---

networks Online Teaching Options

VIDEO **WORKSHEET**

Bush and Obama Tax Cuts

Analyzing the impact of tax cuts
Have students watch the video about tax policies made by Presidents Bush and Obama. Then have them write a paragraph comparing and contrasting the goals and the effects of each set of policies. **Verbal/Linguistic**

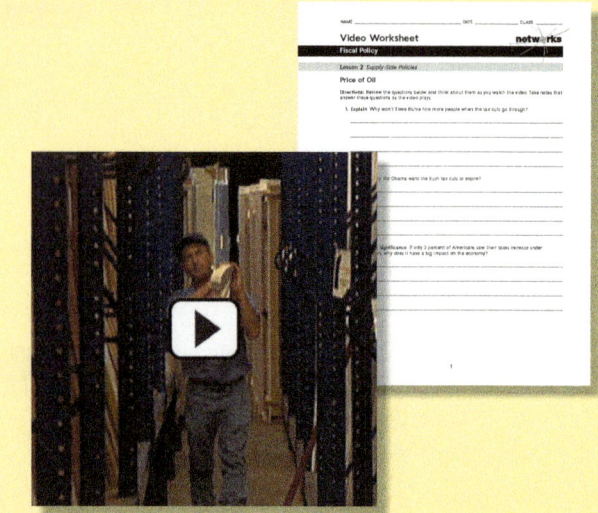

The Laffer Curve

The Laffer curve shown in **Panel A** of Figure 15.1 illustrates a possible $0.2 billion gain in tax revenues after a reduction in income tax rates, shown on the horizontal axis. Tax relief, in theory, would move the economy from point **a** to point **b** and the Internal Revenue Service (IRS) would collect more taxes, despite lower rates.

The theory provided a seemingly sound reason for lower marginal tax brackets. In 1981 President Reagan and Congress cut individual income tax rates 25 percent over a three-year period. As **Panel B** in Figure 15.1 shows, individual income tax receipts adjusted for inflation actually *declined* from 2000 to 2004, even though personal income rose in each of those years. Unfortunately, the increased tax revenue collections predicted by the Laffer curve never materialized. On the plus side, it's likely that the annual increases in personal income stimulated economic growth.

Deregulation

Supply-siders also have sought **deregulation**, relaxing or removing government regulations that restrict the activities of firms in certain industries.

Democrats embraced the idea of deregulation as well, for example in 1980, when President Jimmy Carter signed a major Savings and Loan (S&L) deregulation act. President Reagan then took another step by reducing the number of inspectors in the S&L industry, with the idea that competition would do the job.

deregulation relaxation or removal of government regulations on business activities

EXPLORING THE ESSENTIAL QUESTION

Many people favor deregulation, arguing that competition in a free market is enough to keep firms in line. They believe that consumers will avoid firms that act unfairly and force them to correct their ways or go out of business. Do you agree? Are there situations where the government needs to regulate an industry? Explain.

However, the S&Ls at the time were severely underfunded, and in the late 1980s and early 1990s approximately one-quarter of the country's S&Ls failed. Federal S&L insurance was used to repay money that depositors lost, but American taxpayers had to bail out the S&L insurance fund.

Despite this major crisis, the American economy has seen a flood of deregulation in industries ranging from airlines and banking to telecommunications and interstate trucking.

✓ **READING PROGRESS CHECK**

Identifying When did supply-side economic policies begin to grow in popularity?

Impact and Limitations of Supply-Side Policies

GUIDING QUESTION *How does increasing supply help improve the economy?*

Supply-siders believe that their policies have never been fully tested. For example, deregulation, affecting such industries as oil and gas, cable television, and long-distance phone service, was offset by increased federal spending. The smaller government that supply-siders imagined did not materialize. Hence we don't know whether a smaller government sector would make the economy more efficient.

It's also true that tax collections didn't rise when tax rates were lowered. This dampened support for the supply-side argument.

CHAPTER 15, LESSON 2
Supply-Side Policies

W Writing Skills

Creating a dialogue about supply-side policy effects Have students form groups. Challenge groups to write a dialogue that addresses a drawback of supply-side economics that affects people in their community. Have groups perform their dialogues for the class. **Verbal/Linguistic, Interpersonal**

C Critical Thinking Skills

Analyzing opinions about tax cuts Organize the class into groups of three students each. Instruct groups to interview at least 20 people about income taxes. Tell students to ask their subjects if they believe the current tax rates are satisfactory or if they think the rates should be changed. Direct students to also ask interviewees the primary reason for their opinions about tax rates. Ask groups to prepare a chart that organizes their findings by category (for example, charts could have three columns titled "Favors lower taxes," "Favors higher taxes," and "Favors no change in tax rates"; rows in the chart could then list the different reasons for these opinions). Have groups present their data to the class. Lead a discussion about how public opinion on taxation can impact the government's economic policies. **Verbal/Linguistic, Interpersonal**

ANSWERS, p. 448

CRITICAL THINKING In supply-side policies, the government's role is to increase production by reducing intervention in markets. This is accomplished by cutting taxes and regulations and increasing incentives for investment. In demand-side policies, the government's role is to stimulate consumption and demand by finding ways to give consumers more to spend through cutting taxes or increasing federal spending.

W President Reagan's Budget Priorities

For example, President Reagan cut domestic programs by about $39 billion during his first year in office. But he also expanded expenditures on national defense and in several other categories.

The net result: a yearly *increase* in government spending of about 2.5 percent.

Tax Rates and Economic Growth

Supply-siders predicted that lower tax rates and reduced government regulation would provide a climate for strong economic growth. The performance of the economy during Reagan's first two terms in office partly backed them up: real GDP, or GDP adjusted for inflation, started to grow in late 1982 and continued to grow for 92 months. This peacetime post-World War II record easily shattered the previous 58-month record.

C

However, extensive military spending provided economic stimulus, so the record growth was not entirely due to supply-side policy.

Tax Rates and Tax Revenues

As we saw in Panel B of Figure 15.1, President Reagan's tax rate cuts lowered revenues. When President Bush reduced rates again in 2001, revenues also fell. Thus one of the main foundations of the supply-side school—that tax cuts would lead to higher tax revenues—has been proven false.

Deregulation and Economic Growth

Even so, policies that promote productivity, reduce unnecessary paperwork, or otherwise stimulate the economy to grow to its maximum potential are certainly worthwhile. Almost everyone, including demand-siders, favors policies that make production more efficient.

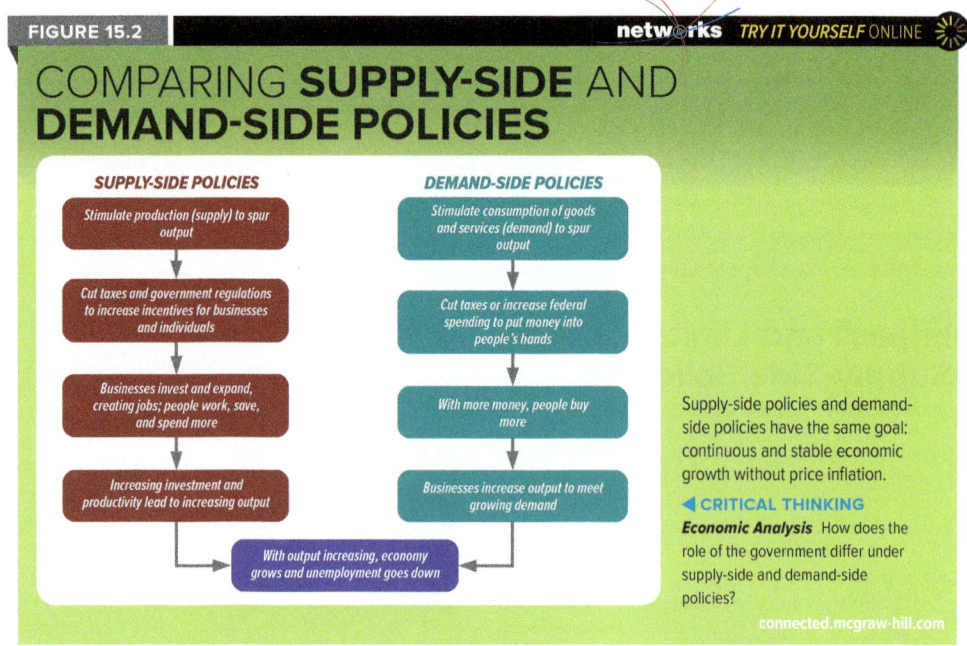

FIGURE 15.2 COMPARING SUPPLY-SIDE AND DEMAND-SIDE POLICIES

Supply-side policies and demand-side policies have the same goal: continuous and stable economic growth without price inflation.

◀ **CRITICAL THINKING**
Economic Analysis How does the role of the government differ under supply-side and demand-side policies?

448

networks Online Teaching Options

CHART

Comparing Supply-Side and Demand-Side Policies

Comparing supply-side and demand-side policies Have students carefully study the comparison of supply-side and demand-side policies in Figure 15.2. Then have them create a political cartoon that illustrates the similarities and differences between the two policies. **Visual/Spatial**

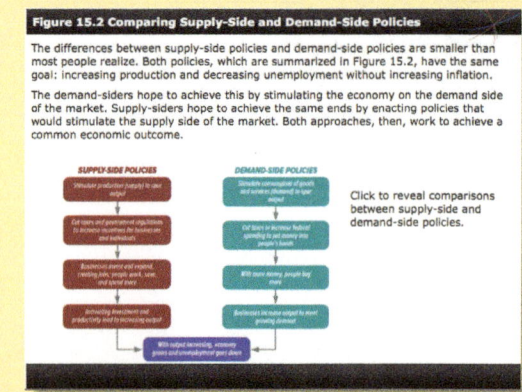

Ronald Reagan's inauguration in 1981 started an emphasis on supply-side economic policies. Reagan moved quickly to deregulate several different industries.

Many economists believe that supply-side policies during both the Reagan and Bush presidencies made the economy less stable: the federal tax structure became less progressive and "safety net" programs were weakened. But we should note that supply-side economic policies are designed to **promote** economic growth, not provide stability.

promote to advance or support

Supply- and Demand-Siders—A Final Comparison

The differences between supply-side policies and demand-side policies are smaller than most people realize. Both policies, which are summarized in **Figure 15.2**, have the same goal: increasing production and decreasing unemployment without increasing inflation.

The demand-siders hope to achieve this by stimulating the economy on the demand side of the market. Supply-siders hope to achieve the same ends by enacting policies that would stimulate the supply side of the market. Both approaches, then, work to achieve a common economic outcome.

✓ **READING PROGRESS CHECK**

Interpreting What are the main goals of supply-side economists?

LESSON 2 REVIEW

Reviewing Vocabulary
1. *Explaining* What does the Laffer curve show?
2. *Describing* What effect does deregulation have on an industry? Specifically, what effect did deregulation of the airline industry have on airfares?

Using Your Notes
3. *Explaining* How would a supply-sider explain how reducing taxes would increase revenue?

Answering the Guiding Questions
4. *Explaining* In what ways are supply-side and demand-side policies different?

5. *Explaining* How does increasing supply help improve the economy?

Writing About Economics
6. *Argument* A friend declared that the biggest problem limiting our country's economic prosperity is the continued application of supply-side economic policy. Make a case for supply-side policy.

CHAPTER 15, LESSON 2
Supply-Side Policies

V Visual Skills

Creating a political cartoon about deregulation
Have students draw a cartoon illustrating one or more of the concepts related to supply-side economics. Inform students that they may include relevant people (Reagan, for example) or events (savings and loan deregulation, for example) in their cartoons. **Verbal/Linguistic, Visual/Spatial**

C Critical Thinking Skills

Comparing demand-side and supply-side policies
Ask: *How are supply-side policies and demand-side policies similar?* (Both may use tax cuts, both intend for people to spend more money, and both have the goal of creating economic growth through higher output and lower unemployment.)

CLOSE & REFLECT

Expressing opinions on supply-side economics
Have students write an opinion essay stating whether they support the idea of using supply-side economics, and give details of its successes or failures to support their opinions. **Verbal/Linguistic**

LESSON 2 REVIEW ANSWERS

Reviewing Vocabulary
1. The hypothetical relationship between federal income tax rates and tax revenues
2. By relaxing or removing government regulations, the industry is free to operate as it chooses with less government oversight. Deregulation of the airline industry resulted in lower airfares.

Using Your Notes
3. Reducing taxes would stimulate additional business activity, leading to greater production and higher tax collections.

Answering the Guiding Questions
4. Under supply-side economics, the government's role in the economy is limited. With demand-side economics, the role of the government is expanded.
5. Smaller government and lower tax rates would stimulate the economy by leaving more money in the hands of consumers and business who would spend the money on consumer products and expansion, thereby initiating more economic growth.

Writing About Economics
6. Students should demonstrate how lower taxes, smaller government, and deregulation of business could encourage economic growth.

ANSWERS, p. 449

✓ **READING PROGRESS CHECK** Lower taxes and less government regulation, increased investing and business expansion, more jobs and more consumer spending, increased economic productivity and economic growth, less unemployment

CHAPTER 15, LESSON 3
Macroeconomic Equilibrium

ENGAGE

C Critical Thinking Skills

🔔 **Evaluating equilibrium** **Ask:** Have you ever experienced one of those rare moments when you feel completely satisfied and do not want to change anything that you are doing? Tell students that this is called a "state of equilibrium," and in this lesson they will find out how the economy, too, occasionally reaches a state of equilibrium. **Intrapersonal**

English Language Proficiency

Beginning As you read portions of the text aloud, ask questions with one-word answers to identify areas in the text that are confusing to students. Help students by asking and writing single-word questions that are aimed at clarifying comprehension.

ANSWERS, p. 450

ESSENTIAL QUESTION ACTIVITY

Remind students to include the proposal, supporters' rationale for the proposal, criticism for the proposal, and whether the proposal was ultimately adopted.
TAKING NOTES
Lower energy prices
Lower interest rates
Lower production costs and higher labor productivity

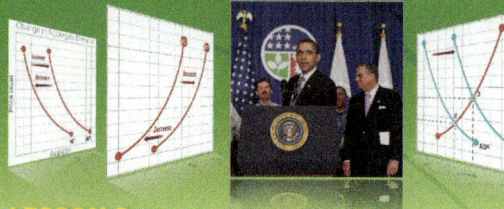
Interact with these digital assets and others in lesson 3
✓ INTERACTIVE GRAPH
  The Economy in Equilibrium
✓ SLIDESHOW
  Great Recession of 2008–2009
✓ SELF-CHECK QUIZ
✓ VIDEO

networks
TRY IT YOURSELF ONLINE

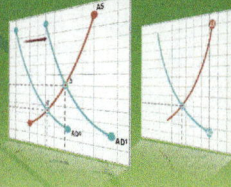

LESSON 3
Macroeconomic Equilibrium

Reading Help Desk

Academic Vocabulary
- framework
- unduly

Content Vocabulary
- macroeconomics
- equilibrium price
- aggregate supply
- aggregate supply curve
- aggregate demand
- aggregate demand curve
- macroeconomic equilibrium

TAKING NOTES:

Key Ideas and Details
ACTIVITY As you read, complete the graphic organizer below by listing at least three factors that could lead to an increase in aggregate supply.

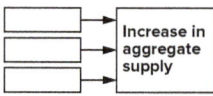

ESSENTIAL QUESTION

C How do we know if macroeconomic equilibrium has been achieved?

The Great Recession in 2008–2009 was the worst economic downturn the United States had seen since the 1930s. And it could have been worse. Many economists believe that we just missed "the big one"—another Great Depression.

In a severe economic downturn—a bad recession or depression—prices fall. Stocks, bonds, real estate, and commodities like oil all become cheaper. Despite the opportunity for investment, firms and consumers are often reluctant to take advantage of these low prices for fear of what might happen next. Consumers may be afraid of losing their jobs. Companies may fear lower profits. But the tendency not to invest or spend but simply pile up money can cause demand and prices to fall even further.

In such times, many people look to government intervention to halt the downward spiral. During the Great Recession, politicians and business leaders put forward different proposals about how the government could help set the economy on the right track.

Use Internet news sites to research one of these proposals. How did its supporters believe their plan would help end the recession? What criticism did the plan receive? Was it ultimately adopted by lawmakers?

Aggregate Supply

GUIDING QUESTION *How is the aggregate supply curve for the economy related to the supply curves of individual producers?*

Macroeconomics focuses on the economy as a whole and decision making by large units. It uses ideas you've studied before—supply and demand. When we study specific markets, supply and demand determine the

---

networks **Online Teaching Options**

BELLRINGER
Macroeconomic Equilibrium

Understanding equilibrium price Have students look at the supply and demand curves in the Bellringer. **Ask: Where is the equilibrium price located on these curves?** *(at the intersection of the curves)* Have students brainstorm reasons why equilibrium pricing is so difficult to achieve. **Verbal/Linguistic**

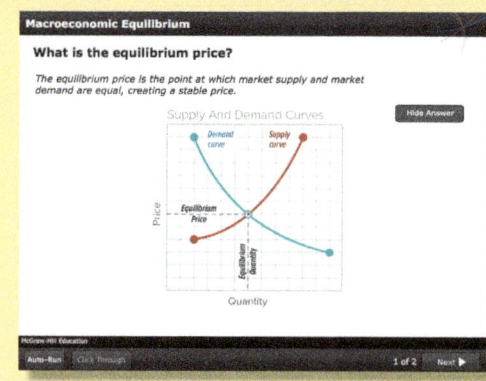

FIGURE 15.3

THE AGGREGATE SUPPLY CURVE

The aggregate supply curve shows the amount of real GDP that would be produced at various price levels. An increase in aggregate supply occurs when production cost decreases for all individual producers. When economists use 2 curves to show changes in aggregate supply, they label the first curve AS^0 and the second AS^1.

▶ **CRITICAL THINKING**
Economic Analysis What causes a decrease in aggregate supply?

Change in Aggregate Supply

connected.mcgraw-hill.com

---

equilibrium price and how much is produced. When we study the economy as a whole, supply and demand work in much the same way.

The Aggregate Supply Curve

In a previous chapter, supply was defined as the amount of a particular product companies will offer for sale at all possible prices. When analyzing the economy as a whole, economists like to look at **aggregate supply**, the total value of goods and services that all firms would produce, in a specific period of time, at various price levels. Note that the *price level* includes the price of everything produced in the economy. The word *price*, by contrast, refers to just one good or service.

Over one year, assuming all production takes place within a country's borders, aggregate supply is the same as gross domestic product, or GDP.

The concept of aggregate supply assumes that the money supply is fixed and the price level stays the same during the period. If the price level changes, firms are likely to adjust their output, which leads to a different GDP. If it were somehow possible to keep adjusting the price level to observe how total output changed, we could then construct an **aggregate supply curve**, which shows the amount of real GDP that would be produced at various price levels.

macroeconomics the branch of economic theory focused on the economy as a whole and decision making by large units, such as governments and unions

equilibrium price price when quantity supplied equals quantity demanded; price that clears the market

aggregate supply the total value of all goods and services that all firms would produce in a specific period of time at various price levels

aggregate supply curve hypothetical curve showing different levels of real GDP that would be produced at various price levels

---

FIGURE 15.4

AGGREGATE DEMAND CURVE

The aggregate demand curve shows the amount of real GDP the economy would demand at all possible price levels. Aggregate demand, like aggregate supply, can either increase or decrease. When economists use two curves to label demand, they label the first AD^0 and the second AD^1.

▶ **CRITICAL THINKING**
Economic Analysis In what ways is the aggregate demand curve similar to an individual demand curve?

Change in Aggregate Demand

connected.mcgraw-hill.com

Fiscal Policy 451

GRAPHS

Aggregate Supply Curve

Interpreting graphs showing aggregate supply changes Have students explore Figure 15.3. Review with students the factors of production—land, labor, capital. Explain that an increase in "cost" of these factors causes the aggregate supply curve to shift to the left. Ask students to give specific examples of each factor. **Logical/Mathematical**

Figure 15.3 The Aggregate Supply Curve

Figure 15.3 shows how an aggregate supply curve for the whole economy might look. Like the supply curve of an individual firm or the market supply curve, it slopes upward from left to right. To distinguish the aggregate supply curve from other supply curves, it is labeled AS.

In Figure 15.3, note that the vertical axis of the graph is labeled "Price level" rather than just "Price," as you have seen in earlier chapters. Economists often use aggregate measures like the price level rather than a single price to better explain changes in the economy. Finally, note that the horizontal axis is labeled "Real GDP," the value of all goods and services produced. Click twice to see the change in Aggregate Supply and learn more.

Aggregate supply, like the supply of an individual firm or the supply of a single product, can increase or decrease. It tends to go up when the cost of production declines. For example, when energy prices fall, most, if not all, firms will produce more, and real GDP rises. This increase in output would happen at all price levels, so it would shift the original aggregate supply curve AS^0 to the right, creating AS^1.

Increases in the cost of production tend to decrease aggregate supply. The cause could be higher oil prices or interest rates, or less productive labor. Any increase in cost that leads firms to offer fewer goods and services for sale at each and every price would shift the aggregate supply curve to the left.

CHAPTER 15, LESSON 3
Macroeconomic Equilibrium

TEACH & ASSESS

W Writing Skills

Defining *aggregate* Instruct students to write a definition of the word *aggregate* based on how it is used in the text. Next, have students look up the dictionary definition of the word *aggregate* and compare it with their own definitions. *(collectively, total)* Finally, ask students to write a sentence using the word *aggregate* to refer to something other than supply or demand. *(Possible sentence: The company's aggregate profits this quarter exceeded expectations.)* **ELL** Verbal/Linguistic

R Reading Skills

Understanding price level and aggregate supply
Ask: **Why is the term *price level* used instead of *price* when discussing aggregate supply?** *(because price level includes everything produced in the economy; price refers to just one good or service)* **What is another way of looking at aggregate supply, assuming all "supply" occurs within a country's borders?** *(gross domestic product, or GDP)* Verbal/Linguistic

C Critical Thinking Skills

Assessing the aggregate demand curve Ask: **Why is the aggregate demand curve a hypothetical curve?** *(because desire, ability, and willingness to purchase a product are abstract concepts that are not easily quantified, especially across an entire population)* Have students name factors in purchasing a product that are not abstract. Verbal/Linguistic

---

ANSWERS, p. 451

CRITICAL THINKING

Decreases in aggregate supply are caused by factors that increase the cost of production for individual firms; for example, higher oil prices, higher interest rates, lower labor productivity.

CRITICAL THINKING

The AD curve and individual demand curve are both downward-sloping. They are different in the way the axes are labeled. The individual demand curve vertical axis represents various prices of a single product, whereas the AD's vertical axis represents various price levels. The horizontal axis for individual demand represents various quantities of a single good, whereas the horizontal axis for the AD curve represents various levels of total output.

Fiscal Policy 451

CHAPTER 15, LESSON 3
Macroeconomic Equilibrium

C1 Critical Thinking Skills

Analyzing causes of increases in aggregate supply Have students identify factors from the text that increase aggregate supply. *(declining costs of production, declining interest rates, more productive labor)* Have them consider at least three additional factors that might increase aggregate supply. Ask them to think about actions or activities that would cause lower costs of inputs. *(increased immigration, decreased regulation, lower taxes)*
Logical/Mathematical

C2 Critical Thinking Skills

Relating underemployment to aggregate supply Point out that underemployment is a growing problem for the U.S. economy. In this situation, workers are employed, but they have jobs that demand fewer skills and less training than they possess. Examples of underemployed workers include carpenters or bricklayers who work as servers at fast-food restaurants, and taxicab drivers who have doctoral degrees. Ask students to give examples of underemployment in their community and explain the impact that it has on aggregate supply. *(Examples will vary. Aggregate supply will decrease because resources are not fully utilized.)*

W Writing Skills

Creating questions about aggregate demand Instruct students to write a five-question quiz about aggregate demand. After they finish writing their quizzes, ask students to write an explanation for why they chose to ask each question. **Verbal/Linguistic, Logical/Mathematical**

ANSWERS, p. 452

✓ **READING PROGRESS CHECK** The aggregate supply economic measure allows economists to study and better explain the economy as a whole.

CRITICAL THINKING
The price level comes down.

Figure 15.3 shows how an aggregate supply curve for the whole economy might look. As does the supply curve of an individual firm or the market supply curve, it slopes upward from left to right. To distinguish the aggregate supply curve from other supply curves, it is labeled **AS**.

In Figure 15.3, note that the vertical axis of the graph is labeled "Price level" rather than just "Price," as you have seen in earlier chapters. Economists often use aggregate measures like the price level rather than a single price to better explain changes in the economy.

Finally, note that the horizontal axis is labeled "Real GDP," the value of all goods and services produced.

Changes in Aggregate Supply

C1 Aggregate supply, like the supply of an individual firm or the supply of a single product, can increase or decrease. It tends to go up when the cost of production declines. For example, when energy prices fall, most, if not all, firms will produce more, and real GDP rises. This increase in output would happen at all price levels, so it would shift the original aggregate supply curve AS^0 to the right, creating AS^1.

C2 Increases in the cost of production tend to decrease aggregate supply. The cause could be higher oil prices or interest rates, or less productive labor. Any increase in cost that leads firms to offer fewer goods and services for sale at each and every price would shift the aggregate supply curve to the left.

✓ **READING PROGRESS CHECK**

Identifying What is the benefit of the aggregate supply economic measure?

aggregate demand the total value of all goods and services demanded at different price levels

aggregate demand curve hypothetical curve showing different levels of real GDP that would be purchased at various price levels

W Aggregate Demand

GUIDING QUESTION *How is aggregate demand related to individual demand?*

In a previous chapter, you learned that demand is the desire, ability, and willingness to purchase a product. If it were possible to add up everyone's demand for every good and service in the economy, we would have a measure of total demand. Economists call this concept **aggregate demand**. You can also think of this number as the total value of all goods and services that would be bought at different price levels.

The Aggregate Demand Curve

Like aggregate supply, aggregate demand can be represented as a graph, and it can either increase or decrease. It shares many similarities with individual demand, so the concept is easy to understand.

The **aggregate demand curve**, labeled **AD**, appears in **Figure 15.4**. It represents the sum of all consumer, business, government, and net foreign demand at various price levels. We measure how much people would buy at every possible price level in terms of real GDP. The curve slopes downward to the right as do the individual and the market demand curves.

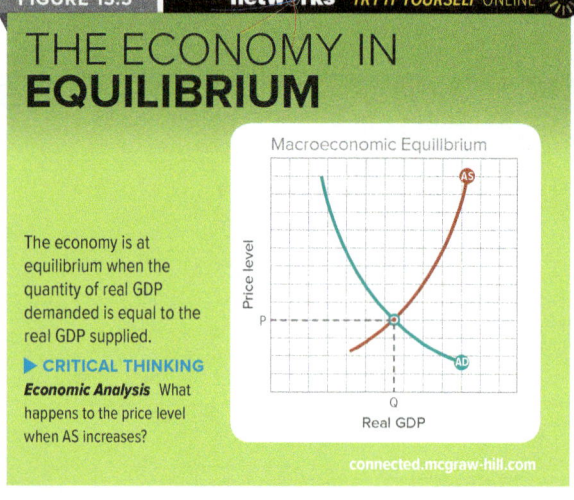

FIGURE 15.5 networks TRY IT YOURSELF ONLINE

THE ECONOMY IN EQUILIBRIUM

The economy is at equilibrium when the quantity of real GDP demanded is equal to the real GDP supplied.

▶ **CRITICAL THINKING**
Economic Analysis What happens to the price level when AS increases?

452

---

networks Online Teaching Options

GRAPHS

Economy in Equilibrium

Describing a graphic representation of macroeconomic equilibrium Have students explore Figure 15.5. Then have them write a summary of how the graph shows changes in the economy due to periods of inflation and recession, defining the term *macroeconomic equilibrium*, and explaining why it is difficult to achieve. **Verbal/Linguistic, Logical/Mathematical**

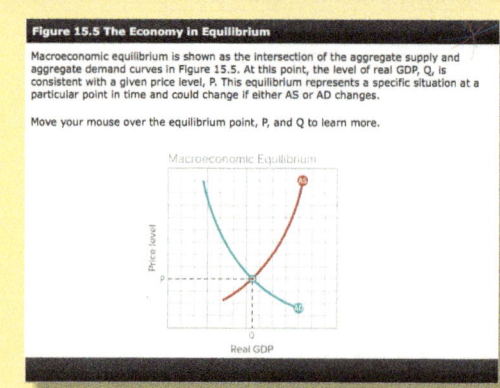

Figure 15.5 The Economy in Equilibrium

Macroeconomic equilibrium is shown as the intersection of the aggregate supply and aggregate demand curves in Figure 15.5. At this point, the level of real GDP, Q, is consistent with a given price level, P. This equilibrium represents a specific situation at a particular point in time and could change if either AS or AD changes.

Move your mouse over the equilibrium point, P, and Q to learn more.

Changes in Aggregate Demand

Aggregate demand can increase or decrease depending on certain factors. For example, if consumers decide to spend more and save less, the increase in consumer spending also increases aggregate demand, shifting the original aggregate demand curve AD^0 to the right to form the new aggregate demand curve AD^1.

A decrease in aggregate demand can occur if the same factors act in an opposite manner. If people were to spend less and save more, the aggregate demand curve would shift to the left. Higher taxes and lower transfer payments could also reduce aggregate spending. Such decisions shift the aggregate demand curve to the left because all sectors of the economy collectively buy less GDP at all price levels.

✓ **READING PROGRESS CHECK**

Comparing How do changes in AS and AD relate to the changes in individual supply and demand curves?

Macroeconomic Equilibrium

GUIDING QUESTION *What is macroeconomic equilibrium?*

Aggregate supply and demand curves are useful concepts because together, they provide a **framework** to analyze how proposed policies might affect growth and price stability. They help us understand inflation and recessions and suggest how the economy might change. They also help us understand how a particular policy might work. However, they can't provide exact predictions.

framework point of reference

macroeconomic equilibrium amount of real GDP consistent with a given price level; intersection of aggregate supply and aggregate demand

Macroequilibrium with AS-AD

Macroeconomic equilibrium is shown as the intersection of the aggregate supply and aggregate demand curves in **Figure 15.5**. The level of real GDP, **Q**, is consistent with a given price level, **P**. This equilibrium represents a specific situation at a particular point in time and could change if either AS or AD changes.

AS and AD help us explain, and understand, two of the major problems in macroeconomics—inflation and recessions. For example, inflation is a steadily increasing price level, which is measured on the vertical axis. A recession or even a depression is represented by steady decreases in real GDP, which is measured on the horizontal axis.

Economic policymakers must decide whether to stimulate changes in AD (demand side) or AS (supply side) in order to keep the economy growing and stable.

Demand-Side Policies Affect AD

These concepts help us see the effect of demand-side policy. **Figure 15.6** shows a single aggregate supply curve and two aggregate demand curves. When aggregate demand is weak, the economy would be at point **a**, where AD^0 intersects AS. Expansionary demand-side fiscal policies such as increases in government spending or tax reductions could shift aggregate demand to AD^1 and move the economy to point **b**, where both real GDP and the price level are higher.

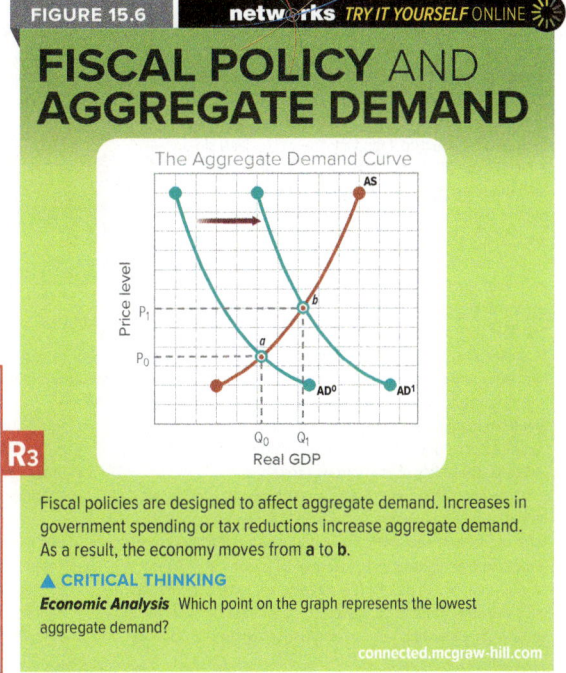

FIGURE 15.6

FISCAL POLICY AND AGGREGATE DEMAND

Fiscal policies are designed to affect aggregate demand. Increases in government spending or tax reductions increase aggregate demand. As a result, the economy moves from **a** to **b**.

▲ **CRITICAL THINKING**

Economic Analysis Which point on the graph represents the lowest aggregate demand?

CHAPTER 15, LESSON 3
Macroeconomic Equilibrium

C Critical Thinking Skills

Predicting changes in aggregate demand Ask: **How would increased competition in the economy likely affect aggregate demand?** *(Increased competition would lower prices and thus increase aggregate demand.)*

R1 Reading Skills

Comparing aggregate demand and the market demand curve Have students identify three causes of a decrease in aggregate demand. *(saving more and spending less, higher taxes, lower transfer payments)* Ask students to recall the factors that cause a change in the market demand curve. *(changes in consumer income, consumer tastes, price of related goods, consumer expectations, and the total number of consumers)* Discuss which factors create both a decrease in aggregate demand and the market demand curve. *(changes in consumer income, consumer expectations)*

R2 Reading Skills

Relating inflation and recessions to macro equilibrium Ask: **How is inflation shown on a graph combining aggregate demand and aggregate supply?** *(Inflation is a steadily increasing price level, which is measured on the y-axis.)* **How is a recession shown on a graph combining aggregate demand and aggregate supply?** *(A recession is represented by steady decreases in real GDP, which is the quantity measured on the x-axis.)*

R3 Reading Skills

Understanding how demand-side policies affect AD Ask: **How does increased government spending affect the aggregate demand (AD) curve?** *(It shifts the AD curve to the right, increasing aggregate demand to a higher level of real GDP.)* **How does increased aggregate demand affect the equilibrium price?** *(Assuming that aggregate supply remains the same, the equilibrium price rises to a higher level, signifying inflation.)*

ANSWERS, p. 453

✓ **READING PROGRESS CHECK** Students should make clear that aggregate supply and demand measure changes across every sector of an entire economy, whereas individual supply and demand relate to one specific sector, consumer, firm, product, etc.

CRITICAL THINKING

Point **a** represents the lowest aggregate demand.

GRAPHS

Fiscal Policy and Aggregate Demand

Exploring the benefits and drawbacks of shifting aggregate demand Have students explore Figure 15.6 showing the effect of fiscal policy on aggregate demand. Then have them write a paragraph describing a benefit of demand-side fiscal policy shown by the graph, and what the drawback might be.
Logical/Mathematical

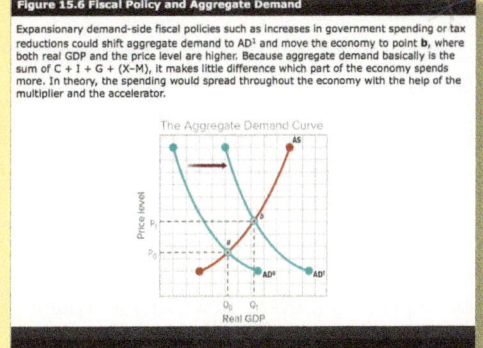

Figure 15.6 Fiscal Policy and Aggregate Demand

Expansionary demand-side fiscal policies such as increases in government spending or tax reductions could shift aggregate demand to AD^1 and move the economy to point **b**, where both real GDP and the price level are higher. Because aggregate demand basically is the sum of C + I + G + (X−M), it makes little difference which part of the economy spends more. In theory, the spending would spread throughout the economy with the help of the multiplier and the accelerator.

CHAPTER 15, LESSON 3
Macroeconomic Equilibrium

C Critical Thinking Skills

Understanding AD and AS Write the following on the board: Increase in Aggregate Supply, Decrease in Aggregate Supply, Increase in Aggregate Demand, Decrease in Aggregate Demand. Call on students to identify factors that would cause these four situations to occur and note their responses under the appropriate heading. Then ask students to select one factor from each heading and illustrate the shift of the curve graphically.

R Reading Skills

Understanding how supply-side policies affect AS
Ask: **How might lower taxes affect the aggregate supply (AS) curve?** *(Lower taxes, a reduced cost of input, shifts the AS curve to the right, increasing aggregate supply to a higher level of real GDP.)*

Because aggregate demand basically is the sum of C + I + G + (X − M), it makes little difference which part of the economy spends more. In theory, the spending will spread throughout the economy with the help of the multiplier and the accelerator.

For example, if a new fiscal policy caused the aggregate demand curve AD to shift to the right, the new equilibrium would land at a higher level of real GDP and prices. This is one of the dilemmas facing economic policy makers—how to make real GDP grow without prompting rises in the inflation rate, or in other words, **unduly** increasing the price level.

unduly too much

Supply-Side Policies Affect AS

The aggregate supply and demand curves can also be used to illustrate the impact of supply-side policies. As **Figure 15.7** shows, when aggregate supply is low, the economy is at point **a**. This is the point where the original aggregate supply curve AS^0 intersects with the aggregate demand curve AD.

THE GLOBAL ECONOMY & YOU

The National Debt

A government that spends more money than it collects must cover this deficit, or budget shortcoming, with a new source of revenue. Typically, budget deficits in the United States have been caused by wars, recessions, and increased spending on entitlement programs such as Medicare.

To raise money to pay the government's obligations, politicians could vote to increase taxes, but this decision would be unpopular and would likely slow growth. As an alternative, the Federal Reserve could print more money and simply give it to the government, but this option is also undesirable, because it would lead to high inflation and price increases.

As a third way to raise revenues, the United States and other governments often issue debt. Just like corporations, governments raise money by selling bonds in the credit market. Bonds, like IOUs, are a promise to repay a certain amount, plus interest, at a later date. Investors who buy bonds either hold them and wait to be repaid, or resell the bonds to other investors to make a profit. In the free market, the value of bonds goes up and down depending on many factors, including the ability of the borrower to repay.

Ordinary citizens, companies, and people all over the world—including foreign governments—hold U.S. government debt in the form of Treasury securities. Currently, Japan and China are the two largest foreign holders, with just over $1 trillion each. These amounts can make people feel uneasy, but most economists consider some debt to be a good thing for nations. Debt ensures stability by allowing crucial government programs to continue

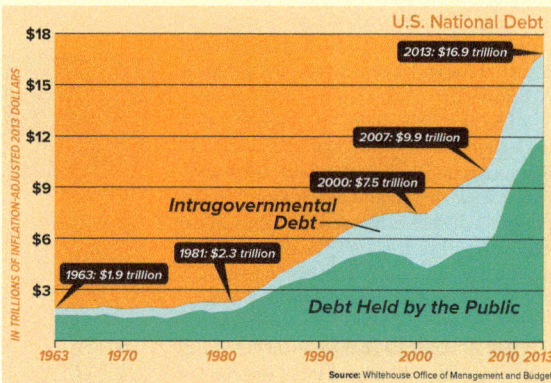

▲ CRITICAL THINKING
Identifying Cause and Effect How could U.S. government debt affect trade relations with other nations?

during hard times. It also increases partnerships between nations that might otherwise become enemies if it were not for their financial relationships.

On the other hand, if a government takes on too much debt that it cannot repay, it might default on its bonds. A government default shakes investor confidence and can lead to financial crisis. Economists debate the issue, but no one really knows what level of national debt is sustainable. To date, the United States has never defaulted on its Treasury bonds.

---

networks Online Teaching Options

GRAPHS

Supply Side Policies and Aggregate Supply

Interpreting changes in equilibrium with changes in aggregate supply Have students explore Figure 15.7 showing changes in aggregate supply and the resulting change in equilibrium. Then have them explain what could possibly prevent the equilibrium point from being lower. **Logical/Mathematical**

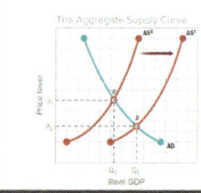

ANSWERS, p. 454

CRITICAL THINKING
Student answers may indicate that national debt tends to strengthen trade relations between countries because the debtor and creditor become mutually dependent. However, students may also point out that a government default could lead to financial crisis and lower trade overall.

If supply-side policies succeed, more output is produced at every price level. The aggregate supply curve shifts to AS¹, and the point of equilibrium moves to point **b**. As long as aggregate demand doesn't fall, real output will grow, and the price level will come down.

Maintaining a Healthy Equilibrium

The economy needs both demand- and supply-side policies. While both strategies have their advantages, a combination of the two is usually best.

For example, some of the most effective fiscal policies used to prevent recessions are demand-side automatic stabilizers. They act quickly, because the legislation has already been approved. If the stabilizers can cushion an early decline in real GDP, we can avoid more aggressive demand-side policies later on.

Effective supply-side policies such as less regulation and more efficient production can, simultaneously, help the economy expand without increasing the price level—the situation shown in Figure 15.7. Less government intervention also means that people are less dependent on federal spending.

A stable macroeconomic equilibrium is difficult to achieve, but we should try. The benefits of higher real GDP without more inflation are huge.

✓ **READING PROGRESS CHECK**

Explaining How does the macroeconomic equilibrium work? How is it used?

FIGURE 15.7

SUPPLY SIDE POLICIES AND AGGREGATE SUPPLY

Supply-side policies are designed to increase aggregate supply through decreased government spending and involvement as well as lower taxes.

◀ **CRITICAL THINKING**
Economic Analysis What happens to the price level when the aggregate supply curve shifts to the right?

LESSON 3 REVIEW

Reviewing Vocabulary
1. *Identifying* What is macroeconomics concerned with?
2. *Explaining* How is aggregate supply related to GDP?

Using Your Notes
Use the information you jotted down in the graphic organizer to answer this question.

3. *Speculating* Of the three factors you found that could lead to an increase in aggregate supply, which do you think would be the easiest one for the government to influence? Explain your answer.

Answering the Guiding Questions

4. *Summarizing* Why do economists find aggregate supply, aggregate demand, and macroeconomic equilibrium to be useful concepts?

5. *Identifying* What happens to the aggregate supply curve during a period of high inflation?

6. *Explaining* How does the concept of macroeconomic equilibrium relate to the goals of policy makers?

7. *Contrasting* Which type of economic policy, supply-side or demand-side, do you think has the most advantages and fewest disadvantages? Explain your answer.

Writing About Economics

8. *Applying* Imagine you are an adviser to the president, and the economy is headed into recession. Which policy changes would you recommend to halt the downturn? Why is your plan the best? Write a memo explaining your recommendations in terms of aggregate supply and aggregate demand. Be sure to use correct grammar, spelling, and punctuation.

CHAPTER 15, LESSON 3
Macroeconomic Equilibrium

R **Reading Skills**

Finding real examples of AS and AD Direct students to scan the business pages of a newspaper or online news source for stories that detail conditions that might cause a change in aggregate supply or aggregate demand. Have students summarize the articles they find, focusing on how aggregate supply or aggregate demand will change.

CLOSE & REFLECT

Creating policy changes Have students design a policy change they feel would bring the country's economy closer to macroeconomic equilibrium. Have them create a brochure that describes how their policy change would be different from past policy changes, and what benefits it would bring to the economy. Remind students to use standard grammar and sentence structure when creating their brochures.

ANSWERS, p. 455

CRITICAL THINKING
The price level comes down.

✓ **READING PROGRESS CHECK**
Macroeconomic equilibrium is the intersection of aggregate supply and aggregate demand; it refers to the amount of real GDP that can be produced at a given price level. Economists use this measure to study the impact of policies and to maintain a stable, healthy economy.

LESSON 3 REVIEW ANSWERS

Reviewing Vocabulary

1. Macroeconomics is the part of economics concerned with the economy as a whole and decision making by large units.

2. Like GDP, aggregate supply measures the total value of goods and services produced by all firms in a specific period of time. If the period is exactly one year and all production took place within a country's borders, then aggregate supply would be equal to GDP.

Using Your Notes

3. Students might point to taxes as the easiest factor for a government to influence. However, any response is acceptable as long as the factor would increase aggregate supply and students justify their choices.

Answering the Guiding Questions

4. Economists find these concepts useful because they allow them to study the impact of policies on the entire economy.

5. An increase in demand across all sectors of the economy will shift the aggregate demand curve to the right. Unless the aggregate supply curve also shifts, this change will result in higher prices and inflation.

6. Students should indicate that policy makers seek to achieve macroeconomic equilibrium in a way that grows GDP without causing excess inflation.

7. Either supply-side or demand-side is acceptable, so long as students highlight the advantages of their chosen policy and support their answer with reasoning. Students may also mention that a balance of supply- and demand-side policies is most effective.

Writing About Economics

8. Students may recommend supply- or demand-side policies, or a blend, so long as they accurately describe these policies and their effects on aggregate supply and aggregate demand.

CHAPTER 15
Debate

ENGAGE

C Critical Thinking Skills

Identifying types of debt Have students brainstorm types of debt that the government carries. Then ask students to create a table listing three types of debt in the first column and a description of the party to whom the money is owed in the second column. **Logical/Mathematical**

TEACH & ASSESS

R1 Reading Skills

Taking notes on each side of the debt debate
Ask students to create a T-chart graphic organizer to take notes about each side of the Debate. Direct them to write notes for the Yes position on the left side of the chart, and notes for the No position on the right side of the chart. Have them write bulleted phrases describing the opinion expressed for each position, a summary of the quote given for each position, and examples to support each side of the argument. Remind students to cite their sources. **Verbal/Linguistic**

R2 Reading Skills

Summarizing sides of the debt debate
Have students read the two sides of the Debate about government debt. Then have them write a short summary of each side of the Debate in their own words. **Verbal/Linguistic**

Making Connections

Effects on the Community After students read both sides of the debt Debate, have them write one benefit and one drawback to their local community that would result from each side's claim about how government debt should be handled.
Verbal/Linguistic, Logical/Mathematical

Debates

C Should the government make major changes in federal spending and taxation to deal with the growing national debt?

R1

For most of American history, the federal government has spent more than it has gathered in taxes. To cover the shortfall, officially called the "deficit," we can raise money in a number of ways. The government can sell bonds called treasury bills, which function as IOUs. It pays interest on this debt to people who buy the bonds and must also pay back the full value of the bill after a set period of time.

Businesses and governments often carry some debt, which can help the economy grow when it is managed well. But as the total sum of the United States' public debt from Treasury bonds and other forms of borrowing approaches nearly 20 trillion dollars, people have grown worried. They wonder whether the United States is headed for a crisis and one day may fail to make payments, or default.

R2

Some economists say that the debt problem may grow too large to solve unless quick action is taken. Others say that big tax increases and spending cuts would do more economic harm than good.

456

YES The national debt...

- REQUIRES MORE TAXPAYER MONEY TO MAKE INTEREST PAYMENTS
- WEAKENS THE VALUE OF THE DOLLAR AROUND THE WORLD
- WILL EVENTUALLY GROW LARGER THAN THE GDP
- SLOWS ECONOMIC GROWTH

> I have long argued that paying down the national debt is beneficial for the economy: it keeps interest rates lower than they otherwise would be and frees savings to finance increases in the capital stock, thereby boosting productivity and real incomes.
>
> —Alan Greenspan, former Federal Reserve Board Chairman

▲ The national debt clock in New York City.

---

networks   Online Teaching Options

DEBATE

Debate: Should the government make major changes in federal spending and taxation to deal with the growing national debt?

Explaining positions regarding debt Have students work in pairs to read the two positions on government debt. Then have each student choose a different side of the Debate. Ask students to create a dialogue with each other, using their chosen positions to direct their thoughts on how to handle increasing government debt. Have them write their dialogue and present it to the class aloud. **Verbal/Linguistic, Interpersonal**

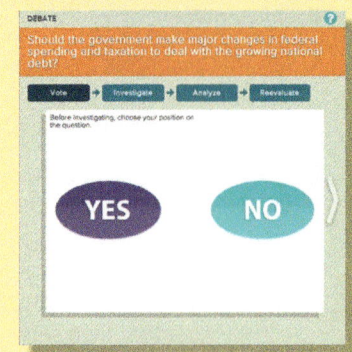

NO The national debt...

- FINANCES ECONOMIC **GROWTH**
- CAN BE MANAGED **WITHOUT** MAKING **DRASTIC** CHANGES
- PAYS FOR **CRITICAL** GOVERNMENT PROGRAMS
- **HAS NOT** PUSHED FOREIGN INVESTORS **AWAY** FROM THE DOLLAR

> National income will be greater tomorrow than it is today because government has had the courage to borrow idle capital and put it and idle labor to work.... Our national debt after all is an internal debt owed not only by the Nation but to the Nation. If our children have to pay interest on it, they will pay that interest to themselves. A reasonable internal debt will not impoverish our children or put the Nation into bankruptcy.

—Franklin D. Roosevelt "Address Before the American Retail Federation, Washington, D.C." May 22, 1939.

▲ Is borrowing money to fund necessary work a bad thing?

networks
TRY IT YOURSELF ONLINE
For an interactive version of this debate go to connected.mcgraw-hill.com

ANALYZING the issue

1. **Analyzing Visuals** How are levels of U.S. public debt tied to significant events like wars and recessions?

2. **Exploring Issues** Some people argue the U.S. government should be required to balance its budget just like an ordinary household. Do you agree? Why or why not?

3. **Evaluating** Which arguments do you find most compelling? Explain your answer.

457

CHAPTER 15
Debate

W Writing Skills

Defending opinions in the debt debate Have students create an oral presentation for the Debate position with which they agree. After students present their opinions to the class, have everyone use sticky notes to vote for the presenter who gave the most compelling argument for each side of the Debate. Tell students to write one reason for their choice on each sticky note. **Verbal/Linguistic, Intrapersonal**

CLOSE & REFLECT

C Critical Thinking Skills

Predicting the effects of actions to reduce debt Have students pick one side of the Debate about debt and imagine that all of the solutions this side proposes have been put in place. Have them write a paragraph describing what the economy will be like after these solutions have been enacted. **Verbal/Linguistic, Logical/Mathematical**

GRAPHIC ORGANIZER

Main Idea Chart

Exploring changes to government spending Distribute copies of the graphic organizer. Have students read both sides of the Debate. Then ask them to identify the benefits and drawbacks of government spending cuts. **Ask: What kinds of cuts do you think would be helpful? What kinds of cuts do you think would harm the economy?** *(Cuts that streamline programs to make them more efficient would be helpful; cuts that hurt people's ability to be contributing taxpayers would be harmful.)* Have students list information in the graphic organizer, and then discuss their notes as a class. **Verbal/Linguistic, Logical/Mathematical**

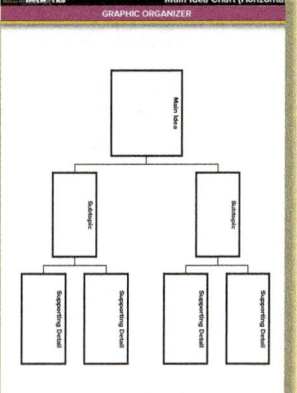

ANSWERS, p. 457

ANALYZING the issue

1. Responses should indicate that levels of U.S. public debt tend to spike during periods of war or recession.
2. Students should take a position and give facts and reasons based on the debate to support their response.
3. Students should summarize an argument made in the debate and explain why they find it compelling.

Fiscal Policy **457**

Chapter 15
Study Guide

W Writing Skills

Simulating Provide students with the following scenario: *The United States is experiencing a severe recession. Nationwide unemployment is at 10 percent, but in some regions it stands at 25 percent. Inflation, however, is running at an annual rate of 3 percent. Consumer and business spending are down. GDP has fallen 5 percent over the last 3 quarters, and government revenues have declined.* Have students select an economic policy—demand-side or supply-side—to bring the United States out of the recession. Direct students to write a brief report detailing and justifying the actions they would take. **Logical/Mathematical**

C Critical Thinking Skills

Analyzing Remind students that both supply-side policies and demand-side policies can impact the macroeconomic equilibrium. **Ask: Which direction would the macroequilibrium point move on the graph if supply-side policies were successful?** *(down and to the right)* **Which direction would the macrequilibrium point move on the graph if demand-side policies were successful?** *(up and to the right)*

STUDY GUIDE

LESSON 1

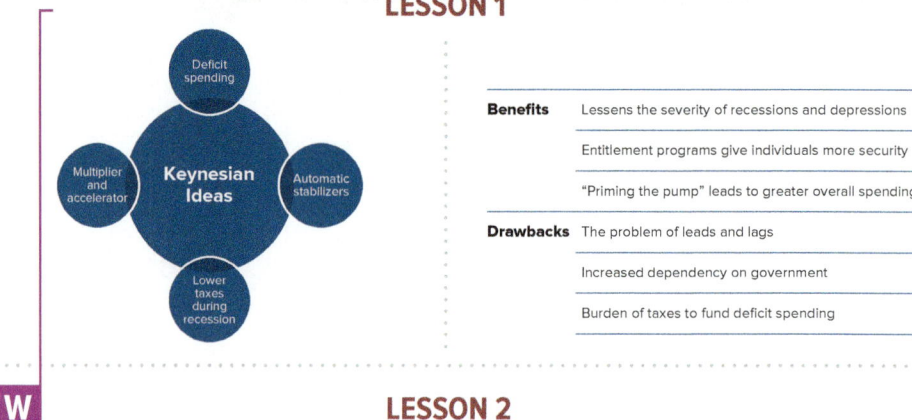

LESSON 2

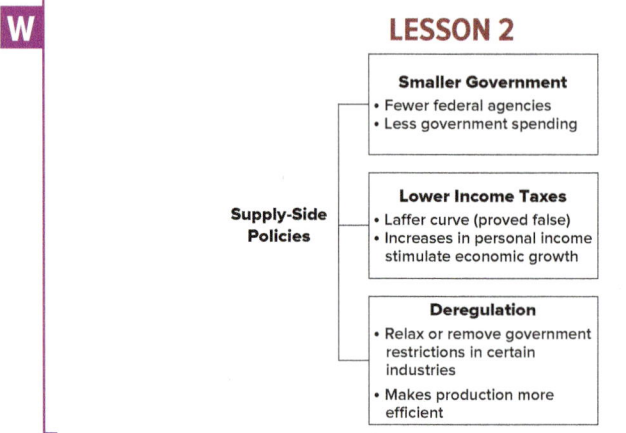

LESSON 3

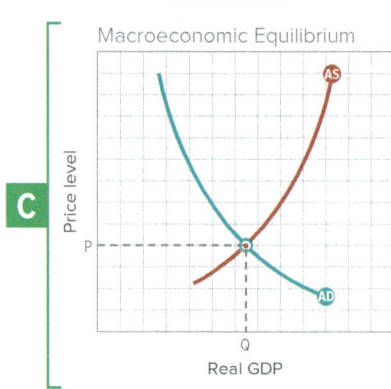

networks Online Teaching Options

WORKSHEET

Enrichment Activity

Examining John Maynard Keynes's demand-side economics
Assign the Enrichment Activity worksheet. Have students read the excerpt from John Maynard Keynes's *General Theory*. Then have them write a list of what Keynes considers to be wasteful loan expenditures on the left side of one page. Tell students to write a list of what Keynes would consider to be useful loan expenditures on the right side of the same page. Have them choose one expenditure from each side of the page to compare and contrast in a one-page essay.

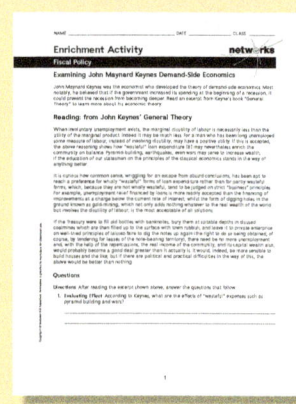

CHAPTER 15 Assessment

Directions: On a separate sheet of paper, answer the questions below. Make sure you read carefully and answer all parts of the questions.

Lesson Review

Lesson 1

1 *Identifying* What is the primary goal of Keynesian economic policies?

2 *Explaining* How could demand-side policies increase people's dependence on government?

Lesson 2

3 *Contrasting* How do supply-side policies differ from demand-side policies?

4 *Identifying* What are some of the shortcomings of supply-side policies?

Lesson 3

5 *Explaining* How is aggregate demand related to individual demand?

6 *Analyzing* Why do macroeconomists use the concepts of aggregate demand and aggregate supply?

7 *Explaining* Why are automatic stabilizers like unemployment insurance some of the most effective fiscal policies in preventing recessions?

Critical Thinking

8 *Analyzing* Why has it been difficult to test key supply-side policies, including reducing the size of government?

9 *Assessing* During a severe recession, your town is considering an increase in property taxes to pay for essential services like schools and fire departments. What effect do you think this policy change will have on demand in the local economy? Explain your answer.

10 *Constructing Arguments* Suppose economists agree that the country has recently entered a recession. To promote growth and end the recession, the president proposes a tax cut for all Americans. Meanwhile, Congress votes for more federal spending on roads and bridges. Write an article for the opinion column in your local newspaper explaining the benefits and drawbacks of each policy, and what you think should be done. Use standard grammar, spelling, sentence structure, and punctuation.

Analyzing Visuals

Use the graph below to answer the following questions about aggregate demand.

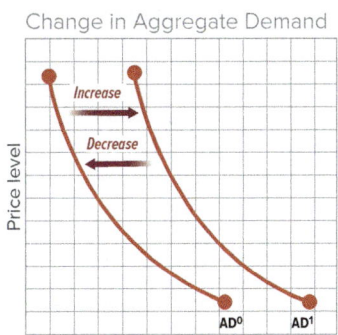

Change in Aggregate Demand

11 *Analyzing Visuals* What change in fiscal policy could explain the change in aggregate demand from AD^0 to AD^1? Explain your answer.

12 *Analyzing Visuals* Which aggregate demand curve represents the higher-performing economy? How can you tell?

ANSWERING THE ESSENTIAL QUESTIONS

Review your answers to the introductory questions at the beginning of each lesson. Then answer the Essential Questions on the basis of what you learned in the chapter. Have your answers changed?

13 *Explaining* How does the government promote price stability, full employment, and economic growth?

14 *Explaining* How do we know if macroeconomic equilibrium has been achieved?

Need Extra Help?

If You've Missed Question	1	2	3	4	5	6	7	8	9	10	11	12	13	14
Go to page	438	442	445	447	452	450	455	447	454	446	451	451	438	453

Chapter 15 Assessment Answers

Lesson Review

Lesson 1

1 The primary goal of Keynesian economic policies is to lower unemployment and stimulate aggregate demand through government spending and taxation.

2 Students should mention the possibility that people could increasingly rely on government measures like transfer payments, rather than their own initiative, to help them when the economy is weak. Additionally, government stimulus that is intended to be temporary may become permanent.

Lesson 2

3 Students may mention the tendency of demand-side policies to increase the scope of government, while supply-side policies seek to decrease it. They may also mention how each type of policy affects aggregate demand or aggregate supply.

4 Students may mention the difficulty politicians have had with actually shrinking the size of government, citing Ronald Reagan as an example. They may also mention the negative consequences of deregulation and the failure of the Laffer Curve.

Lesson 3

5 Aggregate demand is the sum total of goods and services demanded by all individuals, firms, governments, and sectors of the economy. Individual demand is a small component of aggregate demand.

6 The concepts of aggregate demand and aggregate supply allow macroeconomists to better study how policies affect the economy as a whole.

7 Because automatic stabilizers have already been passed into law at the time an economic downturn starts, these fiscal policies do not suffer as much from the problem of lags and leads.

Critical Thinking

8 Students should mention that spending on national defense increased at a time when President Reagan instituted supply-side policies intended to shrink the government.

9 A tax increase will tend to decrease aggregate demand and depress local economic activity even more. Students might mention that this effect could be offset by increased government spending on schools and fire departments.

10 Students may take a variety of positions. In their op-ed they should use economic terminology and display an understanding of the effects each policy will likely have on aggregate supply and aggregate demand.

Analyzing Visuals

11 Any fiscal policy that tends to increase spending across all sectors of the economy could explain the change shown. Examples include a tax decrease or an increase in transfer payments. Students should explain how the policy leads to increased spending by governments, firms, or consumers.

12 The curve labeled AD^1 represents the higher-performing economy because it produces more real GDP at every price level.

Answering the Essential Questions

13 The government uses a variety of supply-side and demand-side policies to promote these goals. Students should say so, and give at least one example of a policy and how it supports one of the goals.

14 A healthy macroeconomic equilibrium has been achieved when GDP output increases without the price level being driven up.

Chapter 15
Assessment Answers

21st Century Skills

15 Students should mention that the Economic Stimulus Act contained a tax rebate for individuals and a temporary change in tax law that benefited businesses. Because the 2008 Stimulus Act dealt exclusively with taxes, students may argue it was a supply-side policy. They could also point to the tax rebate as a Keynesian fiscal stimulus, or they may consider the Act a blended policy, so long as they justify their view with evidence.

16 Students may agree or disagree. They should use economic terminology related to fiscal policy to justify their responses.

17 Students' charts should identify increased government spending, transfer payments, and automatic stablizers as demand-side policies. Shrinking the role of government and deregulation are supply-side policies. Tax policies may be placed in either category, depending on how they are justified.

Building Financial Literacy

18 Students should use economic terminology. They may suggest a variety of ways consumers can plan for a recession, including saving a cushion of cash as a safety net in case of job loss. They may point out that recessions can actually be good times to buy cars, stocks, real estate, or to make other major expenditures, because prices tend to be low.

Analyzing Primary Sources

19 A variety of responses are possible. Students may mention tax revenue and deficit spending. By choosing to spend taxpayer funds to stimulate the economy, the government forgoes other ways in which it could save or invest these funds. On the other hand, if government chooses not to stimulate the economy, a recession could spiral into a depression, leading to a great loss in future tax revenue.

20 Fiscal stimulus is intended to stimulate demand. An increase in aggregate demand, without a commensurate increase in aggregate supply, will raise the price level and result in inflation.

21 Students should indicate that a targeted stimulus will provide resources to people who most need them and who will spend the stimulus funds rather than save them. A variety of targeted policies are possible, including unemployment insurance and tax rebates for people with low incomes.

CHAPTER 15 Assessment

Directions: On a separate sheet of paper, answer the questions below. Make sure you read carefully and answer all parts of the questions.

21st Century Skills

15 Understanding Relationships Among Events Research the Economic Stimulus Act of 2008, which was designed to end the most recent recession. In a few paragraphs, analyze the strategies in the legislation and whether they were supply- or demand-side policy.

16 Identifying Perspectives and Differing Interpretations Your friend listens to a radio talk show host who claims the government should have no role in managing the economy. According to your friend, the host says the failure of communism proves governments make poor economic decisions. What would you say in response?

17 Creating and Using Charts Create a chart showing the different ways that economists believe governments can stimulate economic growth. Organize your chart in a way that lets you categorize each method as supply side or demand side. Then on a separate sheet of paper, explain why you categorized each method as you did.

Building Financial Literacy

18 Planning Recessions are a normal part of the economic cycle. Because you know that another recession is bound to come, it makes sense to organize your finances with that in mind. Think about the relationship among aggregate demand, price, and economic recession. How might smart consumers plan ahead so they can weather the storm? How might they benefit from recessions? Create an oral presentation using correct economic terminology.

Analyzing Primary Sources

Read the excerpt and answer the questions that follow.

PRIMARY SOURCE

"*Fiscal stimulus can raise output and incomes in the short run when the economy is operating below its potential. To have the greatest impact with the least long-run cost, the stimulus should be timely, temporary, and targeted. It should be timely so that its effects are felt while economic activity is still below potential; when the economy has recovered, stimulus becomes counterproductive. It should be temporary to avoid raising inflation and to minimize the adverse long-term effects of a larger budget deficit. And it should be well targeted to provide resources to people who most need them and will spend them: for fiscal stimulus to work, it is essential that the funds be spent, not saved.*"

—Douglas Elmendorf, "Economic Stimulus: What characteristics make fiscal stimulus most effective?" Tax Policy Center, February 7, 2008. From *The Tax Policy Briefing Book: A Citizen's Guide for the 2012 Election and Beyond*, by the Staff and Affiliates of the Tax Policy Center

19 Considering Advantages and Disadvantages Explain the opportunity costs of fiscal stimulus.

20 Identifying Cause and Effect How could fiscal stimulus increase inflation?

21 Exploring Issues According to Elmendorf, fiscal stimulus funds must be "targeted" to succeed. What does he mean? What kind of policy could ensure "targeted" funds? Write a paragraph or two describing it.

Need Extra Help?

If You've Missed Question	15	16	17	18	19	20	21
Go to page	440	446	438	450	453	454	440

460

---

networks Online Assessment Options

WORKSHEET

Chapter Tests and Lesson Quizzes

Chapter 15 Tests Forms A and B Have students complete the Chapter Tests and Lesson Quizzes to assess student understanding throughout the chapter. Print and online assessment tools offer chapter and lesson evaluation through a variety of question formats, including document-based questions.

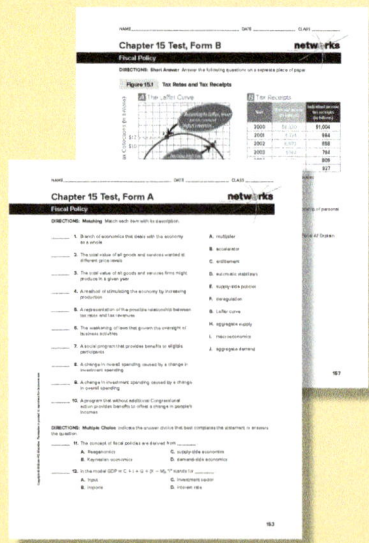

CHAPTER 16
Monetary Policy Planner

UNDERSTANDING BY DESIGN®

Enduring Understanding
- Governments are formed to maintain order and regulate activities in a geographic area.

Essential Question
- How does the government promote the economic goals of price stability, full employment, and economic growth?

Predictable Misunderstandings
Students may think:
- *The Federal Reserve System is an agency of the federal government.* Explain that the Fed is actually owned by private member banks, so it is a private institution, not a government agency. However, it is controlled by a board of governors appointed by the president, so the federal government does control it.

Assessment Evidence
Performance Task
- Hands-On Chapter Project with Technology Extension

Other Evidence
- Guided Reading Activities
- Vocabulary Activity
- Lesson Quizzes
- Self-Check Quizzes
- Chapter Assessment
- Chapter Tests, Forms A and B

Council for Economic Education

Below are the Council for Economic Education Voluntary National Content Standards in Economics covered in the *Monetary Policy* chapter.

Content Standard 11: Money makes it easier to trade, borrow, save, invest, and compare the value of goods and services. The amount of money in the economy affects the overall price level. Inflation is an increase in the overall price level that reduces the value of money.

Content Standard 19: Unemployment imposes costs on individuals and the overall economy. Inflation, both expected and unexpected, also imposes costs on individuals and the overall economy. Unemployment increases during recessions and decreases during recoveries.

Content Standard 20: Federal government budgetary policy and the Federal Reserve System's monetary policy influence the overall levels of employment, output, and prices.

SUGGESTED PACING

Introducing the Chapter: ½ Day	Lesson 3: Economics and Politics. 1 Day
Lesson 1: Structure and Responsibilities of the Fed . 1 Day	Debate . ½ Day
Case Study . ½ Day	Study Guide, Chapter Assessment and Wrap-Up . ½ Day
Lesson 2: Monetary Policy . 1 Day	

TOTAL 5 Days

Key for Using the Teacher Edition

SKILL-BASED ACTIVITIES

Types of skill activites found in the Teacher Edition.

V Visual Skills require students to analyze maps, graphs, charts, and photos.

R Reading Skills help students practice reading skills and master vocabulary.

C Critical Thinking Skills help students apply and extend what they have learned.

W Writing Skills provide writing opportunities to help students comprehend the text.

T Technology Skills require students to use digital tools effectively.

*Letters are followed by a number when there is more than one of the same type of skill on the page.

DIFFERENTIATED INSTRUCTION

All activities are written for the on-level student unless otherwise marked with the leveled labels below.

BL Beyond Level
AL Approaching Level
ELL English Language Learners

All students benefit from activities that utilize different learning styles. Many activities are marked as below when a particular learning style is highlighted.

Intrapersonal
Logical/Mathematical
Visual/Spatial
Verbal/Linguistic
Naturalist
Kinesthetic
Auditory/Musical
Interpersonal

CHAPTER 16: MONETARY POLICY

CHAPTER OPENER PLANNER

Students will know:
- the structure and functions of the Federal Reserve System, and the role it plays in the American economic system.
- how the Fed uses its tools of monetary policy to promote price stability, full employment, and economic growth.

Students will be able to:
- *explain* the idea that the Fed is privately owned but publicly controlled.
- *identify* the responsibilities of the Federal Reserve System.
- *list* the tools the Fed uses to expand and contract the money supply.
- *explain* how monetary policy works.

UNDERSTANDING BY DESIGN®

☑ Print Teaching Options

R Reading Skills

☐ **p. 463 Identifying monetary tools** Students discuss the Fed tools of monetary policy.

C Critical Thinking Skills

☐ **p. 461 Discussing monetary policy** Students discuss actions the Fed takes to expand or contract the money supply.

☐ **p. 461 Interest Rates and Your Future** Students discuss how monetary policy affects saving money, getting a credit card, and borrowing money.

☐ **p. 463 Examining the effect of interest rates on saving** Students discuss how low interest rates encourage spending.

☐ **p. 463 Examining the effect of interest rates on investment** Students discuss how interest rates affect spending and investment.

☑ Online Teaching Options

V Visual Skills

☐ **IMAGES Chapter opener**—Students discuss how monetary policy affects people.

C Critical Thinking Skills

☐ **INFOGRAPHICS Economic Perspectives**—Students explore facts about the Federal Reserve.

☐ **DEBATES Should the Federal Reserve be abolished?**—Students read two views about the Fed.

☐ **INTERACTIVE FEATURES Case Study: Changes in the U.S. Economy: Growth in Government Spending**—Students discuss whether private investors can be convinced to pay for infrastructure.

☑ Printable Digital Worksheets

C Critical Thinking Skills

☐ **WORKSHEET Chapter Summary**—Content is condensed into manageable chunks.

☐ **WORKSHEET Vocabulary Activity**—Students use content and academic terms.

☐ **WORKSHEET Assessing Background Knowledge Activity**—Target misconceptions you can address when teaching the lessons.

Project-Based Learning

Hands-On

WORKSHEET Hands-On Chapter Project
In this workshop, students work in groups to conduct research on how the Fed was created. They learn about its structure and about actions it has taken recently to achieve its economic goals. Groups will then create a news report on their findings. The report will take the form of either a news article, radio report, or television news report. Groups will discuss how their presentations were similar and different.

Digital Hands-On

Create Online Projects

Find an additional activity online that incorporates technology for the Hands-On Project. Visit the EdTech Teacher Web sites for more links, tutorials, and other resources.

Print Resources

ANCILLARY RESOURCE
This ancillary is available for every chapter and lesson.
- Chapter Tests and Lesson Quizzes

PRINTABLE DIGITAL WORKSHEETS
These printable digital worksheets are available for every chapter and lesson.
- Reading Essentials & Study Guide
- Vocabulary Activities
- Chapter Summaries
- Economic Simulations
- Math Practice for Economics
- Reinforcing Economic Skills
- Personal Finance Activities
- Enrichment Activities
- Reteaching Activities
- Guided Reading Activities
- Video Worksheets
- Lesson Quizzes and Chapter Tests (English and Spanish)

More Media Resources

SUGGESTED READING
- For students at a Grade 10 reading level: *From Seashells to Smart Cards: Money and Currency,* by Ernestine Giesecke
- For students at a Grade 11 reading level: *Money Business: Banks and Banking,* by Ernestine Giesecke
- For students at a Grade 12 reading level: *The House of Morgan: An American Banking Dynasty and the Rise of Finance,* by Ron Chernow

SUGGESTED VIDEOS
Find these documentaries yourself online. NOTE: McGraw-Hill Education does not endorse these resources. Preview clips for age-appropriateness.
- *97% Owned* (2 hr. 10 min.)
- *RBS: Inside the Bank That Ran Out of Money* (59 min.)

LESSON 1 Planner

STRUCTURE AND RESPONSIBILITIES OF THE FED

Students will know:
- the structure and functions of the Federal Reserve System, and the role it plays in the American economic system.
- how the United States Federal Reserve System oversees the banking system and regulates the quantity of money in the economy

Students will be able to:
- **explain** the idea that the Fed is privately owned but publicly controlled.
- **identify** the responsibilities of the Federal Reserve System.
- **describe** the principle of monetary expansion under a fractional reserve system.

UNDERSTANDING BY DESIGN®

✓ Print Teaching Options

V Visual Skills

- **p. 465 Analyzing a diagram of the Federal Reserve System** Students analyze a diagram to discuss member bank functions and who decides on monetary policy. **Visual/Spatial**

R Reading Skills

- **p. 465 Making inferences about the Fed** Students infer why the Fed is "publicly controlled." **Verbal/Linguistic**
- **p. 466 Monitoring student understanding about the Fed** Students use flash cards to identify aspects of the Fed. **AL Verbal/Linguistic**
- **p. 467 Understanding changes in Fed advisory groups** Students discuss why some consumer protection issues were removed from the Fed's control in 2011.
- **p. 467 Identifying Fed services to the government** Students identify the financial services the Fed provides to government.
- **p. 468 Drawing conclusions from the lesson** Students answer the question: How does the Fed's structure enable it to carry out its responsibilities effectively?

C Critical Thinking Skills

- **p. 464 Asking questions about the Fed's goals** Students consider the Fed's goals of price stability, full employment, and economic growth. **Verbal/Linguistic**
- **p. 467 Drawing conclusions about the Federal Advisory Council** Students consider why members of the Federal Advisory Council must be from a member bank. **Verbal/Linguistic**
- **p. 468 Identifying effects of Fed responsibilities** Students identify how the Fed's role in financial literacy and consumer protection contributes to economic growth. **Logical/Mathematical**

✓ Online Teaching Options

V Visual Skills

- **GRAPHIC ORGANIZER** **Features of the Federal Reserve System**—Students note details about the structure of the Fed. **Visual/Spatial**
- **IMAGES** **Structure of the Federal Reserve System**—Students explore components of the Fed. **Verbal/Linguistic**
- **CHART** **Responsibilities of Federal Reserve**—Students view a chart about the Federal Reserve's responsibilities. **Verbal/Linguistic**
- **SLIDE SHOW** **Consumer Protections from the Federal Reserve System**—Students give examples of when they have witnessed or benefited from consumer protections. **Verbal/Linguistic**
- **VIDEO** **Stock Options and Executive Greed in Enron and Worldcom**—Students view executive greed. **Verbal/Linguistic**

C Critical Thinking Skills

- **BELLRINGER** **Structure and Responsibilities of the Fed**—Students identify the functions of Fed District Banks. **Verbal/Linguistic**
- **ESSENTIAL QUESTION** **Exploring the Essential Question**—Students discuss how politics can interfere with the management of our financial system. **Interpersonal**

T Technology Skills

- **SELF-CHECK QUIZ** **Lesson 1**—Students receive instant feedback on their mastery of lesson content.
- **GAME** **Lesson 1**—Students solve clues to review lesson content.
- **INTERACTIVE WHITEBOARD ACTIVITY** **Structure of the Federal Reserve System**—Students work together to learn lesson content.

✓ Printable Digital Worksheets

R Reading Skills

- **WORKSHEET** **Guided Reading Activity**—Students use the Guided Reading Activity worksheets to review their comprehension of the content.
- **WORKSHEET** **Reading Essentials and Study Guide**—Students complete the study guide and answer Reading Progress Check and vocabulary questions.

C Critical Thinking Skills

- **WORKSHEET** **Vocabulary Activity**—Students answer questions using vocabulary words from the lesson on the worksheet.
- **WORKSHEET** **Stock Options and Executive Greed in Enron and Worldcom Video Activity**—Students answer questions about stock options and executive greed. **Verbal/Linguistic**

LESSON 2 Planner

MONETARY POLICY

Students will know:
- how the Fed uses its tools of monetary policy to promote price stability, full employment, and economic growth
- the basic tools used to implement U.S. monetary policy, including reserve requirements, the discount rate, and the federal funds rate target, and open-market operations.

Students will be able to:
- **list** the tools the Fed uses to expand and contract the money supply.
- **explain** how monetary policy works.
- **discuss** the importance of timing in the use of monetary policy.

UNDERSTANDING BY DESIGN®

☑ Print Teaching Options

V Visual Skills
- ☐ **p. 471 Calculating fractional reserves** Students calculate the size of the money supply with different reserve requirements.

R Reading Skills
- ☐ **p. 470 Discussing the money supply and fractional reserve system**
- ☐ **p. 470 Explaining how fractional reserve banking increases the money supply**
- ☐ **p. 475 Identifying who borrows from the Fed**
- ☐ **p. 475 Identifying effects of the discount rate**
- ☐ **p. 475 Evaluating monetary policy** Students discuss monetary policy problems.
- ☐ **p. 476 Defining the quantity theory of money** Students illustrate the theory. *Verbal/Linguistic*

C Critical Thinking Skills
- ☐ **p. 471 Predicting the money supply** Students respond to the Fed increasing or decreasing the reserve requirement.
- ☐ **p. 473 Determining cause and effect** Students look at an easy and a tight money policy.
- ☐ **p. 473 Drawing conclusions about the reserve requirement** Students consider other monetary policy tools. *Logical/Mathematical*
- ☐ **p. 474 Simulating open market operations** Students exchange currency and bonds. **ELL**
- ☐ **p. 475 Relating the discount rate to the prime rate**
- ☐ **p. 476 Deciding on policy and timing** Students expand or contract the money supply. **BL**

W Writing Skills
- ☐ **p. 471 Writing to persuade** Students state their opinion of the fractional reserve system.
- ☐ **p. 472 Writing a persuasive essay** Students argue for a rise/drop in the reserve requirement.

T Technology Skills
- ☐ **p. 474 Explaining open market operations** Students use computer software to make a graphic aid.

☑ Online Teaching Options

V Visual Skills
- ☐ **GRAPHS Fractional Reserves and the Money Supply**—Students discuss how fractional reserve requirements can be used to manage the money supply.
- ☐ **GRAPHS Short-Run Impact of Monetary Policy**—Students explore the effects of changes in the money supply. *Logical/Mathematical*
- ☐ **GRAPHS The Reserve Requirement as a Tool of Monetary Policy**—Students explain why a smaller reserve requirement results in a larger amount of money in circulation, and vice versa.
- ☐ **CHARTS Monetary Policy Tools**—Students discuss the effect of the Fed's actions on excess reserves and the money supply. *Logical/Mathematical*
- ☐ **VIDEO Bernanke on the Recovery**—Students learn about Bernanke's monetary policies. *Verbal/Linguistic*
- ☐ **POLITICAL CARTOON Federal Reserve**—Students analyze how Fed actions are perceived by others. *Visual/Spatial*

R Reading Skills
- ☐ **BIOGRAPHY Janet Yellen**—Students read about Janet Yellen's focus in economics.

C Critical Thinking Skills
- ☐ **BELLRINGER Monetary Policy**—Students discuss the effects of monetary policy on interest rates. *Verbal/Linguistic*
- ☐ **ESSENTIAL QUESTION Exploring the Essential Question**—Students read about economic growth and discuss its effects on tax revenue and entitlement programs.

T Technology Skills
- ☐ **SELF-CHECK QUIZ Lesson 2**—Students receive instant feedback on their mastery of lesson content.
- ☐ **GAME Lesson 2**—Students solve clues to review lesson content.
- ☐ **INTERACTIVE WHITEBOARD ACTIVITY Calculating a Car Loan**—Students work together to learn lesson content.

☑ Printable Digital Worksheets

R Reading Skills
- ☐ **WORKSHEET Guided Reading Activity**—Students review their comprehension of the content.
- ☐ **WORKSHEET Reading Essentials and Study Guide**—Students complete the study guide and answer Reading Progress Check and vocabulary questions.

C Critical Thinking Skills
- ☐ **WORKSHEET Bernanke on the Recovery Video Activity**—Students answer questions about Bernanke's monetary policies. *Verbal/Linguistic*
- ☐ **WORKSHEET Math Practice for Economics**—Students calculate how much the bank can lend out with a reserve of 20 percent. *Logical/Mathematical*

LESSON 3 Planner

ECONOMICS AND POLITICS

Students will know:
- how the government influences the economy through discretionary, passive, or structural fiscal policies.
- how current economic and political conditions shape the views of economists and policy makers.

Students will be able to:
- **state** reasons why the use of fiscal policy has declined.
- **examine** ways in which the prevailing economic theory is a product of the times.
- **explain** why the opinions and theories of economists may differ.

UNDERSTANDING BY DESIGN

✓ Print Teaching Options

R Reading Skills

- ☐ **p. 478 Making inferences about business cycles GDP** Students track the business cycle phases during the Great Recession.
- ☐ **p. 479 Creating a recession time line** Students sequence events and policies during the Great Recession. **Visual/Spatial**
- ☐ **p. 479 Defining the word *lag*** Students consider lags in monetary policy. **ELL Verbal/Linguistic**
- ☐ **p. 480 Identifying cause and effect** Students discuss why the Fed took a larger role in managing the economy. **Verbal/Linguistic**
- ☐ **p. 481 Summarizing macro policies of the Great Recession** Students create a concept web showing the policies taken.
- ☐ **p. 482 Predicting consequences of baby boomer retirement**

C Critical Thinking Skills

- ☐ **p. 478 Assessing the effects of economic policies** Students decide whether economic policies improved the economy. **Verbal/Linguistic**
- ☐ **p. 481 Defining supply-sider policies** Students discuss the arguments supply-siders make.
- ☐ **p. 482 Assessing the likelihood of another Great Depression**
- ☐ **p. 483 Understanding the goals of the Council of Economic Advisers** Students discuss the "war against the business cycle." **AL Verbal/Linguistic**

W Writing Skills

- ☐ **p. 482 Writing a letter to the editor** Students research news articles about the Fed's recent policies. **Verbal/Linguistic**

✓ Online Teaching Options

V Visual Skills

- ☐ **INTERACTIVE FEATURE** **Careers**—Students explore the career of Chief Plant Engineer, U.S. Mint. **Verbal/Linguistic**
- ☐ **VIDEO** **Congressional Budget Office**—Students watch a video about the CEA and CBO.

C Critical Thinking Skills

- ☐ **BELLRINGER** **Economics and Politics**—Students discuss the phrase "too big to fail," which was widely used during the financial crisis of 2008–2009. **Verbal/Linguistic**
- ☐ **ESSENTIAL QUESTION** **Exploring the Essential Question**—Students identify ways government activity contributed to the economy. **Verbal/Linguistic**
- ☐ **INTERACTIVE FEATURE** **Global Economy & You**—Students learn about the global effects of the Fed's actions. **Verbal/Linguistic**

T Technology Skills

- ☐ **SELF-CHECK QUIZ** **Lesson 3**—Students receive instant feedback on their mastery of lesson content.
- ☐ **GAME** **Lesson 3**—Students solve clues to review lesson content.
- ☐ **INTERACTIVE WHITEBOARD ACTIVITY** **Types of Economic Policy**—Students work together to learn lesson content.

✓ Printable Digital Worksheets

R Reading Skills

- ☐ **WORKSHEET** **Guided Reading Activity**—Students use the Guided Reading Activity worksheets to review their comprehension of the content.
- ☐ **WORKSHEET** **Reading Essentials and Study Guide**—Students complete the study guide and answer Reading Progress Check and vocabulary questions.
- ☐ **WORKSHEET** **Reteaching Activity**—Use this worksheet with students who need additional help with difficult content concepts.

C Critical Thinking Skills

- ☐ **WORKSHEET** **Reinforcing Economic Skills**—Students compare British and U.S. viewpoints on the 2008 financial crisis.
- ☐ **WORKSHEET** **Enrichment Activity**—Students discuss the financial crisis as a class.
- ☐ **WORKSHEET** **Congressional Budget Office Video Activity**—Students answer questions about the roles of the Council of Economic Advisers and the Congressional Budget Office.

CHAPTER 16 Monetary Policy

INTERVENTION AND REMEDIATION STRATEGIES

LESSON 1 Structure and Responsibilities of the Fed

Reading and Comprehension

Write these questions on the board and instruct students to find the answers by reviewing the lesson:

What does the text mean in describing the Fed as "privately owned, but publicly controlled"?

What is the role of the Board of Governors?

What is the role of the Federal Open Market Committee?

What are some of the ways in which the Fed maintains the payments system?

How does the Fed work to protect consumers in their financial transactions?

How does the Fed serve as the "government's bank"?

Text Evidence

Ask students to write two or three paragraphs answering this question: How does the structure of the Fed enable it to promote the economic goals of price stability, full employment, and economic growth? Have students cite facts and other details from the lesson to support their answer.

LESSON 2 Monetary Policy

Reading and Comprehension

Ask students to imagine that they have a younger friend who knows they have been studying economics and the Fed. On a newscast, the friend has heard the term "monetary policy" being used by commentators. In an email, the friend asks, What is monetary policy and how does the Fed use it to manage the economy? Have students write an email message to their friend that answers the friend's question.

Text Evidence

Share this scenario with students:

The GDP has been slowing for the last 12 months and this last quarter stumbled along at just 0.5 percent. Economists are beginning to worry about a recession. Meanwhile unemployment has continued to rise and sits at about 7 percent. The Fed raised the discount rate to 2.5 percent two years ago and hasn't changed it since.

Ask students to write a recommendation of actions the Fed should take and explain how they would expect these actions to affect the economy. Tell them to cite details from the text to support their ideas.

LESSON 3 Economics and Politics

Reading and Comprehension

Ask students to work in pairs to review the lesson. Tell them to write three questions with the answers about the main ideas of each of the two main sections. Then call the class together and guide a discussion by asking students to share their questions. Ask other students to give the answers.

Text Evidence

Ask students to write an essay giving their opinion on this question: How is the changing nature of our economic policies a result of a change in political views? Have students cite details from the lesson to support their ideas.

Online Resources

Assessing Background Knowledge Use this worksheet to pre-assess students' background knowledge before they start the chapter.

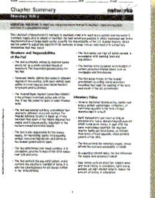

Chapter Summaries Have students use the summary as a pre-reading activity or as a post-reading review to check the main ideas covered in each lesson.

Guided Reading Activities Have students complete these activities as they read each lesson. They provide reading notes the student can use for review and to prepare for assessments.

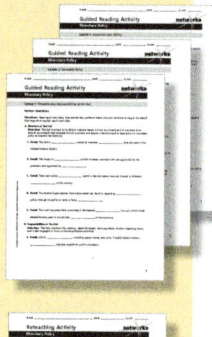

Reteaching Activities Have students complete the Reteaching Activity for remedial practice and review of vital content.

Self-Check Quizzes These quizzes provide instant feedback on areas the students may need to re-read to understand a main idea.

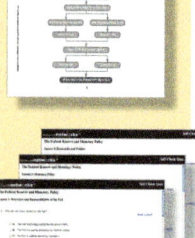

Reading Essentials and Study Guide This resource offers writing and reading activities for the approaching-level student.

Approaching Grade Level Reader This reader presents all of the content of the Online Student Edition but at a lower reading level.

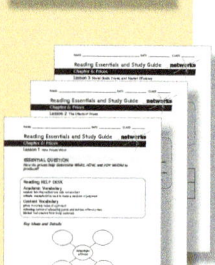

English Language Learner Reader Provide additional reading support for ELL students. Find this tool online.

Monetary Policy

ESSENTIAL QUESTION
How does the government promote the economic goals of price stability, full employment, and economic growth?

networks
www.connected.mcgraw-hill.com
There's More Online about monetary policy.

CHAPTER 16

Economic Perspectives
The Lesser Known Parts of the Federal Reserve

Lesson 1
Structure and Responsibilities of the Fed

Lesson 2
Monetary Policy

Lesson 3
Economics and Politics

CHAPTER 16
Monetary Policy

ENGAGE

🔔 Call students' attention to the photo and ask them to describe what it shows. Guide them to recognize that a financial advisor is counseling a client about financial matters. **Ask: Why is this image a good one to symbolize the chapter titled *Monetary Policy*?** *(Monetary policy affects everyone because it determines interest rates and attempts to maintain a stable economy. A financial advisor is sometimes helpful to people who want to save and invest money for their future.)* **Visual/Spatial**

Discussing monetary policy Remind students that among the government's goals for the economy are stable prices, full employment, and economic growth. The government has many tools to use in pursuing these goals, but one of the most important is monetary policy. Invite students to offer a definition of *monetary policy*. Guide them to understand that it is the actions the Fed takes to expand or contract the money supply in order to increase or reduce the cost and availability of credit. Explain that this, in turn, can affect employment, inflation, GDP, and many other aspects of the economy. **Verbal/Linguistic**

Making Connections

Interest Rates and Your Future Explain to students that if they have not already done so, they will in time be saving money, getting a credit card, borrowing money to buy a car or pay for college, and eventually perhaps taking out a mortgage to buy a house. **Ask: How will monetary policy affect all of these actions?** *(Monetary policy strongly affects interest rates, which will determine how much interest students will earn on their savings and how much they will have to pay in interest on their credit card, auto and school loans, and home mortgage.)*

Letter from the Author

Dear Economics Teacher,

The Federal Reserve System is unique in the American economy. It was set up as an independent agency with several powerful tools that it can use to influence the economy. The Fed's independence means that it is largely free of the political gridlock that seems to afflict Congress, and its independence is truly refreshing in its simplicity. Of course there are always some politicians who would like to have control over the Fed, but we are extremely fortunate to have such a powerful independent agency whose primary agenda is economic stability and growth—an agenda that is free of political ideology.

Gary E. Clayton

Go to the Foldables® library for a cumulative chapter-based Foldable® activity that your students can use to help take notes and prepare for assessment.

CHAPTER 16
Economic Perspectives

TEACH & ASSESS

V Visual Skills

Examining a dollar bill for evidence Have students view an older dollar bill and explain the features that provide information about the Fed. The face of the dollar bill features information that reveal its Federal Reserve origins. On the front of the dollar bill, the Federal Reserve Seal sits on the left side of the bill, which is a letter encircled by an insignia. On the right side, there's a Federal Reserve District Number. Letter codes range from A to L, while number codes range from 1 to 12; both designations refer to which of the 12 Federal Reserve District Banks printed the bill. **Visual/Spatial**

Making Connections

Tight Money Policy Guide students to understand that an advantage of tightening the money supply is to reduce consumer spending, which in an overheated market can slow inflation. The disadvantage of tightening the money supply is that it can slow the economy too much and lead to a recession. **Logical/Mathematical**

Content Background Knowledge

Alan Greenspan Former Federal Reserve Chair Alan Greenspan served as the Federal Reserve Chair under four different presidents: Ronald Reagan, George H.W. Bush, Bill Clinton and George W. Bush. Greenspan held this position just over 18 years.

Economic Perspectives

THE LESSER KNOWN PARTS OF THE FEDERAL RESERVE

Most people only know about the Federal Reserve Board Chair and that person's role in advising the president and Congress. But there is much more to the Federal Reserve than that individual. The Federal Reserve is made up of an executive board, a board of governors, the Federal Open Market Committee, the Federal Advisory Committee, and thousands of federal and member banks. This network of economists, government employees, and bankers work to maintain a predictable money supply for the United States.

V

Executive Board

Board of Governors

Federal Open Market Committee

Federal Advisory Committee

Federal & Member Banks x 3,198

---

networks Online Teaching Options

INFOGRAPHIC

Economic Perspectives: The Lesser Known Parts of the Federal Reserve

Identifying clues about the Fed Have students view the infographic. **Ask:** Who reports to Congress? *(the Federal Reserve Chair—currently Janet Yellen)* Who advises the Fed Board of Governors? *(12 representatives of the banking industry)* How many Federal Reserve District Banks are there? *(twelve)* What is the federal funds rate? *(The federal funds rate is the interest rate at which Federal Reserve depository institutions lend money to other banks. These short-term loans take place overnight, and are available only to the most creditworthy institutions. The federal funds rate is very important because it influences monetary and fiscal conditions in the United States, which ultimately shape the entire economy.)* **Visual/Spatial**

462

CHAPTER 16
Economic Perspectives

Federal Reserve Chair
1 Member

The Chair of the Federal Reserve System's Board of Governors is essentially the head of America's central banking system. The Chair must report the Fed's monetary policy objectives to Congress twice a year, but he or she also meets with the Treasury Secretary and testifies before Congress on various fiscal issues during the year.

Board of Governors
7 Members

The Board of Governors of the Federal Reserve System is the Fed's governing body. The Board has the authority to oversee Federal Reserve Banks and also to execute the country's monetary policy. The Board has seven members, who are designated by Presidential appointment and then confirmed by the Senate. Board members serve 14-year terms. The Board of Governors is led by a Chairman and Vice-Chairman; both of these are selected from sitting Board members and appointed directly by the U.S. president.

Federal Open Market Committee
12 Members
+ 7 BOG
  5 Federal Bank Presidents

The Federal Reserve controls 3 tools of monetary policy: open market operations, discount rate, and reserve requirements. The FOMC is responsible for open market operations, which is when a central bank buys and sells bonds in the open market. The Fed uses open market transactions to keep the federal funds interest rate close to the target rate it has established. Open Market Operations are done by the Trading Desk of the Federal Reserve Bank of New York, under the authority of the Federal Reserve Act.

Federal Advisory Committee
12 Members

The members of the Federal Advisory Committee are twelve representatives of the banking industry from around the country. This group advises the Federal Reserve Board of Governors on the scope of its duties. The Committee is required to meet at least four times per year, and the meetings take place in Washington, D.C. Reserve Banks choose one representative to go to the FAC to represent that Reserve Bank's district for a one-year term. Most of these representatives serve three terms.

THINK ABOUT IT!
In what way is the Federal Reserve influenced by partisan politics?

R Reading Skills

Identifying monetary tools Ask: **What Fed tools of monetary policy are mentioned in the infographic?** *(open market operations, discount or federal funds rate, reserve requirements)* **Verbal/Linguistic**

C1 Critical Thinking Skills

Examining the effect of interest rates on saving Point out to students that expanding the money supply may be useful for encouraging businesses and consumers to borrow and spend, but it can discourage saving. Ask: **If interest rates are low, will you want to spend or to save? Why?** *(Spend, because money that is saved earns very little interest income.)* **Logical/Mathematical**

C2 Critical Thinking Skills

Examining the effect of interest rates on investment Ask: **How do low and high interest rates affect investment?** Lead students to understand that low interest rates encourage investment and spending because money is "cheap" to borrow. High interest rates will reduce investment and spending. **Logical/Mathematical**

CLOSE & REFLECT

Have students answer the *Think About It!* questions.

GRAPHIC ORGANIZER

Cause-and-Effect Chart

Introducing monetary policy basics Have students view the infographic. Ask: **Why would the Fed want to increase the supply of money?** *(More money makes it cheaper to borrow, so consumers and businesses borrow more to use for purchasing goods and expanding businesses. This economic activity helps the economy grow.)* **Why would the Fed want to decrease the supply of money?** *(Less money makes borrowing more expensive, so consumers and businesses borrow less. This helps slow down a market that is growing too fast and reduces the risk of inflation.)* Have students use the graphic organizer to help visually display this information. **Verbal/Linguistic**

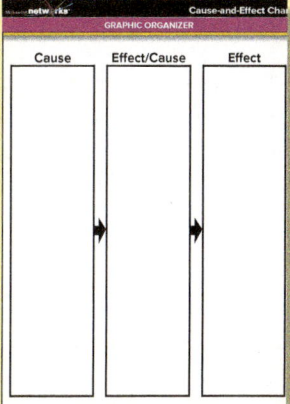

ANSWERS, p. 463

THINK ABOUT IT!

The Board of Governors' members are appointed by the president and confirmed by the Senate. The Fed Chair and Vice-Chair are also appointed by the president. But the Federal Reserve is an independent body that tries not to be influenced by partisan politics.

CHAPTER 16, LESSON 1
Structure and Responsibilities of the Fed

ENGAGE

C Critical Thinking Skills

Asking questions about the Fed's goals
Before students begin the lesson, tell them that the Fed's major goals are to achieve price stability, full employment, and economic growth. Have students write two questions about these goals. Invite students to share some of their questions. Discuss them as a class. Then tell students to keep their questions and to look for answers as they read the lesson. **Verbal/Linguistic**

ANSWERS, p. 464

ESSENTIAL QUESTION ACTIVITY

Answers will vary. Have students support their opinions with sound reasoning.

TAKING NOTES
Sample responses: Privately owned, Directed by a board of governors, Served by district banks, Has a policy-making body, Has advisory committees

---

Interact with these digital assets and others in lesson 1
- ✓ INTERACTIVE CHART
  Structure of the Federal Reserve System
- ✓ SLIDESHOW
  Consumer Protections from the Federal Reserve System
- ✓ SELF-CHECK QUIZ
- ✓ VIDEO

networks
TRY IT YOURSELF ONLINE

LESSON 1
Structure and Responsibilities of the Fed

Reading Help Desk

Academic Vocabulary
- aspects
- functions

Content Vocabulary
- member bank
- currency
- coins
- bank holding companies

TAKING NOTES:

Key Ideas and Details
ACTIVITY Use a graphic organizer like the one below to describe the features of the Federal Reserve System.

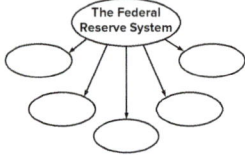

ESSENTIAL QUESTION

C How does the government promote the economic goals of price stability, full employment, and economic growth?

Among our government's chief priorities is maintaining a strong economy and an efficient, dependable financial system. Congress and the president have major roles and great responsibilities in furthering these priorities, but these branches of government are political bodies. They are occupied by members of political parties who are almost continually watching polls for public approval or disapproval while planning for the next round of elections. Operating as an important counterweight to these political bodies is the Federal Reserve System. Although the leadership includes appointed positions, the Fed operates largely independent of the political branches. It can plan far ahead and make logical decisions based on the best economic data and thinking, and then it can take action without further approval.

- Is it good to have an independent body like the Fed watching over the economy? Why or why not?
- Should the Fed be more responsive to the public, Congress, and the presidency?

Structure of the Fed

GUIDING QUESTION *In what ways is the Fed privately owned but publically controlled?*

The main components of the Fed, shown in **Figure 16.1**, have remained practically unchanged since the Great Depression. Even so, the current structure of the Fed works well to help achieve the economic goals of price stability, full employment, and economic growth.

---

networks *Online Teaching Options*

BELLRINGER

Structure and Responsibilities of the Fed

Thinking about money Ask: **Where does the currency in your wallet come from?** *(Lead students to identify the Federal Reserve Bank for your district.)* Show students the Bellringer and ask them to identify the functions of Fed District Banks as they relate to private banks, and the types of currency and coins produced by the U.S. Bureau of Engraving and Printing. Ask students how often they use currency or coins. Ask: **Do you frequently use other forms of money, such as checks and credit cards?** **Verbal/Linguistic**

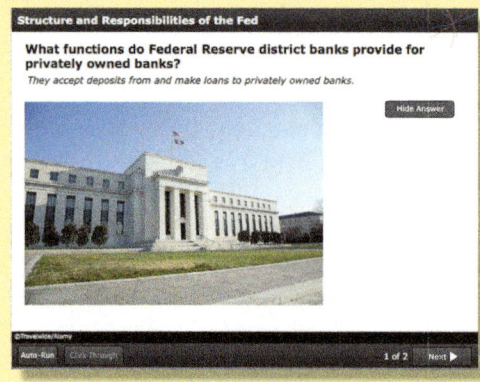

Private Ownership

One of the unique features of the Fed is that it is privately owned by its member banks. A **member bank** is a commercial bank that is a member of, and holds shares of stock in, the Fed. All national banks—those chartered by the national government—must belong to the Fed. State banks—those receiving their charters from state governments—have the option to belong or not. Today, all the large banks, and almost 40 percent of all U.S. banks, are members of the Fed.

The decision to make the Fed a stock corporation was a matter of necessity because the government did not have enough money to set up a new banking system. Instead, banks were required to purchase shares when they joined. This process made the banks part owners of the Fed, just as someone might own shares in a private company. Private individuals are not allowed to buy shares in the Fed, although they become indirect owners by buying shares of stock in a Fed-member bank. The stock ownership feature of the Fed by private banks means that the government does not own the Fed.

Board of Governors

The Fed is led by a seven-member Board of Governors who are appointed by the president and approved by the Senate to serve a single 14-year, non-renewable term of office. One of the governors is appointed as the chair and he or she has a four-year renewable term. The appointments are staggered, so that one appointment becomes vacant every two years. Care is taken to appoint people who will govern the Fed in the public interest. So it is said that the Fed is "privately owned, but publicly controlled."

The board is primarily a regulatory and supervisory agency. It sets general policies for its member banks to follow and regulates certain **aspects** of state-chartered member banks' operations. It helps make policies that affect the level of interest rates and the general availability of credit. The board reports annually to Congress and puts out a monthly bulletin that covers national and international monetary matters.

member bank bank belonging to the Federal Reserve System

aspects parts, phases

Federal Reserve District Banks

The Fed was originally intended to operate as a system of 12 independent and equally powerful banks. Each reserve bank was responsible for a district, and some Federal Reserve notes today still have the district bank's name in the seal to the left of the portrait. More recently, advances in

FIGURE 16.1

STRUCTURE OF THE FEDERAL RESERVE SYSTEM

The Board of Governors supervises the Federal Reserve System. The Federal Open Market Committee (FOMC) has primary responsibility for monetary policy. The Federal Advisory Council (FAC) advises the Board of Governors on economic conditions. The district banks are located throughout the nation, near the institutions they serve. Member banks contribute a small amount of funds and receive stock ownership shares in return.

▲ **CRITICAL THINKING**
Economic Analysis What functions does the Board of Governors perform?

Monetary Policy **465**

CHAPTER 16, LESSON 1
Structure and Responsibilities of the Fed

TEACH & ASSESS

R Reading Skills

Making inferences about the Fed Ask: **Why is it said that the Fed is "publicly controlled"?** *(Members are appointed by the president and approved by the Senate; they serve for 14 years, have staggered appointments, and exhibit characteristics of governing the Fed in the public interest.)* **Verbal/Linguistic**

V Visual Skills

Analyzing a diagram of the Federal Reserve System Ask: **What are two functions that member banks perform?** *(contribute funds to the 12 district banks and receive stock)* **Who is in charge of deciding monetary policy?** *(the Federal Open Market Committee)* **Visual/Spatial**

Content Background Knowledge

The First Central Bank The Bank of Amsterdam was established in Holland in 1609. At that time, Amsterdam was a center of world trade. More than 340 different kinds of silver coins and about 500 types of gold coins circulated throughout the city. Dutch merchants had little idea of how much these coins were worth, so the Bank of Amsterdam was set up under a charter from the city to standardize the currency. The Bank of Amsterdam operated as Holland's central bank for more than 200 years. After making a series of bad loans, however, it failed and went out of business in 1819—almost 100 years *before* America's central bank was founded.

DIAGRAM
Structure of the Federal Reserve System

Understanding components of the Fed
Ask students to explore the components of the Fed by clicking on each part in turn. Ask: **How does having 12 district banks affect the Fed's performance and decisions?** *(Possible answer: Having district banks close to member banks they serve allows the Fed to be more responsive to changing economic conditions within specific districts, which may differ from those of other districts.)* **Why is the Federal Advisory Council considered the most important committee in the Fed?** *(It advises the Board of Governors on the health of the economy.)* **Why is the Federal Open Market Committee important to the functioning of the Fed?** *(It sets interest rates, enabling the Fed to influence national economic conditions.)* **Verbal/Linguistic**

ANSWERS, p. 465
CRITICAL THINKING
It supervises and regulates the Fed.

CHAPTER 16, LESSON 1
Structure and Responsibilities of the Fed

R Reading Skills

Monitoring student understanding about the Fed
Make flash cards that detail some aspect of the Federal Reserve System that is described in the section. After students read the section, hold up the flash cards, one at a time, and call on students to identify what aspect of the Fed is being described. If students struggle, direct them to review the text to find the answer. **AL** Verbal/Linguistic

Content Background Knowledge

Large Denominations of U.S. Currency
Point out that other denominations of currency have been produced in the past. At one time currencies were available in $500, $1,000, $5,000, and $10,000 denominations. The last of these bill denominations was printed in 1945, although the bills were in use until 1969 when the Fed discontinued them because they were not being used. These bills are still legal tender, however, and can be circulated, although most are now in private collections and not in use. In 1934 and 1935, a $100,000 gold certificate was also available. It was the largest denomination ever printed. These particular notes were backed by gold bullion and were only used in transactions among Federal Reserve banks.

English Language Proficiency

Advanced Before students read the lesson, help them develop background knowledge. Ask them what they know about the Fed. Next, have them read, view, and think about the subheadings and visuals. Then tell them to scan for key words, dates, and names. Model how to connect information gained from visual and contextual support with prior knowledge. Provide a graphic organizer such as a KWL chart and model its use before, during, and after reading.

ANSWERS, p. 466

CRITICAL THINKING
Students should recognize that consumer protection laws are put in place to ensure that companies are providing adequate information to consumers allowing them to make informed financial decisions.

---

technology have minimized the need for a regional structure, so the new Fed seal on our currency does not incorporate any mention of the district banks.

Today the 12 Federal Reserve district banks and their branches are strategically located to be near the institutions they serve. The district banks provide many of the same **functions** for banks and depository institutions that banks provide for us. For example, the district banks accept deposits from, and make loans to, privately owned banks and thrift institutions.

functions roles or purposes

R Federal Open Market Committee
The Federal Open Market Committee (FOMC) is the Fed's primary monetary policy-making body because it has the power to raise or lower interest rates. It has 12 voting members: the seven-member Board of Governors, the president of the New York district Fed, and four district Federal Reserve Bank presidents from the other 11 districts who serve one-year rotating terms.

How does the Federal Reserve provide . . .

THE FEDERAL RESERVE BOARD HELPS REGULATE CREDIT AND DEBIT CARD TRANSACTIONS

Consumer Protection in the United States

The Federal Reserve Board does not only worry about manipulating the value of national currency and interest rates. It also plays a role in providing consumer protections. For instance, financial transactions with ATM cards, mortgages, and loans are all regulated by the Federal Reserve. The Truth in Lending Act, for instance, demands that consumers have accurate information about the terms of credit cards, loans, and other financial products.

▲ **CRITICAL THINKING**
Analyzing What is the purpose of consumer protection laws?

---

networks Online Teaching Options

SLIDE SHOW

Consumer Protections from the Federal Reserve System

Understanding the Fed's role in consumer protection Tell students that one of the Fed's responsibilities that directly affects them is its role in consumer protection. Show students the slide show and call on a student to read aloud the text for each slide. Ask students to give examples of when they have witnessed or benefited from any of these protections. Verbal/Linguistic

The FOMC meets eight times a year to review the economy and to evaluate factors such as trends in construction, wages, prices, employment, production, the stock market, and consumer spending. Its decisions have a direct impact on the cost and availability of credit. Although decisions are made in private, they are announced to the public, almost immediately following the FOMC meetings.

Advisory Committees

Historically, several advisory committees have advised the Board of Governors. The most important committee is the Federal Advisory Council, which consists of one representative from each of the 12 district banks. It meets four times a year and provides advice to the Federal Reserve Board on matters concerning the overall health of the economy.

Other advisory groups advise the Fed on matters relating to savings and loan associations, savings banks, credit unions, and matters pertaining to bank solvency. The Fed also had control of many consumer protection issues until they were transferred to the Consumer Financial Protection Bureau (CFPB) in 2011. The CFPB is a separate bureau in the Treasury created as a direct result of lending abuses that helped cause the Great Recession of 2008–2009.

✓ **READING PROGRESS CHECK**

Explaining What is the purpose of the Federal Open Market Committee?

Responsibilities of the Fed

GUIDING QUESTION How does the Fed regulate banks?

The Federal Reserve has other responsibilities as well. These include maintaining the money supply and the payments system, regulating and supervising banks, preparing consumer legislation, and serving as the federal government's bank.

Maintaining the Currency

Today's **currency**, the paper and coin part of the money supply, is largely made up of Federal Reserve notes that are printed by the U.S. Bureau of Engraving and Printing. The paper component, issued in amounts of $1, $2, $5, $10, $20, $50, and $100, is distributed to the Fed's district banks for storage until it is needed by the public.

The Bureau of the Mint produces **coins**—metallic forms of money—such as pennies, nickels, dimes, quarters, and the presidential dollar coin. After the coins are minted, they are also shipped to the Fed district banks for storage. When member banks need additional currency, they contact the Fed to fulfill their needs.

When banks come across coins or paper currency that are mutilated or cannot be used for other reasons, they return them to the Fed for replacement. The Fed then destroys the old money so that it cannot be put back into circulation.

currency paper and coin component of the money supply, today consisting largely of Federal Reserve notes

coins metallic forms of money such as pennies, nickels, dimes, and quarters

Maintaining the Payments System

The payments system involves more than the money supply. It also covers the electronic transfer of funds among businesses, state and local governments, financial institutions, and foreign central banks. In addition, specialized operations called *clearinghouses* process the billions of checks that are written every year. The Fed works with all of these agencies to ensure that the payments system operates smoothly.

Next to cash, checks are the most popular form of payment in the United States. A 2003 law, however, has changed the way checks are processed. Checks used to be returned to the person who wrote them; now only electronic images of the checks are returned to the issuer.

Online banking is another major innovation in the banking system. Now that people can open an account anywhere in the country using the Internet, the Fed is supervising procedures to make sure that no abuses occur.

connected.mcgraw-hill.com   Monetary Policy **467**

VIDEO | **WORKSHEET**

Stock Options and Executive Greed in Enron and Worldcom

Analyzing Enron and Worldcom
Show students the video on stock options and executive greed. Discuss what these cases mean for them. **Ask: Do you think enough has been done to prevent events like these from happening again? How will these actions affect your approach to investing when you begin working and saving?** Verbal/Linguistic

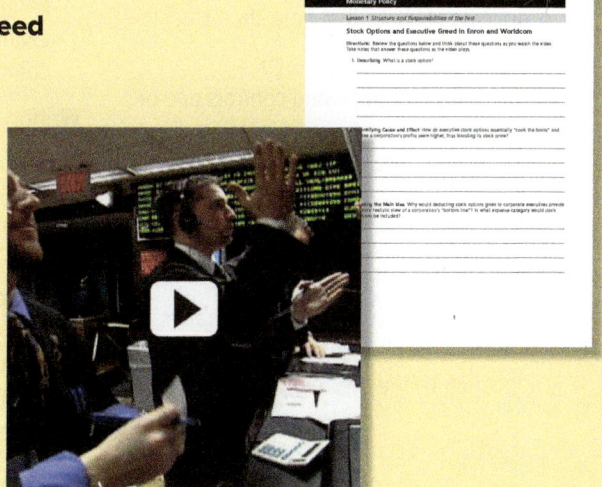

Video Supplied by BBC Worldwide Learning

CHAPTER 16, LESSON 1
Structure and Responsibilities of the Fed

C Critical Thinking Skills

Drawing conclusions about the Federal Advisory Council Ask: Why is it important that members of the Federal Advisory Council be from each member bank? *(Possible answers: They provide insight into the economy of their district. They offer different perspectives on the overall health of the economy.)* Verbal/Linguistic

R1 Reading Skills

Understanding changes in Fed advisory groups Ask: Why were some consumer protection issues removed from the Fed's control in 2011? *(They were transferred to the Consumer Financial Protection Bureau, part of the Treasury Department, as a result of lending abuses that helped cause the Great Recession.)*

T Technology Skills

Debating the penny Have students research to discover various economists' opinions about the penny, and whether the United States should continue to mint it. Ask students to research which countries have done away with their "penny" coin.

V Visual Skills

Using shredded money Most Fed district banks shred old money when they take it out of circulation. Have students agree on a fundraiser that utilizes free shredded currency. Then have volunteers email the nearest Fed bank to obtain shredded money for their fundraiser. Kinesthetic

R2 Reading Skills

Identifying Fed services to the government Ask: What financial services does the Fed provide to the government? *(conducts nationwide auctions of Treasury securities such as T-bills, T-notes, and bonds; also issues, services, and redeems these securities on behalf of the Treasury; maintains the demand deposit accounts for the Treasury; clears checks drawn on those accounts; processes savings bonds; issues federal agency checks, such as Social Security checks; moves money from one part of the country to another)*

ANSWERS, p. 467

✓ **READING PROGRESS CHECK** It evaluates economic factors to determine if interest rates should be raised or lowered.

Monetary Policy **467**

CHAPTER 16, LESSON 1
Structure and Responsibilities of the Fed

C Critical Thinking Skills

Identifying effects of Fed responsibilities Ask: How does the Fed's role in financial literacy and consumer protection contribute to economic growth? *(Sample answer: Educated consumers who are provided with reasonable financial protection will buy and sell goods with greater confidence, thereby contributing to economic growth.)* Logical/Mathematical

CLOSE & REFLECT

R Reading Skills

Drawing conclusions from the lesson Write this question on the board: How does the Fed's structure enable it to carry out its responsibilities effectively? Then organize students into groups to discuss the answer. Tell them to find details in the lesson that support and explain their answers. Invite groups to share their answers in a concluding class discussion.

ANSWERS, p. 468

EXPLORING THE ESSENTIAL QUESTION

A stable banking system allows businesses and consumers to borrow, lend money, and exchange money with confidence, which encourages the investing and spending of money, which in turn promotes economic growth. Economic growth requires higher employment.

✓ **READING PROGRESS CHECK** The Fed regulates all federally chartered banks, many state banks, bank holding companies, foreign branches of its member banks, and U.S. branches of foreign-owned banks.

---

bank holding companies company that owns and controls one or more banks

EXPLORING THE ESSENTIAL QUESTION

After the financial crisis of 2007–2009 and earlier crises, such as the Savings and Loan crisis of the late 1980s and early 1990s, it seems obvious why the Fed regulates and supervises banks. How does this oversight contribute to economic growth and full employment?

Regulating and Supervising Banks

The Fed is responsible for establishing specific guidelines that govern banking behavior. It also has the responsibility for monitoring, inspecting, and examining various banking agencies to verify that they comply with existing banking laws.

The Fed watches over foreign branches of its own member banks and U.S. branches of foreign-owned banks. The Fed has jurisdiction over many activities of state banks, including the operations of **bank holding companies**—firms that own and control one or more banks. Banks that the Fed does not directly inspect and regulate are examined by the Federal Deposit Insurance Corporation (FDIC), the Comptroller of the Currency, or various state banking authorities.

Financial Literacy and Consumer Protection

Although some of the Fed's consumer protection activities have been transferred to the Consumer Financial Protection Bureau (CFPB) in the department of the Treasury, the Fed still supplies a wealth of information on almost everything financial. The Federal Reserve Board of Governors website, for example, offers reports, calculators, and numerous other helpful guides on topics ranging from credit reports and scores to identity theft to mortgages and foreclosures.

If you buy furniture or a car on credit, you will discover that the seller must disclose several items before you make the purchase. These items include the size of the down payment, the number and size of the monthly payments, and the total amount of interest over the life of the loan. All the disclosures that the seller makes were determined by the Fed.

Acting as the Government's Bank

A final Fed function is the range of financial services it provides to the federal government and its agencies. For example, the Fed conducts nationwide auctions of Treasury securities. It also issues, services, and redeems these securities on behalf of the Treasury. In the process, it maintains numerous demand deposit accounts for the Treasury.

Because the Fed acts as a bank for the government, any check written to the U.S. Treasury is deposited in the Fed. Any federal agency check, such as a monthly Social Security payment, comes from accounts held at the Fed. The Fed can also move money from one part of the country to another so that the government can make payments wherever and whenever needed.

Conducting Monetary Policy

Although all the above functions are an important part of the Fed's role in the economy, its most important responsibility is conducting monetary policy.

✓ **READING PROGRESS CHECK**

Summarizing What kind of banks does the Fed regulate?

LESSON 1 REVIEW

Reviewing Vocabulary
1. *Identifying* Who are the member banks of the Fed?
2. *Defining* What is a bank holding company?

Using Your Notes
3. *Explaining* What functions do the Board of Governors perform?

Answering the Guiding Questions
4. *Describing* In what ways is the Fed privately owned but publicly controlled?
5. *Explaining* How does the Fed regulate banks?

Writing About Economics
6. *Argument* Why is the Fed's role in maintaining the payments system a vital part of our national financial system? What would happen if it did not perform this service?

LESSON 1 REVIEW ANSWERS

Reviewing Vocabulary
1. Commercial banks that hold shares of stock in the Fed.
2. A company that owns and controls one or more banks

Using Your Notes
3. It supervises and regulates the Fed.

Answering the Guiding Questions
4. The Fed is owned by its member banks, but all members of the Board of Governors are appointed by the president.
5. It establishes guidelines to govern banking behavior and monitors, inspects, and examines banking agencies to ensure they comply with banking laws.

Writing About Economics
6. Students should demonstrate a clear understanding of how people and financial institutions rely upon the ability to make rapid, predictable payments and exchanges of money across long distances and political boundaries. They might say the financial system would become less certain, reliable, and secure without the Fed's role.

Case Study

CHANGES in the U.S. ECONOMY: GROWTH in GOVERNMENT SPENDING

In 2013, total federal government expenditures—about $3.4 trillion—equaled about 21 percent of GDP. This is a controversial subject in the country. Growth in government spending means either increasing taxes or borrowing more money and increasing the national debt. Those defending the increase in government spending point out that most of the money goes to entitlement programs like Social Security and Medicare. Spending in these programs has to continue as the population ages. Those opposing the increase in government spending want, for example, the government to stop funding items like infrastructure programs. They want private funds to develop infrastructure programs such as cleaning up local water supplies.

An example of the federal government funding a state infrastructure project is the recent grant from the Federal Clean Water Act program to fund a project in Minnesota. The project is to address nonpoint-source (NPS) water pollution. Work on the project began in the spring of 2013 and will last three years. The funding will support studies of specific bodies of water in Minnesota being polluted and help fund development of an action plan to resolve the problem. The project will include 16 sites in Minnesota.

Those who oppose the government funding such a project want private funds to be used. One plan in Congress is to create private funds for infrastructure projects by issuing new infrastructure bonds and working to attract corporate funding. The proposed plan wants companies that buy the bonds to receive a tax break on earnings from overseas profits. Meanwhile, Minnesota moves forward with its project.

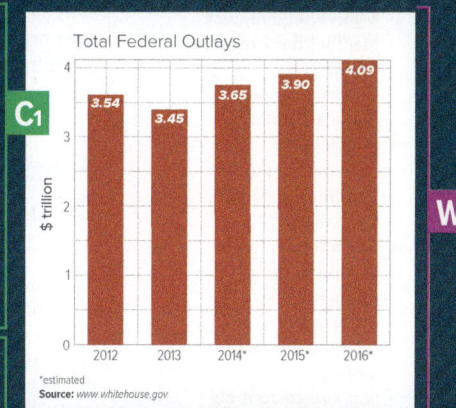

Total Federal Outlays
2012: 3.54
2013: 3.45
2014*: 3.65
2015*: 3.90
2016*: 4.09
*estimated
Source: www.whitehouse.gov

CASE STUDY REVIEW

1. **Analyzing** How is infrastructure spending different from spending in the entitlement programs of Social Security and Medicare?
2. **Assess** Politicians who think the government should fund infrastructure programs are following what overall economic philosophy? In your discussions, cite a time in U.S. history when this philosophy was prevalent.

CHAPTER 16 Case Study

C1 Critical Thinking Skills

Expressing opinions on government spending Ask students what they know about federally sponsored projects in their area. Ask whether the projects are a legitimate way to spend taxpayer money or if the expense should be borne by state or local government or by private companies.

W Writing Skills

Writing a proposal to cut spending Ask students to do research to learn more about federal taxes and the specific areas where increases are occurring. Then ask them to write a proposal suggesting how the government should rein in spending. Remind students that their proposals should identify options, predict consequences, and outline the actions to implement. **Verbal/Linguistic**

C2 Critical Thinking Skills

Discussing the role of government Tell students that the nonpoint-source water pollution project is essentially a state issue. **Ask: Why should this state project be funded by federal tax dollars?** *(States do not have the revenue to fund major projects like this. If the federal government does not do it, problems like this one will not be addressed.)*

R Reading Skills

Explaining a plan for private funding Ask: **How does the plan in Congress propose to engage private companies in funding infrastructure projects?** *(The plan calls for selling federal infrastructure bonds to private companies who would receive a tax break on overseas profits.)* Tell students that this still requires some government funding through the taxes it does not collect, but it can save a large portion of the cost. **Verbal/Linguistic**

ANSWERS, p. 469

Case Study Review

1. Social Security and Medicare are transfer payments that people pay into through FICA taxes, and people receive direct benefits under these programs. Infrastructure programs benefit a regional population.
2. Student answers should show they know about Keynesian, or demand-side fiscal policy, and the New Deal and its massive government spending.

---

networks Online Teaching Options

INTERACTIVE FEATURE

Case Study: Changes in the U.S. Economy: Growth in Government Spending

Evaluating private ownership of infrastructure Ask students if they think private investors can be convinced to pay for infrastructure. Have them discuss how this investment could be profitable to private companies. Explain that toll roads in many states are built and operated by private investors. Likewise, state buildings have occasionally been sold to private companies and then leased (rented) by the state so that the state does not have the ongoing costs associated with owning buildings. **Interpersonal**

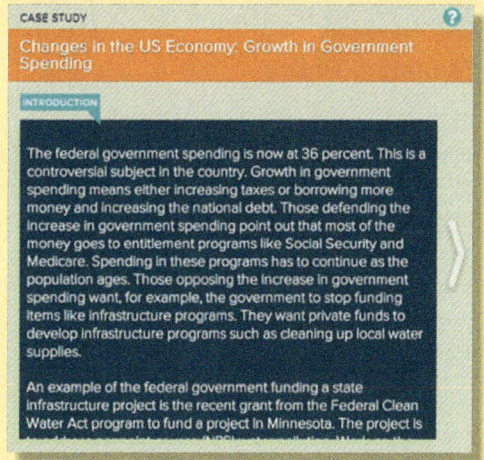

CHAPTER 16, LESSON 2
Monetary Policy

ENGAGE

R1 Reading Skills

Discussing the money supply and fractional reserve system Before students begin the lesson, ask them to summarize what they know about how the availability of more or less money affects the economy. Tell students that the Fed can manage the supply of money in a number of ways, and that one way is through the fractional reserve system. **Verbal/Linguistic**

TEACH & ASSESS

R2 Reading Skills

Explaining how fractional reserve banking increases the money supply Have students explain in their own words how the Fed's policy of fractional reserve banking (set at 20 percent) can increase the amount of money in the economy by 500 percent. *(Answers will vary but should note that banks must keep 20 percent of each deposit and then can lend out the rest. As borrowers pay back loans, or banks get additional deposits, banks can continue to lend out money.)* **Verbal/Linguistic**

ANSWERS, p. 470

EXPLORING THE ESSENTIAL QUESTION

Economic growth reduces the need for entitlement programs.

TAKING NOTES
Policy: Easy Money Policy
Effect: Lower interest rates and greater access to credit; expanded money supply
Policy: Tight Money Policy
Effect: Higher interest rates and restricted access to credit; contraction of the money supply

470

Interact with these digital assets and others in lesson 2

- ✓ INTERACTIVE GRAPH Fractional Reserves and the Monetary Policy
- ✓ INTERACTIVE GRAPH Short Run Impact of Monetary Policy
- ✓ SELF-CHECK QUIZ
- ✓ VIDEO

networks TRY IT YOURSELF ONLINE

LESSON 2
Monetary Policy

Reading Help Desk

Academic Vocabulary
- explicit

Content Vocabulary
- fractional reserve system
- legal reserves
- reserve requirement
- member bank reserve (MBR)
- excess reserves
- monetary policy
- interest rate
- easy money policy
- tight money policy
- open market operations
- discount rate
- prime rate
- monetarism
- quantity theory of money
- wage-price controls

TAKING NOTES:

Key Ideas and Details
ACTIVITY As you read this section, complete a graphic organizer like the one below to describe the effects of each monetary policy discussed.

Effects of Monetary Policies

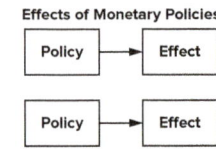

470

ESSENTIAL QUESTION

How does the government promote the economic goals of price stability, full employment, and economic growth?

Why is it in government's interest to create monetary policies that promote economic growth? Write a short paragraph to explain your answer.

Fractional Reserves and Deposit Expansion

GUIDING QUESTION *How do fractional reserves allow the money supply to grow?*

To understand how monetary policy works, we must first understand how a fractional reserve system allows the money supply to expand or contract so easily. Under a **fractional reserve system**, banks are required to keep a portion of their total deposits in the form of legal reserves. This is a feature of banking systems all over the world, and it is the foundation of banking in the United States.

Whenever a bank accepts a deposit, it must keep some of it as **legal reserves**, coins and currency that banks hold in their vaults, plus deposits at the Fed. The size of the reserves is determined by a **reserve requirement**, the percentage of every deposit that must be set aside as legal reserves. The bank can then lend out the rest, which results in a money supply that is several times larger than the initial deposit.

Banking with Fractional Reserves

To see how a fractional reserve system works, we need to expand on an example we started in Chapter 10. In it, a depositor named Kim opened a demand deposit account (DDA) by depositing $1,000 in a bank that is subject to a 20 percent reserve requirement. If we also assume that no one else has any money, the size of the entire money supply is also $1,000. **Figure 16.2** illustrates the monetary expansion process that takes place under these conditions.

- **Monday**—Because of the 20 percent reserve requirement, $200 of Kim's deposit must be set aside as a reserve in the form of vault cash

---

networks Online Teaching Options

BELLRINGER

Monetary Policy

Thinking about monetary policy Ask students what effect interest rates have in their lives. Encourage students to talk about how the rates influence both borrowing and saving. Then show students the Bellringer. Ask: **What effects do the Fed's monetary policy changes have on interest rates?** Ask students to infer what monetary policy the Fed may be following that is influencing the current interest rate. **Verbal/Linguistic**

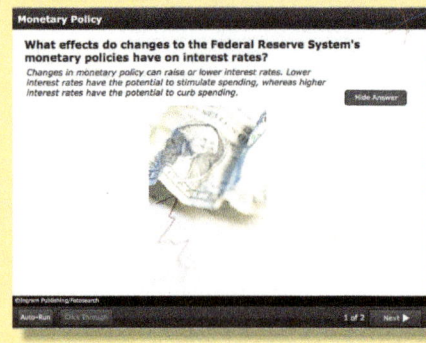

or as a **member bank reserve (MBR)**—a deposit a member bank keeps at the Fed to satisfy reserve requirements. The remaining $800 of **excess reserves**—legal reserves beyond the reserve requirement—represents the bank's lending power and can be loaned out. At the end of Monday the total money supply in the hands of the public amounts to Kim's $1,000 checking account.

- **Tuesday**—The bank lends its $800 excess reserves to Bill. Bill decides to take the loan in the form of a DDA so that the cash never leaves the bank. Even so, the bank treats Bill's DDA as a new deposit, so 20 percent, or $160, must be set aside as a reserve. This leaves $640 of excess reserves to be lent to someone else. By the end of Tuesday, the total money supply in the hands of the public amounts to $1,800—the sum of Kim's and Bill's DDAs.
- **Wednesday**—Maria enters the bank and borrows the $640 excess reserves. If she also takes the loan in the form of a DDA, the bank treats it as a new $640 deposit, 20 percent of which must be set aside as a required reserve, leaving $512 of excess reserves. By the end of the day, the money supply in the hands of the public (DDAs and cash) has grown to $2,440—the sum of the DDAs owned by Kim, Bill, and Maria.

The $2,440 result would be exactly the same if Maria had borrowed the bank's $640 excess reserves in cash. Had she done so, the money supply in the hands of the public would have consisted of the $1,800 in Kim's and Bill's checking accounts, plus Maria's $640.

Limits on Monetary Expansion

The money expansion process will now come to a temporary halt until the $640 cash returns to the bank as a deposit. If Maria spends the money, and if the person who receives it opens a new deposit so that additional excess reserves are created, the expansion process can resume.

The expansion in Figure 16.2 will continue as long as the bank has excess reserves to lend and as long as lenders deposit part or all of that money. In fact,

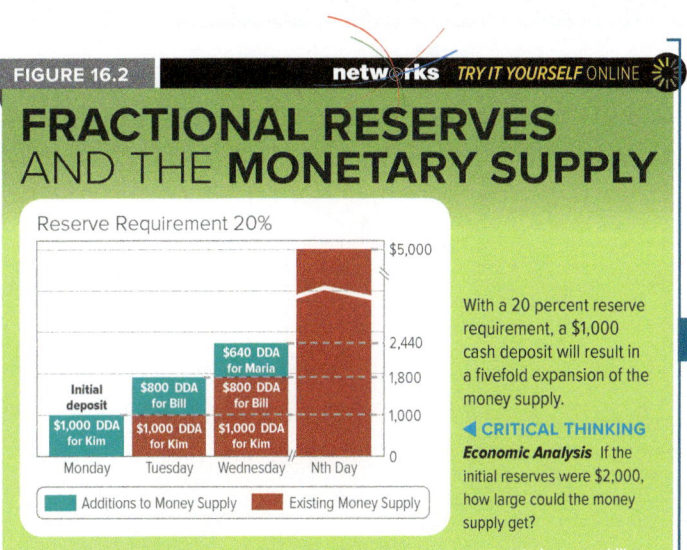

FIGURE 16.2 FRACTIONAL RESERVES AND THE MONETARY SUPPLY

With a 20 percent reserve requirement, a $1,000 cash deposit will result in a fivefold expansion of the money supply.

◀ **CRITICAL THINKING**
Economic Analysis If the initial reserves were $2,000, how large could the money supply get?

fractional reserve system system requiring financial institutions to set aside a fraction of their deposits in the form of reserves or vault cash

legal reserves currency and deposits used to meet the reserve requirements

reserve requirement formula used to compute the amount of a depository institution's required reserves

member bank reserves (MBR) reserves kept by member banks at the Fed to satisfy reserve requirements

excess reserves financial institution's cash, currency, and reserves in excess of required reserves; potential source of new loans

---

CHAPTER 16, LESSON 2
Monetary Policy

C Critical Thinking Skills

Predicting the money supply Have students predict what will happen to the money supply if the Fed increases the reserve requirement to 40 percent *(This increases the amount that must be held aside, and therefore reduces the amount that can be loaned, thus decreasing the money supply.)*, or reduces it to 10 percent *(This reduces the amount that must be held aside, and therefore increases the amount that can be loaned out and, thus, increases the money supply.)* Remind students that changing the reserve requirement is only one of the ways the Fed controls the money supply through monetary policy.

W Writing Skills

Writing to persuade Have students write a paragraph stating their opinion of the fractional reserve system. **Ask: Is it a fair or an unfair practice from the point of view of depositors?** Invite volunteers to share their opinions in a class discussion. **Verbal/Linguistic**

V Visual Skills

Calculating fractional reserves Direct students to Figure 16.2. **Ask: What would be the eventual size of the money supply if there was a 25 percent reserve requirement?** *($4,000)* **A 15 percent reserve requirement?** *($6,666.67)*

GRAPHS

Fractional Reserves and the Money Supply

Examining fractional reserves Emphasize to students that fractional reserve requirements can be used to manage the money supply. Display Figure 16.2 and ask students to read the first paragraph. Then click on Monday and explain that there was only $1,000 in the entire money supply, and Kim deposits that amount into the bank. Now the bank has the $1,000. Explain that the bank has to keep a reserve of 20 percent, but it can loan the rest. Click on Tuesday and read the text aloud. **Ask: How can there now be $1,800 in the money supply when initially there was just $1,000 total?** *(The bank received $1,000 from Kim, held back $200, and lent $800 to Bill, so now there is $1,800 in the money supply.)* Click Wednesday and Nth Day and continue to clarify the expansion of the money supply. **Visual/Spatial, Logical/Mathematical**

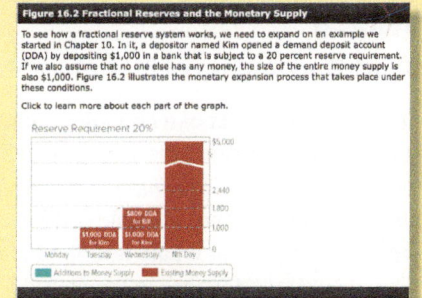

ANSWERS, p. 471

CRITICAL THINKING
$10,000

CHAPTER 16, LESSON 2
Monetary Policy

W Writing Skills

Writing a persuasive essay Have students write a letter to the editor of the local newspaper arguing for a rise or a drop in the Fed's reserve requirement. If necessary, give students an editorial letter to follow as a model. Remind them to support their opinions with facts. **Verbal/Linguistic**

Content Background Knowledge

Y2K and the Panic That Didn't Happen At the end of 1999, the Y2K problem—or millennium bug—affected older computer systems, which used just the last two digits of the year ('99) instead of the full four digits (1999). Some people worried that bank computers would think the year 2000 was the year 1900, and feared that the Y2K problem would affect depositors' ability to withdraw money from their banks. In the last week of 1999, the Fed made about $20 billion in short-term loans to member banks to make sure they had enough reserves in case customers withdrew large amounts of cash. Most banks fixed their computers by the end of 1999 and reassured the public, however, so few people withdrew their money.

ANSWERS, p. 472

✓ **READING PROGRESS CHECK** The expansion is limited when people hold more cash.

CRITICAL THINKING
The supply curve is a vertical line because the supply of money is fixed at any given time.

---

monetary policy actions by the Federal Reserve System to expand or contract the money supply to affect the cost and availability of credit

interest rate the price of credit to a borrower

as long as every dollar of DDAs is backed by 20 cents of legal reserves, the total amount of DDAs would be:

$$\frac{\text{Total MBRs}}{\text{Reserve Requirement}} = \frac{\$1,000}{.20} = \$5,000$$

People will always keep some cash, of course, so the maximum size of the DDAs may never reach $5,000. Even so, fractional reserve banking allows the sum of everyone's DDAs to grow several times larger than the initial deposit.

✓ **READING PROGRESS CHECK**

Describing What happens to the monetary expansion if people decide to hold cash in their pockets?

Conducting Monetary Policy

GUIDING QUESTION What tools does the Fed use to expand and contract the money supply?

One of the most important functions of the Fed is to conduct **monetary policy**—changes in the money supply that affect the availability and cost of credit. This in turn affects interest rates and influences economic activity.

How Monetary Policy Works

Monetary policy is based on the mechanism of supply and demand. **Figure 16.3** shows that the demand curve for money has the usual shape, which illustrates that more money will be demanded when the **interest rate**, or the price of credit to a borrower, is low. However, the supply curve does not have its usual shape. Instead, its vertical slope indicates that the supply of money is fixed at any given time.

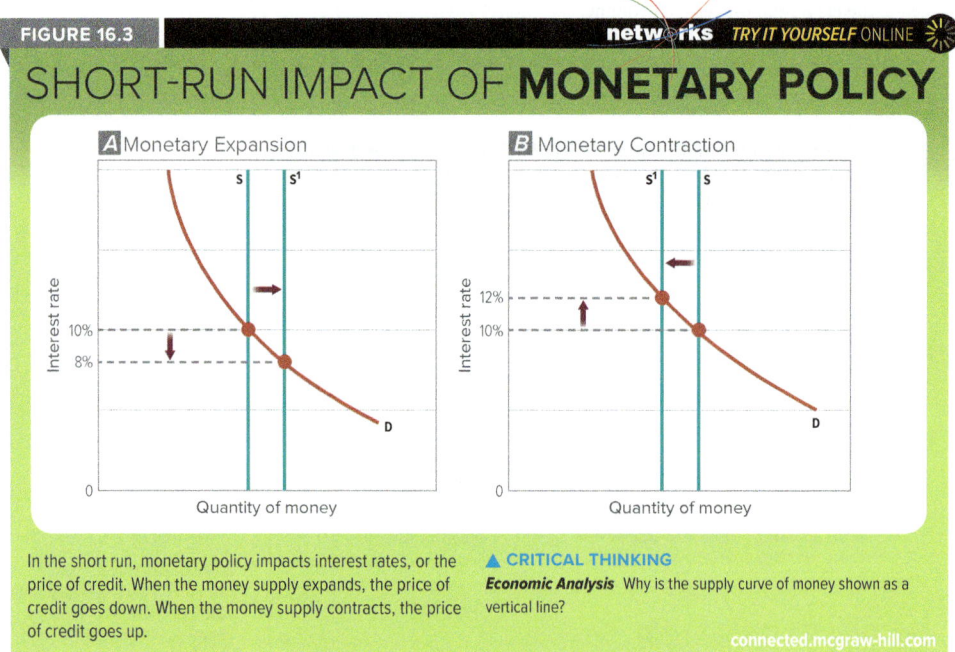

FIGURE 16.3 SHORT-RUN IMPACT OF MONETARY POLICY

In the short run, monetary policy impacts interest rates, or the price of credit. When the money supply expands, the price of credit goes down. When the money supply contracts, the price of credit goes up.

▲ **CRITICAL THINKING**
Economic Analysis Why is the supply curve of money shown as a vertical line?

---

networks Online Teaching Options

GRAPHS

Short-Run Impact of Monetary Policy

Analyzing the effect of a changing money supply Have students view the first slide of Figure 16.3 and ask a student to tell what it shows. *(the interest rate as it relates to a particular supply of money)* **Ask: If the Fed expanded the money supply, what would happen to interest rates?** *(They would fall.)* Advance to the next slide and discuss how it reflects their answer. **Why would the Fed expand the money supply?** *(to encourage companies and individuals to borrow money and then spend it on business expansion, new homes, and so on, which would stimulate economic growth)* **What would happen if the Fed reduced the money supply?** *(Interest rates would rise.)* Advance to the next slide and discuss what it shows. **Under what condition might the Fed want to increase interest rates?** *(Possible response: If inflation is rising, raising interest rates will help reduce inflationary tendencies.)* **Logical/Mathematical**

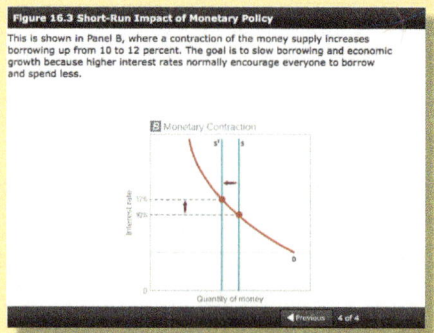

When the Fed conducts its monetary policy, it changes interest rates by changing the size of the money supply. Under an **easy money policy**, the Fed expands the money supply, causing interest rates to fall. Such a policy stimulates the economy because people and businesses borrow more at lower interest rates. This is illustrated in **Panel A**, where a larger money supply lowers the rate from 10 to 8 percent.

Under a **tight money policy**, the Fed restricts the size of the money supply. This is shown in **Panel B**, where a contraction of the money supply drives the cost of borrowing up from 10 to 12 percent. This tends to slow borrowing and economic growth because higher interest rates normally encourage everyone to borrow and spend less.

The Fed can use three major tools to conduct monetary policy. Each tool works in a different way to change the amount of excess reserves—the amount of money a bank can lend to others.

The Reserve Requirement

The first tool of monetary policy is the reserve requirement. Within limits that Congress sets, the Fed can change this requirement for all checking, time, and savings accounts.

For instance, in Figure 16.2 we assumed that a 20 percent reserve requirement applied to the DDAs held by Bill, Maria, and other depositors. In the figure, an initial deposit of $1,000 could expand to as much as $5,000 in total bank deposits. However, the Fed could also lower the reserve requirement to 10 percent or increase it to 40 percent.

- **A lower reserve requirement**—Figure 16.4 shows the results of such changes with the same initial deposit of $1,000. In **Panel A**, the 10 percent reserve requirement means that $900 of excess reserves could be lent out on the second day, $810 on the third day, and so on. Excess reserves are available until the DDAs reach a maximum of:

$$\frac{\text{Total MBRs}}{\text{Reserve Requirement}} = \frac{\$1,000}{.10} = \$10,000$$

- **A higher reserve requirement**—In **Panel B**, the reserve requirement increases to 40 percent. The result is that $600 of excess reserves are available for the first loan, $360 of excess reserves are available for the second loan, and so on until $2,500 of DDAs are generated.

$$\frac{\text{Total MBRs}}{\text{Reserve Requirement}} = \frac{\$1,000}{.40} = \$2,500$$

Historically, the Fed has been reluctant to use the reserve requirement as a policy tool, in part because other monetary policy tools work better. Even so, the reserve requirement can be powerful should the Fed need to use it more frequently.

Open Market Operations

The second tool of monetary policy is **open market operations**—the buying and selling of government securities in financial markets. This method is the Fed's most popular tool. In practice, every day the Fed buys and sells billions of dollars of government securities through dealers. The impact on the money supply is described below:

- **Fed BUYS securities**—The Fed can pay for the securities by writing a check drawn on itself, or it can pay the seller an equivalent amount of cash. Either way, the seller—usually a securities dealer—deposits the

easy money policy
monetary policy resulting in lower interest rates and greater access to credit; associated with an expansion of the money supply

tight money policy
monetary policy resulting in higher interest rates and restricted access to credit; associated with a contraction of the money supply

open market operations
monetary policy in the form of U.S. Treasury bill, or notes, or bond sales and purchases by the Fed

---

CHAPTER 16, LESSON 2
Monetary Policy

C1 Critical Thinking Skills

Determining cause and effect Ask: **Under what conditions might the Fed want to institute an easy money policy? Why?** *(The Fed might ease money policy if economic growth is slow; expanding the money supply increases business activity.)* **Under what conditions might the Fed want to institute a tight money policy? Why?** *(The Fed might tighten money policy if inflation is rising; it restricts the money supply to slow economic growth.)*
Logical/Mathematical

C2 Critical Thinking Skills

Drawing conclusions about the reserve requirement Ask: **Why do you think other monetary policy tools work better than the reserve requirement?** *(Possible answer: It may be difficult to predict the amount of change to make, and it takes time for the changes to take effect.)*
Logical/Mathematical

English Language Proficiency

Advanced High Provide students with a challenging selection to read. Point out the visual and contextual support provided. Circle, highlight, or list challenging vocabulary words. Tell them to use a graphic organizer to take notes as they read, including the vocabulary words in their notes. After they finish reading, have them write a paraphrased retelling of the information and include all of the vocabulary words in the retelling.

WORKSHEET

Math Practice for Economics

Calculating reserves and money supply Read the directions on the Math Practice for Economics worksheet aloud to students, and then ask them to work individually to complete the first half of the worksheet to figure out how much the bank can lend out with a reserve of 20 percent. Discuss students' work and ensure that everyone understands how the calculations are made. Then ask students to complete the remainder of the page. **Logical/Mathematical**

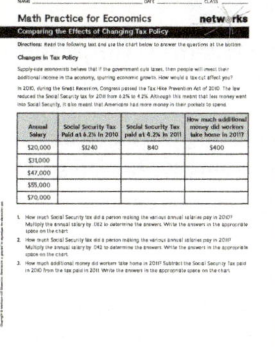

CHAPTER 16, LESSON 2
Monetary Policy

C Critical Thinking Skills

Simulating open market operations Conduct the following simulation of open market operations. Organize students into two groups to represent the public and the Fed. Give 10 slips of paper, each representing $1,000, to each member of the public. Count the money and record the total amount in circulation on the board. Next, give 10 whole sheets of paper, each one depicting a $1,000 bond, to each person representing the Fed. Announce that a new issue of bonds is available for purchase at a good interest rate from the Fed. Have the public buy some. Count and record the money in circulation. Ask the class what happened to the money supply. *(It decreased.)* Next, have the Fed buy back some of the bonds. Count and record the money now in circulation among buyers. Ask students what has happened to the money supply. *(It increased.)* Have students explain open market operations in their own words. **ELL Kinesthetic**

T Technology Skills

Explaining open market operations Have students use computer software to make a table, chart, or other graphic aid that explains how the Fed increases or decreases the money supply using open market operations. Ask students to share their graphic aids in a class discussion. **Logical/Mathematical**

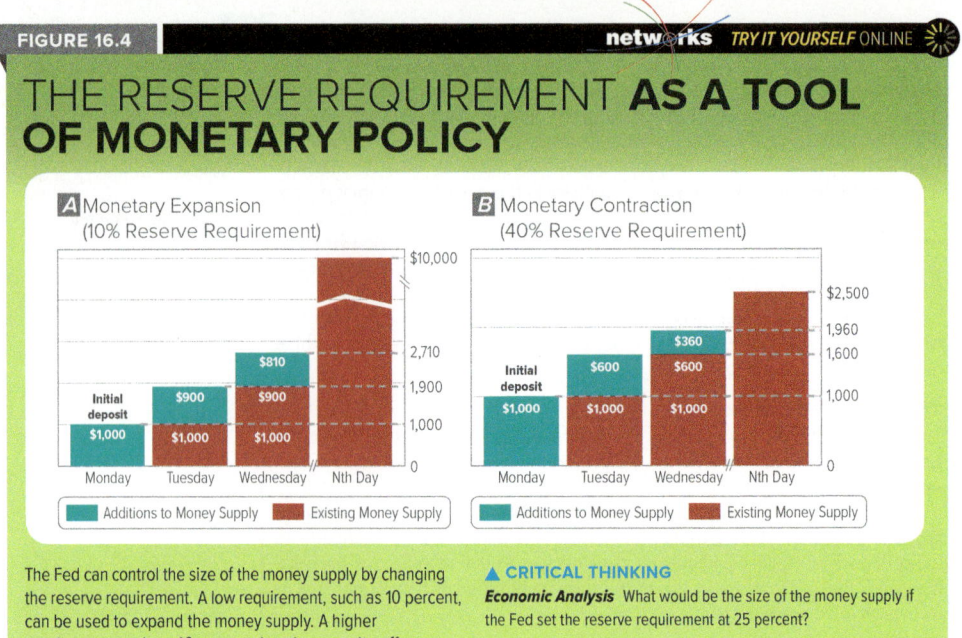

FIGURE 16.4

THE RESERVE REQUIREMENT AS A TOOL OF MONETARY POLICY

The Fed can control the size of the money supply by changing the reserve requirement. A low requirement, such as 10 percent, can be used to expand the money supply. A higher requirement, such as 40 percent, has the opposite effect.

▲ **CRITICAL THINKING**
Economic Analysis What would be the size of the money supply if the Fed set the reserve requirement at 25 percent?

connected.mcgraw-hill.com

discount rate interest rate that the Federal Reserve System charges on loans to the nation's financial institutions

prime rate best or lowest interest rate commercial banks charge their customers

monetarism school of thought stressing the importance of stable monetary growth to control inflation and stimulate long-term economic growth

check or cash in a bank—thereby increasing MBRs and creating excess reserves that can be loaned out. The result is that whenever the Fed *buys* government securities, excess reserves are created and the money supply *expands*. If the Fed buys $200 of securities, the money supply in Figure 16.2 would be $6,000:

$$\frac{\text{Total MBRs}}{\text{Reserve Requirement}} = \frac{\$1,000 + \$200}{.20} = \$6,000$$

C • **Fed SELLS securities**—Suppose the Fed were to sell some of its government securities. When a buyer takes money out of the banking system to pay for the securities, member bank reserves go down, forcing the money supply to contract. If the Fed were to *sell* $400 of securities after allowing the money supply to reach $6,000, the size of the money supply in the equation above would be $4,000:

$$\frac{\text{Total MBRs}}{\text{Reserve Requirement}} = \frac{\$1,200 - \$400}{.20} = \$4,000$$

T The 12-member Federal Open Market Committee (FOMC) is the part of the Fed that supervises the buying and selling of government securities. Normally, the FOMC decides whether interest rates are too high, too low, or just right. After the committee votes to set a target, it directs the New York Fed to buy or sell enough government securities to achieve the desired interest rate. A larger money supply, as we saw in Panel A of Figure 16.3, lowers the interest rate. A smaller money supply raises the interest rate.

---

networks Online Teaching Options

GRAPHS

The Reserve Requirement as a Tool of Monetary Policy

Examining the Fed's use of the reserve requirement Remind students that fractional reserve requirements can be used to manage the money supply. Display Figure 16.4 and ask students to compare it to Figure 16.2. Have students visually compare the length of the bars on the Nth Day of Figure 16.4 for both panel A and B. Ask them to explain why a *smaller* reserve requirement results in a *larger* amount of money in circulation, and vice versa. **Visual/Spatial, Logical/Mathematical**

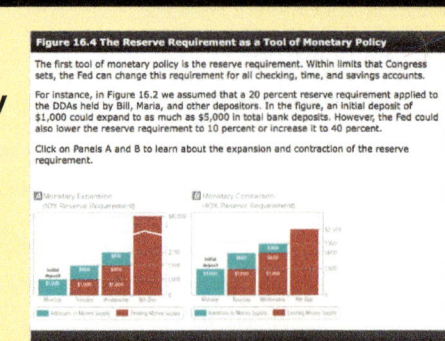

ANSWERS, p. 474

CRITICAL THINKING
The money supply would expand to $1,000/.25 or $4,000.

The Discount Rate

As a central bank, the Fed can make loans to depository institutions. The **discount rate**—the interest the Fed charges on loans to financial institutions—is the third major tool of monetary policy. Only financial institutions can borrow from the Fed; private individuals and companies are not allowed to do so.

- **Raising the discount rate**—If the discount rate goes up, fewer banks will want to borrow from the Fed, and banks will have fewer excess reserves available to loan out. A higher discount rate usually raises all interest rates and makes all borrowing more expensive, thus slowing the pace of economic growth.
- **Lowering the discount rate**—A bank may want to borrow reserves from the Fed if it has an unexpected drop in its reserves. Or a bank could also have high seasonal demands for loans. For example, a bank in an agricultural area might face heavy demand during the planting season. If enough banks were to take advantage of a lower discount rate, total MBRs would increase, which would expand the money supply.

While the Fed directly sets just the discount rate, its monetary policy actions influence other interest rates. For example, changes can directly affect the **prime rate**—the lowest rate of interest commercial banks charge their best customers. At many large banks, the prime rate is linked to other interest rates, so banks usually adjust their prime rate up or down whenever the Fed changes the discount rate.

✓ **READING PROGRESS CHECK**

Examining Why does the Fed use open market operations?

Monetary Policy Dilemmas

GUIDING QUESTION *Why is timing important for the use of monetary policy?*

The Fed uses its monetary policy tools to promote price stability, full employment, and economic growth. This may seem like an easy task, but the impact of monetary policy is complex and sometimes creates a dilemma for Fed policy makers.

Leads and Lags

One problem is that the Fed never knows for sure how long it will take for a particular policy to take effect. Lower interest rates today may stimulate investment spending next week, next month, next year, or even well after that. As a result, it is often difficult for the Fed to know exactly when it should pursue a policy or when it should abandon it.

One solution is to simply let the money supply grow at a steady rate, thereby avoiding alternating periods of easy and tight money. This is the rule-based solution offered by **monetarism**, a philosophy that places primary importance on the role of money in the economy. Monetarists believe that fluctuations in the money supply can be a destabilizing element that leads to unemployment and inflation. Therefore, they favor rule-based policies that lead to stable, long-term monetary growth at levels low enough to control inflation.

Monetarism is an important economic philosophy that competes with the demand-side policies and supply-side policies discussed in the last chapter. While both of these approaches are concerned with stimulating production and employment, neither assigns much importance to the money supply and monetary policy.

BIOGRAPHY

Janet L. Yellen
ECONOMIST (1946–)

Janet Yellen became Chair of the Board of Governors of the Federal Reserve System in February 2014. Yellen had been a Vice Chair on the Board of Governors and a professor of business and economics at the University of California at Berkeley. She has served on the Federal Reserve as a member of the Board of Governors and also as the chair of the Council of Economic Advisors under President Clinton.

Dr. Yellen has written many books on macroeconomic topics and the causes and impacts of unemployment. There is speculation that Yellen may not emphasize manipulating the economy through interest rate adjustments. Rather she may allow inflation to rise a bit higher than past Fed Chairmen to prevent an increase in unemployment numbers. One of Dr. Yellen's first problems as Fed Chair is helping guide the U.S. through the slow recovery following the 2008–2009 credit crisis. She was in favor of President Obama's use of stimulus money to invigorate the lagging economy.

Yellen is the first woman to serve as Fed Chair. Her initial term is scheduled to run for four years.

▲ **CRITICAL THINKING**
Interpreting How can Yellen's support of Obama's stimulus efforts define her role as Fed Chair?

CHAPTER 16, LESSON 2
Monetary Policy

C Critical Thinking Skills

Deciding on policy and timing Organize students into several groups to role-play members of the Federal Reserve Board of Governors. Tell half the groups that they must decide on a policy to expand the money supply, and the other half to develop a policy to restrict the growth of the money supply. Have groups consider the following: What tools of monetary policy should be used? How should they be used? Why should they be used? What is the time frame for results? Call on group representatives to explain their plans to the class. **BL Verbal/Linguistic**

R Reading Skills

Defining the quantity theory of money Ask: **What is the quantity theory of money?** *(a hypothesis that the supply of money directly affects the price level over the long run)* Ask students to cite examples and explain how they illustrate the theory. **Verbal/Linguistic**

Content Background Knowledge

Mansa Musa and Monetary Policy One of the richest and most powerful kings of Mali in West Africa was Mansa Musa, who ruled from 1307 to 1337. He doubled the size of the kingdom of Mali and created a strong central government. After he felt secure, he decided—as a devout Muslim—to make a pilgrimage to Makkah. No ordinary pilgrim, Mansa Musa was joined by thousands of servants and soldiers. Accompanying the people were hundreds of camels carrying gold, as well as food, clothing, and other supplies. Everywhere he went, Mansa Musa lavished gold gifts on his hosts and made hundreds of purchases with gold from merchants. By putting so much gold into circulation in such a short time, he caused the value of gold to fall for decades afterward.

ANSWERS, p. 476

EXPLORING THE ESSENTIAL QUESTION

The correct answer is a.

CRITICAL THINKING

The Fed lowers the reserve requirement to expand the money supply and raises it to contract the money supply.

476

EXPLORING THE ESSENTIAL QUESTION

Monetary policy is designed to help the economy in a variety of ways. Which of the following statements is true?

a. The amount of time for a policy change to affect the economy is difficult to predict.

b. The Fed is able to predict exactly how and when its policies will affect the economy.

quantity theory of money hypothesis that the supply of money directly affects the price level over the long run

Monetary Policy and Public Opinion

Monetary policy can change interest rates, but sometimes the economy is not all that responsive. For example, when the Fed aggressively lowered interest rates in 2001, and again in 2008 to move the economy out of the Great Recession, it took several years for the unemployment rate to come back down.

Of course, reductions in unemployment would be much more difficult to achieve without a monetary policy that reduces interest rates, but we have to realize that interest rates can only do so much. Meanwhile, the Fed will have to endure the clamor of politicians to do more about a situation that it can only influence marginally.

Money Supply Growth and Inflation

Another problem is that in the long run, the money supply also affects the general price level. If the money supply were to expand for a prolonged period of time, we would have too many dollars chasing too few goods, and demand-pull inflation would result. The effect of the money supply on the general price level is the basis for what is known as the **quantity theory of money**, and it often has been observed in history.

When the Spanish brought gold and silver back to Spain from the Americas in the 1500s, for example, the increase in the money supply started an inflation that lasted for 100 years. During the Revolutionary War, the economy suffered severe inflation when the Continental Congress issued $250 million of currency. The country saw similar effects during the Civil War when the Union printed nearly $500 million in greenbacks.

FIGURE 16.5

MONETARY POLICY TOOLS

Summary of Monetary Policy Tools

Tool	Fed Action	Effect on Excess Reserves	Money Supply
Reserve requirement	Lower	Frees excess reserves because fewer are needed to back existing deposits in the system.	Expands
	Raise	More reserves are required to back existing deposits. Excess reserves contract.	Contracts
Open market operations	Buy securities	Checks written by the Fed add to reserves in the banking system.	Expands
	Sell securities	Checks written by buyers are subtracted from bank reserves. Excess reserves in the system contract.	Contracts
Discount rate	Lower	Additional reserves can be obtained at lower cost. Excess reserves expand.	Expands
	Raise	Additional reserves through borrowing are now more expensive. Excess reserves are not added.	Contracts

The Federal Reserve uses monetary policy tools to promote price stability, full employment, and economic growth. Such tools as the reserve requirement, open market operations, and discount rate can either expand or contract the amount of money available in the nation's economy. This can be done as needed to speed up or slow down the economy.

▲ **CRITICAL THINKING**

Economic Analysis How does the Fed use the reserve requirement to affect the money supply?

476

---

networks Online Teaching Options

CHARTS

Monetary Policy Tools

Examining the monetary policy tools of the Fed Explore Figure 16.5 with students, reading each Fed action and discussing each effect on excess reserves and the money supply. Review student understanding by creating index cards with Fed actions on each tool, and quizzing students as to whether the money supply expands or contracts.

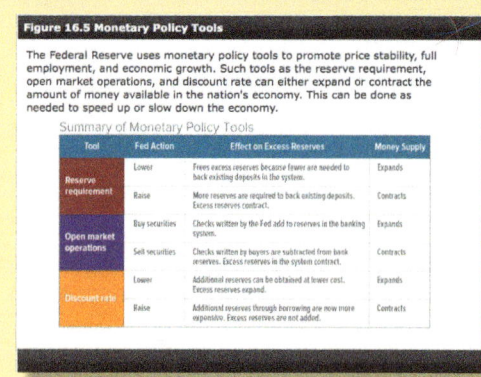

THE FEDERAL RESERVE

This cartoon indicates a few of the perceptions (and misperceptions) of how the Federal Reserve decides to take actions and what impacts these actions have on the economy.

◀ **CRITICAL THINKING**
Evaluating Counter Arguments
This example of how the Federal Reserve makes decisions is an obvious exaggeration. Explain why this exaggeration has come to pass in people's minds.

While these historical examples may seem extreme, they illustrate the inflationary dangers the Fed still faces. To illustrate, when the Fed countered the Great Recession of 2008–2009 by pushing interest rates to record lows, it accomplished this by causing a rapid expansion of the money supply. The low interest rates provided an important boost to the economy, but the rapid and prolonged expansion of the money supply might become a threat to inflation later on.

It is important to control inflation, because it is difficult to control once it gets started. In the early 1970s, for example, President Richard Nixon attempted to stop inflation by imposing **wage-price controls**—regulations that make it illegal for businesses to give workers raises or to raise prices without the **explicit** permission of the government. Most monetarists at the time said the controls would not work. Events soon proved them correct, as prices rose despite the legislated controls.

☑ **READING PROGRESS CHECK**

Summarizing What problems are associated with expansionist monetary policy?

wage-price controls policies and regulations making it illegal for firms to give raises or raise prices without government permission

explicit openly and clearly expressed

LESSON 2 REVIEW

Reviewing Vocabulary
1. *Defining* Explain in your own words what wage-price controls do.

Using Your Notes
2. Use your notes to explain the policies that help the government promote price stability.

Answering the Guiding Questions
3. *Explaining* How do fractional reserves allow the money supply to grow?

4. *Evaluating* What tools does the Fed use to expand and contract the money supply?

5. *Drawing Conclusions* Why is timing important for the use of monetary policy?

Writing About Economics
6. *Informative/Explanatory* Write a paragraph in which you compare and contrast "tight money" and "easy money" policies. How does each policy impact the economy?

connected.mcgraw-hill.com   Monetary Policy **477**

CHAPTER 16, LESSON 2
Monetary Policy

R Reading Skills

Understanding wages, prices, and raises Explain to students that wage-price controls are regulations that make it illegal for businesses to give workers raises or to raise prices without the permission of the government. Make sure that students understand the meanings of the terms *wage*, *price*, and *raise* as they are used in the context of wage-price controls. **Ask: What is a wage?** *(payment received for work that is performed)* **Ask: What is a raise?** *(an increase in pay)* Explain that to give workers raises means to increase their wages. **ELL** Verbal/Linguistic

CLOSE & REFLECT

C Critical Thinking Skills

Asking and answering questions about monetary policy **Ask: What are the two greatest benefits of monetary policy? What are the two biggest weaknesses of monetary policy?** Have students find details in the text to support their answers. Then guide a class discussion of the questions.

LESSON 2 REVIEW ANSWERS

Reviewing Vocabulary
1. Wage-price controls require businesses to get permission from the government before increasing wages or prices.

Using Your Notes
2. Answers should include the federal reserve requirement, open market operations, and the discount rate.

Answering the Guiding Questions
3. By allowing banks to lend out a percentage of each deposit, the money supply is larger than the actual deposits.

4. Fractional reserve banking, federal reserve, discount rate, and open market operations.

5. Because it is difficult to predict how long the economy will take to respond to policies.

Writing About Economics
6. Students should understand that with a tight money policy, the Fed restricts the size of the money supply. Students should understand that in an easy money supply, the Fed expands the money supply, causing interest rates to fall.

ANSWERS, p. 477

CRITICAL THINKING
The Fed's actions sometimes take time for results, and the public often is confused by the lags.

☑ **READING PROGRESS CHECK** Timing is difficult to predict, the economy does not always respond to monetary policy, and prolonged expansion can lead to inflation.

Monetary Policy **477**

CHAPTER 16, LESSON 3
Economics and Politics

ENGAGE

C Critical Thinking Skills

Assessing the effects of economic policies
Before students begin the lesson, ask them what they know or have heard about the economic events from 2007 through 2009. Explain that during that time, the Great Recession lasted for 18 months, with high unemployment and a large decline in real GDP. **Ask: What conclusions can you reach about economic policies during this time? Have economic policies since then improved the economy? Why do you think so?** Explain that students will learn more about the decisions made during and after the Great Recession in this lesson. **Verbal/Linguistic**

TEACH & ASSESS

R Reading Skills

Making inferences about business cycles GDP
Remind students about the phases of the business cycle: trough, expansion, peak, contraction. **Ask: How long did the contraction last during the Great Recession?** *(18 months)* **When did real GDP hit the "trough"?** *(in the eighteenth month)* **How do we know?** *(That is when real GDP stopped declining.)*

ANSWERS, p. 478

ESSENTIAL QUESTION ACTIVITY

Encourage students to think about the specific roles that federal, state, and local governments had in promoting growth. Ask students to identify specific ways in which government activity contributed to the economy, such as through jobs created or increased opportunities for business development.

TAKING NOTES
Changes in U.S. Economic Policy:
- Popularity of demand-side policies erode in favor of monetarism and supply-side policies
- Popularity of fiscal policies diminish
- Rise of monetary policy
- Supply-side policies gain popularity
- Variety of macro policies used to combat the Great Recession (monetary policy, quantitative easing, fiscal policies, and passive fiscal policies)

Economics and Politics Today:
- Economic politics—politicians are concerned with the economic consequences of their action
- Economic theories are a product of their times
- Council of Economic Advisers
- Campaign promises can prevent politicians from following economic advisers
- Increased public understanding

Interact with these digital assets and others in lesson 3
✓ TABLE Monetary Policy Tools
CAREERS Chief Plant Engineer, U.S. Mint
✓ SELF-CHECK QUIZ
✓ VIDEO

networks TRY IT YOURSELF ONLINE

LESSON 3
Economics and Politics

Reading Help Desk

Academic Vocabulary
- ideology
- advocates

Content Vocabulary
- quantitative easing (QE)
- passive fiscal policies
- baby boomers
- Council of Economic Advisers

TAKING NOTES:

Key Ideas and Details
ACTIVITY As you read the section, use the graphic organizer to summarize the changing nature of U.S. economic policy and economics and politics today.

Changes in U.S. Economic Policy	Economic and Politics Today

ESSENTIAL QUESTION

How does the government promote the economic goals of price stability, full employment, and economic growth?

The U.S. government promotes economic growth throughout the country. Think of ways the U.S. government has stimulated economic growth in your community or state in the last two years. Have you read or seen on TV that the government funded road and bridge repair, or did the government help a bank in your state? Write a paragraph describing one way the government has promoted economic growth in your community or state.

Changing Nature of Economic Policy

GUIDING QUESTION *Why has the use of fiscal policy declined?*

In early 2007, it seemed as if times were better than ever. Inflation was largely under control and the economy, while growing somewhat slowly, was larger and more efficient than at any time in the past. The recession of 2001 had been exceptionally mild, but recent economic expansions were getting longer and longer. On top of that, housing prices were rising to record heights and consumers felt wealthier than they ever had been in the past.

Everything changed in December 2007. The Great Recession of 2008–2009 arrived and lasted for a post-1930s record of 18 months. Real GDP declined slightly more than 4.5 percent, and the unemployment rate more than doubled. If there was ever a time to test the efficiency of our macroeconomic policies—demand-side, supply-side, or monetarist—this was it.

Until the recent Great Recession, the popularity of demand-side policies had eroded in favor of monetarism and supply-side policies. However, it took components of all three policies to keep us from sliding into what many people feared might be another Great Depression.

478

networks *Online Teaching Options*

BELLRINGER
Economics and Politics

Evaluating policies on "too big to fail" banks
Tell students that the phrase "too big to fail" was widely used during the financial crisis of 2008–2009 when the government stepped in to save the largest banks and financial institutions as well as the auto industry from financial collapse.
Ask: What do you think this phrase meant? *(The firms were very large, employed many people, and affected many people in many different industries. Allowing these firms to fail would cause massive damage to the economy.)* Guide students to discuss the questions on the slide. **Verbal/Linguistic, Logical/Mathematical**

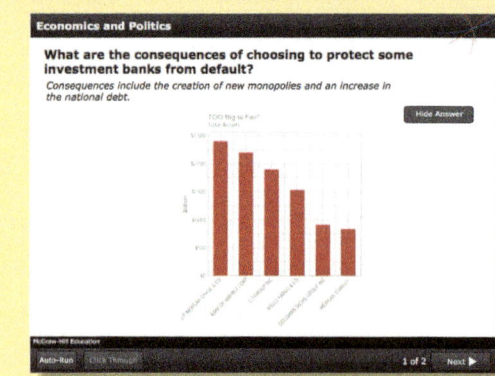

Decline of Discretionary Fiscal Policy

Discretionary fiscal policies that require an action by Congress, the president, or a government agency to take effect had been popular in the post–World War II period. Massive government spending for the war helped pull the economy out of the Great Depression. In the 1960s, President Kennedy used large cuts in income tax rates to get a sluggish economy moving again. In the early 1980s, President Reagan again tried to stimulate the economy with large cuts in marginal income tax rates.

For several reasons, however, popularity of fiscal policy seemed to diminish after President Reagan took office. One relates to the various lags—the recognition lag, the legislative lag, and the implementation lag—that occur between the recognition of a problem and actually doing something about it. After all, the typical recession, which historically lasted for less than a year, would probably be over by the time the spending begins to stimulate the economy.

The second reason for the decline of discretionary fiscal policy is the gridlock that occurs when the political parties in Congress oppose each other's budget views. In both 1995 and 1996, for example, Congress shut down the federal government when Republicans and Democrats could not agree on the federal budget. Even after the Great Recession was over, government was again shut down because of disagreement among politicians.

Ideology is the third reason. President Bush's tax cuts, for example, were based on the belief that the American economy needed a structural change. As a result, in 2001, Bush proposed cuts in tax rates that would extend to the year 2010 and beyond. Some politicians seemed so sure that their policies were the only correct ones that compromise with different points of view seemed almost impossible.

ideology a set of beliefs

THE GLOBAL ECONOMY & YOU

The Global Effects of the Fed's Actions

The Fed's monetary policies affect the global economy as well as the U.S. economy. This is because the U.S. dollar is often used in international transactions, like buying and selling crude oil. In fact, the value of the U.S. dollar has a circular effect on the purchasing power of countries around the world, which in turn affects the global economy.

When the Fed raises interest rates, it usually raises the foreign exchange value of the dollar. This increases the amount of goods the dollar can purchase in other countries. By the same token, when the value of the dollar goes down, Americans can buy fewer imported products. When the value of the dollar is combined with increased prices, this problem is exacerbated. For example, when gas prices increase, it causes Americans to spend less in general on all other goods. If Americans are purchasing fewer goods from other countries, it can affect the economies in those countries as well. In turn, consumers in those countries will be able to buy fewer American exports. This can sometimes create a vicious cycle of global economic downturn.

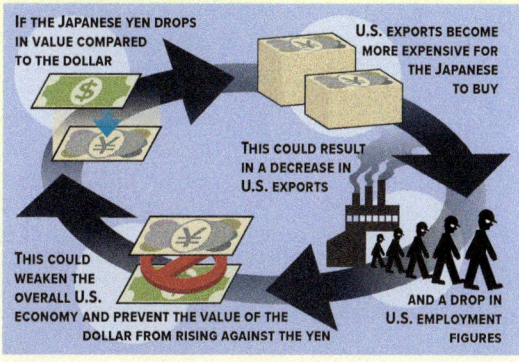

▲ CRITICAL THINKING
Explaining Explain how increasing interest rates in the United States affect the global economy.

CHAPTER 16, LESSON 3
Economics and Politics

R Reading Skills

Identifying cause and effect Ask: How did the declining popularity of discretionary fiscal policy force the Fed to take a larger role in managing the economy? *(Fiscal policy—raising or lowering taxes and government spending—was a way for Congress to stimulate the economy, so when Congress no longer followed this strategy, it left a void in the management of the economy. The Fed had the responsibility to conduct monetary policy, which enabled it to fill this void.)* **Verbal/Linguistic**

Rise of Monetary Policy

R The declining popularity of discretionary fiscal policy left a void filled by the Federal Reserve System, which has the responsibility for conducting monetary policy. As you learned earlier, monetary policy involves changing the amount and availability of credit to influence interest rates—the price you pay for borrowed money.

Monetary policy was believed to be less political and could be implemented with minimum delays. So, while the politicians argued over fiscal policy measures, the Fed could deal with a problem almost immediately.

Such a situation occurred during the recession of 2001. That recession was so short—lasting about eight months—that policymakers altogether ignored discretionary fiscal policy. However, the Fed actively lowered interest on an almost monthly basis to stimulate the economy, and eventually lowered the Fed Funds rate from 6.5% all the way to 1%. The policy worked, and the Fed took much of the credit for preventing a much worse situation.

Of course, even the Fed is not above criticism. For example, the Fed's efforts to prevent inflation by raising interest rates in 2000 may have contributed to the 2001 slowdown. Later, the lowering of interest rates in 2004 to historically low levels may have contributed to the housing boom and bust. Even so, most members of Congress believe that the power to create money and to manage the money supply should remain with an independent agency rather than with elected officials.

CAREERS | Chief Plant Engineer, U.S. Mint

Is this Career for you?

 Do you have strong decision-making skills?

 Do you have an interest in problem-solving?

 Do you enjoy working collaboratively and have strong interpersonal skills?

Working at the U.S. Mint
The U.S. Mint produces and stores monetary coins for the United States. It is organized into six departments: Finance; Information Technology; Manufacturing; Protection; Sales and Marketing; and Workforce Solution Department (Human Resources). The Mint is a federal bureau, so all workers receive a variety of federal benefits, including medical insurance, retirement plans, wellness programs, life insurance, and regular holiday and sick-time benefits. The Mint's six facilities are located in Washington, D.C., Pennsylvania, Colorado, California, New York, and Kentucky.

Salary
$114,468–$148,806 per year

Job Growth Outlook
The number of plant engineers is not expected to change in the coming years.

Profile of Work
Plant engineers, also called industrial engineers, design, install, test, and maintain production equipment. Chief plant engineers oversee the manufacture of precious metal, collectible coins, and national coins. They also consult with management on engineering operations and systems and on the modification of systems.

480

networks Online Teaching Options

INTERACTIVE FEATURE

Career: Chief Plant Engineer, U.S. Mint

Investigating the career of chief plant engineer
Ask a student to read aloud the Profile of Work.
Ask: Why does a plant engineer need strong-decision making skills? *(Sample answer: He or she must make frequent decisions about manufacturing processes and procedures that will determine the quality of the metals and coins produced.)* **Why is an interest in problem-solving an important qualification?** *(Problems will occasionally develop with any manufacturing process. The plant engineer must like finding solutions.)* **Why are collaboration and interpersonal skills important?** *(A plant engineer does not work alone but must coordinate efforts with others and manage a team.)* Ask students to consider all aspects of the career and then discuss whether it is a job they have an interest in, and why or why not. **Verbal/Linguistic**

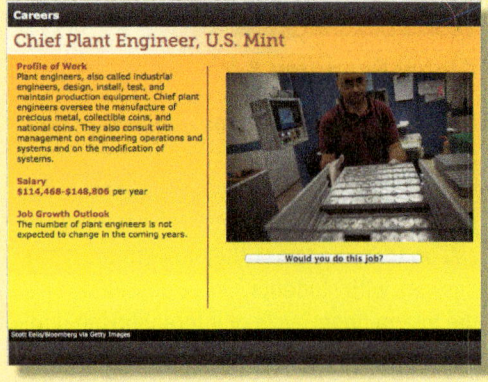

Popularity of Supply-Side Policies

Supply-side policies were also gaining popularity. These policies were structural in the sense that things like fewer government regulations and smaller government expenditures did not have to be managed to compensate for changing economic conditions. Instead, supply-side supporters argued that you could put the economy on a faster growth path by shrinking government, lowering tax rates, and reducing government regulations.

Some of the popularity of the supply-side policies was probably due to people's dislike for taxes, so lower taxes seemed appealing. Likewise, some people may have liked the philosophy of having a smaller government and fewer regulations. Either way, however, there are strong arguments supporting the supply-side position.

Supply-side policies were not designed to deal with the short-term fluctuations of the business cycle. Instead, they were designed to promote growth and economic efficiency. As a result, supply-side policies, while popular, had little to offer when the economy slumped in 2008.

EXPLORING THE ESSENTIAL QUESTION

You have held a part-time job at the local supermarket for the past two years, and the supermarket has to lay off people during a downturn in the economy. You are one of those laid off. What passive fiscal policy will help you replace the income you lost in being laid off? Write two paragraphs identifying and explaining how this passive fiscal policy works.

Macro Policies and the Great Recession

The severity of the Great Recession was a major surprise. Because the economy was declining in all of 2008 and half of 2009, it is called the recession of 2008–2009. It also lasted 18 months, a record not seen since the 1930s, with real GDP declining by about 4.5 percent. In addition, more than 8,400,000 jobs were lost, which drove the unemployment rate to 10 percent in October 2009.

In the banking sector, there was almost a complete meltdown of trust. Banks were unwilling to lend because they worried about getting repaid, and businesses couldn't borrow to cover their bills. All of these factors made the recession the worst since the Great Depression of the 1930s.

Given the severity of the problem, a variety of policies were used:

- **Monetary policy** was used extensively by the Fed to keep interest rates as low as possible. The Fed managed to lower interest rates on Treasury securities to less than 0.45 percent in 2009—and then kept the rates there for a five-year period.
- **Quantitative easing (QE)** was a new tool used by the Fed to keep interest rates low. Rather than buying high-quality government Treasury securities to expand the money supply, the Fed purchased large quantities of riskier securities and other investments from private banks. This had two effects. First, the money that was pumped into the economy helped keep interest rates low. Second, the Fed absorbed some of the risk that banks held so that banks would be more inclined to lend again.
- Congress and the president responded with surprising speed despite widely differing political philosophies when the following fiscal policies were implemented:
  - In **March 2008**, President Bush sponsored and Congress passed a $700 billion Troubled Asset Relief Program (TARP) that was designed to purchase potentially bad loans and investments from banks.

quantitative easing (QE) technique used by the Federal Reserve to keep interest rates low and encourage banks to take on more loans to stimulate the economy

---

CHAPTER 16, LESSON 3
Economics and Politics

C Critical Thinking Skills

Defining supply-sider policies Ask: **What arguments did supply-siders make to put the economy on a faster growth path?** *(shrinking government, lowering tax rates, reducing government regulations)*

R Reading Skills

Summarizing macro policies of the Great Recession Have students create a concept web, with "Ending the Great Recession" in the middle oval. In the outer ovals, have students list the policies taken by the Fed, Congress, and the president to end the Great Recession.

WORKSHEET

Enrichment Activity: Assessing the Fed's Action

Evaluating events of the 2007–2008 financial crisis Distribute copies of the Enrichment Activity worksheet to students and ask them to work on their own to read the text and answer the questions. When they finish, have students meet in small groups to share their responses. Call on students to contribute what they have learned about the financial crisis as the class discusses the lesson. **Verbal/Linguistic**

ANSWERS, p. 481

EXPLORING THE ESSENTIAL QUESTION

Student answers should show an understanding that unemployment insurance is a passive fiscal policy. It is run and administered by each state.

CHAPTER 16, LESSON 3
Economics and Politics

W Writing Skills

Writing a letter to the editor Instruct students to search for recent news articles about the Fed in magazines, newspapers, and news Web sites. Ask students to write a letter to the editor expressing their opinions about the Fed's recent policies. Tell students to support their points with facts and convincing arguments from their source material. Remind students to check the validity of their sources for propaganda and frame of reference. **Verbal/Linguistic**

C Critical Thinking Skills

Assessing the likelihood of another Great Depression Ask: **Do you think the United States could enter another Great Depression today? Why or why not?** *(Students answering "no" may point out that economists now have a better understanding of how the economy works. Students answering "yes" may suggest that events overseas could trigger a depression.)* **Verbal/Linguistic**

R Reading Skills

Predicting consequences of baby boomer retirement Review with students the general concerns related to the issue of retiring baby boomers. Ask: **What economic problems do you think economists have been focusing on since 2010?** *(Answers may include the bankruptcy of Social Security, the massive national debt, and large trade deficits.)* **Verbal/Linguistic**

ANSWERS, p. 482

✓ **READING PROGRESS CHECK** Discretionary fiscal policy is used less frequently for a few reasons. The popularity of discretionary fiscal policy diminished after Reagan was elected. Gridlock that occurs in Congress when political parties oppose each other over budgetary issues is another reason. And ideology, the belief that the American economy needed a structural change, was yet another reason.

---

passive fiscal policies fiscal actions that do not require new actions to go into effect

- In **February 2009**, President Obama sponsored and Congress passed the $787 billion American Recovery and Reinvestment Act (ARRA), which helped finance ailing firms like General Motors, Chrysler, and AIG, one of the biggest insurance companies in the world.
- Finally, **passive fiscal policies**, those that do not require new or special legislative action to go into effect, also played a major stabilizing role. Automatic stabilizers fall into this category because they respond automatically when the economy weakens. Many of the newly unemployed received financial support from state unemployment programs; others tried to retrain to learn new skills. Older workers who could not find a job could collect Social Security if they were eligible.

The combination of the above policies prevented the economy from getting worse, and by 2012, real GDP had recovered to its pre-recession high.

✓ **READING PROGRESS CHECK**

Summarizing Why is discretionary fiscal policy used less frequently today than in the past?

Economics and Politics Today

GUIDING QUESTION *In what ways is the prevailing economic theory a product of the times?*

The choice of which economic policies work best is difficult during periods like the Great Recession—but that time it turned out that we needed a combination of everything. The differences of opinions among economists, however, are smaller than most people realize.

Economic Politics

In the 1800s, the science of economics was known as "political economics." After a while, economists broke away from the political theorists and tried to establish economics as a science in its own right.

In recent years, the two fields have merged again. This time, however, they have done so in a way better described as "public choice economics." Today, politicians are concerned largely with the economic consequences of what they do. Most of the major debates in Congress are over spending, taxes, and other budgetary measures.

Why Economists Differ

Economists who choose one policy over another normally do so because they think that some problems are more critical than others. For example, one economist might think that unemployment is the crucial issue, while another believes that inflation is.

Also, most economic theories are a product of their times. The unemployment and other problems that occurred during the Great Depression influenced a generation of demand-side economists. Because the government sector was so small during the 1930s, supply-side policies designed to make government's role even smaller probably would not have helped much then.

Later, from the 1960s through 1980s, the monetarists gained influence because of the slow decline in popularity of discretionary fiscal policy and because of a decade or more of high and variable inflation. Then, by the 1980s, the ideological rejection of "big government" created a generation of supply-siders who thought that the key to economic growth was a smaller government.

baby boomers people born in the United States during the historically high birthrate years from 1946 to 1964

As we look ahead, the large population of retired **baby boomers**, who were born between 1946 and 1964, will have their own unique set of problems when they retire. The problems facing this group may well prompt another generation of economists to focus on a whole new set of issues. In the end, then, the views of economists are very much affected by the problems of the current period.

---

networks Online Teaching Options

VIDEO **WORKSHEET**

Congressional Budget Office

Examining the Congressional Budget Office Tell students to keep in mind the makeup and purpose of the Council of Economic Advisers as they watch the video on the Congressional Budget Office. Guide them in discussing how these two bodies are alike and how their roles contribute to the economic policies of the country and add to the public's understanding of the economy. **Visual/Spatial, Verbal/Linguistic**

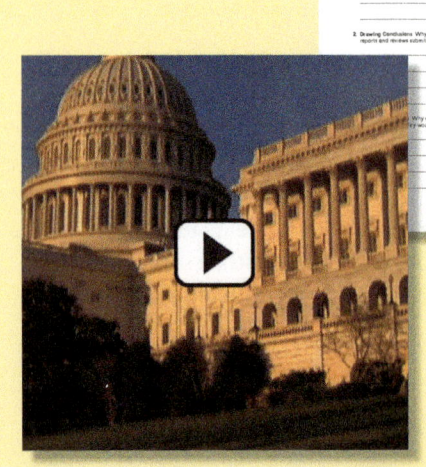

Council of Economic Advisers

Generally, economists and politicians work together fairly closely. To help keep track of the economy, the president has a **Council of Economic Advisers**, a three-member group that reports on economic developments and proposes strategies. The economists are the advisers, while the politicians direct or implement the policies. In its role as "the president's intelligence arm in the war against the business cycle," the council gathers information and makes recommendations.

Many of the economists who have served on the Council of Economic Advisers have moved on to other important positions. For example, Ben Bernanke was chair of President George Bush's Council of Economic Advisers before he went on to be Chair of the Fed's Board of Governors. Likewise, Janet Yellen was chair of President Bill Clinton's Council of Economic Advisers and has now moved on to the Fed as Ben Bernanke's successor.

The president listens to the economists' advice but may not be willing or able to follow it. For example, if the president **advocates** a balanced budget, the economic advisers may recommend raising taxes to achieve this goal. If one of the president's campaign pledges was not to raise taxes, however, the president might reject the advisers' suggestion and let a deficit develop.

Council of Economic Advisers three-member group that devises strategies and advises the President of the United States on economic matters

advocates supports; speaks in favor of

Increased Public Understanding

Despite disagreeing on some points, economists have had considerable success with the description, analysis, and explanation of economic activity. They have developed many statistical measures of the economy's performance. Economists also have constructed models that are helpful with economic analysis and explanation. All of these tools are necessary if we are to understand the opportunity costs of the trade-offs we must make when we select one policy over another.

In the process, economists have helped the American people become more aware of the workings of the economy. This awareness has benefited everyone, from the student just starting out to the politician who must answer to the voters.

As we saw during and after the Great Recession, economists today know enough about the economy to prevent a depression like the one in the 1930s. It is doubtful that economists know enough—or can persuade others that they know enough—to avoid minor recessions. Even so, they can devise policies to stimulate growth, help disadvantaged groups when unemployment rises or inflation strikes, and generally make the American economy more successful.

✓ **READING PROGRESS CHECK**

Interpreting What is the role of the Council of Economic Advisers?

LESSON 3 REVIEW

Reviewing Vocabulary
1. *Defining* Explain what quantitative easing is and what government office initiates it.

Using Your Notes
2. *Summarizing* Use your notes to summarize the U.S. economic policy today.

Answering the Guiding Questions
3. *Considering Advantages and Disadvantages* Why has the use of fiscal policy declined since the recession of 2001?

4. *Evaluating* In what ways are prevailing economic theories the product of their times?

Writing About Economics
5. *Argument* After reading about the changes in the government's role in the economy, write a one-page essay arguing whether you think those changes are helpful or harmful to the U.S. economy. Give your reasons.

CHAPTER 16, LESSON 3
Economics and Politics

C Critical Thinking Skills

Understanding the goals of the Council of Economic Advisers Ask: **What is meant by the Council of Economic Advisers' "war against the business cycle"?** *(The Council of Economic Advisers seeks to minimize the swings in economic health and limit the damage caused by downturns.)*
AL Verbal/Linguistic

CLOSE & REFLECT

R Reading Skills

Summarizing the lesson Have students write two or three paragraphs summarizing the connection between politics and economics and describing its effects on the economy.

ANSWERS, p. 483

✓ **READING PROGRESS CHECK** The role of the Council of Economic Advisers is to gather information and make recommendations to the president.

LESSON 3 REVIEW ANSWERS

Reviewing Vocabulary
1. Quantitative easing is a tool used by the Federal Reserve to keep interest rates low.

Using Your Notes
2. The economic policy today is dominated by major debates in Congress over spending taxes and other budgetary measures. Also, economists disagree over economic policy. The president now has a Council of Economic Advisers, and the American public are more informed about economic issues than previously.

Answering the Guiding Questions
3. There are several reasons why, including the diminishing of its popularity after Reagan was elected, the gridlock in Congress as politicians disagree on budgets, and the rise of monetary policy.

4. Students should discuss the differences of theories between economists and that economic theory is very much affected by the problems of the current moment.

Writing About Economics
5. Student answers should show that they can identify the changes, including the decline in discretionary fiscal policy, the rise of monetary policy, the popularity of supply-side policies, and macro policies that were used during the Great Recession.

CHAPTER 16
Debate

ENGAGE

C1 Critical Thinking Skills

Expressing opinions about the Fed Tell students that the Federal Reserve Bank is one of the three most powerful institutions for managing the economy in the U.S. The other two are Congress and the president, but those two branches of government are often locked in political disagreements that prevent quick and forceful responses during economic crises. The Fed, however, can act quickly and decisively to stem market downturns or other negative economic events. **Ask: Why would some people advocate abolishing the Fed?** *(Some students may say the Fed should be abolished because it is too powerful and it is not a democratic institution.)* Encourage students to discuss the issue, and then to read the rest of the Debate feature to learn more.

TEACH & ASSESS

C2 Critical Thinking Skills

Examining arguments Divide students into groups and assign each group to discuss the bulleted lists of Yes and No arguments. In class, discuss each of the points, calling on groups to contribute their understanding of what each point means. Ask students to tell which points they think are most important and to explain why.
Interpersonal, Logical/Mathematical

Debates

C1 Should the Federal Reserve Bank be abolished?

The Federal Reserve was established by Congress in 1913 in response to a bank panic in 1907. The Fed has had its critics ever since, many wanting to abolish it altogether.

The debate intensified during the financial crisis of 2007–2009 during which the Fed used a range of monetary policies to try to stimulate the economy, reduce unemployment, control inflation, and otherwise stabilize and restore the economy.

Critics claim the policies didn't work and may have even made the situation worse. Proponents of the Fed claimed the actions did work and saved the United States from falling into another Great Depression.

C2 YES — We would be better off without the Fed because . . .

- RETURNING TO THE GOLD STANDARD WOULD STABILIZE THE DOLLAR'S VALUE
- FREED FROM THE FED, MARKETS WOULD REGULATE THE ECONOMY
- FED POLICIES HAVE CAUSED LONG-TERM DEPRECIATION OF THE DOLLAR
- FED POLICIES OF EASY CREDIT AND LOW INTEREST RATES ENCOURAGE BUBBLES, BOOMS, AND BUSTS

> A monetary policy of easy credit and artificially low interest rates was the main source of the financial bubble, and the correction is always trying to fix what the Federal Reserve has done. The only way you can address the business cycle and prevent wild swings in the business cycle is by addressing the Federal Reserve and how they cause nothing but mischief.

—Congressman Ron Paul. Interview with Jennifer Schonberger, "Should We Abolish the Federal Reserve?" *The Motley Fool*, September 25, 2009

▲ Would a return to the gold standard stabilize the economy better than the Federal Reserve?

---

networks — Online Teaching Options

DEBATE

Debate: Should the Federal Reserve Bank be abolished?

Evaluating expert opinions on the Fed Ask students to read the quotations and compare the main points they make.
Ask: Which individual makes the stronger argument? Why do you think so? *(Students should give reasons for their responses.)* **How do these arguments correspond with what you already know about the Fed?** *(Guide students in recalling what they have already studied about the role and responsibility of the Fed.)* Logical/Mathematical

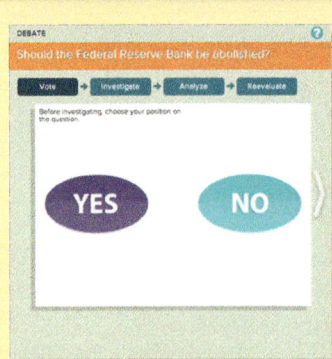

NO We would not be better off without the Fed because...

- CHANGING THE CURRENCY SYSTEM COULD DESTABILIZE THE WORLD'S ECONOMIES
- FED MONETARY POLICIES CAN STIMULATE GROWTH DURING RECESSIONS OR DEPRESSIONS
- SOME AGENCY HAS TO OVERSEE BANKS, MAINTAIN PAYMENTS SYSTEMS, AND SO ON
- FED POLICIES EVEN OUT TURBULENCE IN U.S. AND INTERNATIONAL ECONOMIES

networks
TRY IT YOURSELF ONLINE
For an interactive version of this debate go to connected.mcgraw-hill.com

R
" The Federal Reserve is the agency best equipped for the task of supervising the largest, most complex firms.... It is the only agency with broad and deep knowledge of financial institutions and the capital markets necessary to do the job effectively.... In addition, the Fed's role as lender of last resort depends importantly on its supervision of the largest, most interconnected firms. Supervision gives it deep understanding and timely access to information about the banking sector, payments systems, and capital markets."

—Deputy Secretary Neil S. Wolin, Remarks to the American Bar Association's Banking Law Committee, November 13, 2009

▲ Neil Wolin supports the operation of the Federal Reserve.

ANALYZING the issue

1. Analyzing Reread the first quotation. Congressman Paul claims that easy credit and artificially low interest rates were a main cause of the financial bubble. How can the Fed create easy credit? How can it create artificially low interest rates?

2. Making Generalizations Review the arguments and the quotations in support of the role of the Federal Reserve. What generalizations can you make about the Fed from the points made in this argument?

3. Defending Which argument do you find most compelling? Explain your answer.

485

CHAPTER 16
Debate

R Reading Skills

Considering open market operations Remind students about the Fed's ability to increase or decrease the money supply through open market operations. **Ask: How does this demonstrate the value of the Fed?** *(It demonstrates how the Fed can increase the money supply rapidly in a crisis.)* **What other group could have a similarly rapid response? Explain.** *(None. Congress and the president are too politically engaged to implement responses this quickly.)* **Logical/Mathematical**

CLOSE & REFLECT

C Critical Thinking Skills

Summarizing the main arguments Draw a T-graph on the board. Label one column "Yes" and the other "No." Call on students to list the main points given in the feature that support the two sides of the Debate.

GRAPHIC ORGANIZER
Table

Preparing and defending arguments Divide the class into groups for and against the issue, and distribute the graphic organizer. Ask students to follow these steps in preparing their arguments:

1. Write *Arguments* as the header for the first column. Have students list four reasons that support their position.
2. Write *Counterarguments* as the second column header. Have students come up with points their opponents could use to minimize their arguments.
3. Write *Refutations* as the final column header. Have students write down ways that they can refute, or prove the opponents' counterarguments are wrong.
4. Have students rank arguments from strongest to weakest.

Interpersonal, Visual/Spatial

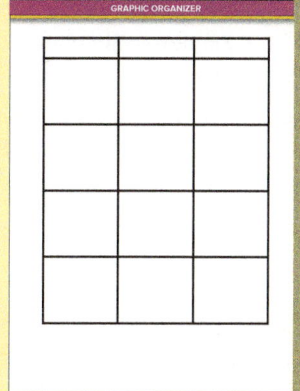

ANSWERS, p. 485

ANALYZING the issue

1. Through the Open-Market Committee, the Fed can reduce the interest rates it charges member banks. The rates are artificial because they're not a result of market competition but a result of the Fed's arbitrary decision based on analysis of economic events. Credit becomes easier because, with lower rates, banks can charge lower rates and are encouraged to make more loans.
2. The Fed can act rapidly, making changes that will almost immediately begin affecting the economy in response to negative or positive events. The Fed may be able to smooth out swings in market conditions and public confidence.
3. Students may choose either of the arguments, but should explain why they feel the argument is most compelling.

Monetary Policy

Chapter 16
Study Guide

R Reading Skills

Summarizing information Refer students to the diagram in the center of this page. Have students create an outline that has each Fed responsibility as a major heading. Then ask students to review the textbook and find supporting details for each heading. They should include these details as bullet points on their outlines. Finally, ask students to create a classroom outline by sharing their bullet points. **Interpersonal**

C Critical Thinking Skills

Determining Cause and Effect Ask students to speculate on when most borrowing occurs. *(Students should recognize that most borrowing occurs when interest rates are low.)* Then lead a class discuss on how consumer borrowing affects the Fed's decisions to use a policy tool. **Ask:** What tools might the Fed use to slow consumer borrowing? *(Possible answer: open market operations to lower bank reserves, or the discount rate to raise the interest rate)* What tools might the Fed use to encourage consumer borrowing? *(Possible answer: open market operations to add to bank reserves, or the discount rate to lower the interest rate)* **Verbal/Linguistic**

STUDY GUIDE

LESSON 1

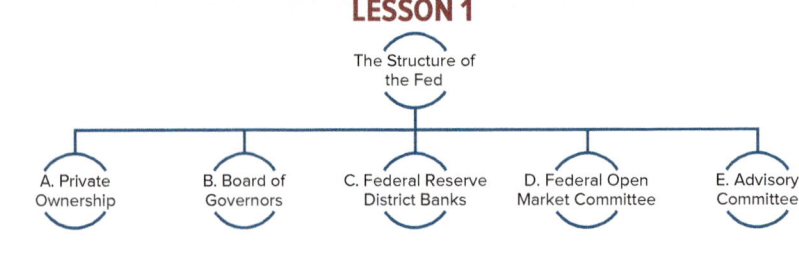

The Structure of the Fed
- A. Private Ownership
- B. Board of Governors
- C. Federal Reserve District Banks
- D. Federal Open Market Committee
- E. Advisory Committee

LESSON 2

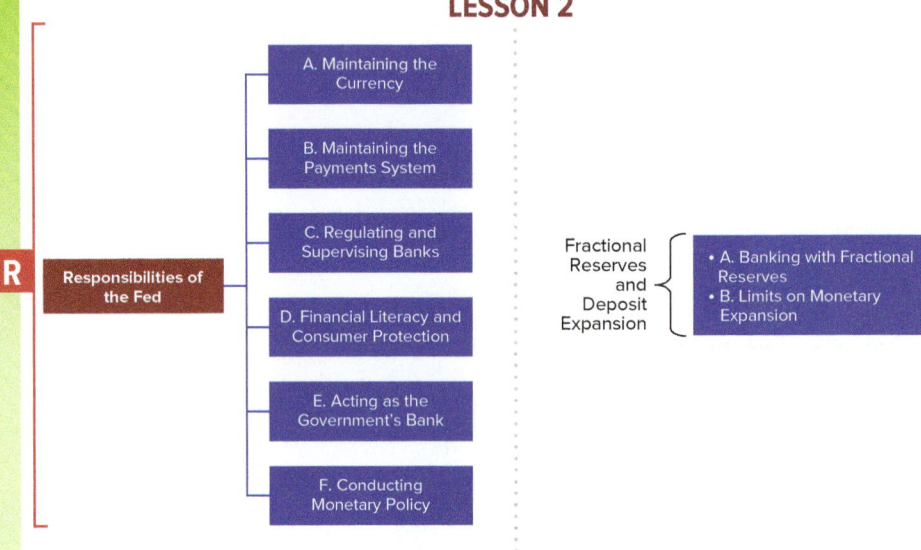

R Responsibilities of the Fed
- A. Maintaining the Currency
- B. Maintaining the Payments System
- C. Regulating and Supervising Banks
- D. Financial Literacy and Consumer Protection
- E. Acting as the Government's Bank
- F. Conducting Monetary Policy

Fractional Reserves and Deposit Expansion
- A. Banking with Fractional Reserves
- B. Limits on Monetary Expansion

LESSON 3

Changing Nature of Economic Policy
- Decline of Discretionary Fiscal Policy
- Popularity of Supply-Side Policies
- Macro Policies and the Great Recession

Economics and Politics Today
- Economic Politics
- Why Economists Differ
- Council of Economic Advisors
- Increased Public Understanding

C **Conducting Monetary Policy**
- How Monetary Policy Works
- The Reserve Requirement
- Open Market Operations
- The Disount Rate

Monetary Policy Dilemmas
- Leads and Lags
- Monetary Policy and Public Opinion
- Money Supply Growth and Inflation

486

networks Online Teaching Options

WORKSHEET

Economic Simulation
In this Economic Simulation worksheet, students role-play economists who make recommendations on an aspect of Fed policy intended to keep the economy on a path of steady, stable growth.

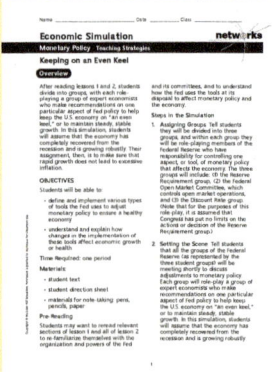

486

CHAPTER 16 Assessment

Directions: On a separate sheet of paper, answer the questions below. Make sure you read carefully and answer all parts of the questions.

Lesson Review

Lesson 1

1 **Describing** In what ways are member banks part of the Federal Reserve System?

2 **Specifying** What is the Federal Reserve System's primary monetary policy-making body, and what does that body do?

Lesson 2

3 **Cause and Effect** What is the effect of a fractional reserve system?

4 **Identifying** What is the economic philosophy that places primary importance on the role of money in the economy? Explain what solution this philosophy offers to promote price stability, full employment, and economic growth.

Lesson 3

5 **Explaining** What two policies were used by the Fed in the Great Recession? Explain what the Fed does in implementing these two policies.

6 **Assess** What was the passive fiscal policy that helped stabilize the economy during the Great Recession? Give an example.

Critical Thinking

7 **Identifying Central Issues** Identify the Fed's primary overseer and what its powers are.

8 **Constructing Arguments** Write a blog post in which you argue whether or not the Fed should have the major job of making changes in the money supply to affect the availability and cost of credit working in the current economy.

9 **Speculating** Assume that management of the economy still relied only on discretionary fiscal policies. Given the issues you have seen Congress struggle with, what would be the consequences of such a policy?

10 **Explaining** What is the relationship between the Fed and bank-holding companies?

Analyzing Visuals

Use the graphs below to answer the following questions.

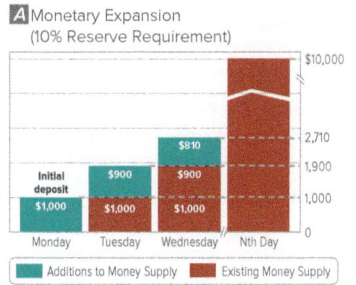

A Monetary Expansion (10% Reserve Requirement)

B Monetary Contraction (40% Reserve Requirement)

11 **Identifying Graphs** In Graph A Monetary Expansion, with the Fed keeping interest rates low, what is the total addition to the money supply on Wednesday?

12 **Reading Graphs** In Graph B Monetary Contraction, what is the amount of money added to the money supply by Wednesday? Why is that less than in Graph A?

Need Extra Help?

If You've Missed Question	1	2	3	4	5	6	7	8	9	10	11	12
Go to page	465	466	470	475	481	482	465	472	478	465	472	472

Chapter 16 Assessment Answers

Lesson Review

Lesson 1

1 Member banks are commercial banks that hold shares of stock in the Fed.

2 The Federal Open Market Committee is the Fed's primary monetary policy-making body. It has the power to raise or lower interest rates, thus having a direct impact on the cost and availability of credit.

Lesson 2

3 The fractional reserve system allows the money supply to expand or contract easily.

4 The economic philosophy is monetarism. This philosophy offers the solution of expanding or contracting the money supply to affect the cost and availability of credit.

Lesson 3

5 The Fed used a monetary policy to keep interest rates as low as possible. It also implemented quantitative easing by swapping its holdings of government securities for riskier securities and loans that banks held, absorbing some of the risk banks held so they would begin lending again.

6 These policies included automatic stabilizers that are ready automatically when the economy weakens. State unemployment programs are examples of such policies.

Critical Thinking

7 The Fed's primary overseer is the Board of Governors. It is mostly a regulatory and supervisory agency.

8 Student answers should demonstrate there is a debate about the role of the Fed affecting the availability of credit in the current economy. Student answers should give reasons for their opinions on this issue.

9 Student answers should show they understand the gridlock that occurs in Congress over monetary and budgetary policy.

10 The Fed has jurisdiction over the operations of bank-holding companies that are firms that own or control one or more banks.

Analyzing Visuals

11 $2,710

12 It expanded only to $1,960. The Fed raised the reserve requirement.

Chapter 16
Assessment Answers

Answering the Essential Questions

13 The government promotes its economic goals by lowering or raising interest rates and by implementing quantitative easing, preventing banks from going bankrupt.

14 Student answers should show they realize the President's Council of Economic Advisers is made up of economists, but that politicians implement the decisions the president ultimately makes about the economy. Students should also know that recently gridlock has occurred in Congress over financial policies.

21st Century Skills

15 Student answers should show they understand monetarism and whether they agree the Fed should implement that philosophy.

16 Student presentations should include that the Fed lowered interest rates and implemented quantitative easing and passive fiscal policy. The summary of the results should show an awareness that together, all those policies helped alleviate the Great Recession.

17 Student graphs should show that interest rates dropped greatly during the Great Recession and are now slowly recovering.

Building Financial Literacy

18 a. Student answers should show that if the Fed raised interest rates to stem inflation, it would not be a good time to buy a house. b. Student answers should show some understanding of the risks involved by taking any financial risk even if interest rates are low and there is low unemployment.

Analyzing Primary Sources

19 Bernanke is saying that the Fed has to do more than just put out fires during a recession.

20 Given the gridlock in Congress over monetary and budgetary issues, Bernanke's remarks would not be welcomed by all members of Congress.

21 Because Bernanke mentioned the New Deal in which the government played a major role in managing the economy, student answers should predict that Bernanke would lead the Fed to an even greater role in managing the economy than it presently does.

CHAPTER 16 Assessment

Directions: On a separate sheet of paper, answer the questions below. Make sure you read carefully and answer all parts of the questions.

ANSWERING THE ESSENTIAL QUESTION

Review your answers to the introductory questions at the beginning of each lesson. Then answer the Essential Question on the basis of what you learned in the chapter. Have your answers changed?

13 **Summarizing** What are two ways the government promotes the economic goals of price stability, full employment, and economic growth?

14 **Understanding Relationships** What role do you think politics plays in the government's promotion of its economic goals? Explain your opinion.

21st Century Skills

15 **Defending** Under what circumstances, if any, do you think it is appropriate for the Fed, an appointed board of economists, to manipulate the supply of money? Write a one-page position statement, supporting your opinion with reasons.

16 **Presentation Skills** Using credible resources, research the actions the Fed took to alleviate the Great Recession. Summarize the results of the Fed's actions. Make a multimedia presentation that includes the Fed actions and your summary of the results and present it to the class.

17 **Creating and Using Graphs** Use the Internet or a newspaper to find the Fed's interest rates within the last 10 years. Then, graph your results.

Building Financial Literacy

18 **Decision Making** Understanding how the government promotes price stability, full employment, and economic growth will help you make better decisions through life, such as choosing what work you will seek, when it is a good time to buy a home, and how to invest your monetary resources.

   a. What facts about the Fed's decisions would affect whether, after you are settled in a job, you decide to buy a home? Give reasons.

   b. Identify a way that a Fed policy of low interest rates and low unemployment would affect your economic decisions. Would you take economic risks or be more cautious? Give reasons.

Analyzing Primary Sources

Read the excerpt and answer the questions that follow.

PRIMARY SOURCE

"*The Fed's many liquidity programs played a central role in containing the crisis of 2008 to 2009. However, putting out the fire is not enough; it is also important to foster a financial system that is sufficiently resilient to withstand large financial shocks. Toward that end, the Federal Reserve, together with other regulatory agencies and the Financial Stability Oversight Council, is actively engaged in monitoring financial developments and working to strengthen financial institutions and markets. The reliance on stronger regulation is informed by the success of New Deal regulatory reforms, but current reform efforts go even further by working to identify and defuse risks not only to individual firms but to the financial system as a whole, an approach known as macroprudential regulation.*"

– Ben S. Bernanke, former Federal Reserve Board Chairman, in a speech at a conference sponsored by the National Bureau of Economic Research, Cambridge, Massachusetts, July 10, 2013

19 **Analyzing** What is Ben Bernanke saying about the role of the Fed during the Great Recession?

20 **Draw Conclusions** Do you think Ben Bernanke's comments would be welcomed by all members of Congress? Give reasons for your opinion.

21 **Making Predictions** From what Ben Bernanke said about the New Deal, in what direction do you predict he and his successors will lead the Federal Reserve Board? Explain your answer.

Need Extra Help?

If You've Missed Question	13	14	15	16	17	18	19	20	21
Go to page	478	482	478	481	473	473	481	482	482

---

networks Online Assessment Options

WORKSHEET

Chapter Tests and Lesson Quizzes

Chapter 16 Tests Forms A and B Have students complete the Chapter Tests and Lesson Quizzes to assess student understanding throughout the chapter. Print and online assessment tools offer chapter and lesson evaluation through a variety of question formats, including document-based questions.

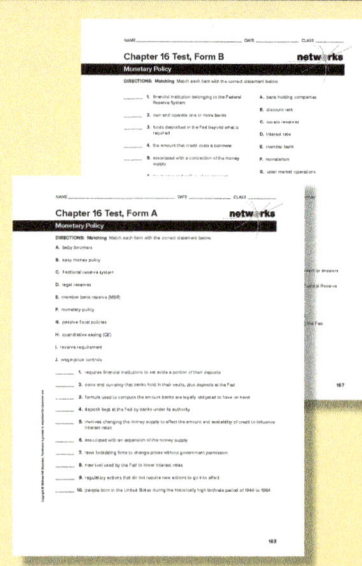

UNIT 7
THE GLOBAL ECONOMY Planner

UNDERSTANDING BY DESIGN®

Enduring Understanding
- The movement of people, goods, and ideas causes societies to change over time.

Essential Questions
- How does trade benefit all participating parties?
- Why is the economic health of all nations important in a global economy?
- What are the challenges associated with globalization?

Students will know:
- when individuals, regions, and nations specialize and then trade with others, production and consumption increase.
- when imports are restricted by public policies, consumers pay higher prices, and job opportunities and profits in exporting firms may decrease.
- international trade relies on the exchange of foreign currencies, but when the exchange rate changes, the relative prices of goods and services traded change; as a result, some groups gain and others lose.
- how investments in factories, equipment, education, new technology, training, and health improve economic growth.
- how countries are economically interdependent.
- the importance of natural resources in modern economic decision-making.

Students will be able to:
- **compare** the concepts of absolute advantage and comparative advantage.
- **describe** the restrictions governments place on international trade.
- **list** the arguments of protectionists and free traders.
- **evaluate** the advantages and disadvantages of trade agreements.
- **analyze** the national and international effects of the strength of the dollar.
- **list** the stages of economic development.
- **name** major obstacles to economic growth in developing countries.
- **explain** how agreements for regional cooperation help member nations develop economically.
- **define** globalization.

Predictable Misunderstandings
Students may think:
- The main reason for tariffs on foreign goods is to protect domestic industries.
- A strong dollar is preferable to a weak dollar on the international market.
- Nuclear energy is a renewable energy source.
- Pollution fees do not help reduce pollution because companies are happy to pay the fees in order to stay in business.

Assessment Evidence
Performance Task
- Hands-On Chapter Projects with Technology Extensions
- Economic Simulations
- Math Practice for Economics
- Personal Finance Activities
- Reinforcing Economic Skills Activities

Other Evidence:
- Guided Reading Activities
- Vocabulary Activities
- Lesson Quizzes
- Chapter Tests, Forms A and B

Key for Using the Teacher Edition

SKILL-BASED ACTIVITIES
Types of skill activities found in the Teacher Edition.
- **V** **Visual Skills** require students to analyze maps, graphs, charts, and photos.
- **R** **Reading Skills** help students practice reading skills and master vocabulary.
- **C** **Critical Thinking Skills** help students apply and extend what they have learned.
- **W** **Writing Skills** provide writing opportunities to help students comprehend the text.
- **T** **Technology Skills** require students to use digital tools effectively.

*Letters are followed by a number when there is more than one of the same type of skill on the page.

DIFFERENTIATED INSTRUCTION
All activities are written for the on-level student unless otherwise marked with the leveled labels below.
- **BL** Beyond Level
- **AL** Approaching Level
- **ELL** English Language Learners

All students benefit from activities that utilize different learning styles. Many activities are marked as below when a particular learning style is highlighted.

- Intrapersonal
- Logical/Mathematical
- Visual/Spatial
- Verbal/Linguistic
- Naturalist
- Kinesthetic
- Auditory/Musical
- Interpersonal

SUGGESTED PACING GUIDE—Semester
Introducing the Unit . . . . ½ Day
Chapter 17: International Trade . . . . 4 Days
Chapter 18: Economic Development and Globalization . . . . 4 Days
Chapter 19: Personal Financial Literacy . . . . 3 Days

UNIT 7: THE GLOBAL ECONOMY

Planner

☑ Print Teaching Options

C Critical Thinking Skills

☐ **p. 489 Analyzing the impact of imported goods** Students skim through these periodicals to locate advertisements for foreign goods and answer a series of questions about why U.S. consumers purchase the imports. **Verbal/Linguistic**

☐ **p. 489 Role-playing a Congressional meeting on tariffs** Students role-play a congressional subcommittee meeting on a plan to raise tariffs on imported products—athletic shoes, for example. Expert witnesses make presentations to the subcommittee for or against the raise in tariffs. **Interpersonal**

☐ **p. 490 Using mathematical skills to interpret economic information** Students learn concepts of percentages and averages. They learn to compute the average by using the mean and the median. **Logical/Mathematical**

W Writing Skills

☐ **p. 489 Reporting on loans to developing nations** Students research and write short reports with graphs showing trends in assistance offered from organizations such as the Ford Foundation, the International Finance Corporation (IFC), and agencies of the United Nations (UN) that offer loans or grants to economically developing nations. **Interpersonal**

☑ Online Teaching Options

☐ **ANIMATION Coffee & Fair Trade: An International Gateway**—Students view the animation about the benefits of fair trade and whether it can encourage political stability and economic growth.

☐ **APPROACHING GRADE LEVEL READER Alternative Student Edition narrative**—You can assign your students who are struggling to read on grade level the Approaching Grade Level version of the Online Student Edition. This reader presents all of the content in the On Grade Level version of the Online Student Edition at a lower reading level.

☐ **ENGLISH LANGUAGE LEARNER READER Alternative Student Edition narrative with ELL support**—Use the Online English Language Learner reader to provide additional reading support for ELL students. You can find this tool in the Online Student Edition.

☑ Printable Digital Worksheets

R Reading Skills

☐ **WORKSHEET Guided Reading Activity**—Students use the Guided Reading Activities worksheets to review their comprehension of the content.

☐ **WORKSHEET Reading Essentials and Study Guide**—Students complete the study guide and answer Reading Progress Check and vocabulary questions.

C Critical Thinking Skills

☐ **WORKSHEET Coffee & Fair Trade: An International Gateway Animation Activity**—Students answer questions about fair trade and whether it can encourage political stability and economic growth.

☐ **WORKSHEET Assessing Background Knowledge Activity**—Students should complete the Assessing Background Knowledge Activity before they study each chapter. Students' responses will give you a good idea of the kinds of misconceptions you can address when teaching the lessons.

☐ **WORKSHEET Chapter Summary**—Summaries are provided for each chapter and thoroughly condense core content into manageable chunks.

☐ **WORKSHEET Vocabulary Activity**—Students apply their knowledge of content and academic vocabulary words.

UNIT 7
The Global Economy

CHAPTER 17
International Trade

ESSENTIAL QUESTION

How does trade benefit all participating parties?

CHAPTER 18
Global Economic Development

ESSENTIAL QUESTIONS

Why is the economic health of all nations important in a global economy?

What are the challenges associated with globalization?

CHAPTER 19
Personal Financial Literacy

ESSENTIAL QUESTIONS

How can financial institutions help you increase and better manage your money?

What are the different types of business organizations?

How can you take control of your own money?

IT MATTERS BECAUSE . . .

International trade agreements, globalization, social networking and marketing, multinational corporations, outsourcing, online retailers and shopping, and more . . . these are just a few of the many reasons why the global economy is at the heart of our modern economic system. In essence, the entire globe is connected through people, resources, products, and via the Internet at the intersection of international trade. What you purchase and sell today indeed has a global stage, and understanding this dynamic will put you on the right track to thinking about economic prosperity and the challenges we face around the world.

ANIMATIONS **WORKSHEET**

Coffee & Fair Trade: An International Gateway

Analyzing the animation After students view the animation, guide a discussion of these questions:

- What are the benefits of fair trade for economic development?
- How can global trade encourage political stability?
- How can global trade encourage economic growth?
- What comparative advantages does the United States have that promote global trade?

UNIT 7
The Global Economy

ENGAGE

🔔 **Analyzing the impact of imported goods** Provide students with copies of newspapers and news magazines. Direct them to skim through these periodicals to locate advertisements for foreign goods. Encourage students to ask themselves the following questions about the advertisements:

- What good is advertised?
- Where is it made?
- How was it transported to the United States?
- Do American companies make this good?
- If so, why do you think we buy it from other countries?

Have students discuss their answers. Conclude by pointing out that the chapters in this unit deal with such topics as international trade and the growing interconnectedness of the world's economies. **Verbal/Linguistic**

Role-playing a Congressional meeting on tariffs Have the class role-play a congressional subcommittee meeting on a plan to raise tariffs on imported products—athletic shoes, for example. Select several students to act as subcommittee members and four or five others to act as the following witnesses: consumer advocates, workers in the shoe-making industry, executives from American shoe manufacturers, and executives from foreign shoe manufacturers. Encourage expert witnesses to make presentations to the subcommittee for or against the raise in tariffs, and have subcommittee members ask them questions. Have the rest of the class act as reporters and write summaries of the procedures. **Interpersonal**

Reporting on loans to developing nations Have students research organizations such as the Ford Foundation, the International Finance Corporation (IFC), and agencies of the United Nations (UN) that offer loans or grants to economically developing nations. Have students write short reports with graphs showing trends in assistance offered. Suggest that students combine their reports into a pamphlet titled *International Organizations and Economic Development*. **Interpersonal**

UNIT 7
The Global Economy

DEVELOP YOUR SKILLS ONLINE

Using Mathematical Skills to Interpret Economic Information

Help students understand the concepts of percentages and averages. Tell students that stores often advertise sale prices as a percent of regular prices—for example, "30 percent off." Remind students that percent means "parts per hundred." So 30 percent means the same thing as 30/100 or 0.30. Expressing change as a percentage allows a consumer to analyze the relative size of the change.

Emphasize to students that the most commonly used summary statistic is the average. Tell students that there are two ways to compute the average: by using the mean or the median. The *mean* is the average of a series of items. Explain to students that when a teacher computes the class average, he or she is really computing the mean. Sometimes using the mean to interpret statistics is misleading, however. This is especially true if one or two numbers in the series are much higher or lower than the others. The median can be more accurate. The *median* is the midpoint in any series of numbers arranged in order.

To give students an opportunity to practice their math skills in an economic context, distribute the Chapter 17 Math Practice worksheet (The Cost of a Pair of Shoes). Read the introductory text, the objective, and the background information aloud to students. Then ask students to work independently to complete the worksheet. When they finish, discuss the activity with the class. Call on volunteers to share their work and ask them to explain how they arrived at the answers. Resolve any misunderstandings. **Logical/Mathematical**

Develop your Skills Online

Use Appropriate Mathematical Skills
to Interpret Economic Information

Economists use their mathematical abilities to interpret and analyze data frequently. Taking every opportunity to improve your mathematical skills is useful to a better understanding of economics and is certainly applicable to many parts of your daily life. This economics program provides opportunities to work on your mathematical skills while examining charts of data or completing worksheets.

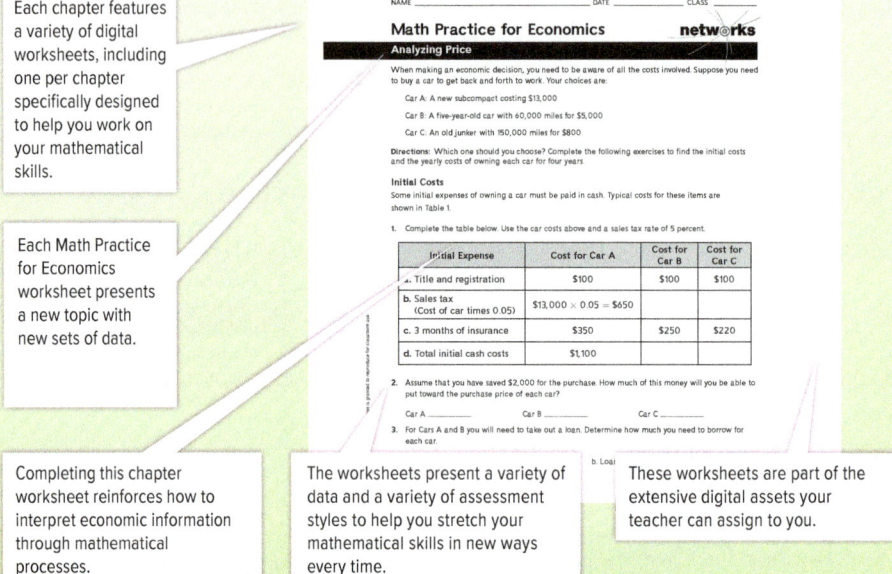

Each chapter features a variety of digital worksheets, including one per chapter specifically designed to help you work on your mathematical skills.

Each Math Practice for Economics worksheet presents a new topic with new sets of data.

Completing this chapter worksheet reinforces how to interpret economic information through mathematical processes.

The worksheets present a variety of data and a variety of assessment styles to help you stretch your mathematical skills in new ways every time.

These worksheets are part of the extensive digital assets your teacher can assign to you.

Find all your interactive resources for each chapter online. **TRY IT YOURSELF ONLINE**

Chapter 17 Resources for Global Trade
READING A BAR GRAPH
Reinforcing Economics Skills worksheet

Chapter 18 Global Economic Development
POPULATION GROWTH
Math Practice for Economics worksheet

490

networks Online Teaching Options

WORKSHEET

SAMPLE Math Practice for Economics

Calculating reserves and money supply Read the directions on the Math Practice for Economics worksheet aloud to students, and then ask them to work individually to complete the first half of the worksheet to figure out how much the bank can lend out with a reserve of 20 percent. Discuss students' work and ensure that everyone understands how the calculations are made. Then ask students to complete the remainder of the page.
Logical/Mathematical

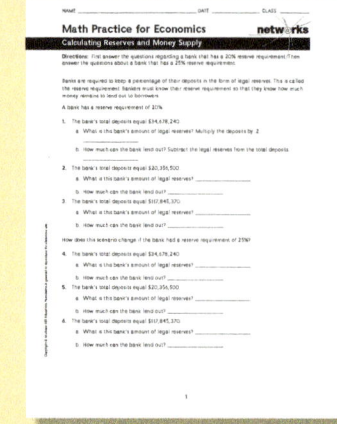

CHAPTER 17
Resources for Global Trade
Planner

UNDERSTANDING BY DESIGN®

Enduring Understanding
- The movement of people, goods, and ideas causes societies to change over time.

Essential Question
- How does trade benefit all participating parties?

Predictable Misunderstandings
Students may think:
- The main reason for tariffs on foreign goods is to protect domestic industries. Explain that while tariffs are sometimes used for that reason, before the Civil War tariffs were used more to generate revenue for the federal government than to protect domestic industries. More recently, tariffs have been used to protect selected domestic groups at the expense of other domestic groups.
- A strong dollar is preferable to a weak dollar on the international market. Explain that a strong dollar is good because it encourages imports; a weak dollar is also good because it makes U.S. goods and services more affordable for the rest of the world, which increases demand for them.

Assessment Evidence
Performance Task
- Hands-On Chapter Project with Technology Extension

Other Evidence
- Guided Reading Activities
- Vocabulary Activity
- Self-Check Quizzes
- Lesson Quizzes
- Chapter Assessment
- Chapter Tests, Forms A and B

SUGGESTED PACING

Introducing the Chapter: ½ Day	Lesson 3: Foreign Exchange and Trade Deficits . . . . 1 Day
Lesson 1: Absolute and Comparative Advantage . . . . . 1 Day	Debate . . . . ½ Day
Case Study . . . . ½ Day	Study Guide, Chapter Assessment and Wrap-Up . . . . ½ Day
Lesson 2: Barriers to International Trade . . . . 1 Day	

TOTAL 5 Days

Key for Using the Teacher Edition

SKILL-BASED ACTIVITIES

Types of skill activities found in the Teacher Edition.

V Visual Skills require students to analyze maps, graphs, charts, and photos.

R Reading Skills help students practice reading skills and master vocabulary.

C Critical Thinking Skills help students apply and extend what they have learned.

W Writing Skills provide writing opportunities to help students comprehend the text.

T Technology Skills require students to use digital tools effectively.

*Letters are followed by a number when there is more than one of the same type of skill on the page.

DIFFERENTIATED INSTRUCTION

All activities are written for the on-level student unless otherwise marked with the leveled labels below.

BL Beyond Level
AL Approaching Level
ELL English Language Learners

All students benefit from activities that utilize different learning styles. Many activities are marked as below when a particular learning style is highlighted.

Intrapersonal
Logical/Mathematical
Visual/Spatial
Verbal/Linguistic
Naturalist
Kinesthetic
Auditory/Musical
Interpersonal

Council for Economic Education

Below are the Council for Economic Education Voluntary National Content Standards in Economics covered in the *Resources for Global Trade* chapter.

Content Standard 5: Voluntary exchange occurs only when all participating parties expect to gain. This is true for trade among individuals or organizations within a nation, and among individuals or organizations in different nations.

Content Standard 6: When individuals, regions, and nations specialize in what they can produce at the lowest cost and then trade with others, both production and consumption increase.

CHAPTER 17: RESOURCES FOR GLOBAL TRADE

CHAPTER OPENER PLANNER

Students will know:
- when individuals, regions, and nations specialize in what they can produce at the lowest cost and then trade with others, both production and consumption increase.
- the methods used by the government to restrict trade.
- the arguments for and against free trade.

Students will be able to:
- **explain** how international trade allows for specialization.
- **compare** the concepts of absolute advantage and comparative advantage.
- **describe** the restrictions governments place on international trade.
- **explain** the difference between fixed exchange rates and flexible exchange rates.
- **analyze** the national and international effects of the strength of the dollar.

UNDERSTANDING BY DESIGN

☑ Print Teaching Options

R Reading Skills
- ☐ **p. 493 Identifying additional WTO functions** Students identify functions of the World Trade Organization.

C Critical Thinking Skills
- ☐ **p. 491 Exploring international trade** Students discuss international trade's importance to the the U.S. economy.
- ☐ **p. 492 Interpreting GDP per capita data** Students answer questions about GDP and GDP per capita.

T Technology Skills
- ☐ **p. 493 Researching the WTO** Students identify areas of WTO dispute.

☑ Online Teaching Options

V Visual Skills
- ☐ **IMAGES Chapter opener**—Students analyze a photo for clues about international trade.

C Critical Thinking Skills
- ☐ **INFOGRAPHICS Economic Perspectives**—Students read about trade among regional partners.
- ☐ **DEBATES Should the euro be abolished?**—Students analyze two views about the euro.
- ☐ **INTERACTIVE FEATURES Case Study: Three Ways 9/11 Affected the Economy**—Students study the ways 9/11 affected the economy, both locally and nationally.

☑ Printable Digital Worksheets

C Critical Thinking Skills
- ☐ **WORKSHEET Economic Simulation**—Students set up an American-based and an international business.
- ☐ **WORKSHEET Chapter Summary**—Content is condensed into manageable chunks.
- ☐ **WORKSHEET Vocabulary Activity**—Students use content and academic terms.
- ☐ **WORKSHEET Assessing Background Knowledge Activity**—Target misconceptions you can address when teaching the lessons.

Project-Based Learning

Hands-On

WORKSHEET Hands-On Chapter Project
In this activity, students will choose a nation and take the role of its trade representative. They will then research important facts about the nation's trade and its products, evaluate the effect of trade barriers on one of the nation's products, and investigate trade surpluses and deficits. Finally, they will produce a trade profile using a medium of their choice.

Digital Hands-On

Create Online Projects

Find an additional activity online that incorporates technology for the Hands-On Project. Visit the EdTech Teacher Web sites for more links, tutorials, and other resources.

Print Resources

ANCILLARY RESOURCE
This ancillary is available for every chapter and lesson.
- Chapter Tests and Lesson Quizzes

PRINTABLE DIGITAL WORKSHEETS
These printable digital worksheets are available for every chapter and lesson.
- Reading Essentials & Study Guide
- Vocabulary Activities
- Chapter Summaries
- Economic Simulations
- Math Practice for Economics
- Reinforcing Economic Skills
- Personal Finance Activities
- Enrichment Activities
- Reteaching Activities
- Guided Reading Activities
- Video Worksheets
- Lesson Quizzes and Chapter Tests (English and Spanish)

More Media Resources

SUGGESTED READING
- For students at a Grade 10 reading level: *India: A Study of an Economically Developing Country*, by David Cumming
- For students at a Grade 11 reading level: *Voyaging to Cathay: Americans in the China Trade*, by Alfred Tamarin & Shirley Glubok
- For students at a Grade 12 reading level: *Ghana: A Study of an Economically Developing Country*, by Steve Brace

SUGGESTED VIDEOS MOVIES
Find these documentaries yourself online. NOTE: McGraw-Hill Education does not endorse these resources. Preview clips for age-appropriateness.
- *Flowing Through* (54 min.)
- *Santa's Workshop: Inside China's Slave Labour Toy Factories* (33 min.)
- *TED Talks: Actually, the World Isn't Flat* (17 min.)

LESSON 1 Planner

ABSOLUTE AND COMPARATIVE ADVANTAGE

Students will know:
- how specialization and voluntary exchange between buyers and sellers lead to mutually beneficial outcomes.
- individuals and nations have a comparative advantage in the production of goods or services if they can produce a product at a lower opportunity cost than other individuals or nations.

Students will be able to:
- *explain* how international trade allows for specialization.
- *compare* the concepts of absolute advantage and comparative advantage.
- *discuss* non-production gains from international trade.

UNDERSTANDING BY DESIGN®

☑ *Print Teaching Options*

V Visual Skills

☐ **p. 495 Using a chart to learn about dependence on trade** Students examine the U.S. dependence on international trade. Logical/Mathematical

☐ **p. 496 Using a chart to learn about trade partners** Students discuss U.S. trade partners. Logical/Mathematical, Visual/Spatial

R Reading Skills

☐ **p. 496 Defining terms** Students define *absolute advantage* and *comparative advantage.* ELL Verbal/Linguistic

☐ **p. 497 Comparing absolute and comparative advantage** Students apply information about absolute and comparative advantages. Verbal/Linguistic

☐ **p. 498 Explaining assumptions** Students explain the assumption on which comparative advantage is based. Verbal/Linguistic

☐ **p. 499 Explaining how trade produces economic growth**

C Critical Thinking Skills

☐ **p. 494 Expressing ideas about imported goods** Students identify their non-U.S.-made products. Interpersonal

☐ **p. 495 Analyzing the relationship between exports and specialization** Students analyze why their states specializes in some exports. Verbal/Linguistic

☐ **p. 499 Debating which comes first** Students debate which takes precedence—international economic cooperation or political cooperation.

☑ *Online Teaching Options*

V Visual Skills

☐ **CHARTS American Dependence on Trade**—Students review how our economy would suffer if certain resources were not available. Visual/Spatial

☐ **MAPS U.S. Merchandise Trade by Area**—Students discuss U.S. exports and imports and the trade deficit. Visual/Spatial, Logical/Mathematical

☐ **GRAPHS Gains from Trade**—Students discuss how comparative advantage benefits countries. Visual/Spatial

☐ **MAPS Increased Political Stability**—Students discuss the political benefits of trade. Visual/Spatial

☐ **VIDEO New Balance in International Trade**—Students watch a video about the impact New Balance's commitment to American workers has on American consumers. Verbal/Linguistic

R Reading Skills

☐ **BIOGRAPHY Paul Krugman**—Students read about Paul Krugman and comparative advantage. Verbal/Linguistic

C Critical Thinking Skills

☐ **BELLRINGER Absolute and Comparative Advantage**—Students discuss how U.S. exports affect U.S. trading partners. Visual/Spatial, Verbal/Linguistic

☐ **ESSENTIAL QUESTION Exploring the Essential Question**—Students discuss why knowing a country's laws would be beneficial to a business hoping to expand into that country. Logical/Mathematical

T Technology Skills

☐ **SELF-CHECK QUIZ Lesson 1**—Students receive instant feedback on their mastery of lesson content.

☐ **GAME Lesson 1**—Students solve clues to review lesson content.

☐ **INTERACTIVE WHITEBOARD ACTIVITY Economic Advantage**—Students work together to learn lesson content.

☑ *Printable Digital Worksheets*

R Reading Skills

☐ **WORKSHEET Guided Reading Activity**—Students use the Guided Reading Activity worksheets to review their comprehension of the content.

☐ **WORKSHEET Reading Essentials and Study Guide**—Students complete the study guide and answer Reading Progress Check and vocabulary questions.

C Critical Thinking Skills

☐ **WORKSHEET New Balance in International Trade Video Activity**—Students answer questions related to the Trans-Pacific Trade Agreement. Verbal/Linguistic

LESSON 2 Planner

BARRIERS TO INTERNATIONAL TRADE

Students will know:
- the methods used by the government to restrict trade.
- the arguments for and against free trade.
- the impact of international organizations including, but not limited to, NAFTA, WTO, GATT and EEC, on the United States economic policy.

Students will be able to:
- **describe** the restrictions governments place on international trade.
- **list** the arguments of protectionists for placing restrictions on international trade.
- **evaluate** the advantages and disadvantages of trade agreements.

UNDERSTANDING BY DESIGN®

✓ Print Teaching Options

V Visual Skills
- **p. 503 Using geography skills** Students determine how the country's resources might allow it to prepare for war. *Visual/Spatial, Verbal/Linguistic*

R Reading Skills
- **p. 501 Summarizing the goals of tariffs** Students read a protective tariff and a revenue tariff. *Verbal/Linguistic*

C Critical Thinking Skills
- **p. 501 Speculating on tariffs and quotas** Students decide when to impose a tariff or quota. *Verbal/Linguistic*
- **p. 502 Interpreting government decisions on tariffs** Students discuss why the U.S. government might pursue a trade policy that raises costs. *Verbal/Linguistic*
- **p. 503 Recognizing barriers to trade** Students identify which barrier to trade is at work.
- **p. 504 Analyzing point of view about protecting domestic jobs** Students explain whether they will impose a tariff increase. **AL** *Verbal/Linguistic*
- **p. 506 Drawing conclusions about most favored nations** Students discuss a country's decision to offer a most favored nation clause. *Verbal/Linguistic*
- **p. 507 Comparing NAFTA to the EU**

W Writing Skills
- **p. 502 Writing an evaluation of tariffs** Students evaluate a tariffs' effectiveness in reaching the government's goals. *Verbal/Linguistic*
- **p. 505 Writing to persuade** Students research trade protection. *Verbal/Linguistic*
- **p. 506 Researching the WTO** Students report on WTO's role in international trade. **ELL** *Verbal/Linguistic*
- **p. 507 Debating free trade** Students debate whether the U.S. should promote free trade.

✓ Online Teaching Options

V Visual Skills
- **BELLRINGER** **Barriers to International Trade**—Students list the pros and cons of free trade. *Verbal/Linguistic*
- **GRAPHIC ORGANIZERS** **Protectionists and Free Traders**—Students take notes on the opposing views of protectionism and free trade. *Verbal/Linguistic*
- **POLITICAL CARTOON** **International Trade**—Students discuss whether protectionism is fair. *Visual/Spatial*
- **VIDEO** **Fair Trade**—Students view a video on fair trade. *Verbal/Linguistic*
- **SLIDE SHOWS** **The WTO**—Students discuss the pros and cons of the WTO. *Visual/Spatial*

C Critical Thinking Skills
- **ESSENTIAL QUESTION** **Exploring the Essential Question**—Partners consider the benefits of buying American-made products. *Verbal/Linguistic*
- **INTERACTIVE FEATURE** **Career: Foreign Service Agricultural Attaché**—Students learn about a Foreign Service Agricultural Attaché. *Verbal/Linguistic*

T Technology Skills
- **SELF-CHECK QUIZ** **Lesson 2**—Students receive instant feedback on their mastery of lesson content.
- **GAME** **Lesson 2**—Students solve clues to review lesson content.
- **INTERACTIVE WHITEBOARD ACTIVITY** **Barriers to Trade**—Students work together to learn lesson content.

✓ Printable Digital Worksheets

R Reading Skills
- **WORKSHEET** **Guided Reading Activity**—Students use the Guided Reading Activity worksheets to review their comprehension of the content.
- **WORKSHEET** **Reading Essentials and Study Guide**—Students complete the study guide and answer Reading Progress Check and vocabulary questions.

C Critical Thinking Skills
- **WORKSHEET** **Math Practice for Economics**—Students answer questions about the cost of manufacturing a pair of shoes overseas. *Logical/Mathematical*
- **WORKSHEET** **Fair Trade Video Activity**—Students summarize a video on fair trade. *Verbal/Linguistic*

LESSON 3 Planner

FOREIGN EXCHANGE AND TRADE DEFICITS

Students will know:
- international trade relies on the ability to exchange foreign currencies.
- the characteristics of flexible and fixed exchange rates, and the advantages and disadvantages of each.

Students will be able to:
- **explain** the difference between fixed exchange rates and flexible exchange rates.
- **analyze** the national and international effects of the strength of the dollar.

UNDERSTANDING BY DESIGN

✓ Print Teaching Options

V Visual Skills

- **p. 511 Using graphs showing flexible exchange rates** Students study the supply and demand of currencies. **AL** Verbal/Linguistic

- **p. 513 Illustrating a chain reaction** Students show effects of a strong and weak dollar on U.S. exports and imports.

R Reading Skills

- **p. 509 Understanding exchange rates** Students interpret a chart of foreign exchange rates. Logical/Mathematical

- **p. 510 Defining *fixed exchange rates*** Students learn the concept of fixed exchange rates.

- **p. 510 Using the Big Mac Index** Students use a graph about undervalued and overvalued currencies. Logical/Mathematical

- **p. 512 Defining economic terms** Students define *trade deficit* and *trade surplus*. **ELL** Verbal/Linguistic

C Critical Thinking Skills

- **p. 508 Discussing the valuation of the dollar** Students discuss how market forces influence the value of the dollar. Verbal/Linguistic

- **p. 512 Analyzing effects of exchange rates on imports and exports** Students connect a nation's currency and costs of exported and imported goods. Verbal/Linguistic

W Writing Skills

- **p. 510 Writing about the gold standard price** Students explain why the U.S. dropped the gold standard. Verbal/Linguistic

- **p. 511 Tracing the effects of flexible exchange rates** **BL** Verbal/Linguistic

✓ Online Teaching Options

V Visual Skills

- **VIDEO** The European Crisis and Its Impact on the United States—Students view a video about the EU's monetary problems.

R Reading Skills

- **INTERACTIVE FEATURE** The Global Economy & You—Students learn about the Big Mac Index. Verbal/Linguistic

C Critical Thinking Skills

- **BELLRINGER** Trade Deficit—Students discuss the trade imbalance between the U.S. and China. Logical/Mathematical

- **CHARTS** Foreign Exchange Rates—Students explore exchange rates to compare units of foreign currency. Logical/Mathematical

- **GRAPHS** Flexible Exchange Rates—Students interpret exchange rates between the yuan and the dollar. Logical/Mathematical

- **GRAPHS** International Value of the Dollar—Students study the changes in the international value of the dollar. Logical/Mathematical

- **ESSENTIAL QUESTION** Exploring the Essential Question—Students recognize the broad effects of foreign trade. Verbal/Linguistic

T Technology Skills

- **SELF-CHECK QUIZ** Lesson 3—Students receive instant feedback on their mastery of lesson content.

- **GAME** Lesson 3—Students solve clues to review lesson content.

- **INTERACTIVE WHITEBOARD ACTIVITY** Strong Dollar vs. Weak Dollar—Students work together to learn lesson content.

✓ Printable Digital Worksheets

R Reading Skills

- **WORKSHEET** Guided Reading Activity—Students use the Guided Reading Activity worksheets to review their comprehension of the content.

- **WORKSHEET** Reading Essentials and Study Guide—Students complete the study guide and answer Reading Progress Check and vocabulary questions.

- **WORKSHEET** Reteaching Activity—Students use the worksheet to interpret a graph to answer questions about the trade deficit.

C Critical Thinking Skills

- **WORKSHEET** The European Crisis and Its Impact on the United States Video Activity—Students answer questions about the EU's financial problems.

CHAPTER 17 Resources for Global Trade

INTERVENTION AND REMEDIATION STRATEGIES

LESSON 1 Absolute and Comparative Advantage

Reading and Comprehension

Organize students into groups of three. Assign students in each group one of these questions:

- How does trade enable a country to specialize, and what is the advantage of specialization?
- What is the difference between absolute advantage and comparative advantage?
- How does international trade promote countries' economic growth?

Tell students to study the text to learn all about their question. Then have them explain the answer to members of their group.

Text Evidence

Tell students that they have been asked to write an essay for the school economics blog about the importance of expanding world trade. Tell students to comb through the lesson to find facts, reasons, and other details that support this position. Then ask them to write a three- or four-paragraph blog explaining the issue.

LESSON 2 Barriers to International Trade

Reading and Comprehension

Write these questions on the board:

- What are the differences among tariffs, quotas, and embargoes and why are they used?
- What are the main arguments for protection?
- Which do you think is the strongest argument for protection? Why?
- What are the economic arguments in favor of free trade?

Allow students a few minutes to find the answers to the questions. Then explore the answers in class discussion.

Text Evidence

Share this scenario with students:

A fifth grade class has been studying history and the subject of international trade has come up. The class is confused by some of the trade disagreements among nations. They do not understand the various barriers to trade that countries have imposed on each other. They do not understand the purposes of the barriers or how they impact economies.

Ask students to prepare an outline of a teaching plan they can use to explain barriers to trade to this class. Tell them to use facts and details from the lesson in their plans.

LESSON 3 Foreign Exchange and Trade Deficits

Reading and Comprehension

Assign students to work in small groups of two or three and to outline the lesson. Tell them to use the headings to organize their outlines and to identify at least two important details to add to the outlines for each heading.

Text Evidence

Tell students that every so often, someone in Congress declares that the United States should return to the gold standard. Ask them to imagine that it is one of their representatives this time. Have them write a letter to the representative explaining why they either support or oppose the proposition because of the effects it would have on international trade. Remind students to use facts and details from this lesson to support their persuasive letters.

Online Resources

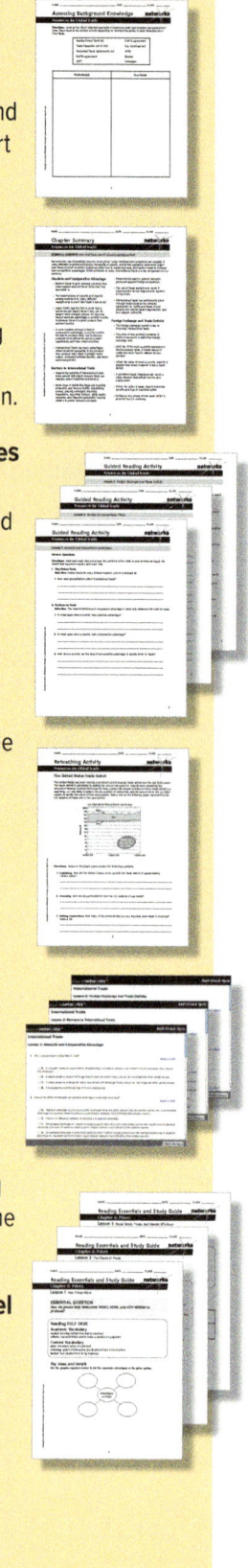

Assessing Background Knowledge

Use this worksheet to pre-assess students' background knowledge before they start the chapter.

Chapter Summaries

Have students use the summary as a pre-reading activity or as a post-reading review to check the main ideas covered in each lesson.

Guided Reading Activities

Have students complete these activities as they read each lesson. They provide reading notes the student can use for review and to prepare for assessments.

Reteaching Activities

Have students complete the Reteaching Activity for remedial practice and review of vital content.

Self-Check Quizzes

These quizzes provide instant feedback on areas the students may need to re-read to understand a main idea.

Reading Essentials and Study Guide

This resource offers writing and reading activities for the approaching-level student.

Approaching Grade Level Reader

This reader presents all of the content of the Online Student Edition but at a lower reading level.

English Language Learner Reader

Provide additional reading support for ELL students. Find this tool online.

Resources for Global Trade

ESSENTIAL QUESTION
How does trade benefit all participating parties?

networks
www.connected.mcgraw-hill.com
There's More Online about resources for global trade.

CHAPTER 17

Economic Perspectives
What Is the World Trade Organization?

Lesson 1
Absolute and Comparative Advantage

Lesson 2
Barriers to International Trade

Lesson 3
Foreign Exchange and Trade Deficits

ENGAGE

Call students' attention to the photo and ask them to describe what it shows. Guide them to recognize that this businessman sells fabrics. **Ask: Why is this image a good one to symbolize the chapter titled *International Trade*?** *(Many of these fabrics have been imported from abroad because of trade agreements. Trade agreements help fuel imports and exports among the United States, India, China, Mexico, and other countries. Imports allow Americans to have a larger variety of products to choose from, and the competition among producers keeps prices lower.)* In a discussion, lead students to understand that international trade is an important component of our free enterprise system.

Exploring international trade Discuss ways in which the United States engages in international trade and why it is important to the growth of our economy. **Ask: Who are a few of our major international trade partners?** *(Students might suggest China, Japan, Germany, Canada, and Mexico, but many others are possible as well.)* **What kinds of products does the U.S. export?** *(Sample answer: vehicles, agricultural products, technology products, aircraft, medical equipment, pharmaceuticals)* Discuss how trade benefits the United States, pointing out that people in retail, wholesale, importing, exporting, and shipping businesses benefit as well as the farmers, factory workers, and others who produce the goods that are exported. Emphasize that their salaries, the goods and services they buy as a result of their salaries, the taxes they pay, and the money they save all contribute to our economic growth. Then discuss the impact of U.S. exports on its trading partners. Point out that many countries rely on American products and resources. **Logical/Mathematical**

Letter from the Author

Dear Economics Teacher,

International trade combines a challenging mix of established ideas and contemporary challenges. Trade with other nations has been popular for centuries because of the desire to have new or scarce and exotic commodities. Trade takes place today because of the need for necessities like oil, food, and some manufactured goods. The challenges to all nations come from the displaced workers who lose jobs because so many products can be produced abroad at a lower cost. We have to remember that international trade does not benefit everyone, so we have to be sensitive to those who are hurt by it.

Gary E. Clayton

Go to the Foldables® library for a cumulative chapter-based Foldable® activity that your students can use to help take notes and prepare for assessment.

CHAPTER 17
Economic Perspectives

TEACH & ASSESS

C Critical Thinking Skills

Interpreting GDP per capita data Ask students to study the GDP and GDP per capita data on the infographic. **Ask: What are the top three trade organizations as measured by GDP?** *(NAFTA, European Union, Shanghai Cooperation Organisation)* **What are the top three trade organizations as measured by GDP per capita?** *(NAFTA, EU, Arab League)* Discuss with students how the GDP per capita for the Arab League can be higher than many other trade regions because the countries in the Arab League have smaller populations than other regions. Explain that GDP per capita is calculated by dividing total GDP by the total population. **Logical/Mathematical**

Content Background Knowledge

From GATT to WTO The General Agreement on Tariffs and Trade (GATT) was signed by 23 nations in 1947. GATT's purpose was to establish tariff rules for trade negotiations. GATT was revamped in 1994 and, after one year of transitioning, became the World Trade Organization. The newest members of the WTO joined in 2012 and 2013, and they include Tajikistan, Lao People's Democratic Republic, Montenegro, Samoa, and Vanuatu.

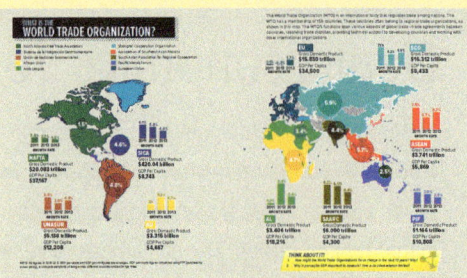

Economic Perspectives: What is the World Trade Organization?

Drawing conclusions about trade relationships among economies Read the introductory text aloud and then discuss the infographic data.
Ask: What is the WTO? *(World Trade Organization; an international body that regulates trade among nations)* Review the list of regional organizations and have students identify the corresponding countries and their location on the map. Ask students to speculate how global trade among these regional partners produces economic benefits. **Ask: Which two regional trade organizations experienced the highest percentage of growth in 2013?** *(Shanghai Cooperation Organisation, Association of Southeast Asian Nations)* **What was the highest percentage of growth for a given year, and where did it occur?** *(2012; The Arab League experienced a growth rate of 8.6%.)*
Logical/Mathematical

492

CHAPTER 17
Economic Perspectives

The World Trade Organization (WTO) is an international body that regulates trade among nations. The WTO has a membership of 159 countries. These countries often belong to regional trade organizations, as shown in this map. The WTO's functions span various aspects of global trade—trade agreements between countries, resolving trade disputes, providing technical support to developing countries, and working with other international organizations.

EU
Gross Domestic Product $15.830 trillion
GDP Per Capita $34,500
Growth Rate: 0.1% (2011), -0.3% (2012), 1.7% (2013)

SCO
Gross Domestic Product $16.312 trillion
GDP Per Capita $8,433
Growth Rate: 7.1% (2011), 5.2% (2012), 5.9% (2013)

ASEAN
Gross Domestic Product $3.741 trillion
GDP Per Capita $5,869
Growth Rate: 7.8% (2011), 4.7% (2012), 5.7% (2013)

AL
Gross Domestic Product $3.406 trillion
GDP Per Capita $18,216
Growth Rate: 0.1% (2011), 8.6% (2012), 3.4% (2013)

SAARC
Gross Domestic Product $6.090 trillion
GDP Per Capita $4,300
Growth Rate: 6.2% (2011), 6.0% (2012), 4.4% (2013)

PIF
Gross Domestic Product $1.166 trillion
GDP Per Capita $10,808
Growth Rate: 4.1% (2011), 3.0% (2012), 2.5% (2013)

Map growth rates: 0% (Europe), 5.9% (Asia), 3.4% (Africa), 4.4% (South Asia), 5.7% (SE Asia), 4.7% (sub-Saharan Africa), 2.5% (Oceania)

THINK ABOUT IT!
1. How might the World Trade Organization's focus change in the next 10 years? Why?
2. Why is per capita GDP important to measure? How is its interpretation limited?

Resources for Global Trade 493

R Reading Skills

Identifying additional WTO functions   Ask: **What are some broad functions of the WTO?** *(It oversees trade agreements between countries, resolves trade disputes, provides technical support to developing countries, and works with other international organizations.)*

T Technology Skills

Researching the WTO   Divide students into four groups and tell them to research online the four major "areas of activity" of the WTO: Trade negotiations, Implementation and monitoring, Dispute settlement, and Building trade capacity. Ask groups to also identify and summarize one or two current areas of dispute that appear on the WTO Web site home page. Have groups report their findings to the class.

CLOSE & REFLECT

Have students answer the *Think About It!* questions.

WORKSHEET

Reinforcing Economic Skills

Reading a bar graph about U.S. trading partners   Distribute the worksheet to students. Students will read a bar graph to answer questions about U.S. trade partners, imports, and exports. Then they will make inferences about the U.S. economy based on the graph. **Logical/Mathematical**

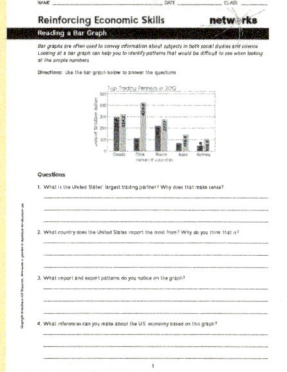

ANSWERS, p. 493

THINK ABOUT IT!

1. Answers will vary. Students may reflect on the changes that globalization and interdependence has had on trade, as well as the economic sanctions that result from political actions.
2. Per capita GDP gives a clearer picture of the distribution of wealth in a country. Even so, it may give a false impression of a country's standard of living if only a small percentage of people hold the majority of wealth while the rest of the people live in poverty.

CHAPTER 17, LESSON 1
Absolute and Comparative Advantage

ENGAGE

C Critical Thinking Skills

🔔 **Expressing ideas about imported goods** Ask students to look through the possessions they have with them. **Ask: Where were those items made?** List the countries they name on the board. Ask students how they would replace those items if they could only buy U.S.-made products. Would they be as satisfied with their choices? With the prices? **Interpersonal**

Making Connections

Benefiting from International Trade Guide students in appreciating how international trade benefits them directly and indirectly. **Ask: What goods do you regularly use that were produced in other countries?** *(Sample answer: cell phones and other electronic products, clothes, gas, vehicles, fresh produce)* **When you purchase one of these products, who profits from it?** *(Retailer, manufacturer, employees of the store and manufacturer, truck drivers, and so on)* Guide students to understand how all the businesses and workers who handle the product in the United States benefit from the sale. Likewise, when the United States manufactures a product and exports it, everyone who has a role in the process benefits economically. Encourage students to think about how they or their parents or friends benefit from international trade indirectly.

ANSWERS, p. 494

ESSENTIAL QUESTION ACTIVITY

You would need to know information about the country's laws, customs, and consumer preferences before exporting your products there. International trade provides currency flow, jobs, and economic growth.

TAKING NOTES

Absolute Advantage Definition: A country's ability to produce more of a given product than another country can produce
Example: Alpha can produce 40 pounds of coffee while Beta produces 6 pounds using the same amount of resources

Comparative Advantage Definition: The ability to produce a product relatively more efficiently, or at a lower opportunity cost
Example: If Alpha has a higher opportunity cost to produce coffee than Beta, then Beta has the comparative advantage for coffee

---

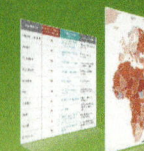

Interact with these digital assets and others in lesson 1

✓ INTERACTIVE GRAPH
U.S. Merchandise Trade by Area
✓ INTERACTIVE MAP
Increased Political Stability
✓ SELF-CHECK QUIZ
✓ VIDEO

networks
TRY IT YOURSELF ONLINE

LESSON 1
Absolute and Comparative Advantage

Reading Help Desk

Academic Vocabulary
- volume
- enabled

Content Vocabulary
- exports
- imports
- absolute advantage
- production possibilities curves
- comparative advantage
- opportunity cost

TAKING NOTES:

Key Ideas and Details
ACTIVITY As you read, complete the graphic organizer below by defining each term and providing an example.

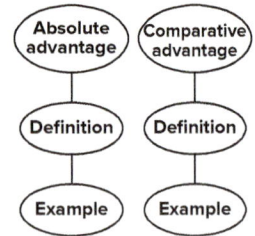

ESSENTIAL QUESTION

How does trade benefit all participating parties?

The largest businesses in the world are often called "multinational corporations" because they operate in many different countries at the same time. These corporations can employ hundreds of thousands or even millions of people. Some chief executives manage multinational corporations whose economies are bigger than those of small countries. They play an influential role in trade and other world affairs.

Imagine that you are the owner of a much smaller business. Currently, you manufacture goods for sale only in the United States, but you want to increase sales of your products by exporting them to another country.

What information would you need to know about this country before exporting your products there? Why would the government of one country encourage its businesses to trade with other nations?

Why Nations Trade

GUIDING QUESTION *How does trade allow for specialization?*

Nations trade for the same reasons that individuals do—because they believe that the products they receive are worth more than the products they give up. International trade is partially responsible for the incredible variety of goods we use every day.

For example, we purchase clothing made in China, oil from the Middle East, bananas from Honduras, and coffee beans from Colombia and Brazil. We consume a service when we vacation in the Caribbean or in Europe. The shoppers in Moscow are doing the same thing: enjoying the goods produced in France, Sweden, and Japan.

---

networks *Online Teaching Options*

BELLRINGER

Absolute and Comparative Advantage

Discussing international trade Have students view the Bellringer. Ask students to list items or categories of goods they think the United States exports (in addition to aircraft engines). Explain that leading U.S. exports (of goods) include industrial supplies, such as petroleum products and chemicals; capital goods, such as computers and machinery; vehicles and car parts; foods and animal feed; and consumer goods. Discuss how these U.S. exports impact U.S. trading partners. **Visual/Spatial, Verbal/Linguistic**

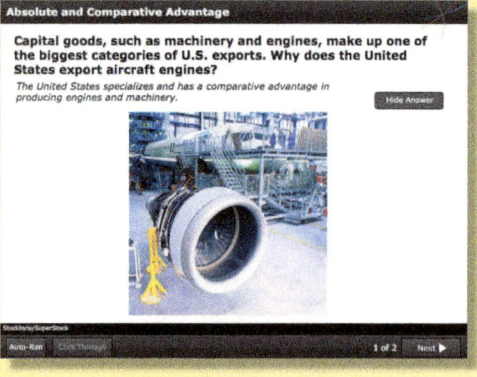

Some trade takes place because countries lack goods at home. **Figure 17.1** shows some essential raw materials used in the United States that come from abroad.

Specialization

An important reason for trade—whether among people, states, or countries—is specialization. When people specialize, they produce the things they do best and exchange those products for the things that other people do best.

States also specialize. For example, New York is a financial center for stocks and bonds, while automobiles are a major industry in Michigan. Texas is known for oil and cattle, while Florida and California are famous for citrus fruit.

Countries specialize in different goods and services in much the same way. If you want to find out what a country specializes in, look at its **exports**—the goods and services that it produces and sells to other nations. If you want to see what a country would like to have but does not produce as efficiently, look at its **imports**—the goods and services that the country buys from other countries.

exports the goods and services that a nation produces and then sells to other nations

imports the goods and services that a nation buys from other nations

Extent of Trade

International trade is important to all nations, even a country as large as the United States. Most of the products that countries exchange are goods. However, trade in services such as banking and insurance is increasing as well.

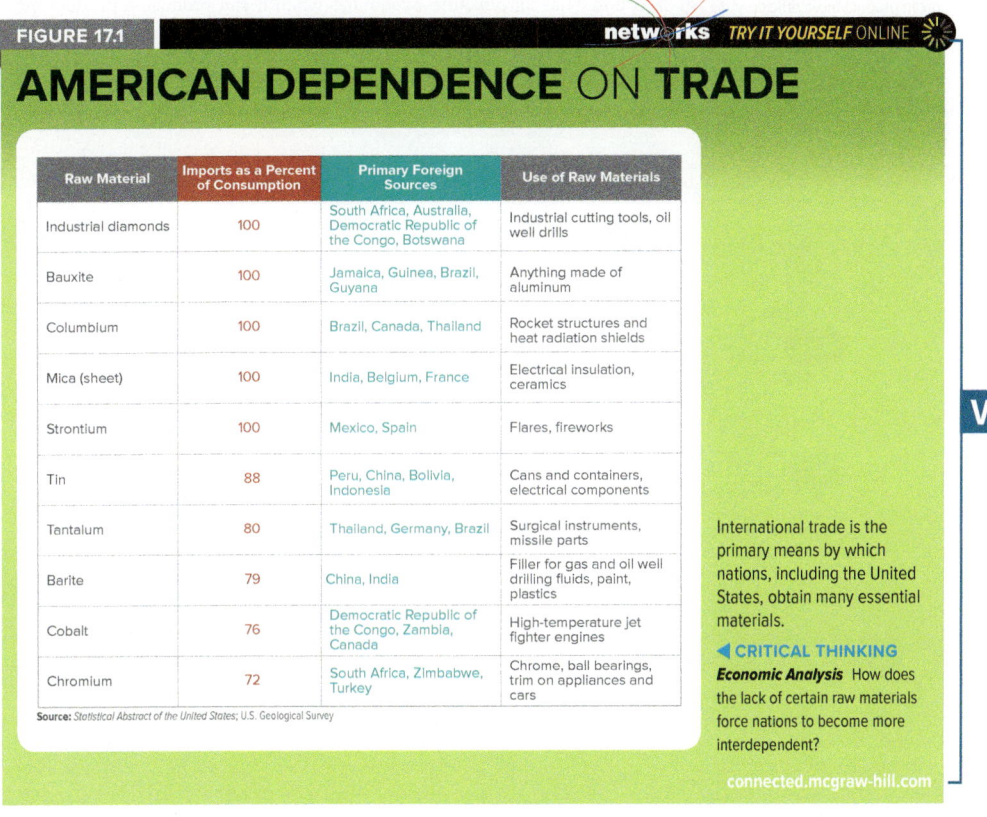

FIGURE 17.1 AMERICAN DEPENDENCE ON TRADE

Raw Material	Imports as a Percent of Consumption	Primary Foreign Sources	Use of Raw Materials
Industrial diamonds	100	South Africa, Australia, Democratic Republic of the Congo, Botswana	Industrial cutting tools, oil well drills
Bauxite	100	Jamaica, Guinea, Brazil, Guyana	Anything made of aluminum
Columbium	100	Brazil, Canada, Thailand	Rocket structures and heat radiation shields
Mica (sheet)	100	India, Belgium, France	Electrical insulation, ceramics
Strontium	100	Mexico, Spain	Flares, fireworks
Tin	88	Peru, China, Bolivia, Indonesia	Cans and containers, electrical components
Tantalum	80	Thailand, Germany, Brazil	Surgical instruments, missile parts
Barite	79	China, India	Filler for gas and oil well drilling fluids, paint, plastics
Cobalt	76	Democratic Republic of the Congo, Zambia, Canada	High-temperature jet fighter engines
Chromium	72	South Africa, Zimbabwe, Turkey	Chrome, ball bearings, trim on appliances and cars

Source: *Statistical Abstract of the United States*; U.S. Geological Survey

International trade is the primary means by which nations, including the United States, obtain many essential materials.

◀ **CRITICAL THINKING**
Economic Analysis How does the lack of certain raw materials force nations to become more interdependent?

connected.mcgraw-hill.com

Resources for Global Trade **495**

CHAPTER 17, LESSON 1
Absolute and Comparative Advantage

TEACH & ASSESS

C Critical Thinking Skills

Analyzing the relationship between exports and specialization Ask: **What is the relationship between a state or nation's exports and its specialization?** *(A state or nation's main exports reflect what the place produces best and at a quantity that allows the products to be sold to other regions or countries; this indicates that the state or nation has an economic advantage related to the manufacturing and sale of these goods.)* Invite students to research exports produced in their state and then analyze why the state might specialize in those items. **Verbal/Linguistic**

V Visual Skills

Using a chart to learn about dependence on trade Ask: **From which countries does the United States import tin?** *(Peru, China, Bolivia, Indonesia)* **What percent of U.S. tin consumption do these imports represent?** *(88 percent)* **Visual/Spatial**

CHARTS

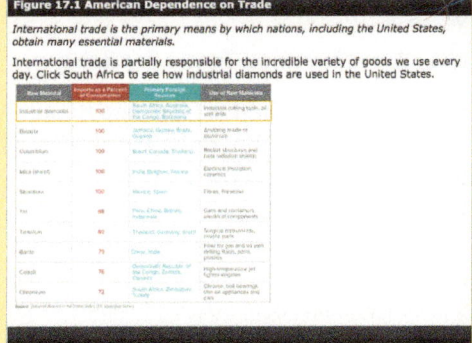

American Dependence on Trade

Assessing the importance of imported raw materials Display Figure 17.1. Discuss how industrial diamonds are used in the United States. Emphasize that much of our trade for raw materials is caused by their limited availability in the United States. Guide students to understand that our economy would be severely handicapped if trade did not make these resources available to U.S. manufacturers. **Visual/Spatial**

ANSWERS, p. 495

CRITICAL THINKING

Countries must become interdependent with one another in order to acquire the raw materials they need.

Resources for Global Trade **495**

CHAPTER 17, LESSON 1
Absolute and Comparative Advantage

R Reading Skills

Defining terms Explain that *absolute* means "ultimate or unquestionable," whereas *comparative* means "related to a comparison between things." Model the use of these terms in sentences for students. Stress that *absolute advantage* is the ability of one country, using the same amount of resources as another country, to produce a particular product at a lower absolute cost. Stress that *comparative advantage* is the ability of a country to produce a product more efficiently—or at a lower *opportunity* cost—than another country. Then ask students to explain the meanings in their own words.
ELL Verbal/Linguistic

V Visual Skills

Using a chart to learn about trade partners
Ask: What percentage of the U.S. GDP do exports represent? *(9.2 percent)* **What is the difference in value between U.S. imports and exports with Mexico?** *(The United States imports $96 billion more from Mexico than it exports to Mexico.)*
Logical/Mathematical, Visual/Spatial

Figure 17.2 shows the patterns of merchandise trade for the United States with the rest of the world. The import of goods alone amounts to $2,240 billion, or about $7,100 per person. The numbers in the figure would be even larger if we included the value of services.

In the end, international trade is much more than a way to obtain exotic products. The sheer **volume** of trade between nations with such different geographic, political, and religious characteristics is proof that trade is beneficial.

volume amount; quantity

✓ **READING PROGRESS CHECK**

Explaining Why is specialization a good idea in trade?

The Basis for Trade

GUIDING QUESTION How does trade result in greater overall output?

In 1776, Adam Smith, in his *Wealth of Nations*, was the first to write that a country should import products if they could be made more cheaply abroad than at home. This was an important departure from prevailing economic thought at the time. Smith was also the first writer to discuss the concept of absolute advantage, which was later refined to a doctrine called *comparative advantage*.

absolute advantage
country's ability to produce a given product more efficiency than can another country

R Absolute Advantage

A country has an **absolute advantage** when it can produce a product more efficiently than can another country. For example, take the hypothetical case of

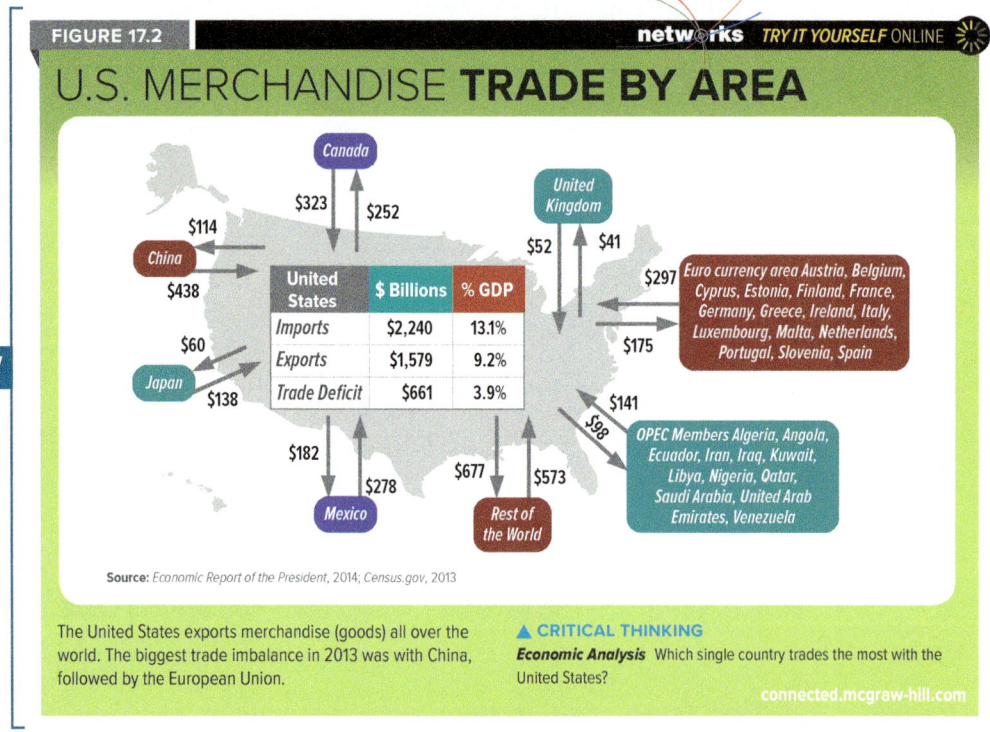

FIGURE 17.2
U.S. MERCHANDISE TRADE BY AREA

United States	$ Billions	% GDP
Imports	$2,240	13.1%
Exports	$1,579	9.2%
Trade Deficit	$661	3.9%

Source: *Economic Report of the President*, 2014; Census.gov, 2013

The United States exports merchandise (goods) all over the world. The biggest trade imbalance in 2013 was with China, followed by the European Union.

▲ **CRITICAL THINKING**
Economic Analysis Which single country trades the most with the United States?

496

---

networks Online Teaching Options

MAPS

U.S. Merchandise Trade by Area

Using a map and chart to learn about trade
Have students view Figure 17.2 and discuss the table. **Ask: What was the value of all U.S. imports in 2013?** *($2,240 billion)* **What percent of our GDP did this represent?** *(13.1 percent).* Have students compare the value of U.S. exports and imports and discuss the trade deficit. Then invite students to identify the countries from which the United States imports the most goods. Continue by discussing exports and the trade deficit. Visual/Spatial, Logical/Mathematical

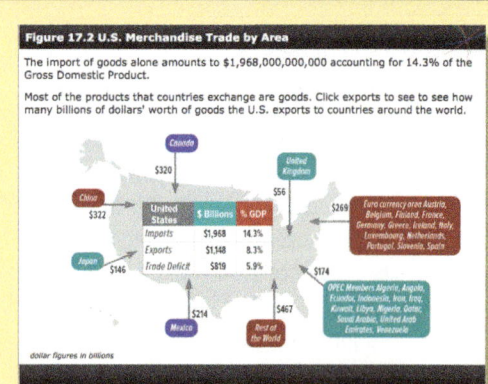

ANSWERS, p. 496

✓ **READING PROGRESS CHECK** It allows people to produce the things they do best and exchange those products for the things that other people do best.

CRITICAL THINKING
Canada trades the most with the United States.

496

two countries—Alpha and Beta—which are the same size in terms of area, population, and capital stock. Only their climate and soil fertilities differ. In each country, only two crops can be grown—coffee and cashew nuts.

In **Figure 17.3** you see an illustration of the **production possibilities curves** (frontiers) for Alpha and Beta. Note that if both countries devote all of their efforts to producing coffee, Alpha could produce 40 pounds and Beta 6 pounds—giving Alpha an absolute advantage in coffee production. If both countries concentrate on producing cashew nuts, Alpha could produce 8 pounds and Beta 6 pounds. Alpha, then, also has an absolute advantage in the production of cashew nuts because it can produce more than Beta.

For years, people thought that absolute advantage was the basis for trade because it **enabled** a country to produce enough of a good to consume domestically while leaving some for export. However, the concept of absolute advantage did not explain how two countries could benefit from an exchange in which a country with a large output, like Alpha, traded with a country with a smaller output, like Beta.

production possibilities curves diagram representing maximum combinations of goods and/or services an economy can produce when all productive resources are fully employed

enabled made possible

Comparative Advantage

Even when one country enjoys an absolute advantage in the production of all goods, as in the case of Alpha above, trade between it and another country is

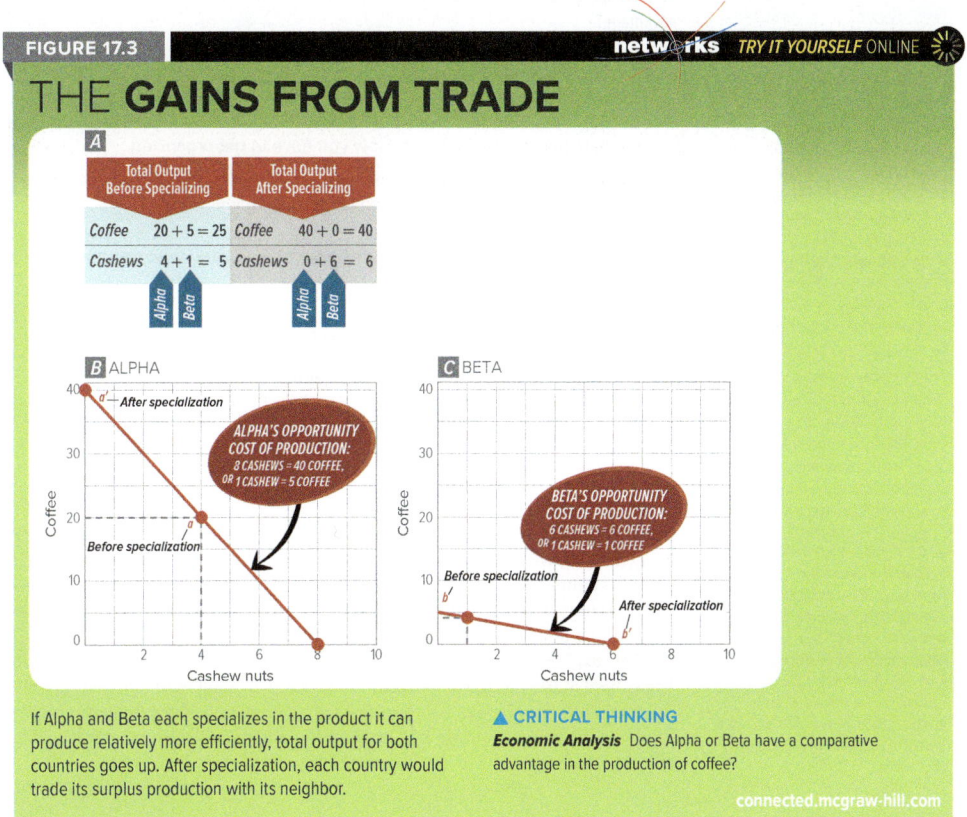

FIGURE 17.3

THE GAINS FROM TRADE

If Alpha and Beta each specializes in the product it can produce relatively more efficiently, total output for both countries goes up. After specialization, each country would trade its surplus production with its neighbor.

▲ **CRITICAL THINKING**
Economic Analysis Does Alpha or Beta have a comparative advantage in the production of coffee?

Resources for Global Trade **497**

CHAPTER 17, LESSON 1
Absolute and Comparative Advantage

R Reading Skills

Comparing absolute and comparative advantage
Ask: What did the theory of absolute advantage fail to explain? *(how two countries could benefit from an exchange in which a country with a large output traded with a country with a smaller output)* **How does the concept of comparative advantage explain the benefits of a large-output country trading with a smaller-output country?** *(It reveals when a country has the ability to produce a good relatively more efficiently or at a lower opportunity cost than another country.)* **ELL**
Verbal/Linguistic

Content Background Knowledge

Comparative Advantage Explain to students that British economist David Ricardo first advanced the theory of comparative advantage in 1817. He used a mathematical example involving the production of wine and cloth in Portugal and England. In England, it might take 100 workers to make a set amount of cloth and 120 workers to make a set amount of wine. In Portugal, it might take 90 workers to make the same amount of cloth, while the same amount of wine might take 80 workers. Ricardo observed that it would be in the interest of England to focus on making cloth, using the finished product to buy wine. By employing its capital in wine production, Portugal could obtain more cloth from England that it could produce by diverting some capital to cloth manufacturing.

GRAPHS

The Gains from Trade

Using graphs to understand comparative advantage Display the first slide and read and discuss the text. **Ask: How much coffee is produced individually and in total by Alpha and Beta?** *(Alpha: 20 pounds, Beta: 5 pounds, total 25 pounds)* Discuss how students know Alpha has a comparative advantage in the production of coffee. **Ask: What happens to coffee production when the countries specialize?** *(Alpha produces 40 pounds of coffee whereas Beta produces none. Total production has increased from 25 to 40.)* **If Alpha produced 30 pounds of coffee, how many pounds of cashews could it produce?** *(2 pounds)* View the Beta graph and discuss how this graph demonstrates the advantage to Beta of specializing. **Visual/Spatial**

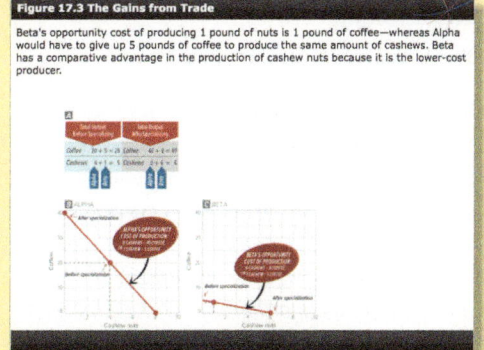

Figure 17.3 The Gains from Trade

Beta's opportunity cost of producing 1 pound of nuts is 1 pound of coffee—whereas Alpha would have to give up 5 pounds of coffee to produce the same amount of cashews. Beta has a comparative advantage in the production of cashew nuts because it is the lower-cost producer.

ANSWERS, p. 497

CRITICAL THINKING

Alpha has a comparative advantage in coffee production.

CHAPTER 17, LESSON 1
Absolute and Comparative Advantage

R Reading Skills

Explaining assumptions Ask: **What is the assumption on which the concept of comparative advantage is based?** *(The concept is based on the assumption that everyone will be better off specializing in the products they produce best.)*
Verbal/Linguistic

English Language Proficiency

Advanced Model using visual and contextual support during prereading, reading, and post-reading of this lesson. Point out and model the use of such supports as illustrations, graphic aids, captions, bold-face terms, the title, and section headings. Think aloud as you use them to make predictions. Provide students with a three-column chart headed **What I See, What I Think It Means**, and **What I Know**. Model the use of the first two columns to make predictions, and the third column to record information during and after reading.

ANSWERS, p. 498

☑ **READING PROGRESS CHECK** Absolute advantage is a country's ability to produce more of a given product than another country can produce. Comparative advantage is a country's ability to produce a given product more efficiently than another country by doing it at a lower opportunity cost.

EXPLORING THE ESSENTIAL QUESTION

Students might list tasks such as *mowing, trimming, bookkeeping, advertising, customer service, equipment maintenance*, and so on. Students should make the connection with comparative advantage by explaining that they would assign tasks on the basis of which worker could perform them most efficiently and at the lowest opportunity cost.

CRITICAL THINKING

1. Responses should indicate that Krugman's theories explained how trade benefited consumers because it produced a greater variety of products at cheaper prices, while earlier trade theories explained how comparative advantage benefited nations that could produce certain products more efficiently and trade for others.
2. Students may mention benefits such as availability of a greater variety of products and negative effects such as limited availability of needed products if two countries go to war, but a variety of responses are acceptable so long as students take positions and justify them with facts and reasons.

498

BIOGRAPHY

Paul Krugman
ECONOMIST (1953–)

Paul Krugman was awarded the 2008 Nobel Prize in Economics for his work studying international trade patterns. After receiving degrees from Yale and the Massachusetts Institute of Technology, Krugman has spent most of his career teaching economics and public policy. His Nobel prize–winning research centered on globalization—an increase in worldwide trade and interdependence—in the post–World War II era. Before Krugman, trade theories used comparative advantage to explain why nations specialized in producing certain types of goods. However, comparative advantage could not explain why one country might import and export variations on the same type of product.

Krugman developed a trade theory that showed how consumers' desire for more choices and varieties of products led to larger economies and the establishment of new trading arrangements between nations.

▲ **CRITICAL THINKING**
Finding the Main Idea How did Paul Krugman's ideas about trade differ from earlier theories?
Exploring Issues Think about globalization—the increasing tendency of the world to be interconnected. What are some positive effects of globalization? What are some negative effects? Explain your answer.

---

still beneficial. This happens whenever a country has a **comparative advantage**—the ability to produce a product relatively more efficiently, or at a lower opportunity cost.

To illustrate, because Alpha can produce either 40 pounds of coffee or 8 pounds of cashew nuts, the **opportunity cost** of producing 1 pound of cashew nuts is 5 pounds of coffee (40 pounds of coffee divided by 8). At the same time, Beta's opportunity cost of producing 1 pound of cashew nuts is 1 pound of coffee (6 pounds of coffee divided by 6). Beta is the lower-cost producer of cashew nuts because its opportunity cost of producing 1 pound of nuts is 1 pound of coffee—whereas Alpha would have to give up 5 pounds of coffee to produce the same amount of cashews.

If Beta has a comparative advantage in producing cashews, then Alpha must have a comparative advantage in coffee production. Indeed, if we calculated each country's opportunity cost of producing coffee, we would see that Alpha's opportunity cost of producing 1 pound of coffee is 1/5 of a pound of cashews (8 pounds of cashews divided by 40). Using the same computations, Beta's opportunity cost is 1 pound of cashews (6 pounds of cashews divided by 6). Alpha, then, has a comparative advantage in coffee production, because its opportunity cost of production is lower than Beta's.

☑ READING PROGRESS CHECK

Summarizing What is the difference between comparative advantage and absolute advantage?

EXPLORING THE ESSENTIAL QUESTION

Imagine that you and a partner are starting a lawn-service business. You will each contribute an equal amount of money to buy a mower, a trimmer, gas, and other materials for the business. Now you have to get organized.

- Make a list of the different tasks associated with your business. Keep in mind that these tasks will not all be related to lawn work.
- Explain how you could use what you have learned about comparative advantage to divide up these jobs between you and your partner.

The Gains from Trade

GUIDING QUESTION What are the gains resulting from trade?

The concept of comparative advantage is based on the assumption that everyone will be better off by specializing in the products they produce best. This applies to individuals, companies, states, and regions as well as to nations.

Greater World Output

If we look at the final result of trade between Alpha and Beta, shown in **Panel A** of Figure 17.3, we can see that specialization and trade increased the total world output. Without trade, both countries together produced 25 pounds of coffee and 5 pounds of cashews. After trade, total world output grew to 40 pounds of coffee and 6 pounds of cashews.

This explains why countries such as the United States and Colombia trade. The United States has the resources to produce farm equipment efficiently, while Colombia has the resources to produce coffee efficiently. Because each country has a comparative advantage in a product the other country wants, trade will be beneficial to both and will lead to economic growth.

498

---

networks Online Teaching Options

BIOGRAPHY

Biography: Paul Krugman

Examining the influence of Paul Krugman
Display the biography feature and call on students to read each of the paragraphs. Read and discuss the questions. Ask: **How does comparative advantage lead to cheaper production costs?** *(Countries can specialize in products they make more efficiently and thereby produce more at lower costs per unit.)* **How does comparative advantage lead to a greater variety of products in the market?** *(Rather than trying to produce everything for its domestic market, a country specializes and imports other goods from many places, providing a wide variety of products from many countries.)*
Verbal/Linguistic

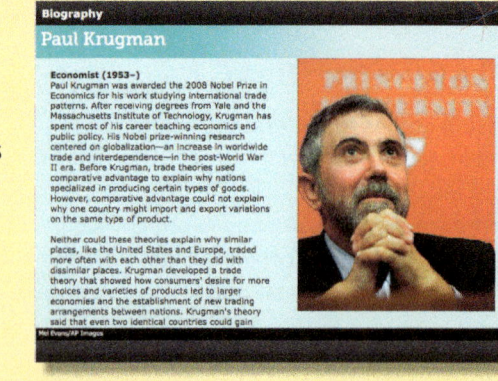

Increased Political Stability

The benefits of trade are not limited to the increased world output only, as there are non-production benefits as well. One of the most important is an increase in political stability between nations that have strong trade relations.

For example, the United States and England were bitter enemies of Japan and Germany during World War II. Since then, these countries have become strong allies that usually support each other in political as well as economic matters. These partnerships started with more international trade and ended up with more political cooperation. In the case of England and Germany, tighter economic and political integration took place because of the Common Market, the predecessor of the European Union.

Economists argue that cooperation in international economic affairs precedes political cooperation. For example, countries that are at war with each other are usually ones that have the least amount of international trade between them. Consequently, economists like to see increased trade between nations because this may tend to lower potential hostilities between nations.

Faster Economic Growth

The gains from trade also help an economy to grow. The growth comes from two sources: a bigger market for the country's manufactured goods and services, and the ability to secure needed inputs for production. Without access to the vital raw materials shown in Figure 17.1, for example, many large-scale manufacturing operations would have to shut down.

A bigger market for the country's manufactured goods and services allows greater specialization at home. This specialization is good for an economy because it allows people and firms to produce even more output—output that can be exchanged for other items the country desires. All of these things increase economic growth, which generates more jobs, and produces more income than ever before.

READING PROGRESS CHECK

Summarizing Why is it beneficial for a country to trade with another when it has a comparative advantage?

comparative advantage country's ability to produce a given product relatively more efficiently than another country; production at a lower opportunity cost

opportunity cost cost of the next best alternative use of money, time, or resources when one choice is made rather than another

---

LESSON 1 REVIEW

Reviewing Vocabulary
1. *Explaining* What does a production possibilities curve show?
2. *Contrasting* Explain the difference between imports and exports.

Using Your Notes
Use the information you jotted down in the graphic organizer to answer this question.

3. *Explaining* Give an example of how one country can hold an absolute advantage in producing a certain product, while another country holds a comparative advantage in producing the same thing.

Answering the Guiding Questions
4. *Evaluating* Consider the reasons why countries trade, and give two examples of how your life would be different if the United States did not trade with other countries.

5. *Predicting* Suppose a nation has a great deal of human capital but few natural resources. In what kinds of products might the nation specialize?

6. *Listing* Identify four reasons that nations trade with one another.

7. *Explaining* Why does total world output increase as countries specialize to engage in trade?

Writing About Economics
8. *Expository* Review the information about production possibilities curves. Then write a paragraph that identifies the information contained in Figure 17.3, and explain how to interpret the graphs. Include brief descriptions of how these visuals can be used to pinpoint opportunity cost.

CHAPTER 17, LESSON 1
Absolute and Comparative Advantage

C Critical Thinking Skills

Debating which comes first Have students debate the statement: *Cooperation in international economic affairs precedes political cooperation.* Ask students to give examples that support their arguments.

R Reading Skills

Explaining how trade produces economic growth
Ask: How does trade help an economy grow? *(It provides a bigger market for a country's goods and services and it provides a source for inputs for production.)* How does a bigger market help a country? *(It enables a country to specialize, which increases its efficiencies and allows it to produce more output that can be exchanged for other items the country needs. These advantages promote economic growth, which generates jobs and income.)* Verbal/Linguistic

CLOSE & REFLECT

Summarizing main ideas Tell students that many people oppose free trade agreements because they think such agreements cost American jobs. Ask students to write six statements based on information in this lesson that support strengthening free trade agreements with other countries. Ask them to share some of their statements in class discussion.

ANSWERS, p. 499

 READING PROGRESS CHECK It can trade a product it produces best in exchange for a product it wants that another country produces best.

LESSON 1 REVIEW ANSWERS

Reviewing Vocabulary
1. A production possibilities curve shows the different amounts of goods and services an economy can produce at its full potential.
2. Imports are goods and services that a nation buys from other nations, while exports are goods and services that a nation sells to other nations.

Using Your Notes
3. If country A is larger and has more people and natural resources than does country B, it may hold an absolute advantage in producing cars because it can make more of them. However, country B could still hold a comparative advantage if it can produce cars more efficiently than can the larger country.

Answering the Guiding Questions
4. Student answers may indicate that many of the products they use on a day-to-day basis come from other countries. Students may also mention political stability and economic growth as benefits of global trade.
5. Student answers should mention services provided by people, such as skilled labor, financial consulting, insurance, and so on.
6. Answers include the lack of goods at home; the need for raw materials; specialization; desire for exotic products; and profit.
7. Because specialization allows countries to concentrate on making the things they produce most efficiently, thereby increasing total output.

Writing About Economics
8. Student responses should explain how the graphs show the different amounts of cashews and coffee that can be produced by each country, depending on how it uses its resources. The opportunity cost of producing each resource can be found by measuring the slope of the graph.

CHAPTER 17
Case Study

C Critical Thinking Skills

Reviewing the history of 9/11 Guide students in a discussion of the 9/11 terrorist attack. Ask them to talk about its causes and when and where it occurred. **Ask: Why was the attack given the name 9/11?** *(Explain that the attack is known as 9/11 because it occurred on September 11, 2001.)* **Interpersonal**

R Reading Skills

Identifying effects of 9/11 Ask: How did 9/11 affect America? *(It affected U.S. security, privacy, national pride, and the economy.)* Guide students to discuss specific ramifications in each of these areas. Ask them if they think these ramifications are continuing to affect us, and why, after so many years. **Verbal/Linguistic**

Content Background Knowledge

Effects of 9/11 The 9/11 terrorist attacks changed many aspects of life in America. Among them were protracted wars in Iraq and Afghanistan that cost American lives, injuries, and billions of dollars. Travelers must go through heightened security checks at airports, many public events, and in public buildings like courthouses. There has been greater intolerance for immigrants, especially those from the Middle East. It has resulted in a loss of privacy in many ways. Invite students to identify other consequences of 9/11, including changes to society, privacy, and the economy.

ANSWERS, p. 500

Case Study Review

1. The new security measures slowed imports to and exports from the United States and increased costs. The slow-down of imports also affected other industries that rely on imports of raw materials or manufactured goods. Some U.S. manufacturers benefited from the delay and increased cost of imported goods.
2. Students should note that if the United States imports critical goods, such as oil, or many goods from the attacked country, the attacks could have negative effects on the U.S. economy. If the attacked country imported a lot of goods from the United States, the impact would likely be negative. Other responses might include the effects of diplomatic actions, changes to import/export costs or timing due to measures taken or infrastructure issues, and the amount of trade between countries.

500

Case Study

THREE WAYS 9/11 AFFECTED the ECONOMY

The terrorist attacks of September 11, 2001, had far-reaching implications for Americans in areas of security, privacy, and national pride. It also had effects on the economy both at home and abroad. Changes occurred for a number of reasons, including consumer confidence, new security regulations, and concessions made for diplomatic purposes.

Following the attacks, new security measures affected how goods were shipped and inspected. Bottlenecks in shipping slowed the movement of both manufactured goods and raw materials. The delay in shipment of raw materials led to slow-downs in manufacturing for several industries, including the automobile industry. Increased inspections also brought increased costs. These increases have a damaging effect on all industries that ship internationally, and may be particularly challenging for small companies. On the other hand, some U.S. manufacturers may benefit because of delays or increased costs on imports from other countries.

As part of its response to 9/11 and as part of the war on terror, the United States changed its diplomatic and political relationships with several countries in the Middle East and Central Asia. Sanctions put in place in reaction to nuclear tests by Pakistan and India were lifted, changing the trade relations between these countries. For example, the lifted sanctions opened the door for more imports of Pakistani apparel.

There are, of course, many other economic impacts of the 9/11 attacks. Looking at the effects of the attacks on September 11th requires examining many angles and aspects of the economic picture.

Flood lights mark the absence of the Twin Towers in the days after September 11th.

CASE STUDY REVIEW

1. **Analyzing** How did security actions in the United States affect imports and exports in both the United States and other parts of the world?
2. **Speculating** What kind of impact do you imagine an attack in another country would have on the economy of the United States? Explain your response.

500

---

networks Online Teaching Options

INTERACTIVE FEATURE

Three Ways 9/11 Affected the Economy

Assessing the effects of trade restrictions Display the Case Study and guide a discussion of how the 9/11 terrorist attacks resulted in costly restrictions on trade. **Ask: What trade restrictions were imposed?** *(Increased security measures for shipping and inspections)* **What were the consequences for business?** *(Bottlenecks due to increased inspections slowed shipping, raising costs to manufacturers because they could not get needed raw materials. The costs of inspections increased.)* **How do you think these events affected consumers?** *(The increased costs to business were passed along to consumers in the form of higher prices.)* **Verbal/Linguistic**

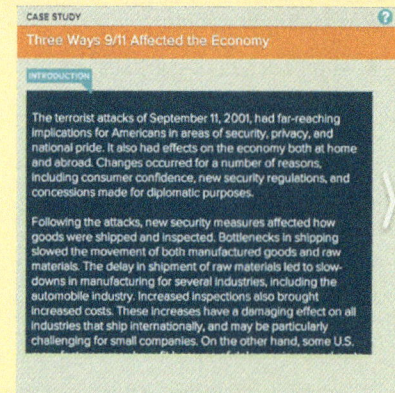

Interact with these digital assets and others in lesson 2

✓ POLITICAL CARTOON
International Trade
✓ SLIDESHOW
The WTO
✓ SELF-CHECK QUIZ
✓ VIDEO

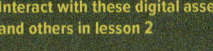
TRY IT YOURSELF ONLINE

Reading Help Desk

Academic Vocabulary
- justify

Content Vocabulary
- tariff
- quota
- protective tariff
- revenue tariff
- embargo
- protectionists
- free traders
- infant industries argument
- balance of payments
- most favored nation clause
- General Agreement on Tariffs and Trade (GATT)
- World Trade Organization (WTO)
- North American Free Trade Agreement (NAFTA)

TAKING NOTES:

Key Ideas and Details
ACTIVITY As you read the lesson, complete the graphic organizer below by describing the arguments of protectionists and free traders.

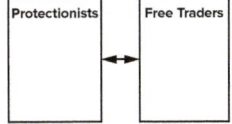

LESSON 2
Barriers to International Trade

ESSENTIAL QUESTION

How does trade benefit all participating parties?

Suppose you choose products made in the United States when possible to support American industries. How might buying a product made elsewhere support American industries?

a. Cheap exports drive down prices at home, which benefits the consumer.

b. Products made elsewhere could be made with American goods or technology.

c. Buying imported goods means somebody else is buying American goods.

Restricting International Trade

GUIDING QUESTION *Why does the government place restrictions on international trade?*

While free markets and international trade can bring many benefits, some people still object, because trade can displace selected industries and groups of workers. When these people object to trade, they look for ways to prevent it, or to at least slow the rate of growth. Historically, trade has been restricted in two major ways. One is through a **tariff**—a tax placed on imports to increase their price in the domestic market. The other is with a **quota**—a limit placed on the quantities of a product that can be imported.

Tariffs

Governments generally levy two kinds of tariffs—protective tariffs and revenue tariffs. A **protective tariff** is a tariff high enough to protect less-efficient domestic industries. Suppose, for example, that it costs $1 to produce a mechanical pencil in the United States, while the same product can be imported for 35 cents from another country. If a tariff of 95 cents is placed on each imported pencil, the cost for these imports climbs to $1.30 per pencil—more than the cost of the American-made one. The result of the tariff is that a domestic industry is protected from being undersold by a foreign one.

The **revenue tariff** is a tariff high enough to generate revenue for the government without actually prohibiting imports. If the tariff on imported mechanical pencils were 40 cents, the price of the imports would be 75 cents,

connected.mcgraw-hill.com   Resources for Global Trade **501**

CHAPTER 17, LESSON 2
Barriers to International Trade

ENGAGE

C Critical Thinking Skills

Speculating on tariffs and quotas Before students begin the lesson, define *tariff* and *quota*. **Ask: What might be an appropriate situation to impose a tariff on a particular good? What about a quota?** Encourage students who oppose trade limitations to give their reasons. **Verbal/Linguistic**

TEACH & ASSESS

R Reading Skills

Summarizing the goals of tariffs Ask: What are the goals of a protective tariff and revenue tariff? *(A government levies a protective tariff to raise costs of imports so that domestic industries are protected from being undersold. A revenue tariff generates government revenue without prohibiting imports.)* **Verbal/Linguistic**

ANSWERS, p. 501

ESSENTIAL QUESTION ACTIVITY

Answer a. may be true, but it is a benefit for consumers, not industries. Answer c. is not necessarily true. Choice b. is the correct answer. Although products made elsewhere are not necessarily made with American goods or technology, they could be, thus benefiting American industries.

TAKING NOTES
Protectionists:
- Protect domestic producers against foreign competition with tariffs, quotas, and other trade barriers
- A country could become so specialized that it would become too dependent
- Some industries need to gain strength and experience before they can compete
- Protect domestic jobs from cheap foreign labor
- Restrictions on imports reduce trade deficits and thus help the balance of payments

Free Traders:
- Favor fewer or no trade restrictions
- Admit that national security is a compelling argument for trade barriers
- Industries accustomed to protection are often unwilling to give it up
- The profit-and-lost system, a major feature of the American economy, should be allowed to work
- Money that goes abroad generally returns

BELLRINGER

Barriers to International Trade

Identifying reasons for and against free trade Have students view the Bellringer. Then draw a T-chart on the board and label one column *Yes* and the other *No*. Have students list as many arguments in favor of free trade as they can, and as many arguments against it as they can. Tell students to keep these arguments in mind as they study the lesson. **Verbal/Linguistic**

Resources for Global Trade **501**

CHAPTER 17, LESSON 2
Barriers to International Trade

W Writing Skills

Writing an evaluation of tariffs Have students research a time in which the U.S. government used tariffs prior to 1913. Tell students to write a short essay evaluating the government's use of the tariffs they researched. Instruct them to categorize the tariffs as either protective or revenue tariffs, and discuss whether the tariffs were successful in achieving the government's goals. **Verbal/Linguistic**

C Critical Thinking Skills

Interpreting government decisions on tariffs
Ask: Why might the U.S. government pursue a trade policy that would raise the costs of products for American consumers? *(to protect domestic industries and the jobs of workers in those industries)* **Verbal/Linguistic**

---

or 25 cents less than the American-made ones. As long as the two products are identical, consumers would prefer the imported one because it is less expensive, so the tariff would raise revenue for the government rather than protect domestic producers from foreign competition.

Traditionally, tariffs were used more for revenue than for protection. Before the Civil War, tariffs were the chief source of revenue for the federal government. From the Civil War to 1913, tariffs provided about one-half of the government's total revenue. After the federal income tax became law in 1913, the government had a new and more lucrative source of revenue. Since then tariffs—also called customs duties—have accounted for only a small portion of total government revenue, as shown earlier in Figure 14.5.

A tariff also gives protection to selected groups at the expense of others. In 2002, for example, the Bush administration imposed a 30 percent tariff on foreign steel imports. The tariff preserved some jobs during an election year, but it also raised the price of domestic steel by 20 to 30 percent to U.S. consumers. In 2009, the Obama administration imposed a 35 percent tariff on Chinese tires to protect union jobs—thereby raising the price of tires to U.S. consumers.

tariff tax placed on an imported product

quota limit on the amount of a good that is allowed into a country

protective tariff tax on an imported product designed to protect less efficient domestic producers

revenue tariff tax placed on imported goods to raise revenue

Quotas

Foreign goods sometimes cost so little that even a high tariff on them might not protect the domestic market. In such cases, the government can use a quota to keep foreign goods out of the country. Quotas can even be set as low as zero to keep a product from ever entering the country. More typically, quotas are used to reduce the total supply of a product to keep prices high for domestic producers.

CAREERS | Foreign Service Agricultural Attaché

Is this career for you?

 Do you understand scientific and technical materials?

 Are you culturally and politically savvy?

 Do you work well with people and other agencies?

 Are you willing to live in other countries and move every few years?

Interview with a professional **Foreign Service Agricultural Attaché**

> " Every day, our office has to think about how 1.1 billion people are going to eat. "

—Holly Higgins, Embassy New Delhi's Minister Counselor for the Office of Agricultural Affairs

Salary
Varies on the basis of assignment and experience

Job Growth Potential
The Foreign Agricultural Service is a relatively small agency, so unless the service is enlarged, the job growth potential remains static.

Profile of Work
Foreign Agricultural Service attachés focus on food security issues. They help administer food aid programs, report on crops and weather, issue press releases about food safety, and promote exchanges of information on science and best practices related to food safety. They work with many other U.S. government agencies and the private sector to achieve goals.

502

---

networks Online Teaching Options

INTERACTIVE FEATURE

Career: Foreign Service Agricultural Attaché

Assessing a career as a Foreign Service Agricultural Attaché Ask a student to read aloud the primary source excerpt and the Profile of Work. Then discuss the questions that will help students decide if the career is for them. **Ask:**

- Why does an agricultural attaché need to understand scientific and technical materials? *(Agriculture is a highly science-based field and an agricultural attaché must be able to understand it.)*
- Why does an agricultural attaché need to be savvy about culture and politics? *(The attaché works in a foreign country among citizens and their political leaders and must know how to understand their background and how to communicate effectively with them.)*
- Why must an agricultural attaché be prepared to live in foreign countries and move every few years? *(Foreign Service Agricultural Attachés live and work abroad and serving where needed in the world is part of the job.)*

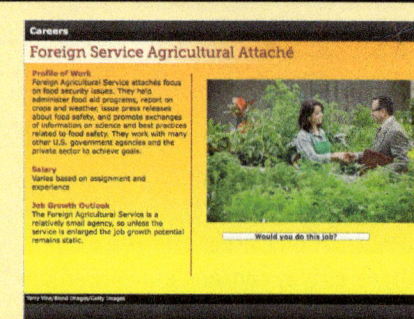

In 1981, for example, domestic automobile producers faced intense competition from lower-priced Japanese imports. Rather than lower their own prices, domestic manufacturers wanted President Ronald Reagan to establish import quotas on Japanese cars. The Reagan administration agreed. As a result, Americans had fewer cars from which to choose, and the prices of all cars were higher than they otherwise would have been.

More recently, the threat of a quota has been used as a way to persuade other nations to change their trade policies. For example, the United States became concerned when the low prices China charged for its textiles exports created problems for the domestic textile industry. In order to make China raise prices, in 2005 the government threatened China with quotas on these textiles. While it may seem odd to have the U.S. government pursue policies that would raise the cost of products to American citizens, the real purpose of the quota was to protect domestic industries and the jobs in those industries.

Other Barriers

Tariffs and quotas are not the only barriers to trade. Many other barriers are more subtle, but are just as effective. Some of the more popular ones are listed below:

- **Embargos**—Sometimes a country will place an **embargo**, or a government order prohibiting the movement of goods to a country. For example, the United States placed an embargo on goods going to Cuba in 1962.
- **Inspections**—Many imported foods are subject to health inspections that are far more rigorous than those given to domestic foods. For years, this tactic was used to keep beef from Argentina out of the United States.
- **Licenses**—Another effective method is to require a license to import. If the government is slow to grant the license, or if the license fees are too high, international trade is restricted.
- **Health concerns**—Some nations use health issues to restrict trade. Several European countries, for example, refuse to import genetically altered crops grown in the United States. While this may or may not be a legitimate argument, they do restrict trade.
- **Nationalism and culture**—Cultural factors also play a role as a trade barrier. Europeans frequently claim that they prefer regional and traditional foods to foods grown elsewhere.

✓ READING PROGRESS CHECK

Comparing How do tariffs and quotas differ?

Arguments for Protection

GUIDING QUESTION On what major points do protectionists and free traders disagree?

Freer international trade has been a subject of debate for many years. **Protectionists** are people who favor trade barriers to protect domestic industries. Other people, known as **free traders**, prefer fewer or even no trade restrictions. The debate between the two groups usually centers on the six arguments for protection discussed below.

Aiding National Defense

The first argument for trade barriers centers on national defense. Protectionists argue that without trade barriers, a country could become so specialized that it would end up becoming too dependent on other countries.

embargo government order prohibiting the movements of goods to a country

protectionists people who want to protect domestic producers against foreign competition with tariffs, quotas, and other trade barriers

free traders people who favor fewer or no trade restrictions

CHAPTER 17, LESSON 2
Barriers to International Trade

C Critical Thinking Skills

Recognizing barriers to trade Write *Tariff*, *Quota*, and *Embargo* on the board. Then provide the following actions to students and have them identify which barrier to trade is at work: The United States limits lumber imports. *(quota)* The European Union halts oil from Syria. *(embargo)* The United States bans trade with Iran. *(embargo)* Japan taxes rice importers. *(tariff)* France limits the number of American films coming into its country. *(quota)* The United States forbids imports of Cuban sugar. *(embargo)* Argentina taxes imports of auto parts. *(tariff)* The United States pressures Japan to limit car exports. *(quota)* The United States taxes sugar from Honduras. *(tariff)*

V Visual Skills

Using geography skills Have students use library and Internet resources to locate resource maps of the United States. Direct them to study the maps and evaluate how the nation's resources might enable it to prepare for war. Then have students use the maps to explain why the United States might seek to institute trade protection for the purpose of national defense. **Visual/Spatial, Verbal/Linguistic**

WORKSHEET

Math Practice for Economics

Calculating the cost of a pair of shoes Remind students that one reason proponents of tariffs cite in arguing for protection of American manufacturers is the low price of labor and production overseas, which siphons off well-paying manufacturing jobs. Provide students with copies of the Math Practice worksheet. When students finish, discuss the answers and clarify how the calculations were done. **Ask: How much did labor cost for each shoe made?** *($2.75)* **How much did it cost for rent and equipment?** *($4.00)* Invite students to speculate on what these costs would have been if the shoes had been manufactured in the U.S. For reference, compare the manufacturing costs for labor and rent to the retailer's costs for these same items. **Ask: What can you conclude from these costs about why some American companies manufacture their products overseas?** *(Most students will conclude that it makes sound business sense to manufacture products where it is cheaper.)* **Logical/Mathematical**

ANSWERS, p. 503

✓ **READING PROGRESS CHECK** A tariff is a tax placed on an imported product, while a quota is a limit on the amount of a good that is allowed into the country.

CHAPTER 17, LESSON 2
Barriers to International Trade

C Critical Thinking Skills

Analyzing point of view about protecting domestic jobs Provide students with the following scenario: You are the president of a nation with a relatively healthy economy. However, one of your major industries—computer parts—is in decline, largely because of foreign competition. Members of your political party who represent districts where computer parts are the major industry want a high tariff on imported computer parts. In addition, workers in the computer parts industry have launched a huge publicity campaign in support of a tariff increase. At the same time, many people are calling for no tariff because they want to be able to buy inexpensive computer parts. Have students explain what they, as leaders, intend to do and why. Have them write their decision in the form of a speech to be made to the nation. **AL Verbal/Linguistic**

English Language Proficiency

Intermediate Have students make word cards with vocabulary used in this lesson. Group students and have group members review the words quickly. Then have groups members take turns holding a word card above another student's head. Other group members provide clues to help the student guess the word.

ANSWERS, p. 504

CRITICAL THINKING

Students' answers will vary but should indicate that the cartoon shows a free trade bias. Evidence for this is seen in that only the drawbacks of protectionism are described.

This cartoon portrays some of the possible benefits and drawbacks of protectionism.

▶ **CRITICAL THINKING**
Identifying Bias Explain whether this cartoon is biased in favor of free trade or protectionism. What evidence is there to support your explanation?

During wartime, protectionists argue, a country might not be able to get critical supplies such as oil and weapons. As a result, some smaller countries, such as Israel and South Africa, have developed large armaments industries to prepare for such crises. They want to be sure they will have a domestic supply should hostilities break out or other countries impose economic sanctions such as boycotts.

Free traders admit that national security is a compelling argument for trade barriers. They believe, however, that the advantages of having a reliable source of domestic supply must be weighed against the disadvantages that the supply will be smaller and possibly less efficient than it would be with free trade.

The political problem of deciding which industries are critical to national defense and which are not must also be considered. At one time, the steel, automobile, ceramic, and electronics industries all have argued that they are critical to national defense and so should receive some protection.

infant industries argument argument that new and emerging industries should be protected from foreign competition until they are strong enough to compete

justify to defend as warranted or necessary

Promoting Infant Industries

The **infant industries argument**—that new or emerging industries should be protected from foreign competition—is also used to **justify** trade barriers. Protectionists claim that some industries need to gain strength and experience before they can compete against established industries in other countries. Trade barriers, they argue, would give them the time they need to develop.

Many people are willing to accept the infant industries argument, but only if protection will eventually be removed so that the industry is forced to compete on its own. The problem is that industries that become accustomed to having protection are often unwilling to give it up, making for difficult political decisions later on.

 To illustrate, some Latin American countries have used tariffs to protect their own infant automobile industries, with tariffs as high as several hundred percent. In some cases, the tariff raised the price of used American-made cars to more than double the cost of new ones in the United States. In spite of this protection, no country in Latin America has been able to produce a globally competitive automobile on its own. To make matters worse, governments have come to rely on the revenue supplied by tariffs, so prices for automobiles remain high for their citizens.

Protecting Domestic Jobs

A third argument—and the one used frequently—is that tariffs and quotas protect domestic jobs from cheap foreign labor. Workers in the shoe industry,

504

---

networks   Online Teaching Options

POLITICAL CARTOON

International Trade

Interpreting a political cartoon Show students the cartoon and have them read and think about it on their own. **Ask: What is the message in this cartoon?** *(Protectionism may protect a country's industry from outside competition, but it also cuts the industry off from trade with the outside world.)* **Is this a fair commentary? Why or Why not?** *(Students should give sound reasons and facts based on their reading.)* **Visual/Spatial**

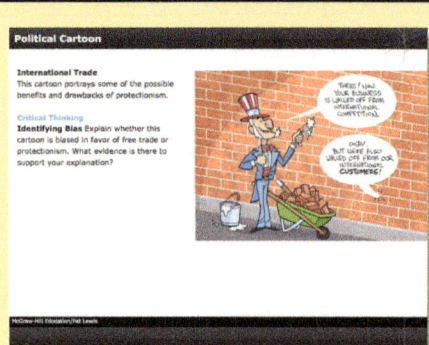

for example, have protested the import of lower-cost Italian, Spanish, and Brazilian shoes. Garment workers have opposed the import of lower-cost South Korean, Chinese, and Indian clothing. Some steelworkers have even blocked foreign-made cars of coworkers from company parking lots to show their displeasure with the foreign-made steel components in the cars.

In the short run, protectionist measures provide temporary protection for some domestic jobs. This is especially attractive to people who want to work in the communities where they grew up. In the long run, however, industries find it difficult to compete today will find it even more difficult to compete in the future unless they change the way they operate. As a result, most free traders believe that it is best not to interfere, thereby keeping the pressure on threatened industries to modernize and improve.

When inefficient industries are protected, the economy produces less and the standard of living goes down. Because of artificially high prices, people buy less of everything, including those goods produced by the protected industries. If the prices of protected products get too high, people look for substitute products, and the jobs that were supposed to be protected will still be lost. Free traders argue that, because the profit-and-loss system is one of the major features of the American economy, it should be allowed to work. Profits reward the efficient and hard-working, while losses eliminate the inefficient and weak.

Keeping the Money at Home

Another argument for trade barriers claims that limiting imports will keep American money in the United States instead of allowing it to go abroad. Free traders, however, point out that the American dollars that go abroad generally come back again. The Japanese, for example, use the dollars they receive for their automobiles to buy American cotton, soybeans, and airplanes. These purchases benefit American workers in those industries.

The same is true of the dollars used to buy oil from the Middle East. The money comes back to the United States when oil-wealthy foreigners buy American-made oil technology. Keeping the money at home, then, hurts those American industries that depend on exports for their jobs.

Helping the Balance of Payments

Another argument in the free trade debate involves the **balance of payments**—the difference between the money a country pays out to, and receives from, other nations when it engages in international trade. Protectionists argue that restrictions on imports reduce trade deficits and thus help the balance of payments.

Protectionists, however, overlook the fact that dollars that return to the United States stimulate employment in other industries. As a result, most economists do not believe that interfering with free trade can be justified on the grounds of helping the balance of payments.

Supporting National Pride

A final argument for protection is national pride. France, for example, is proud of its wines and cheeses and protects those industries for nationalistic reasons. In the 1980s, the United States gave temporary protection to Harley-Davidson, an American icon. Whether this is a good idea depends on how long the protection lasts. If it is permanent, then the government is simply protecting inefficient producers.

✔ READING PROGRESS CHECK

Synthesizing Do you agree with the protectionists' arguments or those of the free traders? Why?

EXPLORING THE ESSENTIAL QUESTION

Suppose you were running for office. You have been asked how removing trade barriers helps your constituents. Would it be easier to answer that question in a community dominated by a protected industry or a community based on other industries? Explain. Why might you recommend removing trade barriers?

balance of payments difference between money paid to and money received from other nations in trade; balance on current accounts includes goods and services, but merchandise trade balance counts only goods

---

CHAPTER 17, LESSON 2
Barriers to International Trade

R Reading Skills

Outlining the main ideas and details Direct students to reread the information in the Arguments for Protection subsection. Ask them to produce an outline that organizes the main ideas and important details from the subsection. Remind students that their outlines should be written in their own words and should not include complete sentences. Have students compare their completed outlines with those of partners, making revisions if necessary. **AL** Verbal/Linguistic

W Writing Skills

Writing to persuade Ask students to write a brief persuasive essay in which they argue either for or against trade protection on the basis of national pride. Direct them to support their arguments using evidence from the text or other reference materials. Remind students to cite their sources and to also evaluate their sources for bias. Verbal/Linguistic

ANSWERS, p. 505

EXPLORING THE ESSENTIAL QUESTION

It would be easier to answer that question in a community that was not dominated by a protected industry because a protected industry is more likely to be threatened by the removal of trade barriers. Possible reasons for removing trade barriers are to lower costs for consumers and to create a stronger economy by forcing industries to be more efficient.

✔ **READING PROGRESS CHECK** Those who agree with protectionists believe in protecting domestic producers using trade barriers. Those who agree with free traders favor few restrictions to allow the system to weed out inefficiencies and weaknesses. Students may agree with either protectionists or free traders, but should give valid reasons for their answers.

VIDEO **WORKSHEET**

Fair Trade

Evaluating the Fair Trade Foundation
Show students the video on the fair trade system. After they view the video, allow them a few minutes to take notes summarizing what they have seen and heard. Then guide students in discussing it. Prompt discussion by asking questions such as: **Is this a good deal for farmers? Why? Is it a good deal for consumers? Why? How does it assist schools?** Verbal/Linguistic

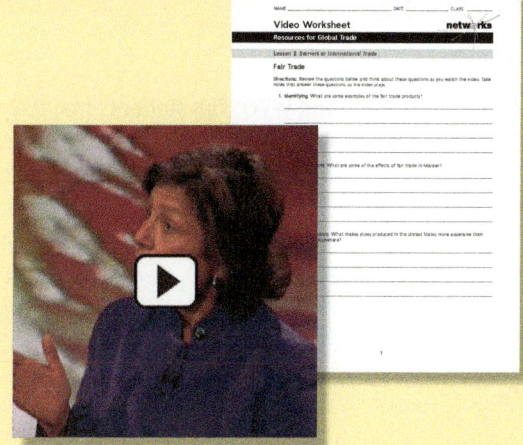

Video Supplied by BBC Worldwide Learning

CHAPTER 17, LESSON 2
Barriers to International Trade

C Critical Thinking Skills

Drawing conclusions about most favored nations
Ask: What do you think might prompt a country like the United States to offer a most favored nation clause to another nation? *(Possible answer: The United States would likely offer the clause because the nation is a major trading partner, and the United States wants to preserve a beneficial trading relationship with the nation.)* **Verbal/Linguistic**

W Writing Skills

Researching the WTO Ask students to research the World Trade Organization, including its members, structure, and key responsibilities. Direct students to use their findings to produce a report on the WTO and its role in international trade. Encourage students to include charts, graphs, or other visuals that they feel may enhance their essays.
ELL **Verbal/Linguistic**

ANSWERS, p. 506

CRITICAL THINKING
Students' answers will vary, but may include the idea that the WTO opening up trade and allowing outsourcing of labor to poorer countries without monitoring human rights abuses or insisting on fair prices can negatively affect workers in those countries.

In 1995, the World Trade Organization (WTO) was formed to administer trade agreements signed under GATT and settle trade disputes between nations. The WTO also organizes trade negotiations and provides technical assistance and training for developing countries. Critics of the WTO say the organization only benefits large corporations and rich countries.

▶ **CRITICAL THINKING**
How might the activities of the WTO negatively impact smaller countries?

most favored nation clause trade law allowing a third country to enjoy the same tariff reductions the United States negotiates with another country

General Agreement on Tariffs and Trade (GATT) an international agreement signed in 1947 among 23 countries to extend tariff concessions and reduce import quotas

World Trade Organization (WTO) international agency that administers trade agreements, settles trade disputes between governments, organizes trade negotiations, and provides technical assistance and training for developing countries

The Free Trade Movement

GUIDING QUESTION *What are the advantages and disadvantages of trade agreements?*

The use of trade barriers to protect domestic industries and jobs works only if other countries do not retaliate with their own trade barriers. If they do, all countries suffer, because they have neither the benefits of efficient production nor access to less costly products and raw materials from other nations.

Tariffs During the Great Depression

In 1930, the United States passed the Smoot-Hawley Tariff Act, one of the most restrictive tariffs in history. It set import duties so high that the prices of many imported goods rose nearly 70 percent. When other countries did the same, international trade nearly came to a halt.

Before long, most countries realized that high tariffs hurt more than they helped. As a result, in 1934 the United States passed the Reciprocal Trade Agreements Act, which allowed it to reduce tariffs up to 50 percent if other countries agreed to do the same. The act also contained a **most favored nation clause**—a provision allowing a country to receive the same tariff reduction that the United States gives to any third country.

Suppose, for example, that the United States and China have a trade agreement with a most favored nation clause. If the United States then negotiates a tariff reduction with a third country, such as Canada, the reduction would also apply to China. This clause is very important to China, because its goods will then sell at an even lower price in the American market.

The World Trade Organization

In 1947, 23 countries signed the **General Agreement on Tariffs and Trade (GATT)**. Under GATT, nations agreed to extend tariff concessions and worked to eliminate import quotas. Later, the Trade Expansion Act of 1962 gave the president of the United States the power to negotiate further tariff reductions. As a result of this legislation, more than 100 countries agreed to reduce the average level of tariffs by the early 1990s.

More recently, GATT has been administered by the **World Trade Organization (WTO)**, an international agency that enforces trade agreements signed under GATT and settles trade disputes between nations. The WTO also organizes trade negotiations and provides technical assistance and training for developing countries. Today, 159 countries are members of the GATT and the WTO.

---

networks **Online Teaching Options**

SLIDE SHOW

The WTO

Discussing GATT and WTO Tell students that the General Agreement on Tariffs and Trade and the later evolution of the World Trade Organization are two of the more important free trade organizations. Show them the slide show and ask and discuss the pros and cons of the WTO. **Visual/Spatial, Verbal/Linguistic**

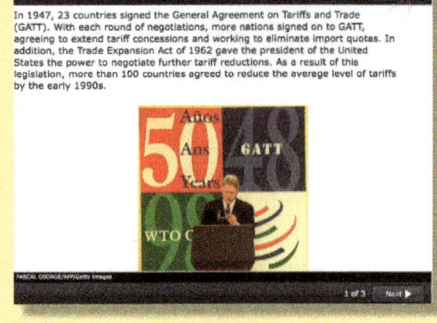

Because so many countries have been willing to reduce tariffs and quotas under GATT and the WTO, international trade is flourishing. Tariffs that in the past nearly doubled the price of many goods now increase prices by only a small percentage. Other tariffs have been dropped altogether. As a result, stores are able to offer a wide variety of industrial and consumer goods from all over the world.

NAFTA

The **North American Free Trade Agreement (NAFTA)** is an agreement to liberalize free trade by reducing tariffs and quotas among three major trading partners: Canada, Mexico, and the United States. It was a bipartisan agreement proposed by President George H. W. Bush and concluded by the Clinton administration in 1993.

Before NAFTA, U.S. goods entering Mexico faced tariffs averaging 10 percent. At the same time, approximately half of the goods entering the United States from Mexico were duty free, while the other half faced taxes averaging only 4 percent. Under NAFTA, the three countries agreed to a phase-out of tariffs and quotas over a 15-year period.

The phase-out was complete by 2008, making NAFTA the world's largest free trade area. The area now links over 470 million people who produce about $19 trillion of goods and services. Because of NAFTA, Canada and Mexico are usually the top two countries that export products to, and import products from, the United States.

Free trade is beneficial in general, but it is not painless. NAFTA was controversial specifically because some workers would be displaced when trade barriers were lowered. Opponents predicted that some high-paying American jobs would be lost to Mexico. Proponents predicted that trade among all three nations would increase dramatically, stimulating growth and bringing a wider variety of lower-cost goods to everyone.

Some of the costs and benefits identified during the NAFTA debate actually occurred, but not to the extent originally predicted. Some jobs were lost, but trade among the three countries has grown steadily since NAFTA was created. In the end, freer trade has allowed the NAFTA partners to capitalize on their comparative advantages for everyone's benefit—making NAFTA an unqualified success.

✓ **READING PROGRESS CHECK**

Recalling How did the WTO help international trade?

North American Free Trade Agreement (NAFTA) agreement signed in 1993 to reduce tariffs among the United States, Canada, and Mexico

---

LESSON 2 REVIEW

Reviewing Vocabulary

1. *Defining* Explain in your own words how free traders feel about tariffs.

Using Your Notes

2. Use your notes to cite details that explain why protectionists may be less likely to believe that trade benefits all involved parties.

Answering the Guiding Questions

3. *Explaining* Why does the government place restrictions on international trade?

4. *Explaining* On what major points do protectionists and free traders disagree?

5. *Comparing* What are the advantages and disadvantages of trade agreements?

Writing About Economics

6. *Persuasive/Explanatory* Suppose you were in charge of trade policy for the United States. Would you recommend that we increase or decrease trade barriers on athletic shoes? Write a memo making your recommendation and explaining why you want to increase or decrease specific trade barriers.

CHAPTER 17, LESSON 2
Barriers to International Trade

C **Critical Thinking Skills**

Comparing NAFTA to the EU Ask: **How is NAFTA similar to the EU?** *(NAFTA has increased the economic interdependence of the United States, Canada, and Mexico. Like the European Union, it is an important economic interconnection.)* **How is NAFTA different from the EU?** *(Unlike the European Union, NAFTA does not allow the free flow of labor among member countries.)*

CLOSE & REFLECT

W **Writing Skills**

Debating free trade Write this proposition on the board: The United States should promote free trade whenever agreements can be worked out with other nations. Then assign half of your students to write two or three paragraphs in opposition to the proposition, and the other half to write two or three paragraphs in support of it. Tell them to draw on facts, reasons, and other details in the lesson. When students finish, have them break into mixed pro- and con- groups to compare and discuss their arguments.

ANSWERS, p. 507

✓ **READING PROGRESS CHECK** The WTO helped countries reduce tariffs and quotas, which has allowed international trade to flourish. Stores can now offer a wide variety of industrial and consumer goods from all over the world.

LESSON 2 REVIEW ANSWERS

Reviewing Vocabulary

1. Free traders believe that tariffs are unnecessary and interfere with the profit-loss system.

Using Your Notes

2. Protectionists believe that fledgling industries need protection to become competitive and that free trade may encourage the nation to become too dependent on other countries for critical supplies.

Answering the Guiding Questions

3. Possible reasons include to aid national defense, protect infant industries, protect domestic jobs, boost national pride, or keep money at home.

4. Protectionists disagree with free traders over the best way to protect a country's independence, industries, and workers. Protectionists believe trade barriers are necessary to protect these things, while free traders believe that the free trade system works best with few barriers.

5. Trade agreements help maintain conditions that benefit all of the nations involved. Raising costs or displaced workers can occur when trade barriers are dropped.

Writing About Economics

6. Students should clearly state an opinion on increasing or decreasing barriers. Those in favor of increasing barriers might cite the need to protect domestic industries and jobs. Those in favor of decreasing barriers might note that costs would be lower for consumers, and that the competition would force out inefficient companies or processes and perhaps promote innovation. They might also consider that American goods or technology might be used in that industry even if the shoes are imported.

CHAPTER 17, LESSON 3
Foreign Exchange and Trade Deficits

ENGAGE

C Critical Thinking Skills

🔔 **Discussing the valuation of the dollar** Point out that the dollar is, in many ways, a commodity that is subject to the market forces of supply and demand. Challenge students to explain this analogy. Then ask them to consider how international market forces would influence the value of the dollar. **Ask: How would this way of valuing the dollar affect international trade?** *(Answers will vary, but encourage students to include the forces of supply and demand in their reasoning.)* Tell students to look for answers as they study this lesson. **Verbal/Linguistic**

ANSWERS, p. 508

ESSENTIAL QUESTION ACTIVITY

- Students should recognize that foreign trade increases the variety of products available to them, lowers the cost of some goods, and creates jobs.
- Students should recognize that they would have a more limited choice of goods, and many goods might cost more due to reduced competition.
- Students should recognize that people in other countries would have access to fewer goods, and reduced competition might increase prices.
- Students may support or approve more international trade, but they should give reasons to support their views.

TAKING NOTES

Sample answers: The foreign exchange market is flooded with dollars.
The dollar loses some of its value.
Imports become more expensive for Americans.
Exports become less expensive for foreigners.

508

Interact with these digital assets and others in lesson 3
✓ INTERACTIVE TABLE
   Foreign Exchange Rates
✓ INTERACTIVE GRAPH
   International Value of the Dollar
✓ SELF-CHECK QUIZ
✓ VIDEO

netw rks
TRY IT YOURSELF ONLINE

Reading Help Desk

Academic Vocabulary
- secure
- persistent

Content Vocabulary
- foreign exchange
- foreign exchange rate
- fixed exchange rates
- flexible exchange rates
- floating exchange rates
- trade deficit
- trade surplus
- trade-weighted value of the dollar

TAKING NOTES:

Key Ideas and Details
ACTIVITY Use the graphic organizer below to describe the effects of trade deficits.

Lesson 3
Foreign Exchange and Trade Deficits

ESSENTIAL QUESTION

How does trade benefit all participating parties?

The United States trades with most of the countries in the world. You can see clear evidence of it in almost any store you walk into. There are products made in China, India, Canada, Mexico, Japan, Germany, and on and on. Likewise, if you paid a visit to another country, you would find American-made products on their shelves. Consider the impact of all this international trade.

- What are the benefits of foreign trade for people in this country?
- How would your life be different without foreign-made goods?
- How do you think having access to American-made goods affects the lives of people in other countries?
- Do you think the United States should trade more, or less, with other countries?

Financing International Trade

GUIDING QUESTION *How are flexible exchange rates and fixed exchange rates different?*

C The forces of supply and demand can be found everywhere, especially in financial markets where the U.S. dollar is traded. After all, not everyone in the world uses the American dollar, so there are markets where dollars can be exchanged for pesos, euros, yen, pounds, and yuan. International trade is not possible without well-functioning markets, and that's where we will start.

Scenarios like the following occur every day around the globe. A clothing firm in the United States wants to import business suits from a company in Great Britain. Because the British firm pays its bills in the British currency, called *pound sterling*, it also wants to receive all of its payments in pound sterling. Therefore, the American firm must sell its American dollars to buy British pounds.

508

---

netw rks *Online Teaching Options*

BELLRINGER

Trade Deficit

Analyzing trade with China Show students the Bellringer and ask them what they know about trade between the United States and China. Guide students to understand that the United States imports more from China than China imports from the United States. Read and discuss the questions on the slide. Then invite students to offer solutions to the trade imbalance and guide them in considering the consequences for consumers, workers, businesses, and the economy.
Logical/Mathematical

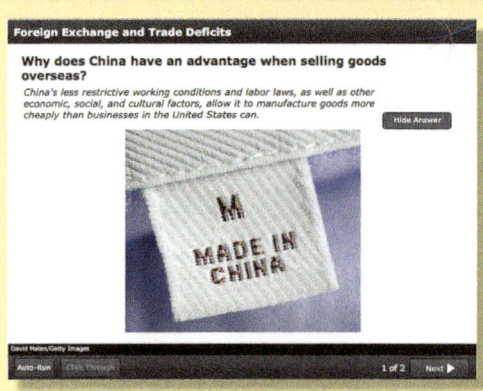

Foreign Exchange

In the field of international finance, **foreign exchange**—different currencies used to facilitate international trade—are bought and sold in the foreign exchange market. This market includes banks that help **secure** foreign currencies for importers, as well as banks that accept foreign currencies from exporters.

Suppose that one pound sterling, or £1, is equal to $1.6359. If the business suits are valued at £1,000 in London, the American importer can go to a U.S. bank and buy a £1,000 check for $1,635.90 plus a small service charge. The American firm then pays the British merchant in pounds, and the suits are shipped.

American exporters sometimes accept foreign currency or checks written on foreign banks in exchange for their goods. They deposit the payments in their own banks, which helps the U.S. banking system build a supply of foreign currency. This currency can then be sold to American firms that want to import goods from other countries. As a result, both the importer and the exporter end up with the currency they need.

The **foreign exchange rate** is the price of one country's currency in terms of another country's currency. The rate can be quoted in terms of the United States dollar equivalent, as in $1.6359 = £1, or in terms of foreign currency units per United States dollar, as in £0.6113 = $1. The rate is reported both ways, as shown in the foreign currency listings in **Figure 17.4**.

foreign exchange foreign currencies used by countries to conduct international trade

secure obtain

foreign exchange rate price of one's country's currency in terms of another currency

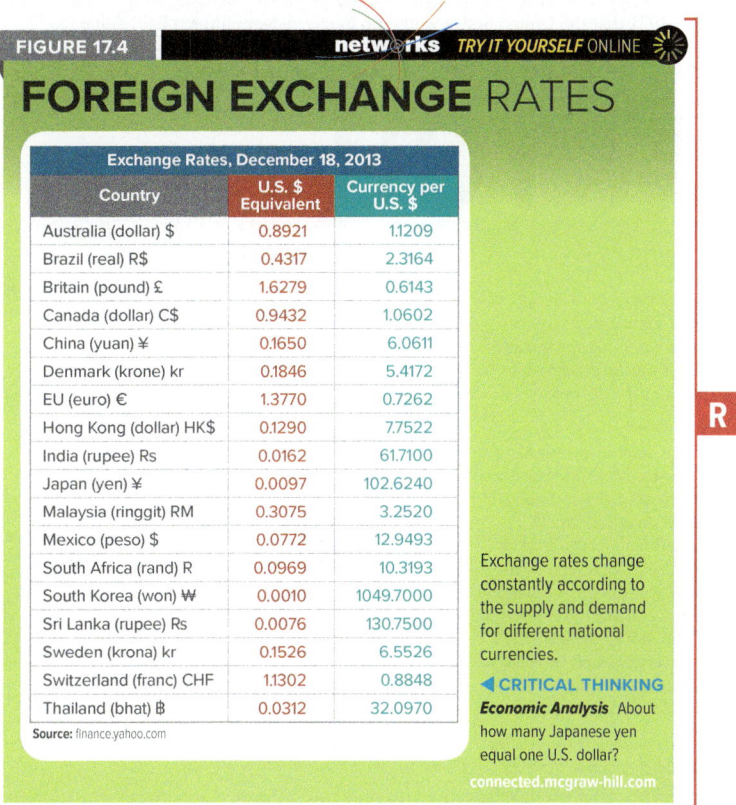

FIGURE 17.4

FOREIGN EXCHANGE RATES

Exchange Rates, December 18, 2013

Country	U.S. $ Equivalent	Currency per U.S. $
Australia (dollar) $	0.8921	1.1209
Brazil (real) R$	0.4317	2.3164
Britain (pound) £	1.6279	0.6143
Canada (dollar) C$	0.9432	1.0602
China (yuan) ¥	0.1650	6.0611
Denmark (krone) kr	0.1846	5.4172
EU (euro) €	1.3770	0.7262
Hong Kong (dollar) HK$	0.1290	7.7522
India (rupee) Rs	0.0162	61.7100
Japan (yen) ¥	0.0097	102.6240
Malaysia (ringgit) RM	0.3075	3.2520
Mexico (peso) $	0.0772	12.9493
South Africa (rand) R	0.0969	10.3193
South Korea (won) ₩	0.0010	1049.7000
Sri Lanka (rupee) Rs	0.0076	130.7500
Sweden (krona) kr	0.1526	6.5526
Switzerland (franc) CHF	1.1302	0.8848
Thailand (bhat) ฿	0.0312	32.0970

Source: finance.yahoo.com

Exchange rates change constantly according to the supply and demand for different national currencies.

◀ **CRITICAL THINKING**
Economic Analysis About how many Japanese yen equal one U.S. dollar?

CHAPTER 17, LESSON 3
Foreign Exchange and Trade Deficits

TEACH & ASSESS

R Reading Skills

Understanding exchange rates Have students study the chart showing foreign exchange rates. **Ask: Which foreign currency has a value most similar to that of the U.S. dollar?** *(Swiss franc)* **Which type of foreign currency has the lowest value?** *(South Korean won)* **The highest value?** *(British pound)* **Logical/Mathematical**

CHARTS

Foreign Exchange Rates

Converting currencies Have students view Figure 17.4 and explain that the middle column indicates how many U.S. dollars are required to purchase one unit of a foreign currency. The right column shows how many units of the foreign currency are required to purchase one American dollar. **Ask: If you exchange $100 U.S. dollars for Indian rupees, how many rupees will you get?** *(6,171 rupees)* **If a Swiss tourist to the United States exchanges 1,000 francs for U.S. dollars, how many dollars will she get?** *($1,130.20)* **Logical/Mathematical**

ANSWERS, p. 509

CRITICAL THINKING
About 97 Japanese yen

CHAPTER 17, LESSON 3
Foreign Exchange and Trade Deficits

R1 Reading Skills

Defining *fixed exchange rates* Guide English language learners in understanding the term *fixed exchange rates*. Point out that in addition to meaning "repaired or mended," the term *fixed* also means "to set absolutely or definitely." Invite volunteers to repeat this definition and apply it to the concept of fixed exchange rates. **ELL** Verbal/Linguistic

W Writing Skills

Writing about the gold standard Have students review the information in the text about the use of a gold standard. Direct them to write a paragraph that explains the concept of a gold standard and describes why the United States dropped the gold standard. Students should also explain why this change proved upsetting to many foreign governments. Verbal/Linguistic

R2 Reading Skills

Using the Big Mac Index Ask: According to the Global Economy & You feature, the currency of which country is more undervalued—India or Japan? *(India)* Which areas discussed in the feature and on the map have currencies that are currently overvalued? *(Euro area, Sweden, Switzerland, Australia, Norway)* Logical/Mathematical

---

fixed exchange rates system under which the values of currencies are fixed in relation to one another; the exchange rate system in effect until 1971

R1 Fixed Exchange Rates

Historically, two major kinds of exchange rates have existed—fixed and flexible. For most of the 1900s, the world depended on the use of **fixed exchange rates**—a system under which the price of one currency is fixed in terms of another currency so that the exchange rate does not change.

Fixed exchange rates were popular when the world was on a gold standard. Gold served as the common denominator that allowed comparisons of currencies, and it kept exchange rates in line. For example, suppose that a country allowed its money supply to grow too fast and that some of the money was spent on imports. Under a gold standard, the countries receiving the currency had the right to demand that it be converted into gold. Because no country wanted to lose its gold, each country worked to keep its money supply from growing too fast.

W

This practice worked until the early 1960s when the United States developed a huge appetite for imports. During that time, American consumers bought large quantities of foreign goods with dollars. At first, foreign countries willingly held U.S. dollars because the dollars were accepted throughout the world as an international currency. This meant that only a portion of these dollars came back when other countries bought American exports.

As dollars began to pile up in the rest of the world, many countries wondered if the United States could honor its promise that the dollar was "as good as gold." Eventually, several countries started redeeming their dollars for gold, which drained U.S. gold reserves. As a result, President Richard Nixon announced in 1971 that the United States would no longer redeem foreign-held dollars for gold.

THE GLOBAL ECONOMY & YOU

The Big Mac Index

Exchange rates should adjust to even out the cost of a market basket of goods and services, wherever it is bought around the world. For example, if you use Canadian dollars to buy a sandwich at a Tim Horton's restaurant in Canada, it should cost about the same as if you bought the same sandwich using U.S. dollars at a Tim Horton's in the United States.

R2

One way to see whether a currency is devalued or overvalued against the U.S. dollar is to use the "Big Mac Index" developed by *The Economist* magazine in 1986. Economists compare the price of a Big Mac hamburger in the United States to what it costs in another country's local currency. Converting the foreign price to U.S. dollars shows whether the price of a Big Mac is undervalued or overvalued against the U.S. dollar. In July 2013, the cheapest burger on the chart was in India, where it cost $1.50, in comparison with an average American price of $4.56. This implies that India's currency, the Indian rupee, is 67 percent undervalued. On the other hand, people of Norway pay the highest price for a Big Mac, a whopping $7.51, which is 65 percent overvalued.

Keep in mind that the Big Mac Index is an imprecise evaluative tool that reflects a secondary level of interpretation of primary source data. As such, you should carefully examine this secondary data for clues as to point of view and potential bias. Measuring the value of a currency through the price of a Big Mac cannot, of course, give a precise evaluation of another nation's currency.

Cost of a BURGER across the GLOBE

- Sweden $6.16
- China $2.61
- U.S.A. $4.56
- Euro area $4.66
- Switzerland $6.72
- Japan $3.20
- Mexico $2.86
- Egypt $2.39
- Argentina $3.88
- Australia $4.62

▲ **CRITICAL THINKING**
Drawing Inferences Would you expect to see other products reflect the same differences in values? Why or why not?

510

---

networks Online Teaching Options

INTERACTIVE FEATURE

Global Economy & You

Understanding the Big Mac Index Have students view the Global Economy & You feature and ask them to read the text. Then ask each student to write one question about the feature on a small piece of paper. Collect the questions and choose ones to discuss with the class.
Verbal/Linguistic

ANSWERS, p. 510

CRITICAL THINKING
Other products would probably reflect a similar difference in value because while the index measures the price of Big Macs, what it is actually showing is differences in exchange rates.

FIGURE 17.5

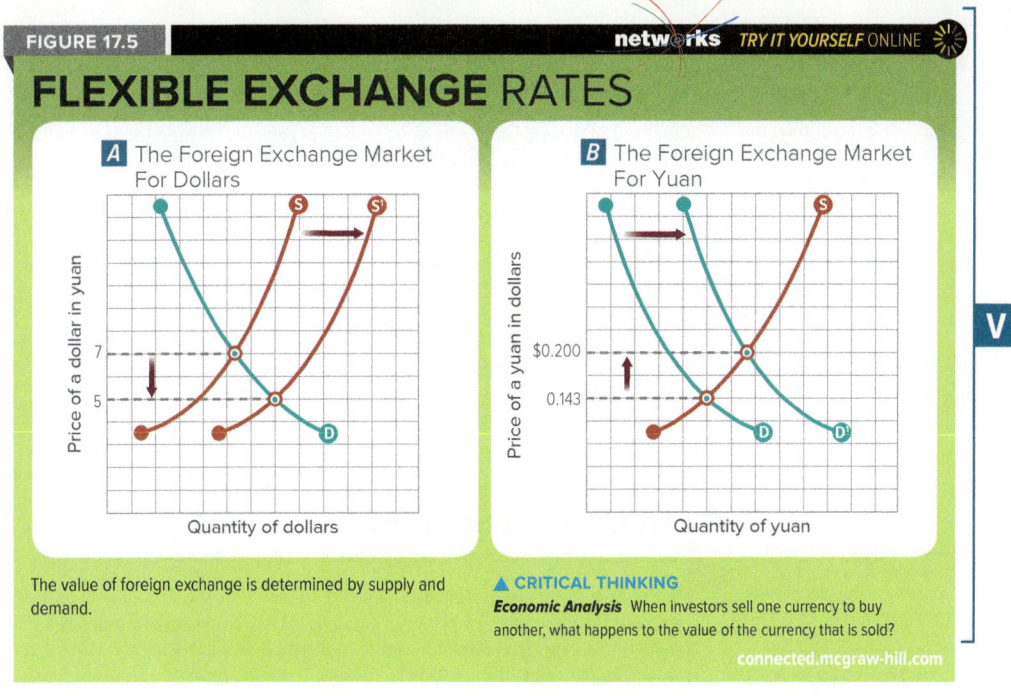

FLEXIBLE EXCHANGE RATES

A The Foreign Exchange Market For Dollars

B The Foreign Exchange Market For Yuan

The value of foreign exchange is determined by supply and demand.

▲ **CRITICAL THINKING**
Economic Analysis When investors sell one currency to buy another, what happens to the value of the currency that is sold?

connected.mcgraw-hill.com

This action saved the gold stock, but it also angered many foreign governments that had been planning on cashing their American dollars into gold.

Flexible Exchange Rates

As soon as the United States stopped redeeming foreign-held dollars for gold, the world monetary system shifted to a floating, or flexible, rate system. Under **flexible exchange rates**, also known as **floating exchange rates**, the forces of supply and demand establish the value of one country's currency in terms of another country's currency.

Figure 17.5 shows how flexible exchange rates work. For example, in a recent year the price of the dollar was 7 yuan, as shown in **Panel A**. Alternatively, we could say that the price of 1 yuan was $0.143, as shown in **Panel B**, because the two numbers are reciprocals of each other.

Suppose now that an American importer wanted to purchase sandals that could be bought for 35 yuan in China. The American importer would have to sell $5 in the foreign exchange market to obtain the 35 yuan needed to buy the sandals. If this continued over a long period of time, the increased supply of dollars in Panel A, shown as a shift in supply from **S** to S^1, would drive the price of the dollar down to 5 yuan. The dollar is now cheaper because one dollar costs only 5 yuan rather than 7. At the same time, the increased demand for yuan, shown in Panel B by the shift of the demand curve from **D** to D^1, would raise the price of a single yuan from $0.143 to $0.200. The yuan is now more expensive because it costs more in terms of U.S. currency.

When the yuan reaches $0.200, the price of a pair of sandals is less competitive. This is because the importer now has to pay $7 (or 35 times $0.200) to obtain enough yuan to purchase a pair of sandals. Excessive imports by the United States thus can cause the value of the dollar to decline, making imports cost more.

flexible exchange rates system that relies on supply and demand to determine the value of one currency in terms of another; exchange rate system in effect since 1971

floating exchange rates system that relies on supply and demand to determine the value of one currency in terms of another; exchange rate system in effect since 1971

CHAPTER 17, LESSON 3
Foreign Exchange and Trade Deficits

V Visual Skills

Using graphs showing flexible exchange rates
Ask: Which type of currency shown in the graphs experienced an increase in demand? How did this influence the supply of that currency? *(The yuan experienced an increase in demand. This caused the supply of that currency to increase.)*
AL Verbal/Linguistic

W Writing Skills

Tracing the effects of flexible exchange rates Have students draw a series of cause-and-effect graphic organizers that trace the effects of flexible exchange rates on the values of currencies for two trading partners over a long period of time. Remind students to consider how supply and demand cause the value of items, such as currency, to change. Tell students to clearly label their organizers so that they can be easily understood.
BL Verbal/Linguistic

GRAPHS

Flexible Exchange Rates

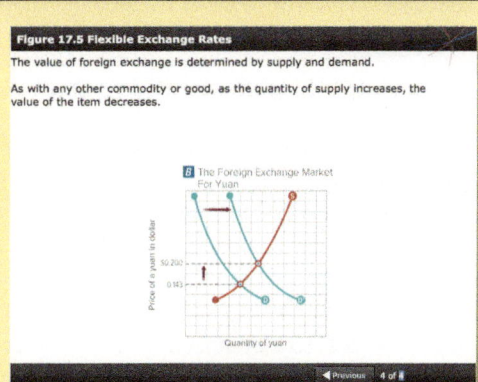

Using exchange rate graphs Have students view Figure 17.5 and discuss the first slide. **Ask: What does the graph show?** *(the price of a dollar in yuan when a certain supply of dollars is available)* **How many yuan does it take to buy one dollar?** *(7 yuan)* Now advance to the second slide. **Ask: What has happened?** *(The supply of dollars has increased.)* **What has happened to the value of the dollar versus the value of the yuan?** *(The value of the dollar has fallen.)* Advance to the next graph. **Ask: What does this graph show?** *(The value of the yuan in dollars when a certain supply of yuan are available.)* **What is the price of one yuan?** *(14.3 cents)* Move to the final slide. **Ask: What has happened?** *(The demand for yuan has increased.)* **What has happened to the value of the yuan?** *(It has increased to 20 cents.)* Logical/Mathematical

---

ANSWERS, p. 511

CRITICAL THINKING
It eventually decreases.

CHAPTER 17, LESSON 3
Foreign Exchange and Trade Deficits

R Reading Skills

Defining economic terms Ask students to explain the definitions of *trade deficit* and *trade surplus*. Then have them describe in their own words the relationship between these concepts and the international value of a nation's currency.
ELL Verbal/Linguistic

Content Background Knowledge

Trade-Weighted Value of the Dollar
The International Value of the Dollar graph represents a trade-weighted average of the value of the dollar in relation to the value of the currencies of a group of major U.S. trading partners. Among these are the Euro Area, Canada, Japan, China, the United Kingdom, and Brazil. A value of 100 represents a base value, measured in 1997 on this graph. A value of 120 would represent an increase of 20 percent over the base.

C Critical Thinking Skills

Analyzing effects of exchange rates on imports and exports Ask: **When a nation's currency becomes stronger, or appreciates, what happens to the cost of its goods in other countries?** *(They become more expensive.)* **What happens to the cost of products imported into that nation?** *(They become cheaper.)* **When a nation's currency becomes weaker, or depreciates, what happens to the cost of its goods in other countries?** *(They become cheaper.)* **What happens to the cost of products imported into that nation?** *(They become more expensive.)* Verbal/Linguistic

---

ANSWERS, p. 512

EXPLORING THE ESSENTIAL QUESTION

The weaker yuan makes China's goods cheaper so it can sell more goods abroad, which keeps its factories busy and its economy growing. However, a cheaper yuan makes foreign goods more expensive for Chinese consumers and businesses to purchase.

✓ **READING PROGRESS CHECK** by purchasing these currencies on the foreign exchange market

CRITICAL THINKING
Imports become more expensive for Americans.

EXPLORING THE ESSENTIAL QUESTION
For many years, China's economy has been growing faster than the economies of much of the rest of the world, and yet it continues to resist international pressure to allow its currency to float. What benefit is China getting from keeping its currency inflexible? How is this policy also hurting China's economy?

This is bad news for U.S. firms that import products from China, because the yuan needed to pay for the imports is more expensive. But it is good news for U.S. exporters. This is because a Chinese firm that bought American soybeans at $6 a bushel before the decline in the value of the dollar would have paid 42 yuan (or $6/0.143) per bushel. Afterward, it had to pay only 30 yuan (or $6/0.200) per bushel. Soybeans became cheaper for Chinese buyers, and U.S. farmers could sell more abroad.

Whenever the dollar falls, exports tend to go up and imports go down. If the dollar rises, the reverse will occur.

The system of flexible exchange rates has worked relatively well. More importantly, the switch to flexible rates did not interrupt the growth in international trade as many people had feared. China is not yet on a system of flexible rates, but it is selling so many products abroad that the yuan is under intense pressure to revalue upward, thus becoming more expensive as in the example above.

✓ **READING PROGRESS CHECK**
Summarizing How do U.S. banks build a supply of foreign currency?

Trade Deficits and Surpluses

trade deficit balance of payments outcome when spending on imports exceeds revenues received from exports

trade surplus situation occurring when the value of a nation's exports exceeds the value of its imports

trade-weighted value of the dollar index showing strength of the United States dollar against a market basket of other foreign currencies

R GUIDING QUESTION *How does the strength of the dollar affect U.S. trade deficits?*

A country has a **trade deficit** whenever the value of the products it imports exceeds the value of the products it exports. It has a **trade surplus** whenever the value of its exports exceeds the value of its imports. Each is dependent on the international value of its currency.

International Value of the Dollar

C Since the dollar started to float in 1971, the Fed has kept a statistic that measures the strength of the dollar. Figure 17.6 shows the **trade-weighted value of the dollar**, an index displaying the strength of the dollar against a group of major foreign currencies. When the index falls, the dollar is weak in relation to other currencies. When the index rises, the dollar is strong.

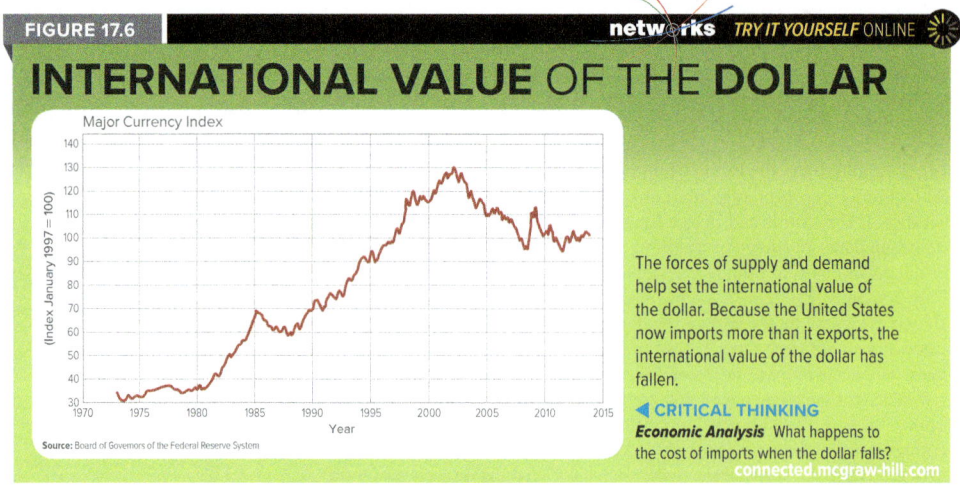

FIGURE 17.6
INTERNATIONAL VALUE OF THE DOLLAR

The forces of supply and demand help set the international value of the dollar. Because the United States now imports more than it exports, the international value of the dollar has fallen.

◄ **CRITICAL THINKING**
Economic Analysis What happens to the cost of imports when the dollar falls?

connected.mcgraw-hill.com

---

networks Online Teaching Options

GRAPHS

International Value of the Dollar

Interpreting changes in the international value of the dollar Display Figure 17.6 and ask students to read the text and click on the graph to reveal the callouts. Ask: **Why did coming off the gold standard cause the value of the dollar to decline?** *(People did not trust the dollar to the same degree, so they valued it less.)* **Why would a boom in the IT industry cause the dollar to strengthen?** *(The boom is an indicator of economic growth, which makes the dollar more valuable.)* **Why would large U.S. trade deficits cause the dollar to weaken?** *(More U.S. dollars were in circulation, making them less valuable.)* Logical/Mathematical

When the dollar is strong, as it was in 1985 and 2002, foreign goods become less costly and American exports become more costly for the rest of the world. As a result, imports rise, exports fall, and trade deficits result. With more dollars going abroad, the value of the dollar then goes down, as it did after 2003.

Effects of a Trade Deficit

A **persistent** trade imbalance can cause a chain reaction that affects income and employment. To illustrate, large U.S. trade deficits from 2003 to 2006 flooded the foreign exchange markets with dollars. The increase of dollars on world markets caused the dollar to lose some of its value, making imports more expensive for Americans and exports less expensive for foreigners. When exports surge, employment and income is generated in the export-oriented industries.

The persistent U.S. trade deficit since 2003 has helped domestic U.S. export industries by driving down the value of the dollar. This has caused the price of Japanese and other foreign-built products to increase in relation to American-built ones. As long as the dollar continues to weaken, export industries will benefit, while import industries will suffer.

When the value of the dollar gets low enough, the process will reverse. Foreigners will sell their currency so that they can buy more American dollars, which they will use to purchase American products. This will drive the value of the dollar up, making it more difficult for American export industries and better for import industries.

persistent continuous, without signs of weakening

A Strong vs. A Weak Dollar

Changes in the international supply and demand for dollars cause the value of the dollar to change daily. But which is best—a strong dollar or a weak dollar?

The answer is: neither!

Under flexible exchange rates, trade deficits tend to correct themselves automatically through supply, demand, and the price system. A strong currency generally leads to a deficit in the balance of goods and services and a subsequent decline in the value of the currency. This is because a strong dollar encourages imports—thereby increasing the supply of dollars in financial markets. A weak currency tends to cause a trade surplus, which eventually pulls up the value of the currency. This is because a weak dollar makes U.S. goods and services cheaper for the rest of the world to buy—thereby increasing their demand for dollars.

Because one sector of the economy is hurt while another is helped, there is no net gain in having either a strong or a weak dollar. As a result, the United States and many other countries no longer design economic policies just to improve the strength of their currency on international markets.

☑ **READING PROGRESS CHECK**

Describing Why did the value of the dollar fall in 2005 and 2006?

LESSON 3 REVIEW

Reviewing Vocabulary
1. ***Identifying*** What does the foreign exchange rate measure?
2. ***Explaining*** What happens when a country has a trade surplus?

Using Your Notes
3. ***Explaining*** Why do imports become more expensive and exports less expensive during a prolonged trade deficit?

Answering the Guiding Questions
4. ***Contrasting*** How are flexible exchange rates and fixed exchange rates different?

5. ***Identifying Cause and Effect*** How does the strength of the dollar affect U.S. trade deficits?

Writing About Economics
6. ***Argument*** You are listening to a political debate between two contenders for a U.S. Senate seat. One candidate complains about her opponent's support of a trade agreement that contributed to a weakening of the dollar. Write one or two paragraphs explaining why a weak dollar is or is not a problem.

connected.mcgraw-hill.com   Resources for Global Trade **513**

LESSON 3 REVIEW ANSWERS

Reviewing Vocabulary

1. The price of one country's currency in terms of another currency
2. The value of the country's exports exceeds the value of its imports.

Using Your Notes

3. During a prolonged trade deficit, the value of the dollar drops in relation to other currencies. The dollar will purchase fewer imported goods, making them more expensive. The weaker dollar makes it cheaper for other countries to buy U.S. goods.

Answering the Guiding Questions

4. With fixed exchange rates, the values of currencies do not change in relation to each other. With flexible exchange rates, supply and demand for currencies determines their relative value.
5. A strong dollar results in fewer exports, which generally leads to a deficit in the balance of goods. A weak dollar generally leads to a trade surplus.

Writing About Economics

6. A weak dollar will lead to a trade surplus. It will make U.S. goods cheaper to buy, which will enable U.S. businesses to increase production and sell more goods abroad.

CHAPTER 17, LESSON 3
Foreign Exchange and Trade Deficits

V Visual Skills

Illustrating a chain reaction Have students create a diagram that illustrates the chain reaction of a strong dollar on U.S. exports and imports. *(When the dollar is strong, export industries suffer and import industries benefit.)* Then have them illustrate the chain reaction of a weak dollar on U.S. exports and imports *(When the dollar weakens, export industries benefit and import industries suffer.)* **Visual/Spatial, Kinesthetic**

C Critical Thinking Skills

Synthesizing information on currencies Ask: **Why might many countries have decided against designing economic policies in order to improve the international strength of their currencies?** *(These countries may have decided against this practice because doing so often benefits one sector of a nation's economy while having a negative impact on other sectors of the economy.)* **Verbal/Linguistic**

CLOSE & REFLECT

R Reading Skills

Reviewing the main ideas Assign students to small groups and ask each group to write three questions about the main ideas in each of the main sections of the lesson. Have them write the answers to their questions on a separate sheet of paper. Then have each group exchange questions with another group and discuss the answers.

ANSWERS, p. 513

☑ **READING PROGRESS CHECK** because a large U.S. trade deficit flooded the foreign exchange markets with dollars

CHAPTER 17
Debate

ENGAGE

C Critical Thinking Skills

Recognizing the advantages and disadvantages of a common currency Ask students to review obstacles to international trade presented by the existence of multiple currencies. **Ask: What solutions have countries found?** *(establishing foreign exchange markets to expedite the exchange of currencies)* **What are the disadvantages of this strategy?** *(Businesses pay a fee for the exchange. They risk losing money as the valuation of currencies float.)* Point out that one solution tried by some European nations is for trading partners to adopt a common currency. Tell students that this step has always been controversial.

TEACH & ASSESS

R1 Reading Skills

Examining motives for adopting the euro
Ask: Why was the euro adopted in 1999? *(to promote trade among members of the eurozone and to eliminate currency exchange fees)* **How does the euro promote trade?** *(It is easier for businesses to buy and sell goods if they do not have to exchange currencies to carry out the transaction. Plus, they save money due to avoiding a bank's exchange fees and fluctuations in the value of floating currency.)* **Verbal/Linguistic**

R2 Reading Skills

Understanding causes for reconsidering the euro
Ask: Why were people beginning to consider abolishing the euro? *(The 2011–2012 debt crisis brought on demands for severe austerity measures and accusations of blame. The euro was endangered and people questioned whether it should be abolished.)* **Logical/Mathematical**

Debates

Should the euro be abolished?

R1 The euro was created in 1999 to strengthen economic ties among members of the European Union. The euro replaced the individual currencies of these nations. It was effective in promoting trade among eurozone nations by eliminating the need for exchange rates for different currencies.

R2 The global economic crisis of 2008–2009 led to severe economic problems in Greece, Ireland, Portugal, and Spain in 2011 and 2012. This resulted in some demands for severe austerity measures as well as accusations of blame over who should be responsible for the losses.

Many people, from political leaders to ordinary citizens in the eurozone, began to think the currency was endangered and started wondering whether or not it should be abolished altogether.

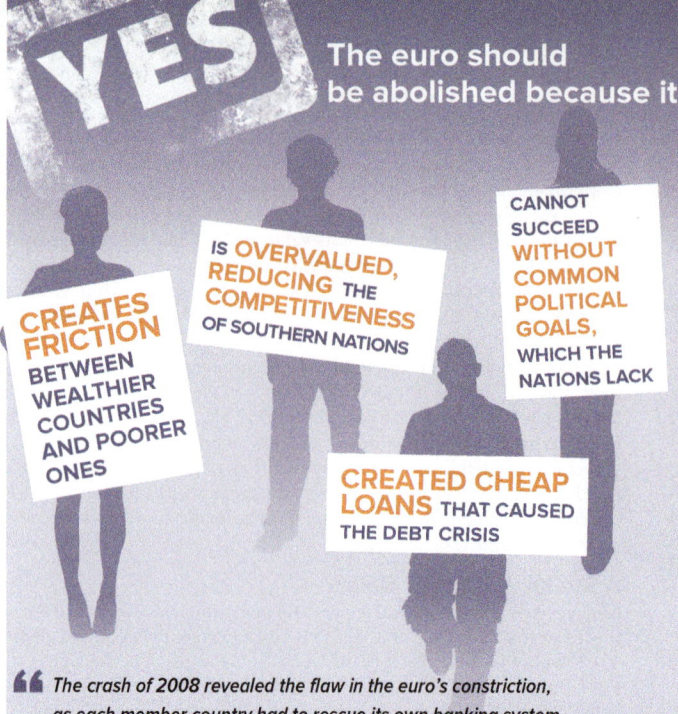

YES The euro should be abolished because it...

- CREATES FRICTION BETWEEN WEALTHIER COUNTRIES AND POORER ONES
- IS OVERVALUED, REDUCING THE COMPETITIVENESS OF SOUTHERN NATIONS
- CANNOT SUCCEED WITHOUT COMMON POLITICAL GOALS, WHICH THE NATIONS LACK
- CREATED CHEAP LOANS THAT CAUSED THE DEBT CRISIS

> The crash of 2008 revealed the flaw in the euro's constriction, as each member country had to rescue its own banking system instead of doing it jointly. The Greek debt crises brought matters to a climax. If member countries cannot take the next steps forward, the euro may fall apart, with adverse consequences for the EU.

—George Soros, Chairman of Soros Fund Management

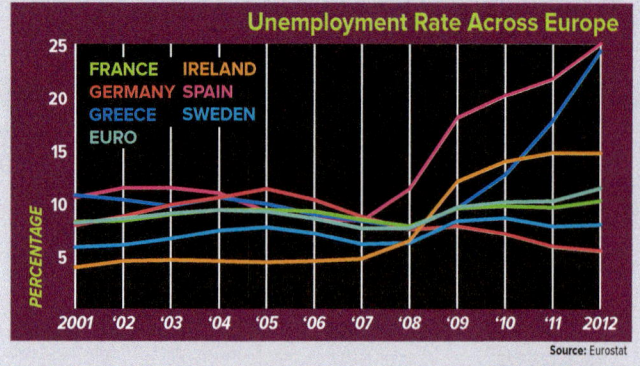

Unemployment Rate Across Europe (FRANCE, GERMANY, GREECE, IRELAND, SPAIN, SWEDEN, EURO), 2001–2012. Source: Eurostat

514

---

networks Online Teaching Options

DEBATE

Debate: Should the euro be abolished?

Understanding arguments for and against the euro Have students read the introductory text. Then ask a student to read the Yes quotation aloud. **Ask: What details does Soros give to support the argument to abolish the euro?** *(The crash of 2008 revealed problems with the euro. Each country had to rescue its own banking system, but countries in great debt that could not move forward with economic recovery threatened the security of the euro.)* Now ask a student to read the No quotation aloud. **Ask: What details does Verhofstadt give in defending the euro?** *(The euro keeps inflation low; creates economic stability; keeps costs of borrowing low; contributes to economic growth and employment; and has become attractive to foreign governments so foreign traders price goods in euros, which enhances trade.)* **Verbal/Linguistic**

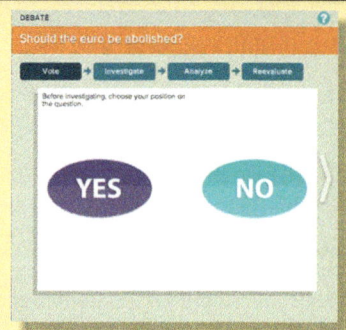

NO The euro should not be abolished because it...

- IS NOT THE PROBLEM; A **LACK OF** POLITICAL AND ECONOMIC **UNITY** IS
- CAN BRING ABOUT **NEEDED** STRUCTURAL **ECONOMIC CHANGES** IN POORER COUNTRIES
- **STABILIZED** THE **EUROPEAN ECONOMY,** EVEN DURING THE 2008 **FINANCIAL CRISIS**
- **OPENS BORDERS** FOR TRADE WHILE **REDUCING** MONETARY OBSTACLES

networks
TRY IT YOURSELF ONLINE
For an interactive version of this debate go to connected.mcgraw-hill.com

> The success of the ECB in keeping inflation low has been a source of stability and has made it possible to keeping borrowing costs low for both the private and the public sectors, thereby contributing to more economic growth and employment. The euro is also attractive to foreign governments as a reserve currency. This is of benefit to the whole euro-zone economy because widespread holdings and a high demand for euros encourages third countries to price their exports in the single currency—thus reducing costs to euro-zone members as there are no exchange-rate costs.

—Guy Verhofstadt, former prime minister of Belgium, "The euro and Europe," *The Economist*, July 26, 2011

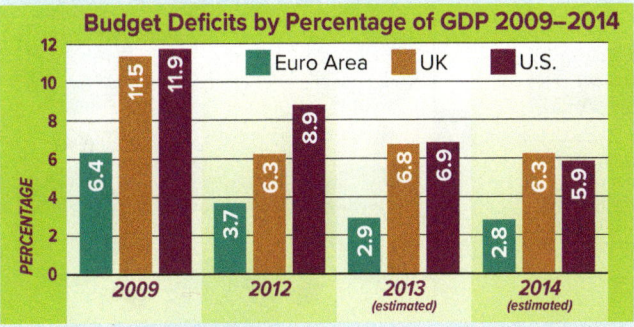

Budget Deficits by Percentage of GDP 2009–2014

Year	Euro Area	UK	U.S.
2009	6.4	11.5	11.9
2012	3.7	6.3	8.9
2013 (estimated)	2.9	6.8	6.9
2014 (estimated)	2.8	6.3	5.9

Source: euroeconomics

ANALYZING the issue

1. **Interpreting** What does Verhofstadt suggest are good things about the state of the euro and its marketplace?

2. **Drawing Conclusions** Review the second graph, "Budget Deficits by Percentage of GDP 2009–2014." What conclusion can you draw from the graph about the eurozone economy?

3. **Defending** Which arguments do you find most compelling? Explain your answer.

515

DEBATE

Analyzing graphs Ask students to study the two graphs above and then write an analysis of what they show. Ask them to write a closing statement in which they draw conclusions about the euro. Have students exchange their analyses with a partner and compare their ideas. **Verbal/Linguistic**

CHAPTER 17
Debate

Content Background Knowledge

European Union Despite the debt crisis of 2011 and 2012, confidence in the euro remains high. There are 28 countries in the European Union, 19 of which have adopted the euro. Lithuania, which joined the EU in 2004, joined the eurozone in January 2015.

CLOSE & REFLECT

R Reading Skills

Reviewing the feature Ask students to share their responses to the *Analyzing the Issue* questions. Have students cite reasons and facts in the feature that support their opinions.

ANSWERS, p. 515

ANALYZING the issue

1. Verhofstadt suggests that because the euro keeps inflation low, the resulting stability keeps borrowing costs low and contributes to economic growth and employment. He also points out that foreign demand for euros encourages countries to price their exports in euros, thus eliminating exchange-rate costs for the whole eurozone.
2. Despite the economic crisis, the budget deficits of all countries covered by the graph showed improvements, but the eurozone nations did the best. The euro, therefore, must be functioning effectively in aiding those nations in controlling debt.
3. Students should give facts and reasons based on the debate to support their response.

Resources for Global Trade 515

Chapter 17
Study Guide

W Writing Skills

Synthesizing information Ask students to conduct a survey of other students in school or of adults they know on the question of buying American-made goods versus buying imported goods. Have them ask each person to state the most important reason for their choice. Ask students to combine their poll results and report their findings to class.

C Critical Thinking Skills

Summarizing information Ask students to write a summary of the debate between protectionists and free traders. In their summaries, they should explain the effect of each of the elements on short-term and long-term economic growth.

V Visual Skills

Illustrating information Ask students to create a political cartoon that convey the same information about a strong and weak dollar as shown in the flow diagram for Lesson 3.

STUDY GUIDE

LESSON 1

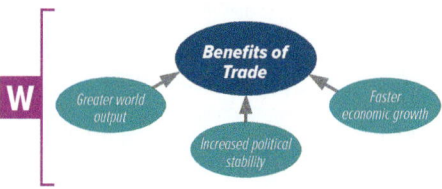

LESSON 2

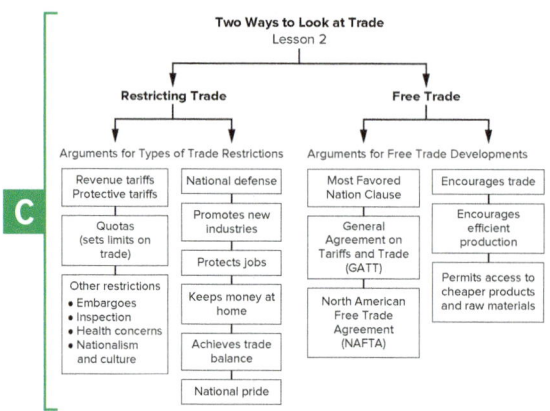

LESSON 3

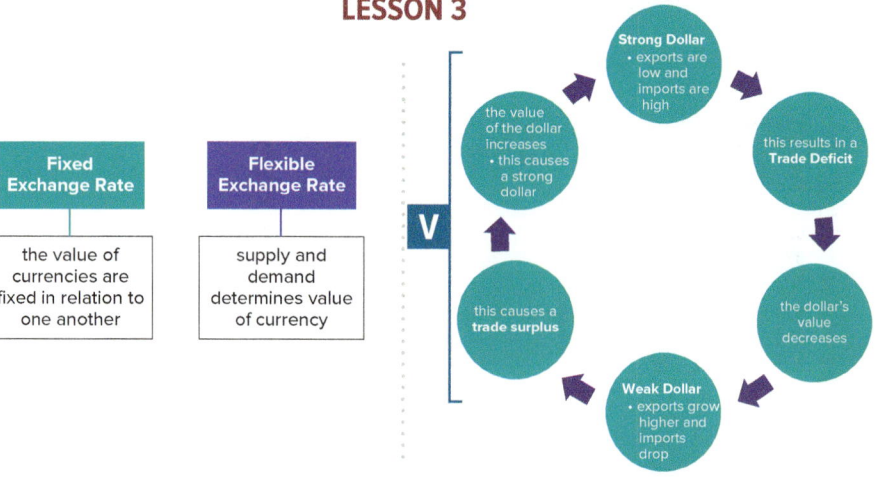

networks Online Teaching Options

WORKSHEET

Personal Finance Activity
Students use information about the cost of activities in several countries and information on exchange rates to determine where they could visit to get the most value for their dollar.

CHAPTER 17 Assessment

Directions: On a separate sheet of paper, answer the questions below. Make sure you read carefully and answer all parts of the questions.

Lesson Review

Lesson 1

1. **Drawing Conclusions** What can you learn about a nation's specialization by studying what it exports?
2. **Explaining** How does comparative advantage help nations acquire goods, services, and resources they lack?
3. **Explaining** Why is international trade important to today's economy?
4. **Explaining** How do the exports of the United States give other countries a comparative advantage?

Lesson 2

5. **Analyzing** Why would a government choose to introduce a protective tariff on certain goods, but apply a revenue tariff to most other goods?
6. **Summarizing** How do tariffs and quotas protect American jobs?

Lesson 3

7. **Describing** How is the value of the dollar established under a flexible exchange rate?
8. **Explaining** Why did the United States leave the gold standard in 1971 and adopt a flexible exchange rate?
9. **Explaining** What will happen to the value of the dollar if the United States has a trade deficit with a country? How will this affect U.S. consumers and employment?

Critical Thinking

10. **Drawing Inferences** How does comparative advantage make trade between countries of different sizes and economic prosperity possible?
11. **Constructing Arguments** When NAFTA was being debated in Congress, many Americans were forming their own opinions. Many workers and unions were strongly opposed to it, claiming it would ship American jobs to Canada and Mexico. Manufacturers often supported it because of the enhanced trade they expected. Do you think NAFTA was a good idea or a bad idea? Write a short essay defending your point of view. Be sure to take into account reasons that support the opposite view.
12. **Exploring Issues** Some people think the United States should return to a system of fixed exchange rates. Defend or oppose this view. Cite examples to support your position.

Analyzing Visuals

Use the graph below to answer the following questions about foreign exchange rates.

A The Foreign Exchange Market For Dollars

13. **Analyzing Visuals** Assume that American imports from China rise over an extended period of time. In which direction will the supply curve for dollars move? What will this mean for the value of the dollar in comparison with the yuan?
14. **Drawing Conclusions** If imports from China continue to grow, what will this mean for the price of the Chinese goods in relation to the price consumers will pay for similar American goods? How will this affect trade?
15. **Analyzing Visuals** What will happen to American exporters to China if the trend continues and imports from China continue to grow? In which direction will the demand curve move?

Need Extra Help?

If You've Missed Question	1	2	3	4	5	6	7	8	9	10	11	12	13	14	15
Go to page	495	498	498	498	501	501	511	510	512	498	507	510	511	511	511

TAKE THIS TEST ONLINE AT connected.mcgraw-hill.com

9. The dollar will lose some of its value, making imports more expensive and exports less expensive. Consumers will pay more for imported goods, but there will be higher employment as manufacturers hire more workers to keep up with higher demand for products to be exported.

Critical Thinking

10. Specialization allows a country to focus on producing and exporting goods it produces efficiently and to import goods it does not produce efficiently. Even countries with large differences in size and prosperity can find products to trade that meet these criteria.

11. Students may take either position but should demonstrate a clear and thorough understanding of NAFTA as well as of the benefits and costs of tariffs and of international trade.

12. Students may argue either point of view but should cite specific facts, reasons, and examples.

Analyzing Visuals

13. The supply curve will move to the right. This will mean that the price of the dollar will decline in comparison with the yuan.

Chapter 17 Assessment Answers

Lesson Review

Lesson 1

1. A nation's chief exports are evidence of what it produces most efficiently and in which it consequently specializes in.
2. It allows countries to trade the items they produce most efficiently in exchange for goods and resources they need.
3. It raises the total world output and standard of living.
4. U.S. exports are purchased by other countries, which allows them to put their resources into developing different products more efficiently, giving them a comparative advantage in those products.

Lesson 2

5. A government might impose a protective tariff on certain goods because similar domestic products cost too much to produce and need to be protected from cheaper imports. Revenue tariffs would be used to contribute to the nation's revenues.
6. They prevent American industries from being undersold by foreign companies so they can continue to operate.

Lesson 3

7. Supply and demand for the dollar establish its value in relation to the value of another country's currency.
8. Nations tried to redeem dollars for gold, which began draining the U.S. gold supply.

14. The price of Chinese goods will increase in relation to American goods. The higher-priced Chinese goods will mean that imports from China will decrease.
15. The price of American exports to China will be cheaper, causing an increase in exports. The demand curve will then move to the left.

Chapter 17
Assessment Answers

Answering the Essential Question

16 Students should demonstrate an understanding of the benefits that trading partners receive regardless of the size of the economies.

21st Century Skills

17 Students should demonstrate an understanding of comparative advantage and apply it correctly in analyzing a project and identifying more efficient ways of completing it.

18 Students should demonstrate an understanding of the effects of trade barriers and the value of international trade to all partners.

19 Students should explain that a stronger dollar means that they will pay less for food and other items in Europe than they would if the dollar stayed the same or fell.

Building Financial Literacy

20 Students should understand that a weak dollar would give Firm Y a trade advantage, so it would probably be able to sell more to the United States than Firm Z can sell to Country A. The free-trade agreement will alter the trade relationship, which might make it difficult to know for certain which company will then have the advantage.

Analyzing Primary Sources

21 Trade sanctions would reduce trade, make it difficult for China to export goods to the United States, and thereby reduce its economic growth. U.S. consumers would pay more for goods produced in China.

22 The undervaluation of the yuan makes Chinese products cheap in relation to U.S. products, so the United States would import more goods from China than it could sell to China.

CHAPTER 17 Assessment

Directions: On a separate sheet of paper, answer the questions below. Make sure you read carefully and answer all parts of the questions.

ANSWERING THE ESSENTIAL QUESTION

Review your answers to the introductory question at the beginning of each lesson. Then answer the Essential Question on the basis of what you learned in the chapter. Have your answers changed?

16 *Explaining* How does trade benefit all participating parties?

21st Century Skills

17 *Problem Solving* Think of a project or assignment you recently completed with a friend. Apply the principle of comparative advantage to the way you and your friend worked. How could you have completed the project more efficiently? Explain.

18 *Identifying Cause and Effect* A number of members of Congress have been increasingly upset over the U.S. trade deficit. They believe Americans are being taken advantage of by numerous countries whose workers have lower wages than do American workers. As a result, American workers are losing their jobs. These representatives claim America cannot compete and we should act to raise protective tariffs to protect our workers. Write a letter to your Congressional representatives explaining why consumers benefit and how tariffs will work against Americans in the long term.

19 *Understanding Relationships Among Events* You and a friend are talking about joining a school-sponsored trip to Europe this summer. Your friend has just read that the dollar has been growing stronger against the euro. He wonders if he needs to make extra money or even cancel his plans altogether. What advice would you give him?

Building Financial Literacy

20 *Analyzing* You have inherited a small sum of money and want to invest it. An uncle urges you to invest it in Firm Y, which operates chiefly in Country A. It exports most of its products to the United States. Another uncle urges you to invest in Firm Z, which exports most of its goods to Country A. Both companies seem equally successful and well run. Consider these factors before making your decision.

- The dollar has been historically weak in comparison with the currency of Country A.
- Country A and the United States will be finalizing a free-trade agreement in the next month.
- Country A's tariffs are currently somewhat lower than U.S. tariffs.

How will you invest your money? Why?

Analyzing Primary Sources

Read the excerpt and answer the questions that follow.
Alan J. Auerbach and Maurice Obstfeld, both professors of Economics at Berkeley, have written about the impact of China's valuation of the yuan. They note that China's trading partners do not like that the yuan is weak, especially as unemployment remains high and economic recovery is slow.

PRIMARY SOURCE

" *Threats of trade sanctions by the U.S. Congress have resulted in periods of measured and limited [yuan] appreciation—most recently, a 2.3% rise against the dollar between early September and mid-October 2010. But such gestures by the Chinese authorities fall short of the 20%-or-better, maxi-revaluation demanded by China's critics in the US and elsewhere.* "

—Alan J. Auerbach and Maurice Obstfeld, "Too much focus on the yuan?" *Vox*, October 23, 2010

Other new market economies have kept their currencies weak, following China's lead. This further increases international unease. But Auerbach and Obstfeld believe that increasing our own economic growth by devaluing the currency of other countries could lead to barriers that would impede international trade.

21 *Analyzing Primary Sources* Why would China be influenced by Congress's threat of trade sanctions? What would be the cost to the United States if these sanctions were imposed?

22 *Exploring Issues* How would a 20 percent undervaluation of the yuan in comparison with the dollar affect U.S. trade with China?

Need Extra Help?

If You've Missed Question	16	17	18	19	20	21	22
Go to page	498	498	501	509	501	505	511

518

---

networks Online Assessment Options

WORKSHEET

Chapter Tests and Lesson Quizzes

Chapter 17 Tests Forms A and B Have students complete the Chapter Tests and Lesson Quizzes to assess student understanding throughout the chapter. Print and online assessment tools offer chapter and lesson evaluation through a variety of question formats, including document-based questions.

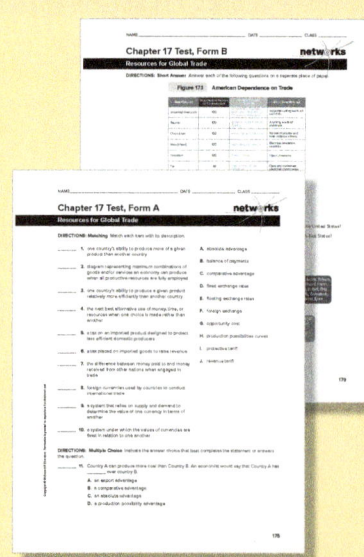

518

CHAPTER 18
Global Economic Development
Planner

UNDERSTANDING BY DESIGN®

Enduring Understanding
- The movement of people, goods, and ideas causes societies to change over time.

Essential Question
- Why is the economic health of all nations important in a global economy?
- What are the challenges associated with globalization?

Predictable Misunderstandings
Students may think:
- *Nuclear energy is a renewable energy source.* Explain that because it requires uranium, which takes millions of years to form, nuclear energy is considered nonrenewable.
- *Pollution fees do not help reduce pollution because companies are happy to pay the fees in order to stay in business.* Explain that the purpose of the fees is to encourage the companies to reduce their emissions, and that as the fees gradually become higher, the incentive to reduce emissions becomes greater. In the end, pollution fees do a considerable amount to reduce pollution.

Assessment Evidence
Performance Task
- Hands-On Chapter Project with Technology Extension

Other Evidence
- Guided Reading Activities
- Vocabulary Activity
- Lesson Quizzes
- Self-Check Quizzes
- Chapter Assessment
- Chapter Tests, Forms A and B

SUGGESTED PACING

Introducing the Chapter: ½ Day	Lesson 3: Global Problems and Economic Incentives . . . ½ Day
Lesson 1: Economic Development . . . 1 Day	Debate . . . . . ½ Day
Case Study . . . ½ Day	Study Guide, Chapter Assessment and Wrap-Up . . . ½ Day
Lesson 2: Globalization: Characteristics and Trends . . . ½ Day	

TOTAL 4 Days

Key for Using the Teacher Edition

SKILL-BASED ACTIVITIES
Types of skill activities found in the Teacher Edition.

V Visual Skills require students to analyze maps, graphs, charts, and photos.

R Reading Skills help students practice reading skills and master vocabulary.

C Critical Thinking Skills help students apply and extend what they have learned.

W Writing Skills provide writing opportunities to help students comprehend the text.

T Technology Skills require students to use digital tools effectively.

Letters are followed by a number when there is more than one of the same type of skill on the page.

DIFFERENTIATED INSTRUCTION
All activities are written for the on-level student unless otherwise marked with the leveled labels below.

BL Beyond Level
AL Approaching Level
ELL English Language Learners

All students benefit from activities that utilize different learning styles. Many activities are marked as below when a particular learning style is highlighted.

Intrapersonal
Logical/Mathematical
Visual/Spatial
Verbal/Linguistic
Naturalist
Kinesthetic
Auditory/Musical
Interpersonal

Council for Economic Education

Below are the Council for Economic Education Voluntary National Content Standards in Economics covered in the *Global Economic Development* chapter.

Content Standard 1: Productive resources are limited. Therefore, people cannot have all the goods and services they want; as a result, they must choose some things and give up others.

Content Standard 4: People usually respond predictably to positive and negative incentives.

Content Standard 5: Voluntary exchange occurs only when all participating parties expect to gain. This is true for trade among individuals or organizations within a nation, and among individuals or organizations in different nations.

Content Standard 6: When individuals, regions, and nations specialize in what they can produce at the lowest cost and then trade with others, both production and consumption increase.

Content Standard 7: A market exists when buyers and sellers interact. This interaction determines market prices and thereby allocates scarce goods and services.

Content Standard 14: Entrepreneurs take on the calculated risk of starting new businesses, either by embarking on new ventures similar to existing ones or by introducing new innovations. Entrepreneurial innovation is an important source of economic growth.

Content Standard 15: Investment in factories, machinery, new technology, and in the health, education, and training of people stimulates economic growth and can raise future standards of living.

Content Standard 16: There is an economic role for government in a market economy whenever the benefits of a government policy outweigh its costs. Governments often provide for national defense, address environmental concerns, define and protect property rights, and attempt to make markets more competitive. Most government policies also have direct or indirect effects on peoples' incomes.

CHAPTER 18: GLOBAL ECONOMIC DEVELOPMENT

CHAPTER OPENER PLANNER

Students will know:
- the impact of world demographics on economic systems
- the stages of economic development and the key characteristics of each stage.
- the obstacles to economic growth in developing countries.
- globalization involves the global spread of products, markets, and production.

Students will be able to:
- **discuss** the importance of economic development for all nations.
- **list** the stages of economic development.
- **define** globalization.
- **explain** how agreements for regional cooperation help member nations develop economically.
- **discuss** the importance of conserving nonrenewable resources.

UNDERSTANDING BY DESIGN®

☑ Print Teaching Options

R Reading Skills

☐ **p. 520 Identifying statistics about women** Students identify what percentage of women receive microloans.

C Critical Thinking Skills

☐ **p. 519 Evaluating the effect of instant news** Students discuss a "smaller world."

☐ **p. 520 Comprehending collateral** Students discuss why microloans are important.

☐ **p. 521 Borrowing Out of Necessity** Students consider whether a minimum wage could repay a microloan.

☑ Online Teaching Options

V Visual Skills

☐ **IMAGE Chapter opener**—Students discuss a cook's role in a global economy.

C Critical Thinking Skills

☐ **INFOGRAPHIC Economic Perspectives**—Students discuss microfinance institutions.

☐ **DEBATE** Are the world's wealthiest nations obligated to aid in the economic development of poor nations?

☐ **INTERACTIVE FEATURE Case Study: A Solar-Powered Nepal**—Students analyze how Nepal is initiating solar power.

☑ Printable Digital Worksheets

C Critical Thinking Skills

☐ **WORKSHEET Economic Simulation**—Students develop a business plan with a microloan or crowdfunding.

☐ **WORKSHEET Personal Finance Activity**—Students analyze outsourced U.S. jobs.

☐ **WORKSHEET Assessing Background Knowledge**—Target misconceptions you can address when teaching the lessons.

☐ **WORKSHEET Chapter Summary**—Content is condensed into manageable chunks.

Project-Based Learning

Hands-On

WORKSHEET Hands-On Chapter Project
In this activity, students will create several maps to examine various aspects of globalization and consider how it is changing world economies. Students will map:
- industrialized and developing economies
- where World Bank money goes
- where in the world a specific corporation has operations
- which countries participate in various trade unions and organizations
- global population concentration
- the locations of nonrenewable natural resources

Students will use these maps to focus their ideas for a one-page paper on worldwide economic development. They will also deliver their findings using posters or multimedia presentations.

Digital Hands-On

Create Online Projects

Find an additional activity online that incorporates technology for the Hands-On Project. Visit the EdTech Teacher Web sites for more links, tutorials, and other resources.

Print Resources

ANCILLARY RESOURCE
This ancillary is available for every chapter and lesson.
- Chapter Tests and Lesson Quizzes

PRINTABLE DIGITAL WORKSHEETS
These printable digital worksheets are available for every chapter and lesson.
- Reading Essentials & Study Guide
- Vocabulary Activities
- Chapter Summaries
- Economic Simulations
- Math Practice for Economics
- Reinforcing Economic Skills
- Personal Finance Activities
- Enrichment Activities
- Reteaching Activities
- Guided Reading Activities
- Video Worksheets
- Lesson Quizzes and Chapter Tests (English and Spanish)

More Media Resources

SUGGESTED READING
- For students at a Grade 10 reading level: *Globalization,* by Adam Hibbert
- For students at a Grade 11 reading level: *Globalize It!: The Stories of the IMF, the World Bank, and the WTO,* by Brendan January
- For students at a Grade 12 reading level: *The Internet,* by Helen Cothran

SUGGESTED VIDEOS
Find these documentaries yourself online. NOTE: McGraw-Hill Education does not endorse these resources. Preview clips for age-appropriateness.
- *Getting Rich* (53 min.)
- *Phoning from the Philippines* (25 min.)
- *TED Talks: The Power of the Informal Economy* (12 min.)

LESSON 1 Planner

ECONOMIC DEVELOPMENT

Students will know:
- the stages of economic development and the key characteristics of each stage.
- the obstacles to economic growth in developing countries.
- how international organizations can help fund economic development through aid and loan programs.

Students will be able to:
- **discuss** the importance of economic development for all nations.
- **describe** the impact of economic growth.
- **list** the stages of economic development.
- **name** major obstacles to economic growth in developing countries.
- **describe** several ways in which economic growth can be financed in developing countries.
- **define** globalization.

UNDERSTANDING BY DESIGN

☑ Print Teaching Options

V Visual Skills

☐ **p. 529 Visualizing outcomes** Students draw a political cartoon of one nation granting aid to another. *Visual/Spatial*

R Reading Skills

☐ **p. 522 Defining *globalization*** Students predict characteristics of globalization.

☐ **p. 524 Calculating crude birthrate** Students divide births by total population.

☐ **p. 529 Summarizing the lesson** Students list the stages and obstacles of economic development.

C Critical Thinking Skills

☐ **p. 522 Comparing GNP among countries** Students speculate on a nation's economic future.

☐ **p. 524 Identifying cause and effect** Students apply development stages.

☐ **p. 525 Comparing natural resources and geography** Students calculate value of imports/exports for landlocked countries.

☐ **p. 525 Exploring issues** Students discuss how epidemics could impact a nation's economy.

☐ **p. 528 Speculating about micro loan businesses** Students identify how a micro loan might help someone start a small business.

W Writing Skills

☐ **p. 526 Writing a narrative** Students research examples of corruption. *Verbal/Linguistic*

☐ **p. 526 Mapping corruption** Students map levels of perceived corruption. *Visual/Spatial*

☐ **p. 529 Summarizing costs and benefits** Students research a project financed by the International Bank for Reconstruction and Development.

☑ Online Teaching Options

V Visual Skills

☐ **CHART Corruption Perception Index chart**—Students compare countries listed as the least and most corrupt.

☐ **VIDEO Gaza Micro Credit**—Students discuss challenges women have faced in Gaza's economy. *Verbal/Linguistic*

R Reading Skills

☐ **GRAPHIC ORGANIZER Five Stages of Economic Growth**—Students identify the five stages of economic growth.

☐ **GRAPHIC ORGANIZER Concept Web**—Students identify the eight obstacles faced by developing countries. *Visual/Spatial*

C Critical Thinking Skills

☐ **BELLRINGER Economic Development**—Students discuss challenges to economic development faced by nations. *Verbal/Linguistic*

☐ **ESSENTIAL QUESTION Exploring the Essential Question**—Students analyze extreme.

T Technology Skills

☐ **SELF-CHECK QUIZ Lesson 1**—Students receive instant feedback on their mastery of lesson content.

☐ **GAME Lesson 1**—Students solve clues to review lesson content.

☐ **INTERACTIVE WHITEBOARD ACTIVITY The Stages of Economic Growth**—Students work together to learn lesson content.

☑ Printable Digital Worksheets

R Reading Skills

☐ **WORKSHEET Guided Reading Activity**—Students review their comprehension of the content.

☐ **WORKSHEET Reading Essentials and Study Guide**—Students complete the study guide and answer Reading Progress Check and vocabulary questions.

C Critical Thinking Skills

☐ **WORKSHEET Gaza Micro Credit Video Activity**—Students answer questions about microloans in Gaza.

☐ **WORKSHEET Economic Simulation**—Students go through the steps to develop a business plan and budget for starting and running a small business. *Logical/Mathematical, Interpersonal*

LESSON 2 Planner

GLOBALIZATION: CHARACTERISTICS AND TRENDS

Students will know:
- regional economic agreements foster trade and economic growth among member nations.
- globalization involves the global spread of products, markets, and production.
- international organizations are formed to facilitate trade among countries.

Students will be able to:
- **explain** how agreements for regional cooperation help member nations develop economically.
- **analyze** globalization trends.
- **explain** how economic incentives relate to population growth.

UNDERSTANDING BY DESIGN®

✓ Print Teaching Options

V Visual Skills

- **p. 534 Identifying EU members** Students examine a map of the EU.
- **p. 535 Identifying ASEAN members** Students study a map of ASEAN.
- **p. 536 Identifying members of COMESA** Students examine a map of COMESA.
- **p. 537 Identifying members of OPEC** Students identify members of OPEC.
- **p. 538 Creating diagrams of interdependence** Students illustrate global trade.

C Critical Thinking Skills

- **p. 532 Evaluating multinationals** Students discuss advantages and disadvantages.
- **p. 533 Drawing conclusions about the importance of computers** Students tie globalization to computers.
- **p. 533 Debating the U.S. role in financial aid** Students debate whether U.S. foreign aid would be better spent at home.
- **p. 535 Speculating about rationales for joining the EU** Students discuss why not all European nations want to join the EU.
- **p. 535 Contrasting customs unions** Students discuss the future of COMESA.
- **p. 540 Speculating about OPEC member nations** Students discuss why only three of the top ten oil producers are OPEC members.

W Writing Skills

- **p. 533 Supporting a viewpoint** Students write about outsourcing.
- **p. 534 Comparing free trade and customs unions** Students identify which is most desirable to member nations.

T Technology Skills

- **p. 531 Researching global franchises** Students look for examples of globalization.

✓ Online Teaching Options

V Visual Skills

- **MAP European Union**—Students examine how the EU developed over time.
- **MAP ASEAN**—Students determine how ASEAN nations strengthen their internal network. *Visual/Spatial*
- **MAP COMESA**—Students explore how COMESA nations work together.
- **MAP OPEC**—Students determine how OPEC nations are a cartel. *Visual/Spatial*
- **VIDEO Brazil**—Students view Brazil's economic interdependence.

R Reading Skills

- **GRAPHIC ORGANIZER Global Institutions**—Students identify key global institutions and their functions.

C Critical Thinking Skills

- **BELLRINGER Globalization Characteristics**—Students discuss ways two multinational corporations may have to adjust their products.
- **ESSENTIAL QUESTION Essential Question**—Students discuss barriers that might interfere with economic interdependence.
- **INTERACTIVE FEATURE Global Economy & You**—Students discuss the true costs of products in a global market. *Visual/Spatial*
- **INTERACTIVE FEATURE Careers**—Students discuss the values of the World Bank.

T Technology Skills

- **SELF-CHECK QUIZ Lesson 2**—Students receive instant feedback on answers.
- **GAME Lesson 2**—Students solve clues to review lesson content.
- **INTERACTIVE WHITEBOARD ACTIVITY International Relationship**—Students work together to learn lesson content.

✓ Printable Digital Worksheets

R Reading Skills

- **WORKSHEET Guided Reading Activity**—Students review their comprehension.
- **WORKSHEET Reading Essentials and Study Guide**—Students complete the study guide and answer Reading Progress Check and vocabulary questions.
- **WORKSHEET Personal Finance: Get a Job**—Students analyze data on outsourcing to better understand globalization's impact on the U.S. job market.

C Critical Thinking Skills

- **WORKSHEET Brazil Video Activity**—Students review Brazil's economy.
- **WORKSHEET Personal Finance Activity**—Students analyze data on outsourcing.

LESSON 3 Planner

GLOBAL PROBLEMS AND ECONOMIC INCENTIVES

Students will know:
- the impact of world demographics on economic systems.
- the connection between population growth and the misuse of natural resources.
- measures taken by international governing agencies to control and reduce pollution.

Students will be able to:
- *explain* how economic incentives relate to population growth.
- *discuss* the importance of conserving nonrenewable resources.
- *list* renewable and nonrenewable resources.
- *evaluate* conservation and pollution control efforts.

UNDERSTANDING BY DESIGN

✓ Print Teaching Options

V Visual Skills

☐ **p. 545 Analyzing energy flows** Students discuss where the U.S. could reduce its energy use.

R Reading Skills

☐ **p. 546 Relating oil prices to energy alternatives** Students discuss how supply and demand have influenced the price of oil.

☐ **p. 547 Exploring solutions for pollution prevention** Students create word webs for *legislated standards* and *pollution permits*.

C Critical Thinking Skills

☐ **p. 541 Relating population growth to scarcity** Students discuss how people affect resources.

☐ **p. 541 Considering the natural increase rate** Students calculate the natural increase rate.

☐ **p. 542 Recognizing regional similarities** Students name five countries growing the fastest and five losing population. **Visual/Spatial**

☐ **p. 544 Evaluating power sources** Students discuss whether nuclear risks are manageable.

☐ **p. 548 Understanding pollution permits** Students discuss how pollution permits limit pollution through supply and demand.

☐ **p. 549 Evaluating economic responsibilities** Students discuss the responsibilities businesses have toward the planet.

W Writing Skills

☐ **p. 541 Distinguishing between terms** Students explain *population* and *population growth rate*. **Verbal/Linguistic**

☐ **p. 542 Understanding population as a push factor of migration**

☐ **p. 543 Applying incentives to high/low population growth** Students list the incentives and disincentives on deciding to have children.

☐ **p. 544 Arguing a point of view** Students discuss government funding for renewable energy.

✓ Online Teaching Options

V Visual Skills

☐ **GRAPH World Population Growth Rates**—Students discuss the growth rate.

☐ **MAP World Population Growth Rates By Country: 1970 and 2013 map**—Students identify where the population growth rate is the lowest and highest.

☐ **GRAPH Energy Flows in the United States**—Students predict how energy use may change in the future. **Visual/Spatial**

☐ **SLIDE SHOW Renewable Resources: Alternatives to Fossil Fuel**—Students identify renewable resources.

☐ **VIDEO Air Pollution in the U.S.A.**—Students consider actions to reduce pollution.

☐ **POLITICAL CARTOON Sources of Energy**—Students discuss 20th century attitudes toward energy and how they have changed. **Visual/Spatial**

R Reading Skills

☐ **BIOGRAPHY Thomas Malthus**—Students read the biography and discuss what events influenced Malthus and if his theories changed attitudes. **Interpersonal**

☐ **GRAPHIC ORGANIZER Types of Resources**—Students identify renewable and nonrenewable resources. **Verbal/Linguistic**

C Critical Thinking Skills

☐ **BELLRINGER Global Problems and Economic Incentives**—Students discuss conflicts between economic and environmental goals. **Verbal/Linguistic**

☐ **ESSENTIAL QUESTION Exploring the Essential Question**—Students discuss how scarcity affects students on a personal level and on national and global levels.

T Technology Skills

☐ **SELF-CHECK QUIZ Lesson 3**—Students receive instant feedback on answers.

☐ **GAME Lesson 3**—Students solve clues to review lesson content.

☐ **INTERACTIVE WHITEBOARD ACTIVITY Global Energy Consumption**—Students work together to learn lesson content.

✓ Printable Digital Worksheets

R Reading Skills

☐ **WORKSHEET Reteaching Activity**—This worksheet can be used with struggling students who need additional help with difficult content concepts.

C Critical Thinking Skills

☐ **WORKSHEET Air Pollution in the U.S.A. Video Activity**

☐ **WORKSHEET Math Practice for Economics**—Students compare two nations' population growths.

CHAPTER 18 Global Economic Development

INTERVENTION AND REMEDIATION STRATEGIES

LESSON 1 Economic Development

Reading and Comprehension

Divide the class into four groups and assign one of the questions below to each group. Have groups answer the questions and find details to support their responses. Then ask students to share their answers and reasons with the class.

- How does population growth harm developing countries? Why is it not as much of a concern in industrialized nations?
- What is capital flight? What causes it and how can nations prevent it?
- How does ending disease and poverty in developing countries help the economies of industrialized nations?
- Why do some cultures in developing nations resist economic development?

Text Evidence

Have student pairs work together to answer these questions: Which two international agencies offer the most economic advice and aid to developing countries? How do they work with developing nations to solve their problems? Ask students to explain their answers, citing details from the text. Ask each pair of students to present their answers in a group discussion.

LESSON 2 Globalization: Characteristics and Trends

Reading and Comprehension

Divide the different examples of free trade areas and customs unions among students. Ask each student to review his or her economic group and to write a paragraph explaining what makes it successful or not successful. Students should use facts and reasons from the text to support their ideas. After completing their paragraphs, ask students to share their ideas in a class discussion.

Text Evidence

Ask students to prove or disprove these statements using quotations from the text:

- Outsourcing is a short-term solution that often damages the domestic economy in favor of international trade. *(Disprove: "[T]he lower costs of production, and the lower prices that consumers pay, are benefits that more than offset the lost jobs.")*
- Customs unions are typically more restrictive toward nonmember countries than free-trade areas. *(Prove: "The free-trade area does not set uniform tariffs for nonmembers... [A] customs union [is] an agreement in which two or more countries... adopt uniform tariffs for nonmember countries.")*
- A Greek teacher can get a job in Sweden without any special work permit. *(Prove: "Citizens of EU member nations hold common passports and can travel anywhere in the EU to work, shop, save, and invest.")*
- Globalization makes industrialized nations wealthy while harming the economies of developing nations. *(Disprove: "...economic cooperation among countries usually leads to increased political cooperation. Thus, globalization will likely enhance economic growth and political stability among all nations.")*

LESSON 3 Global Problems and Economic Incentives

Reading and Comprehension

Ask students to imagine that a bicycle company is considering opening a local manufacturing facility by renovating an abandoned factory in your community. While most citizens welcome the boost the company will give to the local economy, some long-time residents are concerned because the old factory was a major polluter. Have students write a letter to the city council outlining measures they can take to control pollution at the new factory. Remind students to use facts from the lesson to support their suggestions.

Text Evidence

Ask students to write one or two paragraphs responding to this question: Why are families in developing countries typically larger than families in industrialized nations? Ask students to give details from the text to support their answers. Have students compare their responses in small group discussions.

Online Resources

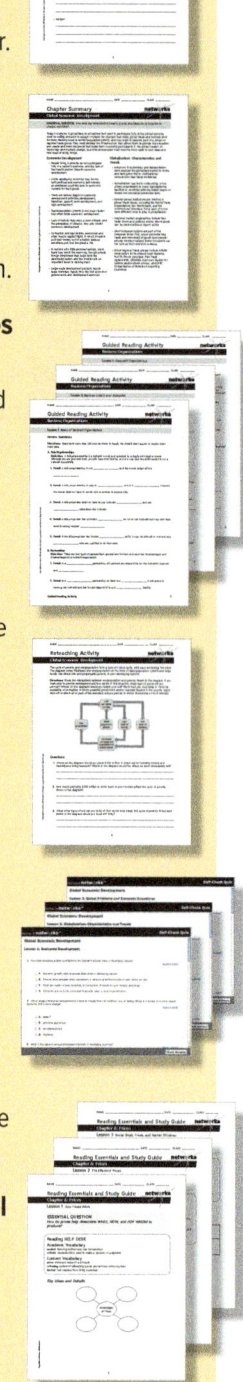

Assessing Background Knowledge

Use this worksheet to pre-assess students' background knowledge before they start the chapter.

Chapter Summaries

Have students use the summary as a pre-reading activity or as a post-reading review to check the main ideas covered in each lesson.

Guided Reading Activities

Have students complete these activities as they read each lesson. They provide reading notes the student can use for review and to prepare for assessments.

Reteaching Activities

Have students complete the Reteaching Activity for remedial practice and review of vital content.

Self-Check Quizzes

These quizzes provide instant feedback on areas the students may need to re-read to understand a main idea.

Reading Essentials and Study Guide

This resource offers writing and reading activities for the approaching-level student.

Approaching Grade Level Reader

This reader presents all of the content of the Online Student Edition but at a lower reading level.

English Language Learner Reader

Provide additional reading support for ELL students. Find this tool in the Online Student Edition.

Global Economic Development

ESSENTIAL QUESTIONS
- Why is the economic health of all nations important in a global economy?
- What are the challenges associated with globalization?

networks
www.connected.mcgraw-hill.com
There's More Online about global economic development.

CHAPTER 18

Economic Perspectives
Micro-lending: Building Economies One Small Loan at a Time

Lesson 1
Economic Development

Lesson 2
Globalization: Characteristics and Trends

Lesson 3
Global Problems and Economic Incentives

CHAPTER 18
Global Economic Development

ENGAGE

Ask students to describe the photo. Guide them to recognize that the man is a cook from Rajasthan, India. **Ask: Why is this man's business important to the global economy?** *(Possible response: He contributes to his own nation's economy, which benefits his region as well as the global economy.)* Lead students to understand that in a global economy, the economic health of all nations is important.

Evaluating the effect of instant news Ask students to name ways they learn about events that happen in other countries. Most will mention television and the Internet. **Ask: How are we affected by our ability to learn, almost instantly, about an event that occurs anywhere in the world?** *(Most students will say that this capability makes the world seem much smaller than it did a generation ago.)* **What effect do you think this "smaller world" will have on the world economy?** *(Many students will say that economic changes in one part of the world will more readily cause changes in other parts of the world.)* Tell students that this chapter examines the ways a "smaller world" has influenced—and will continue to influence—the global economy. **Interpersonal**

Making Connections

Globalization and Career Choices Organize students into small groups of three or four to discuss their future careers. Tell them to include answers to these questions in their discussion: What factors must they consider when making plans for the future? Which careers interest them the most? How will they decide which career to choose? Have each student list the advantages and disadvantages of their top two career choices. Regroup students for a class discussion in which students share their ideas and reasoning. Explain that in Chapter 18 they will find out how globalization affects their own personal choices as well as those of businesses and nations. **Interpersonal**

Letter from the Author

Dear Economics Teacher,

One thing we know is that students have a boundless degree of optimism. Very soon it will be their turn to try to make the world a better place to live. This is where teachers come in, and this is why we have such an important role—because it is *our* job to tell students how the world works and to prepare them for it. When we look at the world today, we should see how markets and prices are involved in a fascinating collage of events. If we can help our students understand how these forces work, they will have a much better chance of success. This is our responsibility, and we can't take it lightly.

Gary E. Clayton

FOLDABLES
Study Organizer

Go to the Foldables® library for a cumulative chapter-based Foldable® activity that your students can use to help take notes and prepare for assessment.

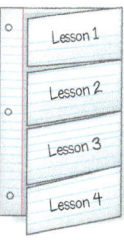

CHAPTER 18
Economic Perspectives

TEACH & ASSESS

C Critical Thinking Skills

Comprehending collateral To give students an understanding of why microloans are important to those with little means (and thus no collateral), have students suppose that they want a loan. **Ask: What could you use for collateral to secure the loan?** *(Assuming that students live with their parents or guardians, lead students to consider using their electronic devices or perhaps a vehicle as collateral.)* **How difficult might it be to survive if your computer or vehicle were taken or repossessed because you defaulted on your loan?** *(Without a means of communication, any future business and income would diminish. As a result, obtaining another loan would be difficult.)*

R Reading Skills

Identifying statistics about women **Ask: What percentage of the world's impoverished people are women?** *(70 percent)* **What percentage of those receiving microfinance services are women?** *(67 percent)*

Content Background Knowledge

SBA Microloans The average microloan administered by the U.S. Small Business Administration is $13,000, whereas nonprofit lenders usually make loans of a few thousand dollars. Globally, microloans tend to be much smaller, usually a few hundred dollars.

Economic Perspectives

MICRO-LENDING:
BUILDING ECONOMIES ONE SMALL LOAN AT A TIME

The microlending industry provides small, low-cost loans to entrepreneurs who don't have access to traditional lenders because they have little or no collateral or credit history. Micro-loans enable borrowers to develop small businesses that empower them financially and in turn, bolster the local economies. Microlending falls under the umbrella of microfinance, a range of financial services provided to those with little or no financial means. Microfinance has become increasingly instrumental in socio-economic growth, particularly in the impoverished communities of developing countries.

MICROLENDING INSTITUTION

37-125% interest rates

MICROLOAN RECIPIENT

$17 Billion in Microloans operating worldwide

Who uses microloans?

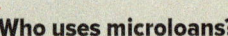

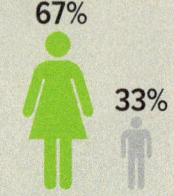
67% / 33%

The gender ratio of microfinance clients varies by region, but on average, 67% of those receiving microfinance services are women, while 33% are men.

Who are microfinance lenders?

There are a number of lenders around the world that administer microloans. In the U.S., the federal government's Small Business Administration oversees its own Microloan Program, which is administered in conjunction with SBA-approved banks and credit unions nationwide. There are also other regional, state and local organizations, like Opportunity Fund, Kiva and Grameen America that offer micro-loans to individual entrepreneurs.

Women, who represent 70% of the world's impoverished people, are the most common recipients of microloans. The rates of loan default/write-off are lower for women borrowers --- to the extent that some microfinance institutions deem lending to male borrowers too risky.

---

networks Online Teaching Options

INFOGRAPHIC

Economic Perspectives: Micro-Lending: Building Economies One Small Loan at a Time

Understanding the impact of microlending
Have students analyze the infographic. Explain that, according to Women's World Banking, 74% of microfinance institutions target women borrowers. In areas of the world where women have limited rights or mobility, microlending empowers women by giving them an avenue to become more productive and autonomous. Nonfinancial services such as literacy and business training, which also give access to financial mobility, are often a part of what microfinance institutions offer. **Ask: What are microloans used for?** *(anything from the purchase of inventory, wages, machinery, or diversity into another business)* **Visual/Spatial**

CHAPTER 18
Economic Perspectives

Making Connections

Borrowing Out of Necessity Discuss the minimum wage with students, and have them consider whether someone working at minimum wage could start a business and repay a microloan. Explain that in 2013, the U.S. federal minimum wage of $7.25 was the seventh highest minimum wage among countries that have a minimum wage. Australia had the highest minimum wage at $16.88, followed by France ($12.09), New Zealand ($11.18), the United Kingdom ($9.83), Canada ($9.75), and Japan ($8.17). Countries with the lowest minimum wage include Sierra Leone ($0.03), India ($0.28), Afghanistan ($0.57), the Philippines ($0.62), Mexico ($0.66), China ($0.80), and Russia ($0.97).

CLOSE & REFLECT

Have students answer the *Think About It!* questions.

WORKSHEET

Economic Simulation

Simulating microfinance Distribute the Economic Simulation worksheet. In it, students are asked to develop a business plan and a budget for starting and running a small business, capable of being started with a microloan or crowdfunding. Read the overview as a class, and then direct students through the steps of the simulation to develop a business plan and budget for starting and running a small business. **Logical/Mathematical, Interpersonal**

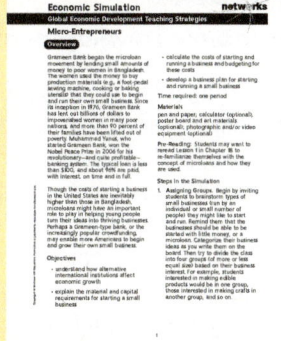

ANSWERS, p. 521

THINK ABOUT IT!

Answers will vary. Students may infer that because microloans are the sole capital these borrowers receive, the borrowers will not jeopardize their future economic growth by not repaying the loans.

CHAPTER 18, LESSON 1
Economic Development

ENGAGE

R1 Reading Skills

Defining globalization Before students begin the lesson, ask them to define *globalization*. Then have students predict what they will learn in the text about the advantages and disadvantages of globalization. Remind students to check their predictions as they read the text.

TEACH & ASSESS

C Critical Thinking Skills

Comparing GNP among countries Instruct students to research a nation's geography and natural resources. Then ask students to explain how these factors impact the nation's per capita gross national product (GNP). Students should speculate about the future of the country. Will it stay in the same GNP per capita range, or will the GNP per capita rise or fall?

R2 Reading Skills

Visualizing proportion Direct students to study the sentence containing the word *proportion*. Ask students to draw a picture or diagram illustrating the concept described in the sentence.
Verbal/Linguistic, Visual/Spatial

ANSWERS, p. 522

ESSENTIAL QUESTION ACTIVITY

Sample response: Yes. Political instability in developing countries greatly affects life in the United States by increasing U.S. defense and security spending and making it that much harder for U.S. companies to invest in and develop markets in developing countries, which in turn hinders U.S. economic growth.

TAKING NOTES:
Primitive equilibrium: A society has no formal economic organization; the economy is stagnant.
Transition: A society moves toward economic and cultural changes; a country does not grow economically in this stage.
Takeoff: A country begins to grow more quickly; people put aside customs to seek new and better ways of doing things. **Semidevelopment:** The makeup of the country's economy changes; national income grows faster than population.
High Development: Efforts for food, shelter, and clothing are more than successful; people turn their attention to services and consumer goods.

Interact with these digital assets and others in lesson 1

- ✓ INTERACTIVE GRAPH
  The Corruption Perception Index
- SLIDESHOW
  Microloans
- ✓ SELF-CHECK QUIZ
- VIDEO

TRY IT YOURSELF ONLINE

LESSON 1
Economic Development

Reading Help Desk

Academic Vocabulary
- proportion
- primary
- ethic
- duration

Content Vocabulary
- developing countries
- primitive equilibrium
- crude birthrate
- life expectancy
- zero population growth (ZPG)
- external debt
- default
- capital flight
- micro loans
- International Monetary Fund (IMF)
- World Bank
- soft loans
- expropriation

TAKING NOTES:

Key Ideas and Details
ACTIVITY Use the graphic organizer below to identify the five stages of economic growth a developing country usually passes through.

Five Stages of Economic Growth

Stages	Characteristics
Primitive equilibrium	
Transition	
Takeoff	
Semi-development	
High development	

ESSENTIAL QUESTION

Why is the economic health of all nations important in a global economy?

Most of the people in the world today live in **developing countries**—countries whose average per capita GNP is a fraction of that in more industrialized countries. Extreme poverty is rampant in most of these countries, with almost 1 billion people worldwide now living on the equivalent of less than $1.25 per day.

Poverty in a developing country often causes social unrest and political instability. Does political instability in developing countries also affect life in the United States? Answer yes or no, and write one or two sentences explaining your answer.

The Importance and Process of Economic Development

R1 GUIDING QUESTION *Why is it important for all nations to develop economically?*

Poverty, whether domestic or global, is more than an economic problem—it is also a source of social discontent and political unrest. It can even threaten the very stability of a country. Fortunately, however, economic development has made significant reductions in the poverty numbers.

Impact of Economic Growth

C In 1990, 1.9 billion people, or about 43 percent of the people living in developing countries, lived below the $1.25/day poverty line. That number fell below 1.2 billion in 2010, and the World Bank estimates that the number could fall to single digits by 2020. Even if it reaches 9 percent by 2020, however, there would still be 690 million people living in extreme poverty.

R2 This progress is due largely to the economic growth that has occurred since 1981. In fact, economists found that a 1 percent increase in the per capita income of developing countries reduces the **proportion** of people in

522

---

networks *Online Teaching Options*

BELLRINGER

Economic Development

Activating prior knowledge Use the Bellringer to initiate a class discussion about the challenges to economic development faced by nations. Explain that the photo was taken in Bangladesh, a nation in South Asia. Guide students to understand that Bangladesh is a developing nation, and that developing nations face challenges to development, such as lack of education and technology. Bangladesh often faces flooding during monsoons, which severely disrupts the economy. The nation struggles to build infrastructure, international trade, and investment. Guide students to understand that other developing countries face both similar and unique challenges. **Verbal/Linguistic**

those countries living on less than $1 a day by about 2 percent. Economic growth thus is the most effective way of dealing with global poverty.

Concern for Developing Countries

The international community shares humanitarian as well as economic concern for the developing countries. For example, many people in the more developed countries believe that it is their moral responsibility to help those who have less income and wealth than they do.

The concern for the welfare of developing countries is also rooted in self-interest. After all, the developed industrial nations need a steady supply of critical raw materials from the developing nations. In turn, developing countries provide markets for the products of industrial nations.

Political considerations also play a role. Despite the dramatic failure of communism in most countries, various political ideologies wage a continuing struggle for the allegiance of developing countries. Countries that develop strong market economies will not only grow faster; they will also find it both necessary and easier to cooperate with developed countries in world markets. Global economic cooperation, in turn, leads to a more stable political climate.

Stages of Economic Development

Some economists have suggested that developing countries normally pass through several stages of economic development. While the boundaries between these stages are not always clear-cut, nor is it clear that all countries progress in this manner, it is still helpful to think of economic development as occurring in stages.

- **Primitive equilibrium**—The first stage is **primitive equilibrium**—"primitive" in the sense that society has no formal economic organization, and "equilibrium" because nothing measurable changes. An example would be the Inuits of the 1800s, who shared the spoils of the hunt with other village families. In this stage, rules are handed down from one generation to the next, with culture and tradition usually directing economic decision making.
- **Transition**—The second stage is a period of transition from the primitive equilibrium to a society that is moving toward economic and cultural changes. The break may be brief and sudden, or it may take years. A country does not grow economically in this transitional stage, but old

developing countries nonindustrial nations marked by extremely low gross national product (GNP), high poverty rates, and economic instability

proportion comparative relationship between things in terms of size, quantity, etc.

primitive equilibrium first stage of economic development during which the economy is stagnant

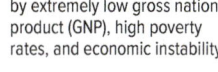

The shift from the more rudimentary types of economy to the most complex ones involve a transition through several stages of development. Earlier stages do not demonstrate much formal organization and tend to be individually centered. As a country develops through the stages, more organization, bureaucracy, and complexity are typically added.

◀ **CRITICAL THINKING**
Understanding This Peruvian man and his burro most likely represent which of the stages of economic development? Explain your answer.

CHAPTER 18, LESSON 1
Economic Development

R Reading Skills

Identifying perspectives Ask: **Why might people in a primitive equilibrium society prefer to remain in that stage?** *(Answers may include fear among elites that economic change will threaten their position, fear of violating tradition or religious beliefs, lack of understanding about the effects of technology, or contentment with current system.)* Have students consider that powerful elites may use propaganda (fear of change) to keep society and the economy from changing.

Content Background Knowledge

Modernization Theory W.W. Rostow, a 20th-century economist, invented a model to explain how countries develop in five stages. His model is sometimes called Modernization Theory. Have students compare his stages to those in the text.

I. Traditional Society: This is a pre-industrial economy that marked all societies prior to ca. 1750. It is characterized by primitive technology and a hierarchical social structure with monarchies.

II. Preconditions for Takeoff: There is a rise in rates of investment, an increase in infrastructure, and the development of a more centralized state that is growth oriented. The first country to enter this stage was Great Britain between 1700 and 1800.

III. Takeoff to Sustained Growth: Growth dominates society but there is a special concentration in lead sectors of the economy (such as cotton textiles in Britain). The rate of new investment rises continuously as productivity improves. This stage is also associated with major technological advances. Great Britain entered this stage during its Industrial Revolution from 1780 to 1820.

IV. Drive to Maturity: The economy enjoys self-sustaining growth as it broadens to include several different sectors. More products are manufactured at home and more consumer goods are made available to a rising middle class, which becomes an engine of future economic growth through increased consumption.

V. Age of Mass Consumption: This stage is marked by steady increases in the size of the economy. Economic growth is often lower than during the two earlier stages, but it initiates from a much greater base. Overall, the economy relies a great deal on middle-class consumption, so consumer spending and confidence are key.

GRAPHIC ORGANIZER

Five Stages of Economic Growth

Taking notes about the five stages of economic growth Have students complete the graphic organizer by identifying the five stages of economic growth and listing the characteristics of each stage. Review and explain difficult or unfamiliar vocabulary from the stages and descriptions, such as *primitive, equilibrium,* and *formal.* Have students look up the prefix *semi-*, then determine which meaning applies to the word *semidevelopment,* as used in this activity. Ask students to brainstorm other words using the same prefix.

AL ELL Verbal/Linguistic, Visual/Spatial

ANSWERS, p. 523

CRITICAL THINKING

Transition stage; Although traditions are still followed, the country does have economic organization as well as elements of change.

CHAPTER 18, LESSON 1
Economic Development

C Critical Thinking Skills

Identifying cause and effect Ask: **What is an example of a national trend or achievement that could help a country advance from semi-development to the high development stage?** *(Answers may include mass production of profitable export goods, implementation of a fair tax system, or adoption of more advanced machinery for factories.)*

Content Background Knowledge

Overlapping Stages of Development Economic growth is often uneven. As a result, some countries may be in several stages of development at the same time. For example, many developing nations in Asia went from having no telephones to widespread use of cell phones. At the same time, people in those countries continue to base other parts of their daily lives on customs and traditions.

R Reading Skills

Calculating crude birthrate Explain to students that the crude birthrate of an area is the number of births divided by population. Birthrates of 10 are low, and birthrates of 35 are high. Provide the following calculations: If your country has 2 million people and 40,000 births per year, the birthrate is 20 per one thousand. Show the calculations on the board:

Number of births ÷ total population = Crude birthrate

40,000 ÷ 2,000,000 = 0.02 = 20 per 1,000

Provide students with other hypothetical figures so they can calculate crude birthrates in class.
AL Logical/Mathematical

ANSWERS, p. 524

✓ **READING PROGRESS CHECK** Economic growth brings about political and economic stability. It pulls populations out of poverty and famine and gives national economies the opportunity to participate in world markets.

---

customs begin to crumble. Societies that enter this stage begin to question their traditions and try new patterns of living.

- **Takeoff**—The third stage of development is reached when the barriers of primitive equilibrium are overcome. A country begins to grow more rapidly as people put customs aside to seek new and better ways of doing things. People begin to imitate the new or different techniques learned from outsiders. During takeoff, a country starts to save and invest more of its national income. New production techniques help industries grow rapidly, and agricultural productivity improves.
- **Semidevelopment**—The fourth stage is semidevelopment. During this stage, the makeup of the country's economy changes. National income grows faster than population, which leads to higher per capita income. At the same time, the country builds its core industries, spends more heavily on capital investment, and makes technological advances.
- **High Development**—This is the final stage where efforts to obtain food, shelter, and clothing are more than successful. Because most people have satisfied their basic needs and wants, they turn their attention to services and consumer goods such as dishwashers, cell phones, and video equipment. Less emphasis is placed on industrial production, while more services and public goods are provided. Mature service and manufacturing sectors are signs of this stage.

✓ **READING PROGRESS CHECK**

Interpreting Why is economic growth so important to developing countries?

Obstacles to Development

GUIDING QUESTION *What are the major obstacles to economic growth in developing countries?*

In many ways, developing countries are similar to other economies of the world. The major difference, however, is that their problems are much greater.

Population Growth

One obstacle to economic development is excessive population growth. The populations of most developing countries grow at a rate much faster than the populations of industrialized countries. When a population grows rapidly, there are more people to feed, and a greater demand for services such as education and health care exists.

One reason for this growth is the high **crude birthrate**—the number of live births per 1,000 people. People in many developing countries are also experiencing an increase in **life expectancy**—the average remaining lifetime in years for persons who reach a certain age. Longer life expectancies, coupled with high crude birthrates, make it difficult for developing countries to increase per capita GNP.

As a result of population pressures, some countries have officially encouraged lower birth rates and smaller families. China has dramatically reduced its population growth with its thirty-year-old "one child per family" policy. Other people even feel that societies should work for **zero population growth (ZPG)**—the condition in which the average number of births and deaths balance.

It is not always possible to restrict population growth, however. In some cultures, large families are valued for economic and personal reasons. In other cultures, efforts to disrupt population growth are considered morally wrong for religious reasons.

crude birthrate number of live births per 1,000 people

life expectancy average remaining life span in years for persons who attain a given age

zero population growth (ZPG) condition in which the average number of births and deaths balance so that population size is unchanged

---

networks Online Teaching Options

GRAPHIC ORGANIZER

Concept Web

Identifying obstacles to development Have students create a concept web by identifying the eight obstacles faced by developing countries. The inner circle should read "Obstacles to Development." Outer ovals should list the eight obstacles (students will need to add two outer ovals). Students can write supporting details in or around the outer ovals, as space allows. **Visual/Spatial**

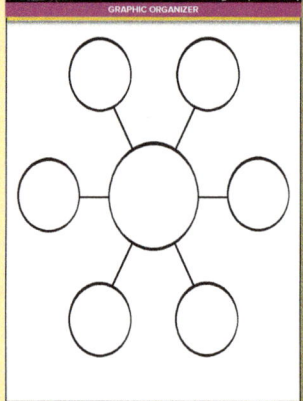

Every country has its own combination of natural resources that can contribute to its economic opportunities. Abundant water sources can provide the opportunity for fishing that can be exported to other nations lacking access to water.

◄ **CRITICAL THINKING**
Understanding Concepts Which of the four factors of production is represented by this picture?

Natural Resources and Geography

Limited natural resources, such as unproductive land, harsh climates, and scarce energy needed for industry, also can hinder economic growth. Even a limited supply of land becomes critical if a country faces a growing population.

In some cases, countries with limited natural resources can make up for the deficiency by engaging in international trade, as Japan has done. However, if a country is landlocked, such as Paraguay, Nepal, or Chad, trade is more difficult. It is no accident that all of the major economic powers today have long had coastal cities with access to major trade routes.

Disease and Substance Abuse

For many developing nations, health has become a major problem. The HIV/AIDS epidemic has been especially devastating in Africa, with some countries experiencing infection rates as high as 20 percent. Because AIDS generally affects young adults, many families have lost their parents and their **primary** income providers, leaving grandparents and neighbors to raise the children.

In parts of Asia, infectious diseases such as bird flu are a constant concern. When even a minor infestation of this disease occurs, entire stocks of poultry have to be destroyed to prevent its spread. In some areas of Asian and South American nations where illegal drugs are grown, high rates of drug addiction among the local population severely impede the prospects for growth.

primary most important

Education and Technology

Still another obstacle is a lack of appropriate education and technology. Many developing countries lack the literacy and the high level of technical skills needed to build an industrial society.

Many developing countries also cannot afford free public education for children. In those that can, not everyone is able to take advantage of it because children must work to help feed their families.

External Debt

Another major problem facing the developing nations today is the size of their **external debt**—money borrowed from foreign banks and governments. Some nations have borrowed so much that they may never be able to repay these loans.

external debt borrowed money that a country owes to foreign countries and banks

connected.mcgraw-hill.com Global Economic Development **525**

CHAPTER 18, LESSON 1
Economic Development

C1 Critical Thinking Skills

Comparing natural resources and geography Direct students to make a list of 10 landlocked countries and a list of 10 countries with an ocean coastline. Have students record the total value of imports and exports for each nation using the most recent data available. Ask students to then calculate the average value of imports and exports for each group. Discuss how (or whether) the averages differ.
Logical/Mathematical

C2 Critical Thinking Skills

Exploring issues Ask: What are some of the ways that an HIV/AIDS epidemic could impact a nation's economy? *(Possible answers: deaths and illnesses of workers reduce productivity; money spent on healthcare lowers consumer spending; deaths and illnesses slow the transfer of job skills and technical knowledge from one generation to the next)*
Logical/Mathematical

W Writing Skills

Supporting an argument Have students write an essay explaining why it is important for people in all nations, including those who are wealthy, to work together to try to end poverty around the world.
Verbal/Linguistic

WORKSHEET

Reteaching Activity

Examining the cycle of poverty and overpopulation
Have students use the Reteaching Activity Global Economic Development worksheet to examine the cycle of poverty and overpopulation, and to consider how to break the cycle. **Visual/Spatial**

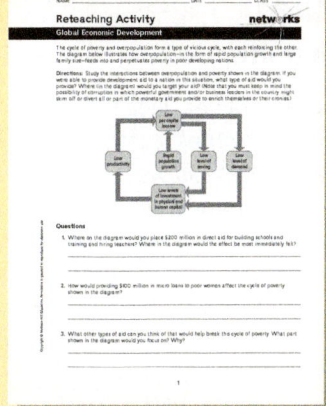

ANSWERS, p. 525

CRITICAL THINKING
Students should readily name land and labor. They may also argue for capital in the intricate nets. Entrepreneurship may be argued if students cite the inventor of the nets.

Global Economic Development **525**

CHAPTER 18, LESSON 1
Economic Development

R Reading Skills

Understanding academic vocabulary Inform students that they may use a dictionary and thesaurus for this activity. **Ask: What are four words that, like *default*, relate to the issue of a nation being unable to repay a large external debt?** *(Possible answers: overspend, nonpayment, bankrupt, failure)* Ask students to write a paragraph using the word *default* and the other words they listed. ELL Verbal/Linguistic

W1 Writing Skills

Mapping corruption Organize the class into five groups. Assign a continent to each of the groups: North and Central America (group together for the purposes of this activity), South America, Europe, Africa, and Asia. Instruct students to visit transparency.org to access the corruption perception index for all the nations of the world. Next, have groups use a mapmaker program (or, if unavailable, distribute a line drawing of each continent) to create a map that illustrates the corruption rankings for the countries on their continent. Suggest that students use a color-coding system to differentiate the levels of perceived corruption. For example, countries ranked 1–20 could be blue, countries ranked 21–40 could be green, and so on. Have students display their maps to the class. When students are finished, combine the continents to create a global map.
Visual/Spatial

W2 Writing Skills

Writing a narrative Have students select one of the 20 nations currently perceived as having the most corruption. Direct students to use reliable library or online resources to investigate examples of corruption that have occurred in their chosen country. Ask students to write a short story illustrating this corruption. Student stories should be fictional, but should be based on factual events.
Verbal/Linguistic

ANSWERS, p. 526

CRITICAL THINKING

Countries with higher poverty rates are often perceived as having more corruption.

---

default act of not repaying borrowed money

R When a country's debt gets too large, it will have trouble just paying interest on the loans. As a result, some developing nations have teetered on the brink of **default**, or not repaying borrowed money. Even this outcome is dangerous, however, because a country that defaults on its loans may not be able to borrow again.

Corruption

Government corruption can be an obstacle to economic progress. Corruption can occur on a massive scale, or it can take the form of minor officials requiring modest bribes to get small things done.

W1 Figure 18.1 shows the 20 countries in the world that are perceived to be the least corrupt, along with the 20 considered most corrupt. A casual look at the list reveals that the countries with the least corruption are more developed than those with the most corruption. Corruption is harmful because it redirects resources into less productive uses. It also makes a few people rich while robbing everyone else.

For example, Iraq has enormous oil reserves and is one of the 12 members of the Organization of Petroleum Exporting Countries (OPEC). Despite its vast natural wealth, decades of corruption and mismanagement by government officials, not to mention war and regime change, have left it relatively poor.

War and Its Aftermath

Unfortunately, many of the developing nations of the world—Angola, Afghanistan, Ethiopia, Cambodia, Somalia, and Vietnam, to name just a

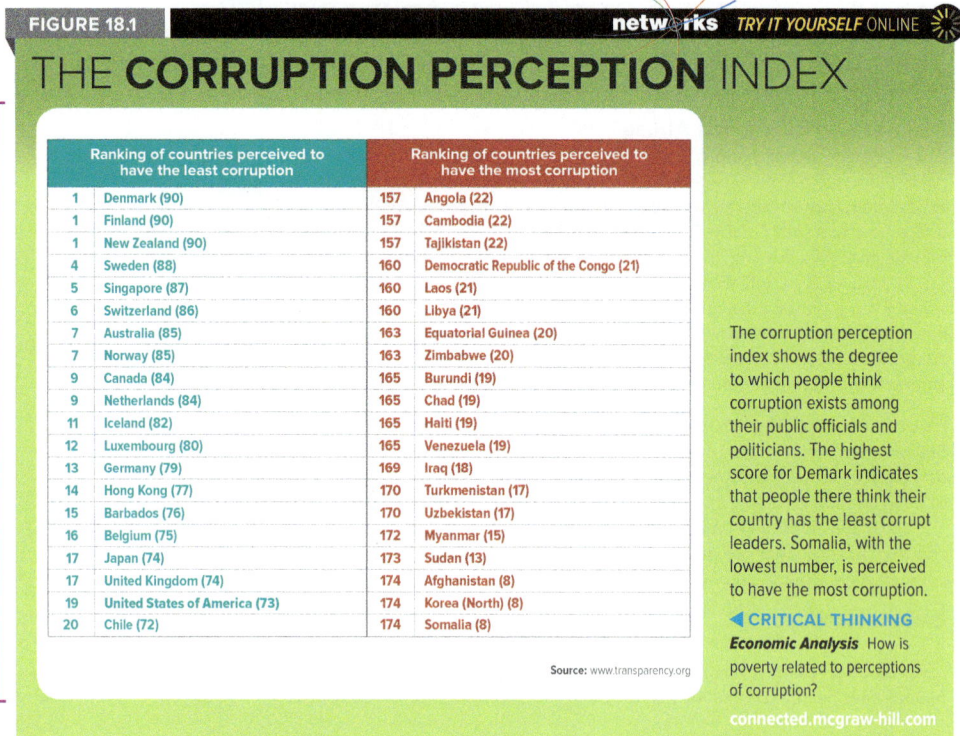

FIGURE 18.1

THE CORRUPTION PERCEPTION INDEX

	Ranking of countries perceived to have the least corruption		Ranking of countries perceived to have the most corruption
1	Denmark (90)	157	Angola (22)
1	Finland (90)	157	Cambodia (22)
1	New Zealand (90)	157	Tajikistan (22)
4	Sweden (88)	160	Democratic Republic of the Congo (21)
5	Singapore (87)	160	Laos (21)
6	Switzerland (86)	160	Libya (21)
7	Australia (85)	163	Equatorial Guinea (20)
7	Norway (85)	163	Zimbabwe (20)
9	Canada (84)	165	Burundi (19)
9	Netherlands (84)	165	Chad (19)
11	Iceland (82)	165	Haiti (19)
12	Luxembourg (80)	165	Venezuela (19)
13	Germany (79)	169	Iraq (18)
14	Hong Kong (77)	170	Turkmenistan (17)
15	Barbados (76)	170	Uzbekistan (17)
16	Belgium (75)	172	Myanmar (15)
17	Japan (74)	173	Sudan (13)
17	United Kingdom (74)	174	Afghanistan (8)
19	United States of America (73)	174	Korea (North) (8)
20	Chile (72)	174	Somalia (8)

Source: www.transparency.org

The corruption perception index shows the degree to which people think corruption exists among their public officials and politicians. The highest score for Demark indicates that people there think their country has the least corrupt leaders. Somalia, with the lowest number, is perceived to have the most corruption.

◄ **CRITICAL THINKING**
Economic Analysis How is poverty related to perceptions of corruption?

connected.mcgraw-hill.com

---

networks Online Teaching Options

TABLE

The Corruption Perception Index

Analyzing tables Ask: Where are the least corrupt countries located? *(Europe, North America, Australia, Asia)* **Where are the most corrupt countries?** *(Africa, the Middle East, Asia)* **How can you explain this difference?** *(Possible response: The least corrupt countries seem to be in areas that have had relative political and economic stability.)* **Why does the chart rank perceived corruption, rather than just corruption?** *(Possible answer: Corruption is hard to prove and document.)* **Why are countries with higher poverty rates perceived as having more corruption?** *(Possible response: Corrupt governments impede development that might help people rise out of poverty.)*

few—suffered through bloody civil wars. The immediate impact of war is the devastating loss of lives and property, not to mention the damage to the country's infrastructure.

The aftermath of war can linger for decades. Poland lost virtually all of its *intelligentsia*—its scientists, engineers, and most of its merchant class—to the gas chambers and concentration camps in World War II. The loss of this talent contributed to the slow recovery of the Polish economy after the war, and even hindered its economic development after the fall of communism.

The widespread use of chemical weapons and land mines makes simple activities like farming extremely difficult in many areas. Moreover, many of the people injured by toxic residue and unexploded weapons, such as children playing in fields, were not participants in the war in the first place. The result is that the weapons of war often impede economic development long after the war is over.

Capital Flight

Finally, developing nations also face the problem of **capital flight**—the legal or illegal export of a nation's currency and foreign exchange. Capital flight occurs because people lose faith in their government or in the future of their economy. When capital flight occurs, businesses and even governments often face a cash shortage. At a minimum, capital flight limits the funds available for domestic capital investment.

Private citizens can even contribute to capital flight. Suppose that someone in Moscow wants to turn rubles into dollars. The person would first purchase traveler's checks in rubles. Next, the individual would destroy the checks and fly to New York. There the person would declare the checks lost or stolen and get replacement checks in dollars, thereby completing the conversion of rubles into dollars.

capital flight legal or illegal export of a nation's currency and foreign exchange

✓ **READING PROGRESS CHECK**

Recalling What are the major obstacles to economic growth in developing countries?

Funding Economic Development

GUIDING QUESTION How is economic development in developing countries financed?

The funding for economic development can come from a number of sources. Some sources are internal, while other sources are external, but all are important.

Importance of Savings

Internally generated funds in many cases are the only source of capital for a developing country. To generate these internal funds, an economy must produce more than it consumes.

If a developing country has a market economy, the incentive to save stems from the profit motive. Firms often try to borrow funds for various projects. Banks in turn pay interest rates on savings that are set by the forces of supply and demand. If the demand for money is high, the interest rate will rise, encouraging savings that can be used for investments by firms.

If a developing country has a command economy, its government may still be able to force saving by requiring people to work on farms, roads, or other projects. However, most command economies do not always mobilize resources to promote economic growth. All too often, resources are instead used for political reasons or personal gain. In addition, forced mobilizations fail to instill long-term incentives or a work **ethic** in people.

ethic moral principles; generally recognized rules of conduct

---

CHAPTER 18, LESSON 1
Economic Development

Content Background Knowledge

UN Human Development Index The United Nations has come up with several ways to gauge a country's progress. One measurement is the Human Development Index, or HDI. To decide where a country falls on the HDI, the UN looks at how much money the average person makes in a year; the cost of goods and services in the country; how many people work in primary, secondary and tertiary jobs; how productive workers are; and the availability of consumer goods. Added to that, the UN measures the health of the people in a country by analyzing their access to medical care and quality schools. In 2011, the UN ranked Norway first, and the United States fourth on the HDI. One problem with using only the HDI as a measurement is that if a few billionaires live in a developing country, the data becomes unbalanced and may look promising. And yet the majority of people might live in extreme poverty. In other countries, the data becomes skewed because minorities and females do not have the same access to education. They cannot compete for higher paying jobs, and the data does not show this.

R Reading Skills

Understanding the importance of the profit motive
Ask: *What motivates people to save, and thus ensure financial capital for economic development?* (Earning interest motivates people to save.)

English Language Proficiency

Advanced High To build academic language proficiency, assign each student a topic related to economic development and a list of grade-level content area vocabulary appropriate to the topic, such as the following terms: developing countries, primitive equilibrium, crude birthrate, life expectancy, zero population growth, external debt, default, capital flight, and micro loans. Have each student use all of the assigned words in the oral report.

WORKSHEET

Guided Reading Activity

Summarizing economic development Ask students to complete the Guided Reading Activity worksheet for Lesson 1: Economic Development. When students finish, read the questions aloud and ask volunteers to share their responses. Encourage discussion among students with different responses. **Verbal/Linguistic**

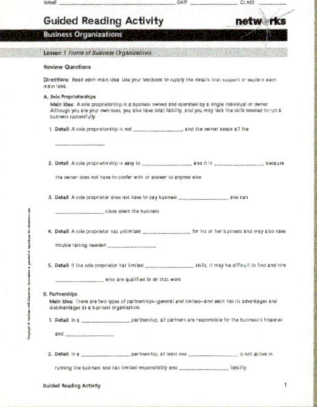

ANSWERS, p. 527

✓ **READING PROGRESS CHECK** Excessive population growth, limited natural resources, disease and substance abuse, lack of appropriate education and technology, external debt, and corruption. War and its aftermath and capital flight or the legal or illegal export of a nation's currency are also problems developing countries face.

CHAPTER 18, LESSON 1
Economic Development

C Critical Thinking Skills

Speculating about micro loan businesses
Ask: What is an example of how a micro loan might help someone start a small business in Africa today? *(Possible answers: a woman receives a small loan to buy a cart from which she will sell vegetables; a woman receives a small loan to purchase materials needed to make wind chimes that she will sell.)* **Logical/Mathematical**

Content Background Knowledge

Grameen Bank and Micro Loans The most famous microloan lender is the Grameen Bank. This organization and its founder Muhammad Yunus, an economist from Bangladesh, won the Nobel Peace Prize in 2006. Similar organizations concentrate on loaning money specifically to women so they can start small businesses making baskets, jewelry, or other items to sell. A drawback is that unscrupulous traders may buy up products for very little money and then sell the items for much more in developed countries. How can you tell whether the hand-woven basket or beaded bracelet you want to buy was made by children in a sweatshop or by fairly paid workers in safe factory conditions? One way is to look for a "fair trade" logo.

R Reading Skills

Activating Prior Knowledge Ask: What was happening in 1944 when the World Bank was founded? How might this have influenced the desire to form an organization like the World Bank? *(World War II was coming to an end; the soon-to-be-victorious Allies might have wanted an organization in place that could help newly independent nations develop.)* **Logical/Mathematical**

Content Background Knowledge

Charitable Organizations There is much debate on what kind of charity to offer developing countries. Some charities—like the Heifer Project—give poor families animals to raise on their farms, or bicycles to help them get to work. Other charities set up schools and provide books. Doctors-Without-Borders provides medical care, and still other organizations meet basic needs with donations of food and clothing.

ANSWERS, p. 528

CRITICAL THINKING

They provide capital to people who could not get it through traditional means, allowing the borrower to undertake an income-generating project.

---

micro loans small, unsecured loans made primarily to women to help them undertake an income-generating project in a developing country

duration length of time

International Monetary Fund (IMF) international organization that offers advice, financial assistance, and currency support to all nations

World Bank international agency that makes loans to developing countries; formally the International Bank for Reconstruction and Development

Microfinance

One of the more successful approaches to economic development in developing countries is the use of **micro loans**. A micro loan is a small unsecured loan, often as small as $50, made primarily to women who want to undertake an income-generating project. Because more than two-thirds of the GDP in a developing country is produced in activities that are not serviced by banks, the loans provide a way to extend the features of capitalism to the poorest of the poor.

For example, in Africa today, a woman might get the equivalent of a $50 loan to buy a hybrid goat that produces a higher milk yield. Since the borrower would be too poor to supply collateral, she would get several other women to cosign the loan in case she defaulted. The loan might have a three-month **duration** and require small weekly payments on the principal. To make the payments, the woman would charge a small fee to other villagers to breed her goat with other goats and thus improve the stock of the whole village. Such loans have been enormously popular, and repayment rates in some areas have been as high as 98 percent.

International Agencies

The problems of the developing countries have not gone unnoticed by the developed countries of the world. Two agencies established by the developed nations work directly with developing nations to help solve their problems.

The **International Monetary Fund (IMF)** is an international organization that offers advice to all countries on monetary and fiscal policies. The IMF also helps support currencies so that the countries can compete in an open market and attract foreign investors.

For example, after the Soviet Union collapsed, a number of former Soviet-bloc countries wanted to trade their currencies on global exchanges. The IMF provided loans to help with the conversion. This is important because investors must be able to purchase the currencies of these countries to conduct international trade with them.

The second important international agency is the World Bank Group, more commonly known as the World Bank. The **World Bank** is an international corporation that makes loans and provides financial assistance and advice to developing countries. The World Bank is owned by IMF member nations, but it operates as a separate organization. The World Bank has undertaken projects to improve broadband connectivity in Mauritania. It also has funded projects to develop inland water transportation in Bangladesh, rural transportation systems in Vietnam, and even tax modernization in Kazakhstan.

The non-profit organization Kiva finds microloan lenders over the Internet to help fight poverty in 73 countries. Kiva has 450 volunteers around the world and a 99 percent repayment rate. In Rwanda, this food stall was set up through one of Kiva's microloans.

▶ **CRITICAL THINKING**
Explaining How do organizations like Kiva help developing nations overcome obstacles to economic growth?

528

---

networks Online Teaching Options

VIDEO   WORKSHEET

Gaza Micro Credit

Analyzing a video about microfinance Show the Gaza Micro Credit video, and guide students in discussing the challenges women have faced in taking part in Gaza's economy, as well as the benefits the microcredit has given to them. **Ask: Why is it better for these women to take micro loans than government subsidies?** *(Possible answer: People take more responsibility and make wiser business decisions when they are expected to pay back a loan than they do when money is just given to them.)* Guide students in a discussion of whether they think micro loans have been a substantial or limited influence on economic development in Gaza. **Verbal/Linguistic**

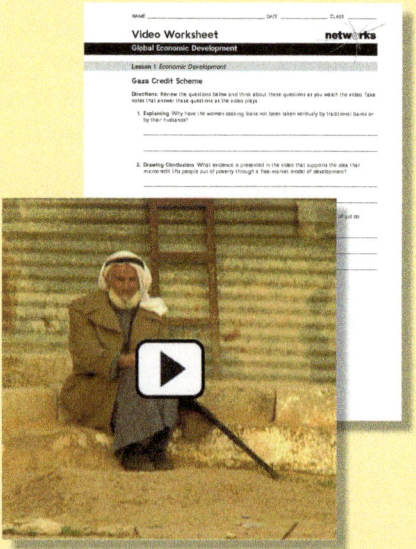

The International Bank for Reconstruction and Development (IBRD)—part of the World Bank Group—helps developing countries with loans and guarantees of loans from private sources. Many of these loans paid for projects such as dams, roads, and factories. Loans are also made to encourage developing nations to change or improve their economic policies.

Another part of the World Bank Group is the International Finance Corporation (IFC), an agency that invests in private businesses and other enterprises. Finally, the International Development Association (IDA) makes **soft loans**—loans that might never be paid back—to the neediest countries. IDA loans are interest-free and may be for periods of 35 or 40 years.

Government Aid Grants

Developing countries can also obtain external funds by borrowing from foreign governments. The United States, Canada, and several countries in western Europe provide this type of aid.

Political considerations usually play a large role in these grants, so the neediest nations do not always receive the funds. For example, the largest recipient of U.S. government aid is Israel. Pakistan also receives financial help from the United States because of its assistance in the war on terrorism.

The former Soviet bloc also gave economic assistance to developing countries. More than half of its aid, however, went to allies such as Cuba, Ethiopia, and Iraq. Like most other foreign aid, it was given to promote political, rather than economic, ends.

Private Foreign Investment

Another way to obtain funds is to attract private funds from foreign investors who might be interested in a country's natural resources. For example, vast oil reserves drew the interest of investors to the Middle East, while copper attracted them to Chile, and mahogany and teakwood to Southeast Asia. In each case, foreign investors supplied the financial capital needed to develop those industries.

If foreign investments are to work, the arrangement must be beneficial to both the investor and the host country. Many investors are unwilling to take major financial risks unless they are sure that the country is politically stable. Developing countries that follow a policy of **expropriation**—the taking over of foreign property without some sort of payment in return—make it harder for all developing nations to attract foreign capital.

☑ **READING PROGRESS CHECK**

Contrasting How do private foreign investments differ from aid through international agencies?

soft loans loans that may never be paid back; usually involves loans to developing countries

EXPLORING THE ESSENTIAL QUESTION

The United States provides funds for development to various foreign governments. If you were employed by the U.S. government and were in charge of identifying nations to receive grant funds, how would you go about choosing? If you had to convince your colleagues to agree with your choices, how would you persuade them on your point of view?

expropriation government confiscation of private- or foreign-owned goods without compensation

---

LESSON 1 REVIEW

Reviewing Vocabulary
1. *Defining* Explain in your own words what the term *soft loans* means.

Using Your Notes
2. *Summarizing* Use your notes to identify two stages of economic development.

Answering the Guiding Questions
3. *Explaining* Why is it important for all nations to develop economically?
4. *Evaluating* What are the major obstacles to economic growth in developing countries?
5. *Describing* How is economic development in developing countries financed?

Writing About Economics
6. *Informative/Explanatory* Select a developing country. Research the major problem that hinders economic growth in that country. Describe the problem and the efforts that have been made to overcome that problem. Predict what you think the outcome will be in five years. Be sure to include the reasons for your prediction.

connected.mcgraw-hill.com Global Economic Development **529**

CHAPTER 18, LESSON 1
Economic Development

W Writing Skills

Summarizing costs and benefits Have students use online or print resources to research a project currently financed by the International Bank for Reconstruction and Development. Ask students to write a paper describing the project and the benefits it will create. Remind students to cite their sources.
Verbal/Linguistic

V Visual Skills

Visualizing outcomes Have students draw a political cartoon based on an example of one nation granting aid to another. Inform students that they may choose an example from the past (for example, Soviet aid to Cuba) or the present (for example, U.S. aid to Pakistan). Instruct students to incorporate the granting nation's motives into their cartoons.
Visual/Spatial

CLOSE & REFLECT

R Reading Skills

Summarizing the lesson Have students list the stages of economic development and describe the main characteristics of each stage. Then ask students to list obstacles to development and give examples of how public and private funds can help developing countries overcome the obstacles.

ANSWERS, p. 529

EXPLORING THE ESSENTIAL QUESTION

Students should outline the rationale behind their decision-making process. Reasons for choosing candidate nations should at least highlight the economic and political reasons alluded to in the lesson. An economic reason could be that the United States is evaluating fiscal policy that has identified an important natural resource as a raw material important to U.S. economic growth, and perhaps that raw material exists in abundance in the candidate nation. Politically, the candidate nation could be persuaded with development funds to assist the United States with military conflicts abroad, as is the case with Pakistan. Students should also demonstrate an ability to persuade others with their points of view.

☑ **READING PROGRESS CHECK** Private investors are usually interested in mutually beneficial financial investments.

LESSON 1 REVIEW ANSWERS

Reviewing Vocabulary
1. Soft loans are made to developing countries and probably will never be paid back.

Using Your Notes
2. Students should identify two of the following: primitive equilibrium, transition, takeoff, semidevelopment, high development.

Answer the Guiding Questions
3. Student should realize that economic well-being creates political and social stability.
4. Excessive population growth, limited natural resources, disease and substance abuse, lack of education and technology, external debt, corruption, war, capital flight
5. organizations such as the International Monetary Fund (IMF) and the World Bank; private investment; foreign government grants

Answer the Guiding Questions
6. The problem, attempted solutions, and predictions should reference the terms and material in the lesson.

Global Economic Development **529**

CHAPTER 18
Case Study

R Reading Skills

Activating prior knowledge Ask: **In what stage of economic development is rural Nepal? Explain.** *(takeoff; people are putting aside old ways and trying new; they are accepting help and adopting technology from outside)* **Logical/Mathematical**

W Writing Skills

Problem solving Ask students to identify two obstacles to development facing people in rural Nepal. In a short oral or written report, have students summarize how the solar power initiative is helping people overcome those obstacles, and then propose at least one other possible solution. **Logical/Mathematical, Verbal/Linguistic**

C1 Critical Thinking Skills

Drawing conclusions Ask: **How can people in rural Nepal afford solar PV systems for their homes when many Americans find this technology financially out-of-reach?** *(Possible answer: They get loans or subsidies from domestic and international private and public institutions.)* **Logical/Mathematical**

C2 Critical Thinking Skills

Predicting outcomes Lead a classroom discussion of whether students think the solar initiative will succeed or fail in Nepal. If it is successful, could similar initiatives work in other developing countries? Or, might Nepal have unique characteristics that do not exist in other countries? If the initiative is a failure, how might similar initiatives in other countries succeed despite the lack of success in Nepal?

ANSWERS, p. 530

Case Study Review

1. The smoke from the fires that Nepalese villagers traditionally use for cooking, heating, and light is hazardous to the villagers' health. Solar-powered energy will help eliminate that problem.
2. Teaching the villagers how to manage the solar-energy program themselves will help them to be self-sufficient. That way, the society will be able to contribute to its own learning, development, and growth.

Case Study

A SOLAR-POWERED NEPAL

For an interactive version of this case study go to connected.mcgraw-hill.com

Nepal's economy has many traditional elements, such as animal herding.

R A small village in rural Nepal is changing the face of that developing nation. In a country where 80 percent of the rural population lives without electricity, the villagers of Khaladig have renewable-energy technology that most people even in developed nations don't have: solar power.

W / C1 The smoke from fires traditionally used for light, cooking, and heating is often hazardous to health, particularly for women and children. Various organizations have worked to solve this problem in Nepal by attempting to supply electricity—and thus modern cooking and heating technology—to its rural villages. In Khaladig, the plan was to install individual solar photovoltaic systems at each home. A solar photovoltaic (PV) system is designed to use the sun as a power source to supply usable electric power.

Once the needs of the community were established, villagers were then taught about the PV system. Each home received components of the system—things such as batteries, chargers, and controllers—which meant there had to be on-the-job training so that the village men and women would know how to assemble and install PV systems in each villager's home. Once this was done, villagers learned how to maintain the systems and how to complete basic repairs.

C2 Today, Khaladig is one of many examples of societies in transition. For this village in rural Nepal, it is solar power. But it may be educational programs for another country in a different part of the world or access to clean water in yet another. Each of these kinds of developments brings societies and nations closer to participating with the global markets that already tie many nations together.

The inclusion of solar panels marks this Nepalese village as one in transition.

CASE STUDY REVIEW

1. **Summarizing** Why are organizations working to install solar energy in villages in Nepal?
2. **Analyzing** What are the benefits of teaching the villagers how to assemble, install, maintain, and repair the PV systems themselves, rather than just doing all that for them?

---

networks Online Teaching Options

INTERACTIVE FEATURE

Case Study: A Solar-Powered Nepal

Evaluating Nepal Have students read the Case Study. Locate Nepal on a world map, and ask students to brainstorm reasons why Nepal is considered a developing country. Encourage classroom discussion by asking the following questions:

- **Why might rural populations in Nepal still live without electricity?**
- **Why are modern cooking and heating important to Nepal?**
- **Why might solar PV (photovoltaic) systems be a more desirable solution than other energy sources?**

Have students work independently to answer the Case Study questions. **Logical/Mathematical, Verbal/Linguistic**

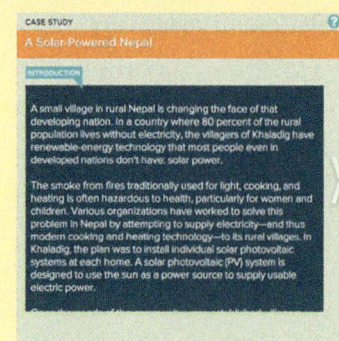

Interact with these digital assets and others in lesson 2
- ✓ INTERACTIVE MAP The European Union
- ✓ INTERACTIVE MAP ASEAN
- ✓ SELF-CHECK QUIZ
- ✓ VIDEO

networks TRY IT YOURSELF ONLINE

Reading Help Desk

Academic Vocabulary
- strategy
- context

Content Vocabulary
- globalization
- multinationals
- outsourcing
- General Agreement on Tariffs and Trade (GATT)
- World Trade Organization (WTO)
- free-trade area
- customs union
- European Union (EU)
- European Coal and Steel Community (ECSC)
- euro
- ASEAN
- Common Market for Eastern and Southern Africa (COMESA)
- cartel
- Organization of Petroleum Exporting Countries (OPEC)
- division of labor

TAKING NOTES:

Key Ideas and Details
ACTIVITY Use the graphic organizer below to identify key global institutions that promote trade and to identify one function of each.

LESSON 2
Globalization: Characteristics and Trends

ESSENTIAL QUESTION

What are the challenges associated with globalization?

One of the most important trends in the world today is **globalization**—the movement toward a more integrated and interdependent world economy. Globalization is taking place because of the voluntary decisions we make as consumers. People today are buying more foreign products, and firms are extending their operations on an international scale. Before you prepare to read more about the challenges of globalization, consider what you know about it:

a. What might be the benefits of globalization?

b. What might be the disadvantages of globalization?

Characteristics of Globalization

GUIDING QUESTION *How would you define globalization?*

There was a time when most markets were local. As transportation and communication improved and populations grew, markets expanded to nearby communities. Later, local markets expanded into regions, then the nation, and today the world.

As a result of this progress, many economists view globalization as a natural, almost inevitable, process. Globalization involves more than markets, however. We also see the globalization of production, institutions, and even culture.

Global Products and Markets

Today you can find specific goods, such as products from McDonald's, KFC, Pizza Hut, Starbucks, or Pepsi, all over the globe. This would have been news just a few decades ago, but today the global presence of a product is the rule rather than the exception.

connected.mcgraw-hill.com *Global Economic Development* **531**

CHAPTER 18, LESSON 2
Globalization: Characteristics and Trends

ENGAGE

R Reading Skills

🔔 **Analyzing globalization** Before students begin the lesson, ask them to list characteristics of globalization in their own words. As they craft their lists, ask students to take notes on the challenges and benefits of an integrated and interdependent world economy. Have students share their lists and insights. **Verbal/Linguistic, Interpersonal**

TEACH & ASSESS

T Technology Skills

Researching global franchises Have students key in a U.S. business plus the term "worldwide" into a search engine (for example, McDonald's worldwide). Ask students to find a link that lists the countries in which the business is located. For each list, have students create miniature logos (or various colored pushpins or toothpicks) to attach to those countries on a world map. Discuss with students if any of the locations of the these businesses surprised them. Why or why not?

ANSWERS, p. 531

ESSENTIAL QUESTION ACTIVITY

Sample answer: Globalization provides more goods and services, more jobs, and regional economic and political cooperation. Globalization also makes countries interdependent, which means that a problem in one country could affect many other countries. In addition, jobs move to countries that have lower wages, taking employment away from the United States.

TAKING NOTES

General Agreement on Tariffs and Trade (GATT): extends tariff concessions and does away with import quotas; resolves trade disputes among members

World Trade Organization (WTO): successor to GATT; resolves trade disputes

International Monetary Fund (IMF): provides advice and financial assistance to nations so that their currencies can compete in open markets

World Bank: provides financial assistance and advice to developing nations

United Nations (UN): promotes economic-development projects; promotes peaceful relations between countries

---

BELLRINGER

Globalization Characteristics and Trends

Activating background knowledge Have students view the Bellringer and answer the questions. Discuss ways in which the two multinational corporations may have to adjust the features of their products in order to do business in other countries.

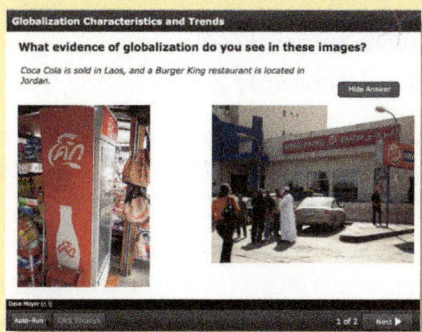

Global Economic Development **531**

CHAPTER 18, LESSON 2
Globalization: Characteristics and Trends

R Reading Skills

Defining multinational Have a volunteer define the term *multinational*. (*a company that does business in many different countries*) Then ask students to speculate on what the prefix *multi-* means. (*many*) Have students list words with this prefix and explain their meanings. (*Possible answers: multiply, multitalented, multicultural, multilingual, multiple, multiplex, multipurpose*)

C Critical Thinking Skills

Evaluating multinationals Ask: **What are some advantages and disadvantages that a multinational gains by being large and operating in many different countries?** (*Possible advantages: ability to draw talent from many different countries, chance to spread risk. Possible disadvantages: risk of political and social unrest in other countries, difficulty in communicating and coordinating, language and social problems, unfamiliarity with other cultures.*)

Making Connections

Globalization of textiles Discuss the following globalization of textiles with students. **Cotton:** Cotton is grown in countries and regions with warm climates, such as India, China, and the southern United States. **Thread:** Spinning cotton into thread is labor intensive. Because it costs more to transport bulky bales of cotton than to transport spools of thread, spinning is often done as close to the source of the cotton as possible, usually in a country that pays low wages to its workers. China makes more than two-thirds of the cotton thread in the world. **Cloth:** Weaving is also a very labor intensive activity. As a result, cloth is usually woven in developing countries where labor costs are low. Almost 90 percent of the cotton cloth made today is woven in China and India. **Garment:** More than two-thirds of the shirts and blouses in the world are sewn in developing countries, although the United States also ranks highly in this category. Indonesia, Bangladesh, and Brazil make a large number of clothes, but China comes in first among developing countries. **Store:** Finally, the shirt is shipped to the United States to a distribution center, which trucks the garment to your local store.

ANSWERS, p. 532

CRITICAL THINKING
Students should provide reasons and details to address each part of the question.

Many of the products we use are made by **multinationals** that produce and sell without regard to national boundaries. Some of these giant corporations, such as British Petroleum (United Kingdom), Ford Motor Company (United States), and Shell Oil Company (United Kingdom and the Netherlands) are well known to most people. Others, such as News Corporation (Australia), Kyocera (Japan), and Vodaphone (United Kingdom), are less well known but make products that millions of Americans use every day.

As a result of globalization, stores are stocked with a wide variety of products from other countries. Switzerland's Nestlé provides us with chocolate bars, coffee, and Stouffers frozen foods. The Citgo gas station you might use is owned by a Venezuelan company, and the 7-Eleven stores by a Japanese firm. The products these companies offer have the same features regardless of the country in which they are sold. This similarity makes selling in a global market easy.

globalization movement toward a more integrated and interdependent world economy

multinationals corporations producing and selling without regard to national boundaries and whose business activities are located in several different countries

Global Production

Globalization means more than having standardized products all over the world, though. It extends to production as well. In some cases, multinationals move their production facilities to be nearer to customers. For example, firms such as Toyota, Nissan, and Honda have opened manufacturing operations in the United States. Others, such as IBM, Boeing, and Intel, moved production facilities abroad to be closer to less expensive sources of labor and raw materials.

THE GLOBAL ECONOMY & YOU

How Much Did Your T-Shirt Cost to Make?

Manufacturers are always seeking ways to lower their costs. So it makes sense from a manufacturer's point of view to make products wherever it can be done less expensively. Also, consumers generally like to pay less for products—when manufacturers lower costs, they can also sell for less.

That's why American and European firms often move production to places such as China, Pakistan, and Bangladesh, where costs—especially labor costs—are much lower. For example, labor costs for a T-shirt in Bangladesh are around $0.22 per shirt. If the same shirt were made in the United States, the labor costs would be more than 30 times that: $7.47. That means that you, as a consumer, would pay much more for a T-shirt manufactured in the United States.

Workers in the United States and Europe fight against their jobs being outsourced overseas, but it's simple to see a manufacturer's motivation, from an economic standpoint. Plus, countries like China and Pakistan compete for the opportunity to manufacture products for companies such as Old Navy, Kohl's, and others, because those opportunities bring jobs and money into their countries.

However, the desire for countries to attract U.S. business and the desire for U.S. business to lower costs can sometimes have negative consequences. In 2013, a garment factory in Bangladesh collapsed, killing more than 1,129 workers and injuring more than 2,500. Two weeks later, a fire in a sweater factory in the same country cost eight lives. These tragedies are not uncommon in Bangladesh and other developing countries.

▲ **CRITICAL THINKING**
Problem Solving Propose a solution to the very low wages and dangerous working conditions in factories in developing countries. In your answer, consider who's responsible for making these changes. Is it the responsibility of countries to better regulate their production facilities? Is it the responsibility of American and European retailers? Is it the responsibility of the workers to demand changes?

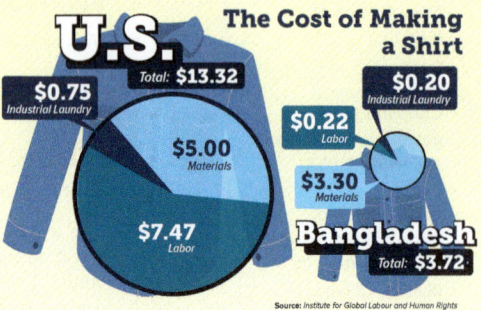

The Cost of Making a Shirt

U.S. Total: $13.32
- Industrial Laundry: $0.75
- Materials: $5.00
- Labor: $7.47

Bangladesh Total: $3.72
- Industrial Laundry: $0.20
- Labor: $0.22
- Materials: $3.30

Source: Institute for Global Labour and Human Rights

---

networks Online Teaching Options

INTERACTIVE FEATURE

Global Economy & You

Exploring issues of global markets Display the Global Economy & You feature. To assess background knowledge, ask:

- How many of you are wearing T-shirts?
- How much do new T-shirts cost at local stores?
- Where do you think your T-shirt was produced?
- How much do you think your T-shirt cost to produce?

Have students read the text and then discuss the true costs of products in a global market. Click on the image to explore how much tax revenue is collected by different governments around the world. Then discuss the questions in the feature.

Visual/Spatial

Most global manufacturing operations are highly sophisticated. For example, Dell uses the Internet to track production and shipping in its plants around the world. By keeping close watch on its operations, Dell is able to keep a modest three-day inventory in its assembly plants. If conditions in one location should suddenly change, Dell can either speed up or slow down shipments of parts to keep production flowing smoothly.

One of the more controversial aspects of global production is **outsourcing**—hiring outside firms for non-core operations to lower operating costs. Many Americans consider outsourcing a controversial issue because they fear losing their jobs to overseas workers. While this is a concern to many workers, in the long run, the lower costs of production, and the lower prices that consumers pay, are benefits that more than offset the lost jobs.

This is little comfort to those who lose their jobs. Yet it is likely that these workers have benefited from and contributed to globalization by buying low-priced clothes made in Indonesia, TV sets from Korea, or other products made abroad.

Global Institutions

Another aspect of globalization is the growth of international organizations that promote trade between nations. Several of the most important ones are described below:

- **GATT**—One early institution that promoted trade is the **General Agreement on Tariffs and Trade (GATT)**, an international agreement signed in 1947 among 23 countries to extend tariff concessions and do away with import quotas. If countries dispute a tariff or other trade issue, they can take it to the World Trade Organization for resolution.
- **WTO**—The success of the GATT led to its successor, the **World Trade Organization (WTO)**. Today more than 150 countries belong to the WTO and turn to it whenever international trade disputes arise between member countries. For example, in 2013 Panama claimed that Colombia placed an unfair tariff affecting the importation of textiles, apparel, and footwear made in Panama.
- **IMF**—The International Monetary Fund (IMF) offers advice and financial assistance to nations so that their currencies can compete in open markets. Without the IMF, many countries would be unable to engage in international trade because their money would not be accepted by other nations. The IMF also extends zero-interest loans to bolster macroeconomic policies and projects in low-income countries. For example, the IMF gave Malawi a $156 million loan to help revive its economic growth after the recent global recession, and $4 billion was provided to Côte d'Ivoire to help it reduce its external debt.
- **World Bank**—The World Bank is another global agency that helps developing countries join global markets as part of their economic development **strategy**. It provides technical assistance, financial support, and grants for infrastructure to help even the poorest of nations join the growing globalization movement. For example, the World Bank is helping enhance irrigation projects in Armenia to make rural farmers more productive.
- **United Nations**—Finally, the United Nations has a role to play in preserving peace through international cooperation and economic development projects that affect farming, entrepreneurship, and young women's employment prospects.

✓ **READING PROGRESS CHECK**

Analyzing How do multinational firms contribute to globalization?

EXPLORING THE ESSENTIAL QUESTION

Despite the benefits of global production that shifts jobs to places where greater efficiencies are available, workers who lose their jobs suffer, especially those who lack the job skills or education to move into other jobs. Does the government have a role to play in helping these workers? What can or should the government do?

outsourcing hiring outside firms to perform non-core operations to lower operating costs

General Agreement on Tariffs and Trade (GATT) international agreement signed in 1947 between twenty-three countries to extend tariff concessions and reduce import quotas

World Trade Organization (WTO) international agency that administers trade agreements, settles trade disputes between governments, organizes trade negotiations, and provides technical assistance and training for developing countries

strategy plan or method

CHAPTER 18, LESSON 2
Globalization: Characteristics and Trends

C1 Critical Thinking Skills

Drawing conclusions about the importance of computers **Ask:** *Do you think globalization would have been possible without computers? Why or why not?* (Most students will say no based on the speed with which modern telecommunications takes place.)

W Writing Skills

Supporting a viewpoint Have students write a paragraph stating whether they agree or disagree that lower costs and prices more than offset jobs lost to outsourcing. Have volunteers read their paragraphs.

C2 Critical Thinking Skills

Debating the U.S. role in financial aid Tell students that the United States is a major financial contributor to international aid organizations such as the IMF and World Bank. Then ask students to argue for or against this statement: *U.S. foreign aid to developing countries is a waste of money and would be better spent fighting problems at home.* Have students debate the topic, citing evidence from the text and current events.

VIDEO | WORKSHEET

Brazil

Analyzing a video Show the Brazil video and guide students in discussing Brazil's economic interdependence. **Ask:** *What obstacles to economic development did Brazil overcome?* (Possible answers: poor transportation and energy infrastructure, lack of education, extreme poverty.) Have students use the worksheet to analyze the Brazil video. **Verbal/Linguistic**

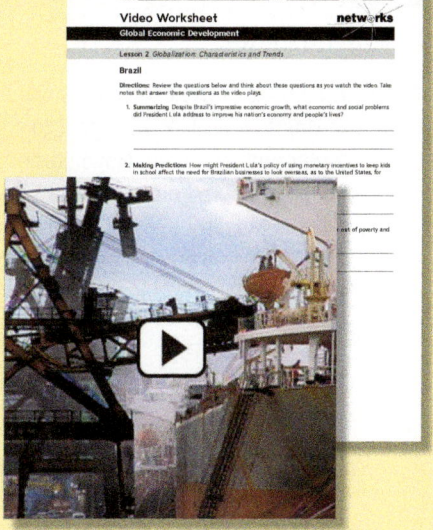

ANSWERS, p. 533

EXPLORING THE ESSENTIAL QUESTION

Many students will say that the government should play a role, but they may differ on the extent of that aid. They may suggest making job training, education, or extended unemployment benefits available.

✓ **READING PROGRESS CHECK** They produce and sell items around the world.

CHAPTER 18, LESSON 2
Globalization: Characteristics and Trends

W Writing Skills

Comparing free trade and customs unions Have students create a Venn diagram to compare and contrast free trade areas and customs unions. **Ask: Which type of economic cooperation is most desirable to member nations?** *(customs unions)* **Why don't more nations create such trading blocs?** *(Possible answer: political instability and international tensions are obstacles to the formation of trading blocs.)*

V1 Visual Skills

Previewing maps Students with various reading and organizational difficulties may have problems relating graphics and the main text. When students encounter a map, have them first identify what the map illustrates by studying the map title and key. Then direct students to read the lesson, restate how each map supports the text, and suggest reasons why the maps were included in the section.

V2 Visual Skills

Identifying EU members Ask: According to the map, which nations are members of the EU? *(Austria, Belgium, Bulgaria, Croatia, Cyprus, Czech Republic, Denmark, Estonia, Finland, France, Germany, Greece, Hungary, Ireland, Italy, Latvia, Lithuania, Luxembourg, Malta, Netherlands, Poland, Portugal, Romania, Slovakia, Slovenia, Spain, Sweden, United Kingdom)*

ANSWERS, p. 534

CRITICAL THINKING
There are no internal barriers regulating the flow of workers, financial capital, or goods and services between EU member nations. Citizens of EU member nations hold common passports and can travel anywhere in the EU to work, shop, save, and invest.

534

---

free-trade area group of countries that have agreed to reduce or remove trade barriers among themselves, but lack a common tariff barrier for nonmembers

customs union group of countries that have agreed to reduce or remove trade barriers and have uniform tariffs for nonmembers

European Union (EU) established in 1993 by the Maastricht Treaty, its 28 member countries make it the largest single unified market in the world in terms of population and output

European Coal and Steel Community (ECSC) group of six European countries formed in 1951 to coordinate iron and steel production to ensure peace among member countries; eventually evolved into the EU

Regional Economic Cooperation

GUIDING QUESTION *How do agreements for regional cooperation help member nations?*

An important step on the way to globalization is the creation of regional trading blocs to promote trade between nations. Most trading blocs start out with a small number of countries, and then they add members to become larger. Eventually they will tend to merge with others, thus paving the way for even more globalization.

One important type of economic cooperation is the **free-trade area**—an agreement in which two or more countries reduce or remove trade barriers and tariffs among themselves. The free-trade area does not set uniform tariffs for nonmembers. Another cooperative structure is the **customs union**—an agreement in which two or more countries abolish tariffs and trade restrictions among themselves and adopt uniform tariffs for nonmember countries. The customs union has more uniformity than a free-trade area, so it represents a higher level of economic integration.

The European Union

The most successful example of regional cooperation in the world today is the **European Union (EU)**. The EU started out as a free-trade area and evolved into a customs union consisting of the member nations shown in **Figure 18.2**.

The EU had its roots in the **European Coal and Steel Community (ECSC)**. The ECSC consisted of Belgium, France, Germany, Italy, Luxembourg, and the

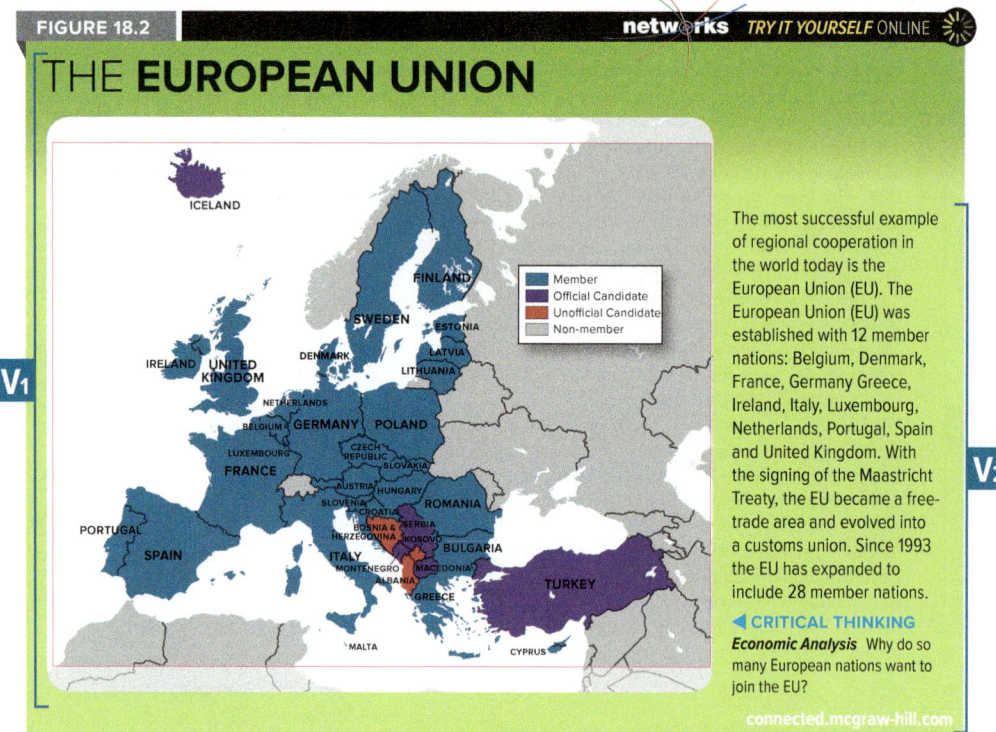

FIGURE 18.2
THE EUROPEAN UNION

The most successful example of regional cooperation in the world today is the European Union (EU). The European Union (EU) was established with 12 member nations: Belgium, Denmark, France, Germany Greece, Ireland, Italy, Luxembourg, Netherlands, Portugal, Spain and United Kingdom. With the signing of the Maastricht Treaty, the EU became a free-trade area and evolved into a customs union. Since 1993 the EU has expanded to include 28 member nations.

◀ **CRITICAL THINKING**
Economic Analysis Why do so many European nations want to join the EU?

534

---

networks Online Teaching Options

MAP

European Union

Analyzing a map of the EU Display the map of the European Union, and click through it to show how the EU developed over time. Have students answer the question to ensure comprehension. Ask students to research the Maastricht Treaty and write a short summary of its history and objectives. Encourage students to share their findings in class.
Visual/Spatial

Netherlands. It was organized in 1951 to coordinate iron and steel production so that it would be difficult for any of the nations to ever again go to war with one another. The ECSC was enormously successful, and over the years, the cooperation evolved into the EU.

In January 1993, the EU became the largest single unified market in the world in terms of population and output, although the EU and the United States now have about the same size GDP. The EU is a single market because there are no internal barriers regulating the flow of workers, financial capital, or goods and services. Citizens of EU member nations hold common passports and can travel anywhere in the EU to work, shop, save, and invest.

A major step in European integration occurred in 2002 with the introduction of the **euro**—a single EU currency. About half of the member nations have adopted it to replace their national currencies. The European Union has not yet achieved complete economic integration because many differences remain; still, the EU is one of the largest unified markets in the world.

euro single currency of the European Union

ASEAN

The success of the EU has encouraged other countries to try regional cooperation. In 1967 five nations—Indonesia, Malaysia, Singapore, the Philippines, and Thailand—formed the Association for Southeast Asian Nations, or ASEAN. **ASEAN** today, shown in **Figure 18.3**, is a 10-nation group working to promote regional peace and stability, accelerate economic growth, and liberalize trade policies in order to become a free-trade area.

ASEAN group of ten Southeast Asian nations working to promote regional cooperation, economic growth, and trade

The region appears to be largely on track to eliminate tariffs and other non-tariff barriers. However, the financial crisis spurred by the Great Recession in the United States weakened the demand for ASEAN's exports. As a result, ASEAN has increased efforts to build a stronger and more unified internal market, one that will place less emphasis on exports.

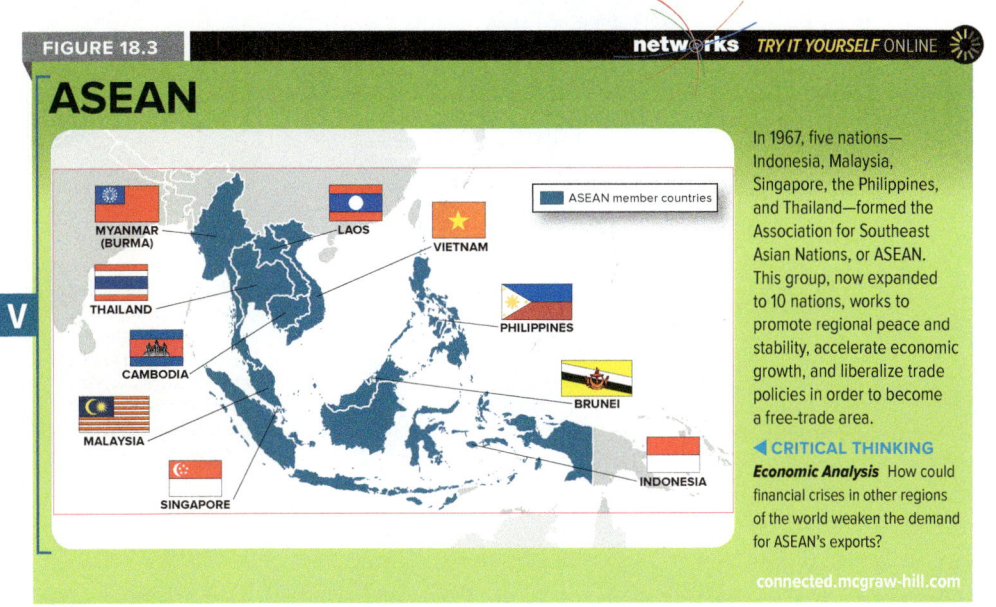

FIGURE 18.3

ASEAN

In 1967, five nations—Indonesia, Malaysia, Singapore, the Philippines, and Thailand—formed the Association for Southeast Asian Nations, or ASEAN. This group, now expanded to 10 nations, works to promote regional peace and stability, accelerate economic growth, and liberalize trade policies in order to become a free-trade area.

◀ **CRITICAL THINKING**
Economic Analysis How could financial crises in other regions of the world weaken the demand for ASEAN's exports?

MAP

ASEAN

Analyzing a map of ASEAN Display the ASEAN interactive map and click through the onscreen text with students to explore how the ASEAN nations are working together to strengthen their internal network. Have students answer the question to ensure comprehension. Ask students to research tariffs and non-tariff barriers that Southeast Asian nations face and how ASEAN works to eliminate them. Have students display their findings in a poster or present a brief oral report, including visuals. **Visual/Spatial**

CHAPTER 18, LESSON 2
Globalization: Characteristics and Trends

Making Connections

The ECSC in Context Ask: **What important event ended in Europe only six years before the founding of the ECSC?** *(World War II)* Have students speculate on why nations like France, Italy, and West Germany might have wanted to encourage closer economic cooperation among nations. *(Possible answer: They may have felt that closer economic integration was a good way to prevent another catastrophic war.)* Ask students to survey older family members for their recollections or stories about the relationships among these countries during this time in history.

C1 Critical Thinking Skills

Speculating about rationales for joining the EU Ask: **Why don't all European nations want to be part of the European Union?** *(Possible answers: Countries with strong independent economies may fear that uniting with weaker economies might drag down their own. Non-EU nations do not want to be subject to EU policies, such as allowing the unregulated flow of workers.)* Ask: **Why doesn't the European Union accept all nations that want to join?** *(Possible answer: The EU may fear that uniting with weaker economies or politically unstable countries might drag down the Union.)*

C2 Critical Thinking Skills

Predicting possible outcomes Ask: **What might happen if Russia joined the European Union, or China joined ASEAN?** *(Possible answer: The new trade unions might become incredibly powerful and create a trade imbalance with the United States and other nations.)*

V Visual Skills

Identifying ASEAN members Ask: **According to the map, which nations are members of ASEAN?** *(Brunei Darussalam, Cambodia, Indonesia, Laos, Philippines, Malaysia, Myanmar, Singapore, Thailand)*

ANSWERS, p. 535

CRITICAL THINKING

Foreign financial crises have the potential to decrease the demand for ASEAN exports forcing ASEAN nations to strengthen internal markets.

CHAPTER 18, LESSON 2
Globalization: Characteristics and Trends

C Critical Thinking Skills

Contrasting customs unions Ask: What challenges might the member countries of COMESA face that the EU nations in Europe did not face? *(Answers will vary depending on students' knowledge of Europe and Africa but may include extreme poverty, ethnic and tribal rivalries, different colonial histories, civil wars, and lack of resources and infrastructure.)* Then have students make and justify predictions about the future of COMESA.

V Visual Skills

Identifying members of COMESA Ask: Which African nations are members of COMESA? *(Burundi, Comoros, Congo, Djibouti, Egypt, Eritrea, Ethiopia, Kenya, Libya, Madagascar, Malawi, Mauritius, Rwanda, Seychelles, Sudan, Swaziland, Uganda, Zambia, Zimbabwe)*

NAFTA

The North American Free Trade Agreement, or NAFTA, was another successful step on the way to globalization. NAFTA was signed into law in 1993 and was designed to completely remove tariff barriers and quotas among Canada, the United States, and Mexico. The goals of the agreement were complete by 2008 and have been directly responsible for significant increases in trade among the three countries.

COMESA

A 1994 effort to copy the remarkable success of the EU was the formation of the **Common Market for Eastern and Southern Africa (COMESA)** shown in **Figure 18.4**. COMESA has 19 member countries. Progress toward a common market has been slow, however, due to a number of issues.

One problem was the way the countries were spread out across Africa, ranging from Swaziland in the south to Libya in the north. Also, several countries suffered from the lack of infrastructure needed for good communication and transportation. Finally, regional wars and the political upheavals in Libya and Egypt during the "Arab spring" further complicated economic cooperation.

Still, the model for cooperation is there, and the countries hope to benefit from it in the future.

Common Market for Eastern and Southern Africa (COMESA) a trading organization consisting of nineteen nations that pools its resources to produce peace and security

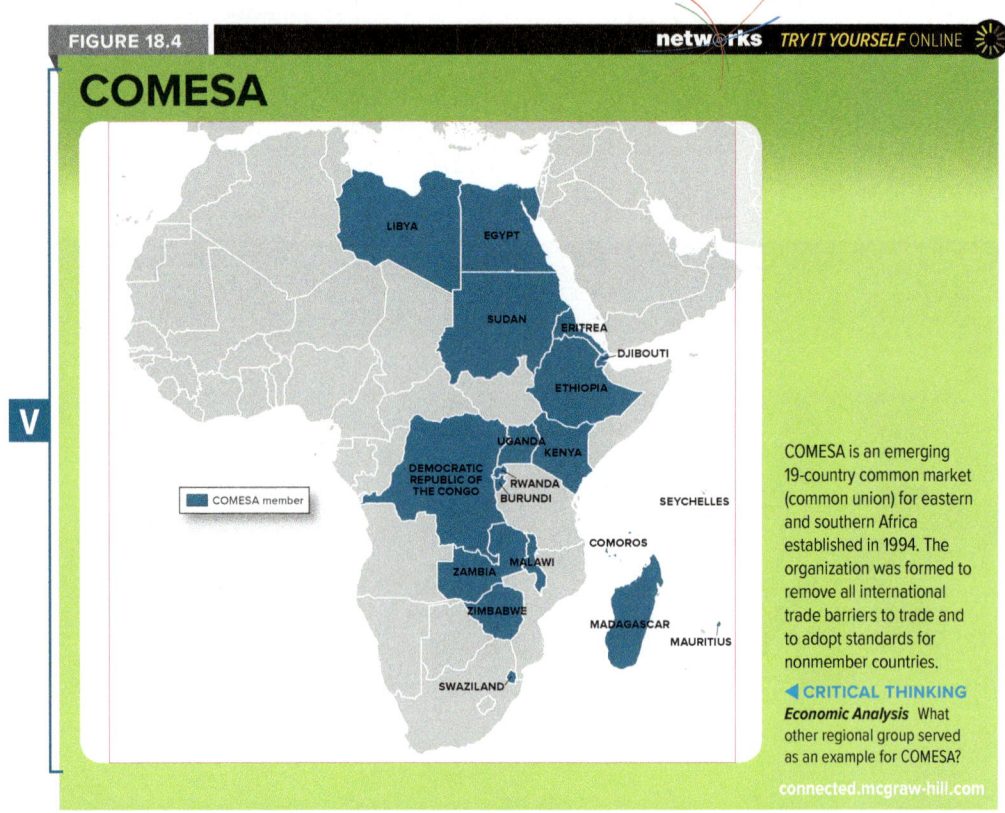

FIGURE 18.4
COMESA

COMESA is an emerging 19-country common market (common union) for eastern and southern Africa established in 1994. The organization was formed to remove all international trade barriers to trade and to adopt standards for nonmember countries.

◀ CRITICAL THINKING
Economic Analysis What other regional group served as an example for COMESA?

connected.mcgraw-hill.com

536

networks Online Teaching Options

MAP

COMESA

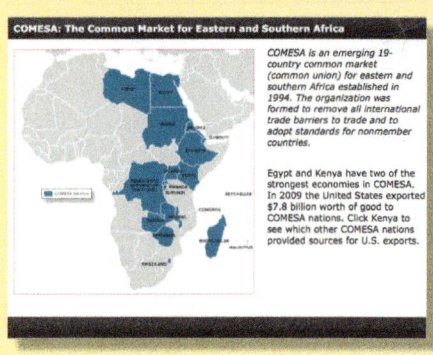

Analyzing a map of COMESA Display the COMESA interactive map and click through the onscreen text with students to explore how the COMESA nations are working to strengthen their internal network. Have students answer the question to ensure comprehension. Ask students to research the top COMESA exports to the United States. Assign one nation to each student. Have students display their findings in a poster or present a brief oral report, including visuals. **Visual/Spatial**

ANSWERS, p. 536

CRITICAL THINKING
The European Union (EU)

FIGURE 18.5

OPEC

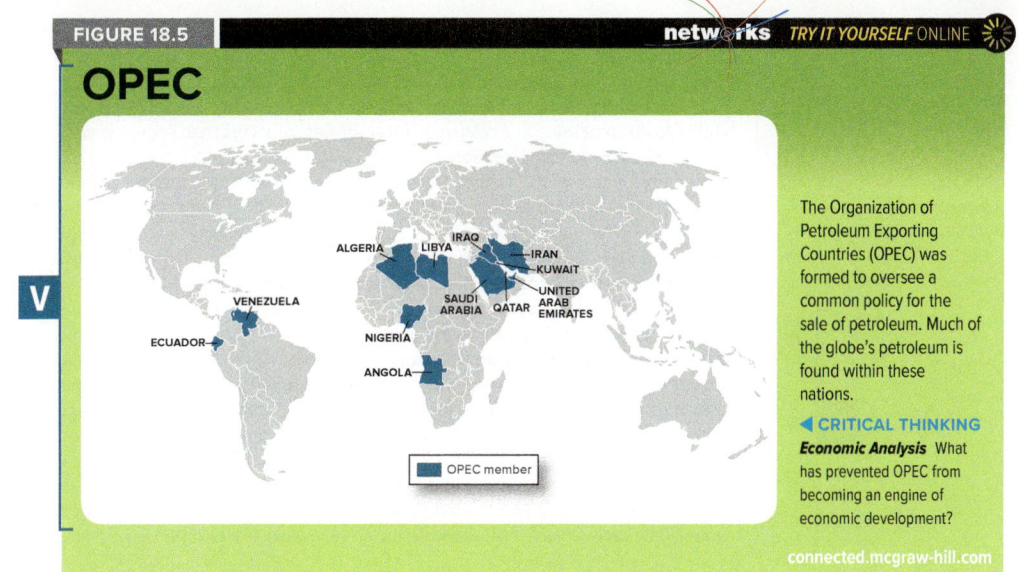

The Organization of Petroleum Exporting Countries (OPEC) was formed to oversee a common policy for the sale of petroleum. Much of the globe's petroleum is found within these nations.

◀ **CRITICAL THINKING**
Economic Analysis What has prevented OPEC from becoming an engine of economic development?

OPEC

In 1960, a number of oil-producing nations formed a **cartel**—a group of producers or sellers who agree to limit the production or sale of a product in order to control prices. The members of the **Organization of Petroleum Exporting Countries (OPEC)**, shown in **Figure 18.5**, tried to create the equivalent of a monopoly and push up world oil prices. While initially successful, higher oil prices have transferred trillions of dollars from industrialized nations to OPEC member countries.

Even with all this financial capital, most OPEC nations have grown slowly by most standards. In Iran, revolution interrupted the development of the domestic economy. In Nigeria, corruption siphoned off most of the oil profits that could have been used for economic development. High oil prices returned in 2006 and 2008, but were then battered down again by the Great Recession of 2008–2009. As a result, OPEC has generally failed to turn the oil cartel into an engine of economic development.

cartel group of sellers or producers acting together to raise prices by restricting availability of a product

Organization of Petroleum Exporting Countries (OPEC) organization formed to oversee a common policy for the sale of petroleum

☑ **READING PROGRESS CHECK**

Describing How do agreements for regional cooperation help member nations?

Globalization Trends

GUIDING QUESTION *Why is economic integration important in a global economy?*

As globalization continues, different trade blocs like free-trade areas and customs unions may merge into even larger global markets. This will have additional benefits, because economic cooperation among countries usually leads to increased political cooperation. Thus, globalization will likely enhance economic growth and political stability among all nations.

Even with continued globalization, however, two trends stand out. The first is the growing economic interdependence among nations. The second is growing regional economic integration around the world.

CHAPTER 18, LESSON 2
Globalization: Characteristics and Trends

V Visual Skills

Identifying members of OPEC Ask: **Which nations are members of OPEC?** (Algeria, Angola, Ecuador, Iran, Kuwait, Libya, Nigeria, Qatar, Saudi Arabia, United Arab Emirates, Venezuela) **Geographically speaking, how is OPEC different from the EU, ASEAN, and COMESA?** (OPEC nations are not all from the same geographic region.)

C Critical Thinking Skills

Speculating about OPEC member nations Ask: **Only three of the top ten oil producers are OPEC members. Why?** (Possible answers: The cartel does not have much power; other nations are OPEC's competitors; other nations are not politically friendly with OPEC nations.)

Content Background Knowledge

Oil Production The top ten oil-producing nations, in millions of barrels per day (2012):

1. Saudi Arabia (11.73)
2. United States (11.11)
3. Russia (10.40)
4. China (4.4)
5. Canada (3.9)
6. Iran (3.6)
7. United Arab Emirates (3.2)
8. Iraq (3.0)
9. Mexico (2.9)
10. Kuwait (2.8)

SOURCE: U.S. Energy Information Administration

MAP
OPEC

Analyzing a map of OPEC Have student pairs look up the word *cartel* in the dictionary. After writing down a definition of *cartel*, have them investigate the word's origin at etymonline.com or a similar Web site. Ask a volunteer to share the definition and etymology with the class. Explain to the class that a word's *connotation* is the feeling the word evokes, and ask for a show of hands from students who think *cartel* has a positive, a negative, or a neutral connotation. Discuss with students why the word tends to have such negative connotation in the United States. Display the OPEC interactive graphic and click through the onscreen text with students to explore how the OPEC nations are working to strengthen their internal network. Have students answer the question to ensure comprehension. **AL** **Visual/Spatial, Verbal/Linguistic**

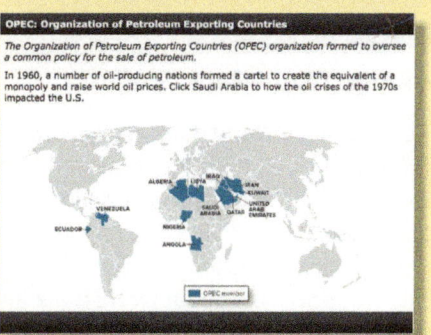

ANSWERS, p. 537

CRITICAL THINKING
Political instability

☑ **READING PROGRESS CHECK** The reduction of trade barriers increases trade among member nations.

CHAPTER 18, LESSON 2
Globalization: Characteristics and Trends

R Reading Skills

Previewing globalization trends Have students preview the Globalization Trends subsection by looking at headings and definitions. Then have them write a sentence describing what they expect to learn in the subsection.

V Visual Skills

Creating diagrams of interdependence Have students create a diagram that illustrates the interdependent nature of global trade involving industrialized countries like Japan and resource-rich countries like Saudi Arabia.

---

division of labor division of work into a number of separate tasks to be performed by different workers; same as specialization

context circumstances surrounding a situation or event

Growing Interdependence

As markets develop, producers become more specialized in their activities. Specialization and the **division of labor** lead to higher levels of productivity. If producers who perform a specialized task have a comparative advantage, or the ability to do something at a relatively lower opportunity cost than someone else, they will be able to compete more effectively in the market.

In the **context** of the family, this usually means that the strongest person handles those tasks that require the most strength. In a global context, the countries most effective at using capital and technology are the ones manufacturing products such as automobiles and construction equipment, which they then exchange for the raw materials of other nations.

The result is an incredible amount of interdependence. This means that we depend on others, and others depend on us, for almost everything we do. On a global scale, it allows a country such as Japan, which has almost no domestic energy resources, to become an advanced industrial nation. It also allows other countries with little manufacturing capacity, such as Saudi Arabia, to exchange their energy resources for a wide range of consumer and other manufactured goods.

The weakness of interdependence is the possibility that a breakdown anywhere in the global system could affect everyone. This is certainly a question that will be on everyone's mind as the progress toward globalization continues.

CAREERS | World Bank Staff

Is this career for you?

 Are you interested in working on global economic issues?

 Are you a self-starter and a problem solver?

 Are you good in math, finance, or economics?

 Are you willing to travel domestically or internationally?

Salary
Financial Analysts median pay: **$74,350**
$35.75 per hour

Job Growth Outlook
Faster than average

Profile of Work

As an organization, the goal of the World Bank is to end extreme poverty around the globe by encouraging the growth of income amongst the poorest people in countries around the world. But the World Bank cannot change the economic policies of individual nations, which is the responsibility of those national governments. So, the World Bank gathers financial and technical data that is then analyzed and evaluated to be offered to governments fighting to end poverty.

World Bank staffers may be asked to analyze a country's economic system, projecting costs for a water system in a remote village or the building of a modern landfill. There is no limit to the kind of projects overseen by the World Bank. Its staff possess a wide range of skills and education and a talent for identifying and creating roles for themselves.

---

networks Online Teaching Options

INTERACTIVE FEATURE

Career: World Bank Staff

Researching a World Bank staff member
Have students read the Profile of Work of a World Bank staff member. Then have students read and analyze Sanjay Pradhan's description of the current World Bank team. **Ask: What does the makeup of this group suggest about World Bank Institute values?** *(Possible answer: The World Bank Institute is a racially diverse organization that values diverse talents and passion for the many types of projects involved.)*

Will Globalization Continue?

Despite the growth and support for globalization, progress has not always been smooth. Change can be threatening to established ways of doing business. Clashes erupt when people fear that not just their jobs but their way of life is at risk. Problems can arise on a small scale when western companies such as McDonald's or KFC open a store in a scenic European location and people feel that the heritage of a location is being compromised. These problems can also happen when Walmart decides to place a new store in England, China, or any other country where it might force local "mom and pop" businesses to close.

Such problems are not only confined to the retail segments of an economy. These concerns apply to service industries as well. France has rules that protect domestic filmmakers by restricting the number of American movies that can be shown. Canada requires its radio stations to reserve a certain amount of airtime for music performed by Canadian artists.

Politics can also play a role in helping or hindering globalization. When nations get along well with one another, they are more likely to cooperate by forming free-trade areas or customs unions. If nations do not get along well, or if an international conflict should erupt, then the opposite result could occur. For example, a dispute with the United States over the future of Taiwan could interrupt China's globalization process. If this happens, trade will likely fall off between the two nations, dealing a severe blow to globalization.

Finally, some radical political organizations oppose the capitalism that drives globalization. Before World War I broke out in 1914, Russian revolutionaries known as Bolsheviks fought against capitalism. Now fundamentalist extremists such as al-Qaeda oppose globalization.

In short, while globalization can lead to great economic gains, these gains may not be equally important to everyone. Even a perceived threat to culture, politics, or religion can slow or halt the process of globalization.

✓ **READING PROGRESS CHECK**

Describing What characteristics show that the European Union is successful at regional integration?

LESSON 2 REVIEW

Reviewing Vocabulary
1. **Comparing and Contrasting** How are a free-trade area and a customs union alike and different?

Using Your Notes
Refer to this lesson's graphic organizer when answering the following question.
2. **Explaining** Name three global institutions and briefly describe how they each affect the global market.

Answering the Guiding Questions
3. **Defining** How would you define globalization?
4. **Explaining** How do agreements for regional cooperation help member nations?
5. **Identifying Cause and Effect** Why is economic integration important in a global economy?

Writing About Economics
6. **Argument** You hear two people arguing over an economic policy that promotes global production. One is strongly against it, arguing that it allows outsourcing of jobs. The other defends the policy because of its overall benefits for the economy. Present your view on global production and give reasons for your position.

CHAPTER 18, LESSON 2
Globalization: Characteristics and Trends

C Critical Thinking Skills

Identifying cause and effect Ask: **What is the relationship between globalization and interdependence?** *(Possible answer: Nations play to their strengths, specializing in different aspects of their shared market; nations become interdependent on each other to supply what they lack.)*

CLOSE & REFLECT

C Critical Thinking Skills

Summarizing Have students identify obstacles to world economic integration and suggest ways of resolving them.

LESSON 2 REVIEW ANSWERS

Reviewing Vocabulary
1. Both comprise countries that have agreed to reduce trade barriers. Members of a free-trade area group do not have a common tariff barrier for nonmembers, but members of a customs union do have uniform tariffs for nonmembers.

Using Your Notes
2. For example, WTO, IMF, UN, and World Bank. They help resolve disputes, reduce tariffs, administer trade agreements, provide loans and technical assistance, and otherwise promote international trade.

Answering the Guiding Questions
3. The movement toward a more integrated and interdependent world economy.
4. They open up markets within the member nations by reducing trade barriers and encouraging cooperation.
5. It allows nations and businesses to specialize, producing what they can produce most efficiently, which leads to global growth.

Writing About Economics
6. Students may take either position but should give facts and reasons for their position, using information provided in the lesson.

ANSWERS, p. 539

✓ **READING PROGRESS CHECK** common currency and movement of workers, capital, goods, and services

CHAPTER 18, LESSON 3
Global Problems and Economic Incentives

ENGAGE

C Critical Thinking Skills

Brainstorming scarcity Before students begin the lesson, ask them to brainstorm ways in which people experience scarcity on a personal level. Write their ideas on the board. **Ask: How do shortages on a personal level affect everyone in your community?** *(Possible answers: When jobs are scarce, people have less money to spend, so the local economy can become depressed. When water is scarce, local governments may restrict usage—for example, not allowing people to water their lawns or wash their cars.)* **How does scarcity on a local level affect the national economy?** *(Possible answer: If local or state economies are depressed, federal tax revenues decrease, causing a budget deficit that may necessitate cuts to federal programs.)* Lead students in a discussion of how national economic health, in turn, influences the global economy as well.

TEACH & ASSESS

R Reading Skills

Skimming text passages Students who have trouble reading a passage may benefit from skimming it before reading to develop a time frame for the events or ideas that are presented. Have students skim the subsection "Global Population Growth" for time markers such as "1798" and "from 1950 to 2050." Have them point out similar markers in other subsections. **ELL AL** Visual/Spatial

---

ANSWERS, p. 540

ESSENTIAL QUESTION ACTIVITY

Most students will recognize that the need for scarce resources causes people to overuse those available to them, causing environmental damage, such as deforestation and the use of controversial methods of extracting gas and oil. Students may suggest it is a global problem because many of these problems, such as air pollution, have far-reaching effects.

TAKING NOTES:
Renewable Resources: Natural resource that can be replenished for future use; Less harmful to the environment than the use of nonrenewable resources; Examples: Hydropower, biomass, solar power, wind power
Nonrenewable Resources: Resources that cannot be replenished once they are used; Source of most of the energy used today; Examples: coal, petroleum, natural gas, nuclear energy

540

Interact with these digital assets and others in lesson 3
- ✓ INTERACTIVE CHART
  Energy Flows in the United States
- ✓ POLITICAL CARTOON
  Sources of Energy
- ✓ SELF-CHECK QUIZ
- ✓ VIDEO

networks TRY IT YOURSELF ONLINE

LESSON 3
Global Problems and Economic Incentives

Reading Help Desk

Academic Vocabulary
- compounded
- successive

Content Vocabulary
- scarcity
- subsistence
- renewable resource
- hydropower
- biomass
- gasohol
- solar power
- nonrenewable resources
- glut
- pollution
- acid rain
- pollution permits

TAKING NOTES:

Key Ideas and Details
ACTIVITY Use a graphic organizer like the one below to identify the two types of resources economists generally recognize.

Renewable Resources	Nonrenewable Resources

ESSENTIAL QUESTIONS

Why is the economic health of all nations important in a global economy? What are the challenges associated with globalization?

C The fundamental economic problem of **scarcity**, the condition that results from not having enough resources to produce all of the things people would like to have, is always with us. We experience scarcity at the personal level, and we experience it at the national level—even in relatively prosperous nations such as the United States. At the global level, scarcity reveals itself through food, energy, and other resource shortages, all of which are **compounded** as world population grows.

As populations increase while countries try to grow their economies, yet another problem surfaces—how to use increasingly scarce resources without harming the environment. These two problems are closely connected at the national and global levels.

a. How does the scarcity of resources cause environmental damage? Give some examples.

b. Why is environmental damage a global problem?

Global Population Growth

R **GUIDING QUESTION** *How do economic incentives relate to population growth?*

Population growth has fascinated the world ever since Thomas Malthus published *An Essay on the Principle of Population* in 1798. His views, written over two hundred years ago, are still relevant today.

---

networks *Online Teaching Options*

BELLRINGER

Global Problems and Economic Incentives

Exploring issues Have students view the Bellringer. Discuss the conflicts between economic and environmental goals. **Ask: Why would wind turbines be effective in coastal areas? Why might some people oppose the turbines?** Verbal/Linguistic

Malthus: Views on Population

Thomas Malthus argued that a population would grow faster than its ability to feed itself. The problem, he stated, was that population tended to grow geometrically, as in the number sequence 1, 2, 4, 8, 16, 32, 64, and so on. The ability of the earth to feed its people, however, would grow at a slower and more constant rate, such as 1, 2, 3, 4, 5, and so on. Eventually, according to Malthus, the masses of the world would be reduced to a condition of **subsistence**—the state in which a population produces only enough to support itself.

Poverty is widespread in many developing countries. Whether in the African country of Somalia or the Indian city of Kolkata (Calcutta), thousands of street dwellers search for food in refuse piles by day and sleep in the streets at night. Similar conditions exist in other parts of the world. In these places, the Malthusian prediction of a subsistence standard of living is a cruel reality.

World Population Growth Rates

Despite the dire predictions, population growth appears to be slowing. **Figure 18.6** shows the estimated rate of world population growth from 1950 to 2050. According to the figure, population grew the fastest in the early 1960s, but the rate of growth has declined, or is expected to decline, steadily thereafter.

According to the U.S. Census Bureau, the world population is currently growing at slightly more than 1 percent per year and is expected to fall below 1 percent by 2017. If the world population keeps growing at the rates shown in the figure, it will reach 8 billion in 2026, and then hit 9 billion by 2042.

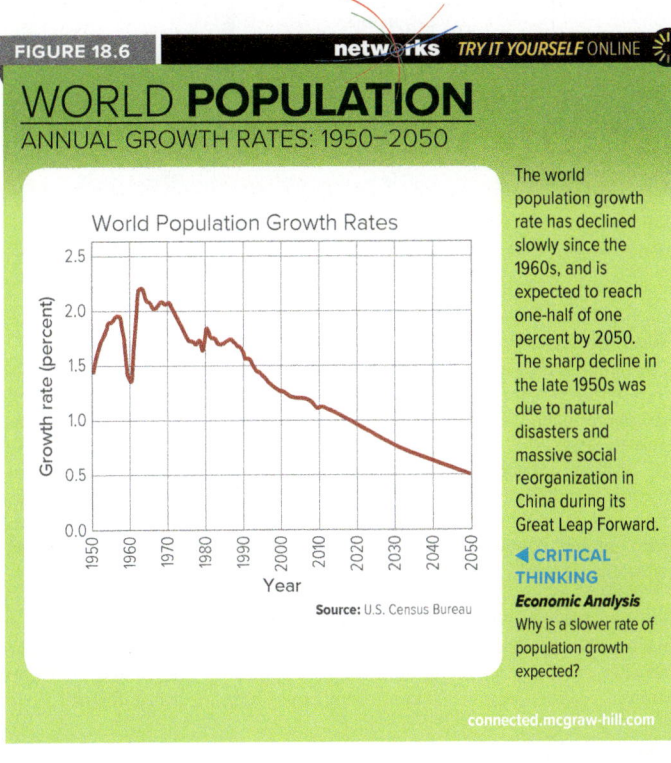

FIGURE 18.6

WORLD POPULATION
ANNUAL GROWTH RATES: 1950–2050

Source: U.S. Census Bureau

The world population growth rate has declined slowly since the 1960s, and is expected to reach one-half of one percent by 2050. The sharp decline in the late 1950s was due to natural disasters and massive social reorganization in China during its Great Leap Forward.

◄ **CRITICAL THINKING**
Economic Analysis
Why is a slower rate of population growth expected?

scarcity fundamental economic problem facing all societies that results from a combination of scarce resources and people's virtually unlimited wants

compounded increased, made worse

subsistence state in which a society produces barely enough to support itself

---

CHAPTER 18, LESSON 3
Global Problems and Economic Incentives

C Critical Thinking Skills

Relating population growth to scarcity Ask: **How does population growth affect world resources? How does this relate to the fundamental economic problem of scarcity?** *(As the human population grows, more people compete for the limited resources, sometimes fiercely. People have virtually unlimited wants with scarce resources.)* **AL**

W Writing Skills

Distinguishing between terms Have students write a paragraph explaining the difference between population and population growth rate. Ask them to make clear how the latter can be falling while the former is rising. **Verbal/Linguistic**

Making Connections

Considering the natural increase rate Explain to students that the natural increase rate for a place is calculated by subtracting the crude death rate from the crude birthrate. The crude death rate is similar to the crude birthrate in that it is the number of deaths per 1,000 people. The natural increase rate is given as a percentage rather than as a rate per thousand, however. The lower the natural increase rate, the more years it takes for that population to double. The higher the rate, the less time it takes for the population to double. Ask: **What would happen to your classroom or school if its population doubled tomorrow? Next year? In four years?** **Logical/Mathematical**

GRAPHS

World Population Growth Rates

Analyzing population growth rates Have students view Figure 18.6. Ask: **When did the population growth rate peak?** *(around 1962–1963)* **When will it be at its lowest?** *(2050)* **With the population growth rate dropping, why is the population still a concern?** *(Although the growth rate is slowing, the population is still growing, meaning there will be more people competing for limited resources.)* **Visual/Spatial**

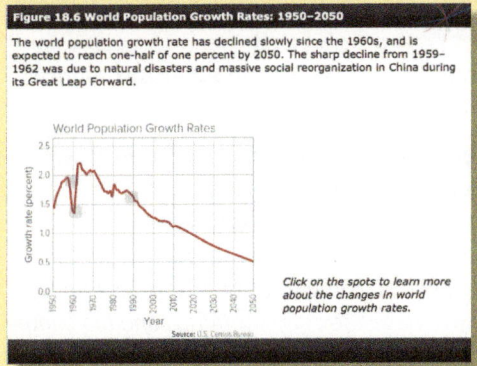

ANSWERS, p. 541

CRITICAL THINKING

Growth rates in developed countries are low and falling; economic incentives push people away from having children.

CHAPTER 18, LESSON 3
Global Problems and Economic Incentives

C Critical Thinking Skills

Recognizing regional similarities Have students compare the World Population Growth Rates map with a world atlas to name five countries that are growing the fastest and five that are losing population. Then ask students to speculate on what each group of countries has in common. *(Students may note that the countries losing population are located in Europe and are mostly developed nations, whereas those growing the fastest are in Africa or the Middle East.)* **Visual/Spatial**

W Writing Skills

Understanding population as a push factor of migration Have students write a paragraph explaining how population pressures are leading to increased emigration to developed countries. *(Explanations should note that rising populations in developing countries cause competition for resources and jobs, and lead people to seek these resources in richer countries.)* **Verbal/Linguistic**

FIGURE 18.7

WORLD POPULATION GROWTH RATES BY COUNTRY: 2013

Population Growth Rate, 2013
-10.88%   0%   13.51%
No data
SOURCE: U.S. Census Bureau, 2014

The world population growth rate has declined slowly since 1960. However, population growth varies from country to country. This map shows the growth rates by country in 2013.

▲ **CRITICAL THINKING**
Economic Analysis What might cause one country's growth rate to be so very different from another country's population growth rate?

connected.mcgraw-hill.com

Was Malthus Wrong?

Population is growing at different rates around the world. As **Figure 18.7** shows, industrialized nations have some of the lowest rates of population growth, while the poorer nations in the developing world tend to have the highest population growth rates.

Malthus did not foresee the enormous advances in productivity that allowed a rising standard of living to accompany a growing population. He also did not foresee that families might choose to have fewer children. This is especially true for a number of industrialized countries, including Japan, Russia, and Germany, which have shrinking populations.

Malthus's predictions may not have been entirely accurate for the industrialized countries, but they still have long-term consequences for all nations. Today, for example, population pressures in the developing world are causing problems for many industrialized countries. The United States, for example, is filled with illegal immigrants from China, Mexico, and Haiti.

542

---

networks Online Teaching Options

MAP

World Population Growth Rates By Country: 1970 and 2013

Identifying high and low population growth countries Display the map and have students read the onscreen text. **Ask: Where is the population growth rate the lowest?** *(Russia and much of Europe)* **Where is the population growth rate the highest?** *(Africa and the Middle East)* Allow students to work in small groups to discuss the Critical Thinking question before regrouping to discuss it as a class. **Visual/Spatial**

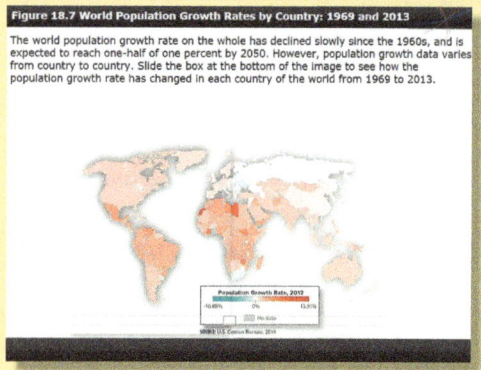

Figure 18.7 World Population Growth Rates by Country: 1969 and 2013
The world population growth rate on the whole has declined slowly since the 1960s, and is expected to reach one-half of one percent by 2050. However, population growth data varies from country to country. Slide the box at the bottom of the image to see how the population growth rate has changed in each country of the world from 1969 to 2013.

ANSWERS, p. 542

CRITICAL THINKING

Countries that are poorer tend to have higher population growth rates than industrialized nations.

Economic Incentives

Economic incentives play a role in population growth. For example, children are relatively expensive to raise in an industrialized country. Medical costs at birth, health insurance, larger homes, cars, and college expenses add to the cost of raising children. In addition, one parent bears a sizeable opportunity cost if he or she forgoes a career while staying home to raise the children.

If a family wants to minimize these costs, as they might other costs, part of the answer is to have fewer children.

The opposite happens in the developing world because children there are regarded as an asset. Medical expenses are minimal or nonexistent, insurance is rare, homes are often shared, and cars and college educations are seldom available. Even young children are likely to help with housework or farm work.

Since developing countries do not have retirement programs like Social Security, parents tend to have large families in hopes that some of the children will care for them in their old age.

The result is predictable. If children are an asset to the family rather than a cost, then parents will try to have as many children as they can. This explains the high rate of population growth in developing countries and the declining—or negative—rate of population growth in the developed world.

✓ **READING PROGRESS CHECK**

Explaining Why might Malthus have been wrong in his predictions?

The Demand for Productive Resources

GUIDING QUESTION Why is it important to conserve nonrenewable resources?

Population pressures add to the depletion of many important resources. Some of these resources are in the form of raw materials, minerals, arable land, and energy. Energy is especially important because it is necessary for the production of the technological goods that make our lives more comfortable.

Renewable Resources

Economists recognize two general types of resources, renewable and nonrenewable. The **renewable resource** is a natural resource that can be replenished for future use. Four main sources of renewable resources are used today.

renewable resource natural resource that can be replenished for future use

RENEWABLE RESOURCES: ALTERNATIVES TO FOSSIL FUELS

Renewable resources, natural resources that can be replenished for future use, are increasingly used as alternatives to fossil fuels because they will not run out, and because they have less of a harmful impact on the environment.

◄ **CRITICAL THINKING**
How might the government encourage the use of renewable resources for businesses?

CHAPTER 18, LESSON 3
Global Problems and Economic Incentives

W Writing Skills

Applying incentives to high/low population growth Have students draw charts that show the effects of incentives and disincentives on the decision to have children in developed and developing nations.
Visual/Spatial

R Reading Skills

Using word parts Have students identify the prefix *(re-)* and suffix *(-able)* used in the term *renewable*. Have them give the meanings of each *(again; ability to be or do something)* and name other words they know that use *re-* or *-able*. **ELL** **Verbal/Linguistic**

SLIDE SHOW

Renewable Resources: Alternatives to Fossil Fuels

Analyzing renewable resources Have students view the slide show and read the text that accompanies each image. Remind students of the previous interactive graphic, which showed renewable energy accounting for a little under 6% of the U.S. energy supply. **Ask: Which renewable resource has been used for the longest time?** *(hydropower)* **Which renewable resource is most limited?** *(biomass)* Conclude the activity by discussing whether economic incentives used for businesses should be used to encourage residential use of renewable resources. **Visual/Spatial, Interpersonal**

ANSWERS, p. 543

✓ **READING PROGRESS CHECK** He did not anticipate the enormous increase in productivity, and he did not expect families to choose to have fewer children.

CRITICAL THINKING
Students' answers will vary, but may include the idea that economic incentives usually encourage businesses to adopt new practices.

CHAPTER 18, LESSON 3
Global Problems and Economic Incentives

W Writing Skills

Arguing a point of view Have students write a letter to the editor of your local newspaper or online news media outlet supporting government funding for research in one of the renewable sources of energy discussed in this section. Have them do research as necessary to support their recommendations. Remind students to evaluate the validity of their sources for frame of reference, and to cite their sources. Ask volunteers who support several different energy sources to share their letters with the class. **Verbal/Linguistic**

C Critical Thinking Skills

Evaluating power sources Point out that nuclear power has been much in the news lately as an alternative to fossil fuels, especially in the discussion of how to reduce greenhouse gases that contribute to global warming. **Ask: Do you think the risks of nuclear power should be reevaluated due to the need to reduce emissions that cause climate change? Are these risks more manageable now, considering what we know about the risks of continuing to burn fossil fuels?** *(Answers will vary but should be logical and supported by facts.)*

---

hydropower power or energy generated by moving water

biomass energy made from wood, peat, municipal solid waste, straw, corn, tires, landfill gasses, fish oils, and other waste

gasohol mixture of 90 percent unleaded gasoline and 10 percent grain alcohol

solar power energy harnessed from the sun

- **Hydropower**—The most important renewable resource today is **hydropower**, power or energy generated by moving water. Hydropower dates from the 1800s when it propelled mills and factories in the Northeast. The power was reliable, abundant, and free. Today, many countries are trying to harness the power of moving water found in ocean waves and tides.
- **Biomass**—**Biomass** is biological material derived from living, or recently living, organisms such as wood and wood waste, peat, municipal solid waste, straw, corn, tires, landfill gases, and fish oils. Ethanol, grain alcohol that is made from corn or other crops, is used to make **gasohol**—a fuel that is a mixture of 90 percent unleaded gasoline and 10 percent ethanol. Since 1998, some American cars have also been designed to run on E85, a mixture of 85 percent ethanol and 15 percent gasoline.
- **Solar Power**—An important source of renewable energy is **solar power**, or energy that is harnessed from the sun. Solar power is relatively new and did not get much attention when the price of oil was low. While it holds much promise, it accounts for only a fraction of the renewable energy used today.
- **Wind Power**—Another growing source of renewable energy is wind-generated electricity. Since the early 1980s, wind farms have been producing enough electricity to power a medium-sized city. California is the largest producer of wind-generated energy, but wind farms can be found in many other states as well.

Nonrenewable Resources

nonrenewable resources resources that cannot be replenished once they are used

Most of the energy we use today comes from **nonrenewable resources**—resources that cannot be replenished once they are used. The major nonrenewable resource category—fossil fuels—is being consumed at an alarming rate, and at current consumption levels may only last for a few more generations.

- **Coal**—Coal was the first nonrenewable fuel to be used on a large scale. It was easy to acquire and is both inexpensive and plentiful. Nearly two-thirds of the world's known coal deposits are in the United States, Russia, and China, with reserves estimated to last about two hundred years.
- **Petroleum**—Oil is the biggest nonrenewable energy source in use today, primarily because it was so inexpensive during much of the 1900s. Petroleum-based products like gasoline are much more convenient to use than natural gas or coal, especially when used for transportation.
- **Natural Gas**—Historically, natural gas was more difficult to transport and use than oil, so it did not become an important energy source until much later. Eventually, inexpensive natural gas became popular as an industrial fuel, so many factories and industrial sites were built to use it.
- **Nuclear Energy**—Nuclear energy is the newest and most powerful source of nonrenewable energy in the United States. The growth of nuclear power has been slowed, however, for a number of reasons. Cost is one, as nuclear reactors are expensive to build and maintain. Second, nuclear energy produces highly hazardous by-products, which are difficult to dispose of safely. Finally, there is always a chance that a nuclear plant will fail, or that an accident would happen. High-profile events such as the 1979 near-meltdown at Three Mile Island in Pennsylvania, the 1986 meltdown of the Chernobyl reactor in the Ukraine, and the failure of Japan's Fukushima power plant when it was hit by an earthquake and tsunami in 2011 serve as constant reminders of the possible dangers of

544

---

networks *Online Teaching Options*

WORKSHEET

Reinforcing Economic Skills

Interpreting graphs and diagrams Students will analyze a diagram of the different costs that make up the price of gasoline in the U.S. and a graph of projected global energy demand, and then speculate about how developing countries may affect the global energy supply.

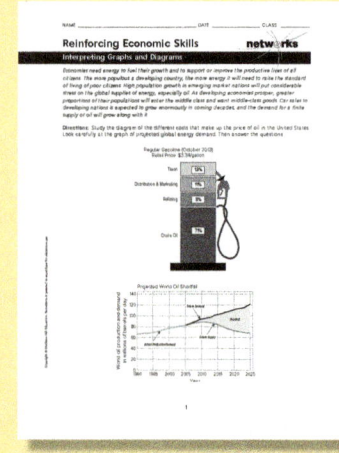

544

nuclear power. These are daunting problems, but safety issues need to be addressed before nuclear power becomes more widespread.

Energy Flows in the United States

Figure 18.8 shows the sources and uses of energy in the United States. Most of the energy we produce, or 78.1 percent, is in the form of coal, natural gas, crude oil, liquid gas, nuclear power, and renewable energy sources. Some of the domestic production, or 10.4 percent, is exported. The remaining 29.6 percent is imported from abroad, mostly in the form of petroleum.

The figure also shows that industry is the biggest domestic consumer of energy, followed by transportation, residential, and commercial needs. Petroleum is again the biggest component of the energy we consume, with only a relatively small component coming from nuclear power and renewable energy resources.

Nonmarket Conservation Efforts

With resources becoming increasingly scarce, efforts are underway to find the best ways to use and preserve them. One way is to appeal to everyone's sense of civic responsibility. For example, in the case of energy, we could ask people to drive their automobiles less, to turn off the lights when they leave a room, or to adjust thermostats when they are not at home.

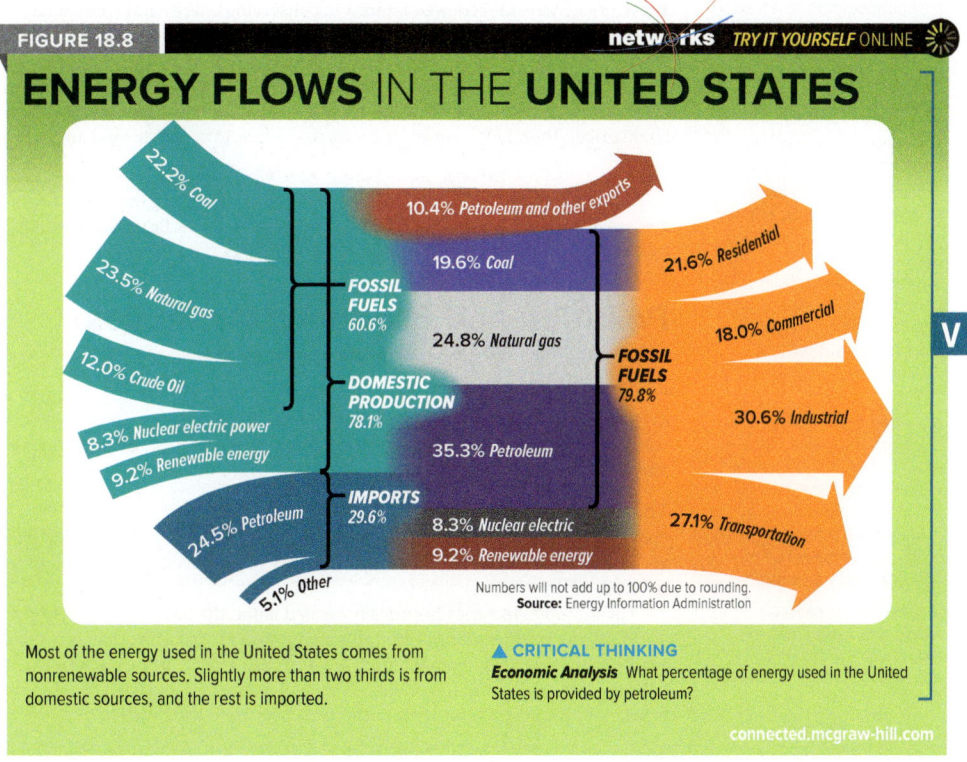

FIGURE 18.8

ENERGY FLOWS IN THE UNITED STATES

Numbers will not add up to 100% due to rounding.
Source: Energy Information Administration

Most of the energy used in the United States comes from nonrenewable sources. Slightly more than two thirds is from domestic sources, and the rest is imported.

▲ **CRITICAL THINKING**
Economic Analysis What percentage of energy used in the United States is provided by petroleum?

CHAPTER 18, LESSON 3
Global Problems and Economic Incentives

C Critical Thinking Skills

Developing alternative energy Have students work in teams to create posters or storyboards that describe a new energy source. Ask them to include diagrams that show how the new energy source will be developed, distributed, and beneficial to the global environment. Explain that the energy sources may be real or fictional, such as harnessing the power of ocean waves or moonlight, for example, or requiring all classroom desks to incorporate treadmills connected to generators. Have teams share their ideas. **Kinesthetic**

V Visual Skills

Analyzing energy flows Refer students to the right side of the chart in the Energy Flows in the United States graphic. **Ask:** *In which of the four sectors do you think the United States could most easily reduce its energy use? Why? (Answers will vary, but students should be able to provide data to support their views.)* **Visual/Spatial**

GRAPHS

Energy Flows in the United States

Evaluating energy use in the United States
Have students study Figure 18.8. **Ask:** *What does the left side of the graphic show? (percentage of the U.S. energy consumption by source) What does the right side of the graphic show? (where energy is used in the United States)* Tell students to click on the energy sources in the central part of the graphic to read the captions. Include in the class discussion students' predictions of how these percentages may change in the future as nonrenewable sources become more scarce. **Visual/Spatial**

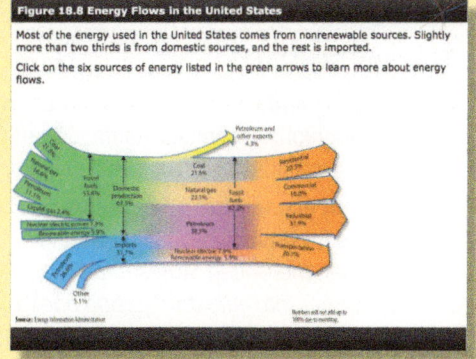

ANSWERS, p. 545
CRITICAL THINKING
35.3 percent

CHAPTER 18, LESSON 3
Global Problems and Economic Incentives

Content Background Knowledge

Thomas Malthus Thomas Malthus, the pioneer of modern population study, was born in England in 1766. At age 18, he became a student at Cambridge University and studied mathematics and classical languages. While at the university, he wrote letters to his father. One subject they discussed was the optimistic view, then popular, that a future of peace, prosperity, and equality awaited the world. Malthus disagreed and wrote his father a 50,000-word letter arguing against this utopian vision. His father was so impressed with his son's reasoning that he encouraged him to publish his ideas. The resulting book was *An Essay on the Principle of Population As It Affects the Future Improvement of Society*. This book changed forever the way people would think about population. Its gloomy predictions led Malthus himself to call economics "the dismal science," a label it has retained ever since.

R Reading Skills

Relating oil prices to energy alternatives Ask: **How have supply and demand influenced the price of oil and the interest in developing energy alternatives?** *(When oil prices have been high, oil producers increase supply, but people use less and have more interest in finding alternatives. When prices are low, people use more oil, production and exploration fall, and there is less interest in finding alternatives.)*

ANSWERS, p. 546

✓ READING PROGRESS CHECK Many factories and cars are built to run on fossil fuels. We have large reserves of these fuels, and renewable sources tend to be expensive.

CRITICAL THINKING
Population pressures and food shortages are important issues in many parts of the world.

BIOGRAPHY

Thomas Malthus
ECONOMIST (1766–1834)

Thomas Malthus, an English economist, gathered statistics on births, deaths, and life spans, among other demographic data. This focus led him to consider the relationship between population growth and growth of the food supply. He observed, "I had for some time been aware that population and food increased in different ratios; and a vague opinion had been floating in my mind that they could only be kept equal by some species of misery or vice." R

Malthus believed that food production could never keep up with population growth. He was convinced, however, that people would not starve or die off, because they would contain population growth through measures such as delaying marriage and through warfare or disease.

Apart from his careful investigation into population growth, Malthus did important early work on demand curves and the relationship between long-term and short-term trends, which he believed were influenced by cyclical events.

▲ **CRITICAL THINKING**
Making Connections Why does Malthus's work continue to have meaning for the study of economics today?

Such measures have been tried, but generally they fail to work. Even the 55-mile-per-hour speed limit, which was instituted to conserve gasoline, did not work. Not only did drivers routinely ignore the law, most individual states eventually repealed the lower speed limits.

Markets and Price Incentives

People seem to be much more responsive to changes in prices. When oil was cheaper before 1973, few countries were willing to devote large resources to retrieving it. In 1973, however, the OPEC oil embargo dramatically raised the price of oil. When the price increased sharply, many countries increased their production almost overnight. At the same time, interest in alternative energy sources soared, and countries poured billions into energy-research projects ranging from shale oil to solar power.

By 1981, oil prices had dropped considerably because of a worldwide **glut**—a substantial oversupply—of oil. At the same time, a worldwide recession and efforts at energy conservation further reduced the demand for oil. Oil prices were then kept low after the first Gulf War in the early 1990s because some OPEC members increased production to replenish their financial reserves, which had been depleted during the war.

Lower oil prices had several consequences. First, the search for alternative energy sources began to wane. Second, the exploration for new oil reserves slowed dramatically. Third, consumers changed their spending habits again, buying large houses and low-mileage SUVs. Increasing demand caught up with stable supply, and energy prices peaked first in 2006 and then again in 2008. These price increases renewed interest in conserving energy and stimulated the development of alternative energy sources and new products such as hybrid and all-electric cars.

In the end, the price system that encourages people to conserve energy when oil prices are high does exactly the opposite when oil prices go down. High prices thus help conserve resources, while low prices tend to do the opposite.

✓ READING PROGRESS CHECK

Analyzing Why is the percentage of renewable energy sources in the United States relatively low?

Pollution and Economic Incentives

GUIDING QUESTION What measures can be taken to control pollution?

Economic incentives can help solve the global problem of pollution. **Pollution** is the contamination of air, water, or soil by the discharge of a poisonous or noxious substance. Most economists argue that the best way to attack the problem is to attack the incentives that caused pollution in the first place.

The Incentive to Pollute

Pollution does not occur on its own: it occurs because people and firms have an incentive to pollute. If that incentive can be removed, pollution will be reduced.

For example, factories historically located along the banks of rivers so they could discharge their refuse into the moving waters. Factories that generated smoke and other air pollutants often were located farther from the water with tall smokestacks to send the pollutants long distances. Others tried to avoid the problem by digging pits on their property to bury their toxic wastes.

546

---

networks Online Teaching Options

BIOGRAPHY

Thomas Malthus

Analyzing the impact of Thomas Malthus Have students read the biography of Thomas Malthus. Then divide students into groups to discuss these questions:

• **What great economical change took place during Malthus's lifetime?** *(The Industrial Revolution transformed the United States and Europe from agrarian, rural societies into industrial, urban ones.)*

• **To what "misery or vice" might Malthus have been referring?** *(Possible answers: disease, wars, overpopulation)*

• **Did Malthus's predictions influence behavior?** *(Possible answers: Yes, governments took heed and looked for ways to slow population growth and increase food production. No, the population and food production trends occurred naturally.)*

Have groups share their ideas and conclusions. **Verbal/Linguistic**

In all three situations, factory owners were trying to lower production costs by using the environment as a giant waste-disposal system. From a narrow viewpoint, the reasoning was sound. Firms increased their profits when they lowered production costs. Those who produced the most at the least cost made the most profits.

The cost of pollution to society as a whole, however, is enormous. For example, **acid rain**—a mixture of water and sulfur dioxide that makes a mild form of sulfuric acid—falls over much of North America, damaging forests and rivers. Fertilizer buildup and raw sewage runoff poison ecosystems in other areas. The damage caused by pollution is extensive, but it can be controlled. One way is through government standards passed by law. Another way is through economic incentives.

Legislated Standards

Legislated standards include laws that specify the minimum levels of purity for air, water, and auto emissions. These government standards can be effective, but they are generally inflexible. Once a standard is set, a firm has to meet it or be penalized. Because of this, many firms lobby extensively to exempt their industry from pollution-control standards.

Congress has declared that all automobiles sold in the United States cannot exceed certain maximum emission standards. Once these standards have been set, the Environmental Protection Agency (EPA) tests random vehicles in every model line of cars. It also samples random cars on the road to ensure that they adhere to the emission controls.

Another pollution-control program was the Superfund that Congress established in 1980 to identify and clean up some of the most hazardous waste sites in the country. The intent was to track down the original polluters and make them pay for the cleanup. When it was discovered that many of the original polluters had gone out of business and could not be forced to pay, the law was amended to force existing businesses to help with the cleanup costs. This was not popular with businesses because some firms were forced to pay for the cleanup of wastes that others left behind.

glut substantial oversupply of a product

pollution contamination of air, water, or soil by the discharge of a poisonous or noxious substance

acid rain pollution in the form of rainwater mixed with sulfur dioxide to form a mild form of sulfuric acid

SOURCES OF ENERGY

This cartoon shows how the perception of economic progress has changed over time.

◀ **CRITICAL THINKING**
Recognizing Counter Arguments In what ways could the man on the left argue that economic progress is best served by using coal instead of developing renewable sources of energy?

CHAPTER 18, LESSON 3
Global Problems and Economic Incentives

C Critical Thinking Skills

Expressing views about pollution Discuss instances of pollution that students have seen or read about, ideas they have for preventing or cleaning up pollution, and any other aspects of the topic that occur to students. Then have students write a journal entry that describes their ideas.

Content Background Knowledge

Union Carbide Gas Tragedy in Bhopal, India Many multinational companies locate in developing countries because they can hire workers and buy land more cheaply, evade pollution and safety standards, and sometimes employ children. This can be a recipe for disaster, as was the case of the Union Carbide factory in Bhopal, India. In 1984, the factory was producing pesticides by a process that was forbidden in other countries. Toxic gases escaped, killing between 3,000 and 8,000 people, and injuring many thousands more.

R Reading Skills

Exploring solutions for pollution prevention To help students understand the material in the subsection on pollution and economic incentives, have them create word webs for each of these three ways of controlling pollution: *legislated standards, pollution fees,* and *pollution permits*. Have students evaluate each method and then contribute their ideas to a class web on the board.

POLITICAL CARTOON

Sources of Energy

Identifying perceptions of energy use Ask: **What do the two men represent?** *(a peasant/farmer and an industrialist)* **Why does the industrialist encourage the farmer to use coal?** *(Coal is a cheap, plentiful resource that has helped the nation industrialize and make the industrialist rich.)* Discuss with students whether this is a fair characterization of 20th century attitudes toward energy. Ask: **How have the conditions of the two men changed in the second panel?** *(The farmer is now prosperous while the industrialist is poor.)* **Why have their positions reversed?** *(Coal is no longer as popular; renewable energy sources are presented as the wave of the future.)* Remind students that this cartoon represents the perspective of industrialized nations, and that they should consider how developing nations may hold a different perspective on renewable energy sources. **Visual/Spatial**

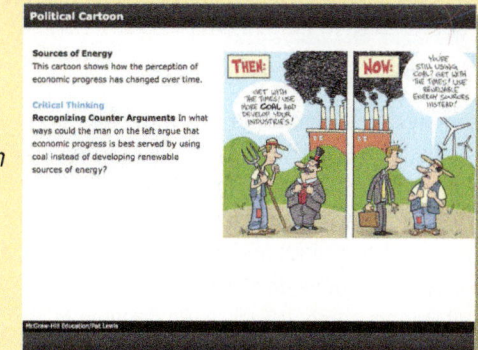

ANSWERS, p. 547

CRITICAL THINKING
Student answers will vary. One answer is that, in many developing nations, coal is cheaper and easier to use than renewable sources of energy. The technology is well-established and readily available. As such, it can lead to faster increases in the standard of living for people in those nations than a conversion to renewable sources, many of which require significant up-front investments in new technologies.

CHAPTER 18, LESSON 3
Global Problems and Economic Incentives

R Reading Skills

Making inferences about pollution fees Ask: **Why might a company want to pay a fee on some pollution it causes but choose to clean up another kind of pollution?** *(For each type of company, some types of pollution disposal are easier and more cost-effective to clean up than others. The company would perform cost and benefit calculations for each type of pollution and choose the more cost-effective solution for each.)*

C1 Critical Thinking Skills

Opposing pollution fees Ask: **Why might a supporter of strong environmental regulation oppose pollution fees?** *(He or she might feel that the fees do not eliminate pollution, but just reduce it. The fees allow companies to continue to pollute if they are willing to pay money to do so.)*

C2 Critical Thinking Skills

Understanding pollution permits Ask: **How do pollution permits limit pollution through supply and demand?** *(Because the supply of permits is limited, their price will rise as they become more scarce. When the price is higher than the cost of eliminating the pollution, companies will choose the cheaper alternative.)*

ANSWERS, p. 548

ESSENTIAL QUESTION ACTIVITY

Students should understand that reducing pollution is a costly enterprise, one that poorer countries can least afford. But because environmental degradation in one country can have global repercussions, it is in the interest of wealthy nations to help poorer countries find solutions.

Pollution Fees

A more market-based approach is to tax or charge firms in proportion to the amount of pollutants they release. Depending on the industry, the size of the tax would depend on the severity of the pollution and the quantity of toxic substances being released. A firm can then either pay the fees or take steps to reduce the pollution.

For example, suppose a community wants to reduce air pollution caused by four factories, each of which releases large quantities of coal dust. A $50 tax on every ton of coal dust released into the air might be applied to each factory. Devices attached to the top of the factory's smokestacks would measure the amount of dust released during a given period, and the factory would be billed accordingly.

Under these conditions, some firms might choose to pay the $50 tax. Others, however, might decide to spend $10, $20, or $30 to clean up a ton of pollution. As long as it is cheaper to clean up the pollution than to pay the tax, individual firms will have the incentive to clean up and stop polluting.

This tax approach does not try to remove all of the pollution, but it can remove a significant amount. In addition, it provides flexibility that legislated standards lack by giving individual firms freedom of choice.

Real-world examples of pollution fees are more complicated than this hypothetical example, but they all work the same way. In addition, firms that pay the tax also help defray some of the costs of the program, which is a relief to taxpayers.

EXPLORING THE ESSENTIAL QUESTION

While most highly industrialized countries are making progress in reducing pollution, much less is being accomplished in developing countries. In fact, those that are in early stages of industrialization are almost entirely dependent upon nonrenewables and rank among some of the world's heaviest polluters, China being an example. Why are developing nations so far behind? Why is it in the interest of wealthy countries to help them develop?

Tradeable Pollution Permits

pollution permits federal permit allowing a public utility to release pollutants into the air; a form of pollution control

An expanded version of pollution fees is the EPA's use of **pollution permits**—federal permits allowing public utilities to release specific amounts of emissions into the air—to reduce sulfur dioxide emissions at coal-burning electric utilities that contribute to the problem of acid rain.

Under this program, the EPA awards a limited number of permits to all utilities. If reducing or cleaning up one ton of emissions costs a utility $300, and if it can sell a permit for $350, the firm will decrease its own emissions and sell the unused permit to another utility whose cleanup or reduction costs are higher. If removing a ton of pollutants would cost the second utility $400, then that company would be better off buying the permit for $350 from the first utility. In either case, one of the utilities has the incentive to clean up a ton of pollutants.

If the level of pollutants is still too high, the EPA can distribute fewer permits. A smaller number of permits will make each one worth more than before, which will again cause firms to redouble their efforts to reduce pollution. In the end, the market forces of supply and demand will provide the encouragement to reduce pollution.

The first set of pollution permits went on sale in March 1993 at the Chicago Board of Trade. The one-ton permits brought prices ranging from $122 to $450.

548

---

networks Online Teaching Options

VIDEO | WORKSHEET

Air Pollution in the U.S.A.

Analyzing air pollution Show the Air Pollution in the U.S.A. video, and guide students in discussing the problem of air pollution and the measures the government is taking to control and reduce it. Have students choose an artistic medium to illuminate some aspect of the problem of air pollution in the United States. Examples include a monologue, dialogue, or play about the effects of air pollution on individuals or communities; a poem or short story; or a mural, collage, video, or other visual.
Visual/Spatial

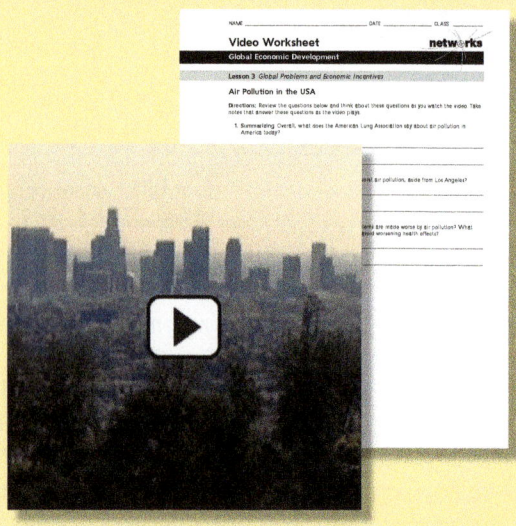

548

The EPA then planned to issue additional, but fewer, permits in **successive** years in an effort to make them scarcer and more expensive. A variation of this is called "cap and trade"—where the cap is the maximum pollution allowed at any one utility and the unused permits can be "traded" or sold. Ultimately, higher prices for the permits will give more utilities the incentive to spend larger amounts of money on antipollution devices.

The system also has advantages for environmentalists who want utilities to reduce pollution at even faster rates. Several environmental groups have purchased pollution permits with their own funds, making them scarcer and therefore more expensive for the utilities.

successive consecutive

Coping with the Future

Everyone wants to know what will happen to the economy in the future. How will it adjust and what course will it take? The answer depends on the type of economic system we have today.

Fortunately, most of the major economies in the world have a healthy mix of relatively free market capitalism. The price system is an important part of the system because prices act as signals to both producers and consumers. If an unforeseen event should occur, the economy has the ability to adjust to change gradually, without having to lurch from one crisis to the next.

Capitalism has evolved over the years, and it shows every sign of continuing to do so in the future. In this regard, capitalism will adjust to change the same way a market adjusts to small changes in supply and demand—incrementally with adjustments so small that they are hardly noticed.

Globalization is one of the more significant events in your lifetime, and it too is happening incrementally, at a pace so subtle that most people are hardly aware that change is taking place. Globalization is also taking place because of the voluntary decisions that millions of people are making independently, decisions that people make because they feel that they will be better off for having made them. So, the next time you buy clothing made in Indonesia, or chocolate from a Swiss-owned company, or even an automobile made by a South Korean manufacturer, just remember that the decisions you make are helping to further the process and inroads of globalization.

✓ **READING PROGRESS CHECK**

Summarizing In which ways can governments control pollution?

LESSON 3 REVIEW

Reviewing Vocabulary
1. *Explaining* In what way is gasohol a biomass resource?

Using Your Notes
2. *Evaluating* What are the two most effective solutions to problems of scarcity?

Answering the Guiding Questions
3. *Explaining* How do economic incentives relate to population growth?
4. *Explaining* Why is it important to conserve nonrenewable resources?

5. *Specifying* What measures can be taken to control pollution?

Writing About Economics
6. *Argument* Should the federal or state governments do more to control pollution or to encourage greater use and more development of alternative energy sources? Why or why not? Give facts, reasons, and other details.

CHAPTER 18, LESSON 3
Global Problems and Economic Incentives

CLOSE & REFLECT

C Critical Thinking Skills

Evaluating economic responsibilities Have students discuss, from both economic and environmental perspectives, the responsibilities businesses have toward the planet.

ANSWERS, p. 549

✓ **READING PROGRESS CHECK** Legislative standards, pollution fees, tradable pollution permits

---

LESSON 3 REVIEW ANSWERS

Reviewing Vocabulary
1. Gasohol is 10 percent ethanol, which is grain made from corn or other crops.

Using Your Notes
2. Market and price incentives, and government regulations and taxes

Answering the Guiding Questions
3. The cost of raising children induces many people in developed nations to have fewer children, and the value of having children in developing countries induces many people to have more.

4. Present consumption levels cannot be continued because the supply of nonrenewables will be depleted and cannot be replaced.

5. The government can pass laws and regulations establishing pollution standards, assess taxes and fees, and sell tradable pollution permits.

Writing About Economics
6. Students may agree or disagree with the role government should play in controlling pollution or in encouraging use of alternative energy, but they should provide facts and details to support their opinions.

CHAPTER 18
Debate

ENGAGE

C1 Critical Thinking Skills

Expressing opinions Millions of people worldwide live on less than $1.25 per day. UNICEF states that individuals can save a child's life with just 50 cents a day. Initiate a class discussion about extreme poverty in developing nations. **Ask:**

- What are the problems the world's poor face?
- What can we do to help them?
- Is sending money the solution?
- Is it our moral duty to help?
- Do we better the situation by providing aid, or does that make things worse?

Remind students of the obstacles to economic growth and ways international organizations can help fund economic development (discussed in Lesson 1). Have students share their ideas in a class discussion. **Verbal/Linguistic, Interpersonal**

TEACH & ASSESS

C2 Critical Thinking Skills

Analyzing arguments After reading the quotation by President Obama, review the bulleted list of Yes arguments. **Ask: Which two arguments in favor of foreign aid are reflected in the quote from President Obama?** *(poverty breeds instability and terrorism that spills across borders; trade with prosperous nations helps our own economy grow)*

C3 Critical Thinking Skills

Constructing arguments Organize students into three groups. Assign two groups the Yes or No position on the following proposition: *Wealthy nations should aid in the development of poor nations.* Instruct the two groups to review the relevant content from the text regarding their assigned positions. Encourage group members to conduct additional research to strengthen their arguments in preparation for the debate. Have the third group act as moderators for the debate. Tell these students to study the important issues related to foreign aid and prepare a series of debate questions that address the topic. When students have completed their preparations, carry out the debate by having the group of moderators take turns asking questions of the other two groups. Assign specific amounts of time for groups to respond to the questions, as well as to offer rebuttals to the opposing teams' responses. Have the moderators declare a winner and explain how they arrived at their decision. **Visual/Spatial**

550

Debates

C1 Are the world's wealthiest nations obligated to aid in the economic development of poor nations?

There is a wide gap between the rich nations of the world and the poorest. Many around the world remain impoverished. They need clean drinking water, sufficient food, medicines and health care, and education. Some governments lack the resources to provide many of the basic necessities of their people.

C3
Most of the wealthy nations of the world have felt the obligation to try to improve these conditions and have given much aid to improve economic conditions in poor countries. In some cases, the aid appears to have been worth it, but in many others, little seems to change despite economic aid.

So a debate arises. Do wealthy nations have a continuing obligation to provide aid to these countries?

YES Wealthy nations should aid in the development of poor nations because . . .

- WE HAVE A **MORAL OBLIGATION** TO **HELP** POORER NATIONS
- WE NEED THE **RESOURCES** AND THE **MARKETS** IN THESE COUNTRIES
- POVERTY BREEDS **INSTABILITY** AND **TERRORISM**, WHICH SPILL ACROSS BORDERS
- **TRADE** WITH PROSPEROUS NATIONS **HELPS** OUR OWN ECONOMY **GROW**

C2
" *I suspect that some in wealthier countries may ask, with our economies struggling, so many people out of work, and so many families barely getting by, why a summit on development? And the answer is simple. In our global economy, progress in even the poorest countries can advance the prosperity and security of people far beyond their borders, including my fellow Americans.* "

—President Barack Obama, speech before the United Nations General Assembly, September 23, 2010

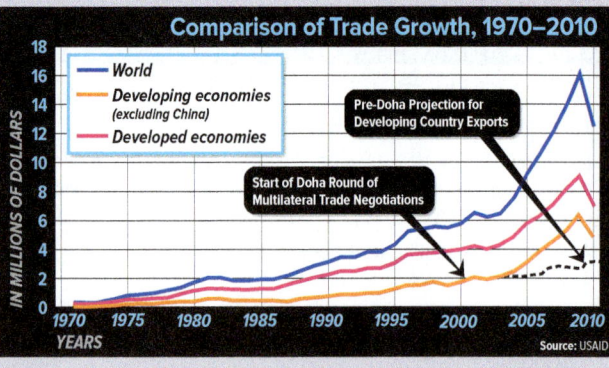

Comparison of Trade Growth, 1970–2010
Source: USAID

550

---

networks Online Teaching Options

DEBATE

Debate: Are the world's wealthiest nations obligated to aid in the economic development of poor nations?

Analyzing foreign aid Display the Debate. After reading the Yes arguments, direct students to analyze the line graph. Have students describe what the graph shows. **Ask: How does this graph support the argument that wealthy nations should aid poorer countries?** *(The graph shows that trade in developing countries increased in 2000, the year when trade agreements brought aid to developing nations. Before 2000, trade growth lagged far behind.)* Next, have a student read the arguments against foreign aid, and then examine the chart. **Ask: How does this chart support the argument that wealthy nations should NOT aid poorer countries?** *(The chart shows that despite international aid, these countries still suffer from extreme poverty and a low GDP growth rate.)* **Visual/Spatial**

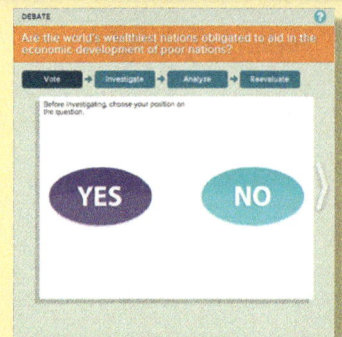

NO Wealthy nations are not obligated to aid in the development of poor nations because...

- WE SHOULD SEE TO THE **NEEDS** OF OUR **CITIZENS FIRST**
- AID **HURTS** COUNTRIES BY CREATING A **CULTURE OF DEPENDENCE**
- THE PROBLEMS ARE **INTERNAL POLITICAL** AND **INSTITUTIONAL** ISSUES
- **CORRUPTION IS** RAMPANT; MUCH OF THE **AID** IS TOTALLY **WASTED**

> Development is something largely determined by poor countries themselves, and outsiders can play only a limited role. Developing countries themselves emphasize this point, but in the rich world, it is often forgotten. So too is the fact that financial aid and the further opening of wealthy countries' markets are tools with only a limited ability to trigger growth, especially in the poorest countries.

—Nancy Birdsall, Dani Rodrik, and Arvind Subramanian, "How to Help Poor Countries," *Foreign Affairs*, July/August 2005

networks TRY IT YOURSELF ONLINE
For an interactive version of this debate go to connected.mcgraw-hill.com

ANALYZING the issue

1. **Interpreting** President Obama says that because we live in a global economy, the progress of even the poorest countries can influence our American economy. How is this possible?

2. **Drawing Conclusions** Review the second graph, "Economic Statistics for Select African Nations." What conclusion can you draw about the effectiveness of the international aid to these countries? Explain your answer.

3. **Defending** Which arguments in this debate do you find most compelling? Explain your answer.

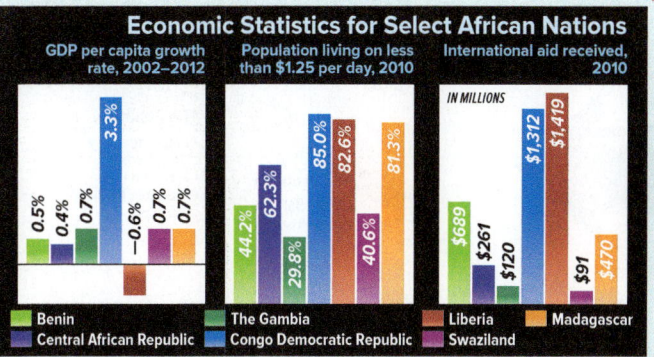

CHAPTER 18
Debate

R Reading Skills

Reading charts Have students examine the chart. **Ask: Which country's data best supports the No argument? Why?** *(Liberia; it receives the highest amount of international aid, yet still has a negative GDP growth rate and the second highest percentage of population living on less than $1.25 per day.)*

Content Background Knowledge

Liberia According to the CIA World factbook, a 1980 military coup began a period of major upheaval in Liberia. After nearly a decade of authoritarian rule, a 1989 rebellion began a prolonged civil war, which destroyed much of the country's economy. The 2006 election of President Ellen Johnson Sirleaf did much to slow the economic slide, encouraging the return of businesses that had fled the country as well as support from international donors. Democratic elections and the cessation of fighting have also encouraged renewed private investment and a lifting of trade embargos. Despite growth and optimism, Liberia does still have the highest ratio of direct foreign investment to GDP in the world.

CLOSE & REFLECT

Summarizing After the debate, discuss as a class students' opinions about the strengths and weaknesses of the experience and what they learned about economic aid to developing countries.

GRAPHIC ORGANIZER

Table

Preparing and defending arguments Divide the class into groups for and against the issue, and distribute the graphic organizer. Ask students to follow these steps in preparing their arguments:

1. Write *Arguments* as the header for the first column. Have students list four reasons that support their position.
2. Write *Counterarguments* as the second column header. Have students come up with points their opponents could use to minimize their arguments.
3. Write *Refutations* as the final column header. Have students write down ways that they can refute, or prove the opponents' counterarguments are wrong.
4. Have students review the graphic organizer and rank arguments from strongest to weakest.

ANSWERS, p. 551

ANALYZING the issue

1. Students should recognize that in a global economy, all countries are interconnected and that the level of prosperity of one affects all others. Some students may also note political instability, terrorism, and other related issues and how they can spill over to other nations.
2. Students may conclude that the data suggest that the economic aid is having little if any effect. They may also question whether the aid is being used effectively.
3. Students may find either side of the debate more convincing but should cite reasons and details to support their answers.

Global Economic Development

Chapter 18
Study Guide

C Critical Thinking Skills

Problem solving Divide the class into eight discussion groups. Assign each group one of the obstacles to development shown in the center graphic. Have groups write a one-sentence statement summarizing the obstacle. Then have them list possible solutions that developed countries, international organizations, and developing countries could take to address each problem. Have each group report to the class on the problem and solutions it identified. After all the groups have reported, conclude by having the class discuss this question: **What is likely to happen if these problems are not solved?**

W Writing Skills

Predicting information Ask students to write a summary answering this question: What will the U.S. economy and world economy look like in the future? Have students consider the impact of changes in technology, an aging population, foreign economic competition, the environment, renewable and nonrenewable resources, and other factors that could affect the American economy and the global economy. Tell students to make predictions about 10 years, 25 years, and 50 years into the future. Call on volunteers to share their predictions with the class.

STUDY GUIDE

LESSON 1

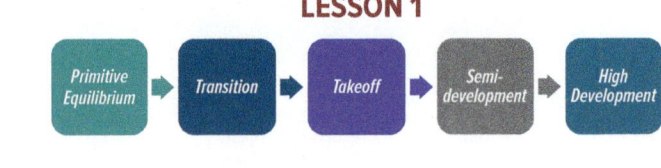

LESSON 2

LESSON 3

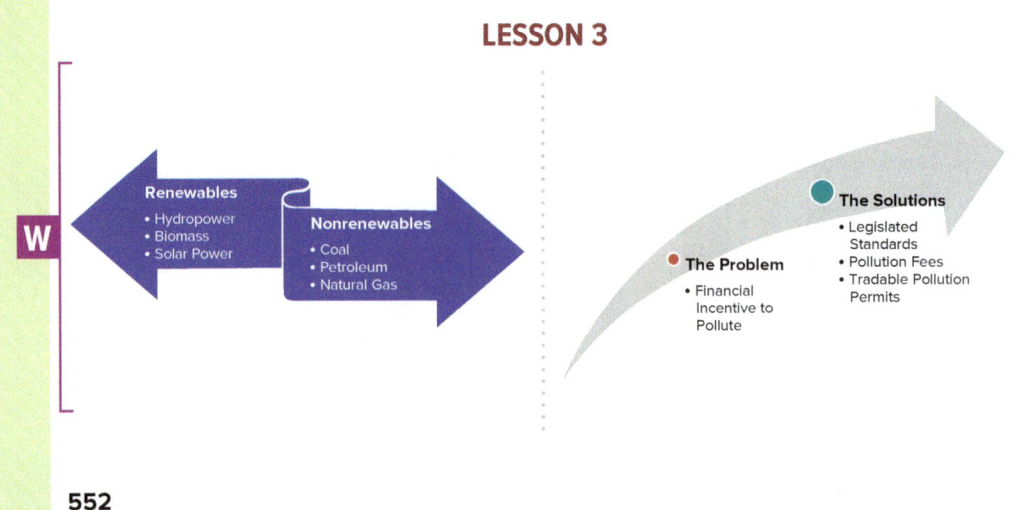

networks Online Teaching Options

WORKSHEET

Enrichment Activity: Global Economic Development

Understanding population effects on global economic development Assign the Enrichment Activity worksheet. Students will read about the effects of human population on global economic development. They will learn about factors such as birth rate, longevity, and death rate and the consequences when any one (or more) of these factors is unbalanced. Students will compare population distribution in West Africa and Western Europe by viewing population pyramids. They will check their understanding of the issues and apply critical reading skills to answer questions about the negative consequences of large populations that are too young or too old to contribute significantly to the economy. Finally, students will research negative growth in advanced industrialized countries, writing an essay that outlines the problem and summarizes opposing viewpoints on a proposed solution.

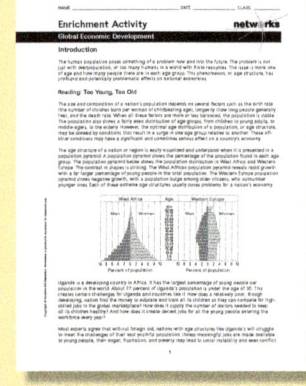

CHAPTER 18 Assessment

Directions: Answer the questions below. Make sure you read carefully and answer all parts of the questions.

Lesson Review

Lesson 1

1. **Explaining** Why do wealthy countries try to improve economic conditions in developing countries?
2. **Problem Solving** What is one key obstacle to development in a developing economy? How might that obstacle be overcome?
3. **Explaining** How does a large population create problems for a developing country?

Lesson 2

4. **Specifying** How does membership in the European Union benefit member countries?
5. **Analyzing** How do markets, products, and production increase globalization?

Lesson 3

6. **Explaining** How have wealthy countries like the United States and those in Europe managed to achieve increasing prosperity despite Malthus's dire predictions?
7. **Explaining** How do pollution permits help to reduce pollution?
8. **Describing** How did the United States, American consumers, and the oil industry react to the oil price increases of the 1970s?

Critical Thinking

9. **Drawing Inferences** Studies indicate that, in general, landlocked nations tend to have lower per capita income levels than surrounding nations that are bordered by oceans and seas. Why do you think this is the case?
10. **Exploring Issues** Do you think globalization is inevitable? Do you think it is desirable? Write one or two paragraphs to answer the questions and explain your reasoning.
11. **Considering Advantages and Disadvantages** If you had to choose between legislated standards or a pollution tax to reduce pollution, which would you choose? In your response, explain the pros and cons of each approach.

Analyzing Visuals

Use the diagram below to answer the following questions about energy flows.

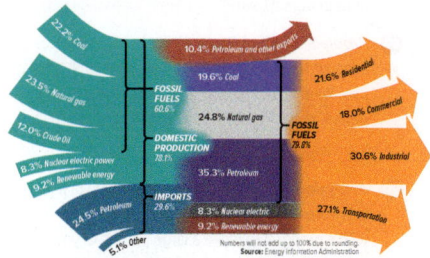

12. **Analyzing Visuals** How do we get most of our petroleum?
13. **Analyzing Visuals** How much of our energy is used for transportation?
14. **Drawing Inferences** We export over 10 percent of our energy while importing almost 30 percent. Why don't we stop exporting energy and then import less?

ANSWERING THE ESSENTIAL QUESTIONS

Review your answers to the introductory questions at the beginning of each lesson. Then answer the Essential Questions on the basis of what you learned in the chapter. Have your answers changed?

15. **Explaining** Why is the economic health of all nations important in a global economy?
16. **Describing** What are the challenges associated with globalization?

Need Extra Help?

If You've Missed Question	1	2	3	4	5	6	7	8	9	10	11	12	13	14	15	16
Go to page	523	524	524	534	531	541	548	546	525	531	542	545	545	545	522	531

Chapter 18 Assessment Answers

Lesson Review

Lesson 1

1. They often feel a humanitarian obligation to help people who are struggling economically, and they also want access to those nations' resources and markets.
2. Students should demonstrate an understanding of obstacles to development and offer a reasonable solution. Obstacles include population growth, disease and substance abuse, corruption, war and its aftermath, capital flight, natural resources and geography, lack of access to education and technology, and external debt.
3. Increased demand for goods can strain the country's resources.

Lesson 2

4. Trade is improved through lack of barriers to the flow of workers, capital, and goods and services. A common currency makes transactions easy and less expensive. Uniform tariffs for nonmembers protect members.
5. Markets expand beyond national boundaries; products from many different countries become available and standardized; production tends to migrate to be near customers and the cheapest resources.

Lesson 3

6. They have increased productivity, which enables an increasing standard of living while also reducing family size by having fewer children.
7. Permits allow a company to pollute, but if the permit is worth more than it will cost to clean up the pollution, the company may clean up its own pollution and sell the permit to another company.
8. Oil producers (specifically those in non-OPEC nations) increased domestic production, while interest in alternative energy sources surged. Countries poured billions into energy-research projects. Consumers demanded more fuel-efficient cars.

Critical Thinking

9. Students should recognize that landlocked nations do not have access to oceanic trade routes and thus have more difficulty generating trade revenue.
10. Most students will agree that globalization is inevitable. There may be more disagreement over whether it is desirable. Students should give details from the lesson to support their responses.
11. Students may choose either but should demonstrate understanding of the pros and cons of each.

Analyzing Visuals

12. From imports
13. 27.1 percent
14. Supply and demand dictate where and how much energy is purchased. In certain cases, it is more profitable to export some energy.

Answering the Essential Questions

15. Students should demonstrate understanding of the economic interconnectedness of all nations.
16. Students should demonstrate understanding of how globalization affects different nations and different groups in many ways. Specific challenges may overlap with the obstacles to development studied in the chapter. Other challenges include the debate around outsourcing, and the sometimes negative consequences (such as hazardous working conditions) associated with hiring overseas.

Chapter 18
Assessment Answers

21st Century Skills

17 Students should demonstrate understanding of how issues relating to developing countries affect people in other nations.

18 Unions oppose outsourcing because it costs American workers their jobs. Consumers and businesses benefit from outsourcing because it results in lower prices for goods and reduces production costs.

19 Answers may include government incentives, government support for research and development of renewable energy resources, and infrastructure developments to support their use.

Building Financial Literacy

20 Students should demonstrate understanding that a CEO has a responsibility to stockholders to maximize the profit of the company. They should also recognize that while outsourcing of the jobs will harm workers, it will also benefit consumers, among whom are those same workers. Students should fully explain the basis for their final decision.

Analyzing Primary Sources

21 "Governments increasingly pick and choose whom they trade with, what sort of capital they welcome and how much freedom they allow for doing business abroad," according to the article. Students should recognize that these aren't "official" barriers like tariffs or embargoes, but rather they're cautious responses to the 2008–2009 financial crisis. Students should also note that these behaviors will effectively slow the growth of developing nations.

CHAPTER 18 Assessment

Directions: Answer the questions below. Make sure you read carefully and answer all parts of the questions.

21st Century Skills

17 *Understanding Relationships Among Events* How do you think the economic growth of developing countries will affect you and your family in the future?

18 *Identifying Perspectives and Differing Interpretations* Why will unions generally condemn outsourcing? What other groups will benefit from it? Why?

19 *Problem Solving* Renewable energy resources account for only a small portion of our total energy use. What changes will need to be made before people make greater use of renewable energy?

Building Financial Literacy

20 *Analyzing* Imagine that you are the CEO of a large U.S. corporation. Your staff has come to you with a proposal to move a large portion of your manufacturing business to China, where your labor costs will be dramatically lower and where you will be closer to many Asian markets that you wish to enter. You're considering the recommendation. Upon hearing rumors of a possible move, a union representative has met with you and encouraged you to consider how your decision will affect American workers. Before you make your final decision, consider these factors:

- your chief responsibilities as CEO of the firm
- the broad effects of globalization
- how your decision will affect families and your community

What will be your decision? What will be the basis for your decision?

Analyzing Primary Sources

After growing for more than 20 years, world exports as a share of the world's GDP began to plateau in 2008. Some economists take it as a sign that globalization efforts have slowed down since the Great Recession of 2008–2009. Read the excerpt below and answer the question that follows.

PRIMARY SOURCE

" *Although they did not retreat into the extreme protectionism of the 1930s, the world economy has certainly become less open [since the Great Recession of 2008–2009]. After two decades in which people, capital and goods were moving ever more freely across borders, walls have been going up, albeit ones with gates. Governments increasingly pick and choose whom they trade with, what sort of capital they welcome and how much freedom they allow for doing business abroad.* . . . "

—"The Gated Globe," *The Economist*, October 12, 2013

21 *Analyzing Primary Sources* What kinds of "walls" have governments built since the Great Recession, according to this source? Are these "trade barriers" in the traditional sense, and why do you think they arrived after the Great Recession? What effect might these restrictions have on economic growth in developing countries?

Need Extra Help?

If You've Missed Question	17	18	19	20	21
Go to page	522	533	543	532	524

---

networks Online Assessment Options

WORKSHEET

Chapter Tests and Lesson Quizzes

Chapter 18 Tests Forms A and B Have students complete the Chapter Tests and Lesson Quizzes to assess student understanding throughout the chapter. Print and online assessment tools offer chapter and lesson evaluation through a variety of question formats, including document-based questions.

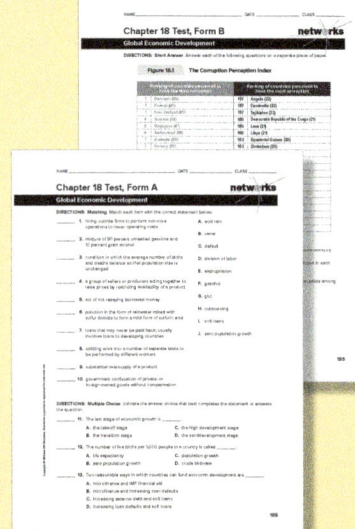

CHAPTER 19
Personal Financial Literacy

UNDERSTANDING BY DESIGN®

Enduring Understanding
- Resources are limited, so people must make choices.

Essential Question
- How can financial institutions help you increase and better manage your money?
- What are the different types of business organizations?
- How can you take control of your own money?

Predictable Misunderstandings
Students may think:
- *Their personal savings has no effect on the overall financial system.* Explain that by saving, each individual makes funds available for other people to use, which is an important part of the financial system and economic growth.
- *Investing requires thousands of dollars.* Explain that some forms of investment, such as CDs and government savings bonds, require relatively small initial investments. Government savings bonds are available for as little as $25.

Assessment Evidence
- Lesson Quizzes
- Chapter Assessment
- Chapter Tests, Forms A and B

SUGGESTED PACING

Introducing the Chapter: ½ Day	Lesson 3: Personal Money Decisions . . . . 1 Day
Lesson 1: Financial Institutions and Your Money . . . . 1 Day	Study Guide, Chapter Assessment and Wrap-Up . . . . . ½ Day
Lesson 2: Business Organizations and Your Money . . . . 1 Day	

TOTAL 4 Days

Key for Using the Teacher Edition

SKILL-BASED ACTIVITIES

Types of skill activities found in the Teacher Edition.

V Visual Skills require students to analyze maps, graphs, charts, and photos.
R Reading Skills help students practice reading skills and master vocabulary.
C Critical Thinking Skills help students apply and extend what they have learned.
W Writing Skills provide writing opportunities to help students comprehend the text.
T Technology Skills require students to use digital tools effectively.

*Letters are followed by a number when there is more than one of the same type of skill on the page.

DIFFERENTIATED INSTRUCTION

All activities are written for the on-level student unless otherwise marked with the leveled labels below.

BL Beyond Level
AL Approaching Level
ELL English Language Learners

All students benefit from activities that utilize different learning styles. Many activities are marked as below when a particular learning style is highlighted.

Intrapersonal
Logical/Mathematical
Visual/Spatial
Verbal/Linguistic
Naturalist
Kinesthetic
Auditory/Musical
Interpersonal

Council for Economic Education

Below are the Council for Economic Education Voluntary National Content Standards in Economics covered in the *Personal Financial Literacy* chapter.

Content Standard 2: Effective decision-making requires comparing the additional costs of alternatives with the additional benefits. Many choices involve doing a little more or a little less of something; few choices are "all or nothing" decisions.

Content Standard 10: Institutions evolve and are created to help individuals and groups accomplish their goals. Banks, labor unions, markets, corporations, legal systems, and not-for-profit organizations are examples of important institutions. A different kind of institution, clearly defined and enforced property rights, is essential to a market economy.

Content Standard 11: Money makes it easier to trade, borrow, save, invest, and compare the value of goods and services. The amount of money in the economy affects the overall price level. Inflation is an increase in the overall price level that reduces the value of money.

Content Standard 15: Investment in factories, machinery, new technology, and in the health, education, and training of people can raise future standards of living.

CHAPTER 19: PERSONAL FINANCIAL LITERACY

Chapter Opener Planner

Students will know:
- the importance of budgeting.
- the role of financial institutions in saving, borrowing, and capital formation.
- the importance of saving now.

Students will be able to:
- *practice* setting up a budget.
- *explain* why saving and becoming creditworthy are good ideas for everyone.
- *explain* various methods of paying for college.

UNDERSTANDING BY DESIGN®

☑ Print Teaching Options

R Reading Skills

☐ **p. 556 Identifying the timeliness of the process** Students identify the dates to complete the FAFSA.

☐ **p. 557 Identifying the types of federal financial aid** Students identify aid provided by government.

C Critical Thinking Skills

☐ **p. 555 Analyzing recent purchases** Students discuss their purchasing behavior.

☐ **p. 556 Sequencing priorities** Students identify actions before applying for financial aid.

☐ **p. 557 Budgeting at college** Students identify figure out how to manage on $350 a month.

☑ Online Teaching Options

V Visual Skills

☐ **IMAGE Chapter opener**—Students discuss their financial futures.

☐ **GRAPHIC ORGANIZERS Time Line**—Students mark specific dates for filling out the FAFSA.

C Critical Thinking Skills

☐ **INFOGRAPHICS Economic Perspectives**—Students learn about the steps to take when filling out the FAFSA and college expenses.

☑ Printable Digital Worksheets

C Critical Thinking Skills

☐ **WORKSHEET Personal Finance Activity: Risk and Return**—Students compare and contrast types of investments, explaining advantages and disadvantages. They consider the risks involved, the earnings potential, and whether they can withdraw their money without a penalty

Project-Based Learning

Hands-On

Students have $10,000 to invest. They can invest some, but not all, of their money one of these savings accounts:
- a savings account that pays 0.6% interest compounded monthly, with no minimum deposit and no limitations on availability of funds
- a pension plan requiring annual deposits of $1,000, collecting simple interest at 0.9% monthly, in which funds cannot be withdrawn until retirement
- a certificate of deposit that pays 3.5% annually, with a minimum deposit of $1,500 and a maturity of one year

Have students create a fact sheet that identifies the plan they selected, how much they invested, and the reasons for their choices. Students should also calculate and show in a graph or table the value of their investment after 6 months.

Print Resources

ANCILLARY RESOURCE
This ancillary is available for every chapter and lesson.
- Chapter Tests and Lesson Quizzes

PRINTABLE DIGITAL WORKSHEETS
These printable digital worksheets are available for this chapter.
- Reading Essentials & Study Guide
- Personal Finance Activities
- Lesson Quizzes (English and Spanish)
- Chapter Tests (English and Spanish)

More Media Resources

SUGGESTED READING
- For students at a Grade 10 reading level: *Street Wise: A Guide for Teen Investors,* by Janet Bamford
- For students at a Grade 11 reading level: *The Wealthy Barber,* by David Chilton
- For students at a Grade 12 reading level: *Everyone's Money Book,* by Jordan E. Goodman

SUGGESTED VIDEOS
Find these documentaries yourself online. NOTE: McGraw-Hill Education does not endorse these resources. Preview clips for age-appropriateness.
- *Not Business as Usual* (62 min.)
- *Million Dollar Traders* (59 min.)

LESSON 1 Planner

FINANCIAL INSTITUTIONS AND YOUR MONEY

Students will know:
- the major methods of accessing funds in checking, savings, and credit accounts.
- the advantages and disadvantages of using credit cards.
- the costs and benefits of declaring personal bankruptcy.
- the basic considerations when investing money, including the risk-return relationship.

Students will be able to:
- **evaluate** bank services to determine which bank would work best for them individually.
- **explain** why saving and becoming creditworthy are good ideas for everyone.
- **explain** the role of savings in the financial system.

UNDERSTANDING BY DESIGN®

✓ Print Teaching Options

R Reading Skills
- ☐ p. 560 Identifying reasons to save
- ☐ p. 561 Asking questions before selecting a bank
- ☐ p. 562 Opening a savings account
- ☐ p. 566 Differentiating secured and unsecured loans
- ☐ p. 566 Explaining the responsibilities and obligations of borrowing money
- ☐ p. 567 Evaluating the costs and benefits of declaring personal bankruptcy

C Critical Thinking Skills
- ☐ p. 558 Recognizing prevalence/lack of savings
- ☐ p. 558 Considering ways to save
- ☐ p. 559 Analyzing the role of interest
- ☐ p. 561 Comparing compound & simple interest
- ☐ p. 562 Determining higher/lower interest rates
- ☐ p. 562 Clarifying the maturity factor on CDs
- ☐ p. 563 Examining debit cards
- ☐ p. 564 Reconciling a bank statement
- ☐ p. 565 Providing examples of creditworthiness
- ☐ p. 565 Analyzing credit risk behaviors
- ☐ p. 565 Examining credit cards
- ☐ p. 566 Evaluating credit card interest rates

W Writing Skills
- ☐ p. 560 Explaining how financial institutions affect households and businesses
- ☐ p. 562 Examining types, risks, costs, and benefits of savings accounts
- ☐ p. 563 Practicing writing a check
- ☐ p. 566 Avoiding/eliminating credit card debt

✓ Online Teaching Options

V Visual Skills
- ☐ **CHART** **Building Your Budget**—Students set up a personal budget that reflects their spending and earnings. *Logical/Mathematical*
- ☐ **CHART** **Simple vs. Compound Interest**—Students learn about compound interest. *Logical/Mathematical*
- ☐ **DIAGRAM** **How to Write a Check**—Students discuss checking account maintenance. *Logical/Mathematical*
- ☐ **CHART** **Credit Basics**—Students analyze credit card offers for examples of the terms and conditions. *Interpersonal*
- ☐ **CHART** **How Do You Score?**—Students access their credit report.

R Reading Skills
- ☐ **GRAPHIC ORGANIZER** **Types of Savings Accounts**—Students explain the differences among types of savings accounts. *Logical/Mathematical*

C Critical Thinking Skills
- ☐ **BELLRINGER** **Credit and You**—Students discuss responsibilities and consequences of taking on debt. *Verbal/Linguistic*
- ☐ **ESSENTIAL QUESTION** **Exploring the Essential Question**—Students discuss the best methods to get their money to work for them and list advantages and disadvantages for each.

✓ Printable Digital Worksheets

R Reading Skills
- ☐ **WORKSHEET** **Reading Essentials and Study Guide**—Students complete the study guide and answer Reading Progress Check and vocabulary questions.

C Critical Thinking Skills
- ☐ **WORKSHEET** **Personal Finance Activity: What to Spend Money On**—Students decide what their needs and wants are and allocate their money accordingly.
- ☐ **WORKSHEET** **Personal Finance Activity: Help from the Fed**—Students explore how two programs run or overseen by the Federal Reserve inform them of their rights as a consumer and user of financial products. *Logical/Mathematical*
- ☐ **WORKSHEET** **Personal Finance Activity: Saving Up for Purchases**—Students discuss which type of savings account would be most beneficial for their short-term and long-term savings goals. *Logical/Mathematical*
- ☐ **WORKSHEET** **Personal Finance Activity: Comparing Credit Card Offers**—Students use a chart to compare terms on credit card offers. *Logical/Mathematical*
- ☐ **WORKSHEET** **Personal Finance Activity: Cash, Debit, or Credit**—Students analyze the pros and cons of using cash, debit cards, and credit cards.

LESSON 2 Planner

BUSINESS ORGANIZATIONS AND YOUR MONEY

Students will know:
- how the amount of savings in an economy is the basis of capital formation.
- the characteristics, advantages, and disadvantages of sole proprietorships, partnerships, and corporations in the United States economy.
- how small businesses and corporations raise capital.

Students will be able to:
- *describe* how various types of businesses are formed and how they grow.
- *discuss* the advantages and disadvantages of sole proprietorships, partnerships, and corporations.

UNDERSTANDING BY DESIGN®

☑ Print Teaching Options

R Reading Skills
- ☐ p. 568 Explaining capital formation
- ☐ p. 568 Relating financial institutions to capital formation
- ☐ p. 570 Identifying capital formation for small businesses
- ☐ p. 570 Identifying capital formation for corporations
- ☐ p. 570 Understanding bonds
- ☐ p. 570 Understanding stocks
- ☐ p. 572 Understanding mutual funds
- ☐ p. 572 Relating the advantages of municipal bonds

C Critical Thinking Skills
- ☐ p. 568 Comprehending the big picture of the financial system
- ☐ p. 569 Analyzing responsibilities and rights of businesses
- ☐ p. 571 Evaluating financial assets
- ☐ p. 571 Diversifying risk
- ☐ p. 572 Considering financial goals
- ☐ p. 573 Discussing reasons for investing

W Writing Skills
- ☐ p. 568 Learning prior knowledge of stocks and bonds
- ☐ p. 569 Analyzing characteristics, advantages, and disadvantages of business organizations
- ☐ p. 571 Evaluating considerations before investing
- ☐ p. 572 Evaluating bonds
- ☐ p. 573 Examining investment options available in IRAs

☑ Online Teaching Options

V Visual Skills
- ☐ **CHART** **Reading Stock Market Reports**—Students explore how to read stock market reports. **Logical/Mathematical**

R Reading Skills
- ☐ **GRAPHIC ORGANIZER** **Comparing Financial Assets**—Students select three investment options and compare their levels of risk and returns. **Logical/Mathematical**

C Critical Thinking Skills
- ☐ **BELLRINGER** **Dow Jones Industrial Average**—Students identify the companies listed on the Dow and research the stock for several companies, deciding which is the best investment. **Verbal/Linguistic**
- ☐ **ESSENTIAL QUESTION** **Exploring the Essential Question**—Students read about economic growth and discuss its effects on tax revenue and entitlement programs. **Logical/Mathematical**

☑ Printable Digital Worksheets

R Reading Skills
- ☐ **WORKSHEET** **Reading Essentials and Study Guide**—Students complete the study guide and answer Reading Progress Check and vocabulary questions.

C Critical Thinking Skills
- ☐ **WORKSHEET** **Personal Finance Activity: Assessing the Competition**—Students learn about sole proprietorships and explore how their "business" fits into the financial system. **Verbal/Linguistic**
- ☐ **WORKSHEET** **Personal Finance Activity: Evaluating Stocks**—Students follow a stock for several weeks and write a summary of how their stock performed. **Logical/Mathematical**
- ☐ **WORKSHEET** **Personal Finance Activity: Risk and Return**—Students explain the advantages and disadvantages of some investments and calculate the earnings of a savings account and a stock. **Visual/Spatial**
- ☐ **WORKSHEET** **Math Practice for Economics**—Students study a corporation on the NYSE Euronext and follow its stock for several weeks or months, graphing the performance and comparing results.

LESSON 3 Planner

PERSONAL MONEY DECISIONS

Students will know:
- the various methods available to pay for college.
- the costs and benefits of buying insurance, renting a home, buying a home, and charitable giving.

Students will be able to:
- *explain* various methods of paying for college.
- *compare* the advantages and disadvantages of renting versus buying a home.
- *identify* the necessity of buying insurance.
- *appreciate* the value of charitable giving.

UNDERSTANDING BY DESIGN

✓ Print Teaching Options

V Visual Skills
- ☐ p. 574 Filling out the FAFSA

R Reading Skills
- ☐ p. 575 Analyzing federal student loan options
- ☐ p. 575 Identify federal student loan amounts
- ☐ p. 577 Researching work-study opportunities
- ☐ p. 578 Understanding the rental ratio
- ☐ p. 579 Understanding the mortgage ratio
- ☐ p. 580 Transitioning from renting to ownership
- ☐ p. 581 Explaining how insurance works
- ☐ p. 582 Listing ways to lower insurance rates
- ☐ p. 583 Identifying benefits of charitable giving

C Critical Thinking Skills
- ☐ p. 576 Examining scholarship responses
- ☐ p. 576 Researching federal grant options
- ☐ p. 577 Nontraditional paying for college
- ☐ p. 581 Evaluating costs/benefits of insurance
- ☐ p. 583 Measuring the costs of charitable giving
- ☐ p. 583 Revising a budget

W Writing Skills
- ☐ p. 576 Charting private loans and federal loans
- ☐ p. 579 Listing renting advantages/disadvantages
- ☐ p. 579 Listing advantages and disadvantages of buying a house

T Technology Skills
- ☐ p. 575 Comparing private/federal student loans
- ☐ p. 576 Researching scholarship opportunities
- ☐ p. 576 Evaluating nonfederal grant options

✓ Online Teaching Options

V Visual Skills
- ☐ **GRAPH** **Unemployment and Earnings**—Students consider the relationship between increased level of education and increased earnings. *Visual/Spatial*
- ☐ **VIDEO** **College Debt**—Students view a video about the cost of college and the difference between federal loans and private loans.
- ☐ **VIDEO** **Decision Making**—Students view a video about the costs and benefits of making decisions.
- ☐ **CHART** **Types of Car Insurance**—Students view Figure 19.10 and learn how insurance companies classify drivers. *Logical/Mathematical*

R Reading Skills
- ☐ **GRAPHIC ORGANIZER** **Paying for College**—Students take notes about loans, work-study programs, and nontraditional ways of paying for college.

C Critical Thinking Skills
- ☐ **BELLRINGER** **Consumer Rights and Responsibilities**—Students explain or provide examples of each consumer right and responsibility listed on the Bellringer. *Verbal/Linguistic*
- ☐ **ESSENTIAL QUESTION** **Exploring the Essential Question**—Students debate the costs and benefits of buying a home versus renting. *Verbal/Linguistic*

✓ Printable Digital Worksheets

R Reading Skills
- ☐ **WORKSHEET** **Reading Essentials and Study Guide**—Students complete the study guide and answer Reading Progress Check and vocabulary questions.

C Critical Thinking Skills
- ☐ **WORKSHEET** **Personal Finance Activity: Get a Job**—Students read about outsourcing and discuss job security. *Verbal/Linguistic*
- ☐ **WORKSHEET** **Personal Finance Activity: Changing Jobs**—Students discuss the necessity of financial stability before changing jobs.
- ☐ **WORKSHEET** **Personal Finance Activity: Who Needs Insurance?**—Students discuss why certain types of insurance are important.
- ☐ **WORKSHEET** **Personal Finance Activity: Tracking Your Spending**—Students decide which items on the budget could be replaced with charitable giving and apply opportunity cost to their decisions. *Logical/Mathematical*
- ☐ **WORKSHEET** **College Debt Video Activity**—Students answer questions about the cost of college and the difference between federal loans and private loans.
- ☐ **WORKSHEET** **Decision Making Video Activity**—Students answer questions about the costs and benefits of making decisions.

CHAPTER 19 Personal Financial Literacy

INTERVENTION AND REMEDIATION STRATEGIES

LESSON 1 Financial Institutions and Your Money

Reading and Comprehension

To have students utilize words in context, have groups create some form of visual advertisement that encourages people to deposit funds into and/or borrow from one of the financial institutions discussed in this lesson. Inform groups that their advertisements should include the APR, annual fees (if any), minimum deposit, and so on. Visuals might take the form of posters, billboards, bumper stickers, buttons, or T-shirt designs. Have groups use their finished products to create an "advertisement corner" in the classroom.

Text Evidence

Have students read the section of text under the heading "Checking Accounts." To have students determine the central ideas of the text, write the following questions on the board for them to write and answer in their notebooks. **Ask: What is a demand deposit account?** *(an account—in this case, a checking account—that allows customers the easiest access to their money for daily and monthly use)* **What are some ways that customers can "demand" their money?** *(Answers may include by filling out a deposit or withdrawal slip in a bank, by writing a check, or by using a debit card.)* Discuss answers with students.

LESSON 2 Business Organizations and Your Money

Reading and Comprehension

To have students determine the meanings of a word in context, have them write the word *maturity* in their notebooks. Tell students that in relation to economics, this word has a specific meaning. Write on the board "life of a bond, length of time funds are borrowed." Have students write a sentence using the word *maturity* as it is used in economics in their notebooks.

Text Evidence

Have students read the section under "Investment Risks vs. Returns." To help them determine the central idea of the text, ask students to list these assets in order of risk (put the assets out-of-order on the board): stocks, mutual funds, corporate bonds, government bonds, savings accounts.

LESSON 3 Personal Money Decisions

Reading and Comprehension

To have students determine the meaning of a phrase as used in the text, have them consider the term *work-study*. Tell students that this is a financial aid option for college students. Have students read the information about "Work-Study Programs" and write a short paragraph explaining how the two programs (FWS and non-FWS) are similar and different.

Text Evidence

Have students read the text under "Insurance." Ask them to create a cause-and-effect diagram explaining how insurance works. **Ask: What is the trade-off for a low deductible?** *(a high premium)* Have students write a short paragraph explaining the importance of health and auto insurance.

Online Resources

Reading Essentials and Study Guide

This resource offers writing and reading activities for the approaching-level student.

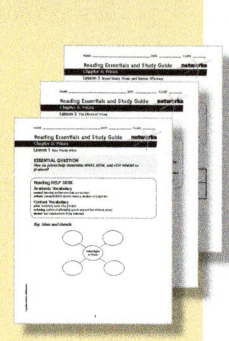

Approaching Grade Level Reader

This reader presents all of the content of the Online Student Edition but at a lower reading level.

English Language Learner Reader

Provide additional reading support for ELL students. Find this tool in the Online Student Edition.

Personal Financial Literacy

ESSENTIAL QUESTIONS
- How can financial institutions help you increase and better manage your money?
- What are the different types of business organizations?
- How can you take control of your own money?

networks
www.connected.mcgraw-hill.com
There's More Online about personal financial literacy.

CHAPTER 19

Economic Perspectives
FAFSA: Free Application for Federal Student Aid

Lesson 1
Financial Institutions and Your Money

Lesson 2
Business Organizations and Your Money

Lesson 3
Personal Money Decisions

CHAPTER 19
Personal Financial Literacy

ENGAGE

🔔 Call students' attention to the photo and ask them to describe what it shows. **Ask: How many of you plan on graduating from college and saving money? What other goals do you have?** In a discussion, lead students to think about the necessity of planning their futures now. Encourage students to continually think about how the Personal Financial Literacy content can apply to their lives, both today and in the years to come.

Analyzing recent purchases Ask students to identify a product they have recently purchased. Then ask them to write answers to the following questions: Before making your purchase, what questions did you ask yourself or others, and what information did you look for? Why did you buy this particular item? Do you think you acted wisely in making your purchase? Why or why not? Call on volunteers to share their responses with the class. Then point out that by seeking information before making purchases, students are developing strategies that will help them act wisely as consumers and savers. **Verbal/Linguistic**

Making Connections

Consumer Behavior Briefly discuss the following questions with students: **How many credit cards do you think the average American holds? Do you compare prices when you shop? How much of your income do you save? Are you curious about purchasing stocks or bonds? Have you studied ways to pay for college? What do you know about purchasing health and auto insurance?** Conclude by mentioning that although these questions may not seem connected, they all address some aspect of consumer behavior with which students should be aware.

Letter from the Author

Dear Economics Teacher,

Your students are about to discover that it soon will be their turn to earn a living. They hopefully have been fortunate enough until now to have had someone help with basic needs—their food, their clothing, and their shelter. But soon this support comes to an end, and when that happens, your students will be the ones responsible for providing for their needs. As their teacher, you've done about all you can do to make them ready for the next big step, so what can you give them by way of useful parting advice? Just remind them of **TINSTAAFL**—**T**here **I**s **N**o **S**uch **T**hing **A**s **A** **F**ree **L**unch!

Gary E. Clayton

FOLDABLES Study Organizer

Go to the Foldables® library for a cumulative chapter-based Foldable® activity that your students can use to help take notes and prepare for assessment.

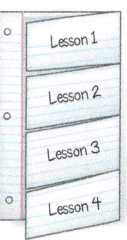

CHAPTER 19
Economic Perspectives

TEACH & ASSESS

R Reading Skills

Identifying the timeliness of the process Ask: **When should you complete the FAFSA?** *(in January of each year a person is in college)*

Content Background Knowledge

Number of FAFSA Applicants Around 14 million FAFSA forms are submitted each year and account for about $80 billion in financial aid.

C Critical Thinking Skills

Sequencing priorities Ask: **What three actions should you perform before applying for financial aid?** *(begin saving, look for scholarships, and ask a guidance counselor or college financial aid office for information about state college funding programs)* **AL**

Making Connections

Eligibility for Federal Student Aid Explain to students that to receive federal student aid, they will need to have a high school diploma or GED certificate, or have completed a high school education in a homeschool setting approved under state law. They must also be enrolled or accepted for enrollment as a regular student in an eligible degree or certificate program. Males between the ages of 18 and 25 must be registered with the Selective Service. Students must have a valid Social Security number unless they are from the Republic of the Marshall Islands, Federated States of Micronesia, or the Republic of Palau. And students must maintain satisfactory academic progress in college or career school to continue to receive federal financial aid.

Economic Perspectives

FAFSA: Free Application for Federal Student Aid

R The process of applying:

The FAFSA is available between January and June of each year, but certain kinds of federal financial aid are on a first come, first served basis. The FAFSA form can be completed online at http://www.fafsa.gov--- or a paper version can be downloaded and mailed. Also, some high school financial aid offices have software for completing the application.

Who is eligible for federal financial aid?

STUDENT APPLICANT

- High School Diploma or GED
- Acceptance into a degree or certificate program
- Registration with Selective Service
- Valid SS#
- Statement of non-default
- U.S. Citizenship
- Maintain Academic Progress

C **1** PIN — Get a PIN from the FAFSA Web site

5  Gather student applicant's and parents' tax information and documents

4  Gather financial/banking information on income, assets and investments for the student applicant and parents

What does federal financial aid pay for?

Federal student financial aid can be used to pay various expenses related to attending school. These expenses could include:

 Tuition & Fees    Room & Board    Books & Supplies    Transportation    Computers    Child Care

---

networks *Online Teaching Options*

INFOGRAPHIC

Economic Perspectives: FAFSA: Free Application for Federal Student Aid

Identifying steps in the financial aid process Display the infographic to start a discussion about paying for college. Ask students to take turns reading the steps of the financial aid process. Invite your school's guidance counselor to visit the class and provide more information about filling out the FAFSA. Have interested students do online research for state funding programs, grants, and scholarships. Have a contest to see which student can identify the most state scholarships available. **Visual/Spatial, Interpersonal**

CHAPTER 19
Economic Perspectives

FAFSA is the application for grants, loans and work-study funds from the federal government, as well as certain state, institution-based and private financial aid. The information provided by the applicant enables financial aid officers to determine how much of which kind of assistance students can receive.

Gather necessary documents (including social security numbers and driver's license numbers)

Prepare a list of colleges or universities that will receive FAFSA information

Complete the FAFSA form: go to http://www.fafsa.gov

Attend College!

Other Financial Options:

grants (which don't require repayment unless you leave school)

loans (money lent by the government)

work-study (students earn money to pay for their education through job programs)

States, colleges, and private organizations also offer forms of financial aid. Check their information to see what types of aid are available, how to qualify, and the proper method for applying.

THINK ABOUT IT!
Understanding List the items needed to complete the FAFSA. How would you explain the application process to someone else?

Personal Financial Literacy 557

C Critical Thinking Skills

Budgeting at college Tell students to suppose they are freshmen at college and have a part-time job that earns $350 a month. They live in a dorm and have a paid meal plan at the college cafeteria. Have student pairs identify three needs they will have. Then have them identify three wants they might have as college freshmen. Finally, have pairs work out how those needs (not already paid for) and wants could be managed on $350 a month.
Logical/Mathematical, Interpersonal

R Reading Skills

Identifying the types of federal financial aid
Ask: **What are the three types of financial aid provided by the federal government?** *(grants, loans, and work-study funds)*

CLOSE & REFLECT

Have students answer the *Think About It!* questions.

GRAPHIC ORGANIZER

Time Line

Logging dates in the financial aid process Distribute the time line graphic organizers to students. Ask them to use the infographic and a calendar to mark specific dates on the time line for each step in filling out the FAFSA form. **Visual/Spatial, Interpersonal**

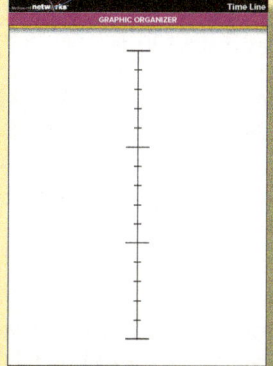

ANSWERS, p. 557

THINK ABOUT IT!

Driver's license and Social Security number; parents' tax forms and financial information about income, assets, and investments

Explaining the application process to someone else should start with going to the government Web site and obtaining a FAFSA pin.

CHAPTER 19, LESSON 1
Financial Institutions and Your Money

ENGAGE

C1 Critical Thinking Skills

Recognizing the prevalence or lack of savings Before students begin the lesson, write the following sentence on the board: *Just 51% of Americans have more emergency savings than credit card debt.* Have a student read the sentence aloud. Ask students whether they think that sentence is true or false, and to give reasons for their opinions. Explain that the statement is true. Discuss the uncertainty faced by the other 49% who have higher credit card debt than savings, or no savings at all.

TEACH & ASSESS

C2 Critical Thinking Skills

Considering ways to save Have students list five ways they can start saving money. **Ask:** How much could you save in a year by cutting these costs?
AL Verbal/Linguistic

ANSWERS, p. 558

ESSENTIAL QUESTION ACTIVITY

Answer 3 is the best way to make your money work for you. Make sure students understand that a certificate of deposit, or CD, is a time deposit account rather than a demand deposit account, which is why the interest rate is higher.

TAKING NOTES
Type of Account: Passbook/Savings Account
Risk: No risk
Amount of Interest: Low and fixed
Deposit Requirements: Low minimum balance

Type of Account: Money Market Deposit Account
Risk: No risk
Amount of Interest: Higher interest, variable based on markets
Deposit Requirements: Higher minimum balance

Type of Account: Money Market Mutual Fund
Risk: Minimal risk
Amount of Interest: Higher interest, variable based on markets
Deposit Requirements: Longer deposit requirements

Type of Account: Certificate of Deposit (CD)
Risk: No risk
Amount of Interest: Higher fixed interest rates
Deposit Requirements: Longer, higher deposit requirements

Interact with these digital assets and others in lesson 1
- ✓ INTERACTIVE CHART Building Your Budget
- ✓ INTERACTIVE CHART Simple vs. Compound interest
- ✓ INTERACTIVE CHART Credit Basics
- ✓ SELF-CHECK QUIZ

networks TRY IT YOURSELF ONLINE

LESSON 1
Financial Institutions and Your Money

Reading Help Desk

Academic Vocabulary
- risk

Content Vocabulary
- financial institution
- savings
- interest
- interest rate
- Federal Reserve System (Fed)
- Federal Deposit Insurance Corporation (FDIC)
- credit unions
- demand deposit account (DDA)
- creditors
- collateral
- secured
- unsecured

TAKING NOTES:

Key Ideas and Details
ACTIVITY Use a graphic organizer like the one below to explain the differences among savings accounts.

Type of Account	Risk	Amount of Interest	Deposit Requirements

ESSENTIAL QUESTION

How can financial institutions help you increase and better manage your money?

When you turned sixteen, your parents promised that you could get an after-school job to start earning your own money. You have worked at this job, getting regular paychecks for three months. You plan to use the money you earn from this job to buy a used car, but your salary is not high enough to save enough money by the target date of the start of your junior year in high school.

Which of the following methods do you think is the best way to put your money to work for you?

1. Keep all of your money in a shoebox in your closet. Promise yourself that you won't spend any money on other things until you reach your goal.
2. Put your money in a bank savings account. It'll earn some interest and you can withdraw what you need at any point.
3. Place your earnings in a certificate of deposit account. It'll raise higher interest, but you will be limited in the flexibility of withdrawing funds.

Budgeting

GUIDING QUESTION What is the value of learning how to properly budget your money?

Nearly everything you do is influenced by money—where you live, how you get around, what you do with your free time, and whether and what kind of job you have. When managed well, money makes your life easier. When managed poorly, it can cause great stress and create significant obstacles. Getting control of what you spend—or budgeting—will prevent a downward spiral into debt that may take decades to overcome.

Many people have no idea what happens to their money. It just seems to "disappear." Here's how to find out where *your* money goes:

558

---

networks Online Teaching Options

BELLRINGER

Credit and You

Identifying a poor credit risk Display the Bellringer as students enter the classroom. Discuss the young man's "thoughts" on the Bellringer, and then have students answer the questions. Explain to students that after they have applied for credit and obtained it, they have taken on certain responsibilities. If they do not pay their credit card bill on time, they get a bad credit history, which may make it difficult or impossible to get credit when they really need it—to purchase a house, for example. And it is the borrower's responsibility to control spending, to keep a record of all the charges made, and to pay more than the minimum payment, or it will take years to reduce the debt. **Verbal/Linguistic**

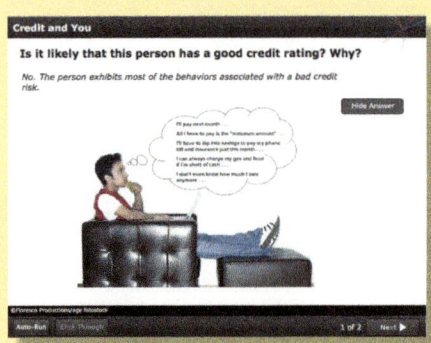

1. List the bills you pay every month (cell phone, Internet access, and car insurance, for example).
2. For one month, list everything you buy, including the price you paid—no matter how little an item costs.

At the end of the month, group everything on your list into categories: Food, Transportation, Entertainment, and Personal Care. Now you can see where your money goes.

Here's how to get a handle on your spending: Write down your income and your expenses into a chart like **Figure 19.1**. Look at each expense in column 2 and think of ways to reduce that payment. Enter the smaller amount in column 3—your New Budget. Total the expenses in column 3 to see if your New Budget matches your income.

You've probably heard again and again about the importance of making wise decisions. This is especially true when you make financial decisions. The wisest financial decision you will ever make is to start a budget now and save a percentage of all money you receive—including cash in birthday cards as well as the pay from your part-time job. The second-wisest decision is to deposit what you save into a financial institution.

✓ **READING PROGRESS CHECK**
Explaining Why is it important to live on a budget?

Financial Institutions

GUIDING QUESTION *How do financial institutions affect your own budget?*

A **financial institution** is an organization that channels **savings** to investors. How does this process work? Essentially, financial institutions make money by "selling" money. You deposit money into an account. In return, the financial institution pays you a certain percentage of that money for keeping it in an account. That payment to you is called **interest**. The financial institution then loans a portion of your original deposit to other people. Those borrowers pay back their loans plus interest (at a higher percentage) to the bank, which keeps the profit.

The amount of interest depends on the **interest rate**, a percentage a bank will pay to depositors or charge to borrowers. Interest rates are determined by the central bank of each country. The **Federal Reserve System (Fed)** acts as our central bank in setting the *discount rate*, which is the interest rate that influences all other interest rates charged by financial institutions.

Commercial Banks

Commercial banks are the most common and safest financial institutions. In addition to accepting deposits and lending or transferring funds, commercial banks help their customers manage day-to-day transaction needs such as paying bills, withdrawing cash, and paying for purchases via debit cards or by check. Many commercial banks have

financial institution group that channels savings to investors; includes banks, insurance companies, savings and loan associations, credit unions

savings the dollars that become available for investors to use when others save

interest payment made for the use of borrowed money

interest rate the price of credit to a borrower

Federal Reserve System (Fed) privately owned, publicly controlled, central bank of the United States

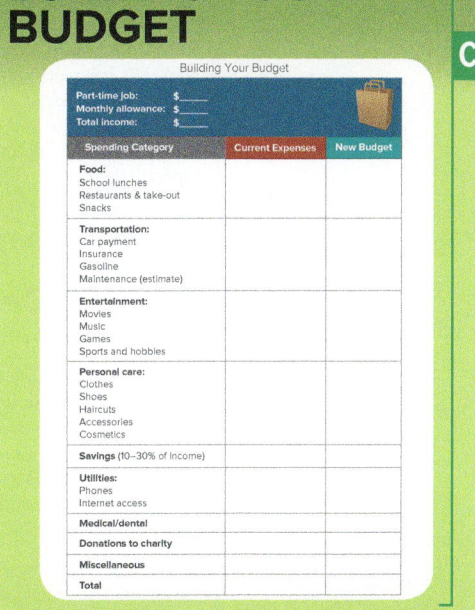

FIGURE 19.1 networks TRY IT YOURSELF ONLINE

BUILDING YOUR BUDGET

Building a budget involves categorizing your income and expenses carefully in order to track how your money is spent. Then you can understand how to accurately plan for the future.

▲ **CRITICAL THINKING**
Economic Analysis Are there any parts of your budget where you spend more money than you expected? How could you reduce spending in those areas?

connected.mcgraw-hill.com Personal Financial Literacy 559

CHAPTER 19, LESSON 1
Financial Institutions and Your Money

C1 Critical Thinking Skills

Creating a budget based on a future career Tell students to choose a career they like and research its average annual salary. Ask students to use that salary to construct a one-year budget plan based on the categories in the Building Your Budget chart.
BL Logical/Mathematical

C2 Critical Thinking Skills

Cutting expenses Have students add a column to the budget chart they completed. Tell students to use the new column to list ways that they will cut expenses in each spending category. Intrapersonal

Making Connections

Autonomy Trumps Wealth According to the American Psychological Association, popularity, influence, money, and luxury do NOT contribute the most to happiness. What does? Autonomy (feeling that your activities are self-chosen), feeling that you are effective in your activities, a sense of closeness with others, and self-esteem. Ask students if they agree or disagree, and why.

R Reading Skills

Explaining the function of financial institutions Ask: What is the main function of financial institutions? *(to channel savings to investors)*
AL Verbal/Linguistic

C3 Critical Thinking Skills

Analyzing the role of interest Ask: What role do you think interest plays in allocating savings to its most productive use? *(Answers may refer to financial institutions paying higher rates of interest to depositors for the long-term use of their deposits. Financial institutions, in turn, charge borrowers higher interest rates on loans from the bank. As a result, entrepreneurs and businesses must feel confident that their endeavor will profit, and they will work hard to produce profits. Similarly, investors channel savings into corporate stocks and bonds that pay high returns, as well as government bonds that are secure.)* Verbal/Linguistic

---

CHARTS

Building Your Budget

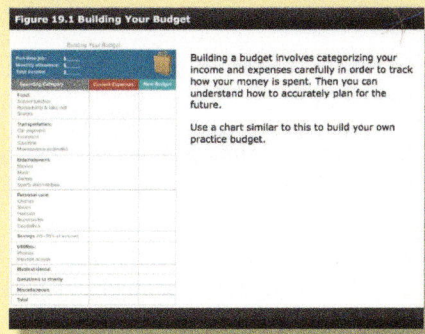

Creating a budget Have students view Figure 19.1 and determine whether they want to set up their budget on a weekly, monthly, or yearly basis. If students get paid every two weeks, they might want to set up an annual budget with 26 biweekly columns. Explain that students should record their net income—the income received after taxes have been taken out, and then to fill in the budget categories with actual figures. Tell students to monitor their budgets to make sure that the amounts they have allotted for each expenditure are reasonable. If they find that a category does not reflect their actual spending, they should adjust it. **Logical/Mathematical**

ANSWERS, p. 559

✓ **READING PROGRESS CHECK** Without a budget, a person can more easily fall into debt.

CRITICAL THINKING
Students' answers will vary, and will likely center around food, entertainment, and personal care.

Personal Financial Literacy **559**

CHAPTER 19, LESSON 1
Financial Institutions and Your Money

W Writing Skills

Explaining how financial institutions affect households and businesses Have students draw a diagram illustrating how financial institutions affect households and businesses. Prompt students to include as the central focus of the diagram all of the financial intermediaries they can think of. Remind students to add the circular activity of households and businesses providing savings (surplus funds) to financial intermediaries in exchange for interest payments, as well as providing savings to government and businesses directly in the form of stock and bond purchases. **Visual/Spatial, Logical/Mathematical**

R1 Reading Skills

Comparing the functions of financial institutions Have students create a chart comparing and contrasting the functions of commercial banks, credit unions, and nonbank financial institutions (finance companies, life insurance companies, investment banks). Have students identify the types of loans available to consumers from each institution. **Verbal/Linguistic**

Content Background Knowledge

Finance Companies Finance companies charge much higher interest rates than banks or credit unions, which makes their loans much more expensive. Assume you want a 60-month car loan for $6,000. A bank loan with an 8 percent interest rate would cost you $1,300 in interest over the life of the loan. Interest on the same loan at a finance company charging 12 percent interest would total $2,008, or at 16 percent, $2,755. A few percentage points make a big difference.

R2 Reading Skills

Identifying reasons to save Ask: **What are three benefits to opening a savings account?** *(Savings earn interest at no risk. Saving improves your credit rating. Savings are your only safety net in financial emergencies.)* **AL Verbal/Linguistic**

ANSWERS, p. 560

CRITICAL THINKING
It keeps depositors from worrying about losing their money should their bank fail and prevents bank runs. The FDIC guarantees deposits and steps in if a bank is in danger of collapse.

✓ **READING PROGRESS CHECK** to channel savings to investors

560

You shouldn't worry about depositing your hard-earned money in the bank. What makes commercial banks safe? The money that you deposit in a single bank is insured for up to $250,000 by an independent agency of the federal government called the Federal Deposit Insurance Corporation (FDIC). The FDIC was created during the Great Depression after so many people lost their bank savings due to bank runs.

▶ **CRITICAL THINKING**
Economic Analysis Why would insuring deposits be beneficial to banks as well as depositors?

online services, and some charge fees for services such as Automated Teller Machines (ATMs). What makes commercial banks safe? The money deposited in a single bank—up to $250,000—is insured (or guaranteed) through an independent agency of the federal government called the **Federal Deposit Insurance Corporation (FDIC)**.

Credit Unions

Credit unions typically are not-for-profit banks that have been organized for a specific group of people. State employees, school districts, or big companies, for example, might have their own credit union. The benefit of a credit union is that its goal is to share its profits with members (customers) by offering perks such as lower fees and lower interest rates on loans. Because of government laws regarding nonprofit organizations and income tax exemption, credit unions often can offer certain benefits that larger banks cannot.

Nonbank Financial Institutions

Some financial institutions do not accept deposits, yet still channel savings to borrowers. *Finance companies*, for example, make loans directly to consumers who want to pay for large items—such as vehicles or appliances—on an installment plan. *Life insurance companies* also lend their surplus funds. *Investment banks* buy and sell stocks and bonds, also known as "securities." At one time, investment banks and commercial banks existed together in the same bank. After the stock market crash of 1929, Congress passed the Glass-Steagall Act to separate them.

✓ **READING PROGRESS CHECK**

Summarizing What is the goal of financial institutions?

You as a Depositor

GUIDING QUESTION *What is the value of learning to save your money at an early age?*

It is true that you have the right to keep your savings in a box under your bed. If someone steals it or if your house catches on fire, however, your money is gone forever. It is safer to deposit your savings in a bank. Earning interest on savings carries no **risk** and requires no extra effort on your part beyond making the deposits. Having a savings account also improves your credit rating, which is vital if you want to borrow money in the future. In addition, your savings are your only safety net in financial emergencies.

Why Start Saving NOW?

Saved money grows, and with an early start you can amass huge amounts of money over time. How? Through a very important concept: compounding. This process results in your interest earning interest.

As you can see from **Figure 19.2**, compound interest is different from simple interest. For example, if you deposited $10,000 and earned *simple* interest of 5%, you would earn $500 a year for a total of $1,500 interest in 3 years.

In contrast, if you deposited $10,000 and earned *compound* interest of 5% annually, you would earn $500 the first year. But in the second year, you would earn interest not on $10,000 but on $10,500—your original deposit *plus* the first

Federal Deposit Insurance Corporation (FDIC) the U.S. government institution that provides deposit insurance on the depositor's account

credit unions nonprofit service cooperative that accepts deposits, makes loans, and provides other financial services

risk a situation in which the outcome is not certain, but the probabilities can be estimated

560

---

networks Online Teaching Options

WORKSHEET

Personal Finance Activity: What to Spend Money On

Considering spending habits Have students complete the Personal Finance Activity, which will give them a chance to decide what their needs and wants are and to allocate their money accordingly. At the end of this activity, they will be able to look at their own spending habits more objectively.
Logical/Mathematical

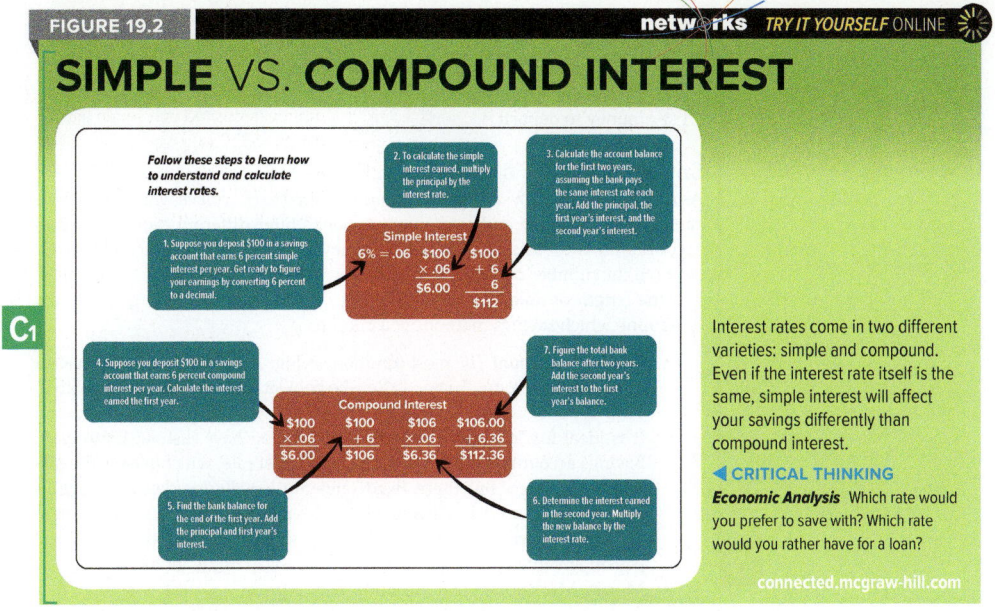

FIGURE 19.2

SIMPLE VS. COMPOUND INTEREST

Interest rates come in two different varieties: simple and compound. Even if the interest rate itself is the same, simple interest will affect your savings differently than compound interest.

◀ **CRITICAL THINKING**
Economic Analysis Which rate would you prefer to save with? Which rate would you rather have for a loan?

year's interest—which would total $525. In the third year, you would earn interest on $11,025, which is $551.25. With compound interest, then, your initial $10,000 would grow to $11,576.26 in three years, instead of $11,500 with simple interest. That may seem like a minor difference, but it can become a major difference as your balance grows over the years.

Interest for some accounts is compounded more often than annually. Some accounts are compounded semi-annually, quarterly, monthly, daily, or even continuously. The more frequently an account is compounded, the more interest you earn.

And the longer you leave your money in an account, the better compounding works—especially in an account with frequent compounding. For example, if you left $10,000 in an account for 10 years, with interest compounded *quarterly*, you'd have almost $16,500—without ever adding another cent!

Opening an Account

People choose a particular bank for various reasons. Some decide to go to the bank their parents use, or they might choose a bank because it's convenient or has a good reputation. Some banks offer better service or lower fees than others. Whatever bank you choose, there are a number of questions you can ask to make sure the bank is right for you.

- **Does it require a minimum balance?** Some banks charge you a fee if you do not keep a certain dollar amount in your account; other banks do not.
- **What are the fees?** It's good to know up front what services you will and won't be charged for.
- **What interest rates does the bank offer?** Even though the Fed determines the initial interest rate, banks have the ability to offer a particular range for various accounts.

You might already have a bank account that someone opened jointly for you (for your education, for example), but you must be age 18 to open an account of your own. Other items you will need to open an account at a bank include:

connected.mcgraw-hill.com   **Personal Financial Literacy 561**

CHAPTER 19, LESSON 1
Financial Institutions and Your Money

C1 Critical Thinking Skills

Applying knowledge about compound interest
Ask: If given a choice, would you rather have a savings account with interest compounded annually, quarterly, monthly, daily, or continuously? *(continuously)* What is the reason for your answer? *(More frequent compounding yields more interest.)* **Logical/Mathematical**

C2 Critical Thinking Skills

Comparing compound and simple interest Use the following activity to guide students through the mathematics for calculating simple and compound interest. Have students imagine that they have $100 to deposit in a savings account. They can place the money in an account that pays 5 percent compound interest or an account that pays 6 percent simple interest. Lead them through the steps of calculating the total savings per year at 5 percent interest on $100 compounded annually for eight years: $105, $110.25, $115.76, $121.55, $127.63, $134.01, $140.71, $147.75. Then guide students to calculate that 6 percent simple interest over eight years would amount to $48, for a total savings of $148. Help students conclude that the first account would be more profitable for long-term savings, and the second would be more profitable for short-term savings. **AL Logical/Mathematical**

R Reading Skills

Asking questions before selecting a bank   Ask: What questions should you ask a potential bank? *(Does it require a minimum balance? What are the fees? What interest rates does the bank offer?)*
AL Verbal/Linguistic

CHARTS

Simple vs. Compound Interest

Understanding how to calculate simple and compound interest Have students follow the steps on Figure 19.2 sequentially. Remind students that simple interest is figured only on the principal, or original deposit, not on any interest earned. Compound interest is paid on the principal plus any interest that has been earned. Point out that the amount of interest earned on a deposit is expressed as a percent, such as 6 percent as shown, for a time period, such as per year. **Ask:** What would be the impact of compounding interest on a daily basis rather than an annual basis? *(Students should realize that compounding interest daily earns more interest.)* **Logical/Mathematical**

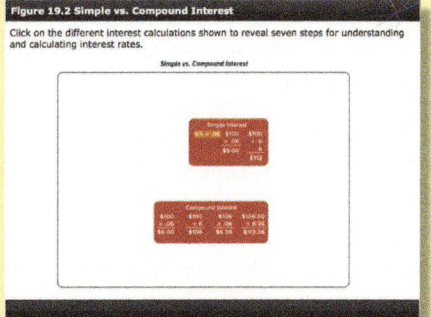

ANSWERS, p. 561

CRITICAL THINKING
Compound; simple

Personal Financial Literacy 561

CHAPTER 19, LESSON 1
Financial Institutions and Your Money

R Reading Skills

Opening a savings account Ask: **How does one begin a savings program?** *(After selecting a bank, at age 18 one can open a savings account with an initial deposit, a photo ID, proof of address, and Social Security card. Make a commitment to put a certain percentage of each paycheck or monetary gift into savings.)*

W Writing Skills

Examining types, risks, costs, and benefits of savings accounts Ask: **What are four types of savings accounts available to consumers from financial institutions?** *(traditional or passbook savings account, money market deposit account, money market mutual fund, certificate of deposit account)* **Which has the most risk?** *(money market mutual fund)* **What three factors affect the return on various types of savings accounts?** *(the minimum balance, or how much money you must keep in the account; the frequency and availability of transactions, or how often you are allowed to deposit or withdraw funds; the length of time you keep the money in the account)* **Verbal/Linguistic**

C1 Critical Thinking Skills

Clarifying the maturity factor on CDs Ask: **What type of person would most likely be interested in opening a CD account?** *(someone seeking to save money over a long period of time)* **What type of person would NOT likely be interested in opening a CD account?** *(someone who needs quick access to his or her money; for example, a person who will soon be buying a car or a house)* **Verbal/Linguistic**

C2 Critical Thinking Skills

Determining higher or lower interest rates Have each student hold a piece of paper with a large arrow on it. As you list a factor that affects interest rates for different types of savings accounts—such as "requires higher minimum balance" or "fast access to cash"—ask students to turn their arrow in the direction of the corresponding interest rate—pointing up for higher interest, and down for lower interest. **BL Kinesthetic, Logical/Mathematical**

ANSWERS, p. 562

CRITICAL THINKING

Students should consider the various deposit requirements with each type of savings account and whether or not they will need to access the money in that account and, if so, how often.

- a photo ID,
- proof of address (this can be on your driver's license; a utility bill with your name and address is also acceptable),
- your Social Security card,
- money to deposit.

Savings Vehicles and Risks vs. Returns

As its name suggests, a savings account is intended to be a place where customers can save their money and earn interest. Banks offer different types of savings accounts on the basis of how much money you keep in your account (your *balance*), the number of times you deposit or withdraw funds (your *transactions*), and the length of time you keep the money in the account. Your goals should determine which savings methods you choose.

- **Passbook Account** The most common savings account is sometimes called a "passbook account," named after the booklet that originally came with it. This type of account usually allows a low minimum balance, and it is ideal for "emergency funds" because you have fast access to cash. Savings accounts typically have a fixed interest rate, which means the rate will not change. But these fixed rates are usually low because savings accounts have no risk. Therefore, you also need to utilize other accounts—including investments—to receive enough interest to offset the taxes you'll pay on any interest earned, and to remain ahead of the inflation rate.
- **Money Market Deposit Account** This type of account is similar to a savings account in that it is safe (FDIC-insured), with easy but infrequent withdrawals. These accounts pay slightly higher interest because they have various deposit requirements, usually requiring a higher minimum balance. The interest rate on money market deposit accounts can change on the basis of the markets.
- **Money Market Mutual Fund** These accounts are relatively low risk because deposits are invested in a pool in short-term financial vehicles. Terms—or the amount of time you cannot withdraw your deposit—are from 90 days to 13 months. Interest rates on these accounts are comparable to money market deposit accounts.
- **Certificate of Deposit (CD)** This type of account has higher interest rates than a traditional savings account. Depositors "purchase" a CD of a certain amount ($100, $1,000, $5,000, $10,000, etc.) with a fixed rate (3.5%, 5%, etc.) with a set time period (1 year, 18 months, etc.). Making an early withdrawal before the "maturity date" can result in a penalty charge.

TYPES OF SAVINGS ACCOUNTS

There are many different types of savings methods available to depositors. Each method has its own set of advantages and disadvantages.

▶ **CRITICAL THINKING**
Economic Analysis You have saved up $1000, and now you wish to use a savings account to earn interest. Consider what your needs are and discuss what options you have for your money.

Certificate of Deposit (CD)
No risk
Higher interest
Longer, higher deposit requirements

Money Market Mutual Fund
Minimal risk
Higher interest
Longer deposit requirements

Money Market Deposit
No risk
Higher interest
Deposit requirements

Savings Account
No risk
Low interest
Easily accessible

562

---

networks Online Teaching Options

WORKSHEET

Personal Finance Activity: Saving Up for Purchases

Determining how long it takes to save Present the Personal Finance Activity, which will help students see how long it might take with a minimum wage job to save up for a large purchase. Have students discuss which type of savings account would be most beneficial for their short-term and long-term savings goals. Review with students the meanings of *disposable income* and *discretionary income*. **Logical/Mathematical**

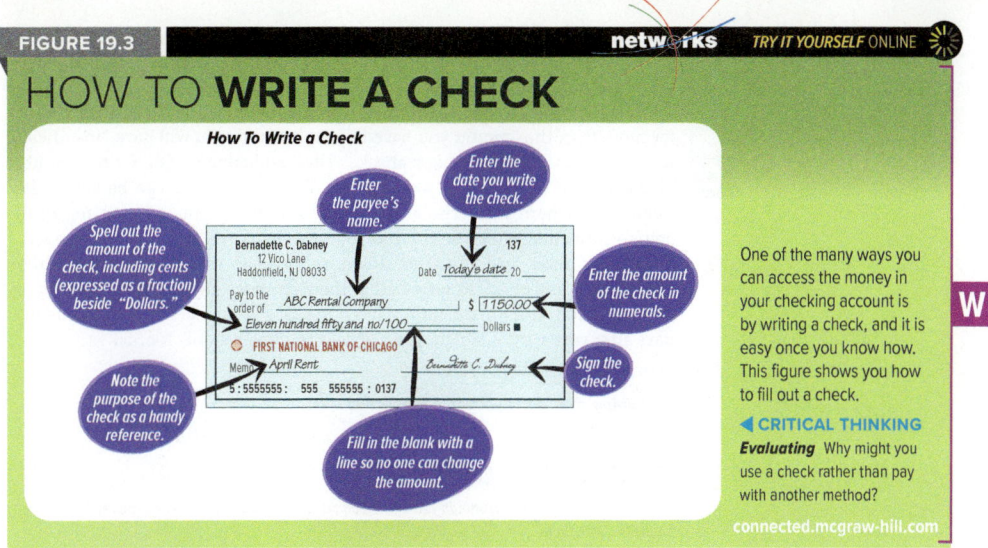

FIGURE 19.3 HOW TO WRITE A CHECK

One of the many ways you can access the money in your checking account is by writing a check, and it is easy once you know how. This figure shows you how to fill out a check.

◀ **CRITICAL THINKING**
Evaluating Why might you use a check rather than pay with another method?

Checking Accounts

A checking account is a **demand deposit account (DDA)**. This kind of account allows customers the easiest access to their money for daily and monthly use. Customers can access their money by walking into the bank and filling out a deposit or withdrawal slip, by writing a check, or by using a debit card. If the account earns any interest at all, it is usually minimal because the balance can change so much.

Demand deposit account (DDA) account whose funds can be removed by writing a check and without having to gain prior approval from the depository institution

Ways to deposit money into your checking account include:

1. Go to the bank, endorse checks (personal checks or paychecks) by signing your name to the back of them, fill out a deposit slip, and hand to a teller.
2. Put endorsed checks and a deposit slip into an ATM. Tellers will make the deposit during banking hours.
3. Transfer funds from a savings or other account to your checking account online.

Ways to access the money in your checking account include:

1. Withdraw cash from an ATM.
2. Use a debit card at a store.
3. Write a paper check (or read numbers from a paper check to a vendor over the phone). (See **Figure 19.3**)
4. Go to the bank, fill out a withdrawal slip, and receive cash from a teller.
5. Pay bills with a bill-paying service through your bank online.

Keep a personal record of every transaction you make—deposits, checks written, and ATM withdrawals. Each month, your bank sends you a *statement*, which is a record of all of the transactions (deposits and withdrawals) you have made in a month. Many banks also allow you to view your activity online through their Web site.

Included in your monthly bank statement is a form that allows you to "reconcile" your account each month. This means that you compare your own personal records with those of the bank to make sure there are no errors. If you

---

CHAPTER 19, LESSON 1
Financial Institutions and Your Money

W Writing Skills

Practicing writing a check Have students practice writing a check. Point out the need to spell out the dollar amount correctly. For example, on the sample check shown in the text, if students spelled out "Eleven fifty" instead of "Eleven hundred fifty" or "One thousand one hundred fifty," the bank might pay only $11.50—not $1,150.00. Remind students to be sure the numerals and longhand version are the same amount. **Kinesthetic**

C Critical Thinking Skills

Examining the positive and negative aspects of debit cards **Ask:** What are the positive aspects of debit cards? *(efficiency, ease of transactions, provides option for not carrying cash)* **Ask:** What are the negative aspects of debit cards? *(tempting to make spontaneous purchases; must be disciplined with keeping and tallying receipts to balance checking account; easier to defraud than a paper checking account)*

English Language Proficiency

Intermediate Provide students with simple sentence frames to help them identify key ideas in the text. Provide a word bank from the text to complete the frames as they read. As more English is learned, decrease the use of linguistic accommodations. Provide only sentence starters to direct students' attention to key ideas.

DIAGRAM

How to Write a Check

Inspecting how to write a check Display Figure 19.3, which shows how to write a check. Have students take turns reading aloud the instructions. Take a poll in the class of those who have a checking account or have written a check. Then take a poll of those who have a debit card or have used one. Explain that the two are the same account. Tell students to get into the habit of logging their debit transactions in a way similar to that of writing a physical check number, date, and amount into a check register. Because of online banking, many people receive their monthly bank statement electronically, as well as a daily list of transactions. Tell students to check their pending payments online every day to stay in control of their balance and to spot fraud early. Remind students to retain all receipts and ATM transactions to keep track of their balance. **Logical/Mathematical**

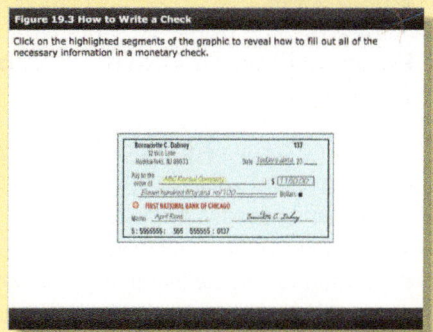

Figure 19.3 How to Write a Check
Click on the highlighted segments of the graphic to reveal how to fill out all of the necessary information in a monetary check.

ANSWERS, p. 563

CRITICAL THINKING

Answers will vary, but students could note that checks are useful in transferring money between individuals or businesses, such as a rental office, that may not be set up to take debit or credit payments.

CHAPTER 19, LESSON 1
Financial Institutions and Your Money

C Critical Thinking Skills

Reconciling a bank statement Stress to students that, after writing a check to someone or making a deposit into their checking account, they need to write the check number, date, and amount in their check register. When they receive their monthly bank statement, they must balance their checkbook by following these steps: 1. Sort the checks by number. Mark off each one in the checkbook. 2. Mark off the deposit slips. 3. Deduct service charges and bank fees from the checkbook balance. 4. Add to the bank statement balance any deposits that have not yet cleared. 5. Total the amount of checks that have not yet cleared. Subtract this total from the amount on the bank statement. **Logical/Mathematical**

W Writing Skills

Appreciating the importance of credit Help students understand the importance of credit in the economy by asking them to discuss what life would be like if all purchases had to be paid for with cash. Begin the discussion by listing on the board the types of purchases people often make with credit—houses, automobiles, home improvement, college tuition, and vacations, for example. Have students use the point developed in the discussion to write a brief essay titled "Life Without Credit." **Verbal/Linguistic**

Making Connections

Becoming Creditworthy Some students may not appreciate how actions taken today can have an impact on creditworthiness. To help students see the connection, provide the following example: If a person is chronically late with payments, defaults on a credit card account, or fails to fulfill other credit obligations, such facts will be reported on his or her credit history. Several years later, potential lenders will read this history and turn down that person's request for a loan or a credit card. Ask students to offer ideas on how a person might keep his or her credit history sound. Then have students construct a credit plan for purchasing a major item. **AL Verbal/Linguistic**

ANSWERS, p. 564

✓ **READING PROGRESS CHECK** Saving now allows your deposits to grow through compound interest.

CRITICAL THINKING

It could negatively impact the ability to repay debt, especially if one's budget is tight to begin with.

---

find a discrepancy, contact your bank's customer service right away to determine the problem. If you fail to report a discrepancy on your statement within 60 days, you could be held responsible.

C It is important to pay attention to your account balance. If you write a check for more than the amount you have in your account, you will have "insufficient funds," also called "bouncing a check." This can happen if you write a number of checks and lose track of your balance. Bouncing checks can be very costly. Vendors to whom you write a bad check will charge you a fee on top of the amount you already owe them. And your own bank will also charge you a fee.

If your debit card is lost or stolen, report it to your financial institution immediately and check to see whether there has been any unauthorized activity on your account. If any unauthorized purchases are made within two business days after your card is stolen, you are held responsible only for $50.

✓ **READING PROGRESS CHECK**

Explaining Why is it important to start saving now?

You as a Borrower

GUIDING QUESTION *What should you understand about the rules of borrowing money from financial institutions?*

W Our society depends more and more on credit, or borrowing, to pay for purchases, which is why it is important to establish and then maintain good credit. Paying cash for everything does not make you a good credit risk. To prove you're responsible enough to get credit, you have to establish a credit history and a credit score. About 15% of a credit score is based on how long you've had credit, so it's important to establish credit as soon as possible.

Are You Creditworthy?

creditors persons or institutions to whom money is owed

Creditors decide whether to lend you money and how much interest to charge by looking at three things:

1. **Can you pay them back?** Add your monthly income to your bank account balances to find your total assets. Then total your monthly expenses, including debts or obligations. Compare the two to see if you're able to take on more debt.

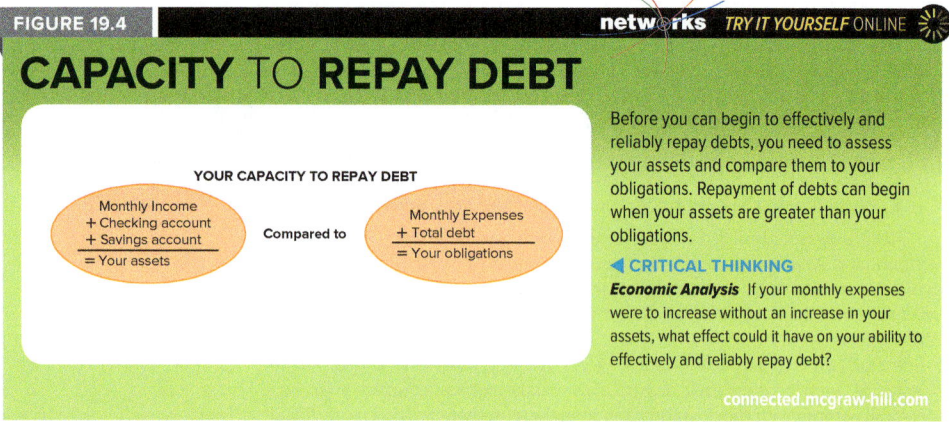

FIGURE 19.4

CAPACITY TO REPAY DEBT

Before you can begin to effectively and reliably repay debts, you need to assess your assets and compare them to your obligations. Repayment of debts can begin when your assets are greater than your obligations.

◀ **CRITICAL THINKING**
Economic Analysis If your monthly expenses were to increase without an increase in your assets, what effect could it have on your ability to effectively and reliably repay debt?

564

---

networks Online Teaching Options

WORKSHEET

Personal Finance Activity: Comparing Credit Card Offers

Comparing credit card offers Students will analyze the advantages and disadvantages of various credit card offers by comparing of each card's features, including APR, annual fees, payment dates, and rewards programs. Students will use a chart to find the information that answers a series of questions about each card. When they are done with each step, the will have the information needed to make an informed decision about which credit card is right for their needs and financial situation. **Logical/Mathematical**

2. **Do you have a good credit rating?** Lenders want to know if you've repaid previous debts on time.

3. **Do you have collateral? Collateral** is used mostly to buy homes or cars. If you don't make the payments, the lender takes back the house or car.

collateral something of value that a borrower lets the lender claim if a loan is not repaid

Credit Cards

When you use a credit card, you're borrowing money from a creditor that must be paid back—*plus interest*. Lenders make their profits on the interest their customers owe. Unlike a friend who loans you money and would prefer to have it all back at once, credit card companies set a low "minimum monthly payment" amount. The longer it takes you to pay off your balance, the more they are able to charge you. This is good for the lender, but ultimately detrimental to you.

Recall that you can earn money on your savings through compounding interest. Most savings accounts earn a low percentage (1% to 3%). In contrast, lenders charge compounding interest that is much higher (15% to 25%). That means if you run up a balance of $1,000 on a credit card and pay only the minimum payment each month (around $25.00), it will take you 22 years to pay off the credit card, and you will end up paying $3,000 total, which is three times the amount you initially borrowed.

Not all banks and credit cards are the same. If you have good credit, you can negotiate a lower interest rate, or annual percentage rate (APR). Be careful that it's not just an "introductory rate," which increases after a certain period of time. Credit card companies often set up information tables on campuses to attract college students. These can be great opportunities to establish your credit, but be sure you ask about the interest rate. If it is too high, keep shopping for a lower APR.

Every month, you'll get a statement listing everything you bought with your credit card the previous month, the payments you made, and the balance. Be sure to pay your credit card bill on time. And do not fall into the credit card trap of paying only the minimum payment.

Building Credit and Your Credit Score

Every time you buy something with a credit card or pay a bill, your activity is being recorded by a credit bureau, which issues each person a credit rating. Companies and banks that loan money can access that credit rating and use it to determine how likely you are to repay a loan.

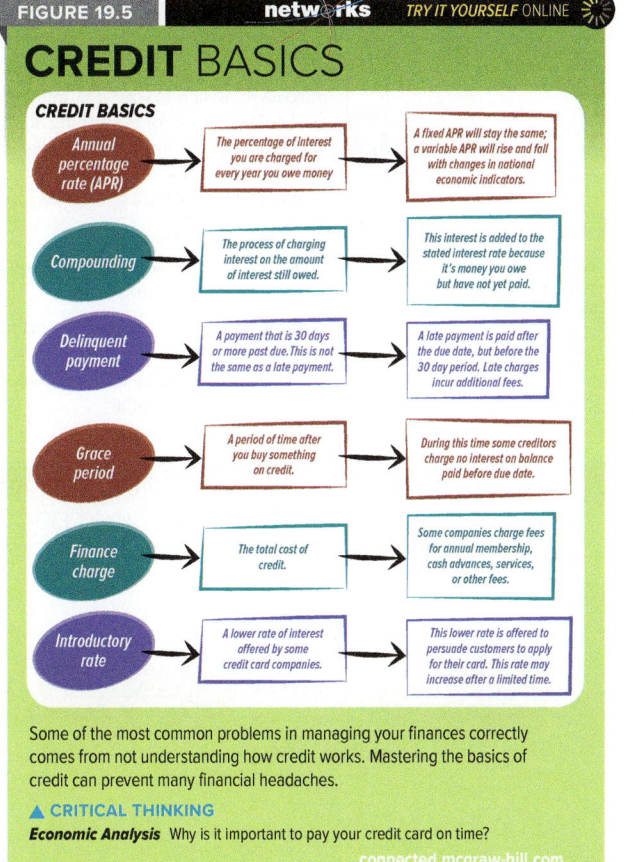

FIGURE 19.5 **CREDIT BASICS**

Some of the most common problems in managing your finances correctly comes from not understanding how credit works. Mastering the basics of credit can prevent many financial headaches.

▲ **CRITICAL THINKING**
Economic Analysis Why is it important to pay your credit card on time?

Personal Financial Literacy **565**

CHARTS

Credit Basics

Understanding terms that apply to credit cards Have students view and study Figure 19.5. Ask volunteers to read each term, definition, and additional information. Bring to class various credit card offers that come in the mail, or go online and print out several. Have students analyze them for examples of the terms and conditions. Have students suppose that they have purchased an item for $2,000 using one of the credit cards offered. Have them calculate how long it would take to pay off the debt making only minimum payments. Students should make their calculations using the APR, compounding, and finance charges.
Interpersonal

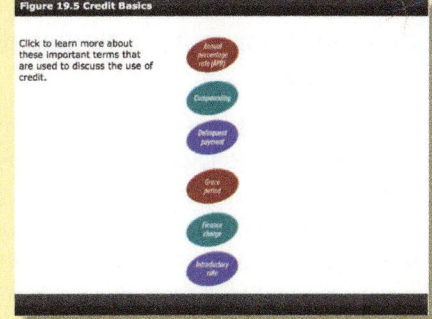

CHAPTER 19, LESSON 1
Financial Institutions and Your Money

C1 Critical Thinking Skills

Providing examples of creditworthiness On the board, draw a table with "Capacity to Pay," "Credit Rating," and "Collateral" as row headings. Add "Good Risk" and "Bad Risk" as column headings. Call on students to come to the board and enter examples of good risks and bad risks in the appropriate cells. **Verbal/Linguistic**

C2 Critical Thinking Skills

Examining the positive and negative aspects of credit cards Ask students to create a T-chart listing the positive aspects of credit card on the left, and the negative aspects on the right. Discuss students' responses in a class discussion.

C3 Critical Thinking Skills

Analyzing credit risk behaviors Ask students to imagine that they have been asked to cosign a loan. Have them list reasons why they would or would not be willing to be a cosigner. **Ask: Do you think you are creditworthy enough for someone else to cosign a loan for you? Why or why not? What type of behavior should a responsible borrower exhibit?** AL **Verbal/Linguistic**

Content Background Knowledge

Credit Score Killers A person's credit score is determined by a mixture of five elements. In order of importance, these elements are payment history, debt, length of credit history, new credit, and types of credit used. A person's amount of income is not figured into their credit score. For example, if someone has a large income but never pays bills on time, he or she will have a low credit score. According to *FDIC Consumer News*, people commonly make seven simple mistakes that lower their credit scores: 1. Paying bills after the due date; 2. Not paying the minimum amount required; 3. Keeping high credit card balances; 4. Owning too many credit cards; 5. Not regularly checking your credit report; 6. Not using your full legal name in bank accounts and financial documents; 7. Not alerting creditors when moving to a different address.

ANSWERS, p. 565

CRITICAL THINKING
Paying your credit card on time prevents late fees.

Personal Financial Literacy **565**

CHAPTER 19, LESSON 1
Financial Institutions and Your Money

C Critical Thinking Skills

Reconciling a bank statement Stress to students that, after writing a check to someone or making a deposit into their checking account, they need to write the check number, date, and amount in their check register. When they receive their monthly bank statement, they must balance their checkbook by following these steps: 1. Sort the checks by number. Mark off each one in the checkbook. 2. Mark off the deposit slips. 3. Deduct service charges and bank fees from the checkbook balance. 4. Add to the bank statement balance any deposits that have not yet cleared. 5. Total the amount of checks that have not yet cleared. Subtract this total from the amount on the bank statement. **Logical/Mathematical**

W Writing Skills

Appreciating the importance of credit Help students understand the importance of credit in the economy by asking them to discuss what life would be like if all purchases had to be paid for with cash. Begin the discussion by listing on the board the types of purchases people often make with credit—houses, automobiles, home improvement, college tuition, and vacations, for example. Have students use the point developed in the discussion to write a brief essay titled "Life Without Credit." **Verbal/Linguistic**

Making Connections

Becoming Creditworthy Some students may not appreciate how actions taken today can have an impact on creditworthiness. To help students see the connection, provide the following example: If a person is chronically late with payments, defaults on a credit card account, or fails to fulfill other credit obligations, such facts will be reported on his or her credit history. Several years later, potential lenders will read this history and turn down that person's request for a loan or a credit card. Ask students to offer ideas on how a person might keep his or her credit history sound. Then have students construct a credit plan for purchasing a major item. **AL Verbal/Linguistic**

ANSWERS, p. 564

✓ **READING PROGRESS CHECK** Saving now allows your deposits to grow through compound interest.

CRITICAL THINKING
It could negatively impact the ability to repay debt, especially if one's budget is tight to begin with.

---

find a discrepancy, contact your bank's customer service right away to determine the problem. If you fail to report a discrepancy on your statement within 60 days, you could be held responsible.

C It is important to pay attention to your account balance. If you write a check for more than the amount you have in your account, you will have "insufficient funds," also called "bouncing a check." This can happen if you write a number of checks and lose track of your balance. Bouncing checks can be very costly. Vendors to whom you write a bad check will charge you a fee on top of the amount you already owe them. And your own bank will also charge you a fee.

If your debit card is lost or stolen, report it to your financial institution immediately and check to see whether there has been any unauthorized activity on your account. If any unauthorized purchases are made within two business days after your card is stolen, you are held responsible only for $50.

✓ **READING PROGRESS CHECK**

Explaining Why is it important to start saving now?

You as a Borrower

GUIDING QUESTION *What should you understand about the rules of borrowing money from financial institutions?*

W Our society depends more and more on credit, or borrowing, to pay for purchases, which is why it is important to establish and then maintain good credit. Paying cash for everything does not make you a good credit risk. To prove you're responsible enough to get credit, you have to establish a credit history and a credit score. About 15% of a credit score is based on how long you've had credit, so it's important to establish credit as soon as possible.

Are You Creditworthy?

creditors persons or institutions to whom money is owed

Creditors decide whether to lend you money and how much interest to charge by looking at three things:

1. **Can you pay them back?** Add your monthly income to your bank account balances to find your total assets. Then total your monthly expenses, including debts or obligations. Compare the two to see if you're able to take on more debt.

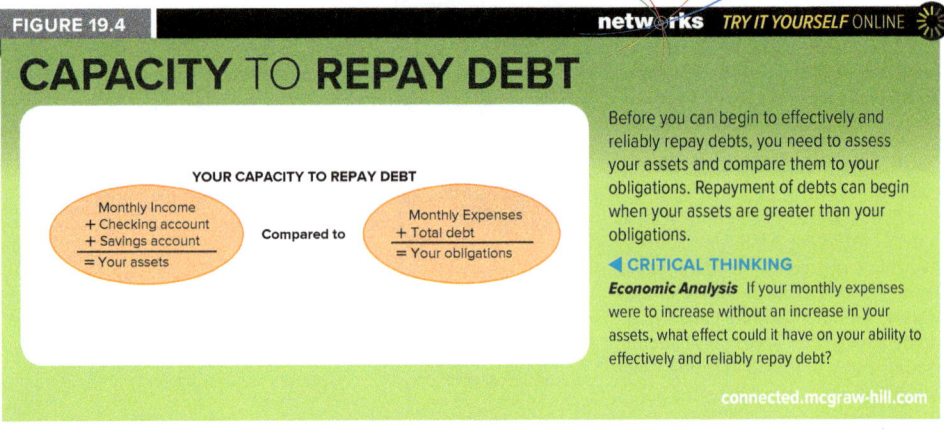

FIGURE 19.4

CAPACITY TO REPAY DEBT

Before you can begin to effectively and reliably repay debts, you need to assess your assets and compare them to your obligations. Repayment of debts can begin when your assets are greater than your obligations.

◀ **CRITICAL THINKING**
Economic Analysis If your monthly expenses were to increase without an increase in your assets, what effect could it have on your ability to effectively and reliably repay debt?

Online Teaching Options

WORKSHEET

Personal Finance Activity: Comparing Credit Card Offers

Comparing credit card offers Students will analyze the advantages and disadvantages of various credit card offers by comparing each card's features, including APR, annual fees, payment dates, and rewards programs. Students will use a chart to find the information that answers a series of questions about each card. When they are done with each step, the will have the information needed to make an informed decision about which credit card is right for their needs and financial situation. **Logical/Mathematical**

as you will be bound by law to the terms laid out in the contract. Be sure to read the fine print on all contracts.

Failure to meet the terms of a loan can lead to legal action, including taking you to court. Lenders can "garnish your wages," meaning your employer will pay the creditor out of your future paychecks. If the loan is for a piece of property, such as a home or a car, the creditor can *repossess* them, or take them from you.

Declaring Bankruptcy

If you have trouble repaying a loan, there are things you can do to get help. Contact your creditor right away. Many creditors are willing to work with you if you lose your job. Credit counselors and other services also are available. There may come a time when income cannot keep up with the accumulation of monthly bills. A person can "declare" bankruptcy by filing a petition with the courts. Some people view bankruptcy as a "clean slate," but it stays on a credit record for a long time and can make moving forward very challenging. It should be the option of last resort.

The rules of bankruptcy vary from state to state. There are two main parties in a bankruptcy, the *debtor* (the party who owes) and the *creditor* (the party that is owed). Most bankruptcy cases involve one debtor (or two if married) and multiple creditors.

Several types of bankruptcies exist. The circumstances determine which "chapter" of the Bankruptcy Code a person should file under. Most personal bankruptcies are one of the following:

- **Chapter 7** is the most common form of bankruptcy. A trustee from the court is appointed to evaluate the debtor's assets and use them to pay a portion of the debt. Money owed on student loans, child support, and taxes will not be dismissed, however. Those with lower incomes and few assets typically choose this option.
- **Chapter 13** bankruptcy allows the debtor to keep some or all of his or her property. A trustee is appointed to create an appropriate repayment plan with lowered payments. The court collects future payments from the debtor to pass onto creditors.

After the debtor has completed the requirements spelled out by the court, he or she is relieved of the debt previously accumulated.

✓ **READING PROGRESS CHECK**

Summarizing Why is a good credit score important?

LESSON 1 REVIEW

Reviewing Vocabulary

1. *Defining* Explain the differences between a secured credit card and an unsecured credit card.

Using Your Notes

2. *Summarizing* Use your notes to explain the methods available for depositing money into a personal checking account.

Answering the Guiding Questions

3. *Explaining* What is the value of learning how to properly budget your money?

4. *Discussing* How do financial institutions affect your own budget?

5. *Describing* What is the value of learning to save your money at an early age?

6. *Prioritizing* What should you understand about the rules of borrowing money from financial institutions?

Writing About Economics

7. *Informative/Explanatory* Write a two-page essay explaining the concept of bankruptcy. When does bankruptcy occur? What benefits does bankruptcy provide to the person or institution? What risks does declaring bankruptcy bring?

CHAPTER 19, LESSON 1
Financial Institutions and Your Money

R Reading Skills

Evaluating the costs and benefits of declaring personal bankruptcy Ask: **What are the costs of declaring bankruptcy?** *(Declaring bankruptcy stays on a credit record for a long time, and can make it difficult to receive credit in the future. The debtor's assets may be used to pay a portion of the debt if Chapter 7 of the Bankruptcy Code is filed.)* **What are the benefits of declaring bankruptcy?** *(If Chapter 13 of the Bankruptcy Code is filed, the debtor has lower payments.)*

W Writing Skills

Researching and writing about bankruptcy Tell students that some Americans think filing for bankruptcy has become too easy. These people want the bankruptcy laws to be revised. They suggest that Chapter 7 bankruptcy—where all debts except taxes, mortgages, student loans, child support, and alimony are wiped out—should be limited to people with low incomes. Anyone earning above the national median income would have to file for bankruptcy under Chapter 13. This entails the setting up of a repayment schedule designed to retire at least a third of the debt. Have students interview a local financial attorney or reseach personal bankruptcy online. Have students investigate the steps in a bankruptcy case, including the schedule of priorities. They should summarize their findings in a short report.

CLOSE & REFLECT

Making wise credit choices Tell students that they have been invited to write an article titled "How I Make Wise Credit Choices" for a consumer magazine. Then ask students to develop an outline for this article explaining the responsibilities of borrowing money. Share the outlines in class.

LESSON 1 REVIEW ANSWERS

Reviewing Vocabulary

1. A secured credit card is limited to the amount one deposits in an account. An unsecured credit card is not limited to the balance of any account.

Using Your Notes

2. Give endorsed check and deposit slip to a bank teller or into an ATM. Or transfer funds online from savings to checking.

Answering the Guiding Questions

3. control your finances, make life less stressful, prevent debt

4. Financial institutions pay interest on savings, and charge interest on borrowed funds. Borrowers must include interest on installment payments.

5. the more your interest will earn interest through compounding

6. keep a good credit rating to negotiate a lower interest rate, pay more than the minimum monthly payment, pay on time, check the monthly statement for errors

Writing About Economics

7. Benefits: dismiss certain loans (Chapter 7) or pay reduced payments (Chapter 13); Risks: bankruptcy stays on a credit record for a long time, obtaining loans in the future is challenging

---

ANSWERS, p. 567

✓ **READING PROGRESS CHECK** A good credit score determines the likelihood of receiving a loan, and a lower interest rate if a loan is granted.

CHAPTER 19, LESSON 2
Business Organizations and Your Money

ENGAGE

W Writing Skills

🔔 **Learning prior knowledge of stocks and bonds** Write the words *Stocks* and *Bonds* on the board. Before students begin the lesson, ask volunteers to come to the board and list what they think they know about these financial assets (in general) under the appropriate heading. Erase anything that is not true, and tell students that personal financial literacy involves becoming more familiar with stocks and bonds.

TEACH & ASSESS

R1 Reading Skills

Explaining capital formation Ask: **What is capital formation?** *(It is a term used by economists to describe the transfer of money from individuals or households to businesses and government through investments and loans.)* Have students explain how the amount of savings in an economy is the basis of capital formation. **Verbal/Linguistic**

R2 Reading Skills

Relating financial institutions to capital formation Ask: **What role do financial institutions play in capital formation?** *(Financial institutions turn the collective savings of all their customers into investments that help many new businesses in the United States get started each year.)* **Verbal/Linguistic**

ANSWERS, p. 568

ESSENTIAL QUESTION ACTIVITY

Both the traditional IRA and the Roth IRA allow the investor to make yearly deposits. The traditional IRA does not take taxes from the contributions until withdrawals are made during retirement. A Roth IRA takes the taxes out during the contribution period rather during the withdrawal period.

TAKING NOTES

Preferred stock: receive dividends after bondholders are paid; no say in how the company is run; need a broker. **Common stock:** allowed a say in how the company is run; earn dividends last, need a broker. **Mutual fund:** reduced risk; returns are tied to the market, need a broker. **Corporate bonds:** moderate risk; interest payments are taxed. **Municipal bonds:** low risk, no federal tax; lower interest. **Treasury instruments:** low risk; lower interest

568

Interact with these digital assets and others in lesson 2
- ✓ INTERACTIVE IMAGE
  Raising Capital
- ✓ INTERACTIVE CHART
  Common Investments
- ✓ INTERACTIVE CHART
  Reading Stock Market Reports
- ✓ SELF-CHECK QUIZ

networks TRY IT YOURSELF ONLINE

Reading Help Desk

Content Vocabulary
- capital formation
- sole proprietorship
- unlimited liability
- limited life
- partnership
- limited partnership
- corporation
- stockholders
- stocks
- dividends
- preferred stock
- common stock
- portfolio diversification
- mutual fund
- stockbroker
- maturity
- municipal bonds
- Treasury bills
- Treasury notes
- Treasury bonds
- savings bonds
- Individual Retirement Accounts (IRAs)

TAKING NOTES:

Key Ideas and Details
ACTIVITY Use the graphic organizer below to describe the advantages and disadvantages of the financial assets listed.

Financial asset	Advantages	Disadvantages
Preferred stock		
Common stock		
Mutual fund		
Corporate bonds		
Municipal bonds		
Treasury instruments		

568

LESSON 2
Business Organizations and Your Money

ESSENTIAL QUESTION

What are the different types of business organizations?

W It's never too early to start thinking about retirement. By disciplining yourself to set aside some of your salary from each paycheck, you can begin saving money and using interest to build up money that you will need later in life when you aren't working for a salary any longer.

Explain the differences between a traditional Individual Retirement Account (IRA) and a Roth IRA.

Business Organization and Ownership

GUIDING QUESTION *How do the different types of business organizations change the amount of financial risk assumed by the individual investor?*

R1 **Capital formation** is a term used by economists to describe the transfer of money from individuals or households to businesses and government through investments and loans. Capital formation depends on savings and borrowing, and the smooth flow of these funds through the financial system benefits everyone. How so? Financial institutions turn the collective savings of all their customers into investments that result in more jobs, which result in more goods and services being produced. Rising employment also increases demand for more goods and services. Countries with good capital formation experience economic growth.

R2 Capital formation helps many of the nearly 600,000 new businesses in the United States get started each year. For many people—and perhaps you in the future—owning a business is a way to fulfill a lifelong passion. For others it is a way to have more control over their professional goals, the people they work with, and personal life balance. Just as there are different motivations for starting a business, there are different ways to organize a business.

Sole Proprietorships

A **sole proprietorship** is a business owned by one person. It is the most common form of business organization. To get started, the owner needs to

---

networks Online Teaching Options

BELLRINGER

Dow Jones Industrial Average

Identifying symbols of the financial market
After displaying the Bellringer, ask students what the image represents. *(Students should recognize that Wall Street symbolizes finance in the United States.)* Then have students categorize the companies listed on the Dow. Categories could include credit card companies, pharmaceuticals, oil companies, communications, and so on. Then organize students into small groups and divide the 30 companies among the groups. Have groups conduct online research to find the current stock price of their companies, as well as the high and low stock prices during the past year. Have each group present this information visually to the class. Ask the class as a whole to identify the two companies that would have been the best investments for the year. **Verbal/Linguistic**

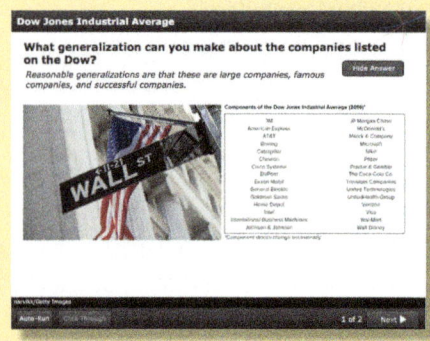

obtain all of the required permits, registrations, and licenses, which vary depending on the state and the kind of business. The U.S. Small Business Administration (SBA) Web site has a listing of these requirements.

Sole proprietorships are easy and often inexpensive to set up, and they have the lowest tax rate of the different types of businesses. All of the decisions are made by one person, who gets all of the profits.

Sole proprietorships also experience disadvantages. Because the business is not separate from the individual who owns it, he or she holds **unlimited liability** for debt and other obligations. It may be difficult to raise money from investors. Sole proprietorships also have **limited life**.

Partnerships

A **partnership** is a business owned by two or more people. Together they divide all profits, and they are responsible for all debts. To get started, the partners sign an agreement as to how they will run the business. A partnership must register with the state, establish a business name, and register with the Internal Revenue Service (IRS) to obtain a tax ID number. The partners also must obtain required permits, registrations, and licenses. Many law offices or doctors' practices are partnerships.

Essentially three types of partnerships exist:
- **General Partnership** In this type of partnership, management of the business, liability, and profits are split equally among partners.
- **Joint Venture** This type of partnership is like a general partnership, but it is typically set up for a single project or for a limited time span.
- **Limited Partnership** This type of partnership allows for certain partners to have less input—less money invested or fewer decision making powers, for example—in exchange for less profit. The percentages of profits are decided in advance and documented in a legal agreement.

Partnerships hold certain advantages. They are relatively easy to form. They utilize the resources and strengths of the partners, and additional partners who have specialized skills may be added.

Disadvantages of partnerships mirror the struggles common whenever people work together. There may be disputes over the direction of the company, day-to-day duties, and the amount of effort. In addition, all partners are liable for the mistakes of the other partners.

Corporations

A **corporation** is a business that is legally separate from its owners. It is made up of **stockholders** (shareholders) who invest money and, in return, receive profits that the corporation earns. Setting up a corporation requires a number of complicated and costly legal prerequisites. Corporations must register with the state, establish a business name, and register with the IRS to obtain a tax ID number. They must acquire permits, registrations, and licenses. Shareholders create a *board of directors*, a group of people who oversee the management of the corporation.

Advantages of a corporation are many. It provides limited liability, meaning that the corporation itself, not its owners, is fully responsible for its obligations. Shareholders are not responsible for the debts of a corporation, and they file their personal taxes separately. Ownership of a corporation can change easily from person to person and outlive the original shareholders. Corporations can raise money for the business, including offering stock, which can be a way to recruit high-quality employees.

---

capital formation the transfer of money from households to businesses and government through investments and loans

sole proprietorship unincorporated business owned and run by a single person who has rights to all profits and unlimited liability for all debts of the firm; most common form of business organization in the United States

unlimited liability requirement that an owner is personally and fully responsible for all losses and debts of a business; applies to proprietorships, general partnerships

limited life situation in which a firm legally ceases to exist when an owner dies, quits, or a new owner is added; applies to sole proprietorships and partnerships

partnership unincorporated business owned and operated by two or more people who share the profits and have unlimited liability for the debts and obligations of the firm

limited partnership form of partnership where one or more partners are not active in the daily running of the business, and whose liability for the partnership's debt is restricted to the amount invested in the business

corporation form of business organization recognized by law as a separate legal entity with all the rights and responsibilities of an individual, including the right to buy and sell property, enter into legal contracts, and to sue and be sued

stockholders persons who own a share or shares of stock in a corporation; same as shareholder

---

CHAPTER 19, LESSON 2
Business Organizations and Your Money

C Critical Thinking Skills

Analyzing responsibilities and rights of businesses Have students discuss the legal responsibility that sole proprietorships and general partnerships have with unlimited liability. Next, ask students to analyze other responsibilities that businesses have regarding their goods and services as they pertain to economic, social, and environmental issues. Then have students recall the rights held by businesses in the United States, such as the right to earn and keep profits, private property rights, and so on.

W Writing Skills

Analyzing characteristics, advantages, and disadvantages of business organizations Have students create a chart with these column headings: Characteristics, Advantages, Disadvantages. Then tell them to add these row headings: Sole Proprietorships, Partnerships, Corporations. Ask students to fill in the chart by first explaining the characteristics of sole proprietorships, partnerships, and corporations. Finally, have students analyze the advantages and disadvantages of each type of business organization. **Visual/Spatial**

WORKSHEET

Personal Finance Activity: Assessing the Competition

Going into business Discuss the characteristics, advantages, and disadvantages of the sole proprietorship. Ask students to consider ways that sole proprietors obtain the capital funds they need to open for business. Then have students complete the Personal Finance Activity and relate how their "business" fits into the financial system. **Verbal/Linguistic**

CHAPTER 19, LESSON 2
Business Organizations and Your Money

R1 Reading Skills
Identifying capital formation for small businesses
Ask: What types of capital are available for sole proprietorships and partnerships? *(start-up loans; Small Business Administration Loan, lines of credit)*
AL Verbal/Linguistic

R2 Reading Skills
Identifying capital formation for corporations
Ask: What are four general ways for corporations to raise capital? *(selling bonds, issuing stocks, borrowing directly from financial institutions, and converting profits)* **AL** Verbal/Linguistic

R3 Reading Skills
Understanding bonds Ask: Why do investors like purchasing bonds? *(Bonds are not very risky, and corporations must pay bondholders even if the company has not made a profit.)* Why do corporations like issuing bonds? *(The interest rate paid to bondholders is lower than that of a bank loan, and the interest paid is tax deductible for the corporation.)*

R4 Reading Skills
Understanding stocks Have students explain how corporations raise money through stocks. *(A corporation offers stocks, or part ownership of the company, to investors. Investors purchase shares of stock and receive dividends—often quarterly—that represent a portion or percentage of profits.)* **Ask:** What is the difference between preferred stock and common stock? *(Preferred stockholders receive dividends after bondholders are paid but have no say in how the company is run. Common stockholders earn dividends last but are allowed a certain say in how a company is run.)*

ANSWERS, p. 570

✓ **READING PROGRESS CHECK** Limited liability prevents corporate owners from being held personally responsible for the debts and obligations of the company.

CRITICAL THINKING
To purchase property and inventory, or to pay start-up fees

✓ **READING PROGRESS CHECK** A bond is a loan repaid regardless of profits and at a lower interest rate. Stocks are loans repaid based on profits, and some stockholders have a say in how the company is run.

570

Partnerships and sole proprietorships have several means of raising capital, including start-up loans, SBA loans, and lines of credit.

▲ **CRITICAL THINKING**
Economic Analysis What is a start-up loan typically used for?

stocks certificates of ownership in a corporation; common or preferred stock

dividends checks paid to stockholders, usually quarterly, representing portion of corporate profits

preferred stock form of stock without vote, in which stockholders get their investments back before common stockholders

common stock most common form of corporate ownership, with one vote per share for stockholders

570

Disadvantages also exist, however. Start-up costs can be very high. Because corporations require more regulation, recordkeeping and other obligations can be burdensome and time consuming.

✓ **READING PROGRESS CHECK**

Evaluating Why is limited liability advantageous for a business organization?

Raising Capital

GUIDING QUESTION *How can small business owners find ways to raise the investment capital they need to start a business?*

All business organizations face a similar need: obtaining capital to develop their business. As you will see, corporations have several options unavailable to sole proprietorships and partnerships.

Small Business Loans
Small businesses such as sole proprietorships and partnerships may obtain *start-up loans* to establish their businesses. These funds typically are used to purchase property and inventory, or to pay start-up fees. Another type of loan for small business owners is a *Small Business Administration loan*. These are funded by the U.S. Small Business Administration and administered through participating banks. *Lines of credit* are loans designed to help with cash flow during slow periods or negative growth. They allow a business to draw from a set amount of funds without having to go through the loan application process over and over again.

Corporate Capital
There are four general ways for corporations to raise capital: selling bonds, issuing stocks, borrowing directly from financial institutions, and converting profits.

- **Selling Bonds** Bonds are like loans from individuals. A corporation offers bonds for sale, and then pays installments of interest to the bondholders. Eventually, the bond itself is repaid. Bondholders do not have any say in how the company is run, yet investors like bonds because they are not very risky; corporations must pay bondholders even if the company has not made a profit. Corporations like bonds because the interest rate is lower than that of a bank loan. The interest paid to bondholders is also tax deductible for the corporation.
- **Issuing Stocks Stocks** are also like loans from individuals. Unlike bondholders, purchasers of stock receive **dividends** representing a portion of corporate profits. There are generally two types of stock. Purchasers of **preferred stock** receive dividends after bondholders are paid but have no say in how the company is run. Purchasers of **common stock** earn dividends last but are allowed a certain say in how a company is run. For instance, they are allowed to vote for the board of directors who manage the corporation.
- **Borrowing Directly** Businesses can get loans from banks or other lenders. The interest rates typically are higher than those for bonds and stocks.
- **Converting Profits** Some corporations use all of their profits to pay their shareholders. Other corporations, called "growth companies," put their profits toward expanding the business in new directions or investing in research that relates to their industry.

✓ **READING PROGRESS CHECK**

Comparing In general, how is a bond different from a stock?

---

net works Online Teaching Options

WORKSHEET

Personal Finance Activity: Evaluating Stocks

Evaluating Stocks Tell students to study the categories and their definitions on the worksheet. After students answer the questions, ask them to find real stock indexes online or in a financial newspaper. Have them select one of the stocks and follow it for several weeks. Then ask them to write a summary of how their stock performed. **Logical/Mathematical**

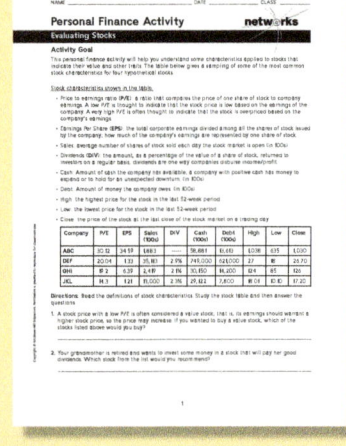

You as an Investor

GUIDING QUESTION *Why is the role of an investor an important part of the economy?*

Investing is not just for the rich. A little extra is all it takes to begin using your money to make more money. All investments, however, involve two unknowns: the possibility of making money—the return—and the risk of losing it. In deciding to invest, you are always balancing these two factors.

Investment Risks vs. Returns
There are two types of financial risk involved when investing:
- **Undiversifiable risk** is also called "systematic" or "market risk." This type of risk affects all companies. Situations like inflation, interest rates, political instability, natural disasters, exchange rates, and wars are examples of undiversifiable risks.
- **Diversifiable risk** is also called "unsystematic." This type of risk is specific to each company or industry. A company being poorly managed, a factory burning down, or new technology replacing another technology are examples of diversifiable risks.

The riskiest investments usually provide the highest returns. The best way to reduce risk is to practice **portfolio diversification**, which means investing in a wide range of assets that would not all be affected in the same way. This is especially wise advice when dealing with stock market investments.

portfolio diversification strategy of holding different investments to protect against risk

Investing in Stocks
As you learned earlier, stocks are shares of a company's assets and are considered a good long-term investment. However, stocks are also the investments with the largest amount of risk. A company might suffer any number of setbacks, and you could lose some or all of the money you invested. To reduce risk, many people buy a collection of stocks called a **mutual fund**. This is a pool of money from

mutual fund company that sells shares of a portfolio of securities, e.g., stocks and bonds issued by other companies

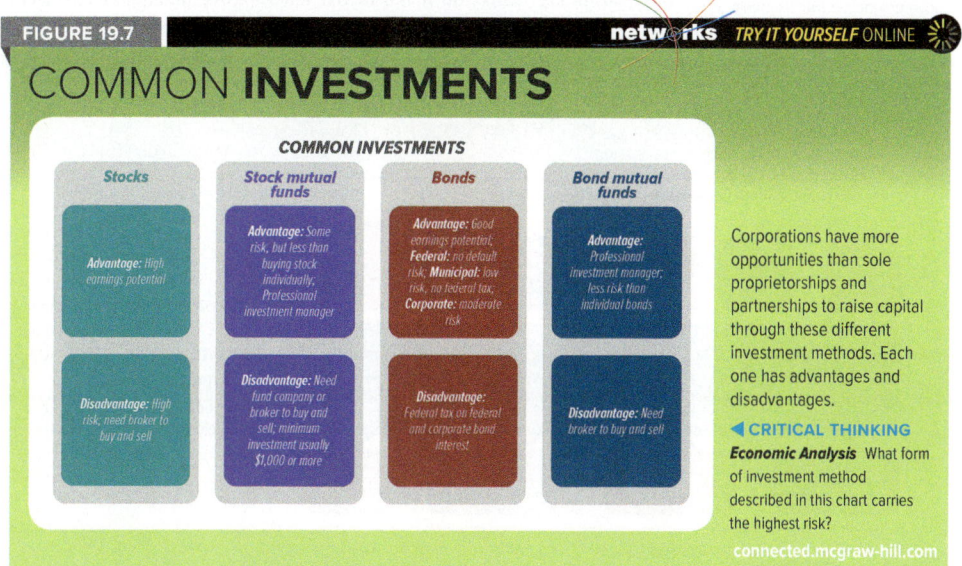

FIGURE 19.7 COMMON INVESTMENTS

Corporations have more opportunities than sole proprietorships and partnerships to raise capital through these different investment methods. Each one has advantages and disadvantages.

◀ **CRITICAL THINKING**
Economic Analysis What form of investment method described in this chart carries the highest risk?

CHAPTER 19, LESSON 2
Business Organizations and Your Money

C1 Critical Thinking Skills
Evaluating financial assets Ask students to consider which financial assets (bonds or stocks) they would prefer to invest their savings in. Have them explain their choices using the terms *risk* and *return*. **Verbal/Linguistic, Logical/Mathematical**

C2 Critical Thinking Skills
Diversifying risk **Ask:** In what ways can an investor reduce risk when allocating savings among assets? *(Investors practice portfolio diversification to reduce risk. U.S. government bonds are investments safe from even undiversifiable risk. Carefully analyzing diversifiable risk for individual corporations is a must for smart investors.)*

W Writing Skills
Evaluating considerations before investing Tell students to suppose they have a friend who asks them if she should invest money she recently inherited in the stock market. **Ask:** What factors should you consider before advising your friend? *(Possible answers: financial goals—the length of time she can leave the money in an investment; current market trends—is it a bull or bear market?; and personal tolerance for risk—will she panic if stock prices drops?)* Finally, ask students to write a response in which they attempt to convince their friend as a potential investor in the stock market to practice portfolio diversification. Encourage students to highlight the benefits of diversification and propose a general strategy through which an investor might assemble a diverse stock portfolio. **Interpersonal**

WORKSHEET
Personal Finance Activity: Risk and Return

Comparing types of investments Distribute the Personal Finance Activity and explain to students that it will help them compare and contrast types of investments. They will explain the advantages and disadvantages of some investments and calculate the earnings of a savings account and a stock.
Visual/Spatial

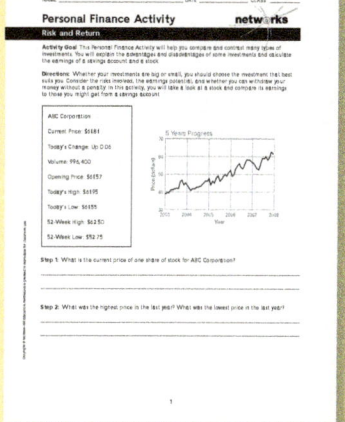

ANSWERS, p. 571
CRITICAL THINKING
Stocks

CHAPTER 19, LESSON 2
Business Organizations and Your Money

R1 Reading Skills

Understanding mutual funds Ask: **What is a mutual fund?** *(a company that sells stock in itself and uses the proceeds to buy stocks and bonds issued by other companies)* Be sure students understand that investing in a share of mutual fund stock does not mean the investor is part owner of the corporations the mutual fund invests in. The mutual fund itself owns shares of the corporate stocks and/or bonds, but the investor owns shares of the mutual fund. Ask: **Why does this fact make mutual funds so attractive?** *(The mutual fund invests in many stocks, bonds, or other assets; therefore, the diversity allows for less risk.)* Explain that because mutual funds do carry some risk, however, investors often purchase shares in different mutual funds. Direct students to key "mutual fund" into a search engine to view the many types of mutual funds available.

C Critical Thinking Skills

Considering financial goals Have students consider what their lives will be like 10 years from now. Ask them to list the types of savings accounts and investments they think they will have at that time. Then ask students to do the same thing for their lives 25 years and 50 years from now. After students have finished their lists, discuss as a class how saving and investing goals change as a person grows older.

W Writing Skills

Evaluating bonds Direct students to research a bond they might consider purchasing. Have them find the Standard & Poor's and Moody's ratings for the bonds and research how these corporations evaluated the bonds. Students should write a brief summary about their findings.

R2 Reading Skills

Relating the advantages of municipal bonds Ask: **What are some of the factors that make municipal bonds attractive investments?** *(Possible answers: regarded as safe investments; presumed that governments will be able to pay interest and principal because of power to tax; municipal bonds are tax-exempt; states at times exempt the interest payments from state taxes)* **Verbal/Linguistic**

ANSWERS, p. 572

CRITICAL THINKING
Google Inc.; Intel Corp.

---

stockbroker person who buys or sells securities for investors

maturity life of a bond, length of time funds are borrowed

municipal bonds a type of investment, often tax exempt, issued by state and local governments; known as munis

---

R1 many people and invested together in a variety of stocks and bonds. It is administered by an investment manager.

To purchase stock, you need to establish an account with a **stockbroker**, either in person or online. There are "full-service" brokers who offer investment advice but also charge higher fees or work on "commission," receiving a percentage of what you earn. Online brokers are becoming more and more popular. They also charge fees, but the fees can be less than those of full-service brokers. Before setting up an account and making any transactions, it is important that you do your research about the broker and know what fees are charged.

C To set up an account, you must be 18 years old, or you can set up a custodial account with your parents. Similar to setting up a checking account, you need two sets of identification, a Social Security number, a W-9 form, and the initial deposit.

Tell your broker your short-term and long-term goals, which will affect the risks and returns on your investments. If you want to select your own stocks, be sure to do your homework: What does the company produce? How profitable is it? What is its earnings history? How has its stock fared recently and over the past year? Join an investment club to help you answer these questions—and to learn what questions to ask.

Patience is the key to successful stock investing. The stock market (where stocks are bought and sold) may go up and down, but the return on stocks over the past 50 years has been consistently higher than for other types of investments.

Investing in Corporate and Government Bonds

W Like stocks, bond transactions can be completed through full-service brokers as well as online brokers. Recall that corporations offer bonds to raise capital for developing or expanding a business. Governments, too, sell bonds. They offer the bonds to raise money for particular projects, such as building bridges.

In general, as a bondholder you will receive scheduled interest payments as well as the repayment of your loan at a specified time in the future—the bond **maturity** date. Maturity dates vary widely, however.

State and local governments sell **municipal bonds** known as munis. *Treasury instruments* are loans you make to the federal government. They include R2

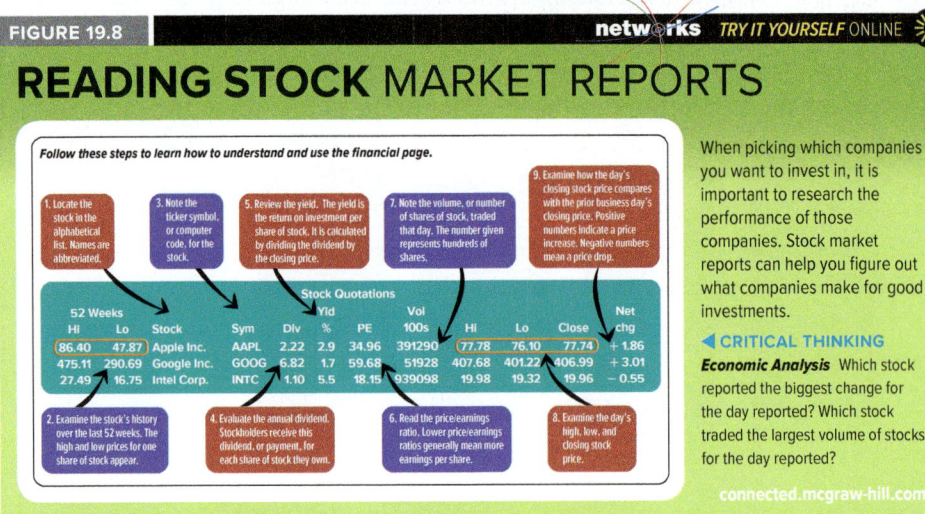

FIGURE 19.8
READING STOCK MARKET REPORTS

When picking which companies you want to invest in, it is important to research the performance of those companies. Stock market reports can help you figure out what companies make for good investments.

◄ **CRITICAL THINKING**
Economic Analysis Which stock reported the biggest change for the day reported? Which stock traded the largest volume of stocks for the day reported?

connected.mcgraw-hill.com

572

---

networks Online Teaching Options

CHARTS

Reading Stock Market Reports

Analyzing a stock market report Display Figure 19.8 and ask students to click on the column headings and circled items to learn more. Explain that a stock market report alphabetically lists stocks and provides information about stock prices and trades. At the beginning of each trading day, stocks open at the same prices they closed at the day before. Prices generally go up and down throughout the day as the conditions of supply and demand change. **Logical/Mathematical**

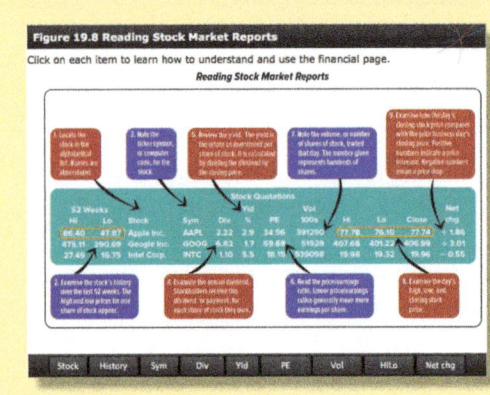

Treasury bills (T-bills), Treasury notes (T-notes), Treasury bonds, (T-bonds), Treasury Inflation-Protected Securities (TIPS), and several series of savings bonds. They have various interest rates and maturity dates. These types of federal bonds offer different payment plans depending upon the maturity date. Because they are issued and backed by the government, Treasury instruments offer low risk. They can be bought directly from the government online, or through banks or brokers. Minimum investments for most are $100–$10,000, but some savings bond minimums are much lower.

Companies such as Standard & Poor's and Moody's rate bonds on their level of risk. Most bonds are considered less risky than stocks, and government bonds are less risky than corporate bonds. In addition, the interest payments on munis are tax-exempt, whereas the interest payments from corporate bonds are taxed.

Investing in "Yourself" with IRAs

Individual Retirement Accounts (IRAs) can be considered both investments and savings. They are savings accounts because you deposit money into them, which you do not access until you reach retirement. They are investments because you (or financial advisors) select the stocks and bonds into which you want your deposits directed. Again, do your homework before you invest your IRA funds. When you're young, you can choose riskier assets to get a higher return because if you lose your investment, you still have many years to recoup your losses. As you near retirement age, you want to transfer your deposits into safer assets.

Some employers offer IRAs. Banks also offer IRAs for those who don't have access to employer-sponsored accounts or who want to save independently for retirement. There are many different types of IRAs. The most common are Traditional and Roth. The differences are in how you pay taxes on the deposits.

- **Traditional IRA** In a traditional IRA, you can make yearly contributions (deposits) into the account up to a certain limit determined by the government. These contributions are not taxed when they are deposited, but you have to pay tax on the whole amount (as income) when you withdraw the funds upon retirement. In theory, by then you might be in a lower tax bracket and won't pay as much in taxes.
- **Roth IRA** The Roth IRA was created as part of the Taxpayer Relief Act of 1997. With this type of account, you have taxes taken out before you make deposits so you do not have to pay taxes when you withdraw the money at retirement.

✓ **READING PROGRESS CHECK**
Summarizing How can you make buying stocks less risky?

Treasury bills United States government obligation with a maturity of a few days to 52 weeks

Treasury notes United States government obligation with a maturity of 2 to 10 years

Treasury bonds United States government bond with maturity of 30 years

savings bonds low-denomination, non-transferable bond issued by the federal government, usually through payroll savings plans

Individual Retirement Accounts (IRAs) retirement account in the form of a long-term time deposit, with annual contributions not taxed until withdrawn during retirement

LESSON 2 REVIEW

Reviewing Vocabulary
1. *Defining* What is a sole proprietorship?

Using Your Notes
2. *Summarizing* Use your notes to compare and contrast the different types of Treasury instruments that can be used to invest in government.

Answering the Guiding Questions
3. *Explaining* How do the different types of business organizations change the amount of financial risk assumed by the individual investor?

4. *Examining* How can small business owners find ways to raise investment capital they need to start a business?

5. *Describing* Why is the role of an investor an important part of the economy?

Writing About Economics
6. *Informative/Explanatory* Write a two-page essay explaining the advantages that a corporation has over a small business. What vehicles for investment does a corporation have access to that a small business does not? At the same time, what risks and challenges does a corporation take on that a small business does not?

CHAPTER 19, LESSON 2
Business Organizations and Your Money

W Writing Skills

Examining investment options available in IRAs
Ask students to explain how a person sets up an IRA. *(contact a financial institution that offers IRAs, or set up one through an employer—a 401(k)* Have students research online the various companies that offer IRAs. **Ask: What kinds of investments choices do people usually make for their IRAs?** *(The choices are varied and may include stocks, bonds, CDs, mutual funds, and even property and gold.)* Explain that when people set up an IRA, they are given choices about what percentage of their funds they want to go into a specific asset. Have students create a mock IRA, listing the percentages of funds they want to allocate for separate assets. Tell them to create a circle graph to illustrate where their funds are allocated. **Interpersonal, Visual/Spatial**

CLOSE & REFLECT

Discussing reasons for investing **Ask: At what age do you plan to start saving for retirement? How much money do you think you will need to have saved so you can live comfortably when you retire?** Create a table on the board that compares students' responses.

ANSWERS, p. 573

✓ **READING PROGRESS CHECK** through portfolio diversification; buy stocks through a mutual fund

---

LESSON 2 REVIEW ANSWERS

Reviewing Vocabulary
1. unincorporated business run by a single owner who has rights to all profits and unlimited liability for all debts of the firm

Using Your Notes
2. They include Treasury bills (T-bills), Treasury notes (T-notes), Treasury bonds, (T-bonds), Treasury Inflation-Protected Securities (TIPS), and several series of savings bonds. They have various interest rates and maturity dates. These types of federal bonds offer different payment plans depending upon the maturity date. Because they are issued and backed by the government, treasury instruments offer low risk. They can be bought directly from the government online, or through banks or brokers. Minimum investments for most are $100–$10,000, but some savings bond minimums are much lower.

Answering the Guiding Questions
3. Sole proprietors and general partners assume risk because of the unlimited liability feature of those business organizations. Corporate bondholders have some risk based on bond ratings, but bondholders also receive dividends before stockholders. Preferred stockholders receive dividends after bondholders are paid, followed by common stockholders.

4. Small businesses (sole proprietorships and partnerships) may obtain start-up loans to establish their businesses. They may also apply for a SBA Loan and Lines of Credit.

5. Investors provide funds for capital, which businesses use to produce goods and to hire workers. Rising employment increases demand for more goods and services, which results in economic growth.

Writing About Economics
6. Advantages: limited liability and unlimited life, separate personal taxes for shareholders, ease of raising capital. Unlike small businesses, corporations raise capital by selling bonds, issuing shares of stock, borrowing from banks and other lenders, and converting profits toward expanding the business. Disadvantages: high start-up costs, regulatory and legal prerequisites, burdensome recordkeeping and other obligations.

CHAPTER 19, LESSON 3
Personal Money Decisions

ENGAGE

C Critical Thinking Skills

Considering future paths Before students begin the lesson, ask if any of them know where they want to go to college after high school graduation. Discuss career choices and expectations about college life and future earnings. Have them analyze the chart on page 575 showing unemployment and earnings by degree. **Ask: Based on your career and degree choices, about how much will you be earning a year after college graduation?** Intrapersonal

TEACH & ASSESS

R Reading Skills

Understanding the requirements for the FAFSA
Ask: What are three requirements necessary to qualify for federal financial aid? *(Answers may include being a U.S. citizen, having a Social Security number, having a high school diploma or GED, and not been found guilty of the sale or possession of illegal drugs.)* **What are three pieces of information you need to complete the FAFSA worksheet?** *(Answers may include most recent tax return, current bank statements, driver's license, and Social Security number.)*

V Visual Skills

Filling out the FAFSA Bring to class copies of the FAFSA form. Walk through each step with students, or have a guidance counselor visit the class to do so, to help students understand how to complete the form.

ANSWERS, p. 574

ESSENTIAL QUESTION ACTIVITY

Sample answer: building credit and equity

TAKING NOTES
Financial Aid: low-interest loans, grants, and work-study programs. **Student Loans:** loans to cover the cost of education; must be repaid. **Scholarships and Grants:** outright gifts that you do not have to pay back. **Work-Study Programs:** part-time employment through the university. **Advance Placement (AP) courses:** college level course offered at the high school level. **College-Level Exam Program:** standardized tests that count towards college credits. **Employer Reimbursement:** tuition reimbursements through employer. **Military:** offers a number of ways to pay for college

---

Interact with these digital assets and others in lesson 3

- ✓ INTERACTIVE GRAPH
  Unemployment and Earnings
- ✓ INTERACTIVE CHART
  Types of Car Insurance
- ✓ INTERACTIVE IMAGE
  Achieving Your College Goals
- ✓ SELF-CHECK QUIZ

networks TRY IT YOURSELF ONLINE

Reading Help Desk

Content Vocabulary
- defaulted
- premiums
- deductible

TAKING NOTES:

Key Ideas and Details
ACTIVITY Use the graphic organizer below to describe various methods available to pay for college.

Method	Description

LESSON 3
Personal Money Decisions

ESSENTIAL QUESTION

How can you take control of your own money?

It is unavoidable that we must spend the money we earn. But learning how to spend it carefully and effectively is the important trick that you should learn. One of your biggest expenses is paying for your own place to live.

What are the financial benefits of buying a home?

Funding Your Education

GUIDING QUESTION *Why are there so many different methods available to help you fund more education?*

You graduate from high school. Then what? Although the workplace has changed over the years, one fact remains constant: what you learn determines what you earn. Workers with bachelor's degrees have greater lifelong earning power than do workers with only a high school diploma, and are less likely to be unemployed.

Financial Aid

Many families cannot afford to pay cash for students to go to college. Instead, they acquire loans and other financial aid. To be considered for financial aid—including low-interest loans, grants, and work-study programs—you must complete a FAFSA form. FAFSA stands for the Free Application for Federal Student Aid. It is the form created by the U.S. Department of Education and managed by the Office of Federal Student Aid. It is used by nearly every college and university to determine eligibility for financial aid and how much you or your family must contribute. Around 14 million FAFSA forms are submitted each year and account for about $80 billion in financial aid. Deadlines vary from college to college, but the form should be filled out in January, as soon as you and your parents receive all tax information from the previous year.

To qualify for financial aid, you must:

- Be a U.S. citizen
- Have a valid Social Security number
- Have a high school diploma or GED

---

networks Online Teaching Options

BELLRINGER

Consumer Rights and Responsibilities

Identifying consumer rights and responsibilities
Ask students to provide examples of each consumer right and responsibility listed on the Bellringer. Explain that these also apply when students purchase student loans, housing, and insurance. Tell them that in 1962 President Kennedy sent the first consumer protection message to Congress. He stated four consumer rights: (1) safety—protection against goods that are dangerous to life or health; (2) informed—information for use not only as protection against fraud but also as the basis for reasoned choices; (3) to choose—the need for markets to be competitive, and for government to protect consumers in markets where competition does not exist; (4) to be heard—the guarantee that consumer interests will be listened to when laws are being written. President Nixon later added the right to redress—to obtain from the manufacturers adequate payment in money or goods for financial or physical damages caused by their products.

- Be registered with the U.S. Selective Service (if you are a male 18 to 25 years old)
- Promise to use federal aid only for educational purposes
- Not owe refunds on any federal student grants
- Not have **defaulted** on any student loans
- Not have been found guilty of the sale or possession of illegal drugs

Documents you need to complete the FAFSA form:

- Most recent income tax return (or your parents' tax return if you are a dependent)
- Current bank statements
- Investment records
- Records of any untaxed income
- Driver's license
- Social Security number
- Alien registration or permanent resident card (if not a citizen)

Student Loans

About half of all financial aid is in the form of loans, which must be repaid—with interest. For most student loans, you must start paying them back nine months after you graduate from college. A few of the most common federal student loans include:

- Direct Subsidized Loan
- Direct Unsubsidized Loan
- Direct PLUS Loan (Parent Loans for Undergraduate Students)
- Direct Consolidation Loan
- Federal Perkins Loan Program

defaulted act of not repaying borrowed money

Go to studentaid.ed.gov to learn how to apply for federal student loans. The advantages to student loans offered by the federal government are lower interest

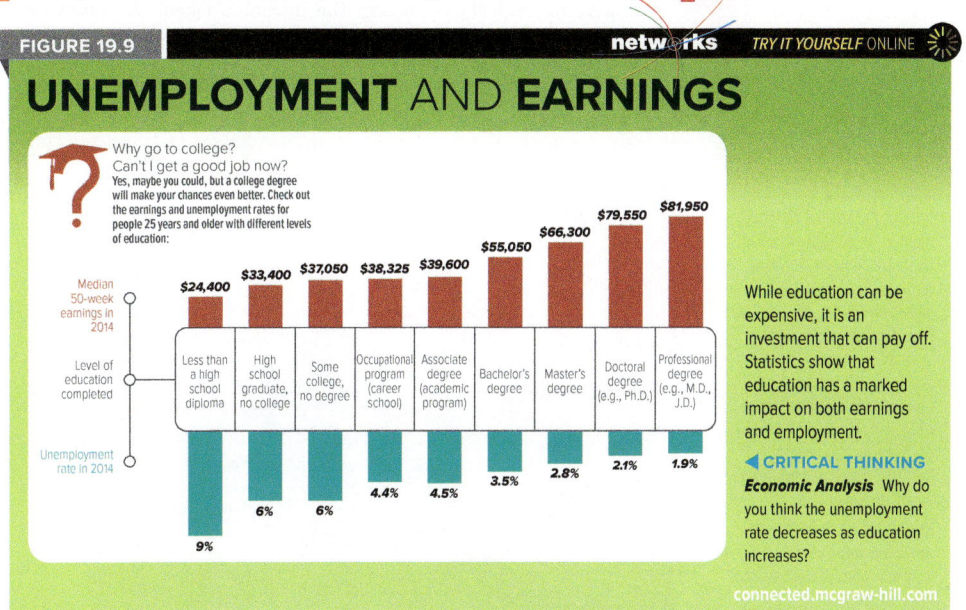

FIGURE 19.9 UNEMPLOYMENT AND EARNINGS

GRAPHS

Unemployment and Earnings

Examining the relationship between education and earnings Have students view Figure 19.9. Ask them to consider the relationship between increased level of education and increased earnings. **Ask: What happens to income as education level rises?** *(income increases)* **If you have some college but no degree, what can you expect your average earnings to be?** *($37,050)* **Where does the biggest jump in earnings occur?** *(from an Associate degree to a Bachelor's degree)* **Visual/Spatial**

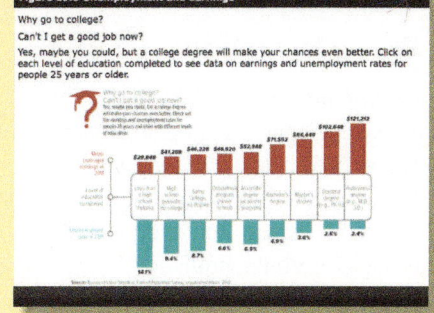

CHAPTER 19, LESSON 3
Personal Money Decisions

R1 Reading Skills

Analyzing federal student loan options Have students visit the financial aid site at studentaid.ed.gov to learn more about federal student loans. **Ask: Which type of loan is available to eligible undergraduate students who demonstrate financial need?** *(Direct Subsidized Loan)* **Which type of loan is available to eligible undergraduate students without regard to financial need?** *(Direct Unsubsidized Loan)* **Which type of loan is available to graduate or professional students and parents of undergraduate students to help pay for education expenses not covered by other financial aid?** *(Direct PLUS Loan)* **Which type of loan allows one to combine all federal student loans into a single loan?** *(Direct Consolidation Loan)* **What are some characteristics of the Federal Perkins Loan Program?** *(The college or university is the lender, and it is available for undergraduate and graduate students with exceptional financial need.)*

R2 Reading Skills

Identify federal student loan amounts Have students visit studentaid.ed.gov to identify how much can be borrowed utilizing the various federal student loan programs. **Ask: How much can an eligible undergraduate student borrow?** *(Up to $5,500 per year in Perkins loans depending on financial need; $5,500 to $12,500 per year in Direct Subsidized Loans and Direct Unsubsidized Loans)* **How much can the parents of an eligible undergraduate student borrow?** *(the remainder of their child's college costs not covered by other financial aid)*

T Technology Skills

Analyzing and comparing private student loans to federal loans Have students find interest rates and repayment plans for student loans from various banks. Then have them visit studentaid.ed.gov to identify the interest rates for Direct Subsidized Loans and Direct Unsubsidized Loans. *(In 2014, the interest rates were 3.86%, plus a 1.072% loan fee.)* **Ask: How do federal interest rates compare to private loans?** *(Federal rates should be lower.)* **How do the federal loan repayment plans compare to private loans?** *(Answers will vary for private loans. The federal repayment options also vary, but generally students have 10 to 25 years to repay loans.)*

ANSWERS, p. 575

CRITICAL THINKING
Education provides skills that employers value.

CHAPTER 19, LESSON 3
Personal Money Decisions

W Writing Skills

Charting private loans and federal loans Ask students to create a chart with the information they find in their research comparing private loans and federal loans. Column headings may include: Financial Institution, Interest Rates, Amount Available, Repayment Plan. The first few rows should list information about federal student loans, followed by private bank loans in the remaining rows.

T1 Technology Skills

Researching and evaluating scholarship opportunities Have students research online for scholarships for high school seniors or juniors. Tell students to identify at least 10 scholarships they are qualified for or are interested in.

C1 Critical Thinking Skills

Examining scholarship responses Invite the guidance or financial counselor to visit the classroom and discuss how to find and complete scholarship opportunities online or in the library. Also ask the counselor to discuss how to avoid scams when searching for scholarships.

C2 Critical Thinking Skills

Researching and evaluating federal grant options Have students visit studentaid.ed.gov to learn more about Federal Pell Grants. **Ask: What qualifications are taken into account to be awarded a Federal Pell Grant?** *(your financial need, your cost of attendance, your status as a part-time or full-time student, your plans to attend school for a full academic year of less)* **What qualifications are necessary to be awarded a Federal Supplemental Educational Opportunity Grant (FSEOG)?** *(exceptional financial need)*

T2 Technology Skills

Researching and evaluating nonfederal grant options Have students do online research for grants offered by their state and local government, individual universities and colleges, and nonprofit organizations. Tell students to create a spreadsheet listing the information for easier evaluation, including the Web site, name of grant, amount available, and requirements to submit.

ANSWERS, p. 576

CRITICAL THINKING
Federal Work-Study

---

rates and flexible repayment plans. Private loans are available from banks and other financial institutions. And some colleges sponsor loans. Interest rates are generally higher for these loans than for federal loans.

Scholarships and Grants

Unlike loans, scholarships and grants are outright gifts that you do not pay back. Both vary in the requirements, dollar amount, and expectations of the recipient. There are key differences between the two, however. A grant is tax exempt and not always related to academics. It is often given on the basis of financial need alone. Scholarships almost always are related to academic scores. They are typically more selective and competitive.

Your high school, your parents' employers, your state government, local companies, and even some nonprofit organizations offer grants and scholarships. Go online to research what is available, and begin reading about the requirements necessary for you to apply. Many applications ask you to submit a short essay about yourself and why you believe you deserve the grant or scholarship.

Work-Study Programs

Work-study programs are part-time employment at the university you attend. The benefits of these types of jobs are that the employers typically are more understanding of your college life and are more likely to consider your class schedule when assigning work hours.

There are two general types of work-study programs:

- **Federal Work-Study (FWS)** The FWS is based on financial need. Jobs can be either on campus (in one of the administrative offices, for example) or off campus. Jobs that are off campus are typically in community service in fields related to your major. You can sign up for these programs by filling out a FAFSA form and checking a box asking for interest in student employment. The employer will pay up to 50% of your wages, and the government will pay the rest. The amount of money you earn cannot exceed your financial aid award. Average work hours are 10–15 a week.
- **Non-Federal Work-Study (non-FWS)** This type of work-study is not based on financial need. Most schools offer student employment

---

FEDERAL WORK-STUDY

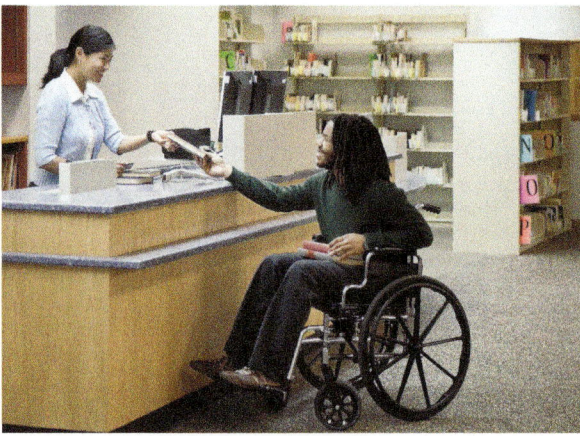

Federal Work-Study is based on financial need. You may request this type of work while completing the FAFSA form and checking a box asking for interest in student employment. You may be employed in administrative offices or libraries on campus, or in the local community off campus. Average work hours are 10-15 a week.

▶ **CRITICAL THINKING**
Economic Analysis Which work-study program is based on financial need?

---

networks — Online Teaching Options

GRAPHIC ORGANIZER

Paying for College

Finding alternative ways to pay for college Display the graphic organizer and have students complete it as they work through the lesson. After discussing loans and work-study programs, discuss nontraditional ways of paying for college. **Verbal/Linguistic**

ACHIEVING YOUR COLLEGE GOALS

There are many ways to acquire the money needed to pay for a college education. Scholarships, tuition-free schools, work-study programs, and many forms of financial aid are possibilities. Earning a college degree can mean significant improvements in job options and earnings potential.

◄ **CRITICAL THINKING**
Economic Analysis Research some of the options available to you to help pay for education, and then write up a paragraph on the results.

R2 opportunities in places like the dining halls, library, and offices of various academic departments. These jobs offer more convenience and flexibility than do off-campus jobs. **R1**

Nontraditional Methods of Paying for College

There are ways to obtain college credits before you enroll in a university. In addition, some other avenues may pay for most if not all of your college education.

- **Take an Advanced Placement (AP) course.** These are college-level courses you can take in most high schools. Every spring, AP students may sign up for the AP exam for certain courses and receive college credits by scoring high on the exams.
- **Sign up for the College-Level Examination Program® (CLEP).** Like AP exams, the CLEP consists of standardized tests that determine your knowledge of subjects at a college level. You may obtain college credits if you pass a test for a particular course. Passing several tests could save you a year or more in college tuition.
- **Apply for employer reimbursement.** As part of workplace benefits, some employers offer tuition reimbursement to their employees. This process requires the worker to pay upfront for college classes, but then he or she is paid back later by the company. The employer may require proof of good grades for one to receive the reimbursement.
- **Join the military.** Each of the Armed Forces offers a number of ways to pay for college.
- **Attend a tuition-free school.** Although the number of schools that do not charge tuition is small, they do exist. Many have strict requirements.
- **Enroll in a Public Service Loan-Forgiveness Program after graduation.** This program allows borrowers to work off their loans after college by getting hired as public service employees. Some examples of public service programs are the National Health Service Corps, National Association of Public Interest Law, Peace Corps, AmeriCorps, and Volunteers in Service to America.

C

✓ **READING PROGRESS CHECK**

Identifying What is the first step you should take when applying for financial aid for college?

connected.mcgraw-hill.com **Personal Financial Literacy** 577

CHAPTER 19, LESSON 3
Personal Money Decisions

R1 Reading Skills

Researching and evaluating work-study program opportunities Have students visit studentaid.ed.gov to learn more about the Federal Work-Study program. **Ask: How much can you earn in a Federal Work-Study program?** *(at least the current federal minimum wage and perhaps more, depending on the type of work and necessary skills)* **Why is it important to apply early for a Federal Work-Study program?** *(These programs are awarded on a first come, first served basis.)*

R2 Reading Skills

Comparing work-study program opportunities
Ask: What is the difference between a Federal Work-Study (FWS) and Non-Federal Work-Study (non-FWS) program? *(The FWS is based on financial need. Jobs can be either on campus or off campus, typically in community service in fields related to your major. Non-FWS is not based on financial need and offer employment in places like the dining halls, library, and offices of various academic departments.)* **What type of work-study would you be most interested in? Why?**

C Critical Thinking Skills

Investigating nontraditional methods of paying for college Have students discuss nontraditional ways of paying for college. Point out that many college freshman and sophomores spend the first two years of study at a local community college while living at home. **Ask: How can this save money?** *(Students should recognize that completing core courses that transfer, as well as avoiding room and board costs, can save a significant amount of loans.)*

VIDEO WORKSHEET

College Debt

Examining college debt Have students watch the video. Then have a class discussion about the benefit of federal loans versus private loans for college. Have small groups research reliable Internet sources to find current information about student loans. They should note whether Congress is considering legislation regarding government student loans and whether student groups are lobbying for specific student loan information. Each group should create a multimedia presentation and present it to the class.

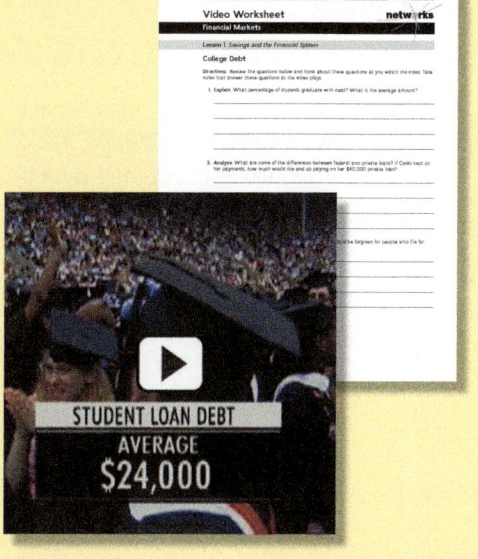

ANSWERS, p. 577

CRITICAL THINKING
Students' answers will vary, but should consider options such as work-study, scholarships and grants, loans, and earning credits through AP courses and CLEP testing.

✓ **READING PROGRESS CHECK** Fill out the FAFSA form.

Personal Financial Literacy **577**

CHAPTER 19, LESSON 3
Personal Money Decisions

C Critical Thinking Skills

Predicting rental payments Have students think about when they will be ready to rent their first apartment. **Ask: How much do you think you will need to pay each month to live in an apartment?** *(Answers will vary based on local rent rates. Students should also remember to consider the security deposit and the utilities that renters are responsible for paying.)* **AL**

R Reading Skills

Understanding the rental ratio Ask: How much should one pay in rent each month? *(The general rule is the amount spent on rent should equal what one earns in a week.)* **What expenses must be paid monthly in addition to rent?** *(utilities such as gas, electric, and water; cable, phone, renters insurance)* **Logical/Mathematical**

Making Connections

Walk-Through Checklist Tell students that, before signing a lease, they should "walk through" the apartment with the landlord and note its condition. To safeguard the deposit, make sure any damages are listed on the lease. Take dated photos before moving in and when moving out. A checklist of items to note include: study door and window locks; working smoke and carbon monoxide detectors; fire exits in front and back; any broken kitchen appliances or bathroom fixtures; any stains, loose tiles, or large scratches on floors; any cracks in windows or walls; and stained or peeling wallpaper.

ANSWERS, p. 578

CRITICAL THINKING
You should have enough to pay the security deposit and the first and last month's rent.

578

Housing

GUIDING QUESTION *What information do you need to be aware of when preparing to rent housing?*

After paying for college, buying a house will probably be one of your biggest expenses. It makes sense that you should put some serious thought into the details. One of the first decisions is whether you will rent or buy.

C Costs and Benefits of Renting

Moving into an apartment can be exciting. Finding and renting one takes work, however. Before you begin searching for an apartment, first consider these items:

- **How much should you pay?** In general, what you spend each month on rent should equal what you earn in one week. For example, if you earn $300 a week, you should consider having a roommate or two who can help make up the difference on an apartment that rents for $800 a month.
- **R Add other expenses.** Some apartments include utilities (gas, electric, water) as part of the rent payment, but many do not. In addition to your monthly rent, you may be responsible for monthly utility bills, including cable, phone, and renters insurance.
- **Consider location and amenities.** There are many factors to consider about location: how close the apartment is to your job, school, family, and friends. Also consider whether the landlord, or property owner, provides security and amenities (laundry, storage, access to a pool or gym). Ask about the pet policy and perhaps handicap accessibility.
- **Save for the security deposit and first and last months' rent.** Many landlords require that you pay a security deposit, which is a set amount of money paid up front that goes toward any repairs for damages you might cause. If you cause no damage, you will get your deposit back. Many property owners also ask for the first and last months' rent.
- **Read the lease carefully before signing.** This is the legal contract that all landlords require before you move in. It lays out the terms of your rental agreement. Particularly note the length of the lease. If you sign a one-year lease and then lose your job after 10 months, you are still

RENTING

Renting provides many benefits. The money you save on not paying property tax and perhaps utilities can be saved or invested. You do not have to perform maintenance or upkeep on the property. It is also easier to move because you only have to get out of a lease. But renters cannot invest in the equity of a home. Also, a landlord can raise the rent on your next lease or balk at making repairs.

▼ **CRITICAL THINKING**
Economic Analysis How much should you save before renting?

578

---

networks — Online Teaching Options

WORKSHEET

Personal Finance Activity: Get a Job

Evaluating job security Tell students that in order to get approved for a mortgage, banks and other finance companies check their work history. Distribute the worksheet and analyze the types of jobs that typically do not get outsourced. Have a class discussion about the most secure jobs in the United States. **Verbal/Linguistic**

responsible for two months' rent. Some leases are for 18 months or two years, while some are month-to-month. The landlord cannot raise your rent within the term of the lease.

- **Select the right roommates.** If you plan to share an apartment with others, make sure they can afford the rent. They should sign the lease to ensure legal responsibility, and understand that everyone is responsible for paying their share of the rent until the lease is up. It is also a good idea to have house rules about chores, parties, overnight guests, and so on.
- **Understand your rights and responsibilities.** Even though a rental is where you live, it belongs to the property owner. Both of you have particular rights and responsibilities. Landlords are responsible for keeping the property structurally safe and sanitary. Prospective landlords are allowed to check your references (the names of people who know you and can vouch for you), your employment history, and credit history. They are allowed to enter your apartment to make repairs and to show the apartment to prospective renters if you are moving out. They are not allowed to discriminate on the basis of race, nationality, religion, gender, or disability. You are responsible for paying your rent on time, not causing damage to the property, being considerate of your neighbors, and following any other terms that are spelled out in the lease.

Renting provides many benefits. The money you save on not paying property tax and perhaps utilities can be saved or invested. You do not have to perform maintenance or upkeep on the property. And if your circumstances change (you find a better job in another state, for example), it is easier to move because you don't have to worry about selling a house, only trying to negotiate out of a lease.

Renting also has several negative aspects. By renting, you are not investing in the equity, or value, of a piece of property. You have less control over your living situation. Because the property does not belong to you, you are limited in remodeling. A landlord can raise the rent on your next lease or balk at making repairs. Although you have rights that protect you, you may need to hire an attorney to assert them.

Costs and Benefits of Buying a House

Owning a house is a good investment but a big commitment. There are different types of properties to choose from when you're looking to purchase: single family homes, condominiums (condos), or cooperatives (owning a share of a building).

A loan undertaken for the purchase of a home is called a mortgage. In general, your monthly mortgage payment—including property tax and homeowners insurance—should be about 30 percent or less of your gross monthly income. Making sure you understand the basics of your mortgage is important. Types of mortgages include:

- **Fixed Rate Mortgage** On these loans, the interest rates don't change, and the mortgage is issued typically for either 15 or 30 years. The advantage is that your monthly payments stay the same.
- **Adjustable Rate Mortgage (ARM)** The interest rates on an ARM vary over time. Although there are greater risks, some people prefer these interest rates because it is typical for the first few years to have lower rates.
- **Hybrid** This type of mortgage combines features of both a fixed rate and an adjustable rate.

Buying a home provides many benefits. In general, houses are a good investment because their values go up. Sometimes they go down, as they did during the collapse of the "housing bubble" of 2007, but houses overall are worth considerably more than they were 50 years ago. Buying a home also helps you

---

CHAPTER 19, LESSON 3
Personal Money Decisions

W1 Writing Skills

Listing advantages and disadvantages of renting Have students create a T-chart, listing disadvantages of renting on the left, and advantages of renting on the right.

R Reading Skills

Understanding the mortgage ratio **Ask:** How much should one's monthly mortgage payment be? *(The general rule is the amount spent on the monthly mortgage should be about 30 percent or less of one's gross monthly income.)* What expenses are included in the mortgage payment? *(property tax and homeowners insurance)* **Logical/Mathematical**

W2 Writing Skills

Listing advantages and disadvantages of buying a house Have students create a T-chart, listing disadvantages of purchasing a home on the left, and advantages on the right.

English Language Proficiency

Intermediate Read a text passage aloud and have students raise their hands when they hear a word they don't know. Help students complete a four square with these words, using pictures, short phrases, examples, and definitions. After the reading, have students review the words with peers.

WORKSHEET

Personal Finance Activity: Changing Jobs

Preparing ahead of time Tell students that before they switch jobs, they should create a plan to make sure they are financially stable between jobs. This Personal Finance Activity will help students understand the factors to consider when switching to a new career.

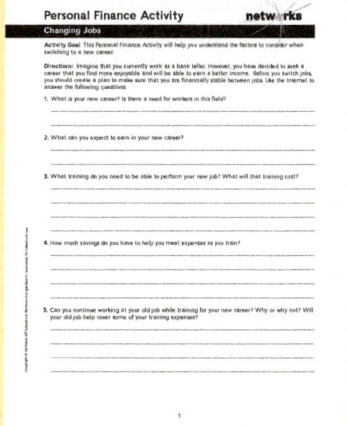

CHAPTER 19, LESSON 3
Personal Money Decisions

Content Background Knowledge

Purchasing a House A mortgage usually involves a down payment and interest. In addition to the cash down payment, homebuyers will need money for closing costs involved in arranging for a mortgage or in transferring ownership of the property. Closing costs can include fees for such items as the title search, legal costs, loan application, credit report, house inspections, and taxes. Although the person buying the house usually pays these fees, the seller may agree to pay part or all of them if this will make it easier to sell the house. It is also important to know about points, which are the fees paid to the lender and computed as a percentage of the loan. Each point the lender charges equals 1 percent of the amount borrowed. Lenders charge points—usually one to four—when they believe that the current interest rate is not high enough to pay the expenses involved in handling the mortgage and still make a profit.

C Critical Thinking Skills

Creating a pamphlet for first-time home buyers Tell students to suppose that they are real estate specialists at a consumer information service. Have them prepare an illustrated pamphlet titled "Buying a Home—What You Need to Know." Inform students that the information contained in their pamphlets should be suitable for first-time buyers and should focus on strategies to prepare renters to transition to home ownership. **Visual/Spatial**

R Reading Skills

Transitioning from renting to home ownership
Ask: What are four ways to prepare yourself to go from renting to buying? *(saving money for a larger down payment, establishing good credit, researching the real estate market, and considering roommates)*

ANSWERS, p. 580

CRITICAL THINKING
The interest rates for adjustable-rate mortgages vary over time, unlike fixed-rate mortgages.

☑ **READING PROGRESS CHECK** Costs: rent, security deposit, renters insurance, limits on renovations; Benefits: a landlord is responsible for upkeep, freedom to move after the lease is up. Home ownership costs more in upkeep but offers equity, tax deductions, and the freedom to renovate.

HOME OWNERSHIP

Houses are a good investment because their values generally go up. Buying a home also helps you build equity, which can be used to borrow money for other large purchases when you are ready. Home owners also receive tax deductions each year. Home ownership also has several negative aspects. It is a huge financial responsibility. Houses also require a great deal of upkeep, which may be time-consuming and add more expense. And if home owners want to move, the process of selling a house is time-consuming and complicated.

▶ **CRITICAL THINKING**
Economic Analysis What is the difference between a fixed-rate mortgage and an adjustable-rate mortgage?

build equity, which can be used to borrow money for other large purchases when you are ready. In addition, you receive tax deductions. The interest you pay on your mortgage and your property tax can be applied to your income tax return. And finally, you can make whatever renovations, alterations, or maintenance to your property you wish (as long as it's legal).

Home ownership also has several negative aspects. First, it is a huge financial responsibility. There are many costs beyond the mortgage. Application and appraisal fees, inspections, real estate agent commissions, and title insurance are some of them. Don't forget property taxes and homeowner's insurance. Second, houses require a great deal of upkeep, which may be time-consuming. There might be rules about maintaining your property if you live in a neighborhood with a homeowner's association. And finally, you have less mobility. If you want to move, the process of selling your house is much more involved than giving notice to a landlord.

Transition from Renting to Buying

When you're ready to consider home ownership, there are ways to prepare yourself to go from renting to buying.

- **Start saving money.** Having money for a down payment lowers the amount you'll need to borrow.
- **Establish good credit.** Recall that good credit lowers your interest rates.
- **Research the market.** Knowing what you want, what's available, and how much you can afford will help you make the right choice at the right time.
- **Consider roommates.** Buying a house could become more affordable if you had an extra room that a friend might be interested in renting until you become more financially stable.

☑ **READING PROGRESS CHECK**

Explaining What are the costs and benefits of renting? How might these be different if you owned a home?

---

networks Online Teaching Options

VIDEO **WORKSHEET**

Decision Making

Understanding economic decision making Have students watch the Decision Making video again, which they watched in Chapter 1. Tell students there are big decisions and small decisions to make in life, but a good guide for making decisions is comparing the additional costs of that decision with the benefits of that decision. Assign students a decision—the decision could be a big decision, such as what education to pursue after high school, or a smaller decision, such as whether to buy a particular brand of running shoes. Have students write a scenario of two friends discussing the assigned decision. Student groups should present their scenarios to the class. **Intrapersonal**

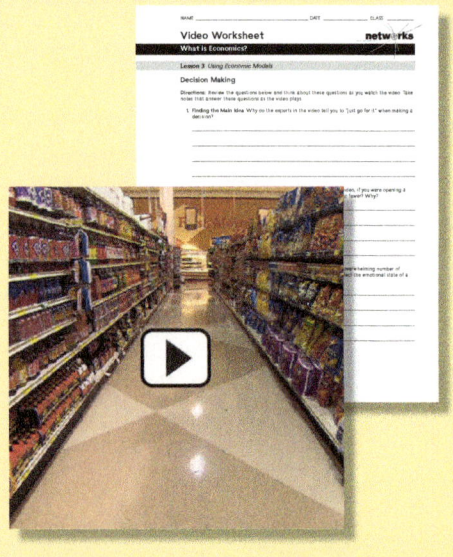

Insurance

GUIDING QUESTION *Why do we purchase insurance?*

Insurance is like a life raft—you don't want to need it, but you're glad it's there in an emergency. You pay an insurance company monthly or quarterly **premiums** for a policy detailing what items are covered and under what conditions. Then if something bad happens—such as a traffic accident, an illness, or an apartment fire—the insurance company will pay a portion or the entirety of what is covered in your policy.

Many policies include a **deductible**, or an amount you pay before the insurance company pays. Deductibles are ways for insurance companies and customers to negotiate the premium. For example, if you have car insurance with a $1,000 deductible and you're involved in a collision, you will have to pay the first $1,000 to fix the car. The insurance company will pay the rest, up to the amount of insurance you've purchased. If you had chosen a $500 deductible, you'd pay only the first $500, but your premiums would be higher.

premiums monthly, quarterly, semiannual, or annual price paid for an insurance policy

deductible an amount you pay before the insurance company pays

Health Insurance

Health insurance pays for hospitalization, visits to the doctor, surgery, exams, and preventative care such as physicals. Many businesses offer to pay for some of the cost of insurance for their employees and their families. By doing so, the business can get a discounted rate for being a part of a group. Some policies include co-pays (a small payment) for services such as doctor visits. Insurance companies allow children to be included on their parents' health insurance to the age of 26.

If you are not covered on a parents' policy or through your employment, you must purchase health insurance. You can do this through any private insurance company, but you may also purchase insurance from the Health Insurance Marketplace at www.healthcare.gov. You may decide to choose a policy with a low monthly premium. In exchange, you will accept a higher deductible, taking the chance that nothing will harm your health.

Auto Insurance

You have the option of buying various types of auto insurance—see **Figure 19.10**. At minimum, you must purchase basic liability insurance, which covers damage you might do to others. It is illegal in most states to drive without it. But having a policy that also covers you and your car is a good idea, too. If you are hurt in an accident you caused, and you don't have enough coverage, you could be required by law to pay for damages out of your own pocket.

Property Insurance

What would it cost to replace everything you own: computer, TV, clothes, furniture? It's more than you can afford, you should insure your possessions against theft, fire, and other dangers. Renters insurance covers the contents of rented property. Homeowners insurance covers belongings as well as damage to the home itself. Both types cover injury to visitors. Separate insurance is needed for flood or earthquake damage.

Other Insurance

Insurance companies offer a variety of different types of insurance policies to meet the specific needs of their customers. The most popular types of coverage include:

- **Disability** This insurance partially replaces income for those who can't work due to an illness or injury.

CHAPTER 19, LESSON 3
Personal Money Decisions

R Reading Skills

Explaining how insurance works Have students explain in a paragraph or through a series of storyboards how insurance works. Direct students to use the terms *premium, policy, coverage, and deductible* in their explanations. **Verbal/Linguistic, Visual/Spatial**

C1 Critical Thinking Skills

Evaluating the costs and benefits of buying insurance Have students create a T-chart, listing costs of purchasing insurance on the left, and benefits on the right.

C2 Critical Thinking Skills

Applying types of insurance Have students suppose that they were driving a car that was hit by a car driven by someone with no car insurance. Tell students that their car was totaled and they suffered a broken arm in the accident. **Ask: Which types of insurance would likely apply in this scenario?** *(collision, medical, personal injury protection, uninsured motorist, rental reimbursement)*

WORKSHEET

Personal Finance Activity: Who Needs Insurance?

Exploring Insurance Have students work in pairs to complete the worksheet, which will guide students to understand why certain types of insurance are important in a free market capitalist economy. Then encourage students to discuss their experiences with insurance. Do they know of situations where people have had to make claims after a storm or other natural disaster harmed their property? **Interpersonal**

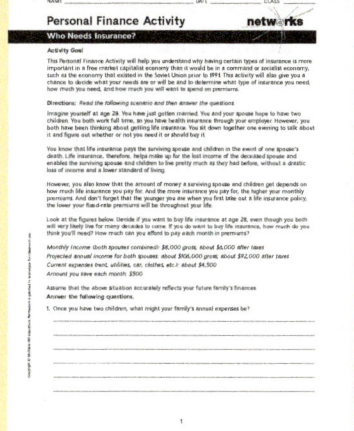

CHAPTER 19, LESSON 3
Personal Money Decisions

Making Connections

Factors Affecting Auto Insurance Rates Explain to students that when they buy auto insurance, the rate they are charged is determined not only by their age and sex but also by the following:

1. The type of car they drive. Insurance companies consider the safety record of a car and the costs to repair it if it is involved in an accident.

2. Where they drive. If the rate of thefts and accidents is high in an area, the risk to the insurance company is greater. A city, for example, would have more thefts and accidents than would a rural area. Therefore, the rate the insurance company charges in a city will be higher.

3. What they use the car for. If drivers use their car for business on a daily basis, the rate will be higher than if they use it only for errands and occasional trips.

4. Marital status. In general, married men and women have lower accident rates than single men and women and, therefore, pay lower insurance rates.

5. Safety record. If a driver has a history of accidents and traffic tickets, he or she will be charged a high rate. Whether a new driver has had driver education is often considered in determining a rate.

6. Number of drivers. The number of drivers using a car increases the insurance rate.

R Reading Skills

Listing ways to lower insurance rates Have students identify three ways they can lower their insurance rates. *(Answers may include opting for a high deductible, maintaining a good credit rating, taking advantage of discounts such as "nonsmoker," and buying several types of insurance from the same company.)* **Verbal/Linguistic**

ANSWERS, p. 582

CRITICAL THINKING
Answers will vary, but students should justify why they chose more or less coverage, and the effect that that coverage could have on their finances in the event of an accident.

✓ **READING PROGRESS CHECK** higher monthly premiums

FIGURE 19.10

TYPES OF CAR INSURANCE

TYPES OF CAR INSURANCE

Collision: Damage to your car, regardless of who caused the accident.

Comprehensive: Damage to your car not caused by an accident, such as theft, vandalism, and natural disasters.

Liability: Bodily injury and property damage to others, plus legal costs. State laws determine how much coverage you must have.

Medical: Medical expenses for everyone injured, regardless of fault.

Personal injury protection: Medical expenses for the insured driver, regardless of fault.

Uninsured motorist: Damage to your car in an accident caused by a driver with no liability insurance.

Underinsured motorist: Damage to your car in an accident caused by someone with insufficient liability insurance.

Rental reimbursement: Car rental if your vehicle cannot be driven after an accident.

At minimum, car operators must purchase basic liability insurance, which covers damage you might do to others. It is illegal in most states to drive without it. Purchasing a car insurance policy that also covers you and car repairs is also a smart use of your money. If you are hurt in an accident you caused, and you don't have enough coverage, what you would be required by law to pay for damages could really hurt your personal finances.

▲ **CRITICAL THINKING**
Economic Analysis What types of car insurance would you consider for yourself? Explain your answer.

connected.mcgraw-hill.com

- **Long-term Care** This insurance pays expenses for the care of those living in nursing homes or similar facilities.
- **Life** This type of insurance provides financial support to the loved ones of a person who dies. Some types of life insurance offer lending or retirement income features.

R **Shopping for Insurance**
Comparison shop among different insurance companies. Low premiums are usually the goal, but this may mean less coverage than you want. Always read the fine print before signing a policy. Maintain a good credit rating—an insurance company may give you a better rate. Ask about and take advantage of discounts for which you might qualify, such as "good student," "nonsmoker," and "good driver." Consider buying several types of insurance—car and rental, for example—from the same company to qualify for a multiple-policy discount.

✓ **READING PROGRESS CHECK**

Drawing Conclusions What is the trade-off for a low deductible?

Charitable Giving

GUIDING QUESTION *What are some benefits of giving to charitable organizations?*

Remember the budget you created at the beginning of *Personal Financial Literacy*? There was a line in it allotted for charitable giving. A charity is an organization

---

networks Online Teaching Options

CHARTS

Types of Car Insurance

Understanding various types of auto insurance Have students view Figure 19.10. Explain that insurance companies classify drivers in various ways, usually according to age, gender, and marital status. Rates depend on the category into which a person fits. The categories, in turn, are based on statistics showing that different types of drivers have different accident rates. **Logical/Mathematical**

Research shows that people who give to charity or who participate in volunteer activities show consistent high levels of self-esteem and generally feel good about themselves. Also, charitable giving can be deducted from taxes.

that has been created for the purpose of helping others, usually a specific group of people who share a common circumstance. Charitable giving is also called *philanthropy*. Some of the most popular charitable organizations are the Red Cross, Susan G. Komen®, and the American Cancer Society®.

People give to charity for a number of reasons. For many, they have a personal connection to the organization's mission—a family member has a condition that is supported by a charity, for example. Others want to make a difference in the world. Still others give because contributions are tax deductible, or can be claimed on an income tax return.

Research shows that those who regularly contribute to a charitable organization have higher self-esteem and developed social skills. You may think that you don't have much to give, but you can always start with acts that don't require money. Volunteer your time. Contact Habitat for Humanity to see if you can help in your area, for example. Donating toys and clothing is also a good way to give back to the community. Find a nonprofit organization that interests you, and phone or email its headquarters for ideas to help.

☑ **READING PROGRESS CHECK**

Explaining What can you do if you have no money to donate to a charitable organization?

LESSON 3 REVIEW

Reviewing Vocabulary
1. *Defining* What does it mean to default on a loan?

Using Your Notes
2. *Summarizing* Use your notes to compare and contrast the differences between a Federal Work-Study program and a non-Federal Work-Study program.

Answering the Guiding Questions
3. *Explaining* Why are there so many different methods available to help you fund more education?
4. *Examining* What information do you need to be aware of when preparing to rent housing?
5. *Describing* Why do we purchase insurance?
6. *Evaluating* What are some benefits of giving to charitable organizations?

Writing About Economics
7. *Informative/Explanatory* Write a two-page essay describing the role of charitable organizations in the capitalist economy. Also, what benefits both financial and non-financial can an individual receive through charitable giving?

CHAPTER 19, LESSON 3
Personal Money Decisions

C Critical Thinking Skills

Measuring the costs of charitable giving Have students discuss what they would have to give up in order to donate $10 a month to a charity.
Verbal/Linguistic, Interpersonal

R Reading Skills

Identifying the benefits of charitable giving Ask: What are the benefits of charitable giving? *(higher self-esteem, better social skills)* Mention to students that many college scholarships and grants they apply for also want to know about student involvement in charitable or community events. Greater involvement now will benefit students later.

CLOSE & REFLECT

Revising a budget Have students review the budget they created earlier. Ask them to add rows for rent; utilities such as gas, electric, and water; renters insurance; student loans; and charitable giving (if omitted earlier). Then have students consider their career and salary goals and whether these will help students match their expenses.
Intrapersonal

ANSWERS, p. 583

☑ **READING PROGRESS CHECK** Donate time

LESSON 3 REVIEW ANSWERS

Reviewing Vocabulary
1. the borrower has not repaid the borrowed money

Using Your Notes
2. The FWS is based on financial need and are awarded after filling out the FAFSA. Jobs can be either on campus or off campus. The employer will pay up to 50% of your wages, and the government will pay the rest. The amount of money you earn cannot exceed your financial aid award. Average work hours are 10-15 a week. The non-FWS is not based on financial need. Most schools offer student employment opportunities in places like the dining halls, library, and offices of various academic departments.

Answering the Guiding Questions
3. Answers will vary but should mention that the differing levels of incomes in the country require differing options of funding education. One goal of government is to invest in human capital by providing education. More education also leads to higher salaries, higher tax bases, and a potentially growing economy.
4. how much to pay for rent, additional expenses such as utilities, amenities, the amount of the security deposit and whether the first and last months' rent are required, the length of the lease
5. Insurance pays for emergency repairs and expensive procedures if something bad happens—such as a traffic accident, an illness, or an apartment fire. The insurance company will pay a portion or the entirety of what is covered in your policy.
6. Benefits include higher self-esteem and social skills, knowing that one is making a difference in the world, and receiving tax deductions on an income tax return.

Writing About Economics
7. Answers should mention the support that charitable organizations provide for the safety and security of many citizens. Essays should also mention the financial benefits of gaining a deduction to apply to yearly tax returns, and non-financial benefits such as improved self-esteem.

Chapter 19
Study Guide

C1 Critical Thinking Skills

Developing a game with steps to pay off debt
Have students work in groups to create a board game titled "Credit Crunch." Indicate that the object of the game is to pay off crushing debt. Each person begins with 3 maxed-out credit cards for a total debt of $10,000. Each credit card has a different APR. At the beginning of the game, students have $200 of discretionary income per month, a car payment, apartment rental, student loan payment, and typical monthly bills. Have students create a "path" to debt freedom, with each step along the path noting changes the player will make to first reduce and then eliminate debt. Point out that lucky breaks (a pay raise or birthday money, for example) and bad breaks (rising energy costs or unexpected repair bills, for example) might advance or stall a player's progress. Explain that the first player to retire his or her debt wins the game.

W Writing Skills

Paying for college Discuss as a class the information presented in this chapter about paying for college. Ask students to write a persuasive essay describing the accessibility of higher education in the United States today. Students should defend a position such as "through financial aid, a college education is still widely attainable today" or "spiraling costs have shut the door on too many young Americans seeking a college education."

C2 Critical Thinking Skills

Determining entrance requirements Have students research the academic requirements of five colleges of their choosing. Ask students to create a chart comparing the requirements of the different schools. Students should include information such as minimum high school GPA, class rank, minimum ACT or SAT score, and any other academic requirements the chosen colleges may have. Students should also make a separate chart that lists due dates for admissions, financial aid, housing, and parking applications. Finally, students should obtain campus maps from the Web sites or catalogs of their five colleges. Students should circle or highlight the college administration offices on the maps. Tell students that, although applying for college includes many deadlines and applications, organizing the necessary information, and planning out beforehand where to file the applications will make the process much easier and less overwhelming.

STUDY GUIDE

LESSON 1

LESSON 2

LESSON 3
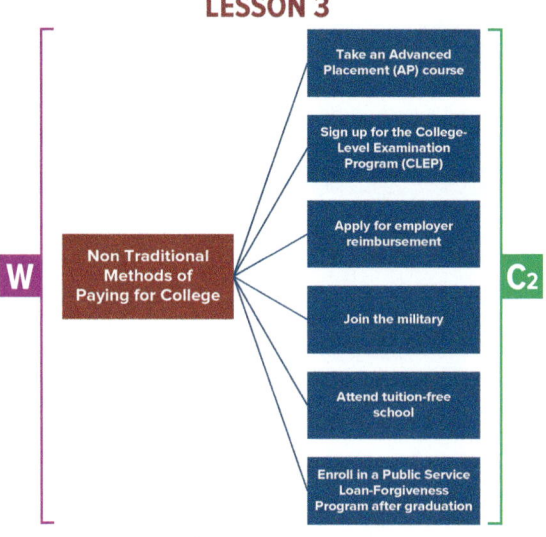

networks Online Assessment Options

WORKSHEET

Personal Finance Activity: Cash, Debit, or Credit

Analyzing advantages and disadvantages of using cash, debit, and credit Students will analyze the pros and cons of using cash, debit cards, and credit cards. This activity will also help them to decide which ways of using money are best for them and why. *Logical/Mathematical*

CHAPTER 19 Assessment

Directions: Answer the questions below. Make sure you read carefully and answer all parts of the questions.

Lesson Review

Lesson 1
1. How does one begin a savings program?
2. Why is it important for you to reconcile your checking account each month?
3. What are your responsibilities as a borrower?
4. How is a credit card finance charge different from its annual percentage rate (APR)?

Lesson 2
5. How do savings form the basis of capital formation?
6. What are four ways for corporations to raise capital?
7. What do you need to do to start investing in stocks?
8. Why are munis attractive to many investors?
9. What is the difference between a traditional IRA and a Roth IRA?

Lesson 3
10. In what three ways might the federal government award you aid after you fill out the FAFSA?
11. As a renter, what are your rights and responsibilities?
12. Explain the advantages and disadvantages of both fixed rate and adjustable rate mortgages.
13. Describe how insurance works.
14. What are the costs and benefits of charitable giving?

Critical Thinking
15. **Calculating Interest** If your bank pays 5.5 percent interest on savings deposits, what is the simple interest paid in the third year on an initial $100 deposit? What is the total amount in the account after three years? What is the amount after three years if the interest was compounded annually?
16. **Making Decisions** List your short-term savings goals, such as saving to buy a new cell phone. Explain the typical ways in which you can save for such a purchase. Then list your long-term savings goals, such as saving for a house or retirement. Explain how you can achieve these goals. What is the major difference between the two ways of saving?

Need Extra Help?

If You've Missed Question	1	2	3	4	5	6	7	8	9	10	11	12	13	14	15	16
Go to page	560	563	564	565	568	570	571	572	573	575	578	579	581	582	560	559

Chapter 19 Assessment Answers

Lesson Review

Lesson 1
1. Start setting aside 10 to 30 percent of your income as savings. Select a bank. Ask questions such as: Does the bank require a minimum balance? What are the fees? What interest rates does the bank offer? Decide which type of savings vehicle you want—one with easy access and low interest, or one with deposit requirements and higher interest.
2. to make sure there are no errors; If you fail to report a discrepancy on your statement within 60 days, you could be held responsible.
3. You are responsible for understanding the terms of the loan and repaying the loan on time.
4. The finance charge is the total cost of credit. It includes interest but also fees for annual membership, transactions, and other services. The APR is the percentage of interest you are charged for every year you owe money.

Lesson 2
5. Financial institutions turn the collective savings of all their customers into investments that result in more jobs, which result in more goods and services being produced.
6. selling bonds, issuing stocks, borrowing directly, converting profits
7. Establish an account with a stockbroker, either in person or online, after researching the broker and knowing what fees are charged. You need to be 18 (or have a custodial account), have two sets of identification, a Social Security number, a W-9 form, and the initial deposit. Know your short-term and long-term goals. Research the potential stock's profits and earnings history.
8. Interest payments on munis are tax-exempt.
9. In a traditional IRA, contributions are not taxed when they are deposited, but you have to pay tax on the whole amount (as income) when you withdraw the funds upon retirement. In a Roth IRA, you have taxes taken out before you make deposits so you do not have to pay taxes when you withdraw the money at retirement.

Lesson 3
10. with a grant, with a low-interest loan, with a work-study program
11. Rights: a safe and sanitary property maintained and repaired by the landlord; nondiscrimination on the basis of race, nationality, religion, gender, or disability; payment of the same amount of rent within the term of the lease. Responsibilities: paying your rent on time, not causing damage to the property, being considerate of your neighbors, and following any other terms that are spelled out in the lease
12. Fixed rate: advantage is that monthly payments stay the same; disadvantage is that the interest rate does not change, even if market rates decline. Adjustable rate: advantage is that interest rates may lower when market rates do; disadvantage is that there is risk if market rates rise
13. You pay an insurance company monthly or quarterly premiums for a policy detailing what items are covered and under what conditions. Then if something bad happens, the insurance company will pay a portion or the entirety of what is covered in your policy, usually after you pay a deductible amount.
14. Costs include the opportunity cost of not spending the charitable amount on something else. Benefits include higher self-esteem and social skills, knowing that one is making a difference in the world, and receiving tax deductions on an income tax return.

Critical Thinking
15. $5.50; $116.50; $117.42
16. Answers will vary but should reflect that short-term savings plans focus on flexibility, whereas long-term savings plans focus on earnings from higher-risk, higher-interest funds.

Chapter 19
Assessment Answers

17 Answers will vary. Banks and large credit unions offer mortgages and other loans, but credit unions would have lower interest rates for auto loans, and finance companies offer installment loans for vehicles at higher interest rates.

18 The benefit of buying on credit is establishing credit history, increasing your credit score, and being able to enjoy the good or service now rather than later. The cost is whatever the borrower must pay in interest or lost opportunities to buy other items. The benefit of buying with cash or using a debit card is that the borrower does not incur debt. The costs are the time the buyer may have to wait to buy while saving, and the lost opportunities to purchase other items. However, if you use a debit card without enough money in your account to back it up, you may incur a fine and other purchases will cause an overdraw on your account.

19 Mortgage payments should be less than 30 percent of monthly take-home pay. Because 30 percent of $2,400 is $720—much less than $900—the lender should not grant the mortgage.

Building Financial Literacy

20 Apply for a secured credit card at a bank or credit union. Use the card to make purchases, and make the monthly payments on time. Later, apply for an unsecured credit card. In addition, apply for a retail store credit card, use it, and make payments on time. Stay in the same job for a while. Pay service providers on time.

21 Answers will vary.

22 Students' choices will vary but may include stocks, bonds, mutual funds, and U.S. Treasury instruments to provide for diversification.

23 Answers will vary.

CHAPTER 19 Assessment

Directions: Answer the questions below. Make sure you read carefully and answer all parts of the questions.

17 **Comparing** Imagine that you need both a car loan and a home mortgage. Use a chart like the one below to help decide which type of lending institution would be most appropriate for each loan.

Financial Institution	Services	Car or Home Loan?

18 **Considering Advantages and Disadvantages** In deciding whether to pay cash or use credit for a purchase, what are the costs involved and the benefits of each choice?

19 **Synthesizing** Suppose you are applying for a mortgage. The mortgage payment will be $900, whereas your monthly take-home income is $2,400. Should the lender grant you the mortgage? Why or why not?

Building Financial Literacy

20 **Decision Making** How do you build credit and improve your credit score?

21 **Planning** Obtain various credit card applications from several retail stores and gas stations. Analyze the applications and prepare a database that organizes the answers to the following questions:

- What questions asked on each application are virtually the same?
- What questions asked on the gas station applications are different from those asked on the retail store applications?
- What are the differences in finance charges and APR?

22 **Identifying Alternatives** Suppose that you have $100,000 in savings. Create a chart like the one below to list the investments you might make and what percentage of the $100,000 you would invest in each. In the last column, explain how your choices will achieve investment diversification.

Investment Type	% of Funds	Diversification

23 **Making Comparisons** Search the Internet for information on car insurance in your area. Write a summary about the companies that sell insurance and analyze the factors they use in determining what to charge for drivers in your age group.

Need Extra Help?

If You've Missed Question	17	18	19	20	21	22	23
Go to page	559	565	579	564	565	562	582

---

networks Online Assessment Options

WORKSHEET

Chapter Tests and Lesson Quizzes

Chapter 19 Tests Forms A and B Have students complete the Chapter Tests and Lesson Quizzes to assess student understanding throughout the chapter. Print and online assessment tools offer chapter and lesson evaluation through a variety of question formats, including document-based questions.

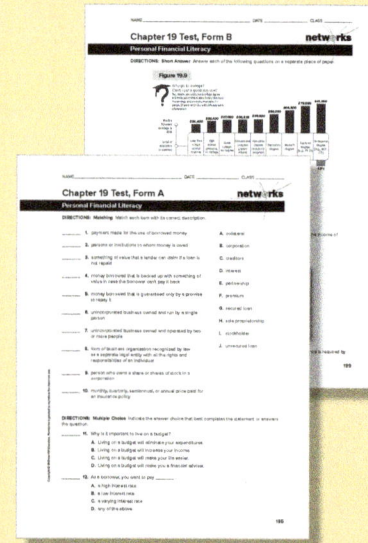

DATA BANK

The American People
U.S. Population Projections............ 588
Civilian Labor Force 588
Hours and Earnings in Private Industries .589

The U.S. Economy
Gross Domestic Product 590
A Look at Stock Market History
    (S&P 500)........................ 590
Real Personal Consumption
    Expenditures 591
Personal Consumption Expenditures 591
Average Prices of Selected Goods..... 592
Annual Changes in Consumer Price
    Indexes 593
Inflation in Consumer Prices........... 593

The Government Sector
Federal Government Expenditures..... 594
Total Government Expenditures........ 594
Federal Government Total Receipts
    and Total Outlays 595
Federal Debt Held by the Public 595
Federal Debt Held by the Public
    Per Capita....................... 595
Federal Budget Receipts.............. 596

The Financial Sector
Interest Rates....................... 597
Consumer Credit Outstanding 597
Personal Saving..................... 598
Money Stock........................ 598

The Global Economy
Population........................... 599
Gross National Income................ 599
Gross Domestic Product 599
World Population by Age.............. 600
Countries Ranked by Population....... 600
Aging Index in Selected Nations of
    the Americas 601
Median Age, World................... 601
U.S. Exports and Imports.............. 602
Inflation and Unemployment,
    Selected Economies 602

The American People

U.S. Population Projections, 2015–2060

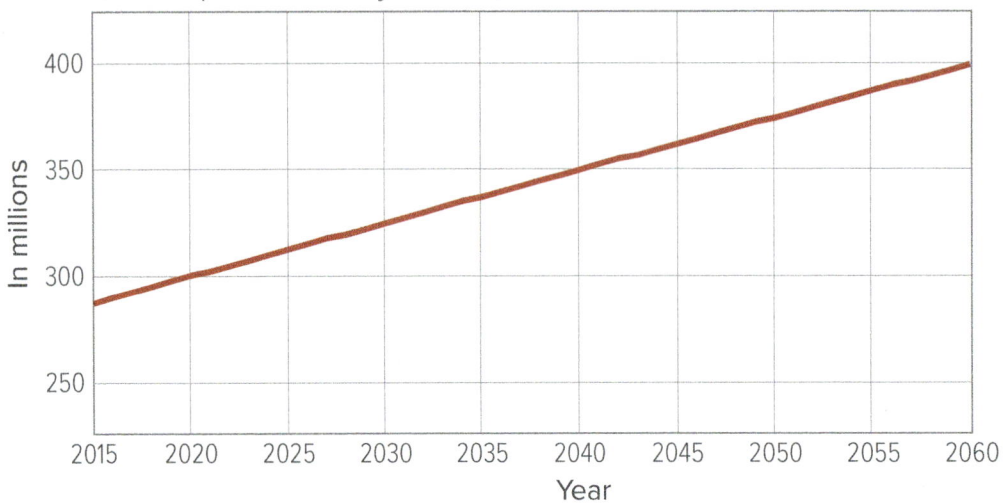

Source: U.S. Census Bureau

Civilian Labor Force, 1950–2025

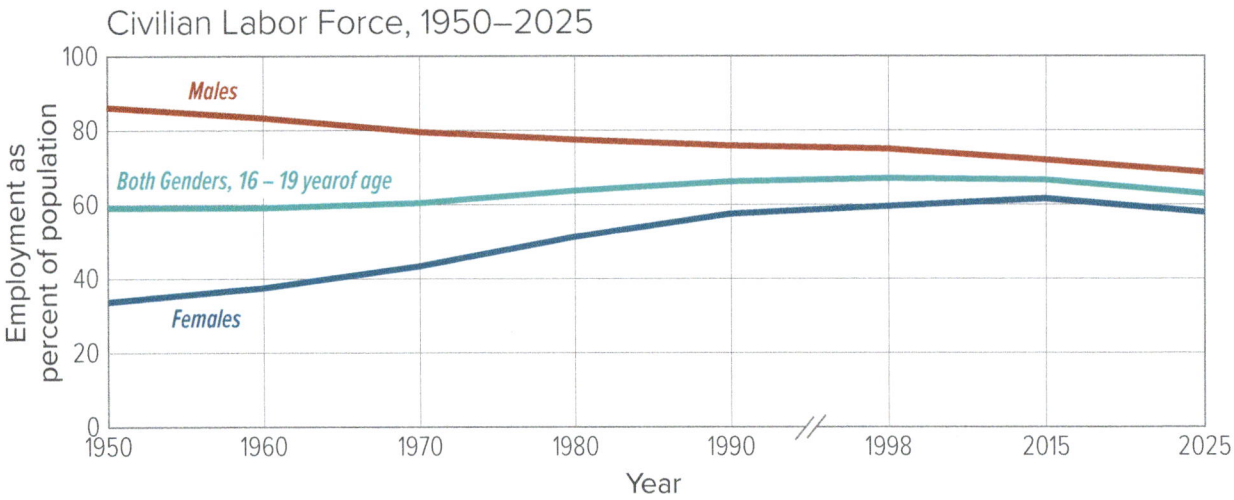

Source: Department of Labor, Bureau of Labor Statistics

The American People

Hours and Earnings in Private Industries, 1960–2014

A Average Weekly Hours of Production Workers

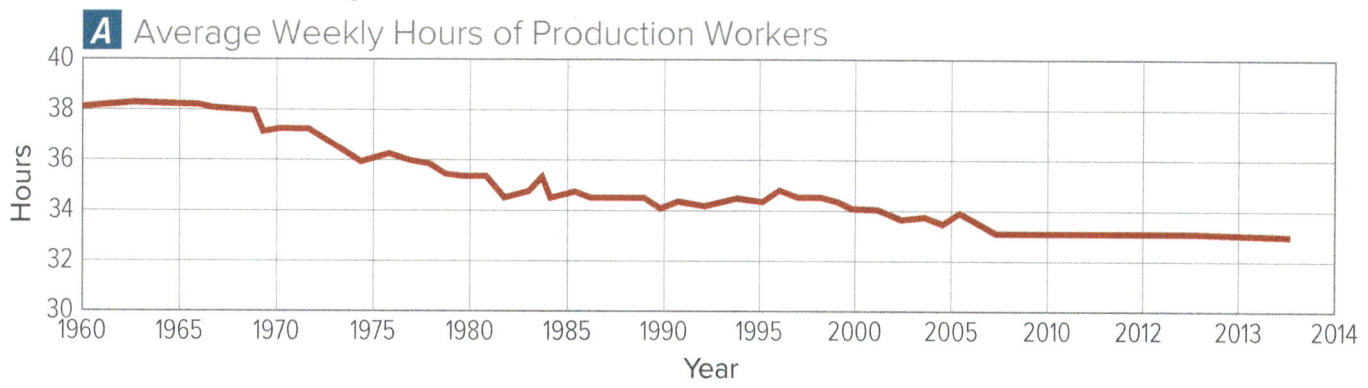

B Average Weekly Earnings of Production Workers, Current Dollars

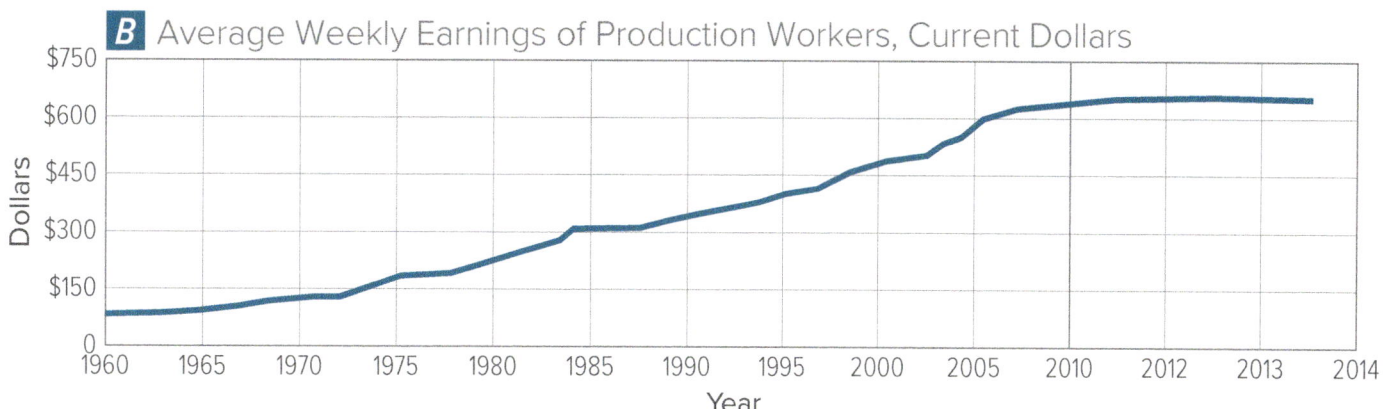

C Average Weekly Earnings, 1982 Dollars

Source: U.S. Department of Labor, Bureau of Labor Statistics

The U.S. Economy

Average Prices of Selected Goods, 2004–2014

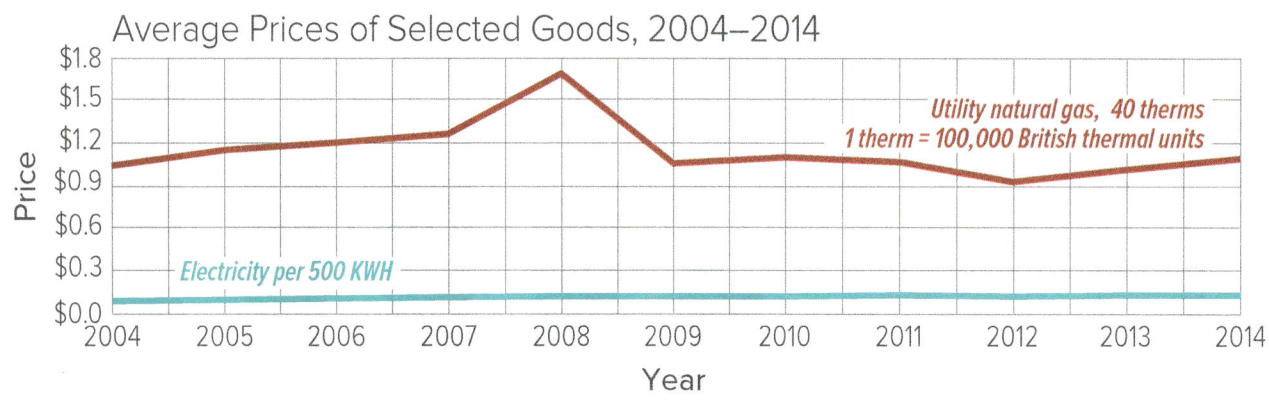

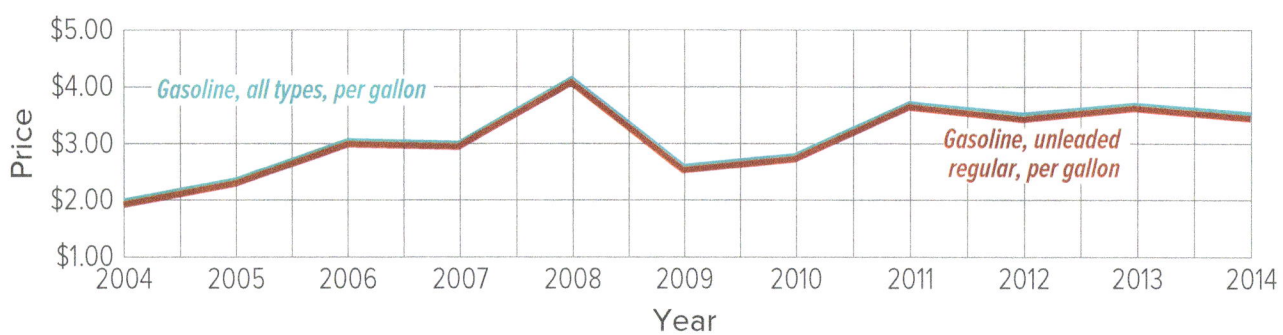

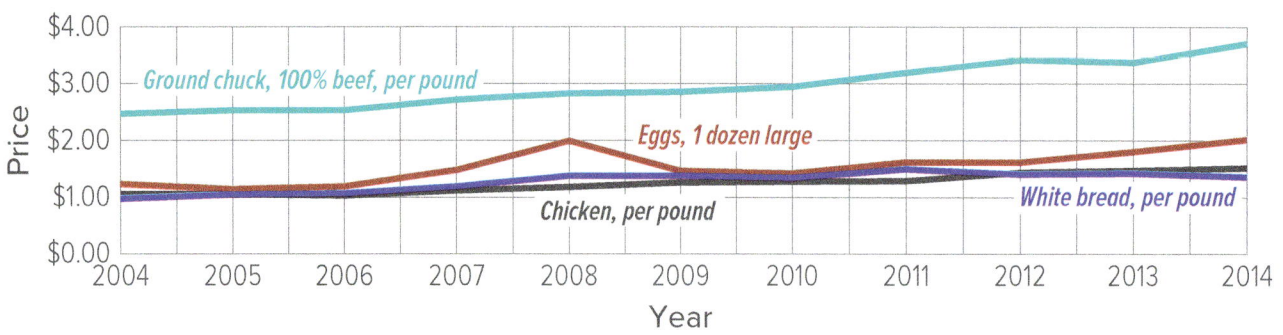

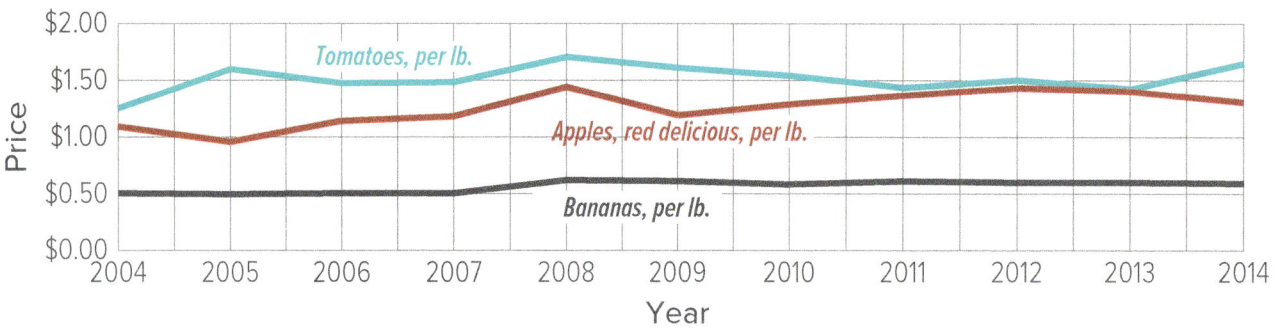

The American People

Hours and Earnings in Private Industries, 1960–2014

A Average Weekly Hours of Production Workers

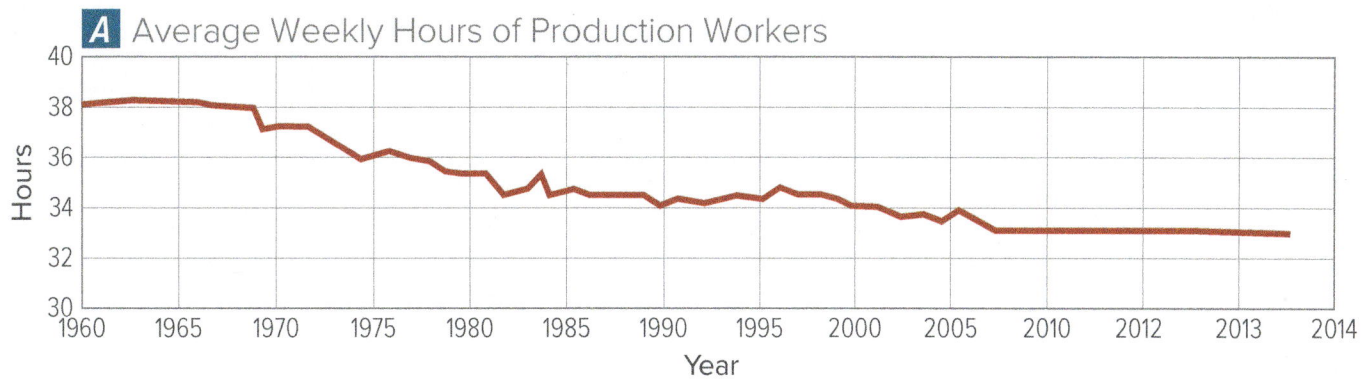

B Average Weekly Earnings of Production Workers, Current Dollars

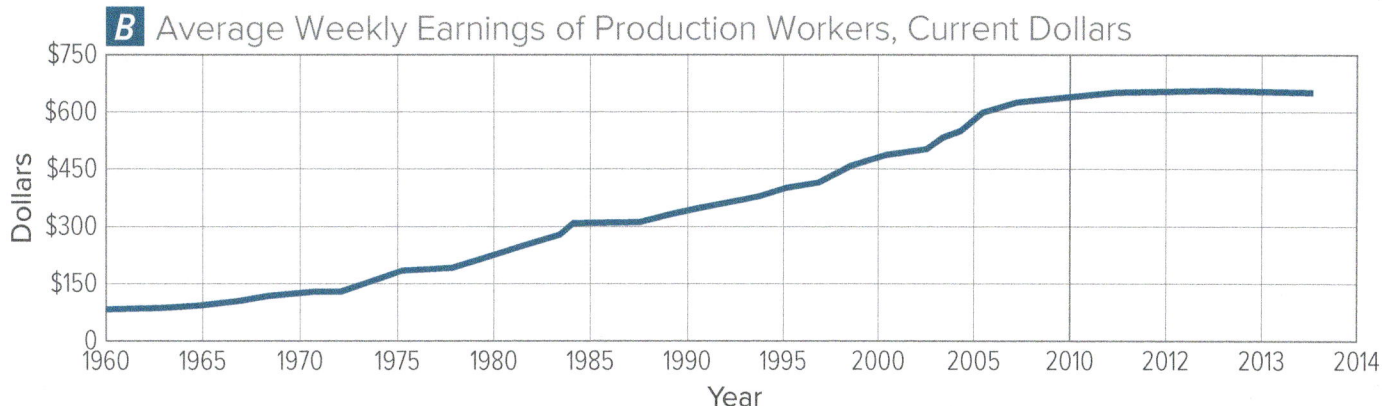

C Average Weekly Earnings, 1982 Dollars

Source: U.S. Department of Labor, Bureau of Labor Statistics

The U.S. Economy

Gross Domestic Product, 1950–2013
Billions of current dollars
18,000
16,000
14,000
12,000
10,000
8,000
6,000
4,000
2,000
0
1950
1955
1960
1965
1970
1975
1980
1985
1990
1995
2000
2005
2010
2011
2012
2013
Year

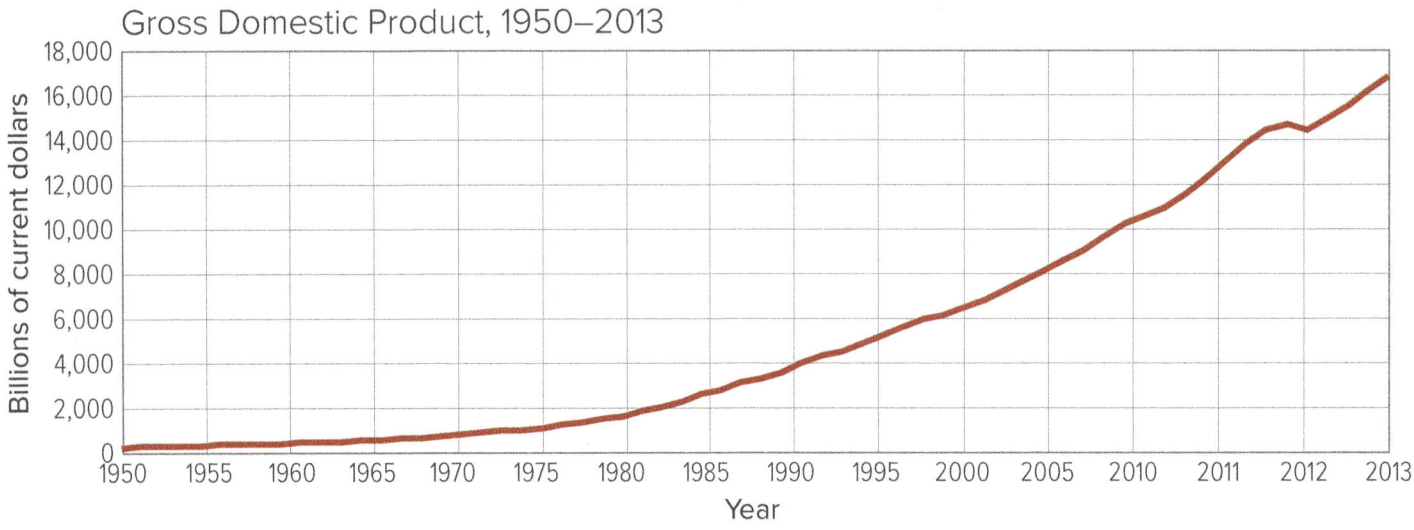

Source: *U.S. Department of Commerce, Bureau of Economic Analysis*

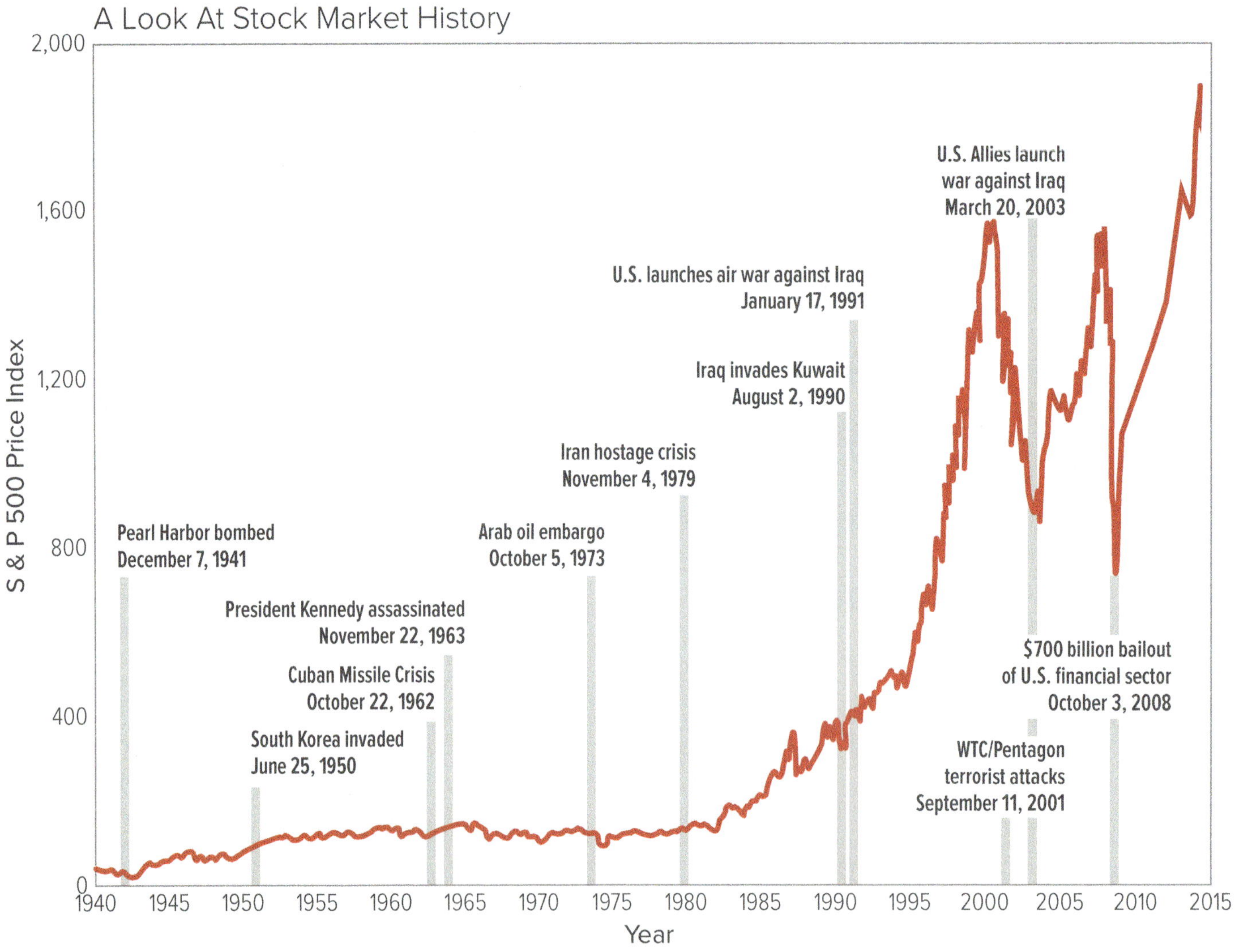

A Look At Stock Market History
S & P 500 Price Index
2,000
1,600
1,200
800
400
0
Pearl Harbor bombed December 7, 1941
South Korea invaded June 25, 1950
Cuban Missile Crisis October 22, 1962
President Kennedy assassinated November 22, 1963
Arab oil embargo October 5, 1973
Iran hostage crisis November 4, 1979
Iraq invades Kuwait August 2, 1990
U.S. launches air war against Iraq January 17, 1991
WTC/Pentagon terrorist attacks September 11, 2001
U.S. Allies launch war against Iraq March 20, 2003
$700 billion bailout of U.S. financial sector October 3, 2008
1940
1945
1950
1955
1960
1965
1970
1975
1980
1985
1990
1995
2000
2005
2010
2015
Year

Source: *Standard & Poor's, Board of Governors of the Federal Reserve System*

The U.S. Economy

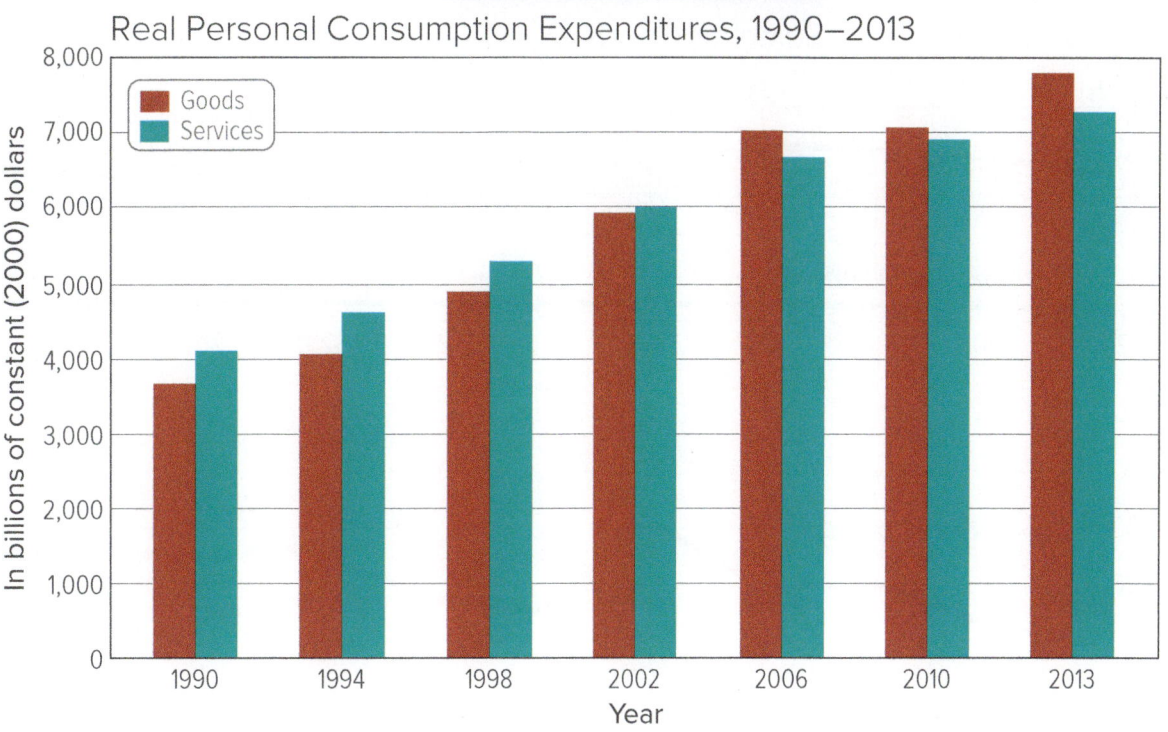

Real Personal Consumption Expenditures, 1990–2013

Source: U.S. Department of Commerce, Bureau of Economic Analysis

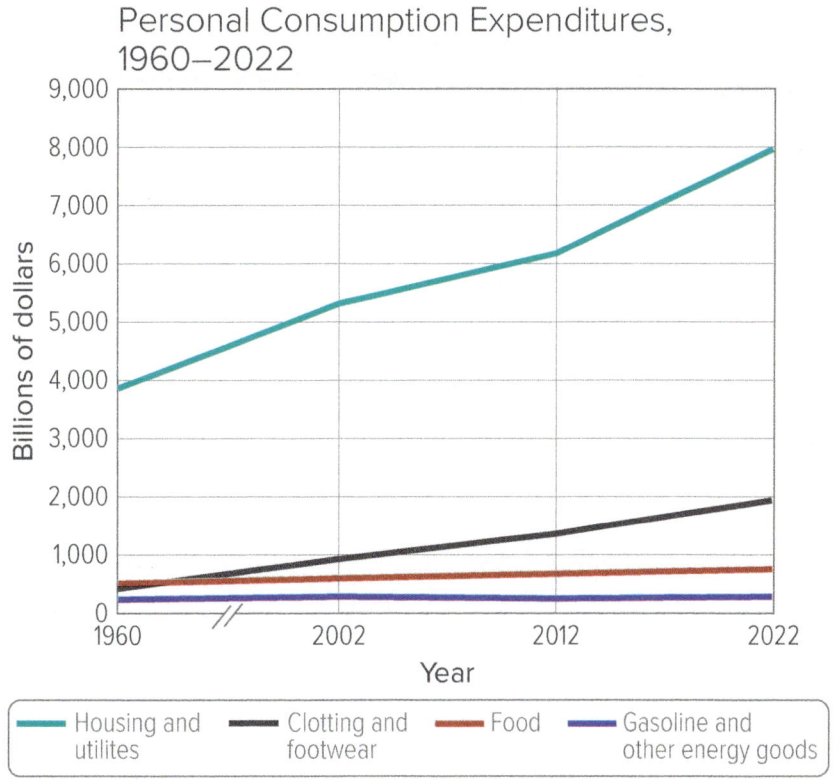

Personal Consumption Expenditures, 1960–2022

Source: U.S. Department of Commerce, Bureau of Economic Analysis; U.S. Department of Labor, Bureau of Labor Statistics

The U.S. Economy

Average Prices of Selected Goods, 2004–2014

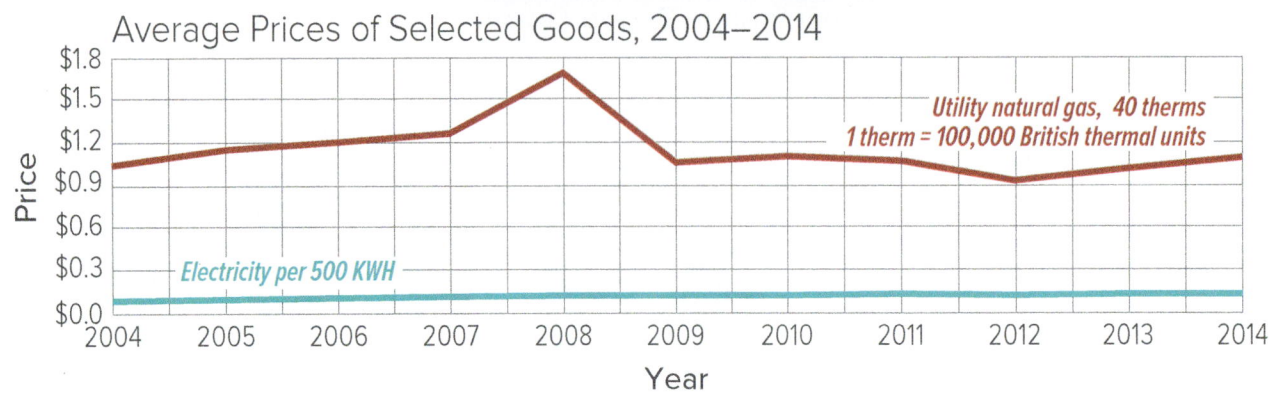

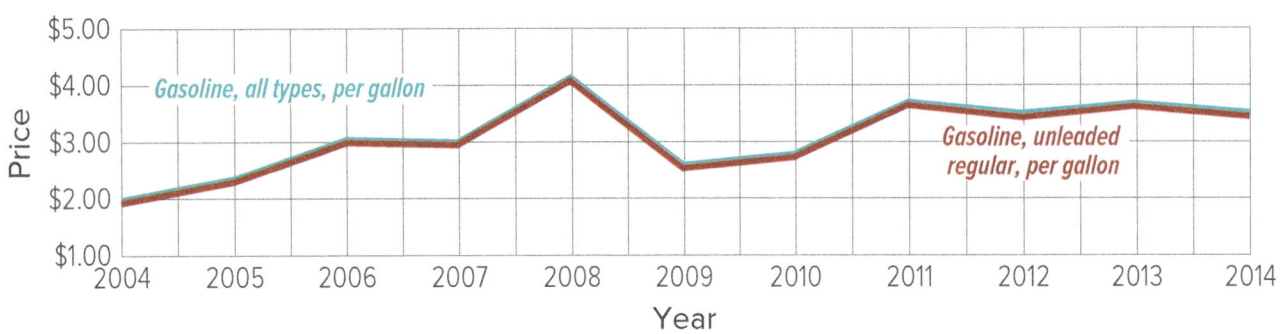

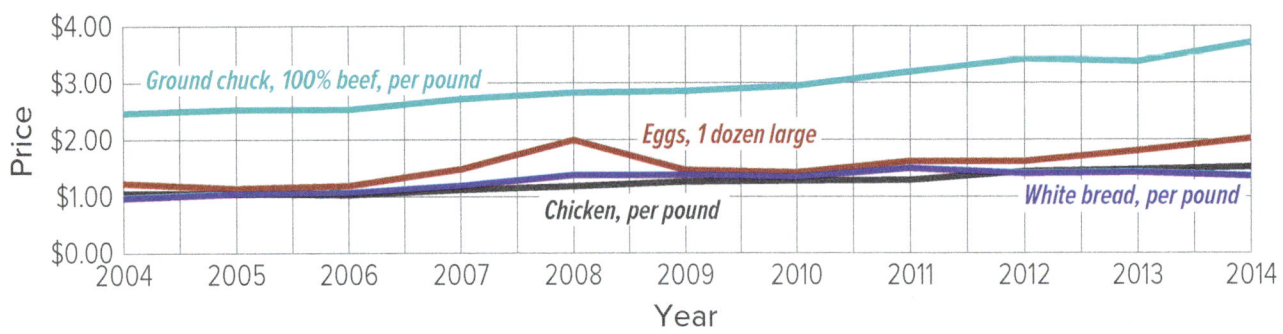

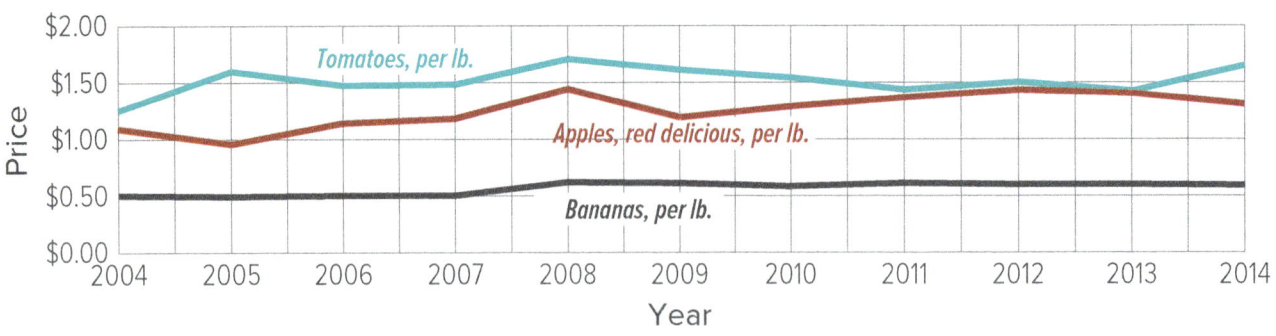

The U.S. Economy

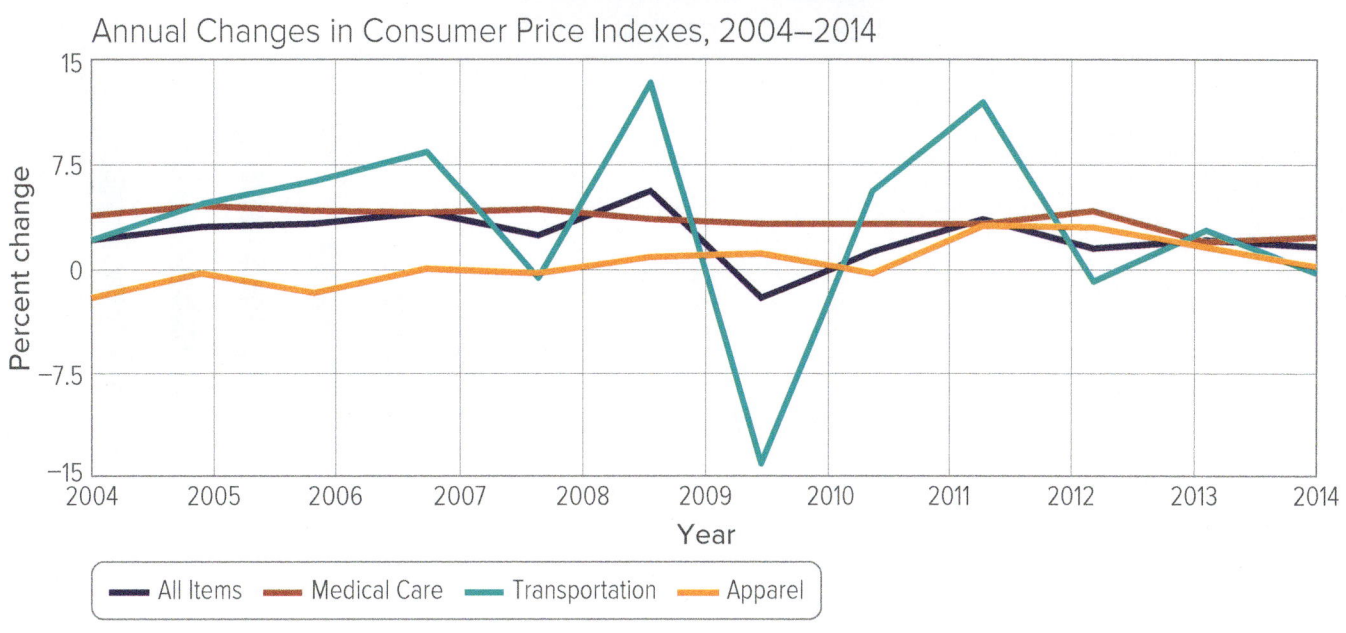

Source: Bureau of Labor Statistics

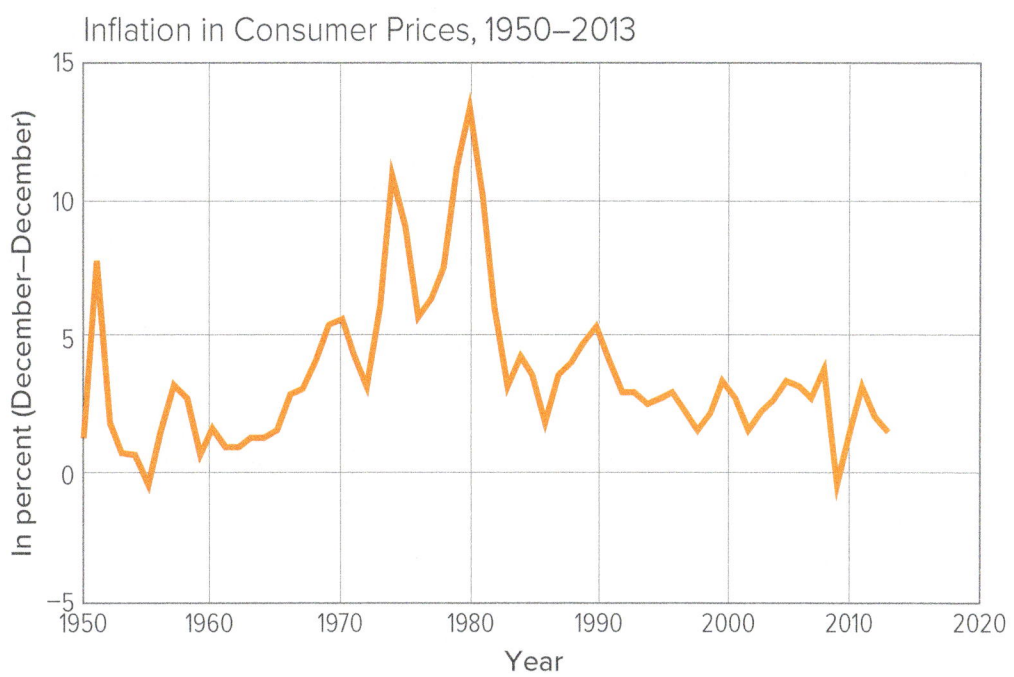

Source: Bureau of Labor Statistics

DATA BANK

The Government Sector

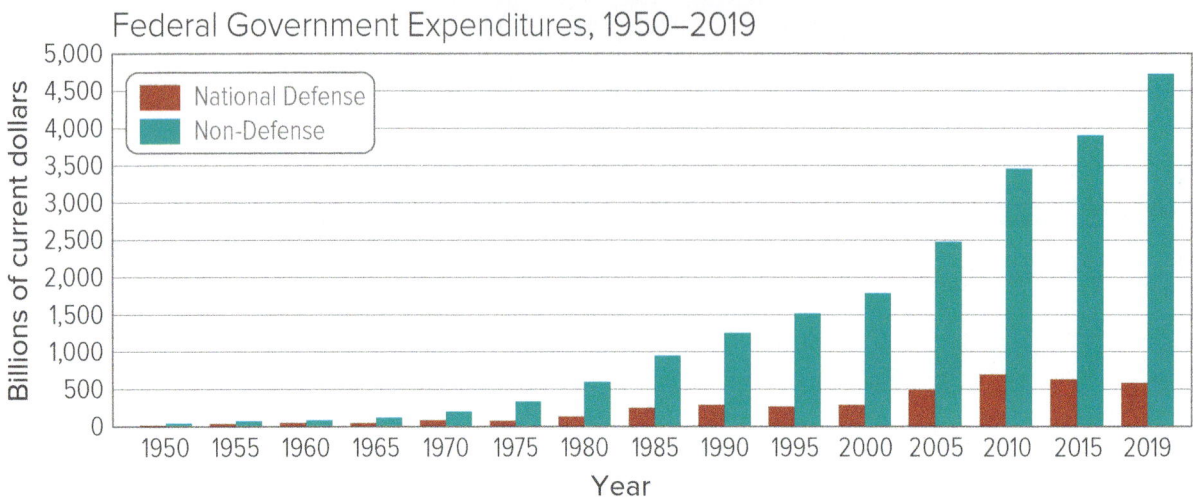

Source: *The Federal Budget for Fiscal Year* 2014, Historical Tables

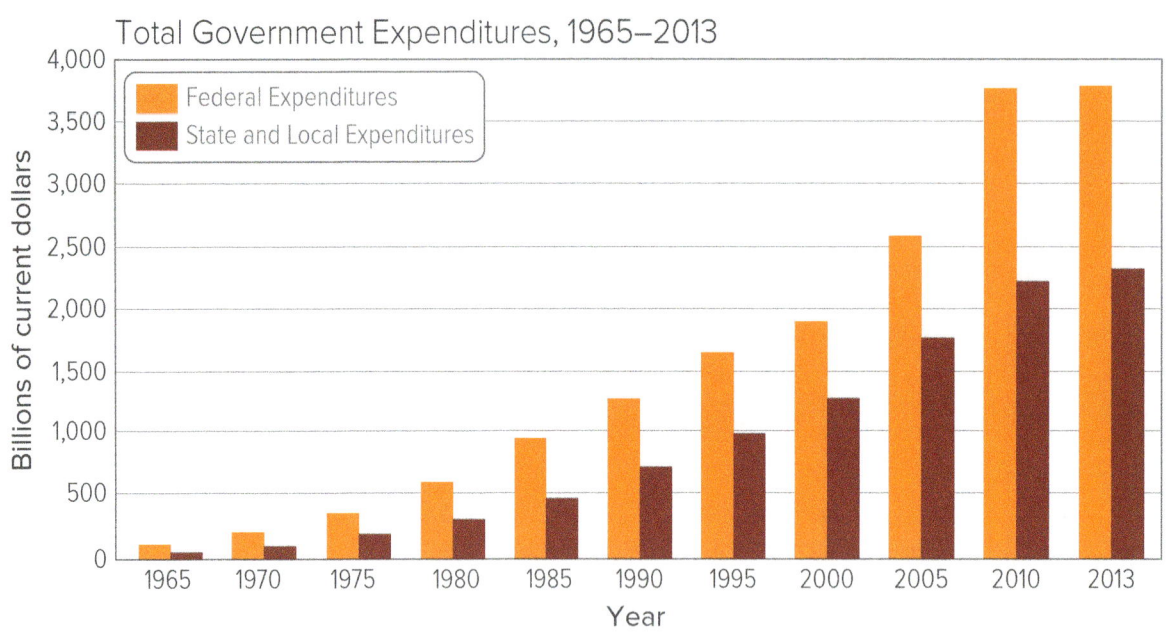

Source: *Economic Report of the President*, 2014

The Government Sector

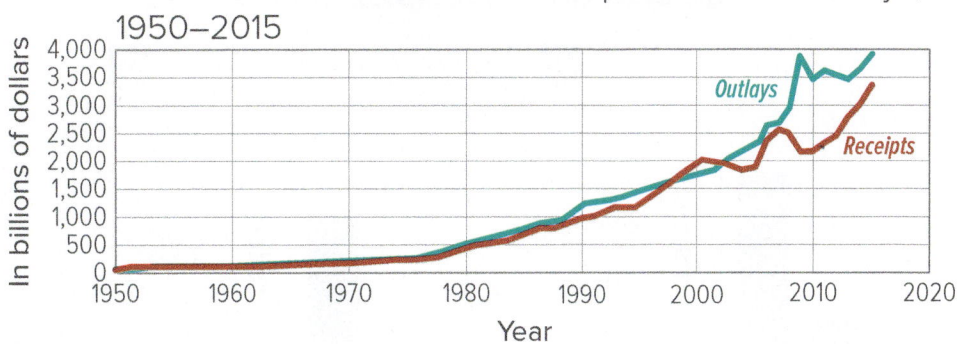

Federal Government Total Receipts and Total Outlays, 1950–2015

Source: *Economic Report of the President,* 2014

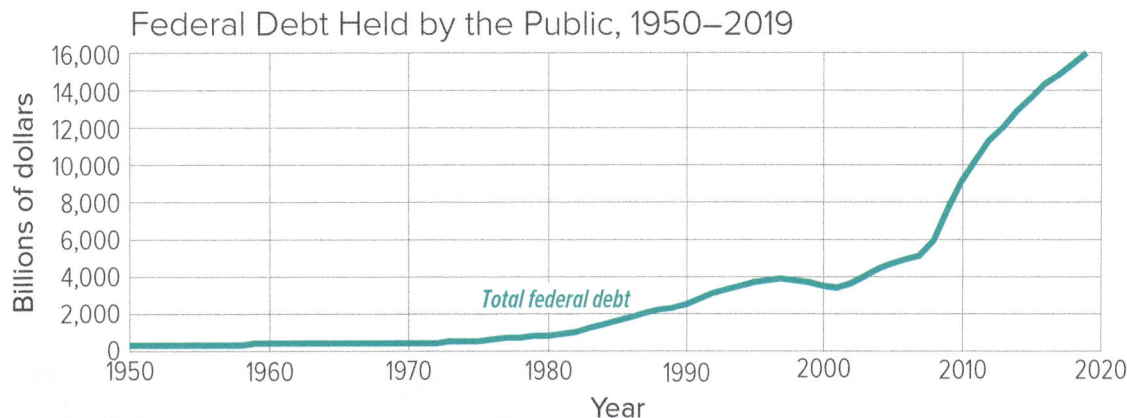

Federal Debt Held by the Public, 1950–2019

Source: *The Federal Budget for Fiscal Year* 2014, Historical Tables

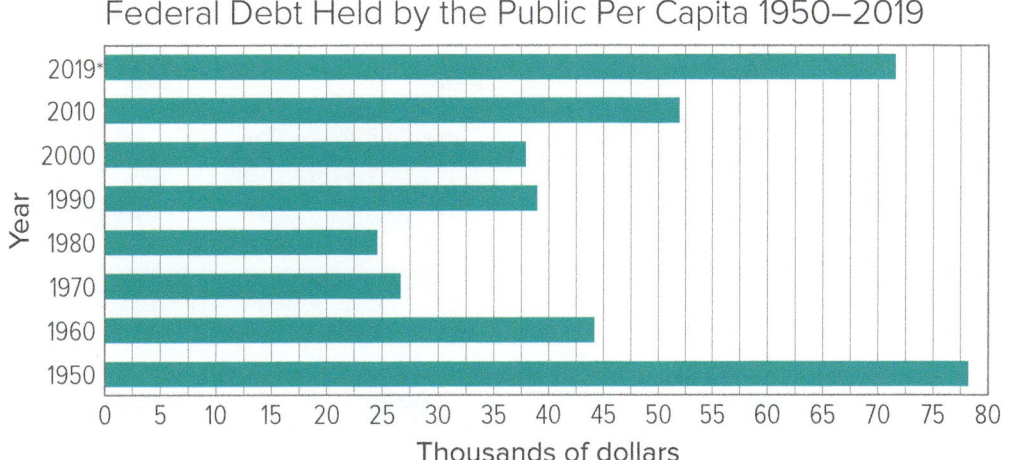

Federal Debt Held by the Public Per Capita 1950–2019

Source: *The Federal Budget for Fiscal Year* 2014, *Historical Tables; United States Census Bureau*
*Estimate

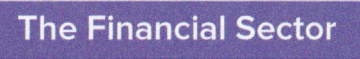

The Financial Sector

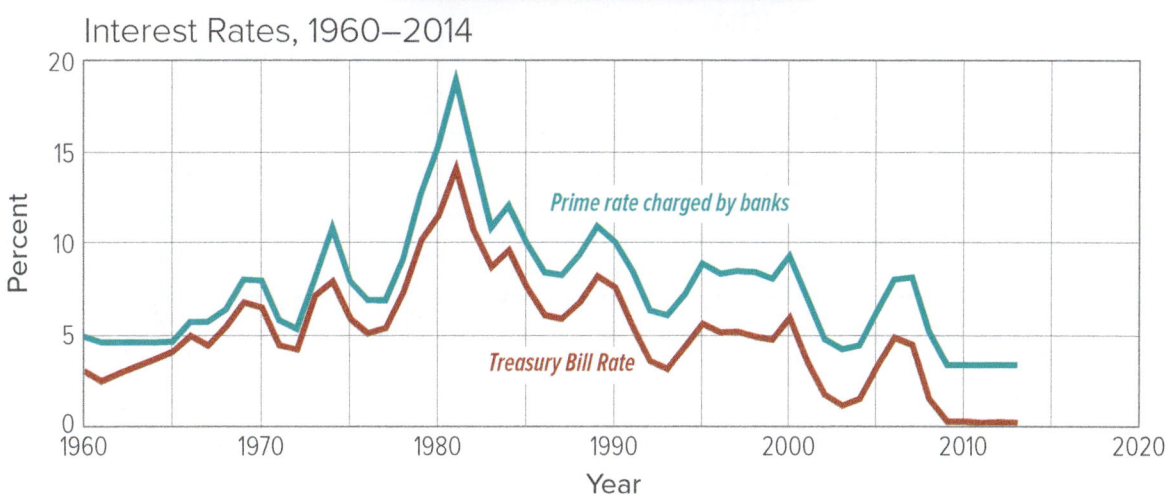

Interest Rates, 1960–2014

Consumer Credit Outstanding, 1985–2014

Total Consumer Credit	
1985	$599.7 billion
1995	$1,141.4 billion
2005	$2,147.9 billion

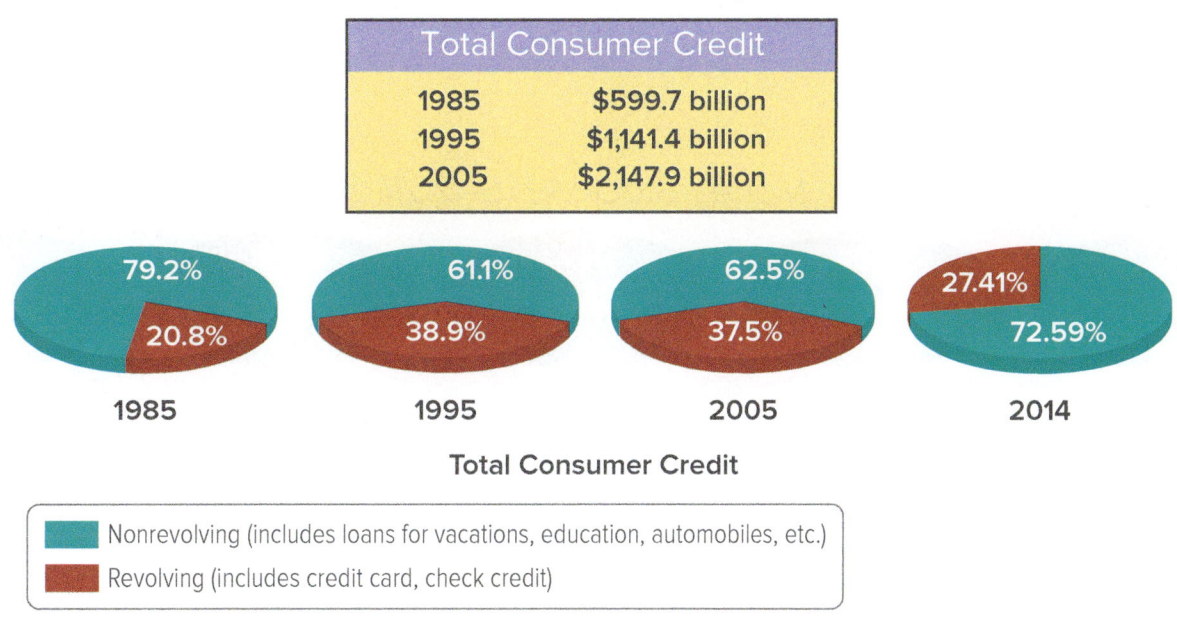

Total Consumer Credit

- Nonrevolving (includes loans for vacations, education, automobiles, etc.)
- Revolving (includes credit card, check credit)

Source: *Board of Governors of the Federal Reserve System*

The Financial Sector

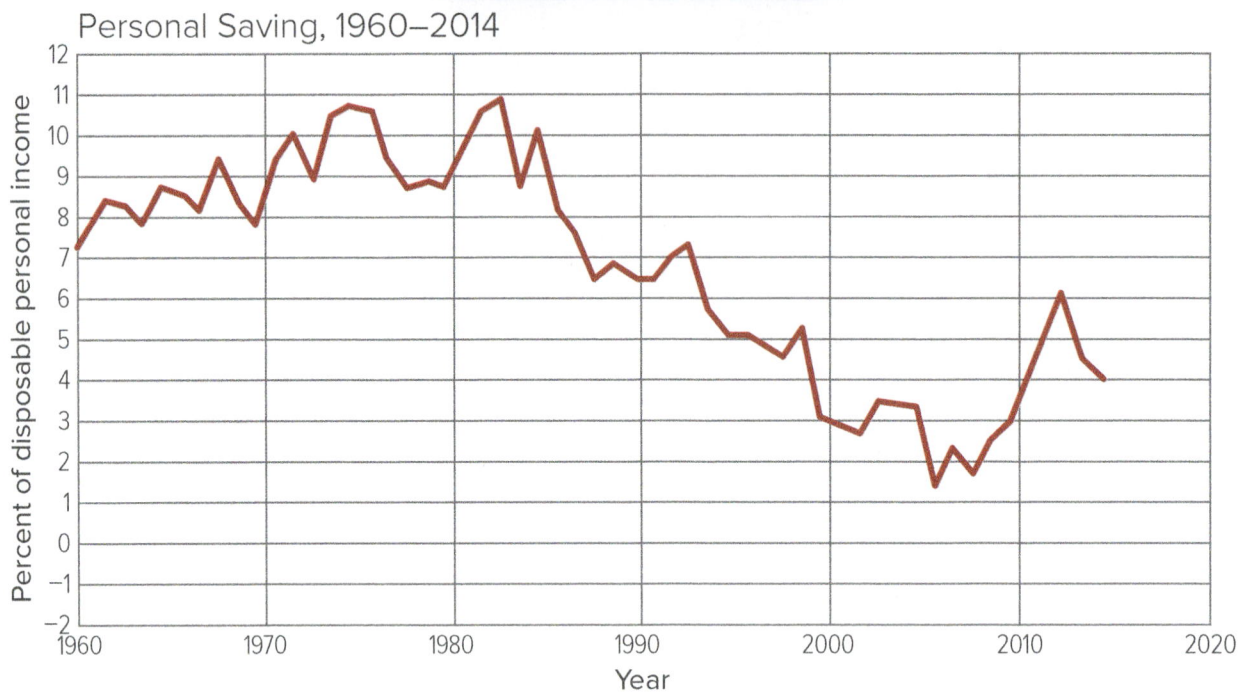

Source: U.S. Department of Commerce, Bureau of Economic Analysis

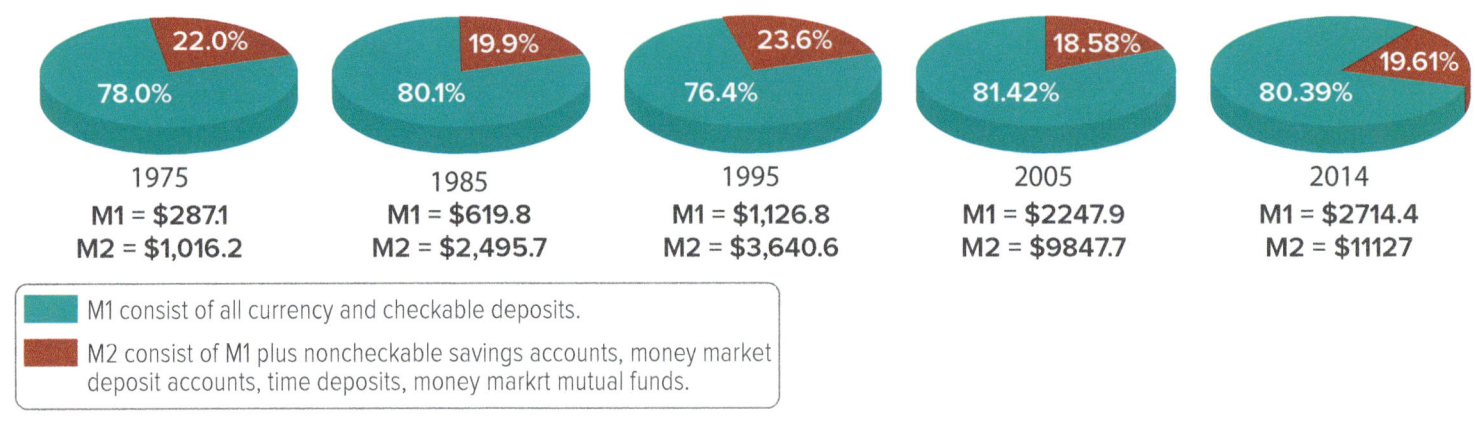

- M1 consist of all currency and checkable deposits.
- M2 consist of M1 plus noncheckable savings accounts, money market deposit accounts, time deposits, money markrt mutual funds.

Source: Board of Governors of the Federal Reserve system

The Global Economy

Population

	Population (in millions)	Population Density (people per sq. km)
Low-income countries (43 countries)	~800	~55
Middle-income countries (101 countries)	~4,850	~75
High-income countries (66 countries)	~1,250	~25

Legend: Population, Population Density

Source: World Bank

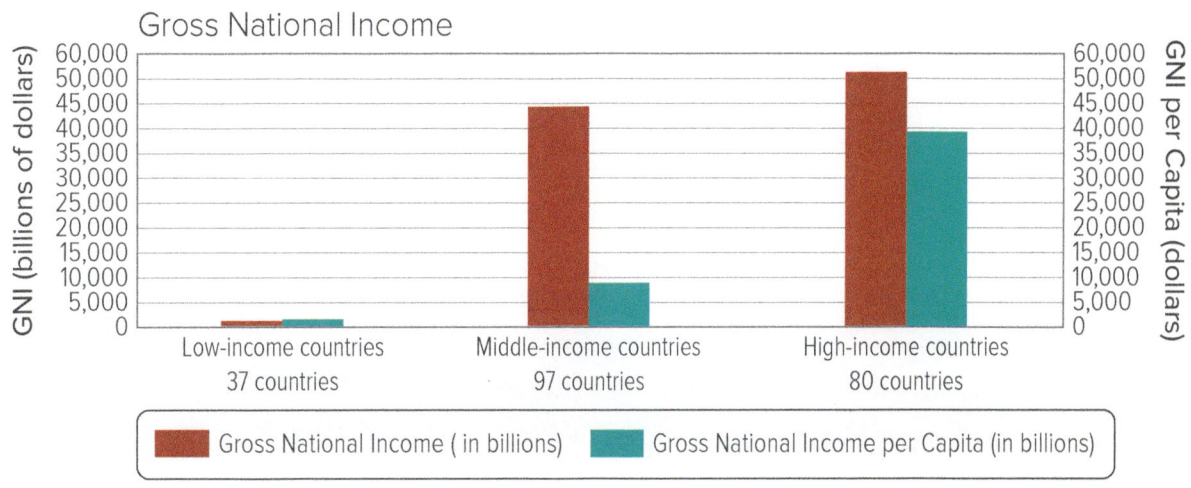

Gross National Income

	GNI (billions of dollars)	GNI per Capita (dollars)
Low-income countries (37 countries)	~500	~1,500
Middle-income countries (97 countries)	~44,000	~8,500
High-income countries (80 countries)	~51,000	~39,000

Legend: Gross National Income (in billions), Gross National Income per Capita (in billions)

Source: World Bank

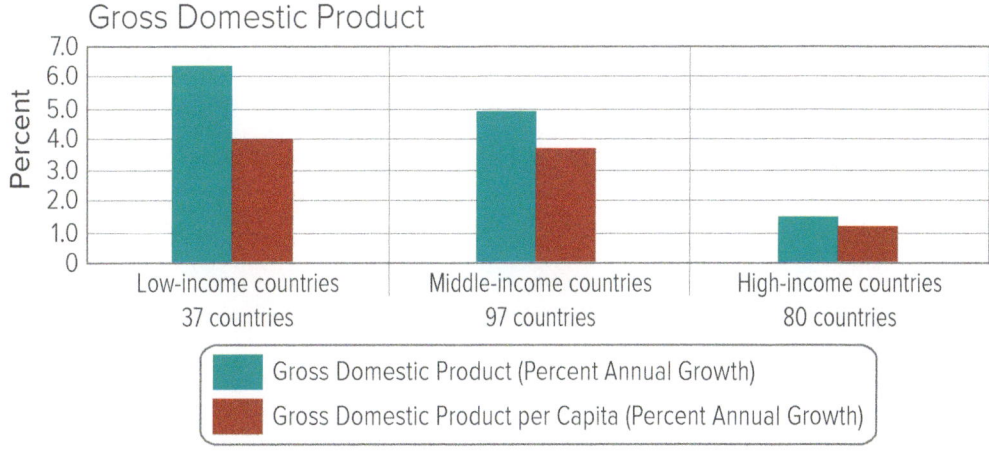

Gross Domestic Product

	GDP (Percent Annual Growth)	GDP per Capita (Percent Annual Growth)
Low-income countries (37 countries)	~6.3	~4.0
Middle-income countries (97 countries)	~4.9	~3.7
High-income countries (80 countries)	~1.5	~1.2

Legend: Gross Domestic Product (Percent Annual Growth), Gross Domestic Product per Capita (Percent Annual Growth)

Source: World Bank

The Global Economy

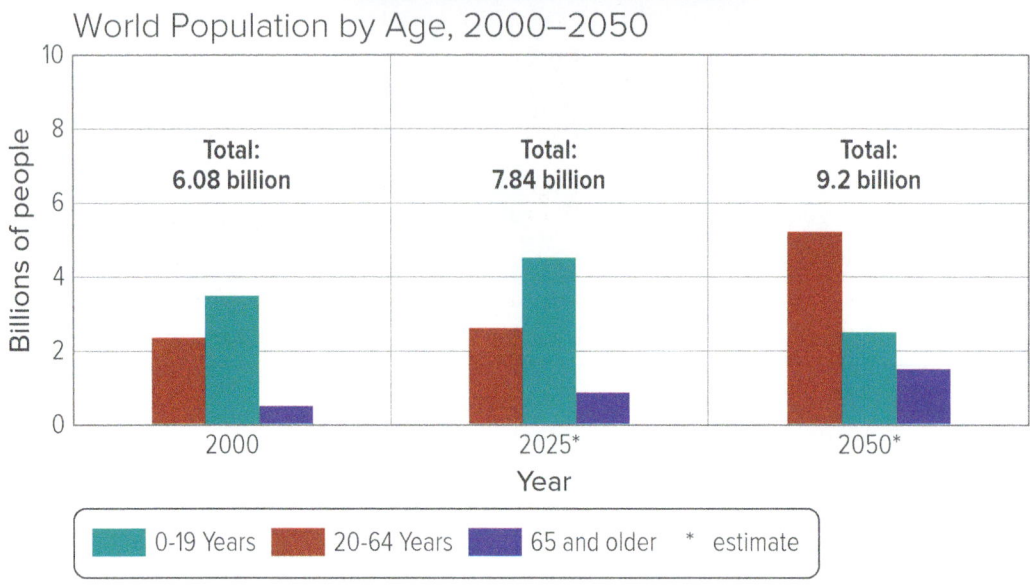

World Population by Age, 2000–2050

- 0-19 Years
- 20-64 Years
- 65 and older
- * estimate

Source: *U.S. Census Bureau*

Countries Ranked by Population, 2000 and 2050

Country	Year 2000		Year 2050*	
	Population (in thousand)	Rank	Population (in thousand)	Rank
China	1,263,638	1	1,303,723	(2)
India	1,006,300	2	1,656,554	(1)
United States	282,162	3	399,803	(3)
Indonesia	214,091	4	300,183	(5)
Brazil	174,315	5	232,304	(8)
Pakistan	152,429	6	290,848	(6)
Russia	147,054	7	129,908	(14)
Bangladesh	132,151	8	250,155	(7)
Japan	126,776	9	107,210	(17)
Nigeria	123,945	10	391,297	(4)
Mexico	99,775	11	150,568	(11)

Source: *U.S. Census Bureau*

The Global Economy

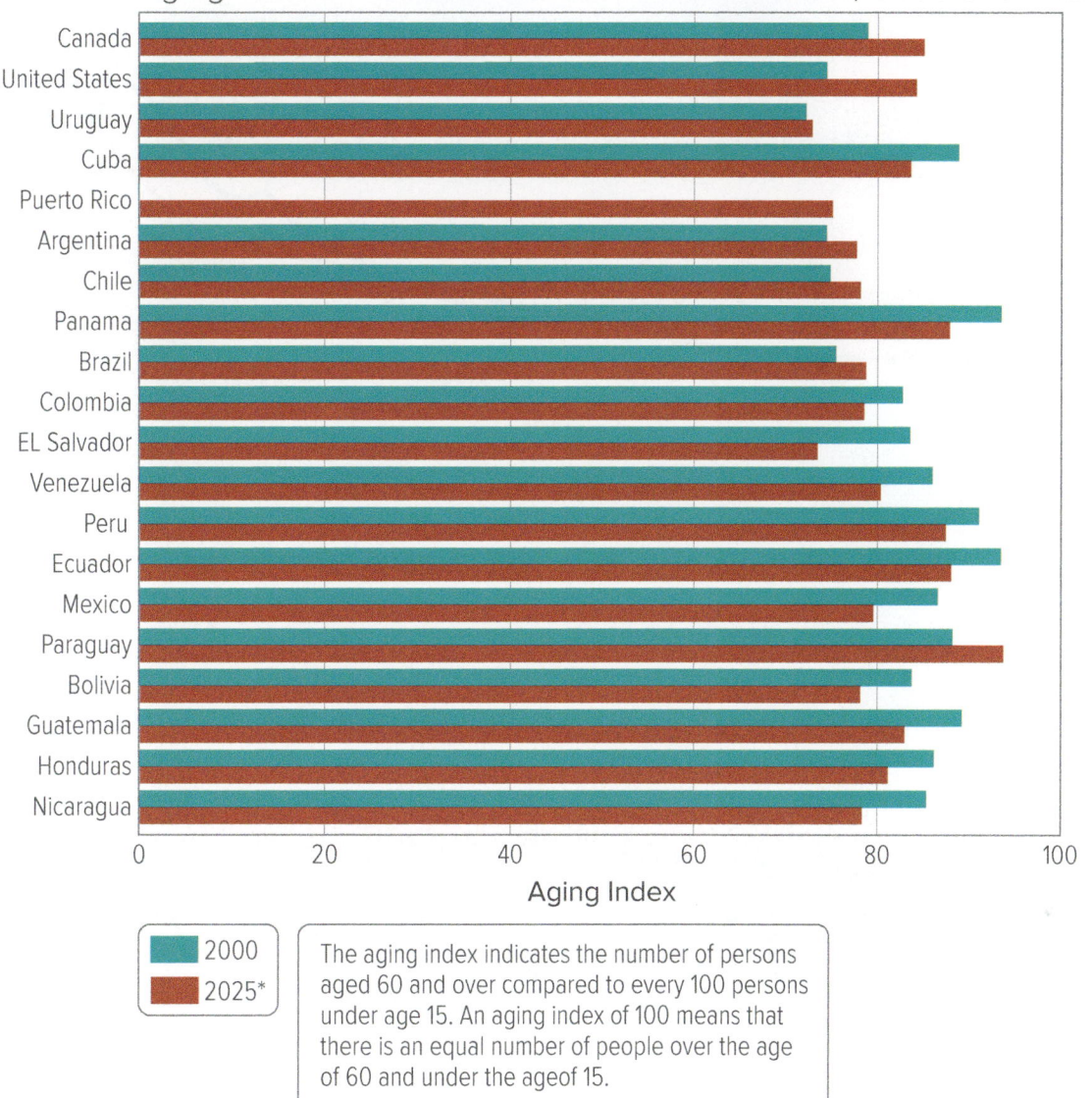

Aging Index in Selected Nations of the Americas, 2000 and 2025

■ 2000
■ 2025*

The aging index indicates the number of persons aged 60 and over compared to every 100 persons under age 15. An aging index of 100 means that there is an equal number of people over the age of 60 and under the age of 15.

Source: U.S. Census Bureau

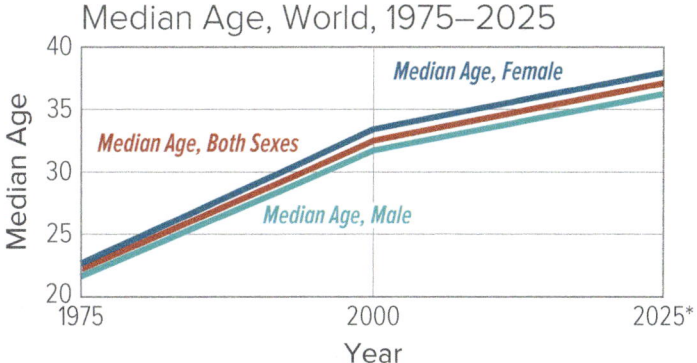

Median Age, World, 1975–2025

Source: U.S. Census Bureau; *estimate

The Global Economy

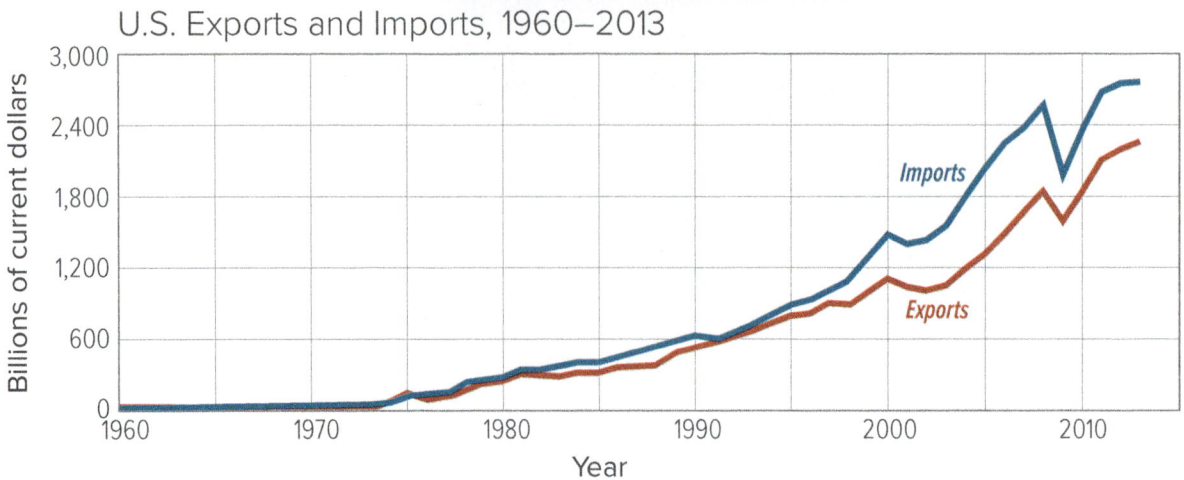

Inflation and Unemployment, Selected Economies 1990–2019

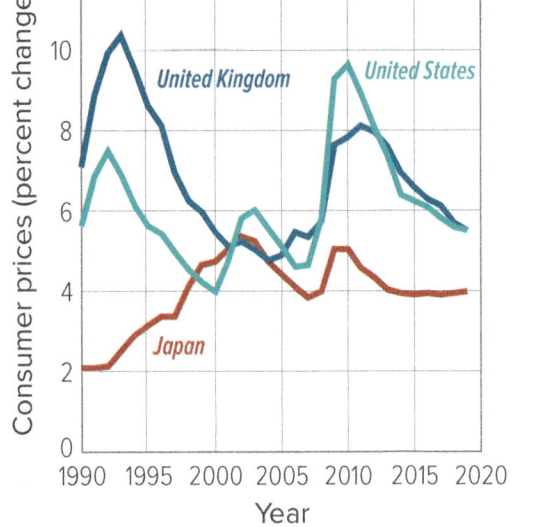
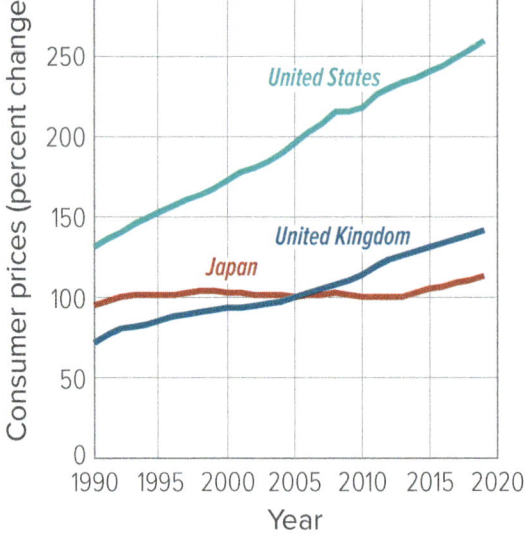

Source: *International Monetary Fund; U.S. Bureau of Labor Statistics*

Reference Atlas

World: Political 604–605
U.S. Political: Political 606–607
World: Land Use 608–609
World's People 610–611
World GDP: Cartogram 612–613
World Population: Cartogram 614–615
North America: Physical 616

ATLAS KEY

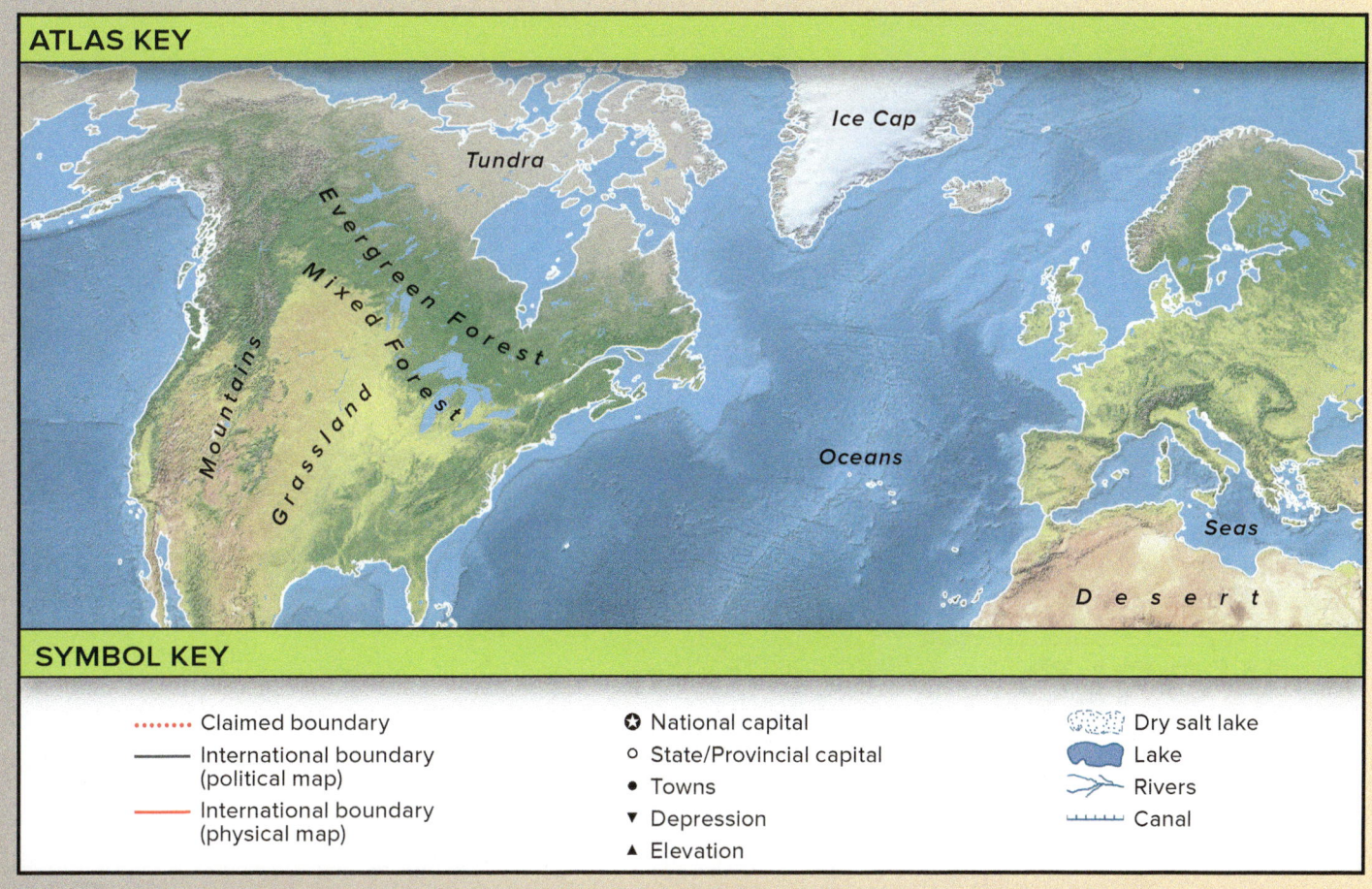

SYMBOL KEY

- .... Claimed boundary
- ——— International boundary (political map)
- ——— International boundary (physical map)
- ✪ National capital
- ○ State/Provincial capital
- • Towns
- ▼ Depression
- ▲ Elevation
- Dry salt lake
- Lake
- Rivers
- Canal

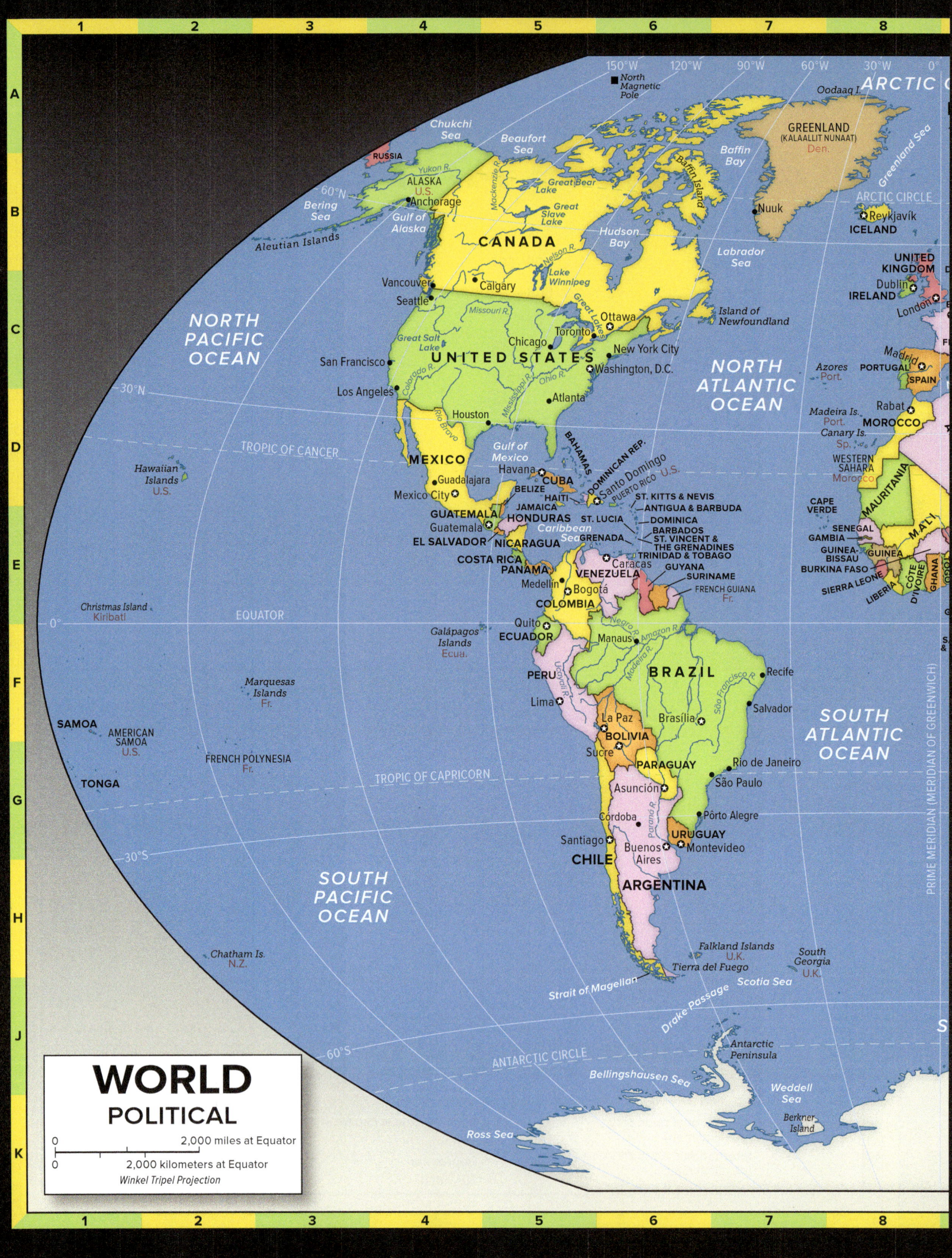

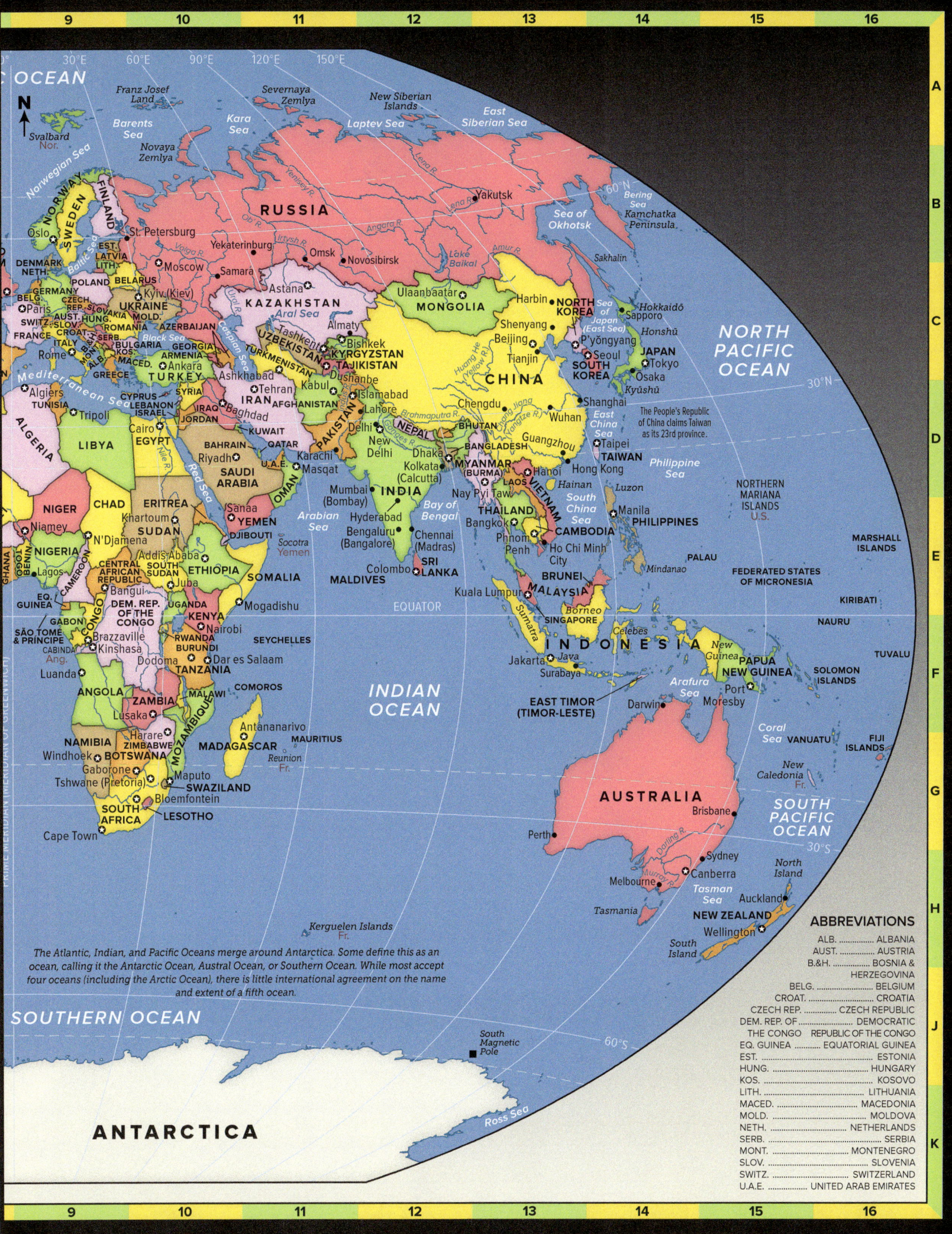

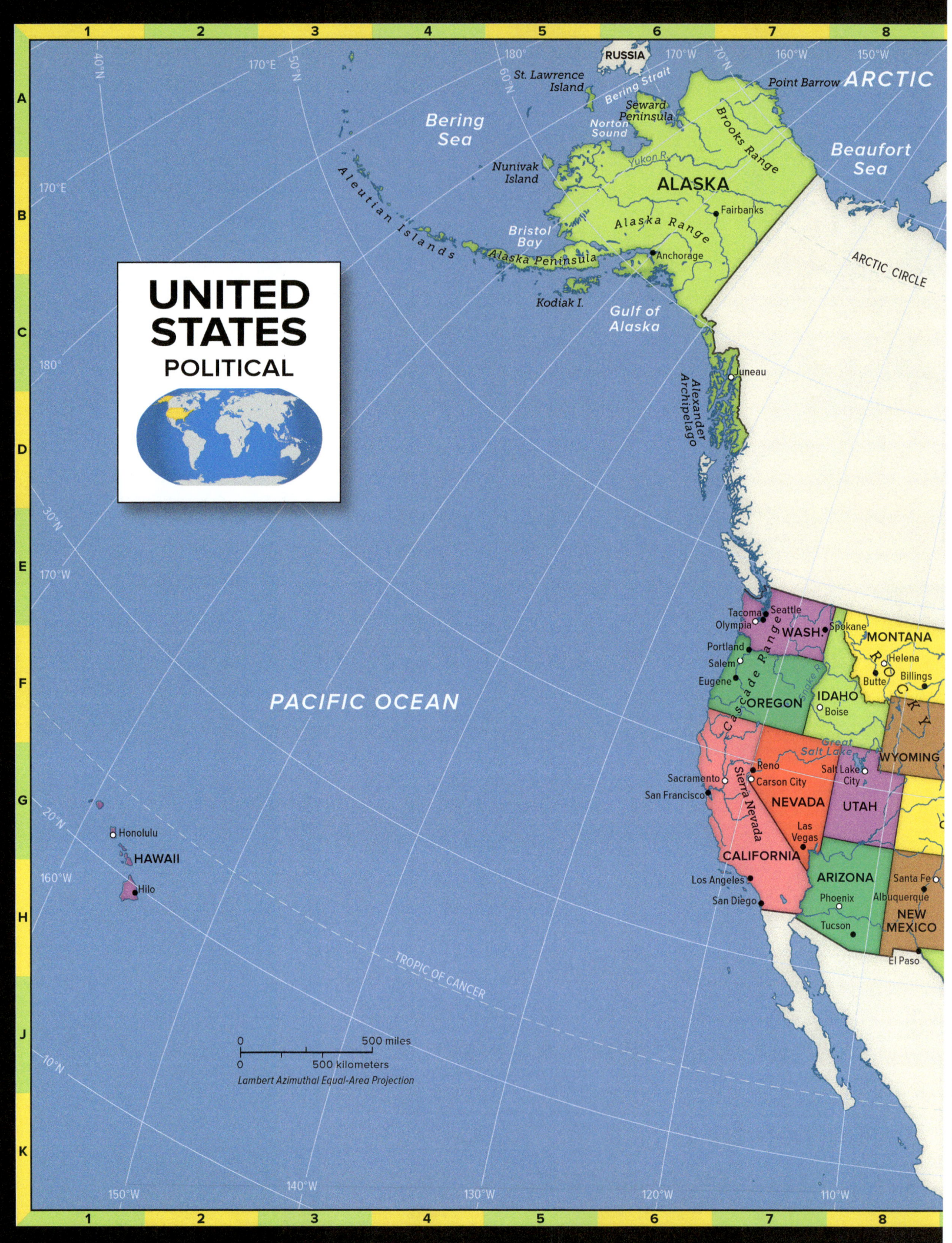

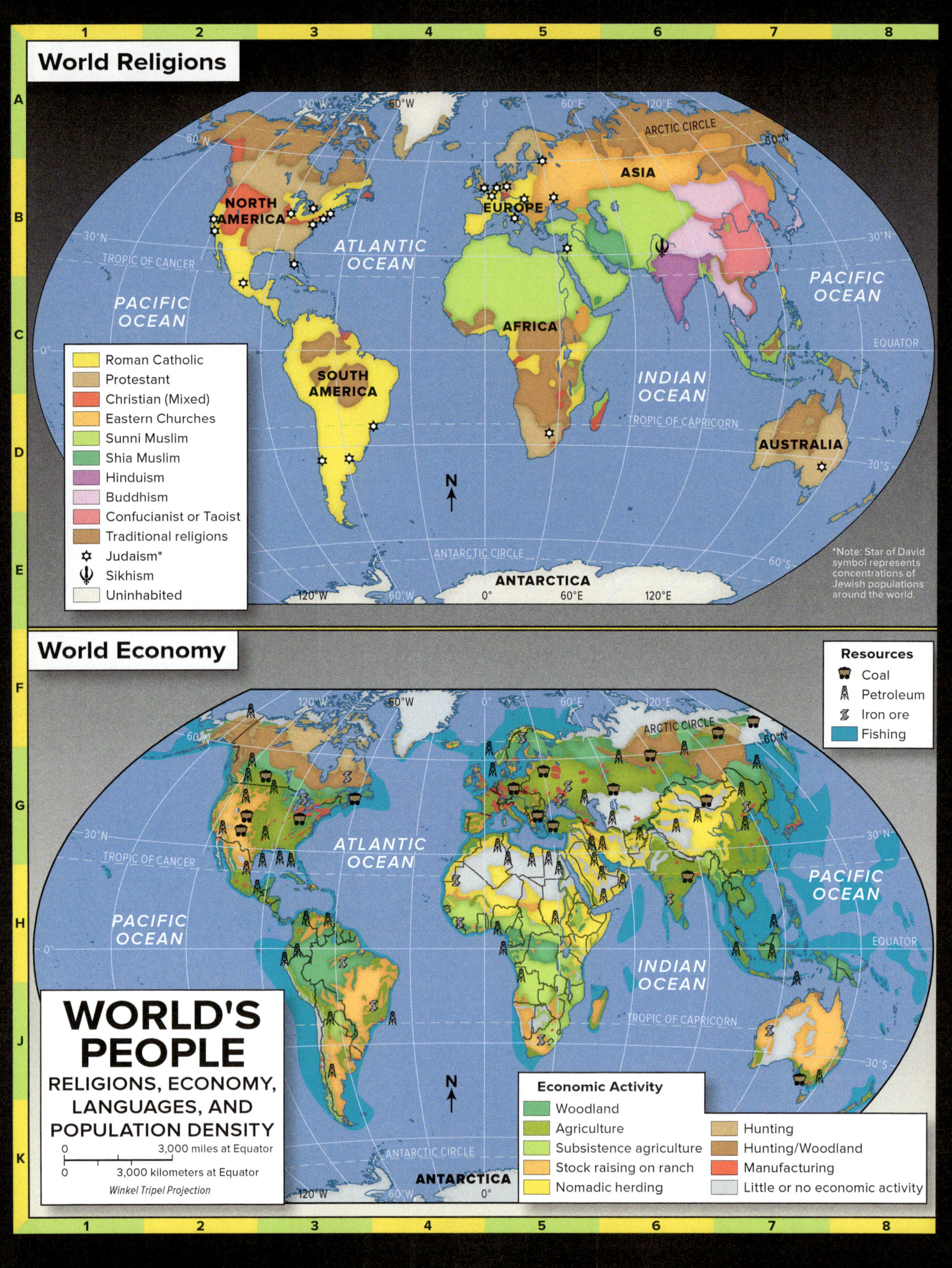

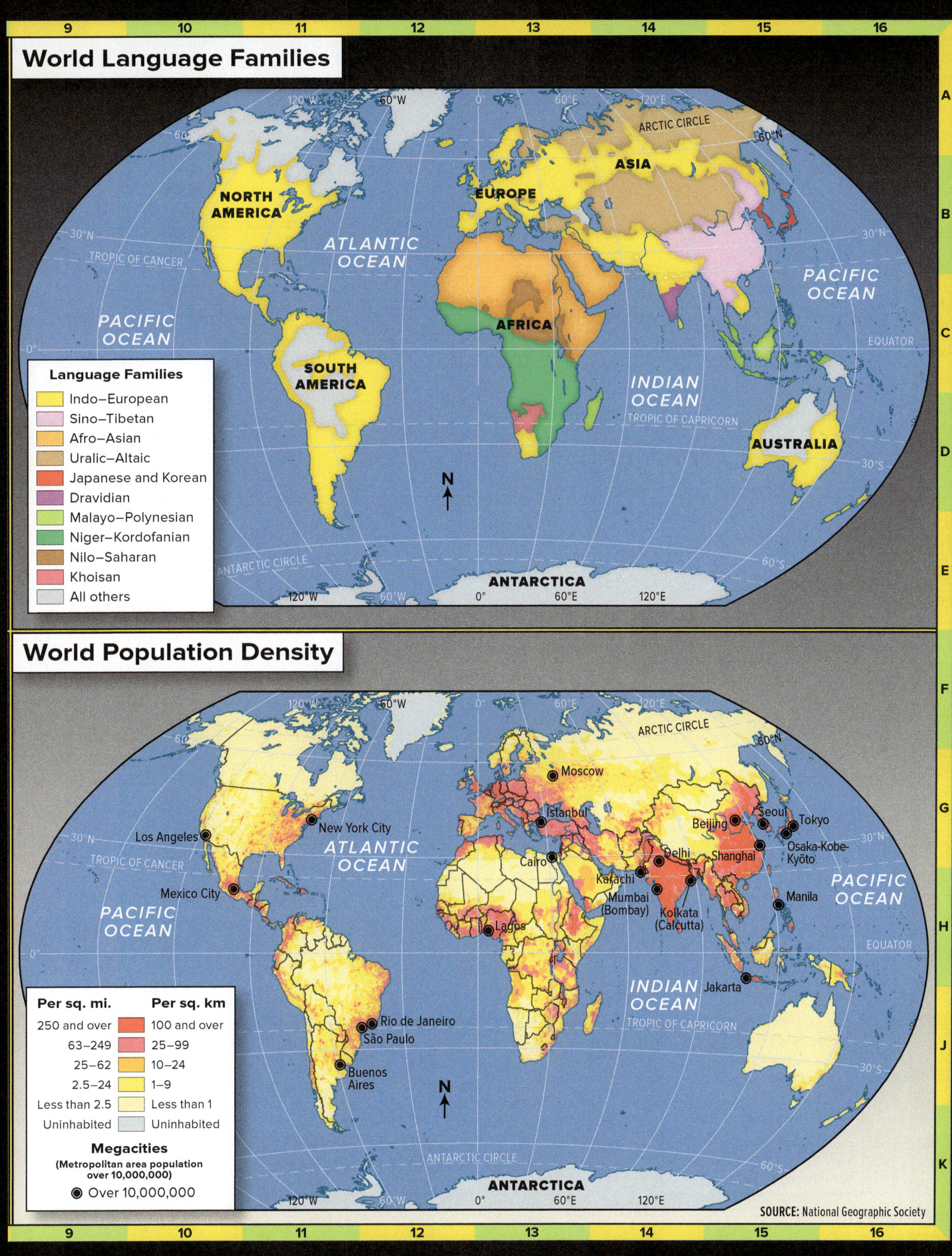

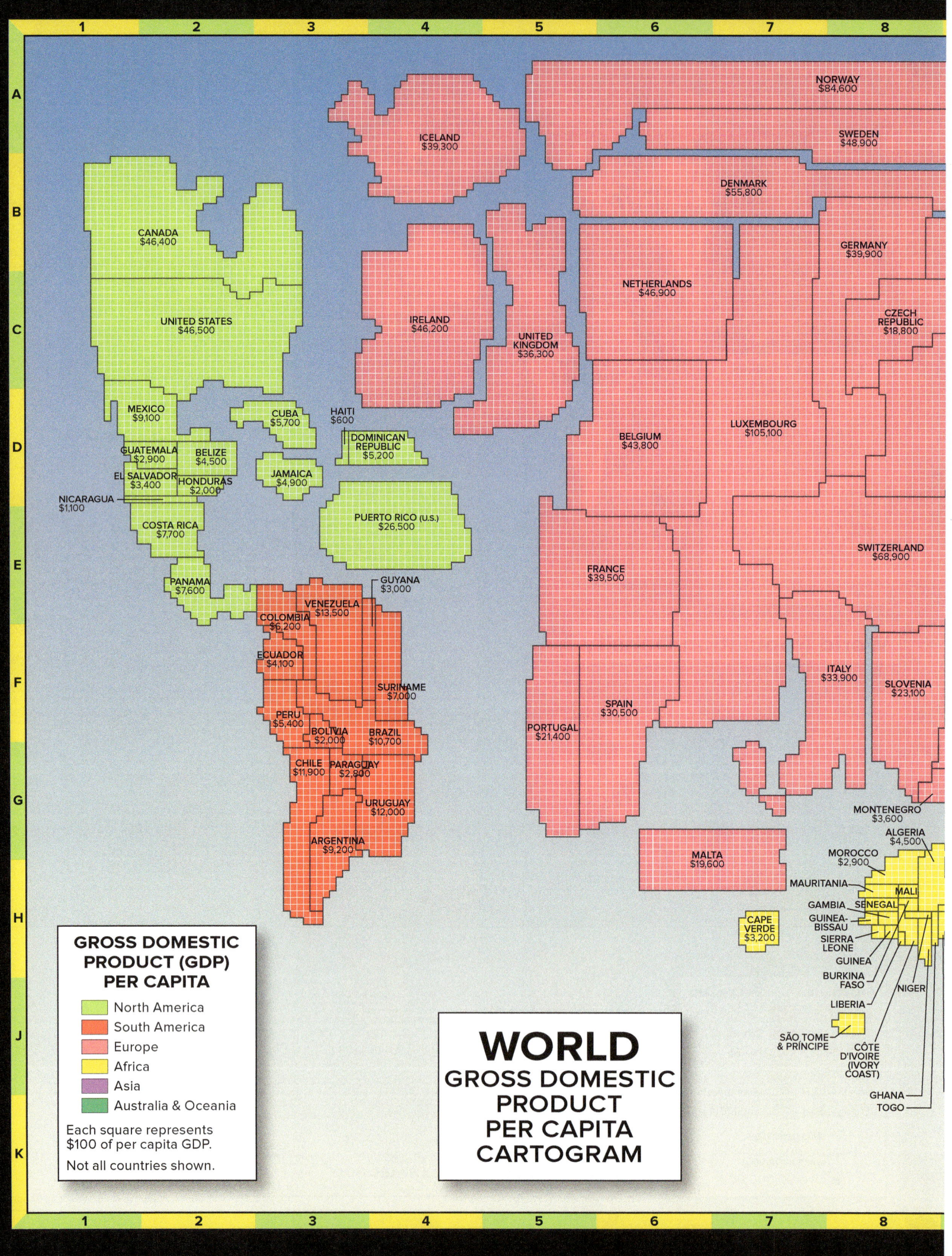

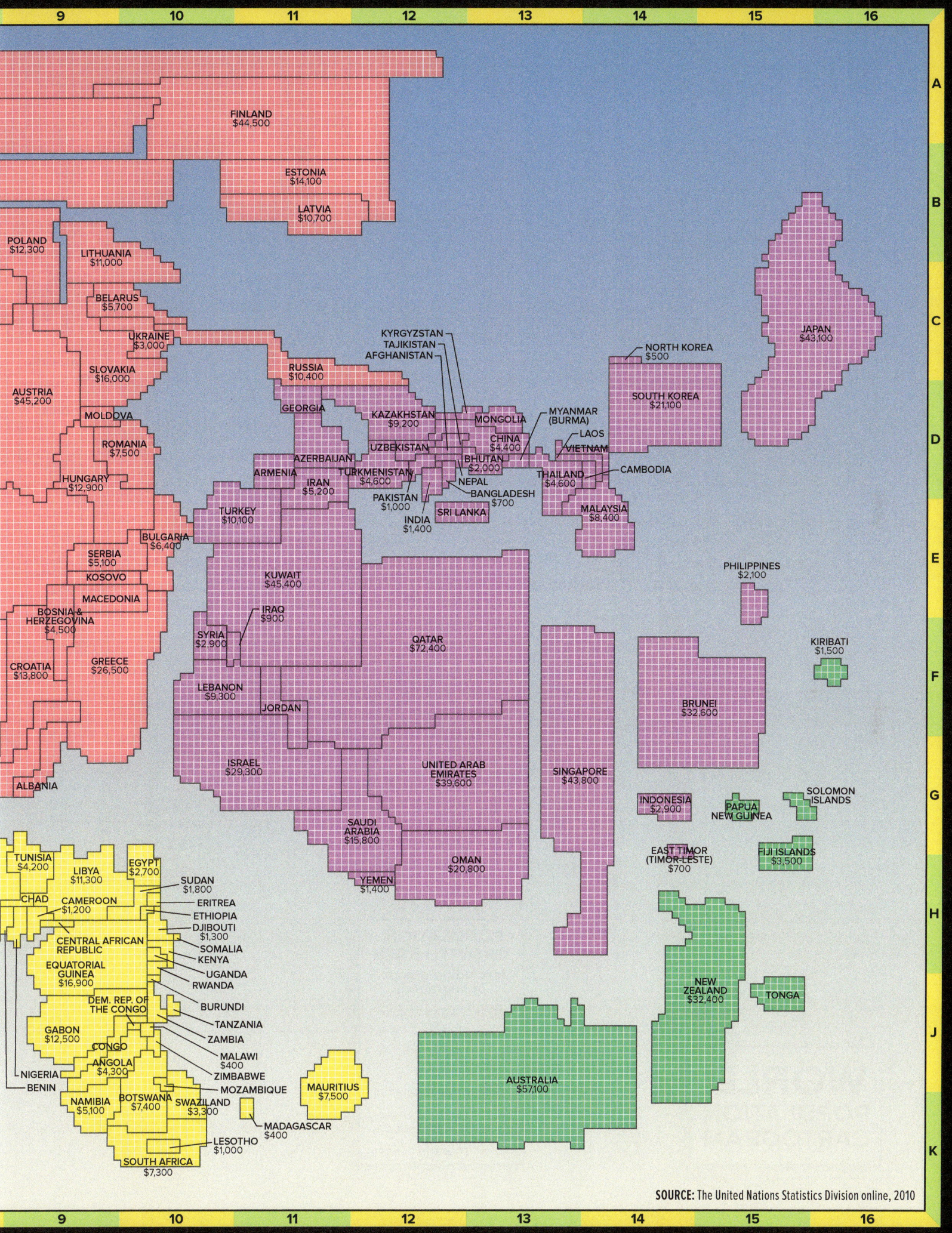

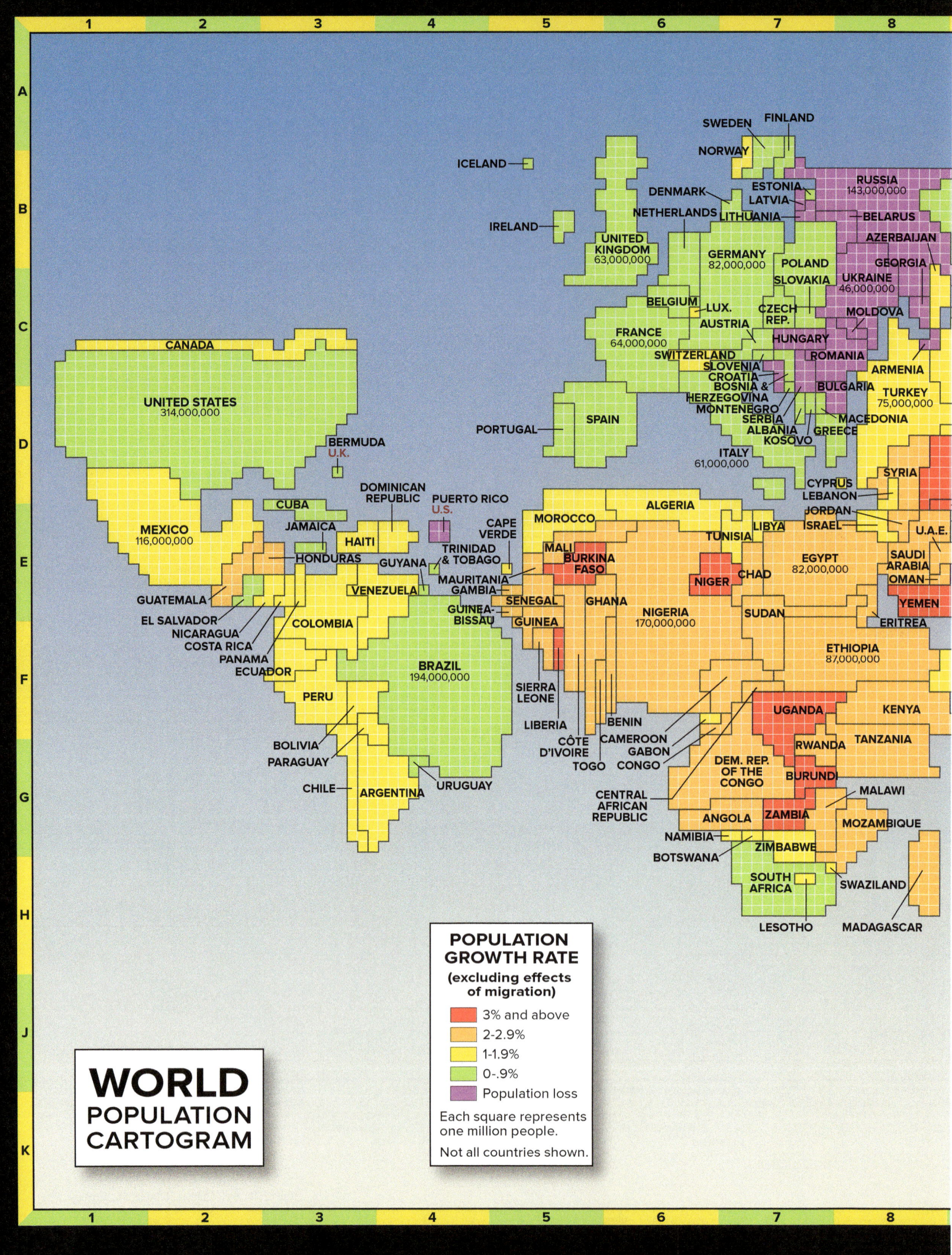

GLOSSARY/GLOSARIO

- Content vocabulary are words that relate to world geography content.
- Words that have an asterisk (*) are academic vocabulary. They help you understand your school subjects.
- All vocabulary words are **boldfaced** or highlighted in yellow in your textbook.

401(k) plan • aggregate supply

A

ENGLISH

401(k) plan: a tax-deferred investment and savings plan that acts as a personal pension fund for employees (p. 322)

ability-to-pay: principle of taxation based on belief that taxes should be paid according to level of income regardless of benefits received (p. 404)

absolute advantage: country's ability to produce a given product more efficiently than can another country (p. 496)

accelerator: change in investment spending caused by a change in overall spending (p. 440)

***accommodate:** to allow for (p. 91)

***accumulation:** gradual collection of goods (p. 9)

acid rain: pollution in the form of rainwater mixed with sulfur dioxide to form a mild form of sulfuric acid (p. 547)

***adequate:** just enough to satisfy a requirement (p. 118)

***adverse:** unfavorable or harmful (p. 88)

***advocates:** supports; speaks in favor of (p. 483)

agency shop: arrangement under which nonunion members must pay union dues (p. 250)

aggregate demand: the total value of all goods and services demanded at different price levels (p. 452)

aggregate demand curve: hypothetical curve showing different levels of real GDP that would be purchased at various price levels (p. 452)

aggregate supply: the total value of all goods and services that all firms would produce in a specific period of time at various price levels (p. 451)

ESPAÑOL

plan 401(k): plan de ahorro e inversiones con impuestos diferidos que funciona como un fondo de pensiones personal para los empleados (p. 322)

capacidad de pago: principio tributario basado en la creencia de que los impuestos deberían pagarse según el nivel de ingresos independientemente de los beneficios recibidos (p. 404)

ventaja absoluta: capacidad de un país de producir un producto dado más eficazmente que otro país (p. 496)

acelerador: cambio en los gastos de inversión a causa de un cambio en los gastos generals (p. 440)

***tener en cuenta:** tener presente, dejar un margen (p. 91)

***acumulación:** recogida gradual de bienes (p. 9)

lluvia ácida: contaminación en forma de agua de lluvia mezclada con dióxido de azufre para crear una forma suave de ácido sulfuric (p. 547)

***adecuado:** lo suficiente como para satisfacer un requisite (p. 118)

***adverso:** desfavorable o prejudicial (p. 88)

***defiende: apoya;** habla a favor de alguien (p. 483)

taller agencial: acuerdo según el cual los miembros no sindicalizados deben pagar la cuota syndical (p. 250)

demanda global: valor total de todos los bienes y servicios para los que hay demanda a diferentes niveles de precios (p. 452)

curva de demanda global: curva hipotética que muestra diferentes niveles de PIB real que se compraría a diferentes niveles de precios (p. 452)

oferta global: valor total de todos los bienes y servicios que todas las empresas producirían en un período específico a varios niveles de precios (p. 451)

Glossary 617

aggregate supply curve • average tax rate

ENGLISH

aggregate supply curve: hypothetical curve showing different levels of real GDP that would be produced at various price levels (p. 451)

***allocation:** distribution (p. 50)

alternative minimum tax: personal income tax rate that applies to cases where taxes would otherwise fall below a certain level (p. 408)

***analyze:** to break down into parts to study how each part relates to another (p. 233)

angel investors: informal and usually affluent investors who provide funds to less-promising start-ups (p. 228)

***anticipate:** to expect or be sure of in advance (p. 256)

appropriations bill: legislation authorizing spending for certain purposes (p. 413)

***arbitrarily:** randomly or by chance (p. 170)

arbitration: agreement by two parties to place a dispute before a third party for a binding settlement; also called binding arbitration (p. 256)

ASEAN: group of ten Southeast Asian nations working to promote regional cooperation, economic growth, and trade (p. 535)

***aspects:** parts, phases (p. 454)

***assumptions:** something taken for granted; something we think is true (p. 26)

automatic stabilizers: programs that automatically provide government benefits during an economic downturn; unemployment, insurance, and entitlement programs (p. 441)

average revenue: average price that every unit of output sells for (p. 144)

average tax rate: total taxes paid divided by the total taxable income (p. 404)

ESPAÑOL

curva de oferta global: curva hipotética que muestra diferentes niveles de PIB real que se producirían a varios niveles de precios (p. 451)

***asignación:** distribución (p. 50)

impuesto mínimo alternativo: tasa de impuesto personal sobre la renta que se aplica a casos en los que de otro modo los impuestos caerían por debajo de cierto nivel (p. 408)

***analizar:** separar en partes para estudiar cómo se relaciona cada parte con otra (p. 233)

inversionistas providenciales: inversionistas informales y por lo general acaudalados que proporcionan fondos a empresas emergentes poco alentadoras (p. 228)

***anticipar:** esperar o estar seguro de algo por adelantado (p. 256)

proyecto de ley de asignación: legislación que autoriza gastos para ciertos fines (p. 413)

***arbitrariamente:** aleatoriamente o por casualidad (p. 170)

arbitraje: acuerdo entre dos partes de presentar un conflicto ante un tercero para llegar a una solución vinculante; también llamado *arbitraje vinculante* (p. 256)

ASEAN: grupo de diez países del Sudeste asiático que trabajan para la promoción de la cooperación regional, el crecimiento económico y el comercio (p. 535)

***aspectos:** partes, fases (p. 454)

***supuestos:** algo que se da por hecho; algo que se piensa que es verdad (p. 26)

estabilizadores automáticos: programas que proporcionan beneficios automáticamente durante un período de desaceleración económica; programas de desempleo, seguros y subsidios (p. 441)

ingresos medios: precio promedio al que cada unidad producida se vende (p. 144)

tasa impositiva promedio: total de los impuestos pagados dividido entre el ingreso total sujeto a impuestos (p. 404)

baby boom • Better Business Bureau

ENGLISH

baby boom: historically high birthrate years in the United States from 1946 to 1964 (p. 349)

baby boomers: people born in the United States during the historically high birthrate years from 1946 to 1964 (p. 482)

balance of payments: difference between money paid to and money received from other nations in trade; balance on current accounts includes goods and services, but merchandise trade balance counts only goods (p. 505)

balanced budget: annual budget in which expenditures equal revenues (p. 418)

balanced budget amendment: constitutional amendment requiring government to spend no more than it collects in taxes and other revenues, excluding borrowing (p. 426)

bank holding companies: company that owns and controls one or more banks (p. 468)

bank holiday: brief period during which all banks or depository institutions are closed to prevent bank runs (p. 287)

bank run: sudden rush by depositors to withdraw all deposited funds, generally in anticipation of bank failure or closure (p. 287)

barter economy: moneyless economy that relies on trade or barter (p. 276)

base year: year serving as a point of comparison for other years in a price index or other statistical measure (p. 264, 339, 376)

bear market: period during which stock market prices move down for several months or years in a row (p. 325)

beneficiary: person designated to take ownership of an asset if the owner of the asset dies (p. 314)

Better Business Bureau: business-sponsored nonprofit organization providing information on local companies to consumers (p. 235)

ESPAÑOL

baby boom: años de históricamente alta tasa de natalidad en Estados Unidos de 1946 a 1964 (p. 349)

niños del baby boom: personas nacidas en Estados Unidos durante los años de históricamente alta tasa de natalidad de 1946 a 1964 (p. 482)

balanza de pagos: diferencia entre el dinero pagado y el dinero recibido de otros países por el comercio; la balanza de cuentas corrientes incluye bienes y servicios, pero la balanza comercial incluye solo bienes (p. 505)

presupuesto equilibrado: presupuesto anual en el cual los gastos son iguales a los ingresos (p. 418)

regla de oro presupuestaria: enmienda constitucional que exige que el gobierno no gaste más de lo que recauda en impuestos y otros ingresos, excluyendo los préstamos (p. 426)

sociedades de cartera bancaria: empresas que son propietarias y tienen el control de uno o más bancos (p. 468)

feriado bancario: período breve durante el cual todos los bancos o instituciones de depósito están cerrados para impedir pánico bancario (p. 287)

pánico bancario: apuro súbito por parte de los depositantes por retirar todos sus fondos depositados, generalmente con anticipación al cierre o la quiebra de un banco (p. 287)

economía de trueque: economía en la cual no se usa dinero que depende del intercambio o el trueque (p. 276)

año base: año que sirve como punto de comparación para otros años en un índice de precios u otra medida estadística (p. 264, 339, 376)

mercado bajista: período durante el cual los precios del mercado de valores bajan durante varios meses o años seguidos (p. 325)

beneficiario: persona designada para tomar posesión de un bien si muere el dueño del mismo (p. 314)

Oficina de Buenas Prácticas Comerciales: organización sin fines de lucro patrocinada por empresas que proporciona información sobre empresas locales a los consumidores (p. 235)

ENGLISH

biofuels: fuel made from wood, peat, municipal solid waste, straw, corn, tires, landfill gases, fish oils, and other waste (p. 77, 159)

biomass: energy made from wood, peat, municipal solid waste, straw, corn, tires, landfill gasses, fish oils, and other waste (p. 544)

black market: market in which goods and services are sold illegally (p. 61)

bond: formal contract to repay borrowed money and interest on the borrowed money at regular future intervals (p. 218, 310)

boycott: protest in the form of refusal to buy, including attempts to convince others to take their business elsewhere (p. 246)

break-even point: production level where total cost equals total revenue; production needed if the firm is to recover its costs (p. 146)

budget deficit: a negative balance after expenditures are subtracted from revenues (p. 413)

budget surplus: a positive balance after expenditures are subtracted from revenues (p. 413)

bull market: period during which stock market prices move up for several months or years in a row (p. 324)

business cycles: systematic changes in real GDP marked by alternating periods of expansion and contraction (p. 366)

business fluctuations: changes in real GDP marked by alternating periods of expansion and contraction that occur on an irregular basis (p. 366)

ESPAÑOL

biocombustibles: combustibles hechos de madera, turba, residuos sólidos urbanos, paja, maíz, neumáticos, gases de vertederos, aceites de pescado y otros residuos (p. 77, 159)

biomasa: energía hecha de madera, turba, residuos sólidos urbanos, paja, maíz, neumáticos, gases de vertederos, aceites de pescado y otros residuos (p. 544)

mercado negro: mercado en el cual se venden bienes y servicios ilegalmente (p. 61)

bono: contrato formal para devolver dinero que se pidió prestado e intereses sobre el dinero que se pidió prestado en futuros intervalos regulares (p. 218, 310)

boicot: protesta en forma de rechazo a comprar, incluyendo intentos por convencer a otros de que hagan sus transacciones en otro lado (p. 246)

punto de equilibrio: nivel de producción en el cual los costos totales son iguales a los ingresos totales; producción necesaria si la empresa quiere recuperar sus costos (p. 146)

déficit presupuestario: saldo negativo después de que los gastos se han restado de los ingresos (p. 413)

superávit presupuestario: saldo positivo después de que los gastos se han restado de los ingresos (p. 413)

mercado alcista: período durante el cual los precios del mercado de valores suben durante varios meses o años seguidos (p. 324)

ciclos económicos: cambios sistemáticos en el PIB real marcados por períodos de expansión y contracción alternados (p. 366)

fluctuaciones económicas: cambios en el PIB real marcados por períodos de expansión y contracción alternados que ocurren de forma irregular (p. 366)

C

call option: futures contract giving investors the option to cancel a contract to buy commodities, equities, or financial assets (p. 325)

capital: tools, equipment, and factories used in the production of goods and services; one of the four factors of production (p. 15)

opción de compra: contrato de futuros que da a los inversionistas la opción de cancelar un contrato para comprar mercancía, títulos valores o activos financieros (p. 325)

capital: herramientas, equipo y fábricas usados en la producción de bienes y servicios; uno de los cuatro factores de producción (p. 15)

ENGLISH

capital flight: legal or illegal export of a nation's currency and foreign exchange (p. 527)

capital formation: the transfer of money from households to businesses and government through investments and loans (p. 568)

capital gains: profits from the sale of an asset held for 12 months or longer (p. 408)

capital good: tool, equipment, or other manufactured good used to produce other goods and services; a factor of production (p. 8)

capital market: market in which financial capital is loaned and/or borrowed for more than one year (p. 315)

capital-intensive: requiring large amounts of capital in relation to labor. (p. 62)

capitalism: economic system in which private citizens own and use the factors of production in order to generate profits (p. 45)

cartel: group of sellers or producers acting together to raise prices by restricting availability of a product (p. 537)

cash flow: total amount of new funds the business generates from operations; broadest measure of profits for a firm because it includes both net income and noncash charges (p. 224)

***catalyst:** something that stimulates activity among people or forces (p. 83)

cease and desist order: ruling requiring a company to stop an unfair business practice that reduces or limits competition (p. 199)

census: complete count of population, including place of residence (p. 347)

center of population: point where the country would balance if it were flat and everyone weighed the same (p. 347)

central bank: a bank that can lend to other banks in times of need, or a "bankers' bank" (p. 286)

ESPAÑOL

evasión de capitales: exportación legal o ilegal de la moneda y divisas de un país (p. 527)

formación de capital: transferencia de dinero de familias a empresas y el gobierno mediante inversiones y préstamos (p. 568)

ganancias de capital: beneficios obtenidos por la venta de un bien que se tuvo durante 12 meses o más (p. 408)

bien de capital: herramienta, equipo u otro bien fabricado que se usa para producir otros bienes y servicios; factor de producción (p. 8)

mercado de capital: mercado en el cual el capital financiero se presta y/o toma prestado por más de un año (p. 315)

de capital intensivo: que requiere grandes cantidades de capital en relación a la mano de obra (p. 62)

capitalismo: sistema económico en el cual ciudadanos privados son dueños y usan los factores de producción para generar ganancias (p. 45)

cartel: grupo de vendedores o productores que actúan juntos para subir los precios al limitar la disponibilidad de un producto (p. 537)

flujo de caja: cantidad total de nuevos fondos que una empresa genera con sus operaciones; medida más amplia de las ganacias para una empresa, ya que incluye tanto los ingresos netos como los cargos que no implican el intercambio de dinero en efectivo (p. 224)

***catalizador:** algo que estimula la actividad entre personas o fuerzas (p. 83)

orden de cesar y abstenerse: sentencia que exige que una empresa abandone una práctica comercial injusta que reduce o limita la competencia (p. 199)

censo: conteo completo de la población, incluyendo el lugar de residencia (p. 347)

centro de población: punto donde el país estaría en equilibrio si fuese plano y todos pesaran lo mismo (p. 347)

banco central: banco que puede prestar a otros bancos en períodos de necesidad, o el "banco de los banqueros" (p. 286)

ENGLISH

certificates of deposit/CDs: receipt showing that an investor has made an interest-bearing loan to a financial institution (p. 291, 304)

chamber of commerce: nonprofit organization of local businesses whose purpose is to promote their interests (p. 234)

change in demand: different amounts of a product are demanded at every price, causing the demand curve to shift to the left or to the right (p. 110)

change in quantity demanded: movement along the demand curve showing that a different quantity is purchased in response to a change in price (p. 108)

change in quantity supplied: change in the amount offered for sale in response to a price change; movement along the supply curve (p. 130)

change in supply: different amounts offered for sale at each and every possible price in the market; shift of the supply curve (p. 130)

charter: written government approval to establish a corporation; includes company name, address, purpose of business, number of shares of stock, and other features of the business (p. 217)

civilian labor force: noninstitutionalized part of the population, aged 16 and over, either working or looking for a job (p. 250, 383)

*****clauses:** a stipulation, usually in a legal document (p. 283)

closed shop: arrangement under which workers must join a union before they are hired; usually illegal (p. 250)

*****coincide:** to happen or exist at the same time or in the same position (p. 412)

coins: metallic forms of money such as pennies, nickels, dimes, and quarters (p. 467)

collateral: something of value that a borrower lets the lender claim if a loan is not repaid (p. 565)

ESPAÑOL

certificados de depósito/CD: recibo que muestra que un inversor ha dado un préstamo que genera intereses a una institución financiera (p. 291, 304)

cámara de comercio: organización sin fines de lucro de empresas locales cuya finalidad es promover sus intereses (p. 234)

cambio en la demanda: distintas cantidades de un producto son demandadas con cada precio, causando que la curva de demanda se desplace hacia la izquierda o la derecha (p. 110)

cambio en la cantidad demandada: movimiento a lo largo de la curva de demanda que muestra que se compra una cantidad diferente en respuesta a un cambio en el precio (p. 108)

cambio en la cantidad ofertada: cambio en el volumen que se ofrece para la venta en respuesta a un cambio en el precio; movimiento a lo largo de la curva de oferta (p. 130)

cambio en la oferta: distintas cantidades ofertadas para la venta a cada precio posible en el mercado; desplazamiento de la curva de oferta (p. 130)

acta constitutiva: aprobación gubernamental escrita para establecer una corporación; incluye el nombre de la empresa, su dirección, la finalidad del negocio, la cantidad de acciones y otros elementos de la empresa (p. 217)

mano de obra civil: parte de la población que no está recluida ni internada, de 16 años o más, que está trabajando o buscando un empleo (p. 250, 383)

*****cláusulas:** estipulaciones, usualmente en un documento legal (p. 283)

taller cerrado: acuerdo según el cual los trabajadores deben hacerse miembros de un sindicato antes de ser contratados; usualmente es ilegal (p. 250)

*****coincidir:** suceder o existir al mismo tiempo o en la misma posición (p. 412)

monedas: formas metálicas de dinero, como las monedas de un centavo o cinco, diez y veinticinco centavos (p. 467)

garantía: algo de valor que un prestatario permite que reclame un prestamista si no se devuelve un préstamo (p. 565)

ENGLISH	ESPAÑOL
collective bargaining: process of negotiation between union and management representatives over pay, benefits, and job-related matters (p. 234, 256)	**negociación colectiva:** proceso de negociación entre representantes sindicales y empresariales sobre el pago, los beneficios y asuntos relacionados con el trabajo (p. 234, 256)
collectivization: forced common ownership of factors of production; used in the former Soviet Union in agriculture and manufacturing (p. 58)	**socialización:** propiedad común forzada de los factores de producción; se usó en la ex Unión Soviética en la agricultura y la fabricación (p. 58)
collusion: illegal agreement among producers to fix prices, limit output, or divide markets (p. 187)	**colusión:** acuerdo ilegal entre productores para fijar precios, limitar la producción o dividir mercados (p. 187)
command economy: economic system characterized by a central authority that makes most of the major economic decisions (p. 39)	**economía planificada:** sistema económico caracterizado por una autoridad central que toma la mayoría de las decisiones económicas importantes (p. 39)
commodity money: money that has an alternative use as an economic good; gunpowder, flour, corn, etc. (p. 277)	**dinero mercancía:** dinero que tiene un uso alternativo como bien económico; pólvora, harina, maíz, etc. (p. 277)
Common Market for Eastern and Southern Africa (COMESA): a trading organization consisting of nineteen nations that pools its resources to produce peace and security (p. 536)	**Mercado Común de África Oriental y Austral (COMESA):** organización de comercio que consta de diecinueve países que aportan sus recursos para producir paz y seguridad (p. 536)
common stock: most common form of corporate ownership, generally with one vote per share for stockholders (p. 217, 570)	**acciones ordinarias:** forma más común de propiedad corporativa, generalmente con un voto por acción por cada accionista (p. 217, 570)
communism: economic and political system in which factors of production are collectively owned and directed by the state; a theoretically classless society in which everyone works for the common good (p. 50)	**comunismo:** sistema económico y político en el cual los factores de producción se poseen de modo colectivo y están dirigidos por el estado; sociedad teóricamente sin clases en la cual todos trabajan por el bien común (p. 50)
company unions: unions organized, supported, or run by an employer (p. 246)	**sindicatos de empresas:** sindicatos organizados, apoyados o dirigidos por un empleador (p. 246)
comparative advantage: country's ability to produce a given product relatively more efficiently than another country; production at a lower opportunity cost (p. 17, 498)	**ventaja comparativa:** capacidad de un país de producir un producto dado de forma relativamente más eficaz que otro país; producción a un costo de oportunidad más bajo (p. 17, 498)
*** compensation:** something, such as money, given or received as an equivalent for goods or services, injury, debt, or high risk (p. 309)	*** compensación:** algo, como dinero, que se da o se recibe como equivalente por bienes o servicios, perjuicio, deuda o gran riesgo (p. 309)
competition: the struggle among sellers to attract consumers (p. 74)	**competencia:** lucha entre vendedores por atraer consumidores (p. 74)
complements: products that increase the use of other products; products related in such a way that an increase in the price of one reduces the demand for both (p. 112)	**complementos:** productos que aumentan el uso de otros productos; productos relacionados de tal modo que el aumento del precio de uno reduce la demanda de ambos (p. 112)

ENGLISH

***compounded:** increased, made worse (p. 540)

***comprehensive:** covering many or all areas (p. 10)

***comprise:** to be composed of (p. 212)

***concept:** general idea (p. 406)

***conducted:** handled by way of (p. 146)

***confined:** kept within (p. 383)

conglomerate: firm with four or more businesses making unrelated products, with no single business responsible for a majority of its sales (p. 226)

***considerably:** to a noticeable or significant extent (p. 425)

***constituents:** persons who are represented by an elected official (p. 423)

***construction:** creation by assembling individual parts (p. 375)

consumer good: good intended for final use by consumers other than businesses (p. 8)

consumer price index (CPI): index used to measure price changes for a market basket of frequently used consumer items (p. 375)

consumer sovereignty: role of consumer as ruler of the market in determining the types of goods and services produced (p. 83)

consumerism: a social movement that was aimed at promoting the interests of consumers (p. 20)

***context:** circumstances surrounding a situation or event (p. 538)

continuing budget resolution: an agreement to fund a government agency at certain levels (p. 413)

***contributes:** gives time, money, or effort (p. 138)

***controversial:** disputed (p. 406)

ESPAÑOL

***agravado:** aumentado, empeorado (p. 540)

***amplio:** que cubre muchas o todas las áreas (p. 10)

***constar de:** estar compuesto de (p. 212)

***concepto:** idea general (p. 406)

***conducido:** manejado por medio de (p. 146)

***confinado:** mantenido dentro (p. 383)

conglomerado: empresa que tiene cuatro o más negocios que hacen productos no relacionados, sin que sea un negocio solo responsable por la mayoría de las ventas (p. 226)

***considerablemente:** hasta un punto significativo o notorio (p. 425)

***electores:** personas que son representadas por un funcionario electo (p. 423)

***construcción:** creación mediante el ensamblaje de partes individuales (p. 375)

bien de consumo: bien destinado al uso final por parte de consumidores que no sean empresas (p. 8)

índice de precios al consumo (IPC): índice usado para medir cambios en los precios de una canasta familiar de productos de consumo usados con frecuencia (p. 375)

soberanía del consumidor: función del consumidor como soberano del mercado en la determinación de los tipos de bienes y servicios producidos (p. 83)

consumismo: movimiento social que tenía como finalidad promover los intereses de los consumidores (p. 20)

***contexto:** circunstancias que rodean una situación o un suceso (p. 538)

resolución continua presupuestaria: acuerdo para financiar un organismo del gobierno a ciertos niveles (p. 413)

***contribuye:** da tiempo, dinero o esfuerzo (p. 138)

***controvertido:** debatido (p. 406)

cooperative, or co-op • crowdfunding

ENGLISH

cooperative, or co-op: nonprofit association performing some kind of economic activity for the benefit of its members (p. 233)

corporate income tax: tax on corporate profits (p. 415)

corporation: form of business organization recognized by law as a separate legal entity with all the rights and responsibilities of an individual, including the right to buy and sell property, enter into legal contracts, and to sue and be sued (p. 216, 291, 569)

cost-benefit analysis: comparison of the cost of an action to its benefits (p. 26, 195)

cost-push inflation: explanation that rising input costs, especially energy and organized labor, drive up the cost of products for manufacturers and thus cause inflation (p. 379)

Council of Economic Advisers: three-member group that devises strategies and advises the President of the United States on economic matters (p. 483)

coupon rate: stated interest on a corporate, municipal or government bond (p. 311)

craft union: labor union whose members perform the same kind of work; same as trade union (p. 245)

credit union: nonprofit service cooperative that accepts deposits, makes loans, and provides other financial services (p. 233, 290, 307)

creditors: persons or institutions to whom money is owed (p. 381, 564)

creeping inflation: relatively low rate of inflation, usually 1 to 3 percent annually (p. 377)

*criteria: characteristics used to make a decision or judgment (p. 156)

crowdfunding: using social networking to appeal to potential investors (p. 229)

ESPAÑOL

cooperativa: asociación sin fines de lucro que desarrolla algún tipo de actividad económica en beneficio de sus miembros (p. 233)

impuesto sobre la renta de sociedades: impuesto que se cobra por las ganacias corporativas (p. 415)

corporación: forma de organización comercial reconocida por la ley como una entidad legal aparte con todos los derechos y responsabilidades de una persona, incluyendo los derechos a comprar y vender propiedad, firmar contratos legales y demandar y ser demandado (p. 216, 291)

análisis de costos y beneficios: comparación de los costos de una acción con sus beneficios (p. 26, 195)

inflación de costos: explicación de que los costos crecientes de los insumos, especialmente la energía y la mano de obra organizada, hacen subir el costo de producción a los fabricantes y así se causa inflación (p. 379)

Consejo de Asesores Económicos: grupo de tres miembros que concibe estrategias y aconseja al Presidente de Estados Unidos sobre temas económicos (p. 483)

tasa de emisión: interés establecido en un bono corporativo, municipal o gubernamental (p. 311)

sindicato de oficio: sindicato cuyos miembros realizan el mismo tipo de trabajo; es lo mismo que *sindicato profesional* (p. 245)

cooperativa de crédito: cooperativa de servicios sin fines de lucro que acepta depósitos, otorga préstamos y proporciona otros servicios financieros (p. 233, 290, 307)

acreedores: personas o instituciones a quienes se les debe dinero (p. 381, 564)

inflación progresiva: tasa de inflación relativamente baja, usualmente del 1 al 3 por ciento anual (p. 377)

*criterio: características usadas para tomar una decisión o emitir un juicio (p. 156)

micromecenazgo: uso de las redes sociales para atraer a inversionistas potenciales (p. 229)

ENGLISH | ESPAÑOL

crowding-out effect: higher than normal interest rates and diminished access to financial capital faced by private investors when government increases its borrowing in financial markets (p. 420)

efecto de expulsión: tasas de interés más altas de lo normal y acceso reducido al capital financiero que deben enfrentar los inversionistas privados cuando el gobierno aumenta sus solicitudes de préstamos en los mercados financieros (p. 420)

crude birthrate: number of live births per 1,000 people (p. 524)

tasa bruta de natalidad: número de nacimientos con vida por cada mil personas (p. 524)

currency: paper and coin component of the money supply, today consisting largely of Federal Reserve notes (p. 467)

papel moneda: componente en papel de la masa monetaria, consistente en la actualidad en los billetes de la Reserva Federal (p. 467)

current dollars: dollar amounts or prices that are not adjusted for inflation (p. 264)

dólares corrientes: cantidades o precios en dólares sin ajuste por inflación (p. 264)

current GDP: gross domestic product measured in current prices, unadjusted for inflation (p. 339)

PIB actual: producto interior bruto medido con los precios actuales, sin ajuste por inflación (p. 339)

current yield: bond's annual coupon interest divided by purchase price; measure of a bond's return (p. 312)

rendimiento corriente: intereses del cupón anual de un bono divdos entre el precio de compra; medida del rendimiento de un bono (p. 312)

customs duty: tax on imported products (p. 416)

derechos arancelarios: impuesto sobre los productos importados (p. 416)

customs union: group of countries that have agreed to reduce trade barriers and have uniform tariffs for nonmembers (p. 534)

unión aduanera: grupo de países que han acordado reducir los obstáculos al comercio internacional y tienen aranceles uniformes para los países no miembros (p. 534)

cyclical unemployment: unemployment directly related to swings in the business cycle (p. 387)

desempleo cíclico: desempleo directamente relacionado con cambios en el ciclo económico (p. 387)

D

debt ceiling: total amount of money the federal government is allowed to borrow (p. 422)

límite de endeudamiento: cantidad total de dinero que el gobierno federal tiene permitido pedir prestado (p. 422)

debtors: persons or institutions that owe money (p. 381)

deudores: personas o instituciones que deben dinero (p. 381)

deductible: an amount you pay before the insurance company pays (p. 581)

deducible: cantidad que se paga antes de que pague la empresa de seguros (p. 581)

default: act of not repaying borrowed money (p. 526, 575)

incumplimiento: acción de dejar de devolver el dinero que se pidió prestado (p. 526, 575)

deficit spending: annual government spending in excess of taxes and other revenues (p. 417)

gastos deficitarios: gastos anuales del gobierno por encima de los impuestos y otros ingresos (p. 417)

deflation: sustained decrease in the general level of the prices of goods and services (p. 375)

deflación: disminución sostenida del nivel general de los precios de los bienes y servicios (p. 375)

demand • developing countries

ENGLISH

demand: combination of quantities that someone would be willing and able to buy over a range of possible prices at a given moment (p. 102)

demand curve: graph showing the quantity demanded at each and every possible price that might prevail in the market at a given time (p. 104)

demand deposit account (DDA): account whose funds can be removed from a bank or other financial institution by writing a check or using a debit card (p. 281, 563)

demand elasticity: the extent to which a change in price causes a change in the quantity demanded; demand elasticity has three cases: elastic, inelastic, or unit elastic (p. 114)

demand schedule: listing showing the quantity demanded at all possible prices that might prevail in the market at a given time (p. 103)

demand-pull inflation: explanation that prices rise because all sectors of the economy try to buy more goods and services than the economy can produce (p. 378)

demographers: people who study growth, density, and other characteristics of the population (p. 350)

dependency ratio: ratio of the population aged under 15 or 65 and over to the population aged 15 to 65 (p. 349)

depreciation: gradual wear on capital goods (p. 223)

depression: state of the economy with large numbers of unemployed, declining real incomes, overcapacity in manufacturing plants, and general economic hardship (p. 367)

depression scrip: currency issued by towns, chambers of commerce, and other civic bodies during the Great Depression of the 1930s (p. 369)

deregulation: relaxation or removal of government regulations on business activities (p. 447)

developing countries: nonindustrial nations marked by extremely low gross national product (GNP), high poverty rates, and economic instability (p. 522)

ESPAÑOL

demanda: combinación de cantidades que alguien estaría dispuesto y sería capaz de comprar en un rango de precios posibles en un momento dado (p. 102)

curva de demanda: gráfico que muestra la cantidad demandada con cada uno y todos los precios posibles que podrían imponerse en el mercado en un momento dado (p. 104)

cuenta corriente: cuenta cuyos fondos pueden retirarse de un banco u otra institución financiera extendiendo un cheque o usando una tarjeta de débito (p. 281, 563)

elasticidad de la demanda: punto hasta el cual un cambio en el precio provoca un cambio en la cantidad demandada; la elasticidad de la demanda tiene tres casos: elástica, inelástica o elasticidad unitaria (p. 114)

tabla de demanda: lista que muestra la cantidad demandada con todos los precios posibles que podrían imponerse en el mercado en un momento dado (p. 103)

inflación de demanda: explicación de que los precios suben porque todos los sectores de la economía tratan de comprar más bienes y servicios de los que la economía puede producir (p. 378)

demógrafos: personas que estudian el crecimiento, la densidad y otras características de la población (p. 350)

tasa de dependencia: índice de población de menos de 15 años o de 65 años o más con respecto a la población de entre 15 y 65 años (p. 349)

depreciación: deterioro gradual de los bienes de capital (p. 223)

depresión: estado de la economía con grandes cantidades de desempleados, ingresos reales en descenso, exceso de capacidad en las plantas de fabricación y dificultades económicas en general (p. 367)

vale de la depresión: papel moneda emitido por pueblos, cámaras de comercio y otras entidades cívicas durante la Gran Depresión de la década de 1930 (p. 369)

liberalización: mitigación o eliminación de las reglamentaciones gubernamentales a las actividades económicas (p. 447)

países en desarrollo: países no industriales que se distinguen por el extremadamente bajo producto nacional bruto (PNB), índices altos de pobreza e inestabilidad económica (p. 522)

devote • duration

ENGLISH

***devote:** give time or attention (p. 233)

diminishing marginal utility: decrease in additional satisfaction or usefulness as additional units of a product are acquired (p. 105)

diminishing returns: stage of production where output increases at a decreasing rate as more units of variable input are added (p. 138)

discount rate: interest rate that the Federal Reserve System charges on loans to the nation's financial institutions (p. 475)

discretionary spending: spending for federal programs that must receive annual authorization (p. 417)

disposable personal income (DPI): personal income less individual income taxes; total income available to the consumer sector after income taxes (p. 341)

ature*distorted: not truthfully represented (p. 256)

distribution of income: the way in which income is allocated among families, individuals, or other groups (p. 401)

diversification: the technique of spreading funds over a large number of investments to reduce the portfolio's overall risk (p. 308)

dividend: check paid to stockholders, usually quarterly, representing a portion of corporate profits (p. 217, 570)

division of labor: division of work into a number of separate tasks to be performed by different workers; same as specialization (p. 23, 538)

double taxation: feature of taxation that allows stockholders' dividends to be taxed both as corporate profit and as personal income (p. 219)

Dow Jones Industrial Average (DJIA): an index of 30 representative stocks used to monitor price changes in the overall stock market (p. 324, 373)

durable good: good that lasts for at least three years when used regularly (p. 8)

duration:* length of time (p. 528)

ESPAÑOL

consagrarse:* dedicar tiempo o atención (p. 233)

utilidad marginal decreciente: disminución en utilidad o satisfacción adicional al adquirirse unidades adicionales de un producto (p. 105)

rendimiento decreciente: etapa de la fabricación en la cual aumenta la producción a una tasa decreciente al agregarse más unidades de insumos variables (p. 138)

tasa de descuento: tasa de interés que la Reserva Federal cobra por préstamos a las instituciones financieras del país (p. 475)

gasto discrecional: gastos para programas federales que deben recibir autorización anualmente (p. 417)

ingreso personal disponible: ingresos personales menos los impuestos sobre los ingresos de las personas físicas; ingresos totales disponibles para el sector de los consumidores después de los impuestos sobre los ingresos (p. 341)

distorsionado:* no representado verazmente (p. 256)

distribución de los ingresos: manera como los ingresos se distribuyen entre las familias, las personas u otros grupos (p. 401)

diversificación: técnica de distribuir los fondos en un número grande de inversiones para reducir los riesgos generales de una cartera (p. 308)

dividendo: lo que se les paga a los accionistas, por lo general trimestralmente, que representa una porción de las ganancias de la empresa (p. 217, 570)

división del trabajo: división de las operaciones en una cantidad de tareas distintas a ser realizadas por distintos trabajadores; lo mismo que *especialización* (p. 23, 538)

doble imposición: característica impositiva que permite que a los dividendos de los accionistas se les impongan impuestos como ganancias corporativas y como ingresos personales (p. 219)

índice Dow Jones: índice de 30 acciones representativas usado para hacer el seguimiento de los cambios en los precios del mercado de valores en general (p. 324, 373)

bien duradero: bien que dura al menos tres años cuando se usa con regularidad (p. 8)

duración:* espacio de tiempo (p. 528)

earmarks, or pork • Efficient Market Hypothesis (EMH)

ENGLISH

earmarks, or pork: a line item budget expenditure that circumvents normal budget building processes and procedures and benefits a small number of people or businesses (p. 416)

Earned Income Tax Credit (EITC): federal tax credits and cash payments for low-income workers (p. 358)

easy money policy: monetary policy resulting in lower interest rates and greater access to credit; associated with an expansion of the money supply (p. 473)

e-commerce: electronic business or exchange conducted over the Internet (p. 146)

econometric model: macroeconomic expression used to describe how the economy is expected to perform in the future (p. 373)

economic growth: increase in a nation's total output of goods and services over time (p. 21)

economic interdependence: mutual dependence of the economic activities of one person, company, region, or nation on those of another person, company, region, or nation (p. 24)

economic model: simplified version of a complex concept or behavior expressed in the form of a graph, figure, equation, or diagram (p. 26, 161)

economic systems: organized way a society provides for the wants and needs of its people (p. 39)

economics: social science dealing with how people satisfy seemingly unlimited and competing needs and wants with the careful use of scarce resources (p. 7)

economies of scale: increasingly efficient use of personnel, plant, and equipment as a firm becomes larger (p. 199)

EE savings bonds: low-denomination, non-transferable bond issued by the federal government, usually through payroll savings plans (p. 314)

Efficient Market Hypothesis (EMH): argument that stocks are always priced about right, and that bargains are hard to find because they are closely watched by so many investors (p. 321)

ESPAÑOL

barril de tocino: gasto en partidas específicas de un presupuesto que elude los procesos y procedimientos normales de creación de un presupuesto y beneficia a un número pequeño de personas o empresas (p. 416)

crédito tributario por ingresos del trabajo (EITC): pagos en efectivo y créditos impositivos federales para trabajadores de bajos ingresos (p. 358)

política presupuestaria expansiva: política monetaria que resulta en tasas de interés más bajas y mayor acceso al crédito; se asocia con una expansión de la masa monetaria (p. 473)

comercio electrónico: intercambio o comercio realizado por Internet (p. 146)

modelo econométrico: expresión de la macroeconomía que se usa para describir cómo se espera que la economía se desempeñe en el futuro (p. 373)

crecimiento económico: aumento en la producción total de bienes y servicios de un país con el paso del tiempo (p. 21)

interdependencia económica: dependencia mutua de las actividades económicas de una persona, una empresa, una región o un país y los de otra persona, empresa, región o país (p. 24)

modelo económico: versión simplificada de un comportamiento o concepto complejo expresado en forma de gráfico, figura, ecuación o diagrama (p. 26, 161)

sistemas económicos: forma organizada como una sociedad prevé los deseos y necesidades de sus personas (p. 39)

economía: ciencia social que se ocupa de cómo la gente satisface deseos y necesidades aparentemente ilimitados e irreconciliables con el uso cuidadoso de recursos escasos (p. 7)

economías de escala: uso cada vez más eficiente del personal, la planta y los equipos al hacerse una empresa cada vez más grande (p. 199)

bonos de ahorro serie EE: bonos no transferibles de valor bajo emitidos por el gobierno federal, usualmente mediante planes de ahorro por nómina (p. 314)

hipótesis del mercado eficiente: argumento de que las acciones siempre tienen un precio bastante real, y de que las gangas son difíciles de hallar porque las siguen de cerca muchos inversionistas (p. 321)

ENGLISH

elastic: type of elasticity in which a change in the independent variable (usually price) results in a larger change in the dependent variable (usually quantity demanded or supplied) (p. 114)

elasticity: a measure of responsiveness that tells us how a dependent variable, such as quantity demanded or quantity supplied, responds to a change in an independent variable such as price (p. 114)

embargo: government order prohibiting the movements of goods to a country (p. 503)

***emphasizing:** stressing (p. 41)

***enabled:** made possible (p. 497)

enterprise zones: areas free of local, state, and federal tax laws as well as other operating restrictions (p. 358)

entitlements: program or benefit using established eligibility requirements to provide health care, food, or income supplements to individuals (p. 421, 441)

***entity:** unit or being (p. 213)

entrepreneurs: risk-taking individuals who introduce new products or services in search of profits; one of the four factors of production (p. 16, 82)

***equate:** to represent as equal or equivalent (p. 189)

equilibrium price: price when quantity supplied equals quantity demanded; price that clears the market (p. 161, 451)

equilibrium quantity: quantity of output supplied that is exactly equal to the quantity demanded at the equilibrium price (p. 161)

equilibrium wage rate: wage rate leaving neither a surplus nor a shortage of workers in the market (p. 253)

equities: stocks that represent ownership shares in corporations (p. 318)

***equivalent:** equal in value (p. 263)

ESPAÑOL

elástica: tipo de elasticidad en la cual un cambio en la variable independiente (usualmente el precio) da como resultado un cambio más grande en la variable dependiente (usualmente la cantidad demandada u ofertada) (p. 114)

elasticidad: medida de la sensibilidad que nos indica cómo responde una variable dependiente, como la cantidad demandada o la cantidad ofertada, a un cambio en una variable independiente, como el precio (p. 114)

embargo: orden gubernamental que prohíbe el movimiento de bienes y servicios hacia un país (p. 503)

***enfatizando:** dando énfasis (p. 41)

***facilitó:** hizo posible (p. 497)

zonas de promoción industrial: áreas donde no se aplican las leyes impositivas locales, estatales y federales así como otras restricciones para las operaciones (p. 358)

subsidios: programa o beneficios que usan requisitos de elegibilidad establecidos para proporcionar asistencia sanitaria, alimentos o complementos al ingreso a personas (p. 421, 441)

***entidad:** unidad o ser (p. 213)

empresarios: personas que se arriesgan para introducir productos o servicios nuevos con el fin de obtener ganancias; uno de los cuatro factores de producción (p. 16, 82)

***equiparar** representar como igual o equivalente (p. 189)

precio de equilibrio precio cuando la cantidad ofertada es igual a la cantidad demandada; precio que despeja el mercado (p. 161, 451)

cantidad de equilibrio: cantidad de producción ofertada que es exactamente igual a la cantidad demandada al precio de equilibrio (p. 161)

escala salarial de equilibrio: escala salarial que no deja excedente ni escasez de trabajadores en el mercado (p. 253)

títulos valores: acciones que representan la propiedad en una corporación (p. 318)

***equivalente:** igual en valor (p. 263)

ENGLISH

estate tax: tax on the transfer of property when a person dies (p. 415)

*ethic: moral principles; generally recognized rules of conduct (p. 527)

euro: single currency of the European Union (p. 535)

European Coal and Steel Community (ECSC): group of six European countries formed in 1951 to coordinate iron and steel production to ensure peace among member countries; eventually evolved into the EU (p. 534)

European Union (EU): established in 1993 by the Maastricht Treaty, its 28 member countries make it the largest single unified market in the world in terms of population and output (p. 61, 534)

*evolved: developed gradually (p. 404)

excess reserves: financial institution's cash, currency, and reserves in excess of required reserves; potential source of new loans (p. 471)

excise tax: general revenue tax levied on the manufacture or sale of selected items (p. 415)

*excluded: not counted or included (p. 337)

expansion: period of uninterrupted growth of real GDP, industrial production, real income, and employment lasting for several years or more; recovery from recession (p. 367)

*explicit: openly and clearly expressed (p. 477)

exports: the goods and services that a nation produces and then sells to other nations (p. 495)

expropriation: government confiscation of private- or foreign-owned goods without compensation (p. 529)

external debt: borrowed money that a country owes to foreign countries and banks (p. 525)

externalities: economic side effects that affect an uninvolved third party (p. 193)

ESPAÑOL

impuesto sobre la herencia: impuesto sobre la transferencia de propiedad cuando muere una persona (p. 415)

*ética: principios morales; reglas de conducta generalmente reconocidas (p. 527)

euro: moneda única de la Unión Europea (p. 535)

Comunidad Europea del Carbón y del Acero (CECA): grupo de seis países europeos formado en 1951 para coordinar la producción de hierro y acero de modo de asegurar la paz entre los países miembros; con el tiempo evolucionó hasta ser la UE (p. 534)

Unión Europea (UE): establecida en 1993 por el Tratado de Maastricht, sus 28 países miembros hacen que sea el mercado unificado más grande del mundo en términos de población y producción (p. 61, 534)

*evolucionó: se desarrolló gradualmente (p. 404)

reservas en exceso: reservas, divisas y efectivo que una institución financiera mantiene por encima de las reservas requeridas; fuente potencial de nuevos préstamos (p. 471)

impuesto especial: impuesto general sobre los ingresos que se recauda por la fabricación o venta de productos seleccionados (p. 415)

*excluido: sin contar o incluir (p. 337)

expansión: período de crecimiento ininterrumpido del PIB real, la producción industrial, el ingreso real y el empleo que dura varios años o más; recuperación de la recesión (p. 367)

*explícito: expresado abierta y claramente (p. 477)

exportaciones: bienes y servicios que un país produce y luego vende a otros países (p. 495)

expropiación: confiscación sin compensación por parte del gobierno de bienes de propiedad privada o extranjera (p. 529)

deuda externa: dinero prestado que un país debe a otros países y bancos extranjeros (p. 525)

externalidades: efectos secundarios económicos que afectan a un tercero no involucrado (p. 193)

F

ENGLISH

fact-finding: agreement between union and management to have a neutral third party collect facts about a dispute and present nonbinding recommendations (p. 256)

factor markets: markets in which productive resources are bought and sold (p. 24)

factors of production: productive resources needed to produce goods; the four factors are land, capital, labor, and entrepreneurship (p. 14)

family: two or more people living together that are related by blood, marriage, or adoption (p. 342)

Federal Deposit Insurance Corporation (FDIC): The United States government institution that provides deposit insurance on the depositor's account (p. 287, 560)

Federal Reserve notes: paper currency issued by the Fed that eventually replaced all other types of federal currency (p. 276)

Federal Reserve System (Fed): privately owned, publicly controlled, central bank of the United States (p. 276, 559)

fertility rate: number of births that 1,000 women are expected to undergo in their lifetime (p. 350)

fiat money: money by government decree; has no alternative value or use as a commodity (p. 277)

FICA: Federal Insurance Contribution Act; tax levied on employers and employees to support Social Security and Medicare (p. 415)

finance company: firm that makes loans directly to consumers and specializes in buying installment contracts from merchants who sell on credit (p. 307)

financial assets: stocks or documents that represent a claim on the income and property of the borrower; CDs, bonds, Treasury bills, mortgages (p. 304)

ESPAÑOL

determinación de hechos: acuerdo entre el sindicato y la gerencia para que un tercero neutral recopile datos sobre un conflicto y presente recomendaciones no vinculantes (p. 256)

mercado de factores de producción: mercados en los cuales se compran y venden recursos productivos (p. 24)

factores de producción: recursos productivos necesarios para producir bienes; los cuatro factores de producción son tierra, capital, mano de obra e iniciativa empresarial (p. 14)

familia: dos o más personas que viven juntas y tienen relación de sangre, matrimonio o adopción (p. 342)

Corporación Federal de Seguro de Depósitos (FDIC): institución del gobierno de Estados Unidos que proporciona seguro de depósitos para la cuenta del depositante (p. 287, 560)

billetes de la Reserva Federal: papel moneda emitido por la Reserva Federal que con el tiempo reemplazó todos los otros tipos de papel moneda del gobierno federal (p. 276)

Reserva Federal: banco central de propiedad privada y control público de Estados Unidos (p. 276, 559)

tasa de fertilidad: número de nacimientos que se espera que tengan mil mujeres en el transcurso de su vida (p. 350)

dinero fiduciario: dinero decretado por el gobierno; no tiene valor alternativo ni uso como mercancía (p. 277)

FICA: *Federal Insurance Contribution Act* (ley de contribución al seguro social); impuesto que se recauda de empleadores y empleados para financiar la Seguridad Social y Medicare (p. 415)

sociedad financiera: empresa que otorga préstamos directamente a los consumidores y se especializa en comprar contratos de venta a plazos de comerciantes minoristas que venden a crédito (p. 307)

activos financieros: acciones o documentos que representan una reivindicación sobre el ingreso y la propiedad del prestatario; certificados de depósito, bonos, letras del Tesoro, hipotecas (p. 304)

financial institution • fluctuate

ENGLISH

financial institution: group that channels savings to investors; includes banks, insurance companies, savings and loan associations, credit unions (p. 559)

financial intermediaries: institutions that channel savings to investors; banks, insurance companies, savings and loan associations, credit unions (p. 305)

financial system: network of savers, investors, and financial institutions that work together to transfer savings to investment uses (p. 306)

fiscal policy: use of government spending and revenue collection measures to influence the economy (p. 438)

fiscal year: 12-month financial planning period that may coincide with the calendar year; October 1 to September 30 for the federal government (p. 412)

Five-Year Plan: comprehensive, centralized economic plan used by the Soviet Union and China to coordinate development of agriculture and industry (p. 58)

fixed costs: costs of production that do not change when output changes (p. 142)

fixed exchange rates: system under which the values of currencies are fixed in relation to one another; the exchange rate system in effect until 1971 (p. 510)

fixed income: income that does not increase over time (p. 89)

flat tax: proportional tax on individual income after a specified threshold has been reached (p. 406)

flexible exchange rates: system that relies on supply and demand to determine the value of one currency in terms of another; exchange rate system in effect since 1971 (p. 511)

floating exchange rates: system that relies on supply and demand to determine the value of one currency in terms of another; exchange rate system in effect since 1971 (p. 511)

***fluctuate:** to rise and fall uncertainly (p. 164)

ESPAÑOL

institución financiera: grupo que canaliza ahorros hacia inversionistas; incluye bancos, empresas de seguros, asociaciones de ahorro y crédito, cooperativas de crédito (p. 559)

intermediarios financieros: instituciones que canalizan ahorros hacia inversionistas; bancos, empresas de seguros, asociaciones de ahorro y crédito, cooperativas de crédito (p. 305)

sistema financiero: red de ahorristas, inversionistas e instituciones financieras que colaboran para transferir ahorros hacia usos en inversiones (p. 306)

política fiscal: uso del gasto gubernamental y disposiciones para el cobro de las rentas para influir en la economía (p. 438)

año fiscal: período de planificación financiera de 12 meses que puede coincidir con el año calendario; va del 1.° de octubre al 30 de septiembre para el gobierno federal (p. 412)

plan quinquenal: plan económico centralizado y amplio usado por la Unión Soviética y China para coordinar el desarrollo de la agricultura y la industria (p. 58)

costos fijos: costos de fabricación que no cambian cuando cambia el nivel de producción (p. 142)

tasas de cambio fijas: sistema bajo el cual los valores de las divisas se fijan en relación entre las mismas; sistema de tasa de cambio en vigor hasta 1971 (p. 510)

ingresos fijos: ingresos que no aumentan con el transcurso del tiempo (p. 89)

impuesto fijo: impuesto proporcional sobre los ingresos personales después de que se ha alcanzado un umbral específico (p. 406)

tasas de cambio flexibles: sistema que depende de la oferta y la demanda para determinar el valor de una divisa en relación a otra; sistema de tasa de cambio en vigor desde 1971 (p. 511)

tasas de cambio flotantes: sistema que depende de la oferta y la demanda para determinar el valor de una divisa en relación a otra; sistema de tasa de cambio en vigor desde 1971 (p. 511)

***fluctuar:** subir y bajar de forma indeterminada (p. 164)

ENGLISH

food stamps: government-issued coupons that can be exchanged for food (p. 357)

foreclosure: process in which a lender reclaims the property due to a lack of payment by the borrower (p. 200)

foreign exchange: foreign currencies used by countries to conduct international trade (p. 509)

foreign exchange rate: price of one's country's currency in terms of another currency (p. 509)

fractional reserve system: system requiring financial institutions to set aside a fraction of their deposits in the form of reserves or vault cash (p. 470)

***framework:** point of reference (p. 453)

franchise: business investment that involves renting or leasing another successful business model (p. 220)

franchisee: person that invests in the business model of the franchisor with his or her own money and start-up costs (p. 222)

franchisor: creator and owner of the business model that is rented or leased by investors (p. 220)

free enterprise: an economic system in which privately owned businesses have the freedom to operate for a profit with limited government intervention (p. 72)

free enterprise economy: market economy in which privately owned businesses have the freedom to operate for a profit with limited government intervention (p. 28)

free traders: people who favor fewer or no trade restrictions (p. 503)

free-trade area: group of countries that have agreed to reduce trade barriers among themselves, but lack a common tariff barrier for nonmembers (p. 534)

frictional unemployment: unemployment caused by workers changing jobs or waiting to go to new ones (p. 386)

***functions:** roles or purposes (p. 466)

ESPAÑOL

cupones para alimentos: cupones emitidos por el gobierno que pueden cambiarse por alimentos (p. 357)

ejecución hipotecaria: proceso por el cual un prestamista reclama la propiedad debido a la falta de pago por parte del prestatario (p. 200)

divisas: monedas extranjeras usadas por los países para comerciar internacionalmente (p. 509)

tasa de cambio de divisas: precio de la moneda de un país en relación con una moneda extranjera (p. 509)

sistema de reserva fraccional: sistema que exige que las instituciones financieras guarden una fracción de sus depósitos en forma de reservas o efectivo (p. 470)

***marco:** punto de referencia (p. 453)

franquicia: inversión comercial que implica alquilar o arrendar otro modelo de negocios exitoso (p. 220)

franquiciado: persona que invierte con su propio dinero y costos iniciales en el modelo de negocios de un franquiciador (p. 222)

franquiciador: creador y propietario del modelo de negocios que inversionistas alquilan o arriendan (p. 220)

libre empresa: sistema económico en el cual empresas de propiedad privada tienen la libertad de operar con la finalidad de obtener ganancias con intervención limitada del gobierno (p. 72)

economía de libre empresa: economía de mercado en la cual empresas de propiedad privada tienen la libertad de operar con la finalidad de obtener ganacias con intervención limitada del gobierno (p. 28)

librecambistas: personas que están a favor de que haya poca o ninguna restricción al comercio (p. 503)

zona de libre comercio: grupo de países que han acordado reducir los obstáculos al comercio entre ellos pero que no tienen obstáculos comunes en forma de aranceles para los países no miembros (p. 534)

desempleo friccional: desempleo causado por trabajadores que están cambiando de empleo o esperando por empezar uno nuevo (p. 386)

***funciones:** tareas u objetivos (p. 466)

fundamental • glut

ENGLISH

*fundamental: basic; an essential part (p. 386)

futures contract: an agreement to buy or sell at a specific date in the future at a predetermined price (p. 325)

G

gasohol: mixture of 90 percent unleaded gasoline and 10 percent grain alcohol (p. 544)

GDP gap: difference between what the economy can and does produce; annual opportunity cost of unemployed resources (p. 387)

GDP per capita: gross domestic product on a per person basis; can be expressed in current or constant dollars (p. 56)

General Agreement on Tariffs and Trade (GATT): an international agreement signed in 1947 among 23 countries to extend tariff concessions and reduce import quotas (p. 506, 533)

general partnership: form of partnership where all partners are equally responsible for management and debts (p. 215)

*generates: produces or brings into being (p. 144)

geographic monopoly: market structure in which a firm has a monopoly because of its location or the small size of the market (p. 188)

gift tax: tax on donations of money or wealth that is paid by the donor (p. 415)

giveback: wage, fringe benefit, or work rule given up when renegotiating a contract (p. 260)

glass ceiling: seemingly invisible barrier hindering advancement of women and minorities in a white male-dominated organization (p. 262)

globalization: movement toward a more integrated and interdependent world economy (p. 531)

glut: substantial oversupply of a product (p. 546)

ESPAÑOL

*fundamental: básico; parte esencial (p. 386)

contrato de futuros: acuerdo para comprar o vender en una fecha específica en el futuro a un precio predeterminado (p. 325)

gasohol: mezcla de 90 por ciento de gasolina sin plomo y 10 por ciento de etanol (p. 544)

brecha del PIB: diferencia entre lo que la economía puede producir y produce; costo de oportunidad anual de los recursos inactivos (p. 387)

PIB per cápita: producto interior bruto medido por persona; puede expresarse en dinero corriente o ajustado por inflación (p. 56)

Acuerdo General sobre Aranceles Aduaneros y Comercio (GATT): acuerdo internacional firmado en 1947 entre 23 países para ampliar las concesiones arancelarias y reducir los cupos de importación (p.506, 533)

sociedad colectiva: forma de sociedad en la que todos los socios son responsables por igual de la administración y las deudas (p. 215)

*genera: produce o crea (p. 144)

monopolio geográfico: estructura del mercado en la cual una empresa tiene un monopolio debido a su ubicación o el tamaño pequeño del mercado (p. 188)

impuesto sobre donaciones: impuesto que se aplica a donaciones de dinero o patrimonio que paga el donante (p. 415)

concesión: salario, beneficio adicional o reglamentación laboral a los que se renuncia al volver a negociar un contrato (p. 260)

techo de cristal: barrera supuestamente invisible que dificulta el ascenso de mujeres y minorías en una organización dominada por hombres blancos (p. 262)

globalización: movimiento hacia una economía mundial más integrada e interdependiente (p. 531)

sobreproducción: exceso significativo de oferta de un producto (p. 546)

Gold Certificates • household

ENGLISH

Gold Certificates: paper currency backed by gold; issued in 1863 and popular until recalled in 1934 (p. 285)

gold standard: a system in which the basic unit of currency is equivalent to, and can be exchanged for, a specific amount of gold (p. 285)

good: tangible economic product that is useful, transferable to others, and used to satisfy wants and needs (p. 8)

Gosplan: central planning authority in the former Soviet Union that devised and directed Five-Year Plans (p. 58)

government monopoly: monopoly created and/or owned by the government (p. 189)

Great Depression: worst period of economic decline in U.S. history, lasting from approximately 1929 to 1939 (p. 49, 247)

Great Leap Forward: China's second Five-Year Plan, begun in 1958, which forced collectivization of agriculture and rapid industrialization (p. 59)

Great Recession: severe economic downturn that lasted from late 2007 through mid-2009 (p. 79)

grievance procedure: provision in a contract outlining the way future disputes and grievance issues will be resolved (p. 256)

gross domestic product (GDP): monetary value of all final goods, services, and structures produced within a country's national borders during a one-year period (p. 10, 337)

gross national product (GNP): the market value of goods and services produced by labor and property supplied by U.S. residents (p. 341)

H

horizontal merger: combination of firms producing the same kind of product (p. 225)

household: basic unit of consumer sector consisting of all of the people who occupy a house, apartment, or separate living quarters (p. 342)

ESPAÑOL

certificados de oro: papeles moneda respaldados por oro; emitidos en 1863 y populares hasta que fueron retirados en 1934 (p. 285)

patrón oro: sistema en el cual la unidad monetaria básica es equivalente a, y puede intercambiarse por, una cantidad específica de oro (p. 285)

bien: producto económico tangible que es útil, transferible a los demás y usado para satisfacer deseos y necesidades (p. 8)

Gosplan: autoridad central de planificación en la ex Unión Soviética que elaboraba y dirigía los planes quinquenales (p. 58)

monopolio estatal: monopolio creado y/o de propiedad del gobierno (p. 189)

Gran Depresión: peor período de deterioro económico en la historia de Estados Unidos, que duró aproximadamente de 1929 a 1939 (p. 49, 247)

Gran Salto Adelante: segundo plan quinquenal de China, que comenzó en 1958 y forzó la socialización de la agricultura y una rápida industrialización (p. 59)

Gran Recesión: gran desaceleración económica que duró desde finales de 2007 hasta mediados de 2009 (p. 79)

procedimiento conciliatorio: cláusula en un contrato que resume la manera como se resolverán futuros conflictos y reclamos (p. 256)

producto interior bruto (PIB): valor monetario de todos los productos, servicios y estructuras finales producidos dentro de las fronteras nacionales de un país durante un período de un año (p. 10, 337)

producto nacional bruto (PNB): valor de mercado de bienes y servicios producidos por la mano de obra y la propiedad aportados por residentes de Estados Unidos (p. 341)

fusión horizontal: combinación de empresas que producen el mismo tipo de producto (p. 225)

hogar: unidad básica del sector de los consumidores que consiste en todas las personas que ocupan una casa, un apartamento o locales habitados separados (p. 342)

human capital • independent unions

ENGLISH

human capital: sum of people's skills, abilities, health, and motivation (p. 22)

hydropower: power or energy generated by moving water (p. 544)

hyperinflation: abnormal inflation in excess of 500 percent per year; last stage of monetary collapse (p. 377)

***hypothetical:** assumed but not proven (p. 136)

***ideology:** a set of beliefs (p. 479)

***illustrated:** shown with an image or example (p. 109)

***impact:** effect (p. 356)

***implemented:** put into effect (p. 424)

***implication:** something suggested to be naturally understood (p. 321)

implicit GDP price deflator: index used to measure price changes in gross domestic product (p. 378)

imports: the goods and services that a nation buys from other nations (p. 495)

***incentive:** something that motivates (p. 73, 103)

incidence of a tax: the final burden of the tax (p. 402)

income effect: that portion of a change in quantity demanded caused by a change in a consumer's income when the price of a product changes (p. 109)

income statement: report showing a business's sales, expenses, and profits for a certain period, usually three months or a year (p. 223)

incubators: places where entrepreneurs can receive the training and other assistance to build a successful start-up business (p. 228)

independent unions: labor unions not affiliated with the AFL-CIO or the Change to Win Coalition (p. 249)

ESPAÑOL

capital humano: suma de las destrezas, capacidades, salud y motivación de las personas (p. 22)

energía hidráulica: electricidad o energía generada por agua en movimiento (p. 544)

hiperinflación: inflación anormal por encima del 500 por ciento al año; última etapa del colapso monetario (p. 377)

***hipotético:** supuesto pero no probado (p. 136)

***ideología:** conjunto de creencias (p. 479)

***ilustrado:** que se muestra con una imagen o ejemplo (p. 109)

***impacto:** efecto (p. 356)

***implementado:** llevado a cabo (p. 424)

***sobrentendido:** algo que se sugiere que es naturalmente entendido (p. 321)

deflactor del PIB: índice que se usa para medir cambios de los precios en el producto interior bruto (p. 378)

importaciones: bienes y servicios que un país compra a otros países (p. 495)

***incentivo:** algo que motiva (p. 73, 103)

incidencia de un impuesto: carga final del impuesto (p. 402)

efecto ingreso: porción de un cambio en la cantidad demandada causado por un cambio en el ingreso de un consumidor cuando cambia el precio de un producto (p. 109)

estado de resultados: informe que muestra las ventas, los gastos y las ganacias de una empresa durante cierto período, usualmente de tres meses o un año (p. 223)

incubadoras de empresas: lugares donde los empresarios pueden recibir capacitación y otro tipo de asistencia para crear una empresa nueva exitosa (p. 228)

sindicatos independientes: sindicatos no afiliados con AFL-CIO ni con Change to Win Coalition (p. 249)

ENGLISH	ESPAÑOL
indexing: adjustment of tax brackets to offset the effects of inflation (p. 414)	**indización:** ajuste de las categorías impositivas para compensar por los efectos de la inflación (p. 414)
individual income tax: tax levied on the wages, salaries, and other income of individuals (p. 403)	**impuesto sobre los ingresos de las personas físicas:** impuesto que se recauda por los sueldos, salarios y otros ingresos de las personas (p. 403)
Individual Retirement Accounts (IRAs): retirement account in the form of a long-term time deposit, with annual contributions not taxed until withdrawn during retirement (p. 314, 573)	**cuentas de ahorro para jubilación (IRA):** cuentas para la jubilación en forma de depósito a largo plazo, con contribuciones anuales no sujetas a impuestos hasta el retiro durante la jubilación (p. 314, 573)
industrial union: labor union whose members perform different kinds of work in the same industry (p. 246)	**sindicato de industria:** sindicato cuyos miembros realizan distintos tipos de trabajos en la misma industria (p. 246)
industry: the supply side of the market (p. 182)	**industria:** parte del mercado que crea la oferta (p. 182)
inelastic: case of demand elasticity where the percentage change in the independent variable (usually price) causes a less than proportionate change in the dependent variable (usually quantity demanded or supplied) (p. 115)	**inelástica:** tipo de elasticidad de la demanda en la cual el cambio porcentual en la variable independiente (usualmente el precio) causa un cambio menos que proporcional en la variable dependiente (usualmente la cantidad demandada u ofertada) (p. 115)
infant industries argument: argument that new and emerging industries should be protected from foreign competition until they are strong enough to compete (p. 504)	**argumento de la industria naciente:** argumento que dice que las industrias nuevas y emergentes deberían ser protegidas de la competencia extranjera hasta que sean lo suficientemente fuertes como para poder competir (p. 504)
inflation: sustained rise in the general level of prices of goods and services (p. 89, 375)	**inflación:** aumento sostenido en el nivel general de los precios de bienes y servicios (p. 89, 375)
infrastructure: the highways, levees, mass transit, communications, power, water, sewerage, and other public goods needed to support a population (p. 348)	**infraestructura:** carreteras, diques, transporte público, comunicaciones, energía, agua, alcantarillado y otros bienes públicos necesarios para el mantenimiento de la población (p. 348)
*__initially:__ originally; at the beginning (p. 284)	*__inicialmente:__ originalmente; al comienzo (p. 284)
injunction: court order issued to prevent a company or union from taking or not taking action during a labor dispute (p. 257)	**medidas cautelares:** orden de un tribunal emitida para evitar que una empresa o un sindicato actúen o no actúen durante un conflicto laboral (p. 257)
*__instituted:__ put into action (p. 421)	*__instituido:__ puesto en marcha (p. 421)
*__intangible:__ not physical; something that cannot be touched (p. 9)	*__intangible:__ no físico; algo que no puede tocarse (p. 9)
interest: payment made for the use of borrowed money; usually paid at periodic intervals for long-term bonds or loans (p. 218, 559)	**interés:** pago hecho por el uso de dinero que se pidió prestado; usualmente se paga en intervalos periódicos para los préstamos o bonos a largo plazo (p. 218, 559)

interest rate • justify

ENGLISH

interest rate: the price of credit to a borrower (p. 472, 559)

intergovernmental expenditures: funds that one level of government transfers to another level for spending (p. 426)

intergovernmental revenue: funds that one level of government receives from another level of government (p. 424)

intermediate products: products that are components of other final products already included in the GDP; for example, new tires and radios for use on new cars (p. 337)

Internal Revenue Service (IRS): branch of the U.S. Treasury Department that collects taxes (p. 403)

*__internally:__ existing or occurring from within (p. 225)

International Monetary Fund (IMF): international organization that offers advice, financial assistance, and currency support to all nations (p. 528)

*__intervention:__ involvement in a situation to alter the outcome (p. 203)

inventory: stock of goods held in reserve; includes finished goods waiting to be sold and raw materials to be used in production (p. 214)

*__inversely:__ in the opposite way (p. 104)

*__isolationism:__ national policy of avoiding international alliances and economic interactions (p. 60)

ESPAÑOL

tasa de interés: precio del crédito para un prestatario (p. 472, 559)

gastos intragubernamentales: fondos que un nivel del gobierno transfiere a otro nivel para gastos (p. 426)

ingresos intragubernamentales: fondos que un nivel del gobierno recibe de otro nivel del gobierno (p. 424)

productos intermedios: productos que son componentes de otros productos finales ya incluidos en el PIB; por ejemplo, nuevos neumáticos y radios para usar en carros nuevos (p. 337)

Servicio Federal de Rentas Internas (IRS): rama del Departamento del Tesoro de Estados Unidos que cobra impuestos (p. 403)

*__internamente:__ que existe u ocurre dentro (p. 225)

Fondo Monetario Internacional (FMI): organización internacional que ofrece consejos, asistencia financiera y apoyo a la moneda a todos los países (p. 528)

*__intervención:__ participación en una situación para alterar el resultado (p. 203)

inventario: existencia de bienes que se mantienen en reserva; incluye bienes finales que están para la venta y materias primas que se van a usar en la producción (p. 214)

*__inversamente:__ en el modo opuesto (p. 104)

*__aislacionismo:__ política nacional que evita las alianzas internacionales y las interacciones económicas (p. 60)

J

junk bonds: exceptionally risky bond with a Standard & Poor's rating of BB or lower that carries a high rate of return as compensation for the higher possibility of non-payment (p. 313)

*__justify:__ to defend as warranted or necessary (p. 504)

bonos basura: bonos muy riesgosos que tienen la calificación BB o menor de Standard & Poor's y que cuentan con una tasa alta de rentabilidad como compensación por la mayor posibilidad de falta de pago (p. 313)

*__justificar:__ defender como justificado o necesario (p. 504)

K

ENGLISH

keiretsu: independently owned group of Japanese firms joined and governed by an external board of directors in order to regulate competition (p. 63)

Keynesian economics: government spending and taxation policies suggested by John Maynard Keynes to stimulate the economy; synonymous with fiscal policies or demand-side economics (p. 438)

L

labor: people with all their abilities and efforts; one of the four factors of production; does not include the entrepreneur (p. 16)

labor union: organization that works for its members' interests concerning pay, working hours, health coverage, fringe benefits, and other job-related matters (p. 234)

Laffer curve: a hypothetical, or possible, relationship between federal income tax rates and tax revenues (p. 447)

laissez-faire: philosophy that government should not interfere with business activity (p. 188)

land: natural resources or "gifts of nature" not created by human effort; one of the four factors of production (p. 15)

Law of Demand: rule stating that more will be demanded at lower prices and less at higher prices; an inverse relationship between price and quantity demanded (p. 104)

Law of Supply: principle that more will be offered for sale at higher prices than at lower prices (p. 128)

leading economic index (LEI): monthly statistical series that uses a combination of ten individual indicators to forecast changes in real GDP (p. 373)

leading economic indicator: statistical series that normally turns down before the economy turns down or turns up before the economy turns up (p. 372)

legal reserves: currency and deposits used to meet the reserve requirements (p. 470)

ESPAÑOL

keiretsu: grupo de empresas japonesas de propiedad independiente asociadas y gobernadas por una junta de directores externa para regular la competencia (p. 63)

economía keynesiana: políticas impositivas y de gastos del gobierno sugeridas por John Maynard Keynes para estimular la economía; sinónimo de políticas fiscales o economía de demanda (p. 438)

mano de obra: personas con todas sus capacidades y esfuerzos; uno de los cuatro factores de producción; no incluye al empresario (p. 16)

sindicato: organización que trabaja por los intereses de sus miembros en lo que respecta al pago, las horas de trabajo, la cobertura de la salud, beneficios adicionales y otros asuntos relacionados con el empleo (p. 234)

curva de Laffer: relación hipotética, o posible, entre las tasas federales de impuestos sobre la renta y los ingresos fiscales (p. 447)

laissez-faire: filosofía que dice que el gobierno no debería interferir en las actividades de las empresas (p. 188)

tierra: recursos naturales o "dones de la naturaleza" no creados por el esfuerzo humano; uno de los cuatro factores de producción (p. 15)

ley de la demanda: regla que dice que se demandará más si los precios son más bajos y menos si los precios son más altos; relación inversa entre el precio y la cantidad demandada (p. 104)

ley de la oferta: principio que indica que se ofertará más si los precios son más altos que si los precios son más bajos (p. 128)

índice económico adelantado (LEI): serie estadística mensual que usa una combinación de diez indicadores individuales para predecir cambios en el PIB real (p. 373)

indicador económico adelantado: serie estadística que normalmente baja antes de que la economía baje o sube antes de que la economía suba (p. 372)

reservas legales: papel moneda y depósitos que se usan para cumplir con los requisitos de reserva (p. 470)

legal tender • M2

ENGLISH

legal tender: currency that must be accepted for payment by decree of government (p. 284)

***legislation:** laws enacted by the government (p. 244)

life expectancy: average remaining life span in years of a person who has reached a specified age (p. 350, 524)

limited life: situation in which a firm legally ceases to exist when an owner dies or quits, or a new owner is added; applies to sole proprietorships and partnerships (p. 214, 569)

limited partnership: form of partnership where one or more partners are not active in the daily running of the business, and whose liability for the partnership's debt is restricted to the amount invested in the business (p. 215, 569)

line-item veto: power to cancel specific budget items without rejecting the entire budget (p. 421)

lockout: management refusal to let employees work until company demands are met (p. 246)

long run: production period long enough to change amount of variable and fixed inputs used in production (p. 137)

long-term unemployed: workers who have been unemployed for twenty-seven weeks or more (p. 384)

Lorenz curve: graph showing how much the actual distribution of income differs from an equal distribution among the five quintiles (p. 354)

ESPAÑOL

dinero de curso legal: papel moneda que debe aceptarse como pago por decreto del gobierno (p. 284)

***legislación:** leyes sancionadas por el gobierno (p. 244)

esperanza de vida: promedio de la duración de vida restante en años de una persona que ha llegado a una edad especificada (p. 350, 524)

duración limitada: situación en la cual una empresa deja de existir legalmente cuando un propietario muere o renuncia, o se agrega un nuevo dueño; se aplica a empresas individuales y sociedades (p. 214, 569)

sociedad comanditaria: forma de sociedad en la que uno o más socios no se ocupan de las operaciones diarias de la empresa, y cuya responsabilidad por la deuda de la sociedad está limitada a la cantidad invertida en la empresa (p. 215, 569)

veto de partidas específicas: poder de suprimir partidas específicas del presupuesto sin rechazar el presupuesto en su totalidad (p. 421)

cierre patronal: rechazo de la dirección a permitir que los empleados trabajen hasta que se cumpla con las demandas de la empresa (p. 246)

largo plazo: período de producción lo suficientemente largo como para cambiar las cantidades de los insumos fijos y variables que se usan en la producción (p. 137)

desempleado de larga duración: se dice de los trabajadores que han estado desempleados por 27 semanas o más (p. 384)

curva de Lorenz: gráfico que muestra cuánto difiere la distribución real del ingreso de una distribución equitativa entre los cinco quintiles (p. 354)

M

M1: narrow definition of money supply conforming to money's role as medium of exchange; components include coins, currency, checks, other demand deposits, traveler's checks (p. 281)

M2: broad definition of money supply conforming to money's role as a medium exchange and a store of value; components include M1 plus savings deposits, time deposits, and money market funds (p. 281)

M1: definición restringida de la oferta de dinero ajustada a la función del dinero como medio de cambio; entre sus componentes se incluyen monedas, divisas, cheques, otros depósitos en cuenta corriente y cheques de viajero (p. 281)

M2: definición amplia de la oferta de dinero ajustada a la función del dinero como medio de cambio y reserva de valor; entre sus componentes se incluyen M1 más depósitos en caja de ahorros, depósitos a plazo fijo y fondos del mercado monetario (p. 281)

ENGLISH

macroeconomic equilibrium: amount of real GDP consistent with a given price level; intersection of aggregate supply and aggregate demand (p. 453)

macroeconomics: the branch of economic theory focused on the economy as a whole and decision making by large units, such as governments and unions (p. 450)

mandatory spending: federal spending authorized by law that continues without the need for annual approvals of Congress (p. 416)

marginal cost: extra cost of producing one additional unit of production (p. 143)

marginal product: extra output due to the addition of one more unit of input (p. 137)

marginal revenue: extra revenue from the sale of one additional unit of output (p. 144)

marginal tax rate: tax rate that applies to the next dollar of taxable income (p. 405)

marginal utility: additional satisfaction or usefulness obtained from acquiring or consuming one more unit of a product (p. 105)

market: meeting place or arrangement through which buyers and sellers interact to determine price and quantity of an economic product; may be local, regional, national, or global (p. 24, 45)

market basket: representative collection of goods and services used to compile a price index (p. 375)

market demand curve: demand curve that shows the quantities demanded by everyone who is willing and able to purchase a product at all possible prices at one moment in time (p. 105)

market economy: economic system in which supply, demand, and the price system help people allocate resources and make the WHAT, HOW, and FOR WHOM to produce decisions; same as free enterprise economy (p. 45)

market failure: condition where any of the requirements for a competitive market—usually adequate competition, knowledge of prices and opportunities, mobility of resources, and competitive profits—leads to an inefficient allocation of resources characterized by too much or too little being produced (p. 192)

ESPAÑOL

equilibrio macroeconómico: cantidad de PIB real consistente con un nivel de precios dado; intersección entre la oferta global y la demanda global (p. 453)

macroeconomía: rama de la teoría económica que se enfoca en la economía como un todo y la toma de decisiones por parte de grandes unidades, como los gobiernos y los sindicatos (p. 450)

gasto obligatorio: gasto federal autorizado por la ley que puede continuar sin necesidad de aprobación anual por parte del Congreso (p. 416)

costo marginal: costo extraordinario de producir una unidad adicional de producción (p. 143)

producto marginal: producción extraordinaria debido al agregado de una unidad más de insumo (p. 137)

ingreso marginal: ingreso extraordinario por la venta de una unidad adicional producida (p. 144)

tasa impositiva marginal: tasa impositiva que se aplica al siguiente dólar de ingreso sujeto a impuestos (p. 405)

utilidad marginal: satisfacción o utilidad adicional que se obtiene al adquirir o consumir una unidad más de un producto (p. 105)

mercado: lugar de reunión o mecanismo mediante el cual compradores y vendedores interactúan para determinar el precio y la cantidad de un producto económico; puede ser local, regional, nacional o global (p. 24, 45)

canasta familiar: grupo representativo de bienes y servicios usados para recopilar un índice de precios (p. 375)

curva de demanda del mercado: curva de demanda que muestra las cantidades demandadas por todos quienes están dispuestos y tienen la capacidad de comprar un producto con todos los precios posibles en un momento dado (p. 105)

economía de mercado: sistema económico en el cual la oferta, la demanda y el sistema de precios ayudan a la gente a asignar recursos y tomar decisiones acerca de QUÉ, CÓMO y PARA QUIÉN producir; lo mismo que economía de libre empresa (p. 45)

falla del mercado: situación en la que cualquiera de los requisitos de un mercado competitivo—generalmente competencia adecuada, conocimiento de precios y oportunidades, movilidad de los recursos y ganancias competitivas—conducen a una asignación ineficiente de recursos caracterizada por una producción excesiva o escasa (p. 192)

market structure • micro loans

ENGLISH

market structure: market classification according to number and size of firms, type of product, and type of competition; nature and degree of competition among firms in the same industry (p. 182)

market supply curve: supply curve that shows the quantities offered at various prices by all firms that sell the same product in a given market (p. 129)

market theory of wage determination: explanation stating that the supply and demand for a worker's skills and services determine the wage or salary (p. 253)

maturity: life of a bond or length of time funds are borrowed (p. 311, 572)

measure of value: one of the three functions of money that allows it to serve as a common denominator to measure value (p. 280)

*mechanism: process or means by which something can be accomplished (p. 24)

mediation: process of resolving a dispute by bringing in a neutral third party to help both sides reach a compromise (p. 256)

Medicaid: joint federal-state medical insurance program for low-income people (p. 358, 417)

Medicare: federal health insurance program for senior citizens, regardless of income (p. 88, 405)

medium of exchange: money or other substance generally accepted as payment for goods and services; one of the three functions of money (p. 280)

member bank: bank belonging to the Federal Reserve System (p. 465)

member bank reserves (MBR): reserves kept by member banks at the Fed to satisfy reserve requirements (p. 471)

*merger: combination of two or more business enterprises to form a single firm (p. 224)

micro loans: small, unsecured loans made primarily to women to help them undertake an income-generating project in a developing country (p. 528)

ESPAÑOL

estructura del mercado: clasificación del mercado según la cantidad y el tamaño de las empresas, el tipo de producto y el tipo de competencia; naturaleza y grado de competencia entre empresas en la misma industria (p. 182)

curva de oferta del mercado: curva de oferta que muestra las cantidades ofertadas con varios precios por todas las empresas que venden el mismo producto en un mercado dado (p. 129)

teoría de mercado en la determinación de los salarios: explicación que dice que la oferta y la demanda de las destrezas y servicios de un trabajador determinan el sueldo o salario (p. 253)

vencimiento: duración de un bono o período por el que se piden fondos prestados (p. 311, 572)

medida de valor: una de las tres funciones del dinero que permite que sirva como denominador común para medir el valor (p. 280)

*mecanismo: proceso o medio por el cual algo puede lograrse (p. 24)

mediación: proceso de resolución de un conflicto que implica traer a un tercero neutral para que ayude a ambas partes a llegar a un compromiso (p. 256)

Medicaid: programa conjunto federal-estatal de seguro médico para personas de bajos ingresos (p. 358, 417)

Medicare: programa federal de seguro de salud para ancianos, independientemente del ingreso (p. 88, 405)

medio de cambio: dinero u otra sustancia generalmente aceptada como pago por bienes y servicios; una de las tres funciones del dinero (p. 280)

banco miembro: banco que está en el Sistema de la Reserva Federal (p. 465)

reserva de un banco miembro: reservas que mantienen bancos miembros en la Reserva Federal para satisfacer requisitos de reserva (p. 471)

*fusión: combinación de dos o más empresas para formar una sola (p. 224)

microcréditos: préstamos pequeños y sin garantía que se otorgan principalmente a mujeres para ayudarlas a emprender un proyecto que genera ingresos en un país en desarrollo (p. 528)

ENGLISH

microeconomics: branch of economic theory that deals with behavior and decision making by small units such as individuals and firms (p. 102)

minimum wage: lowest legal wage that can be paid to most workers (p. 88, 263)

misery index: unofficial statistic that is the sum of monthly inflation and the unemployment rate (p. 388)

mixed economy: economic system that has some combination of traditional, command, and market economies; also see modified free enterprise economy (p. 48, 86)

modified free enterprise economy: free enterprise market economy where people carry on their economic affairs freely, but are subject to some government intervention and regulation; also see mixed economy (p. 86)

modified union shop: arrangement under which workers have the option to join a union after being hired (p. 250)

monetarism: school of thought stressing the importance of stable monetary growth to control inflation and stimulate long-term economic growth (p. 475)

monetary policy: actions by the Federal Reserve System to expand or contract the money supply to affect the cost and availability of credit (p. 472)

monetary unit: standard unit of currency in a country's money supply; American dollar, British pound, etc. (p. 278)

money market: market in which financial capital is loaned and/or borrowed for one year or less (p. 315)

monopolistic competition: market structure having all conditions of pure competition except for identical products; a form of imperfect competition (p. 184)

monopoly: market structure characterized by a single producer; form of imperfect competition (p. 188)

mortgage: legal document that pledges ownership of a home to a lender as security for repayment of borrowed money (p. 200)

ESPAÑOL

microeconomía: rama de la teoría económica que trata sobre el comportamiento y la toma de decisiones por parte de unidades pequeñas, como personas y empresas (p. 102)

salario mínimo: salario legal más bajo que puede pagarse a la mayoría de los trabajadores (p. 88, 263)

índice de miseria: estadística no oficial que es la suma de la tasa de desempleo y la inflación mensual (p. 388)

economía mixta: sistema económico que tiene algún tipo de combinación de economías tradicional, planificada y de mercado; véase también *economía modificada de libre empresa* (p. 48, 86)

economía modificada de libre empresa: mercado de libre empresa en el cual las personas llevan a cabo sus asuntos económicos libremente, pero están sujetas a algo de intervención y reglamentación gubernamental; véase también *economía mixta* (p. 86)

taller sindicalizado modificado: acuerdo según el cual los trabajadores tienen la opción de hacerse miembros de un sindicato después de ser contratados (p. 250)

monetarismo: corriente de pensamiento que enfatiza la importancia del crecimiento monetario estable para controlar la inlación y estimular el crecimiento económico a largo plazo (p. 475)

política monetaria: acciones por parte de la Reserva Federal para expandir o contraer la masa monetaria y afectar el costo y la disponibilidad del crédito (p. 472)

unidad monetaria: unidad estándar de papel moneda en la masa monetaria de un país; dólar estadounidense, libra esterlina británica, etc. (p. 278)

mercado monetario: mercado en el cual el capital financiero se presta y/o se pide prestado por un año o menos (p. 315)

competencia monopolística: estructura del mercado que tiene todas las condiciones de competencia pura salvo para los productos idénticos; forma de competencia imperfecta (p. 184)

monopolio: estructura del mercado caracterizada por un solo productor; forma de competencia imperfecta (p. 188)

hipoteca: documento legal que promete la propiedad de una casa a un prestamista como forma de garantía por la devolución del dinero que se pidió prestado (p. 200)

ENGLISH	ESPAÑOL
most favored nation clause: trade law allowing a third country to enjoy the same tariff reductions the United States negotiates with another country (p. 506)	**cláusula de la nación más favorecida:** ley de comercio que permite que un tercer país disfrute de las mismas reducciones arancelarias que Estados Unidos negocia con otro país (p. 506)
multinational: corporation producing and selling without regard to national boundaries and whose business activities are located in several different countries (p. 226, 532)	**multinacional:** corporación que produce y vende sin tomar en cuenta las fronteras nacionales y cuyas actividades comerciales se encuentran en varios países (p. 226, 532)
multiplier: change in overall spending caused by a change in investment spending (p. 439)	**multiplicador:** cambio en los gastos generales a causa de un cambio en los gastos de inversión (p. 439)
municipal bonds: a type of investment, often tax exempt, issued by state and local governments; known as munis (p. 313, 572)	**bonos municipales:** tipo de inversión, con frecuencia exenta de impuestos, emitida por gobiernos estatales y locales; se conocen como *munis* (p. 313, 572)
mutual fund: company that sells shares of a portfolio of securities, e.g., stocks and bonds issued by other companies (p. 321, 571)	**fondo mutuo:** empresa que vende acciones de una cartera de valores, como acciones y bonos emitidos por otras empresas (p. 321, 571)

N

ENGLISH	ESPAÑOL
national bank: a commercial bank chartered by the National Banking System (p. 284)	**banco nacional:** banco comercial cuya acta constitutiva emite el Sistema de Bancos Nacionales (p. 284)
national currency: currency backed by government bonds and issued by commercial banks in the National Banking System (p. 284)	**papel moneda nacional:** papel moneda que tiene el respaldo de bonos del gobierno y que emiten bancos comerciales que están en el Sistema de Bancos Nacionales (p. 284)
national debt: the total amount borrowed from investors to finance the government's deficit spending (p. 418)	**deuda pública:** cantidad total que se ha pedido prestado a inversionistas para financiar los gastos deficitarios del gobierno (p. 418)
national income (NI): net national product less indirect business taxes; measure of a nation's income (p. 341)	**ingreso nacional:** producto nacional neto menos impuestos indirectos sobre la actividad empresarial; medida de los ingresos de una nación (p. 341)
nationalization: shift of an economy, or part of an economy, from private ownership to government ownership (p. 61)	**nacionalización:** cambio de una economía, o parte de una economía, de propiedad privada a propiedad gubernamental (p. 61)
natural monopoly: market structure in which average costs of production are lowest when all output is produced by a single firm (p. 188, 428)	**monopolio natural:** estructura del mercado en la cual los costos promedio de producción son más bajos cuando toda la producción la hace una sola empresa (p. 188, 428)
need: basic requirement for survival, including food, clothing, and shelter (p. 8)	**necesidad:** requisito básico para sobrevivir, que incluye alimento, ropa y alojamiento (p. 8)

ENGLISH

negative income tax: tax system that would make cash payments in the form of tax refunds to individuals when their income falls below certain levels (p. 358)

net asset value (NAV): the market value of a mutual fund share determined by dividing the value of the fund by the number of shares issued (p. 322)

net exports of goods and services: net expenditures by the output-expenditure model's foreign sector; equal to total exports less total imports (p. 343)

net immigration: net population change after accounting for those who leave as well as enter a country (p. 351)

net income: measure of business profits determined by subtracting all expenses, including taxes, from revenues (p. 223)

net national product (NNP): gross national product minus depreciation charges for wear and tear on capital equipment; measure of net annual production generated with labor and property supplied by a country's citizens (p. 341)

***neutral:** favoring neither one side nor another (p. 155)

nondurable good: item that wears out or lasts for fewer than three years when used regularly (p. 8)

nonmarket transactions: economic activity not taking place in the market, and therefore, not included in GDP; examples include services of homemakers and work done around the home (p. 338)

nonprice competition: competition based on a product's appearance, quality, or design, rather than its price (p. 185)

nonprofit organization: economic institution that operates like a business but does not seek financial gain; schools, churches, and community-service organizations are examples (p. 232)

nonrecourse loan: loan that carries neither penalty nor further obligation to repay (p. 170)

ESPAÑOL

impuesto negativo sobre la renta: sistema impositivo que hace pagos en efectivo en forma de reintegros de impuestos a personas cuando sus ingresos están por debajo de ciertos niveles (p. 358)

valor activo neto: valor de mercado de una acción de un fondo mutuo que se determina dividiendo el valor del fondo entre el número de acciones emitidas (p. 322)

exportaciones netas de bienes y servicios: gastos netos por parte del sector externo del modelo de producción-gastos; es igual a las exportaciones totales menos las importaciones totales (p. 343)

saldo migratorio: cambio neto de población después de tener en cuenta a quienes se van así como a quienes entran a un país (p. 351)

ingreso neto: medida de las ganancias de una empresa determinada al restar todos los gastos, incluyendo los impuestos, de las ganancias (p. 223)

producto nacional neto: producto nacional bruto menos cargos de depreciación por el desgaste de los bienes de capital; medida de la producción neta anual generada con mano de obra y propiedad suministrada por los ciudadanos de un país (p. 341)

***neutral:** que no favorece ni a una parte ni a otra (p. 155)

bien no duradero: producto que se deteriora y dura menos de tres años cuando se usa con regularidad (p. 8)

transacciones fuera del mercado: actividad económica que no tiene lugar en el mercado y que por lo tanto no está incluida en el PIB; son ejemplos servicios de amas de casa y tareas realizadas en el hogar (p. 338)

competencia no basada en el precio: competencia basada en la apariencia, la calidad o el diseño de un producto en vez de en su precio (p. 185)

organización sin fines de lucro: institución económica que opera como una empresa pero que no busca ganancias financieras; escuelas, iglesias y organizaciones de servicio comunitario son ejemplos (p. 232)

préstamo sin aval personal: préstamo que no tiene penalidad ni obligación futura de devolución (p. 170)

ENGLISH

nonrenewable resources: resources that cannot be replenished once they are used (p. 544)

North American Free Trade Agreement (NAFTA): agreement signed in 1993 to reduce tariffs among the United States, Canada, and Mexico (p. 507)

O

*offset: to balance higher levels of risk with a larger payoff (p. 313)

oligopoly: market structure in which a few large sellers dominate and have the ability to affect prices in the industry; form of imperfect competition (p. 186)

open market operations: monetary policy in the form of U.S. Treasury bills, or notes, or bond sales and purchases by the Fed (p. 473)

opportunity cost: cost of the next best alternative use of money, time, or resources, when one choice is made rather than another (p. 498)

option: contract giving investors an option to buy or sell commodities, equities, or financial assets at a specific future date using a price agreed upon today (p. 325)

Organization of Petroleum Exporting Countries (OPEC): organization formed to oversee a common policy for the sale of petroleum (p. 537)

output-expenditure model: macroeconomic model describing aggregate demand by the consumer, investment, government, and foreign sectors; GDP = C + I + G + F (p. 343)

outsourcing: hiring outside firms to perform non-core operations to lower operating costs (p. 386, 533)

overhead: broad category of fixed costs that includes interest, rent, taxes, and executive salaries (p. 142)

ESPAÑOL

recursos no renovables: recursos que no pueden reponerse una vez que se usan (p. 544)

Tratado de Libre Comercio de América del Norte (TLCAN): acuerdo firmado en 1993 para reducir los aranceles entre Estados Unidos, Canadá y México (p. 507)

*compensar: equilibrar niveles altos de riesgo con mayores beneficios (p. 313)

oligopolio: estructura del mercado en la cual unos pocos vendedores grandes dominan y tienen la capacidad de afectar los precios en la industria; forma de competencia imperfecta (p. 186)

operaciones de mercado abierto: política monetaria en forma de ventas y compras de letras o notas o bonos del Tesoro de Estados Unidos por parte de la Reserva Federal (p. 473)

costo de oportunidad: costo del mejor uso alternativo siguiente del dinero, el tiempo o los recursos cuando se hace una elección en vez de otra (p. 498)

opción: contrato que da a los inversionistas una opción de comprar o vender mercancía, títulos valores o activos financieros en una fecha futura específica usando un precio acordado hoy (p. 325)

Organización de Países Exportadores de Petróleo (OPEP): organización formada para fiscalizar una política común para la venta de petróleo (p. 537)

modelo de producción-gastos: modelo macroeconómico que describe la demanda global de los sectores de consumidores, inversionistas, el gobierno y externo; PIB = C + I + G + E (p. 343)

tercerización: contratación fuera de las empresas para realizar operaciones no esenciales con el fin de bajar los costos operativos (p. 386, 533)

gastos generales: categoría amplia de costos fijos que incluye intereses, alquiler, impuestos y salarios de los ejecutivos (p. 142)

P

par value: principal of a bond or total amount borrowed (p. 310)

paradox of value: apparent contradiction between the high value of a nonessential item and the low value of an essential item (p. 8)

partnership: unincorporated business owned and operated by two or more people who share the profits and have unlimited liability for the debts and obligations of the firm (p. 214, 569)

passive fiscal policies: fiscal actions that do not require new actions to go into effect (p. 482)

"pay-as-you-go" provision: requirement that new spending proposals or tax cuts must be offset by reductions elsewhere (p. 421)

payroll tax: tax on wages and salaries to finance Social Security and Medicare costs (p. 415)

payroll withholding system: method of automatically removing deductions from a paycheck (p. 414)

peak: point in time when real GDP stops expanding and begins to decline (p. 367)

pension: regular allowance for someone who has worked a certain number of years, reached a certain age, or who has suffered from an injury (p. 307)

pension fund: fund that collects and invests income until payments are made to eligible recipients (p. 307)

per capita: per person basis; total divided by population (p. 419)

perestroika: fundamental restructuring of the Soviet economy; policy introduced by Gorbachev (p. 58)

perfect competition: theoretical market structure characterized by a large number of well-informed independent buyers and sellers who exchange identical products and have freedom of entry and exit (p. 183)

*persistent: continuous, without signs of weakening (p. 513)

---

valor nominal: capital de un bono o cantidad total que se pidió en préstamo (p. 310)

paradoja del valor: contradicción aparente entre el valor elevado de un producto no esencial y el valor bajo de un producto esencial (p. 8)

sociedad: empresa sin personalidad jurídica cuya propiedad y operaciones corresponden a dos o más personas que comparten las ganancias y tienen responsabilidad ilimitada por las deudas y obligaciones de la empresa (p. 214, 569)

política fiscal pasiva: acciones fiscales que no necesitan nuevas acciones para entrar en vigor (p. 482)

cláusula de pago financiado: requisito de que las nuevas propuestas de gastos o recortes de impuestos deben compensarse con reducciones en otro lado (p. 421)

impuesto sobre la nómina: impuesto sobre los sueldos y salarios para financiar los costos de Seguridad Social y Medicare (p. 415)

sistema de retención por nómina: método de sacar automáticamente las deducciones de un cheque de pago (p. 414)

pico: punto en el tiempo en el que el PIB real deja de expandirse y comienza a decaer (p. 367)

pensión: prestación regular para alguien que ha trabajado cierta cantidad de años, llegado a cierta edad o sufrido una lesión (p. 307)

fondo de pensiones: fondo que recauda e invierte ingresos hasta que se hacen pagos a beneficiarios que cumplen con los requisitos (p. 307)

per cápita: por persona; total dividido entre la población (p. 419)

perestroika: reestructuración fundamental de la economía soviética; política introducida por Gorbachov (p. 58)

competencia perfecta: estructura teórica del mercado caracterizada por una gran cantidad de compradores y vendedores independientes bien informados que intercambian productos idénticos y tienen la libertad de entrar y salir (p. 183)

*persistente: continuo, sin mostrar signos de debilitamiento (p. 513)

personal income (PI) • price floor

ENGLISH

personal income (PI): total amount of income going to the consumer sector before individual income taxes are paid (p. 341)

picket: demonstrate or march before a place of business to protest a company's actions or policies (p. 246)

pollution: contamination of air, water, or soil by the discharge of a poisonous or noxious substance (p. 546)

pollution permits: federal permit allowing a public utility to release pollutants into the air; a form of pollution control (p. 548)

population density: number of people per square mile of land area (p. 63)

population pyramid: diagram showing the breakdown of population by age and gender (p. 349)

portfolio diversification: strategy of holding different investments to minimize risk (p. 321, 571)

poverty guidelines: administrative guidelines used to determine eligibility for certain federal programs (p. 354)

poverty threshold: annual dollar income used to determine poverty (p. 353)

preferred stock: form of stock without vote, in which stockholders get their investments back before common stockholders (p. 217, 570)

premium: monthly, quarterly, semiannual, or annual price paid for an insurance policy (p. 307, 581)

*prevail: to predominate (p. 103)

price: the monetary value of a product (p. 154)

price ceiling: the highest legal price that can be charged for a product (p. 168)

price discrimination: practice of charging different customers different prices for the same product; usually illegal (p. 199)

price floor: the lowest legal price that can be paid for a product (p. 169)

ESPAÑOL

ingresos personales: cantidad total de ingresos que van al sector de los consumidores antes de que se paguen los impuestos sobre los ingresos de las personas físicas (p. 341)

hacer un piquete: demostrar o marchar frente a un establecimiento comercial para protestar por las acciones o políticas de una empresa (p. 246)

contaminación: alteración del aire, el agua o la tierra por el vertido de una sustancia tóxica o perjudicial (p. 546)

permisos de contaminación: permisos federales que autorizan a una empresa de servicios públicos a emitir sustancias contaminantes en el aire; forma de control de la contaminación (p. 548)

densidad de población: cantidad de personas por milla cuadrada de superficie de la tierra (p. 63)

pirámide de población: diagrama que muestra el desglose de la población por edad y sexo (p. 349)

diversificación de la cartera: estrategia de tener diferentes inversiones para minimizar los riesgos (p. 321, 571)

guías de pobreza: directrices administrativas usadas para determinar la elegibilidad para ciertos programas federales (p. 354)

umbral de pobreza: ingresos anuales usados para determinar la pobreza (p. 353)

acción preferente: forma de acción sin voto por la cual a los accionistas se les devuelve su inversión antes que a los poseedores de acciones ordinarias (p. 217, 570)

prima: precio mensual, trimestral, semestral o anual pagado por una póliza de seguro (p. 307, 581)

*prevalecer: predominar (p. 103)

precio: valor monetario de un producto (p. 154)

precio máximo: precio legal más alto que puede cobrarse por un producto (p. 168)

discriminación de precios: práctica de cobrar precios distintos a distintos clientes por el mismo producto; usualmente es ilegal (p. 199)

precio mínimo: precio legal más bajo que puede pagarse por un producto (p. 169)

ENGLISH	ESPAÑOL
price index: statistical series used to measure changes in the price level over time (p. 375)	**índice de precios:** serie estadística que se usa para medir cambios en el nivel de precios con el paso del tiempo (p. 375)
price-fixing: illegal agreement by firms to charge a uniform price for a product (p. 187)	**acuerdo de precios:** acuerdo ilegal entre empresas para cobrar un precio uniforme por un producto (p. 187)
***primary:** most important (p. 218, 525)	***principal:** más importante (p. 218, 525)
primary market: market in which only the original issuer can sell or repurchase a financial asset; government savings bonds, IRAs, small CDs (p. 316)	**mercado primario:** mercado en el cual solo el emisor original puede vender o volver a comprar un activo financiero; bonos de ahorro del gobierno, IRA, CD pequeños (p. 316)
prime rate: best or lowest interest rate commercial banks charge their customers (p. 475)	**tasa preferencial:** mejor o más baja tasa de interés que los bancos comerciales cobran a sus clientes (p. 475)
primitive equilibrium: first stage of economic development during which the economy is stagnant (p. 523)	**equilibrio primitivo:** primera etapa del desarrollo económico durante la cual la economía está estancada (p. 523)
principal: amount borrowed when getting a loan or issuing a bond (p. 218)	**capital:** cantidad que se obtiene prestada al recibir un préstamo o emitir un bono (p. 218)
***principle:** a fundamental law or idea (p. 108)	***principio:** idea o ley fundamental (p. 108)
private property rights: fundamental feature of capitalism, which allows individuals to own and control their possessions as they wish; includes both tangible and intangible property (p. 73)	**derechos a la propiedad privada:** característica fundamental del capitalismo, que permite que las personas sean propietarias y controlen sus posesiones de la manera que quieran; incluye la propiedad tangible y la propiedad intangible (p. 73)
private sector: that part of the economy made up of private individuals and businesses (p. 420)	**sector privado:** parte de la economía formada por personas y empresas privadas (p. 420)
privatization: conversion of state-owned factories and other property to private ownership (p. 57)	**privatización:** conversión de fábricas y otra propiedad perteneciente al estado en propiedad privada (p. 57)
producer price index (PPI): index used to measure prices received by domestic producers; formerly called the wholesale price index (p. 378)	**índice de precios industriales:** índice usado para medir los precios recibidos por productores domésticos; antes se llamaba *índice de precios al por mayor* (p. 378)
product differentiation: real or imagined differences between competing products in the same industry (p. 185)	**diferenciación del producto:** diferencias reales o imaginadas entre productos que compiten en la misma industria (p. 185)
product markets: market in which goods and services are bought and sold (p. 25)	**mercados de productos:** mercados en los cuales se compran y venden bienes y servicios (p. 25)
production function: graphic portrayal showing how a change in the amount of a single variable input affects total output (p. 136)	**función de producción:** representación gráfica que muestra cómo un cambio en la cantidad de un solo insumo variable afecta la producción total (p. 136)

production possibilities curve • protectionists

ENGLISH

production possibilities curve: diagram representing all possible combinations of goods and/or services an economy can produce when all productive resources are fully employed (p. 16, 497)

productivity: measure of the amount of output produced in a specific time period with a given amount of resources; normally refers to labor, but can apply to all factors of production (p. 22)

***products:** things that are sold (p. 290)

profit: difference between the revenue from sales and the full opportunity cost of resources involved in producing the sales (p. 73)

profit motive: driving force that encourages people and organizations to improve their material well-being; characteristic of capitalism and free enterprise (p. 74)

profit-maximizing quantity of output: level of production where marginal cost is equal to marginal revenue (p. 145)

progressive tax: tax where percentage of income paid in tax rises as level of income rises (p. 405)

***prohibited:** prevented or forbade (p. 247)

***promote:** to advance or support (p. 449)

property tax: tax on tangible and intangible possessions such as real estate, buildings, furniture, stocks, bonds, and bank accounts (p. 427)

***proportion:** comparative relationship between things in terms of size, quantity, etc. (p. 522)

proportional tax (or flat): tax in which percentage of income paid in tax is the same regardless of the level of income (p. 404)

protectionists: people who want to protect domestic producers against foreign competition with tariffs, quotas, and other trade barriers (p. 503)

ESPAÑOL

frontera de posibilidades de producción: diagrama que representa todas las combinaciones posibles de bienes y/o servicios que puede producir una economía cuando todos los recursos productivos están a pleno empleo (p. 16, 497)

productividad: medida de la cantidad de producción obtenida en un período específico con una cantidad dada de recursos; normalmete se refiere a la mano de obra, pero puede aplicarse a todos los factores de producción (p. 22)

***productos:** cosas que se venden (p. 290)

ganancias: diferencia entre los ingresos por ventas y el costo de oportunidad total que implicó producir las ventas (p. 73)

afán de lucro: fuerza impulsora que estimula a las personas y las organizaciones a mejorar su bienestar material; característica del capitalismo y la libre empresa (p. 74)

cantidad de producción que maximiza las ganancias: nivel de producción en el cual el costo marginal es igual al ingreso marginal (p. 145)

impuesto progresivo: impuesto según el cual el porcentaje de los ingresos que se paga como impuestos sube al subir el nivel de los ingresos (p. 405)

***prohibió:** impidió o evitó (p. 247)

***promover:** fomentar o apoyar (p. 449)

impuesto sobre el patrimonio: impuesto que se aplica sobre posesiones tangibles e intangibles, como bienes inmuebles, edificios, muebles, acciones, bonos y cuentas bancarias (p. 427)

***proporción:** relación comparativa entre cosas en términos de tamaño, cantidad, etc. (p. 522)

impuesto proporcional (o fijo): impuesto según el cual el porcentaje de los ingresos que se paga como impuestos es el mismo sin importar el nivel de los ingresos

proteccionistas: personas que quieren proteger a los productores nacionales contra la competencia extranjera con aranceles, cupos y otros obstáculos al comercio (p. 503)

protective tariff • real GDP per capita

ENGLISH

protective tariff: tax on an imported product designed to protect less efficient domestic producers (p. 501)

public disclosure: requirement forcing a business to reveal information about its products or its operations to the public (p. 200)

public good: economic products that are paid for and consumed collectively, such as highways, national defense, police and fire protection (p. 193)

public sector: that part of the economy made up of the local, state, and federal governments (p. 416)

pure competition: a theoretical market structure that requires three conditions: very large numbers, identical products, and freedom of entry and exit (p. 182)

put option: futures contract giving investors the option to cancel a contract to sell commodities, equities, or financial assets (p. 325)

Q

quantitative easing (QE): technique used by the Federal Reserve to keep interest rates low and encourage banks to take on more loans to stimulate the economy (p. 481)

quantity supplied: specific amount offered for sale at a given price; point on the supply curve (p. 130)

quantity theory of money: hypothesis that the supply of money directly affects the price level over the long run (p. 476)

quota: limit on the amount of a good that is allowed into a country (p. 501)

R

rationing: system of allocating goods and services without prices (p. 156)

real GDP: gross domestic product after adjustments for inflation; same as GDP in constant dollars (p. 339)

real GDP per capita: gross domestic product on a per person basis† (p. 339)

ESPAÑOL

arancel protector: impuesto que se aplica a un producto importado que fue diseñado para proteger a los productores nacionales menos eficientes (p. 501)

divulgación pública: requisito que obliga a una empresa a revelar información acerca de sus productos o sus operaciones al público (p. 200)

bien público: productos económicos que se pagan y consumen colectivamente, como las carreteras, la defensa nacional, la policía y la protección contra los incendios (p. 193)

sector público: parte de la economía formada por los gobiernos local, estatal y federal (p. 416)

competencia perfecta: estructura teórica del mercado que requiere de tres condiciones: cantidades muy grandes, productos idénticos y libertad de entrar y salir (p. 182)

opción de venta: contrato de futuros que da a los inversionistas la opción de cancelar un contrato para vender mercancía, títulos valores o activos financieros (p. 325)

flexibilización cuantitativa: técnica usada por la Reserva Federal para mantener bajas las tasas de interés y alentar a los bancos a tomar más préstamos para estimular la economía (p. 481)

cantidad ofertada: cantidad específica que se ofrece a la venta a un precio dado; punto en la curva de oferta (p. 130)

teoría cuantitativa del dinero: hipótesis que dice que la oferta de dinero afecta directamente el nivel de precios a largo plazo (p. 476)

cupo: límite en la cantidad de un bien que se permite que entre a un país (p. 501)

racionamiento: sistema de distribución de bienes y servicios sin precios (p. 156)

PIB real: producto interior bruto después del ajuste por inflación; lo mismo que PIB a valores constantes (p. 339)

PIB real per cápita: producto interior bruto por persona (p. 339)

real or constant dollars • savings

ENGLISH

real or constant dollars: dollar amounts or prices that have been adjusted for inflation (p. 264)

recession: decline in real GDP lasting at least two quarters or more (p. 367)

*recover: to get back (p. 379)

regressive tax: tax where percentage of income paid in tax goes down as income rises (p. 405)

*regulator: someone or something that controls activities (p. 85)

renewable resource: natural resource that can be replenished for future use (p. 543)

reserve requirement: formula used to compute the amount of a depository institution's required reserves (p. 291, 470)

*residence: the place where a person lives (p. 347)

*restrained: limited the activity or growth of (p. 199)

revenue tariff: tax placed on imported goods to raise revenue (p. 501)

*revolution: an overthrow of government (p. 278)

right-to-work law: state law making it illegal to require a worker to join a union (p. 248)

*risk: a situation in which the outcome is not certain, but the probabilities can be estimated (p. 308, 560)

rural population: those people not living in urban areas, including sparsely populated areas along the fringes of cities (p. 347)

ESPAÑOL

dólares constantes: cantidades o precios en dólares que han sido ajustados por inflación (p. 264)

recesión: deterioro del PIB real que dura al menos dos trimestres o más (p. 367)

*recuperar: recobrar (p. 379)

impuesto regresivo: impuesto según el cual el porcentaje de los ingresos que se paga como impuestos baja al subir los ingresos (p. 405)

*regulador: alguien o algo que controla actividades (p. 85)

recurso renovable: recurso natural que puede reponerse para su uso en el futuro (p. 543)

tasa de encaje: fórmula que se usa para calcular la cantidad de reservas que debe tener una institución de depósito (p. 291, 470)

*residencia: lugar donde vive una persona (p. 347)

*contuvo: limitó la actividad o el crecimiento (p. 199)

arancel fiscal: impuesto que se aplica a bienes importados para aumentar los ingresos (p. 501)

*revolución: derrocamiento del gobierno (p. 278)

ley de derecho al trabajo: ley estatal que hace que sea ilegal exigir a un trabajador que se afilie a un sindicato (p. 248)

*riesgo: situación en la cual el resultado es incierto pero se pueden estimar las probabilidades (p. 308, 560)

población rural: personas que no viven en áreas urbanas, incluyendo zonas escasamente pobladas a lo largo de la periferia de las ciudades (p. 347)

S

sales tax: general state or city tax levied on a product at the time of sale (p. 403)

savings: the dollars that become available for investors to use when others save (p. 304, 559)

impuesto sobre las ventas: impuesto general estatal o de la ciudad que se recauda sobre un producto en el momento de la venta (p. 403)

ahorros: dinero que queda disponible para que los inversionistas usen cuando otros ahorran (p. 304, 559)

ENGLISH	ESPAÑOL
savings bonds: low-denomination, non-transferable bonds issued by the federal government, usually through payroll savings plans (p. 314, 573)	**bonos de ahorro:** bonos no transferibles de valor bajo emitidos por el gobierno federal, usualmente mediante planes de ahorro por nómina (p. 314, 573)
scarcity: fundamental economic problem facing all societies resulting from a combination of scarce resources and people's virtually unlimited needs and wants (p. 7, 540)	**escasez:** problema económico fundamental que enfrentan todas las sociedades como consecuencia de una combinación de recursos escasos y las necesidades y los deseos prácticamente ilimitados de las personas (p. 7, 540)
seasonal unemployment: unemployment caused by annual changes in the weather or other conditions that prevail at certain times of the year (p. 387)	**desempleo estacional:** desempleo causado por cambios anuales en el clima u otros factores que prevalecen en ciertos momentos del año (p. 387)
secondary market: market in which all financial assets can be sold to someone other than the original issuer; corporate bonds, government bonds (p. 316)	**mercado secundario:** mercado en el cual todos los activos financieros pueden venderse a alguien que no sea el emisor original; bonos corporativos, bonos gubernamentales (p. 316)
secondhand sales: sales of used goods; category of activity not included in GDP computation (p. 338)	**ventas de artículos de segunda mano:** ventas de bienes usados; categoría de actividad no incluida en el cálculo del PIB (p. 338)
***secure:** obtain (p. 509)	***obtener:** conseguir (p. 509)
secured loan: loan that is backed up by collateral (p. 566)	**préstamo garantizado:** préstamo que tiene el respaldo de una garantía (p. 566)
seizure: temporary government takeover of a company to keep it running during a labor-management dispute (p. 257)	**confiscación:** asunción temporal del control de una empresa por parte del gobierno para mantenerla funcionando durante un conflicto entre el personal y la administración (p. 257)
seniority: length of time a person has been on a job (p. 255)	**antigüedad:** período durante el cual una persona ha estado en un empleo (p. 255)
sequester: a law that required automatic budget cuts (p. 422)	*sequester:* ley que exigía recortes automáticos del presupuesto (p. 422)
***series:** group of related things or events (p. 372)	***serie:** grupo de cosas o sucesos relacionados (p. 372)
service: work or labor performed for someone; economic product that includes haircuts, home repairs, and forms of entertainment (p. 8)	**servicio:** trabajo realizado por alguien; producto económico que incluye cortes de pelo, reparaciones en el hogar y formas de entretenimiento (p. 8)
set-aside contract: guaranteed contract or portion of a contract reserved for a targeted group, usually a minority (p. 263)	**contrato reservado:** contrato garantizado o parte de un contrato que se reserva para un grupo objetivo, usualmente una minoría (p. 263)
shareholder: person who owns a share or shares of stock in a corporation; same as stockholders (p. 290)	**accionista:** persona a quien pertenece una o más acciones en una corporación (p. 290)
short run: production period so short that only variable inputs (usually labor) can be changed (p. 136)	**corto plazo:** período de producción tan breve que solo los insumos variables (usualmente la mano de obra) pueden cambiar (p. 136)

ENGLISH

shortage: situation where quantity supplied is less than quantity demanded at a given price (p. 163)

signaling theory: theory that employers are willing to pay more for people with certificates, diplomas, degrees, and other indicators of superior ability (p. 255)

Silver Certificates: paper currency backed by, and redeemable for, silver from 1878 to 1968 (p. 285)

sin tax: a relatively high tax designed to raise revenue while reducing consumption of a socially undesirable product (p. 401)

Social Security: federal program of disability and retirement benefits that covers most working people (p. 88)

socialism: economic system in which government owns some factors of production and has a role in determining what and how goods are produced (p. 39)

soft loans: loans that may never be paid back; usually involves loans to developing countries (p. 529)

solar power: energy harnessed from the sun (p. 544)

sole proprietorship: unincorporated business owned and run by a single person who has rights to all profits and unlimited liability for all debts of the firm; most common form of business organization in the United States (p. 212, 568)

Solidarity: independent Polish labor union founded in 1980 by Lech Walesa (p. 61)

specialization: assignment of tasks to the workers, factories, regions, or nations that can perform them most efficiently (p. 23)

specie: money in the form of gold or silver coins (p. 278)

spending caps: limits on annual discretionary spending (p. 421)

spillover effects: unintended side effects that either benefit or harm a third party not involved in the activity that caused it (p. 193)

ESPAÑOL

escasez: situación en la que la cantidad ofertada es menor a la cantidad demandada con un precio dado (p. 163)

teoría de señalización: teoría que dice que los empleadores están dispuestos a pagar más a personas que tienen certificados, diplomas, títulos y otros indicadores de capacidad superior (p. 255)

certificados de plata: papel moneda respaldado, y canjeable, por plata de 1878 a 1968 (p. 285)

impuesto sobre el pecado: impuesto relativamente alto diseñado para generar ingresos reduciendo al mismo tiempo el consumo de un producto socialmente no deseado (p. 401)

Seguridad Social: programa federal de beneficios por discapacidad y jubilación que cubre a la mayoría de las personas que trabajan (p. 88)

socialismo: sistema económico en el cual el gobierno es el dueño de algunos factores de producción y cumple la función de determinar qué y cómo se producen los bienes (p. 39)

préstamos blandos: préstamos que es posible que nunca se devuelvan; usualmente se trata de préstamos a países en desarrollo (p. 529)

energía solar: energía que se obtiene del sol (p. 544)

empresa individual: empresa sin personalidad jurídica que pertenece y es llevada por una sola persona que tiene derecho a todas las ganancias y responsabilidad ilimitada por todas las deudas de la empresa; forma más común de organización empresarial en Estados Unidos (p. 212, 568)

Solidaridad: sindicato polaco independiente fundado en 1980 por Lech Walesa (p. 61)

especialización: asignación de tareas a los trabajadores, las fábricas, las regiones o las naciones que pueden realizarlas de forma más eficiente (p. 23)

metálico: dinero en forma de monedas de oro y plata (p. 278)

límites de gastos: límites de los gastos discrecionales anuales (p. 421)

efectos expansivos: efectos secundarios no intencionales que pueden beneficiar o perjudicar a terceros no involucrados en la actividad que los causó (p. 193)

ENGLISH

spot market: market in which a transaction is made immediately at the prevailing price (p. 325)

*stabilize: to make steady or unchanging (p. 169)

stages of production: phases of production that consist of increasing, decreasing, and negative returns (p. 138)

stagflation: combination of stagnant economic growth and inflation (p. 378)

*stagnant: not changing (p. 356)

*stagnation: lack of movement (p. 39)

Standard & Poor's 500 (S&P 500): an index of 500 stocks used to monitor prices on the NYSE, American Stock Exchange, and the OTC market (p. 324)

standard of living: quality of life based on ownership of necessities and luxuries that make life easier (p. 28)

state bank: a bank that receives its charter from the state in which it operates (p. 283)

state-chartered bank: bank that receives its charter from the state in which it operates (p. 290)

stock: certificate of ownership in a corporation; can be either common or preferred stock (p. 217, 291, 570)

stock or securities exchange: physical place where buyers and sellers meet to exchange securities (p. 323)

stockbroker: person who buys or sells securities for investors (p. 318, 572)

stockholders: people who own a share or shares of stock in a corporation; same as shareholders (p. 217, 569)

stocks: certificates of ownership in a corporation; common or preferred stock (p. 570)

store of value: one of the three functions of money allowing people to preserve value for future use (p. 280)

ESPAÑOL

mercado al contado: mercado en el cual una transacción se realiza de inmediato al precio prevalente (p. 325)

*estabilizar: hacer estable o invariable (p. 169)

etapas de la producción: fases de la producción que consisten en ingresos negativos, decrecientes y crecientes (p. 138)

estanflación: combinación de inflación y crecimiento económico estancado (p. 378)

*estancado: que no cambia (p. 356)

*estancamiento: falta de movimiento (p. 39)

índice Standard & Poor's 500 (S&P 500): índice de 500 acciones que se usa para hacer el seguimiento de precios en la Bolsa de Valores de Nueva York, la American Stock Exchange y el mercado extrabursátil (p. 324)

nivel de vida: calidad de la vida basada en la propiedad de productos necesarios y lujosos que hacen que la vida sea más fácil (p. 28)

banco estatal: banco que recibe su carta constitutiva del estado en el cual opera (p. 283)

banco con autorización estatal: banco que recibe su carta constitutiva del estado en el cual opera (p. 290)

acción: certificado de propiedad en una corporación; puede ser una acción ordinaria o preferente (p. 217, 291, 570)

bolsa de valores: lugar físico donde compradores y vendedores se encuentran para intercambiar valores (p. 323)

corredor de bolsa: persona que compra o vende valores para inversionistas (p. 318, 572)

accionistas: personas que poseen una o más acciones en una corporación (p. 217, 291, 569)

acciones: certificados de propiedad en una corporación; acciones ordinarias o preferentes (p. 570)

reserva de valor: una de las tres funciones del dinero, que permite que la gente mantenga el valor para su uso en el futuro (p. 280)

strategy • sustain

ENGLISH

*strategy: plan or method (p. 533)

strike: union-organized work stoppage designed to gain concessions from an employer (p. 246)

structural unemployment: unemployment caused by a fundamental change in the economy that reduces the demand for some workers (p. 386)

subsidy: government payment to encourage or protect a certain economic activity (p. 133)

subsistence: state in which a society produces barely enough to support itself (p. 541)

substitutes: competing products that can be used in place of one another; products related in such a way that an increase in the price of one increases the demand for the other (p. 111)

substitution effect: the portion of a change in quantity demanded that is due to a change in the relative price of the good (p. 109)

*successive: consecutive (p. 549)

supply: amount of a product a producer or seller would be willing to offer for sale at all possible prices in a market at a given point in time (p. 128)

supply curve: a graph that shows the quantities supplied at each and every possible price in the market (p. 129)

supply elasticity: responsiveness of quantity supplied to a change in price (p. 134)

supply schedule: a table showing the quantities that would be produced or offered for sale at each and every possible price in the market at a given point in time (p. 128)

supply-side policies: economic policies designed to stimulate the economy by removing government regulations and lowering marginal tax rates to increase production (p. 445)

surplus: situation where quantity supplied is greater than quantity demanded at a given price. (p. 162)

*sustain: to support or hold up (p. 193)

ESPAÑOL

*estrategia: plan o método (p. 533)

huelga: cese del trabajo organizado por un sindicato diseñado para obtener concesiones de un empleador (p. 246)

desempleo estructural: desempleo causado por un cambio fundamental en la economía que reduce la demanda de algunos trabajadores (p. 386)

subsidio: pago del gobierno para estimular o proteger cierta actividad económica (p. 133)

subsistencia: estado en el cual una sociedad produce apenas lo suficiente como para mantenerse a sí misma (p. 541)

bienes sustitutivos: productos que compiten y pueden usarse uno en lugar del otro; productos relacionados de tal forma que un aumento en el precio de uno aumenta la demanda del otro (p. 111)

efecto de sustitución: porción de un cambio en la cantidad demandada causada por un cambio en el precio relativo del producto (p. 109)

*sucesivo: consecutivo (p. 549)

oferta: cantidad de un producto que un productor o un vendedor estaría dispuesto a ofrecer para la venta con todos los precios posibles en un mercado en un momento dado (p. 128)

curva de oferta: gráfico que muestra las cantidades ofertadas con cada uno y todos los precios posibles en el mercado (p. 129)

elasticidad de la oferta: sensibilidad de la cantidad ofertada a un cambio en el precio (p. 134)

tabla de oferta: tabla que muestra las cantidades que se producirían u ofertarían para la venta en cada uno y todos los precios posibles en el mercado en un momento dado (p. 128)

políticas de oferta: políticas económicas diseñadas para estimular la economía al quitar las regulaciones gubernamentales y bajar las tasas impositivas marginales para aumentar la producción (p. 445)

excedente: situación en la que la cantidad ofertada es mayor que la cantidad demandada con un precio dado (p. 162)

*aguantar: soportar o resistir (p. 193)

target price • total revenue

ENGLISH — T — ESPAÑOL

target price: price floor for agricultural products set by the government to stabilize farm prices (p. 170)

precio indicativo: precio mínimo para productos agrícolas que fija el gobierno para estabilizar los precios agrarios (p. 170)

tariff: tax placed on an imported product (p. 501)

arancel: impuesto que se cobra sobre un producto importado (p. 501)

tax assessor: person who examines and values property for tax purposes (p. 428)

tasador de hacienda: persona que examina y tasa propiedades con fines impositivos (p. 428)

tax loopholes: exceptions or oversights in the tax law allowing taxpayer to avoid taxes (p. 403)

laguna tributaria: excepciones u omisiones en la ley impositiva que permiten que los contribuyentes eviten pagar impuestos (p. 403)

tax return: annual report filed with local, state, or federal government detailing income earned and taxes owed (p. 403)

declaración de impuestos: informe anual que se presenta ante el gobierno local, estatal o federal detallando los ingresos obtenidos y los impuestos que se deben (p. 403)

tax-exempt: not subject to tax by federal or state governments (p. 314)

exento de impuestos: no sujeto a impuestos por parte de los gobiernos federal o estatal (p. 314)

*technical: related to a particular subject such as art, science, or trade (p. 116)

*técnico: relacionado con un tema en particular, como el arte, la ciencia o el comercio (p. 116)

technological monopoly: market structure in which a firm has a monopoly because it owns or controls a manufacturing method, process, or other scientific advantage (p. 189)

monopolio tecnológico: estructura del mercado en la cual una empresa tiene un monopolio debido a que posee o controla un proceso, un método de fabricación u otra ventaja científica (p. 189)

technological unemployment: unemployment caused by technological developments or automation that make some workers' skills obsolete (p. 386)

desempleo tecnológico: desempleo causado por desarrollos tecnológicos o automatización que hacen que resulten obsoletas las destrezas de algunos trabajadores (p. 386)

*theoretical: existing only in theory; not practical (p. 182)

*teórico: que existe solo en teoría; no práctico (p. 182)

theory of negotiated wages: explanation of wage rates based on the bargaining strength of organized labor (p. 254)

teoría de salarios negociados: explicación que dice que las escalas salariales se basan en el poder de negociación de los sindicatos (p. 254)

tight money policy: monetary policy resulting in higher interest rates and restricted access to credit; associated with a contraction of the money supply (p. 473)

política monetaria restrictiva: política monetaria que resulta en tasas de interés más altas y acceso restringido al crédito; se asocia con una contracción de la oferta de dinero (p. 473)

total cost: sum of variable cost plus fixed cost; all costs associated with production (p. 143)

costo total: suma de los costos variables más los costos fijos; todos los costos relacionados con la producción (p. 143)

total product: total output or production by a firm (p. 137)

producto total: producción total de una empresa (p. 137)

total revenue: total amount earned by a firm from the sale of its products; average price of a good sold times the quantity sold (p. 144)

ingresos totales: cantidad total ganada por una empresa por la venta de sus productos; precio promedio de un bien vendido por la cantidad vendida (p. 144)

trade deficit • trust funds

ENGLISH

trade deficit: balance of payments outcome when spending on imports exceeds revenues received from exports (p. 512)

trade surplus: situation occurring when the value of a nation's exports exceeds the value of its imports (p. 512)

trade-offs: alternative that must be given up when one choice is made rather than another (p. 18)

trade-weighted value of the dollar: index showing strength of the United States dollar against a market basket of other foreign currencies (p. 512)

traditional economy: economic system in which the allocation of scarce resources, and other economic activity, is the result of ritual, habit, or custom (p. 38)

transfer payments: payments for which the government receives neither goods nor services in return (p. 417)

*transferable: capable of being passed from one person to another (p. 8)

*transformed: to change the nature of something (p. 16)

Treasury bills: short-term United States government obligation with a maturity of 4, 13, 26, or 52 weeks and a minimum denomination of $100 (p. 314, 573)

Treasury bonds: United States government bond with maturity of 30 years (p. 314, 573)

Treasury notes: United States government obligation with a maturity of 2 to 10 years (p. 314, 573)

*trend: a pattern or general tendency (p. 259)

trend line: growth path the economy would follow if it were not interrupted by alternating periods of recession and recovery (p. 367)

trough: point in time when real GDP stops declining and begins to expand (p. 367)

trust funds: special account used to hold revenues designated for a specific expenditure such as Social Security, Medicare, or highways (p. 418)

ESPAÑOL

déficit comercial: resultado de la balanza de pagos cuando el gasto en importaciones excede los ingresos recibidos de las exportaciones (p. 512)

superávit comercial: situación que ocurre cuando el valor de las exportaciones de un país excede el valor de sus importaciones (p. 512)

compromiso: alternativa a la que debe renunciarse cuando se toma una decisión en vez de otra (p. 18)

valor comercial ponderado del dólar: índice que muestra la fortaleza del dólar de Estados Unidos en contraste con una canasta de otras divisas (p. 512)

economía tradicional: sistema económico en el cual la distribución de recursos escasos, y otra actividad económica, es el resultado de la costumbre, hábito o un ritual (p. 38)

pagos de transferencia: pagos por los cuales el gobierno no recibe ni bienes ni servicios a cambio (p. 417)

*transferible: capaz de ser pasado de una persona a otra (p. 8)

*transformado: que ha cambiado su naturaleza (p. 16)

letra del Tesoro: obligación a corto plazo del gobierno de Estados Unidos con un vencimiento de 4, 13, 26 o 52 semanas y un valor mínimo de $100 (p. 314, 573)

bono del Tesoro: bono del gobierno de Estados Unidos que tiene un vencimiento de 30 años (p. 314, 573)

nota del Tesoro: obligación del gobierno de Estados Unidos que tiene un vencimiento de 2 a 10 años (p. 314, 573)

*tendencia: patrón o propensión general (p. 259)

línea de tendencia: trayectoria de crecimiento que seguiría la economía si no fuese interrumpida por períodos alternados de recesión y recuperación (p. 367)

valle: momento en que el PIB real deja de bajar y comienza a aumentar (p. 367)

fondos fiduciarios: cuenta especial usada para mantener ingresos designados para un gasto específico, como Seguridad Social, Medicare o carreteras (p. 418)

trusts • unlimited liability

ENGLISH	ESPAÑOL
trusts: illegal combinations of corporations or companies organized to suppress competition (p. 199)	**trust:** combinaciones ilegales de corporaciones o empresas organizadas para suprimir la competencia (p. 199)
two-tier wage system: wage scale paying newer workers a lower wage than others already on the job (p. 261)	**sistema de salarios de dos niveles:** escala salarial por la que se paga a los nuevos empleados salarios más bajos que a otros que ya están empleados (p. 261)

U

ENGLISH	ESPAÑOL
underground economy: unreported legal and illegal activities that do not show up in GDP statistics (p. 338)	**economía subterránea:** actividades legales e ilegales no declaradas que no aparecen en las estadísticas del PIB (p. 338)
***undertaking:** entering into an activity (p. 57)	***emprendiendo:** involucrándose en una actividad (p. 57)
***unduly:** too much (p. 454)	***excesivamente:** demasiado (p. 454)
unemployed: state of working for less than one hour per week for pay or profit in a non-family-owned business, while being available and having made an effort to find a job during the past month (p. 383)	**desempleado:** situación en la que se trabaja menos de una hora a la semana por un pago o una ganancia en una empresa que no pertenece a la familia mientras se está disponible y se ha hecho un esfuerzo por hallar un empleo durante el mes anterior (p. 383)
unemployment insurance: government program providing payments to the unemployed; an automatic stabilizer (p. 441)	**seguro de desempleo:** programa del gobierno que proporciona pagos a los desempleados; es un estabilizador automático (p. 441)
unemployment rate: ratio of unemployed individuals divided by total number of persons in the civilian labor force, expressed as a percentage (p. 383)	**tasa de desempleo:** razón de las personas desempleadas divididas entre el número total de personas que forman la mano de obra civil, expresada como porcentaje (p. 383)
***unfounded:** not based on fact (p. 387)	***infundado:** no basado en hechos (p. 387)
***uniform:** even or consistent (p. 357)	***uniforme:** constante o consistente (p. 357)
union shop: arrangement under which workers must join a union after being hired (p. 250)	**taller sindicalizado:** acuerdo según el cual los trabajadores deben hacerse miembros de un sindicato después de ser contratados (p. 250)
unit elastic: elasticity where a change in the independent variable (usually price) generates a proportional change of the dependent variable (quantity demanded or supplied) (p. 115)	**elasticidad unitaria:** elasticidad según la cual un cambio en la variable independiente (usualmente el precio) genera un cambio proporcional en la variable dependiente (cantidad demandada u ofertada) (p. 115)
unlimited liability: requirement that an owner is personally and fully responsible for all losses and debts of a business; applies to proprietorships, and general partnerships (p. 214, 569)	**responsabilidad ilimitada:** requisito de que un propietario sea personal y totalmente responsable por todas las pérdidas y deudas de una empresa; se aplica a empresas individuales y sociedades colectivas (p. 214, 569)

660

unrelated individual • voluntary

ENGLISH

unrelated individual: person living alone or with nonrelatives even though that person may have relatives living elsewhere (p. 342)

unsecured loan: loan guaranteed only by a promise to repay it (p. 566)

*****unstable:** unsteady (p. 439)

urban population: those people living in incorporated cities, towns, and villages with 2,500 or more inhabitants (p. 347)

user fee: fee paid for the use of a good or service; form of a benefit tax (p. 416)

utility: ability or capacity of a good or service to be useful and give satisfaction to someone (p. 8)

V

*****validity:** justification (p. 401)

value: monetary worth of a good or service as determined by the market (p. 8)

value-added tax (VAT): tax on the value added at every stage of the production process (p. 406)

variable cost: production cost that varies as output changes; labor, energy, raw materials (p. 143)

*****various:** different (p. 128)

venture capitalist: lender of investment funds to a start-up business in exchange for partial ownership of the business (p. 228)

vertical merger: combination of firms involved in different steps of manufacturing, marketing, or sales (p. 225)

vesting: the length of time you need to work at the company before you can take the employer's matching contribution with you (p. 322)

*****volume:** amount; quantity (p. 496)

*****voluntary:** done or brought about by free choice (p. 161)

ESPAÑOL

persona no relacionada: persona que vive sola o con personas que no son sus parientes aunque pueda tener parientes que vivan en otro lado (p. 342)

préstamo no garantizado: préstamo garantizado solo por una promesa de devolución (p. 566)

*****inestable:** inseguro (p. 439)

población urbana: personas que viven en villas, pueblos o ciudades constituidas con 2,500 habitantes o más (p. 347)

tarifa de utilización: tarifa pagada por el uso de un bien o servicio; forma de impuesto sobre beneficios (p. 416)

utilidad: capacidad o aptitud de un bien o servicio de ser útil y dar satisfacción a alguien (p. 8)

*****validez:** justificación (p. 401)

valor: a cuánto llega en términos monetarios un bien o servicio según lo determina el mercado (p. 8)

impuesto sobre el valor agregado (IVA): impuesto que se cobra sobre el valor agregado en cada etapa del proceso de producción (p. 406)

costo variable: costo de fabricación que varía cuando cambia el nivel de producción; la mano de obra, la energía y la materia prima (p. 143)

*****variado:** diferente (p. 128)

inversor de capital de riesgo: prestamista de fondos de inversión para una empresa nueva a cambio de la propiedad parcial de la empresa (p. 228)

fusión vertical: combinación de empresas involucradas en distintas etapas de la fabricación, el mercadeo o las ventas (p. 225)

adquisición de derechos: período que es necesario trabajar en una empresa antes de poder quedarse con la contribución de contrapartida del empleador (p. 322)

*****volumen:** cantidad (p. 496)

*****voluntario:** hecho u ocasionado con libertad de elección (p. 161)

voluntary exchange • zero population growth (ZPG)

ENGLISH | ESPAÑOL

voluntary exchange: act of buyers and sellers freely and willingly engaging in market transactions; a characteristic of capitalism and free enterprise (p. 73)

intercambio voluntario: acto de compradores y vendedores de dedicarse libre y voluntariamente a realizar transacciones del mercado; característica del capitalismo y la libre empresa (p. 73)

vouchers: certificates that could be used to purchase government-owned property during privatization (p. 57)

cupones: certificados que podían usarse para comprar propiedad que poseía el gobierno durante la privatización (p. 57)

W

wage rate: prevailing pay scale for work performed in an occupation in a given area or region (p. 252)

escala salarial: escala de pagos imperante por trabajo realizado en una ocupación en un área o región dada (p. 252)

wage-price controls: policies and regulations making it illegal for firms to give raises or raise prices without government permission (p. 477)

control de precios y salarios: políticas y normas que hacen que sea ilegal que las empresas aumenten los salarios o suban los precios sin tener permiso del gobierno (p. 477)

want: something we would like to have but is not necessary for survival (p. 8)

deseo: algo que nos gustaría tener pero que no es necesario para sobrevivir (p. 8)

wealth: sum of tangible economic goods that are scarce, useful, and transferable from one person to another; excludes services (p.9)

patrimonio: suma de bienes económicos tangibles que son escasos, útiles y transferibles de una persona a otra; no incluye los servicios (p.9)

welfare: government or private agency programs that provide general economic and social assistance to needy individuals (p. 357)

beneficios sociales: programas de organismos gubernamentales o privados que proporcionan asistencia general económica y social a personas necesitadas (p. 357)

workfare: program requiring welfare recipients to work in exchange for benefits (p. 358)

beneficios sociales condicionados: programa que requiere que los destinatarios de beneficios sociales trabajen a cambio de los beneficios (p. 358)

World Bank: international agency that makes loans to developing countries; formally the International Bank for Reconstruction and Development (p. 528)

Banco Mundial: organismo internacional que da préstamos a países en desarrollo; es el antiguo Banco Internacional de Reconstrucción y Fomento (p. 528)

World Trade Organization (WTO): international agency that administers trade agreements, settles trade disputes between governments, organizes trade negotiations, and provides technical assistance and training for developing countries (p. 506, 533)

Organización Mundial del Comercio (OMC): organismo internacional que administra acuerdos comerciales, resuelve conflictos comerciales entre gobiernos, organiza negociaciones comerciales y proporciona asistencia técnica y capacitación a los países en desarrollo (p. 506, 533)

Z

zero population growth (ZPG): condition in which the average number of births and deaths balance so that population size is unchanged (p. 524)

crecimiento cero de la población: situación en la que el número promedio de nacimientos y muertes mantienen el equilibrio, de modo que el tamaño de la población no cambia (p. 524)

INDEX

The following abbreviations are used in the index: m = map; F = feature (photography infographic, painting, cartoon, chart); q = quote

A

Ability-to-pay, 404
"Ability-to-Repay" rule, 200
Absolute advantage, 496–497
Accelerator, 440
Accumulation, 9
Acid rain, 547
Adjustable-rate mortgage (ARM), 579
Advanced Placement (AP) courses, 577
Advocates, 483
African Mbuti, traditional economy of, 38
Age, census and, 349
Agency shop, 243, 250–251
Aggregate demand, 452–453
    changes in, 453
    defined, 452
    effect of demand-side policies on, 453–454
Aggregate demand curve, 452
Aggregate output expenditure model, 439
Aggregate supply, 450–452
    changes in, 452
    effect of supply-side policies on, 454–455
    supply side policies and, 455
Aggregate supply-aggregate demand, macroeconomic equilibrium with, 453
Aggregate supply curve, 451–452
Agriculture prices, stabilization of, 169
AirTran Holdings Corporation, 226
Akerson, Dan, 138
Allocation, 50
Alternative minimum tax, 408
Amalgamated Association of Iron and Steel Workers, 258
American Bar Association (ABA), 234
American Cancer Society, 583
American Federation of Labor (AFL), 248
American Federation of Labor-Congress of Industrial Organizations (AFL-CIO), 234, 248–249
American free enterprise system, 69–93 economic and social goals of, 87–90 resolving trade-offs among goals, 90–91 social goals of, 171–172
American Medical Association (AMA), 234
American Red Cross, 232
American Stock Exchange (AMEX), 323
AMEX-NASDAQ, 323
Analysis in economics, 11
Angel investors, 211, 228–229
Annual percentage rate (APR), 565
Antipoverty programs, 357
Antitrust laws, 237
Anti-union backlash, 248
Appropriations bill, 413
Arab spring, 536
Arbitration, 256
Argentina, transition to, in capitalism, 61
Assets, financial, 304–305, 310–311
Association of South East Asian Nations (ASEAN), 535
Assumptions, 26
AT&T, 180, 187, 226
Australia, market economy in, 45
Australian Aborigines, traditional economy of, 38
Auto insurance, 581, 582
Automatic stabilizers, 441
Automatic teller machines (ATMs), 292, 560
Average per-capita income, 88
Average revenue, 144
Average tax rate, 404

B

Baby boom, 349, 482
Balance, 562
Balanced budget, 418
Balanced Budget Agreement (1997), 421
Balanced budget amendment, 426
Balanced Budget and Emergency Deficit Control Act (1985), 421
Balance of payments, 505
Bank(s), 293, 306
    central, 286
    consumer fees charged by, 292
    early, in America, 282–285
    with fractional reserves, 470–471
    national, 284
    role of Fed in regulating and supervising, 468
    selecting, 292–293
    state-chartered, 290
Bank accounts, opening, 561–562
Bank holding companies, 468
Bank holiday, 287
Banking Act (1933), 287
Bank of Manhattan, 224
Bank run, 287
Bankruptcy
    Chapter 7, 567
    Chapter 13, 567
    declaring, 567
Barriers to entry, 181
Barter economy, 276
Base year, 264, 339, 376
Bear markets, 325
Behavior adjustment, 401
Benefit principle, 404
Bernanke, Ben, 483
Better Business Bureau (BBB), 235
Bezos, Jeff, 83
"Big Mac" Index, 510
Biofuels, 77, 159
Biomass, 544
Black market, 61
BLADE, 317
Boeing, 532
Boesky, Ivan, 303
Bonds, 218, 302
    components of, 310–311
    computer trading of, 311
    corporate, 303, 313, 572–573
    defined, 310
    as financial assets, 310–311
    foreign government, 303
    government, 314, 318, 572–573
    junk, 303, 313
    kinds of, 303
    municipal, 303, 313–314, 572
    prices of, 311
    ratings of, 312–313
    savings, 573
    selling, 570
    Treasury, 303, 314, 573
    yields from, 312
    zero-coupon, 303
Borrowing, 305, 414–415, 564–567
Boycott, 242, 246
Brazil, as developing economy, 28
Break-even, profit maximization and, 144–146
Break-even analysis, 145–146
Break-even point, 146
British Petroleum (BP), 226, 532
Bubbles, 368
Budget(s)
    balanced, 418
    being smart about, 5
    elements of, 4
Budget deficit, 413
Budgeting, 426, 428, 558–559

Index **663**

**Budget surplus, ** 413
**Buffett, Warren, ** 430
**Bulgaria, ** economy in, 61
**Bull markets, ** 324–325
**Burton Snowboards, ** 147
**Bush, ** George H. W., 449, 507
Business
    fluctuations in, 366
    in free enterprise capitalism, 80
    mergers in, 224–227
    reinvestment in, 223–224
    starting your own, 70–71
**Business association, ** 234–235
Business cycles
    after World War II, 371
    characteristics and causes of, 366–368
    defined, 366
    economic instability and, 366–373
    phases of, 367
    predicting next, 372–373
    recovery and legislative reform, 370–371
    in United States, 369–372
**Business organization, ** 209–237
    corporations, 216–219
    ownership and, 568–570
    partnerships, 214–216
    sole proprietorship, 212–214, 568–569
**Business sales, ** 116–117
**Buying, ** transition from renting to, 580

C

**Call options, ** 325
**Canada, ** market economy in, 45
Capital defined, 15
    as factor of production, 15
    importance of human, 22–23 raising, 570
**Capital flight, ** 527
**Capital formation, ** 306, 568
**Capital gains, ** 408
**Capital goods, ** 8, 15
**Capital-intensive, ** 62
**Capitalism, ** 549. *See also* Free enterprise capitalism
    China transition to, 59–60
    defined, 45, 72
    in generating wealth, 57
    global transition to, 56–65
    in Japan, 62–63
    in Poland, 61
    in Russia, 58–59
    in Singapore, 64
    in South Korea, 63–64
    in Sweden, 65
    in Taiwan, 64–65
**Capital markets, ** 315
Careers
    chief plant engineer, U.S. Mint, 480
    consumer advocate lawyer, 202
    corporate auditor, 216
    cost estimator, 172
    credit counselor, 446
    financial clerks, 293–294
    foreign service agricultural attaché, 502
    franchise business owner, 78
    human resources specialist, 385
    National Labor Relations Board (NLRB) administrative law judge, 255
    painting contractor, 145
    physician's assistant, 41
    retail business manager, 27
    retail buyer, 112
    social worker, 350
    stockbrokers and investment bankers, 319
    tax attorney, 409
    World Bank staff, 538
**Carnegie, Andrew, ** 258
**Carnival Cruise Lines, ** 79–80
**Cartel, ** 537
**Carter, Jimmy, ** 447
Case studies
    changes in U.S. economy, 469
    coming to America, 197
    day in traditional, command, and market economies, 47
    drought and scarcity, 13
    Greek tragedy, 374
    holiday demand, 107
    Homestead Strike, 258
    instant snowboard, 147
    modern currency design, 289
    need for forests, 352
    New York and the National Stock Exchanges, 317
    powder pollution, 222
    President's Point of View, 411
    public versus private ownership, 81
    9/11 effect on economy, 500
    solar-powered Nepal, 530
    Super Bowl advertising, 167
    Tennessee Valley Authority (TVA), 444
**Cash flows, ** 224
    estimating, 223
    reinvesting, 224
**Cease and desist order, ** 199
**Census, ** 347
**Census, U.S. Bureau of, ** 334–335, 347
**Center of population, ** 347, 348
**Central bank, ** 286
**Certificates of deposits (CDs), ** 291, 304, 305, 313, 562
**Chamber of commerce, ** 234
**Change in demand, ** 110–111
**Change in quantity demanded, ** 108–109
**Change in quantity supplied, ** 130–131, 132
**Change in supply, ** 131
    comparing change in quantity supplied, 132
    factors that can cause, 132–134
Changes
    adapting to, in free enterprise capitalism, 76–77
    in demand, 165–166
    reasons for, in prices, 164–166
    in supply, 164–165
**Change to Win Coalition, ** 249, 250
**Charitable giving, ** 582–583
**Charter, ** 217
**Chase Manhattan Bank of New York, ** 224
**Chase Manhattan Corporation, ** 225
**Chase National Bank, ** 224
**Chávez, César, ** 246
**Chavez, Hugo, ** 41, 43, 50, 61
**Checking accounts, ** 293, 563–564
**Checks, ** writing, 563
Chile
    economic development in, 60
    market-oriented economy, 60
China
    confronting pollution in, 60
    debt of, 437
    as developing economy, 28
    economy growth in, 53
    gross domestic product in, 77
    mixed socialism in, 51
    shadow banking system in, 437
    transition to capitalism in, 59–60
Choices made by consumers, 18–20
    made by producers, 14–16
**Cigar Makers' Union, ** 245–246
**Cincinnati Stock Exchange (CSE), ** 317
**Circular flow of economic activity, ** 24–26, 305, 342
    diagram of, 26
    factor markets in, 24
    product markets in, 25
    role of markets in, 25–26
**Citgo, ** 532
**Citizenship, ** economics for, 29
**Civilian labor force, ** 251, 383
**Civil Rights Act (1964), ** Title VII, 263
**Clamp-OnTools, ** 220, 221
**Clayton Antitrust Act (1914), ** 199, 247
**Clean Air Act regulations, ** 222
**Clearinghouses, ** 467
**Clinton, William, ** 257
**Closed shop, ** 243, 250
**Coal, ** 544
**Coins, ** 467
**Collateral, ** 565
**Collective bargaining, ** 234, 256
**Collectivization, ** 58
**College-Level Examination Program (CLEP), ** 577
**College scholarships, ** 237
    paying for, 577
**Collusion, ** 181, 187
**Command economy, ** 37, 39–44
    advantages of, 41, 44

Commercial banks

characteristics of, 39–40
disadvantages of, 42–44
examples of, 40–41
typical day in, 47
Commercial banks, 559–560
Commodity money, 277
Common Market for Eastern and Southern Africa (COMESA), 536
Common stock, 217, 570
Communism, 50–51
Community organizations, 232–233
Company unions, 246
Comparative advantage, 496, 497–498
Compensation, 309
Competition
capitalism and, 74–75
defined, 74
ensuring, 199
in free enterprise capitalism, 74–75
nonprice, 185
as reason for market failure, 192
Competitive markets, 155, 166
Complements, 112
Compound interest, 308, 541, 560
Comprehensive measure, 11
Comptroller of the Currency, Office of (OCC), 280
Conduct, 146
Conglomerate, 226
Congressional action, 413
Congressional Budget Office (CBO), 413
Congress of Industrial Organizations (CIO), 248–249
Consistency, 308
Constant dollars, 264
Constitution, U.S., 85
Construction, 376
Consumer(s)
choices made by, 18–20
demand and tastes of, 111
measuring discomfort, 388
number of, and demand, 113
opportunity cost for, 19
responsibilities of, 20
rights of, 19
role of, in free enterprise economy, 83–84
role of government as, 85
Consumer cooperative, 233
Consumer Financial Protection Bureau (CFPB), 200, 201
role of Fed in, 468
Consumer goods, 8
Consumer income, demand and, 110–111
Consumerism, 20
Consumer price index (CPI), 375, 376–377
Consumer Product Safety Commission, 80
Consumer protection, role of Fed in, 468
Consumer sovereignty, 83
Continental Carbon, 222
Continental dollars, 277, 278, 282–283
Continuing budget resolution, 413
Contract, set-aside, 263
Control of prices, 168–169
Cooperatives (co-op)
consumer, 233
defined, 233
producer, 233
service, 233
Copyright Act (1976), 190
Copyright protection, 190–191
Corporate bonds, 303, 313, 572–573
Corporate capital, 570
Corporate identity, 226
Corporate income taxes, 415
Corporations, 216–219
advantages of, 218–219
defined, 216, 290, 569–570
disadvantages of, 219
forming, 217
Corruption, 526
Corruption Perception Index, 526
Cost(s)
fixed, 142–143
marginal, 142–144
total, 143
underestimating, 58
variable, 143
Costa Cruises, 79
Cost-benefit analysis, 26–27
defined, 195
using, 195–196
Cost-push inflation, 379
Council of Economic Advisers, 483
Coupon rate, 311
Craft unions, 242, 245
Credit, building, 565–566
Credit bureaus, 566
Credit cards, 294, 565
Creditors, 381, 564, 567
Credit reporting companies, 566
Credit score, building, 565–566
Credit unions, 233, 290, 306, 307, 560
Creditworthiness, 295, 564–565
Creeping inflation, 377, 378
Crowdfunding, 210–211, 229
Crowding-out effect, 420
Crude birthrate, 524
Cuba
command economy in, 42
mixed economy in, 52, 53
mixed socialism in, 51
socialism in, 41
Culture as trade barrier, 503
Currency
defined, 467
federal, 284–285
fiat, 279
national, 284
problems with, 283
role of FED in maintaining, 467
Current dollars, 264
Current GDP, 339
Curry, Thomas J., 280
Customs duty, 416
Customs union, 534
Cyclical unemployment, 387
Czechoslovakia, loss of political power in, 57
Czech Republic
economy in, 61
vouchers in, 57

D

Danbury Hatters, 247
Debates
abandonment of gold standard, 296–297
abolishment of Euro, 514–515
abolishment of Federal Reserve Bank, 484–485
duty of multinational corporations to keep base of operations in home countries, 140–141
economic stability as the key to world peace, 390–391
ethics in outsourcing jobs to foreign countries, 230–231
government provision of health care, 54–55
harm versus good of copyright laws, 190–191
insider trading, 326–327
national debt, 456–457
obligation of wealthiest nations to aid in economic development, 550–551
payment of higher taxes by the rich, 430–431
raising minimum wage, 174–175
raising prices on basic items needed during natural disasters, 120–121
rewarding students for good grades, 92–93
success of U.S. economy without manufacturing, 344
worth of senior business executives, 266–267
Debit cards, 293–294
Debt
capacity to repay, 564
national, 418
Debt ceiling, 422
Debtors, 381, 567
Decreasing marginal returns, 138
Deductible, 581
Default, 526
Deficits, reducing, 421
Deficit spending, 417–418, 440
Deflation, 375
Deforestation, 352
Dell, 533
Demand, 99–121
aggregate, 452–453
changes in, 110–111, 165–166
complements, 112
consumer income and, 110–111
consumer tastes, 111
defined, 102, 128
differences between supply and, 128

Demand curve

elastic, 116
expectations, 112–113
factors affecting, 108–112
for goods, 111–112
holiday, 107
illustration of, 102–103
incentives and, 103
income effect, 109
individual schedule for, 103
inelastic, 115, 116
law of, 100–101, 104–105
marginal utility and, 105–106
in market economy, 102
number of consumers, 113
prices and, 153
substitution effect, 109, 111–112
supply and, 161
unit elastic, 115, 116

Demand curve, 104
aggregate, 451, 452–453
individual, 104
market, 105

Demand deposit accounts (DDAs), 280, 293, 563

Demand elasticity, 114–115
business sales, 116–117
determinants of, 117–119
income used for, 119
substitutes and, 118–119
total expenditures test, 115–117

Demand-pull inflation, 378
Demand schedule, 103
Demand-side policies
comparing with supply-side policies, 448
effect on aggregate demand, 453–454
impact of, 440–441
limitations of, 441–443

Demographers, 350
Denmark, mixed market economy in, 51
Dependency ratio, 349
Depositor, 560–564
Depreciation, 223–224
Depression, 367. *See also* Great Depression
Depression-era economics, 439
Depression scrip, 369
Deregulation, 365, 447
economic growth and, 449
Description in economics, 11
Developing countries
concern for, 523

defined, 522
Developing economies, countries with, 28
Diminishing marginal utility, 105
Diminishing returns, 138
Diminishing satisfaction, 105–106
Direct tax, 402
Disability insurance, 581
Discount brokerages, 318
Discount rate, 475
Discretionary fiscal policy, 479
Discretionary spending, 417
Discrimination, 262, 356–357
Disposable personal income (DPI), 341
Distorted incentives, 158
Distribution of income, 401
Diversifiable risk, 571
Diversification, 226
Dividend, 217, 570
Divisibility as characteristic of money, 280
Division of labor, 23–24, 538
Dollars
Continental, 278
in decline, 279
inflation in eroding value of, 380
international value of, 512–513
strong versus weak, 513
Domestic jobs, protecting, 504–505
Dot-com bubble (2000), 364, 368
Double taxation, 219
Dow Jones Industrial Average (DJIA), 324, 373
Drought and scarcity, 13
Due Process clause of Fourteenth Amendment, 73
Durability as characteristic of money, 280
Durable good, 8

Earmarks, 416
Earned Income Tax Credit (EITC), 358
Earning, unemployment and, 575
Eastern Europe, transition to capitalism in, 61–62

Easy money policy, 473
E-commerce, 146
Economic activity, circular flow of, 24–26, 342
Economic bubbles, 364–365
Economic development
funding, 527–529
importance and process of, 522–524
obligations in aiding poor nations in, 550–551
obstacles to, 524–527
stages of, 523–524
Economic efficiency, 87
Economic equity, 88
Economic freedom, 72–73, 87
Economic goals of free enterprise economy, 87–90
Economic growth, 21–24
deregulation and, 449
describing, 22
division of labor and specialization, 22–23
economic interdependence in, 24
effect of, 22
in free enterprise capitalism, 79
human capital in, 22–23
impact of, 522–523
productivity and, 22
risks and sacrifices in, 21
savings and, 304–307
tax rates and, 448
Economic incentives, 420, 543
Economic instability, 363–391
Economic interdependence, 24
Economic models, 26, 161, 373
Economic perspectives
bankrolling start-ups, 210–211
budgeting lifestyles, 4–5
economic bubbles, 364–365
economic systems around the world, 36–37
Federal Reserve, 463–464
federal revenue and expenditures, 398–399
Free Application for Federal Student Aid (FAFSA), 556–557
gas prices--, 152–153

Economies of scale

law of demand, 100–101
law of supply, 126–127
limitations of supply and demand side economics, 436–437
micro-lending, 520–521
monopolies and oligopolies, 180–181
polymer banknotes, 274–275
starting your own business, 70–71
stocks and bonds, 302–303
unions, 242–243
U.S. Bureau of Census, 334–335
World Trade Organization, 491–492
Economic policy, 478–480
Economic politics, 482
Economic Recovery Tax Act, 408
Economic Report of the President, 411
Economics
analysis in, 11
choices in, 14–16
for citizenship, 29
defined, 7, 11
demand-side, 438–443
description in, 11
explanation in, 11
goods and services in, 8
needs and wants in, 8
paradox of value in, 8–9
prediction in, 11–12
scarcity in, 6–9, 14
scope of, 11–12
as social science, 105
studying, 6–7, 27–28
supply-side, 446–449
utility in, 8
wealth in, 9
Economic security,
measures of, 88
Economic systems
advantages of, 45–46
around the world, 36–37
characteristics of, 45
comparing, 44
defined, 39
disadvantages of, 46
examples of, 45
per capita gross domestic product, 62
Economies of scale, 181, 199, 226

Economists
differences in, 482
thinking like, 26–27

Economy
barter, 276
in equilibrium, 452
free enterprise, 28
laissez-faire, 188
services-based, 344–345
underground, 338–339
Education, 355
elementary and secondary, 429
factors of production and, 16
funding your, 574–577
payoffs for investments in, 23

EE savings bonds, 314
Efficiency, 403
prices and, 156
Efficient market hypothesis, 321
Efficient markets, stock markets and, 318–322
Elastic demand, 114–115, 116
Elasticity, 114
demand, 114–115
estimating, 115–116
of supply, 134–135
Elastic supply, 135
Electronic funds transfer (EFT), 294
Embargo, 503
Emergencies, raising prices on basic items during natural disasters or other, 120–121
Employee retirement, 424, 426
Employer reimbursement, 577
Employer resistance, 246
Energy flows in United States, 545
Engels, Friedrich, 50
Enterprise zones, 358
Entitlements, 421, 441
Entrepreneurial education, 228
Entrepreneurial funding for start-ups, 228–229
Entrepreneurs, 16, 82
as factor of production, 16
in free enterprise economy, 82–83
Environmental Protection Agency (EPA), 222, 547

Equal Employment Opportunity Commission (EEOC), 263
Equal Pay Act (1961), 263
Equifax, 566
Equilibrium, economy in, 452
Equilibrium price, 161, 164, 451
Equilibrium quantity, 161
Equilibrium wage rate, 253
Equities, buying or selling, 318–319
An Essay on the Principle of Population (Malthus), 540, 541
Estate tax, 415
Estonia, economy in, 61
Ethic, 527
Ethnicity, census and, 349–350
Euro, 535
abolishment of, 514–515
Euronext, 323
European Coal and Steel Community (ECSC), 534
European Union (EU), 61, 514, 534–535
Eurozone, 514
Excessive monetary growth, 379–380
Excess reserves, 471
Excise tax, 415
Expansion, 367
Expectations
changes in supply and, 133–134
demand and, 112–113
Expenses
fixed, 4
planned, 4
variable, 4
Experian, 566
Explanation in economics, 11
Exports, 495
Expropriation, 529
Extent of trade, 495–496
External debt, 525–526
Externalities, 193
External shocks, 368

Facebook, 229
Fact-finding, 256–257
Factor markets, 24

Factors of production, 14–16
Failure, market, 192–194
Fair Labor Standards Act (1938), 247
Fairness, rationing and, 157–158
Familiarity, prices and, 156
Federal Aviation Administration (FAA), 201
Federal budget, establishing, 412–413
Federal currencies, 284–285
Federal deficit, national debt and, 418
Federal Deposit Insurance Corporation (FDIC), 201, 236, 287, 291, 371, 468, 560
Federal Express (FedEx), 236
Federal government
expenditures of, 416–417
revenue sources of, 414–416
Federal Insurance Corporation Association (FICA), 415
Federal minimum wage, 263–265
Federal Open Market Committee (FOMC), 466–467, 474
Federal regulatory agencies, 200–201
Federal Reserve Board, 289
Federal Reserve Notes, 276, 286, 288
Federal Reserve System (FRS), 201, 286
advisory committees, 467
Board of Governors, 463, 465
chair of, 463
creation of, 286–287
defined, 276, 559
Executive Board, 463
Federal Advisory Committee, 463
Federal and Member banks, 463
Federal Open Market Committee, 463, 466–467
Federal Reserve District Banks, 465–466
global effects of actions of, 476

responsibilities of, 467–468
structure of, 464–466
Federal Society of Journeymen Cordwainers (shoemakers), 242
Federal Trade Commission (FTC), 199, 200, 201
Federal Work-Study (FWS), 576
Fertility rate, 350
Fiat currency, 279
Fiat money, 277
Finance companies, 307, 560
Financed payments, 4
Financial aid, 574–575
Financial assets, 304–305
bonds as, 310–311
characteristics of, 313–315
markets for, 315–316
Financial institutions, 559–560
borrowers at, 564–567
depositors at, 560–564
nonbank, 560
Financial intermediaries, 305, 306–307
Financial literacy, 294–295
role of Fed in, 468
Financial markets, 301–327
bonds in, 302–303, 310–313
financial assets in, 313–316
insider trading and, 326–327
investments in, 307–309
options in, 325
savings in, 304–306
stocks in, 302, 318–325
Financial system, 305
role of savings in, 304
Fiscal policy, 368, 435–457
decline of discretionary, 479
defined, 438
demand-side economics and, 437, 438–443
macroeconomic equilibrium and, 450–455
passive, 482
supply-side economics and, 436, 446–449
Fiscal-policy shocks, 368
Fiscal year, 412
Fiscal year budget (2014), 413
Five-year plan, 58

Index

Fixed costs, 142–143
Fixed exchange rates, 510
Fixed expenses, 4
Fixed income, 89
Fixed price policies, 169–172
Fixed rate mortgage, 579
Flat tax, 406
Flexibility, prices and, 155–156
Flexible exchange rates, 511–512
Floating exchange rates, 511
Fluctuation, 164
Food and Drug Administration (FDA), 201
Food stamps, 354, 357, 417
Ford, Henry, 16, 24
Ford Motor Corporation, 532
Foreclosures, 200, 365
Foreign exchange, 509
Foreign exchange rate, 509
Foreign government bonds, 303
Formosa. *See* **Taiwan**
401(k) plans, 322
Fourteenth Amendment, Due Process clause of, 73
Fracking, 15, 30–31
Fractional reserves, 291
   banking with, 470–471
France, mixed market economy in, 51
Franchisee, 220
Franchises, 212, 220–221
   advantages of, 220–221
   defined, 220
   disadvantages of, 221
Franchisor, 220
Fraternal Order of Police, 250
Free Application for Federal Student Aid (FAFSA), 556–557, 574
Free enterprise, 36, 72
Free enterprise capitalism
   adapting to changes in, 76–77
   benefits of, 75–78
   characteristics of, 72–75
   competition in, 74–75
   creation of wealth in, 77–78
   disadvantages of, 78–80
   economic freedom in, 72–73
   economic growth in, 79
   gaps between rich and poor in, 79
   private property in, 73
   profit motive in, 73–74
   promoting progress in, 77
   rights and responsibilities of business in, 80
   supply side tendencies in, 79–80
   variety of goods in, 76
   voluntary exchange in, 73
Free enterprise economy, 28
   benefits of, 82–86
   consumers in, 29, 83–84
   entrepreneurs in, 82–83
   government in, 85
   privately-owned businesses in, 29
Free-trade area, 534
Free trade movement, 506–507
Free traders, 503, 504
Frick, Henry C., 258
Frictional unemployment, 386
Friedman, Milton, 170
Full employment, 89
Fully employed resources, 17
Functions, 466
Fundable, 229
Fundamental, 386
Futures contracts, 325

G

Galbraith, John Kenneth, 357
Gasohol, 544
Gasoline taxes, 404
Gates, Bill, 430
Gender, census and, 349
General Agreement on Tariffs and Trade (GATT), 506, 533
General Motors (GM), 226
General partnership, 215, 569
Geographic monopoly, 180, 188
Germany, mixed market economy in, 51
Gift tax, 415–416
Girl Scouts, 232
Giveback, 260
Glass ceiling, 262
Glass-Steagall Act (1933), 560
Global economic development, 519–551
Global effects of Fed's actions, 476
Global institutions, 533
Globalization, 549
   characteristics of, 531–533
   continuance of, 539
   defined, 531
   regional economic cooperation in, 534–537
   trends in, 537–539
Global population growth, 540–543
Global production, 532
Global transition
   to capitalism, 56–65
   countries and regions in, 58
   problems of, 56–58
Glut, 546
Goals
   future, 90
   resolving trade-offs among, 90–91
Gold Certificates, 285, 288
Gold prices, rise in, 173
Gold standard, 285–286, 510
   debate over, 296–297
Gold Standard Act (1900), 285
Goods, 8
   capital, 8, 15
   consumer, 8
   demand for, 111–112
   durable, 8
   nondurable, 8
   public, 193
   variety of, in free enterprise capitalism, 76
Gorbachev, Mikhail, 58–59
Gosplan, 58
Government, 236–237
   in correcting market failures, 198
   in dealing with spillovers, 196
   direct role of, 236–237
   in free enterprise economy, 85
   increased dependency on, 442
   indirect role of, 237
   provision of health care by, 54–55
   role of, with demand-side policies, 440–441
   social goals and, 171–172
Government aid grants, 529
Government bonds, 318, 572–573
Government monopoly, 180, 189
Government regulations, changes in supply and, 133
Government savings bonds, 314
Government spending, 469
Graham-Willis Act (1921), 187
Grameen America, 520
Grameen Bank, 521
Gramm-Rudman Hollings Act (GRH) (1985), 421
Grants, 576
   in financial aid, 557
Great Britain, market economy in, 45
Great Depression, 89, 369–371, 389, 438, 479
   banking in, 287
   bank runs of, 285
   causes of, 369–370
   costs of capitalism during, 58
   defined, 49, 247
   labor in, 247
   start of, 287
   tariffs during, 506
Great Leap Forward, 59
Great Recession (2008-2009), 79, 371–372, 450
   buying up of bonds following, 279
   economic growth since, 354
   economic instability during, 389
   interest rates at record lows during, 477
   loss of jobs during, 387
   lower tax collections during, 415
   macro policies and, 481–482
   public understanding of, 483
   reducing federal government tax revenues during, 410
   severity of, 383
   unemployment rate during, 478

Greece, economic crisis in, 374
Greenbacks, 283–284, 288
Greenspan, Alan, 456
Grievance procedure, 256
Gross domestic product (GDP)
 comparing, by system, 36
 current versus real, 339
 defined, 11, 337
 in free enterprise system, 77–78
 macroeconomic instability and, 375
 as measure of national output, 336–340
 measuring current, 337
 tax burden ratio of tax revenues to, 425
Gross domestic product (GDP) gap, 387–388
Gross domestic product (GDP) per capita, 56
Gross income, 4
Gross national product (GNP), 341, 375
Growth companies, 570

H

Habitat for Humanity, 583
Harley-Davidson, 505
Hayek, Friedrich August von, 225
Head Start, 354
Health care, government provision of, 54–55
Health concerns as trade barrier, 503
Health insurance, 581
Healthy equilibrium, maintaining, 455
Higher education, 426
Holiday demand, 107
Holland America, 79
Honda, 532
Horizontal merger, 225
Hospitals, 429
Household, 342
Housing, 578–580
 costs and benefits of buying, 579–580
Housing bubble, 368
Human capital, 22–23
Hungary
 loss of political power in, 57
 transition to market economy, 61
 vouchers in, 57
Hybrid, 579
Hydropower, 544
Hyperinflation, 377–378

I

IBM, 532
Ideology, 479
Immigration, net, 351
Immigration and Nationality Act (INA), 80
Implementation lag, 442
Implicit GDP price deflator, 378
Imports, 495
Incentives, 73, 103
 demand and, 103
 distorted, 158
 responding to new, 58
Incidence of tax, 402
Income, 4
 consumer, 110–111
 distorted distribution of, 381
 distribution of, 354–355
 fixed, 89
 gross, 4
 national, 341
 net, 4
 personal, 341
Income assistance, 357
Income effect, demand and, 109
Income inequality, reasons for, 355–357
Income redistribution, 401
Income security, 417
Income statement, 223
Income taxes, 415
 individual, 414, 425
 negative, 358–359
Incorporation, 217
Increasing marginal returns, 138
Incubators, 210, 228
Independent unions, 249–250
Indexing, 414
India as developing economy, 28
Indigenous people, traditional economy of, 38
Indirect tax, 402
Individual demand, analysis of, 103
Individual demand curve, 104
Individual freedom, 75–76

Individual income taxes, 403, 414, 425
Individual retirement accounts (IRAs), 314–315, 573
Individual schedule for demand, 103
Individual supply curve, 129
Industrial union, 246
Industry, 182
Inelastic demand, 115, 116
Inelastic supply, 135
Infant industries argument, 504
Inflation, 264, 375–381
 causes of, 378–380
 consequences of, 380–381
 cost-push, 377
 creeping, 377
 defined, 89, 375
 demand-pull, 378
 domino effect of U.S., 377
 in eroding value of dollar, 380
 higher rates of crime and poverty and, 389
 measuring, 375–378
 money supply growth and, 476–477
Information, not enough as reason for market failure, 192–193
Infrastructure, 348
Initial public offerings (IPOs) of stock, 211, 228, 364
Injunction, 257
An Inquiry into the Nature and Causes of the Wealth of Nations (Smith), 182
Insider trading, 326–327
Inspections as trade barrier, 503
Instability
 costs of, 387–388
 political, 389
Insurance, 581–582
 automobile, 581, 582
 disability, 581
 health, 581
 life, 582
 property, 581
 shopping for, 582
 unemployment, 441
Intangible, 9
Intel, 532
Interdependence, 181
 economic, 24

Interest
 compound, 560
 defined, 218, 559
 simple, 560
Interest rate, 472, 559
Intergovernmental expenditures, 426
Intergovernmental revenues, 424, 427
Intermediate products, 337
Internal Revenue Service (IRS), 403
International agencies, in finding economic development, 528–529
International Bank for Reconstruction and Development (IBRD), 529
International Development Association (IDA), 529
International Finance Corporation (IFC), 529
International Monetary Fund (IMF), 528, 533
International trade. *See* **Trade**
International value of the dollar, 512–513
Interstate Commerce Commission (ICC), 180, 201
Intervention, 203
Intrinsic motivation, 93
Inuit, traditional economy of, 38–39
Inventory, 214
Investment banks, 560
Investments
 basic considerations in, 307–309
 objectives of, 309
 options for, 310
Investment spending, 368
Investors, 571–573
Isolationism, 60

J

Japan
 capitalist economy in, 62–63
 keiretsu structure in, 63
 market economy in, 45
Jefferson, Thomas, 334
Jobs, Steve, 16, 83
Joint venture, 569
JPMorgan Chase, 225
Junk bonds, 303, 313

K

Keiretsu, 63
Kennedy, John F., consumer rights and, 19
Keynes, John Maynard, 438, 439, 440
  legacy of, 443
Keynesian economics, 438–440
KFC, 531, 539
Khaladig, 530
Kia, 197
Kickstarter, 229
Kiva, 520
Komen, Susan G., 583
Krugman, Paul, 498
Kyocera (Japan), 532

L

Labor
  defined, 16
  division of, 23–24
  as factor of production, 16
  semiskilled, 252
  since the 1930s, 247–250
  skilled, 253
  unskilled, 252
Labor disputes, resolving, 256
Labor force
  civilian, 251, 383
  unionized workers in, 251
Labor-Management Relations Act, 248, 249, 250
Labor Management Reporting and Disclosure Act (1959), 248
Labor Statistics, Bureau of (BLS), 376
Labor unions, 234
Laffer curve, 447
Lags, 475
  implementation, 442
  legislative, 441
  recognition, 441
Laissez-faire economy, 188
Land, 15
Landrum-Griffin Act (1959), 248
Latin America, transition to capitalism in, 60–61
Latvia, economy in, 61
Law of demand, 100–101, 104–105
Law of supply, 126–127, 128
Leading economic index (LEI), 373
Leading economic indicator, 372–373
Leads, 475
Legal reserves, 470
Legal tender, 284
Legislated standards, 547
Legislation, 244
Legislative lag, 441
Lewis, John L., 248
Licenses as trade barrier, 503
Life expectancy, 350, 524
Life insurance, 582
Life insurance companies, 307, 560
Limited liability, 218
Limited life, 214, 569
Limited natural resources, 525
Limited partnership, 215–216, 569
Line-item veto, 421
Lines of credit, 570
LinkedIn, 229
Linton, Brian, 90
Lithuania, economy in, 61
Loans, 291
  in financial aid, 557
  nonrecourse, 170
  secured, 566
  small business, 570
  unsecured, 566
Local government
  expenditures of, 428–429
  revenue sources of, 427–428
Lockout, 242, 246
Long run, 137
Long-term care, 582
Long-term unemployed, 384
Lorenz curve, 354–355
Low-quality goods, production of, in command economies, 42
Ludlow Massacre (1914), 246

M

M1, 280
M2, 280
Macroeconomic equilibrium, 450–455, 453–455
  with aggregate supply-aggregate demand, 453
  defined, 453
Macroeconomy, 336, 341
  consumer sector in, 342
  defined, 450
  government sector in, 343
  investment sector in, 342–343
  net foreign sector in, 343
  output-expenditure model in, 343
Macro policies, Great Recession and, 481–482
Major League Baseball Players Association, 250
Malthus, Thomas, 540, 541, 546
  predictions of, 542
Mandatory spending, 416
Manufacturing wages, 265
Maori people, traditional economy of, 38, 47
Marginal analysis, 184
Marginal cost (MC), 143, 189
  finding, 142–144
Marginal product, 137
Marginal returns
  decreasing, 138
  increasing, 138
  negative, 139
Marginal revenue (MR), 144, 189
Marginal tax rate, 405
Marginal utility, 105
  demand and, 105–106
  diminishing, 105
Market(s)
  black, 61
  defined, 24, 45
  factor, 24
  for financial assets, 315–316
  price incentives and, 546
  prices and, 160–161
  primary, 316
  product, 25
  role of, 25–26
  secondary, 316
  "talking" of, 172–173
Market basket, 375–376
Market demand curve, 105
Market economies
  advantages, 44
  defined, 45
  demand in, 102
  disadvantages, 44
  Hungary transition to, 61
  market structures impact on prices in, 182
  mixed, 51
  prices in, 155–156, 167
  support for nonprofit organizations, 232
  typical day in, 47
Market failures
  defined, 192
  government in correcting, 198
  reasons for, 192
  types of, 192–194
Market remedies, 263
Market structures, 179–203
  characteristics of, 186
  defined, 182
  impact on prices in a market economy, 182
Market supply curve, 129–130
Market theory of wage determination, 253–254
Marx, Karl, 50, 51
Maturity, 311, 572
McDonald's, 531, 539
Measure of value, 280
Mechanism, 24
Mediation, 256
Medicaid, 358, 417
Medicare, 88–89, 405, 414, 415, 417
Medium of exchange, 280
Member bank, 465
Member bank reserve (MBR), 471
Menger, Carl, 105
Mergers, 224
  growth of business through, 224–227
  horizontal, 225
  reasons for, 225–226
  types of, 225
  vertical, 225
Mexico, as developing economy, 28
Microeconomics, 102
Microfinance, 520, 528
Microlending, 520
Micro-loans, 520, 528
Microsoft, 187
Milken, Mike, 303
Minimum wage, 88, 90, 263, 265, 370
  debate over, 263
  federal, 263–265
  raising the, 174–175

**Misery index, ** 388–389
**Mitsubishi, ** 226
**Mixed economies, ** 48–53
  advantages of, 52–53
  characteristics of, 48–50
  defined, 36, 86
  disadvantages of, 53
  emergence of, 86
  examples of, 50–52
  reasons for existence of, 48–49
**Mixed socialism, ** 51
**Modified free enterprise, ** 86, 203
**Modified union shop, ** 243, 250
**Monetarism, ** 475, 477
**Monetary expansion, ** 471–472
**Monetary growth, excessive, ** 379–380
**Monetary policy, ** 461–485, 472, 481
  changes in, 368
  conducting, 468, 472–475
  dilemmas in, 475–476
  public opinion and, 476
  rise of, 480
  short-run impact of, 472
  structure of the Fed, 464–466
**Monetary unit, ** 278
Money
  characteristics and functions of, 278–281
  commodity, 276
  evolution of, 276–278
  fiat, 277
  quantity theory of, 476, 477
  responsibilities and obligations of borrowing, 566–567
  source of, for banks, 290–291
**Money market deposit account, ** 562
**Money markets, ** 315
**Money supply, ** growth and inflation, 476–477
**Monopolies, ** 188–189
  breaking up, 199
  geographic, 180
  government, 180
  natural, 180, 428
  preventing, from forming, 199
  profit maximization and, 189
  regulating existing, 199
  technological, 180
  types of, 188
**Monopolistic competition, ** 184–186
**Monopoly power, ** 356
**Moody's, ** 312, 573
**Mortgage, ** 200
  adjustable-rate, 579
  fixed rate, 579
**Mortgage-backed securities, ** 303
**Most favored nation clause, ** 506
**Motivation, intrinsic, ** 93
**Multinational corporations, ** 140–141, 187, 494
**Multinationals, ** 226–227, 532
**Multiplier, ** 439
**Municipal bonds, ** 303, 313–314, 572
**Mutual funds, ** 321–322, 571–572

**Nabisco, ** 226
**National Aeronautics and Space Administration (NASA), ** 81
**National bank, ** 284
**National Banking System (NBS), ** 284
**National Bank Notes, ** 288
**National Basketball Association, ** 246
**National currency, ** 284
**National debt, ** 418, 454, 456–457
  federal deficit and, 418
  impact of, 420
  making changes in dealing with growing, 456–457
  views of, 419
**National defense, ** 416–417
  aiding, 503–504
**National Education Association (NEA), ** 234
**National Football League, ** 246
**National Highway Traffic Safety Administration (NHTSA), ** 201
**National income, ** 341, 524
  measures of, 340–341
**National Income and Product Accounts (NIPA), ** 336
**Nationalism as trade barrier, ** 503
**Nationalization, ** 61
**National Labor Relations Act (1935) (NLRA), ** 247
**National Labor Relations Board (NLRB), ** 201, 247
**National output, ** GDP as measure of, 336–340
**National pride, ** 505
**National Stock Exchange (NSE), ** 317
**Nations, ** reasons for trade between, 494–496
**Natural disasters, ** raising prices on basic items during, 120–121
**Natural gas, ** 544
**Natural monopolies, ** 180, 188, 428
**Natural resources, limited, ** 525
**Need, ** 8
**Negative externality, ** 194
**Negative income tax, ** 358–359
**Negative marginal returns, ** 139
**Negative spillover, ** 194
**Negotiated wages, ** theory of, 254–255
**Nestlé, ** 532
**Net asset value (NAV), ** 322
**Net exports of goods and services, ** 343
**Net immigration, ** 351
**Net income, ** 4, 223
**Net national product (NNP), ** 341
**Neutrality, ** prices and, 155
**News Corporation, ** 532
**New York City Opera, ** 246
**New York Stock Exchange (NYSE), ** 317, 323
**Nissan, ** 532
**Nixon, Richard M., ** 19, 170, 477, 510
**Nonbank financial institutions, ** 560
**Noncompeting categories of labor, ** 252–253
**Nondurable good, ** 8
**Non-Federal Work-Study (non-FWS), ** 576–577
**Nonmarket conservation efforts, ** 545–546
**Nonmarket transactions, ** 338
**Nonprice competition, ** 185
**Nonprofit organizations, ** 232
**Nonrecourse loan, ** 170
**Nonrenewable resources, ** 544
**Norris-LaGuardia Act (1932), ** 247
**North American Free Trade Act (1993), ** 338
**North American Free Trade Agreement (NAFTA), ** 507, 536
North Korea
  command economy in, 40, 41, 42, 47
  mixed economy in, 51, 52
**Norway, ** mixed market economy in, 51
**Nuclear energy, ** 544–545
**Nuclear Regulatory Commission (NRC), ** 201

Obama, Barack
  election of, in 2008, 410
  Great Recession and, 389
  passing of American Recovery and Reinvestment Act (ARRA) and, 482
  tax code changes and, 430
**Occupational Safety and Health Administration (OSHA), ** 417
**Office of Management and Budget, ** United States (OMB), 413
**Oil prices, ** rise in, 173
**Oklahoma Department of Environmental Quality (ODEQ), ** 222
**Oligopolies, ** 181, 186–188
  competition in, 187
  interdependence behavior in, 186–187
  profit maximization and, 188
**Open market operations, ** 473–474
**Opportunity cost, ** 17, 498
  for consumers, 19

of idle-resources, 17–18
production possibilities and, 17–18
of time, 19
Opportunity Fund, 520
Options, 325
Organization of Petroleum Exporting Countries (OPEC), 526, 537
Orman, Suze, 313
Output-expenditure model, 343
Outsourcing, 386, 532, 533
Overhead, 142
Ownership
business organization and, 568–570
private, 465

P

Paper currency, 277–278, 289
Paradox of value, 8–9
Partnerships, 214–216
advantages of, 215
defined, 214, 569
disadvantages of, 215–216
forming, 215
general, 215, 569
limited, 215–216
types of, 214–215
Par value, 310–311
Passbook account, 562
Passive fiscal policies, 482
Patents, 189
Pay-as-you-go provision, 421
Payments system, role of FED in maintaining, 467
Payroll taxes, 415
Payroll withholding system, 414
Peak, 367
Pension funds, 307
Pensions, 307
Pepsi, 531
Per capita, 419
Per capita gross domestic product, 62
Perceived value, 163
Perestroika, 58
Perfect competition, 183
Personal financial literacy, 555–583
Personal income, 341
Personal income tax rates and receipts, 442

Pesos, 278
Petroleum, 544
Philanthropy, 583
Picket, 242, 246
Pizza Hut, 531
Planned expenses, 4
Poland
loss of political power in, 57
transition to capitalism in, 61
vouchers in, 57
Police and fire protection, 429
Political instability, 389
Political power, loss of, 57
Pollution, 546
confronting, 60
incentives in, 546–547
Pollution fees, 548
Pollution permits, 548–549
Polymer banknotes, 274–275
Population, 346–348
center of, 347, 348
counting, 347
projected trends in, 349–351
rural, 347
urban, 347
Population density, 63
Population growth, 352, 524
Population pyramid, 349
Pork, 416
Portability as characteristic of money, 280
Portfolio diversification, 321, 571
Positive externality, 194
Positive spillover, 194
Postal Service, United States (USPS), 236
Poverty, 353–355
Poverty guidelines, 354
Poverty threshold, 353
Powis-Dow, Tina, 446
Preferred stock, 217, 570
Premium, 307, 581
Presidential intervention, 257
President's Council of Economic Advisors, 411
Price(s), 151–175
adjustments in, 160–164
advantages of, 155
change in quantity demanded, 108
in competitive market economy, 155
competitive markets and, 166
controlling, 168–169
defined, 154
demand and, 153
equilibrium, 161, 164, 451
factors affecting, 168
importance of, 154–158
in market economy, 155–156, 167
markets and, 160–161
market structures impact on, in a market economy, 182
measuring, 375–377
nonexistence of, 156–158
raising, on basic items needed during natural disaster or other emergencies, 120–121
rationing, 156–157
reasons for changes in, 164–166
shortages and, 163
as signals, 154–155
supply and, 152
surpluses and, 162–163
as system, 158–159
talking of markets and, 172–173
target, 170
Price ceilings, 168–171
Price discrimination, 199
Price-fixing, 181, 187
Price floors, 169–170
Price gouging, 120
Price incentives, markets and, 546
Price index, 375
Price stability, 89
Price supports, 170
Price taker, 183
Primary, 525
Primary markets, 316
Prime rate, 475
Priming the pump, 440–441
Primitive equilibrium, 523
Princess Cruises, 79
Principal, 218
Private foreign investment, 529
Private ownership, 81, 465
Private property in free enterprise capitalism, 73
Private property rights, 73
Private sector, 420

Privatization, 57
in Russia, 58–59
of state-owned property, 57
Procter & Gamble, 225
Producer(s)
choices made by, 14–16
opportunity costs for, 19
Producer cooperative, 233
Producer price index (PPI), 378
Product differentiation, 185
Production, questions on, 9–11
Production function, 136–138
Production period, 136–137
Production possibilities, 16–18
fully employed resources, 17
identifying possible alternatives, 16–17
opportunity cost and, 17–18
Production possibilities curves, 16–17, 26, 497
Production possibilities frontier, 17
Productions, stages of, 138–139
Productive resources,
demand for, 543–546
Productivity
changes in supply and, 133
defined, 22
growth and, 401
increases in, 22
Product markets, 25
Products, 128, 290
marginal, 137–138
total, 137
Professional associations, 234
Profit(s), 73–74, 82
converting, 570
higher, 181
Profit maximization, 145, 183, 185–186
break-even and, 144–146
monopolies and, 189
oligopoly and, 188
quantity of output, 145
Profit motive, 73–74
Progress, promoting, in free enterprise capitalism, 77
Progressive tax, 405
Property insurance, 581
Property taxes, 427–428

**Proportion, **522–523
**Proportional tax, **404
**Proprietorship, **212–213
**Protectionism, **503–505
**Protective tariff, **501
**Protector, **role of government as, 85
**Pro-union legislation, **247
**Provider, **role of government as, 85
**Public debt, **418–419
**Public disclosure, **200
**Public good, **193
**Public opinion, **monetary policy and, 476
**Public ownership, **private ownership versus, 81
**Public sector, **416
**Public Service Loan-Forgiveness Program, **577
**Public understanding, **increased, 483
**Public welfare, **426
Purchase
  delay of, 117–118
  portion of income used for, 119
**Purchasing power, **380, 420
**Purchasing power parity (PPP), **88
**Pure competition, **182
**Putin, Vladimir V., **59, 436
**Put options, **325

**Quantitative easing (QE), **481
**Quantity, equilibrium, **161
**Quantity demanded, **change in, 108–109
**Quantity supplied, **130–131
**Quantity theory of money, **476, 477
**Quotas, **501, 502–503

**Race, **census and, 349–350
**Railway Labor Relations Act (1926), **257–258
Rationing
  abuse and misuse and, 158
  administrative cost of, 158
  defined, 156
  problems with, 157–158
**Reagan, Ronald Wilson, **170, 436, 449
  budget priorities of, 448
**Real dollars, **264
**Real GDP, **339
**Real GDP per capita, **339
**Recession, **366, 367, 389. *See also* Great Recession (2008-2009)
**Recognition lag, **441
**Red Cross, **583
**Regional economic cooperation, **534–537
**Regressive tax, **405–406
**Regulator, **85
  role of government as, 85
**Reinvestment, **growth of business through, 223–224
**Renewable resources, **543–544
Rent(s)
  costs and benefits of, 578–579
  transition from, to buying, 580
  using price ceilings to control, 170–171
**Reserve Bank, **debate over abolishing, 484–485
**Reserve requirement, **291, 470
  as tool of monetary policy, 473
**Residence, **347
**Resource allocation, **400
Resources
  cost in, and changes in supply, 132
  fully employed, 17
  nonrenewable, 544
  opportunity cost of idle, 17–18
  renewable, 543–544
**Retail buyer, **112
**Retirement, **money at, 323
**Revenue Act (1861), **398
Revenues
  average, 144
  intergovernmental, 427
  marginal, 144
  raising, 421
  total, 144
  utility, 428
**Revenue tariff, **501–502
**Revolution, **278
**Rights and responsibilities of business, **in free enterprise capitalism, 80
**Right-to-work law, **248, 249
**Right to work states, **243, 249
**Risk, **560
  defined, 308–309
  diversifiable, 571
  undiversifiable, 571
**Risk-return relationship, **308–309
**Rival firms, **181
**Rivals, **elimination of, 226
**Robinson-Patman Act (1936), **199
**Rockefeller, John D., **199
**Romania, **economy in, 61
**Roosevelt, Franklin D., **457
**Rosenfeld, Irene, **371
**Roth IRA, **573
**Royal Caribbean Cruises, **226
**Royal Dutch Shell, **226
**Rural population, **347
Russia. ***See also* **Soviet Union
  as developing economy, 28
  mixed economy in, 52
  supply side economics and, 436
  transition to capitalism in, 58–59

**Sales taxes, **403, 424–425, 428
**Satisfaction, diminishing, **105–106
**Savings, **305, 559
  defined, 304
  economic growth and, 304–307
  in funding economic development, 527
  reasons for, 294–295, 560–561
  role of, in financial system, 304
**Savings accounts, **293, 562
**Savings bonds, **314, 573
Scarcity
  as basic economic problem, 6–9
  as characteristic of money, 280
  coping with problem of, 14, 21
  defined, 7, 541
  drought and, 13
  reasons for, 7
**Scholarships, **576
**Seabourn, **79
**Seasonal unemployment, **387
**Secondary markets, **316
**Secondhand sales, **338
**Secured loan, **566
**Securities and Exchange Commission (SEC), **200, 201, 219, 370–371
**Seizure, **257
**Sellers, **number of, and changes in supply, 133
**Semidevelopment, **524
**Semiskilled labor, **252
**Senior business executives,, **compensation for, 266–267
**Seniority, **255
**September 11, 2001, **impact on economy, 500
**Sequester, **422
**Series, **372
**Service, **8
**Service cooperative, **233
**Services-based economy, **28, 344–345
**Set-aside contract, **263
**7-Eleven stores, **532
**Shadow banking, **437
**Shareholder, **290
**Shell Oil Company, **532
**Sherman Antitrust Act (1890), **180, 199, 237, 247
**Shortages, **163
**Short run, **136–137
**Short-run impact of monetary policy, **472
**Signaling theory, **255
**Signals, **prices as, 154–155
**Silver Certificates, **285, 288
**Simple interest, **560
**Simplicity, **308
Singapore
  capitalist economy in, 64
  market economy in, 45
**Sin tax, **401
**Sixteenth Amendment, **398
**Skilled labor, **253
**Slovak Republic, **economy in, 61

Small Business Administration (SBA), 520, 569
Small business loans, 570
Smart card, 294
Smith, Adam, 8–9, 182, 438, 496
Smithsonian Institution, 232
Social goals
  of free enterprise economy, 87–90
  government and, 171–172
Socialism, 39
  mixed, 51
Socialist economies, 40, 42
Social science, economics as, 11
Social Security, 88, 91, 370
  increased government spending and, 414
  largest expenditures in federal budget for payments to, 416
  payments of, 237
Social Security Act (1935), 370
Societies, questions faced by all, 9–11
Soft loans, 529
Solar power, 544
Sole proprietorship, 212–214
  advantages of, 213
  defined, 212, 568–569
  disadvantages of, 214
Solidarity, 61
Sony, 226
South Africa, mixed economy in, 36
South Korea
  capitalist economy in, 63–64
  market economy in, 45
Soviet Union. See also Russia
  command economy in previous, 41, 43
  mixed economy in, 53
  socialist economy of former, 50
Specialization, 23–24, 495
Specie, 278
Speculation, 368, 381
Spending
  caps on, 421
  deficit, 417–418
  discretionary, 417
  patterns in, 381
  unexpected, 421–422
Spillovers, 193, 194–196
Spot markets, 325
Stabilization of agriculture prices, 169
Stages of production, 138–139
Stagflation, 378
Stagnation, 39, 356
Standard of living, 28
Standard Oil Company, 199
Standard & Poor's (S & P), 312, 324, 573
Starbucks, 531
Start-up loans, 570
Start-ups
  bankrolling, 210–211
  entrepreneurial funding for, 228–229
State banks, 283
State-chartered bank, 290
State government
  expenditures of, 426–427
  revenue sources of, 424–425
State-owned property, privatization of, 57
Stiglitz, Joseph, 193
Stock(s), 217, 290, 302, 570
  common, 217
  computer trading of, 311
  fall in prices of, 173
  investing, 571–572
  issuing in, 570
  performance of, 320–321
  preferred, 217
Stockbrokers, 318, 572
Stock exchanges, 323
Stockholders, 217, 569
Stock market reports, reading, 572
Stock markets
  efficient markets and, 318–322
  performance of, 323–325
Stock ownership, 217
Store of value, 280
Stouffers, 532
Strikebreakers, 258
Strikes, 242, 246, 247
Structural unemployment, 386
Student loans, 575–576
Students, rewarding, for good grades, 92–93
Subsidies, 133
Subsistence, 541
Substitutes, 111–112
  availability of adequate, 118–119
  demand and, 111–112
Substitution effect, 109
Sugar prices, using price floors to support, 169–170
Supplemental Nutrition Assistance Program (SNAP), 357
Supplemental Security Income program (SSI), 357, 417
Supply, 125–147
  aggregate, 450–452
  basic differences between demand and, 128
  change in, 130–134, 164–165
  defined, 128
  demand and, 161
  elastic, 135
  elasticity of supply, 134–135
  inelastic, 135
  prices and, 152
  unit elastic, 135
Supply and demand, 158, 166
Supply curve, 129
  aggregate, 451–452
  individual, 129
  market, 129–130
Supply elasticity, 134
  cases of, 135
  determining, 135
Supply schedule, 128–129
Supply side economics, 436
Supply side of market, 79–80
Supply-side policies, 446–449
  aggregate supply and, 455
  comparing with demand-side policies, 448
  defined, 446
  effect of, on aggregate supply, 454–455
  federal taxes and, 446
  in free enterprise capitalism, 79–80
  goals of, 446–447
  impact and limitations of, 447–449
  origins of, 446–447
  popularity of, 481
  role for government, 446
Surplus, 162–163
Sweden
  mixed market economy in, 51
  transition to capitalism in, 65
Synergy, 226

Taft-Hartley Act (1947), 248, 249, 250
Taiwan, capitalist economy in, 64–65
Takeoff, 524
Target price, 170
Tariffs, 501
  during Great Depression, 506
  protective, 501
  revenue, 501–502
Tax assessor, 428
Tax cuts (of 2011), 410
Taxes
  alternative minimum, 408
  changes in supply and, 133
  corporate income, 415
  criteria for effective, 403
  in dealing with spillovers, 194–196
  direct, 402
  double, 219
  economic impact of, 400–402
  estate, 415
  excise, 415
  flat, 406
  gasoline, 404
  gift, 415–416
  incidence of, 402
  indirect, 402
  payroll, 415
  principles of, 404
  progressive, 405
  property, 427–428
  proportional, 404–405
  regressive, 405–406
  sales, 424–425, 428
  sin, 401
  types of, 404–406
  value-added, 406–407
Tax-exemptions, 314
Tax loopholes, 403
Tax rates
  economic growth and, 448
  tax revenues and, 448
Tax reforms
  of 1981, 407–408
  of 1986, 408
  of 1993, 408

of 1997, 408–409
of 2001, 409
of 2003, 409–410
of 2013, 410
Tax return, 403–404
Tax revenues, tax rates and, 448
Technological monopoly, 180, 189
Technological unemployment, 386
Technology
advances in, 356
changes in supply and, 133
Temporary Assistance to Needy Families (TANF), 357, 417
Tennessee Valley Authority (TVA), 81, 236, 444
3M Corporation, 226, 227
Three-dimensional printing, 147
Tight money policy, 473
Time, opportunity cost of, 19
Time deposits, 293
TINSTAAFL, 9, 44
Tipping point, reaching, 442–443
Total cost, 143
Total expenditures, determining, 115
Total expenditures test, 115–117
Total product, 137
Total revenue, 144
Toxic Asset Relief Program (TARP), 198
Toyota, 532
Tradable pollution permits, 548–549
Trade
American dependence on, 495
arguments for protection, 503–505
basis for, 496–498
extent of, 495–496
financing, 508
gains from, 497, 498–499
restricting, 501–503
volume of, 496
Trade deficit, 512, 513
Trade-offs, 18–19
reasons for, 494–496
resolving, among goals, 90–91
Trade surplus, 512
Trade-weighted value of the dollar, 512

Traditional economy, 38–39
advantages of, 39, 44
characteristics of, 38
disadvantages of, 39, 44
examples of, 38–39
typical day in, 47
Traditional IRA, 573
Transactions, 562
Transferable, 8
Transfer payments, 417
Transition, 523–524
Transparency, 200
TransUnion, 566
Treasury bills (T-bills), 303, 314, 573
Treasury bonds (T-bonds), 303, 314, 573
Treasury Inflation-Protected Securities (TIPS), 573
Treasury instruments, 572–573
Treasury notes (T-notes), 303, 314, 573
Trend, 259
Trend line, 367
Triangular trade, 278
Troubled Asset Relief Program (TARP), 481
Trough, 367
Trust funds, 418
Trusts, 199
Truth in Lending Act (1968), 466
Tuition-free schools, 577
Two-tier wage system, 261

Uncertainty, 389
Underemployment, 384–385
Underground economy, 338–339
Undertaking, 57
Undiversifiable risk, 571
Unemployment, 382–389
cyclical, 387
defending against, 385
defined, 383
earnings and, 575
frictional, 386
measuring, 382–385
programs for, 370
seasonal, 387
sources of, 386–387
structural, 386
technological, 386–387
uneven burden of, 383–384
Unemployment insurance, 441
Unemployment rate, 383, 384
Unexpected spending, 421–422
Unionized workers in labor force, 251
Unions
activities of, 246
attitude of the courts to, 246–247
birth of, 242
craft, 242
decline of, 356
decline of influence of, 259–261
early development of, 244–245
independent, 249–250
kinds of, 250
reasons for decline, 260
tools of, 242
types of, 245–246
Union shop, 243, 250
Union wages, renegotiating, 260–261
United by Blue, 90
United Farm Workers (UFW), 246
United Hatters Union, 247
United Kingdom, market economy in, 47
United Mine Workers of America, 248
United Nations, 533
United Parcel Service (UPS), 236
United States
confronting pollution in, 60
housing bubble in, 365
mixed market economy in, 51–52
U.S. Airline Pilots Association, 250
U.S. Government Securities, 303
U.S. Olympic Committee, 232
U.S. Steel Corporation, 225
United Way, 232
Unit elastic, 115
Unit elastic demand, 115, 116
Unit elastic supply, 135
Unlimited liability, 214, 569
Unrelated individual, 342
Unsecured loan, 566

Unskilled labor, 252
Urban population, 347
User fee, 416
Utilities, 8, 429
Utility revenues, 428

Validity, 401
Value, 8
perceived, 163
Value-added tax (VAT), 406–407
ValuJet, 226
Variable costs, 143
Variable expenses, 4
Venezuela
command economy in, 43
socialism in, 41, 50
Venture capitalists, 211, 228
Verizon, 180
Vertical merger, 225
Vesting, 322
Vietnam
mixed economy in, 53
socialism in, 41
Vodaphone, 532
Volume, 496
of trade, 496
Voluntary, 161
Voluntary exchange, 73
Voucher, 57

W

Wage(s)
manufacturing, 265
renegotiating union, 260–261
theory of negotiated, 254
Wage determination, 252–255
market theory of, 253–254
Wage-price controls, 477
Wage-price spiral, 379
Wage rate, 252
equilibrium, 253
Wagner Act (1935), 247
Wal-Mart, 539
Wampum, 277, 280
Wannski, Jude, 436
Want, 8
Washington, George, 334
Water resources, fracking and, 30–31
Wealth, 9, 355–356
capitalism in generating, 57

Welfare
creation of, in free enterprise capitalism, 77–78
The Wealth of Nations (Smith), 8, 9, 496
Welfare, 357
Werfel, Daniel, 415
Wind power, 544
Women
lower pay for, 261–263
as recipients of microloans, 520
Worker productivity, 264
Workfare, 358
Work-study programs, 557, 576–577
World Bank, 528, 533
World population growth rates, 541
World Trade Organization (WTO), 492–493, 506–507, 533
World War II, business cycles after, 371

Yellen, Janet L., 475, 483
Yeltsin, Boris, 59
Yunus, Muhammad, 521

Zero-coupon bonds, 303
Zero population growth (ZPG), 524
Zoning, 201–202, 203
Zuckerberg, Mark, 83